Oxford Dictionary of
National Biography

Volume 31

Oxford Dictionary of National Biography

IN ASSOCIATION WITH
The British Academy

From the earliest times to the year 2000

Edited by
H. C. G. Matthew
and
Brian Harrison

Volume 31
Kebell–Knowlys

OXFORD
UNIVERSITY PRESS

OXFORD

UNIVERSITY PRESS

Great Clarendon Street, Oxford OX2 6DP

Oxford University Press is a department of the University of Oxford.
It furthers the University's objective of excellence in research, scholarship,
and education by publishing worldwide in

Oxford New York

Auckland Bangkok Buenos Aires Cape Town
Chennai Dar es Salaam Delhi Hong Kong Istanbul Karachi
Kolkata Kuala Lumpur Madrid Melbourne Mexico City Mumbai Nairobi
São Paulo Shanghai Taipei Tokyo Toronto

Oxford is a registered trade mark of Oxford University Press
in the UK and in certain other countries

Published in the United States
by Oxford University Press Inc., New York

British Library Cataloguing in Publication Data
Data available

Library of Congress Cataloging in Publication Data
Data available: for details see volume 1, p. iv

ISBN 0-19-861381-4 (this volume)
ISBN 0-19-861411-X (set of sixty volumes)

Text captured by Alliance Phototypesetters, Pondicherry
Illustrations reproduced and archived by
Alliance Graphics Ltd, UK
Typeset in OUP Swift by Interactive Sciences Limited, Gloucester
Printed in Great Britain on acid-free paper by
Butler and Tanner Ltd,
Frome, Somerset

LIST OF ABBREVIATIONS

1 *General abbreviations*

AB	bachelor of arts
ABC	Australian Broadcasting Corporation
ABC TV	ABC Television
act.	active
A$	Australian dollar
AD	*anno domini*
AFC	Air Force Cross
AIDS	acquired immune deficiency syndrome
AK	Alaska
AL	Alabama
A level	advanced level [examination]
ALS	associate of the Linnean Society
AM	master of arts
AMICE	associate member of the Institution of Civil Engineers
ANZAC	Australian and New Zealand Army Corps
appx *pl.* appxs	appendix(es)
AR	Arkansas
ARA	associate of the Royal Academy
ARCA	associate of the Royal College of Art
ARCM	associate of the Royal College of Music
ARCO	associate of the Royal College of Organists
ARIBA	associate of the Royal Institute of British Architects
ARP	air-raid precautions
ARRC	associate of the Royal Red Cross
ARSA	associate of the Royal Scottish Academy
art.	article / item
ASC	Army Service Corps
Asch	Austrian Schilling
ASDIC	Antisubmarine Detection Investigation Committee
ATS	Auxiliary Territorial Service
ATV	Associated Television
Aug	August
AZ	Arizona
b.	born
BA	bachelor of arts
BA (Admin.)	bachelor of arts (administration)
BAFTA	British Academy of Film and Television Arts
BAO	bachelor of arts in obstetrics
bap.	baptized
BBC	British Broadcasting Corporation / Company
BC	before Christ
BCE	before the common (*or* Christian) era
BCE	bachelor of civil engineering
BCG	bacillus of Calmette and Guérin [inoculation against tuberculosis]
BCh	bachelor of surgery
BChir	bachelor of surgery
BCL	bachelor of civil law
BCnL	bachelor of canon law
BCom	bachelor of commerce
BD	bachelor of divinity
BEd	bachelor of education
BEng	bachelor of engineering
bk *pl.* bks	book(s)
BL	bachelor of law / letters / literature
BLitt	bachelor of letters
BM	bachelor of medicine
BMus	bachelor of music
BP	before present
BP	British Petroleum
Bros.	Brothers
BS	(1) bachelor of science; (2) bachelor of surgery; (3) British standard
BSc	bachelor of science
BSc (Econ.)	bachelor of science (economics)
BSc (Eng.)	bachelor of science (engineering)
bt	baronet
BTh	bachelor of theology
bur.	buried
C.	command [identifier for published parliamentary papers]
c.	*circa*
c.	*capitulum pl. capitula*: chapter(s)
CA	California
Cantab.	Cantabrigiensis
cap.	*capitulum pl. capitula*: chapter(s)
CB	companion of the Bath
CBE	commander of the Order of the British Empire
CBS	Columbia Broadcasting System
cc	cubic centimetres
C$	Canadian dollar
CD	compact disc
Cd	command [identifier for published parliamentary papers]
CE	Common (*or* Christian) Era
cent.	century
cf.	compare
CH	Companion of Honour
chap.	chapter
ChB	bachelor of surgery
CI	Imperial Order of the Crown of India
CIA	Central Intelligence Agency
CID	Criminal Investigation Department
CIE	companion of the Order of the Indian Empire
Cie	Compagnie
CLit	companion of literature
CM	master of surgery
cm	centimetre(s)

Cmd	command [identifier for published parliamentary papers]
CMG	companion of the Order of St Michael and St George
Cmnd	command [identifier for published parliamentary papers]
CO	Colorado
Co.	company
co.	county
col. *pl.* cols.	column(s)
Corp.	corporation
CSE	certificate of secondary education
CSI	companion of the Order of the Star of India
CT	Connecticut
CVO	commander of the Royal Victorian Order
cwt	hundredweight
$	(American) dollar
d.	(1) penny (pence); (2) died
DBE	dame commander of the Order of the British Empire
DCH	diploma in child health
DCh	doctor of surgery
DCL	doctor of civil law
DCnL	doctor of canon law
DCVO	dame commander of the Royal Victorian Order
DD	doctor of divinity
DE	Delaware
Dec	December
dem.	demolished
DEng	doctor of engineering
des.	destroyed
DFC	Distinguished Flying Cross
DipEd	diploma in education
DipPsych	diploma in psychiatry
diss.	dissertation
DL	deputy lieutenant
DLitt	doctor of letters
DLittCelt	doctor of Celtic letters
DM	(1) Deutschmark; (2) doctor of medicine; (3) doctor of musical arts
DMus	doctor of music
DNA	dioxyribonucleic acid
doc.	document
DOL	doctor of oriental learning
DPH	diploma in public health
DPhil	doctor of philosophy
DPM	diploma in psychological medicine
DSC	Distinguished Service Cross
DSc	doctor of science
DSc (Econ.)	doctor of science (economics)
DSc (Eng.)	doctor of science (engineering)
DSM	Distinguished Service Medal
DSO	companion of the Distinguished Service Order
DSocSc	doctor of social science
DTech	doctor of technology
DTh	doctor of theology
DTM	diploma in tropical medicine
DTMH	diploma in tropical medicine and hygiene
DU	doctor of the university
DUniv	doctor of the university
dwt	pennyweight
EC	European Community
ed. *pl.* eds.	edited / edited by / editor(s)
Edin.	Edinburgh
edn	edition
EEC	European Economic Community
EFTA	European Free Trade Association
EICS	East India Company Service
EMI	Electrical and Musical Industries (Ltd)
Eng.	English
enl.	enlarged
ENSA	Entertainments National Service Association
ep. *pl.* epp.	*epistola(e)*
ESP	extra-sensory perception
esp.	especially
esq.	esquire
est.	estimate / estimated
EU	European Union
ex	sold by (*lit.* out of)
excl.	excludes / excluding
exh.	exhibited
exh. cat.	exhibition catalogue
f. *pl.* ff.	following [pages]
FA	Football Association
FACP	fellow of the American College of Physicians
facs.	facsimile
FANY	First Aid Nursing Yeomanry
FBA	fellow of the British Academy
FBI	Federation of British Industries
FCS	fellow of the Chemical Society
Feb	February
FEng	fellow of the Fellowship of Engineering
FFCM	fellow of the Faculty of Community Medicine
FGS	fellow of the Geological Society
fig.	figure
FIMechE	fellow of the Institution of Mechanical Engineers
FL	Florida
fl.	*floruit*
FLS	fellow of the Linnean Society
FM	frequency modulation
fol. *pl.* fols.	folio(s)
Fr	French francs
Fr.	French
FRAeS	fellow of the Royal Aeronautical Society
FRAI	fellow of the Royal Anthropological Institute
FRAM	fellow of the Royal Academy of Music
FRAS	(1) fellow of the Royal Asiatic Society; (2) fellow of the Royal Astronomical Society
FRCM	fellow of the Royal College of Music
FRCO	fellow of the Royal College of Organists
FRCOG	fellow of the Royal College of Obstetricians and Gynaecologists
FRCP(C)	fellow of the Royal College of Physicians of Canada
FRCP (Edin.)	fellow of the Royal College of Physicians of Edinburgh
FRCP (Lond.)	fellow of the Royal College of Physicians of London
FRCPath	fellow of the Royal College of Pathologists
FRCPsych	fellow of the Royal College of Psychiatrists
FRCS	fellow of the Royal College of Surgeons
FRGS	fellow of the Royal Geographical Society
FRIBA	fellow of the Royal Institute of British Architects
FRICS	fellow of the Royal Institute of Chartered Surveyors
FRS	fellow of the Royal Society
FRSA	fellow of the Royal Society of Arts

FRSCM	fellow of the Royal School of Church Music	ISO	companion of the Imperial Service Order
FRSE	fellow of the Royal Society of Edinburgh	It.	Italian
FRSL	fellow of the Royal Society of Literature	ITA	Independent Television Authority
FSA	fellow of the Society of Antiquaries	ITV	Independent Television
ft	foot *pl.* feet	Jan	January
FTCL	fellow of Trinity College of Music, London	JP	justice of the peace
ft-lb per min.	foot-pounds per minute [unit of horsepower]	jun.	junior
FZS	fellow of the Zoological Society	KB	knight of the Order of the Bath
GA	Georgia	KBE	knight commander of the Order of the British Empire
GBE	knight or dame grand cross of the Order of the British Empire	KC	king's counsel
GCB	knight grand cross of the Order of the Bath	kcal	kilocalorie
GCE	general certificate of education	KCB	knight commander of the Order of the Bath
GCH	knight grand cross of the Royal Guelphic Order	KCH	knight commander of the Royal Guelphic Order
GCHQ	government communications headquarters	KCIE	knight commander of the Order of the Indian Empire
GCIE	knight grand commander of the Order of the Indian Empire	KCMG	knight commander of the Order of St Michael and St George
GCMG	knight or dame grand cross of the Order of St Michael and St George	KCSI	knight commander of the Order of the Star of India
GCSE	general certificate of secondary education	KCVO	knight commander of the Royal Victorian Order
GCSI	knight grand commander of the Order of the Star of India	keV	kilo-electron-volt
GCStJ	bailiff or dame grand cross of the order of St John of Jerusalem	KG	knight of the Order of the Garter
		KGB	[Soviet committee of state security]
GCVO	knight or dame grand cross of the Royal Victorian Order	KH	knight of the Royal Guelphic Order
		KLM	Koninklijke Luchtvaart Maatschappij (Royal Dutch Air Lines)
GEC	General Electric Company	km	kilometre(s)
Ger.	German	KP	knight of the Order of St Patrick
GI	government (*or* general) issue	KS	Kansas
GMT	Greenwich mean time	KT	knight of the Order of the Thistle
GP	general practitioner	kt	knight
GPU	[Soviet special police unit]	KY	Kentucky
GSO	general staff officer	£	pound(s) sterling
Heb.	Hebrew	£E	Egyptian pound
HEICS	Honourable East India Company Service	L	lira *pl.* lire
HI	Hawaii	l. *pl.* ll.	line(s)
HIV	human immunodeficiency virus	LA	Lousiana
HK$	Hong Kong dollar	LAA	light anti-aircraft
HM	his / her majesty('s)	LAH	licentiate of the Apothecaries' Hall, Dublin
HMAS	his / her majesty's Australian ship	Lat.	Latin
HMNZS	his / her majesty's New Zealand ship	lb	pound(s), unit of weight
HMS	his / her majesty's ship	LDS	licence in dental surgery
HMSO	His / Her Majesty's Stationery Office	*lit.*	literally
HMV	His Master's Voice	LittB	bachelor of letters
Hon.	Honourable	LittD	doctor of letters
hp	horsepower	LKQCPI	licentiate of the King and Queen's College of Physicians, Ireland
hr	hour(s)	LLA	lady literate in arts
HRH	his / her royal highness	LLB	bachelor of laws
HTV	Harlech Television	LLD	doctor of laws
IA	Iowa	LLM	master of laws
ibid.	*ibidem*: in the same place	LM	licentiate in midwifery
ICI	Imperial Chemical Industries (Ltd)	LP	long-playing record
ID	Idaho	LRAM	licentiate of the Royal Academy of Music
IL	Illinois	LRCP	licentiate of the Royal College of Physicians
illus.	illustration	LRCPS (Glasgow)	licentiate of the Royal College of Physicians and Surgeons of Glasgow
illustr.	illustrated		
IN	Indiana	LRCS	licentiate of the Royal College of Surgeons
in.	inch(es)	LSA	licentiate of the Society of Apothecaries
Inc.	Incorporated	LSD	lysergic acid diethylamide
incl.	includes / including	LVO	lieutenant of the Royal Victorian Order
IOU	I owe you	M. *pl.* MM.	Monsieur *pl.* Messieurs
IQ	intelligence quotient	m	metre(s)
Ir£	Irish pound		
IRA	Irish Republican Army		

m. *pl.* mm.	membrane(s)		ND	North Dakota
MA	(1) Massachusetts; (2) master of arts		n.d.	no date
MAI	master of engineering		NE	Nebraska
MB	bachelor of medicine		*nem. con.*	*nemine contradicente*: unanimously
MBA	master of business administration		new ser.	new series
MBE	member of the Order of the British Empire		NH	New Hampshire
MC	Military Cross		NHS	National Health Service
MCC	Marylebone Cricket Club		NJ	New Jersey
MCh	master of surgery		NKVD	[Soviet people's commissariat for internal affairs]
MChir	master of surgery			
MCom	master of commerce		NM	New Mexico
MD	(1) doctor of medicine; (2) Maryland		nm	nanometre(s)
MDMA	methylenedioxymethamphetamine		no. *pl.* nos.	number(s)
ME	Maine		Nov	November
MEd	master of education		n.p.	no place [of publication]
MEng	master of engineering		NS	new style
MEP	member of the European parliament		NV	Nevada
MG	Morris Garages		NY	New York
MGM	Metro-Goldwyn-Mayer		NZBS	New Zealand Broadcasting Service
Mgr	Monsignor		OBE	officer of the Order of the British Empire
MI	(1) Michigan; (2) military intelligence		obit.	obituary
MI1c	[secret intelligence department]		Oct	October
MI5	[military intelligence department]		OCTU	officer cadets training unit
MI6	[secret intelligence department]		OECD	Organization for Economic Co-operation and Development
MI9	[secret escape service]			
MICE	member of the Institution of Civil Engineers		OEEC	Organization for European Economic Co-operation
MIEE	member of the Institution of Electrical Engineers			
			OFM	order of Friars Minor [Franciscans]
min.	minute(s)		OFMCap	Ordine Frati Minori Cappucini: member of the Capuchin order
Mk	mark			
ML	(1) licentiate of medicine; (2) master of laws		OH	Ohio
MLitt	master of letters		OK	Oklahoma
Mlle	Mademoiselle		O level	ordinary level [examination]
mm	millimetre(s)		OM	Order of Merit
Mme	Madame		OP	order of Preachers [Dominicans]
MN	Minnesota		op. *pl.* opp.	opus *pl.* opera
MO	Missouri		OPEC	Organization of Petroleum Exporting Countries
MOH	medical officer of health		OR	Oregon
MP	member of parliament		orig.	original
m.p.h.	miles per hour		OS	old style
MPhil	master of philosophy		OSB	Order of St Benedict
MRCP	member of the Royal College of Physicians		OTC	Officers' Training Corps
MRCS	member of the Royal College of Surgeons		OWS	Old Watercolour Society
MRCVS	member of the Royal College of Veterinary Surgeons		Oxon.	Oxoniensis
			p. *pl.* pp.	page(s)
MRIA	member of the Royal Irish Academy		PA	Pennsylvania
MS	(1) master of science; (2) Mississippi		p.a.	per annum
MS *pl.* MSS	manuscript(s)		para.	paragraph
MSc	master of science		PAYE	pay as you earn
MSc (Econ.)	master of science (economics)		pbk *pl.* pbks	paperback(s)
MT	Montana		*per.*	[during the] period
MusB	bachelor of music		PhD	doctor of philosophy
MusBac	bachelor of music		pl.	(1) plate(s); (2) plural
MusD	doctor of music		priv. coll.	private collection
MV	motor vessel		pt *pl.* pts	part(s)
MVO	member of the Royal Victorian Order		pubd	published
n. *pl.* nn.	note(s)		PVC	polyvinyl chloride
NAAFI	Navy, Army, and Air Force Institutes		q. *pl.* qq.	(1) question(s); (2) quire(s)
NASA	National Aeronautics and Space Administration		QC	queen's counsel
NATO	North Atlantic Treaty Organization		R	rand
NBC	National Broadcasting Corporation		R.	Rex / Regina
NC	North Carolina		*r*	recto
NCO	non-commissioned officer		*r.*	reigned / ruled
			RA	Royal Academy / Royal Academician

RAC	Royal Automobile Club
RAF	Royal Air Force
RAFVR	Royal Air Force Volunteer Reserve
RAM	[member of the] Royal Academy of Music
RAMC	Royal Army Medical Corps
RCA	Royal College of Art
RCNC	Royal Corps of Naval Constructors
RCOG	Royal College of Obstetricians and Gynaecologists
RDI	royal designer for industry
RE	Royal Engineers
repr. *pl.* reprs.	reprint(s) / reprinted
repro.	reproduced
rev.	revised / revised by / reviser / revision
Revd	Reverend
RHA	Royal Hibernian Academy
RI	(1) Rhode Island; (2) Royal Institute of Painters in Water-Colours
RIBA	Royal Institute of British Architects
RIN	Royal Indian Navy
RM	Reichsmark
RMS	Royal Mail steamer
RN	Royal Navy
RNA	ribonucleic acid
RNAS	Royal Naval Air Service
RNR	Royal Naval Reserve
RNVR	Royal Naval Volunteer Reserve
RO	Record Office
r.p.m.	revolutions per minute
RRS	royal research ship
Rs	rupees
RSA	(1) Royal Scottish Academician; (2) Royal Society of Arts
RSPCA	Royal Society for the Prevention of Cruelty to Animals
Rt Hon.	Right Honourable
Rt Revd	Right Reverend
RUC	Royal Ulster Constabulary
Russ.	Russian
RWS	Royal Watercolour Society
S4C	Sianel Pedwar Cymru
s.	shilling(s)
s.a.	*sub anno*: under the year
SABC	South African Broadcasting Corporation
SAS	Special Air Service
SC	South Carolina
ScD	doctor of science
S$	Singapore dollar
SD	South Dakota
sec.	second(s)
sel.	selected
sen.	senior
Sept	September
ser.	series
SHAPE	supreme headquarters allied powers, Europe
SIDRO	Société Internationale d'Énergie Hydro-Électrique
sig. *pl.* sigs.	signature(s)
sing.	singular
SIS	Secret Intelligence Service
SJ	Society of Jesus

Skr	Swedish krona
Span.	Spanish
SPCK	Society for Promoting Christian Knowledge
SS	(1) Santissimi; (2) Schutzstaffel; (3) steam ship
STB	bachelor of theology
STD	doctor of theology
STM	master of theology
STP	doctor of theology
supp.	supposedly
suppl. *pl.* suppls.	supplement(s)
s.v.	*sub verbo* / *sub voce*: under the word / heading
SY	steam yacht
TA	Territorial Army
TASS	[Soviet news agency]
TB	tuberculosis (*lit.* tubercle bacillus)
TD	(1) *teachtaí dála* (member of the Dáil); (2) territorial decoration
TN	Tennessee
TNT	trinitrotoluene
trans.	translated / translated by / translation / translator
TT	tourist trophy
TUC	Trades Union Congress
TX	Texas
U-boat	*Unterseeboot*: submarine
Ufa	Universum-Film AG
UMIST	University of Manchester Institute of Science and Technology
UN	United Nations
UNESCO	United Nations Educational, Scientific, and Cultural Organization
UNICEF	United Nations International Children's Emergency Fund
unpubd	unpublished
USS	United States ship
UT	Utah
v	verso
v.	versus
VA	Virginia
VAD	Voluntary Aid Detachment
VC	Victoria Cross
VE-day	victory in Europe day
Ven.	Venerable
VJ-day	victory over Japan day
vol. *pl.* vols.	volume(s)
VT	Vermont
WA	Washington [state]
WAAC	Women's Auxiliary Army Corps
WAAF	Women's Auxiliary Air Force
WEA	Workers' Educational Association
WHO	World Health Organization
WI	Wisconsin
WRAF	Women's Royal Air Force
WRNS	Women's Royal Naval Service
WV	West Virginia
WVS	Women's Voluntary Service
WY	Wyoming
¥	yen
YMCA	Young Men's Christian Association
YWCA	Young Women's Christian Association

2 *Institution abbreviations*

All Souls Oxf.	All Souls College, Oxford
AM Oxf.	Ashmolean Museum, Oxford
Balliol Oxf.	Balliol College, Oxford
BBC WAC	BBC Written Archives Centre, Reading
Beds. & Luton ARS	Bedfordshire and Luton Archives and Record Service, Bedford
Berks. RO	Berkshire Record Office, Reading
BFI	British Film Institute, London
BFI NFTVA	British Film Institute, London, National Film and Television Archive
BGS	British Geological Survey, Keyworth, Nottingham
Birm. CA	Birmingham Central Library, Birmingham City Archives
Birm. CL	Birmingham Central Library
BL	British Library, London
BL NSA	British Library, London, National Sound Archive
BL OIOC	British Library, London, Oriental and India Office Collections
BLPES	London School of Economics and Political Science, British Library of Political and Economic Science
BM	British Museum, London
Bodl. Oxf.	Bodleian Library, Oxford
Bodl. RH	Bodleian Library of Commonwealth and African Studies at Rhodes House, Oxford
Borth. Inst.	Borthwick Institute of Historical Research, University of York
Boston PL	Boston Public Library, Massachusetts
Bristol RO	Bristol Record Office
Bucks. RLSS	Buckinghamshire Records and Local Studies Service, Aylesbury
CAC Cam.	Churchill College, Cambridge, Churchill Archives Centre
Cambs. AS	Cambridgeshire Archive Service
CCC Cam.	Corpus Christi College, Cambridge
CCC Oxf.	Corpus Christi College, Oxford
Ches. & Chester ALSS	Cheshire and Chester Archives and Local Studies Service
Christ Church Oxf.	Christ Church, Oxford
Christies	Christies, London
City Westm. AC	City of Westminster Archives Centre, London
CKS	Centre for Kentish Studies, Maidstone
CLRO	Corporation of London Records Office
Coll. Arms	College of Arms, London
Col. U.	Columbia University, New York
Cornwall RO	Cornwall Record Office, Truro
Courtauld Inst.	Courtauld Institute of Art, London
CUL	Cambridge University Library
Cumbria AS	Cumbria Archive Service
Derbys. RO	Derbyshire Record Office, Matlock
Devon RO	Devon Record Office, Exeter
Dorset RO	Dorset Record Office, Dorchester
Duke U.	Duke University, Durham, North Carolina
Duke U., Perkins L.	Duke University, Durham, North Carolina, William R. Perkins Library
Durham Cath. CL	Durham Cathedral, chapter library
Durham RO	Durham Record Office
DWL	Dr Williams's Library, London
Essex RO	Essex Record Office
E. Sussex RO	East Sussex Record Office, Lewes
Eton	Eton College, Berkshire
FM Cam.	Fitzwilliam Museum, Cambridge
Folger	Folger Shakespeare Library, Washington, DC

Garr. Club	Garrick Club, London
Girton Cam.	Girton College, Cambridge
GL	Guildhall Library, London
Glos. RO	Gloucestershire Record Office, Gloucester
Gon. & Caius Cam.	Gonville and Caius College, Cambridge
Gov. Art Coll.	Government Art Collection
GS Lond.	Geological Society of London
Hants. RO	Hampshire Record Office, Winchester
Harris Man. Oxf.	Harris Manchester College, Oxford
Harvard TC	Harvard Theatre Collection, Harvard University, Cambridge, Massachusetts, Nathan Marsh Pusey Library
Harvard U.	Harvard University, Cambridge, Massachusetts
Harvard U., Houghton L.	Harvard University, Cambridge, Massachusetts, Houghton Library
Herefs. RO	Herefordshire Record Office, Hereford
Herts. ALS	Hertfordshire Archives and Local Studies, Hertford
Hist. Soc. Penn.	Historical Society of Pennsylvania, Philadelphia
HLRO	House of Lords Record Office, London
Hult. Arch.	Hulton Archive, London and New York
Hunt. L.	Huntington Library, San Marino, California
ICL	Imperial College, London
Inst. CE	Institution of Civil Engineers, London
Inst. EE	Institution of Electrical Engineers, London
IWM	Imperial War Museum, London
IWM FVA	Imperial War Museum, London, Film and Video Archive
IWM SA	Imperial War Museum, London, Sound Archive
JRL	John Rylands University Library of Manchester
King's AC Cam.	King's College Archives Centre, Cambridge
King's Cam.	King's College, Cambridge
King's Lond.	King's College, London
King's Lond., Liddell Hart C.	King's College, London, Liddell Hart Centre for Military Archives
Lancs. RO	Lancashire Record Office, Preston
L. Cong.	Library of Congress, Washington, DC
Leics. RO	Leicestershire, Leicester, and Rutland Record Office, Leicester
Lincs. Arch.	Lincolnshire Archives, Lincoln
Linn. Soc.	Linnean Society of London
LMA	London Metropolitan Archives
LPL	Lambeth Palace, London
Lpool RO	Liverpool Record Office and Local Studies Service
LUL	London University Library
Magd. Cam.	Magdalene College, Cambridge
Magd. Oxf.	Magdalen College, Oxford
Man. City Gall.	Manchester City Galleries
Man. CL	Manchester Central Library
Mass. Hist. Soc.	Massachusetts Historical Society, Boston
Merton Oxf.	Merton College, Oxford
MHS Oxf.	Museum of the History of Science, Oxford
Mitchell L., Glas.	Mitchell Library, Glasgow
Mitchell L., NSW	State Library of New South Wales, Sydney, Mitchell Library
Morgan L.	Pierpont Morgan Library, New York
NA Canada	National Archives of Canada, Ottawa
NA Ire.	National Archives of Ireland, Dublin
NAM	National Army Museum, London
NA Scot.	National Archives of Scotland, Edinburgh
News Int. RO	News International Record Office, London
NG Ire.	National Gallery of Ireland, Dublin

NG Scot.	National Gallery of Scotland, Edinburgh
NHM	Natural History Museum, London
NL Aus.	National Library of Australia, Canberra
NL Ire.	National Library of Ireland, Dublin
NL NZ	National Library of New Zealand, Wellington
NL NZ, Turnbull L.	National Library of New Zealand, Wellington, Alexander Turnbull Library
NL Scot.	National Library of Scotland, Edinburgh
NL Wales	National Library of Wales, Aberystwyth
NMG Wales	National Museum and Gallery of Wales, Cardiff
NMM	National Maritime Museum, London
Norfolk RO	Norfolk Record Office, Norwich
Northants. RO	Northamptonshire Record Office, Northampton
Northumbd RO	Northumberland Record Office
Notts. Arch.	Nottinghamshire Archives, Nottingham
NPG	National Portrait Gallery, London
NRA	National Archives, London, Historical Manuscripts Commission, National Register of Archives
Nuffield Oxf.	Nuffield College, Oxford
N. Yorks. CRO	North Yorkshire County Record Office, Northallerton
NYPL	New York Public Library
Oxf. UA	Oxford University Archives
Oxf. U. Mus. NH	Oxford University Museum of Natural History
Oxon. RO	Oxfordshire Record Office, Oxford
Pembroke Cam.	Pembroke College, Cambridge
PRO	National Archives, London, Public Record Office
PRO NIre.	Public Record Office for Northern Ireland, Belfast
Pusey Oxf.	Pusey House, Oxford
RA	Royal Academy of Arts, London
Ransom HRC	Harry Ransom Humanities Research Center, University of Texas, Austin
RAS	Royal Astronomical Society, London
RBG Kew	Royal Botanic Gardens, Kew, London
RCP Lond.	Royal College of Physicians of London
RCS Eng.	Royal College of Surgeons of England, London
RGS	Royal Geographical Society, London
RIBA	Royal Institute of British Architects, London
RIBA BAL	Royal Institute of British Architects, London, British Architectural Library
Royal Arch.	Royal Archives, Windsor Castle, Berkshire [by gracious permission of her majesty the queen]
Royal Irish Acad.	Royal Irish Academy, Dublin
Royal Scot. Acad.	Royal Scottish Academy, Edinburgh
RS	Royal Society, London
RSA	Royal Society of Arts, London
RS Friends, Lond.	Religious Society of Friends, London
St Ant. Oxf.	St Antony's College, Oxford
St John Cam.	St John's College, Cambridge
S. Antiquaries, Lond.	Society of Antiquaries of London
Sci. Mus.	Science Museum, London
Scot. NPG	Scottish National Portrait Gallery, Edinburgh
Scott Polar RI	University of Cambridge, Scott Polar Research Institute
Sheff. Arch.	Sheffield Archives
Shrops. RRC	Shropshire Records and Research Centre, Shrewsbury
SOAS	School of Oriental and African Studies, London
Som. ARS	Somerset Archive and Record Service, Taunton
Staffs. RO	Staffordshire Record Office, Stafford
Suffolk RO	Suffolk Record Office
Surrey HC	Surrey History Centre, Woking
TCD	Trinity College, Dublin
Trinity Cam.	Trinity College, Cambridge
U. Aberdeen	University of Aberdeen
U. Birm.	University of Birmingham
U. Birm. L.	University of Birmingham Library
U. Cal.	University of California
U. Cam.	University of Cambridge
UCL	University College, London
U. Durham	University of Durham
U. Durham L.	University of Durham Library
U. Edin.	University of Edinburgh
U. Edin., New Coll.	University of Edinburgh, New College
U. Edin., New Coll. L.	University of Edinburgh, New College Library
U. Edin. L.	University of Edinburgh Library
U. Glas.	University of Glasgow
U. Glas. L.	University of Glasgow Library
U. Hull	University of Hull
U. Hull, Brynmor Jones L.	University of Hull, Brynmor Jones Library
U. Leeds	University of Leeds
U. Leeds, Brotherton L.	University of Leeds, Brotherton Library
U. Lond.	University of London
U. Lpool	University of Liverpool
U. Lpool L.	University of Liverpool Library
U. Mich.	University of Michigan, Ann Arbor
U. Mich., Clements L.	University of Michigan, Ann Arbor, William L. Clements Library
U. Newcastle	University of Newcastle upon Tyne
U. Newcastle, Robinson L.	University of Newcastle upon Tyne, Robinson Library
U. Nott.	University of Nottingham
U. Nott. L.	University of Nottingham Library
U. Oxf.	University of Oxford
U. Reading	University of Reading
U. Reading L.	University of Reading Library
U. St Andr.	University of St Andrews
U. St Andr. L.	University of St Andrews Library
U. Southampton	University of Southampton
U. Southampton L.	University of Southampton Library
U. Sussex	University of Sussex, Brighton
U. Texas	University of Texas, Austin
U. Wales	University of Wales
U. Warwick Mod. RC	University of Warwick, Coventry, Modern Records Centre
V&A	Victoria and Albert Museum, London
V&A NAL	Victoria and Albert Museum, London, National Art Library
Warks. CRO	Warwickshire County Record Office, Warwick
Wellcome L.	Wellcome Library for the History and Understanding of Medicine, London
Westm. DA	Westminster Diocesan Archives, London
Wilts. & Swindon RO	Wiltshire and Swindon Record Office, Trowbridge
Worcs. RO	Worcestershire Record Office, Worcester
W. Sussex RO	West Sussex Record Office, Chichester
W. Yorks. AS	West Yorkshire Archive Service
Yale U.	Yale University, New Haven, Connecticut
Yale U., Beinecke L.	Yale University, New Haven, Connecticut, Beinecke Rare Book and Manuscript Library
Yale U. CBA	Yale University, New Haven, Connecticut, Yale Center for British Art

3 Bibliographic abbreviations

Adams, *Drama* W. D. Adams, *A dictionary of the drama*, 1: *A–G* (1904); 2: *H–Z* (1956) [vol. 2 microfilm only]

AFM J O'Donovan, ed. and trans., *Annala rioghachta Eireann | Annals of the kingdom of Ireland by the four masters*, 7 vols. (1848–51); 2nd edn (1856); 3rd edn (1990)

Allibone, *Dict.* S. A. Allibone, *A critical dictionary of English literature and British and American authors*, 3 vols. (1859–71); suppl. by J. F. Kirk, 2 vols. (1891)

ANB J. A. Garraty and M. C. Carnes, eds., *American national biography*, 24 vols. (1999)

Anderson, *Scot. nat.* W. Anderson, *The Scottish nation, or, The surnames, families, literature, honours, and biographical history of the people of Scotland*, 3 vols. (1859–63)

Ann. mon. H. R. Luard, ed., *Annales monastici*, 5 vols., Rolls Series, 36 (1864–9)

Ann. Ulster S. Mac Airt and G. Mac Niocaill, eds., *Annals of Ulster (to AD 1131)* (1983)

APC *Acts of the privy council of England*, new ser., 46 vols. (1890–1964)

APS *The acts of the parliaments of Scotland*, 12 vols. in 13 (1814–75)

Arber, *Regs. Stationers* F. Arber, ed., *A transcript of the registers of the Company of Stationers of London, 1554–1640 AD*, 5 vols. (1875–94)

ArchR *Architectural Review*

ASC D. Whitelock, D. C. Douglas, and S. I. Tucker, ed. and trans., *The Anglo-Saxon Chronicle: a revised translation* (1961)

AS chart. P. H. Sawyer, *Anglo-Saxon charters: an annotated list and bibliography*, Royal Historical Society Guides and Handbooks (1968)

AusDB D. Pike and others, eds., *Australian dictionary of biography*, 16 vols. (1966–2002)

Baker, *Serjeants* J. H. Baker, *The order of serjeants at law*, SeldS, suppl. ser. 5 (1984)

Bale, *Cat.* J. Bale, *Scriptorum illustrium Maioris Brytannie, quam nunc Angliam et Scotiam vocant: catalogus*, 2 vols. in 1 (Basel, 1557–9); facs. edn (1971)

Bale, *Index* J. Bale, *Index Britanniae scriptorum*, ed. R. L. Poole and M. Bateson (1902); facs. edn (1990)

BBCS *Bulletin of the Board of Celtic Studies*

BDMBR J. O. Baylen and N. J. Gossman, eds., *Biographical dictionary of modern British radicals*, 3 vols. in 4 (1979–88)

Bede, *Hist. eccl.* *Bede's Ecclesiastical history of the English people*, ed. and trans. B. Colgrave and R. A. B. Mynors, OMT (1969); repr. (1991)

Bénézit, *Dict.* E. Bénézit, *Dictionnaire critique et documentaire des peintres, sculpteurs, dessinateurs et graveurs*, 3 vols. (Paris, 1911–23); new edn, 8 vols. (1948–66), repr. (1966); 3rd edn, rev. and enl., 10 vols. (1976); 4th edn, 14 vols. (1999)

BIHR *Bulletin of the Institute of Historical Research*

Birch, *Seals* W. de Birch, *Catalogue of seals in the department of manuscripts in the British Museum*, 6 vols. (1887–1900)

Bishop Burnet's History *Bishop Burnet's History of his own time*, ed. M. J. Routh, 2nd edn, 6 vols. (1833)

Blackwood *Blackwood's [Edinburgh] Magazine*, 328 vols. (1817–1980)

Blain, Clements & Grundy, *Feminist comp.* V. Blain, P. Clements, and I. Grundy, eds., *The feminist companion to literature in English* (1990)

BL cat. *The British Library general catalogue of printed books* [in 360 vols. with suppls., also CD-ROM and online]

BMJ *British Medical Journal*

Boase & Courtney, *Bibl. Corn.* G. C. Boase and W. P. Courtney, *Bibliotheca Cornubiensis: a catalogue of the writings … of Cornishmen*, 3 vols. (1874–82)

Boase, *Mod. Eng. biog.* F. Boase, *Modern English biography: containing many thousand concise memoirs of persons who have died since the year 1850*, 6 vols. (privately printed, Truro, 1892–1921); repr. (1965)

Boswell, *Life* *Boswell's Life of Johnson: together with Journal of a tour to the Hebrides and Johnson's Diary of a journey into north Wales*, ed. G. B. Hill, enl. edn, rev. L. F. Powell, 6 vols. (1934–50); 2nd edn (1964); repr. (1971)

Brown & Stratton, *Brit. mus.* J. D. Brown and S. S. Stratton, *British musical biography* (1897)

Bryan, *Painters* M. Bryan, *A biographical and critical dictionary of painters and engravers*, 2 vols. (1816); new edn, ed. G. Stanley (1849); new edn, ed. R. E. Graves and W. Armstrong, 2 vols. (1886–9); [4th edn], ed. G. C. Williamson, 5 vols. (1903–5) [various reprs.]

Burke, *Gen. GB* J. Burke, *A genealogical and heraldic history of the commoners of Great Britain and Ireland*, 4 vols. (1833–8); new edn as *A genealogical and heraldic dictionary of the landed gentry of Great Britain and Ireland*, 3 vols. [1843–9] [many later edns]

Burke, *Gen. Ire.* J. B. Burke, *A genealogical and heraldic history of the landed gentry of Ireland* (1899); 2nd edn (1904); 3rd edn (1912); 4th edn (1958); 5th edn as *Burke's Irish family records* (1976)

Burke, *Peerage* J. Burke, *A general [later edns A genealogical] and heraldic dictionary of the peerage and baronetage of the United Kingdom* [later edns *the British empire*] (1829–)

Burney, *Hist. mus.* C. Burney, *A general history of music, from the earliest ages to the present period*, 4 vols. (1776–89)

Burtchaell & Sadleir, *Alum. Dubl.* G. D. Burtchaell and T. U. Sadleir, *Alumni Dublinenses: a register of the students, graduates, and provosts of Trinity College* (1924); [2nd edn], with suppl., in 2 pts (1935)

Calamy rev. A. G. Matthews, *Calamy revised* (1934); repr. (1988)

CCI *Calendar of confirmations and inventories granted and given up in the several commissariots of Scotland* (1876–)

CClR *Calendar of the close rolls preserved in the Public Record Office*, 47 vols. (1892–1963)

CDS J. Bain, ed., *Calendar of documents relating to Scotland*, 4 vols., PRO (1881–8); suppl. vol. 5, ed. G. G. Simpson and J. D. Galbraith [1986]

CEPR letters W. H. Bliss, C. Johnson, and J. Twemlow, eds., *Calendar of entries in the papal registers relating to Great Britain and Ireland: papal letters* (1893–)

CGPLA *Calendars of the grants of probate and letters of administration* [in 4 ser.: *England & Wales, Northern Ireland, Ireland*, and *Éire*]

Chambers, *Scots.* R. Chambers, ed., *A biographical dictionary of eminent Scotsmen*, 4 vols. (1832–5)

Chancery records chancery records pubd by the PRO

Chancery records (RC) chancery records pubd by the Record Commissions

CIPM	*Calendar of inquisitions post mortem*, [20 vols.], PRO (1904–); also *Henry VII*, 3 vols. (1898–1955)
Clarendon, *Hist. rebellion*	E. Hyde, earl of Clarendon, *The history of the rebellion and civil wars in England*, 6 vols. (1888); repr. (1958) and (1992)
Cobbett, *Parl. hist.*	W. Cobbett and J. Wright, eds., *Cobbett's Parliamentary history of England*, 36 vols. (1806–1820)
Colvin, *Archs.*	H. Colvin, *A biographical dictionary of British architects, 1600–1840*, 3rd edn (1995)
Cooper, *Ath. Cantab.*	C. H. Cooper and T. Cooper, *Athenae Cantabrigienses*, 3 vols. (1858–1913); repr. (1967)
CPR	*Calendar of the patent rolls preserved in the Public Record Office* (1891–)
Crockford	*Crockford's Clerical Directory*
CS	Camden Society
CSP	*Calendar of state papers* [in 11 ser.: *domestic, Scotland, Scottish series, Ireland, colonial, Commonwealth, foreign, Spain* [at Simancas], *Rome, Milan,* and *Venice*]
CYS	Canterbury and York Society
DAB	*Dictionary of American biography*, 21 vols. (1928–36), repr. in 11 vols. (1964); 10 suppls. (1944–96)
DBB	D. J. Jeremy, ed., *Dictionary of business biography*, 5 vols. (1984–6)
DCB	G. W. Brown and others, *Dictionary of Canadian biography*, [14 vols.] (1966–)
Debrett's Peerage	*Debrett's Peerage* (1803–) [sometimes *Debrett's Illustrated peerage*]
Desmond, *Botanists*	R. Desmond, *Dictionary of British and Irish botanists and horticulturists* (1977); rev. edn (1994)
Dir. Brit. archs.	A. Felstead, J. Franklin, and L. Pinfield, eds., *Directory of British architects, 1834–1900* (1993); 2nd edn, ed. A. Brodie and others, 2 vols. (2001)
DLB	J. M. Bellamy and J. Saville, eds., *Dictionary of labour biography*, [10 vols.] (1972–)
DLitB	Dictionary of Literary Biography
DNB	*Dictionary of national biography*, 63 vols. (1885–1900), suppl., 3 vols. (1901); repr. in 22 vols. (1908–9); 10 further suppls. (1912–96); *Missing persons* (1993)
DNZB	W. H. Oliver and C. Orange, eds., *The dictionary of New Zealand biography*, 5 vols. (1990–2000)
DSAB	W. J. de Kock and others, eds., *Dictionary of South African biography*, 5 vols. (1968–87)
DSB	C. C. Gillispie and F. L. Holmes, eds., *Dictionary of scientific biography*, 16 vols. (1970–80); repr. in 8 vols. (1981); 2 vol. suppl. (1990)
DSBB	A. Slaven and S. Checkland, eds., *Dictionary of Scottish business biography, 1860–1960*, 2 vols. (1986–90)
DSCHT	N. M. de S. Cameron and others, eds., *Dictionary of Scottish church history and theology* (1993)
Dugdale, *Monasticon*	W. Dugdale, *Monasticon Anglicanum*, 3 vols. (1655–72); 2nd edn, 3 vols. (1661–82); new edn, ed. J. Caley, J. Ellis, and B. Bandinel, 6 vols. in 8 pts (1817–30); repr. (1846) and (1970)

DWB	J. E. Lloyd and others, eds., *Dictionary of Welsh biography down to 1940* (1959) [Eng. trans. of *Y bywgraffiadur Cymreig hyd 1940*, 2nd edn (1954)]
EdinR	*Edinburgh Review, or, Critical Journal*
EETS	Early English Text Society
Emden, *Cam.*	A. B. Emden, *A biographical register of the University of Cambridge to 1500* (1963)
Emden, *Oxf.*	A. B. Emden, *A biographical register of the University of Oxford to AD 1500*, 3 vols. (1957–9); also *A biographical register of the University of Oxford, AD 1501 to 1540* (1974)
EngHR	*English Historical Review*
Engraved Brit. ports.	F. M. O'Donoghue and H. M. Hake, *Catalogue of engraved British portraits preserved in the department of prints and drawings in the British Museum*, 6 vols. (1908–25)
ER	The English Reports, 178 vols. (1900–32)
ESTC	*English short title catalogue, 1475–1800* [CD-ROM and online]
Evelyn, *Diary*	*The diary of John Evelyn*, ed. E. S. De Beer, 6 vols. (1955); repr. (2000)
Farington, *Diary*	*The diary of Joseph Farington*, ed. K. Garlick and others, 17 vols. (1978–98)
Fasti Angl. (Hardy)	J. Le Neve, *Fasti ecclesiae Anglicanae*, ed. T. D. Hardy, 3 vols. (1854)
Fasti Angl., 1066–1300	[J. Le Neve], *Fasti ecclesiae Anglicanae, 1066–1300*, ed. D. E. Greenway and J. S. Barrow, [8 vols.] (1968–)
Fasti Angl., 1300–1541	[J. Le Neve], *Fasti ecclesiae Anglicanae, 1300–1541*, 12 vols. (1962–7)
Fasti Angl., 1541–1857	[J. Le Neve], *Fasti ecclesiae Anglicanae, 1541–1857*, ed. J. M. Horn, D. M. Smith, and D. S. Bailey, [9 vols.] (1969–)
Fasti Scot.	H. Scott, *Fasti ecclesiae Scoticanae*, 3 vols. in 6 (1871); new edn, [11 vols.] (1915–)
FO List	*Foreign Office List*
Fortescue, *Brit. army*	J. W. Fortescue, *A history of the British army*, 13 vols. (1899–1930)
Foss, *Judges*	E. Foss, *The judges of England*, 9 vols. (1848–64); repr. (1966)
Foster, *Alum. Oxon.*	J. Foster, ed., *Alumni Oxonienses: the members of the University of Oxford, 1715–1886*, 4 vols. (1887–8); later edn (1891); also *Alumni Oxonienses … 1500–1714*, 4 vols. (1891–2); 8 vol. repr. (1968) and (2000)
Fuller, *Worthies*	T. Fuller, *The history of the worthies of England*, 4 pts (1662); new edn, 2 vols., ed. J. Nichols (1811); new edn, 3 vols., ed. P. A. Nuttall (1840); repr. (1965)
GEC, *Baronetage*	G. E. Cokayne, *Complete baronetage*, 6 vols. (1900–09); repr. (1983) [microprint]
GEC, *Peerage*	G. E. C. [G. E. Cokayne], *The complete peerage of England, Scotland, Ireland, Great Britain, and the United Kingdom*, 8 vols. (1887–98); new edn, ed. V. Gibbs and others, 14 vols. in 15 (1910–98); microprint repr. (1982) and (1987)
Genest, *Eng. stage*	J. Genest, *Some account of the English stage from the Restoration in 1660 to 1830*, 10 vols. (1832); repr. [New York, 1965]
Gillow, *Lit. biog. hist.*	J. Gillow, *A literary and biographical history or bibliographical dictionary of the English Catholics, from the breach with Rome, in 1534, to the present time*, 5 vols. [1885–1902]; repr. (1961); repr. with preface by C. Gillow (1999)
Gir. Camb. opera	*Giraldi Cambrensis opera*, ed. J. S. Brewer, J. F. Dimock, and G. F. Warner, 8 vols., Rolls Series, 21 (1861–91)
GJ	*Geographical Journal*

Gladstone, *Diaries* — *The Gladstone diaries: with cabinet minutes and prime-ministerial correspondence*, ed. M. R. D. Foot and H. C. G. Matthew, 14 vols. (1968–94)

GM — *Gentleman's Magazine*

Graves, *Artists* — A. Graves, ed., *A dictionary of artists who have exhibited works in the principal London exhibitions of oil paintings from 1760 to 1880* (1884); new edn (1895); 3rd edn (1901); facs. edn (1969); repr. [1970], (1973), and (1984)

Graves, *Brit. Inst.* — A. Graves, *The British Institution, 1806–1867: a complete dictionary of contributors and their work from the foundation of the institution* (1875); facs. edn (1908); repr. (1969)

Graves, *RA exhibitors* — A. Graves, *The Royal Academy of Arts: a complete dictionary of contributors and their work from its foundation in 1769 to 1904*, 8 vols. (1905–6); repr. in 4 vols. (1970) and (1972)

Graves, *Soc. Artists* — A. Graves, *The Society of Artists of Great Britain, 1760–1791, the Free Society of Artists, 1761–1783: a complete dictionary* (1907); facs. edn (1969)

Greaves & Zaller, *BDBR* — R. L. Greaves and R. Zaller, eds., *Biographical dictionary of British radicals in the seventeenth century*, 3 vols. (1982–4)

Grove, *Dict. mus.* — G. Grove, ed., *A dictionary of music and musicians*, 5 vols. (1878–90); 2nd edn, ed. J. A. Fuller Maitland (1904–10); 3rd edn, ed. H. C. Colles (1927); 4th edn with suppl. (1940); 5th edn, ed. E. Blom, 9 vols. (1954); suppl. (1961) [see also *New Grove*]

Hall, *Dramatic ports.* — L. A. Hall, *Catalogue of dramatic portraits in the theatre collection of the Harvard College library*, 4 vols. (1930–34)

Hansard — *Hansard's parliamentary debates*, ser. 1–5 (1803–)

Highfill, Burnim & Langhans, *BDA* — P. H. Highfill, K. A. Burnim, and E. A. Langhans, *A biographical dictionary of actors, actresses, musicians, dancers, managers, and other stage personnel in London, 1660–1800*, 16 vols. (1973–93)

Hist. U. Oxf. — T. H. Aston, ed., *The history of the University of Oxford*, 8 vols. (1984–2000) [1: *The early Oxford schools*, ed. J. I. Catto (1984); 2: *Late medieval Oxford*, ed. J. I. Catto and R. Evans (1992); 3: *The collegiate university*, ed. J. McConica (1986); 4: *Seventeenth-century Oxford*, ed. N. Tyacke (1997); 5: *The eighteenth century*, ed. L. S. Sutherland and L. G. Mitchell (1986); 6–7: *Nineteenth-century Oxford*, ed. M. G. Brock and M. C. Curthoys (1997–2000); 8: *The twentieth century*, ed. B. Harrison (2000)]

HJ — *Historical Journal*

HMC — Historical Manuscripts Commission

Holdsworth, *Eng. law* — W. S. Holdsworth, *A history of English law*, ed. A. L. Goodhart and H. L. Hanbury, 17 vols. (1903–72)

HoP, *Commons* — *The history of parliament: the House of Commons* [1386–1421, ed. J. S. Roskell, L. Clark, and C. Rawcliffe, 4 vols. (1992); 1509–1558, ed. S. T. Bindoff, 3 vols. (1982); 1558–1603, ed. P. W. Hasler, 3 vols. (1981); 1660–1690, ed. B. D. Henning, 3 vols. (1983); 1690–1715, ed. D. W. Hayton, E. Cruickshanks, and S. Handley, 5 vols. (2002); 1715–1754, ed. R. Sedgwick, 2 vols. (1970); 1754–1790, ed. L. Namier and J. Brooke, 3 vols. (1964), repr. (1985); 1790–1820, ed. R. G. Thorne, 5 vols. (1986); in draft (used with permission): 1422–1504, 1604–1629, 1640–1660, and 1820–1832]

IGI — *International Genealogical Index*, Church of Jesus Christ of the Latterday Saints

ILN — *Illustrated London News*

IMC — Irish Manuscripts Commission

Irving, *Scots.* — J. Irving, ed., *The book of Scotsmen eminent for achievements in arms and arts, church and state, law, legislation and literature, commerce, science, travel and philanthropy* (1881)

JCS — *Journal of the Chemical Society*

JHC — *Journals of the House of Commons*

JHL — *Journals of the House of Lords*

John of Worcester, *Chron.* — *The chronicle of John of Worcester*, ed. R. R. Darlington and P. McGurk, trans. J. Bray and P. McGurk, 3 vols., OMT (1995–) [vol. 1 forthcoming]

Keeler, *Long Parliament* — M. F. Keeler, *The Long Parliament, 1640–1641: a biographical study of its members* (1954)

Kelly, *Handbk* — *The upper ten thousand: an alphabetical list of all members of noble families*, 3 vols. (1875–7); continued as *Kelly's handbook of the upper ten thousand for 1878* [1879], 2 vols. (1878–9); continued as *Kelly's handbook to the titled, landed and official classes*, 94 vols. (1880–1973)

LondG — *London Gazette*

LP Henry VIII — J. S. Brewer, J. Gairdner, and R. H. Brodie, eds., *Letters and papers, foreign and domestic, of the reign of Henry VIII*, 23 vols. in 38 (1862–1932); repr. (1965)

Mallalieu, *Watercolour artists* — H. L. Mallalieu, *The dictionary of British watercolour artists up to 1820*, 3 vols. (1976–90); vol. 1, 2nd edn (1986)

Memoirs FRS — *Biographical Memoirs of Fellows of the Royal Society*

MGH — Monumenta Germaniae Historica

MT — *Musical Times*

Munk, *Roll* — W. Munk, *The roll of the Royal College of Physicians of London*, 2 vols. (1861); 2nd edn, 3 vols. (1878)

N&Q — *Notes and Queries*

New Grove — S. Sadie, ed., *The new Grove dictionary of music and musicians*, 20 vols. (1980); 2nd edn, 29 vols. (2001) [also online edn; see also Grove, *Dict. mus.*]

Nichols, *Illustrations* — J. Nichols and J. B. Nichols, *Illustrations of the literary history of the eighteenth century*, 8 vols. (1817–58)

Nichols, *Lit. anecdotes* — J. Nichols, *Literary anecdotes of the eighteenth century*, 9 vols. (1812–16); facs. edn (1966)

Obits. FRS — *Obituary Notices of Fellows of the Royal Society*

O'Byrne, *Naval biog. dict.* — W. R. O'Byrne, *A naval biographical dictionary* (1849); repr. (1990); [2nd edn], 2 vols. (1861)

OHS — Oxford Historical Society

Old Westminsters — *The record of Old Westminsters*, 1–2, ed. G. F. R. Barker and A. H. Stenning (1928); suppl. 1, ed. J. B. Whitmore and G. R. Y. Radcliffe [1938]; 3, ed. J. B. Whitmore, G. R. Y. Radcliffe, and D. C. Simpson (1963); suppl. 2, ed. F. E. Pagan (1978); 4, ed. F. E. Pagan and H. E. Pagan (1992)

OMT — Oxford Medieval Texts

Ordericus Vitalis, *Eccl. hist.* — *The ecclesiastical history of Orderic Vitalis*, ed. and trans. M. Chibnall, 6 vols., OMT (1969–80); repr. (1990)

Paris, *Chron.* — *Matthaei Parisiensis, monachi sancti Albani, chronica majora*, ed. H. R. Luard, Rolls Series, 7 vols. (1872–83)

Parl. papers — *Parliamentary papers* (1801–)

PBA — *Proceedings of the British Academy*

Pepys, *Diary*	*The diary of Samuel Pepys*, ed. R. Latham and W. Matthews, 11 vols. (1970–83); repr. (1995) and (2000)
Pevsner	N. Pevsner and others, Buildings of England series
PICE	*Proceedings of the Institution of Civil Engineers*
Pipe rolls	*The great roll of the pipe for . . .*, PRSoc. (1884–)
PRO	Public Record Office
PRS	*Proceedings of the Royal Society of London*
PRSoc.	Pipe Roll Society
PTRS	*Philosophical Transactions of the Royal Society*
QR	*Quarterly Review*
RC	Record Commissions
Redgrave, *Artists*	S. Redgrave, *A dictionary of artists of the English school* (1874); rev. edn (1878); repr. (1970)
Reg. Oxf.	C. W. Boase and A. Clark, eds., *Register of the University of Oxford*, 5 vols., OHS, 1, 10–12, 14 (1885–9)
Reg. PCS	J. H. Burton and others, eds., *The register of the privy council of Scotland*, 1st ser., 14 vols. (1877–98); 2nd ser., 8 vols. (1899–1908); 3rd ser., [16 vols.] (1908–70)
Reg. RAN	H. W. C. Davis and others, eds., *Regesta regum Anglo-Normannorum, 1066–1154*, 4 vols. (1913–69)
RIBA Journal	*Journal of the Royal Institute of British Architects* [later *RIBA Journal*]
RotP	J. Strachey, ed., *Rotuli parliamentorum ut et petitiones, et placita in parliamento*, 6 vols. (1767–77)
RotS	D. Macpherson, J. Caley, and W. Illingworth, eds., *Rotuli Scotiae in Turri Londinensi et in domo capitulari Westmonasteriensi asservati*, 2 vols., RC, 14 (1814–19)
RS	Record(s) Society
Rymer, *Foedera*	T. Rymer and R. Sanderson, eds., *Foedera, conventiones, literae et cuiuscunque generis acta publica inter reges Angliae et alios quosvis imperatores, reges, pontifices, principes, vel communitates*, 20 vols. (1704–35); 2nd edn, 20 vols. (1726–35); 3rd edn, 10 vols. (1739–45); facs. edn (1967); new edn, ed. A. Clarke, J. Caley, and F. Holbrooke, 4 vols., RC, 50 (1816–30)
Sainty, *Judges*	J. Sainty, ed., *The judges of England, 1272–1990*, SeldS, suppl. ser., 10 (1993)
Sainty, *King's counsel*	J. Sainty, ed., *A list of English law officers and king's counsel*, SeldS, suppl. ser., 7 (1987)
SCH	Studies in Church History
Scots peerage	J. B. Paul, ed. *The Scots peerage, founded on Wood's edition of Sir Robert Douglas's Peerage of Scotland, containing an historical and genealogical account of the nobility of that kingdom*, 9 vols. (1904–14)
SeldS	Selden Society
SHR	*Scottish Historical Review*
State trials	T. B. Howell and T. J. Howell, eds., *Cobbett's Complete collection of state trials*, 34 vols. (1809–28)
STC, 1475–1640	A. W. Pollard, G. R. Redgrave, and others, eds., *A short-title catalogue of . . . English books . . . 1475–1640* (1926); 2nd edn, ed. W. A. Jackson, F. S. Ferguson, and K. F. Pantzer, 3 vols. (1976–91) [see also Wing, *STC*]
STS	Scottish Text Society
SurtS	Surtees Society
Symeon of Durham, *Opera*	*Symeonis monachi opera omnia*, ed. T. Arnold, 2 vols., Rolls Series, 75 (1882–5); repr. (1965)
Tanner, *Bibl. Brit.-Hib.*	T. Tanner, *Bibliotheca Britannico-Hibernica*, ed. D. Wilkins (1748); repr. (1963)
Thieme & Becker, *Allgemeines Lexikon*	U. Thieme, F. Becker, and H. Vollmer, eds., *Allgemeines Lexikon der bildenden Künstler von der Antike bis zur Gegenwart*, 37 vols. (Leipzig, 1907–50); repr. (1961–5), (1983), and (1992)
Thurloe, *State papers*	*A collection of the state papers of John Thurloe*, ed. T. Birch, 7 vols. (1742)
TLS	*Times Literary Supplement*
Tout, *Admin. hist.*	T. F. Tout, *Chapters in the administrative history of mediaeval England: the wardrobe, the chamber, and the small seals*, 6 vols. (1920–33); repr. (1967)
TRHS	*Transactions of the Royal Historical Society*
VCH	H. A. Doubleday and others, eds., *The Victoria history of the counties of England*, [88 vols.] (1900–)
Venn, *Alum. Cant.*	J. Venn and J. A. Venn, *Alumni Cantabrigienses: a biographical list of all known students, graduates, and holders of office at the University of Cambridge, from the earliest times to 1900*, 10 vols. (1922–54); repr. in 2 vols. (1974–8)
Vertue, *Note books*	[G. Vertue], *Note books*, ed. K. Esdaile, earl of Ilchester, and H. M. Hake, 6 vols., Walpole Society, 18, 20, 22, 24, 26, 30 (1930–55)
VF	*Vanity Fair*
Walford, *County families*	E. Walford, *The county families of the United Kingdom, or, Royal manual of the titled and untitled aristocracy of Great Britain and Ireland* (1860)
Walker rev.	A. G. Matthews, *Walker revised: being a revision of John Walker's Sufferings of the clergy during the grand rebellion, 1642–60* (1948); repr. (1988)
Walpole, *Corr.*	*The Yale edition of Horace Walpole's correspondence*, ed. W. S. Lewis, 48 vols. (1937–83)
Ward, *Men of the reign*	T. H. Ward, ed., *Men of the reign: a biographical dictionary of eminent persons of British and colonial birth who have died during the reign of Queen Victoria* (1885); repr. (Graz, 1968)
Waterhouse, *18c painters*	E. Waterhouse, *The dictionary of 18th century painters in oils and crayons* (1981); repr. as *British 18th century painters in oils and crayons* (1991), vol. 2 of *Dictionary of British art*
Watt, *Bibl. Brit.*	R. Watt, *Bibliotheca Britannica, or, A general index to British and foreign literature*, 4 vols. (1824) [many reprs.]
Wellesley index	W. E. Houghton, ed., *The Wellesley index to Victorian periodicals, 1824–1900*, 5 vols. (1966–89); new edn (1999) [CD-ROM]
Wing, *STC*	D. Wing, ed., *Short-title catalogue of . . . English books . . . 1641–1700*, 3 vols. (1945–51); 2nd edn (1972–88); rev. and enl. edn, ed. J. J. Morrison, C. W. Nelson, and M. Seccombe, 4 vols. (1994–8) [see also *STC, 1475–1640*]
Wisden	*John Wisden's Cricketer's Almanack*
Wood, *Ath. Oxon.*	A. Wood, *Athenae Oxonienses . . . to which are added the Fasti*, 2 vols. (1691–2); 2nd edn (1721); new edn, 4 vols., ed. P. Bliss (1813–20); repr. (1967) and (1969)
Wood, *Vic. painters*	C. Wood, *Dictionary of Victorian painters* (1971); 2nd edn (1978); 3rd edn as *Victorian painters*, 2 vols. (1995), vol. 4 of *Dictionary of British art*
WW	*Who's who* (1849–)
WWBMP	M. Stenton and S. Lees, eds., *Who's who of British members of parliament*, 4 vols. (1976–81)
WWW	*Who was who* (1929–)

Kebell, Thomas (*c*.1439–1500), lawyer, was the third son of Walter Kebell and his second wife, Agnes, daughter of John Folville of Rearsby in Leicestershire. His father's background is hazy but from at least 1420 Walter was steward of the honour of Abergavenny, the dower of Joan Beauchamp, Lady Bergavenny. He later served the lord treasurer, Richard, Lord Cromwell, but it was probably the Beauchamp connection that secured his marriage to Agnes, the daughter of the royal coroner for Leicestershire, and eventually half the estates of her long-established county family. About 1454 Thomas Kebell entered the Inner Temple, and his name came to figure prominently in records connected with the educational work of the inn. He became a bencher, and a partial text of what is probably his second law reading exists in the British Library (BL, Hargrave MS 87, fols. 302–8). Kebell built a highly successful midlands practice upon service to the locally dominant Hastings retinue, as both attorney-general to the family and as the counsel of choice to the Hastings affinity. He remained a client of the Hastings family until his death.

From 1477 Kebell was retained by the duchy of Lancaster. In 1483, probably through the influence of William, Lord Hastings, Kebell replaced Richard Empson as duchy attorney-general but was promoted serjeant-at-law in 1486 to allow Empson to be restored to office. Commissioned as justice of assize on the northern circuit from February 1494, Kebell became second justice at Lancaster in 1495. In June of that year he took the oath as a royal counsellor and in November became a king's serjeant, sitting in the Lords in that capacity in 1497. In 1499 he was appointed justice at Chester.

Inheriting no land himself, Thomas Kebell was the fortunate beneficiary of a gift in the late 1460s of a sizeable estate in and around Great Stretton near Leicester. The donor was a distant relative, Richard Hotoft, esquire, of Humberstone, who may already have financed Kebell's training at the Inner Temple, and it was probably this new status (in addition to the support of William, Lord Hastings) that accounted for his appointment as a Leicestershire JP in 1474. Thereafter by careful investment of his 'winnings' from the law—and shrewd if not sharp speculation—Thomas Kebell built up a substantial estate in some twenty villages in the county, with possibly other property outside. In 1476 or 1477 he purchased the Hotoft manor and house at Humberstone near Leicester which he made his home, a substantial two-storied building of fourteen rooms, with offices. Much of his estate was devoted to sheep farming and after his death his flock was inventoried at over 3500.

Although never a judge at Westminster, Kebell is of unique interest among late medieval common lawyers because of the comprehensive documentation that has survived about him. As well as the law reading, this includes his will, inventory, inquisition post mortem and a very large number of his law opinions which throw considerable light on contemporary legal ideas and practice; Kebell is, indeed, the most reported serjeant-at-law of his day. In court he showed a boundless confidence coupled with a style aggressive and humorous, and in the year-books he comes over as well educated and of real intellectual strength. He was fluent in French and Latin, expert in rhetoric, and his inventory, which details his farming and his affluent lifestyle, also lists thirty-six books, both manuscript and print, an impressive collection covering religion, general knowledge, the classics, literature, and a little law.

Thomas Kebell married three times. Margery Palmer probably belonged to a Northamptonshire legal family. His second wife and the mother of his minor heir, Walter, was Agnes Flower, *née* Saltbie, the widowed daughter-in-law of Roger Flower, four times speaker of the House of Commons; they were married in 1483. Kebell died on 26 June 1500. Despite his planning, the crown established a claim to the wardship of the heir, but although this was then purchased by Kebell's patron, Lady Mary Hastings, and Walter later made two advantageous marriages, he died young leaving a two-year-old son in royal wardship and an estate encumbered with charges. One of these was to the serjeant's third wife, Margaret Basset (whom he had married in 1498), the heir of Ralph Basset of Blore in Staffordshire, who continued to collect a jointure of £40 for thirty-four years, despite having married Sir Ralph Egerton of Ridley in Cheshire, Henry VIII's standard-bearer; she died in 1534. The death of Walter's own son was followed by a third minority and more encumbrances, and by the time his male line died out in 1571 most of the serjeant's estate had been liquidated. A memorial tomb in Humberstone church with Kebell's effigy in robes was destroyed between 1638 and 1795.

E. W. IVES

Sources E. W. Ives, *The common lawyers of pre-Reformation England* (1983) · Baker, *Serjeants* · Sainty, *King's counsel* · E. W. Ives, '"Against taking aweye of women": the inception and operation of the Abduction Act of 1487', *Wealth and power in Tudor England: essays presented to S. T. Bindoff*, ed. E. W. Ives, R. J. Knecht, and J. J. Scarisbrick (1978), 21–44 · E. W. Ives, 'A lawyer's library in 1500', *Law Quarterly Review*, 85 (1969), 104–16 · *CIPM, Henry VII*, 2, no. 497
Archives Wilts. & Swindon RO, 88:5/17a
Wealth at death £796 15s. 2½d.—moveable property: inventory, Wilts. & Swindon RO, 88:5/17a

Keble, John (1792–1866), Church of England clergyman and poet, was born at Fairford, Gloucestershire, on 25 April 1792. The Kebles had deep roots in the countryside on the eastern side of the Cotswolds. Keble's father, also John (1745–1834), was vicar of Coln St Aldwyn, a village 3 miles north of Fairford, where he served for fifty-two years. His mother, Sarah (1758–1823), the daughter of John Maule, rector of Ringwood in Hampshire, was, however, of Scottish descent. The second child and eldest son in the family of two sons and three daughters, John Keble grew up at Court Close, the family house built by his grandfather (another John, but not a parson) about 1772. His childhood was a happy one and the family close-knit.

Education and Oxford career All the Keble children were educated at home, initially by aunts, but principally by their father. A diligent country parson of the old-

John Keble (1792–1866), by George Richmond, 1844

fashioned type (cavalier and nonjuring traditions were strong), his influence proved deep and lasting. John and his brother Thomas *Keble (1793–1875) both became priests, and John especially never outgrew what principal John Shairp called 'the absolute filial reverence' for their father and an intense loyalty to the tradition he stood for (Shairp, 31). In later life Keble was apt to convey his approval of some point of doctrine with the telling remark 'that seems to me just what my father taught me' (Coleridge, 564).

Having failed to gain a demyship at Magdalen College, Oxford, Keble was admitted as a Gloucestershire scholar at Corpus Christi College, Oxford, where his father had been a scholar and fellow. He went up at the age of fourteen in January 1807. In 1811, just after his eighteenth birthday, he gained double first-class honours, a distinction achieved only once before, two years earlier, by the twenty-year-old Robert Peel. Almost a year later, with Richard Whately, he was elected to an open fellowship at Oriel College, then the intellectually pre-eminent college in the university. In 1812 he won university prizes for the English and Latin essays, took private pupils, was appointed public examiner in the classical school, and, more significantly perhaps, was appointed a college tutor at Oriel in 1817.

Although a friend of the new provost, Edward Copleston, and especially John Davison, the leading tutor, Keble was not wholly at ease with the intellectual atmosphere of a college later famous as the home of the Noetics. However, he saw his college tutorship as a unique opportunity for influencing students, regarding it as a distinctive pastoral charge. He had been ordained deacon to the title of his fellowship on Trinity Sunday 1815 and priest a year later, also taking temporary charge of two neighbouring villages, Eastleach and Burthorp, near his father at Coln St Aldwyn.

Oxford, 1821–1833 Already writing poems, later to be published in *The Christian Year* (1827), Keble was asked to stand for the Oxford chair of poetry in 1821 but he declined. He was anxious to leave Oxford for a country parish. 'I get fonder and fonder of the country and of poetry and of such things every year of my life' he wrote in 1822 (Lock, 15). In 1823 he accepted a college living at Coleby, Lincolnshire. On the death of his mother in May he withdrew his acceptance; while continuing at Eastleach and Burthorp he became curate at Southrop to be near his father at Fairford, a pastoral charge of about 1000 folk. Keble remained a fellow of Oriel, although he seldom visited the college. He kept his links with Oxford, with pupils occasionally joining him for reading parties at Southrop in the vacation. These included young men later significant in the Oxford Movement: Robert Wilberforce, Isaac Williams, and Richard Hurrell Froude.

In 1827, however, Copleston was appointed bishop of Llandaff. Keble's former pupils were anxious that he should succeed to the provostship, but the majority of fellows—including Pusey and Newman—favoured Edward Hawkins; so, in December, Keble withdrew his candidacy. 'You know we are not electing an Angel, but a Provost,' was Newman's quip to a hesitant fellow (*The Letters and Diaries of John Henry Newman*, ed. C. S. Dessain and others, 31 vols., 1–10, 2nd edn, 1978–, 3.107). Keble's precise relationship with Newman, both intellectual and emotional, is hard to evaluate. Initially shy and suspicious of one another, they became friends shortly after Hawkins became provost, when Newman was moving away from his early liberalism and evangelicalism. Froude afterwards maintained that it was he who had brought them together, and at the end of his life declared that if asked what good deed he had ever done he would say that he brought Keble and Newman to understand each other (Church, 28).

Their relationship was cemented by the struggle to oust Peel as burgess for the university after the 'betrayal' of Catholic emancipation in 1829, when Keble took the younger fellows of Oriel with him into the high tory camp in defiance of the Liberal tradition of the college. This crucial realignment was arguably the true beginning of the Oxford Movement. From then on Newman stood in awe of Keble, captivated by this living embodiment of the Caroline tradition. But his praise for the older man has masked the reality that, for much of the 1830s and as late as 1843, it was Keble who was under Newman's spell. This dependence was deeply resented by the more traditional 'country' wing of the movement, the Bisley school, which included Keble's brother Tom.

It is significant that Keble himself later admitted this dependence had, to an extent, forced him off course. 'I look upon my time with Newman and Pusey as a sort of parenthesis in my life, and I have now returned again to my old views such as I had before', he told Isaac Williams in 1854 (*Autobiography of Isaac Williams*, 118). This is obviously not completely true in that Keble did alter his theological opinions on some matters, notably in a sharpening of his understanding of the real presence. But there is truth in it.

Poetry, 1821–1827 Keble's best known work, *The Christian Year*, was probably the widest selling book of poetry in the nineteenth century. Its diverse readership went well beyond the high-church element within the Church of England, and well beyond the Church of England itself. Published anonymously in July 1827, when Keble was in his thirty-fifth year, a first edition of 500 was soon followed by a second edition in November. Six additional poems were added to the third edition in 1828. By 1837 there had been sixteen editions and by Keble's death there were ninety-five. When copyright expired in 1873 there were 158 editions and copyright sales stood at 379,000. Characteristically the phenomenal success distressed its reticent author, who devoted the profits to the restoration of Hursley church. Its popularity waned sharply in the twentieth century, though several poems remain famous as hymns, including 'Blest are the pure in heart' and 'New every morning is the love'.

Keble had found emotional relief in writing poetry since student days, but would never have ventured into publishing his poems had others not pressed him. The preface, or 'Advertisement', to *The Christian Year* provides an important insight into his intentions: he aimed to make more accessible 'the sober standard of feeling' of the liturgical year and to illustrate the 'soothing' tendency of the prayer book offices. As Stephen Prickett has pointed out in *Romanticism and Religion: the Tradition of Coleridge and Wordsworth in the Victorian Church* (1976) 'soothing' meant more than 'calming', and in Keble's own aesthetic theory was closer to the Aristotelian notion of catharsis. 'Soothing' also carried with it the older meaning of asserting or upholding a truth. The poems undoubtedly diffused the spirit of Caroline piety among many within the church. As Newman later put it, 'his happy magic made the Anglican Church seem what Catholicism was and is' (J. H. Newman, *Essays: Critical and Historical*, 2nd edn, 1872, 2.444). But they were in no sense 'high and dry'; indeed, Hurrell Froude playfully characterized them as 'methodistical'. In linking creed and feeling, Keble witnessed to (and himself furthered) the change in sensibility we associate with Romanticism. By bringing the dangers of Romanticism under the discipline of religious self-control Keble contributed to what one historian has aptly described as 'the Victorian

Churching of Romanticism'. It is not surprising, therefore, that Wordsworth, despite his radical past, was Keble's chief influence. Keble had been introduced as an undergraduate to his poetry by Coleridge's nephew, the future Lord Justice Coleridge, and its impact upon him was both lasting and profound. Nevertheless, his essentially sacramental approach to nature—which he saw as the repository of types and symbols of the unseen and the spiritual—owed even more to patristic theology; his sense of nature as a sacrament of a divine indwelling may well have derived, too, from Bishop Joseph Butler's influential *Analogy of Religion* (1736), which established a harmony between natural and revealed religion and natural phenomena.

Oxford Movement, 1833–1836 In 1824 Keble declined the offer of the archdeaconry of Barbados. The following year he took sole charge of the parish of Hursley, 5 miles from Winchester, on the recommendation of his former pupil Sir William *Heathcote. Hursley was united to the rectory of Otterbourne, and the incumbent was Sir William's elderly and infirm uncle, Archdeacon Gilbert Heathcote. In 1826, however, Keble's younger sister Mary Anne died, and since an older sister, Elizabeth, was an invalid he felt duty bound to return to Gloucestershire and assist his elderly father. Despite this pastoral commitment in the country Keble was to be crucial in the foundation of the Oxford Movement: indeed, for Newman, Keble was its 'true and primary author'. He regarded Keble's assize sermon preached on 14 July 1833 (later published as *National Apostasy*, 1833) as the movement's starting point. R. W. Church's classic history, *The Oxford Movement* (1891), followed Newman, and so influenced subsequent historiography, though the significance of the sermon as a call to arms has been questioned, notably by F. L. Cross in 1933. It certainly attracted scant contemporary attention, while Isaac Williams records that in the opinion of many the sermon was 'indiscreet and fruitless' (*Autobiography of Isaac Williams*, 95–6). Despite its analysis of the 'apostate mind' of the times, applying the text 1 Samuel 12:23 to the contemporary scene, it suggested no practical course of action. However, the preface of the sermon, dated 22 July and corrected for the press by Newman, was more pointed in its reference to the usurpation by the state in the matter of the Irish Temporalities Bill: it thus played a part in stirring concerned churchmen into action.

Although invited, Keble was unable to attend the Hadleigh conference (25–29 July 1833) when the more staid high-churchmen and Hurrell Froude met at Hugh James Rose's Suffolk rectory to discuss future courses of action. He none the less exercised an influence behind the scenes. The conference disclosed a division of opinion between the high-churchmanship of William Palmer, A. P. Perceval, and Rose, whom Froude dubbed the 'Z's', and the younger 'apostolicals'. Keble's subsequent support for the radical stance of Froude allied him thereafter with the more uncompromising group. Confronted by the perceived threat to the church in the 1830s, the orthodox political theology in which Keble had been reared now seemed to him woefully inadequate. Following Froude, Keble was even prepared by the mid-1830s to countenance disestablishment, despite having criticized Whately's *Letters of an Episcopalian* (1826) for just such a suggestion.

Poetry, 1831–1839 In 1831 Keble was elected professor of poetry at Oxford University without opposition, his poetic reputation having been established with the publication of *The Christian Year*. He held the non-resident post for ten years. As professor of poetry Keble delivered the Creweian oration in 1839, when Oxford University bestowed an honorary degree on his hero Wordsworth. His own lectures delivered during the ten-year tenure of the poetry professorship (1832–41) were published (in Latin) in 1844, and dedicated to the poet in a fulsome and carefully phrased dedication, which significantly called attention to Wordsworth's championing of 'the cause of the poor and simple', and paying tribute to him as a Christian poet.

Being in Latin (they were translated into English in 1912) the influence of Keble's *praelectiones* on critical theory was inevitably limited. Entitled *De poeticae vi medica* (the healing power of poetry), they were devoted almost entirely to a discussion of classical poetry. Keble took Wordsworth's principle of poetry as the spontaneous overflow of feeling but went beyond it. For him poetry was a disguised rather than direct form of self-expression, and poetic creation arose from the conflict this repression involved. Poetry was therefore seen as release and relief, hence the 'healing power' of a divinely bestowed medicine. Keble was even prepared to describe poetry as 'a safety valve, preserving men from actual madness' (J. Keble, *De poeticae vi medica*, 1844, 1.55). Poets were divided into primary and secondary. Primary poets were those 'who spontaneously moved by impulse, resort to composition for relief and solace of a burdened or overwrought mind' (ibid., 1.53–4); the secondary are those who imitate the ideas and expression of the former. Adapting Quintilian's rhetorical distinction, Keble also divided poetry into two genres: 'ethos', which displayed long-term character traits and which encompassed the epic, dramatic, and narrative forms, and 'pathos', which expressed a passing, though intense and overpowering, impulse and which comprised the lyric, elegy, and some modes of satire. For M. H. Abrams in his seminal study of Romantic critical theory, *The Mirror and the Lamp* (1953), Keble's proto-Freudian theory made the lectures 'under their pious and diffident surface, the most sensationally radical criticism of their time' (Abrams, 45). They also provide an important insight into Keble's character.

Keble published a metrical translation of the Psalms in 1839, carefully vetted by E. B. Pusey, though this appears never to have been widely used. In 1846 he published (again anonymously and to raise money for restoration) another volume of poetry, *Lyra innocentium: Thoughts in Verse on Christian Children, their Ways and their Privileges*. This also lacked wide appeal, though it displays more metrical variety, greater lyricism, and in many respects a brighter tone than his earlier poetry.

Marriage and life at Hursley In 1836 Sir William Heathcote again offered Keble the living of Hursley (he had previously done so in 1829 on the death of Archdeacon Heathcote but Keble had demurred on the ground that he must continue to help his father). This time Keble accepted and was instituted on 9 May 1836. His father had died in 1835, his ninetieth year, and on 10 October 1835, shortly before moving to Hursley, Keble married Charlotte Clarke (1806–1866), the younger sister of his brother's wife. Her father, the Revd George Clarke (d. 1809), had been rector of Maisey Hampton near Fairford; the Keble and Clarke families were old friends as well as near neighbours. George Clarke had been up at Oxford with John Keble senior in the 1760s, and the Keble and Clarke children had been friends since childhood. The marriage raised a few eyebrows, especially at Oxford, where some thought the marriage unsuitable. Keble was forty-three and Charlotte fourteen years his junior. It would seem that the marriage was a perfectly happy one, although there were no children and Mrs Keble was throughout life a delicate woman, frequently ill. Keble's invalid sister, Elizabeth, lived with them at Hursley until her death in 1860 and John appears to have been devoted to both, referring to them frequently as his 'two wives' without embarrassment.

Keble remained as vicar of Hursley for thirty years until his death. It was from the relative obscurity of the country parish, an obscurity admittedly somewhat 'cultivated', that Keble achieved his fame both as poet and as protagonist in the ecclesiastical events of the day. His keen and active interest in church affairs never abated. He visited Oxford or London when necessary and published forceful tracts and letters on doctrinal issues and matters of church and state.

At Hursley, Keble endeavoured to implement Tractarian pastoral ideals in a quiet yet firm manner, working under the watchful eye of his patron who, as Tractarian squire at Hursley Park, ensured no dissenting tenants rented land in the village. New churches were built for the outlying hamlets of Ampfield and Otterbourne; Hursley church was completely rebuilt and daily services were introduced. Keble was assiduous in parish visiting, especially the sick, and took very seriously the duty of catechizing and confirmation preparation. His preaching followed the liturgical pattern of the prayer book. He was not an eloquent preacher and certainly not a demonstrative one. To his friend Sir John Coleridge it was rather the 'affectionate almost plaintive earnestness' which made his sermons moving (Coleridge, 556–7). Eleven volumes of sermons were published posthumously (1875–80), with a further volume, *Sermons, Occasional and Parochial* (1867), and *Village Sermons on the Baptismal Service* (1868).

Keble quietly urged the practice of sacramental confession and became Pusey's confessor in 1846. He exercised a valued personal ministry to many others who sought it, including the novelist Charlotte Mary Yonge, whom he prepared for confirmation. Examples of his teaching can be found in the posthumously published *Letters of Spiritual Counsel and Guidance* (1870), edited by R. F. Wilson, a former curate. But his Tractarian priorities also included a strong commitment to revivify rural paternalism. As parish priest Keble was concerned with such matters as the provision of allotments, and the setting up of a friendly and medical society and a blanket club, as well as ensuring wholesome recreation as an antidote to the temptations of the beer house. Keble was not indifferent to matters such as the implications of the price of bread or poor harvests, farmers' grievances or the poor rates. There was a gritty realism in his pastoral ministry that is often lost in conventional accounts which romanticize the Tractarian pastoral idyll. Keble was revered by many in his lifetime and after as a saintly example of the Anglican country parson.

Oxford Movement, 1836–1841 Being out of Oxford, Keble could give little active support to the events unfolding there. He was, in any case, much concerned with his scholarly three-volume edition of the works of Richard Hooker, the Elizabethan divine (and former Corpus man), which he published with a long introduction in 1836. Owen Chadwick has described this as 'the work of a careful editor, an antiquarian rather than a historian, but a genuine critic of the first rank' (Chadwick, 60). With Keble's other scholarly work, notably *On Eucharistical Adoration* (1857) and his *Life of Thomas Wilson, Bishop of Sodor and Man* (1863), it shows that, despite a narrow range and limited sympathies, he was not without intellectual ability once he had become galvanized.

Keble's sermon *Primitive Tradition Recognised in Holy Scripture*, preached on 27 September 1836 at Archdeacon William Dealtry's visitation in Winchester Cathedral, aroused controversy when it was published. Some found its uncompromising defence of apostolic tradition distasteful, despite the author's subsequent claim—in a postscript to the third edition—that he was defending the rule of the Church of England 'as distinguished on the one hand from Romish usurpation and on the other from rationalistic licentiousness' (J. Keble, *Primitive Tradition*, 3rd edn, 1837, p. 4). The rationalistic licentiousness Keble had in mind could well have been the Bampton lectures of Renn Dickson Hampden, recently elevated to the regius chair of divinity. The lengthy postscript was a reply to critics and included Tract 78, a *catena patrum* of Anglican testimony to the Vincentian canon.

Keble contributed nine of the Tracts for the Times: numbers 4, 13, 40, 52, 54, 57, 60, 78, and 89. Tract 4, *Adherence to the Apostolical Succession the Safest Course*, epitomized the early Tractarian programme and demonstrated Keble's own allegiance to the strictest episcopalian theory which, he had accepted in his introduction to Hooker, was not shared by the Elizabethan divine. Tracts 52, 54, and 57 also concerned the ministry. Tract 13 was a plea against change in the lectionary, while Tract 62 argued the need for personal devotion to be supported by sound doctrine. Tract 89, published in 1841, shortly before the series ended, was nearly 200 pages long and collected together material given elsewhere to uphold the value of the patristic method of the mystical interpretation of holy scripture.

Keble was joint author with Newman and Pusey from 1836 of the Library of the Fathers. But his main contribution to the project probably lay in his reputation, securing the patronage of Archbishop William Howley, to whom the volumes were dedicated. His translation of St Irenaeus's five books against heresy was not published until after his death. He was also on the committee of the Library of Anglo-Catholic Theology, which between 1841 and 1863 reprinted eighty-three volumes of mostly seventeenth-century Anglican divinity, including his work on Thomas Wilson.

Keble's part in the publication of Hurrell Froude's notorious *Remains*, which he edited with Newman in 1838, aroused deep disquiet and marked a crucial stage in the movement's repudiation of the Reformation. Keble felt unable to subscribe to the martyr's memorial in Oxford lest in doing so he appeared to repudiate Froude, although he was concerned at the growth of a definite pro-Roman party among the younger men. He recommended the publication of Newman's Tract 90 in an effort to retain their loyalty to the Church of England, and because of this felt its condemnation and the subsequent secessions all the more acutely.

The later movement, 1841–1866 The refusal of the bishop of Winchester in 1841 to priest Keble's curate, the Revd Peter Young, on the grounds of his 'unsound' eucharistic beliefs, showed that Keble was a marked man in the eyes of ecclesiastical authority. The failure of Isaac Williams to succeed Keble as professor of poetry early the next year, the increasingly Romeward trend of the *British Critic*, and the censure of Pusey's university sermon *The Holy Eucharist, a Comfort to the Penitent* in 1843 all testified to the disintegration of the Tractarian party. Keble nevertheless defended W. G. Ward's right to speak in a forceful pamphlet in 1844 and felt his subsequent degradation by the university keenly. More devastating was the loss of Newman through his conversion to Roman Catholicism in 1845, a 'thunderbolt', as he put it in a letter to his old friend, and a cause of deep personal grief.

Keble was not the man to marshall Tractarian sympathizers shaken by Newman's secession. Nevertheless he did not withdraw from public controversy, and sought to reassure those who, like himself, felt it impossible to desert the Church of England. He helped Pusey in opposing Hampden's elevation to the bishopric of Hereford in 1847 and threw himself actively into the controversy relating to the Gorham judgment in 1850. He later defended the doctrines of the real presence and eucharistic sacrifice in the trials of Archdeacon G. A. Denison (1853) and Bishop A. P. Forbes of Brechin (1858), which led to the publication of his *On Eucharistical Adoration* (1857). For many high-churchmen Keble's principles remained the significant criterion by which to judge affairs. As H. P. Liddon declared 'people would wait and see what came from Hursley before making up their minds as to the path of duty' (Battiscombe, 354).

Character assessment To assess Keble's life is difficult. No adequate biography exists: the official memoir (1869) by Lord Justice Coleridge, a friend since undergraduate days, is a rambling and disorganized affair. Newman, when asked to portray Keble with his pen, pointedly replied 'How can I profess to paint the portrait of a man who will not sit for his picture?' (J. H. Newman, *Occasional Papers and Reviews*, 1877, xiii).

Keble's famous 'reserve' stemmed from a theologically grounded frame of mind that invested submission to authority and self-restraint with an intense moral seriousness. But reserve was also rooted in the structure of his personality: he was a shy man, awkward with strangers, diffident, self-effacing, apparently devoid of ambition. Yet paradoxically the man who so feared the impact of his personality on others had an astonishing impact on those few intimates who breached his defensive exterior and those, priest and lay, who looked to him as spiritual guide. Interestingly, too, he felt at ease with children, who responded to his playfulness and simplicity. Isaac Williams recorded Keble's gardener at Southrop as saying 'Master is the greatest boy of the lot' (*Autobiography of Isaac Williams*, 18). Short in stature, there remained well into middle life a boyishness about him which is well captured by George Richmond's first portrait (1844), when Keble was a little over fifty.

Posterity's assessment of Keble has often been influenced by the charges of narrow-mindedness, obscurantism, and laziness levelled by James Anthony Froude, Tom Mozley, and Francis Newman. These supposed limitations have been sensitively addressed by Owen Chadwick in a character study of Keble (*The Spirit of the Oxford Movement*, 54–62). Yet Keble's personality remains elusive. He could be by turns affectionate and enthusiastic, and maddeningly slow and stubborn. Gentleness and severity seemed to exist within him in a curious juxtaposition. He had a temper, Dean Church put it, 'of singular sweetness and modesty, capable at the same time when necessary, of austere strength and strictness of principle' (Church, 23). Too often the 'fiery eagerness, the indignant remonstrances poured out, and the sternness of his judgment when he thought Church doctrine was being endangered', which Catherine Moberly recalled, have been overlooked (Moberly, 77–8).

Death and Keble College Keble died on 29 March 1866 at Bournemouth, where he had gone for the sake of his wife's health; Charlotte Keble died soon after him, on 11 May. Both were buried at Hursley. On 12 May 1866 a meeting at Lambeth Palace resolved to build a college in Keble's memory at Oxford which would offer an education at moderate costs in strict fidelity to the teaching of the Church of England. Keble College was opened in 1870.

Preaching at the opening of the chapel in 1876, Pusey chose as his text the beatitude 'Blessed are the meek'. It was an apt text, though meekness is an often misunderstood grace. It is perhaps properly constituted by considerable powers held in deliberate limitation and reserve. Keble knew early what he wanted in life: to be a country parson as his father had been before him and to be a poet. Unlike many people he never deviated from these objectives and he achieved what he wanted. What Keble was,

was important for the development of the Oxford Movement and for nineteenth-century Anglicanism. At the time of the Gorham case he is said to have observed 'If the Church of England were to fail, it should be found in my parish' (Chadwick, 62). This was surely the most characteristic of all his sayings.

PERRY BUTLER

Sources J. Coleridge, *Life of the Rev. John Keble* (1869) · G. Battiscombe, *John Keble: a study in limitations* (1963) · W. Lock, *John Keble: a biography* (1892) · O. Chadwick, 'The limitations of Keble', *The spirit of the Oxford Movement: Tractarian essays* (1990) · S. Prickett, *Romanticism and religion: the tradition of Coleridge and Wordsworth in the Victorian church* (1976) · S. Gilley, 'John Keble and the Victorian churching of Romanticism', *An infinite variety: essays in Romanticism*, ed. J. R. Watson (1983) · G. Rowell, introduction, *A speaking life: John Keble and the Anglican tradition of ministry and art*, ed. C. R. Henry (1995) · R. W. Church, *The Oxford Movement: twelve years, 1833–1845*, ed. G. Best, new edn (1970) · M. H. Abrams, *The mirror and the lamp* (1952) · *The autobiography of Isaac Williams*, ed. G. Prevost, [2nd edn] (1892) · C. A. E. Moberly, *Dulce domum: George Moberly … his family and friends* (1911) · J. C. Shairp, *John Keble: an essay on the author of the 'Christian year'* (1866)

Archives Bodl. Oxf., essays for the chancellor's prize; corresp. · Hants. RO, corresp. · Keble College, Oxford, corresp. and papers · LPL, corresp. · Pusey Oxf., diaries and corresp. | Archives of the British Province of the Society of Jesus, London, corresp. with William Henry Bliss · Birmingham Oratory, corresp. with John Henry Newman · BL, corresp. with W. E. Gladstone, Add. MSS 44208–44409 · Bodl. Oxf., letters to Jane Martha Hicks Beach; letters to Lord Blachford; corresp. with John Taylor Coleridge; letters to George, Hubert, and Robert Cornish; corresp. with H. E. Manning; letters to Lord Nelson and William Edward Heygate; letters to C. A. Ogilvie; letters to William Ashmead Pruen, Mrs Pruen, and Jane Martha St John; letters to R. A. Wilberforce; letters to Samuel Wilberforce · Glos. RO, letters to Sir George Prevost · Hants. RO, letters to Sir William Heathcote · LPL, letters to Charles Thomas Longley; letters to John Frewer Moor and Charles Marriott; letters from Isaac Williams; letters to Christopher Wordsworth; letters to Cecil Wray · Oriel College, Oxford, letters to John Davison and others; letters to Edward Hawkins; letters to James Endell Tyler · Oxon. RO, letters to Hubert Kestell Cornish · Pembroke College, Oxford, letters to G. W. Hall · Pusey Oxf., letters to Sir William Heathcote and Lady Heathcote; letters to John Henry Newman; corresp. with E. B. Pusey; letters to E. T. Richards; letters to H. A. Woodgate · University of British Columbia Library, special collections and university archives division, letters mainly to Katherine Hedger · University of Dundee, archives, letters to Alexander Forbes

Likenesses G. Richmond, watercolour drawing, 1844, Keble College, Oxford [*see illus.*] · G. Richmond, chalk drawing, 1863, NPG · T. Woolner, bust, 1872, Westminster Abbey, London · G. Richmond, marble bust, 1874, Keble College, Oxford · G. Richmond, oils, 1876, Keble College, Oxford · R. H. Preston, photograph, NPG · Preston & Poole, photograph, NPG · G. Richmond, chalk drawing, Walsall Museum and Art Gallery

Wealth at death under £16,000: resworn probate, March 1867, *CGPLA Eng. & Wales* (1866)

Keble, Joseph (1632–1710), lawyer and writer, was born in the parish of St Giles-in-the-Fields, London, the fourth and youngest son of Richard *Keble (d. 1683/4), commissioner of the great seal from 1649 to 1654, and his wife, Mary, *née* Sicklemor. He was educated at the parish school of St Andrew's, Holborn, and afterwards proceeded to Jesus College, Oxford, where he was made a fellow by the visitors appointed by parliament in 1648. He matriculated at All Souls on 22 March 1651 and graduated BCL in 1654. Meanwhile, he had been admitted to Gray's Inn on 6 May 1647, on the same day as his elder brother Thomas, and was called to the bar on 29 June 1653. After a spell of travelling in Europe about 1660, Keble returned to England and embarked on a remarkable regime of study. He attended the court of king's bench from 1661, but he had no legal practice, being content to report the cases before the court. Keble's contemporary biographer noted that he rose before six o'clock, studied until eleven, then met 'company in the walks', had dinner, studied, and then at six went to the walks again. In vacation times he walked to Hampstead where he had purchased a small estate, but even there he still studied. He noted over 4000 sermons that were preached twice daily at Gray's Inn chapel. The first fruit of Keble's labour was a new table to the statute book which appeared in print in 1674 and for which he was paid £300. Other works followed, such as *An Explanation of the Laws against Recusants* (1681), and *An Assistance to Justices of the Peace* (1683). Of more substance was his *Reports in the court of queen's bench … from the 12th to the 30th year of the reign of Charles II* (1685). He also published several works on 'human nature'.

Keble died on 28 August 1710 at Gray's Inn Gate, Holborn, while awaiting a coach to Hampstead, and was buried at Tuddenham, near Ipswich, where he held some property. His will also referred to his house in Hampstead and his chambers in Gray's Inn, which were occupied by his sister's daughter. Much of his will dealt with his unpublished work, which consisted mainly of legal notes in manuscript. He left twenty volumes of notes to Gray's Inn 'as a testimony of the honour and thanks I owe to their worthy countenance' of his labours. The remainder he left to Samuel Keble, a bookseller. Keble died unmarried, but there is a reference, in the papers of Sir John Reresby, to Diana (1622–1674), fifth daughter of Sir George Reresby, who reportedly married 'one Keble', the son of a great lawyer, but 'she approved so little of her husband the next day that she would never own him for her husband' (*Memoirs of Sir John Reresby*, xl).   STUART HANDLEY

Sources *A brief account of Joseph Keble, with a catalogue of his writings* [1710] · Wood, *Ath. Oxon.*, new edn, 4.575, 581 · J. W. Wallace, *The reporters*, 4th edn (1882), 315–26 · A. Kippis and others, eds., *Biographia Britannica, or, The lives of the most eminent persons who have flourished in Great Britain and Ireland*, 2nd edn, 4 (1789), 2800 · Foster, *Alum. Oxon.*, 1500–1714 · J. Foster, *The register of admissions to Gray's Inn, 1521–1889, together with the register of marriages in Gray's Inn chapel, 1695–1754* (privately printed, London, 1889), 245 · R. J. Fletcher, ed., *The pension book of Gray's Inn*, 1 (1901), 404 · will, PRO, PROB 11/516, sig. 181 · *Memoirs of Sir John Reresby*, ed. A. Browning, 2nd edn, ed. M. K. Geiter and W. A. Speck (1991), xl · *DNB*

Keble, Richard (d. 1683/4), judge, was the seventh son of Giles Keble (d. 1626) of Old Newton, Suffolk, and his wife, Anne, *née* Went, of Woodbridge, in that county. Giles Keble was himself a second son, descended from a family that was long settled around Ipswich. Admitted to Gray's Inn on 7 August 1609, Keble displayed an aptitude for legal study that brought him to be called to the bar on 4 August 1614, and to recognition at his inn with appointments as ancient on 4 May 1632 and as Lent reader on 2 November 1638. He was admitted to the Suffolk commission of the peace on 19 September 1634. As a barrister he began to be

noted in law reports from 1636, and at Gray's Inn he was one of a number of Suffolk lawyers associated with an uncompromising protestantism out of sympathy with the innovations of Archbishop Laud. This circle of godly lawyers provided the context for his marriage before 16 February 1635 to Mary Sicklemor, daughter of an Ipswich alderman who in 1637 formed part of a delegation to the king against the Laudian Bishop Wren of Norwich.

After the outbreak of civil war, Keble's father-in-law was appointed to Suffolk and Ipswich parliamentarian committees, and although there is no record of political activity by Keble himself, there can be no doubt of his sympathies in the conflict. His appointment as recorder of Orford in the 1640s was further evidence of his political leanings, and on 4 October 1647 he was succeeded in the office by his brother-in-law. Gray's Inn provides the most plausible link between the East Anglian lawyer and the Welsh judgeship to which Keble was appointed on 18 March 1647 by a vote in the House of Lords. Sir Thomas Myddelton, whose army under Thomas Mytton had reduced north Wales to submit to parliamentary authority during 1646 and 1647, remained 'the inevitable pillar of the six North Wales committees' (Dodd, 125); he had been admitted to Gray's Inn two years before the Suffolk man.

In October 1648 Keble was eleventh in the list of serjeants-at-law created that month, and was admitted to Serjeants' Inn, Chancery Lane. His sponsors at the creation ceremony were Lord Grey of Wark, speaker of the House of Lords and commissioner of the great seal, and Sir John Danvers, a future regicide. Initially posted to the Anglesey circuit, Keble was chief justice of north Wales until 1649, when on 8 February he became the third and least experienced commissioner of the great seal under the Commonwealth. According to Bulstrode Whitelocke, the senior commissioner, Keble and John Lisle, their colleague, tried unsuccessfully to combine against him. Keble presided at the trial in October 1649 of John Lilburne, and generally proved patient in the face of the Leveller leader's provocations. In his refutation of Lilburne's claim that juries were historically judges of law as well as of fact, Keble was determined not to allow him to make 'ciphers' (*State trials*, 4.1314) of the judges. Keble was also president at the trials for treason of the presbyterians Christopher Love and John Gibbons, in which he admitted that presbyterianism, if shorn of the covenant with the Scots, would 'tend to the peace of this nation' (ibid., 5, col. 171). He was the first named among the commissioners for a high court of justice in March 1650, and helped plan, but did not act in, a high court to try Norfolk rebels in December. Hilkiah Bedford, the biographer of Dr John Barwick, dean of St Paul's, describes Keble as an 'insolent mercenary pettifogger' for presiding in courts without juries, but the Lilburne and Love trials were examples of traditional common-law procedures at work, and the high courts of justice were a response to civil emergencies. Keble did not find favour under the protectorate, and lost his office on 3 April 1654. His disappearance from commissions of the peace for Welsh counties was complete by the end of 1655. After his repeated petitioning for arrears of salary as a commissioner of the great seal, a letter of privy seal was granted him on 6 April 1658 for the £1050 owing. At the Restoration he was voted on 13 June 1660 by the Commons to be excepted from the Act of Indemnity and Oblivion in its second category of offenders, probably as the result of petitions by victims of the high courts of justice. In his will, dated April 1683, Keble left £1000 to his daughter, Mary, and the remainder of his estate to his son, Joseph *Keble. It was proved on 2 August 1684, probably soon after his death at Old Newton.　STEPHEN K. ROBERTS

Sources State trials, vols. 4–5 · Baker, Serjeants · W. H. Rylands, ed., The visitation of the county of Suffolk, begun … 1664, and finished … 1668, Harleian Society, 61 (1910) · Miscellanea Genealogica et Heraldica, 5th ser., 5 (1923–5) · Report on manuscripts in various collections, 8 vols., HMC, 55 (1901–14), vol. 4 [Orford] · Seventh report, HMC, 6 (1879), 1–182 [House of Lords] · The diary of Bulstrode Whitelocke, 1605–1675, ed. R. Spalding, British Academy, Records of Social and Economic History, new ser., 13 (1990) · W. R. Williams, The history of the great sessions in Wales, 1542–1830 (privately printed, Brecon, 1899) · J. R. S. Phillips, ed., The justices of the peace in Wales and Monmouthshire, 1541 to 1689 (1975) · Birm. CA, MSS 602725/193, 603503/312 · J. Foster, The register of admissions to Gray's Inn, 1521–1889, together with the register of marriages in Gray's Inn chapel, 1695–1754 (privately printed, London, 1889) · R. J. Fletcher, ed., The pension book of Gray's Inn, 2 vols. (1901–10) · Fragmenta Genealogica, 10 (1904), 65 · Report of the Deputy Keeper of the Public Records, 5 (1844), appx 2, p. 271 · A. H. Dodd, Studies in Stuart Wales, 2nd edn (1971) · will, PRO, PROB 11/377, sig. 103
Likenesses R. Walker, oils, c.1652, Palace of Westminster, London
Wealth at death left £1000 to daughter; remainder to son: will, PRO, PROB 11/377, sig. 103

Keble, Thomas (1793–1875), Church of England clergyman, was born at Court Close, Fairford, on 25 October 1793, the younger son of John Keble, vicar of Coln St Aldwyns, and his wife, Sarah, daughter of John Maule. John *Keble, one of the major figures in the Oxford Movement, was his elder brother. Like his brother, Thomas was educated entirely by his father; he was elected Gloucestershire scholar of Corpus Christi College, Oxford, on 31 March 1808. In 1811 he graduated BA, taking a second class in classics and a third (then called a second below the line) in mathematics. He was made deacon in December 1816, and ordained priest the following year. From April 1817 to October 1818 he was curate of Sherborne with Windrush, Gloucestershire, but, after the first of several serious illnesses, he returned to Oxford in the autumn of 1819 to become college tutor at Corpus. At the time he headed the list of scholars and, according to a contemporary at Corpus, accepted the post reluctantly. In 1820 Keble was elected probationary fellow, the following year fellow, and in 1822 junior dean of the college, a position he held until he left Oxford two years later, by which time he had also gained his BD degree. While at Oxford he shared with his brother the curacy of Eastleach Turville and Eastleach Martin (formerly Burthorpe), near Fairford, until 1824, when he became curate of Cirencester. The following year, on 14 June, he married Elizabeth Jane Clarke (1804–1870), elder daughter of the Revd George Clarke, an old family friend and rector of Meysey Hampton near Cirencester.

In 1827 Keble was instituted to the living of Bisley, Gloucestershire, a large and scattered parish on the Cotswolds above Stroud, with a number of outlying hamlets inhabited mainly by very poor and neglected labourers' families. During his forty-six years at Bisley, Keble persevered, in spite of many set-backs, to improve the physical, moral, and spiritual welfare of his people, organizing self-help and emigration schemes, and building churches with districts assigned to them from the old parish, in addition to a chapel of ease and several schools. A high-churchman of the old school, whose manner could at times be autocratic, Keble was, nevertheless, an exemplary and devoted pastor, his whole life being one of concern for his parish and people. He was one of the first in England to revive daily services in church, a feature of his work made the subject of a poem by his friend Isaac Williams. Keble's example was taken up, through Williams, by John Henry Newman at St Mary's, Oxford, and at Littlemore, from where it spread through England. As one of the original Tractarians, Keble was closely involved in the early years of the Oxford Movement, his contribution to which has not always been fully appreciated or acknowledged. His opinions were highly regarded by many friends and contemporaries, and his judgement on spiritual questions was frequently sought by his elder brother. Keble was particularly identified with the 'country' wing of the movement, and through a notable succession of curates—known as the Bisley school, and including Isaac Williams, Sir George Prevost, and Robert Gregory—his orthodox views became established in many Gloucestershire parishes and further afield.

For much of his life Keble was dogged by poor health, and the demands of his parish left him little time for literary work. Among his published writings are four of the Tracts for the Times, numbers 12, 22, 43, and 84, the last being completed by Prevost. The first three belong to the Richard Nelson series, later published separately. Keble also wrote fifty-five of the Plain Sermons, by Contributors to the Tracts (1839–48), the publication of which was probably first suggested by him. He translated the Homilies of St John Chrysostom on the epistle to the Hebrews for the Library of the Fathers (revised by J. Barrow, 1877), and in 1872 published a short tract, Considerations on the Athanasian Creed. He also edited a translation of Thomas a Kempis's Of the Imitation of Christ by J. Worthington (1841), and assisted his brother in his edition of the works of Richard Hooker (1831–5). Thomas Keble died at Bisley vicarage on 5 September 1875, and was buried in All Saints' churchyard, Bisley, on 11 September. He left three daughters and one son, also Thomas, who had succeeded him as vicar of Bisley in 1873.

J. H. OVERTON, rev. HUGH J. GREENHALF

Sources J. T. Coleridge, A memoir of the Rev. John Keble (1869) · R. W. Church, The Oxford Movement: twelve years, 1833–1845, ed. G. Best, new edn (1970) · O. W. Jones, Isaac Williams and his circle (1971) · G. Battiscombe, John Keble: a study in limitations (1963) · The autobiography of Isaac Williams, ed. G. Prevost, 3rd edn (1893) · H. J. Greenhalf, Shining pastors: Thomas Keble, the Bisley School and the

Oxford Movement [forthcoming] · R. Gregory, *Robert Gregory, 1819–1911: being the autobiography of Robert Gregory, DD*, ed. W. H. Hutton (1912) · C. Hole, *The life of the Rev. and Ven. W. W. Phelps* (1871) · G. Sanders, *The younger brother* (1975) · family correspondence, Keble College, Oxford · parish register, All Saints, Bisley, 5 Sept 1875, Glos. RO [death] · parish register, All Saints, Bisley, 11 Sept 1875, Glos. RO [burial]

Archives Glos. RO, corresp. · Keble College, Oxford, family corresp. · LPL, corresp., letter-books, and papers | Bodl. Oxf., Keble–Coleridge corresp. · Glos. RO, Keble–Prevost letters · Oxon. RO, letters to Hugh Kestell Cornish

Likenesses group photograph, *c.*1863 (with family); copy, priv. coll. · photograph, *c.*1870; copy, priv. coll.

Wealth at death under £60,000: probate, 18 Oct 1875, *CGPLA Eng. & Wales*

Keck, Sir Anthony (*bap.* 1630, *d.* 1695), lawyer and politician, was born at Mickleton, Gloucestershire, and baptized there on 28 March 1630, the fifth son of Nicholas Keck of Old Cowcliffe, Oxfordshire, and Long Marston, Gloucestershire, and Margaret (*bap.* 1590), daughter of John Morris of Bretforton, Worcestershire. He was admitted to the Inner Temple in 1653, and called to the bar in 1659. Keck married, on 11 June 1660, Mary (*d.* 1702), daughter of Francis Thorne. He was made a bencher of his inn in 1677. In 1680 he was the busiest counsel in chancery, where he presumably specialized. No doubt this expertise was the reason why Keck was employed by William III on 4 March 1689 as one of three commissioners of the great seal. He was knighted on 15 March 1689, but retired as commissioner in May 1690 following the dismissal of Sir John Maynard. One contemporary saw his resignation as 'a great act of self denial in him, but his relations will suffer by it' (*The Portledge Papers*, 74).

On 20 April 1691 Keck was elected to the House of Commons as MP for Tiverton, but he seems to have felt little affection for the chamber, describing it as 'a bear garden' (*Diary of Sir Richard Cocks*, 23). He made a notable speech on 9 February 1693 in support of the Triennial Bill, in which he decried criticism of the measure as invading the royal prerogative. This lends some support to Roger North's view that Keck believed the best form of government to be 'a republic, or, which was the same thing, a king always in check'. North described him as 'a person that had raised himself by his wits, and, bating some hardness in his character, which might be ascribed to his disease, the gout, he was a man of a polite merry genius' (North, 3.169). Keck did not stand for parliament in 1695, and died in December of that year in Bell Yard, Chancery Lane, Luttrell reporting his death at the very end of the month. His will bears testimony to his wealth, for after referring to property at Blunsdon, Wiltshire (where he was buried), purchased for £11,000, he decreed that a further purchase of land be made for £29,000 by his executors, pursuant to the marriage settlement of his son, Francis. At his death Keck left nine daughters; the four remaining unmarried were to receive portions of £4000 apiece.

In 1697 there was published anonymously *Cases argued and decreed in the high court of chancery from the 12th year of Charles II to the 31st*, which according to Sir Edward Ward,

chief baron of the exchequer, was Keck's. He certainly collected reports, as among the manuscripts of the earl of Ashburnham are two volumes of chancery cases from Charles I to William III.

STUART HANDLEY

Sources HoP, *Commons, 1690–1715* [draft] · *Le Neve's Pedigrees of the knights*, ed. G. W. Marshall, Harleian Society, 8 (1873) · R. North, *The lives of … Francis North … Dudley North … and … John North*, ed. A. Jessopp, 3 (1890), 169 · D. Lemmings, *Gentlemen and barristers: the inns of court and the English bar, 1680–1730* (1990), 160, 288 · *The parliamentary diary of Narcissus Luttrell, 1691–1693*, ed. H. Horwitz (1972), 413 · *The parliamentary diary of Sir Richard Cocks, 1698–1702*, ed. D. W. Hayton (1996), 23 · will, PRO, PROB 11/435, sig. 238 · will, PRO, PROB 11/514, sig. 70 [Mary Keck, wife] · *The Portledge papers: being extracts from the letters of Richard Lapthorne … to Richard Coffin*, ed. R. J. Kerr and I. C. Duncan (1928), 74 · W. H. Shawcross, *A transcript of the register of the parish church, Bretforton* (1908), 9, 78 · N. Luttrell, *A brief historical relation of state affairs from September 1678 to April 1714*, 3 (1857), 567 · IGI

Wealth at death considerable; estate valued at £11,000, plus £29,000 to purchase land for son, plus four marriage portions of £4000 each for daughters: will, PRO, PROB 11/435, sig. 238

Keck, Anthony (1726/7–1797), architect, was first recorded in the register of Lugwardine parish, Herefordshire, on 29 June 1761, when he married Mary Palmer by special licence. He was said to be of Randwick, Gloucestershire, and was probably engaged at this time in the rebuilding of the central section of Longworth Hall, in the same parish. Randwick remained his home until 1768 when he moved to Beech House, King's Stanley, where he lived for the rest of his life. Nothing else is known about Keck's background but it seems likely that he was a member of a minor gentry family settled at Great Tew in Oxfordshire or Mickleton in north Gloucestershire, and came to his profession as a gentleman rather than an artisan. During the next three decades he was, according to his obituary in the *Hereford Journal* of 11 October 1797, the most 'celebrated architect' in Gloucestershire, Worcestershire, Herefordshire, and south Wales.

Much of Keck's earliest recorded work around Stroud is of a minor character. He provided new pews for Standish church in 1764 and new wings for Bownham Park (1766–70); his first complete house was the modest Ferney Hill (1768), near Dursley. Keck's career developed beyond Gloucestershire with the support of the Revd Dr Treadway Nash, the author of *Collections for the History of Worcestershire* (1781–2). Nash was a powerful force in Worcestershire in the late eighteenth century, an indefatigable promoter of public works who was a member of an influential group of local gentry. About 1758 he acquired an estate at Bevere, north of Worcester, where Keck was employed to convert his farmhouse into a neat Palladian villa. Thereafter, Nash assiduously promoted Keck's skills among his friends. In 1764, for instance, he was vice-president of a committee established to build a new infirmary in Worcester, which chose Keck as its architect from a shortlist of four architects which included the nationally respected Henry Keene. Nash's influence probably enabled Keck to secure his next commission, St Martin's Church, Worcester (1768–72), where he was once again in competition with Keene and may eventually have worked to his design. Nash was also a trustee for the rebuilding of the Severn Bridge: in August 1770 Keck was paid £50 'for his plans and estimate' (Bridge book of orders, 1 Aug 1770, Worcs. RO), presumably for a scheme to repair the old bridge which Nash was promoting.

Nash's influence can next be detected at Upton-on-Severn, where the lord of the manor was John Martin of Ham Court, Nash's brother-in-law: Keck provided a lead-covered cupola for the parish church (1769) and rebuilt the court (1772). With its end-on bows, pedimented centre-piece, and austere treatment, it was the prototype for several of Keck's later houses. Another of Nash's close acquaintances was the Revd Dr Davenport, rector of Bredon, who seems to have employed Keck in 1771 to add a bay to his rectory. In August, Davenport's former pupil Thomas Mansel Talbot stayed at Bredon; on returning to south Wales in November, he made a note to himself to write to 'Mr. Keck' (Martin, 30). The result was Keck's finest house, Penrice Castle, Glamorgan (1775–80). Like his earlier houses, the façade is sparsely ornamented, but a single sea-facing bow runs from basement to attic; inside, the simple but refined rooms are arranged around a top-lit staircase following the typical villa plan.

Two years before work commenced at Penrice, in April 1773, Keck refurbished Kentchurch Court, a medieval manor in west Herefordshire for John Scudamore MP. His neighbour was Sir George Cornewall of Moccas Court, where Keck stepped into the shoes of Robert Adam, exploiting his design but also repeating his own success at Penrice. This is one of several projects where Keck seems to have been employed to adapt the design of a more eminent architect for his patron. By the mid-1770s Keck had established himself as the premier architect in the region: houses in his individual style—bows or canted bays, crisp façades, and chaste interiors—appear throughout the Cotswold–Severn area. But some are poorly documented and can only be connected to Keck by style or his association with Nash. Works at Castleditch, Underdown, Canon Frome Court, Hanbury Hall, Burghill Court, and Sufton Court, all in Herefordshire and Worcestershire, have been attributed to Keck; better-documented are Forthampton Court, near Tewkesbury, for the daughter of Bishop Isaac Maddox, and the great bows of Longworth Hall, about 1788. In south Wales there is one documented work, the magnificent Margam orangery, designed in 1787 for Thomas Mansel Talbot. Meanwhile, several commissions are recorded in Gloucestershire: Flaxley Abbey (1777), Moreton in Marsh church (1790), Barnsley Park (c.1780), alterations to Batsford Park (1778–81), and finally, his most important Cotswold commission, the rebuilding of Hill House (1784–92; now Rodborough Manor) for Sir George Paul.

Towards the end of his life Keck was increasingly involved in institutional work. Earlier in 1779 he had designed a new lock on the Stroudwater Canal; between 1784 and 1788 £3431 was spent providing a 'thorough and complete repair' (V. Green, *History and Antiquities of the City of Worcester*, 2, 1796, 28–9) of Worcester gaol, where Nash was on the restoration committee.

On the day after the collapse of Hereford Cathedral in April 1786, Keck was on the scene providing plans for temporary repairs to the cathedral. In August 1788 the *Hereford Journal* announced that Keck was to provide plans for the restoration of the county gaol, but owing to illness they did not materialize until July 1789; by this time the justices had decided to build a new gaol to the designs of John Nash. Keck and Nash were jointly consulted in September 1793 by the trustees of the new asylum in Hereford, where Nash also succeeded as architect. A stone in King's Stanley churchyard recorded Keck's death on 4 October 1797, aged seventy. A daughter was also buried in the same churchyard: Mary, wife of Samuel Sadler, vicar of Sandhurst, Gloucestershire, who died in August 1790.

DAVID WHITEHEAD

Sources Colvin, *Archs.* · N. Kingsley, 'Modelling in the provinces: the work of Anthony Keck', *Country Life* (20 Oct 1988), 138–41 · N. Kingsley, 'Visions of villas: the work of Anthony Keck', *Country Life* (27 Oct 1988), 126–9 · D. Whitehead, 'Georgian Worcester', MA diss., U. Birm., 1976 · D. Whitehead, 'John Nash and Humphry Repton: an encounter in Herefordshire, 1785–98', *Transactions of the Woolhope Naturalists' Field Club*, 47 (1991–3), 210–36 · T. Lloyd, *The lost houses of Wales* (1986) · J. Martin, ed., *The Penrice letters, 1768–95* (1993) · D. C. Cox, 'This foolish business': Dr Nash and the Worcestershire collections, Worcestershire Historical Society, 7 (1993) · correspondence, *Country Life* (12 Jan 1989), 112 · G. W. Beard, 'Nash, historian of Worcestershire', *Transactions of the Worcestershire Archaeological Society*, new ser., 33 (1956), 14–22, esp. 14–16 · *Hereford Journal* (1788–97) · parish register, Lugwardine, 29 June 1761, Herefs. RO [marriage] · Hereford Cathedral Library, 5695 account, April 1786 · account book, Moccas Court, Herefs. RO, J56/IV/2 · quarter sessions records, 1782–91, Worcs. RO, fols. 267, 359 · R. Bigland, *Historical, monumental and genealogical collections, relative to the county of Gloucester*, ed. B. Frith, 3 (1992), 1138
Archives NRA, priv. coll.

Keck [*née* Hamilton], **Lady Susanna** [Susan] (*bap.* 1706, *d.* 1755), political manager, was baptized on 26 September 1706 at Canongate, Edinburgh, the seventh and youngest child of James *Hamilton, fourth duke of Hamilton and first duke of Brandon (1658–1712), and his second wife, Elizabeth Gerard (c.1682–1744), only daughter and heir of Digby Gerard, fifth Baron Gerard of Gerard's Bromley, Cheshire, and his wife, Elizabeth, daughter of Charles Gerard, first earl of Macclesfield. As a duke's daughter, Lady Susan's formal education would have taken place at home, but no governess succeeded in making her quick-witted articulacy insipid, or her handwriting legible. Her portrait at Stanway House, Gloucestershire, suggests that she was never a beauty like her mother; however, her correspondence indicates that she inherited her mother's forthright and spirited confidence, and her intelligence. Growing up as she did in one of Britain's leading territorial and political families during the age of party, she developed an intimate understanding of the political world and a clear-sighted, even cynical, appreciation of human nature. The unashamedly opportunistic politics of her father and her eldest brother undoubtedly contributed to this. Both held important positions at the British court in London yet, like a number of other ambitious noblemen at the time, both also flirted with the exiled Stuart court. This may explain her conviction that Jacobitism was a real threat and that tories were little more than Jacobites in disguise. It may also lie behind her lifelong allegiance to the whigs.

Lady Susan's whiggism was reinforced by her marriage on 3 August 1736 to the whig squire of Great Tew, Oxfordshire, Anthony Tracy Keck (1708–1767). Born Anthony Tracy, he was the second son of John Tracy of Stanway and Anne, daughter of Sir Robert Atkyns MP and chief baron of the exchequer. He received the estate at Great Tew and took the name Keck after 1729 in accordance with the will of his great-uncle Francis Keck. Marrying into a gentry family, even a highly respectable old Gloucestershire family such as the Tracys, was a significant step down the social ladder, but the marriage seems to have been happy. Even Lady Susan's political opponents, when searching for ammunition against her during the 1754 election, did not cast aspersions on it. Indeed, they did little more than charge the easy-going Keck with being 'hen-peck'd' by his dynamic wife—a charge which may well have been true. Although Keck was elected to parliament in 1754 for the duke of Marlborough's pocket borough of New Woodstock, he was a sportsman not a politician. His main passion was horseracing, and several winners emerged from his stables. Racing, however, was inseparable from gambling in the eighteenth century, which may explain jibes about the precarious nature of the Kecks' finances in old interest (tory) broadsheets and squibs during the 1754 election. The Kecks had two children: Henrietta Charlotte (c.1744–1817), who took back the name of Tracy by an act of parliament in 1774 in accordance with her uncle's will, and who married on 2 June 1774 Edward Devereux, twelfth Viscount Hereford (1741–1783); and Susan (c.1745–1835), who married on 18 July 1771 Francis Charteris, Lord Elcho (1749–1808). After their parents' deaths, both girls held positions at court until they married, thanks no doubt to the patronage of Lady Susan's sister, Lady Charlotte Edwin, a longstanding lady of the bedchamber to Augusta, princess dowager of Wales.

As the wife of a squire and justice of the peace, and an aristocratic woman with influential political and court connections of her own, Lady Susan had busied herself with pardons, patronage, and electoral politics well before she decided to take an active role in the 1754 Oxfordshire election. In 1750, for instance, she sought a pardon for a woman who she believed had been wrongly accused of murder, used her political connections to seek patronage for Theophilus Leigh, master of Balliol College, Oxford, and solicited the support of Simon Harcourt, first Earl Harcourt, for Sir Edward Turner in his bid for election at Oxford, albeit only after deciding not to use her own interest at court.

Turner's failure to win the by-election of 1750 was the catalyst for Lady Susan's high-profile involvement in the election of 1754. She was convinced that Turner had lost because of the new interest (whig) gentlemen's lax campaigning and general lack of political sense. She was appalled 'That any sett of Men cou'd have combined together to act against their wishes, and proclaim Themselves Idiots'. She was annoyed that she had believed these 'fools' knew what they were doing (Bodl. Oxf., Dep. c. 576,

4. ii. 1750/51, fol. 111*r–v*). Consequently, when it became clear in 1752 that the local whig magnate, Charles Spencer, third duke of Marlborough, was going to sponsor a new interest opposition with the support of Lord Harcourt and George Parker, second earl of Macclesfield, she decided to take an active part. She knew that securing the victory would mean taking an organizational role herself, as well as snapping at the heels of the new interest peers. She knew from the outset that this might make her the new interest's 'Raw head and Bloody Bones' (Bray papers, Exeter College, Oxford, L. IV. 7. C. fol. 27)—something which did not happen—but it was a chance she was willing to take. She also knew that the demands of an extended campaign would place a strain on her already fragile health. Unfortunately she was all too correct in 1752 when she predicted to her nephew James Hamilton, sixth duke of Hamilton, that her 'ancient Gambol … will even make me extinct, but I shall make my exite in the midst of loud acclamations' (*Hamilton MSS*, 177).

Lady Susan's involvement in the election was celebrated and criticized in the scores of squibs and broadsheets generated by the hack journalists of the respective camps over the next two years. It is a mark of her dynamism and force of character that it was she, rather than either of the candidates, that the new interest writers elevated as the 'real' opposition to the leading old interest candidate, Sir James Dashwood. Ballads regularly included cheers for 'my Lady S[ue]' and chortled over her ability to 'unman' the opposition. They even suggested mischievously that the 'Grey Mare' was the 'Better Horse' and that she would be the best member for the county.

That Lady Susan was able to play as large a part in the campaign as she did, and that men from all levels of society seemed to have little difficulty working with her or under her instruction, was due in part to her ability to interact easily with people of all ranks. It also drew on a general acceptance, even an expectation, of aristocratic women's involvement in eighteenth-century electoral politics. Most importantly, she got results.

By December 1752 Lady Susan had already turned her home at Great Tew into the new interest's social and political headquarters, frequented alike by peers, candidates, agents, local gentlemen, freeholders, and their wives. She knew the importance of social politics and was convinced that the new interest could win if they could out-flatter, out-treat, and out-canvass the opposition. She also gathered as much information as possible from as wide a range of sources as possible in order to monitor the political situation in the county. She then either took action herself, or had any of a number of agents across the county carry out her instructions, or informed the relevant new interest peer of what needed to be done.

A consummate politician, Lady Susan was both a good strategist and a successful canvasser. She ensured that voters were located, canvassed, and secured; waverers were wooed; country gentlemen's egos were stroked; and lazy or untrustworthy agents were identified, their areas being re-canvassed if necessary (sometimes by Lady Susan herself). She was not the only aristocratic woman who canvassed for the new interest, but she did so more flamboyantly and more successfully than others. While old interest propagandists attempted to shame her out of canvassing by telling her that she was too old, or by claiming that all the riding she was doing would make both her bum and her complexion peel, their efforts were futile. Moreover, the election results from the areas that she canvassed suggest that she generally won votes.

After more than two years of intense campaigning and phenomenal expenditure (reputedly £20,000) on each side, the election of April 1754 ended inconclusively in a double return. Thus Lady Susan turned from electioneering to securing witnesses for the scrutiny. Immediately afterwards she had to find yet more witnesses for the subsequent coroner's inquest. This resulted from the shooting of a chimney sweep by a new interest gentleman whose carriage was in danger of being thrown off Magdalen Bridge by an old interest mob at the end of the scrutiny. Finally, in late July 1754 she was implicated in the Rag plot, the new interest's last attempt to smear the old interest with charges of Jacobitism before the election petitions were taken up by parliament. As a known poet and someone who had written and published at least one poem and an address to the voters during the election campaign, she was suspected of having written the notorious pro-Jacobite verses which lay at the heart of the plot.

Lady Susan's health appears to have declined rapidly after the election. She continued, however, to follow the progress of the case in parliament. Finally, on 23 April 1755, all of her efforts were vindicated when the Commons decided the Oxfordshire election in favour of the new interest candidates. Six weeks later, on 3 June 1755, she died at her country home in Great Tew, Oxfordshire. Her obituary, in the *London Evening-Post* of 6 June 1755, reprinted in *Jackson's Oxford Journal* of 7 June 1755, commended her 'publick-spirited Sentiment', 'her flowing Generosity of Temper', and her dignity. It also, revealingly, emphasized those other characteristics which had contributed so much to her political and personal success: 'with an uncommon Quickness of Apprehension, and Sagacity of Judgment, a chearful lively Wit, with an happy Facility of Expression, she was ever the Delight and Joy of all she conversed with'.   E. H. CHALUS

Sources IGI • GEC, *Peerage*, new edn, 266–9 • *Scots peerage*, 4.383–92 • *Collins peerage of England: genealogical, biographical and historical*, ed. E. Brydges, 9 vols. (1812) • *GM*, 1st ser., 6 (1736), 292, 487 • *Pedigree of Keck of Long Marston, co. Glouc. & Great Tew, co. Oxon.* (1857) • *London Evening-Post* (6 June 1755); repr. in *Jackson's Oxford Journal* (7 June 1755) • *VCH Oxfordshire*, 2.230–31 • Bray papers, Exeter College, Oxford • Blenheim papers, BL, Add. MS 61670, vol. DLXX • *The election magazine, or, The Oxfordshire register, being a compleat collection of all the pieces in prose and verse lately published in favour of the old and new interest* (1753) • *The Oxfordshire contest, or, The whole controversy between the old and new interest* (1753) • *Oxfordshire in an uproar, or, The election magazine* (1753) • *The old and new interest, or, A sequel to the Oxfordshire contest* (1753) • *Jackson's Oxford Journal* (1753–5) • R. J. Robson, *The Oxfordshire election of 1754* (1949) • *An eighteenth-century correspondence*, ed. L. Dickins and M. Stanton (1910) • *Poll of the freeholders of Oxfordshire, taken at the county court held in Oxford on the 17th of April, 1754, by Tho. Blackall, esq. high sherriff* (1754) • *Informations and other papers relating to the treasonable verses found at Oxford, July 17, 1754*

(1755) • L. B. Namier, 'Three eighteenth-century politicians', *EngHR*, 42 (1927), 408–13 • L. B. Namier, 'Keck, Anthony', HoP, *Commons, 1754–90* • W. Wing, *Oxfordshire in the eighteenth century and the county election of 1754* (1881) • W. Wing, *The great Oxfordshire election of 1754* (1881) • W. R. Ward, *Georgian Oxford* (1958) • *The Oxfordshire election of 1754*, Oxfordshire county council, record publication no. 6 (1970) • NRA • J. Brooke, 'Oxfordshire', HoP, *Commons, 1754–90*, 1.356 • *The manuscripts of the duke of Hamilton*, HMC, 21 (1887)
Archives BL, Blenheim papers, corresp. with third duke of Marlborough, Add. MS 61670 • Exeter College, Oxford, letters to Thomas Bray relating to Oxfordshire election • NL Scot., Hamilton papers, corresp. with fifth duke of Hamilton and sixth duke of Hamilton
Likenesses group portrait, oils, 1740–49 (with family), Stanway House, Gloucestershire

Keddie, Henrietta [*pseud.* Sarah Tytler] (**1827–1914**), novelist, was born on 4 March 1827 at Cupar in Fife, one of the large family of a lawyer, Philip Keddie (1793/4–1852), and his wife, Mary, *née* Gibb (*d.* 1869). With her sister Jessie, she was educated by her eldest sister, Margaret; she was a keen reader from the age of six, enjoying the novels of Walter Scott and *Blackwood's Magazine*. Later she and Jessie were sent to a school in Leith, and they continued to educate themselves at home afterwards. The Keddie family often spent the summer at Grange Farm, an isolated house near some mines, of which Philip Keddie had become proprietor. This enterprise proved financially unsuccessful and in the 1840s most of the six surviving children left home to work to support the family. In 1848, with three of her sisters, Henrietta Keddie established a school in Cupar, taking day pupils and later boarders. In 1852 her first novel was published, followed swiftly by a second; both fell flat. A short story, based on a Selkirk local tradition and entitled 'Meg of Elibank' met with more success: published in *Fraser's Magazine* in November 1856, it was her first paid work and initiated a career as a contributor to the journal which lasted seventeen years. She also contributed to the *Cornhill Magazine*, *Good Words*, and the *Sunday Magazine*. Her literary work introduced her to leading figures in Scottish intellectual circles, including Dr John Brown, the author of *Rab and his Friends* (1859), the traveller and writer Isabella Bird (later Bishop), A. H. K. Boyd, and Margaret Oliphant.

By 1869 Henrietta Keddie's parents and most of her siblings were dead; with her sister Margaret, she decided to move to London to further her literary career. Settling at Blackheath and then Kensington, she mixed with a wide range of literary figures, including J. A. Froude, George Macdonald, Dinah Mulock Craik, Mrs Henry Wood, Jean Ingelow, Dora Greenwell, and Anna Maria Hall.

Under the pen name Sarah Tytler, Keddie was an extremely prolific novelist who worked largely within the mid-century tradition of domestic realism. Many of her publications were historical novels, often with an eighteenth-century background: they ranged from the early *Citoyenne Jacqueline* (1865), a slightly precious but atmospheric tale of the French Revolution, to such later and lighter romances as *In Clarissa's Day* (1903) and *Innocent Masqueraders* (1907). Other more nostalgic novels—such as

Logie Town (1887), which describes the Fife of her childhood, and *A Daughter of the Manse* (1905), a romance focusing on the Disruption of 1843—were set in mid-nineteenth-century Scotland. A novel such as *Beauty and the Beast* (1884), the contemporary tale of a soldier in the ranks who unexpectedly inherits a baronetcy, shows Keddie at her best: although the plot is often sensational, her talent for original and sympathetic characterization is considerable and her perception of the problems of social divisions keen and realistic.

Keddie also wrote children's stories, such as the enjoyable seventeenth-century tale *At Lathom's Siege* (1903); young women were another favourite audience. *Papers for Thoughtful Girls* (1862), which consisted of essays on such subjects as intellect, friendship, self-sacrifice, and fashion, illustrated with short stories, revealed her moderately progressive views on women's roles: she favoured professional careers and public service at a local government level. She also wrote popular history books, usually women's biographies, such as *The Songstresses of Scotland* (with J. L. Watson, 1871) and *Six Royal Ladies of the House of Hanover* (1898). Although lively and not devoid of insight, these works rarely exhibited any research beyond the most obvious secondary sources.

In 1880 Margaret Keddie died and left her sister Henrietta 'stripped indeed' (Keddie, 345). Leaving England in 1884, Henrietta Keddie spent some time travelling on the continent with a group of friends and her adopted daughter. On her return, she moved to Oxford to be close to her friends Professor William Wallace (1844–1897) and his wife (both natives of Fife); she remained there for twenty years. In 1904 she received a pension from the Royal Literary Fund. After then living in Bristol for two years in a joint household with the family of Lees Smith, a professor of economics, she returned to London. Henrietta Keddie died on 6 January 1914 at her home, 68 Belsize Park Gardens, London.   ROSEMARY MITCHELL

Sources H. Keddie, *Three generations: the story of a middle-class Scottish family* (1911) • *WWW* • J. Sutherland, *The Longman companion to Victorian fiction* (1988) • *Wellesley index* • d. cert.

Kedermyster, Richard. *See* Kidderminster, Richard (*c*.1461–1533/4).

Kedington, Roger (1711/12–1760), Church of England clergyman, was born at Acton, Suffolk, the son of Ambrose Kedington (*b*. 1678), and his wife, Judith Brinkley. He was educated at Bury St Edmunds grammar school and at Gonville and Caius College, Cambridge (1729–36), where he became a fellow. Kedington graduated BA in 1733, MA in 1737, and DD in 1749. He was ordained deacon in March 1734, and priest in March 1736. From 1738 to 1742 he was vicar of Fordham, Cambridgeshire, and from 1750 to 1760 rector and patron of Kedington, Suffolk.

Kedington published a number of works on scriptural interpretation and religious inquiry. These included an account of heathenism (1753), and *Christianity as Taught in Scripture: Sermons on Public Occasions* (1754). In 1759 his *Critical Dissertations on the Iliad of Homer* was published. The Revd William Cole described Kedington as a 'tall, jolly, and well-looking Person', but wrote that he destroyed himself in a fit of insanity (BL, Add. MS 5874, fol. 37). He died at the rectory, Kedington, on 25 March 1760.

    GORDON GOODWIN, *rev.* ROBERT BROWN

Sources Venn, *Alum. Cant.* • *GM*, 1st ser., 30 (1760), 202 • BL, Add. MS 5874, fol. 37

Kedourie, Elie [*known as* Eliahou Abdallah Khedhouri] (1926–1992), historian and political scientist, was born in Baghdad on 25 January 1926, the son of Abdallah Eliahou Khedhouri (*d*. 1964), an employee of the Iraq currency board, and his wife, Loulou Moshi, *née* Dangour (*d*. 1980). Both parents were Jewish. He was educated at the Collège A-D Sasson and then the Shamash School before going in 1947 to the London School of Economics (LSE) to study for the BSc (Econ). His graduate work was at St Antony's College, Oxford, between 1951 and 1953. From 1953 he taught at the LSE, becoming professor of government in 1965 and retiring in 1990. On 3 August 1950, at the Spanish and Portuguese Synagogue, London, he married Sylvia Gourgi Haim, a student of Semitic languages, and daughter of Gourgi Abraham Haim, a company director; they had two sons and one daughter.

Kedourie's academic career began dramatically when in 1953 he withdrew his Oxford doctoral thesis, later published as *England and the Middle East: the Destruction of the Ottoman Empire, 1914–1921* (1956). Kedourie's history offended the Oxford examiner Sir Hamilton Gibb, of whose standards of historical scholarship Kedourie was still contemptuous when, in a second edition of the book in 1978, he wrote an introduction recounting this now famous event. Kedourie's lifelong study of the Middle East challenged the idea that British and French imperial dominance of Arab countries had been a unique oppression generating an irresistible demand for national self-determination. He believed that a culturally misconceived imperial remorse had facilitated the emergence of unscrupulous despotisms in Arab countries. The spread of Western ideologies had led to a way of talking about politics in the Middle East which persuaded Western statesmen, quite wrongly, that they understood what was actually going on. *In the Anglo-Arab Labyrinth* (1976) is regarded by some as Kedourie's masterpiece. This was a detailed examination of the history of Anglo-French relations with the Arabs during and immediately after the First World War which led Kedourie to conclude:

> Some sixty years or so after the exchanges between McMahon and the Sharif, then, there was in Britain a miasm of guilt and self-incrimination, of penitence and breast-beating which hung over relations with the Arab world. It has been chiefly generated by officials hopelessly lost in the labyrinth of their own files.   (*In the Anglo-Arab Labyrinth*, 318)

One of the most notable features of Kedourie's work was a lucid and witty style which could bring out the grand significance of political activity without sacrificing its contingent character.

Kedourie and his wife, Sylvia (herself a notable scholar of Arab affairs), were convivial hosts, and Kedourie was meticulous in performing administrative duties such as

Elie Kedourie (1926–1992), by unknown photographer

being convenor of his department at the LSE. He and Sylvia founded the journal *Middle Eastern Studies* in 1964. Four years previously Kedourie's *Nationalism* appeared. It had a dramatic effect on historical scholarship. Kedourie destroyed the idea that nationalism was an immemorial political passion. Rather, it was a specific doctrine created around the turn of the nineteenth century. Resisting the strong contemporary impulse to blame Hegel for all dangerous ideas, Kedourie found one source of nationalist ideas in Kant's doctrine of self-determination. He later developed these ideas in the long introduction to an anthology, *Nationalism in Asia and Africa* (1971).

Kedourie took a close historian's interest in the detail of politics, and sometimes became involved in public policy. He had a number of conversations with Margaret Thatcher. He was especially alarmed by the degradation of British universities as they expanded during and after the 1960s, and wrote two brilliant pamphlets on the theme: *Diamonds into Glass: the Government and the Universities* (1988) and *Perestroika in the Universities* (1989).

Kedourie's work was governed by two basic understandings. The first was a philosophical sophistication which treated history as the evidential study of events. This was in part developed from association with his friend Michael Oakeshott, who had been responsible both for appointing him to the LSE and for publishing his early work. The second was a realistic view of the mechanics of government as quite different from the moralistic justifications of policy advanced in public discourse. Kedourie immersed himself in the documents, and was alert to what could not be known. He eschewed the mechanical value-freedom on which, for example, students of Soviet politics often fatally prided themselves, but his judgements were always closely aligned to evidence.

Kedourie's education in Baghdad had been French, but he had acquired a great admiration for England, an England which he believed had been corrupted by a false interpretation of recent history. He talked of 'scrupulosity' replacing 'scruple'. One specific target of his criticism was Arnold Toynbee, and one book of essays was entitled *The Chatham House Version* (1970). He was also a mordant critic (in *The Crossman Confessions and other Essays*, 1984) of

what Oakeshott called 'rationalism in politics', mocking, for example, the insouciant objectives (such as building half a million houses) conjured by the Wilson government of the 1960s out of nothing more substantial than abstract desirability.

Kedourie was made a fellow of the British Academy in 1975 and a CBE in 1991. He died of heart failure at the Adventist Hospital, Tacoma Park, Montgomery county, Maryland, USA, on 29 June 1992, while on a visit to Washington, DC. He was buried on 2 July at Edgware Spanish and Portuguese cemetery, London. He was survived by his wife and three children. A memorial service was held at the Bevis Marks Synagogue, London, on 24 September 1992, and a memorial meeting was held at the London School of Economics on 20 January 1993. Kedourie generally had several projects going at the same time, so that at his death a book, *Hegel and Marx* (1996) (typically developed from lectures), was virtually complete. It was published posthumously, edited by his wife. She also edited *Elie Kedourie, CBE, FBA, 1926–1992: History, Philosophy, Politics* (1998), an indispensable source of knowledge about Kedourie.   KENNETH MINOGUE

Sources S. Kedourie, *Elie Kedourie, CBE, FBA, 1926–1992: history, philosophy, politics* (1998) · *WWW*, 1991–5 · personal knowledge (2004) · private information (2004) [S. Kedourie] · *The Times* (3 July 1992) · *The Independent* (3 July 1992) · m. cert. · *CGPLA Eng. & Wales* (1993)
Archives SOUND BL NSA, 'The politics of Elie Khedhouri', BBC Radio 3, 25 Aug 1995 · BL NSA, performance recording
Likenesses photograph, repro. in *The Times* · photograph, repro. in *The Independent* · photograph, priv. coll. [*see illus.*]
Wealth at death £154,419: probate, 9 Feb 1993, *CGPLA Eng. & Wales*

Keeble. For this title name *see* McCarthy, Lila Emma [Lila Emma Keeble, Lady Keeble] (1875–1960).

Keeble, Sir Frederick William (1870–1952), botanist and scientific adviser, was born at 9 Rupert Street, Westminster, London, on 2 March 1870, the second son of Francis Henry Keeble (1839–1923), furniture manufacturer, and his wife, Annie Eliza Gamble (1847–1910). He was educated at Alleyn's School, Dulwich, and at Gonville and Caius College, Cambridge. He obtained a first class in part one of the natural sciences tripos in 1891 and a second in part two in 1893, being appointed Frank Smart student in the latter year. He then spent a year researching plant physiology in Ceylon, and in 1897–8 was an assistant lecturer in botany at the Victoria University of Manchester.

On 9 July 1898 Keeble married Mathilde Marie Cécile (d. 1915), daughter of Louis Maréchal, a Parisian engineer; they had one daughter. In 1902 he was appointed lecturer in botany and director of the horticultural department at University College, Reading, where he became professor in 1907, and was dean of the faculty of science from 1907 to 1909. During his years at Reading, Keeble's main scientific publications were two series of papers in experimental biology. The first, in collaboration with F. W. Gamble, professor of zoology at the University of Birmingham, was on the physiology and ecology of marine plants and animals. The second, in collaboration with the industrial chemist E. F. Armstrong and Christine Pellew, at the John Innes Horticultural Institution, was on the formation and inheritance of floral pigments. He was an early champion of the Mendelian theory of heredity and a founding member of the Genetical Society.

In 1914 Keeble became director of the Royal Horticultural Society's gardens at Wisley, Surrey, but almost at once, on the outbreak of war, he was transferred to the Board of Agriculture and Fisheries. He became controller of horticulture (1917–19) in the food production department, and, in 1919, an assistant secretary to the board. In this position he was able to facilitate the setting up of the East Malling Research Station as an independent government-funded institute for horticultural research. For his services in the war he was appointed CBE in 1917, and knighted in 1922.

Keeble returned to academic life in 1920 as Sherardian professor of botany at Oxford. On 27 March 1920 he married his second wife, the actress Lillah *McCarthy (d. 1960); they had no children. Together they created the beautiful house and gardens at Hammels on Boars Hill, near Oxford, where they entertained extensively. Among their guests was Sir Alfred Mond (later Lord Melchett), head of the firm Brunner Mond, which had developed the process for producing nitrogenous fertilizers from atmospheric nitrogen. He persuaded Keeble to relinquish his chair in 1927 to become agricultural adviser to Imperial Chemical Industries, which had taken over the process following its creation from the merger of Brunner Mond and Nobel Industries.

Keeble entered with enthusiasm into the task of organizing research into the use of nitrogenous fertilizers. A station was set up at Jealott's Hill, near Bracknell in Berkshire, and a staff assembled under his directorship. His programme of research was based on the belief that the use of fertilizers could, with proper management, lead to greatly increased yields on arable and grass land. By the time Keeble relinquished his post as director in 1932, the reputation of Jealott's Hill as a centre of research was firmly established. After an interval, during which he continued to advise Imperial Chemical Industries, Keeble took up his final appointment as Fullerian professor of the Royal Institution (1938–41).

Keeble's interest in applied botany led to his position as editor (1908–19), and thereafter scientific adviser, of the *Gardeners' Chronicle*. He was also successively president of the botany and agricultural sections (1912 and 1920) of the British Association. He was elected FRS in 1913.

Besides his technical papers, Keeble published several books. The first, *Practical Plant Physiology* (1911), with M. M. C. Rayner, is notable for a lengthy preface which stresses the value of its subject as an instrument of education. It was not commercially successful. *The Life of Plants* (1926) was a short and readable account of its subject, and *Science Lends a Hand in the Garden* (1939) was a collection of his more notable contributions to the *Gardeners' Chronicle*. *Polly and Freddie* (1936), which has been described as an 'imaginative autobiography', included tales of biology told to his grandchildren.

In Keeble the training of a scientist sat uneasily with the temperament of an artist. In later life he argued that biology could afford to dispense with the exactitudes of the physical sciences, for which he seems to have had no patience. Thus, for example, he became quite critical of the Mendelian theory of heredity as overly reductive, preferring instead the older, natural historical approach. It may be for this reason that his own work has left little mark on the development of modern biology. His part was that of stimulant and irritant to others. It is said that he was warmhearted and a witty conversationalist. After his retirement he and Lady Keeble lived for a while at Fowey, Cornwall; but they returned eventually to London, where he died at his home, Flat 6, Cranley Mansion, 160 Gloucester Road, on 19 October 1952.

W. O. JAMES, *rev.* PAOLO PALLADINO

Sources V. H. Blackman, *Obits. FRS*, 8 (1952–3), 491–501 · *The Times* (21 Oct 1952) · V. H. Blackman, 'Sir Frederick Keeble', *Nature*, 171 (1953), 63 · private information (1971) · b. cert. · m. certs. · d. cert. · *CGPLA Eng. & Wales* (1953)

Archives Royal Horticultural Society, London, papers | BL, corresp. with Marie Stopes, Add. MS 58539

Likenesses W. Stoneman, two photographs, 1917–31, NPG · F. Dobson, bronze bust, ICI Ltd, London

Wealth at death £10,320 4s. 5d.: probate, 26 Jan 1953, *CGPLA Eng. & Wales*

Keeble, John (1711–1786), organist, was, according to Burney, born in Chichester in 1711. The identity of his parents is unknown. He was brought up as a chorister under Thomas Kelway, organist of the cathedral there from 1720 until his death in 1744.

By 1736 Keeble had made his way to London, where, in August of that year, he was an unsuccessful candidate for the post of organist at St Bride's, Fleet Street. By this date too, it seems, he had already made the acquaintance of the celebrated Dr Pepusch, whose antiquarian researches were to inspire his own lifelong interest in Greek musical theory. This was later to bear fruit in Keeble's *Theory of Harmonics, or, An Illustration of the Grecian Harmonica*, published in 1784 and reviewed at considerable length not only in the *European Magazine* of April–June 1785 but also, somewhat harshly, by Charles Burney in the *Monthly Review* six months later. Having settled in the metropolis, it was not long before Keeble began to acquire a reputation as a fine harpsichord player and teacher, and particularly 'among the first nobility and gentry of his time' (*GM*, 581). Among his pupils were the bluestocking Mrs Anne Ord (*née* Dillingham) and, as formal apprentices, John Burton and Jacob Kirkman (a nephew of the great harpsichord maker of the same name). Keeble was an original subscriber (from 1738) to the Fund for the Support of Decay'd Musicians or their Families, later the Royal Society of Musicians, and was the first organist of Ranelagh Gardens (opened in 1742). In April 1744 he was appointed as assistant to the ailing Thomas Roseingrave, official organist of St George's, Hanover Square; the salary of £45 p.a. they shared between them.

On 1 September 1747 Keeble married Hannah Painter of New Bond Street, described in the *Whitehall Evening-Post* of 8 September 1747 as 'a very agreeable young Lady with a handsome Fortune'; the wedding took place at St Botolph without Bishopsgate, a church in which, somewhat surprisingly perhaps, there was as yet no organ. By 1750 Keeble was generally recognized as *de facto* organist of St George's, and two years later he successfully applied for an increase in salary (from £20 to £30 p.a.); this became £50 p.a. after Roseingrave died (in 1766). Apart from the *Theory of Harmonics*, his chief published work is a set of twenty-four *Select Pieces for the Organ* (4 vols., 1777–8). Shortly after his death there also appeared a book of *Forty Interludes to be Played between the Verses of the Psalms*, twenty-five of which are by Keeble, and the remaining fifteen by Jacob Kirkman, who had succeeded him at St George's. Keeble died on 24 December 1786 at his house in Conduit Street and was buried, as he had wished, at his wife's side in the parish church of Ramsholt in Suffolk.

H. DIACK JOHNSTONE

Sources Burney, *Hist. mus.*, new edn • *GM*, 1st ser., 78 (1808), 581 • *Monthly Review*, 73 (1785), 343–56, 441–7 • *European Magazine and London Review*, 7 (1785), 186–90, 353–61, 431–41 • Highfill, Burnim & Langhans, *BDA*, vol. 8 • *DNB* • D. Dawe, *Organists of the City of London, 1666–1850* (1983) • vestry minutes of St George's, Hanover Square, Westminster Public Library • *ABC dario musico* (privately printed, Bath, 1780) • M. Sands, *Invitation to Ranelagh* (1946) • *New Grove* • B. Matthews, ed., *The Royal Society of Musicians of Great Britain: list of members, 1738–1984* (1985)
Wealth at death see will, summarized, Highfill, Burnim & Langhans, *BDA*

Keeble, Samuel Edward (1853–1946), Wesleyan Methodist minister and social reformer, was born at 1 Regent Terrace, City Road, London, on 20 July 1853, son of Robert Keeble, brazier and coppersmith, and his wife, Harriet, *née* Hunt. One of nine children, he was educated at St Thomas Charterhouse School, London, where he was taught by the former Chartist leader, William Lovett. After some years in business in Liverpool and London, he trained for the Wesleyan Methodist ministry at Didsbury College, Manchester, from 1876 to 1879. He then served as a minister for three-year periods in Ripley, Nottingham, Leeds, Chester, Sheffield, Liverpool, two circuits in Manchester (1902–8), Southport, Llandudno, Southsea (1914–18), and Maidstone, retiring from circuit work in 1921. On 6 March 1883 he married Lucy Jane (1853–1903), daughter of James Warriner, postmaster at Ripley, Derbyshire. They had five sons, only two of whom survived infancy. After his wife's death in 1903 he married, on 9 October 1906, Jessie (*b.* 1874), daughter of Edward Potts, an architect. She shared her husband's social concerns to the full, and survived him.

Keeble was one of the leaders of the Forward Movement in Wesleyan Methodism, a pioneer of democratic socialism in the British free churches, and a proponent of 'social Christianity': he rejoiced greatly at the electoral victory of the Labour Party in 1945. With men like F. D. Maurice, Charles Kingsley, and John Ruskin as his mentors, Keeble made himself a master of economics and sociology, and published three notable books. In the most influential of these, *Industrial Day Dreams* (1896), he sought to show that economics could not be divorced from ethics, and provided a summary of socialist thought (including an analysis of Marx) and an outline of democratic socialist principles. *The Ideal of a Material Life* (1908) had striking parallels to the ideas of the Webbs on the need for social engineering to benefit the unemployed and the elderly, and *Christian Responsibility for the Social Order* (the Fernley lecture for 1922) corresponded closely with the ideas of William Temple and R. H. Tawney. It is largely a historical survey of Christian social involvement, with many pungent judgements including a gloomy view of the consequences of the industrial revolution. The book is based on a firm respect for personality and the need for co-operation rather than competition, typified by public ownership of key industries. In it Keeble asserted that 'a Christian spirit of love, good will and brotherhood is capable of transforming all the wrong relationships of men in society, local, industrial and international'.

Keeble was more radical than his friends Hugh Price Hughes and John Scott Lidgett, moving from support for Liberalism to open endorsement of the Labour Party, and influenced leaders like Philip Snowden. He was a prolific journalist, contributing to Hughes's *Methodist Times* under the pseudonym Labour Lore. Articles included a trenchant attack on the Leeds city council for permitting jerry-building (1890). From 1900 to 1903 he floated his own paper, the *Methodist Weekly*, which was notable for its full support for the free church case on the Education Act of 1902, opposition to the Second South African War, and vitriolic attacks on the policies of Joseph Chamberlain. In a clear parallel to the Anglican Christian Social Union and the work of Henry Scott Holland and Charles Gore, Keeble was one of the founders of the Wesleyan Methodist Union for Social Services (WMUSS) in 1905, acting as chairman with W. F. Lofthouse as secretary. Its magazine, *See and Serve* (1906–17), edited by Henry Carter, was influenced by Keeble, and its publications, including *The Citizen of Tomorrow* (1906), *Social Science and Service* (1909) and, most notably, *The Social Teaching of the Bible* (1909)—which included contributions from Lofthouse, J. H. Moulton, Scott Lidgett, Maldwyn Hughes, and J. E. Rattenbury—were all edited by Keeble. A further development in 1909 was the smaller Sigma Club, which was more overtly socialist than the WMUSS.

Keeble was no mere social activist, for he was known to be a faithful minister, notable for his inspirational work with young people. His sermons were not political speeches, but careful expositions of scripture with prophetic insight. Even those most opposed to his politics honoured him as a pastor. A pacifist in the First World War, he was a pioneer in setting up the Wesleyan Methodist Temperance and Social Welfare Department in 1918 (later the Division of Social Responsibility). He also took a leading role at the conference on politics, economics, and citizenship in 1924. The next year he persuaded J. C. Beckly to endow the Beckly lecture on social science, still given annually at the Methodist conference by an expert in the field.

In appearance Keeble was short and stocky with a large

moustache. He never sought high office, turning down the chair of a Methodist district. There is perhaps some parallel here with Tawney's lack of insight into power and its uses. In his retirement, which was long and active, he played a notable role behind the scenes in Methodism. He has been described as 'the rejected prophet', a harsh assessment in the light of the increasing support for the Labour Party which he witnessed in his church, especially among the ordained ministry. His *Christian Responsibility for the Social Order* was one of the most notable pleas for Christian socialism from a free church source. He died at the age of ninety-three at St Luke's Hospital, Guildford, on 5 September 1946.   JOHN MUNSEY TURNER

Sources M. L. Edwards, *S. E. Keeble: pioneer and prophet* (1949) · M. S. Edwards, *S. E. Keeble: the rejected prophet* (1977) · *The minutes of the annual conference of the Methodist church* (1946) · b. cert. · m. cert. · *CGPLA Eng. & Wales* (1946)
Archives JRL, Methodist Archives and Research Centre, corresp. and papers
Likenesses photograph, repro. in Edwards, *S. E. Keeble: pioneer and prophet* (1949)
Wealth at death £888 9s. 5d.: probate, 15 Nov 1946, *CGPLA Eng. & Wales*

Keegan, John [J. K.; *pseud.* Steel Pen] (1809–1849), poet and writer, was born in a small farmhouse on the banks of the Nore, in Queen's county, Ireland, 3 miles from Abbeyleix. He was the younger of two sons, and, his father dying when John Keegan was just a boy, his education was conducted by his maternal uncle, Thomas Maloney, the brother of Bridget Maloney. Thomas Maloney was a man of some learning, and ran a school for the children of farmers and nearby residents. At the request of the vicar of Killeaney, Maloney began to travel to the village to teach in the vestry there, and classes often conducted outside meant that Keegan later described his schooling as that of a 'hedge school' (O'Donoghue, xii), although a permanent school building was later constructed, at which Keegan himself taught as a young man.

Keegan began to write verses when he was very young, and the influence of his affection for local legends and ballads can be traced throughout his work. He was also something of a musician, playing the violin and the trombone in the local village band. His verse was first published in 1837 in the *Leinster Express* under his initials, or the pseudonym Steel Pen, and he went on to publish in a variety of journals including *Dolman's Magazine*, *The Nation*, the *Irish Penny Magazine*, and the *Dublin University Magazine*. Generally speaking he wrote for the Catholic press, stating that 'though the labours of Catholic writers are little requited, I would prefer a guinea earned *honourably* to the wealth of Angela Burdett Coutts if acquired by disreputable or recreant practices' (O'Donoghue, xxiii–xxiv). His sentimental ballads were immensely popular during his lifetime.

Despite his literary success, Keegan referred to himself as an 'Irish peasant' (O'Donoghue, xviii), and he was never wealthy. About 1840 he married Bridget Collins (*b. c.*1810), the daughter of a nearby small farmer and country carpenter. Her parents were opposed to the match, and so the couple eloped, both being about thirty years of age at the time. The marriage was unhappy, however, partly because

of temperamental differences between them, and partly because of the friction between the two families caused by the marriage. After a short time they separated, and his wife returned with their daughter (*d.* 1896) to the Collins family home.

Keegan was employed as a clerk to one of the many relief committees established to assist the poor during the 1846–7 famine. His own health suffered, and his poetry of this period displays a deep concern with the famine's ravages. He went to Dublin in May 1847, and took up cheap lodgings there, in 8 Lower Bridge Street, where he earned a living through his literary work. He contracted cholera in 1849 and was moved to temporary wooden sheds designed for the reception of cholera patients near the Rialto Bridge. It is likely that he died there, and was moved to Glasnevin for burial on the same day in late June or early July of 1849. Keegan had been preparing a collected edition of his poems, which was never finished. His work nevertheless remained popular long after his death, and appeared in several compilations, such as Edward Hayes's *The Ballads of Ireland* (1855). Keegan's collected legends and poems were published in Dublin in 1907, with a memoir by D. J. O'Donoghue.   M. CLARE LOUGHLIN-CHOW

Sources R. Welch, ed., *The Oxford companion to Irish literature* (1996) · R. Hogan, ed., *Dictionary of Irish literature*, rev. edn, 1 (1996) · *The Irishman* (14 July 1849) · *The Irishman* (10 Oct 1876) · D. J. O'Donoghue, 'Memoir', in J. Keegan, *Legends and poems*, ed. J. O'Hanlon (1907) · E. Hayes, *The ballads of Ireland*, 2 vols. (1855) · A. J. Webb, *A compendium of Irish biography* (1878) · Ward, *Men of the reign*
Archives NL Ire., commonplace book | NL Ire., letters to John Daly

Keeley [*née* Goward], **Mary Ann** (1805–1899), actress, was born in Orwell Street, Ipswich, on 22 November 1805, one of a family of four sisters and five brothers. Her mother's maiden name was Plannen. Mary Ann studied singing from 1817 to 1824 with a Mrs Smart and made her début in York as a concert artist. She also acted in Norwich and Dublin. On 15 June 1824 she was at Ipswich playing Diana Vernon in *Rob Roy* and on 19 June had her first benefit, at which she spoke an address by Jane Cobbold which she could still repeat by heart at the age of ninety. She made her first appearance in London at the Lyceum on 2 July 1825, as Rosina in William Shield's comic opera of that name, and Little Pickle in *The Spoiled Child*. Here and at Covent Garden she met Robert *Keeley (*d.* 1869), with whom she appeared on 7 September 1825. She was at that time considered second only to Madame Vestris and Fanny Kelly, whose pupil she was. She married Keeley on 26 June 1829 in London. They had two daughters, Mary (*b.* 1831), who married the humorist entertainer Albert Richard Smith, and Louise (*b.* 1835), later an actress with the stage name of Louisa Miller, who became the wife of Montagu Williams QC.

Mary Ann Keeley returned to the stage in 1834 at the Adelphi as comic support to J. B. Buckstone. On 8 June 1835 she and her husband appeared at Fanny Kelly's farewell benefit at Drury Lane. They then went on a tour to America. They had been invited by Stephen Price to play the parts in which they had already successfully appeared in

England at the Park Theatre in New York, where they were given benefit performances in June 1837. They also performed in Philadelphia, Boston, Niagara, and Mobile, where Mary Ann contracted a fever from a rat bite. By November 1838 she was back at the Adelphi, where she had the greatest successes of her career as Smike in *Nicholas Nickleby* and as Jack Sheppard. With W. C. Macready at Drury Lane from 1842 she played many parts with varying success, Polly Pallmall (in Douglas Jerrold's *The Prisoner of War*) being well received and nightly encored, but as Audrey in *As You Like It* 'the sprightly Mrs Keeley could by no means assume the stolidity' required. The Keeleys' only benefit performance in London took place on 19 May 1842 at Drury Lane, Robert Keeley not being in favour of making their London audience pay enhanced prices to see them. They managed the Lyceum in 1844, and in 1846 Mary Ann was playing mainly in Albert Smith's adaptations of Dickens's novels. The *Illustrated London News* published an engraving of them in *The Battle for Life* at the Lyceum in 1846. In 1848 she played Nerissa in *The Merchant of Venice* before the queen and prince consort. She was with Charles Kean and Benjamin Webster at the Haymarket, and from 1850 to 1855 at the Adelphi, in the course of which she played to much acclaim a great variety of parts. Her salary at this time never exceeded £20 a week. In 1856 the Keeleys and their daughter Louisa appeared in Edinburgh and Glasgow.

Mary Ann Keeley retired at the same time as her husband in 1859, but often reappeared for benefit performances. Robert Keeley died in 1869 and both her daughters predeceased her. She gave afternoon performances at the Gaiety and in 1880 was again in America. In 1888 her portrait by W. Goodman was exhibited at the Royal Academy. During the sittings for the portrait she had gossiped with Goodman about her life and family, which provided the basis for his book *The Keeleys on the Stage and at Home* (1895). She had revisited Ipswich several times during her career and was there for the last time on 29 March 1891, at the opening of the New Lyceum. She met 'Wild (Buffalo) Bill' Cody and saw his Wild West show in London in 1892. At the request of Queen Victoria she was received at Buckingham Palace on 5 March 1895 wearing her 'best black silk'. Her ninetieth birthday was celebrated on 22 November 1895 at the Lyceum by a miscellaneous entertainment, patronized by the queen, given by many leading actors, an indication of the general affection with which she was regarded by the public. She died on 12 March 1899 at 10 Pelham Crescent, Brompton, where she had lived since 1867, of pneumonia following influenza. She left the substantial sum of £17,812 17s. 2d. Her funeral was at Brompton cemetery on 16 March and was almost a public ceremonial. She was a small, neatly made person, not beautiful, but an actress of wonderful variety, with a 'laughing devil in her eye'. She was also a promising amateur painter: one of her landscapes was owned by the Savage Club.

JOSEPH KNIGHT, *rev.* J. GILLILAND

Sources W. Goodman, *The Keeleys on the stage and at home* (1895) · Mrs C. Baron-Wilson, *Our actresses*, 2 vols. (1844) · C. Tomalin, *The invisible woman: the story of Nelly Ternan and Charles Dickens*, new edn (1991) · C. Tomalin, *Mrs Jordan's profession* (1994) · *The Era* (18 March 1899) · *The Athenaeum* (18 March 1899), 348 · J. R. Planché, *The recollections and reflections of J. R. Planché*, 2 vols. (1872) · J. W. Marston, *Our recent actors*, 2 vols. (1888) · P. Hartnoll, ed., *The concise Oxford companion to the theatre* (1972) · W. Archer, *William Charles Macready* (1890), vol. 1 of *Eminent actors*, ed. W. Archer (1890–91) · Boase, *Mod. Eng. biog.* · Hall, *Dramatic ports.*

Archives Theatre Museum, letters | BL, letters to J. M. Kemble, Add. MSS 42975–42995, *passim*

Likenesses T. H. Wilson, watercolour, 1845, Garr. Club · W. Goodman, oils, *c.*1888 · photograph, *c.*1897, NPG · J. B. Folkard, oils, 1898, NPG · J. Holland, portrait?, 1898, NPG · Fradelle & Marshall, photograph, NPG · J. Smart, portrait (aged fourteen) · C. F. Tomkins, sepia drawing (as Lurline), BM · Walker & Sons, photograph, NPG · engravings?, repro. in *ILN* (26 Dec 1847) · engravings?, repro. in *ILN* (18 April 1891) · four photographs, repro. in Goodman, *The Keeleys* · photographs, NPG · portrait, repro. in R. Mander and J. Michenson, *A picture history of the British theatre* (1957) · theatrical prints, BM, NPG · twenty-two items, Harvard TC

Wealth at death £17,812 17s. 2d.: probate, 7 April 1899, CGPLA Eng. & Wales

Keeley, Robert (1793–1869), actor, one of a family of sixteen children, was born in London at 3 Grange Court, Carey Street, Lincoln's Inn Fields. After the death of his father, who had been a watchmaker, he was apprenticed to Hansard the printer, but ran away to join a strolling company of actors. Not discouraged by one or two failures as an amateur, in 1813 he joined the Richmond Theatre in the humblest capacity. From there he proceeded to Norwich, and remained on that circuit under John Brunton for four years, after which he joined Henry Roxby Beverley at the West London Theatre (subsequently the Prince of Wales's) in Tottenham Street. R. W. Elliston saw him in Birmingham and engaged him for the Olympic, where he made what was practically his début in London in 1818, as the original Leporello in *Don Giovanni in London*, based on Mozart's opera; the part of Simpkins was played by his brother, who died shortly afterwards. When, in 1819, Elliston took Drury Lane, Keeley went with him, but not many opportunities were afforded him there. He appeared at the Adelphi as the original Jemmy Green in W. T. Moncrieff's *Tom and Jerry*, which ran for two seasons in 1821 and 1822. At the end of the first he went to Sadler's Wells under Daniel Egerton, and in April 1822 played Jerry in Pierce Egan's own version of his *Life in London*.

Charles Kemble then engaged Keeley for Covent Garden, where he first appeared in October 1822. The following February he made a decided hit as Rumfit, a tailor, in Peake's *Duel, or, My Two Nephews*. In the summer, at the English Opera House, he was the original Fritz in Peake's *Frankenstein* and the Gardener in Planché's *Frozen Lake*, both parts having been written for him. In November 1824, at Covent Garden, Keeley had one of his greatest successes, as Master Innocent Lambskin in *A Woman Never Vext, or, The Widow of Cornhill*, Planché's adaptation of Rowley's *A New Wonder*. He also played Master Matthew in Ben Jonson's *Every Man in his Humour* and Bob Acres in Sheridan's *The Rivals*. He remained at Covent Garden for several years, performing a great variety of roles, from Shakespearian characters to many parts in forgotten works by Isaac Pocock, Planché, Edward Fitzball, and other dramatists. On 26 June 1829 he married Mary Ann Goward (1805–

1899), who, as Mrs *Keeley, was associated with him in many of these pieces. The couple also appeared at the English Opera House.

In June 1833 Keeley and his wife were engaged by Abbott and Daniel Egerton for the Coburg (renamed the Victoria), and on the failure of that experiment went to America in 1837. That trip was not too successful either, and in 1838 they returned to join Madame Vestris at the Olympic, where they stayed until 1841. In 1841–2 they were with W. C. Macready at Drury Lane, and in 1844 joined Strutt in the management of the Lyceum. They played there until 1847, producing burlesques and adaptations of novels by Dickens. In August 1850 Keeley joined Charles Kean in the management of the Princess's, beginning with a revival of *Twelfth Night*, in which Keeley played Sir Andrew Aguecheek. He was a carrier and Mrs Keeley Dame Quickly in a performance of *Henry IV* at Windsor by royal command. At the close of the season Keeley retired from the management partnership. He played, however, in November 1852, Sir Hugh Evans in *The Merry Wives of Windsor*, Mrs Keeley being Mrs Page, and one of their daughters, Mary Lucy, playing Anne Page. The Keeleys then went in turn to the Haymarket, the Adelphi, and the Olympic, and in September 1856 appeared at Drury Lane under E. T. Smith in a burlesque of Sheridan's *Pizarro*. Keeley's last appearance before retirement was made at Drury Lane in March 1857, in Thomas Morton's *A Cure for the Heartache*, in which he played Old Rapid to the Young Rapid of C. Mathews and the Frank Oatlands of Mrs Keeley. For the benefit of the Royal Dramatic College, however, he appeared in May 1861 as Touchstone in a scene from *As You Like It* at Covent Garden, and for that of E. T. Smith, in March 1862, he was Euclid Facile in Oxenford's farce *Twice Killed*. He died on 3 February 1869, at 10 Pelham Crescent, Brompton, where he had lived for seven years in failing health. He was seen to have been a prudent man as he left a handsome provision for his family. One of his daughters, Mary Lucy, who made her début at the Lyceum in 1845, married the humorist Albert *Smith, and died on 19 March 1870, aged thirty-nine. Another, Louise, married Montagu *Williams, QC, a police magistrate; she appeared at Drury Lane on 12 July 1856 as Gertrude in Planché's *The Loan of a Lover*, and died on 24 January 1877, aged forty-one. Mrs Keeley died in 1899.

Keeley was a genuine comedian. His height was only 5 feet 2 inches; he had when young red hair, a high-coloured, handsome, but in repose inexpressive face, and a slight limp. He had a good deal of mannerism, and, like most comedians, an individuality recognizable through all his roles. In the expression of semi-idiocy or rustic wonderment, or as the suffering victim of unjust fate, he had few equals. Among his best parts were Master William Waddilove in Tom Taylor's *To Parents and Guardians*, Diego in Beaumont and Fletcher's *The Spanish Curate*, Dolly Spanker in Boucicault's *London Assurance*, and Mr Bounceable in *What Have I Done?*

JOSEPH KNIGHT, rev. NILANJANA BANERJI

Sources *The life and reminiscences of E. L. Blanchard, with notes from the diary of Wm. Blanchard*, ed. C. W. Scott and C. Howard, 2 vols. (1891) • T. A. Brown, *History of the American stage* (1870) • T. Marshall, *Lives of the most celebrated actors and actresses* [1846–7] • *Oxberry's Dramatic Biography*, 5/73 (1826), 145–55 • *Actors by Daylight* (2 June 1838) • Hall, *Dramatic ports.* • *The biography of the British stage, being correct narratives of the lives of all the principal actors and actresses* (1824) • C. E. Pascoe, ed., *The dramatic list* (1879) • C. E. Pascoe, ed., *The dramatic list*, 2nd edn (1880) • Genest, *Eng. stage* • J. W. Marston, *Our recent actors*, 2 vols. (1888) • *CGPLA Eng. & Wales* (1869)

Likenesses H. O'Neil, oils, exh. RA 1863, Garr. Club • T. H. Wilson, watercolour drawing, 1865, Garr. Club • O. J. Rejlander, two photographs, NPG • Wageman, sketch, repro. in *Oxberry's Dramatic Biography*, 145 • T. H. Wilson, watercolour drawing (as Billy Black in *The £100 note*), Garr. Club • pencil drawing, priv. coll. • portrait, repro. in *Actors by daylight* • portrait, repro. in *Theatrical Times* (27 June 1846) • portrait, repro. in *Thespian and Dramatic Record* (29 July 1857) • portrait, repro. in J. Cumberland, *Minor theatre* (1831) • prints, Harvard TC • theatrical prints, BM, NPG

Wealth at death under £18,000: probate, 20 March 1869, *CGPLA Eng. & Wales*

Keeling, Dorothy Clarissa (1881–1967), social worker, was born at Grammar School House, Manor Row, Bradford, on 2 December 1881, the seventh of nine children of the Revd William Hulton Keeling (1840–1916), for many years headmaster of Bradford grammar school, and his wife, Henrietta Frances Gedge (d. 1905). Keeling was educated at home and at a girls' grammar school, but physical weakness in childhood barred her from serious academic work and deterred her from following the family vocation of teaching. She had, however, 'an intense interest from childhood in people', and while she continued to live at home after leaving school at the age of eighteen, she overcame the reservations of her overprotective family and a severe stammer to become involved in voluntary social work. After some experience with workhouse visiting, in 1907 she joined the staff of the Bradford Guild of Help, which had been founded in 1905. Drawing on the model of the 'Elberfeld system' in Germany, the Edwardian Guilds of Help promoted a vision of social betterment that drew on ideals of cross-class 'friendship' and civic participation; Guild volunteers visited needy or distressed families, less to dispense relief than to help the family devise a strategy for rehabilitation. Keeling held the position of honorary assistant secretary for the Bradford Guild of Help for ten years, undertaking 'an immense amount' of visiting and supervising both the work of the Guild's district heads and the practical training of students from the Leeds University school of social work.

After her father's death in 1916 Keeling became self-supporting, accepting first a salary for her work in Bradford and then the secretaryship of the National Association of Guilds of Help, headquartered in Manchester. It was with this background that she was hired in 1918 as the first secretary of the newly established personal services committee of the Liverpool Council of Voluntary Aid, a position she held until the Second World War. The Personal Services Society (PSS), as the committee was renamed in 1922, was set up by those Liverpool municipal reformers and social workers—among them Eleanor Rathbone (1872–1946), Elizabeth Macadam (1871–1948), and F. G. D'Aeth (1875–1940)—who saw the need for a new society to carry on the work of 'friendly visiting', which had been pioneered by the settlement houses and expanded during the First World War. The first years of the society were, however, rocky ones. Many of the established philanthropic societies in Liverpool saw no need for another organization, especially one determined to dispense advice but not material aid, while Keeling's weak health and subsequent leave delayed the society's effective operation for almost a year.

Over time, however, the PSS did establish itself as the premier social work organization in Liverpool. Although Keeling herself seems to have been somewhat shy and personally timid (she admitted in her autobiography that she had never been 'quite brave enough' to live among the poor), she guided the society with some skill for almost two decades. Organized on a ward basis and enrolling voluntary workers responsible individually for only a small number of families, the society proved flexible enough to develop innovative responses to new social needs. Thus, while the society did establish clothing clubs, boot clubs, a loan fund, and other schemes intended to ease the effects of the chronic poverty and unemployment of the interwar years, and from 1932 administered aid on behalf of the very philanthropic society (the Central Relief Society) which had initially opposed its creation, it also inaugurated many other services, establishing advice bureaux for tenants on new housing estates, pioneering a scheme of marriage counselling, offering legal advice in cases ranging from marital disputes to money claims, organizing holidays for 'tired mothers' and city children, and providing various forms of care and visiting to old, ill, and disabled people. This record of work and Keeling's officially non-partisan but generally progressive leadership strengthened the society's reputation as a leader in the development of family casework and as a reliable resource for those in need of advice and aid. Thus, while the society had initially dealt largely with referrals from other statutory or voluntary bodies, by 1935 about three-quarters of the year's caseload of 9000 families had come to the society of their own accord. By the outbreak of the war, the society was providing a wide array of services, had trained many dozens of students in the methods of social work, and drew on the services of some 560 voluntary workers.

Keeling left Liverpool during the Second World War to work more closely with the London-based National Council of Social Service (NCSS), with which the PSS had close ties. Convinced that voluntary workers could help with many of the problems caused by the war, she expanded the number and scope of the Citizens' Advice Bureaux, which she had helped to organize under the aegis of the NCSS in 1938, and developed new council services for the elderly. Made an OBE in 1946 for her work with the Citizens' Advice Bureaux, Keeling returned to Liverpool at the end of the war, resuming both her central role in voluntary social work there and her domestic partnership with Ellinor Black, then senior lecturer in the department of social science at Liverpool University, with whom she had lived since 1926. In 1950 Black was appointed director of the Sheffield School of Social Work and Keeling left Liverpool with her, taking a position on the management committee of the Middlewood Mental Hospital and serving on the Sheffield Council of Social Service. Keeling returned to Liverpool after Black's death in 1956, and for several years remained active in social work with old and mentally handicapped people, and in the work of the Citizens' Advice Bureaux. She died on 27 March 1967 at 66 West Heath Road, Hendon, London.

SUSAN PEDERSEN

Sources D. C. Keeling, *The crowded stairs: recollections of social work in Liverpool* (1961) · M. E. Brasnett, *The story of the Citizens' Advice Bureaux* (1964) · M. Brasnett, *Voluntary social action: a history of the National Council of Social Service, 1919–1969* (1969) · H. R. Poole, *The Liverpool Council of Social Service, 1909–1959* (1960) · J. Lewis, 'The boundary between voluntary and statutory social service in the late nineteenth and early twentieth centuries', *HJ*, 39 (1996), 155–77 · b. cert. · d. cert.
Archives Liverpool, Liverpool Council for Voluntary Aid MSS
Likenesses D. Valentine, photograph, repro. in Keeling, *Crowded stairs* [frontispiece]
Wealth at death £4923: probate, 11 May 1967, *CGPLA Eng. & Wales*

Keeling, Enoch Bassett (1837–1886), architect, was born on 15 March 1837 in Sunderland, the son of Isaac Keeling (1789–1869), a Wesleyan minister there, and his wife, Esther. He was baptized on 16 June 1837 at Sans Street Wesleyan Chapel, Bishopwearmouth. He was articled in 1852 to the Leeds architect Christopher Leese Dresser, and attended Leeds School of Practical Art. Keeling established himself in London in 1857 and was elected an associate of the Royal Institute of British Architects in 1860, the year of his marriage to Mary Newby Harrison (1841–1882).

Keeling quickly picked up substantial church-building commissions, most notably St Mark's, Notting Hill (1862–3), St George's, Campden Hill (1864–5), and St Paul's, Upper Norwood (1864–6). Relatively inexpensive, freely planned, highly eclectic in their Gothic, these churches combined strident polychromy and unconventional decoration with new structural materials, especially iron. Critics acknowledged their ingenuity, but deplored their eccentricity. Reaction to Keeling's first major secular building, the Strand Music Hall (1863–4), was intensely hostile. Though remarkably innovative, with such features as overhead lighting from a multicoloured glass ceiling, its wild medley of ornament was ridiculed and condemned. Worse still, the Strand was a commercial disaster: heavily implicated financially, Keeling was declared bankrupt in 1865. He apparently abandoned architecture for a while, and quit the Royal Institute of British Architects in 1872, but re-emerged in the late 1870s to design commercial buildings in the City, their functionalism strikingly different from his churches; examples include 18 Tokenhouse Yard (1880) and Tokenhouse Buildings (1882). Combining property development with architecture, he also produced the ponderous apartment block of Prince's Mansions, Westminster (1884–6). But personal problems overwhelmed him: his wife died in childbirth in 1882, their infant son in 1884. Keeling drank excessively, and died at his home, Dunwood House, Paradise Row, Stoke Newington, of cirrhosis of the liver on 30 October

Enoch Bassett Keeling (1837–1886), by unknown photographer, c.1884

1886; he was buried in November in Abney Park cemetery, Stoke Newington.

Although H. S. Goodhart-Rendel considered him a 'rogue' architect (Goodhart-Rendel, 251), Keeling's idiosyncrasies were dynamically related to central developments in high Victorian Gothic: this has not saved his buildings, most of which have been destroyed or radically altered. CHRIS BROOKS

Sources J. S. Curl and J. Sambrook, 'E. Bassett Keeling, architect', *Architectural History*, 16 (1973), 60–69 · J. S. Curl and J. Sambrook, 'E. Bassett Keeling: a postscript', *Architectural History*, 42 (1999), 307–15 · J. S. Curl and J. Sambrook, 'Gothic freely treated: a look at the career of E. Bassett Keeling', *The Architect*, 2 (1972), 40–42 · J. S. Curl, 'Acrobatic Gothic, freely treated', *Country Life*, 180 (1986), 1030–32 · H. S. Goodhart-Rendel, 'Rogue architects of the Victorian era', *RIBA Journal*, 56 (1948–9), 251–9 · *The Builder*, 51 (1886), 753 · M. B. Adams, 'Architects from George IV to George V', *RIBA Journal*, 19 (1911–12), 643–54, esp. 652 · R. H. Harper, *Victorian architectural competitions: an index to British and Irish architectural competitions in The Builder, 1843–1900* (1983) · *London: south*, Pevsner (1983) · *Northumberland*, Pevsner (1992)

Likenesses photograph, c.1884, repro. in Curl, 'Acrobatic Gothic' [see illus.]

Wealth at death £209 0s. 6d.; plus interest in property: Curl and Sambrook, 'E. Bassett Keeling', 67

Keeling, Frederic Hillersdon [Ben] (1886–1916), social reformer, was born in Colchester, Essex, on 28 March 1886, the elder of the two sons of Frederic John Keeling (d. 1901), a well-to-do and cultivated solicitor and Conservative, and his third wife, Alice May Mildred Chapman (d. 1903). Educated at a Wokingham preparatory school and at Winchester College (1899–1904), Ben Keeling was unhappy and rebellious as a child. As a teenager he became a socialist, joined the Fabian Society and induced his mother to buy everything from the Co-op. At Winchester (also attended by his brother Guy) he was hardworking, fearlessly combative in declaring his opinions, but not good at games and not popular. His father died when he was fourteen, and his mother three years later. His father bequeathed him £300 a year, together with much guilt, which he henceforth assuaged with personal austerities and many gifts to those he thought less privileged than himself.

At Trinity College, Cambridge (1904–7), Keeling at last found happiness—relishing the relative freedom and the serious conversations with congenial friends spiced by his candour and punctuated by his roars of laughter. It was when reading Shaw's *Man and Superman* at Cambridge that 'the whole conception of the solubility of property and marriage came on me like a flash', and several years later he claimed that 'it has been the main driving force of my thought ever since' (*Keeling Letters and Recollections*, 142–3). He won first-class honours in both parts of the historical tripos, spoke memorably at the Union, and established a university Fabian branch. It was Keeling's skilful subterfuge that enabled Keir Hardie to outwit hostile undergraduates and address his legendary meeting at Cambridge in February 1907. Keeling's driving energy and flamboyant daring made him well-known among his contemporaries, themselves a notable generation, with Hugh Dalton not least among them.

After staying on at Cambridge for a year to study economics, Keeling impressed Beatrice Webb in September 1908 with his 'generous vitality and incontinent intelligence' (*Diary*, 3.98). At the Webbs' suggestion he moved to Walworth in London, joined a London County Council care committee, and read for the bar. He was, H. G. Wells recalled, 'a copious, egotistical, rebellious, disorderly, generous, and sympathetic young man' (*Keeling Letters and Recollections*, ix), 'a wild, loose thing' (ibid.) whose egotism led him to fire off many letters largely about himself, leaving us unusually well-informed about what motivated a young Edwardian left-wing idealist who would otherwise have remained obscure. Repudiating religious belief, he was engulfed by successive waves of ideals, impressions, and ideas—all of them interacting continuously with his volatile moods, his boyish enthusiasms, and his intense energies and emotions. He sought periodic relief through energetic walks and climbs at home and abroad, during which he soaked up new thoughts and experiences—relishing the beauty of nature and the goodness of life.

On 15 May 1909 Keeling married Rachel Susanna Townshend, who had been imprisoned the year before as a suffragette. Their daughter Joan was born late in 1909, but Keeling did not live with his wife. Instead he regularly visited her when she set up house near Leeds with their daughter, and in March 1912 they had a son, Bernard. Eventually Rachel divorced him, but her socialist mother Emily Townshend—attractive to young men—was for him a mother figure, and in his many introspective letters to her his ideas tumbled out indiscriminately, ever in search of a creed and a role in life. Keeling's was an unconventional personal life: it puzzled his contemporaries and still seems surprising. Less surprising are his occasional comments in letters at this time about the tension between his rather abstract benevolence and the need to tackle the pressing problems of the individuals around him.

The Webbs' contacts had meanwhile enabled Keeling to

work for the Board of Trade in 1909, and then in January 1910 he became an enthusiastic manager of Leeds labour exchange. His 76-page booklet on *The Labour Exchange in Relation to Boy and Girl Labour* (1910) is thoroughly Fabian in its practical tone, its firm grasp of empirical detail, and its alertness to German experience; it is dedicated to his contemporary Ashley Dukes, with whom he had shared rooms in Walworth: 'one of the very small minority of Englishmen who make our forms of Government actually workable in practice' (*Keeling Letters and Recollections*, 64). In February 1911 Keeling moved on again, helping to improve the organization of the boy labour market through juvenile advisory committees, and at the same time collecting material for a projected book on industrial regulation. He resigned from the civil service, which had in some ways cramped his style, and left Leeds in summer 1912.

After travels in Europe Keeling settled in London and worked for the *New Statesman* with furious energy, eventually becoming assistant editor. A recognized authority on young people's employment, he published his *Child Labour in the United Kingdom* in February 1914. Again severely practical in its concerns, it is indigestibly replete with tables and statutory detail, and emerged from a committee appointed by the British section of the International Association for Labour Legislation conference at Zürich in 1912. By 1914 Keeling was settling into a Liberal pragmatism, shedding his more revolutionary ideas, and coming to terms with the Colchester of his childhood that he had earlier repudiated.

At the end of August 1914 Keeling enlisted as a private in the 6th battalion of the Duke of Cornwall's Light Infantry. In view of his enthusiasm for German social-welfare legislation, Britain seemed to him somehow to have taken on the wrong enemy, and a crudely anti-German chauvinism was not for him. He admitted that 'sheer egotistical adventurousness' was one component of his decision to enlist (*Keeling Letters and Recollections*, 222), and he relished the hardships and the classless, semi-socialist companionship of army life. His articles from the front in the *New Statesman* evocatively captured its austerities and excitements, attacked conscription and dreamed of 'a really big international democratic movement after the war' (*Keeling Letters and Recollections*, 240). His private letters confront the truth with Orwellian honesty and directness. They repudiate wartime sentimentality and anti-German press stunts, and hint at the grim scenes he witnessed. Yet he retained his zest for life, and remained alive to the beauties of nature on a fine day. He records his programme of serious reading and longs for peace—though not before victory has been secured.

Rapidly promoted through the ranks to sergeant, Keeling several times refused a commission. His appearance changed markedly during his short adulthood: lean and 6 foot tall, he had decided in 1908 to disguise his weak chin by growing a handsome, rather unkempt beard and moustache, but by the end of his life he was balding, his facial hair had become neatly trimmed, and his moustache had become decidedly twirly. In May 1915 his battalion went to

France, where he was wounded on 29 July and hospitalized. 'It is dying, not death, that one fears', he wrote in August (*Keeling Letters and Recollections*, 239). Having returned to the trenches in September, he was brave, alert to the welfare of his men, and greatly respected by them. By December he had become a sergeant-major of a new grenadier or bomber company. On 18 August 1916, at Delville Wood on the Somme, he was shot while leading his bombers along a German trench and died instantly. He was awarded the Military Medal posthumously.

H. G. Wells, whose Ted Hatherleigh in *The New Machiavelli* (1911) was modelled on Keeling, wrote a preface to the remarkable collection of his letters and recollections which Emily Townshend edited and published in 1918; it reveals much but conceals more. Rachel Townshend's divorce had the effect of denying her a state pension, but she later concealed the divorce and described herself as a widow. She eventually settled for an austere and prolonged rural existence in the Chilterns, then became active as Labour representative for Bethnal Green on London County Council (1934–41). With no career of her own and socially somewhat difficult, she became rather embittered in later life, and died in 1969. Her daughter Joan married E. A. Radice, the Fabian economist, and her son Bernard spent his career in the iron and steel industry. Few members of the 'lost generation' showed Keeling's promise, but we will never know whether his brave intellect and fierce loyalties could ultimately have disciplined his superabundant energy, his impulsiveness, and his questing temperament. All that this notable member of the 'lost generation' left behind was the memory of a short and wayward but in many ways brilliant and courageous life that had been lived to the full.   BRIAN HARRISON

Sources D. Hopkinson and D. E. Martin, 'Keeling, Frederic Hillersdon', *DLB*, vol. 7 · *Keeling letters and recollections*, ed. E. T. [E. Townshend] (1918) · *The diary of Beatrice Webb*, ed. N. MacKenzie and J. MacKenzie, 4 vols. (1982–5), vol. 3 · private information (2004) [Mrs Joan Radice]
Likenesses photographs, repro. in E. T., ed., *Keeling letters*
Wealth at death £5297 14s. 5d.: probate, 8 Dec 1916, *CGPLA Eng. & Wales*

Keeling, Josiah (*fl.* 1679–1691), conspirator, was a white salter or oilman of East Smithfield, London, in the parish of St Botolph, Aldgate. Although his parentage and birthplace are unknown, Keeling had been concerned in a coalworks in Warwickshire as late as April 1679. He is known to have been married. At the time of the parliaments of 1679–81, his brother John, a smith of St Ann Blackfriars, lived near the whig activist Steven College, the 'Protestant Joiner', who was executed for treason in 1681. The Keeling brothers may have been within College's political circle. A Baptist, Josiah was also a parish constable. As the court-inspired harassment of dissenters mounted in 1682, he opposed loyalist JPs who sought to suppress dissenting meetings. When the court intervened in the corporation of London in 1682 to ensure the election of tory sheriffs, Keeling was among those whig citizens who signed petitions in protest. Like more prominent City whigs, he regarded the court's imposition of loyalist sheriffs, and also of a loyalist lord mayor, as an 'invasion' of civic rights. Keeling stood bail for the unknown printer of Robert Ferguson's *The Second Part of the Growth of Popery and Arbitrary Government* (1682). However, by 1683 he was in financial difficulty and had reportedly been expelled from his congregation.

Keeling's actions and beliefs brought him to the attention of the circle of lawyers, dissenters, and Cromwellian officers who were plotting an April 1683 assassination of Charles II and the duke of York. Keeling agreed to participate in an attempt on their lives at Rye House in Hertfordshire. His knowledge of the whig underworld of plebeian activists enabled him to assist such plot principals as Robert West and Richard Goodenough in recruiting other men. According to West, Keeling was motivated by his desire to 'save the city charter and the nation', but Keeling was also described by one acquaintance as having 'had always the character of an ambitious man' (*State trials*, 9.391, 980). When the initial plan miscarried, Keeling remained in touch with the plot's ringleaders. Goodenough pressed him into service again on 24 April 1683, when Keeling served as a special bailiff in the whig arrest of Lord Mayor Sir William Prichard. The loyalist Prichard had refused to respond to king's bench suits, brought by the London whigs, that challenged the election of the tory sheriffs. Whatever its precise relationship to the Rye House plot, this escapade collapsed after a few hours with the lord mayor's release.

In May and June 1683 West and Goodenough resumed their conspiracy and recruited leaders for a London insurrection. Expected to employ his Wapping contacts on behalf of a rising, Keeling became anxious about the design. 'If it were a sin in David to cut off the hem of Saul's garment', he recalled thinking, 'it was a sin in me much more to kill my king'. His tavern fellows later remembered that a 'disturbed or distracted' Keeling had spoken of rewards he might receive from 'great men' for discoveries he could make (*State trials*, 9.535, 974). Becoming suspicious, his fellow conspirators considered murdering Keeling, but they instead sought to retain his allegiance with a loan. Keeling had, however, already commenced the revelations to Secretary of State Sir Leoline Jenkins that initiated the government's unravelling of the plot. Keeling was pardoned and employed as a witness in the treason trials of Thomas Walcott, William Hone, Algernon Sidney, and Charles Bateman. He was eventually awarded £500 and a place in the victualling office on Tower Hill. Named an assistant in the Broderers' Company in the remodelling of the London livery, he also provided the government with additional information about disaffected dissenters in the eastern out-parishes at the time of Monmouth's rebellion. Keeling lost his place during the 1689 parliamentary investigation of the conspiracy trials and turned Jacobite. In 1691 he was fined £500 for drinking James II's health, and he disappears from the historical record thereafter.   GARY S. DE KREY

Sources DNB · BL, Middleton MSS, Add. MS 41803 · *State trials*, vols. 9, 11 · *CSP dom.*, 1683; 1685 · BL, Add. MS 38847 · R. L. Greaves, *Secrets of the kingdom: British radicals from the Popish Plot to the revolution of 1688–89* (1992) · N. Luttrell, *A brief historical relation of state affairs from September 1678 to April 1714*, 1 (1857), 266–8, 289, 364–5; 2 (1857), 211, 234, 307, 310 · 3 Oct 1682, CLRO, sessions file 301, recognizance 46 · *Burnet's History of my own time*, ed. O. Airy, new edn, 2 (1900), 360 · ward assessment books for six-months tax, 1680, CLRO · R. North, *The life of the Lord Keeper North*, ed. M. Chan (1995), 99, 101 · R. North, *Examen, or, An enquiry into the credit and veracity of a pretended complete history* (1740), 378–9

Likenesses R. White, engraving, 1793, BL, Add. MS 32352, fol. 26 · R. White, line engraving, BM, NPG

Keeling, William (1577/8–1620), naval officer in the East India Company, is of unknown parentage, his date of birth being calculated from his supposed age of forty-two at death. His ability to deal with eastern potentates suggests that he was 'socially a cut above the average sea captain' (Strachan and Penrose, 4). He spoke Arabic and Malay well. Given his skill in merchandising, he may have served an apprenticeship with a London livery company. He is also said to have served the Levant Company.

Keeling was appointed captain of the *Susan* in the second East India Company voyage under Sir Henry Middleton, which sailed on 25 March 1604. They arrived at Bantam on 23 December 1604, with crews much reduced and enfeebled by sickness. Middleton sailed for the Moluccas on 18 January 1605, leaving two ships, the *Susan* and the *Hector*, to load pepper. When the captain of the *Hector* died Keeling transferred to her, and the two ships left Bantam for England on 4 March 1605. Nine months elapsed before the *Hector* reached the Cape of Good Hope, by which time the crew was reduced to fourteen and the *Susan* had disappeared. They were fortunate to meet and obtain help there from Middleton. The fleet reached the Downs on 6 May 1606.

Keeling had done well, and while still in his twenties was appointed general of the third East India Company voyage, with detailed orders to continue trade with Java and to open up commerce with India and Aden. Though Keeling's original journal of the voyage is lost, a drastically abridged version was published by Samuel Purchas (Purchas, 2.502–49). Three ships left Tilbury on 12 March 1607 and were almost immediately scattered by storms. David Middleton made a fast voyage in the *Consent* to the Moluccas and back, but Keeling and William Hawkins, in the *Dragon* and *Hector* respectively, had a much harder and slower voyage; in the course of it the crews allegedly staged early performances of *Hamlet* and *Richard II*. Though an attempt to reach Aden failed, the *Hector* under Hawkins became the first English ship to reach India. The crew of the *Dragon* frustrated Keeling's plan to sail to the Moluccas, but on meeting the *Hector*, Keeling transferred to her, obtained a cargo of cloves in the Banda Islands despite Dutch opposition, stirred up local resistance to the Dutch, and discovered the Cocos (or Keeling) Islands in 1609; he arrived back in England on 10 May 1610.

Keeling married Ann Broomefield (d. 1631), possibly his second wife, on 25 September 1610. No more is heard of him until September 1614 when the East India Company appointed him for five years to reorganize their trading establishments in Asia, preferring him, in view of his skill in merchandise, to Thomas Best, a difficult man but the better navigator and commander. Christopher Newport went as vice-admiral to supplement navigational expertise. Keeling wished to take his pregnant wife with him and smuggled her aboard, but was refused permission and threatened with dismissal until he put her ashore. The fleet left the Downs on 23 February 1615, carrying Sir Thomas Roe to be first ambassador to the Mughal emperor. Keeling worked hard in the East, and established a factory at Teko in Sumatra. Keeling badly missed his wife, however, suffered ill health, and was relieved when the company reluctantly agreed to his return though the work of reorganization was still incomplete. He reached England in May 1617.

Keeling was subsequently appointed captain of Cowes Castle and groom of the bedchamber to James I. Sir John Oglander described him as a brave and noble fellow, noted for his hospitality. Keeling made his will on 6 October 1620 and was buried in Carisbrooke church three days later, leaving at least three children. His curious monument, erected by his 'loveing & sorrowfvll wife', wrongly stated his date of death as 19 September 1619. A rich widow, according to Oglander, she remarried on 9 April 1621.

J. K. LAUGHTON, rev. G. G. HARRIS

Sources M. Strachan and B. Penrose, eds., *The East India Company journals of Captain William Keeling and Master Thomas Bonner, 1615–1617* (1971), 4–6, 22–6, 31, 34, 41–2, 44, 59–60 · W. Foster, ed., *The voyage of Sir Henry Middleton to the Moluccas, 1604–6*, Hakluyt Society (1943), xvi, xviii, xx, xxix, xxx, xxxiii, 5, 61, 150 · *CSP col.*, vols. 2–3 · S. Purchas, *Hakluytus posthumus, or, Purchas his pilgrimes*, bk 2 (1625); repr. Hakluyt Society, extra ser., 15 (1905), 502–49 · W. Keeling's letter-book, 1616–20, University of Indiana, Bloomington, Lilly Library [cited in Strachan and Penrose] · *The embassy of Sir Thomas Roe to India, 1615–19*, ed. W. Foster, rev. edn (1926), xxv, 9–10, 361–2 · J. D. Jones, *Isle of Wight curiosities* (1989), 46 · T. D. S. Bayley and F. Steer, 'The Keeling memorials in Carisbrooke church', *Mariner's Mirror*, 42 (1956), 235–8 · F. C. Danvers and W. Foster, eds., *Letters received by the East India Company from its servants in the east*, 6 vols. (1896–1902), vol. 4, pp. 64–6 · F. C. Danvers and W. Foster, eds., *Letters received by the East India Company from its servants in the east*, 6 vols. (1896–1902), vol. 6, pp. 199, 202 · parish register, Carisbrooke church, Isle of Wight RO · PRO, PROB 11/136, fol. 369 · *A royalist's notebook: the commonplace book of Sir John Oglander*, ed. F. Bamford (1936), 153–4
Archives Indiana University, Bloomington, Lilly Library, letter-book · University of Minnesota, Minneapolis, James Ford Bell Library, journal of his voyage taking Sir Thomas Roe as ambassador to the great Mughal [formerly Phillipps MS 8650]
Likenesses stamps, issued 1984 (artist's impression of William Keeling) · memorial tablet, Carisbrooke church, Isle of Wight; repro. in Jones, *Isle of Wight curiosities*, 46
Wealth at death substantial: will, PRO, PROB 11/136, fol. 369 · widow wealthy: Oglander, *Royalist's notebook*

Keeling, William Hulton (1840–1916), headmaster, was born on 8 February 1840 at the parsonage, Blackley, near Manchester, Lancashire, one of several children of the Revd William Robert Keeling (1807/8–1869), rector of Blackley (1838–69)—where he rebuilt the church and promoted the building of three sets of schools—and his wife, Susan, daughter of Charles Nevill. He was a scholar of Manchester grammar school (1849–59) and exhibitioner of Wadham College, Oxford (1859–62) where he took a first in classical moderations (1859) and a second in *literae*

humaniores in 1862 (BA, 1862; MA, 1865). He took holy orders in 1864 and became a schoolmaster. From 1865 until 1867 he was headmaster's assistant at Rossall School, Fleetwood. In 1867 he became headmaster of Northampton grammar school. He married on 21 April 1870 Henrietta Frances (*d.* 1905), daughter of the Revd Sydney Gedge. In 1871 he was appointed headmaster of Bradford grammar school and held that post until his death.

At Northampton, Keeling already showed those qualities of energy and purpose which are necessary to revive a failing school. That is why he was appointed to Bradford. Bradford in 1871 was a dynamic city, commercial and largely nonconformist. Its medieval grammar school was under-endowed, classical, high-church, and effete. An alliance of Jacob Behrens, the prominent woollen merchant, William Byles, editor of the *Bradford Observer*, and Vincent William Ryan, the evangelical vicar of Bradford (and formerly bishop of Mauritius), seized the opportunity provided by the endowed schools commission to set about its reform as a school of the first grade, authorized to teach Greek and to teach pupils up to the age of nineteen and prepare them for entry to the universities. This premier status was not achieved without a struggle, such was the school's decay. The reforming governors were required to sell the school's landed estates and invest the income in government securities. Keeling often complained in the following years that his school was inadequately endowed. Under his direction, however, the reconstituted school flourished. Keeling, although a classicist himself, created a modern side more suited to Bradford's needs, specializing in languages, mathematics, science, and commercial subjects. The school became liberal in its curriculum and its sympathies, and its attendance and reputation increased rapidly until by 1895 it was cited by a royal commission as an example that 'local schools are no whit inferior to great Public Schools' (headmaster's report for 1895, governors' minute books, 3 March 1896). Keeling's personal contribution was recognized in 1912 when the freedom of the city was conferred upon him.

The personal qualities which underlay this achievement can be surmised to some extent from contemporary portraits. An etching of 1882 reveals a burly man with a clear gaze and a firmly set jaw. Not the face of a poet or an artist, it is pre-eminently that of a man with a clear conscience who knows his own mind. The Sichel portrait presented in 1912 adds the distinction of forty years of headmastership. To schoolboys of course the headmaster cuts a less heroic figure. Humbert Wolfe described 'a huge square face like that of a tin statue of Thor which had been left to rust in some abandoned garden' with 'a voice as rusty-red as his face' (H. Wolfe, *Yorkshire Observer*, 20 April 1939) which read prayers 'as though he were pelting the school with the words' (Wolfe, 135–6). The artist William Rothenstein on the other hand remembered Keeling telling him 'You will have to earn your living with your hands, you will never do it with your head' (W. Rothenstein, *Yorkshire Observer*, 17 Aug 1939), but then clearing the way for him to concentrate entirely upon his art. Keeling himself enjoyed a happy family life among his five sons—all educated at the grammar school—and his four daughters, educated at the girls' grammar school which his wife, Henrietta, helped to found in 1875.

Keeling's genius as a headmaster was in his energy, his clear vision, and the determination with which he realized it. He never neglected the classical side, which was the high road to Oxford and Cambridge, where 280 scholarships gained a national reputation for the school. At the same time he developed the modern side. Above all he resolved to open the school to clever boys of every class— what he described as 'the genius of the grammar school throughout the ages' (W. H. Keeling, *Bradford Observer*, 21 May 1897)—and exerted relentless pressure upon the city fathers to provide the funds. The first council scholarship boys entered the school in 1892. Bradford took notable advantage of the Liberal government's grant regulations in 1907 when the numbers were increased from less than 50 to 125, or a quarter of the school. In pursuit of this strategy Keeling did his best to stifle the development of secondary education elsewhere in the city, a development which earned him critics, notably in the Independent Labour Party and Bradford Trades Council where he was described as 'the bitterest enemy in the cause of education for the mass of the poorest children in the city' (T. Brown, *Forward*, July 1905). When Keeling was granted the freedom of the city however it was the Labour leader on the council, William Leach, himself a former pupil, who commented that:

> We remember Keeling as the friend of the scholarship boy. We remember how often you have advocated the cause of parents who have children to educate and little money wherewithal to do it. We remember further that the public schools are far too largely the homes of priggism and snobbery and that it is chiefly due to Dr. Keeling that Bradford Grammar School is an honourable exception to that. (*Bradford Observer*, 11 Oct 1912)

William Keeling died peacefully at his home, 25 Hampton Road, Southport, Lancashire, on 30 March 1916, a few months before his retirement became effective, and was buried at Blackley, near Manchester. The length of his headmastership and what he did for Bradford and its grammar school give him a place in the history of the city. His educational aims and the success with which he pursued them combine to award him a larger place in the national history of grammar school education. Keeling spent little time away from his school but from 1894 to 1897 he was a member of the committee of the Headmasters' Conference. His obituarist wrote:

> In the Headmasters' Conference, that body of indecisive compromise, he was always eagerly listened to because he knew what he wanted. His ability to foresee the effect and future developments of any policy was remarkable and Bradford Grammar School was generally found to have anticipated the progressive regulations of the Board of Education. (*Bradford Observer*, 31 March 1916)

DAVID SMITH

Sources D. Smith, 'A Victorian headmaster', W. Yorks. AS, Bradford [unpublished monograph] · governors' minute books, 1871–1925, Bradford grammar school · miscellaneous press cuttings, Bradford grammar school · *The Bradfordian* [Bradford grammar school magazine] · W. Claridge, *Origin and history of the Bradford grammar school* (1882) · H. Wolfe, *Now a stranger* (1933) · copies of articles by Old Bradfordians, Bradford grammar school archive · Venn, *Alum. Cant.* · Foster, *Alum. Oxon.* · *CGPLA Eng. & Wales* (1916) · m. cert. · b. cert.
Archives Bradford grammar school, reports and speeches
Likenesses E. Sichel, oils, 1912, Bradford grammar school · portrait, repro. in Claridge, *Origin and history*, frontispiece
Wealth at death £3447 2s. 11d.: probate, 18 May 1916, *CGPLA Eng. & Wales*

Keeling, William Knight (1807–1886), painter, was born in Cooper Street, Manchester, and apprenticed to a wood-engraver. He moved to London to be assistant to the portrait painter William Bradley, whom he helped in the painting and engraving of some portraits. About 1835 he returned to Manchester and worked as a portrait painter and drawing-master. Some of his drawings from *Gil Blas* were engraved in *Heath's Picturesque Annual*. Many of his earlier works, especially his illustrations for the novels of Sir Walter Scott, showed the influence of his friend Henry Liverseege. He first exhibited at the Royal Manchester Institution in 1831, when he showed an illustration to Scott's novel *The Betrothed*, and he exhibited there regularly, winning the Heywood silver medal in 1833 for an oil painting, *The Bird's-Nest*.

Keeling was a member of the original Manchester Academy, was one of the founders of the Manchester Academy of Fine Arts, and president from 1864 to 1877. He was a regular contributor to exhibitions there until 1883. He was elected an associate of the New Society of Painters in Watercolour in 1840, and a full member in 1841, and exhibited sixty paintings at their exhibitions. He exhibited once at the Royal Academy in 1855, and once at the British Institution. Three of his paintings, *Water Carrier, Seville, Spanish Muleteer*, and *Touchstone, Audrey, and William* (1839) are in the Victoria and Albert Museum, London. Keeling died at his home, 56 Canal Bank, Barton upon Irwell, near Manchester, on 21 February 1886. He was survived by his wife, Mary Ann, and at least one son.

ALBERT NICHOLSON, *rev.* ANNE PIMLOTT BAKER

Sources *Manchester Guardian* (24 Feb 1886) · Graves, *RA exhibitors* · Wood, *Vic. painters*, 3rd edn · Mallalieu, *Watercolour artists* · L. Lambourne and J. Hamilton, eds., *British watercolours in the Victoria and Albert Museum* (1980) · private information (1891) · *CGPLA Eng. & Wales* (1886) · d. cert.
Wealth at death £110: probate, 16 Aug 1886, *CGPLA Eng. & Wales*

Keen, Arthur (1835–1915), iron and steel manufacturer, was born in Cheshire, possibly at Weston, near Nantwich, on 23 January 1835, the son of Thomas Keen (1792/3–1867), a yeoman farmer and innkeeper. He had apparently received little education before joining the London and North Western Railway (LNWR) at Crewe, probably as a clerk. Promotion at the age of about twenty brought him to Smethwick as LNWR goods agent as the first stations opened there. The job gave him contact with local businessmen, including Thomas Astbury, a wealthy Smethwick ironfounder and cannon manufacturer, who introduced Keen to his first business partner, an American,

Francis Watkins, probably in 1856. On 2 September 1858 Keen married Astbury's daughter, Hannah, at Smethwick, an important step for Keen as Astbury 'improved his worldly prospects very notably' (Jones, *History of GKN*, 166). The couple lived in Edgbaston, Birmingham, for fifty years, and had ten children; four sons and five daughters outlived Keen, and the tenth child died before Hannah Keen in 1904.

Astbury recognized the potential of the patent for a nut-making machine that Watkins was trying to sell in Britain in 1856. With funding from Astbury, the firm of Watkins and Keen was established at Victoria works, Rolfe Street, Smethwick, with a dozen employees. The potential was realized rapidly; two years later, the workforce was 500 and by 1880 over 1000, a quarter of them female. The parallel with Nettlefold and Chamberlain is remarkable in several ways.

The next step was a move about 1860 to London works, Cranford Street, Smethwick, built in 1840 and vacated by Fox, Henderson & Co. on their failure in 1856. Thomas Astbury & Sons had taken over part of the famous works in 1858 but by the mid-1860s were pushed out by the burgeoning Watkins and Keen.

In 1864 Watkins and Keen was floated as a limited company as the Patent Nut and Bolt Company. The capital was £200,000 with Arthur Keen and Francis Watkins as joint managing directors though Watkins withdrew after a few years. Soon afterwards, Keen merged with Weston and Grice of Stour works, West Bromwich, and their associate, the Cwm-Bran Iron Company of Monmouthshire. Patent Nut's share capital doubled to provide the £50,169 purchase price and additional building at Cwmbrân to house more nut production.

In 1865 *The Engineer* (15 September 1865, 161) commented on the 'fruitful principle of the division of labour' driving London works, with 'upwards of 1000' employed there, and at Stour works, many of whom were mere boys and girls as the machinery was 'self-acting'. To cut costs, new plant was regularly installed and each works concentrated on different products with Stour works principally making railway fastenings. Keen sought to dominate the nut, bolt, and rivet trade through price-cutting and takeovers to obtain economies of scale or eliminate competitors but did not succeed in this to the extent of Nettlefold and Chamberlain, possibly because the nut and bolt trade was more diverse, competitors such as Garringtons were tougher, or Keen was less ruthless. Keen became chairman in 1895, succeeding his son-in-law Sir Joseph Dodge Weston (1822–1895). In 1899 he negotiated with Ivor Guest, Viscount Wimbourne, to take over the Dowlais Iron Company and the newly built integrated steelworks at East Moors, Cardiff. This big step involving £1.5 million, was achieved in 1900 to form Guest, Keen & Co. (GK) with an issued capital of £2.53 million.

Keen became chairman of GK, assisted by two of his sons, Arthur Thomas Keen (1861–1918) and Francis Watkins Keen (1863–1933), as joint managing directors and E. P. Martin, the existing general manager at Dowlais. The aim of the merger was 'to give the company a position of complete independence and to enable it to hold its own in competition with the whole world' (Macrosty, 38) and to do this out of retained profits. Not all Keen's ambitions were satisfied. Mergers proposed—in 1900 with the United States Steel Corporation; in 1905 with the Ebbw Vale Steel, Iron, and Coal Company; and in 1914–15, just before his death, with Dudley Docker's Metropolitan Carriage Company in Birmingham—were all abortive.

The next target of the greatly enlarged Keen empire was Smethwick neighbour Nettlefolds (the Chamberlains having withdrawn). In 1902 Guest, Keen, and Nettlefolds was created, ostensibly to remove competition, though the reality of this was exaggerated. In 1902 the Crawshay Brothers' Cyfarthfa steelworks in Merthyr Tudful were acquired to push issued capital up to £4.5 million. Keen kept the head office at the London works in Smethwick in order to have the group under his control. Profits of £400,000 per annum were consistently earned in the 1900s, representing a return of 10 per cent on issued capital.

Outside his group Keen was (understandably) recognized as a leading industrialist and investor. An early line of interest carried him into banking, as director of the Birmingham and Midland Bank from 1880, positively contributing to the bank's emergence as a national concern. He was chairman from 1898 to 1908 of what had become the London, City, and Midland Bank. He was also chairman of Muntz Metal, in Smethwick, for many years and of the New Cransley Iron and Steel Company, Kettering, from 1890 to 1915. He was director of Loddington Ironstone Company from 1891 to 1915 and of Bolckow, Vaughan & Co., Middlesbrough, until a few years before his death.

Keen was a member of the Iron and Steel Institute from 1885, and its vice-president from 1895 to 1915. A member of the Institution of Mechanical Engineers from 1869, he joined the council in 1891 and was vice-president from 1897 to 1911. He was an 'indefatigable' member of the midland iron and steel wages board for many years, promoting a 'Birmingham alliance' with Richard Juggins's National Amalgamated Nut and Bolt Makers Association to fight underselling, particularly from Darlaston in 1889–90, with a closed shop first set up in 1885.

Keen served 'unostentatiously' (*Birmingham Gazette and Express*, 7 March 1907) for twenty-five years on the local board of health in Smethwick, including fifteen years as its chairman. This period saw considerable activity in the provision of a public baths (1888), a library (1880), and municipal gas supplies (1881), and the acquisition of Victoria Park (1887–8). Keen became one of the first aldermen on Staffordshire county council in 1888 but refused to be the first mayor of Smethwick in 1899. He was also involved, in 1899–1900, with Joseph Chamberlain, in the foundation of Birmingham University as chairman of the canvassing committee and, later, as a life governor. He was a JP for Staffordshire.

Politically, Keen supported the Liberals, being treasurer

of the East Staffordshire Liberal Association, but, dis-agreeing with home rule, he helped, in 1886, to form the Handsworth Liberal Unionist Association and the Edgbaston Liberal Unionist Association, though he refused to stand for parliament. He believed in Joseph Chamberlain's tariff reform movement of the 1900s and was a member of the tariff commission's iron and steel committee from 1904 to 1911.

While the *Birmingham Gazette and Express* referred to 'a Dr. Smiles' temperament' (*Birmingham Gazette and Express*, 7 March 1907), Jones's summing up of Keen seems excellent:

> a self-made man of great determination and energy, he was both the creator of Guest, Keen and Nettlefolds and one of its outstanding chairmen. Neither an innovative engineer nor an expert in the manufacture of steel, Keen was in essence a tough businessman with a passion for growth whether internally generated or by acquisition. He possessed a shrewd eye for take-overs and through his network of contacts in industry, finance and the various professional bodies, Keen was able to build a mighty empire from modest beginnings. (*DBB*)

Jones notes a failing in that Keen left no obvious successor to take over the chairmanship. His son Arthur Thomas Keen 'found the pressures intolerable' (he died after three years as chairman) and 'Francis W. Keen refused the post' (*DBB*). Obviously his sons failed to inherit his 'extraordinary will-power' and drive.

Keen died unexpectedly at his home, Sandyford, 33 Augustus Road, Edgbaston, on 8 February 1915, aged eighty. He left £1 million. He was buried on 11 February at Harborne parish church. It was assumed, by the *Birmingham Gazette and Express* of 7 March 1907, that he had refused a deserved knighthood. *The Birmingham Post* (9 February 1915) pronounced him the:

> architect of his own fortune, possessing a combination of acute business instinct with abounding energy and steady perseverance, which enabled him to foresee and make the most of every opportunity that came within his reach … cautious to a degree and yet always enterprising.

He was the 'animating spirit of the business' in the 1860s and later. He was 'no ordinary man of business'.

BARBARA M. D. SMITH

Sources E. Jones, *A history of GKN, 1: Innovation and enterprise, 1759–1918* (1987) • E. Jones, 'Keen, Arthur', *DBB* • *The Engineer* (15 Sept 1865) • H. W. Macrosty, *The trust movement in British industry* (1907) • directories, Birmingham • directories, Staffordshire • *Birmingham Daily Post* (9 Feb 1915) • *Birmingham Daily Post* (12 Feb 1915) • 'Midland captains of industry', *Birmingham Gazette and Express* (7 March 1907) • *The Ironmonger* • B. M. D. Smith, 'Bibliography of Birmingham industrial history, 1860–1914', Birm. CL [esp. refs. to *The Ironmonger*] • *VCH Staffordshire*, vol. 17
Archives GKN, London, Guest, Keen, and Nettlefolds archives
Likenesses group photograph (with family), repro. in Jones, *History of GKN* • portrait, repro. in Jones, 'Keen, Arthur'
Wealth at death £1,000,000: probate, 1 April 1915, *CGPLA Eng. & Wales*

Keenan, Sir Patrick Joseph (1826–1894), educationist and educational administrator, was born, probably in Dublin, the son of John Keenan of Phibsborough, Dublin, and his wife, Mary, daughter of Patrick Sherlock of Dublin. He had at least one sister. He was educated at Ratoath national school, Meath, and trained as a teaching monitor at the Central Model Schools of the Board of National Education, Marlborough Street, Dublin. In 1845 he was appointed headmaster of the Central Model Schools and in 1848 a district inspector of the national board. He rose through the ranks to become head inspector (1855), chief of inspection (1859), and resident commissioner of national education (1871–94).

Keenan's knowledge and experience of Irish education were widely recognized. He was both the child of the national education system and its architect. In 1857 he published a pamphlet *Model Schools—a Sketch of their Nature and Objects*, and in 1868 was called as a leading witness to the royal commission on primary education (Ireland). As a Catholic and exemplar civil servant he acted as adviser to and mediator between the government and the Catholic church authorities. He was an acknowledged expert in the system of 'payment by results' which was introduced into Irish national schools in 1872, and as such was appointed by the British government to report on the education system of Trinidad in 1869 and that of Malta in 1878. In both colonies his Irish experience of the problems of language and religion in education proved invaluable.

Among Keenan's main achievements as resident commissioner were: the passing of the Intermediate Education Act (1878) which established a system of payment by results for secondary schools, based on success in public examinations; the recognition of the Irish language as an 'extra' subject (for result fees) in national schools from 1879; the provision of state grants for denominational teacher training colleges; and the introduction of compulsory free education by the 1892 Irish Education Act. He also gained popularity with national schoolteachers by his official recognition of their newly formed union—the Irish National Teachers' Organization. He gave evidence on Irish education to both the royal commission on technical instruction (1881–4) and the royal commission on the workings of the Elementary Education Act (England and Wales) (1886–8).

Keenan married Elizabeth Agnes, daughter of Michael Quin JP of Waterville, co. Limerick, in 1860. They had a son and a daughter. In his later years he suffered ill health and his work was curtailed. He was appointed CB (1871), KCMG (1881), a member of the Royal Irish Academy, and JP for co. Dublin; in 1885 he was sworn of the privy council. He was president of the education department of the social science congress held in Dublin in 1881. Keenan died at Delville, Glasnevin, near Dublin, on 1 November 1894 and was buried at Glasnevin cemetery. S. M. PARKES, *rev.*

Sources F. O'Dubhthaigh, 'A review of the contribution of Sir Patrick Keenan, 1826–1894, to the development of Irish and British colonial education', MEd diss., TCD, 1974 • *Thom's directory: Dublin*, various edns • *Irish Times* (4 Nov 1894) • Boase, *Mod. Eng. biog.*
Archives BL, corresp. with Arthur James Balfour, Add. MSS 49818–49819 • NL Ire., letters to Lord Emly
Likenesses T. H. Farrell, memorial bust, 1899, Tyrone House, Dublin

Wealth at death £10,729 0s. 2d.: probate, 20 Nov 1894, *CGPLA Ire.*

Keene, Sir Benjamin (1697–1757), diplomat, was born in King's Lynn, the eldest son of Charles Keene, mercer and alderman, and Susan (d. 1753), daughter of Edmund Rolfe, election agent in King's Lynn for Sir Robert Walpole. His younger brother was Edmund *Keene (1714–1781), bishop of Ely. He was educated at King's Lynn grammar school and at Pembroke College, Cambridge, where he was admitted on 8 April 1713 and graduated LLB in 1718. He continued his legal studies at the University of Leiden.

Keene's Norfolk connections, particularly with Edmund Rolfe, gained him Walpole's patronage and through him his appointment in 1723 as agent for the South Sea Company. He continued to hold this position until 1739. In 1724 he was appointed consul-general at Madrid, and in 1727 he was promoted to minister-plenipotentiary, in which capacity he was involved in negotiating the treaty of Seville in 1729. In 1734 he became envoy-extraordinary at the Spanish court. During his first period of residency in Madrid his principal achievement was the negotiations that led to the convention of Prado in January 1739, which sought a peaceful conclusion to the dispute provoked by British contraband and privateering activities in the Gulf of Mexico.

The convention was unpopular in Britain and failed to prevent wars from breaking out with Spain; on his return home in 1739 Keene encountered much criticism for his role in the negotiations. He was briefly threatened with impeachment after the fall in 1742 of his protector and patron, Walpole, who found him a seat in the Commons as MP for Maldon (1740–41) and then for West Looe (1741–7). His support for the ministry earned him in 1741 appointment as a lord of trade, and in December 1744 promotion to the office of paymaster of pensions. However, Keene found parliamentary life dull and aspired to a return to diplomatic duties. He therefore welcomed the opportunity to exchange offices with Charles Compton, the British envoy at the Portuguese court. The secretary of state for the south, the duke of Newcastle, sanctioned the move, and in summer 1746 Keene took up his new position as envoy-extraordinary and plenipotentiary in Lisbon. His residency was enjoyable but short-lived. Following the end of hostilities in the War of the Austrian Succession in 1748, Spain assumed greater importance as a sphere of influence for British diplomacy and Keene was seen as the best qualified to advance British interests in Spain. Accordingly, he was sent to Madrid in 1749 as ambassador.

Keene's second mission to Spain (1749–57) was the most important and successful part of his career. He was given a twofold commission: first, to restore British trading privileges with Spain and her overseas empire or, failing this, to negotiate a new treaty of commerce. Second, he was to attempt to detach Spain from the family compact with the French Bourbons and to substitute an alliance with Britain. The obstacles, principally irreconcilable commercial and colonial interests, to an alliance proved insurmountable despite Keene's best efforts. None the less, he achieved some successes, notably in persuading Ferdinand VI's government to sign a commercial treaty whereby Britain abandoned demands to renew the *asiento* of 1713 to supply slaves to Spanish America, and received £100,000 as compensation to the South Sea Company. Moreover, British traders regained the privileges they had enjoyed during the reign of Carlos II (1665–1700), including their exemption from any new customs tolls, taxes, and duties other than those levied on Spanish traders.

The treaty was warmly welcomed in Britain and Keene was disappointed not to receive the Order of the Bath, the customary reward for a successful diplomat. He had been instrumental in drawing up the treaty of Aranjuez between Spain, Austria, and Sardinia, in June 1752, which was seen as an important step in weakening the family compact. He played an influential role in the downfall in July 1754 of the marqués d'Ensenada, the staunchly pro-French and anti-British minister, and secured the appointment as Ensenada's replacement of Ricardo Wall, the Spanish ambassador to Britain since 1750. He was now rewarded with the Order of the Bath, and was invested at a ceremony performed by Ferdinand VI on 23 September 1754. His objective in the final two years of his embassy was to maintain Spanish neutrality in the Seven Years' War, in which he succeeded, thanks in part to the blunders of his French counterpart, Duras, who offended and antagonized Ferdinand by his imperious behaviour. According to Lodge, Keene was largely responsible for the resulting break-up of the family compact.

Keene's health began to deteriorate rapidly from 1754, but his requests to be allowed home were continually denied. Unmarried, he died in Madrid on 15 December 1757. His body was brought home in March 1758 and buried in St Nicholas's Church in King's Lynn in the following month. Highly regarded in Madrid, Keene was instrumental in improving Britain's relations with Spain at a critical time and has justifiably been described as belonging to 'that small band of diplomatists who became a real force in the country to which they were accredited' (Lodge, 42).

M. J. MERCER

Sources *The private correspondence of Sir Benjamin Keene*, ed. R. Lodge (1933), xi–xxxi · R. Lodge, 'Sir Benjamin Keene, K.B.: a study in Anglo-Spanish relations', *TRHS*, 4th ser., 15 (1932), 1–43 · A. N. Newman, 'Keene, Benjamin', HoP, *Commons, 1715–54* · Venn, *Alum. Cant.* · *GM*, 1st ser., 4 (1734), 108 · *GM*, 1st ser., 10 (1741), 31 · *GM*, 1st ser., 11 (1742), 220 · *GM*, 1st ser., 14 (1744), 677 · *GM*, 1st ser., 15 (1745), 444 · *GM*, 1st ser., 19 (1749), 333, 478, 526 · *GM*, 1st ser., 20 (1751), 974 · *GM*, 1st ser., 23 (1753), 148 · *GM*, 1st ser., 24 (1754), 388 · *GM*, 1st ser., 28 (1758), 46

Archives BL, corresp. and papers, Add. MSS 43412–43443, 49621 | BL, corresp. with Lord Grantham, Add. MSS 23780–23789, 23821, 32760–32764, 32849–32861, *passim* · BL, corresp. with Lord Holland, Add. MS 51388 · BL, corresp. with duke of Newcastle, Add. MSS 32722–32992, *passim* · BL, corresp. with Sir John Norris, Add. MSS 23627–23628, 28149, 32794 · BL, corresp. with Lord Tyrawly, Add. MSS 23627–23629, 28149, 32760–32801, *passim* · BL, corresp. with first Earl Waldegrave, Add. MSS 32754–32801, *passim* · BL, corresp. with Horatio Walpole, Add. MSS 32752–32801, *passim* · CUL, letters to Sir Robert Walpole · Hunt. L., letters to duke of Newcastle and duke of Bedford · NRA, priv. coll., corresp. with first Earl Waldegrave · U. Nott. L., corresp. with duke of Newcastle · W. Yorks. AS, Leeds, corresp. with Lord Grantham

Likenesses copper medal, BM • oils, Pembroke Cam. • oils (after L. M. van Loo, type of 1736), town hall, King's Lynn, Norfolk • sculpture, BM

Keene, Charles Samuel (1823–1891), illustrator and etcher, was born in Duvals Lane, Hornsey, Middlesex, on 10 August 1823, one of the sons of Samuel Browne Keene (*d.* 1838), a solicitor of Furnival's Inn, London, and Ipswich, and Mary Sparrow (*d.* 1881), the daughter of John Sparrow of the old Ipswich family of Sparrow's House, Buttermarket. He was educated in London and at the grammar school in Foundation Street, Ipswich, and on leaving it in 1839 he entered his father's old office. Finding the law uncongenial and actively encouraged to draw by his mother, he entered the employ of the architect William J. Pilkington of Scotland Yard. This was found no more satisfactory and about 1842 he left to be apprenticed to Messrs Whymper Brothers, the celebrated wood-engravers. It has always been considered that the wood-engraving studio was beneficial to his work, imposing a professionalism and discipline which many other illustrators lacked. However, in a letter to his illustrator nephew in 1871, he asserted, 'I don't think drawing on wood is a good road to stand on as an artist', adding 'This is how I began, and have been sorry for it ever since' (J. A. Hammerton, *Humorists of the Pencil*, 1905, 132).

Keene must have begun to work as an independent illustrator while still at Whympers; his frontispiece to *The Adventures of Dick Boldero* is dated 1842 and was engraved by J. D. Cooper, a fellow apprentice with whom he collaborated. At the end of his apprenticeship he produced designs for his first major book, *The Life and Surprising Adventures of Robinson Crusoe* (1847), very much under the influence of John Tenniel and John Gilbert. He was employed to work up sketches by Samuel Read for the *Illustrated London News* in 1853 and he prepared subjects on Sevastopol for Messrs Dickinsons' publications during the Crimean War. Keene began to contribute to *Punch* anonymously in 1851, though he signed with his initials from 1854, but he did not join the *Punch* 'Table' until 1860. In 1864, following the death of John Leech, he succeeded to his place as chief social cartoonist. He contributed regularly to the magazine for the next thirty years but remained somewhat detached from the 'Table', eschewing the radical politics of his older colleagues as well as the social ambitions of the younger ones. Never a humorous draughtsman, but a draughtsman of humorous situations, he chose to illustrate the comedy of the street and the country, usually leaving the drawing-room to George Du Maurier. He relied heavily for subjects on his friend Joseph Crawhall (1821–1896), who supplied him with albums of incidents! His collected *Punch* work appeared as a volume, *Our People*, in 1881.

Keene's fine line and skill with gradations of colour in sepia, achieved with his home-made pens and self-mixed inks, made him a more serious artist than some of his *Punch* contemporaries. This is apparent in his illustrations of fiction in *Punch*'s sister paper *Once a Week* in which he illustrated stories by George Meredith and Mrs Henry Wood. The same vivid and intense interpretation of

Charles Samuel Keene (1823–1891), by Horace Harral, 1860s

nineteenth-century life is found in his pages and vignettes for Herbert Vaughan's *The Cambridge Grisette* (1862), the original drawings for which are masterpieces of Victorian sensitivity.

Keene's stylistic development can be divided into four phases: the first youthful drawings when he was influenced by Tenniel; the early magazine work when he was inspired by German illustration, particularly that of Adolph Menzel; a strong debt to the Pre-Raphaelite illustrators in the 1860s; and finally a triumphant attempt in the 1880s to bend traditional black and white work towards atmosphere and mood. His Germanic style can be seen in the pages of Charles Reade's 'A Good Fight' in *Once a Week* (1859), while his last *Punch* contribution, 'Arry on the Boulevards' (15 August 1890), reflects a loose treatment akin to contemporary French artists such as Jean-Louis Forain. Keene was unique among his confrères in having an international reputation among artists, admired by such diverse figures as Whistler, Menzel, Edgar Degas, and Camille Pissarro.

Keene worked as an etcher from the 1870s but published few of his plates, mainly landscapes and figures, regarding the results as a mere hobby. Through his contact with the etcher Edwin Edwards, his etched work reached a wider circle. Mrs Edwards printed his plates and entered his works for the Paris Exhibition in 1889, where they won a gold medal.

From early manhood Keene lived a life apart as an eccentric bachelor, accommodated in London in various dilapidated rooms and lodgings often separated from a permanent studio. He moved from an attic above the Strand to Clipstone Street, then to 55 Baker Street, 11 Queen's Road, west Chelsea, and King's Road, Chelsea. In each of these addresses he surrounded himself with a jumble of artistic props, books, flints, and memorabilia, cooking meat to a cinder on an open fire. He had musical talent, joined a group of round singers, and learned to play the Northumbrian bagpipes with considerable competence, featuring them in some of his *Punch* jokes.

A tall, gangling figure in untidy clothes, Keene would frequently walk between Chelsea and the West End with a haversack and with his favourite clay pipe between his teeth filled with dottles—a lethal blend of used quids which helped him to draw! Domiciled in London, he took a cottage at Witley, Surrey, for some years, but his spiritual home was undoubtedly Suffolk, where he spent long holidays in rented rooms. He was an observer who liked to draw from nature in country and town. Even in late middle age he regularly attended the weekly life class at the Langham Sketch Club. He was a considerable antiquary, able letter-writer, and something of an intellectual, which accounted for his close friendship with the poet Edward FitzGerald at Woodbridge, Suffolk.

Keene's excessive smoking and poor diet led to the gradual onset of heart disease in 1890 and he died at his home, 112 Hammersmith Road, London, on 4 January 1891; he was buried in Hammersmith cemetery, attended by all his *Punch* friends. He left over £30,000, a sum which astonished his friends but included an annuity for his servant.

SIMON HOUFE

Sources G. S. Layard, *The life and letters of Charles Keene* (1892) · J. Pennell, *The work of Charles Keene with an introduction and comments on the drawings illustrating the artist's methods* (1897) [bibliography of bks and catalogue of essays] · D. Hudson, *Charles Keene* (1947) · S. Houfe, *Charles Keene* (1991) [exhibition catalogue, Christies] · S. Houfe, *The work of Charles Samuel Keene* (1995) · F. L. Emanuel, *Charles Keene, etcher, draughtsman and illustrator, 1823–1891* (1932) · F. Reid, 'Charles Keene, illustrator', *Print Collector's Quarterly*, 17 (1930), 23–47 · M. H. Spielmann, *The history of 'Punch'* (1895) · M. H. Spielmann, 'Introduction', in *Twenty-one etchings by Charles Keene* (1903) · *Catalogue of the works of Charles Keene*, Fine Art Society (1891) · Arts Council, *Drawings by Charles Keene* (1952) · *Catalogue of the Lindsay collection of drawings by Charles Keene* (1952) [exhibition catalogue, Leicester Galleries, London] · *CGPLA Eng. & Wales* (1891) · Henry Silver diary, *Punch* Library and Archives, London

Archives *Punch* Library and Archive, London · FM Cam., MSS | BL, letters to A. J. Hipkins and his wife, Add. MSS 41637–41639 · FM Cam., letters to Edwin Edwards and his wife

Likenesses C. S. Keene, self-portrait, oils, c.1860, Tate collection · H. Harral, photograph, 1860–69, NPG [*see illus.*] · D. W. Wynfield, photograph, c.1862–1864, NPG · C. S. Keene, self-portrait, pen, ink, and wash drawing, c.1865, AM Oxf. · D. W. Wynfield, albumen print, c.1865, NPG · A. W. Cooper, pencil drawing, 1866, NPG · G. Reid, portrait, 1881, Aberdeen Art Gallery · C. S. Keene, three self-portraits, pencil drawings, 1883–5, Tate collection · C. S. Keene, self-portrait, pen-and-ink drawing, c.1885, NPG · G. Frampton, bronze memorial bas-reliefs, 1896, Shepherd's Bush Library, London · G. Frampton, bronze memorial bas-reliefs, 1896, Tate collection · W. Corbould, watercolour drawing, NPG · G. Frampton, plaster model of memorial bas-reliefs, Tate collection · H. Furniss, pen-and-ink caricatures, NPG · C. S. Keene, self-portrait, pen-and-ink drawing, Tate collection · C. S. Keene, self-portrait, pencil sketch, Tate collection · photograph, repro. in Layard, *Life and letters* · print, NPG

Wealth at death £34,174 8s. 6d.: probate, 4 Feb 1891, *CGPLA Eng. & Wales*

Keene, Edmund (1714–1781), bishop of Ely, was born at King's Lynn, Norfolk, the third son of Charles Keene, mercer and in 1714 mayor of King's Lynn, and Susan (d. 1753), daughter of Edmund Rolfe. His elder brother was Sir Benjamin *Keene, ambassador to Spain, who later left him the bulk of his fortune. He was educated at Mr Horne's school in King's Lynn and at Charterhouse School. He matriculated at Gonville and Caius College, Cambridge, on 2 July 1730 and graduated BA in 1734; he proceeded MA in 1737 and DD in 1749. He was made fellow of Caius in 1736 and in 1739 a fellow of Peterhouse, where he served as master from December 1748 to 1754. He was ordained deacon by the bishop of Norwich on 18 July 1736 and was appointed a Whitehall preacher in 1738. In 1740 he became chaplain to a regiment of marines.

Keene's progress was helped by his brother's connection with Sir Robert Walpole, who in 1740 secured him the lucrative rectory of Stanhope, co. Durham. Walpole's son Horace later told William Cole, the antiquary, that Sir Robert, having an illegitimate daughter whom he wished to provide for, acquired a rectory worth £600 and offered it to Keene on the condition that he promised to marry her. Keene accepted but when, after Sir Robert's death, the lady came of age he rejected her. He had by then made other connections and the lady was, according to Cole, who had met her, of a 'squat, short gummy Appearance … by no means deformed, or mishapen, but rather undersized' (Cole, BL, Add. MS 5847, fol. 205r). Horace Walpole claimed that he found her with her mother in a starving condition, rescued her, and wrote to Keene on her behalf; thus pressed Keene agreed to pay her the £600 or interest on the sum. Cole was not however entirely convinced by this story; he knew well Walpole's hostility to bishops and observed: 'Mr. Walpole is one of the most sanguine Friends or Enemies that I know. He has had a long Pique against the Bishop' (ibid.). Cole knew both men and, writing in 1774, sought to give a balanced view:

> The Bp. I allow, is as much puffed up with his Dignities and Fortunes as any on the Bench … The Bp. was ever esteemed a most chearful, generous and good-tempered Man. Great fortune with a Wife and great Dignity in the Church often make the wisest Men forget themselves.   (ibid.)

Whatever the truth of this story, in May 1752 Keene married Mary (bap. 1725, d. 1776), only daughter of Launcelot Andrewes of Edmonton, formerly a linen draper in Cheapside, and from her inherited a considerable fortune. The couple had one son and one daughter. Mary Keene died on 24 March 1776.

Following the fall of Walpole, Keene continued as an ally of Henry Pelham and his brother Thomas Pelham-Holles, duke of Newcastle. Keene's election as vice-chancellor of Cambridge University in 1749 followed Newcastle's election as chancellor the previous year. Newcastle shared the desire of some of his parliamentary colleagues for some measure of university reform and in Keene he found a willing ally. In 1749 Keene and the heads of houses drew up new regulations, which were amended and approved by Newcastle. They forbade undergraduates and BAs to be out of college after 11.00 p.m., to frequent coffee houses or places of amusement in the morning, to visit the town brothels, or to dice or play cards in the taverns. Students were required to attend sermons in the university church and to refrain from rioting and extravagant dress. Although the measures were moderate and drawn up entirely within the existing constitution of the university they were brought forward at the same time as reformers among Newcastle's supporters in parliament were proposing a bill to establish a committee of parliamentary visitation for the universities of Oxford and Cambridge. Consequently many members of the senate felt 'the liberties of the University were in danger' (Searby, 324) and it was only with great difficulty that Keene forced the regulations through on 26 June 1750. He was much reviled and ridiculed for this but Newcastle congratulated him on 'the Zeal you show'd for the Discipline and Honor of the University' (Keene, correspondence, BL, Add. MS 32723, fol. 330*v*) and demonstrated his gratitude by ensuring Keene's re-election as vice-chancellor for another year, hinting at a richer reward to follow. Samuel Johnson, in a bitter attack on Keene, accused him directly of self-seeking: 'all your pretended Services were Projects to promote your own base Interest' (Johnson, *Occasional Letter*, 9). In November 1750 the new regulations were flouted when some students, late of Westminster School, were discovered by a proctor in the Three Tuns tavern after 11.00 p.m., celebrating the anniversary of their school's patron with some fellows of Trinity College and the regius professor of Greek. Keene admitted privately to Newcastle that he believed the gathering harmless but he felt he had to support the proctor. During the prolonged enquiry and public proceedings Keene was savagely lampooned but Newcastle continued to support him, and his praises gave Keene more satisfaction 'than all the Ribaldry thrown on me has given me pain' (Keene, correspondence, BL, Add. MS 32723, fol. 358).

Keene did not continue as vice-chancellor for the year 1751/2, but was rewarded by Newcastle in March 1752 with the see of Chester, where he rebuilt the bishop's palace. In 1764 he turned down a move to the archbishopric of Armagh and was criticized for telling his friends of the offer. Keene was through and through a Cambridge man and he made no secret of the fact that the bishopric of Ely was his 'great object, the aim and end of his ambition' (Nichols, *Lit. anecdotes*, 4.323). In January 1771 he won translation to Ely, whereupon he gave up his rectory at Stanhope and thereafter sought no further advancement. The major event of his episcopate was the sale for £11,000 of the old Ely House in Holborn, London, and the building of a new palace on Dover Street to replace it. Contemporaries noted with amusement that he stripped the see of the strawberries of Holborn noted in Shakespeare (*Richard III*, III.iv); he replaced the old mansion with a new one in Portland stone and a revenue of £5000 to keep it warm and in good repair. He also made alteration to the bishop's palace at Ely.

Keene's move to Ely brought him into close partnership with Philip Yorke, second earl of Hardwicke, the principal whig magnate in Cambridgeshire and high steward of the university from 1764. Keene adopted a policy of deference, acceding to Hardwicke's request in 1771 that he sit on the commission of the peace for the Isle of Ely. He recommended few of his fellow clergy to the bench, protesting that he had 'ever been of opinion that if the Gentlemen of the County would act in the capacity of Justices, it wd. be proper not to employ the clergy in that office' (Keene, letters, BL, Add. MS 35680, fol. 87). He stressed later that he had 'no object in view but to have men of integrity, of some property, and who are on the spot to execute the business of the Isle, for ease and accommodation of the inhabitants' (ibid., fol. 296). Hardwicke later helped Keene's son Benjamin to win election to the Commons for the borough of Cambridge in 1776. Keene returned the favour by meeting Hardwicke's constant demands for livings for his protégés; in a letter of September 1779 he complained that after many years as a bishop he had not yet been able to advance any of his own relatives.

Keene's support for the North ministry caused Richard Watson, prebendary at Ely from 1774 and archdeacon from 1779, to consider him 'as guilty of "apostasy from Whiggism"' (Gascoigne, 215) on the grounds that North endorsed the extension of the prerogatives of the crown in a way alien to Cambridge's whig tradition. Keene's identification with the ministry was compatible with his established interpretation of the constitution. He accepted the balance between king, lords, and Commons but feared that 'there may be great reason to suspect that the liberties, or rather the licentiousness of the people, may overwhelm all authority, and abolish government' (Keene, *A Sermon Preached before the Rt. Hon. the Lords*, 23). However he recognized that 'Men unite in Society, and mutually concur in establishing the Security, and advancing the Happiness of the Government they live under' (Keene, *A Sermon Preached before the Society*, 10) and observed that 'Happiness is to the social Body, what Health is to the natural one' (ibid., 15).

In 1780 Keene showed signs of ill health. Despite visits to Brighton, where he delighted in 'the fine air with the Sea breezes, and pleasing walks and rides' (Keene, letters, BL, Add. MS 35681, fol. 312), he died, aged sixty-seven, on 6 July 1781 in Ely House, Dover Street, of a dropsy in the breast. He was buried near his wife's grave in Ely Cathedral.

ROBERT HOLE

Sources Nichols, *Lit. anecdotes*, vols. 4, 8 • P. Searby, *A history of the University of Cambridge*, 3: 1750–1870, ed. C. N. L. Brooke and others (1997) • *GM*, 1st ser., 51 (1781), 343–4 • *GM*, 1st ser., 66 (1796), 902 • Venn, *Alum. Cant.*, 2/4 • E. Keene, letters to the second earl of Hardwicke, BL, Add. MSS 35613, fols. 158, 162, 309, 311, 314; 35616, fols. 21, 183; 35680, fols. 87, 296, 383; 35681, fols. 292, 312 • E. Keene, correspondence with the duke of Newcastle, BL, Add. MSS 32723, fols. 330–38, 357–8; 32724, fol. 236 • W. Cole, to Strawberry Hill to visit Horace Walpole, BL, Add. MS 5847, fol. 205 • S. Johnson, *An occasional letter to the Revd. Dr. Keen* (1750) • S. Johnson, *The friendly and honest advice of an old tory to the vice-chancellor of Cambridge* (1751) • E. Keene, *A sermon preached before the Rt. hon. the Lords … Jan 30, 1753* (1753) • E. Keene, *A sermon preached before the society corresponding with the Incorporated Society in Dublin for promoting English protestant working schools in Ireland* (1755) • *The works of Thomas Gray in prose and*

verse, ed. E. Gosse, 4 vols. (1884) · J. Gascoigne, *Cambridge in the age of the Enlightenment* (1989), 106, 108, 215 · *IGI*
Archives BL, corresp. with earls of Hardwicke and Charles Yorke, Add. MSS 35596–35681, *passim* · BL, corresp. with duke of Newcastle, Add. MSS 32714–32934, *passim* · BL, letters to the duke of Newcastle, Add. MS 35418, fol. 69; Add. MS 35596, fols. 329, 355 [copies] · BL, *Suit v. Wray*, Add. MS 36225, fols. 350, 361 · BL, memorial for the prosecution of Revd R. Bulcock, Add. MS 33055, fol. 308
Likenesses C. Turner, mezzotint, pubd 1812 (after J. Zoffany), BM · oils, bishop's house, Chester

Keene, Henry (1726–1776), architect and surveyor, was born in Ealing on 15 November 1726, the son of Henry Keene and Elizabeth Elkins. His father is thought to have been the carpenter who worked on Ealing parish church, which was designed by James Horne and built in 1739–40. Keene has traditionally been described as 'bred to the profession of architecture' (Colvin, *Archs.*, 572) and in 1746, aged only twenty, he became surveyor to the dean and chapter of Westminster Abbey. In 1752 James Horne resigned as surveyor to the fabric of Westminster Abbey in Keene's favour. (Keene was possibly a pupil of Horne's, although there is no documentary evidence to support this.) Keene held both surveyorships until his death in 1776. Keene's major contribution to Westminster Abbey was to remodel the Jerusalem Chamber in 1769 in Gothic style, although his work there no longer survives. In 1775 he also designed Gothic-style choir furniture which could be temporarily removed when public occasions required. The choir furniture is no longer located there but is illustrated in J. P. Neale and E. W. Brayley, *The History and Antiquities of the Abbey Church of St Peter, Westminster*, of 1823 (vol. 2, pl. 30). Two gates designed by him in the cloister do survive.

Keene married Anne Martha Deval, said to be the daughter of a French refugee. According to the *Dictionary of National Biography*, the marriage took place in 1762, but this date seems unlikely given that their eldest son, Theodosius, also an architect, exhibited at the Society of Artists in 1770. Their other son, Thomas, married Jane Harris, sister of the first Lord Harris; their son Henry became a famous Persian scholar. Keene's only daughter, Elizabeth, married the Royal Academician and portrait painter William Parry.

In addition to his work at Westminster Abbey, Keene received commissions for country houses, Oxford colleges, and London developments. His earliest recorded works include the Flesh Market in Westminster, a Doric colonnaded square, fronted by town houses, built in 1749–50, and a house in South Square, Gray's Inn (both dem.). He also designed 17–18 Cavendish Square. A petition of 1757 in the Foundling Hospital papers describes Keene as having 'attended this Hospital ten y[ea]rs past in the business and Quality of surveyor'. It also refers to Keene as having taken instruction, since 1747, from the governors and guardians and Theodore Jacobsen—the amateur architect responsible for the overall design of the charity's buildings in Bloomsbury, London—and having executed several buildings, making 'a present of such his Time and Labour and attendance' (LMA, A/FH/M01/6). A 1760 conversation piece by Robert Pyle (des. 1940; illustrated in *Country Life*, 30 March 1945, 556) shows Keene surrounded by his principal craftsmen, all named. They include Euclid Alfray (Keene's clerk), Ben Carter (a statuary mason), and Thomas Gayfere (master mason at Westminster Abbey).

In the 1750s Keene and John Sanderson (who had also worked at the Foundling Hospital) were both paid for providing the working drawings for the classical west front of Trinity College, Dublin, to a design by Jacobsen. In 1761 Keene travelled to Ireland with George Dunk, second earl of Halifax, the newly appointed lord lieutenant, and he is referred to in 1763 as 'architect to the barrack board' in Ireland. There are no identified works by Keene in Ireland from this period, although it has been suggested that he may have provided designs for the Provost's House, Dublin, and in 1764 he was paid for work at the college. In 1766 he resigned from the barrack board and was replaced by Christopher Myers.

Keene received several notable classical country house commissions in which his hallmarks were a rococo liveliness in elevation and roofline, and a distinctive use of canted bays. In 1755–60 he enlarged Bowood House in Wiltshire (dem. 1955) for Henry Petty, first earl of Shelburne. The same patron commissioned the classical guildhall in High Wycombe in Buckinghamshire (1755–7), which survives largely unaltered. Also in Buckinghamshire, Keene rebuilt the east front of Hartwell House in 1759–63 for Sir William Lee, fourth baronet, for whom he also designed, partly as an eye-catcher from the house, an octagonal Gothic revival church at Hartwell (now derelict).

While most of his surviving works are classical, Keene is best-known for contributing to the Gothic revival in the mid-eighteenth century. Indeed, Sir Howard Colvin remarks, 'it is only in the history of the Gothic revival that he [Keene] has a place of some importance' (Colvin, *Archs.*, 572). As surveyor to Westminster Abbey, Keene had regular contact with the finest Gothic architecture in the country, and details drawn from the abbey appear frequently in his work. For example, the fan-vaulting both of Hartwell church and of a garden temple attributed to Keene built *c.*1750 for Harry Grey, fourth earl of Stamford (now the Enville Museum), were derived from that of the famous Henry VII Chapel at Westminster Abbey. Keene provided working drawings for Gothic revival pioneer Sanderson Miller in the 1740s. Keene's first important Gothic revival commission was for Isaac Maddox, bishop of Worcester, to remodel and refit the chapel at Hartlebury Castle (completed by 1750), the official seat of the bishops of Worcester.

Between 1762 and 1776 Keene made a major contribution towards redesigning the interiors of Arbury Hall, Warwickshire, one of the most significant Gothic revival houses of the mid- to late eighteenth century. The patron, with whom he presumably collaborated closely, was another important figure in the taste for Gothic, Sir Roger Newdigate, bt, the high tory MP for Middlesex and later for Oxford. Keene's precise contribution at Arbury is unclear. He is first mentioned in the accounts for 'drawing, etc.' in 1762 for which he received 15 guineas; in 1771 he was paid £24 for the 'Front and Hall, &c.'. However, Keene probably designed the dining-room at Arbury, with its impressive fan-vaulted plaster ceiling and three oriel windows. His too is the drawing-room chimney-piece, carved by Richard Hayward and modelled on the medieval tomb of Aymer de Valence, earl of Pembroke (d. 1260), one of Westminster Abbey's most admired monuments. In 1768 Keene also added a Gothic revival chancel arch and altar to Harefield parish church in Middlesex, for Newdigate.

Keene was one of the dominant architects in Oxford during the 1760s and 1770s: this was thanks in part to Newdigate, who, as MP for Oxford (1750–80), was an influential patron. In a letter dated 16 July 1768 Keene wrote to Newdigate: 'they keep me employed in that Univ[ersit]y for all which I am obliged to you as my kind Introducer' (quoted in Nares, 1212). In 1766 Keene remodelled the interior of the hall of University College in the Gothic style (his work there was dismantled in 1904, but is illustrated in Ackermann's *History of the University of Oxford*, 1814). The chimney-piece was a gift from Newdigate and, like that he designed for Arbury's drawing-room, it was modelled on the thirteenth-century tomb of Aymer de Valence in Westminster Abbey. Keene worked for Christ Church, where he designed the anatomy school in 1766–7 and altered the library in 1769–72. He was also employed by Magdalen and at Balliol. One of his significant surviving commissions is the classical rococo provost's lodgings at Worcester College, built between 1773 and 1776. Keene produced a design for the Radcliffe Observatory, Oxford, which was begun in 1772. After adverse criticism of that design—especially by Edward Statham in *Oxonian explicate et ornate* (1773)—the trustees chose another design by James Wyatt, which Keene had to execute; it was completed after his death by his son Theodosius.

Keene's late monuments show confidence and originality, as with the rococo monument to George Henry Lee, third earl of Lichfield, at Spelsbury church, Oxfordshire (1772), with its striking cutaway perspective view of the urns in the base. One of his last buildings was the Gothic-style Vandalian Tower for a whig patron, Sir Matthew Fetherstonhaugh, bt, at Uppark in Sussex (1774), to commemorate a utopian settlement in America called Vandalia. However, by his death on 8 January 1776, Keene's career seems to have been in decline, certainly in Oxford, where Wyatt had eclipsed him. He died at his country house at Drayton Green, Ealing, though his main residence was at 13 Golden Square, London, and he also owned further property in London, Middlesex, and Oxford.

Some thirty architectural drawings by Keene are preserved in the Victoria and Albert Museum. These are principally undated and unexecuted proposals for country houses in the classical rococo style, several of them on a palatial scale, with a distinctive use of canted bays, low porticoes, and Diocletian and Serlian windows. There is a handful of designs for Gothic revival garden pavilions, one of which bears a close comparison to Hartwell church. Another drawing is for a Turkish tent, thought to be that built at Painshill Park, Surrey, for the Hon. Charles Hamilton. These Victoria and Albert drawings illustrate Keene's architectural range and ambition and perhaps his limitations. Despite some ambitious remodellings of houses, he does not seem to have had an opportunity to build a major new country house from scratch.

JEREMY G. D. MUSSON

Sources Colvin, *Archs.* · T. Mowl, 'Henry Keene', *The architectural outsiders*, ed. R. Brown (1985), 82–97, 200 · M. McCarthy, *The origins of the Gothic revival* (1987), 119–20, 128–40, 154–162 · H. Clifford Smith, 'A Georgian architect', *Country Life*, 98 (1945), 556–60 · C. Hussey, *English country houses: early Georgian, 1715–1760* (1955), pp. 31, 200–01 · T. Davies, *The Gothick taste* (1974), 52–60, 64 · C. Brooks, *The Gothic revival* (1999), pp. 65–7, 101 · G. Nares, 'Arbury Hall, Warwickshire: II', *Country Life* (15 Oct 1953), 1203–13 · M. Hall, 'Arbury Hall, Warwickshire: I and II', *Country Life* (7 Jan 1999), 30–35; (14 Jan 1999), 40–43 · G. Jackson-Stops, 'Hartwell, Buckinghamshire', *Country Life* (22 Nov 1990), 69–73 · M. Collier and D. Wrightson, 'The recreation of the Turkish tent at Painshill', *Garden History*, 21/1 (1993), 46–59 · *VCH Middlesex*, 3.255 · E. McParland, 'An academic palazzo in Ireland', *Country Life* (14 Oct 1976), 1034–7 · E. McParland, 'Cherishing a Palladian masterpiece', *Country Life* (21 Oct 1976), 1066–1109 · A. Crookshank and D. Webb, *Paintings and sculptures in Trinity College, Dublin* (1990), 77 · *Biographical index of Irish architects*, The Irish Architectural Archive, Dublin
Archives BL, journal of a tour through the Netherlands, Add. MS 60356 · Bodl. Oxf., estimate, order, and letter relating to building of Radcliffe Observatory | LMA, letters to Sir Roger Newdigate relating to repairs and alterations to Harefield church; also drawings, sketches, and specifications
Likenesses R. Pyle, group portrait, oils, 1760, repro. in Clifford Smith, 'Henry Keene: a Georgian architect', *Country Life* (30 March 1945), 556; destroyed, 1940 · portrait, oils, 1760–99, TCD, Provost's lodgings

Keene, Henry George (1781–1864), orientalist, was born on 30 September 1781, the only son of Thomas Keene, and grandson of Henry *Keene. His mother was Jane, sister of George Harris, first baron of Seringapatam and Mysore. He was educated privately, partly by Menon, afterwards one of Napoleon's generals. He went to India as a cadet in the Madras army in 1796 or 1798, and shortly after became adjutant of a Sepoy regiment, which formed part of the brigade commanded by Colonel Arthur Wellesley. In May 1799 the brigade took part in the siege of Seringapatam, where Keene led the company carrying the scaling-ladders for the storming party (4 May).

The stresses of Indian campaigning having affected his health, Keene obtained an appointment in the Madras civil service through his uncle, Lord Harris, the commander-in-chief, in February 1801. After a short visit to England he entered Fort William College, Calcutta, then newly established by Marquess Wellesley for the training of young civil officers. In January 1804 he obtained a first-class honours degree in Persian and Arabic, with prizes in classics, English composition, and French, and a gold medal in Islamic law, having held public disputations in Arabic and Persian. He joined the service at Madras and became in turn registrar of the district court at Rajahmundry, and assistant registrar to the sudder courts at the presidency. He wrote a book on law in

Arabic, for which the government awarded him 10,000 rupees. In 1805 he went to Europe. After his return in 1809 he soon incurred the displeasure of Sir George Barlow, the governor. He consequently resigned and left India that year.

On 13 November 1811 Keene matriculated at Sidney Sussex College, Cambridge, where he graduated in 1815 as eighth senior optime. He was admitted fellow of his college on 13 November 1817, and took holy orders. About this time he visited the continent, in Lord Stanhope's company, and became the friend of Archduke John and of Baron von Hammer, the orientalist, with both of whom he kept up a constant correspondence for many years. In March 1819 he unsuccessfully contested the Arabic professorship of Cambridge University.

In 1824 Keene became professor of Arabic and Persian at the East India College at Haileybury, near Hertford, of which he was afterwards appointed registrar. In the same year he married Anne, daughter of Charles Apthorp Wheelwright, formerly of Boston, Massachusetts, a royalist refugee; they had two sons and two daughters. At Haileybury he received visits from many famous men, and employed his leisure in literary work, among other things assisting his friend Adam Clarke in the philological part of his Commentary on the Bible. He had written a Persian grammar, but destroyed the manuscript on learning that a similar work had been undertaken by the Mirza Muhammad Ibrahim, his assistant. In 1834 he resigned his positions at Haileybury, and went to live at Tunbridge Wells, where he spent the rest of his life in local work, and in writing extensively on the ancient history of Persia, though his work was never published. He died at 3 Mount Ephraim, Tunbridge Wells, on 29 January 1864.

Keene translated a small number of books from Persian. His book of Persian Fables was translated into Tamil in 1840. His translations are literal and clear.

H. G. KEENE, rev. PARVIN LOLOI

Sources personal knowledge (1891) · private information (1891) · Boase, Mod. Eng. biog. · Allibone, Dict. · C. E. Buckland, Dictionary of Indian biography (1906) · Venn, Alum. Cant. **Archives** BL OIOC, commonplace book, MS Eur. C 813 · CUL, travel journal in Germany and Austria · Flintshire RO, Hawarden, corresp. and papers | NL Scot., corresp. with Lord Melville **Wealth at death** under £2000: probate, 11 March 1864, CGPLA Eng. & Wales

Keepe, Henry (1652–1688), antiquary, was born in 1652 in Fetter Lane in the parish of St Dunstan-in-the-West, London, the son of Charles Keepe, a member of Sir William Courtney's cavalry regiment during the civil war and later employed in the exchequer. Keepe went to New Inn Hall, Oxford, as a gentleman commoner in 1668 but left without taking a degree and returned to London to study law at the Inner Temple. To this, however, he had a 'natural aversion' and, left to his own devices through his father's death which had occurred while he was still at Oxford, Keepe abandoned the law also. Later he related how:

my genius and inclination leading almost from my cradle for solitude … I gave myself the liberty of pleasing my own fancy … [in the pursuit of knowledge which is] … not only

the chiefest accomplishment of a gentleman but highly satisfactory in itself.   (BL, Sloane MS 1011, fol. 1v)

For eighteen years a member of Westminster Abbey's choir, Keepe published Monumenta Westmonasteriensia, or, An Historical Account of the Abbey Church of Westminster in 1682. This was reprinted in slightly expanded form the following year, but a prospectus for a fuller version illustrated by copperplate-engravings failed to elicit sufficient subscriptions and the larger project had to be abandoned. Keepe's other published works were The Genealogies of the High-Born Prince and Princess George and Anne of Denmark (1684) and A true and perfect narrative of the strange and unexpected finding of the crucifix and gold chain of that pious prince St. Edward, the king and confessor, which was found after 620 years interment (1688), the latter under the pseudonym Charles Taylour and describing his discovery of the two splendid objects which he had presented to James II in 1685. Keepe also began (c.1684) a manuscript survey of York, concentrating on a detailed description of the coats of arms in the city churches, a work acknowledged for its heraldic information by Francis Drake in his Eboracum (1736).

Keepe wrote an incomplete and undated manuscript account of his life but as much of it is little more than a rambling recollection of an encounter with a group of beggars, it reveals virtually nothing of his personality beyond a certain priggishness, while of his individual circumstances there is only Anthony Wood's statement that 'This person had changed his name with his religion for that of Rome, in the reign of King James II, his lodgings also several times, and died, as I have heard, but in a mean condition' (Wood, Ath. Oxon., 4.239). This occurred at his lodgings in Carter Lane, near St Paul's, in early June 1688; Keepe was buried on 11 June in St Gregory by Paul adjoining the cathedral.

Keepe's claim that Monumenta Westmonasteriensia was both more comprehensive and accurate in its details than the earlier accounts by Camden, Stow, and Weever has some substance. Its combination of evidence from 'authentick records and Testimonies' with first-hand observation of a building he knew well for many years makes it a unique and useful record of the abbey immediately prior to the extensive repairs carried out by Wren after 1698. Importantly, Keepe was the first of the abbey's historians to comment on the preservation of the great pavement in front of the high altar, 'that noble and most glorious inlaid floor still remaining intire … so laid and wrought to the Spectator's satisfaction that you are unwillingly drawn from the sight thereof' (H. Keepe, Monumenta Westmonasteriensia, 1683, 32). But it is chiefly for the accurate recording of the church's many monuments, complete with their heraldry, several of which have subsequently been destroyed or displaced, that his work remains of enduring value.

NICHOLAS DOGGETT

Sources E. W. Brayley and J. P. Neale, The history and antiquities of the abbey church of St Peter, Westminster, 2 (1823), esp. n. 71 · Gillow, Lit. biog. hist., 3.677 · Wood, Ath. Oxon., new edn, 4.238–9 · R. G. [R. Gough], British topography, [new edn], 1 (1780), 762; 2 (1780), 423 · T. Moule, Bibliotheca heraldica Magnae Britanniae (privately printed, London, 1822), 222 · F. Drake, Eboracum, or, The history and antiquities *of the city of York* (1736), preface · BL, Sloane MS 1011 [autobiography] · parish register, St Gregory by Paul, London [burial] **Archives** BL, incomplete MS autobiographical account, Sloane MS 1011

Keetley, Charles Robert Bell (1848–1909), surgeon, born on 13 September 1848 at Grimsby, was the son of Robert Keetley and his wife, Elizabeth, *née* Waterland, both of seafaring stock. When his father, a shipbuilder and a mayor of Grimsby, fell into financial straits, he was brought up mainly by his grandparents and an uncle, T. Bell Keetley MRCS, a medical practitioner. Educated at Browne's School, Grimsby, he acted as 'surgery help' or unarticled apprentice to his uncle during his last years at school, and then attended lectures on botany and anatomy at Hull Infirmary. He entered St Bartholomew's Hospital in 1871, matriculating at London University, and in 1874 he obtained gold medals at the intermediate MB examination, one for anatomy and the other for chemistry and materia medica; curiously he never took a final degree. Keetley was admitted MRCS and LRCP in 1873 and FRCS in 1876. After serving in 1875 as house surgeon to the Queen's Hospital, Birmingham, he worked in general practice at Bungay in Suffolk. In 1876 he was appointed an assistant demonstrator of anatomy at St Bartholomew's Hospital, where he achieved recognition for stimulating lectures enlivened by coloured chalk drawings. He was married to Anna, daughter of Henry Holmes Long of the East India Company; they had no children.

In 1878 Keetley was elected assistant surgeon at the West London Hospital, Hammersmith, where he remained until his death. During his thirty years' service, and mainly by his exertions, the hospital grew from a small suburban venture into a major institution. At the outset Keetley introduced antiseptic methods of surgery into the wards and operating theatre, before they were adopted significantly by other London hospitals. He was an energetic and conscientious surgeon, who was prepared to undertake emergency operations all night, even when seriously ill before his death. It was said he gave every hospital patient deliberate and prolonged attention, often putting a hand in his pocket to help them financially. Beneath a sometimes combative exterior, there was an attractive geniality, a ready wit, and a shrewdness which often proved prophetic.

Keetley's vision and initiative promoted the foundation of the West London Medico-Chirurgical Society in 1881; his presidential address, 'On surgery of the knee-joint' (1887), was a powerful defence of antiseptic surgery. An enthusiasm for teaching generated *The Student's Guide to the Medical Profession* (1878) and *An Index of Surgery* (1881). He was co-editor of the *Annals of Surgery* (1885–91), a fellow of the Medical Society of London and of the Royal Society of Medicine, a corresponding member of the American Orthopaedic Association, and a founder member of the British Orthopaedic Society. Based on vast experience, he wrote *Orthopaedic Surgery* (1900) partly illustrated with his own line drawings. He gave a Harveian lecture on plastic surgery, and in 1907 a Cavendish lecture on conservative abdominal surgery, in which he advised an interval or delayed appendicostomy, rather than radical appendicectomy, in the belief that appendicitis and other ills were related to that grisly spectre of the day, chronic constipation. None the less he counselled immediate operation for gastric haemorrhage and perforation. His contributions to medical journals, particularly *The Lancet*, were numerous and wide-ranging. In 1883 he wrote *Kallos: a Treatise on the Scientific Culture of Personal Beauty and the Cure of Ugliness*, which concentrated on the influence of Hellenic culture on concepts of beauty. Keetley was a member of the Savage Club and a president of the Lincolnshire Society of London. With Mr Herbert Chambers he originated and organized an Army Medical Civilian Reserve, later merged into the Territorial Army as the 3rd London General Hospital.

Contemporaries said Keetley was easily first in the second rank of London surgeons and would have achieved more but for a slight but incurable deafness, lack of punctuality, and want of business aptitude. A keen athlete in early life, he was well known as a footballer, boxer, and oarsman; he was a skilful artist and caricaturist with pen and pencil, and he had a gift for impromptu rhymes. Troubled by a cardiac condition in late 1909, he went to Brighton hoping to shake off a harassing cough, but he died there of sudden heart failure, at 11 Oriental Place, on 4 December 1909. He was buried in Kensal Green cemetery on the 8th.   D'A. POWER, *rev.* JOHN KIRKUP

Sources *The Lancet* (11 Dec 1909), 1788–9 · *BMJ* (11 Dec 1909), 1721–2 · *West London Medical Journal*, 15 (1910), 69–72 · V. G. Plarr, *Plarr's Lives of the fellows of the Royal College of Surgeons of England*, rev. D'A. Power, 2 vols. (1930) · personal knowledge (1912) · private information (1912) · CGPLA Eng. & Wales (1910) · b. cert. **Likenesses** photograph (in later life), Mora Ltd, Brighton and Southsea · portrait, repro. in *The Lancet* · portrait, repro. in *BMJ* · portrait, repro. in *West London Medical Journal* **Wealth at death** £2267 10s. 4d.: probate, 17 Feb 1910, CGPLA Eng. & Wales

Keightley, Sir Charles Frederic (1901–1974), army officer, was born at Anerley, near Croydon, on 24 June 1901, the only surviving child of Charles Albert Keightley, vicar of Anerley, and his wife, Kathleen Ross. He just missed service in the First World War. Because of his ability he was accelerated in promotion from the outset of the Second World War, successfully commanding a division, corps, and army without having commanded a squadron or regiment. Having been educated at Marlborough College (1914–18) and the Royal Military College, Sandhurst, he was commissioned into the 5th dragoon guards in 1921, a tall, well-built young man with a direct yet friendly manner and a strong sense of humour.

The regiment was then serving in the Middle East, where it was uneasily amalgamated with the 6th Inniskilling dragoons. Difficult days there were mitigated by removal to India and, later, operations on the north-west frontier. When the 5th Inniskilling dragoon guards returned to York in 1929 Lieutenant Keightley had made a name for himself as 'an exceptionally capable officer who has excelled in a range of duties'. He had also excelled in polo, playing on occasion for the army in India. In 1932 he married Joan Lydia, daughter of Brigadier-General George

Sir Charles Frederic Keightley (1901–1974), by Elliott & Fry

Nowell Thomas Smyth-Osbourne, of Ash, Iddesleigh, north Devon; they had two sons.

At York the regiment was in danger of becoming a drafting unit for overseas requirements. It fell to a dynamic commanding officer with Keightley as his adjutant to preserve regimental identity and expertise, activity in which Keightley again enhanced his reputation. He passed competitively into the Staff College at Camberley for the 1934–5 course, unaware that his regimental service had ended.

After passing out with high marks in 1935 he became staff officer to the director-general, Territorial Army (1936), and brigade-major to the cavalry in Cairo (1937–8) before returning to instruct at Camberley in 1938. At short notice, early in 1940, he was detached assistant adjutant and quartermaster-general (principal administrative staff officer) of 1st armoured division in France and Belgium. Among many critical problems he dealt with in the ensuing defence and withdrawal operations was the replacement of armoured vehicles in units, developing and implementing an embryo scheme which was adopted subsequently for the army as a whole. His work came to the notice of General Alan Brooke who drew him out of the administrative staff stream first to a brigade command and later in 1941 to direct, as a major-general, all Royal Armoured Corps training in the United Kingdom. When a force was formed to land in French north Africa, Keightley was chosen to command the 6th armoured division within it. He was then forty-one.

During the fleeting opportunities of late 1942 and the trials of 1943 Keightley demonstrated sound judgement in tactics and in the nurturing and driving of his command. By the time of the allied advance in Italy in the latter part of the year his standing was such that he was moved to command 78th infantry division when the opportunity for armoured warfare had diminished. He quickly won the support of this famous battleworthy formation, taking them through the Cassino operations in the following year, when he was promoted to command 5th corps. He continued no less successfully at this level, notably in the Argenta Gap operations leading to the final collapse of the German forces in Italy.

The war ended on 9 May. In north-east Italy, as elsewhere, Anglo-American relations with communist allies at once became tense. Southern Austria apart, Keightley's corps embraced Venezia Giulia, Istria, and Trieste, all of which Marshal Tito threatened to annex. It seemed possible that forces of the Russian Balkan front under Marshal Tolbulkhin might support him. At the same time the corps fighting troops were substantially diverted in superintending half a million German prisoners of war, including some 40,000 Russians—Cossacks who had fought with the German army—and a growing swarm of refugees and stragglers.

The Yalta agreement required the return of all Soviet citizens in the Anglo-American zones to their motherland, notably from Italy the Cossacks and their families. On 13 May Harold Macmillan, resident political adviser to Field Marshal Alexander, informed Charles Keightley of British governmental policy concerning Tito's claims in north-east Italy (and southern Austria) concluding briefly with the anticipated disposal of the Cossacks and other Russians in his charge. The two matters were interconnected: if 5th corps was obliged to thwart Tito's territorial ambitions by force, he needed to clear his ground of prisoners and refugees. The requirement was pressed up the chain of command to theatre headquarters, from which it was confirmed that the repatriation should take place.

What was not made clear was the exemption of some 'Russians' from the claims of the Yalta agreement. For example, a fraction of the refugees assembled in northeast Italy had left Russia before the Soviet Union was established. Many of these were none the less exchanged as 'Soviet' citizens. All those returned were either killed outright by the Soviet authorities, or perished later as prisoners.

Long after the anxieties of May 1945 had fallen away concerning Tito's threat to north-east Italy, suggestions were made that Keightley was precipitate in beginning the prisoner exchange and negligent in failing to identify those who had valid claims to remain as refugees in the 5th corps area. Following investigation, however, he was cleared on all counts.

With the end of the war and rapid demobilization, there were too many temporary lieutenant-generals for a shrinking army. Some retired, some reverted, but Keightley retained his rank, becoming director-general of military training in 1946 and military secretary in 1948. When Lieutenant-General Sir Brian Horrocks fell ill Keightley was sent to replace him, embarking on a series of commands-in-chief overseas for a span of almost ten years: the British army of the Rhine (1948–51), the Far East land forces (1951–3), and the Middle East land forces (1953–7).

Keightley's time in the Middle East was prolonged because of the Suez crisis, in which he found himself in the worst of positions as the responsible army commander; with a shifting political concept, inter-allied plans of which he had no knowledge until a late stage, a protracted delay in mounting operations because of logistic factors, and the absence of a unified commander. From this misconceived venture Keightley emerged with credit. He coped readily with order and counter-order, insisting that any landing must be properly supported and maintained. In the political aftermath of the operations, his departure at last from the Middle East in 1957 was falsely rumoured in London to stem from mismanagement. The story took no root in the army and was dissipated by his appointment as governor and commander-in-chief, Gibraltar—a post from which he finally retired in 1962 after more than forty years of service. He had become a general in 1951.

Keightley persistently regretted that circumstances prevented him from commanding his regiment, and was proud to own that his ideas of soldiering had been shaped principally by it. Thence came his belief that every man, however junior, must be expected and encouraged to think for himself, whether alone or part of a team. Yet, though a cavalryman to the core, he acquired a remarkable insight into—not simply a knowledge of—the infantry art, the potential and the burdens of the infantry soldier. This was an important factor in his success as a commander.

Keightley's honours and appointments were many. Admitted to the DSO (1944) and the American Legion of Merit (1942), appointed OBE (1941), CB (1943), KBE (1945), KCB (1950), he was advanced to GCB in 1953 and GBE in 1957 and made a grand officer of the Légion d'honneur in 1958. From 1953 to 1956 he was aide-de-camp general to the queen. He was colonel of his regiment for ten years (1947–57) and colonel-commandant of the Royal Armoured Corps (cavalry wing) (1958–68).

Keightley died on 17 June 1974 at Salisbury General Infirmary.   ANTHONY FARRAR-HOCKLEY

Sources personal knowledge (2004) · private information (1986) · A. Horne, *Macmillan*, 1: *1894–1956* (1988) · W. S. Churchill, *The Second World War*, 6 (1954) · H. Macmillan, *Tides of fortune, 1945–1955* (1969) [vol. 3 of autobiography] · *The London Irish at war* (1946) · *CGPLA Eng. & Wales* (1974)
Archives FILM BFI NFTVA, documentary footage · IWM FVA, documentary footage
Likenesses photograph, 1956, Hult. Arch. · portrait, 1959 (after photograph), Royal Dragoon Guards · Elliott & Fry, photograph, NPG [*see illus.*]
Wealth at death £46,421: probate, 20 Nov 1974, *CGPLA Eng. & Wales*

Keightley, Thomas (*c.*1650–1719), government official, was the only son of William Keightley (*b. c.*1621) of Hertingfordbury, Hertfordshire, and his wife, Anne, daughter of John Williams of London. Nothing is known of Keightley's early years or education, but on 3 May 1672 he was appointed a gentleman usher to James, duke of York. On 9 July 1675 he married Lady Frances (*b.* 1658, *d.* after 1723), youngest daughter of Edward Hyde, first earl of Clarendon, and sister of the duke of York's first wife. Although the Keightleys had seven sons and two daughters, by the late 1680s only a daughter, Catherine, survived, and the marriage had broken down. In 1713, when the couple met at Somerset House, London, they had not seen each other for 27 years. The Hyde family did not impute any blame to Keightley, and rather viewed Frances as the source of the problem.

Soon after his marriage Keightley sold his property in Hertfordshire, and emigrated to Ireland. In the 1680s his family connections resulted in the duke of York granting annual rents of £238 from his Irish estate to Keightley for thirty-one years, while Charles II granted him a yearly pension of £400. Keightley's involvement in Irish government commenced with the appointment of his brother-in-law Henry Hyde, second earl of Clarendon, as lord lieutenant of Ireland. In early 1686 he was appointed Irish vice-treasurer, normally a lucrative post, but the grant applied only to the judicial role, with a yearly salary of £20. Clarendon, believing Keightley had a good understanding of revenue matters, hoped to get him appointed to the Irish revenue commission, which paid £1000 a year, but feared pressing the issue owing to the potential for accusations of nepotism. In July Clarendon sent him to England, ostensibly on private business, but in reality to keep Keightley's other brother-in-law, Laurence Hyde, earl of Rochester and lord high treasurer, informed on Irish affairs.

Keightley's lengthy career in Irish government commenced in earnest in 1692, with his appointment as a revenue commissioner and privy councillor. Prior to these appointments Keightley had commenced proceedings for recovering the rents and pension granted to him in the 1680s, but by 1694 he was petitioning for a custodiam of Irish forfeited lands. William III looked favourably upon the petition, initially granting him a three-year custodiam of lands to the yearly value of £674, and later a ninety-nine-year grant to the same value. However, events in England altered the significance of these grants following the report by the English parliamentary commissioners of inquiry in December 1699. Keightley was named in the report as one of sixteen grantees to benefit most from the seventy-six grants in being at that time. Likewise he was one of the five named grantees who had sold substantial parts of their lands. The English Act of Resumption in 1700 caused problems for Keightley, as the loss of his grant could have been financially ruinous. However, in 1701 Rochester secured a re-grant of Keightley's 1680s pension, while in 1702 Keightley succeeded in getting an English act passed for confirming his grant of forfeited lands.

Keightley was a member of the Irish House of Commons from 1695 to 1714, and although at times he was alienated from the Irish court party, he remained a loyal government supporter. He also managed to retain his revenue post for twenty-two years, and received other benefits, primarily owing to his relationship with Rochester. In 1700 Rochester was appointed lord lieutenant of Ireland, and prior to his arrival there in 1701 kept up a regular correspondence with Keightley, treating him as his personal agent and his mouthpiece in government. On Rochester's return to England in 1702 his dissatisfaction with his Irish lords justices found expression on the accession of Queen Anne in March, when Keightley was appointed as one of two new lords justices. Rochester now looked to Keightley for advice on all issues relating to government, while still relying upon him as his private agent and friend. However, the replacement of Rochester as lord lieutenant in 1703 by James Butler, second duke of Ormond, heralded the end of Keightley's brief foray into the realms of the chief governor's office. For the remainder of Anne's reign he continued to serve as a commissioner, and, although being suggested for the post of lord justice in 1706, and serving for a brief period in 1710 as a commissioner for the great seal, he did not progress again within government. In 1714 he was removed from the revenue commission as part of a political reformation in government following the Hanoverian succession. The previous year he had received a pension of £1000 for his long and faithful service. He did not serve in public office again, and died on 19 January 1719.   C. I. McGrath

Sources NL Ire., Inchiquin MSS, Keightley MSS · C. I. McGrath, 'The Irish revenue system: government and administration, 1689–1702', PhD diss., U. Lond., 1997 · *GM*, 1st ser., 99/1 (1829) · *The state letters of Henry, earl of Clarendon*, ed. [J. Douglas], 2 vols. (1765) · J. L. Chester and J. Foster, eds., *London marriage licences, 1521–1869* (1887) · *Report of the commissioners appointed by parliament to enquire into the Irish forfeitures … 1699* (1700) · J. E. Cussans, *History of Hertfordshire*, 2/2 (1874) · H. Chauncy, *The historical antiquities of Hertfordshire* (1700); repr. in 2 vols., 1 (1826) · G. Agar-Ellis, ed., *The Ellis correspondence: letters written during the years 1686, 1687, 1688, and addressed to John Ellis*, 2 vols. (1829), vol. 1 · J. G. Simms, *The Williamite confiscation in Ireland, 1690–1703* (1956) · *Eighth report*, 1, HMC, 7 (1907–9) · R. Lascelles, ed., *Liber munerum publicorum Hiberniae … or, The establishments of Ireland*, later edn, 2 vols. in 7 pts (1852), vol. 1, pt 2 · *DNB*
Archives NL Ire., corresp. | BL, letters to John Ellis, Add. MSS 28880–28894 · BL, letters to earl of Rochester, Add. MS 15895

Keightley, Thomas (1789–1872), historian and author, was born in Dublin on 17 October 1789, the eldest son of Thomas Keightley of Newtown, co. Kildare; he claimed relationship with Thomas Keightley (1650?–1719). He entered Trinity College, Dublin, in July 1803, aged fourteen, and graduated BA in 1808, but ill health made him abandon a design of going to the Irish bar. By 1824 he had settled in London and was engaged in literary and journalistic work. A fellow Anglo-Irishman, Thomas Crofton Croker, was one of his earliest London friends, and Keightley contributed materials to Croker's *Fairy Legends of South Ireland* (1825), for, brought up in Ireland, he had listened eagerly to the tales that circulated there. Out of this collaboration grew his own folkloric books, starting with *The Fairy Mythology* (1828), which assembled European peasant stories and was praised by Jacob Grimm. Its methods showed an advance over Crofton's, particularly in its respect for the nature of oral story-telling. Keightley also

contributed to periodicals, such as the *Foreign Quarterly Review* (1827–35). His *Mythology of Ancient Greece and Italy* appeared in 1831 (enlarged edn, 1838). In it, he established parallels between classical myths and later legends, an approach he developed further in his *Tales and Popular Fictions: their Resemblance, and Transmission from Country to Country* (1834), the first English book to demonstrate the widely scattered appearances of common folk-tale plots and incidents. The preface announced that his enquiries into popular superstitions and traditions were at an end; but he had provided enough insights to prepare the way for successors in comparative folklore.

The remainder of Keightley's life went into other labours. He had already embarked on historical manuals for educational or popular purposes, several of which long held their place in schools. His *Outlines of History*, thrown off at speed, was a one-volume history of the world, issued in Lardner's Cabinet Cyclopaedia in 1830 and frequently revised. His *History of the War of Greek Independence* (2 vols., 1830) was succeeded by *The History of Greece* (1835), and *The History of Rome to the End of the Republic* (1836). In *The History of England* (2 vols., 1837–9), one of his aims was to counteract biases of the Roman Catholic divine John Lingard, on whose work the book was largely based. Keightley himself was an Anglican, and professed little interest in party politics. A *History of the Roman Empire* came in 1840; and finally *A History of India* in 1847. Keightley's main other historical writings were *The Crusaders* (1834), and *Secret Societies of the Middle Ages* (1837), dealing with the assassins of the East, the knights templars, and the secret tribunals of Westphalia.

Having previously produced an edition of Ovid's *Fasti* (1839), and elaborate *Notes on the 'Bucolics' and 'Georgics' of Virgil* (1846), Keightley now turned to editing further Latin classics, and brought out the following editions: *Bucolics and Georgics* (1847), the *Satires and Epistles* of Horace (1848), and the *Catilina and Jugurtha* of Sallust (1849). Moving on to English classics, he followed a succinct *Account of the Life, Opinions, and Writings of John Milton* (1855) with editions of Milton (2 vols., 1859, with good notes), and of Shakespeare's plays (6 vols., 1864). In the latter his attitude to emendation was eccentric, but his *Shakespeare Expositor* (1867) won commendation.

Keightley tended to trumpet his own merits, but also confessed to leading the existence of a London hack. Little is known of the incidents of his life, though he refers to having spent time in Italy. He claimed to have read in some twenty languages and dialects, including Hebrew, and issued *The Manse of Mastland* (1860), a translation from the Dutch of a novel by C. E. van Koetsveld. He was industrious, with an ability to compress bulky material into an easy synopsis. His folkloric works were innovative; many of his subsequent books went into several editions, and some into other languages. But his literary earnings were modest. From July 1854 he received a civil-list pension of £100, 'in consideration of his Services to Historical Literature & of the straitened circumstances to which he is reduced'. During his later years he lived at Belvedere,

Erith, in Kent, with a sister who helped him in his writings. He died there on 4 November 1872, of senile dementia, and was buried in Erith churchyard—'the last male of his branch of an ancient family', according to the tombstone.   ANGUS FRASER

Sources R. M. Dorson, *The British folklorists: a history* (1968) · *DNB* · *The Times* (7 Nov 1872) · C. R. Smith, *Retrospections, social and archaeological*, 3 vols. (1883–91) · Civil list ledger · d. cert.

Keigwin, John (*bap.* **1642**, *d.* **1716**), scholar of the Cornish language, was born at Mousehole, Cornwall, from a long line of merchants and minor gentry, and was baptized at Paul on 7 January 1642, the only surviving son of Martin Keigwin (*bap.* 1595, *d.* 1667) and his second wife, Elizabeth (*bap.* 1606, *d.* 1677), daughter of Robert Scawen of St Germans. John was thus the nephew of William Scawen, vice-warden of the stannaries, who was a passionate advocate for the preservation of the Cornish language. He married Mary (*d.* 1690), daughter of John Penrose and the niece of Frances Penrose, his father's first wife, at Sithney in Cornwall on 10 July 1666; they had at least eight and most probably ten children. John, baptized at Paul on 30 May 1682, was probably their last-born child and seems to be the only son to have continued the family line, assuming that he was the John Keigwin who migrated to America and married Hannah Brown on 10 October 1700 in Stonington, Connecticut, falsely adding ten years to his age to assert his majority.

It was upon being chided about the decay of the language by Sir Francis North at the Launceston assizes in 1678 that Scawen sought Keigwin's help in translating into English his original copy of 'Pascon agan Arluth' ('The passion of Our Lord'), now in the British Library (Harley MS 1782) and often referred to as 'Mount Calvary' or the passion poem. Scawen acknowledged both John Keigwin and his father, Martin, in his essay on the decline of Cornish, written just before his death in 1689, noting that Martin had spent periods in Wales and Brittany and had some understanding of those varieties of Celtic speech. Both John and his father appear to have been native speakers of Cornish. William Pryce (perhaps paraphrasing some lost statement of Thomas Tonkin) claimed that they had both 'sucked in the broken dialect with their milk' (Pryce, [5]).

Keigwin's translation of 'Pascon agan Arluth' was completed in 1682, that of William Jordan's 'Creation of the world' was commenced in 1691 at the request of Jonathan Trelawney, bishop of Exeter, and completed in 1693, and the three dramas of the *Ordinalia* cycle were translated about 1695. In addition Keigwin translated some other Cornish pieces and assisted the linguist Edward Lhuyd with word lists as well as copies of these translations during and after the latter's visit to Cornwall in 1700. His translations have been criticized for being over-literal and at times confused, but it must be remembered that there were no grammars or vocabularies of Cornish accessible at the time Keigwin was writing. He must have worked from the spoken Cornish he knew to an interpretation of the late medieval Cornish of the written texts, which were often difficult to read. Every scholar who came after him is

thus in his debt. While John played down his abilities in the translator's preface to the passion poem, Scawen judged both him and his father as 'pretty good grammarians' (Hawke, 'Manuscripts', 23), and John Boson's poem written at Keigwin's death claimed that he was knowledgeable in Latin, Greek, Hebrew, and French as well as Cornish. Edward Lhuyd said of him that he was 'without any comparison, the most skilfull judge of our age in the Cornish Language' (Pryce, [8]). Keigwin said of himself in 1702 that he was 'of his country and race the dearest lover' (Davies, 10). This patriotism explains his labours in preserving the Cornish language, and his encouragement in the same task of others such as Edward Lhuyd, William Gwavas, and Thomas Tonkin. Keigwin was buried on 20 April 1716 at Paul, where Mary had been buried on 29 March 1690.   MATTHEW SPRIGGS

Sources parish register, Paul, Cornwall RO · J. Burke, *History of the commoners of Great Britain and Ireland* (1838), 4.287–91 · A. Hawke, 'The manuscripts of the Cornish passion poem', *Cornish Studies*, 9 (1981), 23–8 · B. O. Murdoch, *The medieval Cornish poem of the passion* (1979), 5–9 · W. L. Davies, *Cornish manuscripts in the National Library of Wales* (1939), 8–11 · W. Pryce, *Archaeologia Cornu-Britannica* (1790), 4–5, 8 (unpaginated) · W. Scawen, 'Antiquities Cornu-Britannick', [n.d., *c*.1678–1689], Royal Institution of Cornwall · A. Hawke, 'A lost manuscript of the Cornish Ordinalia?', *Cornish Studies*, 7 (1979), 45–60 · O. Padel, *The Cornish writings of the Boson family* (1975), 24–37, 59 · A. L. Holman, *Blackman and allied families* (Chicago, 1928), 114–20 · R. T. Gunther, *Life and letters of Edward Lhuyd* (1945), 309, 370, 483–8, 494, 548 · P. A. S. Pool, *The death of Cornish (1600–1800)* (1982), 11–12, 14–15 · N. H. Nicholas, 'Memoir of John Keigwin', in D. Gilbert, *Mount Calvary* (1826), xi–xxii · D. Gilbert, *The creation of the world* (1827) · P. Neuss, 'The creacion of the world': a critical edition and translation (1983), lxxvi–lxxviii · R. M. Nance, 'John Keigwin's translation of King Charles I's letter of thanks', *Old Cornwall*, 1/4 (1926), 35–40 · E. G. R. Hooper, 'More about Keigwin's Cornish', *Old Cornwall*, 9/6 (1982), 284–5 · parish register, St Germans, Cornwall, 7 Oct 1606 [baptism, mother] · parish register, Sithney, Cornwall, 10 July 1666 [marriage]

Keigwin, Richard (*d.* **1690**), naval and army officer in the East India Company, was the third son of Richard Keigwin (1605–1647) of Penzance and Margaret, daughter of Nicholas Godolphin of Trewarveneth. In 1665 he was appointed lieutenant of the *Santa Maria*, one of the Blue squadron in the Four Days' Battle (1–4 June 1666). He was promoted by Prince Rupert to command the flagship *Eagle* in 1672 but was soon afterwards moved into *Assistance* under Commodore Munby. In an attack on the island of St Helena the following year he led the men who landed in Prosperous Bay at the spot since known as Keigwin's Rock. Keigwin subsequently served as governor of the island but was recalled after a few months by the East India Company. His merits were recognized and he was promoted and sent out to Bombay, where he was appointed commandant of the garrison and of the company's land and sea forces. As commandant he insisted on the need for energetic restraint of the threatening attitude of the Marathas, and on 18 October 1679, commanding the company's ship *Revenge*, he led a successful action with Sirajee's fleet of some forty or fifty ships; some of them were sunk, while others fled.

Before news of this affair reached England orders had

arrived in Bombay to reduce the garrison and Keigwin was recalled. However, he returned to Bombay in 1681 holding the rank of captain-lieutenant and third in the council. Once again the directors chose to cut military expenditure and reduced the salaries of the soldiers including Keigwin, who also lost his seat in the council. The soldiers were angry and broke into open revolt in December 1683. Keigwin threw in his lot with the troops. The conspirators seized the deputy governor and several members of his council, annulled the authority of the company, and declared Bombay Island to be directly under the king's protection. The garrison and the inhabitants of the island elected Keigwin as governor. He took possession of the *Return* and the frigate *Hunter* as well as the treasure found on board, amounting to between 50,000 and 60,000 rupees, and declared that it should be used to strengthen the defence of Bombay. Keigwin and his associates addressed letters to the king and the duke of York expressing their determination to maintain the island for the king, until his wishes should be known.

On 31 January 1684 John Child, the president of the company's settlement in Surat, arrived off Bombay. He held conferences with the mutineers, promising to pardon their actions if they surrendered, but in vain. The animosity of Keigwin and his adherents was directed against the president and Sir Josiah Child, one of the company's directors in London, whom they held responsible for reducing military expenditure. The company could not take the island by force and was perturbed by the growing activity of English interlopers. Two leading company servants, Bowcher and Petit, had assisted them and were dismissed from the service. There were frequent reports concerning the creation of a new East India Company in England and Child feared that interlopers could gain possession of Bombay if they co-operated with the rebels.

Interloping activity rapidly increased, with English ships being fitted out in Ostend and sailing to India. The king, however, ordered them to be intercepted and supported the company. In a report to Charles II the company repudiated the accusations, made by Keigwin in his letters to the king and the duke of York, that Bombay was badly maintained, reported that some £300,000 had been spent on fortifications and improvements, and claimed that interlopers were the real source of the rebellion. These interlopers wanted to establish a factory in India and had inspired the rebels to act. The king was advised to restore Bombay to the company and to pardon the rebels with the exception of the leaders, including Keigwin. This request was granted.

On 7 March 1684 the company's forces captured the *Return*, which Keigwin had sent to Petit, the chief of the interlopers at Surat, indicating the existence of a connection between the rebels in Bombay and the interlopers. However, with the arrival of Sir Thomas Grantham, the king's officer, on 10 November 1684 Keigwin agreed to surrender Bombay on condition that both he and his adherents were granted a free pardon. Keigwin arrived in England in July 1685 under Grantham's protection and he was not prosecuted.

In May 1689 Keigwin was appointed captain of the frigate *Reserve*; he moved soon afterwards into *Assistance*, and early in 1690 was sent to the West Indies under Commodore Lawrence Wright. At the attack on St Kitts on 21 June he landed at the head of his marines and was killed in action leading his men on the assault on Basseterre.

J. K. LAUGHTON, *rev.* SØREN MENTZ

Sources J. Bruce, *Annals of the honorable East-India Company, from their establishment by the charter of Queen Elizabeth, 1600, to the union of the London and English East-India companies, 1707–8*, 3 vols. (1810), 2.512–17, 522–8, 536–42 · *The diary of William Hedges … during his agency in Bengal; as well as on his voyage out and return overland (1681–1687)*, ed. R. Barlow and H. Yule, 2, Hakluyt Society, 75 (1888), 168–84 · J. Keay, *The honourable company: a history of the English East India Company* (1991), 137–40
Wealth at death see administration, PRO, PROB 6/66, fol. 167v

Keilin, David (1887–1963), biochemist and parasitologist, was born in Moscow on 21 March 1887, the second son in the family of seven children of Hirsh Davidoff Keilin, a businessman and small landowner from Warsaw, and his wife, Rachel Strelsin. Keilin was educated by a governess until the age of ten and he then attended the Górski Gymnasium, a private high school in Warsaw. After leaving school in 1904 he attended and completed a pre-entry course in medicine at the University of Liège in Belgium, but as he suffered from asthma he felt that it would be unwise to follow a medical career. From Belgium he moved to Paris where he attended lectures in philosophy at the Collège de France and learned about the arts by visiting museums and galleries. One day he attended a lecture on entomology given by Maurice Caullery, who, on seeing Keilin's enthusiasm for the subject, invited him to complete a biology course at the Laboratoire d'Évolution des Êtres Organisés and then stay on to carry out research. Here Keilin specialized in entomology, particularly the dipterous larvae, and his work involved the study of the life cycles of parasitic insects and protists, which include micro-organisms that can parasitize insect larvae. He carried out research on the fly *Pollenia rudis* which parasitizes the earthworm *Allolobophora chlorotica* and published his first paper on this in 1909. Further papers on other diptera followed. In 1914 he was awarded the Prix Passet of the Société Entomologique de France for his researches, which also formed the basis for his thesis for a DSc degree at the Sorbonne.

In 1915 Keilin came to Britain and took up the post of research assistant to George H. F. Nuttall, the first Quick professor of biology at Cambridge. Here his parasitological work continued, notably with a study on lice (which were a serious problem during the First World War). He also studied morphology and continued with his researches on the dipterous larvae and parasitism, and also on insect respiration.

In 1920 Keilin became Beit memorial research fellow, a post he held for several years. He carried out significant work on the life cycle of the horse bot-fly (*Gasterophilus intestinalis*), and found that the red bot-fly larvae, which live in the stomach of the horse, contain haemoglobin—the red pigmentation in blood. This research led to his important discovery of cytochrome, an intracellular pigment consisting of three haemochromogen compounds which he called cytochromes *a*, *b*, and *c*. He found that cytochrome was present not only in animal tissues, but also in plants, yeast, and bacteria, and by studying it further, was able to observe its oxidation and reduction in living cells and thus establish its important catalytic function in cell respiration. For its spectroscopic study he used a microspectroscope ocular and a Hartridge reversion spectroscope, and later emphasized the importance of having used a *low dispersion* spectroscope to find the accurate absorption band spectra of its components. His paper 'On cytochrome, a respiratory pigment, common to animals, yeast, and higher plants' appeared in the *Proceedings of the Royal Society* (*B Series*) in 1925. In 1938–9 Keilin demonstrated the existence of the enzyme cytochrome oxidase, and in papers (written with E. F. Hartree) of 1940 and 1945 he described the properties and purification of cytochrome *c*, the only component of cytochrome to be obtained at the time in a highly purified state, thus allowing it to be extensively studied.

In 1925 Keilin became university lecturer in parasitology, and in 1931 he was appointed Quick professor of biology and director of the Molteno Institute as Professor Nuttall's successor. Keilin remained director of the institute until his official retirement in 1952, but afterwards he continued to work there on various projects until his death. He maintained his extensive knowledge of parasitology as editor of the journal *Parasitology* from 1934 to 1963, and his interest in the history of biological science was evident in his Leeuwenhoek lecture, 'The problem of anabiosis or latent life: history and current concept' given before the Royal Society and published in the *Proceedings* in 1959.

In Paris in 1913 Keilin had married Anna Hershlik, who later practised as a doctor in Cambridge. They had one child, a daughter, Joan, who became a biochemist and completed and edited Keilin's book *The History of Cell Respiration and Cytochrome* (1966). In this book Keilin indicated that his discovery of cytochrome had been an advance on the researches carried out on myohaematin and histohaematins in 1884–7 by a medical practitioner, Charles Alexander MacMann.

Keilin was a man of small stature. He had a round face with a moustache, and wore glasses. He was fluent in several languages and spoke English with a distinctive French/Polish accent. For relaxation he read great works of literature and enjoyed modern detective novels, which he often read at night when his asthma was troublesome. He travelled infrequently because of his health, but served on several Cambridge University committees and boards and some government and Royal Society committees. Above all he was a dedicated, practical research worker who always had a fund of ideas with which to develop his studies. He took great care in the preparation of his lectures for students, and his scientific papers were written with elegance and clarity. In personality he was optimistic and cheerful with a good sense of humour, and always inspired confidence in his colleagues.

During his life Keilin published nearly 200 scientific papers. Apart from those on cytochrome and entomological subjects, they included several on the enzymes catalase and peroxidase, carbonic anhydrase, and glucose oxidase (notatin), and others on haemoglobin and its derivatives. His work on carbonic anhydrase eventually led to the development of a drug to treat glaucoma. The awards he received were numerous. He was elected a fellow of the Royal Society in 1928, he gave the Croonian lecture in 1934, and he received the society's royal medal in 1939 and Copley medal in 1952. He was very proud to be elected a *membre correspondant* (1947) and *membre associé étranger* (1955) of the Académie des Sciences de l'Institut de France. Honorary degrees of the universities of Brussels (1946), Bordeaux (1947), Liège (1951), and Utrecht (1957) were given to him, and he received an honorary fellowship of Magdalene College, Cambridge, in 1957.

Keilin died suddenly of a heart attack on 27 February 1963 while attending a meeting at the Old Schools, in Cambridge, about the future of the Molteno Institute. He was survived by his wife. Keilin is chiefly remembered for his work on cytochrome and the discovery of its essential role in cell respiration. He was instrumental in bringing molecular biology to Cambridge and, as director of the Molteno Institute, was responsible for the training of many outstanding scientists of different nationalities in biochemical research, thereby developing this important branch of science. After his death the Biochemical Society endowed a biennial Keilin lecture and medal in his honour.   CHRISTOPHER F. LINDSEY

Sources T. Mann, *Memoirs FRS*, 10 (1964), 183–205 · *Journal of General Microbiology*, 45 (1966), 159–85 · D. Keilin, *The history of cell respiration and cytochrome*, ed. J. Keilin (1966) · E. F. Hartree, *Biochemical Journal*, 89 (1963), 1–5 · *Parasitology*, 55 (1965), 1–28 · *DNB* · R. A. Klein, ed., 'The Molteno Institute, University of Cambridge, 1921–1987', *The Biochemist*, 14/1 (1992), 3–20; 14/2 (1992), 15–30 · *The Times* (2 March 1963) · *The Times* (6 March 1963) · F. McD. C. T., 'In memoriam: D. K. and W. B. R. K.', *Magdalene College Magazine and Record*, new ser., 7 (1962–3), 13–16 · T. Mann, *Nature*, 198 (1963), 736 · R. A. Klein, 'Magdalene and the Molteno Institute', *Magdalene College Magazine and Record*, new ser., 31 (1987), 20–22
Archives Biochemical Society, London, Keilin archive · CUL, corresp. and papers · Magd. Cam. · Medical Research Council, London, corresp. · U. Oxf., department of zoology, drawings and papers | CAC Cam., corresp. with A. V. Hill
Likenesses H. A. Freeth, drawing, 1952, Magd. Cam. · H. A. Freeth, ink and wash drawing, 1952, NPG · photograph, repro. in Keilin, *History of cell respiration* · photographs, CUL, Keilin's archive file
Wealth at death £26,766 7s. 0d.: probate, 1 Aug 1963, *CGPLA Eng. & Wales*

Keill, James (1673–1719), physician and anatomist, was born in Edinburgh on 27 March 1673, the younger son of Robert Keill, admitted as a writer to the signet on 29 November 1673, and his wife, Sarah Cockburn (*d.* 1697), a draper. Sarah Cockburn's uncle was Patrick Scougall (1607–1682), bishop of Aberdeen, and her brother was John Cockburn (1652–1729), a noted Scottish Episcopalian clergyman. (William Cockburn MD was apparently not a relation.) James Keill's older brother John *Keill (1671–1721) was a mathematician and natural philosopher.

Keill enrolled at the University of Edinburgh in 1688,

and he and his brother studied mathematics there with David Gregory. There is no evidence that he obtained a degree. Keill then travelled on the continent for some years. In Paris he attended the chemistry lectures of Nicolas Lemery and possibly the anatomy lectures of Joseph-Guichard Duverney. He enrolled as a medical student at the University of Leiden on 26 October 1696 but did not take a degree. On his return to Britain in 1698 he joined his brother John at Oxford, where he supported himself by lecturing on anatomy. He may also have lectured at Cambridge. In 1698 he published his *Anatomy of the Humane Body Abridg'd*, an anatomy textbook, largely translated from the French *Nouvelle description anatomique* (1679) of Amé Bourdon. Keill dedicated it to Edward Tyson. In the same year he published a translation of the eighth edition of Nicolas Lemery's *Cours de chymie*, which supplanted Walter Harris's translations of earlier editions and was often reprinted.

Keill did not formally attend medical school. Probably through his brother's influence he obtained the degree of MD from King's College, Aberdeen, in May 1699, but this did not involve a course of study. Through the patronage of Hans Sloane he obtained the degree of MD (*comitiis regiae*) from Cambridge University on 16 April 1705. Around 1703 Sloane helped Keill enter into medical practice in Northampton, where he remained for the rest of his life.

As a student of Gregory, Keill was introduced to the 'iatro-mathematical' ideas of Archibald Pitcairne of Edinburgh. Pitcairne attempted to revise Cartesian mechanical physiology with reference to Newtonian mathematics and methods. The writings on chemistry and mathematics of Keill's brother John also influenced his work. In the second edition of his *Anatomy of the Humane Body Abridg'd*, published in 1703, Keill revised the text based on his iatromechanical reading and his anatomical experience. He introduced in this work his concept of secretion, based on the velocity of the blood, which he envisaged as a congeries of particles. In different parts of the body the differing speed of the blood's flow would cause its constituent particles to cohere into larger particles of differing sizes, which would then pass through appropriately-sized orifices into the correct gland.

With the exception of a paper in the *Philosophical Transactions* on the autopsy of a Northamptonshire man reported to have been 130 years old, Keill published nothing between 1703 and 1708, when he issued a third, unrevised edition of his *Anatomy*. In this year also appeared his most important work, *An Account of Animal Secretion, the Quantity of Blood in the Humane Body, and Muscular Motion*. The first essay in this volume was Keill's most original contribution to physiology. He elaborated on the account of secretion in his *Anatomy*, both by employing Newton's concept of a short-range chemical attraction analogous to gravity to explain the cohesion of the particles of blood, and by developing a mathematical model of the circulatory system which would support his hypothesis. Although his mathematics were faulty, he has been credited with 'the first attempted use of a geometrical series to estimate a

property of a bifurcating network (in this case total time for blood to flow from the heart to the terminal branches of the mesenteric artery)' (Woldenburg, 249).

Keill's other two essays in the volume were less original, but notable for their application of mathematics to problems of physiology. In 1717 this work was issued in a second edition, *Essays on Several Parts of the Animal Oeconomy* (translated into Latin as *Tentamina medico-physica*, 1718), with a new essay on the force of the heart. This new essay provoked a debate in the pages of *Philosophical Transactions* with another Newtonian, James Jurin, who questioned Keill's calculations. Keill replied, and Jurin's response appeared shortly after Keill's death. Appended to the 1718 *Tentamina* was Keill's *Medicina statica Britannica*, an attempt to duplicate the work of the Italian physician Sanctorius on human intake and excretion, using himself as the experimental subject.

Keill was a successful medical practitioner, whose noble patients included Lord Leominster, the duke of Leeds, and Earl Ferrers, all referred to him by Sloane, with whom he kept an extensive correspondence on clinical matters.

Keill never married. Beginning in 1716 he suffered from what appears to have been cancer of the mouth. Although a tumour was cauterised the affliction spread, and a hard swelling of the face and neck caused Keill's death by suffocation on 16 July 1719. He may have been killed by the tumour, or by an infection of the lymph nodes. Keill was buried in the churchyard of St Giles's Church, Northampton, where his brother John erected a monument in his memory.

Keill died a wealthy man and left the bulk of his estate to his brother John. He also left £800 to one sister, Magdalen Murray, specifying that it should be out of her husband's control, and £150 'to my Muse Dr Cockburn', which may refer either to William Cockburn MD, or to his uncle John Cockburn DD. He left his books and microscopes to Matthew Lee, later a prominent physician.

ANITA GUERRINI

Sources F. M. Valadez and C. D. O'Malley, 'James Keill of Northampton, physician, anatomist, and physiologist', *Medical History*, 15 (1971), 317–35 · A. Guerrini, 'Newtonian matter theory, chemistry, and medicine, 1690–1713', PhD diss., Indiana University, 1983 · A. Guerrini, 'The tory Newtonians: Gregory, Pitcairne, and their circle', *Journal of British Studies*, 25 (1986), 288–311 · M. J. Woldenburg, 'James Keill (1708) and the morphometry of the microcosm', *Process and form in geomorphology*, ed. D. R. Stoddart (1997), 243–64 · Venn, *Alum. Cant.* · *Biographia Britannica, or, The lives of the most eminent persons who have flourished in Great Britain and Ireland*, 4 (1757) · will, PRO, PROB 11/570, sig. 165

Archives BL, letters to Sir Hans Sloane, MSS 4039–4045, 4059, 4078

Wealth at death bequests totalling £1000; bulk of estate inherited by John Keill: will, PRO, PROB 11/570, sig. 165

Keill, John (1671–1721), mathematician and natural philosopher, was born in Edinburgh on 1 December 1671, the son of Robert Keill, later a writer to the signet, and his wife, Sarah Cockburn (*d.* 1697), a draper. Her uncle was Patrick Scougall (1607–1682), bishop of Aberdeen, and her brother was John Cockburn (1652–1729), episcopalian clergyman and nonjuror. In 1692, when Keill moved to

Oxford, Cockburn wrote a letter recommending him to his fellow nonjuror, Thomas Smith of Magdalen. James *Keill (1673–1719), the Newtonian physician, was John's younger brother.

Teaching Newton's principles Keill entered the University of Edinburgh in 1688 and gained distinction in mathematics and natural philosophy under David Gregory (1661–1708). He was one of Gregory's most accomplished students and, having graduated MA, he followed his preceptor to Balliol College when Gregory became Savilian professor of astronomy at Oxford in 1691. Keill was incorporated MA on 2 February 1694, having been awarded a 'Scotch exhibition' to help him pay his way. Gregory already had a reputation as a committed and pedagogically gifted Newtonian, and his influence upon Keill was manifest. After developing ways of expounding Newtonian principles by experimental demonstrations in his room at Balliol, Keill was appointed as a lecturer in experimental philosophy at Hart Hall. He therefore offered the first course on Newtonian natural philosophy, and the first reputedly based on 'experimental demonstrations', at either of the English universities. Judging from the published version of his lectures (*Introductio ad veram physicam*, Oxford, 1701), many of his demonstrations were mathematical rather than experimental, being based on 'thought experiments' (imagined experiments) rather than real manipulations. Nevertheless, some of Keill's demonstrations called for real apparatus, and the innovatory nature of his teaching, continued after 1710 by his student John Theophilus Desaguliers (1683–1744), should be recognized.

Keill began his publishing career while at Oxford with his *Examination of Dr Burnet's Theory of the Earth* (1698), which used Burnet's *Sacred Theory of the Earth* as an occasion to attack modern 'world-makers' who endeavour to show 'how, by the necessary laws of Mechanisme, without any extraordinary concurrence of the Divine Power, the world and all that therein is might have been produced' (2nd edn, 1734, 12). Blaming in the most contemptuous terms the great French philosopher René Descartes for this trend, Keill also attacks Baruch de Spinoza (1632–1677), Henry More (1614–1687), Thomas Hobbes (1588–1679), Richard Burthogge (1638?–1694?), Nicolas Malebranche (1638–1715), Richard Bentley (1662–1742), and even William Wotton (1666–1727) for his praise of Descartes, before focusing his attention on Burnet (1635–1715). Although Keill begins from the same premise as Burnet, that true philosophy does not contradict scripture, he insists that where Burnet and similar thinkers have gone wrong is by mistaking the true philosophy, which must be based upon observations and calculations. Although Keill praises Newton and his refutation of Descartes, and sees Newton's philosophy as the only one which is based upon observation and calculation, he does not attempt to substitute a Newtonian account of the Noachian flood for Burnet's Cartesian account. He simply insists that 'a much easier and shorter account' can be given by referring to the 'Omnipotent hand of God, who can do whatsoever he pleases' (*Examination*, 1734, 26–8). The *Remarks on Mr Whiston's New Theory of the Earth*, which followed on, were more deferential to William Whiston's Newtonian approach but took issue with numerous points of detail in order to undermine Whiston's naturalistic account of biblical events which Keill saw as playing into the hands of atheists. In the following year Keill published an *Examination of the Reflections on the Theory of the Earth*, in response to an anonymous defender of Burnet, and *A Defense of the Remarks Made on Mr. Whiston's New Theory*, in response to Whiston himself.

Shortly after this, in 1699, Keill began to fulfil the duties of the Sedleian professor of natural philosophy as deputy to Sir Thomas Millington (1628–1704), who preferred to occupy himself with his duties as president of the Royal College of Physicians in London and as royal physician. Keill now published his lecture course on Newtonian physics. He became a fellow of the Royal Society in April 1701 and became a regular contributor to its *Philosophical Transactions*. When his Scotch exhibition expired in 1703 he moved to Christ Church, again following Gregory, who had transferred there two or three years before, presumably because he found the high-church ethos of the college under its dean, his friend Henry Aldrich, more congenial than Balliol. Keill failed to win the Sedleian chair after Millington's death and was similarly unlucky in his pursuit of the Savilian professorship after Gregory's death. At this point he sought instead a government post. In 1709 Robert Harley, lord treasurer, helped him to become appointed treasurer of the palatines, that is to say treasurer of the fund subscribed for protestant refugees from the Palatinate. He conducted a party of exiles to New England, returning at the beginning of 1711. Despairing of a new preferment in England, Keill was about to take up an offer as mathematician to the Republic of Venice when Harley finally offered him the post of decipherer to Queen Anne (although, at £100 per annum, at only half the salary of his predecessor, William Blencowe). In 1712 the Savilian chair of astronomy was vacated once again by the death of John Caswell (or Carswell), Gregory's successor. This time Keill was unanimously elected to the post. He was awarded the degree of MD by public act in July 1713.

By now Keill was one of the most influential natural philosophers in Britain, helping to establish and disseminate Newtonian principles. His influence derived not just from his published lecture course but from an important paper published in 1708 in the *Philosophical Transactions of the Royal Society* on the laws of attraction and other physical properties ('Epistola … in qua leges attractionis aliaque physices principia traduntur'). Keill had already signalled the importance of the Newtonian principle of attraction between particles in his *Examination of Dr Burnet's Theory of the Earth* when he took the Cartesians to task for believing that they could explain all the phenomena of nature by the principles of matter and motion 'without the help of attraction and occult qualities' (1734 edn, 12). Now, further inspired by Newton's suggestions in the 'Queries' which he added to the end of his *Opticks* (1704, and revised Latin edition, 1706), Keill became one of the first to use the notion of attractions between the constituent invisibly small particles of bodies to explain phenomena such as cohesion, fluidity, elasticity, crystallization, dissolution, fermentation (which was then seen as a purely chemical phenomenon, not as a result of biological processes), effervescence, precipitation, and so on. These ideas were immediately taken up by John's brother James, who tried to develop them in physiology and medicine, and by his friend and fellow student of Gregory's, John Freind (1675–1728), who developed them in chemistry. The theories soon became highly influential, particularly among British thinkers, and led to a thriving Newtonian chemistry in the eighteenth and nineteenth centuries.

The use of attractive forces, which looked very much like the occult qualities which Descartes had proudly boasted to have driven out of natural philosophy, attracted a good deal of criticism from continental readers, however. The leading continental philosopher, G. W. Leibniz, writing in the *Acta Eruditorum* in 1710, rejected these tendencies of 'Keill and his followers', likening talk of attractions to magical talk of sympathy and antipathy, and even linking Keill's name to the notorious early seventeenth-century 'enthusiast', Robert Fludd. These criticisms have been seen as an explanation for the attack on Leibniz which Keill now launched, and which was to initiate and foster bitterness and recrimination between the two leading philosophers of the day, Leibniz and Newton, until their deaths. In another article for *Philosophical Transactions* ('Epistola … de legibus virium centripetarum'), which appeared in 1710, Keill took the opportunity to suggest that Leibniz had taken Newton's unpublished mathematical technique of 'fluxions', changed the name and the symbolism, and published it as his own (as what is now known as differential calculus).

Dispute over the invention of calculus The ensuing priority dispute over the invention of differential calculus, or fluxions, was extremely rancorous and it is hardly possible now to be sure what was said in good faith, and what was said with rhetorical intentions variously motivated. Accordingly, it is one of those episodes which has divided historians. Sir David Brewster, Newton's first biographer, says nothing of Leibniz's attack on Keill and explains Keill's accusation as a justifiable and perfectly reasonable *tu quoque* in response to a supposed earlier accusation by Leibniz that Newton had plagiarized from him (Brewster, 2.43). Professor A. R. Hall—one of the twentieth century's leading Newton scholars and author of *Philosophers at War* (1980), the fullest examination of the dispute—by contrast suggests that John Keill was the creator of the rift between the two great philosophers. The accusation of plagiarism allegedly made against Newton by Leibniz appeared in the *Acta Eruditorum* of January 1705 and was not even noticed as in any way insulting, by Newton or anyone else, until Keill brought it to Newton's attention in 1711, when he (Keill) was called upon to justify his charge against Leibniz. In fact what Leibniz had said in 1705 was that instead of using differentials, Newton had always made elegant use of fluxions, just in the same way that Honoré Fabri had 'substituted the advance of movements

for the method of Cavalieri'. It is certainly possible to read this as merely a comment on the close equivalence of the two pairs of techniques, Fabri's and Bonaventure Cavalieri's on the one hand, and Leibniz's and Newton's on the other. Keill, however, pointed out that it was possible to read this as a suggestion that Fabri's technique can be seen as a way of taking one of the infinite number of lines in a geometrical shape which Cavalieri's technique supposed, and making it move across the shape, and so is derivative upon Cavalieri's technique. And that, by the same token, Newton's fluxions can be seen merely as flowing versions of Leibniz's differentials.

Leibniz wrote to Hans Sloane, secretary of the Royal Society, on 4 March 1711 asking that Keill publicly deny the injurious sense which his words in *Philosophical Transactions* might be taken to have. Keill's response, seen as all but a denial of the charge of plagiarism by Brewster and as a 'counterattack' by Hall, did not placate Leibniz, who now asked that Newton should be brought in to tell the upstart Keill to back down. Instead, Newton drafted a report, usually known by its short title, *Commercium epistolicum*, supposedly written by a committee appointed by the society but in fact written by Newton himself, which insisted upon Newton's prior invention of the new mathematical technique. This was distributed to suitable recipients early in 1713. It has previously been suggested that Keill edited this report for the committee, even though he was not a member of it, but this is incorrect: Newton had no need of Keill's help. Keill did, however, publish a popularization in French of the *Commercium epistolicum* in the *Journal Literaire de la Haye* of May–June 1713. Similarly, in the summer of 1714 he published in the same journal another response to a defence of Leibniz but was unable to add anything new.

During this time Keill also took it upon himself to defend Newton's *Principia mathematica* against a criticism levelled at it by Johann Bernoulli (*Philosophical Transactions*, July–September, 1714). In response Bernoulli sought to demonstrate Keill's incompetence in mechanics in an anonymous reply in the *Acta Eruditorum* (July 1716). Disputes between these two mathematicians continued until Keill's death, and meanwhile Keill continually tried to poison relations between Newton and Bernoulli by reminding Newton of Bernoulli's earlier support of Leibniz. Bernoulli, however, was anxious to forge friendly links with Newton and it is perhaps a sign of Newton's increasing resentment and distrust of Keill that he reconciled himself to Bernoulli in a friendly letter sent in September 1719.

It is hardly surprising that many on the continent regarded Keill as a truculent polemicist and it seems fair to say that he emerges from the calculus priority dispute with even less credit than any of the other protagonists. Evidently he did not allow his championing of Newton to take up all his time. He married in 1717, although his choice of wife was regarded as something of a scandal— Mary (or Moll) Clements (*b. c.*1696) was held to be of very inferior rank, being the daughter of James Clements, an Oxford bookbinder. Perhaps the attraction for Keill was the fact that she was twenty-five years younger. They had a son who became a linen draper in London (perhaps reverting to the Keill family trade). The year after his marriage Keill published a second set of his lectures, this time on astronomy, *Introductio ad veram astronomiam* (Oxford, 1718). It is perhaps significant that when this appeared in English translation in 1721 Keill announced in the dedication that it was published 'at the Request, and for the Service of, the Fair Sex' (sig. A3r). He went on to say that 'It was no Flattery to the Ladies, to say, that such of them as delight in Arts and Sciences, as to the Quickness of Perception and Delicacy of Taste, are equal, if not superior to Men' (sig. A3r–v). Perhaps he had learned something from his new wife.

Keill died at his house in Holywell Street in Oxford on Thursday 31 August 1721, as the result of a 'violent fever' which struck him a few days after entertaining the vice-chancellor and other dignitaries of the university with wine and punch. He was buried at nine o'clock in the evening on 2 September, at St Mary's Church. He evidently died intestate even though he had been left a supposedly large fortune by his brother James.   JOHN HENRY

Sources A. R. Hall, *Philosophers at war: the quarrel between Newton and Leibniz* (1980) · A. Guerrini, 'James Keill, George Cheyne, and Newtonian physiology, 1690–1740', *Journal of the History of Biology*, 18 (1985), 247–66 · A. Guerrini, 'The tory Newtonians: Gregory, Pitcairne, and their circle', *Journal of British Studies*, 25 (1986), 288–311 · R. E. Schofield, *Mechanism and materialism: British natural philosophy in an age of reason* (1970) · A. Thackray, *Atoms and powers: an essay on Newtonian matter-theory and the development of chemistry* (1970) · A. Thackray, '"Matter in a nut-shell": Newton's *Opticks* and eighteenth-century chemistry', *Ambix*, 15 (1968), 29–53 · *DNB* · D. Brewster, *Memoirs of the life, writings, and discoveries of Sir Isaac Newton*, 2 vols. (1855) · D. Kubrin, 'Providence and the mechanical philosophy: the creation and dissolution of the world in Newtonian thought', PhD diss., Princeton University, 1968 · M. Feingold, 'The mathematical sciences and new philosophies', *Hist. U. Oxf.* 4: *17th-cent. Oxf.*, 359–448 · J. Gascoigne, *Cambridge in the age of the Enlightenment* (1989) · J. E. Force, *William Whiston, honest Newtonian* (1985) · A. Kippis and others, eds., *Biographia Britannica, or, The lives of the most eminent persons who have flourished in Great Britain and Ireland*, 2nd edn, 4 (1789)

Archives CUL, letters, notes | CUL, Lucasian papers, letters, drafts of lectures, notebooks, inventory of his library

Wealth at death a large fortune, chiefly inherited from his brother James: *DNB*

Keiller, Alexander (1889–1955), archaeologist, was born at Binrock House, Dundee, on 1 December 1889, the only child of John Mitchell *Keiller (1851–1899), master grocer and JP, and his wife, Mary Sime Greig (1862–1907), of the esteemed Dundee medical family. His parents were both Scottish, with his family heritage firmly rooted in Dundee. The company James Keiller & Sons was established in 1797, initially concentrating on the production of marmalade, but by the time Alexander was born they had a worldwide reputation not only for marmalade but for confectionery as well.

On the death of his father in 1899, Alexander Keiller, at the age of nine, became sole heir to the great marmalade fortune. He was educated first at Hazelwood preparatory school in Limpsfield, Surrey, and from there went on to Eton College. He left Eton following the death of his

mother in 1907, when he had just turned seventeen. Little is known of the interim years from leaving school until his twenty-first birthday (when he came into his inheritance), except that he spent some time involved with the family business, and there served an apprenticeship as a draughtsman.

On 2 June 1913 Keiller married Florence Marianne Phil-Morris (1883–1955), daughter of the artist Philip Richard Morris, and they moved into Keiller's London house at 13 Hyde Park Gardens. Later the same year he founded and financed the Sizaire-Berwick motor company, which produced a Rolls-Royce lookalike. After the outbreak of the First World War he joined the Royal Naval Volunteer Reserve as a temporary lieutenant, moving to the Royal Naval Air Service in December 1914 to work with the armoured car division. At Chingford in 1915 he obtained his aviator's licence, but shortly afterwards was invalided out of the service. In 1918 he joined air intelligence, with which he remained until the end of the war.

After the war Keiller divorced his first wife, and began to pursue his interest in archaeology. In 1922 he approached O. G. S. Crawford of the Ordnance Survey, suggesting an aerial survey of archaeological sites in south-west England. This project culminated in the publication of *Wessex from the Air* (1928), the first book of aerial archaeology to be published in the UK.

On 29 February 1924 Keiller married Veronica Mildred Liddell (1900–1964). Veronica had a keen interest in archaeology, and visited Avebury in Wiltshire with him later that year. This was to be a turning point for Keiller. He decided to buy up Windmill Hill and undertake a series of excavations on the site, which was known to be neolithic. Between 1925 and 1929 excavations proved the site to be a causewayed enclosure. It became a type-site for many years to follow.

Following a separation, Keiller divorced Veronica in 1934. In the same year he began a two-year programme excavating another area in Avebury: the West Kennet Avenue, which led south from the stone circle. Buried stones were uncovered and re-erected, and stone-holes marked with pillars. He procured a lease on Avebury Manor, and further land purchases strengthened his commitment to the village.

The first major excavation of Avebury stone circle was in 1937, the first of three seasons over the ensuing years. Each concentrated on a quadrant of the circle, restoring and preserving the site for future generations. The first season was concentrated on the north-west quadrant, which includes the great Diamond stone. The whole area was covered with bracken and trees, which were removed as the work progressed. Eight stones, some up to a metre below the ground, were uncovered and re-erected in their original stone-holes, and as with the avenue, concrete pillars were used to denote missing stones.

The second season, in 1938, was in the south-west quadrant. At the outset only one stone was standing, with a further three visible, in this sector. In the first ten days five buried stones were uncovered, and on day fifteen the famous barber–surgeon skeleton was discovered, lying where it had been since the stone toppled on the unfortunate man in the middle ages. (Over sixty years later, the skeleton of the barber–surgeon, thought to have been lost during the blitz, was discovered in the archives of the Natural History Museum.) By the end of this season, eleven stones were standing in the quadrant and stone-holes duly marked. The excavations in 1939 concentrated on the south-east quadrant, where the Obelisk stone described by Stukeley had once stood. Work was concentrated on the inner circle, and a curious rectangular setting of eight small stones, named the z-stones, was discovered to the west of the Obelisk site. These can now be seen close to the plinth (designed by Keiller) which marks the site of the Obelisk.

As Avebury was a site of national interest, the project maintained a high profile in the public eye. A museum was opened in June 1938, displaying finds from the Windmill Hill, West Kennet, and Avebury stone circle excavations. On 16 November 1938 Keiller was married for a third time; his new wife was Doris Emerson Chapman (*b.* 1901), an artist, who had joined the Morven Institute of Archaeological Research, founded by Keiller, in 1937.

The outbreak of war ended excavations at Avebury. Keiller joined the special constabulary at Marlborough, and was soon promoted to inspector. His duties left little time for other works, and the museum was closed to the public. In 1943, following negotiations with the office of works and the National Trust, Keiller sold his properties and land in Avebury to the National Trust for £12,000, which was the agricultural value of the 950 acres. He did not ask for any reimbursement for the vast sum (today equivalent to over £2 million) which he had spent on excavating and restoring the circle.

Both Keiller and his wife had brief affairs during and shortly after the war, but it was only in 1948, when he met Gabrielle Muriel Styles, *née* Ritchie (1908–1995), the champion golfer and art collector, that he sought a divorce. Doris refused. In 1951 he had an operation for throat cancer, and shortly afterwards Doris granted him a divorce on 16 June 1951, leaving him free to marry Gabrielle the following day. He was her third husband. The couple moved into Telegraph Cottage, Kingston Hill, Surrey, where he died on 29 October 1955. His ashes were interred in the wall of Gairn Castle, Morven, Ballater, Aberdeenshire, where he had once had a major landholding.

Keiller was described as 'a tall, well-built man, brown hair and good shaped head; an interesting somewhat furrowed face … distinguished and speaks with distinction, decision and confidence' (King diary, 1938, 27). His main interests throughout life were archaeology, photography, racing cars, and skiing, all of which his considerable fortune allowed him to indulge. Skiing had been a lifelong pastime, particularly cross-country and ski-jumping, for which he had won many honours in St Moritz and further afield. In 1931 he was elected president of the Ski Club of Great Britain. He had more than a passing interest in witchcraft and criminology, and in exploring the range of sexual practices. He did not have any strong religious or political beliefs, but was very patriotic.

In 1966 the museum at Avebury and its contents were gifted to the nation by his widow, Gabrielle. Avebury (together with Stonehenge and associated sites) was inscribed a world heritage site in 1986, and by 2000 received over 350,000 visitors a year.

LYNDA J. MURRAY

Sources L. J. Murray, *A zest for life* (1999) · Alexander Keiller Museum Archive, Avebury · W. Young diaries, Devizes Museum, Wiltshire · D. G. King diaries, Alexander Keiller Museum Archive, Avebury · I. F. Smith, *Windmill Hill and Avebury: excavations by Alexander Keiller, 1925–1939* (1965) · A. Burl, *Prehistoric Avebury* (1979) · C. Malone, *Book of Avebury* (1989) · *The Independent* (12 Jan 1996) [obit. of Gabrielle Keiller] · *The Eton register*, 8 vols. (privately printed, Eton, 1903–32) · NA Scot. · d. cert.
Archives Alexander Keiller Museum, Avebury, corresp. and papers · English Heritage, Swindon, National Monuments record, air photo notebook |FILM Alexander Keiller Museum, Avebury, home footage |SOUND Alexander Keiller Museum, Avebury, dictaphone recording of letter dictation
Likenesses photograph, *c.*1920–1929, Ski Club of Great Britain, London · D. Chapman, pencil drawing, 1934, NPG · Lafayette, photograph, 1940, Alexander Keiller Museum, Avebury
Wealth at death £106,798 14s. 11d.: probate, 22 June 1956, CGPLA Eng. & Wales

Keiller, John Mitchell (1851–1899), preserves and confectionery manufacturer, was born at 3 Nelson Street, Dundee, on new year's day 1851, the only child of Alexander Keiller (1821–1877), a preserves and confectionery manufacturer, and his wife, Elizabeth Mitchell (1813–1871). He came from a long line of Keillors, Kelers, and Killers, resident in the town for centuries, mainly in modest mercantile capacities. His formal education started at the proprietary school in Dundee, and continued, with considerable success, in the Greek-revival surroundings of the Dundee high school. At Edinburgh University he won prizes, but left before graduation to pursue—as a prelude to commercial work—two years of language studies in France and Germany. At the age of twenty he was back home, in the family firm. Six years later, in 1877, his father died, and he became the youthful and third-generation inheritor of the largest and most successful business of its kind in Britain. In 1883 he married Mary (1862–1907), the daughter of David Grieg MD, of Dundee: a son, Alexander *Keiller, was born in 1889.

The confectionery firm was set up around 1800 by John's grandfather James Keiller (1775-1839) in Seagate, near a sugar refinery and the busy waters of the Tay. As a young unmarried grocer, he worked in close association with his enterprising mother, Janet Mathewson. Business was initially local, but rapidly expanded as a result of harbour and transport improvements, a population explosion in and around Dundee, and the coastal probings of the London retail and entrepôt markets. James Keiller's special offering was chip (shredded-peel) marmalade, a supposedly warming breakfast spread, in place of the beaten (pulped-peel) marmalade of English desserts. After his death his widow, Margaret Spence (1800–1850), took over the business, maintaining its by then famously high standards. She was followed, after her own death, by three sons: Alexander (1821–1877), William (1829–1899), and Wedderspoon (1835–1866). Wedderspoon and William successively ran new factories in Guernsey, set up in 1857 to bypass sugar duties, which left Alexander as sole manager of the Dundee firm, by that time called James Keiller & Son. By the mid-1870s it was lodged in spacious buildings off Albert Square.

When John Keiller took control in 1877, output ranged from marmalade, jellies, and jams, through lozenges, comfits, and jujubes, to candied peels and bottled fruits. He greatly expanded the enterprise, with a 'characteristic pushfulness' (*Dundee Advertiser*, 6 Jan 1899), but refrained from radical innovation. Items on the firm's 1887 price list were identical to those of twenty years earlier—chocolate and cocoa products being added only in the 1890s. Keiller did, however, travel the world, 'ever on the alert to widen the industry by opening up new markets' (ibid.). Exhibition medals from Vienna (1873) and Cape Town (1877) were supplemented by new marmalade awards from Sydney (1879), Melbourne (1881), and Calcutta (1884). Of importance, too, was Keiller's transfer in 1879 of English production (following the repeal of sugar duty) from Guernsey to Silvertown, London. His junior co-partner, James Boyd, assisted, becoming manager of the new, markedly self-sufficient, factory on the Thames—'mammoth works … declared a study of marvellous perfection' (*Dundee Courier & Argus*, 6 Jan 1899). In 1893 the decision was taken to make James Keiller & Son a limited-liability company. John Keiller became chairman, though he used the juncture to begin a progressive withdrawal from direct business activity.

Unlike his modest predecessors, Keiller seemed happy to divert profits into conspicuous personal expenditure and to break out of the limits imposed by his ancestral town. Outlays included the purchase of Binrock House, Dundee, about 1880, and (on the sale of Binrock) 9 Cavendish Square and 13 Hyde Park Gardens, London; the 10,000 acre Morven and Gairnside shooting estate (with the later Craigendarroch Lodge) on Deeside in 1886; the ocean-going yacht *Erl King*; and, for the 1887 jubilee, the donation of more than 3000 books to the Dundee Free Library and the clearance of the Albert Institute's £9500 debt (opening the way for the Victoria Galleries extension to Sir George Gilbert Scott's original building). These last gestures, combined with other gifts, a lively patronage of the fine arts, some limited public service, and a local magistracy, secured his good name in Dundee—despite the place having latterly 'seen or heard very little of him' (*Dundee Advertiser*, 6 Jan 1899).

In politics, Keiller was conservative; in religion, Church of Scotland. He suffered poor health in his last years, and died on his yacht, in tempestuous seas between Madeira and the West Indies, on 2 January 1899, aged only forty-eight. He was buried in the western cemetery, Dundee. An annuity was bequeathed to his widow, Mary, and a £20,000 pension fund was set up for his workforce. The bulk of his estate passed, in trust, to his son.

W. M. MATHEW

Sources Catalogue of books presented to the reference department of the Dundee free library (part of a jubilee gift from John M. Keiller, Esq., of Morven, 1887), Dundee public libraries, D8406 · 'The history of Keiller', 1972, Dundee public libraries, DO7151 · James Keiller & Son, price lists, 14 May 1885 and 10 March 1887, Dundee public libraries, 29, (1) and (2) · Keillor family genealogy, Dundee public libraries, 391(38) · I. Fleet, letter to Miss M. Sheppard, 21 May 1991, Dundee public libraries, 200A(69) · extracts from Lockit book of the burgh of Dundee, Dundee public libraries, 391(39) · Stones in Howff with the name Keiller, Dundee public libraries, 391(39) · *Dundee Advertiser* (6 Jan 1899) · *Dundee Courier and Argus* (6 Jan 1899) · *People's Journal for Dundee* (7 Jan 1899) · *Scottish Trader* (7 Jan 1899) · trade directories, Dundee, 1809–1902 · D. Bremner, *The industries of Scotland: their rise, progress, and present condition* (1869) · P. Collins, 'Keiller, John Mitchell', *DSBB* · C. A. Wilson, *The book of marmalade* (1985) · *Dundee Yearbook* (1898), 58–9 · C. McKean and D. Walker, *Dundee: an illustrated introduction* (1984) · A. H. Millar, *Glimpses of old and new Dundee* (1925) · A. M. Sandeman, *Dundee delineated* (1822) · D. Scruton, *The Victoria Galleries: art and enterprise in late nineteenth century Dundee* (1989) · J. Keay and J. Keay, eds., *Collins encyclopaedia of Scotland* (1994) · birth register, General Register Office for Scotland, Edinburgh · W. M. Mathew, *Keiller's of Dundee: the rise of the marmalade dynasty, 1800–1879* (1998) · W. M. Mathew, *The secret history of Guernsey marmalade: James Keiller & Son offshore, 1857–1879* (1998)

Archives Archive and Record Centre, Dundee · Dundee public libraries

Likenesses J. M. Brown, drawing, 1888 (after photograph), repro. in Scruton, *Victoria Galleries*, 7

Wealth at death £435,367 11s. 5d.: confirmation, 13 March 1899, *CCI*

Keilwey, Robert (1496/7–1581), lawyer, came of a family long settled in Dorset and Hampshire, where his kinsman Sir William Keilwey (d. 1569) was seated at Rockbourne. In a moot book which he possessed as a student he described himself as 'Kydwelle alias Kelwey alias Kelowey alias Kelway alias Robertus Kylwey de Nova Sarum in comitatu Wilts. armiger' (Harvard law school, MS 183, final leaf), suggesting that he may have regarded the family surname as being a corruption of Kidwelly. The inscription also confirms the supposition that he was the son of Robert Keilwey, sometime mayor of Salisbury, Wiltshire, who served as member of parliament for that city in 1523.

Keilwey the lawyer was appointed to the commission of the peace for Wiltshire in 1543, and was still 'of Salisbury' in 1547. Nothing is known of him before 1534, when he appears as a member of the Inner Temple. He became a bencher in 1542, pointing to a probable date of admission in the second half of the 1520s. He must therefore have spent an unusually long period in an inn of chancery, or have pursued some other occupation before turning to the law. In 1545 he became member of parliament for Bristol, and recorder of the same city, serving in parliament again in 1547 and (as member for Steyning) in 1559. He was an adviser to Edward Seymour, earl of Hertford and later duke of Somerset, who obtained for him the important appointment of surveyor-general of the court of wards in 1546 and intervened in 1548 to secure his discharge from reading in the Inner Temple. He retained his office as surveyor of the wards until his death, though he became embroiled in a heated dispute with the previous holder, John *Hynde, who twice tried to thwart Keilwey's tenure by having him made a serjeant-at-law against his will. A serjeant's writ was indeed issued to Keilwey in July 1552, whereupon he gave up his recordership of Bristol, but his excuses were accepted and he never did take the coif. During the reign of Edward VI, Keilwey and Sir Walter Mildmay were charged with the task of saving the grammar schools which were being threatened by the dispersal of chantry funds, and many of the schools were refounded in the king's name. It is a testament to Keilwey's ability and moderation that he retained his office under four sovereigns, through various changes in religion, and despite the fall of his patron Somerset in 1549. He remained active in the public administration until old age.

Keilwey's public duties must have curtailed his private practice at the bar, though he was evidently still able to report cases in the time of Edward VI. Sir Simonds D'Ewes (1602–1650) possessed a manuscript of 'Keilweies reportes Edward. 6. penned by himselfe', but these are no longer to be found. Keilwey's name is, however, well known in the legal profession by reason of its association with a volume of earlier law reports printed in 1602 and usually cited as 'Keilwey'. The title was 'reports of certain cases selected from the books of Robert Keilwey' (*Relationes quorundam casuum selectorum ex libris Roberti Keilwey*), and no claim was made that Keilwey was the author, as indeed he could not have been. The reports cover the period from 1496 to 1522 and were in fact written by John *Caryll (*d*. 1523), serjeant-at-law. Keilwey was a close friend of the reporter's son John, a fellow Inner Templar, and borrowed Serjeant Caryll's autograph manuscript from him some time before 1538, when he cited it in court. Keilwey's manuscript passed to his relative John *Croke (*d*. 1620), who shared his chambers in Fig Tree Court, and it was Croke who saw it through the press in 1602, leaving out terms which he thought were adequately covered by the printed year-books, and interpolating some eyre reports from Edward II's reign (including the only known reports from the 1309 eyre of Guernsey) and eight *quo warranto* cases from the reign of Edward I. The work was reprinted in 1633 and 1688, and a new edition of Caryll's reports was published by the Selden Society in 1999–2000.

Keilwey married Cecily, daughter of Edward Bulstrode of Hedgerley and Upton, Berkshire, and they had one daughter, Anne, who married Sir John Harrington of Exton, Rutland. He became a justice of the peace for Berkshire in 1549, and it may have been through his marriage around this time that he acquired property at Shellingford in that county, where he probably lived until he obtained a lease of Coombe Abbey, Warwickshire, in 1556. Besides these residences he also had a house in Fleet Street and another at Stepney. Keilwey died on 21 February 1581, aged eighty-four, and was buried at Exton, where there is a handsome monument bearing his effigy and an inscription praising him as a distinguished esquire of the long gown ('insignis dum vixit inter togatas armiger').

J. H. BAKER

Sources HoP, *Commons, 1509–58*, 2.458–9 · HoP, *Commons, 1558–1603*, 2.389–90 · J. H. Baker, introduction, in *Reports of cases by John Caryll*, ed. J. H. Baker, 1, SeldS, 115 (1999) · Baker, *Serjeants*, 170 · H. E. Bell, *The court of wards and liveries* (1953), 20–21 · CPR, *1547–8*, 154 · L. W. Abbott, *Law reporting in England, 1485–1585* (1973) · F. A. Inderwick and R. A. Roberts, eds., *A calendar of the Inner Temple records*, 1 (1896) · A. G. Watson, *The library of Sir Simonds D'Ewes* (1966), 284 ·

moot book, Harvard U., law school, MS 183 · will, PRO, PROB 11/63, sig. 9 · monumental inscription, Exton Church, Rutland
Likenesses alabaster effigy on monument, *c*.1581, Exton, Rutland

Keimer, Samuel (1689–1742), printer, was born on 11 February 1689, probably in the parish of St Thomas's, Southwark, London, the son of Samuel Keimer, a blacksmith. He enrolled in the Merchant Taylors' School, in Suffolk Lane, London, on 11 September 1699. Keimer was apprenticed to Bryan Mills, printer, on 6 December 1703 and made free by Mills on 4 February 1712. About 1707, according to his own later account, Keimer had become associated along with his mother and sister Mary with the so-called French Prophets, a millenarian group who were gaining notoriety in London by prophesying and speaking in tongues. By 1713 he had set up his own printing office and the earliest known imprint from his press was a 500-page work, *The General Delusion of Christians*, by a leading preacher of the group, John Lacy. The early output of his press was eclectic however, and his association with the prophets has perhaps been unduly stressed, although through all his adult life he wore a full beard in accordance with the book of Leviticus. He was made a liveryman of the Stationers' Company in April 1714. During the Jacobite rising of 1715 some imprudent issue of the press caused him to be imprisoned for seditious libel. However, he was able to print during the following year a number of pamphlets since attributed to Daniel Defoe, as well as two plays by Susannah Centlivre, and to publish a newspaper, the *London Post*. His press went silent after 1716, perhaps because of financial improvidence. At some time before 1718 he had married.

In 1718 there appeared *A Brand Pluck'd from the Burning* and *A Search after Religion*, both identified as Keimer's on the title-page. Both treat Keimer's life and thought, and have constituted principal sources of biographical information, sometimes contradictory, on Keimer to that point. However, it should be emphasized that here and elsewhere when Keimer is speaking of himself, as he frequently does, his statements must be treated with caution.

Nothing is known of Keimer between 1718 and 1722. When he emerges again from the shadows in 1723 it is in Philadelphia, where he was conducting a small bookselling business and operating a printing press, having left his wife behind in England. His only competitor in the book trades of the growing city was Andrew Bradford, son of the first printer in the colony, William Bradford. Benjamin Franklin appeared in Philadelphia seeking employment and was introduced by the senior Bradford, whom he had met in New York, to Keimer; Keimer took on the seventeen-year-old journeyman as his assistant, with results well known to readers of Franklin's *Autobiography*.

Although Franklin did not respect Keimer's skills as a printer, Keimer was a more innovative bookseller and publisher than either of the Bradfords. For example, he printed and sold a translation of Epictetus, the earliest edition of a classical author published in the American colonies. He showed his sense of timing, and his political colours, by republishing Trenchard's and Gordon's the *Independent Whig*, first as a weekly magazine (another innovation in America) and then in book form. His edition of a Welsh concordance to the Bible (1730) was apparently the earliest colonial publication in that language, and at 232 folio pages must have engendered some problems in the composition.

When Franklin went on his famous first voyage to England in 1724, he at some time met Keimer's wife and 'heard a bad Character of him … from his Wife and her Friends' (*Autobiography*, 108). Somewhat reluctantly, then, he returned to Keimer's printing office in 1727 as foreman but in the next year quarrelled with his cantankerous employer and departed to found his own printing business.

In an effort to compete with Bradford's *American Weekly Mercury*, and to forestall Franklin's attempt to found a newspaper, Keimer began his own in 1728, the *Universal Instructor in All Arts and Sciences, and, Pennsylvania Gazette*. In this weekly he serialized Defoe's *Religious Courtship* and began reprinting, issue by issue, the contents of Chambers's *Cyclopedia*, starting from the letter A. When Keimer reprinted the article on abortion in late January 1729, Franklin was waiting to pounce. Two letters were published in the next issue of Bradford's *Mercury*, affecting to be from the morally offended ladies Martha Careful and Caelia Shortface, advising Keimer to desist further publishing of the sort. Thus was opened Franklin's Busy-Body series, so-called from the superintending persona, aimed principally at Keimer. Keimer attempted to reply—in Hudibrastic verse on one occasion—but the battle of wits was no contest. Whether the Busy-Body papers brought about or only assisted in Keimer's financial ruin is uncertain. What is known is that he announced his intention to leave Pennsylvania in September 1729, having already been gaoled by his creditors, and sold the *Instructor* to Franklin and his partner that month. Franklin shortened the title to *Pennsylvania Gazette* and soon made it the leading newspaper in the colonies.

Keimer settled in Barbados and there founded the *Barbados Gazette* in 1731, the colony's first newspaper and one that evidenced a substantial interest in literature on the part of its editor. Selections from the paper were published in London in two volumes under the title *Caribbeana* (1741). This anthology has been found significant, both in its own right and as a primary source of Barbados cultural and social history. Keimer died in Barbados on 20 August 1742 and was buried there at the parish church of St Michael, Bridgetown.

Franklin's evaluation of Keimer cannot be bettered, that 'he did not profess any particular Religion, but something of all on occasion; was very ignorant of the World, and had … a good deal of the Knave in his Composition' (*Autobiography*, 79). He may now also be seen as an innovative bookseller and printer in two colonies.

CALHOUN WINTON

Sources H. Amory and D. D. Hall, eds., *The colonial book in the Atlantic world* (2000) · *The autobiography of Benjamin Franklin*, ed. L. Labaree (1964) · H. Schwartz, *The French prophets* (1980) · *ESTC* · I. Thomas, *The history of printing in America*, rev. 2nd edn (1970) · J. Handler, *A guide to source materials for the study of Barbados history* (1971) · I. Maxted, *The British book trades, 1710–1777* (1983) · C. L. Carlson, 'Samuel Keimer', *Pennsylvania Magazine of History and Biography*, 61 (1937), 357–86 · J. A. Sappenfield, *A sweet instruction* (1973) · *London Post* (1716) · S. Keimer, *A brand pluck'd from the burning* (1718) · S. Keimer, *A search after religion* (1718) · C. J. Robinson, ed., *A register of the scholars admitted into Merchant Taylors' School, from AD 1562 to 1874*, 2 vols. (1882–3) · D. F. McKenzie, ed., *Stationers' Company apprentices*, [3]: *1701–1800* (1978)

Keir, Sir David Lindsay (1895–1973), university teacher and administrator, was born on 22 May 1895 at Bellingham, Northumberland, the eldest in the family of two sons and three daughters of the Revd William Keir, Presbyterian minister, of Aberuthven, Perthshire, and his wife, Elizabeth Craig. The family moved from Bellingham to Newcastle upon Tyne, to Birkenhead, and later to Glasgow, where Keir attended Glasgow Academy. In 1913 he won a bursary to Glasgow University. War intervened in his second year: he was commissioned in 1915 in the King's Own Scottish Borderers, and rose ultimately to the rank of captain. He was wounded on the Somme and again at Arras; he also served in Ireland, and this laid the foundations of a long affection for that country.

In 1919, after the war, Keir entered New College, Oxford, and in 1921 he obtained an outstanding first in history. University College immediately elected him to a fellowship. There he served as dean (1925–35) and as estates bursar (1933–9). In 1930 he married Anna Clunie, daughter of Robert John Dale, shipping underwriter, of Montreal; they had a son and a daughter. His very happy marriage and his wife's great charm were pit props of his successful career. From 1931 to 1939 Keir was university lecturer in English constitutional history. These Oxford years were productive: in 1928 he published with F. H. Lawson *Cases in Constitutional Law* and in 1938 *The Constitutional History of Modern Britain*. The latter book bears witness to his special talents as a legal historian: clear and thorough, with a humane sense of perspectives in legal history and a meticulous mastery of detail.

In 1939 Keir was appointed to the vice-chancellorship of Queen's University, Belfast. He was particularly well fitted for this post: Oxford had given him a sound training in academic administration, and his Scottish upbringing and his knowledge of Ireland gave him a sympathetic understanding of the problems of Ulster and of Ulstermen. Liked and trusted, he became widely involved in the life of the province. From 1942 to 1949 he was chairman of the Northern Ireland Regional Hospital Board, and his appointment to the Northern Ireland Planning Advisory Board made him contacts in government that were supremely useful to his university. He was instrumental in securing in 1945 an invitation to visit Queen's from the Northern Ireland government to the University Grants Committee, and the results of that visit ensured funding comparable with that of other British universities. This paved the way for post-war expansion, and the years 1945 to 1949 saw a successful appeal and a new building programme, a substantial increase in staff, and a steady growth in student numbers. Under Keir's stewardship, for which he was awarded a knighthood in 1946, Queen's University was set on the path towards a new and substantial role in post-war Ulster. In 1949 he resigned the vice-chancellorship to become master of Balliol College, Oxford.

The debates preceding Keir's election at Balliol were protracted and at times bitter, and he found there a fellowship whose members were able, outspoken, undocile, and who disagreed easily on college policy. They were not a comfortable body to lead, and, besides, Keir was not much in sympathy with some developments in Oxford in the 1950s and 1960s, such as the rapid growth of graduate studies and the looming prospect of co-education. Where he was most successful was in reaffirming links between Balliol and its old members, and in maintaining its position as a cosmopolitan institution which admitted a high proportion of students from overseas. His chairmanship of the advisory committee on overseas colleges of arts, science, and technology (1954–64), and his membership of numerous committees on higher education overseas gave him influence in this area, as it gave him also a role in shaping the future of academic institutions in Africa and Asia in the post-colonial era. He maintained his interest in medical affairs, and from 1950 to 1958 was chairman of the United Oxford Hospitals Trust. The greatest triumph of his Balliol years was, however, the launching of the college's septcentenary appeal, which raised more than £1 million and freed Balliol from the constraints of the comparative indigence that had dogged its history from the foundation to his time. He retired in 1965.

In politics Keir was a liberal conservative, in religion a sincere Christian, and in his ways methodical and very careful. He did not relish the cut and thrust of controversy, and made his mark by the weight of mature and benign influence rather than by dramatic initiatives. Outwardly dignified and decorous, he had a generous spirit and a sense of fun, which, alas, invariably left him when speaking in public. He had a real love of the countryside, of cricket, football, and boating, and of the 'old ways'. He received many honorary degrees and was created an honorary DCL at Oxford in 1960. He held honorary fellowships at University College, Balliol College, and New College, Oxford, and was an honorary FRIBA (1948). He died at his home, Hillsborough, in Lincombe Lane, Boars Hill, Oxford, on 2 October 1973. M. H. KEEN, *rev.*

Sources *University College Record* (1974) · R. Meiggs, 'Sir David Lindsay Keir', *Balliol College Record* (1974) · *The Times* (4 Oct 1973) · *The Times* (10 Oct 1973) · personal knowledge (1986) · private information (1986) · J. Jones, *Balliol College: a history*, 2nd edn (1997), 290–91 · *CGPLA Eng. & Wales* (1974)

Archives BLPES, corresp. with Lord Beveridge · Bodl. RH, Colonial Office Advisory Committee on Arts, Science and Technology MSS

Likenesses W. Stoneman, two photographs, 1946–58, NPG · A. Gwynne-Jones, oils, 1960, Balliol Oxf.

Wealth at death £4795: probate, 7 March 1974, *CGPLA Eng. & Wales*

Keir, James (1735–1820), chemist and industrialist, was born on 29 September 1735 at Edinburgh, the youngest of eighteen children of John Keir (1686–1743), landowner of Muirton and Queenshaugh, Stirlingshire, and his wife, Magdaline, *née* Lind (1691–1775). His mother was the sister of George Lind of Gorgie, lord provost of Edinburgh in 1760–62 and one-time MP for the city. A portrait of his father in 1708 shows him in the robes of a town councillor of Edinburgh.

Keir was educated at the high school, Edinburgh, in 1742–8 and then privately until entering the University of Edinburgh in 1754 to study medicine. Although he had plainly benefited from his chemistry classes and established a lifetime friendship with Erasmus Darwin (1731–1802), he abandoned medicine for the army in 1757. He served in the West Indies in the 61st foot but, missing intellectual stimulation from other officers, he resigned his commission as a captain in 1768. In the previous year he had visited Birmingham and the west midlands, drawn by Darwin, then a doctor at Lichfield, and his lively friends in the Lunar Society, and also by the business opportunities that the expanding west midlands seemed to offer someone who had to make a living. In 1771 he married Susanna Harvey (1747–1802) in Birmingham.

Keir progressed through six distinct business ventures over the next forty or so years. In 1770 he commenced glass manufacture at Holloway, Amblecote, in Stourbridge, about 5 miles from Birmingham, in partnership with Samuel Skey and 'old' John Taylor. He lived nearby, and in 1772 started chemical operations at the glass house. A laboratory facilitated his ongoing experiments, notably in alkali manufacture, on which he published a paper in 1776. He invested in the new Stourbridge Navigation Company in 1775.

Meanwhile, Keir became involved with Boulton and Watt at Soho, first offering advice in 1775 and then as unpaid manager of the business in Matthew Boulton's too regular absences. He found 'great abuses' in the management (Moilliet and Smith, 19) and gave up glass making in 1778, moving to Winson Green so as to be near Soho. There was talk of a partnership up to 1778 but finances at Soho soon clearly precluded that, though for two years Boulton failed to find time to discuss the arrangements. Finally, in 1781, Keir withdrew from the Soho works though he became a quarter-partner in Watt's letter-copier venture.

Keir's hopes of adding his chemical business to Soho's diversity had come to nothing, as did commercial hopes for Keir's metal, patented in 1779, an alloy of copper and zinc intended for sheathing ships' bottoms. He, therefore, needed a livelihood. The opportunity seemed to lie in caustic alkali manufacture as previous sources of supply were cut off by the American War of Independence. Several Lunar Society members were seeking solutions in the 1770s and, in 1780, Keir, in partnership with Alexander Blair, an officer friend from his army days, started manufacturing alkali at Bloomsmithy, Tipton; later, and more effectively, came the manufacture of soap and white and red lead. Beside Factory Bridge over the Birmingham Canal and alongside the River Tame in Bloomfield Road, a site estimated to be 20 acres, including two pools and a building of 20,000 sq. ft with water and fire engines, is thought to have been developed, producing an estimated

1 million pounds of soap a year. It became a showplace, second only to Soho, as the first soap factory in the world. This was Keir's greatest accomplishment; he designed the factory, developed the chemical engineering, and trained the workers for their new industry. The business was profitable. Keir was still involved in 1807 and even 1814, though in poor health. His final business venture took him apparently unwillingly (*Letters from England*, 173) into coalmining 3 miles away at Tividale in 1794, again with the Blairs, senior and junior, as partners. The mine was beside what is now misspelt as Kier's Bridge over the canal.

Keir had other diverse activities. In 1785 he became a fellow of the Royal Society, and he also belonged to the Society of Antiquaries and the Society for the Encouragement of the Arts, Manufactures, and Commerce. He wrote several poems and many papers on a wide range of subjects from geology to warfare, helped Darwin improve his poem, *The Botanic Garden*, in 1787, wrote a memoir of Lunar Society member Thomas Day in 1791, a *Memoir of Matthew Boulton* in 1809, and a *Dictionary of the Art of War Ancient and Modern* about 1792 (though no copy has survived). His first publication, in 1771, was a translation of Macquer's *Dictionnaire de chymie* with added notes. However, his plans for his own *Dictionary of Chemistry* in 1789 failed with the first volume. In a lower key, he prepared 'Dialogues on chemistry between a father and his daughter' (though his daughter, Amelia, was grown up and married) probably in 1805–6. It remained in manuscript, throwing light on his views of Lavoisier and others. Perhaps his most important chemical work was *A Treatise on the Various Kinds of Permanently Elastic Fluids or Gases* (1777) which may have introduced the word gas into the English language. Like Joseph Black, he distinguished carbon dioxide from ordinary air.

Keir had firm political views. An industrialist whig, he sympathized with the French and American revolutions. He proposed the toast at the dinner in Birmingham on 14 July 1791 that was the pretext for the subsequent Church and King riots. He contributed to Earl's *Authentic Account* of the riots and he is now accepted as the author of a pamphlet on them, *A letter from Timothy Sobersides, extinguisher-maker, at Wolverhampton, to Jonathan Blast, bellows-maker, at Birmingham*, that appeared in 1792. He also strove to advise, and obtain justice for, Joseph Priestley, whose house was destroyed by the rioters.

A notable chemist, outstanding technologist and successful industrialist, Keir was active and influential in public affairs and a considerable pamphleteer with some literary talent. Versatile and gifted, he had considerable influence on his friends Darwin, Watt, Priestley, and Boulton, and was actively involved in the Lunar Society. Letters reveal a lively personality of charm and amiability but caution in business. His contribution to chemistry, in which he supported Priestley's phlogiston theory against the 'new chemistry' of Lavoisier, was rapidly overtaken by events.

He and his wife, Susanna, had a son who died young (though alive in 1776–7) and a daughter, Amelia (1780–1857) who, in 1801, married John Lewis Moilliet, a wealthy young Birmingham banker and merchant (his bank became part of Lloyds). In 1790, Keir moved to The Woodlands, Hill Top, West Bromwich (and after the house burned down in 1807 lived nearby). He suffered grievously from rheumatism from at least 1804 though he managed to 'join Mrs. Siddons and a haunch of venison' (Moilliet and Smith, 59) at Boulton's house in 1807 and to attend the final allocation of the Lunar Society library in 1813. He died at West Bromwich on 11 October 1820 and was buried at West Bromwich church on 19 October.

BARBARA M. D. SMITH

Sources J. L. Moilliet and B. M. D. Smith, *A mighty chemist: James Keir of the Lunar Society* (privately printed, 1982) • *DNB* • A. Moilliet and J. K. Moilliet, *Sketch of the life of James Keir, Esq., FRS* (1868) • J. L. Moilliet, 'Keir's "Dialogues on chemistry"—an unpublished manuscript', *Chemistry and Industry* (19 Dec 1964), 2081–3 • J. L. Moilliet, 'Keir's caustic soda process—an attempted reconstruction', *Chemistry and Industry* (5 March 1966), 405–8 • B. M. D. Smith and J. L. Moilliet, 'James Keir of the Lunar Society', *Notes and Records of the Royal Society*, 22 (1967), 144–54 • B. M. D. Smith, *James Keir, 1735–1820: entrepreneur and scientist* (1966) • S. Shaw, *The history and antiquities of Staffordshire*, 2 vols. (1798–1801) • E. Curran, communication, 7 Nov 1997, Birm. CL [copy] • *Maria Edgeworth: letters from England, 1813–1844*, ed. C. Colvin (1971)

Archives priv. coll. | Birm. CA, corresp. with Matthew Boulton and others

Likenesses L. de Longastre, pastel drawing, *c*.1805, priv. coll. • W. H. Worthington, line engraving (after Longastre), BM • portraits, repro. in Moilliet and Smith, *Mighty chemist*, frontispiece

Wealth at death £250,000

Keir, Thelma Cazalet- (1899–1989), politician, was born on 28 May 1899 at 4 Whitehall Gardens, London, the third of four children, the eldest of whom was killed in action in 1916, and only daughter of William Marshall Cazalet (1865–1932), a man of hereditary wealth and standing, whose family origins were Huguenot, and his wife, Maud Lucia (*d*. 1952), daughter of Sir John Robert Heron-Maxwell, seventh baronet, of Springkell, Dumfriesshire, who was of modest means. The mother was the dominant parental influence: from her Thelma derived her worldly sophistication and love of the arts; also her feminism and Christian Science, two creeds to which she held firmly throughout her life. In London and at the Cazalets' country house, Fairlawne in Kent, she was introduced as a child to many leading figures in politics and literature, including Rudyard Kipling, J. M. Barrie, the Pankhursts, and Sidney and Beatrice Webb. After being taught at home by governesses, she attended lectures at the London School of Economics.

The lure of politics was already strong, and in the years immediately following the First World War Thelma Cazalet became an accepted member of the Lloyd George family circle, through her close friendship with the prime minister's youngest child, Megan. She entered politics by way of local government, first in Kent and then as a member of the London county council (LCC) for seven years (1924–31), after which she became an alderman. Despite her radical connections her party allegiance was Conservative, though her outlook was never narrowly partisan. In 1931 she unsuccessfully contested the parliamentary seat of East Islington at a by-election, but in the general

Thelma Cazalet-Keir (1899–1989), by Elliott & Fry

election held later in the year she was returned as National Conservative MP for the same constituency with a majority of over 14,000.

In the House of Commons Thelma Cazalet joined her brother Victor, who was MP for Chippenham. (He was killed in 1943 in an air crash with the Polish general Sikorski.) Her best subject in parliament was education, with which she had been particularly concerned on the LCC. She was a regular speaker on the education estimates, and from 1937 to 1940 was parliamentary private secretary to Kenneth Lindsay, when he was parliamentary secretary to the Board of Education. She married, in August 1939, David Edwin, son of the Revd Thomas Keir. Her husband was lobby correspondent of the *News Chronicle*. He died in 1969, and there were no children. On her marriage she changed her surname to Cazalet-Keir.

In March 1944, as a member of the Tory Reform Committee, Thelma Cazalet-Keir was put in charge of an amendment to the Education Bill introduced by R. A. Butler providing that there should be equal pay for men and women teachers. When the amendment was carried by the margin of a single vote, Churchill's wartime coalition suffered its only defeat. Greatly angered, Churchill insisted that the clause be deleted, making the issue one of confidence in himself; and she then felt she had no option but to vote against her own amendment. An important point had been made, however, and Churchill announced the setting up of a royal commission to consider the question of equal pay for equal work (1944–6). From 1947 she was

chairman of the Equal Pay Campaign Committee, and eventually saw the principle enshrined in legislation in 1970. Meanwhile Churchill had made personal amends by appointing her in May 1945 parliamentary secretary for education in his short-lived caretaker government. The 1945 general election, which swept that government away, also cost her her seat and ended her parliamentary career.

For some time Thelma Cazalet-Keir remained active in public life outside parliament. From 1946 to 1949 she was a member of the Arts Council, of whose precursor, the Council for the Encouragement of Music and the Arts, she had been a founder member in 1940. She was also on the executive committee of the Contemporary Art Society, and from 1956 served a five-year term as a governor of the BBC. She was a keen supporter of the Fawcett Library, and in 1964 was president of the Fawcett Society. She was appointed CBE in 1952. A friend of most of the prime ministers during her life, she was a special confidante of Edward Heath throughout his premiership, though their relations later cooled when she rebuked him for his attitude to Margaret Thatcher. Rather surprisingly, she was never recommended for a life peerage.

After losing her parliamentary seat Thelma Cazalet-Keir started market gardening at her home in Kent, Raspit Hill, and for a time ran a flower shop in London. When she sold Raspit Hill, deliberately for much less than its true value, to an old friend, Malcolm MacDonald, she moved to a flat in London. During her last years her sight failed, a particularly sad affliction for one who was, perhaps above all, a visual aesthete. She had a valuable collection of works by modern British artists including Augustus John, who knew her well; his portrait of her in a bright yellow dress, with a piano—which she played more than adequately—behind her, is one of his finest. (It was painted in 1936, and is privately owned.)

In 1967 Thelma Cazalet-Keir published a short volume of memoirs, *From the Wings*, notable especially for its vivid description of Lloyd George. She died on 13 January 1989 at her London flat at 90 Eaton Square.

JOHN GRIGG, *rev.*

Sources *The Times* (16 Jan 1989) · T. Cazalet-Keir, *From the wings* (1967) · personal knowledge (1996) · private information (1996) **Likenesses** photograph, 1931, Hult. Arch. · A. John, portrait, 1936, priv. coll. · Elliott & Fry, photograph, NPG [*see illus.*] **Wealth at death** £584,273: probate, 3 May 1989, *CGPLA Eng. & Wales*

Keir, William. *See* Grant, Sir William Keir (1771–1852).

Keith. For this title name *see* individual entries under Keith; *see also* Elphinstone, George Keith, Viscount Keith (1746–1823); Elphinstone, Hester Maria, Viscountess Keith (1764–1857); Flahault de la Billardrie, Margaret de, *suo jure* Lady Nairne and *suo jure* Baroness Keith, and Countess de Flahault de la Billardrie in the French nobility (1788–1867).

Keith family (*per. c.*1300–*c.*1530), nobility, may have taken its surname from the lands of Keith in eastern Lothian. From the end of the twelfth century its members held the hereditary office of marischal of Scotland, which entailed responsibility for the service and victualling arrangements in the king's hall. Some judicial function seems also to have fallen to the marischal, whose court dispensed immediate justice during wartime, and he shared some ceremonial duties with the constable, including the organization of tournaments and trial by battle.

Sir Robert Keith (d. 1343/4) succeeded to the lands and office of marischal in 1293. He was appointed warden of the forest of Selkirk in August 1299, and in the same year he joined in the raid into that forest, acting in the interests of the guardians of Scotland against the English. In 1300 Keith was captured during a skirmish in Galloway, and he submitted to Edward I in 1303, receiving the office of sheriff of Aberdeen in 1304. In 1305 he was one of ten Scots chosen to represent Scotland in the English parliament held by Edward I at Westminster, and on 26 October 1305 Edward I appointed him one of four deputy wardens of Scotland, with the office of justiciar north of Forth. Keith was ordered to aid the English against Robert Bruce in September 1307, but he had espoused King Robert's cause by Christmas 1308, and attended his first parliament at St Andrews in 1309. According to Barbour, Keith commanded the Scottish cavalry, consisting of 500 light horse, at Bannockburn, where he led a fierce charge which broke the ranks of the English archers. In the Perth parliament of 1320 Robert I rewarded the marischal with a substantial grant, consisting of the forest of Kintore and of lands in Buchan forfeited by the Comyns, while his brother, Edward Keith (who succeeded him as marischal), also received lands in Buchan. As a result, the Keiths' landed influence shifted to the north-east of Scotland.

Keith was a signatory to the declaration of Arbroath on 6 April 1320, and was later involved in helping the young David II to escape to France, accompanying him there in May 1334 and returning with him in June 1341, although he was back in Scotland in the interim, as his name appears frequently in the records as sheriff of Aberdeen between 1335 and 1342. He married Barbara Douglas, and had a son, John, who, however, was dead by November 1324. As a result it was Sir Robert's grandson, another Robert, who was designated the marischal's heir, although he did not survive his grandfather who appears to have died in either 1343 or 1344, when he was succeeded by his brother, **Sir Edward Keith** (d. 1346). The latter had married Isabella Sinton, thereby acquiring the lands of Sinton, before July 1305, and held the office of sheriff of Selkirk in 1328, while in 1341 he was named as one of the jurors in an inquisition held at Aberdeen before his elder brother. Sir Edward's death at the battle of Nevilles Cross, on 17 October 1346, is recorded by the English chronicler Henry Knighton, and also by Fordun.

Sir William Keith (d. in or after 1407), Sir Edward's eldest son and heir, is recorded as marischal in 1354. He was named as one of the commissioners negotiating for the release of David II in 1357 and travelled to England on the king's business in 1358. On 5 June that year he witnessed a charter of King David's at Edinburgh. Keith was present at the coronation of Robert II at Scone in 1371, and was one of the signatories to the second Act of Settlement in 1373. In August 1390 Keith was a witness, as both marischal and a significant member of the north-eastern nobility, to Earl Alexander of Buchan's conditional release from the excommunication which he had incurred for his attacks on Elgin and Forres earlier that year.

Keith acquired the barony and castle of Dunnottar in Kincardineshire, probably at the time of his marriage (which had taken place by 1359) to Margaret Fraser, daughter and heir of John Fraser and Mary Stewart, sister of Robert I. Dunnottar had been owned by William, fifth earl of Sutherland; Keith and Margaret subsequently granted it to Sir William *Lindsay of the Byres [see under Lindsay family of the Byres], probably as part of their daughter Christian's dowry when she married Lindsay before 27 December 1375. On 8 March 1392 Keith and Margaret agreed with Lindsay to exchange the lands of Pittendreich and West Markinch for Dunnottar, which became thereafter the Keith family's principal seat. However, Keith's construction of a tower on the rocky promontory led Walter Trail, bishop of St Andrews, to excommunicate him on the grounds that he had encroached upon consecrated ground, previously occupied by a parish church, even though this had been moved elsewhere by the end of the fourteenth century. Keith protested that his tower at Dunnottar was necessary for securing the safety of his people and possessions, in view of the tribulations and hostility faced by him at the time, and that his use of Dunnottar was in no way harmful either to the new church or to its rector. His excommunication was rescinded on 14 June 1395 by a papal bull issued by the Avignon pope Benedict XIII.

The tribulations alluded to by Keith involved a conflict between Sir James Lindsay and Robert Keith, son of the marischal, which caused considerable disruption in the north-east at this time; Wyntoun describes a battle fought at Bourtrie in the Garioch in 1395, when Lindsay, leading a force of 400 men, sought to rescue his wife, besieged in Fyvie Castle by her nephew, Robert Keith. Keith's force was defeated, but the local feuding had national repercussions, as both men had close associations with rival factions in the royal household—Keith with Robert *Stewart, earl of Fife, later duke of Albany, who had married, as his second wife, William Keith's daughter Muriel and Lindsay with Fife's nephew, John Stewart, earl of Carrick, later King Robert III. When the council ordained in 1399 that Robert III's eldest son, David, duke of Rothesay, was to govern with the advice of twenty-one wise councillors, the composition of the council represented a distinct bias towards those with northern interests and connections with the duke of Albany. The choice of William Keith, although a reasonable one by virtue of his marischal's office, certainly demonstrated this bias. On 2 May 1407 Keith granted a charter for the lands of Aboyne, and probably died soon afterwards.

Robert Keith (d. in or before 1430) had succeeded his father before 1410. One of the commissioners chosen to treat for the release of James I in 1424, he was sent as a hostage for the king's ransom on 28 March, his estate being valued at 800 merks. He was in the hands of John Langton, warden of the castle of York, on 16 June 1425, when he was given leave to return to Scotland until the following Martinmas. He died before 20 July 1430.

William Keith, first Earl Marischal (*b.* after 1425, *d.* 1483), had succeeded his father by 20 July 1430, when he witnessed a charter as marischal. The genealogy of the fifteenth-century Keiths has suffered confusion in the past as a result of the measures which William Keith took to safeguard the descent of the family's lands. In 1442 he granted all his lands to his son Robert, but when Robert died in 1446, the lands reverted to William. The latter was created a lord of parliament, probably before 10 April 1450, and was styled William, Lord Keith, in charters granted by James II on 6 July 1451. He was one of the guarantors of the truce with England in 1457, and his elevation to an earldom, with a title—that of Earl Marischal—which derived from his hereditary judicial office rather than his estates, occurred between 20 March and 4 July 1458. This elevation, like that of the constable, William Hay, to the earldom of Erroll, gave increased status to a family with a convincing pedigree of loyal support for the crown, without this entailing any significant alienation of crown resources. Keith appears on a number of parliamentary sederunt lists during the reign of James III, but died in 1483. He had married Marjorie, daughter of Alexander Fraser.

William Keith, second Earl Marischal (*d.* 1526/7), is recorded as sitting in parliament, as master of Keith, on 18 March 1482, and he spoke for his father to the lords auditors on 10 December 1482. He was styled Earl Marischal following the death of his father in 1483, and was a loyal supporter of James III, aiding the king in raising an army in 1488. The Marischal was with James III at Aberdeen in April 1488, and was one of the six royal commissioners involved in drawing up the Aberdeen articles, proposals for a settlement between King James and his opponents, but the king's repudiation of them may have disappointed him sufficiently to keep him from accompanying James back south in May. He was one of the king's representatives chosen to treat with the rebels after the confrontation at Blackness, but following the death of James III at Sauchieburn, on 11 June 1488, he seems to have withdrawn temporarily from political involvement.

The Earl Marischal was absent from the coronation of James IV at Scone on 24 June 1488, although he was in parliament on 6 October. His commitment to the new regime was, at best, lukewarm, and he was not elected to the lords of the articles, although he was permitted to sit with Bishop Elphinstone of Aberdeen among the lords auditors. Discontent with the government resulted early in 1489 in an uprising led by the earl of Lennox and Lord Lyle in the south of Scotland, and when George Gordon, master of Huntly, and Alexander, Lord Forbes, rebelled in the north, the Marischal joined forces with them. In September 1489 Keith and the master of Huntly swept south through Angus, causing great damage, but on 11 October the Marischal was on the losing side at the encounter at the field of the Moss, although he did not remain long in

disgrace, as he was chosen to serve on the new privy council in the parliament held in February 1490.

In April 1502 the Earl Marischal received one of the letters sent by James IV requesting support for King Hans of Denmark against a Swedish rising, and in 1504 he was made one of the commanders of the forces which took part in James IV's highland campaigns. On 15 October 1504 the Marischal entertained James IV at Dunnottar, and he attended the parliament held in Edinburgh in 1510. Following the battle of Flodden, the Earl Marischal was one of those given custody of the young King James V during the governorship of John Stewart, duke of Albany, when the latter was absent in France between 1517 and 1520. In recompense for substantial sums advanced to the treasury, Albany granted the Marischal the ward of the heiress of Inverugie; and on 24 July 1527, after he had come of age, James V confirmed the ward to the second earl's grandson. William Keith had married Elizabeth Gordon, third daughter of George *Gordon, second earl of Huntly, on 11 January 1482, so linking two important north-eastern noble families. He died before 2 May 1527, and was succeeded by his grandson, another William.

C. A. McGLADDERY

Sources *CDS*, vols. 2–4 · Rymer, *Foedera*, new edn, vol. 4 · J. M. Thomson and others, eds., *Registrum magni sigilli regum Scotorum / The register of the great seal of Scotland*, 11 vols. (1882–1914), vol. 2 · C. Innes, ed., *Registrum episcopatus Aberdonensis*, 1, Spalding Club, 13 (1845) · J. Robertson, ed., *Illustrations of the topography and antiquities of the shires of Aberdeen and Banff*, 4, Spalding Club (1862) · J. Stuart, ed., *The miscellany of the Spalding Club*, 5, Spalding Club, 24 (1852) · J. Barbour, *The Bruce: selections for use in schools*, ed. W. M. Mackenzie (1909) · G. Burnett and others, eds., *The exchequer rolls of Scotland*, 23 vols. (1878–1908), vols. 1, 9 · *RotS*, vol. 1 · [T. Thomson], ed., *The acts of the lords of council in civil causes, 1478–1495*, 1, RC, 41 (1839) · *Scots peerage*, vol. 4 · GEC, *Peerage*, 8.464–77 · F. M. Powicke and E. B. Fryde, eds., *Handbook of British chronology*, 2nd edn, Royal Historical Society Guides and Handbooks, 2 (1961), 483

Keith, Alexander (*d.* 1758), celebrant of clandestine marriages and excommunicated Church of England clergyman, claimed to have been ordained by the bishop of Norwich on 13 June 1731 and to have been a reader at the Rolls Chapel in Chancery Lane. He also claimed the degree MA but it is unclear where this came from. When St George's Chapel, Hyde Park Corner, was built in the early 1730s to cater for the growing population in the new squares and streets in the parish of St George's, Hanover Square, Keith was appointed incumbent. An eloquent preacher, he soon attracted a large congregation and began to build up a flourishing trade in clandestine marriages. Such marriages—which, although recognized by the church as valid, contravened church law in one or more respects—had been conducted for many years in the area around the Fleet prison but Keith's chapel attracted a more fashionable clientele, which had many reasons for wanting quick and secret marriages. He conducted 117 such marriages in 1741, and 723 in 1742, when Dr Trebeck, rector of St George's, Hanover Square, concerned at his loss of business, took Keith to the ecclesiastical court, arguing that all marriages in his parish should take place in the parish church. The court upheld this claim; Keith was excommunicated by Edmund Gibson, bishop of London, on 27 October 1742 and, after he had in return excommunicated the bishop, the judge, and Dr Trebeck at his chapel, Keith was committed to the Fleet prison in April 1743 for contempt of the church.

Undaunted, Keith opened his own chapel, close to St George's Chapel, employing Fleet parsons to conduct the marriages, while he signed the licences in prison. He advertised 'Mr Keith's Little Chapel in May-Fair, near Hyde Park Corner, opposite the Great Chapel, within 10 yards of it. There is a porch at the door like a country church porch' (*Daily Advertiser*, 23 Jan 1750) in the leading London newspapers, pointing out the advantages of a Mayfair wedding and assuring the public that his imprisonment had not caused the suspension of business. When his wife, whom he had married on 23 July 1729, died in 1749 he had her body embalmed and announced that she would remain unburied until he would be free to attend the funeral; when one of his sons died the funeral procession carried a placard setting out Keith's grievances against the ecclesiastical authorities and asking the public to carry on having their weddings at his chapel. Over 5000 marriages were held there between 1744 and 1749, 1136 between October 1753 and March 1754, and 61 on Lady day 1754, the day before the new Marriage Act came into force. Although some of those married in Keith's chapel were members of fashionable society—including James, sixth duke of Hamilton, who married Elizabeth Gunning at 12.30 on the night of 14 February 1752, after their parson had refused to marry them; Bysshe Shelley (the poet's grandfather) and Mary Catherine Michell (30 June 1752); and Lord George Bentinck (29 June 1753)—Keith was happy to marry anyone who came along. He claimed that most of those who were married there had known each other for less than a week: 'happy is the wooing that is not long a-doing' (A. K.).

For eleven years Keith lived in luxury in the Fleet on the proceeds of his marriage business until the government, led by the lord chancellor, Philip Yorke, first Baron Hardwicke, and encouraged by the church, decided to put an end to clandestine marriages and passed the Marriage Act of 1753. This made marriage according to the law of the church the only valid form of marriage recognized by the state, and offending clergymen were to be sentenced to fourteen years' transportation. Keith had not put any money aside and spent the rest of his life in poverty in a shared attic in the Fleet. In an appeal 'to the Compassionate' for donations he said that the act had reduced him to a deplorable state of misery, living on bread and water. Keith published a pamphlet, *Observations on the Act for Preventing Clandestine Marriages*, in 1753, in which he claimed that the sole purpose of the act was to suppress his chapel. He argued that marriage was good for society, as the strength of a state depended on a large population, whereas any restriction on marriage would lead to an increase in immorality: 'hasty and precipitant marriage

… is the very foundation of our present happiness and prosperity' (A. K., 25). Keith died on 13 December 1758 in the Fleet prison.

ANNE PIMLOTT BAKER

Sources R. B. Outhwaite, *Clandestine marriage in England, 1500–1800* (1995) · R. Lee Brown, 'The rise and fall of the Fleet marriages', *Marriage and society*, ed. R. B. Outhwaite (1981), 117–36 · J. C. Jeaffreson, *Brides and bridals* (1872), 2.158–66 · P. C. Yorke, *The life and correspondence of Philip Yorke, earl of Hardwicke*, 2 (1913), 58–75 · J. Southerden Burn, *The Fleet registers* (1833), 96–104 · J. Ashton, *The Fleet: its river, prison, and marriages* (1888), 356–61 · W. Eden Hooper, *The history of Newgate and the Old Bailey* (1935), chap. 4, 148–52 · R. Lee Brown, *A history of the Fleet prison, London* (1996) · A. K. [A. Keith], *Observations on the Act for Preventing Clandestine Marriages* (1753) · IGI

Likenesses engraving, repro. in A. K., *Observations*

Wealth at death died in penury

Keith, Alexander (1737–1819), antiquary and benefactor, was born on 27 December 1737, the son of Alexander Keith (1705–1792), depute-clerk of session, and his wife, Johanna Swinton (*d.* 1792) of Swinton, Peeblesshire. The fortunes of his family evidently rose from the seventeenth century onwards; Keith's grandfather, Alexander, acquired the estate of Ravelston, near Edinburgh, in 1726, while his father bought the lands and castle of Dunnottar, Kincardineshire, from the last Earl Marischal in 1766. His father claimed the headship of the Keith family by reason of his descent from Alexander Keith of Pittendrum, fourth son of the third Earl Marischal. Robert Keith, bishop of Fife, disputed this claim and challenged it in print. However, it seems that the last Earl Marischal, who sold Dunnottar to Keith's father, recognized the claim because he sent the elder Keith all the family records as well as the 'black stock of Dunnottar', an ancient oak table which was an important Keith heirloom.

Keith was trained as a writer to the signet and was admitted into the Society of Writers on 29 November 1763, but his main interests were antiquarian. These interests may have led him to conduct excavations on his lands, and on 28 November 1784 he read to the Society of Antiquaries of Scotland a paper entitled 'An account of the discovery of two ancient instruments of a deep coloured brass, resembling the heads of small hatchets, dug up on the estate of Ravelston' (Smellie, 156). Other papers presented by Keith to this society dealt with the coronation of Charles I at Holyrood and the Scottish regalia. Besides belonging to the Society of Antiquaries, Keith was also a member of the Royal Society of Edinburgh, to which he likewise presented various papers. He was a friend of Sir Walter Scott, to whom he was related through the Swintons and who shared his antiquarian interests. Scott remembered him affectionately as rather indecisive, especially about spending money. Like his father, Keith was interested in the connection with the earls Marischal and at one point wished to repair their family vault in Dunnottar churchyard. However, he dithered for years about the money needed for this task, while the vault continued to deteriorate. When he finally sent the required sum the edifice had collapsed.

Keith married Margaret Oliphant (*b.* 1770, *d.* in or after 1847), youngest daughter of Laurence Oliphant of Gask, on 24 April 1811; the couple had no children. Keith died on

26 February 1819, leaving £1000 in his will for the promotion of science. His trustees decided to use £600 for founding a biennial prize, to be awarded for scientific discoveries made internationally but submitted to the Royal Society of Edinburgh and first published in their *Transactions*. The remainder of the bequest was used to found the Keith prize in the Royal Society of Arts of Edinburgh.

Keith's nephew, Alexander (*b.* 1780), the son of his brother William, acted as knight marshal during the visit of George IV to Edinburgh in 1822. He admitted that another branch of the Keith family had a better claim to its headship than his own.   ALEXANDER DU TOIT

Sources R. Douglas, *The peerage of Scotland*, 2nd edn, ed. J. P. Wood, 2 (1813), 191 · *The Society of Writers to His Majesty's Signet with a list of the members* (1936), 210 · *Transactions of the Royal Society of Edinburgh*, 9 (1823), 259–61 · J. G. Lockhart, *Memoirs of the life of Sir Walter Scott*, [new edn] (1845), 479 · W. Smellie, *Account of the institution and progress of the Society of Antiquaries of Scotland* (1832), 156, 168, 170, 196 · L. R. Timperley, ed., *A directory of landownership in Scotland, c.1770*, Scottish RS, new ser., 5 (1976), 130, 181 · W. Anderson, *The Scottish nation*, 2 (1868), 588, 592 · T. L. Kington-Oliphant, *The Jacobite lairds of Gask* (1870), 373 · R. Douglas and others, *The baronage of Scotland* (1798), 132, 589

Archives NL Scot., Melville MSS

Wealth at death £435 estates in Corstorphine parish, near Edinburgh: valuation roll, 1771 · £1292 13*s*. 4*d*. estates in Dunnottar parish: valuation roll, 1771 · left £1000 for promotion of science in Scotland: *Transactions*

Keith, Alexander (1792–1880), Free Church of Scotland minister and writer on prophecy, was born in Keith Hall, Aberdeenshire, on 13 November 1792 (*Scot. Fasti*; *DNB* gives 30 Nov 1791), the second son of George Skene *Keith (1752–1823), minister of the same place, and his wife, Helen Simpson (*d.* 1798). He was educated from 1805 at Marischal College, Aberdeen, where he graduated MA in 1809, before proceeding to the study of divinity. Licensed by the presbytery of Garioch on 17 March 1813, he was ordained to the parish of St Cyrus, Kincardineshire, on 27 August 1816. Keith married, on 10 December 1816, Jane Blaikie (*d.* 1837), with whom he had a daughter and seven sons, including Alexander (1817–1880), who became his assistant at St Cyrus.

Keith established his reputation through the *Evidence of the Truth of the Christian Religion from the Fulfilment of Prophecy*, designed as a refutation of the views of David Hume, the first of many editions of which appeared in 1823. It was widely translated, and an enormously popular and influential work—'known as a household word throughout the land', according to Thomas Chalmers (*DNB*). But equally, it was one that Keith never surpassed. Later works, such as *The Signs of the Times* (1832), covered similar ground to less effect. Marischal College, Aberdeen, conferred the degree of DD on him in 1833.

His reputation as 'Prophecy Keith' (*Annual Register*) made him a natural choice to form part of the Church of Scotland's mission of inquiry to the Jews, which was dispatched to the Holy Land in 1839. Keith and Alexander Black were the senior members of the party and they separated from R. M. McCheyne and A. A. Bonar to return through Europe, along the Danube. They broke their journey at Pest, where both fell ill, with Keith exhibiting signs

of cholera. The attack was nearly fatal and he was detained for six months before he was fit enough to return to Scotland. During this time he developed a warm friendship with the Archduchess Marie Dorothea, who suggested Pest as a site for the establishment of a mission to the Jews. A mission station was duly established there in 1841.

Keith retired from pastoral work on his return to Scotland, but he was convener of the Jewish Mission Committee, both in the Church of Scotland and in the Free Church of Scotland (which he joined in 1843) until 1847. He returned to the Holy Land in 1844 with his son George Skene Keith and took daguerreotype views of notable places in Syria. Keith apparently declined the moderatorship of the Free Church general assembly on a number of occasions, citing poor health, and devoted the remainder of his long life to literary pursuits. After 1840 he appears to have resided in Edinburgh, and published an account of his experiences in Pest in the periodical *Sunday at Home* in 1867.

Although he often spent the summer in Scotland, at Bridge of Allan, Keith was latterly resident at Buxton, Derbyshire. He died at Aberdeen House, 56 West Street, Buxton, on 8 February 1880, and was buried in the graveyard of the Congregational church at Chinley, Chapel-en-le-Frith, Derbyshire, on 12 February. A tall, dramatic, and revered figure within the Free Church, whose oldest minister he was at the time of his death, Keith was seen with a more sceptical eye by his nephew William Garden Blaikie, who considered that 'He had a remarkably enthusiastic temperament, so much so, that it was irksome to him to concentrate attention on subjects that lay outside his hobbies' (*Blaikie*, ed. Walker, 7).

LIONEL ALEXANDER RITCHIE

Sources *Fasti Scot.* · J. A. Wylie, *Disruption worthies: a memorial of 1843*, ed. J. B. Gillies, new edn (1881), 331–8 · *Men of the time* (1879), 583–4 · *Aberdeen Journal* (12 Feb 1880) · *Annual Register* (1880), 149–50 · *High Peak News* (14 Feb 1880) · *The Times* (13 Feb 1880) · *William Garden Blaikie: an autobiography*, ed. N. L. Walker (1901) · *Fasti academiae Mariscallanae Aberdonensis: selections from the records of the Marischal College and University, MDXCIII–MDCCCLX*, 2, ed. P. J. Anderson, New Spalding Club, 18 (1898) · private information (1891) · *DSCHT* · *DNB* · *High Peak News* (14 Feb 1880)

Likenesses lithograph, BM · portrait, repro. in Wylie, *Disruption worthies*, facing p. 331 · woodcut, NPG; repro. in *Christian Herald* (April 1880)

Wealth at death £105 12*s*. 1*d*.: confirmation, 16 July 1880, *CCI*

Keith, Alexander (1895–1978), author and farmer, was born on 18 August 1895 in The Square, Kintore, Aberdeenshire, the son of Alfred George Keith, chemist, and his wife, Janet Greig, *née* Wishart. Janet Keith was the daughter of a local farmer and butcher, and brought up the family single-handed, running both the business and the local savings bank after her husband's early death. Alexander was educated at Kintore and Strichen parish schools, winning a bursary which enabled him to gain an honours MA in English from Aberdeen University in 1916. After brief experience of keeping the pedigree records of the Brucklay Castle herd of Aberdeen Angus, he joined the editorial staff of the *Aberdeen Daily Journal* (later *Press and Journal*) in

1917, and was assistant editor from 1929 until 1944. In 1943 he bought the farm of Eigie, by Balmedie, north of Aberdeen, which he worked until 1971, when he retired to Stonehaven in Kincardineshire. He specialized in breeding Aberdeen Angus cattle, and was secretary of the Aberdeen-Angus Cattle Society from 1944 to 1955. He was also a member of the council of the Aberdeen chamber of commerce in 1954, becoming president in 1957, and he travelled all over the world to promote the interests of both bodies. In 1967 Aberdeen University awarded him an LLD *honoris causa*, describing him as 'the universal man of the North-East' (*Aberdeen University Review*, 42). He married twice, first on 5 August 1922, Agnes Roberta MacDougall, and second on 16 January 1957, Lewella Agnes Mackay.

Throughout his life Keith was a prolific writer, publishing eight books, well over seventy articles, countless editorials and reviews, and almost a hundred BBC scripts and talks. The diversity of his subject matter was also great, ranging from local histories of banking, cattle-breeding, distilling, printing, and business, to works on Burns, Shakespeare, and Byron, together with studies of men and women eminent in the history of the north-east of Scotland, from poets to professors, soldiers to singers. He was one of the first to broadcast from the new BBC station in Aberdeen (2BD), established in 1923. He broadcast throughout his life, especially on horticulture and gardening, and spoke on air in America in the 1940s on behalf of the war effort.

In publishing, Keith's local fame derived from *The North of Scotland Bank Limited, 1836–1936*, *The Aberdeen-Angus Breed: a History* (1958), *Families of the Aberdeen-Angus Breed* (1959), and his final history, *A Thousand Years of Aberdeen* (1972); it was increased by the posthumous publication of his collected essays from the *Aberdeen Chamber of Commerce Journal*, entitled *Eminent Aberdonians* (1984). 'A. K.' became a legend in his own time, a member of clubs and associations with intriguing names such as the Sit Siccars, the Calm Soughers, the Club of Deer, and the Life Preserving Society, together with characters such as Charles Murray, David Rorie, J. B. Tocher, William Tawse, Lord Boyd Orr, and William Walker. He was highly popular as a man of charm and tact, common sense and worldly wisdom, of sheer readability and sense of fun (though he characteristically requested a private funeral).

Keith's international fame stemmed from *Last Leaves of Traditional Ballads and Ballad Airs Collected in Aberdeenshire by the Late Gavin Greig and Edited, with an Introductory Essay, Collations and Notes by Alexander Keith*, published by the Buchan [Field] Club in 1925. The title was doubly misleading: the contents represented only about 13 per cent of the huge collection (some 3500 songs) made in the decade before the First World War from a rich living tradition (which continued to thrive); it was amassed not only by Gavin Greig, an Aberdeenshire parish schoolmaster, but also by the Revd James Bruce Duncan, a local minister. They were overwhelmed by the size of their collection, and it was not ready for publication before their deaths (Greig's in 1914; Duncan's in 1917). Their papers went to Aberdeen University Library where they were examined by the great ballad

authority William Walker. Greig and Duncan had scrupulously taken down everything their informants had given, from music-hall songs to great ballads, mingling 'dross' with material of the highest quality. Walker did not recommend publication, but when friends in the Buchan Field Club later suggested publication of the songs of Bell Robertson (Greig's most prolific informant) Walker proposed that they print instead the annotated compilation of great 'traditional' ballads in the collection, which Greig and Duncan had almost completed.

Too old at eighty-five for the task, Walker proposed the young Alexander Keith as editor, although other than publishing *Burns and Folksong* in 1922 (six articles originally suggested by Walker, mostly from Keith's weekly newspaper column, 'From a Scottish study'), Keith had no experience in this field. He was guided and advised by Walker, who also chose the elegiac title and ensured that the introduction was used to rescue the battered reputation of his favourite, an earlier local collector, Peter Buchan. The sheer quality of Greig's and Duncan's material, both tunes and texts, brought international acclaim for *Last Leaves*, and lasting fame to Keith who, for the rest of his life, pursued an interest in folk song, especially of the north-east. Keith died on 5 October 1978 in Woodcot Hospital, Stonehaven, Kincardineshire, and was buried in Stonehaven.   IAN A. OLSON

Sources W. Witte, 'Alexander Keith', *Aberdeen University Review*, 42 (1967–8), 155–6 · H. M. R. Watt, 'Tribute', *Journal* [Aberdeen Chamber of Commerce], 48 (1967), 899–902 · I. D. B. Bryce and C. Graham, 'Alexander Keith: a valediction', *Leopard*, 44 (1978), 23–5 · H. M. R. W. [H. M. R. Watt], 'Alexander Keith: a bibliography', *Aberdeen University Review*, 48 (1979–80), 61–7 · I. A. Olson, 'Scottish traditional song and the Greig–Duncan collection: last leaves or last rites?', *The history of Scottish literature*, 4: *Twentieth century*, ed. C. Craig (1987), 37–48 · I. A. Olson, 'Editing the Glenbuchat ballads: David Buchan's legacy', *Aberdeen University Review*, 57 (1997–8), 29–45 · b. cert. · d. cert. · CCI (1979)
Archives U. Aberdeen L., ballad collections, letters, and papers | Surrey HC, corresp. with Lucy Broadwood | SOUND School of Scottish Studies, Edinburgh
Likenesses photographs, Aberdeen City Libraries
Wealth at death £74,140.74: corrective estate, 15 Nov 1979, CCI

Keith, Sir Arthur (1866–1955), museum curator and palaeoanthropologist, was born on 5 February 1866 at Old Machar, Aberdeenshire, the sixth of the ten children of John Keith, a farmer, and his wife, Jessica (Jessie) Macpherson. To prepare for a medical education he went to Gordon's College, Aberdeen, for a grounding in Latin and Greek, and in 1884 entered Marischal College. It was here that he came under the influence of James Trail, the botanist, and John Struthers, the anatomist, both of whom inspired him with the resolve ultimately to seek an academic career. He was also captivated by his professor of surgery, Alexander Ogston, one of Lister's early followers, who had a particular interest in military surgery. Keith experimented with the effects of rifle bullets fired at close range on tin cans filled with water and on animal thigh bones, and was able to demonstrate to Ogston the explosive effect of high-velocity missiles.

Keith qualified MB with first-class honours in 1888. After a term as demonstrator in physiology, and brief periods as

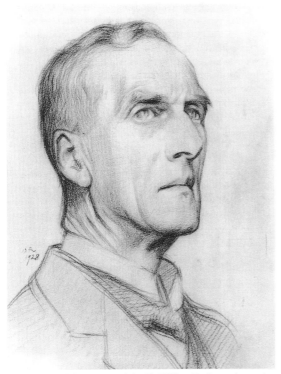

Sir Arthur Keith (1866–1955), by Sir William Rothenstein, 1928

assistant at the Murray Asylum, Perth, and as a general practitioner in Mansfield, a critical period in his career opened when he accepted a post as medical officer to a mining company in Siam, with a commission to collect botanical specimens for Kew Gardens. His collection was later used by H. N. Ridley in his comprehensive work on the *Flora of the Malay Peninsula*. But Keith himself became more interested in field and anatomical studies of the local monkeys and gibbons, and it was these activities which first began to focus his attention on the comparative anatomy of the primates, the evolution of man, and physical anthropology in general.

After three years in Siam, Keith returned home and in 1894 was awarded the degree of MD of Aberdeen University with the Struthers medal for a thesis on the myology of caterrhine monkeys, and in the same year he passed the examination for the fellowship of the Royal College of Surgeons. In the following year he was appointed senior demonstrator in anatomy at the London Hospital medical school, subsequently becoming lecturer. He married, in 1899, Cecilia Caroline (*d.* 1934), daughter of artist Tom Gray. In 1902 there appeared his well-known book *Human Embryology and Morphology*, which reached a sixth edition in 1948. Of his earlier research work that dealing with the anatomy of the heart won him the greatest distinction, and in seeking for one of the basic causes of cardiac arrhythmia he discovered (with his colleague Martin Flack) the sinoatrial node, or pacemaker, of the human heart, a small condensation of specialized tissue of immense importance for the initiation and control of the normal rhythmic contraction of the heart. This important finding was published in *The Lancet* in 1906.

In 1908 Keith was elected to the conservatorship of the Royal College of Surgeons, and his inspired direction revived the somewhat somnolent scientific side of the college's work both by his own research and by attracting surgeons, anatomists, and anthropologists to work with him for longer or shorter periods in the museum and its laboratories. As a result the Hunterian Museum of the college came to be recognized as one of the finest records of the structure and history of the human body, with particular reference to the anatomical and embryological basis of the surgical disabilities and disorders which may affect it. One of Keith's main duties at the college was to conduct courses of lectures, and he rapidly acquired a high reputation as a gifted lecturer. Soon after assuming his new office he began to give his attention much more actively to problems of human evolution and the diversification of the modern races of mankind. There followed a number of palaeoanthropological studies, as a result of which Keith claimed a much higher antiquity for *Homo sapiens* than had hitherto been accepted. His conclusions have proved to be partly correct—but not entirely, for some of the fossil skeletons on which he relied for his evidence were later demonstrated by modern techniques of dating to be more recent than he had supposed.

The publication of the alleged discovery of the Piltdown skull in 1912 led Keith into serious controversy with those who claimed that the skull (as well as the jaw) displayed remarkable simian characters, and he was able to show that, if properly reconstructed, the skull was in fact quite like that of *Homo sapiens*. Nevertheless, though he expressed doubts as to the interpretation of this 'fossil', Keith thought that Piltdown man was indeed akin to a very early ancestor of modern man. The exposure that the skull and its related artefacts were, in fact, fraudulent was distressing to him in his last years. The tragedy to him, he said, was 'the loss of faith in the testimony of our fellow-workers'.

In 1915 *The Antiquity of Man* was published—a widely read book reviewing all the fossil remains of man at that time known. It was brought up to date in 1931 by a supplementary volume, *New Discoveries Relating to the Antiquity of Man*. During the First World War Keith was occupied with problems of surgical anatomy related to war injuries, and published a number of lectures on the anatomical and physiological principles underlying the treatment of wounds involving muscles, bones, and joints. Some of his wartime lectures appeared in book form as *Menders of the Maimed* (1919). In 1913 he was elected to the presidency of the Royal Anthropological Institute, a position which he held for four years, and in 1916 he was invited to give the Christmas juvenile lectures at the Royal Institution; these were later published in a book entitled *The Engines of the Human Body* (1919), a second edition of which appeared in 1925. His writings made his name familiar to the lay public, for he was one of the last, and among the greatest, of the Victorian popularizers of science in the tradition of Thomas Huxley.

During the years following the war Keith's interests turned more to the general themes of medical history and to somewhat speculative considerations of evolutionary processes in relation to the origin of man; at the same time he was always busy revising some of his books for new editions. He was elected FRS as early as 1913, in 1921 he was knighted, and from 1918 to 1923 he occupied the position of Fullerian professor of physiology at the Royal Institution. He was elected to the presidency of the British Association for 1927. His presidential address, 'Darwin's theory of man's descent as it stands today', presented an affirmation of Darwin's general conclusions on the evolutionary derivation of the Hominidae from an ancestry in common with the anthropoid apes, amplified by references to the accumulation of comparative anatomical and palaeontological evidence since Darwin's time. One result of this meeting of the British Association was the immediate response to Keith's appeal for the preservation of Darwin's home at Downe in Kent.

In 1930 Keith was elected rector of Aberdeen University and in his rectorial address he developed the thesis that the spirit of nationalism is a potent factor in the evolutionary differentiation of human races. This thesis, later expanded in a book entitled *A New Theory of Human Evolution* (1948), met with some criticism. Keith received honorary degrees from Aberdeen, Durham, Manchester, Birmingham, and Oxford. He was an honorary fellow of the Royal Societies of Edinburgh and New Zealand, and honorary member of the United States National Academy of Sciences and the New York Academy of Sciences.

In 1933, after a severe illness, Keith retired from the Royal College of Surgeons and went to live at the Buckston Browne Research Institute in Downe. A year later he suffered the loss of his wife; they had no children. Except for his *Autobiography* (1950) which he published at the age of eighty-four, Keith's last work of importance was a comprehensive study of the skeletal remains of palaeolithic man found in the caves of Mount Carmel. The results of this work appeared in the treatise, *The Stone Age of Mount Carmel* (1939, with T. D. McCown).

Keith died suddenly at his home, Homefield, Downe, on 7 January 1955, and was buried in Downe churchyard. Apart from his claims to distinction as a scientist, he was a much loved man, kindly and gentle in manner, friendly and unassuming, and of a somewhat retiring disposition. It seemed entirely fitting that this devoted student of human evolution should himself spend the latter part of his long life in the countryside where his great predecessor Charles Darwin had once lived.

W. E. LE GROS CLARK, rev. HAROLD ELLIS

Sources R. H. O. B. Robinson and W. R. Le Fanu, *Lives of the fellows of the Royal College of Surgeons of England, 1952–1964* (1970) · A. Keith, *An autobiography* (1950) · J. C. Brash and A. J. E. Cave, *Journal of Anatomy*, 89 (1955), 403–18 · Z. Cope, *The Royal College of Surgeons of England: a history* (1959) · W. E. Le G. Clark, *Memoirs FRS*, 1 (1955) · *The Times* (8 Jan 1955)
Archives Medical Research Council, London, corresp. · RCS Eng., corresp., diaries, papers · Royal Institution of Great Britain, London, letters | RCS Eng., corresp. with Margaret Willis, Rupert Willis, and J. W. Nicholson · Royal Anthropological Institute, London, corresp. with Royal Anthropological Institute · UCL, letters to Karl Pearson · W. Yorks. AS, Leeds, letters to William Hornsby [photocopies]
Likenesses W. Stoneman, photograph, 1921, NPG · W. W. Ouless, oils, c.1928, RCS Eng. · W. Rothenstein, pencil drawing, 1928, NPG [*see illus.*] · M. Hoffman, plaster bust, 1930, RCS Eng. · R. T. Mackenzie, bronze medallion, 1930, U. Aberdeen, department of anatomy; plaster bust, RCS Eng. · K. Parbury, bronze bust, 1935, RCS Eng. · J. Pannett, chalk drawing, 1954, NPG · K. Panbury, bronze bust, RCS Eng.
Wealth at death £11,778 3s. 9d.: probate, 14 April 1955, CGPLA Eng. & Wales

Keith, Arthur Berriedale (1879–1944), Sanskritist and jurist, was born on 5 April 1879 at 3 Abercorn Terrace, Portobello, Edinburgh, the fourth of six talented children and the third son of Davidson Keith (1842–1921), advertising agent, and Margaret Stobie Keith, *née* Drysdale (1851–1911). His father came from a Caithness family, his mother from Dunfermline. Following his older brothers, William John *Keith and Robert Charles Steuart Keith, he studied at the Royal High School, Edinburgh (1887–94), and Edinburgh University (1894–7), taking an MA there before going to Balliol College, Oxford, as classical scholar and Boden scholar (Sanskrit). At every stage he displayed academic excellence and intellectual brilliance, setting record marks in examinations, receiving several bursaries, and winning scholarships including both the Ferguson and the Guthrie. While his early prominence was in classics, he added Sanskrit during his final year at Edinburgh. At Oxford he set numerous academic records to the astonishment of examiners. He gained firsts in classical moderations (1899), in Sanskrit and Pali in the school of oriental studies (1900), and in *literae humaniores* (1901). He graduated BA in 1900, and in the same year published his first scholarly article, in the *Journal of the Royal Asiatic Society*. He was admitted to the Inner Temple in 1900 and called to the bar in 1904. He took a BCL in 1905 and a DCL in 1911, both at Oxford, for the latter offering his study, *The Theory of State Succession* (1907). In 1921 he became a member of the Faculty of Advocates in Scotland.

Shortly after Keith went to Balliol, his mother moved to Oxford, leaving his father in Edinburgh. She established a household for him and his brother, Robert, including, as well, the two younger children, Annie (Nan) Balfour and Alan Davidson. From that time until her death in 1911, his mother, a strong, dominant person, ran his domestic affairs.

Again following the lead of his older brothers, Keith took the home and Indian Civil Service examinations in 1901. He established the record score which no one in that year neared. In October 1901 he entered the Colonial Office as clerk, second class. Shortly after his appointment the examinations were reformed. He served in the Colonial Office in several departments until 1914, though from 1903 to 1905 he transferred to the crown agents for the colonies. He was assigned to the dominions department, created in 1907, and completed his service (1912–14) as private secretary to the permanent under-secretary, Sir John

Anderson. He served on the staff of several colonial conferences, of many inter-departmental committees, and of the Imperial Conference. He was valued as an assiduous, prodigious, and rapid worker, although, on occasion, his superiors found him contentious. An articulate analyst, especially of complex colonial and imperial constitutional issues, he wrote several specialist papers in the Confidential Print Series. He also liaised on behalf of the Colonial Office with the International Colonial Institute, an organization based in Brussels that included representatives of the principal colonial powers and existed to share information on comparative colonial practices.

In 1914, after several unsuccessful attempts to find an academic position, Keith was named regius professor of Sanskrit and comparative philology at Edinburgh University, a position he held for the rest of his life. In that same year he took the degree of DLitt at Edinburgh, for which he offered two published translations from Sanskrit. He arranged for his courses and lectures to be given during the first two terms, thus allowing him six months each year for research, an arrangement he maintained even after 1927 when he took the additional post of lecturer on the constitution of the British empire. At first he was active in discussions of academic issues in the university, and, as an Asquithian Liberal, represented Scottish universities in the Scottish Liberal Federation. Gradually, however, he withdrew into teaching, writing, examining, and corresponding. Over a period of more than forty years he published fifty-six books (some of which went through several editions), pamphlets, and hundreds of articles and reviews, and wrote numerous letters to newspapers. Beyond this he carried on an extensive correspondence; some seven hundred persons are included in extant materials. His publications ranged across classics, Sanskrit language and literature, oriental philosophy and religion, constitutional law of England and of the British empire, history, geography, and international affairs in the fields of both law and diplomacy.

From the prodigious production of this polymath a few works may be cited, to illustrate the range. In oriental studies Keith's best-regarded publications were predominantly on the Vedic period, beginning with a translation of, and masterly introduction to, *Aitareya Aranyaka* (1909). His *Vedic Index of Names and Subjects* (1912), written with A. A. Macdonnell, was for a time indispensable. Further Vedic translations followed and two volumes entitled *The Religion and the Philosophy of the Veda and Upanishads* (1925) rounded off his Vedic studies, which had rendered accessible large tracts of the literature until then hardly more than surveyed. In the field of classical Sanskrit his publications included works on philosophy (*Indian Logic and Atomism*, 1921; *Buddhist Philosophy in India and Ceylon*, 1923) and two substantial volumes surveying with full documentation and critical appreciation the history of Sanskrit drama and literature. He had an interest in tracing religious origins, which led to *Indian Mythology* in 1917. His translations and editions of Sanskrit works have remained important, although some of his judgements, especially in philosophy, became dated; his catalogues of

manuscripts in the Bodleian Library and elsewhere are likely to remain essential.

Keith's legal publications included several works on the law of the dominions, the most important being *Responsible Government in the Dominions* (1909, 1912, 1928). He wrote a lucid *Constitutional History of the First British Empire* (1930) for which he received the gold prize of the Royal Empire Society. He edited and revised A. V. Dicey's classic, *A Digest of the Law of England with Reference to the Conflict of Laws* (1922, 1927, 1932). In public affairs his contributions included letters to *The Scotsman* and other newspapers, first collected in *Letters on Imperial Relations* (1935). He assembled essential documents in *Selected Speeches and Documents on British Colonial Policy, 1763–1917* (1918) and published a book on the causes of the Second World War in 1940. His publications in law and public affairs show him to be more emotionally exposed there than in his oriental studies. He was prone to sharp and sometimes prejudiced judgement, and aroused controversy. None the less his works were authoritative, and were often quoted on both sides of a constitutional crisis within the Commonwealth. His *Responsible Government* was for many years the classic exposition of the constitutional position of the dominions. His histories and collections of documents continue to be consulted and valued, and in many areas his works are the starting place for scholarly research.

Several illustrations from the 1930s indicate the range of Keith's involvements. From 1930 to 1934 he worked for the associated chambers of commerce of India and Ceylon in the Indian round-table conferences. In 1932–3 he advised on the differences between English and Scottish law in the divorce proceedings of Janet Aitken Campbell, Lord Beaverbrook's daughter. From 1935 he joined Sylvia Pankhurst and others in criticizing the government's stance on the Abyssinian crisis, through strategy meetings and articles in the *New Times and Ethiopia News*. In 1936 he was asked by America's National Broadcasting Company to explain for Americans the constitutional issues raised by Edward VIII's marriage proposal. In 1938 he presented both written and oral arguments in an appeal from Malta to the judicial committee of the privy council. In 1939 he assisted Chief Sobhuza II, paramount chief of the Swazi, to petition the king on alleged injustices committed by the Union of South Africa against Swaziland.

Through extensive scholarly production and active participation Keith embodied his commitment to the rule of law as the appropriate way to restrain arbitrary actions by individuals, institutions, and governments. He was generous with time, advice, and information. Often he took positions that were unpopular, for example, defending the legality of Éire's neutrality in 1939 as fully consistent with dominion status. Brilliant yet at times quixotic, he continued an active public and scholarly life almost until his final year.

Keith married Margaret Balfour Allan (1874–1934) at the parish church in Bathgate on 1 June 1912. They had no children. From 1920 they lived at 4 Crawfurd Road, Edinburgh. Following her death in 1934, which he felt deeply, he invited his younger sister Nan Dewar, by that time widowed, to join him there. Both his wife and his sister greatly assisted him, and he acknowledged their help in dedications and prefaces to his books. Especially, they helped by organizing all details of the house so that he was completely freed for his work. Fond of detective stories, he often had his wife, or later his sister, read to him while he engaged in scholarly work. He had a wry sense of humour—for example, turning to broad Scots for some oral examinations while at Oxford. He rejected offers of other appointments from Oxford and from Harvard, preferring to remain at Edinburgh. Indeed, unlike all his siblings, whose careers and lives took them to Burma or India, he lived within the triangle of Edinburgh–Oxford–London. He accepted only one honorary degree, an LLD from Leeds University in 1936. He was elected FBA in 1935 but resigned in 1939. Following a series of strokes he died at home on 6 October 1944 and was buried on 9 October in Grange cemetery, Newington, Edinburgh.

RIDGWAY F. SHINN, JUN.

Sources R. F. Shinn, Jr, *Arthur Berriedale Keith: 'the chief ornament of Scottish learning'* (1990) · R. F. Shinn, Jr, 'Guide to Arthur Berriedale Keith papers and correspondence, 1896–1941', 1981, U. Edin. L., Gen 140–153 · R. F. Shinn, Jr and R. A. Cosgrove, *Constitutional reflections: the correspondence of Albert Venn Dicey and Arthur Berriedale Keith* (1996) · *The Times* (7 Oct 1944) · *The Scotsman* (7 Oct 1944) · *The Scotsman* (9 Oct 1944) · *Daily Telegraph* (11 Oct 1944) · *TLS* (14 Oct 1944) · *New Times and Ethiopia News* (14 Oct 1944) · *University of Edinburgh Journal*, 13 (1944–5), 47 · *Yearbook of the American Philosophical Society* (1945), 377 · minute, Senatus Academicus, 8 Nov 1944, U. Edin. · *Journal of Comparative Legislation* (1944), 61–2 · cabinet papers, related to Keith's work, PRO · colonial office files, related to Keith's work, 1901–14, PRO · foreign office files, especially related to Peace Handbooks, PRO · U. Edin. L., Keith collection · *DNB* · b. cert. · d. cert. · d. cert. [Margaret Keith] · *The Scotsman* (3 June 1912)
Archives Oxford University Press, archives · U. Edin. L., corresp. and papers | Bodl. Oxf., Sir Louis Stuart MSS · NA Scot., corresp. with Lord Lothian · NA Scot., corresp. with Viscount Novar · NL Aus., James Bryce MSS, Lewis Harcourt MSS · priv. coll., Dewar collection | SOUND Museum of Broadcasting, New York, current affairs footage, 2281, pt 1, 2284, pt 1, 2285, pt 1, all Box E 36–5
Likenesses W. Stoneman, photograph, 1935, NPG · photograph, *c*.1942, U. Edin., Sanskrit department · photographs, repro. in Shinn, *Arthur Berriedale Keith*, ii, pp. 5, 10, 14
Wealth at death £19,769 5s. 9d.: confirmation, 10 Nov 1944, CCI

Keith, Sir Edward (d. **1346**). *See under* Keith family (*per. c.*1300–*c.*1530).

Keith, George, fourth Earl Marischal (1549/50–1623), magnate and founder of Marischal College, Aberdeen, was the eldest son of William, master of Marischal (*c.*1530–1580), and his wife, Elizabeth Hay (*b. c.*1530), daughter of George, seventh earl of Erroll. He was educated with his younger brother William in Paris and at the academy in Geneva, where he studied under the Calvinist theologian Theodore Beza, who held his pupil in high regard; he was schooled in the Latin, Greek, and Hebrew languages, and in ancient history, geography, politics, and rhetoric. After the death of his brother in 1577, during a brawl in the countryside near Geneva, he abandoned his studies to tour the courts of Italy and Germany, and returned to Scotland from France in May 1580. His father died in August, and on 24 October he was appointed a gentleman of the king's bedchamber. He succeeded as Earl Marischal on the death of his grandfather William *Keith, third Earl Marischal, on 7 October 1581, inheriting great estates in the rich farmlands of the north-east. These were reckoned to produce an annual income of 270,000 merks and were regarded as 'the revenue greatest of any earl of Scotland' (Rogers, 8). The third earl's testament was valued at the exceptionally high sum of £44,664 Scots. This huge wealth had accrued through the Keith estates remaining concentrated in the hands of the earls Marischal. As a result the lairds of the Keith kindred were relatively few in number, and Marischal's following was considered small.

A committed protestant, in November 1581 Marischal was elected to a committee to establish a presbytery in the Mearns. The following April the general assembly appointed him a commissioner to investigate Roman Catholic observance in Aberdeenshire. Marischal was married in February 1581 to Margaret (*c.*1565–1598), daughter of Alexander, fifth Lord *Home, and his wife, Margaret, daughter of Sir Walter Ker of Cessford. They had a son, William *Keith, who became fifth Earl Marischal, and two daughters, Anne and Margaret, who married respectively the seventh earl of Morton and Sir Robert Arbuthnott of Arbuthnott.

Marischal attended the convention which met at Holyrood in October 1582 following the Ruthven raid, and was nominated to the privy council. When James VI evaded his captors at Falkland in June 1583 to reach St Andrews Castle, Marischal joined him there. But as he was opposed to the earl of Arran, who was then recalled to government, Marischal left court to avoid offending the king. He resisted initial calls to return to court, but arrived at Stirling in December and was well received by James. When Colonel William Stewart led the king's guard into the Tolbooth during the sitting of the Edinburgh parliament of May 1584, Marischal protested that this action was injurious to his office. On 8 June 1585 he and his brother John were granted a remission for their part in the murder of their kinsman William Keith, eldest son of the laird of Ludquhairn. Marischal favoured *entente* with the English and on 31 July 1585 he voted with the convention in favour of an Anglo-Scottish protestant alliance. When the lords exiled after the collapse of the Ruthven raid returned across the border to march on Stirling in November, Marischal was charged with the defence of the town's West Port, which he conducted with restraint. The following May he was appointed to meet with Elizabeth's commissioners. It is doubtless significant that an anonymous list of the Scottish earls drawn up in this year does not name the thirty-six-year-old Marischal among the many 'malcontents'. On 14 May 1587 he attended a banquet of reconciliation hosted by the king in Edinburgh Castle.

Marischal enjoyed varying relations with his territorial rival, the sixth earl of Huntly, and made constant requests to be exempted from the jurisdiction of the latter's commissions of lieutenancy in the north of Scotland. A tryst between Marischal and Huntly in early 1587 broke down in violence, during which John Keith was slain by

William Gordon of Gight. In March 1589 the earls were called to submit all their feuds to the decision of the king, who formally reconciled them at a dinner in Huntly's Edinburgh lodgings.

On account of his rank and learning Marischal was chosen to lead the embassy sent to arrange James VI's marriage to Anne of Denmark. His great wealth must also have influenced the decision, for he bore most of the initial cost of the embassy. Two ships had been made ready to sail from Leith by May 1589, but when royal orders to embark failed to materialize Marischal dismissed the ships. However, James allowed the ambassadors to sail early the following month and they landed at Copenhagen on 29 June. In the ensuing negotiations the Danes proved unreceptive to the Scots' demands for an exorbitant dowry and Marischal declined to proceed without further instruction from the king. Having dispatched his nephew Lord Dingwall back to Scotland for this, he set off to visit the neighbouring German cities. On Dingwall's return with directions to accept the Danish proposals, negotiations moved apace and the wedding contract was celebrated at Kronburg Castle on 20 August 1589 with Marischal acting as the king's proxy. The Scots and their new queen set sail for Scotland on 5 September, but were prevented from making passage by successive storms, and out of concern for Anne's health the decision was taken to winter in Oslo. The impatient James, writing to Marischal at this point for news of progress, addressed him disparagingly as 'my little fat pork' (Letters of King James VI and I, 95). The king decided to join his bride in Norway and was married to her on 24 November. The following day he issued an act exonerating Marischal from his services. Part of the rest of the Scots' stay in Norway was taken up by a dispute over precedence between Marischal and Sir John Maitland of Thirlestane, which the chancellor won. On his return to Scotland the earl was compensated for his considerable expenses by confirmation of a grant, first made in July 1587, erecting the abbacy of Deer into the lordship of Altrie. The lordship was to be held during his lifetime by the commendator, Marischal's uncle Robert Keith, with remainder to the earl and his heirs.

In July 1591 Marischal was warded in Edinburgh Castle on suspicion of intriguing with the earl of Bothwell, whom he had visited with Lord Home at Crichton Castle. In 1593 he accompanied the king during his campaign against the rebellious northern lords, assisting with the reduction of their houses. While the king was at Aberdeen he lodged at the earl's house in the city. The lieutenancy of the north was divided between Marischal and the earl of Atholl, though Marischal was latterly accused of not exercising his authority sufficiently. At the October convention he was appointed to a commission to try the earls of Angus, Huntly, and Erroll for treason, and during the May parliament of 1594 he was one of the five lords of the articles who voted against their forfeiture.

On 2 April 1593 Marischal founded Marischal College in Aberdeen, endowing the college with the former property of the town's Dominican and Carmelite friars. The foundation charter records that the college was established to counter the lack of education among the young in the north of Scotland. It has been argued that the earl's decision to establish the college as a firmly protestant institution, teaching along humanist lines and using a professorial system, arose from his dissatisfaction at the failure of King's College in Old Aberdeen to reform itself thus. Ten years earlier he had been keenly involved in the promotion of Andrew Melville's 'new foundation' at King's, but royal and parliamentary opposition had frustrated progress there. None the less it seems that aspects of Melville's programme were introduced, and Marischal's agreement to take part in a visitation of the college ordered by the assembly at the end of April 1593 does not suggest that he had despaired of its capacity to reform further. It is more likely that Marischal College was intended to present a challenge to the Catholic party of the northeast, and in particular to its leader Huntly, whose influence in Aberdeen was now in decline. In this remarkable project Marischal received firm support from the Aberdeen ministers David Cunningham and Peter Blackburn, while the burgh, recognizing the prestige the college would bring, offered the old Franciscan buildings to help house it. The foundation was ratified by parliament on 21 July 1593, and the appointment of the college's professors was vested in the earl's family, an arrangement that lasted until the forfeiture of the ninth Earl Marischal in 1716.

Marischal dictated the administrative and academic establishment to be adopted by the college in great detail in its foundation charter. A principal and three rectors were to teach a curriculum composed of the liberal arts and divinity, one designed to equip graduates to become protestant ministers. Concerned that scholars without means should not be deprived of an education, Marischal provided for six bursaries and exempted the poor from all fees. In a bid to secure the goodwill of King's College he invited its principal to assist in the selection of staff, but this overture was rebuffed and thereafter the two colleges remained separate institutions until united as Aberdeen University in 1860. Marischal retained a proprietorial interest in the college's affairs for the rest of his life. In 1619, for instance, he had the college gates locked against a visitation party investigating misconduct alleged against the principal. He also showed his commitment to learning by supporting Thomas Cargill's translation of Hesiod.

Marischal's wife, Margaret Home, died in May 1598. According to tradition she took great pleasure in the news that her half-brother, the sixth Lord Home, had murdered William Lauder, a Lauder bailie who had slighted her, but after a great fit of laughter she developed a swelling in her throat and died within a day. Marischal subsequently married Margaret (b. c.1570), daughter of James, fifth Lord Ogilvy of Airlie. They had four children: James, laird of Benholm, and Alexander, John, and Mary. Both Alexander and Mary died young.

On 14 December 1598 the privy council passed an act regulating attendance at its sessions, dictating that absences without leave extending beyond four days would result in expulsion. Marischal fell foul of this rule the following May, when he failed to reappear after an authorized absence of forty days, exclusion on his estates clearly proving preferable to matters of state. However, he had been readmitted to the council by February 1601, and in 1604 parliament appointed him a commissioner to discuss union with England. In January 1606 the earl and his son Lord Keith were called before the council to account for challenges sent on their instructions to Francis Sinclair, son of the fifth earl of Caithness.

In the same year a dispute arose between Marischal and his cousin, the ninth earl of Erroll, concerning the rights and privileges which attached to their respective offices as high marischal and high constable of Scotland, when both men claimed the right to keep the keys of the parliament house. The controversy was no doubt precipitated by other disagreements between them nearer home. After deliberation the council decided that the keeping of the outer bar was the responsibility of the constable, while that of the inner bar fell to the marischal. The matter was raised again by Erroll the following July, but the earlier decision was upheld.

Marischal was one of the assessors who in March 1609 participated in the underhand treason trial of Lord Balmerino at St Andrews. On 6 June the king chose him to replace the late earl of Montrose as his commissioner to the Scottish parliament. When the privy council was restructured to have thirty-five members in February 1610 Marischal was renominated to it. That same year the general assembly appointed him to sit in the new court of ecclesiastical high commission for the diocese of St Andrews, and he continued to be a member of the commission after its courts were unified in 1615. At the Perth general assembly of 1618 he voted for the changes in worship embodied in King James's five articles of Perth. In his last years Marischal retired from public life to Dunnottar Castle, Kincardineshire. He died there on 2 April 1623 and was buried locally, in the parish church. On 30 June a funeral oration was delivered at Marischal College by the professor of moral philosophy, William Ogston, who praised the college's founder as a religious man, devoted to Bible reading and meditation, prayer, and good works. His king remembered him as 'that man, who had to our honour and contentment served us at home and abroad in greatest charges' (*Reg. PCS*, 13.591).

JOHN SIMMONS

Sources CSP Scot., 1547–1603 · Reg. PCS, 1st ser., 13.591 · G. D. Henderson, *The founding of Marischal College Aberdeen* (1947) · GEC, *Peerage* · Scots peerage, 6.46–54 · D. Calderwood, *The history of the Kirk of Scotland*, ed. T. Thomson and D. Laing, 8 vols., Wodrow Society, 7 (1842–9) · J. M. Thomson and others, eds., *Registrum magni sigilli regum Scotorum / The register of the great seal of Scotland*, 11 vols. (1882–1914), vols. 4–8 · D. Stevenson, *Scotland's last royal wedding: the marriage of James VI and Anne of Denmark* (1997) · P. J. Anderson and J. F. K. Johnstone, eds., *Fasti academiae Mariscallanae Aberdonensis: selections from the records of the Marischal College and University, MDXCIII–MDCCCLX*, 3 vols., New Spalding Club, 4, 18–19 (1889–98) · *Letters of King James VI & I*, ed. G. P. V. Akrigg (1984) · A. Hay, *Estimate of the Scottish nobility during the minority of James the Sixth*, ed. C. Rogers, Grampian Club (1873)

Likenesses C. Alexander, portrait, U. Aberdeen

Keith, George (1638?–1716), Quaker schismatic and Church of England clergyman, was born in Aberdeenshire; the names of his parents are unknown, though he may have been given his Christian name after his father. He attended Marischal College, Aberdeen, where he graduated MA in 1657. Gilbert Burnet, later bishop of Salisbury, was one of his classmates. Keith made his way to Edinburgh for a while, where he became a tutor in a nobleman's family. He stayed in contact with Burnet, though, and together they explored the writings of the Cambridge Platonists. These works—especially those of Henry More—encouraged both men to seek a closer relationship with God, and both deserted presbyterianism because of them. More was himself aghast to learn later that one of his books had influenced Keith to become a Quaker, as Keith maintained. Though George Fox had not made it as far into Scotland as Aberdeen, there was a small circle of Friends there led by Alexander Jaffray and Robert Barclay. Keith eventually fell in with this circle, and was the first in the region to publish an apology for Quakerism.

Keith had turned Quaker just in time for the fury of Restoration persecution, and he was expelled from Aberdeen for his refusal to conform. He returned, and was imprisoned in the Tolbooth and beaten in 1664. This treatment seems only to have strengthened his resolve: while 'prisoner for the truth' (as he himself put it), he wrote several books, notably *Immediate Revelation* (1668), which was intended to prove that direct revelation was still possible. This was one of the earliest systematic writings of the Quakers. Since the sect emphasized experience rather than doctrine, most Quaker writings were emotive rather than systematic. But Keith had been trained as a logician, and was loath to abandon the tradition entirely. So he used his training in the service of Quakerism. Not long after he was released from the Tolbooth, Keith was emboldened to preach at the cathedral in Aberdeen, only to be rewarded for his efforts afterwards by being knocked to the ground by the bell-ringer. In the late 1660s Keith returned to Edinburgh and continued to defend Quaker ideas and write apologies for the sect. He worked closely with Robert Barclay, travelling around the countryside proselytizing, and was imprisoned at least once more during this period.

In 1670 Keith was released on condition that he leave Edinburgh. He obeyed, and made his way to London. This opened up a whole new chapter in his life. In London, Keith fell in with William Penn and George Whitehead as well as George Fox, and developed a close working relationship with these Quaker leaders that would last for two decades. He befriended Henry More, who liked Keith and called him 'the best Quaker of them all' (*Conway Letters*, 307). He was also part of Lady Conway's circle at Ragley, and spent time there with Francis Mercury von Helmont, the German philosopher–mystic. He and von Helmont speculated about the possibility of the transmigration of souls. In London, moreover, Keith began a career of controversial writing. He evidently relished controversy, for he was engaged in many pamphlet wars over his lifetime.

More noted that Keith was 'rudely and unjudiciously schismaticall' (ibid., 307). The first salvo was an attack by Robert Gordon, cousin of Robert Barclay, over Christology. Gordon charged the Quakers with Socinianism. Keith answered him in *The Light of Truth Triumphing* (1670) and *Universal Grace* (1671).

In 1671 Keith married Elizabeth Johnston, a gentlewoman, whose mother had been among the first converts in Aberdeen. She was evidently a faithful companion to her husband, a good mother (and bore at least three daughters), and even converted to Anglicanism when George did. Keith travelled a good deal during these years: he visited Ireland; accompanied George Fox, William Penn, and Robert Barclay to the Netherlands and Germany; and was often in Scotland (he was in Aberdeen for the formal organization of a Friends meeting, and was persecuted in Edinburgh). He was frequently in the company of Robert Barclay, and the two had a major debate with theological students at the University of Aberdeen in 1675. Barclay seems to have been influenced by Keith's arguments, for he took many of them for his own. And always there was controversy. Keith wrote against the Baptists in London, and felt that he had to respond to the charges of the clergymen of Edinburgh that Quakers were crypto-Catholics. In the early 1680s Keith was master of the Quaker school at Waltham Abbey. Since he was not licensed by the bishop of London, however, legal proceedings were brought against him. This was simply one more in a long line of prosecutions against Keith. He, like the other Quakers, had suffered often for his beliefs. With the exception of a brief window of toleration around the declaration of indulgence of 1672, Keith was in and out of prison and was often fined for his activities. Since he refused on principle to pay the fines, the penalty amounted to the same thing as imprisonment, as he was incarcerated for refusing the fines. In 1682 he and seven others refused the oaths and were hauled into gaol. In February 1684 he was moved to Newgate in London, and was not released until August of that year.

In 1684, however, a new opportunity offered itself. Shortly after he was released from Newgate, Keith was appointed as the surveyor-general of the colony of East Jersey. Though his life in America was much more tranquil than that in England and Scotland, he succeeded in stirring up controversy there as well: the boundary line he established between East and West Jersey was bitterly disputed and successfully challenged. Further, Keith could not resist railing against a sect of Ranters, or even criticizing the new generation of Quakers, who were, he believed, in danger of departing from orthodoxy because of their careless disregard of doctrine and teaching. He also tried to goad the Boston clergy (Cotton Mather, Samuel Willard, James Allen, and Joshua Moody) into debate, but they would not take their cue from him. Thus thwarted, he finally published a repudiation of their doctrines in *The Presbyterian and Independent visible churches in New England and elsewhere brought to the test* (1689). In 1689 he accepted a position as schoolmaster in Philadelphia, but did not stay long in this position. He was evidently preparing to leave the New World soon after, when he precipitated a new controversy that would eventually end in his repudiation of Quakerism altogether. Keith had decided that it was important for Quakers to develop a creed that would place them within acceptable bounds of Christological orthodoxy, and tried to foist such a creed on his brethren, but they baulked since this was contrary to Quaker tradition and practice.

Schism Whether it was a long-brewing dispute or a short-term conflict is debated, but at the yearly meeting of Quakers in Philadelphia in 1691 a row occurred that caused much acrimony between Keith and his Quaker brethren. William Stockdale, one of the early Quaker settlers, accused Keith of heresy, of preaching two Christs because he overemphasized the two separate natures of the Saviour. The issue arose because of Keith's public dispute with a Rhode Island physician, Christian Lodowick, who claimed that Quakers did not recognize the human Christ. In his reply to Lodowick, *The Christian faith of the people of God called Quakers, vindicated from the calumnies of Christian Lodowick* (1691), Keith had emphasized that Quakers accepted the historic, physical Christ. This led Stockdale to criticize him for advocating a dualistic Christology. Keith was, as always, ready for a fight, and he struck back with counter-charges against Stockdale. He demanded that a series of Quaker meetings be held to establish whether he or Stockdale was the heretic. The meetings, however, failed to arrive at any definitive answer.

At the January 1692 monthly meeting in Philadelphia, Keith discovered that a new charge was levelled against him for 'denying the Sufficiency of the Light' within (G. Keith, *Some Reasons and Causes of the Late Separation*, 1692, 8). This charge was taken seriously, but was not proven. But the episode exacerbated the acrimony, and polarized the Quakers into two hostile groups. In the spring Keith's opponents secretly changed the meeting time and locked him and his followers out of the meeting-house, an action which Keith maintained was the cause of the schism (ibid., 15–16). Keith also published his account of the controversy in *Some Reasons and Causes*, thereby making the dispute public, and was more and more vociferous about the errors of the Friends. The issues were taken up again at the yearly meeting of 1692. Though approximately a quarter of those present backed Keith, the meeting officially branded Keith a schismatic and condemned him in strong terms. Keith was livid and vowed to appeal to the London yearly meeting. He had one more trial to endure in Pennsylvania before he returned to England, however: he was accused of libelling Quaker magistrates who had found it necessary to send an armed expedition against a group of pirates. Keith maintained that Quakers should stay out of government because they inevitably would have to act contrary to their beliefs. For his intemperate speech, Keith was fined.

While this was going on, Keith and his adherents managed to keep meeting with the other Quakers, but they were relegated to the rear of the meeting-house. But Keith could not be clearly heard from this vantage point. His followers, therefore, built a gallery that raised him off the floor and made it impossible for him to be ignored. Eventually, a group of Friends who were piqued by this insolence tore down the gallery. From this time on, Keith and his followers met separately, distinguishing themselves as 'Christian Quakers'. Keith had previously used the term to emphasize the fact that the Quakers were true Christians, but now he began to use it to designate his splinter group.

The Christian Quaker Keith returned to England in 1693, where the controversy dragged on. The London yearly meeting tried for nearly two years to reconcile the two parties, but finally realized that this was impossible. At the 1694 yearly meeting Keith was expelled. After this Keith's (as well as the Quakers') pugnacity knew no bounds: he bitterly attacked the Quaker leaders, such as George Whitehead, called them heretics, and claimed that they 'pretended' to infallible teachings to gain absolute authority, were motivated by 'the Praise of Men', and had endangered the souls of their followers (G. Keith, *Gross Error and Hypocrisie Detected, in George Whitehead, and Some of his Brethren*, 1695). He came to believe that Christian Lodowick's claims were true of most of the Quaker leaders: they had departed from Christian orthodoxy by emphasizing the inner light at the expense of the historic and physical nature of Christ. Keith attacked William Penn, too, and maintained that he was virtually a deist or a pagan because he said 'that there is one general Rule of Faith and Life to all Mankind' (G. Keith, *The Deism of William Penn and his Brethren … Laid Open*, 1699). He also wrote a massive answer to Robert Barclay's *Apology*, averring that it was the 'most Heterodox and unsound, of any System, that ever I think in this Age was Published' (G. Keith, *The Standard of the Quakers Examined, or, An Answer to the Apology of Robert Barclay*, 1702, 507).

Keith had held separate meetings for his partisans even before his excommunication, but afterwards he redoubled his efforts. He created a centre for them at Turner's Hall in London and tried to maintain a separate organization of 'Christian Quakers'. But the tendency to drift into other established Christian organizations was too strong; though the Turner's Hall meetings continued, most of Keith's adherents conformed to more established groups. Keith himself accepted the invitation of the Society for Promoting Christian Knowledge, and wrote and travelled for the SPCK around England, preaching the errors of Quakerism. He caused a stir in London with his constant badgering of Quakers: he wrote pamphlets and personally interrupted their meetings. He was known for attracting huge crowds and befuddling his Quaker opposition. Though he had already made an alliance with the SPCK, it still remained for him to conform officially. This he did in February 1700. And only three months after that, he was ordained deacon by the bishop of London. The news of his conformity stunned the public. One pamphlet trumpeted it under the title *One Wonder More Added to the Seven Wonders of the World* (1700).

Anglican missionary In 1702 Keith was ordained priest. Soon after, he was sent back to America as an Anglican missionary under the auspices of the fledgeling Society for the Propagation of the Gospel in Foreign Parts. Keith made Boston his headquarters and, predictably, quickly ran into opposition. He stirred up no less an adversary than Increase Mather, who criticized him for having left one error only to fall into another one equally great. He also sparred with Samuel Willard, president of Harvard College, but his main target was the Quakers, and he harried them with all of his energy. Keith was tireless, riding from town to town, preaching and disputing. His favourite trick was to attend Quaker meetings and bait the attendees into answering his queries. Keith attracted crowds wherever he went—he always provided a good show—but it is not clear how successful he was or how many conversions he obtained. He did manage to baptize a good number of people, but many of these had already been his partisans. Certainly he found most Quakers steadfast in their resistance. But the Society for the Propagation of the Gospel was very happy with his labours and made him a member for life. He continued to be a popular consultant on Quakers and Quakerism for the society until his death.

Keith returned to England in the summer of 1704. He kept himself busy with publications until, in 1705, he was granted the living of St Andrew's Church in Edburton, Sussex, by the archbishop of Canterbury. So he and his two daughters, Elizabeth and Margaret, moved to the rectory there. For the first few years he continued his crusade against Quakerism by sponsoring meetings locally and by writing for the SPCK. But by 1710 Keith had succumbed to illness, and it dogged him the rest of his life. He tried valiantly to continue his duties as a pastor, but was sometimes so poorly that he had to be carried to church. Keith died in March 1716 and was buried at Edburton on 29 March, leaving all his worldly goods to his daughters.

Assessment There is something of a mystery about Keith's disenchantment with, and conversion from, Quakerism, and his subsequent zeal for the established church. After all, he turned against his friends, colleagues, and confidants of nigh on thirty years. Despite the fact that Keith himself wrote down explanations, historians have disagreed about what motivated him. Edward J. Cody saw the flare-up in Pennsylvania simply as a result of Keith's drive for religious purity (Cody, 1–19), but this ignores the question of why it took thirty years for such intractable hostilities to develop. Ethyn Kirby, Keith's biographer, maintained that he had always been different from the Friends' norm, and that it was only a matter of time until he stretched his Quakerism too far. Gradually he saw the need to rein in the excesses of those who emphasized the inner light to the exclusion of the historic 'outer' nature of Christ and the gospel. He himself had never denied the externals, even if he had revelled a bit too much in the idea of the inner light. It was a gradual change in emphasis rather than a radical shift of perspective. When Keith tried to rein in the worst excesses, he encountered resistance and, ultimately, an explosion (Kirby, 46, 53, 55). Frederick Storrs Turner had a view similar to that of Kirby, but differed in that he maintained that while George Fox lived Keith was overpowered by his vision and charisma. After Fox died, however, Keith quickly saw things in a different light, and was very soon striving with his erstwhile brethren (Turner, 253–60). But Gary Nash found the causes of the conflict in a very different realm: he suggested that the controversy that ended in Keith's schism was less a religious issue than the result of the tumultuous environment of political and economic divisions in Pennsylvania (Nash, 144–60). Jon Butler countered that none of these perspectives is correct. He argued that Keith did indeed change, and that when he proposed his *Gospel Order Improved* he threatened not only the non-creedal tradition of Quakerism but also the developing leadership of the Pennsylvania group. Though Quakers had abandoned the idea of formal clergy, the Quakers in Pennsylvania had been evolving leadership with tighter control and authority—the so-called 'Public Friends' (Butler, 431–52). This theory gives credence to Keith's claim that the leaders had arrogated to themselves arbitrary power by claiming they had the 'Light Within'.

Keith himself, however, would have been most happy with Kirby's analysis. He claimed that he had erred in his early Quaker years in emphasis, but not in fundamentals. He was humble enough to admit that he had in those days overemphasized the inner light and had slighted scripture as a primary rule, but he steadfastly maintained that he had never veered so far from the truth as had the Quakers of the late seventeenth and early eighteenth centuries. It is also likely that Keith, with his combative nature, was the sort who needed an 'enemy' to oppose. It may not be a coincidence that soon after the persecution of the Quakers declined because of toleration, he found enemies within his own camp.

J. S. CHAMBERLAIN

Sources E. W. Kirby, *George Keith, 1638–1716* (1942) · J. W. Frost, *The Keithian controversy in early Pennsylvania* (1980) · *The Conway letters: the correspondence of Anne, Viscountess Conway, Henry More, and their friends, 1642–1684*, ed. M. H. Nicolson, rev. edn, ed. S. Hutton (1992) · M. Nicolson, 'George Keith and the Cambridge Platonists', *Philosophical Review*, 39 (Jan 1930), 36–55 · J. Butler, 'Gospel order improved: the Keithian schism and the exercise of Quaker ministerial authority', *William and Mary Quarterly*, 31 (1974), 431–52 · C. Leslie, *The snake in the grass or Satan transform'd to an angel of light, discovering the deep and unsuspected subtilty which is couched under the simplicity, of many of the principal leaders of those people call'd Quakers*, 3rd edn (1698), 61–76, 111–12, 259–61, 281–3, 332ff. · E. J. Cody, 'The price of perfection: the irony of George Keith', *Pennsylvania History*, 39 (1972), 1–19 · W. C. Braithwaite, *The beginnings of Quakerism*, ed. H. J. Cadbury, 2nd edn (1955) · J. Gough, *A history of the people called Quakers, from their first rise to the present time*, 4 vols. (1789–90) · BL, Dunkin MSS, Add. MS 32326, fol. 54 · abstract letter-book, Society for Promoting Christian Knowledge, London, CRI 1:1374, 1392, 1464, 1830, 2312, 2763 · *A journal or historical account of … George Fox*, ed. [T. Ellwood], 1 (1694), 433, 435, 452, 454, 521 · G. Keith to T. Bradbury, 1697, BL, Add. MS 4276, fol. 8 · BL, Stowe MS 305 [Latin epigram on George Keith], fol. 241b · G. Keith to Lady Conway, 6 day, 3d month, 1677, BL, Add. MS 23217, fol. 21 · F. S. Turner, *The Quakers: a study historical and critical* (1889) · G. B. Nash, *Quakers and politics: Pennsylvania, 1681–1726* (1968)

Archives Bodl. Oxf., Harley MS 3778 · Bodl. Oxf., Rawlinson MS 743 · Bodl. Oxf., Walker MS C.3.32 · Bodl. RH, letters to SPG · LPL, corresp. with SPG

Keith, George, styled tenth Earl Marischal (1692/3?–1778), Jacobite army officer and diplomatist in the Prussian service, was the eldest son of William *Keith, ninth Earl Marischal (c.1664–1712) [*see under* Drummond, Lady Mary] and Lady Mary *Drummond (1675–1729), eldest daughter of James Drummond, fourth earl and Jacobite first duke of Perth, chancellor of Scotland. Although he stated in the preface to his memoir that he was born in 1689, he was described as being in his eighty-sixth year at death, suggesting that he was born in 1692 or 1693; the birth probably took place at Inverugie Castle, Aberdeenshire.

At some point between 1708 and 1711 Keith served under the duke of Marlborough in Flanders. He succeeded to the earldom on his father's death, 27 May 1712. On 3 February 1714 he was appointed captain of the Scottish troop of Horse Grenadier Guards. After the death of Queen Anne he nearly proclaimed her half-brother James Francis Edward Stuart, the Pretender, as James VIII and III before his troop, but the council of his fearful fellow Jacobites dissuaded him. After resigning or being deprived of his commission, Marischal returned to Scotland. On the way north he met his brother James Francis Edward *Keith, who was heading to London to lobby for a promotion, and persuaded him to reverse his steps. Marischal attended the meeting convened by John Erskine, twenty-third or sixth earl of Mar, at Aboyne on 27 August 1715, when some of the Scottish Jacobites decided to rise on behalf of the Pretender. At the tactically indecisive but strategically disastrous battle of Sheriffmuir, he commanded two squadrons of horse. Marischal's house at Newburgh provided the Pretender with a place to sleep on his second night in Scotland, 23 December, and he hosted James's first privy council on Scottish soil at his mansion of Fetteresso, Kincardineshire. Marischal and Mar accompanied James when he made his entry into Dundee. As the Jacobites retreated from Perth to Montrose, Marischal supposedly was to accompany James to France, but the plan went awry and the Pretender sailed without him. After the Jacobite army dispersed, he made his own way to the continent.

In 1716 the Hanoverian government attainted Marischal for treason and forfeited his estates to the crown: he was one of the few Scots to suffer such a heavy penalty for resisting the new dynasty. Marischal remained a devoted Jacobite, living in Paris and then in Madrid. In 1719 he received command of the Spanish expedition to impose James on Scotland. It landed first (4–5 April) on the island of Lewis, off the west coast of Scotland. A plan rapidly to seize Inverness failed when disputes between Marischal and William Murray, marquess of Tullibardine, with whom he shared command, caused delays fatal to achieving that end. Eventually the Jacobites reached Wester Ross, where on 10 June General Joseph Wightman, deputy commander-in-chief in Scotland, attacked them near the

George Keith, styled tenth Earl Marischal (1692/3?–1778), by John Simon (after Pierre Parrocel, c.1716)

pass of Glenshiel. In the ensuing battle the Scots highlanders fled into the hills and the Spanish surrendered. Marischal, severely wounded, escaped to the Western Isles, where he hid for several months before embarking in disguise for Spain. He lived there for some years, chiefly at Valencia, although he attended the Jacobite court at least once (in 1732). During those years he was a major adviser of the Pretender and one of his ambassadors to the Spanish court, for which he became a Jacobite knight of the Thistle in 1725. He remained involved in the numerous, but futile, plans to restore the Stuarts. Following the outbreak of war between Spain and Britain, in 1740 he was sent by the Pretender to Madrid to persuade the Spanish to sponsor another expedition to Britain. He remained sceptical of Spanish interest in the scheme, of which nothing in fact came.

In 1744, when France planned a major attack on Britain, Marischal was to be commander-in-chief in Scotland. During the wait for the embarkation Marischal became well acquainted with Charles Edward Stuart, the Pretender's heir. It was the start of an extremely sour relationship. Marischal's proud, distant, arrogant, and pessimistic manner contrasted entirely with the needs of the optimistic princeling, and Marischal came to hate the younger man. The French abandoned the attempt, much to Marischal's relief and Charles Edward's disgust. Marischal headed to the papal enclave of Avignon, having persuaded the French court that service by Charles in Flanders against the British would be unwise. As a result his credit

with both James and his son plummeted. However, in summer 1745 he was back at Versailles negotiating on behalf of the Jacobites and was still the prospective Jacobite captain-general in Scotland, but took no part in the 1745 rising there.

After returning to Spain, Marischal then went to Vienna, and in 1747 proceeded to Prussia to join his brother, who had just left the Russian army. In April 1749 he rejected the post of secretary of state to Charles, pleading ill health. In February 1751 he arranged a meeting between Charles and Frederick II (the Great) of Prussia in Berlin, laying the groundwork for an episode of Jacobite-Prussian scheming, but more importantly heralding a fresh start to his career. On 28 August Marischal left Potsdam to become Prussian ambassador to France. The appointment of a notorious Jacobite and forfeited traitor infuriated the British government. However, the situation was far more complex than it seemed. While Marischal had refused to undertake any commission from the Jacobite court after Culloden, he assiduously carried out the orders of the Prussian king. Marischal's insistence that the English Jacobites should act for the cause only at his approval led him to sabotage the plans of Charles. In 1752 Frederick gave him the order of the Black Eagle and made him governor of Neufchâtel; his secretary of the legation, Baron Knyphausen, succeeded him as envoy in Paris. Throughout his embassy he had played an intimate, yet undermining role in the Jacobite Elibank plot, named after the Jacobite agent Alexander Murray of Elibank.

Marischal's conversion from Scot to Prussian is apparent from his career after 1753. In a letter of 15 April 1754, responding to Charles's request for a meeting, he refused, stating that his duty was entirely to Frederick and not the Jacobites. On the death of his brother Marshal Keith at the battle of Hochkirch on 13 October 1758, Frederick sent him a letter of condolence signed 'your old friend till death'. From 1759 to 1761 he served Frederick as Prussian ambassador to Spain, where he reputedly informed the Hanoverian government (which, although Frederick's ally, he should, if a loyal Jacobite, have treated as an implacable enemy) of the Spanish preparations to enter the war as a French ally. As a result of this signal service, he was pardoned by George II on 29 May 1759, but he remained attainted and was unable to use his title formally in Great Britain. In 1760 the British parliament passed an act allowing him to inherit the estate of his kinsman William Keith, fourth earl of Kintore, which he did on 22 November 1761, but his attainder prevented him from inheriting the earldom. Marischal returned to Scotland, but was back in Neufchâtel by April 1762, where he entertained Jean-Jacques Rousseau. In August 1763 he again left Potsdam, going to Scotland with the intention of reviving his estates. While in Scotland he bemused opinion by taking 'about with him a young ex-Mohammedan girl whom every one believed to be his mistress' (Greig, 357). In 1761 parliament had passed a special act concerning his forfeited estates, which had been sold in 1720 for £3618 sterling. Marischal was granted the sale price plus interest on the sum accrued from Whitsunday 1721. On 20

February 1764 he purchased the Marischal estates centring on Dunnottar for £31,320 at auction against no other bidders. Some weeks later he received a letter from Frederick, written on 16 February, promising peace, friendship, liberty, and philosophy if he returned to Prussia. Finding the Scottish climate disagreeably harsh, and Frederick's pleas pleasing, Marischal left his native land for good. In 1766 he sold the recovered Marischal lands to Alexander Keith of Ravelston. Frederick had a villa cottage built for him near the palace at Potsdam. Marischal lived there, a close and valued friend of the king until his death at Potsdam on 28 May 1778. He never married, and a kinsman, Anthony Falconer, seventh Lord Falconer of Halkertoun, inherited the Kintore estate and earldom. He maintained a friendship with Voltaire and impressed Rousseau with his noble face. Marischal's lengthy devotion to the Stuart cause appears to have been sustained entirely by principle, but his later career in the service of the Prussian royal house, although characterized by the esteem and friendship of Frederick, and loyalty to his brother Marshal Keith, reflected more closely the demands of self-interest. EDWARD M. FURGOL

Sources *Calendar of the Stuart papers belonging to his majesty the king, preserved at Windsor Castle*, 7 vols., HMC, 56 (1902–23) · *A fragment of a memoir of Field-Marshal James Keith, written by himself, 1714–1734*, ed. T. Constable, Spalding Club, 8 (1843) · GEC, *Peerage*, new edn, vol. 8 · F. McLynn, *Charles Edward Stuart* (1991) · *The Jacobite attempt of 1719: letters of James Butler, second duke of Ormonde, relating to Cardinal Alberoni's project for the invasion of Great Britain on behalf of the Stuarts, and to the landing of a Spanish expedition in Scotland*, ed. W. K. Dickson, Scottish History Society, 19 (1895) · T. Carlyle, *History of Friedrich II of Prussia, called Frederick the Great*, new edn, 6 vols. (1858–65) · DNB · J. Y. T. Greig, 'Two fragments of autobiography by George Keith, 10th Earl Marischal of Scotland', *Miscellany … V*, Scottish History Society, 3rd ser., 21 (1933), 355–74
Archives NA Scot., corresp. and papers · NL Scot., corresp. and papers · U. Aberdeen L., corresp. and papers · U. Aberdeen L., letters | Royal Arch., Stuart papers, corresp. with duke of Mar and the Old Pretender, James Stuart · U. Aberdeen L., letters to George Keith Elphinstone
Likenesses P. Parrocel, oils, c.1715–1720, U. Aberdeen, Marischal College; version, Scot. NPG · attrib. P. Costanzi, oils, NPG · J. Simon, mezzotint (after P. Parrocel, c.1716), BM, Scot. NPG [see illus.] · relief ivory medallion, BM · two portraits, U. Aberdeen

Keith, George Skene (1752–1823), Church of Scotland minister and writer, was born on 6 November 1752 in the Old House of Aquhorsk in Mar, near Aberdeen, the eldest son of James Keith, and grandson of Professor Thomas Keith of Marischal College, Aberdeen. He was the lineal representative of the Keiths of Aquhorsk, descendants of Alexander Keith, third son of the second Earl Marischal. He took the degree of MA from Marischal College, Aberdeen, in 1770, and was licensed by the presbytery of Aberdeen on 14 July 1774.

Keith was presented by the commissioners for George Keith, tenth Earl Marischal, to the living of Keith Hall and Kinkell, Caskieben, Aberdeenshire, on 9 May 1776, but the next day the Earl Marischal, who was living in Potsdam, gave a presentation to Thomas Tait, minister of Old Machar. After legal proceedings before the church courts and the court of session, the case was finally decided in

Keith's favour by the House of Lords in April 1778, and Keith was ordained to the living on 14 May 1778. He contributed an account of the parishes of Keith Hall and Kinkell to Sir John Sinclair's *Statistical Account of Scotland* (1791), edited the *Lectures on Ecclesiastical History* by his friend Professor George Campbell, principal of Marischal College, with a memoir (1800), and published several sermons. He never completed his 'System of political philosophy' which he began in 1797. Keith was awarded the degree of DD from Marischal College in 1803.

On 26 August 1783 Keith married Helen (*d*. 1798), daughter of James Simpson, merchant of Old Meldrum; they had four sons and three daughters. Their eldest son, James, was killed during the retreat from Kabul in 1839; their son Alexander *Keith (1792–1880) wrote on the fulfilment of prophecy; and their son John succeeded his father as minister at Keith-Hall, following Keith's move to the living of Tulliallan, Perthshire, in 1822.

For over thirty years Keith investigated methods for equalizing weights and measures, and strongly supported the adoption of the seconds pendulum as a standard. His plan was laid before a committee of parliament in January 1790 by Sir John Riggs Miller MP, who intended to bring in a bill on the subject; but it came to nothing because of the dissolution of parliament. Keith's pamphlet, *Synopsis of a System of Equalization of Weights and Measures of Great Britain* (1791), was praised by Sir Joseph Banks, and in 1817 Keith published *Different Methods of Establishing an Uniformity of Weights and Measures*.

Keith was much interested in agricultural matters. In 1798 he gave evidence before the Scottish distillery committee of the House of Commons on the malt tax. In 1799, at the request of the committee and of the Scottish board of excise, he did a series of experiments on distillation. His results were printed in the appendix to the committee's report, 1798–9. Keith did more experiments in 1802–3 for the commissioners of excise in Scotland. In 1803 he again gave evidence before a committee of the House of Commons on the proportion of the malt tax levied in England and Scotland, and in 1804 he took part in a discussion about the distilling experiments that had been undertaken for the Scottish commissioners. The House of Commons voted Keith £500 to pay for his experiments. In 1800 he drew up the main points for a new Corn Bill, which was handed to the corn committee of the House of Lords by Sir W. Pulteney.

Keith's most important publication was *A General View of the Agriculture of Aberdeenshire* (1811), drawn up under the direction of the board of agriculture, with 'Observations on British grasses' and a 'Short account of two journeys undertaken with a view to ascertain the elevation of the principal mountains in the division of Marr' in the appendix. His other works included *Tracts on the Reform of the British Constitution* (1793), *An Impartial and Comprehensive View of the Present State of Great Britain* (1797), *Observations on the Bill for the Sale of Corn by Weight* (1797), and *Dissertation on the Excellence of the British Constitution* (1800).

Keith died on 7 March 1823 at his home, Tulliallan

House, Perthshire, and was buried in the churchyard of Keith Hall. A large white marble tablet was erected in his memory.   BERTHA PORTER, *rev.* ANNE PIMLOTT BAKER

Sources Desmond, *Botanists*, rev. edn · R. Douglas, *The peerage of Scotland*, 2nd edn, ed. J. P. Wood, 2 vols. (1813) · *Fasti Scot.* · private information (1886) · *Edinburgh Magazine and Literary Miscellany*, 91 (1823), 647 · 'Report of the committee to consider the state of the distillery in Scotland', *British Sessional Papers: Reports*, 24 (1798–9), 360–62, no. 156 · 'Select committee … on rate of duty on malt', *Parl. papers* (1803–4), 5.16–29, no. 129 · *Monthly Review*, new ser., 6 (1791), 95–7 · *Monthly Review*, new ser., 10 (1793), 93, 191
Archives U. Aberdeen L., letters to Lord Keith
Likenesses miniature, priv. coll.

Keith, James, Baron Keith of Avonholm (1886–1964), judge, was born on 20 May 1886 at Hamilton, the eldest child of Sir Henry Shanks Keith, merchant and authority on local government, and his wife, Elizabeth, daughter of John Hamilton. Educated at Hamilton Academy and Glasgow University, where he graduated MA with first-class honours in history (1908) and thereafter LLB (1908), Keith was admitted to the Faculty of Advocates in 1911 and rapidly acquired a large practice before its interruption by war service. He was commissioned in the Seaforth Highlanders in 1914 and served in France, where a wound put an end to his active service. In 1915 he married Jean Maitland, daughter of Andrew Bennet, solicitor, of Arbroath; they had one son and two daughters.

Later in the war, having been attached to the Egyptian army, Keith held official appointments under the Sudan government. So attracted was he by Sudan that he seriously considered making his career in that country's service, but eventually decided to return to practice at the Scottish bar. He recovered at once his extensive junior practice in all types of work, and especially work concerned with local government, licensing, and property law. He took silk in 1926. His advocacy was notable for its masterly presentation of law and fact and was marked by integrity, perception, and contempt for the verbose. He was elected dean of the Faculty of Advocates, the chosen leader of the Scottish bar, in 1936.

In 1937 Keith was appointed lord commissioner of justiciary and senator of the college of justice, and took his seat upon the bench with the judicial title of Lord Keith. This appointment was warmly welcomed by the profession as a whole. A strong, conscientious, and hardworking judge of independent mind, both in the outer house and subsequently in the inner house, Lord Keith manifested in his opinions the same forthright and lucid presentation reinforced by cogent powers of reasoning as had distinguished his advocacy. When in due course he came to sit in the first division, that court was presided over by Lord Cooper, a profound scholar and an innovator impatient of the obsolete or pettifogging. While Lord Keith was his colleague, the lord president presided, but did not necessarily dominate. Keith was noted for his independence of approach, and his not infrequent dissenting opinions still illuminate the law no less than do the opinions he delivered when concurring with the majority.

Keith was a very effective member of the royal commission on marriage and divorce (the Morton commission) to which he was appointed in 1951, and his incisive and independent views are reflected in the report. His preference for a clean break on divorce so far as property rights are concerned, although not a popular view, has practical social advantages. On another major social issue he had the courage to change his mind. Before the royal commission on capital punishment reported, Keith supported the retention of the death penalty for deliberate murder; after the Homicide Act, 1957, he advocated the abolition of this punishment.

In 1953, when Lord Normand retired as lord of appeal in ordinary, Keith had to make another crucial decision affecting his career. Although judicial office in the House of Lords is perhaps the highest aspiration of an English lawyer, this is not necessarily true of Scottish judges who have spent their professional lives in Edinburgh and who have over the years developed strong social, cultural, and personal ties in Scotland. Keith was essentially a Scot in speech, outlook, and lifestyle, and, of course, a member of the close-knit community—geographically and professionally—of the Scottish bench and bar. It was no easy matter to decide to move to London from the Georgian New Town of Edinburgh, with easy access to Muirfield, where he could find relaxation in golf. However, since a strong Scottish judge was required in London to replace Normand, Keith consented to be 'drafted', and found perhaps more fulfilment as lord of appeal in ordinary from 1953 to 1961 than he had anticipated. On being created a life peer in 1953 he took the title of Keith of Avonholm. In the same year he was sworn of the privy council, and, when he sat in the judicial committee of the privy council, earlier interests in the law and administration of other countries overseas were revived. Even after he retired as lord of appeal in ordinary he continued to sit from time to time on the judicial committee of the privy council. In the highest courts in London he was both liked and respected by his English colleagues, and in 1953 he was elected an honorary bencher of the Inner Temple. His contributions in the highest appellate courts were fresh, original, and not infrequently dissenting. Several of his dissenting speeches, such as in *White and Carter (Councils) Ltd.* v. *McGregor* (1962), a case on anticipatory breach of contract, point to the solutions which may well eventually prevail. It was said that there was a kind of perennial youth about Keith. He changed little over the years and despite his interest in outdoor sports he seemed to walk alone. His mind was independent, always alert to consider an argument, and his speech direct. There was nothing superficial in his legal thinking.

A man of exceptional physical and mental energy, with a special interest in scholarship and the young, throughout his professional life in Scotland Keith gave freely of his time and counsel to various aspects of public service. He was a trustee of the National Library of Scotland from its foundation in 1925 to 1937, and succeeded Normand as convener of the standing committee of trustees. From 1942 to 1946 he was chairman of the Scottish youth advisory committee appointed by the secretary of state for

Scotland, and in 1943–9 was chairman of the Scottish Probation Council. Other bodies on which he served included the Scottish advisory committee on physical training and recreation, the Scottish Council for National Parks, the Red Cross Society, and the Scottish Youth Hostels' Association.

About two years before he died Keith lost completely the use of his legs, an affliction which was particularly grievous to one of his interests and temperament. He accepted his condition with his accustomed courage and without self-pity. His son, Henry Shanks Keith, in 1971 took his seat as a senator of the college of justice and lord commissioner of justiciary with the judicial title of Lord Keith. Baron Keith of Avonholm died in Edinburgh on 30 June 1964.   T. B. SMITH, *rev.*

Sources *The Times* (1 July 1964) · *Scots Law Times: News* (22 Feb 1936), 45 · *Scots Law Times: News* (29 May 1937), 117 · *Scots Law Times: News* (14 Nov 1953), 205 · *Glasgow Herald* (1 July 1964) · private information (1981) · personal knowledge (1981) · NA Scot., SC 70/5/334/78
Wealth at death £48,115 2s. 0d.: confirmation, 11 Aug 1964, NA Scot., SC 70/5/334/78

Keith, James Francis Edward [*known as* Marshal Keith] **(1696–1758)**, army officer in the Russian and Prussian service, was born on 11 June 1696 at Inverugie Castle near Peterhead, the second son and fourth and youngest child of William *Keith, ninth Earl Marischal (*c.*1664–1712) [*see under* Drummond, Lady Mary], and his wife, Lady Mary *Drummond (1675–1729), daughter of the first earl of Perth. Keith's father was episcopalian and his mother Roman Catholic. James left an autobiography, whose opening sentence runs:

> Memoires are commonly so tedious in the beginning, by the recital of genealogies, trifling accidents which happen'd in the childhood, and relatione of minucies (hardly fit to be imparted to the most intimate friend), that it renders them not only uninstructive to the reader, but often loathsome to those who wish to employ their time in any usefull way. (Keith, 1)

Keith begins his own story at the death of Queen Anne, making it necessary to piece together his early life from other sources. Along with his elder brother, George *Keith, the tenth and last Earl Marischal (1692/3?–1778), he appears to have been educated by a kinsman, Robert Keith, later bishop in turn of Caithness and Fife, and William Meston, later professor of philosophy at Marischal College, Aberdeen's second university. According to some accounts Keith became MA of Marischal College, but there is no official record of this, nor of alleged legal studies in Edinburgh. Both James and George participated in the Jacobite rising of 1715, including the defeat at Sheriffmuir, following which they were forced to flee via the Western Isles to exile in Europe.

In Paris Keith continued his education under the patronage of James II's widow. Having failed in an attempt to enter the service of Peter the Great during the Russian tsar's visit to Paris in 1717 he soon left for Spain, where he became involved in the unsuccessful Jacobite expedition to Scotland in 1719. He spent the following years mainly in France and Spain, participating as colonel in the Spanish army's siege of Gibraltar from 1726 to 1727. Finding his

James Francis Edward Keith (1696–1758), by Allan Ramsay, 1740

protestant religion a bar to further promotion, he set out for service in Russia in 1728 under the patronage of the Spanish ambassador there, the duke of Liria—his fellow Jacobite, James Fitzjames, son of the duke of Berwick, himself the illegitimate son of James II.

In the succession crisis following the unexpected death of Peter II in 1730 Keith was surprised to be made lieutenant-colonel in Empress Anna's newly created Izmaylovsky guards regiment, and to find himself a centre of attention from seekers after court patronage. Avoiding high politics, in 1732 he became inspector-general of the military districts along the rivers Don and Volga and near Smolensk. He spent the whole year reviewing more than thirty regiments and travelling several thousand miles. In 1733 the Polish king died, and Russia became involved in the War of the Polish Succession. Keith was sent with a force of infantry to Ukraine, and soon participated in an invasion of Poland. His memoirs give out at the end of 1734, but other sources indicate that he continued to play an important part in the war under the command of the Irish general Peter Lacy until it was brought to an end in 1736.

No sooner was the War of the Polish Succession over than another conflict broke out with Turkey. Now a lieutenant-general, Keith was actively involved in the defence of Ukraine against incursions from the Turks and their Crimean Tartar allies. However, he was wounded during a lengthy siege of the Black Sea fortress of Ochakov in 1737, and had to withdraw from fighting for two years. During this time he was taken to France by his brother for successful treatment, and paid a visit to London in autumn 1739. Early in the following year Keith was presented to George II, who received him with all the grace and ceremony owed to an outstanding general in full-dress uniform. He was also made provincial grand master of Russia by his kinsman John Keith, earl of Kintore, grand master mason of England. Peace with Turkey was drawn up in 1739. On his return to Russia, Keith was presented by the empress with a bejewelled sword and with the governorship of Ukraine. The story goes that, during negotiations with the Turks, he realized that his opposite number was the son of a former bellringer in Kirkcaldy.

Further service and advancement was to come soon after the death of Empress Anna in 1740 with another succession crisis and yet another war breaking out, this time with Sweden. Keith was made second in command to General Lacy. For his part in the victory at Wilmanstrand in August 1741 he received a considerable increase in pay. After the accession of the Empress Elizabeth in December 1741 Keith played a leading part in the advance into Finland. In 1743 he was sent to Stockholm at the head of a military and diplomatic mission requested by the Swedish king, Frederick, who feared an attack from Denmark, and helped to set up a Swedish masonic lodge. Keith received ceremonial swords and money from both Frederick and Elizabeth. The empress also presented him with the order of St Andrew and an estate in Livonia. Two years later, he was too busy to contemplate making any contribution to the Forty-Five Jacobite rising. For in the same year he was ordered to go to the assistance of Poland, which was under the threat of invasion from Prussia.

The man himself made no mention of this possibility in a letter of March 1749 to the earl of Kintore, giving his reasons for leaving Russian service in 1747: his correspondence had been intercepted, and he had found it very difficult to keep in touch with his beloved brother, George, who had been refused permission to come to live in Russia. Moreover, some of the most important court officials had looked upon him with suspicion and jealousy, and conspired to block his further promotion. And so, after nearly twenty years there, he had sought and eventually obtained leave to depart from what he deemed to be 'a country dangerous to all foreigners, and where innocence is no security against punishment'.

Keith's new employer, Frederick the Great of Prussia, immediately made him a field marshal and, two years later, governor of Berlin, where, near to the centre, there is now a street named after him. The Keith brothers both entered Frederick's intimate circle and participated in many of his projects, while James was made honorary member of the Academy of Sciences. Undoubtedly, although plagued by bad health, Keith was at his busiest and most effective in the first campaigns of the Seven Years' War which broke out in 1756, for example at the victories of Lobositz and Rossbach, the defence of Leipzig, and the unsuccessful sieges of Prague and Olmütz. In December 1757 he wrote to his brother George: 'We give battles here, as people elsewhere give operas.'

Ten months later, during the battle of Hochkirch, Keith suffered a gunshot wound in the abdomen on 14 October 1758. He refused to leave the field, and was later hit a second time in the chest as a cannonball knocked him from his horse, mortally wounded. Unmarried, he was survived by Eva Merthens, his companion of several years, who managed a successful claim to the major share of a small inheritance following a dispute with Keith's brother. His body was recovered later, and given a solemn military funeral in Berlin. Voltaire was among those who sent condolences to Frederick the Great, while George supplied the epitaph to be seen on a memorial statue in Potsdam, a copy of which, presented in 1868 by William I of Prussia, may be found in Peterhead: *Probus vixit, fortis obiit* ('He lived honestly and died bravely'). There is also a memorial to Keith in the church at Hochkirch, which in its walls and door still bears the marks of the battle.

It is difficult to find anything but praise for Keith in the accounts of the period. He appears to have enjoyed good relations with King Frederick and most of his fellow officers, and to have been respected and obeyed by the lower ranks. Among other achievements, he devised a precursor of the war game, the *Kriegsschachspiel*. Somewhat aloof and reserved in temperament, he was a knowledgeable man as well as an outstanding soldier, and probably deserved the characterization given him by Thomas Carlyle:

A man of Scotch type; the broad accent, with its sagacities, veracities, with its steadfastly fixed moderation, and its sly twinkles of defensive humour, is still audible to us through the foreign wrappages; not given to talk unless there is something to be said, but well capable of it then. (Carlyle, 4.389)

PAUL DUKES

Sources DNB · *A fragment of a memoir of Field-Marshal James Keith, written by himself, 1714–1734*, ed. T. Constable, Spalding Club, 8 (1843) · K. A. Varnhagen von Ense, *Leben des Feldmarschall Jakob Keith*, 3rd edn (Leipzig, 1888) · R. Wills, *The Jacobites and Russia, 1715–1750* (2000) · T. Carlyle, *History of Friedrich II of Prussia, called Frederick the Great*, new edn, 6 vols. (1858–65)
Archives BL, journals of campaigns in Finland, Kings MS 234 [copies] · NA Scot., corresp. and papers · NL Scot., memoirs · U. Aberdeen, special libraries and archives, corresp. and papers, MSS 2703, 2704, 2707, 2708, 2709, 2710, 2711, 3064/329, 3295, 3500/2
Likenesses A. Ramsay, oils, 1740, Staatliche Schlossen und Garten, Berlin [see illus.] · statue, 1868, Peterhead, Aberdeen · A.-S. Belle, oils, U. Aberdeen, Marischal College · J. Given, line engraving, Scot. NPG · A. van Haecken, mezzotint (after A. Ramsay), Scot. NPG · Miller, line engraving, Scot. NPG · A. Pesne, oils, Scot. NPG · double portrait, oils (with Frederick II), Scot. NPG · engravings, Scot. NPG
Wealth at death little: Varnhagen von Ense, *Leben*

Keith, John, first earl of Kintore (d. 1715), politician, was the fourth son of William *Keith, fifth Earl Marischal (c.1585–1635), and his wife, Lady Mary, daughter of John *Erskine, earl of Mar; William *Keith, sixth Earl Marischal (1614–1671), was his eldest brother. In the winter of 1651–2, during the siege of Dunnottar Castle, Keith, although still a youth, played an important role in preventing the Scottish regalia, stored there for safety by the Scottish estates, from falling into the hands of English soldiers. In a scheme said to have been hatched by his mother, he acted as a decoy while the regalia were taken from the castle and hidden in Kinneff church, and on the surrender of the castle swore that he had taken them to France and delivered them to Charles II. Accepting his story, the Cromwellian regime stopped their search. In return for this, at the Restoration, Keith was appointed knight marischal of Scotland, and the office was made hereditary in his family. In 1661 he had a charter of the lands of Caskieben, Aberdeenshire. On 24 April 1662 he married Lady Margaret (b. 1641), posthumous daughter of Thomas *Hamilton, second earl of Haddington; they had three sons and two daughters.

On 26 June 1677 Keith was created earl of Kintore, and Lord Keith of Inverurie and Keith Hall. From this time he was politically active both as a privy councillor and in parliament. A commissioner for the suppression of conventicles in Banffshire and Aberdeenshire from 4 August that year, on 14 May 1678 he was included on a committee for trying rebels against the established religion. In 1679, 1680, and 1681 he received orders for calling out the militia in the same counties. He attended the 1678 convention of estates and on 10 July was appointed a commissioner of supply for Kincardineshire; in 1680 he was included on a privy council committee for encouraging the export of cattle and linen, and was named an excise commissioner for Aberdeenshire. He attended the parliament of 28 July to 17 September 1681, signing on the opening day a declaration by the clergy and nobility acknowledging that it was illegal to take up arms against the king under any circumstances. Having, like other privy councillors, subscribed the controversial Test Act on 22 September, he was ordered to oversee its subscription in the burghs of Kintore and Inverurie and to administer it to the colleges of Aberdeen.

Following a couple of years in which he had a lower profile on the council, in 1684 Kintore resumed a more active role on committees. In December he was appointed as treasurer-depute and to suppress religious disaffection and conventicles in Morayshire. In 1685 he signed the Test Act, sat on several commissions, and attended the parliament, but early in March 1686 he and the duke of Queensberry were called to account for the state of the Treasury and their commissions were revoked. Kintore attended the parliament of 29 April to 15 June 1686, but in September was, with others, removed by the king from the privy council.

The revolution returned Kintore to prominence. He was present on 14 March at the opening day of the 1689 convention of estates, and although he did not subscribe to the 16 March declaration that the meeting was free and legal, he did set his name to its letter to William of 22 March promoting the cause of union between Scotland and England. He was appointed a commissioner of supply for Aberdeenshire in April and a privy councillor in May, being formally admitted when he swore the oath of allegiance to William and Mary on 14 June. By this time evidently fully committed to the Williamite cause, he was entrusted in the months that followed with various military, political, and administrative tasks, including the administration to the Earl Marischal of the oath of allegiance. On 21 January 1690, with two other 'persones of knowen loyaltie and integritey' (Reg. PCS, 15.30), he became a commissioner of the privy seal.

Kintore attended nine of the ten sessions of the Williamite parliament between 1689 and 1702, sitting on several commissions and committees, and on 10 September 1696 he signed the Association. He was likewise active during the union parliament of 1703 to 1707, aligning himself to the court party and supporting the union. He also voted on 12 November 1706 in favour of the act for the security of religion. He died on 12 April 1715.

JOHN R. YOUNG

Sources Scots peerage, vol. 5 · APS, 1670–86; 1689–1707 · Reg. PCS, 3rd ser., vols. 5–7, 9–16 · P. W. J. Riley, The Union of England and Scotland (1978)

Archives NL Scot., papers · U. Aberdeen, special libraries and archives, letters

Keith, Mary. See Drummond, Mary, Countess Marischal (1675–1729).

Keith, Sir Robert (d. 1343/4). See under Keith family (per. c.1300–c.1530).

Keith, Robert (d. in or before 1430). See under Keith family (per. c.1300–c.1530).

Keith, Robert (1681–1757), Scottish Episcopal bishop and historian, was born on 7 February 1681 at Uras, Dunnottar, Kincardineshire, the younger son and fifth child of Alexander Keith (d. 1683), a small landowner, and his wife, Marjory (c.1638–1707), daughter of Robert Arbuthnot. His father, whose Jacobite sympathies had forced him to sell some of his hereditary estate, was descended through the younger line of the third Earl Marischal (d. 1581). Both the allegiance and the lineage would inform Keith's life and activities. His father having died when he was not quite two, Keith was brought up by his mother in Aberdeenshire, where he attended Aberdeen grammar school, c.1692–1696, and then, from 1696 to 1700, Marischal College, which had been founded by his ancestor George, the fifth earl. From 1703 to 1710 he was tutor to his young kinsmen George, later the tenth earl, and his brother James, later a field marshal in the service of Prussia.

Keith was made deacon on 16 August 1710 and served two years as domestic chaplain to the thirteenth earl of Erroll. After accompanying Erroll to Europe he narrowly escaped shipwreck on his way home. Back in Scotland he was ordained priest on 18 August 1713 and ministered for the rest of his life to an Episcopal congregation in Barrenger's Close, in the burgh of Canongate, Edinburgh. Having refused to swear an oath to Queen Anne under the Toleration Act (1712) Keith continued to promote the Jacobite cause and was denied the liberty of public worship granted to other compliant episcopalians. Yet even within their own small ranks the nonjurors were divided on the twin issues of episcopal authority and liturgical practice. Keith, holding the controversial opinion that the Erastian authority of James Stuart, the chevalier and Jacobite claimant to the throne, was no longer practical or wise, accepted, on 18 June 1727, consecration as coadjutor bishop of Edinburgh at the hands of those bishops who shared his views. Nonjurors were also divided over the issue of usages, involving both eucharistic custom and differences over whether to use the English Book of Common Prayer or the Scottish liturgy of 1637. Keith played the major role in formulating the concordats of 1727 and 1731 which resolved both of these disputes. Henceforth bishops were elected by the clergy without reference to James. According to Michael Russell, Keith's prudence and moderation in these matters could 'not be too highly extolled' (Keith, *Historical Catalogue*, xxix). Even James's agent, George Lockhart of Carnwath, approved of Keith personally, calling him 'the best character of any' in the factious party (Lockhart, 2.327). Keith was a handsome man of striking appearance, with a strong jaw and well-set eyes. At some point, probably in the 1720s, he married Isobell Cameron (*d.* after 20 Jan 1757). Their son died young but their daughter, Catherine (*d.* 1793), survived him.

As bishop, Keith looked after the clergy in the ancient dioceses of Caithness and Orkney. Although the full extent of Keith's activity remains obscure, there is evidence of his ordaining in Orkney as late as 1751. From July 1733 he added the bishopric of Fife, describing himself as 'the first to exercise a diocesan superintendence' there (Keith, *Historical Catalogue*, 548); from 1741 William Falconer served as his coadjutor. Keith resigned the see in August 1743 and his fellow bishops immediately elected him *primus episcopus inter pares*, a ninth-century Scottish office revived in the eighteenth century. As such he presided over the episcopal synod and was responsible for the public business of the church.

Both as bishop and as primus, Keith upset those closest to him, the presbyters of Edinburgh, who resented the practical authority he exercised. In 1738 he had objected to their election of Nathaniel Spens as a moderator in a practice he called uncanonical. As primus he was mainly responsible for the canons of 1743, strengthening episcopal jurisdiction and again offending the Edinburgh clergy. The canons regulated the practice and obedience of the church without requiring the advice or concurrence of presbyters. Bypassing Keith's authority as primus the Edinburgh clergy approached the nonjuring English bishop George Smith to consecrate one of their number to the vacant bishopric of Edinburgh. Keith, who had been corresponding with Smith for many years, objected to his appointment in a letter of 22 May 1744, while conceding that Scottish presbyters did 'not like to be imperiously dealt with' (NA Scot., CH 12/16).

But larger matters than these, in Keith's words, 'silenced even the voice of controversy' (Keith, *Historical Catalogue*, xxxiii). Even before the second Jacobite rising of 1745 resulted in severe penal legislation against nonjurors, Keith, in a shorthand letter to Bishop John Alexander, had declared, 'I can't hope to see a legal settlement', and lamented that he now 'felt ald farran'd like other folk' (24 April 1744, NA Scot., CH 12/23). The elderly primus would not live to see better days in the reign of George III, but his scholarly research had always offered him consolation and did so especially in his declining years.

In 1734 Keith published in Edinburgh the *History of the Affairs of Church and State in Scotland*, covering the years 1542 to 1568. This work has claims to be the first history of the period based on original research, and its collection of supporting documents was considerably augmented in the Spottiswoode Society's edition of 1844. In a letter of 15 April 1736 Bishop Smith said it would 'stand the test of ages because no part is related but on the best authority' (NA Scot., CH 12/23). This was generous praise from a man with whom Keith frequently clashed on issues of episcopal authority and liturgical worship. Each respected the other's robust scholarship, and neither was afraid of being dictatorial in his convictions. In old age—they died within a few weeks of each other—each must have derived some scholarly pleasure from their postal polemics, Keith on one occasion even threatening not to receive Smith's next letter.

In 1738 Keith was invited by his fellow bishops to make a register of all the Scottish bishops since 1688. This encouraged him to produce a list of all Scottish bishops prior to 1688, which was published in 1755 as *A Large Catalogue of Bishops*. The work also contains a note on post-1688 bishops, a historical account of the early church in Scotland, and an entertaining correspondence between Keith and his old pupil Field Marshal James Keith, to whom the book is dedicated. It has the merit of being a pioneering work but has needed much correction and alteration by scholars since the 1860s. An enlarged edition of 1824 contained a brief biography by its editor, Bishop Michael Russell, who said that Keith, to the end of his life, valued 'his relationship with the noble and the great' (Keith, *Historical Catalogue*, xx). Keith fiercely defended that relationship in a pamphlet of 1750, vindicating his right 'to the honour of lineal descent from the noblehouse of the earls of Marischal'. His other writings include manuscripts on mysticism and the Scottish liturgy, and he also had scholarly interests in archaeology and numismatics.

The most distinguished scholar among the Scottish nonjurors, Keith was a man of principle and uncompromising orthodoxy. George Grub believed that 'during a trying and calamitous period, he presided over the church with great prudence and ability' (Grub, 4.47). Keith's relative unpopularity with the Edinburgh clergy stemmed simply from his assertion of episcopal authority at a time when many of the rank and file clearly differed little from their Presbyterian counterparts in desiring parity rather than hierarchy. But even they respected Keith for his learning and personal worth. His near contemporary Bishop John Skinner called his character irreproachable. After serious illnesses in 1748 and 1751, Keith, suffering from failing eyesight and constant headaches, retired to his villa at Bonnyhaugh, Bonnington, Leith, in 1752. Nominally, at least, he continued to care for his congregation in the Canongate up to the time of his death, after a day's illness, on 20 January 1757. He was buried in Canongate churchyard.

GERALD M. D. HOWAT

Sources Alexander letters, Episcopal chest, NA Scot., CH 12/23 · miscellaneous letters, Episcopal chest, NA Scot., CH 12/16 · R. Keith and J. Spottiswoode, *An historical catalogue of the Scottish* *bishops, down to the year 1688*, new edn, ed. M. Russel [M. Russell] (1824) [incl. memoir, pp. xvii–xliii] · J. F. S. Gordon, *Scotichronicon*, 2 vols. (1867) · R. Keith, J. P. Lawson, and C. J. Lyon, *History of the affairs of church and state in Scotland from the beginning of the Reformation to the year 1568*, 3 vols., Spottiswoode Society (1844–50) · G. T. S. Farquhar, *Three bishops of Dunkeld* (1915) · G. Grub, *An ecclesiastical history of Scotland*, 4 vols. (1861) · W. Stephen, *History of the Scottish church*, 2 vols. (1894–6) · T. Lathbury, *A history of the nonjurors* (1845) · *Scots Magazine*, 19 (1757), 54 · G. Lockhart, *The Lockhart papers: containing memoirs and commentaries upon the affairs of Scotland from 1702 to 1715*, 2 vols. (1817) · J. Skinner, *Ecclesiastical history of Scotland* (1788) · J. B. Craven, *History of the church in Orkney* (1883) · W. Anderson, *The Scottish nation*, 3 vols. in 9 (1865) · *Records of Marischal College, Aberdeen* (1898)

Archives NA Scot., letters · University of Dundee, archives, catechetical instructions | NA Scot., corresp. with John Alexander · NA Scot., corresp. with George Smith

Likenesses T. A. Dean, stipple, pubd 1834, BM · H. Adlard, vignette, stipple, BM · engraving, repro. in Gordon, ed., *Scotichronicon*, 152

Wealth at death under £450: Keith, *Historical catalogue*; Gordon, *Scotichronicon*, 267

Keith, Robert (*c*.1697–1774), diplomatist, was the only son of Colonel Robert Keith of Craig, Kincardineshire, and Agnes, daughter of Robert Murray of Murrayshall, Stirlingshire. His father was descended from John Keith, fourth son of William, second Earl Marischal. Little is known about his early life except that by 1730 he was married to Margaret, second daughter of Sir William Cunningham, second baronet, of Caprington, Ayrshire, in which year their eldest son, Sir Robert Murray *Keith (1730–1795), was born. They had two other children: Sir Basil Keith (*d.* 1770), who served in the navy and became governor of Gibraltar, and Anne Murray Keith (1736–1818), who appeared under the name Mrs Bethune Baliol in Scott's *Introduction to the Chronicles of Canongate*.

Keith served for some time as secretary to the forces under the earl of Stair. About August 1746 he was made secretary to John Montagu, fourth earl of Sandwich, went with him to The Hague, and accompanied him to the congress of Aix-la-Chapelle. In August 1748 he was appointed British minister at Vienna in succession to Sir Thomas Robinson, and conducted with credit, though without much success, the negotiations regarding the imperial election of 1752, and the alliances which preceded the Seven Years' War. He was throughout a firm friend to Newcastle. At the end of 1753 he was raised to the rank of minister-plenipotentiary. In 1757 he was transferred to St Petersburg and arrived in March 1758; he remained there throughout the revolution of 1762 and left in October when the government of the new empress, Catherine II, requested that a nobleman should take his place. Rumours that he had been Catherine's lover, which were encouraged by some of the diplomatic corps in St Petersburg, appear to have been groundless. He was apparently granted a pension of £1000 a year, and obtained supporters to his arms on 17 March 1769.

For the first ten years of his retirement Keith lived at The Hermitage, near Edinburgh, and devoted himself to gardening. His large circle of friends included David Hume and William Robertson, with whom, as Ambassador Keith, he was very popular. Shortly before his death he moved to a house in St Andrews Square, Edinburgh, and he died there on 21 September 1774.

W. A. J. Archbold, *rev.* R. D. E. Eagles

Sources *Memoirs and correspondence (official and familiar) of Sir Robert Murray Keith*, ed. Mrs G. Smyth, 2 vols. (1849) · D. B. Horn, ed., *British diplomatic representatives, 1689–1789*, CS, 3rd ser., 46 (1932) · W. Coxe, *Memoirs of the administration of the Right Honourable Henry Pelham*, 2 vols. (1829), vol. 1, pp. 452, 465; vol. 2, p. 118 · Walpole, *Corr.*

Archives BL, corresp. and letter-books, Add. MSS 35461–35495 · BM, Add. MS 32814, fols. 59, 93 · NL Scot., corresp. | BL, corresp. with Lord Holdernesse, Egerton MSS 3414–3415, 3455, 3463 · BL, corresp. with Lord Hyndford and duke of Newcastle, Add. MSS 45117–45121 · BL, letters to Thomas Robinson, Add. MSS 23829–23830 · U. Nott. L., corresp. with Henry Pelham and duke of Newcastle

Keith, Sir Robert Murray, of Murrayshall (1730–1795), diplomatist and army officer, was born in Edinburgh on 20 September 1730, the eldest child of the diplomat Robert *Keith (*c*.1697–1774), of Craig, Kincardineshire, and his wife, Margaret Cunningham, daughter of Sir William Cunningham of Caprington, second baronet, who died when Keith was eleven. Keith received his early education at Edinburgh high school. He inherited the estate of Murrayshall (formerly Halmyre) at the death of his great-uncle Robert Murray on 8 February 1743, and accordingly added the name of Murray to his own. He was evidently destined for a military career from an early age, because about 1745 he was sent to a military academy in London, where he learned fencing, riding, and fortification, as well as some 'polite' subjects such as music and drawing. He also learned French at this time, and in later life was to be a gifted linguist, speaking fluent Dutch, German, and Italian.

Keith received a cornet's commission in the 6th (Lord Rothes) dragoons in 1747, and served with that regiment at Breda in the Netherlands. On 2 June 1747 he accepted a commission from James Douglas, earl of Drumlanrig, in the latter's regiment of the Scots brigade, in the Dutch service, in which he was made a captain on 10 October 1748. When this regiment was reduced in 1752, Keith returned to Britain with a small pension. Failing to obtain a commission in the British army, he went abroad with his friend Frederick Campbell (later lord clerk register) in order to visit his father (at that time on diplomatic service in Vienna) and to investigate the possibility of military employment in Germany. He was recalled to the Scots brigade in 1755, becoming a captain in Halkett's regiment on 27 July 1756. He remained with this regiment until September 1757, when he rejoined the British army as a captain in the 73rd foot. On the recommendation of his friend Colonel Henry Seymour Conway, he was made an aide-de-camp to the British commander Lord George Sackville, and in November 1758 was serving under Prince Ferdinand of Brunswick. He fought in the battle of Minden on 1 August 1759 and later in that month he carried the resignation of the disgraced Sackville (the 'coward of Minden') to London. This brought Keith into contact with the elder

William Pitt, who thought highly of him. Accordingly, when it was decided to raise companies of Highland Volunteers (later the 87th foot) for service in Europe, Pitt appointed Keith as their major-commandant. The companies joined Prince Ferdinand's allied army in late 1759. Keith was promoted to colonel-commandant in May 1760, and his highlanders served with distinction in numerous battles between 1760 and 1762, including Warburg, Zeirenberg, Fellinghausen, Grabenstein, and Brunker-Muhl. He plainly took an active part in the fighting, because rumours of his death at Fellinghausen were current in London in 1761. When war ended in 1763, the highlanders were disbanded, and Keith was once again unemployed and on half pay. He visited Paris briefly in 1764, and in 1765 settled in London. While there he became a member of The Gang, a social club of younger politicians with whom he remained close throughout his life, and who were sometimes of use to him in his future career.

The end of his military service, the friendship of Pitt and Conway, his father's diplomatic position, and his knowledge of Germany probably turned Keith's mind in the direction of a diplomatic career. With the assistance of Conway, Keith became envoy-extraordinary to the court of Saxony at Dresden, where he arrived on 19 May 1769. He was then transferred to Copenhagen, and took up his ambassadorial duties there on 24 June 1771, having first paid a visit to his father in Vienna.

It was while at Copenhagen that Keith achieved real prominence. In early 1772 there was a general political reaction against the minister Johan Friedrich Struensee, who ruled Denmark in the name of the insane King Christian VII. Struensee and his adherents—among them the queen, Caroline Matilda—were arrested and confined. As the queen was the sister of George III, the matter was one of great concern to the British government. Owing to the slowness of communication, Keith could not hope to receive timely instructions from London, and so appears to have acted on his own initiative in the face of the worsening situation. He forced his way into the council which was discussing the problem of the queen and threatened a British naval bombardment of Copenhagen if Caroline Matilda was harmed. This frightened the Danes and earned Keith the gratitude of George III, who made him a knight of the Bath on 29 February 1772, despite there being no vacancy in the order. The Bath insignia were sent to him in Denmark, with instructions to invest himself as there was no monarch available to perform this task. The Danes had meanwhile agreed to allow the queen to go into peaceful exile in Hanover, and Keith had the task of persuading her that there was no possibility that she could re-establish herself in Denmark. On 1 May 1772 Keith was ordered to escort her to Germany and then return to London.

As a further reward for his conduct in Denmark, Keith was made envoy-extraordinary and plenipotentiary to the imperial court in Vienna (a position which he was to hold for twenty years), and he took up his post there on 20 November 1772. In 1773 Thomas Bradshaw, an MP and fellow member of The Gang, proposed that Keith should become MP for Peeblesshire, even though he was not in Britain. Keith was favourable to the idea, but the project required the co-operation of the local electoral patron, William Douglas, third earl of March. As March proved awkward, the scheme was abandoned. In July 1774 Conway arrived in Vienna, and Keith set out on a tour of Hungary with him, returning to Vienna in late August or early September. At the death of his father on 21 September 1774, Keith obtained leave of absence to return home and settle his affairs. He was preparing to return to Vienna in November 1775 when the death of Adam Hay, MP for Peeblesshire, made it feasible to revive the scheme of putting Keith in parliament. Keith returned to Scotland but March remained hostile. The prime minister, Lord North, and the northern secretary of state, Henry Howard, twelfth earl of Suffolk, persuaded March that in asking him to endorse Keith they were not trying to reduce his power in the county, and Keith was returned as MP for Peeblesshire on 14 December 1775. He remained MP until 1780, though he returned to Vienna in June 1776 and never attended the Commons in person.

Keith proved to be an extremely able diplomat in Vienna and was well thought of, both by his own government and by Empress Maria Theresa and Emperor Joseph II, both of whom he admired. However, he was subject to many inconveniences. He was obliged to entertain British visitors at his own expense, and had continual financial trouble, at one stage contemplating the sale of his Murrayshall estate. This was only slightly alleviated when he was appointed colonel in the 10th foot in 1781, and lieutenant-general in 1782. He was irritated by elaborate Viennese court etiquette, and the slowness and inefficiency of British foreign policy was a constant annoyance. When an alliance was made between Britain and Prussia, which had immense implications for British imperial relations, Keith learned about it from the Prussian ambassador rather than his own government. In the 1780s, when war between the Habsburg dominions and Turkey had made relations between Vienna and London especially difficult, Keith received no instructions for five months. By his own estimate he received one reply from London to every forty dispatches he sent there. In these circumstances Keith's duties were not easy, but he seems to have performed them ably, and his correspondence suggests an astute and conscientious diplomat, constantly alert to shifting European politics and his own country's interests therein. His private correspondence suggests that he was well regarded by significant literary figures. David Hume recommended him as a man worth knowing, and the Scottish historian William Robertson sometimes asked him for assistance with research material in Europe. He has been credited with *The Caledoniad*, a collection of poems published in 1775.

The fall of North caused Keith to worry about the security of his position in Vienna, but he retained it under succeeding administrations, which gave him several indications of his worth to them. He went home in October 1788, and while there was appointed a privy councillor on 29 April 1789. He returned to Vienna in September 1789, and his salary was substantially increased. One of his last duties as ambassador was to attend the congress of Sistovo in 1790–91, which brought an end to the war between imperial and Turkish forces, a result greatly desired by the British government.

Keith retired in 1792 and returned to London with a handsome pension; he eventually settled in Hammersmith. He died at his house there very suddenly on 22 June 1795, collapsing into the arms of a servant after having entertained some guests for dinner, possibly from a stroke or heart attack consequent from his obesity. Keith never married, though he seems to have had an illegitimate daughter, about whom nothing is known.

ALEXANDER DU TOIT

Sources *Memoirs and correspondence (official and familiar) of Sir Robert Murray Keith*, ed. Mrs G. Smyth, 2 vols. (1849) · E. Haden-Guest, 'Murray Keith, Sir Robert', HoP, *Commons, 1754–90* · Anderson, *Scot. nat.* · D. B. Horn, ed., *British diplomatic representatives, 1689–1789*, CS, 3rd ser., 46 (1932), 5, 39, 65 · J. Ferguson, ed., *The Scots brigade in Holland*, 3 vols. (1899–1901) · *The correspondence of King George the Third from 1760 to December 1783*, ed. J. Fortescue, 6 vols. (1927–8), vol. 2, pp. 337–40, 354, 358, 729; vol. 4, pp. 480, 524–5; vol. 5, pp. 15–16, 152, 155, 162, 203, 267; vol. 6, p. 55 · *The later correspondence of George III*, ed. A. Aspinall, 5 vols. (1962–70), vol. 1, pp. 68, 73, 411, 413 · Walpole, *Corr.*, 9.379; 11.2; 23.373, 375, 387; 24.398; 35.310; 38.354, 365; 39.537–8 · W. E. H. Lecky, *A history of England in the eighteenth century*, 2nd edn, 8 vols. (1882–90), vol. 5, pp. 239, 559, 591, 593–4 · D. Stewart, *Sketches of the character, manners, and present state of the highlanders of Scotland: with details of the military service of the highland regiments*, 2 (1822), 68–80 · J. H. Burton, *The Scot abroad*, 2nd edn (1881), 423–32 · P. Mackesy, *The coward of Minden: the affair of Lord George Sackville* (1979), 13, 118, 136, 151, 154 · *GM*, 1st ser., 65 (1795), 535 · J. W. Buchan and H. Paton, *History of Peeblesshire*, 3 vols. (1927), 3.37–8 · L. R. Timperley, ed., *A directory of landownership in Scotland, c.1770*, Scottish RS, new ser., 5 (1976), 254 · E. Kilmurray, *Dictionary of British portraiture*, 3 (1981), 124 · GEC, *Baronetage*, 4.273 · *The letters of David Hume*, ed. J. Y. T. Greig, 2 (1932), 264 · H. M. Scott, *British foreign policy in the age of the American revolution* (1990)
Archives Österreichische Staatsarchiv, Vienna, diplomatic corresp. · BL, corresp. and papers, Add. MSS 6806–6825, *passim*, 35503–35583 · BL, letters, Add. MSS 24157–24158 · BL, letters, Add. MS 24173 · NL Scot., corresp. and papers · PRO NIre., corresp. and papers | Beds. & Luton ARS, corresp. with Lord Grantham · BL, letters to Lord Auckland, Add. MSS 34431–34445 · BL, Berkeley papers · BL, corresp. with Lord Grenville, Add. MSS 34437–34444, *passim* [copies] · BL, corresp. with Richard Grenville, Add. MSS 70956–70983, 70992–70997 · BL, official copies of dispatches between Baron Grenville and others, Add. MS 36814 · BL, Greville diary · BL, corresp. with Sir Robert Gunning, Egerton MSS 2697–2703, *passim* · BL, Hamilton and Greville papers · BL, Hardwicke papers · BL, letters to Lord Holdernesse, Add. MSS 32849–32907, *passim* [copies] · BL, corresp. with duke of Leeds, Add. MSS 28060–28066, 344430–344436, Egerton MS 2501 · BL, Liverpool papers · BL, letters to A. Mitchell, Add. MSS 6810, 6860 · BL, corresp. with duke of Newcastle, Add. MS 32854 · BL, letters to Lord Mountstuart, Add. MS 38774 · BL, official and private letters to Lord Mountstuart, Add. MS 36806 · BL, corresp. of F. G. Osborne, Add. MSS 28060–28066 · BL, corresp. of T. Pelham, Add. MS 33090 · BL, corresp. of General Rainsford, Add. MS 23669 · BL, Stowe collection · CKS, corresp. with third duke of Dorset · Hunt. L., letters to Frances Murray · NL Scot., R. Liston papers · NL Scot., Melville papers · NL Scot., Stuart-Stevenson papers · NRA, priv. coll., letters to Lord Cathcart · NRA, priv. coll., letters to Lady Mary Coke · NRA, priv. coll., corresp. with Joseph Ewart · NRA, priv. coll., corresp. with Lord Stormont · Suffolk RO, Ipswich, letters to Alexander Straton · U. Hull, Brynmor Jones L., letters to Charles Hotham-Thompson

Likenesses J. Jacobie, mezzotint, 1788 (after A. Graaff), BM, NPG · stipple, pubd 1848, NPG; repro. in Gillespie-Smyth, ed., *Memoirs and correspondence*, vol. 2, frontispiece · J. Opie, oils, Gov. Art Coll.
Wealth at death £322 13s.: valuation roll, 1761, Timperley ed., *Directory*, 254

Keith, Robert William

Keith, Robert William (1787–1846), composer, was born in Stepney, London, on 20 March 1787. He was the eldest son of Cornelius Keith, organist of St Peter's, Cornhill, and the Danish Chapel in Wellclose Street, and the grandson of William Keith (*d.* 1800), organist of West Ham church. His grandfather taught him the rudiments of music, and he then went to F. H. Barthélémon and Joseph Diettenhofer for tuition on the violin and for lessons in harmony and composition. Later he presided over a music and musical instrument warehouse at 131 Cheapside, London, and prepared many of his own publications. These included mainly short sacred pieces and pedagogical writings. Some of his sacred music was published by Clementi.

While organist and composer to the New Jerusalem Church in Friars Street, Keith published *A selection of sacred melodies … to which is prefixed instructions for the use of young organists* (1816), followed by *A musical vade mecum, being a compendious introduction to the whole art of music; Part I, containing the principles of notation, etc., in an easy categorical form, apprehensible to the meanest capacity* (1820?) and *Part II, Elements of Musical Composition*. He also compiled instruction books for piano, flute, and Spanish guitar (using the name 'Paulus Prucilli'), and *A Violin Preceptor on an Entire New Principle* (1813?), which was very popular in its time and went through many editions. On the death of the Princess Charlotte Augusta in 1817 he set to music some elegiac verses, *Britannia, Mourn*; he also arranged the overture and other extracts from Weber's *Der Freischütz* as a duet for two violins (1830?), and edited *Favourite Airs with Variations, for the Violin* (1821, *c.*1825). Keith died on 19 June 1846.

L. M. MIDDLETON, rev. DAVID J. GOLBY

Sources [J. S. Sainsbury], ed., *A dictionary of musicians*, 2 vols. (1824) · Brown & Stratton, *Brit. mus.* · private information (1891) · *GM*, 1st ser., 86/1 (1816), 346–7

Keith, Thomas

Keith, Thomas (*bap.* 1759, *d.* 1824), writer on mathematics and teacher, was born at Winestead, near Patrington, the son of Thomas Keith, a labourer, and his wife, Elizabeth, and was baptized at Brandesburton, near Beverley, East Riding of Yorkshire, on 22 September 1759. His father died soon after.

Keith began his career as a teacher in his home area of east Yorkshire, where he worked at least until 1781. By 1784 he had a naval and military academy in Woolwich; in 1788 he was in Bromley, and by 1794 in Swallow Street, London. At that time he was still teaching, while writing several very successful textbooks.

The first, *Short and Easy Introduction to … Geography* (1787), had at least seven editions. The next, *Complete Practical Arithmetician* (1788), had fifteen and one at Philadelphia, an abridgement. His most popular book, *New Treatise on the Use of the Globes* (1805), had at least twenty-five editions by 1875, including three at New York. He also wrote *Introduction to Trigonometry* (1801) and *Elements of Plane Geometry*

(1814). His 'Synopsis of logarithmical arithmetic' (1788) was printed in the *Mathematical Repository* in 1791, and he edited various works, including William Hawney's *Complete Measurer* (1798).

Keith's growing reputation led to his appointment in 1804 as secretary to the master of the king's household. In 1810 he became geography tutor to Charlotte Augusta, daughter of the prince of Wales, and he also taught Princess Sophia Matilda. Through Charles Abbot, later first Lord Colchester, he was appointed in 1814 accountant to the British Museum. His address was then 1 York Buildings, New Road, Marylebone, where he died on 29 June 1824. It is not known whether he ever married.

W. A. J. ARCHBOLD, rev. RUTH WALLIS

Sources *GM*, 1st ser., 94/2 (1824), 279–80 · private information (1891) · private information (2004) · *Lady's and Gentleman's Scientifical Repository*, 221

Keith, Sir William (d. in or after **1407**). *See under* Keith family (*per. c.*1300–c.1530).

Keith, William, first Earl Marischal (b. after **1425**, d. **1483**). *See under* Keith family (*per. c.*1300–c.1530).

Keith, William, second Earl Marischal (d. **1526/7**). *See under* Keith family (*per. c.*1300–c.1530).

Keith, William, third Earl Marischal (c.**1510–1581**), magnate, was the eldest son of Robert, master of Marischal (d. 1524/5), and his wife, Elizabeth (or Beatrice) Douglas (d. after 1527), daughter of John, second earl of Morton. He was still a minor when he succeeded to the title on the death of his grandfather between 24 November 1526 and 2 May 1527. He was identified as the fourth earl until 1927, when the sequence was revised by Thomas Innes; since then William Keith has been generally accepted as the third Earl Marischal. He was also the hereditary sheriff of Kincardineshire, and on 27 January 1532 he had a charter erecting Kincardine as the head burgh of the shire. In April 1531 he performed the marischal's traditional office of keeping order within the hall in which parliament was sitting, perhaps to mark his coming of age, but otherwise he acted through deputies until 1535. Also in 1531, or soon afterwards, he married Margaret (b. c.1518, d. in or before 1563), granddaughter and coheir of Sir William Keith of Inverugie, who brought great wealth of her own into the family; Marischal paid large sums to the crown for his wife's lands, at least £2200, and possibly more than £6000. They had twelve children—nine daughters and three sons—including William, master of Marischal, and Robert, Lord Altrie.

Marischal accompanied James V in 1536 when he went to France to marry Madeleine, daughter of François I, and also on his expedition to the isles in 1540. On 2 July 1541 he was appointed an extraordinary lord of session. As early as 1542 he showed sympathy for ideas of religious reform, and in 1544 he was among those who were favourably impressed by George Wishart's preaching in Dundee. The parliament of March 1543 appointed him to the privy council and as one of the keepers of the young Queen Mary. From 1545 (when the records begin) to 1566 he frequently attended council meetings. In June 1544 he signed the agreement to support Mary of Guise, the queen dowager, as regent against the earl of Arran, but he also supported an English alliance, so long as the sovereignty of Scotland could be preserved. In 1545 he was apparently involved in a plot to attack Cardinal Beaton in Glasgow. He was active in defending Scotland against England in 1547, and on 10 September fought at the battle of Pinkie. In September 1550 he accompanied the queen dowager on her trip to France. He was one of those who were moved by Knox's preaching in Edinburgh in May 1556 and who urged Knox to write to the queen regent to convert her to the cause of reform; the subsequent letter was printed in 1558. Marischal's strong ties to the queen regent were shown at her deathbed when she appointed him as her executor testamentary, but Marischal, pleading ill health, refused to act, though he did offer to do anything he could in an informal manner to recover her debts. Despite his evangelical sympathies, Marischal provided no military support for the 1559–60 uprising that with English help established protestantism in Scotland. At the Reformation Parliament of July and August 1560 he subscribed the confession of faith and the Book of Discipline, but baulked at such secular measures as subscribing the treaties of Berwick and Edinburgh with England.

When Queen Mary returned to Scotland in 1561 Marischal was appointed to her privy council and was one of those who rotated in and out of personal attendance on her. He was also reappointed an extraordinary lord of session in 1561, a position he retained until 1573. In 1563 the general assembly of the kirk appointed him to a committee to revise the Book of Discipline, even though he had earlier opposed depriving the queen of the mass. Marischal's eventual withdrawal from public life about 1566–7 can be attributed to both his temperament and his declining health. Sir Ralph Sadler in 1543 called him 'a goodly young gentleman' (Clifford, 1.99), but subsequent English observers emphasized his caution and conservatism. In 1561 Randolph wrote that Marischal 'is fearful and loath to enter into any matter of controversy' (*CSP for.*, *1560–61*, 230). A later observer in 1577 called him 'a favourer of all present authorities' (*CSP Scot.*, 5, 1577, 253). On the other hand, contemporaries invariably identified him as a committed protestant. In the 1559 English debate over whether to intervene in Scotland, Marischal was deemed to be favourable in religion, and an English report in 1577 described him as 'very religious' (ibid., 256). A later manuscript history of the Keith family called him 'one of the greatest men of his age for his personall merit' (NL Scot., MS 21187A, fol. 25r).

Marischal's caution and conservatism, therefore, were focused on the secular world, not the religious. The two, however, could overlap: thus Marischal's speech to the Reformation Parliament concerning the confession of faith emphasized that the failure of 'my lord bishops' to speak against it was an important factor in his subscription, and he therefore expressed himself in unambiguous terms: 'Farther, I protest, if anie persons ecclesiasticall sall heerafter oppone themselves to this our Confessioun, that they have no place nor credite' (Calderwood, 2.38). The tension between his religious conviction and his secular conservatism was apparent in a report of 1566 to the pope, in which he was said to be heretical but willing to fight for Queen Mary. After the death of Darnley and Mary's marriage to Bothwell in 1567, Marischal did come out in opposition to his queen, but the conflict of loyalties and a desire for peace and safety may well account for his subsequent retirement, especially since it was his son-in-law, James Stewart, earl of Moray, who became regent. The other contributing factor was probably ill health, which was first referred to in 1560 when Marischal refused to act as executor for Mary of Guise. In 1565 Marischal's son Robert supplied his place in the army, and after 1567 his parliamentary duties were once more carried out by deputies. In 1576 a minister's testimonial excused him from a summons before the privy council because of his inability to travel, and in 1577 an English report referred to his 'great infirmities and sickness' (CSP Scot., 5, 1577, 253). His eldest son, William, was held a prisoner in England from 1558 to about 1568: once he returned he took his father's place in national affairs, but died a year before him in 1580.

Marischal had the reputation of being the wealthiest man in Scotland, his yearly rental being estimated at 270,000 merks; so widely was his property scattered that it was said that he could journey from Berwick to the northern limits of the country, eating his meals and sleeping every night on his own estates. He died on 7 October 1581, probably in Dunnottar Castle, near Stonehaven. In his later years he spent so much of his time there that he was known as William of the Tower. At his death his movable estate was valued at £44,664 7s. 6d. Scots. His heir was his grandson George *Keith.   MICHAEL WASSER

Sources Scots peerage, 6.46–51 • CSP for., 1558–68 • APS, 1124–1592 • CSP Scot., 1547–81 • J. M. Thomson and others, eds., Registrum magni sigilli regum Scotorum / The register of the great seal of Scotland, 11 vols. (1882–1914), vols. 3–5 • M. Livingstone, D. Hay Fleming, and others, eds., Registrum secreti sigilli regum Scotorum / The register of the privy seal of Scotland, 8 vols. (1908–82) • Reg. PCS, 1st ser., vols. 1–2 • D. Calderwood, The history of the Kirk of Scotland, ed. T. Thomson and D. Laing, 8 vols., Wodrow Society, 7 (1842–9), vols. 1–2 • commissariot court of Edinburgh, NA Scot., CC8/8/11, fols. 53r–59r • Third report, HMC, 2 (1872) [Sir Patrick Keith Murray (Ochteryre MSS)] • GEC, Peerage, new edn, 8.477–9 • NL Scot., MS 21187A, fols. 25r–26r • J. Cameron, James V: the personal rule, 1528–1542, ed. N. Macdougall (1998) • The state papers and letters of Sir Ralph Sadler, ed. A. Clifford, 1 (1809), vol. 1 • N. Tranter, The fortified house in Scotland (1966), vol. 4 • M. Lee, James Stewart, earl of Moray: a political study of the Reformation (1953) • T. Innes, 'The first earl marischal', SHR, 24 (1926–7), 280–97 • John Knox's History of the Reformation in Scotland, ed. W. C. Dickinson, 2 vols. (1949)
Archives NL Scot., Acc. 6026, 11041
Wealth at death £44,664 7s. 6d. Scots—moveable estate: NA Scot., CC 8/8/11, fols. 53r–59r

Keith, William, fifth Earl Marischal (c.1585–1635), naval official, was the eldest son of George *Keith, fourth Earl Marischal (1549/50–1623), and his wife, Margaret (d. 1598), daughter of Alexander *Home, fifth Lord Home. In 1601 Keith travelled abroad to further his education, visiting Paris, Orléans, Tours, and Saumur. On 21 January 1608 he was, along with his father, summoned to answer for his conduct towards Francis Sinclair, son of the earl of Caithness. On 12 October 1609 he was contracted to marry Lady Mary Erskine, daughter of John Erskine, earl of Mar and his second wife, Lady Mary Stuart.

Keith acted as his father's deputy in the Scottish parliament in June 1621. He purchased the lands of Kinellar and others in the thanage of Kintore from his brother James in February 1623, and succeeded to the earldom on the death of his father on 2 April the same year. On 1 October he granted a charter, ratifying his father's erection of Marischal College, Aberdeen, and mortification therefore of the lands of the black and the white friars, and in the same year became a justice of the peace for Kincardineshire. The earl soon became involved in litigation against his stepmother, Dame Margaret Ogilvie, and her new husband, Alexander Strachan, laird of Thornton. Marischal accused her of theft of silver work, tapestry, and other goods belonging to his father's estate. The controversy was eventually resolved by the king's intervention.

Marischal was present at the funeral of James VI and I at Westminster Abbey, on 5 May 1625. At the end of the same month he was made a baronet of Nova Scotia with a land grant of 48,000 acres there. Charles I continued to favour him. During the restructuring of the new Scottish privy council in March 1626, Charles included him as a member of it. This was a position which he would continue to occupy and participate in until his death. The entry of Christian IV of Denmark–Norway into the Thirty Years' War and conflicts with France and Spain saw Charles I place Scotland on a martial footing, and the earl received an appointment to the Scottish council of war on 12 July 1626. When Charles I that year bought three ships for securing the Scottish coasts, the Earl Marischal was made commander of them. Controversy ensued, arising largely from the jealousy of Scotland's lord high admiral, Alexander, earl of Linlithgow. Complaints were received by the privy council but Charles I seemed satisfied with Marischal and personally intervened to settle the dispute. Marischal put the ships to use convoying Scottish soldiers for service under the king's uncle, Christian IV of Denmark–Norway. He also ordered privateers to attack enemy shipping on the coast of France, where they had some success. Another dispute arose with Linlithgow as to who had jurisdiction over the ships brought home as prizes. On 9 July 1631 such disputes were finally resolved when Marischal was confirmed as the commander of the king's navy in Scotland. This force consisted of six ships contributed by Marischal and one supplied by Charles I.

When Charles entered Edinburgh after his coronation in 1633 the Earl Marischal received him at the High Tolbooth. In the following year he fitted out a fleet, which he sent to the assistance of Uladislaus VII, king of Poland. Marischal died at his castle of Dunnottar on 28 October 1635, just one month after his last engagement with the privy council in Edinburgh. He was buried in the church at Dunnottar on 26 December. He was survived by his wife, and by eight of their children: William *Keith, sixth Earl

Marischal (1614–1671), George Keith, seventh Earl Marischal, Sir Robert Keith, Alexander Keith (d. in or before 1654), John *Keith, first earl of Kintore (d. 1715), Mary, married in 1633 to John, Lord Kinpont, Jean married to Alexander, Lord Forbes of Pitsligo, and Anne. His widow married, on 15 July 1639, Patrick Maule, earl of Panmure; she was still living in March 1665.

T. F. HENDERSON, rev. STEVE MURDOCH

Sources Reg. PCS, 1st ser., vol. 13 · Reg. PCS, 2nd ser., vols. 1–4 · Scots peerage · J. Spalding, Memorialls of the trubles in Scotland and in England, AD 1624 – AD 1645, ed. J. Stuart, 2 vols., Spalding Club, [21, 23] (1850–51) · P. J. Anderson and J. F. K. Johnstone, eds., Fasti academiae Mariscallanae Aberdonensis: selections from the records of the Marischal College and University, MDXCIII–MDCCCLX, 3 vols., New Spalding Club, 4, 18–19 (1889–98) · P. Buchan, An historical and authentic account of the ancient and noble family of Keith, Earls Marichal of Scotland (1820) · A. K. Merrill, The Keith book (1934) · GEC, Peerage

Keith, William, sixth Earl Marischal (1614–1671), nobleman, was the son of William *Keith, fifth Earl Marischal (c.1585–1635), and Lady Mary, daughter of John Erskine, earl of Mar. He entered Marischal College, Aberdeen (founded by his grandfather), in 1631, and subsequently travelled on the continent, being in France when his father died on 28 October 1635. The new earl spent some time at court in England before returning to Scotland, where in 1637 he married Lady Elizabeth (1621–1650), daughter of George *Seton, third earl of Winton. His attitude to the resistance to Charles I over religious and other grievances which emerged in Scotland in 1637 was ambiguous. In November 1637 he gave his 'promise to subscryve' a petition to the king against his policies, his wife 'shedding of tears' in support of his resolution (Diary of Sir Archibald Johnston, 272–3). But he avoided open involvement in opposition, and on 2 July 1638 he was sworn of the Scottish privy council, indicating that it was believed he could be relied upon to support royal policies. On 22 September 1638 he signed the king's covenant whereby Charles tried to rally support against the national covenant, but on 15 February 1639 he welcomed a covenanting committee to his stronghold of Dunnottar Castle, and thus 'declairit him self cleirlie to be ane covenanter, quhilk wes doubtful befoir', and he began to muster men for their forces (Spalding, 1.138).

Marischal's support was of great importance to the covenanters as his power and influence in north-east Scotland countered that of the royalist marquess of Huntly. On 30 March he and his men formed part of the army under the earl of Montrose which advanced northwards through Aberdeen to Turriff to overawe Huntly. Marischal returned to Aberdeen on 25 April and took measures to secure the town for the covenanters, acting as governor. But when, after victory at the Trot of Turriff on 14 May, the royalists Lord Aboyne and Sir George Ogilvie of Banff occupied Aberdeen, Marischal failed to oppose them, choosing to remain in Dunnottar. It was said that he persuaded the royalists to disband their forces by promising not to act against them unless he received direct orders from the covenanters to do so, but he subsequently denied this, and it is more likely that the royalists retired out of

William Keith, sixth Earl Marischal (1614–1671), by George Jamesone, 1636

reluctance to make war on so important a lord as Marischal without the permission of Huntly—who was by this time a prisoner of the covenanters. Once the royalists had disbanded, Marischal raised his own men and reoccupied Aberdeen on 23 or 24 May, being reinforced by Montrose with about 4000 men on 25 May. The covenanters' forces moved on to subdue the countryside, and though Aboyne again managed to occupy Aberdeen, Marischal, 'who wanted not courage' (J. Gordon, 2.270), beat off his attempt to seize Stonehaven, near Dunnottar. Marischal and Montrose then retook Aberdeen, after fighting at Brig of Dee on 18 and 19 June. The allegation that Marischal urged Montrose to burn the town (ibid., 2.281–2) is implausible. At this point the complex manoeuvrings of this first bishops' war were ended by the news that Charles I had agreed the treaty of Berwick with the covenanters.

In the second bishops' war of 1640 Marischal was again active on behalf of the covenanters. He entered Aberdeen on a number of occasions to enforce subscription of the national covenant, and he accompanied the covenanters' commander in the north-east, Colonel Robert Monro, when he entered the town on 28 May, allowing him to use his house, 'the most conspicuous lodging in Aberdene', as his headquarters (J. Gordon, 2.168). Marischal went south to Edinburgh to attend parliament in June, but returned to Aberdeen on 2 July and accompanied Monro in an expedition which occupied Huntly's castle of Strathbogie (Huntly Castle). In July and August the general assembly of the Church of Scotland met in Aberdeen, symbolizing the covenanters' triumph in the former centre of resistance to them, and Marischal provided guards and made his house available for committee meetings. Now they were not needed locally, men recruited by Marischal were sent to join the Scottish army which had occupied the north of England, and he visited the army at Newcastle.

A royalist source described Marischal as 'a gentleman not ill disposed if left to himselfe, and at that time too young to see the deepth of thes courses that he was ledd upon' by the influence of the earl of Argyll. His actions were 'much against the good lyckings of his mother', the dowager Countess Marischal, 'who laboured much (but in vaine), to reclaime her son to the King's partye' (J. Gordon, 3.160). However, the doubts which had delayed Marischal's joining of the covenanters soon re-emerged. He was alienated by the covenanters' refusal to accept his demand that his domination of Aberdeenshire—his rivals Huntly and the Gordons now being defeated royalist 'rebels'—be recognized by giving him command of all regiments raised there. In August 1640 he was one of a group of discontented covenanting nobles (including Montrose) who signed the Cumbernauld bond which (though vague in wording) reflected growing fears of Argyll's increasing ambition and power, and on 6 December he signed a bond of friendship with Montrose. Once knowledge of the Cumbernauld bond became public, Marischal lost the trust of the covenanter leaders. In 1641 he was further embittered by failure to gain payment for expenses incurred in the bishops' wars, and after a dispute over the right to the customs of Aberdeen in 1642 he 'went to dur [hard] malcontent' (Spalding, 2.96).

When, late in 1643, the covenanters began to levy a new army, to enter England to help the English parliament in the civil war against the king, Marischal became embroiled in a new dispute over status. Lord Gordon, Huntly's eldest son, had agreed to co-operate with the covenanters, and it was decided that the north-east should, for recruiting purposes, be divided between him and Marischal. Months of bickering over the precise division followed, though Marischal did raise a regiment which served in the Scottish army in England in 1644–7. His disillusionment with the covenanters' treatment of him did not lead him to royalism, however. When Huntly halfheartedly attempted a royalist rising in March 1644, occupying Aberdeen, he sent to Marischal at Dunnottar asking what his intentions were, and received the reply that the earl was 'myndit not to stur, except he was compellit thairto' (Spalding, 2.331). Argyll moved north against Huntly, and Marischal raised men and co-operated with him in suppressing the north-eastern royalists, but thereafter he relapsed into trying to avoid involvement in civil war. When the marquess of Montrose brought his royalist army north after his first victory (at Tippermuir on 1 September 1644), Marischal made no attempt to oppose him. As was commented on by both royalist and covenanter historians: 'he lay still in Dunnotar when most was ado' (ibid., 2.405); 'Marischall, being malcontent, satt still in Dunotter' (*Letters and Journals of Robert Baillie*, 2.234). In the campaigning that followed, the earl ventured out of his stronghold on a number of occasions to meet covenanting nobles and gentry, but then retired home without action. In March 1645 the committee of estates informed him that parliament had given him the chief command of the shires of Kincardine, Aberdeen, and Banff, promising that all his expenses (and those of previous campaigns) would be paid, but he did nothing. In the same month Montrose, still hoping to persuade Marischal to join the royalist cause, wrote to him, but he refused to reply—on the advice, it was said, of his wife and the sixteen or so covenanter parish ministers who had taken refuge at Dunnottar. Montrose reacted to his silence by burning Stonehaven, but the royalists still hoped to win his support, and when, in one of his ventures out of Dunnottar (in August or September 1645), he was captured by Lord Aboyne he was quickly set free to avoid alienating him.

Marischal's inactivity in the mid-1640s was partly based on personal grievances, but it also reflected the unease shared by many nobles who had formerly been active covenanters at military intervention in England against the king, an unease that his mother's unswervingly royalist stance must have intensified. The emergence in 1647–8 of the engager regime in Scotland, combining moderate royalists with moderate covenanters and dedicated to opposing the English parliament in the name of both the imprisoned Charles I and the covenants, gave Marischal a cause he could support wholeheartedly. On 4 May he was commissioned to raise a troop of horse, while his brother George commanded a regiment of foot. Marischal led his troop into England with the duke of Hamilton's army, but fled back to Scotland as the army disintegrated in August after the battle of Preston. Under the kirk party regime which then seized power, engagers such as Marischal were excluded from public life, and only once Oliver Cromwell occupied Edinburgh after the battle of Dunbar was it conceded that the military services of engagers could be accepted, provided they admitted their former conduct to be sinful. On 14 December 1650 Marischal was referred to the presbytery of Aberdeen to give satisfaction for his support for the engagement, and on 20 December he was appointed a colonel of horse and foot. Charles II visited Dunnottar in July 1650 and February 1651, and on 22 May 1651 Marischal was ordered to be ready to lead all the landowners of Kincardineshire, with horses, arms, and provisions, against the English. However, on 31 July, before marching into England, Charles ordered Marischal and his friends to remain behind, and to 'draw togidder all the men they are aibill … for defence of our kingdome and offending the enemie' (NA Scot., GD 22/1/519). Marischal was also a member of the committee of estates left to govern the kingdom, and with many other members of it he was captured by the English at Alyth in Forfarshire on 28 August 1651.

Through his office as marshal of Scotland the earl had responsibility for the honours of Scotland—the crown, sceptre, and sword—during sessions of parliament, and when the final parliament of the covenanters adjourned at Perth on 6 June 1651 he had been instructed to take them to safe-keeping in Dunnottar Castle. Charles II also sent property, which he valued at £20,000 sterling, to Dunnottar for safety. On his capture at Alyth, Marischal managed to send a messenger to his mother, the dowager countess, with a key to the strongroom in which he had concealed the honours. She immediately went to Dunnottar and passed custody of them to the commander of the garrison, George Ogilvie of Barras. When the castle was besieged by the English he arranged for them to be smuggled out and hidden in Kinneff church, where they remained until the restoration of monarchy in 1660.

Marischal was sent to London, where his imprisonment in the years that followed varied in degree of confinement. Some of the time he was detained within the Tower, but on others given freedom within London or even within 20 miles of the city. Pressure was put on him to order the surrender of Dunnottar, and on 4 May 1652 he wrote to Ogilvie with the necessary orders. The letter, with its fulsome praise of the English, had clearly been extorted under pressure, but Ogilvie was reaching the end of his ability to resist, and Dunnottar surrendered on 24 May, the last garrison in Scotland to fall to Cromwell. In April 1654 Marischal had sufficient freedom to get married, to Lady Anne (d. c.1689), daughter of Robert Douglas, eighth earl of Morton (his first wife, Elizabeth, having died in June 1650), and in July he was given an allowance of £3 sterling a week, later raised to £5, to support himself and his wife. He petitioned for a month's liberty in November 1655, as his health had been ruined by four years of restraint, eighteen months of it in the Tower. This was allowed, and extended several times. Marischal was excluded from the Scottish Act of Pardon of 1654 and his property confiscated, though he claimed that he had never been in arms against the English Commonwealth and when captured in 1651 had been travelling peacefully from his home to Alyth. In 1657 a fine of £9793 sterling was substituted for confiscation. The date of his release from imprisonment is unknown, but by July 1659 he was back at Dunnottar, and in September he signed a new undertaking not to act against the regime, under threat of being again imprisoned if he refused.

On 8 October 1660, monarchy having been restored, Marischal took over custody of the honours, 'the antient monuments of this kingdome', from George Ogilvie. The triumph of their preservation was, however, marred by a bitter dispute betwen Ogilvie and Marischal's mother over who should have credit—and therefore reward—for having concealed them. As the earl told his mother disapprovingly, 'it hes bene an Uglye and Unhandsom busines' (NL Scot., MS 21174, fol. 99). Marischal was appointed a privy councillor (13 February 1661) and keeper of the privy seal of Scotland, but is said to have spent much of his final years in London. Nearly all the furnishing and his other property in Dunnottar had been sold off in 1652, and he had had to sell off much of his land in the 1650s to meet debts and pay his fine. He never recovered from these financial losses, which makes the story that 'he reduced himself and his successors to absolute poverty' by 'his

extravagant habits' (Scots peerage, 6.57) seem unduly harsh. He died at Inverugie in March 1671 'after a chronick mallady' (Fraser, 480).   DAVID STEVENSON

Sources DNB · GEC, Peerage · Scots peerage · J. Spalding, Memorialls of the trubles in Scotland and in England, AD 1624 – AD 1645, ed. J. Stuart, 2 vols., Spalding Club, [21, 23] (1850–51) · The letters and journals of Robert Baillie, ed. D. Laing, 3 vols. (1841–2) · J. Gordon, History of Scots affairs from 1637–1641, ed. J. Robertson and G. Grub, 3 vols., Spalding Club, 1, 3, 5 (1841) · P. Gordon, A short abridgement of Britane's distemper, ed. J. Dunn, Spalding Club, 10 (1844) · R. Gordon and G. Gordon, A genealogical history of the earldom of Sutherland … with a continuation to the year 1651 (1813) · D. G. Barron, ed., In defence of the regalia, 1651–2 (1910) · E. M. Furgol, A regimental history of the covenanting armies, 1639–1651 (1990) · F. D. Dow, Cromwellian Scotland, 1651–1660 (1979) · P. Buchan, An historical and authentic account of the ancient and noble family of Keith, Earls Marichal of Scotland (1820) · CSP dom., 1651–9 · Reg. PCS, 2nd ser., vol. 7 · Diary of Sir Archibald Johnston of Wariston, 1, ed. G. M. Paul, Scottish History Society, 61 (1911) · NA Scot., GD 220/3/180; RH 4/57/85 · NA Scot., PA 11/4, fol. 9r · A. F. Mitchell and J. Christie, eds., The records of the commissions of the general assemblies of the Church of Scotland, 3, Scottish History Society, 58 (1909) · D. Stevenson, ed., The government of Scotland under the covenanters, Scottish History Society, 4th ser., 18 (1982) · The Clarke Papers, ed. C. H. Firth, 4, CS, new ser., 62 (1901), 27, 41 · NA Scot., GD 22/1/519 · NL Scot., MS 21174, fol. 99 · J. Fraser, Chronicles of the Frasers: the Wardlaw manuscript, ed. W. Mackay, Scottish History Society, 1st ser., 47 (1905), 480

Archives NL Scot., corresp. and papers | NL Scot., letters to Robert Farquhar

Likenesses G. Jamesone, oils, 1636, Scot. NPG [see illus.]

Keith, William (c.1664–1712). See under Drummond, Mary, Countess Marischal (1675–1729).

Keith, Sir William, fourth baronet (c.1669–1749), colonial governor, was the son of Sir William Keith, third baronet (d. c.1721), and Jean, née Smith. He was baptized in the Scottish Episcopal church on 16 February 1680 at Peterhead, Aberdeenshire. He obtained an MA degree at Marischal College, Aberdeen, in 1687. Keith went to the exiled Jacobite court at St Germain, apparently shortly after the revolution of 1688, for by 1704 he had 'been long at that court, he had free access to that queen and prince, and hoped they would have made him under-secretary for Scotland' (Bishop Burnet's History, 5.124). He was implicated in the 'Scotch Plot' of 1703–4. In July 1704 he entered the Middle Temple, London, and about the same time married a wealthy widow, Ann Newbury, née Diggs (1675–1740). In 1710 he stood as a parliamentary candidate in Aberdeenshire, and solicited the support of the prime minister, Robert Harley, protesting his loyalty to the queen.

Although he failed in 1710, Keith successfully petitioned Harley in 1713 for the post of surveyor-general of the customs in the southern colonies of North America. He arrived in Virginia in August 1714 to take up his duties. He had begun to undertake them vigorously when the whig purge of supporters of Anne's last ministry led to his dismissal in July 1715. In the following year Keith was in Philadelphia, where he persuaded the agents of William Penn, the proprietor of Pennsylvania, that he would make an admirable replacement for the deputy governor, William Gookin, whose unbalanced behaviour was causing problems. He promptly went to England to solicit the appointment from Penn and to have it endorsed by the privy council, after which he returned to Philadelphia in May 1717.

Keith at first impressed Penn's friends in Pennsylvania, giving them 'a very favourable opinion of his good sense, sweetness of disposition, and moderation in his former post' (*Pennsylvania Archives*, 11.53). His reputation rose further when he successfully resolved the issues raised by the Quaker practice of affirming rather than swearing, and the resentment this had incurred among Anglicans. But the Quakers of Pennsylvania came to regret Keith's appointment when 'he surprised his friends … who had recommended him and had conceived very different hopes and expectations of him by discovering his fondness of absolute power' (Logan to Joshua Gee, 1 Oct 1724, Logan MSS, American Philosophical Society, fol. 277). One of the ways in which he displayed this penchant was by distinguishing between his appointment to the governorship of Pennsylvania and that of the three lower counties which became known as Delaware. The first was without limitation, but the second was during the king's pleasure. Keith interpreted this to indicate that Delaware was now regarded as a crown colony, and proceeded to act as if he were the king's rather than the proprietor's deputy. Thus he called himself 'Excellency', and issued a charter to New Castle in 1724 with no reference to the proprietor.

After Penn died, in 1718, Keith even began to assert his own authority in Pennsylvania, where he seemed 'to be very much in a state of independency, being neither under the immediate cognisance of the Crown, in which the Government is not vested, nor under any Proprietor, the right not being yet determined' (*Pennsylvania Archives*, 11.77). Keith built up a power base in the assembly, cultivating especially the members for Philadelphia city and county. The issue of paper currency in 1723 was apparently in response to the wishes of the tradesmen and merchants in these constituencies, but contrary to those of the landowners, including the Penns, whose quit-rents fell in value by 12 per cent. Keith's policies alienated the proprietary faction on the council, who complained to Penn's widow about it. She wrote to Keith requiring him to consult the council before accepting bills from the assembly. He countered this move to restrain him by publishing the letter, and accusing those who had solicited it of trying to turn the council into an upper chamber. Since by the frame of government issued by Penn the legislative functions of the council had been abolished, the Pennsylvania legislature was unicameral. Keith was therefore appealing to it over the heads of the proprietorial family and the provincial council. In 1726, however, the Penns thwarted his ambitions when he was dismissed as governor and replaced by Patrick Gordon.

Keith then sought to keep control of the assembly in order to use its authority against the new governor. The elections of 1726 and 1727 were consequently among the fiercest fought in eighteenth-century Pennsylvania. In so far as there was a serious issue at stake, it was the question of paper money. Keith had incurred the support of the Philadelphian business community for his approval of the currency, and built it up by establishing the 'tiff' or 'leather apron club' and the gentleman's club in the city. Governor Gordon found his chief support in the rural counties of Bucks and Chester. Although those counties returned a majority to the assembly, Keith capitalized on his interest with the Philadelphia assemblymen by getting them to boycott the assembly, making it non-quorate and thereby bringing legislative business to a standstill.

When this stratagem failed to paralyse the provincial government Keith sought to exploit his interest at Whitehall, and therefore left Pennsylvania and sailed to England. There he tried to persuade the king to grant him the governorship of the three lower counties, but the Penn family showed that it had too strong an interest at court for a successful challenge to be mounted against them there. Keith tried to obtain other colonial favours from the government. In 1728 he petitioned for the governorship of New Jersey, and in 1731 he proposed to the Board of Trade the creation of a new colony west of the Blue Ridge mountains to be called Georgia. Neither bid was successful. By then Keith was desperately in debt. He had always been spendthrift, and his extravagance and shady speculations to recover his losses had aggravated the case against him in Pennsylvania. He spent the years 1734 and 1735 in the Fleet prison. In the late 1730s he became a journalist, published pamphlets and a history of Virginia, and launched a weekly paper, *The Citizen*. When he died, on 18 November 1749, in London, the *London Magazine* observed that he had been 'well known to the projecting part of the world' (Horle and others, 2.584). W. A. SPECK

Sources 'Keith, Sir William', *Lawmaking and legislators in Pennsylvania: a biographical dictionary*, ed. C. W. Horle and others, 2 (Philadelphia, 1991), 561–89 · *Pennsylvania Archives*, 2nd ser., 19 vols. (1874–90), vol. 11 · American Philosophical Society, Philadelphia, Logan MSS · Hist. Soc. Penn., Logan papers · CSP col., vols. 1, 5, 7, 9–45 · *The case of the heir at law and executrix of the the late proprietor of Pensylvania etc, in relation to the removal of Sir William Keith* (1726); repr. (1923) · *Bishop Burnet's History*, vol. 5 · C. P. Keith, 'The wife and children of Sir William Keith', *Pennsylvania Magazine of History and Biography*, 56 (1932)

Keith, Sir William John (1873–1937), administrator in Burma, was born at Portobello, Edinburgh, on 13 April 1873, the eldest of six children of Davidson Keith, an advertising agent of Edinburgh, and his wife, Margaret Stobie Drysdale. All six children built their lives around Britain's Indo-Burmese empire. Of Keith's three brothers, Arthur Berriedale *Keith (1879–1944) became regius professor of Sanskrit and comparative philology at the University of Edinburgh; Steuart was a sessions judge in Burma at the time of his death in 1919, aged forty-two; and Alan Davidson, a barrister who spent all his professional life in Burma, was nearing elevation to the Rangoon high court when he died in February 1928, also aged forty-two. Of Keith's sisters, one married R. W. Adamson, director of the Burmah Oil Company, and the other married Frank Dewar of the Indian Civil Service.

Keith was educated at the Royal High School, Edinburgh, and Edinburgh University, where he graduated with first-class honours in classics in 1895. In August 1895 he joined the Indian Civil Service. He spent a year's probation at Christ Church, Oxford, and arrived in Burma in November 1896.

In 1899, after short postings in Kyaukse, Meiktila, and Shwebo, Keith was appointed secretary to the financial commissioner of Burma, in which post he set about standardizing the district revenue manuals, a work of exacting precision which was to become his hallmark. In December 1907 he was appointed settlement officer of Minbu in Upper Burma, and in 1911 published his *Report on the Second Settlement of the Meiktila District, Upper Burma*.

In July 1912 Keith was appointed revenue secretary, which post he continued to hold for the next seven years, exerting a formidable control over other government departments. During this period Keith was also a member of the Burmese legislative council. In May 1915 he married Isabel, only daughter of Sir Harvey Adamson, lieutenant-governor of Burma, who herself had been born in Burma.

In January 1921, after two years as commissioner of Magwe division, Keith went to Delhi as a nominated member of the newly constituted Indian legislative assembly. In August 1922 he regained his control over the purse strings of Burmese government as financial commissioner, and in the following January, when the Montagu–Chelmsford system of diarchy was introduced to Burma, he was made first member and vice-president of the executive council, again in charge of the revenue and finance departments.

Keith's work was marked by inexhaustible attention to detail and a readiness to interfere at the lowest levels of administration, characteristics which did not endear him to other civil servants or the expatriate commercial community. He was known for his wordy, sometimes pompous, minutes and was easily caricatured as a humourless Scot. Whatever the irritation suffered by his European colleagues, however, his patience and lack of grandeur made him popular with the first Burmese politicians who tasted power under diarchy. In an era when most Europeans thought the Burmese incapable of any form of self-government, Keith was one of the few prepared to treat his Burmese colleagues as intimates.

Keith was appointed knight bachelor in 1925, and for four months of that year was acting governor of Burma. Although it was generally held that he and his retiring wife were too homely to seek high office, Keith had hoped to see out his career as governor and was disappointed in 1927 not to be chosen as Sir Harcourt Butler's successor.

Keith retired in April 1928, having been appointed KCSI, the only such honour for service exclusively in Burma. Settling at St Margaret's, Dunbar, he served on the burgh council (1929–32) and as bailie and magistrate (1931). He died at St Margaret's on 22 January 1937, and was survived by his wife, a son, and two daughters. He was buried at St Margaret's on 26 January.   KATHERINE PRIOR

Sources *Rangoon Gazette* (7 May 1928) • *The Times* (25 Jan 1937) • A. J. S. White, *The Burma of 'A. J.': memoirs of A. J. S. White* (1991) • BL OIOC, Halifax MSS, vol. 21 • *WWW, 1929–40* • *DNB*

Likenesses W. Stoneman, photograph, 1930, NPG • photograph, repro. in *Rangoon Gazette*, 15
Wealth at death £7241 17s. 8d.: confirmation, 14 Feb 1937, *CCI*

Kekewich, Sir Arthur (1832–1907), judge, was born on 26 July 1832 at Peamore, Exeter, the second son of Samuel Trehawke Kekewich of Peamore, MP for Exeter in 1826 and for South Devon in 1858, and his first wife, Agatha Maria Sophia, daughter of John Langston of Sarsden, Oxfordshire. Kekewich came from an old Devon family and his elder brother Trehawke Kekewich (1823–1909) took a prominent part in county affairs. Sir George William *Kekewich (1841–1921) was his half-brother and Major-General Sir Robert George *Kekewich (1854–1914) was his nephew.

Kekewich was educated at Eton College and Balliol College, Oxford, where he matriculated on 11 March 1850. He was awarded a second class by the mathematical moderators in 1852, and graduated BA in 1854 with a first class in *literae humaniores* and a second in the final school of mathematics. In the same year he was elected to a fellowship at Exeter College, which he held until his marriage on 23 September 1858 to Marianne, daughter of James William Freshfield. He took an MA in 1856.

Having entered as a student at Lincoln's Inn on 8 November 1854, Kekewich was called to the bar on 7 June 1858. The connections he had through his wife with the prestigious firm of Freshfield & Son, solicitors, gave him an excellent start, and led to his becoming at an early stage junior standing counsel to the Bank of England. For many years he enjoyed one of the largest junior practices at the Chancery bar. He was made QC on 4 May 1877 and a bencher of Lincoln's Inn on 4 May 1881. Though he possessed a sound knowledge of law and practice, he lacked the qualities of a good leader. He never obtained a firm footing in any of the chancery courts, and his practice withered. He stood unsuccessfully for parliament as a Conservative candidate for Coventry in 1880 and Barnstaple in 1885.

On the retirement of Vice-Chancellor Bacon in November 1886, to the surprise of the bar Kekewich was appointed by Lord Halsbury to fill the vacancy. He was knighted early in 1887. On the bench Kekewich showed a briskness and speed not usual in Chancery proceedings. He had a thorough knowledge of the minutiae of equity practice, especially the administration of estates in Chancery. But his quickness of perception and his speed of decision sometimes impaired his judgments, and he failed to curb his natural tendency to exuberance of speech. He was also apt to be irritable on the bench. His judgments were appealed against with uncomplimentary frequency, and he was often reversed in the Court of Appeal though occasionally upheld by the House of Lords. Several of his juniors on the bench were promoted over his head to the Court of Appeal.

Kekewich was a strong churchman and Conservative. A man of fine physique and active habits, he was a keen shot and fisherman, and became in later life an enthusiastic

Sir Arthur Kekewich (1832–1907), by Barraud, pubd 1891

golfer. He died after a very short illness at his house at Devonshire Place, London, on 22 November 1907, and was buried in Exminster, near Exeter. He was survived by his wife, two sons, and five daughters.

J. B. ATLAY, rev. HUGH MOONEY

Sources *The Times* (23 Nov 1907) · **Archives** Bodl. Oxf., case papers · **Likenesses** Barraud, photograph, NPG; repro. in *Men and Women of the Day*, 4 (1891) [see illus.] · Spy [L. Ward], chromolithograph caricature, NPG; repro. in *VF* (24 Jan 1895) · **Wealth at death** £60,364 10s. 4d.: probate, 14 Dec 1907, CGPLA Eng. & Wales

Kekewich, Sir George William (1841–1921), civil servant and politician, was born on 1 April 1841, the fourth son of Samuel Trehawke Kekewich (1796–1873), landowner and MP for South Devon, and his second wife, Louisa, only daughter of Lewis William Buck, MP for North Devon. He had three brothers and seven sisters. He was educated at Eton College and at Balliol College, Oxford, taking a second-class degree in *literae humaniores* in 1863. Rejecting the possibility of a career in the church, Kekewich started reading for the law at Lincoln's Inn but in 1867 readily accepted an appointment to the education department as an examiner through the patronage of Sir Stafford Northcote, a distant relative. He was promoted to senior examiner in 1871 and in 1890 Lord Cranbrook appointed him permanent secretary on Patrick Cumin's death, being impressed by his grasp of departmental matters as well as his liberal education views.

Kekewich desired equity in education and believed that schoolteachers should be free to implement the task entrusted to them. The education code of 1890 reflected his views and initiated the demise of the Draconian system of payment by results introduced by Robert Lowe in 1861. Similarly, the establishment of the principle of free elementary education in the 1891 Education Act owed much to his success in circumventing the more reactionary aims of Lord Salisbury. From 1892 to 1895 he enjoyed a harmonious working relationship with the Liberal vice-president A. H. D. Acland and their adjustments to the annual education department Code effected a liberalization of the elementary school curriculum. The Code was used also to force incompetent schools to improve and the issuing of Circular 321 in 1893 enforced adherence to the required standards for buildings and facilities. Innovations were made in the education of handicapped children, while steps were taken to initiate reform of the secondary school system. These changes were the necessary precursors to a more fundamental overhaul of the system, but one consequence of the election of Lord Salisbury's Unionist government in 1895 was that Kekewich would not oversee this.

An initial rapport with his two new political masters, the eighth duke of Devonshire and Sir John Gorst, allowed Kekewich to continue to contribute to policy formulation and in 1900 he was appointed secretary of the newly created Board of Education. Thereafter he found it difficult to accept policies designed to establish new local education authorities based upon the county and county borough councils and involving the demise of the *ad hoc* school boards, which he had encouraged since their inception in 1870. His opposition alienated him from the government and he was deemed unfit to ensure the successful implementation of the 1902 Education Act. His premature retirement was enforced in October 1902, with Robert Morant succeeding him. Kekewich's feeling of injustice was so strong that his first act was to resign from the Junior Carlton Club and thereafter he campaigned vigorously against the act. In 1906 he was elected as Liberal MP for Exeter, a seat he held until 1910; but his hopes that the Liberal governments would redress the imbalances of the 1902 act remained unfulfilled. His lively memoir, *The Education Department and After* (1920), provides useful insights about the governance of English education in the late nineteenth century but has to be treated with caution because of its embittered mien.

Kekewich's achievements in education reform have been overshadowed by those of his more charismatic successor but his administration was beneficent. By 1900 he could see the promised land and, while he did not enter it, his efforts earned him the gratitude of many teachers; in 1903 he was made the first honorary member of the National Union of Teachers. A devotee of salmon fishing, which he believed to be a panacea for all human ills, Kekewich was also a keen gardener. He was married twice: first, on 19 November 1863, to Hannah (d. March 1890), daughter of George Lovegrove; and then, on 10 June 1890, to Agnes Jane (d. 1931), daughter of William Symmons. He died at 6 Sackville Gardens, Hove, Sussex, on 5 July 1921. He was appointed CB in 1891, KCB in 1895, and was awarded the honorary degree of DCL by Durham University in 1897.   N. D. DAGLISH

Sources *The Times* (7 July 1921), 15 · *The Times* (11 July 1921), 13 · Burke, *Gen. GB* · *WWW* · G. W. Kekewich, *The education department and after* (1920) · *The diary of Gathorne Hardy, later Lord Cranbrook, 1866–1892: political selections*, ed. N. E. Johnson (1981) · G. Sutherland, *Policy-making in elementary education, 1870–1895* (1973) · 'Celebrities at home, no. 1232: Sir George William Kekewich', *The World* (22 Jan 1902), 6–7 · *CGPLA Eng. & Wales* (1922)
Archives BLPES, letters · Duke U., Perkins L., corresp. | PRO, Education Department MSS
Likenesses WHO, portrait, repro. in *VF* (26 July 1911); copy, Hult. Arch.
Wealth at death £1762 4s. 10d.: probate, 17 June 1922, *CGPLA Eng. & Wales*

Kekewich, Robert George (1854–1914), army officer, was born on 17 June 1854 at Brampford Speke, near Exeter, the second son of Trehawke Kekewich (1823–1909) of Peamore, Exeter, and nephew of the judge Sir Arthur Kekewich. His mother was Charlotte (d. 1879), daughter of Captain George Peard RN. He was educated at Marlborough College and entered the army (102nd regiment) in 1874. He was transferred to the Buffs (East Kent regiment) in the same year, however, and soon saw active service, going to the Malay peninsula with the Perak expedition of 1875–6. In 1883 he received his captaincy, and afterwards served with the Sudan expedition of 1884–5 as deputy assistant adjutant and quartermaster-general. For his services there he was promoted brevet major. In 1888 he served as deputy assistant adjutant-general of British troops at Suakin, in the eastern Sudan. He was awarded the Mejidiye (fourth class). In 1890 he was made major in the Royal Inniskilling Fusiliers, and the following year he was appointed military secretary to the commander-in-chief, Madras, a post which he held until 1897. He served in Burma on the Chin hills expedition, 1892–3, and was promoted lieutenant-colonel in command of the 1st battalion, Loyal North Lancashire regiment, in 1898.

In the Second South African War of 1899–1902 Kekewich served as lieutenant-colonel, commanding all the troops in Griqualand West and Bechuanaland. He gained his fame as the commander of the diamond-mining town of Kimberley, which was besieged by the Boers from 15 October 1899 to 15 February 1900. With a small garrison—half a battalion of his own regiment, some Cape police, and the rest local volunteers—Kekewich improvised effective fortifications. His skilful conduct of the defence won the praise of Roberts and Kitchener. His problems were exacerbated by Cecil Rhodes. Kimberley was largely a De Beers company town, its garrison was largely De Beers employees, and Rhodes dominated De Beers. Domineering, energetic, volatile, and sometimes irresponsible and abusive, Rhodes, who thought Kekewich lacked drive and did not know his job, quarrelled with him and challenged his authority. At one meeting Rhodes exclaimed, 'You low, damned, mean cur, Kekewich, you deny me at your peril' (Pakenham, 322) and tried to punch him. Kekewich was

Robert George Kekewich (1854–1914), by W. & D. Downey

tactful, but Rhodes's hostility continued until and after the relief of Kimberley (15 February). French then, influenced by Rhodes, sacked Kekewich as garrison commander. Yet Kekewich's military reputation continued high, and he was created CB in 1900.

After the relief of Kimberley, Kekewich returned to the command of his battalion, which formed part of the column under Methuen. From December 1900 to January 1902 he commanded a mobile column. In February 1902 he was given a group of columns to command. He took a prominent part in the actions of Moedville (30 September 1901) and Rooiwal (11 April 1902), and as a reward for his services was made major-general (1902). Kekewich retired in March 1904, and was colonel of the Buffs from October 1909 until his death. He never married. He died on 5 November 1914 at his home, Whimple rectory, Whimple, near Exeter.   C. V. OWEN, rev. M. G. M. JONES

Sources *The Times* (6 Nov 1914) · W. A. J. O'Meara, *Kekewich in Kimberley* (1926) · T. Pakenham, *The Boer War* (1979) · *Army List* · Burke, *Gen. GB* · *Standard and Digger's News* (10 Nov 1899) · private information (1927) · C. N. Robinson, *Celebrities of the army*, 18 pts (1900) · *WWW* · N. B. Leslie, *The succession of colonels of the British army from 1660 to the present day* (1974) · J. G. Lockhart and C. M. Woodhouse, *Rhodes* (1963)
Archives Queen's Lancashire Regimental Museum, Fulwood barracks, Preston, Lancashire, diary
Likenesses W. & D. Downey, photograph, NPG [see illus.]
Wealth at death £23,743 1s. 6d.: probate, 3 Feb 1915, *CGPLA Eng. & Wales*

Kelburn, Sinclare (1753/4–1802), minister of the Presbyterian General Synod of Ulster, was the only surviving son of the Revd Ebenezer Kelburn (d. 1776), minister of Plunket Street Presbyterian Church, Dublin, and Martha Sinclare. He was educated at Trinity College, Dublin, from 1769 to 1774 when he graduated BA, and then went to Edinburgh and Glasgow universities to study theology and medicine. Having been licensed to preach he received a call from the Third Presbyterian Congregation of Belfast (now Rosemary Presbyterian Church), and on 8 February 1780 was ordained as assistant and successor to the Revd William Laird.

The volunteer movement was then at its height, and Kelburn became one of its most ardent promoters, sometimes appearing in his pulpit on Sundays in the uniform of his corps, with his musket standing beside him. On one occasion 450 volunteers were quartered all night in his church, and he preached to them on the following day. His first publication, *The Morality of the Sabbath Defended* (1781), was a rejoinder to a sermon preached by his neighbour, the Revd Dr James Crombie, in which the volunteers had been recommended to meet on Sundays for drill. He soon acquired a high reputation as a preacher. In 1790 he published *The Duty of Preaching the Gospel Explained and Recommended* (1790). His largest and most important work was *The divinity of our Lord Jesus Christ asserted and proved, and the connection of this doctrine with practical religion pointed out* (1792). It reached a second edition.

In April 1797 Kelburn was arrested and lodged in Kilmainham prison on suspicion of being connected with the United Irishmen. On his liberation, after six months' incarceration, his health deteriorated and in November 1799, at the request of his congregation, he resigned his pastoral charge. He died, aged forty-eight, at Beersbridge, Belfast, on 31 March 1802, and was buried in the burial-ground of Castlereagh Presbyterian Church, co. Down. His widow, Frances, died on 21 August 1834.

THOMAS HAMILTON, rev. DOUGLAS ARMSTRONG

Sources *Records of the General Synod of Ulster, from 1691 to 1820*, 3 vols. (1890–98), vols. 2, 3 · S. Kelburn, 'Memoir', *The divinity of our Lord Jesus Christ asserted and proved … in five sermons*, 2nd edn (Lexington, KY, 1805) · minutes of the Rosemary Presbyterian Church committee, 1774–1835, office of Rosemary Presbyterian Church, Ekenhead Memorial Halls, North Circular Road, Belfast · pulpit record of Rosemary Presbyterian Church, 1761–1812, office of Rosemary Presbyterian Church, Ekenhead Memorial Halls, North Circular Road, Belfast · *Belfast News-Letter* (2 April 1802) · *Belfast News-Letter* (26 Aug 1834) · R. S. J. Clarke, ed., *Baronies of upper and lower Castlereagh* (1966), vol. 1 of *Gravestone inscriptions: County Down* (1966–89), 10 · W. I. Addison, ed., *The matriculation albums of the University of Glasgow from 1728 to 1858* (1913) · *Northern Star* (21 April 1797) · Burtchaell & Sadleir, *Alum. Dubl.* · T. Witherow, *Historical and literary memorials of presbyterianism in Ireland, 1731–1800* (1880) · D. Armstrong, *Rev. Sinclare Kelburn, 1754–1802: preacher, pastor, patriot* (2001)

Keldeleth, Robert. *See* Kenleith, Robert (d. 1273).

Kelham, Robert (1717–1808), legal antiquary, was baptized on 12 December 1717 at Billingborough, Lincolnshire, the son of Robert Kelham (c.1676–1752), vicar of Billingborough, Threckingham, and Walcot, Lincolnshire. Admitted a member of Lincoln's Inn on 8 July 1734, he practised as an attorney in the court of king's bench until

1792. Kelham married Sarah (1720/21–1774), youngest daughter of Peter and Joanna Gery of Bilstone, Leicestershire, who died on 28 September 1774 at the age of fifty-three. He subsequently erected a monument to her and four infant children in the church of St Michael Royal, College Hill, London. As well as founding a school at Great Gonerby, Lincolnshire, Kelham was a member of Staple Inn.

Kelham died at Bush Hill, Edmonton, Middlesex, where he had lived, on 29 March 1808, in his ninety-first year, and was buried at St Michael Royal, London. He was survived by a son, Robert Kelham (1755–1811), an attorney of the king's bench, and a daughter.

Kelham was a noted legal antiquary, publishing annotated translations of John Selden's *Dissertatio ad Fletam*—*The Dissertation of John Selden, Annexed to Fleta, Translated, with Notes* (1771)—and of part of the thirteenth-century treatise known as *Britton*: *Britton, containing the antient pleas of the crown: translated, and illustrated with references, notes, and antient records* (1762). He compiled *A Dictionary of the Norman or Old French Language* (1779), which he published together with an edition of David Wilkins's translation of the laws of William the Conqueror, and a companion to Domesday Book, *Domesday Book Illustrated* (1788). His *Alphabetical Index to All the Abridgments of Law and Equity* (1758) was a valuable aid to users of the *Abridgment* of Charles Viner, and was incorporated into the second edition of Viner's work. DAVID IBBETSON

Sources *GM*, 1st ser., 78 (1808), 370 · will, PRO, PROB 11/1477 fol. 352 · father's will, PRO, PROB 11/794 fol. 332 · W. P. Baildon and R. Roxburgh, eds., *The records of the Honorable Society of Lincoln's Inn: the black books*, 5 vols. (1897–1968) · *IGI* · Nichols, *Lit. anecdotes* · W. P. Baildon, ed., *The records of the Honorable Society of Lincoln's Inn: admissions*, 2 vols. (1896) · W. Robinson, *The history and antiquities of the parish of Edmonton, in the county of Middlesex* (1819) · J. G. Marvin, *Legal bibliography, or, A thesaurus of American, English, Irish and Scotch law books* (1847)

Wealth at death legacies to the amount of approx. £7000 in goods and land, but will dates from twenty years before death: will, PRO, PROB 11/1477, fol. 352

Kelk, Sir John, first baronet (1816–1886), builder and public works contractor, was born in Compton Street, Soho, London, on 16 February 1816, the son of John Kelk (1781–1848) and his wife, Martha (d. 1861), daughter of Jacob Germain of Bloomsbury. The Kelk family came from Carlton in Lindrick, in north Nottinghamshire. Though his father was a prosperous Soho ironsmith, Kelk was admired by his contemporaries as a man, who 'without powerful or wealthy connections … by a combination of industry, intelligence and integrity' had become wealthy and successful (*PICE*). After a good commercial education, Kelk was apprenticed to the builder and developer Thomas Cubitt, a connection strengthened by the marriage of a sister of his to Cubitt's nephew, J. C. Cuthell. Kelk first went into partnership with William Newton of Margaret Street, Cavendish Square, working in Mayfair, St James's, and Belgravia. On Newton's retirement, he amalgamated with John Elger, another Mayfair builder. Kelk carried out a wide variety of contracts, including the rebuilding of houses in Grosvenor Square and the construction of a number of churches, including St Michael's, Chester Square, and All Saints, Margaret Street, for which his work was praised by the architect, William Butterfield. He built Kneller Hall in Twickenham, the Museum of Practical Geology in Jermyn Street (1849–51), to the design of James Pennethorne, and carried out the reconstruction of the Carlton Club in Pall Mall in 1854.

Kelk's real wealth, however, was made in the construction of public works such as railways and docks, where increasingly he was a promoter rather than the contractor, handing over his firm to his foremen, Smith and Taylor, in 1862. He built the Commercial Dock Company's south dock in Rotherhithe and was a partner in the Thames Iron Works and Shipbuilding Company of Blackwall. This firm, from which the British navy's first seagoing ironclad, *Warrior*, was launched in 1860, was the biggest and most important shipbuilding enterprise on the Thames. It also produced ironwork for Blackfriars railway bridge and Hammersmith Bridge, and for many of Kelk's enterprises such as the building for the 1862 exhibition and the Alexandra Palace.

To contemporary obituarists, Kelk's most impressive railway enterprise was the building of the Victoria Station and Pimlico Railway across the Thames from Battersea into the centre of London in 1858–60, a project on which he worked with the engineer, John Fowler. This railway route was opposed by Thomas Cubitt, a dominant developer in the area, but his death in 1855 removed a major obstacle. Kelk, who had substantial works in the Grosvenor basin, conceived the idea of bringing the railway along the Grosvenor Canal and using the basin as the site of Victoria Station. Kelk worked with Fowler on other projects, including the enlargement of Farringdon Station in 1863 for the Metropolitan Railway, and the Smithfield meat market goods depot. Both Kelk and Fowler were concerned with Peto and Betts, and Waring Brothers, in the building of railways in Kensington, involving the lines for the Metropolitan Railway and the Metropolitan District Railway, respectively from South Kensington to Paddington, and from Tower Hill to South Kensington, from 1864 until 1871.

Kelk undertook a development with Elger in Prince's Gate, Kensington, somewhat prejudiced by the presence of the Crystal Palace in Hyde Park. Wentworth Dilke, secretary to the commission for the 1851 exhibition, recommended him as agent in the purchase of the Gore House estate. Further involvement in the commissioners' estate in South Kensington followed. His firm, seen as a 'thoroughly responsible contractor' (Survey of London, 38.100), was employed to erect the early buildings for the South Kensington Museum, today the Victoria and Albert Museum, a difficult matter because of the unpredictable nature of Treasury contributions. Kelk built the Sheepshanks, Turner (1857), and Vernon (1858–9) galleries, the north court (1859–62), part of the south court (1862), and the lecture range in 1864–6.

Kelk assisted the promoters of the 1862 exhibition, by offering, with the firm of Lucas Brothers, to construct the exhibition building for a figure lower than the anticipated cost. He was a very substantial guarantor, and when it appeared that the ill-fated exhibition, shorn of its figurehead by the death of Prince Albert, was likely to make a loss, he offered to meet the shortfall. He reused elements of the building in the development of the Alexandra Palace, which was intended as a north London rival to the Crystal Palace, providing a venue for exhibitions, concerts, and other occupations contributing to the 'stock of harmless amusements' (*PICE*). Owen Jones had designed the original building but he was succeeded as architect by John Johnson. Lucas and Kelk provided one-third of the finance, together with the London Finance Association and an entrepreneur called Rodonachi, who later withdrew. The palace's destruction by fire in June 1873, less than a month after its opening, damaged Kelk's fortune considerably, but it was rebuilt and opened again on 1 May 1875.

Kelk's firm was the main contractor for the Albert Memorial, a task which he carried out with his usual efficiency, striking terror into at least one of the sculptors. He carried out the work at cost and when the memorial was inaugurated in 1872, like G. G. Scott, the architect, he was offered a knighthood but refused (Scott accepted). This may have been because, like many successful Victorians, he hankered for a baronetcy, which he eventually obtained from Disraeli in 1874. He sat in the House of Commons as Conservative MP for Harwich from 1865–8, but did not make much of a parliamentary career.

Though Kelk became extremely wealthy, not all of his enterprises were successful. In 1863, he was involved in a partnership with John Aird & Sons, to build the Millwall docks, a development in which Fowler and his associate William Wilson were also involved. The financing was somewhat difficult, and Kelk turned to 'Baron' Albert Grant and his Crédit Foncier et Mobilier. The Overend and Gurney crash of 1866 affected the project badly, and it was only completed satisfactorily through the efforts of Acton Smee Ayrton (1816–1886), Liberal MP for Tower Hamlets, and chairman of the Millwall Freehold Land and Docks Company in 1866–8.

Kelk married his cousin Rebecca Anne (*d.* 1885), third daughter of George Kelk of Braehead House, Ayr, on 5 September 1848; they had a son, John William, who inherited the baronetcy, and a daughter. Kelk's wealth was reflected in his lifestyle. He bought Bentley Priory at Stanmore, and later the famous sporting estate of Tidworth in Hampshire, where he employed John Johnson to extend Tedworth House, and to rebuild South Tidworth church in 1878–9. Kelk also rebuilt 3 Grosvenor Square for his own occupation in 1875–7, again employing Johnson, with whom he had worked as a contractor. Kelk became a member of the Institution of Civil Engineers in 1861, magistrate and deputy lieutenant for Middlesex, and a magistrate and sheriff for Hampshire. Despite occasional financial setbacks, he died a very wealthy man, providing substantially for his children. He died at home at Tedworth House, on 12 September 1886; he was mourned locally as a generous host to both sporting associates and learned societies. He was buried in Kensal Green cemetery under a ledger-stone of the pink granite used in the Albert Memorial.   HERMIONE HOBHOUSE

Sources PICE, 87 (1886–7), 451–5 · The Times (14 Sept 1886) · Salisbury & Winchester Journal (18 Sept 1886) · 'The International Exhibition', ILN (10 May 1862) · 'The works of the Metropolitan railway extension in Smithfield', ILN (17 Dec 1864) · 'Commercial docks, Rotherhithe', The Builder, 13 (1855), 323 · 'The new dock of the commercial docks, Rotherhithe', The Builder, 13 (1855), 388 · Principal Registry of the Family Division, London [will granted 9 Nov 1886] · Boase, Mod. Eng. biog. · Burke, Peerage (1916) · The parish of St James, Westminster, 2 pts in 4 vols., Survey of London, 29–32 (1960–63) · S. Porter, ed., Poplar, Blackwall and the Isle of Dogs: the parish of All Saints, 2 vols., Survey of London, 43–4 (1994) · H. Hobhouse, ed., Southern Kensington: Kensington Square to Earl's Court, Survey of London, 42 (1986) · F. H. W. Sheppard, ed., The Grosvenor estate in Mayfair, 2 vols., Survey of London, 39–40 (1977–80) · The museums area of South Kensington and Westminster, Survey of London, 38 (1975) · D. J. Croman, A history of Tidworth and Tedworth House (1991) · CGPLA Eng. & Wales (1886) · The Post Office directory (1846)
Archives City Westm. AC, Grosvenor estate records · Hants. RO, deeds relating to the Tidworth estate
Wealth at death £408,821 4s. 9d.: resworn probate, Dec 1887, CGPLA Eng. & Wales (1886)

Kelke, Roger (1523/4–1576), college head, was the fourth son of Christopher Kelke (c.1491–1524) of Barnetby-le-Wold and Great Kelk, Lincolnshire, and his wife, Isabell (c.1495–1559/60), daughter of Robert Girlington of Frodingham, Lincolnshire. He graduated BA at Cambridge in 1543–4, became a fellow of St John's College in 1545, and proceeded MA in 1547. He was preacher of St John's from 25 April 1552 and was elected a senior fellow of the college on 19 October.

After Mary I's accession Kelke followed the reformer Thomas Lever, master of St John's, to the continent: in Zürich by 13 October 1554, he moved to Basel in 1555. Having returned to Cambridge upon Elizabeth I's accession, he became Lady Margaret preacher in October 1559, though not as yet a bachelor of theology, and on 9 November he was re-elected a senior fellow of St John's. Ever a place-seeker, he wrote in the same month to Sir William Cecil, principal secretary, requesting an archdeaconry. Cecil, chancellor of the university and himself a member of St John's and Kelke's near contemporary, seems to have been responsible for the latter's appointment in November by the visitor, Thomas Howard, fourth duke of Norfolk, as master of Magdalene College, replacing the deprived Richard Carr. Kelke was ordained priest by Edmund Grindal, bishop of London, on 14 January 1560 at the age of thirty-six, having perhaps retained his fellowship at St John's for a period after becoming master of Magdalene. He took the BTh degree in the same year and on 10 June was elected preacher of Ipswich, Suffolk, where two years later the great court cleared him of charges that he was a 'liar, and … a preacher of no true doctrine' (Richardson, 263). In 1561 he wrote again to Cecil seeking an archdeaconry, and at last on 22 January 1563 came royal presentation to the archdeaconry of Stow, in the diocese of Lincoln. In the same year he was again Lady Margaret preacher. A return to St John's as master seemed possible upon Leonard Pilkington's resignation, and

indeed the majority of the fellows initially elected Kelke, but Richard Longworth, Pilkington's candidate, supported by Cecil and royal letters, became master in May 1564. In the same year Kelke took the degree of DTh and was among those who participated in the theology disputation when Elizabeth visited Cambridge; he was also appointed 'to set forth and to teach such plays as should be exhibited before her grace' (Nichols, 1.26). In November 1565, with Robert Beaumont, the vice-chancellor, Longworth, Matthew Hutton, master of Pembroke College, and John Whitgift, Kelke signed a letter to Cecil, as chancellor, against the enforcement of the national vestment regulations in Cambridge, following a revolt among the more radical protestants against cap and surplice at St John's. In June 1567 Beaumont died in office and was temporarily replaced as vice-chancellor by Kelke, who in the following year became rector of Sproughton, Essex. The headship of St John's, split by faction, again became vacant in 1569 upon Longworth's expulsion by Richard Cox, bishop of Ely, who wrote to the fellows suggesting Kelke 'as a fitting man for the place: being indifferent to either side, zealous and not unlearned' (Strype, Whitgift, 15). On 18 November 1569 John May, vice-chancellor, and four other heads of colleges wrote to Cecil recommending Kelke as 'most meet for that place', 'for his experience in that house, indifferency towards all parties, and other aptness in government' (BL, Lansdowne MS 11, fol. 183r). However, upon Cecil's recommendation the mastership went to Nicholas Shepherd, fellow of Trinity College.

In 1570 Kelke, though master of a college more puritan than Church of England, and a town preacher clearly sympathetic to the reformed religion, was among the nine heads of colleges who deprived Thomas Cartwright of his professorship and forbade him to preach in the university. In 1571–2 he was again vice-chancellor. Ipswich provided him with a deputy, though he nevertheless spent time away from Cambridge: as he explained to Lord Burghley in July 1572, 'I was resident upon my cure in all the late disorders, and could not at that time be resident upon mine office' (BL, Lansdowne MS 15, fol. 111r). In August 1572 he was appointed to the rectory of Teversham, Cambridgeshire, and in 1575 he was offered £40 a year to continue as preacher and to reside in Ipswich. Though 'undoubtedly overbearing and awkward' (Cunich and others, 67) and a careless manager not infrequently absent, Kelke's relationship with the fellows of Magdalene seems in general to have been amicable, despite the college's financial difficulties. He resented, however, external interference in the appointment of fellows, a matter which came to a head with his expulsion of Elias Newcomen, a royal nominee, whom he was subsequently forced to reinstate, protesting to Burghley in 1574 that the college had been 'a virgin unspotted and free from all contention these fourteen years (for so long have I been master)' (Lansdowne MS 16, fol. 30r). This was not the last external interference over fellowships, and acquiescence in another external demand proved Kelke's downfall at Magdalene.

In January 1575 Kelke wrote to Burghley, assuring his patron that the 'College have acted according to your request respecting Mr Spinola'. On 13 December, 'the most important date in [Magdalene's] entire history' (Cunich and others, 215), the college granted to the queen, for an annual rent-charge of £15, 7 acres of freehold land in the parish of St Botolph, Aldgate, London, part of the endowment bequeathed by Thomas Audley, Baron Audley, in 1544; the grant was conditional upon a conveyance by 1 April 1575 to Benedict Spinola, a Genoese moneylender. Though satisfactory in the short term, the disastrously improvident nature of the deal rapidly became apparent as Spinola developed the land and sold it to Edward de Vere, seventeenth earl of Oxford. Subsequent generations' attempts to recover the endowment as unlawfully alienated were to no avail, and for centuries Magdalene's problems were to be quintessentially financial.

The date of Kelke's marriage to his wife, Rose, who survived him, is unknown. Their only child, Abigail, married Nicholas Farrer of Pinner, Middlesex. Kelke died on 6 January 1576, 'before the consequences of his actions could catch up with him' (Cunich and others, 83), and was buried two days later in the church of St Mary the Great, Cambridge, leaving a house in Ipswich and land at Sproughton to his wife for life and thereafter to their daughter, together with gifts to the poor of Teversham and Sproughton and to the hospital at Ipswich, and £20 to Magdalene College.   N. G. JONES

Sources P. Cunich and others, *A history of Magdalene College, Cambridge, 1428–1988* (1994) · Venn, *Alum. Cant.*, 1/3 · A. R. Maddison, ed., *Lincolnshire pedigrees*, 4 vols., Harleian Society, 50–52, 55 (1902–6) · will, PRO, PROB 11/57, sig. 56 · Cooper, *Ath. Cantab.* · *CSP dom.*, 1547–80 · C. H. Cooper and J. W. Cooper, *Annals of Cambridge*, 5 vols. (1842–1908) · W. H. Richardson, ed., *The annals of Ipswich* (1884) · S. M. Leathes, ed., *Grace book A* (1897) · M. Bateson, ed., *Grace book B*, 2 vols. (1903–5) · J. Venn, ed., *Grace book Δ* (1910) · J. Strype, *The life and acts of … John Whitgift* (1718) · J. Nichols, ed., *The progresses and public processions of Queen Elizabeth*, 3 vols. (1788) · BL, Lansdowne MSS 11, 15,16 · C. H. Garrett, *The Marian exiles: a study in the origins of Elizabethan puritanism* (1938) · J. Strype, *The history of the life and acts of … Edmund Grindal* (1710)
Wealth at death significant; left house in Ipswich, and at Sproughton, Essex; various gifts incl. £20 to his college: will, PRO, PROB 11/57, sig. 56

Kell, Reginald Clifford (1906–1981), clarinettist, was born on 8 June 1906 at 164 Bishopthorpe Road, York, the eldest in the family of two sons and one daughter of Frederick Kell, a theatre music director, and his wife, Edith Porter. As a child he studied the violin, but after leaving school at fourteen he taught himself the clarinet, and joined his father's band. Within a year of taking up the clarinet he was playing in the orchestra at the Opera House, Harrogate, for the silent films, and in 1929 he won an open scholarship to the Royal Academy of Music to study with Haydn Draper, and moved to London. While still a student he played in the Royal Philharmonic Orchestra from 1930 to 1931, and on leaving the Royal Academy in 1932 he was invited by Sir Thomas Beecham to take the position of principal clarinettist in his newly formed London Philharmonic Orchestra, chosen because his tone was similar to that of the principal oboist, Leon Goossens. At the same

time he was principal clarinettist of the Covent Garden Opera House orchestra, from 1932 to 1936, and from 1935 to 1939 he taught at the Royal Academy; he was made FRAM in 1941. On 23 August 1936 he married Diana Gabrielle (*b.* 1915/16), daughter of the composer Joseph *Holbrooke (1878–1958) and sister of Gwydion Brooke, principal bassoonist in the London Philharmonic Orchestra. They had one son.

Kell left the London Philharmonic Orchestra in 1936 after a financial disagreement with Beecham, and for the next twelve years continued to pursue a busy orchestral career. From 1936 to 1939 he was principal clarinettist of the London Symphony Orchestra, finding time also to adjudicate at the international festival of woodwind playing in Vienna in 1938, played in the Toscanini International Orchestra at the Lucerne festival in 1939, and then joined the BBC Salon Orchestra, formed in 1939 to broadcast high-quality light music during the war. The Salon Orchestra was based in Bristol until 1941, when it moved to Evesham, and before it was disbanded in July 1942 Walter Legge, recording manager of EMI, recorded several works with some of the leading players, including Kell; his first recordings of the Mozart and Brahms clarinet trios date from 1941. Kell was principal clarinettist of the Liverpool Philharmonic Orchestra from 1942 to 1945. When Walter Legge founded the Philharmonia Orchestra in 1945, he appointed Kell principal clarinettist, and at the orchestra's first public concert, in the Kingsway Hall on 27 October 1945, Kell played the Mozart clarinet concerto in an all-Mozart programme conducted by Beecham. He also became principal clarinettist of Beecham's new orchestra, the Royal Philharmonic Orchestra, in 1946, while remaining at the Philharmonia until 1948.

After touring the United States with the Busch Quartet in November 1948, Kell decided to give up orchestral playing in order to pursue a solo and chamber music career, and emigrated to the United States, where his style of playing became very popular. As well as performing in the United States and Canada, he was a professor at the Aspen Music School in Colorado from 1951 to 1957. He spent 1958 to 1959 in England, teaching at the Royal Academy, where his pupils included Harrison Birtwistle and Alan Hacker, and gave his last solo performance in 1959 at the Bath Festival, playing the Mozart clarinet concerto conducted by Yehudi Menuhin. He then took up an administrative appointment as a director of the band instrument division of the musical instrument distributors Boosey and Hawkes in New York, from 1959 to 1966.

Kell made many fine recordings; one of his most famous was that of the Brahms clarinet quintet, with the Busch Quartet, recorded in 1937, and his recording of Schubert's 'Der Hirt auf dem Felsen' with Elizabeth Schumann in 1936 was a landmark. Other recordings included the first complete version of Schumann's *Phantasiestücke*. In 1939 he recorded one of the two clarinet quintets composed by his father-in-law, Joseph Holbrooke. He had a very sweet and expressive tone, influenced by the oboe playing of Leon Goossens, and used a lot of vibrato, in contrast to the firm, clear tone of his contemporary Frederick Thurston, the other leading British clarinettist of his generation, although there were some who found his use of vibrato and his free use of rhythm excessive. *17 Staccato Studies* (1958) and a clarinet tutor, the *Kell Method* (1968), were published in New York.

In 1971 Kell returned to live in England, and in his retirement took up watercolour painting, but in 1975 he moved back to America. In 1978 he exhibited a one-man show during the Aspen music festival. He died on 5 August 1981 in Frankport, Kentucky, USA. He was survived by his wife. ANNE PIMLOTT BAKER

Sources P. Weston, *Clarinet virtuosi of today* (1989), 12–13 · *The Times* (22 Aug 1981) · *New Grove*, 2nd edn · S. J. Pettitt, *Philharmonia Orchestra* (1985) · C. Lawson, ed., *The Cambridge companion to the clarinet* (1995) · J. Sclater, 'Reginald Kell—clarinettist without a country', *The Clarinet* (March–Dec 2001) · 'Memories of Reginald Kell', *Clarinet and Saxophone*, 7 (Jan 1982) · b. cert. · m. cert.

Likenesses photograph, repro. in *Penguin Music Magazine*, 6 (1968), following p. 64

Kell, Sir Vernon George Waldegrave (1873–1942), intelligence officer, was born on 21 November 1873 at the barracks, South Town, Matford, Suffolk, the only son of Major Waldegrave Charles Vernon Kell of the South Staffordshire regiment and his wife, Georgiana Augusta Konarska. Kell's skill as a linguist led at first to thoughts of the diplomatic service, but in 1892 he entered the Royal Military College at Sandhurst and two years later joined his father's old regiment. Here he continued his study of languages, qualifying as an interpreter in French and German and, after studying in Moscow in 1898, in Russian. In 1900 he married Constance Rawdon Scott, whose drive and ambition were in marked contrast to his natural reserve. He was afterwards posted to Shanghai to learn Chinese, but he became caught up in the Boxer uprising and was unable to qualify as a Chinese interpreter until 1903. He then returned to London to a post in the German intelligence section of the War Office, but in 1905 he transferred to the Far Eastern section, and in 1907 moved to the committee of imperial defence (CID), where he was involved in writing the official history of the Russo-Japanese War.

In 1909 the CID was asked to investigate the danger of German espionage and, influenced by widespread fears of invasion, recommended the establishment of a new secret service bureau. Kell agreed to retire from the army to become its military representative, although, as his wife recalled, he was warned by his friends 'that he would find himself thrown over, if he were to make the slightest slip' (Kell). His chronic asthma and limited budget kept him from active enquiries, but he began the methodical collection of suspicious reports, and gradually gained the confidence of a select group of chief constables and government officials. Kell was convinced that the German army was already planning invasion, and arranged for the secret registration of more than 30,000 resident aliens, who he was convinced formed the basis of a network of military agents and saboteurs. He also detected a small

Sir Vernon George Waldegrave Kell (1873–1942), by F. A. Swaine, *c*.1920

group of German naval agents who were seeking technical information about the Royal Navy, and marked them down for arrest on the outbreak of war. This was the total extent of German espionage in Britain, but the efficient destruction of this network in August 1914 was overshadowed by Kell's redoubled efforts to locate the non-existent army of German saboteurs who he was convinced were still at large.

During the war Kell's counter-espionage department, rechristened MI5, brought thirty-one German agents to trial, but its principal work remained the hunt for wider and more subtle conspiracies. When full conscription was introduced in May 1916 Kell accepted that the British peace movement had now to be 'classed as pro-German' and MI5 began the intensive surveillance of more than 5000 individuals (memo by Major V. Ferguson, 14 June 1916, PRO, HO 45/10801/307402, file 75). By October 1917 its registry contained almost 40,000 personal files, and 1 million cross-index cards, and its principal work had become the collection and analysis of information on a vast range of innocent individuals and organizations. Kell was appointed CB in 1917 and KBE in 1919.

By the end of the war in November 1918 Kell had a staff of 850 and an annual budget of £100,000 devoted to this work, but the intelligence reorganization of 1919 saw many of MI5's responsibilities transferred to the special branch of Scotland Yard. Kell's budget was cut to £35,000, his staff was reduced to just thirty, and his duties were confined to counter-espionage and the combating of communism within the armed forces. Over the next six years he fought a running battle with the special branch and MI6, the foreign intelligence service, simply to preserve the existence of his unit.

The post-war 'red scare' seemed ideal for MI5, as it demanded the cross-checking of vast numbers of suspects, and apparently confirmed that democracy required strengthening from outside by determined men such as Kell. However, financial constraints prevented MI5 from recruiting young staff and forced Kell to rely heavily on personal links with business and political organizations, often on the far right. Yet he continued to inspire loyalty in his hand-picked staff, and with their help managed to double the size of his bizarre 'precautionary index', which by February 1925 included more than 25,000 supposedly dangerous individuals, carefully classified by blood, by racial interests, and by sympathy and friendship. MI5's official historian considered it 'a tribute to Sir Vernon Kell's personality that the organisation was kept in being under such conditions', and gradually his obsessive search for disloyalty gained official backing (Curry, 66). In October 1931 MI5, now known as the 'security service', was given responsibility for investigating communism throughout the United Kingdom, using staff transferred from the special branch and MI6, and in 1934 it also gained the task of investigating fascism. This produced a rapid increase in MI5's resources and, although in 1935 Kell's staff numbered just over ninety, within four years it had grown to 330, with an annual budget of more than £90,000 and a secret registry containing some 250,000 personal files.

Unfortunately MI5's obsessive indexing of possible suspects revealed almost nothing about actual secret service operations in Britain, and on the outbreak of war in September 1939 its ramshackle registry was overwhelmed by requests for security clearance. Kell, whose health had begun to fail, no longer enjoyed the confidence of senior officials, and when Winston Churchill became prime minister in May 1940 he dismissed both Kell and his deputy, Eric Holt-Wilson. Constance Kell informed MI5 staff that 'your precious Winston has sacked the General' (West, 153), and insult was added to injury through the granting of an ungenerous pension.

According to Sir Dick White, Kell was 'a calm, modest and patient man, which made it seem obvious that fly-fishing was his chosen hobby' (DNB). He retired to a small rented cottage, Stonepits, Emberton, Olney, in Buckinghamshire, where he died on 27 March 1942; he was survived by his wife.   NICHOLAS HILEY

Sources C. R. Kell, 'Secret well kept: an account of the work of Sir Vernon Kell', [n.d.], IWM, Kell MS PP/MCR/120 · N. Hiley, 'The failure of British counter-espionage against Germany, 1907–1914', *HJ*, 28 (1985), 835–62 · N. Hiley, 'Counter-espionage and security in Great Britain during the First World War', *EngHR*, 101 (1986), 635–70 · J. Curry, 'The security service, its problems and organisational adjustments, 1908–1943', 1945, PRO, KV/1, vol. 1 · *DNB* · F. H. Hinsley and C. A. G. Simkins, *British intelligence in the Second World War*, 4: *Security and counter-intelligence* (1990) · *CGPLA Eng. & Wales* (1942) · b. cert. · d. cert. · N. West, *MI5: British security service operations, 1900–1945* (1981) · 'Field security police and their employment on military intelligence duties', PRO, WO 33/1025 · memo by Major V. Ferguson, 14 June 1916, PRO, HO 45/10801/307402, file 75, 2

Archives IWM, lectures, reports, and biography by his widow [microfilm] | FILM BFI NFTVA, documentary footage

Likenesses F. A. Swaine, photograph, c.1920, Hult. Arch. [see illus.]

Wealth at death £11,723 9s. 8d.: probate, 3 July 1942, *CGPLA Eng. & Wales*

Kelland, Gilbert James (1924–1997), police officer, was born on 17 March 1924 at Pickwell, near Georgeham, Devon, the only child of Edith Kelland, an unmarried domestic servant. Brought up by his grandparents, he attended Georgeham village school and Braunton secondary school before starting work at fourteen as a clerk at a local firm of agricultural merchants.

The Second World War took Kelland away from his rural background. He joined the Fleet Air Arm in May 1942 and served as a mechanic with 824 squadron aboard HMS *Striker* on Atlantic convoy duty. At demobilization, his career choice was made: he went to London to be sworn in as a constable of the Metropolitan Police on 1 July 1946. Kelland passed his probationary period on the Whitehall beat and became station cyclist at Rochester Row. Lean, dark, and over 6 feet tall, he excelled at long-distance running for the Metropolitan Police Athletic Club (which he chaired from 1964 to 1984). He was advanced to sergeant after four years and on 12 August 1950 married Edith Ellen Marshall (b. 1927/8), a typist, with whom he had two daughters.

From 1950 to 1955 Kelland worked in south London, initially in the Elephant and Castle area. He was dissuaded from writing his thesis on corruption when he attended the National Police Staff College in 1955 before being appointed an inspector. There was no busier police station than West End central, Savile Row, his posting from December 1955. Mayfair and Soho were notorious for a high incidence of shoplifting, drunkenness, and living off immoral earnings. Some 5000 prostitutes operated there before the Street Offences Act (1959). Inspector Kelland looked on his chief superintendent, Arthur Townsend, as a role model. His own reputation for fair and fearless policing was made as a chief inspector in Notting Hill between June 1959 and September 1961. Feeling still ran high after the race riots of 1958, but he encouraged stability by improving police relations with West Indian immigrants, closing illegal drinking dens, and trying to curb the profiteering slum-landlord Peter Rachman. The High Court case *Kelland v. de Freitas* (1961) was concerned with defining a landlord.

After two months at Lavender Hill station, Kelland returned to West End central as a superintendent in November 1961 and took charge of its anti-vice unit, the clubs office (1962–4). 'Clip joints' and gambling rackets were the latest problems in Soho; *Kelland v. Raymond* (1964) exposed loopholes in the Betting and Gaming Act (1960). He amassed evidence for the Denning inquiry into the Profumo affair (1963). Promoted to commander in 1965, Kelland combated violent crime in Tower Hamlets, worked in the management services department at Scotland Yard

(1968–70), and led all uniformed police in the West End, before being transferred in June 1971 to the Criminal Investigation Department (CID) as commander of north-west London. He became the deputy assistant commissioner responsible for south London six months later.

On 19 April 1973 Kelland was chosen by Commissioner Sir Robert Mark to investigate charges of corruption against the obscene publications squad (OPS), which had failed to halt the proliferation of pornographic bookshops in Soho. Jailed pornographer Jimmy Humphreys alleged that OPS officers had connived at his trade in return for large bribes. It took Kelland and his team of eight detectives almost three years to find independent corroboration. Their dogged struggle against insidious obstruction exposed a long-established criminal conspiracy. Of seventy-four policemen examined, twelve resigned, twenty-eight retired, and eight were dismissed. The biggest scandal in the Metropolitan Police for a century saw a dozen officers—including a chief superintendent and a commander—sentenced to prison in three highly publicized trials (1976–8).

Praised for his thoroughness, Kelland became one of the top five policemen in London on 1 February 1977 when he was appointed as assistant commissioner 'A' department, responsible for uniformed policing. Maintaining order at the mass picket of Grunwick Processing Ltd was a major task. Fears that OPS corruption might have infected other units of the CID prompted the new commissioner, David McNee, to transfer him to assistant commissioner (crime) on 1 August 1977. This placed him in control of over 3500 detectives, some of whom did not welcome his appointment. His fatherly demeanour and readiness to delegate won over subordinates, however, while his unforgiving glance was usually enough to silence the merest suggestion of rule bending. If anyone protested that his anxiety about misconduct verged on obsession, Kelland took it as a compliment. He reformed the drugs squad and flying squad, secured closer liaison between uniformed and plain-clothed officers, and devised formal codes of procedure to regulate potentially compromising operations. The careful use of resident informants ('supergrasses') led to signal successes against organized crime, especially armed robbery. Voluntary blackouts of news proved helpful in kidnap cases. IRA bombing campaigns were a grave concern. Controversially, he published a racial breakdown of reported crime in March 1982 as a contribution to the public debate on policing and the black community which followed the Brixton riots of 1981.

Kelland was the longest serving officer in the metropolitan force by his retirement on 16 March 1984. He had received the queen's police medal in 1975 and a CBE in 1978. A member of the Parole Board (1986–9), he aided an Amateur Athletic Association inquiry into drug abuse in 1988 and advised Consolidated Safeguards, a private security firm. He died of prostate cancer at his home, 9 Croft Lane, Henfield, Sussex, on 30 August 1997.

With his erect carriage, immaculate uniform, and neat moustache, Gilbert Kelland appeared a copper of the old school. He was an unashamed patriot and an active free-mason who feared that modern youngsters lacked a proper sense of shame. His traditional ideas of service and undisputed integrity helped to restore confidence in the Metropolitan Police during a troubled period in its history. JASON TOMES

Sources G. Kelland, *Crime in London* (1986) · *The Guardian* (2 Sept 1997) · *The Times* (5 Sept 1997) · B. Cox, J. Shirley, and M. Short, *The fall of Scotland Yard* (1977) · R. Mark, *In the office of constable* (1978) · *WWW* · b. cert. · d. cert.

Wealth at death £180,000: probate, 24 Oct 1997, *CGPLA Eng. & Wales*

Kelland, Philip (1808–1879), mathematician, was born in the parish of Dunster, Somerset, where his father, the Revd Philip Kelland (d. 1847), was curate. Though Kelland's father was an Oxford man he sent his son to Queens' College, Cambridge, where he graduated BA in 1834 as senior wrangler and first Smith's prizeman. After taking holy orders he was for three years a tutor in his college, graduating MA in 1837. A year later his reputation was already such that he was invited to apply for the vacant chair of mathematics at Edinburgh, in competition with Duncan Gregory, Edward Sang, and others. He was strongly supported by the professor of natural philosophy, James D. Forbes, who believed there was a need to appoint a mathematician from outside the very philosophical Scottish tradition represented by Gregory. The outcome was a narrow majority in favour of Kelland, who became the first Englishman with an entirely English education elected to a chair in the university. He knew that he was by no means unreservedly welcome in Edinburgh, but, as Davie points out, 'before many years had elapsed, [he] took very effective steps to undermine the local legend that Cambridge analysts like himself were poor hands at the philosophy of mathematics' (Davie, 123).

While at Cambridge Kelland had published *Theory of Heat* (1837) in which he dismissed Fourier's application of sine and cosine series (Fourier series) to the conduction of heat as mostly erroneous; in 1841, however, the seventeen-year-old William Thomson (later Lord Kelvin) published his first scientific paper showing that Kelland's criticisms were unjustified. In the meantime the latter had published a successful textbook, *The Elements of Algebra* (1839), and from then on he devoted more of his time to teaching and educational reform than to mathematical research. He was very popular with his students, and it was said of him that his function was less to make discoveries than to methodize, adapt, and disseminate the discoveries of others. He thoroughly identified himself with the Scottish university system, and took an active part in the movement for reform which resulted in the appointment of an executive commission to implement the provisions of the Universities (Scotland) Act, which included the ultimate release of the University of Edinburgh from the control of the town council. Kelland was twice married; first to a Miss Pilkington of Dublin and second, on 30 April 1846, to Alexandrina Janetta Donaldson, only daughter of Captain Boswell RN of Wardie, Edinburgh.

On 6 December 1838 Kelland was elected a fellow of the

Royal Society, and in 1839 a fellow of the Royal Society of Edinburgh, of which he was president from November 1878 to his death; he contributed numerous papers to its *Transactions* over forty-one years. When Forbes became incapacitated through illness, Kelland, with the assistance of Balfour Stewart, assumed the duties of the natural philosophy chair at intervals from 1852 until 1856. He also took much interest in the Life Association of Scotland, of which he was one of the founders, and conducted the septennial investigation of its affairs from the actuarial point of view. In this connection he made a tour in Canada and the United States in 1858. Occasionally he officiated in St James's and other episcopal churches in Edinburgh, but it was the opinion of his friends that preaching was one of the few accomplishments in which he did not excel. In physical science he wrote on the motion of waves in canals and on various questions of optics, but he mainly devoted his investigations to pure mathematics; one of his most important papers was his 'Memoir on the limits of our knowledge respecting the theory of parallels', in which he dealt with non-Euclidean geometry. Almost his last work, and that which is most worthy of his reputation as a mathematician, was the article 'Algebra' in the ninth edition of the *Encyclopaedia Britannica* (1875).

Kelland was a kindly and congenial man, ever ready to help deserving students. His wide knowledge and the quickness of his perception made him an excellent conversationalist, and he was also a fine musician, playing the cello and the flute. He died at his home, Balmoral Cottage, Bridge of Allan, Stirlingshire, on 7 May 1879, from kidney disease. He was survived by his wife, three sons, and two daughters.   RONALD M. BIRSE

Sources *Proceedings of the Royal Society of Edinburgh*, 10 (1878–80), 208–11, 321–9 • *The Scotsman* (9 May 1879) • *DNB* • *PRS*, 29 (1879), vii–x • *The Times* (10 May 1879) • *The Times* (10 June 1879) • A. Grant, *The story of the University of Edinburgh during its first three hundred years*, 2 (1884), 304–5 • G. E. Davie, 'The 1838 contest for the Edinburgh mathematical chair', *The democratic intellect: Scotland and her universities in the nineteenth century* (1961), 105–26 • d. cert. • IGI • CCI (1879)
Archives U. Edin. L., letters to David Ramsay Hay • U. St Andr. L., corresp. with James David Forbes
Likenesses W. Hole, etching, NPG; repro. in W. B. Hole, *Quasi Cursores: portraits of the high officers and professors of the University of Edinburgh at its tercentenary festival* (1884) • J. W. Slater, pencil and watercolour drawing, Queens' College, Cambridge • T. C. Wageman, watercolour drawing, Trinity Cam.
Wealth at death £20,964 11s. 8d.: confirmation, 12 June 1879, CCI • £79 8s. 4d.—Scotland: eik additional estate, 4 July 1879, CCI

Kellas, Alexander Mitchell (1868–1921), chemist and mountaineer, was born on 21 June 1868 at 28 Regent Quay, Aberdeen, the son of James Fowler Kellas, secretary to the local marine board, and his wife, Mary Boyd, *née* Mitchell. He was educated at Aberdeen grammar school and then attended Aberdeen University, Heriot-Watt College in Edinburgh, and Heidelberg University, where he gained a PhD. He was for a period assistant to Sir William Ramsay at University College and taught chemistry to medical students at the Middlesex Hospital. Kellas was keenly interested in chemistry and even more enthusiastic for mountaineering. The two interests combined to make him pre-

eminent for a time in the field of high-altitude physiology. He was able to combine research at low pressure in the laboratory with practical studies at altitude in the Himalayas.

Kellas had a great love for wild mountain places. He was not given to technical climbing but was supremely interested in mountain geography and exploration, in the course of which he reached numerous unclimbed Himalayan summits. He began mountaineering in the Cairngorms while a student at Aberdeen University. During the next few years he came to know most of the highlands and at the same period climbed in Switzerland.

In his late thirties Kellas made his first visit to the Himalayas. He made six expeditions to Sikkim from 1907 to 1920. He did a phenomenal amount of climbing and yet very little is known about him because he was of a retiring nature and wrote so little of his remarkable, if not unique, achievements. Unusual in that he generally climbed without European companions, he was accompanied by an ever loyal group of local porters whom he trained in the basic alpine skills. He possessed phenomenal energy and tenacity: during one season in 1910 he made ten first ascents above 20,000 feet, including Sentinel Peak (21,292 feet), Pauhunri (23,375 feet), and Chomoyummo (22,400 feet). In 1909 he had twice attempted to climb Pauhunri, getting within 200 feet of the top. The summit was obviously important enough for him to return in the following year in order eventually to reach it.

During the First World War, Kellas channelled all his energies into high-altitude research and the effect of diminished atmospheric pressure on human physiology, a subject of great importance to the Air Ministry. Several papers were published in the *Geographical Journal*, including 'A consideration of the possibility of ascending the loftier Himalaya', which concluded that 'a man in first-rate training, acclimatized to maximum possible altitude, could make the ascent of Mount Everest without adventitious aids, provided that the physical difficulties above 25,000 feet are not prohibitive' (*Geographical Journal*, 49, January 1917). Seventy years later this observation became reality, with Messner and Habeler making the first ascent of Everest without 'canned' oxygen.

In 1919 Kellas suffered a breakdown in health from overwork, resigned his lectureship in London, and returned to Aberdeen. To the surprise of his friends he recovered the following year and set out again for the Himalayas to carry out more experiments at altitude on himself and his high-altitude porters (or 'coolies' as they were termed at the time). He reached a height of 23,622 feet on Kamet. Although he reached Mead's Col, he could not persuade his porters to pitch camp in the intense cold. After several months in the Garhwal he travelled over to Sikkim, where in November 1920 he climbed north of the Kang La to obtain photographs of the peaks north of Everest that were then unknown.

Amazingly Kellas returned to the Kang La region in April 1921 and climbed a higher peak to see more of Everest's north side. He then climbed Narsingh (19,110 feet) before turning his attention to working out a way through the icefall on Kabru. He had time to reach only 21,000 feet. He returned to Darjeeling just one week before he was to join the first expedition to Mount Everest, led by Charles Kenneth Howard-Bury.

Kellas was chosen to be a member of the climbing team of four. This may seem surprising considering he was fifty-three. The Everest committee had few reservations, despite his age, because he had far more experience of high-altitude climbing than any contemporary. No other climber had such a grasp of the mysteries of the effects of rarefied air upon humans. He had alone built up a good rapport with the Sherpa Bhotias hill men and, by emphasizing the importance of adequate training and of treating them with respect, had shown their value to any mountaineering enterprise.

After only a week of rest from his attempts to see more of the Everest region and his prolonged work on Kabru, Kellas had no time to recuperate properly for the rigours of the Tibetan plateau. He went down with dysentery and had to be carried on a stretcher. Just before Kampa Dzong the accumulated strain of his spring climbing, the biting cold of the plateau, and rampant dysentery overtaxed his heart. He died, on 5 June 1921, among his faithful porters, as he had insisted his countrymen went on ahead. 'The old gentleman (such he seemed) was obliged to retire a number of times en route and could not bear to be seen in this distress' as Mallory, appalled at the situation, wrote at the time (Unsworth, 37).

Kellas was buried on a hillside to the south of Kampa Dzong in sight of the peaks of Sikkim, where he had made so many first ascents. From the same place the summit of Everest was visible 100 miles to the west. Howard-Bury concluded, 'He lies, therefore, within sight of his greatest feats in climbing and within view of the mountains that he had longed for so many years to approach—a fitting resting place for a great mountaineer' (Howard-Bury, 54).

DOUG SCOTT

Sources *GJ*, 58 (1921), 73–5 · *Alpine Journal*, 34 (Nov 1921), 145–7 · W. Unsworth, *Everest* (1991) · C. K. Howard-Bury, *Mount Everest: the reconnaissance, 1921* (1922) · b. cert. · *WWW*

Kellaw, Richard (d. 1316), bishop of Durham, was a member of a local family with lands in Kelloe and Old Park on Spennymoor. His parents seem to have been named Thomas and Agnes. He was professed a monk at Durham Cathedral priory, where he was third prior by 1300, when he witnessed the appeal against a visitation by Bishop Antony (I) Bek (d. 1311) that May. By 1302 he was sub-prior and vicar-general of Prior Richard Hoton (d. 1308), who was absent in pursuit of his appeal to the pope against the bishop. In 1305 he was prior of Holy Island. Following Bishop Bek's death Kellaw was chosen in succession by the monks on 31 March 1311, despite an attempt by Edward II to nominate a kinsman of Antonio Pessagno, his newly acquired Genoese banker. The royal assent was given on 11 April, and the temporalities restored on 20 May. He was consecrated at York on 30 May, and enthroned at Durham on 4 September. This rapid acceptance of a Durham monk—one who was not even prior of the house—as bishop must be seen in the context of the conflict between Edward II and the lords ordainer, when the usual royal control of canonical elections could not be maintained.

While Kellaw was a conscientious diocesan, he had to meet the secular problem of defence of his lands against Robert Bruce, who in his fight to consolidate his claim to the Scottish throne as Robert I, was raiding increasingly deeply into northern England. Kellaw was excused attendance at the Council of Vienne in 1311 on the grounds that his presence was needed to defend the Scottish border. To regular summonses to parliament Kellaw as regularly explained his absence on account of Scottish inroads, and sent proctors. His strategy, however, was to support the practice of buying off the Scots for short truces. The leading member of his council, Richard Marmaduke, was also a retainer of Thomas, earl of Lancaster (d. 1322), and frequently served as negotiator for payment of the Scottish blackmail. When Piers Gaveston was besieged at Scarborough in 1312 Kellaw refused him refuge; and it has been said that in consequence Edward II tried unsuccessfully to have him translated to another see. In 1314 the bishop was required to pay the king 1000 marks, and to supply 1500 men from his palatinate for the royal invasion of Scotland. The practice of paying 'blackmail' to the Scots continued for the rest of his episcopate.

As regards his episcopal activities, Kellaw issued *Constitutiones synodales* in 1312, and attempted a visitation of Northumberland. In November 1314 he visited his cathedral chapter. His register is the earliest to have survived for Durham, providing information about ordinations, indulgences, licences to study, loans, and grants. He died at Bishop Middleham in co. Durham on 9 October 1316, and was buried in his monastic habit in the apse of the chapter house of Durham, with a replica wooden crozier beside him. He was commemorated by a brass, set in Frosterley marble, now destroyed. The contemporary Durham chronicler, Robert Graystanes (d. 1336), described him as well-lettered, fit to govern, and mindful of his monastic origins, with monks serving him as chancellor, steward, and chaplain. This statement does not seem to be supported by the actual personnel appointed. Neither William Denum nor Robert Brompton, chancellors, appears on the list of Durham monks in 1310, and Richard Marmaduke, the bishop's steward, was a layman. But there does seem to be truth in Graystanes's statement that Kellaw relied heavily on his kinsmen. Patrick Kellaw, his brother, held military command in Norham; Peter Kellaw was granted the valuable rectory of Sedgefield in 1311; and William Kellaw was constable of Durham Castle and receiver of the Durham exchequer. Kellaw's register was removed from its proper custody in the seventeenth century, and eventually accompanied the Rawlinsonian collection to the Bodleian Library. It was returned to Durham in 1812, and later passed with other documents of the palatinate to the Public Record Office, London. It was published in the Rolls Series, under the title *Registrum palatinum Dunelmense*, in four volumes edited by Sir Thomas Duffus Hardy between 1873 and 1878.

C. M. FRASER

Sources *'Registrum palatinum Dunelmense': the register of Richard de Kellawe, lord palatine and bishop of Durham*, ed. T. D. Hardy, 4 vols., Rolls Series, 62 (1873–8) · U. Durham L., miscellaneous charter 5523 (22) [DCD/ Locellus 7, *passim*] · J. Scammell, 'Robert I and the north of England', *EngHR*, 73 (1958), 385–403 · *Historiae Dunelmensis scriptores tres: Gaufridus de Coldingham, Robertus de Graystanes, et Willielmus de Chambre*, ed. J. Raine, SurtS, 9 (1839), 92–8 · D. Wilkins, ed., *Concilia Magnae Britanniae et Hiberniae*, 2 (1737), 416–19 · *CEPR letters*, 2.87, 93 · *CClR*, 1305–42, p. 568 · *RotS*, 2.127 · R. Surtees, *The history and antiquities of the county palatine of Durham*, 1 (1816), xxxv–xxxvii, 64–5 · [J. T. Fowler], ed., *Rites of Durham*, SurtS, 107 (1903), 55, 243 · J. T. Fowler, 'An account of the excavations made on the site of the chapter house of Durham Cathedral in 1874', *Archaeologia*, 45 (1880), 385–404, esp. 387, 393–4 · W. Greenwell, 'Durham seals', *Archaeologia Aeliana*, 3rd ser., 14 (1917), 221–91, esp. 242–3
Archives PRO, Durham register 3/1
Likenesses seal, repro. in Greenwell, 'Durham seals', 242–3
Wealth at death see will, Hardy, ed., *Registrum*, vol. 3, p. liv

Kellaway, Charles Halliley (1889–1952), physiologist and medical research administrator, was born on 16 January 1889 in Melbourne, Australia, the eldest son in a family of five children of the Revd Alfred Charles Kellaway (*b.* 1856), curate to the dean of the pro-cathedral church of St James, who emigrated from Dorset, England, as a child. His mother was Anne Carrick (*b.* 1854), daughter of Richard Roberts and Frances Halliley, the daughter of a north of England manufacturer who was interested in chemistry and was a friend of John Dalton. Kellaway was taught at home by his father up to the age of eleven, attended Caulfield Grammar School for a year, and won a scholarship to the Melbourne Church of England grammar school, where he studied until 1906. He passed the senior public examination with first-class honours in physics and chemistry and won the Clarke scholarship to Trinity College, Melbourne University, where he initially intended to become a medical missionary. He qualified MB BS in 1911.

After resident appointments at the Royal Melbourne Hospital (1911–13), Kellaway became tutor in physiology at Trinity College, and acting professor of anatomy at the University of Adelaide in 1915. He left Australia in 1915 as a captain in the Australian Army Medical Corps associated with the Australian expeditionary force then fighting in Gallipoli, though there is no evidence from the available army records that he served there; his first post was in the laboratory of the 3rd Australian General Hospital in Cairo. There, he worked on the bacteriology of dysentery under the guidance of Charles J. Martin, director of the Lister Institute in London. Kellaway then went with the Australian forces to France, and received the Military Cross for tending the wounded after the battle of Zonnebeke in September 1917. He was gassed by phosgene and judged unfit for active service. He was sent to London early in 1918 and was a specialist officer on the medical boards for the Australian Flying Corps. On Martin's recommendation he worked in Sir Henry Dale's department of the projected National Institute for Medical Research, which was temporarily housed at the Lister Institute. Here he undertook research into the physiological effects of sudden lack of oxygen, which was experienced in high altitude flying.

In 1920 Kellaway became acting professor of physiology in Adelaide, and married Eileen Ethel, the youngest daughter of G. J. Scantlebury, a Melbourne physician. It was a happy marriage and they had three sons. Kellaway was appointed Foulerton research student of the Royal Society in 1920; he worked with Dale on the nature of anaphylaxis at the National Institute for Medical Research, which was then in Hampstead, London. After a brief time in Sir Charles Sherrington's physiology department at Oxford, he moved to T. R. Elliott's medical unit at University College Hospital, London. There he worked with S. J. Cowell on the role of the adrenal cortex in resistance to histamine and other toxic products of tissue damage.

Kellaway was director of the Walter and Eliza Hall Institute, Melbourne, from 1923 to 1944. He modelled the institute on the Lister Institute and the National Institute for Medical Research. Kellaway changed the institute from a laboratory service to the Melbourne Hospital to the main research institute in Australia, which influenced medical research throughout the country. Kellaway's own research with his immediate collaborators included important analysis of the physiological effects of the venoms of Australian snakes and other indigenous fauna, and of the toxins of pathogenic bacteria. He found, in collaboration with William Feldberg, that snake venoms caused the release of histamine, although they had other modes of action. He developed specific antibodies (antitoxins) against various snake toxins and his own life was probably saved by one of these.

In his role as adviser to the federal government Kellaway was chairman of the commission, set up in 1928, to investigate the Bundaberg disaster in Queensland. Twelve children, injected with diphtheria vaccine from a multidose container, died from toxin produced by staphylococci which had grown in the vaccine. Frank MacFarlane Burnet showed that these containers were dangerous, as bacteria introduced accidentally while withdrawing doses of vaccine could grow to dangerous levels. Subsequently, preservatives were always used in these containers to prevent bacterial growth; this practice was incorporated into the provisions of the Therapeutic Substances Act in Great Britain. Kellaway was elected FRCP (1929), founder fellow of the Royal Australasian College of Physicians (1938), and FRS (1940). He was on the council of the Royal Society in 1947–9.

At the outbreak of the Second World War, Kellaway, with the rank of colonel, became director of pathology to the Australian Army Medical Service, and was involved with staffing and equipping the pathological services, including blood transfusion. The Hall Institute did much of the background work in blood transfusion. In 1941 he visited the USA and was with Dale at the time of the Japanese attack on Pearl Harbor in December 1941. In 1942, with the rank of brigadier-general, he served as scientific liaison officer to the director-general of the Australian Army Medical Service. In 1944 Burnet, his assistant director, succeeded him as director of the Hall Institute.

Kellaway then accepted Dale's offer of the position of director-in-chief of the research laboratories of the Wellcome Foundation in the United Kingdom and the

American branch at Tuckahoe, New York state. His task was difficult. Sir Henry Wellcome had set up his company with many autonomous units. He had made the Wellcome Research Laboratories comparable to the National Institute for Medical Research and the Lister Institute as the main institutes for fundamental medical research in Great Britain; the Wellcome laboratories were not regarded as 'industry'. However, there was virtually no cross-communication between departments, and little commercial use was made of the superb talents available. This structure functioned while Wellcome was directing it, but after his death the autonomous departments were very difficult to co-ordinate and no attempt was made to do so. The Wellcome Foundation wholeheartedly supported the war effort, and made anti-gas gangrene serum, which was little used, and penicillin, whose production was abandoned because the initial surface growth technique could not compete with the American deep fermentation method. The financial returns were nugatory and in 1947 the Wellcome Foundation had an overdraft of £2,640,000, which was more than the annual turnover. In the event the foundation was greatly aided by its American operation in Tuckahoe.

Kellaway was appointed to reorganize the Wellcome Foundation. He was a new broom in a complex organization which was out of touch with commercial realities. His Australian manner with 'no side' and his intolerance of obstacles to good research were a culture shock to an organization in which everyone knew both their place and the unwritten conventions. Moreover, Kellaway had long experience of financial problems at the Hall Institute, and did not avoid difficult decisions. Inevitably, the necessary rationalization and financial stringency made Kellaway the best-hated man in the organization.

Kellaway pushed for further collaboration with Tuckahoe. In early April 1948 he visited Tuckahoe, and informed the managing director, Howard Fonda, that he would be replaced by William N. Creasy. During this time, Kellaway exposed George Brownlee to his American counterparts before revealing to Brownlee, and management, his plan to make him head of the physiological research division at Beckenham. He encouraged funds to go to the future Nobel prizewinning chemist, George Hitchings, at Tuckahoe, and later visited Tuckahoe with John Boyd and Len Goodwin to facilitate drugs being flown to London for testing in the Wellcome Laboratory for Tropical Medicine; the anti-malarial pyrimethamine (Daraprim) was selected for development in this way.

Kellaway knew the importance of promoting gifted young scientists. He made appointments based on his realization that the future lay in chemotherapy (which at that time referred to the treatment of infection and not tumours) and synthetic drugs and not in the area of anti-sera. He wrote of the need to 'investigate the activity of all new classes of compounds … on as wide a range of organisms and physiological processes as possible'. He increased co-ordination and fluidity within the foundation, so that staff could be concentrated on urgent problems. He retained Wellcome's tradition of undertaking and publishing independent fundamental research (Kellaway).

Kellaway was a chain smoker. He pushed himself hard and his deteriorating health became apparent to his intimates, but not to most of his staff, in 1949. He had failed to convert the older staff and by March 1950 he had abandoned his plan to retire John William Trevan, who was head of the Beckenham laboratories, with consequent delay in moving the thrust of research from anti-sera and vaccines to chemotherapy and synthetic drugs. Hospital investigation of his intractable colitis in 1951 revealed an inoperable carcinoma of the lung, and with the diagnosis his élan disappeared. Kellaway returned to the religious convictions of his upbringing, and related his belief in the resurrection to Brownlee a fortnight before his death. He died at his home, 2 Grove Terrace, Hampstead on 13 December 1952, working almost to the end. His wife survived him.

Kellaway did important research on histamine, SRS-A and snake venoms. His organizational skills, often used to provide research opportunity for others, and his eye for talented scientists, in particular Burnet, established a leading role for the Hall Institute. Finally he moved the Wellcome Foundation into the modern world, despite its cash flow problems. Kellaway's success was based on enthusiasm for listening to the research of others and then looking ahead imaginatively, his drive to support good research, and his genius for making contacts and friends. He enjoyed the success of the scientists he selected. He was a cultured man who appreciated literature and music, with a liking for narrative verse and biblical quotations, which he revealed only to his friends. He loved life and enjoyed angling.

GEOFFREY L. ASHERSON

Sources *The Lancet* (27 Dec 1952) • *BMJ* (27 Dec 1952), 1421–3 • F. M. Burnet, 'Charles Halliley Kellaway', *Medical Journal of Australia*, 1 (7 Feb 1953), 203–7 [incl. bibliography] • H. H. Dale, *Obits. FRS*, 8 (1953) [incl. bibliography] • A. R. Hall and B. A. Bembridge, *Physic and philanthropy: a history of the Wellcome Trust, 1936–1986* (1986) • R. R. James, *Henry Wellcome* (1994) • C. H. Kellaway, 'The Wellcome Research Institution', *PRS*, 135B (1947–8), 259–70 • C. Sexton, *The seeds of time: the life of Sir Macfarlane Burnet* (1991) • J. W. Trevan, *Nature*, 171 (1953), 107–8 • *DNB* • *CGPLA Eng. & Wales* (1953) • private information (2004) [G. Brownlee, L. G. Goodwin, P. O. Williams] • L. G. Goodwin and E. Beveridge, *Wellcome's legacies: Sir Henry Wellcome and tropical medicine* (1998) • G. Brownlee, videotape, 1997, Oxford Brookes University, Oxford Centre for Twentieth Century Biography
Archives RS | CAC Cam., corresp. with A. V. Hill
Likenesses W. Stoneman, photograph, 1945, NPG • W. Stoneman (signed by Kellaway), repro. in Dale, *Obits. FRS*, 503–21 • photograph (signed by Kellaway), repro. in G. R. Cameron, *Journal of Pathology and Bacteriology*, 66, frontispiece • photograph, repro. in Burnet, *Medical Journal of Australia*
Wealth at death £6104 17s. 9d.: probate, 29 Aug 1953, *CGPLA Eng. & Wales*

Kellawe, Richard de. *See* Kellaw, Richard (d. 1316).

Keller, Godfrey [Gottfried] (d. **1704**), composer and keyboard player, was presumably of German origin and may have been in England by about 1680, as Edward Lowe (c.1610–1682) copied music by him. He had certainly settled in London by 23 June 1694, when he was granted a pass to visit Holland. Keller was to have taught the organ and harpsichord in the abortive royal academies of 1695 along with two distinguished musicians, Henry Purcell and Giovanni Battista Draghi—apparently some measure of the standing he had already achieved in the London musical community. On 31 March 1698 he married Mary Goodrick at St James's, Duke's Place, London. They had two sons, Godfrey and Edward.

Pedagogy is Keller's chief claim to fame. He was the author of a posthumously published treatise on basso continuo playing, *A compleat method for attaining to play a thorough bass upon either organ, harpsicord or theorbo-lute … with variety of proper lessons and fuges, explaining the several rules throughout the whole work* (1705), which also included directions for tuning the harpsichord. The first such work to be published in England since Matthew Locke's pioneering *Melothesia* (1673), it went through several editions and was also printed as an appendix in the 1731 edition of William Holder's *A Treatise of the Natural Grounds, and Principles of Harmony.*

Keller was also an important composer of chamber music. His works demonstrate contrapuntal skill, imaginative harmony (particularly in the slow movements), and a love for the trumpet idiom even in music written for woodwind instruments. About 1697–8 Étienne Roger in Amsterdam published a collection of six sonatas for two recorders, two oboes or violins, and basso continuo: four by Gottfried Finger and two by Keller. This association of composers suggests that Keller may have been serving as the keyboard player for Finger's public concert series at York Buildings, London, in conjunction with or after Draghi. Two years later Roger published another collection of six sonatas by Keller (three for trumpet or oboe, two violins, tenor violin, and basso continuo; three for two recorders, two oboes or violins, and basso continuo), dedicating them to Princess Anne, with whose court he claimed familiarity. They were written for the famous trumpeter John Shore and the 'hautboys' (chamber band) of Anne and her consort, Prince George of Denmark. Thus Keller may have acted as a house composer to Princess Anne and Prince George, or have been angling for such a position, although his name is not found in court records.

The dedication of Keller's next collection (four sonatas for two recorders or violins and basso continuo; three sonatas for recorder, violin or oboe, and basso continuo) in 1700 to Robert Orme, esquire, and the inclusion in the collection of a sonata by Orme himself suggest a connection with the public concerts of John Banister the younger, for which Orme also wrote pieces. Keller may also have been connected with the band at the Theatre Royal, Drury Lane, or even been a member of it, as on 19 and 27 April 1703 'the whole band' there performed 'a new entertainment of instrumental music' by Keller in which James Paisible played the recorder, Banister the violin, and Peter Latour the oboe. These three men and other performers associated with the theatres took part in two concerts of music by Keller at York Buildings on 11 December 1703 and 28 April 1704, the second being for the benefit of Banister.

According to Sir John Hawkins, Keller died 'an immature death' (Hawkins, 822). He made his will on 7 November 1704, bequeathing his estate to his wife and sons. Godfrey also received his father's 'best fidle and spinnett', and Keller's brother Frederick was the executor. Keller had died, probably in London, by 25 November, when a collection of music that he and Banister had purchased from Finger—presumably when the latter left England in 1701—was advertised for sale by Banister and the publisher Henry Playford. A collection of six sonatas for two recorders and basso continuo by Keller was published posthumously by Roger in 1706.   DAVID LASOCKI

Sources J. Hawkins, *A general history of the science and practice of music*, new edn, 3 vols. (1853); repr. in 2 vols. (1963) · D. Lasocki, 'Professional recorder players in England, 1540–1740', PhD diss., University of Iowa, 1983 · M. Tilmouth, 'The royal academies of 1695', *Music and Letters*, 38 (1957), 327–34 · private information (2004) [P. Holman] · IGI

Keller, Hans Heinrich (1919–1985), broadcaster and writer on music, was born at Nusswaldgasse 13, Döbling, Vienna, Austria, on 11 March 1919, the son of the architect Fritz Keller (d. 1939) and his wife, Grete Grotte (1883–1959); he had one half-sister, Gertrud Franey (d. 1998). Raised in the well-to-do suburb of Döbling, he passed his Abitur at the local Landerziehungsheim (1935–8) while benefiting from involvement in his parents' cultural circle, which included the composer Franz Schmidt. He was imprisoned, interrogated, and released by the Nazis (he described himself as an 'unpious Jew'), an episode movingly recalled in his 'Vienna 1938' (published in *The Listener* on 28 March 1974), and on 20 December 1938 he fled to join his relatives in England. After internment on the Isle of Man, he settled in London for the rest of his life and formed a partnership with the German artist Milein Cosman (b. 1921), whom he eventually married on 27 March 1961.

A brilliant but unconventional writer (he was a self-styled 'anti-critic'), Keller drew on an unusual range of experience. In the 1940s he took his licentiate of the Royal Academy of Music, played violin in string quartets and orchestras, and later became a coach (or 'anti-coach') of string quartets; he reviewed film music, and in a book's worth of polemical notices, essays, and pamphlets related practice to (his own) theory; he began to champion the music of Benjamin Britten, on whom he edited an influential collection of essays (1952); he wrote music and dramas (though little remains) as well as the librettos for Benjamin Frankel's opera *Marching Song* and Josef Tal's *Der Turm*. He later taught composition and translated librettos; in 1949–52 he emerged as a forceful critic through his contributions to *Music Review*; and with Donald Mitchell he also edited the lively *Music Survey*. Indeed, such was the impact of his intense, witty, companionable, yet highly combative personality that in 1959 he joined the BBC at the suggestion of William Glock. There he worked for twenty years in various senior capacities and helped to establish the European Broadcasting Union; he also set new standards with his short talks, interviews, programme booklets, and extended analyses of classical chamber music.

Hans Heinrich Keller (1919–1985), by George Newson, 1984

After his retirement from the BBC in March 1979 he became visiting professor at McMaster University, Hamilton, Ontario, which he revisited during a tour of Canada and the United States in 1980. Until 1985 he also coached string quartets at the Yehudi Menuhin School and the Guildhall School of Music and Drama, and spoke in many other venues. On 30 September 1985 the president of Austria awarded him the Ehrenkreuz für Wissenschaft und Kunst, 1. Klasse, and on 23 February 1986 Channel 4 showed a posthumous documentary, *The Keller Instinct*.

His unpublished papers in the university library, Cambridge, show the origins of his thought. During the 1940s he worked closely with sociologists, and in his reactions to both their investigations into small-group psychology and his own into fire brigades, tank crews, clubs, schools, prostitutes, and string quartets he drew on an informed understanding of psychoanalysis. This he acquired partly through self-analysis and partly through the works of Sigmund Freud, Alfred Adler, Ernest Jones, Edward Glover, and J. C. Flugel. In addition, he developed a crystalline prose style in which paradox and aphorism held pride of place. For example, he wrote that 'Art arises where the arbitrary and the predictable are superseded by unpredictable inevitability' (Keller, 'Quotation', 25). He was thus well equipped to comment lucidly and provocatively on any issue of the day—from the need to abolish capital punishment to Hitler, women's liberation, and the individual merits of members of the Brazilian football team. Some of these topics, together with a typically astute appraisal of the contemporary music scene, reappeared in Keller's book *1975 (1984 minus 9)* (1977). The psychosociological perspective also emerged in his exploration of the 'artistic personalities' of composers from Haydn to his own day, and in his analyses of opera

(mainly by Schoenberg and Britten). His understanding of culture emerged in *The Jerusalem Diary* (2001) and his sustained and formidable critique of critics and audiences found full expression in *Criticism* (1987).

Psychological concerns also informed his purely musical writings. Keller drew on the analytical models of Arnold Schoenberg (who had promoted a 'physiological', organic awareness rather than a dryly 'anatomical' one), and devised a series of fifteen 'functional analyses' of music, mainly by Haydn, Mozart, and Beethoven, to show how 'latent' unity lay behind 'manifest' contrast. These Spenglerian demonstrations eschewed words on the grounds that musical and conceptual logic are unrelated. He devised a 'two-dimensional theory of music' to show how the 'foreground' of what composers did was projected against the 'background' of what they or others had done before ('form is the sum total of our expectations'); he then pursued this theory in all musical dimensions—rhythm, pitch, key, timbre, and form. He also championed Schoenberg's twelve-note method of composing, and related classical to modern practice. His principal works were *The Great Haydn Quartets: their Interpretation* (1986) and *Stravinsky Seen and Heard* (in collaboration with Milein Cosman, 1982); he wrote voluminously on Mozart and Schoenberg in scattered articles, and sustained important columns on 'The new in music' and 'Truth and music'. A bibliography appeared in *Music Analysis*, 5.2/3 (1986), and was followed by selected *Essays on Music* (1994).

Hans Keller had a conspicuous appearance, with a thin, short-to-medium physique, a high forehead, an aquiline nose, a moustache, a measured, unfaltering diction, and penetrating eyes. According to his *Times* obituarist:

> he could be aggravatingly contradictory and/or challenging, never allowing any statement to pass without a challenge from his active thoughts on the matter. Though superficially prickly, he was—to those who knew him well—kind and considerate. He was a great soccer enthusiast and loved to talk about the game almost as much as music. (*The Times*, 7 Nov 1985)

He died childless from motor neurone disease at his home, 3 Frognal Gardens, Hampstead, on 6 November 1985 and was cremated at Golders Green crematorium. He was one of many distinguished Austro-German émigrés who enriched British musical culture in the post-war years.   CHRISTOPHER WINTLE

Sources C. Wintle, ed., 'Hans Keller (1919–85): a memorial symposium', *Music Analysis*, 5/2–3 (July–Oct 1986) · private information (2004) [Milein Keller] · m. cert. · d. cert. · 'The Keller instinct', BFI NFTVA, Channel 4, 23 Feb 1986 · *The Times* (7 Nov 1985) · H. Keller, 'The question of quotation', *Music Survey*, 2/1 (1949), 25 · *CGPLA Eng. & Wales* (1986) · H. Keller, *The Jerusalem diary: music, society and politics, 1977 and 1979*, ed. C. Wintle and F. Williams (2001) · H. Keller, *Music and psychology: from Vienna to London 1939–52*, ed. C. Wintle (2003) · A. Garnham, *Hans Keller and the BBC* (2003)

Archives CUL, music department | BL, letters to Bernard Stevens, Add. MSS 69027–69028 | FILM BFI NFTVA, 'The Keller instinct', Channel 4, 23 Feb 1986 | SOUND BBC WAC · BL NSA, oral history interview · BL NSA, recorded talk · BL NSA, current affairs recording · BL NSA, 'The time of my life', 20 Dec 1973, T6548/W TR1 · BL NSA, *Reputations*, BBC Radio 3, 2 Oct 1996, H78193

Likenesses G. Newson, photograph, 1984, NPG [*see illus.*] · M. Cosman, drawing, NPG · M. Cosman, portrait, McMaster University, Ontario, Canada · photograph, repro. in H. Keller, *Essays on music*, ed. C. Wintle, B. Northcott, and I. Samuel (1994), jacket · portrait (with his wife), repro. in *MT* (Aug 1994) · portraits, priv. coll.
Wealth at death £200,112: probate, 18 Aug 1986, *CGPLA Eng. & Wales*

Kellett, Edward (*c.*1580–1641), Church of England clergyman and religious writer, was born in the parish of St Olave, Southwark, Surrey, probably the son of Robert Kellett (*d.* in or before 1612), citizen and joiner of London and Southwark. Educated at Eton College from about 1594, he was admitted as a king's scholar to King's College, Cambridge, on 25 August 1598. There, as he later recalled, Richard Mountague, future bishop of Norwich, was his 'chamber-fellow' (E. Kellett, *Miscellanies of Divinitie*, 1633, 2.11). Kellett became a fellow of his college in 1601, graduated BA early in 1603, and proceeded MA in 1606. On 22 December of that year, aged twenty-six or in his twenty-sixth year, he was ordained priest in the diocese of London. In 1608 he resigned his fellowship and on 28 May was presented by the crown to the rectory of West Bagborough, Somerset. He proceeded BD in 1613 and on 6 November 1615 was presented by George Harrison to the rectory of Crowcombe in the same county; he remained in possession of both benefices until his death. He proceeded DD in 1621, and on 4 August 1630 he was appointed a prebendary of Exeter. At some point he married Julian, whose other name is unknown. They had no children.

Kellett's first publication was *A Returne from Argier* (1628), a sermon preached at Minehead at the request of William Laud, bishop of Bath and Wells, on the readmission into the Church of England of an English sailor who had been taken prisoner by Turkish pirates, sold into slavery, and forced to become a Muslim. In a letter to Samuel Ward, archdeacon of Taunton, Kellett complained that several passages in his sermon had been removed or altered by the ecclesiastical licenser, and declared: 'heerafter if I print any thing, I intend by gods grace to come or send to Cambridge, where I shall have sound and learned judges' (Bodl. Oxf., MS Tanner 72, fols. 292, 293). His second book, *Miscellanies of Divinitie* (1633), a wide-ranging work of speculative theology on 'the estate of the Soul in her origination, separation, particular judgement and conduct to eternal blisse or torment', was duly printed at Cambridge, though the unsold stock was reissued in 1635 with the imprint of a London bookseller. Kellett observed that 'the nature of my Miscellanies [gives] me licence to travel farre and neare' (E. Kellett, *Miscellanies of Divinitie*, 1633, 2.174), and the work covers a remarkably wide range of subjects, including some of the controversial points which had been censored in *A Returne from Argier*. It is particularly notable for its daring speculations on original sin. Kellett argued that original sin did not result from sexual intercourse; that it did not enter the human embryo at the moment of conception; and that it was committed by Adam, not by Eve, for 'I think I may be bold to averre, that Christ would have taken on him the feminine sex, if by Eve we had fallen' (ibid., 1.42).

In his *Miscellanies* Kellett stated that he planned to write 'a second Tractate' on the state of human souls between Christ's second coming and the resurrection of the dead. This was never published, but shortly before his death he brought out another major work: *Tricoenium Christi in nocte proditionis suae* (1641), dedicated to Sir John Finch, baron of Forditch, originated as a series of communion sermons preached to his parishioners. The word 'tricoenium' (threefold supper) was Kellett's own coinage, which he justified by declaring that every author 'frameth some words to his present occasions; every wit inventing and adding somewhat'. The main proposition of the book was that the last supper could be interpreted in three separate ways: as the eating of the paschal lamb, as the eating of an ordinary communal meal, and as the institution of the eucharist. This theory enabled Kellett to argue that although the disciples had shared their communal meal sitting or reclining, it was proper for Christians to receive the sacrament kneeling in recognition of its eucharistic nature. In an appendix Kellett acknowledged that his threefold theory had been anticipated by two Jesuit authors, Theophilus Raynaud in his *Optimae vitae, finis pessimus* (Lyons, 1634) and Jan Wauters van Vieringen in his *De triplici coena Christi agni, vulgari, eucharistica* (Antwerp, 1617), but insisted that he had not seen or heard of these works before completing his own, 'nor since took so much as one line, or any one testimony from either of them'.

The most significant aspect of *Tricoenium Christi* was its attempt to establish a theological rationale for Archbishop Laud's 'beauty of holiness' programme. Kellett supported the placing of the communion table at the east end of the chancel, defended the use of lawful recreations on the sabbath, praised cathedral music for its 'joyfull quickening and reviving of devout affections' (E. Kellett, *Tricoenium Christi in nocte proditionis suae*, 1641), and bitterly denounced the inhabitants of Exeter for urinating against the cathedral walls, a practice which provoked him to express his feelings in rhyme:

> The Church-yard is a sacred place;
> Who pisseth there, is voyd of grace.
> (ibid.)

When Kellett dedicated his *Miscellanies* to Laud, he described himself as a 'crazie, old, retired man, who never saw you but once, and that long since', but declared that he wished the book to be a 'testimoniall to the world' of his admiration for the archbishop (E. Kellett, *Miscellanies of Divinitie*, 1633, dedication). Kellett's concern with order and reverence in church worship was also reflected in his will, in which he bequeathed £40 towards the restoration of St Paul's Cathedral, £20 to Exeter Cathedral to be spent on a 'faire font', and £20 each to the parish churches of West Bagborough and Crowcombe to be spent on 'a faire Chalice guilded for the Administration of the sacrament'. The parish of West Bagborough still possessed at the beginning of the twenty-first century the chalice and flagon that were bought with Kellett's bequest.

Some sources state that Kellett was ejected from his livings; this statement apparently derives from Anthony Wood, who described Kellett as 'a sufferer, if I mistake not, in the time of the rebellion, which began 1642' (*Fasti Angl.* (Hardy), 1.368). However, Kellett, who wrote that he suffered from gout and kidney stones, was alive at or shortly before the publication of *Tricoenium* in 1641 but must have died before 29 May 1641, when his will was proved by his widow Julian. Kellett had appointed Laud, together with Joseph Hall, bishop of Exeter, and William Piers, bishop of Bath and Wells, as overseers of his will, enjoining them to look after his wife in her widowhood; and commended his soul to God, 'desiring him by the prayers of his Church to bless me with what my soul hath desired'.   ARNOLD HUNT

Sources will, PRO, PROB 11/186, sig. 60 · E. Kellett, letter to Samuel Ward, 7 Aug 1628, Bodl. Oxf., MS Tanner 72, fols. 292–3 · T. Scott Holmes, *A report to the convocation of the province of Canterbury on the ecclesiastical records of the diocese of Bath and Wells* (1914) · F. W. Weaver, ed., *Somerset incumbents* (privately printed, Bristol, 1889) · *Fasti Angl.* (Hardy) · Venn, *Alum. Cant.* · Foster, *Alum. Oxon.* · W. Sterry, ed., *The Eton College register, 1441–1698* (1943), 195 · GL, MS 9535/2, fols. 141v–142r

Wealth at death over £100; incl. major bequests of £100: will, PRO, PROB 11/186, sig. 60

Kellett, Ernest Edward (1864–1950), schoolmaster and writer, was born at 21 Brewer Street, Maidstone, Kent, on 23 August 1864, the third son of the Revd Featherstone Kellett, Wesleyan minister, and his wife, Ellen, *née* Harrison. His Methodist upbringing was a profound cultural influence, and furnished raw material for much of his later writing, especially for his *Religion and Life in the Early Victorian Age* (1938), whose sympathetic tone was not then in fashion. Kellett's lifelong love of books began with the 2000 books in his father's study, and he chronicled his reading life in remarkable detail in his *Ex libris: Confessions of a Constant Reader* (1940). After attending Kingswood School, Bath, he entered Wadham College, Oxford, in 1882 and gained a first in mathematics moderations in 1883 and a second in classics in 1886. At the Wesleyan Chapel, Chorlton, Manchester, on 9 August 1907 he married Josephine (*b.* 1878/9), a fellow of the Victoria University and younger daughter of Joseph Laidler, a physician, of Stockton-on-Tees; they had one daughter.

From 1889 to 1924 Kellett was senior English master at the Leys School, Cambridge—a calling that he thought kept him young. 'I have not yet lost the feeling', he wrote in 1936, 'that I am a contemporary of a generation forty years junior to myself' (*As I Remember*, 16). He published two volumes of *Musa Leysiana*: school songs and poems typical of the late-Victorian public school. He was no good on the sports field, but his wide interests, skill at story-telling, quick wit, and shrewd judgement lent him considerable impact; a colleague recalled that 'his very presence in the Common Room at once diverted and re-vitalised it' (Bisseker and Jenkins, 85).

Teaching did not preclude publishing widely. Kellett's translation (with E. W. Naylor) of the *History of the Pianoforte*, from the German of Oscar Bie, appeared in 1897, followed in 1901 by his translation (with F. H. Marseille) of *Monasticism*, by Adolf Harnack. German culture remained with him a continuing interest, as did the related subject of myth: in 1914 he published *The Religion of our Northern Ancestors: a Study of Teutonic Religious Belief and Practice*, and in 1927 a collection of talks entitled *The Story of Myths*, subtitled 'for the use of students in training colleges, and others'; quotations from German often recur in his later publications. After publishing some light fiction and poetry, he edited *A Book of Cambridge Verse* (1911): a book of poems relevant (as were many of his own poems published earlier) to Cambridge University. There followed a thin stream of spin-offs from his teaching: guides for students, and books and essays on literary and historical topics. His books were not tautly written, nor was he shy of repeating the same anecdote or reflection from one book to the next. In 1938 he published *Aspects of History*, a collection of somewhat trite essays on objectivity in history; though the book was based on wide reading, it was not clear why and for whom it was written.

In *Who's Who* Kellett listed his recreation as chess, but among his long-standing literary interests was the history of changes in taste, the theme of his *The Whirligig of Taste* (1929) and his *Fashion in Literature* (1931). As literary critic he saw it as his role to introduce others to the many pleasures he had himself enjoyed. He urged his readers

> to cultivate a catholic and generous taste; to read widely if not voraciously, and to welcome works of all kinds and of almost every rank; to find room in our sympathies not merely for the great but for the little, not merely for the exquisite but for the rough.   (*Fashion in Literature*, 353)

Kellett's interest in shifting fashion led him ineluctably, in the 1930s, into defending the Victorians, and this he did most effectively in his autobiographical *As I Remember* (1936); 'I cannot expect the public to take notice of so obscure and undistinguished a life as mine', he wrote in its preface. Instead, he aimed in the book 'to play … the part of a traveller who happens to have seen a country not familiar to the majority of his audience and to describe it for their benefit'. The tone of his civilized, discursive, good-humoured, and broadly tolerant autobiographical-historical writing is conversational in its easy and unpretentious accessibility. It links up casual encounters, anecdotes, and stray thoughts with serious intellectual concerns, and ruminatively tackles important theoretical issues: how can the historian hope to capture the sheer diversity of human experience and character in a past society? And how can any long-lived person hope to re-create for younger people the subtle ways in which modes of thinking have changed during his or her lifetime?

Kellett's rarely footnoted but intelligent, observant, fair-minded reflectiveness, his cultural breadth, and his limpid style all call to mind G. M. Young, who was writing at about the same time, and whose aim was the same: to rescue the Victorians for history from debunking fashion. Lytton Strachey's portrait of Thomas Arnold was, for Kellett, a 'libel' (*Religion and Life*, 25). 'Having spent many of my best and happiest years in the Victorian age', he wrote, 'I do not quite like to hear it disparaged' (*As I Remember*, 17), and he went on to emphasize the Victorians' humanitarian, cultural, and economic achievement. When confronted with a hostile comment on the Victorians, he repeatedly applied it to somebody he had known, and found the generalization wanting. Impressionistic and aware that his experience had been untypical, Kellett resembled Young in his serious-minded concern with the importance but also with the difficulty of recovering for the present the elusive mood and tone of a disappearing past—of thinking himself into lost modes of speech and thought. Also like Young, he was by then a master of the intriguingly informative but slightly tangential footnote. Not surprisingly Young approved of Kellett, whose memoirs he reviewed and pronounced 'of real historical value', as well as incidentally providing 'abundant entertainment' (Young, 161). It was Kellett who wrote the substantial essay on the press in Young's important collection *Early Victorian England, 1830–1865* (1934).

At the end of his life Kellett lived at 82 Somerset Road, Redhill, Surrey, and died at Moana, The Cutting, Redhill, on 23 October 1950, his wife surviving him. He was a fine example of nonconformist culture's potential for a principled breadth of sympathy that radiated outwards into society at large. 'Justice will be done', he wrote, when discussing the Victorians, 'but not yet' (*As I Remember*, 13). His own efforts contributed in their quietly unpretentious way towards that outcome.　　　　　　BRIAN HARRISON

Sources E. E. Kellett, *As I remember* (1936) · E. E. Kellett, *Ex libris: confessions of a constant reader* (1940) · H. Bisseker and J. H. Jenkins, *The Fortnightly* [Leys School] (1950), 85–7 · G. M. Young, 'Tempus actum', *Victorian essays* (1962), 158–62 · *The Times* (24 Oct 1950) · *WWW* · J. Foster, *Oxford men, 1880–1892: with a record of their schools, honours, and degrees* (1893) · b. cert. · m. cert. · d. cert. · *CGPLA Eng. & Wales* (1950)
Wealth at death £3965 12s. 11d.: probate, 12 Dec 1950, *CGPLA Eng. & Wales*

Kellett, Sir Henry (1806–1875), naval officer, son of John Dalton Kellett of Clonacody in co. Tipperary, Ireland, was born on 2 November 1806. He entered the navy in 1822, and after five years' service in the West Indies was appointed to the *Eden* with Captain William Fitzwilliam Owen, going out to the coast of Africa, and being more especially employed in the scheme for the colonization of Fernando Po. Kellett was promoted lieutenant on 15 September 1828, but continued in the *Eden* during a very trying commission, until she was paid off in the summer of 1831. He was then appointed to the surveying vessel *Aetna* with Captain Edward Belcher, and, after she was paid off in 1835, to command the cutter *Starling*, employed on the survey of the west coast of South America. In 1840 he took this little vessel across the Pacific to China, where as surveyor and pilot he played a very important part in the operations in the Canton and Yangtze (Yangzi) Rivers. He was promoted commander on 6 May 1841, but continued in the *Starling*, which was afterwards officially rated as a sloop of war, in order to give him the sea time necessary for promotion to post rank on 23 December 1842. He was at the same time made a CB.

Kellett returned to England in the summer of 1843, and in February 1845 was appointed to command the *Herald*, a small frigate commissioned as a surveying vessel in the Pacific. Her most important work there was the exact survey of the coast of Colombia between Guayaquil and Panama, but this was interrupted by three summer voyages, in 1848–50, through the Bering Strait to co-operate with the Franklin search expeditions. She afterwards returned home across the Pacific, via Hong Kong, Singapore, and the Cape of Good Hope, and arriving in England in the summer of 1851.

In February 1852 Kellett commissioned the *Resolute* for the search for Franklin, and sailed under the orders of his former captain, Sir Edward Belcher. Going up Baffin's Bay and through Lancaster Sound, the *Resolute* wintered at Melville Island. In August 1853 she was driven out of her winter quarters and passed the next winter in the ice pack. On 15 May 1854 she was abandoned by Belcher's orders, contrary to Kellett's strongly expressed views, with which naval opinion has generally concurred. The ship's company, after a fortnight's journey over the ice, were received on the *North Star* and returned to England in September 1854. The *Resolute*, left to herself, passed uninjured through Lancaster Sound, down Baffin's Bay, and on 16 September 1855 was picked up by Captain Buddington of the American whaler *George Henry*, who brought her to New London. Mr Crampton, the British minister, waived all claim to her. She was then bought by the United States government, refitted, and sent to England. She anchored at Spithead on 12 December 1856, and was formally presented to 'the Queen and people of Great Britain'. She was, however, never again commissioned, though her name continued on the list of the navy until 1879.

On his return to England from Arctic service, Kellett was immediately appointed commodore at Jamaica, where he served from 1855 to 1859. On 16 June 1862 he was promoted rear-admiral, and from 1864 to 1867 he was superintendent of Malta Dockyard. On 8 April 1868 he became vice-admiral, and on 2 June 1869 was made KCB; he was commander-in-chief in China from 1869 to 1871. Kellett died at his home, Clonacody House, co. Tipperary, on 1 March 1875.　　　J. K. LAUGHTON, *rev.* ANDREW LAMBERT

Sources G. S. Ritchie, *The Admiralty chart: British naval hydrography in the nineteenth century* (1967) · G. S. Graham, *The China station: war and diplomacy, 1830–1860* (1978) · Boase, *Mod. Eng. biog.* · *Annual Register* (1875) · O'Byrne, *Naval biog. dict.* · B. Seeman, *Narrative of the voyage of HMS Herald, 1845–51*, 2 vols. (1853)
Archives Admiralty House, London, log of HMS *Herald* · NA Canada, records left in Arctic during search for Franklin · Naval Historical Library, London · NMM, letter-book
Likenesses I. S. Pearce, oils, 1856, NPG; replica, NPG · wood-engraving (after photograph by Kilburn), NPG; repro. in *ILN* (24 April 1852)
Wealth at death £6000: probate, 16 Aug 1875, *CGPLA Ire.*

Kelley, Sir Edward (1555–1597/8), alchemist, was born at Worcester on 1 August 1555. Little is known of his background and early life but he was said by Ashmole to have been at first an apothecary. In 1583 he married the widowed Jane Weston, *née* Cooper (1563–1606) of Chipping Norton, whose children he later helped to educate. Anthony Wood believed he had studied at Gloucester Hall, Oxford, perhaps under the alias of Talbot, though this cannot be confirmed. Colourful traditions about his early years were current in the seventeenth century, mostly gathered in Morhof (Morhof, 152–8) and since repeated in popular works on alchemists. Allegedly his ears were cropped about 1580 (Nash, 446), perhaps for a forgery of ancient title-deeds, and he was said to have exhumed a corpse to 'question the dead' about a gentleman's prospects (Weever, 46).

In 1582, when the mathematician and astrologer Dr John Dee sought a new medium for angel séances, Kelley began working for him. For the next seven years they would conduct sessions, with prayers for enlightenment and in the spirit of Dee's ecumenical hopes that alchemy and angelic knowledge would heal the rift of Christendom. Along with Kelley's wife and Dee's whole household, the two left England in September 1583, funded by the Polish nobleman Albrecht Laski, and settled eventually in Bohemia under the patronage of Vilem Rožmberk at Trebon in 1586. In the séances, Dee took notes of Kelley's spirit messages, including the code of an angelic language. In one of the extant copies of Dee's *Book of Enoch* (BL, Sloane MSS 3189, 3191), Kelley's skilled draughtsmanship is evident in hundreds of diagrams; its care suggests that he was, at least initially, committed to the spiritual enterprise of angel séances that Dee directed. Whatever had been Kelley's initial attitude, he later repeatedly tried to end the sessions but Dee insisted on continuing, even to the extent of acting upon the supposed order of a spirit 'Madimi' that the two men have intercourse with each other's wives.

Kelley, who had access to gold and silver mines, worked on his alchemy until various noblemen believed that he was 'projecting' gold. Rudolph II knighted him as Sir Edward Kelley of Imany and New Lüben. The official decision was recorded in 1589, though there are indications that he actually received his knighthood a few years earlier. Also in 1589, Kelley left Dee at Trebon, probably to join the emperor's court at Prague, and the latter returned to England. Several of Kelley's writings survive, including two alchemical verse treatises in English (in E. Ashmole, *Theatrum*, 1651, 324–33, and in the Royal Library, Copenhagen, Old Royal Coll., MS 242, p. 240), and the three treatises he dedicated to Rudolph II from prison were published as *Tractatus duo egregii de lapide philosophorum una cum theatro astronomiae* (1676). The treatises have been translated as *The Alchemical Writings of Edward Kelley* (1893).

The long-standing view of Kelley as a charlatan corrupting a credulous and innocent Dee is not supportable in the light of new scholarly study of the papers documenting their careers, and their tense, quarrelsome, highly eroticized partnership. Whatever Kelley's opportunism, both men viewed alchemy and angelology as enterprises that were at once physical and spiritual. To Elizabeth Jane *Weston (*bap.* 1581?, *d.* 1612), a widely admired neo-Latin poet, Kelley was a 'kind stepfather' (Bassnett) who took her in after the deaths of her two grandmothers; the poet celebrates the Latin tutor Kelley hired for her, one John Hammond, noted by Dee as tutor earlier to his children.

In 1591 the emperor imprisoned Kelley on a charge of killing an official named Jiri Hunkler in a duel, and perhaps also to ensure that he did not leave with his supposed alchemical secrets. At the time, Elizabeth I of England was trying to persuade him to return home, using Sir Edward Dyer as her intermediary. Kelley was released in 1593 and resumed his alchemical metallurgy. In 1595 he was again imprisoned, this time in Most, where his wife and stepdaughter sought help from the imperial counsellor Jindrich Domináček z Pisnic, whose relative Ludmila or Lydia had married Kelley's brother Thomas. Kelley died, still a prisoner in Most, in either late 1597 or 1598, reportedly of injuries sustained in an escape attempt.

LOUISE SCHLEINER

Sources *The private diary of Dr John Dee*, ed. J. O. Halliwell, CS, 19 (1842) · R. J. W. Evans, *Rudolf II and his world: a study in intellectual history, 1576–1612* (1973) · M. Casaubon, ed., *A true and faithful relation of what passed for many years between Dr John Dee and … some spirits* (1659) · *Elias Ashmole (1617–1692): his autobiographical and historical notes*, ed. C. H. Josten, 5 vols. (1966 [i.e. 1967]) · *The alchemical writings of Edward Kelly*, ed. and trans. [A. E. Waite] (1893) · S. Bassnett, 'Revising a biography: a new interpretation of the life of Elizabeth Jane Weston (Westonia), based on her autobiographical poem on the occasion of the death of her mother', *Cahiers Elisabethains*, 37 (1990), 1–8 · A. Bauer, *Die Adelsdocumente österreichischer Alchymisten* (1893) · W. P. W. Phillimore, ed., *Oxford parish registers* (1909) · E. J. Weston, *Parthenicon libri tres* (*c.*1607–1610) · A. Truhlář and K. Hrdina, eds., *Enchiridion renatae poesis Latinae in Bohemia et Moravia cultae* (1982) · K. Hrdina, 'Dvě práce z dějin českého humanismu', *Listy filologické*, 55 (1928), 14–19 · J. Svatek, *Anglicky alchymista Kelley v Čecach: obrazy z kulturnich dějin Čech. Dil. prvni* (1891) · C. Fell-Smith, *John Dee, 1527–1608* (1909) · private information (2004) · D. G. Morhof, *De metallorum transmutatione ad Joelum Langelottum epistola* (1673) · J. Weever, *Ancient funerall monuments* (1631) · T. Nash, *Collections for the history of Worcestershire*, 1 (1781) · Wood, *Ath. Oxon.* · Johann, von Tetzen, 'Des Weltberuehmten Engellaenders Edoardi Kellaei ausfuehrlicher Tractat dem Kayser Rudolpho zugeschrieben', *Drey Vortreffliche und noch nie im Druck gewesene Chymische Bücher* (Hamburg, 1670)
Archives BL, Sloane MSS 3179, 3181 · Bodl. Oxf., Ashmole MSS · Kongelige Bibliotek, Copenhagen
Likenesses portrait, repro. in Casaubon, *True and faithful relation*, frontispiece

Kellie. For this title name *see* Erskine, Thomas, first earl of Kellie (1566–1639); Erskine, Thomas Alexander, sixth earl of Kellie (1731–1781); Erskine, Thomas, ninth earl of Kellie (1745/6–1828).

Kellison, Matthew (1561–1642), Roman Catholic priest, was born at Harrowden, Northamptonshire, into a family of tenants of Lord Vaux. Taking refuge in France from the persecution that broke out on the arrest of Edmund Campion in 1581, Kellison entered the English College, Rheims, on 13 June that year, and went on to the English College, Rome, in November 1582. During the troubles that broke out in August 1585 he sided with the Jesuit administration and was one of fifty students who signed a petition to the cardinal protector on their behalf. After being ordained priest at the Lateran on 1 May 1587 he was invited to lecture on theology at Rheims from 23 October 1589, and he accompanied the English College on its return to Douai in August 1593. About this time he was awarded a doctorate of theology by the University of Rheims.

After returning to Rheims as regius professor of the university on 21 September 1601 he published his first book, *A Survey of the New Religion*, in 1603 with a dedication to the new king, appealing to him for a relaxation of the penal laws against Catholics and even hoping to convince him of the truth of the Catholic religion. After his appointment as rector magnificus or chancellor of the University of Rheims on 30 January 1606 Kellison published his *Reply to Sotcliffes Answer* (1608), a response to two publications directed against his work by Matthew Sutcliffe, dean of Exeter. Sutcliffe was behind the project to establish the college of controversy at Chelsea. Its Catholic counterpart, attached to the College of Arras in Paris, was established in 1611 with Kellison among its first fellows, though he remained at Rheims. He brought out a Latin version of his original book as *Examen reformationis novae* (1616).

Meanwhile the English College, Douai, was involved in the continuing troubles between the secular clergy and the Jesuits, with the president, Thomas Worthington, being accused of being too subservient to the latter. In 1613 Worthington was summoned to Rome and Kellison was invited, as one likely to be accepted by both sides, to take over provisional government of the college on 10 June. Then, after resigning his position at Rheims, he was appointed president of the English College and proceeded to sever the close connections of that college with the Jesuits. From now on in the eyes of the secular clergy he seemed an ideal candidate for the appointment of bishop over English Catholics, and on three occasions he was recommended by them for this position, but each time, as Dodd comments, 'Doctor Kellison's humility was an obstruction to his preferment' (Dodd, 3.90).

A further controversy which now occupied Kellison's attention was on the oath of allegiance, supported, despite papal condemnation, by some secular priests and the Benedictine Thomas Preston (alias Roger Widdrington), who published a *Responsio apologetica* under his pseudonym in 1612 against the arguments of Cardinal Bellarmine. Kellison undertook to answer him in *The Right and Jurisdiction of the Prelate and the Prince* under the initials I. E. in 1617, while treading carefully so as to incur the wrath of neither king nor pope. Preston's response appeared in 1620, only to elicit a further reply from Kellison in the form of an augmented second edition of his former book.

Another major controversy occurring in the new reign of King Charles involved Kellison ostensibly (as in his first book) 'against the anarchie of Calvin' but really in defence of the claims of Bishop Richard Smith to ordinary episcopal authority over all English Catholics, including the religious orders. His book, *A Treatise of the Hierarchie* (1629), incurred prompt rebuttal by two eminent Jesuit authors, Edward Knott and John Floyd, and the controversy ended only when Pope Urban VIII imposed silence on both sides with his brief *Britannia* of 9 May 1631.

Kellison was long supposed the author of *The Gagge of the New Gospel* (1623), which, when answered in 1624 by the Anglican divine Richard Montague with a work usually known as *A New Gagg for an Old Goose*, led to Montague's

being attacked by a host of puritans for his Arminian ideas and his leniency towards Catholics. As Dodd remarks, 'this was a bone of dissension thrown among the Protestant divines' (Dodd, 3.91), but it was thrown not by Kellison but by the learned printer of the St Omer press, John Heigham.

Meanwhile Kellison was not without other, more practical problems as president of Douai, not the least being financial. To relieve the debts of his college he went on two fund-raising journeys, one to England from October 1623 to April 1624, and the other to Brussels in July 1625, but without success. Subsequently Douai was on three occasions afflicted with the plague, which increased the cares of the president and the debts of the college. Finally, after a long presidency of twenty-seven years Kellison died at the college on 21 January 1642. He is described by Dodd as 'above the common size, with a majestick carriage; and though his countenance was somewhat forbidding, affability and an agreeable conversation took off the aversion that might be conceived on that account' (Dodd, 3.89). In the controversies in which he became involved, however, his affability and his desire to please all parties led to his being compared by John Floyd to 'the sea-crab which looketh one way and goeth another' (J. Floyd, *An Apology of the Holy Sea Apostolicks Proceeding*, 1630).

PETER MILWARD

Sources Gillow, *Lit. biog. hist.*, 3.677–85 · C. Dodd [H. Tootell], *The church history of England, from the year 1500, to the year 1688*, 3 (1742), 88–91 · G. Anstruther, *The seminary priests*, 1 (1969), 193–4 · H. Foley, ed., *Records of the English province of the Society of Jesus*, 6 (1880), 156, 506 · A. F. Allison, 'Richard Smith's Gallican backers and Jesuit opponents [pt 1]', *Recusant History*, 18 (1986–7), 329–401 · A. F. Allison, 'John Heigham of S. Omer (*c*.1568–*c*.1632)', *Recusant History*, 4 (1957–8), 226–42 · A. F. Allison, 'The later life and writings of Joseph Cresswell, SJ (1556–1623)', *Recusant History*, 15 (1979–81), 79–144 · P. Milward, *Religious controversies of the Jacobean age* (1978), 40, 105–6, 137–9, 174, 199–200

Kellner, Ernest Augustus (1792–1839), singer, was born on 26 January 1792 at Windsor, Berkshire, the son of an oboist from Saxe-Weimar in Queen Charlotte's private band. He began to learn the piano from his father before he was two years old, and at five he played one of Handel's organ concertos in front of the royal family at Windsor. He had a beautiful voice as a boy, and, at the king's wish, was trained by Sir William Parsons. Kellner first sang at a court concert when he was eight years old. He continued under the immediate patronage of royalty until his father made engagements for him to sing in public. After this he was heard at the Glee Club, the Catch Club, and the Ancient Concerts (as soloist, 1802).

In 1805 Kellner was a midshipman on HMS *Plover*, and afterwards on the *Acasta*, but when the ship was ordered to a West Indies station his parents persuaded him to leave the navy. By this time his voice had changed to a baritone. In 1809–10 he had some lessons from Venanzio Rauzzini at Bath, and sang at the theatre. He toured with Charles Incledon, and was engaged in 1813–14 for concerts in London. In 1815 he married, went to Italy, and studied under Porri at Florence, in 1817 under Pietro Casella and Nozzari at Naples, where he gave two concerts, and under

Girolamo Crescentini at Bologna. When passing through the main towns of Switzerland, Bavaria, and Saxe-Weimar, he gave successful musical soirées.

Kellner settled in London as a teacher in December 1820, and sang during the following three seasons at the Philharmonic and other London concerts, but his voice had lost some of its strength. He sang in the provinces with Angelica Catalani in 1822. Kellner was also appointed choirmaster at the Bavarian Chapel, but in 1824 he left England for Venice, where he sang at La Fenice with success. Illness forced him to cancel an engagement at Parma, but a mass he had composed was performed at the archduchess's chapel, and he was appointed court pianist there. He taught music in Florence for some time. In the course of a concert tour in 1828 he visited Odessa and St Petersburg, then spent the next few years in Paris. He returned to London in 1834, and spent the rest of his life teaching and writing. He died on 18 July 1839.

Kellner's hundred or more manuscript compositions include several masses performed at the Bavarian Chapel, an unfinished dramatic piece founded on the revolution in Poland, some lyrical and other poems, and essays on musical education. His published songs include 'County Guy' and 'The Lasses with a Simpering Air' (1824?), 'The Blind Mother', 'Speak on', 'Shepherd's Chief Mourner', 'Medora's Song', and 'Though all my dreams' (1835–9). While at Bologna he composed a symphony and fugue for voices for which he was awarded membership of the Philharmonic Society of Bologna.

L. M. MIDDLETON, *rev.* ANNE PIMLOTT BAKER

Sources [J. S. Sainsbury], ed., *A dictionary of musicians*, 2 vols. (1824) · *Musical World* (22 Aug 1839), 259–62 · 'Sketch of the state of music in London', *Quarterly Musical Magazine and Review*, 2 (1820), 373–91, esp. 391

Kello, Esther. *See* Inglis, Esther (1570/71–1624).

Kello, Samuel (*d.* 1680). *See under* Inglis, Esther (1570/71–1624).

Kelly. For this title name *see* individual entries under Kelly; *see also* Erskine, Thomas Alexander, sixth earl of Kellie [Kelly] (1731–1781).

Kelly, (Margaret) Ann Davidson (1912–1989), medical social worker, was born on 1 February 1912 at Manley House, Bridge of Allan, Stirlingshire, the second daughter and youngest of the five children of John Davidson Kelly (1861–1928), schoolmaster, and his wife, Ann (1875–1937), daughter of John Barnes JP of Bunker's Hill, Cumberland. John Norman Davidson *Kelly (1909–1997), patristic scholar, was her immediate sibling. One of a gifted family, she was taught at home to university level by her father, who in true Scots fashion encouraged intellectual rigour and developed her capacity for disciplined and independent thought. In 1934 she graduated from Glasgow University with an MA honours degree in history and proceeded to a diploma in social studies.

Kelly gained the certificate of the Institute of Hospital Almoners (IHA) in 1937 and was appointed assistant almoner at St Thomas's Hospital and later at Westminster Hospital. In 1940 she was elected honorary secretary of the Hospital Almoners' Association (HAA), and when in 1943 its membership grew too large to be managed by volunteers she was appointed its first paid secretary. For the next two and a half years she laid the foundations of the kind of service required by a body of professional workers. Having played a major part in the planning and negotiations which resulted in the fusion of the HAA and the IHA to form the Institute of Almoners in 1945, she decided to return to the field and chose a municipal hospital rather than another teaching hospital. As head almoner of the North Middlesex County Hospital she experienced the differences between statutory and voluntary hospitals.

In 1951 Kelly became head almoner at King's College Hospital, a post she held until 1962. Never an easily satisfied boss, she promoted a stimulating milieu, establishing high standards for work with patients and excellent training facilities for students and staff, earning their lasting respect and affection. During those years she continued to make important contributions to the development of the profession and services to patients. She served on numerous committees, was chairman of the Institute of Almoners education committee, and in 1962 was vice-chairman of the institute's council.

A woman of conviction and enthusiasm, Kelly came firmly to the view that social work in hospitals must become part of a much wider profession founded on a shared philosophy and values and pursuing common goals. She supported the recommendations of the Younghusband *Report on Social Workers in the Local Authority Health and Welfare Services* (1959) and encouraged colleagues to accept the challenge of integrating these new workers, generically trained at different levels. In the late 1950s social workers at King's College Hospital took part in a project with the local Family Welfare Association (FWA) on co-operation between agencies to redefine casework and to consider how family casework could be used in the preventive field. Kelly worked closely with Florence Mitchell, FWA district secretary, who became a lifelong friend.

From 1962 Kelly spent two years as a regional welfare officer for the Ministry of Health. These were not particularly happy years, partly because she was prohibited from being involved in the activities of her professional association. None the less she gained experience of central government which proved useful when she became the first and only general secretary of the Institute of Medical Social Workers, as the Institute of Almoners was renamed in 1964. Over the next six years she set about confirming the institute as a fully professional body, negotiating an improved salary structure within the Whitley Council, and helping to ensure that its qualifying courses reflected good standards of practice. She became nationally known for her thoroughness in preparing for the major legislative, organizational, and professional changes ahead. The Social Work (Scotland) Act of 1968, the Local Authority Social Services Act of 1970, the inception of the British Association of Social Workers (BASW) in 1970, and the establishment of the Personal Social Services Council and of the Central Council for Education and Training in Social Work in 1971 were all developments which demanded her attention and used to the full her abilities to speak and negotiate on behalf of workers and patients.

Having believed for years in the merits of a unified social work profession, Kelly set about the task of preparing the institute and its members for change. Arrangements were made for the institute's training school to be incorporated in courses at the London School of Economics, and the institute's offices at 42 Bedford Square became the first home of the British Association of Social Workers. Kelly herself was one of the first three assistant general secretaries of the new association until her retirement in February 1972. Those first years of professional and organizational unification were fraught with uncertainties and tensions, which Kelly handled with humour and trenchant argument. When she retired, the debate about the future of social work in the National Health Service was nearing its peak, generating many divided loyalties.

It was typical of Kelly that while enjoying the pleasures of retirement, through visits to France, cooking, and gardening, she found time in the next two years to return to part-time work, first on models for health-related social work in a local authority and then as a practitioner in a small geriatric hospital, thus bringing her career full circle. In 1973 she was awarded an OBE in recognition of her achievements. A woman with 'a first class brain with an enviable clarity of mind coupled with a phenomenal memory and Churchillian courage', she was remembered for 'her wisdom, warm concern, sense of humour and the generosity which she has shown to her patients, her staff and her colleagues', truly 'one of the pillars of the association' (*Social Work Today*, 2/24, 1971, 2). She died on 18 February 1989 at the Royal Sussex County Hospital, Brighton, having lived in Kingston, near Lewes, for many years. She was a committed Anglican and her funeral was held on 24 February at St Michael's Church, Lewes, where she had worshipped regularly; following cremation at Brighton on the same day, her ashes were interred at St Michael's on 26 February. JOAN BARACLOUGH

Sources Yearbooks of Hospital Almoners' Association (1937–41) • *HAA Almoners News Sheets* (1942–8) • *The Almoner* (1964–) • *Medical Social Work*, 1–22 (1948–70) • *Social Work Today*, 1–4 (1970–74) • *The Guardian* (28 Feb 1989) • J. Baraclough and others, *100 years of health related social work* (1996) • personal knowledge (2004) • private information (2004) • b. cert. • d. cert.

Archives University of Warwick, archives of British Association of Social Workers predecessor organisations | FILM NFTA: video: 100 years of health related social work—BASW: producer K. Richards, 1995

Likenesses photograph, repro. in *The Guardian*

Wealth at death £28,334: probate, 1989, *CGPLA Eng. & Wales*

Kelly, Benedictus Marwood (1785–1867), naval officer and benefactor, was born at Holsworthy, Devon, on 3 February 1785, and baptized on 1 September 1790 (the date sometimes given for his birth), the second son of Benedictus Marwood Kelly (d. 1836) of Holsworthy, attorney, and

his wife, Mary, daughter of Arscott Coham. Educated at Exeter, he entered the navy on 19 October 1798 on the *Niger* (32 guns). In November 1798 he joined the *Gibraltar* (80 guns), commanded by his uncle, Captain William Hancock Kelly, and later by Captain G. F. Ryves. Kelly assisted at the capture on 19 June 1799 of Rear-Admiral Perrée's squadron, served on the expeditions to Ferrol (1800) and Egypt (1801), and was wounded while serving in the boats in a successful attack on the French at Elba. In 1804 he joined the *Temeraire* (98 guns, later immortalized as Turner's *Fighting Temeraire*). In January 1805 he was made sublieutenant in the schooner *Eling* (14 guns) and so missed Trafalgar. Promoted lieutenant on 31 January 1806, he served on the *Adamant* (50 guns) in the Caribbean and on the west African coast. From August 1807 he served on the frigate *Daedalus* (32 guns) and was at the capture in December 1808 of the fort and town of Samana, San Domingo, a privateer base, and led a detachment which pursued, fought, and captured the crews of two privateers. In March 1810 he became first lieutenant of the *Polyphemus* (64 guns), flagship of Vice-Admiral Bartholomew Samuel Rowley. In 1811 Kelly commanded the sloop *Dasher* (18 guns) in the expedition which captured Java.

Kelly was promoted commander on 28 November 1811 but, despite repeated requests for employment, was on half pay until appointed on 28 September 1818 to command the sloop *Pheasant* (22 guns). He served on the African coast against the slave trade until February 1822, gaining over £800 in prize money, and for much of the period was senior officer of the squadron there. He was promoted captain on 19 July 1821, but then retired from ill health; he was made rear-admiral in March 1852, vice-admiral in October 1857, and admiral in April 1863.

Kelly suffered from ill health—'internal troubles' and a resultant 'nervous condition'. He married at St Margaret's Church, Westminster, on 31 August 1837 Mary Ann, eldest daughter and heir of Richard Price, banker, of Duke Street, Westminster, and Highfields Park, Withyham, Sussex. She died in childbirth on 14 July 1838. After leaving the navy Kelly became involved in the City, and was a director of the London Brighton and South Coast Railway and the Bristol and Exeter Railway, and for some time chairman of the Royal Mail Steam Packet Company. Between the death of his first wife and his second marriage he lived very frugally, with only one room, and his laundry and darning done by relatives, which caused comment. In 1855 he married Juliana (1803–1896), eldest daughter of William Boyd, banker and coal owner, of Burfield Priory, Gloucestershire; they left no children. After this marriage Kelly bought Saltford House, Saltford, near Bath, above the Box Tunnel, and resided there until his death there on 26 September 1867. He was buried at Holsworthy, Devon.

By his will dated 29 September 1866 Kelly left money and other property for trustees (including the earl of Devon and Thomas Dyke Acland) to found an Anglican boys' school in western Devon with foundationerships for his kin (lineal descendants of his paternal grandfather Arthur Kelly of Kelly, Devon, d. March 1762) and sons of naval officers. He reportedly bequeathed £132,000 (but this may have been exaggerated), to which approximately £20,000 was added after his widow's death on 4 December 1896. The Kelly College charitable trust was approved in August 1872, and the eighth duke of Bedford gave land near Tavistock. Kelly College was opened in September 1877, and 'although on a smaller scale, became at one time to the Royal Navy what Wellington was to the Army' (Gardner, 192). It is now co-educational.

ROGER T. STEARN

Sources O'Byrne, *Naval biog. dict.* · A. O. V. Penny, ed., *Kelly College register, 1877–1927* (1930) · L. G. Pierson and T. L. Stoddard, eds., *Kelly College centenary register* (1977) · *GM*, 4th ser., 4 (1867) · Boase, *Mod. Eng. biog.* · W. L. Clowes, *The Royal Navy: a history from the earliest times to the present*, 7 vols. (1897–1903), vol. 5 · B. Lavery, *Nelson's navy: the ships, men, and organisation, 1793–1815*, rev. edn (1990) · P. Mackesy, *The war in the Mediterranean, 1803–1810* (1957) · R. Muir, *Britain and the defeat of Napoleon, 1807–1815* (1996) · J. Egerton, *Turner: the fighting Temeraire* (1995) · B. Gardner, *The public schools* (1973)
Likenesses bust, Kelly College, Tavistock
Wealth at death under £70,000: probate, 11 Nov 1867, *CGPLA Eng. & Wales* · reportedly bequeathed £132,000

Kelly, Sir David Victor (1891–1959), diplomatist, was born on 14 September 1891 in Adelaide, South Australia, the only child of David Frederick Kelly (1849–1894), professor of classics at the University of Adelaide, and Sophie Armstrong (*d.* 1933), daughter of the Revd Ignatius George Abeitshauer d'Arenberg of Trinity College, Dublin. Both parents were Irish; his father's family were protestant landowners in co. Londonderry, while his mother was descended from a member of a Rhenish ducal house who emigrated to southern Ireland at the end of the Napoleonic wars. After his father's death, the family returned to Ireland, and thence to England, where Kelly was educated at St Paul's School, London, and Magdalen College, Oxford. The traditional St Paul's diet of Latin and Greek did little to enthuse him, but in his final school years, under the challenge of the Oxford scholarship exams, Kelly's passion for history flourished, and his waxing appetite for politics found expression in letters to various national newspapers, though not always on subjects about which he was entirely conversant. As a demy (scholar) at Magdalen, he obtained first-class honours in modern history in 1913, fenced for the university, and became 'a devoted admirer of Germany, a slave to French literature and cooking, a philosophic English tory and a delighted reader of Kipling' (Kelly, *Ruling Few*, 71–2). But it was the experience of foreign travel during this time, especially long meandering car journeys through Europe, Russia, and north Africa with his future stepfather, and son of his former school headmaster, Richard Johnson Walker, which perhaps had the biggest influence on the direction of Kelly's future career.

It was on the advice of Sir Herbert Warren, president of Magdalen, that Kelly sat the Foreign Office entrance examination, which he passed in 1914. However, war intervened before he could take up his appointment and he immediately volunteered for active service, winning a commission in the Leicestershire regiment. It was also at

Sir David Victor Kelly (1891–1959), by Walter Stoneman, 1949

this time that he became a devoted Roman Catholic. Kelly's activities as a brigade intelligence officer won him an MC in 1917, and were described in his book *39 Months* (1930), a work written largely as a corrective to the distorted representation of warfare which coloured popular literature on the subject.

When Kelly finally commenced his diplomatic career in 1919, his first posting was to Argentina, where he met and married, on 17 April 1920, Isabel Adela, daughter of Henry Maynard Mills of Buenos Aires. She died in 1927, leaving a son and daughter, and two years later, on 4 June 1929, Kelly married his second wife, (Renée Octavie Ghislaine) Marie-Noële de Jourda de Vaux [*see below*]. They had two sons.

After a succession of postings in Lisbon (1923–5), Mexico (1925–7), Brussels (1927–9), and Stockholm (1929–31), and service in the American department of the Foreign Office (1922–3 and 1931–4), Kelly was appointed counsellor, acting high commissioner, and chargé d'affaires in Cairo. He retained this position until 1938, when he returned to head the Egyptian department in the Foreign Office. It was in Cairo that Kelly's innate abilities as a diplomatist began to show. British relations with Egypt during these years were strained owing to the power struggle between King Fuad and the Wafd, the negotiations leading to the Anglo-Egyptian treaty in 1936, and the threat of war caused by

Mussolini's attack on Abyssinia in 1935. Kelly argued persuasively for a treaty settlement with Egypt, and was one of the first to advocate a withdrawal of British troops from Cairo to the canal zone. His keen sense of Britain's military weakness in the eastern Mediterranean made him counsel against provoking Italy over the Abyssinian crisis. Kelly's firm handling of affairs in Cairo, especially during the absences of the high commissioner, Sir Miles Lampson, and his management of Egyptian affairs in London, marked him out as one of the Foreign Office's 'rising stars' before the war.

In January 1940 Kelly was appointed envoy-extraordinary and minister-plenipotentiary at Bern. The unexpected allied collapse in the summer of 1940 left Switzerland completely surrounded by hostile powers. The presence of Kelly's small legation in Bern kept the union flag flying in the heart of Nazi Europe, and enabled Britain to organize espionage and smuggling activities which proved invaluable to Britain's beleaguered war effort. Kelly's success in these endeavours gained him the dubious honour of having the high command of the German armed forces (OKW) draw up plans for his assassination in late 1940. Skills of a rather more genteel fashion were needed to stiffen the Swiss government's resolve in the face of mounting axis pressures, and Kelly's friendship with Marcel Pilet-Golaz, the federal president and foreign minister, was critical in preventing a rupture in Anglo-Swiss diplomatic relations over the winter of 1940–41 after the accidental bombardment of Swiss territory by the Royal Air Force. Kelly found life as minister in Bern, protecting British interests without endangering Swiss neutrality or falling victim to the numerous agents provocateurs, an exhilarating experience. Communication with London was erratic and restricted to telegrams whose security could never be guaranteed, and as a result it was almost inevitable that Kelly's attitude towards such sensitive issues as German peace overtures occasionally diverged from those of his superiors in London. On the whole Kelly's record in Bern was admirable, and when he left in early 1942 he was promoted to KCMG, having already been appointed CMG in 1935.

In June 1942 Kelly returned to Buenos Aires as ambassador, a position he held until May 1946. His period of service there saw the beginnings of the Peronist revolution and America's efforts to impose its political and economic influence on the region. Kelly's careful nurturing of Argentina's political and business élites did much to defend Britain's traditional standing in the country, but the distraction of war in Europe and the need to act in tandem with the Americans meant that Kelly frequently found his hands tied. The obstinate refusal, as he saw it, of British companies to respond flexibly to the changing circumstances in Argentina did nothing to lighten his task. His next posting, as ambassador in Ankara from May 1946 until April 1949, presented him with a similar problem of managing relations with rapidly diminishing resources at his disposal. Britain's decision to reduce its military and economic assistance to Turkey in early 1947 prompted the American administration into enunciating the famous

'Truman doctrine' and stepping up its involvement in this region. On a personal level, Kelly's three years in Turkey proved to be some of the most enjoyable for himself and his family. They travelled widely and immersed themselves in the country's language, literature, and culture. Kelly's penchant for direct personal diplomacy suited the Turkish temperament, and his close relations with the 'ruling few' were of no small influence at a time when parliamentary government was still in its infancy, and the country's security hung so much in the balance.

It was a mark of the regard with which Kelly was held in the Foreign Office that he was chosen to represent British interests in the Soviet Union for his last posting, as ambassador in Moscow from June 1949 to October 1951. The severe restrictions imposed on foreign diplomats and the secrecy and fear which permeated Soviet society made fostering normal social contacts with Soviet officials almost impossible and thus made many of Kelly's diplomatic skills redundant. Undeterred, Kelly threw himself into the job, and his shrewd, balanced dispatches did much to guide British policy in the years in which the Soviet atomic test, the outbreak of the Korean War, and the subsequent Soviet 'peace offensive' in western Europe brought Soviet–Western relations to their nadir. In recognition of his service, Kelly was advanced to GCMG in January 1950.

Having spent thirty-five years tutoring government officials in the intricacies of the foreign societies in which he had served, it was typical that in retirement Kelly turned his attention to educating the wider public on matters of Anglo-Soviet affairs. This was no easy task, but Kelly's cool, measured columns in leading newspapers did much to elucidate many points of detail, and to clarify opinions on a range of issues affecting the Soviet regime. These articles were published as a collection entitled *Beyond the Iron Curtain* in 1954. He also composed a philosophical tract, *The Hungry Sheep* (1955; translated into German with a preface by the Swiss scholar and diplomatist Carl Jacob Burckhardt in 1959), in which he drew on his experience in public affairs and devout religious beliefs to warn against the decline of values in modern society. His wide range of contacts, sensitivity to foreign societies, and healthy but constructive scepticism were put to good use as president of the Anglo-Turkish Society and the British Atlantic Committee, and later as chairman of the British Council.

In his memoirs, *The Ruling Few, or, The Human Background to Diplomacy* (1952), Kelly distilled many of his thoughts on diplomacy, particularly the need, as he saw it, for diplomatists to combine traditional interpersonal skills with an acute understanding of the importance of commercial and financial affairs. Kelly's involvement with the British Council also reflected a long-held belief in the value of information, ideas, and, in wartime, propaganda, in international relations. As ambassador he had frequently berated London for failing to keep his embassy supplied with newsreels, films, and papers, and he showed more alacrity than most in responding to Foreign Office requests for views on how British policies could best be presented abroad. As the diplomatic service was only just coming to terms with the importance of economics in diplomacy, Kelly's awareness of the power of the media showed great foresight, and was evidence of a distinctly more 'modern' approach to his profession than the old school image for which he was often known. Kelly died of a brain haemorrhage on 27 March 1959 at his home, Tara House, Inch, co. Wexford, shortly after returning from a British Council mission to India and Pakistan. A funeral service was held at St Patrick's Church, Castletown, co. Wexford, on 30 March.

Kelly's second wife, **(Renée Octavie Ghislaine) Marie-Noële Kelly** [*née* de Jourda de Vaux], Lady Kelly (1901–1995), traveller and hostess, was born in Belgium on 25 December 1901, the eldest of three daughters of Charles de Jourda de Vaux, comte de Vaux. Her maternal grandfather was Baron George Snoy, author of a series of travel guides. On her father's side her ancestors included Maréchal Charles Noël de Jourda, comte de Vaux, who conquered Corsica for Louis XV. Educated at a Belgian convent and in England, she met her future husband at a dinner party at her grandparents' house near Waterloo in 1928. Ten years his junior, she shared Kelly's love for travel and life on the diplomatic circuit. Her vivaciousness and panache made her an excellent companion and hostess. She was a close friend of Rebecca West and Freya Stark. Her first book, *Turkish Delights* (1951), included detailed descriptions of many hitherto neglected Byzantine and Turkish monuments. *Mirror to Russia* (1952) and *Picture Book of Russia* (1952)—illustrated with her own photographs—benefited from the unusual freedom to travel accorded her and her husband by the Soviet authorities. She also published *This Delicious Land Portugal* (1956) and her autobiography, *Dawn to Dusk* (1960), with an introduction by Rebecca West. After her husband's death she maintained a cottage in co. Wexford, but lived mainly in a large flat in Carlyle Square, London, where she 'continued to keep open house with great dash and, sometimes slapdash, élan' (*The Times*, 24 Feb 1995). She died on 22 February 1995, and was buried in co. Wexford. She was survived by her two sons.

NEVILLE WYLIE

Sources DNB · D. Kelly, *The ruling few, or, The human background to diplomacy* (1952) · M.-N. Kelly, *Dawn to dusk* (1960) · D. V. Kelly, *39 months* (1930) · D. V. Kelly, *The hungry sheep* (1955) · K. Urner, *Die Schweiz muss noch geschluckt werden! Hitlers Aktionspläne gegen die Schweiz* (1990) · M.-N. Kelly, *Turkish delights* (1951) · M.-N. Kelly, *Mirror to Russia* (1952) · D. V. Kelly, *Beyond the iron curtain* (1954) · *The Times* (28 March 1959) · *The Times* (3 April 1959) · *The Times* (17 April 1959) · *The Times* (5 May 1959) · *The Times* (16 July 1959) · *Sunday Times* (29 March 1959) · *FO List* (1950) · N. Wylie, 'Pilet-Golaz, David Kelly and British policy towards Switzerland, 1940', *Diplomacy and Statecraft*, 8/1 (1997), 49–79 · Foreign Office MSS, PRO · *CGPLA Eng. & Wales* (1959) · *The Times* (24 Feb 1995) · *Daily Telegraph* (23 Feb 1995) · *The Independent* (15 March 1995)
Archives PRO, diplomatic dispatches, FO 371 series
Likenesses W. Stoneman, photograph, 1949, NPG [*see illus.*] · photograph, 1949, Hult. Arch. · D. Glass, photograph, repro. in Kelly, *Ruling few*, frontispiece · J. R. Renard-Goulet, bronze bust, priv. coll.
Wealth at death £37,863 11s. 4d.—in England: probate, 8 July 1959, *CGPLA Eng. & Wales* · £11,985—in Ireland: *The Times* (16 July 1959)

Kelly, Edward [Ned] (*c.*1854–1880), bushranger, was born at Beveridge, Victoria, Australia, about 1854. One of eight children, he was the eldest son of John (Red) Kelly, an ex-convict transported from Ireland to Van Diemen's Land in 1842 for stealing two pigs. Red Kelly was freed in 1848 and travelled to Victoria, where at Melbourne in 1850 he married Ellen Quinn, a member of the Quinn clan from co. Antrim, Ireland. Ned Kelly received his only schooling at Avenel School at Hugh's Creek, Victoria (*c.*1864–1866). In 1866 his father died and, with Ned as the male head, the indigent family moved into an old hut on a land selection of 88 acres at Lurg in the Greta district of north-east Victoria. This was Quinn clan country, and Kelly was here influenced by the bog-Irish element, where internal clan arguments and criminal activity were common, and police and other authority figures were disdained. At Lurg he had his first brush with the law when he was charged and acquitted in 1869 for an alleged assault on a Chinese man. This was followed by arrests for robbery, when he was again discharged, and sending an indecent letter—when he was sentenced to three months in gaol.

In 1871 Kelly was sentenced to three years' imprisonment for receiving a stolen horse. After being released from Pentridge gaol in February 1874 he took a job timber milling, then later went panning for gold and bush mustering. His next encounter with the police was not until 1877, when he was arrested and fined for being drunk and disorderly and assaulting policemen.

Members of the Quinn–Kelly clan were constantly coming under police suspicion—sometimes justifiably but very often not—for horse stealing and similar offences. A turning point for the family occurred on 15 April 1878, when Constable Alexander Fitzpatrick, described by his chief commissioner as 'a liar and larrikin' and by himself as 'not fit to be in the police force', attended alone at the Kelly home on Eleven Mile Creek, ostensibly to arrest Ned's brother Dan, who was wanted on warrant for horse stealing. Fitzpatrick did not have the warrant with him and made no arrest, but he sparked what is generally known as the 'Fitzpatrick affair'. Accounts of what occurred differ greatly: Fitzpatrick claimed that while trying to arrest Dan he was assaulted by a number of the Kelly clan, then shot in the wrist by Ned. The Kelly version was that Ned was not present and that Fitzpatrick was ushered from the premises without the use of firearms. Whatever the truth, the incident made Ned an outlaw. Arrest warrants were issued against Ned, Dan, and Ellen Kelly, Bill Skillion, and Brickey Williamson. The latter three were quickly arrested and in October 1878 Ellen was sentenced to three years' hard labour and the two men to six years. Ned and Dan evaded capture and, joined by two friends, Steve Hart and Joe Byrne, this foursome were pursued by the police as the Kelly Gang.

In October 1878 the police mounted a pincer movement to hunt the gang, but at Stringybark Creek the Kellys ambushed a police patrol camp, killing three policemen. This put the gang on the path to infamy, and during a period of twenty months the four bushrangers, led by Ned, were pursued by police through a labyrinth of rural

Edward [Ned] Kelly (*c.*1854–1880), by unknown photographer, *c.*1874

sympathizers in an outbreak of social banditry that included spectacular bank robberies at Euroa and Jerilderie. At the scene of the second crime Kelly left a handwritten manuscript of about 8000 words detailing his view of the world—the 'Jerilderie letter'—which was published in a limited edition in 1942. The Kelly outbreak reached its climax in a hotel siege at Glenrowan, where on 28 June 1880 Hart, Byrne, and Dan Kelly were killed, and Ned, wearing a suit of body armour made from steel plough mould boards weighing almost 100 lbs, was shot and captured. In Melbourne on 28–9 October 1880 he was tried for the murder of Constable Thomas Lonigan at Stringybark Creek. He was hanged at the Melbourne gaol on 11 November and was buried in an unmarked grave in the gaol grounds. He was already a legendary figure, and he remains Australia's best-known folk hero. His exploits were commemorated in a notable series of paintings by Sidney Nolan and formed the basis for Peter Carey's Booker prize-winning novel, *True History of the Kelly Gang* (2001).   ROBERT HALDANE

Sources R. Haldane, *The people's force* (1986) · J. McQuilton, *The Kelly outbreak, 1878–1880* (1979) · J. Molony, *I am Ned Kelly* (1980) · C. Turnbull, *Kellyana* (1943) · Public Records Office, Victoria, Australia, Kelly Historical Collection, VPRS 4965–4969 · Victoria Police Historical Unit Archives, Victoria, Australia, The Kelly Papers · *Royal commission of enquiry into the circumstances of the Kelly outbreak: minutes of evidence and second progress report* (1881) · *Ned Kelly, being his own story of his life and crimes*, ed. C. Turnbull (1942) ['Jerilderie letter']
Archives Public Records Office, Victoria, Australia, Victoria Archives, Crown Law Department · Victoria Police Historical Unit Archives, Victoria, Australia
Likenesses photograph, *c.*1874, State Library of New South Wales, Mitchell Library [*see illus.*] · photograph, *c.*1880, Victoria Police Historical Unit Archives, Victoria, Australia

Kelly, (Martha) Emily [Pat] (1872/3–1922), mountaineer, was the eldest sibling in a large family; details of her birth, parentage (and hence her maiden name), and education are not known. Growing up, she found herself responsible for 'more than the average girl's share of domestic duties' (*Pinnacle Club Journal*), and all her life she was known for her capacity for hard work combined with a natural organizational flair. These abilities stood her in good stead when later she became a businesswoman. By February 1917, when her will was drawn up, she was married to the celebrated cragsman Harry Mills Kelly (1884–1980), with whom she was living at Levenshulme, Manchester. She shared an office in Manchester with her husband, an insurance clerk.

Pat Kelly began climbing at the beginning of 1914 and was apparently a graceful and bold balance climber. Her husband remarked that most of their climbing on local gritstone was done solo. She did so from choice—wishing, as she said, 'to develop her own technique in her own way' (Clark and Pyatt, 159). Harry Kelly thought one of her most outstanding achievements was to climb solo Jones's route from Deep Ghyll in the Lake District; observers on Scafell pinnacle told him of their consternation on seeing this lonely figure coming up the arête. Friends described her 'indomitable will' and 'almost inexhaustible vitality', but also noted her warm-heartedness (*Pinnacle Club Journal*).

Pat Kelly was dedicated to encouraging other women to overcome their natural timidity on rock. The idea of a women's rock-climbing club germinated naturally from this, and her drive and enthusiasm gradually brought it to fruition. Harry Kelly recalled how by 1920 their 'small office at 29 Fountain Street, Manchester, had become the seat of operations' (Angell, 3). A letter in the *Manchester Guardian* announcing the proposed formation of a club for women rock-climbers was boosted by an appreciative leader written by C. E. Montague (himself a climber). The inaugural meeting of the Pinnacle Club, the first dedicated rock-climbing club for women, was held at Pen-y-Gwryd in north Wales on 26 March 1921; its entry requirement was the ability to lead a 'difficult' rock climb. The club started out with more than sixty members; its first honorary secretary was Pat Kelly, and Mrs Eleanor Winthrop Young its president.

As a young woman in the early 1890s Pat Kelly had readily identified with the mood of awakening feminine consciousness. Influenced by such writers as George Eliot, the Brontës, and Olive Schreiner, she read a paper on Eliot before a local literary society in which she defended 'her kind from the cheap male sneer that woman's only place is at home looking after the baby' (*Pinnacle Club Journal*). But contemporaries took pains to stress that no sex antagonism or rivalry fuelled her convictions. It was just that, when climbing with men, women hardly ever got to lead or to master the finer points of route finding, technique, or responsibility. Mrs Kelly's ambition was to provide an atmosphere of encouragement in which women and girls could discover and develop their own skills.

The accident which killed Pat Kelly occurred on 17 April, the last day of a club meet in north Wales at Easter 1922. No one saw what happened. She was discovered with head injuries at the foot of Tryfan, and with one boot missing, having fallen from apparently easy ground after other climbers had packed up for the night. She was taken to the Carnarvonshire and Anglesey Infirmary, Bangor, where she died from a fractured base of the skull on 26 April 1922, aged forty-nine.

It mystified all who knew her how so sure-footed a climber as Kelly could have fallen in this way. But sixty-six years later, when the history of the Pinnacle Club came to be written, an explanation finally emerged. Its author, Shirley Angell, was told that some months after the accident friends of Pat Kelly found the missing boot jammed immovably in rocks by one of its front nails. She was known to be experimenting with a new pattern of nails that day. Unused to them, she must have caught her foot during descent and been thrown off balance. The boot was clearly wrenched from her as she pitched headlong. Those who made the discovery vowed never to speak of it during the lifetime of Harry Kelly or of the friend who had supplied the new nails for his wife.   AUDREY SALKELD

Sources *Pinnacle Club Journal*, 1 (1924) • R. W. Clark and E. C. Pyatt, *Mountaineering in Britain* (1957) • S. Angell, *Pinnacle Club: a history of women climbing* (1988) • G. W. Young, G. Sutton, and W. Noyce, *Snowdon biography: 200 years of achievement* (1957) • W. Birkett and W. Peascod, *Women climbing* (1989) • W. Birkett, *Lakeland's greatest pioneers: 100 years of rock climbing* (1983) • d. cert. • will, 23 Feb 1917
Archives Alpine Club, London, letter
Likenesses photograph; priv. coll. • photographs, Fell and Rock Climbing Club, Cumbria
Wealth at death £1282 16s. 7d.: probate, 27 June 1922, *CGPLA Eng. & Wales*

Kelly, Sir Fitzroy Edward (1796–1880), judge, was born on 9 October 1796 in London, the second son of Captain Robert Hawke Kelly RN (*d.* in or before 1807) and his wife, Isabella, *née* Fordyce (*bap.* 1759, *d.* 1857) [*see* Kelly, Isabella]. He was educated privately at a school in Chelsea kept by the Revd Mr Farrer. Afterwards his mother, by then a widow, placed him in the office of Robert Brutton, an attorney in practice in the City, with a view to his obtaining articles. Brutton found him to be so talented that he advised that Kelly should read for the bar. On 31 March 1819 Kelly was admitted as a student of Lincoln's Inn where he was a pupil of T. Abraham and of G. H. Wilkinson, who were special pleaders, and he practised for some time as a special pleader before being called to the bar on 6 May 1824.

Kelly was a member of the home circuit for about a year, but by 1826 he had joined the Norfolk circuit where he was immediately successful. At the same time he rapidly built up a London practice on which he soon concentrated. He was a specialist in commercial law and was standing counsel for the East India Company and the Bank of England. As an advocate he was almost unrivalled in his ability to make an intricate case intelligible to a jury. At the height of his practice his annual earnings reached £25,000—a figure believed to have been exceeded among his contemporaries only by Roundell Palmer. In 1834, only ten years after his call, Kelly was made king's counsel and on 23 January 1835 was elected a bencher of his inn. All this was achieved, as *The Times* (20 September 1880) acknowledged at his death, not by introductions or influence, but solely by 'his own fearless energy, sound learning, and unwearied combativeness'.

Kelly supported the Conservative interest in politics. From 1830 he made various unsuccessful attempts to

Sir Fitzroy Edward Kelly (1796–1880), by John & Charles Watkins

enter parliament, which included being unseated at Ipswich on a petition in 1835. In 1837 he was defeated at Ipswich in the poll but came in next year on a petition. He stood again for Ipswich in the general election of 1841 but was defeated. From 1843 until 1847 he represented the town of Cambridge. In May 1852 he was elected for East Suffolk, where he owned considerable estates (at Sproughton, near Ipswich), and which he represented for the rest of his parliamentary career.

On 17 July 1845 Kelly was made solicitor-general in Peel's administration and was shortly afterwards knighted. Following Lord George Bentinck and the protectionists after 1846, he was again solicitor-general in Derby's first administration from February to December 1852. Under Derby's second administration (February 1858–June 1859) Kelly was attorney-general. In July 1866, immediately after the formation of Derby's third administration, Sir Frederick Pollock resigned the office of lord chief baron of the exchequer and the vacant post was conferred on Kelly.

Kelly's reputation has suffered from Holdsworth's judgement, based on the memoirs of Serjeant Ballantine and of Lord Justice Rolt, that he 'was not an admirable character' (Holdsworth, *Eng. law*, 484). Both Ballantine and Rolt are unreliable sources. Ballantine had a dubious reputation, and his own biographer, Thomas Seccombe, described his memoirs as 'an uncritical farrago of newspaper and club gossip' (*DNB*). Rolt's memoirs are unreliable for a different reason. They were almost entirely written at a time when Rolt had been forced through sudden ill health, involving what he described as 'a severe Paralytic attack', to retire permanently from the bench, and when, as the text shows, it is likely that he was suffering from a degree of depression that would now be seen to require medical treatment. If one looks beyond these sources a different picture of Kelly emerges. On the bench he was precise and painstaking and his demeanour was remarkably dignified and courteous. According to Sir Henry Hawkins, 'whatever his decision, you went away satisfied that you had been fairly dealt with … [Y]ou never smarted under a sneer, or had to put up with a mediocre jest' (*Reminiscences*, 1.153). Kelly's reputation for considerate behaviour is supported by Sir Edward Clarke, who recalled how, at a time of anxiety as a bar student, he was helped and shown kindness by Kelly.

Kelly was never a mere technical lawyer. He would judge on the merits of the case and was distinguished from some younger judges by his ability to look beyond decided cases to general principles. His own decisions were rarely upset on appeal, and on several occasions his dissenting judgment was upheld by the House of Lords. Unfortunately, his powers began to fail towards the end of his life and he became very slow.

For many years Kelly tried to achieve law reform. In doing so he ignored the traditional boundaries of party politics, giving generous support to reforms promoted by his political opponent Sir Richard Bethell. Kelly was completely opposed to capital punishment on the simple grounds that it led to the deaths of innocent people and failed to have any significant deterrent effect. He advocated a better system of appeals in criminal cases and the extension of the right to testify to the accused. He supported the consolidation of statute law and in 1856 became a member of the statute law commission set up by Lord Cranworth two years earlier. In 1878 Kelly engaged in public controversy with Lord Cairns over the right, claimed by Kelly as a member of the privy council, to be open about the fact that an opinion of that body in a judicial matter had not been unanimous.

Kelly was married twice. In January 1821 he married Agnes Scarth, daughter of Captain Mason of Leith. There was one daughter of the marriage who survived to adulthood but who predeceased her father. Kelly's first wife died in 1851 and in January 1856 he married Ada, daughter of Mark Cunningham of co. Sligo. There were five daughters of this marriage, which ended with Ada Kelly's death in 1874. Kelly did not receive the peerage which might have been expected, possibly as a result of his controversy with Cairns or else on account of the financial losses he was believed to have sustained in his later years. He died on 17 September 1880 at the Bedford Hotel, King's Road, Brighton, and was buried at Highgate cemetery on 22 September.   C. J. W. ALLEN

Sources *The Times* (20 Sept 1880), 8 · *Law Times* (25 Sept 1880), 367–8 · *Solicitors' Journal*, 24 (1879–80), 861 · Lord chief baron of the exchequer [F. Kelly], *A letter to the lord high chancellor* (1878) · *Hansard 3* (1844), 75.14–15; (1856), 140.718–38 · 'Capital punishment commission', *Parl. papers* (1866), 21.122ff., no. 3590 [minutes of evidence] · Holdsworth, *Eng. law*, 15.482–6 · *The memoirs of the Right Honourable Sir John Rolt* (privately printed, 1939), 14, 139–49, 175, 178–9 · [W. D. I. Foulkes], *A generation of judges* (1886), 38–53 · E. Clarke, *The story of my life* (1918), 66–7 · *The reminiscences of Sir Henry Hawkins*, ed. R. Harris, 1 (1904), 153 · T. A. Nash, *The life of Richard, Lord Westbury*, 1 (1888), 1.209 · W. Ballantine, *Some experiences of a barrister's life*, 8th edn (1883) · *DNB* · F. W. Ashley, *My sixty years in the law* (1936), 31–9 · d. cert.

Archives BL, corresp. with Sir Robert Peel, Add. MSS 40510–40576 · Bodl. Oxf., letters to Benjamin Disraeli · Herts. ALS, letters to Lord Lytton · Lpool RO, letters to fourteenth earl of Derby · Niedersächsisches Hauptstaatsarchiv Hannover, corresp. with duke of Cumberland · Som. ARS, letters to Sir William Jolliffe

Likenesses Kilburn, daguerreotype, 1851, repro. in *ILN* (17 Nov 1866) · D. Pound, stipple and line engraving, 1858 (after photograph by Mayall), NPG · E. Walker, oils, c.1866, Lincoln's Inn, London · portrait, oils, c.1870, Inner Temple, London · S. Bull, stipple and line engraving (after S. Lane), NPG · J. & C. Watkins, photograph, NPG [*see illus.*] · Lock & Whitfield, photograph, NPG · London Stereoscopic Co., photograph, NPG · S. Marks, mezzotint (after A. Lucas), BM · E. Walker, miniature, Lincoln's Inn, London · W. Walker, engraving (after F. Hudson), Lincoln's Inn, London · W. Walker, mezzotint, BM · caricature, repro. in *Punch* (28 April 1866)

Wealth at death under £60,000: probate, 8 Dec 1880, *CGPLA Eng. & Wales*

Kelly, Frances Maria [Fanny] (**1790–1882**), actress and singer, was born at Brighton on 15 October or 15 December 1790. Her father was Mark Kelly (1767–1833), originally from Dublin, where he was master of ceremonies at Dublin Castle. Mark Kelly was one of a very large family, a minor actor who had a varied career, including service in the navy. His brothers included the actor and composer Michael *Kelly. Fanny's mother, Mary Singleton (d. 1827), was the daughter of a country physician and the widow of a Mr Jackson, with whom she had a daughter, Anne, the wife of the actor Charles Mathews, the elder. Mark Kelly incurred heavy debts and deserted his wife in 1795. The family was given help by a relative, Annie Ross, the sister of the singer and actor David Ross.

Fanny was articled to her uncle Michael Kelly for nine years. She proved an apt and willing pupil, although he did not devote much time to her. She was then enrolled with the singer Anna Maria Crouch, with whom Michael Kelly had a long friendship. This arrangement was not successful owing to the jealousy of the older woman. Fanny made her stage début at the age of seven at Drury Lane, in her uncle's opera *Bluebeard* (16 January 1798). When she was ten she was enrolled in the Drury Lane company as a chorister and appeared under John Kemble's management as the Duke of York in *Richard III* and as Prince Arthur in *King John*, where her performance came to the attention of Sheridan and C. J. Fox; they predicted that she would reach the head of her profession. Sarah Siddons, who gave a moving performance as Constance in the same piece—always remembered by the child—was equally impressed. Fanny was the Barbara of the essay 'Barbara S …' by Charles Lamb (published in the *London Magazine*, 1 April 1825), in which he introduced an incident of this period showing her honesty in financial matters. As a girl she

Frances Maria Kelly (1790–1882), by Thomas Uwins, 1822

played parts previously undertaken by Nancy Storace and a little later those of Dorothy Jordan, 'the goddess of her idolatry'.

From 1800 to 1806 Fanny Kelly played at Drury Lane and the Italian Opera, where she learned Italian. Later she also acquired French and Latin. She had lessons on the guitar from Ferdinand Sor and the harp from Philip Meyer. In the summer of 1807 she moved to the Queen Street Theatre, Glasgow. After a poor start she was well received, and later toured nearly all the chief provincial theatres. The following year George Colman engaged her for the Haymarket, in 1809 she was at the Lyceum, and thereafter appeared at Drury Lane under Samuel Arnold, a life-long friend. After the fire at that theatre she migrated with the company to the Lyceum. Her suitor at that time was Thomas Phillips of Dublin, a celebrated singer, but she refused him. She had a personal success in 1811 in *MP, or, The Blue Stocking*, which was not generally well received. In 1812 she played Ophelia to Edmund Kean's Hamlet at the newly constructed Drury Lane Theatre. With occasional appearances elsewhere she remained at Drury Lane for thirty-six years.

On Saturday 17 February 1816, when Kelly was playing in *Modern Antiques, or, The Merry Mourners* at Covent Garden, a member of the audience, George Barnett, fired a pistol at her from the pit, having previously written her letters offering marriage but complaining about her appearing 'in breeches parts'. The shot missed her and some of it fell into the lap of Mary Lamb, who was there with her brother Charles. Barnett was tried and acquitted on grounds of insanity. When the Lyceum reopened on 15 June 1816 Kelly was chosen to deliver the inaugural address. In 1818 she was at the Theatre Royal in Dublin with F. E. Jones, and on

16 February had £500 benefit from a viceregal command performance. She took part in the Dublin music festival, singing in the Easter oratorio. Another attack on her, probably at her Dublin lodgings in Westmorland Street, and possibly associated with local protests at the employment of an actress from England, is recorded. At this time she was being pursued by Lord Essex, who showered her with gifts. She refused his advances on the grounds of her friendship with his wife.

On 20 July 1819 Kelly received a proposal of marriage from Charles Lamb, who frequently reviewed plays in which she appeared, and who wrote sonnets to her. This she refused, probably on the grounds of his family's history of mental illness. She remained, however, on good terms with the Lambs and was a regular visitor to their home. Her mother died in 1827 and her father, whom she had continued to support financially, met a violent end, probably suicide, in Paris in 1833. On 5 April 1829 Mary Ellen Thatcher Gerbini was born in Edinburgh, and lived thereafter with Kelly. The child became generally known as Miss Greville. Opinions differ as to whether she was an illegitimate daughter, possibly by Samuel Arnold, or adopted, perhaps at the behest of the clown, Grimaldi, in whose welfare Kelly had taken an interest. In any event her intimate friendship with the Lambs seems to have lessened at this time, attributed by some to possible notoriety associated with the child.

Kelly gave her farewell performance at Drury Lane on 8 June 1835, when she chose to act Lisette in *The Sergeant's Wife*, with Miss Peggy in *The Country Girl* as a curtain-raiser. By this time she had amassed a sum of £20,000 and wanted to set up a dramatic school for training young women. While working on this project she was also making extended tours with her *Dramatic Recollections*, for which she had first taken the New Strand Theatre in 1833. In 1839, with the patronage of the duke of Devonshire, she began building at the back of her house, 73 Dean Street, Soho, a model theatre, first called Miss Kelly's Theatre and then the Royalty, which opened on 24 May 1840 but soon closed owing to the failure of some machinery. The dramatic school flourished, and Kelly reopened the theatre, which was used by the first amateur company in the United Kingdom—the Amateurs, of which Dickens was a leading light—to produce *Everyman* before a very distinguished audience. The next production, on 3 January 1846, was a benefit for her by the same company, for which Dickens wrote a prologue to be spoken by her. However, despite an appeal to the duke of Devonshire which resulted in a £200 loan, she soon fell into debt when the theatre was, she was assured illegally, seized by the landlord. She lost £16,000 on the venture.

Kelly continued to give Shakespearian readings and to receive a few pupils when she moved with Mary Greville to 30 Moscow Road, Bayswater, then considered 'out of town'. In 1853 an attempt was made for another benefit, to be supported by Devonshire, the queen, and some members of the royal family, but it fell through. The play was not ready in time and Dickens and Kelly were both ill. Later, in increasing financial difficulties, Kelly moved to

Feltham, Middlesex, where she named her house Ross Cottage after the aunt who had been so supportive earlier in her life, and where she was visited by Kent, Irving, and Toole, the latter two telling her that they, along with other leading actors, had petitioned Gladstone, as prime minister, for financial aid for her, which she at first refused. However, she was finally given a royal grant of £150, on a memorial signed by Lord Lytton and other distinguished persons, which arrived only very shortly before her death, at Feltham on 6 December 1882. She was buried at Brompton cemetery and the grant was used to cover the expenses of the funeral and erect a memorial over her grave. She left £3037 13s. 10d.

Kelly was of average height, with a symmetrical and beautiful figure, a round face, which Lamb described as her 'divine plain face', light blue eyes, long glossy black hair admired by Byron, a low forehead, and an exceedingly beautiful smile. She was described as very 'ladylike' in her private social life, contrasting with her emotional acting, which earned her the name the 'Child of Nature'. *The Times* obituary referred to her as the last survivor of a great school of actresses.

CHARLES KENT, *rev.* J. GILLILAND

Sources B. Francis, *Fanny Kelly of Drury Lane* (1950) · L. E. Holman, *Lamb's Barbara S…* (1935) · Mrs C. Baron-Wilson, *Our actresses*, 2 vols. (1844) · Highfill, Burnim & Langhans, *BDA* · *Oxberry's Dramatic Biography*, 1/13 (1825) · C. Tomalin, *The invisible woman: the story of Nelly Ternan and Charles Dickens*, new edn (1991) · M. Kelly, *Reminiscences*, 2 vols. (1826) · E. Stirling, *Old Drury Lane*, 2 vols. (1881) · S. D'Amico, ed., *Enciclopedia dello spettacolo*, 11 vols. (Rome, 1954–68) · Boase, *Mod. Eng. biog.* · Hall, *Dramatic ports.* · P. Hartnoll, ed., *The concise Oxford companion to the theatre* (1972) · *CGPLA Eng. & Wales* (1883)
Archives BL, working copies of stage parts, Egerton MSS 3282–3287 · Hunt. L., corresp. and memoirs · Theatre Museum, London, letters
Likenesses S. De Wilde, watercolour, 1809, Garr. Club · W. Foster, watercolour, 1811, Garr. Club · J. Slater, drawing, 1813, Hunt. L. · T. Uwins, chalk, 1822, NPG [*see illus.*] · F. W. Wilkin, lithograph (as Lady Savage), Harvard TC · engraving, repro. in Baron-Wilson, *Our actresses* · portrait, repro. in *ILN* (3 Jan 1846), 9 · portrait, repro. in *ILN* (23 Dec 1882) · portrait, repro. in *Theatrical Inquisitor* (1874) · portrait, repro. in *Illustrated Sporting and Dramatic News* (1880) · portrait, repro. in R. Mander and J. Mitchenson, *A picture history of the British theatre* (1957) · portraits, Harvard TC · prints, NPG · prints, BM
Wealth at death £3037 13s. 10d.: probate, 9 March 1883, *CGPLA Eng. & Wales*

Kelly, Frederick Septimus (1881–1916), composer and oarsman, was born on 29 May 1881 at 47 Phillip Street, Sydney, Australia, the seventh child and fourth son of Thomas Hussey Kelly (1830–1901) of Glenyarrah, Double Bay, Sydney, an Irish-born businessman with interests in wool and tin who founded the Sydney smelting company (private information), and his Australian wife, Mary Ann Dick (1842–1902). Nicknamed Sep, or Cleg after S. R. Crockett's *Cleg Kelly: Arab of the City* (1896), he was educated at Sydney grammar school (1891–2), Eton College (1893–9), Balliol College, Oxford (Lewis Nettleship musical scholar, 1909–11), and the Hochschule Konservatorium, Frankfurt (1912–14). Widely travelled, he lived at Bisham Grange, Marlow, Buckinghamshire, from 1905. Likenesses reveal

pale, determined features and a powerful physique; contemporaries noted his vitality and contradictory personality. Blunt and irritable, he rolled on the ground or indulged in war-dances and animal impressions when overcome by high spirits.

Kelly's diaries also chart the ascetic self-discipline which refined flair in the disparate spheres of rowing and music. He remains a sporting legend: a fine oar, and one of the greatest scullers of all time. Kelly learned aquatic skills on family yachts in Sydney harbour, stroked the Eton eight in 1899, rowed for Oxford in 1903, won the Grand Challenge Cup at Henley, 1903–5, and the Stewards' Cup in 1906, and rowed in the veteran English crew which won the Olympic eights in 1908. His sculling was beautiful to see: unspoilt by professional coaching he sculled as he rowed, and his natural sense of poise and rhythm made his boat a live thing under him, perfectly controlled. Few scullers have ever equalled the precision of his blade work and the perfect counterpoise of the two sides of his body. His style was so easy that when going his fastest at the hardest moment of a race it looked as if he were paddling. He first won the Diamond sculls at Henley as a novice in 1902, the final heat being probably the finest race of his life. He won again in 1903, lost in 1904 when improperly trained, and won in 1905, lowering the record by 13 seconds to 8 minutes 10 seconds, a time which fell only in 1938. In 1903 he won the Wingfield sculls easily, and contributed an illustrated chapter to *The Complete Oarsman* (1908). He was also a capable mountaineer and skater, and a fine tennis, football, and fives player.

Although Kelly memorized Mozart piano sonatas at five and published improvisations aged eleven, his parents vetoed private studies in France and Germany. Active involvement in Oxford music crystallized his ambition 'to be a great player and a great composer' (Kelly, diaries, 4 Dec 1907). His Frankfurt professors were Ernst Engesser and Iwan Knorr; creativity was also stimulated by a quarrelsome friendship with Donald Francis Tovey. Athletic achievement and private means cast the seriousness of Kelly's music-making into doubt but he served a conscientious apprenticeship of provincial British appearances before giving seven concerts at Sydney in 1911. Critics hailed 'an Artist of the First Rank' (*Sydney Morning Herald*, 10 July 1911) and noted the first Australian performances of Skryabin and Debussy. John Lemmoné, Nellie Melba's flautist, première Kelly's *Serenade*, op. 7 (published by Schott in 1914). The string trio, op. 8, 1909–11 (NL Aus., MS 3095), and *A Cycle of Lyrics* for piano, op. 4 (1910), were also introduced.

Kelly programmed *Waltz-Pageant*, op. 2b (1913), *Allegro de concert*, op. 3 (1913), and test pieces by Beethoven, Brahms, Chopin, and Liszt in his début London season. *The Times* complimented 'the completeness of his technical equipment' (21 Feb 1912) although a 'hampering nervousness' (28 Feb 1912) caused concern. As chairman of the Classical Concerts Society (1912–14), Kelly sought security in chamber performance. He played publicly with Jelly d'Arányi and Pablo Casals and informally with Frank Bridge, Edward Elgar, and Percy Grainger. Compositions mirror this change, bravura piano solos yielding to *Theme, Variations and Fugue* for two pianos, op. 5 (1913), *Two Songs*, op. 1 (1912), *Six Songs*, op. 6 (1913), and a violin sonata, 1915–16 (Stadtbibliothek, Frankfurt, MS Mus Hs 2394).

Kelly joined the Royal Naval division in September 1914 and sailed with Rupert Brooke and William Denis Browne for the Dardanelles. Under Brooke's influence he matured personally and musically:

> Kelly was freeing himself, finding himself—throwing off in his playing some hampering restrictions that had clung to him through a long routine and habit of practice, and gaining for his composition not only greater vigour and freshness in the ideas but a new judgment and discrimination in the use of all resources, particularly those of form. (*Balliol College War Memorial Book*, 318)

The *Elegy* for strings and harp (1926), inspired by Brooke's burial at Skyros on 23 April 1915, moves farthest from Kelly's conformist idiom:

> The modal character of the music seems to be suggested by the Greek surroundings as well as Rupert's character & some passage-work by the rustling of the olive tree which bends over his grave. (Kelly, diaries, 21 May 1915)

Twice mentioned in dispatches, Kelly gained the DSC during the Gallipoli evacuation in January 1916. Promoted lieutenant-commander in May, he boosted morale on the Somme by leading community singing of folksongs and shanties, and directing the Hood battalion band in Tchaikovsky's '1812' during a real bombardment in Noulette Wood. He was shot in the head while rushing a German machine-gun at Beaucourt-sur-Ancre on 13 November. He was buried at Martinsart British cemetery and commemorated by an Eric Gill Calvary in Bisham.

HAROLD HARTLEY, *rev.* RHIAN DAVIES

Sources R. Davies, 'Composers of the Great War', MA diss., U. Wales, Aberystwyth, 1985 · F. S. Kelly, diaries, 1907–15, NL Aus., MS 6050 · private information (2004) · R. Davies, 'Kelly, Frederick Septimus', *New Grove* · [H. B. Hartley and L. Borwick], 'Frederick Septimus Kelly', *Balliol College war memorial book, 1914–1919*, 1 (1924), 314–21 · C. Page, *Command in the royal naval division* (1999) · *Sydney Morning Herald* (4 June 1881) · *Sydney Morning Herald* (10 July 1911) · *The Times* (1912–17) · J. Carmody, 'Kelly, Frederick Septimus', *AusDB*, 9.554–5 · 'In memoriam Lieut. F. S. Kelly', *Eton College Chronicle* (7 Dec 1916) · S. Banfield, *Sensibility and English song: critical studies of the early twentieth century* (1985) · R. Davies, 'Two more corners, two more foreign fields: Rupert Brooke and the Gallipoli composers', *British Music*, 12 (1990), 41–3 · F. S. Kelly, 'Sculling', *The complete oarsman*, ed. R. C. Lehmann (1908), 157–77 · *CGPLA Eng. & Wales* (1917) · Commonwealth War Graves Commission, Maidenhead · G. P. Walsh, 'Kelly, Thomas Hussey', *AusDB*, 5.9 · King's AC Cam., MS Xc 13

Archives NL Aus., compositions and drafts · NL Aus., diaries · priv. coll., letters to his family · priv. coll., scrapbooks

Likenesses photographs, 1900–03, Balliol Oxf. · Royal Central Photo Co., photograph, 1914, King's Cam. · J. S. Sargent, charcoal drawing, 1914, priv. coll.; repro. in R. Davies, 'Brother officers: F. S. Kelly and Rupert Brooke', *Armistice festival … complete programme guide*, ed. T. Cross (1988), 50 · photographs, repro. in Lehmann, ed., *The complete oarsman*

Wealth at death £17,291 19s. 9d.: resworn probate, 31 Jan 1917, *CGPLA Eng. & Wales*

Kelly, George (*b.* **1688**, *d.* in or after **1747**), Jacobite agent, was born in St John, co. Roscommon, into the protestant branch of a Roman Catholic family. He was the third son of Edward Kelly, whose profession is described as that of *centurio* (Burtchaell & Sadleir, *Alum. Dubl.*, 457). George was educated at Mr Thules's school in Athlone and then matriculated on 7 May 1702 as a pensioner at Trinity College, Dublin, where his tutor was Thomas Squire. He graduated BA in the spring term of 1706 and was ordained deacon. According to Captain John Ogilvie, he became 'a preacher in Dublin and was suspended for getting a woman with child' (*Stuart Papers*, 6.330). By his own account he fled in 1718 from Ireland to France when he was threatened with prosecution after a sermon preached on some public occasion in Dublin caused offence (Kelly, 22–3). As well as becoming a successful speculator in John Law's Mississippi scheme, Kelly was employed by English Jacobites in France to carry messages to sympathizers in England. At this stage of his career, as later, Kelly was not trusted by some Jacobites. This feeling of distrust is epitomized by Captain John Ogilvie's letter to Lord Mar, dated 12 May 1718, in which he alleges that Kelly's activities were calculated to harm Jacobite interests abroad (*Stuart Papers*, 6.429).

Kelly arrived in England from France in 1720 and he was soon drawn into the plot focused upon Francis Atterbury, bishop of Rochester, for the restoration of the Stuarts. This involvement led to his being taken up by the authorities in May 1722. Kelly was released but seized a second time in October 1722. He was accused of complicity in the plot and a bill of pains and penalties was moved against him in parliament by Philip Yorke, the solicitor-general, and Samuel Sandys, member of parliament for Worcester, and passed. Kelly was then imprisoned in the Tower of London, where he was supported financially by the Jacobite member of parliament Watkin Williams Wynn, and enjoyed a number of privileges as a prisoner of honour. Gradually, and despite the intervention of Sir Hans Sloane, those privileges were withdrawn, and, resenting the conditions under which he was held, Kelly escaped to France on 26 October 1736.

Once in France, Kelly was befriended by James Butler, second duke of Ormond, who, as well as appointing him his secretary, introduced him to those Jacobites who were plotting the rising attempted in 1745. He entered the service of Prince Charles Edward Stuart in 1744, and with the prince and his six other companions he embarked on board *La Doutelle* at Nantes on 22 June 1745. When they had landed in Scotland 'Mr. Kelly's chief employment was to go betwixt his young master in Scotland and the French ministry, with some of whom he was very intimate' (Paton, 1.284). While great confidence was shown in Kelly's ability to obtain French military support for the rising (James Gilchrist to Viscount Irwin, 20 Oct 1745, *Various Collections*, 8.113), he was unable, as the speech attributed to the duke of Perth and published in the *Edinburgh Evening Courant* on 7 January 1747 suggests, to fulfil his promise of securing 10,000 of the best troops of France to support the landing of Jacobite forces (Blaikie, 85).

Kelly remained in the prince's service after the defeat at Culloden, becoming his sole secretary in 1747. His influence over the prince was regarded by some Jacobites as baneful. As William MacGregor of Balhaldy wrote of him to James Edgar on 31 May 1747, 'trick, falsehood, deceit, and imposition, [are] joined to those qualities that make up a sycophant' (Bell, 372). A juster estimate may be that of Speaker Onslow, who, in contrasting his abilities with those of his master, Atterbury, in prosecuting the eponymous scheme, wrote: '[he was] a man of far more temper, discretion and real art, and indeed in all respects a very proper instrument for such a work' (*Buckinghamshire MSS*, 512). The date of Kelly's death is unknown, but he survived at least until 1747.   ROGER TURNER

Sources *Memoirs of the life, travels and transactions of the Revd. Mr. G. K.* (1736) · Burtchaell & Sadleir, *Alum. Dubl.*, 2nd edn, 457 · *The manuscripts of the earl of Buckinghamshire, the earl of Lindsey … and James Round*, HMC, 38 (1895), 512, 514 · *Calendar of the Stuart papers belonging to his majesty the king, preserved at Windsor Castle*, 7 vols., HMC, 56 (1902–23), vol. 5, p. 53; vol. 6, pp. 330, 429 · *Report on manuscripts in various collections*, 8 vols., HMC, 55 (1901–14), vol. 8, pp. 111, 113 · W. B. Blaikie, ed., *Itinerary of Prince Charles Edward Stuart*, Scottish History Society, 23 (1897) · R. Forbes, *The lyon in mourning, or, A collection of speeches, letters, journals … relative to … Prince Charles Edward Stuart*, ed. H. Paton, 1, Scottish History Society, 20 (1895), 284 · *Memorials of John Murray of Broughton*, ed. R. F. Bell, Scottish History Society, 27 (1898) · Bodl. Oxf., Carte MS 114, fol. 374 · BL, Sloane MS 4051, fol. 182 · *A catalogue of books … being the library of Mr. George Kelly* (1737) · E. Cruickshanks, *Political untouchables: the tories and the '45* (1979), 20

Archives BL, Sloane MS 4051, fol. 182 · Bodl. Oxf., Carte MSS

Kelly, Sir Gerald Festus (1879–1972), portrait painter, was born in Paddington, London, on 9 April 1879, the youngest of three children and only son of Frederic Festus Kelly and his wife Blanche, daughter of Robert Bradford of Farningham in Kent but, like her husband, of Irish descent. His father was a curate in Paddington but, in the year after Kelly's birth, became vicar of St Giles, Camberwell, London, where he served for thirty-five years and Gerald spent his boyhood. Gerald Kelly, a sickly child, was on his own admission rather spoiled but, encouraged by his father, he developed a love of watching cricket and, through being taken to Dulwich College Picture Gallery, an interest in pictures which led to his trying his hand with watercolours. His schooling at Eton College was ended abruptly through illness and a winter's convalescence in South Africa. He then, in 1897, entered Trinity Hall, Cambridge, where he read much poetry and took a poll degree.

Although without any formal training in art, Kelly had decided by this time to become a painter and, with this in mind, moved to Paris in 1901 whence, helped by the art dealer Paul Durand-Ruel, he visited Monet, Degas, Rodin, and Cézanne, among others, and made friends with Walter Sickert, J. S. Sargent, and, in particular, W. Somerset Maugham. Fired by this background, his own experiments enabled him to develop meticulous craftsmanship with great attention to detail, as is shown by his immense care in painting hands, following an overheard criticism. He became, in 1904, a member of the Salon d'Automne and his work soon gained for him the patronage of Sir Hugh Lane and, in 1908, election as an associate of the Royal Hibernian Academy. Then, having been deserted by his dancer girlfriend, he spent a year in Burma, thrilled by its colour and lifestyle.

Kelly settled down in London, at his parents' house in Gloucester Place, in 1909 although, thereafter, he made many study visits to Spain. During the First World War he joined the intelligence department of the Admiralty. By 15 April 1920, when he married a young model from a working-class family, namely Lilian (*b.* 1898/9; although he always called her Jane), the fifth daughter among Simon Ryan's eight children, he was becoming well established as a portrait painter. Donning his boiler suit, he worked hard each day not only at his easel but, as a connoisseur of wines, in preparing them for the frequent and lively dinner parties at the house. The couple had no children.

This busy period, during which Kelly was elected associate of the Royal Academy in 1922 and academician in 1930, culminated in his being commissioned, in 1938, to paint the state portraits of King George VI and Queen Elizabeth. Following the outbreak of the Second World War he worked on them at Windsor Castle; they were not completed until 1945, when they were exhibited at the Royal Academy, and Kelly was knighted. In the same year he undertook to be honorary surveyor of Dulwich College Picture Gallery and soon he was in the forefront of a major argument on what he, and many others, considered to be too drastic cleaning of paintings in the National Gallery. He was a member of the Royal Fine Arts Commission from 1938 to 1943.

At seventy years of age, in December 1949, Kelly was elected president of the Royal Academy and devoted most of his time to its loan exhibitions, including 'Holbein and other Masters' and 'European Masters of the Eighteenth Century', not only persuading owners to lend works but becoming the star of related television programmes. Five years later he had to retire under the academy's age limit and in 1955 was appointed KCVO. He remained active for much longer but, after an unsuccessful eye operation in his ninetieth year, he had to give up painting. Among his honours he was made Royal Hibernian academician (1914), honorary Royal Scottish academician (1950), and honorary fellow of the Royal Institute of British Architects (also 1950), and received honorary degrees of LLD (1950) from Cambridge and Trinity College, Dublin.

Kelly was a charmer, both in speech and in his letters, and of indomitable spirit, but he was often petulant and tactless. Hardly 5 ft 6 in. in height, he darted in thought and action at most things, though he was completely methodical and painstaking at his easel. His output of portraits and many landscape studies was considerable, the latter owing much to the influence of J. A. M. Whistler. Among his best early works are pictures of his father, entitled *The Vicar in his Study* (1912), and of W. Somerset Maugham, called *The Jester* (1911), which many years later was purchased through the Chantrey bequest and placed in the Tate collection. He never tired of painting his wife and perhaps the finest portrait of her is *Jane XXX* (1930), deposited in the Royal Academy as his diploma work. Among his other portraits were *Hugh Walpole* (1925), *Dr. M. R. James* (1937), *Sir Malcolm Sargent* (1948), and *Dr. Ralph Vaughan Williams* (1953; Royal College of Music, London), and he painted many versions of beautiful Asian dancing girls. He died at his home, 117 Gloucester Place, Portman Square, London, on 5 January 1972. The contents of his studio were sold at Christies on 8 February 1980.

S. C. HUTCHISON, *rev.*

Sources D. Hudson, *For love of painting: the life of Sir Gerald Kelly* (1975) · records, 1922–72, RA · *Exhibition of works by Sir Gerald Kelly* (1957) [exhibition catalogue, RA, 12 Oct – 15 Dec 1957] · personal knowledge (1986) · S. C. Hutchison, *The history of the Royal Academy, 1768–1968* (1968) · *CGPLA Eng. & Wales* (1972) · m. cert.
Archives BL, corresp. with Marie Stopes, Add. MS 58543 · TCD, corresp. with Thomas Bodkin | FILM BBC, 13 Jan 1953 commentated on *Dutch pictures* exhibition
Likenesses O. Birley, oils, 1920, NPG · D. Low, pencil caricature, NPG
Wealth at death £178,222: probate, 9 March 1972, *CGPLA Eng. & Wales*

Kelly, Herbert Hamilton (1860–1950), founder of the Society of the Sacred Mission and theologian, was born on 18 July 1860 at St James's vicarage, George Street, Manchester, the son of the Revd James Davenport Kelly (1829–1912) and his wife, Margaret Alice Eccles (1846–1912). His father was rector of St James's; his mother was the daughter of a prosperous mill owner near Blackburn. He was educated at Manchester grammar school following which he enrolled as an officer cadet in the Royal Military Academy, Woolwich, in 1877. It was soon evident that he was not suited to this profession and in 1879 he went up to Queen's College, Oxford.

E. B. Pusey was still alive, but Kelly was less impressed by the Tractarians than by F. D. Maurice, from whom he learnt something about the way in which God may be perceived in history. Kelly was not impressed with the history taught at Oxford (he got a fourth) but he did begin to understand the way in which a society and culture create propositions about God, and then create a church 'system' that follows from those propositions. Kelly wished to distinguish both the propositions and the system from the reality that lies behind them—a fundamental distinction between 'God' and 'religion'. He was ordained in 1883 and went as a curate to St Paul's, Wimbledon Park, where he was not a great success. 'I preached occasionally but they petitioned that the curate should not preach' (Kelly, *No Pious Person*, 39).

It was in 1890 that Kelly responded to an invitation from Charles Corfe, bishop in Korea, to take charge of half a dozen young men who had volunteered for missionary work. Kelly's analysis of the missionary situation at the end of the nineteenth century was that institutional religion was in transition: the church was working 'with ideas which not only do not fit the world around us, but which we no longer think ourselves and are even indignant at being told that we do' (Kelly, lecture notes). He concluded that the church system based on these ideas needed radical revision.

In a house in Vassall Road, London, Kelly first interviewed and then trained a succession of candidates, first for Korea and then for other missionary ventures, especially in Africa. There were three conditions: acceptance did not necessarily mean ordination, there was to be no pay, and therefore no marriage. The period of preparation was to be four years, during which students could think through their faith in a community of work, study, and prayer. Living in this way brought Kelly to the idea of a religious community, the concept having been revived in the Church of England fifty years earlier. This community, to be called the Society of the Sacred Mission, was given a constitution written by Herbert Kelly; and he and Herbert Woodward made their profession in 1894. From that point some men came to train and join the society while others came to share the life of the community in their training, but would be free to work overseas or in an English parish at the end of it.

The basis of the theological course as it emerged was the historical theology with which Kelly had been wrestling; so that students, discerning the purposes of God in different ages and places, might attain a vision of God in their own lives and for the world of their day. The integration of study and worship was vital to the development of this vision. A significant innovation was that recruitment included men whose background gave them neither the educational nor financial means to offer themselves for ordination through the normal route of university and theological college. The numbers of students increased and the college moved first to Mildenhall in Suffolk and then to the Gilbert Scott mansion at Kelham in Nottinghamshire in 1903, where it continued to train students until 1971.

In 1910 H. K. (as he had become known) ceased to be director of the Society of the Sacred Mission and head of the house and college at Kelham. Between 1913 and 1919 he was in Japan as professor of apologetics at the Anglican central theological college, and here he wrote a series of seminal articles. Instead of parishes being supplied from outside with a paid professional and college-bred priesthood, or as in the mission field with qualified catechists having a missionary behind them and supported by a foreign source, Herbert Kelly wished to see every congregation choosing a spiritual leader from their own number. Kelly believed that locally ordained ministers should replace the system of professional stipendiaries that had already outlived its effectiveness.

On his return, Kelly continued to give some lectures at Kelham until 1943 when he was over eighty. Long before that he had become 'the old man', a deaf and eccentric figure asking questions about God and writing theological letters and lectures on scraps of paper designed for another purpose. He nevertheless continued to be sought by a wide range of people with whom he corresponded. He died on 31 October 1950 at Kelham Hall and was buried there, probably on 4 November, in the society's cemetery, ten years before the society reached its numerical peak of eighty-three. Its members continue to offer educational and pastoral work in different parts of the world.

VINCENT STRUDWICK

Sources Archives of the Society of the Sacred Mission, Milton Keynes, Buckinghamshire · G. Every, autobiographical sketch, priv. coll. [in possession of Vincent Strudwick] · H. H. Kelly, *No pious person*, ed. G. Every (1960) [autobiographical sketches] ·

A. Mason, *History of the Society of the Sacred Mission* (1993) • H. H. Kelly, 'Church in the 19th century', lecture notes (annotated), undated, Archives of the Society of the Sacred Mission, Milton Keynes, Buckinghamshire • personal knowledge (2004)

Archives Society of the Sacred Mission, Milton Keynes, papers and corresp.

Wealth at death £2537 8s. 0d.: probate, 1951, *CGPLA Eng. & Wales*

Kelly, Hugh (1739–1777), writer and attorney, was born in Killarney, the son of a Dublin tavern keeper. Little is known about Kelly's life beyond the material collected in early biographies, which began appearing after Kelly's first theatrical success in 1768. He married in 1761 Elizabeth and was the father of numerous children, only one of whom appears to have survived to adulthood: Bartlett Hugh Kelly (d. 1818), who became an army officer stationed in India. Kelly, who had little education, was apprenticed to a staymaker before leaving Ireland in 1760 for London, where he began a career in journalism with Charlotte Lennox's *Ladies' Museum* and Israel Pottinger's *Court Magazine*. In addition, Kelly wrote news for Charles Say's *Gazetteer*, to which he also contributed verse. In 1763 Kelly wrote a series of essays under the pseudonym 'The Babler' which were reminiscent of Addison and Steele's *Spectator* essays. In 1767, 123 of Kelly's approximately 200 essays were collected by John Newbery and published as *The Babler*. Late in spring 1767 Kelly began writing for Newbery's *Public Ledger*, and continued to do so until 1772.

In 1766 Kelly published the first part of *Thespis, or, A critical examination into the merits of the principal performers belonging to Drury-Lane theatre*, completed in February 1767. Long held to be in imitation of Charles Churchill's poem, *The Rosciad*, Kelly's couplet poem was meant to give him authority as a theatre critic. As a result of publishing this poem, Kelly met David Garrick, who became a key figure in Kelly's career. In 1767 Kelly published his only novel, *Memoirs of a Magdalen, or, The History of Louisa Mildmay* (2 vols.), the story of a young woman seduced by a rake and kidnapped. Out of shame she voluntarily commits herself to a magdalen house, where her repentant lover finds her and they marry. Kelly's novel is indebted to Samuel Richardson's *Clarissa* in its epistolary form and seduction-shame plot. Kelly may also have been the editor of *The beauties of the magazines, and other periodical works, selected for a series of years: consisting of essays, moral tales … (2 vols., 1772).*

Kelly's first play, *False Delicacy*, opened in January 1768 and ran for twenty nights. Garrick's preference for Kelly's play over Oliver Goldsmith's *The Good Natur'd Man*, written on a similar theme, sparked enmity between Kelly and Goldsmith, which Goldsmith describes in his poem, *The Retaliation*. Kelly embarked on a new form of drama just as audience tastes were changing and when writers were becoming self-conscious about their abilities to meet the demands of the theatregoing public. Kelly uses the traditional complications in courtship as his plot and his theme in *False Delicacy*, with the breaches in politeness or 'delicacy' making his comic points. His contemporaries Goldsmith, R. B. Sheridan, and Samuel Foote, for example, were still using class and wealth as their comic resources for scenes of duplicity and deception. Though *False Delicacy* was successful initially, it was performed only sporadically through the 1780s.

Kelly began legal studies at Temple Bar on 11 April 1768 in the hope of securing a better source of income for his large family. He was called to the bar on 22 May 1773 and he was involved in at least two high-profile cases. The first, in 1773, involved an inheritance dispute and the second, in October 1776, was a forgery case. Between 1768 and 1775 Kelly made enemies among those theatre critics who did not share his support for Garrick. Kelly was also attacked in the *Middlesex Journal* for his opposition to radical views such as those espoused by John Wilkes. Such was the radical opposition to Kelly that in March 1770 Kelly's second drama, *A Word to the Wise*, caused riots when Garrick tried to stage it at Drury Lane. Afterwards, Kelly published his next three works anonymously, beginning with *Clementina* (1771), his only tragedy. Bearing a notable similarity to Thomas Otway's *Venice Preserv'd*, the play ran for nine nights. It is the story of a young Italian girl forced to disobey her father to marry her lover. Kelly's third play, *The School for Wives* (1774), was the most successful drama in Drury Lane's 1773–4 season. Another comedy involving marriages and disguises, the play ran for twenty-four nights. It was printed in five editions and was seen in 1805 in Bath. In February 1773 Kelly began writing for the *General Evening Post*. Kelly's next drama was *The Romance of the Hour* (1774). After the play closed, Kelly continued to write for periodicals in support of the government during the trial of Warren Hastings, while publishing, under the pseudonym Numa, a series of letters in the *Public Advertiser* supporting Britain's colonial policies. Kelly remained the subject of radical attacks in the newspapers and was often the victim of rumour and false reports about his political loyalties. His final, and unsuccessful, production was *The Man of Reason* (1776). By late eighteenth-century standards, Kelly was financially successful, earning between £200 and £300 a year.

In January 1777 the newspapers reported Kelly's fatal illness as an 'abscess in his side, accompanied by fever', and hinted that his corpulence and sedentary life were the causes of his illness. Kelly underwent an operation at the Newgate Street Bagnio to remove the growth but this failed and he died on 3 February 1777 at his home in Gough Street. He was buried in the vault of St Dunstan-in-the-West on 8 February 1777.

An anonymous poem, 'Sacred to the Memory of Hugh Kelly, Esq' appeared in the *General Evening Post* of 13–15 February 1777. *The Works of Hugh Kelly, to which is Prefixed the Life of the Author* was published in 1778 for the benefit of his widow.

BEVERLY E. SCHNELLER

Sources R. Bataille, *The writing life of Hugh Kelly: politics, journalism and theater in late-eighteenth-century London* (2000) • *The plays of Hugh Kelly*, ed. L. Carver and M. Cross (1980) • I. Donaldson, 'Drama, 1710–1780', *Dryden to Johnson*, ed. R. Lonsdale (1971) • A. Kendall, *David Garrick: a biography* (1985) • R. Welch, ed., *The Oxford companion to Irish literature* (1996) • *DNB* • will, PRO, PROB 11/1029/119, fol. 177 • private information (2004) • ESTC

Archives V&A NAL, corresp. with David Garrick

Likenesses J. Boydell, mezzotint, 1778 (after H. Hamilton), BM, NPG; repro. in H. Kelly, *Dramatic works* (1778) · line engraving, NPG

Kelly [*née* Fordyce; *other married name* Hedgeland], **Isabella** (*bap.* **1759**, *d.* **1857**), poet and novelist, was born at Cairnburgh Castle and baptized on 4 May 1759, the youngest of the three daughters of William Fordyce of Aberdeen, and his wife, Elizabeth Fraser (*d.* 1785), niece of Alexander Fraser, Lord Strichen. Her grandfather William Fordyce of Anchorthies was a figure of scandal: a successful merchant and sometime baillie of Aberdeen, he was eventually convicted for his part in a kidnapping ring. Her parents were both cut off by their wealthy families, following a clandestine marriage in the early 1750s. Her father served with the Royal Marines, was promoted to captain by 1761, and later became groom of the bedchamber to George III, though in time he fell from favour at court.

In December 1789 Isabella married Robert Hawke Kelly, the son of Colonel Robert Kelly of the East India Company. The younger Kelly had served in Madras before his marriage, and he apparently died there by 1807 with the rank of major. In 1794 Isabella Kelly published her first book, a *Collection of Poems and Fables*, although if her claim that '[s]everal of the pieces' in it 'were written before … her fourteenth year' (p. iii) is true, she had started writing much earlier. Kelly had by that time suffered 'a variety of domestic calamities' (ibid.), including—if the poems are read autobiographically—marital unhappiness, possible desertion by her husband, and the death of a child.

In an attempt to support her two surviving children, Kelly began writing Gothic fiction, publishing her first novel, *Madeline*, in 1794, and writing nine more between 1795 and 1811. The novels, which are full of both Gothic paraphernalia and fashionable sentiment, were moderately successful; the *Critical Review* thought *Madeline* 'entitled to a decent rank in the circulating libraries' (Kelly, *Abbey of St Asaph*, viii), and Kelly's later work received some aristocratic patronage. In addition to her fiction, Kelly wrote educational books, including a French grammar for children, and a rather eccentric collection of miscellaneous information, *Instructive Anecdotes for Youth* (1819). In the preface of that book, which is dated from the King's Road, Chelsea, she implies that she has been a teacher.

By 1816 Isabella Kelly had married Joseph Hedgeland, a wealthy merchant who was dead by 1820, possibly having lost his money in speculation. In 1819 her son, Sir Fitzroy *Kelly (1796–1880), entered Lincoln's Inn and subsequently enjoyed a distinguished legal career. Her last book, *A Memoir of the Late Mrs. Henrietta Fordyce*, was published anonymously in 1823, perhaps in an attempt to silence rumours that she had taken advantage of a generous elderly relative. Said to have been ninety years old in 1849, she died at 20 Chapel Street, London, on 25 June 1857.   RICHARD GREENE, rev. PAM PERKINS

Sources R. Lonsdale, ed., *Eighteenth-century women poets: an Oxford anthology* (1989) · I. Kelly, *Collection of poems and fables* (1794) · I. Kelly, *Poems and fables* (1807) · I. Kelly, *the Abbey of St Asaph*, ed. D. Varma (1975) · J. Shattock, *The Oxford guide to British women writers* (1993) · J. Todd, ed., *A dictionary of British and American women writers, 1660–1800* (1984) · d. cert. · bap. reg. Scot.

Kelly, James Fitzmaurice- (1857–1923), historian of Spanish literature, was born in Glasgow on 20 June 1857, the eldest son of Colonel Thomas Kelly, then of the 40th foot but formerly of the Egyptian police, and his wife, Catherine, *née* Fitzmaurice. As he was a Roman Catholic and three-parts Irish, he can be said to have inherited sociability, wit, and feelings of sympathy with Spain. From his French maternal grandmother he obtained an exact command of French and the discipline of French literary taste. His mother, who died abroad while he was still a boy, remained such a powerful influence on his life that he later prefixed her surname to his own.

Educated at St Charles's College, Kensington, he learned some Spanish from a schoolfellow of that nationality, and later taught himself to read *Don Quixote*. At first he was destined for the priesthood, but he was deterred partly through the study of Pascal, although he retained the affectionate esteem of leading Catholics. He started to study medicine but realized that he had no vocation for that profession. He was greatly attracted by art, music, and literature, particularly by the writings of Cervantes. He went to Spain in 1885, acting as tutor to Don Ventura Misa in Jerez de la Frontera and forming friendships with Juan Valera, Gaspar Núñez de Arce, and other leading men of letters.

On his return to London in 1886 Fitzmaurice-Kelly began to make a name for himself as an authority on Spain and as a reviewer for *The Spectator*, *The Athenaeum*, and *Pall Mall Gazette*. He was influenced by William Ernest Henley, who said that Fitzmaurice-Kelly appeared 'to have read everything' and that he wrote 'with any amount of brio and gest and style' (*Selected Letters*, 283). In 1892 he made his mark on Spanish studies with his *Life of Miguel de Cervantes Saavedra*. But it was with the issue of his *History of Spanish Literature* in 1898 that he came to occupy a position of authority in this subject, not seriously challenged before his death. He was contemporary with, and kept abreast of, decisive advances in the knowledge of Spanish literature. Through his friendship with Raymond Foulché-Delbosc and Archer Huntington (of New York), he constituted one of a triumvirate of foreign scholars influential in guiding the new studies. The value of his work was early recognized by learned bodies. He was elected a corresponding member of the Spanish Academy (1895), a fellow of the British Academy (1906), a member of the academies of history (Madrid, 1912), of *buenas letras* (Barcelona, 1914), and of sciences (Lisbon, 1922). He was a member of council and medallist of the Hispanic Society of America (1904) and was created a knight of the order of King Alfonso XII (1905). For many years Fitzmaurice-Kelly maintained himself by his pen. But he then became increasingly active as a lecturer, at, for example, Oxford (1902), the British Academy (1905 and 1916), Harvard, Yale, and other American universities (1907), London University,

James Fitzmaurice-Kelly (1857–1923), by Sir John Lavery, 1898

and Cambridge (1908). In 1909 he was chosen by the University of Liverpool as its first Gilmour professor of Spanish language and literature. He held the chair with distinction, and entered actively into the life of the university for seven years. In 1916 he accepted the Cervantes chair of Spanish language and literature at King's College, London. Although Fitzmaurice-Kelly lacked a formal academic education, 'he created important cadres of specialists' at Cambridge and Liverpool universities and at King's College, London (Ward, 212–13).

On 5 July 1918 Fitzmaurice-Kelly married Julia Kate Harriett (b. 1877/8), third daughter of the Revd Henry William Sanders, curate of St Nicholas's Church, Nottingham. His wife was a gifted Spanish scholar. They had no children. Fitzmaurice-Kelly's health began to fail in 1920, and he retired from teaching, although continuing his literary work.

Fitzmaurice-Kelly's general works on Spanish studies apart from the *History* (revised in 1913 and 1926) include *Chapters on Spanish Literature* (1908), thirty-nine articles on Spanish literature and authors in the *Encyclopaedia Britannica* (11th edn, 1910), *The Oxford Book of Spanish Verse* (1913), and *Cambridge Readings in Spanish Literature* (1920). They brought into focus the great advance in Spanish studies made since the days of the American scholar George Ticknor, and in particular the gains due to the creative criticism of Marcelino Menéndez y Pelayo; they also stimulated fresh investigations. Omnivorous reading, wide sympathy, balance, and wit made Fitzmaurice-Kelly's *History* unique as well as an accurate practical guide to the subject. He worked on the *History* continually until

three days before his death. His wife said that it 'accompanied him everywhere' as he revised and corrected it (J. Fitzmaurice-Kelly, vii). As for the *Oxford book of Spanish Verse*, this long remained a standard collection. Introducing the second edition in 1940, J. B. Trend observed that 'the name of Fitzmaurice-Kelly, his preferences and his prejudices', were as inseparable from the anthology as 'those of Palgrave from *The Golden Treasury*' (Trend, xxxiv). Fitzmaurice-Kelly did not research very deeply or evolve new theories; but he had a remarkable gift for extracting from various sources what represented permanent additions to knowledge, and for ascertaining to what extent they intensified enjoyment of literature. His devotion to Cervantes gave rise to *Miguel de Cervantes Saavedra* (1913, the older *Life* rewritten in the light of Pérez Pastor's documents) which remained definitive for many years. He collaborated with John Ormsby on a monumental edition of *Don Quixote* (1898–9), and edited the English *Complete Works* of Cervantes in 1901–3. He summarized Cervantine studies for the *Year Book of Modern Languages* (1920). A selection from his delightful letters appeared in the *Revue Hispanique*, 74, 1928. All his principal works were translated into Spanish, and long remained as standard texts in Spain.

Fitzmaurice-Kelly died of pneumonia at his house at 1 Longton Avenue, Sydenham, Kent, on 30 November 1923 and was buried in Norwood cemetery on 4 December. He was survived by his wife.

W. J. ENTWISTLE, *rev.* DONALD HAWES

Sources *The Times* (1 Dec 1923) · J. Fitzmaurice-Kelly, preface, in J. Fitzmaurice-Kelly, *A new history of Spanish literature* (1926) · P. Ward, ed., *Oxford companion to Spanish literature* (1978), 212–13 · *Selected letters of W. E. Henley*, ed. D. Atkinson (2000), 283–4 · J. B. Trend, 'Note', in J. Fitzmaurice-Kelly, *Oxford book of Spanish verse*, 2nd edn (1940) · J. Fitzmaurice-Kelly, 'Preface', *Miguel de Cervantes Saavedra* (1913) · CGPLA Eng. & Wales (1924) · m. cert. · d. cert.
Archives King's Lond., letters to David Hannay · NL Ire., letters to Alice Stopford Green · NL Scot., letters to R. B. Cunninghame Graham · U. Leeds, Brotherton L., letters to Sir Edmund Gosse
Likenesses J. Lavery, oils, 1898, NPG [*see illus.*] · group portrait, oils, 1917 (The faculty of Arts), U. Lpool
Wealth at death £220: administration with will, 9 Jan 1924, CGPLA Eng. & Wales

Kelly, John (c.1684–1751), writer, was probably born in Port Royal, Jamaica, the son of Smith Kelly, a planter and merchant who became provost marshal of Jamaica in 1686 and was killed by French invaders in 1693, and his wife, Susan (d. in or before 1708), who was in England with her son when her husband died. Descended probably from the O'Kellys of Aughrim, co. Galway, Kelly entered the Inner Temple in 1712 as 'son and heir of Smith Kelly, late of Aughrim in the island of Jamaica', and signed himself 'John O'Kelly Esq. of the Inner Temple' when dedicating to the future Queen Caroline, two or three years later, his manuscript comedy 'The Islanders, or, Mad Orphan' (BL, Kings MS 301).

Evidently autobiographical (and including thinly veiled representations of prominent Jamaicans, including Colonel Peter Beckford as Colonel Blithe), Kelly's 'Islanders' follows the orphaned Infaustus as he returns to Jamaica to confront the guardian, Lucre, who has stolen his inheritance. Scathing in its representation of the planters as base, mercenary, and brutal to their slaves, the play reflects Kelly's unsuccessful efforts to retrieve his estate from a group of London merchants alleged to have conspired with his father's West Indian executors (including Beckford himself) to defraud him of £30,000. Having returned to Jamaica for some years following his marriage in 1700 to Elizabeth Lane (b. c.1679; two sons from the marriage were living in 1717), he settled in the parish of St James, Westminster, by 1710, and was fruitlessly embroiled in chancery proceedings until 1718. Thereafter his finances were permanently rocky, and he spent at least two periods in the Fleet, once in 1727–8, and again (after his second marriage on 5 November 1735 to Mary Boucher) in 1738–9.

Though posthumously described in the *London Magazine* as 'an eminent counsellor, in the Temple' (July 1751), Kelly does not appear to have been called to the bar. He may have attempted a career as a merchant, but by the later 1720s was writing for a living. A translation from Bandello which he projected in 1728 seems not to have been carried out, but in 1732–3 he was translating the opening volume of Rapin's history of England in fifty-three weekly numbers (alongside the rival version by Nicholas Tindal), and later undertakings included *Nature Delineated* (2nd edn 1740), part of the original by Abbé Pluche, and a new version of Fénelon's *Telemachus* (1742). Other works drawing on his facility with languages are *French Idioms* (1736), in which he recalls learning French 'almost as early as my Mother-Tongue' and using the language at home and abroad for forty-five years (p. vi), and *A New, Plain and Useful Introduction to the Italian* (1739). As a journalist he was one of the early contributors to Henry Baker's *Universal Spectator* (1728–46), writing at least twenty-four leaders in 1729–30 and later receiving credit for the collected reprint of 1747. In March–April 1732 his comedy *The Married Philosopher* had five performances at Lincoln's Inn Fields, bringing Kelly benefit night receipts of £85 10s. Based on Destouches's *Le philosophe marié* (1727), the play has been credited with introducing the French *comédie larmoyante* to the English stage. It was followed by a more modest success, *Timon in Love* (again based on a French original, *Timon le misanthrope*, 1722, by the sieur de la Drevetières de Lisle), which played at Drury Lane for three nights in December 1733.

Whether from conviction or opportunism, Kelly was also a prolific (and sometimes inflammatory) partisan writer. His pamphlets of 1727, *The Hotch-Potch* and *The History of the Fall of Count Olivarez, Sole Minister to Philip IV*, were anti-ministerial satires which attracted government scrutiny, the latter being identified in an official memorandum as 'done by one Kelly in the Fleet—a West Indian who understands Spanish, Italian and French and gets his living by translating' (PRO, SP 36/5, 181). *Timon in Love* had a mildly oppositional colouring, and Kelly's later plays *The Plot*, performed three times at Drury Lane in January 1735, and *The Fall of Bob, or, The Oracle of Gin* (which in January 1737 was picked by Fielding at Haymarket to lead off the season that was to culminate in the Licensing Act) were more blatantly anti-Walpole. So was *Desolation, or, The Fall of Gin*, a verse satire published as the Gin Act passed into law in May 1736. A year later, as the Licensing Act was debated, Kelly was paid a guinea a week to revive the seditious newspaper *Fog's Weekly Journal*, which he did with incendiary verve. After only his seventh number (a lightly encoded attack on the late Queen Caroline, appearing on 16 July 1737 and given added venom, one might speculate, by Kelly's earlier failure to win Caroline's patronage), he was arrested. His abject plea 'that he had no design to give Offence to the Government in the said paper, but only to procure Subsistence for himself and family … being by reiterated misfortunes reduced to write for his Daily bread' (PRO, SP 36/41, 133) seems to have helped him to avoid the severe punishment inflicted on other opposition agitators at the time (notably Henry Haines, printer of *The Craftsman*), and he was bound over to attend the king's bench for four terms. His undertaking not to reoffend was broken when, as the campaign against Walpole entered its endgame in November 1741, he published his last play, *The Levee*, advertised on its title-page as having been 'accepted for Representation … in Drury-Lane, but by the Inspector of Farces denied a Licence'.

Deprived of his livelihood as an anti-Walpole polemicist and playwright, Kelly turned (like Fielding) to the expanding market for prose fiction. *The Third Volume of Peruvian Tales* (1739) is his continuation of the original by Thomas Gueulette (first translated in 1734), and in 1741 he was commissioned to write *Pamela's Conduct in High Life*, the first of several spurious continuations of Richardson's best-selling novel. Originally published in May, this work was successful enough to be extended to a second volume in September, and forced Richardson to produce a sequel of his own. Kelly may later have written *The Memoirs of the Life of John Medley, Esq.* (1748), a novel billed as 'by the Author of *Pamela's Conduct in High Life*', though some doubt is cast on his authorship by the appearance of a second volume in 1756, five years after his death. He died on 15 July 1751 at the Inner Temple, and was buried at St Pancras on 21 July.

THOMAS KEYMER

Sources T. Keymer, 'Introduction', in J. Kelly, *Pamela's conduct in high life* (2001), vols. 4–5 of *The Pamela controversy: criticisms and adaptations of Samuel Richardson's Pamela*, ed. P. Sabor and T. Keymer, vol. 4, pp. vii–xliii · PRO, state papers, 36/5, fols. 135, 177–182; 36/41, fols. 91, 133, 206, 240; 36/45, fol. 326 · T. Lockwood, 'John Kelly's "lost" play *The fall of Bob* (1736)', *English Language Notes*, 22/1 (1984), 27–32 · M. Harris, *London newspapers in the age of Walpole* (1987) · A. H. Scouten, ed., *The London stage, 1660–1800*, pt 3: *1729–1747* (1961) · T. C. D. Eaves and B. D. Kimpel, *Samuel Richardson: a biography* (1971) · W. J. Graham, *English literary periodicals* (1930) · admissions register, Inner Temple, London [information from Michael Frost, Inner Temple Library] · J. Kelly, 'The islanders, or, Mad orphan', BL, King's MS 301 · J. Kelly, 'Preface', *French idioms* (1736) · *Selected letters of Samuel Richardson*, ed. J. Carroll (1964) · *London Magazine*, 20 (1751)

Kelly, John (1750–1809), Manx scholar, the only son of William Kelly, farmer and wine cooper, and his wife, Alice Kewley, was born on 1 November 1750 on his father's property of Algare, in Baldwin, Isle of Man. He was educated by the Revd Philip Moore at Douglas grammar school, where he was soon noted for his intelligence and industry. Before his seventeenth birthday Kelly began the difficult task of writing a grammar of the Manx language, his only sources being the gospel of St Matthew published by Bishop Thomas Wilson in 1748, and the native speech of his fellow Manxmen. This grammar was intended as an aid to those engaged in translating the scriptures. Kelly sent the fair copy to the duke of Atholl, asking permission to dedicate the work to him. The duke neither replied nor returned the manuscript. It was ultimately rescued in 1802 and published in 1804. The grammar's main defect is that it attempts to describe Manx inflection as though it were Latin. At the same time as he began his grammar, Kelly was engaged by Mark Hildesley, the then bishop of Sodor and Man, to assist Philip Moore with the task of producing a Manx version of the Bible. The scriptures had been distributed by Hildesley in portions to various members of his clergy for them to translate. Moore was the general editor and Kelly his amanuensis. The first of two parts (Genesis to Esther) appeared in 1771 and again in 1772. The second part (from Job to the end of the Old Testament, together with the Wisdom of Solomon and Ecclesiasticus from the Apocrypha) was printed in 1773. It fell to Kelly to take the finished manuscript of the second part to the printers, John Ware & Son, in Whitehaven. He was shipwrecked *en route* but it is said that he managed to save the manuscript by holding it above the water for five hours until rescued from the sinking ship. He also transcribed the third volume containing the New Testament and corrected the proofs of the entire Old Testament. The Old Testament was almost complete by 1772 and Kelly, having received a gratuity from the Society for Promoting Christian Knowledge, was able to fulfil his desire of entering the church.

Kelly went to England where he was ordained deacon at Chester on 4 August 1776 and priest in Carlisle on 31 August 1777. In 1776 he accepted an invitation from the episcopalian church in Ayr in Scotland to become their pastor. In 1779 he was appointed tutor to George Gordon, marquess of Huntly, son of the duke of Gordon. He continued to supervise the young nobleman's education at Eton College and at Cambridge, where tutor and pupil both studied at St John's College, and on a tour of the continent. Kelly had previously matriculated from Queen's College, Oxford, in 1782, but he matriculated from St John's, Cambridge, in 1794, and proceeded LLB (1794) and LLD (1799). It was to the marquess that he dedicated his grammar. In April 1791 the duke of Gordon obtained for him the vicarage of Ardleigh near Colchester in Essex, a living which he held until 1800, when he was promoted to the more valuable benefice of Copford nearby. He was of some importance in Essex, being a justice of the peace for the county. Two of his sermons were published. In the years 1779–90 he accomplished the bulk of his major work, the triglot dictionary of the three Gaelic languages, Scottish Gaelic, Irish, and Manx, with the meanings given in English. The dictionary was unwieldy, being arranged

in four columns and containing much fanciful etymology. The printing had proceeded as far as the letter L, when a fire in the printing shop destroyed all but a few copies. The Manx–English portion was published for the Manx Society together with an English–Manx section in 1866 by the Revd William Gill, vicar of Malew.

In 1785 Kelly married Louisa, daughter of Peter *Dollond [*see under* Dollond family], optician, of St Paul's Churchyard, London, and granddaughter of John Dollond FRS, the inventor of the achromatic telescope. The couple's only child was Gordon William Kelly, afterwards recorder of Colchester, who was baptized at Eton on 18 February 1786. Kelly contracted typhus fever in November 1809 and died on 12 November at Copford rectory. He was buried in his own parish church on 17 November. In 1858 Mrs Gordon Kelly, the widow of John Kelly's son, gave £1000 to Douglas grammar school for an exhibition to the universities and £100 for an annual Manx prize, both in memory of her father-in-law. A memorial to Kelly, his wife, and son, was set up in the old church of Kirk Braddan on the island.   N. J. A. WILLIAMS

Sources GM, 1st ser., 80 (1810), 84–5 · A. W. Moore, *Manx worthies, or, Biographies of notable Manx men and women* (1901) · W. Cubbon, *A bibliographical account of works relating to the Isle of Man*, 2 (1939) · R. L. Thomson, *The study of Manx Gaelic* (1969) · G. Price, *The languages of Britain* (1984) · Venn, *Alum. Cant.* · IGI · DNB

Kelly, John (1801–1876), Congregational minister, was born in Edinburgh on 1 December 1801, educated at Heriot's Hospital, and converted under the preaching of Dr Robert Gordon. He studied for the Independent ministry at Vint's academy, Idle, Yorkshire. In January 1827 he went to Bethesda Chapel, Hotham Street, Liverpool, to preach in place of the Revd P. G. Charrier who had just died. He received a call to this church, and on completion of his studies was ordained there in September 1829. The building quickly became too small for his congregation, and Crescent Chapel was built in the developing area of Everton Brow in 1837, with day schools added in William Henry Street in 1846. Kelly's congregation was wealthy and powerful, and included John Hope Simpson, the doyen of Liverpool Congregationalism. By the time of Kelly's death, however, Crescent was already an inner-city church. Kelly sent out a large number of members to revitalize old causes or establish new ones, and encouraged many young men to join the ministry. He served the London Missionary Society, the Lancashire Congregational Union, and the Lancashire Independent college, and was chairman of the Congregational Union in 1851 and 1852. Between 1838 and 1843 he took part in pamphlet controversies with local Anglican clergy over the voluntary principle, yet his *Church Principles* (1863) developed the idea of all the churches in an area such as Liverpool being branches of a single local church. A man of strongly Calvinistic principles, he was the chief antagonist of Samuel Davidson in the bitter dispute of 1856–7, about which he wrote an *Explanation* (1857). His wife, formerly a Miss Dunbar, with whom he had at least one son, died in 1870; he retired on 28 September 1873 and died at his home, 18 Richmond Terrace, Liverpool, on 12 June 1876; he was buried in the city's necropolis.

G. C. Boase, rev. Ian Sellers

Sources E. Hassan, *The Rev. John Kelly: a memorial* [1876] · *Congregational Year Book* (1877) · *Liverpool Mercury* (13 June 1876) · J. Waddington, *Congregational history*, 5 (1880)
Likenesses portrait, repro. in Hassan, *Memorial*
Wealth at death under £5000: probate, 19 July 1876, CGPLA Eng. & Wales

Kelly, Sir John Donald (1871–1936), naval officer, was born at Southsea in Hampshire on 13 July 1871, the second son of Lieutenant-Colonel Henry Holdsworth Kelly, Royal Marine Artillery, and his wife, Elizabeth, daughter of John Collum of Bellevue, co. Fermanagh. Entering the Royal Navy in 1884 his initial service was not particularly promising. At Dartmouth his commanding officer reported on Kelly as 'doubtful' (under the service usefulness category) and he gained only a second-class certificate on promotion to lieutenant in 1893. None the less he clearly demonstrated practical command and leadership qualities as, after service on the Australia, Cape, and China stations, he was promoted captain in 1911. His subsequent appointment, from 1913–14, as superintendent of physical training was consistent with his serious interest in training and personnel matters. In 1915 he married Mary (*d. c.*1937), daughter of Thomas Hussey Kelly, of Glengarrah, Sydney, New South Wales; they had one daughter, Antonia, who launched the destroyer HMS *Kelly* named after her father in 1938. This ship later became famous as the wartime command of Earl Mountbatten of Burma.

From the outbreak of the First World War to 1917 Kelly commanded, in succession, the cruisers *Dublin*, *Devonshire*, and *Weymouth*. While commanding the *Dublin* in the Mediterranean he and his brother, Captain William Archibald Howard Kelly, commanding the cruiser *Gloucester*, came the closest of the pursuing Royal Navy ships to intercepting the German battle cruiser *Goeben* on its passage to Turkey. From 1917 to the end of the war Kelly commanded the battle cruiser *Princess Royal*. For his war service he was appointed CB in 1919.

Kelly's career followed a conventional post-war path with an appointment to the naval staff in 1919, promotion to rear-admiral in 1921, and command of the 4th battle squadron in 1922–3. In subsequent appointments he served as fourth sea lord in 1924–7, second in command of the Mediterranean Fleet in 1927–9, and admiral commanding reserves in 1929–31. He received promotions to vice-admiral in 1926 and to admiral in 1930. He was advanced to KCB in 1929. He was considered for the post of second sea lord but was not selected, and in 1931 was on the point of retiring.

However, a reliable flag officer was needed to restore morale and discipline after the mutiny at Invergordon in 1931 and Kelly was invited by the Admiralty, with some urging from George V, to assume command of the Atlantic (later Home) Fleet. His appointment reflected confidence in his personnel management abilities. Kelly restored discipline in the fleet very quickly by removing 121 ratings and some officers and he kept the crews busy with rigorous exercises. He was also required by a 'secret' letter of 31 October 1931 from Sir Vincent Baddeley, assistant secretary to the Admiralty board, 'to make careful examination of the discipline' (Coles, 137–8) and all the relevant circumstances relating to the mutiny. But he was forbidden to call this investigation a court of inquiry. In his sixty-four section report he expressed the view that the Admiralty board should have accepted greater responsibility for the rising because of its inept handling of pay cuts and the general neglect of personnel issues. He was also concerned about disaffection caused by the spread of radical political ideas among the ratings. His report considered the naval schoolmaster branch officers to be 'of a type which is frankly socialistic in outlook' (Carew, 168).

Kelly received due acknowledgement from the king for his services after the mutiny by the personal appointment as GCVO in 1932 and as first and principal naval aide-de-camp to the king from 1934 to 1936. He was also advanced to GCB in 1935. Kelly's last post was as commander-in-chief, Portsmouth, and he received special promotion to admiral of the fleet the day before he reached the compulsory retiring age of sixty-five in June 1936.

Retirement was brief for Kelly, at his home, Greenham Hall, Wellington, near Taunton in Somerset, as he died in a nursing home at 23 Bentinck Street, St Marylebone, London, on 4 November 1936 and after a service at St Martin-in-the-Fields he was taken to Portsmouth for burial at sea from HMS *Curacoa* on 7 November. He was one of that select band of naval 'characters' immortalized in Geoffrey Lowis's *Fabulous Admirals* (1959). In Kelly's case, being a character who could command the respect of sailors was an important factor in his successful handling of the aftermath of the Invergordon mutiny.

F. E. C. Gregory

Sources DNB · G. Lowis, *Fabulous admirals* (1959) · *The Times* (5 Nov 1936) · D. Divine, *Mutiny at Invergordon* (1970) · A. Coles, *Invergordon scapegoat* (1993) · A. Ereira, *The Invergordon mutiny* (1981) · A. Carew, *The lower deck of the Royal Navy, 1900–39* (1981) · WW · W. S. Chalmers, *The life and letters of David, Earl Beatty* (1951) · C. Owen, *Plain tales from the fleet* (1997) · CGPLA Eng. & Wales (1936)
Archives NMM, corresp., journals, and papers | BL, corresp. with Lord Keyes · NMM, corresp. with Lord Chatfield · NMM, corresp. with Sir Julian S. Corbett | SOUND IWM SA, oral history interviews
Likenesses J. Broome, sketch, repro. in Lowis, *Fabulous admirals*, 241 · photograph, repro. in *The Times* (7 Oct 1931) · photograph, NPG
Wealth at death £24,081 17s. 3d.: probate, 31 Dec 1936, CGPLA Eng. & Wales

Kelly, John Norman Davidson (1909–1997), patristic scholar and college head, was born on 13 April 1909 at Bridge of Allan, Perthshire, the fourth of the five children of John Davidson Kelly (1861–1928), schoolmaster, and his wife, Ann (1875–1937), daughter of John Barnes JP of Bunker's Hill, Cumberland, and his wife, Catherine. His father was Scottish and his mother was English. (Margaret) Ann Davidson *Kelly was his younger sister. When Kelly was born his father was headmaster of Stanley House School for Boys; but during the First World War the school ran into financial difficulties. His father's connection with it was severed. Despite financial stringency, he never again worked full time but devoted himself to the education of his children at home, with the family eventually settling in Glasgow. From his father Kelly acquired a commitment to academic excellence and to hard work; but he regretted that education at home deprived him of the social life and sporting opportunities of the normal schoolboy.

The elder Kelly destined his son to graduate at Glasgow University, then to proceed by means of a Snell exhibition to Balliol College, Oxford, and ultimately to join the Indian Civil Service. Kelly duly went to Glasgow University in 1925, graduating with first-class honours in classics in 1929, but chance circumstances denied him a Snell exhibition. Instead he entered Queen's College, Oxford, with an open scholarship which, together with a succession of university prizes, made Oxford financially possible. His father's death left him free to shape his career. By 1933 he gained first-class honours in classical moderations, Greats, and theology, besides being president of the junior common room. By upbringing a presbyterian, he was confirmed in the Church of England. Having decided to enter its ministry, he proceeded to St Stephen's House, Oxford. In 1934, he was made deacon to serve in the parish of St Andrew's, Northampton, where his assiduous house-to-house visiting was remembered.

Kelly did not complete his deacon's year there, for the principal of St Edmund Hall, A. B. Emden, invited him to return to Oxford as chaplain and tutor in theology and philosophy at the hall. Thus began an association with the hall that was maintained for sixty-two years. In 1937 Emden made Kelly vice-principal, and he served as such throughout the Second World War years. Because of his own wartime commitments Emden did not release Kelly to be the services chaplain that he wished to be; but he undertook work for Chatham House, which placed his linguistic skills at the service of the Foreign Office. In 1951, when ill health enforced Emden's retirement, he was the almost inevitable choice for the principalship, which he held until his retirement in 1979; he was thereafter an honorary fellow.

Kelly became principal at a critical point in St Edmund Hall's seven centuries of history. Since 1937 Emden had been working to secure its independence of Queen's College; but neither by temperament nor by conviction could he contemplate a transition from aularian to collegiate status. Kelly had long perceived that the transition must be made, and his first concern as principal was to secure, with the generous co-operation of Queen's, a charter of incorporation as a college, which the duke of Edinburgh presented in 1958. No less far-seeing was Kelly's purpose, in his last years as principal, of extending membership of the college to women; he oversaw all the necessary steps. The middle years of his principalship were marked, largely through his negotiating and fund-raising skills, by a programme of building and extension. But the most memorable features of his principalship arose from his own personality. A natural communicator, he knew by name, subject of study, and personal interests virtually every member of what became a large student body. His legendary concern for the sporting life of the hall was, perhaps, in part a compensation for his deprivation of games in boyhood and also of national service; he was also active in promoting the arts, particularly acting and the visual arts, in a community of all-round achievement.

Kelly was less involved in university life and business. When, in 1966, the vice-chancellorship came to him under the then prevailing system of rotation, an untimely attack of jaundice compelled him to relinquish it almost immediately. But he remained prominent in the theological faculty; after being speaker's lecturer in biblical studies from 1945 to 1948, he held until 1976 a university lecturership in patristic studies. During and after his tenure of it, he maintained a flow of authoritative publications which fall into three broad groups. The first concerned the development of patristic theology. *Early Christian Creeds* (1950; 3rd edn, 1972) was complemented by a book on Rufinus's *Commentary on the Apostles' Creed* (1955) and by *The Athanasian Creed* (1964). *Early Christian Doctrines* (1963; 5th edn, 1977) studied the development of doctrines from the end of the New Testament period to the council of Chalcedon in 451. Second, Kelly turned to the New Testament, with commentaries on the pastoral epistles (1963) and the epistles of Peter and Jude (1969). Kelly's cast of mind was not speculative or innovatory; his approach was historical and expository, and he offered masterly evaluations of fresh developments and directions in Christian thought. His conclusions tended to be conservative; thus he upheld St Paul's authorship of the pastoral epistles. Some thought that the mastery and orderliness of his work belied the gaps and uncertainties of interpretation that remained, and that he underrated the critical approach of such scholars as Harnack and Loofs. However, especially in the patristic field, the comprehensiveness, insight, and lucidity of his books won them a lasting place both as student textbooks and as authoritative scholarly works.

The last decades of Kelly's life witnessed a shift in his interests from ideas to people, and especially to the inner springs of their beliefs and activities. A third group of his publications was biographical; its high points were his studies of St Jerome (1975) and St John Chrysostom (1995). The intervening years had been occupied partly by the preparation of *The Oxford Dictionary of Popes* (1986), a universally acclaimed survey of each papal career from St Peter to John Paul II. He maintained his scholarly work until the end of his long life, and was known in the Bodleian Library as its most regular reader. In due course he left the library a handsome bequest of some of his collection of pictures.

Kelly was only occasionally drawn into wider church life. He refused an early invitation to become senior chaplain at Lambeth Palace because he did not feel that he could work with Archbishop Fisher; but under the more congenial Michael Ramsey he was from 1964 to 1968 chairman of the archbishop's commission on Roman Catholic relations; in 1966 he accompanied Ramsey to Rome on his historic visit to Pope Paul VI. He greatly valued his association with Chichester Cathedral, of which he was a canon from 1948 until 1993.

Kelly was a master of the spoken as well as of the written word, both formally as in lectures and sermons and informally as in after-dinner speeches and general conversation. His disciplined life combined an outgoing, even flamboyant, public personality with a fondness for solitude and privacy. He won deep affection. His honours included an Oxford doctorate of divinity (1951) and fellowship of the British Academy (1965). He never married. He died at Sir Michael Sobell House, Oxford, on 31 March 1997. He was cremated on 8 April at Oxford crematorium and on 21 June his ashes were interred in the antechapel of St Edmund Hall.   H. E. J. COWDREY

Sources *The Times* (3 April 1997) · *The Independent* (4 April 1997) · *The Guardian* (5 April 1997) · *Daily Telegraph* (3 April 1997) · H. E. J. Cowdrey, 'John Norman Davidson Kelly, 419–37', *PBA*, 101 (1999), 419–37 · private information (2004) · personal knowledge (2004)
Archives St Edmund Hall, Oxford, archives
Likenesses R. Buhler, oils, 1959, St Edmund Hall, Oxford · S. Prawer, crayon sketch, *c.*1990, St Edmund Hall, Oxford
Wealth at death £1,659,278: probate, 27 June 1997, *CGPLA Eng. & Wales*

Kelly, (Renée Octavie Ghislaine) Marie-Noële, Lady Kelly (1901–1995). *See under* Kelly, Sir David Victor (1891–1959).

Kelly, Mary Elfreda (1888–1951), founder of the Village Drama Society, was born on 25 March 1888 at Salcombe vicarage, Devon, the second of the four children of the Revd Maitland Kelly (1842–1929), from 1900 squire of Kelly, Devon, and his second wife, Elfreda Blanche Carey (*d.* 1891). After her mother's death Ella Carey, her aunt, acted as housekeeper and mother to the younger children. Mary spent a happy childhood at Kelly House—'filled with sunshine, green grass and blue skies' (Kelly, 183)—as one of the 'Little Ones', who looked upon their six stepsiblings more or less as adults. Educated at home by a governess until the age of sixteen, Mary then attended school at The Halsteads, East Sheen. It is believed that at some time during the 1920s she attended art school. During the First World War she worked as a cook in a VAD hospital in Exeter and then at the War Office as a clerk. She loved London, where her intellect was stimulated. After the war she returned home to Kelly House, where in 1918 she founded the Village Drama Society (VDS).

Mary Kelly began the VDS at home, where there had been family theatricals since Victorian days. A little bored as a pampered young gentrywoman, yet also conscious of the democratic upheaval that came in the wake of the war, she now endeavoured to include local people in such activities. She developed plans for a Kelly Dramatic Society, which should include all the people in the parish, of whatever class or age. But there was a specific potential that she wanted to develop. The Revd Hugh Maitland and his wife had mounted a modest annual missionary festival in the parsonage garden. After the Maitlands left in 1905,

the young Margaret and Dorothea Kelly continued it, moving it to Kelly House grounds and introducing a small pageant.

On 15 January 1919 Mary Kelly called a meeting to announce her plans. While some of the tenant farmers and their families were immediately enthusiastic, others were much less so. But the squire's social writ—the Kelly estate comprised the whole parish: all the farmers were tenants—ensured that the whole village pulled together. Quite soon, the dramatic society established itself as something of a community.

Mary Kelly wrote a Bible story play, *Joseph*, which was performed on Ascension day 1919. Impressed by the emergence of talent from unexpected places, she went on to write and mount such plays each Ascensiontide, eventually moving the performances into the tithe barn. Maitland Kelly directed that a stage be built there. Emphatically Christian as well as communal in emphasis, the annual event—which included a special service and a feast—raised £100 per annum for the Society for the Propagation of the Gospel medical mission that Mary's sister Ursula and her husband, Frank Drewe, had established at Holy Cross, Pondoland, in southern Africa.

Mary Kelly's religious plays—she wrote others—were written around the village players, to suit their own characteristics. They adhered to their Devon dialect. An ethos of simple dignity was maintained. Gradually the Kelly play became famous, especially for its simplicity and the sincerity of the players. Leonard and Dorothy Elmhirst, who arrived at Dartington in 1925, were friends and regular visitors, bringing a crowd with them.

The idea of the Village Drama Society was to encourage similar experimentation in other villages. Visits by the Kelly players indeed encouraged other societies to form, and Mary was soon busy fielding requests for advice. Kelly being remote, she moved to Camberwell in the 1920s—but returned to Kelly to produce the Ascensiontide play for seven or eight years. The society grew rapidly and Mary travelled the country speaking at Women's Institute meetings arguing for better drama—but a mixed reception eventually made her decide to sever links with the institute. The VDS affiliated to the British Drama League (founded 1919), becoming absorbed by it in 1932. Mary continued to work for the league, and by 1939 over 600 village societies had formed.

Mary wrote and produced pageants at Selborne (1926), Rillington (1927), Bradstone (1929), Launceston (1931), Bude, and Exeter Cathedral ('The Pitifull Queene', 1932). The Selborne play dramatized parts of Gilbert White's *Antiquities* and letters, to evoke and construct an easeful, gentrified village summer. 'The Pitifull Queene' dealt with Henrietta Maria. Her major emphasis elsewhere is on the life of common folk, sometimes, as at the opening of the Rillington drama, achieving a domestic focus centred on women and children. The Launceston pageant sharply dramatized the distinct cultural and racial identity of the Cornish. Bradstone is the tiny hamlet neighbouring Kelly. As the squire's daughter, Mary could for this event forgo the business of financial guarantees that beset most pageant makers. Her father had a grandstand built. The bishop of Exeter attended.

Mary handled the pageant form distinctively and well. In *How to Make a Pageant* (1936) she drew on her own experiences and her witnessing of similar events in other countries to argue for its reform. By then an outmoded cultural form, characterized by apathy, embarrassment, and at best a vague sense of nationhood, the pageant had, she argued, the potential to show 'the slow unfolding and growth of ideal which history reveals', 'the conflict between the individual and the mass', so that 'the raw crowds [of performers] will lose all self-consciousness and be lifted together into a strongly felt and sincerely acted emotion' (pp. 6–9). The coexistence in the ostensibly 'non-political' Kelly of royalist sentiment on the one hand and enthusiastically progressive—to some extent democratic—impulses on the other was not unusual in the inter-war period.

Mary Kelly's early success with village drama depended on much more than her class and her father's power. It rested on her good nature and her enthusiasm. Roy Johns (*b.* 1913), who got involved aged six along with his tenant-farmer father, Abel, and played for the Kelly Drama Society into the 1950s, recalled both her intellect and her 'wonderful sense of humour'. She involved herself fully in the village and insisted that any member might chair a meeting of the society. This outgoing woman, who could readily drop into dialect, was so well liked that 'people couldn't refuse her'. Plump, homely, and physically comfortable, she laughed easily, her laughter moving both her whole body and then others to laughter.

Between the wars Kelly House filled again with children, as nephews and nieces from two families moved back from Africa. Mary loved and understood the younger generation, and took especial care of her godson Michael. His wife, Margery, who arrived at Kelly in 1937 recalled Mary as lively, full of fun, artistic, and a rebel: 'There was a rather outrageous occasion when she used face powder! Ye Gods!' (private information). To all the younger generation at Kelly she was fun and a great friend. Her stepsister Margaret praised the way she continued working despite ill health, and overcame all obstacles; but also noted that she did not suffer fools gladly. Of her various publications—including plays and pageants, *On English Costume* (1932), and *Group Play Making* (1948)—the most significant are *How to Make a Pageant* (1936) and *Village Theatre* (1939). 'The book of the Kellys' (1954) is an unpublished family history researched by Mary and completed by her stepsister Margaret.

When war broke out in 1939, Mary Kelly moved back to the south-west to live in Exeter and to work for the drama and music committee of the Devon education department, visiting schools in the county. However, following two major operations, she retired and moved to South Africa later in 1939 to join her great friend Joanna Elder at Kokstad, East Griqualand. There she painted and helped both Africans and Europeans with their drama. On 9 June 1949 she was appointed OBE for her services to the British Drama League. Her life was again full of interest; but she

fell ill and was hospitalized with dysentery, and while convalescing died suddenly on 5 November 1951 at Ikopo, Natal. At her memorial service in 1951 Ian Kelway, who succeeded Mary as Devon county drama adviser, declared that it was she 'who began again to give back to the ordinary village people what was their birthright' by reviving village drama (private information).   MICK WALLIS

Sources M. Kelly and M. Kelly, 'The book of the Kellys', 1954, Theatre Museum, London · private information (2004) · D. Matless, *Landscape and Englishness* (1998) · A. Nicoll, *English drama, 1900–1930* (1973) · G. Tayler, *History of the amateur theatre* (1976) · *CGPLA Eng. & Wales* (1952)

Wealth at death £3714 9s. 1d. in England; South African probate sealed in England, 4 Nov 1952, *CGPLA Eng. & Wales*

Kelly, Matthew (1814–1858), historian and Roman Catholic priest, born in Maudlin-Street, Kilkenny, on 21 September 1814, was the eldest son of James Kelly and Margaret Sauphy. An uncle, Patrick Kelly, was bishop of Waterford. Kelly was taught in very early years by M. S. Brennan, author of the *Ecclesiastical History of Ireland*. When about seven years of age he entered the Kilkenny diocesan seminary, and in 1831 he began professional studies at St Patrick's College, Maynooth, where he was elected a Dunboyne student in 1836 and ordained priest in 1838. From 1839 to 1841 he was professor successively of philosophy and theology in the Irish College at Paris, and on 5 November 1841 was appointed to the chair of English and French at Maynooth; on 20 October 1857 he became professor of ecclesiastical history there. In 1854 he was made DD by the pope, and about the same time a canon of Ossory. He died at Maynooth on 30 October 1858 from tuberculosis, and was buried in the cemetery of Maynooth.

Kelly was an enthusiastic student of Irish antiquities and ecclesiastical history. At his death he had made large collections for a work on the ecclesiastical annals of Ireland from the invasion to the Reformation, as a continuation of the work of John Lanigan. His editions of John Lynch's *Cambrensis eversus* (3 vols., 1848–52), Stephen White's *Apologia pro Hibernia* (1849), and Philip O'Sullivan's *Historiae catholicae Iberniae compendium* (1850) remained in use throughout the twentieth century. His was the first edition of the *Calendar of Irish Saints: the Martyrology of Tallagh* (1857), and although it has been superseded, it was an important work of scholarship in its day. Kelly contributed to various periodicals, notably the *Dublin Review*, and an uneven collection of his essays, *Dissertations Chiefly on Irish Church History* (1864), was edited, with a memoir, by Dr Daniel McCarthy.

W. A. J. ARCHBOLD, *rev.* PATRICK J. CORISH

Sources St Patrick's College archives, Maynooth [esp. MS diary of Revd Dr McCarthy] · 'Memoir', M. Kelly, *Dissertations chiefly on Irish church history*, ed. D. M'Carthy (1864) · J. Healy, *Maynooth College: its centenary history* (1895), 593–8 · N. Murphy, 'The Very Rev. Matthew Kelly, DD, professor, Maynooth College, and Canon of Ossory', *Irish Ecclesiastical Record*, 3rd ser., 17 (1896), 704–13 · Wellesley index

Archives St Patrick's College, Maynooth | BL, letters to John Daly, Add. MS 43685

Likenesses portrait, St Patrick's College, Maynooth; repro. in Healy, *Maynooth College*

Wealth at death under £450: probate, 30 July 1859, *CGPLA Ire.*

Kelly, Michael (1762–1826), singer and composer, was born on 25 December 1762 in Dublin, the eldest of the fourteen children of Thomas Kelly and his wife, a Miss McCabe from co. Westmeath. His father was master of ceremonies at Dublin Castle and a wine merchant.

Kelly was brought up in a musical household. He had piano lessons from Morland and Cogan and singing tuition from Passerini, Peretti, and San Giorgio. He attended Italian operas and performed in amateur musical theatricals. He made his professional début as a treble in 1777, replacing an indisposed castrato as the Count in Piccinni's *La buona figliuola*. That summer he also took the title role in Michael Arne's *Cymon* for three nights at the Crow Street Theatre, followed by a benefit performance as Master Lionel in Charles Dibdin's *Lionel and Clarissa*. The famous castrato Venanzio Rauzzini gave Kelly lessons during a visit to Dublin in 1778 and advised his father to send him to Italy to study singing.

Kelly set sail on a Swedish merchant ship on 1 May 1779 and arrived on 30 May in Naples, where he lived under the patronage of Sir William Hamilton (1730–1803), British envoy to the court of Naples, and in the care of Father Dolphin, a Dominican. He studied at the conservatory of San Maria di Loreto. In 1780 he continued his studies with the castrato Giuseppe Aprile, who took him to Palermo; there his voice matured into a tenor. In 1780 or early 1781 in Livorno he met the young English composer Stephen Storace and his younger sister Nancy, a *buffa* singer, with both of whom he formed a lifelong friendship. He accepted various singing engagements in Italy, including Florence and Venice, and he went briefly to Graz.

In 1783 Kelly, along with Nancy Storace, Francesco Benucci, and Stefano Mandini, was offered a contract by Emperor Joseph II to sing *opera buffa* at the Burgtheater in Vienna. He sang secondary roles in works by composers such as Paisiello, Martín y Soler, Salieri, Sarti, and Storace, and took the double role of Don Curzio and Don Basilio in Mozart's *Le nozze di Figaro* in 1786. Kelly devoted almost a hundred pages of his *Reminiscences* to his four years in Vienna, providing a lively account of the cultural and social whirl, with personal recollections of the musicians and passing comments about the music he heard and performed.

On 24 February 1787 Kelly set off for London in the company of Stephen and Nancy Storace, their mother Elizabeth, Harry Vane (later Lord Barnard), and the young composer Thomas Attwood. They travelled through Salzburg, where they visited Mozart's father Leopold, and Paris, where they went to the opera and probably acquired opera scores. Kelly arrived in London for the first time on 18 March.

Kelly joined the company at the Theatre Royal, Drury Lane. He made his début there on 20 April 1787 as Lionel in *A School for Fathers* [*Lionel and Clarissa*], partnered by Anna Maria *Crouch (1763–1805) as Clarissa. That summer, after receiving news of his mother's death, Kelly and the Crouches travelled to Dublin, then toured the English provincial theatre circuit. For the remainder of their professional lives Kelly and Anna Crouch performed at Drury Lane during the London theatre season and toured professionally during the summers; in some years they included a visit to France, where Kelly attended the opera and purchased opera scores for use in London.

In 1787 Kelly began to share accommodation with Anna Crouch and her husband in a seemingly amicable arrangement. The Crouches separated in 1791; Kelly and Anna Crouch performed together until she retired in 1801, and lived together until her death in 1805. He had no children; his niece, Frances Maria *Kelly (1790–1882), became an actress and singer.

Most of Kelly's new roles at Drury Lane were composed for him by Storace, who was acting house composer between 1788 and 1796. When Kelly played Sir William in Storace's *The Haunted Tower* (1789) he was partnered by Anna Crouch and joined by Nancy Storace and Jack Bannister as the principal comic characters. For the next seven years these four singers played together in almost all of Storace's mainpiece operas, including *The Siege of Belgrade* (1790), *The Pirates* (1792), *The Cherokee* (1794), and his posthumous work *Mahmoud* (1796), which Kelly may have helped to complete.

On 16 April 1790 Kelly gave the première of Storace's afterpiece *No Song, No Supper* for his benefit performance because John Philip Kemble had rejected it for inclusion in the regular repertory; it became a staple of the theatre well into the nineteenth century. In 1793 Kelly and Storace became joint acting managers of the Italian Opera company at the King's Theatre; Kelly then continued as stage-manager for most of his professional life.

In 1789 Kelly earned £11 a week at Drury Lane; by 1795–6 this had risen to £16, where it remained for at least ten years. He increased this substantial income by performing in concert series such as the Academy of Ancient Music, the Concerts of Ancient Music, and the annual Handel celebrations at Westminster Abbey. He also made occasional appearances with the Italian Opera company.

After Storace died in 1796, Thomas Linley's son William was appointed as house composer at Drury Lane. When he proved unsuccessful, Kelly began to compose for the theatre, starting with *A Friend in Need* and *Blue Beard* (both 1797) and *Of Age Tomorrow* (1800). Some of his musical manuscripts were destroyed in the fire that demolished Drury Lane in 1809. He claimed to have written sixty-two operas, though not all were entirely his own work. He had a lyric gift but little technical skill, and sometimes allowed others to harmonize or orchestrate his melodies. Kelly was an adherent of the simpler style of English opera, in which the action takes place in the spoken dialogue and is interspersed with songs and simple ensembles.

1802 was a busy year for Kelly. On 1 January he opened a music shop and publishing business at 9 Pall Mall (next door to the King's Theatre), which went bankrupt in 1811. He also took over supervision of the music at Drury Lane and, in the summer season, at the Little Theatre in the Haymarket.

When Kelly retired from the stage on 17 June 1808, he included *No Song, No Supper* in his final performance. He continued to manage the King's Theatre and direct the music at Drury Lane until 1820. In his last years, immobilized by severe gout, he lived under the friendship and patronage of George IV.

Kelly was remarkable for using full voice at the top of his range rather than the falsetto favoured by other English tenors. Boaden described its 'amazing power and steadiness; his compass was extraordinary' (Boaden, 1.350–52); other commentators were less enthusiastic. His acting was not notable but he was a popular performer, and retained his Irish accent. He was a very personable character: in Boaden's words, 'a very kind and friendly man', popular for his good humour and cheerful spirit. His most important legacy is his *Reminiscences* (1826), ghosted by Theodore Hook, and generally accurate and detailed. His errors, for which he has sometimes been criticized, are, in the generous words of John Taylor, 'all of a trifling nature, and hardly worth notice' (*Records of my Life*, 302–9). The *Reminiscences* give an invaluable picture of eighteenth-century musical life and personalities.

Kelly died on 9 October 1826 in Margate, and was buried in London in the churchyard of St Paul's, Covent Garden. He left no will. JANE GIRDHAM

Sources M. Kelly, *Reminiscences*, 2nd edn, 2 vols. (1826); repr., R. Fiske, ed. (1975) · M. Kelly, *Reminiscences*, 2nd edn, 2 vols. (1826); repr. (1968) · A. H. King, 'Kelly, Michael', *The new Grove dictionary of opera*, ed. S. Sadie, 2 (1992) · Highfill, Burnim & Langhans, *BDA*, 8.291–300 · J. Taylor, *Records of my life*, 2 (1832), 302–9 · J. Boaden, *Memoirs of the life of John Philip Kemble*, 2 vols. (1825), vol. 1, pp. 350–52
Likenesses J. Neagle, line engraving, repubd 1796 (after T. Lawrence), BM · H. Meyer, stipple, pubd 1825 (after A. Wivell), BM; repro. in Kelly, *Reminiscences* (1826), frontispiece; versions, NPG, NG Ire. · C. Turner, mezzotint, pubd 1825 (after T. Lawrence), BM, NG Ire. · C. Turner, mezzotint, pubd 1825 (after J. Lonsdale), BM, NG Ire. · S. De Wilde, oils (as Cymon), Garr. Club · S. De Wilde, watercolour, Harvard TC · T. Hook, pen-and-ink drawing, BM · W. Loftis, watercolour (as the Mask in *The island of St Marguerite*), Folger · W. Loftis, watercolour (as William in *The haunted tower*), Folger · J. Lonsdale, oils, Garr. Club · ten prints, Harvard TC · theatrical prints, BM, NPG

Kelly, Patrick (1755/6–1842), mathematician and astronomer, was for many years master of the Finsbury Square Academy, London. Nothing is known of his parentage or early life; on 1 August 1789 he married Ann Plomley, who predeceased him. Their son, later the Revd Anthony Plomley Kelly (b. 1797), survived him. The Finsbury Square Academy, a finishing school teaching commercial and mathematical subjects, comprised a boarding-house, schools, and an observatory. Kelly published for the use of his students *Practical Introduction to Spherics and Nautical Astronomy* (1796), which reached a fifth edition; *Elements of Book-Keeping* (1802), which reached a seventh edition; and *The Ship-Master's Assistant and Owner's Manual* (1803), which continued to a twentieth edition, latterly in other hands.

He was appointed mathematical examiner at Trinity House, and in 1809 the degree of LLD was conferred on him by the University of Glasgow.

The series of works for which Kelly was best known dealt with the rates of exchange of currencies, and the equivalence of weights and measures employed in different countries. At the end of the eighteenth century English merchants lacked any reliable guide to rates of exchange comparable with J. E. Kruse's *Allgemeiner und besonders Hamburgischer Contorist* (1753) prepared for the Hamburg merchants. The Bank of England in 1796 declined to undertake a similar task, and in 1804 Kelly submitted a prospectus for an expanded and updated version of Kruse's work. The bank then agreed to support Kelly, as did the Board of Trade, East India Company, and leading mercantile houses. His *Universal Cambist* (1811) dealt with the moneys, coins, weights, and measures 'of all trading nations', and surpassed Kruse by including the East and West Indies and America. The Bank of England had assayed the gold and silver content of the coins, but Kelly could not procure foreign standards of weight and measure during the war years, and had perforce to rely on the equivalents provided by merchants. When peace came, the government issued a circular to all British consuls to obtain standards; these were compared at the Royal Mint. The first edition of the *Cambist* showed up the earlier defective exchange rates, especially in Spanish and French currencies, which had cost England dear, and these new and corrected values were published in the second edition in 1821.

The East India Company then agreed to provide Kelly with examples of the weights and measures in regions under its control; his work was completed in 1823; his comparisons were then verified, the weights at the mint, the measures by the instrument maker Edward Troughton. Kelly submitted several requests for payment for this exercise, but this was at first refused, the company declaring that it would subscribe to forty copies but that Kelly should expect nothing more. In the end a small payment was made, rather less than Kelly had received for his calculations made for a House of Commons committee. The material was appended to the chapter on the East Indies in the *Cambist*, and a separate *Oriental Metrology* was published in 1832.

Kelly enjoyed the friendship of astronomers and mathematicians, schoolmasters, and men of science of the day, among them Nevil Maskelyne, William Herschel, Samuel Vince, Charles Hutton, and Matthew Raine. His opinions were sought by committees of both houses of parliament on matters of currency and exchange. In retirement Kelly lived at Western Cottages, Brighton, Sussex, where he died on 5 April 1842.

R. E. ANDERSON, *rev.* ANITA MCCONNELL

Sources *GM*, 2nd ser., 18 (1842), 434–5 · *Annual Register* (1842) · D. Vaughan, 'Patrick Kelly and the Castlereagh Collection', *Science Museum Review 1989* (1989), 40–42 · W. I. Addison, *A roll of graduates of the University of Glasgow from 31st December 1727 to 31st December 1897* (1898), 303 · East India Company court minutes, BL OIOC, B/176–7,

179–80 · parish register (marriage), London, Lothbury, St Margaret, 1 Aug 1789
Likenesses T. Woolnoth, stipple (after H. Ashby), BM, NPG

Kelly, Richard John (1860–1931), journalist, was born in Tuam, co. Galway, Ireland, the eldest son of Jasper Kelly (*d.* 1873), newspaper editor, and his wife, Delia, daughter of John Daly. He was descended from the Ouseley family of Courteen Hall, Northampton, through Margaret Ouseley, who married his great-grandfather Anthony Kelly of Castle Park, near Mount Talbot. Richard Kelly was educated in Blackrock and at the Queen's College, Galway, and entered the King's Inns, Dublin, in 1883. He spent a term at the Middle Temple in the autumn of 1884. Called to the Irish bar in 1886, he took silk in 1914. Kelly married Edith, a daughter of Bryan Mackey of Southampton, a distant cousin of Dame Sybil Thorndike; they had one son and five daughters.

Kelly's grandfather, also Richard John Kelly, was a follower of Daniel O'Connell, and founded the *Tuam Herald* in May 1837. Jasper Kelly succeeded him as proprietor in 1864, and his son succeeded in turn, in 1868. In 1851 the paper was described as Liberal, and claimed to represent the Roman Catholic church in the district. Richard Kelly attended the inaugural meeting of the Land League in Irishtown, co. Mayo, in April 1879, and he was a long-standing and trusted friend of Charles Stewart Parnell and Michael Davitt. By the 1880s the *Tuam Herald's* politics were nationalist. After the split in the Irish parliamentary party, and the death of Parnell, Richard Kelly supported John Redmond.

Despite his work on the newspaper Kelly also had a considerable career as a lawyer. He was a revising barrister for Dublin city, co. Cork, co. Armagh, and co. Donegal, and was crown prosecutor for co. Sligo. The author of a number of books on the law of newspaper libel and landlord and tenant legislation, he also edited volumes of Irish patriotic poetry and a life of Charles Kickham. He became vice-president of the Galway Archaeological and Historical Society and wrote a history of Tuam.

In the latter part of his life Kelly lived in Dublin, where he was a governor of Richmond Hospital, a member of the Statistical Society and the Royal Society of Antiquaries of Ireland. He was a governor of the National Bank. He died in Dublin on 3 September 1931 and was buried at Glasnevin cemetery. He was survived by his wife.

MARIE-LOUISE LEGG

Sources WWW · *Tuam Herald and Western Advertiser* (21 May 1988) [150th anniversary suppl.] · *Tuam Herald* (Sept 1931) · CGPLA *Éire* (1931)
Likenesses photograph, repro. in *Tuam Herald* (21 May 1988), iii
Wealth at death £12,509 0s. 4d.: probate, 2 Dec 1931, CGPLA *Éire*

Kelly, Thomas (1769–1855), hymn writer and founder of the Kellyites, was born at Kellyville, Queen's county, on 13 July 1769, the only son of Thomas (*d.* 1809), the Rt Hon. Chief Baron Kelly of Kellyville, Queen's county, justice of the Irish court of common pleas. He was educated at Portarlington and Kilkenny before entering Trinity College, Dublin, on 14 November 1785 and taking his BA degree in 1789. Initially Kelly intended to practise law. While studying for the bar in London he attracted the attention of Edmund Burke, in whose house he was a frequent guest. He was admitted to the Middle Temple on 4 July 1786. Back in Dublin, after being challenged by John Walker on the necessity of inward conversion, he passed through an ascetic period, eventually emerging as an articulate exponent of the tenets of 'serious religion'. Against the wishes of his family Kelly then decided to abandon law in favour of ordination in the Church of England, which occurred in 1792. Three years later, in July 1795, he married Elizabeth, eldest daughter of William Tighe (*d.* 1782), MP (and Irish patron of John Wesley), of Rosanne, co. Wicklow, who brought a sizeable fortune to the marriage. They had at least one daughter.

Inspired by the visit of the English evangelical Rowland Hill in 1793, Kelly began preaching the 'doctrines of grace' in and around Dublin. In early 1794, together with three clerical allies, Kelly began preaching the Sunday afternoon sermon at St Luke's, Dublin, until his success awakened the opposition of the rector. Soon afterwards they were inhibited by Robert Fowler, the archbishop of Dublin, for preaching 'certain strange and pernicious doctrines'. The focus of their spiritual efforts then began to disperse throughout the country, Kelly abandoning Dublin for Athy. After his marriage he migrated to Blackrock, outside Dublin, preaching at an Anglican chapel of ease recently constructed from his own resources. Here Kelly appeared, as Walker described it, 'all on fire, as if he would set the world in a blaze' (*Evangelical Magazine*).

For some years Kelly continued to preach at the principal evangelical churches and chapels throughout Ireland. In 1802 he founded the Kellyites, a religious connexion based on a congregational plan. Although the precise details of the Kellyites remain uncertain, it is known that congregations were founded at New Ross, Waterford, Blackrock, Dublin, Athy, Kilkenny, Cork, Limerick, Portarlington, and Wexford. Some pulpits were filled by laymen and local ministers, others with students from the academy formed by Robert and James Alexander Haldane in Scotland. In 1803, concluding that a national establishment of religion was incompatible with New Testament principles, Kelly severed his relationship with the Church of England.

At first glance Kelly's secession and the advancement of his connexion outside the established church appear a mere episode in the complex religious history of Ireland; yet when they are considered within the overall context, occurring simultaneously with John Walker's spectacular secession and the founding of his connexion, the Walkerites, they take on added significance.

Kelly continued to minister to the bodies meeting at Dublin and Athy until his death in Dublin on 14 May 1855. By the following year a number of the chapels had closed. Congregations still met at Dublin, Waterford, New Ross, Athy, and perhaps elsewhere, but the number of adherents had begun to diminish considerably. Kelly published a number of controversial religious tracts, although he is best known as the author of some 765 sacred hymns which appeared in three principal volumes: *A Collection of Psalms and Hymns Extracted from Various Authors* (1802), *Hymns on Various Passages of Scripture* (1804), and *Hymns by Thomas Kelly, not before Published* (1815).

One of the outstanding figures in early Irish evangelicalism, Kelly was a deeply learned man, skilled in oriental languages; his friends and acquaintances alike found him a likeable man, frank and generous in manner.

GRAYSON CARTER

Sources 'Memoir of the late Rev. Thomas Kelly, Dublin', *Evangelical Magazine and Missionary Chronicle*, new ser., 34 (1856), 61–71 · J. Julian, ed., *A dictionary of hymnology*, rev. edn (1907) · J. Miller, *Singers and songs of the church*, 2nd edn (1869), 337–9 · G. Carter, 'Evangelical seceders from the Church of England, c.1800–1850', DPhil diss., U. Oxf., 1990 · D. J. O'Donoghue, *The poets of Ireland: a biographical and bibliographical dictionary* (1912), 228 · *IGI* · Burke, *Gen. GB* [Elizabeth Kelly] · H. Farrer, *Irish marriages*, 2 vols. (1897) · H. A. C. Sturgess, ed., *Register of admissions to the Honourable Society of the Middle Temple, from the fifteenth century to the year 1944*, 2 (1949), 400 · Burtchaell & Sadleir, *Alum. Dubl.* · Boase, *Mod. Eng. biog.* · J. Hall, *The memory of the just: a tribute to the memory of the late Thomas Kelly* (1855)

Kelly, William (1821–1906), member of the (Plymouth) Brethren and biblical scholar, only son of William Kelly, an Ulster squire, was born at Millisle, co. Down, in May 1821. His only sister married a Canadian clergyman. He was educated at Dr Nelson's academy, Downpatrick, and at Trinity College, Dublin (1836–41), where he graduated BA with the highest honours in classics. Left fatherless at an early age, he became tutor in the family of Ernest le Pelley, seigneur of Sark. Probably brought up in a Presbyterian family, and a practising Anglican in Sark, he became a member of the (Plymouth) Brethren in 1841, and shortly after left Sark for Guernsey. Like many other evangelicals he was at first attracted by the Tractarian movement, but soon became disillusioned. At the age of twenty-four he met John Nelson Darby, leader of the Darbyite Brethren, became his ablest interpreter, and edited his collected writings (34 vols., 1867–83). In 1879 Kelly supported Edward Cronin, who was excommunicated, in his dispute with Darby on a question of church discipline. Kelly and his party maintained the superiority of individual conscience over church control in matters not fundamental, but they remained true to Darby's basic doctrinal views with the partial exception of baptism, on which subject Kellyites inclined towards the baptism of believers. C. H. Spurgeon said of Kelly that he was 'born for the universe', but 'narrowed his mind by Darbyism'.

After nearly thirty years (1844–71) in Guernsey, Kelly spent his last thirty-five years at Blackheath. He married first Elizabeth Montgomery (d. c.1850) of Guernsey, and secondly Elizabeth Emily (d. 2 Feb 1884), daughter of H. Gipps, rector of St Peter's, Hereford. Kelly presented his library of 15,000 volumes to the town of Middlesbrough shortly before his death at The Firs, Denmark Road, Exeter, on 27 March 1906. He was buried near his second wife in Charlton cemetery.

Kelly was a prolific writer and lecturer on scriptural subjects. From 1848 to 1850 he edited *The Prospect* and from 1856 to his death the *Bible Treasury*, periodicals devoted to

the discussion of scriptural topics from a dispensationalist point of view. From 1854 to 1856 he contributed to the *Christian Annotator*, for which Samuel Prideaux Tregelles and Philip Henry Gosse also wrote. As editor he came into contact with theologians of many schools of thought, including Dean Alford and Principal Thomas Charles Edwards. A keen critic and controversialist and an uncompromising opponent of radical forms of higher biblical criticism, he obtained wide recognition as a scholar. The value of his critical Greek text published as *Revelation of St John* (1860), the first Greek work printed in Guernsey, was approved by Heinrich von Ewald, the German theologian. He corresponded with members of the New Testament Revision Committee. His published works, which fill almost four pages of the British Library catalogue, include expositions of each New Testament and most Old Testament books, as well as theological studies. Outstanding among them, in addition to his work on the Greek text of Revelation, are the following: *Lectures on the Book of Revelation* (1861) and *The Revelation Expounded* (1901), which contain his understanding of biblical prophecy still to be fulfilled; *Six Lectures on the Church of God* (1865), which sets out with striking clarity his views on the subject; *The Gospel of John Expounded* (1898), which exemplifies the devotional tone as well as the exegetical qualities of his biblical expositions; and *The Powers that Be* (1854), which reveals his advocacy of capital punishment. *The Creation* (1869) and *In the Beginning and the Adamic Earth* (1894) engage with evolutionary theories. *Lectures Introductory to the Study of the Pentateuch* (1871) and *The Higher Criticism* (1906) represent his response to current biblical criticism. Kelly's writings constitute the finest literary achievement of those Brethren who—broadly speaking—followed the teachings of J. N. Darby.

W. B. OWEN, *rev.* HAROLD H. ROWDON

Sources *The Times* (31 March 1906) · H. Wreford, *Memories of the life and last days of William Kelly* (1906) · 'William Kelly as a theologian', *Expositor*, 7th ser., 17 · F. R. Coad, *A history of the Brethren movement* (1968) · private information (2004) · M. L. Taylor, '"Born for the universe": William Kelly and the Brethren mind in Victorian England', MPhil diss., University of Teesside, 1993

Likenesses portrait, repro. in Wreford, *Memories*

Wealth at death £5891 16s. 9d.: probate, 25 April 1906, *CGPLA Eng. & Wales*

Kelman, John (1864–1929), United Free Church of Scotland minister, was born on 20 June 1864 in the Free Church manse, Dundonald, Ayrshire, the only son of John Kelman (1830–1907), minister of Dundonald Free Church of Scotland, and his wife, Margaret Harper Urquhart. His only sister, Janet Harvey Kelman, became a children's writer and was the first principal (1925) of the YWCA College at Selly Oak, Birmingham. After his father's translation in 1866 to St John's Free Church, Leith, John was educated at Leith high school, Royal High School, Edinburgh, and Edinburgh University, where he matriculated in 1879, and graduated MA in 1884, and where he particularly appreciated J. S. Blackie in Greek and David Masson in English literature.

Kelman's training at New College, Edinburgh, for the

Free Church ministry (1884–5, 1888–90) was interrupted by illness. Three recuperative years in Australia included a session (1887–8) in Ormond (Presbyterian) College in Melbourne. The enterprising openness of Australian society no doubt fostered Kelman's easy sociability and confidence in human potential. In June 1890 he was licensed to assist George Adam Smith at Queen's Cross, Aberdeen. Kelman wrote up his later travels with Smith in *The Holy Land* (1902), and with other companions in *From Damascus to Palmyra* (1908). In October 1891 he was ordained to Peterculter Free Church, Aberdeenshire, and on 18 May 1892 married Ellin Runcorn Bell, daughter of William Hamilton Bell of Edinburgh.

Kelman's Edinburgh ministry began on 4 March 1897 as colleague and successor to Dr Robert Gordon Balfour (who soon demitted) in New North Free Church, which he led into the United Free Church in the church union of 1900. Its poky, unattractive building in Forrest Road (subsequently the Bedlam Theatre) became the centre of an influential apologetic-cum-evangelistic outreach to thousands of students, using also the capacious Operetta House in nearby Chambers Street. Working almost like an early university chaplain, Kelman also held classes on the religious message of the poets. The honorary DD of 1907 from Edinburgh University recognized his involvement with the university settlement. On 5 March 1907 Kelman became junior colleague to Alexander Whyte in the prestigious pulpit of St George's United Free Church in Edinburgh's West End. His more liberal evangelicalism co-existed harmoniously with Whyte's deeper conservatism. When war broke out Kelman quickly volunteered as a chaplain, but illness again intervened. He later worked with the YMCA in France and Italy (1916–17), became an OBE (1917), and was commissioned by the government to advocate the allied cause in America, where he travelled widely with much acceptance.

In November 1919 Kelman moved to Fifth Avenue Presbyterian Church, New York. He accepted numerous invitations to preach, including the Lyman Beecher lectures on preaching at Yale in 1919, published as *The War and Preaching* (1919). In the following year he delivered the Mendenhall lectures, De Pauw, Indiana, which appeared in book form as *Some Aspects of International Christianity* (1920). Kelman's 1924 series of William Belden Noble lectures at Harvard, devoted to Thomas Carlyle, Matthew Arnold, and Robert Browning, was published under the title of *Prophets of Yesterday* (1924). Yet despite being in such demand Kelman lacked popular appeal as a preacher. He was honoured by Yale (DD, 1917), Princeton (DD, 1921) and Lafayette (LittD, 1920). His health collapsed again, and yet again after he returned to Britain to become minister of Frognal St Andrews Presbyterian Church, Hampstead, in April 1924. He retired in September 1925 to Edinburgh, where he died on 3 May 1929 at his home, 7 Inverleith Place. His wife survived him.

As a writer Kelman was more productive than distinguished. He assisted Alexander Whyte and Marcus Dods in editing handbooks for Bible classes, and displayed his literary interests in *The Faith of Robert Louis Stevenson* (1903) and other works. He excelled in the pulpit, whence he became 'a living force in Edinburgh' (*The Scotsman*). Moving away from his father's reformed faith he espoused a more optimistic, generous, refined, and thoughtful brand of evangelical liberalism.

D. F. WRIGHT

Sources J. A. Lamb, ed., *The fasti of the United Free Church of Scotland, 1900–1929* (1956) · *WWW, 1929–40* · E. J. Hagan, 'The late Dr. Kelman', *Record of the Home and Foreign Mission Work of the United Free Church of Scotland*, new ser., 29 (1929), 257–9 · *The Scotsman* (4 May 1929) · *Who was who in America*, 1 (1943), 664 · E. de W. Jones, *The royalty of the pulpit: a survey and appreciation of the Lyman Beecher lectures on preaching* [1951], 89–95 · *CCI* (1929)

Archives NL Scot., corresp. · U. Edin. L., corresp. · U. Edin., New Coll. L., corresp.

Likenesses A. Swan Watson, photograph, repro. in Hagan, 'The late Dr. Kelman', 258

Wealth at death £9489 10s. 6d.: confirmation, 13 July 1929, *CCI* · £1039 14s. 10d.: eik additional estate, 4 Oct 1929, *CCI*

Kelsall, Charles (1782–1857), traveller and architect, was baptized on 1 August 1782 at Greenwich, Kent, the son of Thomas Kelsall, a member of the council of the East India Company and his wife, Sarah. He was educated at Eton College and Trinity College, Cambridge, where he became a fellow-commoner in 1800. He left in 1803 without taking a degree and spent three years in a Wiltshire militia regiment. In subsequently adopting the life of a travelling scholar, he was doubtless influenced by the academic study of Greece being undertaken about 1800 by a remarkable group of Cambridge scholars. He first visited Sicily while he was still an undergraduate, and it was on a second visit to the island in 1808–9 that he wrote the first of his many privately published books, a translation of Cicero's *The Last Two Pleadings … Against Caius Verres* (1812). He unexpectedly appended to this a 'Post script containing remarks on the state of modern Sicily' in which his sympathy with contemporary trends in secular rationalist thought led him to argue that Sicily was in need of drastic modernization along liberal and democratic lines.

Kelsall adopted the cause of Greek independence in *A Letter from Athens Addressed to a Friend in England*, a lengthy poem published in 1812, the same year as *Childe Harold* by Lord Byron. In a footnote he held up the Greek Doric style as the model for a reformed modern architecture. In idealist language derived from J. J. Winckelmann, he praised Doric for its permanence and longevity, recording 'the rapid progress of the present age to the attainment of true taste in architecture'. He admired recent Greek revival buildings in St Petersburg, Berlin, Trieste, London, and Cambridge, but reserved his greatest praise for Paris, where 'grecian architecture triumphs' and was consequently 'a better school for young architects than either Rome or Venice'.

Kelsall designed buildings in various styles, including Grecian, of which he published engravings by Henry Moses and other artists in *Phantasm of an University* (1814), a book which has something in common with Claude-Nicolas Ledoux's *L'architecture considérée sous le rapport de l'art, des mœurs, et de la législation* (1804), with the proposals of Thomas Jefferson for the University of Virginia, and with the founding of London University. Kelsall argued for the fundamental reform, academically and architecturally, of Oxford and Cambridge, urging them to 'Take at last measures to keep peace with the improvements made in the present age, in all the departments of science and art.' Denying that 'universal science is centred in mathematics, in the classics', he proposed as fields of study civil policy and languages, fine arts, agriculture and manufactures, natural philosophy, moral philosophy, and mathematics. The course would be followed by a world tour. The university buildings were themselves instructive, incorporating all the 'orders to be seen in the ruins of Greece and Italy' as well as English medieval styles.

In his *Classical Excursion from Rome to Arpino* (1820) Kelsall published designs for a monument to Cicero in the Amalthea at Arpino. In 1841 he acquired a villa called Knightons in Hythe, Hampshire, which he renamed the Villa Amalthea, setting up busts of poets and scholars in the garden. His *Remarks Touching Geography Especially that of the British Isles* (1822) proposed the introduction of Napoleonic departments, while his *Horae viaticae* (1836) included a novel about a radical reforming pope. Kelsall also published *Esquisse de mes travaux, de mes voyages, et de mes opinions* (1830). On his death in 1857 he left his books and manuscripts to Morden College, Blackheath, London, where a building was designed to house them by Philip Hardwick.   DAVID WATKIN, *rev.*

Sources D. J. Watkin, 'Charles Kelsall: the quintessence of neoclassicism', *ArchR*, 140 (1996), 109–12 • D. Watkin, *Thomas Hope and the neo-classical idea* (1968) • IGI

Kelsall, John (1683–1743), Quaker minister and diarist, the son of John Kelsall (1650–*c*.1684), a tailor and later proprietor of an ale house, and Elizabeth, *née* Cragg (1660–*c*.1685), was born at Hart Street, near Covent Garden, London, on 18 September 1683. His parents died soon after, and with Joseph, his brother, he was 'left fatherless and motherless among strangers, very few or none of our kindred living in the City, but Friends were careful over us' (RS Friends, Lond., S.194/1). In May 1687 his grandmother took charge of the boys and settled them initially at Quernmore, near Lancaster. During 1687–9 Kelsall was locally educated before attending Abbeystead School in 1690. After his grandmother's death in 1699 Kelsall lived with an uncle at Wiersdale, where he continued his education. In April 1700 he briefly taught at a Friends' school at Yelland, but felt he had insufficient appreciation of Quaker doctrines. After this Kelsall went to Lancaster, where he fell into 'many troubles, temptations and exercises' (ibid.), but from June 1700 he underwent a spiritual conversion which was assisted with his removal to Penketh School. He remained here until May 1701 before accepting a teaching post at Dolobran Friends' school, near Welshpool, Montgomeryshire. From 1704 Kelsall became a regular representative to the London yearly meeting, but was not impressed by what he saw as the 'many spacious works and curious contrivances of men. … Pride and vanity are very regent and the glory of this world hath blinded the eyes of many' (ibid.).

On 3 May 1711 Kelsall married Susannah (1688–1767), the daughter of Amos Davies of Coed Cowryd, and between 1713 and 1733 they had ten children. From 1713 he lived in the Dolobran meeting-house, but it was a difficult time. The school numbers had significantly dropped, and he was forced to sell his stock and equipment. He also considered emigrating to Pennsylvania with other Friends, in spite of his earlier protestations concerning Friends leaving Wales. In late 1713 the Quaker industrialist Abraham Darby offered him the position of clerk at the Dolgyn ironworks near Dolgellau, Merioneth, but Kelsall found that he could not be 'easie in my mind to be too hard and screwing with people in bargaining or agreements' (RS Friends, Lond., S.194/1). Later in 1719 he was dismissed by the works' new owner, Samuel Milner of Bewdley, but was appointed in April 1720 to a similar position at Dolobran by Charles Lloyd. After Lloyd was declared bankrupt Kelsall returned as clerk at the Dolgyn furnace under the Paytons of Dudley, where he remained until the works closed in 1734. During the next year Kelsall taught at Welshpool, but by June 1735, in an impoverished condition, he was forced to seek employment as a teacher in Cork, from where he returned in February of the following year. After another spell in Dublin, Kelsall accepted a teaching post in Chester before moving to Boughton in January 1740. From then until his death in 1743 he sought work wherever he could find it, but his poor health increasingly assisted his fall into poverty.

Kelsall's diaries, now held at the Religious Society of Friends Library in London, provide insight into the hardships faced by, and lifestyle of, eighteenth-century Quakers in north-west England and Wales. While working for Charles Lloyd at Dolobran, for example, Kelsall commented on his disputes with non-Quakers and the difficulties faced by his employers and his family. Elsewhere, he recorded the numerous visitors to the Dolobran meeting, among them Quaker ministers from Pennsylvania. His religious beliefs were also expressed in his diaries, letters, and in the local meeting minutes. In 1705 he warned members about sleeping in meetings, while in April 1731 he complained that Friends 'unwilling to give … offence' were not testifying against the 'lifeless superstitious ministry of the Priests' (RS Friends, Lond., S.194/1). Kelsall may have also foreseen the rise of Methodism; it was, he wrote,

> my belief God will raise in due time a people out of Friends or others who will be commissioned to strike at the Root and Branch of Antichrist without Regard to the Frowns or Favours of High or Low Clergy or others.   (ibid.)

Apart from his journals Kelsall also engaged in a sizeable correspondence and compiled two volumes of unpublished poetry. In 1726 his *The Faithful Monitor, or, An Earnest Exhortation to Sobriety and Holiness* was published. In June 1737 he penned 'An alarm sounded to the sinners in Sion and all such as hold the truth in unrighteousness' and a 'List of such publick Friends and some others that I have known and had acquaintance withal since the year 1700' (RS Friends, Lond., S.191, 23 May 1736). These brief papers, however, were not published. Kelsall died on 1 August 1743 at Boughton, and was buried two days later at Newton, Cheshire.   RICHARD C. ALLEN

Sources J. Kelsall, diaries, letters, and poetry, RS Friends, Lond., MSS S.185, S.193/1–4, S.194/1–3 · H. G. Jones, 'John Kelsall: a study in religious and economic history', MA diss., U. Wales, Bangor, 1938 · DWB, 532 · E. R. Morris, 'The Dolobran family in religion and industry in Montgomeryshire', Montgomeryshire Collections, 56 (1959–60), 124–47 · T. M. Rees, A history of the Quakers in Wales (1925), 138, 140, 141, 213 · G. H. Jenkins, 'Quaker and anti-Quaker literature in Wales from the Restoration to Methodism', Welsh History Review / Cylchgrawn Hanes Cymru, 7 (1974–5), 403–26 · W. Rees, Industry before the industrial revolution, 1 (1968), 319–25 · R. C. Allen, 'The Society of Friends in Wales: the case of Monmouthshire, c.1654–1836', PhD diss., U. Wales, Aberystwyth, 1999, chaps. 6, 9
Archives RS Friends, Lond., diaries, letters, and poetry

Kelsey, Henry (c.1667–1724), explorer in Canada and Hudson's Bay Company official, is of uncertain origins, although he may have been the son of John Kelsey, mariner, of East Greenwich, Kent, a location with which Henry Kelsey is known to have been associated. He enters the historical record on 15 March 1684, when he apprenticed to the Hudson's Bay Company for a term of four years. He may have been in the company's service as early as 1677, and had sailed to Hudson Bay before he went out in the Lucy in 1684. In that year he was posted at the fort at Nelson River (later resited and styled York Fort). Weeks after his arrival French forces attacked it but without success. Kelsey travelled from the fort to New Severn in the winter of 1688–9. He became known to the London committee of the Hudson's Bay Company as 'a very active Lad Delighting much in Indians Compa., being never better pleased than when Hee is Travelling amongst them' (Davies, 'Kelsey, Henry', 2.308).

In 1689 Kelsey was sent to Churchill River in order to attract northern Indians. On this expedition he at first travelled under sail, in the Hopewell, but this was unsuccessful; accordingly he suggested an expedition by land. Accompanied by an Indian boy he went north 138 miles over difficult ground, encountered musk ox, and returned without having found any. On 12 June 1690 he left York Fort to encourage native peoples to trade with the Hudson's Bay Company. He took trade items and gifts in order to promote the fur trade but he also had instructions to look for mines, minerals, and medicines. He endeavoured to keep the peace among the tribes for the company regarded war as detrimental to trade.

Kelsey's travels took him from York Fort 600 miles south west to a place he called Dering's Point, named for Sir Edward Dering, the company's deputy governor. The location was most likely 12 miles below The Pas, Manitoba, on the Saskatchewan River. On 15 July 1691 he travelled west, went up the Saskatchewan River, then abandoned his canoes and went overland to the Red Deer River, where he met the Eagle Creek Assiniboines. He crossed a plain abounding with buffalo, or bison, and in the wooded highlands beyond recorded descriptions of the buffalo and grizzly bear, being the first to do so in the Canadian west. He may have met Sioux and Atsinas, and he attempted to play the role of peacemaker. With a sizeable party of Indians he returned to York Fort in the summer of 1692, ending a most remarkable land voyage notable for its extent and its consequences. Aided by Indians his solo sortie was none the less a triumph of nerve and of technique; nerve because of the courage required, and technique because of the requirement to win the confidence of the native people among whom he travelled and traded. His written observations on Indian life and beliefs are a significant ethnographic record.

Kelsey re-enlisted in the Hudson's Bay Company on 25 April 1694 and began the second phase of his career in the Canadian north, as a trader and administrator. When two French vessels under Pierre le Moyne d'Iberville invested York Fort, Kelsey negotiated its surrender, on 4 October 1694. Having been taken prisoner he was released and was back in England by early 1696. He sailed for Canada on 2 June and was present at the retaking of York Fort. Again the French attacked by sea. Again the place was surrendered to Iberville, on 2 September. On 7 April 1698 Kelsey married Elizabeth Dix of East Greenwich, with whom he had one son and two daughters.

From 1701 to 1703 and from 1707 to 1709 he was a shipmaster and trader, promoting trade and encouraging discoveries of Hudson Bay shores. He was out of the service of the Hudson's Bay Company for a few years, perhaps on grounds of health. He returned as chief trader, at Albany, and on 11 September 1714 was back at York Fort when the French returned it to the company after the peace of Utrecht. He was second in command (1715–18) to Governor James Knight; he took command of York Fort in 1717; and in 1718 he became governor over all settlements of the company. He went on voyages of trade and discovery northwards to 62°40′ N (in 1719) and 64° N (in 1721). On the latter voyage he searched for minerals, especially copper, for the north-west passage, and for whales. The intention was also to develop trade with the Inuit.

Kelsey returned to Britain on 31 October 1722. He applied but was not given command of the Hudson's Bay Company ship Hannah; perhaps James Knight's earlier charge (unsubstantiated) that Kelsey had been engaging in private trade stood in his way. He died at East Greenwich on 2 November 1724 and was buried the same day at St Alfege's Church. He was survived by his wife. Registrations of the baptisms of his first two children (in 1704 and 1706) describe him as 'mariner', that of the third child (1713) as a 'gentleman'. His papers, journals, and memoranda are fragmentary and incomplete. The Kelsey Papers, edited by A. G. Doughty and Chester Martin, published in 1929, includes a selection of his texts, some written in poetic verse. BARRY M. GOUGH

Sources K. G. Davies, 'Kelsey, Henry', DCB, vol. 2 · K. G. Davies, ed., Letters from Hudson Bay (1965), 376–94 · Kelsey papers, ed. A. Doughty and C. Martin (1929) · J. Warkentin, Introduction, in Kelsey papers, ed. A. Doughty, C. Martin, and J. Warkentin, new edn (1994)
Archives Provincial Archive of Manitoba, Winnipeg, Hudson's Bay Company archives, MSS

Kelsey, Thomas (d. in or after 1676), parliamentarian army officer and major-general, was a younger son of Thomas Kelsey (d. in or before 1630), yeoman farmer, of Shere in

Surrey, and Mary Willet (d. in or after 1621). He was apprenticed to Henry Graunt on 20 October 1630, and made free of the London Drapers' Company on 15 May 1639, and he married one of the daughters of his master. Wood talked of him as 'a mean trader' and a 'godly button maker' (Wood, *Ath. Oxon.: Fasti*, 2.111). Kelsey joined the parliamentarian cause as a major in the New Model foot regiment of Colonel Edward Montague, and signed the articles for the surrender of Langford House in October 1645. In 1646 he became a lieutenant-colonel in the regiment of Richard Ingoldsby, and from 1646 to at least 1650 served as deputy governor of Oxford. He supported the parliamentarian visitation of the university, and was awarded an honorary MA in 1648, the year in which he helped to foil a royalist plot in the city. In November 1648, as a member of the general council of officers, he helped to prepare the officers' *Agreement of the People*, and the famous remonstrance presented to parliament on 20 November. In January 1649 he participated in the Whitehall debates, casting doubt on the prophetess Elizabeth Poole. He played no part in the trial of Charles I but supported the new regime, and oversaw the taking of the engagement in Oxford.

In May 1651 Kelsey was made colonel of a regiment of dragoons, and was ordered to march to Dover, where he was immediately commissioned as lieutenant of Dover Castle and governor of the garrison. He proved zealous in providing news, in examining suspects and prisoners, and in overseeing naval matters, particularly during the First Anglo-Dutch War. After the dissolution of the Rump Parliament in 1653 he was seconded to a number of council of state committees and became a commissioner for the navy, a position he was able to retain as a supporter of the protectorate in December 1653. Although he attended the congregation of the Fifth Monarchist John Simpson, Kelsey evidently supported a national church, and served as a commissioner for scandalous ministers in Kent in 1654. His concern for the purity of the church was evident following his election to parliament for Sandwich in 1654, and he was involved in committees dealing with the ejection of scandalous ministers, the enumeration of heresies, the investigation of the Socinian John Biddle, and the preparation of a bill regarding the Quakers.

Although Kelsey was considered for a military command in Ireland in the summer of 1655, on account of his 'valour and discreet courage' (Thurloe, *State papers*, 3.567), he remained in England, and in August was appointed one of the major-generals, for the counties of Kent and Surrey. He displayed both puritan zeal and political radicalism, banning Whitsun celebrations, endeavouring to uncover the Gerard plot, and arresting royalist delinquents such as the earl of Southampton, and Ranters such as Richard Coppin. He sought to purge royalists from local office, and was an enthusiastic supporter of widespread decimation. He proved less successful in relation to the 1656 parliamentary elections, and complained about the efforts of the 'rabble' to secure the election of George Cony at Dover, and about the spirit of opposition that was manifest in attempts to prevent the election of swordsmen, decimators, and courtiers. Kelsey responded by proposing

a ruthless policy of exclusions from the parliament, through an oath of recognition designed to keep out 'rigid fellows' (Thurloe, *State papers*, 5.384). He considered that the interest of God's people was to be preferred before one thousand parliaments, in order to prevent a return to slavery to 'Egyptian taskmasters' (*CSP dom.*, 1656–7, 87).

Kelsey was himself returned in 1656 at both Guildford and Dover, although he naturally opted to represent the latter. In the lengthy debates on the punishment of the Quaker James Nayler, he revealed his opposition to the death penalty, and his support for giving Nayler a hearing, religious counsel, and the opportunity to recant. He spoke of the need to mix mercy with judgment, and questioned parliament's jurisdiction in the case. An Independent in religion, Kelsey supported preachers such as Philip Nye and John Owen, and sought to protect dissenting ministers who agreed on matters of faith but differed over discipline and worship. With his ally John Disbrowe he also opposed the introduction of a bill for catechizing, and the imposition of fines for those who refused to engage in the practice. Later he supported harsh measures against the Quakers, albeit for disturbing the peace rather than for refusing to take oaths. Kelsey mixed this tolerant attitude with a hardline policy towards royalists, including those returned to the Commons, and also opposed the award of large sums of money and tracts of land to prominent political figures, particularly Lord Broghill.

Kelsey gradually emerged as a leading critic of the political conservatism that became increasingly evident during the protectorate, his disillusionment probably sparked by the overthrow of the major-generals in January 1657. Although he was involved in committees relating to 'The humble petition and advice' in the spring of 1657, which proposed offering the crown to Cromwell, he sought to persuade the protector to reject the proposals, and he would later make it clear that he opposed the reform of the constitution along the lines proposed. He emerged in Richard Cromwell's parliament in 1659 as a prominent opponent of the protectorate and took a stand against plans for the introduction of, and transactions with, the 'other house'. He was particularly hostile to the idea of recognizing the legal right of the old peers to sit in parliament, which would 'lay a foundation for Charles Stuart's coming over' and imply that 'all hath been a mere usurpation of the House of Commons' (Rutt, 3.408, 407).

Kelsey supported the dissolution of the protectorate in May 1659 and was confirmed as a navy commissioner, and as governor of Dover, by the restored Rump. He emerged alongside Disbrowe as a prominent member of the Wallingford House party during the ensuing months, but was one of the officers whose commission was revoked for circulating petitions in the army in October, prompting the army's interruption of parliament. When the Commons returned in December 1659, he was deprived of his position at Dover, and was briefly arrested in January 1660. Shortly after March 1660 he fled to the Low Countries with Disbrowe, where he was kept under close observation as a suspected plotter against Charles II. In 1666 he was ordered to return to England, possibly in order to be tried for treason, but he remained abroad until securing a pass to return in November 1671, and a pardon in February 1672. Kelsey lived out the rest of his life in relative obscurity, perhaps as a brewer. He was still alive in February 1676, when he reportedly attended a dissenting congregation in Leadenhall Street, along with former major-generals James Berry and Disbrowe. However, the date and place of his death remain unknown. J. T. PEACEY

Sources CSP dom., 1648–76 · Diary of Thomas Burton, ed. J. T. Rutt, 4 vols. (1828) · Thurloe, State papers, vols. 3–7 · Calendar of the Clarendon state papers preserved in the Bodleian Library, 4–5, ed. F. J. Routledge (1932–70) · The Clarke papers, ed. C. H. Firth, 4 vols., CS, new ser., 49, 54, 61–2 (1891–1901) · C. H. Firth and R. S. Rait, eds., Acts and ordinances of the interregnum, 1642–1660, 3 vols. (1911) · Sixth report, HMC, 5 (1877–8) · Seventh report, HMC, 6 (1879) · JHC, 7 (1651–9) · C. Durston, Cromwell's major-generals (2001) · B. S. Capp, The Fifth Monarchy Men: a study in seventeenth-century English millenarianism (1972) · London, Drapers' Company Archive · Wood, Ath. Oxon.: Fasti (1820), 111

Keltie, Sir John Scott (1840–1927), geographer, was born on 29 March 1840 in Dundee, the son of David Keltie, a builder and stonemason in Perth, and his wife, Christian, the daughter of William Scott of Crieff. The family returned to Perth shortly after John's birth and he attended school there. At the age of fourteen he became a pupil teacher in the old school in Watergate, and four years later he entered St Andrews University. In 1860 he transferred to Edinburgh University, where he studied intermittently until 1867 without taking a degree. He also trained for the ministry of the United Presbyterian church at Theological Hall in Edinburgh, but did not present himself for ordination. Instead he continued the journalism he had practised as a student, and in 1861 joined the editorial staff of W. and R. Chambers in Edinburgh, where he worked on the first edition of their *Encyclopaedia*.

In 1865, in Edinburgh, Keltie married Margaret (*d.* 1922), the daughter of Captain John Scott of Kirkwall; they had one daughter. In 1871 they moved to London, where Keltie joined Macmillan and worked on *Nature*, to which he often contributed more than a quarter of the items in an issue. He also edited books, from 1875 contributed regularly to *The Times*, and in 1883 became editor of the *Statesman's Year Book*, a position he held until the end of his life. These last two activities whetted his appetite for gathering and explaining geographical information and developed his professional attitude towards publishing, which he later put to good use in the Royal Geographical Society (RGS).

In 1883 Keltie became a fellow of the RGS and the following year he was appointed its inspector of geographical education, with the task of reporting on geographical teaching in British public schools and universities. The initiative was inspired by Douglas Freshfield as a first step towards enabling the society to improve such teaching. Keltie spent a year visiting British institutions and gathering data about overseas institutions, in person or by correspondence. His report on *Geographical Education* (1886) revealed the lamentable state of geographical teaching in

Sir John Scott Keltie (1840–1927), by James Russell & Sons

British schools and its almost complete absence from British universities. A well-attended touring exhibition which he organized showed the wall maps, textbooks, and atlases which were common in continental, particularly German, schools, but which were unmatched by their dismal British counterparts in their ability to engage, enlighten, and excite pupils. Keltie's cogent arguments, publicity campaigns, lectures, and enthusiasm, combined with Freshfield's persistence, succeeded where the society's previous efforts to stimulate geographical teaching had failed. In 1887 a readership in geography was established at the University of Oxford with financial support from the RGS. Its first holder was Halford Mackinder, who attributed his interest in geography to meeting Keltie at his touring exhibition. The University of Cambridge established a lectureship, again supported by the RGS, in 1888. Geography gradually, although not smoothly, became established at these and other universities, which provided high quality schoolteachers who, with their new equipment, gradually transformed the subject in schools.

In 1885 Keltie became librarian of the RGS, in 1892 its assistant secretary, and in 1896 its secretary. He played an important role in organizing the sixth International Geographical Congress in London in 1895, and in planning and effecting the society's move from Savile Row to far larger premises in Kensington Gore in 1913. He was never president of the society, but through his geniality, tenacity, and tact was often an important policy maker, not least because his long period in office allowed him to bide his time and press his ideas at favourable moments. He expanded the society's role as the natural London home for British and visiting explorers. Unusually, he was also active in and, in 1913, president of the Geographical Association, the society which promoted geography in schools. Its membership included many female professional teachers and differed markedly from that of the RGS, which was dominated by male amateurs and explorers. The service of Keltie to both societies helped prevent the distinction from becoming too great a rift. Within the RGS Keltie was a consistent supporter of the admission of women fellows, and once their election had been secured in principle he quietly invited some distinguished women to stand for election and supported the candidature of others. He regarded a contribution to geographical education, for example from schoolmistresses, as qualification enough, but also assisted explorers such as Gertrude Bell gain election. In 1893 he initiated publication of, and for twenty-four years edited, the RGS's *Geographical Journal*, helping to ensure that the society's publications fully reflected progress in the new academic, scientific geography, as well as in exploration and travel. He resigned as secretary of the RGS with effect from 1915 and as editor of the *Journal* in 1917.

Keltie was rewarded with honorary membership of numerous foreign geographical societies, gold medals from those of America, Paris, and Scotland, the Victoria medal of the RGS, decorations from Sweden, Finland, and Norway, and in 1918 a British knighthood. He died at his home, 88 Brondesbury Road, Kilburn, London, on 12 January 1927 after a sudden attack of bronchitis.

Keltie's contribution to British geography is universally acknowledged. His written legacy was modest, although not negligible for one who was not primarily a scholar. He was neither the first nor the only person to hope that geography might assume an important place in the school and university curriculum, or to see that continued exclusive concern with exploration would condemn the RGS to a marginal and anachronistic position among international geographical societies as the turn of the century approached. But through his good-humoured persistence, quiet conviction, and journalist's sense of opportunism he succeeded where others failed, and the 1886 report, now always known as the Keltie report, is universally recognized as a turning point in the history of the subject.

ELIZABETH BAIGENT

Sources L. J. Jay, 'John Scott Keltie', *Geographers: Bibliographical Studies*, 10 (1986), 93–8 · P. Coones, 'The centenary of the Mackinder readership at Oxford', *GJ*, 155 (1989), 13–22 · M. J. Wise, 'The Scott Keltie report, 1885, and the teaching of geography in Great Britain', *GJ*, 152 (1986), 367–82 · D. I. Scargill, 'The RGS and the foundations of geography at Oxford', *GJ*, 142 (1976), 438–61 · D. R. Stoddart, 'The RGS and the foundations of geography at Cambridge', *GJ*, 141 (1975), 216–39 · H. R. Mill, *The record of the Royal Geographical Society, 1830–1930* (1930) · M. Bell and C. McEwan, 'The admission of women fellows to the Royal Geographical Society, 1892–1914: the controversy and the outcome', *GJ*, 162 (1996), 295–312 · M. J. Wise, 'The campaign for geography in education: the

work of the Geographical Association, 1893–1993', *Geography*, 78 (1993), 101–9 · *CGPLA Eng. & Wales* (1927) · *The Times* (13 Jan 1927) · T. H. Elkins, 'Germany, J. Scott Keltie and British geographical education', *Materialen zur Didaktik der Geographie*, 16 (1992), 137–50 **Archives** Scott Polar RI, corresp. and literary papers | BL, corresp. with Macmillans, Add. MS 55042 · Bodl. Oxf., corresp. with Sir Aurel Stein · NL Scot., corresp. with Bartholomew & Son · NL Scot., corresp. with Sir Patrick Geddes · RGS, letters to H. R. Mill · RGS, corresp. with Royal Geographical Society **Likenesses** J. Russell & Sons, photograph, NPG [*see illus.*] · photograph, repro. in Jay, 'John Scott Keltie', 93 **Wealth at death** £4044 0s. 4d.: probate, 23 Feb 1927, *CGPLA Eng. & Wales*

Kelton, Arthur (d. 1549/50), verse chronicler, was probably a native of Shrewsbury. His parents and date of birth are unknown. Wood says he was thought to be Welsh, but Kelton himself seems to have been uncertain about his national identity. In his first published work he refers to the Welsh as 'they', but in the second he writes from the perspective of 'we Welshmen'; probably he was English by birth and language, but Welsh by descent. He was apparently a student at Oxford, though his name does not appear in the registers. He married Matilda Strange, with whom he had four children. A grandson born in 1541 was also named Arthur, and is sometimes confused with his grandfather. In 1543 he was granted a thirty-year lease of the deanery and tithings of the collegiate church of St Mary, Shrewsbury, possibly in reward for his services as a Tudor propagandist.

Kelton applied himself to the study and popularization of ancient British history, in the fabulous form received from Geoffrey of Monmouth. His two published works, both in old-fashioned verse, are *A Commendacion of Welshmen* (1546) and *A chronycle with a genealogie declaryng that the Brittons and Welshemen are lineallye dyscended from Brute* (1547). The latter is dedicated to Edward VI, though written in the reign of Henry VIII. Although Kelton made some attempt to reconcile Geoffrey's stories with the accounts of Roman historians, his learning was not deep and most of the sources he cites are either secondhand or fabricated. His works are devoted to the celebration, in roughly equal measure, of British antiquity, the Tudor dynasty, the Reformation, and the union of England and Wales. Kelton's originality lies in the way he fused these disparate strands into a grand historical narrative. Although he had no great influence, he inaugurated a theme that would later be developed by Edmund Spenser, among others. Kelton also probably provided a source for George Owen Harry's *Genealogy of the High and Mighty Monarch, James* (1604). Kelton was still living in 1549, but was mentioned as deceased in a record of 30 September the following year (Owen and Blakeway). He was buried at St Mary's Church, Shrewsbury.

PHILIP SCHWYZER

Sources H. Owen and J. B. Blakeway, *A history of Shrewsbury*, 2 (1825), 329–31 · Wood, *Ath. Oxon.*, new edn, 1.73 · A. H. Dodd, 'A commendacion of Welshmen', *BBCS*, 19 (1960–62), 235–49 · W. O. Ringler, 'Arthur Kelton's contributions to early British history', *Huntington Library Quarterly*, 40 (1976–7), 353–6 · Tanner, *Bibl. Brit.-Hib.* · J. Ames, *Typographical antiquities, or, An historical account of the* *origin and progress of printing in Great Britain and Ireland*, ed. W. Herbert, 3 vols. (1785–90) · *DNB*

Keltridge, John (*bap.* 1553, *d.* 1582×1604), Church of England clergyman, was baptized at St Michael Cornhill, London, on 22 May 1553. He was probably the eldest son of William Keltridge and Agnes Kelsay, and the half-brother of Samuel and Sidney Keltridge who both attended St John's College, Cambridge. John, however, was a scholar of Trinity College, where he matriculated in 1566; he graduated BA in 1572, proceeded MA in 1575, and was incorporated in that degree at Oxford on 14 July 1579.

Ordained deacon and priest in the diocese of Lincoln in 1576, Keltridge was called upon to give the ordination sermon at Fulham Palace on Ascension day (16 May) 1577 by John Aylmer, bishop of London. Here he 'addressed himself to his lordship against the vicious old popish clergy', urging him to 'rub and raze out the stock of Jezebel' in a thorough purge (Strype, 22). Perhaps it was Keltridge's aggressive approach which provoked the angry factional struggle which followed his institution to Dedham, Essex, on 20 July 1577. In the following June he recalled a year scarred with 'contentions', a 'troublesome and perilous time' of 'tossings and tumblings wherein I am sweltered and overcome' (Keltridge, *Exposition*; Strype, preface). Keltridge's book, in a judgement which perhaps rests partly on personal disappointment, laments the numbers of university trained ministers with no preferment.

Keltridge resigned from Dedham about this time, and on 2 September 1578 was instituted rector of Capel St Andrew, Suffolk, at the presentation of John Tyler. From there he was sent by Aylmer to Cookham, Berkshire, to replace a puritan minister earlier removed by an ecclesiastical commission. Once more Keltridge encountered entrenched opposition, for his institution was blocked altogether by 'one Welden', as Strype reports. This was probably Sir William Welden of Cannon Court, Cookham, a powerful local gentleman who held patronage rights both at Cookham and at nearby Shottesbrooke. Welden is reported to have boasted that 'though the bishop himself should come to sit with Keltridge in Cookham church, he should have a very warm seat' (Strype, 23).

Keltridge continued in Aylmer's favour, however, for before March 1580 he had been appointed one of his twelve examiners of ordinands. On 25 February 1581 Christopher Hoddesdon, governor of the Merchant Adventurers at Antwerp, wrote to Walsingham concerning a successor to Walter Travers, the preacher there; Keltridge had shown an interest in the place but Hoddesdon considered him too young. Later in 1581 Keltridge was at Holborn, from where, on 10 June, he dedicated to Walsingham *Two Godlie and Learned Sermons*. As the preface explains, his conference with Jesuits, the 'instruments of Satan' imprisoned in the Tower of London, had not gone well, since he found them 'stiffened in their errors'. This may perhaps be attributed to his sermons preached before them on 7 and 21 May, rather apt to offend than to persuade, and much later dubbed 'indiscreet ebullitions of exuberant zeal' (Cooper, *Ath. Cantab.*, 1.449). In 1582 the

Roman Catholic Gregory Martin denounced him as ignorant of Greek and Hebrew, and William Fulke offered only the most grudging defence of his co-religionist. That same year he was instituted rector of Reydon, Suffolk, compounding for the benefice on 15 September. After this nothing is known of his life, except that he was dead by 18 July 1604, when his father left £25 to John Keltridge's son William, to be paid him when he reached the age of twenty-five, and £5 to an unnamed daughter. The identity of John's wife is unrecorded.   STEPHEN WRIGHT

Sources Cooper, *Ath. Cantab.*, 1.449 · *Exposition and readynges of John Keltridge* (1578) · *VCH Berkshire*, vol. 3 · J. Strype, *Historical collections of the life and acts of … John Aylmer*, new edn (1821) · H. G. Owen, 'The London parish clergy in the reign of Elizabeth I', PhD diss., U. Lond., 1957 · J. Keltridge, *Two godlie and learned sermons* (1581) · A. F. S. Pearson, *Thomas Cartwright and Elizabethan puritanism, 1535–1603* (1925) · W. Fulke, *A defence of the sincere and true translations* (1583); [new edn], ed. C. H. Hartshorne, Parker Society, 17 (1843) · institution to Capel St Andrew, Suffolk, Norfolk RO, Reg/14/20, fol. 29*v* · composition record for Reydon, Suffolk, PRO, E 334/10, fol. 21*r* · Venn, *Alum. Cant.*, 1/3.4 · will, PRO, PROB 11/104, fols. 198–9

Kelty, Mary Ann (1789–1873), writer, was the daughter of Peter Kelty of Peas Hill, Cambridge, an Irish surgeon. Her father was particularly irritable towards her mother during the pregnancy and was always estranged from his precocious daughter. Her older brother, Sterling (1781–1827), was a fellow of King's College, and Kelty had many mentors from the university who encouraged her to develop her musical and literary talents. In 1821 she published anonymously *The Favourite of Nature*, dedicating it to Joanna Baillie. It was favourably reviewed as a 'well written novel, in which female character and an intimate knowledge of the human heart are ably pourtrayed' and praised as 'a tale which no mother need be afraid to place in the hands of her daughter' (*Monthly Magazine*, 269–70). Harriet Martineau called it 'the first successful religious novel' (Wilson, 174).

On 16 August 1822 Kelty's father dropped dead at the auction mart, Bartholomew Lane, London, where he had gone for the purpose of showing his daughter the building (*The Times*, 17 Aug 1822); her mother also died in 1821 or 1822. Determined against marriage and in possession of a comfortable private income, Kelty took rooms with a follower of the evangelical preacher Charles Simeon. Despite an attempt by her university friends to remove her from evangelical influence, she renounced her novelistic career after further efforts in the genre (*Osmond*, 1823, *The Story of Isabel*, 1826) and began a series of religious tracts with *Religious Thoughts* (1827) and *The Speculator and the Believer* (1828). Simeon was displeased that 'a woman, and a hearer of his, should legislate for herself in the kingdom of thought' (Wilson, 186), but she persisted until severe haemorrhaging from the throat put her life in danger. She fell under still more extreme religious influences, including Edward Irving and Mary Campbell, a 'prophetess', and burnt all her piano music and other symptoms of worldly pleasure. Gradually she recovered a calmer sense of spirituality through the writings of William Law (a selection of whose work she edited in 1838) and Isaac Pennington. She took up needlework for charitable purposes.

Finally Kelty left Cambridge, and after an uncomfortable winter in the country settled at 5 Hanover Street, Rye Lane, Peckham. She was an attender at the Friends' Meeting at Peckham but never took membership. She wrote on Quaker themes in *Early Days in the Society of Friends* (1840) and *Memoirs of the Lives and Persecutions of the Primitive Quakers* (1844), and explored the workings of religion in individual lives in *Facts and Feelings* (1841). Over the last thirty years of her life she produced numerous 'devotional diaries', reflections on spirituality in the domestic sphere, and a small volume of poetry 'addressed to the thoughtful and suffering' (*Waters of Comfort*, 1856). Her autobiographical testimonies, *Reminiscences of Thought and Feeling* (1852) and *The Solace of a Solitaire* (1869), are still of interest. Kelty sent the first of these to Harriet Martineau, who shied away from a meeting, but was:

> glad to have read the memoir; and glad that it exists,— painful as it is: for it is a striking emanation of the spirit of the time, and illustration of its experiences. Of the ability, courage and candour of the writer there can be no question. (Wilson, 171–2)

Kelty died at her house in Hanover Street on 8 January 1873 aged eighty-four.   PAUL BAINES

Sources M. A. Kelty, *Reminiscences of thought and feeling* (1852) · M. A. Kelty, *The solace of a solitaire* (1869) · M. Wilson, *These were muses* (1924) · *Harriet Martineau's autobiography*, ed. M. W. Chapman, 3 vols. (1877) · Blain, Clements & Grundy, *Feminist comp.* · W. S. Ward, *Literary reviews in British periodicals, 1821–1826: a bibliography* (1977) · *Monthly Magazine*, 51 (1821), 269–70 · Venn, *Alum. Cant.*, 2/5 · *The Times* (17 Aug 1822) · CGPLA Eng. & Wales (1873)
Archives CUL, letters | BL, receipt to R. Bentley, Add. 46616
Wealth at death under £450: probate, 22 Jan 1873, CGPLA Eng. & Wales

Kelvin. For this title name *see* Thomson, William, Baron Kelvin (1824–1907).

Kelway [Kellaway, Kellway], **Joseph** (*c*.1702–1782), musician, was probably born in Chichester, Sussex, the younger brother of Thomas *Kelway; his parents are believed to have been either Thomas Kelway and his wife, Ann Crosfield, of Chichester, or Jasper Kellway and his wife, Mary Brathwait, of Windsor. He studied under his elder brother, was apprenticed to a dancing-master in Bath, and received instruction from Chilcot and the eminent Francesco Geminiani. The Italian became a close friend, confidant, and business partner in later life. Chosen in preference to William Boyce, Kelway succeeded Obadiah Shuttleworth as organist of St Michael Cornhill, London, in 1730, and resigned in 1736 to succeed John Weldon at St Martin-in-the-Fields (his post at St Michael was then taken by Boyce). Kelway's 'extempore flights' (Burney, *Hist. mus.*, 214) in performance on the organ were the match of any contemporary. His 'bold, rapid, and fanciful' voluntaries were judged to resemble the 'wild and desultory style of Geminiani' (ibid., 214, 1009). According to Burney, Handel himself, among others, frequented St Martin's Church to hear the 'masterly and original' Kelway and the 'fire and precision' (ibid., 214) of his performances. Also, around this time, evidence emerges of 'Kelway' selling Geminiani's works from a 'Mr. Brigg's', a coach painter in Princes Street, near Leicester Fields, and in 1739, the year in which (on 28 August) he became a founding governor of the Royal Society of Musicians, he sold the Italian's sonatas op. 4 from near Depuis's Coffee House in Conduit Street (see Careri, 30–31). Geminiani's sole extant autograph, a letter from Hollard to 'Kalloway' dated 20 January 1747 (now in the British Library) and addressed to Upper Grosvenor Street, London, maintains their friendship and business relationship (ibid., 36–7). Indeed, in May of that year Kelway advertised some more of Geminiani's works, obtainable from Upper Grosvenor Street.

In addition to his achievements on the organ, Kelway was esteemed as a performer on the harpsichord and as a teacher. Among his pupils were Charles Wesley, Mrs Mary Delany, and Queen Charlotte, wife of George III, to whom he was appointed harpsichord master and chamber musician around the time of her arrival in England in 1761. According to his will, Kelway also became harpsichord maker to the queen. Delany (then Mrs Pendarves) wrote in 1736 to Ann Granville:

> My brother has tied me down at last to learn of Kellaway; he has paid him the entrance money, which is two guineas, and has made me a present of Handel's 'Book of Lessons'. I don't find Kellaway's method difficult at all.   (*Autobiography ... Mrs Delany*, 1.579)

And Ann Granville asks Lady Throckmorton, in August 1739: 'Have you heard Mr. Kellaway upon the harpsichord? He is at Scarborough, and a most delightful player, very little inferior to Handel' (*Autobiography ... Mrs Delany*, 2.61). Kelway was evidently a brilliant exponent of Scarlatti's most difficult sonatas, and Burney praised his 'neat and delicate' execution and places him at the 'head of the Scarlatti sect' (Burney, *Hist. mus.*, 1009).

Kelway's ability and prominence earned him the patronage of Richard, seventh Viscount Fitzwilliam of Merrion. Burney was, however, not so complimentary with respect to Kelway's compositions. Perhaps it was his determination to be novel, but Kelway's works were seen as wanting in 'grace, melody, and experience' (Burney, *Hist. mus.*, 214). He composed a few harpsichord lessons and other small pieces and some vocal music but it was the arrival of J. C. Bach and his appointment at court that prompted Kelway to publish his *Six Sonatas for Harpsichord* (1764). Influenced by Scarlatti and certainly bold and original, these were severely and famously, if perhaps unfairly, criticized by Burney as perhaps 'the most crude, awkward, and unpleasant pieces of the kind that have ever been engraved' (ibid., 1009).

Towards the end of Kelway's life, J. C. Bach introduced a new *galant* style, the pianoforte gained in popularity as a concert instrument and began to rival the harpsichord in the home, and Kelway's musical 'sect' (Careri, 19) did not survive the changes in public taste. Nevertheless, he had been one of the most highly esteemed English keyboard players of his day.

There is little information on Kelway's later life,

although he appears to have suffered from 'a mental illness' (Lincoln). His portrait, by J. Russell, shows him to have been a man of large and dignified stature.

Kelway died, probably during May and in London, in 1782. His will (signed on 14 April 1779 and proved on 5 June 1782) provided for his grandnephew, William Kelway, and for four grandnieces: Ann Branch (née Kelway); Elizabeth Kelway; Ann Heather (née Snapes); and Elizabeth Smith (née Snapes), wife of the musician John Stafford Smith. To Elizabeth Smith and Ann Heather he left his harpsichord (by Petrus Joannes Couchet), his Cremonese violin, and all his other instruments and books of music. The collection was sold within the year. He had given his picture of Geminiani and his own portrait to his 'faithful servant', Ann Phillips, to whom he also granted during her lifetime the use of his house in King's Row, Upper Grosvenor Street, where he had lived at least from January 1747, and his household goods. After Ann's death, they were to go to the grandnephew and nieces. To his brother William, Joseph left £10, and to each of his children, 1s. Robert Heather, coach builder, and John Stafford Smith were the executors.   L. M. MIDDLETON, *rev.* DAVID J. GOLBY

Sources Highfill, Burnim & Langhans, *BDA* • Burney, *Hist. mus.*, new edn, 2.214, 1009 • E. Careri, *Francesco Geminiani (1687–1762)* (1993) • S. Lincoln, 'Kelway, Joseph', *New Grove* • *The autobiography and correspondence of Mary Granville, Mrs Delany*, ed. Lady Llanover, 1st ser., 3 vols. (1861)
Likenesses J. Russell, pastel drawing, 1776?, NPG; repro. in Highfill, Burnim & Langhans, *BDA*, 301
Wealth at death see will, Highfill, Burnim & Langhans, *BDA*

Kelway, Thomas (*c*.1695–1749), organist and composer, was born at Chichester, Sussex, probably the son of Thomas Kelway and his wife, Ann Crosfield, of Chichester, or of Jasper Kellway and his wife, Mary Brathwait, of Windsor. Joseph *Kelway was his younger brother. He was a member of the cathedral choir at Chichester, and was seemingly a pupil of John Weldon or his master John Walter of Eton, since his compositions are said to bear traces of Weldon's influence. He received tuition on the organ from John Reading and became an apprentice organist at Chichester Cathedral in 1720 and full organist in 1733. He appears to have retained this position until his death. He may have been the Thomas Kelway who married Sarah Slaterford at St Peter the Great, Chichester, on 14 February 1726.

Kelway's printed music includes three evening services in A minor, B minor, and G minor, the last of which survives in twentieth-century editions, and two anthems, 'Not unto us' and 'Unto thee'. The library of Chichester Cathedral houses these works in manuscript, together with services in F, C, and A, and the anthems 'O praise the Lord', 'Sing we merrily', 'Sing unto God', 'The Mighty God', 'Blessed be the Lord God', and 'Let the words of my mouth'. The library of Christ Church Cathedral, Oxford, also contains two evening services in A and B minor respectively and four chants. In 1886 J. D. Brown praised the quality of Kelway's music and testified to its continued and frequent use in cathedrals and churches.

Kelway died in Chichester on 21 May 1749. After his gravestone was rediscovered a century later it was restored and placed in the south aisle of the cathedral. It is possible that Kelway had a son called Joseph, whose daughter Elizabeth is named as a grandniece in the will of his brother Joseph Kelway.   L. M. MIDDLETON, *rev.* DAVID J. GOLBY

Sources S. Lincoln, 'Kelway, Thomas', *New Grove* • J. D. Brown, *Biographical dictionary of musicians: with a bibliography of English writings on music* (1886), 355 • *MT*, 5 (1862), 134 • *IGI*

Kelynack, Theophilus Nicholas [Theo] (1866–1944), physician, was born at High Street, Wells, Somerset, on 26 June 1866, the son of a Wesleyan minister, Nicholas Kelynack, and his wife, Anne Wesley Doré. Educated at University College School, London, he studied medicine at Manchester University, graduating MB ChB with distinction in 1889. Four years later he was awarded the gold medal for his MD thesis on the pathology of the vermiform appendix. He gained the MRCP in 1895. In Manchester he served as house physician, pathologist, and medical registrar at the Manchester Royal Infirmary, as well as demonstrator and assistant lecturer in pathology and assistant to the professor of pathology and medicine at the university. It was here that he launched his writing career with a book on renal growths in 1898 and the *Pathologist's Handbook* in 1899.

After returning to London, Kelynack was appointed honorary visiting physician to the Mount Vernon Hospital for Consumption and Diseases of the Chest. His active association lasted for many years, latterly as a governor. Through his work at Mount Vernon he became an acknowledged expert on tuberculosis. Kelynack was particularly interested in the welfare of children, and he became honorary medical adviser to the Shaftesbury Society (for socially handicapped children), the Ragged School Union, the National Association for the Feeble Minded, and the National Children's Home. He was also honorary visiting physician to the home's sanatorium at Harpenden, Hertfordshire, and the Infant Hospital, Westminster. On 27 April 1904 Kelynack married Clara Violet McLaren MB ChB (1875/6–1940), daughter of James Grieve McLaren, tea broker. She later became medical secretary of the Medical Women's Federation and also assisted Kelynack in his editorial work. They had a daughter.

Kelynack's major contribution to medicine came through skilled editorship and an ability to collate current research and other useful information and make it publicly accessible. He edited the *British Journal of Tuberculosis* (1907–34), the *British Journal of Inebriety* (1903–41), and *The Child* (1910–27). In 1907 he edited *The Drink Problem of To-Day in its Medico-Sociological Aspects*; this went into a second edition in 1916 and became a classic on the subject. Among his edited volumes was *Medical Examination of Schools and Scholars* (1910), a guide for school medical officers, educationists, and others involved in child welfare. From 1910 to 1914 he edited four *National Health Manuals*. Covering infancy, childhood, school life, and youth, these presented social workers with governing principles in simple non-technical words. He did the same for those involved

Theophilus Nicholas Kelynack (1866–1944), by Lafayette, 1932

in tuberculosis work with his *Tuberculosis Year Book and Sanatoria Annual* (1913). This comprised papers on current medical research and a guide to treatment centres and preventive organizations. *The Yearbook of Open Air Schools and Children's Sanatoria* followed in 1914. In the same year he edited *Human Derelicts*, a collection of medico-sociological studies for teachers of religion and social workers.

Kelynack's own contributions to his edited volumes were based on a thorough knowledge of the subject area, and always included extensive bibliographies. Not only was he widely read but he also made a point of visiting relevant centres before writing about them. He was especially interested in the social aspects of disease, and he possessed, as his obituary in the *British Medical Journal* noted, a deep feeling of social responsibility. This was complemented by his warm, friendly, and sympathetic personality. While he believed that poverty was a predisposing factor in tuberculosis, he did not press for social or political reform.

Kelynack was elected a fellow of the Royal Society of Medicine, a member of council of the Royal Institute of Public Health and Hygiene, and he was for a number of years secretary of the institute. For many years he was honorary secretary to the Society for the Study of Inebriety, and was appointed vice-president in 1941. As justice of the peace for the county of London from 1919 he carried out his duties with the thoroughness for which he was

renowned. Kelynack died at his home, 9 Arden Grove, Harpenden, Hertfordshire, on 23 December 1944. He was survived by his daughter, Agnes, who was assistant secretary to the British Medical Association at the time of her father's death.   LINDA BRYDER

Sources *BMJ* (6 Jan 1945), 29 · *The Lancet* (13 Jan 1945), 67–8 · *The Times* (28 Dec 1944), 6 · *BMJ* (20 Jan 1945), 101–2 · b. cert. · m. cert. · d. cert.
Likenesses Lafayette, photograph, 1932 [*see illus.*]
Wealth at death £12,352 16s. 7d.: probate, 8 March 1945, *CGPLA Eng. & Wales*

Kelyng, Sir John (*bap.* 1607, *d.* 1671), judge and politician, was baptized on 19 July 1607 at All Saints', Hertford, the only son of John Kelyng (*d.* 1642), a barrister of Hertford, and his wife, Alice, daughter of Gregory Waterhouse of Halifax, Yorkshire. He matriculated from Trinity Hall, Cambridge, in 1623, and clearly decided to follow the same profession as his father, entering the Inner Temple on 22 January 1624, and being called to the bar on 10 February 1632. He practised at first in the forest courts, and soon after he became a barrister he married Martha (*d.* 1660), daughter of Sir Thomas Boteler of Biddenham, Bedfordshire. Six children of the marriage were baptized at All Saints', Hertford, between February 1634 and August 1641; three died in infancy. In 1637 Kelyng became steward of Hertford. In 1642 he refused the protestation and presided at the Hertford quarter sessions, where he urged the grand jury to present men for illegally drilling after the promulgation of the militia ordinance. When the foreman of the jury complained to the House of Commons, Kelyng was imprisoned in Ely House. He was still in prison in August 1644 when he wrote to the Bedfordshire sequestration committee to point out that he had never borne arms in the conflict. He had certainly been released by 1647, when he was acting as an attorney and living at Southill under the protection of his brother-in-law, Sir William Boteler, a member of the Bedfordshire committee.

All Kelyng's tribulations came to be an asset after the Restoration. Clarendon described him as 'a person of eminent learning [and] eminent suffering, [who] never wore his gown after the rebellion, but was always in gaol' (*HoP, Commons, 1660–90*). Kelyng's first wife died on 18 July 1660, and at some point he married Mary (*d.* 1667), daughter of William Jesson, a London draper, and the widow of Oliver Boteler of Harrold, Bedfordshire. Also in July 1660 he was one of the first group of serjeants-at-law created after the Restoration. In October 1660 Kelyng acted for the prosecution at the trials of the regicides Francis Hacker and William Heveningham. In January 1661 he presided at Bedfordshire quarter sessions which ordered the imprisonment of John Bunyan, who subsequently characterized Kelyng as 'Lord Hategood'. On 25 March 1661 Kelyng was elected to parliament for Bedford, and although his return was disputed he was allowed to take his seat. On 6 November 1661 he became a king's serjeant, and on 9 November he prosecuted John James, a Fifth Monarchist, for high treason. Kelyng was knighted on 22 January 1662. He was

Sir John Kelyng (*bap.* 1607, *d.* 1671), by Sir Peter Lely and studio, *c.*1666

appointed to many parliamentary committees, particularly on ecclesiastical matters, and was responsible for drawing up the Act of Uniformity (1662). In June 1662 he prosecuted Sir Henry Vane, to whom he exhibited 'a very snappish property' (*State trials*, 6.171).

Kelyng's career in the House of Commons was brought to an end by his elevation on 18 June 1663 to be a judge of king's bench. It proved to be a controversial appointment. He was one of the judges at the treason trials in York after the abortive rising in that county in 1663. In 1664 he outraged the Quakers so much during a trial for attending conventicles that they printed a rebuttal of the 'evil surmises, false aspersions, and unrighteous suggestions of Judge Keeling' (Stockdale, 47). On 21 November 1665 Kelyng was made chief justice of king's bench. As such he was appointed in the following year by Charles II to inquire into the origins of the great fire of London. He also sat extensively on the fire court set up to hear disputes between the lessors and lessees of damaged buildings. Kelyng's conduct as a judge has been characterized as excessively intemperate, especially towards juries, and on one occasion in 1667 this landed him in trouble with the Commons. Having disapproved of a Somerset grand jury's findings, he fined them £20 each and had an altercation with the chair of the jury, Sir Hugh Wyndham MP. Wyndham duly reported the judge to the Commons and a committee was appointed to look into 'innovations of late', including restraints upon juries and his apparently disparaging comments on Magna Carta. Kelyng was heard before the committee, but the affair was put off until after the end of term. Kelyng appeared before the house on 13

December 1667, where he acknowledged 'the failings of a man, but I cannot accuse myself of injustice, bribery or perverting or acting against the known laws' (*The Diary of John Milward*, ed. C. Robbins, 1938, 166–70). The Commons duly voted the fining and imprisoning of jurors illegal, ordered a bill to be brought in to confirm this, but agreed that no further proceedings should be taken against Kelyng 'out of particular respect to him and the mediation of a great many' (Pepys, *Diary*, 8.578). It was Kelyng's treatment of juries which led to his modern reputation as 'authoritarian' (Cromartie, 120, 238), but before the Commons he had defended the legality of his legal decisions, while remaining reticent about his treatment of Wyndham.

The death of Kelyng's second wife on 24 September 1667 had been followed on 23 March 1668 by his marriage to Elizabeth (1637/8–1691), daughter of Sir Francis Bassett of Tehidy, Illogan, Cornwall. In 1668 Kelyng presided over the trial of rioters who had destroyed some houses of ill repute, arguing that such actions were high treason because in attempting a public reformation the rioters had usurped the regal authority. On 8 November 1670 it was reported that Kelyng 'has been so ill that he has not sat on the bench this term' (*Hastings MSS*, 2.324). However, he still managed to incur the wrath of Lord Holles, who on 1 March 1671 complained to the House of Lords 'of some indignities put upon him by' Kelyng in king's bench. Kelyng was forced to apologize.

Kelyng died at his house in Hatton Garden, London, at 2 a.m. on 10 May 1671, 'after a long weakness and decay' (Campbell, 511). Kelyng's will, made on 23 January 1671 when he was already 'under some indisposition of body', referred to his two surviving younger sons from his first marriage, Thomas and Charles; four daughters from that marriage had already received their portions; it also referred to his daughter by his second marriage. Kelyng was buried on 13 May at St Andrew's, Holborn. He left a manuscript collection of reports, part of which was published by the direction of Sir John Holt as *A report of divers cases in the pleas of the crown adjudged and determined in the reign of the late King Charles* (1708, reprinted 1739 and 1789). A complete edition was published by Richard Loveland in 1873, *Sir John Kelyng's Reports of Crown Cases in the Time of King Charles*. His eldest son, Sir John *Kelyng (*bap.* 1634, *d.* 1680), became a barrister, king's counsel, and serjeant-at-law.

STUART HANDLEY

Sources HoP, *Commons, 1660–90* · E. Stockdale, 'Sir John Kelyng, chief justice of the king's bench, 1665–1671', *Miscellanea*, Bedfordshire Historical RS, 59 (1980), 43–53 · Sainty, *Judges* · Sainty, *King's counsel* · Baker, *Serjeants* · Venn, *Alum. Cant.* · will, PRO, PROB 11/336, sig. 54 · Foss, *Judges*, 7.137–40 · *Le Neve's Pedigrees of the knights*, ed. G. W. Marshall, Harleian Society, 8 (1873), 150 · John, Lord Campbell, *The lives of the chief justices of England*, 1 (1849), 503–11 · *State trials*, 5.1177, 1229; 6.76, 171 · A. F. Havighurst, 'The judiciary and politics in the reign of Charles II [pt 1]', *Law Quarterly Review*, 66 (1950), 62–78, esp. 69 · A. Cromartie, *Sir Matthew Hale, 1609–1676: law, religion and natural philosophy* (1995), 120, 133, 186, 238 · T. A. Green, *Verdict according to conscience: perspectives on the English criminal trial jury, 1200–1800* (1985), 208–21 · *Report on the manuscripts of the late Reginald Rawdon Hastings*, 4 vols., HMC, 78 (1928–47), vol. 2

Likenesses P. Lely and studio, oils, *c.*1666, Plymouth City Museum and Art Gallery [*see illus.*]

Kelyng, Sir John (*bap.* **1634**, *d.* **1680**), lawyer, was baptized on 16 February 1634 at All Saints', Hertford, the son of Sir John *Kelyng (*bap.* 1607, *d.* 1671), lord chief justice, and his wife, Martha Boteler (*d.* 1660). He was admitted to the Inner Temple in 1653 and called to the bar on 10 July 1660. By 1663, when his son John was baptized, Kelyng had married Philippa, daughter of Alessandro *Antelminelli, the resident of the duke of Tuscany at the court of Charles II. They had three sons and five daughters.

Kelyng became a bencher of the Inner Temple on 28 October 1677. His political acceptability was recognized by his appointment on 5 February 1679 as a deputy lieutenant for Bedfordshire. He was knighted on 26 October 1679, and on 24 November he became king's counsel. In February, Kelyng was mentioned as the man most likely to succeed Sir Francis Pemberton on the bench. In May 1680 he was made a serjeant-at-law, his sponsors being the earls of Ailesbury and Kent, in company with George Jeffreys and Robert Wright, and on 13 May he became king's serjeant. In August, Kelyng was rumoured to be in line to replace Lord Chief Justice Scroggs, but again he was passed over. Kelyng's elevation to the bench never in fact occurred, as he died, apparently predeceased by his wife, at his house in Southill, Bedfordshire, on 29 December 1680. He was succeeded by his son John.

STUART HANDLEY

Sources Sainty, *King's counsel* · Baker, *Serjeants* · IGI · will, PRO, PROB 11/387, sig. 50 · J. E. Martin, ed., *Masters of the bench of the Hon. Society of the Inner Temple, 1450–1883, and masters of the Temple, 1540–1883* (1883), 48 · *Le Neve's Pedigrees of the knights*, ed. G. W. Marshall, Harleian Society, 8 (1873), 150 · *CSP dom.*, 1679–80, pp. 70, 397, 597 · N. Luttrell, *A brief historical relation of state affairs from September 1678 to April 1714*, 1 (1857), 43 · *Calendar of the manuscripts of the marquess of Ormonde*, new ser., 8 vols., HMC, 36 (1902–20), vol. 5, p. 275 · W. H. Cooke, ed., *Students admitted to the Inner Temple, 1547–1660* [1878], 335

Kem, Joseph [Teddy] (*bap.* **1700**, *d.* **1780**), miser and farmer-weaver, was baptized on 14 May 1700 at Wolvey, Warwickshire, the younger son of Joseph Kem (*c.*1680–*c.*1730), butcher, and his wife, Frances (*c.*1680–1731). He was the great-great-grandson of Samuel Keme, the puritan divine and spy. Joseph's elder brother, Daniel, became a yeoman farmer at Smockington, Leicestershire, a few miles distant from Wolvey. Joseph remained in the Wolvey–Monks Kirby area of Warwickshire until he married Mary Butler on 10 April 1722 at St Mary de Castro Church in Leicester. Within a year mother and child had died during childbirth, and were interred at the parish church of St Margaret, Leicester.

Kem's early career was that of both a 'customer-weaver', with independent status in the village and making up customers' orders, and a 'smallholder weaver', working part-time at the loom. In his later life the erratic nature of the local weaving industry may have given him the status of a superior artisan, self-employed and working by the 'piece' for a choice of masters. By 1763 Kem was proprietor and farmer at Sinney Fields (valued at £3 17s. 7d.), Burton Hastings, near Attleborough. He had probably moved by 1767 and was then associated with Daniel Leigh (who managed Lord Pagett's Attleborough lands).

In 1772 and 1773 Kem was brought before the local court for failing to clean ditches and cut hedges, which was part of his tenancy agreement. This was a serious offence because the local rivers rose seasonally and the ditches were essential to flood relief. The punishments varied from public humiliation to fining. Kem was threatened twice with fines of £1 10s. 0d., a sum which no tenant farmer could have paid unless he earned extra income. The fine was not paid but Kem relented and thereafter undertook his specified duties. It was believed that he made a great deal of money, but that he hid the coins in the walls or chimney of his house while continuing to maintain a frugal lifestyle.

In 1774 Kem voted in the Warwickshire elections, giving his place of abode as Nuneaton. His voting status implied he was a 'forty-shilling freeholder', or yeoman, farming his own land and enjoying parliamentary franchise. He voted for Skipwith the whig and Mordaunt the tory. He died in February 1780 and on Tuesday 29 February was buried at St Nicolas parish church, Nuneaton, in an unmarked grave, leaving no will or descendants.

Kem's life history became well known in the nineteenth century and historians made references to this miserly character. Such austere behaviour was influenced by the *Whole Duty of Man* (1658). By 1861 George Eliot had developed the story into *Silas Marner*, with the help of her father, Robert Evans. Alfred Scrivener, a local historian and journalist, drew on literary and historical sources for his article in the *Nuneaton Observer*, on 27 December 1878. The story was reprinted in 1909 emphasizing the gold hoarding of the hermit. The local public reaction was unexpected; many people then scoured the site, looking for gold coins. Kem's farm was cited on Ordnance Survey maps from 1887 to 1966 as Teddy Kem's Heaven. The name Teddy was a local corruption of 'tedder', a person who cut grass and laid it out to dry. The farm was demolished about 1970, and the site was later developed for housing. In 2002 the local authority agreed to place a commemorative tablet there, marking the site.

ALAN F. COOK

Sources Nuneaton suit rolls and presentments, 1772 and 1773, Warks. CRO, Jodrell papers, 1765–74, Box 1 (79A) · Birm. CL, The poll of the freeholders of Warwickshire taken at Warwick, October 1774 · parish register (burials), St Nicolas, Nuneaton, Warwickshire, Nuneaton Library, 29 Feb 1780 · parish register, Wolvey, Warwickshire, 14 May 1700, Warks. CRO [baptism] · parish register, Leicester, St Margaret, 10 April 1722, Leics. RO [marriage] · parish register, Leicester, St Mary de Castro, 1723, Leics. RO [burial] · A. L. Scrivener, 'Teddy Kem's Heaven', *Nuneaton Observer*, 61 (27 Dec 1878) · A. F. Cook, 'Kem dynasty: the Hanoverian remnants in the Hinckley–Nuneaton area', *Hinckley Historian*, 32 (1993), 3–8 · A. F. Cook, *The mystery of Teddy Kem: the Attleborough recluse* (1988) · A. F. Cook, *The story of Teddy Kem's Heaven*, Attleborough (1990); rev. (1992) · G. Eliot, *Silas Marner* (1861) · Warks. CRO, Coton enclosures, 1763 (1765) · IGI

Kem, Samuel (**1604–1670**), Church of England clergyman and army officer, was born in London, the son of a cooper.

This doth but speak his outside to the eye,
Nor can express ought but Humanity:
He that surveyes his Intellect, shall finde
Health for his Soule: and Knowledge for his Minde.

Samuel Kem (1604–1670), by George Glover, 1638

Having matriculated at Oxford as a commoner of Magdalen Hall on 23 June 1621, he was elected to a demyship at Magdalen College in 1624, and graduated BA on 19 February 1625. He resigned his demyship in 1626 on being presented to a college living, and in 1628 became vicar of Newark, Nottinghamshire. In 1630 he was appointed rector of Little Chart, Kent. Created BD on 13 August 1636, he shortly afterwards became rector of Albury, Oxfordshire, and, according to Anthony Wood, chaplain to its patron, Edward Wray.

On 11 August 1640 Kem preached in St Saviour, Southwark, to the soldiers 'exercising armes in the Martiall Garden', a sermon subsequently printed as *The New Fort of True Honour Made Impregnable* (1640), urging godly life by way of a series of military metaphors. While vehement in tone, its content was conventionally reformist, but it showed that Kem was already familiar with and enamoured of military discipline. At the outbreak of the civil war he apparently put a curate into his livings and became chaplain first to the earl of Essex and then in the earl of Denbigh's regiment, where he was soon also captain of a troop of horse. He preached assiduously in support of parliament and against suspected papists and a king in thrall to evil advisers. Rising to the rank of major, he was at one time quartermaster-general to Sir Thomas Myddelton. Royalists claimed that he would preach in the morning and plunder indiscriminately in the afternoon and that he

was 'a saint in the pulpit and a devil out of it' (Wharton, 1.210).

By 1643 Kem was vicar of Low Leyton, Essex. In November 1644 he accompanied the earl of Denbigh and other parliamentary commissioners to treat with the king at Oxford, where he preached *The Messengers Preparation for an Addresse to the King for a Well-Grounded Peace*, which looked forward to a time when 'killing [could] come to kissing' (p. 10); when printed in 1644 and 1646 it included an impressively regal portrait of Charles I. Having taken the covenant, Kem revealed himself as a moderate: already by December 1645 he complained of lay preaching and strange doctrine.

When Bristol was held by parliament Kem took charge of the City regiment. His *The King of Kings* (1646), preached on 28 February 1646, urged the choice of godly burgesses in impending elections. Later that year the garrison was reduced and Kem was ordered to service at sea. His farewell sermon, *Orders Given out; the Word, Stand Fast* (1647), preached on 8 November 1646, reveals pride in his professional skill in shaping a good regiment. In Bristol he is said to have preached in a buff coat and scarlet cloak with pistols on the cushions beside him.

At sea Kem became the ally and agent of Vice-Admiral William Batten, apparently sharing his fear that the old constitution would be overthrown by the Independents and the army. After a stormy voyage to Tynemouth in January 1647 he acted as Batten's intermediary to the Scots and was invited to preach by the captive king. *An Olive Branch Found after a Storme in the Northern Seas* (1647) deplored the self-destructive divisions of the godly, proffered possible reconciliation, and pleased Charles but aroused suspicion in London. In a letter of 30 January 1647 Kem defended himself against charges of clandestine communication with a royalist agent.

In August 1647 Batten and Kem, now also parson of Deal, Kent, abetted presbyterian MPs in their flight to France after the army had driven them from parliament. In the spring and summer of 1648 Kem was in touch with the leaders of rebellion in Kent, and was instrumental in fomenting and managing the revolt of a significant portion of the parliamentary fleet in the Downs. If he accompanied Batten when he took his ships to join the prince of Wales off the Netherlands in July 1648, it would seem that he eventually played a double game, for in December 1648 he reported from Rotterdam on royalists' movements, and in May 1649 was employed by the council of state on unspecified state business. On 18 November 1650 he was arrested for corresponding with Major James Greenstreet, 'a traitor', but released on 28 November. By 1651 Kem had resigned his living of Low Leyton, while retaining Albury. Continuing in his dual character of 'parson Major Kem' (Powell and Timings, 285), he served in Scotland as major of a regiment of horse in 1654 and was incorporated BD at Cambridge in 1658.

In April 1660 Kem preached in Gloucester on the Sunday before the elections *King Solomon's Infallible Expedient for Three Kingdoms Settlement* (1660), declaring that 'Monarchy

[was] the very best Government ... to the People's Security, Peace and Indemnity' (*King Solomon's Infallible Expedient*, 2). In June and July he was commissioned chaplain in two foot regiments. Conforming in 1662, he kept his living of Albury, although he was absent during the 1665–7 Dutch War, commanding a privateer. Anthony Wood attributed the twists and turns of Kem's durable career to servility, greed, and general bad character, but while he was a restless and acquisitive pluralist who found his true metier as a soldier, Kem's progression from parliamentary enthusiasm through disillusion to endorsement of the Restoration was typical of many of his contemporaries. He died at Albury on 22 October 1670, and was buried two days later in the church near an inscription to the three wives who had predeceased him, Anne, daughter of John Ball, citizen and skinner of London, Jemima, said by Anthony Wood to be the daughter of Herbert Pelham of Lincolnshire and Essex and Jemima Waldegrave, and Mary, daughter of Samuel Bridger of Dursley, Gloucestershire. He left a young widow, Elizabeth, two sons, and two daughters.   BARBARA DONAGAN

Sources Wood, *Ath. Oxon.*, new edn · *Mercurius Aulicus* (20 July 1644) · *Mercurius Aulicus* (27 July 1644) · *CSP dom.*, 1641–3; 1649–50 · A. Laurence, *Parliamentary army chaplains, 1642–1651*, Royal Historical Society Studies in History, 59 (1990) · B. Capp, *Cromwell's navy: the fleet and the English revolution, 1648–1660* (1989) · J. R. Powell and E. K. Timings, eds., *Documents relating to the civil war, 1642–1648*, Navy RS, 105 (1963) · Fourth report, HMC, 3 (1874) [earl of Denbigh, pt 1] · H. Wharton, ed., *The history of the troubles and tryal of ... William Laud*, 1 (1695) · *The diary of Ralph Josselin, 1616–1683*, ed. A. MacFarlane, British Academy, Records of Social and Economic History, new ser., 3 (1976), 399n. · Venn, *Alum. Cant.* · A. R. Maddison, ed., *Lincolnshire pedigrees*, 3, Harleian Society, 52 (1904), 768
Likenesses G. Glover, line engraving, 1638, BM, NPG [*see illus.*]
Wealth at death small estate with no real property: will, PRO, PROB 11/334

Kemball, Sir Arnold Burrowes (1820–1908), army officer, born in Bombay on 18 November 1820, was one of five sons of Surgeon-General Vero Clarke Kemball of the Bombay medical staff and his wife, Marianne, daughter of Major-General Shaw of the Black Watch. Kemball's brothers all served in the Bombay presidency: George and Alick in the Bombay cavalry, Vero Seymour in the Bombay artillery, Charles Gordon in the civil service, and John in the 26th Bombay infantry.

Educated at the military college at Addiscombe (1836–7), Kemball was commissioned second lieutenant in the Bombay artillery on 11 December 1837. He served in the First Anglo-Afghan War, and was at the capture of Ghazni (28 July 1839) and the occupation of Kabul. On the march back to Bombay he took part in the capture of the fortress of Kalat.

After Kemball's return to the Bombay presidency he was promoted first lieutenant (17 August 1841), passed his examinations in oriental languages, and was appointed assistant political agent in the Persian Gulf. He remained in the region from 1842 until the close of his military career in 1878. He was promoted captain on 28 February 1851, took part in the Anglo-Persian War of 1856–7, and was mentioned in the dispatches of Sir James Outram, who

had applied for his services. Lord Canning, the governor-general of India, especially commended his share in the expedition against Ahvaz. For the Persian campaign Kemball received the brevet of major (19 January 1858) and the CB.

At the close of the war Kemball resumed his political duties in the gulf, and in 1859 was appointed consul-general at Baghdad. He took a particular interest in schemes for the construction of a railway from Constantinople to the Persian Gulf, and was involved with the Euphrates valley scheme. He became lieutenant-colonel on 11 April 1860, and on 1 September 1863 attained the rank of colonel in the Royal Artillery. He was appointed KCSI in 1866, and major-general on 6 March 1868.

On 29 December 1868 Kemball married his cousin Anna Frances (Fanny), daughter of Alexander Nesbitt Shaw of the Bombay civil service. They had three daughters, of whom only one, Wynford Rose, survived. She married Bentley Lyonel, third Baron Tollemache, in 1902. Kemball's wife survived him.

In 1873 Kemball was attached to the shah of Persia during his visit to England. In 1875 he served as British delegate on the international commission on the Turco-Persian frontier. On the outbreak of the war between Turkey and Serbia in July 1876 he was appointed military commissioner with the Turkish army in the field. He was present at all the operations in the vicinity of Nisch and Alexinatz, and at the close of the campaign was nominated president of the international commission to delimit the frontiers between Turkey and Serbia. His knowledge of the Turkish language and calmness under fire endeared him to the Turkish soldiery.

In the spring of 1877, on the outbreak of the Russo-Turkish War, Kemball was appointed military commissioner with the Turkish army in Asia. The Turks continued to show the fullest confidence in him, and he was praised by the British press: 'Wherever the fire was hottest ... there ... [was] invariably to be found ... Lieutenant-General Sir Arnold Kemball' (*The Times*, 20 July 1878). The Russians knew his reputation with the Turks and, like the Serbians previously, assumed he commanded the Turkish forces. After the battle of Tahir on 16 June 1877 they attempted to capture him. Cossacks pursued him over 20 miles, and he daringly swam across the Araxes River to find shelter in a Turkish camp. He protested against Kurdish atrocities, and urged the Ottoman commander-in-chief to suppress them. He was made KCB (29 July 1878) and was promoted lieutenant-general on 1 October 1877.

On Kemball's return to England in 1878, he was made colonel-commandant of the Royal Artillery at Woolwich. He was designated military adviser to Lord Beaconsfield's special mission to the Berlin congress that year, but his uncompromising objection to the cession of Batumi to Russia led to the withdrawal of this offer. He was promoted full general (retired list) on 26 February 1880.

After retiring from active service Kemball was prominently associated with Sir William Mackinnon and others in the development of east Africa, and was one of the founders and first directors in 1888 of the Imperial British

East Africa Company. After the cost of the expedition led by Frederick Lugard nearly bankrupted the company, Kemball argued strongly for a British protectorate in Uganda. He was also prominent in support of the extension of the Uganda Railway from Mombasa to Lake Victoria. Kemball died at his London residence, 62 Lowndes Square, Knightsbridge, on 21 September 1908, and was buried in Kensal Green cemetery.

C. B. NORMAN, rev. ALEX MAY

Sources Army List · Hart's Army List · Indian Army List · The Times (10 Jan 1878) · The Times (21 June 1878) · The Times (20 Sept 1892) · The Times (22 Sept 1908) · E. Lodge, Peerage, baronetage, knightage and companionage of the British empire, 81st edn, 3 vols. (1912) · F. W. M. Spring, The Bombay artillery (1902) · J. C. Dalton, 'The Bombay horse artillery in Persia and the mutiny, 1857–59', Journal of the Royal Artillery, 52 (1926), 556–61 · G. H. Hunt, Outram and Havelock's Persian campaign (1858) · Civil Service List · F. J. Goldsmid, James Outram: a biography, 2nd edn, 2 vols. (1881) · C. B. Norman, Armenia and the campaign of 1877 (1878) · C. Williams, The Armenian campaign (1878) · J. S. Galbraith, Mackinnon and east Africa, 1878–1895: a study in the new imperialism (1972) · P. L. McDermott, British East Africa (1893) · E. R. Vere-Hodge, Imperial British East Africa Company (1960) · H. M. Vibart, Addiscombe: its heroes and men of note (1894)

Archives Staffs. RO, corresp. as estate commissioner | BL, corresp. with Sir A. H. Layard, Add. MSS 38942–39147 · Bodl. RH, corresp. with Lord Lugard · NL Scot., letters to Sir Henry Elliot · SOAS, corresp. with Sir William Mackinnon

Likenesses C. Silvy, photograph, 1860, NPG · Ape [C. Pellegrini], chromolithograph caricature, NPG; repro. in VF (1878) · wood-engraving, NPG; repro. in ILN (29 Sept 1877)

Wealth at death £61,735 14s. 11d.: resworn probate, 21 Oct 1908, CGPLA Eng. & Wales

Kemball-Cook, Sir Basil Alfred. See Cook, Sir Basil Alfred Kemball- (1876–1949).

Kemble, Mrs. See Furnival, Elizabeth (fl. 1731–1752).

Kemble [married name Sartoris], **Adelaide** (1815–1879), singer and author, was born into a celebrated theatrical family in London on 6 November 1815, the youngest of the five children of Charles *Kemble (1775–1854) and his wife, Maria Theresa *Kemble, née De Camp (1777–1838). She was six years younger than her only sister, the actress Fanny *Kemble (1809–1893), who followed Adelaide's career with solicitude and described various episodes in their childhood in her Records of a Girlhood (1878).

Adelaide Kemble, who studied music with John Braham, sang professionally for the first time at a Concert of Ancient Music on 13 May 1835 and appeared at the York festival in the following September; her performance of Handel's music was affected by nerves, and she went to Paris for further training before visiting Germany in 1837. She remained on the continent until 1841, studying in Italy with the composer Saverio Mercadante and the soprano Giuditta Pasta. She sang at La Scala, Milan, in 1838, and made her first appearance in opera at La Fenice, Venice, in the same year, as Norma. She was extremely well received, and began to be compared with Pasta; although her soprano voice lacked the weight of the Italian singer, she was to be praised for the intelligence of her interpretation and her powers as an actress. She went on to perform to great acclaim in other Italian cities, until in 1841 the serious illness of her father returned her to England.

Adelaide Kemble (1815–1879), by Camille Silvy, 1860

Kemble sang at a charity concert at Stafford House, London, in June 1841, and appeared in an English version of Norma on 2 November 1841 at Covent Garden. She received even greater praise for Mercadante's Elena da Feltre in January 1842, an opera which had failed in Italy but which her performance carried through triumphantly in the English version. During the 1842 season she sang Susanna in The Marriage of Figaro and Caroline in Cimarosa's Il matrimonio segreto, as well as appearing in La sonnambula and Semiramide at Covent Garden, and at the Philharmonic and Ancient concerts. She retired from the stage at the end of the year, her final performance being as Norma at Covent Garden on 23 December 1842.

Kemble's retirement was occasioned by her marriage, to Edward John Sartoris (1814–1888), in Glasgow on 25 July 1842. His father was a wealthy French banker, while his mother came from the English landed gentry, and the demands of respectability barred Adelaide from further professional appearances, although she continued to sing privately in fashionable drawing-rooms. She found a further outlet as an author: 'A Week in a French Country House', published in Cornhill and in book form in 1867, was appreciated for its humour and freshness. Medusa and other Tales appeared in 1868, and was republished in 1880 as Past Hours. Adelaide and Edward Sartoris and their three children spent much of their time at their house near the

Trinità dei Monti in Rome, but it was at their English home, Warsash House, Titchfield, Hampshire, that she died on 6 August 1879.

Adelaide Kemble had, in her youth, an imposing figure, with classical, finely chiselled features, and wore her hair in a Renaissance bun with elaborate ornaments. She attracted many admirers, including Frederic Leighton and the fifth duke of Portland. In maturity, like her sister Fanny, she became stout. Her short career was a source of chauvinistic pride to British audiences, who rejoiced in finding so technically accomplished a singer among their compatriots at a time when the operatic stage was dominated by continental performers.

L. M. MIDDLETON, rev. K. D. REYNOLDS

Sources F. A. Kemble, *Record of a girlhood*, 3 vols. (1878) · *The Athenaeum* (3 July 1841), 510 · *The Athenaeum* (16 Aug 1879), 208 · Mrs C. Baron-Wilson, *Our actresses*, 2 vols. (1844) · P. Fitzgerald, *The Kembles: an account of the Kemble family*, 2 vols. (1871) · *Morning Chronicle* (3 Nov 1841) · C. B. Hogan, 'The Kemble family: a genealogical record, 1704–1925', *Theatre Notebook*, 30 (1976), 103–9 · S. D'Amico, ed., *Enciclopedia dello spettacolo*, 11 vols. (Rome, 1954–68) · J. R. Planché, *The recollections and reflections of J. R. Planché*, 2 vols. (1872) · H. F. Chorley, *Thirty years' musical recollections*, 2 vols. (1862) · C. E. Pascoe, ed., *The dramatic list*, 2nd edn (1880) · F. A. Kemble, *Records of later life*, 3 vols. (1882) · F. A. Kemble, *Further records, 1848–1883: a series of letters*, 2 vols. (1890) · d. cert. · *CGPLA Eng. & Wales* (1879) · L. Ormond and R. Ormond, *Lord Leighton* (1975)

Archives Ches. & Chester ALSS, letters to Rhoda Broughton

Likenesses C. Silvy, photograph, 1860, NPG [*see illus.*] · F. L. Rhys, portrait?, 1895 · J. & C. Cook, engraving (after photograph by J. M. Wright), repro. in *Ladies Companion*, 2nd ser., 3 (1853), 133 · J. & C. Cook, engraving (after photograph by J. M. Wright), repro. in *The Court Magazine and Belle Assemblée*, 18 (1843), 1 · Dantan, bust; formerly in possession of the marquess of Titchfield, 1843 · F. Leighton, pencil study · L. & R. Ormond, caricature · J. G. & E. Short, photograph, NPG · eighteen prints, Harvard TC · lithograph, NPG · miniatures; formerly in possession of the marquess of Titchfield, 1843 · portrait, repro. in *Cruickshank's omnibus* (1842), 238 · portrait?, repro. in Baron-Wilson, *Our actresses* · prints, BM, NPG

Wealth at death under £2000: probate, 21 Aug 1879, *CGPLA Eng. & Wales*

Kemble, Charles

Kemble, Charles (1775–1854), actor, theatre manager, and playwright, was born on 25 November 1775 in Brecon, south Wales, the eleventh child of Roger *Kemble (1722–1802) and his wife, Sarah, *née* Ward (1735–1807), respectively manager and leading actress of a company of strolling players. In a family which also contained two of the greatest performers of their generation, Sarah *Siddons and John Philip *Kemble, and three other siblings engaged in stage careers, including Ann Julia *Hatton and Stephen George *Kemble, the theatrical milieu was inescapable. Yet John Kemble, eighteen years Charles's senior and effectively his mentor and surrogate father, whose influence extended well into adulthood, in an attempt to quell any theatrical ambitions, sent him when he was thirteen to his old school, the Jesuit college in Douai, France, to receive the classical education befitting a gentleman rather than a player. When Charles left Douai at the age of sixteen, John found him employment in the Post Office; but he was restless, and a year later, resisting all contrary advice, took to the stage. His first recorded

Charles Kemble (1775–1854), by Henry Perronet Briggs, 1830s

appearance was at Sheffield in late 1792 as Orlando in *As You Like It*, which was followed by performances in Newcastle, Edinburgh, and elsewhere; but within a year he migrated to Drury Lane.

Kemble's London début (21 April 1794), as Malcolm in his brother's production of *Macbeth*—John played the title role and Sarah Siddons Lady Macbeth—earned him, according to Robson (a self-confessed 'warm partizan of the Kemble school of acting'), despite his classic good looks, the description of 'a *complete stick*' (Robson, 6, 41). Although he lacked early promise, his possession of the Kemble name proved to be his passport to theatrical opportunity; but it was also a limitation in that professionally he lingered under John's shadow for more than twenty years. None the less Kemble's early career benefited enormously from his brother's supervision, which demanded of him 'a probation as strict and regular' as prescribed 'to the least gifted of his associates' (Donne, 158–9). Much attracted to Shakespeare, Kemble soon graduated at Drury Lane to Bassanio, Laertes, and Hotspur (1795–6), followed by Ferdinand (1796–7) and Prince Hal (1797–8), complementing in each case his brother's principal roles. An early and continuing success was Cassio (Drury Lane, September 1797), which even W. C. Macready came to admire for the drunk scene. In 1799 Kemble, supporting his brother and sister, acted Alonzo in Drury Lane's runaway success, Sheridan's adaptation from Kotzebue, *Pizarro*. Reviewing a revival, the *Monthly Mirror* (November 1807) remarked on the 'good sense, judgment, and correctness, [which] wait upon [Kemble's] acting, and where he fails 'tis nature's fault'. On 2 July 1806, after an engagement lasting six years, Kemble married the Drury

Lane actress Maria Theresa De Camp (1777–1838) [*see* Kemble, Maria Theresa] at St George's, Bloomsbury. They had five children, of whom four survived infancy: John Mitchell *Kemble, Frances Anne (Fanny) *Kemble, Henry Vincent James Kemble (1812–1857), and Adelaide *Kemble.

Although it began uncertainly, and although he was reluctant to compete with his brother in the principal Shakespearian roles, Kemble's career was one of continuous development: in 1825 he was regarded as having 'improved in his acting, every season, for the last thirty years' (*Oxberry*, 3). His Jaffeir in *Venice Preserv'd* (first attempted in 1805) was described by Hazlitt as having 'very considerable effect' at Covent Garden in 1815 (*Complete Works*, 5.262); indeed, he rivalled Edmund Kean in the role. At his Drury Lane benefit (19 May 1803), Kemble made a 'chaste and animated' Hamlet (*Monthly Mirror*, June 1803). Even though he did not play the part regularly until after his brother's retirement in 1817, the same character delighted audiences in New York and elsewhere in 1832, when Kemble was nearly sixty; and at the Haymarket in 1835 Marston was impressed at his harmony of the 'contrasts of impetuosity and inaction, of pensiveness and passion, of amiability and irony' (Marston, 79). Kemble also achieved acclaim for Mark Antony, Faulconbridge, and an animated Mercutio; but Donne suggests that Hamlet was 'perhaps [his] greatest achievement as an actor' (Donne, 175).

Although he had serious competitors in Junius Brutus Booth, Thomas Cooper, and James Wallack, after the death in 1823 of his brother Kemble was usually ranked third, after Kean and Macready, especially in tragedy. While contemporary comedy was reportedly 'too light for him' (*Oxberry*, 12), he was unrivalled in the legitimate comic repertory, in roles as varied as Mirabel, Dorimant, Jack Absolute, and Charles Surface.

As a playwright Kemble's success was more uneven. His drama *The Point of Honour* (from Mercier, *Le déserteur*, modified to provide a happy ending) came out in 1800 (Haymarket, 15 July), with Kemble as the hero, Durimel, and his wife as Bertha Melfort. The most powerful of Kemble's dramatic pieces, certainly the strongest written—'vigorous and elegant', said *Biographia dramatica*—it was several times revived up to 1849 in Britain and the USA. In 1808 *The Wanderer* (from Kotzebue) was staged at Covent Garden (12 January), which, after objections from the censor, Kemble translated from the politically sensitive Scotland of the Young Pretender to Sweden. It was revived in its original Scots colours as *The Royal Fugitive* (26 November 1829). His farce *Plot and Counterplot, or, The Portrait of Michel Cervantes* (Haymarket, 30 June 1808), adapted from Dieulafoi, had the longest run of all. Several other pieces—*Kamchatka, or, The Slave's Tribute* (16 October 1811), *The Child of Chance* (8 July 1812), *The Brazen Bust* (29 May 1813), *Proof Presumptive* (20 October 1818)—had no success on the stage and were never printed. A condensed version of Shakespeare's tripartite *Henry VI*, never performed, was published posthumously in 1890. The farce *A Budget of Blunders* (Philadelphia, 1811, 1823) is a spurious attribution.

With the exception of provincial engagements from 1813 to 1815, the occasional continental tour, and summer seasons at the Haymarket, from 1804 Kemble was for more than thirty years associated with Covent Garden, of which his brother John owned one-sixth of the share capital. In November 1820 this was given to Kemble, and on 11 March 1822, after Henry Harris resigned, he headed a new management committee of principal shareholders. Thus he became fatally involved as actor–manager in a theatre financially on its knees and morally bankrupted by its continued defence of the indefensible principle of the patent-theatre monopoly. His aggressive strategy to reduce day-to-day expenses and the crippling debts meant that authors were not properly paid and actors' salaries were cut. Several leading performers, including Macready, quit in disgust. One bright spot was Kemble's pioneering production of *King John* (November 1823), which, in collaboration with J. R. Planché, was dressed with historical accuracy, thereby setting a fashion for antiquarianism in Shakespearian production. In October 1829 the theatre, on the brink of financial catastrophe, was temporarily saved by a triumphant *Romeo and Juliet*, with Kemble's daughter Fanny making her astonishing stage début as heroine and her father, for propriety, playing Mercutio for the first time instead of the leading role, normally another of his great successes. After his recovery from a life-threatening lung infection in 1831, he relinquished management duties at the close of the season and began a highly successful tour of North America (September 1832–June 1834) to restore the family's fortunes. Father and daughter were mobbed by enthusiastic audiences and, as in London, circulated in the most fashionable society.

Kemble's appointment as examiner of plays on 27 October 1836, succeeding George Colman junior, led the manager of Drury Lane, Alfred Bunn, to object angrily to 'a performer and proprietor of the rival house [being] deputed to sit in judgment upon the *productions of this*' (Bunn, 2.151). But two months later Kemble terminated his professional engagements with a witty, tender farewell performance as Benedick in *Much Ado about Nothing* (23 December). Kemble believed at least in political censorship—he claimed in 1832 that audiences 'are better guardians of their own moral and religious sentiments than anybody can be for them' ('Select committee', question 708)—but, in the event, as censor, did not interfere at all. It seems he regarded the examinership as a reward for family services to the theatre. Dogged by illness, he was abroad for long periods (including most of 1838) to recover his health, while his son John Mitchell Kemble deputized for him. After more illness in late 1839 Kemble petitioned the lord chamberlain in January to keep the office in the family by transferring it to his son. This was effected on 22 February 1840. That year Kemble made his last formal appearance on stage, at Covent Garden, in a series of favourite characters at the special request of the queen.

Against all advice, Kemble resumed management of Covent Garden for a short time during the 1842–3 season, notable for a grand though damagingly costly production of *The Tempest*, but his theatrical career was nearly over. During his last years in public life he read *Cymbeline* before the queen at Buckingham Palace in April 1844 and in May gave a series of popular readings of Shakespeare in Willis's Rooms, London, which were repeated on several occasions between 1845 and 1848. These were collected and published posthumously in 1870.

Kemble was about 5 feet 11 inches tall, proportionately built, with the 'decidedly Roman countenance' (*Oxberry*, 14) that tended to characterize the family. A classical actor like his brother, Kemble lacked John's grandeur, but also some of his stiffness. While having little of Kean's physicality, he was known for his expressiveness and a quality of introspection suited equally to the title character in Thompson's *The Stranger* or to Hamlet. Overall his range of success in comedy and tragedy was considerable—the widest, said Donne, since Garrick. Although Macready despised him as 'a mere actor, *and not a very good one*, of *second and third rate parts*' (*Diaries*, 1.383), most contemporaries saw him as a dignified and worthy representative of the great Kemble–Siddons tradition.

Like his elder brother, Kemble had a reputation as a womanizer, even after his marriage. Off stage Kemble was courteous, urbane, even old-fashioned in manners: his assault in 1830 on Charles Molloy Westmacott, editor of *The Age*, for libel on Fanny, was uncharacteristic. A good modern linguist and a great traveller, he had a wide circle of friends, drawn mostly from scholarly and artistic society. He was a keen member of the Garrick Club. After 1848 advancing deafness, however, isolated him from many social pleasures. He died at home in Savile Row, London, on 12 November 1854 and was buried at Kensal Green cemetery.   JOHN RUSSELL STEPHENS

Sources *Oxberry's Dramatic Biography*, 3/33 (1825), 1–14 · D. E. Baker, *Biographia dramatica, or, A companion to the playhouse*, rev. I. Reed, new edn, rev. S. Jones, 1 (1812), 421–2 · *The Times* (15 Nov 1854) · *ILN* (18 Nov 1854) · *GM*, 2nd ser., 43 (1855), 94–6 · W. B. Donne, 'Charles Kemble', *Fortnightly Review* (Dec 1854); repr. in *Essays on the drama* (1858), 156–86 · J. W. Marston, *Our recent actors*, new edn (1890), 74–98 · W. Robson, *The old play-goer* (1846), [40]–50 · J. Williamson, *Charles Kemble: man of the theatre* [1970] · 'Select committee on dramatic literature', *Parl. papers* (1831–2), 7.1–252, no. 679 · *The complete works of William Hazlitt*, ed. P. P. Howe, 5 (1930) · *The complete works of William Hazlitt*, ed. P. P. Howe, 18 (1933) · *The diaries of William Charles Macready, 1833–1851*, ed. W. Toynbee, 2 vols. (1912) · *ILN* (15 Oct 1842), 364 · J. R. Stephens, *The censorship of English drama, 1824–1901* (1980) · A. Bunn, *The stage: both before and behind the curtain*, 3 vols. (1840) · A. Nicoll, *Early nineteenth century drama, 1800–1850*, 2nd edn (1955), vol. 4 of *A history of English drama, 1660–1900* (1952–9); repr. (1967–76) · J. Shattock, ed., *The Cambridge bibliography of English literature*, 3rd edn, 4 (1999) · Hall, *Dramatic ports.* · Highfill, Burnim & Langhans, *BDA* · *Henry James: letters*, ed. L. Edel, 3: *1883–1895* (1980), 400

Archives BL, accounts and memoranda, Add. MS 31976 · Folger, promptbooks · Harvard TC, letters · Hunt. L., Larpent MSS, licensing copies of plays · Theatre Museum, London, letters | BL, letters to George Colman, Add. MSS 42865–42901 *passim* · BL, letters to third Lord Holland and Lady Holland, Add. MSS 51834–51856 · BL, letter-book of Henry Robertson, containing letters from Kemble to performers and others, Add. MS 29643

Likenesses H. P. Briggs, oils, *c*.1830–1839, NPG [*see illus.*] · T. Sully, oils, 1833 (as Fazio in *Fazio*), Pennsylvania Academy of Fine Arts, Philadelphia · E. Davis, bust, 1836 · R. J. Lane, sixteen lithographs, 1840 · W. H. Nightingale, pencil drawing, 1840, Harvard TC · T. Butler, bust, 1844 · H. Andrews, double portrait (with Fanny Kemble), Royal Shakespeare Company Picture Gallery, Stratford upon Avon, Warwickshire · P. Audinet, engraving (as Young Wilmot in *The Fatal Curiosity*; after Roberts), repro. in Cawthorne, *British Library* (1796) · H. P. Briggs, oils, Dulwich Picture Gallery, London · H. P. Briggs, two oil portraits, Garr. Club · T. Chapman, engraving (as Lorenzo in *The mistake*; after Moses), repro. in *British Drama* (1808) · T. Clark, portrait (as Laertes?) · G. Clint, oils (as Charles II in *The merry monarch*), Garr. Club · H. R. Cook, engraving (as Giraldi Fazio in *Fazio*), repro. in *The Drama, or, Theatrical Pocket Magazine* (1821) · H. R. Cook, engraving (as Sebastian in *The renegade*; after S. De Wilde), repro. in *Theatrical Inquisitor and Monthly Mirror*, 9 (1816) · G. Cruikshank, engraving (as Giraldo Fazio in *Fazio*), repro. in *British Stage* (March 1818) · I. R. Cruikshank, engraving (as Friar Michael in *Maid Marion*), repro. in *Mirror of the Stage* (1 April 1823) · J. L. Dantan, bust; formerly in possession of the marquess of Titchfield, 1843 · S. De Wilde, engraving (as Sigismund in *The wanderer*), Harvard TC · S. De Wilde, pencil and chalk drawing, BM · S. De Wilde, watercolour, Harvard TC · G. H. Harlow, group portrait, oils (*Court for the trial of Queen Catherine*), Royal Shakespeare Company Picture Gallery, Stratford upon Avon, Warwickshire · T. Kearsley, portrait (as Hamlet), Garr. Club · R. J. Lane, engraving (as Don Felix; after R. J. Lane), repro. in *ILN* (15 Oct 1842) · L. MacDonald, bust · A. Mortimer, oils (as Macbeth), Garr. Club · A. Morton, oils (as Macbeth), Garr. Club · W. T. Page, engraving (as Pierre in *Venice preserv'd*; after R. Cruikshank), repro. in *Figaro in London* (14 Jan 1837) · W. Ridley, engraving (as Laertes; after T. Clark), repro. in *Monthly Mirror* (May 1802) · J. Rogers, engraving (as Romeo; after R. Page), repro. in *Oxberry's Dramatic Biography* · J. Thomson, engraving, repro. in *European Magazine* (1822) · J. Thomson, engraving (as Romeo; after Cowell), repro. in *Oxberry's New English Drama*, 6 (1819) · J. Thomson, engraving (as Vincentio [error for Romeo]; after A. Wivell), repro. in W. Oxberry, ed., *The new English drama*, 14 (1821) · A. Wivell, oils (as Romeo), Garr. Club · T. Woolnoth, engraving (as Faulconbridge; after drawing by T. Wageman), repro. in W. Oxberry, ed., *The new English drama*, 7 (1819) · H. Wyatt, oils, Royal Shakespeare Company Picture Gallery, Stratford upon Avon, Warwickshire · engraving (after bust by T. Butler), repro. in *ILN* (8 Nov 1854) · prints, BM, NPG · silhouette, Garr. Club · watercolour (as Malcolm or Macbeth), Garr. Club · watercolours, Garr. Club · watercolours, Harvard TC

Kemble [*née* Satchell], **Elizabeth** (1762/3–1841), actress, born in Great Pulteney Street, Golden Square, London, was the daughter of a musical instrument maker named John Satchell, of Great Pulteney Street, Golden Square. She had at least three sisters, all of whom made attempts on the stage. Her first recorded appearance took place at Covent Garden, on 21 September 1780, as Polly in *The Beggar's Opera*. She also played Patty in *The Maid of the Mill*, and other parts. In the following season she was promoted to Margaret in Philip Massinger's *A New Way to Pay Old Debts*, Juliet, Ophelia, and Celia in *As You Like It*, and took several characters of some importance in new pieces.

On 24 September 1783, after she had begun to play leading business, Elizabeth Satchell appeared as Desdemona to the Othello of Stephen George *Kemble (1758–1822). They were married two months later, on 20 November 1783, at St George's, Bloomsbury. The favour Mrs Kemble won in public estimation was not shared by her husband, whom, to the regret of the management and the town, she accompanied on his enforced migrations. Her career consisted indeed in playing to and eclipsing her husband, with whom she appeared in Edinburgh, Glasgow, Newcastle, and other towns. She spent summer seasons at the Haymarket from 1787 to 1796. On 4 August 1787 she was the first Yarico in the younger George Colman's *Inkle and*

Elizabeth Kemble (1762/3–1841), by Samuel De Wilde, in or before 1791 [as Imoinda in *Oroonoko, or, The Royal Slave* by Thomas Southerne]

Yarico, and on 10 July 1788 she played the original Harriet in *Ways and Means*.

Mrs Kemble's repertory in London and the country was very large and consisted of more than 150 roles. She played characters as diverse as Lady Teazle in *The School for Scandal*, Cowslip in *The Agreeable Surprize*, Roxalana in *The Sultan*, and Portia in *The Merchant of Venice*. By her prudence and exertions she contributed to her husband's fortune.

James Boaden supplied a pleasing picture of the actress:

> The stage never in my time exhibited so pure, so interesting a candidate as Miss Satchell. … No one ever like her presented the charm of unsuspecting fondness or that rustic simplicity which, removed immeasurably from vulgarity, betrays nothing of the world's refinement. (*Siddons*, 1.214)

Equally favourable testimony is borne by John Wilson in *Blackwood's Magazine* (April 1832), who said there were few more delightful actresses, and declared that her eyes 'had an unconsciously alluring expression of innocence and voluptuousness'. He further claimed for her genius rather than talent, spoke of her clear, silvery voice, and praised her Katherine in *Katherine and Petruchio* and her Ophelia. She sang with much feeling, but was less gentle than she appeared. Displays of temper on the stage were not unknown, and she once almost bit a piece out of the shoulder of Henry Erskine Johnston, who was acting with her.

Elizabeth and Stephen Kemble had three children:

George Kemble, who died in infancy, Frances Crawford Kemble (1787–1849), who acted for some years before marrying Robert Arkwright in 1805, and Henry Stephen *Kemble (1789–1836), who performed in London during the first decades of the nineteenth century.

On 20 January 1841, nineteen years after the death of her husband, Elizabeth Kemble died, in retirement, at the Grove, near Durham, and was buried on 25 January by his side in Durham Cathedral.

JOSEPH KNIGHT, *rev.* K. A. CROUCH

Sources Highfill, Burnim & Langhans, *BDA* · C. B. Hogan, ed., *The London stage, 1660–1800*, pt 5: *1776–1800* (1968) · J. Boaden, *Memoirs of Mrs Siddons*, 2nd edn, 2 vols. (1831) · T. Plain [M. Thriepland], *Letters respecting the performances at the Theatre Royal, Edinburgh, originally addressed to the editor of the Scots Chronicle* (1800) · *Thespian Magazine* (Sept 1972) · *GM*, 2nd ser., 15 (1841), 331 · J. Wilson, 'Miss Fanny Kemble's tragedy', *Blackwood*, 31 (1832), 673–92 · T. Wilkinson, *The wandering patentee, or, A history of the Yorkshire theatres from 1770 to the present time*, 4 vols. (1795) · *The thespian dictionary, or, Dramatic biography of the present age*, 2nd edn (1805) · T. Gilliland, *The dramatic mirror, containing the history of the stage from the earliest period, to the present time*, 2 vols. (1808)

Likenesses S. De Wilde, oils, in or before 1791 (as Imoinda in *Oroonoko*), Garr. Club [*see illus.*] · Barlow, double portrait, engraving (as Yarico with J. Palmer as Inkle; after Cruikshank), repro. in J. Roach (1790) [an edition of Colman's play *Inkle and Yarico*] · J. Goldar, line engraving, BM; repro. in *General Magazine and Impartial Review* (1790) · W. Leney, engraving (as Imoinda; after S. De Wilde), repro. in J. Bell, ed., *Bell's British theatre* (1791) · M. A. Shee, oils (as Cowslip), repro. in Highfill, Burnim & Langhans, *BDA* · C. H. Sherwin, line engraving (as Juliet in *Romeo and Juliet*; after J. H. Ramberg), BM; repro. in *Bell's British Theatre* (1785) · four prints, Harvard TC

Kemble [*married name* Butler]**, Frances Anne** [Fanny] (1809–1893), actress and author, was born on 27 November 1809 in Newman Street, London, not far from Covent Garden, the centre of the life of her theatrical family. Her parents were Charles *Kemble (1775–1854) and Maria Theresa *Kemble, *née* De Camp (1777–1838), both prominent actors, and her father was also the manager of Covent Garden Theatre. She was their second child and the elder daughter among four children. Her father's elder brother was John Philip *Kemble, the foremost male tragedian of his generation, and his sister was Sarah *Siddons, one of the most famous English-speaking actresses of all time. At least twenty-two of their close relatives were occupied full time in the theatre, and a dozen of them had entries in the *Dictionary of National Biography*. The talents of Fanny Kemble and her brothers and sister were particularly noticeable: she herself reigned for several years as the brightest of the young actresses of her day before beginning a brilliant career as monologist and a whole new life as a writer; her younger sister Adelaide *Kemble was widely accounted one of the greatest singers England had ever produced; her elder brother John Mitchell *Kemble was an eminent Anglo-Saxon scholar; and—not too surprisingly in this flamboyant family—her younger brother, Henry, distinguished chiefly for his personal beauty, died in a lunatic asylum, perhaps of venereal disease. The parents and children were fond of each other, but Fanny's father and mother seemed hopelessly unable to squeeze their

Frances Anne Kemble (1809–1893), by Thomas Sully, 1833

oversized personalities into the same house with any comfort.

Education and early career Fanny Kemble was educated partly at schools in Bath, Boulogne, and Paris, but learned even more in her irregular reading with her odd but highly intelligent and literate family. Surprisingly, she was not familiar with Shakespeare's works as a teenager. When her father was threatened with bankruptcy in 1829 in the impending financial crash of his theatre, he suggested to his nineteen-year-old daughter that she become an actress rather than a governess; on 5 October, only three weeks later, never having acted before on a public stage, she made her début in Covent Garden as Juliet, with her parents playing Mercutio and Lady Capulet. She was a stupendous success, and she thereafter so consistently filled the theatre on the nights she was acting that its crash was postponed. She was unusually short for a star, never conventionally beautiful, although she could create the illusion of being so; much of her effect on others came from her vivid dark eyes and velvety deep voice (baritone, she called it). In middle age, like all the women of her family, she became too stout to be convincing on stage as the impetuous girlish heroines in which she had once specialized, but she still moved with the grace of a dancer. She relied too heavily on the inspiration of the moment to create characters; her total innocence of learned technique was particularly noticeable when she played the grand Shakespearian roles she inherited from her aunt Mrs Siddons, to whom she was constantly compared.

Fanny Kemble was always phenomenally quick at learning parts and began playing a new role each month, among others, the leading parts in *Venice Preserv'd*, *The Grecian Daughter*, and *The Provoked Husband* (as Lady Townly).

When the theatres in London closed for the summer, she and her father made a profitable tour of the provinces and Ireland. In following seasons, besides Lady Macbeth, Portia, Beatrice, and Constance, she performed in an adaptation of Kotzebue's *The Stranger*. Julia in Sheridan Knowles's *The Hunchback*, written especially for her, was perhaps her most consistently successful part, although she felt that she was least at home in comedy. Even her presence in the cast was not enough to make a success of *Francis the First*, one of two historical plays she wrote and appeared in.

The truth was that, in spite of her startling success, Fanny Kemble always despised acting as distinctly inferior to poetry and novels, and planned on leaving the stage when she could afford to. In 1831 she wrote, 'I do not think it is the acting itself that is so disagreeable to me, but the public personal exhibition, the violence done … to womanly dignity and decorum in thus becoming the gaze of every eye and theme of every tongue' (*Record of a Girlhood*, 432). She was already a pet of London society, almost a daughter to many hostesses, for she was that rarity, an intelligent and attractive young woman who could hold her own at their parties with the great conversationalists of the day. She was also a magnet to hordes of young men pursuing her. She fell in love with one of them, Augustus Craven, an ineffectual charmer of illegitimate but noble birth who was more interested in marrying money than in making a career of his own; she was devastated when the engagement was broken (for unspecified reasons), and as an old woman she indicated that it had been the most important single event in her life.

In 1831 the London theatre suffered from political discontent with such inherited privileges as Covent Garden Theatre's royal licence. Revenues fell drastically; the audiences began deserting Covent Garden for the music halls; newspapers for the first time seemed cutting in their criticism of Fanny's acting; the Kemble family finances were overstretched. In 1832, after her engagement was broken and her father was replaced as manager of Covent Garden, Fanny reluctantly agreed to accompany him to the United States on a two-year barnstorming tour; she was his leading lady despite their family relationship and the considerable difference in their ages. Her chaperone and dresser was her aunt Adelaide De Camp (who died in America after a carriage accident).

In America: acting and marriage The Kembles' American débuts were in the Park Theatre in New York in September 1832. The critics complained that Charles was not slim enough to play Hamlet, but the notices of both Kembles were good, as they were elsewhere, and it was generally acknowledged that they were the first truly great actors to take the American stage. The next two years were a triumphal tour of the major cities of the eastern seaboard, as well as New Orleans and Montreal and a host of lesser places; their repertory was chosen to exhibit Fanny, who now usurped her father's place as their chief attraction.

Fanny was young, still somewhat gauche socially, and she made many visitor's gaffes, criticizing the manners of Americans, their government, food, and intelligence, the looks and dress of the women, even the way their horses were trained. Like most English travellers after Mrs Trollope, she complained of the incessant spitting, but when she had travelled more in Europe she made a handsome, spontaneous apology for thinking the habit was confined to one country. In 1835 she made her position in America difficult by publishing two volumes of her journal, detailing her introduction to America, which many of its citizens found hard to forgive, despite the dashes that partly concealed the names of those whom Fanny had encountered—and dissected. It remains notable for the freshness of its style and the penetrating unconventionality of its observations, rather than for anything shocking or coarse.

From their opening in New York the Kembles went to Philadelphia, a city that Fanny at first preferred considerably. However, she soon saw that she made the inhabitants nervous socially because she was impossible to place exactly, either as the descendant of strolling players or as a dazzling actress and habituée of the great English houses. Among those intrigued by her was a well-born Philadelphian, Pierce Butler (1807–1867), the indolent heir to vast plantations in North Carolina and Georgia and potentially a very wealthy man. He was at first more interested in Fanny than she was in him, but he followed her and her father around the country paying his suit until his persistence (hardly patience) was finally rewarded. Their wedding was on 7 June 1834 in Christ Church, Philadelphia, a ceremony that took place in part because Charles Kemble had decided to return to England, and Fanny could scarcely stay on without a chaperone after her aunt's death. Fanny turned over to her father the considerable sum they had managed to save in America, thinking it would not be necessary for the wife of a man as rich as Pierce Butler. The marriage was so hurried that she had no time even to buy shoes for her wedding outfit. She honoured her agreement to act for another fortnight, and then retired from the stage with profound relief.

Fanny Butler and her new husband first lived with his brother and sister-in-law in Philadelphia, then moved to a generous family farm some 5 miles north of the city, where their two daughters, Sarah and Frances, were born. Clearly, Fanny knew little more about Butler before their marriage than she had known of Augustus Craven; he was clever and handsome—or at least very attractive to women—and she made the fundamental mistake of thinking that he would accept guidance from a wife. Nor did she know anything of his womanizing or even, as she claimed, that the source of the family fortune was slavery. The Butler family distrusted her for not being an aristocrat and, even more, for being an actress and abolitionist. Almost from the first the marriage was a disaster, although mutual passion seems to have helped them to paper over the cracks in its early days.

Slavery and authorship In 1838 Fanny with husband and children went to Georgia to spend the winter on their plantations. From apparently knowing nothing of slavery, she was thrown into the thick of the problem. Butler was moderately considerate to his slaves, but nothing could disguise the horrors of a system in which one man lived by owning others, treating them precisely as he fancied in order to get the best investment out of them. Worst of all, Fanny recognized that the considerable wealth the Butlers enjoyed, and to which she owed every mouthful she ate, came from the hated system. As it turned out, she spent less than four months on the plantations, but that was enough to stoke her moral indignation over the atrocities she saw. Once more, as she had done on first going to America, she kept a journal of her experiences, which in 1863 finally saw print as *Journal of a Residence on a Georgian Plantation in 1838–1839*. It is a small masterpiece of generous outrage, arguing from the amply and sympathetically documented details of what she had seen, to generalized indignation that such treatment could be tacitly encouraged by part of a civilized nation. Although it was deliberately not published in the American south, copies soon found their way there and scarcely increased admiration for the meddling of an outsider who expressed herself on what was regarded as an indigenous issue.

Back in Britain It had taken a quarter of a century for the Georgian *Journal* to appear, largely because Pierce Butler adamantly opposed its publication. In retrospect this seems symptomatic of what had gone wrong with the marriage: their deep division over slavery, the position of women (and particularly writers), and the necessity of independence of mind as well as of body. Fanny travelled to England between 1840 and 1843, then again in 1845, in an attempt to let the marriage breathe, for she still felt affection of a kind for her husband. Unfortunately, she kept stumbling over evidence of his infidelity, and by 1847 she was seeking ways to support herself should the marriage not be rehabilitated. She acted for a time in the English provinces, then went to London as leading lady to the most exciting Shakespearian actor of the day, W. C. Macready, with whom she was moderately successful, although their relationship was constantly threatened by outbursts of mutual disapproval. *Punch* noted that she was paid £100 a performance (an exaggeration of the truth) for her 'priceless abilities', and concluded sourly that, 'as long as that lady asks £100 per night, we think they are likely to remain so' (13 Feb 1847).

In April 1848 Fanny gave her first solo public reading of a Shakespearian play, following the precedent of her father and her aunt Siddons. Once more she was a thorough success, if on a more limited scale than at her Covent Garden début, and for fifteen years she toured up and down England and the United States giving her one-woman versions of Shakespeare. They were particularly popular in puritanical America because they brought an exhilarating whiff of drama and artifice with none of the obviously tawdry associations of the stage. She was neither the first nor the last to give public readings, but she was probably the most skilful solo reader of them all. Her income, although as volatile as one would expect of such a tempestuous woman, kept her comfortably until her retirement from the reading platform in 1863.

Return to America: divorce Less than a month after her first reading in London, Fanny had been summoned to America, where her husband filed divorce proceedings on the grounds of desertion; batteries of expensive lawyers were hired on both sides; but Butler finally agreed to a settlement without the formality of a trial, to prevent revelation of evidence extremely embarrassing to him. It was a long and bitter divorce, but it was settled with surface amicability; Fanny was to have $2500 a year and access to the children, who were to live with their father. Butler tried every stratagem to keep from fulfilling the conditions, to the extreme pain of Fanny, who resumed her maiden name.

Final years and death Fanny Kemble divided her time for the next three decades between England, Philadelphia, and the cottage she bought in Lenox, Massachusetts, a part of the country she loved. In 1877–8 she returned to London to live alternately with her two daughters and their families and to retake her place in London society that had been disrupted by moving to America. She knew everyone who counted, and she once reminded a caller who was on the point of departing early that he would never again have a chance 'to talk with a woman who had sat at dinner alongside of Byron, who has heard Tom Moore sing, and who calls Tennyson, Alfred' (E. Earnest, *S. Weir Mitchell*, 73). He stayed. Not surprisingly, one of her best friends in old age was a fellow Anglo-American much her junior, Henry James, to whom she passed several incidents from life that he used as the matrices of stories and novels. He commemorated their friendship with a splendid obituary of his old friend. 'The great thing', he wrote, 'was that from the first she had abundantly lived'.

Fanny Kemble wrote many plays and poems and a novel, but the most solidly enduring of her works are autobiographical: the two journals of her arrival in America and of her plantation life in Georgia, and also *Record of a Girlhood* (1878; 2nd edn, 1880) and *Records of Later Life* (1882). She died peacefully, apparently of a heart attack, on 15 January 1893 at 86 Gloucester Place, London, the home of her daughter, Frances, by now the Hon. Mrs Leigh, and was buried at Kensal Green cemetery. It was a quiet end, very unlike both her life and what she had hoped would be its conclusion: to 'break my neck off the back of my horse at a full gallop on a fine day'.

Robert Bernard Martin

Sources F. A. Butler [F. A. Kemble], *Journal of Frances Anne Butler*, 2 vols. (1835) · F. A. Kemble, *Journal of a residence on a Georgian plantation in 1838–1839*, ed. J. A. Scott, 2 vols. (1961); repr. (1984) [incl. bibliography] · F. A. Kemble, *Record of a girlhood*, rev. edn, 3 vols. (1879) · F. A. Kemble, *Records of later life*, 3 vols. (1882) · F. A. Kemble, *Further records, 1848–1883: a series of letters*, 2 vols. (1890) · M. Bell, *Major Butler's legacy* (1987) · Highfill, Burnim & Langhans, *BDA* · J. Williamson, *Charles Kemble: man of the theatre* [1964] · L. Kelly, *The Kemble era* (1980) · J. C. Furnas, *Fanny Kemble* (1982) · L. S. Driver, *Fanny Kemble* (1933) · P. Fitzgerald, *The Kembles: an account of the Kemble family*, 2 vols. (1871) · H. James, 'Frances Anne Kemble', *Temple Bar*, 97 (1893), 503–25
Archives BL, MS autobiography, Add. MSS 55048 [fragment] · Folger · Harvard TC · Harvard U., Houghton L. · Hist. Soc. Penn., corresp. and papers · Hunt. L., letters and literary papers · NL Scot. · University of Illinois Library, Urbana-Champaign, letters | BL, corresp. with Edward Fitzgerald, Add. MSS 45097–45098 · Borth Inst., letters to Lady Georgina Grey · Col. U., Rare Book and Manuscript Library, letters to Charles Sedgwick and his wife · Eton, letters, mostly to Lady Anne Ritchie · NL Scot., corresp. with George Combe · NYPL, Berg MSS · RA, corresp. with Thomas Lawrence
Likenesses T. Lawrence, drawing, 1830, NPG · H. Andrews, group portrait, oils, c.1831 (*The trial of Queen Katherine*), Royal Shakespeare Theatre, Stratford upon Avon, Warwickshire · H. R. Cook, coloured stipple, pubd 1831 (after J. Jenkins), NPG · M. Gauci, lithograph, pubd 1832, NPG · T. Sully, oils, 1833, Pennsylvania Academy of the Fine Arts, Philadelphia [*see illus.*] · P. F. Rothermel, oils, 1849, NPG · J. Doyle, pencil caricature, 1851, BM · J. Bishop, line and stipple engraving, NPG · de Lemercier, coloured lithograph (after Gigoux), NPG · H. Inman, oils, Brooklyn Museum, New York · A. William-Wolfe, coloured stipple and line engraving (as Julia in *The hunchback*), NPG · aquatint and etching (as Juliet), Harvard TC · coloured lithograph, NPG · double portrait (with Mrs Siddons), Boston Athenaeum · pencil and watercolour drawing (after T. Lawrence), Courtauld Inst. · pencil drawing (after T. Lawrence), Metropolitan Museum of Art, New York · theatrical prints, BM, Harvard TC, NPG · watercolour, Garr. Club
Wealth at death £205: administration, 28 July 1893, *CGPLA Eng. & Wales*

Kemble, Henry (1848–1907), actor, born in London on 1 June 1848, was the son of Henry Kemble, captain of the 37th foot. Charles *Kemble was his grandfather. He was educated at Bury St Edmunds and at King's College School, London. In 1865 he entered the privy council office, but devoted most of his time to amateur theatricals. Yielding to the hereditary bias, he made his professional début on the stage at the Theatre Royal, Dublin, on 7 October 1867, and for a year and a half remained a minor member of Harris's stock company there. He then acted old men and character parts at Edinburgh, Glasgow, Scarborough, and Newcastle upon Tyne. On 29 August 1874 he made his first appearance in London at Drury Lane, under Chatterton's management, as Tony Foster in a revival of Andrew Halliday's *Amy Robsart*. He was the original Philip of France in the same author's *Richard Coeur de Lion*, and later was favourably received as Dr Caius in *The Merry Wives of Windsor*. In 1875 he joined John Hare's company at the Court Theatre, and was seen to advantage as Dr Penguin in J. Palgrave Simpson's *A Scrap of Paper*. In September 1876 he appeared at the Prince of Wales's as Crossby Beck in *Peril*, by Bolton Rowe and Saville Rowe, thus beginning his long association and friendship with the Bancrofts. Among his later characters there were Sir Oliver Surface in *The School for Scandal* and the original Mr Trelawney Smith in *Duty*, an adaptation by Albery from Sardou.

Having followed the Bancrofts to the Haymarket, Kemble appeared there on the opening night of their management (31 January 1880) as Mr Stout in Bulwer-Lytton's *Money*. He spent the next two years alternating between the Haymarket and touring the provinces, first with Ellen Terry and then with Mrs Scott-Siddons. In February 1882 he reappeared at the Court in two new characterizations—as the Revd Mr Jones in Dion Boucicault's adaptation *My Little Girl* and Mr Justice Bunby in F. C. Burnand's farce *The Manager*. Other original characters followed. On 20 July 1885 he played his old part of Mr Snarl in *Masks and*

Faces, by Charles Reade and Tom Taylor, at the Bancroft farewell.

A variety of engagements of little importance at West End theatres occupied Kemble for the next fifteen years, during which he also played small Shakespearian roles at the Haymarket. In September 1891 he made an acceptable Polonius at the Theatre Royal, Manchester, in Herbert Beerbohm Tree's first performance of *Hamlet*. He was first engaged by Tree to play the original Mr Parr in Robert Buchanan's *Partners* at the Haymarket in 1888, and later became a leading member of Tree's Crystal Palace company. After joining Tree at Her Majesty's, Kemble was, on 1 February 1902, the original Ctesippus in Stephen Phillips's *Ulysses*. His last appearance on the stage was made at the Criterion in April 1907, as Archibald Coke in a revival of Henry Arthur Jones's *The Liars*. He died, unmarried, at 29½ Harve des Pas, St Helier, Jersey, on 17 November 1907.

Kemble was an excellent comedian, and revelled in strongly marked character parts. His stout figure and somewhat short stature enhanced the comicality of his mien. Much beloved by his associates, he was affectionately known at the Garrick Club as 'the Beetle' on account of his early habit of wearing a long brown cloak with a large collar, which he pulled over his head in cold weather. W. J. LAWRENCE, rev. NILANJANA BANERJI

Sources B. Hunt, ed., *The green room book, or, Who's who on the stage* (1906) · J. Parker, ed., *The green room book, or, Who's who on the stage* (1907) · *Era Almanack and Annual* (1896), 49–50 · C. E. Pascoe, ed., *The dramatic list*, 2nd edn (1880) · P. Hartnoll, ed., *The Oxford companion to the theatre* (1951); 2nd edn (1957); 3rd edn (1967) · M. E. Bancroft and S. Bancroft, *The Bancrofts: recollections of sixty years* (1909) · E. Terry, *The story of my life* (1908) · W. Archer, *The theatrical 'World' of 1896* (1897) · C. Brookfield, *Random reminiscences* (1902) · *Dramatic notes* (1881–6)
Archives Theatre Museum, London, diary of parts played and letters
Likenesses H. Allen, oils, 1908, Garr. Club · Spy [L. Ward], caricature, NPG; repro. in *VF* (24 April 1907)
Wealth at death £1255 9s.: probate, 29 Jan 1908, *CGPLA Eng. & Wales*

Kemble, Henry Stephen (1789–1836), actor, was the son of Stephen George *Kemble (1758–1822) and Elizabeth *Kemble, *née* Satchell (1762/3–1841), both celebrated performers. He was born on 15 September 1789 in Villiers Street, Strand, London, where his mother was carried when she went into labour after acting the role of Queen Margaret in *The Battle of Hexham*, on the closing night of the Haymarket Theatre. He was educated at Winchester College and Trinity College, Cambridge, which he left after two years to try his fortune on the stage. His first appearance was made at Whitehaven in Cumberland, under his father's management, as Frank Heartall in Andrew Cherry's comedy *The Soldier's Daughter*. Under his father he acted in various northern towns, and married, in opposition to parental wishes, a Miss Freize, a member of the company. After his father gave up management in the north, Kemble joined the Southampton and Portsmouth circuit under Maxfield, Kelly, and Collins. In 1814, as Octavian in George Colman's *The Mountaineers* to the Agnes of

his wife, he made his first appearance at the Haymarket, where the family name secured him a favourable reception. He was then engaged by Palmer of the Bath Theatre, and played under the same management in Bristol. He made his first appearance in Bath in November 1816, as Bertram in C. R. Maturin's tragedy of the same name. He was also seen as Bajazet in Nicholas Rowe's *Tamerlane* and as Gambia in Thomas Morton's *The Slave*. One reviewer at the time called him boisterous, and a Bath paper said of his De Zelos in *Manuel* that it was received 'with peals of derision, although entitled to shouts of disgust'.

Kemble's father caused much murmuring during his one year's management of Drury Lane (1818–19), by sending for him and entrusting him with many parts of importance for which he was wholly unqualified. When he made his first appearance, on the opening night of the theatre, as Romeo, he shouted and ranted, and it was said of him that he had promised to be heard in Bath. During this time at Drury Lane, Kemble was the first exponent of some dozen characters, among which were Giafar in Milner's *Barmecide, or, The Fatal Offspring*, Sextus in Howard Payne's *Brutus*, and Manfredi in Bucke's *The Italians, or, The Fatal Accusation*. He also played Marmion in *Flodden Field*, an adaptation from Scott by himself and his father, staged in December 1818. At about this time, Mrs Henry Kemble made a successful début at the English Opera House (later known as the Lyceum) as Polly in *The Beggar's Opera*. At the close of this season Kemble seems to have dropped into the minor theatres. For the Coburg he altered *Flodden Field* into *The Nun of St Hilda's Cave*. Here, and at the Surrey, Astley's, and east London theatres, he acted principal parts, incurring the censure that he possessed the strongest lungs and weakest judgement of any performer in his station. He was, however, generous, although self-indulgent, and was widely popular. He died on 22 June 1836.
JOSEPH KNIGHT, rev. NILANJANA BANERJI

Sources *Oxberry's Dramatic Biography*, new ser., 1 (1827), 146–55 · *The biography of the British stage, being correct narratives of the lives of all the principal actors and actresses* (1824) · Hall, *Dramatic ports.* · Genest, *Eng. stage* · *GM*, 2nd ser., 6 (1836), 219 · *General Magazine* (1789)
Likenesses portrait, repro. in *Oxberry's Dramatic Biography* · prints (as Giafar in *Barmecide* and other characters) · thirteen prints, Harvard TC

Kemble, John [St John Kemble] (1599–1679), Roman Catholic priest, was the son of John Kemble, gentleman, and Anne Kemble (*née* Morgan) of Rhyd y Car, St Weonards, Herefordshire. He went to St Gregory's College, Seville, Spain, about 1620, and was ordained priest at Douai on 23 February 1625; on 4 June was sent on the mission in Herefordshire. In 1678, at the time of the Popish Plot, he was seized at Pembridge Castle, Herefordshire, where he was living as chaplain to the Scudamore family. He was tried at the summer assizes of 1679 at Hereford, convicted as having said mass at Pembridge, and executed at Widemarsh Common, near the town, on 22 August 1679; he was buried that day at Welsh Newton churchyard. There is a tradition that he smoked a pipe on the way to execution. His hand is kept at the church of St Francis Xavier, Hereford, and a piece of linen dipped in his blood is at Downside Abbey.

Pilgrimages were made to the grave, and miracles were, it is asserted, wrought there. Charles Kemble, who claimed to be the priest's great-great-nephew, paid a visit to the churchyard with Mrs Siddons, and some verses on the occasion are printed in the life by M. V. Lovejoy. He was canonized by Pope Paul VI on 25 October 1970.

W. A. J. ARCHBOLD, rev. G. BRADLEY

Sources M. V. Lovejoy, *Blessed John Kemble* [n.d., *c.*1960] · B. Camm, 'Pembridge Castle', *Forgotten shrines: an account of some old Catholic halls and families in England* (1910), 333–42 · G. Anstruther, *The seminary priests*, 2 (1975) · Gillow, *Lit. biog. hist.*, 3.685 · R. Challoner, *Memoirs of missionary priests*, ed. J. H. Pollen, rev. edn (1924), 555–7 · D. H. Farmer, *The Oxford dictionary of saints* (1978), 230–31 · M. Murphy, *St Gregory's College, Seville, 1592–1767*, Catholic RS, 73 (1992)
Archives U. Hull, Everingham MSS, speech at his execution
Likenesses portrait, St Francis Xavier Church, Broad Street, Hereford · portrait, St Mary's Church, Monmouth

Kemble, John Mitchell (1807–1857), philologist and historian, was born on 2 April 1807, the elder surviving son of the actor Charles *Kemble (1775–1854) and his wife, Maria Theresa *Kemble, *née* De Camp (1777–1838). He was a nephew of John Philip Kemble (1757–1823) and of Sarah Siddons (1755–1831), and a brother of the singer Adelaide *Kemble and Frances Anne (Fanny) *Kemble (1809–1893), an actress and writer, whose *Record of a Girlhood* provides lively glimpses of his youth. Kemble's early passion for grammar and language, kindled by his father and his uncle John, was reinforced by his early education at the school run by the lexicographer Charles Richardson at Clapham. As a boy he acquired a taste for chemistry, and enjoyed making toy theatres, and acting plays with Fanny. He then went to King Edmund's Grammar School at Bury St Edmunds, under Dr Benjamin Heath Malkin, where among his contemporaries were Malkin's son Frederick, Edward Fitzgerald, James Spedding (the later biographer of Bacon), and William Bodham Donne, Kemble's lifelong friend. In June 1824 he was admitted as a pensioner to Trinity College, Cambridge, but did not go into residence until the Michaelmas term of 1825. He held a Hewer exhibition from his school and great things were expected of him.

At Cambridge, Kemble's enthusiasm for rifle-shooting, rowing, and fencing was matched by the attractions of speaking in the union club (of which he was president in Lent 1828) and the private debating society. His fine physique, handsome appearance, expressive voice, and brilliant talk made him extremely popular. He contributed verse and prose to *The Athenaeum* and in 1826 became a member of the celebrated Apostles (officially the Cambridge Conversazione Society, founded in 1820). His friends, here and later, included, according to Fanny, 'Arthur Hallam, Alfred Tennyson and his brothers, Frederick Maurice, John Sterling, Richard Trench, William Bodham Donne, the Romillys, the Malkins, Edward Fitzgerald, James Spedding, William Thackeray and Richard Monkton Milnes' (Kemble, *Record*, 1.299). Eleven of these were Apostles, who exalted liberalism, imagination, and friendship, maintained by annual dinners and copious correspondence.

At Cambridge, Kemble's strongly independent spirit was shown in his neglect of mathematics, his devotion to language studies, and his passionate involvement in radical politics, including a 'fanatical admiration for Jeremy Bentham, and Mill' (Kemble, *Record*, 1.293). He entered at the Inner Temple in June 1827 and worked alongside F. D. Maurice but confined his studies to those parts of English law that illustrated history or ancient customs. This academic independence and his reference to Paley as 'a miserable sophist' and to Locke's 'loathsome infidelity' led the Cambridge examiners early in 1829 to defer his degree. During the long vacation of 1829 he visited Germany with his Trinity friend Charles Barton, and having left him at Heidelberg went on to Munich and the Tyrol, and began a serious study of German philology. In early 1830 Kemble was impelled to return home, partly by reading of Fanny's triumph as Juliet (in a successful bid to rescue the desperate family fortunes), and partly by his father's securing for him an opportunity in the church. He took his degree on 25 February, rejected a career at the bar, and determined to take orders (an aspiration pleasing to Fanny and to his father), but found he would have to wait for divinity lectures until the Michaelmas term. He spoke frequently in the union, and in March acted Dogberry in *Much Ado*, with Hallam as Verges and Milnes as Beatrice. Kemble's priestly aspiration prompted Tennyson's sonnet 'To J.M.K.', which sees him as 'a latter Luther, and a soldier-priest' (*The Poems of Tennyson*, ed. C. Ricks, 1972, 1.280). In July 1830, however, he joined an ill-fated Spanish expedition designed to topple Ferdinand VII, launched by Sterling's cousin, John Boyd, Richard Chenevix Trench, and other young Englishmen. (The affair is described in Thomas Carlyle's *Life of John Sterling*, ix, x, xiii.) By October, Kemble was with Trench in Gibraltar, where he spent his leisure discussing German metaphysics. From the beginning the uprising was a miserable failure; Trench returned in February 1831. Kemble held on another three months but returned to London on 21 May. Eventually, in December 1831, Torrijos and fifty-two of his followers, including John Boyd, were captured and shot.

Having abandoned his idea of taking orders, Kemble spent the period from Michaelmas 1832 to the summer of 1835 mostly in Cambridge, 'acquiring a more intimate knowledge of the manuscript sources for Old English literature and history than any scholar had since Wanley' (Dickins, 11). His vacations were spent in the British Museum, where he studied Jacob Grimm's *Deutsche Grammatik*. He opened his academic career with a somewhat premature edition of *Beowulf* (1833), and in 1834 personally arranged a course of language lectures at Cambridge. His enthusiasm and eloquence initially attracted a large audience, but his Germanic rigour deterred all but the more serious students. In a review of Benjamin Thorpe's *Analecta Anglo-Saxonica* (which he commended), he launched a scathing but intemperate attack on the current state of Anglo-Saxon studies in Oxford, complaining of its 'idle and ignorant scholars' (*GM*, 1834, 1.391). This provoked a caustic counter-attack in a pamphlet entitled *The Anglo-Saxon Meteor*, possibly emanating from the

Netherlands and Joseph Bosworth, in which Kemble's credentials are questioned and he is depicted as slavishly following the Danes and the Germans. Letters by Sir F. Maddem and Dr Ingram continued the controversy (*GM*, 1834, 2.483; 1835, 3.43). Bosworth's detailed attack on Kemble's treatment of verbs was not well based and Kemble's reputation survived. Yet Kemble's career prospects were fatally blighted. No professorship of Anglo-Saxon was forthcoming, and at Cambridge he later failed to obtain the post of principal librarian, and that of regius professor of modern history.

Kemble wrote to Jacob Grimm on 30 June 1832, opening a scholarly correspondence which lasted until 1852, and in August 1834 spent three weeks with him in Göttingen, Grimm finding him very learned in the Anglo-Saxon tongue. On this visit he met his future wife, Natalie Auguste (*d.* after 1857), daughter of Professor Amadeus Wendt (1783–1836) and Henriette, *née* Dölitzch (1789–1859). In March 1835 Kemble wrote to her father, asking for Natalie's hand in marriage, and on a later visit he married her by special licence in a Lutheran house ceremony at Göttingen on 24 July 1836 (Wiley, 12). They had three children: Gertrude, who was to marry Charles Santley, the singer; Henry Charles, who later became a colonel in the 2nd Bengal cavalry; and Mildred, who became the first wife of the Revd C. E. Donne, son of her father's friend.

Since 1836 Kemble had deputized for his ailing father as examiner of plays, and in 1840 he was appointed to this post, which he held until his death. Kemble was then living in London, engaged in literary work, and researching, in the British Museum and various college and cathedral libraries, the Anglo-Saxon charters that formed the basis of his major work, the *Codex diplomaticus* (6 vols., 1839–48), containing over 1400 documents. This was a foundational work, which well displays Kemble's mastery of Anglo-Saxon and his skill in deciphering documents. It provided the sound basis for his next and most popular major work, *The Saxons in England* (2 vols., 1849). This had its faults, but benefited from Kemble's ability to relate his findings to the work of German scholars on other branches of the Germanic family of languages.

For its first few years Kemble's marriage appears to have been happy, but in 1847 he parted from his wife. In letters to Grimm he attributes this to drunkenness and repeated adultery on her part (Wiley, 31–3, 36). At this time he was living with his children in a small house near Rickmansworth in Hertfordshire and was advertising for pupils, since he was earning little from his publications. These were to include many editions and translations of Anglo-Saxon texts and a variety of articles in such periodicals as the *British and Foreign Review* (which he edited from 1835 to 1844), *Archaeologia*, and latterly *Fraser's Magazine*. This editorship, which he used to foster the work of his friends, brought him £400 a year, and when it ended he was in dire poverty. The Apostles rallied to his support and paid the premium of his life insurance policy, but he had to sell his library.

From 1848 Kemble moved to Hanover, seeking a divorce, which presumably he obtained. (The records were destroyed in wartime action.) He delegated his duties as examiner to Bodham Donne, who performed them gratis. Donne became acting examiner in 1849, and succeeded to the post in 1857. At Hanover in 1854 Kemble turned his attention to prehistoric archaeology, and rearranged and catalogued the collections in the Royal Museum, the curators of which employed him for five months to excavate funeral barrows on Lüneburg Heath and its environs. He took to archaeology ardently and, though untutored as a draughtsman, rapidly acquired the requisite skills. He made a large number of careful drawings of prehistoric antiquities in the museums of Munich, Berlin, and Schwerin. By this time he was a member of numerous European learned societies. On his return to England he sent accounts of his discoveries to the Society of Antiquaries and the Archaeological Institute, and issued the prospectus of a book to be published by subscription, with the title *Horae ferales*. This was intended to provide a systematic account of northern archaeology, and supply the means of relating it to other ages and countries.

At this point the committee of the Manchester Art Treasures Exhibition employed Kemble to collect and arrange Celtic and Roman antiquities, and in February 1857 he delivered an address, 'On the utility of antiquarian collections', before the Royal Irish Academy in Dublin. While there he caught cold, developed an inflammation of the lungs, and died at the Gresham Hotel on 26 March 1857. He was buried in the cemetery of Mount Jerome. His wife survived him for some years. Several Apostles contributed to a fund for the care of his children. It remained for R. G. Latham to edit *Horae ferales* from Kemble's incomplete papers. The work appeared in 1863, with an introduction by A. W. Franks to the splendid collection of plates, along with translations of Kemble's lecture at the opening of the Hanoverian Museum, and his address to the Royal Irish Academy.   JOHN D. HAIGH

Sources DNB · private information (1891) [C. E. Donne] · R. A. Wiley, ed., *John Mitchell Kemble and Jakob Grimm: a correspondence, 1832–1852* (1971) · W. B. Donne, *Fraser's Magazine*, 55 (1857), 612–18 · F. A. Kemble, *Record of a girlhood*, 3 vols. (1878) · F. A. Kemble, *Records of later life*, 2 (1882), 28 · F. A. Kemble, *Further records, 1848–1883: a series of letters*, 2 vols. (1890), 151, 158 · W. C. Lubenow, *The Cambridge Apostles, 1820–1914* (1998) · J. R. Stephens, *The censorship of English drama, 1824–1901* (1980) · *Richard Chenevix Trench: letters and memorials*, ed. [M. Trench], 2 vols. (1888), vol. 1, pp. 11, 22, 30, 46, 57, 61, 91, 162 · GM, 2nd ser., 1 (1834), 391–3 · GM, 2nd ser., 2 (1834), 483 · GM, 2nd ser., 3 (1835), 43–4 · GM, 3rd ser., 2 (1857), 439 · *The Anglo-Saxon meteor, or, Letters in defence of Oxford treating of the wonderful Gothic attainments of J. M. K.* [n.d., c.1835] · B. Dickins, 'J. M. Kemble and Old English scholarship', *PBA*, 25 (1939), 51–84 [incl. bibliography of his writings] · F. M. Brookfield, 'John Mitchell Kemble', *The Cambridge Apostles* (1906), 159–87 · C. B. Johnson, *William Bodham Donne and his friends* (1905) · T. W. Reid, *The life, letters, and friendships of Richard Monckton Milnes, first Lord Houghton*, 1 (1890); 2 (1890), 161 · *The Athenaeum* (28 March 1857), 406 · *The Athenaeum* (4 April 1857), 439

Archives BL, papers, Add. MSS 32126–32131, 36531 · Bodl. Oxf., corresp. · Duke U., Perkins L., corresp., notebooks, and papers · S. Antiquaries, Lond., notes and papers relating to excavations in Germany · Trinity Cam., Johnson papers, letters from John Mitchell Kemble and William Bodham Donne · Yale U., Beinecke L., archaeological notes and sketches | BL, corresp. with John Allen, Add. MS 52184

Likenesses T. Woolner, marble bust, *c*.1865, Trinity Cam. · Lady Eastlake, drawing, priv. coll. · H. Lane, double portrait, medallion (with his wife) · H. Lane, engraving (in youth) · S. Morton, drawing, repro. in Johnson, *William Bodham Donne*, facing p. 27 · drawing, repro. in Brookfield, 'John Mitchell Kemble', facing p. 160 · sketch, repro. in Kemble, *Record*, 2.293–4; priv. coll.

Kemble, John Philip (1757–1823), actor, was born in Prescot, then a small Lancashire town between Liverpool and Warrington, on 1 February 1757, the second child and first son of Roger *Kemble (1722–1802) and Sarah Ward (1735–1807).

The Kembles and the Wards Although Kemble's parents owe their posthumous recognition to their children, they were not undistinguished in their own time. Roger Kemble was the son of a Hereford barber and the inheritor of a notable Roman Catholic tradition. A recent ancestor, Father John Kemble, had been executed in 1679 for his supposed part in the Popish Plot, and the Captain Richard Kemble who was with Charles II's army at the battle of Worcester in 1651 was Roger Kemble's grandfather or great-grandfather. Roger Kemble was already thirty when he abandoned barbering for the theatre. In 1752–3 he joined a company of players under the management of John and Sarah Ward. Ward was an Irishman with a reputation as a disciplinarian. His company, though sometimes known as the Warwick Players, toured extensively: to Coventry, Worcester, Leominster, Hereford, Gloucester, Brecon (where Roger Kemble's first child, later famous as Mrs Siddons, was born in 1755), Carmarthen. Surprisingly, in view of the later reputation of Methodists, he was also an early supporter of John Wesley's call for spiritual renewal. By 1753 he was entrusting the female juvenile leads to his daughter Sarah, already tall, stately, and refined while still in her teens. Like most of the children she would later have, young Sarah Ward was headstrong on the matter of marriage. Her father may have wanted a fine husband for her, may even have extracted a promise that she would never marry an actor, but her head was quickly turned by the handsome bachelor from Hereford. On 6 June 1753, evidently without parental approval and perhaps after the sentimental romance of an elopement, they were married in Cirencester.

According to Kemble family legend, John Ward comforted himself by saying that Roger Kemble was no actor. If that is true, it is all the more surprising that he took the young couple back into his company. The probability is that he needed them. He had expansive ambitions. During the 1750s his company performed as far south as Bath and as far north as Liverpool. The birthplaces of the first five of the Kembles' children (Brecon, Prescot, Kington, Hereford, Warrington) chart the itinerary of touring players. But Roger Kemble had ambitions of his own. From 1761 to 1763 he broke away from his father-in-law to set up a company of his own, and in 1766, when Ward retired, he took over the management, sustaining it to general approval until his own retirement in 1781. The Kemble children were born into the theatre; and they were born, also, into

John Philip Kemble (1757–1823), by Sir Thomas Lawrence, 1801 [as Hamlet]

a family of religious compromise. Their parents agreed that the sons would be brought up in Roger's faith and the daughters in Sarah's. It was from their mother that the best-known of the children inherited their strong features and physical grace, but an inbred awareness of alternative and equally powerful pulls is a discernible influence on their approach to dramatic character.

Early years and theatrical apprenticeship Roger Kemble did not intend his eldest son for the theatre, though the exigencies of management led him to cast the ten-year-old John as the young Duke of York in William Havard's *King Charles the First* at the King's Head in Worcester on 12 February 1767. Discretion may have been overruled by necessity on other occasions, but a Catholic education was the priority. In November 1767 Kemble entered Sedgley Park School, near Wolverhampton, to begin a period of intense study that would culminate at the English College in Douai from 1771 to 1775. Fluent in French, and grounded in Latin and Greek, he developed literary ambitions rather than the calling to the priesthood that his father had probably envisaged. When he returned to England in 1775, it was with a determination to act and to write. It was probably his sister Sarah *Siddons (1755–1831), already making her way in the theatre, who negotiated his engagement with a minor touring company, and he made his adult début at Wolverhampton on 8 January 1776 in the purple-versed title role of Nathaniel Lee's *Theodosius*. Over the next eighteen months he had first-hand experience of the strolling player's hand-to-mouth rootlessness and developed the habit of palliative drinking that was his lifelong bugbear.

Kemble's first secure employment was with Joseph Younger's company, based in Liverpool. Younger had the wit to recognize the young actor's hunger and the acumen to exploit it. Between June 1777, when he and Sarah (already married to William Siddons) went together to Liverpool, and September 1778, Kemble accumulated an impressive portfolio of roles in tragedy and comedy, including Othello (to Sarah's Desdemona), Laertes (to Sarah's Hamlet), King Lear, Brutus, Shylock, Posthumus in *Cymbeline*, Pierre in Thomas Otway's *Venice Preserv'd*, Ranger in Benjamin Hoadly's *The Suspicious Husband*, and Archer in George Farquhar's *The Beaux' Stratagem*. All these were listed in the repertory of 126 roles (sixty-eight in tragedy, fifty-eight in comedy) that he sent to Tate Wilkinson at York in a letter of application dated 21 June 1778. (The letter is now in the collection of manuscript letters in the Folger Shakespeare Library.)

The shrewdest of all provincial managers, Wilkinson had already benefited from the quality of Mrs Siddons, and he cherished his reputation as a starmaker. He would come to value Kemble as 'a choice root from my botanical garden' (Wilkinson, 4.75), but the relationship over the three years from 1778 to 1781 was not uniformly easy. Kemble's quest for personal dignity made him prickly, even as a young man, and his response to anything he considered an insult was unyielding. Wilkinson recounts a potentially dangerous confrontation in the York theatre in April 1779. A Mrs Mason was making her début opposite Kemble in Arthur Murphy's *Zenobia*, and their performances were audibly derided by the daughter of a local baronet in the stage-box. With her continuing laughter accompanying the death throes of the final act, Kemble 'made a full and long stop' and, when urged to go on, 'with great gravity, and a pointed bow to the stage-box, said he was ready to proceed with the play as soon as *that* lady had finished her conversation, which he perceived the going on with the Tragedy only interrupted' (Wilkinson, 2.20–21). Confident of support from most of the audience, Kemble refused the call for an apology clamorously led by officers of the North Riding militia. The scandal rumbled on for a week, though Kemble knew well that he could bring it to an end by apologizing for the *lèse-majesté* of a mere player. But he, not the lady, was the aggrieved party. In the end, to his gratification, the York audience exonerated him without an apology. By the time he left Wilkinson's company he had won the admiration of audiences at York, Leeds, Hull, and, briefly, Edinburgh. He had also presented himself as a playwright, with his tragedy *Belisarius* (manuscript in the Huntington Library), which had been earlier performed in Liverpool, and a farce called *The Female Officer*, first performed for his own benefit at Manchester on 25 March 1778. A small collection of his poetic

Fugitive Pieces was published in York in 1780, to his later, justifiable, embarrassment.

Kemble had still a lot to learn about his own strengths and limitations when he left York in the winter of 1781 to work for £5 per week with Richard Daly's company at the Smock Alley Theatre, Dublin. He was tall, dark-eyed, strong-featured, and athletically graceful. Importantly, too, he had acquired a habit of diligent study in preparation for the performance of major roles, which he would always copy out for himself. Tate Wilkinson was one of the earliest to observe that he excelled 'where sternness is requisite, more than in the tender passions' (Wilkinson, 2.6). Romeo, then, was not a part for him, but neither, in general, was he suited to comedy. Perhaps envious of Garrick's famed versatility, or that of his own near-contemporary John Henderson, Kemble would never abandon comedy, but it was as Hamlet that he made his Dublin début on 2 November 1781, to modest approval. As Sir George Touchwood, though, in Hannah Cowley's *The Belle's Stratagem*, he was at best damned with faint praise. Significantly, it was as Raymond in *The Count of Narbonne*, Robert Jephson's dramatic treatment of Horace Walpole's Gothic novel *The Castle of Otranto*, that Kemble first caught the imagination of the Dublin public. The Gothic was a mode that suited him well—he was a master in the portrayal of brooding intensity, as he later demonstrated in roles he made his own: Penruddock in Richard Cumberland's *The Wheel of Fortune*, Octavian in the younger George Colman's *The Mountaineers*, above all the eponymous Stranger in Benjamin Thompson's version of a play by Kotzebue, in which, according to James Boaden, 'he bore … a living death about him' (Boaden, 2.215). Kemble's friendship with Jephson gave him access to the cream of Dublin society, and his stock rose higher in the wake of Mrs Siddons's trumpeted triumph at Drury Lane in October 1782. These were early signs of a durable social acceptability.

The Dublin company included such seasoned professionals as West Digges and Anne Crawford, but it was with younger members that Kemble's future would be linked. His sentimental attachment to Elizabeth Inchbald, which dated back to his earliest year on the stage, had matured into mutual admiration. She later painted an impressionistic portrait of him as Dorriforth in her novel *A Simple Story* (1791), a portrait that would mingle with the Byronic hero in influencing Charlotte Brontë's creation of Mr Rochester in *Jane Eyre*. A much better actress than Inchbald, though never so sterling a friend to Kemble, was the youthful Dorothy Francis—soon, as Dorothy Jordan, to become the acknowledged queen of English comedy. Never assured in his relationships with women, Kemble was too solemnly self-important for her taste. Nor did he succeed in his pursuit of the young singer Anna Maria Phillips. In her years of fame, when, as Mrs Crouch, she was the acknowledged mistress of the brilliant tenor Michael Kelly, she was Kemble's hostess on many a convivial evening, but in Dublin she was the resistant partner in what even James Boaden, a reticent biographer, admits was 'a very zealous friendship, perhaps a little romantic on his side' (Boaden, 1.46). On balance, though, the Dublin seasons served Kemble's career well. By the end of the theatrical year 1782–3 Daly had doubled his salary, and he was ready to join his sister in London.

Kemble at Drury Lane Mrs Inchbald was away from London when Kemble arrived in mid-August 1783, but she made her rooms in Leicester Fields available to him for the preparation of his Drury Lane début as Hamlet on 30 September 1783. It was not the most sensational of occasions, but most critics were respectful, and the rival theatre in Covent Garden felt sufficiently challenged to put up its star, John Henderson, as an oppositional Hamlet. Compared with Henderson, Kemble was slow and deliberate, his speaking of the familiar lines punctuated with pauses, designed to carry the meaning across to the audience. 'To be critically exact', wrote Boaden, 'was the great ambition of his life' (Boaden, 1.158). Always indolent in his management of Drury Lane, Sheridan allowed his new acquisition a range of Shakespearian opportunities: not only Hamlet, but also Richard III, King John (with Mrs Siddons as Constance), and Shylock. His benefit on 13 April 1784 brought him £290, less house charges of £107. There were, as there would always be, cavillers. People who looked back to Garrick, or across to Henderson at Covent Garden, complained of a lack of fire, of a studiousness that toppled sometimes into tedium. Already as Hamlet, Kemble was developing his own particular style, which Bertram Joseph has defined as 'his way of working himself into a part, of pulling it together into one overwhelmingly concentrated and classical drive forward' (Joseph, 214), and not everyone had the patience to wait to see what he was driving towards.

Even so, it was undeniable that Kemble had made an auspicious beginning, and his second Drury Lane season maintained the momentum. After returning to Liverpool and Joseph Younger for the summer of 1784, he negotiated with Sheridan a salary increase to 10 guineas per week, and opened as Hamlet on 21 September 1784. Equally significant was his success in the title role of Joseph Addison's *Cato*, the first of the Roman heroes with whom he became increasingly identified. Hazlitt, with a mixture of exasperation and admiration that characterized his commentaries on Kemble's acting, later described his Cato as 'a studied piece of classical costume—a conscious exhibition of elegantly disposed drapery, that was all: yet, as a mere display of personal and artificial grace, it was inimitable' (Rowell, 17). Not short of the necessary vanity of the major actor, Kemble not only looked good but also knew he looked good in a toga. He had the Roman nose and handsome head to match it. He also had the confidence to put himself forward as an adapter of plays. The 1784–5 season saw the first of well over thirty performed reworkings of 'old' English plays, most of them Shakespearian. Twenty-six were published in the collected edition of 1815.

Towards the end of his second season at Drury Lane, Kemble played a 'not easily moved' Othello to his famous sister's Desdemona, and, for his benefit on 31 March 1785, Macbeth to her Lady Macbeth. The production coincided with the publication of Thomas Whately's influential *Remarks on some of the Characters of Shakespeare*. Kemble was sympathetic to Whately's argument that the individual is a product of the interplay between a predominant principle of behaviour and coincidental subsidiary qualities. He made no secret of the fact that his study of Shakespearian character aimed to identify the leading passion of each tragic hero. But he disagreed with Whately's presentation of Macbeth as the 'type' of a coward. The Scottish tyrant was, for him, a victim of his own unvarying intrepidity: his crimes were consistent with his acts of heroism. Kemble's publication of *Macbeth Reconsidered* in 1786—an articulate, if sometimes confused, rebuttal of Whately—added to his scholarly reputation. Henderson's untimely death in 1785 had made Kemble the almost undisputed leading tragedian of the London stage, though he had not yet played either King Lear (21 January 1788) or the role which was, by general consensus, his finest, Coriolanus (7 February 1789). But he did not wish to be confined to tragedy, and his new roles in the 1786–7 season were mostly in comedy. In General John Burgoyne's *Richard Coeur de Lion* (24 October 1786) he even sang, though the popularity of this piece owed more to the voices of Mrs Crouch and Mrs Jordan. In *Cymbeline* on 29 January 1787, with his sister as Imogen, he played 'by a thousand degrees, the best Posthumus of my time' (Boaden, 1.344) and, on 14 April 1787, another Gothic brooder in Robert Jephson's *Julia*.

At the age of thirty Kemble was near the top of his stressful world. There were, however, problems. His winter performances were particularly affected by a troublesome cough and his summer performances by asthma, and he dosed himself with alcohol and opium. Furthermore, Sheridan's erratic management led often to the nonpayment of wages; a few years later, according to a manuscript in the British Library, Kemble was owed £1367 in back pay. And, though convivial outside the theatre, he was lonely. It was probably this last condition that lay behind his precipitate marriage on 8 December 1787. The wife he chose was an undistinguished Drury Lane actress, the widow of William Brereton and the daughter of a Drury Lane prompter, William Hopkins. The marriage survived until Kemble's death, but the overwhelming impression is that Priscilla *Kemble (1758–1845) never deeply engaged her husband's emotions. He did nothing to promote her career, and did not oppose—indeed, he may even have proposed—her retirement from the stage in 1796. If he were to continue to rise in society he needed a hostess, and that is a job the childless Priscilla managed tidily. Marriage to Kemble was a step up for her, and his awareness of that was evidently important to him. But the theatre was more important. Drury Lane needed him, and when, at the end of the 1787–8 season, Sheridan's exasperated acting manager Thomas King resigned, Kemble agreed to replace him. In his manuscript journal he wrote against the date of 23 September 1788, 'This day I undertook the management of D. L. Theatre' (BL, Add. MS 31972).

As acting manager of Drury Lane, Kemble had every intention of restoring the glory of the Garrick years. It was to be the home of the classic drama, above all of Shakespeare. The new drama mattered much less to him. Kemble signalled his intentions on 25 November 1788 with a lavish production of *Henry VIII*. In his own performance (initially as Thomas Cromwell, later as Cardinal Wolsey), in the demands made on scene and costume designers, and in his careful disposal of the hoards of extras he was at last able to experiment with 'visual rhetoric' (Bate and Jackson, 99). Odell's claim that Kemble was 'the first great "producer" of Shakespeare on the English stage' (Odell, 2.85) has substance. There was further evidence of that with the opening of *Coriolanus* on 7 February 1789. There was virtual unanimity of acclaim for Kemble's playing of the title role, and he would certainly have repeated it throughout the 1790s had not political events in France rendered the play unpalatable to the English censors.

Henry VIII and *Coriolanus* were by no means isolated triumphs of Kemble's management. Joseph Donohue has itemized his opulent 1794 production of *Macbeth* (Donohue, 'Kemble's production of *Macbeth*'), with its sixteen painted scenes and seven scene painters, and David Rostron has shown the care he took over the 1795 staging of *King Lear* (Richards and Thomson, 149–70). Despite the cares of management, he continued his private study of the roles he assumed. He was playing to audiences who applauded the detailed 'points', vocal and gestural, of leading actors, and it was in detail that he excelled. 'He never pulls out his handkerchief without a design upon the audience', wrote Leigh Hunt (Rowell, 11). But the decorum he valued in performance and in his public life concealed personal stress. There was the rebuilding of the condemned theatre to cope with, and the rehousing of the company from 1791 until the reopening on 12 March 1794. It was a period of extreme national tension, and Kemble was anathema to whigs and radicals. His Shakespearian productions implicitly harnessed the national poet to traditional values, and his personal aloofness often offended. Try as he might, he could not avoid scandal. He fought a farcical duel with the actor James Aickin in 1792, outraged the whig Sheridan by cancelling a performance on 25 January 1793 as a sign of respect to the executed Louis XVI, and lapsed all too frequently into bouts of excessive drinking that exacerbated the gout from which he was beginning to suffer. The abiding problem, though, was Sheridan, whose interventions at Drury Lane were as unpredictable as his failures to act in a crisis were predictable. With the grand new theatre opened in March 1794, and the style of spectacular staging that its massiveness demanded launched, Kemble was approaching the end of his tether.

The problems were not immediately apparent. On 9 June 1794 Kemble's own musical afterpiece *Lodoiska* began a successful run which continued into the 1794–5 season. It is a Gothic farrago which, while pandering to popular taste, reveals more of Kemble's own taste than is generally recognized. His Penruddock in Cumberland's *The Wheel of Fortune* belongs to the same genre. Before that play's triumphant opening on 28 February 1795, Kemble had been forced to make a public apology for his assault,

perhaps attempted rape, of a young actress. Undoubtedly he was drunk on that evening in January 1795, and certainly he was ashamed of himself, but the episode had a disturbing sequel. Maria De Camp, victim of the assault, fell in love with Kemble's younger brother Charles *Kemble (1775–1854). Their betrothal was announced in 1800, but it is claimed that Kemble opposed the match, forcing a delay until Charles reached the age of thirty. The couple were eventually married on 2 July 1806. Whatever the detailed facts, behind this broad outline there is an emotionally troubled man. Kemble escaped to Ireland with his wife at the end of the 1794–5 season, earning, as he had felt forced to do every summer, a star's money in the provincial theatre. 'Though he is not a miser', wrote Tate Wilkinson, 'yet I believe he will own he does not *hate* money' (Wilkinson, 3.66).

When he returned to London in August 1795 Kemble was about to experience the worst year of his theatrical life so far (worse was to come with the Old Price riots). Beset by debts, Drury Lane was in crisis, and the season was a flat one until the opening of the younger Colman's *The Iron Chest* on 12 March 1796. Kemble and Colman had been friends at least since 1793, when the playwright's *The Mountaineers* had provided the actor with one of his finest roles, but Kemble found nothing to please him in the Gothic guilt of Sir Edward Mortimer in *The Iron Chest*. Disdain as well as illness and opium contributed to his disastrous performance, and Colman was probably justified in attacking him in print when the second edition of the play was published. Kemble did not defend himself, but the episode took the heart out of his resistance to Sheridan's determination to stage *Vortigern*. This Shakespearian manuscript, 'discovered' by a youthful admirer of Chatterton called William Henry Ireland, had been denounced as a forgery by Kemble's friend the Shakespeare scholar Edmund Malone, but Sheridan cared more about the publicity than the manuscript. Bound by contract to play the title role, Kemble mischievously suggested that they should open on April fool's day, but it was on 2 April 1796, before a crowded house, that the travesty was enacted. According to eyewitnesses, Kemble's weighty delivery of the fifth-act line 'And when this solemn mockery is o'er' convulsed the audience, but he was sensitive to the insult to his status as a Shakespearian. He had been threatened with imprisonment for debts that were properly Sheridan's at the end of the previous year. *Vortigern* was the last straw. At the end of the 1795–6 season Kemble resigned from management and sailed for Dublin.

This was not the end of Kemble's Drury Lane career. He bargained with Sheridan for a weekly salary of £24 and continued as leading actor until the end of the 1801–2 season. He was even enticed, by promises of the right to purchase a share, to resume the management in 1800. During his final season he faced, for the first time since the death of Henderson, serious competition from Covent Garden in the person of the erratic George Frederick Cooke. His annual money-making forays into the provinces augmented a Drury Lane salary that, in 1799–1800, amounted to £1112. Openly ambitious to share the financial control of one of the patent theatres, he was bent on building his resources, and when his negotiations with Sheridan fell through he accepted the offer of a one-sixth share in Covent Garden, then under the principal management of Thomas Harris. The price was £22,000, of which £10,000 was to be paid in cash (borrowed from his banker friend Robert Heathcote) and the remaining £12,000 set against salary and future profits.

Kemble at Covent Garden Kemble's years at Covent Garden ought to have been, and in some ways were, his finest. He was a partner in, as well as acting manager of, a strong company which he had the personal pull to augment almost at will. To begin with, though, he needed a holiday. Leaving his wife to care for his ageing parents (her widowed mother had died in October 1801) and to manage the fine house in Great Russell Street that he had bought some years earlier, he set off with Robert Heathcote in July 1802 for a tour of the continent that would last until March 1803. The trip included a visit to the sadly dilapidated college at Douai, the start of an abiding friendship with the leading French actor Talma, hobnobbing with the nobility in Paris (since the revolution there were more English than French aristocrats there), and crossing the Pyrenees to visit Madrid and to sojourn with Lord Holland in Valencia. He was in Spain when he heard news of the death of his venerable father, and there is genuine affection in the letters he wrote to his brother Charles in response. The Kembles were a close family, so ready to promote each other's interests as to stimulate critics into charges of nepotism.

On his return to London, Kemble completed negotiations with Thomas Harris that would assure him a management salary of £200 per year and an acting salary of nearly £38 per week. Since the season would not open until September 1803 he spent part of the summer performing in Bath and Bristol and part, according to Boaden, buying books. Over the years Kemble accumulated a theatrical library that was unrivalled. After his retirement he sold his collection of 4000 plays and forty volumes of playbills to William Cavendish, sixth duke of Devonshire, and they now provide the nucleus of the Devonshire collection at the Huntington Library. A residue of 1677 titles, 181 prints and drawings, as well as manuscripts and notebooks, was auctioned by Evans in Pall Mall over ten days from 26 January 1821.

Kemble made his Covent Garden début as Hamlet on 24 September 1803. He later played Richmond to Cooke's Richard III, the King in *2 Henry IV*, Ford in *The Merry Wives of Windsor* (still hankering after versatility), and Antonio to Cooke's Shylock. Despite a tactful preparedness to play second fiddle to Cooke, Kemble could not win over all of the Covent Garden old guard. Theatres are jealous places, and there was predictable hostility to his importation of his brother Charles and his nephew and niece Henry and Harriet Siddons. No one, surely, would have dared voice an objection to the additional presence in the company of Henry's mother.

It was evidently among the Covent Garden employees that the nickname Black Jack began to stick to Kemble, whose pleasure in his second season was seriously marred by the craze for the Young Roscius, Master Betty. His motives for promoting the thirteen-year-old Betty at Covent Garden were solely commercial, and he was taken aback by the public's adulation of the beautiful boy. The seasons of 1805–6 and 1806–7 were largely devoted to re-establishing for Kemble and his theatre a reputation for serious devotion to the classics. It was as Prospero in his own mangled version of *The Tempest* (8 December 1806) that he risked the ridicule of audiences by insisting on pronouncing 'aches' ('Fill all thy bones with aches') as a two-syllable word, 'aitches'. The reason, as with most of the curious pronunciations for which he was notorious, was metrical, but his stubbornness was ominous. As his health failed through the 1807–8 season, when gout and the telling cough—or the alcohol and opiates he consumed to appease them—reduced his appearances, there were signs that his popularity was on the wane. The new century, as the old king's hold on reality weakened and the heir to the throne caroused with the whigs, was less wedded to decorum and propriety than the old one had been under the eyes of Beau Nash and the earl of Chesterfield. Kemble, perhaps, suffered by association: 'his patrician air became less representative as England became more industrial' (Bartholomeusz, 150).

Disaster may have been imminent, but when it struck it was by accident. On 20 September 1808 Covent Garden was destroyed by fire. Insurance covered less than half of the £100,000 loss. It was the generosity of friends and their own Sheridan-free speed of reaction that saved the proprietors. Just less than a year later, on 18 September 1809, a new Covent Garden, designed to represent Kemble's classical taste by the Greek revivalist Robert Smirke, was ready to open with Kemble and Mrs Siddons in *Macbeth*.

The sixty-seven nights that followed are famous in the history of popular intervention as the Old Price riots. They followed the decision of the proprietors, taken on the grounds of predictable income, to raise prices for the pit and boxes and, with a dangerous hint of élitism, to reduce the capacity of the gallery by introducing an additional twenty-six private boxes. Marc Baer selects, as the two key elements in gathering support for the rioters, 'the sense that an important didactic function of theatre was being undermined; and that something of the English character was at stake in this conflict' (Baer, 192). Not immediately, but increasingly and then almost exclusively, Kemble became the object of mob hatred and mass ridicule among the astonishingly well-organized rioters. He was caricatured as King John and Black Jack in the viciously satirical prints that proliferated. Popular songs were rewritten to incorporate him:

Your displeasure and groans he regards as mere trash,
And he spits in your face while he pockets your cash.
(Baer, 71–2)

His hunger for aristocratic recognition was pilloried:

With Lord O'Straddle I drink hop and nob,
And I am hand and glove with my Lord Thingumbob.
(ibid., 72)

Confronted each night by a mob set on drowning the play with their chanting, Kemble did his best to respond with dignity, but his body language was read as disdain. It was like York in 1779, but on a much larger scale and without the assured support of the majority of the audience. What had begun as a theatrical dispute had developed into a trial of the nation's liberty, and the outcome, however long delayed by Kemble's stubbornness, was inevitable. On 14 December 1809 Kemble formally accepted the demands of the rioters at a banquet in the Crown and Anchor tavern. The Old Price riots had widened the split between whigs and tories, and it was only the whig papers that announced John Bull's triumph over King John.

It took all of Kemble's considerable courage to play out the remnant of the 1809–10 season. Over the summer he rested and drank with his friend Francis North, fourth earl of Guilford, in the North family's opulent home, Wroxton Abbey, near Banbury. Kemble was gratified by the warm reception given him at Covent Garden in 1810–11, but the season was essentially one of recuperation and the playing of familiar roles. It was not until 29 February 1812 that he attempted his next, and last, new role, that of Brutus in *Julius Caesar*. As always with Shakespeare, Kemble radically reworked the text in order to present it in the shape he had predetermined, but the outcome, however questionable by Shakespearians, was 'one of the most significant revivals in the play's history. … Throughout the next eighty years audiences saw no production which did not owe a direct and profound debt to the 1812 revival' (Ripley, 73). Kemble's intelligence may not have been strictly literary, but it was still formidable. Mrs Siddons retired at the end of the 1811–12 season, making her farewell as Lady Macbeth opposite her brother. Kemble's tears on the occasion may have been tinged with envy. He was about to resign from active management and take two years leave from Covent Garden. Apart from a short visit to Paris in autumn 1813 it was not a leave from acting. Having failed to find a buyer for his share in Covent Garden he filled his purse with provincial appearances in Liverpool, Edinburgh, Dublin, Bath, Bristol, and Dublin again. He was preparing for retirement, and his final seasons at Covent Garden had a valedictory air. Even fully fit, he would have been hard-pressed to meet the challenge of Edmund Kean at Drury Lane. Only twelve days separated Kemble's return to Covent Garden as Coriolanus on 15 January 1814 from Kean's sensational début as Shylock on 27 January. For Leigh Hunt, under the spell of Kean, Kemble 'appears to submit everything to his judgement, and exhibits little of the enthusiasm of genius' (Rowell, 8). For his farewell performance as Coriolanus on 23 June 1817, Kemble shrugged off the ill health that had dogged him. Rapturous applause and shouts of 'No farewell!' followed the fall of the curtain. Four days later there was a dinner in his honour at the Freemasons' Tavern (Kemble had been a mason since 1808): 336 people paid 2 guineas each for a ticket.

Mostly through sheer hard work, Kemble had saved enough for a comfortable retirement. After some months of travel in Scotland and through France, he and his wife settled in Toulouse early in 1819. His fragile health improved: 'I have never had a cough since I have been at Toulouse', he wrote on 27 February 1820, 'my spitting of blood has, I am willing to persuade myself, entirely ceased; and my fits of the gout have been for this twelve-month past so slight, that I make a pish at the sufferance' (Boaden, 2.566). Relations between France and England, though, were still tense in 1820, and the Kembles thought it prudent to move to Lausanne in the spring. The death of Thomas Harris in November 1820 brought Kemble back to London, where he took the opportunity to make his will. The disposal of his Covent Garden interests, though, was not so easy. In the event he made a gift of his share to his brother Charles. 'My father received the property with cheerful courage and not without sanguine hopes of retrieving its fortunes', wrote Fanny Kemble many years later, 'instead of which it destroyed him and his family' (Ransome, 11). There was no malice in the gift, but it was typically canny of Kemble to rid himself of an awkward entanglement. He was back in Lausanne for Christmas 1820, settling in to a routine of reading, gardening, and receiving occasional visitors. In autumn 1822 he paid a reverential first visit to Rome, but the trip tired him. Back in Lausanne he suffered a stroke on 24 February 1823, and he died there on 26 February. Boaden, on no very convincing evidence, believes that he had converted to protestantism before his death (Boaden, 2.580). He was buried in the Lausanne cemetery, and a statue in the character of Cato, after Flaxman, was erected in Westminster Abbey, where it remained until 1865. His widow received an annuity of £1000 per annum and the interest from £17,000 as well as household goods. After her husband's death she returned to England, where she lived in comparative seclusion until her death in 1845.

Kemble and the theatre Because he came between Garrick and Kean, Kemble has suffered by comparison with both, not least because historians have tried to pin him to a single style. He is presented as coldly classical, surrounded on either side by 'hot' actors:

Precise in passion, cautious ev'n in rage,
Lo Kemble comes, the Euclid of the stage.
(Kelly, 193)

His mastery of Roman characters has counted against his posthumous reputation, spreading a picturesque stillness that is wholly imaginary over every role he performed. The probability is that he adapted his technique to the vast new Drury Lane in 1794. Audibility was a problem there, even for actors untroubled by breathing difficulties and a persistently threatening cough. The energetic movement that characterized his early performances would have made things worse.

A hugely attractive subject for painters, Kemble came to represent the transition from Reynolds to Lawrence. He was, at his most tragically impressive, both representative of what is typical in human nature and what is splendid. At a time when history painting was rated above all other kinds, he pictorialized himself as history in an honest quest for the sublime, and if he sometimes mistook Gothic gloom for sublimity he was not alone in that.

Kemble was an immensely thoughtful actor, but his thinking preceded his playing. Leigh Hunt, who found much in his acting to criticize, conceded that 'no player, perhaps, understands his author better' (Rowell, 11). But it is important to recognize the aim of Kemble's study. Believing that all human behaviour is explicable, he sought to discover the ruling passion that dictated the reactions (more often than the actions) of the character he was to play. Once that discovery had been made, he reshaped the text to show that passion in conflict with circumstance. It was an intensifying of human experience, but representative of it. As Hazlitt recognized, Kemble aimed always to build intensity towards an explosive climax. Psychologically drawn and physically suited to stoical Romans, he excelled also where pathos and melancholy were dominant and with the fierily single-minded (he was a fine Hotspur). As Joseph Donohue has keenly argued, Kemble strove, both as actor and producer of plays, to present in dramatic form the essence of human nature and its relationship to the outside world as the Romantic age consistently viewed it. No actor is for all time, but Kemble was the supreme actor for an age.

PETER THOMSON

Sources J. Boaden, *The life of John Philip Kemble*, 2 vols. (1825) · H. Baker, *John Philip Kemble: the actor in his theatre* (1942) · T. Wilkinson, *The wandering patentee, or, A history of the Yorkshire theatres from 1770 to the present time*, 4 vols. (1795) · Highfill, Burnim & Langhans, *BDA* · M. Baer, *Theatre and disorder in late Georgian London* (1992) · J. Donohue, *Dramatic character in the English romantic age* (1970) · D. Bartholomeusz, *Macbeth and the players* (1969) · J. Ripley, *Julius Caesar on stage in England and America, 1599–1973* (1980) · L. Kelly, *The Kemble era* (1980) · J. Williamson, *Charles Kemble: man of the theatre* [1964] · E. Ransome, ed., *The terrific Kemble* (1978) · G. Rowell, ed., *Victorian dramatic criticism* (1971) · G. C. D. Odell, *Shakespeare from Betterton to Irving*, 2 (1920) · K. Richards and P. Thomson, eds., *The eighteenth century English stage* (1972) · J. Bate and R. Jackson, *Shakespeare: an illustrated stage history* (1996) · B. Joseph, *The tragic actor* (1959) · J. Donohue, 'Kemble's production of Macbeth', *Theatre Notebook*, 21 (1966–7), 63–74 · S. West, *The image of the actor* (1991) · A. Sprague, *Shakespeare and the actors* (1944) · E. Inchbald, *A simple story*, ed. J. M. S. Tompkins (1967) · MS journal of John Philip Kemble, BL, Add. MS 31972
Archives BL, professional memoranda, Add. MSS 31972–31975 · Bodl. Oxf., transcripts of documents relating to theatre · Folger, annotated plays and papers · Harvard TC, MSS · Harvard U., Houghton L., papers | BL, letters to third Lord Holland and Lady Holland, Add. MSs 51821–51825, 51846–51848 · BL, corresp. with Samuel Ireland, Add. MS 30348 · Bodl. Oxf., letters to William Godwin · Hunt. L., Devonshire MSS · RA, corresp. with Thomas Lawrence · U. Hull, Brynmor Jones L., letters to Sir Charles Hotham-Thompson · V&A, letters to Elizabeth Inchbald
Likenesses oils, 1794, V&A · T. Lawrence, oils, exh. 1798, Guildhall Art Gallery, London · T. Lawrence, oils, 1801, Tate collection [*see illus.*] · T. Lawrence, pencil study, 1801, NPG · H. Hone, copper miniature, 1809, Garr. Club · G. H. Harlow, oils, exh. 1815, Royal Shakespeare Memorial Theatre Museum, Stratford upon Avon · J. Flaxman, sculpture, 1826, Westminster Abbey · W. Beechey, oils, Dulwich Picture Gallery, London · R. Cosway, miniature, V&A · S. De Wilde, oils (as Penruddock in *The wheel of fortune*), Garr. Club · J. Flaxman, bust, Sir John Soane's Museum, London · J. Gibson, bust, Sir John Soane's Museum, London · J. Gibson, pencil drawing, BM · G. H. Harlow, group portrait, oils (*Court for the trial of Queen Catherine*), Royal Shakespeare Memorial Theatre Museum, Stratford upon Avon · T. Lawrence, oils (as Cato), Garr. Club · W. Owen, oils, Graves Art Gallery, Sheffield · G. Stuart, oils, NPG · theatrical prints, BM, NPG · theatrical prints, Theatre Museum, London
Wealth at death considerable: will, Boaden, *Life* vol. 2, pp. 589–94

Kemble [*née* De Camp], **Maria Theresa** (1777–1838), actress, was born in Vienna on 17 January 1777, the eldest of the six children of George Lewis De Camp, a musician, and his wife, Jeanne Adrienne Dufour, a dancer. She was brought to England as a child, and at the age of eight appeared at the King's Theatre as Cupid in a ballet of Noverre. After playing in a theatre directed by M. Le Texier Zélie in a translation of Madame de Genlis's *La Colombe*, she was engaged to dance for the Royal Circus. On the alleged recommendation of the prince of Wales she was subsequently engaged by Colman for the Haymarket, where she appeared in a ballet entitled *Jamie's Return*. She was then secured for Drury Lane, where, as Miss De Camp, on 24 October 1786, she played Julie in Burgoyne's *Richard Coeur de Lion*. She remained there for the following five seasons, performing in speciality dances and other small parts, though she also appeared at the Haymarket during the summers. Her father, who died in Germany in 1787, had taught her no English, and the few words she spoke were acquired by imitation. According to the *Biographia dramatica*, reading, writing, and arithmetic were taught her by Viscountess Perceval, and music and Italian by a Miss Buchanan.

Maria Theresa first attracted public attention on 15 August 1792 at the Haymarket, when, in *The Beggar's Opera*, she performed Macheath to John Bannister's Polly, in one of the experiments of changing the sex of the exponents then in vogue at that theatre. Biddy in *Miss in her Teens*, Adelaide in *The Count of Narbonne*, and Gillian in *The Quaker* were then assigned her; and she also played some original parts, including Lindamira in Cumberland's *Box Lobby Challenge*, Judith in *The Iron Chest*, and Irene in *Blue Beard*. In singing parts she was allowed at times to replace Anna Storace and Anna Maria Crouch, and was considered a pleasing vocalist. She continued performing at Drury Lane in the winters, but did not appear at the Haymarket after 1800, travelling instead to theatres in Birmingham, York, Edinburgh, and other towns. In 1795 she received a public apology in the newspapers from her London manager, John Kemble, for his attempt to rape her behind the scenes. Rescued by her theatrical colleagues, De Camp was vindicated in the press and by Kemble himself, who acknowledged her character to be irreproachable.

For her benefit, on 3 May 1799, De Camp gave at Drury Lane her own unpublished play *First Faults*. In the same year William Earle jun. printed in octavo a poor piece called *Natural Faults*, and accused De Camp in the preface of having stolen his plot and characters. In a letter to the *Morning Post*, dated 10 June 1799, she positively denied the charge, and asserted that her play was copied by Earle from recitation. In *Some Account of the English Stage*, Genest

Maria Theresa Kemble (1777–1838), by Samuel De Wilde [as Patie in *The Gentle Shepherd* by Allan Ramsay, adapted by Richard Tickell]

observed that Earle's statement 'has the *appearance of truth*'.

After a lengthy courtship, and some delay given the disapproval of his family, Maria Theresa De Camp married Charles *Kemble (1775–1854) on 2 July 1806 at St George's, Bloomsbury. She then accompanied him, and the rest of the Kemble clan, to Covent Garden, where she made her first appearance as Maria in *The Citizen*; she remained there for the rest of her acting career. During the years that followed, she wrote three additional comedies, and performed in them for either her own or her husband's benefits. Only *The Day after the Wedding, or, A Wife's First Lesson* and *Smiles and Tears, or, The Widow's Stratagem* were printed, but critical comment about these and her other works was gentle. Genest described the latter's comic scenes as good, but thought 'the serious scenes … rather disgusting than pleasing'. Among the parts assigned to her were Ophelia, Violante in *The Wonder*, Beatrice in *Much Ado about Nothing*, and Mrs Ford in *The Merry Wives of Windsor*. An admirable actress of chambermaids, she was also excellent as Mrs Oakley and Lucy Lockit. She was good-looking, intelligent, and so industrious that she was said in her early life to have almost lived at Drury Lane. A writer for *Blackwood's Magazine* (April 1832) spoke of her as 'a delightful dark-eyed, dark-haired girl, whose motion was itself music ere her voice was heard', and commented on her remarkable charm.

Mrs Kemble performed rarely after 1814–15, but did not officially retire until she played Lady Julia in *Personation* (9 June 1819). A single reappearance was made at Covent Garden as Lady Capulet on the début of her daughter Fanny *Kemble as Juliet, on 5 October 1829. Maria Theresa Kemble died at Addlestone, near Chertsey, Surrey, on 3 September 1838. She was survived by her husband and their four surviving children: John Mitchell *Kemble, Henry Vincent James Kemble (1812–1857), Fanny, and Adelaide *Kemble.　　　JOSEPH KNIGHT, *rev.* K. A. CROUCH

Sources Highfill, Burnim & Langhans, *BDA* · C. B. Hogan, ed., *The London stage, 1660–1800*, pt 5: 1776–1800 (1968) · Genest, *Eng. stage*, vol. 8 · D. E. Baker, *Biographia dramatica, or, A companion to the playhouse*, rev. I. Reed, new edn, rev. S. Jones, 1/2 (1812), 427–9 · *Thespian Magazine*, 2 (Dec 1793), 360 · *Thraliana: the diary of Mrs. Hester Lynch Thrale (later Mrs. Piozzi), 1776–1809*, ed. K. C. Balderston, 2nd edn, 2 (1951), 911 · *GM*, 2nd ser., 10 (1838), 565 · M. T. Kemble, *Day after the wedding, or, A wife's first lesson* (1808) · M. T. Kemble, *Smiles and tears, or, The widow's stratagem* (1815) · J. Wilson, 'Miss Fanny Kemble's tragedy', *Blackwood*, 31 (1832), 673–92 · [J. Haslewood], 'Mrs E. Kemble', *The secret history of the green rooms: containing authentic and entertaining memoirs of the actors and actresses in the three Theatres Royal*, 2 (1790), 253–63 · J. Roach, *Roach's authentic memoirs of the green room* (1796) · *The thespian dictionary, or, Dramatic biography of the present age*, 2nd edn (1805) · A. Pasquin [J. Williams], *The pin-basket to the children of Thespis* (1797) · T. Holcroft, *Theatrical Recorder*, 2 (1805)

Likenesses R. M. Paye jun., stipple, pubd 1805 (after E. A. Paye), BM · S. De Wilde, watercolour, 1808, Garr. Club · Cardon, engraving (as Catherine in *Catherine and Petruchio*; after S. De Wilde), repro. in Cawthorne, *Minor British theatre* (1806) · A. E. Chalon, pen and watercolour drawing, NPG · J. Condé, engraving, repro. in *Thespian Magazine* · S. De Wilde, black and red chalk drawing, V&A · S. De Wilde, oils (as Patie in *The gentle shepherd*), Garr. Club [*see illus.*] · Mackenzie, engraving (after Dighton), repro. in *Thespian dictionary* · W. Ridley, engraving (after J. Barry), repro. in *Monthly Mirror* (1801) · silhouette, Garr. Club · theatrical prints, BM, NPG · twenty prints, Harvard TC

Kemble [*née* Hopkins; *other married name* Brereton], **Priscilla** (1758–1845), actress, was born in London on 17 December 1758, the younger daughter of two struggling actors, William Hopkins (*d.* 1780) and Elizabeth Barton (1731–1801). It was not until after her birth that her father became established as prompter to, and her mother as an actress in, the Drury Lane company. It was at her parents' benefit on 19 April 1773 that she made her first appearance on the Drury Lane stage, delivering a specially composed 'Address to the town' at the conclusion of *As You Like It*. In his final season of 1775–6, Garrick employed her fairly regularly in minor roles, most challengingly as Celia in William Whitehead's *The School for Lovers*, but also as the young Prince Edward for his own final appearances as Richard III. At the end of her second season, 1776–7, she and her sister were awarded a joint benefit, where receipts amounted to a gratifying £237 (less house charges of £65). While she was not an outstanding beauty, Priscilla Hopkins was petite and lively enough to win a summer engagement at the increasingly fashionable theatre in Bath, principally as a soubrette. She was probably already infatuated with the talented but erratic William Brereton (1751–1787), some eight years her senior. In August 1777 what may have been an attempted elopement on her part, and a mere seduction on his, was foiled, and the couple

Priscilla Kemble (1758–1845), by Richard James Lane, pubd 1830 (after Sir Thomas Lawrence)

were formally married in Bath on 24 September 1777. Just what should be read in her continuing to perform as Miss Hopkins during the 1777–8 season at Drury Lane is uncertain. The marriage was probably doomed from the start, but the Breretons acted together at the Crow Street Theatre in Dublin during the summer of 1778, and it was as Mrs Brereton that Priscilla appeared during the next eight seasons at Drury Lane. Substantial roles included Mistress Ford in *The Merry Wives of Windsor* and the widowed Anne in *Richard III*.

By 1784, with Brereton drinking heavily, increasingly unstable, and probably desperately in love with an unmoved Sarah Siddons, the marriage was effectively over. He attempted suicide more than once, and was finally incarcerated in the Hoxton Lunatic Asylum when he threatened Priscilla's life. He died there on 17 February 1787. Presumably consolable, his young widow continued her engagement at Drury Lane, and on 8 December 1787 she made a second startling marriage. Her new husband, John Philip *Kemble (1757–1823), was the leading tragedian of his generation, and could certainly have found a more impressive partner.

None of Kemble's biographers has had much to say about the marriage. James Boaden, who knew the couple best, credits the wife whom Kemble generally called Pop with 'quiet manners, steady principle, and gentle temper' (Boaden, 1.374), and the survival of the partnership, despite Kemble's frequently disorderly drinking, occasional philandering, and tumultuous theatrical career, must say something about her tolerance. What is surprising, given the Kembles' preparedness to promote each other's careers, is Priscilla's lack of advancement, even after her husband's promotion to manager of Drury Lane in September 1788. There is an odd perfunctoriness even about the wedding day: that same evening Priscilla appeared as Louisa Dudley in Richard Cumberland's *The West Indian*. If she had talent as a performer, it would seem almost as if Kemble, either carelessly or intentionally, suppressed it. If she had not, he was never so starry-eyed as to deceive himself. By the season of 1795–6 her salary at Drury Lane had risen to £6 per week, but that was her last year as an actress. On 23 May 1796 she made her farewell appearance, as Flavia in her husband's adaptation of Dryden and Cibber's *The Comical Lovers*: the play was sufficiently altered to merit the new title of *Celedon and Florimel*. From then until Kemble's death in 1823, Priscilla seems to have been content to serve as a prop to his glittering social and theatrical career, accompanying him on most, but not all, of his travels until his retirement in 1817. There were social advantages, certainly. Neither as Miss Hopkins nor as Mrs Brereton would she have been invited to Wroxton Abbey as a guest of the earl of Guilford or to Haddo House, Lord Aberdeen's Scottish home. A sense of social achievement breathes through the letter she wrote to Elizabeth Inchbald after her 'every way triumphant' management of the marquess of Abercorn's amateur theatricals at Bentley Priory in 1802 (Kelly, 143–4), while Kemble was in Paris with his banker friend Robert Heathcote.

From 1818 to 1820, doctors having advised the asthmatic John Philip to escape the English damp, the Kembles lived in Toulouse, and from 1820 until his death in Lausanne. They had sold their house in Great Russell Street and could afford to live comfortably. After Kemble died his widow returned to England, assured of a £1000 annuity and the income from any goods and properties she chose to sell. She lived initially at Heath Farm in Hertfordshire, where she was visited by her niece Fanny Kemble. Fanny enjoyed the riches of her aunt's library, reading Byron and Jeremy Taylor 'on the mossy-cushioned lawn under a beautiful oak tree, with a cabbage leaf of fresh-gathered strawberries and a handful of fresh-blown roses beside me' (Ransome, 19). At some time in the 1830s Priscilla moved to Leamington, where she devoted herself to good works and continued to read avidly. She died there on 13 May 1845, at the age of eighty-six, and was buried in the private chapel of the Greatheed family in St Mary's, Warwick. Her principal beneficiary was her brother-in-law Charles Kemble.   PETER THOMSON

Sources Highfill, Burnim & Langhans, *BDA* · H. Baker, *John Philip Kemble* (1942) · J. Boaden, *Memoirs of the life of John Philip Kemble*, 2 vols. (1825) · L. Kelly, *The Kemble era* (1980) · J. Williamson, *Charles Kemble: man of the theatre* [1964] · E. Ransome, *The terrific Kemble* (1978)

Likenesses Walker, line engraving, pubd 1776 (after J. J. Barralet), NPG · line engraving, pubd 1776 (after J. Roberts), NPG · J. Collyer, line engraving, pubd 1777 (after D. Dodd), repro. in *The new English theatre*, 12 vols. (1776–7) · Pollard, line engraving, pubd 1778 (after J. Roberts), NPG · J. Thornthwaite, line engraving, pubd 1778, NPG · coloured line engraving, pubd 1778, NPG · R. J. Lane, lithograph, pubd 1830 (after T. Lawrence), BM, NPG [*see illus.*] · T. Lawrence, pencil and chalk drawing · theatrical prints, BM, NPG
Wealth at death not known but not inconsiderable; residue of estate went to Charles Kemble: *GM* (July 1845)

Kemble, Roger (1722–1802), actor and theatre manager, was born in Hereford on 1 March 1722, the son of Roger Kemble, a tolerably prosperous barber, respected in Hereford despite the family's Roman Catholicism and rumoured Jacobite sympathies. The Father John Kemble who was executed in 1679 for suspected complicity in the Popish Plot was probably the barber's great-uncle. Nothing, beyond the fact that she had at least four children, is known of the elder Roger Kemble's wife, and it is only supposition that his parents were opposed to the younger Roger's decision, in 1752, to abandon the barber's trade for the stage.

Kemble's first known engagement was with a company based in Canterbury, where he soon formed a liaison with the actress Elizabeth (Fanny) *Furnival (*fl.* 1731–1752). Although she called herself Mrs Kemble (sometimes Campbell), it is unlikely that the couple married, and they were anyway separated when Kemble joined a Warwick-based company under the management of John Ward. The details of the whirlwind romance between the thirty-year-old Kemble and the manager's tall and handsome daughter Sarah (1735–1807) are obscure. According to Jane Williamson, drawing on unpublished family memoirs, they eloped (Williamson, 12). They were certainly married in Cirencester on 6 June 1753. Sarah was seventeen, headstrong and in love, and her father, however angry, was sufficiently fond (as well, perhaps, of her acting talent as of herself) to receive the young couple back into the company. The probability is that Kemble was a lesser actor than his wife, and that the theatrical dynasty they founded owed more to her than to him. The first five of their twelve children were born between 1755 and 1761, while they were touring with John Ward's company, and their various birthplaces (Brecon, Prescot, Kington, Hereford, Warrington) record a theatrical itinerary. Briefly, from 1761 to 1763, the Kembles set up a touring company of their own, but they were with Ward again from 1763 to 1766, when Ward retired and Kemble took over the management.

For the next fifteen years the Kemble company toured, predominantly in the Worcester region and along the Welsh border, straying occasionally into Wales. The playwright, novelist, and radical Thomas Holcroft, who was with the company in 1771–2, and whose novel *Alwyn* draws on the experience, describes a travelling company of comedians as 'a small kingdom, of which the manager is the monarch' (*Memoirs of Thomas Holcroft*, 93), but his *Memoirs* acknowledges that the Kemble company 'was more

Roger Kemble (1722–1802), by William Ridley, pubd 1791

respectable than many other companies of strolling players'. Even so, 'it was not in so flourishing a condition as to place the manager beyond the reach of the immediate smiles or frowns of fortune' (ibid., 90). It is doubtful whether Kemble would have been able to retire in 1781, having sold his theatrical stock and interests to John Boles Watson, had it not been for the prospect of future support from his two eldest children, soon to be famous as Sarah *Siddons and John Philip *Kemble. His daughter Ann Julia *Hatton became an actress and writer.

The marriage of Kemble and Sarah Ward seems to have been a harmonious one, despite the fact that he was Catholic and she protestant. Their sons, it was agreed, would be brought up in their father's faith, and their daughters in their mother's. All the evidence suggests that the children retained love and respect for their parents and did their best to ensure that their retirement would be a comfortable one. Kemble was at Drury Lane on 10 October 1782 to see Mrs Siddons triumph as Isabella in Garrick's adaptation of Thomas Southerne's *The Fatal Marriage*, and dined with her after the performance, as she gushingly recalls in her *Reminiscences*:

> My Father enjoyed his refreshments, but occasionally stop'd short, and laying down his knife and fork, and lifting up his beautiful and venerable face, which was partly shaded by his silvered hairs hanging about it in luxuriant curls, let fall such abundant showers of delicious tears, that they actually poured down into his plate.   (Kelly, 20)

On 26 August 1788, for the benefit of his son Stephen *Kemble's wife at the Haymarket Theatre, Kemble came out of retirement for his only known London performance in a forgotten trifle called *The Miller of Mansfield*. Outshone as an actor by most of his children, he was staunchly supported by his wife. James Boaden, who visited the Kembles in their old age at their cottage in Kentish Town, was informed by Sarah that her husband was 'the only *gentleman* Falstaff that I have ever seen' (Boaden, 1.6). He recalls Kemble, his silver curls covered by a quaint silken cap to protect him against catching a cold, as a man of great polish and exquisite manners.

Basking in the reflected glory of his eminent elder children, Kemble had applied for, and been granted, a coat of arms in 1792, no longer a strolling player but a gentleman. He died on 6 December 1802 in John Philip Kemble's grand house at 89 Great Russell Street. It is not known where he was buried, but a letter from John Philip Kemble (who was in Madrid when his father died) to his younger brother Charles *Kemble agreed that 'his remains should be protected by a simple stone; but I beg that in the plain memorial inscribed on it, his AGE may be mentioned. Long life implies virtuous habits, and they are real honours' (Boaden, 2.367). In a will dated 14 January 1802 he left his stocks, his household goods, his money out on mortgages, and his five renter's shares in the Drury Lane Theatre Royal to his widow, with instructions on the disposal of the property to their surviving eight children after her death. Sarah died on 24 April 1807 and was buried at the church of St Marylebone on 29 April.

PETER THOMSON

Sources Highfill, Burnim & Langhans, *BDA* · J. Boaden, *Memoirs of the life of John Philip Kemble*, 2 vols. (1825) · L. Kelly, *The Kemble era* (1980) · J. Williamson, *Charles Kemble: man of the theatre* [1964] · *Memoirs of Thomas Holcroft*, ed. W. Hazlitt (1926) · M. Denning, *Theatre in the Cotswolds* (1993)
Archives Harvard TC, company records written by him
Likenesses T. Beach, oils, 1787, Victoria Art Gallery, Bath · W. Ridley, stipple, pubd 1791, BM, NPG [*see illus.*] · G. H. Harlow, group portrait, oils (*Court for the trial of Queen Catherine*), Royal Shakespeare Memorial Theatre Museum, Stratford upon Avon, Warwickshire · O. Humphry, watercolour miniature, Royal Shakespeare Memorial Theatre Museum, Stratford upon Avon, Warwickshire · Indian ink and wash, BM
Wealth at death stocks, household goods, money out on mortgages, five renter's shares at Drury Lane: will proved, 6 April 1803

Kemble, Stephen George (1758–1822), actor and theatre manager, was born on 3 April 1758 at Kington, Herefordshire, the second son of the eight surviving children of Roger *Kemble (1722–1802) and his wife, Sarah (1735–1807), the daughter of the theatre manager John Ward and Sarah Butcher. Both his parents were performers in John Ward's touring company, which Roger managed from 1766. Because of this peripatetic beginning Stephen received little formal education, although his brothers John Philip *Kemble and Charles *Kemble were educated at Douai. At the age of fourteen he was briefly apprenticed to a chemist in Coventry, 'but stimulated by the example of his brothers and sisters, then on the stage, sought for theatrical glory in an itinerant company' (*Thespian Dictionary*). He appears to have served his theatrical apprenticeship with Mark Moore's troupe at Painswick. In 1781 he

Stephen George Kemble (1758–1822), by James Heath, pubd 1808 (after John Raphael Smith)

joined Tate Wilkinson's company, and played the Earl of Essex at Doncaster in October and the title role in *St Ignatius* at York in December. In 1782 he toured to Cork, playing Pyrrhus in Ambrose Philips's *The Distrest Mother* and Wellborn in Philip Massinger's *A New Way to Pay Old Debts*, before transferring to the Capel Street Theatre, Dublin.

On 24 September 1783 Kemble made his London début, as Othello, at Covent Garden. Sardonic biographers suggest he was employed in error for his elder brother, John Philip, who joined Sarah *Siddons at the rival house in Drury Lane. The author of *The Secret History of the Green Rooms* was less than charitable about his Othello:

> Never was the heroic Moor so literally murdered. Many exclamations excited laughter; and so fond was he of Miss Satchell, the gentle Desdemona, that in embracing her he would have a kiss; the collision left one side of her face quite black, much to the entertainment of the audience. (Haslewood, 248)

The managers at Covent Garden were not taken with him, but Elizabeth Satchell (1762/3–1841) [*see* Kemble, Elizabeth] was. She married him on 20 November 1783 at St George's, Bloomsbury. Kemble saw out the season playing Bajazet in Nicholas Rowe's *Tamerlane*, Richmond in *Richard III*, Colredo in Henry Jones's *The Heroine of the Cave*, and other minor roles, and was paid a modest £95 for 190 performances. He fared best with the critics as Sealand in Richard Steele's *The Conscious Lovers*. The *Theatrical Review* thought 'his countenance … manly, agreeable, and expressive; and his voice particularly adapted to give energy to such paternal feelings, as Sealand is described to have. His greatest deficiency is—a taste of manner, and elegance of person' (Highfill, Burnim & Langhans, *BDA*). These criticisms were to be repeated throughout his career.

The Kembles left London and toured the provinces, making their début at Edinburgh, as Othello and Desdemona, on 23 February 1786. Stephen played several leading roles, including King John, Chamont in Thomas Otway's *The Orphan*, Don Carlos in Edward Young's *The Revenge*, and Old Norval in John Home's *Douglas*, in a season marred by the death of the couple's first child, George. The Kembles established a regular pattern of winter seasons in Edinburgh and summer seasons at George Colman's Haymarket in London, where 'he [was] merely useful in sentimental *Old Men*' (Haslewood, 248), including Dominick in Dryden's *The Spanish Fryar*, Bonniface in Farquhar's *The Beaux' Stratagem*, Mr Sturdy in *Half an Hour after Supper*, and a favourite, Sir Christopher Curry in Colman the younger's *Inkle and Yarico*.

In 1790, with two small children to support, Kemble began his management career at Coventry. The following spring the Kembles played Freeport and Amelia in the elder Colman's *The English Merchant*, at the new Theatre Royal in Newcastle, managed by his brother-in-law, Charles Edward Whitlock. Kemble assumed the management of Newcastle and the circuit of Chester, Lancaster, and Sheffield theatres in March 1791 for £300 a year rent and £1000 for properties. He enthusiastically programmed new plays and enticed London performers north, but without permission to raise house prices to cover the increased expenses. He escaped to the Haymarket for the summer, where Elizabeth Kemble chose his two-act farce entitled *The Northern Inn, or, The Days of Good Queen Bess*, adapted from Heywood, as her much needed benefit.

Back in Newcastle for the autumn and unperturbed by initial set-backs, Kemble expanded and leased the Edinburgh and Glasgow theatres from John Jackson for £1350 a year. The *Newcastle Chronicle* (5 November 1791) thought this would enable 'the manager, whose spirited exertions have always kept pace with the contingencies of his situation, to maintain a better company, and pay greater salaries, than any other connection out of London could support' (Robinson, 138). Initially Edinburgh promised much, netting more than £470 over its first four nights, but Kemble and Jackson, the previous manager, fell out over the terms of the lease and patent. The arguments are documented in such publications as *A Statement of Facts ... Relative to the Theatre Royal of Edinburgh* (1792) and *A Comparative View of the Rights and Merits of Mrs Harriet Esten and Mr Stephen Kemble* (1793). In brief, when Kemble reneged on the terms of his one-year lease, Jackson agreed to lease the theatre for the 1793 season to Mrs Esten, a popular actress, and one of the patentees, the duke of Hamilton, allowed her the patent. Denied lease and patent on the Theatre Royal, Edinburgh, Kemble opened a rival theatre in the quickly refitted Circus on 12 January 1793. His success, £180 on the first night, was quashed when Mrs Esten enforced her patent and had the new theatre temporarily closed on 6 February, and allowed only 'amusements of

various kinds', including concerts and 'imitations'. Reconciliation must have occurred during the spring, because by June 1793 Mrs Esten was performing for Kemble at Newcastle, and he advertised his sole management of the Theatre Royal, Edinburgh, in 1794.

Even while the debate over Edinburgh raged, Kemble had run a full touring season out of Newcastle and seen off a printed complaint from John Edwin about his poor salary, benefits, and excessive travelling expenses. He continued to expand, opening theatres at Berwick upon Tweed in 1794, Aberdeen in 1795, and Alnwick in 1796. In 1799 he leased the Durham circuit, with Scarborough, North and South Shields, and Sunderland. This final acquisition may have been to offset the decline at Edinburgh, where as Timothy Plain (otherwise Moncrieff Thriepland) complained to the *Scots Chronicle* (later published as *Letters on the Theatre in Edinburgh*), Kemble was passing off 'the *dross* of all theatres, merely because the Manager now and then treats us with a peep of his sister, the Siddons, and his brother John' (Plain, 8). Kemble himself took on more and more roles, although he was primarily suited to 'plain sentimental characters' (ibid., 22), and his modest abilities were not aided by his enormous size: by the 1790s he weighed 18 stone. The critic also accused him of letting the theatre fall into disrepair. Matters were so bad at Edinburgh that his farewell speech as manager in July 1800 was hissed off the stage. Kemble continued his management of the Newcastle and Durham circuits, but here too he was beset by criticism of the company and the condition of the theatres' fabric. In 1804 the proprietors of Newcastle were so exasperated that they advertised the theatre to let. Even the once loyal *Newcastle Chronicle* only advertised shows with London performers. In November 1806 Kemble yielded the management of Newcastle to William Macready.

Kemble continued to act and returned to Drury Lane in 1802 in the character of Falstaff. He composed a poem to mark his arrival:

> ... all good honest flesh, and blood, and bone,
> And weighing, more or less, some thirty stone!
> Upon the northern coast by chance we caught him,
> And hither in a broad-wheeled waggon brought him;
> ... Blest with unwieldiness (at least), his size
> Will favour find in every critic's eyes;
> (Kemble, *Odes*, 26)

Although the *Monthly Mirror* felt he was 'merely reciting the text, in the habit of Falstaff, instead of entering into the true jovial spirit of the character' (Highfill, Burnim & Langhans, *BDA*), the role became a speciality and he performed it at Manchester in 1804 and at Covent Garden in 1806. His performance record is patchy after this. In 1809 he brought out *Odes, Lyrical Ballads, and Poems*, a collection of his songs, addresses, and miscellaneous poems, including an intriguing pair: the pro-trade 'On the Slave Trade' (1784) and the counter-poem of 1808, 'Being fully convinced of my former errors'. Many of the addresses are topical, and the tone of the collection is overwhelmingly patriotic, revealing his keen ear for audience-rousing oratory.

Kemble returned to management briefly at Whitehaven in 1814, and as stage manager at Drury Lane in 1818, when he took the opportunity to cast his son, Henry Stephen *Kemble, in many unsuitable leading roles and to produce *Flodden Field*, a romantic drama, written by father and son. The following season Kemble returned to acting, but stepped down with the arrival of the acting phenomenon Edmund Kean in the company. His final performance was as the Miller in *The King and the Miller of Mansfield*, by Robert Dodsley, on 26 April 1820. Kemble died on 5 June 1822 at The Grove, near Durham, and was buried on 11 June in the chapel of nine altars in Durham Cathedral. His wife survived him by nineteen years, and both his children, Frances Crawford Kemble (1787–1849) and Henry Stephen Kemble (1789–1836), became performers.   J. MILLING

Sources Highfill, Burnim & Langhans, *BDA* · K. E. Robinson, 'Stephen Kemble's management of the Theatre Royal, Newcastle-upon-Tyne', *Essays on the eighteenth-century stage: proceedings of a symposium sponsored by the Manchester University dept. of drama*, ed. K. Richards and P. Thomson (1972), 137–48 · *The thespian dictionary, or, Dramatic biography of the eighteenth century* (1802) · [J. Haslewood], *The secret history of the green rooms: containing authentic and entertaining memoirs of the actors and actresses in the three Theatres Royal*, 2 (1790), 2 · J. Edwin, *To the public* (1793) · S. Kemble, *To the public* (1793) · J. Jackson, *A statement of facts, explanatory of the dispute between John Jackson and Stephen Kemble* (1792) · *Answers for Robert Playfair … to petition of Stephen Kemble* (1793) · *A comparative view of the rights and merits of Mrs. Harriet Pye Esten, &c. and of Mr. Stephen Kemble* (1793) · S. Kemble, *Petition of Stephen Kemble, manager of the New Theatre of Edinburgh, against Lord Swinton's interlocutor* (1793) · T. Plain [M. Thriepland], *Letters respecting the performances at the Theatre Royal, Edinburgh, originally addressed to the editor of the Scots Chronicle* (1800) · S. G. Kemble, *Odes, lyrical ballads, and poems on various occasions* (1809) · *Oxberry's Dramatic Biography*, 2/17 (1825)
Archives U. Durham L., account of performances at Sunderland Theatre
Likenesses R. Dighton, caricature engraving, pubd 1794, Harvard TC; repro. in Highfill, Burnim & Langhans, *BDA* · R. Dighton, coloured etching, pubd 1794, BM · drawing, 1802, V&A, Beard collection · C. Warren, engraving, pubd 1804 (after De Wilde) · S. De Wilde, watercolour, 1805, Garr. Club · S. Freeman, engraving, 1807 (after T. Kearsley), repro. in *Monthly Mirror* (1807) · J. Heath, engraving, pubd 1808 (after J. R. Smith) [*see illus.*] · J. Downman, portrait, 1812 · S. De Wilde, red chalk, Indian ink, and watercolour wash, 1817, BM · Meyrion, engraving, 1825 (as Falstaff in *The merry wives of Windsor*; after Singleton), repro. in *Oxberry's Dramatic Biography* · J. Rogers, engraving, 1825 (as Falstaff in *The merry wives of Windsor*; after G. H. Harlow), repro. in *Oxberry's Dramatic Biography* · S. De Wilde, watercolour (as Falstaff in *The merry wives of Windsor*), Harvard TC · G. H. Harlow, group portrait, oils (*Court for the trial of Queen Catherine*), Royal Shakespeare Memorial Theatre Museum, Stratford upon Avon; copy, Garr. Club · W. Loftis, watercolour (as Falstaff in *1 Henry IV*), Folger · J. R. Smith, stipple, BM, NPG · engraving, repro. in *British Stage and Literary Cabinet*, 4 (1820) · miniature, oil on wood panel (as Falstaff in *The merry wives of Windsor*), priv. coll. · stipple, BM

Kemeys family (*per. c.1570–1747*), landowners, were allegedly descended from Stephen de Kemeys who owned land in Monmouthshire about 1234. Between 1576 and 1783 nine members of the Kemeys family were sheriffs of Glamorgan while several represented the borough or the county of Monmouth in parliament. **Edward** [i] **Kemeys** (*d. c.*1607) held the estate in the late sixteenth and early seventeenth centuries. He was married first to Elizabeth, daughter of Rowland Morgan of Machen, and second to Catherine, daughter of William Kemeys of Llanrhymney and widow of Henry Morgan, the second son of Rowland Morgan of Machen. Between 1573 and 1608 he was on the commission of the peace and was four times sheriff of Glamorgan. According to contemporary reports, he was unscrupulous and 'abused every function which it was left to him as sheriff to commit'. In 1585, the Star Chamber indicted him for accepting a bribe and releasing a prisoner, selling offices, and imprisoning the county gaoler. In mid-1595 he handpicked a coroner's court jury in a murder case to save the life of a friend, and in 1599 he was fined £500 and 100 marks damages. This action also led to his removal from the commission of the peace 'until his right honourable the Lord Keeper should be better satisfied of his behaviour' (Williams, 107). He died about 1607 and his will was proved in March 1610.

In the seventeenth century the Cefn Mabli estate was owned by **David Kemeys** (*d.* 1617), a nephew of Edward [i] Kemeys. In 1616 he married Rachel, daughter of Sir Robert Hopton and coheir of her brother, Ralph, Lord Hopton. He was sheriff of Glamorgan in 1616–17. After his death by drowning in 1617 his son **Edward** [ii] **Kemeys** (*d.* 1637) gained ownership of the estate. He married Theodosia, daughter of Sir Henry Capel. Theodosia died on 1 January 1636 and Edward died one year later, on 12 January 1637. His daughter Elizabeth briefly succeeded him before dying on 31 January 1637. The title of the estate then passed to Elizabeth's great-uncle **Sir Nicholas Kemeys**, first baronet (*d.* 1648), of Llanfair Castle. In 1628 he was elected member of parliament for the borough of Monmouth, and in 1631–2 was appointed sheriff of Monmouthshire, and in 1638–9 high sheriff of Glamorgan. On 13 May 1642 he was created a baronet by Charles I and became the MP for Glamorgan. He was an ardent royalist commander during the first civil war. He raised a regiment of horse and was appointed governor of Cardiff Castle. On 25 May 1648 he died defending Chepstow Castle for three weeks after refusing to surrender to Cromwell's forces. His body was dismembered and parts of it later adorned the hats of his roundhead attackers. A later poem described Kemeys's brave defence of the castle:

> Let us Sir Nicholas Kemeys' name rehearse,
> Let not our bards his noble deeds forget!
> Perchance his bright example may be yet
> A beacon to some hero yet unborn!
> Our land may yet by cival war be torn
> Perchance some valiant Welshman yet may rise
> To emulate the deeds of our Kemeys!
> (Rowlands, 25)

Nicholas's son **Sir Charles** [i] **Kemeys**, second baronet (*c.*1614–1658), studied at Jesus College, Oxford, where he matriculated on 3 February 1632, and in 1634 he was a student at Gray's Inn. On 13 June 1643 he was knighted at Oxford, and on the death of his father in 1648 succeeded him as second baronet. He was similarly a staunch royalist who attacked Cardiff in 1646 and later defended Pembroke Castle. Upon its surrender he was fined £5262 and exiled for two years. He married twice; his first wife was Blanche, daughter of Sir Lewis Mansel of Margam, and his second wife was Margaret, daughter of Sir George Whitmore, lord mayor of London in 1631-2. He died in 1658 and was succeeded by his son **Sir Charles** [ii] **Kemeys**, third baronet (1651/2–1702). On 26 May 1669 he matriculated at Wadham College, Oxford, and on 9 July 1669 he was awarded the degree of MA. He was MP for Monmouthshire in 1685-7 and 1695-8, and for Monmouth borough in 1690–95. He also held the office of sheriff of Glamorgan about 1689, and he was the governor of Cardiff Castle in 1702. He married twice, but the indications are that he was a less than affectionate husband as he 'worshipped the bottle rather than his wife and proved demonstrably neglectful of her feelings' (Jenkins, 101). He died on 22 December 1702.

Sir Charles [ii] Kemeys's son **Sir Charles** [iii] **Kemeys**, fourth baronet (1688-1735), was born on 23 November 1688. He entered Trinity College, Cambridge, on 17 June 1706. In 1702 he became fourth baronet of Cefn Mabli, and he was sheriff of Glamorgan between 1712 and 1713 and MP for Monmouthshire in 1713–15 and for Glamorgan from 1716 to 1734. There were a number of political intrigues involving Charles [iii] Kemeys, notably concerning election expenses, and there is one tale of his friendship with George, the elector of Hanover, and his reluctance to accept him as the king of Great Britain. In spite of Kemeys' support for the Stuart cause, the king sought to renew his friendship with Sir Charles and allegedly remarked 'Send for him—tell him he must come. I long to smoke a pipe with him'. Kemeys nevertheless proved his loyalty to the Stuarts by stating, 'I should be happy to smoke a pipe with him as Elector of Hanover, but I cannot think of it as king of England' ('Cefn Mably', *South Wales Daily News*, Jan–Feb 1910). With his death, without issue, on 29 January 1735 the baronetcy became extinct.

In 1704 **Jane Kemeys** (*d.* 1747), the sister of Sir Charles [iii] Kemeys, married Sir John Tynte, second baronet (1683-1710), of Halswell, Somerset. They had three sons, Halswell (1705-1730), John (1707-1740), and Charles (1710-1785), and one daughter, Jane (1708-1741). The early deaths of their male grandchildren meant that the estate devolved to their granddaughter Jane Hassell (1738-1824). On 19 February 1765 she married Lieutenant-Colonel John Johnson of Glaiston, Rutland (*d.* 1806), and by royal licence granted on 28 October 1785 took the family name of Kemeys-Tynte. Jane Kemeys-Tynte died on 29 January 1824, and the male issue of the Kemeys-Tynte family throughout the nineteenth century then inherited the estate.   RICHARD C. ALLEN

Sources *A great overthrow given to the kings forces in Wales under the command of Sir Charles Kemish and Kerne the sheriff* (1645) • *DWB* • G. Williams, ed., *Glamorgan county history*, 4: *Early modern Glamorgan* (1974), 79, 82, 107, 111, 169–71, 174, 189, 191, 196, 199, 234, 237, 238, 260, 266, 273, 275, 277, 280, 389, 397–9, 404, 406–8, 410, 583 • 'Cefn Mably', *South Wales Daily News* (29 Jan 1910) • 'Cefn Mably', *South Wales Daily News* (5 Feb 1910) • J. Rowlands, *Welsh royalists: Sir Nicholas Kemeys, bart. Cefn Mably* (1879) • J. A. Bradney, *A history of Monmouthshire*, ed. M. Gray, vol. 5: *The hundred of Newport* (1993), 104–6 • G. T. Clark, *Limbus patrum: Morganiae et Glamorganiae* (1886), 413–15 • D. Morganwg, *Syr Nicholas Kemeys Gorchfygwr ac Amddiffynwr Casgwent* (1881) • Foster, *Alum. Oxon.* • Venn, *Alum. Cant.*, 1/3.5 •

M. Powell Siddons, *Visitations by the heralds in Wales* (1996), p. 194 • J. R. Phillips, *Memoirs of the civil war in Wales and the marches, 1642–1649*, 2 vols. (1874), vol. 2 • J. G. Jones, *Early modern Wales, c.1525–1640*, 11, 34, 205, 206 • A. Bielski, *The story of St Mellons* (1985), chaps. 10–11 • 'Glamorgan calendar rolls and gaol-files (1542–1830)', J. H. Matthews, *Cardiff records*, vol. 2, chap. 5, 171 • G. H. Jenkins, *The foundations of modern Wales* (1987), 18, 96, 101, 149–50 • P. D. G. Thomas, 'Jacobitism in Wales', *Welsh History Review / Cylchgrawn Hanes Cymru*, 1 (1960–63), 279–300, esp. 282 • W. S. K. Thomas, *Stuart Wales* (1988), 26, 45, 115, 184 • P. Gaunt, *A nation under siege: the civil war in Wales, 1642–48* (1991), 71, 73

Archives Glamorgan RO, Cardiff, Kemeys-Tynte MSS, estate and family MSS, D/D KT • Gwent RO, Cwmbrân, Monmouthshire, deeds and documents relating to family, NPT MSS M000-M469.5 • Gwent RO, Cwmbrân, Monmouthshire, family and estate MSS, D337-D1228 • NL Wales, Kemeys-Tynte MSS, estate and political corresp. | Bodl. Oxf., Tanner MSS • NL Wales, MSS 5172, 5178, 5181, 6535, 6546, 6548, 6587, 6588, 6594, 6610, 6611, 9263 • NL Wales, Penrice and Margam MSS, corresp.

Kemeys, Sir Charles, second baronet (*c.*1614-1658). *See under* Kemeys family (*per. c.*1570–1747).

Kemeys, Sir Charles, third baronet (1651/2–1702). *See under* Kemeys family (*per. c.*1570–1747).

Kemeys, Sir Charles, fourth baronet (1688-1735). *See under* Kemeys family (*per. c.*1570–1747).

Kemeys, David (*d.* 1617). *See under* Kemeys family (*per. c.*1570–1747).

Kemeys, Edward (*d. c.*1607). *See under* Kemeys family (*per. c.*1570–1747).

Kemeys, Edward (*d.* 1637). *See under* Kemeys family (*per. c.*1570–1747).

Kemeys, Jane (*d.* 1747). *See under* Kemeys family (*per. c.*1570–1747).

Kemeys, Sir Nicholas, first baronet (*d.* 1648). *See under* Kemeys family (*per. c.*1570–1747).

Kemnal, Sir James Herman Rosenthal (1864-1927), engineering manufacturer, was born James Hermann Rosenthal in London on 16 August 1864, the son of David Ferdinand Rosenthal and his wife, Elizabeth, *née* Marshall. His father, a naturalized British subject, was a glass and china dealer; his mother was of Scottish descent. Probably educated in London, he later studied at Cologne University, before undertaking an apprenticeship at the works of the Belgian State Railways. His first job was at the Anderston Foundry Company Ltd, Glasgow.

About 1883 Rosenthal joined a branch of Babcock and Wilcox, a firm based in New York, which manufactured water-tube boilers. In the 1880s Rosenthal supervised the London office, where he impressed the American owners both as an engineer and as a salesman. When a completely independent British firm of the same name was formed in 1891 (the New York parent had grown so fast that it had outrun its available capital), Rosenthal became the London managing director. Increasingly under Rosenthal's direction, the company expanded rapidly, especially into the European market. The use of electricity was growing swiftly, so increasing the demand for larger and more efficient boiler plant. The introduction of the steam turbine in 1884 not only resulted in a rapid expansion of electricity, particularly in the field of power as against lighting, but also ensured the water-tube boilers' adoption for marine purposes because of its savings in weight and space. In 1898 branch companies were opened in France and Germany; then before the First World War in Poland, Italy, and Japan. In 1900 Babcock and Wilcox was re-registered with an authorized and issued capital of £630,000, with Rosenthal as the managing director, a position he held until 1927.

Rosenthal's first marriage in 1889 was to Amelia, daughter of Richard Marshall, a manufacturer; they were later divorced. In 1905 he married Linda Larita, daughter of August de Leuse, of Nyallo, Victoria, formerly of Nice; they had one son. An autocrat and a hard taskmaster, Rosenthal—who changed his name to Kemnal in 1915—dominated Babcock and Wilcox with his energy, linguistic abilities (he was fluent in French and German), and salesmanship. Under his direction, the company was extremely profitable. Between 1898 and 1914 dividends never fell below 14 per cent, while only on six occasions was the rate below about 20 per cent (and this was aside from bonus issues in 1905 and 1912). The company grew to include, besides overseas subsidiaries and a Renfrew works, a tube works at Dumbarton, and boiler works in Oldbury and Lincoln. By Kemnal's death, capital had increased to £4.6 million and Babcock and Wilcox had over 10,000 employees worldwide.

In addition to Babcock and Wilcox, Kemnal also served on the boards of the Power Securities Corporation, Balfour, Beatty & Co. Ltd, and the Power and Traction Company (Poland) Ltd. He was chairman of Worthington-Simpson Ltd of London and of Newark, as well as undertaking the presidency of the British and Latin American chamber of commerce. A member of various technical societies—such as the Institution of Marine Engineers and the Institution of Mechanical Engineers—in the 1920s Kemnal presented numerous papers on steam-generating practice and became one of the earliest advocates of higher working pressures.

Kemnal was knighted in 1920. He was a liveryman of the Worshipful Company of Shipwrights, a freeman of the City of London, and a JP for Glasgow; had he lived an LLD would have been bestowed on him by Glasgow University. He was taken ill at his home, Kemnal Manor, Chislehurst, in 1926 and died on 8 February 1927 at Stormbanks Road, near Poole, Dorset. His second wife survived him.

GEOFFREY TWEEDALE

Sources G. Tweedale, 'Kemnal, Sir James', *DBB* · *The Engineer* (11 Feb 1927) · *Journal of the Institution of Electrical Engineers*, 65 (1927) · H. E. Metcalf, *On Britain's business* (1943) · *WWW*, 1916–28 · d. cert. · *CGPLA Eng. & Wales* (1927)
Archives U. Glas., Archives and Business Records Centre, Babcock and Wilcox records, UGD/309
Likenesses photograph, repro. in Tweedale, 'Kemnal, Sir James'
Wealth at death £452,726 3s. 9d.: probate, 2 July 1927, *CGPLA Eng. & Wales*

Kemp. *See also* Kempe.

Kemp [*née* Marshall]**, Elizabeth** [*known as* Lizzie Berry] (1847–1919), poet, was born in Great Bowden, Leicestershire, the daughter of Jeremiah Marshall (*b.* 1822), labourer, and his wife, Elizabeth (*b.* 1824), a dressmaker. She attended the village national school briefly. At the age of nineteen she was in Islington, London, possibly in service, and on 29 October 1866 was married there to John Archie Berry, plasterer. Their first child died in infancy. Two sons, Archie and Frank, were subsequently born, and soon afterwards the father died. She then married Edmund Kemp, a railway signalman, moving to Far Cotton near Northampton, and later to Watford. They had a daughter and two sons. But Kemp proved an errant husband and the stormy marriage ended in separation. By 1891 Lizzie was back in a cottage in Great Bowden with the three Kemp children, maintaining them all by her dressmaking. Her sons Archie and Frank Berry predeceased her, Frank dying in her arms at twenty-four as she took him home from the Brompton Consumptive Hospital. The other sons, Sidney and William Kemp, emigrated to Canada. Thereafter, for almost half her life, Lizzie lived alone, known always as Mrs Berry, dressmaker. She also published under the name Lizzie Berry.

Documentary records of Lizzie Berry's life are scanty. Its course and quality have to be gathered from the poems. For, despite her humble origin and sketchy schooling, Lizzie Berry became a prolific poet, highly regarded in her own sphere. Her first poems were published in the weekly *Midland Times* of Rugby and were collected into two volumes, *Poems* (1877) which contains eighty-seven poems and *Poems Volume II* (1879) with a further sixty-eight poems. She then started contributing to the *Wharfedale and Airedale Observer* and for some thirty-eight years between 1880 and 1918 she supplied a poem virtually every week, in addition to writing short stories and other poems. The newspaper paid her half a guinea a month, just the rent of her cottage.

Two collected volumes were published by the Yorkshire paper: *Heart Echoes* (1886), which contained 269 poems and reached a third edition by 1901, and *Day Dreams* (1893) which had 257 poems. Shortly before her death she was in correspondence with the same publisher about a possible third volume but 1918 was not a propitious time and it never appeared. However, she left two privately printed volumes, *The Tramp* and *The Wayside Inn*, as well as a scrapbook with 319 further poems pasted into it. These have been arranged with evident care, grouped sometimes by subject, sometimes by stanza form or metre, and it seems likely that this was her text for the projected third volume.

Lizzie Berry is a notable poet with a remarkable facility and technical skill in verse, who gained a wide and appreciative readership, as evidenced by the letters that came to the paper when she announced her retirement in 1918. She writes as a woman who knows pain and loss but also passionate love and the joys and exasperations of motherhood. She knows the corrosive power of betrayal and anger in marriage; she knows poverty; she deplores, sometimes with irony, sometimes savagely, hypocrisy and social pretension, the insensitivity of the comfortably off, and the airs of ladies of fashion whom she no doubt met in her trade. The poems also reveal a deep religious faith. Images abound of the pilgrim's steep and stony path and of storms breaking over defenceless heads. But God is always near and she draws on His strength to accept His will. Her many devotional poems affirm her Anglican faith; and her theological insight, unexpected in the light of her upbringing and hard-pressed life, is often striking.

Lizzie Berry took her role as poet seriously, using it to work through the trials of her life. The portraits in her books show a strong but rather plain face, hair tightly drawn back, but with large and expressive eyes which indicate the passionate, sensitive, independent character that the poems reveal. She died on 13 July 1919, in the influenza epidemic, at her home at 17 The Green, Great Bowden, and was buried four days later at Dingley Road cemetery. Appropriately the Yorkshire newspaper carried a dignified *In Memoriam* which was of her own composition. HENRY ARTHUR JONES

Sources L. Berry, *Heart echoes: miscellaneous and devotional poems* (1886) · L. Berry, *Heart echoes: miscellaneous and devotional poems*, 3rd edn (1901) · private information (2004) · m. cert. [John Archie Berry] · *Wharfedale and Airedale Observer* (18 July 1919) · d. cert.
Likenesses engraving, Bodl. Oxf.; repro. in L. Berry, *Poems*, 2 (1879) · photograph, Bodl. Oxf.; repro. in Berry, *Heart echoes* (1886) · photograph, repro. in L. Berry, *Day dreams: a collection of miscellaneous poems* (1893) · photograph, repro. in *Wharfedale and Airedale Observer*
Wealth at death £209 13s. 11d.: probate, 25 March 1920, *CGPLA Eng. & Wales*

Kemp, George Meikle [*pseud.* John Morvo] (1795–1844), architect, was born on 26 May 1795, at Hillriggs Farm, near Biggar, Lanarkshire, the son of James Kemp, a shepherd, and his wife, Jean Mulberry or Mowbray (d. c.1827), a family frequently on poor relief. Showing an early fondness for drawing, carving, and woodwork (he made furniture throughout his life), he was apprenticed as a carpenter to Andrew Noble of Redscaurhead (where his 1932 memorial was erected) before joining a millwright's shop in Galashiels in 1813 (part of his journey being a lift on Sir Walter Scott's coach). In 1815 he joined John Cousin, builder and joiner of Leith, as a journeyman carpenter, and he may periodically have returned to Cousin's firm whenever work was short elsewhere. In 1817 he moved to Lancashire, where he worked as a carpenter while studying Gothic architecture; he also practised as a carpenter in 1820 in Glasgow while attending evening classes. He moved to London in 1824, failed to find a permanent position, and travelled into France. Kemp considered emigrating to Canada, but returned to Scotland upon his mother's death. In 1827 he became a freemason of St Andrew's Lodge, Edinburgh. Probably through his brother Thomas, clerk of works to the duke of Buccleuch 1821–40, he was employed by William Burn on drawings for Bowhill, Selkirk, perhaps as clerk of works; he also worked extensively with John Smith of Darnick. In 1831 he constructed a large wooden model of proposals for Dalkeith by William Burn. In 1832 he married Elizabeth (Betsy)

George Meikle Kemp (1795–1844), by William Bonnar

Bonnar, daughter of an Edinburgh house painter and decorator.

After his views of Melrose were exhibited at the Royal Scottish Academy in 1830, Kemp was invited by a Mr Johnstone to prepare drawings for a proposed publication on 'Scottish cathedrals and antiquities'. He was still working on this in 1838, but the project foundered thereafter. By 1836 there was confusion about Kemp's profession. The antiquarian Revd John Sime called him an 'architectural artist', whereas, when completing the West Church in Maybole that year, Kemp referred to himself as an architect. Wholly absorbed in the rediscovery and recreation of the glories of medieval Scotland, Kemp may be compared to an architectural Thomas Chatterton. He drew a proposed restoration of Melrose Abbey, and (unless this was the work of his son Thomas) of Roslin Chapel, Midlothian, and a relocation of Trinity College Church, Edinburgh. His largest project at the time was the restoration of Glasgow Cathedral for Archibald MacLellan; but his drawings were published and forwarded to the Treasury in 1836 without any credit. Kemp presented a set to James Skene of Rubislaw, each drawing annotated 'John Morvo Archt' to underline his authorship. (Morvo was his pseudonym for his greatest work, the Scott monument commission.) Perhaps thinking that Kemp, however good an illustrator, had inadequate credibility as architect, MacLellan commissioned Gillespie Graham for new proposals. Mortified, Kemp exhibited drawings for the cathedral, with sketches for three original windows, and a model, with costs obtained from John Cousin in Edinburgh in 1838. In vain.

In 1836 Kemp was persuaded to enter the competition for a memorial in Edinburgh to Sir Walter Scott. For one of three premiated designs, he was awarded 50 guineas. The competition was rerun in 1838, and Kemp's design won for its 'strict conformity with the purity and style of Melrose Abbey' (Bonnar, 85). There was probably nobody in Scotland as familiar with Melrose Abbey as Kemp, and he won with a vertical and slender design which John Britton praised as a 'florid cenotaph' (Bonnar, 93). 'The whole building being composed of a substantial collection of buttresses and piers … a feature in which it is well known that the principal beauties as well as strength of gothic architecture resides', wrote Kemp, there were no walls at all (Bonnar, 97). The monument—perhaps the most striking commemoration of an individual in any British city—dominates Princes Street and contrasts with the classicism of the nearby art galleries. There was fierce controversy. William Burn admired 'the purity of Gothic composition and more particularly the constructive style', but then attempted to persuade Kemp to accept £100 and give the commission to him (Bonnar, 98).

Kemp's family moved in 1837 from Stockbridge to 'the land of Canaan', Bloomberry Cottage, Canaan Lane, Morningside. Contemplating entering partnership with John Cousin's son David, he demurred once he had decided to undertake the additional role of supervisor of the building works of the monument at 2 guineas a week. He passed on to David Cousin the proposed 'cheap church' that a Mr Blackie had offered him, and eventually sent his son Thomas to train with him. The foundation-stone of the Scott monument was laid on 15 August 1840. On 5 April 1843 Kemp was elected affiliate member, operative lodge journeyman, Edinburgh; but on 6 March 1844 he tumbled into the Union Canal at Fountainbridge, on his way home, and drowned. He was buried in St Cuthbert's churchyard, Edinburgh. At his death, it was thought he had achieved 'a prosperous position in business', but he died intestate, leaving assets of £202 and the model of Glasgow Cathedral 'which has proved unsaleable'. His wife survived him.

Kemp was excellent company, a prolific poet, devoted to his family, and had good rapport with his workmen, who regarded him as a role model. He never appears to have made the full transition from joiner to architect that, say, had been achieved only recently by Archibald Elliot. He is reputed to have had a hand in the design of the spiky churches of Millburn Free, Renton (1843), and St John's Free, George Street, Glasgow, designed by J. T. Rochead. But, besides the Scott monument and West Church, Maybole, the only buildings reliably attributed to him are the south wing at Woodhouselee, Midlothian, for James Tytler, and perhaps Gothic Bank, Morningside, fees for both of which were still owing at his death.   CHARLES MCKEAN

Sources T. Bonnar, *Biographical sketch of George Meikle Kemp* (1892) · Colvin, *Archs.* · *Plans of the proposed restorations and alterations to the cathedral of Glasgow*, Royal Incorporation of Architects of Scotland (1836) [G. M. Kemp's signed copy of this] · sheriff court records, commissariat of Edinburgh, NA Scot., SC 70/1/60, p. 354 · MSS and clippings in Bonnar volume, NA Scot., GD 327/5/1–12; GD 327/61– 161; GD 314/555/6 · index, National Monuments Record of Scotland · MSS by Thomas Bonnar, sketches possibly by Thomas Kemp, Edinburgh Central Reference Library, ECL/WNA/997 K 32 · *Edinburgh*, Pevsner (1984) · M. Glendinning, R. MacInnes, and A. MacKechnie, *A history of Scottish architecture* (1996) · J. Macaulay, *The Gothic revival* (1975) · J. Macaulay, 'The demolition of the western towers of Glasgow Cathedral', *The architecture of Scottish towns and cities*, ed. D. Mays (1997), 115–24 · C. McKean, ed., *Illustrated architectural guides to Scotland* (1982–)

Archives Edinburgh Central Reference Library, notebooks | Dalkeith Palace, Midlothian, model of proposals to Dalkeith Palace · National Monuments Record of Scotland, Edinburgh, Royal Incorporation of Architects in Scotland collection, Scott monument, proposed restoration of Melrose Abbey, and copy drawing of proposed completion of Roslin Chapel, possibly by son Thomas · Royal Incorporation of Architects in Scotland, Edinburgh, proposals for Glasgow Cathedral

Likenesses W. Bonnar, oils, Scot. NPG [*see illus.*] · D. O. Hill, calotype, Scot. NPG · D. O. Hill, sketch · D. Hunter, portrait · J. Hutchison, bust · A. H. Ritchie, plaster bust, Scot. NPG

Wealth at death £202 18s. 6d.: NA Scot., SC 70/1/60 p. 354, valuation

Kemp, Johannes Theodorus van der (1747–1811), missionary, was born on 7 May 1747 in Rotterdam, the Netherlands, the second son of Cornelius van der Kemp, the town's leading reformed clergyman, and Anna Maria van Teylingen. After attending the Latin schools of Rotterdam and Dordrecht, he enrolled in the University of Leiden in 1763. In part because he was rejecting reformed Christianity for deism, he studied medicine, but he soon became contemptuous of that science. The appointment of his elder brother, Didericus, as professor of church history was the spur which led him to abandon his studies and join the dragoon guards, as he did not wish to remain his brother's inferior. Both as a student and as an army officer he lived a libertine life, fathering an illegitimate child, Johanna ('Antje'), whom he brought up himself. In 1778 he fell in love with Christina ('Styntje') Frank (d. 1791), and he lived with her for a year before a reprimand from the prince of Orange on this irregular state of affairs caused him both to marry Styntje, on 29 May 1779, and quit the army.

Van der Kemp took up his medical studies again, in Edinburgh, and in two years had completed his degree, rounded off with some significant experiments into asphyxiation (entailing the drowning of cats). He also prepared for publication a treatise in Latin on cosmology, entitled *Parmenides* (1781), which was apparently well received by those few who read it. He then returned to the Netherlands, where he practised as a doctor first in Middelburg and then near Dordrecht. Then, on 27 June 1791, his wife and daughter Antje were drowned in a yachting accident from which van der Kemp himself barely escaped. As a result he experienced an emotional conversion back to the reformed Christianity of his family. On the one hand he justified his faith in substantial intellectual works on the epistle to the Romans, in which he used his knowledge of some thirteen languages (Xhosa and Khoekhoe he learnt later); on the other he felt the need to engage in missionary work. In this he was influenced by the Moravian Brethren and by the prevailing millenarian ideas. He contacted the newly founded London Missionary

Society (LMS), inspired the initiation of a Dutch counterpart, and was sent out to South Africa as leader of the first party of LMS missionaries; they arrived in March 1799.

Once in South Africa, van der Kemp journeyed beyond the eastern frontier of the colony to work among the Xhosa under Chief Ngqika. From them he received the name Jank' hanna ('the bald man'), and for several generations Christians were known as the followers of Jank'hanna. War between the Cape Colony and the Xhosa soon drove him back, though, and from 1801 onwards van der Kemp worked exclusively within the colony, mainly with dispossessed Khoi-Khoi. He was initially in Graaff-Reinet and later at Bethelsdorp, the mission station he founded in 1802 near what was to become Port Elizabeth. He was able to gather together a congregation of African converts whom he imbued with his belief that they, not the colony's white inhabitants, were the true Christians, and that God's wrath would descend on the colony's many sinners. At the same time he rejected the outward signs of respectability, once famously declaring that all civilization came from the devil.

Together with his marriage on 7 April 1806 to Sara Janse, a freed slave forty-five years his junior with whom he was to have four children, van der Kemp's attitudes caused great opposition from within the colony, and he was for a time ordered by the government to leave Bethelsdorp. He died a few years later, in Cape Town, on 18 December 1811, of fever, and was survived by his widow. Despite the controversy he caused, however, his agitation together with that of his colleague James Read lead to the institution of a more regularized system of justice in the colony, and his campaigning Christianity began a strain which has lasted to this day.   ROBERT ROSS

Sources I. H. Enklaar, *Life and work of J. Th. van der Kemp* (1988) · E. Elbourne, 'Concerning missionaries: the case of Van der Kemp', *Journal of South African Studies*, 17 (1991), 153–64
Archives Netherlands Missionary Society, Oegstgeest · SOAS, London Missionary Society Archives
Likenesses engraving, repro. in *Evangelical Magazine* (April 1799)
Wealth at death see will, Cape Archives, MOOC 7/1/63, 22

Kemp [Kempe], **John** (1380/81–1454), administrator, cardinal, and archbishop of York and of Canterbury, was born at Olantigh by Wye, near Ashford, Kent, perhaps the second son of Thomas Kemp (*d.* 1428), sometime escheator of the county, and Beatrice, daughter of Sir Thomas Lewknor, a Sussex landowner. His brother, Sir Thomas, had at least two sons, Sir William, the archbishop's named heir, and Thomas, whom the bishop patronized extensively, to the extent of securing the see of London for him in 1448 in the face of the duke of Suffolk's candidate.

Early career in England and Normandy Kemp was a fellow of Merton College, Oxford, from 1395 to 1407, serving as senior bursar in 1403–4. He was ordained subdeacon on 14 April 1403 and finally priested on 21 May 1407, at the time he was preferred to the rectories of St Michael, Crooked Lane, London (often connected with personnel of the court of arches), and Southwick, Sussex. He was BCL by 1407 and DCL by 1413.

John Kemp (1380/81–1454), seal [kneeling below]

Kemp's early career was evidently in one of the courts of the archbishop of Canterbury, to which Archbishop Thomas Arundel attracted notable talent. On 13 September 1409 he accompanied the archbishop as one of his clerks on a visitation of Glastonbury Abbey. He was appointed as examiner-general in the court of Canterbury on 30 January 1413 and was on the tribunal for the second session of the famous trial of the Lollard Sir John Oldcastle on 25 September. He became dean of the court of arches by 21 February 1414, which explains why he was no longer the examiner-general by June. He was said to be still dean in 1428, but this is impossible. His preferment was modest for his position: the rectory of Hawkhurst and a prebend in Wingham collegiate church (both in Kent) only replaced his previous benefices. Even when he was collated to the archdeaconry of Durham, on 13 October 1417, he was obliged on papal instruction to give up the rectory.

Between 26 April 1414 and 13 July 1416 Kemp was appointed several times to hear appeals from the court of admiralty, and four more times before 1425, even though his career had moved on. On 25 July 1415 he was appointed to an embassy to treat with Aragon, and was engaged thus from 8 September 1415 to 13 June 1416. He was a receiver of the Canterbury convocation's first subsidy in support of its delegation to the Council of Constance, and by 1416, but probably much earlier, was on the council of Christ Church, Canterbury.

Henry V's campaigns in France stretched his administrative resources and brought several Canterbury officials into major royal service. On 20 July 1417 Kemp was appointed to exercise the jurisdiction of the archbishop of Canterbury overseas, which meant chiefly in those parts of France that the king was slowly acquiring by conquest. It was a key step in his career. On 7 July he had been granted letters of protection as a member of the king's retinue, and on 1 October was included for the first time in a delegation to treat with the French crown. On 6 November 1417 he was appointed—perhaps worthy of note, perhaps a mere formality—to hear confessions in the king's army. With hindsight, perhaps it is not a matter for surprise that by the end of 1417 he was Henry's chancellor of Lancastrian Normandy, a position he retained until September 1422, but in the immediate context the recognition of his ability and his swift rise to such prominence are as impressive as they are undocumented. In 1418, besides the general creation and ordering of the chancery, Kemp helped array troops in Normandy, treated with Burgundy (appointed 28 April), and travelled extensively on the king's business in the duchy.

Diplomatic employment On 3 October 1418 Kemp was appointed keeper of the privy seal, a rise to chief office that meant his return to England to replace Henry Ware, a close colleague in still recent days in the archbishop's administration, who had just become a bishop and now crossed to France to join the king's immediate circle of government. Kemp was now fully engaged in the government of England in the king's absence, but still much involved in the prosecution of the war. On 24 September 1418 he had been appointed to treat with the house of Anjou, a commission that perhaps lapsed; on 21 January 1419 he was appointed in a top-rank delegation to treat with the French crown, and another on the 22nd with the dauphin, the other leading members of the embassy all being in France, but with Kemp presumably included to co-ordinate with the administration at home. With the treaty of Troyes in the making, Kemp received a rapid series of appointments to treat for peace on 23 February, 28 March, and 22 April. It seems almost certain that he was expected to be in France when he was appointed to a highest-level delegation on 28 May, to receive the oaths of Charles VI, Queen Isabella, and Philip of Burgundy that they would keep the treaty.

So high and fast had Kemp climbed in the king's estimation that in this spring of 1419 he was on the shortlist of those whom Henry V discussed seriously with Henry Beaufort as the latter's successor to Winchester, the richest see in the realm. In the event, Kemp received much less. On 21 June 1419 he was provided to the meagre see of Rochester (of which the archbishop of Canterbury was patron), receiving custody of the temporalities on 27 July and being consecrated at Rouen on 3 December. From July 1419 to May 1420 he was still in France, engaged in the negotiations surrounding the definitive treaty. He then returned to England, but had letters on 30 October and 6 November 1420 to go to the king in France once more. Kemp resigned as keeper of the privy seal on 25 October 1421, and just three days later was translated to Chichester; he received the temporalities formally only on 21 August, but had had a grant of £650 p.a. out of them since 25 December previously. However, he was already intent on climbing higher, and is known to have intrigued in the papal curia for the see of London, to which he was translated on 17 November 1421 against the king's nominee and elect of the chapter, Thomas Polton of Hereford. On 22 May 1422 Kemp was given the spiritualities, signalling that he had won the contest, and the temporalities followed on 20 June. Polton had to settle humblingly for succeeding to Chichester. On 26 October, Kemp would enjoy the novel experience of being enthroned in one of his sees.

Meantime Kemp had been back in France. He surrendered the great seal of Normandy to the new regent in France, the duke of Bedford, after Henry V's death on 31 August 1422, but remained on the council in France until mid-October, when he returned to England to join the regency council there. On 22 February 1423 the bishop was present at this body to receive orders to resume his service to the council in France. On 14 May he received the customary commission to array troops, and left for France in the next two or three days. By 26 November 1423 he had returned to England and was appointed on 28 January to a weighty delegation to discuss the liberation of James I with the Scots at Durham. He remained fully engaged in council business, but found time to take on a commission to repair the condition of St Mary's Hospital, Ospringe, in Kent, on 16 February 1424, a reminder of the enduring interest in his native county that perhaps had made his frequent commuting between England and France less wearying to him than it was to others. Shortly after 2 July 1425 Kemp went over to France once more. There he undertook the unpalatable task of representing Humphrey of Gloucester in Paris, in the question of Humphrey's proposed duel with the duke of Burgundy. Fortunately, this failed to happen, and Kemp himself, who had perhaps helped ensure that it did not, certainly gained the good opinion of the duke of Bedford, for whom the quarrel between his brother and brother-in-law was a grave crisis in his regency.

Archbishop and chancellor Kemp's ambition to advance himself beyond London is witnessed by the correspondence between himself and his proctor in the papal curia, William Swan (preserved in the latter's letter-book, BL, Cotton MS Cleopatra C.iv). He watched the health of elderly bishops with interest. The archbishopric of York, where Henry Bowet was bedridden, did not feature on his list, perhaps because Kemp believed the council had already earmarked the succession, but it was thither that he was translated on 20 July 1425, a third choice at best, and perhaps engineered with Bedford's support after deadlock between the pope's nominee, Richard Flemming of Lincoln, and that of the council in England, Philip Morgan of Worcester. If his promotion was not immediately accepted in England, this was probably because the hostility between Beaufort and Gloucester was making any government decision impossible. It was only on 22 April 1426 that the temporalities were restored to him, immediately after Bedford had returned to England to resolve the political crisis.

As part of Bedford's general settlement of affairs, Kemp was appointed chancellor of the realm on 18 March 1426, not the last time that he would be called upon to take up the reins in a crisis not of his making. Bedford returned to France very quickly, and left Kemp to make what he could of a still simmering and factionalized regime. The archbishop endured it for nearly six years. On 13 July 1428, 25 October 1429, and 21 February 1431 he personally pressed the Canterbury convocation for urgently needed funds. Throughout, he is to be found at the centre of conciliar activity, seeking to respond to the deteriorating fortunes of the war in France, and to the continuing animosity between Gloucester and the majority of the council. Kemp had no faction of his own. In January 1431 he was unable to open parliament because of illness, although he attended later. By the end of that year he was finding Gloucester's attitude intolerable, especially as the duke's influence waxed against the background of defeats abroad. He connived urgently with Swan for a papal mandate ordering him to Rome, although when this was finally issued in June 1432 he had already had to resort to another pretext, that of ill health, to resign the great seal by 26 February; perhaps, in terms of stress, it is even unfair to call it pretext.

Kemp retired to his York diocese, which hitherto had seen him for only a few weeks each August and September, although he had taken care to make a primary visitation of his cathedral, and then a close one of the powerful archdeaconry of Richmond in 1428. After just seven months, however, Kemp was back in his Westminster inn and able to make regular trips to Olantigh by Wye, now that he was free to pursue his plan to create a school and collegiate church in his birthplace. The convenient call to Rome went unheeded. With Swan's assistance Kemp had always enjoyed the regard of the papacy as a strong supporter of its authority against proponents of conciliar reform, and he was now courted for his influence in England. Indeed, he was appointed as a royal envoy to the Council of Basel on 28 November 1432, and as late as 17 March 1433 payments were arranged for his journey, but he never went, and returned the instalment, being diverted by decision of the government to talks with France. According to his York register he was at Calais in May.

Further embassies The archbishop had never formally left the council, even while generally absenting himself while Gloucester briefly held sway. He was negotiating with French envoys in England in July 1433. On 9 November 1434 Bedford named him as an executor. Kemp was now the closest colleague of Cardinal Beaufort in the direction of English policy, and headed the crown's delegation from 25 July 1435 until the latter's arrival at the Congress of Arras on 31 August. Ordered to take a hard line by the government, Kemp assumed a stance towards a peace settlement that was twice rebuked formally by the papal legates who were trying to mediate. Beaufort did not soften the position and withdrew the English delegation on 6 September. Kemp's diocese forfeited his annual visit. On the other hand, in 1436 he was unusually active in the north, helping to relieve the siege of Roxburgh.

In April 1437 the two prelates went to negotiate with the Lancastrian chancellor in France. On 9 April 1438 they and the earls of Warwick and Suffolk headed as weighty a delegation as England could produce to treat with the enemy, indeed empowered on the twentieth to treat for a marriage settlement. From 20 November 1438 to 26 February 1439 they were at Calais, engaged in long but ultimately fruitless negotiations with the duchess of Burgundy, Kemp crossing to and fro in December and February to liaise with the king and council at home. About 23 May 1439 Kemp was appointed to lead the delegation to yet another peace conference with Charles VII's envoys at Calais. Thomas Beckington, the king's secretary, has left a detailed record of this mission. Kemp left London four days after his appointment but did not cross to Calais until 26 June. Talks began on 6 July and were uneasy and mutually distrustful throughout. He returned to Westminster to report the lack of progress on 8 September, before going back for one final effort which failed inside a week. On 29 September he did at least achieve a commercial treaty with Flanders (the duke of Burgundy's county). Kemp was more ready than Beaufort to consider a surrender of the Lancastrian claim to the French throne if the territorial concessions were good enough, but the time was far from ripe to sell such a humiliation to English political opinion. Both were, besides, of a generation that conducted talks with Frenchmen in tones of deep and open distrust. He returned to London on 7 October.

Although the government's fortunes were failing, Kemp's status was enhanced by his creation on 18 December 1439 as cardinal-priest of St Balbina. He was licensed by the king to accept the red hat on 14 February 1440, despite furious protests from the aged Archbishop Chichele of Canterbury about the superior legatine authority Kemp might thereby seek to exercise in the southern province. Twenty years earlier Chichele had nearly ruined Beaufort over the latter's similar promotion, and at least delayed it for seven years. This time, his protests were treated with contempt. Crown and papacy were in agreement over Kemp's merits and position; he thus became the first cardinal-archbishop in England.

Political eclipse However, the failure of English policy in France led to Kemp's implication in Gloucester's furious attack in January and February 1441 on Beaufort's record and even loyalty. Although Beaufort was fully protected by the crown, and Kemp was never indicted directly, rising figures around the king, notably the earl of Suffolk, seem to have felt that the two cardinals had had their day. Although there is no specific evidence at the time, it might be thought likely that this shadow was a contributory factor to Kemp's being passed over in favour of John Stafford, bishop of Bath and Wells and chancellor, for the succession to Canterbury in 1442–3. Kemp loved Kent and would not have seen age as an issue, nor his dreadful absenteeism from his diocese (which Stafford at least equalled) as an indictment. It seems more than coincidence that, for the first time ever, Kemp's customary August visit to his diocese in 1443 extended into a stay of sixteen months, save only for limited periods of attendance at Westminster in January–February and June–July 1444, no doubt in connection with the French expedition funded by Cardinal Beaufort under the leadership of the latter's nephew, the duke of Somerset. Kemp had by now a solid group of very long-standing officials (some of them even student friends) entrenched in the York chapter and provincial administration, and his secular officers became involved in such serious friction with the earl of Northumberland's men around Knaresborough as to engage the direct attention of the crown in 1442 and 1443. Perhaps this too was an incentive to Kemp to spend time fighting his own corner rather than serve an ungrateful government.

Kemp was clearly not now a part of the narrowing circle around the king that actually ran the government and, as in the time of his chancellorship, there was only limited use of formal council meetings where men such as he might give their opinion. However, he was urgently required in Westminster in 1445 when relations with France entered a crucial phase, and he was needed to provide status, experience, and overt commitment to the great delegation that received a French embassy in the wake of the marriage of Henry VI and Margaret of Anjou. The business done, he was free to return to York from August 1446. On 20 January 1447 he was named as a principal executor of Cardinal Beaufort's will, and spent some time in April and May in Winchester on that business. In that same year, and curiously late in life, he became a member of the confraternity of Christ Church, Canterbury, and was in Kent for much of the autumn, probably to enjoy opening his school in Wye.

If it is clear that Kemp and his close friend and political colleague, Ralph, Lord Cromwell, were by no means close to the duke of Suffolk's ruling circle, yet they came to lend their attendance and reputation to the king's faltering government so far as they were allowed. During 1449 the archbishop managed only one brief trip to his diocese, in July, as the crisis of war and finance came to a head. However, it may have been a more personal matter that had principally kept Kemp at Westminster of late. It is generally held that Suffolk made a serious political mistake in pressing for the promotion to the see of London of Marmaduke Lumley, bishop of Carlisle and treasurer of the realm, refusing to give government approval to the appointment of the cardinal's nephew, Thomas Kemp, who had received the formal support of the king for his candidacy and consequently papal provision to the see on 21 August 1448. The cardinal had actually lived in the bishop of London's palace in Fulham for much of the previous six months, even though his own was perfectly inhabitable, while old Bishop Robert Gilbert's life was

maddeningly prolonged by intensive nursing at Much Hadham, Hertfordshire. The fact that Thomas Kemp was a meritless candidate, as he was to prove comprehensively over the next forty years, while Lumley was making impressive steps in recovering the crown's financial stability, does not remove the question mark over Suffolk's belated obstruction. However, if it helped distance Kemp publicly and probably in fact from Suffolk just when the duke needed him, the cardinal rallied none the less to the government's aid, and thus also to the duke's, when crisis came.

Pillar of the government When Suffolk was impeached early in 1450, all the chief officers of state perforce resigned or were dismissed. The king and government were in disarray as the Commons in parliament closed in on those they hated. It was in such circumstances, on 31 January 1450, that Kemp was recalled as chancellor. As had happened twenty-four years earlier, he was being asked to remedy a crisis caused by others, and as he had then he responded with loyalty to the crown, ability, and no little courage. Naturally, within a week his nephew had firm possession of the see of London. There is no doubt that the cardinal was a prime maker as well as mouthpiece of the bold strategy that saved Suffolk from judicial condemnation. Then, on 6 July 1450 Kemp helped negotiate the withdrawal from London of Jack Cade and his followers from the south-eastern counties. However, between August and September he led unsympathetic inquiries in person in Kent into the causes and nature of the revolt. Towards the end of the year, when the duke of York's attempts to involve himself in government caused grave concern in the court, the Commons in parliament demanded (and obtained) some purging of the household and resumption of royal revenues, and the duke of Somerset and others faced threats of lynching, Kemp maintained some semblance of authority and competence for the government. He himself faced no criticism from any quarter, and by May 1451 the crown had shrugged off its various critics. Although the duke of Somerset is seen, especially in retrospect when civil wars broke out, as emerging rapidly as the strongman of the regime, there does seem to have been broader-based policy making at this time, with finances stabilized and some sound preparation for the relief of Gascony. Kemp played his part in this restoration of respect for the crown. In February 1452 he acted as a mediator between York and the king, when the duke backed down from his attempt at an armed coup to bring Somerset to trial.

Kemp was even able to secure Canterbury at last. After the death of John Stafford on 25 June 1452, Kemp was elected just three days later, and his translation by the pope followed as soon as 21 July, with the enhanced title of cardinal-bishop of St Rufina. The first cardinal-archbishop of Canterbury received his temporalities on 6 September and the pallium from his nephew on the twenty-fourth. He was enthroned at Canterbury on 11 December. His health was not good by now, but it is inconceivable that anyone else could have been promoted at that time. Indeed, whether inspired specifically by achieving his home diocese and primacy of all England, he found novel enthusiasm for ecclesiastical duties. Ill health prevented his attending convocation in February 1453, so he brought the assembly to himself at Lambeth and invited open discussion on possible reforms of the church in the province, an initiative all too soon overtaken by the usual agenda of taxation. As early as September 1452 he had prepared a fascinatingly detailed itinerary for a primary visitation of his diocese, promising personal inspection of each parish and setting out his mealtimes and places each day; ill health and government business inevitably aborted the plan.

The collapse of the king's mental health in early August 1453 brought Kemp to his last and greatest crisis. It seems that, for as long as the king was alive, the majority of the Lords proposed simply to group around him and exercise collective authority in the king's name, allowing no one even the name of protector, still less regent. When Henry VI's only child, Edward, was born on 13 October, Kemp stood as godparent, despite his advanced age and frail health, alongside the dukes of Somerset and Buckingham, a firm public statement of the boy's heritage. That same month the lords in council, who had been hanging fire over the vacation but had now to come to at least implicit terms with the king's incapacity, called for York to join them and subsequently concurred in the imprisonment of Somerset until he should answer charges laid against him. In December, leading lords led by Kemp explicitly admitted to the king's illness and undertook to rule. It was said that the queen requested she be made regent, but no formal response has been found.

Death of a statesman   It was resolved that parliament must be recalled on 14 February 1454, having been twice prorogued since the king's collapse. Amid open tension and rumours that armed factions were being called up by various magnates, the duke of Norfolk was warned by a servant that he should hide his own such preparations from Kemp and other lords of the council, if he was to avoid sanctions. The cardinal himself prepared an armed bodyguard. When the assembly opened, Kemp was fully active in attendance, and called publicly for prayers for the king's health on 2 March 1454. There is no convincing sign of any move to establish a protectorate, only speculation through hindsight by some historians. Then, with no warning, Kemp died at Lambeth Palace on 22 March. The Lords moved at once to send a forlorn but necessary delegation to Windsor to seek guidance from the king as to a new chancellor and new archbishop. In its nervously detailed report on its failure, this delegation never mentioned the idea of a protectorate, but this was what the Lords now moved to establish. Those who had been named as councillors before Kemp's death demanded to reconsider their position now that their service was to be under York's leadership, and there was widespread (if sometimes nominal) reluctance. This seems to confirm that the arrangement had not been planned at all before the cardinal died, and that he was irreplaceable in moral as well as official authority in the turbulent body politic of the time. There were significantly contradictory rumours after his demise. One allegation was that Norfolk had

wanted him dismissed as chancellor, presumably as an obstacle to York's advance, or as a deeply cautious obstacle to Somerset's being brought to trial; a contrary scandal claimed that Somerset had had him poisoned. The first has a note of credibility; the latter testifies more to Somerset's deep unpopularity. Together they indicate Kemp's position above faction. Had he survived until the king recovered his health, the civil wars might not have happened; with his death, they were certain.

There is no will extant. Kemp was buried on the south side of the presbytery in Canterbury Cathedral, where his handsome tomb survives. On the completion of his school and college project at Wye, his birthplace, in 1447, Kemp had recommended that, if possible, a fellow of his own alma mater, Merton College, should always be appointed as provost. The archbishop was given to such long-standing affections, in both his personal and public lives. His letters to Swan have made him appear notably avaricious, but it is only their survival that is unusual. His record of absenteeism from his diocese has been held against him and cannot be gainsaid, but it was never lazy. His ascent to eminence was based on pure ability and a willingness to shoulder burdens that had broken others; no political favours or sinecures came his way, and indeed at times he was rewarded ungenerously. He affected no asceticism or high-profile piety, but likewise acquired no image of corruption, flamboyance, or avarice. He was not so much a politician as the ablest administrator of his time, always loyal to the crown and rallying a consensus around it when factionalism had overtaken. He had few if any friends among those born to the purple, and they did little to win his respect. His officials were his old friends, and his family came above all else. He earned squarely the status and honours that came his way. He died peerless as cardinal-archbishop of Canterbury; he would have liked that. He was buried in Kent; he would have liked that even more.

R. G. DAVIES

Sources   register as bishop of London, GL, MS 9531/4, fols. 192–213v · register as archbishop of York, Borth. Inst., Register 19 · register of John Stafford and John Kemp, LPL, latter fols. 210–347v · Emden, *Oxf.*, 2.1031–2 · R. G. Davies, 'The episcopate in England and Wales, 1375–1443', PhD diss., University of Manchester, 1974, 3.cl–clvi · *DNB* · BL, Cotton MS Cleopatra C.iv [William Swan's letter-book] · William Swan's letter-book, Bodl. Oxf., MS Arch. Selden B.23 · J. Haller, ed., *Piero da Monte: ein Gelehrter und päpstlicher Beamter des 15. Jahrhunderts* (Rome, 1941) · *Memorials of the reign of Henry VI: official correspondence of Thomas Bekynton, secretary to King Henry VI and bishop of Bath and Wells*, ed. G. Williams, 2 vols., Rolls Series, 56 (1872)

Archives   Borth. Inst., register, register 19 · GL, register, MS 9531/4, fols. 192–213v · LPL, register of John Stafford and John Kemp | BL, corresp., Cotton MS Cleopatra C.iv · Bodl. Oxf., corresp., MS Arch. Selden B.23

Likenesses   J. Swaine, line engraving (after A. Martin), BM, NPG; repro. in *GM*, 2nd ser., 24 (1845), facing p. 481 · seal, BL; Birch, *Seals*, 2331 [*see illus.*] · window, Bolton Percy church, near York

Kemp, John (1665–1717), antiquary, details of whose origins and upbringing are unknown, was possessed of private means, and resided in the parish of St Martin-in-the-Fields, Westminster. He owned a fine museum of antiquities, chiefly formed by the French educational writer Jean

Gailhard, who was governor to George, first Baron Carteret (1667–1695). Gailhard sold it to Lord Carteret for an annuity of £200, and Kemp subsequently purchased it after Carteret's death in 1695. Kemp was elected a fellow of the Royal Society on 20 March 1712 and died, unmarried, on 19 September 1717. By his will he directed that the museum (with books) should be offered to Robert Harley, earl of Oxford, or his son for £2000. However, the proposal was declined. The lexicographer Robert Ainsworth drew up an elaborate account of Kemp's antiquities, *Monumenta vetustatis Kempiana, ex vetustis scriptoribus illustrata, eosque vicissim illustrantia* (2 pts, 1719–20). John Ward, professor of rhetoric at Gresham College, provided Ainsworth with descriptions of the statues and lares, with the discourse *De vasis et lucernis, de amuletis, de annulis et fibulis*, and with the *Commentarius de Asse et partibus ejus*, printed in 1719.

Kemp's collection was eventually sold by auction at The Phoenix tavern in Pall Mall, Westminster, on 23–5 and 27 March 1721, in 293 lots, for £1090 8s. 6d. Six ancient inscriptions, bought by the antiquary Richard Rawlinson, form part of his collection at the Bodleian Library, Oxford, and appear in Richard Chandler's *Marmora Oxoniensia* (1763). GORDON GOODWIN, rev. PHILIP CARTER

Sources Nichols, *Lit. anecdotes*, 5.249, 519 · R. G. [R. Gough], *British topography*, [new edn], 2 vols. (1780) · M. Maty, *Authentic memoirs of the life of Richard Mead* (1755) · *The diary of Ralph Thoresby, 1677–1724*, 2 vols. (1830) · will, PRO, PROB 11/559, fols. 286v–288r

Kemp, John (1763–1812), mathematician, was born at Auchlossen, Aberdeenshire, on 10 April 1763, the son of John Kemp. In 1779 he matriculated at Marischal College, Aberdeen, where he won a Gray mathematical bursary in 1782 and graduated MA in 1783. In the latter year he emigrated to America, where he taught at the academy at Dumfries, Virginia, for two years before moving to New York, where in 1785 he was appointed teacher, and in 1786 professor, of mathematics in Columbia College. In 1795 he was transferred to the chair of geography, history, and chronology. He received the degree of LLD from King's College, Aberdeen, in 1787 and was elected to a foreign fellowship by the Royal Society of Edinburgh in 1792. One of his pupils, and a personal friend, De Witt Clinton, mayor of New York, frequently consulted him on municipal business. In 1810 Kemp visited Lake Erie, and in advance of the surveys pronounced the projected canal to be entirely practicable. Kemp, who married twice, died in New York on 15 November 1812. A daughter from his first marriage survived him.

GORDON GOODWIN, rev. M. C. CURTHOYS

Sources Irving, *Scots.* · *DAB*
Likenesses portrait, Col. U.

Kemp, Joseph (1778–1824), organist and composer, was born in Exeter. He was the brother of James Kemp, the author of the poem *Northernhay* (1808). Kemp was a chorister at Exeter Cathedral and a pupil of William Jackson during and after his time in the choir. In 1802 he was appointed organist of Bristol Cathedral, a post he retained until 1807, when he resigned and settled in London. He had married the daughter of Henry John of Cornwall in 1805.

In London he sold music at a warehouse at 43 Old Bond Street between 1807 and 1809 and edited the monthly *Musical Magazine, Review and Register* from 1809 to 1810. He took his MusB degree at Sidney Sussex College, Cambridge, in 1808, submitting a war anthem, 'A Sound of Battle is in the Land' (composed 1803), as his exercise. He became MusD in 1809 with an anthem entitled *The Crucifixion*.

Kemp produced a couple of pieces for the theatre in London in 1809 and 1810, and in 1810 began a series of public lectures on musical education, in which he advocated, perhaps for the first time in England, the teaching of music in classes and the playing of exercises by pupils in concert. These were given at the Russell Institution, Great Coram Street, Russell Square, and formed the basis of *The new system of musical education, being a self instructor and serviceable companion to music masters* (c.1821) and *Upwards of 100 cards, containing more than 500 points in music, connected with the new system of musical education* (c.1821). Kemp's non-pedagogical works include songs, glees, chants, anthems, *Sonatas or Lessons for the Pianoforte* (c.1814), and *Musical Illustrations of the Beauties of Shakespeare* (c.1820).

Kemp is reported to have lived at 20 Kenton Street, Russell Square, in 1811. In 1814, on account of failing health, he returned with his wife and family to Exeter, where he founded a music college and resided until 1824, although he spent the period 1818–21 in France. A journey to London in April 1824 proved too much for Kemp, then in a weak state of health, and he had a relapse 'of his former complaint, and after acute suffering in his head for upwards of three weeks' (Kassler, 1.626) died in his lodgings on 22 May. He left a widow, two sons, and a daughter.

L. M. MIDDLETON, rev. DAVID J. GOLBY

Sources J. C. Kassler, *The science of music in Britain, 1714–1830: a catalogue of writings, lectures, and inventions*, 1 (1979), 625–32 · W. H. Husk, 'Kemp, Joseph', *New Grove*

Kemp, Joseph William (1872–1933), Baptist minister, was born on 16 December 1872 at Windsor Street, Hull, the son of Joseph William Kemp, a policeman, and his wife, Mary Hopkin. In 1880 his father was drowned and two years later his mother died, leaving Joseph as one of six young orphans. After minimal education he was befriended by a businessman, J. H. Russell, and found employment at a local post office in Hull. Having discovered a lively Christian faith, after studying at night school Kemp was able in 1892 to enter the Bible Training Institute, Glasgow, and after two years he graduated with a diploma of merit. He had been helped by Presbyterians, but in 1896 he was baptized in Cambridge Street Baptist Church, Glasgow.

After mission work in Ayrshire and other parts of the west of Scotland, Kemp was inducted as minister to the Kelso Baptist Church on 4 April 1897. While there he met Winifred Binnie, and they married in June 1897. From Kelso he moved to Hawick Baptist Church in July 1898. After a successful ministry Kemp was called to Charlotte Baptist Chapel, Rose Street, Edinburgh, early in February 1902. This church had been founded in 1808, but had dwindled in size and influence by the end of the nineteenth century. A back-street site and a dilapidated building were obstacles for a new minister to overcome, and there were only thirty-five people at his induction. Nevertheless, at a time of great evangelical revival in Wales and elsewhere, Kemp led his church to remarkable growth. Vigorous evangelism both in the church and out of doors led to the need for a much larger building, which was opened in October 1912. A home for fallen women was opened and mission work set up in Edinburgh's High Street and Jamaica Street. A number of his church members subsequently joined missionary organizations, both at home and overseas; and by the close of Kemp's ministry there were 875 members of his church.

In September 1915 Kemp left for New York, where he served as minister of Calvary Baptist Church until 1917 and then of the Metropolitan Tabernacle (1917–19). This was a less happy experience, and difficulties in the churches led to a severe breakdown in his health. Yet in 1920 he moved to New Zealand to undertake another large city centre church, the Auckland Baptist Tabernacle, founded by Thomas Spurgeon, son of Charles Spurgeon of the Metropolitan Tabernacle, London. Here some of the success of the Edinburgh years followed him, and the church became a centre of evangelistic activity. In 1922 Kemp created a Bible Training Institute, becoming its honorary principal. In the following year the New Zealand Baptist Theological College was formed in the buildings of the tabernacle with the active co-operation of Kemp. He was elected president of the Baptist Union of New Zealand in 1929. However, his previous illness returned and he died on 4 September 1933 in Auckland, where he was buried in the Hillsborough cemetery. The membership of the tabernacle was by that time over 1000, but the church declined after his death. According to a contemporary, Professor E. M. Blaiklock, who taught classics at the University of Auckland, the Bible Training Institute was Kemp's greatest achievement in New Zealand (private information).

A forceful man, opinionated and difficult to work with, Kemp was described as 'erratic in temperament' (private information). Conservative in his view of the Bible, he preached much on revival, the second coming, and the dangers of the cinema, the theatre, and other 'worldly' entertainments. He also attacked what he saw as liberalism and modernism in the churches. He wrote a number of small books, including *The Soul Winner and Soul Winning* (1916), which, though derivative from other authors, were simple and straightforward. He was also the author of *Outline Studies on the Tabernacle* (1913). DEREK B. MURRAY

Sources [W. Kemp], *Joseph W. Kemp: the record of a spirit-filled life* [1936] · W. Whyte, *Revival in Rose Street* [n.d., 1953?–1960?] · private information (2004) [G. Pound] · b. cert. · *DSCHT* · D. W. Bebbington, ed., *The Baptists in Scotland: a history* (1988) · G. Yuille, *History of the Baptists in Scotland* (1927)
Likenesses photograph, Charlotte Baptist Chapel, Rose Street, Edinburgh

Kemp, Peter Mant MacIntyre (1915–1993), intelligence officer and journalist, was born on 19 August 1915 in Bombay, India, the younger son of Sir Norman Wright Kemp (d. 1937), chief judge of the small cause court and later chief judge of the high court, Bombay, who listed his interests as ju-jitsu and boxing, and his wife, Olivia Mary, daughter of C. W. Martin. Sent back to England at the age of four, Kemp was educated at a preparatory school in Sussex, Wellington College, and Trinity College, Cambridge, where he lived life to the full and scraped a third in classics and law. Reluctantly he began to read for the bar.

Kemp was a romantic adventurer and a convinced anti-communist; the outbreak of the Spanish Civil War steered him away from a legal career for ever. In November 1936, aged twenty-one, he joined a Carlist cavalry regiment on Franco's side. After taking part in close-quarter street fighting in Madrid he transferred to the élite Spanish foreign legion, in which he was decorated for gallantry and served as an officer, a rare distinction for a non-Spaniard. Several times wounded, he was finally put out of action in the summer of 1938 by a mortar bomb that almost killed him.

Kemp combined his hatred of communism with an equal hostility to Nazism. Commissioned in 1940, he served with the Special Operations Executive (SOE) and its forerunner, military intelligence (research) known as MI(R), for most of the Second World War. In 1942, as a member of the small-scale raiding force, he took part in night raids on the German-held Channel Islands and continental coast. In August 1943 he parachuted into occupied Albania, where he spent many months working with communist and anti-communist guerrilla groups, was in contact with Enver Hoxha, the communist guerrilla leader and future dictator of Albania, and had several narrow escapes from death.

After his evacuation from Montenegro in February 1944, Kemp at the end of that year parachuted into occupied Poland, where he and his SOE mission, under the command of Colonel D. T. ('Marko') Hudson, were overrun and imprisoned by the advancing Red Army, to be released only several weeks later. He then volunteered for service with Force 136, SOE's Far East section, and in the last days of the war against Japan was dropped into Thailand, where he ran arms across the border to the French in Laos. He ended his service commanding the Japanese garrison in Bali before the Dutch authorities arrived. For his work with SOE he was awarded a DSO in 1945. 'There may be braver men than Peter Kemp', recalled one SOE colleague, 'but I am not certain that I have met any of them' (Howarth, 75).

Tuberculosis contracted in the Far East forced Kemp's retirement from the army and he subsequently embarked on an occasional career as an author and a journalist. He wrote three fine memoirs about his Spanish and wartime exploits: *Mine were of Trouble* (1957), *No Colours or Crest* (1958), and *Alms for Oblivion* (1961); he later combined these in an autobiography, *The Thorns of Memory* (1990). As a journalist, he reported from Hungary in 1956, from Congo, Vietnam, and Rhodesia, and on revolutions in central and South America; and towards the end of his life he revisited Kosovo, where he had last been in the winter of 1943–4. This work he complemented with a job as an insurance salesman for Imperial Life. The irony that his own life was virtually uninsurable was not lost on him.

Kemp was tall, slim, and fair; the shattered jaw and other wounds he received in Spain gave him a delicate, distinct jawline, and pain for the rest of his life. Charming, generous, and self-deprecatingly modest, he was a man with extraordinary reserves of energy and courage and a wide circle of friends, though also a certain weakness for drink. He was twice married and twice divorced.

Peter Kemp died of septicaemia following a chest infection at Chelsea and Westminster Hospital, London, on 30 October 1993.   RODERICK BAILEY

Sources *Daily Telegraph* (3 Nov 1993) · *The Independent* (4 Nov 1993) · *The Times* (6 Nov 1993) · P. Howarth, *Undercover: the men and women of the special operations executive* (1980) · J. Keene, *Fighting for Franco: international volunteers in nationalist Spain during the Spanish civil war, 1936–39* (2001) · P. Toynbee, *The distant drum: reflections on the Spanish civil war* (1976) · *The Spectator* (17 Aug 1985) · private information (2004) · d. cert.

Kemp, Stanley Wells (1882–1945), zoologist and oceanographer, was born at 84 Lansdowne Road, Kensington, London, on 14 June 1882, the second of the six children (three sons and three daughters) of Stephen Benjamin Kemp (1849–1918), professor of pianoforte at the Royal Academy of Music and the Royal College of Music, and his first wife, Clara Wells Beasley (*d.* 1891?), daughter of Frederick Beasley, of London. He was educated at St Paul's School, Hammersmith, London, and at Trinity College, Dublin, whence he graduated in 1903 with a first senior moderatorship (gold medal) in natural science, with zoology as his special subject. He obtained the degree of ScD in 1919.

From early childhood Kemp had been interested in entomology, but although it remained a lifelong interest, it was his first appointment, in marine biology, which determined the course of his career. After graduation he became assistant naturalist in the fisheries branch of the department of agriculture for Ireland under Ernest W. L. Holt, a pioneer of fisheries research. With Holt, Kemp took part in cruises to explore the life of the continental slope to the west and south-west of Ireland. He wrote many papers on the results of these dredgings and trawlings, became an authority on the decapod Crustacea, and in 1905 was elected a fellow of the Challenger Society.

In 1910 Kemp was appointed senior assistant superintendent of the zoological and anthropological section of the Indian Museum, which later became the zoological survey of India. He continued to work on the Crustacea, and between 1910 and 1925 published thirty-three papers on the group, in addition to several other zoological papers, and a monograph on *The Crustacea Stomatopoda of the Indo-Pacific Region*. In 1913, in Colombo, he married Agnes Sharwood Green (1879–1978), daughter of the Revd William Spotswood Green, government inspector of Irish fisheries. They had one daughter.

While working for the Indian Museum, Kemp took part in many collecting expeditions. In 1912, while with the Abor expedition in north-east India, he discovered the first onychophoran (Peripatus-like animal) to be found in

Stanley Wells Kemp (1882–1945), by Walter Stoneman, 1933

Asia. Much of his work was done in marine or freshwater environments, including the Kumaon lakes (1911), the coasts of southern India, and Chilka Lake in Orissa (1913–14), the coral reefs of the Andaman Islands (1915–1922), and the Sundarbans of the Ganges delta. Here he discovered some remarkable new fish and Crustacea with a striking resemblance to deep-water forms. He became superintendent of the zoological survey in 1916 and carried out extensive wartime researches to allay anxieties that Indian freshwater snails might become second hosts for the human parasite *Schistosoma* (bilharzia). In 1922 Kemp made an outstanding exploration of the Siju cave in the Garo hills of Assam. Throughout this period he was an active fellow of the Asiatic Society of Bengal.

Kemp left India in 1924 to become the first director of the *Discovery* investigations, set up by the Colonial Office to gain knowledge that could permit stocks of Antarctic whales to be conserved by regulating, according to scientific findings, the rapidly developing 'fishery'. Kemp was responsible for planning these researches, which soon developed into a wide-ranging survey of the physical and biological conditions of the Southern Ocean. He himself led the first two major expeditions, the voyage in 1925–7 of the *Discovery*—Captain Scott's famous ship re-equipped for oceanographic work—and that of the *Discovery II* in 1929–31. The latter ship was newly built to Kemp's design and incorporated improvements based on experience gained on the first expedition. The many volumes of the *Discovery Reports* recording the results of these and subsequent expeditions are a monument to Kemp's vision and energetic leadership. As was stated in his obituary in *The Times*: 'No finer leader and no better companion for a long and lonely voyage in sub-Antarctic waters could be imagined'. In 1931 Kemp was elected FRS and in 1938 he was president of the zoology section of the British Association. He received the Victoria medal of the Royal Geographical Society in 1936.

Kemp was reluctant to abandon his Southern Ocean work, but the *Discovery* investigations had never enjoyed a secure future. Thus, when the post of secretary of the Marine Biological Association and director of its laboratory at Plymouth became vacant in 1936, Kemp successfully applied for the post. His characteristic energy and forceful personality contributed to the further development of the Plymouth laboratory, but his work was interrupted by the outbreak of war. In March 1941 the laboratory was hit by incendiary bombs. Kemp directed the salvage attempts, sacrificing in the process his own adjoining house and personal possessions. He continued to plan for the future both at Plymouth and further afield, as a member of the *Discovery* committee and of a committee planning postwar fisheries research in British colonies. Colleagues, however, believed that the trauma of the bombing of the laboratory contributed to his decline in health and relatively early death.

As well as being an outstanding field naturalist, Kemp was a first-class scientific administrator who made good use of his talents in the different positions he occupied. He was tall and well proportioned and combined modesty and a dislike for publicity with a powerful personality; he had also a sense of humour and a gift for genuine friendship. He inherited his father's musical ability and was also a skilled cabinet-maker. He died at the Prince of Wales Hospital, Plymouth, on 16 May 1945, and was buried at the Efford cemetery, Plymouth on the 19th.

A. C. HARDY, rev. MARGARET DEACON

Sources A. C. Hardy, 'Stanley Wells Kemp, 1882–1945', *Journal of the Marine Biological Association of the United Kingdom*, 26 (1946), 219–34 · W. T. Calman, *Obits. FRS*, 5 (1945–8), 467–76 · R. B. S. Sewell and N. A. Mackintosh, 'Stanley Wells Kemp', *Proceedings of the Linnean Society of London*, 157th session (1944–5), 113–19 · S. L. Hora, 'Stanley W. Kemp, DSc, FRS, FRASB (1882–1945)', *Yearbook of the Royal Asiatic Society of Bengal*, 12 (1947), 165 · N. A. Mackintosh, 'Dr Stanley W. Kemp', *Nature*, 156 (1945), 41–2 · *The Times* (18 May 1945) · A. Hardy, *Great waters: a voyage of natural history to study whales, plankton and the waters of the Southern Ocean* (1967) · J. Coleman-Cooke, *Discovery II in the Antarctic: the story of British research in the southern seas* (1963) · A. Savours, *The voyages of the Discovery: the illustrated history of Scott's ship* (1992) · *WWW* · *The Times* (21 May 1945) · C. Moriarty, 'William Spotswood Green, marine scientist', *More people and places in Irish science and technology*, ed. C. Mollan, W. Davis, and B. Finucane (1990) · private information (2004) · personal knowledge (2004) · b. cert. · d. cert. · *CGPLA Eng. & Wales* (1945)

Archives Marine Biological Association, Plymouth, corresp. | Marine Biological Association laboratory, Plymouth, director's office MSS · Marine Biological Association laboratory, Plymouth, corresp. with E. T. Browne · NL Scot., corresp. relating to the *Discovery* committee and with Sir James M. Wordie · PRO, Colonial Office MSS · Scott Polar RI, *Discovery* committee MSS · Southampton Oceanography Centre, National Oceanographic Library, Challenger Society archive · Southampton Oceanography Centre, National Oceanographic Library, George Deacon MSS · Southampton Oceanography Centre, National Oceanographic Library, *Discovery* committee MSS

Likenesses W. Stoneman, photograph, 1933, NPG [see illus.] · J. H. Welsh, photograph, 1937, repro. in Calman, *Obits. FRS*, facing p. 467

Wealth at death £17,396 15s. 3d.: probate, 4 Sept 1945, *CGPLA Eng. & Wales*

Kemp, Thomas Read (1782–1844), property speculator, was born on 23 December 1782, at 169 High Street, Lewes, Sussex, the younger surviving child and only son of Thomas Kemp (*bap.* 1745, *d.* 1811), wool merchant and MP, and his wife, Anne (1748/9–1807), daughter of Henry Read, grazier, of Brookland, Kent. He attended Westminster School and was admitted to St John's College, Cambridge, in 1800, where he graduated BA in 1805, and to the Middle Temple in 1804. On 12 July 1806 he married Frances (1783–1825), fourth daughter of Sir Francis *Baring bt, with whom he had four sons and six daughters. In the following year he purchased Herstmonceux Place, Sussex, where they lived until he sold it in 1819, and they moved to The Temple, Montpelier Road, Brighton. A drawing by Sir Thomas Lawrence in 1808 shows a handsome, fashionable gentleman.

Having stood unsuccessfully for a county seat in 1807, Kemp was returned unopposed as MP for Lewes in the by-election following his father's death in 1811. In 1816 he resigned his seat. He served as vice-president of the Church Missionary Society from 1812 to 1816. Under the influence of his wife's sister Harriet Wall, he joined with her brother George Baring to found an evangelical sect, set up chapels in Lewes and Brighton, and preached regularly. In 1823 he returned to the Church of England, to fashionable society and an extravagant style of living, and to politics, by being elected MP for Arundel. In the general election of 1826 he regained a seat at Lewes, serving in five successive parliaments until 1837. A whig, he was a champion of parliamentary reform and also supported several radical measures, particularly free trade. He seldom took part in debates, except on local issues. In Brighton and Lewes he was a prominent figure, for example acting as a town commissioner in Brighton, receiving the king and queen on their visit to Lewes in 1830, supporting many charities, and riding with the Brighton Union hunt.

Kemp's wealth was founded on lands which his father had inherited from an uncle in 1774. The most valuable part was the freehold of nearly half the parish of Brighton outside the old town, onto which housing for the burgeoning resort had been spreading, piecemeal, since the 1770s. In 1823 he initiated the development of Kemp Town, on 40 acres a mile east of the old town. His intention was to profit from providing what Brighton lacked, houses of the size and distinction as, for example, were being built in terraces around Regent's Park in Marylebone. To plans by Charles Augustin Busby and Amon Henry Wilds, the sites for 106 houses were laid out. A square opened from the centre of a crescent which was terminated by terraces parallel with the cliff, and communal gardens and esplanades gave access to the beach. Kemp financed the external construction of ninety-two houses, which had been erected by the end of 1828; they were let on ninety-nine-year building leases with the option to purchase at a fixed price. He also fitted out and occupied one, 22 Sussex Square, where he entertained in grand style. He gave the site of the Sussex County Hospital and £1000 towards the hospital. But with the collapse of the 1824–8 building boom tenants were slow in completing their houses, and it was only, for Kemp too late, in the 1840s that the development was counted a success. The flow of income was far below what was needed to support the expenditure incurred.

Kemp's wife died in 1825. On 26 November 1832 he married Frances Margaretta, daughter of Charles Watkin John Shakerley, of Somerford Park, Cheshire, and widow of Vigors Harvey, of Killiane Castle, Wexford. They had one son, Frederick (*b.* 1833).

In April 1837 Kemp resigned his seat in the Commons, let his houses in Kemp Town and in London (at 24 Belgrave Square, Chelsea), and left Britain to live on the continent for the rest of his life except for a visit in 1840–41. The principal reason was financial: his extravagance and the failure so far of Kemp Town had overwhelmed him. Mortgages secured on his first marriage settlement and on Kemp Town amounted to at least £84,000. His finances continued to deteriorate. Land in Brighton was auctioned in 1842, as was his London house early in 1844.

Kemp died on 20 December 1844 at 64 rue du Faubourg St Honoré, Paris, and was buried in the cemetery of Père Lachaise. His wife returned to spend most of her remaining years in Kemp Town, before dying in Tunbridge Wells in 1860.   JOHN H. FARRANT

Sources A. Dale, *Fashionable Brighton, 1820–1860*, 2nd edn (1967), chap. 4 · *GM*, 2nd ser., 23 (1845), 441–3 · H. Hobhouse, *Thomas Cubitt: master builder* (1971) · will, PRO, PROB 11/2010/90 · ING Barings, London, Barings archives, AC35; DEP 193.40 · HoP, *Commons, 1790–1820*, vol. 4 · particulars of sale, Herstmonceux Place estate, E. Sussex RO, AMS 6314 · Venn, *Alum. Cant.*

Likenesses T. Lawrence, drawing, 1808, repro. in Dale, *Fashionable Brighton*, pl. 36 · T. Illman, stipple, pubd *c.*1812 (after T. Lawrence), BM · G. Hayter, group portrait, oils (*The House of Commons, 1833*), NPG

Kemp [Kempe], **William** (1554/5–1628), landowner and sufferer from melancholia, was the eldest son of Robert Kemp of Spain's Hall, Finchingfield, Essex, and his wife, Elizabeth Heigham. He had at least two younger brothers and two sisters. Under a contract dated 10 October 1588 he married Philippa Gunter of London and Aldbury, Hertfordshire. They had one daughter, Jane, who married John Burgoyne of Sutton, Bedfordshire. In December 1604 Kemp was among the Essex gentry who pleaded poverty as an excuse for not contributing to a loan to James I. Although in 1615 his brother Robert bequeathed him money and hawks, which suggests that he was then taking part in country sports, at some point William suffered the psychological trauma which precipitated his sole claim to fame: a retreat into silence which lasted for seven years, 'so swallowed up with a melancholy phrensie, that he neither went to Church nor spake to any person for several years, but always signified his mind by Writing' (Firmin, 2). Seventeenth-century sources, the earliest of them Kemp's own monument in the family chapel in Finchingfield church, offer no reason for his affliction, but family legend attributed his silence to remorse after he had drunkenly insulted his wife, and added that he occupied the years which followed by making fishponds, each one bigger than the last. Local myth-makers elaborated the story with tales of additional misfortunes, including the drowning in the fishponds of three of his servants.

If Kemp's lengthy abstinence from speech was indeed caused by an altercation with his wife, it none the less continued after her death, since Philippa's burial is recorded in Finchingfield church as 21 August 1623. His depression may well have been religious in origin, since it was spiritual counselling that released him from it, at least two years after Philippa died. In September 1625 the vicarage of Finchingfield, worth £200 per annum, fell vacant by the death of Thomas Pickering. Kemp was the patron, and though he received several applications he showed his puritan sympathies by insisting—always in writing—on presenting Stephen Marshall, a leading figure among the godly of Essex, to the living. Marshall was instituted on 25 October 1625, and soon persuaded Kemp to re-enter society by engaging in conversation and by going to church. Thereafter Kemp took part in local government and ecclesiastical business, the latter in co-operation with Marshall. He administered funds for the repair of the church and relief of the poor, and at the time of his death was acting as a surveyor of the highway. His monumental inscription records his burial on 10 June 1628 at the age of seventy-three. He left no will, and since his daughter declined to act the administration of his goods was entrusted to his nephew Robert Kemp, who also inherited Spain's Hall.   HENRY SUMMERSON

Sources F. Hitchin-Kemp, *A general history of the Kemp and Kempe families* (1902) · G. Firmin, *A brief vindication of Mr Stephen Marshal: appendix to The questions between the conformist and nonconformist* (1681) · J. Duport, *Musae subsecivae* (1676) · T. Webster, *Stephen Marshall and Finchingfield* (1994) · E. Vaughan, *Stephen Marshall: a forgotten Essex puritan* (1907) · *VCH Essex*, vol. 2 · PRO, PROB 6/13, fol. 102v

Kemp [Kempe], **William** (*c.*1560–1601), writer on education, was the son of Walter Kempe of Devon or Cornwall. He is not to be confused with another William Kempe, master of Colchester grammar school between 1598 and 1637. Kemp the writer was very probably educated at Plymouth grammar school under William Minterne. In June 1578 he matriculated as a pensioner at Christ's College, Cambridge, but migrated to Trinity Hall, where he graduated BA in 1580/81 and MA in 1584. From 1581 to 1601 Kemp acted as master of Plymouth grammar school, where he was paid a salary of £20.

Kemp is remembered chiefly as the author of pioneering works on the theory and practice of education. He was an apostle of the systems of Ramus, fashionable at Cambridge in the 1560s and 1570s, and his work also bears the influence of Plutarch. It has been very plausibly supposed that William Minterne, himself a graduate of Christ's, had brought Ramism from the college to Plymouth and that it was he who introduced Kemp to the doctrine even before the boy went up to his former college. Kemp's most notable book was *The Education of Children in Learning*

(1588), dedicated to the mayor and corporation of Plymouth. He was concerned for the education of boys (not girls) from yeoman and merchant, as well as landed backgrounds. Kemp was extremely keen that schooling should be both accessible and challenging, and hoped his book 'may teach the unlearned with some delight and not be tedious to those that are learned' (Kempe, *Education*, sig. A3). But he also believed, as in the book of Proverbs, that 'Foolishness is tied in the heart of the child, but the rod of discipline shall drive it away' (ibid., title-page).

There are several indications of Kemp's preference for broadening the traditional curriculum, though classical studies remained central. 'What is music in sounds, in harmony, and in their spaces, concords and divers sorts, but only arithmetic in hearing?', he asked, though music found no more place in his school curriculum than anywhere else (Watson, 212). He recommended that for three years from the age of twelve boys should study logic and rhetoric. The bulk of their time, however, should be spent not on learning theoretical systems but in reading such authors as Cicero, Virgil, and Horace. Kemp was unusual in recommending the intensive study of arithmetic and geometry for six months, at the age of fifteen. He produced the only contemporary translation of Ramus's arithmetical texts into English, enthusiastically describing the author as 'that worthy ornament of arts and all good learning in our time' (Kempe, *Art of Arithmetic*, A3r).

In addition to his works on education Kemp produced *A Dutiful Invective Against the Moste Haynous Treasons of Ballard and Babington* (1587), which contains a preface addressed to George Barne, lord mayor of London, inveighing against 'the treacherous dealing of that ungodlie disposed woman, the Scottish queen, with the sentence pronounced against her at Fotheringhay and confirmed by her majesty'. His patriotism was of a deeply Calvinist colour, full of confidence that (as he wrote in his will) God 'hath beautified me with the merits of our Lord Jesus Christ, and so made me an heir of thy blessed life to come'. Kemp acquired several properties in Plymouth and furnished his executors with an inventory of his estate, which, after payment of his debts, he estimated to be worth £540. Dividing it into seven parts, he left two parts to his wife and five to be held in trust for his children, to be allocated when they reached adulthood, with no distinction of age or gender. In the meantime, careful provision was made for 'the good education of my children in the fear of God'. Kemp died between 24 July 1601, when he signed his will, and the grant of probate on 18 November; his wife, whose name was Joan, and five of their children survived him.   STEPHEN WRIGHT

Sources R. D. Pepper, ed., *Four Tudor books on education* (1966) • will and inventory, PRO, PROB 11/98, sig. 79 • W. Kempe, *The education of children in learning* (1588) • W. S. Howell, *Logic and rhetoric in England, 1500–1700* (1956) • F. Watson, *The English grammar schools to 1660: their curriculum and practice* (1908); repr. (1968) • R. N. Worth, *History of Plymouth from the earliest period to the present time* (1890) • W. Kempe, *The art of arithmetic* (1592) • W. Kempe, *A dutiful invective against the moste haynous treasons of Ballard and Babington* (1587) • Venn, *Alum. Cant.*

Wealth at death £540—net of debts: will, PRO, PROB 11/98, sig. 79

Kemp, William (*fl.* 1585–1602), actor, was the most important stage clown working in the late Elizabethan period. He was the original performer of some of Shakespeare's most famous comic roles, but contemporaries knew him best as a maker of jigs and merriments, of which the most celebrated was his feat, performed in 1600, of dancing a morris from London to Norwich. Of unknown origins and parentage, he adopted a comic persona—the plain man of low status—that reflected the sphere in which his social allegiances lay.

Early career Kemp's earliest notices link him to the Earl of Leicester's Players in the 1580s. He was not, as sometimes stated, the 'Mr Kempe' to whom the corporation of Ipswich sent a letter in 1580 at about the date that Leicester's Men were performing there (Eccles, 293). He did, though, perform with the earl's company at Leicester House in London in May 1585, and was one of fifteen players who travelled to the Netherlands in November, when Leicester took up his post as general of English forces in the Netherlands. Kemp seems to have contributed to the general air of ostentation that marked Leicester's disconcertingly regal entourage. He would have performed in shows such as 'The Forces [=Labours?] of Hercules' at Utrecht in April 1586, but he also provided special feats of impromptu clowning and athleticism. One record has him leaping into a ditch while the earl was out walking with Prince Maurice: presumably this was some kind of tumbling trick. Leicester had already singled Kemp out for an individual reward of 10s. in May 1585, and he received further special payments in the Netherlands. The earl's nephew Sir Philip Sidney called him 'William, my Lord of Leicester['s] jesting player', and used him in January 1586 to carry correspondence home to Lady Sidney (*The Complete Works of Sir Philip Sidney*, ed. A. Feuillerat, 4 vols., 1912–26, 3.167). Unfortunately Kemp embarrassed Sidney by delivering his letters to Lady Leicester, who was the subject in them of some undiplomatic remarks.

Returning to London in May 1586, Kemp immediately embarked on a second continental journey by joining five other English 'instrumentalists and tumblers' in the entourage of the Danish ambassador, Henrik Ramel (Sjogren, 121). This group, which included two future members of Shakespeare's company, George Bryan and Thomas Pope, accompanied Ramel home to the Danish court at Elsinore and worked for three months in the employ of Frederick II. There they probably provided music and pastimes for banquets and other social occasions. When Kemp next becomes locatable, in 1592, he was again in company with Bryan and Pope, performing in England with Lord Strange's Men. However, in the interim he had pursued his own way, for he did not follow the others to Dresden but left Elsinore in August, a month before the rest, and with a month's wages as a gift. Travelling independently with his 'boy', Daniel Jones, Kemp may still have been operating essentially as a solo entertainer.

By 1590 Kemp had begun to amass a considerable reputation as a comic performer. Richard Tarlton, the revered clown of the Queen's Men, died in 1588, and Kemp rapidly replaced him in public esteem as the most admired comedian of the next decade. The earliest testimony to his popularity comes in Thomas Nashe's *An Almond for a Parrat* (1590). This satirical tract opens with a mock dedication from 'Cuthbert Curry-knave' to 'that most comical and conceited cavalier, Monsieur du Kemp, jestmonger and vice-gerent general to the ghost of Dick Tarlton', asking Kemp to receive his pamphlet and 'with the credit of thy clownery protect thy Cuthbert from carpers'. Cuthbert claims that during a visit to Bergamo he had met 'that famous francatrip Harlicken [i.e. Harlequin]', who asked 'if I knew any such parabolano here in London as Signior Ciarlatano Kempino', adding that 'for the report he had heard of his pleasance, he could not but be in love with his perfections'. This was an elaborate spoof designed to preface the ensuing pamphlet with a disclaimer of serious intent, but it signalled how famous in London Kemp's 'pleasances' had become. Two years later, another of Nashe's pamphlets twitted Gabriel Harvey by suggesting that his actions would 'fall to [Kemp's] lot for a merriment' (*Works of Thomas Nashe*, 1.287, 3.342–3).

Kemp's merriments Kemp's merriments were of two kinds. The anonymous play *A Knack to Know a Knave*, printed in 1594 with 'Kemp's applauded merriments of the men of Gotham' (title page), indicates that in some plays he provided independent comic episodes, self-contained farcical skits with minimal integration into the surrounding action. In the play the 'madmen' of Gotham, a cobbler, a miller, and a smith, squabble over who is to present a petition at King Edgar's visit. With much malapropism and absurd logic they compete over who will do it most wisely, but when the petition is read, it is a ridiculous request that travellers arriving in their town be compelled to purchase ale. It is easy to see how, through improvisation and by-play, this inconsequential scene could be elaborated beyond its intrinsic interest into a clowning routine that temporarily hijacked the action. It has been plausibly suggested that the semi-detached scene in Shakespeare's *Titus Andronicus* involving a common man who mistakes words, and who is sent on a fool's errand resulting in his execution, was an episode written in for Kemp (Wiles, 34). A reference in Ben Jonson's *Every Man out of his Humour* (1599) to Kemp throwing his shoe at another player perhaps preserves a memory of one more merriment. In the anonymous play *The Return from Parnassus*, part 2 (performed at St John's College, Cambridge, at Christmas 1601–2), in which Kemp is brought on stage as a character, his comic turn is a speech parodying a foolish justice of the peace.

Kemp's other speciality was the jig or comic afterpiece, a song-and-dance routine that was customarily performed at the end of a play by up to five actors led by the clown: as Nashe explained, 'the quaint comedians of our time ... when their play is done do fall to rhyme' (*Works of Thomas Nashe*, 1.244). Danced to ballad tunes and rooted in folk culture and popular story-telling, jigs were a distinctly low form of comedy. Their rambunctious and frequently bawdy humour often contrasted radically with the plays to which they were attached, and they acquired a reputation for coarseness and scandal. When, in *Hamlet* (II.ii), Polonius interrupts the first player's tragical 'Pyrrhus' speech, the prince's put-down—'he's for a jig or a tale of bawdry'—is meant to be cutting. None the less, jigs had a loyal audience following, and some spectators would arrive at a play's close simply for the sake of the ensuing afterpiece.

At least six of Kemp's jigs had reached print by 1595, and he must have been responsible for more of which we have no record. Four survive, two of which are in German (the jig being a European, and not a narrowly English, form). In the jig *Rowland*, extant only in German, the clown has been cheated of his mistress by a sexton, but wins her back by lying in one of the sexton's graves and surprising the couple with his resurrection. In a German companion piece, *Von den Mannern*, the clown's wife catches him out by playing the same trick on him, pretending she has died and punishing him for the infidelities on which he at once embarks. In *Rowland's Godson*, the servant John has seduced his master's wife, and by a cunning plot he simultaneously dispels his master's suspicions and arranges for him to be beaten. And in *Singing Simpkin*, Simpkin uses a contrivance involving concealment in a chest to enable him to cuckold an old man and outwit a blustering soldier who is trying to seduce the same woman. It will be seen that Kemp's jigs were neatly ironical domestic farces featuring sexual competition and comical violence. Their hero was an ordinary but resourceful man who generally managed to win through despite the odds stacked against him. In the 1590s these beautifully focused and ingenious skits earned Kemp the adulation of the playhouses, though not the approval of more sedate spectators. As one satirist complained in 1598:

whores, beadles, bawds and sergeants filthily
Chant Kemp's jig.
(Baskerville, 110)

The Lord Chamberlain's Men The 1590s saw Kemp's career at its height. In 1592–4, and probably earlier, he worked with Strange's Men, at this time England's most successful playing company. Led by Edward Alleyn, Strange's performed (when in London) at the Rose in Southwark, and here Kemp would have acted in Kyd's *Spanish Tragedy*, Marlowe's *Jew of Malta*, and, perhaps, *Titus Andronicus*. Then in 1594 the London companies were completely reorganized. In the new groupings, Kemp emerged with the Lord Chamberlain's Men (Burbage and Shakespeare's company), playing at the Theatre and the Curtain in Shoreditch, with whom he created his remarkable sequence of Shakespearian clowns. He must have become a considerable force in the company. In March 1596, he (together with Shakespeare and Richard Burbage) was the payee for the company's court performances during Christmas 1595–6, and in February 1599 he was one of five players invited by Richard and Cuthbert Burbage to help finance the building of the Globe, in return for a share of the profits. In *The Return from Parnassus* (1601–2), Kemp is brought on stage as one of London's two most famous stars: 'He's not counted a gentleman that knows not Dick Burbage and Will Kemp' (Leishman, 339).

Kemp's parts for the Chamberlain's Men are a litany of famous roles: Costard in *Love's Labour's Lost* (1594), Peter, the Nurse's servant, in *Romeo and Juliet* (*c*.1595)—the 1599 quarto includes the direction 'Enter Will Kemp'—Bottom in *A Midsummer Night's Dream* (1595–6), Lancelot in *The Merchant of Venice* (1597), Dogberry in *Much Ado about Nothing* (1598), and Cob in Ben Jonson's *Every Man in his Humour* (1598). Some scholars think he also created Falstaff, and Lance in *The Two Gentlemen of Verona*. *The Two Gentlemen* is an early play, and Lance could easily have been written in later, though Kemp is not otherwise known for a double act with a dog. Falstaff is a difficult case. He has self-evident clown features, such as direct audience address and farcical misadventures, but his role is much more developed than Kemp's usual parts, and his age, size, and gentility do not match Kemp's athleticism and plainness. It is significant that John Lowin, the Falstaff of the next generation, was not a clown but a tragedian. All of Kemp's other attested roles are unpretentious men who plough a fine line between vulgar ignorance and demotic cunning. Often intellectually at sea in the complex affairs into which they stray, they none the less possess a shrewd common sense that allows them more insight into their world than that possessed by their betters—the classic instances being Bottom and Dogberry, who are their plays' real, if unofficial, heroes. All have Kemp's trade marks to a greater or lesser degree: verbal mistaking (such as Dogberry's malapropisms), upside-down epiphany (as in Bottom's 'dream'), direct audience address, puzzled soliloquy, and scope for improvisation. Without Kemp in his company, Shakespeare's output in the 1590s—though not unimaginable—would clearly have been significantly different.

The nine days' wonder and after Yet despite these glorious roles, Kemp left the company some time in 1599 to resume a career of solo clowning. He sold his share soon after its purchase, and was a conspicuous absentee from the cast of Jonson's *Every Man out of his Humour* (late 1599). Possibly he stayed in Shoreditch when the Chamberlain's Men moved to the Globe, for in September the German traveller Thomas Platter saw a clown performing at the Curtain with an unnamed company. His next certain appearance was the famous morris dance from London to Norwich, a 130-mile journey begun on 11 February 1600 and completed a month later. This small-scale but fantastic adventure seems to have combined financial speculation with canny self-advertisement. Travelling with an overseer whose job was to certify he really did dance all the way, Kemp laid money with backers, who promised to return three times the sum should he complete the feat, and gave further small gifts as financial pledges to sympathetic spectators *en route*. In the pamphlet he wrote to publicize his achievement, *Kemp's Nine Daies Wonder* (1600), he described in picaresque detail his encounters along the

road, the amusement, companionship, and occasional competition he provoked. He also complained that many who wagered against his reaching Norwich failed to pay up when he returned, and threatened to publish their names in a supplement. None the less, the preface suggests that the journey was sufficiently successful to encourage him to attempt another solo continental tour.

During the ensuing year Kemp made his way into Germany and Italy, eventually arriving at Rome, where he met the English traveller Sir Anthony Shirley, an encounter dramatized after his death in Day, Rowley, and Wilkins's play about the Shirley family, *The Travailes of the Three English Brothers* (1607). He may also have been the 'Johann Kemp' who in November 1601 was leading an English troupe that had reached Munster by way of Amsterdam and Cologne. But these sparsely documented ventures do not seem to have helped him financially. He was at home in September 1601, complaining of having fallen prey to misfortunes, and in March 1602 he borrowed money from Philip Henslowe, the impresario of Worcester's Men. By this time he had accepted a position with Worcester's Men and was one of their most senior players: he and the dramatist Thomas Heywood were payees for the company's court performance in January 1602. Still, he was probably earning far less from this company than the income he would have received had he remained a sharer at the Globe. Although he had garnered incomparable fame and popular acclaim, the dazzling financial rewards that some contemporary actors acquired largely eluded him.

Why did Kemp leave the Chamberlain's Men? It has frequently been supposed that in 1599 he was the victim of a company coup, for about the time of his departure Chamberlain's recruited a new comedian in Robert Armin. Armin's line was quite different from Kemp's robust athleticism. More witty, musical, and philosophical, he played fools rather than clowns and was less given to improvisation. Not only did Shakespeare reflect Armin's specialisms in the changed character of his subsequent comic parts, but new departures seem to be signalled in *Hamlet* (1600). The prince's advice to the players includes severe censure of clowns who 'speak more than is set down for them', intrude laughter into serious passages, and endlessly recycle their 'one suit of jests' (III.i). If, as this suggests, Chamberlain's were trying to move upmarket, Kemp may indeed have felt unwelcome at the new Globe.

Yet the surviving evidence is not clear-cut. Had the Burbages wanted to force Kemp out, they would hardly have offered him a share, as this made him one of the company's most powerful members. For his part, Kemp may not have seen the break as final. At Norwich in 1600 he was still travelling under the title of 'the Lord Chamberlain his servant' (D. Galloway, ed., *Norwich, 1540–1642*, 1984, 115), and his pairing with Burbage in the Cambridge *Return from Parnassus* perhaps indicates that at some point after returning from Italy he briefly rejoined the Globe company. Still, the tide was against him and the jigs that were his forte. In the next reign a separation started to emerge between the old-style open-air amphitheatres and the much smaller and more exclusive indoor playhouses that were gradually being built. In this new landscape, jigs were increasingly associated with playhouses like the Fortune and the Red Bull, where audiences were overwhelmingly plebeian and the repertoire had failed to move on. In Richard Brome's *The Antipodes* (1638), a character directing a play within the play rebukes his clown for disrupting the performance with impromptu jokes. That, he says, was the way:

> of Tarlton and Kemp,
> Before the stage was purged from barbarism
> And brought to the perfection it now shines with.
> (Wiles, 35)

In the more fashionable and socially segregated theatres of Stuart London, nostalgia for jigs connoted a taste for outmoded and inferior dramatic forms.

Kemp's most important roles with Worcester's Men would have been in Dekker and Webster's *Sir Thomas Wyatt* (1602) and Heywood's *A Woman Killed with Kindness* (1603). His last certain mention comes in a costume payment in Henslowe's accounts for September 1602. He may or may not have been 'Kemp, a man' who was buried at St Saviour's, Southwark, on 2 November 1603.

MARTIN BUTLER

Sources D. Wiles, *Shakespeare's clown: actor and text in the Elizabethan playhouse* (1987) · E. K. Chambers, *The Elizabethan stage*, 4 vols. (1923) · C. R. Baskerville, *The Elizabethan jig and related song drama* (1929) · W. Kemp, *Nine daies wonder*, ed. G. B. Harrison (1923) · C. Sutcliffe, 'Kemp and Armin: the management of change', *Theatre Notebook*, 50 (1996), 122–34 · G. Sjogren, 'Thomas Bull and other "English instrumentalists" in Denmark in the 1580s', *Shakespeare Survey*, 22 (1969), 119–24 · R. C. Strong and J. A. van Dorsten, *Leicester's triumph* (1964) · R. C. Bald, 'Leicester's Men in the Low Countries', *Review of English Studies*, 19 (1943), 395–7 · *Henslowe's diary*, ed. R. A. Foakes and R. T. Rickert (1961) · *A knack to know a knave* (1594) · J. B. Leishman, ed., *The three Parnassus plays* (1949) · *The works of Thomas Nashe*, ed. R. B. McKerrow, 5 vols. (1904–10); repr. with corrections and notes by F. P. Wilson (1958), vols. 1, 3 · *DNB* · M. Eccles, 'Elizabethan actors, III: K—R', *N&Q*, 237 (1992), 293–303
Likenesses stipple, pubd 1793, BM, NPG · woodcut, repro. in Kemp, *Nine daies wonder*, title-page

Kempe, Sir Alfred Bray (1849–1922), lawyer and mathematician, was born on 6 July 1849 in Kensington, London, the fourth of five children of Prebendary John Edward Kempe, rector of St James's, Piccadilly, and his wife, Harriet, daughter of the Revd Robert Serrell Wood. He was educated at St Paul's School, London, where he was Camden exhibitioner, and at Trinity College, Cambridge, where he was twenty-second wrangler in mathematics in 1872.

On leaving Cambridge, Kempe embarked on a legal career, becoming a barrister of the Inner Temple and practising on the western circuit in 1873. He quickly established a reputation for clarity of mind and scrupulous fairness. From 1881 to 1883 he was secretary of the royal commission on the ecclesiastical courts, and came to be respected as a recognized authority on ecclesiastical law. He was

Sir Alfred Bray Kempe (1849–1922), by unknown photographer

appointed to six diocesan chancellorships, Newcastle, Southwell, St Albans, Peterborough, Chichester, and finally London in 1912. He received an honorary doctorate of civil laws from Durham University in 1908, and in the following year was elected a bencher of the Middle Temple.

Throughout his life Kempe sustained a passionate interest in mathematics, writing his first paper in 1872, the year in which he received his degree. His mathematical contributions, although few in number, were highly regarded by his contemporaries and he was elected fellow of the Royal Society on 2 June 1881 and was president of the London Mathematical Society from 1892 to 1894. His first mathematical paper concerned the solution of equations by mechanical means. This work arose from his interest in kinematics, and in particular from the construction of mechanical linkages for drawing various curves, a subject stimulated by Peaucellier's discovery of a linkage that traces a straight line. He presented some popular lectures on the subject in Kensington, which led in 1877 to the publication of a celebrated memoir entitled *How to Draw a Straight Line*.

Kempe's best-known paper is probably his incorrect solution in 1879 of the map colour theorem, that the countries of any map can be coloured with just four colours so that neighbouring countries are differently coloured; this paper was commissioned by James Joseph Sylvester for his newly founded *American Journal of Mathematics*. Although Kempe's solution proved to be deficient, as demonstrated by Percy Heawood in 1890, it contained important ideas that were to resurface in the eventual solution by Kenneth Appel and Wolfgang Haken in 1976. Another of his mathematical writings was 'A memoir introductory to a general theory of mathematical form', published in the *Philosophical Transactions of the Royal Society* in 1886. This work on the fundamental nature of mathematics, together with its successor in the *Proceedings of the London Mathematical Society* in 1890 relating the logical theory of classes to the geometrical theory of points, led to a set theory (now called multisets) more general than that of George Cantor, and contains a novel use of tree diagrams to represent mathematical form; it was to influence particularly the American philosopher C. S. Peirce. Such considerations enabled Kempe to fill some lacunae in W. K. Clifford's posthumous papers on the theory of algebraic invariants; indeed, in many ways he can be regarded as Clifford's mathematical successor.

In 1898 Kempe was elected treasurer and a vice-president of the Royal Society, posts he held with distinction for twenty-one years. He played a major role in the administration of the British National Antarctic Expedition of 1901–4, and Mount Kempe and Kempe glacier in South Victoria Land are named after him. He was also involved in the establishment and building of the National Physical Laboratory, a massive project undertaken by the Royal Society in 1902, and with the eventual transference of its control to the state in 1918. Much of the credit for the early development and success of this institution is due to Kempe. His legal expertise, his clearness of judgement in administrative matters, and his conciliatory nature in matters of dispute proved to be of immense value in negotiations between the Royal Society and other parties, particularly in his frequent disputes with government agencies over funding. He was knighted in 1912 in recognition of his contributions to the society.

Kempe was married twice: first in 1877 to Mary, daughter of the oculist Sir William Bowman, who died in 1893 leaving no children, and second in 1897 to Alice Ida Meadows, daughter of Judge Meadows White, who survived him and with whom he had two sons and a daughter. His main relaxations were in mountain walking and music. He was a keen alpinist and visited Switzerland over forty times to admire the scenery and enjoy the alpine flora. As a musician he was blessed with a fine countertenor voice, singing with the Bach Choir and the Moray Minstrels (a men's glee club) and occasionally helping the Westminster Abbey choir at evening services.

Kempe's health broke down in 1917, possibly due to the immense strain caused by his many duties, and in 1919 he felt compelled to resign the treasurership of the Royal Society, while remaining on the council. Eventually, pneumonia overtook him, and he died peacefully at his home, 50 Sussex Gardens, Hyde Park, London, on 21 April 1922.

ROBIN J. WILSON

Sources A. Geikie, *PRS*, 102A (1922–3), i–x · *DNB* · W. Sussex RO, Kempe family papers · election certificate, RS · N. L. Biggs, E. K. Lloyd, and R. J. Wilson, *Graph theory, 1736–1936* (1976)
Archives W. Sussex RO, corresp. and papers
Likenesses photograph (as young man), London Mathematical Society, Burlington House, Piccadilly, London, Tucker collection · photograph, repro. in Geikie, *PRS* · photogravure?, NPG [*see illus.*]
Wealth at death £3456 17s. 4d.: probate, 17 June 1922, *CGPLA Eng. & Wales*

Kempe, Alfred John (*c.*1785–1846), antiquary, was born in London, the only son of John Kempe (1749/50–1823), descended from an old Cornish family, who had succeeded his father as *porteur d'or*, or gentleman porter, at the Royal Mint. His mother, Ann (*d.* 1835), was the youngest daughter of James Arrow of Westminster, a descendant of a Berkshire family, which still retained a small estate there. Kempe was educated by two French refugees, from whom he and his sister Anna Eliza [*see* Bray, Anna Eliza] received a good grounding in literature and the arts, and he was able to benefit from the family's wide circle of artistic acquaintances. He seems to have had no settled employment, although for a short time he too held an appointment at the mint. For some years he was a staff writer for the *Gentleman's Magazine*, for which he produced over two hundred articles on numerous subjects, mainly antiquarian and archaeological; from about 1840 to 1845 he was employed at the state paper office in transcribing and calendaring.

On 3 October 1808 Kempe married Mary, the daughter of J. Prior, a captain in the merchant navy, at Leyton, Essex; they had eleven children. Around 1809 he made the acquaintance of Charles Alfred *Stothard (1786–1821), who married his sister Anna Eliza, and he was drawn into sharing Stothard's enthusiasm for antiquities. With him Kempe explored the district of Keston, in Kent, to which he moved in 1813. These investigations were continued with Thomas Crofton Croker (1798–1854), and led to an article by Kempe, 'An investigation of the antiquities of Holwood Hill, in the parish of Keston', which appeared in the *Military Register* for 1814, and was also appended to John Dunkin's *Outlines of the History and Antiquities of Bromley in Kent* of 1815. Kempe returned to the subject again in an article entitled 'An account of some recent discoveries at Holwood Hill, in Kent', printed in the *Archaeologia* of the Society of Antiquaries of 1829, to which he had contributed since 1816. He became a fellow of the society in 1828, and from among its members, with Crofton Croker, formed the select Society of Noviomagus, which took its name from the Roman city supposed to have been sited at Holwood Hill.

Kempe helped his sister in the posthumous production of C. A. Stothard's *Monumental Effigies of Great Britain* by writing the introduction and descriptions for this beautifully illustrated work, which came out in parts between 1823 and 1832. Apart from this, and a translation in 1820 of a two-volume work by Baron von Odeleben which had appeared in French in 1817 (although originally written in German), published as *Circumstantial Narrative of the Campaign in Saxony in the Year 1813*, his published work consists of short miscellaneous papers, some of them reprints of his articles for the *Gentleman's Magazine*. Kempe died at Stamford Villas, Fulham Road, London, on 21 August 1846 and was buried in Fulham churchyard on 27 August.

W. P. COURTNEY, rev. SHIRLEY BURGOYNE BLACK

Sources J. M. Kuist, *The Nichols file of the Gentleman's Magazine: attributions of authorship and other documentation in editorial papers at the Folger Library* (1982) · *Autobiography of A. E. Bray*, ed. J. A. Kempe (1884) · A. E. Bray, *Memoirs*, ed. C. A. Stothard (1823) · J. Maclean, *The parochial and family history of the deanery of Trigg Minor in the county of Cornwall*, 1 (1873), 78 · private information (1891)
Archives Canterbury Cathedral, archives, memoranda book, notes, sketches | Bodl. Oxf., letters to John Dunkin
Likenesses J. B. Swaine, mezzotint (after miniature by W. Patten), BM, NPG

Kempe, Charles Eamer (1837–1907), artist in stained-glass and church decoration, was born on 29 June 1837 at Ovingdean Hall, Sussex, the fifth son and seventh and last child of Nathaniel Kemp JP, who died when his son was six, and his second wife, Augusta Caroline, the daughter of Sir John Eamer, a former lord mayor of London. Kempe (he added the 'e' in the 1860s) was educated at Rugby School, and Pembroke College, Oxford (MA 1862).

A severe stammer prevented his taking holy orders, and Kempe determined to devote his Anglo-Catholic fervour to the cause of ecclesiastical art. He gained practical experience and made designs for embroidery and furniture in the office of the young G. F. Bodley, son of the Kemp family physician, and a leading figure in the later phase of the Gothic revival in architecture. He studied briefly in the London stained-glass studios of Clayton and Bell, and in 1866 set up his own business in stained-glass and church decoration. Three years later he received his first major commission, to decorate Bodley's new church of St John, Tue Brook, Liverpool.

Thereafter Kempe's business prospered, and his work graces many cathedrals, including those in Wells, Lichfield, Southwark, Winchester, Durham, Gloucester, Canterbury, and York Minster. Of his many foreign commissions one of the most prestigious was the window ordered in 1877 by Princess Alice, grand-duchess of Hesse and by Rhine, for the royal mausoleum in Darmstadt, in commemoration of the death of her young son.

In 1875 Kempe bought an Elizabethan house, Old Place, Lindfield, Sussex, which he greatly enlarged and decorated lavishly with his growing collection of furniture and works of art. Although he is often characterized as retiring and eccentric, he entertained distinguished visitors in style, and studio staff were frequently welcomed to Old Place and treated with considerable generosity.

Never more than competent as a draughtsman himself, Kempe was adept at selecting and training young designers and craftsmen to carry out schemes under his direction. His early work was inspired by English fifteenth-century glass, and he was a pioneer in his appreciation of late medieval styles. By 1880 he was turning to German models, and as business increased (he is believed to have employed as many as a hundred men) production became stereotyped. In 1882 the eighteen-year-old (John) Ninian Comper was Kempe's pupil and already anticipated the view of most subsequent critics with his preference for Kempe's early work.

Kempe died, unmarried, at his home, 28 Nottingham Place, London, on 29 April 1907, and was buried in the family vault at Ovingdean. The business passed to his cousin, Walter E. Tower, and the weak derivatives of the Kempe formula produced until the studio's demise in 1934 did little to advance Kempe's reputation. Yet his role in the advancement of late nineteenth-century art and architecture was an important one. His adaptations of late Gothic and northern Renaissance styles were influential and had many admirers. That he had established an alternative path to Pre-Raphaelite styles was recognized by W. Owen Chadwick, who suggested in *The Victorian Church* (1966) that 'the art of stained glass reached its zenith, not with the innovations of William Morris and Edward Burne-Jones, but in the tractarian artist, Charles Eamer Kempe'.

MARTIN HARRISON, rev.

Sources M. Harrison, *Victorian stained glass* (1980) · M. Stavridi, *Master of glass* (1988) · *CGPLA Eng. & Wales* (1907)
Wealth at death £62,802 5s. 5d.: resworn probate, 1 July 1907, *CGPLA Eng. & Wales*

Kempe, Dorothy. *See* Gardiner, Dorothy (1873–1957).

Kempe, Harry Robert (1852–1935), electrical engineer and journal editor, was born at 12 Addison Terrace, Kensington, London, on 1 March 1852. He was the youngest in the family of four sons and one daughter of the Revd John Edward Kempe, later rector of St James's, Piccadilly (1853–95), prebendary of St Paul's, and chaplain-in-ordinary to Queen Victoria (1864–1901), and his wife, Harriet, daughter of the Revd R. Wood, of Osmington House, Dorset. One of his older brothers was Alfred Bray *Kempe, an ecclesiastical lawyer. He was educated at Westminster School (1865–7) and at King's College, London (1867–70), where he studied applied science, but took no degree. His autobiographical reminiscences mention two years spent in the laboratory of Sir Charles Wheatstone. He worked for three years with Sir Samuel Canning, engineer-in-chief of the Telegraph Construction and Maintenance Company, and was involved with the laying of the Malta–Gibraltar cable in 1870. He also had a working association with the civil engineer Robert Sabine, one of the pioneers of transatlantic telegraphy.

Kempe moved to Southampton to work with William H. Preece, divisional engineer in the postal telegraph department, on 1 April 1872. Preece was appointed electrician to the postmaster-general in 1877 and Kempe was subsequently transferred to London on 2 March 1878 to act as his assistant. On 8 July 1880 he married Helen Catherine (d. 1932), daughter of Major-General Byng of the Madras light infantry. They had one daughter.

During the 1890s Kempe worked on inductive telegraphy, which was particularly important for communication with lighthouses and lightships. He was responsible for many telegraph and telephone services used by the Post Office (including sending keys, and postal pneumatic extensions) and his design of the Dover–Calais cable for the London–Paris telephone was an acknowledged success. He succeeded Preece, becoming principal technical officer on 15 March 1900 and electrician on 1 August 1907, a position from which he retired in 1913. During the First World War he was examiner to the inventions committee of the Air Ministry.

While still living with his family in London in 1871, he was among the first associate members of the newly formed Society of Telegraph Engineers (later the Institution of Electrical Engineers). From 1872 onwards he contributed student articles to the *Telegraphic Journal*, which later became the *Electrical Review*. He became the editor and one of the proprietors, retaining full control of the journal until 1931. His major written works include *A Handbook of Electrical Testing* (1876), *Alternating Currents* (1916), *The Electrical Engineers' Pocket-Book* (1890), and a contribution on telephony and telegraphy for the eleventh edition of the *Encyclopaedia Britannica*. His *Engineer's Year-Book*, first produced with W. Hannaford-Smith, was a major achievement and a project which he steered for thirty-six years.

Kempe lived for many years at Lavethan, Brockham, Betchworth, Surrey, and died there on 10 April 1935. He was buried on 15 April 1935 at Brockham church.

D. DE COGAN, rev.

Sources *Post Office Electrical Engineers' Journal*, 5 (1912–13), 498–503 · *The Electrician* (19 April 1935), 522 · *Electrical Review*, 116 (1935), 577–8 · *Journal of the Institution of Electrical Engineers*, 77 (1935), 893 · b. cert. · m. cert. · d. cert. · *The Times* (12 April 1935), 18e · biography, 1990, Inst. EE [prepared by family]
Likenesses two photographs, repro. in *Electrical Engineers' Journal* [Post Office], 5 (1912–13), facing p. 498, p. 501
Wealth at death £3370 2s. 4d.: family biography

Kempe [*née* Brunham], **Margery** (*b. c.*1373, *d.* in or after 1438), visionary, was the author of the earliest surviving autobiography in English. She was born at Bishop's Lynn, Norfolk, the daughter of John Brunham (*d.* 1413), merchant, who was five times mayor and six times MP for Lynn between 1364 and 1391. The identity of Kempe's mother is unknown. At about twenty she married John Kempe, the younger son of a Lynn skinner, also called John (*d. c.*1393). John Kempe the younger was admitted to the freedom in 1393, and was a chamberlain of Lynn in 1394. He is recorded as a brewer in 1403–5. Margery Kempe became pregnant soon after their marriage, and when the child was born she experienced a severe post-partum depression, lasting for eight and a half months. She was finally cured when Jesus appeared and sat at the end of her bed, speaking words of comfort. This marked the beginning of her conversion, though Kempe continued for several years in her old way of life: she ran a brewing business which collapsed, and then a short-lived horse-mill. These failures convinced her that she was being punished for her sinfulness, and she embarked on a life of penance.

Almost everything known about Margery Kempe derives from her *Book*. Kempe could not write, but determined in the early 1430s to record her spiritual autobiography. She employed as amanuensis an Englishman who

had lived in Germany, but he died before the work was finished, and his writing was anyway illegible. Kempe persuaded a local priest to begin rewriting on 23 July 1436, and on 28 April 1438 he started work on an additional section covering the years 1431–4. Only one manuscript survives, now in the British Library (Add. MS 61823), and previously in the possession of the Butler-Bowdon family of Lancashire. It was copied about 1450 by an East Anglian scribe named Salthows, and later in the century was owned by the Yorkshire Carthusian priory of Mount Grace. Until the manuscript was identified by Hope Emily Allen in 1934, Kempe's *Book* was known only from excerpts printed by Wynkyn de Worde *c.*1501, and by Henry Pepwell in 1521 (where the author is described as 'a devoute ancres'). The *Book* was first published complete in 1936, in a version in modern English by William Butler-Bowdon. A critical edition for the Early English Text Society by Sanford Brown Meech and Hope Emily Allen followed four years later. Other versions have followed since, including one in the Penguin Classics series in 1985.

The chronology of Kempe's life is unclear from her *Book*, and few events, including her encounters with authority, can be documented from other sources. She had another thirteen children before she finally persuaded her husband, in the summer of 1413, to agree that they should live chastely. Kempe then sought permission from Philip Repingdon, bishop of Lincoln, to become a vowess and wear the characteristic mantle and ring, to which she proposed adding white clothes symbolizing her spiritual purity. Repingdon sent her to Thomas Arundel, archbishop of Canterbury, who received her kindly, but it is not certain that she took a formal vow. Possibly that year, Kempe visited Julian of Norwich to seek reassurance about the authenticity of her visions. Later in 1413 she left Yarmouth on a pilgrimage to the Holy Land, via Constance and Venice, living on alms. After reaching Jerusalem, she visited Calvary and the holy sepulchre, where she first manifested the uncontrollable crying which for many years was to be the hallmark of her devotion. She travelled in the Holy Land before re-embarking for Venice, and then went to Assisi and Rome, where she wore white clothing, and where her roaring in church caused much hostility. Throughout this period Kempe had frequent visions, which included a mystical marriage to the Godhead in Rome. While there she met a former servant of the visionary St Bridget of Sweden. She returned to England after Easter 1415.

Back in Lynn, Kempe was a source of scandal, with her white clothing and noisy weeping. In 1417 she set off again on pilgrimage to Santiago de Compostela. While waiting for a ship in Bristol she was welcomed into the household of Thomas Peverel, bishop of Worcester, who had known her father and treated her as a holy woman. On her return from Spain she visited the shrine of the holy blood at Hailes, in Gloucestershire, and then went on to Leicester. The political climate, in the aftermath of Oldcastle's revolt of 1414, was not favourable to unusual styles of religion. Earlier, in Canterbury, Kempe had been called a Lollard and threatened with burning by people in the street;

here she was brought before the mayor, charged with Lollardy, and imprisoned. After being harassed, verbally and sexually, by the steward of Leicester, she was examined on the eucharist in the mayor's presence by the abbot of the town's Augustinian house, and by the dean of Leicester. She was pronounced orthodox, and made her way to York. Here her white clothing, her sobbing during communion, and her following in the city once more made her suspect. She was examined by minster clergy and then brought before the archbishop of York, Henry Bowet, at Cawood, where she was again accused of heresy and again found to be orthodox. Bowet had her escorted out of the area, but she was rearrested by royal authorities and taken to Beverley. Bowet released her again and gave her a letter certifying her orthodoxy. Once across the Humber she was arrested yet again and released, before going to London to secure a letter from Henry Chichele, archbishop of Canterbury, allowing her frequent access to confession and communion. She returned to Lynn some time in 1418.

Several years of painful illnesses followed, which made Kempe less mobile than before. The intense spiritual life recorded in her *Book* includes extended visions, conversations with Jesus, and bouts of noisy crying. A priest read works of contemplation to her over a period of years, including the Bible and commentaries, the *Revelations* of St Bridget, Walter Hilton's translation of the *Stimulus amoris*, and the *Incendium amoris* of Richard Rolle. She also knew of Marie d'Oignies (d. 1213) and Elizabeth of Hungary (d. 1231). Although much criticized, she always had supporters among the clergy, including the Dominican anchorite of Lynn, himself a visionary, her parish priest, Robert Springolde, who succeeded the anchorite as her principal confessor, Thomas Hevingham, prior of the Benedictine monastery in Lynn, Richard Caister, vicar of St Stephen's, Norwich, and William Southfield, Carmelite of Norwich, also a visionary.

In the 1420s Kempe lived apart from her husband. When he was accidentally injured, and later became senile, she nursed him until his death about 1431, in penance for her pleasure in his body when young. Their son, who lived in Germany, returned to Lynn with his wife and died, shortly before his father. In April 1433 Kempe left Ipswich, without her confessor's permission, to accompany her daughter-in-law back to Danzig. Their ship was blown off course to Norway, but eventually reached Danzig, from where Kempe travelled with difficulty to Wilsnack in Brandenburg to see the miraculous Holy Blood. Then she went to Aachen and its holy relics, and returned via Calais to London. She visited the Bridgettine abbey at Syon, probably in August 1434, where she received the Lammastide indulgence for pilgrims, and then returned to Lynn to be reconciled with her confessor. In 1438, when the *Book* was completed, a Margeria Kempe, who may be its author, was admitted to the prestigious Trinity Guild of Lynn. The date of Kempe's death is unknown.   FELICITY RIDDY

Sources *The book of Margery Kempe*, ed. S. B. Meech and H. E. Allen, EETS, 212 (1940) · *The book of Margery Kempe*, ed. B. A. Windeatt, pbk edn (1985) · C. W. Atkinson, *Mystic and pilgrim: the book and the world of Margery Kempe* (1983) · D. M. Owen, ed., *The making of King's Lynn*

(1984) · S. E. Holbrooke, 'Margery Kempe and Wynkyn de Worde', *The medieval mystic tradition in England* [Exeter 1987], ed. M. Glasscoe (1987), 27–46
Archives BL, Add. MS 61823 · CUL, 'A shorte treatyse of contemplacyon', (1501?; STC 14924) · Hunt. L., 'A shorte treatyse of contemplacyon', (1501?; STC 14924)

Kempe, Ursley (d. 1582). *See under* Essex witches (*act.* 1566–1589).

Kempenfelt, Richard (1718–1782), naval officer, was born at Westminster, the son of Magnus Kempenfelt (b. 1664/5, d. c.1727), a native of Sweden, and Anne Hunt (b. 1678/9). His father is said to have been in the service of James II and followed him to France, later returning to England where he entered the army, and gained the rank of lieutenant-colonel. In 1725–6 Magnus was lieutenant-governor of Jersey; he died about 1727, and was survived by two daughters and two sons, including Richard.

Richard Kempenfelt entered the navy, served in the West Indies at the celebrated taking of Portobello, and on 14 January 1741 was promoted lieutenant of the *Strafford*, then carrying his flag, by Edward Vernon. After the failure at Cartagena, Kempenfelt was moved into the *Superbe*, and again into the frigate *Seahorse*. He returned to England towards the end of 1746. In September 1748 he was appointed to the *Anson*, first with Captain Nutt, and afterwards with Captain Charles Holmes. In January 1755 he joined the *Lichfield* under the command of Captain Charles Steevens whom in April he followed to the *Orford* as first lieutenant. On 5 May 1756 he was promoted to command the fireship *Lightning*, and on 17 January 1757 he became captain of the *Elizabeth*, bearing the broad pennant of Captain Steevens, and went out to the East Indies as commodore and second in command.

In the *Elizabeth*, Kempenfelt played a role in the distinguished actions of 29 April and 3 August 1758. He was then appointed to the frigate *Queenborough* in which he convoyed troops of Colonel William Draper's regiment to Madras where their prompt landing, when the French under Count Lully were on the point of assault, prevented its falling to the enemy. A few months later he rejoined Steevens, now a rear-admiral, on the *Grafton*, which he commanded in the action of 10 September 1759. On Steevens's becoming commander-in-chief, Kempenfelt accompanied him to the *Norfolk*, and took part in the capture of Pondicherry; Kempenfelt's account of the action was reprinted in the *Gentleman's Magazine* for 1846. When Steevens died Rear-Admiral Samuel Cornish hoisted his flag in the *Norfolk*; he retained Kempenfelt as his flag captain, and put him in charge of landing troops at Manila; after its capture he was detached to take possession of the Spanish naval station at Cavite, and was specially requested by Sir William Draper to act as its governor. Kempenfelt was then sent home with dispatches. After his return to the East Indies he resumed command of the *Norfolk*, and brought her to England in 1764. He is said to have spent a considerable part of the following years travelling in France and elsewhere on the continent, where he made a special study of French shipbuilding techniques.

It remains unclear when Kempenfelt developed his

evangelical Christian convictions, but one of his short poems was written at sea near the island of Sicily, on 20 May 1769, when he was on half pay, and his collected *Original Hymns and Poems* were published in 1777. Apart from his personal spirituality he shared a conviction, growing among officers in the fleet, that restoration of religious observances could support the structure of naval discipline. In 1779 he wrote to Admiral Charles Middleton (later Lord Barham): 'Don't let anyone imagine that this discipline [of daily prayers] will disgust the men and give them a dislike to the service, for the very reverse will be the consequence' (*Letters and Papers*, 1.308). Two years later he had the first consignment of bibles supplied by the Bible Society placed on board his flagship, the *Royal George*.

During the dispute with Spain over the Falkland Islands in 1770 Kempenfelt commanded the *Buckingham*, which was paid off in the following year. In October 1778 he was appointed to the *Alexander*, and in April 1779 he sat as a member of the court martial on Sir Hugh Palliser. Afterwards, on the recommendation of George III as 'a great friend of Lord Clarendon, [and] much respected by all parties and one well qualified to heal all little breaches' (*Correspondence*, ed. Fortescue, no. 2209, 9 March 1779), Kempenfelt was appointed captain of the fleet first to Sir Charles Hardy the younger, and, in 1780, to Sir Francis Geary and Vice-Admiral George Darby. As a loyal subordinate to a succession of elderly commanders-in-chief, Kempenfelt worked to overcome the tactical limitations of the fleet which had been brought to his attention during Palliser's trial. During the crisis of 1779, when a large but inefficient Franco-Spanish fleet was in the channel and threatening invasion, Kempenfelt expressed a belief that a smaller but tactically more efficient British fleet should be able, if not to dominate the situation, at least to make invasion impossible. However, his efforts to drill the fleet met with little success, his difficulties having been increased initially by Admiral Hardy's obstinacy. Despite his extensive experiments with new signal books and his practical skill as a tactician, his ability as a theoretician who needed to overcome service conservatism to effect reform proved to be somewhat limited.

On 26 September 1780 Kempenfelt was advanced to rear-admiral of the blue; he continued with Darby until towards the end of 1781 when, with his flag in the *Victory*, he was directed to put to sea in command of twelve ships of the line and some frigates, and intercept a French squadron and convoy, reported bound for the West Indies. He was instructed that the escort would consist of not more than seven ships; but when he sighted it, on 12 December, some 50 leagues to the south-west of Ushant, he found it consisting of nineteen. Every available ship had been sent, under the command of De Guichen, who was reputedly one of the most skilful tacticians in the French navy. Kempenfelt at once saw that it was impossible for him to attack such a superior force. He formed line abreast and followed the French until he noticed that their van and centre had drawn too far ahead to be any longer able to support the convoy. Turning into line ahead, he engaged the French rear and, brushing it aside,

closed with the convoy, twenty of which he captured; he sank the four frigates of the close escort. Forming two divisions, one of which took the prizes in tow and the other of which covered their rear, he ran into Plymouth under a press of sail and hotly engaged by two of De Guichen's ships and a few of the transports.

On Lord Howe's taking command of the fleet in April 1782, Kempenfelt hoisted his flag in the *Royal George* as one of the junior admirals, and continued with the fleet during the summer cruise. On 15 August the fleet anchored at Spithead, and was ordered to refit with all possible haste and proceed to the relief of Gibraltar. As part of this process it was necessary to give the *Royal George* a slight heel to get at a leak a few inches below the water-line. This was done on 29 August by running her guns over to the other side. While she was so heeled supply boats came alongside to transfer casks through the depressed lower gun ports; the additional weight allowed an inrush of water which immediately capsized and sank her. Besides the crew, a very large number of tradesmen, women, and children were on board; it was estimated that more than 800 lost their lives. Kempenfelt was at the time in his cabin, and died in the accident. The master, gunner, and boatswain were all ashore in violation of orders, and the carpenter had been unable to find the officer of the watch to warn him. At the court martial, however, the crew were absolved of all blame.

After the conservatism of previous commanders the appointment of Earl Howe had brought a sympathetic commander with whom Kempenfelt had been able to work. Because Kempenfelt died so soon afterwards it was left to Howe to provide the fleet with a numerically based flag system capable of transmitting a rapid succession of complex tactical instructions; and it fell upon Sir Home Popham to equip it with a 'marine telegraph' capable of two-way communication of intelligence.

J. K. LAUGHTON, *rev.* NICHOLAS TRACY

Sources B. Tunstall, *Naval warfare in the age of sail: the evolution of fighting tactics, 1650–1815*, ed. N. Tracy (1990) · *Letters and papers of Charles, Lord Barham*, ed. J. K. Laughton, 3 vols., Navy RS, 32, 38–9 (1907–11) · *The correspondence of King George the Third from 1760 to December 1783*, ed. J. Fortescue, 6 vols. (1927–8) · R. F. Johnson, *The Royal George* (1971) · *Naval Chronicle*, 7 (1802), 365–71 · R. C. Blake, 'Transmission of the faith and transformation of the fleet: the religious education of the Royal Navy, 1770–1870', *Foi chrétienne et milieux maritimes, XVe–XXsiècle*, ed. A. Cabantous and F. Hildesheimer (1987)
Archives NMM, letters to Sir Charles Middleton
Likenesses T. Kettle, group portrait, oils, exh. Society of Artists 1768, priv. coll.; *see illus. in* Cornish, Sir Samuel, baronet (*c.*1715–1770) · T. Kettle, oils, exh. RA 1782, NMM · R. Earl, oils, 1783, NPG · print (after T. Kettle), BM
Wealth at death see will, PRO, PROB 11/1095, fol. 177

Kempster, Frederick John [Fred] (1889–1918), giant, was born at 5 East Block, Chapel Side, Paddington, London, on 13 April 1889, the youngest in the family of two sons and three daughters of Joseph Kempster, a milk carrier, and his wife, Jane, *née* Price. His parents were of normal height, although his sister Ruth was over 6 feet tall when she married. His father died when he was a child. Although Fred Kempster was originally a basket maker by trade, it became impossible to carry on doing this for a living as he could not stand upright in a normal room and his hands became too large to handle any tools, but he worked for a time as a gardener in Devizes, Wiltshire, sometimes staying in Weston, near Bath, with his sister Ruth and her husband, James Rayner, a gardener.

In 1910, when Kempster was 7 feet 9½ inches (236 centimetres) tall, and still growing, he joined a travelling circus, with a manager, William Thompson, and went on his first European tour, billed as 'Frederick the Great, the English Giant', and 'The World's Tallest Man'. He appeared with the German giantess Brunhilde, who was 4 inches taller than he. In between tours, he lived with his sister and brother-in-law, who had moved to Worton, Wiltshire. He had to enter their house on his hands and knees, and played darts in the pub kneeling. He lit his cigarettes from the gas street lights and shook hands with people through their first-floor bedroom windows, and it was said that you could cover a single bed with his shirt. The Worton village blacksmith later sold picture postcards of him taken in Germany in 1910.

Fred Kempster was touring in Germany at the outbreak of war in 1914, and was sent to an internment camp where he remained until 1916, when he was released with the help of the American ambassador in Berlin. He returned to England in poor health, and moved to Seend Cleeve, Wiltshire, where his sister and brother-in-law now ran The Barge inn. He became a tourist attraction, with sightseers coming from far and wide to pay 6*d.* to sit in the pub with 'the Avebury Giant' and hear him talk about his life and the problems posed by his height. Several people remembered him passing a half-crown through the gold ring he wore on his little finger. Although children were frightened of him at first, they later happily sat on his knee, and he had the reputation of being kind and mild-mannered, known as the 'gentle giant'.

Kempster continued to tour as a fairground attraction, but he never recovered his health, and collapsed in a Blackburn street while on a tour of the north of England. It took eight men to carry him in a fireman's jumping blanket to an ambulance, and when he was admitted to hospital, where three beds were lashed into one for him, he was found to be suffering from pneumonia. Kempster died in the union workhouse infirmary, Blackburn, on 15 April 1918. According to the undertaker's records he was 8 feet 4½ inches (255 centimetres) tall at his death and weighed 27 stone (171 kilos). Ten pall bearers were needed to carry the coffin at his funeral on 19 April in Blackburn cemetery. It is almost certain that he suffered from gigantism, caused by over-production of the growth hormone somatotrophin.   ANNE PIMLOTT BAKER

Sources C. Alexander-Jones, *An introduction to Frederick, the English giant* (1998) · *Avebury before today* (1978) · D. Buxton, *Around Devizes: old photographs* (1990), 140 · private information (2004) [from Great Barn Museum of Wiltshire Rural Life, Avebury, Wiltshire] · b. cert. · d. cert.

Likenesses photograph, 1910, repro. in Buxton, *Around Devizes*, 140 · photographs, repro. in Alexander-Jones, *Introduction to Frederick*, 9

Kempt, Sir James (1763/4–1854), army officer and governor-in-chief of British North America, was born between December 1763 and December 1764 in Edinburgh, the son of Gavin Kempt and his wife, the daughter of Alexander Walker of Edinburgh. Although nothing is known about his early life, he was gazetted ensign in the 101st foot in March 1783 and lieutenant the following year. After the regiment's disbandment in 1785, Kempt remained on half pay until 1794, when he was commissioned captain and then major in the 113th foot. When that regiment was broken up, he served briefly as inspecting field officer of recruiting at Glasgow, and in 1796 was again placed on half pay. In 1799 he became aide-de-camp to Sir Ralph Abercromby, commander of troops in north Britain, whom he accompanied with expeditionary forces to Holland and the Mediterranean. On Abercromby's death in 1801, Kempt joined the staff of John Hely-Hutchinson for the rest of the Egyptian campaign. In 1803 he was appointed aide-de-camp to David Dundas, commanding the southern district in England; later that year he obtained the lieutenant-colonelcy of the 81st foot, and served in 1805–6 in Naples and Sicily under Sir James Henry Craig. From 1807 to 1811 Kempt was quartermaster-general in British North America and in 1809 advanced to colonel. Between 1811 and 1814 he served on the staff of Wellington's army in Spain and France, with the rank of major-general. In June 1814 he commanded one of the brigades dispatched from Bordeaux to reinforce British troops in the Canadas during war with the United States. Kempt returned to Europe on Napoleon's escape from Elba and commanded the 8th brigade at the battle of Waterloo. In acknowledgement of his wartime services he received a string of British and foreign decorations, the KCB and GCB in 1815, and the GCH in 1816. He held the lieutenant-governorship of the garrison at Fort William from 1813 and at Portsmouth from 1819. He was colonel successively of the 60th foot (1813), the 3rd West India regiment (1818), the 81st foot (1819), and the 40th foot (1829). He was promoted lieutenant-general in 1825 and general in 1841.

Like other Wellingtonian officers, Kempt was drawn into the post-war colonial service. He was appointed in 1819 lieutenant-governor of Nova Scotia on the promotion of his friend Lord Dalhousie to governor-in-chief of British North America. Although Dalhousie forewarned him of conflict with provincial politicians, particularly over financial matters, Kempt's conciliatory manner enabled him to preserve harmonious relations with the legislature. He managed to postpone serious consideration of the British government's disruptive proposal in 1825 that the assembly should be invited to vote a civil list, covering the salaries of leading officials, in exchange for control over crown revenues. Religious disputes, especially over higher education, proved more troublesome. The Anglican exclusiveness of King's College, Windsor, had been challenged by Dalhousie's inauguration in 1818 of a non-sectarian college in Halifax, modelled on the University of Edinburgh. Although a building was begun in 1820, the debt-ridden institution remained moribund. In vain Kempt urged the colonial secretary, Lord Bathurst, a fervent Anglican, to sanction a special grant from crown revenues. Kempt also failed to secure funds from a legislature facing similar demands from King's College and Presbyterian Pictou Academy. His constructive initiative to amalgamate King's and Dalhousie won local endorsement in 1824 but was vetoed by the archbishop of Canterbury, with Bathurst's acquiescence.

In 1828 Kempt was dispatched by the British authorities on a military mission to inspect the building of the Rideau Canal in Upper Canada, where the expenditures contracted by the chief engineer, Lieutenant-Colonel John By, had spiralled alarmingly out of control. On his return to Halifax that summer, Kempt received word of his appointment as governor-in-chief, following the hasty removal of Dalhousie amid a political storm in Lower Canada and at Westminster, where a Commons select committee was investigating his conduct. Kempt viewed with mixed feelings the promotion he had long expected and the task of dealing with a formidable crisis arising chiefly from a protracted, bitter dispute over the appropriation of revenues. He temporarily eased the deadlock by practising calm forbearance and by making tactical concessions to the legislature in the hope that parliament would soon provide a permanent settlement. The recipient of vague, contradictory instructions and much criticism from the Colonial Office, he was relieved to surrender his responsibilities to Lord Aylmer in October 1830. Kempt's success as governor in cultivating a degree of harmony stemmed in part from qualities of character and personality and from a deliberately non-partisan approach to colonial politics. An affable and highly sociable individual, his tact and common sense won widespread respect and co-operation. Kempt was also favoured by circumstances, administrating both colonies during interludes between political strife.

On arrival in England, Kempt became master-general of the Board of Ordnance, with a seat on the privy council, but determined to stay out of parliament and party politics. In addition to departmental duties, he served on royal commissions in 1833–4 to investigate military punishments and the civil administration of the army, objecting in the latter instance to any change in the powers of the Ordnance. He retired from public life in December 1834, though his name was mentioned in 1835 and again in 1837 for a Canadian appointment. He died, unmarried, in South Audley Street, London, on 20 December 1854, leaving in his will gifts totalling £59,800 and £675 in annuities to various relatives and friends. PETER BURROUGHS

Sources The Times (22 Dec 1854) · GM, 2nd ser., 43 (1855), 188–9 · Army List (1783–1854) · PRO, Colonial Office Records, CO 42/217–30, CO 43/27–28 (Lower Canada), CO 217/138–48, CO 218/29–30 (Nova Scotia) · H. J. Morgan, Sketches of celebrated Canadians, and persons connected with Canada (1862), 266–8 · H. T. Manning, The revolt of French Canada, 1800–1835 (1962) · P. A. Buckner, The transition to responsible government: British policy in British North America, 1815–1850 (1985) · W. S. MacNutt, The Atlantic provinces: the emergence of colonial

society, 1712–1857 (1965) · G. A. Raudzens, The British ordnance department and Canada's canals, 1815–1855 (1979) · R. Christie, A history of the late province of Lower Canada, 3 (1850); 6 (1855)
Archives Claydon House, Buckinghamshire, letter-book · NA Canada, letter-books | All Souls Oxf., corresp. with Charles Richard Vaughan · BL, corresp. with Sir James Willoughby Gordon, Add. MS 49512 · Derbys. RO, letters to Sir R. J. Wilmot-Horton · NA Scot., corresp. with Lord Dalhousie · NL Scot., corresp. with Edward Ellice · U. Durham L., letters to second Earl Grey · U. Southampton L., letters to first duke of Wellington · W. Sussex RO, letters to duke of Richmond
Likenesses S. Bellin, mezzotint, pubd 1841 (after R. McInnes), NPG · W. Salter, group portrait, oils (Waterloo banquet at Apsley House), Wellington Museum, London · W. Salter, oils (study for Waterloo banquet), NPG
Wealth at death gifts totalling £59,800; £675 in annuities: will, PRO, PROB 11/2204, fols. 392–3

Kempthorne, Sir John (c.1620–1679), naval officer, was the second son of John Kempthorne, attorney, of Ugborough, Devon, and his wife, Agnes Simon. John senior served as a royalist cavalry officer in the civil wars, by which time his son seems already to have been at sea for several years, beginning as apprentice to the master of a Topsham vessel and eventually commanding Levant Company ships in the Mediterranean trade. About 1649 Kempthorne married Joanna (d. 1691), a servant to Lady Bendish, the wife of the ambassador to Constantinople from 1647 to 1661. In 1657 his ship, probably the Eastland Merchant, was captured after a hard fight by the Spanish privateer Papachino, who showed great kindness to his prisoner—a generosity of spirit which Kempthorne reciprocated when Papachino was imprisoned in the Tower of London in 1658, eventually procuring the Spaniard's release. On 17 November 1660 John Kempthorne 'of Poplar' was elected a brother of Trinity House, and in 1662–3 he was commanding the merchantman Maidenhead, still in the Mediterranean trade, when she was requisitioned by the Turks to transport troops to Candia (Crete). The ambassador at Constantinople, the earl of Winchilsea, noted at the time that 'the captain has always been a man of loyal principles' (Finch MSS, 1.180).

The mobilization for the Second Anglo-Dutch War in 1664 brought Kempthorne his first naval command, probably through the auspices of his father's old commanding officer, Prince Rupert of the Rhine. He was captain of the Kent from June to October 1664, transferring from her to the Dunkirk and then, on 26 November, to the first-rate Royal James, which he commanded in the battle of Lowestoft on 3 June 1665 as flag captain to Rupert. On 19 July he transferred to the Old James, whose captain, the earl of Marlborough—a distant relative of the Kempthorne family—had been killed in the action. Kempthorne moved from her to the Royal Charles in February 1666, commanding her as flag captain to the duke of Albemarle in the Four Days' Fight of 1–4 June before moving to the Defiance on 10 June, becoming rear-admiral of the Blue squadron in her in September. He stayed in the same ship until the end of 1667 and during this period commanded one of the 'flying squadrons' sent out by the bankrupt government instead of a main fleet. His ships convoyed the Mediterranean trade between February and May 1667, then remained in south-western waters, based at Plymouth, during the Dutch attacks on the English and Scottish coastlines in the summer. At the end of June the squadron sailed for Ireland, where it remained until the end of September, usually cruising off the north-west coast between Blackrock and Rockall. After leaving the *Defiance* in December 1667, he commanded the *Warspite* during the summer of 1668.

Early in 1669 Kempthorne took command of the *Mary Rose*, the ship intended to carry Lord Howard as ambassador to Morocco. After landing him at Tangier, Kempthorne collected under his escort a multinational convoy of six merchantmen, only to be attacked north of Cadiz on 18 December by seven Algerine corsairs. The *Mary Rose* engaged without hesitation. The fighting lasted that day and much of the next, with six of the Algerine force attacking Kempthorne's single warship. Despite severe damage to her masts and rigging, the *Mary Rose* managed to disable the enemy admiral's vessel, at which point the whole Algerine force withdrew. Kempthorne's squadron arrived safely in Cadiz Bay on the 20th. The event was immortalized by the engraver Wenceslaus Hollar, a passenger on the *Mary Rose*, and it earned a knighthood for Kempthorne on 24 April 1670. When the Third Anglo-Dutch War began in 1672 he became rear-admiral of the blue once more, flying his flag in the *St Andrew*, in which he fought at the battle of Solebay on 28 May 1672. The blue bore the brunt of the fighting and Kempthorne's unsuccessful efforts to relieve his doomed admiral, the earl of Sandwich, brought him high praise: 'he … fought till eight with as much conduct and bravery as ever man in the world did, continually engaged on both sides almost the whole day' (Thomas Lucas to Nathaniel Herne, PRO, SP 29/310/35). Kempthorne's own account tells of his day-long running battle with the Dutch admiral De Ruyter, who was to regard this action as the hardest he ever fought. Kempthorne subsequently became rear-admiral of the red, and remained in the *St Andrew* for the 1673 campaign, serving under Sir Edward Spragge as vice-admiral of the blue. As such, he took part in the two indecisive battles of the Schooneveld on 28 May and 4 June, as well as in the battle of the Texel/Kijkduin on 11 August 1673. Spragge's deliberate decision to detach his squadron from the main fleet to pursue his private vendetta with the Dutch admiral Tromp led to bitter recriminations: Kempthorne criticized the conduct of his rear-admiral, Thomas Butler, earl of Ossory, but subsequently retracted the charges. His own part in the action, primarily against Tromp's vice-admiral, Sweers, and Tromp himself, centred on the relief of the severely damaged *Royal Prince*.

After leaving the *St Andrew* in October 1673 Kempthorne drew a flag officer's pension of £200 per annum, and served both as master of Trinity House in 1674-5 and as the first steward of the club for naval captains set up in 1674. Early in 1675 he was appointed resident commissioner of the navy at Portsmouth, forming a close relationship with the governor there, Colonel George Legge, later Lord Dartmouth, a fellow naval veteran of the Dutch wars. During the naval mobilization which occurred in 1678

(when there was a threat of war with France), Kempthorne held his last seagoing command, in the post of vice-admiral of the narrow seas and flying his flag in the *Royal Charles*. In February 1679, through Legge's good offices, he was returned as one of the MPs for Portsmouth in the elections for a new parliament, despite the government's attempts to secure the seat for the chancellor of the exchequer. Kempthorne's parliamentary career was short-lived as he died at Portsmouth on 19 October 1679. He was buried in St Thomas's Church there, where a memorial was erected to him.

All three of Kempthorne's sons had naval careers. His eldest surviving son, John, was born in 1651, followed by Morgan, born at Leghorn in 1655, and Rupert. An unnamed daughter married a protégé of Prince Rupert, Sir William Reeves, who died of wounds received at the battle of the Texel on 11 August 1673 when in command of the *Sovereign*. Kempthorne's son John joined the East India Company's service in 1682 and died in 1692. Morgan was killed in command of the *Kingfisher* in 1681 in an engagement with seven Algerine pirates, an action reminiscent of his father's fight in the *Mary Rose*. Rupert commanded a fireship in 1690 but was killed in a tavern brawl in 1691, a fate which took an evidently unruly son from his 'tender but grossly abused mother' (BL, Egerton MS 928, fol. 268). In his will Kempthorne left land in Bigbury, Devon, and shares in five merchantmen: he had remained a prominent owner of merchant ships throughout his naval career, hiring the *Turkey Merchant* to the navy in 1666, in the Third Anglo-Dutch War, and in 1678, as well as being a part owner of the privateer *Jamaica Merchant* in the third war. Throughout his naval career he had remained popular with the mariners of his native Devon, who often flocked to serve with him.   J. D. DAVIES

Sources BL, Egerton MS 928 · G. A. Kempthorne, 'Sir John Kempthorne and his sons', *Mariner's Mirror*, 12 (1926), 289-317 · will, 1 June 1679, PRO, PROB 11/361, fol. 152 · PRO, ADM 10/15, 75-6 · *Report on the manuscripts of Allan George Finch*, 5 vols., HMC, 71 (1913-2003), vol. 1 · PRO, ADM 7/630, fol. 13 · GL, Trinity House MSS · P. Watson, 'Kempthorne, Sir John', HoP, *Commons, 1660-90* · *CSP dom., 1658-79* · R. C. Anderson, ed., *Journals and narratives of the Third Dutch War*, Navy RS, 86 (1946) · J. D. Davies, *Gentlemen and tarpaulins: the officers and men of the Restoration navy* (1991) · J. D. Davies, 'Devon and the navy in the civil war and the Dutch wars', *The new maritime history of Devon*, ed. M. Duffy and others, 1 (1992)

Archives BL, corresp. and papers, Egerton MS 928 · PRO, Admiralty MSS, ADM 106

Wealth at death lands in Bigbury, Devon; fee farm rent at Long Bennington, Lincolnshire; shares in five merchant ships: will, 1 June 1679, PRO, PROB 11/361, fol. 152

Kemsley. For this title name *see* Berry, (James) Gomer, first Viscount Kemsley (1883-1968).

Kemys, Lawrence. *See* Keymis, Lawrence (1564/5-1618).

Ken, Thomas (1637-1711), bishop of Bath and Wells and nonjuror, was born at Little Berkhamsted in July 1637, the son of Thomas Ken (d. 1651), attorney of Furnival's Inn and clerk of assize in Glamorgan, Radnorshire, and Brecon, and his second wife, Martha (d. 1641), daughter of the poet John Chalkhill (fl. 1600). After his father's death in 1651 he lived with his half-sister, Ann (b. 1610), whose husband,

Thomas Ken (1637–1711), by F. Scheffer, c.1700

Isaak *Walton (1593–1683), a literary figure of pronounced Laudian views, doubtless had great influence on the young Ken's spiritual and literary development.

Education and early career Ken was educated at Winchester College, where he was elected scholar on 26 September 1651 and admitted the following January. In autumn 1656 he was elected to New College, Oxford, and he entered there in 1657 after a brief spell at Hart Hall. At Winchester and New College he developed a lifelong friendship with Francis Turner, another future nonjuror. At Oxford he also probably began his association with George Hooper, whose life was to interweave with his and to whom in 1704 he gladly ceded his bishopric of Bath and Wells. New College was deeply permeated with puritanism during the interregnum. It is for this reason that Ken may have joined a group which, led by John Fell, met for Anglican worship at the house of Thomas Willis. Music was a favourite recreation all Ken's life and at Oxford, as a skilful lutenist, he took part in a musical society. He also reportedly gave alms to the poor. He graduated BA on 3 May 1661 and proceeded MA in January 1664. In 1661 and 1662 he was lector in logic, and possibly mathematics, at New College.

After ordination in 1661 or 1662 Ken was instituted on 17 August 1663 into the rectory of Little Easton, Essex, where he was spiritual counsellor to the devout Margaret, Lady Maynard (d. 1682); she seems to have had a lasting spiritual influence on him. Her husband had attended Charles II on his entry into London and served at the coronation, and was to become comptroller of the royal household and a privy councillor in 1672. It was perhaps Ken's intimacy with the Maynards, coupled with Isaak Walton's friendship with Bishop George Morley of Winchester, that

brought Ken early promotion. Early in 1665 he resigned his living and moved to Winchester as Morley's chaplain. Living in the close he took unpaid charge of the parish of St John in the Soke, where he frequently preached, and reportedly converted many Anabaptists. In December 1666 he was elected fellow of Winchester, resigning his fellowship at New College, where he gave £103 10s. towards new buildings. On 6 July 1667 Morley instituted him to the rectory of Brighstone, on the Isle of Wight. Here he remained until spring 1669, when he was clearly intended for the rectory of Bishop's Waltham—on 11 April that year Ken subscribed for that living, but was never instituted. Instead, on 28 May he became rector of East Woodhay. In parallel, on 12 April 1669 he became prebendary of Winchester, moving from one prebend to another in May. In autumn 1672 he resigned his living to make way for George Hooper, his fellow chaplain, who moved from Havant, where the damp was affecting his health. Ken now lived in Winchester, fulfilling his duties as cathedral prebendary, college fellow, and bishop's chaplain, and in St John's parish. Music was still an important part of his life; he had an organ of his own, and frequently accompanied himself for morning and evening prayers on the lute. In 1674 he published his *Manual for Winchester Scholars*, but without his three hymns added later. In 1675 he went on a tour of Europe with his nephew, Isaac Walton the younger. In Rome, where it was jubilee year, papal grandeur was at its zenith. This was enough to alert him to the imperfections of Rome and to confirm him in his adherence to Anglicanism as the purest form of the church catholic, albeit that on his return some said he was 'tinged with popery' (Wood, *Ath. Oxon.*, 4.546). On 6 July 1678 Ken was created BD and on 30 June 1679 DD.

The Hague and Tangier Late in 1679 Henry Compton, bishop of London, appointed Ken to succeed George Hooper as chaplain to Mary, wife of the future William III. From now onwards Ken was increasingly involved in the turbulent events of the 1680s that engulfed the royal family and the realm. The task at The Hague was not easy, as Hooper had unpleasantly discovered; the chaplain's role was to protect Mary's Anglicanism from William's dour and boorishly combative Calvinism. Ken himself was 'horribly unsatisfied with the Prince', thought he was 'not kind to his wife', and decided to speak to him 'though he kicks him out of doors' (*Diary of … Sidney*, 2.19–20). William's threats prompted Ken to offer his resignation, but Ken's firmness impressed William enough to persuade him to stay. When Compton asked Ken to enquire into the possibility of Anglican union with Dutch protestants, Ken advised against proceeding further, because of the questionable validity of Dutch ordination. Nevertheless, he scored a notable coup in securing the conversion from Catholicism of Colonel Edward Fitzpatrick, a scion of a noble Irish family and nephew of the duke of Ormond. In September 1680 Ken was able to report that Fitzpatrick had received 'the Holy Eucharist in our chapel' (Plumptre, 1.152–3). This conversion at the time of the Popish Plot was doubly significant, for some had suspected Ken himself of harbouring popish sympathies.

On his return to England in 1680 Ken was appointed one of the king's chaplains, but continued to live in Winchester. Three years later, in summer 1683, Charles made one of his frequent visits with the royal court to Winchester to oversee the construction of his magnificent new palace. Ken stubbornly refused requests to accommodate the king's mistress, Nell Gwyn, in his prebendal house. Instead she had to stay in the deanery. Charles, typically accepting this rebuff, respected Ken for his views and his boldness; later he reportedly declared 'I must go and hear little Ken tell me of my faults' (Plumptre, 1.159).

Ken's next assignment was to Tangier, granted as a Portuguese marriage dowry to Charles II in 1661. Originally attractive, its possession proved a costly burden, and the government decided to send a taskforce to withdraw the garrison and destroy the fortifications. In August 1683 at short notice Lord Dartmouth, the fleet commander, on Samuel Pepys's advice appointed Ken, a man of 'piety, authority and learning', as senior chaplain of the fleet (*Life, Journals*, 2.149–50). His task included oversight of other chaplains, who were said to be little better than the current decadent state of the navy. Rough weather made the voyage in their ship, the *Grafton*, long and arduous; it took five weeks, during which Ken was in frequent discussion with Pepys and Dartmouth. In Tangier all three were appalled by its depravity. Pepys himself noted 'nothing but vice in the whole place of all sorts, for swearing, cursing, drinking and whoring' (*Tangier Papers*, 89). Ken courageously preached in the Anglican church 'particularly in reproof of the vices of this town' (*Life, Journals*, 1.374), sometimes in the presence of officials including the governor, Colonel Percival Kirke, a capable, if brutal, soldier once described as a 'foul-mouthed, drunken, bullying sensualist' (Rice, 59). Dining quietly in Pepys's cabin Ken and Pepys one evening discussed the 'viciousness of this place and its being time for God Almighty to destroy it' (*Tangier Papers*, 49). On another occasion they had an angry confrontation with Kirke about the 'excessive liberty of swearing and blaspheming we observe here' (ibid., 50). With Kirke as an uncongenial companion they embarked, after long delays, on the return journey on 8 March. This proved extremely hazardous in one of the worst gales for decades. Arriving at Portsmouth in April, six months later than originally intended, they brought with them the Tangier church silver, later given to Portsmouth for use in the parish church, now the cathedral. This prolonged naval episode, unsought and unwelcome as it was, amply demonstrated Ken's devotion to duty and his moral and physical courage in confronting both Tangier's depravity and the terrors of the sea.

Bishop of Bath and Wells, 1685–1688 Ken clearly had so impressed the king and his brother, James, by his work at The Hague and in Tangier that, when in November 1684 the see of Bath and Wells fell vacant, Charles was eager to appoint him. Allegedly Charles declared 'Odd's fish! Who shall have Bath and Wells but the little fellow who would not give poor Nelly a lodging' (Bowles, 2.66). The king pressed to have the processes completed rapidly. Elected

by the Wells chapter on 16 December, Ken was consecrated by Sancroft, with Turner as a co-consecrator, at Lambeth on 25 January 1685. When the king fell ill only a few days later, significantly Ken was one of four bishops summoned to his deathbed. Ken was present for three days and nights. Though the junior bishop there, he 'was the most in favour with (the king) of all the bishops' (*Burnet's History*, 392), and took the lead. Speaking with 'an elevation of thought and expression like a man who was inspired' (ibid., 218), he tried to awaken the king's conscience. Although he had received communion from Ken himself as recently as Christmas, the king now stubbornly refused the sacrament. Despite receiving a mere nod regarding penitence, Ken absolved the clearly adamant king. Courageous as ever, he demanded the removal of the king's mistress, the duchess of Portsmouth, from the bedchamber and the admission of the queen. Eventually it was Father John Huddleston who, with the king's active consent, administered the last rites. Charles died on 6 February, a Catholic, despite all Ken's efforts. Apparently none of the bishops attended the royal funeral in Henry VII's chapel on 14 February.

Enthroned by proxy on 6 February 1685, Ken instituted his first incumbent to a benefice six days later, but it was the national scene that soon came to dominate his brief tenure of the see. On 23 April he fulfilled the historic role of the bishop of Bath and Wells at the coronation as one of the king's supporters, while Turner, now bishop of Ely, preached. A mere six weeks later Monmouth landed at Lyme Regis to set his rebellion in motion. On 13 June local Monmouth sympathizers rioted near Wells Cathedral; by 30 June horses were stabled there and on 1 July the mob broke in and ransacked the building. In almost daily attendance at the Lords, and loyal to the king, Ken was in London during these tumultuous events and was still away when Monmouth was defeated at Sedgemoor (6 July) and subsequently captured. On 13 and 14 July Ken and Turner, chosen specifically by James, were in the Tower of London with Monmouth. They told him of his impending execution, obtained from him a declaration of his illegitimacy, and prepared him for death. On 15 July, after passing the night with the duke, they, with Hooper and Tenison, accompanied him to the scaffold.

Ken then journeyed to Somerset and, appealing to James, tried to halt the appalling carnage being perpetrated under the military commanders Feversham and Kirke. Accordingly several hundred prisoners were saved from death. After unsuccessfully interceding with Judge Jeffreys, Ken spent his time day and night visiting prisoners at Wells, Taunton, and Bridgwater, supplying their wants where possible. At the Bloody Assize that followed at Wells, 97 of 500 prisoners were condemned to death and 385 to transportation.

The king and Ken held each other in considerable esteem. James seemed to respect the bishop's boldness, his deep faith, his ascetic way of life, his preaching skills as 'the best preacher among the Protestants' (Wood, *Ath. Oxon.*, 4.548), and the work he had done in The Hague and in Tangier, while Ken also admired James. This went beyond his natural respect for an anointed monarch. He was also a friend who not only appreciated James's genuine affection for his children, but had pastoral concern for his soul. Nevertheless James's maladroit and politically insensitive Romanist policies thrust Ken into opposition.

The tide of Romanism was now gathering pace. In November 1685 the papal nuncio arrived. In March 1686 James issued a declaration of indulgence for Scotland, and in July set up the commission for ecclesiastical causes. Though by nature no controversialist, as part of the growing campaign of anti-Catholic preaching Ken felt increasingly fired to protest with a series of sermons, and he had the temerity to do so. In March 1687, for instance, at Whitehall in Princess Anne's presence he preached on 'the blasphemies, perfidy, wresting of scriptures, preference of traditions before it, spirit of persecution, legends and fables of the scribes and pharisees' (Evelyn, *Diary*, 4.541) as an obvious allusion to the current situation with the Romanists. He followed this with another on the following Sunday at St Martin-in-the-Fields. There was sensation in London. Anne was even keen enough to request a special invitation to listen to Ken in Turner's London chapel. Soon afterwards James issued his first declaration of indulgence in England. In May Ken again preached fervently before the queen at Bath, where she was taking the waters. An Irish Jesuit's pamphleteering reply met with no response from Ken. Later the same month the king, discourteously without Ken's knowledge, touched for the king's evil in Bath Abbey, using a specially revived Romish rite. It was not a good year; by December Compton had been suspended and Sancroft was banned from court.

In 1688 Ken resumed his passionate preaching. On 1 April in Anne's presence he preached 'with his accustomed action, zeal and energy' (Evelyn, *Diary*, 4.578) and again people flocked to hear him. This sermon in the royal court was audacious, drawing a parallel between the English church and ancient Judah and Israel in captivity, as they patiently awaited the arrival of a saviour. In the face of Romish dangers Ken called for collaboration with dissenters, though not for comprehension. James, not present at the time, was nettled enough to request a discussion afterwards. In April the king issued his second declaration of indulgence in England. Whereas this in itself posed no real problem for the bishops, the subsequent order in council, enforcing it to be read publicly in late May or early June, certainly did, for this active element implied approval of the king's dispensing power.

On 18 May under Sancroft's leadership Ken and other bishops drew up and signed a moderate, but firm, petition opposing the dispensing power. This they delivered personally by barge to Whitehall that evening, but almost immediately, to the bishops' shocked surprise, it was leaked to the popular coffee houses. When the king consequently demanded the bishops' appearance at the privy council on 8 June they, as peers, refused to enter into recognizances and were committed to the Tower. After a trial in the king's bench they were acquitted on 30 June amid great rejoicing.

Ken stayed on in London briefly as adviser to the ailing Sancroft. When news of William's preparations for invasion reached England, Ken and other prelates met James several times at his request. On 3 October Ken and Sancroft again visited the king with further suggestions to alleviate political tension, but it was fruitless. This was Ken's final meeting with James, and he left for Wells soon afterwards. Little is known of Ken's part in the discussions which soon led to James's abject capitulations to the Anglican episcopate in what has been dubbed 'the Anglican revolution' (Goldie, 108). On 23 September Ken had declared his constant readiness to serve the king 'as far as can be consistent with my superior duty to God' (Plumptre, 2.11–12). William landed at Brixham on 5 November. By 24 November the Dutch were seizing houses in the Wells neighbourhood. Because Ken knew William and Mary personally, he decided to retire to the countryside, probably to Poulshot. On 18 December James left the kingdom.

Ministry under William III and deprivation After Christmas in Wells, which included his Advent ordination two days beforehand, Ken reached London on 10 January 1689 and had discussions with other bishops about issues arising from William's arrival. In the Convention, meeting first on 22 January, Ken consistently voted for a regency, against declaring William and Mary king and queen, and against taking new oaths to the new monarchs. On 12 February Ken left the Lords, never to return, and went back to Wells.

Ken now had to make the hard decision about personally swearing the oaths, but, unlike some, he hesitated. Despite his personal vow to James II and his denial of parliament's claim to deprive clergy of preferments, he realized that many of James's policies had been misconceived. He refused to trim to William for office like some but, shrinking from the prospect of permanent schism, he distanced himself from the bitterness and scurrilous libels that future nonjurors indulged in. To hard-liners he was a waverer. To Henry Dodwell he was 'fluctuating' (Plumptre, 2.41); to Francis Turner, his friend, he was 'warping from us … towards a compliance with the new government' (ibid., 40). Indeed, George Hooper at Lambeth, with whom he stayed before Ascensiontide 1689, 'so superfined' upon him that he all but persuaded him to take the oaths (Marshall, 52). In July Ken announced his decision to refuse them, and was officially suspended on 1 August. He was not finally deprived, however, until mid-April 1691. Before leaving he protested formally from his throne in the cathedral, asserting his canonical rights and his continuing readiness to perform his pastoral duty. He then left the cathedral for the last time.

Though his tenure had been so short and his attention inevitably so distracted by the national scene, Ken was much loved in his diocese. Records show that, except during his almost daily parliamentary attendance up to July 1685, he personally instituted to benefices until February 1690 and confirmed regularly until his final deprivation over a year later. He carried out visitations in 1686 and

1689 and starting in May 1686 he ordained regularly, usually at Trinity and Michaelmas, though his last was in Advent, on 23 December 1688. All ordinations took place in Wells, in the palace chapel or the cathedral.

In his diocese, calling himself 'Thomas, unworthy bishop of Bath and Wells', Ken was essentially a pastor and teacher (Ken, *Prose Works*, ed. Round, 445). Simple in his own lifestyle, his holiness and asceticism impressed all and won the love of the people. At Wells he frequently had twelve poor people to dine with him, and tried unsuccessfully to establish a workhouse for the poor. After his consecration he typically refused to hold an extravagant banquet, but instead gave £100 to the building of St Paul's. Appealing to his clergy in 1686 to support the Huguenots recently expelled from France, he himself contributed substantially from episcopal funds.

Ministering in his first year to prisoners after Monmouth's rebellion, Ken was appalled by 'a lamentable ignorance and forgetfulness of God' which he found among them (Plumptre, 1.237), and accelerated publication of his *Practice of Divine Love*. This was soon followed by the simpler *Directions for Prayer for the Diocese*, and plans to found schools in several Somerset towns. He also wrote a manual for those rich and poor taking the waters at Bath. In February 1688 he published instructions on how to keep Lent.

But Ken's deprivation caused a sea change in his life. When Richard Kidder was consecrated as his successor in August 1691, Ken could only refer to him, with unusual bitterness, as 'my successor, or rather supplanter ... He is a person of whom I have no knowledge' (Plumptre, 2.52). Ken himself had lost his role, not only his beloved diocese with its pastoral care and its income, but also his place in national affairs. While James and his ministers had often called upon him for advice, Ken, with the familiar cry of the role-loser, now found he was 'wholly in the dark', knowing nothing (ibid., 2.39).

Ken the nonjuror Though Lord Weymouth was himself no nonjuror, he had been a friend of Ken's since their Oxford days, and was sympathetic to the group. He now offered Ken a home at Longleat. Ken left Wells with a mere £700 from the sale of his possessions, in exchange for which Lord Weymouth granted him a life annuity of £80. From now onwards he lived mainly at Longleat, also spending time in other places—Poulshot, where his nephew, Isaac Walton, was rector, Leweston, the Thynne family home, and Naish Court, near Portishead, with the Kemeys sisters. His relationship with his nonjuring colleagues, apart from two moderates, Robert Frampton and John Fitzwilliam, was never happy. Nevertheless, when abusive pamphleteering hounded the nonjurors in 1690 soon after the English fleet's defeat off Beachy Head, Ken closed ranks with them in denying any part in conspiracies. Later, however, he characteristically distanced himself from the other more belligerent nonjurors, including Turner, as they developed closer contacts with James II in France. Still tortured in conscience, Ken above all abhorred anything that seemed to perpetuate the schism

between the nonjurors and the church, and thus vigorously opposed the clandestine consecration of two nonjurors as bishops in February 1694.

Ken was still prepared to come out of obscurity when necessary. In December 1694 Queen Mary died, but nonjurors had never been happy with her part in superseding her father. Consequently in March 1695 Ken wrote to Archbishop Tenison, condemning his naïve attendance at the queen's deathbed and his subsequent adulatory sermon. In April, fully robed, Ken—on the only occasion he did so after his deprivation—officiated at All Hallows Barking at the funeral of the nonjuring devotional writer John Kettlewell, a moderate like himself. Soon afterwards, with others, he supported Kettlewell's plan to establish a charity for deprived nonjuring clergy. Kettlewell's death affected Ken profoundly, and from then onwards he sought to minimize and, if possible, end the division they both hated so much. In the confused aftermath of the 1696 plot to assassinate William, Ken was arrested with others, but after being summoned before the council and interrogated he was released.

Meanwhile the breach with other nonjurors widened. In 1701, after several nonjuring prelates had died, Ken, still in search of an end to the schism, proposed to Lloyd that they, as the two surviving prelates, should renounce the canonical claims to their bishoprics. This created further offence.

In 1702 the new queen, Anne, offered to restore Ken to Bath and Wells by translating Kidder to Carlisle, but he refused; he felt unable to take the new oath of abjuration, and was also in poor health. Kidder died in the great storm of October 1703. Nonjuring extremists regarded this as an act of providence, but not so Ken. Mixed though his feelings must have been it was to him a 'deplorable calamity'. He was filled with a natural awe and pity. Anne now offered Hooper the bishopric, which out of deference for Ken he initially refused. Ken, however, persuaded him to accept, and agreed to cede his rights to him, as a means of stopping 'a Latitudinarian traditour' (Plumptre, 2.133) from taking the see. Ken now significantly abandoned his episcopal signature 'Tho: Bath and Wells'. Lloyd and other nonjurors condemned Ken for treachery, while Anne granted him a pension of £200.

With Lloyd's death in January 1710 Ken, now the only surviving nonjuring prelate, told Robert Nelson, a moderate nonjuring layman, philanthropist, and writer, that he thought the schism should end. In line with Ken's wishes, from Lent 1710 onwards moderate nonjurors started attending their parish churches. Soon afterwards Ken announced his intention of receiving the sacrament from Hooper in Wells Cathedral, but it was probably his rapidly declining health that prevented this significant step from happening. After a period at Bristol Hotwells from April to November 1710, he visited Leweston, where he succumbed to paralysis and dropsy. The following March he reached Longleat, but died soon afterwards, on 19 March. Two days later he was buried modestly at sunrise, as he wished, in Frome parish churchyard beneath the east window of St John's Church, his coffin being draped in a plain black cloth instead of a funeral pall. In his will he declared:

> I die in the holy catholic and apostolic faith, professed by the whole church before the disunion of east and west; more particularly I die in the communion of the Church of England, as it stands distinguished from all papal and puritan innovations, and as it adheres to the doctrine of the cross. (will, fol. 289v)

Among Ken's legacies were a number of small bequests to family members; Viscount Weymouth was left all those books of Ken's of which Weymouth did not already have copies. He left £500 to the deprived English clergy, £40 to deprived officers of the church, and £50 to the deprived Scottish clergy. He also bequeathed a wooden cup with gold lining and Lord Clarendon's *History of the Rebellion* to his friend Mrs Margaret Mathew of Cardiff, and a chalice to the parish where he was buried, for the use of sick persons desiring the sacrament.

Ken's writings Ken's important writings were devotional, written in his earlier days. His *Manual of Prayers for the Use of Winchester Scholars* (1674), intrinsically valuable, is primarily noteworthy for the three *Hymns for Morning, Evening and Midnight*, written about 1670 but first appended to the eighth edition of 1695. They were 'Awake, my soul, and with the sun', 'Glory to thee, my God, this night', and 'Lord, now my sleep does me forsake'. These hymns, memorable to this day, were probably inspired by canticles from the Roman breviary. Ken himself sang them daily to the accompaniment of lute or organ; he hoped Winchester scholars and others would do the same.

Ken's *Practice of Divine Love* (1685), a devotional exposition of the catechism, was written for his diocese and republished in the following year with *Directions for Prayer*. In Rupp's words 'No other contemporary catechism has such a "devotion of rapture"' which, though redolent of the medieval mystics, 'is an authentically seventeenth-century devotion—Puritan as well as Caroline' (Rupp, 14). Its affective mystical character is encapsulated in these words from the catechism itself: 'Thou, Lord, art my hope, my trust, my life, my joy, my glory, my God, my all, my love' (T. Ken, *Practice of Divine Love*, 1685, 2).

Ken's only other contemporary publications were few, but included three of his sermons, *Sermon Preached at the Funeral of Lady Mainard* (1682), *Sermon Preached at Whitehall* (1685), and another at Whitehall on Passion Sunday 1688. Rupp has described his preaching style as belonging 'to an older generation, and the beautiful passages, in which he loves to repeat a key word, have a haunting and melodic quality unlike that of the new preaching age' (Rupp, 13). Other prose works include his *Pastoral Letter* in support of the French protestants (1686) and his *Letter to* (Archbishop Tenison) *on his Sermon Preached at the Funeral of her Late Majesty* (1695), but two works, *Ichabod*, otherwise known as *Expostularia*, and *The Royal Sufferer*, are no longer attributed to him.

After Ken's death William Hawkins, his nephew, found Ken to have been also a prolific, if clandestine, writer of poetry, and published his works in four volumes containing 2058 pages. Apart from the hymns, his poetry, probably written as a private therapy to alleviate the frustrations of his later life, was poor in quality and clearly not intended for publication; even Ken's greatest admirers are uncharacteristically critical. One work, 'Edmund', a long epic, probably written in his last years, was a reflection on his life's vicissitudes, while 'Hymnotheo' was a thinly veiled autobiography.

Appearance and character Though small, sparely built with dark hair and eyes, Ken had a powerful personality. Endowed with 'a very lively temper, but too hot and sudden' (*Burnet's History*, 382), he was a fiery, passionate preacher, drawing large crowds in the 1680s. He could be venomous when, for instance, attacking Dutch Calvinists or latitudinarians, but was always ready to ask for forgiveness for any hurt caused. Not a great intellectual, he was nevertheless scholarly and read French, Spanish, and Italian. Ascetic in his lifestyle and generous with his income, Ken was never wealthy, finding it necessary to borrow even for his consecration expenses. In London, while other bishops used coaches, Ken went on foot.

The holiness of Ken's life was paramount. To the twenty-first-century observer he initially may seem sanctimonious. The tone of his letters, headed constantly by 'All Glory Be To God', chimes uneasily in a materialistic age, but a study of his life reveals a man of genuine holiness rooted in the practicalities of life. A devotional writer, his spirituality is reminiscent of the French and Spanish mystics, whose books furnished his library.

With conscience as his guide Ken showed remarkable physical and moral resilience. No seaman, he endured uncomplainingly the rigours of the hazardous journeys to and from Tangier. He displayed moral audacity in speaking his mind whether to William at The Hague, to the people of Tangier, the royal court in London, or to Charles II or James II in person. He was never bitter in confronting wrong, whether political, ecclesiastical, or ethical, except perhaps when Kidder 'supplanted' him, but he could not condone Mary's apparent frivolity when taking over her father's inheritance at Whitehall. Not a typical nonjuror, he was equally firm with his nonjuring colleagues, and had no truck with the rancorous controversy they provoked. A moderate in all his dealings, his opposition to the new oaths was tempered by his paramount desire for the peace, unity, and welfare of the church. Ken suffered the full agony caused by the dichotomy of his stance. Though always ready, when necessary, to fight and preach vigorously for what he felt to be right, he found it more important to welcome Hooper as his successor and thus defend the church's truths than to encourage permanent schism by prolonging the nonjuring protest. An ascetic, courageous, saintly figure, living always true to his love for God and his fellow men, and to his principles, he justly deserves a high place in the annals of church and nation.

WILLIAM MARSHALL

Sources [J. L. Anderdon], *The life of Thomas Ken*, 2nd edn (1854) · E. H. Plumptre, *The life of Thomas Ken*, 2 vols. (1888) · G. Rupp, *Religion in England, 1688–1791* (1986) · W. Hawkins, *A short account of the life of* the Rt. Revd. father in God Thomas Ken DD, sometime bishop of Bath and Wells (1713) · H. A. L. Rice, Thomas Ken, bishop and nonjuror (1958) · The prose works of Thomas Ken, ed. J. T. Round (1838) · W. M. Marshall, George Hooper (1976) · J. H. Overton, The nonjurors: their lives, principles, and writings (1902) · The Tangier papers of Samuel Pepys, ed. E. Chappell, Navy RS, 73 (1935) · Bishop Burnet's History of his own time, new edn (1857) · The prose works of Thomas Ken, ed. W. Benham (1889) · M. Goldie, 'The political thought of the Anglican revolution', The revolutions of 1688, ed. R. Beddard (1991), 102–36 · episcopal register, Morley, Hants. RO, 21M65/A1/33 · subscription books, Hants. RO, Winchester diocesan records, 21M65/F1/2 · Kenn episcopal register, Som. ARS, D/D/B Register 23 (Kenn 1684–1691) · Sheldon to Henchman, episcopal register, 1660–75, GL, MS 9531/16 · Sancroft archiepiscopal register, LPL, Sancroft 1 · S. H. Cassan, The lives of the bishops of Bath and Wells, 2 vols. (1829–30) · Diary of the times of Charles the Second by the Honourable Henry Sidney (afterwards earl of Romney), ed. R. W. Blencowe, 2 vols. (1843) · The life, journals and correspondence of Samuel Pepys, ed. J. Smith, 2 (1841) · T. F. Kirby, Winchester scholars: a list of the wardens, fellows, and scholars of … Winchester College (1888) · Evelyn, Diary, vol. 4 · W. L. Bowles, The life of Thomas Ken (1830) · JHL, 14 (1685–91) · Wood, Ath. Oxon., new edn, 4.547 · will, PRO, PROB 11/520, fols. 289v–290r

Archives BL, letters, MSS Index VI 1985 · Longleat House, Wiltshire, Thynne MSS, corresp. · LPL, MS 2872, MS 3171 | Yale U., Beinecke L., letters to William Lloyd, FB 78

Likenesses G. Bower, silver medal, 1688, NPG · J. Drapentier, line engraving, c.1688 (The seven bishops), BM · F. Scheffer, oils, c.1700, NPG [see illus.] · circle of G. Kneller, portrait, c.1700–1710, Longleat House, Wiltshire · F. Scheffer, oils, version, c.1700–1710, New College, Oxford · F. Scheffer, oils, version, 1707, Bishop's Palace, Wells · F. Scheffer, portrait, c.1710, Winchester College, Hampshire · G. Vertue, line engraving (after F. Scheffer), BM, NPG; repro. in Hawkins, Short account · engraving (after portrait at CCC Oxf.) · group portrait, oils (The seven bishops committed to the Tower in 1688), NPG · oils, NPG · portrait, CCC Oxf. · portrait, Oriel College, Oxford

Wealth at death over £440: will, PRO, PROB 11/520, fols. 289v–290r

Kendal. For this title name see Schulenburg, (Ehrengard) Melusine von der, suo jure duchess of Kendal and suo jure duchess of Munster (1667–1743).

Kendal, Dame Madge [real name Margaret Shafto Robertson; married name Margaret Shafto Grimston] (**1848–1935**), actress, was born on 15 March 1848 at Grimsby, Lincolnshire, the youngest of (allegedly) twenty-two children of William Robertson (d. 1872) and his wife, the actress Margharetta Elisabetta Robertson (d. 1876), née Marinus, whose parents had moved to England from their native Netherlands. Well educated and literary in his tastes, William Robertson gave up his apprenticeship with a Derby solicitor to join the family's Lincolnshire theatrical circuit, of which he became manager in the early 1830s. By then he had met and—in 1828—married Miss Marinus, who on 9 January 1829 gave birth to their first child, Thomas William *Robertson, who became the founder of the naturalistic school of drama in the 1860s. In his apocryphal phrase, T. W. Robertson was 'nursed on rose-pink and cradled in properties', as evidently were his siblings, certainly Madge, who appeared on the stage as a babe in arms.

Early days on the stage Madge Robertson's first known speaking part was as Marie in Edward Stirling's nautical drama The Struggle for Gold, on 20 February 1854 at the Marylebone Theatre, of which her father was then

Dame Madge Kendal (1848–1935), by Sir William Orpen, c.1927–8

co-lessee with J. W. Wallack. Five days later she appeared as the blind Jeannie in an adaptation of Dickens's The Seven Poor Travellers, in a cast consisting largely of members of her family.

In 1855 the Robertsons repaired to Bristol, where they were engaged by J. H. Chute. As Eva in an adaptation of Uncle Tom's Cabin, Madge revealed an exceptional singing ability in her rendition of 'I see a land of spirits bright' and other songs, though sadly diphtheria and the removal of her tonsils prevented her voice from reaching its potential. Nevertheless, when Chute opened the new Bath Theatre in March 1863 with a production of A Midsummer Night's Dream, Madge was cast as Second Singing Fairy— 'Over hill, over dale', 'I know a bank' in Mendelssohn's settings—alongside Ellen Terry as Titania and Kate Terry as Oberon. Throughout her apprenticeship in Bristol and Bath, Madge, already tall for her age, was rigorously coached by her father, who taught her the value of contrast by the repetition of Viola's tender and pathetic 'She never told her love' from Twelfth Night and Queen Constance's vehement 'Gone to be married, gone to swear a peace' from King John.

A developing reputation Technically skilled beyond her years, Madge Robertson made her London adult début with Walter Montgomery at the Haymarket Theatre and created a favourable impression as Ophelia (29 July 1865), Blanche in King John (10 August), and Desdemona (21 August). She returned to the provinces initially with Montgomery and in 1866 for William Brough at the Theatre Royal, Hull, where Samuel Phelps had been engaged for three nights during fair week. The stock company's Lady Macbeth being unwell, Madge was thrust into the role, and met her Thane for the first time after her delivery of the letter scene, not having had the benefit of rehearsing with him. The young actress's technique stood her in good stead and Phelps subsequently invited her to appear as Lady Teazle to his Sir Peter in Sheridan's *The School for Scandal* at the Standard Theatre, Shoreditch. In old age Madge Kendal drew upon her youthful experience to give an imitation of Phelps as Macbeth.

After provincial and metropolitan engagements (for F. B. Chatterton at Drury Lane, E. A. Sothern at the Haymarket, and John Hollingshead at the new Gaiety Theatre) Madge Robertson joined J. B. Buckstone's company, initially on tour and thereafter at the Haymarket, where she remained until 1874. On 7 August 1869, at St Saviour's Church, Manchester, she married an actor from Buckstone's company, William Hunter Grimston, whose stage name of Kendal she adopted professionally. The couple had wrung from William Robertson his reluctant consent to their marriage on the condition, which they consistently observed, that they would always act together—in Shaw's words, 'a Perpetual Joint' (*Dame Madge Kendal*, 70).

William Hunter Kendal (1843–1917), actor and theatre manager, was born in London on 16 December 1843, the eldest son of Edward Hunter Grimston and his wife, Louisa Rider. Grimston, whose maternal grandfather was a painter, showed early talent in that art, but was intended for medicine until his regular visits to the Soho Theatre to sketch the performers led to his appearance on stage in *A Life's Revenge* (6 April 1861), using the stage name Kendall (he subsequently dropped the second l). Kendal remained at the Soho Theatre for two years before seeking experience in the provinces, notably Glasgow, where he remained for four years. In 1866 he joined J. B. Buckstone's company.

At the Haymarket, Madge Kendal enjoyed a string of successes, notably as Lilian Vavasour in Tom Taylor's *New Men and Old Acres* (25 October 1869), Lydia Languish in *The Rivals* (24 October 1870), Rosalind in *As You Like It* (9 October 1871), and Mrs Van Brugh in W. S. Gilbert's *Charity* (3 January 1874). Following engagements at the Opéra Comique and the Court Theatre she joined the Bancrofts at the Prince of Wales's Theatre, where her roles included Dora in *Diplomacy* (12 January 1878), adapted from Sardou's *Dora* by B. C. Stephenson and Clement Scott. Her husband having refused to play Bassanio in *The Merchant of Venice*, Madge Kendal—true to her father's injunction and in keeping with the spirit of the caskets—declined the Bancrofts' invitation to play Portia, thereby leaving the way clear for Ellen Terry to play the role.

A tall, very good-looking man, W. H. Kendal had a gift for light comedy but was stilted and unnatural in more serious roles. His repertory, which was almost invariably determined by the opportunities offered to his wife, included Colonel Blake, resplendent in a full-length bearskin coat, in J. Palgrave Simpson's *A Scrap of Paper*, Orlando, Captain Beauclerc in *Diplomacy*, William in *William and Susan*, W. G. Wills's customized rewriting of Douglas Jerrold's *Black-Eyed Susan*, and Aubrey Tanqueray to his wife's Paula in Pinero's *The Second Mrs Tanqueray*. Kendal's real skills were managerial and financial. His wife recalled that, at the end of each season during their partnership with Hare at the Court in the 1870s, Kendal invested his share of the profits, always leaving enough over for some jewellery for her and a painting for himself. With his flair for art Kendal assembled a fine collection of contemporary paintings, which was housed in their increasingly grand dwellings—Taviton Street, Harley Street, and Portland Place, plus The Lodge, Filey, Yorkshire. Madge Kendal gave Hugh Walpole's portrait of her husband to the Garrick Club, of which he had been a member (he was also a member of the Junior Carlton, Beefsteak, Arts, Cosmopolitan, and AA clubs).

From 1879 to 1888 the Kendals shared the management of the St James's Theatre with John Hare, with whom Kendal had previously entered into a 'silent' partnership at the Court Theatre. At the St James's, Madge Kendal's successes included Lady Giovanna in Tennyson's *The Falcon* (18 December 1879), Susan in *William and Susan*, Kate Verity in Pinero's *The Squire* (29 December 1881), and a reprise as Rosalind (24 January 1885). Her Rosalind had always been noted for her vivacity, irony, and pathos rather than her tenderness and lyricism, but with advancing years impulse, spirit, and spontaneity had fallen victims to calculated points of business and over-deliberate delivery of speeches. Of Madge Kendal's acting at this time, W. E. Henley wrote: 'How carefully she constructs a part, and how consummately she executes! Voice, face, presence, habit, disposition—everything is turned to account' (*The Stage*, 17 April 1886).

A national figure By the mid-1880s the Kendals were benefiting from the improvements in the status of the theatre to which they had significantly contributed. In *Society in London* (1885, 295), T. H. S. Escott wrote: 'Mrs Kendal, one of the best artists of her sex on the London stage, is in private life the epitome of all domestic virtues and graces.' W. H. Kendal epitomized the gentrified theatre of the late nineteenth and early twentieth century; of him Herbert Beerbohm Tree said, 'when I look at Kendal I know acting is the profession of a gentleman' (*Dame Madge Kendal*, 30). On 23 September 1884 Madge Kendal addressed the Congress of the National Association for the Promotion of Social Science in Birmingham with a paper entitled 'The drama', in which she robustly proclaimed the advances in her profession, though she made some barbed allusions to certain fairly easily identifiable members of it of whom she disapproved. In 1886, like much of fashionable London, the Bancrofts interested themselves in the case of John Merrick, the Elephant Man, as a consequence of which Madge Kendal herself eventually achieved the status of a dramatic character, in Bernard Pomerance's 1979 play and the subsequent film. In February 1887 the Kendals were commanded to perform before the queen and court at Osborne, the first such entertainment since the prince consort's death. The queen sent Mrs Kendal a diamond brooch as an expression of her appreciation, and the actress received a similar token of esteem from Joseph Chamberlain at a farewell banquet on 16 July 1889, before an American tour. The Kendals spent most of the next five years in the United States, very much to their financial advantage.

When Madge Kendal returned to the London stage in the 1890s her accomplishments were relished by Shaw, who wrote in the *Saturday Review* of her performance in Sydney Grundy's *The Greatest of These* at the Garrick Theatre (10 June 1986): 'her finish of execution, her individuality and charm of style, her appetisingly witty conception of her effects, her mastery of her art and of herself … are all there, making her still supreme among English actresses in high comedy' (Shaw, 2.157). This supremacy was put to the test when Herbert Beerbohm Tree invited Madge Kendal and Ellen Terry to appear together in *The Merry Wives of Windsor*, as Mistress Ford and Mistress Page respectively, at His Majesty's Theatre in 1902. Tree allegedly observed the on-stage reunion of the two actresses, hidden in a box. Madge Kendal always proclaimed the mutual affection between the two women from their teenage years in Bath, but her saccharine recollection of 'Nellie' buying apples and generously sharing them with 'Madge' turns sour when she describes Ellen Terry as 'a real daughter of Eve' (*Dame Madge Kendal*, 26). In the event, as Mistress Ford Madge Kendal shed some of her customary artifice and displayed an unwonted exuberance and apparent spontaneity, though whether this was in any way connected with the fact that for the only time since her marriage she was performing without her husband can only be a matter of speculation. The Kendals renewed their professional partnership for the remaining years of their careers until they retired from the stage in 1908, though Madge did return—as Mistress Ford—for the coronation gala of 1911.

Family life, retirement, and death Though they were such a devoted couple, the Kendals' family life was deeply troubled, and in her memoirs Madge recurrently refers to herself as 'Mater Afflicta'. The Kendals—or the Grimstons as they were always known in family and social life— became estranged from their four surviving children; William observed at the grave of their first-born, Margaret: 'All the children that loved us, Madge, lie under this stone' (*Dame Madge Kendal*, 85). Madge Kendal attributed her husband's death on 6 November 1917 to a broken heart and wounded pride caused by their children's behaviour, in particular the divorce of their youngest daughter, Dorothy, in 1913 from the manager Bertie A. Meyer. During her lengthy retirement and widowhood Madge Kendal, always resolutely Victorian in her appearance and opinions, maintained a public presence. She supported the Actors' Association, the Royal General Theatrical Fund, the Royal Academy of Dramatic Art, and Denville Hall, the actors' retirement home, of which she became president. In 1926 she was appointed DBE and in 1927 GBE; for her eightieth birthday she sat for a portrait by Sir William Orpen and recorded a speech from *As You Like It* for the BBC; in 1932 she became the first woman to receive the freedom of Grimsby, which, after a lifetime's uncertainty, had been established as her birthplace; and in 1933 she published her memoirs, *Dame Madge Kendal by Herself*, written with the assistance of Rudolf de Cordova.

Dame Madge Kendal died at her home, Dell Cottage, Chorleywood, Hertfordshire, on 14 September 1935. By her own wish only her doctor and a nurse were present at her bedside, and her funeral—at St Marylebone cemetery, East Finchley—was private. The obituary in *The Times* (16 September 1935) spoke of Dame Madge's 'very unhistrionic coldness of temperament and … superficiality of thought' as 'the barriers between her acting and any form of greatness'. The actress and the woman are inseparable, and these characteristics also formed a barrier between Madge Kendal and her children, as a consequence of which, her closing years, her death, and her funeral were acted out in isolation from her family. Intentional or not, the ambiguity in the title of Madge Kendal's memoirs was sadly apt.   RICHARD FOULKES

Sources *Dame Madge Kendal by herself*, ed. R. de Cordova (1933) · T. E. Pemberton, *The Kendals: a biography* (1900) · C. E. Pascoe, ed., *The dramatic list*, 2nd edn (1880) · J. Parker, ed., *Who's who in the theatre*, 5th edn (1925) · B. Hunt, ed., *The green room book, or, Who's who on the stage* (1906) · *The Era* (1865–1935) · *The Stage* (1880–1935) · *The Times* (16 Sept 1935) · B. Duncan, *The St James's Theatre: its strange and complete history, 1835–1957* (1964) · J. Gielgud, J. Miller, and J. Powell, *An actor and his time*, rev. edn (1981) · S. Hicks, *Me and my missus* (1939) · J. Gielgud, *The Times* (28 Jan 1978) · G. B. Shaw, *Our theatres in the nineties*, rev. edn, 3 vols. (1932) · M. Kendal, *Dramatic opinions* (1890) · B. Pomerance, *The elephant man* (1979)
Archives Theatre Museum, London
Likenesses V. Prinser, oils, exh. RA 1883, Garr. Club · lithograph, pubd 1883 (after W. & D. Downey), NPG · J. Collier, group portrait, oils, 1904, repro. in G. Ashton, *Shakespeare* (1990) · W. Orpen, oils, *c*.1927–1928, Tate collection [*see illus.*] · Barraud, photograph, NPG; repro. in *Men and women of the day* (1888) · W. & D. Downey, photograph, NPG; repro. in W. Downey and D. Downey, *The cabinet portrait gallery*, 2 (1891) · H. Walpole, portrait (William Kendal), Garr. Club · photographs, repro. in *Dame Madge Kendal* · theatrical prints, BM, Harvard TC, NPG
Wealth at death £4835 12*s*. 9*d*.: resworn probate, 30 Jan 1936, CGPLA Eng. & Wales · £66,251 17*s*. 9*d*.—William Kendal: probate, 27 Dec 1917, CGPLA Eng. & Wales

Kendal [Kendale], **Richard** (*d.* 1431?), grammarian, is recorded in the catalogue of the library of Syon Monastery, Isleworth, Middlesex (now Cambridge, Corpus Christi College, MS 141), as the author of a grammatical work which had apparently been lost from the library by 1526. In his index of British writers the sixteenth-century bibliographer John Bale gives the titles of six grammatical works by Kendal from a book that he says he saw at the Benedictine monastery of Horsham St Faith, Norfolk. Since none is now extant, Bale's attributions cannot be tested. Nor is there confirmation for the date of Kendal's death, given as 1431 by Thomas Tanner. Nothing links Richard Kendal with a certain Kendale, a monk of Sherborne, who is credited as the author of a short verse treatise on music in a collection of such treatises originally belonging to John Wylde, precentor of Waltham Abbey (*fl.* *c*.1460), and now in the British Library (Lansdowne MS 763, fols. 52–3; an eighteenth-century transcript of this manuscript is BL, Add. MS 4912, fols. 81–2).

                                    MARIOS COSTAMBEYS

Sources R. Sharpe, *A handlist of the Latin writers of Great Britain and Ireland before 1540* (1997) · M. Bateson, ed., *Catalogue of the library of Syon Monastery, Isleworth* (1898) · H. Ellis and F. Douce, eds., *A catalogue of the Lansdowne manuscripts in the British Museum*, 2 (1819) · Tanner, *Bibl. Brit.-Hib.*, 452 · Bale, *Cat.*, 1.566–7 · A. Hughes, 'Kendale, Richard', *New Grove*

Kendal, William Hunter (1843–1917). *See under* Kendal, Dame Madge (1848–1935).

Kendale, Richard. *See* Kendal, Richard (d. 1431?).

Kendall family (*per. c.*1700–1807), ironmasters, of Staffordshire, Furness, and Brecknockshire, together with the kindred families of *Cotton and *Hall, played a leading role in the development of the iron industry in Britain between the mid-seventeenth and the early nineteenth centuries. Members of the family were closely involved in the extended partnerships which dominated iron production in Staffordshire, Cheshire, and the north-west of England.

The family came to prominence with **Edward [i] Kendall** (1684–1746), the fourth son, but ultimate heir, of Jonathan Kendall (1648–1716) of Austrey, Warwickshire, and of his wife, Jane, daughter of Edward Dyson of Inkberrow, Worcestershire. By 1702 he was an agent under John Wheeler in the Foley partnership for the Stour valley and forest of Dean ironworks. In 1710 he became, with William Rea of Monmouth, joint manager of the Staffordshire ironworks, and the far-flung nature of his family's later interests was foreshadowed in 1712. In that year he married Anna Cotton (1685–1763), daughter of the former Yorkshire ironmaster William *Cotton (1648/9–1703), of Haigh Hall [*see under* Cotton family]; they had two sons and two daughters. In common with the Cotton family, Kendall was staunchly nonconformist, and he led those who petitioned quarter sessions to license a new meetinghouse in Stourbridge in 1715, after the original one was destroyed by a mob. In 1743 the congregation built a house for the new minister at Stourbridge on land conveyed to them by Kendall and his wife.

In Shropshire, together with his brother-in-law William Westby *Cotton (*bap.* 1689, *d.* 1749) [*see under* Cotton family], Kendall acquired Kemberton furnace in 1714. In 1724 he leased Cradley ironworks on the Stour and from there he supplied pig iron to the Stour valley forges, especially during the 1740s. In Staffordshire in the 1720s he was probably involved in Rushall furnace. Anna *Cotton (*d.* 1721) [*see under* Cotton family], widow of William Cotton, assigned Colnbridge forge in Yorkshire to her son William Westby Cotton in 1716, and further assignees were Kendall and another son-in-law, William Vernon, a move which probably marked Anna Cotton's retirement from active participation in management. By 1718 Kendall was involved as partner of Edward Hall and Daniel Cotton at Cunsey furnace in Furness. This had been built in 1711 so that some of the haematite ores of the area could be smelted on the spot, rather than after shipping to furnaces on the Cheshire plain. The building of a second northern furnace on the River Duddon in 1736 endorsed this move.

Kendall died in February 1746. He willed his ironworks to be continued for six years by his widow, who survived her husband until 1763, and his son **Jonathan Kendall** (1714–1791), with his servant Samuel Hopkins as manager. Meanwhile the Cheshire–Staffordshire works were deprived by death of all managing partners: Thomas *Hall of the Hermitage, son of the senior partner Edward *Hall of Cranage [*see under* Hall family], died in 1748; Thomas *Cotton of Eardley End [*see under* Cotton family] followed in 1749; and then Edward Hall himself died in 1750. Because their heirs were not interested in iron, Jonathan Kendall was left as senior partner, assisted by Samuel Hopkins, now also one of Cotton's executors. In 1741 Kendall married Elizabeth Smith of Birmingham, but the marriage did not produce any children.

Major difficulties impended. In Furness seven furnaces were now in competition, forcing up the price of the most expensive raw material, charcoal, and in the nail trade, cheap coke-smelted rod iron was soon to replace rod made from cold-short charcoal-smelted iron. It made sense to concentrate on tough pig iron, convertible into best merchant bar at the forge, and also suitable for making tin plate. The manufacture of tin plate spread rapidly about 1740, especially within south Wales; but its shipping in small quantities down the Weaver Navigation during the 1740s by Thomas Cotton suggests that the company's forge at Oakamoor was then already producing tin plate.

To escape rising charcoal prices a Welsh furnace, situated on the Conwy, ideally placed to smelt haematite ore shipped from Furness, had already been erected in 1748. It could ship its product to the company's own forges in Cheshire, to south Wales, or to the Severn valley. In 1755 another Welsh furnace was built at Dyfi, where Kendall's partner was his cousin Ralph Vernon, while at the still more remote Scottish furnace, built the same year at Goatfield on Loch Fyne, Jonathan's younger brother **Henry Kendall** (1718–1787) was involved. Henry matriculated at Glasgow University in 1740 and married Ellen Jacques; they had four sons and one daughter. He was established at Ulverston by 1750 and in the north he was partnered by the manager at Duddon, William Latham, another Austrey man. Jonathan's partner in Staffordshire was Samuel Hopkins; banking was provided by Jonathan's brother-in-law Samuel Notton, a London grocer, husband of Elizabeth Kendall.

Meanwhile, the furnaces at Cunsey, at Carr mill in south Lancashire, and at Lawton in Cheshire were closed about 1750. Mear Heath in Staffordshire closed before 1763. Cranage forge had also closed, so smelting was concentrated at Doddington and Madeley furnaces, with Cumbrian haematite ores being used at Doddington after carriage across the Cheshire plain. The two furnaces were close to the company's small forges at Lea, Norton, and Winnington, and not far from the forges at Warmingham and Consall, which with annual outputs of 300 tons of bar iron were among the largest in Britain. Tin-plating at Oakamoor was joined by an iron and tin plate works in Aston, where the Kendalls were partnered by Thomas Hopkins, lessee of Cannock forge from 1775.

William Latham's Duddon furnace account books show that, to coordinate the affairs of such widely scattered works, company meetings were held regularly in Cheshire, the places mentioned including Warrington (1775), Middlewich (1760), Hilcot (in Staffordshire, 1762), and Holmes Chapel (1763). Managing personnel were compelled to move too: Henry Kendall's son Edward replaced Ralph Vernon as manager at Warmingham forge before 1773; by 1762 Jonathan Kendall had established himself at Hilcot, but by 1779 he had moved on to Market Drayton; by 1790, when he made his will, he had moved back to Stourbridge, where he died on 7 March 1791.

In 1779, in a complete break with the past, members of the Kendall family showed their usual flexibility by building the coke-fuelled Beaufort furnace above Ebbw Vale in south Wales, on land leased from the duke of Beaufort. The Cheshire forges were not maintained beyond 1784. Conwy furnace had closed by 1774, Dyfi continued in 1794 but was abandoned during the next ten years, Goatfield was blown out in 1813, and though William Latham's sons, Joseph and Richard, continued to operate Duddon, it too was sold to Harrison, Ainslie & Co. in 1828.

Beaufort furnace produced 1500 tons of pig iron per year; the addition of a second furnace in 1798 and of steam-powered blast enabled production to soar to 7000 tons in 1825. **Edward** [ii] **Kendall** (1750–1807), who had formerly been at Warmingham, was the driving force at Beaufort. His first wife was Elizabeth, daughter of Samuel Irton, of Irton Hall, Cumberland; they had one son. His second wife, whom he married in 1801, Elizabeth Bevan of Crickhowell, was a widow who had two sons by her former marriage. Kendall was chairman of the Monmouthshire Canal, which afforded transport for his iron to Newport. He also interested himself closely in local affairs, perhaps more so than any other ironmaster of Brecknockshire, was a justice of the peace, and ultimately became high sheriff of the county. 'Nothing like iron', he thought, and he fenced the river front land of the estate which he acquired in 1804 at Dan y Parc, on the Usk near Crickhowell, with a massive iron deer fence, which still stood unimpaired in 1906.

Edward Kendall died suddenly on 7 March 1807. Since his own son, Edward [iii] Kendall (b. 1789), showed little interest in the works, he wished his stepson William Hibbs Bevan to succeed him. During Bevan's minority Joseph Latham carried on as manager until retirement in 1816, when Bevan, now Latham's son-in-law, succeeded him.

In 1833 the concern was taken over by its near neighbours, Joseph and Crawshay Bailey of Nant-y-glo ironworks, and Edward [iii] Kendall disposed of his remaining share in the works, so ending an involvement of well over a century, during which, rather unusually, his family had successfully negotiated all the technical, commercial, and logistical problems entailed in the changeover from charcoal smelting of iron to smelting with coke.

BRIAN G. AWTY

Sources J. Lloyd, *The early history of the old south Wales ironworks, 1760–1840* (1906) · A. Fell, *The early iron industry of Furness and district* (1908) · B. G. Awty, 'Charcoal ironmasters of Cheshire and Lancashire, 1600–1785', *Transactions of the Historic Society of Lancashire and Cheshire*, 109 (1957), 71–124 · H. E. Palfrey, 'Early non-conformity in Stourbridge', *Transactions of the Unitarian Historical Society*, 6 (1935–8), 293–309 · P. Riden, *A gazetteer of charcoal-fired blast furnaces in Great Britain in use since 1660* (1987) · H. J. B. Kendall, *The Kendalls of Austrey, Twycross and Smithsby* (1909) · *Northowram register* [n.d.] · will, PRO, PROB 11747/155, 1745 · parish register, Old Swinford, Worcestershire, 10 Feb 1746 [burial] · Burke, *Gen. GB* · parish register, Ulverston, Lancashire, 12 May 1787 [burial]
Archives Lancs. RO, Duddon furnace account books

Kendall, Edward (1684–1746). *See under* Kendall family (*per. c.*1700–1807).

Kendall, Edward (1750–1807). *See under* Kendall family (*per. c.*1700–1807).

Kendall, Edward Augustus (1775/6–1842), writer, of whose life very little is known, had a varied literary output, which divides into four categories: his serious ideas and proposals for political and social reforms, for example his letters on the state of Ireland; his weekly 'popular' journalism which, ambitiously, might be described as a forerunner of Harmsworth; his translations from the French; and his children's books.

In 1809 Kendall published an account of his travels in North America, having previously been 'employed in a civil capacity in Canada' (Watkins and Shoberl). In 1817 he issued proposals for the Patriotic Metropolitan Institution in London for the assistance of new settlers in the colonies and for the encouragement of new branches of colonial trade. He also proposed the establishment of new colonies for the Eurasians of India and metis of the West Indies. And he urged the benefits to be derived from establishing in England free drawing schools and schools of chemistry and mathematics.

Aiming to provide cheap and good literature for the people, Kendall started in London in 1819 the *Literary Chronicle and Weekly Review*, which lasted until 1828, when he started a new series which was shortly to be incorporated with *The Athenaeum*. There is also an edition entitled the *Country Literary Chronicle*, beginning in 1820 with a part numbered 59. The *Literary Chronicle* was succeeded by another popular miscellany projected by Kendall, called *The Olio, or, Museum of Entertainment* (11 vols., 1823–33). These efforts at periodical literature were described in Kendall's *Gentleman's Magazine* obituary as having originated 'the present deep and deservedly popular race of weekly issues from the press' (*GM*). Kendall also wrote the more weighty *Letters to a friend on the state of Ireland, the Roman Catholic question, and the merits of constitutional religious distinctions* (1826), in which he argued that Ireland enjoyed a vigorous and paternal government, whose duty it was to repress Roman Catholicism there, and in Great Britain as well.

Kendall's most attractive works, however, are his books for children, some of which were still being reprinted fifty years after his death, especially *Keeper's Travels in Search of his Master* (1799); *The Crested Wren* (1799); and *Burford Cottage and its Robin Red Breast* (1835), the last of which is a long novel narrated by a robin, who discourses on natural history and other improving topics. Kendall's educative impulses can also be seen in his earlier *Parental Education, or, Domestic Lessons: a Miscellany Intended for Youth* (1803). His children's books are generally marked, however, by a sentimental style which has now long been out of fashion, although his lengthy *The English Boy at the Cape: an Anglo-African Story* (1835) is more mature and less sentimental than his other children's books.

Kendall was also a member of the Society of Antiquaries, and his more scholarly work included translations from the French such as Saint-Pierre's *The Indian Cottage* (1791); *Beauties of Saint-Pierre, Selected from his 'Studies of Nature'* (1799); and *The Travels of Denon in Egypt* (2 vols., 1802).

Kendall died at Pimlico, London, on 14 October 1842, aged sixty-six, and was buried there.   GUY ARNOLD

Sources *GM*, 2nd ser., 18 (1842), 671 • [J. Watkins and F. Shoberl], *A biographical dictionary of the living authors of Great Britain and Ireland* (1816) • Watt, *Bibl. Brit.* • Allibone, *Dict.* • *DNB*

Kendall, George (*bap.* 1611, *d.* 1663), clergyman and religious controversialist, was the eldest son of George Kendall of Cofton, Dawlish, Devon, collector of customs for Exeter and Dartmouth, and Katharine Moor. He was baptized in Exeter Cathedral on 16 April 1611. He was educated at Exeter grammar school and Exeter College, Oxford, where he matriculated on 18 February 1627. He proceeded BA in 1630, MA in 1633, BD in 1642, and DD on 31 May 1654. He was a fellow of Exeter College from 1630 to 1647, and was ordained priest in Exeter Cathedral on 4 January 1637. It is said that Charles I wished him to succeed John Prideaux as rector of Exeter College in 1642, but he was not elected.

On 24 August 1643 Kendall was instituted as rector of St Nicholas, Abingdon, the king being the patron. He never seems to have taken up residence and in 1655 the churchwardens presented him at the Berkshire sessions: 'hath not been amongst us these 10 or 11 years'. Meanwhile two ministers had in turn been intruded into the cure (*Calamy rev.*, 304). In any case he was presented in 1643 by the crown to the rectory of Blisland, Cornwall, despite his strong presbyterian sympathies. He became a prebendary of Exeter Cathedral in February 1645, and in 1648 he was appointed to the sequestered living of Bodmin. Since Bodmin is only 5 miles from Blisland and he continued to ascribe his books from the latter, it is probable that he held the two parishes in plurality.

In 1653 Kendall moved to be rector of St Benet Gracechurch, London, seemingly to be able the more effectively to oppose the anti-Calvinist preaching and writing of John Goodwin at the neighbouring St Stephen, Coleman Street. He was admitted a member of the fourth London classis on 21 November 1653 and immediately elected a delegate to the provincial assembly; he took a leading part in the work of the classis in 1654, presiding, for instance, over nine meetings for an ordination in May. His last appearance at the classis was in 1655 and he may thereafter have returned to Devon as he was one of the moderators at the first meeting of the Devon association of ministers in

October 1655. During these years he was engaged in controversy with John Goodwin, whose *Redemption Redeemed* appeared in 1651, and to a lesser extent with Richard Baxter. Kendall's *Vindication of the Doctrines Commonly Received in the Reformed Churches* was dated from Blisland 14 September 1652. *Sancti sanciti*, which appeared in 1654, was effectively a continuation of the *Vindication*, since it, too, was a detailed reply to Goodwin's book. Goodwin was espousing the familiar 'Arminian' position that Christ died for all men 'sufficiently', but only 'efficaciously' for those who responded in faith. For Kendall, Christ died only for those who were elect from all eternity: 'we deny … that he intended to purchase eternal salvation for them all' (G. Kendall, *Vindication*, 1652, 2nd pagination, 93). To preach 'universality' is to 'befriend the devil' (ibid., 3rd pagination, 30). In defence of this position Kendall comes near to a *reductio ad absurdum*: 'To provide for the salvation of all men would have been no grace' (ibid., 3rd pagination, 73). To the question does our doctrine raise 'jealousies and, hard thoughts' about God (ibid., 3rd pagination, 52), Kendall has one invariable reply: man can neither understand nor question the dispositions of God; man is 'no competent judge of what makes for God's honour' (ibid., 2nd pagination, 25). Goodwin, in a long digression, had attacked the Calvinist doctrine of the perseverance of the saints as leading to antinomianism, charging that 'our doctrine asserts the saints are in no possibility of falling away finally or totally, continue they never so loose and exhorbitant' (G. Kendall, *Sancti sanciti*, 1654, xxiv). To Kendall 'this doctrine of perseverance lieth very near the fundamental article of the reformed religion' (ibid., 3rd pagination, 132). He believes that it was essential for the saints' assurance of salvation and, far from leading to antinomianism, inspired such love in the believer's heart that he advanced in sanctity. He allows that there are 'stumblings' and 'ebbs and floods', but asserts that the Christian learns from them. If the seeming Christian falls finally from grace this is 'apostasy', and shows he has never been a true believer. Goodwin had attacked the doctrine of personal election and claimed that the scriptural passages on perseverance and election applied to the church at large rather than to individual Christians; this arouses Kendall to especial wrath: 'I have resolved not to be angry; else I should fall foul on you for throwing this dirt so shamelessly in our faces' (ibid., 1st pagination, 60). In each of the books Kendall turns aside to tangle with a more doughty opponent, Richard Baxter, 'a man whom I very much respect … but the truth is he stands so full in my way that I cannot pass on without a friendly scuffle with him' (ibid., xxxx).

In his *Aphorismes of Justification* (1649) Baxter had sought to find a middle way between antinomianism, the result of which he had seen in the civil war, and Arminianism, a cause which he hesitated fully to embrace. For Kendall, Baxter's apostasy in the *Aphorismes* centres in his belief that new 'immanent acts of God' are possible: election is an immanent act decreed by God from eternity, and Baxter's teaching is an attack on divine providence. For Baxter this belief, found in the teaching of William Twisse, led to 'that error and pillar of antinomianism, viz. justification from Eternity' (Baxter, *Aphorismes*, 173). Kendall replies (G. Kendall, *Vindication*, 1652, 1st pagination, 133) that any new immanent act must be in God's will or understanding and in either case God would be shown to be fallible. This analysis he argues against Baxter's position that 'this (new act) doth make no change in God'. God can make 'a moral change in our relation' to himself without that being a new immanent act; 'the proper effect of the immanent act (in eternity) is to lay the foundation from which the (new) relation (of justification) can arise' (Baxter, *Aphorismes*, 175). There can in any case be a delay between an original act and its fulfilment, just as there is between the drawing up of a deed of gift and its implementation. But as to the small print Baxter says 'I dare not be too confident in so dark a point'—an admission which from his entrenched position Kendall could not make (ibid., 176). Baxter accepted the distinction between sufficient grace for all men and efficient grace for salvation and attempted to hold the two in balance. For instance he maintained that common grace enables men to live in society, but is not sufficient for salvation. To Kendall this is anathema: 'surely the schools of Pelagius owe you a doctorate the next commencement' (G. Kendall, *Sancti sanciti*, 1654, 2nd pagination, 105). Baxter replied to the *Vindication* in 1654 with *The Reduction of a Digressor*, covering much the same ground as the *Aphorismes*. The controversy between the two men features frequently in Baxter's *Correspondence*, with his friends writing to commiserate with him. The hatchet was finally buried thanks to Archbishop Ussher's intervention. Kendall was appointed to the vacant vicarage of Kenton in Devon in 1656. From there he produced in the following year his third major book. This was *Fur pro tribunali*, a collection of works, all in Latin. Most important was his defence of the doctrine of predestination, written in the form of a dialogue, against an anonymous work, *Fur praedestinatus*. There were also an exegesis of the 1595 Lambeth articles, an oration against neo-pelagianism, and finally a life of his hero and mentor, William Twisse.

In October 1662 Kendall was ejected both from his vicarage at Kenton and his prebend in Exeter Cathedral. He retired to Cofton and died there on 19 August 1663, being buried in a chapel adjoining his house. His wife, Mary (*d.* 1676), daughter of Periam Pole of Tallaton, Devon, licensed the house as a meeting-place in 1672. One of Baxter's correspondents, Henry Bartlett, advised Baxter that to answer Kendall in full would be 'too voluminous and too tedious' and recommended only a brief reply without 'particular repeating and answering' (*Correspondence of Richard Baxter* 1.141, letter 184); he had clearly recognized the obsessive streak in Kendall's character. Baxter himself, who believed that Kendall 'thought to get an advantage for his reputation by a triumph over John Goodwin and me', was somewhat more generous: 'he was a little quick-spirited man, of great ostentation and a considerable orator and scholar' (*Reliquiae Baxterianae*, 1.110).

BARRY TILL

Sources DNB · *Calamy rev.* · *Walker rev.* · W. M. Lamont, *Puritanism and the English revolution*, 3: *Richard Baxter and the millennium* (1963);

repr. (1991) · J. Goodwin, *Redemption redeemed* (1651) · R. Baxter, *Aphorismes of justification* (1649) · R. Baxter, *The reduction of a digressor* (1654) · *Calendar of the correspondence of Richard Baxter*, ed. N. H. Keeble and G. F. Nuttall, 2 vols. (1991) · register of the fourth London classis, DWL, MS 38.27 · *Reliquiae Baxterianae, or, Mr Richard Baxter's narrative of the most memorable passages of his life and times*, ed. M. Sylvester, 1 vol. in 3 pts (1696) · A. E. Preston, *The church and parish of St Nicholas, Abingdon: the early grammar school, to end of sixteenth century*, OHS, 99 (1935)

Wealth at death widow to pay creditors

Kendall, George

Kendall, George (1808/9–1886), Chartist and trade unionist, was baptized in the village of Hoton on the Hill near Loughborough on 26 July 1811, the son of George and Sarah Kendall. Starting work in the local hosiery industry at the age of five years, he moved to Sutton in Ashfield as a young man and worked as a framework knitter, making stockings and socks on a hand frame. He married, and with his wife, Sarah, had two children, Elizabeth, born in 1834, and George, born in 1836.

Industrial villages like Sutton were the location of most organized Chartist activity and Kendall became a recognized leader of the Sutton framework knitters during the early 1840s. He spoke at or presided over many of the larger meetings in the locality, and represented his village at delegate meetings. In addition he was called to give evidence to the 1845 commission on the condition of the framework knitters.

The origins of Nottinghamshire discontent sprang from a depression in the framework knitting trade. The introduction of new marketing techniques and the pressure to reduce standards of work, together with a labour force for which there was not enough work in times of slack trade, had led to the continual lowering of wages and speeding up of work. The operatives had, by the Chartist period, been involved in machine breaking and in various forms of trade union activity in their attempts to reverse the continual downward trend of their wages and conditions, but without success.

As well as pursuing the political programme of the six points of the People's Charter, Kendall and his group campaigned against wage reductions and against the 'truck system' (the payment of wages in goods). In his evidence before the commission of 1845 Kendall stressed the evils of this system. He became the secretary of an anti-truck association formed by some of the local Chartists which took many employers to court. The result of his activity led to his being blacklisted by employers in the locality, but had little effect on reducing the prevalence of truck payment.

In the second half of the century the hosiery trade began to improve, and trade union organization became more possible. Kendall became the secretary of the local wide-hand framework knitters' trade society. His first wife died of tuberculosis and he married his second wife, Mary Ann, who was eighteen years his junior. There were two more children from this marriage, Eliza, born in 1859, and William, born in 1861.

During the 1850s and 1860s the Sutton operatives, under

Kendall's continued leadership, took part in an experiment in industrial relations: this involved the establishment of an arbitration board on which workers and employers could discuss problems before they reached a phase of industrial dispute. The first chairman of the board was A. J. Mundella, the radical politician and hosiery manufacturer. The board seems to have maintained a degree of tranquillity in the relations between the two sides of the industry, and truck payment was finally abolished altogether. Unfortunately, the experiment did not establish a model for other industries as its originators had hoped, and it broke down in the harsher competitive conditions of the 1870s, finally coming to an end in 1884.

Apart from his political and industrial activities, Kendall, like many other ex-Chartists, was an active supporter of the 1870 Education Act. He served on the local school board for eight years, using his position to make the service available to the poorer children by the waiving of fees and encouraging families to keep the children in full- or half-time education in spite of the availability of juvenile employment. In 1879 when illness forced him to give up his work in the hosiery trade, Kendall resigned his chairmanship of the Sutton school board in order to become its employee as a school caretaker. He worked in this post for seven years, but continued his association with his trade and with local affairs generally.

Kendall died of cancer on 14 October 1886 at 21 Union Street, Sutton in Ashfield, and was buried in the churchyard of St Mary's Church, Sutton, on 16 October. He was survived by his wife.   DOROTHY THOMPSON

Sources J. Rowley, 'Kendall, George', *DLB*, vol. 6 · *Northern Star* (1841–6), *passim* · *Nottingham Review* (1839–70) · d. cert. · parish registers, Hoton on the Hill, Leics. RO · newspaper cuttings, Notts. Arch.

Kendall, Henry (1718–1787). *See under* Kendall family (*per. c.*1700–1807).

Kendall, (Thomas) Henry [*later* Henry Clarence Kendall] (1839–1882), poet, was born in Kirmington, near Milton, in the Ulladulla district of New South Wales, Australia, on 18 April 1839, one of the twin sons of Basil Kendall (*d.* 1852) and his wife, Melinda, *née* M'Nally. His father, who had been an officer in the Chilean navy, a flour factor, a farmer, and a shepherd, was the son of Thomas Kendall, a missionary to Australia under Samuel Marsden. After Basil Kendall died, while running a school at Grafton, New South Wales, his widow and children moved to her father's home at Wollongong, south of Sydney.

Henry Kendall received little formal education. He went to sea on the whaling vessel *Waterwitch* in September 1855, and upon his return to Australia in March 1857 set up a house for his mother, twin brother, and sisters at Newtown, in Sydney. In 1859 he began to contribute poetry to *The Month*, whose editor consequently introduced him to literary men such as James Lionel Michael, a lawyer who in 1860 employed Kendall as a clerk and allowed him to use his extensive library.

In 1862 Kendall sent a parcel of manuscript verses to *The Athenaeum* in London, whose editor sufficiently appreciated their promise to publish three poems dealing with the scenery of the Australian bush, noting that although Kendall had 'much to learn', his poems possessed a 'wild, dark … power of landscape-painting' (*The Athenaeum*, 27 Sept 1862, 394). Encouraged by this recognition Kendall had a volume, *Poems and Songs*, printed in Sydney in 1862; but he suppressed it in 1865 on grounds of its immaturity and issued, without date, another volume, *At Long Bay: Euroclydon: Poems*. At the same time Henry Parkes encouraged him to contribute verse to *The Empire*, his newspaper.

Kendall entered the public service of New South Wales in 1863 as clerk in the lands department, with a salary of £150, and in 1866 was transferred to the colonial secretary's office, where he earned a salary of £200 a year. In March 1868 he married Charlotte, the eighteen-year-old daughter of John Yates Rutter, a medical officer of Woolloomooloo, Sydney. About this time he added 'Clarence' to his name, after the Clarence River, but continued to sign letters and publish poetry as Henry Kendall. His domestic circumstances were strained, however, as he was often in debt to friends and moneylenders, largely because of his sisters' extravagance and his brother's fiscal dishonesty. His second volume of poetry, *Leaves from an Australian Forest* (1869), was well received but was not a financial success. The combined pressure of this commercial failure, the debts incurred by his mother and siblings, and the death of his one-year-old daughter Araluen in 1870 worsened an existing problem with alcohol. Fearing bankruptcy and dismissal, on 31 March 1869 he resigned from the civil service, and attempted to make a living in Melbourne as a journalist. Things became worse, however, and in December 1870 he was charged with forging and uttering a cheque, a charge of which he was found not guilty by reason of insanity. His wife returned to her mother and Kendall became a derelict, finally being committed to the Gladesville Hospital for the Insane in Sydney from April to July 1873.

Later in 1873, however, Kendall was befriended by William and Joseph Fagan, who allowed him to live with their family at Gosford, New South Wales, as he recovered his health, and in 1875 gave him a job in their timber business. In May 1876 his wife and children rejoined him, and he began to rebuild his family life, slowly supplementing his income with occasional publications. They moved to Camden Haven, and in 1879 he wrote the words for a cantata and hymn of praise sung at the Sydney International Exhibition, and he also won the *Sydney Morning Herald*'s prize of 100 guineas for a poem on the exhibition.

Kendall's third volume of poetry, *Songs from the Mountains*, was published in December 1880 to critical acclaim and popular success. In 1881 the post of inspector of forests was offered to him by Sir Henry Parkes, a former patron whom he had previously offended on several occasions, even as late as 1879, with his satiric poem 'The Gagging Bill'. He was grateful for the job, but his health made him unable to cope with its requisite long rides in all kinds of weather, and he collapsed in June 1882 at Wagga Wagga.

He was taken to William Fagan's house in Bourke Street, Surry Hills, Sydney, and died there of phthisis on 1 August 1882. His wife survived him, as did three sons, Frederick (b. 1870), a second son (b. 1873), and Æthelstan (b. 1877), and two daughters, Evelyn Persia (b. 1878) and Roma (b. 1879). He was buried in the Waverley cemetery near Sydney, and in 1886 a monument was erected to his memory. After his death £1200 was raised by public subscription for the support of his wife and family.

The twentieth-century critic T. Inglis Moore has noted that 'as a poet, Kendall was over-praised in his own day, then suffered an undue depreciation'. Although he lacked discipline and economy and tended at times towards an excess of sentiment, he had a 'gift of song' and 'a rich variety of verse forms, subjects and moods' and was an 'accomplished painter' of Australian scenes (Moore, ix–x). He was one of the first Australian-born writers to gain a significant reputation outside his own country.

MEGAN A. STEPHAN

Sources T. T. Reed, 'Kendall, Thomas Henry', AusDB, 5.13–14 · T. I. Moore, ed., Australian Poets: Henry Kendall (1963) · W. H. Wilde, Henry Kendall (1976) · Henry Kendall: poetry, prose, and selected correspondence, ed. M. Ackland (1993) · F. Johns, An Australian biographical dictionary (1934), 189 · R. McDougall, ed., Henry Kendall: the muse of Australia (1992) · The Athenaeum (27 Sept 1862), 394–5 · The Athenaeum (9 Sept 1882), 339 · D. B. W. Sladen, 'A study of Henry Kendall as a bush poet', Australian ballads and rhymes: poems inspired by life and scenery in Australia and New Zealand (1888), 277–301 · A. H. Miles, ed., The poets and the poetry of the nineteenth century, 7 (1906), 11–16 · P. J. Holdsworth, 'Henry Kendall: a prefatory note', in H. Kendall, Poems (1886) · P. Serle, Dictionary of Australian biography, 2 vols. (1949) · D. W. B. Sladen, Australian poets, 1788–1888 (1888), 280–81 · DNB

Kendall, Henry Edward (1776–1875), architect, was born on 23 March 1776 in York. A pupil of Thomas Leverton (1743–1824), who was helped early in his career by Kendall's banker father, he may also have worked in the office of John Nash (1752–1835) before entering the barrack department of the War Office, where he remained until appointed (1823) surveyor to the districts of St Martin-in-the-Fields and St Anne, Soho, positions he held for half a century. He was a regular exhibitor at the Royal Academy (1799–1843). Twice married, his first wife, Ann (1793/4–1863), bore him four children: two sons, Henry Edward Kendall junior (1805–1885) and Charles (b. c.1840), and two daughters, one of whom, Sophia, married his pupil Lewis Cubitt. He married secondly, Matilda Alice Clowser (d. 1876), daughter of Samuel Clowser, on 1 March 1866.

In 1825–7 Kendall completed the Gothic church of St George, Ramsgate, Kent, commenced in 1824 to designs by Henry Hemsley (d. 1825): its west tower was derived from Boston Stump, Lincolnshire. This was followed by: Christ Church, Cockfosters, Middlesex (1829); Holy Trinity Church, Claygate, Surrey (1840; exhibited RA, 1841); the remodelling of Bedford Chapel, Bloomsbury Street, London (1846; dem.); and a church at Bantry, co. Cork, Ireland (1840s).

Kendall's output was stylistically varied, rising occasionally to distinction: the Greek-Doric sessions-house and house of correction (1824–6) at Spilsby, Lincolnshire, plans of which were published in Christopher Davy's

Architectural Precedents: with Notes and Observations, 1841, is a good example of his work. He also designed two other Lincolnshire houses of correction, at Spalding (1824) and Louth (1828; exhibited RA, 1829). In 1828 he submitted Classical and Gothic entries for the competition to build the sessions-house at Sleaford, Lincolnshire, winning with a Tudor Gothic essay (completed 1831), and, in the same town, designed the east range and chapel of the Tudor Gothic Carr's Hospital almshouses (1830), and (probably) the south range (1841–6). In 1832 he won the competition for the design of the buildings at Kensal Green cemetery, Middlesex, with proposals in the Gothic style which were published in *Sketches of the Approved Designs of a Chapel and Gateway Entrances … at Kensal Green* (1832) with lithographs by Thomas Allom, but Gothic met with opposition, and the buildings later erected to designs by John Griffith of Finsbury (1796–1888) were in the Greek revival style.

With John Douglas Hopkins (d. 1869) Kendall entered Gothic proposals for the Houses of Parliament competition (1835), won by Charles Barry. By the early 1830s his son Henry Edward Kendall junior was working with him, and together they carried out various schemes, including: the esplanade and tunnel, Kemp Town, Brighton (1828–30); houses at Brighton, including 19–20 Sussex Square (1829–31); and the hotel, pier, and gardens at Rosherville, Northfleet, near Gravesend (1837). Kendall designed the workhouses at Uckfield, Sussex, and Semington, Wiltshire (1836–9); the school for blind children in St John's Wood, London (1838); the corn exchange, Sudbury, Suffolk (1841–2); the rectories at Tillington, near Petworth, Sussex (1817–18; exhibited RA, 1818), and Fishtoft, Lincolnshire (1826; dem.); 24 Belgrave Square, London, a handsome Greek-Ionic composition (1827–33); the remodelling of Haverholme Priory, Lincolnshire (1830; dem.; exhibited RA, 1830); Ashurst Lodge, Surrey (c.1835; exhibited RA, 1838); additions to The Castle, Chiddingstone, Kent (1837–8; exhibited RA, 1838); and sundry works at Wimpole Hall, Cambridgeshire (1842–5).

With his son Henry, Kendall helped to found the Institute of British Architects; early meetings to that end were held in his house, 17 Suffolk Street, Pall Mall, London, in 1834, the year in which he was elected a fellow of the institute.

Tall, handsome, generous, with refined and gentlemanly manners, Kendall was personally successful. A competent architect, his houses were among the finest of his time, and he was a master of scenic and picturesque effects, as his developments at Brighton and Rosherville demonstrated. In old age he was called the Nestor of British architecture (*The Builder*, 33, 9 Jan 1875, 33). He died at home at 78 Dean Street, Soho, London, on 4 January 1875 and was buried on 12 January 1875 in Kensal Green cemetery.

JAMES STEVENS CURL

Sources Colvin, Archs. · J. S. Curl, A celebration of death: an introduction to some of the buildings, monuments, and settings of funerary architecture in the western European tradition (1993) · D. Brock, 'The competition for the design of Sleaford sessions house, 1828', Architectural History, 27 (1984), 344–55 · The Builder, 4 (1846), 79–80 · The Builder,

33 (1875), 33, 60 • *The Builder*, 48 (1885), 883–4 • A. Dale, *Fashionable Brighton* (1947) • F. W. Leakey, 'Beaudelaire et Kendall', *Revue de littérature comparée*, 30/1 (1956) • F. W. Leakey, *Baudelaire: text and context: essays, 1953–1988* (1989) • C. Davy, *Architectural precedents* (1841) • *The watering places of Great Britain and fashionable directory* (1831–3) • *CGPLA Eng. & Wales* (1875) • d. cert. • m. cert. [Matilda Alice Clowser]

Archives Lincs. Arch. • RIBA BAL, Nomination papers | Suffolk RO, minutes of Sudbury Market House Company
Likenesses J. B. Black, lithograph, 1852, NPG
Wealth at death under £100: probate, 8 Feb 1875, *CGPLA Eng. & Wales*

Kendall, John (*d.* 1485), administrator, may have been the son of John Kendall of Gloucester (*d.* July 1447) and Elizabeth, his wife; and if so he was the eldest son and was of age in 1447. The younger John Kendall received legal training, possibly studying at Barnard's Inn, and is described as an attorney in 1479. He made his career as secretary to Richard, duke of Gloucester, being first recorded in that capacity in a document dated 22 December 1474. As secretary he gradually increased his power and influence, becoming in 1482 clerk of returns of the writs in the castle and county of York, and in 1483 keeper of the writs and rolls of the common bench.

Kendall's influence increased after his master became king as *Richard III. As secretary he received his livery of 6 yards of scarlet at the coronation in 1483, and he accompanied the post-coronation progress. His many grants included his appointment in 1483 as controller, changer, and assayer of the mints in the Tower of London and at Calais for life, and keeper of the prince's wardrobe in the city of London. After the rebellions of that year he was given lands worth £80 per annum from forfeitures in Berkshire and Oxfordshire. In December 1484 he was on the commission of the peace for Middlesex as secretary (together with a namesake 'of Westminster'), and possibly on the commissions in December 1483 and April 1485. He may also have been on the commissions of the peace in the East Riding of Yorkshire in June and December 1483 and September 1484. By February 1485, in a grant of the office of master forester in the king's park of Havering atte Bower, Essex, he was being described as king's councillor and secretary, and he also became steward of the abbey of Waltham Holy Cross. In July 1485 he accompanied Richard III to Nottingham, and on 1 August was one of the witnesses in the chapel of the castle when the great seal was handed over to Richard by Thomas Barowe, keeper of the rolls. Kendall undoubtedly fought with the king on 22 August 1485 at Bosworth, and was probably killed there. He was attainted afterwards and his lands confiscated. He was certainly married, but it is not known to whom, and he probably had a son.

Another **John Kendall** (*fl.* 1476–1486) was a vicar-choral at Southwell Minster, admitted on 16 March 1476. His parentage is not known. His career was inglorious (something he shared with several of his colleagues) and included fighting and taking women of bad character to his chantry. He resigned on 16 August 1486. Nothing further is known of him.   P. W. HAMMOND

Sources A. F. Sutton, 'John Kendale: a search for Richard III's secretary', *Richard III: crown and people*, ed. J. Petre (1985), 224–38, esp. 231–3 • R. Horrox, 'John Kendale, secretary, and wife', *The Ricardian*, 7 (1985–7), 230 • R. Horrox, 'Sons of John Kendale and Sir Robert Brackenbury', *The Ricardian*, 7 (1985–7), 335 • C. Ross, *Richard III* (1981), 156 n. 32 • A. F. Leach, ed., *Visitations and memorials of Southwell Minster*, CS, new ser., 48 (1891)
Wealth at death approx. £450 p.a.; three manors valued at £15: Ross, *Richard III*, *CIPM* Henry VII, 3, no. 654

Kendall, John (*d.* 1501), administrator and prior in England of the knights of St John, probably born into a Norfolk or Yorkshire family, entered the order of the knights of the hospital of St John of Jerusalem at an early age. He began his career in the convent on Rhodes where he was retained by the master until May 1465. In 1466–7 he acted as proctor of the English tongue (the English brethren in the convent) at the order's chapter general at Rome. After the chapter he returned to Rhodes where he ran into unknown difficulties, but on 21 August 1474 he was in Westminster, when Brother Robert Multon, who was afterwards replaced, was presented to Edward IV as the new prior of England. Kendall returned again to Rhodes where on 28 April 1477 he was elected turcopolier, that is conventual bailiff, and commander of the lighter mercenary troops. On 7 November 1478, during a general chapter on Rhodes, he also became proctor-general at the Roman curia, and on 20 January 1479 he was named proctor and lieutenant of the master, Pierre d'Aubusson, of the convent and treasury for Italy, Burgundy, the Netherlands, England, and Ireland. Probably from mid-1479 onwards he took up residence at Rome. When Rhodes was besieged by the Ottomans in 1480, he had to gather men and money from the West, which suggests that he was not on the island during the siege. Again in Westminster on 29 and 30 April 1480, Kendall gained royal protection for the order and two letters of recommendation (one for a visit to Ireland). In England he also sold indulgences, including one for Dame Joan Plumpton. He was in Rome on 6 May 1484 when he was granted by Sixtus IV the first year's fruits of the order's benefices in England for the rearmament of the English part of the city walls and for the rebuilding of the house of the English tongue in Rhodes (on which Kendall's arms were probably still to be found in 1826), and in 1485 he was a member of the order's legation to the new pope, Innocent VIII.

On 22 June 1489 Kendall was elected prior of England and resigned the office of turcopolier. In August 1490 he was allowed to leave Rome for England, and on 1 March 1491—as a sign of their deep personal relationship—the pope made him a member of his own family, the Cibò of Genoa, and took him under papal protection. On 5 January 1492 Kendall was pardoned by Henry VII for having acted as prior of England without royal permission, and afterwards became involved in English politics. In June 1492 he took part in peace negotiations with France, in February 1496 he was one of the envoys to Archduke Philip, the son of Maximilian I, and in June 1500 he accompanied Henry VII to a meeting with Philip in Calais. In September 1492 and in June 1496 he is mentioned as justice of the peace for Essex (and Middlesex), in June 1497 he was one of the commissioners to inquire concerning insurrections in Cornwall and elsewhere, and in November 1499 he participated in a grand jury that found Edward, earl of Warwick, one of the heirs presumptive of Richard III, guilty of high treason. It seems that Kendall remained in the king's favour throughout (obtaining a general pardon on 18 June 1496), though in March 1496 he had been accused of having sided with another of the Yorkist pretenders, Perkin Warbeck. Kendall remained prior of England until his death which occurred between 20 January and 6 April 1501. The lease-book from his administration of the hospitaller houses in England survives (BL, MS Lansdowne 200). Although he was probably not on Rhodes during the siege, he was honoured by a contemporary Italian medal (now in the British Museum). It bears a bust on one side and his arms on the other with the inscriptions 'Io. Kendal Rhodi Tvrcvpellerivs' and, on the obverse, 'Tempore Obsidionis Tvrchorvm MCCCCLXXX' ('at the time of the siege [of Rhodes] by the Turks, 1480').

JÜRGEN SARNOWSKY

Sources National Library of Malta, Valletta · *CEPR letters*, vols. 13–15 · CPR · CClR · J. Gairdner, ed., *Letters and papers illustrative of the reigns of Richard III and Henry VII*, 2 vols., Rolls Series, 24 (1861–3), 1.402, 2.87, 2.318–26 · Rymer, *Foedera*, 12.112, 253, 481, 579 · T. Stapleton, ed., *Plumpton correspondence*, CS, 4 (1839), 119–20, 143 · E. Hawkins, *Medallic illustrations of the history of Great Britain and Ireland to the death of George II*, ed. A. W. Franks and H. A. Grueber, 1 (1885), 17–18 · B. E. A. Rottiers, *Description des monumens de Rhodes*, 2 (Brussels, 1828) · N. Davis, ed., *Paston letters and papers of the fifteenth century*, 2 (1976) · J. Riley-Smith, *The knights of St John in Jerusalem and Cyprus, c.1050–1310* (1967), 280, 325 · H. J. A. Sire, *The knights of Malta* (1994), esp. 182–6 · A. Luttrell, *The hospitallers of Rhodes and their Mediterranean world* (1992)

Archives BL, Lansdowne MS 200

Likenesses medal, 1480, BM

Kendall, John (*fl.* 1476–1486). *See under* Kendall, John (*d.* 1485).

Kendall, John (1726–1815), Quaker minister and writer, was born on 6 March 1726 at Colchester, one of six sons of John Kendall (*d.* 1752?), printer and bookseller, and his wife, Elizabeth Yarritt (*c.*1704–1773). John and Elizabeth Kendall belonged to the Society of Friends in a town with a large congregation and two meeting-houses. Kendall himself became a minister in the society at the age of twenty-one. He travelled extensively in the ministry for some years, his first tour of religious visits taking him, in 1750, to the north of England and Scotland as companion to Daniel Stanton. Two years later, in July 1752, he set out for the Netherlands, which he revisited on four further occasions. A group of Friends, by then dwindling in numbers and including the parents of the Quaker historian William Sewel, was at that time established in Amsterdam and in the neighbouring town of Twisk. Kendall, who had some knowledge of Dutch, was always welcomed at both places.

After the death of his father, Kendall took responsibility for his mother, his five brothers, and the business which he inherited. He prospered, and on 17 July 1764 he married Ann Havens (1734?–1805), daughter of Philip and Ann Havens of Colchester; they had no children. His time and

money were thenceforth spent in religious visits to various towns, sometimes as part of extensive tours, in philanthropic pursuits, and in study. He attended the yearly meeting of Friends in London over a long period. With his wife he founded, in 1791, Kendall's almshouses at Colchester, for eight poor widows. The rules and original minutes are in his own handwriting, and the former were subsequently printed. He was also involved with the short-lived Friends' school at Ipswich, which was in existence from 1790 to 1800. His bequest of £2000 set up Kendall's Trust, which provided for the distribution of a certain number of religious books every year, and Kendall's Foundation, a school at Colchester, to which his cousin Francis Freshfield also bequeathed money. Six poor boys, preferably the sons of Quakers, were to receive a free education, and a valuable library of 1030 volumes was left for the use of the master and assistants. Since this consisted chiefly of Greek, Latin, and Dutch books, it proved unserviceable and was by consent of the charity commissioners sold, with its furniture, by Sothebys in 1865, the net benefit of £270 going to the school. From 1746 Kendall also undertook clerical work for the Quakers in Colchester, and he appears to have been clerk of Colchester monthly meeting between 1757 and 1791.

Kendall's kindly disposition and personal influence caused him to be received with courtesy wherever he went. It is said that he attended the theatre in Colchester one Saturday night, at the start of the performance, and persuaded both actors and audience quietly to disperse. He called at public houses in Colchester to admonish people against the evils of intemperance, and visited other places of public entertainment for similar purposes. He published his views on the wasting of time in a pamphlet, addressed to all Christians, entitled *Remarks on the prevailing custom of attending stage entertainments: also on the present taste of reading romances and novels* (1794).

Kendall was a prolific author and editor of Quaker literature. His most printed work was *Some principles and precepts of the Christian religion explained, by way of question and answer, for the use of children* (1783), of which five editions were printed in his lifetime and further reprints went on into the mid-nineteenth century. Rearranging the entries chronologically he edited the Quaker devotional standard collection of obituaries, *Piety Promoted* (1789). Sharing the quietist enthusiasm for continental devotional writing, he also edited *Extracts from the writings of Francis Fénelon, Archbishop of Cambray, with some memoirs of his life* (1797). Outside the Quaker tradition he published an abstract of *The Imitation of Christ* (1805). A work much used in Quaker families early in the nineteenth century was his abstract, in two volumes, *The Holy Scriptures of the Old and New Testament* (1800). Other devotional publications included anthologies of poems on religious subjects (in three parts, 1775–1807) and two volumes of Quaker letters (1802–5).

Kendall more than once visited George III and Queen Charlotte, and, when with his regiment in Colchester, the prince of Wales called on Kendall at the king's request. Kendall died at Colchester on 27 January 1815 and was buried there, in the Quaker burial-ground, on 3 February. The posthumous *Memoirs of the Life and Religious Experience of John Kendall*, containing a short autobiographical sketch and a number of letters, was published in 1815.

DAVID J. HALL

Sources DNB · *Memoirs of the life and religious experience of John Kendall* (1815) · 'Dictionary of Quaker biography', RS Friends, Lond. [card index] · J. Smith, ed., *A descriptive catalogue of Friends' books*, 2 (1867) · S. H. G. Fitch, *Colchester Quakers* [1962] · C. B. Rowntree, 'Friends' schools at Ipswich (1790–1800) and Colchester (1817–1917)', *Journal of the Friends' Historical Society*, 35 (1938), 50–64 · *Annual Monitor* (1816), 20–24
Archives Religious Society of Friends, Birmingham, papers
Wealth at death £2000—one bequest: Rowntree, 'Friends'

Kendall, John (1768/9–1829), architect and stonemason, was the youngest of four children of Edward Kendall (d. 1796) of Exeter, monumental sculptor and mason, and his wife, Mary (*bap.* 1738, *d.* 1831), daughter of James and Elizabeth Rennel of Kingsteignton. He probably attended Exeter grammar school with his elder brother William (1767–1832), later praised as a poet, amateur architect, and local philanthropist. Kendall's interest in medieval architecture and his practical skills as a craftsman owed much to his father, who had been employed as stonemason to Exeter Cathedral since 1766. The family's separate statuary business provided Kendall's first commissions: he designed and carved funeral monuments for the cathedral from 1791, and continued until his last years. On Edward Kendall's death in November 1796 John was appointed stonemason to Exeter Cathedral.

On 30 July 1798 Kendall married Grace Luxmore (*bap.* 1770) of Okehampton. Seven daughters and one son, John Henry (later vicar of Treneglos, Cornwall), were born between 1799 and 1809. Kendall's large young family and the chapter's annual settlement of accounts probably contributed to his bankruptcy in 1811. Soon at work again, he embarked on a major expansion of the cathedral restoration programme that had begun with repairs to the west front in 1805. Fifteen years of hectic activity followed on the cathedral surveyor's 1812 report describing Exeter's crumbling structure. From then until 1827 Kendall prepared plans and estimates and personally carried out all the main stonework repairs. Decayed pinnacles, parapets, windows, and buttresses were restored or replaced, many of the west front image screen figures repaired or reinstated. The restored chapter house became the cathedral library's new home and the lady chapel, freed of books, was returned to its proper use. It was, however, Kendall's new Gothic reredos, erected in 1818 (removed by Sir George Gilbert Scott) that was commended by contemporary visitors as his finest achievement. His similar screen (1821) at Haccombe church, Devon, survives. Kendall followed in the tradition of the medieval master masons, combining the skills of designer and builder. Some of his detailed drawings of the cathedral interior (1805–6) he later used as illustrations for his treatise *An Elucidation of the Principles of English Architecture, Usually Denominated Gothic* (1818). Of his designs prepared for the dean and chapter, only his 1818 design for the new reredos has survived.

After a protracted illness Kendall died on 24 September 1829, aged sixty, at Longbrook Street, Exeter, where he lived; he was buried on 29 September in St David's churchyard, Exeter. His wife survived him.

L. H. CUST, rev. ANGELA DOUGHTY

Sources chapter act books, 1765–1829, Exeter Cathedral, dean and chapter archives, D & C Exeter 3570–3580 · fabric accounts, 1766–1829, Exeter Cathedral, dean and chapter archives, 3776/3–5 · extra-ordinary solutions accounts, 1774–1819, Exeter Cathedral, dean and chapter archives, 3791 · fabric papers, new altar screen, 1811–19, Exeter Cathedral, dean and chapter archives, 7063/1 · parish registers, 1799–1829, St David, Exeter · parish register, 28 June 1770, Okehampton, Devon [baptism] · parish register, 30 July 1798, Okehampton, Devon [marriage] · apprenticeship books, 1778, PRO, IR 1/29, xxix f206 · *Exeter Flying Post* (1 Dec 1796) · *Trewman's Exeter Flying Post* (7 Nov 1811) · *Trewman's Exeter Flying Post* (1 Oct 1829) · *Trewman's Exeter Flying Post* (1849–50) [edns with G. Oliver's 'Biographies of Exonians'] · V. Hope, Exeter Cathedral monumentarium, handwritten list of monumental inscriptions, 1956 · J. Kendall, plan and elevation of proposed new reredos, Jan 1818, Exeter Cathedral, dean and chapter archives, ref P2/3 · folio of original drawings by J. Kendall, presented 1935, Exeter Cathedral Library · P. Leach, *James Paine* (1988) · Colvin, *Archs.* · Graves, *RA exhibitors* · J. N. Brewer, *The history and antiquities of the cathedral church of Exeter* [n.d., 1814?]; repr. [n.d., 1819?] · *Devon*, Pevsner (1989)
Archives Exeter Cathedral, drawings and papers

Kendall, Jonathan (1714–1791). *See under* Kendall family (*per. c.*1700–1807).

Kendall, Kay [*real name* Justine Kay Kendall McCarthy] (1927–1959), actress, was born on 21 May 1927 at Stanley House, Hull Road, Withernsea, near Hull in Yorkshire, the youngest child in the family of two daughters and one son of Justin McCarthy, professionally known as Terry Kendall, and his wife, Gladys Drewery, both entertainers. Kay's paternal grandmother, Marie Kendall (1873–1964), was a great star of the music-hall, married to Stephen McCarthy, a Canadian. When her father formed a song and dance team with his sister Pat, they retained their mother's famous name, performing in revue as Pat and Terry Kendall.

At the outbreak of war in 1939 Kay and her sister Kim, who was two years older, were evacuated to a convent school in Oban, Scotland. The family had often been separated through work, and in 1940 their parents divorced. The girls joined their mother in London, where, having the height and looks to find work as chorus girls, they followed their parents into show business. Kim appeared in revue at the Holborn Empire with Ben Lyon, Bebe Daniels, and Tommy Trinder, and she went with them to the London Palladium in a new review, *Gangway* (1941). Kay joined her in the chorus. After two years, touring in George Black revues, the sisters formed a double act, appearing in troop shows and on the variety circuit. Kay also worked as a fashion model, and in 1944 began to get small parts in films—*Fiddlers Three* and *Champagne Charlie*, both with Trinder; *Dreaming* with Bud Flanagan and Chesney Allen; and then *London Town* (1946), a reckless attempt by Rank Studios to emulate the Hollywood musical. It starred another comic, Sid Field, and Kendall was his leading lady. The film was a

Kay Kendall (1927–1959), by Sir Cecil Beaton, 1957

disaster, and 'when it flopped—I flopped with it' said Kendall (*Films and Filming*, vol. 2, no. 6, March 1956, 10).

With this set-back Kendall returned to the stage, entertaining the troops in Europe and learning her craft in provincial repertory theatres. Trying films again she could only get small roles, until an admired performance on television—in the play *Sweethearts and Wives*—was seen by Frank Launder and Sidney Gilliatt, who cast her in *Lady Godiva Rides Again* (1951); she got good notices and more offers. Under contract to Rank, her first picture was *Genevieve* (1953). Kendall's performance as a trumpet-playing fashion model, taken along by Kenneth More on the London to Brighton vintage car rally, was widely praised and the film a massive hit. The part was tailor-made and the first to exploit her gift 'for remaining soignée while being bumped or slapped around' (Shipman, *Story of Cinema*, 807). But she was unlucky with her next few films and the momentum was lost. She returned to the stage playing Elvira in Noël Coward's *Blithe Spirit* with Dennis Price and Irene Handl, a performance that pleased the author, and began to fight for better film roles. Suffering salary suspension for her pains, she was finally loaned to London Films to appear as one of the wives of Rex Harrison [*see* Harrison, Sir Reginald Carey] in *The Constant Husband* (1955). This was a role she would soon play out in life, as she and Harrison began to live together.

In Hollywood Kendall scored a huge success in a musical with Gene Kelly, *Les Girls* (1957); the critics compared her to Carole Lombard, she was flooded with offers, and finally she was a star. But Kay Kendall was already ill with leukaemia, a fact kept from her by her doctors and by Harrison. He had remained married to the actress Lilli Palmer (his second wife), but confronted with this knowledge she

agreed to a divorce to allow Harrison and Kendall to marry, which they did in New York on 25 June 1957. Kendall made one more good film, *The Reluctant Débutante* (1958), with her husband, and he directed her in a play, *The Bright One*, which closed after a few days. She had been undergoing treatment, as she thought for anaemia, for some years; admitted to the London Clinic, Devonshire Place, London, she died there on 6 September 1959. She was buried in St John's churchyard, Church Row, Hampstead, London. Her relationship with Harrison was the basis of the play *After Lydia* by Terence Rattigan. The Withernsea lighthouse (her maternal grandfather, a fisherman, had helped in its construction) is home to the Kay Kendall Memorial Museum.

Kendall's premature death robbed the cinema of a uniquely gifted comedienne. Elegant, witty, and zany, she was a sophisticated clown; the studios did not know what to do with her, but in her few films of quality she made an indelible impression.   ALEX JENNINGS

Sources D. Shipman, *The great movie stars: the international years* (1972) · R. Harrison, *Rex* (1974) · R. Harrison, *A damned serious business* (1990) · R. Moseley, *Rex Harrison* (1987) · J. P. Wearing, *The London stage … a calendar of plays and players*, 9 vols. (1984–90) [vols. covering 1920–58] · D. Shipman, *The story of cinema*, 2 (1984) · L. Palmer, *Change lobsters and dance* (1976) · D. Bogarde, *Snakes and ladders* (1978) · E. Katz, *The film encyclopedia*, 3rd edn (1998) · *The Noël Coward diaries*, ed. G. Payn and S. Morley (1982) · G. Wansell, *Terence Rattigan* (1995) · *CGPLA Eng. & Wales* (1960) · private information (2004) · *The Times* (7 Sept 1959)
Archives FILM BFI, London
Likenesses C. Beaton, photograph, 1957, NPG [*see illus.*] · F. W. Daniels, photograph, NPG · photographs, Hult. Arch.
Wealth at death £2313 16s. 7d.: probate, 3 March 1960, *CGPLA Eng. & Wales*

Kendall, Larcum (1719–1790), watchmaker, was born on 21 September 1719 at Charlbury in Oxfordshire, the elder of two sons of Moses Kendall, mercer and linen draper, and Anne, *née* Larcum, of Chipping Wycombe, Buckinghamshire. His parents were both Quakers. On 7 April 1735 Larcum was apprenticed to the watch, clock, and repeating-motion maker John Jefferys for seven years, at which time he was living with his parents in St Clement Danes in Westminster. In 1736 his maternal grandfather, Nicholas Larcum, a salesman of Chipping Wycombe, left property in trust for him, through his mother, and he inherited a reasonable private income.

In 1742, immediately after his apprenticeship had ended, Kendall set up on his own, working almost exclusively for the great watch and clock maker George Graham (1685–1751) as an escapement maker specializing in the horizontal (cylinder) escapement. Kendall was brought up a Quaker, but once his own master he no longer stayed as one of their brethren, though, according to his obituary in the *Gentleman's Magazine*, he 'never quitted that simplicity of manners for which that sect is so generally admired; and a man more inflexibly upright, either in person, word or deed, perhaps scarcely ever lived'. He was highly respected as a craftsman, too: working under Graham and with his contemporary Thomas Mudge, he was part of the finest watchmaking team of the day. He appears, though, to have remained something of a loner in the trade; he was not a member of the Clockmakers' Company and probably not among the group of talented London watchmakers who met at the Devil tavern during the last quarter of the eighteenth century.

Through Jefferys and Graham, Kendall had connections with John Harrison, the great pioneer and inventor of the marine timekeeper and precision watch. In June 1765, by which time he was established at 6 Furnival's Inn Court, near Holborn Bars, the board of longitude selected him as one of six experts to witness the explanation by Harrison of the construction of his fourth timekeeper (H4), an event which took place between 14 and 22 August that year. During these deliberations the board also decided that a copy of the timekeeper must be made and Harrison recommended Kendall, who may have contributed to the making of the fourth timekeeper itself in the preceding years. Kendall agreed to make the copy 'part for part', but made it clear he had little faith in its design; he would make no guarantees of its good performance. The copy (later known as K1) was completed in 1769 and the following year was inspected by the same group as before, including Harrison's son William, who admitted that it was even better made than his father's original. Kendall was paid the agreed £450, plus an *ex gratia* payment of £50 for 'the extraordinary trouble in adjusting it for 9 months' and taking it and H4 to pieces. In 1772 K1 was sent for trials with James Cook on his second voyage of discovery to the south seas (1772–5), during which time it performed so well that Cook learned to rely on his 'trusty friend the watch', his 'never failing guide'.

Nevertheless, Harrison's design was too complex and expensive and in 1769 the board commissioned Kendall to create a simplified version. The result, K2 of 1771, which cost £200, was later famous for being on the *Bounty* when the notorious mutiny took place. The watch was taken to Pitcairn Island, only returning to England in 1840. It employed many of the features of H4, but Kendall omitted the essential remontoir mechanism, thus prejudicing its chances of success, and it never performed well. Further simplified designs by Kendall, including a type of escapement said to be his own invention, resulted in K3 of 1774 (costing £100), which was sent with Cook on his third, ill-fated voyage (1776–9). This watch also failed to perform as well as Harrison's, being fundamentally no better than K2. (These three timekeepers were all preserved at the National Maritime Museum, Greenwich.)

After this Kendall, following the lead of the great pioneer John Arnold, began making pocket timekeepers with 'detached' (pivoted detent) escapements; the collection of the Clockmakers' Company, Guildhall, London, included an example. The quality of his work was second to none, as is shown by the few watches, signed by him, which survive, but he never showed any real ingenuity of his own. He was primarily a watchmaker to the top retail trade, producing first-rate products to the design of those with greater imagination; the majority of his work, which also included some clocks and precision regulators, would appear to have been sold under other retailers' names.

Kendall died at Furnival's Inn Court on 22 November 1790. Although his obituary states that the Quakers 'received his body into the bosom of their church at his death', this does not in fact appear to have been the case; no record of his burial can be found in either nonconformist or Anglican cemeteries in London or Charlbury. As well as leaving a large sum in trust for his brother Moses and his family, his will, written on 6 November 1790 and proved on 8 December, also leaves his 'implements in trade' and personal effects to Moses, who arranged for them to be sold by auction; the contents of his workshop, and his household furniture and other effects, were sold by Christies on 23 December that year. It is not known whether Kendall ever married. No wife or children are mentioned in his will and the furniture and effects sold strongly suggest the home of a lifelong bachelor.

JONATHAN BETTS

Sources R. T. Gould, *The marine chronometer: its history and development* (1923) • *GM*, 1st ser., 60 (1790), 1213 • D. Howse, 'Captain Cook's marine timekeepers [pt 1]', *Antiquarian Horology and the Proceedings of the Antiquarian Horological Society*, 6 (1968–70), 190–205 • J. Harrison, *The principles of Mr Harrison's timekeeper* (1767) • C. Clutton, 'Larcum Kendall's pivoted detent escapement', *Antiquarian Horology and the Proceedings of the Antiquarian Horological Society*, 3 (1959–62), 172 • G. L'E. Turner, 'The auction sale of Larcum Kendall's workshop, 1790', *Antiquarian Horology and the Proceedings of the Antiquarian Horological Society*, 5 (1965–8), 269–75 • M. Quill, *John Harrison, the man who found longitude* (1966) • Mr Christie, *A catalogue … the property of Mr Larcum Kendall* (23 Dec 1790) • *Digest registers of births, marriages and burials for England and Wales, c.1650–1837* [1992] [Berkshire and Oxfordshire quarterly meeting; microfilm]
Archives BL, corresp., deeds, and papers, Add. MS 39822; Add. Ch 62374–62384 • BM, documents relating to the making of 'K1' • BM, family papers and contracts • CUL, board of longitude MSS (RGO), letters, and accounts, esp. RGO 14 • NMM, timekeepers
Wealth at death £1200 consolidated bank annuities: will • £243 from sale of effects: Christie, *Catalogue*

Kendall, Sir Maurice George (1907–1983), statistician, was born on 6 September 1907 in Kettering, Northamptonshire, the only child of John Roughton Kendall, engineering worker, of Kettering, and his wife, Georgina, of Standon in Hertfordshire. At matriculation stage in the Derby central school he was primarily interested in languages but, becoming interested in mathematics, he won a scholarship to St John's College, Cambridge, where he was a keen cricketer and chess player. He obtained a first class in part one of the mathematical tripos (1927) and was a wrangler in part two. He entered the civil service in 1930, and was employed at the Ministry of Agriculture on statistical work. This led to his becoming co-author with George Udny Yule for the eleventh to fourteenth editions of Yule's *An Introduction to the Theory of Statistics*, which had first been published in 1911.

In 1941 Kendall became statistician to the British chamber of shipping, and in the following years published many papers in the theory of statistics, primarily in the theory of rank correlation coefficients of paired-comparison experiments, and the analysis of time-series, in the construction of a theory of randomness, and most originally and most intricately in the theory of symmetric functions of the observations in a sample. One of the two most important rank correlation coefficients was named after Kendall, who discovered it in 1938. His two-volume treatise, *The Advanced Theory of Statistics* (1943–6), was followed by the award of a Cambridge ScD in 1949.

In 1949 Kendall was appointed professor of statistics in the University of London, holding this chair at the London School of Economics, where he founded a research techniques division and published the first major dictionary of statistical terms (1957) and the first comprehensive bibliography of statistical literature (3 vols., 1962–8).

In 1961 Kendall again changed the direction of his career by joining the computer consultancy later called Scientific Control Systems Ltd (SCICON), where he was successively scientific director, managing director, and chairman. His interests ranged widely: he was president not only of the Royal Statistical Society (1960–62) and the Institute of Statisticians, but also of the Operational Research Society and the Market Research Society. When he retired from SCICON in 1972 he began yet another, and perhaps his most testing, career as the first director of the World Fertility Survey, a very large multinational sample survey project, from which illness forced his retirement in 1980. Kendall was twice married. On 11 February 1933 he married Sheila Frances Holland (*b.* 1908/9), daughter of Percy Holland Lester, rector of Ashton upon Mersey. They had two sons and a daughter. After they were divorced in 1947 he married, on 1 March of the same year, Kathleen Ruth Audrey (*b.* 1904/5), the divorced wife of Frank Whitfield and daughter of Roland Abel Phillipson, dentist. They had one son.

Kendall had an orderly mind and an enormous capacity for hard work. He was at his best in the organization of research, where he had an almost infallible capacity to delegate responsibility. He wrote seventeen books and about seventy-five papers in statistics alone; a memorial volume, *Statistics: Theory and Practice* (ed. Alan Stuart, 1984), reprints seventeen of his papers and contains a select bibliography. Perhaps the greatest influence that he exerted was through *The Advanced Theory of Statistics*, which was revised into a three-volume work (1958–66), later retitled *Kendall's Advanced Theory of Statistics*, and became the leading treatise on the subject.

Kendall's literary style, lucid, balanced, and sometimes ironical, reflects his early interest in language. He constantly played with words, writing sometimes under the anagrammatic names Lamia Gurdleneck and K. A. C. Manderville, and many pastiches, of which the best known is 'Hiawatha Designs an Experiment'. His inaugural lecture, 'The statistical approach', and his presidential address to the Royal Statistical Society, 'Natural law in the social sciences', demonstrated that it was possible to write interestingly of statistical matters. Kendall was a tall, good-looking, and friendly man, who managed to get on with all those with whom he worked.

Many honours came to Kendall. In 1968 the Royal Statistical Society awarded him its highest distinction, the Guy medal in gold. He received doctorates from the universities of Essex (1968) and Lancaster (1975). In 1970 he became a fellow of the British Academy, and in 1974 a knighthood was conferred on him for services to the theory of statistics. When, finally, he retired from the World Fertility Survey, his exceptional work there was recognized by the award of a United Nations peace medal. Kendall died in Redhill General Hospital, Redhill, Surrey, on 29 March 1983.   ALAN STUART, *rev.*

Sources A. Stuart, *Journal of the Royal Statistical Society*, 147 (1984), 120–22 · *The Times* (31 March 1983), 16g · personal knowledge (1990) · private information (1990) · m. certs. · d. cert.
Wealth at death £119,503: probate, 25 Aug 1983, *CGPLA Eng. & Wales*

Kendall, Timothy (*fl.* 1572–1577), translator and poet, son of William and Alice Kendall, was raised in North Aston, Oxfordshire. Very few personal details about his life are known. He was educated at Eton College and went on to Oxford where he was a member of Magdalen Hall in or before 1572. He left the university without a degree and became a student at Staple Inn where he compiled the verse work *Flowers of epigrammes, out of sundrie the moste singular authours selected, as well auncient as late writers* (1577). Kendall lists the authors he translates on the reverse of the title-page and dedicates his work to Robert Dudley, earl of Leicester. The translated epigrams are followed by Kendall's compositions entitled 'Trifles by Timothe Kendall devised and written (for the most part) at sundrie tymes in his yong and tender age. Tamen est laudanda voluntas' and include 'Verses Written to his Father when he was Scholler at Æton', 'Preceptes written in his friend Richard Woodwards praier booke, sometime his companion in Oxford', 'Verses written at the request of his cosen, Mary Palmer, in her praier booke called The Pomander of Praier', and some epitaphs on his father and mother. Many of the pieces are taken verbatim from Martial, some, without acknowledgement, are from George Turberville's collections. Despite the substantial dependence of *Flowers of Epigrammes* on Martial's work, Francis Meres describes Kendall as one of the English epigrammatists, along with John Heywood, Thomas Drant, Thomas Bastard, and Sir John Davies (*Palladis tamia*, 1598). *Flowers of Epigrammes* was reprinted by the Spenser Society in 1874. The manner, place, and date of Kendall's death are unknown and there is no evidence of a will having been proved.

A. H. BULLEN, *rev.* JANICE DEVEREUX

Sources *STC, 1475–1640* · Foster, *Alum. Oxon.* · T. Kendall, *Flowers of epigrammes* (1874) [repr. of original 1577 edn for the Spenser Society] · *Prose and poetry: Sir Thomas North to Michael Drayton* (1909), vol. 4 of *The Cambridge history of English literature*, ed. A. W. Ward and A. R. Waller (1907–27); repr. www.bartleby.com/cambridge/index. html, 2000 · T. Corser, *Collectanea Anglo-poetica, or, A … catalogue of a … collection of early English poetry*, 11 vols., Chetham Society (1860–83) · Wood, *Ath. Oxon.*, new edn, 1.484–7

Kendrew, Sir John Cowdery (1917–1997), molecular biologist, was born on 24 March 1917 in Oxford, the only son of Wilfrid George Kendrew (*d.* 1962), reader in climatology at the University of Oxford, and his wife, Evelyn May Graham, *née* Sandberg (*d.* 1961), art historian, for many years resident in Florence, where she published under the name of Evelyn Sandberg-Vavalà; Kendrew was brought up by his father. Kendrew was educated at the Dragon

Sir John Cowdery Kendrew (1917–1997), by Nick Sinclair, 1993

School, Oxford (1923–30), and at Clifton College, Bristol (1930–36), where he became interested in chemistry. He entered Trinity College, Cambridge, as a major entrance scholar, reading chemistry, physics, biochemistry, and advanced mathematics (the latter two as half subjects) for the first part of the natural sciences tripos, and chemistry for the second. In 1938 he was awarded a senior scholarship at Trinity and in 1939 graduated with first-class honours. He then started doctoral research in the department of physical chemistry under E. A. Moelwyn-Hughes.

War service Following the outbreak of the Second World War, Kendrew was told to continue his research, but with most of his colleagues leaving for war-related projects he became increasingly dissatisfied and searched for possibilities actively to join the war effort. In February 1940 he was recruited to the Air Ministry Research Establishment (later the Telecommunication Research Establishment) to work on the development of airborne radar. In September 1940 he was attached to the staff of Sir Robert Watson-Watt for operational research duties, a field then in its infancy. From Royal Air Force Coastal Command (1940–41) he moved to Cairo to build up the operational research section at headquarters RAF Middle East (1941–4), and from there to air command south-east Asia, where he served in India and Ceylon as officer in charge of operational research and as scientific adviser to the allied air commander-in-chief (1944–5). He worked mainly on anti-submarine warfare, bombing accuracy, and radio aids. While at Cairo he produced the very successful *Handbook for Aircrews and Controllers*, often referred to by aircrews as the 'bible'. On his move to south-east Asia he was appointed honorary wing commander. He rejoined the Air Ministry in London in June 1945 after a four-month return trip via Australia, the south-west Pacific, and the USA, which he visited on military mission.

When the war ended Kendrew contemplated a career in the scientific civil service. With others he was convinced that science had an important role to play in post-war reconstruction, and felt that scientists who like him had gained experience of administration and of working alongside government had the moral obligation to remain in government service. However, after some hesitation, he decided to return to academia until career chances in the civil service were more clearly defined.

Protein crystallography In September 1945, having been awarded an ICI research fellowship, Kendrew started research in protein crystallography in the Cavendish Laboratory, under the guidance of Max Perutz and with W. H. Taylor, reader in crystallography, as official supervisor. This represented a clear break from his pre-war research. According to Kendrew's own account it was the crystallographer John Desmond Bernal who, 'in a jungle in Ceylon' while both he and Kendrew were working as advisers to the allied air commander-in-chief, convinced Kendrew that it should be possible to use X-ray diffraction to solve the structure of proteins (video interview with J. Kendrew, 18 June 1997, Laboratory of Molecular Biology Archive). Kendrew also credited the structural chemist Linus Pauling and the embryologist Conrad Waddington, both of whom he had met during the war, with influencing him in his decision to move from chemistry to biology. However, the techniques he employed required a broad range of physical, chemical, mathematical, and organizational skills, for which he was well suited both by education and by talent. He made good use of those skills, thereby making decisive contributions to the new field of protein crystallography.

Kendrew first collaborated with Perutz in the investigation of the structure of haemoglobin, embarking on a comparison of foetal and adult haemoglobin. This work gained him his PhD in 1949. From the beginning, however, he also attempted the crystal analysis of myoglobin, the protein responsible for oxygen storage in muscle. This project was long hampered by the difficulty of growing crystals of a size suitable for X-ray analysis. Once this hurdle was cleared and sperm whale myoglobin identified as ideal source material the project was much aided by the small size of myoglobin (a quarter that of haemoglobin). By this time protein crystallography in the Cavendish under the aegis of W. Lawrence Bragg was put on a more secure footing by the creation, in 1947, of the Medical Research Council unit for the molecular structure of biological systems, with Perutz and Kendrew as only members. Other scientists as well as assistant staff soon joined, among them Hugh Huxley, Kendrew's first PhD student; Francis Crick; James Watson, originally taken on to help Kendrew with his myoglobin project; Vernon Ingram; and Sydney Brenner.

In 1957 Kendrew and his collaborators presented a first molecular model of myoglobin at 6 Ångström resolution. The model, the first of a globular protein ever to be built based on direct structure analysis, was remarkable for the unexpected twists the protein chain performed. It was followed two years later by a 2 Ångström resolution model, built of meccano and 'Kendrew type' skeletal model parts, which indicated the exact position of most of the 1200 atoms of the molecule. This work gained Kendrew, jointly with Perutz, the 1962 Nobel prize for chemistry. The crystallographic calculation for both models relied decisively on the use of the first electronic digital computers built at Cambridge, EDSAC I and II, of which Kendrew made pioneering use. Together with John Bennett of the mathematical laboratory in Cambridge he wrote the first paper on crystallographic computation with electronic digital computers, published in *Acta crystallographica* in 1952. His interest in electronic computers built on his long-standing fascination with information handling systems. This pronounced interest, together with his organizational skills, were crucial for the successful completion of the myoglobin project. In her informed guide to Kendrew's extensive collection of papers, Jeannine Alton observed how an interest in note keeping, filing, and organization, present in the schoolboy and fostered by operational research during the war, found a kind of 'bureaucratic apotheosis in the sustained effort of accuracy required for the long haul to the final successful three-dimensional picture [of the protein molecule]' (Alton, 65).

Kendrew was an active fellow of Peterhouse, where he was first a research fellow (1947–53), then a supernumerary fellow (1953–75), and finally an honorary fellow (1975–97); from 1972 he was also an honorary fellow of Trinity. He was director of studies in natural science for many years and also undertook other college duties, serving successively as librarian, prolector, steward, wine steward, and custodian of the college's paintings. Also from Peterhouse, Kendrew for many years edited the *Journal of Molecular Biology*, founded by him on the initiative of Kurt Jacobi in 1959. The journal contributed decisively to the establishment of molecular biology as a distinctive field of research. Kendrew remained editor-in-chief of the journal until 1987. In 1964 he presented the new biology in a BBC lecture series, later published as a book, *The Thread of Life* (1966). On 1 May 1948 he married Mary Elizabeth Jarvie (b. 1918/19), a widow, and daughter of John Henry Gorvin, civil servant; shortly thereafter she qualified as a medical practitioner. There were no children of the marriage, which was dissolved in 1956.

When Bragg moved to the Royal Institution in 1954 Kendrew became a part-time reader at the Davy–Faraday Laboratory to help build up protein crystallography there, a post he held until 1968. When in 1962 the MRC unit moved from the Cavendish to the new MRC Laboratory of Molecular Biology at Cambridge, he became deputy chairman of the new institution and head of its structural studies division. He continued to work on the refinement of the myoglobin structure, pushing the analysis to 1.4 Ångström resolution. However, this work was never published. While continuing to run his division effectively his own interest in active research began to wane. Instead he took on an increasing number of advisory and organizational functions relating both to military and to civil research.

Wider fields In 1961, on the suggestion of Solly Zuckerman, chief scientific adviser to the Ministry of Defence, who had crossed paths with Kendrew in Cairo during the war, he was appointed part-time scientific adviser to the same ministry. He resigned the position in 1963, but continued to serve as an independent member on numerous defence panels and committees. From 1971 to 1974 he was chairman of the Defence Scientific Advisory Council. Parallel to his military advisory functions he was also involved in civilian science policy. He was a member of the Council for Scientific Policy from its inception under the Labour government in 1964 to its demise in 1972. He served as deputy chairman from 1969. He was also chairman of the standing committee on international scientific relations and chairman or member of many of the council's working groups, notably one on molecular biology.

In December 1962 Kendrew became involved in the first informal discussions regarding the creation of a European molecular biology laboratory on the model of Conseil Européen de Recherches Nucléaires, a plan which he embraced wholeheartedly. The successful conclusions of the negotiations, which stretched over more than a decade, owed much to Kendrew's perseverance and diplomatic skills. He was a founder member of the European Molecular Biology Organization; he served on its council (1963–71 and 1975–7) and as its secretary-general (1969–74). He was also secretary-general of the European Molecular Biology Conference, the intergovernmental organization for the support of molecular biology (1970–74). He headed the laboratory committee from its inception in 1969, became project leader in 1971, and in 1975 moved to Heidelberg as first director-general of the European Molecular Biology Laboratory. Kendrew's mediation was particularly decisive for the inclusion of Israel, which contributed with a generous gift to the launch of the plan.

On his retirement from Heidelberg in 1982 Kendrew became president of St John's College, Oxford, a post which he filled for five years with his usual dedication and effectiveness. In 1987 he returned to his residence at the Old Guildhall, Linton, near Cambridge.

Among the innumerable other offices he held Kendrew gave particular importance to his long association with the International Council of Scientific Unions, which he served as secretary-general (1974–80), vice-president (1982–3), president (1983–8), and past president (1988–90). He was also a member of the board of governors of the Weizmann Institute of Science (1963–97); a member of the BBC Science Consultative Group (1964–7); president of the International Union for Pure and Applied Biophysics (1969–72); president of the British Association for the Advancement of Science (1973–4); trustee of the British Museum (1974–9); trustee of the International Foundation for Science (1975–8); chairman of the natural sciences advisory board of the United Kingdom National Commission for UNESCO (1976–84); a member of the council, UN University (1980–86; chairman 1983–5); and chairman of the board of governors of the Joint Research Centre, EEC (1985–92). Among the later responsibilities he took on was the chief editorship of the *Encyclopedia of Molecular Biology*, published in 1994.

Kendrew was elected a fellow of the Royal Society in 1960, appointed CBE in 1963, and knighted in 1974. He was a member of numerous societies and academies, including the American Academy of Arts and Sciences (1964) and the Leopoldina (1965). He was a recipient of the royal medal of the Royal Society (1965) and held honorary degrees from several universities, including Cambridge (1997).

Kendrew was highly valued for his sharp intellect, effectiveness, calm judgement, and diplomatic skills, as well as for the breadth of his interests and his sense of humour. Despite being somewhat aloof and reserved he was supportive and encouraging, especially with younger colleagues. He cultivated a deep interest in Renaissance art and music. He was fluent in French, German, and Italian, and spent as much time abroad as at home. A convinced European and socialist, he believed that science could help social development and international relations.

Kendrew died of cancer at the Evelyn Hospital, Cambridge, on 23 August 1997, and was cremated. A large part of his estate formed a bequest to St John's College, Oxford, dedicated to supporting students from the developing world and to promoting music in the college. His papers were deposited at the Bodleian Library, Oxford. Both the 'sausage' and the 'forest of rods' models of myoglobin were given to the Science Museum, London.

SORAYA DE CHADAREVIAN

Sources Bodl. Oxf., MSS Kendrew · J. Alton, ed., Catalogue of the papers and correspondence of Sir John Cowdery Kendrew, 2 vols. (1989) · J. Kendrew, video interview, 18 June 1997, Medical Research Council, London, Laboratory of Molecular Biology Archive · The origins and development of operational research in the Royal Air Force, [Air Ministry] (1963) · J. C. Kendrew, 'Myoglobin and the structure of proteins': Nobel lecture, December 11, 1962', Nobel lectures including presentation speeches and laureates' biographies: chemistry, 1942–1962 (1964), 676–98 · L. K. James, ed., Nobel laureates in chemistry, 1901–1992, American Chemical Heritage Foundation (1993) · The Guardian (27 Aug 1997) · The Times (27 Aug 1997) · Daily Telegraph (3 Sept 1997) · The Independent (12 Sept 1997) · MRC News (autumn 1997) · K. C. Holmes, Memoirs FRS, 47 (2001), 311–32 · WWW · private information (2004) · m. cert.

Archives Bodl. Oxf., corresp. and papers · CUL, papers | CAC Cam., corresp. with A. V. Hill · CUL, corresp. with Peter Mitchell · Sci. Mus., 6 and 2 Ångström resolution models of myoglobin | FILM BFI NFTVA · Medical Research Council, London, Laboratory of Molecular Biology Archive, interview, 1997

Likenesses W. L. Bragg, pencil and chalk drawing, 1964, U. Cam. · R. Speer, oils, 1986, St John's College, Oxford · S. Fisher, charcoal drawing, 1990, Peterhouse, Cambridge · N. Sinclair, photograph, 1993, NPG [see illus.] · photograph, repro. in The Times · photograph, repro. in Daily Telegraph · photograph, repro. in The Guardian · photograph, repro. in The Independent · photographs, Peterhouse, Cambridge · photographs, Hult. Arch.

Wealth at death £1,318,265: probate, 9 Jan 1998, CGPLA Eng. & Wales

Kendrick, Emma Eleonora (1788–1871), miniature painter, was baptized on 22 February 1789 at St Mary Street, St Marylebone Road, Middlesex, the daughter of Joseph Kendrick (b. 1755), sculptor, and his wife, Jane. Her elder brother, Josephus Kendrick (1791–1832), was also a sculptor; in the *Dictionary of National Biography* his identity was confused with that of his father. Josephus Kendrick entered the Royal Academy Schools in 1808, where in 1813 he obtained a gold medal. He exhibited frequently at the Royal Academy and designed two monumental tablets in St Paul's Cathedral. He was described by Gunnis as 'a competent minor sculptor' (Gunnis, 226).

Emma Kendrick became very successful as a miniature painter in watercolour on ivory and obtained a large practice. She later noted that 'Mr. West, the late president of the Royal Academy, said to me when a beginner "Go on and prosper; you are in the right road"' (Kendrick, 111). In 1810–11 she was awarded by the Society of Artists a silver palette for a drawing after Giorgione; in 1812 a silver medal for a miniature copy, after Guercino; and in 1814 the Gold Isis medal for an original figurative miniature, *Religion*. This medal she was again awarded in 1816 for an original miniature of Dido, and in 1817 for an original historical miniature. She exhibited at the Royal Academy, from 1811 to 1840, a total of eighty-three miniatures, including *ad vivum* portraits and copies after works by Sir Joshua Reynolds and Van Dyck, and a similar number at the Society of British Artists in Suffolk Street. From 1815 to 1820 she also exhibited with the Society of Painters in Water Colours. Her portraits in miniature include a three-quarter-length portrait of Lady Caroline Lamb in a white dress and cashmere shawl, holding an open book (exh. RA, 1817; V&A), which is signed on the reverse and also there inscribed by the artist with her address, '6 Upper Marylebone Street / Fitzroy Square'. In keeping with the sitter's pensive expression this miniature is more softly and delicately painted than her hard-edged miniature of Mrs Vanhardt in masquerade dress, signed and dated 1828, also in the Victoria and Albert Museum. Basil Long noted that she 'varied her style a good deal' (Long, 249).

Following the débâcle of her affair of the previous year with the poet Lord Byron, in January 1814 Lady Caroline Lamb stole a miniature of Byron (priv. coll.), painted by George Sanders (c.1812), from the house of the publisher John Murray. Through the intervention of her aunt Lady Melbourne the miniature was eventually returned to Byron, but not before Lady Caroline succeeded in obtaining a secret copy of it, taken by Miss Kendrick, which Lady Caroline enclosed in a large gold locket inscribed with the words 'Ne Crede Byron'. This locket, which still contains the miniature of Byron painted by Miss Kendrick, is now in the Bodleian Library, Oxford. Her miniature of General Matvey Ivanovich Platov, one of the commanding officers of the Russian allies against Napoleon, was sold at Christies (18 December 1974, lot 70). Miss Kendrick painted miniatures of several British officers, including William Carr Beresford, Viscount Beresford, and Sir George Walker. Her portrait of Thomas Erskine, first Baron Erskine of Restormel, was exhibited at the Royal Academy in 1816. In her rectangular miniature of an unknown man (priv. coll., France), inscribed 'Emma Eleonora Kendrick / Pinxit 1825. / 4 Duchess Street / *Portland Place*', Long saw 'the influence of Sir Thomas Lawrence'; 'the features were softly but accurately modelled'; this miniature he considered 'distinctly good' (Long, 250). Many of her miniatures were engraved, including those of Lady Forester, Lady Kirkwall, and Lady Grantham. Miss Kendrick described herself in 1818 as miniature painter to Princess Elizabeth, Landgravine of Hesse-Homburg; in 1831 she was appointed miniature painter to William IV.

Miss Kendrick published in 1830 *Conversations on the Art of Miniature Painting*, in which she describes, in five conversations, her materials and technique. In her advice to Miss Forester, daughter of the duchess of Rutland, to whom she dedicated this work, she upholds the precepts of Sir Joshua Reynolds put forward in his *Discourses*. In particular his endorsement of the generally held belief that artists should study but not slavishly copy the old masters and that 'Nature is still a nobler resource' are two precepts on which Miss Kendrick's advice to her pupil are founded (Kendrick, 37). Hogarth's belief that 'a gentle, waving serpentine line is the line of beauty' also finds expression in her conversations (ibid., 11). In addition to this evidence of Miss Kendrick's theoretical knowledge of her art, however, her belief that 'art [is] poor when compared with the sublime grandeur of Nature' (ibid., 37) and that 'a soul or spirit should breathe through the whole, and it should be rather the expression than the mere lines of a face which you should try to represent' (ibid., 41) places her work (like that of some of her more notable subjects) securely within the context of nineteenth-century Romanticism rather than under the theoretical (or social) constraints imposed on, or by, eighteenth-century portraiture. Among the works that she exhibited at the Royal Academy in the 1820s and 1830s were several with titles indicating that they were based on the works of Byron or Scott. In 1839 the miniature painter James Holmes (who knew both Byron, of whom he painted several portraits, and Lady Caroline Lamb) exhibited at the Royal Academy a portrait of Miss Kendrick.

Miss Kendrick died at her home, 88 Albany Street, Regent's Park, London, where she had lived with her sister, Josephia Jane Mary Kendrick, on 6 April 1871, aged eighty-three.   ANNETTE PEACH

Sources E. Kendrick, *Conversations on the art of miniature painting* (1830) · A. Peach, '"San fedele alla mia Biondetta": a portrait of Lord Byron formerly belonging to Lady Caroline Lamb', *Bodleian Library Record*, 14 (1991–4), 285–95 · A. Peach, 'Portraits of Byron', *Walpole Society*, 62 (2000), 1–144 · *IGI* · artist's folder (MS and typed notes), V&A · B. S. Long, *British miniaturists* (1929) [Long's annotated copy, V&A print room] · C. H. Collins Baker, notes on artists, NPG, archive · *CGPLA Eng. & Wales* (1871) · Graves, *RA exhibitors* · G. Hall and others, *Summary catalogue of miniatures in the Victoria and Albert Museum* (1981) · R. Gunnis, *Dictionary of British sculptors, 1660–1851* (1953); new edn (1968) · R. Walker, *National Portrait Gallery: Regency portraits*, 2 vols. (1985) · R. Walker, *The eighteenth and early nineteenth century miniatures in the collection of her majesty the queen* (1991) · E. C. Clayton, *English female artists*, 2 vols. (1876)

Likenesses J. Holmes, miniature, exh. RA 1839

Wealth at death under £600: administration, 2 June 1871, *CGPLA Eng. & Wales*

Kendrick, James (1771–1847), botanist, was born on 14 January 1771 at Warrington, Lancashire, the town where

both his father and grandfather were born. He was educated at Burtonwood grammar school and at Warrington's free grammar school. On leaving school he was apprenticed to a Mr Hankinson, a local 'practitioner in surgery of some note in his day' (*GM*). He began practising medicine—as a surgeon—about 1793, and together with his friend Thomas Glazebrook Rylands was instrumental in establishing the Warrington Dispensary.

Although a career, medicine was not Kendrick's passion. In his leisure he studied botany and zoology, and was admitted a fellow of the Linnean Society in 1802. In 1811 he and a group of friends started the first literary and scientific institution in Warrington; Kendrick was made vice-president. He was also part of the 'small circle of nature lovers' who founded the Warrington Natural History Society on 23 November 1838. At the time of his death Kendrick was president of the society, which subsequently provided material to form the nucleus of the Warrington Museum and Library. Kendrick was one of the chief founding benefactors of the museum—others included William Beamont, William Robson, and John Fitchett Marsh.

Kendrick was president of the Botanical Society of Warrington, and contributed observations and notes to George Crosfield's *A Calendar of Flora, Composed during the Year 1809, at Warrington, Latitude 53° 30′* (1810). Kendrick was well acquainted with the philanthropist John Howard and gave much assistance to James Baldwin Brown in his *Memoirs of the Public and Private Life of John Howard* (1818)—in which Kendrick was described as 'the successor of Dr [John] Aikin'. The botanist Thomas Nuttall (1786–1859) named the *Rhododendron kendrickii* (imported into England in 1852 from Bhutan) after him. Kendrick's wish 'to die quietly at the close of a day's work' (*GM*) was fulfilled when he died on 30 November 1847, at Stanley Street, Warrington. He was buried on 6 December at St Elphin's Church, Warrington (with the simple inscription 'Kendrick' to mark his grave). He was married and is known to have been survived by two sons and several daughters.

Kendrick's eldest son, **James Kendrick** (1809–1882), local historian and topographer, was born on 7 November 1809, at the corner of Orford and Buttermarket streets, Warrington. He was educated at Mr Davenport's School (then located in Golborne Street), Warrington, and he also attended a school in Mersey Street, which was run by the Revd Topping, curate at the parish church.

Kendrick began his medical career with his father and served an apprenticeship at the Warrington Dispensary in Buttermarket Street. About 1828 he moved to Edinburgh where he graduated MD on 1 August 1833 with a thesis entitled *On the Dependence of Diabetes Mellitus on Disease of the Stomach and Intestines*. Soon after Kendrick returned to Warrington where he began to practise medicine from 1833; about 1850 he acted as physician to Mr Lyon's family, at Appleton Hall. On 21 July 1837 Kendrick married Isabella Anne (d. 23 July 1863), the only child of Robert Berry, a merchant formerly of Port Louis, Mauritius (afterwards consul for Sweden and Norway in China, where he resided at Macao), and his wife, Ann Mary; this marriage resulted in nine children, five of whom survived their father. The year after his first wife's death, on 19 October 1864, he married Martha (*d. c.*1873), third daughter of Thomas Green of Warrington and sister-in-law to Benjamin Pierpoint, of the same town; this marriage was childless. In 1874 he married his third wife, Catherine, daughter of William Burgess of Frodsham, and sister of Alderman John Burgess; their marriage was also childless.

Kendrick had a fondness for antiquities and frequently lectured on local topography and history. He issued a series of 'Contributions to the early history of Warrington' in the *Manchester Courier* (1839–40; 1851) and wrote many papers which appeared in the publications of the Historic Society of Lancashire and Cheshire, Chester Archaeological Society, the *Reliquary*, and the *Warrington Guardian*. In 1853 he became a member of the British Archaeological Association.

Kendrick wrote a number of other publications including: *An Account of Warrington Siege, anno 1643* (1852; 1856); *A Description of Two Ancient Chessmen, Discovered in the Mote Hill, Warrington* (1852); *Profiles of Warrington Worthies* (1853; 1854); *An Account of Excavations Made at the Mote Hill, Warrington* (1853); *Account of the Loyal Warrington Volunteers of 1798* (1854; 1856); *A Morning's Ramble in Old Warrington* (1855); and *The Warrington Blue Coat School Exposure, and its Beneficial Results* (1868).

In 1869 Kendrick wrote *On the Roman Station at Wilderspool, Near Warrington* (1870). He spent much time and money on the excavation of this site and on 15 August 1870 it was reported that Kendrick had presented an extensive collection of Roman artefacts found there to the Warrington Museum. In 1871 he released *On Recent Discoveries at the Roman Site at Wilderspool*, and a year later compiled *A Guide Book to the Roman Remains from Wilderspool*, which was presented to the museum. He was also co-author, with William Robson, of *Memorials of the Late Dr. Robson, of Warrington: his Life and Writings* (1876).

In 1859 Kendrick took charge of the antiquities in the Warrington Museum; he subsequently contributed many items to the collections, including an important series of impressions from German imperial seals. In 1878, he donated some 1000 books and pamphlets to the Warrington Free Library. Kendrick died on 6 April 1882 at his home, 27 Bold Street, Warrington. His remains were interred beside other members of his family in Padgate churchyard on 11 April 1882; present at his funeral were his third wife, two daughters, and two sons.

YOLANDA FOOTE

Sources *Warrington Advertiser* (8 April 1882) · *Warrington Advertiser* (15 April 1882) · *Manchester Guardian* (11 April 1882) [James Kendrick, 1809–1882] · *Journal of the British Archaeological Association*, 38 (1882), 337–8 · GM, 2nd ser., 29 (1848), 313–14 · *Annals and Magazine of Natural History*, 12, 10 · Desmond, *Botanists*, rev. edn · WWW · J. Kendrick, ed., *Profiles of Warrington worthies* (1853) · *Palatine Note-Book*, 2 (1882), 113–16 [James Kendrick, 1809–1882] · H. Wells, *Warrington parish church* (1997) · P. O'Brien, *Warrington Academy* (1989) · J. B. Brown, *Memoirs of the public and private life of John Howard, the philanthropist* (1818) · R. D. Radcliffe, *A memoir of Thomas Glazebrook Rylands* (1901) · *Warrington Guardian* (17 Dec 1898)
Archives Linn. Soc., notes and papers · Warrington Library, corresp. and papers

Likenesses R. J. Lane, lithograph, 1841, BM, NPG · J. Kendrick, silhouette, 1853, repro. in Kendrick, *Profiles* · Crozier, portrait, 1878?, Warrington Museum, Art Gallery · T. Robson, oils, Warrington Museum, Art Gallery; presented in 1877? · portrait (James Kendrick junior), repro. in *Palatine Note-Book*, 179–80
Wealth at death £1362 15s. 8d.—James Kendrick (1809–1882): probate, 30 May 1882, CGPLA Eng. & Wales

Kendrick, James (1809–1882). *See under* Kendrick, James (1771–1847).

Kendrick, John (*bap.* 1574, *d.* 1624), merchant and benefactor, was baptized at St Mary's Church, Reading, Berkshire, on 18 May 1574, the third of probably five children of Thomas Kendrick (*d.* 1588), mercer and mayor of Reading (1580–81), and his wife, Agnes, probably *née* Bye (*d.* 1603), daughter of a Reading clothier.

Kendrick's father appears to have turned to cloth manufacture following marriage, since in 1568 the privy council granted him dispensation to make cloth, although not apprenticed to the trade, because his wife, Agnes, 'had been brought up all her life to clothmaking' (*CPR, 1566–9*, 197). He was clearly prosperous: the family acquired a house and workshops in Minster Street, Reading, and assumed a coat of arms. John Kendrick, the eldest son, was educated probably at Reading Free School and at St John's College, Oxford, where he matriculated on 10 October 1589, aged fourteen. He was a contemporary of William Laud, also of Reading, who matriculated the same year. Kendrick did not take his degree, but returned to Reading to learn the trade of clothmaking, before moving to London about 1595 to serve an apprenticeship in one of the city's livery companies under John Quarles, master draper and merchant adventurer. His younger brother, William, succeeded to the family business and became a leading figure in the town, being elected mayor of Reading for 1630–31.

John Kendrick was admitted to the freedom of the Drapers' Company in 1603 and called to the livery in 1614. In partnership with George Lowe, Richard Bennet, Laurence Halstead, and others, he developed a substantial and profitable trade as a merchant adventurer, exporting dyed and dressed broadcloths to the Low Countries, where he had resident factors in Antwerp, Middleburg, and Delft. He maintained close links with Reading and the neighbouring clothing town of Newbury, whence he obtained a significant proportion of his cloths. By the early 1620s he had amassed a considerable fortune, emerging seemingly unscathed from the commercial dislocation caused by the Cockayne experiment of 1614–17, when Kendrick numbered among the sixty-three merchant adventurers prepared to join the newly formed and short-lived Company of King's Merchant Adventurers. Kendrick's business interests were not merely commercial. He also ran a cloth-finishing operation in London, where cloths were rowed, sheared, pressed, and folded prior to export.

John Kendrick never married. From 1605, possibly earlier, he lived in the parish of St Christopher-le-Stocks in the City of London. He maintained a close interest in both family and friends, providing support in times of hardship, employing at least one of his nephews as an apprentice, and remembering distant relatives in his will.

Thomas Fuller compares John Kendrick's achievement to the mustard seed 'very little at the beginning, but growing so great, that ... he therein made nests for many birds, which either inflamed or maimed, must have been exposed to wind and weather' (Fuller, *Worthies*, 32). The extent of Kendrick's personal fortune is unknown, but the value of bequests made in his will, signed the day before his death, exceeded £32,000. Some £19,000 was bequeathed to charitable purposes in London and Berkshire, with the remainder being carefully divided according to need and desert among family, friends, neighbours, associates, and employees. The residue of his estate was left to his 'loving friend and Partner', Laurence Halstead, described more harshly in 1627 by the earl of Banbury as 'so base a man' (Dormer, 12). Kendrick left substantial funds to relieve the poverty and hardship of the sick and vulnerable, but the bulk of his charitable bequests were designed to provide opportunities for employment and self-betterment for the poor, ranging from the funding of dowries for poor maids and apprenticeships for vagrant boys to the founding of workhouses and establishment of loan schemes for aspirant tradesmen and merchants. His most ambitious projects were reserved for Reading and Newbury, to which towns he left £7500 and £4000 respectively to erect 'fit and commodious' houses 'for setting the poor on worke ... with a common stock to be employed and bestowed in [the] trade of clothing', with further sums to provide interest free loans to clothiers and to finance other charitable works. The bequests were intended to preserve and revitalize cloth manufacture in Reading and Newbury, but the schemes proved too ambitious for the towns to handle and collapsed within a decade amid accusations of peculation and financial loss.

Kendrick appears to have been conventionally devout. He left several bequests to establish morning prayer charities and contributed cash sums towards repairs at his local parish church, St Paul's Cathedral, and St Mary's Church, Reading. The scale and scope of his charitable giving appears to reflect a generosity of spirit exhibited in his own lifetime, since numerous debts and favours are forgiven in his will.

John Kendrick died in the parish of St Christopher-le-Stocks on 30 December 1624 and was buried at the parish church, Threadneedle Street, on 14 January 1625. He was later reinterred at St Margaret's Church, Lothbury, where a plaque marks his beneficence to the poor of the area. William Kendrick's funerary monument in St Mary's Church, Reading, celebrates his brother's good works as well as his own. Two copies of a portrait commissioned after John Kendrick's death by the mayor and burgesses of Reading survive, and reveal a dignified but kindly gentleman, with auburn hair and beard, and affluent but modest clothing. Described as 'the phenix of worthy benefactors' (Crawford, 109), John Kendrick's will was published in 1625 to provide inspiration to future merchant donors.

CHRISTINE JACKSON

Sources will, 1624, Berks. RO • charity, 1625–50, Berks. RO, Kendrick accounts, R/2296 • E. W. Dormer, *John Kendrick of Reading and his benefactions* (1927) • C. Jackson, 'The Kendrick bequests: an experiment in municipal enterprise in the woollen industry in Reading and Newbury in the early seventeenth century', *Southern History*, 16 (1994), 44–66 • A. Friis, *Alderman Cockayne's project and the cloth trade: the commercial policy of England in its main aspects, 1603–1625*, trans. [A. Fausboll] (1927) • G. P. Crawford, ed., *Registers of the parish of St Mary's, 1538–1812*, 2 vols. (1891–2) • J. M. Guilding, ed., *Reading records: diary of the corporation*, 4 vols. (1892–6) • freedom list, 1567–1656, Drapers' Company Archives, F.A.1 • quarterage book, 1605–18, Drapers' Company Archives, QB1 • Foster, *Alum. Oxon.*, 1500–1714 • Fuller, *Worthies* • *CPR, 1566–9*, 197, no. 1132 • guild records, Berks. RO, R/HMC/LVI

Likenesses oils, 1626, Kendrick School, Reading; copy, Reading Borough Council Museum • glass panel, 19th cent., Reading Borough Council Art Gallery • aquatint, 1816, Reading Borough Council Art Gallery • engraving, 1816, Reading Borough Council Art Gallery

Wealth at death over £32,000—bequests: will, 1624, Berks. RO

Kendrick, Sir Thomas Downing (1895–1979), museum director, was born at Handsworth, Birmingham, on 1 April 1895, the eldest child of Thomas Henry Kendrick, a manufacturer of bedsteads, and his wife, Frances Susan Downing, of Stourton Hall, near Stourbridge. His father died in 1902 and his mother remarried in 1905; her husband was Prebendary Sewter.

Kendrick was educated at Charterhouse School and at Oriel College, Oxford. After one year at Oxford he joined the Warwickshire regiment in 1914 and became a captain. Sent to France, he was severely wounded in a hand and a leg. Thereafter he walked with a stiff knee, but rarely talked about his experiences at the Front. He returned to Oxford in 1918 to read chemistry, but turned to anthropology; he received a diploma with distinction in 1919, and graduated BA and proceeded MA in 1920.

Under the influence of R. R. Marett, Kendrick started work on a BSc on the megaliths of the Channel Islands, his research forming the basis of a later book—*The Archaeology of the Channel Isles* (vol. 1, 1928). The Channel Islands work contributed to his qualification for appointment in 1922 as assistant in British and medieval antiquities at the British Museum under the academically formidable keeper O. M. Dalton. Thereafter Kendrick's career lay in the museum: he became assistant keeper in 1928 and keeper in 1938. He was appointed director in 1950 and retired in 1959. He was created KCB in 1951.

Kendrick was a jovial figure, though subject to quick temper. In his later years in the museum he strode, limping, through its galleries, swinging his bunch of keys and joking with members of staff. In formal circumstances he was retiring (he refused to have an official portrait painted), but was a lively and racy correspondent, clubbable, and a hospitable host. Through his many foreign connections he was able to help a number of German refugees during the 1930s. He was a good keeper, bringing modern techniques of display and conservation to his department. Unfortunately he was a strong proponent of the cleaning of antiquities (a problem which bedevilled the 1930s) and as a result many bronze objects in his department were overcleaned. Perhaps his greatest excitement in this post came from his support of the excavations of the great seventh-century ship burial at Sutton Hoo, the rich finds from which he acquired by gift from Edith May Pretty in 1939. This find was central to his own academic interest and he was able quickly to edit two series of papers on it which were published in the first years of the Second World War. When the war was over, he put the find on exhibition in an exemplary fashion and quickly produced a popular, well-illustrated guide.

As director, Kendrick was an adequate and intuitive administrator, although he had not got the strength to carry the Treasury with him in the reconstruction of a much war-torn museum building, particularly at the time of economic cuts in the early 1950s. He was depressed by his seeming failure to influence government and, although quite at home in Whitehall, could not finish the fight and withdrew more and more into his own self. He was, however, a passionate defender of the academic integrity of the museum and of its collections, realizing that, through its universal quality, it was unique in the world and worth fighting for.

As a scholar, Kendrick first made a brief excursion into the Stone Age, which resulted in *The Axe Age* (1925) and in his book on the Channel Islands. This subject was moving very quickly, however, as Gordon Childe, O. G. S. Crawford, Grahame Clark, and Stuart Piggott changed the whole face of the subject in Britain. Kendrick apparently realized this and turned his mind to the viking and Anglo-Saxon periods, perhaps influenced by the appointment of a prehistorian, C. F. C. Hawkes, to the department and the foreseen need to replace the expertise of R. A. Smith in the early medieval field. Kendrick mastered the various sources, both archaeological and historical, and in *The Viking Age* (1930), *Anglo-Saxon Art* (1938), and *Late Saxon and Viking Art* (1950) he presented the history and material culture of early medieval northern Europe in a lively and innovative fashion. The two latter are his most important mainstream books and set a new framework for the study of the art of the British Isles in the period between the Romans and Normans. The last volume, much influenced by Francis Wormald, appeared as his interest in the period began to wane, but is a masterly and still useful survey of a most difficult period.

Kendrick was a major, though not a key, figure in British archaeology of the inter-war years, being one of the two secretaries of the International Congress of Pre- and Proto-historic Sciences in 1932; with his colleague Hawkes he wrote a summary of British archaeology for the congress, which was for many years a much referred to standard work. He was secretary of the Society of Antiquaries from 1940 to 1950 and was elected FBA in 1941.

Always slightly eccentric in his interests (he collected bus tickets, for example, which he mounted in a frame in the hall of his official residence), Kendrick was also innovative in taste; with John Piper, John Betjeman, and a number of friends he fought for the recognition and preservation of the then highly unpopular Victorian stained glass and won some notable battles. He had long been interested in the history of antiquarian thought, and

wrote books on *The Druids* (1927) and *British Antiquity* (1950)—the latter dedicated to Piper and Betjeman. He edited the seven volumes of *The County Archaeologies*. In his later years he published books on *The Lisbon Earthquake* (1956) and other Iberian subjects, as well as a semi-autobiographical novel, *Great Love for Icarus* (1962).

On 25 February 1922 Kendrick married Ellen Martha (Helen; 1898/9–1955), daughter of Louis Henrik Kiek, a merchant banker; she died in 1955 and he married on 14 October 1957 Katherine Elizabeth (1903/4–1980), daughter of Arthur Edward Wrigley. With his first wife he had a daughter, Frances, with whom he was not on good terms. He retired to a comfortable life at Poole, Dorset, and died at Dorchester on 2 November 1979.

DAVID M. WILSON

Sources *DNB* · *The Times* (23 Nov 1979) · R. L. S. Bruce-Mitford, 'Thomas Downing Kendrick, 1895–1979', *PBA*, 76 (1990), 445–71 · private information (2004) · m. certs. · *CGPLA Eng. & Wales* (1980)
Archives BM · S. Antiquaries, Lond., corresp. concerning Scripta Minoa | Bodl. Oxf., letters to O. G. S. Crawford · Lancs. RO, letters to T. H. Floyd
Likenesses D. Glass, photograph, c.1955, BM
Wealth at death £82,624: probate, 6 Feb 1980, *CGPLA Eng. & Wales*

Kenealy, Arabella Madonna (1859–1938), writer and physician, was born on 11 April 1859, at 8 Wellington Road, Portslade, Sussex, the second daughter of Edward Vaughan Kenealy, a barrister, and his wife, Elizabeth, the daughter of William Nicklin of Russell Hall, near Dudley. Educated at home, and at the London School of Medicine for Women, she practised as a doctor in London and Watford between 1888 and 1894 but was forced to retire following a severe attack of diphtheria. She did not marry, listing her recreations as walking, reading, and the study of race improvement. In later years Kenealy became increasingly interested in occultism, especially in the effect of the gyroscopic rotation of the earth on human evolution (Sutherland, 348), which she explored in *Gyroscope* (1934).

Kenealy wrote her first and most successful novel, *Dr Janet of Harley Street*, in 1893. In this work Dr Janet is the wise friend and lesbian lover of the young Phyllis Eve, who escapes sexual violation at the hands of the aged and degenerate marquess of Richeville two hours after marrying him. Adopted by the fifty-year-old Dr Janet, she trains as a doctor and expresses relief when, following an attempt to assert his conjugal rights, Richeville blows off his head in a fit of delirium tremens. Kenealy wrote several further novels and sociological treatises, including *A Semi-Detached Marriage* (1898) which recounts a story of adultery and bigamy, and a number of tracts opposing vivisection; she is best known for her sustained interrogation of female emancipation in *Feminism and Sex-Extinction* (1920).

Kenealy has recently begun to receive critical attention as part of the revival of interest in the 'new woman' of the 1890s. As a physician and novelist who engaged critically with relations between the sexes, she appears to have firm feminist credentials, but Kenealy occupied a contradictory relation to feminism by espousing what might appropriately be termed 'eugenic feminism'. Her interest in marriage and sex was motivated not by feminist concerns but by anxiety over the future of the British race. Like several other women writers and activists of the late nineteenth century, she believed that it was only through women—as 'race-regenerators'—that the race could be salvaged and improved. This agenda was predicated on the conservative ideology that women were innately—biologically—moral and unmotivated by sexual pleasure, while men were reckless pleasure-seekers. In 1891 in the *Westminster Review* she argued that if women were provided with professions and occupations, so that they could be economically independent, the marriage market and therefore the race would benefit. Marriage would not be the only occupation open to women, and thus those women who married would enjoy greater choice in sexual selection and thus prevent the degeneration of the race, 'for women generally are better judges than are men of a suitable life-partner' (Kenealy, 'A new view', 471).

The publisher and critic W. T. Stead, editor of the *Pall Mall Gazette*, noted with approval in *Review of Reviews* Kenealy's insistence that:

> it was a grave mistake, and a crime against the next generation, for women who hope some day to be mothers, to spend in study or labour the physical and nervous vitality which should be stored up as a kind of natural banking account to the credit of their children.

Every woman who used up her 'natural vitality in a profession or business, or in study, will bear feeble, rickety children, and is in fact spending her infant's inheritance on herself' (Stead, 67). An exponent of race motherhood, Kenealy was also a proponent of rational dress, stressing in *The Humanitarian* in 1896 that 'by the fetish of corsets women have deformed and atrophied those capabilities which would have made them efficient mothers of a fine-limbed race' (Kenealy, 'Dignity of love', 435). She believed that women should be able to qualify as doctors only in order to treat female patients; her views were underpinned by the separate-sphere ideology which pervaded Victorian culture and structured relations between the sexes.

Kenealy became increasingly concerned that feminism would lead to the extinction of the female sex: in *Feminism and Sex-Extinction* she wrote that 'nature made women ministrants of Love and Life, for the creation of an ever more healthful and efficient, a nobler and more joyous, Humanity. Feminism degrades them to the status of industrial mechanisms' (Kenealy, *Feminism*, 218). Kenealy died at 29 Devonshire Street, Marylebone, on 18 November 1938 of coronary thrombosis.

ANGELIQUE RICHARDSON

Sources WWW · A. Kenealy, 'A new view of the surplus of women', *Westminster Review*, 136 (1891), 465–75 · A. Kenealy, 'The dignity of love', *The Humanitarian*, 8 (1896), 435–9 · A. Kenealy, *Feminism and sex-extinction* (1920) · W. T. Stead, 'Book of the month: the novel of the modern woman', *Review of Reviews*, 10 (1894), 64–74 · J. Sutherland, *The Longman companion to Victorian fiction* (1988) · A. Richardson, *Love and eugenics in the late nineteenth century: rational reproduction and the new woman* (2003) · L. Pykett, *Engendering fictions: the English novel in the early twentieth century* (1995) · A. Kenealy, 'A study in degeneration', *Eugenics Review*, 3 (1911), 37–45 · b. cert. · d. cert. · CGPLA Eng. & Wales (1938)
Likenesses photograph, repro. in Stead, 'Book of the month'
Wealth at death £45,477 4s. 5d.: probate, 30 Dec 1938, CGPLA Eng. & Wales

Kenealy, Edward Vaughan Hyde (1819–1880), barrister and writer, was born on 2 July 1819 at Nile Street, Cork, the first of four children of William Kenealy, shopkeeper, and his wife, Catherine. His parents were Roman Catholics, but at university he abandoned the Catholic faith. After attending several private schools at Cork, he entered Trinity College, Dublin, on 6 July 1835. In 1840 he graduated BA, in 1846 LLB, and in 1850 LLD. He was called to the Irish bar in 1840, and joined the Munster circuit. He offered to contest the parliamentary representation of Trinity College, Dublin, on repeal principles in June 1847, of Kinsale in February 1848, and of Cork in late 1849, but received too little support to persevere. Meanwhile he became a student of Gray's Inn on 13 January 1838, and paid several visits to London before he was called to the English bar on 1 May 1847. In that year he settled in London, becoming a queen's counsel and a bencher of his inn in April 1868. He joined the Oxford circuit, and attended sessions at Shrewsbury and at the central criminal court. In 1848 he defended Francis Looney and William Dowling on charges of treason-felony, and was subsequently junior counsel for the defence of William Palmer, the Rugeley poisoner. In 1850 he was prosecuted by the guardians of the West London Union for punishing with undue severity Edward Hyde, his six-year-old illegitimate son. He was sentenced to a month's imprisonment. On 29 November 1851 he married Elizabeth, daughter of William Nicklin, a builder, of Tipton, Staffordshire; they had eleven children.

In December 1867 Kenealy defended the Fenians Burke and Casey, but after the Clerkenwell explosion he retired from the case; and in 1869 he led the prosecution of Overend, Gurney, and others for conspiracy to publish a fraudulent banking prospectus. In 1868 he unsuccessfully contested Wednesbury as an independent candidate. In April 1873 he succeeded William Campbell Sleigh as leading counsel for the *Tichborne claimant, whose case he conducted with violent partisanship, which has been sometimes attributed to ill health (he suffered from diabetes). He made groundless imputations against witnesses and various Roman Catholic institutions, treated the bench with contempt, and protracted the case into the longest trial at *nisi prius* on record. The jury appended to their verdict a censure of the language he had employed. He then started a scurrilous paper called *The Englishman*, which attained a large circulation, to plead the cause of the claimant.

Kenealy's conduct during and after the trial was brought before the professional tribunals, and he was expelled from the mess of the Oxford circuit on 2 April 1874, dispatented by the lord chancellor, and disbenched and disbarred by Gray's Inn on 17 August 1874. Intent on publicizing his own and his client's grievances, he founded the Magna Charta Association and toured the country, delivering lectures on the Tichborne trial. After receiving numerous invitations to contest Stoke, Kenealy was actually elected MP for that borough on 16 February 1875, by a majority of nearly 2000 votes. On 18 February he took his seat; contrary to custom, no members introduced him to the house, the ceremony being dispensed with on the motion of Disraeli. On 23 April Kenealy moved for a royal commission of inquiry into the conduct of the Tichborne case, but beyond his own and his co-teller's, he obtained only 1 vote; there were 433 against him. Kenealy cut no figure in parliament; he contested Stoke again at the general election of 1880, and came bottom of the poll. Meanwhile, however, under Kenealy's leadership, the Magna Charta Association became a leading popular radical organization demanding triennial parliaments, votes for women, the abolition of income tax, and duties on tea, coffee, and sugar. Kenealy inspired, among others, the socialist Henry Hyndman.

Kenealy was a great reader and a voluminous writer, of varied and considerable learning. His poems contain translations from Latin, Greek, German, Italian, Portuguese, Russian, Irish, Persian, Arabic, Hindustani, and Bengali, but he was probably not an accomplished scholar in all these tongues. His poems were published both in book form and in leading periodicals such as *Fraser's Magazine*. He carried the extravagance and unconventionality which had wrecked his legal career into his spiritual life, fabricating from ancient texts an extraordinary mystic religion of his own: he believed he was the twelfth messenger of God, part of a line that included Adam, Jesus Christ, and Ghengis Khan. Kenealy wrote a series of theological works starting with *The Book of God: the Apocalypse of Adam-Oannes* in 1866 in which he set out his religious views. A more conventional publication was his biography of *Edward Wortley Montagu* (1869); he was also the editor of a nine-volume edition of the Tichborne trial account.

Kenealy died on 16 April 1880 of heart failure and diabetes at his home, Stoke House, 6 Tavistock Square, London, and was buried on 22 April in the church at Hangleton, Portslade, Sussex. He was survived by his wife. The Magna Charta Association, led by Kenealy's son, Maurice, lasted for another six years. Although Kenealy enjoyed only limited success as a lawyer and littérateur, he became for a brief period one of the most dynamic political demagogues between the end of Chartism and the rise of socialism.   J. A. HAMILTON, *rev.* ROHAN McWILLIAM

Sources M. Roe, *Kenealy and the Tichborne case* (1974) · *Memoirs of Edward Vaughan Kenealy*, ed. A. Kenealy (1908) · R. McWilliam, 'The Tichborne claimant and the people', DPhil diss., U. Sussex, 1990
Archives Hunt. L., letters, literary MSS, and drawings | Bodl. Oxf., letters to Benjamin Disraeli
Likenesses double portrait, corbel, 1876 (with Disraeli), Chester Cathedral · London Stereoscopic Co., photograph, NPG · Spy [L. Ward], watercolour caricature, NPG; repro. in *VF* (1 Nov 1873) · double portrait, caricature chromolithograph (with Mr Hawkins), NPG · illustrations, repro. in E. V. Kenealy, ed., *The trial at the bar of Sir R. C. D. Tichborne* (1875–80) · photograph (aged twenty-six), repro. in *Memoirs of Edward Vaughan Kenealy* · photographs, repro. in Roe, *Kenealy and the Tichborne case* · portrait (aged two), repro. in *Memoirs of Edward Vaughan Kenealy* · wood-engraving (at the trial of the Tichborne claimant), NPG; repro. in *ILN* (23 Aug 1873)
Wealth at death under £3000: probate, 2 July 1880, *CGPLA Eng. & Wales*

Kenealy, William [*pseud.* William of Munster] (1828–1876), journalist, was born in Cloyne, co. Cork, the son of a blacksmith. He became a schoolmaster, but was dismissed for writing an 'inflammatory pamphlet'. He was rescued by Dr Maginn, the coadjutor-bishop of Derry, who made Kenealy a teacher in his diocesan college and then arranged for him to work on *The Lamp*, a Catholic penny journal published in York, which was founded in 1850 and devoted to literature, science, and general instruction. Kenealy returned to Clonmel, co. Tipperary, to edit the *Tipperary Leader*, but in 1855 he was prosecuted by a local protestant clergyman who alleged he had been libelled; Kenealy refused to name the journalist responsible for the article and was sent to gaol and sentenced to pay damages which he was unable to meet.

From gaol Kenealy successfully applied to be editor of the *Kilkenny Journal*, a long-established Liberal newspaper which proclaimed 'Ireland for the Irish' and was owned by Mary Anne Maxwell, the widow of Cornelius Maxwell, who had been a supporter of Daniel O'Connell. A number of men who later became Fenians were employed on the paper, including the foreman printer John Haltigan, who became the printer of the *Irish People*. The writer Charles J. Kickham was another applicant for the post of editor.

In 1858 Kenealy married Rose Maxwell, Mary Anne Maxwell's daughter, and on their marriage he received a half-share in the newspaper. He also had the option to purchase the other half on the decease of his mother-in-law, but in fact he predeceased her. He died in Kilkenny on 5 September 1876, aged forty-eight, and is buried in the churchyard of St Patrick's Church.

Kenealy was not a Fenian; one of his political aims was to achieve tenant-right through constitutional means. He was an accomplished speaker, and his advocacy for tenant-right spread his reputation far beyond Kilkenny. He wrote poetry for *The Nation*, using the pseudonym William of Munster, and he was said to have been the anonymous author of the introduction to Edward Hayes's *Ballads of Ireland* (1856). He was twice mayor of Kilkenny, in 1872 and 1873. After his death, Kickham wrote in the *Kilkenny Journal* on 9 September: 'Though our opinions on some questions were as wide as the poles asunder, I am happy to think that our friendship was never dimmed ... since I first long ago in early manhood made the acquaintance of "William of Munster".'   MARIE-LOUISE LEGG

Sources M. Kenealy, 'Finn's Leinster Journal', *Old Kilkenny Review*, new ser., 15 (1979) · *Kilkenny Journal* (6 Sept 1876) · C. J. Kickham, *Kilkenny Journal* (9 Sept 1876) · *Kilkenny Moderator* (9 Sept 1876) · Gillow, *Lit. biog. hist.* · D. J. O'Donoghue, *The poets of Ireland: a biographical and bibliographical dictionary* (1912); repr. (1970) · 'Court of Exchequer Wednesday "The Tipperary Leader" Henry George Spring v. Wm Kinneally', *Tipperary Free Press and Clonmel General Advertiser* (5 Feb 1856)

Kenilworth. For this title name *see* Siddeley, John Davenport, first Baron Kenilworth (1866–1953).

Keninghale, John (*d.* 1451), theologian, prior of Norwich, and diplomat, was born near Norwich and joined the Carmelite order there. He was ordained acolyte on 8 March 1407, and later studied at Oxford University, where he graduated DTh some time before 1425. As a young theologian, he was a confidant of Thomas Netter (*d.* 1430), on whose behalf he visited Rome several times, being described as 'nuncio to the Apostolic See'. In 1421 he conveyed to the prior-general the response of Netter to certain criticisms that had been made against him, and towards the end of 1425 he was in Rome again, presenting a copy of Netter's *Doctrinale fidei ecclesiae* to Pope Martin V, while in the following year he presented the second volume.

After Netter's death Keninghale was elected provincial in 1430 at Hitchin, and he held office until he resigned in 1444 because of his involvement in affairs of state. Present at the Council of Basel during 1432–4, Keninghale was a conspicuous opponent of the Wycliffite views of Peter Payne (*d.* 1455/1456?), and a sermon he preached to the council has survived (Mansi, 1237). In 1438–9 Keninghale and three other Carmelites were the only English representatives at the Council of Florence and it was while he was there that Keninghale (not Nicholas Kenton, who died in 1468, as in some accounts) visited the tomb of Sant'Andrea Corsini and was 'miraculously cured of a great pain in the head' (BL, Harley MS 3838, fol. 37*v*). In 1443 Keninghale and the French provincial were appointed commissaries by the prior-general to resolve dissensions in the Lower German province.

Keninghale, who was at one time confessor to Richard, duke of York (*d.* 1460), and his wife, Cecily (*d.* 1495), ended his days as prior of Norwich, where he built a library and room for himself. He died on 28 April 1451 and was buried at the priory. His writings included a collection of twelve sermons which were formerly in the Carmelite library at Oxford. In his *Scriptores*, John Bale adds works by Keninghale 'on his travels and legations' and on Aristotle, but these lack incipits. Keninghale is credited by late twentieth-century scholars with being the provincial who played a leading part in bringing together the *Fasciculi zizaniorum*, a Carmelite collection of anti-Wycliffite documents which is a major source of information for this period.   RICHARD COPSEY

Sources J. Bale, Bodl. Oxf., MS Bodley 73 (SC 27635), fols. i, 51*v*, 58, 81*v*, 94*v*(bis), 95, 97, 98, 101*v*, 103, 119*v*, 133*v*, 197 • J. Bale, Bodl. Oxf., MS Selden supra 41, fol. 178*v* • J. Bale, BL, Harley MS 3838, fols. 37–37*v*, 43*v*, 211*v*–212 • Bale, *Cat.*, 1.592–3 • Emden, *Oxf.*, 2.1035 • J. Haller, G. Beckmann, R. Wackernagel, G. Coggiola, and H. Hesse, eds., *Concilium Basiliense: Studien und Quellen zur Geschichte des Concils von Basel*, 8 vols. in 7 (Basel, 1896–1936), vols. 2–4 • J. Greatrex, 'Thomas Rudborne, monk of Winchester, and the Council of Florence', *Schism, heresy and religious protest*, ed. D. Baker, SCH, 9 (1972), 171–6 • B. Zimmerman, 'Alcune osservazioni sul *S. Andrea Corsini* del P. Paolo Caioli, Carm.', *Rivista Storica Carmelitana*, 2 (1930), 37–40 • *Acta sanctorum: Januarius*, 2 (Antwerp, 1643), 1072–3, 1077 • J. D. Mansi, *Sacrorum conciliorum nova, et amplissima collectio*, 30 (Florence, 1792), 1237 • M. Harvey, 'England, the Council of Florence and the end of the Council of Basle', *Christian unity and the Council of Ferrara-Florence, 1438/39–1989*, ed. G. Alberigo (1991), 203–25 • A. N. E. D. Schofield, 'England and the Council of Basel', *Annuarium Historiae Conciliorum*, 5 (1973), 1–117 • J. Bale, *Illustrium Maioris Britannie scriptorum … summarium* (1548), 251*v*–252 • *Commentarii de scriptoribus Britannicis, auctore Joanne Lelando*, ed. A. Hall, 2 (1709), 441–2, 456 • C. H. Lohr, 'Medieval Latin Aristotle commentaries', *Traditio*, 27 (1971), 252–351, esp. 252 • J. Pits, *Relationum historicarum de rebus Anglicis*, ed. [W. Bishop] (Paris, 1619), 646–7 • 'Thomae Rudborne historia major', *Anglia sacra*, ed. [H. Wharton], 1 (1691), 179–286, esp. 268–70 • Tanner, *Bibl. Brit.-Hib.*, 453–4 • C. de S. E. de Villiers, *Bibliotheca Carmelitana*, 2 vols. (Orléans, 1752); facs. edn, ed. P. G. Wessels (Rome, 1927), 20–21

Archives Balliol Oxf., MS 164, pp. 642bis–680; MS 165A, pp. 265–71 • Bibliothèque Municipale, Douai, MS 198 (3), fols. 178–85 • Stadtarchiv, Cologne, W236, fol. 220*r*–*v* • Stadtarchiv, Cologne, GB f° 123, fols. 5*v*–8 | Bodl. Oxf., MS e Museo 86 • PRO, chancery warrants series, 1 C81/1793/24

Keninghale, Peter (*d.* 1494), prior of Oxford and theologian, was born in France of a noble English family. He joined the Carmelites in Oxford, where he incepted as a DTh in 1479–80. He is recorded as being prior there in 1461 and again in 1481, and probably he remained in office until his death. In 1494 he received a bequest of 20*s.* from Master Robert Geffray, a former master of Beam Hall, Oxford, who died as archdeacon of Shropshire. Keninghale passed all his life lecturing in the Carmelite studium in Oxford and when he died, on 10 November 1494, he was buried in the chapel there. Bale ascribes to him a collection of fifty-seven sermons, with incipit, one of which he preached as part of his doctoral examination in 1479, and Leland adds a volume of *disputationes*.   RICHARD COPSEY

Sources J. Bale, Bodl. Oxf., MS Bodley 73 (SC 27635), fols. 135, 197 • J. Bale, BL, Harley MS 3838, fols. 108*v*–109, 220*v* • Bale, *Cat.*, 2.71 • Emden, *Oxf.*, 2.1036 • *Commentarii de scriptoribus Britannicis, auctore Joanne Lelando*, ed. A. Hall, 2 (1709), 456 • *Holinshed's chronicles of England, Scotland and Ireland*, ed. H. Ellis, 6 vols. (1807–8), 543 • J. Bale, *Illustrium Maioris Britannie scriptorum … summarium* (1548), 252 • J. Pits, *Relationum historicarum de rebus Anglicis*, ed. [W. Bishop] (Paris, 1619), 684 • Tanner, *Bibl. Brit.-Hib.*, 452

Kenleith [Keldeleth], **Robert** (*d.* 1273), chancellor of Scotland and abbot of Melrose, was a monk of the Benedictine abbey of Dunfermline and became its abbot in 1240. His name was probably derived from Kinleith in Currie (Midlothian). Wyntoun includes 'Robert of Kydeleth' among the 'mony famows gret persounys' present at the translation of the remains of St Margaret at Dunfermline Abbey in June 1250 (Wyntoun, 2.250–51). He was appointed chancellor of Scotland between 1247 and 1251, perhaps because of his influence at the papal curia, which had been sufficient for him to obtain the erection of Dunfermline into a mitred abbacy in 1245.

In the factional turmoil which characterized the minority of Alexander III, Kenleith took the side of Alan Durward, 'justiciary of the whole of Scotland' (*Chronica gentis Scottorum*, 2.289). On Christmas day 1251 Alexander III was knighted by Henry III in York and on the following day he married Margaret, the English king's daughter. The faction opposing Durward, headed by Walter Comyn, earl of Menteith, and William, earl of Mar, took advantage of the occasion to gain Henry III's assistance to oust the Durward party from power. They seem to have accused

Durward, with Kenleith and other supporters, of plotting to procure from the pope the legitimation of Durward's wife, Marjory, the illegitimate sister of Alexander III, apparently so that in the event of the king's death she might succeed to the crown. Kenleith was said to have used the great seal of Scotland to forward this design. On the coming into power of the Comyn faction Kenleith was removed from the chancellorship (1252), and the great seal was broken and a smaller one given to Gamelin, afterwards (1255) bishop of St Andrews.

Kenleith, apparently in dispute with his monks and out of favour with the king, resigned his abbacy in 1253 and retired into the Cistercian abbey of Newbattle as a simple monk. He did not return to power with his party in 1255, and may have gone into exile in England, since in 1260 he was acting as a messenger for Henry III. In 1268 he was chosen abbot of Melrose, on the retirement or deposition of John of Edrom, which office he held until his death in 1273. He probably died and was buried at Melrose Abbey.

JAMES TAIT, *rev.* NORMAN H. REID

Sources J. Stevenson, ed., *Chronica de Mailros*, Bannatyne Club, 50 (1835), 151, 178–9 · W. Bower, *Scotichronicon*, ed. D. E. R. Watt and others, new edn, 9 vols. (1987–98), vol. 5, pp. 171, 300–03, 399 · Andrew of Wyntoun, *The orygynale cronykil of Scotland*, [rev. edn], 2, ed. D. Laing (1872), 250–51 · C. Innes, ed., *Registrum de Dunfermelyn*, Bannatyne Club, 74 (1842), xi–xiii, no. 279 · *Johannis de Fordun Chronica gentis Scotorum / John of Fordun's Chronicle of the Scottish nation*, ed. W. F. Skene, trans. F. J. H. Skene, 2 vols. (1871–2), vol. 1, pp. 293, 296; vol. 2, pp. 289, 291–2 · J. Morton, *Monastic annals of Teviotdale* (1832), 226–7 · A. A. M. Duncan, *Scotland: the making of the kingdom* (1975), vol. 1 of *The Edinburgh history of Scotland*, ed. G. Donaldson (1965–75), 461, 559, 561–2 · M. Ash, 'The church in the reign of Alexander III', *Scotland in the reign of Alexander III, 1249–1286*, ed. N. H. Reid (1990), 31, 36–7, 38

Kenmure. For this title name *see* Gordon, John, first Viscount Kenmure (*c*.1599–1634); Gordon, Jane, Viscountess Kenmure (*d.* 1675); Gordon, William, sixth Viscount Kenmure and Jacobite marquess of Kenmure (*d.* 1716).

Kenmure [*née* Findlay], **Vera Mary Muir** (1904–1973), Congregational minister, was born on 13 February 1904 at 24 Burnbank Gardens, Glasgow, the only child of John Findlay, measurer, and his wife, Viola Craig. Vera Findlay was slim and elegant, with striking dark hair and eyes. She was educated at Hillhead high school, Glasgow (1916–22), where she was gold medallist (dux) in English, and at Glasgow University. She graduated with honours in classics in 1926. During her student years she began seriously to consider a vocation to ministry in the Congregational Union of Scotland. She was encouraged by the principal of the Scottish Congregational college, where she studied with distinction 1926–8. Even as a student she was recognized as an eloquent preacher, with a clear, compelling voice and lyrical delivery. She so impressed the deacons of Partick Congregational Church, Glasgow, that they called her to be their pastor before she had completed her bachelor of divinity course at Glasgow University. She was ordained and inducted in November 1928. In 1929 she applied for recognition as a minister of the Congregational Union of Scotland, giving rise to considerable debate within the wider Scottish ecclesiastical community about the ordination of women to the ministry of Word and Sacrament. One influential contributor to the discussion wrote: 'We are considering a phase of the long, slow progress of women in the course of civilisation. Our Church boasts its freedom. Let us use it to give full opportunity of survival to the woman ministry' (T. Templeton, *The Scottish Congregationalist*, March 1929). On 29 April 1929 the Congregational Union carried a constitutional amendment which allowed 'Minister' to apply equally to women and men. Vera Findlay was subsequently admitted to the union without opposition. She was thus the first woman ordained to a pastoral charge in the ministry of a mainstream Scottish denomination.

Vera Findlay's pastorate at Partick was innovative and fruitful, and her ministry was characterized throughout her career by an ability to communicate with, support, and befriend people of all ages, classes, and circumstances. Her preaching gifts and espousal of practical Christianity drew large crowds to the church. She married Colin Frame Kenmure, a chartered accountant, on 31 March 1933, and the event was regarded by most members of the congregation as an occasion for jubilation. However, there was controversy the following year, after Vera gave birth to her only child: a son, Alastair (born December 1933). A minority group within the congregation argued that the duties of motherhood were incompatible with those of ministry, and she received many unpleasant anonymous letters (Thomson, 8). On the day of her son's baptism Vera Kenmure announced that she would resign her charge, not because she agreed that she could not combine the roles of wife and mother with church ministry: 'On the contrary, I am convinced that my ministry, and indeed any ministry, will only be enriched and made more useful by the added experiences which these relationships bring.' Her sole reason for resigning was 'my strong feeling that the deep opposition and active hostility of a section of the congregation make honest cooperation impossible, and prevent me from continuing a successful ministry among them' (quoted in *John Bull*, 10 March 1934).

Once more, Vera Kenmure became the focus of national attention and press interest. Several congregations invited her to become their minister, but she established a new church, known as Christ Church Congregational, with a large number of former Partick members. In 1936 Hillhead, the mother church of the Congregational Union of Scotland, asked Mrs Kenmure to accept a call, and proposed that members of her congregation join Hillhead. A congregational meeting decided in favour of both proposals, and Christ Church was dissolved. Vera Kenmure was minister at Hillhead 1936–45. She took a break from pastoral service between 1945 and 1954, but continued to preach in pulpits around the country—including those of the Church of Scotland. She had a particular concern for theological education (as chair of the Scottish Congregational college management committee), and her wider activities included vice-chairmanship of the Glasgow Marriage Guidance Council. During 1951–2 she served as the first female president of the Congregational Union. She returned to the pastorate in 1954, becoming minister of Pollokshields Congregational Church, where she remained until her retirement in 1968. She was devoted to the three children of her son, a consultant cardiologist whose medical career was a source of great pride. She died of cancer on 27 December 1973 at the Royal Infirmary, Aberdeen, during a Christmas visit with his family there, after suffering a year of great pain, borne with fortitude. She was buried at Glasgow.

The length, quality, and diversity of her pioneering ministry (conducted under continuing public interest and scrutiny) and the fact that she exercised her vocation as the first ordained Scotswoman, while fully committed to family life, invested Vera Kenmure with a historical significance well beyond the limited sphere of her own small denomination.   LESLEY ORR MACDONALD

Sources private information (2004) · K. McCarra and H. Whyte, eds., *A Glasgow collection: essays in honour of Joe Fisher* (1990) · J. D. P. Thomson, ed., *Women ministers in Scotland: personal records of experience and discovery* (1963), 8–9 · H. Escott, *A history of Scottish Congregationalism* (1960) · *Scottish Congregational Yearbook* (1974–6), 71–3 · b. cert. · m. cert. · d. cert.
Likenesses photograph, repro. in *Congregational Yearbook* (1951) · photographs, priv. coll.

Kennard, Sir Howard William (1878–1955), diplomatist, was born in Hove, Sussex, on 22 March 1878, the younger son in a family of two sons and two daughters of Arthur Challis Kennard (b. 1831), landowner, of 17 Eaton Place, London, and his wife, Ann Homan, daughter of Thomas Homan Mulock, of Bellair, King's county, Ireland. He was educated at Eton College, from 1891 to 1896, and entered the diplomatic service in August 1901. In April 1902 he was appointed attaché and in August 1903 third secretary at the British embassy in Rome. He was transferred to Tehran in December 1904 and by July 1905 had already been granted an allowance for knowledge of Persian. He returned to the Foreign Office in May 1907, but was moved to Washington, with the rank of second secretary, in October. There he met and, in 1908, married Harriet (d. 1950), daughter of Jonathan Norris, of New York. They had one son. After a short period in charge of the British legation in Havana in 1911, Kennard was moved in August the same year to Tangier, then an important post in view of the rivalry between Germany and the entente powers for control of north Africa and its Atlantic ports. He passed an examination in Arabic a year later. In July 1914 he was promoted first secretary. From July 1916 until June 1919 he worked in the Foreign Office in London; he then went back as counsellor to Rome. He was appointed CMG in January 1923 and CVO in May 1923.

In May 1925 Kennard was moved for the first time to eastern Europe, when he was appointed envoy-extraordinary and minister-plenipotentiary in Belgrade. In the years following the settlements that ended the First World War, the role of British representatives tended to be confined to informing their government of the complex rivalries in the region. The apparent lack of British influence and interest in the region gave local British representatives scope for personal initiatives to keep all doors open. Kennard was appointed KCMG in March 1929 and in September the same year he was made minister in Stockholm, transferring to Bern in April 1931.

In January 1935 Kennard was appointed ambassador in Warsaw. Once more his role was to maintain British influence without making commitments. Poland was considered to be a French sphere of interest. It was this appointment that gave Kennard his permanent position in the history of the origins of the Second World War. When Kennard presented his letters of credence on 14 January 1935 he and the Foreign Office assumed that his task was to prevent the Poles undermining European stability by getting involved in unnecessary conflicts with the Soviet Union, Lithuania, but most importantly with Germany. The signing of the Polish–German agreement in 1934 forecast a new era of co-operation between the hitherto estranged signatories. Nevertheless the issue of the Polish Corridor and continuing rivalry over the city of Danzig contradicted these optimistic hopes. Kennard was to sustain Britain's moderating influence in Poland. This he did with consistency and tenacity. If at times he seemed to fail, the fault did not lie with him.

Kennard's influence in the Foreign Office, and with the cabinet foreign policy committee and the prime minister, Neville Chamberlain, was insignificant. Britain's commitment to the appeasement of Germany left little scope for Kennard's finer arguments, which suggested that Poland was merely seeking security for her borders. His cautionary and invariably well-informed reports were marginalized because departmental heads within the Foreign Office, as well as the prime minister, preferred to take their cue from Nevile Henderson, the British ambassador in Berlin. It was difficult for Kennard to put forward to the cabinet a Polish point of view on conflicts within eastern Europe. Kennard's communications circulated within the Foreign Office, while Henderson communicated directly with Chamberlain. The result was that cabinet discussions took as their starting point Germany's territorial demands in the east and Germany's rationale for them.

Kennard's lowest point came in the wake of the Munich crisis, when Polish troops occupied Czechoslovak territory and seized the district of Teschen (Cieszyn). The rejection by Poland's foreign minister, Colonel Josef Beck, of Kennard's request for moderation, was reported in the newspapers. Undeterred by this calculated slight, Kennard prevailed upon the Foreign Office not to write off Poland. Within Polish ruling circles he detected signs of anxiety, and in the months that followed he sought to reassure Poland's military rulers of Britain's goodwill. By 21 March 1939 the British government had come to the point of discussing the desirability of creating an eastern front against Germany. Poland became the key element in that proposal. Kennard worked hard to give this initially vague idea real substance.

In the course of the negotiations which followed, the Poles had their own ideas, and frequently were their own worst enemies. By May 1939 all decisions on the issue of an eastern front were postponed pending a decision on whether to seek Soviet support. The signing on 25 August of a Polish–British agreement of mutual assistance was largely due to Kennard's persistent efforts. In the face of British Treasury opposition he also succeeded in securing loans for the Poles.

It could be argued that the British commitment to Poland was of little military consequence at the time of the outbreak of the war. It nevertheless formed the basis of future agreements between the British government and the Polish government in exile which emerged in Paris on 26 September 1939. With the same degree of pragmatism displayed throughout his sojourn in Poland, on 25 September Kennard advised the Foreign Office to recognize that government and to proceed to make full use of the Poles' willingness to continue fighting in the west.

Notwithstanding Britain's failure to support the Poles, they respected Kennard, appreciated his efforts, and came to see him as a champion of their cause. The fact that Kennard recognized the importance of presenting British policies separately from French intrigues in the Polish capital allowed him a larger degree of influence over Colonel Beck than was warranted by the lack of British support for Poland.

Kennard left Warsaw on 5 September 1939 to accompany the Polish government when it withdrew from Warsaw. Accompanied by his wife, he followed the government to Romania, where it was interned. His report to the Foreign Office filed from Bucharest gave a firsthand account of indiscriminate German bombing of civilian targets. The Foreign Office first blanched at the political implications of such a shocking report, but finally released its contents to the press.

On 15 October Kennard joined the newly formed Polish government in exile led by General Władysław Sikorski in France. He returned to London in June 1940 and retired in 1941. He had been advanced to GCMG in June 1938, and was sworn of the privy council on his retirement. He settled in Bath, where he died at his home, 20 The Circus, on 12 November 1955.

All papers relating to Kennard's sojourn in Warsaw were either destroyed or lost during the evacuation. All remaining personal papers were destroyed by him during the war in anticipation of a German invasion.

ANITA J. PRAZMOWSKA

Sources PRO, FO 371, 1935–40 · *Diariusz i teki Jana Szembeka*, ed. J. Komarnicki, 1 (1964) · P. Starzeński, *Trzy lata z Beckiem* (1991) · *DNB* · A. Prazmowska, *Britain and Poland, 1939–1943: the betrayed ally* (1995) · *The Times* (14 Nov 1955) · *CGPLA Eng. & Wales* (1956) · *The Eton register*, 8 vols. (privately printed, Eton, 1903–32) · Burke, *Gen. GB*
Likenesses W. Stoneman, photograph, 1933, NPG
Wealth at death £57,191 10s. 1d.: probate, 29 Feb 1956, *CGPLA Eng. & Wales*

Kennaway, Sir Ernest Laurence (1881–1958), pathologist, was born at 16 Velwell Villas, Exeter, on 23 May 1881, the youngest of five children of Laurence James Kennaway, a colonial farmer, and his wife, Mary Louisa Galton. His grandfather, who was twice mayor of Exeter, had been

Sir Ernest Laurence Kennaway (1881–1958), by Walter Stoneman, 1947

prominent in combating the local cholera epidemic of 1832. Kennaway became interested in natural history as a boy when, owing to a childhood illness, he was advised to partake of an open-air life. He received his scientific training at University College, London, and from 1898 at New College, Oxford, with an open scholarship in natural sciences. In 1903 he graduated BA with a first class in the final honours school in physiology. After three years at the Middlesex Hospital, London (at which he held a university scholarship), he qualified MB BCh in 1907. He subsequently worked for short periods at the Lister Institute and University College, London; in 1908 he was a demonstrator in physiology at St Thomas's Hospital. Kennaway was in 1909 a Hulme student at Brasenose College, Oxford, and in 1910 he became a Radcliffe travelling fellow of that university, at Heidelberg and Munich. He passed the DM (Oxford) in 1911, and DSc (London) in physiological chemistry in 1915. On 24 July 1920 he married Nina Marion (1882/3–1969), daughter of William Derry, a bank manager of Edgbaston; there were no children.

Kennaway's career as an experimental and chemical pathologist began at Guy's Hospital, London, where from 1909 to 1914 he was a demonstrator in physiology, and at the Bland-Sutton Institute of Middlesex Hospital where from 1914 to 1921 he was in charge of the department of chemical pathology. In 1921 he joined the research institute of the Cancer Hospital, and in 1931 on the death of Professor Archibald Leitch he became director and professor of chemical pathology in the University of London. On retirement in 1946 he continued his research in the pathological laboratory at St Bartholomew's Hospital—as professor emeritus—in a modest attic laboratory.

Kennaway and his collaborators conducted research into purine metabolism and acetonuria. At the Cancer Hospital he embarked on investigating the malignancy-producing properties of coal tar. In 1915 epitheliomas had been produced in the rabbit ear by long-term applications of this substance, and in 1918 it was shown that mice were peculiarly susceptible to this transformation. In 1921 Kennaway confirmed some observations made at Zürich that the carcinogen in coal tar was probably a cyclic hydrocarbon. Working on the observation that carcinogenic tars are brilliantly fluorescent when exposed to ultraviolet light, in 1927 William Valentine Mayneord (in Kennaway's department) was able to recognize the characteristic three-banded features of the fluorescence spectrum. Israel Hieger then noted this spectrum in 1:2-benzanthracene, and in 1929 Kennaway himself demonstrated cancer-producing activity in the related 1:2:5:6-dibenzanthracene, the first pure compound to manifest pronounced carcinogenic activity. This discovery was to change the face of cancer research. Kennaway and his associates soon demonstrated that the carcinogen in pitch was 3:4-benzpyrene; this team also discovered a range of polycyclic aromatic carcinogenic hydrocarbons of which methylcholanthrene was among the most potent. Six papers relating to these discoveries were published in the *Proceedings of the Royal Society* between 1932 and 1942. Kennaway was also a pioneer in the epidemiology and statistics of malignant disease—especially its relationship with ethnicity and occupation—in particular that involving the lung, larynx, and pharynx. Many of these discoveries, carried out jointly with his wife, were undertaken concurrently with his more widely renowned laboratory-based researches. The Kennaways' 1936 publication was one of the first to focus attention on the rising incidence of lung cancer, especially in men.

For more than thirty years Kennaway suffered from advancing Parkinson's disease (about which he wrote anonymously in *The Lancet* for February 1949), but this did not abort his quest for further scientific knowledge. He also suffered a serious traffic accident in his sixty-fifth year. A profound agnostic, in his latter years he wrote *Some Religious Illusions in Art, Literature and Experience* (1953). He was fond of the music of J. S. Bach, and had many other recreational interests: natural history and the history of medicine, social customs, swimming, and the theatre.

Kennaway's numerous honours included the William Julius Mickle fellowship of London University (1922), fellowship and the Baly medal (1937) of the Royal College of Physicians, the Anna Fuller prize (jointly, 1939), honorary fellowship of New College, Oxford (1942), the Walker prize of the Royal College of Surgeons (1946), the Garton medal of the British Empire Cancer Campaign (1946), honorary membership of the American Association for Cancer Research (1947), honorary fellowship of the New York Academy of Medicine (1954), honorary fellowship of the

Royal Society of Medicine (1952), honorary foreign membership of the Académie Royale de Médecine de Belgique (1954), and the Osler memorial medal of Oxford (1950). Kennaway was elected a fellow of the Royal Society in 1934 and awarded the royal medal in 1941; he was knighted in 1947. He died in London at St Bartholomew's Hospital on 1 January 1958.   ALEXANDER HADDOW, *rev.* G. C. COOK

Sources J. W. Cook, *Memoirs FRS*, 4 (1958), 139–54 · R. E. Waller, '60 years of chemical carcinogens: Sir Ernest Kennaway in retirement', *Journal of the Royal Society of Medicine*, 87 (1994), 96–7 · J. P. Griffin, 'Famous names in toxicology', *Adverse Drug Reactions and Toxicological Reviews*, 13/4 (1994), 175–6 · *The Lancet* (11 Jan 1958), 109 · *BMJ* (11 Jan 1958), 104–6; (15 Feb 1958), 405 · *The Times* (2 Jan 1958), 11a · *The Times* (9 Jan 1958), 14f · *The Times* (13 Jan 1958), 12f · *Munk, Roll* · C. M. Badger, 'Ernest Laurence Kennaway', *Journal of Pathology and Bacteriology*, 78 (1959), 593–606 · A. Haddow, 'Sir Ernest Kennaway', *Nature*, 181 (1958), 309–10 · *CGPLA Eng. & Wales* (1958) · b. cert. · m. cert. · d. cert. · E. Kennaway, 'The identification of a carcinogenic compound in coal-tar', *BMJ* (24 Sept 1955), 749–52
Archives Wellcome L., notebooks
Likenesses W. Stoneman, photograph, 1947, NPG [*see illus.*]
Wealth at death £15,013 5*s*. 7*d*.: probate, 15 April 1958, *CGPLA Eng. & Wales*

Kennaway, James Peebles Ewing (1928–1968), novelist and scriptwriter, was born on 5 June 1928 at Kenwood Park, Auchterarder, Perthshire, the younger of two children of Charles Gray Kennaway (1894–1941) and Marjory, daughter of G. T. Ewing of Pitkellony, Muthill. Both parents were of Perthshire stock. His father was a wealthy lawyer who also acted as factor to several Perthshire sporting estates, while his mother had trained as a medical practitioner. Kennaway was educated at Cargilfield School in Edinburgh (1937–42) and at Trinity College, Glenalmond, Perthshire (1942–6), but the even tenor of his childhood was destroyed by his father's sudden death from tuberculosis of the kidney in January 1941.

The death had a profound effect on the young Kennaway: he claimed that it gave him an early sense of mortality and awakened a need to experience life to the full. As he wrote to his mother in a letter in 1956, having seen his father die young he did not want to suffer the same fate. 'Just now I want to blaze, in every direction, right or wrong, just so I shan't sink with too much left undone, too much never tried, too many sensations missed.'

After leaving school in 1946 Kennaway was called up for national service and was commissioned in the Queen's Own Cameron Highlanders, serving with the 1st Gordon Highlanders in Germany. In 1948 he entered Trinity College, Oxford, to read philosophy, politics, and economics and on graduating in 1951 became a publisher with Longmans, Green. On 6 October 1951 at St Mary Magdalen, Oxford, he married Mary St Joan Howard Edmonds (b. 1930), known as Susan, daughter of Bertram Eric Edmonds of Fairford, Gloucestershire, publisher. They set up home in north London and had four children: Emma (b. 1953), Jane (b. 1955), Guy (b. 1957), and David (b. 1959).

While working as a publisher Kennaway had started writing fiction and had achieved modest success with 'The Dollar Bottom', which was published in the January 1954 issue of *Lilliput*. Suitably encouraged, he completed his first novel, *Tunes of Glory* (1956), which centres on the rivalry between two men from different backgrounds for the command of a highland infantry battalion. It was well received by the critics: writing in the *Daily Mail* Peter Quennell forecast that Kennaway would 'take his place amongst the finest storytellers of the day'. In 1957 he was elected a fellow of the Royal Society of Literature.

The novel's success brought financial as well as critical rewards and in April 1957 Kennaway turned down the opportunity to become manager of the Longmans, Green office in Hong Kong. Instead he decided to concentrate on writing and in 1961 published his second novel, *Household Ghosts*. Set within the claustrophobic confines of an aristocratic Scottish family, it reveals the childhood fantasies and frustrated passions which lie behind an intense relationship between a brother and his sister, and her attempt to find with a lover the sexual satisfaction denied to her by her husband. During the same period Kennaway had begun a second career as a film scriptwriter and his first scripts included *Violent Playground* (1958) and *Tunes of Glory* (1960).

Although Kennaway still considered himself to be primarily a novelist, scriptwriting provided more substantial financial rewards. His script for *Tunes of Glory* proved that he could write commercially successful films, and in 1961 he was invited to work in Hollywood. The experience unnerved him in that it prevented him from concentrating on his novels. Also, away from his wife, he engaged in a number of casual affairs, claiming that an active sex life was the regenerative source of his literary ability. Later, in a diary entry, he characterized the split between the reliable family man and the philanderer as 'James et Jim, man and artist, wild boy and introvert'.

In 1961 and 1962 the Kennaways travelled widely, living at different periods in California, Majorca, and Kashmir. On their return to London, Kennaway completed *The Bells of Shoreditch* (1963), a novel about marital infidelity and scandal in the financial world. The following year his marriage was again shaken when Susan Kennaway began a sexual relationship with David Cornwell (the novelist John Le Carré). The two men were friends and literary rivals. The discovery of the affair led to a period of intense anxiety on Kennaway's part. Throughout the experience, which came to an emotionally violent climax in January 1965 during a skiing holiday at Zell-am-See in Switzerland, Kennaway kept a detailed diary and notes. These were later edited and published by Susan Kennaway in *The Kennaway Papers* (1981). From them it is possible to see the extent to which Kennaway was prepared to dramatize his own life in order to provide material for his fiction. His third novel, *Some Gorgeous Accident* (1967), concerns a triangular relationship and many of its scenes are echoes of the relationship between himself, his wife, and Le Carré.

Following a period of separation, the marriage survived and in 1966 the Kennaways returned to live in Britain at the Manor House, Fairford, Gloucestershire. His other novels are *The Mindbenders* (1963), *The Cost of Living Like This* (1969), and *Silence* (1972). He also continued to write for the cinema, including the script for *The Battle of Britain* (1969) and *Country Dance* (1970), based on his novel *Household Ghosts*.

Kennaway was killed in a motoring accident on 21 December 1968 while returning from London to Fairford. He was subsequently found to have suffered a heart attack at the time of the accident. He was buried in the churchyard of St Mary's, Fairford, Gloucestershire.

TREVOR ROYLE

Sources T. Royle, *James and Jim: a biography of James Kennaway* (1983) · J. Kennaway and S. Kennaway, *The Kennaway papers* (1981) · D. McAra, 'James Kennaway', *London Magazine, a Monthly Review of Literature*, new ser., 17/8 (1978), 37–55 · A. Massie, 'The artful art of James Kennaway', *New Edinburgh Review*, 52 (1980), 13–16 · G. Smith, 'James Kennaway's legacy', *Sunday Times Magazine* (4 Oct 1970) · A. Bold, 'Kennaway and character', *Modern Scottish literature* (1983), 249–50 · m. cert. · b. cert. [Susan Kennaway]
Archives NL Scot., corresp., diary, notebooks, and papers | U. Reading L., letters to the Bodley Head Ltd
Wealth at death £38,384: probate, 10 July 1969, *CGPLA Eng. & Wales*

Kennaway, Sir John, first baronet (1758–1836), army officer in the East India Company and diplomatist, was born on 6 March 1758 in Exeter, the third of six children of William Kennaway (1717–1793), woollen merchant, and his wife, Frances (1722–1788), the daughter of Aaron Tozer. In 1772, after leaving Exeter grammar school, Kennaway obtained the patronage of a near relation of his mother, Robert Palk, former governor of Madras. Having entered the service of the East India Company as a military cadet, Kennaway sailed for India before his fourteenth birthday. On the approach to Calcutta he was shipwrecked and lost all his possessions. His early years in India were marred by ill health and slow career advancement. Only at the insistence of a family friend at Madras did Kennaway stay in India. Of scholarly inclinations, he learned Persian and wrote commentaries on late Roman poetry. A devout Anglican, he also compiled prayers, a habit he followed through the better part of his life. In a letter to his eldest brother, William, on 17 March 1780 Kennaway wrote: 'I am ambitious of acting upon a large scale' and expressed a 'hope to spend the summer of my life in affluence with my friends' (Devon RO, M961 Add. S/F39).

In 1781 opportunity to 'act upon a large scale' presented itself when Kennaway's brigade marched 1700 kilometres from Bengal to the Carnatic to serve in the Second Anglo-Mysore War. He saw action at Cuddalore and made captain's rank in 1783, and his linguistic skills were recognized when he became the brigade's Persian translator. With peace restored in 1784, he briefly returned to Bengal before being sent in 1785 to the Oudh residency as translator. His knowledge of Persian and Indian courtly etiquette was further acknowledged a year later when he was appointed to attend Haidar Beg Khan, Oudh's chief minister, on an embassy from Lucknow to Calcutta to meet the governor-general, Cornwallis, who, impressed with Kennaway, made him his aide-de-camp.

Cornwallis continued to promote Kennaway. In April 1788 he was appointed temporary resident to the court of the nizam of Hyderabad, a lucrative but delicate post charged with obtaining the peaceful cession of the Guntur

Circar. The nizam had, in 1768, promised to cede the area—a strategic coastal region between Bengal and Madras—to the company upon the death of his brother in return for military assistance and annual cash payments. When the nizam's brother died in 1782 and neither party enforced the lapsed treaty, in 1786 the London authorities ordered Cornwallis to acquire Guntur Circar in return for annual rent. Kennaway fulfilled his task, and in September 1788 British forces occupied the area. In 1789 Kennaway's recall from Hyderabad was pre-empted when Tipu Sultan of Mysore attacked Travancore, a company ally, and Kennaway was instructed to negotiate the nizam's participation in a coalition.

By the treaty of Pangal, Kennaway obtained the nizam's co-operation and was awarded a baronetcy on 25 February 1791. In 1792, with the allies encamped before the walls of Mysore's capital, Cornwallis bid him to negotiate peace. By the treaty of Seringapatam, Mysore ceded half its territory to the allies, more than 3 crores of rupees (approximately £3 million) and Tipu Sultan gave two of his sons as hostages against Mysore's default. Kennaway, who enjoyed conducting affairs in Persian, ascribed his success as a diplomat, in a letter to Colonel Harper of 3 May 1787, to an ability to maintain 'an appearance of indifference and total unconcern' (Devon RO, M961 F/2, fol. 114). After negotiating before Seringapatam, Kennaway fell ill and took a leave of absence from his duties as resident. Balding, grey, and commonly thought to be a decade older than he was, Kennaway knew his career was taking a physical toll. None the less his lingering idea of returning to England became a conviction only after learning of his father's death, and in 1794 he left India.

A thrifty man who regularly remitted funds to England, Kennaway fulfilled his youthful hope and lived out his life in congenial affluence. He purchased Escot House, at Ottery St Mary, near Exeter, for £26,000 and became a respected member of the Devon gentry. In 1797 he married Charlotte (1768–1845), daughter of Charles Amyatt, nabob and MP. The couple had seven sons and five daughters, of whom nine survived childhood. Besides being colonel of the local militia for twenty-five years, Kennaway was an avid hunter. He also supported parochial charities, including the Devon and Exeter Society for promoting Christianity among the Jews. By 1826 his eyesight was going. Despite his affliction the blind old baronet kept his morning habit of donning a military greatcoat and riding about his estate. On 26 December 1835 he suffered a paralysing stroke. He died early on new year's day 1836, and was succeeded in his baronetcy by his eldest son, John.

BRENDAN CARNDUFF

Sources Devon RO, Kennaway MS M961 · PRO, Cornwallis MSS, 30/11 · J. Sarkar, ed., *English records of Maratha history: Poona residency correspondence*, 3: *The allies' war with Tipu Sultan, 1790–1793*, ed. N. B. Roy (1937) · J. Kennaway, 'Narrative of the negotiation with Tippoo', BL OIOC, Mack. Gen. 61 · BL OIOC, Malet MSS, MS Eur. F 149 · BL OIOC, Munro MSS, MS Eur. F 151 · BL OIOC, Kennaway MSS, MS Eur. C 156 · J. Philippart, *East India military calendar*, 1 (1823) · *GM*, 2nd ser., 5 (1836), 313 · R. Newton, *Eighteenth-century Exeter* (1984) · *The report of the commissioners concerning charities containing that part which relates to the county of Devon* (1826) · B. Freeman, *The yeomanry of Devon, 1794–1927* (1927)

Archives BL OIOC, Kennaway MSS, journal, MS Eur. C 156 · Devon RO, corresp. and papers · RA, letters and papers | BL OIOC, Malet MSS, MS Eur. F 149 · Devon RO, letters to Sir Thomas Dyke Acland

Likenesses portrait, repro. in *Allies' war with Tipu Sultan*, frontispiece · portrait, repro. in Freeman, *Yeomanry of Devon*, 63

Kennaway, Sir John Henry, third baronet (1837–1919), politician, was born at Park Crescent, London, on 6 June 1837, eldest son and heir of Sir John Kennaway, second baronet (1797–1873), and his wife, Emily Frances (d. 1858), second daughter of Thomas Kingscote. He was educated at Harrow School and Balliol College, Oxford, where he took first-class honours in the law and modern history school (1860). He was called to the bar by the Inner Temple (1864) and for a time practised on the western circuit. He travelled widely, in Greece, the Crimea, Palestine, and the United States. His American travels after the civil war led him to write *On Sherman's Track*, an account of the southern states published in 1866. He married on 27 November 1866 Frances (d. 1922), daughter of Archibald Francis Arbuthnot and granddaughter of Field Marshal Viscount Gough.

Kennaway succeeded to the baronetcy and the family seat, Escot, near Honiton, Devon, in 1873, having become Conservative MP for East Devon at an unopposed by-election in 1870. He sat continuously until 1910, representing the Honiton division of Devon after 1884. When he was opposed by a Liberal candidate at general elections in 1880, 1885, and 1892, he won by large majorities, but in the last election in which he stood, in 1906, his majority over his Liberal opponent was considerably reduced. From 1908 to 1910 he was father of the House of Commons.

Kennaway held strong low-church views and his parliamentary activities were primarily devoted to upholding them. The subjects on which he spoke included education, church discipline, temperance, and missionary work. He was president of the Church Missionary Society and the London Society for Promoting Christianity among the Jews. He was also linked with the Church Association, an organization dedicated to opposing Romanizing tendencies in Anglican services. Although his interventions in the house were neither frequent nor extensive, his length of service and loyalty to his party gave him authority. His evangelical views never made him intolerant towards high-churchmen in his own party nor to the nonconformists on the benches opposite. Speaking on the controversial Public Worship Regulation Bill of 1874, he rejoiced that nonconformists were able to attend Anglican services, but thought it unfair that they should be able to start litigation against Anglican clergymen. He had little sympathy with strident attempts to control ritualism by legislation: thus on a Church Discipline Bill moved from the Liberal benches in 1899 he supported the government position of continuing to maintain the bishops' veto on the initiation of judicial proceedings.

On education Kennaway was a strong upholder of

denominationalism and defender of the Church of England's work in establishing schools. When in 1906 he offered measured and defensive opposition to the Liberal government's Education Bill he was able to remind the house of his experience, reaching back to Forster's act of 1870. When in one of his last speeches, in 1909, he defended the Anglican establishment in Wales he recalled to his audience that he had entered the house immediately after the disestablishment of the Irish church, but that Gladstone had then refused to adopt the same policy for Wales. Among his work for temperance there was an attempt in 1877 to move, jointly with Joseph Chamberlain, a resolution enabling borough councils compulsorily to acquire retail liquor licences, a proposal similar to the well-known Göteborg system. He asked frequent questions on missionary work, especially in Uganda. He had erected, in Escot church, a monument to Lieutenant Shergold Smith, sent to Uganda in 1876 in response to Stanley and killed there.

Kennaway's position as a loyal back-bencher with distinct views but no obvious ministerial ambitions was well appreciated by Salisbury, who offered him a peerage. He preferred to remain in the Commons, however, and was sworn of the privy council in 1897. He was made a Companion in the Order of the Bath in 1902. He was a man of commanding presence and outspoken views, well known in his county of Devon, where he owned over 4000 acres. He was an officer in the Devonshire regiment of volunteers for forty-two years and commanded his battalion from 1896 to 1902. Kennaway died at Escot on 6 September 1919 and was buried five days later. He was survived by his wife, their son, who succeeded to the baronetcy, and two daughters, the second of whom, Joyce Christabel, married Sir Philip Wilbraham Baker-*Wilbraham.

E. J. FEUCHTWANGER

Sources The Times (11 Sept 1919) · Burke, Peerage · I. Elliott, ed., The Balliol College register, 1833–1933, 2nd edn (privately printed, Oxford, 1934) · A. T. C. Pratt, ed., People of the period: being a collection of the biographies of upwards of six thousand living celebrities, 2 vols. (1897) · Men and women of the time (1899) · E. Gaskell, Devonshire leaders (1907) · Hansard 3 (1874), 221.235 · Hansard 4 (1899), 71.231–99 · Hansard 5C (1909), 3.1579–81 · G. I. T. Machin, Politics and the churches in Great Britain, 1869 to 1921 (1987), 232, 246 · E. J. Feuchtwanger, Disraeli, democracy and the tory party: conservative leadership and organization after the second Reform Bill (1968), 216, 236
Archives Devon RO, corresp. and papers | Bodl. Oxf., corresp. with Sir Henry Burdett · LPL, corresp. with Archbishop Benson
Likenesses W. Ouless, oils, 1907, priv. coll. · Spy [L. Ward], watercolour caricature, NPG; repro. in VF (10 April 1886)
Wealth at death £78,732 17s. 9d.: probate, 30 July 1920, CGPLA Eng. & Wales

Kennedy family (per. c.1350–1513), nobility, was important in the history of the Gaelic-speaking province of Carrick in south-west Scotland in the later middle ages, and also assumed national prominence in the mid-fifteenth century. The Kennedys, who were clearly of Gaelic origin, entered Carrick in the retinue of Duncan, earl of Carrick, in the late twelfth century. Under Earl Duncan, Kennedys held the office of steward of Carrick. Members of the family also acquired lands and offices elsewhere in western Scotland under the patronage of the Comyns. The head of

the family from c.1350 was **John Kennedy of Dunure** (d. c.1385), whose chief property was on the north-west coast of Carrick, a few miles south of Ayr; he also held the lands of Kirkintilloch in the Fleming barony of Lenzie north-east of Glasgow, and was steward of Carrick. Other branches of the family were to be found at Blairquhan, Knockdolian, Dalmorton, and Gyltre at this period. John further acquired the Carrick lands of Cassillis on the River Doon by marriage to or purchase from Marjorie Montgomery, and also the nearby estate of Dalrymple. There is evidence of building work at the castles of Dunure and Cassillis in the fourteenth century which may well be attributable to John's growing wealth and power; he also founded a chapel in honour of the Blessed Virgin Mary at the parish of Maybole in Carrick.

By 1372 John Kennedy had also acquired properties and offices which had belonged to the now extinct line of the earls of Carrick descended from Earl Duncan: armorial bearings, lands in Lennox, and the offices of bailie of Carrick and keeper of Loch Doon Castle as well as headship of the kindred (ceann cinneil, 'kenkynnol') of Carrick. Possibly these acquisitions came about through his marriage to an otherwise unidentified Mary who may have been a female descendant of the Carricks. Moreover, John was succeeded by his son Gilbert, a name which may signal a connection with the Carricks inasmuch as it had also been the name of the father of Earl Duncan, progenitor of the Carrick family, and of many subsequent members of the family. On the other hand, John's acquisition of Carrick offices may simply have reflected his political dominance of the province, apparent for example in the submission to his 'captaincy' by the unidentified clan of Muntercasduf (muintir quas Duf, 'the household of the servants of Duf') in the reign of David II.

John Kennedy's successor, **Sir Gilbert Kennedy of Dunure** (d. 1408x29), who had been a hostage in England for King David's ransom in 1357, appears to have been twice married, first to Marion Sandilands of Calder and then to Agnes Maxwell of Pollok, but **Sir James Kennedy** (d. 1408), the eldest son of the second rather than the first marriage, was during his father's lifetime designated as heir to the family's lands and titles, possibly following his marriage to Mary Stewart, a daughter of King *Robert III. This marriage established cousinship with the royal house of Stewart which was to be important in the progress of Kennedy fortunes in the fifteenth century. The offspring of the marriage of Gilbert Kennedy and Marion Sandilands were probably later represented by the Kennedys of Coif, Leffnoll, and Carluke, members of which branches of the family maintained claims to the headship of the kindred and other properties until well on in the fifteenth century. Gilbert was still alive when James was killed on 8 November 1408, perhaps by disinherited members of his kindred—in that year he made an indenture with the duke of Albany, the governor of Scotland, under which in return for the latter's consent to an entail of Kennedy lands, Gilbert became the duke's retainer.

James Kennedy left three infant sons, and during their minority, control of the family patrimony seems to have passed into the hands of his four brothers, in particular Alexander of Ardstinchar, who is described as tutor of James's sons in one source. Alexander is said to have been murdered by his brothers, and Thomas of Kirkoswald and Bargany seems thereafter to have become the most powerful, holding the office of bailie of Carrick until at least 1438. The eldest of James Kennedy's three sons, John, was however designated as of Dunure and Cassillis in 1429, suggesting that he had then succeeded to those parts of the family estates at least. But in 1431 John was arrested for treason and subsequently went into exile, possibly as a result of his connections with Archibald, fifth earl of Douglas, who was arrested at the same time. The precise nature of John's treason remains mysterious, as does his ultimate fate.

John Kennedy's troubles do not seem to have affected either his uncle of Bargany, who continued to hold the office of bailie of Carrick as already noted, or his younger brothers, **Gilbert Kennedy**, first Lord Kennedy (b. c.1407, d. in or after 1479), and James *Kennedy (c.1408–1465), the latter having already commenced an ecclesiastical career which would lead to the bishopric of St Andrews in 1440 and significant political influence in the 1450s and 1460s. In the mid-1440s, perhaps following John's death in exile, Gilbert Kennedy began to play a much more prominent role in both Carrick and national affairs and, with royal support possibly aimed at establishing a counter to Douglas power in the south-west, established himself as the head of his family with all its lands and offices, including the bailie-ship of Carrick, keepership of Loch Doon Castle, and the kenkynnol. In order to do this he had to overcome opposition from within his own kindred. The keepership of Loch Doon Castle was resigned to him by John Kennedy of Coif in 1450; he received a quitclaim of the kenkynnol and his Kirkintilloch lands from Gibboun (that is, Gilbert) Kennedy of Leffnoll in 1454; and in 1465 he entered upon elaborate agreements for the settlement of feud with the Kennedys of Bargany, involving intermarriage between the two families. The family muniments contain many other indentures, bonds of manrent, and letters of retinue between Gilbert and other Kennedys, indicative of the manoeuvres which the former had to undergo to establish and make good his claim to be head of the kindred.

This gradual consolidation of his position in Carrick may have enabled Gilbert Kennedy to commission further building work at Dunure and Cassillis. He also embarked upon lengthy litigation, only concluded in 1466, to recover from Robert, Lord Fleming, the lands of Kirkintilloch in the Fleming barony of Lenzie. In 1458 he was made a lord of parliament; a mark of continued royal favour, not to mention Bishop Kennedy's influence, it also underlines his new prominence in the south-west following the forfeiture of the Douglases in 1455. Significantly, Gilbert Kennedy was also justiciar of the forfeited Douglas estates in Galloway. Following the death of King James II in 1460, the influence of Gilbert's brother Bishop James of St Andrews reached its zenith as guardian of the minor King James III in 1463–5. Gilbert succeeded to this role upon his

brother's death in 1465 (it doubtless helped that as the son of James I's sister he was the young king's closest adult relative), and was also a justiciar and keeper of Stirling Castle in this period. But after the coup by Robert, Lord Boyd, in 1466, he fell from power and was briefly imprisoned in Stirling despite having entered a complex series of bonds of manrent, friendship, and mutual support with Boyd and others in the Boyd camp earlier that year. He continued, however, to attend parliament until 1479, about which time he died. He was twice married: his first wife was Katherine Maxwell, daughter of Herbert *Maxwell, first Lord Maxwell; his second was Isabel Ogilvie, daughter of Walter Ogilvie of Lintrathen and widow of Patrick, Lord Glamis.

Gilbert Kennedy was succeeded as second Lord Kennedy by his eldest son, **John Kennedy** (d. 1508/9), who was four times married. John's eldest son, **David Kennedy** (d. 1513), was made first earl of Cassillis in 1509, perhaps in consequence of his second marriage, which was to Margaret Boyd, daughter of Thomas *Boyd, earl of Arran [see under Boyd family]. His first wife had been Agnes Borthwick, daughter of William, Lord Borthwick. David, earl of Cassillis, was killed at the battle of Flodden on 9 September 1513.

The Kennedys were a Gaelic kindred who from the thirteenth century onwards extended their activities well beyond, but without losing sight of, the Gaelic milieu whence they came. On the evidence of William Dunbar's poem of c.1500, 'The Flyting of Dunbar and Kennedy' (Walter, the Kennedy in question, was a younger son of Gilbert, first Lord Kennedy), the family still spoke Gaelic as well as Scots, and the Gaelic form of lordship exercised by them, the kenkynnol, was clearly still worth contending over in the fifteenth century; indeed, the claim of 'calp' (the chief's entitlement to a gift from those under his protection and maintenance) to which it gave rise was seen as so oppressive as to require parliamentary abolition in 1490. At the same time the leaders of the Kennedy kindred had no difficulty in seeking and exercising power in the non-Gaelic worlds of national and ecclesiastical politics, and do not appear to have seen any contradiction between their Gaelic and their Scottish personas. Members of the family married royalty, became guardians of minor kings, were appointed as bishops and lords of parliament, exercised offices under the crown, and resolved their disputes by litigation, arbitration, and bonds of manrent. The family history is an excellent illustration of the interplay between local and national interests, and the varying traditions, which together constituted the late medieval Scottish noble polity.　　HECTOR L. MACQUEEN

Sources NA Scot., Ailsa muniments, GD 25/1 · J. M. Thomson and others, eds., *Registrum magni sigilli regum Scotorum / The register of the great seal of Scotland*, 11 vols. (1882–1914), vols. 1–2 · *Report on the Laing manuscripts*, 2 vols., HMC, 72 (1914–25) · G. W. S. Barrow and others, eds., *Regesta regum Scottorum*, 6, ed. B. Webster (1982) · G. Burnett and others, eds., *The exchequer rolls of Scotland*, 2–13 (1878–91) · H. L. MacQueen, 'The kin of Kennedy, kenkynnol and the common law', *Medieval Scotland: crown, lordship and community: essays presented to G. W. S. Barrow*, ed. A. Grant and K. J. Stringer

(1993), 274–96 • S. I. Boardman, 'Politics and the feud in late medieval Scotland', PhD diss., U. St Andr., 1989 • M. Brown, *James I* (1994), 125–35 • Acta dominorum concilii et sessionis, NA Scot., CS/2 • *APS*, 1124–1567 • W. S. Cooper, ed., *Charters of the royal burgh of Ayr*, Ayrshire and Wigtonshire Archaeological Association, 12 (1883) • R. Pitcairn, ed., *Historical and genealogical account of the principal families of the name of Kennedy* (1830) • R. Nicholson, *Scotland: the later middle ages* (1974), vol. 2 of *The Edinburgh history of Scotland*, ed. G. Donaldson (1965–75); repr. (1978)
Archives NA Scot., Ailsa muniments, GD 25/1

Kennedy, Alexander (1695–*c*.1785), violin maker, was the first of an eminent family, famous for its prolific output of string instruments. He was born in Scotland and moved to London early in the eighteenth century, and set up business from about 1730 in Oxford market, north of Oxford Street. He made only violins, which he built on the high-arched Stainer model, and varnished with a brownish yellow spirit varnish. He is regarded as 'one of the better London makers' of the mid-eighteenth century, and his instruments are generally well made and with 'well-figured wood' (Harvey, 359). He died about 1785. His nephew **John Kennedy** (1729/30–1816) was apprenticed to him. Remaining in London, John subsequently established himself in Cooper's Gardens, near Shoreditch church; in Houghton Street, then Clement's Lane, Clare Market; and in Long Alley, Sun Street, Moorfields. At the height of his success he employed several assistants making violins and violas of the high German model. His instruments were mainly cheap violins (roughly made and unpurfled) with a light reddish varnish, made principally for the music shops. He died in poor circumstances at Long Alley, Moorfields, in 1816, aged eighty-six, and was buried in Shoreditch churchyard. He was married three times; the eldest son from the third marriage was **Thomas Kennedy** (1784–1870), the best-known maker of the family. He was born in Houghton Street, Clare Market, London, on 21 January 1784. After working for some time in his father's shop, he was apprenticed to Thomas Powell (17 June 1795), and at the beginning of the nineteenth century he worked occasionally for the younger William Forster (whose son was subsequently apprenticed to him). In 1811 he set up his own business at 19 Princes Street, Westminster. From there he moved to 364 Oxford Street, nearby, where he worked for thirty-three years. Like his father, he worked a great deal for the music trade, and, being a rapid and neat (if uneven) workman, was one of the most prolific of English makers. He is credited with about 2000 instruments, including at least 300 cellos based mainly on the Amati model. His best work is of a very high quality and achieves high prices at auction (see Harvey, who also includes a plate of one of Kennedy's violins dated 1844). In June 1849 he retired from business and moved to Cumming Place, Pentonville, London, where he died in 1870. He was married, but had no family. One of his violin-making pupils was James Brown (1759–1834), a former silk weaver, who, like his son and pupil, James Brown the younger (1786–*c*.1860), produced works of a reasonable but variable quality.

EDWARD HERON-ALLEN, *rev.* DAVID J. GOLBY

Sources B. W. Harvey, *The violin family and its makers in the British Isles: an illustrated history and directory* (1995) • W. Sandys and S. A. Forster, *The history of the violin and other instruments played on with the bow from the remotest times to the present* (1864), 352–4 • W. C. Honeyman, *Scottish violin makers*, 2nd edn (1910) • W. Henley, *Universal dictionary of violin and bow makers*, 1 vol. edn (1973)
Wealth at death 'in poor circumstances'; John Kennedy: Sandys and Forster, *History of the violin*

Kennedy, Sir Alexander Blackie William (1847–1928), mechanical and electrical engineer, born at 20 Stepney Green, Stepney, London, on 17 March 1847, was the eldest son of John Kennedy, Congregational minister, and his wife, Helen Stodart, daughter of Alexander Blackie, bank manager, of Aberdeen. He was educated at the City of London School and the School of Mines, which was then in Jermyn Street.

Marine engineering At the age of sixteen Kennedy was apprenticed for five and a half years to the firm of J. and W. Dudgeon at Millwall and gained his first experience in marine engine construction. In 1868 he was made leading draughtsman in the engine works established by Sir Charles Mark Palmer at Jarrow, and here he worked out the designs for the first compound marine engines built on Tyneside. In 1870 he became chief draughtsman to the firm of T. M. Tennant & Co., of Leith, working under Wilson Hartnell, and a year later he went into partnership with H. G. Bennett, a consulting marine engineer in Edinburgh. In 1873, at the request of William Henry Maw, editor of *Engineering*, he went to the Vienna Universal Exhibition. In conjunction with Maw and James Dredge, Kennedy used his fluent French and German to contribute many detailed reports of the international engineering exhibits. In Vienna he met Franz Reuleaux, distinguished German professor of mechanical engineering, and he learned much about continental methods of engineering education at the exhibition. Kennedy continued to contribute regularly to *Engineering* until 1887.

Professorship In 1874 Kennedy was appointed professor of engineering at University College, London, at a drop in salary to less than £200 a year. He had married Elizabeth Verralls (*d.* 1911), eldest daughter of William *Smith (1816–1896), an Edinburgh actuary, in the same year; the marriage produced two sons and one daughter. At University College, Kennedy founded a school of engineering teaching, the principles of which were widely followed in Britain and the United States of America. His lectures were based on Franz Reuleaux's *Theoretische Kinematik*, which he translated and edited as *Kinematics of Machinery: Outlines of a Theory of Machines* (1876). This classic text was read by students of mechanical engineering for several generations thereafter. After four years of planning and fund-raising Kennedy established in University College the first British engineering laboratory, in 1878, following the examples at Berlin and Munich. In this laboratory, between 1881 and 1892, he and his students carried out experiments on the strength and elasticity of materials, on the strength of riveted joints, and on marine engines. Kennedy thereby established the importance of training engineering students in the skills of precise measurement. The year after

Sir Alexander Blackie William Kennedy (1847–1928), by Hugh Goldwin Riviere, exh. RA 1903 [replica]

publishing his textbook, *The Mechanics of Machinery* (1886), which ran to many editions, Kennedy was elected a fellow of the Royal Society.

While professor Kennedy designed the steel arch pier at Trouville and the steel and concrete internal structure of the Hotel Cecil and of the Alhambra Theatre, the latter being probably the first building in which concrete slabs were used on a large scale to carry heavy weights. Between 1887 and 1889, in collaboration with Bryan Donkin, he made exhaustive tests of different types of boilers. Although controversial in method and interpretation, Kennedy's results were published in *Engineering*, and afterwards edited by Donkin under the title *Experiments on Steam Boilers* (1897); they subsequently won wide acceptance.

In 1889 Kennedy resigned his professorship to practise as a consulting engineer at Westminster in partnership with Bernard Maxwell Jenkin, son of Henry Charles Fleeming Jenkin. His seniority in the profession was recognized in 1894 when Kennedy was elected both president of the Institution of Mechanical Engineers, and of section G of the British Association for the Advancement of Science. On Jenkin's retirement in 1908 he went into partnership with his own son, John Macfarlane Kennedy, and Sydney Bryan Donkin, son of Bryan Donkin.

Electrical engineering From 1889, however, Kennedy directed his attention particularly to the fast-growing new field of electrical engineering, joining the Institution of Electrical Engineers in 1890. His interest in electrical matters had been aroused in 1887 by the trials of motors for electric lighting which he had undertaken with John Hopkinson and Beauchamp Tower for the Society of Arts, and by his colleague at University College, John Ambrose Fleming. Although trained as a mechanical engineer, Kennedy soon became competent in electrical engineering, and contributed significantly to the establishment of low power electric stations, in opposition to Ferranti's great project for supplying London. In a few years he built up one of the largest practices in the country. He was engineer to the Westminster Electric Supply Corporation from its foundation in 1889, and planned the whole system and works. Similarly he planned the system and was chief engineer of the Central Electric Supply Company from the start in 1899, and was engineer to the St James' and Pall Mall Electric Light Company, registered in 1888.

Kennedy was also closely connected with the development of electric transport, his early expertise in marine engineering proving of great value in this line of work. On the death of James Henry Greathead, in 1896, he became joint engineer with W. R. Galbraith for the Waterloo and City Railway. Kennedy prepared the whole of the electrical work, substituting for locomotives motors in the front and rear ends of the train, a plan which afterwards came into general use where practicable. In 1899 the London County Council consulted him as to the electrical working of its tramways, and adopted his recommendation of a conduit system for the central district with overhead wiring for the outlying suburbs. As consulting engineer to the Great Western Railway, he prepared the plans for the work of electrification west of Paddington of the Great Western, and of the Hammersmith and City railways. His firm provided consulting electrical engineers to the London and North Western, and London and South Western Railways for their schemes of suburban electrification round London, and later on he carried out similar work for the South Eastern and Chatham Railway. Kennedy was consulting engineer to the Calcutta Electric Supply Corporation until 1928, and to the corporation of Edinburgh. He was also concerned with the construction of electrical stations in Manchester and many other English and Scottish towns, and also in Japan. His public service was recognized by a knighthood in 1905, and in the following year he was president of the Institution of Civil Engineers.

Other interests In his later years Kennedy did work in many diverse fields. From June 1909 he was an associated civil member of the ordnance committee, and in 1913 served on Lord Parker's committee on wireless telegraphy. During the First World War he served on the panel of the munitions invention department, was chairman of the committee on gunsights and rangefinders, and was vice-chairman of the committees on ordnance and ammunition and on anti-aircraft equipment. In 1920 he was chairman of the Ministry of Transport's committee on electrical railways. He was also closely associated with the formation of the London Power Company.

After the war, Kennedy, a widower since 1911, devoted himself to making a detailed photographic record of the scenes of devastation. He therefore made a survey of the western front, publishing his observations and photographs under the title *From Ypres to Verdun* in 1921. At the age of seventy-five he undertook a somewhat perilous exploration of Petra with a view to giving a full description of the remains there. He made a short preliminary visit in 1922 and two long visits in the years following. Husain, king of Nedj and Hejaz, received him kindly, afforded him help, and gave him the title of pasha in 1924. In 1925 he published *Petra: its History and Monuments*, the most complete monograph on the subject and a valuable photographic record.

Kennedy was a musical amateur of taste and enthusiasm, and at his rooms in the Albany, Piccadilly, London, gave private concerts at which chamber music was performed by leading professional musicians. He was president of the London Camera Club, and a member of the Alpine Club, and in 1902 edited and published Adolphus Warburton Moore's diary under the title *The Alps in 1864*. After a lifetime of vigorous and diverse activities in which he influenced the world of British engineering in many important ways, the popular and elegant Kennedy died at his home, 7a Albany, on 1 November 1928.

E. I. CARLYLE, rev. GRAEME J. N. GOODAY

Sources *PICE*, 227 (1928–9), 269–75 · *The Times* (2 Nov 1928), 19 · R. E. D. Bishop, 'Alexander Kennedy, the elegant innovator', *Transactions* [Newcomen Society], 47 (1974–6), 1–8 · A. B. W. Kennedy, 'The use and equipment of engineering laboratories', *PICE*, 88 (1886–7), 1–80 · E. S. Ferguson, 'Kennedy, Alexander Blackie William', *DSB* · b. cert. · d. cert.
Archives CAC Cam., corresp. with A. V. Hill · CUL, corresp. with Lord Kelvin · St Ant. Oxf., Middle East Centre, corresp. with Philby relating to Petra · UCL, letters to Karl Pearson
Likenesses H. G. Riviere, oils, exh. RA 1903 · H. G. Riviere, oils, replica, exh. RA 1903, Inst. CE [*see illus.*] · W. Stoneman, photograph, 1917, NPG · drawing, UCL · ink drawing, repro. in Bishop, 'Alexander Kennedy' · portrait, repro. in *PICE*, 167 (1907), frontispiece
Wealth at death £90,909 11s. 7d.: probate, 17 Dec 1928, *CGPLA Eng. & Wales*

Kennedy, Sir Arthur Edward (1810–1883), army officer and colonial governor, was born at Cultra, co. Down, Ireland, on 9 April 1810, the fourth son of Hugh Kennedy and his wife, Grace Dora, the daughter of John Hughes. He was taught at home and then attended Trinity College, Dublin. In 1827 he joined the army as ensign in the 11th regiment. He served in Corfu, bought a commission, and in 1840 became captain of the 68th regiment; he then served in Canada for three years. On 18 May 1839 he married Georgina Matilda, the daughter of Joseph Macartney of St Helen's, co. Dublin. They had two daughters, one named Georgina Grace Maria, and one son, Arthur Herbert William, who later entered the army.

In 1846 Kennedy was appointed poor law inspector for Ireland; during the famine of 1847 he served on Sir John Burgoyne's relief committee. He retired from the army altogether in 1848.

In 1851 Kennedy received his first appointment in the colonial service as governor of the Gambia. The following year he transferred to the governorship of Sierra Leone, and in 1854 he became consul-general of Sherbro county. He was governor of Western Australia from 1854 to 1862,

when he was made CB. He was moved to Vancouver Island in 1863 and to the west African settlements in 1867, was knighted in 1868, made KCMG in 1871, and in 1872 became governor and commander-in-chief of Hong Kong. Kennedy's wife died on 3 October 1874, and in 1877 he left Hong Kong to take up the post of governor of Queensland. He was made GCMG in 1881 and left Australia for England, aboard the steamship *Orient*, in 1883. He died during this voyage, off the coast of Aden, on 3 June 1883 and was buried at sea in the Gulf of Aden.

THOMAS SECCOMBE, rev. LYNN MILNE

Sources *The Times register of events in 1883* (1884) · R. L. Smith, 'Kennedy, Sir Arthur Edward', *DCB*, vol. 11 · P. Boyce, 'Kennedy, Sir Arthur Edward', *AusDB*, vol. 5 · *Colonial Office List* · d. cert. · *CGPLA Eng. & Wales* (1883) · m. cert.
Archives Bodl. Oxf., corresp. with Lord Kimberley
Wealth at death £10,844 13s. 4d.: probate, 9 Nov 1883, *CGPLA Eng. & Wales*

Kennedy, Benjamin Hall (1804–1889), headmaster and classical scholar, was born at Summer Hill, near Birmingham, on 6 November 1804, the eldest son of Rann *Kennedy (1772–1851) and his wife, Julia (née Hall). Charles Rann *Kennedy was his brother. From 1814 to 1818 he was educated in his father's house and at King Edward's School, Birmingham, and throughout his youth owed much to the encouragement of his father's friends John Johnstone and Samuel Parr. The example of his father early imbued him with a love of learning and passionate admiration for poetry, and he read widely in his father's large library. When a child he thoroughly mastered an edition of *The British Theatre* in thirty volumes, and a love of dramatic literature never left him. In spite, however, of his discursive reading, he worked hard at classics, and when, in January 1819, he went to Shrewsbury School, the composition which he wrote, consisting, as the fashion then was, entirely of original Latin composition in verse and prose, exhibits astonishing command of Latin and power of invention.

Samuel Butler was the headmaster of Shrewsbury, and under him young Kennedy developed rapidly. In a year he became second boy, and in a year and a half, when he was not sixteen, head boy, a position which he held until he left in 1823. Among his schoolfellows were Charles and Erasmus Darwin. While still at school he sent in a copy of iambics for the Porson prize and a Latin ode for Sir W. Browne's medal at Cambridge; in both cases the examiners selected his composition for the prize, and, although he was not eligible for the Browne medal, he received the Porson, and the regulations were in consequence altered, so that he is the only schoolboy who ever won it.

In 1823 Kennedy went to St John's College, Cambridge. Professor J. E. B. Mayor says that the list of what he had then read 'sounds like the record of a Scaliger' (*Classical Review*, 227). In January 1824, when only in his second term, he won the Pitt university scholarship. During the examination Dean Law set Isaiah 14: 6–17 for Greek iambics, and Kennedy's translation was so good that the Greek professor, Dobree, had it printed and circulated. His other university distinctions were the Porson prize for the

Benjamin Hall Kennedy (1804–1889), by Walter William Ouless, 1883

second time in 1824, and for the third in 1826; the prizes for the Greek ode in 1824, for the Latin ode in 1824, and for the epigrams in 1825, and the members' prize in 1828. He graduated BA in 1827, being a senior optime in the mathematical tripos, and senior classic and first chancellor's medallist. Throughout his undergraduate career he was as notable for his wit and his social qualities as for his scholarship. The first Lord Lytton, who for fifty years remained his close friend, recorded the impression produced by 'an ardent, enthusiastic youth from Shrewsbury, a young giant in learning, who carried away the prize from Praed' (Lytton, 1.232). He took frequent part in the union debates and became president in 1825. In 1824 he was also elected a member of the Cambridge Conversazione Society, better known as the Apostles, where he formed a close friendship with F. D. Maurice and John Sterling, and in the same year became an original member of the Athenaeum, at the invitation of Richard Heber. Among his other undergraduate friends and acquaintances were W. M. Praed, Alexander Cockburn, Charles Wordsworth, Charles Buller, and William Selwyn.

In 1827 Kennedy went to Shrewsbury as an assistant master, but, on being elected fellow of St John's in 1828, returned to Cambridge to take pupils. Among them were Richard Shilleto, Charles Merivale (afterwards dean of Ely), Henry Philpott (afterwards bishop of Worcester), and William Cavendish (afterwards seventh duke of Devonshire). He was ordained deacon in 1829 and priest in 1830, and in the latter year accepted a mastership under C. T.

Longley at Harrow, where he had the Grove House. In March 1831 he married Janet (d. 1874), daughter of Thomas Caird, of Paignton, Devon. They were the parents of a son and four daughters Charlotte Amy May *Burbury [see under Kennedy, Marion Grace], Marion Grace *Kennedy, Julia Elizabeth *Kennedy [see under Kennedy, Marion Grace], and Edith Janet. At Harrow discipline was at the time extremely lax, and the general standard of teaching very low, and Kennedy's position as assistant master gave him no effective influence. But early in 1836 Samuel Butler was made bishop of Lichfield, and Kennedy, his former pupil, was nominated his successor in the headmastership of Shrewsbury, greatly to Butler's satisfaction. Although the headmastership of Harrow had fallen vacant at the same time, Kennedy made no concealment of his preference for Shrewsbury. He was also made DD by royal mandate at this time.

Kennedy remained at Shrewsbury until 1866, a period of thirty years, and throughout that time the school maintained an unparalleled reputation for classical training. It was poorly endowed, and could not secure brilliant boys by offers of rich scholarships. Although the headmaster was fairly well paid, there were no means of paying undermasters a good salary, and the whole burden of teaching the upper boys fell upon the headmaster. The buildings of the school, dating from the sixteenth century, were meagre and the accommodation for boarders very defective. Until Kennedy went there was no cricket ground, and the very scanty school grounds possessed a solitary fives court as the sole provision for healthy amusement. The numbers of the school were consequently never large; having inherited a pupil body of nearly 230, at one time Kennedy found their numbers down to about eighty. None the less he regularly sent up to the universities a succession of pupils, who carried all before them. A list of the very numerous distinctions obtained by Shrewsbury men at Oxford and Cambridge between 1840 and 1860 establishes Kennedy's claim to be the greatest classical teacher of the nineteenth century. His success was due to his energetic nature; his enthusiasm, like all genuine enthusiasm, was contagious, and his pupils left him possessed of the true key of knowledge—a genuine and vigorous love of knowledge for its own sake. Yet there is abundant evidence that his teaching methods were erratic and idiosyncratic to a quite remarkable degree.

The veneration in which Kennedy was held by his pupils was shown by the large sum which was raised for a testimonial to him on his retirement in 1866. The money was devoted partly to the building of the chancel of the chapel at Shrewsbury School, and partly to the founding of a professorship of Latin in the University of Cambridge. Kennedy added £500 to the fund, on the condition that the professorship should not be named after him (though since 1911 it has indeed been called the Kennedy professorship). The first occupant of the new chair was one of his former pupils, H. A. J. Munro, and the second was another, J. E. B. Mayor. It was to Kennedy that Munro dedicated his great edition of Lucretius and Mayor his famous edition of Juvenal.

While at Shrewsbury Kennedy was, in 1843, appointed prebendary of Lichfield, and in 1861 select preacher in the University of Cambridge. In 1862 a royal commission sat to inquire into the condition of the nine chief public schools, including Shrewsbury (which would have been inconceivable had it not been for the headmasterships of Samuel Butler and of Kennedy himself). Kennedy's published evidence clearly defined the value of classical study, though he had instituted a 'non-collegiate' class at the school. Among the changes recommended was the use of the same Latin and Greek grammars in public schools, and the headmasters of the nine chief schools unanimously selected as the basis of the new Latin grammar Kennedy's *Elementary Latin Grammar*, originally published in 1847. Accordingly, a small subcommittee (which included Kennedy himself) constructed, on the basis of Kennedy's *Grammar*, *The Public School Latin Primer*, which was published in 1866, but was greeted with widespread hostile comment. Subsequently, however, Kennedy published *The Public School Latin Grammar* (1871), a more thorough and complete work than any which had preceded it in England, and not without value more than a century later. The Latin primer had met with much criticism, but it stood the test of time; however, the revision of 1888, and the *Shorter Latin Primer* of the same year, owed much not only to Kennedy's ex-pupils G. H. Hallam and T. E. Page, but also to his unmarried daughters Marion Grace and Julia, and it is unlikely that Kennedy had any hand in these works.

Before Kennedy left Shrewsbury in 1866 he had accepted the living of West Felton, near Oswestry, vacant by the death of his son-in-law, William Burbury, patron of the living. In 1867 he was appointed regius professor of Greek at Cambridge and canon of Ely, which offices he held until his death. He represented the Ely chapter as proctor in convocation for some years. At Ely he was held in great affection, and helped to break down the barriers which had long separated the cathedral body from the rest of the town. At Cambridge he took a vigorous part in the business of the university, and was elected a member of the council in 1870. With his daughters he took a keen interest in the movement for the education of women, and in an impressive speech in February 1881 he strongly supported the opening of the Cambridge University honour examinations to the women students of Girton and Newnham colleges. He was from 1870 to 1880 a member of the committee for the revision of the New Testament, and took an active part in the work. In 1880 he was elected an honorary fellow of his old college, St John's, and in 1885 an ordinary fellow of it for the second time after an interval of fifty-eight years. In the same year he received from the University of Dublin the honorary degree of LLD. Kennedy died of bronchitis at Shipway House, Torquay, on 6 April 1889.

Kennedy's passionate love of poetry, and not merely their classical perfection, gives his compositions in Greek and Latin their singular charm, seen to best advantage in his *Between Whiles* (1877). In politics he was a Liberal, and in religious matters a staunch supporter of the established church, although intolerant of narrow sectarian prejudices. His general reading was exceptionally wide, and his memory unusually retentive. Of English history his knowledge was profound and minute; his familiarity with naval and military annals was remarkable. He was a brilliant speaker, with a voice and gesture capable of every modulation. His character was notably impulsive. In society he was an excellent conversationalist, overflowing in anecdote and genial humour. He is said to have been a knowledgeable connoisseur of wine.

T. E. PAGE, rev. J. H. C. LEACH

Sources J. E. B. Mayor, *Classical Review*, 3 (1889), 226–7, 278–81 · G. W. Fisher, *Annals of Shrewsbury School*, rev. J. S. Hill (1899) · J. B. Oldham, *Headmasters of Shrewsbury School* (1937) · J. H. C. Leach, *A school at Shrewsbury* (1990) · F. D. How, *Six great schoolmasters* (1904) · private information (1891) · E. R. Bulwer-Lytton, first Earl Lytton, *The life, letters and literary remains of Edward Bulwer, Lord Lytton*, 2 vols. (1883) · Venn, *Alum. Cant.*

Archives BL, corresp. with Samuel Butler, Add. MSS 34585–34592 · Herts. ALS, corresp. with Lord Lytton

Likenesses W. W. Ouless, oils, 1883, St John Cam. [*see illus.*] · photogravure photograph, pubd 1886 (after W. W. Ouless), NPG · E. T. Haynes, portrait (after W. W. Ouless), Shrewsbury School · G. Richmond, crayon drawing, Shrewsbury School · wood-engraving (after photograph by Scott & Wilkinson), NPG; repro. in *ILN* (27 April 1889)

Wealth at death £28,166 3s. 9d.: probate, 31 May 1889, *CGPLA Eng. & Wales*

Kennedy, Catherine Lucy (1851–1910), headmistress, was born on 20 September 1851, the daughter of the Revd William James Kennedy (1814–1891), inspector of schools in the diocese of Manchester, and his wife, Sarah Caroline (d. 1896), daughter of George Kennedy. She had three brothers, including William Rann *Kennedy. Her uncle was the distinguished classical scholar Benjamin Hall *Kennedy, whose daughters Marion Grace *Kennedy and Julia Elizabeth *Kennedy [*see under* Kennedy, Marion Grace] were promoters of Newnham College, Cambridge. Although her three brothers went to Cambridge, Catherine Kennedy was educated at home, then at a private school in London, and finally at Cheltenham Ladies' College, achieving a first class in both groups A and B of the Cambridge higher local examination. In 1874 she became assistant mistress under Miss Dorothea Beale at Cheltenham Ladies' College, and was appointed headmistress of the newly founded Leeds Girls' High School two years later, when still only twenty-four.

In Leeds the grammar school was exceptionally well endowed, but the influence of the endowed schools commission failed to bring any part of these resources to meet the needs of girls in the town. A meeting of representatives of the Yorkshire Ladies' Council of Education and of the Leeds Ladies' Educational Association decided that, in the absence of any available endowment, a joint-stock company should be established to raise the necessary funds and to run a girls' high school. Capital was subscribed and premises were hired, and in June 1876 Catherine Kennedy was selected as headmistress. The personality and qualities of Catherine Kennedy made the project a success, and she was in that sense the actual founder of the school. At an inaugural meeting in September 1876 she outlined her philosophy, explaining that there would be no attempt to concentrate on accomplishments but instead the school would strengthen and develop accurate logical thought, quickness of observation, and the mastery of difficulties by steady persistence. The study of classical languages and of mathematics by the girls would be central to achieving these aims. The third subject which would receive special attention was natural science, especially valuable in promoting habits of reflection and observation. The school opened in rented premises with forty-two pupils. Miss Kennedy remained as head until the death of her father in 1891, when she resigned to care for her widowed mother. By this time Leeds Girls' High School had about 160 pupils and a strong reputation for academic achievement; the first few of a later flow of pupils had made their way to university.

From 1894 to 1896 Catherine Kennedy acted with A. P. Laurie as assistant commissioner for the West Riding of Yorkshire for the royal commission on secondary education (Bryce commission). Her report (published in volume 7 of the commission's report) gives an authoritative account of the provision for girls' education in the area.

After the death of her mother in 1896 Catherine Kennedy became headmistress of the Clergy Daughters' School at Warrington. This school was languishing with only about forty pupils. Catherine Kennedy soon raised its efficiency, reputation, and numbers. During her headship daughters of the laity were admitted and a department for training secondary school mistresses was created. The school moved to larger and better premises at Darley Dale, Derbyshire, purchased in 1905. Additional dormitories, a chapel, a gymnasium, and a sanitorium were added to the now flourishing St Elphin's School, as it was renamed. At Warrington and Darley Dale she succeeded in establishing a girls' school with good academic credentials under the auspices of the Church of England. Catherine Kennedy died of pneumonia and cardiac failure at St Elphin's School on 17 February 1910.   PETER GOSDEN

Sources H. M. Jewell, *A school of unusual excellence: Leeds Girls' High School, 1876–1976* (1976) · K. E. Procter, *A short history of the Leeds Girls' High School*, 2 vols. (1926) · *Guardian* (4 March 1910) · 'Memorial service address, St John's Church, Leeds, 25 February 1910', *Leeds Girls' High School Magazine* (spring 1910) · I. Jenkins, 'The Yorkshire council of education, 1871–91', *Thoresby Society Miscellany*, 17 (1978), 27–71 · *Annual Reports* [Leeds Ladies' Educational Association] · *Annual Reports* [Yorkshire Ladies' Council of Education] · *Leeds Girls' High School Magazine* [relevant issues] · 'Opening of Leeds Girls' High School', *Yorkshire Evening Post* (4 Sept 1876) · Venn, *Alum. Cant.* [material on male members of her family] · d. cert.
Archives Leeds Central Library, Yorkshire Ladies Council of Education minute books and papers
Likenesses photograph, *c*.1870–1879 (in youth), repro. in Procter, *A short history*, pt 1, facing p. 16, pl. 1 · photograph (in later years), repro. in Jewell, *A school of unusual excellence*, facing p. 12
Wealth at death £8306 12*s*. 9*d*.: probate, 24 March 1910, *CGPLA Eng. & Wales*

Kennedy, Charles Rann (1808–1867), lawyer and classical scholar, was the son of Rann *Kennedy (1772–1851), a poet, and his wife, Julia, daughter of the historical engraver John Hall. He was the younger brother of Benjamin Hall *Kennedy. He was educated at Shrewsbury School and at King Edward VI School, Birmingham, before matriculating as an exhibitioner at Trinity College, Cambridge, in October 1827. He was a talented student and won several prizes and scholarships. In 1831 he graduated BA as a senior classicist, and was elected a fellow of Trinity; he proceeded MA in 1834. On 5 February 1835 Kennedy was admitted at Lincoln's Inn. He was called to the bar on 19 November 1836. At first he practised in London and took part in the significant libel actions brought by John Stockdale against Hansard between 1836 and 1840. In connection with this case he published *The Privileges of the House of Commons* (second edition, 1841). In the autumn of 1849 he was elected professor of law in Queen's College, Birmingham, and he asked to join the midland circuit. Unusually, this request was refused, leading Kennedy to publish in 1850 an open letter to the lord chancellor, complaining of the conduct of the circuit leagues. In May 1856 Kennedy became the professional adviser of Mrs Swinfen, the plaintiff in the case of *Swinfen v. Swinfen*, and carried the litigation to a successful conclusion. A dispute, however, arose as to his payment, and on 26 March 1862 he brought an action against Mrs Swinfen for £20,000. Kennedy won in the first instance but this result was overruled in the court of common pleas, the judges holding that a barrister could not sue for his fees. A deed which Kennedy had obtained from Mrs Swinfen, giving him a reversion to the Swinfen Hall estates in Staffordshire, was ordered to be delivered up by a judgment of the master of the rolls on 31 July 1863. Kennedy died at his home, Stapylton House, Harborne, Staffordshire, on 17 December 1867. He was married and left a family.

Kennedy was an accomplished classical scholar and translator. He published translations of the various works of Demosthenes and completed an English translation begun by his father of the last eight books of Virgil's *Aeneid*.   W. A. J. ARCHBOLD, *rev.* ERIC METCALFE

Sources Venn, *Alum. Cant.* · W. P. Baildon, ed., *The records of the Honorable Society of Lincoln's Inn: the black books*, 4 (1902) · *Annals of our time* · *GM*, 4th ser., 5 (1868), 255 · *Law List* (1891) · *Annual Register* (1891) · private information (1891) · *CGPLA Eng. & Wales* (1868)
Wealth at death under £1500: probate, 3 Feb 1868, *CGPLA Eng. & Wales*

Kennedy, David, first earl of Cassilis (*d.* 1513). *See under* Kennedy family (*per. c.*1350–1513).

Kennedy, David (1825–1886), singer, was born in Perth on 15 April 1825, the only son of a weaver, David Kennedy, who was also precentor of a United Secession church, and his wife, Catherine Taylor. At the age of sixteen he was apprenticed to a painter, but he was trained in music by his father and in 1845 became precentor of the South Kirk, Perth. During 1848 he worked at his trade in Edinburgh and London, and returned to Perth to set up in business. There, on 22 December 1848, he married Helen, daughter of Robert Henderson, a brewer, and following her death five years later, on 5 June 1855, Elizabeth, daughter of Charles Fraser, a farm servant. Marjory Kennedy-*Fraser, the folk-song collector, was their second and his fifth child.

Kennedy later obtained a precentorship in Edinburgh,

and in 1859 began a series of weekly concerts. Short concert tours in Scotland followed in 1860 and 1861, and in 1862 he made his first appearance in London, at the Hanover Square Rooms. Between December 1862 and May 1863 he gave a hundred concerts in the Egyptian Hall; and in 1864 and 1865 he was again in London, singing, and reading parts of Walter Scott's *Waverley*. In 1866–8 he toured Canada and the eastern United States, with his eldest daughter, Helen, as his accompanist. In 1869 he went to San Francisco via Panama. While he was in San Francisco the first railway across the continent was opened, and he sang 'The Star-Spangled Banner' at the inaugural ceremony.

After spending three years in Scotland, Kennedy and his family made a tour around the world (1872–6), visiting Australia and New Zealand, the United States, Canada, and Newfoundland. From 1876 to 1879 he toured in the British Isles, and performed two seasons in London; in 1879 he visited South Africa, and in 1879–80, India. On his way home he spent several months in Italy, where several of his children were studying; in 1881 one of his sons and two of his daughters died when the Théâtre des Italiens, Nice, burnt down. In 1881–2 Kennedy was again in Canada and the United States, in 1883–4 in Australia and New Zealand. In March 1886 he appeared in London for the last time and then left for Canada, where he died at Stratford, Ontario, on 12 or 13 October 1886. He was buried in the Grange cemetery, Edinburgh.

Kennedy possessed a rich tenor voice and good dramatic powers, along with a fund of humour, sometimes 'pawky', sometimes broad. He followed the example of John Templeton in concentrating on Scottish songs, and his many tours were prompted largely by a desire to bring his native music to the many expatriate Scots throughout the world. W. D. WALKER, rev. JOHN PURSER

Sources M. Kennedy and D. Kennedy, *David Kennedy, the Scottish singer* (1887) · M. Kennedy-Fraser, *A life of song* (1929) · *The Scottish Musical Monthly*, 1/12 (Sept 1894), 215–16 · m. certs.
Likenesses J. and D. Frater, lithograph (after photograph by W. Crooke), repro. in Kennedy and Kennedy, *David Kennedy* · memorial slab bronze bas-relief, Calton Hill, Edinburgh · portrait, oils, Scot. NPG · print, Harvard TC
Wealth at death £7420 5s. 8d.: confirmation, 10 March 1887, CCI

Kennedy, Douglas Neil (1893–1988), folk musician and dancer, was born on 11 May 1893 at 138 Bruntsfield Place, Edinburgh, the son of John Henderson Kennedy (d. 1912?), solicitor and singing teacher, and his wife, Patricia Grieve Thomson (d. 1906). He was educated at George Watson's College, Edinburgh, from 1899 to 1907, when he moved to London and attended the Mercers' School, Holborn.

While studying science at South-Western Polytechnic in 1911 Kennedy was introduced to folk-dancing by his sister Helen. The polytechnic was home to the core of Cecil Sharp's English Folk Dance Society (EFDS) and Kennedy became the youngest member of the new society's demonstration dance team. Of the seven regular dancers, four were killed in the First World War, and two left the folk-dance movement. Kennedy spent the war first with the

Douglas Neil Kennedy (1893–1988), by unknown photographer

14th battalion London Scottish regiment, then with the Royal Defence Corps, reaching the rank of captain and gaining the MBE. On demobilization in 1918 he was elected an EFDS committee member. Prior to the war he had become first a student, then a demonstrator, in the department of botany, Imperial College. He had married Helen May Karpeles (1888–1976), a founder member of the EFDS, on 29 September 1914, and two sons were born in the immediate post-war period.

Kennedy's life as a scientist whose hobby was folk-dancing changed on Cecil Sharp's death in 1924. Sharp had indicated that he wanted Kennedy to succeed him as director of the EFDS, and Kennedy accepted. Sharp's artistic legacy was maintained through the society's board of artistic control, consisting of Kennedy, Ralph Vaughan Williams, and Maud Pauline *Karpeles. Karpeles, secretary of the society, Sharp's literary executor, and Kennedy's sister-in-law, was the driving force, and this caused tension until 1928, when Karpeles resigned as EFDS secretary, citing difficulty in distinguishing the functions of secretary and director.

Unlike Sharp, Kennedy was primarily a performer; many commented on the litheness of his tall, slender figure when dancing. He led EFDS dance teams to the Basque country, Prague, the United States, and elsewhere; he devised folk ballets, including *The Morning of the Year*, with music by Holst; and he used his talents effectively as director of performances at several national and international festivals. Although he assisted E. K. Chambers in his work on folk plays, edited country-dance books (based on Playford dances) with his wife, and published the North Skelton longsword dance notation in 1927, he was no pedantic scholar: during the 1930s, when disputes arose about the steps of Bampton dances, he adjudicated in favour of artistry above exactitude.

In 1937 Kennedy visited the United States to direct the Pinewoods Camp summer school, and began collecting American square dances. He introduced them into England at the Stratford upon Avon summer school the next year, and published *Square Dances of America* jointly with his wife in 1939. In the same year he and his wife, with Nan and Brian Fleming-Williams, formed the Square Dance Band, comprising drum, guitar, fiddle, and concertina. This was radically different from the genteel piano or violin with small orchestra for dance accompaniment, and it set the standard and pattern for all subsequent folk-dance band playing, to the consternation of the more conservative elements in the society.

In 1938 Kennedy was elected squire (president) of the Morris Ring, formed by men's morris teams partly to encourage dance outside the classroom. He expected to step down after two years, and announced his intention to resign as director of the English Folk Dance and Song Society (as the EFDS had become on merging with the Folk Song Society in 1932) and to emigrate to the United States; but the outbreak of the Second World War thwarted both aims. He remained squire, and was appointed honorary director of the EFDSS during the wartime suspension of activities. During the war he was a flight lieutenant in the Air Ministry, and attributed his survival to his absence on war work when a bomb destroyed the EFDSS headquarters in 1940. His elder son, however, died on active service the same year.

After reviving the Morris Ring in 1947 he resigned as squire, but resumed the full directorship of the EFDSS. He scripted and presented the first regular folk-dance radio programme in 1946. Under his leadership the EFDSS moved away from pedagogy to an emphasis on popular participation, culminating in the abolition of the society's examination structure in 1956. His instructional films were designed to bypass laborious pedagogical methods and to demonstrate dances in their entirety from the start. A singer as well as a dancer, he recorded Scots lowlands ballads for HMV in 1955.

He was appointed OBE in 1952, and continued as director of the EFDSS until the end of 1961, retiring at the EFDSS jubilee to Waldringfield, Suffolk, where he maintained a yacht. Remaining active, he was appointed president of the Folklore Society from 1964 to 1967 and vice-president of the International Folk Music Council in 1975-7. His wife died after a long illness in 1976; and at the end of that year (31 December) he married Elizabeth Ann Ogden (*b.* 1929), a nurse and musician, of Waldringfield. He continued writing and lecturing, and took up painting in 1983.

Douglas Kennedy died from heart disease on 7 January 1988, at his home, the Deck House, Waldringfield, and was buried with his first wife at the church of All Saints, Waldringfield, on 12 January, with a public thanksgiving there on 14 January. With his death the EFDSS lost its last direct contact with its founder. Kennedy had been a survivor in both senses: he survived when most of Sharp's dancers were killed in the trenches, and survived all his contemporaries to lead Sharp's society through thirty-six years, during which he transformed its approach to folk music to ensure its continuing relevance to the young. He survived over a quarter century of retirement, continuing to serve the wider folk movement at the highest level. Throughout he maintained a demeanour of cheerful calm, even when in sometimes fierce dispute with the society's old guard.   MICHAEL HEANEY

Sources *English Dance and Song*, 50/1 (1988), 2-4 · *Folk Music Journal*, 5 (1985-9), 520-36 · *Folklore*, 99 (1988), 127-8 · *Folk Music Journal*, 3 (1975-9), 188-90 · private information (2004) · m. cert. · CGPLA Eng. & Wales (1988)

Archives FILM Morris Ring Archive, 'Traditional teams 1950', film 26 · Vaughan Williams Memorial Library, London, 'The rose tree', film 13a, b; video 9, 9a, 105 | SOUND BL NSA, documentary recordings · BL NSA, performance recordings · Vaughan Williams Memorial Library, London, tapes 135-40 · Vaughan Williams Memorial Library, London, cassettes 106, 147, 259 · Vaughan Williams Memorial Library, London, tape 173

Likenesses W. Fisher Cassie, portrait, 1947, Vaughan Williams Memorial Library, London · R. Adler, oils, *c.*1950, Vaughan Williams Memorial Library, London · P. Kennedy, portrait, 1955, Vaughan Williams Memorial Library, London · photograph, Vaughan Williams Memorial Library, London [see illus.]

Wealth at death £261,666: probate, 18 Aug 1988, CGPLA Eng. & Wales

Kennedy, Edmund Besley Court

Kennedy, Edmund Besley Court (1818-1848), surveyor and explorer, was born on 5 September 1818 at St Peter Port, Guernsey, Channel Islands, the sixth of the eight children of Colonel Thomas Kennedy and Mary Ann, daughter of Thomas Smith, sometime lord mayor of London. After attending Elizabeth College, Guernsey, Kennedy trained as a surveyor and then sailed for Australia, arriving in 1840 and being appointed assistant surveyor in the surveyor-general's department in New South Wales. His first task of surveying, in Victoria, ended with his being recalled after a dispute with a local magistrate and an indiscreet liaison with an Irish immigrant, Margaret Murphy, with whom he had a child.

After spending two years with little surveying work in Sydney, Kennedy was suddenly in 1845 appointed second in command of the last exploring expedition conducted by Sir Thomas Livingstone Mitchell in 1846 in search of a route from Sydney to the Gulf of Carpentaria. After maintaining a base camp for some months, in March 1847 Kennedy volunteered to trace the 'Victoria' River, which was the furthest point touched by Mitchell in 1846. Starting from Sydney with eight mounted men with led horses, and eight months' provisions, he reached Mitchell's furthest point during an exceptionally dry season, descended the Thomson River, and followed the 'Victoria' southwest, showing that it did not flow north-west into the gulf as Mitchell had supposed. After tracing the Warego River and naming the Thomson, Kennedy turned back and reached Sydney in February 1848. Another stream having been named the Victoria, Kennedy renamed Mitchell's 'Victoria' by its Aboriginal name, the Barcoo. The narrative of this journey was published in the *Journal of the Royal Geographical Society* (1852).

In January 1848 Kennedy started on his last expedition for the exploration of Cape York peninsula. The party, consisting of nine men, with horses, and an Aborigine called Jackey Jackey, set out from Rockingham Bay, and found itself beset with misfortune. Mangrove swamps and mountains made progress slow, as did sickness and a growing shortage of supplies. Kennedy had to leave eight of his men sick at Weymouth Bay while the others tried under his leadership to reach the supply ship. On the subsequent journey one man shot himself accidentally, and the two others had to be left to tend him. Kennedy continued his journey with Jackey Jackey, hoping to reach the vessel at the tip of Cape York. Trapped by crocodile-infested mangrove swamp and hostile Aborigines, Kennedy was attacked and speared, dying on 13 December 1848 in the arms of the faithful Jackey Jackey, who thirteen days afterwards brought the tidings to the steamer *Ariel* in Albany Bay. Of the other members of the expedition, only two survived to return to Sydney.

An excellent leader, patient and persevering, Kennedy's important geographical discoveries have too often been overshadowed by the tragedy of his last expedition.

H. M. CHICHESTER, rev. ELIZABETH BAIGENT

Sources *AusDB* · E. Beale, 'Edmund Besley Court Kennedy', *Royal Australian Historical Society Journal and Proceedings*, 35 (1949), 1–25 · J. Macgillivray, *Narrative of the voyage of H.M.S. Rattlesnake … 1846–1850 to which is added an account of Mr E. B. Kennedy's expedition for the exploration of Cape York peninsula* (1852) · W. Carron, *Narrative of an expedition … for the exploration of the country lying between Rockingham bay and Cape York* (1849)
Archives NRA, priv. coll., corresp. and papers
Likenesses monument, St James's Church, Sydney, New South Wales, Australia

Kennedy, Geoffrey Anketell Studdert (1883–1929), Church of England clergyman and poet, was born on 27 June 1883 in Leeds, the seventh child in the family of seven sons and two daughters of the Revd William Studdert Kennedy, vicar of St Mary's, Quarry Hill, Leeds, and his second wife, Jeanette Anketell. There were also one son and four daughters of a first marriage. Educated at Leeds grammar school, he graduated in classics and divinity at Trinity College, Dublin, in 1904, after which he taught for two years at a school in West Kirby in Liverpool. Following a year of ordination training at Ripon Clergy College he was ordained in 1908 to a curacy at Rugby parish church, moving from there in 1912 to be curate at Leeds parish church. In 1914 he married Emily, daughter of Alfred Catlow, coal merchant; they had three sons. Appointed that same year as vicar of St Paul's, Worcester, in 1915 he became a chaplain to the armed forces and began the wartime ministry among the troops in France and Flanders for which he is most remembered.

Studdert Kennedy's considerable natural gifts as a preacher were combined with a talent for poetry, particularly dialect verse in the manner of the barrack-room ballads of Rudyard Kipling. In the carnage and suffering of the trenches his strongly sacramental Christianity was communicated in memorable addresses and in colloquial verse of sometimes powerful simplicity, which brought together the passion of Christ and the doubt, fear, and courage of soldiers caught in the squalid stalemate of the Flanders trenches. Studdert Kennedy preached a suffering God, Christ the revealer, 'pierced to the heart by the sorrow of the sword' (Wilkinson, 138). The experience of war made him question both the metaphysical assumption of an impassible God, and the hortatory patriotic moralism of many contemporary churchmen and political leaders. He could contrast sharply (in *Peace Rhymes of a Padre*) the God of glory in Isaiah's vision with the God revealed in the suffering Christ:

> God, I hate this splendid vision—all its splendour is a lie …
> And I hate the God of power on His hellish heavenly
>   throne …
> Thou hast bid us seek Thy glory, in a criminal crucified …
> For the very God of Heaven is not Power, but Power of Love.
> (Wilkinson, 137)

A bitter poem from the end of the war saw the statesmen who were meeting at Versailles to agree to a peace treaty as those who crucified Christ anew. After the war a number of volumes of Studdert Kennedy's collected poems were published, the most notable being *Rough Rhymes of a Padre* (1918), *Peace Rhymes of a Padre* (1920), *Songs of Faith and Doubt* (1922), and *The Unutterable Beauty* (1927).

Given the nickname Woodbine Willie by the troops, Studdert Kennedy once described his chaplain's ministry as taking 'a box of fags in your haversack, and a great deal of love in your heart' (Mozley, 141) and laughing and joking with those he was called to serve. 'You can pray with them sometimes; but pray for them always' (ibid.). Ministering on the front line under fire he showed conspicuous bravery and was awarded the MC for his tending of the wounded under fire during the attack on the Messines Ridge. He was slightly built and liked to joke in public about his prominent ears and simian features, though contemporaries were much more likely to be arrested by the large and melancholy brown eyes.

Demobilized in 1919, Studdert Kennedy was appointed a chaplain to the king. In 1922 he left his Worcester parish to run the church of St Edmund King and Martyr in Lombard Street in the City of London, a non-parochial cure, which left him free for his major post-war work as 'messenger' of the Industrial Christian Fellowship (ICF), which had come into being in 1920 as a result of the amalgamation of the Christian Social Union and the Navvy Mission Society. Critical alike of Marxist socialism and of capitalism, Studdert Kennedy commanded considerable audiences for his addresses during the ICF's missions and crusades in the years of the depression. He was sure that his Christianity had political consequences, but that it was religion not political panaceas that met human need. Archbishop William Temple, who described him as 'the finest priest I have known' (Mozley, 208), characterized him as evangelical without a trace of puritanism, and fired by a strong Catholic sacramentalism, with the cross at the heart of it all. The suffering of war and the suffering of the depression were alike uniquely met by the crucified God.

Studdert Kennedy was on an ICF crusade at the time of his death, which occurred in Liverpool on 8 March 1929 at St Catherine's vicarage, Abercromby Square; he was survived by his wife.   GEOFFREY ROWELL, *rev.*

Sources J. K. Mozley, ed., *G. A. Studdert Kennedy by his friends* (1929) · G. Studdert-Kennedy, *Dog-collar democracy: the Industrial Christian Fellowship, 1919–1929* (1982) · A. Wilkinson, *The Church of England and the First World War* (1978) · D. Edwards, '"Woodbine Willie" was a true prophet', *Church Times* (24 June 1983), 5, 11 · R. Fuller, 'Woodbine Willie lives', in R. Fuller, *Owls and artificers: Oxford lectures on poetry* (1971), 27–43 · W. Purcell, *Woodbine Willie, an Anglican incident: being some account of the life and times of Geoffrey Anketell Studdert Kennedy, poet, prophet, seeker after truth, 1883–1929* (1983) · *CGPLA Eng. & Wales* (1929)
Wealth at death £5499 13s. 1d.: administration with will, 26 April 1929, *CGPLA Eng. & Wales*

Kennedy, Sir Gilbert, of Dunure (d. 1408×29). *See under* Kennedy family (*per. c.*1350–1513).

Kennedy, Gilbert, first Lord Kennedy (b. *c.*1407, d. in or after 1479). *See under* Kennedy family (*per. c.*1350–1513).

Kennedy, Gilbert, second earl of Cassillis (*c.*1492–1527), magnate, was the eldest son of David *Kennedy, first earl of Cassillis (d. 1513) [*see under* Kennedy family (*per. c.*1350–1513)], and his wife, Agnes Borthwick (b. *c.*1460, d. in or before 1509), daughter of William, third Lord Borthwick. He was the chief of a kindred which had been prominent in southern Ayrshire since the mid-fourteenth century. When his father was killed at Flodden in 1513, Gilbert, who was almost certainly already of age and married to Isobella Campbell (b. *c.*1495, d. in or after 1533), daughter of the second earl of Argyll, succeeded as second earl of Cassillis and fourth Lord Kennedy. He and Isobella had seven sons, including Gilbert *Kennedy, third earl of Cassillis, and Quintin *Kennedy, abbot of Crossraguel, and at least three daughters. Gilbert supported the duke of Albany, governor of Scotland during the earlier years of James V's minority, and in 1515 was among the forces besieging the queen dowager in Stirling Castle. He was one of the ambassadors sent to England in February 1516 and on 14 November that year the town of Maybole was created a free burgh in barony for him. In March 1523 he was paid £150 by parliament for remaining for three months with the young king during Albany's second absence in France.

When Albany finally quit Scotland in May 1524, Cassillis joined the earl of Arran's party, and during the winters of 1524 and 1525 he was again in England negotiating peace. He was acquitted of the murder of Martin Kennedy of Lochland and Gilbert Makilwraith by an assize presided over by his brother-in-law the third earl of Argyll on 13 June 1525 and on 18 June 1526 he was granted a respite, along with many of his kindred and dependants, for the murder of Cornelius Machtema, a Dutch merchant killed during the sitting of parliament, and other offences. In

August, as the Douglases tightened their hold on government, Cassillis withdrew from council. He backed the earl of Lennox's efforts to wrest James V from the control of the sixth earl of Angus and on 4 September was with the army that unsuccessfully opposed Angus and Arran at Linlithgow. His estates were subsequently forfeited and nominally awarded to Arran, but on 25 November he was discharged of treason—a letter from James V enlisting his support was produced in his defence.

A dispute over the ownership of Turnberry and other lands in Carrick caused relations between Cassillis and his territorial rival Sir Hugh Campbell of Loudoun, sheriff of Ayr, to deteriorate. On 11 July 1527 the case was submitted before the lords of council, but on 23 July Cassillis complained that Loudoun, a follower of Angus, had privately persuaded members of council to subscribe a decreet in his favour. Before due process could be exhausted the earl was murdered, at Loudoun's instigation, on the sands beside Prestwick some time between 24 and 31 August 1527. Loudoun was outlawed for the crime on 5 October, but escaped punishment through crown patronage. By tradition the Kennedys swore beneath the dule tree of Cassillis to revenge his death, and in actuality retaliated by killing Robert Campbell of Lochfergus. The second earl was buried in Maybole collegiate church.

JOHN SIMMONS

Sources NA Scot., Ailsa muniments, GD 25 · R. K. Hannay, ed., *Acts of the lords of council in public affairs, 1501–1554* (1932) · *APS, 1424–1567* · M. Livingstone, D. Hay Fleming, and others, eds., *Registrum secreti sigilli regum Scotorum / The register of the privy seal of Scotland*, 1 (1908) · *RotS*, vol. 2 · G. Burnett and others, eds., *The exchequer rolls of Scotland*, 14 (1893); 15 (1895) · J. M. Thomson and others, eds., *Registrum magni sigilli regum Scotorum / The register of the great seal of Scotland*, 11 vols. (1882–1914), vols. 2–3 · GEC, *Peerage*, new edn, 3.74 · *Scots peerage*, 2.464–8 · R. Pitcairn, ed., *Historical and genealogical account of the principal families of the name of Kennedy* (1830) · R. Pitcairn, ed., *Ancient criminal trials in Scotland*, 7 pts in 3, Bannatyne Club, 42 (1833) · justiciary court book, NA Scot., JC 1/3

Kennedy, Gilbert, third earl of Cassillis (*c.*1517–1558), magnate, was the eldest son of Gilbert *Kennedy, second earl of Cassillis (*c.*1492–1527), and his wife, Isobella Campbell (b. *c.*1495, d. in or after 1533). Quintin *Kennedy, who became abbot of Crossraguel, was his brother. The second earl was murdered in late August 1527, and the younger Gilbert's upbringing was entrusted to his uncle William Kennedy, abbot of Crossraguel. According to John Knox, Cassillis was obliged when only twelve or thirteen to subscribe the death warrant of Patrick Hamilton, Scotland's first protestant martyr, who was burnt at the stake at St Andrews on 29 February 1528. This has been interpreted as evidence for the earl's having matriculated at St Andrews University, but he does not appear in its records, and in any case Cassillis was probably only eleven in 1528. On 8 April 1530 he was licensed to go on pilgrimage to France with another uncle, Thomas Kennedy of Coiff. He remained there for about five years, much longer than many Scots spent on the continent, and it was probably then that he received his education. His personal tutor was no less a figure than George Buchanan, who in 1533 dedicated to Kennedy his translation of Linacre's *Latin*

Grammar, published that year in Paris. By 1536 the two men had returned to Scotland; shortly afterwards Buchanan wrote his *Somnium* at Cassillis's family seat in Ayrshire.

Following his return Cassillis emerged as a power to be reckoned with in the west of Scotland, and principally in Ayrshire, where he began a lawsuit against Hugh Campbell of Loudoun, the killer of his father, probably over lands at Turnberry. He was made a member of James V's privy council, attended parliament regularly, and accompanied the king to the Western Isles in 1540. On 3 July 1538, shortly before he came of age, his marriage was granted to Margaret Kennedy of Bargany (*c*.1520–1596), the widow of William Wallace of Craigy, who then married him; they had three sons and two daughters. In November 1538 he received sasine of his earldom, confirmed to him by a charter of entail on 6 February 1541; its revenues have been estimated at about £715 Scots per annum. Cassillis also set about recreating the Kennedy affinity. Many of his kin, surname, and adherents were with him on 25 November 1542, when Sir Thomas Wharton captured him at Solway Moss.

Cassillis was taken to London as an important prisoner of war and initially lodged in the Tower of London. But when news came of James V's death on 14 December, and thus of the accession to the throne of his newly born daughter, Mary, the earl was brought to court and released into the custody of Archbishop Thomas Cranmer. Influenced by both Buchanan and Cranmer, he emerged in 1543 as a firmly committed protestant, ready to sign articles promising to advance by all the means in his power the marriage of Prince Edward to Queen Mary and to help Henry VIII gain the most important Scottish castles. An English pension of 300 marks must have made it easier for him to swallow treason, but he also had to provide hostages for his good behaviour. They were two of his brothers, David and Archibald, and also his uncle Thomas, and they languished in England for a long time, not returning home before February 1545 or later.

Back in Scotland in March 1543 as one of the Assured Lords, Cassillis was active in the protestant cause, ever promoting 'thys godly mariage and union' of Edward and Mary (Merriman, 112). In April 1544 he was apprehended by the governor, the second earl of Arran, at a time when he was collaborating with the earls of Lennox and Glencairn and with Lord Maxwell to undermine Arran's rejection of the English marriage, but was soon released. At the forefront of plots to assassinate Cardinal David Beaton, at the end of May Cassillis approached the English ambassador Sir Ralph Sadler with such a proposal, though he demanded a reward and a written warrant. Henry was reported as 'reputing the fact not meet to be set forward by him, and yet not misliking the offer' (*LP Henry VIII*, 20/1, no. 834), and his councillors tried to forward the scheme, but Cassillis was discouraged and abandoned the idea. When the deed was eventually done by others, on 29 May 1546, so shocking did it appear that on 11 June Cassillis (along with others of the Assured Lords) swore before his peers at Stirling that he had renounced all his contracts with Henry VIII.

Cassillis was not being wholly dishonest. Although he continued to communicate with the English and to receive letters from them (for example, he was sent ten copies of the printed proclamation of September 1547 and the February 1548 *Epistle*), he did little for his former allies. Nevertheless, he remained a committed protestant. Acts of iconoclasm erupted in many of the churches on or near his estates, and he was an early admirer of George Wishart, who in 1545 was invited to preach against the pope and the mass in Ayrshire. Cassillis may have flirted with treason in order to ensure that the government paid well for his support; if so, his tactics paid off, for by 1549 the French had appointed him lieutenant-general of the Scottish army and were paying him a pension to provide 800 light horse. An ally of Mary of Guise, the queen dowager, against Arran in 1544, Cassillis accompanied her to France in 1550 for her meeting with Henri II, and in October 1552 agreed with the earl of Angus and others to support her against Arran (now duc de Châtelherault). After she had become regent on 12 April 1554, Cassillis was rewarded on the 20th with the office of lord treasurer.

Although he was firmly against a war with England in the French interest in 1557, Cassillis was one of the eight Scottish commissioners appointed at the end of that year to negotiate in Paris for the marriage of Mary, queen of Scots, to the dauphin, François. The nuptials were duly celebrated on 24 April 1558 but ultimately proved fatal for several of the Scots who had negotiated them. A dispute as to whether the dauphin should have the Scottish crown matrimonial soured their mission, and as they were returning home four of the commissioners died. Almost inevitably there were suspicions of poison. Cassillis made his will on 8 November and died at Dieppe on the 28th. His body was taken back to Scotland for burial at Maybole, Ayrshire. His eldest son, Gilbert *Kennedy, succeeded to the earldom. MARCUS MERRIMAN

Sources *Scots peerage*, 2.464–71 · GEC, *Peerage*, 3.74–5 · J. Cameron, *James V: the personal rule, 1528–1542*, ed. N. Macdougall (1998) · M. Merriman, *The rough wooings: Mary queen of Scots, 1542–1551* (2000) · *LP Henry VIII*, vols. 17–21 · M. H. B. Sanderson, *Ayrshire and the Reformation* (1997)
Wealth at death £725 Scots: Cameron, *James V* (1998), 155 n. 78

Kennedy, Gilbert, fourth earl of Cassillis [*nicknamed* the King of Carrick] (*c*.1541–1576), nobleman, was the eldest of five children of Gilbert *Kennedy, third earl of Cassillis (*c*.1517–1558), and his wife, Margaret (*c*.1520–1596), daughter of Alexander Kennedy of Bargany. He was under age in November 1558 when his father—in whose absence he first sat in parliament as master of Cassillis—died in France, and he was not served heir until 16 October 1562. On 10 February 1559 he succeeded his father as a gentleman of the bedchamber to Henri II of France. The English ambassador reported him, in August 1561, 'that Sunday at the preaching and the Monday at the Mass: it is said that since he has repented it and this is but Tuesday' (*CSP Scot.*,

1547–63, p. 547). Despite such inconsistency, Cassillis initially resisted reform, guided by his uncle Quintin *Kennedy, abbot of Crossraguel. His eventual conversion to the protestant faith, in August 1566, is attributed to Margaret (*c.*1545–1626), only daughter of John Lyon, seventh Lord Glamis, whom he married on 30 September. They had two sons, John *Kennedy, fifth earl of Cassillis, and Hew, master of Cassillis.

Cassillis's relative youth precluded any significant participation in politics until the later years of Mary Stuart's reign. He sat on the assize which in April 1567 acquitted the earl of Bothwell of Lord Darnley's murder, signed the so-called Ainslie bond shortly afterwards in favour of Bothwell's marriage to Mary, but joined the confederacy opposing the royal couple at Carberry Hill on 15 June. Following Mary's escape from Lochleven Castle on 2 May 1568, he signed the Hamilton bond, and on 13 May fought for her at Langside, where his brother Sir Thomas Kennedy of Culzean was taken prisoner. After the queen's flight to England he remained loyal to her, though he entertained a genuine respect for the regent Moray, and acted as pallbearer at his funeral.

Cassillis achieved notoriety when he attempted to resolve a long-running dispute over the ownership of the lands of Crossraguel Abbey by roasting their commendator (lay proprietor) in the black vault of Dunure Castle. The abbey had been in Kennedy hands since 1524, but following the death of Abbot Quintin in August 1564 the crown intervened to appoint Allan Stewart as commendator. Cassillis held a five-year lease of the abbacy set to expire at Whitsun 1569 and when he attended the 1566 celebration of Candlemas in Holyrood chapel, his display of devotion was rewarded with a further nineteen-year lease, in terms which appeared to contradict the earlier grant to Stewart. However, the new commendator, intent on diverting lands to his brother Sir James Stewart of Cardonald, proved unreceptive to Cassillis's attempts to buy him out. Allan Stewart was lured to Dunure Castle on 29 August 1570. When he refused to dispone the lands in Cassillis's favour, so Stewart alleged, he was carried to the black vault, where he was stripped below the waist and his feet set between an iron chimney and a fire until he complied with the earl's demands. His refusal to ratify the relevant charters a week later saw him put back over the fire. He was finally rescued in November 1570 by men of the sheriffdom led by Cassillis's uncle Sir Thomas Kennedy of Bargany. The leader of King James's party in Carrick, Bargany had himself detained the commendator in the previous year, in pursuit of a share of the Crossraguel lands.

Cassillis's attempts to reassert his authority in Ayrshire were arrested when the regent Lennox descended on Carrick, and he was forced to enter himself in ward at Stirling on 15 April 1571, thus effectively ending his support for the queen. He rejoined the privy council under the regent Mar on 7 September. Cassillis subsequently acquired the Crossraguel estates by purchase. His violence was condemned by opponents of the Marian cause, but his actions consolidated his family's grip on southern Ayrshire, where he

was popularly known as the King of Carrick. He had earlier secured the lands of Glenluce Abbey at the expense of Sir John Gordon of Lochinvar. In 1576 his horse fell with him as it crossed a bridge near Glasgow. He was carried to Edinburgh, where he died on 12 December. He was buried in Maybole collegiate church.   JOHN SIMMONS

Sources F. C. H. Blair, ed., *Charters of the Abbey of Crosraguel*, 2 vols., Ayrshire and Galloway Archaeological Association (1886) · NA Scot., Ailsa MSS, GD 25 · *Reg. PCS*, 1st ser., vols. 1–2 · *CSP Scot.*, 1547–63 · R. Pitcairn, ed., *Historical and genealogical account of the principal families of the name of Kennedy* (1830) · J. Knox, *History of the Reformation in Scotland*, vols. 1–2 of *The works of John Knox*, ed. D. Laing, Wodrow Society, 12 (1846–8) · *Scots peerage*, 2.468–74 · NA Scot., Edinburgh commissary court, CC8/8/29 · D. MacGibbon and T. Ross, *The ecclesiastical architecture of Scotland* (1897) · K. M. Brown, 'A house divided: family and feud in Carrick under John Kennedy, fifth earl of Cassillis', *SHR*, 75 (1996), 168–96

Kennedy, Gilbert (1678–1745), minister of the Presbyterian General Synod of Ulster, son of Gilbert Kennedy (d. 1689), who was successively minister of Girvan, Ayrshire, and Dundonald, co. Down, was born at Dundonald. In 1697 he entered the University of Glasgow. He was probably in Ireland by late 1701 and was licensed by the presbytery of Armagh on 17 November 1701. On 23 March 1704 he was ordained by the presbytery of Armagh as minister of the united charges of Donaghcloney and Tullylish, and, during the first subscription controversy, soon became one of the most prominent men on the orthodox side in the synod of Ulster. In 1720 he was elected its moderator. He was probably the author of *New Light Set in a Clear Light* (1721), published anonymously in Belfast, which was intended as a reply to the *Religious Obedience Founded on Personal Persuasion* of John Abernethy, and James Kirkpatrick's *Vindication of the Presbyterian Ministers in the North of Ireland*. In 1724 was published *A Defence of the Principles and Conduct of the General Synod of Ulster*. It was a reply to Samuel Haliday's *Reasons Against the Imposition of Subscription to the Westminster Confession of Faith*, and appears to have been the work of several hands, but Kennedy's name alone appears on the title-page. In 1727 he issued *A Daily Directory Enlarged* which expanded on the devotional work of the same title published in 1680 by Sir William Waller, the parliamentarian general. It was several times republished. *The Narrative of the Non-Subscribers Examined* (1731) has also been attributed to Kennedy, but on insufficient evidence. A long correspondence between him and John Abernethy is among Wodrow's papers in the National Library of Scotland, Edinburgh. Kennedy married Elizabeth, daughter of the Revd George Lang of Newry; they had four sons and three daughters. He died on 8 July 1745, probably at Tullylish, where he was buried.

THOMAS HAMILTON, *rev.* RAYMOND GILLESPIE

Sources T. Witherow, *Historical and literary memorials of presbyterianism in Ireland, 1731–1800* (1880) · *Records of the General Synod of Ulster, from 1691 to 1820*, 3 vols. (1890–98) · private information (1891) · private information (2004)
Archives PRO NIre., family and estate papers | NL Scot., Wodrow papers

Kennedy, Grace (1782–1825), novelist, was born at Pinmore, Ayrshire, the fourth daughter of Robert Kennedy (d.

1790) and Robina, daughter of John Vans Agnew of Barnbarroch, Galloway. Heavy financial losses forced the family to move to Edinburgh while Grace was still a child. Here she was brought up under the instruction of her mother, a devout evangelical protestant. Being of a very retiring disposition, she took no share in the ordinary amusements of society. But her cheerful temper and intellectual attainments made her a delightful companion among intimate friends. She showed an active interest for many years in the education of children, and was led to writing fiction as a means to serve God.

Grace Kennedy's novels (at least eight) were all published anonymously and rapidly in the early 1820s, and met with considerable success, being reissued late into the nineteenth century, often in religious reprint libraries. The first, addressed to adolescent readers and entitled *The Decision, or, Religion must be All, or is Nothing* (1821), sets a standard. A mixture of conduct-book instruction and dramatically executed scenes, it tells of a young girl's entrance into London society and her rejection of it in favour of religious duty. *Anna Ross: a Story for Children* (1823) replaces the rational Lockean narratives of a previous generation of writers for children, such as Anna Letitia Barbauld and Maria Edgeworth, with an unremitting focus on individual salvation.

1823 also saw the publication of *Father Clement: a Roman Catholic Story*, the book by which she is best known. A controversial novel, it set the fashion for tales of suffering Jesuits that continued throughout the nineteenth century. Though written from the protestant viewpoint, it distinguishes between the system (to be condemned) and the individual, the sympathetic Father Clement, whose faith is at issue in a tearful deathbed conclusion. It reached a twelfth edition in 1858, and was translated into several European languages. The anonymous *Father Oswald: a Genuine Catholic Story* (1842) declares itself an 'antidote' to Kennedy's novel, while *Father Clement*'s reputation was still current in 1857 when Miss Pratt, a character in George Eliot's novella *Janet's Repentance*, refers to it.

In 1824 appeared *Andrew Campbell's Visit to his Irish Cousins* and *Dunallan*, Kennedy's longest tale, written before any of the others. After enjoying uninterrupted good health until 1824, Grace Kennedy died unmarried in Edinburgh on 28 February 1825. *Philip Colville, a Covenanter's Story*, left unfinished at her death, was published posthumously. It attempts to correct the fanatical picture of the Scottish covenanters painted by Sir Walter Scott in *Old Mortality* (1816). A collected edition of Kennedy's works was issued at Edinburgh in 1827 in six volumes, and was reprinted at Brussels in 1836.

W. A. GREENHILL, rev. KATHRYN SUTHERLAND

Sources 'A short account of the author', *The works of Grace Kennedy*, 1 (1827) • R. Jamieson, *Cyclopaedia of religious biography: a series of memoirs of the most eminent religious characters of modern times, intended for family reading* (1853), 295–6

Kennedy, Harry Angus Alexander (1866–1934), biblical scholar, was born at Dornoch, Sutherland, on 4 July 1866, the elder son of George Rainy Kennedy, a Free Church of Scotland minister in Dornoch, and his wife, Mary Margaret McIntyre. He was educated at the Edinburgh Academy (where he won distinction in classics) and at the University of Edinburgh before studying theology at New College, Edinburgh, and at the German universities of Halle and Berlin. In 1893 he married Elisabeth (d. 1928), the daughter of George Gordon, a flax importer, of Donavourd, Perthshire; they had at least three daughters. In the same year Kennedy was ordained minister of the Free church at Callander, where he remained for eight years. He was Cunningham lecturer in Edinburgh until 1905, when he was elected to the chair of New Testament language and literature at Knox College, Toronto. Four years later he returned to Edinburgh, having been called to succeed the well-known biblical scholar Marcus Dods in the chair of New Testament language and literature at New College. He remained in this post until ill health compelled him to take early retirement in 1925. After a period of illness, which prevented him from continuing his scholarship, Kennedy died in Edinburgh on 23 March 1934.

Kennedy first made a name for himself among biblical scholars during his ministry at Callander. His short volume, *The Sources of New Testament Greek*, published in 1895, was a pioneer of its kind. Its thesis was that the language of the Septuagint and of the New Testament was not, as had always been assumed, a Hebraic dialect of the Greek tongue, but the common speech of the contemporary Hellenistic world, a conclusion which was soon to be confirmed by the study of the Greek papyri found in Egypt, and by the further researches of scholars such as Adolf Deissmann, George Milligan, and J. H. Moulton. After contributing a learned article, 'Old Latin biblical versions', to the third volume of James Hastings's *Dictionary of the Bible* (1904), Kennedy turned from the linguistic field to that of biblical ideas. In 1904 he published his Cunningham lectures (delivered in Edinburgh from 1902 to 1904), as *St Paul's Conceptions of the Last Things*, just at the time that the eschatological problem was beginning to occupy the central place in biblical controversy. Kennedy's wide acquaintance with Jewish apocalyptic literature combined with his conscientious New Testament scholarship enabled him to make timely contributions to this debate. Nine years later he published *St Paul and the Mystery Religions* (1913), which was also in tune with a newly fashionable discussion, namely that represented by Richard Reitzenstein and other continental scholars concerning the derivation of the most characteristic features of Paulinism from certain ideas widely current in the contemporary Hellenistic world. Later scholarship has argued strongly for the distinctively Palestinian nature of Paul's thought, and this view has prevailed over Kennedy's. In 1919 *Philo's Contribution to Religion* came out, a piece of research of interest not only to students of Philo but also to those examining the background of New Testament thought. In the same year Kennedy published *The Theology of the Epistles*, a short book hardly surpassed in its field at the time. His last work, a popular book entitled *The Vital Forces of the Early Church*, was published in 1920.

Kennedy's private theological position was that of a liberal evangelical. But his work was praised in the twentieth century for its impartiality; his conscientiousness as a scholar ensured that he did not prejudice his conclusions but followed his evidence wherever it appeared to lead. His integrity and personal warmth gained him the admiration of several generations of Scottish ministers taught by him in Edinburgh.   GERALD LAW

Sources *The Times* (29 March 1934) · *CGPLA Eng. & Wales* (1934) · *DNB*
Wealth at death £4088 10s. 0d.: confirmation, 10 June 1934, *CCI*

Kennedy, Hugh (1698–1764), Church of Scotland minister, was born in the north of Ireland of Scottish parents. Nothing further is known of him until his attendance at Glasgow University, first recorded in 1713. He graduated MA on 9 March 1714. On 16 March 1722 Kennedy married Margaret Scott (*d*. 1746), the second sister of Walter Scott of Crumhaugh, south-west of Hawick, and probably the daughter of Charles Scott (1664–1698). They had at least thirteen children, six of whom survived their father. After serving as chaplain to Archibald Douglas of Cavers, Kennedy was licensed by Jedburgh presbytery on 5 October 1720, ordained to Torthorwald, near Dumfries (7 September 1721), translated to Cavers, near Hawick (13 November 1723), and then to the Scots Kirk in Rotterdam on 25 May 1737, where he joined John Enslie (*d*. 1766) as colleague. After Enslie retired in 1759, Kennedy was assisted by William Walker (1719–1774).

Kennedy was held in high regard in Scotland and Rotterdam. He declined calls to return to Dunfermline in 1742 (to succeed Ralph Erskine) or to Dalkeith in 1746—and thereby won from Rotterdam's city fathers an increased stipend. Marischal College, Aberdeen, made him a DD in 1762. A contemporary called him 'one of the best pulpit-men' in Scotland (Steven, 173). In Rotterdam he energetically reordered the working of the consistory and the role of ministers and elders individually, especially in visitation. Catechizing, admission to the Lord's supper, discipline, and the questions to be put to intending members (in length and density highly taxing) were all reformed.

Kennedy was frequently consulted on theological and ecclesiastical matters, and devoted special interest to two concerns. First, he had the work of Scottish and English divines translated into Dutch, sometimes contributing prefaces, as for Thomas Boston's *Covenant of Grace* (1741) and Thomas Halyburton's *Memoirs* (1746) and *Great Concern of Salvation* (1747). He advised on the best British biblical commentaries for a translation series of 59 volumes (1741–87). Second, Kennedy's ardour for revival ensured that Christians in Scotland and England were informed of Dutch events, especially at Nieuwkerk under Gerard Kuypers, in his *Short Account of the Rise and Continued Progress of a Remarkable Work of Grace in the United Netherlands* (1752), which assembled reports partly printed separately in 1750 and 1751. He also had translated into Dutch narratives of the awakening in Cambuslang and Kilsyth, especially James Robe's *Narrative*. More than once he defended revivals against Dutch critics, particularly one Professor van den Honert. A short collection of sermons published

in Dutch, *De leer en leiding des Evangeliums* (1748), included one address delivered as moderator of Merse and Teviotdale synod which had previously been issued in English (1732). This and his *Discourse Concerning the Nature, Author, Means and Manner of Conversion* (1743) were abridged in his *Remains* (1828), edited by John Brown of Whitburn.

Kennedy was tall and slender with 'a commanding appearance, a fine open countenance and a ruddy complexion' (Steven, 197). To Alexander (Jupiter) Carlyle he was 'popular, and pompous, and political, and an Irishman' (*Autobiography*, ed. Burton, 173). He well exemplified the Scottish evangelical Calvinism of his era. He died in Rotterdam, at his home 'by the dijk gate, over the bridge', on 3 November 1764 and was buried at the city's Laurens Kirk on the 8th.   D. F. WRIGHT

Sources *Fasti Scot.*, new edn, 2.106, 490 · W. Steven, *The history of the Scottish church, Rotterdam* (1832, 1833) · J. Morrison, *Scots on the Dijk: the story of the Scots church, Rotterdam* (1981) · *DSCHT* · R. H. Campbell, 'Kennedy, Hugh', *The Blackwell dictionary of evangelical biography, 1730–1860*, ed. D. M. Lewis (1995) · *The autobiography of Dr Alexander Carlyle of Inveresk, 1722–1805*, ed. J. H. Burton (1910) · private information (2004) [Scottish Borders Archive and Local History Centre, Selkirk; Mrs Sionag Ruymgaart-Marten, church archivist, Rotterdam] · J. van Abkoude, *Naamregister van de … Nederduitsche Boeken … 1600 tot … 1761*, ed. R. Arrenberg (1788) · parish register (marriage), Hawick
Likenesses pencil sketch (after photograph of an earlier portrait); photographic reproduction, priv. coll. · photograph (after portrait); formerly at Scots Kirk, Rotterdam [destroyed May 1940]

Kennedy, Sir James (*d*. 1408). *See under* Kennedy family (*per. c.*1350–1513).

Kennedy, James (*c.*1408–1465), bishop of St Andrews, was the third son of a much married mother, Mary Stewart (*d*. after 1458), daughter of Robert III, and her second husband, Sir James *Kennedy of Dunure (killed 8 November 1408) [*see under* Kennedy family (*per. c.*1350–1513)]. Mary Stewart's various marriages—first to George Douglas, earl of Angus (*d*. 1403), and, after Kennedy, to Sir William Graham of Montrose, and finally to Sir William Edmonstone of Duntreath—meant that, from birth, her sons might expect influential support and rapid advancement. In spite of occasional political reverses, James Kennedy emerged to become an important figure, as ecclesiastical statesman, diplomat, and royal adviser, in the reign of James II and the minority of his son. Being the third son, Kennedy seems to have opted for an ecclesiastical career at an early stage. He entered the University of St Andrews about 1426, supported financially by Bishop John Cameron of Glasgow and by his uncle James I. He duly took his master's degree in 1429 and was holding academic office at St Andrews the following year.

A temporary setback then occurred. In the summer of 1431 the king suddenly arrested Archibald, fifth earl of Douglas, and Sir John Kennedy, James's eldest brother. This royal intervention may have been a drastic solution to a Kennedy family feud in Carrick; and it has recently been suggested that James and his other brother, Gilbert *Kennedy [*see under* Kennedy family (*per. c.*1350–1513)], with no desire to share Sir John's fate—incarceration in Stirling Castle followed by escape into exile—may have assisted the king in undermining John's position. Alternatively, a combination of prudence and fear may have led James to go abroad at this point to the new University of Louvain, where he matriculated in the faculty of law and graduated as bachelor of canon law some time before the end of January 1433. Returning to Scotland, he found himself again in favour, being provided anew to the subdeanery of Glasgow in the spring of 1433. Late in January 1437, when he was aged about twenty-nine, his career appeared at last to have 'taken off': against the wishes of Pope Eugenius IV, the cathedral chapter at Dunkeld, and Walter Stewart, earl of Atholl (d. 1437), James I provided his nephew James Kennedy to the bishopric of Dunkeld.

Almost at once (21 February 1437) James I was assassinated at the instigation of his uncle Atholl, and Kennedy was faced with the problems of gaining acceptance from an initially hostile pope and coping with the political perils associated with a royal minority—for James II, in the care of the widowed queen Joan Beaufort, was only six in 1437. Astutely, the new bishop of Dunkeld threw his support behind Pope Eugenius in his struggle with the Basel conciliarists, a crucial move. By 1439 Kennedy had transformed himself into the leader of the papalist party in Scotland, receiving from a grateful pontiff first the commend of the abbey of Scone (23 September 1439) and then the richest prize of all, the bishopric of St Andrews, following the death of Bishop Henry Wardlaw in 1440. The translation was made on 1 June. Significantly, Kennedy's standing with the pope was such that he was allowed to remit only half the 3300 gold florins in common services payable on entry to St Andrews.

Close association with the queen mother and the rump of James I's administration brought dangers for Kennedy at home, and the bishop found himself on the wrong side in the civil war of 1444–5 which culminated in the collapse of the late king's party, the death of Joan Beaufort, and the dominance of the Douglas–Livingston faction at court. The victors seem to have considered depriving Kennedy of his bishopric; his lands were harried by the earl of Crawford (an incident which led to Kennedy's cursing of Crawford, who died in the 'battle of Arbroath' a year later) and he played no further part in government for four and a half years.

Kennedy re-emerged in the parliament of January 1450, supporting the adult James II in condemning his former keepers, the Livingstons, and lending the king money. Thereafter he went on pilgrimage to Rome to attend the jubilee celebrations, and cannot certainly be found in Scotland between 28 August 1450 and 18 April 1452. Thus he was absent when James II launched the first of his assaults on the Black Douglases, and probably returned to Scotland only after the killing of the eighth earl of Douglas, by James II himself, on 22 February 1452. Kennedy's role as royal counsellor was not therefore a dominant one—Bishop William Turnbull of Glasgow was much more active on the royal side during the 1452 crisis—but he performed the signal service of making St Andrews Castle available to Queen Mary of Gueldres during her third pregnancy, which ended successfully in the birth of a male heir, the future James III (May 1452). For the remaining eight years of James II's life Kennedy was a frequent witness to royal charters, an occasional parliamentarian (1452 and 1454), and an auditor of exchequer in 1452, 1455, and 1456. Yet he appears to have played no part in the king's final defeat of the Black Douglases in 1455, and he was never given a major office of state. On embassy to Bourges to take part in Scoto-Danish negotiations in the summer of 1460 he fell ill at Bruges; at about the same time (3 August 1460) James II was killed at the siege of Roxburgh, aged only twenty-nine.

Kennedy's role in government during the early years of James III's minority was limited; he seems not to have returned to Scotland until after the first parliament of the new reign (February 1461), in which Mary of Gueldres effectively took charge of government. A running battle between the queen mother and the bishop ensued, with the latter attempting to honour his earlier promise to Charles VII of France to pursue a Franco-Lancastrian foreign policy, while Mary of Gueldres, perhaps more realistically, followed a more pragmatic line, balancing Lancaster against York in the English civil wars, and recognizing that the Yorkists were the clear victors by the early 1460s. The death of Mary of Gueldres on 1 December 1463, however, left Kennedy, for the last eighteen months of his life, in charge of the young James III. He took the king on an extended northern progress in the summer of 1464; and before he died, at St Andrews on 24 May 1465, the bishop entrusted the custody of the king to Gilbert Kennedy.

Sixteenth-century writers, starting with John Mair (1521), would exaggerate Kennedy's role as James II's principal adviser in his struggle with the Douglases, largely because the theme of the over-mighty subject, not to mention the wilful queen mother, was one which struck a resonant chord in the troubled minority of James V. Later historians, above all A. I. Dunlop in a biographical work of massive scholarship published in 1950, would echo and develop these claims. Yet it is arguable that the true legacy of Bishop Kennedy did not lie in politics. On 27 August 1450 he founded the college of St Salvator at St Andrews, with the particular intention that it should promote the study of theology in the university. The college was liberally endowed—its provost and twelve scholars were to be supported from the teinds (tithes) of four neighbouring parishes—and was soon attracting members of noble Scottish families, studying at their own expense. Mair, followed by Leslie, Pitscottie, and Buchanan later in the sixteenth century, would remember this as one of Kennedy's three remarkable achievements, along with the erection in 1458 of a magnificent tomb in the chapel of his college and the possession of a huge ship, the *Salvator*, of 500 tons, greatly admired by the water bailiff of Sluys as she rode at anchor in the harbour in 1457.

NORMAN MACDOUGALL

Sources J. M. Thomson and others, eds., *Registrum magni sigilli regum Scotorum / The register of the great seal of Scotland*, 11 vols. (1882–1914), vol. 2 · *APS, 1424–1567* · *A history of greater Britain … by John Major*, ed. and trans. A. Constable, Scottish History Society, 10 (1892) · A. I. Dunlop, *The life and times of James Kennedy, bishop of St*

Andrews, St Andrews University Publications, 46 (1950) · N. Macdougall, 'Bishop James Kennedy of St Andrews: a reassessment of his political career', *Church, Politics and Society: Scotland, 1408–1929*, ed. N. Macdougall (1983), 1–22 · 'Auchinleck Chronicle', *The Asloan manuscript*, ed. W. A. Craigie, 1, STS, 14 (1923), 54–5 · A. I. Dunlop, ed., *Acta facultatis artium universitatis Sanctiandree, 1413–1588*, 2 vols., Scottish History Society, 3rd ser., 54–5 (1964) · J. Lesley, *The history of Scotland*, ed. T. Thomson, Bannatyne Club, 38 (1830), 42–3 · *The historie and cronicles of Scotland … by Robert Lindesay of Pitscottie*, ed. A. J. G. Mackay, 1, STS, 42 (1899) · [G. Buchanan], *The history of Scotland translated from the Latin of George Buchanan*, ed. and trans. J. Aikman, 6 vols. (1827–9), vol. 2 · G. Burnett and others, eds., *The exchequer rolls of Scotland*, 5–6 (1882–3) · *RotS*, vol. 2 · R. G. Cant, *The University of St Andrews: a short history*, rev. edn (1970)

Archives NA Scot., R. M. S. · NA Scot., E. R. · U. St Andr., 'St Andrews acta'

Kennedy, James (*fl.* 1662–1686), Latin poet, was the son of James Kennedy, town clerk of Aberdeen and sheriff clerk from 1661 to 1672, who was dismissed from his post when writs were issued against him for debts he had incurred. Both father and son possessed the title of sheriff clerk when they were admitted burgesses of Aberdeen on 9 June 1668. The son may be identical with the James Kennedy who became conservator of Scottish privileges and Scottish resident in the Low Countries about 1684, and who was knighted in that or the following year. After the departure of Bevil Skelton, Kennedy was also appointed English resident and belatedly received his commission as consul from the states general of the United Provinces at Rotterdam on 16 August 1686, but his time in the town was marred by the antagonism of the English community there. His office brought him great personal expense and he wrote letters to Skelton and Lord Middleton describing the straitened circumstances of his large family, which included his five children (see BL, Add. MS 41820, fols. 28, 35).

Kennedy's first publication, a pastoral with echoes of Virgil's *Eclogues*, emerged in Aberdeen in 1662 entitled *Diadēma kai mitra, seu, Daphnidis et Druydum reditus* ('The Diadem and the Mitre, or, The Return of Daphnis and the Druids'). The poem, which comprises eighty Latin hexameters, takes the form of a conversation between two shepherds, describing the celebrations in Scotland now that Daphnis and the druids have returned from exile. It is a simple allegory on the return of the episcopacy to Scotland: Daphnis represents James Sharp, archbishop of St Andrews, and the druids are the bishops. In the same year Kennedy found in the marriage of Charles II and Catherine of Braganza another reason to rejoice, and published *Gamēlion dōron* ('Wedding present'), a jubilant epithalamium in Latin hexameters. The little volume is rounded off with a prayer in Latin sapphics for the safety of the royal couple and their kingdom.

Kennedy's only other published work was *Aeneas Britannicus* (1663), a poem largely composed of passages culled from the *Aeneid* and pieced together to celebrate Charles II as the 'British Aeneas'. The unique copy of this book, of which only the first few pages (containing 211 hexameters) survive, is in Aberdeen University Library. A couple of lines from the poem, which mimic the beginning of the *Aeneid*, will indicate the style:

Arma virumque cano, Britannis primus ab oris
Gallica qui fato profugus Germanaque venit
Littora.
('Arms I sing and the man, who first left British shores, exiled by fate, and came to the coasts of France and Germany.' Ll. 5–7)

What remains of the poem covers only the battle of Worcester, but the 'argument' attests that it went on to describe Charles's exile, restoration, and marriage, hinting that this was a sizeable production. Although he has been described as a straggler behind the great tradition of Scottish Latin verse (Bradner, 198), James Kennedy was a competent Latin poet, and his letters show him to have been conscientious in his duties as a consul.

Ross Kennedy

Sources W. K. Leask, ed., *Musa Latina Aberdonensis*, 3: *Poetae minores*, New Spalding Club, 37 (1910), 167–85 · D. Littlejohn, ed., *Records of the sheriff court of Aberdeenshire*, 3 vols. (1907) · L. B. Taylor, ed., *Aberdeen council letters*, 6 vols. (1942–61) · L. Bradner, *Musae Anglicanae: a history of Anglo-Latin poetry, 1500–1925* (1940) · BL, Add. MSS 41810–41823

Archives BL, Middleton papers, Add. MSS 41810–41823

Kennedy, James (1784/5–1851), medical bibliographer, was the son of Captain John Kennedy. He was born in Scotland and spent his childhood at Tillyrie, near Kinross. He became librarian to the Glasgow Public Library (a subscription library) and was presumably responsible for the catalogue printed in 1810, which displays his lifelong tendency to over-elaboration. He celebrated his native region in *Glenochel, a Descriptive Poem* (2 vols., 1810), including lengthy scholarly notes, and was editor of a short-lived magazine, *The Druid* (1812). He began to attend medical classes at Glasgow University in 1810 and graduated MD in 1813 with a thesis, *De lingua humana*. He practised as a physician at Dunning, Perthshire, until 1821, then at Glasgow, becoming an ardent phrenologist and friend of George Combe (letters in National Library of Scotland MSS 7215–7269, 7383–7388). His practice at Dunning furnished material for a series of articles in the *London Medical Repository* between 1820 and 1826, and in 1825 he published *Instructions … on the Management of Children*; his 'Instructions … on the management of the female constitution' was described as 'ready for the press' but was never published.

In 1826 Kennedy moved to Tamworth, and in 1827 or 1828 he was invited to Ashby-de-la-Zouch by Edward Mammatt, agent to the marquess of Hastings, who was promoting the town as a spa. Kennedy contributed 'Remarks on the water' to T. Wayte's *Descriptive … Guide* (1831) and in the same year published anonymously *An Exposure of the Unphilosophical and Unchristian Expedients Adopted by Antiphrenologists*, an overblown response to *Anti-Phrenology* (1829), by Dr John Wayte of King's Lynn. He continued to contribute to professional journals and to the *Gentleman's Magazine*, but his only other publication in book form was *A Lecture on … Cholera* (1832). His first wife was Miss Thompson, sister of Lord Hastings's secretary; subsequently he married Charlotte Hawkes of Norton Canes, Staffordshire, on 20 November 1838. There were no children.

In 1842 Kennedy retired to Woodhouse, near Loughborough, retaining some charitable practice and serving as physician to the Loughborough Dispensary, but concentrating on his *Athenae medicae Britannicae*, a long-standing project for an author-bibliography of British medicine to 1800 (including foreign authors published in Britain). The work was accepted for publication by the Sydenham Society and in 1851 Kennedy moved up to London to supervise printing and to work at the British Museum, but he was taken ill in April after delivery of the first thirty-two pages of proofs. He died aged sixty-six on 9 May 1851, at 24 Great Russell Street, from inflammation of the bowels, and was buried at Woodhouse on 15 May. The manuscript of his bibliography, of which only the letter A was in a finished state, was presented to the British Museum by his widow on 5 August 1859 (now British Library Add. MSS 23168–23194). His library was sold at Sothebys on 11–13 December 1851, and realized £330. 4s. 0d.   JOHN SYMONS

Sources *GM*, 2nd ser., 36 (1851), 205–6 · 'Chronological and bibliographical catalogue of literary periodical works published in Glasgow during the present century', *The Ant* (29 Sept 1827), 289–96 · A. C. P. Callisen, *Medicinisches Schriftsteller-Lexicon*, 10 (Copenhagen, 1832), 137–8 · A. C. P. Callisen, *Medicinisches Schriftsteller-Lexicon*, 29 (Copenhagen, 1841), 223–4 · *London and Provincial Medical Directory* (1847–52) · G. G. Meynell, *The two Sydenham societies* (1985) · R. Cooter, *Phrenology in the British Isles: an annotated historical biobibliography and index* (1989) · J. M. Kuist, *The Nichols file of the Gentleman's Magazine: attributions of authorship and other documentation in editorial papers at the Folger Library* (1982) · *Medical Times* (17 May 1851) · m. cert. · census returns, 1841, 1851 · d. cert. · private information (2004)
Archives BL, Add. MSS 23168–23194 | Folger, Nichols MSS · NL Scot., corresp. with George Combe · NL Scot., Dick MSS, 9658

Kennedy, James. *See* Bailie, James Kennedy- (1793–1864).

Kennedy, James (*c*.1793–1827), writer, about whose early life nothing is known, published *Glenochal*, a two-volume poem, in 1811, and, having planned to be a barrister, graduated MD from Edinburgh in 1813. He became an army hospital assistant in 1814, and assistant staff surgeon in 1815.

For most of his life, Kennedy was posted in the Mediterranean, where he was also involved in missionary and educational work. It was in Cephalonia in 1823 that he met Byron. He had received a religious education, but was not a strict Christian until university. Now he undertook to explain his faith to some sceptical friends. Byron was at the first meeting; the two became friends, and Byron subsequently had frequent conversations with Kennedy on the subject. He entrusted a little Turkish girl he intended to adopt to Kennedy and his wife, Hannah Sarah. When the poet died, Kennedy summarized their discussions in *Conversations on Religion with Lord Byron*, published with some success posthumously in 1830.

Kennedy returned to England in 1826, spent time in Ireland, and in December was ordered to the West Indies. He died at Up Park Camp, near Kingston, Jamaica, of yellow fever, on 18 September 1827.

W. A. GREENHILL, *rev.* JESSICA HININGS

Sources J. Kennedy, *Conversations on religion with Lord Byron and others* (1830) · Allibone, *Dict.* · *The life of Lord Byron, with his letters and journals*, ed. T. Moore, new edn (1847) · *North American Review*, 36 (1833) · [J. Watkins and F. Shoberl], *A biographical dictionary of the living authors of Great Britain and Ireland* (1816) · L. A. Marchand, *Byron: a portrait* (1971); another edn (1976) · admin., PRO, PROB 6/204, fol. 53

Kennedy, James (1797–1886), mechanical engineer, born on 13 January 1797 in the village of Gilmerton, near Edinburgh, was apprenticed to a millwright near Dalkeith from 1810 to 1815, after which he took various jobs in Scotland to gain experience in mechanical engineering. In 1824 George Stephenson put him in charge of his engine works in Newcastle upon Tyne, where Kennedy was involved in the design and building of two pairs of stationary engines and the first four locomotives for the Stockton and Darlington Railway. At the end of 1825 he went to Liverpool and shortly afterwards joined the firm of Bury, Edward & Co. at their Clarence foundry in Liverpool as works foreman, supervising the construction of stationary, marine, and locomotive engines. One of his locomotives, the *Liverpool*, was in 1830 the first built in England to have horizontal cylinders linked directly to the crank axle. In 1842 Kennedy was taken into partnership, the firm becoming Bury, Curtis, and Kennedy. For many years the firm concentrated on building four-wheeled locomotives; their designs were sound and their workmanship excellent, but largely because of Bury's conservatism and reluctance to undertake larger locomotives, Kennedy left in 1844, to join Thomas Vernon & Son, shipbuilders in Liverpool, where he introduced the use of iron deck beams for vessels requiring exceptional strength. In 1847 he was elected a member of the Institution of Mechanical Engineers, of which he served as president in 1860. Kennedy died on 25 September 1886 at his home, Cressington Park, Garston, near Liverpool. He was survived by his wife, Adelaide.   RONALD M. BIRSE

Sources *Engineering* (1 Oct 1886), 351 · *Institution of Mechanical Engineers: Proceedings* (1886), 532–3 · M. R. Bailey, 'Robert Stephenson & Co., 1823–1829', *Transactions* [Newcomen Society], 50 (1978–9), 109–38, esp. 112–20 · J. G. H. Warren, *A century of locomotive building by Robert Stephenson & Co., 1823–1923* (1923); repr. (1970) · J. W. Lowe, *British steam locomotive builders* (1975) · d. cert.
Wealth at death £97,780 1s. 11d.: resworn probate, May 1887, CGPLA Eng. & Wales (1886)

Kennedy, James [Jimmy] (1902–1984), popular songwriter, was born on 20 July 1902 at Omagh, co. Tyrone, Ireland, the elder son of Joseph Hamilton Kennedy, of the Royal Irish Constabulary, and his wife, Annie Baskin. He was educated at Trinity College, Dublin, and spent some time as a teacher at Shaftesbury, where he composed songs, before joining the colonial service as a political officer. Bored, he turned to full-time songwriting. He joined Lorraine Music in Greek Street, Soho, London, where he dealt with publicity, but within a few months had his first song published, 'Hear the ukuleles' (1929). 'The Barmaid's Song', a summertime success with Blackpool holidaymakers in 1930, resulted in the London music publisher Bert Feldman offering him a contract as lyric editor. He supplied words for 'Oh Donna Clara' and 'Play to me Gipsy', but it was his lyrics to 'Teddy Bears' Picnic' (1931) that made Kennedy a force in popular music.

Kennedy left Feldman in 1934 to work exclusively for

Peter Maurice until 1940. He worked in collaboration with classically trained Austrian refugee Wilhelm Grosz on 'Isle of Capri', the first of a string of anecdotal songs told with admirable compression, followed by 'Red sails in the sunset' and 'Harbour Lights'. Though primarily a lyricist, he composed the music for 'The Coronation Waltz' (1937), 'My Serenade' (1943), and 'Roll along covered wagon' (1934), with which he liked to accompany himself on halting, self-taught piano. On 11 June 1932 he married Margaret Elizabeth Winifred (b. 1909/10), daughter of a hotelier, Simon Galpin.

It was while with Peter Maurice that Jimmy Kennedy embarked upon a five-year collaboration with the somewhat larger-than-life Tin Pan Alley tunesmith Michael Carr, son of a featherweight boxer, Cockney Cohen. The partnership between the brash Carr and the charming, shy, money-conscious Kennedy worked well while it lasted, and together they became one of the most popular and successful songwriting teams of the century. 'The Chestnut Tree' preceded 'Why did she fall for the leader of the band?' (1935); 'Home Town' (1937), a hit for Flanagan and Allen; 'Stay in my arms, Cinderella' (1938), one of the biggest dance songs of the year; and 'South of the border', their best-selling composition, recorded by Bing Crosby, Frank Sinatra, Perry Como, and Gene Autry. Their swan song was 'We're gonna hang out the washing on the Siegfried Line', a well-known morale-booster which, as Kennedy recalled, enraged Hitler. Following Territorial Army service, he became a captain in the Royal Artillery.

Kennedy's unerring gift for sensing the public taste led to the dance party classic 'The Cokey Cokey' (1942), more commonly called 'The Hokey Cokey'. He rarely misjudged the mood ('The angels are lighting God's little candle' was an exception) and 'An Apple Blossom Wedding' unseasonably helped to celebrate the marriage in November 1947 of Princess Elizabeth. Kennedy also established himself as one of the first songwriters to rewrite or translate continental songs for a British and American market; the most successful of these was 'My Prayer', a reworked version of 'Avant de mourir'. After the war Kennedy lived in the United States for some years following the success of his songs in the American charts (in January 1940 'My Prayer' was at no. 2 with 'South of the border' at no. 1 in America during the same week). His writing was very popular especially with country-music singers. Meanwhile, 'The red we want is the red we've got', a song about the Korean War, became a hit for Eddie Fisher and the bandleader Hugo Winterhalter. His first marriage was dissolved in 1946 and in the same year he married the actress and singer Constance Carpenter (1906–1992), daughter of Harold Carpenter and former wife of Paul Ord Hamilton and John Lucas-Scudmore.

Returning from America, Kennedy lived less happily in politically torn Ireland, then settled in Switzerland as a tax exile when the teenage record-based rock and roll revolution shattered the dominance of Tin Pan Alley and its sheet music industry. ('Better to be rich and miserable in Switzerland than poor and happy in England', Kennedy

told a colleague, without conviction.) In the 1970s he composed a number of melodies, one of which was adopted by the St John Ambulance Brigade, and spent his final years writing music for plays performed in Dublin. In 1977 he won a Dramatists' prize of the year with Stewart Parker for the play Spokesong. More honours came his way: a first Ivor Novello award (1971); an American ASCAP award in 1976 for 'Red sails in the sunset', which was the most played record on American radio in that year; a rare honorary DLitt degree from the University of Ulster (1978), of which, being 'merely a wordsmith', he was justly proud; a second Novello in 1980, and appointment as OBE in 1983. He became a fellow of the Royal Geographical Society and of the Royal Society of Arts. In his later years Kennedy returned to Dublin under an Irish government tax concession, commuting at his own expense to London for meetings of the Songwriters' Guild (later renamed the British Academy of Songwriters, Composers and Authors, BASCA), of which he was the much-loved, conscientious chairman.

After Kennedy's second marriage was dissolved in 1972 he married on 22 July 1976 Elaine Edith Bradbury Pobjoy (b. 1908/9), a widow, daughter of Henry Holloway, solicitor. Kennedy died on 6 April 1984 at the Cotswold Nuffield Nursing Home, Talbot Road, Cheltenham, and he was buried at Staplegrove, near Taunton, Somerset. The eulogy at his memorial service on 2 October 1984 at St Giles-in-the-Fields, London, was given by his wartime colleague Denis Thatcher, husband of the prime minister, Margaret Thatcher. In 1984 the BASCA inaugurated an annual Jimmy Kennedy award and in 1997 he was inducted into the American Songwriters' Hall of Fame, a notable achievement for a British pioneer.

STEVE RACE, rev. CLARE L. TAYLOR

Sources M. White, 'You must remember this …': popular songwriters, 1900–1980 (1983) · N. Harrison, Songwriters: a biographical dictionary with discographies (1998) · E. Rogers, Tin Pan Alley (1964) · C. Larkin, ed., The encyclopedia of popular music (1998) [repr.] · m. certs. [Margaret Galpin, Elaine Pobjoy] · d. cert. · personal knowledge (1990) · private information (1990) [Elaine Kennedy, widow; Derek V. Kennedy; L. Bray; D. Thatcher]
Wealth at death £177,625: probate, 6 July 1984, CGPLA Eng. & Wales

Kennedy, Sir James Shaw (1788–1865), army officer, was born on 13 October 1788 at The Largs, Straiton, Ayrshire, second of the six children of John Shaw (d. 1831), a former captain in the 76th highlanders who had served in the American War of Independence, from Dalton, Kirkcudbrightshire, and his wife, Wilhelmina Hannah Macadam, sister of John Loudon Macadam, the road engineer. James's paternal grandfather, John Shaw, sold the family estate, Dalton in Kirkcudbrightshire, before his son could inherit, and the younger John's family moved from Straiton into an old castle near Maybole, Ayrshire. James Shaw was educated at Maybole parish school and Ayr Academy.

On 18 April 1805 Shaw became an ensign in the 43rd foot (light infantry), which he joined at Hythe, Kent, and which was training under Sir John Moore. William Napier was then a captain in the regiment. Shaw became lieutenant

Sir James Shaw Kennedy (1788–1865), by Jan Willem Pieneman, 1821

on 23 January 1806 and served with the regiment during the 1807 expedition to Denmark in the battle of Kioge and siege of Copenhagen. In 1808 the 43rd sailed for northern Spain under Sir David Baird, advancing to support British troops at Sahagun, shortly before Sir John Moore began his long retreat to Corunna, pursued hotly by the French. Shaw fought with the rearguard, which covered the evacuation. Back in England he suffered from a severe fever whose effects never thereafter fully left him. None the less, he returned to the Peninsula in 1809, marching with the light division from Lisbon to Talavera, where he assumed responsibility as adjutant in the 43rd. During 1809 and 1810 Shaw was aide-de-camp to Brigadier-General Robert Craufurd and took part in several actions between the Coa and Agueda rivers, being severely wounded in the elbow at Almeida on 24 July 1810. Shaw's account of this phase of the Peninsular War, preserved in a journal, has been judged 'most ample and reliable' (Craufurd, 89). During the storming of Ciudad Rodrigo (19 January 1812) he was standing beside Craufurd on the crest of the glacis, when the general fell mortally wounded. He carried Craufurd from the field, and, subsequently, conveyed Wellington's summons to surrender to the French governor. On his return to regimental duty he served with the 43rd at the siege and storming of Badajoz (5–6 April 1812) where he distinguished himself in assaulting a lesser breach, at the battle of Salamanca, and in the advance to Madrid. During Wellington's withdrawal from Madrid to winter quarters at Ciudad Rodrigo, Shaw acted as aide-de-camp to Major-General Charles von Alten, and was

involved in various minor actions *en route*. In July 1812 he was promoted captain. At the close of 1812 Shaw was declared medically unfit, returned home, and suffered another bout of debilitating fever.

On 2 April 1813 Shaw joined the senior department of the Royal Military College, Sandhurst, but in August ill health compelled him to leave. During the 1815 crisis he returned to active service as assistant quartermaster-general with the 3rd division of Lieutenant-General Sir Charles von Alten, at Quatre-Bras and Waterloo. As the only quartermaster-general's staff officer still in action with the division, on 17 June he reconnoitred its detached line of march, separate from the main force, during northwards withdrawal from Quatre-Bras across the Dyle River at Weys, 'a movement of great delicacy … in open day in presence of Napoleon's advance' (Levinge, 320). The following day (when retrospectively he would acquire a brevet majority) at Waterloo, where Alten's division had its left flank resting on the Charleroi–Brussels road above La Haye-Sainte, Shaw 'was allowed, in the presence of the duke of Wellington, to form the division in an order of battle new and unusual, that of oblongs in exchequer, to meet the formidable masses of cavalry seen forming in its front' (Levinge, 320). The oblongs, mostly formed on the two centre companies of battalions, had their faces and flanks four ranks deep; but to preserve the closest affinity to line formation each flank had only the width of a subdivision. Thus drawn up, the division withstood furious enemy cavalry assaults in late afternoon. Struck in the side and disabled for some time, Shaw had one horse killed and another wounded under him during the battle.

For three years (1815–18), Shaw was commandant and military agent as assistant quartermaster-general at Calais with the army of occupation. He had many difficulties with the French garrison, and received the thanks of the tsar, with a diamond ring, for his services in embarking 8000 Russians during October 1818. Having been placed on half pay in the regiment on 25 March 1817, he obtained a brevet lieutenant-colonelcy (21 January 1819) following Wellington's recommendation. In 1820, at Ayr, Shaw married Sir John Whiteford's granddaughter, Mary Primrose Kennedy (d. 1877) of Kirkmichael, an estate close to Maybole. When he succeeded to the estate through his wife, in 1834, Shaw added Kennedy to his surname.

In 1826, after nine years on half pay, Shaw had become assistant adjutant-general in Belfast; later that year he transferred to Manchester, where he remained for nine years during outbreaks of civil disorder, mainly caused by dissatisfaction with working conditions. On leaving the city he was presented with a valuable service of plate by some of the inhabitants, and Sir Charles Napier dubbed his report on general principles for preserving order during periods of labour unrest 'a masterly affair' (DNB). Having declined Sir Robert Peel's offer of the position of first commissioner of the new Metropolitan Police in 1829, Shaw Kennedy accepted the post of inspector-general of the Irish constabulary in 1836. During his two-year tenure he raised and organized a force of 8000 men, devising his own successful system of drill and field exercise. He became a major on the unattached list on 16 July 1830, colonel (10 January 1837), major-general (9 November 1846), and lieutenant-general (20 June 1854). He was appointed colonel, 47th foot, on 27 August 1854, and promoted general on 19 August 1862. Shaw Kennedy became CB on 19 July 1838, and KCB in 1863. He also held the military general service medal (often called the Peninsular silver medal) with three clasps, and the Waterloo medal.

Summoned from St Leonards, on 10 April 1848 Shaw Kennedy was ordered to take charge of troops, under the control of the civil authorities, in Liverpool, where Chartist demonstrations were feared. Later that year he was appointed extra general officer on the Irish staff under Sir Edward Blakeney. Indifferent health caused him to decline that post and the governorship of Mauritius proposed the following year. In 1852 Shaw Kennedy did accept command of the forces of north Britain, but persistent poor health led him quickly to resign and move to Bath. That year Sir William Napier—his close friend whom he considered the greatest genius he had ever personally known—referred to Shaw Kennedy's 'great intelligence, great zeal, and undaunted courage on very many occasions … He is, perhaps, with the exception of Lord Seaton, the very ablest officer in the service' (Craufurd, 8). But his weak constitution prevented any serious suggestion that he succeed Wellington as commander-in-chief or lead the Crimean expeditionary force.

Despite his medical problems Shaw Kennedy remained tall, spare, and erect throughout his life, abstemious in habit, at once reserved and distant in manner but also gentle, kind, and modest. Unlike Napier he eschewed politics and reputedly never voted in an election. With another aide-de-camp to Craufurd, William Campbell, he edited *Standing Orders for the Light Division*, while his Peninsular journal appeared in Lord Frederick Fitzclarence's *Manual of Outpost Duties* (1851); in 1859 he wrote *Notes on the Defence of Great Britain and Ireland*, in 1863 *Notes on Waterloo*, in 1860 a brief autobiography, and in 1862 *Plan for the Defence of Canada*; all were published in 1865.

Shaw Kennedy died of a long-standing liver complaint at 8 Royal Circus, Bath, on 30 May 1865, and was interred in a vault at Kirkmichael parish church, where his widow was also buried in 1877. Two daughters, Henrietta Shaw Kennedy and Wilhelmina Shaw, predeceased their father, but John Shaw Kennedy survived him to succeed as laird of Kirkmichael.   H. M. CHICHESTER, rev. M. R. D. FOOT

Sources DNB · R. G. A. Levinge, *Historical records of the forty-third regiment, Monmouthshire light infantry* (1868) · W. F. P. Napier, *Life of General Sir William Napier*, ed. H. A. Bruce, 2 vols. (1864) · A. H. Craufurd, *General Craufurd and his light division* (1891) · CGPLA Eng. & Wales (1865)
Archives Bodl. Oxf., corresp. with Sir William Napier, MSS Eng. lett. c. 247, d.235, 242, 299
Likenesses J. W. Pieneman, oils, 1821, Wellington Museum, Apsley House, London [see illus.]
Wealth at death under £7000 in England: probate, 17 June 1865, CGPLA Eng. & Wales

Kennedy, John, of Dunure (d. c.1385). See under Kennedy family (per. c.1350–1513).

Kennedy, John, second Lord Kennedy (d. 1508/9). See under Kennedy family (per. c.1350–1513).

Kennedy, John, fifth earl of Cassillis (1574/5–1615), nobleman, was born in Ayrshire between October 1574 and April 1575, the son of Gilbert *Kennedy, fourth earl of Cassillis (c.1541–1576), and his wife, Margaret (c.1545–1626), daughter of John *Lyon, seventh Lord Glamis (b. c.1521, d. in or before 1559). His father dying while he was still a small child, he was placed under the tutorship first of his uncle, John Lyon, eighth Lord Glamis (c.1544–1579), and then of his paternal uncle, Sir Thomas Kennedy of Culzean. In 1597 he married (by contract dated 4 November 1597) Lady Jean *Fleming (1553/4–1609), daughter and heir of James Fleming, fourth Lord Fleming, and widow of John Maitland of Thirlestane, former chancellor. Almost immediately, probably because of her influence at court, he became involved in national politics, being recorded on a sederunt of the privy council in January 1598 and attending conventions of the estates in June and December. In April 1599 he was appointed, through his wife's influence, lord high treasurer to James VI. He was reluctant to accept this office, the privy council charging him on 11 April to come to Edinburgh to take up his duties. Six days later, Kennedy of Culzean appeared before the council in his stead to accept the office formally on the demission of its former holder. Within a few weeks he resigned, already 40,000 merks (£26,666 Scots) out of pocket.

Cassillis was party to the murder in Ayrshire in December 1601 of Gilbert Kennedy of Bargany, in revenge for Bargany's attempt on Cassillis's life in an ambush. In the following May, Kennedy of Culzean was murdered by Bargany's brother and, in 1603, while the earl was in England with James VI, his wife and brother were seized by Bargany's kinsmen because his killer was in their company. Although Cassillis returned on hearing of this outrage, he had little affection for his wife. On 1 November 1604, he was charged to enter Blackness Castle 'for preissing, in presens of the Counsall, to have violentlie tane his wife furth of the counsalhous' during a meeting of the privy council (*Reg. PCS*, 7.16). They were in dispute over the laird of Clerkington's lease of the 'place of Lethington' (now Lennoxlove), Haddingtonshire, which belonged to the countess and which Cassillis was accused of 'violentlie takking and deteaning'. A few weeks later, the king having commended the countess to the care of the privy council, Cassillis had to enter surety of £5000 Scots and was ordered to remain west of Linlithgow (*Reg. PCS*, 7.580). On 23 June 1609 the countess died, aged fifty-five, the marriage having produced no children.

Cassillis remained active, attending conventions of the estates in 1608 and 1609 and regularly appearing on the privy council. In November 1610 he was made a justice of the peace in Wigtownshire and Kirkcudbright, and in Ayrshire. He was also involved in ecclesiastical affairs, attending the general assembly at Linlithgow in December 1606 and being appointed to the court of high commission under the archbishop of Glasgow in March 1610. His last recorded attendance on the privy council was in March 1615 and he died in October 1615. His nephew John Kennedy (1595–1668) succeeded as sixth earl of Cassillis.

ALAN R. MACDONALD

Sources Scots peerage · Reg. PCS, 1st ser. · T. Thomson, ed., Acts and proceedings of the general assemblies of the Kirk of Scotland, 3 pts, Bannatyne Club, 81 (1839–45) · Edinburgh commissary, register of testaments, NA Scot., CC8/8/29, fols. 34–46 · GEC, Peerage
Archives NA Scot., Ailsa muniments | NA Scot., RH 15/204 · NA Scot., Stair muniments, GD 135

Kennedy, John (fl. 1626–1629), poet, a Scot, published two small volumes at Edinburgh in the early part of the seventeenth century. His first work, printed in 1626, was a love tale interspersed with songs and relations in different metres and entitled *The history of Calanthrop and Lucilla, conspicuously demonstrating the various mutabilities of fortune in their loves, with every several circumstance of joyes and crosses, fortunate exploites and hazardous adventures, which either of them sustained before they could attaine the prosperous event of their wished aimes*. The dedication to Sir Donald Mackay, from June 1628 Lord Reay of Stranever, reveals that this was the author's first production: 'the first perspicuous invention of my stirile braine'. Kennedy confesses to being 'meanly acquainted' with Mackay and seeks to mitigate his audacity with allusions to his addressee's learning, virtue, and generosity, and to the poet's own 'dutiebound obligation'. Commendatory verses in Latin were provided by Walter Bellenden and Robert Fairley, and in English by Patrick Mackenzie.

> But view this pamphlet, and thy wilt shall finde
> Wise precepts and instructions for thy minde.
> Sweet peace of thought, the secret joy of heart,
> Chaste modest love, void of all vitious airt.

It was reprinted at London in 1631 as *The Ladies' Delight*. Both editions are very rare, and references to copies can be found in the Huth library catalogue of 1880 and in the catalogue of Heber's collection of early English poetry.

Kennedy also wrote *A theological epitome or divine compend, apparently manifesting Gods great love and mercie towards man* (1629). This short verse exploration of Old Testament narratives dwells on aspects of divine justice and mercy. Kennedy's closing appeal is for unity of purpose:

> What obligation then have we,
> Towards our gracious Lord?
> Who hath from hell thus set us free,
> O then in one accord!
> In faith, and love with hearts contreit,
> Let us our spirits raise,
> And yeeld to Father, Sonne, and Spreit,
> Thanks, Honour, Glorie, praise.

A copy, believed to be unique, is in the British Library.

THOMAS SECCOMBE, rev. ELIZABETH HARESNAPE

Sources STC, 1475–1640 · H. Huth, W. C. Hazlitt, and F. S. Ellis, The Huth library: a catalogue of the printed books, manuscripts, autograph letters, and engravings, collected by Henry Huth, 5 vols. (1880) · W. C. Hazlitt, Hand-book to the popular, poetical and dramatic literature of Great Britain (1867) · J. Payne Collier, ed., A catalogue of Heber's collection [1834] [sale catalogue] · J. Hunter, 'Chorus vatum Anglicanorum: collections concerning the poets and verse-writers of the English nation', 6 vols., 1838–54, BL, Add. MS 24492, fol. 132 · T. Corser, Collectanea Anglo-poetica, or, A … catalogue of a … collection of early English poetry, 8, Chetham Society, 102 (1878)

Kennedy, John, sixth earl of Cassillis (1601×7–1668), politician, was the son of Hew Kennedy (d. 1607), younger son of Gilbert *Kennedy, fourth earl of Cassillis, and his wife, Katherine, daughter of Uchtred Macdowall of Garthland. He succeeded his uncle John *Kennedy, fifth earl of Cassillis (1574/5–1615), in October 1615. On 24 January 1619 he received a royal licence to travel in France, Germany, and the Low Countries 'for his instruction in languages and doing his other lawful affairs' (*Historical Account*, 45). He was served as heir to his uncle on 13 December 1621. He was still under age when he was contracted on 21 December 1621 (at Edinburgh) and on 7 January 1622 (at Whitehall) to marry Lady Jean Hamilton (1607–1642), third daughter of Thomas *Hamilton, first earl of Haddington (1563–1637), and his second wife, Margaret Foulis. They had a son, James, who predeceased his father, dying in 1663. The countess has been identified as the heroine of *The Gypsy Laddie*, but she was dead before some of the events depicted in the song.

Cassillis was known as 'the grave and solemn earl' (GEC, *Peerage*) as befitted, perhaps, a zealous presbyterianism. Indeed, Gilbert *Burnet, whose first wife was one of Cassillis's daughters, talked of his father-in-law's 'obstinate stiffness' (*Bishop Burnet's History*, 1.96). He opposed the religious policies of Charles I in Scotland, but he maintained that this was out of zeal rather than a challenge to royal authority. This was the theme of the instrument of protest unveiled by Cassillis and Archibald Johnston of Wariston at the market cross in Edinburgh on 22 February 1638. However, there is some evidence that even at this early date he was in contact with others of a similar outlook in England with the aim of bringing both kingdoms under one reformed religion.

Although a committed signatory of the national covenant Cassillis had to be convinced by Robert Baillie of the necessity of forcible resistance to the king. Characteristically, once convinced he entered wholeheartedly in covenanting resistance and he was present in the covenanters' camp upon Duns Law in 1639. He was named to the committee of estates appointed on 8 June 1640 to sit in the interval before parliament was due to reconvene in November 1640. When parliament eventually sat Cassillis was named to several important committees and on 17 September 1641 he was nominated by the king to the new privy council of Scotland. Following the end of the parliamentary session he was named to the most important financial interval committees, and also those concerned from January 1642 in supplying troops for the Irish campaign which were to be paid by the English parliament. When the convention of estates met from June to August 1643 Cassillis served on four of its most important committees. He duly signed the solemn league and covenant on 2 November 1643, the first occasion that a privy councillor could do so.

Early in January 1644 the Scottish army crossed into England, where, on 20 February 1644 at 'the Scots league at Heighton', Cassillis, whose first wife had died about 15

December 1642, signed a contract to marry Lady Margaret Hay (d. 1695), daughter of William Hay, earl of Erroll, and the widow of Henry Ker, Lord Ker (d. 1643), eldest son of Robert Ker, first earl of Roxburghe. They had one son and four daughters. Meanwhile Cassillis was very active in the committees of the convention of estates in the first part of 1644 and on the committees of the parliament which met under the terms of the Triennial Act in June 1644. In July 1644 he was named to the army section of the committee of estates, but still attended nearly half of the meetings of the Edinburgh section and most of the privy council meetings.

Cassillis continued to be active in both parliament and the various committees set up in the intervals between sessions. When the president of the parliament, the earl of Crawford-Lindsay, was absent Cassillis was chosen vice-president of the parliament on 26 December 1645. In January 1646 he supported the Act of Classes which set out the punishments for malignants and delinquents. With Crawford-Lindsay again absent Cassillis was elected president of the parliament on 6 February 1647. He was an active attender of the committee of estates between March 1647 and February 1648, although the balance of power had swung towards the duke of Hamilton and the engagement. He was not elected president of the first session of the second triennial parliament in March 1648, but attended and sometimes spoke in support of the marquess of Argyll and Johnston of Wariston. Like Argyll, Cassillis did not vote for the legislation of 11 April which paved the way for the invasion of England. With the changed circumstances following the defeat of the engagers at Preston in August 1648 Cassillis was one of the leaders of the Whiggamores' raid to Edinburgh which secured control of the committee of estates. Cassillis was a leading figure on the revamped committee which met on 14 September 1648. When parliament reassembled in February 1649 Cassillis supported the renewal of the solemn league and covenant and the Act of Classes debarring the engagers from parliament.

Following parliament's proclamation of Charles II in February 1649 Cassillis set sail on 17 March as the only peer among the seven commissioners sent to Charles at The Hague. He reported back to parliament on 11 June on the unsuccessful negotiations with the king. On 29 June 1649 he was admitted lord justice-general and on 3 July 1649 an extraordinary lord of session. Although Cassillis opposed the appointment of commissioners to treat with Charles at Breda in February 1650 he was duly nominated a commissioner, and in fact was elected president of the commission which met Charles II in March. On 29 April 1650 Cassillis signed the invitation to Charles to come to Scotland, but he urged the kirk to prevent the ratification of any agreement with the king because he had not taken the covenants. According to John Lamont, Cassillis attended the coronation of Charles II at Scone on 1 January 1651, but not in his robes. He attended all the meetings of the committee of estates between the coronation and the meeting of parliament in March 1651. The defeat of the Scottish army at Worcester on 3 September 1651 and the incorporation of Scotland into the English Commonwealth in October saw his retirement from political affairs. Oliver Cromwell nominated Cassillis to his other house in 1656–8, but he never took his seat. However, he was placed second behind General George Monck in the commission of assessment for Ayrshire in June 1657, and again in January 1660.

At the Restoration Charles II restored Cassillis to his places as justice-general in August 1660 and as a lord of session. However, when parliament assembled on 1 January 1661 Cassillis declined to take the oath of allegiance unless he could add his own interpretation to it, and particularly objected to the crown's supremacy in ecclesiastical issues. He left the parliament saying 'I resolve to leave his counsels and dominions which is as ill as anything Oliver ever threatened me with' (Young, 321). By an act of 10 April 1661 he was deprived of his office as an extraordinary lord of session and barred from holding any public office. A subsequent trip to London in spring 1661 failed to retrieve his political position, or to prevent the imposition of episcopacy in Scotland, although in August he argued against the establishment of bishops. He returned to Scotland about November 1661, possibly with a royal promise that he and his family would remain unmolested by the government. Certainly in January 1664 the Scottish authorities received orders that Cassillis and his family should not be harassed for a refusal to comply with the law in ecclesiastical matters. Cassillis reciprocated this gesture in 1665 by spurning Dutch approaches to support a rebellion. Cassillis died 'at his own house in the west country', presumably Maybole in Ayrshire, in April 1668, and was succeeded as seventh earl by John *Kennedy (c.1646–1701), his son from his second marriage. His wife died in London and was buried in St Martin-in-the-Fields on 22 April 1695.

STUART HANDLEY

Sources GEC, *Peerage* · *Scots peerage* · J. R. Young, *The Scottish parliament, 1639–1661: a political and constitutional analysis* (1996) · G. Brunton and D. Haig, *An historical account of the senators of the college of justice, from its institution in MDXXXII* (1832), 342–3 · J. Buckroyd, *Church and state in Scotland, 1660–1681* (1980) · O. Airy, ed., 'Letters addressed to the earl of Lauderdale', *Camden miscellany, VIII*, CS, new ser., 31 (1883), 1–10 · *Historical account of the noble family of Kennedy, marquess of Ailsa and earls of Cassillis* (1849), 27–45 · *The letters and journals of Robert Baillie*, ed. D. Laing, 3 vols. (1841–2) · *The life of Mr Robert Blair ... containing his autobiography*, ed. T. M'Crie, Wodrow Society, 11 (1848) · *Bishop Burnet's History*, vol. 1 · *The diary of Mr John Lamont of Newton, 1649–1671*, ed. G. R. Kinloch, Maitland Club, 7 (1830) · M. Steele, 'The "Political Christian": the theological background to the national covenant', *The Scottish national covenant in its British context*, ed. J. Morrill (1990)
Archives BL, letters to Lord Lauderdale, etc., Add. MSS 23114–23128

Kennedy, John, seventh earl of Cassillis (c.1646–1701), nobleman, son of John *Kennedy, sixth earl of Cassillis (1601×7–1668), was born soon after his father's marriage to Lady Margaret (d. 1695), daughter of William Hay, earl of Erroll, and widow of Henry Ker, Lord Ker, eldest son of the first earl of Roxburghe. He succeeded his father in 1668, 'being heir', claimed his brother-in-law Bishop Gilbert Burnet, 'to his stiffness, but not to his virtues' (*Bishop Burnet's History of his Own Time*, ed. G. Burnet and T. Burnet,, 2 vols., 1724–34, 1.292). He was noted for his opposition to the religious policies of Charles II and to Lauderdale's government, and in 1670 was the sole commissioner in the Scottish parliament to vote against the act forbidding field conventicles. Cassillis refused to subscribe the bond stipulating that neither his family nor tenants would attend conventicles and, in 1678, 1500 of the 'highland host' were quartered on his estates. The earl himself was outlawed for declining to give sureties against nonconformity, and gained nothing by two journeys to London with the duke of Hamilton. Owing to financial pressures and debt, he was obliged in 1674 to sell his estates in Wigtownshire to John Hamilton, Lord Bargany, acting for Sir John Dalrymple of Stair.

Cassillis supported William of Orange at the revolution of 1688 and thereafter took a more active part in public affairs, as a member of the privy council and a lord of the Treasury. By a marriage contract dated December 1668 he had married Lady Susan, daughter of James Hamilton, first duke of Hamilton. After her death he married, in February 1698, Mary, daughter of John Fox of Lincoln's Inn Fields. She outlived him, dying on 12 September 1746. Cassillis himself died on 23 July 1701, and was succeeded by his grandson John, eighth earl (son of Cassillis's eldest son from his first marriage).

F. H. GROOME, *rev.* SHARON ADAMS

Sources *Scots peerage* · *Reg. PCS*, 3rd ser., vol. 5 · NA Scot., Ailsa MSS, GD 25 · GEC, *Peerage*
Archives NA Scot., Ailsa MSS
Likenesses J. M. Wright, portrait, Culzean Castle and Country Park, South Ayrshire

Kennedy, John (1698–1782), Church of England clergyman and chronologist, on 10 November 1732 succeeded William Hawford as rector of All Saints', Bradley, near Ashbourne, Derbyshire, a position he retained until his death. He was the author of several controversial works on the chronology of the Bible, the first of which was *A New Method of Stating and Explaining the Scriptural Chronology*, published in 1751. In 1753 he drew attention to what he considered to be the errors and defects of the Revd John Jackson's chronological calculations in a work entitled *Examination of the Reverend Mr. Jackson's 'Chronological Antiquities'*. Kennedy's best-known publication was *A Complete System of Astronomical Chronology, Unfolding the Scriptures* (1762), which contains a dedication to George III written by Samuel Johnson (Boswell refers to Kennedy as the Revd Dr Kennedy in his *Life of Johnson*). In this Kennedy attempted to date some of the most important events of the Bible. However, his calculations and conclusions were challenged by the astronomer James Ferguson and, perhaps more eloquently, by the Revd Thomas Bowen of Bristol in a series of letters in the *Christian Magazine*. Kennedy defended his findings in a publication of 1774 entitled *An Explanation and Proof of 'A Complete System of Astronomical Chronology'*, which took the form of a series of letters to James Ferguson, but he was never able to convince a sceptical public of the reliability and accuracy of his dating.

Kennedy died at Bradley on 4 February 1782 and was buried in the churchyard there. The inscription on his gravestone credits him with the degree of MA but his name does not appear on the lists of graduates from the English or Scottish universities.

W. C. SYDNEY, *rev.* M. J. MERCER

Sources Allibone, *Dict.* · Watt, *Bibl. Brit.* · J. Watkins, *The universal biographical dictionary*, new edn (1821) · *N&Q*, 3rd ser., 8 (1865), 371, 545 · J. C. Cox, *Notes on the churches of Derbyshire*, 3: *The hundreds of Appletree and Repton and Gresley* (1877), 29 · J. Boswell, *Life of Johnson*, ed. R. W. Chapman, rev. J. D. Fleeman, new edn (1970); repr. with introduction by P. Rogers (1980), 259–60

Kennedy, John (1729/30–1816). *See under* Kennedy, Alexander (1695–*c*.1785).

Kennedy, John (1769–1855), textile manufacturer, was born on 4 July 1769 at Knocknalling, Kirkcudbrightshire, a small farm 6 miles from New Galloway which had belonged to the family for over three centuries. John's father inherited the estate from his own father; his mother came from Stirling. Both parents had some education, his father having attended college in Edinburgh. There were seven children, five sons of whom John was third eldest and two daughters. The father died when the children were young. Distance from the local school meant that the children received only occasional teaching from tutors training to be schoolmasters. Through contact with one such occasional teacher, Kennedy recognized his enthusiasm for mechanics, and this was encouraged by his mother who believed that such skills were the key to an independent life. The eldest son took over the running of the farm, and the others had to seek employment elsewhere. In February 1784 John Kennedy moved to Chowbent, near Leigh in Lancashire, to be apprenticed to William Cannan, who came originally from the parish of Kells, and was the son of a neighbour of the Kennedys. Kennedy's training covered the manufacture of textile machinery including carding engines, jennies, and water frames. On completing his apprenticeship in February 1791, he moved to Manchester and formed a partnership with Benjamin and William Sandford, fustian warehousemen, and James M'Connel, a nephew and former apprentice of Cannan, to manufacture textile machinery and undertake cotton spinning. This partnership lasted for four years, the active management of the business being undertaken by M'Connel and Kennedy, the latter taking charge of the machine department. For some years the firm was virtually the only business using Crompton's mule. Kennedy was a skilled and inventive engineer, and has been credited with devising a crucial improvement to fine spinning machinery, called double speed, which enabled much finer thread to be manufactured. This made possible the mechanization of fine spinning, marked an important advance in the quality of production, and formed the basis for the success of the business.

In March 1795 M'Connel and Kennedy formed a new partnership with their share of the profit from the previous partnership, and a little additional capital of their own, in sum £1770, and moved to a new factory in the same Canal Street, where they remained for six or seven years. Then they built the first of their three mills in Union Street. This new partnership formed the basis for the rest of Kennedy's working life, which spanned the next three decades. Initially the firm continued to make cotton-spinning machinery for sale, but this part of the business ended around the turn of the century, although it still manufactured for its own requirements. Thereafter the spinning side of the business became the sole activity, concentrating on the production of the highest quality cotton yarn. In 1815 a survey of firms in Manchester showed that only nine companies employed over 400 workers, the largest being Adam and George Murray with 1215 workers followed by M'Connel and Kennedy with 1020. In 1798 the firm's inventory showed that it had almost 7500 spindles at work valued at £1107. By the time Kennedy retired in 1826 the number of spindles had increased to almost 125,000 and the valuation to £28,540. In 1804 John Kennedy married Mary, daughter of John Stuart of Manchester; they had one son and several daughters. The family lived in Ancoats Lane until 1806, and in Medlock until 1822, when they moved to Ardwick Hall.

M'Connel and Kennedy was thus one of the major pioneering firms in the early phase of the Lancashire cotton industry. The firm was also distinctive in concentrating on the fine-quality market, selling their product mainly in Scotland and Ireland, and later supplying the Nottingham lace trade. Its rise demonstrates one route through the potential minefield of business growth in a volatile market situation propped up by a network of interconnected credits and debits, which brought many businesses to a speedy and inglorious end. The key to the success of this firm appears to have been risk aversion. Manufacturing their own machinery, and initially renting premises, enabled the partners to limit debt by offering discounts for cash or short credit. Vulnerability to market fluctuations was thus minimized. Ironically, such caution allowed the partners to enjoy the massive windfall gains from highly speculative ventures during the Napoleonic wars, when blockades confined trade with Europe to smuggling. This promised substantial gains if successful, but total loss if the cargo was discovered and confiscated. The capital so carefully accumulated allowed M'Connel and Kennedy to venture into this trade, and to profit substantially from it. This mixture of technical expertise, financial prudence, and commercial opportunism brought success and considerable prosperity, and allowed Kennedy to retire from the business while still in his fifties. His only son did not follow him into the firm, which was carried on by M'Connel and his sons, and the Kennedy name disappeared from the business in the 1830s.

Kennedy devoted much of his time subsequently to following his technical and mechanical interests. He was consulted about the Liverpool and Manchester Railway, on the issue of the relative merits of stationary or moving engines, and was an umpire at the Rainhill engine trials in 1830. He was an active member of the Manchester Literary and Philosophical Society, and had four papers published in the transactions of the society on the state of the cotton trade (1815), the poor law (1819), and the influence of machinery on the working classes (1826), and a memoir of Samuel Crompton (1830). Although Kennedy was highly successful in business, Fairbairn's memoir depicts him as a rather retiring individual of a nervous disposition, prone, like his father, to depression, and whose greatest enthusiasm lay in the search for mechanical improvement. He died on 30 October 1855 at home at Ardwick Hall, Manchester, and was buried at Rusholme Road cemetery, Ardwick, Manchester.   C. H. LEE

Sources C. H. Lee, *A cotton enterprise: a history of M'Connel and Kennedy, fine cotton spinners* (1972) · J. Kennedy, 'Brief notice of my early recollections', *Miscellaneous papers on subjects connected with the manufactures of Lancashire* (privately printed, Manchester, 1849), 1–18 · W. Fairbairn, 'A brief memoir of the late John Kennedy, esq.', *Memoirs of the Literary and Philosophical Society of Manchester*, 3rd ser., 1 (1862) · d. cert.
Archives University of Manchester Library, company records

Kennedy, John (1789–1833), poet, was born in Kilmarnock on 3 October 1789, the son of a prosperous hand-loom weaver. After a sound elementary education under a teacher named Thomson he began work with his father. While at his loom, however, during the day he had his book conveniently placed for study, and his evenings also were occupied with literature. From 1807 to 1815 he was in the Royal Ayrshire militia, serving in both Great Britain and Ireland. Having settled again in Kilmarnock he was in frequent collision with the authorities through the vehemence of his political criticisms. In early 1820 he suffered two short periods of imprisonment as a result of his association with radicals who were plotting to muster in arms against the government. Fortunately he managed to prove his innocence.

Eventually Kennedy qualified as a teacher. After a short engagement in Kilmarnock he was appointed schoolmaster at Chapel Green, near Kilsyth, Stirlingshire, where he settled in July 1820 with his young wife, Janet Houston, whom he had married on 14 July. He speedily made a favourable impression as a teacher while, socially, his frankness of utterance both provoked keen opposition and secured him much esteem.

By 1820 Kennedy had published two volumes of verse and poems in several provincial periodicals. In 1826 he published *Fancy's Tour with the Genius of Cruelty, and other Poems*. In the leading piece he studies 'what man has made of man', drawing upon sacred and profane history from the time of Cain to that of Claverhouse. Several other poems are noteworthy: that on Horace for its reminiscences and its critical opinions, while that entitled 'Andra the Bard' is practically a defence of lowland Scots as a literary instrument. All display satirical force rather than poetical grace.

Kennedy died suddenly at Kilsyth on 4 October 1833, leaving a widow and three daughters, from a family of six, unprovided for. *Geordie Chalmers, or, The Law in Glenbuckie*, a satirical novel, was published immediately after his death. Manifestly based on personal experience, this book is valuable as a vivid, if somewhat caustic, delineation of nineteenth-century Scottish rural life.

T. W. BAYNE, *rev.* JAMES HOW

Sources J. Paterson, *The contemporaries of Burns and the more recent poets of Ayrshire* (1840) • private information (1891) • 'Advertisement', J. Kennedy, *Geordie Chalmers, or, The law in Glenbuckie* (1833)
Wealth at death widow and three daughters unprovided for: Kennedy, 'Advertisement', *Geordie Chalmers*

Kennedy, John (1819–1884), Free Church of Scotland minister, was born on 15 August 1819 at the manse at Killearnan, Ross-shire, the son of John Kennedy, Church of Scotland minister of Killearnan and a close friend of John Macdonald of Ferintosh (the Apostle of the North), and his wife, Jessie, the daughter of Kenneth Mackenzie of Assynt, Sutherland. Their fourth son, he was educated at the parish school at Killearnan and at Aberdeen University, where he excelled in mental and moral science and chemistry, and graduated MA in 1840. He proceeded to the Theological Hall of the Church of Scotland in Aberdeen, and while there served as tutor in the family of Dr Henderson of Caskieben, Aberdeenshire. Licensed by the Church of Scotland Presbytery of Chanonry in September 1843 he, like his brother Donald, who succeeded his father at Killearnan, entered the ministry of the Free Church following the Disruption of that year.

In February 1844 Kennedy was inducted to his only pastorate, at Dingwall, Ross-shire. On 28 April 1848 he married Mary (1819–1896), daughter of Major Forbes Mackenzie, at Fodderty. Of their four children, a girl and a boy died in infancy and twin daughters survived. Kennedy was in great demand as a preacher in both Gaelic and English—hundreds of people attended when he participated in communion seasons—and he was loved by young and old alike. P. Carnegie Simpson recalled that, 'As a preacher, he was a king to whom his pulpit was a throne. … His sermons were massive structures … but they literally glowed with Celtic fervour, and, as he poured them forth, he strained and soared heavenward, till at times he broke out at last into impassioned adoration' (P. C. Simpson, *The Life of Principal Rainy*, 1909, 1.442). He declined calls from Dunoon (1853), Australia (1854), Greenock (1857 and again in 1872), Tain (1857), and Renfield church, Glasgow (1863). In 1873 he became a DD (Aberdeen). Kennedy served as clerk to the presbytery of Dingwall and to the synod of Ross. During the winter of 1869–70 his health broke down, and he was off duty for periods in 1872, 1873 (when he visited Canada and America, and was impressed by the prayers of Charles Hodge and disquieted by a sermon by Henry Ward Beecher which, he thought, emphasized the fatherhood of God at the expense of sin and the need of atonement), and 1881. On 17 May 1870 the Baptist Charles Spurgeon, whom Kennedy had met while recuperating in London, preached at the opening of the new Free Church building in Dingwall.

Kennedy's words, 'To be behind an age that is drifting away from truth and godliness is the only safe, the only dutiful position' (J. Kennedy, *The Present Cast and Tendency of Religious Thought and Feeling in Scotland*, 1902, 18), aptly indicate his stance. As his first book, *The Days of the Fathers in Ross-Shire* (1861), makes clear, he was for 'the old paths', and, though not unaware of their weaknesses, his admiration for earlier ministers and Men (a spiritual élite in the highlands comprising elders, schoolmasters, catechists, and others of deep spiritual experience), who combined faith, experience, and practice, was deep and nostalgic; he lamented 'The fathers, where are they?' (*The Days of the Fathers in Ross-Shire*, 84).

Though a reluctant controversialist, many of Kennedy's writings were polemical. He sided with James Begg, and during 1863–73 led the highland opponents of the proposed union of the Free Church with the United Presbyterian church, both because of his commitment to the establishment over against the voluntary principle and because he suspected that the United Presbyterians were unsound on the doctrine of the atonement. He rebuked those who argued for the disestablishment of the Church of Scotland. He opposed the use in worship of 'uninspired hymns' (hymns other than metrical renderings of biblical passages) and instrumental accompaniments to singing; the organized temperance movement; Sunday schools; age- and sex-specific church organizations; soirées; Plymouthism—'the slimiest of all isms'; the critical views of W. Robertson Smith; and the opening of the Highland Railway on Sundays. His theological position is summed up in *Man's Relations to God Traced in the Light of 'the Present Trends'* (1869), and his homiletic method is exemplified in his posthumous *Expository Lectures* (1911). No arch-Calvinist who would offer the gospel to 'sensible sinners' only, Kennedy was no rampant evangelist either, being stoutly opposed to the methods of such revivalists as Dwight L. Moody: he relied on God's enabling grace to draw sinners to the Christ freely offered in the gospel.

On his way home from a visit to Italy, Kennedy died at Bridge of Allan, Stirlingshire, on 28 April 1884, and was buried in the grounds of the Free Church in Dingwall on 1 May, more than sixty ministers and thousands of people being in attendance.

ALAN P. F. SELL

Sources A. Auld, *Life of John Kennedy* (1887) • *In memoriam, Rev. John Kennedy* (1884) • J. Noble, 'Memoir', in J. Kennedy, *The days of the fathers in Ross-shire*, new edn (1897) • A. P. F. Sell, *Defending and declaring the faith: some Scottish examples, 1860–1920* (1987) • G. N. M. Collins, *An orchard of pomegranates* • H. Cartwright, *Monthly Record of the Free Church of Scotland* (Oct 1983), 210–12 • 'Editorial', *Monthly Record of the Free Church of Scotland* (May 1984), 99–101 • *DNB* • A. P. F. Sell, 'Kennedy, John', *DSCHT*
Likenesses photographs, repro. in Auld, *Life of John Kennedy* • photographs, repro. in *In memoriam, Rev. John Kennedy*
Wealth at death £677 19s. 1d.: confirmation, 2 Dec 1884, *CCI* • £35: additional estate, 12 Feb 1896, *CCI*

Kennedy, John Clark- (1817–1867), army officer, descendant of the Kennedys of Knockgray, was the eldest son of Lieutenant-General Sir Alexander Kennedy Clark-Kennedy, a Peninsular and Waterloo veteran who, as Captain Clark, 1st (Royal) Dragoons, distinguished himself at Waterloo by capturing, single-handed, a French 'eagle'. He was colonel 6th dragoon guards 1860–62, and was colonel of the 2nd dragoons from 1862 until his death. He assumed the additional name of Kennedy, dying in London, aged eighty-three, on 30 January 1864.

His son John purchased a cornetcy in the 7th dragoon guards in October 1833, then commanded by his father, a lieutenancy in March 1837, and a captaincy in December

1841. Afterwards exchanging to the 18th (Royal Irish) foot, he served with them in China, including in the China expedition of 1842, when he was present at the attack on Nanking (Nanjing). He was assistant quartermaster-general to the force under Major-General d'Aguilar during the combined naval and military operations in the Canton River in 1847. He served through the Second Anglo-Sikh War as aide-de-camp, including at the siege and capture of Multan, the battle of Gujrat, and the occupation of Peshawar. He married in 1850 Frances Eleanor, only daughter of J. E. Walford of Chipping Hall, Essex; they had two sons, and she died in 1857.

Clark-Kennedy attained the rank of major in December 1854, and served in the Crimea at the siege of Sevastopol, where he commanded the right wing of the 18th (Royal Irish), the leading regiment of Eyre's brigade, in the assault of 18 June 1855, and was wounded in the neck; he was appointed assistant adjutant-general at headquarters on 10 August, and was present in the assault of 8 September 1855. He was awarded the Mejidiye (fifth class), and a CB in February 1860. In 1859 he married Charlotte Isabella, daughter of Colonel Hon. Peregrine Cust; they had three daughters and she survived him. He was afterwards assistant quartermaster-general at Aldershot, and in February 1860 became colonel-commandant of the military train. He went, on special service for the Abyssinian expedition, to Cairo, and died at Alexandria on 18 December 1867 of dysentery.   H. M. CHICHESTER, rev. M. G. M. JONES

Sources Hart's Army List · GM, 3rd ser., 16 (1864), 527 · Burke, Gen. GB · private information (1887) · CGPLA Eng. & Wales (1868)

Wealth at death under £6000 in UK: probate, 17 Jan 1868, CGPLA Eng. & Wales

Kennedy, Sir John Noble (1893–1970), army officer and colonial governor, was born at the manse, Portpatrick, Wigtownshire, Scotland, on 31 August 1893, the eldest of the six children—four sons and two daughters—of James Russell Kennedy (b. 1854), a Church of Scotland minister, and his wife, Sarah Maude Noble. Educated locally at Stranraer, he acquired a lifelong love of fishing and bird-watching. In 1911 he joined the navy as a paymaster-midshipman, but on the outbreak of war in 1914 managed to transfer to the army, fearful he might not see action. From the Royal Military Academy, Woolwich, he was commissioned in 1915 as a (regular army) second lieutenant in the Royal Regiment of Artillery. He was wounded in 1916 and in 1917 won the MC for conspicuous gallantry in action. 'He, with three men, established an observation post in "No-Man's Land" and under a heavy hostile fire directed the fire of his battery most successfully' (London Gazette, 26 March 1917).

From 1919 to 1920 Kennedy served with the British military mission in south Russia, being appointed to the order of St Vladimir for helping to repel a cavalry attack near Moscow. He contributed papers to the Royal Artillery Magazine and was credited with inventing 'a new method of gun-laying ... adopted for field and heavy artillery' (Wigtown Free Press, 5 May 1921). In 1926 Kennedy married Isabella Rosamond Georgiana Joicey-Cecil (d. 1941). They had three sons and two daughters.

Between the wars Kennedy served in Egypt as well as England. In 1921 he was a student, and in the 1930s an instructor, at the Staff College, Camberley. There he caught the eye of the commandant, Sir John Dill, who in 1934 was appointed director of military operations (DMO) and in 1935 brought him into the War Office 'in charge of that section of the General Staff which devilled strategy and war plans for him' (Kennedy, 1). After attending the Imperial Defence College in 1938, Kennedy returned to Whitehall as deputy director of military operations, becoming in the following year director of plans. He had now found his true métier and, apart from two brief periods in France and Ireland and several frustrating months in hospital after being run down in the black-out in December 1939, spent the whole war in Whitehall.

As DMO from 1940 to 1943 and assistant chief of the Imperial General Staff (operations and intelligence) from 1943 to 1945, Kennedy gave loyal support, and was admired by successive holders of the post of chief of the Imperial General Staff, especially Sir Alan Brooke, who described his subordinate as 'a superb DMO gifted with broad strategic vision and the ability to express his thoughts in the clearest language' (Bryant, Triumph in the West, 41n.).

Kennedy's The Business of War (1957), based on notes he made at the time, gives an illuminating insight into the evolution and application of military strategy from 1938 to the end of 1944, and chronicles in detail the constant clashes between Churchill and his army advisers. 'Whenever an idea, however wild, was thrown up, he ordered detailed examinations, or plans, or both to be made at high speed' (Kennedy, 173). The War Office, concluded Kennedy, almost needed 'two staffs: one to deal with the prime minister, the other with the war' (ibid.). It was, Kennedy warned his subordinates, their duty to supply 'the military evidence' for or against any proposal and to resist the 'tendency to modify wording ... of papers submitted to the prime minister with the idea of making them more acceptable to him' (ibid., 93). There was an embarrassing encounter between the two men when in April 1941 Kennedy, in Brooke's words, 'infuriated the PM' by arguing that plans should be prepared for the possible loss of Egypt, 'and was relegated amongst those "many generals who are only too ready to surrender and who should be made examples of like Admiral Byng"' (Bryant, Turn of the Tide, 254). Though shaken, Kennedy bravely stuck to his guns, commenting later: 'The charges of defeatism which Churchill hurled at us all continually and were so resented at first, came to be regarded ... lightheartedly' (Kennedy, 146). A man of generous disposition—his earlier accident had, he insisted, been 'my own fault'—Kennedy took in good part the abuse he had suffered. 'The massive figure of the great prime minister', he insisted, remained undiminished 'by glimpses of his petulance' (ibid., 356). Kennedy's first wife died in 1941 and the following year he married Catherine Fordham (d. 1969).

From December 1944 until the end of the war in August 1945 Kennedy was on sick leave, suffering primarily from exhaustion. In recognition of his contribution to the war effort, he received a knighthood in that year. However, he decided that to return to the army would be 'flogging a dead horse' (Kennedy, 355). Having retired, he was appointed governor of Southern Rhodesia, where he remained until it became part of the Federation of Rhodesia and Nyasaland in August 1953. 'Here was a new world indeed,' he wrote later, 'expanding, growing, buoyant, stimulating, refreshing; inhabited by the kindest people imaginable' (ibid.). These feelings were reciprocated. 'Both he and Lady Kennedy devoted themselves to the welfare of all sections of the community', wrote one local historian (Kane, 239). 'He is regarded as one of the country's more open-minded governors ... noted for his attempts to mix socially with Africans', confirmed another writer (Rasmussen, 130), while his own chief justice considered him 'the best governor we ever had' (Tredgold, 225).

Kennedy makes no mention in his *Business of War* of his brother, James Russell Kennedy (b. 1895), who was commissioned into the Royal Artillery on the same day as himself and also served in Russia and at the War Office, before retiring in 1931 to edit *The Army, Navy and Air Force Gazette* and to write on military subjects. A progressive in military thinking—he was a supporter of the tank enthusiast J. F. C. Fuller—he became a political reactionary and fascist. J R, as he was known, was the author of several books on military matters, including *Modern War and Defence Reconstruction* (1936).

Sir John Kennedy briefly returned to Rhodesia in 1960 to chair a national convention on the country's future, but spent his final years enjoying country life in Scotland. He died at his home, Broxmouth House, Dunbar, East Lothian, on 15 June 1970. Although 'austere', recorded an obituary, and 'meticulous over detail', he remained 'hospitable, kindly and friendly, with'—his most striking characteristic—'a tremendous capacity for work' (*The Times*). The honours Kennedy received for his distinguished service included KCVO (1947), KCMG (1952), and GCMG (1953). NORMAN LONGMATE

Sources J. Kennedy, *The business of war: the war narrative of Major-General Sir John Kennedy*, ed. B. Fergusson (1957) · A. Bryant, *The turn of the tide, 1939–1943: a study based on the diaries and autobiographical notes of Field Marshal the Viscount Alanbrooke* (1957) · A. Bryant, *Triumph in the West, 1943–1946* (1959) · *Wigtown Free Press* (7 Sept 1893) · *Wigtown Free Press* (5 Aug 1915) · *Wigtown Free Press* (24 Aug 1916) · *Wigtown Free Press* (2 Aug 1917) · *Wigtown Free Press* (22 Nov 1917) · *Wigtown Free Press* (26 Dec 1918) · *Wigtown Free Press* (7 Aug 1919) · *Wigtown Free Press* (5 May 1921) · N. S. Kane, *The world's view: the story of Southern Rhodesia* (1954) · R. K. Rasmussen, *Historical dictionary of Rhodesia / Zimbabwe* (1979) · R. C. Tredgold, *The Rhodesia that was my life* (1968) · *WWW, 1961–70* · *The Times* (17 June 1970) · *Daily Telegraph* (17 June 1970) · Burke, *Peerage* (1967) · I. Hancock, *White liberals, moderates and radicals in Rhodesia, 1953–80* (1984) · *Fasti Scot.*, new edn, vol. 2

Archives Bodl. RH, account of establishment of the Central African Federation, MSS Afr. r. 209 · Ewart Library, Dumfries, newspaper entries · King's Lond., Liddell Hart C., papers relating to his career, incl. diaries relating to service with royal artillery, western front, diary of South Russian campaign, and papers concerning his services as director

Likenesses W. Stoneman, photographs, 1941–7, NPG · H. Lamb, oils, 1943, IWM

Wealth at death £69,033: probate, 20 July 1970, *CGPLA Eng. & Wales*

Kennedy, John Pitt (1796–1879), army officer and engineer, fourth son of John Pitt Kennedy, rector of Carn Donagh, co. Donegal, and afterwards of Balteagh, co. Londonderry, and Mary, only daughter of Thomas Cary of Loughash, co. Tyrone, was born at Donagh on 8 May 1796. Tristram Edward *Kennedy was his brother. He was educated at Foyle College, Londonderry, under the Revd James Knox. He entered the Royal Military Academy, Woolwich, on 6 November 1811, passed out fourth of his year in 1813, and was commissioned second lieutenant, Royal Engineers, on 1 September 1815.

Ionian Islands, 1819–1831 Kennedy was employed on the Ordnance Survey in Gloucestershire and Oxfordshire for a short time, and served at Plymouth, Chatham, and Portsmouth until 1819, when he was sent to Malta, and thence to Corfu in the Ionian Islands, a British protectorate from 1815 to 1863. On 6 April 1820 he was made director of public works at Santa Maura. He constructed a small harbour on the eastern side of the island, with a canal from it to the natural harbour on the west, and lengthened the mole. He was promoted lieutenant in the Royal Engineers on 19 June 1821, but went on half pay on 28 May 1822 when the corps was reduced in size.

On the appointment of Major Charles Napier as military resident of Cephalonia in 1822 Kennedy became island secretary and director of public works. He there built the Guardianno and Point Theodore lighthouses, a marine parade, a quay, and a market, and he intersected the island with roads. Napier formed a high opinion of Kennedy's abilities, and wrote of his 'genius' and that he was 'an excellent architect' (W. Napier, 1.389, 318). Kennedy became Napier's best friend—their friendship was to be lifelong—and helped him through difficult times with his tempestuous Cephalonian mistress, Anastasia. Napier continued to attempt to advance Kennedy's career.

Kennedy was brought back to the Royal Engineers from half pay on 23 March 1825, returned to England in 1826, and was sent to Woolwich. To retain his Cephalonia appointment he was, at Napier's request, transferred from the Royal Engineers on 20 April 1826 to the 50th foot, as lieutenant. He ceased duty at Woolwich on 14 May, and on 10 June 1826 purchased an unattached company and returned to Cephalonia. On 3 January 1828 he was appointed sub-inspector of militia in the Ionian Islands, a position he held until 1 March 1831, when he returned home and settled in Ireland. He bought land in Donegal which he believed would be a profitable investment.

Service in Ireland, 1831–1849 Kennedy attempted to remedy the deplorable state of the Irish peasants, and to show by small-scale practical example what might be done for the country. He devoted himself to teaching the farmers the principles of agriculture, and to setting the unemployed to cultivate wastelands. He managed his nephew's property at Lough Ash in co. Tyrone, and the Clogher, co. Tyrone, estate of his future father-in-law, Sir Charles Style of Glenmore, Stranorlat, co. Donegal. Both at Lough Ash and Clogher, Kennedy established a national school, and arranged practical agricultural lessons on a model farm of a few acres. He also divided the wastelands into reclaiming farms, and had great success. In 1833 he visited agricultural schools in Belgium, Germany, and Switzerland. On 19 June 1835 he was brought in from half pay to the 28th foot, and on 26 June he sold out to devote the money from his commission to the furtherance of his schools. Kennedy married Anna (Annie) Maria Style in Dublin on 2 October 1838, and they had three sons and one daughter.

In November 1837 Kennedy was appointed inspector-general in the Irish national education department, on the understanding that practical instruction in agriculture was to become prominent in education. Inspectors were appointed under him for each county by public competition, and he chose 60 acres at Glasnevin, north of Dublin, with a large house and garden, for a central model farm and training establishment for teachers from the district schools, who also were trained in teaching at Dublin. His plan was to have a second-class agricultural school, subordinate to the central school, in each of the four provinces, a third-class school in each county, a fourth-class school in each barony, and a fifth-class school connected with each elementary school. However, his proposals were persistently thwarted by some members of the board, and the board itself, largely officials fully occupied with their particular duties, did so little to advance agricultural and other education that on 18 March 1839 Kennedy wrote a spirited protest, resigned, and returned to Lough Ash.

Napier (now Sir Charles) wrote a pamphlet, *Essay Addressed to Irish Absentees on the State of Ireland*, on the value of Kennedy and of his plan. In January 1838 Kennedy had declined an Australian governorship in order to continue to promote his views on agricultural education in an appointment which he described as neither lucrative nor brilliant. He was self-confident and optimistic and believed in the possibility of progress; 'his promises were alluring, and his views so forcibly stated that they always commanded attention' (Sandes, 106). Napier and his brother, William, continued to believe his potential wasted and that, given the chance, he could have achieved great change in Ireland. In 1844 William Napier wrote to Charles, 'If the government had decided to give Kennedy a free hand in his education and farming schemes in Ireland people would have been well off by now, and O'Connell would have had no following beyond his immediate ones' (P. Napier, *Raven Castle*, 29).

Sir Robert Peel, as part of his Irish 'conciliation' policy, in November 1843 appointed a small royal commission, of Irish landowners chaired by the earl of Devon, on the law and practice of land occupation in Ireland. Kennedy was appointed—'*without any solicitation* from myself or any friend' (Kennedy to Napier, 13 Dec 1843, Napier papers, d. 243/1)—secretary to the Devon commission, which reported in February 1845. It heard many witnesses and received many written submissions, and the work was arduous, resulting in five printed folio volumes, with a mass of data and criticism of the social and economic system and of bad landlords, but only limited proposals for legislation, including compensation for tenants' improvements. In November 1845 Peel, responding to the Irish potato blight, appointed the temporary relief commission, comprising some of the most influential and able members of the Irish administration, to supervise the local relief committees and their distribution of the grain the government had purchased overseas. Possibly because Sir Charles Napier wrote to Peel on behalf of Kennedy, 'a man without a match' (P. Napier, *Raven Castle*, 104), the latter was appointed secretary of the commission.

In 1846 Kennedy was appointed superintendent of the relief works in the western division of co. Limerick under the board of works, an appointment he relinquished in September on becoming agent for Lord Devon's extensive estates in co. Limerick. He was also a director of the Waterford and Limerick Railway. In spring 1848, when excitement was great and a revolution was expected in Dublin, Kennedy volunteered to organize security measures. The city authorities gave him control over the volunteer arrangements. He divided the city into defence districts; maps were distributed showing the key points in each district, the defence of which would secure the whole. At this crisis the Dublin Orangemen offered their services to the lord lieutenant. Lord Clarendon declined, as they had passed resolutions accusing the government of encouraging popery, and demanding that Roman Catholics be suppressed. Kennedy, thinking more of the safety of Dublin than of politics, enrolled them among his volunteers, and gave them £600 to purchase arms. This was to form one of the grounds of an attack on the government in the House of Lords on 18 February 1850, in response to which Lord Clarendon defended the government, and declared that Kennedy had generously provided the money for these arms out of his own pocket without the knowledge of the government, and with the laudable intention of keeping the Orangemen loyal.

Direct and indirect links with India, 1849–1879 When in 1849 Sir Charles Napier was appointed commander-in-chief in India, he offered Kennedy the post of military secretary, and obtained permission for him to re-enter the army. Kennedy was reinstated in the army on 23 March 1849 as ensign in the 25th foot, and on 4 May he was appointed to a cornetcy in the 14th light dragoons, with the local rank of major in the East Indies. He went to India with Napier, and accompanied the expedition to Peshawar to open the pass and relieve the fortress of Kohat in 1850.

Besides his duties as military secretary, Kennedy devoted his spare time to the construction of a great military road from the plains through Simla towards Tibet, and a company of sappers was placed at his disposal. The road bore his name. In November 1850 he was appointed consulting engineer to the government of India for railways, and went to Calcutta to take charge of the railway department. He strongly opposed any break of gauge, and planned a system of railways throughout India.

In September 1852, in a memorandum to the directors, Kennedy made proposals for a general system of railways which, he claimed, would enable reduction in the army and so financial saving, and he criticized the achievement of railway engineers in England. However, his plans were based on incorrect assumptions, one of which was that railways should run almost on a dead level and along coastlines and rivers. His proposals were condemned by the government's railway consulting engineers, who alleged his data were erroneous, he exaggerated the saving on military expenditure, and that the railways could not be built in the way he proposed. According to E. W. C. Sandes, Kennedy's proposals were 'typical of the grandiose schemes which have so often been propounded by imaginative engineers in any new field of endeavour without the collection of sufficient data' (Sandes, 107). However, Kennedy's health failed, and he resigned and returned to Britain in 1852. A minute of the governor-general, Lord Dalhousie, stated that his departure was a public loss to the government. He was promoted lieutenant on 15 March 1853, exchanged into the 42nd foot on 24 June, gazetted lieutenant-colonel in the East Indies, and placed on half pay on 11 November 1853.

On his arrival in England Kennedy became one of the founders and the managing director and chief engineer of the Bombay, Baroda, and Central Indian Railway, and in September 1853 he returned to India, and surveyed the line. An ingenious engineer, he experimented successfully on the Surat–Ahmadabad line with special piers for railway bridges on alluvial soils, and speeded construction by standardizing his iron bridge spans. From 1854 his home was in England, and he continued active on the board of directors for the remainder of his life. In 1859 he induced the court of directors to permit him to extend the railway south to Bombay, building under difficult conditions a succession of bridges, using metal screw piles filled with concrete. An enthusiastic optimist, he underestimated the cost of building the railway. However, largely owing to his energy Bombay gained an additional outlet for trade, and better communications with the hinterlands of Broach and Surat, which produced excellent cotton. Kennedy again visited India for the company in 1863–4. He was elected a member of the Institution of Civil Engineers on 3 March 1868, and in 1872 he promoted a company for building with concrete.

Kennedy's publications Kennedy's publications included many pamphlets on Irish and Indian issues: agriculture, railways, and others. Among them were *Instruct; employ; don't hang them, or, Ireland tranquilized without soldiers and enriched without English capital* (1835); *Analysis of projects proposed for the relief of the poor of Ireland* (1837); *Road-making in the hills. Principles and rules having special reference to the new road from Kalka viâ Simla to Kunawur and Thibet* (1850); *Finances, military occupation, government, and industrial development of India* (1858); *On the financial and executive administration of the British Indian empire* (1859); *National defensive measures, their necessity, description, organization, and cost* (1860); and *Railway gauge, considered in relation to the bulk and weight of goods to be conveyed, more especially in India* (1872). Kennedy died on 28 June 1879 at his residence, 66 St George's Square, Pimlico, London. His wife, one son,

Charles Napier Kennedy, and his daughter, Mrs Florence Martin, survived him. Kennedy was a man of great ability and simplicity, unworldly and disinterested. However, living in an era of impressive technological progress, he was sometimes unrealistic and over-optimistic in his schemes. R. H. VETCH, *rev.* ROGER T. STEARN

Sources C. J. Napier, *The colonies* (1833) • W. Napier, *The life and opinions of General Sir Charles Napier, GCB*, 4 vols. (1857) • *PICE*, 59 (1880), 293–8 • *Royal Engineers Journal*, 9, 169 • *The Times* (8 July 1879) • priv. coll. • Napier papers, Bodl. Oxf., MS Eng. lett. d. 243 • P. Napier, *I have Sind: Charles Napier in India, 1841–1844* (1990) • P. Napier, *Raven Castle: Charles Napier in India, 1844–1851* (1991) • E. W. C. Sandes, *The military engineer in India*, 2 (1935) • T. W. Moody and others, eds., *A new history of Ireland*, 5: *Ireland under the Union, 1801–1870* (1989) • C. Kinealy, *This great calamity: the Irish famine, 1845–52* (1994) • T. Bartlett and K. Jeffery, *A military history of Ireland* (1996) • Boase, *Mod. Eng. biog.* • K. Jeffery, ed., *'An Irish empire'? aspects of Ireland and the British empire* (1996) • CGPLA Eng. & Wales (1879)

Archives Bodl. Oxf., letters to Sir William Napier, MS Eng. lett. d. 243

Wealth at death under £8000: probate, 13 Aug 1879, CGPLA Eng. & Wales

Kennedy, John Stodart (1912–1993), entomologist, was born in Titusville, Pennsylvania, USA, on 19 May 1912, the only son in the family of three children of James John Stodart Kennedy, an Anglo-Scottish engineer, and his American wife, Edith Roberts Lammers. His early childhood was unsettled—his family lived in Hong Kong, Philadelphia, and Toronto—and he attended six different schools. His father was a first-class handyman and imbued him with something of his mechanical ingenuity as well as with his disrespect for people like lawyers and stockbrokers who 'produced nothing'. Both parents were deeply religious; Kennedy's teenage apostasy and later divorce gave them profound unhappiness.

Kennedy was unlike many entomologists: neither he nor any of his family had any particular interest in natural history. At school he 'never excelled at anything in particular, unless it was French, and keeping white mice, and [he] had a habit of wool-gathering' (unpublished autobiographical note). It was not until his last years at Westminster School that he discovered biology, with his enthusiasm fostered by his biology teacher George Pickering. He went on to study zoology at University College, London, where he was deeply influenced by his teachers: simultaneously attracted by the mechanistic approach of J. B. S. Haldane and G. P. Wells, and repelled by E. S. Russell's vitalist animal behaviour lectures. This was the period when his biological and political views both took shape. His politics were characterized by compassion, a concern for social justice, and anti-fascism, articulated for many years as support for the Communist Party. In 1936 he completed his MSc under the eminent physiologist Gottfried Fraenkel, a recent refugee from Hitler's Germany who introduced him to the study of insect behaviour that was to become a passion for the rest of his life. On 20 November the same year he married a fellow student, Dorothy Violet Bartholomew (*b.* 1908/9), daughter of Walter Bartholomew, general merchant; they had one son.

From 1934 to 1936 Kennedy worked as a locust investigator for the Imperial Institute of Entomology at the University of Birmingham, where he studied for his PhD under G. L. Gunn and B. P. Uvarov. In 1936–7 he and Dorothy spent four months in Sudan doing fieldwork. Kennedy was intrigued by the mechanisms locusts used to steer a course towards a stimulus such as a bush, by the conditions of the environment that stimulated them to leave some locales yet remain in others, and by variation in the conditions of the locusts themselves that led to variation in their behaviour. These studies underpinned all his science thenceforth. They led to an understanding of how insects orient to visual and chemical stimuli, to factors underlying migration, to the importance of physiological state in affecting behavioural responses, and to a more general understanding of the causes that underlie the behaviour of insects and other animals. Rigorous experimentation for the interpretation of behaviour and precision in terminology were already his hallmarks. His work led to the award of a PhD in 1938, and to a succession of short-term posts, at the London School of Hygiene and Tropical Medicine (1937–8), the Rockefeller Malaria Research Laboratory, Tirana, Albania (1938–9), and the Wellcome Entomological Field Laboratories, Esher, Surrey (1939–42).

In 1942 Kennedy was given a wartime assignment with the Middle East anti-locust unit and investigated the effectiveness of applying an insecticide to the winged locusts that were devastating food crops in Africa and the Middle East. Eventually he overcame the major logistical difficulties, only to find that it was generally an ineffective method of control. He continued his war work at the chemical defence experimental station, Porton Down (1944–5). Porton Down was already expert at the dissemination of poison from the air. Kennedy helped adapt this expertise to killing disease-carrying mosquitoes as part of the preparation for allied attacks on Japanese-occupied positions. He discovered that the initial effect of DDT is to excite the insect so that it can fly off before receiving a lethal dose, a phenomenon now known to occur with many insecticides.

In 1946 Kennedy took up a research post in V. B. Wigglesworth's newly formed Agricultural Research Council unit of insect physiology in Cambridge, where he remained until 1967. Divorced from his first wife in 1946, he later met Dr Claude Jacqueline (Claudette) Bloch, née Raphäel, a French biologist, at a conference. Widowed by the Holocaust and herself recovering from three years in Auschwitz and other Nazi camps, she brought her ten-year-old son to live with them after they were married in Paris in 1950. They had two further children, a son and a daughter, and established a happy home whence warmth and hospitality were extended to a wide circle of friends and colleagues.

Throughout his period at Cambridge and for five years subsequently, Kennedy studied the behaviour of aphids, and in particular how their flight is related to their leaving and finding host plants. He brought to this work his knack for devising methods and apparatus that could give answers not possible with 'off-the-shelf' equipment. Using a vertical wind tunnel which balanced the speed of the down draft against an aphid's rate of climb towards the light, he showed that the aphid responds primarily to the ultraviolet wavelengths of skylight while dispersing, and that its primary response then shifts to the wavelengths of light corresponding to leaves. Similar techniques enabled him to recognize that host-finding involves the integration of take-off, ascent, migration, descent, landing, probing, and reproduction behaviours. By cutting the stylets of a feeding aphid he confirmed that the turgor pressure of the plant provides a flow of sap to the insect—and incidentally provided plant physiologists with a technique for directly assaying unadulterated plant phloem.

Kennedy realized that generalizations were possible between the behaviour of the aphids during their migratory phase and that of the locusts with which he had worked earlier. Migration could be distinguished by persistent locomotion which is continued even if the insect is presented with a stimulus such as a mate or host plant; the difference between migratory and 'trivial' locomotion lay in the insect's threshold of responsiveness to these types of stimuli. Later Kennedy showed that this was part of an antagonistic system of behaviour: the longer an aphid's flight, the stronger its subsequent response to a leaf, and the stronger the response to the leaf, the stronger any subsequent flight.

When Wigglesworth retired in 1967, the Cambridge Agricultural Research Council unit was disbanded. T. R. E. Southwood then invited Kennedy and his colleague A. D. Lees to move to the department of zoology and applied entomology of Imperial College, where they established the Agricultural Research Council's insect physiology group at the Silwood Park field station. The title of professor of animal behaviour in the University of London was conferred on Kennedy in 1968, but he never really enjoyed the small number of lectures that fell to his lot.

At Silwood, Kennedy's research continued to blossom. In 1973 he returned to investigating insect orientation in flight. Using a large wind tunnel with a moving floor to represent changes in the ground pattern, he demonstrated that male moths tend to 'zig-zag' up odour plumes (pheromones) released by a female, adjusting to the effect of wind drift by reference to the ground and changing their angle of turn according to changes in the strength of the odour. He tested the responses of moths to odour in the field using an ingenious system: pheromone and soap bubbles were released simultaneously from an old tower, allowing the researchers and their videotapes to 'see' the direction of travel of the pheromone and relate it to the moths' flight. He was able to prove that, contrary to previous beliefs, moths did not find the pheromone source by moving up the concentration gradient; instead, the moths primarily track the wind, finding the pheromone within it. Together with his colleagues, Kennedy revolutionized biologists' understanding of the nature of moth orientation to odour sources, and the laboratory attracted visiting scientists from all over the world.

Kennedy continued his research at Silwood (as a senior research fellow and emeritus professor of Imperial College, London) past his retirement in 1977 until 1983, when Southwood, now head of the department of zoology at Oxford, invited him to join as a research associate. In Oxford his main work was his book *The New Anthropomorphism* (1992). In this, his scientific testament, he condemned the description of animal behaviour in teleological terms; this, he powerfully argued, obstructed clear analytical thought.

Kennedy was elected a fellow of the Royal Society in 1965. He was president of the Royal Entomological Society from 1967 to 1969, and was elected an honorary fellow in 1974 and awarded its Wigglesworth medal in 1985. He was awarded the gold medal of the Linnean Society in 1985. On 3 February 1993, while working at the zoology department in Oxford, and just after a discussion with a colleague, he suffered a brain haemorrhage. He died on 4 February at the John Radcliffe Hospital, Oxford. He was survived by his wife and stepson, and his own three children. T. R. E. SOUTHWOOD

Sources J. Brady, *Memoirs FRS*, 41 (1995), 245–60 · unpublished autobiographical note, priv. coll. · *The Times* (26 Feb 1993) · *WWW*, 1991–5 · personal knowledge (2004) · private information (2004) [James Kennedy, Cathy Kennedy] · m. cert. · d. cert.
Archives ICL, corresp. and papers
Likenesses photograph, *c*.1967, repro. in *The Times* · photograph, repro. in *Memoirs FRS*, 244
Wealth at death under £125,000: probate, 22 Feb 1993, *CGPLA Eng. & Wales*

Kennedy, Julia Elizabeth (1839–1916). *See under* Kennedy, Marion Grace (1836–1914).

Kennedy, (Aubrey) Leo (1885–1965), journalist, was born at Brighton on 6 February 1885, the second of the four sons of Sir John Gordon Kennedy (1836–1912), minister-plenipotentiary in Bucharest from 1897 to 1905, and his wife, Evelyn Adela (d. 1939), daughter of Colonel Edward Wilbraham. He was educated at Harrow School (1899–1903) and at Magdalen College, Oxford, receiving his BA in 1906. He joined *The Times* under G. E. Buckle in 1910 and was put in the foreign sub-editors' room to learn something of the working practice in Printing House Square. He was sent to Paris in 1911. When the Balkan wars broke out in 1912 he went to report them from Serbia, Romania, and Albania. During the First World War he served successively in the King's Own Yorkshire light infantry, the intelligence corps, and the Scots Guards; he was mentioned in dispatches and gained the MC. All his three brothers were killed in action; the memory of their deaths strengthened his own determination to do all he could in his writings to avert another war.

In 1919, after Kennedy returned to *The Times*, Henry Wickham Steed, then editor, sent him round Europe to gather all the information he could about the changes brought about by the Versailles treaty. Power politics became Kennedy's main concern, which was never to leave him throughout his working life. The title of his first book, published in 1922, *Old Diplomacy and New, 1876–1922*, could as fitly be applied to scores of the leading articles

which he was to write for *The Times*. His interest led him to be a founder member of the Royal Institute of International Affairs in 1920. On 12 July 1921 he married Sylvia Dorothy (d. 1968), daughter of Arthur Herbert Meysey-Thompson, civil engineer; they had three daughters.

Kennedy's main work began in 1923 when G. Geoffrey Dawson returned for his second period as editor of *The Times*. Dawson appointed Kennedy a foreign leader writer and sent him from time to time as a special correspondent in European capitals. Broadcasting was still only beginning; television news and comment were unknown; *The Times* under Dawson was regarded as the voice of Britain's ruling class. Kennedy—quiet, earnest, dark-haired, courteous, soldierly, with a military officer's sweeping moustache—was an excellent ambassador for the newspaper, and he talked confidentially with many of the European ministers over the years. Whenever he wrote a leader, he used to say, he felt the chanceries of Europe looking over his shoulder. He took his responsibilities seriously, weighing every word, seeking a way out of every problem. He had more than one period of absence through strain.

Kennedy's inner torment increased when Hitler began his aggressive moves. On the one hand he saw the German dictatorship for the evil it was and he maintained that Hitler meant all that he had written in *Mein Kampf* about Germany's need to expand. In 1937 he wrote a forthright book, *Britain Faces Germany*. Here he differed from Dawson and R. M. Barrington-Ward, the deputy editor. He wished them to give clearer warning to the country about the dangers which would arise if Neville Chamberlain's appeasement policy failed. On the other hand, Kennedy, abhorring the thought of another Great War, believed that much of the Versailles treaty had to be rectified. Here he was at one with Dawson and Barrington-Ward, and it was Kennedy who wrote the first draft of the renowned leading article in *The Times* of 7 September 1938.

The leader suggested, as the international tension was coming near to snapping point, that Prague might consider ceding the Sudeten lands and other border areas for the sake of peace. Dawson persuaded Kennedy to rewrite part of the leader and then hastily tinkered with it himself. It emerged ill considered and ill timed. In Britain and abroad it was immediately regarded as an appalling forecast of British official policy, yet the immediate storm of protest did not deter Chamberlain and Daladier from forcing Prague to make the concessions at Munich. In his private diary Kennedy wrote (17 October 1938) that in penning the leader he had been moved by three influences: by the general line of thought in Printing House Square, by Neville Chamberlain's confidential hint the previous May that he would not refuse the cession of the Sudeten lands, and by Lord Halifax's no less confidential remark in a letter to Dawson a little later that he would not rule out a solution by means of a plebiscite.

Little more than a month after Munich, Kennedy returned to the other strand in his thinking. In a personal letter published by *The Times* he gave warning of the dangers of further German expansion. Dawson occasionally allowed him such outlets. Kennedy got on well with Dawson but he and Barrington-Ward found it harder to agree on policy. Barrington-Ward had been editor for less than a month when in October 1941 he suggested that Kennedy should do less work inside the office and be more free to take on outside work. Kennedy, then fifty-six, preferred to leave altogether and went to the European service of the BBC until the end of the war. He lived afterwards for some years in north Yorkshire. He published a life of Lord Salisbury (1953), and edited (1956) for Lady Derby the letters that the fourth earl of Clarendon, foreign secretary from 1865 to 1866 and 1868 to 1870, wrote to Lady Derby's mother, the duchess of Manchester.

Kennedy died in Westminster Hospital, London, on 8 December 1965. He was the archetype of the conscientious, liberal-minded, and deeply troubled intellectual who tried in vain to cope with the evil of Hitlerism without incurring the evil of another Great War.

IVERACH MCDONALD, rev.

Sources News Int. RO, *The Times* archive · [S. Morison and others], *The history of The Times*, 4 (1952) · CAC Cam., Kennedy MSS · personal knowledge (1981) · *The Times* (9 Dec 1965) · Burke, *Peerage* (1967) [Ailsa; Meysey-Thompson, bt] · *CGPLA Eng. & Wales* (1966) **Archives** CAC Cam., journals · News Int. RO, papers **Likenesses** F. Eastman, oils, priv. coll. **Wealth at death** £33,109: probate, 10 Feb 1966, *CGPLA Eng. & Wales*

Kennedy [*née* Doyle; *other married name* Farrell], **Margaret** (*d.* 1793), singer and actress, had an Irish background but, according to Anthony Pasquin, she was born in London and studied music under Gaetano Quilici before becoming a pupil of Thomas Augustine Arne. In his *Musical Memoirs* W. T. Parke claimed that some Covent Garden performers heard her singing when she was waiting on the parlour guests at a public house near St Giles-in-the-Fields and took Arne to hear her. She married Thomas Farrell on 7 August 1774 and in 1775 sang at the Haymarket Theatre in three concerts put on by Arne to display his pupils. Each evening included catches, glees, and Arne's *The Sot*, in which Mrs Farrell played the male role of Fairlove, with the hunting song 'The dusky night rides down the sky'. After another pupils' concert early in 1776 she sang that March in two performances of Arne's *Comus* at Covent Garden.

Mrs Farrell joined the Covent Garden company in December 1776, when she was a principal singer in Arne's music for *Caractacus*. The *Morning Post* praised the duet between Leoni and Mrs Farrell, 'who sung with great taste, and fine execution' (*Morning Post*, 7 Dec 1776). Her Ariel in *The Tempest* later that month was successful vocally, but she was taller and more heavily built than her Prospero. Suited by her appearance and contralto voice for male roles, she sang the title role in Arne's *Artaxerxes* in January and Macheath in John Gay's *The Beggar's Opera* early the next season. The *Morning Post* of 18 October 1777 admired her voice and praised the judgement and spirit of her interpretation, but Macheath's singing of Arne's hunting song was attacked by the *Public Advertiser* as being 'in Defiance of Propriety and Common-Sense' (*Public Advertiser*, 18

Oct 1777). In the summers of 1777 and 1778 she appeared at Ranelagh, performing songs by Arne and James Hook, and in those years, besides her theatre appearances, she sang in festivals in Manchester, Oxford, and Winchester and in the Lent oratorio seasons in London. On 24 January 1779 the widowed Margaret Farrell married an Irish doctor, Morgan Hugh Kennedy (*d.* 1809), and as Mrs Kennedy she remained a leading singer at Covent Garden until 1789.

Mrs Kennedy performed at Vauxhall Gardens every summer from 1781 to 1785, and numerous songs by Hook, Michael Arne, and others were published as sung by her there. She was heard in the oratorio seasons at Drury Lane (1779, 1784) and the Haymarket (1785). In 1791, two years after Mrs Kennedy's retirement from the stage, Mrs Papendiek was moved in a Handel concert at Westminster Abbey by her 'contralto voice melodiously sweet' (*Court and Private Life*, 2.254). At Covent Garden her salary rose from £5 a week to £12 in her last two seasons. She sang much incidental music, and her roles in stock pieces included Don Carlos in Sheridan's comic opera *The Duenna* and later Lucy in *The Beggar's Opera*. She created a large number of roles designed for her, including Cicely in Hook's *Lady of the Manor* (23 November 1778), Orra in Charles Dibdin's *The Islanders* (25 November 1780), Margaret and later Allen-a-Dale in William Shield's *Robin Hood* (17 April 1784; 12 October 1784), and William in his *Rosina* (31 December 1782), the role she played in her final stage appearance on 2 April 1789. The playwright John O'Keeffe gave her the Irish roles of Patrick in *The Poor Soldier* (4 November 1783) and Mrs Casey in *Fontainbleau* (16 November 1784), both with music by Shield, as well as one of her most frequently performed parts, Don Alfonso in Arnold's *The Castle of Andalusia* (2 November 1782). In 1786 the celebrated Mrs Kennedy appeared in her favourite roles in the Edinburgh summer season.

The Secret History of the Green Rooms claimed that Mrs Kennedy left the stage because of a disagreement with the manager, Thomas Harris, and *The Bystander* deplored her departure, praising her 'easy, sweet, natural, and unaffected' singing (*The Bystander*, 1790, 140). It is likely that her health was declining; Parke stated that she was prescribed brandy and water for a medical condition and by 1791 was drinking too much. She died on 23 January 1793 at Bayswater Hall, Bayswater (her husband was physician at the lying-in hospital there), and was buried at St Anne's, Soho, on 3 February. Even in 1821 a writer in the Boston *Euterpeiad* remembered her thrilling voice, a 'sweet counter tenor; a quality so rare in a female, that it charmed by its novelty no less than by its richness of tone' (*Euterpeiad*, 13 Oct 1821, 114).

OLIVE BALDWIN and THELMA WILSON

Sources G. W. Stone, ed., *The London stage, 1660–1800*, pt 4: 1747–1776 (1962) · C. B. Hogan, ed., *The London stage, 1660–1800*, pt 5: 1776–1800 (1968) · church register of St Clement Danes, 7 Aug 1774 [marriage] · church register of St Paul's, Covent Garden, 24 Jan 1779 [marriage] · church register of St Anne's, Soho, 3 Feb 1793 [burial] · *Morning Post* (7 Dec 1776) · *Morning Post* (28 Dec 1776) · *Morning Post* (18 Oct 1777) · *Public Advertiser* (18 Oct 1777) · L. Baillie and R. Balchin, eds., *The catalogue of printed music in the British Library* to 1980, 62 vols. (1981–7) • A. Pasquin [J. Williams], 'The children of Thespis', *Poems*, 2 [1789] • J. O'Keeffe, *Recollections of the life of John O'Keeffe, written by himself*, 2 (1826) • W. T. Parke, *Musical memoirs*, 2 vols. (1830) • 'Juvenile recollections', *Euterpeiad* (13 Oct 1821), 114 • *Court and private life in the time of Queen Charlotte, being the journals of Mrs Papendiek*, ed. V. D. Broughton, 2 vols. (1887) • *The Bystander* (10 Oct 1790), 140 • [J. Haslewood], *The secret history of the green rooms: containing authentic and entertaining memoirs of the actors and actresses in the three Theatres Royal*, 2 (1790) • *Recollections of R. J. S. Stevens: an organist in Georgian London*, ed. M. Argent (1992) • J. Jackson, *The history of the Scottish stage* (1793) • *ABC dario musico* (privately printed, Bath, 1780) • Mr Dibdin [C. Dibdin], *A complete history of the English stage*, 5 (privately printed, London, [1800]) • *GM*, 1st ser., 63 (1793) • *European Magazine and London Review*, 23 (1793)

Likenesses double portrait, engraving (as Artaxerxes in *Artaxerxes*, with Reinhold as Artabanes), BM, Harvard TC • engraving (as Macheath in *The Beggar's Opera*), BM, Harvard TC; repro. in J. Bew, *Vocal Magazine*, 1 (1778)

Wealth at death married at death; no married women's property at this time

Kennedy, Margaret [*married name* Margaret Davies, Lady Davies] (**1896–1967**), novelist and playwright, was born at 14 Hyde Park Gate, London, on 23 April 1896, the eldest of the four children of Charles Moore Kennedy (1857–1934), a barrister descended from a Scottish family settled in Ulster since the seventeenth century. Her mother, Ellinor Edith Marwood (1861–1928), came of a family from Cleveland. Joyce Cary, the novelist, was a cousin on the Kennedy side, but there was little other trace of literary talent in the family. Margaret Kennedy was educated at Cheltenham Ladies' College, where she was taught English by the formidable Elizabeth Guinness, the vice-principal, who had previously taught Ivy Compton-Burnett. Margaret Kennedy did not enjoy her time at Cheltenham, but she none the less won not only the prize for drama but, more impressively, the award for a poem in honour of St Hilda, judged by William Butler Yeats. In 1915 she went up to Somerville College, Oxford, where she had been preceded by such novelists as Vera Brittain and Dorothy Sayers. The First World War took its toll of the Kennedy family; casualties included Tristram Kennedy, next brother to Margaret.

After taking second-class honours in history, Margaret Kennedy cut her teeth as a writer with a historical work, *A Century of Revolution* (1922). Her first novel, *The Ladies of Lyndon* (1923), owed something to the tribal background of her mother's Yorkshire family, and to its tensions. It was to be her second novel, however, that catapulted Margaret Kennedy into best-selling literary celebrity. *The Constant Nymph* (1924) opens in the Austrian Tyrol with which the author had fallen in love. The *ménage* of the priapic composer, Albert Sanger, has been likened to that of the painter Augustus John. Margaret's cousin, George Kennedy, the architect, had connections with the John circle, and as a schoolgirl she had met the painter Henry Lamb at her cousin's house. If John had something in common with Sanger, Lamb was thought to have inspired the character of Lewis Dodd, whose love destroys Tessa Sanger, the 'constant nymph'. Not only was the novel a worldwide best-seller but the dramatization, done in co-operation with Basil Dean, in which Noël Coward, and later John

Gielgud, played Lewis Dodd, was an equal success. Cyril Connolly wrote of the dramatization that 'one wept most of the time … and Tessa died in a tumult of sobs from the audience' (Connolly, 177). Film versions were equally moving.

On 20 June 1925 Margaret Kennedy married David Davies (1889–1964), a barrister who became a county court judge and, later, a national insurance commissioner. He was knighted in 1952. They had a happy family life, with one son and two daughters, one of these, Julia Birley, also becoming a novelist.

After stage success, Margaret Kennedy co-authored three plays that were performed in the West End of London. Most popular was *Escape Me Never* (1934), adapted from *The Fool of the Family* (1930), a sequel to *The Constant Nymph*. In this Elizabeth Bergner played a cunning waif. Relations with Bergner were turbulent, but the play and the subsequent film were generally applauded.

Having become famous, originally, as the author of a tragic fairy-tale was something of a handicap to Margaret Kennedy when it came to gaining a reputation as a novelist to be taken seriously. She was, however, much in demand as a judge of literary prizes, and as an active and forceful member of professional committees. Of her eight pre-1940 novels, *A Long Time Ago* (1932) was one of the most psychologically perceptive, contrasting the disillusions of early middle age with the uncertainties of children struggling towards puberty, their family party on an Irish holiday being disrupted by a seductive prima donna. On the other hand *The Midas Touch* (1938), a *Daily Mail* book of the month, dealt with a money-making gift, passed down through generations with a climax of Gothic disaster.

After the Second World War Margaret Kennedy returned to novel writing with *The Feast* (1950), a Literary Guild choice in the USA. Among her later novels, *Troy Chimneys* (1953) won the James Tait Black memorial prize, while *The Heroes of Clone* (1957) owed much of its dark humour to its author's experience as a scriptwriter for films. Keenly interested in the technique of writing, Margaret Kennedy published a short biography of Jane Austen in 1950, and a study of the art of fiction, *Outlaws on Parnassus* in 1958, both works of percipient criticism. She accepted, in due course, an invitation to become a fellow of the Royal Society of Literature.

Margaret Kennedy was tall and dark; she was a good pianist and had a fine singing voice. Music was a passion which she shared with her husband. They were also fond of mountain walking and were fortunate in finding a house near Cadair Idris in north Wales, from where such walks were inexhaustible. The loss of Sir David Davies, in 1964, left his widow alone to face the debilitating illness of her son, James. In spite of these blows, she continued to make plans for further books until she died in her sleep on 31 July 1967 at the house of a friend, 1 Le Hall Place, Adderbury, Oxfordshire.   VIOLET POWELL

Sources personal knowledge (2004) • private information (2004) [family] • V. Powell, *The constant novelist: a study of Margaret Kennedy* (1983) • C. Connolly, *A romantic friendship: the letters of Cyril Connolly*

to Noel Blakiston (1975) · b. cert. · m. cert. · CGPLA Eng. & Wales (1967)

Archives NRA, corresp. and literary papers · Somerville College, Oxford, papers and corresp. | JRL, corresp. with Basil Dean · Royal Society of Literature, letters to Royal Society of Literature · U. Reading L., corresp. with George Bell & Sons · UCL, letters to Arnold Bennett

Likenesses D. Cooke, oils, c.1921 · H. Coster, photographs, 1931–51, NPG · E. O'Hara, watercolour, 1948 · F. Dobson, bronze bust

Wealth at death £17,582: probate, 1 Dec 1967, CGPLA Eng. & Wales

Kennedy [née Walker], **Margaret Stephen** (1814–1891), missionary in India, was born in Aberdeen on 18 January 1814, the youngest of at least four daughters of John Walker (c.1780–c.1860), a prosperous businessman whose enterprises failed in the 1830s, making it necessary for Margaret to support herself as a teacher. Fortunately she had been sent to one of the best girls' schools in Aberdeen, and had become a voracious reader and competent book-keeper. An elder of his church, Walker dominated his family and was the principal influence on his daughter, together with Mr Aitken, minister of the Old Secession Church of Anti-Burghers, Aberdeen (later united with the Free Church of Scotland). However, she rejected the former's strict sabbatarianism and dour dutiful approach to religion. This was because she experienced, according to an autobiographical fragment left to her children, and quoted extensively in her husband's memoir of her (1892), a direct revelation, 'as if the sun had burst out in the darkness of midnight' (Kennedy, Memoir, 8). Faith was sheer joy and peace, despite great anguish and suffering in India, and the deaths before the age of five of three among her seven children. She loved singing hymns, and made Sunday observance enjoyable for her family. She rejected the strict Calvinist opposition to missions.

Margaret Walker went to India and joined her sister Eliza Ann (d. 1857) and her brother-in-law, the controversial Scottish London Missionary Society (LMS) missionary William Buyers (1804–1865), until 1840, when ill health forced them to leave their work in Benares, but then she married a Scottish LMS colleague, the Revd James Kennedy (1815–1899) from near Aberdeen and she stayed on as an LMS missionary. While always upholding the Westminster confession (1648) and strict evangelical principles, Margaret Kennedy became increasingly ecumenically minded in India. She also initiated work among women. Ill health forced her to go to the Kumaon hills in 1848, where from 1869 to 1877 she and her husband were involved in pioneering work developing the hill station of Ranikhet, building a church and schools and comforting lepers. She had to return to Scotland in the years 1850–53, 1857–9 (after harrowing experiences in the Indian mutiny in which her sister and many friends died), 1862–5, and 1874, when she devoted herself to her children and parish work. Always opposed to women speaking in public, she did no deputation work even though her husband wished her to preach, but conducted women's meetings in Benares and Ranikhet, ran superb Sunday schools, and did much pastoral work as she spoke fluent Hindustani and Hindi. She superintended the LMS orphanage in Benares and organized girls' schools whenever possible, but prejudice against female education made this difficult. Although not medically trained, her ministrations to the constant stream of Indian sufferers were much appreciated. Her effectiveness as an evangelist was indirect, through her friendships with members of different races and classes, even a Coorgi princess. The quality of her life distinguished her—her cheerfulness, patience, and attempts to walk closely with God—rather than the creation of enduring institutions.

In 1877 the Kennedys returned to Scotland. James Kennedy was a Congregationalist minister at Portobello, near Edinburgh, from 1878 to 1882, then retired to Acton, Middlesex. Margaret Kennedy exhausted herself helping others in the extreme winter conditions of 1890–91. Smitten by bronchitis, on 23 May 1891 she died in Acton surrounded by her family. She was buried in Hampstead, London, on 27 May.   E. M. JACKSON

Sources J. Kennedy, Memoir of Margaret Stephen Kennedy (1892) · J. Kennedy, Life and work in Benares and Kumaon, 1839–1877 (1884) · Bengal mission, SOAS, Archives of the Council for World Mission (incorporating the London Missionary Society) [IOC Leiden, microfiche] · D. M. Lewis, ed., The Blackwell dictionary of evangelical biography, 1730–1860, 2 vols. (1995) · Boase, Mod. Eng. biog.

Archives SOAS, LMS archives, husband's letters, colleagues' reports [on microfiche from IOC, Leiden]

Wealth at death thrift and frugality were legendary; living with husband on missionary's pension, and had difficulty finding affordable accommodation in London

Kennedy, Marion Grace (1836–1914), classical scholar, was born at Shrewsbury on 23 November 1836, the second daughter of Benjamin Hall *Kennedy (1804–1889) and his wife, Janet (d. 1874), daughter of Thomas Caird. There were four daughters: Charlotte Amy May [see below]; Marion Grace, known within the family as Maisie; Julia Elizabeth (Poppy) [see below]; and Edith Janet (1842–1922), who later married William Kitson, a west country solicitor; a son, Arthur Herbert (1846–1885), went to Oxford and the bar but subsequently worked in the wine trade. All but the eldest daughter were born while their father was headmaster of Shrewsbury School. He was a benevolent, but fiercely and erratically impulsive man, prone to dismiss whole groups of boys (on one occasion, the entire sixth form), only to forget his decision overnight. He was no manager of money or keeper of records, and it was Janet Kennedy who held the purse strings.

Charlotte Amy May Burbury [née Kennedy] (1832–1895), educationist, the eldest daughter, was born at The Grove, Harrow School. She married on 10 June 1852 William Burbury (1821/2–1865), second master at Shrewsbury School and, from 1861, rector of West Felton, near Oswestry (her father succeeding to the living after her husband's death). They had no children. She was for ten years secretary to the Cambridge Local Examinations Board, and from 1871 to 1876 was secretary to the London National Society for Women's Suffrage, standing unsuccessfully as a candidate for the London school board in 1873. From 1870 until her death she was a member of the committee of the Society for the Employment of Women. She was a governor of the London School of Medicine for Women

Marion Grace Kennedy (1836–1914), by Sir James Jebusa Shannon, 1892

and of the North London Collegiate School. Charlotte Burbury died at 4 Cambrian Villas, Queen's Road, Richmond, Surrey, on 14 November 1895.

Julia Elizabeth Kennedy (1839–1916), supporter of education for women, was born at Shrewsbury on 23 December 1839. She and her sister Marion remained single, and they lived with their parents, moving to Cambridge on their father's election to the regius chair of Greek in 1867. After their mother's death in 1874 they kept house for their father at The Elms, a large house in Bateman Street. The sisters became well-known members of Cambridge society, which from the early 1880s was transformed by the relaxation of celibacy rules for college fellowships. Several young fellows who taught at the new women's colleges (Girton, founded in 1869, and Newnham, founded in 1871) subsequently married their pupils. Marion and Julia were staunch members of the liberal reforming circle in this society; they were probably the two elderly spinsters whom A. N. Whitehead tried to embarrass by announcing advanced Liberal views—only to be told how pleased they were that he shared their own opinions (B. Russell, *Autobiography of Bertrand Russell*, 1975, 130).

Benjamin Kennedy was a firm supporter of women's education and of their admission to university teaching and degrees, and Marion and Julia worked hard for the cause of women's education. Together with the Sidgwicks and the Fawcetts they were among the original supporters of the movement for providing lectures for women students. In 1877 Marion Kennedy became executive secretary of the Association for Promoting the Higher Education of Women in Cambridge, which she supported with a donation of £100; when the association was amalgamated with Newnham Hall in 1880, she became honorary secretary to what was henceforth Newnham College, a post she retained until 1904. In the college's early years, she devoted much time to the pastoral care of its students.

After the family's move to Cambridge, Julia Kennedy began to learn philology from W. W. Skeat, and was the daughter to whom J. E. B. Mayor referred as an intelligent member of his Latin class for ladies in 1871. By the following decade she was sufficiently competent to be asked to give lectures on Anglo-Saxon at Girton College. In 1890 she was elected to membership of the Cambridge Philological Society. This election may have been influenced by local knowledge of her part in writing the *Revised Latin Primer* which had appeared under her father's name in 1888.

The book was prepared when Kennedy himself was in his eighties. The schoolmaster turned professor had not kept up with the progress of comparative philology, being revolutionized in the 1880s by the New Grammarians led by Osthoff and Brugmann. In the surviving correspondence with the publisher Longman, most letters are from the pen of Marion. She wrote as if acting as her father's secretary, but it is noticeable that the book's progress was slowed after Marion had a riding accident. In 1913 a question of copyright payment forced her to inform Longman that she and Julia had written the book themselves, with the help of two of her father's former pupils, G. H. Hallam of Harrow and T. E. Page of Charterhouse. Marion had provided the examples, Julia the philological introduction. In the event they were persuaded by counsel's opinion that they should not risk litigation, since the book had been issued solely under their father's name and they had made no public claim to authorship.

Marion Kennedy died at Torquay, Devon, on 11 January 1914, and Julia Kennedy on 9 December 1916 at Shenstone, 7 Selwyn Gardens, Cambridge, the house which she and Marion had shared after their father's death. Their memory and that of their father survives in the name of Kennedy Hall in Newnham College. In 1888 a fund had been raised by subscription to found a research studentship named after Marion; its first two holders were Mary Bateson and Philippa Fawcett. Marion's support for female suffrage placed her in a minority in the Cambridge Women's Liberal Association and led to her resignation from that body. In 1913, aged seventy-seven, she joined the suffrage procession in London. She and Julia were born just too early to take advantage of the educational provision for girls and women which they so strongly supported. Both in this work, and in their unacknowledged writing of the *Revised Latin Primer*, they devoted themselves loyally to the causes they believed in.   CHRISTOPHER STRAY

Sources A. Gardner, *Newnham College Letter* (1914), 31–3 · *The Athenaeum* (17 Jan 1914), 92 · *The Queen* (1914), 101 · J. M. Smith, *Newnham*

College Letter (1916), 64–6 · *Englishwoman's Review*, 27 (1896), 57 · *CGPLA Eng. & Wales* (1914) · d. cert. [Charlotte Amy Mary Burbury] **Archives** U. Reading L., Longman archive **Likenesses** group photograph, *c.*1860–1869 (with family), Shrewsbury School · J. J. Shannon, oils, 1892, Newnham College, Cambridge [*see illus.*] · photograph, priv. coll. · photograph (Julia Kennedy), Newnham College, Cambridge **Wealth at death** £6050 11*s.* 5*d.*: probate, 3 April 1914, *CGPLA Eng. & Wales* · £9147 16*s.* 10*d.*—Julia Kennedy: probate, 24 April 1917, *CGPLA Eng. & Wales* · £5369 13*s.* 2*d.*—Charlotte Amy May Burbury (*née* Kennedy): probate, 27 June 1896, *CGPLA Eng. & Wales*

Kennedy, Patrick (*d.* 1760), numismatist, was of Scottish birth and may have come from Aberdeen, where he had an uncle. By profession a physician, he was generally known as Dr Kennedy, and he has been referred to as John, not Patrick, apparently erroneously. According to John Nichols he resided for some time at Smyrna but by 1736 he was in London, collecting ancient coins and corresponding with others at home and abroad on numismatics. His collection, augmented by a purchase from Richard Mead, was strong in the coinage of the Hellenistic kingdoms but it was with Roman imperials that Kennedy particularly concerned himself. A special interest in the issues of the third-century British usurper emperors Carausius and Allectus, about which he corresponded with William Stukeley, George North, and others, led him into a rather ridiculous controversy. Kennedy maintained that the female figure named Oriuna on a billon coin of Carausius in Paris was the usurper's patron goddess; Stukeley held her to be his wife. Neither had actually seen the coin in question, relying instead on an engraving; in fact it was a poorly preserved specimen, reading not Oriuna but Fortuna and showing the anodyne image of the goddess Fortune. The debate did however draw attention to the unusually rich imagery of the Carausian coinage, and Kennedy's two principal contributions—*A Dissertation upon Oriuna* (1751) and *Further Observations upon Carausius* (1756)—are still of interest. He also produced a sixpenny *Letter to Dr Stukeley* and an engraved plate of some of his coins of the two usurpers.

Kennedy died 'at an advanced age' (Nichols, *Lit. anecdotes*, 5.451) on 26 February 1760 in the Strand, London, leaving as heirs a sister, her daughters, and two cousins. His will, a highly eccentric document, is chiefly concerned with the disposition of his coins, suggesting that the first pick of his Carausian pieces be given to English buyers, though they would be 'greatly valued abroad by all the powers who collect, as France, Spain, a curious pontiff &c'. The collection was sold by Prestage on 8 and 9 May 1760; the 256 coins of Carausius and 89 of Allectus were purchased by P. C. Webb for £86 10*s.* and afterwards passed into the collection of William Hunter. Kennedy's books and a collection of about 200 pictures, including two portraits of himself by Keysing, had been sold on 30 April.

W. W. WROTH, *rev.* C. E. A. CHEESMAN

Sources Nichols, *Lit. anecdotes*, 2.283; 5.451; 6.219; 9.409–11 · Nichols, *Illustrations*, 4.209 · will, 6 Feb 1760, PRO, PROB 11/853, sig. 64 · *A catalogue of the … collection of Greek and Roman medals and medallions … of the learned Dr Kennedy, deceas'd (etc.)* (1760) · *A collection of … books and … pictures … of the learned Dr Kennedy* (1760) · letters from Kennedy, 1736–7, BL, Egerton MS 22, fols. 35–7 · P. Kennedy, letters, Bodl. Oxf., MS Ballard 40, fols. 137–41 · *GM*, 1st ser., 30 (1760), 102 **Archives** BL, letters, Egerton MS · U. Glas., Hunterian coin collection **Likenesses** Keysing, two heads **Wealth at death** coin collection raised £440: annotated copy of *Catalogue*, BM, dept. of coins and metals

Kennedy, Patrick (1800–1873), antiquarian, was born at Kilmyshall, near Bunclody, co. Wexford, the son of Patrick Kennedy. In 1807 the family moved to Castleboro, with the result that—thanks to the patronage of the Carew family—the boy acquired a sound education in a traditional-style school. The area at this time was rich in folklore and communal harmony, a factor which imbued all his subsequent work with a humane warmth. In 1821 he moved to Dublin to further his education, and two years later became an assistant master with the Kildare Place Society, a pioneering project devoted to interdenominational popular education. Perhaps because of the hostility which the society provoked in certain sectors of Catholic Ireland, Kennedy (a self-effacing man) finally abandoned teaching in 1843, and opened a bookshop-cum-library in Dublin's Anglesea Street. His clients included notable figures such as Sir Charles Dilke.

Amid the modest literary revival stimulated by Isaac Butt, Samuel Ferguson, and others, Kennedy gained a reputation as a repository of folktales and local history. He collected his work using the pseudonym Harry Whitney. His principal publications in this vein are *Legends of Mount Leinster* (1855), *Banks of the Boro: a Chronicle of the County of Wexford* (1867), and *Evenings in the Duffrey* (1869). Kennedy's work with less local material, for example in *Legendary Fictions of the Irish Celts* (1866) and *The Bardic Stories of Ireland* (1871), prefigures the interest of W. B. Yeats, Augusta Gregory, and other writers of the Irish literary renaissance, while lacking their modernist appreciation of myth and the archaic world. His inclusion with Thomas Hood in *The Book of Modern Anecdotes* (1873) encapsulates his mid-Victorian middlebrow conception of the writer as entertainer. Nevertheless, Kennedy was one of the first people in the Anglophone world to recognize the importance of the *Kalevala* for the understanding of western folklore and tradition.

Kennedy's friendship and business relationship with Joseph Sheridan Le Fanu contributed to his material comfort during the 1860s. His many contributions to the *Dublin University Magazine* during Le Fanu's editorship (July 1861 to June 1869) are reflected in *The Wellesley Index to Victorian Periodicals* (1987, 4.657–9) though the list given there includes some items attributed on slender, and often circular, evidential argument. It is certainly striking that the earliest article he claimed, writing to the Royal Literary Fund in April 1871, had appeared in the issue for September 1861, while the latest attributed to him by the Wellesley researchers appeared in May 1873, two months after Kennedy's death and four months after Le Fanu's. Both men were book lovers, with antiquarian interests. Though Kennedy has been cast as a specialist on Irish topics, his range in the *Dublin University Magazine* included

French, Breton, and even Russian literature. His influence on Le Fanu's short fiction is evident in the stories the latter published in *All the Year Round* in 1870. Despite his modest background, his learning was both extensive and innovative, at least in the context of Victorian Dublin.

Patrick Kennedy died of bronchitis at his home, 9 Anglesea Street, Dublin, on 28 March 1873.

RICHARD GARNETT, rev. W. J. MCCORMACK

Sources A. J. Webb, *A compendium of Irish biography* (1878) · C. A. Read, ed., *The cabinet of Irish literature* (1879–80) · *Dublin University Magazine*, 81 · University College, Dublin, Patrick Kennedy MSS · d. cert.

Archives UCL, corresp. with Sir Edwin Chadwick

Likenesses oils, NG Ire.

Kennedy, Quintin (c.1520–1564), abbot of Crossraguel and religious controversialist, was the fourth of the seven sons of Gilbert *Kennedy, second earl of Cassillis (c.1492–1527), and his wife, Isobella Campbell, daughter of Archibald Campbell, second earl of Argyll. Possibly he was taught by George Buchanan, tutor to his eldest brother. He then matriculated at St Salvator's College, St Andrews, in 1540, and is recorded at Paris University in 1542–3. Vicar of Girvan by October 1545, he was also parish clerk of Colmonell and succeeded his brother Thomas, slain at Pinkie in November 1547, as vicar of Penpont (Nithsdale). When his uncle William Kennedy, abbot of Cluniac Crossraguel and commendator of Premonstratensian Holywood, died at some point after 23 May 1547, Quintin succeeded him at Crossraguel. The Cassillis family clearly dominated the church in the Carrick division of Ayrshire: Cassillis and Dunure (seats of the family), Colmonell, and Crossraguel were all in Carrick, and the earl was bailie of Crossraguel.

Quintin Kennedy's election (technically postulation, as he was not a monk though presumably a priest) was confirmed on 1 January 1548 by the father abbot of the Cluniac order in Scotland. On 1 February Kennedy was installed as abbot and acknowledged receipt of all monastic property, as it had been in the keeping of his brother Gilbert *Kennedy, the third earl, since Abbot William's death. On 23 April he received crown admittance to the temporalities. He also resigned his benefices at Girvan, Colmonell, and Penpont, the latter two to his brother Hugh. The evidence for his monastic status, however, is conflicting. The Crossraguel abbacy did not require Roman consistorial provision. Election and confirmation denote a regular abbot, and resigning benefices is a similar indication, but in July 1554 Julius III, at Queen Mary's petition, appointed Kennedy to be commendator of Crossraguel. The inference must be that he had never become a monk and regular abbot.

During the next ten years Kennedy took little part in public life, though he attended the Scottish church council of 1549. He sat in parliament in April 1554, and in May he was recorded as setting out for France to have dealings with the bishop of Ross, who was already there as the queen's envoy. In the years between 1558 and 1563, however, he played an active part in Reformation disputes. In 1558 he published *Ane Compendius Tractive*, dedicated to his nephew, the master of Cassillis, in which he severely criticized abuses in the church, particularly the appointment of unsuitable men and even children to pastoral positions, but insisted that interpretation of scripture and all matters of faith and worship were to be decided by church authority only. The tract was influential and he also circulated a summary.

The protestant John Willock preached at Ayr in the winter of 1558–9 and accepted Kennedy's challenge to a disputation on the mass in early May 1559. It did not take place. Willock claimed his opponent was unpunctual, while Kennedy asserted that Willock arrived with several hundred supporters instead of the agreed twelve on each side, whereupon Kennedy refused to debate and repeated the challenge. He was absent from the church council held at that precise time but soon after was discussing with Archbishop James Beaton means of combating the protestant reformers.

Kennedy did not attend the Reformation Parliament of August 1560 and plainly did not accept its enactments. He was mentioned specifically in the general assembly's complaint in December 1560 about mass still being said in Ayrshire. At this time he composed *Ane Litil Breif Tracteit* aimed at proving Christ's presence in the consecrated elements. This and two other works have survived in manuscripts dated 1561: *Ane Oratioune* to the protestant lords of congregation, warning them against being deceived by the reformed ministers; and *Ane Compendious Ressonyng*, with the theme that the mass was instituted by Christ.

Kennedy was declared an outlaw for non-payment of the tax of a third of the revenues of benefices which was levied in 1561 and 1562 to finance a reformed ministry, and indeed had 'deforced' (resisted) an official sent to uplift the tax. In June or July 1562 he was present at a secret meeting of Roman Catholics in Paisley, planning, it was said, a Catholic rising. In September came the incident for which he is best known: his three-day disputation at Maybole (Carrick) with John Knox on the eucharist. What is known about this comes from Knox's account but neither disputant was able afterwards to claim a clear victory. After a promising start, with Kennedy attempting to prove that the mass is a sacrifice because Christ is a priest according to the order of Melchizedek, the disputation declined into a somewhat sterile debate on the nature of Melchizedek's offering.

At Easter 1563 there was a public celebration of Roman Catholic sacraments in Ayrshire and other western districts, in which Kennedy and Crossraguel monks were involved. Carrick remained a Roman Catholic stronghold, and Crossraguel monks all stayed Catholic. By now Kennedy's health had deteriorated badly; he had been ill the previous year and was not expected to live. He survived for a year, however, and died in July 1564, probably at Crossraguel.

The only accusation to be made against Kennedy's character was John Knox's stricture that he had failed to instruct his flock. In fact Kennedy features little in contemporary sources and he published only one short tract, though three others survived in manuscript. Nineteenth-century publication of sources made him better known, and two tracts, recently rediscovered and printed, have revealed his eucharistic theology. In this area he made a real contribution. Though not an original thinker, he produced a simplification of late medieval theology, citing the fathers not at first hand but from recent works. His approach was less polemical than systematic, aimed at showing that the mass was identical with the last supper and was not a repetition of Calvary, but was rather the means whereby the fruits of Calvary were distributed. He used the concept of bloody and unbloody sacrifice a year before its appearance in the Council of Trent's decree. Kennedy's tracts add significantly to knowledge both of the Scottish Reformation and of literary sixteenth-century Scots. He attempted to bridge the gap between technical theology and its popular expression, and in doing so he used both traditional pulpit oratory and Renaissance rhetoric.

G. W. SPROTT, *rev.* MARK DILWORTH

Sources *Quintin Kennedy, 1520–1564: two eucharistic tracts*, ed. C. H. Kuipers (Nijmegen, 1964) [incl. *Ane litil breif tracteit* and *Ane Compendious ressonyng*] · F. C. H. Blair, ed., *Charters of the Abbey of Crosraguel*, 2 vols., Ayrshire and Galloway Archaeological Association (1886) · M. Dilworth, 'Scottish Cluniacs and the Reformation struggle', Scottish Church History Society [forthcoming] · M. Taylor, 'The conflicting doctrines of the Scottish Reformation', *Innes Review*, 10 (1959), 97–125 · I. B. Cowan, 'Ayrshire abbeys: Crossraguel and Kilwinning', *Ayrshire Collections*, 14/7 (1986), 265–95 · Q. Kennedy, *Ane compendius tractive* (1558); repr. in *The miscellany of the Wodrow Society*, ed. D. Laing, Wodrow Society, [9] (1844) · Q. Kennedy, *Ane oratioune in favouris of all thais of the congregatione*, ed. A. B. [A. Boswell] (1812); repr. in D. Laing, ed., *The works of John Knox*, 1, Wodrow Society, 12 (1846), 157–65 · R. Keith, *History of the affairs of church and state in Scotland from the beginning of the Reformation to the year 1568*, ed. J. P. Lawson and C. J. Lyon, Spottiswoode Society, 1 (1844), Kennedy's letters to Beaton and Willock, 1559 · corresp. Kennedy–Knox, 1562, printed by Knox 1563, repr. by Laing [among Knox's works]

Kennedy, Rann (1772–1851), schoolmaster and poet, was the son of Benjamin Kennedy (*d.* 1784), surgeon, and his wife, the daughter of Illedge Maddox. He was of Scottish origin, being descended from a branch of the Ayrshire Kennedys, who settled at Shenstone, Staffordshire, early in the eighteenth century. His father went about 1773 to America, to introduce inoculation, and settled at Annapolis in Maryland with his family, where they remained during and after the American War of Independence. On his father's death in 1784, Rann returned with his mother, who was of Welsh descent, to her family's estate at Withington, near Shrewsbury, where he was brought up.

In 1791 Kennedy went to St John's College, Cambridge, where he formed a lasting friendship with S. T. Coleridge. After obtaining his degree (BA 1795 and MA 1798) he took holy orders, and accepted a mastership at King Edward's School, Birmingham, where he became second master in 1807. From 1797 to 1817 he was also curate of St Paul's, Birmingham, and from 1817 until about 1847 was its incumbent, his congregation having purchased for him the next presentation.

In 1802 Kennedy had married Julia, daughter of John *Hall (1739–1797), historical engraver, and Mary de Gilles, a French Huguenot. Their four sons also had distinguished

and successful careers at Cambridge and beyond. All won the Porson prize while at university, and the three elder were senior classics (1827, 1831, and 1834). Benjamin Hall *Kennedy (1804–1889) eventually became the regius professor of Greek at Cambridge, and Charles Rann *Kennedy (1808–1867) was a lawyer and a classical scholar. A third son, George John (*d.* 1847), was to become master at Rugby, while the fourth son, William James (1814–1891), was to serve as first secretary of the National Society for the Promotion of Education, as HM inspector of schools (1848–78), and as vicar of Barnwood, Gloucestershire.

Kennedy was earnest and enthusiastic, and a determined enemy of intolerance and bigotry. He was considered to be 'one of the best classical scholars of his time' (Trott, 47), and also published several poetical works, including *A Church of England Psalmbook* (1821), and its companion piece, *Thoughts on the Music and Words of Psalmody as at Present in use among the Members of the Church of England* (1821). He had a great many friends in intellectual circles, chief among them being John Johnstone MD and Samuel Parr, but he also associated with Coleridge, Washington Irving, Wordsworth, James Montgomery, Henry Francis Cary, Charles Kemble, and Sarah Siddons. A poem which he published in 1817 on the death of the Princess Charlotte received the highest praise from Washington Irving, who quotes from it in his 'Sketch-book'. Irving described Kennedy as 'a most eccentric character' and 'a man of real genius … one of the queerest mortals living' (Trott, 47).

Kennedy inherited a small property called the Fox Hollies, near Birmingham, from his cousin John Kennedy, and in March 1835 he retired from his mastership at King Edward's School. Kennedy assisted his son Charles in a translation of Virgil, published in 1849. Several of his poems were published in his sons' volumes, including the much praised lyrical poem 'The Reign of Youth' (1840; reprinted in B. H. Kennedy's *Between Whiles*, 2nd edn 1882). He died at Charles's home, 34 St Paul's Square, Birmingham, on 3 January 1851.

T. E. PAGE, *rev.* MEGAN A. STEPHAN

Sources Allibone, *Dict.* · A. Trott, *No place for fop or idler: the story of King Edward's School, Birmingham* (1992) · B. H. Kennedy, ed., *Between whiles* (1877); 2nd edn (1882) · Boase, *Mod. Eng. biog.* · Brown & Stratton, *Brit. mus.* · d. cert. · *GM*, 2nd ser., 37 (1852), 206
Likenesses portrait (after daguerreotype), repro. in Trott, *No place for fop or idler*

Kennedy, Susanna. *See* Montgomerie, Susanna, countess of Eglinton (1689/90–1780).

Kennedy, Thomas (*d.* 1754), judge, son of Sir Thomas Kennedy of Kirkhill, Ayrshire, provost of Edinburgh in 1685–7, was called to the Scottish bar in 1698, and acquired a considerable practice and a high reputation for forensic eloquence and ingenuity. He held with distinction the office of lord advocate during the temporary disgrace of Sir David Dalrymple, from June to November 1714. On the accession of George I he was raised to a seat on the exchequer bench, which he held thereafter.

Kennedy was an able judge and a man of refined tastes and wide knowledge, and his house was a centre of reunion for the cultivated society of Edinburgh. His modesty and courtesy were as remarkable as his ability. He married, on 19 August 1714, Grizel Kynynmound, widow of Sir Alexander Murray, a lady much admired for her dignity and charm. Kennedy's health declined in his later years. He died on 19 April 1754, and was survived by his wife. J. M. RIGG, rev. ANITA McCONNELL

Sources *Scotland and Scotsmen in the eighteenth century: from the MSS of John Ramsay, esq., of Ochtertyre*, ed. A. Allardyce, 1 (1888), 76–81 · private information (1891) · *Historical notices of Scotish affairs, selected from the manuscripts of Sir John Lauder of Fountainhall*, ed. D. Laing, 2, Bannatyne Club, 87 (1848), 666 · *GM*, 1st ser., 24 (1754), 244

Archives NA Scot., corresp.

Likenesses portrait, Parliament Hall, Edinburgh

Kennedy, Thomas (1784–1870). *See under* Kennedy, Alexander (1695–*c*.1785).

Kennedy, Thomas (1874–1954), socialist organizer and politician, was born at Kennethmont, Aberdeenshire, on 25 December 1874, the son of Thomas Kennedy (1833/4–1917), gamekeeper, and his wife, Ann MacDonald (1835/6–1924). He was educated at Kennethmont public school and Gordon School, Huntly, before settling in Aberdeen. His early working life was spent as a railway clerk, and he became a member of the Social Democratic Federation (SDF) in the mid-1890s. He spent six years as a member of Aberdeen school board, and was also a lecturer on socialism under the auspices of the *Clarion* newspaper. He married a schoolteacher who was also a member of the SDF in Aberdeen, Christian Elizabeth Farquarson (1867/8–1917). The Aberdeen socialist movement was less sectarian than many of the national leaders, and Kennedy from an early stage was one of those who looked to maximize contact with the wider labour movement and the trade unions in particular.

Kennedy soon became SDF organizer in Aberdeen, and from 1903 he was the SDF's paid Scottish divisional organizer. His success here was seen in a significant expansion of the number of SDF branches in Scotland, although he was defeated as SDF parliamentary candidate in North Aberdeen in 1906 and in January 1910. The SDF was subsumed into the British Socialist Party (BSP) in 1912, when Kennedy became the BSP's London organizer. In 1913 he became the BSP's national organizer. He served in the Royal Army Medical Corps throughout the First World War which, apart from a spell in Italy, he spent at an army hospital in Aberdeen. He was a supporter of the patriotic minority within the BSP led by H. M. Hyndman, which was effectively thrown out in 1916.

After the war Kennedy joined, and became the secretary of, Hyndman's new National Socialist Party, which subsequently reverted to the old SDF title, and was affiliated to the Labour Party. His first wife had died in July 1917 and in February 1919 he married Annie Simpson, daughter of G. S. Michie, an Aberdeen fish-curer; they had one son. In 1921 he won a by-election in Kirkcaldy burghs, Fife. He lost the seat in 1922 but regained it in 1923. In the weak Parliamentary Labour Party of the 1918 parliament Kennedy's organizing abilities were a clear asset, and he became the party's Scottish whip, a position he held again between

1923 and 1925. In the first Labour government of 1924 he was lord commissioner of the Treasury and one of the more successful whips. He became deputy chief whip in 1925 and chief whip in 1927. He retained the latter position when Labour returned to office in 1929, assuming the honorific title of parliamentary secretary to the Treasury, and being sworn of the privy council in 1931. This rise up the Labour hierarchy did not meet with total approval in the Fife labour movement. There, he sided with the right-wing miners' leaders who were struggling to keep control of their union in the face of a strong communist offensive, and Kennedy's already strong anti-communism was still further reinforced as a result.

The second minority Labour government's period of office was marked by failure and increasing despair as it proved unable to meet intensifying economic crisis. For Kennedy it was a very difficult period indeed, much of his time being spent on the thankless task of trying to cobble together enough votes to keep the government in office. The result, not surprisingly, was that he came close to a breakdown in March 1931. That August the ministry collapsed in ignominy, and Ramsay MacDonald formed a national government. Kennedy was offered a post in the new administration, but refused, and went into opposition. He lost his seat at the October 1931 general election.

All this time Kennedy had remained a leading figure in the SDF. But it was an organization whose time had passed. Its weekly newspaper, *Justice*, had folded in 1925. A jubilee conference in 1931 to celebrate the organization's sixtieth birthday brought old members of the SDF together, but it was a backward-looking event. By the 1930s the SDF was little more than a dining club for ageing right-wing Labour politicians; its membership was no more than 500 and it finally ceased to exist in 1941.

Kennedy was narrowly defeated in the Montrose burghs by-election of June 1932, but was returned, once more, for Kirkcaldy burghs at the 1935 general election. However, he was in rather poor health and made little impact. In 1940, with many Labour leaders going into the Churchill coalition, he was pressed into service as a member of the Parliamentary Labour Party's administrative committee, but was defeated in the elections for that body in November 1941. His health was continuing to deteriorate and he applied for the Chiltern Hundreds in 1943, finally ceasing to be an MP early in 1944. He died in Lumsden, Aberdeenshire, on 3 March 1954. ANDREW THORPE

Sources W. Knox, ed., *Scottish labour leaders, 1918–39: a biographical dictionary* (1984) · H. W. Lee and E. Archbold, *Social-democracy in Britain: fifty years of the socialist movement*, ed. H. Tracey (1935) · M. Crick, *The history of the social-democratic federation* (1994) · *WWW, 1951–60* · *The Times* (4 March 1954) · C. Tsuzuki, *H. M. Hyndman and British socialism* (1961) · P. Williamson, *National crisis and national government: British politics, the economy and empire, 1926–1932* (1992) · *The diary of Beatrice Webb*, ed. N. MacKenzie and J. MacKenzie, 4 vols. (1982–5), vol. 4 · *The Second World War diary of Hugh Dalton, 1940–1945*, ed. B. Pimlott (1986) · *The Labour who's who* (1927) · *Militant miners: recollections of John McArthur, Buckhaven, and letters, 1924–26, of David Proudfoot, Methil, to G. Allen Hutt*, ed. I. MacDougall (1981) · K. D. Buckley, *Trade unionism in Aberdeen, 1878 to 1900* (1955) · b. cert. · T. Kennedy, *From the kennels to Downing Street: a memoir of Thomas Kennedy (1874–1954)* (privately printed, Staindrop, Durham, 1999)

Archives JRL, corresp. with James Ramsay MacDonald · NML, Labour History Archive and Study Centre, corresp. | BLPES, Social Democratic Federation MSS

Kennedy, Thomas Francis (1788–1879), politician, born at Dalquharran Castle, Ayrshire, on 11 November 1788, was the only son of Thomas Kennedy of Dunure and Dalquharran, and great-nephew of Thomas Kennedy (d. 1754), Scottish judge. His mother was Jane, daughter of John Adam of Blair Adam, Kinross-shire, architect. Kennedy was educated first under James Pillans, afterwards professor of humanity at Edinburgh, then at Harrow School, where he was a contemporary of Byron, and subsequently at the University of Edinburgh, where he attended Dugald Stewart's lectures and studied law, but took no degree. He was called to the Scottish bar in 1811, and in 1818 he entered parliament for Ayr burghs, which he continued to represent until his retirement from political life in 1834. A strong whig, he took from the first a prominent position in the House of Commons. In 1819 he introduced, but failed to carry, a measure for the reform of the Scottish poor law, and subsequent attempts met with no better success. He was more successful with a measure for substituting a system of ballot with peremptory challenge on the part of the prisoner for the arbitrary power which the Scottish judges then possessed, and sometimes abused, of nominating juries in criminal cases. His measure was adopted by the government in 1825 and carried into law (6 Geo. IV c. 22). Kennedy also advocated the abolition of the inquisitorial powers vested by the Scottish law in the public prosecutor, and of the Scottish law of entail. He took great interest in the salmon fisheries of Scotland, and was chairman of a committee appointed in 1824 to inquire into the laws relating to them, which initiated the measure passed in 1828 for their preservation (9 Geo. IV c. 39). In 1831 he piloted through the House of Commons the government bill providing for the eventual extinction of the Scottish court of exchequer.

In general politics Kennedy supported the removal of religious disabilities, the extension of the franchise, and the reduction of the corn duties. He was the close friend of Henry Cockburn, Lord Minto, Jeffrey, and other eminent members of the whig party in Scotland, in concert with whom he prepared in 1830 a scheme for the extension of the franchise in that country, and gave notice of motion on the subject in the House of Commons, but withdrew it on the government's announcing their intention of introducing a comprehensive measure of reform. He forwarded to Lord John Russell for ministers' consideration a memorandum, 'Proposed reform in Scotland', which was adopted as the basis of the government's measure. In recognition of his services to the cause of reform, Grey gave him, in February 1832, the post of clerk of the ordnance, and in the following November promoted him to a junior lordship of the Treasury.

Financial embarrassment, due in great measure to Kennedy's voluntary assumption of responsibility for his father's debts, compelled his retirement from political life in 1834. In 1837 he was appointed to the newly created office of paymaster of the civil services in Ireland, and

Thomas Francis Kennedy (1788–1879), by Sir Henry Raeburn, c.1822

sworn of the Irish privy council. He administered this office with great efficiency until 1850, when he exchanged it for a commissionership of woods and forests. High-handed action against several employees in this department led to complaints to the Treasury. Gladstone, as chancellor, recommended his dismissal and in 1854 Aberdeen dismissed him without a pension, an action which led to a substantial row between Russell and Gladstone. Kennedy's correspondence with Russell on the affair was published as *Letter to … Russell from the Rt. Hon. T. F. Kennedy … with Lord John Russell's reply and remarks and correspondence* (1854).

For the rest of his life Kennedy resided mainly on his Ayrshire estates, occupying himself with county affairs, stock-breeding, sanitation, and the application of science to agriculture. He did not, however, lose interest in politics; he approved of the reform movement of 1867–8, and of the Elementary Education Act of 1870. Kennedy was chosen as an extraordinary director of the Highland Agricultural Society in 1835, and was a deputy lieutenant and a justice of the peace for Ayrshire. He married in 1820 Sophia, only daughter of Sir Samuel *Romilly; they had one son. Congestion of the lungs led to Kennedy's death at his home, Dalquharran Castle, on 1 April 1879.

J. M. RIGG, *rev.* H. C. G. MATTHEW

Sources Boase, *Mod. Eng. biog.* · *The Scotsman* (2 April 1879) · J. B. Conacher, *The Aberdeen coalition, 1852–1855* (1968), 377–82 · Gladstone, *Diaries*

Archives BL, corresp. with Sir Robert Peel, Add. MSS 40519, 40601 · Lpool RO, letters to fourteenth earl of Derby · NL Scot., corresp. with George Combe · NL Scot., corresp., incl. with Lord Rutherford · NRA, priv. coll., corresp. with Lord Dunfermline · PRO, corresp. with Lord John Russell, PRO 30/22

Likenesses H. Raeburn, oils, *c*.1822, repro. in *Country Life* (29 July 1954), 363 [*see illus.*] · G. Hayter, group portrait, oils (*The House of Commons, 1833*), NPG · G. Hayter, oils, Scot. NPG · drawing, NPG · stipple and line engraving, NPG

Wealth at death £12,162 13*s.* 9½*d.*: confirmation, 30 Aug 1879, *CCI*

Kennedy, Tristram Edward (1805–1885), lawyer and politician, was born on 27 June 1805 at Inishowen in Donegal, the twelfth of fourteen children of John Pitt Kennedy (1759–1811), a popular Church of Ireland clergyman, and Mary, only daughter of Thomas Cary of Loughash, in co. Tyrone; both parents were Ulster protestants. His ancestors had left Scotland to settle in Ulster during the early seventeenth century; one of them, Horas Kennedy, was sheriff of Londonderry during the siege of 1688 and took a prominent part in its defence and in the memorable closing of its gates to King James's army.

Educated at Derry Free Grammar School, Kennedy became an attorney and in 1828 was himself made sheriff of Londonderry. In that capacity he won the admiration of both sides when he chaired a lengthy and controversial debate between protestant and Catholic clergymen. In 1829 he had himself struck off the roll of attorneys and then entered Lincoln's Inn and King's Inns, Dublin. Called to the bar in Ireland in 1834, he determined to improve the standard of legal education.

When Kennedy opened the Dublin Law Institute in 1839, he welcomed students to classes in a discipline which had not been taught systematically in Ireland for at least two centuries. It was a historic moment, marking not only a major educational development in legal training in the United Kingdom but also a growth in the confidence of the Irish middle classes. The campaign to reform legal education, on which Kennedy and Thomas Wyse, MP for Waterford City, collaborated closely, was to have effects lasting into the late twentieth century. It stimulated the academic study of English law at universities in Britain and Ireland, hastened the introduction of qualifying examinations for both branches of the profession, and pointed up the overwhelmingly ideological rationale for what was then the requirement that young men attend the English inns before being admitted to practise at the Irish bar. In 1846 the select committee on legal education, chaired by Wyse, produced a report for which the two men were chiefly responsible; it has been described by a modern English authority as being of 'fundamental importance', in that 'the history of legal education in England over the past 120 years is largely an account of the struggle to implement the recommendations of the 1846 committee and the effects of that struggle' (*Report of the Committee on Legal Education* [in England and Wales], HC 1971, 4595, 7–8). The history of legal education in Ireland has been no less influenced by the report.

Kennedy's law school fell victim to the troubled times in which it was founded and it collapsed in 1845. Shortly after its demise Kennedy ended his legal career, taking up

a position as land agent on the Bath estates in co. Monaghan. His reforming work there, which commenced during the great famine, won him the admiration of Catholics and of land reformers in the Tenant League and created the basis for his future election to parliament for the neighbouring county. The Carrickmacross lace industry, which he initiated, is testimony to his achievements.

In 1852 Kennedy was elected to the House of Commons by Catholic voters as an 'independent' representative of co. Louth. His contributions to debates were concerned largely with landlord and tenant matters or with national and industrial education. But the Independent Party to which he belonged was riven by internal divisions and by 1856 had lost two of its principal leaders. Frederick Lucas was dead and Charles Gavan Duffy had emigrated to Australia. He stopped on the way at Kennedy's London house to borrow a mount and the two men rode together in Rotten Row. At the election of 1857 Kennedy lost his seat.

Having failed to be re-elected two years later, Kennedy returned to the fray again in Louth in April 1865. He was privately opposed by Archbishop Cullen, who wanted a candidate who was committed to the educational policy of the Catholic church. Kennedy's subsequent victory was rashly interpreted by some as a rebuff to the Catholic hierarchy. Kennedy then joined with John Blake Dillon to build bridges between Irish Catholics and independent Liberals on the one hand and Irish reformers and English Liberals on the other. In December 1865 the two men acted as joint secretaries for 'a considerable number of Irish representatives' in arranging a personal interview with Gladstone on the land question. Some regarded this development as a significant step towards the creation of a new alliance on Ireland but the initiative was stillborn. Dillon died unexpectedly in 1866 and Kennedy withdrew from the election of 1868 in the face of a blatantly sectarian campaign waged by the Catholic candidate, Matthew O'Reilly Dease. In the election of 1874, aged almost seventy, Kennedy was prevailed upon to stand as a Liberal candidate in Donegal but failed to be returned.

Kennedy was a member of the Dublin Social and Statistical Inquiry Society. He visited Belgium to inspect institutional responses to poverty in that country and in 1855 published with W. K. Sullivan a booklet on industrial training, which was inspired partly by what he had seen there. He also published, in 1877–8, two tracts on the reform of law and legal education.

In 1862, at the age of fifty-seven, Kennedy married Sarah Graham of Cossington, Somerset. The couple had seven children. The family lived in Somerset and London but Kennedy retained his house in Henrietta Street, Dublin, behind the King's Inns. He gradually acquired three-quarters of the property along that elegant Georgian cul-de-sac but failed to persuade the benchers to buy the entire street and to erect a gate so that it might become an area of chambers for the Dublin inn. Kennedy had two distinguished brothers to whom he remained close. John Pitt *Kennedy (1796–1879) had been appointed inspector-general of national schools and was a soldier in arms with Sir Charles Napier; a highway from India towards Tibet bore his name into the twentieth century. Evory Kennedy (1806–1884) was a leading obstetrician and academic, appointed master of the Rotunda Hospital in Dublin at the age of twenty-seven.

On 20 November 1885 Kennedy died in his sleep at his residence, Charleville, The Shrubbery, Weston-super-Mare. He was buried at Cossington village church. Charles Gavan Duffy wrote in sympathy to his family from the south of France, describing him as 'honest and gallant'. The independent opposition which Kennedy, Duffy, and others had initiated came to be highly respected by Parnell.

Kennedy flourished during a period when the movement for repeal of the Act of Union floundered, when the efforts of Irish members to unite in common cause at Westminster were confounded, and when, above all, Ireland was scarred by the holocaust of the great famine and the misery of many Irish tenants. Notwithstanding such discouragements, Kennedy's response was positive and determined, transcending traditional religious boundaries. His contributions to reform were pragmatic, justifying his own description of himself as having been 'always faithful and true to the poor people'. He was one of a small number of Irishmen who provided a tenuous parliamentary link between Daniel O'Connell and Charles Stewart Parnell. His formidable efforts to transcend both of the main cultural traditions in Ireland made him a model of encouragement for those who continued to seek methods of reconciliation in Ireland.   COLUM KENNY

Sources C. Kenny, 'Paradox or pragmatist? "Honest" Tristram Kennedy (1805–85): lawyer, educationalist, land agent and member of parliament', *Proceedings of the Royal Irish Academy*, 92C (1992), 1–35 · 'Select committee on legal education in Ireland', *Parl. papers* (1846), vol. 10, no. 686 · F. M. E. Kennedy, *A family of Kennedy of Clogher and Londonderry, c.1600–1939* (1938) · *The Times* (25 Nov 1885) · *Dundalk Democrat* (28 Nov 1885) · *CGPLA Ire.* (1886) · private information (2004)
Archives King's Inns, Dublin, Dublin Law Institute scrapbook | Bodl. Oxf., letters to Sir William Napier · King's Inns, Dublin, Dublin Law Institute, rules and by-laws · Longleat House, Wiltshire, Bath papers, Irish box · NL Ire., Dublin Law Institute MSS, MS 2987 · NL Ire., William Smith O'Brien MSS, MS 22393
Likenesses photograph, 1865, priv. coll. · H. McManus, oils, priv. coll. · photograph (in old age), priv. coll.
Wealth at death £581 12s. 1d.: probate, 11 Feb 1886, *CGPLA Ire.*

Kennedy, Vans (1783–1846), army officer and Sanskrit and Persian scholar, was born at Pinmore in the parish of Ayr, Scotland, the youngest son of Robert Kennedy of Pinmore and his wife, Robina, daughter of John Vans of Barnbarroch, Wigtownshire, who on marrying his cousin assumed the name of Agnew. Kennedy belonged to an old Ayrshire family and was connected with the houses of Cassillis and Eglintoun. His father was ruined by the failure of the Ayr Bank, and had to sell Pinmore and retire to Edinburgh, where he died in 1790. The care of their numerous children, who included the writer of religious tales Grace *Kennedy (1782–1825), then fell to his widow, who was a woman of great strength and ability.

Kennedy was educated in Edinburgh, at Berkhamsted, and finally at Monmouth and was noted in youth for his studious habits. He was particularly fond of language study, rather in its theoretical and grammatical sides than in the spoken. On the completion of his fourteenth year he returned to Edinburgh, and, having obtained a cadetship in the East India Company's Bombay army, he sailed for Bombay in 1800. Shortly after his arrival he was employed with his corps, the 1st battalion of the 2nd grenadiers, against the people of the Malabar district, and received a wound in his neck, from the effects of which he suffered all his life. In 1807 he became Persian interpreter to the peshwa's subsidiary force at Sirur, then commanded by Colonel W. Wallace (d. 1809). While at Sirur Kennedy had frequent opportunities of meeting Sir Barry Close and Sir James Mackintosh, both of whom greatly admired him. In 1817 he was appointed judge-advocate-general to the Bombay army, and on 30 September of the same year he contributed a paper on Persian literature to the Literary Society of Bombay, forerunner of the Bombay branch of the Asiatic Society. Mountstuart Elphinstone, who described Kennedy as the most learned man of his acquaintance, gave him the appointment of Marathi and Gujarati translator of the regulations of government, but the post was abolished a few months after Elphinstone's retirement. Kennedy was promoted to major in 1820, and held the office of judge-advocate-general until 1835, when as the result of a dispute or misunderstanding he was removed by Sir John Keane. After that he was appointed oriental translator to the government, and he held this office until his death.

Kennedy remained a student throughout his life, and he seems to have belonged to the type of the recluse and self-denying scholar. He was described as working sixteen hours a day, and as spending all his money on manuscripts and munshis, as well as in relieving the wants of others if he felt they were the victims of injustice. He contributed several papers to the Bombay branch of the Asiatic Society, of which he served successively as secretary, president, and honorary president, and in 1824 he published at Bombay a Marathi–English dictionary. In 1828 he published in London a quarto volume entitled *Researches into the Origin and Affinity of the Principal Languages of Asia and Europe*, and in 1831 he followed this with another quarto entitled *Researches into the Nature and Affinity of Ancient and Hindu Mythology*. These were scholarly works for their time and show energetic and independent thinking. Though their findings and hypotheses are now almost entirely superseded, they none the less both deserve attention as documents in the history of western studies in Indology, historical philology, and comparative religion. The first considers both semitic and Indo-European linguistics and makes some corrections to the assertions of other early scholars in these fields. But the erroneous conclusion of the work, based on examination of comparative vocabulary, was that Sanskrit was the parent language of Greek, Latin, and Gothic. In the second work Kennedy similarly tries to derive the Graeco-Roman, Etruscan, and Thracian religious systems from that of India. Kennedy also wrote five letters on the Puranas, and had a controversy with Horace Hayman Wilson and Sir Graves Champney Haughton on the subject of Vedanta philosophy. He published in

Bombay in 1832 a work on military law, of which a second edition appeared in 1847. A list of his principal writings is appended to the biographical memoir by James Bird in the journal of the Bombay branch of the Royal Asiatic Society for 1848. Kennedy died in Bombay on 29 December 1846, and the next day was buried with due military honours at the old European cemetery in Sonepur, Bombay. He does not appear to have married.

HENRY BEVERIDGE, rev. J. B. KATZ

Sources J. Bird, 'Biographical memoir of the late Major General Vans Kennedy', *Journal of the Bombay Branch of the Royal Asiatic Society*, 2 (1844–7), 430–36 · V. N. Mandlik, preface, *Transactions of the Literary Society of Bombay*, 1 (1819), xv; repr. (1877) · 'A short account of the author', *The works of Grace Kennedy*, 1 (1827), ii · *Revised list of tombs and monuments of historical or archaeological interest in Bombay*, Government of Bombay [1912] · Bombay ecclesiastical records, BL OIOC, N/3/20, fol. 437 · Bombay army cadet records, BL OIOC, L/Mil/9/110, fol. 71 · Bombay wills and administrations, BL OIOC, L/AG/34/29/350, 4–5 · Bombay inventories of estates, BL OIOC, L/AG/34/27/397, 21–4

Archives BL, 'Notice respecting the religion introduced into India by the emperor Akbar', Add. MS 25673

Wealth at death in debt in India: administration, BL OIOC, L/AG/34/29/350, 4–5; inventory, BL OIOC, L/AG/34/27/397, 21–4

Kennedy, Walter (1455?–1518?), poet, was a younger son of Gilbert *Kennedy (d. in or after 1479) [see under Kennedy family], first Lord Kennedy of Dunure in Ayrshire, and Katherine, daughter of Herbert *Maxwell, first Lord Maxwell. Descended through his grandmother Mary, countess of Angus, from Robert III, he boasted of his kinship to James IV: 'I am the kingis blude, his trew speciall clerk' (Dunbar and Kennedy, 417). The Kennedy family possessed estates in Carrick and other parts of the southwest of Scotland, where it was very powerful and influential. Walter was the nephew of James *Kennedy, bishop of St Andrews (d. 1465), and his own nephew David *Kennedy [see under Kennedy family] became first earl of Cassillis in 1509.

The earliest reference to Walter names him as the sixth son of Lord Kennedy in 1455 (NA Scot., Ailsa MS 66). He was educated at the University of Glasgow, where he graduated in 1476, and became MA in 1478. On 3 November 1481 he was nominated as one of the examiners for the faculty of arts (Innes, 222, 227, 236). On 24 February 1492 he acted as deputy to his brother John, second Lord Kennedy, in his hereditary office of bailie of Carrick (Thomson, 212). There is no evidence that Kennedy had a degree in law, but on 29 October 1497 he acted as legal representative for the Cluniac abbey of Crossraguel in Ayrshire (Donaldson); and was described as 'attorney' in an instrument of seisin, dated 29 November 1498 (Ailsa MS 166). It was then common for educated laymen to act on behalf of others in the Scottish courts. On 25 September 1498 he was one of the witnesses to a charter granted by Archibald, earl of Angus, to Janet Kennedy (Thomson and others, *Registrum*, no. 2457).

Unpublished charters and documents, dated between 1504 and 1510, indicate that Kennedy possessed Glentig and other estates in Carrick and Galloway; by 1505, and probably much earlier, he was married to Christian Hynd,

and had heirs, of whom two sons (at least) survived him. On 30 July 1510 he was also styled 'parson' of Douglas (NA Scot., Ailsa MS 220). Two years earlier the register of Pope Julius II (23 July 1508) recorded that the prebend of Douglas, together with a canonry at Glasgow Cathedral, were held unlawfully by 'Walter Kennedi, who claims to be a cleric' (*CEPR letters*, no. 38). This evident doubt as to Kennedy's status seems justified; there is no evidence that he was ordained as a priest, and he may have remained in minor orders, which would have permitted him to marry.

A vivid but scurrilous pen-portrait of Kennedy exists, drawn by a contemporary. In *The Flyting of Dunbar and Kennedie*, a verse quarrel (composed before 1505), William Dunbar depicts Kennedy as poor, leprous, and lice-ridden, a thieving highland 'baird', living with his wife in a remote glen. In reply Kennedy's powers of invective match those of Dunbar; he also proudly refers to his substantial properties, and asserts the claim of Erse, or Gaelic, to be 'the gud langage of this land' (Dunbar and Kennedy, 347). Carrick was then still Gaelic-speaking, but Kennedy's own poems are written in lowland Scots.

The Flyting was one of the first works printed in Scotland (*c*.1508); Kennedy's other poems are preserved in the great literary miscellanies, such as the Asloan manuscript, the Bannatyne manuscript, and the Maitland folio. They include a 'ballat' in praise of the Virgin Mary, and three moral lyrics, highly penitential in tone. None can be definitely dated, although two adopt the persona of an old man. Kennedy's most substantial work, containing over 1700 lines, is *The Passion of Christ*, which is preserved in MS Arundel 285, one of the few collections of religious verse to survive from pre-Reformation Scotland. Owing much to the devotional tradition of the pseudo-Bonaventuran *Meditations on the Life of Christ*, it is a learned and complex poem. The story of the crucifixion is related to the hours of the divine office in the week before Easter; and simple narrative is punctuated by highly rhetorical passages, in which the reader is exhorted to feel compassion and contrition through contemplation of Christ's sufferings.

Kennedy's literary reputation is inevitably overshadowed by that of Dunbar, with whom he is often coupled. Yet he was much admired by contemporary poets, such as Gavin Douglas, who styled him 'greit Kennedie' (*Palice of Honour*), and Sir David Lindsay, who praised his 'aureate' diction (*Testament of the Papyngo*). Dunbar himself, despite the insulting tone of *The Flyting*, expressed grief that 'gud maister Walter Kennedie / In poynt of dede [death] lyis veralie' (no. 21: 'I that in heill wes and gladnes'). Past scholars wrongly assumed that Kennedy must have died *c*.1508, when these lines were published. But he seems to have survived until shortly before 18 June 1518; on that date various estates were conveyed to his son, also called Walter Kennedy, who seems, in addition, to have succeeded his father as rector of Douglas and canon of Glasgow Cathedral (NA Scot., Ailsa MS 241).

PRISCILLA J. BAWCUTT

Sources NA Scot., Ailsa MSS, GD 25/1 [sometimes known as the Culzean charters] · C. Innes, ed., *Munimenta alme Universitatis*

Glasguensis | Records of the University of Glasgow from its foundation till 1727, 2, Maitland Club, 72 (1854) · *CEPR letters*, vol. 18 · W. Dunbar and W. Kennedy, *The flyting, The poems of William Dunbar*, ed. P. Bawcutt, no. 65, Association of Scottish Literary Studies, 27–8 (1998), 200–18 · *Scots peerage*, 2.452–6 · *The poems of Walter Kennedy*, ed. J. Schipper, Denkschriften der Kaiserlichen Akademie der Wissenschaften, 48 (1902) · J. A. W. Bennett, ed., *Devotional pieces in verse and prose from MS Arundel 285 and MS Harleian 6919*, STS, 3rd ser., 23 (1955) · J. M. Thomson and others, eds., *Registrum magni sigilli regum Scotorum | The register of the great seal of Scotland*, 11 vols. (1882–1914), vol. 2 · G. Donaldson, ed., *Protocol book of James Young, 1485–1515*, Scottish RS, 74 (1952), no. 962 · [T. Thomson], ed., *The acts of the lords of council in civil causes, 1478–1495*, 1, RC, 41 (1839) · J. A. W. Bennett, *Poetry of the passion* (1982)
Archives NA Scot., Ailsa MSS

Kennedy, William (1799–1871), diplomatist and writer, was born in Scotland on 26 December 1799, the eldest of five sons and a daughter of an Ayrshire man who became a cotton manufacturer in Dublin and his wife, Ann Davis. Kennedy's parents died before he reached adulthood, and the Revd James Bridge, a Presbyterian minister who lived near Aughnacloy, co. Tyrone, was his guardian until Kennedy could take legal responsibility for his siblings. Kennedy attended Belfast Academical Institution, known as a training place for dissenting clergymen. His father's will stipulated that Kennedy could inherit only on becoming a clergyman and Kennedy accordingly undertook a theological course at Dr Lawson's Seminary, Selkirk. He returned to Aughnacloy and was licensed to preach on 17 December 1822, but left the ministry after a year.

By February 1824 Kennedy lived in Dublin, tiring of monotonous Aughnacloy. He supposedly set out for Greece to join Lord Byron, but there is no firm evidence of this. By 1826 Kennedy was established in Paisley, where he became a friend of William Motherwell. In this year he published his first work, *My Early Days*, a moralizing fictional piece for children, reprinted in 1828, 1835, and 1843. On 25 March 1826 Kennedy became editor of the *Paisley Advertiser*, a post he held until 17 May 1828. In 1827 he published his first verse collection, *Fitful Fancies*, and during 1828 he and Motherwell produced the *Paisley Magazine*. Kennedy then moved to London, resolved on becoming an English lawyer. A letter (12 August 1828) reports that 'there are two highly satisfactory things here—constant employment and good pay' (Marshall, 18). By October he had become a student of the Inner Temple, simultaneously working for the *Morning Journal* at 5 guineas a week. The short-lived *Englishman's Magazine* was undertaken with Leitch Ritchie [see Ritchie, (Duncan) Leitch] in 1831. Kennedy also contributed to several annuals, and published a second verse collection, *The Arrow and the Rose* (1830), and another fictional work, *An Only Son* (1831).

Kennedy's historical drama, *The Siege of Antwerp* (1838), was dedicated to the earl of Durham, a whig, who was appointed governor-in-chief of British North America in March 1838. Durham, who had known Kennedy since 1833, appointed him commissioner for inquiring into the municipal institutions of Lower Canada. At some time between 1831 and 1838 Kennedy worked in Hull, where he met his wife, whose identity is unknown. According to family tradition she was socially unacceptable. There

were no children. Kennedy's attachment to his wife is recorded in a poem, 'Alla mia sposa', written on board a New York packet on 25 December 1841:

> And where thou art, the dreariest spot
> Is home, sweet home to me.
> (Marshall, 53)

After Durham's retirement, late in 1838, Kennedy travelled to America, spending some months in Texas, and after his return to England in 1839 he supported the cause of Texas in debates about its independence. In 1841 he published a two-volume work entitled *The Rise, Progress and Prospects of the Republic of Texas*. He offered his services to Lord Aberdeen at the Foreign Office, and visited Texas again, claiming responsibility for the ratification of the slave trade treaty. Kennedy's popularity in Texas is reflected in his appointment as its consul-general in London, soon after his return in the spring of 1842. He resigned when he was offered the post of British consul to Galveston, Texas, in September 1842. Kennedy returned to England in 1847, suffering bad health. He visited Glasgow, undertaking the editorship of the third edition of Motherwell's poems. In 1849 he retired on a government pension, living first in London, then Paris. He became ill again in Paris, and was a patient in the Maison de Santé at Neuilly. He died there in the spring of 1871. He was buried in Paris, but his sister moved his remains to Caen in Normandy. Kennedy's verse was largely of the 'gift book' genre, though a few pieces reflect a more personal involvement, such as his poem 'I love the land'. He is perhaps more entitled to be remembered as a diplomat than a poet.   ROSEMARY SCOTT

Sources J. J. Marshall, *Life of William Kennedy* (1920) · E. D. Adams, *British interests and activities in Texas, 1838–1846* (1910) · *N&Q*, 2nd ser., 1 (1856), 163, 183, 342, 400 · J. G. Wilson, ed., *The poets and poetry of Scotland*, 2 (1877), 213–14 · Ward, *Men of the reign* · Irving, *Scots.*
Archives BL, corresp. with Lord Aberdeen, Add. MS 43126 · Lambton Park, Chester-le-Street, co. Durham, letters to earl of Durham
Likenesses J. Fillans, bust, repro. in Marshall, *Life*, frontispiece

Kennedy, William (1859–1918). *See under* Glasgow Boys (*act.* 1875–1895).

Kennedy, William Denholm (1813–1865), historical genre and landscape painter, was born at Dumfries on 16 June 1813; he received his early education at Edinburgh. At seventeen he moved to London where he entered the Royal Academy Schools in 1833. His lifelong friendship with the artist William Etty began at this time, the older artist influencing both Kennedy's style and his subject matter. The two artists even collaborated on paintings, for example, *A Nymph Reposing* and *A Bather* (ex Christies, 1865).

In 1833 Kennedy sent his first pictures to the Royal Academy, *A Musical Party* and *The Toilet*, and he continued to exhibit there almost every year until his death. In 1835 he won the academy's gold medal for a historical painting with his *Apollo and Idas*. In 1840 he was awarded a travel allowance from the academy and journeyed to Italy, where he spent two years studying in Rome. He returned with many sketches and studies of Italian scenery. Six landscape watercolours in the British Museum relate to his Italian travels: these vibrant, lightly washed paintings are full of light and were deftly painted *en plein air*, for example, *Castel Gandolfo* and *Rainy Day at Baiae, Bay of Naples*. However, it does not seem that Kennedy worked up these watercolours into full studies at a later date.

Kennedy continued to paint Italian genre scenes and literary subjects, including scenes from Byron, Spenser, and Tasso, after he returned from Italy. Pictures such as *The Bandit Mother* (1845), *The Italian Goatherd* (1847), and *The Land of Poetry and Song* (1865) demonstrate the continued impact of his time there. He also made stained glass designs for Thomas Willemont, including those for the windows in St Stephen Walbrook, London, and was a good judge of etchings and engravings. He collected etchings by his contemporaries Sir Edwin Landseer, Sir David Wilkie, and Richard Parkes Bonington, as well as those after the old masters such as Paolo Veronese, Titian, Rubens, and Van Dyck.

Kennedy died of heart disease and dropsy at his home, 26 Soho Square, London, on 2 June 1865. He was a competent but not popular artist of the nineteenth century and consequently, despite exhibiting throughout his life at the British Institution and the Royal Academy, many of his works remained in his studio and were sold after his death by Christies. The sale also included forty-nine etchings by Rembrandt—very fine impressions of *Christ Preaching* (called *The Little La Tombe*) and the *Agony in the Garden*.

LUCY DIXON

Sources J. Halsby, *Scottish watercolours, 1740–1940* (1986) · J. Halsby and P. Harris, *The dictionary of Scottish painters, 1600–1960* (1990) · P. J. M. McEwan, *Dictionary of Scottish art and architecture* (1994) · L. Binyon, *Catalogue of drawings by British artists and artists of foreign origin working in Great Britain*, 3 (1902) · Wood, *Vic. painters*, 3rd edn · Mallalieu, *Watercolour artists* · Graves, *RA exhibitors* · Bryan, *Painters* · d. cert. · *DNB*

Wealth at death under £1000: administration, 23 Dec 1865, CGPLA Eng. & Wales

Kennedy, William Quarrier (1903–1979), geologist, was born on 30 November 1903, at the Orphan Homes of Scotland in Bridge of Weir, Renfrewshire, the youngest of five children of John Gordon Kennedy, headmaster of the Orphan Homes school, and his wife, Peterina, *née* Webster. He had a happy childhood at their riverside home; he idolized his father (a stern Presbyterian who made his family go to church twice on Sundays). It was his father and his elder brother Ian who first made him interested in sciences and literature, especially poetry. He was educated at his father's school and at Glasgow high school, and he entered Glasgow University in 1921 to study agriculture. He graduated in 1926 and he proceeded to an honours degree in geology, graduating with first-class honours in 1927. While a student, Kennedy obtained a Royal Society grant for cave exploration, which led to his first geological publication in 1930. He was a member of council of Glasgow University Geological Society, probably his only ever service on a scientific society council.

On graduating, Kennedy won a J. R. K. Law scholarship for research in applied sciences abroad; he chose Zürich Technische Hochschule. He studied magnetite deposits in Traversella, Piedmont, under Professor Paul Niggli. On his return to England (fluent in German), he applied for a post with the geological survey. Offered appointment in September 1928, he reported at the Edinburgh office the following day, thus joining a group including such outstanding geologists as E. B. Bailey (1881–1965), J. E. Richey (1886–1968), and H. H. Read (1889–1970). Kennedy was assigned to geological mapping in the midland valley and in the highlands.

During his career Kennedy developed two main geological interests; in the Precambrian Moine rocks of the west highlands, and in the processes by which volcanic rocks of the midland valley and Western Isles evolved in the mantle and lower crust. Both were discussed in papers of major significance, and systematically described on geological maps and in memoirs. He made the spectacular discovery of a 65 mile wrench on the Great Glen fault, and recognized the simple domal pattern (displaced by the fault) of metamorphic zones in the highlands.

In 1945 Kennedy left his beloved Scotland to become professor of geology at Leeds University. The department there had concentrated on northern England geology; Kennedy shifted its research emphasis to petrogenesis, tectonics, and global problems. Disliking committee work, or answering letters, he nevertheless obtained staff, equipment, and eventually a new building for a department of earth sciences, which incorporated geophysics, geochemistry, and geology. He attracted a thriving group of research students, for he was an inspiring teacher and a lucid lecturer, and he was always happy to discuss problems with students.

In research, Kennedy continued to think about Scottish problems. In 1953 he read a paper to the Geological Society reinterpreting the Morar structures, an interpretation which was initially rejected and which led to Kennedy's shunning the society thereafter. Later, John Sutton (1919–1992), one of the chief dissenters, acknowledged that Kennedy was right.

In 1951 Kennedy and the Uganda geological survey jointly led an expedition to the formidable Ruwenzori range. However, owing to the complexity of the geology, and the small scale of the expedition, no report resulted. Becoming increasingly interested in research and mineral exploration in Africa, Kennedy established contacts with mining companies. A chance meeting with Sir Ernest Oppenheimer, head of Anglo-American Corporation, resulted in 1955 in the establishment at Leeds of a research institute of African geology, funded by the corporation. Thereafter Kennedy concentrated on African research, initially on Karoo volcanics and mineralization in eastern Rhodesia, on geochemical provinces and minerals in pegmatites, younger granites, and kimberlites.

In 1960 Kennedy spent time in hospital: after a leave of absence from 1965, he retired in 1967. Apart from a brief visiting lectureship at St Andrews and a few papers, ill-health ended his scientific work. Nevertheless his contribution had been outstanding. Through his career he had gained many honours, including the Geological Society's

Bigsby (1948) and Lyell medals (1967), the Geological Society of Edinburgh's Clough medal (1966), and fellowships of the Royal Society of Edinburgh (1948) and the Royal Society (1949).

Kennedy's personal life reflected his temperament; H. H. Read called him sensitive as a ballet dancer. He had an unassuming charm, interest in people, and humility. His first marriage, on 3 October 1933, to Elizabeth Jane Lawson McCubbin (*b.* 1911/12), daughter of Thomas McCubbin, structural engineer, began with éclat; they had a son and two daughters. However, it ended unhappily with separation. After some years of loneliness in his house in Leeds, he married Sylvia Margaret Grieves in 1962; they were happily married and had two children. On his retirement they moved to Elie, Fife. Despite pneumonia and ill-health, he enjoyed golf, gardening, and the odd flutter. He died peacefully, in Harrogate, on 13 March 1979.   ROBERT M. SHACKLETON

Sources J. Sutton, *Memoirs FRS*, 26 (1980), 275–303 · B. J. Bluck, 'W. Q. Kennedy, the Great Glen fault and strike-slip motion', *Milestones in geology: reviews to celebrate 150 volumes of the Journal of the Geological Society*, ed. M. J. Le Bas (1995), 57–65 · b. cert. · m. cert., 1933 · CCI (1979)
Likenesses photograph, repro. in *Memoirs FRS*
Wealth at death £5633.26: confirmation, 16 Aug 1979, CCI

Kennedy, Sir William Rann (1846–1915), judge, was born at 9 Campden Hill Villas, Kensington, on 11 March 1846, the eldest son of the Revd William James Kennedy and his cousin, Sarah Caroline Kennedy. His father, the fourth son of the Revd Rann Kennedy, was successively secretary to the National Society, HM inspector of schools, and vicar of Barnwood, Gloucestershire. Catherine Lucy *Kennedy was his sister.

Kennedy came from a family of distinguished classical scholars, three of his uncles, Benjamin Hall Kennedy, Charles Rann Kennedy, and George John Kennedy, having been senior classics and winners of the Porson prize, while his father was also Porson prizeman as well as Powis medallist. Kennedy himself was educated at Eton College and King's College, Cambridge, and carried on the family tradition by gaining the Craven and Bell scholarships and the Powis and Browne medals, and by becoming senior classic in 1868. He was also president of the Cambridge Union Society. After taking his BA degree in 1868, Kennedy taught the sixth form at Harrow School for a year under Dr Henry Montagu Butler. He was a fellow of Pembroke College, Cambridge, from 1868 until his marriage in 1874 to Cecilia Sarah, daughter of George *Richmond RA, with whom he had four sons and one daughter.

From 1870 to 1871 Kennedy acted as private secretary to George Goschen at the Poor Law Board. He was called to the bar by Lincoln's Inn in 1871 and read in the chambers of R. J. Williams. After call he joined the northern circuit and settled as a 'local' barrister at Liverpool in 1873. He soon acquired a substantial practice, particularly in commercial and shipping cases. He moved to London in 1882 and in 1885 he became queen's counsel. In 1891 he published *The Law of Civil Salvage* which became the recognized authority on the subject.

A keen Liberal in politics, Kennedy made several unsuccessful attempts to enter the House of Commons, contesting Birkenhead in 1885 and 1886 and St Helens in 1892. In 1892, at the unusually early age of forty-six, he was nominated by Lord Herschell to a judgeship in the Queen's Bench Division in succession to Mr Justice Denman, and was knighted. As a judge of first instance he tried two cases which attracted popular interest, *Allen* v. *Flood* (1895) and *Flood* v. *Jackson* (1898), a case on the liability of trade union officials, and *Ashby's Cobham Brewery Co.* (1906), a compensation case under the Licensing Act of 1904. From 1897 onwards he frequently sat in the commercial court set up in 1895.

On the appointment of Lord Cozens-Hardy as master of the rolls in 1907, Kennedy was appointed a lord justice of the Court of Appeal, and was sworn of the privy council. In the Court of Appeal his judicial reputation grew, and some of his dissenting judgments were upheld by the House of Lords.

Kennedy's judgments showed his great experience, learning, and intellect, and lucid expression. He was deeply interested in international law, and played a leading part in the work of the International Law Association, of which he was president from 1908 to 1910. He became a member of the Institut de Droit International in 1913. He kept up his classical scholarship to the end of his life, and published a translation of the *Plutus* of Aristophanes in 1912. He was elected an honorary fellow of Pembroke College, Cambridge in 1893, and a fellow of the British Academy in 1909. He died of heart trouble on 17 January 1915 at his London home, 23 Phillimore Gardens, Kensington.

      DAVID DAVIES, *rev.* HUGH MOONEY

Sources *The Times* (18 Jan 1915) · *Law Quarterly Review*, 31 (1915), 224–7 · *Journal of the Society of Comparative Legislation*, new ser., 15/1 (July 1915) · T. E. Holland, 'Lord Justice Kennedy', *PBA*, [7] (1915–16), 552–4
Likenesses G. Richmond, oils, Lincoln's Inn, London · Spy [L. Ward], chromolithograph caricature, NPG; repro. in *VF* (14 Dec 1893)
Wealth at death £22,327 2s. 8d.: administration, 5 March 1915, CGPLA Eng. & Wales

Kennelly, Arthur Edwin (1861–1939), electrical engineer, was born on 17 December 1861 at Colaba, near Bombay, India, the only son of David Joseph Kennelly and Kathrine (or Cathrine) Heycock. His father, a native of Cork, Ireland, was then harbour master at Bombay; he later became a barrister in England and king's counsel in the province of Nova Scotia, Canada. Kennelly's mother died a few years after her son's birth. Kennelly was educated at University College School, London (1873–6), and at other private schools in England, Scotland, France, and Belgium. He entered the London office of the Society of Telegraph Engineers (later the Institution of Electrical Engineers) as an office boy and, having studied electrophysics in his spare time, was in 1876 appointed a telegraph operator in the Eastern Telegraph Cable Company based in London. For the next ten years he was engaged in submarine cable work, latterly as a chief electrician, for that company.

In 1887 Kennelly went to the United States to join

Thomas A. Edison as principal assistant in his electrical laboratory at West Orange, New Jersey, where he remained until 1894 when he joined a firm of consulting electrical engineers. From 1902, when he was appointed to the chair of electrical engineering at Harvard University, until his retirement in 1930, he devoted all his time to teaching and scientific writing. From 1913 to 1924 he was also professor of electrical communications at the Massachusetts Institute of Technology, where for many years he directed electrical engineering research. On 22 July 1903 he married Julia Grice, a medical practitioner of Philadelphia; they had two children, a daughter who died in infancy and a son, Reginald Grice.

Kennelly's most important contributions lay in the interpretation and explanation of electrical phenomena. His introduction of complex numbers and complex hyperbolic functions in the analysis of alternating currents was an advance on earlier methods, and his postulate of an ionized layer in the upper atmosphere that enabled radio transmissions to be received by reflection over thousands of miles was subsequently verified by Sir Edward Appleton. The same explanation was put forward shortly afterwards independently by Oliver Heaviside and it was named, after both men, the Kennelly—Heaviside layer, now known as the E-layer in the ionosphere.

Widely honoured at home and abroad, Kennelly was president of the American Institute of Electrical Engineers (1898–1900), the British Institution of Electrical Engineers (1916), and several other professional institutions; he served as a member of many national and international organizations, and received honorary degrees from four universities. His publications include twenty-eight books (as author or co-author) and more than 350 technical papers. Kennelly died on 18 June 1939, in Boston, of uraemic poisoning, and his ashes were scattered in Mount Auburn cemetery in Cambridge, Massachusetts.

RONALD M. BIRSE

Sources C. L. Dawes, 'Kennelly, Arthur Edwin', *DAB* • *Who was who in America*, 1 (1968), 668 • V. Bush, 'Biographical memoir of Arthur Edwin Kennelly, 1861–1939', *National Academy of Sciences Biographical Memoirs*, 21 (1941), 83–119 • C. Süsskind, 'Kennelly, Arthur Edwin', *DSB* • *University College School: register for 1860–1931, with a short history* [1931], 29, 163
Likenesses portrait, repro. in *National Academy of Sciences Biographical Memoirs*, 22 (1943), 83

Kennet. For this title name *see* Scott, (Edith Agnes) Kathleen, Lady Scott [(Edith Agnes) Kathleen Young, Lady Kennet] (1878–1947); Young, (Edward) Hilton, first Baron Kennet (1879–1960).

Kenneth I [Cináed mac Alpin, Kenneth Macalpine] (*d.* **858**), king in Scotland, was ruler of the Dalriada in western Scotland from 840, and also ruler of the Picts from 842. In the genealogy of Scottish kings his father, *Alpin, occurs as a son of *Eochaid, son of *Aed Find, a celebrated king of Dalriada [*see under* Dál Riata, kings of]. The Irish synchronisms (based on king-lists), in the undoubtedly correct Edinburgh text, include Alpin among 'kings in

Scotland'; some modern scepticism concerning his kingship, and also concerning Áed Find's own royal descent, is a result of scribal omissions from some texts.

Kenneth himself is first heard of in the seventeenth-century annals of the four masters. Under 835 they say that a lord of Airgialla (perhaps in the Western Isles, not the Airgialla—Oriel—of Ireland) 'went over to Alba [Scotland] to reinforce Dalriada at the bidding of Kenneth, Alpin's son' (Anderson, *Early Sources*, 1.267). This would be more explicable if it were several years after 835. But although some of the four masters' material is in fact pre-dated by as much as five years, there seems to be no textual reason why this entry should not belong, as does the rest of the year-section, to 836. In that year Eoganán, a grandson of Áed Find's brother Fergus, became king of Dalriada. Eoganán's uncle and father had recently been kings of Dalriada and, for a total of more than twenty years, of Picts as well. *Eoganán (or Uven) [*see under* Picts, kings of the] likewise appears in regnal lists for both kingdoms.

In 839 Eoganán died in a disastrous battle against 'heathen' (probably Danes). In the Pictish kingship he was followed by one Urad who reigned for three years. The Dalriadan kingship seems to have been held by Kenneth's father, Alpin, for only one year, 839–40. It is likely enough that he died at the hands of Picts, as the late chronicle of Huntingdon says, but that is a very poor authority. The year 834 which it gives for the death of Alpin was inferred from a faulty king-list, and has no authority at all.

The most substantial source for Kenneth is the Scottish chronicle, a reign-by-reign narrative from Kenneth to the late tenth century. He held Dalriada, it says, for two years (840–42) before he 'came to Pictavia'. Having 'destroyed' the Picts, he reigned over Pictavia for sixteen years, from 842 to 858.

King-lists show that in the year when Kenneth 'came to Pictavia' the Pictish Urad ceased to reign, and that Urad's son Bred, who succeeded him, probably died in the same year. Three further Pictish kings are named by one group of lists, with reigns totalling six years (842–8). The last of them, Drust, was 'killed at Forteviot, or some say at Scone' (Anderson, *Kings and Kingship*, 266). This must refer to the story known in Ireland and Scotland in the twelfth century as 'the treachery of Scone', in which Pictish nobles invited by Scots to a council or feast were treacherously killed. Whatever truth there may have been in the tale, the germ of which is as old as Herodotus, it must be supposed that the death of Drust ended six years of active opposition to Kenneth. To follow tradition by describing Kenneth son of Alpin as the first king to rule over both Picts and Scots would be to simplify greatly a development which extended over more than half a century. His main political achievement should rather be seen as the establishment of a new dynasty which aspired to supremacy over the whole of Scotia, and under which the Scots so dominated Pictland that its native language and institutions rapidly disappeared.

The Scottish chronicle says that in the seventh year of

his reign (848 or 849) Kenneth 'brought relics of Saint Columba to a church that he built' (Anderson, *Early Sources*, 1.288). In 849 relics were taken to Ireland also. Norse raids had by this time made Iona untenable. Kenneth's church was probably at Dunkeld, though later Pictish lists attributed the building of Dunkeld church to the King Constantine (or Causantin) who died in 820. The chronicle lists other events of Kenneth's reign without dates. Six times he invaded Saxonia (Northumbria), and he seized and burnt Dunbar and Melrose. But British (from Strathclyde) burnt Dunblane, while 'Danes' laid Pictavia waste 'as far as Clunie and Dunkeld' (ibid.).

A notice of Kenneth's death in 858 is the only mention of him in the older Irish annals. The Scottish chronicle says that he died of a 'tumour', in February, at Forteviot; perhaps on Tuesday the 8th, but the reading is in doubt. He and most of his successors down to the eleventh century are said by lists to have been buried in Iona. He left two sons, *Constantine I and Áed, who were kings in succession from 862, and at least two daughters: one who married Run, king of the Britons of Strathclyde, and one who married Mael Muire, who died in 913.

Kenneth was succeeded by his brother **Donald I** [Domnall mac Alpin] (*d.* 862), king in Scotland, in whose time (the date is not specified) the Gaels with their king 'made the rights and laws of the kingdom [which were known as the laws] of Áed, son of Eochaid, at Forteviot' (Anderson, *Early Sources*, 1.291). What they then promulgated (rather than created, it may be supposed) was presumably a body of more or less Irish customary law associated with the name of Donald's great-grandfather Áed Find. 'Laws of Macalpine' which were known, or known about, in the thirteenth century may not have been distinct from these laws of Áed. Some writers have been misled by a late group of king-lists into believing that Donald was the father of a famous king, Giric. But in the original source Giric's father was undoubtedly 'Dúngal', not 'Donald'.

Donald mac Alpin died on 13 April 862, *in palacio Cinnbelathoir*, the Scottish chronicle says, but the place has not been identified. Later king-lists say that he died in 'Rathinveramon', 'the fort at the mouth of the [Perthshire] River Almond' (Anderson, *Early Sources*, 1.291), as Skene proposed. The two places are possibly the same and only a few miles from Forteviot, which archaeological remains show could well have been a royal residence at that time. It stands above the right bank of the Water of May, a small river that joins the Earn less than a mile to the north. The chronicle does not mention Forteviot again after Donald's reign.

Forteviot was almost certainly within Fortriu, roughly equatable with the southern half of modern Perthshire. The Irish annalists give the title 'king of Fortriu' to only four Pictish kings: two who died in 693 and 763 respectively, and Kenneth's predecessors Constantine and Oengus in the ninth century. Kenneth I is not called 'king of Fortriu'. He, his brother Donald, and Kenneth's two sons are all called 'king of Picts'. This title had very seldom been used by the annalists when writing of their own

times. It may imply a claim to sovereignty over all Pictish provinces; but there is very little evidence to show how far Kenneth's or Donald's sovereignty actually extended.

MARJORIE O. ANDERSON

Sources *Ann. Ulster* · M. O. Anderson, *Kings and kingship in early Scotland*, rev. edn (1980), 249–91 · A. O. Anderson, ed. and trans., *Early sources of Scottish history, AD 500 to 1286*, 1 (1922); repr. with corrections (1990), 270, 288, 291 · A. Boyle, 'The Edinburgh synchronisms of Irish kings', *Celtica*, 9 (1971), 177 · K. H. Jackson, ed. and trans., *Duan Albanach*, SHR, 36 (1957), 125–37 · *AFM* · W. F. Skene, ed., 'Chronicle of Huntingdon', *Chronicles of the Picts, chronicles of the Scots, and other early memorials of Scottish history*, ed. W. F. Skene (1867), 209–13 · J. Bannerman, *Studies in the history of Dalriada* (1974) · L. Alcock and E. Alcock, 'Reconnaissance excavations on early historic fortifications and other royal sites in Scotland, 1974–1984', *Proceedings of the Society of Antiquaries of Scotland*, 122 (1992), 215–91 · W. F. Skene, *Celtic Scotland: a history of ancient Alban*, 2nd edn, 1 (1886), 381 · M. O. Anderson, 'Dalriada and the creation of the kingdom of the Scots', *Ireland in early mediaeval Europe*, ed. D. Whitelock, R. McKitterick, and D. Dumville (1982), 106–32

Kenneth II [Cináed mac Maíl Choluim] (*d.* 995), king in Scotland, was the son of *Malcolm I (*d.* 954); King *Dubh (*d.* 966) was his older brother. Kenneth, who may have married a daughter of one of the Uí Dúnlainge kings of Leinster, became king after the death of *Culen in battle with the Britons of Strathclyde in 971 and reigned for twenty-four years and two months. He immediately plundered Strathclyde, but suffered a serious defeat at 'Moin Vacornar'. He repeatedly invaded England, on one occasion capturing a 'son of the king of the Saxons' (Anderson, *Early Sources*, 1.512). A contemporary account of the submission of Welsh kings to King Edgar of England at Chester in 973 is elaborated in later versions to include Kenneth as one of the kings who rowed a boat with Edgar at the helm. What is more certain is that *c.*975 King Edgar formally acknowledged Kenneth's rule over Lothian, which may have been annexed to the Scottish kingdom when Edinburgh fell to King Indulf at some time between 954 and 962. It is possible, however, that Lothian was temporarily lost to the earls of Northumbria in the last year of Kenneth's reign, 994–5.

Kenneth killed Olaf (brother of King Culen) in 977, which apparently brought a lull for two decades in the rivalry between the two branches of the royal dynasty—the descendants of Constantine I (*d.* 876), to which Kenneth belonged, and the descendants of King Aed (*d.* 878), to which Kenneth's predecessor, Culen, had belonged. Kenneth was a benefactor of the church, and founded the monastery of Brechin, in Angus, perhaps as a Céli Dé community: there were Céli Dé there until the early thirteenth century. It may, however, be conjectured that Brechin was founded for strategic reasons as much as religious motives. It is situated in the north of Strathmore, the broad and fertile valley which runs north-east from the Gowrie (north of Perth) to the Mearns (in modern Kincardineshire), and may have lain in disputed territory. Kenneth apparently had trouble in Strathmore which led eventually to his death. He allegedly killed the only son of Finguala (Finella), the daughter of Conchobar, earl of

Angus, at Dunsinane in the Gowrie; and, in revenge, Finguala arranged for Kenneth's assassination in 995 at Fettercairn in the Mearns—not 12 miles from Brechin. He was succeeded by *Constantine III [see under Culen].

With his Irish wife, Kenneth had at least one son, *Malcolm II, king of Scots from 1005 to 1034. Boite mac Cinaeda was probably another son of Kenneth II (rather than a son of Kenneth III), but possibly born to a different mother. Boite had a grandson who was killed by Malcolm II in 1032, and he also had a daughter, Gruoch, successively the wife of Gille Comgáin, ruler of Moray (d. 1032), and of Macbeth, ruler of Moray and king of Scots (d. 1057).

DAUVIT BROUN

Sources A. O. Anderson, ed. and trans., *Early sources of Scottish history, AD 500 to 1286*, 1 (1922), 478–84, 511–16 · M. O. Anderson, *Kings and kingship in early Scotland*, rev. edn (1980), 249–53, 265–89 · A. O. Anderson, ed., *Scottish annals from English chroniclers, AD 500 to 1286* (1908), 75–9 · A. A. M. Duncan, *Scotland: the making of the kingdom* (1975), vol. 1 of *The Edinburgh history of Scotland*, ed. G. Donaldson (1965–75), 95–7 · A. P. Smyth, *Warlords and holy men: Scotland, AD 80–1000* (1984), 228, 233

Kenneth III [Cináed mac Duib] (d. **1005**), king in Scotland, was the son of King *Dubh (d. 966). When he killed *Constantine III [see under Culen] in 997 and became king, his victory represented the final demise of the rival branch of the royal dynasty, the descendants of King Aed (d. 878). After Kenneth's triumph competition for the kingship narrowed to rival descendants of Malcolm I. In 1005 Kenneth III was killed in battle at Monzievaird (Perthshire) by his cousin *Malcolm II (d. 1034), who succeeded him. A late (and debatable) source claims that he was buried on Iona. Boite mac Cinaeda, whose son or grandson was killed by Malcolm II, may have been Kenneth III's son, but was more probably the son of Kenneth II. Kenneth III's supposed son Giric was apparently the product of a copyist's error, but Kenneth probably did have a son or sons whose descendants became the *clann* Duib (later Macduff).

DAUVIT BROUN

Sources A. O. Anderson, ed. and trans., *Early sources of Scottish history, AD 500 to 1286*, 1 (1922), 521–4 · M. O. Anderson, *Kings and kingship in early Scotland*, rev. edn (1980), 52, 265–89 · A. A. M. Duncan, *Scotland: the making of the kingdom* (1975), vol. 1 of *The Edinburgh history of Scotland*, ed. G. Donaldson (1965–75), 97, 116

Kenneth, Archibald Graham [Archie] (**1915–1989**), composer and editor of highland bagpipe music, was born on 6 June 1915 at Shirvan, Lochgilphead, Argyll, the son of Archibald Kenneth, a coalmaster, who was killed at Gallipoli on 12 July 1915 while serving as a captain in the 4th battalion, Royal Scots Fusiliers, and his wife, Katherine Louisa, *née* Graham-Campbell, of Shirvan. He was sent to school in England, much to his distaste: he later declared, 'I would rather be a tinker on the roads of Argyll than live in the South of England' (Campbell, 3). On his return he settled as a country gentleman and amateur botanist on his estate at Stronachullin, Ardrishaig, near Lochgilphead, his life there interrupted only by wartime service as an officer in the 8th battalion of the Argyll and Sutherland

Highlanders, during which he was mentioned in dispatches. He married Janet MacMillan, and they had a son, Iain, and a daughter, Mary.

As a botanist, Kenneth specialized in the hawkweeds of Wester Ross and Sutherland and the general flora of Knapdale and Kintyre. He contributed to M. H. Cunningham's *The Flora of Kintyre* (1979), and was the author of *Additions to the Flora of Kintyre* (1985). However, it was as a traditional musician, and more particularly as a composer and editor of pipe music, that Kenneth is mainly remembered. He was born into the tightly knit group of Argyllshire gentry who had founded the Piobaireachd Society in 1903 and it was his maternal uncle, John Graham-Campbell of Shirvan, a founding member of the society and leading judge of piping, who gave him his first instruction, later supplemented by Pipe Major Willie Ross, one of the foremost players and teachers of the twentieth century. Kenneth became in turn a long-serving judge of piping and steward at the Argyllshire Gathering, one of the most important of such events, held annually at Oban, and a regular contributor to the magazine *Piping Times*, mainly on problems of music editing. He was a talented composer of *ceòl beag* (the light music of the pipe) and a number of his pieces, including the jig 'The Lady in the Bottle' and the reel 'The Back of the Moon', became favourites. He published several collections of bagpipe music, including volumes of piobaireachd of his own composition.

In 1947 Kenneth was elected to the music committee of the Piobaireachd Society, which was responsible for producing the society's published *Collection* (15 vols., 1925–). This was to create problems when he became the society's editor in 1963, since the earlier volumes of the series had presented the personal arrangements of his predecessor, Archibald Campbell, Kilberry, as the work of traditional master players, despite the protests of the performers obliged to play the resulting scores at the major competitions. Although he was aware of some of the shortcomings of the previous volumes and expressed concern that proper care had not been taken of the original sources, he was anxious for the reputation of the society and felt that 'to revise over-freely would be rather a confession of inadequacy in the first instance' (Kenneth, 11). He was responsible for completing volume 10 (1961) and then volumes 11–15, the last being published after his death, in 1990. As an editor of piobaireachd, however, Kenneth's musical flair deserted him. He translated a large number of tunes into staff notation from the Nether Lorn canntaireachd, a pioneering system of vocalic notation developed during the closing years of the eighteenth century, but his decision to persevere with the society's unidiomatic and unhistoric house style meant that the results were seldom happy.

Kenneth's interests in traditional music were wide, covering Gaelic song and its putative links with piobaireachd, Scottish fiddle music, even new-wave folk rock; he also played the accordion from childhood. He wielded a vigorous pen, describing one of the longest established piping societies as 'a snob 'n' booze association' and a prominent (male) Piobaireachd Society colleague as 'a litigious wee bitch' ('Letters', NL Scot.).

In his later years Kenneth became increasingly reluctant to leave Argyll to attend conferences and meetings. He died at his home at Stronachullin on 27 July 1989, of lung cancer. He was buried at Lochgilphead, Argyll, on 31 July 1989.   WILLIAM DONALDSON

Sources W. Donaldson, *The highland pipe and Scottish society, 1750–1950* (2000) · J. Campbell, 'The influence of Archie Kenneth', *Proceedings of the Piobaireachd Society Conference*, 17 (1990), 1–8 · A. Kenneth, 'Re-publishing piobaireachd', *Piping Times*, 24/10 (1972), 8–11 · A. G. Kenneth, letters to J. MacFadyen, 1965–75, NL Scot., Acc. 9103/7 · papers, agendas, reports of general committee, reports of music committee, 1902–76, NL Scot., Piobaireachd Society MS Acc. 9103/3 · SM [S. MacNeill], 'A. G. Kenneth', *Piping Times*, 42/1 (1989), 48–9 · *Glasgow Naturalist*, 21/5 (1990), 576 · b. cert. · d. cert.
Archives NL Scot., letters, mostly to John MacFadyen · NL Scot., Piobaireachd Society papers, agendas, accounts, reports of general committee, reports of music committee, Acc. 9103/3
Likenesses photograph, repro. in *Piping Times*, 42/3 (1989)
Wealth at death £569,123.63: confirmation, 28 Dec 1989, *CCI*

Kennett, Basil (1674–1715), antiquary and translator, was born at Postling, Kent, on 21 October 1674, the son of Basil Kennett (d. 1686), vicar of Postling and rector of Dymchurch, and his wife, Mary White. He was educated by his elder brother White *Kennett (1660–1728), bishop of Peterborough, at a school at Bicester, Oxfordshire, and in the family of Sir William Glynne, baronet, at Ambrosden, near Bicester. In 1689 he entered St Edmund Hall, Oxford, under the tuition of his brother, who was then vice-principal. In 1690 he was elected a scholar of Corpus Christi College, Oxford, as a native of Kent, and graduated BA in 1693 and MA in 1696. That year he published his first and most successful work, *Romae antiquae notitia, or, The Antiquities of Rome*. Prefaced by two original essays—'The Roman learning' and 'The Roman education'—it passed through many editions, and as late as 1786 the bookseller William Lowndes purchased a thirty-second share in the rights to the book. Its elegant synthesis of the antiquarian data assembled over the previous 200 years ensured it a leading place among books on the daily life of the Romans until the nineteenth century.

In 1697 Kennett became fellow and tutor of Corpus, and published *The Lives and Characters of the Ancient Greek Poets*. This book, like his earlier one, was dedicated to the duke of Gloucester, son of Queen Anne, and indeed there was some talk (reported in *Biographia Britannica*) of Kennett's becoming tutor to the young prince. Between 1703 and 1705 he published translations of several French works, including *Thoughts upon Religion* (1704, later edns, 1727, 1741) from Pascal's original, and original essays, of which *A Brief Exposition of the Apostles' Creed* (1705, later edns, 1721, 1726) enjoyed some success. He also presided over a collaborative translation of Puffendorf's *Law of Nature and Nations* (1703, later edns, 1710, 1717, 1729, 1749).

In 1705 Kennett's brother White, then a canon at Salisbury Cathedral, presented him to the vicarage of Coombe Bisset, Wiltshire. The following year he agreed, again at the instigation of his brother, a leading figure in the Society for the Propagation of the Gospel in Foreign Parts, to

go as the first chaplain to the British trading factory at Leghorn. Nominated by royal licence dated 8 September 1706, he arrived in December. His appointment attracted attention both in England, where he was awarded an Oxford BD by decree of convocation the following February, and in Italy, where the Inquisition interfered with the execution of his duties and even, his brother's letters relate, with his personal safety. Though he had a firm ally in Henry Newton, British envoy at Florence, the political support needed to make his position tenable was long in coming. Kennett's health suffered, a fact variously ascribed to his scholarly lifestyle and, as suggested in a biographical note by White Kennett, a poison administered by the Inquisition. He soon decided to resign his post although, unwilling to abandon it before the still indecisive government sent out his replacement, he remained until February 1712. Before returning home he visited Florence, Rome, and Naples with the merchant Humphrey Chetham, and spent large amounts of money (much of it his brother's) on books, sculpture, and curiosities. He arrived back in July 1713, and in October took up another appointment arranged by his brother, as chaplain to William Wake, bishop of Lincoln.

During Kennett's absence several smaller works of his had been published, including a translation of selections from Jean-Louis de Balzac's *Aristippus* (1709). This caused some embarrassment for his brother, who had contributed the preface: soon after its publication a pamphlet entitled *French Favourites* appeared, containing extracts from it arranged so as to produce a satirical commentary on the relationship between Queen Anne and the duchess of Marlborough; authorship was attributed to White Kennett, compelling him to issue a swift denial. In May 1714 Basil Kennett was elected president of Corpus Christi College, being made DD the following July. His health had not improved. He fell seriously ill in November and died of a fever in the president's lodgings on 3 January 1715. He was buried in the college chapel on 6 January. Though his will included generous bequests to his college and university, it emerged that he had died in debt, and some of his effects had to be sold. His sermons to the merchants at Leghorn were published in 1715. His letters and unpublished works, including commentaries on the Bible and liturgy, 'Lives of the Latin poets', and notes on English poets, survive in his brother's collections, now subsumed in the Lansdowne manuscripts in the British Library.

C. E. A. CHEESMAN

Sources W. Kennett, 'Minutes of Dr Basil Kennett, president of C.C.C., Oxon who died in 1714', BL, Lansdowne MSS, Add. MS 987 fols. 222–3 [printed in E. Brydges, *Restituta, or, Titles, extracts, and characters of old books in English literature, revived*, 1, 1814, 153–4] · W. Kennett, papers relating to his brother, 1706–15, BL, Lansdowne MS 1041 · W. Kennett, letters to S. Blackwell, 1707–13 [printed in Brydges, 3, 1815, 359–408] · B. Kennett, letters to H. Newton, 1707, BL, Lansdowne MS 927, fols. 118–123v · B. Kennett, letters to S. Blackwell, 1705–14, BL, Lansdowne MS 1019, fols. 2–16 · J. Reynolds, letter to W. Kennett, 1715, BL, Lansdowne MS 989, fol. 43 · W. Newton, *The life of the right reverend Dr White Kennett, late lord bishop of Peterborough* (1730), 52–101 · W. Lowndes, note of purchase of shares in books from the executors of Charles Bathurst, 1786, BL, Add. MS 38730, fol. 16v · will, proved 11 Feb 1715, Oxf. UA, Hyp/

B/28, fols. 61–2 · *Liber admissorum*, CCC Oxf., B/1/3/4, 121 · register of institutions, diocese of Salisbury, 1549–1846, Wilts. & Swindon RO, WSRO/D5/1/2 [Dean's Peculiars] · Royal warrant appointing B. Kennett minister to the English factory at Leghorn, 1706, BL, Add. MS 38889, fol. 130b · J. Ingamells, ed., *A dictionary of British and Irish travellers in Italy, 1701–1800* (1997), 202, 568–9 · *Biographia Britannica, or, The lives of the most eminent persons who have flourished in Great Britain and Ireland*, 4 (1757) · *Remarks and collections of Thomas Hearne*, ed. C. E. Doble and others, 1, OHS, 2 (1885), 285, 295, 311, 332 · *Remarks and collections of Thomas Hearne*, ed. C. E. Doble and others, 2, OHS, 7 (1886), 179, 234 · *Remarks and collections of Thomas Hearne*, ed. C. E. Doble and others, 11 vols., OHS, 2, 7, 13, 34, 42–3, 48, 50, 65, 67, 72 (1885–1921), vol. 5, pp. 9, 11 · T. Rawlinson, untitled obit. book, Bodl. Oxf., MS Rawl. C. 915, see 3 Jan 1714–15
Archives BL, White Kennett MSS, Lansdowne MSS 924–934
Wealth at death £303 12s. 0d.—value of receipts from his estate: BL, Lansdowne MS 1041, 28 April 1715, fols. 273–6; cf. Lansdowne MS 989, fol. 156; Lansdowne MS 987, fol. 222

Kennett, Brackley (*c*.1713–1782), wine merchant and local politician, was born in Putney, Surrey, the son of John 'Kinnick', a waterman in Putney. Little is known about his business career, but it is likely that he began working on the rougher side of the tavern trade. He emerged as a wine merchant in Pall Mall; respectability and civic office came by way of his membership of the Vintners' Company, of which he was master in 1768. He was sheriff of the City of London in 1765–6, and was elected alderman of Cornhill ward in 1767. He was elected lord mayor in 1779, and was thus in office during the Gordon riots of 1780, when a campaign by Lord George Gordon for the repeal of the Catholic Relief Act of 1778 led to a week of mob rule.

The lord mayor's ineffectiveness was unfavourably portrayed by Charles Dickens in *Barnaby Rudge* (1841). The evidence is partial, but it seems that Kennett was timid to the point of indifference. When he was asked on 3 June to protect the Catholics in Moorfields, he is said to have replied: 'You do not know anything of the business. I have orders to employ the military if necessary, but I must be cautious what I do lest I bring the mob to my house. I can assure you that there are very great people at the bottom of the riot' (Castro, 51). Next day, when the mob was destroying the Catholic chapel in Moorfields, he apparently turned a deaf ear to requests for orders from the soldiers and the fire officers in attendance; and when the rioters' work was done he uttered the mildest of rebukes: 'That's pretty well, gentlemen, for one day; I hope you will now go to your own homes' (ibid., 52). On 5 June he is said to have ignored a request from a Catholic merchant for protection for his family in the Mansion House; and he stirred himself only when the Bank of England was reported to be in the mob's sights.

Kennett was charged with criminal neglect of duty, and his case was tried before Lord Mansfield in March 1781. After a little hesitation on the part of the jury, he was found guilty. Another charge, relating to the release of some rioters apprehended during an attack on a prison, was dropped. Kennett died on 12 May 1782 with his sentence for neglect of duty, and a suit for defamation brought by Thomas Howard, third earl of Effingham (whom Kennett had alleged to have been one of the rioters), still outstanding. The possibility of suicide cannot be ruled out. His first marriage was to Frances Boure. He was survived by his second wife, Hannah, and two sons. Two girls took his surname, but were either illegitimate or adopted. He was buried in Putney church.

IAN DOOLITTLE, *rev.* CHRISTINE CLARK

Sources J. P. de Castro, *The Gordon riots* (1926) · 'Rex v. Kennett', F. A. Carrington and J. Payne, *Reports of cases argued and ruled at nisi prius in the courts of the king's bench, and common pleas, and exchequer*, 5 (1833), 282–96 · G. Rudé, *Hanoverian London, 1714–1808* (1971) · CLRO · GL · will, PRO, PROB 11/1090, sig. 235 · A. B. Beaven, ed., *The aldermen of the City of London, temp. Henry III–[1912]*, 2 vols. (1908–13) · A. J. F. Mills, *History of the riots in London in the year 1780* (1883)

Kennett, Robert Hatch (1864–1932), biblical and Semitic scholar, was born at Nethercourt, St Lawrence, Thanet, Kent, on 9 September 1864, the only son of four children of John Kennett, farmer, JP for the Cinque Ports and first mayor of Ramsgate, and his second wife, Jane Hatch, of Ulcombe, Kent. Kennett was educated at Merchant Taylors' School, London, where he was taught Hebrew by Charles James Ball, and fellow students included G. A. Cooke, later regius professor of Hebrew, and Charles Fox Burney, later Oriel professor of the interpretation of holy scripture, both at Oxford. In 1882 he gained a scholarship to Queens' College, Cambridge, whose president was the Syriac scholar George Phillips, and where the orientalist William Wright taught him. He gained a first class in the Semitic languages tripos of 1886, and in 1887, the year in which he was ordained, was awarded the first Tyrwhitt Hebrew scholarship and the Mason prize for biblical Hebrew. Elected a fellow of Queens' College in 1888, Kennett was lecturer in Hebrew and Syriac there from 1887 to 1903, and chaplain from 1887 to 1893 and again from 1902 to 1908. He was also lecturer in Hebrew and Syriac at Gonville and Caius College, Cambridge, from 1891 to 1893. He was appointed Cambridge University lecturer in Aramaic in 1893, and ten years later was elected to the regius professorship of Hebrew (held in conjunction with a canonry of Ely Cathedral). In 1889 he married Emily Augusta, second daughter of Edward William Smythe Scott, major-general in the Bengal artillery, and granddaughter of W. S. Whish (1787–1853). They had two sons and a daughter. Kennett was of medium height and dark-haired with blue eyes. He was a generous and warm-hearted man with great personal charm and wide interests. His health was never good and he died quite suddenly at the priory, Ely, on 15 February 1932. His younger son, Austin, an official in the government of Nigeria, and author of an important book *Bedouin Justice* (1925), survived his father by only a few months.

Kennett's years in Cambridge coincided with a lively period in biblical studies, largely due to the influence of William Smith (1846–1894). Kennett took a prominent part in interpreting the Graf-Wellhausen position in Old Testament criticism which was then winning its way. This approach to biblical studies involved an interest, above all else, in the history of the composition of the Old Testament, which can be very difficult to reconstruct. For forty years Kennett was an earnest evangelical teacher and 'higher critic', and worked to bridge the gulf between conservative and revisionist biblical scholars. As a critic he was independent and original, if not daring; and his studies on the date of Deuteronomy (the first of which was published in the *Journal of Theological Studies* for January 1905) brought him notice, as did his broader treatment of Israelite history during the seventh to the fifth centuries BC, and his defence of a Maccabean date for the Psalms and other parts of the Old Testament. He was twice (1909 and 1931) Schweich lecturer of the British Academy, his lectures being published as *The Composition of the Book of Isaiah in the Light of History and Archaeology* (1910) and *Ancient Hebrew Social Life and Custom as Indicated in Law, Narrative and Metaphor* (1933). His reconstruction of biblical history was the subject of much debate at the time, although in many respects his views were in harmony with certain trends of Old Testament research; many modern scholars would be wary of the confidence he placed in the then new and exciting textual and source critical methods.

S. A. COOK, *rev.* GERALD LAW

Sources F. C. Birkitt, *Cambridge Review* (26 Feb 1932), 287–8 · personal knowledge (1949) · S. A. Cook, introduction, in R. H. Kennett, *The church of Israel* (1933), xv–lvi · b. cert. · m. cert. · *CGPLA Eng. & Wales* (1932)
Archives NL Scot., corresp. with publishers
Likenesses photograph, repro. in Cook, introduction, in Kennett
Wealth at death £5957 17s. 6d.: probate, 8 April 1932, *CGPLA Eng. & Wales*

Kennett, White (1660–1728), historian and bishop of Peterborough, was born in the parish of St Mary, Dover, on 10 August 1660, the eldest of the seven children of Basil Kennett (*d.* 1686) and Mary, eldest daughter of Thomas White, a wealthy shipwright. His father was a storekeeper in the dockyards at Dover, but after the Restoration he was ordained and became in 1668 vicar of Postley and in 1676 rector of Dymchurch, both in Kent.

Education and early career Kennett attended local schools at Elham and at Wye, after which he was sent to Westminster School in London. On contracting smallpox he returned home and after regaining his health he spent a year tutoring the three sons of a family in Beaksbourne, Kent. He matriculated from St Edmund Hall, Oxford, on 25 June 1678. A conscientious student, Kennett was tutored by Andrew Allam and was also taught by Anthony Wood, the celebrated antiquary. At Oxford he developed a life-long fascination with historical and antiquarian scholarship.

It was during the Exclusion crisis, while he was an undergraduate, that Kennett produced his first publication. *A Letter from a Student at Oxford to a Friend in the Country* appeared just before the opening of parliament in 1681. The anonymous pamphlet attacked parliament for its support of exclusion and railed against papists and puritans alike. It aroused parliament's ire to the point that the vice-chancellor was ordered to identify the offending author and punish him. Fortunately for Kennett the king quickly dissolved parliament and the matter was dropped, prompting Kennett to publish a celebratory poem in

White Kennett (1660–1728), by John Faber senior, 1719

which he declared 'that our King's a God on earth' (Bennett, *White Kennett*, 6).

After graduating BA on 2 May 1682, Kennett settled on a career in the church and began to study for his master's degree in January 1684. To support himself, and to make his mark as a scholar, he translated several Latin works into English, most notably Erasmus's *Moriae encomium*, which was published as *Wit Against Wisdom, or, A Panegyric upon Folly*. On 12 October 1684 Kennett became curate and assistant schoolmaster of Bicester, Oxfordshire, where his pupils included his younger brother Basil *Kennett. Having received his MA on 22 January 1685, he was ordained priest by Bishop John Fell in Oxford on 15 March. He was befriended by Sir William Glynne, who presented him to the vicarage of Ambrosden on 3 June 1685. Kennett carried out his clerical duties conscientiously, but it was a small parish and the workload was not taxing. Ambrosden's proximity to Oxford facilitated Kennett's continuing scholarly research. His translation of Pliny contained a dedication to Glynne which reiterated Kennett's arch-royalist views.

Nevertheless, James II's pro-Catholic policies alienated Kennett. Like most of the clergy in the diocese of Oxford he refused in May 1687 to sign an address to the king or to read the second declaration of indulgence in his church. The accession of William and Mary to the throne tested Kennett's loyalty. He eventually decided to take the oaths of allegiance to the new sovereigns, arguing that he could 'abridge' his obedience to James because the king was too far away for Kennett to give him 'just tribute'; motivated also by self-interest, he recognized that his refusal would 'promote my own ruine' (Bennett, *White Kennett*, 12).

Misfortune and marriage The strain imposed on Kennett from these political events was compounded by personal adversity. The barrel of his gun splintered while he was out shooting in January 1689 and a piece of metal fractured his skull. He endured painful surgery and 'a hot and distempered brain' which afflicted him for five weeks (Bennett, *White Kennett*, 11). He had a scar on his forehead and wore a patch over it for the rest of his life. Kennett married Sarah (1674/5–1694), daughter of Robert and Mary Carver of Bicester, on 6 June 1693 at Ambrosden. She died in childbirth on 2 March of the following year. Kennett was devastated and fell seriously ill for several days. He later wrote that he suffered 'so great weakness and decay of spirits that my Physician and my Friends expected nothing but death' (ibid., 256). Fifteen months later, on 6 June 1695, he married as his second wife Sarah Smith (*d.* 1702), the sister of Richard Smith MD, of London and Aylesbury. They had two children: White Kennett (*d.* 1740), who became rector of Burton-le-Coggles, Lincolnshire, and prebendary of Peterborough, and Sarah (*d.* 1756), who married John Newman, of Shottesbrooke, Berkshire.

Advancing career In 1691 Kennett was appointed tutor and vice-principal at St Edmund Hall, Oxford, and moved back to Oxford. In the same year he was chosen as public lecturer and pro-proctor, and named as one of the city lecturers at St Martin's, Carfax; his sermon upon the death of Queen Mary was printed in 1695. In June 1694 he was presented by Francis Cherry, a nonjuring squire, to the rectory of Shottesbrooke, Berkshire, in the diocese of Salisbury; he retained the Ambrosden living. Shottesbrooke was then a haven for nonjurors, such as Henry Dodwell and, briefly, George Hickes, and Kennett found the environment strengthened his opposition to the rigid principles of the nonjurors. His political and theological thinking was moving towards a more latitudinarian stance.

Release from Shottesbrooke came in 1700 when Kennett was appointed curate of St Botolph, Aldgate, by the impropriator of the parish, Samuel Brewster. Kennett secured the cure only after the incumbent, Richard Hollingsworth, was ejected and lost his suit to regain his office. As priest in a large London parish, and still in possession of his two rural livings, Kennett now enjoyed a comfortable income. He sedulously carried out his duties and his sermons were much admired; he preached before the City corporation in 1705, the House of Commons in 1706, and later that year before Queen Anne.

Church politics Kennett's arrival in London coincided with the convocation controversy. Francis Atterbury's *Letter to a Convocation Man* (1697) and *The Rights, Powers, and Privileges of an English Convocation* (1700) made the high-church case that the convocation of Canterbury had legislative authority in ecclesiastical affairs; thus it was not in the power of the king—or of the archbishops—to call or prorogue it. Atterbury's works touched off a battle of books in convocation between 'high-flying' champions of the lower house and whiggish advocates of the episcopal

upper house. The principal critics of Atterbury and his circle were William Wake, Edmund Gibson, and White Kennett. Kennett's several contributions to this debate, most notably his *History of the Convocation of the Prelates and Clergy of the Province of Canterbury* (1702), exposed the flimsy historical basis of Atterbury's arguments and, in particular, vindicated the archbishop's authority over the lower house. He contended that such authority, rather than diminishing the church's standing in society, actually enhanced it.

By the time convocation opened on 30 December 1701 Kennett had won the confidence of Archbishop Thomas Tenison and became his primary adviser and advocate in the lower house. He remained so in the convocations of 1702–5, 1708, and 1710–13. His task was to obstruct the high-church majority in the lower house and uphold the power of the bishops. Dabbling in newspaper journalism, Kennett contributed to the whig *Medley* in 1711, defending the bishops against Jonathan Swift's claim in the *Examiner* that the low-church clergy were crypto-Presbyterians out to subvert the church. The bitter divisions within convocation guaranteed that the meetings would be fruitless, and convocation was suspended in 1717.

Kennett's defence of the upper house won him the favour of Gilbert Burnet, bishop of Salisbury, who collated him to a prebend in the cathedral church of Salisbury in April 1701. And on 16 May Kennett was appointed archdeacon of Huntington, Lincolnshire, an office he held until 1720.

Following the death of his second wife in August 1702, Kennett married Dorcas Havers (*d.* 1743) in 1703. The daughter of Thomas Fuller, rector of Wellinghale, Essex, and the widow of Clopton Havers, a physician, Kennett's new wife proved to be a forceful character. Thomas Hearne's jaundiced view was that Dorcas 'wears the Breeches, and manages him as his Haughty, insolent Temper deserves' (Bennett, *White Kennett*, 257).

State politics In the ideological conflict between whigs and tories Kennett robustly defended in print and from the pulpit the ministry of Marlborough and Godolphin. On 31 January 1704, the fast day to commemorate the execution of Charles I, Kennett delivered a sermon, *A Compassionate Enquiry into the Causes of the Civil War*, which supplied historical justification for the ministry's war against France: he blamed the 'French Interest and Alliance', personified by Queen Henrietta Maria, for causing the civil war (Bennett, *White Kennett*, 91). The publication of this sermon on 19 February 1704 provoked a torrent of pamphlet attacks from tory loyalists. Kennett's views of the civil war were reformulated at length in the *Compleat History of England*, published in 1706. The author's negative portrayals of the early Stuarts and his enthusiasm for the war against France ignited another round of broadsides against Kennett. On 22 November 1709, soon after the costly battle of Malplaquet, Kennett preached a sermon before Queen Anne in which he praised Marlborough's 'unblemishe'd and uninterrupted Honour' and called to task those who 'could be counted to diminish and detract from his merits' (ibid., 106).

Eager to advance his career, Kennett cultivated the favour of whig ministers. In April 1707, angling for the deanery of Peterborough, Kennett asked Bishop William Wake to approach Lord Sunderland on his behalf. In June 1707 Kennett was made a royal chaplain at Windsor. He acquired a reputation for sycophancy, exemplified by the flattering eulogy he delivered at the funeral in Derby of William Cavendish, first duke of Devonshire and a whig grandee, whose licentiousness was notorious. This sermon prompted a new round of salvos against Kennett, most notably one by John Sharp, reader at Stepney, to which Kennett responded in *A Vindication of the Church and Clergy of England*. This anonymously published tract expressed Kennett's opposition to 'Popery and French Power', favoured by 'a Party who have been out of humour ever since the Revolution' (Bennett, *White Kennett*, 101). Kennett's loyalty to the whigs paid off when the second duke of Devonshire successfully pressed Queen Anne to nominate Kennett as dean of Peterborough, which she did on 8 January 1708.

Kennett was drawn into the heated controversy generated by Henry Sacheverell's infamous sermon, *The Perils of False Brethren, both in Church and State* (1709). The high-church Sacheverell identified Kennett by name as the author of the anonymously published *Compleat History of England* and cited the work to support his claim that William of Orange was not bent on resistance to James II when he landed at Torbay in 1688. Kennett retorted, in *A True Answer to Dr Sacheverell's Sermon*, that he had made no such statement. He further defended archbishops Tenison and Tillotson and Bishop Burnet against Sacheverell's aspersions.

The tory electoral victory in 1710 drove Kennett into further activity. His sermons and pamphlets expressed his concern to preserve the Hanoverian succession and the Toleration Act, and to combat the nonjuring doctrines of divine right kingship and non-resistance. Assailed by George Hickes in 1711 as an immoral pluralist, political time-server, and promoter of dissent, Kennett responded with a pamphlet, and retorted that 'I have for many years looked upon Hereditary Succession and Passive Obedience in the rigid Notions of Dr Hickes to have no Foundation in the Christian Gospel or in the English Constitution' (Bennett, *White Kennett*, 117–18).

An embattled whig Kennett was preoccupied with the issue of lay baptism throughout most of 1712. The high-church party had claimed in the previous year that baptism was valid only when it was conferred by an episcopally ordained minister. Such a position, Kennett wrote, constituted 'dangerous Pretensions of unchurching the Foreign Churches, and paganizing Fellow-Christians, and excluding Protestant Heirs to the Crown' (Bennett, *White Kennett*, 122). He undertook historical research to uphold the validity of lay baptism, on behalf of Archbishop Tenison, who met his bishops at Lambeth Palace, where they decided against the high-church position.

On 1 November 1713 Kennett preached a sermon at Windsor 'against Popery and Profaneness' (Bennett, *White*

Kennett, 125). He warned about the danger to the protestant succession before a congregation that included— besides the queen—the earl of Oxford, Viscount Bolingbrooke, and Jonathan Swift. Kennett observed later that Swift 'drew the eyes of many upon him, when I happen'd to mention among other corruptions of the Age, the prevailing foolishness of Wit and Humour so called' (ibid., 125). Kennett's whiggish sermons did not win him any friends at court, but he never compromised his views. A pamphlet in 1713 made the case that a monarch could not name his or her own successor in defiance of parliament. It read like a cautionary warning to Queen Anne.

Kennett's outspokenness made him anathema to the tory high-flyers. In 1714 one of their number, Dr Richard Welton, rector of Whitechapel in London, had an altarpiece placed in his church that depicted the last supper. The painting showed Judas with a mark on his forehead and the face was clearly recognizable as that of White Kennett. People turned out in droves to admire the wicked caricature. Verses appeared lampooning the 'new false Brother' (Bennett, *White Kennett*, 127) and a new round of pamphlets was published, some of which contained images from the painting. Kennett was humiliated. The whig press came to his defence. The *Flying-Post* attacked Dr Welton and the *Daily Courant* offered a reward for information that could lead to the prosecution of those responsible for the altarpiece. The chancellor of the diocese viewed the painting and ordered that it be taken down.

The Hanoverian accession Kennett had great expectations that the accession of George I in 1714 would rapidly advance his career, and he was disappointed when no new offices or rewards came his way. He seems to have been held back by his reputation as a controversialist—even though on behalf of the whigs—and by his ineptness as a courtier. The death of Bishop Burnet and the resignation of the second duke of Devonshire deprived Kennett of his influential patrons. When the see of Lincoln went to Edward Gibson in 1716, instead of to Kennett, the dean's spirits sank and he described himself as 'a forgotten man' (Bennett, *White Kennett*, 135).

Nevertheless Kennett remained a vigorous publicist for a latitudinarian church and whiggish politics. In published sermons he denounced the Jacobite rising of 1715. He continued his attacks on papists and the nonjurors in controversies with Jeremy Collier and Mathias Earbury. He was also drawn into the Bangorian controversy in 1717, when he was accused, plausibly, of having toned down before publication the sermon by Benjamin Hoadly, bishop of Bangor, entitled *The Nature of the Kingdom or Church of Christ*. Kennett vigorously denied the charges in an open letter in the newspapers. He staunchly defended Hoadly against his high-church critics in convocation.

Kennett's opportunity for preferment finally came in 1718 when the bishop of Peterborough, Richard Cumberland, died. William Wake, the archbishop of Canterbury, commended him to the earl of Sunderland and Kennett was nominated to the see of Peterborough on 12 October 1718. Henceforth Kennett faithfully attended the House of Lords, where he became part of Sunderland's circle in that body. Kennett spoke in the Lords in support of the ministry's bill to repeal the Occasional Conformity and Schism Acts. He aspired to be influential at court and hoped that Peterborough would be a stepping-stone to a more prestigious bishopric. But Sunderland's political decline and his death in 1722 meant that Kennett had no entrée to higher office. Although Kennett continued to speak out in favour of whig policies, he now spent more time on historical scholarship and on running his diocese.

Historical works White Kennett made a significant contribution to British historical scholarship. By the early 1690s he had joined a circle of historians at Queen's College, Oxford—led by William Nicholson, and including William Wake, Edmund Gibson, and Thomas Tanner—which conducted pioneering research in medieval and antiquarian studies. While at Oxford Kennett wrote *Parochial antiquities attempted in the history of Ambrosden, Burchester, and other adjacent parts in the counties of Oxford and Bucks* (1695). Tracing the land tenures in north Oxfordshire before and after the Norman conquest, Kennett showed that a new structure of landholding was imposed by William I. The book bolstered the argument of Henry Spelman, Robert Brady, and others that the Norman conquest had produced novel legal and military institutions, namely feudalism. It also discussed lay impropriations, deaneries, and papal policies. It was the first substantial parish history and was well received, but Kennett's proposal that he and his colleagues should write a general history of medieval England fell on deaf ears.

The convocation disputes, based on appeals to history, further propelled Kennett's research. *The Case of Impropriations* (1704) examined the history of lay impropriations. In 1706 Kennett's massive *Compleat History of England* (3 vols.) was published anonymously. The *Compleat History* answered William Temple's call in 1695 for a general history of England from ancient times to the present. It was among the most ambitious and expensive publishing ventures up to that time. Thirteen booksellers collaborated on its publication and requests for subscriptions were sent throughout the provinces. Kennett was paid £150 for the work, which was edited, probably, by John Hughes. The first two volumes consisted of old chronicles; the third offered a narrative of the period from the reign of Charles I to that of William III.

Kennett wrote his *History* in part to refute the tory view of the English revolution and Restoration. The work chronicled the perils of 'popery', especially the arbitrary power that, Kennett argued, always attended it. Kennett made extensive use of Clarendon's recently published *History of the Rebellion* and wanted to show that 'the noble historian' could not be appropriated by the tories (Okie, 28). Although Kennett upbraided Charles I for his laxity towards Catholics and Catholic powers, it is only with the Restoration that the work took on a consistently whiggish tone. Kennett painted a very unflattering picture of Charles II, wrote favourably of the Exclusion Bill, and authenticated the Popish Plot. He argued that the revolution of 1688 was based on 'Church of England principles'

in the face of the popish threat posed by James II (ibid., 29).

Kennett's narrative was embedded in copious documentation. Most of the work consists of state documents, memoirs, histories, newsletters, trials, and so forth, threaded together with the author's level-headed narrative. It broke no new ground and displayed a rather static concept of history, but was notable for its scholarship and its relatively impartial tone, notwithstanding Kennett's whiggish interpretation.

Kennett's *Compleat History* was generally well received, going through four reprints, and a new edition in 1719. Inevitably it provoked hostile reactions from tory writers. As late as 1740 a 700-page critique, *The Examen*, by Roger North, was published to discredit Kennett's 'pretended Complete history' (Okie, 31).

Kennett's final work, *A Register and Chronicle Ecclesiastical and Civil* (1726), was a massive collection of English historical documents which covered the years 1660 to 1662. Kennett intended it as an example of the kind of documentary record which could be continued by future scholars with government support.

Churchman Despite the many hours Kennett devoted to historical and political writing, he did not neglect his considerable pastoral duties. As chaplain at St Botolph, Aldgate, he preached twice every Sunday, visited the sick, and officiated at numerous marriages, baptisms, and funerals. When a less burdensome living at the combined rectory of St Mary Aldermary and St Thomas the Apostle in the City presented itself in 1708, Kennett accepted it.

Kennett was a latitudinarian churchman who encouraged greater toleration of dissenting protestants. Although devout, he was more interested in winning souls and in church administration than he was in theology. He was also one of those churchmen who feared that irreligion, immorality, and lawlessness were on the rise. Hence he became a leader of the Society for Promoting Christian Knowledge (SPCK) and the Society for the Reformation of Manners. He joined the SPCK in 1700 and for several years thereafter attended meetings every week. He was most active during the latter years of Queen Anne's reign in nourishing relations between the SPCK and similar organizations on the continent. He did much to promote charitable giving for the Palatine refugees in 1709 and to defend their cause. The SPCK's project that elicited Kennett's most ardent support was the charity school movement. He promoted the growth of charity schools in Aldgate and wrote a pamphlet for the students there, *The Christian Scholar* (1708), that was adopted by the society for schools elsewhere; it reached its twentieth edition in 1811. Kennett's anti-Catholic views can be seen here as well: 'Every Charity-School is as it were a Fortress and a Frontier Garrison against Popery' (Bennett, *White Kennett*, 190).

Kennett was in 1701 among the first members of the Society for the Propagation of the Gospel in Foreign Parts and of its governing standing committee. His book *An Account of the Society for Propagating the Gospel in Foreign Parts* (1706) related the early history of the society and argued that the American colonies should have a suffragan bishop. He attended meetings of the society regularly even after becoming a bishop, occasionally serving as its vice-president.

As archdeacon of Huntington, Lincolnshire, from 1701 to 1720, and dean of Peterborough from 1708 to 1718, Kennett was a highly conscientious and meticulous administrator. He took it as his mandate to further the 'Apostolical Cause of having All Things done decently and in order' (Bennett, *White Kennett*, 196). He upbraided clergy for their slovenly appearance, closely monitored the financial accounts of his archdeaconry and cathedral, hectored churchwardens to keep their churches in good repair, laid down a code of conduct for all employees of the cathedral church, and imposed fines on those who breached regulations.

Kennett brought his passion for order and discipline to the see of Peterborough, which had been neglected by his predecessor. He complained in 1723 that the clergy of the cathedral church were 'most idle' and that the buildings were in disrepair (Bennett, *White Kennett*, 235). He took it upon himself to see that the cathedral prebends performed their duties faithfully. He had to deal with insubordination by the new dean, Richard Reynolds, and misconduct by the registrar, Thomas Cumberland, whom he dismissed. He undertook three episcopal visitations and several additional tours to confirm lay people. He presided over forty-four ordinations—a higher rate than most bishops—and made every effort to select qualified priests.

Kennett's indefatigable devotion to the church testifies to his boundless energy and to his strong sense of moral purpose. He had firm convictions and harboured few doubts about his personal worth. He was outspoken, combative, and tactless—traits that hindered his career. But he was also empathetic, generous, and not without charm; he had close, lasting friendships, and good working relationships with colleagues and associates.

Final years and death Personal troubles clouded Kennett's last years. He felt pained and humiliated when he found out that his daughter, Sarah, had formed a relationship with his coachman, John Newman. She became pregnant, and in December 1721 clandestinely married Newman. The marriage lasted, and father and daughter were eventually reconciled. Kennett's will designated that she receive half of his money.

Having been unwell for months, White Kennett died on 19 December 1728 of an undisclosed illness at his St James Street town house in Westminster. He was survived by his wife, who died on 9 July 1743. He was buried behind the high altar at the cathedral in Peterborough, where a marble monument was erected in his honour. He bequeathed over 1500 books printed before 1641 to the Peterborough Cathedral Library; they are now on deposit at Cambridge University Library. LAIRD OKIE

Sources G. V. Bennett, *White Kennett, 1660–1728, bishop of Peterborough* (1957) · L. Okie, *Augustan historical writing: histories of England in the English Enlightenment* (1991) · G. V. Bennett, 'Robert Harley, the Godolphin ministry, and the bishoprics crisis of 1707', *EngHR*, 82

(1967), 726–46 · W. Newton, *The life of the right reverend Dr White Kennett, late lord bishop of Peterborough* (1730) · *DNB*
Archives BL, papers and MS collections, Lansdowne MSS 935–1041 · Bodl. Oxf., antiquarian notes · Bodl. Oxf., commonplace book · CUL, extracts from collections in Lansdowne MSS · CUL, historical collections · CUL, transcript of notes | Bodl. Oxf., letters to Arthur Charlett · Bodl. Oxf., corresp. with Humphrey Prideaux and Thomas Tanner · Bodl. Oxf., letters to Anthony Wood · Christ Church Oxf., Wake MSS · LPL, Gibson MSS, Tenison MSS
Likenesses J. Faber senior, mezzotint, 1719, BM, NPG [see illus.] · J. Fittler, engraving, 1818 (after portrait), repro. in Bennett, *White Kennett*

Kenney, Annie (1879–1953), suffragette, was born prematurely on 13 September 1879 in Springhead, Lancashire, the daughter and fifth in a family of eight girls and four boys of Horatio Nelson Kenney and his wife, Ann Wood (d. 1905). Horatio Kenney, a cotton minder at Grotten Hollow spinning mill, was kindly and scrupulously honest, but mismanaged money and occasionally drank too much. He exhibited birds and animals at shows, and his son Rowland (1882–1961) recalled that 'small livestock were … part of the blood and bone of my childhood's existence' (R. Kenney, 4). The Kenneys moved between mill villages seeking space for their children and livestock, and at eighteen Annie Kenney had lived in at least five houses, the last of which was the large and impressive Whams House, Hey. Her mother could not sign her name on Annie's birth certificate, but hers was the strong character in the family. She was a saintly woman, with a strong sense of humour, self-respecting and a strict parent: the Kenney children were packed off early to bed. 'To my mother I owe all that I have ever been, or ever done that has called upon courage of loyalty for its support', Annie Kenney recalled (A. Kenney, 26).

Becoming a suffragette: 1879–1905 Educated in village and Sunday schools, and confirmed at seventeen despite religious doubts, Annie Kenney had begun work on her tenth birthday in 1889 as a half-timer at Henry Atherton & Sons' textile mill, Springhead, and for three years worked from 6 a.m. to 12.30 p.m. At thirteen she left school and from then until twenty-six she worked full-time as a card and blowing room operator from 6 a.m. to 5.30 p.m. The 1901 census found her living at 1 Whams in Springhead with her parents, her brothers Reginald (commercial traveller), Rowland (general labourer), Herbert and Harold (aged twelve and ten respectively), and her sisters Jessie (reeler), and Alice and Jane (both described like Annie as card room hand). Annie Kenney disliked her later propagandist label 'the suffragette mill girl' because her home had been respectable, and it was only unexpected poverty that had driven her temporarily into factory work. Two of her sisters became Montessori teachers, another sister a school secretary, Rowland an author, and another brother a respected Manchester businessman.

Robert Blatchford ('our literary father and mother', A. Kenney, 23), co-founder of the socialist weekly *Clarion*, drew Annie Kenney towards socialism. Yet Blatchford, no feminist, offered no remedy for the fact that she was paid less than the boys and was exposed to higher risk: a whirling bobbin severed a finger. Jane Ogden, a fellow singer in

Annie Kenney (1879–1953), by unknown photographer, 1906

the Oldham Clarion Vocal Club, was on Oldham Trades Council, and invited her to hear the council being addressed on women's suffrage by Teresa Billington and Christabel Pankhurst, Emmeline Pankhurst's eldest daughter. Billington, Kenney recalled, 'used a sledge-hammer of logic and cold reason … I liked Christabel Pankhurst: I was afraid of Theresa Billington' (ibid., 27); yet Kenney was at first more devoted to Billington, more admiring of her speaking style, than her memoirs revealed. None the less Christabel Pankhurst soon became Kenney's heroine; she was perhaps a mother substitute, given that Kenney's mother had died a few months before. With her passionate, impulsive nature, her fair hair, and intense blue eyes Kenney conveyed a misleadingly vulnerable image. Her speaking and organizing talents soon attracted attention, and with her three younger sisters she became active in the Women's Social and Political Union (WSPU). She began regularly visiting the Pankhursts' Manchester home, and with their encouragement she stood for election to the textile union committee, became its first woman member, and began (but did not complete) a correspondence course at Ruskin College, Oxford.

A life in the Women's Social and Political Union: 1905–1918
Manchester's Free Trade Hall on 13 October 1905 saw suffragette militancy launched with the historic moment when Annie Kenney (speaking first) and Christabel Pankhurst interrupted a political meeting. They repeatedly asked Sir Edward Grey and the Liberal candidate Winston Churchill whether they would, if elected, make women's suffrage a government measure. Receiving no answer, they unfurled a flag inscribed 'Votes for women', were driven from their seats by Liberal stewards, and next day were found guilty of obstruction. Refusing to defend themselves or pay their fines, they went to prison, Pankhurst receiving a week and Kenney three days. On 21 December 1905 Kenney was ejected from a Liberal rally at the Albert Hall, London, after asking a similar question, and participated in Keir Hardie's successful election campaign.

After the Liberals had won the general election of 1906 the Pankhursts sent Kenney to reinforce the WSPU's growing support in London. When H. H. Asquith refused to receive a deputation, Kenney and women from the East End persistently rang his doorbell, and she received two months in Holloway prison. The shift in the WSPU's centre of gravity to London from its Lancashire working-class and socialist roots marginalized leading Lancashire WSPU pioneers, some of whom angrily seceded into the Women's Freedom League in 1907. Kenney, by contrast, clung ever more tightly to the Pankhursts and the union—not only seeking a substitute for the family fragmented by her mother's death, but also gaining an income as paid organizer. To the Pankhursts she was increasingly valuable as a symbol of working-class support for militancy, especially as so many more working-class women backed the adult suffragists and the non-militant female suffragists. Painful as she found the WSPU's splits of 1907 and 1912, Kenney remained loyal to Christabel Pankhurst in both.

So, uniquely among working women, Kenney witnessed the WSPU's innermost counsels. Yet she did not directly influence policy: 'to put me on a committee', she recalled, 'was like putting a doll or a dummy there. I had never any suggestions to offer or any ideas to contribute' (A. Kenney, 72). Her value lay in her simplistic contempt for the political process and in her total and almost mystical devotion to Christabel Pankhurst. Together these lent Kenney great courage and determination; hers was, as she later recalled, 'exactly the faith of a child'. An autocracy 'suits my conservative, liberty-loving nature', she wrote; 'I either like to be told what to do, provided I have a deep admiration and profound respect for the one advising me, or I like to be left absolutely alone to act in my own way' (ibid., vi, 73). Pankhurst treated Kenney almost as an instrument, with little sign of tenderness, and Kenney suppressed her private doubts about militancy, especially in its later stages, saying in 1911 that she 'would go through fire for Christabel' (Rosen, 156). To her critics Kenney was 'just a blotter for Christabel', so in letters to her she jokingly signed herself 'the Blotter' (Pankhurst, 245).

Kenney became the right-hand woman of the WSPU's top leadership whenever action was required: protests at meetings, forthright challenges to authority at deputations, drumming up support for the WSPU in the west of

England, overseas missions, election campaigning. Furthermore, her artless appeals could captivate the influential. Emmeline Pethick-Lawrence recalled how Kenney:

> burst in upon me one day in her rather breathless way and threw all my barriers down. I might have been a life-long friend by the complete trust in me that she showed … There was something about Annie that touched my heart. She was very simple and she seemed to have a whole-hearted faith in the goodness of everybody that she met. (Pethick-Lawrence, 147)

This intense emotional attraction between the two women at first frightened Billington as 'something unbalanced and primitive and possibly dangerous to the movement' (Pugh, 149), but it gradually moderated into a friendly working relationship. Kenney also helped produce a second crucial conversion, that of Lady Constance Lytton, whose aristocratic support complemented Kenney's at the opposite social extreme. Gender could be advertised as taking precedence over social class in women's loyalties; walking arm in arm with Lytton at Littlehampton in late summer 1908, Kenney impressed her with a remark made 'in a tone of utmost conviction' that she had 'never known class distinction and class prejudice stand in the way of my advancement, whereas the sex barrier meets me at every turn' (Lytton, 11).

From 1912 Kenney travelled regularly in disguise for more than a year between the movement in London and its leader Christabel Pankhurst, self-exiled in Paris. Kenney was crucial in holding the WSPU together. 'I knew from experience that Annie was the person to hold the fort at headquarters', Pankhurst recalled. 'She had no personal ties that would impose upon her a divided duty', and 'she had earned by her own record … as a militant pioneer the honour of being first in command' (Pankhurst, 208). Often seasick and increasingly exhausted, Kenney did all that was asked of her. In June 1913, after demonstrating at the Albert Hall and from the Ladies' Gallery of the House of Commons, she was given eighteen months in prison, during which she went on hunger strike. There followed a debilitating sequence of arrest and release under the 'Cat and Mouse Act' (1913), involving the repeated adoption of disguises, unexpected appearances at public meetings on a stretcher, and appeals for sanctuary at Lambeth to an embarrassed archbishop of Canterbury.

Nor did Kenney's Pankhurstian loyalties cease in 1914. At the outbreak of war the Pankhursts sent her on an American speaking tour to promote militant suffragism, then brought her back for war work which included encouraging women into making munitions for Lloyd George, outwitting Bolshevik influence on British workers, and visiting Australia in the vain hope of persuading prime minister William Hughes to return to Britain. Then in 1918 she campaigned for Christabel Pankhurst, candidate at Smethwick for the Women's Party, of which Kenney became secretary. But Kenney recalled that thereafter 'I could work no longer. I was exhausted to death, my nervous system called for rest and recuperation' (A. Kenney, 288), and after a long talk with Pankhurst she at last secured her release.

Married life and aftermath: 1918–1953 Annie Kenney's half-entry into public life from 1905 to 1918 thereafter trailed away into a long anti-climactic afterglow. When holidaying in Scotland in 1918 she met James Taylor (1892/3–1974), an engineer, and was drawn towards him by their shared love of singing. They were married on 21 April 1920 at Lytham St Anne's by special licence, he being twenty-seven and she forty. Their son Warwick (named after Shakespeare's Warwick the Kingmaker) was born on 4 February 1921, and took the surname Kenney-Taylor. To his education she devoted enormous care, and her interests focused increasingly on theosophy and the Rosicrucian order. The suffragette and theosophist Clara Codd had been among her most active helpers in the west of England in 1907–8, but Christabel Pankhurst had discouraged Kenney from taking this distracting road—this being 'the one time Christabel grew stern with me' (A. Kenney, 127). Theosophist friends now, however, encouraged the Taylors to settle in Letchworth. There James Taylor got a job as a plumber's mate, and later became an instructor in a government training centre for the unemployed. Ann Taylor, as she had now become—a good cook, fond of music, and sociable—was often visited by her sister Jessie (also in the Rosicrucian order, and a stewardess on the Orient Line), but took no part in local community life. After a long decline Ann Taylor died of diabetes in the Lister Hospital, Hitchin, on 9 July 1953. Her husband lived on in Letchworth, and their son Warwick became a director in a steel firm, Richards and Wallington Ltd, in London.

Among suffragette autobiographies, Kenney's memoirs (1924) were preceded only by Emmeline Pankhurst's (1914). Bound in suffragette colours, they had been 'written under *very* difficult conditions', Kenney recalled; 'some of the best parts were written on a high road in Sussex while I was taking Warwick, as a baby, out for an airing' (Museum of London, David Mitchell collection, 73.83/34: Kenney to C. Pankhurst, endorsed *c.*1942). Drawing more on memory than on documents, they were 'the imperishable record of my own soul' (A. Kenney, 136). They reflect her crusading, apolitical approach to public policy; still star-struck with Christabel, they swallow her tactics whole, and focus largely on daring japes and escapades. Nowhere does Kenney consider the case for party-aligned, adult suffragist, or non-militant options, let alone the objection that her brother Rowland raised in his memoirs: for him, the suffragettes were 'robbing the Socialist movement of its finest elements and wasting them in a fight for the vote, which was of little or no use compared with industrial solidarity and the making of Socialist converts' (R. Kenney, 137). His memoirs mention his sister only twice, and in one of these two instances he expresses resentment at being labelled 'Annie's brother'; he thought she was being exploited as 'a splendid marketable commodity' (Mitchell, *Queen Christabel*, 214). None the less Annie Kenney's memoirs, for all their mysticism and political naïvety, vividly describe how the WSPU and its personalities seemed to a dedicated and strategically placed subordinate. In a letter of 1943 to Christabel Pankhurst, adulatory as usual, Kenney none the less contrasted her memoirs with what could be written 'by *you*, the author and inspirer of the very movement itself' (Mitchell, *The Fighting Pankhursts*, 302). WSPU history must, she thought, be wrested from the sole guardianship of Christabel's younger sister Sylvia, whose published portrait of Kenney had been less than flattering.

Kenney's wider significance depends partly on how far militant tactics are credited with delivering votes for women. To see her as 'after the Pankhursts … the most daring and influential of the Suffragettes' (Liddington, 13) inflates her importance, which is threefold. First, her devotion to Christabel Pankhurst paradoxically nourished autocracy within a movement whose aims were democratic. Second, her role was crucial in recruiting for militancy its two most effective organizers, the Pethick-Lawrences. Third, there was her symbolic role. She resembled Lady Constance Lytton, whose aristocratic backing for militancy she did much to secure, in advertising how the loyalties of social class could give way to those of gender. When the point needed advertising, she would don her mill girl's shawl and clogs and demonstrate the fact in her own person.   BRIAN HARRISON

Sources T. Billington-Greig, *Calling All Women* (Feb 1954), 4 · A. Kenney, *Memories of a militant* (1924) · R. Kenney, *Westering* (1939) · J. Liddington, 'Who was Annie Kenney?', *Spare Rib*, 36 (June 1975), 13–14 · C. Lytton, *Prisons and prisoners: some personal experiences* (1914) · D. Mitchell, *The fighting Pankhursts: a study in tenacity* (1967) · D. Mitchell, *Queen Christabel: a biography of Christabel Pankhurst* (1977) · typescript copy of letter from Kenney to Christabel Pankhurst, endorsed, *c*.1942, Museum of London, David Mitchell collection, 73.83/34 · C. Pankhurst, *Unshackled: the story of how we won the vote* (1959) · E. Pethick-Lawrence, *My part in a changing world* (1938) · M. Pugh, *The Pankhursts* (2001) · A. Rosen, *Rise up, women! The militant campaign of the Women's Social and Political Union, 1903–1914* (1974) · private information (2004) [James Taylor] · b. cert. · m. cert. · d. cert.
Archives University of East Anglia, Norwich, corresp. and papers |FILM BL NSA, 'Shoulder to shoulder', BBC 2, 10 April 1974
Likenesses photograph, 1906, Women's Library, London [*see illus.*] · photographs, Women's Library, London · portrait, repro. in Kenney, *Memories*, frontispiece

Kenney, Arthur Henry (1776/7–1855), Church of Ireland dean of Achonry and religious writer, was the youngest son of Edward Kenney (*d.* 23 April 1818), vicar-choral and prebendary of Cork, and Frances, daughter of Thomas Herbert MP, of Muckross, co. Kerry. In 1790 he entered Trinity College, Dublin, where he was elected a foundation scholar in 1793, and graduated BA in 1795. In 1800 he proceeded to an MA, and was a junior fellow, a post which he left in 1809 to take up the college living of Kilmacrenan, Donegal. He became BD in 1806, and DD in 1812.

On 27 June 1812 Kenney was made dean of Achonry, a post which enabled him to publish *An enquiry concerning some of the doctrines maintained by the Church of Rome: in answer to the charge of intolerance brought by members of that church against members of the Church of England* (1818), and *Principles and Practices of Pretended Reformers in Church and State* (1819). He resigned as dean in May 1821 in order to take up a new appointment as rector of St Olave, Southwark. Here he was popular with his parishioners and,

under the initials A. H. K., edited a fifth edition of Archbishop Magee's *Discourses on the Scriptural Doctrines of Atonement and Sacrifice* (1832) as well as a memoir of Magee, which served as an introduction to the archbishop's *Works* in eight volumes (1842). Under his own name he also published *Documents illustrative of the history of the period immediately preceding the accession of William III* (1827), *The dangerous nature of popish power in these countries, especially as illustrated from awful records of the time of James the Second* (1839), and *A comment, explanatory and practical, on the epistles and gospels for the Sundays of the year, and on those for holy days immediately relating to our Blessed Saviour* (1842). St Olave's eventually got into financial trouble and the post was abolished. He then went to live abroad for the last ten years of his life, dying in Boulogne on 27 January 1855. He was twice married, and had a son and daughter with his first wife; the son was the Revd Arthur Robert Kenney, rector of Bourton-on-Dunsmore, Warwickshire. He also had several sons and one daughter with his second wife.

GORDON GOODWIN, *rev.* DAVID HUDDLESTON

Sources GM, 2nd ser., 44 (1855), 544 · W. B. S. Taylor, *History of the University of Dublin* (1845), 445, 490 · H. Cotton, *Fasti ecclesiae Hibernicae*, 1 (1845), 221 · H. Cotton, *Fasti ecclesiae Hibernicae*, 4 (1850), 105 · Burke, *Gen. GB* (1868) · [J. H. Todd], ed., *A catalogue of graduates who have proceeded to degrees in the University of Dublin, from the earliest recorded commencements to … December 16, 1868* (1869), 317 · *BL cat.*, 173.40 · J. B. Leslie, *Raphoe clergy and parishes* (1940), 97 · Burtchaell & Sadleir, *Alum. Dubl.*
Archives BL, corresp. with Sir Robert Peel, Add. MSS 40261–40526

Kenney, Charles Lamb (1821–1881), author and playwright, was born at Bellevue, France, on 29 April 1821, the last son of the Irish-born playwright James *Kenney (1780–1849) and his wife, Louisa, *née* Mercier (*c*.1780–1853), the widow of the playwright and novelist Thomas Holcroft. He was named after his godfather, the well-known author Charles Lamb, and, according to his acerbic rival in the theatre Sir Francis Burnand, the name 'did a great deal for him' in a public and literary life in which he moved in the most lofty of circles.

Kenney was educated at London's Merchant Taylors' School and in his early working days went through a variety of jobs: as a clerk in the Post Office, as a playreader for Covent Garden Theatre, as an all-purpose reporter and critic for *The Times*, as publicity man for the Great Exhibition (1851), as secretary, first to Sir Joseph Paxton during the Crimean War (1855) and then to Ferdinand de Lesseps in the early days of the Suez Canal project (1856), and latterly as a journalist again, this time on *The Standard*.

Throughout this time Kenney also wrote—or, more accurately, for the most part translated and/or adapted—a number of works, both for the printed page (*Fairy Tales and Romances*, 1849; *Travels in Southern Russia*, 1853) and for the theatre. While still in his early twenties he had a hand in some of the extravaganzas written by Albert Smith and Tom Taylor for the Keeleys at the Lyceum. He also further adapted Nathaniel Thomas Haynes Bayly's adaptation of a French play as *The Spitalfields Weaver*, in which the comic actor Johnnie Toole made his stage début under the Keeleys at the Haymarket in 1852, and which remained a perennial in Toole's repertory for many years. In 1859 Kenney married Rosa Stewart in Paris, and in the same year, with Sutherland Edwards, he provided the St James's Theatre with a burlesque of the Brothers Grimm's Swan Lake tale, *The Swan and Edgar*.

It was another adaptation from the French, however, which gave the multilingual Kenney his most significant success. The English Opera at the Theatre Royal, Covent Garden, had been struggling since the retirement of its famous managers Louisa Pyne and William Harrison, and in October 1864 a limited company fronted by the former concert promoter John Russell took over its management. Russell commissioned adaptations of Charles Gounod's *Le médecin malgré lui* and Jacques Meyerbeer's latest hit *L'Africaine* from Kenney before the limited company went under, at which stage Russell took over the theatre with an ambitious project of his own: the first faithfully adapted English version of a full-sized *opéra bouffe* by Offenbach to be produced in Britain. He entrusted the adaptation of *La grande-duchesse* to Kenney. Russell's production proved a landmark, *opéra bouffe* became the rage of the English and American stage for a decade, and productions of Kenney's highly praised version of *La grande-duchesse* were seen throughout the English-singing world for many years.

Kenney subsequently adapted Offenbach's *Barbe-Bleue* for Russell, *La princesse de Trébizonde* and *La belle Hélène* for John Hollingshead at the Gaiety, Emil Jonas's zany *Le canard à trois becs* for E. P. Hingston at the Opera Comique, and Offenbach's *La jolie parfumeuse* for Russell's erstwhile prima donna, Emily Soldene. At the same time he continued to turn out English versions of French and Italian operas, adding to his list between 1871 and 1875 *Don Pasquale*, *La fille du régiment*, *Lucia di Lammermoor*, *Le nozze di Figaro*, *Un ballo in maschera*, *La muette de Portici*, *La favorita*, *Semiramide*, *Le domino noir*, *Ali Baba*, and *L'elisir d'amore*. He also translated the text to Verdi's Requiem into English. Among his other stage works were an English edition of Léo Délibes' little *opérette Six demoiselles à marier* for Drury Lane, where it was produced with Lydia Thompson in the principal role in March 1867. He revised and modernized one of the old Keeley extravaganzas as a pantomime, *Valentine and Orson, or, Harlequin the Big Bear and the Little Fairy* (music by George Richardson), for Sefton Parry at the Holborn Theatre at Christmas 1867. Kenney's short farcical sketch 'with musical finale' entitled *Our Autumn Manoeuvres* played as a curtain-raiser to Andrew Halliday's long-running adaptation of *Les misérables* at the Adelphi in 1871, with Henry Ashley and Mrs Alfred Mellon featured, and his comedietta *Maids of Honour* was produced by Horace Wigan at the Mirror Theatre in April 1875 with Fred Irish as the attraction.

Kenney was never an enthusiastic worker—Burnand described him as 'epigrammatically brilliant and invariably, because constitutionally, lazy' (Burnand, 2.245)—and the onset of what would be his final illness meant that he produced little in the last five years of his life. By June 1877 he was in such straits that Lord Dunraven, Tom Taylor, and Lord Londesborough organized a benefit matinée on his behalf: Henry Kemble, Henry Neville, Charles Santley, Johnston Forbes Robertson, Henry Irving, Ellen Terry (in her London début), Sims Reeves, Mrs Alfred Mellon, and Mrs Henry Leigh featured in *A School for Scandal* to a packed house at the Gaiety.

Latterly Kenney contributed spasmodically to magazines such as *The Musical World* and published a translation, *The Correspondence of H. de Balzac* (1878), but he spent his final years as an invalid. He died at his home in Eldon Road, Kensington, on 25 August 1881, and was buried in the family grave at Brompton cemetery on 30 August. His two children, Charles Horace Kenney (1857?–1909) and Rosa A. Kenney (1860?–1905), both had careers on the stage.   KURT GÄNZL

Sources K. Gänzl, *The encyclopedia of the musical theatre*, 2 vols. (1994) • F. C. Burnand, *Records and reminiscences, personal and general*, 2 vols. (1904) • *The Era* (3 Sept 1881), 6 • *DNB*

Kenney, James (1780–1849), playwright, was born in Ireland, the son of James Kenney (*fl.* 1760–1800), well known in English sporting circles. Nothing is known of his childhood or education, but his father was for many years manager of Boodle's Club in St James's Street, London, and it was presumably he who placed Kenney in the London banking house of Herries, Farquhar & Co. Despite a diffidence which, in later life, exhibited itself as a nervous inability to make up his mind on even the most trivial issues, Kenney declared his literary ambitions in 1803 by publishing *Society, a Poem in Two Parts, with other Poems*, which made little impact.

Kenney persisted, however, and the production at Covent Garden on 5 November 1803 of his first play, *Raising the Wind*, made his reputation. It remains his strongest claim to a place in dramatic history, above all for its creation of the charming confidence trickster Jeremy Diddler. Before submitting the play to Covent Garden, Kenney had played Jeremy Diddler in an amateur performance, but it was the ageing William 'Gentleman' Lewis who made the part, and the play, famous. *Raising the Wind* ran for thirty-eight nights in its first season, and its success enabled Kenney to abandon the safety of the bank for the danger of a playwright's career. He was already well enough acquainted with the London theatres to have shaped his first play according to the strengths of the Covent Garden company. Not only did Jeremy Diddler slot in to Lewis's line in lounge lizards, but there was also a shrewdly comic Yorkshire servant for the popular tyke John Emery and a female grotesque for Mrs Davenport.

It was by providing such custom-built plays for actors, singers, and theatre managers that Kenney sought to sustain his forty-year career in London. His name is linked to more than fifty pieces, and he had a hand in many others. *Raising the Wind* was followed by three musical pieces, comic operas in the style of the day, with music by Matthew Peter King. The third of these, a comic opera in three acts called *False Alarms*, opened at Drury Lane on 12 January 1807 and ran for twenty-one nights. Its popularity was enhanced by the contribution of the singer–composer John Braham, and in particular by Braham's setting of Kenney's sentimental ballad, 'Said a Smile to a Tear'. When the taste for melodrama declared itself, Kenney supplied Drury Lane with *Ella Rosenberg*, an early example of domestic Gothic, which opened on 19 November 1807 with Mrs Siddons in the title role. On 31 March 1808 the same theatre staged his first comedy, *The World*, which ran for twenty-three nights. 'Ah! where is Kenney's wit?', asked Byron a year later in *English Bards and Scotch Reviewers*, complaining that *The World* 'tires the sad gallery, lulls the listless Pit'. Byron was not alone in perceiving in the play's popularity evidence of the destitution of contemporary comedy, but Kenney made no attempt to answer his critics. He was much liked for his good humour, and for his unwillingness to join in malicious gossip. J. R. Planché, who could not remember Kenney's 'saying a severe thing of or to anyone', recalled an occasion when his nervous friend, startled by a sudden noise, exclaimed, 'Is—*Heaven* broke loose?' (Planché, 1.125–6).

Accepted into literary circles after the success of *The World*, Kenney was a regular guest of Samuel Rogers, and numbered Charles Lamb among his close friends. By 1812 he had become prosperous enough to marry, but not, perhaps, to marry as he did. Louisa Mercier (*c*.1780–1853) had become the fourth wife of the playwright-novelist Thomas Holcroft in April 1799. When Holcroft died in March 1809, Louisa was left in sole charge of their twin daughters and of two daughters from Holcroft's third marriage. She and Kenney were married on 5 March 1812, and had four further children, of whom Charles Lamb *Kenney (1821–1881) is the best-known. The struggle to maintain his extended family was a given circumstance for the rest of Kenney's working life. He continued to write in a variety of dramatic genres, ranging from tragedy (*The Pledge* of 1831 was a version of Hugo's *Hernani* and *The Sicilian Vespers* of 1840 an adaptation of a play by Casimir Delavigne) to burlesque (*Aladdin* at the Lyceum in 1844), but his greatest successes, in association with the actor John Liston, were in farce. *Love, Law and Physic*, which opened at Covent Garden on 20 November 1812, provided Liston with the first, and most enduring, of a string of lower middle-class cockney roles, Lubin Log. It was followed, in 1814, by *Debtor and Creditor*, with Liston as Gosling. The partnership was renewed at the Haymarket on 7 July 1823, when Liston created the lovelorn cockney waiter Billy Lackaday in Kenney's *Sweethearts and Wives*, and continued at Drury Lane, where Liston played Knipper Clipper in *Thirteen to the Dozen* (1826) and the shipwrecked cockney Bowbell in Kenney's unfairly neglected *The Illustrious Stranger*, which opened on 4 October 1827.

At about this time, Kenney was briefly associated with Elliston in the management of Drury Lane, but his nervous disposition was unequal to the strain of theatrical in-fighting. His appearance was so affected by his anxiety that 'he was more than once taken for an escaped lunatic' (*DNB*). After his marriage to Louisa, Kenney lived for several years in St Valéry-sur-Somme, where Louisa may have plumped the family income by instructing private pupils. Kenney died of heart disease at his home, 22 South Terrace, Alexander Square, Brompton, London, on 25 July 1849. That the family was suffering financial hardship is suggested by the staging of a benefit performance at Drury Lane on the day of his death. On 13 October 1849 his widow was awarded a civil-list pension of £40 a year which passed to her dependent daughters on her death on 17 July 1853.

PETER THOMSON

Sources R. C. Leslie, *Autobiographical recollections* (1886) · J. R. Planché, *The recollections and reflections of J. R. Planché*, 2 vols. (1872) · *The letters of Charles Lamb: to which are added those of his sister, Mary Lamb*, ed. E. V. Lucas, 3 vols. (1935); rev. edn, ed. G. Pocock, 2 vols. (1945) · J. Davis, *John Liston, comedian* (1985) · A. Nicoll, *Early nineteenth century drama, 1800–1850*, 2nd edn (1955), vol. 4 of *A history of English drama, 1660–1900* (1952–9) · G. B. Cross, *Next week — East Lynne* (1977) · *Memoirs of the late Thomas Holcroft*, ed. W. Hazlitt, 3 vols. (1816) · M. W. Disher, *Blood and thunder* (1949) · *DNB* · *IGI*

Likenesses J. Heath, stipple, pubd 1809, BM, NPG · attrib. S. De Wilde, watercolour drawing (probably James Kenney), Garr. Club · S. Laurence, chalk drawing, NPG · G. S. Newton, oils, NG Ire.

Wealth at death needy: Disher, *Blood and thunder*; *Letters*, ed. Lucas

Kenney, Peter James (1779–1841), Jesuit, was born in Dublin, probably at 28 Drogheda Street, on 7 July 1779, the son of Peter Kenney (*fl. c*.1740–1810) and his wife, Ellen, *née* Molloy, who ran a small business together. Kenney's known siblings were Anne Mary, who joined the convent of the Sisters of St Clare, and an elder brother, or half-brother, Michael, who set up an apothecary shop in Waterford. Peter was apprenticed for a while to a coach-maker, and was educated in the schools run for poor children and apprentices by the former Jesuit priest Dr Thomas Betagh, in cellars and back lanes in Dublin. He was impressed by Betagh and another former Jesuit, Richard Callaghan, and this influenced his choice of career. The Jesuits had been suppressed in 1773, except in Belorussia; their continuation there was formally recognized by the papacy in 1801, which gave hope of a general restoration of the order. As a result Father Callaghan sent Kenney and some other young men to Carlow College to prepare for the priesthood. From there they were sent to Stonyhurst College in Lancashire, which was run by former English Jesuits, where they commenced their noviciate. Kenney made an impression almost immediately with his ability, sound piety, and eloquence, despite suffering from asthma. Following the recognition of the society in Sicily, Kenney was sent there in 1808 to complete his studies and for the sake of his health.

The island of Sicily was in danger of invasion by Napoleon, and depended on the British navy and British military garrison for its defence. For this reason, Kenney's ordination and that of his colleagues was brought forward: he was ordained on 4 December 1808, but remained in Sicily until 1811. It was a period of cultural and spiritual development, and his ability and general maturity so impressed the Jesuit superior that he termed him 'L'incomparable P. Kenney' (Morrissey, 64). During his time in Sicily he was chosen to act as interpreter in a

British naval expedition to rescue the pope from imprisonment by Napoleon. However, the pope refused to leave Rome. Kenney and an English Jesuit friend, Thomas Glover, also acted as chaplains to Catholic soldiers and sailors in the British force on the island, many of whom were Irish. Their efforts were terminated by the intolerance of 'Scotch generals' (ibid., 58–9). Kenney's and Glover's reports about the matter gave rise to questions in the House of Commons.

Kenney returned to Ireland on 31 August 1811 and found himself much in demand. Dr Daniel Murray, bishop of Dublin, sought his assistance at Maynooth College, the national seminary, where there were problems with morale and discipline. Under Murray as president and Kenney as vice-president, the college was transformed within a year. Kenney's sermons and spiritual meditations were written down by students and passed from hand to hand for years. In 1814 he founded Clongowes Wood College, co. Kildare, which became the leading boarding college for the middle-class Catholic population. Five years later he opened a house at Rahan, near Tullamore, in the midlands, which subsequently became St Stanislaus College, and then a small church in Dublin, which became in turn the forerunner of the large church of St Francis Xavier at Gardiner Street and of the well-known day school Belvedere College. The Jesuit order was restored universally in 1814, and Kenney was appointed superior of the Irish mission. Despite his achievements, he was considered too demanding and strict by some fellow Jesuits and was replaced after four years. His standing with the Jesuit-general, however, led to his being sent in 1819 to North America to sort out the problems of disunity among the Jesuits of different nationalities working there.

Kenney's visitation of the Jesuits, mainly in Maryland, proved successful. He brought order into the temporal administration, introduced customs and structures which promoted order and team effort, revitalized Georgetown University, and prepared for the future by approving the sending of six young men to Rome to further their studies. On his return to Ireland, he was appointed superior once more, and soon achieved further distinction as a preacher and spiritual guide. He played a prominent part in assisting many religious congregations, and was particularly close to the founders of the new religious bodies—the Irish Sisters of Charity, the Irish Christian Brothers, and the Sisters of Loreto. From 1830 to 1833 he went once more to the United States of America on behalf of the Jesuit-general, this time as superior of the entire mission, which by now had spread southward into the vast area then termed Missouri. They were years of endeavour, long journeys, periods of ill health, and eventual achievement. He helped to consolidate the universities at Georgetown and St Louis, promoted harmony and good order across the vast territory, established better management in the estates which had supported much of the early work, improved the living conditions of the slaves who worked the estates, and raised the question of managing without their forced labour. He also laid the ground for the renewal of the society's mission to the North American

Indians. As he left Maryland was raised to the status of a province of the society, and Missouri was acknowledged an independent mission. On the day of his departure, 11 July 1833, the diary for Georgetown University contains the entry: 'Never has a man lived among us whom all without exception so loved and reverenced' (Morrissey, 338). His standing with the diocesan clergy and bishops is indicated by his name's having been put forward at different times for the bishoprics of New York, Philadelphia, and Cincinnati.

When Kenney returned to Ireland, a very tired man, he was appointed once more the overall superior. This post he tried to combine with pastoral work at the Gardiner Street Church. It was too much. Owing to the constant demands from people, clergy, religious, and bishops, for confession, sermons, and spiritual direction, he neglected his reports to Rome and was unable to act adequately as provincial. He was removed from the position, much to his relief, in May 1836. His pastoral endeavours led to his being termed 'the modern apostle of Dublin' and 'to an incalculable extent, of Ireland at large' (Meagher, 93). In 1841 he was chosen by his fellow Jesuits to represent them at a general congregation of the procurators of the society at Rome in October. He set out despite very severe asthma and a strained heart. After a journey marked by rain, floods, and other hardships, he arrived at Rome exhausted, and after some days suffered a stroke. He died on 19 November, and was buried under the high altar at the Jesuit church of the Gesù in Rome. When the news reached Dublin on 3 December, large crowds mourned his passing. Kenney was one of the most eminent preachers, theologians, and spiritual directors in Ireland in the first half of the nineteenth century, and he also had very considerable influence as an educationist and through his foundations. His greatest contribution to the development of the Catholic church, however, was probably in the United States of America. Manuscript copies of his 'Meditations' have been preserved, as have parts of his American diaries.   THOMAS J. MORRISSEY

Sources T. J. Morrissey, *As one sent: Peter Kenney S. J., 1779–1841* (1996) • W. Meagher, *Notice of the life and character of His Grace Most Revd Daniel Murray* (1853) • S. A. [S. Atkinson], *Mary Aikenhead: her life, her work and her friends* (1879) • M. C. Normoyle, ed., *The correspondence of Edmund Rice and his assistants, 1810–1842* (1978) [privately printed] • R. E. Curran, ed., *Bicentennial history of Georgetown University, 1789–1889*, 1 (1993) • Irish Jesuit archives, Leeson Street, Dublin, Kenney MSS • English Jesuit archives, Farm Street, London • Stonyhurst College, Lancashire, English Jesuit archives • St Louis University archives • Vatican Film Library • Maryland province archives • Georgetown University archives • Jesuit archives, Missouri province

Archives Archives of the British Province of the Society of Jesus, Stonyhurst College, Lancashire, letters etc. • Archives of the British Province of the Society of Jesus, London, letters, etc. • Archives of the Irish Province of the Society of Jesus, Dublin, meditations, letters, and diaries • Georgetown University archives • Maryland province archives • Missouri province, Jesuit archives • Vatican Film Library, letters, etc. • Washington University, St Louis, Missouri, letters, etc.

Likenesses portrait, St Patrick's College, Maynooth, co. Kildare, Ireland • portrait, Clongowes Wood College, co. Kildare, Ireland

Kennicott, Benjamin (1718–1783), biblical scholar, was born at Totnes, Devon, on 4 April 1718 and baptized there on 20 April, the son of Benjamin Kennicott (*bap.* 1688, *d.* 1770), barber and parish clerk of Totnes, and his wife, Elizabeth Sage (*d.* 1749/50). He was educated at the town's grammar school for seven years, as a foundation boy. Apart from his books Kennicott as a youth was passionate about bellringing; he drew up regulations for the practice of the Totnes ringers in 1742 and gave a brass eight-light candlestick for the use of the ringers in the belfry. His first appointment was that of master of the blue coat, or charity, school of Totnes, where he attracted notice by some short poems, particularly 'On the Recovery of the Hon. Mrs. Eliz. Courtenay from her Late Dangerous Illness', printed in 1743 and 1747.

Academic and clerical career Subscriptions were opened to finance Kennicott's studies at Oxford, and mainly through the Courtenays of Powderham, Ralph Allen of Bath, and the Revd William Daddo, master of Blundells's School at Tiverton, he matriculated as a servitor from Wadham College, Oxford, on 6 March 1744. His undergraduate notes display a precocious familiarity with a comparative approach to scripture. He was Pigott exhibitioner in 1744 and 1745, Hody (Hebrew) exhibitioner from 1745 to 1747, and Bible clerk from 3 May 1746. In order to be eligible for a fellowship at Exeter College, as he had not resided long enough to qualify in the usual way, he was made (in accordance with the recommendation of the earl of Arran, chancellor of the university) BA, by decree, without examination, on 20 June 1747 and was duly elected to a fellowship, which he held until 1771. His subsequent degrees were MA (4 May 1750), BD (6 December 1761), and DD (10 December 1761); he was elected FRS in 1764. In politics he was loyal to the Pelhamite whigs and benefited from their patronage.

Having taken holy orders Kennicott was Whitehall preacher in 1753, vicar of Culham, Oxfordshire, from 21 September 1753 to 1783, chaplain to Bishop Robert Lowth of Oxford, in 1766, and Radcliffe librarian at Oxford from 27 November 1767 until his death. He initially discharged his librarian's duties conscientiously and helped to remedy the library's state of disrepair; he persuaded the trustees to acquire an illuminated Iberian Bible of 1476, subsequently known as 'Kennicott's Bible' and one of the Bodleian Library's greatest treasures. In July 1770 he was appointed to a canonry at Westminster Abbey but soon resigned it for the fourth stall at Christ Church, Oxford (installed 1 November 1770). On 3 January 1771 Kennicott married Ann (*d.* 1831), sister of Edward Chamberlayne (*d.* 1781), later secretary of the Treasury, and sister-in-law of William Hayward Roberts, provost of Eton College. From 1771 to 1781 Kennicott held the vicarage of Menheniot, Cornwall, which was given to him as a fellow of Exeter College by the dean and chapter of Exeter on the recommendation of Bishop Lowth. He conscientiously resigned this preferment in 1781 because of his inability to reside in the parish. He was also a member of the Royal Society of Science at Göttingen, the Theodore-Palatine academy at

Benjamin Kennicott (1718–1783), by unknown artist

Mannheim, and the Royal Academy of Inscriptions at Paris.

Hebrew scholar Kennicott was instructed in Hebrew by Professor Thomas Hunt, and the greater part of his life was spent in the collation of Hebrew manuscripts with the object of producing a definitive original text of the Old Testament. Robert Lowth, always his major patron, first inspired him with a desire to test the accuracy of the Hebrew text of the Old Testament. With his formidable knowledge of Syriac, early Latin, the Septuagint, and the Samaritan Pentateuch it was recognized that he was very well qualified for the task. His critical examination of manuscripts, initially in the British Museum and the libraries of Oxford and Cambridge, began in 1751, and when Thomas Secker, then bishop of Oxford (and also a member of Exeter College), urged him in March 1758 to undertake their collation he agreed to the request. In return Secker, when archbishop of Canterbury, gave Kennicott his unstinting support and friendship when for a time he nurtured a project for producing a revised Authorized Version of the Bible. Meanwhile in 1753 Kennicott issued *The State of the Printed Hebrew Text of the Old Testament Considered: a Dissertation*, and in 1759 he brought out a second dissertation on the same subject. He identified his object thus:

to compare Scripture with itself, to explain a difficult phrase or passage by a clear one, that bears some relation to it, to consider the natural force of the Original Words, the tendency of the Context, and the Design of the Writer; to compare the most ancient editions of the Original, with one another, and with the best copies of the most celebrated versions. (vol. 1, p. 12)

These volumes were translated into Latin by W. A. Teller

and published at Leipzig, the first in 1756, the second with additions in 1765.

Kennicott's scholarly endeavours attracted support in Britain and beyond. In England subscriptions amounted to £9119 7s. 6d.; in France the duc de Nivernois (a former French ambassador to the court of St James) patronized him and helped him to gain access to Parisian manuscript collections in 1767; the king of Denmark offered him the use of six ancient manuscripts; four quarto volumes of variant readings were sent to him on the king of Sardinia's orders; and the stadholder of the Netherlands made an annual donation of 30 guineas. His first report, *On the Collation of the Hebrew Manuscripts of the Old Testament*, was forwarded to the subscribers in December 1760 and a similar statement appeared each year until 1769. This annual summary afforded him an opportunity to defend the accuracy of his own collations, the Hebraic scholarship of the staff assisting him, and to print lists of subscribers.

Kennicott's labours culminated in the production of his *Vetus Testamentum Hebraicum cum variis lectionibus*, the first volume published at Oxford in 1776, the second in 1780. These were two superb folios complete with parallel Samaritan and Hebrew texts and *apparatus criticus*. To the second volume was annexed *Dissertatio generalis*, on the manuscripts of the Old Testament, which was published separately at Oxford in the same year and reprinted at Brunswick in 1783 by Paul Jacob Bruns, a native of Lübeck, who had been employed by Kennicott in collating manuscripts on the continent. A copy of the entire work was personally presented by Kennicott to George III. Lowth called the 1776 variorum Old Testament 'a work the greatest and most important that has been undertaken and accomplished since the Revolution of Letters' (Hepworth, 145).

Reception of *Vetus Testamentum Hebraicum cum variis lectionibus* Kennicott's second volume, of 1780, concluded that 'none of the variants was a threat to essential doctrine or increase[d] historical knowledge', but none the less his biblical scholarship provoked appreciable controversy. Though he took pains to deny it, his work seemed like a dire threat to the familiar Authorized Version. The first exchanges followed on from publication in 1753 of *The State of the Printed Hebrew Text*. Fowler Comings at once replied with *The printed Hebrew text of the Old Testament vindicated: an answer to Mr Kennicott's dissertation* (1753) and Julius Bate issued *The integrity of the Hebrew text and many passages of scripture vindicated from the objections and misconstructions of Mr Kennicott* (1754). Bate's involvement as a leading Hutchinsonian was indicative of that grouping's concern that the work undertaken by Kennicott ('the English Ezra', as he called him) was destabilizing a time-honoured text with the unintended consequence of fostering unbelief. Kennicott responded anonymously with the pamphlet *A word to the Hutchinsonians, or, Remarks on three extraordinary sermons lately preached before the University of Oxford* (1756), which disparaged contemporary Hutchinsonian politics and refused to take their scholarly endeavours seriously. This work in turn prompted a

defence and counter-attack by George Horne, then a don at University College. Thomas Rutherforth, regius professor of divinity at Cambridge, was also drawn in, producing a pamphlet on the second *Dissertation* (1761), in which he backed a recommendation that senate in Cambridge should support Kennicott's work, yet refrained from retracting earlier claims that the project was 'in many instances injudicious and inaccurate'.

Controversies were also generated on the other side of the channel. In 1771 there appeared *Lettres de M. l'Abbé de — ex-professeur en Hébreu … au Sr Kennicott*, purporting to have been printed at Rome and sold in Paris, and an English translation was produced by William Stevens in 1772. It treated Kennicott and his project with learned disdain and made a particular charge that he had much underestimated the Jewish role in preserving and transmitting the text. It lambasted the imaginary corrections, describing them as 'follies, ignorant productions, omissions … which only deserve contempt and derision' (p. 147). In reply there appeared (possibly by Kennicott himself) *A letter to a friend occasioned by a French pamphlet lately published against Doctor Kennicott etc.* (1772), stating that the *Lettres de M. l'Abbé de —* were the composition of Capuchins in the convent of St Honoré, Paris. It is more likely to have been written by Ignatius Adophus Dumay, Jewish by birth, who had been for four years chief collator to Kennicott and who also produced a powerful manuscript critique of his former employer's project, particularly the quality of the assistance that he had received. Bruns published at Rome in 1782 a Latin version of *A letter to a friend* and added some correspondence of his own. In Italy there appeared a censure upon Kennicott's letters in *Des titres primitifs de la revelation par Gabr. Fabricy, Romae* (2 vols., 1772). Kennicott remained largely aloof from these assaults. Sure of his patrons and his enterprise, he clearly did not feel either would be adversely affected by silence on his part, and he relied on replies by followers and admirers.

Many of Kennicott's chief opponents were Germans, notably J. D. Michaelis, whose *Bibliotheca orientalis* (pt 11) contained a severe criticism of his first volume on the grounds that he too easily disregarded vowel points and accents and had an unfortunate predilection for facilitating readings. Kennicott sent out a long Latin epistle to Michaelis (Oxford, 1777; reprinted Leipzig, 1777) inserted into the twelfth part of the *Bibliotheca orientalis*. After publication of his second volume Kennicott drew up a brief defence in Latin, *Contra ephemeridum Goettigensium criminationes* (1782). The four volumes of J. B. de Rossi's *Variae lectiones veteris testamenti*, published at Parma in 1784–8, with a supplement of 1798, form a supplement to Kennicott's volumes of 1776 and 1780, and include codices which the latter had missed.

Reputation and final years The scale of textual criticism (he had consulted and collated 615 manuscript versions and 52 printed editions) gave Kennicott a European reputation that transcended national and denominational boundaries, his labours constituting a milestone 'in a more systematic and comprehensive examination of the formation of the biblical text and canon by subsequent scholars'

(Ruderman, 23). His pertinacity offset an unpropitious start in life, and through careful organization and working to schedule he completed his great undertaking in his lifetime. But with indomitability went an arrogant streak that repeatedly generated hostility to his scholarship and ambition. He always found it hard to take his detractors and their charges seriously and he relied principally on powerful allies like Secker and Lowth to protect as well as patronize him.

Many of Kennicott's other published works were in response to critical attacks occasioned by his preaching and, in due time, his academic renown. Early in his career he fell foul of William King, the Oxford Jacobite, and caustically defended Exeter College for its pro-whig line in the notorious Oxfordshire election of 1754 in *A letter to Dr. King, occasion'd by his late Apology, and in particular by such parts of it as are meant to defame Mr Kennicott* (1755). Kennicott gave ammunition to his detractors with his *Christian fortitude: a sermon preached before the University at St. Mary's, Oxford, 25 Jan. 1757* (1757), to which there were several fierce replies. He also wrote anonymously *Remarks on the 42 and 43 Psalms* (n.d., 1765?), which was soon followed by a similar treatise on psalms 48 and 89. These, when translated into Latin with an appendix by Bruns, were published by J. C. F. Schultz at Leipzig in 1772. Another anonymous tract was *Critica sacra, or, A Short Introduction to Hebrew Criticism* (1774). *Remarks on Select Passages in the Old Testament. With Eight Sermons* (1787) was published following directions in Kennicott's will.

Kennicott suffered badly from gout towards the end of his life and was walking on two sticks by 1781. After a lingering illness he died at Oxford on 18 August 1783, and was buried in Christ Church Cathedral, close to the grave of Bishop Berkeley, on 21 August. Ann Kennicott long survived her husband, and died on 25 February 1831. She was very friendly with Richard Owen Cambridge, Mrs Garrick, Hannah More, and Fanny Burney, and after marriage had learned Hebrew, in order to assist her husband in his edition of the Bible: 'She was to him hands and feet, and eyes and ears, and intellect' (H. Roberts, 1.291). During her widowhood she had a warm friendship with Bishop Shute Barrington and there was even talk of their marrying after his wife died. She was also on intimate terms with Bishop Beilby Porteus and his wife and she frequently stayed with them at Fulham and in Kent. She moved closer to the evangelical camp in the early nineteenth century and was a strong supporter of the abolition of the slave trade and of the Windsor branch of the Bible Society. In memory of her husband and for the promotion of the study of Hebrew she founded two scholarships at Oxford, and her name is included in the bidding prayer among the benefactors of the university. NIGEL ASTON

Sources *GM*, 1st ser., 17 (1747), 471–2 · *GM*, 1st ser., 38 (1768), 147–9, 203–5, 251–3, 366–8 · *GM*, 1st ser., 41 (1771), 520 · *GM*, 1st ser., 53 (1783), 718, 744 · *GM*, 1st ser., 59 (1789), 289 · *GM*, 1st ser., 61 (1791), 222 · *GM*, 1st ser., 100/1 (1830), 282, 374 · *IGI* · W. McKain, 'Benjamin Kennicott: an eighteenth-century researcher', *Journal of Theological Studies*, 28 (1977), 445–64 · E. Windeath, 'Benjamin Kennicott, D.D.: a biographical sketch', *Report and Transactions of the Devonshire Association*, 10 (1878), 215–22 · Foster, *Alum. Oxon.*, 1715–1886, 2.787 · *Fasti Angl., 1541–1857*, [Bristol], 96 · *Fasti Angl.* (Hardy), 3.310 · *Hist. U. Oxf.* 5: *18th-cent. Oxf.* · I. Guest, *Dr John Radcliffe and his trust* (1991), 160–63 · W. Jones, *The life of George Horne, D.D., late lord bishop of Norwich* (1795), x–xi, 84–109 · W. Roberts, *Memoirs of the life and correspondence of Mrs Hannah More*, 2nd edn, 4 vols. (1834), vol. 1, p. 291 · Nichols, *Illustrations*, 3.482; 4.656; 5.182, 627 · Nichols, *Lit. anecdotes*, 8.230, 239, 242–59 · W. D. Macray, *Annals of the Bodleian Library, Oxford*, 2nd edn (1890); 118, 260, 263, 306, 372 · R. J. Robson, *The Oxfordshire election of 1754: a study in the interplay of city, county and university politics* (1949) · D. S. Katz, 'The Hutchinsonians and Hebraic fundamentalism in eighteenth-century England', *Sceptics, millenarians, and Jews*, ed. D. S. Katz and J. Israel (Leiden, 1990), 237–55 · D. B. Ruderman, *Jewish enlightenment in an English key: Anglo-Jewry's construction of modern Jewish thought* (2000) · N. W. Hitchin, 'The politics of English Bible translation in Georgian Britain', *TRHS*, 6th ser., 9 (1999), 67–92 · B. Hepworth, *Robert Lowth* (1978) · M. H. Goshen-Gottstein, 'Hebrew biblical manuscripts: their history and their place in the HUBP edition', *Biblica*, 48 (1967), 243–90 · F. Deconinck-Brossard, 'England and France in the eighteenth century', *Reading the text: biblical criticism and literary theory*, ed. S. Prickett (1991), 136–81 · B. J. Roberts, *The Old Testament text and versions: the Hebrew text in transmission and the history of the ancient versions* (1951) · *DNB* · parish register, Totnes, 20 April 1718 [baptism] · commonplace book and literary papers, LPL, MSS 1720–1721, 1920–1921, 22243, 2601–2605 · correspondence with Charles Jenkinson, first earl of Liverpool, 1763–80, BL, Add. MSS 38201–38206, 38304–38308, 38457, 38469

Archives Bodl. Oxf., verses and letters, MS Eng. misc. d. 641; MS Don. d. 137; MS Eng. lett. c. 574; MS Eng. misc. c. 399 · Bodl. Oxf., 'Observations on Dr Kennicott's manner of collating Hebrew manuscripts of the Old Testament etc', MS Kennicott c. 43 · LPL, commonplace book and literary papers | BL, Newcastle MS, Add. MS 32902, fols. 104–5, 147 · BL, corresp. with Charles Jenkinson, first earl of Liverpool, Add. MSS 38201–38206, 38304–38308, 38457, 38469, *passim*

Likenesses oils, Exeter College, Oxford [*see illus.*]

Kenning, Sir George (1880–1956), motor car distributor, was born on 21 May 1880 at Clay Cross, Derbyshire, the second son of the eight children of Francis Kenning (*d.* 1905), hardware dealer, and his wife, Ann, *née* Whitworth. Francis Kenning, who came originally from Blyth to work in the Clay Cross mines, set up his hardware and oil business following a coalmining accident in 1878. He was joined in this by the young Kenning, who left school at the age of eleven to sell paraffin, pots, matches, and soap at local markets and from door to door. On the death of his father and elder brother, Kenning assumed control of the business, F. Kenning & Sons. He began to diversify by hiring out bicycles and horses but the opportunities offered by motor vehicles for expanding the business caught his attention.

Although Kennings continued to deal in hardware, the motor business soon became the dominant part of the firm's selling activities. Kenning was appointed a distributor for BSA Royal Enfield motor cycles in 1910; in 1916 he gained a Ford agency and by 1922 was handling Morris, Austin, Guy, Laurin and Clement, and Dennis vehicles in the Derbyshire area. In the 1920s Kenning was the only dealer in Britain to hold both Morris and Austin distributorships. The Morris agency was of particular importance as William Morris emerged as the foremost British car manufacturer, building up distributorships from 400 in 1923–4 to 1750 in 1927. Morris spread the financial risks of his business between his suppliers and his distributors, insisting that, in return for a generous

Sir George Kenning (1880–1956), by Elliott & Fry, 1943

profit margin, dealers should pay for cars before delivery. When Kenning placed his first major fleet order for 140 bullnose Morris Oxfords, Morris was wary of releasing a major part of his production to a single customer, and Kenning wondered whether Morris could handle an order of such size. The two men later developed a firm friendship.

Kennings Ltd was registered as a private company with a capital of £100,000 in 1930. In the later 1930s profits were running at almost £50,000 per annum and in 1939 the firm converted to a public company. By then it claimed to be the largest distributor of cars and commercial vehicles in the provinces, having depots as far afield from its Derbyshire base as Manchester and London. As well as selling cars, Kenning moved into the associated areas of providing services to car owners. He sold petrol, undertook repairs, provided finance, and even introduced car valeting to his major service centres. He was one of the first agents in the UK for Lucas electrical components and the first for the Tyresoles system of remoulding tyres for longer life. He set up the Midlands Counties Motor Finance Company, later acquired by Bowmaker. During the war the company expanded greatly and by 1956, when George Kenning died, it covered eighteen counties, employed over two thousand people and had a turnover of over £20 million.

In the words of an obituary, Kenning was 'gentle and unassertive, humble, astonishingly kind, ready to defer to the judgement of others and at ease in all strata of life'

(*The Times*). He was a notable benefactor in a wide range of causes, a pillar of support to the Methodist church at Clay Cross, a freemason, and chairman of the Alfreton bench. For almost thirty years he was a member and chairman of the Clay Cross urban district council and member and alderman of Derbyshire county council. A prominent Liberal, he declined invitations to stand for parliament. He was knighted in 1943

George Kenning married in 1911 Catherine Bogle Buchanan (who survived him), a local teacher whose family came from near Londonderry. She supported him in both business and public life and was herself a county councillor. They had four sons, three of whom survived his death at his home in Sheffield, Stumperlowe Hall, on 6 February 1956.   FRANCIS GOODALL

Sources D. Kenning and F. Goodall, 'Kenning, Sir George', *DBB* · *The Times* (16 Feb 1956) · *Derbyshire Times* (10 Feb 1956) · *WWW* · R. J. Overy, *William Morris, Viscount Nuffield* (1976) · R. J. Overy, 'Morris, William Richard', *DBB* · d. cert.
Likenesses Elliott & Fry, photograph, 1943, NPG [*see illus.*]
Wealth at death £333,478 6s. 5d.: probate, 17 March 1956, CGPLA Eng. & Wales

Kenningham [Kynyngham], **John** (*d.* 1399), Carmelite friar and theologian, probably came from Suffolk; though his family is unknown, he mentions in one of his surviving works that his father had died when he was a boy. He entered the Carmelite order at the Ipswich convent, but must have been sent to Oxford in the 1360s, since by the time of his determinations against John Wyclif (*d.* 1384) he was already a doctor of theology. In 1393 he was elected prior provincial of the order in England; on 18 May 1399 he was appointed vicar provincial for the Irish province, but six days before this he had died at the York convent and was buried there. He preached before Richard II on All Saints' day 1392. In 1392–3 and 1397–8 he acted as confessor to John of Gaunt, duke of Lancaster, was at various times resident in Gaunt's household, and was witness to his will. On 27 January 1399, shortly before his own death, Kenningham was summoned by Richard II to attend a council at Oxford to advise on possible solutions to the papal schism.

Kenningham disputed with his younger contemporary John Wyclif through a series of exchanges in Oxford, probably conducted about 1372–3. Neither side of the argument survives complete, and aspects of the sequence remain unclear; part of Kenningham's side is preserved in the manuscript of *Fasciculi zizaniorum*, while Wyclif's contributions are found much more fragmentarily in a single copy. It would seem that the early stages on both sides are lost; Kenningham, in the first (perhaps summarized) document, refers to material *in ultima determinatione mea* (*Fasciculi zizaniorum*, 4–13); this was answered by Wyclif (ibid., 453–76), followed by another riposte from Kenningham (ibid., 14–42), and another by Wyclif that in the single manuscript breaks off very early in the argument (ibid., 477–80). In all of the material thus far Kenningham speaks of Wyclif as *magister*, whereas Wyclif refers to his opponent as *doctor*. The third and fourth determinations of Kenningham (ibid., 43–72, 73–103), between which

Wyclif had evidently replied, frequently speak of Wyclif as *doctor*; this makes probable a date of 1372–3 for the sequence. The debate primarily concerned the implications for the study of scripture of Wyclif's views on universals, in particular the problem of the compatibility of Wyclif's insistence that 'si aliquid fuerit vel erit, ipsum est' ('if anything has been or will be, it has real existence at the present'; ibid., 8) with certain biblical passages that seem only intelligible if understood as contingent or indeed temporary. Other topics included the endowment of the church; Kenningham also tantalizingly states that Wyclif 'dicit se non credere quod Christus dixit panem esse corpus suum' ('says that he does not believe that Christ said that the bread is his body'; ibid., 54), and endeavours to enlarge the sense of *esse*, both pointing forward to his final eucharistic views. Though Kenningham nowhere resorts to polemic, his tone often appears slightly patronizing and ironic; he claims that Wyclif was forced to retreat from some of his points, a claim that the fragmentary material from the other side in part bears out.

Whether Kenningham continued to oppose Wyclif in Oxford after 1373 is unclear. On 28 May 1382 he was present at the Blackfriars Council in London when a list of Wyclif's views were anonymously condemned; two days later he preached the sermon after the procession in London, in which, on the commission of the archbishop of Canterbury, he pronounced the conclusions false and all those excommunicate who taught, favoured, or heard them. Ten years later, on 28 May 1392, he was present at the trial of the Cistercian Henry Crump in the Carmelite house at Stamford.

The Carmelite John Bale lists nineteen works of his earlier co-religionist, all but two with incipits. Five of these correspond to the surviving parts of Kenningham's arguments with Wyclif in *Fasciculi zizaniorum* (the last is divided by Bale into two parts). Though no entry appears for Kenningham in Bale's *Index*, the remainder derive from Bale's early access to Carmelite sources; several notes concerning him survive in Bale's notebooks. None of these other works has so far been traced, and there is no reason to connect a commentary on Ecclesiasticus in BL, Royal MS 2 D.iv, ascribed at the start to Kyngisham, with the opponent of Wyclif.   ANNE HUDSON

Sources [T. Netter], *Fasciculi zizaniorum magistri Johannis Wyclif cum tritico*, ed. W. W. Shirley, Rolls Series, 5 (1858), 4–103, 286, 357, 453–80 · J. Bale, notebooks, Bodl. Oxf., MS Bodley 73 · John Bale's notebooks, BL, Harley MSS, 1819, 3838 · G. Wessels, ed., *Acta capitulorum generalium ordinis fratrum B. V. Mariae de Monte Carmelo*, 1 (Rome, 1912), 71, 106, 116, 122 · A. Goodman, *John of Gaunt: the exercise of princely power in fourteenth-century Europe* (1992), 247–8, no. 32 · *Knighton's chronicle, 1337–1396*, ed. and trans. G. H. Martin, OMT (1995), 260–61 [Lat. orig., *Chronica de eventibus Angliae a tempore regis Edgari usque mortem regis Ricardi Secundi*, with parallel Eng. text] · *CCIR, 1396–9*, 367–8 · BL, Add. MS 35115, fol. 33 · Bale, *Cat.*, 1.457–8 · [J. Raine], ed., *Testamenta Eboracensia*, 1, SurtS, 4 (1836), 223–39, esp. 235

Archives Bodl. Oxf., MS e Museo 86, fols. 8v–34

Kennington, Eric Henri (1888–1960), artist, was born on 12 March 1888 in Liverpool, the second of the two sons of Thomas Benjamin Kennington (1856–1916), artist, and his Swedish wife, Elise Nilla Lindahl Steveni (1861–1895). Kennington senior was a well-known portraitist and a founder member of the New English Art Club (1886). In 1922 Eric Kennington married Edith Celandine Hanbury-Tracy, *née* Cecil (1886–1973), daughter of Lord Francis Cecil RN: they had two children, a son and a daughter, and lived first in Chiswick Mall, Chiswick, Middlesex (1922–9), and then in Oxfordshire, at Goring Heath (1929–35) and at Ipsden (1935–60) respectively. Kennington's admiration for all forms of endurance affected everything he did. Arguably the greatest artistic champion of the British First World War infantryman, he was also a close friend and defender of T. E. Lawrence, a determined fund-raiser for the Artists' Benevolent Institution, the rector's warden of Checkendon church, Oxfordshire, and a simple man fascinated by the staying power of Portland stone, nasturtiums, and his 1925 Fiat car.

A vital, independent talent in early and mid-twentieth-century British art, Kennington became a formidable draughtsman-painter, printmaker, and sculptor (his working practice evolved roughly in that order), and a great portraitist: his figures were often somewhat idealized, but always boldly executed, and frequently in pastel crayon, a self-taught medium in which he came to excel. Kennington's best-known graphic works are the many figure studies and portraits he made as an official war artist from 1917 to 1919 (examples of which are in the Imperial War Museum, London, at Manchester City Galleries, the Canadian national war memorial, Ottawa, and elsewhere), and again from 1939 to 1942. They are followed by the fine pastels he made of Arab leaders in the Near East (1921), while art editor of *The Seven Pillars of Wisdom* (1926) for T. E. Lawrence, and by pastels and oil paintings of many other notable figures whom he dignified throughout his career. All of this tends to overshadow Kennington's sculpture, his favoured medium from the 1920s onwards. This gained him high regard and interest in his lifetime, but has since suffered from critical neglect.

Kennington was educated at St Paul's School, London, where the artist Paul Nash remembered him drawing, 'knocking off likenesses of the plaster casts and whistling tunelessly the while' (P. Nash, *Outline*, 1949, 70). After some months with relatives in St Petersburg, Kennington (now seventeen) entered the Lambeth School of Art (1905–7), and then studied at London's City and Guilds Art School, first exhibiting at the Royal Academy and at the Leicester Galleries in 1909. At this time, the milieu of London street traders (called by C. R. W. Nevinson 'the Coster Craze') was enjoying great success in the music halls. Like other young London artists, Kennington was attracted by this theme, and treated it in several attractive but lightweight oils. Then in 1913 he painted *The Costermongers*, his most important treatment of the coster subject. Its uncompromising, statuesque figures and *quattrocento* perspective marked a new phase in Kennington's work, and he gained further attention when Edmund Davies presented the picture to the Luxembourg, Paris.

In 1914 Kennington enlisted as a private in the 1st battalion 13 London regiment (the Kensingtons), and fought with the battalion in France and Flanders from the end of 1914 until June 1915, when he was wounded and invalided out of the army. He spent the rest of 1915 painting an outstanding autobiographical fragment, *The Kensingtons at Laventie* (IWM), in reverse, in oil on to a glass measuring 54 by 63 inches, and exhibited it in May 1916 at the Goupil Gallery, London, to mixed response. *The Kensingtons* is arguably the first great commemorative painting of the First World War. In it, no. 7 platoon (including the tall figure of Kennington himself) is observed assembling in a ruined yard, before a long march to billets after front-line duty. They are battle-weary: one soldier is on the ground, ill and exhausted, but the message is one of endurance. However, *The Kensingtons* was too stark and direct for the Ministry of Information. They would not employ Kennington as an official war artist until pressed to do so by Campbell Dodgson (keeper of prints and drawings at the British Museum), who perceived and promoted Kennington as 'a born painter of the nameless heroes of the rank and file' (Dodgson and Montagu, introduction). Indeed, the public responded well to the bold, linear grandeur of his drawings (1917–18) of the infantrymen he so respected, and, later, to the challenging oil painting *Gassed and Wounded* (1918; IWM). However, Kennington's sour relationship with the Ministry of Information continued unabated until the Canadian war memorials commission requested a commemorative painting from him in 1918. They received *The Victors* (or *The Conquerors*: 1919; Ottawa), a large and imposing *memento mori* laden with equivocal symbolism, the very antithesis of *The Kensingtons*, but just as uncompromising.

Kennington's detailed drawings and paintings of steely-eyed airmen, seamen, and soldiers made in 1939–42 for the War Artists' Advisory Committee during the Second World War were not always appreciated. The superb finish of these images can seem over-idealistic, even monolithic, and the closely observed pastel portraits of the Home Guard (1944), the heroes of Kennington's first war, lack the touch of 1915–19. One cause of this apparent inconsistency was his rapid development as a sculptor between 1920 and 1939.

A modern combination of simple forms, and different from all other idealized commemorative sculpture of the time, the memorial to the 24th division (1924; Battersea Park, London) was Kennington's first major sculptural experiment and his first success, gaining him critical ranking with Frank Dobson, Leon Underwood, John Skeaping, Barbara Hepworth, and Henry Moore. Kennington was quickly convinced that sculpture should be fully integrated with its setting, and his output reflects this conviction: examples range from the memorials, fonts, and gravestones he carved for Checkendon and other churches, through the huge British war memorial, *Missing*, at Soissons, France (1927–8), to *Love, Jollity, Treachery, War*, and *Life and Death* (1928–32), the five integrated reliefs in specially made red brick for Elizabeth Scott's main façades at the Royal Shakespeare Theatre, Stratford upon Avon. All demonstrate Kennington's tremendous breadth of subject matter as a carver, and were interwoven with his own concepts of Englishness and of an English past, and with a profound trust in intuitive working methods. Delicacy, balance, and detail are equally visible in several large works, such as *Man Child* (1925), his full-length bronze of Thomas Hardy (1929; Hardy birthplace, Dorchester), in his effigy of T. E. Lawrence (1939; St Martin's Church, Wareham; copy, Tate collection), and in numerous smaller 1920s bronzes. In a *Studio* article Kennington gave form to his most heartfelt ambitions ('to revive the feeling for monumental sculpture in this country'), his views on the 'right' style for British sculpture ('the heavy form that best suits our misty light and damp, eroding climate'), and the need for sculpture and architecture to be interdependent ('sculpture must be part of a building itself, not something stuck on') ('In the studio of Eric Kennington', 79–85). Throughout and after the Second World War, and with one eye on the rebuilding of Britain, Kennington argued these and similar issues regularly in magazine articles, while drawing and painting portraits 'to pay for the sculpture—which never pays for itself' (C. Kennington, introduction in Hicks, ed., *Eric Kennington*, exhibition catalogue, Maas Gallery, London, 1981, 4).

After years of determined opposition to the Royal Academy, Kennington consented to his election as an associate in 1951, and became a Royal Academician in 1959. He died on 13 April 1960 at 16 Bath Road, Reading, Berkshire, after a long battle with cancer, and was buried on 21 April in the churchyard at Checkendon. Not long before, he had organized the entire village to assist him in carving the decorations for the church's new roof.

JULIAN FREEMAN

Sources E. Hicks, ed., *Eric Kennington: exhibition of drawings, pastels and watercolours, 1905–1930* (1981), introduction by C. Kennington [exhibition catalogue, Maas Gallery, London, 27 April – 15 May, 1981] · correspondence, 1914–18, IWM, department of art, 245(A)/6, 245(B)/6; 1939–45, GP/55/1(A), GP/55/1(B) [3 vols.] · C. Dodgson and C. E. Montagu, *British artists at the front, Eric Kennington*, 4 (1918) · S. Harries and M. Harries, *The war artists* (1983) · B. Read and P. Skipwith, *Sculpture in Britain between the wars* (1986) [exhibition catalogue, Fine Art Society, London, 10 June – 12 Aug 1986] · 'In the studio of Eric Kennington: the man and his work', *The Studio*, 112 (1936), 79–85 · E. Kennington, *Drawing the RAF* (1942) [introduction by R. Storrs] · J. Brophy, *Britain's home guard: a character study, portrayed in colour by Eric Kennington* (1945) · *A concise catalogue of paintings, drawings and sculpture of the First World War, 1914–1918*, Imperial War Museum, 2nd edn (1963) · P. Curtis and J. Lyon, eds., *Modern British sculpture: from the collection* (1988) · CGPLA Eng. & Wales (1960) · d. cert. · private information (2004) [family] · J. Black, *The sculpture of Eric Kennington* (2002)

Archives IWM, MSS · Man. City Gall., MSS | Bodl. Oxf., letters to T. E. Lawrence · King's Lond., Liddell Hart C., corresp. with Sir B. H. Liddell Hart · Ransom HRC, corresp. with T. E. Lawrence · U. Glas. L., letters to Eric Stanford · V&A, questionnaire completed for Kineton Parkes | FILM IWM, two short extracts on 16 mm B/W silent film

Likenesses H. Coster, photographs, NPG · W. Rothenstein, crayon drawing, Man. City Gall. · photograph, repro. in Read and Skipwith, *Sculpture in Britain*, 96 · photograph, repro. in 'In the studio of Eric Kennington'

Wealth at death £23,106 1s. 4d.: probate, 6 Dec 1960, CGPLA Eng. & Wales

Kennion, Charles John (1789–1853). *See under* Kennion, Edward (1744–1809).

Kennion, Edward (1744–1809), landscape painter, was born on 15 January 1744 in Liverpool, the son of James Kennion, a businessman. His grandfather, John Kennion, was a nonconformist minister preaching at the Toxteth Park Chapel, Liverpool. A relative, John Kennion, took charge of Edward's education, placing him at John Holt's school in Liverpool. When Kennion was fifteen he entered Mr Fuller's academy in London, where he learned to draw. Edward Kennion sailed for Jamaica in 1762, and joined the British attack on Spanish Havana under Sir George Pococke and George Keppel, third earl of Albemarle, in which John Kennion was commissary. After the capture of Havana Kennion went briefly to New York to recover his health, and then returned to England in December 1763. In 1765 he again went to Jamaica, where he remained until July 1769, serving as superintendent of John Kennion's estates and aide-de-camp to the commander-in-chief of the island.

In 1769 Kennion returned to London, where he worked in trade until 1782. About 1771 Kennion made the acquaintance of George Barret RA, a landscape painter, and in the following years accompanied him on sketching tours in the Lake District and around Liverpool. On 13 November 1774 Kennion married Ann Bengough, a Worcester woman of some property. None of the couple's several children survived, and Kennion's wife died in 1786. On 10 October 1787 he married Mary Hill of Upton-on-Severn, Worcestershire. In 1782, Kennion had retired from business in London and moved to Rydd-Green, near Malvern in Worcestershire. There he began making drawings for a treatise on landscape painting. In 1784 he published *Antiquities of the Counties of Hereford and Monmouth* which contained five perspective views of ancient castles on the Welsh border, and three ground plans engraved by R. Godfrey, with full descriptions by Kennion. Kennion spent the winters of 1787 and 1788 in London, where he gave drawing lessons. In 1789 Kennion and his family moved to London permanently, and he adopted the profession of teacher and artist.

Kennion was admitted as a fellow to the Society of Artists in 1790. Between 1790 and 1791 he exhibited twenty-four works, including drawings, watercolours, and oil sketches, at its annual exhibitions. He also exhibited eight pictures at the Royal Academy between 1795 and 1807. Several of the works shown at the Society of Artists were designated as studies for a proposed work entitled *Elements of Landscape and Picturesque Beauty*, to be published in four volumes. Kennion's uncle, a Liverpool physician, died in 1791, leaving him enough money to proceed with plans for the book. In 1803 Kennion published a full prospectus of the work, and final arrangements were made for the publication of the first volume early in 1809. However, before the volume was published Kennion died in London on 14 April 1809. He was survived by his wife and four children, including his son Charles John Kennion [*see below*], who was born in 1789.

The only part of Kennion's proposed *Elements of Landscape and Picturesque Beauty* that was complete at his death was entitled *An Essay on Trees in Landscape* and was issued in 1815. Many of the plates for this work were engraved or finished in aquatint and soft ground etching by his son Charles. The volume contains fifty etched and aquatinted plates, a preface and biographical notice, and forty-eight pages of instructional text. A copy in the Manchester Free Library was bound up in 1844 with four large unpublished landscapes said to be by Kennion, and six picturesque studies of trees, etched by H. W. Williams. A critic, Arlunydd Penygarn, wrote: 'He seems to have devoted himself to the representation of the specific growth of trees, and gives studies of a great number, sometimes very good, sometimes not so happy, but it was a thing needed in the art of the time' (Dibdin, 88). Characteristic examples of Kennion's work such as *Landscape with Fishermen* (V&A) show picturesque landscapes populated by figures and animals, and surrounded by soft masses of foliage-laden trees. An engraving by Kennion, after a drawing by Benjamin Ferrey, was included in Ferrey's book *The Antiquities of the Priory of Christ-Church, Hampshire* (1834). According to the preface of *An Essay on Trees in Landscape*, Kennion seldom painted in oils, and his earlier work was executed in India ink and pencil with tints applied later. However, under the tutelage of George Barret he began to paint in watercolours and also learned print-making techniques.

Charles John Kennion (1789–1853), landscape painter, exhibited twenty-six works at the Royal Academy between 1804 and 1853, and five works at the Suffolk Street Gallery. His watercolour paintings were much in the style of his father. Charles Kennion died in Robert Street, Regent's Park, London, on 10 September 1853.

ALBERT NICHOLSON, rev. A. CASSANDRA ALBINSON

Sources E. Kennion, *An essay on trees in landscape, or, An attempt to shew the propriety and importance of characteristic expression in this branch of art, and the means of producing it; with examples* (1815) · Graves, *RA exhibitors* · Graves, *Soc. Artists* · Graves, *Artists*, 3rd edn · E. R. Dibdin, 'Liverpool art and artists in the eighteenth century', *Walpole Society*, 6 (1917–18), 59–91 · L. Lambourne and J. Hamilton, eds., *British watercolours in the Victoria and Albert Museum* (1980) · B. Ferrey, *The antiquities of the priory of Christ-Church, Hampshire: consisting of plans, sections, elevations, details, and perspective viewes, accompanied by historical and descriptive accounts of the priory church; together with some general particulars of the castle and borough* (1834) · *N&Q*, 4th ser., 3 (1869), 263 · *GM*, 2nd ser., 40 (1853), 538 · Boase, *Mod. Eng. biog.* · IGI

Kennish [Kinnish], **William** (*bap.* 1799, *d.* 1862), naval officer and poet, son of Thomas Kennish and his wife, Margaret Radcliffe, was baptized at Kirk Maughold, Isle of Man, on 24 February 1799. He was reared as a ploughboy, but in 1821 entered the navy as a common seaman, where he first learned English, and rose to be a warrant officer. He was ship's carpenter on the *Hussar*, under Admiral Sir Charles Ogle at the North American station, 1829–30. While stationed at Halifax he devised a plan for concentrating a ship's broadside more effectively, which met with encouragement from Captain Edward Boxer of the *Hussar*, and was tried by Sir Charles Napier on board the *Galatea* in 1831. It was recommended to the Admiralty, to which Kennish also submitted a theodolite of his invention. In June 1832 he received the gold Isis medal from the Society of Arts, and he published his essay *A Method for Concentrating the Fire of a Broadside of a Ship of War* in 1837. He subsequently served upon the men-of-war *Tribune* and *Donegal* in the Mediterranean and in the channel, but felt he had not received encouragement from the Admiralty commensurate with the labour and money he had spent on his essay, and he left the navy about 1841.

Three years later Kennish published in London *Mona's Isle and other Poems*, a mine of Manx folklore, with a long subscription list of naval men. Disappointed at the limited circulation of his fame, Kennish went to America and became attached to the United States admiralty, for which he made a survey of the isthmus of Panama. He died at New York city on 19 March 1862, leaving a widow, Mary, in Surrey.

THOMAS SECCOMBE, rev. SARAH COUPER

Sources W. Kennish, preface, *Mona's isle and other poems* (1844) · private information (1901) [R. Cortell Cowell] · *Bibliotheca Monensis*, rev. edn, 24, rev. W. Harrison, Manx Society (1876) · Boase, *Mod. Eng. biog.* · *CGPLA Eng. & Wales* (1863) · IGI
Wealth at death under £300: probate, 21 Dec 1863, CGPLA Eng. & Wales

Kennon, Sidney (d. **1754**), midwife and collector, whose family background and education are obscure, distinguished herself initially in her services to the royal family, especially to Queen Caroline and Augusta, princess of Wales. The infant George III was delivered by her. Kennon was highly respected for her professional acumen and, at the time of her death, could command 50 guineas for attending the birth of a child. Her connections at court gave her some degree of influence. Dinner guests at her home in Jermyn Street, London, often included the titled; Frederick, prince of Wales, is said to have dined with her regularly.

As a result of her professional interests and financial success, Mrs Kennon (as she was known) became an avid collector, beginning perhaps in the early 1740s. The earliest records of her holdings refer to natural history material. She owned worms and polyps and traded them with Martin Folkes, president of the Royal Society, with whom she also engaged in discussions regarding their microscopical anatomy. Her collection also contained human anatomical material, a unique claim for a woman collector of her century.

Kennon's collection expanded to include a great variety of subjects. Horace Walpole laughed about the historic and ethnographic items he purchased at her posthumous sale but then displayed them at Strawberry Hill, noting in the catalogue both her ownership and virtuosity. Mary Delany, an avid collector herself, admired Kennon's collection of shells. Richard Mead, physician-in-ordinary to George II, gave her one of a set of three crocodiles which he received about 1745. Her coins and medals were esteemed very fine by both dealers and collectors.

Kennon died at her home, Clifford Street, Burlington Gardens, London, on 11 December 1754. Her belongings were bequeathed to the Revd Dr Arthur Young, author of

Historical Dissertations on Idolatrous Corruptions in Religion (1734) and father of Arthur Young (1741–1820), the agricultural writer. He sold the natural history books to a relative, while the coins, natural history specimens, and historic and ethnographic curiosities were sold at public sales through the auctioneer Abraham Langford in 1755 and 1756. The sales were frequented by many collectors. The shells alone were valued by one observer at £2500, while another estimated the whole of the estate to be worth about £5000. 'It is said that on her deathbed Kennon gave the physician Frank Nicholls a bank note for £500 for his services to the midwives' cause' (Donnison, 32).

Kennon was an acknowledged expert on childbirth and an opponent of man-midwives and their use of instruments. Despite this apparent acknowledgement of distinct gender roles, Mrs Kennon in both her profession and collections successfully negotiated a territory between such separate spheres.   P. E. KELL

Sources A. Langford, *A catalogue of the genuine and entire collection … of the eminent Mrs. Kennon* (1755) [sale catalogue, London, 24 Feb 1755] · *The autobiography of Arthur Young*, ed. M. Beetham-Edwards (1898) · J. H. Aveling, *English midwives: their history and prospects* (1872) · J. Hervey, *Memoirs of the reign of George the Second*, ed. J. W. Croker, 3 vols. (1884) · Walpole, *Corr.*, 37.439–40 · G. Edwards, 'An account of *Lacerta*', *PTRS*, 49 (1755–6), 639–42 · E. Mendes da Costa, 'Notices and anecdotes of literati', *GM*, 1st ser., 82/2 (1812), 205 · *The autobiography and correspondence of Mary Granville, Mrs Delany*, ed. Lady Llanover, 1st ser., 3 vols. (1861) · J. Westbrook, note to William Hunter, c.1770, U. Glas., Hunter MS H.171 · J. H. Jesse, *Memoirs of the life and reign of King George the Third*, 5 vols. (1901), vol.1, pp. 13–14 · death notice, *London Magazine*, 23 (1754), 572 · J. Donnison, *Midwives and medical men: a history of inter-professional rivalries and women's rights* (1977)
Wealth at death approx. £5000; incl. house contents, collection, and money in funds: *Autobiography*, ed. Beetham-Edwards, 10

Kenny, Courtney Stanhope (1847–1930), jurist, was born at Park House, Ripon, on 18 March 1847, the elder son of William Fenton Kenny, solicitor, and his wife, Agnes Ramsden Ralph, of Halifax. He was educated in Yorkshire at the Heath and the Hipperholme grammar schools, and in 1863 was articled to a Halifax firm of conveyancing solicitors. After his admission to practice in 1869 he worked for two years as a partner in the firm, but in 1871 he decided to leave practice and acquire a university education. He entered Downing College, Cambridge, on 17 May 1871 and in 1872 he was elected to a foundation scholarship. His career as a student was brilliant. In 1874 he was senior in the law and history tripos, won the Winchester reading prize, and was elected president of the union. In 1875 he won the chancellor's medal for legal studies.

Kenny was elected a fellow of Downing College in 1875 and was appointed to a lecturership in law and moral science. In 1876 he married Emily Gertrude Wiseman, of Ossett, Yorkshire; they had two daughters. In three successive years, 1877, 1878, 1879, he submitted an essay which won him the Yorke prize; the essays were on the history of the law of primogeniture, the law relating to married women's property, and the law of charities. In all of these works Kenny wrote both as a legal historian and as a reformer, and his book on charities exercised a direct influence in bringing about the introduction in 1891 of the

Mortmain and Charitable Uses Bill, which Lord Herschell piloted through parliament.

In 1881 Kenny was called to the bar at Lincoln's Inn and joined the south-eastern circuit. In 1885 he was elected member of parliament for the Barnsley division of Yorkshire, and at the general election of June 1886 he was again returned as a Gladstonian Liberal. While in parliament he introduced bills for the abolition of primogeniture and for the amendment of the law relating to blasphemy, which demanded the repeal of the laws restricting the expression of religious opinion.

In 1888, on the election at Cambridge of Frederic William Maitland to the Downing professorship of the laws of England, Kenny succeeded him as university reader in English law, and retired from parliament in order to devote himself exclusively to his academic duties. However, he took part in local affairs and served for several years as a justice of the peace and as vice-chairman of the Cambridgeshire county council; he was also chairman of the Cambridgeshire quarter sessions from 1912 to 1922. The practical experience thus gained proved of great value to him as a lecturer and writer on law. In 1907, on Maitland's death, Kenny was elected to succeed him as Downing professor, and he held the chair until his resignation in 1918. He was also elected a fellow of the British Academy in 1909, and later served as a member of its council.

Kenny was unquestionably the most successful of all the Cambridge law teachers of his time, doing more than anyone else to raise the standard of lecturing. He was one of the first legal scholars to edit collections of judicial decisions, and his *Cases on Criminal Law* (1901) and *Cases on the Law of Torts* (1904) were recognized as models of their kind. Of the former, Maitland once said that he could not imagine a book better fitted to give the freshman his first ideas about law.

Kenny's most important work was his *Outlines of Criminal Law* (1902; 19th edn, 1966; American edition by J. H. Webb, 1907; French edition by A. Poulian, 1921). It became a legal classic, being an indispensable textbook used not only by students but also by the bench and bar. It contains a clear and penetrating exposition of fundamental principles, illustrated by novel and vivid examples, many of them borrowed from continental legal literature, for Kenny had made a study of French, German, and Italian criminal law. His essay *The Law of the Air* (1910) was one of the pioneer contributions to this new subject, and in 1927 he brought out an edition, with introduction and notes, of *Parliamentary Logic*, the title under which the works of William Gerard Hamilton, 'single-speech Hamilton', had been published in 1808 by Edmund Malone.

The rapid change in criminal law since Kenny's death, on 18 March 1930 at the Evelyn Nursing Home, Cambridge, led to a lessening influence of Kenny's work. He is no longer mentioned in the same breath as many of his contemporaries, although any successor to Maitland was bound to suffer by comparison. Kenny should be remembered as a solid contributor to those generations (1880–1930) of English jurists who extracted the fundamental principles of various parts of the law from the previous inchoate mass of reported cases. His reputation as teacher and scholar retain his place in the history of the common law. A. L. GOODHART, *rev.* RICHARD A. COSGROVE

Sources The Times (19 March 1930) · 'In memoriam', *Cambridge Law Journal*, 4 (1930–32), 50 · P. H. Winfield, 'Courtney Stanhope Kenny', *Cambridge legal essays written in honour of and presented to Doctor Bond, Professor Buckland and Professor Kenny*, ed. P. H. Winfield and A. D. McNair (1926), 17–21 · Venn, *Alum. Cant.*
Likenesses C. Wilkinson, oils, Downing College, Cambridge · photograph, Downing College, Cambridge · portrait, repro. in Winfield and McNair, eds., *Cambridge legal essays* (1926)
Wealth at death £50,191 7s. 5d.: probate, 12 June 1930, *CGPLA Eng. & Wales*

Kenny, Elizabeth (1880–1952), nurse and specialist in the treatment of polio, was born on 20 September 1880 at Kelly's Gully, near Warialda, New South Wales, Australia, the daughter of Michael Kenny, an Irish immigrant farm labourer, and his wife, Mary, formerly Moore. Kenny had little formal education and learned her nursing skills through apprenticeship, without formal hospital training or certification. Before the First World War she practised in southern Queensland as a bush nurse, and first encountered children with the symptoms of polio, known as infantile paralysis, in 1911. Told by her mentor, Aeneas John McDonnell, a Toowoomba physician, that the disease had no known effective treatment, Kenny treated the cases symptomatically with heated blankets to ease the pain, and was able to help six children overcome their paralysis. She gained a local reputation for healing muscles that other professionals considered permanently paralysed and for making rehabilitation a critical part of patient care.

In 1915 Kenny joined the Australian army, and made fourteen trips on transport ships between England and Australia. On 1 November 1917 she was promoted to sister, or head nurse, a title she kept all her life. In 1919 she was discharged as medically unfit with viral myocarditis, and went to live with her mother in Nobby, Queensland, where she worked as a private nurse. She supplemented her income with her war pension and patent royalties from a stretcher she invented in 1926.

Sporadic polio epidemics in the 1920s and 1930s renewed her interest in the disease and her conviction that she had a better treatment than did physicians. In 1933, despite growing medical opposition, she set up a small clinic in Townsville, which the following year received state funding. The Queensland government subsequently supported Kenny clinics in Brisbane and Toowoomba, and other states funded clinics in Sydney, Newcastle, Melbourne, and Hobart. Kenny also travelled to London and briefly took charge of two wards at Queen Mary's Hospital for Children, in Carshalton, Surrey.

In 1937 Kenny published her first book, written with the assistance of physician James Guinane, *Infantile Paralysis and Cerebral Diplegia: Methods used for the Restoration of Function*, which began to lay out a theory of polio based on three original concepts: muscle spasm, mental alienation,

Elizabeth Kenny (1880–1952), by unknown photographer, 1942 [receiving the award of the Legion of Merit from Commander William Klatt]

and muscle inco-ordination. In contrast to orthodox medicine, Kenny believed that, in polio cases, muscles considered normal were instead in 'spasm' or involuntary contraction, and the opposing seemingly paralysed muscles were healthy but abnormally stretched and therefore 'alienated' from nerve impulses, leading to inco-ordination. Unlike the standard medical therapy of immobilization and splinting, Kenny began active treatment in the acute stage, with applications of 'hot packs' made of boiled wool, and then gentle muscle therapy. Medical antagonism in Australia worsened with the publication in 1938 of the report of a royal commission set up by the Queensland government three years earlier to investigate Kenny's work, which warned that her methods could lead to deformities. However, with widespread support from the public and local politicians, Kenny was given charge of a ward at the Brisbane General Hospital.

In 1940 Kenny's medical advocates convinced the Queensland state government to send her to the USA, where polio was a significant problem and President Franklin Roosevelt, himself a polio victim, had recently helped to set up the National Foundation for Infantile Paralysis to fund polio rehabilitation. Kenny based herself in Minneapolis after gaining the interest of physicians at the University of Minnesota's medical school, including Wallace Cole, a professor of orthopaedic surgery, and John Pohl, an orthopaedic surgeon who directed the infantile paralysis clinic at the Minneapolis General Hospital. Kenny was offered control of a ward at this hospital and some beds at the University of Minnesota Hospital. She established a training course for nurses and doctors at the medical school, and in 1941 published her second textbook, *The Treatment of Infantile Paralysis in the Acute Stage*. She won increasing popular and medical interest through articles in *Reader's Digest* and *Time Magazine*, accounts published by her Minneapolis supporters in American medical journals, and the decision of the National Foundation to fund her training course.

In 1943 Kenny and Pohl published what became her definitive text: *The Kenny Concept of Infantile Paralysis and its Treatment*, with a preface by the National Foundation's director, Basil O'Connor. In the same year she also published her autobiography *And they Shall Walk: the Life Story of Sister Elizabeth Kenny*, written with novelist Martha Ostenso. Medical opposition increased, however, when she established first the Elizabeth Kenny Institute in Minneapolis, an independent teaching and research institution, and then the Kenny Foundation, whose fund-raising drives competed with the National Foundation's March of Dimes campaigns. In 1944 an American Medical Association investigatory committee issued a critical report, and the National Foundation publicly withdrew its backing (though it continued to fund Kenny methods when recommended by a physician).

During the 1940s Kenny was awarded honorary doctorates by the University of Rochester, Rutgers University, and New York University, and received honorary membership of the American Nurses' Association; she was also among the first to be appointed to the American Legion of Merit in 1942. Her therapy was widely integrated into medical and nursing practice, but was more often known as 'hot packs' than the 'Kenny method'. Although she travelled widely as the guest of health departments and hospitals, Kenny, a flamboyant figure in large hats and dramatic corsages, remained dissatisfied that only elements of her technique—not her concept of the disease—were accepted. Her influence waned in Australia during the war, and the last Australian Kenny clinic closed in 1947; but American clinics were established during and after the war in New York, New Jersey, Illinois, Michigan, Minnesota, and California. She published another book, *Physical medicine: the science of dermo-neuro-muscular therapy as applied to infantile paralysis*, and enthusiastically assisted in the making of the Hollywood film *Sister Kenny* (1946), which starred Rosalind Russell.

In 1949 Kenny retired as head of the Kenny Institute and made her home in Toowoomba, beginning her second autobiography, published posthumously, *My Battle and Victory: History of the Discovery of Poliomyelitis as a Systemic Disease* (1955). In 1950 she became only the second person in American history to be awarded a lifetime visa-free passage by congress. In a Gallup poll in January 1952 she was chosen as the most admired woman in America, ahead of Eleanor Roosevelt. Kenny died on 30 November 1952 in Toowoomba of cerebrovascular disease. She never married, and was survived by her ward, Mary Stewart-Kenny McCracken, who was Kenny's major assistant during the 1940s.   NAOMI ROGERS

Sources V. Cohn, *Sister Kenny: the woman who challenged the doctors* (1975) · J. R. Wilson, *Through Kenny's eyes: an exploration of Sister Kenny's views about nursing* (1995) · E. Kenny and J. Pohl, *The Kenny concept of infantile paralysis and its treatment* (1943) · E. Kenny and M. Ostenso, *And they shall walk: the life story of Sister Elizabeth Kenny* (1943) · J. R. Paul, *A history of poliomyelitis* (1971) · E. Kenny, *The treatment of infantile paralysis in the acute stage* (1941) · E. Kenny, *My battle and victory: history of the discovery of poliomyelitis as a systemic disease* (1955) · Minnesota Historical Society, St Paul, Minnesota, Kenny Collection · State Library of Queensland, Brisbane, Queensland,

Australia, Charles Chuter MSS · private information (2004) [M. K. McCracken]

Archives American Academy of Arts and Sciences, Beverly Hills, California, Margaret Herrick Library · Archives and Resource Center, Master of Dimes, White Plains, New York, Elizabeth Kenny Foundation files · Minnesota Historical Society, St Paul · priv. coll. | Franklin D. Roosevelt Presidential Library, Hyde Park, New York, Franklin D. Roosevelt MSS · New York Academy of Medicine, rare books collection, Philip Stimson MSS · Nursing Archives of Australia, Quoiba, Tasmania · State Library of Queensland, South Brisbane, Charles Chuter MSS
Likenesses photograph, 1942, Hult. Arch. [see illus.]

Kenny, Sir Thomas Kelly- (1840–1914), army officer, son of Mathew Kelly of Tuanmanagh, Kilrush, co. Clare, was born at Tuanmanagh on 27 February 1840. In 1874 he took the additional surname of Kenny. In 1858 he received a commission in the 2nd foot, and in 1860 took part in the Second Opium War, was present at the capture of the Taku (Dagu) forts, and was mentioned in dispatches. He took part as a captain in the Abyssinian expedition of 1867–8 and was again mentioned in dispatches. After twenty-four years of regimental service he was promoted in 1882 to the command of the 2nd battalion of the Queen's regiment, as the 2nd foot had become, and he first attracted notice for the state of efficiency to which he brought the battalion. After this command he had a succession of staff appointments, in which he made a name for himself as an administrator. He was a Catholic, a moderate Irish nationalist of a sort, and a Wolseleyite.

In 1896 Kelly-Kenny was promoted major-general and given command of an infantry brigade at Aldershot, and in the following year he was made inspector-general of auxiliary forces at the War Office. He was holding this position when the Second South African War broke out (1899), and, after the first five divisions had left for South Africa under the command of Sir Redvers Buller, he was chosen to organize and command the 6th division at Aldershot. After the 'black week' (December 1899) of British defeats, and following the appointment of Lord Roberts to the supreme command, Kelly-Kenny took this division to South Africa and led it during the operations for the relief of Kimberley. He was the oldest officer in the army, after Roberts.

Following a night march (14–15 February 1900) the 6th division arrived at Klip Drift on the Modder River and relieved Major-General J. D. P. French's cavalry division, which was thus enabled to gallop through the Boer lines towards Kimberley. On discovering General Piet Cronje's movement eastwards from Magersfontein, Kelly-Kenny followed him up, engaged his rear-guard at Klip Kraal Drift (16 February), and by hampering the Boer retreat enabled Roberts two days later to bring up the 9th division to join the 6th, while French's cavalry returned from Kimberley and prevented Cronje from escaping by the right bank of the Modder. Cronje had entrenched himself in a laager at Vendutie Drift, just east of Paardeberg. During the first attack on the laager (18 February) Kelly-Kenny was the senior general on the spot, but Roberts had sent forward his chief of staff, Lord Kitchener, to co-ordinate the

movements of the various divisions, and ordered that Kitchener, not Kelly-Kenny, command there. This placed Kelly-Kenny in a difficult position, as he did not agree with Kitchener's tactics, believing him recklessly impatient. Kelly-Kenny, no genius but competent and sensible, wanted the infantry to seal off the Boers' position while the artillery bombarded them into surrender: a plan which would probably have succeeded with minimal casualties. Kitchener overruled him and ordered an infantry frontal attack, which failed with relatively heavy casualties, and only after bombardment did Cronje surrender (27 February).

After Cronje's surrender Kelly-Kenny led his division in the action of Poplar Grove (7 March), but the Boers, finding their flank turned by the British cavalry, did not await the attack of the infantry. The failure to trap the Boers, one of the great opportunities of the war, was a bitter disappointment to the British. Roberts blamed French and Kelly-Kenny, the latter for being too slow and cautious in attacking the Boer trenches. Kelly-Kenny admitted he would have attacked sooner if he had realized the Boers were so demoralized, but blamed Roberts for the inadequate supplies which hampered his division.

Three days later (10 March) the Boers made a determined stand at Driefontein, and there the brunt of the fighting fell on the 6th division, which Kelly-Kenny handled with such skill that the Boers never again accepted a pitched battle. After the occupation of Bloemfontein and Roberts's advance to Pretoria, Kelly-Kenny was left in command in the Free State, where his chief function was to protect the long railway communications against de Wet's numerous raids. In the autumn of 1900 he came home with Lord Roberts.

Kelly-Kenny had been promoted lieutenant-general in 1899, and in 1902 he was created KCB for his services in the war. He was adjutant-general of the forces from 1901 to 1904. In 1904 he received the GCB, and he was promoted general in 1905. In the latter year he accompanied Prince Arthur of Connaught on the mission to confer the Garter on the emperor of Japan. He retired in 1907 and died, unmarried, on 26 December 1914 at Hove.

F. B. MAURICE, rev. M. G. M. JONES

Sources J. F. Maurice, ed., *History of the war in South Africa, 1899–1902*, 1 (1906) · *Army List* · personal knowledge (1927) · C. N. Robinson, *Celebrities of the army*, 18 pts (1900) · T. Pakenham, *The Boer War* (1979)
Archives NAM, department of archives, letters to Earl Roberts
Likenesses C. Knight, photograph, c.1899, repro. in Robinson, *Celebrities of the army* · Spy [L. Ward], chromolithograph caricature, NPG; repro. in *VF* (29 Aug 1901)
Wealth at death £78,523 15s.: Irish probate sealed in London, 15 Feb 1915, *CGPLA Eng. & Wales*

Kenny, William Stopford (1787/8–1867), schoolmaster and educational writer, was born in 1787 or 1788. On 1 January 1812 he married, at St Pancras, London, Eliza Adams. For many years he kept a classical school at 5 Fitzroy Street, Fitzroy Square, London, later moving to Richmond, Surrey, where his son, William D. Kenny, ran a boarding-school. In 1856 Kenny stated that he had been a teacher for forty years. An accomplished chess player, his first published works were *Practical Chess Grammar* (1817), *Practical Chess Exercises* (1818), and *Analysis of the Game of Chess* (1819), a translation of Danican Philidor's work. He was later known for his schoolbooks. His most popular work, *Why and because: being a collection of familiar questions and answers on subjects relating to air, water, light and fire* (4th edn, 1830; 18th edn, 1854), translated from a French original, set out in an appealing way answers to children's questions about nature. His *Grammatical Omnibus* (8th edn, 1853) identified and corrected 'improprieties frequent in writing and conversation'. Latterly he was described as a teacher of languages, and he published French and Italian phrase books (1854–6). *Kenny's School Geography* (1856) was a catalogue of facts to be learned by heart, with questions and exercises. He died on 16 November 1867 at 2 York Villas, Richmond.

GORDON GOODWIN, rev. M. C. CURTHOYS

Sources GM, 4th ser., 5 (1868), 113 · Boase, *Mod. Eng. biog.*

Kenrick family (*per. c.*1785–1926), hardware manufacturers, came to prominence with **Archibald** [i] **Kenrick** (1760–1835). Born in 1760 at Wynn Hall, Ruabon, Denbighshire, Archibald was the third eldest son among the seven children of John Kenrick (1725–1803), a small landowner, and his wife, Mary Quarrel or Quarrell.

Archibald's first business venture, which commenced when he moved to Birmingham during the mid-1780s, was in the buckle trade with a distant relation who, like Archibald, was a Unitarian. After acquiring a knowledge of plating, Archibald was able in 1787, with financial support from his father, to enter into partnership with another buckle maker. However, when buttons and laces began to replace buckles Archibald turned to the hardware trade. The finance for this change of direction came from the dowry he received from his father-in-law, Joseph Smith of Staffordshire, on his marriage to Rebecca Smith (1770–1809) in December 1790. In 1791 Archibald set up an iron foundry business in West Bromwich which produced cast ironmongery, beginning with coffee mills, door furniture, cast nails, and mole traps, supplying households and the building trade.

Through patented technical improvements, litigation, and collusion, and by close attention to quality and appearance, which depended on careful control of casting and variation in finishes, Kenrick's tinned hollowware established a reputation for lightweight, attractive, and hygienic cooking utensils of a quality and at a price that enabled them virtually to replace 'black', or untinned, hollowware and to compete with similar vessels made from copper or brass. Growing sales of coffee mills, tinned light cast-iron hollowware, and nails were obtained from an increased asset base and a rise in the number of workers employed, counted in tens before 1815 but in two or three hundreds by the time of Archibald's death on 6 November 1835. Little is known about Archibald's life outside the business. He was a supporter of the Sunday school movement and of the diffusion of knowledge among workers. He established a works library and a savings society for his employees. In 1812 he married his second wife,

Mary Eddowes (1763–1854). There were four sons and three daughters from his two marriages.

Archibald's death left two of his sons, **Archibald** [ii] **Kenrick** (1798–1878) and **Timothy Kenrick** (1807–1885), in possession of equal shares in the partnership. Both were educated at private academies, after which Archibald [ii] studied mechanics in Birmingham while Timothy was apprenticed, probably in the iron trade. Archibald [ii] married Ann (d. 1864), daughter of William Paget, a Unitarian and banker of Leicestershire, whose loans aided the Kenrick enterprise. The couple had four sons and three daughters. The ill health of Archibald and Timothy's extensive business activities outside the firm meant that their involvement in the day-to-day management of the firm declined during the third quarter of the century. Timothy served as chairman of Lloyds Bank, and was a founder of the Nurses' Training Institution in Birmingham, for which he purchased a home. Timothy was married to Maria Paget (1808–1876), and the couple had three sons and six daughters. Archibald [ii] died at Berrow Court, Edgbaston, Birmingham, on 10 March 1878. His brother Timothy died on 23 February 1885 at Maple Bank, Birmingham. Their successors were **John Arthur Kenrick** (1829–1926), the eldest son of Archibald [ii], who joined the company in 1848, and from 1850 his brother **William Kenrick** (1831–1919), who in 1857 became a full partner together with his father, brother, and Timothy. The commercial success of Timothy's 1846 patent for glazing and enamelling the metal surfaces of cast iron led to investment and the growth of home and overseas sales. On incorporation in 1883, still owned and controlled by the family, Archibald Kenrick & Sons Ltd employed roughly 700 workers and was capitalized at £201,700. Capital was increased to £301,700 in 1899, by which time employment had almost doubled since 1883. As one of the two largest British hardware manufacturers, the company had reached its peak.

John Arthur Kenrick was educated at a private school in Handsworth, the Edgbaston proprietary school, and the Hove School. When he was eighteen his father's illness compelled him to withdraw from University College, London, to assist Timothy in the family firm. After similar schooling, William's studies of mathematics and chemistry at University College were completed with distinction. While John Arthur took responsibility for production, William's contribution was in commercial management, though between 1872 and 1911 John Arthur was chairman of the Cast Iron Hollowware Manufacturers' Association which regulated price competition in the home market. From the 1860s both Kenrick brothers became increasingly engaged in other business ventures and in public affairs. John Arthur continued as chairman of the company until 1898, though from the entry into the firm in 1873 of his successor, George Hamilton Kenrick (1850–1939), cousin to the two senior partners, the day-to-day commercial management became his responsibility. After 1868 production management was delegated to Frederick Ryland, a professional engineer who was also the first non-family manager (and from 1883 director) employed in the family firm. John Arthur became a director and chairman of both Nettlefolds Ltd and William Elliott & Sons Ltd, and a director of Lloyds Bank and of the Union Rolling Stock Company. In 1878 he bought the *West Bromwich Free Press* with the intention of restoring its fortunes; this purchase led to the formation of Kenrick and Jefferson, which became a commercial printer on a large scale.

In their public activities, John Arthur and William continued the family tradition. Archibald [ii] had been chairman of the board of commissioners and of the local Liberal Party in West Bromwich. Timothy, too, was a Liberal, both were Unitarians, supported the Education League, and together built a school for the children of local workers. Archibald [ii] was chairman of the Provident Medical Dispensary from 1864, while Timothy was involved in the management of Birmingham General Hospital and a founder of the Nurses' Training Institution. In 1858 the brothers purchased Aston Hall and Park as a place for public recreation.

John Arthur's public activities were concentrated in West Bromwich where he became chairman of the board of guardians, of the highway board, and later of the improvement committee which governed the town's development between 1866 and 1882. He was also president of the West Bromwich Liberal Association. In 1866 he married Clara, daughter of the Revd John Taylor; they had four sons and four daughters. He died at Berrow Court, Edgbaston, Birmingham, on 23 April 1926.

William's public life centred upon Birmingham. In 1862 he married Mary Chamberlain, the elder sister of Joseph *Chamberlain, with whom William became a close political ally. Kenrick and his wife had two sons and two daughters. William's sister Harriet was the first wife of Joseph Chamberlain, and his cousin Florence Kenrick the second wife. A member of the Education League from 1866, in 1869 William represented one of four Unitarian business families, the others being the Nettlefolds, the Martineaus, and the Chamberlains, who together contributed a total of £5000 to launch the National Educational League. Under Joseph Chamberlain's leadership this organization spearheaded the campaign to transform Birmingham nonconformity into a militant, reforming force on a national scale. Between 1866 and 1877 William was also a member of the council of the Midland Institute, though his special interest in technical education was reflected in membership of the managing committee of the Birmingham School of Art, inaugurated in 1874, of which he became chairman in 1883. He was also instrumental in setting up the Jewellers' School and in creating scholarships to promote craft education.

William was chairman of the general committee of the National Liberal Federation from 1882 to 1886 and became MP for North Birmingham in 1885. Before then his public life was dominated by activities related to Birmingham politics. He represented the Edgbaston ward between 1870 and 1911, becoming mayor in 1877. He was a central figure in the progressive, reforming campaigns mounted by the group of predominantly nonconformist businessmen and Liberal town councillors led by Joseph Chamberlain. He was chairman of the watch committee from 1874 to 1876, and of the gas committee from 1880 to 1883, when he assumed responsibility for the continued success of this municipal enterprise, the profitability of which was planned to underpin a civic revolution, transform the urban environment, and enrich the town's cultural and recreational endowments. Progress towards these goals was assisted further by William's position as a member of the free libraries committee and chairman of the museum and school of art committee from 1884, when the school was transferred to the corporation, until 1911. His contribution to museum development began in 1880 when he was a founder member of the Art Gallery purchase committee; from then on donations of pictures and money for further acquisitions enhanced the national reputation of Birmingham Art Gallery. On the national political stage, he was chairman of the general committee of the National Liberal Federation between 1882 and 1886. Between 1885 and 1899 he was the liberal, and subsequently Liberal Unionist, MP for North Birmingham, his contribution at Westminster deriving mainly from his knowledge and experience of local government. In 1911 William received the freedom of the city of Birmingham, an acknowledgement of his role as one of the architects of the social and political character of modern Birmingham. He died on 31 July 1919 at The Grove, Harborne Park Road, Harborne, Birmingham. Later chairmen of the company included Sir George Hamilton Kenrick (1850–1936), Wilfrid Byng Kenrick (1872–1962), and Wilfrid's son William Edmund *Kenrick.

The hardware manufacturing business founded by Archibald [i] Kenrick in the mid-1780s had, a century later, become one of the two largest firms of its kind in the country. Successive members of the family, through technical innovation and shrewd marketing, established a reputation for its light and attractive cast-iron hollowware and hardware. Retaining their Unitarian affiliation, the Kenricks were active in local Liberal politics, and were significant civic and philanthropic figures in the Birmingham and West Bromwich areas. ROY CHURCH

Sources W. Byng Kenrick, ed., *Chronicles of a nonconformist family* (1932) · R. A. Church, *Kenricks in hardware: a family business, 1791–1966* (1969) · *Birmingham Journal* (7 Nov 1835) · *Birmingham Post* (1 Aug 1919) · *Birmingham Mail* (31 July 1919) · WWW · Boase, *Mod. Eng. biog.* · WWBMP · d. certs. · CGPLA Eng. & Wales (1878); (1885); (1919); (1926)

Archives U. Birm.

Wealth at death £168,309 11s. 8d.—William Kenrick: probate, 28 Nov 1919, CGPLA Eng. & Wales · under £90,000—Archibald Kenrick: probate, 29 March 1878, CGPLA Eng. & Wales · £157,838 14s. 8d.—Timothy Kenrick: resworn probate, June 1885, CGPLA Eng. & Wales · £101,775 14s. 8d.—John Arthur Kenrick: probate, 28 May 1926, CGPLA Eng. & Wales

Kenrick, Archibald (1760–1835). *See under* Kenrick family (*per. c.*1785–1926).

Kenrick, Archibald (1798–1878). *See under* Kenrick family (*per. c.*1785–1926).

Kenrick, Daniel (*b.* 1649/50), poet and physician, the son of Samuel Kenrick (*b.* 1602/3), rector of St Mary de Crypt, Gloucester, was born in Gloucestershire, matriculated aged sixteen at Christ Church, Oxford, on 30 May 1666, took his BA in 1670, became MA in 1674, and was later vicar of Kempsey in Worcestershire. His brother Christian was educated at New Hall, Oxford (BA 1679), and later took up the position of vicar of Eckington, Worcestershire, in 1681. It appears that Daniel Kenrick also practised as a physician in Worcester for some time. Kenrick's reputation rests on the poems collected in *The Grove* (1721), which also includes some biographical information:

> Dr Kenrick took his degrees both in Divinity and Physick, and being a Person of Vivacity and wit, entertain'd his Leisure Hours in Poetical Compositions. His Talents seem equal in Panegyrick, satire, and Lyric: There is a Fire and Sprightliness of Thinking which runs thro' all his Copies, and to this, perhaps, he ow'd that haste in his Writing, which made him sometimes negligent of Harmony both in Rhimes and Numbers.

Kenrick had a wide circle of friends including Aphra Behn and Henry Purcell. Some of his work is closely associated with Henry Hall, and it is likely that Kenrick was a high-churchman, and perhaps, Jacobite sympathizer. This would account for the sermon of 1688 (though a difficult attribution to prove beyond all doubt), the argument of which was developed from Romans 31.1, 'Let every Soul be Subject to the Higher Powers'. It is divided into the following arguments:

> I. 'Of the Necessity of our Subjection to the Higher Powers: And then more particularly.'
> II. 'Of the strick Obedience we owe to the higher Powers, or the Kings of this Realm.'
> III. 'Of the Reasonableness of our Obedience to the King in the present juncture of Affairs.'

According to Kenrick, religion was for some:

> the specious Cry, when alas all his Religion is either Pride, Interest, Revenge for lost Honour, or a wild humour for innovation. For 'tis utterly impossible that any Man can have a serious awe of his Maker … and disturb the Peace of the Kingdom in which he lives.   (Kenrick, *Sermon*)

It is a skilfully argued sermon which follows a basically tory stance, yet seeks a religious and political tolerance for Catholics. Kenrick's sermon should be read in the context of the fears concerning the potential for Catholic monarchy and attendant political resurgency in England, which occupied Kenrick's years as a priest, following James II's *His Majesty's Gracious Declaration to All his Loving Subjects for Liberty of Conscience*, issued on 4 April 1687. This allowed Catholics to reassume public office, and permitted them the freedom of religious assembly. Many Anglicans were repulsed by James's use of the royal prerogative to appoint Catholics to positions in the army and the universities. In conclusion Kenrick asks 'Are we afraid of Popery?':

> The King assures us, 'Tis possible to be happy, without being pernicious … Tho seeming clouds appear, let our Fears and Jealousies be laid aside, and fear no Darkness, since God and the King say, *Let there be Light*.   (ibid.)

Kenrick's reputation as a poet rests on work published in *The Grove*, though other poems can be found in manuscript (Harvard UL, MS Eng. 614). As a whole, *The Grove* contains work stretching over a considerable period of time. Kenrick's most widely known work is 'A New Session of Poets'. Occasion'd by the Death of Mr John Dryden', first published in the year of Dryden's death, 1700. It is a playful piece which names many contemporary poets as successors to Dryden, yet finds fault with all of them when judged against Dryden's towering stature. Apollo, called upon as judge, returns to heaven saying:

> Ye sons of Wit, 'tis by your God decreed,
> Till One arise to match the mighty Dead,
> The Wreath shall stay on the De Facto's Head.

There was, however, a sting in the tail since Dryden was criticized for having attempted to consider religion in *The Hind and the Panther* (1687). Kenrick's other work found in *The Grove* is mostly devoted to his muse Sylvia, one of which, 'Upon Visiting Sylvia, on her Death-Bed, as her Physician. An Ode' is a rare, perhaps dramatized, reference to his professional life.   NICHOLAS JAGGER

Sources D. Kenrick, *A sermon preached April 7th 1688* (1688) · Foster, *Alum. Oxon.* · P. J. Wallis and R. V. Wallis, *Eighteenth century medics*, 2nd edn (1988) · D. Kenrick, *The grove* (1721) · private information (2004) [B. Frith]

Kenrick, George (1792–1874). *See under* Kenrick, Timothy (1759–1804).

Kenrick, John (1788–1877), classical historian and tutor, was born on 4 February 1788 at Exeter, the eldest son and second of five children of Timothy *Kenrick (1759–1804), Unitarian minister, and his first wife, Mary (*d.* 1793), the daughter of John Waymouth of Exeter, merchant. His father married second Elizabeth Belsham (1743–1819), sister of Thomas Belsham (1750–1829), who proved a 'conscientious and affectionate' stepmother (Kenrick, 6). He received his early education from his father, and in 1793 was sent to the grammar school conducted by the Revd Charles Lloyd (1766–1829), where, after an initial distaste for classical grammar, he made good progress in Latin and Greek. In 1799 he entered the nonconformist academy conducted by his father and the Revd Joseph Bretland (1742–1819), even though he was only in his twelfth year and considerably below the age of the other students. He studied Greek and Latin, and later Hebrew. Because of his age, his removal from a school discipline was not a success, and his father had already decided to place him at school again when he died suddenly in 1804. Thomas Foster Barham (1766–1844) taught him German, of great importance later for his classical and biblical studies. With Barham he wrote essays and sermons, the only direct training he received for the ministry. After the Exeter Academy closed in March 1805 Kenrick continued his studies at Birmingham under John Kentish, his father's intimate friend, who for two years directed his reading. In 1807, on the advice of Lant Carpenter, Kenrick entered

Glasgow University with a Dr Williams's exhibition, where he studied for three years, graduating MA on 1 May 1810. Although personally obliged to a number of the professors, privately he was to be critical of the quality of instruction, though he did later appreciate the benefits when he began to teach himself. Kenrick's considerable intellectual powers and scholarship were evident while at Glasgow. He was the first prizeman in his class for all three years, won the Gartmore gold medal for an essay on the English constitution in the Tudor period, and a silver medal for an essay on the aberration of light. 'He is spoken in higher terms than were ever bestowed upon a young man' (Charles Wellbeloved, 6 April 1809, Harris Manchester College, Oxford, Wood MS 1, fol. 84r).

In 1809 Kenrick was invited to become classics tutor at Manchester College, York, but he did not take up the appointment until after graduating the following year. Although highly praised by Charles Wellbeloved (1769–1858), the theological tutor, he had little experience of teaching and began to doubt his own abilities. He offered his resignation at Christmas 1810, but was persuaded to withdraw it. In 1817 feelings of personal inadequacy and shyness again led him to offer his resignation with the intention of studying abroad. In 1819 he was given leave of absence to spend a year in Germany. During the winter semester he studied history at Göttingen under A. H. L. Heeren, attending also the lectures of J. G. Eichhorn and J. F. Blumenbach; the following summer semester he devoted to classical study at Berlin under the great philologists, studying Tacitus with F. A. Wolf, Demosthenes with A. Boeckh, and Latin composition and conversation with K. G. Zumpt, and he attended Friedrich Schleiermacher's course of philosophy. After a tour in southern Germany and Switzerland he returned to York in September 1820. This introduction to the main nineteenth-century advances in German historical criticism and philology was of critical importance to his intellectual development.

In 1818 and again in 1825 Thomas Belsham tried to persuade Kenrick to become his assistant at Essex Street Chapel, London; but Kenrick had decided upon an academic career: though an able exponent of his own theological position, he had none of the gifts of a popular preacher. He had also married Wellbeloved's eldest daughter, Laetitia (d. 1879), on 13 August 1821; they had no children.

Kenrick was the greatest scholar among the Unitarians of his day: he was the equal of Eliezer Cogan (1762–1855) in erudition, and his superior in culture. His reputation as a classical scholar was established by his highly popular translations, *Latin Grammar* (1823; 5th edn, 1839), from Zumpt's work, and *Introduction to Greek Prose Composition* (1835; 3rd edn, 1839), from the work by V. C. F. Rost and E. F. Wusteman, and by his own *Exercises on Latin Syntax* (1825; 4th edn, 1838) and pioneering textbooks for schools. He was chosen by Bishop Blomfield to revise the fifth edition of A. H. Matthiae's greatly enlarged *Greek Grammar* (1832).

In 1840, when the college returned to Manchester, Kenrick became professor of history and served also as principal from 1846; he retired from both offices in 1850. He continued to live in York, and travelled to Manchester to deliver his lectures. His later publications were principally historical: *The Egypt of Herodotus* (1841), *Ancient Egypt under the Pharaohs* (1850), and *Phoenicia* (1855). Curator of antiquities for the Yorkshire Museum from 1858 until his death, he also published on Roman York. Kenrick regularly attended the annual meetings of the British Association for the Advancement of Science during the 1830s. Although only marginally concerned with natural science itself, he did help mould Unitarian reactions to the religious controversies over Darwinism and the origins of the earth. His *Essay on Primeval History* (1846) demonstrated how the principles of criticism could be applied to myths and traditions. His theology, while essentially that of the older Unitarian school, was modified in its conservatism by his acceptance of the new standards of biblical criticism. Both his teaching and his writings were characterized by his immense scholarship and 'comprehensive grasp' of the subject's 'whole outline … nothing fragmentary, nothing discursive, nothing speculative, broke the proportions' or disturbed his overall interpretation (Martineau, 408). An outstanding teacher who breathed life into the classics by placing them in their historical contexts, he was, however, a severe critic of those students who fell short of his exacting standards. Through his pupils, most notably John James Tayler (1797–1869), James Martineau (1805–1900), and George Vance Smith (1816–1902), and his writings he was responsible for helping to introduce to Britain the main nineteenth-century advances in German historical criticism and philology. On his death in York on 7 May 1877 *The Times* described him as 'indisputably the greatest nonconformist scholar of our day' (26 May 1877). He was buried in York cemetery on 12 May.

DAVID L. WYKES

Sources J. Kenrick, 'Memoranda of my life', UCL, Sharpe MS 189/2, Dec 1870, 14 Feb 1872 · J. Martineau, 'In memoriam: John Kenrick', *Theological Review*, 14 (1877), 374–97 [repr. 1878 [with full list of publications]; repr. in *Essays, reviews and addresses* (1890), 1.397–421] · *Christian Life* (12 May 1877) · *Christian Life* (11 Oct 1879) · *The Inquirer* (19 May 1877) · *The Times* (26 May 1877) · 'Autobiographical notices of contemporary divines: John Kenrick, M.A.', 15 Jan 1875, DWL, MS 38.64 [collected by T. Hunter (1875–6)] · J. Yates, 'A brief account of those students at the *University of Glasgow*, who went thither on the foundation of Dr *Williams*', 1851, DWL, MS 38.57, pp. 128–9 · W. I. Addison, ed., *The matriculation albums of the University of Glasgow from 1728 to 1858* (1913) · J. Hunter, *Familiae minorum gentium*, ed. J. W. Clay, 1, Harleian Society, 37 (1894), 183, 186

Archives Bodl. Oxf., library catalogue · Borth. Inst., travel journal · DWL, lectures, notebooks, essays and academic papers · Harris Man. Oxf., lecture notes · UCL, lecture notebooks; letters and papers | Harris Man. Oxf., letters to George William Wood and William Rayner Wood · priv. coll., letters to Charles Beard

Likenesses J. Pickersgill, oils, 1837, Harris Man. Oxf. · T. Lupton, mezzotint, 1847 (after G. Patten), BM, NPG · Sarony of Scarborough, photograph, 1866, UCL, Sharpe MSS, MS 190 · G. Patten, oils, Yorkshire Philosophical Society; repro. in Martineau, 'In memoriam: John Kenrick' (1878)

Wealth at death under £45,000: resworn probate, Feb 1878, *CGPLA Eng. & Wales*

Kenrick, John Arthur (1829–1926). *See under* Kenrick family (*per. c.*1785–1926).

Kenrick, Timothy (1759–1804), Unitarian minister and tutor, was born on 26 January 1759 at Wynn Hall in the parish of Ruabon, Denbighshire, one of the four sons of John Kenrick (d. 1803), a landowner, and his wife, Mary, the daughter of Timothy Quarrell of Llanfyllin, Montgomeryshire. The family was Presbyterian, and Timothy was baptized at Chester Street Chapel, Wrexham, on 6 February 1759. His brother Archibald *Kenrick (1760–1835) [*see under* Kenrick family] founded a dynasty of hardware manufacturers in West Bromwich.

In 1774 Kenrick entered the dissenting academy at Daventry, then conducted by Caleb Ashworth and from 1775 by Thomas Robins. At the end of his course in 1779 he was appointed tutor in mathematics and natural philosophy, and on Robins's resignation in 1781 he continued under Robins's successor, Thomas Belsham. He left the academy in January 1784 to take up the post of assistant minister to James Manning at George's Meeting, Exeter, and was ordained there on 28 July 1785. On 24 February 1786, at St Mary Major, Exeter, Kenrick married Mary (d. 1793), the daughter of John Waymouth of the city. They had five surviving children: Lucy, John *Kenrick, Samuel, Mary (b. 1791), and George [see below]; the twin of Samuel, George, died in infancy. In 1794, following Mary's death, Kenrick married the sister of his former tutor, Elizabeth (1743–1819), who was the second daughter of James Belsham (d. 1770), a dissenting minister, and Anne Woodward (d. 1780).

During his ministry in Exeter, Kenrick encountered both religious and political controversy, especially in the years following the French Revolution. Although he worked well with his senior colleague, Manning, they differed theologically, for Manning was an Arian and Kenrick followed Belsham in holding a Unitarian view of Christ's nature. This division was underlined when Kenrick wrote a preamble to the rules of the Western Unitarian Society, which was formed in 1792 and explicitly excluded Arians. News of the Birmingham riots of 14 July 1791 compelled Kenrick to condemn the rioters, who had attacked dissenting chapels, in a sermon preached on 24 July. A number of his congregation gathered to request him to refrain from discussing 'subjects of a political nature … in the pulpit' ('Kenrick letters', 4/1, 69). Kenrick responded by defending his right 'to treat of any Political duty in the Pulpit' should 'a just occasion' arise (ibid., 70), a response that satisfied his congregation. A year later, however, in October 1792, he again courted controversy when he 'prayed for success to those who were endeavouring to promote the liberty & happiness of mankind' (ibid., 80). This apparent expression of support for the French revolutionaries led John Merivale to withdraw from Kenrick's congregation in protest. Although Kenrick was appalled at the violence of the terror in France, he deplored the British government's measures to restrict civil liberties and refused

to observe the general fast on 1 February 1793, the day that Britain went to war with France. Continued criticism led him to offer his resignation in April 1793, but separate petitions of support from the men and women in his congregation persuaded him to withdraw his resignation. He none the less considered escaping the atmosphere of religious and political intolerance in Britain by following the example of his brother-in-law Ralph Eddowes, and emigrating to the United States, yet concern for the health and welfare of his wife and family seems to have dissuaded him. By 1798 he had decided to stay in Exeter, for he declined the invitation to become divinity professor at Manchester Academy.

In October 1799 Kenrick and Joseph Bretland reopened the dissenting academy in Exeter that had flourished under Joseph Hallett and had been revived by Samuel Merivale in the 1760s; it was known as the third Exeter Academy. Three pupils were in attendance by mid-October, and, as Kenrick reported to his father, 'this is but a small beginning, but we hope it may come to something more. A Subscription has been opened & a Society formed for ye support of Divinity Students wch will I hope in time do much good' (Byng Kenrick, 125). Kenrick rented the house adjacent to his own to house boarding pupils, the first of whom, Coffin, was a grand-nephew of Richard Price, and sent for the academy's library, which since 1786 had been loaned to Hackney Academy and was no longer in use, Hackney Academy having closed in 1796. The two tutors divided the teaching between them: Kenrick took responsibility for logic, metaphysics, moral education, the evidences of natural and revealed religion, the New Testament, and Jewish antiquities, and shared the teaching of Latin, Greek, Hebrew, and English composition and elocution. Eleven students, including James Hews Bransby, underwent the whole course, and four others, among them Kenrick's eldest son, John, received a part of their training before the academy closed on 25 March 1805.

While on a preaching tour Kenrick died suddenly, 'as he was walking in the fields, near Wrexham' (Bogue and Bennett, 4.273), on 22 August 1804. He was buried on 26 August in the dissenters' burial-ground at Rhosddu, near Wrexham. In addition to four sermons published separately during his lifetime, two volumes of *Discourses on Various Topics* (1805) were published posthumously, as was Kenrick's most important work, *An Exposition of the Historical Writings of the New Testament* (3 vols., 1807). The *Exposition* demonstrated Kenrick's considerable learning, yet was soon to be superseded by the new methods of historical criticism and philology developed by German scholars.

Kenrick's fourth son, **George Kenrick** (1792–1874), Unitarian minister, was born at Exeter on 28 October 1792 and was educated at the boarding-school established in Exeter by Lant Carpenter, who had succeeded Timothy Kenrick as co-pastor at George's Meeting. He matriculated from Glasgow University in 1808, and from 1810 to 1813 studied under Charles Wellbeloved at Manchester College, York, where his elder brother John was classics tutor. He served as Unitarian minister to congregations at Chesterfield (1813–14), Hull (1815–21), Maidstone (1822–6), Hampstead

(1829–45), and Battle (1845–7). From 1833 to 1860 he was a trustee of Dr Williams's foundations. He published sermons and contributed to the *Monthly Repository* and other periodicals. Of his three marriages, his first, on 10 September 1817, was to Mary Ann, the youngest daughter of Richard Hodgson, Unitarian minister at Doncaster; they had a daughter, Marianne, who married Abraham Champion, a Bristol engineer. His second wife, whom he married at St Leonard's, Exeter, on 11 October 1822, was Margaret (*bap.* 1794, *d.* 1824), the daughter of Charles Bowring, a wool merchant, and his wife, Sarah Jane Anne Lane, and the sister of Sir John *Bowring (1792–1872). Lastly, in May 1848 he married Sarah (*d.* 1888), the daughter of Thomas Walters. In 1860 he retired in considerable ill health to Tunbridge Wells, where he died on 2 December 1874.

ALEXANDER GORDON, rev. S. J. SKEDD

Sources J. Kentish, 'Memoir', in T. Kenrick, *An exposition of the historical writings of the New Testament*, 3 vols. (1807), vol. 1 · Mrs W. Byng Kenrick, ed., *Chronicles of a nonconformist family: the Kenricks of Wynne Hall, Exeter and Birmingham* (1932) · 'The Kenrick letters', *Transactions of the Unitarian Historical Society*, 3/3 (1925), 251–71; 3/4 (1926), 378–9; 4/1 (1927), 66–82; 4/2 (1928), 193–7 · W. F. Carter, 'Notes on Kenrick families', *The Genealogist*, 24 (1908), 15–22, 96–103, 164–72, 244–9; 25 (1909), 15–21, 120–25, 175–81, 215–23 · A. Brockett, *Nonconformity in Exeter, 1650–1875* (1962) · *Monthly Repository* (1818), 229–30 · *Monthly Repository* (1822), 197, 547–8 · J. Murch, *A history of the Presbyterian and General Baptist churches in the west of England* (1835), 406 ff., 507 ff. · D. Bogue and J. Bennett, *History of dissenters, from the revolution in 1688, to the year 1808*, 4 vols. (1808–12) · IGI

Archives DWL, lecture notes; student essays · UCL, corresp. and papers

William Kenrick (1729/30–1779), by Thomas Worlidge

Kenrick, Timothy (1807–1885). *See under* Kenrick family (*per. c.*1785–1926).

Kenrick, William (1729/30–1779), writer and translator, was the son of Robert Kenerick, staymaker, of Hemel Hempstead, Hertfordshire, and his wife, Mary (1708/9–1789). A member of a Baptist family, Kenrick attended probably either Philip James's Baptist school or Thomas Squire's Quaker school. Apprenticed in 1745 to Thomas Bennett, a mathematical instrument maker in London, Kenrick abandoned his apprenticeship after three years, in favour of a career in literature.

Early career Kenrick's verse satire, *The Town* (1748), was followed by the much more complex but still essentially juvenile *Old Woman's Dunciad* (1751). He also issued two equally unmemorable prose satires on his literary contemporaries and a further verse satire, *The Pasquinade* (1753), ridiculing John Hill. Never one to limit his options, Kenrick resorted to panegyric in a bid for patronage, with his *Monody to the Memory of … Frederick Prince of Wales* (1751), but neither abuse nor flattery earned him much public recognition.

However, Kenrick's fluent pen quickly found an appreciative welcome in the periodical press. By 1750 he was editing a monthly literary miscellany, *The Kapélion*, with Francis Stamper. They became embroiled in (or invented) a paper war with Christopher Smart's rival publications, *The Student* and *The Midwife*. Kenrick was also significantly involved in the production of an opposition newspaper, *Old England* (April 1751 – February 1753). His literary and political views came together when he turned to the stage to lampoon Henry Fielding, whose political views had already made him a target for *Old England*. The performance was suppressed by the lord mayor of London, but published under the title *Fun: a Parodi-Tragi-Comical Satire* (1752).

In February 1753 Kenrick published his most popular work, *The Whole Duty of Woman*. Resurrecting a late seventeenth-century title to capitalize on the success of Dodsley's *Oeconomy of Human Life*, Kenrick's guide to female conduct went through at least five editions in his lifetime and remained popular well into the next century. This uncharacteristic work may have been a purely commercial venture undertaken to support his new family. On 12 March 1752 he had married Mary Edge (*b.* 1726/7) with whom he had two daughters and three sons. The eldest son, William Shakespeare Kenrick, succeeded his father as editor of the *London Review* in 1778.

Between 1753 and 1756 Kenrick ventured abroad, though he returned periodically, as the births of his second and third children testify. He may have studied in the Netherlands, and he certainly mastered French and German during this period. He penned a defence of English foreign affairs, *L'Observateur observé, ou, Lettre d'un Hollandois à un de ses amis* (The Hague, 1756), but later complained that his one venture into political writing had proved fruitless.

Perhaps Kenrick's travels inspired him to a more philosophical view, expressed in his *Epistles to Lorenzo* (1756; substantially expanded as *Epistles Philosophical and Moral*, 1759).

The epistles, in blank verse, were initially acclaimed; the *Monthly Review* hailed Kenrick as 'a genius whose temperament and disposition more resembled the immortal Author of the "Essay on Man" than any other poet' (vol. 16, quoted in Brewer, 48). Thus Kenrick was understandably annoyed when his 1759 version met with a far less warm reception. He took the reviewers to task in *A Scrutiny, or, The Criticks Criticis'd* (1759), then abandoned longer poems and turned reviewer in revenge. By July 1759 Kenrick was imprisoned in the king's bench. Since he was taken in by the actress Jane Lessingham upon his release in late 1761 or early 1762, it would appear that his wife had died in the interim.

Reviewer and translator Armed with a good knowledge of European languages and in need of a steady income, Kenrick replaced Oliver Goldsmith as the chief reviewer for Ralph Griffiths's *Monthly Review*. Soon afterwards he wrote an exceptionally cruel review of Goldsmith's *An Enquiry into the Present State of Polite Learning in Europe* (1759) for which Griffiths forced him to apologize. Kenrick also sent an anonymous letter to the *St James Chronicle* in 1767 accusing Goldsmith of plagiarism, a charge Goldsmith successfully refuted. From 1758 to 1766 Kenrick gruellingly subjected almost all foreign-language publications to an 'admirable, if frenzied, astuteness' (Fussell, 43). Kenrick also took over from Robert Lloyd (who was himself imprisoned for debt) as editor of the *St James Magazine* from February 1764 until its demise in June.

While in the king's bench and subsequently immersed in foreign literature for the *Monthly Review*, Kenrick undertook translations to supplement his income. He began with Rousseau's *La nouvelle Héloïse*, published as *Eloisa* in 1761, and by 1767 had translated virtually all of the French philosopher's works (fourteen volumes). Kenrick was clearly interested in Rousseau's ideas, but he and his booksellers were also responding to public demand, which they satisfied with translations of the works of Salomon Gessner (*Rural Poems*, 1762) and of Voltaire (*Treatise on Religious Toleration*, 1764). While translation was standard fare for the denizens of Grub Street, Kenrick was unusually talented: 'Never an enthusiast, he was fully aware of weaknesses in Rousseau's position; but he also saw the futility of dogmatic abuse, and his criticism throughout was the most analytical and unbiased of any of the contemporary commentators upon Rousseau' (Sewell, 62).

These translations represented the zenith of Kenrick's intellectual reputation. As translator, his name clearly had selling power, for in 1771 his name alone adorned the title-page of *Elements of the History of England, from the Invasion of the Romans to the Reign of George II*, even though Gilbert Stuart and John Langhorne each contributed a quarter of the translation from the work by Abbé Millot. Even more significantly, his efforts brought him scholarly acknowledgement when he was created doctor of laws by the faculty of Marischal College, Aberdeen, in February 1772. With John Murdoch he translated *A Natural History of Animals, Vegetables, and Minerals* (1775) from the French of Buffon and at his death he was editor of a fourteen-volume translation of Voltaire's works (1779–81).

Having regained some semblance of financial security through his employment on the *Monthly Review*, Kenrick was able to marry again; on 5 May 1764 he wed Elizabeth Piercy Perrins (*bap.* 1744). The couple had no children, and Elizabeth died two years later. During this period Kenrick often visited Thomas Worlidge, the painter responsible for the only known portrait of Kenrick. When Worlidge died in the same year as Elizabeth, Kenrick published several elegiac poems and composed the artist's epitaph.

Theatrical works and more literary feuds Either distraught from grief or emboldened by an arrangement to edit a ten-volume edition of Shakespeare for 100 guineas per volume, Kenrick forsook the *Monthly Review* for the theatre, presenting a Shakespearian-inspired comedy entitled *Falstaff's Wedding* (1766). Kenrick prefaced his play with a typically arrogant and ironically contemptuous remark to the critics:

> The author foresaw that these mice would necessarily be nibbling; he has therefore, purposely left some rotten holes in the cheese, that the poor little animals may be kept doing; for, considering them as real objects of pity, he would by no means have them starve for want of employment. (p. vi)

Although *Falstaff's Wedding* played only one night, Garrick permitted Kenrick to stage a second comedy, *The Widow'd Wife*, the next season, which ran for nine nights and was translated into German in 1773.

Kenrick's larger ambitions, however, were severely disappointed when George Steevens agreed to compile a Shakespeare edition without payment and Kenrick's lucrative agreement was cancelled. This loss added poignancy to Kenrick's appearance in September 1766 at the Shakespeare jubilee as Shakespeare's ghost. Modest stage successes kept Kenrick solvent through this period, but he returned to periodical publishing in November 1768 with the *Gentleman's Journal*, which survived only a fortnight, and contributed to the *Universal Museum* and, after 1773, to the *Westminster Magazine*. By the end of January 1769 Kenrick was editing *Critical Memoirs of the Time* and was a founding editor of the *Morning Chronicle* that same year. He also published individual poems in literary magazines, many of which were ultimately collected in his *Poems; Ludicrous, Satirical and Moral* (1768; with additions, 1770).

During this period Kenrick also sought to engage Samuel Johnson in controversy. In an exceptionally long review, later published separately, Kenrick meticulously catalogued the imperfections in Johnson's *Dictionary*, then issued his own *Defence of Mr Kenrick's Review* (1766). When Kenrick subsequently published his own *New Dictionary of the English Language* (1773), with a guide to pronunciation, he drew almost entirely on Johnson's efforts and must have further galled the great lexicographer. Kenrick also composed *An Epistle to James Boswell, Esq.* (1768), accusing Johnson of immoral cynicism and offering Rousseau as a moral guide superior to Boswell's admired Pasquale Paoli. In response to these provocations Johnson maintained a stoic silence.

Unable to incite Johnson, Kenrick contemplated a similar assault on William Warburton. In 1769 Kenrick wrote to John Wilkes, with whom he was on good terms, asking for notes on Pope because 'The publication of a new edition affords so fine an opportunity of mauling the Bishop of Gloucester, that I would not lose it for the world' (BL, Add. MS 30870, fol. 116r). Wilkes ultimately passed his notes to Joseph Warton, and Warburton was spared Kenrick's ire.

The sole controversy in which Kenrick's arguments prevailed concerned his views on adultery and divorce, originally published anonymously in 1771 to support Richard Grosvenor's lawsuit against his wife for her liaison with the king's brother, Henry, duke of Cumberland. Kenrick is reputed to have received £500 for this slim volume, probably his most lucrative publication, and later expanded his views in *Observations, Civil and Canonical, on the Marriage Contract* (1775).

During these years Kenrick also continued to write for the stage, though his relations with the dramatic companies were never easy. His plays were all reasonably entertaining, but his incessant arguments with the patentees meant that his productions rarely came to the boards without much delay and rancour. After the production of *Falstaff's Wedding* Kenrick and Garrick disputed the distribution of the final night's proceeds and by 1771 Kenrick was corresponding with George Colman about an opera for Covent Garden, despite having quarrelled with Colman in print a few years earlier. Colman, who had accepted a Kenrick comedy for the 1772–3 season, opted to stage Goldsmith's new play, *She Stoops to Conquer*, instead. Kenrick replied with a libel in the *London Packet* that insulted not only Goldsmith but also a female friend; for this affront Goldsmith assaulted the publisher and had to donate £50 to charity to avoid prosecution, while Kenrick reportedly played the part of innocent bystander. Kenrick's *Duellist* was presented later in 1773, but the first performance was complicated by an argument over Charles Macklin's employment and the play closed, though it too was later translated into German.

Kenrick's most famous, and shameful, controversy arose in 1772, when he published *Love in the Suds*, accusing Garrick of a homosexual relationship with the disgraced Isaac Bickerstaff. The pamphlet went through five editions in the year, until Kenrick, fearing imprisonment for libel, finally suppressed the work and issued an apology in November. Kenrick's resentment stemmed from delays in producing his plays, not from any moral qualms, and the tasteless cruelty of the attack ensured his opprobrium and forced him to confine his opinions to the pages of the *London Review*.

Other schemes Having lost the contract to edit Shakespeare, Kenrick instead collected his friend Robert Lloyd's *Poetical Works* (1774). That same year, unwilling to let his Shakespearian insights languish, Kenrick converted his critical notes into a series of successful lectures on the bard. Although he twice had to move to larger venues to accommodate the crowds, the series faltered after March 1774 and then metamorphosed into a much grander proposal to establish 'A Public Academy, for the Investigation of the English Language, and the Illustration of British Literature' (*Morning Chronicle*, 20 Aug 1774).

The school never eventuated, but its intended curriculum formed the basis for Kenrick's final venture, the *London Review of English and Foreign Literature*, which first appeared in January 1775 and survived its founding editor by six months. As editor and chief writer, Kenrick finally exercised complete sovereignty over a critical empire. Although the magazine did not uphold its initial promise of illustrative plates and coverage of all new publications, it rivalled the established reviews and became known for its extended critiques and philosophical interests.

Amid all these publishing ventures Kenrick also found time to develop his long-standing fascination with perpetual motion. As early as 1761 Kenrick (with the support of Thomas Bennett, his former master) had sought a patent for a perpetual motion machine, but refused to supply the details requested by the attorney-general. He claimed to have experimented with the design for more than fifteen years before he presented his arguments in two publications and displayed his device at a series of three lectures in 1770–71. Even the physics of his day recognized the impossibility of such an invention, and Kenrick found few subscribers for a proposed stock offering, though he attracted much notoriety and ridicule. He none the less remained undaunted, returning to the attorney-general in May 1779, less than a month before he died, still in search of a patent.

Final years Throughout the final decade of his life, incessant financial demands required Kenrick to pursue an impressive variety of undertakings. He needed to sustain a new family with his third partner, Elizabeth (d. 1818), with whom he had three daughters between 1770 and 1775. The two apparently never wed, though her 1818 obituary refers to her as his 'relict' (*GM*, 1818). On 27 June 1776 Kenrick was back at the altar, this time with Frances Gymer. The two had no children, but this may have been just as well since Kenrick spent most of 1777 and half of 1778 in the Fleet prison for debt when a warehouse fire consumed most of an issue of the *London Review*. In 1778 Kenrick finally saw the performance of his only opera, *The Lady of the Manor*, and at the end of the year he closed his theatrical career with a Christmas farce, *The Spendthrift*. By the beginning of 1779 he could no longer sustain the pace and called upon his eldest son to assist him with the *London Review*.

The lingering illness that led to his death, on 10 June 1779, aged forty-nine, remains unidentified. His funeral and burial took place on 13 June, in Chelsea Old Church. The church has been substantially altered and no memorial remains. The probate record a year later lists him as 'late of the parish of St Martin-in-the-Fields'. Frances survived him.

Assessment From his early engagement with his literary contemporaries in the 1751 paper war to his 1778 *Observations on Soame Jenyns's 'View of the Internal Evidence of the Christian Religion'*, Kenrick was rarely without a public enemy. He relished controversy and always sought the last word. If no one would oppose his views, he was not above writing replies to himself, as he did in a theological tract (*The

Grand Question Debated, 1751) and its reply. He dismissively described himself as 'a pretender to almost all kinds of writing' (*The Pasquinade*, 20n.), and his career typified the life of a professional writer, working at various times, frequently simultaneously, as periodical reviewer and editor, translator, dramatist, poet, controversialist, and inventor. Kenrick achieved notoriety in several fields, but sullied his reputation through unjustified attacks on more famous contemporaries. His almost boundless energy and broad learning were impressive, but his unwavering arrogance and irascible temper vitiated his accomplishments. As Alexander Chalmers judiciously concluded almost two centuries ago:

> Dr. Kenrick was really a man of talents, and deficient only in the knowledge of making a proper use of them; it was his misfortune likewise to settle upon no regular plan of study, and to fancy himself equal to any task which his necessities imposed upon him. (Chalmers, 19.324)

C. S. ROGERS and BETTY RIZZO

Sources G. E. Brewer, 'The black sheep of Grub street: William Kenrick LL.D.' (unpubd typescript), Boston PL, MS AM. 1817 RBD 1195 · P. J. Anderson and J. F. K. Johnstone, eds., *Fasti academiae Mariscallanae Aberdonensis: selections from the records of the Marischal College and University, MDXCIII–MDCCCLX*, 3 vols., New Spalding Club, 4, 18–19 (1889–98) · G. E. Brewer and P. Fussell, 'The birth date of William Kenrick', *N&Q*, 195 (1950), 51–2 · W. Kenrick, *The pasquinade* (1753) · P. Fussell, 'William Kenrick, eighteenth century scourge and critic', *The Journal of the Rutgers University Library*, 20 (1957), 42–59 · R. B. Sewell, 'William Kenrick as translator and critic of Rousseau', *Philological Quarterly*, 20 (1941), 58–68 · *GM*, 1st ser., 49 (1779), 327 · *GM*, 1st ser., 88/2 (1818), 376 · M. W. England, *Garrick's jubilee* (1964) · P. A. Tasch, *The dramatic cobbler: the life and works of Isaac Bickerstaff* (1971) · P. Fussell, 'William Kenrick's "courtesy" book', *Publications of the Modern Language Association of America*, 66 (1951), 538–40 · W. R. Irwin, 'William Kenrick: volunteer moralist', *Publications of the Modern Language Association of America*, 67 (1952), 288–91 · W. Zachs, *The first John Murray and the late eighteenth-century London book trade* (1998) · R. Mahony and B. W. Rizzo, *Christopher Smart: an annotated bibliography, 1743–1983* (1984) · A. Chalmers, ed., *The general biographical dictionary*, new edn, 19 (1815), 324 · G. Colman, ed., *Posthumous letters, from various celebrated men: addressed to Francis Colman, and George Colman, the elder, with annotations … by George Colman, the younger* (1820) · *The recantation and confession of Dr William Kenrick* (1772) · IGI

Archives BL, Add. MSS 30870, fols. 116, 209; 30871, fols. 87–8 · Boston PL, Shakespeare edition agreement · PRO, petition for perpetual motion patent, SP 37/1, fol. 85

Likenesses T. Worlidge, engraving, NPG [*see illus.*]

Wealth at death see Brewer, 'Black sheep', 218

Kenrick, William (1831–1919). *See under* Kenrick family (*per. c.*1785–1926).

Kenrick, William Edmund (1908–1981), hardware manufacturer, was born at Edgbaston, Birmingham, on 21 September 1908, the second child and eldest son of Wilfrid Byng Kenrick (1872–1962) and his wife, Norah Beale. William was the fifth generation of the *Kenrick family to head the cast-iron hollowware and hardware firm of Archibald Kenrick & Sons Ltd, established in West Bromwich by Archibald [i] Kenrick in 1791. Educated first at Rugby School, then at Balliol College, Oxford, where he read classical Greats, William proceeded to continue the unitarian family tradition, both in business, by exercising leadership in the trade, and through public service. In 1939 he married Elizabeth, daughter of Lieutenant-Colonel Francis Loveday.

William joined the company in 1930 when the company's fortunes lay in the hands of the chairman, Sir George Hamilton Kenrick (1850–1939), William's cousin, and his father, both of whom were heavily involved in public affairs at a time when the cast-iron hollowware and hardware trade, the mainstay of the business since the mid-nineteenth century, had been in permanent decline for a decade. New cast-iron products which had been added to the company's range in an attempt to enter a growing market, such as electric and gas irons, made no headway, failing to achieve profitability to offset losses in the traditional trade. The exception was the cast-iron bath, which was the largest selling item until the demand for munitions rescued the company after 1939. Hollowware was discontinued.

William began his career in the failing family firm without any guidance or clear responsibility, working in the recently created cost department. In 1937, following the board of directors' rejection of a management consultant's recommendation that professional management should be introduced from outside the Kenrick family, his father appointed William as head of the sales department.

The firm avoided bankruptcy first through government contracts during the war, and after the war by a combination of circumstances and changes in personnel. In 1945 William's father, W. Byng Kenrick, then aged seventy-three, withdrew from day-to-day involvement in management, allowing William to be promoted to managing director. On his father's retirement in 1953, William found himself under a new chairman, Arthur Wynn Kenrick, a distant relative, formerly joint managing director of Kenrick and Jefferson, a successful printing business. Another new element was introduced in the shape of John Donkin, an engineer formerly with GEC, who was appointed to West Bromwich as joint general manager to work with William. At the same time, by chance, an Australian inventor offered William Kenrick the option on a patent (Shepherd's) furniture castor produced by die-casting, which on William's recommendation the board took up. These developments, combined with William's insistence that henceforward sales and the consumer, rather than the plant's capacity to produce, should determine product policy and investment, enabled the firm to survive, though still on the narrow basis of a single product. William retired as managing director and chairman in 1978, a position which he had held since 1963. His son Martin joined the company in 1964 and became chairman in 1978. The company was taken over by a west midlands consortium in 1992.

One of the reasons William succeeded, in the context of the challenges facing him from the 1930s, was his break with the tradition by which the Kenricks looked to their historic leadership in trade associations to sustain the firm's relative position. Even so, he was president of the National Institute of Hardware from 1950 to 1953, and of the National Hardware Alliance in 1957. After the abolition of resale price maintenance during the mid-1960s, however, such associations became defunct.

Kenrick's prominence as a local businessman led to his being president of the Birmingham chamber of commerce in 1962 and vice-president of the Association of British Chambers of Commerce. He was also governor (and chairman of governors) of the College of Art and Design between 1962 and 1970, during which time he played a major role in the formation of Birmingham Polytechnic, of which he was also governing chairman (1971–8). A life governor of the University of Birmingham and a member of convocation of the University of Aston, he received honours from the University of Birmingham (LLD) and from the Royal Society of Arts, to which he was elected as fellow in 1973.

Kenrick was a gifted amateur in business. His readiness to accept non-family expertise and his ability to intuit management skills and exploit chances enabled him to keep alive a company which otherwise might have failed at any time between 1950, when he took charge, and 1978. He was declared dead at the General Hospital, Birmingham, on 21 June 1981, following a road accident. He was survived by his wife.   ROY CHURCH

Sources R. A. Church, *Kenricks in hardware: a family business, 1791–1966* (1969) · *The Times* (9 July 1981) · d. cert.
Archives U. Birm. L., MSS
Wealth at death £101,929: probate, 8 Oct 1981, *CGPLA Eng. & Wales*

Kensit, John (1853–1902), religious controversialist, was born on 12 February 1853 in Bishopsgate in the City of London, the only son of John and Elizabeth Anne Kensit. He was educated at the Bishopsgate Ward Schools, before becoming a draper's assistant with Messrs S. and R. Morley in Wood Street, Cheapside. Despite a brief spell as a choirboy at the ritualist church of St Lawrence Jewry, Kensit soon gave his allegiance to the militant protestant cause. In 1870 he took up Sunday-school work and open-air evangelism in Hackney, and at about the same time he left the drapery business and opened a stationer's shop and subpost office in East Road, Hoxton. He married, on 14 September 1878, Edith Mary, daughter of Alfred Eves of the Corn Exchange, Mark Lane. Their family comprised three daughters and a son.

During the 1870s and 1880s Kensit's business grew, as did his involvement in militant protestantism. In 1885 he opened the City Protestant Book Depot at 18 Paternoster Row, thus uniting his professional and protestant interests, and from 1886 he was a regular attender at the annual church congress. In 1889 Kensit gained some notoriety when two of his publications were censured by *Truth* as 'religious obscenity' (29 Aug 1881, 381). In the same year he acquired the *Churchman's Magazine*, which became a vehicle for vigorous protestant polemic, and founded the Protestant Truth Society, whose work expanded in the early 1890s from literature distribution to the holding of public meetings and services in ritualist parishes. An able propagandist with a flair for publicity and a disregard for respectability, Kensit stood unsuccessfully for election to the London school board in 1894 as part of his campaign against ritualism in the Church of England. As the Protestant Truth Society gained support in this period, and as its secretary moved from the East End to West Hampstead, questions were asked about Kensit's protestant credentials and financial probity.

Kensit was a leading protagonist in the so-called Church Crisis of 1897–1904. In January 1897 he made a formal protest at the confirmation of Mandell Creighton's election to the see of London. Later in the same year he interrupted a service at All Saints', Lambeth, to object to the use of the 'Hail, Mary'. The winter of 1897–8 witnessed persistent protests at St Ethelburga, Bishopsgate, followed by a campaign of disruption during Holy Week 1898. This culminated in a brawl at the veneration of the Cross at St Cuthbert's, Philbeach Gardens, on Good Friday, where Kensit seized the crucifix and said, 'In the name of God I denounce this idolatry in the Church of England; God help me' (*Record*, 15 April 1898, 359). Negotiations with Bishop Creighton led to a temporary truce, but the agitation resumed within a matter of months. Over the next four years Kensit organized bands of Wickliffe Preachers to proclaim the protestant message throughout England, while he continued with public protests and bitter criticism of the episcopate for its apparent failure to suppress ritualism. In the general election of 1900 Kensit polled 4693 votes as a militant protestant candidate for Brighton.

In the course of a turbulent campaign on Merseyside in autumn 1902, Kensit was injured by an iron file thrown by an unknown assailant. At Liverpool Royal Infirmary septic pneumonia and meningitis developed, and Kensit died on 8 October 1902, hailed by his supporters as 'the first Protestant martyr of the twentieth century' (*Churchman's Magazine*, Nov 1902). Funeral services were held at St Clement's, Toxteth Park, Liverpool, and at St Mary's, Kilburn, London, before Kensit was buried in Hampstead cemetery. His son, John Alfred Kensit (1881–1957), succeeded him as secretary of the Protestant Truth Society.

MARTIN WELLINGS

Sources J. C. Wilcox, *John Kensit, reformer and martyr: a popular life* (1903) · M. Wellings, 'The first protestant martyr of the twentieth century: the life and significance of John Kensit, 1853–1902', *Martyrs and martyrologies*, ed. D. Wood, SCH, 30 (1993), 347–58 · DNB · *Churchman's Magazine* (1892), 354–6 · *The Times* (9 Sept 1902) · *The Times* (9 Oct 1902) · *The Times* (13 Oct 1902) · *The Times* (9 Dec 1902) · *The Times* (10 Dec 1902) · *The Times* (12 Dec 1902) · *English Churchman* (9 Oct 1902) · *English Churchman* (16 Oct 1902) · *Truth* (15 Aug 1889) · *Truth* (29 Aug 1889) · *Truth* (5 Sept 1889) · *Truth* (12 Sept 1889) · *Truth* (10 Oct 1889) · *Truth* (28 Dec 1893) · *Truth* (14 Feb 1895) · *Truth* (21 Feb 1895) · *Truth* (2 May 1901) · *Truth* (23 May 1901) · *Truth* (26 Dec 1901) · *Record* (22 Jan 1897) · *Record* (4 Feb 1898) · *Record* (15 April 1898) · C. Mackenzie, *My life and times*, 10 vols. (1963–71), vol. 2, p. 219
Archives Kensit Memorial Bible College, Finchley, London · LPL, corresp. concerning his protests against ritualist practices
Likenesses portrait, Kensit Memorial Bible College, Finchley, London
Wealth at death £2196 7s. 6d.: administration, 20 March 1902, *CGPLA Eng. & Wales*

Kenswood. For this title name *see* Whitfield, Ernest Albert, first Baron Kenswood (1887–1963).

Kent. For this title name *see* Odo, earl of Kent (*d.* 1097); Burgh, Hubert de, earl of Kent (*c.*1170–1243); Margaret, countess of Kent (1187x95–1259); Edmund, first earl of Kent (1301–1330); Holland, Thomas, earl of Kent (*c.*1315–1360); Joan, *suo jure* countess of Kent, and princess of Wales and of Aquitaine (*c.*1328–1385); Holland, Thomas, fifth earl of Kent (1350–1397); Holland, Thomas, sixth earl of Kent and duke of Surrey (*c.*1374–1400); Holland, Edmund, seventh earl of Kent (1383–1408); Neville, William, earl of Kent (1401?–1463); Grey, Edmund, first earl of Kent (1416–1490); Grey, George, second earl of Kent (*d.* 1503); Grey, Richard, third earl of Kent (*b.* in or before 1478, *d.* 1524); Grey, Elizabeth, countess of Kent (1582–1651); Grey, Henry, tenth earl of Kent (*bap.* 1594, *d.* 1651); Grey, Henry, duke of Kent (*bap.* 1671, *d.* 1740); Victoria, Princess, duchess of Kent (1786–1861); George, Prince, first duke of Kent (1902–1942); Marina, Princess, duchess of Kent (1906–1968).

Kent, kings of (*act. c.*450–*c.*590), rulers in Kent, held power in the Anglo-Saxon kingdom roughly coterminous with the modern county of Kent, from its foundation to the accession of King *Æthelberht I (*d.* 616?). The traditional founders of the Kentish royal house are the two brothers **Hengist** (*d.* 488?) and **Horsa** (*d.* 455?). Bede identified them as the leaders of the Germanic forces invited to Britain by Vortigern, as described by Gildas, and he calculated that they had arrived in 449. By the ninth century an elaborate saga existed describing the history of the relations between Hengist, Horsa, and Vortigern which appears in attenuated form in the Anglo-Saxon Chronicle and in rather more detail in a ninth-century Welsh compilation, known as the *Historia Brittonum*, where the defeat of the British is attributed in part to Vortigern's love for Hengist's daughter. Superficially the chronicle narrative in particular appears convincing, with named battles and protagonists. But even stripped of the names of personalities and places, the notion of the originally peaceful settlement of Germanic contingents in a military context may be supported by the archaeological evidence. In Kent, and other parts of southern Britain, apparently peculiarly Germanic inhumation burials can be dated to the first half of the fifth century, and the goods found in them include belt furniture of a kind worn by Germans in Roman military service. That such mercenary captains should turn on their erstwhile employers is highly plausible. The chronicle relates that Hengist and Horsa fought Vortigern at 'Ægelesthrep' in 455, with the result that Hengist became king; Horsa was slain in the battle and Bede reports that a monument bearing his name could be seen in the eastern part of Kent.

In spite of such details it seems very likely that Hengist and Horsa were mythical founders rather than real personages. Their alliterating names recall other founding figures of Indo-European legend such as Romulus and Remus. The names mean 'stallion' and 'horse', and the possibility that they were in origin equine deities receives some support from accounts that in nineteenth-century Saxony protective roof-finials in the shape of horse-heads

were known by their names. The Hengist who appears in Old English poetry as a Jutish leader is no doubt intended to be the same person as the founder of the Kentish royal house, for Bede says that the Germanic settlers in Kent were of Jutish stock. However, the literary references cannot be seen as independent confirmation of Hengist's existence as a real person, as they may have been influenced by the development of his legend within England.

Hengist is said in the Anglo-Saxon Chronicle to have succeeded to the kingdom in 455 with his son **Æsc** (*d.* 512?), and successful battles against the British are recorded at 'Creacanford' in 456, at 'Wippedesfleot' in 465, and in an unrecorded location in 473. In 488 Æsc became king in his own right—presumably Hengist is supposed to have died—and is said to have reigned for twenty-four years. Bede believed that Hengist's son was in fact called Oeric, but that his cognomen was Oisc (cognate with Æsc) and that the kings of Kent were known from him as the Oiscingas. The name Æsc or Oisc seems to mean 'god' and the possibility must therefore be allowed that he too is a thinly disguised deity. Possibly Oeric is a genuine progenitor with whom the name of Oisc (Æsc) came to be associated, but in view of the dubious company he keeps it becomes very difficult to accept the battles cited for him and his equally problematical 'father' in the chronicle as reliable accounts of the early history of the kingdom of Kent. Oeric's son is said by Bede to be **Octa** (*fl.* 512?), although in another version of the Kentish royal pedigree, in the so-called 'Anglian collection' of genealogies, it is Octa (Ocga) who is the son of Hengist and Oisc (Oese) who is the grandson. No activities are recorded for Octa, though his reign would have begun in 512, according to the chronicle reckoning for the length of Æsc's reign.

It is only with the third generation from Hengist that there appears an individual who can with some certainty be identified as a king of Kent. The son of Octa (Bede) or Oese (Anglian collection) was **Eormenric** (*fl.* 550x600) who was the father of Æthelberht, the first king of Kent whom Bede discusses in any detail. Gregory of Tours, writing of the marriage of the Frankish princess Bertha, daughter of King Charibert, to Æthelberht, describes him as 'the son of a certain king in Kent' and that is the only reference which definitely implies that Eormenric ruled as king (Gregory of Tours, 4.26). The marriage is not the only evidence for strong Frankish influence in Kent during the sixth century. Grave-goods from Kentish cemeteries show not only the acquisition of luxury goods made or acquired through Francia, but also the adoption of Frankish fashions of dress and other ways of displaying status. The first element of Eormenric's name is uncommon among Anglo-Saxon personal names, but relatively common in Francia, and so may be further evidence for Frankish influence in the time of his parents. Such influence may have gone beyond that of trade. Various Frankish sources and some of the correspondence connected with the mission sent by Pope Gregory to Kent in 596 may imply a degree of Frankish overlordship of Kent in the second half of the sixth century, perhaps aided by the fact that people from Kent seem to have settled within Francia in the vicinity of Boulogne.

Eormenric's reign cannot be dated precisely. Bede believed that Æthelberht succeeded to the throne in 560, which by implication would be the date of Eormenric's death. But Gregory of Tours's statement that Æthelberht was not yet king of Kent when he married Bertha implies that the 560 date cannot be correct, for Bertha was not born until some time between 561 and 568 and Gregory seems to have believed that Æthelberht was still a *filius regis* ('son of the king') at the time he was writing in 589. Even if it is allowed that Gregory may not have been fully informed on the Kentish succession, Eormenric's reign must be placed in the second half of the sixth century.

BARBARA YORKE

Sources ASC, s.a. 449, 455, 456, 465, 473, 477, 568 · Bede, *Hist. eccl.*, 1.15; 2.5 · D. N. Dumville, 'The Anglian collection of royal genealogies and regnal lists', *Anglo-Saxon England*, 5 (1976), 23–50 · N. Brooks, 'The creation and early structure of the kingdom of Kent', *The origins of Anglo-Saxon kingdoms*, ed. S. Bassett (1989), 55–74 · Gregory of Tours, *The history of the Franks*, ed. and trans. L. Thorpe (1974), bk 4. p.26; bk 9 p. 26 · I. N. Wood, *The Merovingian North Sea* (1983) · B. A. E. Yorke, 'Gregory of Tours and sixth-century Anglo-Saxon England', *The world of Gregory of Tours*, ed. K. Mitchell and I. Wood (Leiden, 2002) · B. A. E. Yorke, *Kings and kingdoms of early Anglo-Saxon England* (1990) · L. Oliver, *The beginnings of English law* (2002)

Kent, Albert Frank Stanley (1863–1958), physiologist, was born on 26 March 1863 at Stratford Tony, Wiltshire, the sixth son of the rector, the Revd George Davies Kent, and his wife, Anne, daughter of William Rudgard of Newland House, Lincoln. He was educated at Magdalen College School and Magdalen College, Oxford, where he obtained a second class in physiology in 1886 and proceeded to his DSc in 1915. He was elected a member of the Physiological Society in 1887 and lived to be its senior member. After demonstrating in physiology at Manchester (1887–9), Oxford (1889–91), and St Thomas's Hospital, London (1891–5), he became professor of physiology at Bristol in 1899.

At St Thomas's, Kent, who was an early worker on X-rays, helped to develop the radiological department; but it was in Bristol that he found full scope for his enthusiastic energies and organizing ability. He founded and for some eight years carried on a clinical and bacteriological research laboratory which later became the city's public-health laboratory and he was for a time bacteriologist to the Royal Infirmary. He was a leading spirit in the movement which led to University College Bristol's becoming a chartered university in 1909 and he designed the university's new department of physiology.

In 1904 Kent married Theodora (d. 1957), daughter of William Henry Hobson, of Great Berkhamsted and Upper Berkeley Street, London. They had a daughter who died in childhood.

During the First World War Kent became interested in problems of industrial fatigue and was responsible for several government publications on the subject. He became editor-in-chief in Great Britain of the *Journal of Industrial Hygiene* and in 1918 he edited *Physiology of Industrial Organization*, a translation of Jules Amar's work. In that year he resigned his chair in order to organize and direct a department of industrial administration in the Manchester Municipal College of Technology.

After his retirement in 1922 Kent returned to the west country and, converting one room in his house into a laboratory, continued his work on cardiac physiology which he had begun at Oxford and for which he is best known. In a series of communications to the Physiological Society (1892–3) he had reported his investigation of the atrioventricular bundle and its properties which formed the basis of the twentieth-century understanding of the normal conduction of the heart beat and of the functional dissociation of ventricles from atria which occurs in heart block. He retained his interest in physiological matters until ill health overtook him, a year or so before he died in St Martin's Hospital, Bath, on 30 March 1958, leaving several thousands of sections representing the work of many years.

Kent was a man of slight build who worked to high standards and drove himself hard. This produced an atmosphere of great intensity which made him appear on first acquaintance as a rather austere man, but to those who came to know him well he was very friendly. He gave the impression of enjoying himself most when in the company of one or two friends with whom he could converse freely on some topic of common interest. In his school and college days he was active in rowing and rifle-shooting and he became a keen photographer. He also enjoyed foreign travel.   R. J. BROCKLEHURST, rev.

Sources *Nature*, 181 (1958), 1240–41 · personal knowledge (1971) · CGPLA Eng. & Wales (1958) · DNB
Wealth at death £4347 14s. 7d.: administration, 29 Sept 1958, CGPLA Eng. & Wales

Kent, (William) Charles Mark [*pseud.* Mark Rochester] (1823–1902), writer and journalist, was born in London on 3 November 1823, the eldest son among five sons and two daughters of William Kent, naval officer, and his wife, Ellen, only daughter of Charles Baggs, judge of the vice-admiralty court, Demerara, and sister of Charles Michael *Baggs (1806–1845), Roman Catholic bishop. He was the grandson of William *Kent (1751–1812), naval officer. Both parents were Roman Catholics, and Kent was educated at Prior Park, Bath, and then in 1838 at St Mary's College, Oscott, where he began writing prose and verse.

In December 1845, when Kent was only twenty-two, he succeeded William Frederick Deacon as editor of *The Sun*, an evening newspaper of liberal politics founded in 1792 by William Pitt. Its circulation had, however, significantly decreased by the mid-nineteenth century. Murdo Young had owned the paper since 1833, and Kent bought it from him in 1850 for £2024. Kent married Murdo Young's daughter Ann (1824–1911) on 27 June 1853; she had been received into the Roman Catholic church earlier that year. Ann also had a literary bent, having produced several novels as a young woman, including *Evelyn Stuart* (1846), which was published under the pseudonym Adrian. The

(William) **Charles Mark Kent** (1823–1902), by John & Charles Watkins

couple had five sons and two daughters, and Ann Kent continued to write for the periodical press until 1906.

The Sun was one of the first journals to publish reviews of books, and Charles Kent was a prolific contributor of these, as well as of leading articles. It was through Kent's review of *Dombey and Son* that he first met Charles Dickens, who had written asking the editor to express his 'warmest acknowledgements and thanks' to the reviewer. Kent's admission of authorship was the beginning of a lifelong friendship. Kent went on to contribute to Dickens's *Household Words* and *All the Year Round*. His articles in the former journal were later collected into a volume entitled *Footprints on the Road* (1864) and dedicated to Dickens, who wrote that it 'most heartily gratifies me, as the sincere tribute of a true and generous heart' (*Letters of Charles Dickens*, 6 Nov 1865). Kent organized the grand public farewell dinner before Dickens's second American public-reading tour in 1867, and wrote of his performances in *Charles Dickens as a Reader* (1872), a work with which Dickens assisted before his death. Kent was the recipient of the last letter that Dickens ever wrote, produced an hour before Dickens's death, which he presented to the British Museum in 1879. He also produced *The Humour and Pathos of Charles Dickens* (1884) and *Wellerisms from Pickwick and Master Humphrey's Clock* (1886).

Kent's other works included *Catholicity in the Dark Ages, by*

an *Oscotian* (1847), and *Aletheia, or, The Doom of Mythology; with other Poems* (1850). This latter volume contained a poem, 'Larmartine in February [1848]', which came to the notice of the French poet and statesman three years after its publication, and elicited from him an enthusiastic letter of gratitude. Kent also collected some twenty poems that he had contributed to the *New Monthly Magazine* and published them as *Dreamland, or, Poets in their Haunts* (1862). Some of his political sketches from *The Sun* were also collected and republished, although under pseudonyms, including *The Derby Ministry* (1858), by Mark Rochester, which was later reissued as *Conservative Statesmen*, and *The Gladstone Government* (1869) by A Templar.

Kent had been called to the bar at the Middle Temple on 10 June 1859, but he never practised law, preferring to focus on his editorial work and writing. His literary circle was wide. In addition to Dickens, he was friends with Leigh Hunt, the first and second Lord Lytton, Charles Reade, Robert Browning, George Meredith, Wilkie Collins, and Matthew Arnold. He arranged for the inscription of Leigh Hunt's line 'Write me as one that loves his fellowmen' to appear on Hunt's tomb at Kensal Green, and later wrote *Leigh Hunt as an Essayist* (1888). He produced the article on Charles Reade for the first *Dictionary of National Biography*.

In spite of Kent's considerable zeal and industry as editor, *The Sun* never regained its late-eighteenth-century popularity, and it ceased publication on 28 February 1871. Kent went on to edit the *Weekly Register and Catholic Standard* from 1874 to 1881, but his later years were devoted largely to preparing popular editions of the works of great writers. He published the collected works of Robert Burns in 1874, and in 1875 published a centenary edition of Lamb's works, the biographical introduction to the latter volume containing, among other new facts, an account of Lamb's relationship with Frances Maria Kelly, based on information from the actress herself. Other editions included the works of Thomas Moore (1879), and Father Prout (1881). Kent also edited a literary curiosity entitled *Corona catholica: de Leonis XIII assumptione, epigramma in 50 linguis* (1880), which supplied translations of an English epigram into fifty languages; among the scholars who supplied the translations were Max Müller and Prince Lucien Bonaparte. The manuscript of the compilation is now held in the British Library.

Kent received a civil-list pension of £100 on 4 January 1887, in recognition of his 'public services to literature as poet and biographer' (*The Times*, 24 Feb 1902). In his final years he was a frequenter of the Athenaeum Club, which he had joined in 1881. Charles Kent died on 23 February 1902 at his home, 1 Campden Grove, Kensington, London. He was buried in Kensal Green Roman Catholic cemetery, London, and was survived by his wife, who died on 16 August 1911.

SIDNEY LEE, *rev.* M. CLARE LOUGHLIN-CHOW

Sources *The Times* (24 Feb 1902) • *WWW* • A. Lohrli, 'Household Words' … *table of contents, list of contributors and their contributions* (1973) • Allibone, *Dict.* • m. cert. • d. cert. • d. cert. [Ann Kent] • J. Foster, *Men-at-the-bar: a biographical hand-list of the members of the various* *inns of court*, 2nd edn (1885) · *The letters of Charles Dickens*, ed. M. House, G. Storey, and others, 12 vols. (1965–2002) · *The letters of Wilkie Collins*, ed. W. Baker and W. M. Clarke, 2 vols. (1999)

Archives BL, *Corona Catholica* and corresp., Add. MSS 35229, 36355, 43457 · Boston PL, corresp. | Durham RO, letters to marquess of Londonderry · Herts. ALS, corresp., mainly with the Bulwer-Lytton family · Herts. ALS, corresp. with first Lord Lytton and second Lord Lytton · NL Scot., letters to Blackwoods **Likenesses** J. & C. Watkins, photograph, NPG [*see illus.*]

Kent, Constance Emilie (1844?–1944?), convicted fratricide, was reportedly born in February 1844, at Sidmouth, ninth child of Samuel Saville Kent (1801–1872), assistant inspector of factories in west England, and his first wife, Mary Ann (1808?–1852), daughter of Thomas Windus, a Bishopsgate coach builder. She had four elder brothers (of whom three died young, and the other in 1858, aged twenty-three), one younger brother, William, whom she adored, and four elder sisters (of whom two died young). Though her mother was stated by Samuel Kent to have become mentally disturbed around 1836, she subsequently bore him four children, each of which died within a year (1837–42); she supposedly became chronically insane after the birth of her tenth child in 1845. In 1843 he recruited Mary Pratt as governess and housekeeper, and in 1853 married her. They had a stillborn daughter (1854), another daughter (1855), a son (1856), and in 1858 a daughter called Emiline. Samuel Kent, who received sympathy from early twentieth-century writers, was subsequently depicted as a sexually dominant tyrant, manipulating other male figures of authority.

Pratt was perhaps affectionate as a governess, but after her elevation to mistress of the household and the birth of her own children she was a neglectful and probably harsh stepmother. Constance, who was headstrong, resolute, and irritable, was sent to boarding-school in Bath in the year of the birth of her first half-sister (1855). During a school holiday in 1856 she ran away from home, cutting her hair, dressing as a boy, and taking her brother William with her. They intended to go to sea from Bristol, but were apprehended at Bath.

On the night of 29–30 June 1860 Constance's half-brother, known as Saville (the favourite child of the family, not yet aged four), went missing from his bed. Some hours later his corpse was found crammed down the vault of a disused privy in the grounds of their home, Road Hill House, North Bradley, a village 4 miles north-east of Frome on the borders of Somerset and Wiltshire. His head was nearly severed from his body by a knife wound; there was another deep wound above the heart, and his tongue was protruding and his mouth blackened as if by suffocation. There was strong evidence that an inmate of Road Hill House rather than an intruder had committed the murder. After an incompetent police investigation Constance was arrested (20 July) at the behest of Inspector Jonathan Whicher of Scotland Yard and taken to Devizes gaol, where she maintained a dogged silence. Whicher fixed on her by a process of elimination, and believed she had been animated by jealous revenge. She was brought

before magistrates, but no real evidence was adduced of her guilt, and she was discharged (27 July). Local rumour-mongers decided that a girl of sixteen was incapable of such a bloodthirsty deed, and insinuated that Samuel Kent or the nursemaid, Elizabeth Gough, were singly or jointly the culprits. It was speculated by Constance's supporters that her father was sleeping with Gough (the second Mrs Kent was heavily pregnant), that Saville had surprised them in the night and had been either accidentally stifled or coldly murdered to protect the lovers' reputations, and that his throat had been cut to disguise the cause of death and the body hidden to divert suspicion. If Constance was innocent, then this alternative remains probable. In September Gough was charged with the murder but was never committed for trial.

About 1861 Constance was settled as a pupil in a convent at Dinan in Brittany, and in 1863 became a paying guest in St Mary's Home, a religious retreat for ladies attached to the Anglo-Catholic church of St Paul's, Brighton. There she fell under the spiritual direction of the Revd Arthur Wagner, to whom in confession she admitted her guilt of the murder. Stimulated by the intensity of her religious surroundings, she resolved to make public confession, and accompanied by Wagner—who had consulted W. E. Gladstone as to the action he should take—delivered herself up in a formal statement at Bow Street court to the police magistrate Sir Thomas Henry (25 April 1865). She stated that she bore no ill will against the little boy except as favourite child of her stepmother, who had spoken derogatorily of the first Mrs Kent. Several details of her account, notably her claim to have used a razor to make the chest wound and the slowness of the blood to flow from Saville's throat, are anomalous. She was at pains to exonerate her father. Her avowal of the crime was not universally accepted, and indeed was never corroborated. There was mistrust of her emotional situation: in the intense religious atmosphere she may have offered herself as a sacrifice. Succoured by her spiritual guardians, who passionately desired to vindicate the high-church confessional, she perhaps confessed to a sin she had not committed as a means of gratifying them. At Wiltshire assizes on 21 July she pleaded guilty to murder and entered no defence. Sir James Willes wept while sentencing her to death.

This capital sentence was commuted to penal servitude for life. Most of Constance's term was served in Portland prison, where she made church mosaics, and at Millbank prison, where she worked as a laundress and infirmary nurse. In Millbank she seemed 'a small mouse-like little creature, with … high cheek-bones, a lowering overhanging brow, and deepset small eyes; but yet her manner was prepossessing, and her intelligence was of a high order' (Griffiths, 10). After release in 1885 she is variously stated to have entered an Anglican sisterhood, to have worked in Canada as a children's nurse called Emilie King, or to have lived under the name of Emily Kaye in Australia, dying there in 1944, but the actual circumstances of her later life and death remain a matter of speculation.

Wilkie Collins used elements of Kent's case in *The Moonstone* (1868); her escapade of 1856 prompted Charles Dickens's handling of the flight of Helena Landless in *The Mystery of Edwin Drood* (1870), and her story inspired James Friel's fine novel *Taking the Veil* (1989).

RICHARD DAVENPORT-HINES

Sources Y. Bridges, *Saint—with red hands?* (1954) · J. Rhode, *The case of Constance Kent* (1928) · M. Hartman, *Victorian murderesses* (1977), 94–101, 107–12, 118–29 · F. T. Jesse, *Murder and its motives* (1924), 74–116 · W. Roughead, *Classic crimes* (1951), 137–70 · J. B. Atlay, 'Famous trials: the Road mystery', *Cornhill Magazine*, [3rd] ser., 2 (1897), 80–94 · J. W. Stapleton, *The great crime of 1860* (1861) · A. Griffiths, *Secrets of the prison house, or, Gaol studies and sketches*, 2 vols. (1894) · *A mid-Victorian Pepys: the letters and memoirs of Sir William Hardman*, ed. S. M. Ellis (1923), 20–24 · *The Times* (1860) · *The Times* (1865) · *Annual Register* (1860) · *Annual Register* (1865) · *Mary Gladstone (Mrs Drew): her diaries and letters*, ed. L. Masterman (1930) **Likenesses** photograph, c.1860, repro. in Hartman, *Victorian murderesses*, 85 · photograph, c.1865, Hult. Arch.; repro. in H. Scott, ed., *The concise encyclopaedia of crime and criminal* (1961), 168

Kent, Edward Thomas. *See* Ceannt, Éamonn (1881–1916).

Kent, Eliza (1765/6–1810), traveller and writer, was born in 1765 or 1766, the daughter of William Kent, of Newcastle upon Tyne. In her youth Eliza described herself as 'destitute of Fortune, Beauty, Sense … and what is worse, bearing the Appellation of a Coquette' (letter to William Kent, 25 April 1788, Mitchell L., NSW, Kent family papers, A3966). Having declined 'several very advantageous offers' (letter to William Kent, 23 Jan 1791, Mitchell L., NSW, Kent family papers, A3967), on 24 November 1791 she was married at Newcastle to her cousin William *Kent (1751–1812), a naval lieutenant. It was now her ambition, she said, 'To retire with the Man of my Choice, far from the Gay, the Giddy, and the Vain' (ibid.). And so she did.

Eliza's first child, also Eliza, was born in September 1792. In January 1795 the family embarked on the *Supply*, bound for New South Wales under William Kent's command. They arrived at Sydney in September. They accompanied his uncle, John Hunter, lately appointed second governor of New South Wales, and Eliza seems to have gone with the intention of presiding at Government House, Hunter being a bachelor. She was thus apparently the first woman to undertake official responsibilities in British Australia and as such was a key figure in Hunter's hopes of establishing a polished civil society.

Within two months of their arrival, a son—John Hunter Kent—was born. He died aged six months and was buried in the grounds of Government House. Another girl, Mary, followed in 1797, and William in 1799. The Kents built a substantial house and garden at the edge of Sydney Cove, but Eliza spent two long periods alone, when her husband was sent by his uncle to the Cape of Good Hope for supplies.

In October 1800 the family sailed with Hunter back to England on the *Buffalo*, under William Kent's command, but William and Eliza immediately returned by the same ship to New South Wales, this time apparently leaving their three children behind. They remained abroad until December 1805, part of that time being spent on a voyage in 1803–4 from Sydney to New Caledonia and Calcutta.

Eliza Kent's early letters show that she was an enthusiastic writer and she became a skilled reporter of life on the far side of the world. In September–October 1807 she published in *The Athenaeum* material taken from letters written to her mother from New Caledonia, and in July 1808 a longer piece dating back to her journey of 1800–01 (part of which was immediately copied by the *Naval Chronicle*). Her published description of New Caledonia was a rare early glimpse of that remote spot, some of it unvisited hitherto by Europeans, and it proves her ambition to rise above the narrow range of expertise prescribed to women. She writes with authority and mentions herself only in the third person. Thus, of their first meeting with a local chief she says, 'A lady on board the Buffalo tied a broad pink sash across his shoulders, which pleased him so much that he sat by her all the time they were at breakfast' ('Account of part of the south-west side of New Caledonia', *The Athenaeum*, 1807, 237–8). Similarly, when other natives came on board, 'They listened attentively to the songs which a lady on board sang to [the violin] … and joined chorus with her in the tune of "tink a tink"' (ibid., 337).

Eliza Kent died in London on 29 January 1810, after 'a lingering illness' (*Naval Chronicle*, 1810, 176). Her age was given as forty-four, although she may have been younger. She was buried on 31 January at St Mary's Church, Paddington. On her gravestone William Kent proclaimed that her 'attachment to a once happy but now afflicted Husband, induced her to visit Countries far remote, and twice to circumnavigate the Globe' (Bonwick transcripts, Mitchell L., NSW, box 8, fol. 301). Her son and two daughters also survived her.

ALAN ATKINSON

Sources Kent family papers, Mitchell L., NSW, A3966, A3967, A3969 · *Historical Records of New South Wales*, 2, 3, 4 (1896) · *The Athenaeum* (1807–8) · *Naval Chronicle* (1808) · *Naval Chronicle* (1810) · Bonwick transcripts, Mitchell L., NSW, box 8, fols. 299–302 · K. M. Thomas, '"Romulus of the southern pole …, [or], Superintendent of pickpockets": a biographical appraisal of John Hunter R.N. (1737–1821)', B.A. hons. thesis, University of New England, 1992 · *Sydney Morning Herald* (16 June 1847) · parish register, St Nicholas's Church, Newcastle upon Tyne · memorial, St Mary's Church, Paddington, London **Archives** Mitchell L., NSW, family papers

Kent, Elizabeth (1790–1861), botanist and writer, was born in Brighton on 13 March 1790, a younger daughter of Ann Kent, court milliner. Nothing is known about her father; when Bessy (as she was known at home) was thirteen her widowed mother married Rowland Hunter, a bookseller in St Paul's Churchyard. Although she had only a dame-school education, Elizabeth Kent had clear intellectual interests, and studied languages and botany. The marriage of her older sister Marianne to Leigh Hunt brought her into lifelong contact with the Romantic writers, including Mary Shelley. She was Hunt's confidante and later his principal correspondent during Hunt's stay in Italy, 1822–5; his sonnet 'To Miss K.' (1818) asks 'what sylvan homage would it please your Leafyship to have?' Until 1836 she lived with her mother and stepfather, where, she later recalled, she passed much of her time in writing.

Elizabeth Kent combined her literary and botanical interests by writing about plants, producing books and essays meant to excite an interest in flowers among those who were otherwise 'deterred by the terms of science which met them at the threshold'. *Flora domestica, or, The Portable Flower-Garden* (1823, 1825) is an engaging book about container-gardening. Addressed to town-dwelling 'lovers of nature', it lists flowers, shrubs, and small trees that can be grown in pots and tubs, gives horticultural tips about soil, cultivation, and watering, and includes anecdotes on topics such as the introduction of species into Europe. Kent cites many verses by classical and contemporary poets, including Keats, Shelley, and Charlotte Smith. Her book represented the contemporary Romantic suburban aesthetic, and was widely praised by Byron, Coleridge, and Clare. In *Sylvan Sketches, or, A Companion to the Park and the Shrubbery* (1825), a compendium of information about trees and shrubs, she celebrates plants because 'there is something beyond mere use, something beyond mere beauty, in their influence upon the human mind'. Her chapter on the maple tree, for example, successfully blends botany and poetry by surveying different species of *Acer*, describing North American sugaring (tapping sap from the sugar maple to make syrup), and interpolating verses from Virgil, Sidney, Cowper, and Clare.

Elizabeth Kent also integrated botany into her other activities. She wrote a series of introductory articles for young people on Linnaean botanical nomenclature and systematics in the *Magazine of Natural History* (1828–30), and advertised lessons for young ladies 'in the science of botany' (*The Times*, 7 Aug 1828). She wrote a section on botany in *The Young Ladies' Book* (1829), and updated Galpine's *Synoptical Compendium of British Botany* (1834) and Irving's *Botanical Catechism* (1835). Other writing included a book of tales for children, reviews for J. C. Loudon's *Magazine of Natural History* during the late 1820s, and many unsigned articles and reviews for Leigh Hunt's *Indicator* (1819–20) and *The Tatler* (1830–32).

Elizabeth Kent was left without provision after the death of her mother and the failure of Hunter's business in 1836. She worked as a governess from 1837 to 1846, and received a legacy of £300 from her employer, Mr Bind. This was followed by a period of illness and an unsuccessful attempt to establish a seaside home for young invalids at St Leonards. By 1849, with impaired sight, she was dependent on friends 'of that class having more mind than money' (Kent to Royal Literary Fund, 1855). She applied to the Royal Literary Fund for assistance in 1855, and detailed her 'extreme privation' and 'delicate circumstances'. She endeavoured to support herself as a writer, but found herself 'a stranger in the literary world'. A second application, in 1858, records a fruitless attempt to interest a publisher in a manuscript about 'a visit to the principal watering-places on the southern coast' with botanical information. Leigh Hunt supplied testimonials about her 'impoverished circumstances' and 'high respectability'. At the time of her last application, in 1860, Kent was living with her nephew Thornton Hunt and his large family at 39 Bedford Street, Strand, with no money for clothing, laundry, and medicine. She died in 1861.

ANN B. SHTEIR

Sources letter, Kent to Royal Literary Fund, 1855, Royal Literary Fund archives, London, no. 1383 · M. Tatchell, 'Elizabeth Kent and *Flora domestica*', *Keats–Shelley Memorial Bulletin*, 27 (1976), 15–18 · M. Tatchell, *Leigh Hunt and his family in Hammersmith* (1969) · K. N. Cameron and D. H. Reiman, eds., *Shelley and his circle, 1773–1822*, 1 (1961) · L. Hunt, *Foliage* (1818)
Archives Royal Literary Fund, London, letters

Kent, Frances (*d.* 1685), midwife, was probably born some time between 1615 and 1640. The details of her birth as well as her maiden name are unknown. Her husband was John Kent of Reading, a clothier and a Quaker, who survived her by two years. The Kents had at least four children. Their daughter Hannah died (unmarried) in 1676. Their daughters Sarah and Mary each married London merchants (John Harwood and Samuel Clay, respectively) that same year. Their son John and his wife Ann had five children between 1682 and 1690.

The exact date of Frances Kent's conversion to Quakerism is unknown. During the 1660s and 1670s she was an active participant in the Quakers' Reading and Warborough monthly meeting. Like other prominent Quakers, she attended local business meetings where she reviewed proposals of marriage by Quaker youth. She also signed Quaker marriage and birth certificates, including those of her own children and grandchildren. During these years, Frances Kent was also gaoled twice at Newgate (in 1663 and 1672) for attending Quaker conventicles.

Despite religious persecution by state officials, Frances Kent was highly sought after as a midwife by prominent non-Quaker families, including the Buckinghamshire and Leicestershire gentry. Only three years after her first imprisonment at Newgate, Edmund Verney, the eldest son of Sir Ralph Verney, invited Frances Kent to be his wife Mary's midwife at Middle Claydon, Buckinghamshire. According to contemporary accounts, Mary Verney was mentally ill. Her husband had engaged the services of local women healers and London gentlewomen to try to cure her. Verney was ambivalent about inviting a Quaker to be his wife's midwife, but the glowing references of local gentlewomen and female relatives convinced him to do so. As Verney commented in a letter to his father, Frances Kent was a midwife 'reputed by all the doctors of Oxford as the best in England' (Hess, *Community Case Studies*, 108). A female cousin ('old lady Woodward') told Verney that 'she had never seen such a learned and adroit midwife, and that anyone would think themselves happy if they could have her, and that one gave her ordinarily £20, £10, and at the least £5 for her pains'. This cousin also reported to Verney that Frances Kent 'never meddled in speaking of her religion to her patients', that 'if she promised to come she is perfectly faithful to her word', and furthermore that 'if the Queen had continued pregnant she would have been her midwife' (ibid., 109). Frances Kent wrote to Verney to decline his offer (like many other Quakers she was fully literate), apologizing:

friend I ame sor[ry], thee hath put thyself to soe much trobell and I not in a Condicion to serve thee for the Ladey davis had layen in in London ... I canot in aney means

disopoint her shee being in a weekley Condicion.
(ibid., 110)

Frances Kent promised that if Lady Davis delivered in time at London then she would 'macke all the hast' she could to attend Mary Verney at Middle Claydon. Whether Frances Kent actually delivered the Verney baby is unknown (ibid., 111).

In addition to being sought out by the royal family and the gentry of Restoration England, Frances Kent was also employed by prominent Quaker families who lived in Buckinghamshire, Hertfordshire, and London. Among them was the wife of William Penn, the founder of Pennsylvania, as well as Sarah Meade, the daughter of Margaret (Fell) Fox and stepdaughter of George Fox, the founder of English Quakerism. Sarah Meade praised Frances Kent in a letter to her mother;

> Frances Kent stayed with me a week after I was laid. She is a fine woman; it was the Lord sent her to me. It was the Lord's mercy to me that I had her, who is a very skilfil and tender woman for that imployment.   (ibid., 113)

On 27 August 1685, the year after she delivered Sarah Meade's baby at London, Frances Kent died at Reading. She was buried by the Quakers on 1 September.

ANN GIARDINA HESS

Sources A. G. Hess, 'Community case studies of midwives from England and New England, c.1650–1720', PhD diss., U. Cam., 1994 · A. G. Hess, 'Midwifery practice among the Quakers in southern rural Europe in the late seventeenth century', *The art of midwifery: early modern midwives in Europe*, ed. H. Marland (1993), 49–76 · Claydon House, Middle Claydon, Buckinghamshire, Verney MSS, Verney letters, 1666–1667 · non-parochial registers and records c.1775–1837, PRO, RG/6/1367; RG/6/1255 · digested copies of registers of births, marriages, and burials of the Society of Friends, 1587–1838, RS Friends, Lond. · 'Sarah Meade to her mother [1684]', *Journal of the Friends' Historical Society*, 30 (1933), 42 · H. Verney, *The Verneys of Claydon* (1968) · F. P. Verney and M. M. Verney, *Memoirs of the Verney family*, 2nd edn, 2 vols. (1904) · N. Penney, ed., *Extracts from state papers relating to Friends, 1654–1672* (1913) · J. Besse, *A collection of the sufferings of the people called Quakers*, 1 (1753) · L. V. Hodgkin, *Gulielma: wife of William Penn* (1947)

Archives PRO, RG/6/1255, 1367, 1378 | Claydon House, Middle Claydon, Buckinghamshire, Verney MSS, corresp. between Edmund Verney and Ralph Verney, and between Edmund Verney and Frances Kent · RS Friends, Lond., Berkshire, and Oxfordshire Quarterly Meeting, births, 1612–1837, marriages 1648–1837, burials 1655–1837

Wealth at death employed by royalty and gentry of Restoration England; charged high fees

Kent, Sir Harold Simcox (1903–1998), lawyer and civil servant, was born on 11 November 1903 at Tientsin (Tianjin), China, the younger son in the family of two sons and one daughter of Percy Horace Braund Kent (1876–1963), a barrister practising in the consular courts at Tientsin, and his wife, Anna Mary (d. 1957), youngest daughter of the Revd Henry Kingdon Simcox, rector of Ewelme, Oxfordshire, and lord of the manor of Harborne, Warwickshire. At the age of eight he travelled with his older brother to preparatory school in Malvern, and he did not see his parents again until 1916, when his father returned to enlist. (The latter served with distinction in the trenches as a captain in the Scots Guards, winning an MC; he then returned to China where he remained, except for a brief spell in the

Sir Harold Simcox Kent (1903–1998), by Walter Stoneman, 1957

Treasury solicitor's department during the Second World War, until 1947.) Kent won scholarships to Rugby School and then Merton College, Oxford, where he obtained seconds in classical moderations (1924) and *literae humaniores* (1926).

After graduating, Kent became a pupil of Sir Donald Somervell, whose practice was in commercial law, but in 1928 (the year in which he was called to the bar by the Inner Temple) he joined common-law chambers when the Wall Street crash was beginning to bite. With the wolf at the door and having on 14 April 1930 made an improvident but very happy marriage to Zillah Lloyd (1905/6–1987), state registered nurse and daughter of Henry Rees Lloyd, cabinet-maker, the impecunious barrister turned, temporarily, to a literary career. *Punch* had been the recipient of Kent's contributions and, while still on honeymoon, he completed a novel about a country house murder and the detective abilities of a young, impoverished barrister on the foggy Cornish coast, with a surprising romantic dénouement. *The Tenant of Smuggler's Rock* (1930) was followed by *The Black Castle* (1931). The publishers were satisfied but the author believed, as he put it, that he would be happier as a 'desk-lawyer'. Moreover, the birth of his daughter, Margaret Anne (1931–1963)—who was later followed by a son, James Michael (b. 1934)—encouraged him to seek a more stable source of income.

In July 1932 Kent was introduced to second parliamentary counsel (then in recruiting mode) and joined his office in January 1933. As a junior draftsman, he showed a clarity of mind and a power of expression which made abstruse provisions comprehensible, together with a creative ability which helped the conception of legislation to grow in his mind so that the strands knitted into a coherent whole. He was allowed real responsibility on the Gas Undertakings Bill of 1934, and in 1936 was counsel's 'devil' on the Budget and Finance Bill. Of more general interest was the abdication that year of Edward VIII—on which Kent expressed the view that had the king married Mrs Simpson privately, he could not have been deposed by legislation which needed the royal assent. In 1938 he undertook the drafting of the Hire Purchase Bill. Powerful vested interests were involved who fought the complex legal issues all the way. Complexity was a subject that interested Kent, who believed that any legal change needed to be expressed exactly and that it should not be left to the courts to fill gaps in order to give effect to broad principles or supposed parliamentary intentions. Ironically, the Civil Defence Act (1939) placed on Kent heavy responsibility for drafting detailed schemes, for example for compulsory air raid shelter provisions, which the home secretary wanted in the bill for all to see.

In 1940 Kent was promoted parliamentary counsel. Wartime was a legal desert for him, but all changed under the post-war Labour administration, when he was asked to draft the first National Health Service Bill providing for a dichotomous system of care for private and state patients. Standing committees considered the bill between May and July 1946, and the legislation was enacted in November 1946. The draftsman's view of the National Health Service thirty years later was that having regard to developments in surgery and medicines it was surprising that it had not broken down completely. The pressure on Kent increased dramatically in the late 1940s with new responsibilities for drafting the legislation for the nationalization of the electricity, gas, and iron and steel industries. Subsequently, he did not regard the unscrambling of the Iron and Steel Act as a pleasant prospect.

In March 1953 another chapter opened when, to Kent's own great surprise, he was offered the post of Treasury solicitor. He was knighted (KCB) in the following year, having been appointed CB in 1946. Leaving a very small office with minimal managerial responsibilities to become head of the biggest solicitors' business in the country was, for one as modest and diffident as Kent, awesome. He was welcomed as a profound lawyer with broad experience, and showed to all his new colleagues the charm, warm humanity, and strong sense of humour for which he was already known. As Treasury solicitor, he was 'hands-on': he took a leading role in the affairs of the tribunal set up in 1963 under the chairmanship of Lord Radcliffe to investigate the circumstances in which John Vassall had been convicted of offences under the Official Secrets Acts, and he interviewed Vassall at the tribunal's request in Maidstone prison. He was advanced to GCB on retirement later that year.

Kent's concern with official secrets did not end with his retirement; between 1965 and 1971, at the height of the cold war, he was a member of the security commission, and he also served as a member of the committee set up to re-examine section 2 of the Official Secrets Act. In retirement he also placed his talents at the disposal of the Church of England, serving as standing counsel to the church assembly and general synod from 1964 to 1972. As dean of the arches of the court of Canterbury from 1972 to 1976 he was, in effect, the church's most senior judge. He took silk (*honoris causa*) in 1973 and was awarded a doctorate of civil law by Lambeth Palace in 1977. Having retired to Chipping Campden, Gloucestershire, he died on 4 December 1998 at Alveston Leys Nursing Home, Kissing Tree Lane, Alveston, Stratford upon Avon, of cancer of the bladder, and was buried at St James's Church, Chipping Campden. He was survived by his son, James, his wife and daughter having predeceased him.   JOHN BAILEY

Sources H. S. Kent, *In on the act* (1979) · *The Times* (1 Jan 1999) · *Daily Telegraph* (16 Feb 1999) · *WWW* · Burke, *Peerage* · personal knowledge (2004) · private information (2004) · m. cert. · d. cert.
Likenesses W. Stoneman, photograph, 1957, NPG [*see illus.*] · photograph, 1973, repro. in *Daily Telegraph*
Wealth at death £404,120—gross; £400,033—net: probate, 9 April 1999, *CGPLA Eng. & Wales*

Kent, James (1700–1776), organist and composer, was born at Winchester on 13 March 1700, the son of a glazier. He was a chorister at Winchester Cathedral (1711–14) and then at the Chapel Royal (1714–18) under Dr William Croft. Through the influence of the subdean, John Dolben, he was appointed organist to the parish church of Finedon, Northamptonshire, in 1718. He resigned in 1731 on being elected organist of Trinity College, Cambridge, remaining there until he succeeded John Bishop as organist of Winchester Cathedral and Winchester College. He was married to Elizabeth, daughter of John Freeman, a singer in the theatre and in the choirs of the Chapel Royal, St Paul's, and Westminster Abbey. He resigned in 1774 and died in Winchester on 6 May 1776.

Kent published *Twelve Anthems* (1773), and after his death *A Morning and Evening Service with Eight Anthems* (c.1777) was edited by Joseph Corfe. He had assisted William Boyce in the preparation of his *Cathedral Music* (1760). His anthem 'Hear my prayer', for two solo trebles, may be taken as representative of his work, which was both extravagantly praised and excoriated: his work drew so heavily from G. B. Bassani and others as to open him to charges of unscrupulous plagiarism.

R. F. SHARP, rev. K. D. REYNOLDS

Sources W. Shaw, 'Kent, James', *New Grove* · 'Kent, James', Grove, *Dict. mus.* (1927)
Likenesses G. M., oils, Winchester College, Hampshire

Kent, John. *See* Siôn Cent (*fl.* 1400–1430).

Kent, Marion (d. 1500). *See under* Women in trade and industry in York (*act. c.*1300–*c.*1500).

Kent, Nathaniel (1708–1766). *See under* Kent, Nathaniel (1737–1810).

Kent, Nathaniel (1737–1810), land agent and writer on agriculture, was the younger son of Ambrose Kent of Penton Mewsey, Hampshire. In 1755 he began work as a clerk at Portsmouth Dockyard, and later he held a secretarial post on the staff of Admiral Geary, at Portsmouth.

From 1762 to 1765 he was in Brussels as secretary to Sir James Porter, minister-plenipotentiary, and while there he studied Flemish farming methods. On his return to England in 1766, he was asked by Sir John Cust, speaker of the House of Commons, to write an account of farming in the Austrian Netherlands, and he was encouraged by Cust and Thomas Anson, MP for Lichfield, to leave the diplomatic service and became an agricultural adviser. He became manager of Anson's property in Norfolk. Soon afterwards he met Benjamin Stillingfleet, the naturalist.

In 1775 Kent published *Hints to Gentlemen of Landed Property*. This was one of the first works to set out detailed plans for model cottages. It also advised landowners to drain their land, and recommended enclosure, favouring either the Flemish eight-course system of crop rotation or the Norfolk six-course system. This work made him famous, and by 1793 he had a land agency in London at Craig's Court, Charing Cross, in partnership with John Claridge and William Pearce; the firm carried out land and rent valuations, and acted as an estate agency. From 1791 Kent managed the royal estates at Windsor Great Park and Richmond Park, and by 1797 he had converted 1400 acres of parkland at Windsor into two farms, one run on the Flemish system and the other on the Norfolk one.

Kent was asked to write a report on Norfolk for the board of agriculture in 1796. His later writings included *The Great Advantage of a Cow to the Family of a Labouring Man* (1797), and *An Account of the Improvements made on the Farm in the Great Park of His Majesty the King at Windsor* (1799).

In 1808 Thomas Coke of Holkham, president of the Norfolk Agricultural Society, presented Kent with a silver goblet in recognition of his services to agriculture. Kent contributed to the progress of the 'agricultural revolution' by making improvements while managing large estates.

Kent is known to have had a wife called Armine, but nothing else is known about his family life. He died of apoplexy at Fulham, Middlesex, on 10 October 1810.

Another **Nathaniel Kent** (1708–1766), scholar, was born on 17 April 1708 at Weedon, Northamptonshire, but his parentage is unknown. He was a king's scholar at Eton College and went to King's College, Cambridge in 1725 as a scholar. He was awarded a BA in 1729, an MA in 1733, and became a fellow of King's College. He was ordained in 1731 and was a priest at Ely from 1732. In 1744 he became insane, but he recovered and by 1748 was headmaster of Wisbech School. Later he became curate of Kersey in Suffolk. While at Cambridge, Kent published an edition of Lucian, *Excerpta quaedam ex Luciani Samosatensis operibus, in usum Tyronum* (1730). Latin notes and a Latin version accompanied the text, and the work was reprinted several times in London. Kent died in 1766.

Ronald Bayne, rev. Anne Pimlott Baker

Sources P. Horn, 'An eighteenth-century land agent: the career of Nathaniel Kent', *Agricultural History Review*, 30 (1982), 1–16 · J. Thirsk, ed., *The agrarian history of England and Wales*, 6, ed. G. E. Mingay (1989) · *GM*, 1st ser., 81/1 (1811), 182–3 · F. W. Steer and others, *Dictionary of land surveyors and local cartographers of Great Britain and Ireland, 1550–1850*, ed. P. Eden, [4 vols.] (1975–9) · G. E. Fussell, 'Nathaniel Kent, 1737–1816', *Journal of the Land Agents' Society*, 46 (1947), 150–52 · F. M. L. Thompson, *Chartered surveyors: the growth of a profession* (1968) · R. A. Austen-Leigh, ed., *The Eton College register, 1698–1752* (1927) · Venn, *Alum. Cant.*

Archives BL, letters to Sir James Porter · BL, corresp. with W. Windham · Holkham Hall, Norfolk, survey of Coke estates · Norfolk RO, corresp. relating to Windham estate · V&A NAL, report on Richmond Park
Likenesses J. Young, mezzotint (after J. Rising), BM
Wealth at death over £24,000: Horn, 'An eighteenth-century land agent'

Kent, Sir Percy Edward [Peter] (1913–1986), geologist, was born on 18 March 1913 in West Bridgford, Nottingham, the youngest of three sons and third of four children of Edward Louis Kent, photo-engraver and commercial artist, of West Bridgford, and his wife, Annie Kate, daughter of Luke Woodward, hosiery machine manufacturer and alderman, of Nottingham. He won scholarships to West Bridgford grammar school (1924) and University College, Nottingham (1931), graduating with first-class honours in the London University BSc degree (1934). He was awarded a Department of Scientific and Industrial Research studentship for postgraduate research and was invited to join the east African archaeological expedition led by L. S. B. Leakey in 1934–5. He was the expedition geologist in western Kenya and northern Tanganyika; his PhD thesis (1941) was based on this work, and his lifelong fascination with east Africa dated from this period. His DSc was awarded for published work in 1959.

Though Kent hankered after the British Geological Survey or an academic career, preferably in the east midlands, this was not to be, and in 1936 he took a temporary job with the Anglo Iranian Oil Company (later BP) and was posted to Eakring, 17 miles from Nottingham. While there he worked on the petroleum prospects of the east midlands (oil was found at Eakring in 1939) and southern England, and then joined the Royal Air Force Volunteer Reserve in 1941, in spite of being in a reserved occupation. From 1941 to 1945 he served with the combined intelligence unit at Medmenham; he was mentioned in dispatches in 1944. After the allied victory in Europe he worked at the US Pentagon on Japanese targets and was awarded the US silver medal of the Legion of Merit (1946). He went to Hiroshima and Nagasaki as a member of the US investigation team—an experience which he kept very much to himself.

On demobilization in 1946 Kent rejoined Anglo Iranian and for the next fifteen years worked in Iran, east Africa, Papua, and North and South America, returning to London in 1960. He became BP's chief geologist in 1966 and, though the title changed, the role did not; he retired from BP in 1973 as assistant general manager (exploration). On retirement from BP he went to the Natural Environment Research Council (NERC), where he was a very active full-time chairman in what was nominally a part-time job (1973–7). He joined NERC at a critical time and played a major part in the implementation of recommendations from the third Baron Rothschild, which transformed relationships between the research council and spending ministries. On completing his term with NERC, in 1977 he returned to industry and was still active as a consultant and company director at the time of his death.

A meticulous field geologist and outstanding stratigrapher, Kent had a gift for the synthesis and interpretation of large masses of geological data. The author of 145 papers, he made major contributions to the understanding of the geology of eastern England, the North Sea basins, and the tectonic evolution of the north-west European continental shelf. His interests were global and his thinking powerfully influenced studies of sedimentary basins worldwide. Dedicated to his science, which was both profession and hobby, he acted throughout his career rather like an international professor of geology. He was demanding but fair, and always ready to discuss problems (when you could catch him in the office). Kent was neat, bespectacled, quietly spoken, and of medium height. Many thought him a retiring man, a listener rather than a talker, but he enjoyed social gatherings and was at his liveliest in the company of women. A landscape painter and gardener, he loved choral singing and he and his first wife were lifelong members of the Friary Congregational Church in West Bridgford; their home at 38 Rodney Road, West Bridgford, was his base through all of his wanderings.

Kent's honours included fellowship of the Royal Society (1966), the Geological Society's Murchison medal (1969), the MacRobert award (1970), a Royal Society Royal medal (1971), a knighthood (1973), and honorary degrees from Leicester (1972), Durham (1974), Bristol (1977), Glasgow (1977), Aberdeen (1978), Cambridge (1979), Hull (1981), and Birmingham (1983).

In 1940 he married Margaret Betty, daughter of George Frederick Hood, science master at Nottingham high school. She was a Nottingham JP for many years and died of cancer in 1974. They had two daughters, the younger of whom became a tutorial fellow in English at University College, Oxford. In 1976 he married Lorna Ogilvie, daughter of Henry James Scott, schoolteacher. As head of BP exploration's information branch, Lorna was a friend of long standing, and this too was a happy marriage. Kent, who had recovered well from an earlier heart attack, died suddenly on 9 July 1986, while on a business trip to Sheffield.   GEOFFREY LARMINIE, rev.

Sources N. L. Falcon and K. Dunham, *Memoirs FRS*, 33 (1987), 343–73 · BP company records · A. J. M., 'Sir Peter Kent', *Annual Report* [Geological Society of London] (1986), 25–7 · *CGPLA Eng. & Wales* (1986)
Archives U. Nott. L., corresp. and papers
Wealth at death £197,368: probate, 25 Nov 1986, *CGPLA Eng. & Wales*

Kent, Thomas (*b.* in or before 1410, *d.* 1469), administrator, was presumably of Kentish ancestry and 'of gentle birth'. He was probably at Oxford before going to Italy, where he lectured on canon and civil law at the University of Pavia in 1440–41, and became a doctor of both laws by 1442. He returned to England soon afterwards and briefly held two London rectories before being appointed in March 1444 to succeed Adam Moleyns (*d.* 1450) as secondary of the privy

seal office and clerk of the king's council. This appointment gave him considerable authority and he frequently signed council warrants. In 1445 he was appointed underconstable of England with a salary of 100 marks a year, and was seen as one of the court faction who in the parliament of November 1450 were alleged to have been 'misbehaving about your royal person', and whose members were to be excluded from the king's presence (*RotP*, 5.216). It had no effect upon Kent, who, apart from his activities at the council, was very frequently sent on diplomatic missions to France, Burgundy, Prussia, Scotland, Brittany, and Spain. In July 1455, for both excessive service and old age, he was granted an indult permitting him to avoid fasting in Lent. He appears to have avoided political involvement, for he retained his appointment under Edward IV, though by 1462 he was ceasing to play any real part in the affairs of the council. He did, however, play an important part in the negotiations of 1467 for the marriage of Edward's sister Margaret (*d.* 1503) to Charles, duke of Burgundy.

Kent lived in the parish of St James Garlickhythe, London, and was a citizen of London. He appears to have married twice—first, by 1451, Isobel, and second, Joan, widow of Thomas Dounton of London, who survived him. His will, made in January 1469, asked that he be buried next to his first wife, Isobel, in St James Garlickhythe. Kent bequeathed a long list of canon- and civil-law books, which he donated to the use of the prerogative court of Canterbury if housed in a suitable building near St Paul's Cathedral: if not, they were to go to All Souls College, Oxford. There is mention in the will of landed property in London and in various places in Kent, including Headcorn, Langley, and Brussyng, and also a tenement and land in Bishop's Lynn, Norfolk. Kent appointed as executors his wife and two former subordinates in the privy seal office, Richard Langport and William Tilghman. He died between 9 January and 15 March 1469: there is no evidence that he left any children.   ROGER VIRGOE

Sources Emden, *Oxf.* · A. L. Brown, *The early history of the clerkship of the council* (1969) · J. F. Baldwin, *The king's council in England during the middle ages* (1913) · will, PRO, PROB 11/5, sig. 26 · N. H. Nicolas, ed., *Proceedings and ordinances of the privy council of England*, 7 vols., RC, 26 (1834–7) · PRO · *Chancery records* · C. L. Scofield, *The life and reign of Edward the Fourth*, 2 vols. (1923) · *CEPR letters* · *Calendar of the fine rolls*, PRO, 18 (1939), 205
Wealth at death very substantial: will, PRO, PROB 11/5, sig. 26

Kent, Thomas (*d.* 1489), astronomer, was elected probationary fellow of Merton College, Oxford, in 1480 and was chaplain of the university at his death. Noted in the college register as 'a good astronomer' (Emden, *Oxf.*, 2.1039), he is said to have issued predictions as to the severe winter and famine of 1490. He died of the plague on 7 September 1489. Later antiquaries recorded his interment in either the college chapel or its burial-ground. He is said to have written treatises on astronomy, but nothing produced by him is known to have survived.   JOHN M. FLETCHER

Sources Emden, *Oxf.* · H. E. Salter, ed., *Registrum annalium collegii Mertonensis, 1483–1521*, OHS, 76 (1923), 16–125 · G. C. Brodrick, *Memorials of Merton College*, OHS, 4 (1885), 241

Kent, William (*bap.* 1686, *d.* 1748), painter, architect, and designer of gardens and interior furnishings, was baptized William Cant in St Mary's Church, Bridlington, Yorkshire, on 1 January 1686, the son of William Cant and his wife, Esther Shimmings.

Family and education In his will registered on 25 June 1739 William Cant senior was described as a joiner, and he may have been responsible for the joinery in his house—Kent's birthplace—at 45 The Toft, Bridlington. Cant was no 'humble' craftsman, but obviously of local standing and some affluence; his son probably attended the town's grammar school in the Bayle. Apprenticeship lists in Hull do not support George Vertue's claim that Kent was apprenticed to a coach and house painter there in 1701; Vertue may be confusing the support given to Kent by friends in Bridlington with an apprenticeship taken out in the City of London. Vertue further reports that Kent broke this apprenticeship in 1706: if true, this may imply a self-willed young man.

The next two years of Kent's life went unrecorded. He may already have met the antiquary John Talman, possibly through Talman's friend and fellow antiquary Samuel Gale, son of the dean of York. However, it was in Bridlington that Kent had, in Vertue's words, 'the Good fortune to find some Gentlemen of that Country to promote his studyes, [who] raisd a contribution and recommended him to propper persons at London to direct him to Italy' (Vertue, *Note books*, 3.139). These included Kent's first patron, Sir William Wentworth of Bretton Park, West Riding, and Sir Richard Osbaldeston of Hunmanby Hall near Bridlington. This local patronage led to the next and formative stage in the young man's career when in July 1709 Kent (no longer Cant) set sail to Italy in the galley *Swallow* accompanied by Talman and the Cambridge virtuoso Daniel Lock. Thus by the age of twenty-five Kent had distanced himself from the circumstances of his provincial birth and become a metropolitan friend of the Italophile son of the distinguished architect William Talman.

The Italian scene The *Swallow* docked at Leghorn on 15 October 1709, and the trio of travellers arrived in Pisa on 20 October for a month's stay. They were in Florence from 18 November and left that city in April 1710. For Kent this Florentine period was one of the discovery and assimilation of Italian art in churches and private collections. Excursions are recorded to Pistoia and Lucca, and the virtuosi, dealers, and artists in Florence whom they met included the painter Giuseppe Scacciati, the sculptor G. B. Foggini, his pupil Agostino Cornacchini, and the antiquary Lorenzo Magnolfi, who acted as Talman's agent. Talman certainly, and maybe Kent and Lock too, then walked to Rome via Siena to save money. Talman lodged with the German dealer Antonio Axer on the Corso, while Kent and Lock shared lodgings with Thomas Edwards the painter, on the strada Paolina off the Corso; by 1717 Kent had moved along the street to lodge with the painter Giuseppe Pesci. On 9 May 1710 Talman wrote to his father, 'we are all in separate lodgings, but agree very well, and every Thursday ["ye couriosty day"] we spend in seeing

William Kent (*bap.* 1686, *d.* 1748), by William Aikman, *c.*1723–5

fine palaces, as last Thursday we saw Borghese Palace' (Parry, letter 78). On 5 July 1710 he wrote again, observing Kent's 'bashful temper and inexperience in writing' (ibid., letter 103). By now Kent had probably entered the studio of Giuseppe Chiari (1654–1727) to start formal training as a painter.

As a pupil of Carlo Maratta, Chiari would have looked up to and taught the classicism of Raphael and his school. There would be extensive copying of old masters, notably Guido Reni and Correggio, and obviously study of Raphael's work in the Vatican Loggia, the Farnesina, and the Villa Madama. In the studio with Kent was the Irish painter Henry Trench, who evoked from Vertue an anecdote that illuminates Kent's friendship with Richard Boyle, third earl of Burlington and fourth earl of Cork: Lord Burlington in Rome, wrote Vertue, 'lookt upon' Kent to be 'the better painter of the two by much'—and because of this Trench 'took an occasion to write an expostulatory letter to this noblemen setting forth the difference of meritt on his side, more than Kent, [but to the only effect that] Lord Burlington would read it to Kent, by way of mortification—and mirth' (Vertue, *Note books*, 4.163). This smacks of a tale humorously related by Kent himself. No drawings survive from this period in Kent's studio training: at this juncture—around 1710–12—his daily tasks must be recreated from the reports and letters of his friends in Rome. He attended Talman's St Luke's feast for the leading virtuosi in May 1711 and observed Talman's project for a monumental painting on the subject of 'Learning & arts are ye chief accomplishments of a Nobleman' (Parry, letter 183) to be executed by Chiari and Trench. He must have made many excursions, although apparently not to Naples between October and December 1710 with Talman and the portrait painter William Aikman. In March 1712 Kent accompanied Humphry Chetham, a merchant, and Lock to the Villa Aldobrandini; in April he went with Chetham to the Villa Borghese. About this time Kent met Talman's friend Burrell Massingberd of South Ormsby in Lincolnshire, initiating his joint support with his friend Sir John Chester of Chicheley, Buckinghamshire, of a gift of £40 a year in hope 'of your becoming a great Painter' (Massingberd to Kent, 14 May 1713, Lincoln Diocesan Archives, 2MM B19A), no less than the *Raphaelus secundus*.

Kent's apogee as Chiari's pupil was in June 1713, when he was placed second in the second tier of painting classes at the Accademia di S. Luca for a drawing of the *Miracle of S. Andrea Avellino*, for which he received a silver medal from the pope. This award was trumpeted in England as if he was indeed the second Raphael. All that Rome has to offer of Kent's sojourn there is his *Glorification of St Julian*, a fresco in the cupola of S. Giuliano dei Fiamminghi in Rome, the contract dated July 1717: it is unknown what Chiari really thought of this decidedly mediocre and conventional composition. However, two British noblemen arrived in Rome who would severally change the whole course of Kent's life, drawing out of him latent interests and passions which hitherto had only been sensed by Talman perhaps. The first was the third earl of Burlington, who was there from 30 September to the end of December 1714, but apparently ill in bed all the time. Apart from Massingberd's exhortation to Kent that 'Lord Burlington is coming full of money … and loves pictures mightily' (Massingberd to Kent, 5 July 1714, Lincoln Diocesan Archives, 2MM B19A), there is no evidence of a meeting then. The second nobleman was Thomas Coke of Holkham, who arrived in Rome on 7 February 1714. Kent's introduction to the young Coke, the self-confessed 'perfect virtuoso and great lover of pictures' (Ingamells, 225) occurred in Chiari's studio, where Coke had engaged the architect Giacomo Mariari to teach him to draw architecture. When Coke and Kent set off for a companionable tour of northern Italy in June 1714, the artist's interests began to broaden. Kent was both bear leader and collector's agent on this expedition. His journal, 'Remarks by way of painting & architecture' (Bodl. Oxf., MS Rawl. D.1162), begun on 6 July 1714, shows him becoming increasingly observant of architecture and gardens, but not yet attracted to the work of Andrea Palladio, to judge by the single day they spent in Vicenza. Unfortunately, Kent's sketchbook, in which he made 'sketches of some piece in every place I came' (Kent to Massingberd, 24 Nov 1714, Lincoln Diocesan Archives, 2MM B19A), is lost. By the time Coke left Italy in June 1717, a lifelong friendship had been cemented.

How Kent began a similar friendship with Burlington is unclear. It is manifest during Burlington's visit to Genoa and the Veneto after August 1719 and when Kent was travelling from Florence to Genoa with Sir William Wentworth on the way home. Writing from Paris on 15 November 1719, Kent recollected his stay with Burlington in Genoa, and in particular how his lordship 'lik'd my designs so well both painting & Archetecture that he would make me promis at least to begin to paint for him the fierst when I come over' (Kent to Massingberd, 15 Nov 1719, Lincoln Diocesan Archives, 2MM B19A). Exactly what Kent meant by 'Archetecture' is unclear, but he probably referred to interior decoration. A year earlier Kent wrote to Massingberd that he was drawing 'continualy ornements and archetecture … things yt I think will be necessary for use in England' (Kent to Massingberd, 15 Nov 1719, Lincoln Diocesan Archives, 2MM B19A), but nearly ten years would pass before he designed an architectural exterior. Nevertheless, Kent, in his plans for the future, must have envisaged architecture proper as a subject for his professional consideration. About October to November 1719 Burlington had told him of plans 'to get architects to draw all the fine buildings of Palladio' (ibid.), and there is acknowledgement of the neo-Palladian reformation in architecture taking place in England in Kent's criticism (1719) of the 'Dam'd Gusto [that is, taste for the baroque] that has been [in England] for this sixty years past' (ibid.).

Kent's character So much of Kent's subsequent artistic achievement can be seen as an extension of his idiosyncratic self, not least in his drawings, and in many of the tasks he was happy to execute: a pram for little Dorothy Boyle, a lady's dress ornamented with the five orders of architecture, so that she appeared a 'walking Palladio in petticoats' (Lord Ilchester, ed., *Lord Hervey and his Friends*, 1950, 115–16), the uniform for the bargemen of Frederick, prince of Wales, a dog kennel, a fantastic silver surtout. This man of humble origins, who could never quite shake off the half-educated idiosyncrasy of his spelling and composition, had already earned the sobriquet of 'il Signor' when he was welcomed into Burlington House, Piccadilly, the most advanced artistic and fashionable household in London. Clearly Kent had established a personal relationship with Burlington before returning to London, for as early as 30 January 1720, hardly unpacked from ten years in Italy, he could refer to Burlington House as 'our house' when reporting Burlington's impending marriage to Lady Dorothy Savile, hoping 'vertu will grow stronger in our house and architecture will flourish more' (Kent to Massingberd, Lincoln Diocesan Archives, 2MM B19A). In London Kent met Handel and the musicians of the Italian opera and the newly formed Royal Academy of Music, the poets Alexander Pope and John Gay, and the painter

Charles Jervas. The prickly Pope and Lady Burlington loved him as much as anyone, and all consorted and lived in harmony.

Kent's easy-going and warm-hearted familiarity and his fundamentally happy temperament inspired quick affection. Some referred to him as 'il Kentino', or 'the Little Rogue Kent', or 'the Honest Signior'. No correspondence better describes Kent's character than that between Kent, Burlington, and Pope. Poet and artist constantly teased each other, variously reporting to each other: Kent to Burlington, November 1738: '[Pope is] … the greatest glutton I know … [he] told me of a soupe that must be seven hours a making' (G. Sherborne, ed., *The Correspondence of Alexander Pope*, 4, 1956, 150); Pope to Burlington: '[Come] and eat a mutton stake in the manner of that great Master, Signior Kent' (ibid., 3, 1956, 517); Pope to Burlington, January 1740: 'If he [Kent] proceeds in his carnality & carnivoracity, he must expect not to imitate Raphael in anything but his untimely end'; and Pope to Burlington, July 1734: '[Kent is] a wild Goth … from a Country which has ever been held no part of christendome' (ibid., 3, 1956, 417). In Benedetto Luti's Roman portrait of Kent in 1718 the soft features, the open eye, and the double chin of the gourmand and *bon-vivant* can be recognized; the chins are accentuated in Bartholomew Dandridge's portrait of *c*.1730, and even more exaggerated in Lady Burlington's sketch of Kent (*c*.1730s) drawing at a table. These images give a sense of the mirthful character reflected in the witticisms of his drawings and his lively bucolic writing which was so often, as Burlington observed, 'more allegorical as ever'.

The impulsive Kent was a perfect foil to the austere lord, who was a rigid theorist and learned scholar, the affection of each man for the other being based on the attraction of opposites. Kent's mistress, the fat Drury Lane actress Elizabeth Butler, and their two children, to whom he bequeathed his moneys, is not proof that Kent was only heterosexual. An agreeable companion to Lady Burlington when her lord was on his travels, he became her drawing master, inundating her with news from town when she was away in the country. Unlike others who were patronized by the great, Kent was no sycophant. Nor was he a political creature; indeed he seemed almost apolitical. He confessed as much when he wrote to Burlington in that troubled Jacobite year of 1745 of his solitary enthusiasm reading a book on the Farnese Gardens and the plans of the Palatine: 'as Politicks are not my Genius, it diverts me much now at nights to look and read of these fine remains of antiquity' (Burlington collection, Chatsworth). If his lord was at least a closet Jacobite—and even this is uncertain—Kent was neither concerned, nor reported as such; there is no evidence that either he or Burlington was a freemason.

Kent as painter   In fulfilment of his prophecy in November 1719 that he would 'feirst' start work at Burlington House, Kent was soon proposing a sketch for the Great Room with ornaments *al Italiano*. By late 1720 a *Banquet of the Gods* was painted for the ceiling and probably grisaille ornaments for the cove: in the adjacent room was an *Assembly of the Gods*. If contrasted with Sebastiano Ricci's oils on the staircase, or the displaced Antonio Pellegrini canvases now at Narford Hall, Norfolk, Kent was immature in composition and figural work. Surprisingly it was not Sir James Thornhill, the king's sergeant painter, but Kent, who in March 1722 was offered the commission to decorate the new Cupola Room in Kensington Palace, followed by the king's drawing-room (1722–3), the privy chamber and king's bedchamber (1723), the presence chamber and council chamber (1724), and the king's gallery, great and little closets, and staircase (1725–7). The commission was Burlington's doing, arousing violent enmity from William Hogarth, Thornhill's son-in-law, and at once set up opposing camps: those committed to Burlington's Italianate programme of reformation appearing on one side, and those promoting Lord Harley's native British one, including the architect James Gibbs, Thornhill, and Charles Bridgeman the gardener, on the other.

The novelty of the Cupola Room was to set above the chimneypiece a marble relief by J. M. Rysbrack of a copy of a Roman marriage in the Palazzo Sacchetti (the reliefs in the stone hall and dining-room at Houghton are distinguished later examples, also by Rysbrack). Both the design for the Kensington drawing-room, and that signed and dated 1725 for the saloon at Houghton, are still late Roman baroque in composition and colouring. However, the ceiling of the Kensington presence chamber (and bedchamber and council chamber; destr.) are in the antique grotesque manner first recommended to Kent by Talman in 1717. Chiari would have approved, for the style is Raphaelesque, deriving from the decoration of the Villa Madama via both Kent's own firsthand study and drawings after antique Roman ceilings by Francesco Bartoli specially commissioned by Coke in 1718. The Kensington ceilings were the first in the eighteenth-century revival of this mode. In the Cupola Room at Kensington (from 1722) and on the king's grand staircase there, and in the king's gallery (1724), at Houghton, Norfolk (from 1726), Raynham Hall, Norfolk (*c*.1728), the Blue Velvet Room, Chiswick (*c*.1728), and at Stowe House, Buckinghamshire (*c*.1730), Kent consistently used grisaille ornaments in grey green enlivened by gilt ornament, often on mosaic grounds based on antique precedent (a technique which he termed *al Italiano*). In this type of decoration he was far more accomplished than in conventional painting: the staircase at Houghton is a *tour de force* of *trompe-l'oeil* grisaille painting. He painted a grotesque ceiling at Rousham as late as 1738 and Bartoli-style coffered ceilings with painted insets at 22 Arlington Street in 1741, and at 44 Berkeley Square in 1743: both are in the style of Giulio Romano. When Kent first took responsibility for the design of the whole room is still unclear: it is not known, for instance, if Colen Campbell was responsible for the architectural wall frames in the Burlington House Great Room. Unfortunately, several of Kent's early commissions are not fully documented: ceilings for Canons, Middlesex, owned by James Brydges, first duke of Chandos; substantial interior work for Thomas Pelham-Holles, fourth duke of Newcastle, at Newcastle House, Lincoln's Inn Fields (1725); and

Wanstead House, Essex (early 1720s?), where Kent painted ceilings and designed furniture and, if Hogarth's *Assembly at Wanstead* (1729) is to be trusted, a complete room. Certainly by 1724 in the hall at Ditchley House, Oxfordshire, and at Houghton Hall, Norfolk, from 1725, Kent was in full command of the architectonic decoration of walls, including chimneypieces and doors, combined with movable wall furniture. Now he was the decorator, furniture designer, and ornamentalist. Attention to interiors and what they contained led in due course to consideration of the architectural whole, and concurrently to the surrounding garden and landscape.

Drawing style Kent attained this achievement through the normal medium of design drawings, but what was abnormal was his mode of presentation. Unfortunately the designs for Burlington House, which would have been most revealing, have disappeared in recent times. To judge by his earliest surviving design—for the Kensington drawing-room ceiling in 1722—his unconventional style was not yet apparent, nor did it appear at Ditchley in 1724 (hence early misattributions to Gibbs of Kent's design for the hall). But it was full-blown by the time he was working on Houghton in 1725 and the dining-room for Charles Fitzroy, second duke of Grafton, in 1728. The idiosyncratic characteristics of his new style were a three-dimensional painterly manner of elevation and section, the employment of a yellowy bistre wash over freehand drawing without use of ruler, and the many witticisms and personal pentimenti added. As if she was looking over his shoulder at him drawing Grafton's dining-room, Kent sketches in the head of Lady Burlington; in views of Chiswick a dog pees against his leg; while a donkey brays under the triumphal arch at Holkham. These amusing pentimenti abound. Kent composed as a painter, and although his office did produce conventional working drawings of plan and elevation for execution at the site, he rarely used the ruler, but in perspective washed his way across paper just like a topographical artist. For an architect this is unique: Burlington, Henry Flitcroft, and Isaac Ware never emulated his picturesque manner. It had several sources. One signal influence was to be found in the early 1720s in the library of William Cavendish, second duke of Devonshire, at nearby Devonshire House in Piccadilly: Claude Lorrain's precious *Liber veritatis*. It is inconceivable that the curious Kent did not examine the bistre-yellow-washed arcadian compositions by a painter familiar to him as a student in Italy. Another influence is the volume of Inigo Jones's masque designs acquired by Burlington about 1724, in which are to be found parallels with the drafting style of Kent's water garden projects for Chiswick in the early 1730s. If Kent's newly invented mode was unconventional for architectural design, it was revolutionary when he turned his mind to landscape.

Furniture and ornamental design Concurrent with mural paintings, Kent soon considered the design of furniture: in this too he struck out in unfamiliar directions. The first evidence of his abilities as a furniture designer is in the Houghton saloon elevation, dated 1725: this showed furniture and pictures in position, as indeed he was to propose at Kensington. Significantly, this mode of presenting a design has precedents in England only in drawings by John Talman. The Houghton side-tables shown in the design are of a scrolled foliate sort, not unlike the Chiswick Gallery tables, which may have first been made for the Old House at Chiswick shortly before 1724. His furniture must be assessed with his drawings made in 1725 for Pope's *Odyssey* (1726), engraved by Peter Fourdrinier. Kent's first attempt at book illustration occurred in 1720 with the frontispiece to *Mr Gay's Poems on Several Occasions*, and significantly this is conventional, with none of the baroque flourishes to be found in the Veneto–Florentine–Roman style furniture and decoration of the *Odyssey* illustrations, and of course likewise in the 1725 Houghton design. What is exceptional in Kent's translation of this Italian style, formulated by such designers as Andrea Brustolon, Giovanni Giardini, and G. B. Foggini, into his own furniture, is his singular incorporation of classical ornament such as Vitruvian scroll, wave moulds, Greek key, enclosed guilloche, interwoven bands, key meander—essentially the vocabulary of Palladio's ornamental trim. It first appears at Kensington, and it is tempting to envisage Burlington and Kent together discovering Jonesian (that is, Palladian) ornament through their joint study of the designs by Palladio, Jones, and John Webb bought by Burlington from John Talman in 1720–21. With this austere classical ornament Kent combined into his furniture compositions, foliate, scallop shell, fish scale, and reversed scroll ornament, using large shells in particular as terminations, as in the green velvet state bed at Houghton (1732), or as focal points on chair rails or table centres.

Although Kent's furniture is strongly sculptural, it is also architectonic. In the same category as furniture must be judged the state barge designed for Frederick, prince of Wales (1732). There was clearly sympathy between prince and artist: in the prince's masquerade of 1731 he was a shepherd attended by eighteen huntsmen 'dressed after a drawing of Kent's, in green waistcoats, leopardskins and quivers at their backs … antique gloves with pikes up to their elbow, and caps and feathers upon their heads like a Harry the 8th by Holbein' (Lord Ilchester, ed., *Lord Hervey and his Friends*, 1950, 115–16). If the design of Kent's furniture is seen as grammatically wilful, and if wilful means breaking the rules, then it has affiliations with the mannerist tendencies to be observed in his architecture after 1730. Not surprisingly, the furniture designer soon turned to consider ornamental items and utensils. The key document for these is a book by Kent's acolyte John Vardy, *Some Designs of Mr. Inigo Jones and Mr. William Kent* (1744). Here are illustrated fourteen designs for chandeliers, tureens, dish covers, candlesticks, cups and covers, and various items of plate that seem mostly to have been made after the mid-1730s: they include a table centre as part of a service for Frederick, prince of Wales (1745–6), Colonel Pelham's gold cup (1736), and silver chandeliers for George II at Herrenhausen.

Kent as architect Kent's education as an architect began at Chiswick, not in Italy, although his sketchbook and what was stored in his memory provided a rich quarry. By 1719 Burlington had determined to be an architect, and by 1721 he was designing Tottenham Park, Wiltshire, for Lord Bruce, and in 1722 the Westminster dormitory. In 1723, with the design for General Wade's house in Old Burlington Street, he was delving into the designs by Palladio. By 1725, when the decision was taken to build his villa at Chiswick, Burlington had established professional drawing offices managed by Henry Flitcroft, his clerk of the works, in Burlington House and at Chiswick: this was Kent's learning ground. Crucial was Burlington's discovery of Jones's ornamental vocabulary through the study of his surviving works and his designs, the first step towards Burlington's emergence as the British Vitruvius—an achievement from which Kent cannot be excluded. The Jonesian vocabulary is evident in Kent's designs for chimneypieces through the 1720s: these were not the literal translations from Jones as favoured by Burlington, but incorporated Jonesian elements and ornament. The real catalyst that converted Kent the decorator into Kent the architect was the task given him by Burlington in 1724 to edit *The Designs of Inigo Jones … with some Additional Designs* (by Burlington and himself), which appeared in two volumes in 1727. The watershed between decorator and architect occurred about 1730, and it is significant that only one design for exterior architecture by Kent survives before that date. By February 1731 Isaac Ware had advertised his *Designs of Inigo Jones and Others*, containing garden buildings by Kent that must all have been designed about 1730: the Temple of Venus at Stowe, Buckinghamshire, a temple and obelisk at Shotover, Oxfordshire, and two garden buildings at Claremont, Surrey. By about 1730, too, Kent had designed the Queen's Hermitage in Richmond Gardens, and at Pope's Twickenham Villa garden ornaments and the Shell Temple. The first architecture of any substance is Kew House, for Frederick, prince of Wales, designed in 1730. The new refronting—incorporating open pediments—derived from the reconstruction drawings by Palladio of the Roman baths, then in Burlington's possession; these were edited by Burlington as *Fabbriche antiche disegnate da Andrea Palladio* (1730), for which Kent provided a title-page and tailpieces and Ware drawings for the engraver.

As this one work transformed Burlington from a Palladian into a proto-neo-classic Vitruvian architect, so too was it a powerful influence upon Kent. This is first manifested in Kent's unexecuted designs for the Painted Chamber at Westminster in 1730, boasting an antique Roman front with a tripartite window set under a Diocletian one, lighting a gallery based upon a Roman reconstruction by Palladio. The encircling ornamental Roman Trajanesque frieze has no precedent in conventional European architecture before 1760. The difficulty of disentangling Kent's work from Burlington's can be seen when this Westminster project is compared with Burlington's Vitruvian York assembly rooms, also begun in 1730. It is even more evident when Burlington, Kent, and Coke (now Lord Lovell) conspired to design Coke's Holkham Hall, Norfolk, from 1733. Holkham was a collaborative effort, demonstrated when Coke wrote to Burlington on 26 November 1736, 'I shall wait on you with my portfeuill and make the Signor scold, for now we must think of the inside of the rooms' (Burlington correspondence, Chatsworth). Kent was directly responsible for the exterior, the hall, and the inside of the south-west pavilion. The executant architect and clerk of the works was Matthew Brettingham, who completed the interior in a less disciplined version of Kent's decorative style long after the deaths of Kent and Burlington—and subsequently claimed the whole as his own in *The Plans and Elevations of the Late Earl of Leicester's House at Holkham* (1761). Holkham is a perfect fusion of Palladian and Jonesian elements: the tower house is derived from Burlington's Tottenham crossed with Jonesian Wilton House, with Palladian windows set in relieving arches, and incorporating many elements from Chiswick. Its columnar hall of imperial Roman grandeur was a worthy successor to the York assembly rooms, and served as a model in private and public works throughout the world for the next two centuries.

The Westminster commission was a result of Kent's membership of the board of works. Through Burlington's influence he had a seat on the board as master carpenter from May 1726. In 1728 he was favoured by a 'new constituted place' of surveyor or inspector of paintings in the royal palaces, and in 1735 became master mason and deputy surveyor of the works. His works in this capacity began in 1731 with the Royal Mews on the site of the present National Gallery and Trafalgar Square. Kent's many designs show him experimenting with mannerist devices, such as keystones breaking up into entablatures or partly rusticated string courses, reflecting his study of Giulio Romano. In the final mews design Kent turned to more conventional sources found in Jones and Campbell, combined with a novel adaptation of the wall of Palladio's nave of San Giorgio Maggiore with Diocletian windows in blank arcading to light the interior of the stalls, themselves based upon what were believed to be Jones's stables at Holland House, Kensington, published by Ware in his 1731 book. The method by which Kent breaks up the façade into separate and sometimes discordant elements has been analysed by Rudolf Wittkower. It occurred in the pavilion fronts at Holkham, in the Link Building added to Chiswick in 1733, in the model for a royal palace in Richmond Gardens (1734), and in many unexecuted designs for buildings, both large and small. But this manner of design is also to be recognized in interiors: notably the mannerist wall elevations of the proposed Westminster Painted Chamber (1730), Queen Caroline's Library in St James's Palace (1736), and in the stringing out of the pavilions of the Horse Guards designed by Kent shortly before he died in 1748. Clearly Kent was the favoured architect of the board, although it is not clear how far the Burlingtonians—Burlington, Kent, Flitcroft, Ware, and Vardy—really were conspiring to establish a national Palladian style for England. Certainly Kent's Mews of 1731 and the Treasury buildings of 1733 stood out as prominent new works on the London scene, in particular the Treasury; this showed Kent departing from the Palladian and Burlingtonian norm in the use of rustication to articulate façades as wall mass, minimizing or eliminating exterior orders.

Had Richmond Palace been built, and Kent's and Burlington's designs for a new houses of parliament, the situation would have been different. In March 1733 Burlington is reported to have a design in hand, following the rejection of designs by Hawksmoor. From then until at least 1739 numerous schemes and more than 100 drawings were produced. Except for one interior of the House of Lords, dated 1735 and idiosyncratically drawn by Kent, many are plans and elevations copied by draughtsmen in the works office. However, the presence of a large number in Kent's hand demonstrates the importance he gave this project, and also shows that he was capable of competing with those in his office as a conventional draughtsman. In effect, they comprise the York assembly rooms, Holkham, and Richmond Palace, writ large on the scale of imperial Rome. In the earlier schemes the purity of Burlington's Vitruvian architecture shines out, but when the project was revived early in 1739, Kent alone was in control, producing more conventional elevations as a worthy successor to the celebrated designs by Jones and Webb for a Whitehall Palace. Like that palace, the houses of parliament designs have entered the mythology of great lost opportunities.

In his late works of the 1740s Kent began to unshackle himself from the Burlingtonian norm. Worcester Lodge at Badminton House, Gloucestershire, completed just after Kent's death, would have received the imprimatur of Giulio Romano as a great work, even if one on a small scale. As David Watkin has percipiently observed, it maintains 'a perfect balance between the opposing tensions of Baroque and Palladian' (Colvin, *Archs.*, 581). This is true too of the Banqueting House at Euston, Suffolk (1746), and if baroque implies movement, nothing could be more baroque than the staircase in 44 Berkeley Square (1742), which would not evoke surprise if found in a Turinese palace by Fillipo Juvarra. The suggestion of a connection with Juvarra is not far-fetched: that architect was in London in 1720, and made a gift of a sketchbook to Burlington in 1730. The staircase at 44 Berkeley Square is a piece of theatre, recognized as such in the words of Horace Walpole: 'as beautiful a piece of scenery and, considering the space, of art, as can be imagined' (H. Walpole, *Anecdotes of Painting*, 1798, 491). Baroque too is the extraordinary vaulted system of the saloon ceiling in 22 Arlington Street (1741). Yet late in life, concurrent with the Worcester Lodge, at Wakefield Lodge, Northamptonshire, the last work for his patron Charles Fitzroy, second duke of Grafton, Kent produced a house that might have found a place in Nicholas Ledoux's Parisian works. Frontally it is a Palladian tower house with Roman bath open pediments. However, the austerity of its elevations, the succession across the second storey of semi-blind lunettes—the huge centre one spanning the width of the single storey portico, and the ground-floor Palladian windows—blind where the outer lights should be, endow this hunting-lodge with qualities that would not look out of place in France in the 1770s.

Among Kent's board commissions the gateway to the Clock Court of Hampton Court Palace (1732) and the screen to Westminster Hall (1739) were Gothic—as too was the Gothic pulpit and choir furniture in York Minster (1741), and the choir screen in Gloucester Cathedral (1741). To these can be added the wings to the Tudor gatehouse of Henry Pelham's Esher Place, Surrey (1732), the wings and fenestration to Rousham House, Oxfordshire (1738), and the attributed Laughton Tower, Sussex, built for Pelham. This phenomenon of the 1730s allowed Kent to play pioneer in the making of an associational Gothic that earlier had occasionally been practised by Wren and Hawksmoor. In Howard Colvin's apt words, these works 'establish him as the creator of an English rococo Gothic happily free from antiquarian preoccupations' (Colvin, *Archs.*, 581). Esher in particular, and Kent's Gothic works engraved by John Vardy, established a Gothic formula adopted throughout the first half of the eighteenth century. Shortly before his death Kent drew upon these Gothic experiences when preparing the illustrations for Thomas Birch's 1751 edition of Spencer's *Faery queen*.

Kent as gardener When, by 1730, Kent had turned to the professional design of architecture he was also ready to consider gardens and parkscape. What he achieved was coloured by his memories of ten years in Italy, the 'garden of the world'. During his Italian years Kent expressed no view of what he saw of gardens. His visual responses then were intuitive rather than based upon book learning, which would come later. The ten years he spent in the Burlington House circles following 1719 were crucial, certainly through his study of Claude's *Liber veritatis*. He may have recorded Italian villa gardens in his sketchbook, but even so, such sketches would have been partial. What he did not see personally, he would have studied in such works as G. B. Falda's *Li giardini di Roma* of 1683. Only later would he have read the English translation in 1707 of J. F. Felibien's *Villas of Pliny* to learn about ancient Roman gardens, and later still Robert Castell's *Villas of the Ancients Illustrated* (1729). It is far more likely that his real education began in England after 1720, observing the revolution that Vanbrugh and Hawksmoor were effecting in the making of the sublime Roman templescapes at Castle Howard with temples, belvederes, pyramids, obelisks, arches, and Roman bridges. So talked of was this garden that surely Kent or Burlington would have gone over to Lord Carlisle's from Burlington's Londesborough, barely 25 miles cross-country. Kent was also aware of the partial emancipation of the old formal gardens once constrained by their walls and avenues that had continued apace during the first twenty years of the century. His view of these old gardens is only recorded through the pen of Lord Lovell, who wrote to Burlington in 1736 about 'those damned dull walks at Jo: Windhams those unpictoresk those cold & insipid strait walks wch make the signor sick' and mischievously referred to Kent as 'Signor Cazzo Vestito' (Burlington correspondence, Chatsworth). What is amazing about Kent the gardener is the burst of activity altering gardens around 1730. He was at Pope's house at Twickenham; at Stowe, Buckinghamshire, from 1730 to 1735, creating the Elysian Fields and at least seven garden buildings; in Richmond Gardens, Surrey, erecting Queen Caroline's Hermitage—and in 1735 Merlin's Cave; at Shotover, Oxfordshire, establishing a new area of landscape garden with a temple and an obelisk; and at Claremont, Surrey, radically altering the formal Vanbrughian gardens and adding three more temples and buildings. By 1733 the renovations at Chiswick had commenced, with Kent now entirely in charge of all buildings and landscape; and the new garden for Frederick, prince of Wales, at Carlton House, Pall Mall, London, was begun with its octagonal domed temple, virtually a Chiswick in miniature. By 1735 the huge Roman layout of Holkham, Norfolk, was commenced as a miniature Castle Howard; and Esher Place, Surrey, was well in progress as perhaps the most complete and satisfying of all Kent's creations: 'Kent is Kentissime there' (Walpole, *Corr.*, 9.71), as Walpole wrote to George Montague in 1748, meaning more perfect perfection. Walpole's rapturous description of Esher (to Montague) on 19 May 1763 evokes more than any other the Georgian aesthetic response to a Kentian garden: 'The day was delightful, the scene transporting, the trees, the lawns, cascades, all is the perfection in which the ghost of Kent would joy to see them … in short it was Parnassus as Watteau would have painted it' (ibid., 10.72). In 1738 Kent began to modify the old formal layout at Rousham, Oxfordshire, to surround the extended house in the Gothick style for his old friend General Dormer. To these must be added work in the 1740s at Badminton, Gloucestershire, Euston, Suffolk, and Horseheath Hall, Cambridgeshire. The list is certainly incomplete. It was Walpole, the first biographer of Kent, who in his essay *On Modern Gardening*, by writing that Kent 'leapt the fence and saw that all Nature was a garden' (H. Walpole, *On Modern Gardening*, ed. W. S. Lewis, 1931, 43–4), first mistakenly set him up as a prologue to Capability Brown. Kent would not have acknowledged this: his stretches of natural landscape were always of limited extent, tied in at their extremities by ha-has, and ornamented with garden buildings scenographically situated. A catalyst was the preparation of the four frontispieces to James Thomson's *The Seasons*, published in 1730: they are Claudian, but Claude with Palladian buildings. As with Kent's response to Italian gardens, he was an intuitive designer whose only grand set piece was Holkham, where no doubt Coke had many a 'scold' with the *signor* in devising this semi-formal layout. Kent did not use measuring rods and line: as Sir Thomas Robinson perciently observed in 1734, 'There is a new taste in gardening just arisen … after Mr Kent's notion of gardening, viz., to lay them out, and work without either level or line' (*Carlisle MSS*, 143–4)—referring to Carlton Garden, Claremont, Chiswick, and Stowe. Kent's drawings bear this out and effect a revolution in the manner by which he literally paints his groves across sheets of paper and transforms them into reality.

Vertue attributed Kent's death to a dropsical inflammation ending in 'a mortification in his bowells & feet especially inflamd'; until the last on 12 April 1748 he was 'attended … with great care at Burlington house'. A week later he was taken to his beloved Chiswick in 'A herse & 9 morning coaches' and buried in the church there 'in his noble patron's vault' (Vertue, *Note books*, 3.140). In his will he stipulated exactly what all his friends were to receive in his memory, and was particularly generous to Elizabeth Butler and their two children. Kent's designs are scattered through many public and private collections. The bulk are held in London by the British Museum, the Public Record Office, the Royal Institute of British Architects, Sir John Soane's Museum, and the Victoria and Albert Museum; in Oxford by the Ashmolean Museum, and in the Devonshire collections at Chatsworth, Derbyshire. John Dixon Hunt's monograph publishes nearly all the garden and landscape designs.

Summary Kent's achievement as painter, designer, architect, and gardener cannot be judged in isolation from his character. One illumines the other. His was a natural genius who broke out of the shackles of a provincial birth. The relationship of this low-born attractive man with the high-born Burlington has encouraged speculation as to the nature of that relationship. Certainly it was unusual and uncommon to have been taken into the household of the Boyles and treated as an equal, until laid to rest in their family vault at Chiswick. Even as early as 1719, barely six months after they had first met, Kent was using the familiar 'we' when referring to his and Burlington's artistic affairs. It was not necessarily a homosexual relationship, but was undoubtedly an attraction of opposites, the love of one man for another. As Pope's letters demonstrate, Kent was beloved by all who came into friendly contact with him.

As a painter Kent was never more than a competent decorator, not of the mettle of a Thornhill. Nevertheless, he struck out in new directions, particularly with the revival of antique-inspired Grotesk ceiling painting. This served him well for the internal embellishment of the neo-Palladian architecture promoted and practised by Burlington from 1720, and after 1730 jointly with Kent. However, only rarely was Kent wholly party to the pedantic sources used by Burlington. His architecture was a far more powerful statement expressed in a language sometimes matching the idiosyncrasies of his writing and personality. He strove for a surface articulation and movement alien to Burlington, who had not studied the mannerist architecture of Giulio Romano in Mantua. This would profoundly affect the later works of James Paine and Robert Adam.

Never did a painter's eye so influence the presentation of architectural designs. Kent was not trained to use the ruler. Instead, his are painterly picturesque compositions enlivened with whimsical pentimenti that have far more client appeal than the conventional orthographic plan, elevation, and section. He revolutionized the making of garden designs. He abandoned the gardener's rod and line and painted his proposed garden scenes for others to transpose into reality.

In all he did in gardens, although Italy was never far from his thoughts, he was also keenly aware of the templescapes of Sir John Vanbrugh and Colen Campbell. He was masterful at adapting and softening earlier layouts of the formal Bridgeman school with his groves and clumps and judiciously sited garden buildings. Some of the episodes of his planting are as natural as anything by Capability Brown. To paraphrase Walpole, Kent did see that all nature could be a garden, one in which he pioneered painterly and graduated flower planting.

Nothing could be described as more idiosyncratically Kentian than the type of furniture he was first designing for Houghton from 1726. Furniture as it had conventionally evolved from that of the late Stuart and Williamite courts reached a juncture, after which Kent created a style of furnishing appropriate for, and integrated into, the neo-Palladian interior. In this, as in everything he designed, the product could not be mistaken for that by any other designer of his time. It is truly Kentian.

JOHN HARRIS

Sources Vertue, *Note books* · M. Jourdain, *The work of William Kent* (1948) · R. Wittkower, 'Lord Burlington and William Kent', *Palladio and English Palladianism* (1974) · K. Woodbridge, 'William Kent as landscape gardener: a re-appraisal', *Apollo*, 100 (1974), 126–37 · H. M. Colvin and others, eds., *The history of the king's works*, 5 (1976) · M. I. Wilson, *William Kent* (1984) · C. M. Sicca, 'On William Kent's Roman sources', *Architectural History*, 29 (1986), 134–57 · J. Dixon Hunt, *William Kent landscape garden designs* (1987) · Colvin, *Archs.* · S. Neave and D. Neave, 'The early life of William Kent', *Georgian Group Journal*, 6 (1996), 4–11 · Bridlington parish registers, Beverley, Humberside county archive office, PE 153/2 · G. Parry, 'The John Talman letter-book', *Walpole Society*, 59 (1997), 3–179 · J. Ingamells, ed., *A dictionary of British and Irish travellers in Italy, 1701–1800* (1997) · D. Watkin, ed., *A house in town: 22 Arlington Street* (1984) · *The manuscripts of the earl of Carlisle*, HMC, 42 (1897) · Burlington correspondence, Chatsworth House, Derbyshire
Archives Bodl. Oxf., Italian notebook, MS Rawl. D.1162 · Lincs. Arch., letters | Bodl. Oxf., sale catalogue, MS Mus. Bibl. III 4 to 17, 8°20 · Chatsworth House, Derbyshire, corresp. with third earl of Burlington and countess of Burlington
Likenesses B. Luti, oils, 1718, Chatsworth House, Derbyshire · W. Aikman, oils, *c.*1723–1725, NPG [*see illus.*] · B. Dandridge, oils, *c.*1730, NPG · G. Hamilton, group portrait, oils, 1735 (*A conversation of virtuosis ... at the Kings Armes*), NPG · A. Bannerman, line engraving (after W. Aikman), BM, NPG; repro. in Walpole, *Anecdotes* (1762) · S. F. Ravenet, line engraving (after W. Aikman), BM · two drawings, Chatsworth House, Derbyshire

Kent, William (1751–1812), naval officer, was the son of Henry Kent of Newcastle upon Tyne and Mary (*b.* before 1734), daughter of William Hunter, shipmaster of Leith, near Edinburgh. His uncle on his mother's side was Vice-Admiral John *Hunter, governor of New South Wales (1795–1800). Kent was educated at home, joined the navy in 1763, and became a lieutenant in 1781. After continuous service in home waters, in 1794 he was appointed to command the *Supply*. He sailed for New South Wales in February 1795, reaching Sydney on 7 September. In 1791 Kent had married his cousin Eliza *Kent (1765/6–1810), daughter of William Kent of Newcastle.

After two trips to Norfolk Island with supplies, in September 1796 Kent took the *Supply* to the Cape of Good Hope to procure livestock, and despite her deplorable condition he successfully completed his mission, returning to Sydney in the following May. In August 1799 he was transferred to the recently arrived *Buffalo* and in 1799–1800 he repeated the South Africa voyage before taking her to England in October 1800. On his return to Sydney in October 1802 Governor King promoted him acting commander, and the next year Kent took the *Buffalo* to survey New Caledonia, where he discovered the magnificent Port St Vincent harbour. Sailing on to Calcutta he again procured a large cargo of livestock which he brought back to Sydney in June 1804. In October he took to Port Dalrymple in Van Diemen's Land the party forming a settlement there, and reported on its harbour; the next year he returned to England with confidential dispatches explaining the seizure of two Spanish ships off Peru by Australian vessels. He arrived at Plymouth on 22 December 1805 with birds and plants for Admiral Lord St Vincent and Sir Joseph Banks, and in January 1806 he was promoted captain. From November 1808 he took command of the *Agincourt* and the *Union*.

Captain Kent was an outstanding officer; governors John Hunter and Philip King both praised his services highly and both recommended his promotion. In the colony he was appointed to the vice-admiralty court, and as a commissioned officer he served in the criminal court, where he helped both governors against the prejudices and self-interest of Judge-Advocate Richard Dore and the officers of the New South Wales Corps. King appointed him a magistrate in 1802 and the following year to a committee investigating court martial procedure. Privately he was a successful settler. In 1800 he had sold the spacious mansion he had built on his land grant in Sydney to the government for £1539; an additional sale of livestock was valued at £407. Even so, in 1805 he held 1200 acres of land, 350 sheep and a few cattle.

Kent's wife, Eliza, died on 29 January 1810, leaving one son and two daughters; all were born in Sydney between 1799 and 1805, but all followed their father to England. Kent died in the *Union* off Toulon on 29 August 1812. His son William junior lived in strangely straitened circumstances in Cheltenham until he visited Australia in 1838 to realize his father's property.

A. G. L. SHAW

Sources 'Kent, William', *AusDB*, vol. 2 · A. G. L. Shaw, 'King, Philip Gidley', *AusDB*, vol. 5 · [F. Watson], ed., *Historical records of Australia*, 1st ser., 2–5 (1914–15); 3rd ser., 1 (1921) · F. M. Bladen, ed., *Historical records of New South Wales*, 2–6 (1893–8) · J. S. Cumpston, *Skipping arrivals and departures, Sydney, 1788–1825* (1963) · *Sydney Gazette* (15 April 1804–26 May 1805) · *GM*, 1st ser., 80 (1810), 288 · *GM*, 1st ser., 82/2 (1812), 400
Likenesses pastel; known to be in family possession in 1892
Wealth at death land and livestock in New South Wales: 'Kent, William', *AusDB*; referring to *Australian* (21 July 1835, 15 Dec 1835, 13 Dec 1838, 3 Jan 1839, and 4 May 1841)

Kent, William Saville- (1845–1908), marine biologist, was born William Savill Kent on 10 July 1845 at Cliff Cottage, Sidmouth, Devon, the youngest of ten children of Samuel Savill Kent (1801–1872), sub-inspector of factories, and his first wife, Mary Ann (1809–1852), daughter of Thomas Windus FSA, coach builder. Both his parents were from London, but the family had moved to Devon in 1833. Between 1849 and 1858 Kent boarded at various schools in Bath, Worcester, and Gloucester; in 1867–8 he studied at King's College, London. His first appointment was as assistant to William Flower in the Royal College of Surgeons, where he met Thomas Huxley. He then moved to the British Museum to work under Sir Richard Owen and John Gray, and in 1870 he received a grant from the Royal Society to survey for sponges and corals in the waters off Portugal in the yacht *Norna*, lent to him by Marshall Hall, a wealthy fellow of the Geological Society. This work initiated his commitment to living marine fauna, and about the same time Frank Buckland introduced him to aquaculture.

A family tragedy led William Kent to change his name. In 1865 his sister Constance Emilie *Kent confessed to the murder of her infant stepbrother Savill, and to distance himself from the light of publicity caused by this event, he adopted Saville Kent, or Saville-Kent, as his surname. His marriage on 11 June 1872 to Elizabeth Susanna Bennett (1850–1875) was registered under his original name of Kent. She was the daughter of Thomas Randle Bennett, a barrister. After her death he married, on 5 January 1876, Mary Ann Livesey (1846–1919), daughter of Thomas Livesey, gentleman.

Frustrated by lack of promotion Saville-Kent left the museum in 1873. He saw in the new public aquariums, then under construction in a number of British towns, great potential for experimental marine biology, and took a position as resident naturalist at the Brighton aquarium. He subsequently held similar posts at Manchester and at the Westminster aquarium in London. From his experience in these facilities grew an ambition to establish a national marine laboratory, and in 1877 he floated a company, backed by Owen and other prominent biologists, to achieve this objective. In 1879 he studied at the Royal College of Science, London. When the company venture and another involving the Brighton aquarium failed, he accepted in 1884 an appointment as superintendent and inspector of fisheries in Tasmania.

In Tasmania Saville-Kent surveyed resources, built a research laboratory, established oyster culture, and revised the legislation. After clashing with those promoting salmonid culture he moved to Victoria where he again surveyed resources and recommended a programme of development. With his established reputation for managing oyster fisheries the Queensland government sought his assistance to address problems in that colony. There he renewed his interest in corals and sponges. After three years in Queensland he was persuaded to accept a similar position in Western Australia. Saville-Kent's twenty years in Australia laid the foundations for fisheries development throughout the continent, excepting only New South Wales and South Australia, and provided the material for two major books: *The Great Barrier Reef* (1893), and *The Naturalist in Australia* (1897). These books remain the only visible memorial of his work in Australia.

In parallel with his official appointments Saville-Kent maintained his private research interests, initially in microscopic forms, then corals and sponges, and finally lizards. His interest in microscopy and lizards was stimulated by Huxley, to whom his three-volume *Manual of the Infusoria* (1882) was dedicated. Saville-Kent published over a hundred papers, books, and reports, in England and Australia. A fellow of the Royal Society of Queensland, after leaving government service he established a company to culture pearls off Somerset, in the far north of Queensland. The secrecy of this endeavour and his sudden death left uncertainty as to whether he should be credited with the discovery of the technique to culture pearls. Saville-Kent had lived in England periodically since the 1890s; he returned there in July 1908 and died in the House of Good Hope Hospital, Bournemouth, on 11 October 1908. He was buried in All Saints' churchyard, Milford-on-Sea, Hampshire, his grave appropriately adorned with corals.

A. J. HARRISON

Sources A. J. Harrison, *The savant of the Australian seas*, Tasmanian Historical Research Association (1997) · J. W. E. Stapleton, *The great crime of 1860* (1861) · B. Taylor, *Cruelly murdered* (1979) · m. cert. · d. cert.

Archives Bournemouth and District Society for Natural History, minute books · Linn. Soc., corresp.; membership registers · Milford-on-Sea History Society · Milford-on-Sea Women's Institute, scrapbooks · NHM, biographical file · Royal Society of Queensland, Brisbane, corresp. and minutes · RS, corresp. · Zoological Society, London, corresp. | Australian Museum, Sydney, letters to the directors, E. P. Ramsay and R. G. Etheridge, G 6401, AMS 6 vol.14, AMS 9/K19 · Mitchell L., NSW, papers of Henry Parkes and John Douglas

Likenesses photograph (pertaining to the Centennial Exhibition), LaTrobe Library, Melbourne, Australia

Wealth at death £166 17s.: probate, 10 Dec 1908, *CGPLA Eng. & Wales*

Kent and Strathearn. For this title name *see* Edward, Prince, duke of Kent and Strathearn (1767–1820).

Kentigern [St Kentigern, Mungo] (d. 612x14), patron of the diocese (later archdiocese) of Glasgow, was allegedly the son of St Thaney, a British princess from Lothian, and a British prince called Owain. The possibility that this parentage is largely, if not completely, fictional must be taken seriously, however. All that can be said with any confidence about Kentigern is that he was a contemporary of King Rhydderch of Strathclyde, who appears as a contemporary of St Columba (d. 597) in the life of Columba written by Adomnán, c.697. Rhydderch may have established the see of his kingdom at Glasgow with Kentigern as its first bishop. It is possible, however, that Glasgow may have acquired this status only in the early twelfth century.

There is very little information for Kentigern's life that can be regarded as contemporary or impartial. The main surviving medieval account is a biography written by the accomplished hagiographer, Jocelin of Furness (probably c.1180). This work was intended to replace a life of the saint commissioned by Herbert, bishop of Glasgow from 1147 to 1164, of which only a fragment survives. Neither

Jocelin of Furness nor the author of the earlier life, however, were primarily concerned to write a factual account of the saint's life as this would be understood today. Other hagiographical material is found in later works (notably the thirteenth-century Sprouston breviary and the Aberdeen breviary, published in 1510). The sources which these medieval accounts drew upon are a matter of scholarly discussion and conjecture, and it is doubtful whether any genuine information about the saint can now be convincingly identified. For instance, medieval accounts agree in making Kentigern receive his education at Culross under St Serf. St Serf, however, is likely to have flourished c.700, a century later than his supposed pupil.

It has been argued 'with some diffidence' that the life of the saint written by Jocelin of Furness contains an account of Kentigern's death which includes enough circumstantial detail to enable a plausible reconstruction of what occurred (McRoberts, 50). Not only are there elements in Jocelin's narrative of Kentigern's death which cramped his literary style, and which he presumably felt obliged to repeat because they were too well known, but there are liturgical aspects which would have become obsolete not long after Kentigern's day. According to this reconstruction, Kentigern's fatal illness struck him when he was performing the annual ceremony of baptism at the cathedral at the feast of the Epiphany. The saint was so decrepit that he had to wear a bandage round his head to support his lower jaw and prevent his mouth from hanging open. After delivering a homily from his ornate stone episcopal throne, he was assisted to the font. The water had been warmed to make the ceremony more tolerable in the midst of winter, and the aged bishop began to baptize the catechumens one by one. The effort was too much for him, however, and he collapsed, dying a week later, on 13 January. He was buried beside the altar of his cathedral.

There is uncertainty about the precise year in which Kentigern died. In *Annales Cambriae* it is recorded as nine years after the '160th year' after 444 but also two years before the '170th year', which would suggest 612 or 613. To add to the confusion, however, *Annales Cambriae* placed the death of Aedán mac Gabrán, one of the most famous kings of Dál Riata, six years earlier than Kentigern's death. Aedán probably died in 608, which would point to 614 as the actual date of Kentigern's death. It may be significant that Irish chronicles which share material with *Annales Cambriae* placed the obits of Aedán and others two years too early, which could reinforce the suggestion that the notice of Kentigern's death in *Annales Cambriae* is as much as two years wide of the mark.

St Kentigern became the focus of a cult centred on Glasgow and was closely associated with the kingdom of Strathclyde. A cluster of dedications to the saint in Cumberland may reflect the recovery of this area by Strathclyde in the tenth century. His cult also spread as far as north Wales, and it has even been suggested that St Machar, patron of the diocese of Aberdeen, is merely St Kentigern in another guise. The existence of a Gaelic pet-form of his name, Mo Choe (or Mo Cha(tha)), besides the well-known Cumbric pet-form Munghu (Mungo), suggests that his cult became current among Gaelic speakers as well as the Britons of Strathclyde in the century after his death. He has remained as a powerful symbol of Glasgow's identity throughout the city's development as a medieval burgh and as a modern commercial centre and Mungo became a popular boy's name in Scotland.

DAUVIT BROUN

Sources E. G. Bowen, *Saints, seaways, and settlements in the Celtic lands*, 2nd edn (1977), 83–93 · A. Boyle, 'St Servanus and the manuscript tradition of the life of St Kentigern', *Innes Review*, 21 (1970), 37–45 · J. Carney, *Studies in Irish literature and history* (1955), 165–88 · A. P. Forbes, ed., *Lives of S. Ninian and S. Kentigern* (1874), 243–52 · K. H. Jackson, 'The sources for the Life of St Kentigern', in N. K. Chadwick and others, *Studies in the early British church* (1958), 273–358 · J. MacQueen, 'A lost Glasgow life of St Thaney', *Innes Review*, 6 (1955), 125–30 · J. MacQueen, 'The dear green place: St Mungo and Glasgow, 600–1966', *Innes Review*, 43 (1992), 87–98 · D. McRoberts, 'The death of St Kentigern of Glasgow', *Innes Review*, 24 (1973), 43–50 · C. Ó Baoill, 'St Machar: some linguistic light?', *Innes Review*, 44 (1993), 1–13 · A. Macquarrie, *The saints of Scotland: essays in Scottish church history, AD 450–1093* (1977), 117–44

Kentigerna [St Kentigerna, Caintigern] (d. **734**), anchorite, was an Irish noblewoman who ended her days as an anchorite on a Scottish island. She owes her fame to her reputation for holiness and to the holiness and status of her male kin: she was the daughter of *Cellach Cualann, king of the Uí Máil of Leinster (d. 715), probably with his fourth wife, Caintigern, and her death merited an entry in the contemporary annals of Ulster. Two of Kentigerna's sisters, according to genealogies based on the annals of the four masters, were wives of Uí Néill kings while a third married a king of the Uí Dúnlainge.

For Kentigerna's own life there are only late traditions, found in the ninth-century Book of Deer and the early sixteenth-century Aberdeen breviary. According to these, Kentigerna, herself the wife of an Irish king, Feriacus of Monchestree, left Ireland on his death in the company of her brother, *Cóemgen and her son, *Fáelán of Cluain Móescna [see under Fáelán Amlabar]. With them she went first to Strathfillan, later moving to the island of Inchcailloch in Loch Lomond to adopt the solitary life. Whatever the historicity of these accounts, those elaborations which credit Kentigerna with St Fursa and St Ultán as further sons should be dismissed as apocryphal.

Kentigerna's travels underline the vitality of the links in the eighth century between south-west Scotland and the Irish coasts of Wicklow and Wexford, links forged both by intermarriages between the aristocracies of these regions as well as by the wanderings of their saints.

HENRIETTA LEYSER

Sources A. O. Anderson, ed. and trans., *Early sources of Scottish history, AD 500 to 1286*, 2 vols. (1922); repr. with corrections (1990) · A. P. Smyth, *Celtic Leinster* (1982)

Kentish, John (1768–1853), Unitarian minister, was born at St Albans, Hertfordshire, on 26 June 1768, the only child (after the death in infancy of a daughter born in 1773) of John Kentish (d. 1814) and his wife, Hannah (d. 1793), daughter and heir of Keaser Vanderplank. The Kentishes were a family of landowners and brewers whose importance in St Albans runs back at least to the fifteenth century. The elder John Kentish, at one time a draper, was the youngest son and ultimately the heir of Thomas Kentish, who in 1723 was high sheriff of Hertfordshire.

Kentish was educated at the school of John Worsley (d. 1807) at Hertford and in 1784 entered Daventry Academy as a divinity student. At Daventry he was a 'parlour boarder', with better accommodation than students on the foundation and with easier access to the chief tutor, Thomas Belsham. In September 1788 with two fellow students, John Corrie (1769–1839) and William Shepherd (1768–1847), he left Daventry for the new college at Hackney, following the prohibition by the Coward trustees, who controlled Daventry, against any use of written prayers; the next year Belsham, having turned Unitarian, also moved to Hackney.

In the autumn of 1790 Kentish left Hackney to become the first minister of a newly formed Unitarian congregation at Plymouth Dock. A chapel in George Street was opened on 27 April 1791 by Theophilus Lindsey, using a prayer book drawn up by Kentish and Thomas Porter, minister of the Treville Street congregation, Plymouth. In 1794 Kentish succeeded Porter, who, like many Unitarians in that repressive period, emigrated to the United States. In 1795 he moved to London as afternoon preacher at the Gravel Pit, Hackney, where Belsham had become the morning preacher in succession to Joseph Priestley in 1794, adding to this office appointment as morning preacher at Newington Green from 1799 to 1802 and at St Thomas's Street, Southwark in 1802–3. On 23 January 1803 he became minister of the New Meeting in Birmingham. On 28 October 1805 he married Mary (1775–1864), daughter of John Kettle of Birmingham (d. 1808); there were no children.

A full-length silhouette, executed in 1851, exhibits Kentish's short stature, portly figure, and old-fashioned costume with knee-breeches. He was a man of great personal dignity, and his weight of character, extensive learning, and ample fortune generously administered, secured him a wide respect rarely accorded a nonconformist minister. He was a sound scholar, versed in oriental languages and familiar with the works of German biblical critics. Relying heavily on biblical exegesis, he was a Unitarian of the most conservative type, holding closely to the miraculous foundation of revelation. His sermons, rigorously non-doctrinal and practical, were remarkable for beauty of style. In politics he was an old whig, as disapproving of radicals in the 1830s as he had been of his more extreme fellow students at Hackney. Until the Reform Act of 1832 deprived him of his vote as a burgess of St Albans, he regularly supported the Spencer family, patrons of the borough, but looked dubiously on the narrow self-interest of other electors.

Kentish published a number of separately printed sermons and a collection in 1848, the second edition of which (1854) carries an admirable memoir by John Kenrick (1788–1877). His most important and characteristic theological work is *Notes and Comments on Passages of Scripture*

(1844; 3rd edn, 1848). His memoir of the Revd Timothy Kenrick (1759–1804) is prefixed to Kenrick's *Exposition* (1807). He was a frequent contributor to the *Monthly Repository* and the *Christian Reformer*, usually with the signature N. In 1832 Kentish declined his stipend but remained a minister, continuing to preach frequently until 1844. He retained his faculties to a great age, but an attack of paralysis in 1850 began a slow decline. He died of pneumonia on Sunday 6 March 1853 at his residence, Park Vale, Edgbaston. On 15 March he was buried in the public general cemetery at Kaye Hill, Hookley, near Birmingham.

R. K. WEBB

Sources [J. Kenrick], 'Memoir of the late Rev. John Kentish', *Christian Reformer, or, Unitarian Magazine and Review*, new ser., 9 (1853), 265–85 · *The Inquirer* (1853), 180 · E. Toms, *The story of St Albans*, rev. edn (1975), 124–5, 146 · *GM*, 1st ser., 63 (1793), 1060 · *GM*, 1st ser., 75 (1805), 1072

Archives DWL, student essays · RS, corresp. | DWL, corresp. with Joshua Wilson

Likenesses T. Phillips, oils, 1840, NPG · silhouette, 1851 · T. Lupton, engraving (after T. Phillips), Harris Man. Oxf.

Wealth at death under £30,000: estate duty register, PC 208, Reg. 1

Kentner, Louis Philip (1905–1987), pianist, was born Lajos Kentner on 19 July 1905 in Karwin, Silesia, Austria–Hungary, the only son and elder child of Julius Kentner, stationmaster, and his wife, Gisela Buchsbaum. He was educated at the *Gymnasium* in Budapest and the Royal Franz Liszt Academy of Music, also in Budapest. This was a remarkable beginning: he was only six years old, and simultaneously a school pupil and an academician. He studied the piano with Arnold Szekely and composition with Hans Koessler, Leó Weiner, and Zoltan Kodály. Both Weiner and Kodály were lifetime influences. He gained a diploma in musical composition.

Composition was Kentner's first ambition. Three sonatinas were published (by Oxford University Press) in the 1930s, and there were later performances of a string quartet and a divertimento for chamber orchestra. But it was the piano that was to become the centre of his musical life. His concert career began with a recital in Budapest when he was thirteen. From the 1920s he undertook a ceaseless round of concerts around the world, his fame spreading rapidly. He went back to Hungary, but with the political situation worsening emigration beckoned, and he decided to move to England in 1935, becoming one of the mid-Europeans who transformed Britain's musical life. He became a British citizen in 1946, and London remained his home until his death.

In an early review (in the *Sunday Referee* of 11 October 1936), headed 'A new—and great—pianist comes to England', Constant Lambert wrote:

> What gives Kentner's playing its exceptional quality, however, is not so much his technical ability, which he shares with several virtuosos, but the remarkable intelligence and musical instinct which direct this ability ... I have never heard a pianist of such power who at the same time has such delicacy and subtlety of tone gradation ... a pianist with a brilliant future.

Lambert immediately discerned Kentner's exceptional

musicianship, as did William Walton and the Sitwells, who were warm supporters and friends. He became an admired performer in solo recitals and concertos—an early Mozart concerto with Sir Thomas Beecham was a landmark—as also in chamber music, a lifelong passion. For some years there was a trio with Yehudi Menuhin and the cellist Gaspar Cassadó. Music-making with Menuhin, who married Kentner's second wife's sister, was an important activity over the years.

Kentner's repertory was enormous and ranged from Bach to Bartók. He was especially noted for his Chopin and Liszt, the latter being most remarkable. Liszt's music had been regarded as superficial and it was 'not done' to perform it. It was largely due to Kentner's championship and deeply felt performances that Liszt came to be treated as a composer of serious beauty. In 1951 he was one of the founders of the Liszt Society, and from 1965 to his death its president.

Kentner gave the first performances of Bartók's second piano concerto (conducted by Otto Klemperer, 1933) and—in Europe—his third concerto (conducted by Sir Adrian Boult, 1946), the first piano concerto of Alan Rawsthorne in 1942, the piano concerto of Michael Tippett (1956), and, with Menuhin, of Walton's sonata for violin and piano. He was gifted with a formidable technique and a faultless memory. But what governed his playing was a constant quest for musical truth and his faithfulness to the composer's intention, with which he wished to identify. So his performances moved one both through their effortlessness—though he never tried to dazzle—and his sensitivity, accuracy, and, above all, musical humility. He seemed to be communing with the composer, and this musicianship transmitted itself to the listener. He was one of the last great romantic pianists and his eightieth birthday concert in the Queen Elizabeth Hall, London, caused a spontaneous standing ovation. Fortunately, a number of splendid recordings were made.

The same qualities inspired Kentner's teaching, whether in master classes at the Yehudi Menuhin School of Music or with individual pupils in his studio. His standards were high and criticisms tough, though spiced with good Hungarian sarcasm ('Why play the wrong note when the right one is next door?'). There was no didactic method, just a search for musical truth. Technique was taught *through* the music, and Kentner could translate brilliantly musical points into words. He wrote: 'no teacher can put anything into a pupil which is not already there. He can only awake what is already lying dormant, and guide it towards possible short cuts, tending and nurturing it as it grows.' And so his pupils were inspired. He also liked writing, and his little book, *Piano* (1976), is necessary reading for any aspiring pianist. He became an honorary member of the Royal Academy of Music in 1970 and was appointed CBE in 1978.

Physically, Kentner was small in build, and he looked even smaller on his very low (collapsible) piano stool. He had a beautiful head, and an ever-hovering smile. A gentle warmth emanated from him, coupled with a special sense of humour, sometimes wicked, always witty. He was a brilliant raconteur, equalled only by his second wife, Griselda. His wide reading made him into a typically cultured mid-European.

In 1931 Kentner married a pianist, Ilona, daughter of Ede Kabos, journalist and writer. They were divorced in 1945 and in 1946 he married Griselda Katharine, sister of Diana, who married Yehudi Menuhin the following year, and daughter of Gerard Louis Eugene Gould (d. 1916), of the special branch in the Foreign Office, and his wife, the pianist Evelyn Suart. There were no children of either marriage. Kentner and Griselda shared the remainder of his life, and he spoke often of how central to his playing and life Griselda was: he wrote of her as 'beautiful, talented, angelic, highly musical withal'. Kentner died at their home at 1 Mallord Street, Chelsea, on 22 September 1987. CLAUS MOSER, rev.

Sources H. Taylor, ed., *Kentner: a symposium* (1987) · *The Independent* (30 Sept 1987) · *The Times* (23 Sept 1987) · personal knowledge (1996)
Likenesses photograph, Hult. Arch.
Wealth at death £259,185: probate, 18 Nov 1987, *CGPLA Eng. & Wales*

Kenton, Benjamin (1719–1800), wine merchant and philanthropist, was born on 19 November 1719 at Fieldgate Street, Whitechapel, London, the son of Benjamin Kenton and his wife, Mary, who kept a small greengrocer's shop. He was educated at the parish charity school and at fifteen he was apprenticed to the landlord of the Angel and Crown inn, Whitechapel. In 1741 he became waiter and drawer at the Crown and Magpie in Aldgate, an inn frequented by sea-captains whose vessels berthed on the Thames. The owner had discovered the technique of bottling beer so that it withstood the high temperatures and rough passage around the Cape, and had built up a substantial export trade. The inn was also famous for its sign of a stone crown surmounted by a magpie carved in pear wood. When the landlord removed the magpie and changed the name of his beer to Crown Beer, the quality is said to have suffered. The loss of the magpie was blamed and trade declined.

Kenton, however, was popular with the seamen. A witty and attentive waiter, contemporaries recalled how he kept two candles constantly burning on the bar to remind him that as they dimmed he needed to attend to every candle in the house. When the owner died, the customers put up the capital for Kenton to take over as landlord. His first task was to restore the magpie and, with it, the inn's reputation. Kenton prospered, and in 1765 moved to new premises in the Minories, where he quickly established himself as a wine merchant. With expert financial guidance from his banker friend, Thomas Harley (1730–1804), alderman of Portsoken ward, his business profits were transformed into a considerable fortune.

Kenton was an active member of the Vintners' Company; in 1768 he was elected to its court and, in 1776, to the position of master. He donated £4250 to enlarge the company's almshouses at Mile End. A trustee of the Sir John

Cass School and governor of the Foundling Hospital, he gave liberally to many charities, including the White-chapel School where he was educated, and a number of other charity schools. He bequeathed £20,000 to Hetherington's charity for the blind, and £5000 each to St Bartholomew's, Christ's, and Bridewell hospitals.

Kenton was a man of solid proportions, with a slight inward squint. He was predeceased by his wife (whose name is not known), and by his children, including at least one son and a daughter. His son became an eminent druggist in Lawrence Lane, Cheapside, and died a wealthy man in his own right. His daughter died from tuberculosis before her intended marriage to David Pike Watts, her father's clerk. Kenton had opposed the engagement, but ultimately the men became close friends and Watts, as Kenton's main beneficiary, reputedly inherited almost £300,000. Kenton died at his home in Gower Street on 25 May 1800 and was buried in St Dunstan and All Saints, Stepney. An annual sermon to commemorate his benefactions to the Vintners' Company was established, and a street near the Foundling Hospital was named after him.

NORMAN MOORE, rev. CHRISTINE CLARK

Sources B. Standring, *Benjamin Kenton, a biographical sketch* (1878) · R. Watson, *A scrapbook of inns* (1949) · W. Herbert, *The history of the twelve great livery companies of London*, 2 (1837) · private information (1892)
Likenesses W. Ridley, stipple, BM, NPG; repro. in *European Magazine and London Review*, 54 (1808), facing p. 331 · Westmacott, monument, St Dunstan's Church, Stepney · portrait, Vintners' Hall, London
Wealth at death over £300,000: Standring, *Benjamin Kenton*

Kenton, Nicholas (d. 1468), Carmelite friar and preacher, was born in Kenton, Suffolk. He joined the order at Ipswich and undertook his early studies in London, where he was ordained subdeacon on 2 March 1420 and priest on 21 December 1420, before attending Cambridge University, where he had graduated DTh by 1444. In the same year he was elected provincial at Stamford, and held this office until he resigned in 1456. But he acted as vicar-general in later years, and in that capacity presided over the provincial chapter held in London in 1468 to elect a successor to John Milverton (d. 1487), who was imprisoned in Rome. Kenton died shortly afterwards on 4 September 1468, in the Carmelite house, London.

John Bale wrote that Kenton was known throughout England for his inspiring sermons and his skill in explaining complicated subjects. Kenton composed a collection of metrical prayers to the saints, written during his travels around the province, and Bale preserves one celebrating the canonization of Sant'Alberto of Sicily in 1453 (Bodl. Oxf., MS Bodley 73, fol. 91v). Other works, now lost, include theological lectures given at Oxford, collections of sermons, the lives of Elijah the Prophet and Cyril of Jerusalem, and a collection of over 212 letters. One letter survives, appealing to the king for the return of an errant friar, and John Bale preserves the text of another recommending Thomas Scrope (d. 1492), along with notes on some others (PRO, C81/1793/25; BL, Harley MS 1819, fols.

196v–197, 200–200v). Kenton has been credited with writing the lessons for the Carmelite feast of Our Lady of Mount Carmel, but this is doubtful. The miraculous cure, through the intercession of Sant'Andrea Corsini, which is said to have happened to Nicholas Kenton at Florence, should more correctly be assigned to John Keninghale (d. 1451), an earlier provincial. RICHARD COPSEY

Sources J. Bale, Bodl. Oxf., MS Bodley 73 (SC 27635), fols. 3, 4v, 50, 51, 68, 81v, 82, 91v, 120v, 133v, 201v, 208v, 217 bis · J. Bale, BL, Harley MS 1819, fols. 196v–197, 200–200v · J. Bale, Bodl. Oxf., MS Selden supra 41, fol. 180v · J. Bale, BL, Harley MS 3838, fols. 37v–38, 43v, 103–104, 212 · Bale, *Cat.*, 1.608–9 · Emden, *Cam.*, 336 · B. Zimmerman, 'Alcune Osservazioni sul "S. Andrea Corsini" del P. Paolo Caioli, Carm.', *Rivista Storica Carmelitana*, 2 (1930), 37–40 · *Acta sanctorum: Januarius*, 2 (Antwerp, 1643), 1072, 1073, 1077 · J. Bale, *Illustrium Maioris Britannie scriptorum … summarium* (1548), fol. 203 · *Commentarii de scriptoribus Britannicis, auctore Leando*, ed. A. Hall, 2 (1709), 459 · J. Pits, *Relationum historicarum de rebus Anglicis*, ed. [W. Bishop] (Paris, 1619), 657–9 · Tanner, *Bibl. Brit.-Hib.*, 453 · C. de S. E. de Villiers, *Bibliotheca Carmelitana*, 2 vols. (Orléans, 1752); facs. edn, ed. P. G. Wessels (Rome, 1927), vol. 2, pp. 499–500
Archives Bodl. Oxf., MS Bodley 73, fol. 91v · Bodl. Oxf., MS Bodley 73, fol. 68

Kenworthy, Joseph Montague, tenth Baron Strabolgi (1886–1953), naval officer and politician, was born at 22 Willes Road, Leamington, Warwickshire, on 7 March 1886, the first son of Cuthbert Matthias Kenworthy (1853–1934), gentleman, and his wife, Elizabeth Florence (d. 1951), daughter of George Buchanan Cooper of Sacramento. Cuthbert Kenworthy claimed the barony of Strabolgi, created in 1318 but in abeyance since 1788. He established his controversial claim in May 1916, becoming ninth baron.

Orginally intended for holy orders, J. M. Kenworthy became fired at preparatory school with the desire to be a polar explorer. A naval career seemed the best way to achieve this ambition and Kenworthy was entered at Eastman's Naval Academy, Winchester, which specialized in preparing boys for the entrance examination to the training ship *Britannia*, which he joined in 1902, completing his cadet training in the cruiser *Isis*. As a midshipman he joined the battleship *Goliath* on the China station, soon transferring to the flagship *Glory*. The station provided much opportunity for his lifelong passion for shooting. He also proved to be a talented boxer and eventually became heavyweight champion of the navy.

After a short time in the Channel Fleet battleship *Montagu* (wrecked very shortly after he left it in 1906), Kenworthy obtained a first-class pass in his examination for sub-lieutenant. His rank became substantive in 1907, after the usual course at the Royal Naval College, Greenwich, and he was posted as first lieutenant in HMS *Hussar*, the commander-in-chief's dispatch vessel in the Mediterranean. After an incident with his admiral over shooting, he exchanged posts with the first lieutenant of the destroyer *Albatross*.

Kenworthy's new ship was a plum command, and the slight cloud on his career did not preclude his promotion to lieutenant in 1908. He remained in flotilla work, commanding a torpedo boat based at Queenstown. After broadening his career in the armoured cruiser *Achilles* and the gunnery training tender at Sheerness, Kenworthy was appointed to command the destroyer *Bullfinch*. He also married, on 4 December 1913, Doris (1888/9–1988), only child of Sir Frederick Whitley Thornson, a Halifax mill owner and Liberal MP for Skipton. They had three sons and a daughter.

After the outbreak of the First World War *Bullfinch* was seriously damaged in collision with a Dutch steamer; Kenworthy was absolved of blame and congratulated on saving his ship. In 1915 he joined the battleship *Commonwealth*, an obsolescent pre-dreadnought of the 3rd battle squadron which was soon redeployed from Scapa to Sheerness. *Commonwealth*'s captain was Herbert Richmond, whom Kenworthy found a kindred spirit and who joined him, Kenneth Dewar, Reginald Plunkett, and others as one of the 'young Turks' critical of what they saw as pusillanimous Admiralty policy. Kenworthy, a lieutenant-commander from 1916, was able to exploit both his location and his connections by marriage to exert behind-the-scenes influence with politicians and the press unusual for an officer of his rank. Through Lord Northcliffe he obtained access to Lloyd George. The prime minister saw Kenworthy on two occasions, on 14 and 20 May 1917, and wrote in his *War Memoirs* his appreciation of Kenworthy's 'making him acquainted at this critical stage with the views of the younger officers in the Navy' (Lloyd George, 1173). The resulting changes in the Admiralty saw Kenworthy temporarily loaned to the operations division of the naval staff, in the section known eventually as 'plans'. His ideas for various offensive operations were overruled and at the end of the year he was transferred to Gibraltar as assistant chief of staff to organize an allied convoy system for the western Mediterranean.

After a bout of influenza, Kenworthy joined the submarine depot ship *Blake*. He had decided to enter politics and was Liberal candidate for Rotherham in the general election of 1918. Soundly defeated, coming third behind the Conservative and Labour candidates, he was appointed to the naval base at Immingham in February 1919 with responsibility for the armoured cruisers *Duke of Edinburgh*, *King Alfred*, *Minotaur*, and *Leviathan*, which were awaiting disposal. He soon took up the offer of another opportunity for a seat in parliament, at a by-election in Central Hull in March 1919. He won an unexpected and sensational victory, overcoming a tory majority of over 10,000 at the general election four months earlier, to defeat the Conservative coalitionist Lord Eustace Percy.

Kenworthy was a popular MP in his constituency and soon made his mark in the House of Commons as a radical and combative back-bencher, fearlessly taking the unpopular side on many issues, such as Versailles and the Irish troubles. Along with Donald Maclean and William Wedgwood Benn he was an energetic member of the Asquithian opposition to Lloyd George's coalition government. During the 1920s he supported improved relations with the USSR, opposed naval competition with the USA, espoused the Zionist cause, and used his sporting and

social relations with the Indian nobility to foster Anglo-Indian constitutional development.

Kenworthy was among the twelve Liberal rebels who voted, on 8 October 1924, against his own party's amendment, supported by the Conservatives, on the Labour government's handling of the prosecution of the communist J. R. Campbell; the carrying of the amendment brought down Ramsay MacDonald's administration. After the ensuing general election Kenworthy belonged to the radical group of seven Liberal MPs who opposed Lloyd George's leadership of the party in the House of Commons. When Lloyd George assumed leadership of the reunited Liberal Party in November 1926, Kenworthy resigned and went over to Labour. Standing as a Labour candidate he retained his Hull seat at a by-election later in the month, gaining an increased majority in a three-cornered contest against both Conservatives and Liberals. One contemporary observer of the House of Commons described him in 1931 as being a 'bruiser' whose 'hectoring style' tended to alienate his fellow parliamentarians (Johnston, 60). He was defeated by a Conservative in a straight fight during the National Government landslide of 1931.

In 1927 Kenworthy published the first of a series of books on contemporary affairs, followed by an entertaining autobiography in 1933. On his father's sudden death in February 1934 he succeeded as tenth Baron Strabolgi. He continued to speak out on issues such as Abyssinia and the Spanish Civil War and joined the front bench for the first time as opposition chief whip in the House of Lords in 1938, a position he held until 1942. Strabolgi joined the parliamentary Home Guard but found time between 1940 and 1944 to publish several books on the war. He was disappointed not to be a member of the post-war Labour government.

Strabolgi's first marriage was dissolved in 1941 to allow him to marry, on 1 February 1941, Geraldine Mary (*b.* 1899/1900), a secretary, daughter of Maurice Francis Hamilton; the marriage produced a daughter. Lord Strabolgi died suddenly of a heart attack at 20B Collingham Gardens, Kensington, London, on 8 October 1953. His second wife survived him.   ERIC J. GROVE

Sources J. M. Kenworthy, *Sailors, statesmen and others: an autobiography* (1933) · *The Times* (9 Oct 1953) · *WWW, 1951–60* · A. G. Marder, *From the dreadnought to Scapa Flow: the Royal Navy in the Fisher era, 1904–19*, 4: *1917, the year of crisis* (1969), vol. 4 · D. Lloyd George, *War memoirs*, 3 (1934) · private information (2004) [eleventh Baron Strabolgi] · J. Johnston, *A hundred commoners* (1930) · Burke, *Peerage* (2000) · b. cert. · m. certs. · d. cert. · *The Labour who's who* (1927) · R. Douglas, *The history of the liberal party, 1895–1970* (1971) · M. Bentley, *The liberal mind, 1914–1919* (1977)
Archives SOUND priv. coll., tape of BBC recording
Likenesses D. Selous, portrait, priv. coll.
Wealth at death £400: private information

Kenyatta, Jomo (*c.*1895–1978), president of Kenya, was born in Ngenda in north-eastern Kiambu district at the inception of British rule in east Africa, the son of Muigai wa Magana. Orphaned early by the death of his father, in a smallpox epidemic during the early stages of colonialism,

The association also sought to represent Kikuyu grievances over land and labour issues, particularly the loss of land to white settlement, to the colonial government, and to various British investigating commissions appointed to study the colony's turbulent affairs.

In 1929–30 Kenyatta made his first visit to Britain to represent Kikuyu interests and grievances directly to the imperial authorities. He was granted only one brief meeting with senior officials at the Colonial Office. He made contact, however, with a wide spectrum of British society and politics, from missionaries to liberal critics of imperialism and many segments of the British left, including the Communist Party. George Padmore, then the highest-ranking black official of the Comintern, befriended him and sponsored his travels in Europe to France, the Netherlands, Germany, and the Soviet Union. He returned to Kenya to become embroiled in 1930 in the controversy over female circumcision, which the Kikuyu Central Association defended against missionary attempts to abolish the custom, and was eventually expelled from the Church of Scotland.

In 1931 Kenyatta returned to Britain with Parmenas Mockerie to present evidence and petitions from the association to the joint parliamentary commission on closer union in east Africa. Denied a chance to testify, Kenyatta stayed on in Britain for more than fifteen years, pursuing a personal and political odyssey, searching for an education and an 'unanswerable argument' that would compel the attention of British authorities to Kikuyu grievances. He spent a term at the Quaker Woodbrook College in Selly Oak, Birmingham, in early 1932, greatly improving his command of written English. He also gave evidence to the Kenya land commission before its departure for Kenya.

In 1932–3 Kenyatta spent a year in the Soviet Union as a student at the Comintern's University of Toilers of the East (KUTV). Nothing in his life is more enshrouded with myth and controversy than this brief period. For the British authorities, it forever marked him with the stigma of communism. The opening of Comintern files in Soviet archives has finally clarified what occurred. While it remains unclear whether Kenyatta ever actually joined the Communist Party of Great Britain, his Comintern instructors regarded him as increasingly hostile to Marxism and Soviet policies, and therefore wholly unsuitable for recruitment as an agent. Had British intelligence known this, the intense suspicion and hostility with which the British dealt with him could well have been avoided.

After returning to London, Kenyatta spent the rest of the 1930s pursuing his education and a growing involvement in African affairs at the fringes of British politics. Penniless and without any prospect of further contributions from the Kikuyu Central Association, he supported himself by becoming a linguistic informant to Lilias Armstrong at University College, London, and contributing significantly to her work on Kikuyu phonology. This involvement in university life culminated in 1935 in his being admitted, without benefit of any university degree,

Jomo Kenyatta (c.1895–1978), by Mohamed Amin, 1973

he lived with his uncle Ngengi. Known as Kamau wa Ngengi, he was raised in a typical Kikuyu farming and herding homestead, and was educated in the indigenous culture, particularly by his grandfather Kongo wa Magana, a noted traditional healer and savant.

In 1909 Kenyatta became one of the first boarding students at the Scottish mission at Thogoto, near Nairobi. He left in 1914 after receiving a rudimentary primary education and vocational training, and being baptized that year as Johnstone Kamau. In 1913 he had gone through a missionary version of traditional Kikuyu initiation into the Mubengi age grade. After moving to Nairobi, he became a well-known young man about town, soon called Johnstone Kenyatta after the brightly beaded belt (kinyatta) he often wore. He held a succession of jobs, notably during the 1920s as a meter reader for the Nairobi water department. He married for the first time in 1919, to Grace Wahu, and they had two children, Peter Muigai and Margaret Wambui (mayor of Nairobi in 1969–76).

As a prominent member of the emerging literate intelligentsia of mission-educated young men (known locally as athomi—'the readers'), Kenyatta became involved in the cultural and political ferment of urban African life in Nairobi. In 1928 he became general secretary of the Kikuyu Central Association and editor of its monthly journal, Muigwithania ('The Reconciler', which was to remain one of his nicknames for the rest of his life). In its columns Kenyatta and athomi debated their role in Kikuyu society, the meaning of Kikuyu karing'a ('authentic Gikuyuness'), and the reconciliation of Kikuyu and European culture.

to the postgraduate diploma course in social anthropology at the London School of Economics as the personal student of Bronislaw Malinowski. Anthropology appeared to provide the authoritative scientific argument that he needed for his representation of the Kikuyu. Teachers and fellow students, including Raymond Firth, Isaac Schapera, Elspeth Huxley, and Prince Peter of Denmark, held him in high esteem. His thesis was revised and published as *Facing Mount Kenya*, which made a notable contribution to the ethnography of the Kikuyu, and was one of the first such studies produced by an African of his own people.

Politically, Kenyatta distanced himself from communist organizations and support, although remaining in touch with the non-communist left, particularly in the Independent Labour Party. His closest associates of this period were among the small black intelligentsia in Britain, particularly a group of pan-Africanists, led by Padmore, with whom he joined in 1937 to found the International African Service Bureau to advance pan-African ideas and colonial freedom. During this period he dropped the name Johnstone in favour of the more African-sounding Jomo that he made up himself. His associates included the celebrated singer and actor Paul Robeson, as well as many who later achieved intellectual and political distinction, such as C. L. R. James, Eric Williams, Peter Abrahams, Kwame Nkrumah, and Ralph Bunche.

By the end of the 1930s Kenyatta had matured politically and intellectually. His qualities of leadership and character, and the measured dignity with which he presented the interests of his people, were widely recognized by his friends and associates in Britain, even if they found his preoccupation with Kikuyu interests and a conservative reconciliation of European and Kikuyu cultures narrow and parochial. During the Second World War he spent several years working on a farm in the Sussex village of Storrington and lecturing for the Workers' Educational Association and to British troops on African affairs. His personal charm and conviviality made him a friend to many in the village, including the composer Arnold Bax. In 1942 he was married a second time, to Edna Grace Clark; their son Peter Magana was born the following year. He also found time to write two pamphlets on Kenyan history and politics, and joined with his International African Service Bureau colleagues to organize the 1945 Pan-African Congress in Manchester. In 1946 Kenyatta married Grace, daughter of Senior Chief Koinange, who died in childbirth. In 1951 he was married for the fourth time, to Ngina, daughter of Chief Muhoho, who survived him. They had two sons and three daughters.

After participating in Fabian Society conferences on post-war colonial affairs, Kenyatta returned to Kenya in September 1946 to resume his political career. The Kikuyu Central Association had been banned in 1940 and its leaders detained for the duration of the war. Kenyatta now assumed leadership of the Kenya African Union (KAU), a colony-wide association founded in 1944. In an environment of rapid economic growth and expanding conflict between Africans, particularly the Kikuyu, and the Kenya government and settler community, the KAU sought constitutional reforms giving Africans increased political representation, and the resolution of socio-economic grievances. By the early 1950s the failure of reformist politics brought Kenyatta under pressure from militants of the secret Mau Mau movement, and counter-pressure from the colonial regime to denounce it. Escalating Mau Mau terrorism and official repression culminated in the declaration of a state of emergency in October 1952. Kenyatta was arrested and charged, along with some of the movement's actual leaders, with organizing Mau Mau. Convicted after a sensational trial marked by perjured testimony and an openly biased judge, he was sentenced to seven years' imprisonment and an indefinite term of restriction in the remote northern desert of Kenya.

After the suppression of Mau Mau, African politics began to revive in Kenya in the late 1950s with a new generation of leaders and growing mass following drawn from all Kenya's major ethnic communities. The imprisoned Kenyatta became the symbol of Kenyan nationalism and unity. When British policy changed in early 1960 to permit Kenya's independence under an African majority government, pressure for his release grew, despite his continued denunciation by the colonial regime as a 'leader to darkness and death'. After his release in August 1961 he quickly assumed leadership of the Kenya African National Union (KANU), formed the previous year in an alliance of the Kikuyu and Luo, the two largest ethnic groups. He entered parliament in January 1962 as leader of the opposition and the following month led KANU at the London constitutional conference. In April 1962 he became a minister in the transitional coalition government and prime minister in June 1963 after KANU won the election for internal self-government. Kenya became independent on 12 December 1963. A year later, the quasi-federal independence constitution was replaced by a unitary republic and Kenyatta became president.

Kenyatta ruled Kenya until his death, which occurred at Mombasa on 22 August 1978. Although he was duly re-elected every five years, he was a patriarchal figure, above electoral competition—a combination of senior elder and governor. He elevated the power of the presidency far above that of parliament or party, relying heavily on the Africanized colonial-era provincial administration as his direct linkage with the people and instrument of control. He ruled, however, with a spirit of conciliation and unity under his motto *Harambee* ('let us pull together'). In a celebrated speech to white settlers in Nakuru shortly before independence, his generosity and spirit of reconciliation offered to his harshest foes turned him from the evil manipulator of Mau Mau to their revered *Mzee* ('old man'). Although Kenya under KANU was a *de facto* one party state, competitive primary elections provided for significant turnover of members of parliament, including cabinet ministers.

Kenyatta's government presided over a conservative capitalist development strategy, despite a commitment to a vaguely defined 'African socialism', and saw members of the African élite, especially from among Kenyatta's own Kikuyu people, move into prominent positions in business. Steady economic growth, however, fuelled by significant foreign investment, was accompanied by widening inequalities of wealth in a rapidly growing population.

Kenyatta was a masterful dispenser of patronage and player of 'carrot and stick' politics, deploying the extensive resources of the Kenyan state to balance the diverse ethnic factions within KANU. However, a breakaway of more radical elements to the Kenya People's Union led by his former vice-president, Oginga Odinga, ended the Luo-Kikuyu alliance. It was suppressed after a violent confrontation of its supporters with police during a Kenyatta speech in Kisumu in November 1969. His administration was also marred by the assassination of prominent political figures Pio Gama Pinto, Tom Mboya and J. M. Kariuki, although Kenyatta himself was not directly implicated.

Internationally, Kenyatta's Kenya was firmly in the Western camp during the cold war. While he was a founding member of the Organisation of African Unity, Kenyatta did not play a significant role in African politics. His two attempts to reconcile internal conflicts, in Congo in 1964 and Angola in 1975, both ended in failure. His central preoccupation and contribution was the establishment of a strong post-colonial state in Kenya, one of the few in modern Africa that has remained under civilian government since independence. His lifelong project of reconciling African and European cultures, symbolized by his lion's tail fly whisk and London School of Economics tie, remained more elusive.

A commanding and charismatic figure who dominated potential rivals, he was a powerful orator in several languages. By his death he was recognized as a leading African statesmen. In 1974 he became life president of KANU. Other honours included an honorary fellowship of the London School of Economics, a knighthood of St John in 1972, the order of the Golden Ark of the World Wildlife Fund in 1974, and the honorary degree of LLD from the University of East Africa (1965) and Manchester University (1966).   BRUCE J. BERMAN

Sources J. Kenyatta, *Facing Mount Kenya* (1938) · C. Rosberg and J. Nottingham, *The myth of 'Mau Mau': nationalism in Kenya* (1966) · J. Murray-Brown, *Kenyatta* (1972) · B. Berman, *Control and crisis in colonial Kenya: dialectic of domination* (1990) · B. Berman and J. Lonsdale, *Unhappy valley: conflict in Kenya and Africa* (1992) · A. Pegushev, 'The unknown Jomo Kenyatta', *Edgerton Journal* [Kenya], 1/2 (1996), 173–98 · B. Berman and J. Lonsdale, 'The labours of Muigwithania: Jomo Kenyatta as author, 1929–45', *Research in African Literatures*, 29/1 (1998), 16–42 · *DNB*

Archives FILM BFI NFTVA, documentary footage · BFI NFTVA, news footage · IWM FVA, documentary footage · IWM FVA, news footage | SOUND IWM SA, oral history interview

Likenesses M. Amin, photograph, 1973, Hult. Arch. [*see illus.*]

Kenyon, Sir **Frederic George** (1863–1952), Greek and biblical scholar and museum director, was born on 15 January 1863, the seventh son and the eleventh of the fifteen children (eleven boys, four girls) of John Robert Kenyon (1807–1880), grandson of the first Baron Kenyon of Pradoe,

Sir Frederic George Kenyon (1863–1952), by Walter Stoneman, 1919

Shropshire, fellow of All Souls and Vinerian professor of law at Oxford, and his wife, Mary Eliza (*d.* 1903), daughter of Edward Hawkins FRS, keeper of antiquities in the British Museum. He was born at his maternal grandfather's house, 6 Lower Berkeley Street, London, but from the age of six was brought up at Pradoe. From his preparatory school he went as a scholar to Winchester College (1875–82), then, again as a scholar, to New College, Oxford (1882–6), where he obtained first classes in both classical moderations (1883) and *literae humaniores* (1886). From schooldays he had shown an interest in biblical study, winning prizes at each school; and at Oxford, besides the chancellor's English essay (1889), he won the Hall-Houghton junior Greek Testament prize (1885) for a study of St Matthew's gospel.

Kenyon obtained a fellowship at Magdalen College in 1888 and in the next year entered the British Museum as an assistant in the department of manuscripts. Shortly afterwards he began to catalogue its collection of Greek papyri, and while he was thus engaged the museum made the remarkable acquisition of papyri which included Aristotle's treatise on the Athenian constitution, the mimes of Herodas, part of the speech of Hyperides against Philippides, a grammatical work by Tryphon, and a long medical treatise by an unknown author, besides known works of Demosthenes, Isocrates, and Homer. Kenyon's publication of the Aristotle (1891; 3rd and revised edn, 1892) brought him honorary doctorates at Durham and Halle, and his election in 1900 as corresponding member of the

Berlin Assembly. In 1891 he published an English translation, and he edited the Greek text for the Berlin Academy's *Supplementum Aristotelicum* (1903) and for the Oxford Classical Texts (1920). The translation appeared in the Oxford translation of Aristotle's works (1920). The other literary papyri, except the medical treatise (copied by Kenyon, edited by Diels), were published or collated in *Classical Texts from Papyri in the British Museum* (1891). In 1896 the museum acquired the lost epinician odes and dithyrambs of Bacchylides, which Kenyon edited in 1897. An essay which won him the Conington prize at Oxford in 1897 was expanded into a volume, *The Palaeography of Greek Papyri* (1899). His work on documentary papyri produced volumes 1 (1893) and 2 (1898) of *Greek Papyri in the British Museum*; in volume 3 (1907) he was assisted by a junior colleague. For the Oxford Classical Texts he edited all the extant works of Hyperides (1907).

Meanwhile Kenyon did much other work, official and private, including the cataloguing of the Hardwicke papers and many manuscripts of the Stowe and royal collections. In 1895 appeared *Our Bible and the Ancient Manuscripts*, a valuable handbook which ran into several editions. This led the firm of Macmillan to commission his *Handbook to the Textual Criticism of the New Testament* (1901). His *Facsimiles of Biblical Manuscripts in the British Museum* appeared officially in 1900. An interest in the Brownings dating from schooldays inspired several volumes, beginning with *The Brownings for the Young* (1896). In 1897 appeared his editions of Elizabeth Barrett Browning's letters in two volumes, and her poetical works in a companion volume to the two-volume edition of Robert Browning's poems (1896) in which Kenyon had written brief notes to *The Ring and the Book*. Other work on the Brownings included the article in the *Times Literary Supplement* for the centenary of their marriage in 1946.

On 6 August 1891 Kenyon married Amy Hunt (*d.* 1938), daughter of Rowland Hunt of Boreatton Park, Shropshire. They had two daughters, the elder of whom, Kathleen Mary *Kenyon, became a well-known archaeologist and principal of St Hugh's College, Oxford. In 1898 Kenyon was promoted assistant keeper of manuscripts and in 1909 succeeded Sir Edward Maunde Thompson as director of the museum, an office he held until 1930. He certainly ranks among the greatest directors. He was at once a scholar and an able administrator, possessing a legal mind which gave him a remarkable grasp of essentials and a judicial temper immune to personal bias; and, scholar though he was, he realized fully the need, in a national institution, to cater for a less instructed public. The antithesis of the pedantic specialist, he did much, including the introduction of guide lecturers and picture postcards, to stimulate popular interest in the collections. His wide interests made him an ideal head of what is both a library and a museum.

Official duties left little time for scholarly work, but this did not wholly cease, and Kenyon was active in many spheres. Not among the original fellows, he had a hand in the foundation of the British Academy in 1901 and became a fellow in 1903, a member of council in 1906, president

(1917–21), and in 1930 succeeded Sir Israel Gollancz as secretary, retiring in 1949; he was honorary treasurer (1940–50), and an honorary fellow (1950). After retiring he wrote *The British Academy: the First Fifty Years* (1952). He was an active member of the Territorial Army, joining in 1899 the Inns of Court corps, in which he received a commission in 1906 (captain, 1912; lieutenant-colonel, 1917); he went to France in 1914 but was recalled at the request of the trustees. From 1917 he served on the Imperial War Graves Commission, visiting cemeteries in France and the Near East. He served on the Council for Humanistic Studies, was vice-president of the Hellenic Society (president, 1919–24), vice-president of the Roman Society, and in 1913 president of the Classical Association. After the war he was a member of the University Grants Committee, and was closely associated from its foundation with the National Central Library. He was a fellow of Winchester College from 1904, and warden in 1925–30. In 1926 he was nominated a fellow, *honoris causa*, of the Society of Antiquaries, and was president in 1934–9.

His retirement in 1930 enabled Kenyon to return full time to scholarly work, and the opportune acquisition by Chester Beatty of a valuable collection of biblical papyri, which Kenyon was asked to edit, provided the material. Hence arose also several other volumes, including *Books and Readers in Ancient Greece and Rome* (1932), *Recent Developments in the Textual Criticism of the Greek Bible* (1933), and *The Text of the Greek Bible: a Student's Handbook* (1937).

Kenyon was often criticized as cold and remote from human contacts, but this was only in part true. His reserved manner, due partly to a certain shyness in personal matters, partly to a legal temperament which would have made him an ideal Chancery judge, hid much genuine kindness, never forgotten by those who benefited by it, and, despite his reserve, he could expand on occasion. He never allowed personal feeling to influence his official conduct or to interfere with his austere sense of duty, and his judicial temper and discriminating judgement made him an admirable chairman of committees. A corresponding member of many foreign academies and the recipient of numerous honorary degrees, he was appointed CB in 1911, KCB in 1912, and in 1925 GBE; in 1918 he was appointed gentleman usher of the purple rod in the latter order. He was an honorary fellow of both Magdalen and New colleges, Oxford. He died on 23 August 1952 at Oxted and Limpsfield Hospital, Oxted, Surrey, and was buried on 27 August at Godstone, Surrey. H. I. BELL, *rev.*

Sources H. I. Bell, 'Sir Frederic George Kenyon, 1863–1952', *PBA*, 38 (1952), 269–94 · Burke, *Peerage* · *The Times* (25 Aug 1952) · *The Times* (28 Aug 1952) · *WW* · Foster, *Alum. Oxon.* · J. B. Wainewright, ed., *Winchester College, 1836–1906: a register* (1907) · M. Caygill, *The story of the British Museum*, 2nd edn (1992) · *CGPLA Eng. & Wales* (1952)

Archives NRA, priv. coll., corresp. and papers | BL, letters to Franz Bucheler relating to Herodas, Add. MS 62551 · BL, corresp. relating to Codex Sinaiticus, Add. MSS 68923–68932 · Bodl. Oxf., letters to W. E. Crum · Bodl. Oxf., corresp. with L. G. Curtis · Bodl. Oxf., corresp. with Gilbert Murray · Bodl. Oxf., corresp. with J. L. Myres · Bodl. Oxf., corresp. relating to Society for Protection of Science and Learning · Bodl. Oxf., corresp. with Sir Aurel Stein · Commonwealth War Graves Commission, corresp. and papers relating to work for Imperial War Graves Commission · LUL, corresp. with Duckworth & Co. · NL Scot., corresp. with Lord Rosebery · NL Wales, letters to Sir Thomas Parry-Williams

Likenesses J. Russell & Sons, photograph, c.1915, NPG · W. Stoneman, photograph, 1919, NPG [see illus.] · J. A. Stevenson, bronze bust, c.1928, BM · A. John, pencil drawing, British Academy, London · photograph, repro. in Bell, PBA, facing p. 269

Wealth at death £20,666 4s. 0d.: probate, 8 Dec 1952, CGPLA Eng. & Wales

Kenyon, George, second Baron Kenyon (1776–1855), activist against Catholic emancipation, was born in the parish of St Giles-in-the-Fields, London, on 22 July 1776, the second son of Lloyd *Kenyon, first Baron Kenyon (1732–1802), lord chief justice of England, and his wife, Mary (1741–1808), third daughter of George Kenyon of Peel Hall, Lancashire. He was educated at Christ Church, Oxford, where he matriculated in 1794, took his BA in 1797, his MA in 1801, and his DCL in 1814. He was called to the bar in 1811 and was *custos brevium* of the court of king's bench.

Kenyon's elder brother, Lloyd, died in 1801, and he accordingly succeeded to the peerage on the death of his father in 1802. On 1 February 1803 he married Margaret Emma (1785–1815), only daughter of Sir Thomas Hanmer, bt, of Hanmer, Flintshire; they had two sons and three daughters. His wife died in 1815, and he did not remarry.

Kenyon appears to have had whiggish inclinations in his youth, but by the second decade of the nineteenth century he had settled into the die-hard toryism to which he adhered for the rest of his life. He was driven, above all, by staunch anti-Roman Catholic views, which led him about 1808 to join the Orange order, believing it to be 'formed for the encouragement, and in Ireland for the protection of the Protestant cause' ('Select committee on Orange institutions', 126). His pamphlet, *Observations on the Roman Catholic Question*, was an incisive statement of the arguments against emancipation, in which he argued that concession would subvert the protestant nature of the government, the basis of the succession to the throne, and the union of church and state. It was first published in 1810 and was reprinted on several later occasions.

In the late 1820s Kenyon was a member of the hard core of ultra-tory peers and played a very active role in last-ditch efforts to mobilize public opinion against emancipation. He wrote four widely circulated 'letters to the Protestants of Great Britain' and was a leader of the Brunswick clubs, which he evidently hoped could become the nucleus of a reconstituted anti-Catholic tory party. By 1827 he had also become deputy grand master of the Orange order for England and Wales and was a key patron of its activities. The grand lodge normally met at his house in Portman Square.

Following the passage of emancipation in 1829 a note of despair and panic was apparent in Kenyon's activities. He gave the Orange order extensive financial backing in the hope of using it as a basis for protestant recovery, and ill-advisedly employed William Blennerhasset *Fairman, a self-important adventurer, to reorganize and expand the institution. Kenyon also participated actively in the protestant campaign in defence of the Church of Ireland in

1834–5, and in the early meetings of the Protestant Association in 1835–6. He was, however, implicated in the disgrace of the Orange order in 1836 when, largely as a result of Fairman's activities, it was pilloried as a secret society possibly conspiring to subvert the succession to the throne. Kenyon's own conduct was imprudent rather than seditious, but his reputation suffered and thereafter he largely withdrew from public life.

Kenyon had a tall and dignified figure and was described in 1837 as possessing 'the appearance of a gentlemanly old Welch clergyman' (*Recollections of Exeter Hall*, 55–6). He did indeed identify himself with Wales, where his estates were located, and died there at his home, Gredington Hall, Flintshire, on 25 February 1855. He was buried at Hanmer. He had been a conscientious but unsophisticated defender of increasingly unfashionable views, whose growing desperation and isolation drove him to some regrettable misjudgements. JOHN WOLFFE

Sources 'Select committee on Orange institutions in Great Britain and the colonies', *Parl. papers* (1835), vol. 17, no. 605 · private information (2004) · H. Senior, *Orangeism in Ireland and Britain, 1795–1836* (1966) · G. I. T. Machin, *The Catholic question in English politics, 1820 to 1830* (1964) · J. Wolffe, *The protestant crusade in Great Britain, 1829–1860* (1991) · *Random recollections of Exeter Hall in 1834–1837, by one of the protestant party* (1838) · [M. P.], *The history of Orangeism: its origin, its rise and its decline* (1882) · Burke, *Peerage*

Archives Lancs. RO, corresp. · priv. coll., corresp. | BL, corresp. with earls of Liverpool, loan 72 · BL, corresp. with second earl of Liverpool, Add. MSS 38247–38328, 38563, 38573, *passim* · BL, corresp. with Sir Robert Peel, Add. MSS 40344–40577, *passim* · NL Wales, corresp. with second earl of Powis relating to dioceses of St Asaph and Bangor · W. Sussex RO, letters to fifth duke of Richmond

Likenesses G. Hayter, group portrait, 1820 (*The trial of Queen Caroline*), NPG

Kenyon, George Thomas (1840–1908), politician, second son of Lloyd Kenyon, third Baron Kenyon, and his wife, Georgina, daughter of Thomas De Grey, fourth Baron Walsingham, was born in London on 28 December 1840. He was educated at Harrow (1854–60), entered Christ Church, Oxford, in 1860, graduated BA with second-class honours in law and history in 1864, and proceeded MA in 1870. In 1869 he became a barrister of the Middle Temple. He contested the Denbigh boroughs unsuccessfully as a Conservative in 1874 and 1880, but won the seat in 1885 and held it until 1895, and again from 1900 to 1905. In 1897 he stood unsuccessfully for East Denbighshire at a by-election, his protectionist views proving unpopular. His chief interest was the promotion of secondary and higher education in Wales, and he played an important part in the passing of the Welsh Intermediate Education Act of 1889, which established a comprehensive system of secondary schools in Wales. Kenyon worked with Sir William Hart-Dyke to facilitate the passing of the bill, a Liberal initiative led by Stuart Rendel. He took an active part in the establishment of the University of Wales in 1893 and was its junior deputy chancellor from 1898 to 1900. He was also the promoter and first chairman (1891–1908) of the Wrexham and Ellesmere Railway. On 21 October 1875 Kenyon married Florence Anna (d. 25 April 1929), daughter of J. H. Leche, of

Carden Park, Chester. They had no children. He died on 26 January 1908, at his seat of Llannerch Banna, near Ellesmere.   J. E. LLOYD, rev. H. C. G. MATTHEW

Sources *The Times* (28 Jan 1908) · K. O. Morgan, *Wales in British politics, 1868–1922* (1963) · *WW*
Archives NRA, papers
Likenesses E. Miller, portrait; formerly at Llannerch Banna, 1912 · Spy [L. Ward], caricature, chromolithograph, NPG; repro. in *VF* (29 Dec 1888)
Wealth at death £10,266 17*s.* 11*d.*: probate, 23 June 1908, *CGPLA Eng. & Wales*

Kenyon, John (1784–1856), patron of the arts and poet, was born in December 1784 in the parish of Trelawney, Jamaica, the eldest of three sons of John Kenyon (Kennion), wealthy sugar plantation owner, and his wife, a daughter of John Simpson of Bounty Hall. After the death of his wife in 1789, Kenyon's father brought John and his brothers Edward and Samuel to England, probably to the vicinity of Chester. On the death of their father about 1792, the boys' uncle Samuel Kenyon became their guardian and custodian of their considerable property. As a youth, John attended schools at Cheshunt (where Robert Browning's father was a fellow student), Fort Bristol, and Charterhouse School, London. He also received tutoring in science by William Nicholson of the Philosophical Institute. Kenyon matriculated at Peterhouse, Cambridge, in 1802, but left without a degree in 1803 or 1808. He entered Lincoln's Inn in 1804.

Kenyon lived at Woodlands, between Alfoxden and Nether Stowey, between 1802 and 1812, and became acquainted with Thomas Poole, S. T. Coleridge, Robert Southey, and William Wordsworth. He also married in this period. His wife's death at Naples in 1818 terminated their European tour, begun in 1815. After his second marriage, to Caroline Curteis of Lewisham in 1822, Kenyon and his wife made Bath their headquarters, with frequent visits to London and the channel resorts until they left for a year in Italy in 1830 when they became acquainted with the Landors at Fiesole. On their return to London, the couple probably established themselves at 39 Devonshire Place, the home of Caroline's wealthy brother John Curteis, until her death on 6 August 1835.

A seasoned traveller and a lion of London society, Kenyon made his home a mecca for the intelligentsia and for foreign travellers, especially Americans. Several names suggest the scope of his guest list: Charles Babbage, Charles Dickens, Benjamin Haydon, Charles Macready, Sir Anthony Panizzi, Bryan Procter, and Henry Crabb Robinson. A close friend of Elizabeth Barrett, his distant cousin, and of Robert Browning, Kenyon was influential in igniting their famous correspondence and courtship and supported their marriage. To Kenyon, Browning dedicated his *Dramatic Romances and Lyrics*. Failing to procure for Kenyon a copy of the picture of *Andrea del Sarto and his Wife* in the Pitti Palace, Browning wrote and sent to him from Florence the poem 'Andrea del Sarto'. When the Brownings visited England, Kenyon offered them his home and there in 1856 Elizabeth Barrett Browning finished 'Aurora Leigh' and dedicated it to Kenyon in grateful

remembrance of a friendship 'far beyond the common uses of mere relationship and sympathy of mind'. Another friend of several years was Sarah Bayley, a prominent Unitarian and intellectual, who aroused feelings of admiration and spiritual kinship in Kenyon on his first meeting her at Rome and Naples in 1840; she was to see him through his painful illness and death.

Kenyon's encounters with George Ticknor and Edward Everett in Paris in 1817 promoted his acquaintance with increasing numbers of Americans whom he entertained and aided with letters of introduction. James T. Fields, George Hillard, Charles Eliot Norton, Ralph Waldo Emerson, Henry Wadsworth Longfellow, and James Lowell were guests at his renowned breakfast and dinner parties, as were Daniel Webster and his family whom Kenyon escorted to Oxford on the occasion of Webster's speech at the agricultural meeting in July 1839. Indeed, his later claim to fame rested largely on his generosity; his favourite role of host fostered his aptitude for arranging fruitful introductions, which in turn contributed to his popularity and extended his influence. Kenyon's reputation as a wealthy dilettante with a genial disposition and generous purse was universally acknowledged. Crabb Robinson's remark about Kenyon's having the 'face of a Benedictine monk and joyous talk of a good fellow' is legendary. The author of the obituary in the *Gentleman's Magazine* (March 1857) emphasizes his acts of charity; George Hillard in his letter to the *Boston Daily Courier* (9 March 1857), while noting him to be 'remembered more for what he did than for what he wrote', stressed his qualities as a scholar and gentleman.

Kenyon published three volumes of poetry: *A Rhymed Plea for Tolerance* (1833), a strong statement of his liberal religious thinking rather than an imaginative effort; *Poems, for the Most Part Occasional* (1838); and *A Day at Tivoli, with Other Verses* (1849). The prefaces and many of the poems, aptly called 'occasional', reflect his inherent modesty and familiarity with English literature and its backgrounds. His poem, 'Champagne rosée' appeared in the *Oxford Book of English Verse* in 1939.

Kenyon's reputation for generosity is confirmed by his will with its lengthy list of legacies which included £5000 to University College Hospital, £10,500 to the Brownings, and £5000 and Lime Cottage at Wimbledon to Miss Bayley.

Kenyon died at his home, 3 Parade, West Cowes, on 3 December 1856, probably of cancer, although the death certificate reads 'natural decay'. His remains were interred in the Curteis family vault in St Mary's churchyard, Lewisham.   MEREDITH B. RAYMOND

Sources M. B. Raymond, 'John Kenyon, the magnificent dilettante', *Studies in Browning and his Circle*, 14 (1986), 32–62 · *The letters of Elizabeth Barrett Browning to Mary Russell Mitford, 1836–1854*, ed. M. B. Raymond and M. R. Sullivan, 3 vols. (1983) · *The Brownings' correspondence*, ed. P. Kelley, R. Hudson, and S. Lewis, [14 vols.] (1984–), esp. vols. 10–13 · Mrs. A. Crosse, 'John Kenyon and his friends', *Red-letter days of my life* (1892), 2.122–86 · J. Marks, *The family of the Barrett* (1938) · T. A. Walker, ed., *Admissions to Peterhouse or St Peter's College in the University of Cambridge* (1912), 376 · Venn, *Alum. Cant.* · *GM*, 3rd ser., 2 (1857), 105, 309–15 · G. Hillard, 'The late John Kenyon', *Boston*

Daily Courier (9 March 1857), 2, col. 3 · John Kenyon's will, PRO · H. C. Kirby and L. L. Duncan, eds., *Memorial inscriptions in the church and churchyard of S. Mary, Lewisham* (1889), 12 · J. Kenyon, letter to H. C. Robinson, 19 Feb 1840, DWL, 138 · *Life, letters, and journals of George Ticknor*, ed. G. S. Hillard and others, 2 vols. (1876), vol. 1, pp. 411n., 418; vol. 2, pp.144, 181–2 · J. Maynard, *Browning's youth* (1977), 395, n.19 · J. Kenyon, *Poems: for the most part occasional* (1838) · *DNB* · C. M. Fuess, *Daniel Webster* (1930), 1.77 · d. cert.

Archives FM Cam., notebook · Harvard U., Houghton L., letters · Hunt. L., corresp. · Mass. Hist. Soc., letters | BL, letters to Sir Richard Owen, Add. MS 39954 · DWL, corresp. with Henry Crabb Robinson · FM Cam., letters to E. B. Browning · Wordsworth Trust, Dove Cottage, Grasmere, letters to Wordsworths

Likenesses E. B. Browning, drawing, Baylor University, Waco, Texas, Armstrong Browning Library · T. Crawford, bust, Baylor University, Waco, Texas, Armstrong Browning Library · A. D. Ingres, photograph (of Kenyon?; after a sketch), Baylor University, Waco, Texas, Armstrong Browning Library; repro. in Raymond, 'John Kenyon, the magnificent dilettante', 44–5 · R. J. Lane, lithograph (after a watercolour by J. C. Moore, 1857), NPG · G. Scharf, pencil sketch (after a marble bust by T. Crawford), NPG · drawing, Baylor University, Waco, Texas, Armstrong Browning Library

Wealth at death approx. £145,000 in gifts outright; plus estates, incl. houses at Cowes, 39 Devonshire Place, and Lime Cottage at Wimbledon: will, PRO

Kenyon, John (1812–1869), Roman Catholic priest and Young Irelander, was born at Thomondgate, Limerick City, Ireland, one of the three sons and three daughters of Patrick Kenyon, owner of marble works and prosperous grocery stores, and Mary, *née* McMahon. One of his brothers, Patrick, became a priest, and his three sisters all became nuns. His other brother, Louis, trained as an engineer and emigrated to the United States. Educated in Limerick, John Kenyon entered Maynooth College in 1829, and was ordained a priest for the diocese of Killaloe in 1835. Having served as curate in various other parishes, he was appointed in December 1842 to a curacy in Templederry, co. Tipperary, where he spent the rest of his life.

A dedicated and popular priest, Kenyon joined the Repeal Association in May 1845, and soon sided with the Young Irelanders. He wrote letters and poems (signed 'N.N.') to *The Nation* and later to John Mitchel's *United Irishman*. His letters to the editor of the *Limerick Reporter* about physical and moral force were later published as a pamphlet. In 1847 he was elected to the council of the Irish Confederation. A highly critical letter in *The Nation* about Daniel O'Connell, in which he stated that his death was no loss for Ireland (*The Nation*, 5/244, 5 June 1847, 553), made him very unpopular among supporters of O'Connell. When he, by his own decision, nominated the Young Irelander Richard O'Gorman against John O'Connell in the general elections in 1847, he was attacked by crowds of O'Connell supporters. Father Kenyon was tall, athletic, and strong, with a wilful and charismatic personality. The learned priest was extremely outspoken and his contemporaries described him as a brilliant orator. According to John Martin, he spoke faultlessly, and his speeches were better than his writings. He knew how to address the rural population and used irony effectively. His Templederry Confederate Club, of which he was the president, was one of the largest and best organized in the country.

Kenyon was a close friend of John Mitchel, who described him as 'the finest fellow, lay or cleric, that I ever knew' (*Templederry, my Home*, 134). He shared Mitchel's views on the necessity for an Irish revolution, and in his speeches he told the people to be prepared for an uprising. Together with another priest, he was suspended by his bishop, Dr Kennedy, for making revolutionary speeches in Templederry on 16 April 1848. In June 1848 'the patriot priest of Templederry' took part in a secret meeting of some confederate leaders to organize the Irish rising. In the following elections for a new council of the confederation, Kenyon topped the poll together with Meagher. However, on returning from Dublin, Kenyon was given an ultimatum from his bishop that he either stop his revolutionary activities, or lose his parish. He made a pact with the bishop that he would not take a leading part in the rising, but apparently reserved himself the right to take his place in the ranks once there was an armed rebellion. He repented openly for his revolutionary speeches in a letter to the bishop, which was published on 14 June 1848, but refuted any claims that he had retired from public life in a letter to the *Limerick Reporter* on 16 June 1848. However, he refused to return to Dublin when summoned by Duffy and Martin, since otherwise he would have lost his parish. When, in July 1848, Dillon and Meagher went to Chapel House and asked him to mobilize his parishioners, and to join forces with Smith O'Brien, he dismissed the idea and criticized Smith O'Brien's revolutionary tactics. After that episode, Duffy was highly critical of Kenyon, but most of the other Young Irelanders were understanding.

After 1848 Kenyon only occasionally got involved in politics, and led a retired life. Many of his friends believed that his talents were wasted in a small country parish. Although he was not openly in favour of the Fenians, since he believed the movement to be a failure, folk legend has it that he hid James Stephens in his house when he was on the run. Father Kenyon was also known as a staunch supporter of religious tolerance, and one of his speeches, asserting that 'an Irish Presbyterian soul was as good in its kind as any Roman Catholic archbishop's' (Kenyon, 24 March 1862, NL Ire., MS 10518), again brought him into difficulties with the church hierarchy in 1862. Kenyon died on 21 March 1869 of haemorrhage after an illness at his home, Chapel House, Templederry. At the request of his parishioners, he was buried in the chapel of Templederry, on 23 March 1869.   BRIGITTE ANTON

Sources L. Fogarty, *Father Kenyon: a patriot priest of forty-eight* (1921) · *Templederry, my home* (1980) · T. F. O'Sullivan, *The Young Irelanders*, 2nd edn (1945) · *The Nation* (1846–7) · four letters, NL Ire. · NL Ire., Hickey MSS · C. G. Duffy, *Young Ireland: a fragment of Irish history, 1840–1845*, rev. edn, 2 vols. (1896) · C. G. Duffy, *Four years of Irish history, 1845–1849: a sequel to 'Young Ireland'* (1883) · C. G. Duffy, *My life in two hemispheres*, 1 (1898); facs. edn (Shannon, 1969) · C. G. Duffy, *My life in two hemispheres*, 2 (1898) · rental of Cloghonane, co. Tipperary, 1853, PRO NIre. · P. J. Hamell, *Maynooth: students and ordinations index, 1795–1895* (1982) · R. J. Hayes, ed., *Manuscript sources for the history of Irish civilisation*, 2 (1965) · R. J. Hayes, ed., *Manuscript sources for the history of Irish civilisation: first supplement, 1965–1975*, 1 (1979)

Archives NL Ire. | NL Ire., Hickey collection

Likenesses group portrait, photograph, 1866 (*The three Johns*), repro. in Fogarty, *Father Kenyon*, 134–5; formerly priv. coll. · commemorative plaque, 1975, Chapel House, Templederry · drawing (as a young man), repro. in Fogarty, *Father Kenyon*, frontispiece

Wealth at death £300: probate, 13 Nov 1869, *CGPLA Eng. & Wales*

Kenyon, Joseph (1885–1961), organic chemist, was born on 8 April 1885 at Blackburn, Lancashire, the eldest child in the family of four sons and three daughters of Lawrence Kenyon, a gardener, of Blackburn, and his wife, Mary Anne Southwarth. Kenyon's was no easy education and it was by his own efforts that he ascended the educational ladder. After leaving the Blackburn secondary higher grade school at the age of fourteen he became a laboratory assistant at the municipal technical school in Blackburn. He continued his education, mainly on a part-time basis but with two years' full-time study while he held the John Mercer FRS scholarship, until he graduated, with honours, as BSc (London) in 1907. He was awarded the degree of DSc (London) in 1914.

Kenyon's first research was done while he was still an undergraduate, when he published three papers with R. H. Pickard, his supervisor in Blackburn. One of these papers, on the resolution of secondary octyl alcohol into its optically active forms, marked the beginning of a lifelong interest in stereochemistry.

At the time of this early work, no general method was available for the resolution of compounds, such as alcohols, which do not form salts with acids or bases. Pickard and Kenyon surmounted this difficulty by converting the alcohol into its half-ester with a dibasic acid, which left one acidic group free in the half-ester, and thus enabled salt formation with optically active bases. The two different (diastereoisomeric) salts could then be separated, and the (+)− and (−)− forms of the *sec*-octyl alcohol obtained from them by hydrolysis. In his subsequent scientific work Kenyon accomplished many resolutions using this technique and attempted to elucidate the relationship (or apparent lack of it) between chemical constitution and optical activity.

Despite his work on optical activity, it is probably for his work on the stereochemistry of nucleophilic substitution reactions that Kenyon is best known. Some of these reactions, but not all, are accompanied by inversion of configuration (the 'Walden inversion'). Kenyon studied reactions in which an optically active compound was converted into its enantiomeric (mirror image) form and sought to identify the stage at which the inversion had occurred. Using techniques which he had previously developed, Kenyon, together with his colleagues, succeeded in doing this by designing reaction cycles such that only one of the whole series involved cleavage of a bond at the centre of the asymmetry in the molecule (the site about which inversion must occur). This breakthrough, taken with the classic work and theories of E. D. Hughes and C. K. Ingold at University College, London, was crucial in determining that inversion always occurs in bimolecular processes at an asymmetric carbon atom, but that in unimolecular processes various stereochemical consequences are possible, racemization being the typical result. This conclusion is fundamental to our understanding of one of the basic processes of organic chemistry. Kenyon made many other contributions to the subject. With various colleagues he published over 160 papers, mainly on stereochemistry and its relationship to reaction mechanisms.

In 1906 Kenyon obtained his first academic post—that of assistant lecturer at Blackburn Technical College. He was promoted to lecturer in 1907. During the First World War he was engaged with H. D. Dakin and J. B. Cohen in war research at Leeds University on the synthesis of chloramine-T as a possible antidote to 'gas gangrene'. From 1916 to 1920 he was at Oxford with W. H. Perkin, working on dyestuffs chemistry in collaboration with the British Dyestuffs Corporation. On 9 April 1917 he married Winefride Agnes, daughter of Cornelius Foley of Cork. They had one daughter, Patricia.

In 1920 Kenyon was appointed head of the department of chemistry at Battersea Polytechnic, where he created one of the best chemistry schools of its day in the country. He remained at Battersea until his retirement in 1950. He was held in high esteem by his contemporaries, not only in his own department but in the chemical community in general. This was particularly true in London, where he served as a member of the university board of studies in chemistry and of the University of London senate, as vice-president and council member of the Chemical Society, and in various capacities for the Royal Institute of Chemistry of which he was a fellow for fifty years. He was elected a fellow of the Royal Society in 1936.

After his retirement from Battersea, Kenyon spent two periods as visiting professor at the University of Alexandria, and one at the University of Kansas. He also continued his research and was for some years still a member of the London University board of studies. Kenyon died at his home, 2 Charmouth Court, Kings Road, Richmond, Surrey, on 12 November 1961. His wife survived him.

G. H. WILLIAMS, *rev.*

Sources E. E. Turner, *Memoirs FRS*, 8 (1962), 49–66 · *Journal of the Royal Institute of Chemistry*, 86 (1962) · *The Times* (17 Nov 1961) · personal knowledge (1981)

Likenesses W. Stoneman, photograph, RS, no. 41688

Wealth at death £180 12s. 11d.: probate, 9 March 1962, *CGPLA Eng. & Wales*

Kenyon, Dame Kathleen Mary (1906–1978), archaeologist, was born on 5 January 1906 in London, the elder daughter (there was no son) of Sir Frederic George *Kenyon (1863–1952), of Pradoe, Shropshire, and London, director and principal librarian of the British Museum, and his wife, Amy (d. 1938), daughter of Rowland Hunt, of Boreatton Park, Shropshire. She was educated at St Paul's Girls' School, where she became head girl, and at Somerville College, Oxford, where she read medieval history, obtaining a third-class degree in 1928. She also took an active interest in sport, gaining a hockey blue, and in the university Archaeological Society, of which she was the first woman to be elected president. Shortly after leaving

The end of the war enabled Kenyon to return to fieldwork, and the next few years saw her active at sites in London, Herefordshire, and Leicester again. She was appointed lecturer in Palestinian archaeology at the Institute of Archaeology (1948–62). The political situation did not permit her to work in this area immediately, and she had to be content with excavating on the Phoenician and Roman site of Sabrathah, in Tripolitania (now Libya) from 1948 until 1951, when she became honorary director of the reconstructed British School of Archaeology in Jerusalem. In 1952 she embarked on what was to be the greatest achievement of her career, the excavation of the mound of Jericho, in the Jordan valley. In *Archaeology in the Holy Land* (1960) she largely rewrote the history of ancient civilization in Palestine. In 1961 she began excavating in Jerusalem and by 1967, when the work ended, much information had been added to the understanding of its ancient topography, although some of her results have been modified by more recent work.

Kenyon was not altogether a popular figure, especially with those of her peers who did not know her well and saw her only as an autocrat. She had a very forceful character and a determination which at times verged on the obstinate. Yet she was never ruthless, and much of her self-sufficiency and brusque manner stemmed from an inherent shyness. Once this was overcome, she was revealed as a kind and warm person, particularly concerned for young people (and animals), greatly loved by all who worked really closely with her. Her direct approach and simplicity of manner were reflected also in her scholarship. She was certainly not a great scholar in the conventional sense, and paradoxically her archaeological interpretations were often marked by a lack of that attention to detail and of precision for which her fieldwork was so famed. She often seemed unaware of the work of other researchers, and her arguments were sometimes too simplistic to be convincing. She was reluctant to delegate, with the result that the publications of the Jericho and Jerusalem excavations were largely unfinished at her death, and were passed to younger scholars to complete.

The final season at Jerusalem in 1967 marked the end of Kenyon's career as an excavator. In 1962 she had left the Institute of Archaeology to become principal of St Hugh's College, Oxford, where, until she retired in 1973, she was an energetic administrator, responsible notably for the ambitious programme of expansion on which the college had embarked. She continued to maintain a close control over the affairs of the British School of Archaeology in Jerusalem, as chairman of the governing body from 1966 until her death, and regularly visited the Near East, while she was also actively involved in the negotiations which eventually, shortly after her death, led to the foundation in Amman, Jordan, of the new British Institute for Archaeology and History (both institutions now amalgamated into the Council for British Research in the Levant). Her years of retirement, when she lived at Rose Hill, Erbistock, near Wrexham in north Wales, were spent mainly on preparing the materials from her excavations at Jericho and Jerusalem for publication, and she was doing this

Dame Kathleen Mary Kenyon (1906–1978), by Jorge Lewinski, 1969

Oxford she joined (in 1929) the British Association's expedition to Zimbabwe in Southern Rhodesia as photographer and assistant to the director, Gertrude Caton-Thompson. In the following year she became a member of the large team excavating the Roman city of Verulamium (St Albans) under Mortimer Wheeler and his wife. She was one of the Wheelers' ablest pupils.

Kenyon participated from 1931 to 1934 in J. W. Crowfoot's expedition to Samaria and was influential in introducing stratigraphical methods, learned from Wheeler, into the region. In 1939 she published a short paper in the *Palestine Exploration Quarterly* on her theory of excavation. Appearing on the eve of the Second World War, however, it had little impact; not until two decades later, with her work at Jericho, did what has come to be known as the 'Wheeler-Kenyon method' begin to have a real influence in Near Eastern archaeology. She also wrote considerable parts of the final report on the Samaria excavations.

Kenyon's experience in Palestine had not alienated her from British archaeology, and in the late 1930s she was actively digging Iron Age and Roman sites in Leicester and Shropshire. Her friendship with Wheeler and her obvious organizational abilities led her in 1937 to be involved with him in founding the University of London Institute of Archaeology, of which she was secretary (1935–48) and acting director (1942–6); that this fledgeling institution survived these troubled times was very largely due to her. The war kept her busy in other ways also, notably with the British Red Cross Society, the youth department of which she directed from 1942 until 1945.

when she died at Erbistock on 24 August 1978. She was unmarried.

Kenyon was appointed CBE (1954) and DBE (1973), and elected FBA (1955) and FSA. She held several honorary doctorates and was an honorary fellow of Somerville (1960) and St Hugh's (1973).

P. J. PARR, *rev.* PIOTR BIENKOWSKI

Sources *The Times* (25 Aug 1978) · personal knowledge (1986) · A. D. Tushingham, 'Kathleen Mary Kenyon, 1906–1978', *PBA*, 71 (1985), 555–82 · 'Kathleen Kenyon in retrospect', *Palestine Exploration Quarterly*, 124 (1992), 91–123 · P. R. S. Moorey, *A century of biblical archaeology* (1991), 94–9, 122–6 · P. Bienkowski and A. Millard, eds., *Dictionary of the ancient Near East* (2000), 165 · *CGPLA Eng. & Wales* (1979)
Archives AM Oxf. · CUL · Manchester Museum · priv. coll., MSS · Royal Ontario Museum, Toronto | BM, Jericho and Jerusalem artefacts · Bodl. Oxf., letters to O. G. S. Crawford · English Heritage, Wroxeter excavations records · U. Cam., Jericho excavation archive, MSS
Likenesses J. Lewinski, photograph, 1969, NPG [*see illus.*] · photographs, Palestine Exploration Fund, London, archives
Wealth at death £262,242: probate, 19 March 1979, *CGPLA Eng. & Wales*

Kenyon, Lloyd, first Baron Kenyon (1732–1802), judge, was born at Gredington, near Hanmer, Flintshire, on 5 October 1732, the second (but first surviving) son, and heir, of Lloyd Kenyon (1696–1773) and Jane (1703–1771), the eldest daughter and coheir of Robert Eddowes, of Eagle Hall, Cheshire, and his wife, Anne. Kenyon's father, the son of a Manchester barrister, was educated at St John's College, Cambridge, and admitted to Gray's Inn, but became a landed gentleman and a justice of the peace. Lloyd, as his younger son, was educated at the village school in Hanmer and then at Ruthin grammar school before being articled to Mr Tomkinson, or Tomlinson, an attorney in Nantwich, Cheshire, for five years. The exact chronology is unclear; Kenyon's elder brother, Thomas, died in 1750, apparently the year after Kenyon began his articles. Kenyon was admitted to the Middle Temple on 7 November 1750 but seems to have remained in Nantwich to finish his articles and probably moved to London in 1753. As a student for the bar he followed the common practice of taking notes of cases in Westminster Hall; they were edited and published after his death as *Kenyon's Reports*, and covered the period from 1753 to 1759. In February 1755 he was living in Bell Yard, Carey Street, near the Temple. He was called to the bar on 9 February 1756, and through his long professional life worked and then presided in the highest courts of equity and the common law.

The bar and politics Kenyon's earnings at the bar rose from £17 to only £80 after seven years, as he followed the north Wales and Oxford assize circuits and attended quarter sessions. He was good friends with John Dunning and came to the notice of Edward Thurlow, both of whom respected his knowledge of the law. In the 1760s they began relying on him heavily, recommending him to solicitors and rapidly forwarding his career. By the late 1770s his income approached £6000; his earnings from chancery business and arguing briefs was almost matched by fees for opinions. In 1778 and 1780 he refused judicial appointment at

Lloyd Kenyon, first Baron Kenyon (1732–1802), by John Opie, 1788

Westminster, which would have ended private practice and probably not led to the highest posts, which usually followed a parliamentary career. His eminence was recognized by Lincoln's Inn, where he was admitted in 1779. When he declined a justiceship of common pleas early in 1780 he was promised the chief justiceship of Chester, which would not have barred him from practice. Thurlow, by then lord chancellor, appointed him to Chester that summer; he had been named king's counsel on 10 July. He defended Lord George Gordon on the charge of high treason in 1781 but the verdict was won by Thomas Erskine, his junior, who made his reputation in the case. Kenyon much preferred office work. His opinions on stated cases were prompt, practical, and succinct—on the game laws for Henry Paget, earl of Uxbridge, patent issues for Richard Arkwright, land titles, conveyancing, divorce, and all the other questions crucial to a wealthy clientele. As counsel and as judge Kenyon was decisive and expeditious, the epitome of a hard-working, practical lawyer. Wilberforce wrote of him bringing home cases to be answered 'as another man would crack walnuts, when sitting tête-à-tête with Lady K. after dinner' (Kenyon, *Life*, 137). 'Lady K.' was Kenyon's wife, his first cousin Mary (1741–1808), the daughter of George Kenyon, of Peel Hall, Lancashire, a barrister, and Peregrina Eddowes; they married at Deane, Lancashire, on 16 October 1773.

Kenyon practised for over twenty-five years before becoming a parliamentary crown lawyer, an unusually long period for a future chief justice. An expected vacancy in the Commons for Flint Boroughs in 1774 disappeared, but in 1780 he was elected for the borough of Hindon, in Wiltshire, where Thurlow managed the interest of the Beckford family. His opponents unsuccessfully alleged bribery. Kenyon seems to have been loyal to the North ministry until after the fall of Yorktown, and from December 1781 opposed the continuation of the American War of Independence in the Commons. In April 1782 the incoming home secretary, William Petty, second earl of Shelburne, offered Kenyon the post of attorney-general in the second Rockingham administration, which he accepted on Thurlow's advice (17 April 1782). As chief law officer, to the dismay of some colleagues, he pursued the former paymaster-general of the forces, Richard Rigby, and the former treasurer of the navy, Welbore Ellis, for failing to account for monies, and advised the prosecution of John Powell and Charles Bembridge, the cashier and accountant in the pay office. The episode provided an opportunity to harass Edmund Burke, whose campaign against Warren Hastings Kenyon deplored. Burke, then paymaster-general, unwisely defended his clerks: one committed suicide and the other was later convicted. Kenyon remained attorney-general in Shelburne's administration, resigned when the Fox–North coalition took office in April 1783, and voted for William Pitt's motion for parliamentary reform in May. When Pitt took office at the end of the year he persuaded a reluctant Kenyon to serve again as attorney-general from 26 December, with the expectation of appointment as master of the rolls, a common reward for politically useful lawyers since it could be held by a member of the Commons. Kenyon spoke rarely in the House, explaining the law with respect to a few proposed tax bills, defending his reputation for giving independent opinions, urging Thurlow's case for a tellership of the exchequer, and calling for an account of monies held by Rigby. His principal role was giving detailed legal advice—as he had done for many years—to Thurlow.

Kenyon gave up the chief justiceship of Chester when he was appointed master of the rolls on 30 March 1784. He was sworn of the privy council on 2 April, elected to the Commons for Tregony, in Cornwall—a Treasury seat—on 5 April, and created a baronet (he was never knighted) on 28 July. He was appointed a lord commissioner of trades and plantations on 6 September 1786. He had a long professional association with the court of chancery, and as master of the rolls he impressed with his speed of decision and his impatience with professional delay: he once struck out an entire list of causes owing to the absence of counsel and solicitors.

Twenty-four of Kenyon's speeches are recorded in the 1784 parliament. Nine dealt with the Westminster scrutiny of 1784, where he defended the government's position vigorously enough to move Charles James Fox to speak scornfully of his 'losing sight of the sanctity of his station both in this House and out of it' (Cobbett, *Parl. hist.*, 24.886). He subsequently was satirized in *The Rolliad*, where a mock portrait enlivens the title-page. In the Commons most of his speeches were legal arguments or assertions of his integrity as a lawyer and judge. He spoke frequently against the impeachment of Hastings and also against the proposed impeachment of Sir Elijah Impey, a friend; Burke referred sarcastically to the evident eagerness of the master of the rolls for elevation. Kenyon also spoke on the Ecclesiastical Courts Bill (with some feeling on the evils of defamatory accusations) and on the shop tax of 1788. He clearly resented the attacks on his integrity that were part of parliamentary debate. His appointment as chief justice of king's bench meant that he never endured such treatment again, and he rarely spoke in the Lords. He surrendered the rolls on 7 June 1788 and, made serjeant-at-law, was appointed lord chief justice; he was created 'Lord Kenyon, Baron of Gredington' on 9 June.

Lord chief justice Kenyon's appointment as lord chief justice had been delayed, and disputed, in spite of Thurlow's and Pitt's support. His predecessor, William Murray, first earl of Mansfield, had wanted Francis Buller, a puisne justice of king's bench, to succeed to the chief justiceship, and stayed on the bench longer than might have been the case had he not wished to exclude Kenyon. *The Times* reflected some of the considerable opposition to Kenyon's appointment, citing his lack of criminal practice and reporting from May 1786 on Mansfield's determination not to resign. In a parody of this jockeying the paper eventually reported the triumph of 'Sir Lloyd Kenyon's *Sound Doctrine*' in 'the King's Bench Plate' (*The Times*, 4 July 1788). That summer James Boswell heard it said that Kenyon did not deserve appointment because he lacked 'elegance of manners and a knowledge of the world'. Boswell differed: Kenyon was a hardworking 'real lawyer' who would be 'a good fuller's mill to thicken and consolidate the law, which was very necessary after the loose texture which Lord Mansfield had given it' (*English Experience*, 234–5). This view of Mansfield, not uncommon, was undoubtedly Kenyon's. He believed law and equity should be entirely distinct in their separate courts, and in a direct criticism of the former chief justice he said 'I confess I do not think that the Courts ought to change the law so as to adapt it to the fashions of the times' (*Ellah* v. *Leigh*, 1794). In his personality as in his traditionalism he also differed greatly from Mansfield. Kenyon was abrupt in speech and temper, often rude to counsel, not given to oratory unless it concerned an issue that touched him deeply. Usually his judgments were relatively short expositions (in part because he was likely to give an immediate and succinct oral judgment) of the technical points at issue, with fairly frequent references to manuscript cases in his own possession.

Concern for moral principle appeared to govern Kenyon's decisions at least as much as concern for the letter of the law. In *Read* v. *Brookman* (1789), he heard arguments that he could have sent to chancery. In *Pasley* v. *Freeman* (1789) he agreed with Sir William Ashhurst and Sir Francis Buller to develop the tort of deceit to allow suits against third parties. The early nineteenth-century lord chancellor John Scott, earl of Eldon, later thought the case undermined distinctions between common law and equity, but the judgment was entirely consonant with Kenyon's great attachment to moral principle. He tried subsequently to extend the doctrine even further, an attempt repudiated by his brethren in *Haycraft* v. *Creasy* (1801), to his great annoyance, Kenyon declaring 'that laws were never so well directed as when they were made to enforce religious, moral, and social duties between man and man'. He reversed a number of Mansfield's decisions in the area of land law. In contract law he strongly upheld the ancient common-law rule against the transferability or assignment of debts, repudiating moves made by Mansfield and Buller (*Johnson* v. *Collings*, 1800). But it was in the law of marriage and that of markets that he most visibly rejected Mansfield's views, in seeking to impose his deeply held moral convictions on English society.

Kenyon abhorred adultery, and in criminal conversation actions he allowed more weight to circumstantial evidence and encouraged juries to award huge punitive damages that effectively turned a civil suit into a criminal punishment. Such cases had been increasing in number before Kenyon was appointed but awards over £2000 increased fourfold while he was chief justice, and the increase in litigation that he encouraged merely reinforced his conviction that sexual misconduct was undermining social order. In 1799 he remarked that he wished adultery was punishable by death; he associated it with revolutionary irreligion and political sedition. His views were shared by many of his brethren on the legal and episcopal benches. By 1800, however, critics of Kenyon's crusade included Sir Richard Pepper Arden (master of the rolls) and Richard Brinsley Sheridan, who declared that exemplary damages in civil suits were exemplary nonsense.

As master of the rolls in the 1780s Kenyon moderated some aspects of the law of dower that had gone against widows' interests in mid-century cases, a reflection of his conservative view of marriage. In 1792 he rejected the idea that a husband could get damages for adultery by his wife after a separate maintenance agreement, a doctrine reversed by his successor. Kenyon's judgment perhaps was influenced by his clear hostility to the implications of separation agreements: he may have thought that a husband willing to make one was inviting betrayal by his spouse. As early as 1797 he expressed doubts about the validity of separation agreements, and in 1800 established a precedent, in the case of *Marshall* v. *Rutton*, that strongly reaffirmed the ancient common-law idea of the legal unity of husband and wife. In doing so he overturned a line of cases by Mansfield in which contract ideology had permeated more traditional notions of marriage, making it possible to enforce separate maintenance agreements that gave the separated wife power to contract, and to sue and be sued for her debts. Kenyon objected that this would:

> place the parties in some respects in the condition of being single, and leave them in others subject to the consequences of being married; and ... would introduce all the confusion and inconvenience which must necessarily result from so anomalous and mixed a character. (*Marshall* v. *Rutton*)

The courts in other areas found no difficulty in making distinctions in such 'mixed' cases; it seems likely that Kenyon reaffirmed marital unity for the same reasons that he deplored the prevalence of divorce. His stance was shared by Eldon and by Kenyon's successor as lord chief justice, Edward Law, first Baron Ellenborough; both subsequently worked from *Marshall* to more refined rules that none the less confirmed the diminished autonomy of the separated wife.

Kenyon's hostility to market reasoning appeared most strongly in the last decade of his life. In 1857 John Campbell, first Baron Campbell of St Andrews, published a hostile biography of Kenyon in the third volume of his *Lives of the Chief Justices*; in it he expressed incredulity that Kenyon had sought in 1801 to reaffirm as common-law offences the crimes of forestalling, regrating, and engrossing foodstuffs, famously compared by Adam Smith to the crime of witchcraft. Kenyon's decision responded to the two great dearths of 1795–6 and 1800–01, which presented courts and parliament with a political as well as a social crisis. Kenyon believed that immoral speculators had driven prices to artificial heights; he deplored the fact that Edmund Burke had led parliament to repeal the old criminal legislation in 1772. The chief justice encouraged successful prosecutions in 1800 of John Rusby, a dealer in the Mark Lane corn market, and Samuel Ferrand Waddington, a dealer in hops in Kent and Worcestershire. Kenyon believed that convictions in these cases would save the poor from starvation, establish precedents for the future, and prevent disorder by showing the mob that the state would protect them. The denunciations of the chief justice and the other judges in fact encouraged the mob. Huge food riots took place in London in September 1800, and the rioters celebrated Lord Kenyon in song and graffiti. Most of the cabinet were horrified by Kenyon's doctrine and its results. As popular disorder and political criticism grew in 1801, the judges began to draw back, and by 1802 the prosecutions still before the courts died with the chief justice, as did his doctrine of market criminality. Kenyon took a similar view of labour markets, in which he denounced the criminality of trade union activity ('combination') but equally strongly condemned combination by masters, and threatened to punish them more severely:

> The law of England held the balance even, upon the scale of Justice, between the rich and poor. Those who were to administer that justice, from their feelings as men, which he hoped he should always carry about him, were naturally led to protect the lower orders of the community, and who, some of them, had perhaps no other protection than the Law. (*Morning Chronicle*, 23 Feb 1799)

Kenyon was acutely aware that it was a revolutionary age. His family's letters express fear of the Jacobin mob, notably during the protests against the so-called Two Acts, in November and December 1795, in May 1796, and in November 1800. Kenyon took precautions: early in 1799 he ordered from Birmingham, presumably for his domestic defence, six huge blunderbusses—'deadly instruments each capable of killing 50 men at a shot (more I believe than his Lordship's mouth ever sent from this world at one judgement)' (Matthew Robinson Boulton to James Watt, 4 Feb 1799, Birmingham City Archives, Boulton and Watt Collection, parcel B). In court he presided at several of the most important state trials of the period. His charge to the jury in *R. v. Stockdale* (1789) gave the whole issue of seditious libel to the jury, an apparent rejection of Lord Mansfield's insistence that libel was a matter of law for the judge, and led to suggestions that he sympathized with the defendant, the bookseller John Stockdale, a supporter of Warren Hastings. His apparent inconsistency in subsequently opposing the Libel Act in 1792—he was joined in a formal protest by Thurlow and several others that it could lead to 'the confusion and destruction of the law of England' (Cobbett, *Parl. hist.*, 29.1537–8)—can probably be explained by his belief that the judges should be able to adapt the doctrine to the necessity of the case, including the dangers of a period of revolution. Among his other state trials were those of John Frith in 1790, for throwing a stone at the king's carriage; of Patrick William Duffin and Thomas Lloyd in 1792, for a satiric squib held to be seditious; of Thomas Paine in 1792, *in absentia*, for *The Rights of Man*, part 2; of John Frost in 1793, for seditious words; of Daniel Isaac Eaton in 1793, for publishing Paine; and of John Lambert, James Perry, and James Gray, also in 1793 (the *Morning Chronicle case*), for advertising a meeting of the Society for Constitutional Information, allegedly constituting a seditious libel. In the *Morning Chronicle case* Kenyon strongly supported the government view of the law of seditious libel and condemned the 'horrid doctrines' (Howell, 22.1017) abroad in the country; the jury none the less acquitted, after prolonged deliberations. In the trial of John Frost of the Corresponding Society for seditious libel, in May 1793, Kenyon supported the argument of the prosecution that words on the face of it seditious threw the burden on the defence to disprove intent. He emphasized also that the seditiousness of particular words changed with the danger of the times; the jury convicted. In the trial of Daniel Isaac Eaton in July 1793, for selling Paine's *Rights of Man*, part 2, in spite of his clear support of the prosecution and a charge arguably contrary to the Libel Act, an acquittal followed.

Kenyon was later criticized for attending the pretrial examinations of Hardy and Horne Tooke by the privy council, but did not sit on the cases, reputedly because of fears that he would be intemperate on the bench. He heard several cases after the passage of the Treasonable Practices Act, in November 1795, and the Seditious Assemblies Act, the so-called Two Acts (36 Geo. III c. 7, 8), which he supported. The law of conspiracy was developed rapidly by the judges in these years, and in the trial in 1796 of William Stone, for treason, justices Sir Nash Grose and Sir Soulden Lawrence, also on the bench, persuaded Kenyon to accept evidence of conspiracy that he was at first inclined to exclude. He also heard the cases of John Reeves in 1796, on the charge of libelling the constitution, and Thomas Williams in 1798, for publishing Paine's *Age of Reason*, in which he advertised his own deep religious beliefs in his charge to the jury. In the trial of John Cuthell for seditious libel (1799) Kenyon denounced the redundancy of the Libel Act, claiming that it added nothing to the existing doctrine of the common law. In 1800 he presided over the acquittal of John Hadfield, on grounds of

insanity, for firing at the king, and had him held until the enactment of statutory authority for such confinements.

Public and private character Chief justices frequently dominate their courts, and Kenyon was no exception, sometimes clearly piqued when his court did not follow him, which happened a half-dozen times in the fourteen years that he was chief justice. His profound Christian beliefs were often expressed in court. He had been a member of the Proclamation Society (founded in 1788 to enforce the proclamation of George III against immorality and idleness) until appointed chief justice, never failed to attend Sunday worship, and invoked the deity frequently in his later cases. Sir Richard Hill, Samuel Glasse, William Wilberforce, and other prominent evangelicals were among his friends and correspondents. Kenyon led a quiet private life, did not fit easily in polite society, and disliked and distrusted the world of fashion. He entertained seldom and rarely invited members of the bar to dine. His religious earnestness, lack of a university education, and parsimony all appeared ridiculous in a wealthy lawyer and leading judge. It was reported in 1786 that:

> The Master of Rolls, says a correspondent, keeps house with even greater strictness than any of the primitive Christians; for in his honour's mansion the domestics experience the Passion all the year in the parlour, and Lent all the year in the Kitchen. (*The Times*, 4 July 1786)

The stories grew with his years, and after his death were preserved in the biography by W. C. Townshend. His unpopularity with many barristers and even more attorneys encouraged anecdotes about his ignorance of Latin, coarseness, and bad temper. His partiality toward some members of the bar, notably Thomas Erskine, was notorious, as was his disdain for other counsel, including Edward Law. On one occasion he was bested. John Horne Tooke had been a companion of Kenyon when they were students at law, and in 1792 (though not a barrister) he defended himself in an action brought by Fox. His wit and subtle insolence toward the bench led Kenyon to shed tears of frustration.

Condemning gaming, aristocratic divorce, and duelling, Kenyon attracted much hostility from the fashionable world. The prince of Wales (afterwards George IV) rebuked him for alluding to his support of a gambling club in 1799. In the same year the barrister Henry Clifford (1768–1813), a nephew of the fourth Baron Clifford of Chudleigh, made a reference to newly created peers in *R. v. Flower*, tried before Kenyon. Kenyon in turn made a slighting allusion to Thomas Clifford, first Baron Clifford of Chudleigh. Clifford retaliated in print:

> we seldom observe in our hereditary peers, those pedantic notions of impracticable morality, or that boisterous impetuosity of manners, which sometimes accompany and disgrace, even in the highest situations, those who have been raised to them from the desk, merely on account of their industry and professional success. (Howell, 27.1066)

In the following year, charging a jury in an adultery case, Kenyon criticized the loose morals of the opponents of the bill to criminalize adultery brought by William Eden, first Baron Auckland. One of them, Frederick Howard, fifth earl of Carlisle, complained of breach of privilege in the Lords. Pitt had to ask the king to restrain the prince of Wales and the royal dukes, who apparently supported Carlisle. Kenyon confided to his diary: 'That puppy and adulterous profligate the Earl of Carlisle was to bring on his Motion … against me for breach of privilege in alluding to his infamous speech on the Bill against adultery, but he withdrew his Motion' (10 June 1800; A. Aspinall, ed., *Later Correspondence of George III*, vol. 3, 1967, 358). George III liked Kenyon and in 1795 asked him whether the coronation oath prevented him assenting to measures for Catholic emancipation from the penal laws (the chief justice thought not); the king appears also to have been sympathetic to Kenyon's stand on the marketing offences.

Kenyon's relationship with his wife was one of great mutual respect and affection. They corresponded frequently when Kenyon was on circuit or when they were apart for other reasons. During the demonstrations against the 'Two Acts' Lady Kenyon wrote from Bath: 'If there are Riots or danger let me come to you directly and share every danger with the Man of my Heart' (25 Nov 1795; Kenyon MSS, Lancashire RO, quarto box 18). She followed his reputation closely in the press and wrote to other members of the family in praise of his jury charges; she particularly admired his rhetoric in the adultery case of Arthur Annesley, ninth Viscount Valentia. In 1796 Kenyon threatened to punish gambling even when committed by the fashionable world, and provoked a spate of caricatures, including several of Lady Buckinghamshire (Albinia Hobart) and Lady Archer in the pillory. Lady Kenyon observed that one of them was 'a very ridiculous good print if it will but deter from deserving the reality of it' (Lady Kenyon to the Hon. George Kenyon, Christchurch, 20 May 1796, misdated 1795; Kenyon MSS, Lancashire RO, quarto box 19). In spite of such satires Kenyon enjoyed good press. His hostility to dishonest attorneys and legal chicanery was frequently praised. He was considerate of the students who attended his court (in Guildhall they sat in a box near the bench) and explained the issues in the record while counsel were speaking. Many men and women of evangelical persuasion wrote to him of their appreciation of a godly chief justice, particularly after his attack on market speculators.

Kenyon made one of the great judicial fortunes. In 1782, when chief justice of Chester and attorney-general, he earned £11,542, £7555 of it from private clients. His earnings—rivalled by very few other lawyers—came largely from opinions on cases, rather than advocacy, for which he had no particular gifts. His judicial posts also were immensely remunerative. The mastership of the rolls was worth between £2500 and £4000 a year in salary and fees. The chief justice of king's bench received £4000 a year and had offices in king's bench worth about £15,000 a year in his gift. Kenyon (like other chief justices) named his sons and other relatives to several: Lloyd (1775–1800) as filazer; George *Kenyon (1776–1855), later second Baron Kenyon, as joint chief clerk. In 1804 Lord Ellenborough appointed Kenyon's youngest son, Thomas (1780–1851), as filazer, and in 1810 shared the post of *custos brevium*, now in

his possession, with George. Members of the family still occupied several offices in the mid-1830s.

Kenyon made shrewd purchases in Flintshire and Denbighshire, and extensively rebuilt Gredington Hall. From 1796 to 1798 he was lord lieutenant of Flintshire, and from 1796 to 1802 *custos rotulorum* of that county. He invested in government securities and lent money to landowners, and was the first judge to invest in canals. At his death, in 1802, his fortune was about £260,000, the sixth largest of the 139 judges for whom figures are available in the eighteenth and nineteenth centuries. The illness and death of his eldest son, Lloyd, who died on 15 September 1800, almost overwhelmed Kenyon with grief. In his will he asked to be buried with him; he left £30,000 to his surviving younger son, Thomas, a jointure of £2500 to his widow, and the rest as a life estate to his elder son, George. His own health and strength declined, and he sat at assizes for the last time, on the home circuit, in the summer of 1801. In the spring of 1802 he went to Bath for the waters, and died there on 4 April. Lady Kenyon died on 8 August 1808 at her home near Ellesmere, Shropshire. They are buried at Hanmer, where a memorial commemorates Lord Kenyon's devotion to 'Religion, Law, and Order'.

DOUGLAS HAY

Sources 'Memoir of the late Lord Kenyon', *Legal Observer*, 1 (Nov 1830–April 1831), 184–5 · 'Life of Lord Kenyon', *Law Magazine, or, Quarterly Review of Jurisprudence*, 17 (1837), 252–96 · 'Life of Lord Kenyon', *Law Magazine, or, Quarterly Review of Jurisprudence*, 18 (1837), 49–85 · 'Lord Kenyon', *Journal of Jurisprudence*, 19 (1875), 464–75 · *A sketch of the life and character of Lord Kenyon* [inaccurate in many particulars] · *Annual Register* (1802) · P. Atiyah, *The rise and fall of freedom of contract* (1979) · Baker, *Serjeants*, 220 · John, Lord Campbell, *The lives of the chief justices of England*, 3 vols. (1849–57); repr. (1971) · C. Catton, *The English peerage, or, A view of the ancient and present state of the English nobility*, 3 vols. (1790) · GEC, *Peerage*, vol. 7 · D. Duman, *The judicial bench in England, 1727–1875* (1982) · Foss, *Judges*, vol. 8 · E. Foss, *Biographia juridica: a biographical dictionary of the judges of England … 1066–1870* (1870) · C. Durnford and E. H. East, *Term reports in the court of king's bench*, 8 vols. (1817) [99–101 ER Reports] · E. H. East, *Reports of cases argued and determined in the court of king's bench*, 16 vols. (1800–12) [102–04 ER] · *GM*, 1st ser., 72 (1802), 377–9 · *The report of the select committee … to enquire into the establishment of the courts of justice in Westminster Hall, the courts of assize, the civil law* (1799) · D. Hay, 'The state and the market: Lord Kenyon and Mr Waddington', *Past and Present*, 162 (1999), 101–62 · D. Hay, 'Moral economy, political economy, and law', *Moral economy and popular protest: crowds, conflict and authority*, ed. A. Randall and A. Charlesworth (1999), 93–122 · T. B. Howell, *A complete collection of state trials*, 20–28 (1816–20) · J. Innes, 'Politics and morals: the reformation of manners movement in later eighteenth-century England', *The transformation of political culture: England and Germany in the late eighteenth century*, ed. E. Hellmuth (1990), 57–118 · G. T. Kenyon, *The life of Lloyd, first Lord Kenyon, lord chief justice of England* (1873) · R. L. Kenyon, *Kenyon family biography* (1920) · *The manuscripts of Lord Kenyon*, HMC, 35 (1894) · manuscript pedigree, priv. coll. [L. Tyrell-Kenyon, sixth Baron Kenyon] · *Notes of cases argued and adjudged in the court of king's bench … by … Lord Kenyon*, ed. J. W. Hanmer (1819) [96 ER Kenyon] · D. Lemmings, *Professors of the law: barristers and English legal culture in the eighteenth century* (2000) · R. A. Melikan, *John Scott, Lord Eldon, 1751–1838: the duty of loyalty* (1999) · J. Brooke, 'Kenyon, Lloyd', HoP, *Commons, 1754–90* · Cobbett, *Parl. hist.*, vols. 21–33 · Lancs. RO, Kenyon papers · Kenyon MSS, priv. coll. · Sainty, *Judges* · Sainty, *King's counsel* · S. Staves, *Married women's separate property in England, 1660–1833* (1990) · L. Stone, *Road to divorce: England, 1530–1987* (1992) · *The Times* (1785–1802) · W. C. Townshend,

The lives of twelve eminent judges of the last and of the present century (1846) · J. B. Williamson, *The Middle Temple bench book*, 2nd edn (1937) · *Boswell: the English experiment, 1785–1789*, ed. I. S. Lustig and F. A. Pottle (1986), vol. 13 of *The Yale editions of the private papers of James Boswell*, trade edn (1950–89) · will, PRO, PROB 11/1373, sig. 289, fols. 86v–87r · Hanmer parish register transcripts, Society of Genealogists, WS/R/67

Archives Flintshire RO, Hawarden, papers · Lancashire RO, Preston, corresp., diaries, accounts, and legal papers · NRA, priv. coll., corresp., legal notes, etc. | BL, Liverpool papers, Add. MSS · Bodl. Oxf., Wilberforce papers · PRO, KB series · Shrops. RRC, papers of Sir Richard Hill

Likenesses J. Gillray, etching, pubd 1787 (*Ancient music*), NPG · J. Opie, portrait, 1788, priv. coll. [*see illus.*] · J. Fittler, line engraving, pubd 1789 (after J. Opie), BM, NPG · W. Holl, stipple, 1804 (as chief justice, 1788; after G. Romney) · W. Davison, oils, *c.*1813–1843 (after G. Romney and M. A. Shee), NPG · W. Holl, stipple, pubd 1832 (after M. A. Shee), BM; repro. in W. Jerdan, *National portrait gallery of illustrious and eminent personages*, 5 vols. (1830–34) · E. Orme, engraving, BM · G. Romney, portrait, priv. coll. · G. Romney and M. A. Shee, oils, Middle Temple, London; copy, NPG

Wealth at death approx. £260,000: D. Duman, *The judicial bench in England, 1727–1875* (1982), 140–43

Kenyon, Lloyd Tyrell-, fifth Baron Kenyon (1917–1993), museum administrator and book collector, was born on 13 September 1917 at 17 Manchester Street, Marylebone, London, the only son of Lloyd Tyrell-Kenyon, fourth Baron Kenyon (1864–1927), a lord-in-waiting to Queen Victoria, Edward VII, and George V, and his wife, Gwladys Julia (1884–1965), the only daughter of Colonel Henry Lloyd Howard, of Wigfair, Denbighshire. He had a twin sister. He succeeded to his father's peerage at the age of ten and was educated at Eton College and Magdalene College, Cambridge. After taking his degree Lord Kenyon's interest in the visual arts led to his appointment as an honorary attaché at the Fitzwilliam Museum, where Louis Clarke had just become director. He joined the Shropshire yeomanry in 1937 and served in the Second World War in the Royal Artillery (Territorial Army) until he was invalided out in 1943 on account of his poor eyesight.

After the war Kenyon married, on 3 June 1946, Leila Mary, *née* Cookson (*b.* 1923), the widow of Lieutenant Hugh Peel of the Welsh Guards; the couple had three sons (one of whom died in the same year as his father) and a daughter. The subsequent pattern of Kenyon's life was set in these post-war years. Motivated by a strong sense of public duty and skilled at leading on a loose rein, he served on Flint county council for ten years, becoming chairman in 1954–5, was president of the University of North Wales at Bangor from 1947 to 1982 (a post his father had held before him), chief commissioner for the Wales Boy Scouts Association from 1948 to 1966 (his mother had been a friend of the Baden-Powells), and a deputy lieutenant for Flint from 1948. He had boundless zest for the constant travelling involved in these duties, but he also found time to look after his own properties and manage his 10,000 acre estate. He was the first farmer to import Charollais cattle into Britain; and he was a keen gardener and plantsman, personally labelling every species in his borders with meticulous care. Unsentimental about what he owned, he had the once fine and elaborately timbered mansion of Kenyon Peel Hall—which had begun to fall apart after coal

extraction in the area had undermined it structurally—pulled down in the 1950s, and Gredington itself, impractically large, he also demolished to be replaced by smaller family houses. He then lived himself in nearby Cumbers House, an attractive late-Victorian red-brick house.

From 1958 Kenyon was closely involved with the Welsh hospital service. He was a member of the Welsh Regional Hospital Board from 1958 to 1963 and of the Council for Professions Supplementary to Medicine from 1961 to 1965, and chairman of the Wrexham, Powys, and Mawddach hospital management committee from 1960 to 1974 and of the Clwyd Area Health Authority from 1974 to 1978. He was also a director of Lloyds Bank from 1962 to 1988 and chairman of its north-west board. But closest to his heart was the world of art and books. At the age of thirty-five he was appointed president of the National Museum of Wales (he had been vice-president since 1947), serving for five years from 1952 to 1957. In the following year he began a seven-year term as a member of the Standing Commission on Museums and Galleries and became a trustee of the National Portrait Gallery, where he remained on the board for five consecutive terms, succeeding Sir Geoffrey Keynes as chairman in 1966 and relinquishing this position only in 1988, when he was finding it increasingly difficult to read.

Kenyon was in his element with historical portraits; he never tired of consulting and quoting from the *Dictionary of National Biography*. As chairman he trusted and supported successive directors and their staff; he always found time to talk and encourage, and if, very rarely, reproof were needed, it might happen over dinner at Brooks's. Crisply but meticulously conducted trustees' meetings were preceded by lunch at the Beefsteak and ended in good time for catching the train at Euston. The most important issues in his time were expansion of the gallery's confined building of 1896 adjoining the National Gallery and the provision of outstations in the regions—chiefly in collaboration with the National Trust—to allow significant parts of the collection to be shown outside London. Kenyon was always prepared to lobby ministers, but he disliked fund-raising, except for important purchases such as the portraits of Handel and Sterne, and the first stage of expansion (1993) did not happen until after his retirement. He did, however, initiate and use his personal authority and his proximity to carry through, with characteristic and tireless energy, a highly successful Victorian outstation as part of Clwyd county council's cultural development at Bodelwyddan Castle in north Wales, opened in 1988. It was perhaps his most remarkable single achievement.

Kenyon's appreciation of the unique significance of the gallery's historic archive and his wise encouragement of research reflected his deep love of books. He helped to relaunch the celebrated Gregynog Press in 1978, and was a passionate collector chiefly of early English liturgical books. His elegant handwriting was that of a calligrapher. Kenyon was a member of the Royal Commission on Historical Manuscripts from 1966 to 1992 and chairman of the friends of the national libraries from 1962 to 1985. His knowledge of rare books was always at the service of others, and it was one of the greatest sadnesses of his life that in his later years he had to sell a large part of his collection.

Kenyon never sought to move in London society, and did not attend the House of Lords. He rarely travelled outside England and Wales except for occasional holidays in the sun and a visit to the United States for the centenary of Kenyon College, Ohio. Although his commitments took him frequently to London, where he greatly enjoyed club life and its rituals and his visits to the bookseller Heywood Hill, he was essentially a man of the shires. In his younger days he enjoyed country pursuits, especially hare-coursing, and for many years he was secretary of Altcar Racing Club. Later he owned one racehorse, Rupertino, but although the Peel estate, which adjoined his own and of which he was a senior trustee, included Bangor-on-Dee (Bangor Is-coed) racecourse, he was not at heart a racing man. Kenyon was sociable and hospitable, and infinitely generous. He bore his troubles and infirmities without complaining and never lost his quiet good humour. He was an old-fashioned aristocrat in his self-confident bearing and affability, his way of life, and his devotion to public service. But he was distinctive, too, in his pebble glasses, bow-tie, light fawn topcoat worn even in extreme weathers, and cultural interests. He was a fellow of the Society of Antiquaries and was appointed CBE in 1972. He died at Cumbers House, Gredington, Shropshire, on 16 May 1993, from lung cancer.   JOHN HAYES

Sources N. Barker, *The Independent* (19 May 1993) · *The Times* (20 May 1993) · *Daily Telegraph* (19 May 1993) · Burke, *Peerage* · *WWW*, 1991–5 · personal knowledge (2004) · d. cert. · m. cert.
Likenesses Bassano, photographs, 1938, NPG · J. Ward, chalk and watercolour heightened with white, 1988, priv. coll. · T. C. Dugdale, oils, priv. coll.
Wealth at death £2,872,423: probate, 3 Dec 1993, *CGPLA Eng. & Wales*

Keogh, Sir Alfred (1857–1936), army medical officer, was born in Dublin on 3 July 1857, the son of Henry Keogh, barrister and magistrate of Roscommon. He was educated at Queen's College, Galway, and Guy's Hospital, London. He continued his medical studies at the Royal University of Ireland, from which he graduated MD in 1878. After working as a house physician at the Brompton Chest Hospital in London, and later as a clinical assistant at the Royal Westminster Ophthalmic Hospital, Keogh joined the Army Medical Service in March 1880 as a surgeon. His unusual breadth of clinical experience stood him in good stead for the medical corps' entrance examination, in which he came second, and he went on to excel academically at the Army Medical College, Netley, gaining the Herbert prize and the Martin memorial medal.

Keogh's first military position was that of surgeon at the Royal Arsenal, Woolwich, and, having distinguished himself in this post, he was quickly promoted to the rank of surgeon-major—the rank he held at the beginning of the Second South African War in 1899. During the war Keogh's reputation continued to soar. He was mentioned in dispatches on a number of occasions and was specially promoted to the rank of lieutenant-colonel, taking charge of No. 3 general hospital near Cape Town. Under Keogh's command the hospital acquired a reputation for efficiency and was one of the few military medical institutions to escape criticism in the British and South African press. The ravages of epidemic disease and neglect of the sick and wounded among the British force in South Africa gave rise to a public outcry in the summer of 1900. Many military doctors were condemned for their passivity and their outdated views but Keogh had demonstrated a talent for cutting through military 'red tape' and often bypassed official channels in order to ensure that his hospital was properly equipped. He was also more diligent than most in the maintenance of hygiene and sanitation, ensuring that his hospital was relatively free from the epidemic diseases which claimed the lives of thousands of British soldiers.

As one of the few senior medical officers to emerge from the Second South African War with his reputation intact, the ambitious, forward-looking Keogh seemed a natural choice for inclusion in the consultative committee on the medical services established in 1901 by the secretary of state for war, St John Broderick (1856–1942). This committee suggested a number of important reforms, including the construction of a new Army Medical College in London and the formation of a permanent advisory board on army medical matters, to which Keogh was later appointed.

Keogh's service to government earned him a CB in 1902 and promotion in 1905 to the post of director-general of the Army Medical Service. In the following year he was created KCB and in 1907 was made an honorary physician to the king. As director-general, Keogh played a crucial role in further reforms of the Army Medical Service. He and other senior medical officers came to the conclusion that any future war between Britain and a major industrial nation would be protracted, placing a severe strain on the country's material and human resources. It was therefore imperative, they believed, to harness the enthusiasm of voluntary medical services such as the Red Cross and to ensure their full co-operation with the armed services. Keogh's views on military–civilian co-operation in wartime were in harmony with those of the Liberal secretary of state for war, R. B. Haldane (1856–1928), under whom was established the Territorial Force (later Territorial Army). Keogh worked closely with Haldane, organizing medical sections for the territorials and the new Officers' Training Corps.

Keogh retired from the post of director-general in March 1910, whereupon he became rector of the Imperial College of Science and Technology in London—a post he held until 1922. On the outbreak of war in 1914, Keogh also took charge of the Red Cross committee which co-ordinated voluntary medical aid in France and Flanders. He was not long in his post before his presence was once again requested at the War Office. The task of organizing military medical provisions for a fast-growing army was proving too much for one person and a decision was made to split responsibility between the current director-general, Sir Arthur Sloggett, who was sent to France as director-general of medical services, and Keogh, who returned to his old post as director-general of Army Medical Services in London. He continued in this office until June 1918, when he was succeeded by Surgeon-General T. H. J. C. Goodwin.

One of Keogh's greatest achievements during the war was to maintain good relations with voluntary bodies supplying medical aid. While there was some tension between regular and voluntary services during the war, the Red Cross and the War Office worked together far more harmoniously than in South Africa. The assistance of bodies such as the Red Cross and the St John Ambulance Brigade, not to mention the female nurses of the voluntary aid detachments, was crucial given that regular medical staff were in increasingly short supply. Keogh also proved adroit in negotiations with government concerning the allocation of medical manpower, gaining priority for military over civilian needs. However, the dispatch to France of Keogh's territorial general hospitals was thwarted until April 1916 by the secretary of state for war, Lord Kitchener, who had an undisguised contempt for the Territorial Force. Indeed, the two men appear to have been intensely suspicious of one another, Kitchener having attempted, unsuccessfully, to remove Keogh to France. In 1916 Keogh also came in for a certain amount of criticism from civilian members of the Howard commission on medical provisions in France and Flanders for his allegedly profligate use of resources. There were also complaints of a breakdown in communication between medical staff in London and those in France. However, Keogh enjoyed the confidence and support of most senior army officers and was able to oppose plans for cuts in medical services. Despite these criticisms, Keogh's wartime work was generally regarded as outstanding, as is evident from the many international honours he received during and after the conflict. He was made GCB in 1917; grand officer of the French Légion d'honneur and of the crown of Belgium in the same year; a Companion of Honour and GCVO in 1918; he also received honorary doctorates from the universities of Oxford, Leeds, Dublin, Edinburgh, and Aberdeen. He was elected a fellow of the Royal College of Physicians in 1914.

Keogh was twice married: first in 1880 to Elizabeth Williams (d. 1887), daughter of George Williams MP, of the Indian Medical Service (IMS), with whom he had one son; second in 1888 to Camilla Porterfield (d. 1948), daughter of Captain William Hamilton Sheriff Hart of the 105th regiment, with whom he had two daughters. Keogh died at his home at 19 Warwick Square, London, on 30 July 1936. He was remembered as a man of strong opinions, although he was said to be highly adaptable and capable of delegation. These characteristics explain his success as an administrator and his ability to reconcile hitherto hostile camps. It was not for nothing that Haldane referred to Keogh as 'one of the finest organisers I ever knew'.

MARK HARRISON

Sources Wellcome L., RAMC collection · war office files, PRO · *The Lancet* (8 Aug 1936) · *BMJ* (8 Aug 1936), 317–18 · *DNB* · *CGPLA Eng. & Wales* (1936)
Archives BL OIOC, corresp. with Sir Walter Lawrence, MS Eur. F 143 · Bodl. Oxf., corresp. with Sir Henry Burdett · NL Scot., corresp. with Lord Haldane · Wellcome L., Royal Army Medical Corps collection
Likenesses A. Hacker, oils, exh. RA 1919, Royal Army Medical College; copy, ICL · Mesurier and Marshall, photogravure, Wellcome L. · Russell, photograph, repro. in *The Lancet* · W. Stoneman, photograph, NPG
Wealth at death £2667 6s. 7d.: probate, 18 Sept 1936, *CGPLA Eng. & Wales*

Keogh, John (*c*.1650–1725), Church of Ireland clergyman and scientist, was born near Limerick at 'Cloonclieve' (probably Clooncleagh in co. Tipperary), the son of Denis Keogh and his wife (*née* Wittington), widow of a clergyman named Eyres. The Keoghs, descended from an old Irish Catholic family, the Mac Eochaidh, had lost their lands near the rivers Shannon and Mulkear during the Cromwellian wars. John Keogh was educated by his protestant mother who kept him at a school in Dublin, where he entered Trinity College in 1669. He was a scholar of the college in 1674, proceeded MA in 1678, and took orders in the episcopal Church of Ireland. He twice competed unsuccessfully for a fellowship of the college. John Hodson, possibly a relative and bishop of Elphin, appointed him to a living in that diocese and he was installed prebendary of Termonbarry in February 1678.

Keogh married in 1679 Avis Clopton, daughter of Dr Rous Clopton, of an old Warwickshire family that had settled under Cromwell near Athlone, and his wife, formerly Mrs Day. The Keoghs may have had as many as twenty-one children. He settled down to a scholar's life at Strokestown, co. Roscommon, where he also kept a school and prepared pupils for the University of Dublin. His favourite studies seem to have been Hebrew and the application of mathematics to mystical religious problems. Keogh wrote a demonstration of the Trinity in Latin verse, which was shown by his son John to Isaac Newton who expressed approval of it. In his 'Scala metaphysica' Keogh attempted a mathematical demonstration of a dependence on God of a scale of beings from the highest angel to the lowest insect. A part of his extensive writings, none of which were published, may have been destroyed by a fire at his residence. However, a number of manuscript works, including a Hebrew lexicon, a work entitled 'De orthographia', Latin and Greek grammars, and an 'Analogy of the four gospels', were saved. Some of Keogh's manuscripts were deposited in the library of Archbishop William King and subsequently sold.

In 1684 and 1685 Keogh was associated with William Molyneux and the Dublin Philosophical Society. He wrote in March 1684 to Molyneux enclosing a detailed description of co. Roscommon intended as a contribution to the Irish part of Moses Pitt's 'English atlas'. In correspondence with Molyneux, Keogh expressed enthusiasm for the aims of the Dublin Philosophical Society and received information on its progress and activities. In December 1684 Keogh informed the society of various investigations including that of a philosophical character or characteristic. He worked on this topic for about a year and at the end of 1685 he presented a discourse to the society, then under the chairmanship of St George Ashe. His philosophical character may have proved a disappointment, however, and no more was heard of the project after 1685. In one respect Keogh stood out among the members of the society, namely in his extensive use of Latin in contributions. When in 1707 and 1708 the Dublin Philosophical Society was revived under its secretary Samuel Molyneux, Keogh was once again a corresponding member reporting on curiosities such as a giant tooth and rare plants grown in greenhouses near Athlone.

Keogh died in 1725 and was survived by six of his children including sons Michael (d. c.1734) and **John Keogh** (1680/81–1754), Church of Ireland clergyman and author of scientific and medical tracts. Like their father both sons entered the church. Michael was beneficed in the diocese of Elphin at Strokestown and John, after acting for some time as chaplain to James King, fourth Lord Kingston, obtained the living of Mitchelstown, co. Cork. John married Elizabeth, daughter of Dr Henry Jennings, a cousin of the duchess of Marlborough, and had three sons and three daughters. He died in 1754 aged seventy-three. His published books, *Botanologia universalis Hibernica, or, A general Irish herbal … giving an account of the herbs, shrubs and trees … in English, Irish and Latin* (1735) and *Zoologica medica Hibernica, or, A treatise of birds, beasts, fishes, reptiles, or insects … in this kingdom, giving … their names in English, Irish and Latin* (1739), emphasized the medicinal value of plants and animals and separate medical tracts were appended to these. A third work, in which he included an account of his family, entitled *A vindication of the antiquities of Ireland and a defense thereof against all calumnies and aspersions cast on it by foreigners* (1748) contains an appended etymological tract on Irish names and is distinctly patriotic in character.   JAMES G. O'HARA

Sources DNB · J. Keogh, *A vindication of the antiquities of Ireland* (1748) · R. Ryan, *Biographica Hibernica: a biographical dictionary of the worthies of Ireland* (1819–21) · A. J. Webb, 'Keogh, John, DD', *A compendium of Irish biography* (1878) · D. J. O'Donoghue, 'Keogh, Rev. John', *The poets of Ireland: a biographical and bibliographical dictionary* (1912) · J. Britten and G. S. Boulger, 'Keogh, Rev. John (1681?–1754)', *A biographical index of British and Irish botanists* (1893), 96 · K. T. Hoppen, *The common scientist in the seventeenth century: a study of the Dublin Philosophical Society, 1683–1708* (1970) · K. T. Hoppen, 'The papers of the Dublin Philosophical Society, 1683–1708', *Analecta Hibernica*, 30 (1982), 151–248 · J. G. Simms, *William Molyneux of Dublin, 1656–1698*, ed. P. H. Kelly (1982) · S. J. Connolly, *Religion, law, and power: the making of protestant Ireland, 1660–1760* (1992) · J. H. Andrews, 'Land and people, c.1685', *A new history of Ireland*, ed. T. W. Moody and others, 3: *Early modern Ireland, 1534–1691* (1976), 454–77 · T. W. Moody and others, eds., *A new history of Ireland*, 9: *Maps, genealogies, lists* (1984)

Archives Royal Irish Acad., herbal [John Keogh] · TCD, letters | BL, botanologia universalis, 1735, Add. MS 25586 [John Keogh]

Keogh, John (1680/81–1754). *See under* Keogh, John (c.1650–1725).

Keogh, John (1740–1817), campaigner for Roman Catholic rights, was born in humble circumstances to Cornelius

Keogh (1708–1774), labourer, and Abigail Keogh (1711–1779) in Dublin. He made his fortune in silk and brewing in Dublin, and from the lease and purchase of land. In addition to his home at Mount Jerome, Harold's Cross, co. Dublin, he acquired property in counties Sligo, Leitrim, and Roscommon which, with investments, reputedly guaranteed him an annual income of between £5000 and £6000 in the late 1790s. He was a proud man, who 'boasted of his Milesian ancestry' (Wall, 164), and his economic achievements served to highlight how unjust it was that Catholics in Ireland had to live their lives under the shadow of the penal laws. He successfully stood for election to the Catholic committee for Enniscorthy in January 1781, and he subsequently represented St Andrew's parish, Dublin, and co. Leitrim. He attended few meetings in 1781 and 1782, but he voted with the majority on 11 November 1783 when the committee controversially asserted that it was the voice of Irish Catholics and effectively invited the volunteer grand national convention to include Catholic enfranchisement in its plan of reform. This did not come to pass, but in 1784 Keogh and a small number of Catholic activists supported the alliance of Dublin and Ulster radicals who advocated a plan of parliamentary reform that promised limited Catholic enfranchisement. This was not popular with the mainstream Catholic leadership, but the committee was able to avoid a split.

The Catholic committee was largely inactive until the election in 1790 of a new committee, in which Keogh was to the fore, energized its ranks. Early in 1791 the committee determined to press actively for the repeal of the remaining penal laws but, on meeting with stiff resistance from the Irish administration, Keogh was authorized to travel to England to lay Catholic grievances before ministers. After three months he returned with a favourable answer, but the prospects of relief were undermined by the secession in December 1791 of Lord Kenmare and his conservative allies, following their failure to convince the committee to leave Catholic relief to Dublin Castle. However, instead of acquiescing in the refusal of the Irish parliament in 1792 to respond sympathetically, Keogh intensified the campaign. He drew on his extensive financial resources, on Wolfe Tone who was recruited as secretary to the committee, and on his own formidable determination, and a Catholic convention was assembled in Dublin on 3 December 1792. Guided by Keogh the convention appointed a deputation, of which he was a member, to present to the king a statement of the grievances under which the Catholics of Ireland laboured. The deputation was favourably received, and the Relief Act of 1793, which gave Catholics the vote, followed directly.

The 1793 Relief Act was the great triumph of Keogh's life, though he did not escape criticism because of his refusal to hold out for full emancipation, his failure to divulge all the details of his dealings with British politicians, and his agreement to dissolve the Catholic committee. He was tempted to take a more radical stand when Catholic expectations of emancipation were dashed by the precipitate recall of the lord lieutenant, Earl Fitzwilliam, in 1795. The subsequent Catholic delegation to London, of which Keogh was a member, was accorded a frosty response. As his membership of the United Irishmen in the early 1790s attests, Keogh shared at least some of their aims, and he may have become an active United Irishman for a time in the mid-1790s. However, his instinct for self-preservation was stronger than his desire for political change. He was arrested and his house searched on a number of occasions, but he kept radicalism at a sufficient distance to safeguard himself against prosecution. With the reanimation of Catholic politics in the aftermath of the Union, his renowned vanity allowed him to be tempted back into the limelight. He participated in the discussions of the merits of presenting a Catholic petition in 1804–5, but was uneasy at what he perceived as the élitism of the organizers and withdrew. He subsequently relented, but by 1810 he was soon eclipsed by younger men, such as Daniel O'Connell, who were not prepared to be guided by him.

Keogh died on 13 November 1817 at Mount Jerome, and was buried beside his parents in St Kevin's churchyard in Dublin. Six years later his wife, Mary Keogh (1757–1823), died and was laid in the same spot.   JAMES KELLY

Sources M. Wall, 'John Keogh and the Catholic committee', *Catholic Ireland in the eighteenth century: collected essays of Maureen Wall*, ed. G. O'Brien (1989) · D. Gwynn, *John Keogh, the pioneer of Catholic emancipation* (1930) · M. Elliott, *Wolfe Tone: prophet of Irish independence* (1989) · T. Bartlett, *The fall and rise of the Irish nation: the Catholic question, 1690–1830* (1992) · *The correspondence of Edmund Burke*, ed. T. W. Copeland and others, 10 vols. (1958–78) · *The Irish Catholic petition of 1805: the diary of Denys Scully*, ed. B. MacDermott (1992) · B. C. MacDermot, ed., *The Catholic question in Ireland and England, 1798–1822: the papers of Denys Scully* (1988) · R. D. Edwards, ed., 'The minute book of the Catholic Committee, 1773–1792', *Archivium Hibernicum*, 9 (1942), 1–172 · headstone, St Kevin's Park, Camden Row, Dublin · *DNB*

Archives Sheffield Central Library, Fitzwilliam MSS · TCD, Tone papers

Likenesses attrib. J. Comerford, watercolour on ivory, NG Ire.

Keogh, William Nicholas (1817–1878),

judge, belonged to a Roman Catholic family formerly settled at Keoghville, co. Roscommon. He was born at Galway on 7 December 1817. His father, William M. Keogh (d. 1865), was a solicitor and sometime clerk of the crown for the county of Kilkenny; his mother was Mary, daughter of Austin Ffrench of Rahoon, co. Galway. He was educated at the Revd Dr Huddard's school in Mountjoy Square, Dublin, and in 1832 entered Trinity College, Dublin, where he obtained honours in science in his first and second years. He left in his third year without having taken a degree. While at Trinity he was a frequent speaker in the debates of the Historical Society, and was awarded the first prize for oratory at the age of nineteen. In 1835 he was admitted a student of the King's Inns, Dublin, and in 1837 of Lincoln's Inn. In 1840 he was called to the Irish bar, and joined the Connaught circuit, where his family connections lay. In the same year he published, with Michael J. Barry, *A Treatise on the Practice of the High Court of Chancery in Ireland*, but he never obtained any considerable practice in that court. His natural gifts were those of an advocate rather than of a lawyer; a

powerful voice, an impressive face, and an impassioned delivery were combined with a ready flow of vigorous and ornate language.

Keogh soon acquired a fair practice, principally on circuit, where, as a junior, he held leading briefs in the most important cases, and his powers of advocacy were considered so formidable that special counsel were sometimes brought down to oppose him. In 1841 he married Kate, daughter of Thomas Roney, surgeon; they had a son and a daughter. At the general election of 1847 he was returned for Athlone as an independent Conservative, the only Roman Catholic Conservative elected to that parliament. After a time he was considered a Peelite. In 1849 he was made a QC. In 1851 he took an active and prominent part in the obstructive parliamentary campaign of the Irish brigade against the Ecclesiastical Titles Bill. This greatly increased his reputation and popularity in Ireland. He was the principal speaker at a mass meeting of Roman Catholics held in Dublin in August 1851 to protest against the measure, and was one of the founders of the Catholic Defence Association established in consequence of it. In the same month, together with the other members of the Irish brigade, he made common cause with the tenant right movement led by Charles Gavan Duffy, and in the session of 1852 seconded in the House of Commons the Tenant Right Bill of William Sharman Crawford. At the general election of 1852 he was again returned for Athlone, and he was subsequently among those MPs who assembled in Dublin and committed themselves to remain independent of, and in opposition to, any and every government that did not concede to their policy demands on land and religion. In December 1852 Keogh and the bulk of the Irish party voted in the majority which overturned Lord Derby's ministry. In the new ministry of Lord Aberdeen (December 1852) Keogh accepted office as solicitor-general for Ireland, while John Sadleir MP for Carlow, became a junior Treasury minister. The two men's names were thenceforth linked in obloquy by nationalist propagandists who accused them of betraying, through personal ambition, a policy and a party to which they were solemnly pledged. Subsequently their defection came to be depicted as the cause of a generation of Irish youth rejecting constitutional politics and embracing Fenianism. At the time Keogh was bitterly assailed by Gavan Duffy in *The Nation* and by Frederick Lucas in *The Tablet*, and his re-election for Athlone was opposed. His appointment was also distasteful to the Conservatives, and was attacked by Lord Westmeath in the House of Lords. At Athlone he was supported by the Catholic bishop (Dr Browne) and clergy, and was re-elected by a large majority. In January 1855 the Aberdeen ministry resigned and in Palmerston's ministry Keogh was appointed attorney-general for Ireland and was sworn of the Irish privy council. He was re-elected at Athlone without opposition. In April 1856, on the death of Mr Justice Torrens, he was appointed a judge of the court of common pleas in Ireland. Among the remarkable cases in which he was counsel while at the bar were *Birch* v. *Somerville* (December 1851), an action by the proprietor of *The World* newspaper against the Irish chief secretary on an alleged agreement to pay him for supporting law and order in his paper; *Handcock v. Delacour*, in the court of chancery (February 1855), a case involving the title to a large estate in Galway, in which Keogh's reply for the plaintiff was so touching and eloquent as to draw tears from the chancellor; and *R. v. Petcherine* (December 1855), the trial of a Redemptorist monk on a charge of profanely and contemptuously burning a copy of the Authorized Version of the Bible; Keogh conducted the prosecution as attorney-general.

On the bench Keogh soon acquired the reputation of a judge of ability and discernment. Though not a profound lawyer, he never failed to appreciate a legal argument, and his judgments were clear and to the point. He excelled in the trial of *nisi prius* cases; his perception was quick, he grasped the facts of the case rapidly, and presented them to the jury with clearness and precision. In 1865 he was appointed, with Mr Justice Fitzgerald, to the special commission for the trial of the Fenian prisoners at Dublin and Cork, and before them Luby, O'Leary, O'Donovan Rossa, and the other principal conspirators were tried. Luby, in his speech after conviction, acknowledged the fairness of Keogh's summing-up to the jury. In 1867 the University of Dublin conferred upon him the honorary degree of LLD. In 1872 the celebrated Galway county election petition was tried before him. The candidates at the election were Captain J. P. Nolan (home-ruler) and Captain Le Poer Trench (Conservative); the former was returned by a large majority. His return was petitioned against mainly on the ground of undue influence exercised on his behalf by the Roman Catholic clergy. The trial lasted from 1 April to 27 May, and resulted in Captain Nolan being unseated, and three Roman Catholic bishops and thirty-one priests were reported to the house as guilty of undue influence and intimidation. That Captain Nolan was properly unseated on the evidence could hardly be contested, but in the course of his judgment Keogh commented on the action of the Roman Catholic bishops and priests in terms of unusual severity. His remarks were deeply resented, and aroused much popular feeling. Meetings were held at which he was denounced, he was burnt in effigy in numerous places, and the excitement became so great that special precautions had to be taken by the government for his protection. In the House of Commons Isaac Butt, the home-rule leader, brought forward a motion impugning the conduct of the judge; it was defeated by a large majority, only twenty-three voting in its favour (9 August 1872). For the remainder of his life Keogh was the subject of constant attack by the Home Rule Party. In 1878 his health began to fail, and he died at Bingen-on-the-Rhine on 30 September that year, some weeks after suffering a wound which may have been self-inflicted. He was buried on 3 October in the Catholic cemetery at Bonn.

During the greater part of his tenure of office, Keogh had been one of the most conspicuous figures on the Irish bench. Genial and good-natured, he was popular in private life, where his ready wit and conversational powers made him an agreeable companion; he possessed an unusually retentive memory, and his fund of anecdotes was varied and entertaining. Although his attitudes had come to be strongly anti-clerical, Keogh's closest friend in the last decade of his life was James Healy, parish priest of Little Bray, co. Dublin, and a celebrated wit, and Keogh is believed to have received the last rites devoutly on his deathbed. J. D. FitzGerald, *rev.* R. V. Comerford

Sources *Freeman's Journal* [Dublin] (2 Oct 1878) · J. H. Whyte, *The independent Irish party, 1850–59* (1958) · *Memories of Father Healy of Little Bray* (1895) · *Irish Times* (2 Oct 1878) · Burtchaell & Sadleir, *Alum. Dubl.* · *Law Magazine*, 4th ser., 4 (1878–9), 62–72 · *The Times* (2 Oct 1878) · Boase, *Mod. Eng. biog.*
Archives NA Ire.
Likenesses H. Furniss, caricature, pen-and-ink sketch, NPG · L. Werner, oils, King's Inns, Dublin · portrait, repro. in *ILN*, 16 (1850), 261 · portrait, repro. in *The Graphic*, 6 (1872), 90, 95 · wood-engraving (after a photograph by Chancellor), NPG; repro. in *ILN* (12 Oct 1878)
Wealth at death under £12,000: probate, 1 Nov 1878, *CGPLA Ire.*

Keon, Miles Gerald (1821–1875), novelist and colonial official, the last male descendant of an old Irish family, was born on 20 February 1821 at Keonbrooke, Leitrim. He was the only son of Myles Gerald Keon (*d.* 1824), a barrister, and Mary Jane (1787–1825), his second wife, who was a daughter of Patrick, Count Magawly, a title bestowed by the kingdom of Sicily. Following the death of his parents, Keon and his younger sister, Ellen Benedicta, were brought up by their maternal grandmother, Countess Magawly, and, after her death, by their uncle, Francis Philip, third Count Magawly, sometime prime minister of Marie Louise in the duchies of Parma, Placentia, and Guastalla.

Keon was educated at the Jesuit Stonyhurst College, which he entered in March 1832. He won many prizes there. He left Stonyhurst in 1839, and after spending some time in France, he crossed to Algeria where he served briefly in the French army. He was admitted to Gray's Inn in 1840, but was never called to the bar. On 21 November 1846 he married Anne de la Pierre Hawkes. They had no children.

For the next twenty years Keon earned his living as a journalist, contributing to *The Tablet* and Colburn's *United Service Magazine*. In 1846 he became editor of *Dolman's Magazine*, and subsequently worked for the *Morning Post* for twelve years. He reported the coronation of Alexander II in St Petersburg in 1856, where he met Boucher de Perthes, who wrote about Keon in *Voyage en Russie* (1859). Keon also wrote a number of popular novels. The most successful was *Dion and the Sibyls: a Romance of the First Century* (1866).

After an unsuccessful short visit to India as editor of *Bengal Hurkaru*, Lord Lytton appointed Keon secretary to the government of Bermuda in March 1859. He served there for the rest of his life. He died on 5 June 1875 at Flatts Village, Hamilton, Bermuda, and was buried at St Edward's Church on the island. Marie-Louise Legg

Sources *Stonyhurst biographical directory*, pt 2 (1826–50) · A. M. Brady and B. Cleeve, eds., *A biographical dictionary of Irish writers*, rev. edn (1985) · *Bermuda Royal Gazette* (8 June 1875) · D. J. O'Donoghue, *The poets of Ireland: a biographical and bibliographical dictionary* (1912); repr. (1970) · J. Foster, *The register of admissions to Gray's Inn, 1521–1889, together with the register of marriages in Gray's Inn chapel, 1695–*

1754 (privately printed, London, 1889) · Burke, *Peerage* (1939) · Gillow, *Lit. biog. hist.*

Archives Herts. ALS, letters to Lord Lytton

Wealth at death £600: administration with will, 4 Nov 1875, *CGPLA Eng. & Wales*

Keper, John (*b. c.*1547?), poet, appears to have been born at Wells, Somerset. He entered Hart Hall, Oxford, in 1564, and graduated BA on 11 February 1569. He was still in residence in the hall in 1572. On 8 July 1580, being then MA of Louvain, he petitioned to be incorporated at Oxford, but the grace was refused, as he was suspected to be a Catholic. Keper's surviving work consists of several lyric poems in three volumes published under the name of Thomas Howell, *The Arbor of Amitie* (1568), *Newe Sonets, and Pretie Pamphlets* (1575?), and *H. his Devises* (1581), in all of which he features as one of Howell's poetic correspondents. It has been conjectured that he was the J.K. who translated from the Italian of Annibale Romei *The Courtiers Academie* (1598), but this seems unlikely.

GORDON GOODWIN, rev. MATTHEW STEGGLE

Sources Foster, *Alum. Oxon.* · *Reg. Oxf.*, 2/1.156, 377; 2/2.29, 35 · Wood, *Ath. Oxon.*, 1st edn · *The poems of Thomas Howell*, ed. A. B. Grosart (1879) · *Thomas Warton's History of English poetry*, ed. D. Fairer, 4 vols. (1998), vol. 3, p. 418 · *Reg. Oxf.*, 1.268 · *Howell's devises, 1581*, ed. W. Raleigh (1906)

Keppel [*née* Edmonstone], **Alice Frederica** (1868–1947), mistress of King Edward VII, was born at Woolwich Dockyard on 29 April 1868, the youngest of the nine children (eight daughters and one son) of William Edmonstone (1810–1888), naval commodore (later admiral), superintendent of Woolwich Dockyard, and later fourth baronet, of Duntreath Castle, Stirlingshire, and his wife, Mary Elizabeth, *née* Parsons (*d.* 1902). Educated at home, Alice early on showed evidence of the beauty, tact, and vivacity for which she was to become renowned. On 1 June 1891 she married George Keppel (1865–1947), third son of William Coutts *Keppel, seventh earl of Albemarle. There were two children: Violet *Trefusis (1894–1972), who later won notoriety for her turbulent love affair with Victoria ('Vita') Sackville-West, and Sonia Rosemary (1900–1986).

Early in 1898 the twenty-nine-year-old Alice Keppel met—and soon became the mistress of—the fifty-six-year-old Albert Edward, prince of Wales [*see* Edward VII]. His accession to the throne in 1901 as King Edward VII in no way diminished her role; not only did she maintain her position as *maîtresse en titre* but she became one of the leading personalities of the Edwardian court, in which environment her daughters were effectively brought up. Throughout the ten years of Edward VII's reign, Mrs Keppel, as she was generally known, was an accepted, respected, and highly visible member of the royal entourage. She often travelled abroad with the court—notably to the king's favourite resort of Biarritz—and remained, in the widely used phrase, 'la favorita'. Her ability to keep the notoriously impatient monarch amused was greatly appreciated in royal and government circles. Baron Hardinge of Penhurst, at that time the permanent undersecretary at the Foreign Office, later paid tribute to her

Alice Frederica Keppel (1868–1947), by Alice Hughes, 1899 [with her daughter Violet Keppel (later Trefusis)]

'excellent influence', notably on occasions when the king was in disagreement with his department:

> … I was able, through her, to advise the king with a view to the policy of Government being accepted … It would have been difficult to have found any other lady who would have filled the part of friend to King Edward with the same loyalty and discretion. (Souhami, 10)

She herself disclaimed the role of royal confidante on constitutional matters; the duchess of Marlborough ascribed the durability of her relationship with the king to shared interests; 'she invariably knew the choicest scandal, the price of stock, the latest political move' (Aronson, 212). She was also an adept card player. Other contemporaries attested to her ability to amuse without malice and to the absence of snobbery from her character; she was, however, fascinated with the power of money and financially astute. She cultivated people like the financier Sir Ernest Cassel and is known to have enriched herself by the sale of shares presented to her by her royal lover.

The widely believed story that as King Edward VII lay dying, his wife, Queen Alexandra, magnanimously sent for Mrs Keppel to take leave of him, is inaccurate. It was much against the will of the queen—who had tolerated the affair in public, but was less forgiving in private—that Alice Keppel saw the dying king, at her own insistence. On being asked to leave the death chamber, she made an embarrassing scene and had to be escorted out; Viscount Esher coldly described it as 'a painful and rather theatrical

exhibition … [which] ought never to have happened'
(Souhami, 91). Afterwards, in an effort to safeguard her
position, Alice claimed that the queen had summoned
her, and promised to look after her in the future. During
the First World War, in which her husband saw active service, Alice Keppel divided her time between entertaining
in her London home, at 16 Grosvenor Street, and staying
in various country houses. She also helped her friend Lady
Sarah Wilson run a hospital for wounded soldiers in Boulogne. In the mid-1920s the Keppels sold their London
house and bought the Villa dell'Ombrellino, Bellos-
guardo, Florence. Celebrated as the ex-mistress of Edward
VII, as an international *grande dame*, and as a matchless
hostess, Alice Keppel reigned like a queen over Florentine
society. During the Second World War the Keppels established themselves at the Ritz Hotel in London. At the end
of the war they returned to the Villa dell'Ombrellino
where Alice died of liver disease on 11 September 1947.
She was buried in a protestant cemetery, I Allori, Florence.
Obituaries made discreet reference to her friendship with
the king and queen; *The Times* recorded her passing as
marking the end of an era, noting obliquely that 'discretion was perhaps her long suit'. George Keppel survived
her by little more than two months, while her devoted
daughter Violet wrote that she had 'lost everything … any
little success I may have is dedicated to her' (Souhami,
290).   THEO ARONSON

Arnold Joost van Keppel, first earl of Albemarle (1669/70–
1718), by Sir Godfrey Kneller, *c.*1700

Sources T. Aronson, *The king in love: Edward VII's mistresses* (1988) ·
W. S. Blunt, diary, FM Cam. · S. Keppel, *Edwardian daughter* (1958) ·
J. Lees-Milne, *The enigmatic Edwardian* (1986) · P. Magnus, *King
Edward VII* (1964) · D. Souhami, *Mrs Keppel and her daughter* (1996) ·
V. Trefusis, *Don't look round* (1952) · R. Lamont-Brown, *Edward VII's
last loves* (1998) · *The last Edwardians: an illustrated history of Violet Tre-
fusis and Alice Keppel*, Boston Athenaeum (1985) · b. cert. · Burke,
Peerage (1924)
Likenesses A. Hughes, double portrait, photograph, 1899, NPG
[*see illus.*] · F. Jenkins, photogravure (after E. Roberts), NPG
Wealth at death £177,637 14s.: probate, 8 March 1948, *CGPLA Eng.
& Wales*

Keppel, Arnold Joost van, first earl of Albemarle
(1669/70–1718), courtier and army officer, was born in
1669 or 1670, probably in Gelderland, United Provinces,
and was probably baptized on 30 January 1670 at Zutphen
in Gelderland, the son of Osewalt van Keppel, lord of
Voorst (d. 1685), and his wife, Reinira Anna Geertruid van
Lintelo tot de Mars. The Keppels were long established in
Gelderland, and were descended from Walter, lord of
Keppel (*fl.* 1179–1223). At his father's death Keppel found
his estates heavily in debt; although he was of high birth,
his prospects would depend on his own abilities.

A page of honour, Keppel accompanied William, prince
of Orange, to England in 1688 and remained with him following his accession to the throne with his wife, Mary II,
in 1689. He came to William's attention in March 1691
when he broke his leg while hunting; William was
impressed with his bravery while the wound was set, and
later that year he appointed him a groom of the bedchamber; he may also have provided funds to redeem the lordship of Voorst from Keppel's creditors. William adopted

Keppel as a protégé. Keppel's outgoing manner made him
many friends, including the king's mistress Elizabeth
Villiers. He emerged as a leading representative of the
younger generation at court and as such William came to
find him more useful than his more withdrawn confidant
William Bentinck, first earl of Portland. After the death of
Mary, Keppel became William's closest companion. In
1695 he was appointed master of the robes and was
installed in a suite communicating with that of William at
Kensington Palace. Although contemporaries and later
writers have inferred a homosexual relationship from this
evidence, this was certainly not the case; William preferred his closest aide to have an adjoining room to his as
his working practices needed his presence well into the
night, and Keppel was renowned for his succession of mistresses. Keppel's loyalty to William was rewarded when
on 10 February 1697 he was created Baron Ashford, Viscount Bury, and earl of Albemarle.

The rise of the apparently frivolous Albemarle infuriated Portland, and Albemarle certainly raised no objections when Portland was sent to Paris as ambassador. Albemarle also used his influence to have John Churchill, earl
of Marlborough, an antagonist of Portland, appointed
governor to William, duke of Gloucester, the only son of
Princess Anne and heir to the British thrones.

In June 1697 Albemarle was made major-general on the
English establishment and appointed colonel of the 1st
troop of Horse Guards (Life Guards), although he sold this
post to Portland in 1710. On 14 May 1700 he was made KG
and became colonel of the first regiment of Swiss in the
Dutch service. The earl later became colonel of the cara-
bineers in the Dutch army, governor of s'Hertogenbosch,

and deputy forester of Holland. In 1701 he married Geertruid Johanna Quirina, the daughter of Adama van der Duyn, lord of St Gravemoer, governor of Bergen op Zoom, and master of buckhounds to the stadholder. There was a son, William Anne *Keppel (1702–1754), and a daughter, Sophia (d. 1773), from the marriage.

Shortly before William III died, and following Louis XIV's seizure of the barrier fortresses in the Spanish Netherlands, promised to the United Provinces at the treaty of Ryswick (1697), Albemarle was sent to the Netherlands to confer with the states general on future strategy against France. This delicate mission was accomplished with great skill, and Albemarle confirmed his friendship with Marlborough during this period. He was at William's side at his deathbed in March 1702, and the king is reputed to have whispered 'You know what to do with them' as he handed him the keys to his private cabinet and drawers. William bequeathed to his favourite 200,000 guilders and the lordship of Breevorst, although legal arguments about this last bequest with members of William's family went on for some years.

Albemarle returned to the Netherlands in 1702, and as a general of horse in the Dutch army had an active part in the duke of Marlborough's campaigns in the Low Countries during the War of the Spanish Succession. In 1703 he was entrusted with the command of a major convoy bringing supplies to the allied forces at Maastricht, and brought off a difficult task with great ability. Marlborough stayed at Albemarle's house just before the march to the Danube began in 1704, an indication of the friendship between the two men. Albemarle was present at the forcing of the lines of Brabant in 1705, and correctly urged an active pursuit of the beaten French and Bavarians, against the wishes of his fellow Dutch commanders. He also fought at Ramillies (1706) and Oudenarde (1708). During the protracted siege of Lille (1708) Marlborough employed him with thirty squadrons of cavalry to cover the progress of a great convoy bringing supplies to the allied siege train from Brussels. The success of this hazardous enterprise, in the face of two powerful French armies, was largely on account of the earl's skilful conduct. In 1709 he was made governor of Tournai, after which he was actively engaged at the sieges of Bouchain and Aire (1711). Following Marlborough's dismissal he was in command of the allied garrison at Denain, when the fortress was stormed by Marshal Villars (24 March 1712). Despite a strenuous defence the Dutch troops were overwhelmed and the earl was taken prisoner. However, he was released soon afterwards; that winter he entertained Prince Eugene of Savoy at his house.

On the death of Queen Anne in 1714 Albemarle was sent by the states general to George I with congratulations on his accession to the throne of Great Britain. He was entrusted with the reception of the king and his entourage at the Dutch border en route for London. Albemarle died at The Hague on 30 May 1718 and was succeeded by his son, William Anne, as second earl. His widow died in December 1741 at The Hague.

Albemarle, who enjoyed a generally wide popularity, was described as a generous and charming man, but was rather absorbed in his own pleasures in youth. William III was very taken with his good looks and fine manners, though more importantly recognized his emerging talents as an administrator and an officer. His early role as royal favourite has overshadowed his undoubted ability as a military commander. This quality, while perhaps not of the first rank, enabled Marlborough to employ Albemarle on important tasks requiring high capability and judgement.　　　　　　　　　　　　　　　　　　　JAMES FALKNER

Sources DNB · Letters and dispatches of John Churchill, ed. G. Murray (1845) · English army commission lists and registers, 1661–1714, ed. C. Dalton (1904) · N. A. Robb, William of Orange, 2 vols. (1966), vol. 2 · S. B. Baxter, William III (1966) · W. S. Churchill, Life and times of Marlborough (1948) · T. B. Macaulay, The history of England from the accession of James II, abridged edn, 2 (1889) · E. Gregg, Queen Anne (1980) · H. Chapman, Queen Anne's son (1954) · D. Chandler, Marlborough as military commander (1973) · N. Henderson, Prince Eugen of Savoy (1964) · J. Kenyon, Robert Spencer, earl of Sunderland (1958) · IGI

Archives BL, letters to earl of Strafford, ADD. MS 22211 · BL, papers incl. letters to William II, Add. MSS 63629–63630 · Longleat House, Wiltshire, corresp. with Matthew Prior · Suffolk RO, Ipswich, corresp. and papers

Likenesses G. Kneller, oils, c.1700, NPG [see illus.] · G. Kneller, oils, 1702, Chatsworth House, Derbyshire · by or after G. Kneller, oils, Woburn Abbey, Bedfordshire · J. Smith, mezzotint (after oil painting, Woburn Abbey), BM, NPG

Keppel, Augustus, Viscount Keppel (1725–1786), naval officer and politician, second son of William Anne *Keppel, second earl of Albemarle (1702–1754), and his wife, Anne (1703–1789), second daughter of Charles *Lennox, first duke of Richmond, was born on 25 April 1725. His family were prominent whigs, and this background would prove highly significant for Keppel's future career.

Early naval career In 1735 Keppel left Westminster School and, when aged ten, entered the navy on board the Oxford and served for two years on the coast of Guinea. There followed three years in the Mediterranean with Commodore Clinton in the Gloucester. Back in England, he moved in 1740 to the Prince Frederick and then to the Centurion (60 guns) with Commodore George Anson on his famous voyage of circumnavigation. Keppel was active in the various landings and captures, including that of the treasure-laden Acapulco galleon. Anson, his ever approving and influential patron, made him an acting lieutenant. On the Centurion's return to England in 1744, Keppel passed his lieutenant's examination on 25 July and was at once confirmed in that rank. Scurvy had deprived him of many teeth and much hair, but he was fit enough to join the Dreadnought on 11 August. On 7 November he was made commander of the sloop Wolf, and on 11 December, when aged nineteen, he was posted to the frigate Greyhound.

In February 1745 Keppel shifted to the Sapphire (40 guns) and cruised off the south of Ireland with some success. From November he commanded the Maidstone (50 guns) and cruised for over a year in the soundings and the Bay of Biscay. Frustrated near Belle Île by the escape of some small French vessels, Keppel, on 29 June 1747, pursued a large one. He ran onto hidden rocks and the Maidstone was wrecked. Having, with most of his crew, been rescued and

Augustus Keppel, Viscount Keppel (1725–1786), by Sir Joshua Reynolds, 1752–3

made prisoner by the French, Keppel wrote with a patrician's easy assurance to Maurepas, the French navy minister, and was politely transported back to England, where he was exchanged. His men also soon returned. On 31 October a court martial acquitted Keppel of blame for the loss of his ship. Meanwhile the *Anson* (60 guns) was being built at Bursledon and in November Keppel was formally appointed to her. Until 21 December he sat on the court martial of Captain Thomas Fox, who had shown inadequate aggression on 14 October 1747. Edward Hawke's victory left few pickings for such as Keppel when cruising with that admiral in 1748.

After peace was concluded in October, Keppel was specially favoured by being appointed in 1749, when aged twenty-four, as commodore commanding in the Mediterranean. He was to apply judicious pressure to the dey of Algiers, ruler of a port that had long been a nest of piratical activity. Wearing his broad pennant in the *Centurion* (now reduced to 50 guns), Keppel took with him a youthful Joshua Reynolds—an act of patronage very welcome at that early stage of the painter's career. He sailed in July, and during the next two years visited Lisbon, Cadiz, Gibraltar, Algiers, and Mahon; and Reynolds wrote to Lord

Edgecumbe: 'I have had the use of his cabin and his study of books, as if they were my own' (Keppel, 1.148). Eventually Keppel concluded an agreement with the dey protective of British commerce. Having also negotiated treaties at Tripoli and Tunis, he returned to England in July 1751.

In 1754 the slide towards a new French war saw Keppel again appointed as a commodore. In February 1755, with the *Centurion* and the *Norwich*, he took General Edward Braddock's transports into Hampton Roads. Late in July he was superseded due to Vice-Admiral Edward Boscawen's arrival on the American coast and on 22 August he returned to England with news of Braddock's defeat and death. Four days later he was ordered to commission the *Swiftsure* of 70 guns. It was in 1755 that he was elected an MP for Chichester, a seat vacated by his elder brother, George *Keppel, on succeeding as third earl of Albemarle.

In June 1756 Keppel moved to the *Torbay* (74 guns), his favourite ship, in which he remained until 1761. By then he was established as one of the most popular and best-regarded captains in the navy—affectionately called 'little Keppel' by the sailors (Keppel, 2.235). There was, wrote Boscawen, 'no better seaman than Keppel, few so good, and not a better officer' (Rodger, *Wooden World*, 260). Meanwhile, having commanded a small squadron off Cape Finisterre and taken three French prizes, he returned in December to Spithead. In January he sat as a member of John Byng's court martial. Surprised by the ineffectiveness of the court's recommendation to mercy, he tried, ultimately without success, to persuade parliament to intervene. On 24 June 1757 he sailed with Boscawen and, having been detached with the *Medway* (60 guns), took a rich prize. In September he took part in the disappointing Rochefort expedition. Nothing that Admiral Hawke and the fleet could do succeeded in persuading the army to land. Again under Hawke, in March 1758 Keppel participated in his foray into the Basque Roads. Later that year he was with the fleet under Anson. In September he was appointed to command the naval side of a joint expedition to Goree, a French settlement of some strategic significance on the west African coast. On 29 December Goree was duly taken.

From May 1759 Keppel participated in Hawke's strategically crucial blockade of Brest, following which the *Torbay* was prominent at the conclusive battle of Quiberon Bay, fought on 20 November in a forty-knot gale. Under attack by the *Torbay*, the *Thesée*, also of 74 guns, foundered with horrifying abruptness. True to what Keppel deemed a very 'English' penchant for 'humanity and pity' (Keppel, 1.446), he immediately hoisted out boats and, despite the perilous conditions, a number of French lives were saved.

The fleet at Brest having been reduced to a remnant, Keppel was in March 1761 chosen to command the naval part of a major joint expedition to take Belle Île. Wearing his broad pennant in the *Valiant* (74 guns), he had his protégé Adam Duncan with him as flag captain. By June the operations had been crowned with success, relations between army and navy—so frequently difficult—having been notably good. Keppel continued to command off Brest and Belle Île until January 1762. Now, with Spain entering the war on the side of France, the cabinet decided to attack Havana. The preliminary planning was done by Anson. Admiral George Pocock was the naval commander and Keppel's elder brother, Lord Albemarle, commanded the army. Augustus Keppel was appointed as commodore and naval second in command. Though rightly dubious about Captain Augustus Hervey's proposal to bombard the fortress El Morro from the sea, Keppel gave solid support. The fortress was taken after six weeks of hard fighting, before yellow fever quite prevailed. On 11 August Havana itself surrendered. The three Keppels—Albemarle, Augustus, and Major-General William—were hugely enriched by their share of the enormous prize money. The commodore received nearly £25,000. However, his health had suffered severely. Overall, the enterprise has been rated a masterpiece of planning, amphibious warfare, and naval prowess. On 21 October 1762 a promotion of captains to flag rank was extended to include Keppel, who at thirty-seven became a rear-admiral of the blue. He remained in command at Jamaica until January 1764 and did not reach England until June.

Political admiral, 1765–1778 By 1765 Keppel, who was an MP for Windsor from 1761 to 1780, had become actively involved in politics. Together with his able cousin, the duke of Richmond, and his friend and legatee Vice-Admiral Sir Charles Saunders, he was attached to the opposition leader, the marquess of Rockingham. In Rockingham's first administration (July 1765 to July 1766) Saunders and Keppel were naval lords at the Admiralty, and when Grafton succeeded Rockingham at the Treasury Saunders became first lord with Keppel now a senior commissioner. Keppel saw the need to improve Portsmouth Dockyard before any new conflict with France and Spain. However, on 27 November, to the king's understandable displeasure, Saunders and Keppel both resigned over the dismissal of Rear-Admiral Lord Edgecumbe, a fellow Rockingham whig, as groom of the bedchamber. While valued primarily for his naval knowledge and reputation, Keppel had become, by 1767, a leading member of the Rockingham faction.

From October 1770 until January 1771 war with France and Spain threatened over the Falkland Islands and Keppel, having been promoted on 18 October 1770 to rear-admiral of the red, was again promoted on the 24th to vice-admiral of the blue, apparently with a view to his commanding the Channel Fleet. However, this did not silence Saunders and Keppel in their parliamentary criticisms of the Admiralty. With Lord Sandwich establishing himself ever more firmly as first lord of the Admiralty in Lord North's administration, Keppel's adherence to the opposition left him awkwardly placed as an admiral should war supervene. In November 1776 the king did ask him, as the obvious candidate (and a vice-admiral of the red since February), to be ready to command the fleet. His cousin Richmond warned Keppel that, however unfairly, blame for any subsequent naval reverse might be laid on

him. The fact that the Rockinghams publicly sympathized with the rebellion of the American colonists did not endear them to the king and his ministers. The matter of Keppel's health also deserves notice. He seems never to have fully recovered from the fevers of Havana. His illnesses are mentioned in letters of 1765 and 1772; and in 1776 Keppel tells Rockingham that, having endured 'torments' from prolonged recourse to the waters of Spa, he is thankful to revert to his 'usual degree of pain' (Keppel, 1.425).

The battle of Ushant, 1778 By early 1778 France and Spain were ready to go to war. Britain, on the other hand, was burdened with heavy American commitments. As Keppel and Richmond had remarked in parliament, these commitments had left the British holding no fleet manoeuvres, whereas the French and Spanish had exercised ships of the line together. The allies, moreover, had overwhelming numbers of ships, many of them ready to fight. Privately, Sandwich and the Admiralty found the situation alarming.

Keppel, having been promoted on 29 January to admiral of the blue, was appointed on 18 March to command the Grand Fleet. Writing to Lord Rockingham, Keppel hoped that his indifferent health would permit him to rise to the unpromising situation. It is a sign of Keppel's continuing naval expertise that he had already, on the 10th, asked for the 42-pound guns on the lower deck of his assigned flagship, the *Victory*, to be replaced by 32-pounders.

On 24 March Keppel went down to Portsmouth and hoisted his flag. He found only six ships of the line, instead of the promised thirty-five, ready for the sea. Men, stores, and provisions were deficient. By May, however, a considerable force had been assembled, but early in June, to the detriment of the Channel Fleet, thirteen of the line were sent away to New York. Meanwhile Keppel had closely questioned Sandwich about the strategic options likely to confront him. The Admiralty's guidance was issued in secret instructions dated 25 April. If, for example, Keppel discovered that the Brest squadron was superior to his, he was to fight if the superiority in numbers was not very apparent. However, should the enemy fleet, whether at sea or in port, prove manifestly superior, he was to retire to St Helens, where reinforcements would be gathering. Again, since neither France nor Spain had actually declared war, Keppel was not to attack their shipping if it was innocuous.

On 13 June Keppel sailed towards Brest with twenty-one of the line. Two French frigates precipitated a brush and the French government dated hostilities from 17 June. From prisoners taken, Keppel concluded that thirty-two ships of the line were ready for sea at Brest and he therefore fell back to St Helens, as instructed. Angry merchants blamed the unreadiness of the Admiralty.

Keppel sailed again on 9 July and by the 11th he had thirty ships of the line. In the *Victory* (100 guns) his estimable old friend Rear-Admiral John Campbell was, at his own request, Keppel's first captain. Robert Harland, a captain under Hawke on 14 October 1747 and now a vice-admiral of the blue, commanded the van division. In command of the rear division was a more junior vice-admiral of the blue, Sir Hugh Palliser. He was a highly competent officer who had been controller of the navy and knew well its material strength and weaknesses. Less fortunate, certainly from Keppel's viewpoint, was Palliser's membership, latterly as senior naval lord, of Sandwich's Board of Admiralty. Should a reverse be suffered, the potential for recrimination was considerable.

On 8 July the French fleet had issued from Brest under the command of the comte d'Orvilliers, furnished with vacillating instructions which induced caution. Owing to thick weather, it was not until the 23rd that d'Orvilliers sighted the British line. Overnight he passed ahead of it to gain the weather gauge, but during the manoeuvre two of his ships became separated to leeward and had to go into Brest. Now he also had thirty of the line and some frigates.

Having been foiled by d'Orvilliers's nocturnal manoeuvre, Keppel had to work from leeward, in foggy, squally, unsettled weather, to close on his enemy. He knew that nothing short of a decisive naval victory could wrest the strategic initiative from the Bourbon powers. On 27 July, with the wind continuing west-south-west, both fleets stood to the north-west. Endeavouring to converge on the now visible French, Keppel, somewhat like Hawke in November 1759, hoisted the general chase signal early in the day. At 9 a.m. the French wore in succession so that their admiral, by closing the gap, could see Keppel's chasing fleet more clearly. Towards 10 a.m. the wind backed southwards by two points (22°), affording Keppel a better chance of closing. Soon afterwards he tacked, still without signalling a line of battle, so as to close on the rear of the enemy. In a squall of rain, the wind veered, making it easier for the British to get within range. Meanwhile, however, hidden in the rain, d'Orvilliers realized that action could no longer be avoided. He again changed course so that the two fleets were now heading towards each other on opposite tacks. D'Orvilliers had thus adroitly avoided Keppel's threatened concentration on his rear. Having at last converged close enough to be able to engage his elusive enemy, Keppel, who had avoided the loss of time consequent on signalling a line of battle, did not hoist that signal now. Improving on Thomas Mathews's notorious failure to cope with a somewhat similar situation in 1744, he simply hoisted the flag to engage. The two fleets, very roughly in a line, but with the French in somewhat better order, approached each other with the French further off the wind (still at west-south-west) than the British, so that Harland's van division was further from the enemy than was Palliser's rear division. Palliser's ships and some of Keppel's, including the *Victory*, therefore received successively the fire of most of the French fleet. Five British ships were crippled and fell away to leeward.

At 1 p.m. d'Orvilliers, having passed clear of the British, signalled to wear in succession, so that, by standing southward, he could engage Keppel, also now standing south, from leeward. Keppel manoeuvred to cover his crippled ships. With a view to counter-attacking the enemy, he signalled for Palliser to come to his support. Palliser's division, endeavouring to repair the considerable damage suffered, was lying to, having by then fallen astern and to windward of Keppel's centre division. Palliser afterwards claimed that the signal was hidden from him. Keppel may well have expressed frustration at the time. He sent a frigate to communicate with Palliser by speaking-trumpet, a fact tellingly (if one-sidedly) confirmed at Keppel's trial. Anyhow, the incident had no bearing on the outcome of the action because d'Orvilliers, having had trouble with his own communications, abandoned his chance to attack Keppel's ships from leeward. D'Orvilliers had had the best of it in terms of manoeuvre and damage to the mobility of the British. He had denied Keppel the decisive victory that could have given Britain the strategic initiative in the war. D'Orvilliers therefore retired to Brest to make good his damages. Because the British, as was their habit, had concentrated their fire on the hulls rather than the masts of their enemy, the French casualties were somewhat heavier—according to John Creswell 163 killed and 573 wounded against 133 killed and 375 wounded in Keppel's fleet. But British hulls had also suffered. The hull of Palliser's flagship, the *Formidable* (90 guns), suffered more than seventy shot-holes, five of them under water.

On 29 July Keppel wrote to Sandwich, with whom he had maintained quite good relations (as indeed he had with Palliser): 'The object of the French was at our masts and rigging, and they have crippled the fleet in that respect beyond any degree I ever saw' (*Private Papers of … Sandwich*, 2.128). Light is thrown on the improved gunnery of the French by Palliser's letter to Sandwich of 10 August, in which he says that the French gunners were more effective than numbers of their often little-trained British counterparts, owing to the French corps of seaman gunners (established in 1767). Palliser also complained of the incomplete work of the Ordnance department when preparing the fleet for sea.

At the battle of Ushant, given that he did not enjoy that clear-cut ship-for-ship superiority that he and most British admirals of the century had been wont to assume, Keppel had, considering his continuing poor health, behaved with obvious spirit. Remembering also some disadvantage by way of previous fleet exercises, his tactical handling of the action against a skilful, evasive foe may be rated as more than adequate.

The Keppel–Palliser affair In August Keppel wrote to Sandwich praising the efforts of all his admirals in getting the fleet ready to sail again from Portsmouth. Keppel, hoping for a more conclusive encounter with the French, sailed again with the fleet on 23 August. He cruised off Ushant without achieving contact with the French. Meanwhile, by 28 October when he returned to Spithead, the fuse for the Keppel–Palliser affair had been lit. An account of Keppel's frustration at the time of Palliser's failure or inability to respond to his signals during the afternoon of the battle had appeared in a newspaper. The sensitive Palliser prepared a laudatory and exculpatory letter for Keppel to sign for publication. This Keppel refused to do.

More papers took up the story, which received mention in the House of Commons. On 9 December Palliser presented to the Board of Admiralty, of which he was still a member, a demand for Keppel's court martial—a demand disastrous for his own career and damaging to the cohesion of the navy.

With Sandwich and the government coming under attack, the Admiralty was perhaps over-prompt in immediately issuing orders for Keppel to be tried. The opposition was much incensed, as indeed were most of the officers in the navy. The five rather absurd but capital charges held that Keppel had improperly and half-heartedly marshalled his fleet, approached the fight in a manner unbecoming an officer, shown undue haste in quitting the conflict, run away from the scene, and failed to pursue the enemy. Until this point the relationship between Keppel and Sandwich had been maintained on a very reasonable footing. Now, at a blow, that mistrust of Sandwich previously expressed to Keppel by such as Richmond was apparently justified. Horace Walpole, himself an opposition whig, makes the most of the affair. Richmond had recently again been hounding Sandwich in parliament. Therefore (writes Walpole) Sandwich, who had been 'cunning' and 'treacherous' towards Wilkes, 'could not resist the impulse of attacking Keppel with the same arms'—that admiral being 'cousin-german and dear friend' of Richmond. In the Commons on 12 December Temple Luttrell moved for Palliser (also an MP) to be court-martialled himself 'for disobedience of signals'. Palliser, for his part, explained that he had waited for five months before charging Keppel because it was only the other day that Keppel 'had declared that he would serve with him no more'. Keppel himself spoke 'with a mixture of pathetic modesty and sublime dignity'. He said that the 'charges attacked both his life and his fame' and he called for the trial 'to clear both, though he lamented the mischiefs' that it might occasion. His 'few sentences were littered with so much majesty and grace that the House melted into tears' (*Last Journals of Horace Walpole*, 2.222–5). Most naval officers, with the venerable Lord Hawke at their head, expressed outrage at the decision to have Keppel tried.

On 9 January 1779 the court martial began at Portsmouth and continued for five weeks. Thirty captains, some lieutenants, and several masters testified. Together with the admirals Harland and Campbell, nearly all the witnesses (with Captain John Jervis particularly effective) refuted the charges to the noisy satisfaction of Keppel's relatives, friends, and political allies who attended each day in his support. Among them were the marquess of Rockingham, two royal dukes, Richmond and two other dukes, and Keppel's second cousin Charles James Fox, together with Richard Brinsley Sheridan and Edmund Burke. During the trial Palliser's manner was 'poor and passionate', while Keppel's was 'cool', 'temperate and modest'. 'Keppel stood to hear his own praises sounded higher even than he had grounds to expect; Palliser saw himself the opprobrium and outcast of his profession' (*Last Journals of Horace Walpole*, 2.245). On 11 February the court pronounced the charges malicious and unfounded. That evening there were riotous celebrations in London and elsewhere. Popular resentment was vented on Palliser's London house and on the gates of the Admiralty. Keppel became a national hero. Palliser had soon to face his own court martial. Though exonerated, he lost all his appointments.

Later years Keppel, whose health had not improved, declined in any case to serve again under Sandwich, and some other flag officers made similar damaging gestures. Although dissension in the service persisted for a time, Keppel began to lose some of his popularity as he continued, despite the war, to denounce the administration. In 1780 Rockingham fruitlessly nominated Keppel (from September MP for Surrey) as first lord of the Admiralty. Finally the news of Yorktown led to Rockingham's second administration and, in March 1782, Keppel became first lord. Having been on 8 April promoted admiral of the white, on 26 April he was raised to the peerage by an unenthusiastic George III as Viscount Keppel and Baron Elden. In office Keppel accomplished little of note. He appointed some of his strong supporters, such as Samuel Barrington and Hyde Parker, to important seagoing commands and gave Harland a seat at the Admiralty. His decision to replace Rodney with Admiral Hugh Pigot proved embarrassing when news soon afterwards arrived of Rodney's victory at the Saints. Despite his diplomatic skills, he found, like other first lords, that he could not work well with that indispensable controller of the navy Charles Middleton. After Rockingham died in April, Keppel remained uncomfortably in Shelburne's administration. Unhappy with the peace preliminaries, he resigned in December, and was replaced at the Admiralty by Lord Howe. From April 1783 he was again first lord until the Fox–North coalition was dismissed in December.

Keppel quite cheerfully bore worsening infirmities until he died on 2 October 1786. He had never married, though he apparently kept mistresses, for instance in 1758 and 1763. His title died with him. Small in stature, with a nose permanently dented by a blow received early on from a footpad, he left an indelible impression of cheerful agreeability and charm, coupled with an underlying firmness in getting his way. By 1778, however, he was corpulent and—often with good reason—more inclined to gloom. Up to 1762 his naval career, especially in combined operations, had been outstanding. Thereafter his political interests complicated and tended to limit his naval achievements.

RUDDOCK MACKAY

Sources T. R. Keppel, *The life of Augustus, Viscount Keppel*, 2 vols. (1842) • GEC, *Peerage* • DNB • *The private papers of John, earl of Sandwich*, ed. G. R. Barnes and J. H. Owen, 4 vols., Navy RS, 69, 71, 75, 78 (1932–8) • J. Creswell, *British admirals of the eighteenth century: tactics in battle* (1972) • B. Tunstall, *Naval warfare in the age of sail: the evolution of fighting tactics, 1650–1815*, ed. N. Tracy (1990) • N. A. M. Rodger, *The wooden world: an anatomy of the Georgian navy* (1986) • N. A. M. Rodger, *The insatiable earl: a life of John Montagu, fourth earl of Sandwich* (1993) • R. F. Mackay, *Admiral Hawke* (1965) • D. Syrett, ed., *The siege and capture of Havana, 1762*, Navy RS, 114 (1970) • *The last journals of Horace Walpole*, ed. Dr Doran, rev. A. F. Steuart, 2 vols. (1910) • E. H.

Jenkins, *A history of the French navy* (1973) · P. Langford, *The first Rock-ingham administration, 1765–1766* (1973) · N. Tracy, *Navies, deterrence and American independence* (1988)

Archives NMM, corresp. and papers · Suffolk RO, Ipswich, naval corresp. and papers · U. Mich., Clements L., official reports | BL, letters to Lord Anson, Add. MS 15956 · BL, corresp. with duke of Newcastle, Add. MSS 32726–33071 · Bodl. Oxf., letters to Lord Shelburne, MSS film dep. 961–1005 · Hunt. L., letters to Sir George Pocock · NMM, letters to duke of Portland · NMM, Lord Rosse's (Hawke) MSS [microfilm] · NMM, corresp. with Lord Sandwich · PRO, Admiralty records · PRO, letters to Lord Rodney, boxes 12, 26 · Sheff. Arch., corresp. with Edmund Burke · Sheff. Arch., letters to Lord Rockingham · W. Yorks. AS, Leeds, corresp. with Lady Rockingham

Likenesses portrait, 18th cent. (after Fisher; after Reynolds), Walmer Castle, Kent · J. Reynolds, oils, 1749, NMM · J. Reynolds, oils, 1752–3, NMM [*see illus.*] · J. Reynolds, oils, 1759, Woburn Abbey, Bedfordshire · J. Reynolds, portrait, *c.*1762–1764, NMM · J. Reynolds, oils, 1764, NPG · J. Ceracchi, marble bust, 1777, Belvoir Castle, Leicestershire · W. Dickinson, mezzotint, pubd 1779 (after G. Romney), BM, NPG · studio of Reynolds, oils, 1779, NPG · J. Reynolds, portrait, 1780, Tate collection · J. Sayers, two caricatures, etchings, pubd 1784, NPG · J. Reynolds, portrait, 1785, Royal Collection · J. Chapman, stipple, pubd 1800 (after J. Reynolds), BM, NPG · J. Scott, mezzotint, pubd 1863 (after J. Reynolds), BM, NPG · J. Caldwall, mezzotint (after J. Tassie), BM, NPG · E. Fisher, mezzotint (after J. Reynolds), BM, NPG · G. Romney, oils, Goodwood, West Sussex · J. Tassie, medallion, BM; plaster replica, Scot. NPG · J. Tassie, medallions, priv. coll.; plaster replicas, 1779, Scot. NPG · mezzotints (after unknown artists), BM, NPG · mezzotints (after J. Reynolds), BM, NPG

Wealth at death very considerable: *DNB*; Keppel, *Life of Augustus Viscount Keppel*; Syrett, ed., *Siege and capture of Havana*

Frederick Keppel (1729–1777), by unknown artist, *c.*1765

Keppel, Frederick (1729–1777), bishop of Exeter, was born on 30 January 1729, the fourth son of William Anne *Keppel, second earl of Albemarle (1702–1754), and his wife, Anne (1703–1789), daughter of Charles Lennox, first duke of Richmond. He was educated at Westminster School and at Christ Church, Oxford, where he graduated BA in 1752, MA in 1754, and DD by diploma on 19 October 1762. One of fifteen children, Keppel sought a career in the church rather than following his brothers into the armed forces and was ordained in February 1753. He married, on 13 September 1758, Laura (1734–1813), eldest natural daughter of Sir Edward Walpole, who in 1784 left her Lacy House, Isleworth, and most of his fortune. The marriage produced one son and three daughters.

Though regarded as an able preacher, Keppel's rise in the church probably owed more to the royal connections of his eldest brother, the third earl of Albemarle, who was a protégé of the duke of Cumberland and a favourite of George II. Keppel's career shows that the support of the duke of Newcastle was not always necessary to success in the mid-eighteenth-century church. He was a chaplain-in-ordinary to both George II and George III, and was appointed by the former to a canonry at Windsor (19 April 1754), despite Newcastle's objection that he was too young. Through his wife Keppel also had close connections to the Walpoles and the Waldegraves.

Keppel's father-in-law, Sir Edward Walpole, wrote to William Pitt the elder in August 1761, asking whether it was 'agreeable to him to make Mr. Keppel a bishop at this juncture' (*Correspondence of William Pitt*, 2.134–5), and

although this application was unsuccessful he was consecrated bishop of Exeter on 8 November 1762. Though it was rumoured that the preferment was bestowed upon him on account of Albemarle's capture of Havana, Horace Walpole, his uncle by marriage, maintained that the see was promised to him the day before the news came. He also held *in commendam* the archdeaconry of Exeter and a prebendal stall in that cathedral, and obtained the promise of translation to the more lucrative bishopric of Salisbury on the next vacancy. In 1765 he relinquished this promise for the deanery of Windsor, to which he was appointed, with the registrarship of the Order of the Garter. Augustus Hervey commented, 'all things are crowded into three or four people's pockets' (Smith, 3.91).

Despite his pluralism, Keppel was an attentive diocesan who gained a reputation for generosity. In 1764 he confirmed almost 24,000 on his first visitation tour. He spent large sums of money improving the episcopal palace at Exeter and in relieving the needs of the poorer clergy in his diocese. Polwhele praised his distribution of patronage, and the philologist Jonathan Toup was among those he promoted.

Keppel was an active member of the House of Lords, especially through 1770, generally following the lead of his brothers, who were allied with the Rockingham whigs from 1765. Keppel thus spent most of his parliamentary career in opposition. Though he seldom spoke, he subscribed to five protests between 1767 and 1775, and often voted against the ministry. In March 1776 he preached a sermon before George III advocating peace with America, and on his deathbed he 'thanked God that he had not given one vote for shedding American blood' (*Last Journals of Horace Walpole*, 2.86). He died at the deanery, Windsor, on 27 December 1777 of 'dropsy of the stomach' (*London Chronicle*) and was buried on 2 January 1778 in St George's Chapel, Windsor. Keppel published little: a set of verses as part of his university's collection of poems on the death of the prince of Wales in 1751 and two sermons. Historiographically, however, he made a major contribution to the study of his era by copying and editing the manuscript memoir of the second Earl Waldegrave, which was entrusted to him by his sister-in-law. It was subsequently published in 1821.

W. P. COURTNEY, *rev.* WILLIAM C. LOWE

Sources A. Warne, *Church and society in eighteenth century Devon* (1969) · Walpole, *Corr.* · N. Sykes, *Church and state in England in the XVIII century* (1934) · *The memoirs and speeches of James, 2nd Earl Waldegrave, 1742–1763*, ed. J. C. D. Clark (1988) · G. Oliver, *Lives of the bishops of Exeter, and a history of the cathedral* (1861) · *The last journals of Horace Walpole*, ed. Dr Doran, rev. A. F. Steuart, 2 vols. (1910) · R. Polwhele, *The history of Devonshire*, 3 vols. (1793–1806) · C. J. Abbey, *The English church and its bishops, 1700–1800*, 2 vols. (1887) · *Correspondence of William Pitt, earl of Chatham*, ed. W. S. Taylor and J. H. Pringle, 4 vols. (1838–40) · *The Grenville papers: being the correspondence of Richard Grenville … and … George Grenville*, ed. W. J. Smith, 4 vols. (1852–3) · GEC, *Peerage* · *London Chronicle* (30 Dec 1777–1 Jan 1778) · Yale U., Lewis Walpole Library, Keppel MSS · portrait, bishop's palace, Exeter

Archives Yale Library, Farmington, Lewis Walpole Library, letters | BL, Newcastle MSS, Add. MSS 32968–32970 · Devon RO, visitation returns

Likenesses portrait, *c.*1765, bishop's palace, Exeter [*see illus.*]

Wealth at death 'immeasurably in debt', owing tailor £1000 and brother £5000: John Baker, *Diary* (1931), 448, quoted in Walpole, *Corr.*, 32.411n. · see of Exeter valued at approx. £1500 p.a., 1762; deanery of Windsor £900: *Correspondence of King George the Third*, ed. J. Fortescue, 6 vols. (1927–8), 1.33–7

Keppel, George, third earl of Albemarle (1724–1772), army officer and politician, was born on 5 April 1724, the eldest son of William Anne *Keppel, second earl of Albemarle (1702–1754), and his wife, Anne (1703–1789), daughter of Charles *Lennox, first duke of Richmond. Viscount Bury, as he was styled until succeeding his father in 1754, was educated at Westminster School from 1732 to 1740.

Bury followed his father—a notorious spendthrift who left little but debts—into a military career. He made effective use of family connections and his friendship with William, duke of Cumberland, George II's favourite son, whom he had met at Westminster. Entering the Coldstream Guards in 1738 as an ensign, he was a lieutenant-colonel by the time he served as one of Cumberland's aides-de-camp at Fontenoy (1745). At Culloden (1746) he drew the first shots of the battle when Cumberland ordered him forward to reconnoitre the Jacobite artillery; later he was almost killed when the finery of his uniform led an errant highlander to mistake him for the duke and narrowly miss at close range. Bury had the honour of carrying the news of the victory to George II. Bury's career continued to prosper. His uncle, Charles *Lennox, second duke of Richmond, returned him to parliament for Chichester in 1746, but he showed little interest in the Commons and continued to rise in the army. He became colonel of the 20th foot (1749), major-general (1756),

lieutenant-general (1759), colonel of the King's Own dragoons (1755), and privy councillor and governor of Jersey (1761). A lord of the bedchamber to Cumberland from 1746, his loyalty to his patron was fierce.

In 1760 Albemarle (as he had become in 1754) accepted a challenge from General George Townshend that arose in part from the latter's caricatures of the duke (the duel was averted by the intervention of another officer). After Cumberland died in 1765, Albemarle was named his executor by George III who instructed him to 'destroy everything that his uncle … might have desired to keep concealed' (Whitworth, 238). To the regret of later historians Albemarle effectively culled the duke's papers of politically sensitive material.

Albemarle's success at advancing his military career through connections at court drew criticism from some contemporaries. Wolfe lumped him with his father as 'showy men who are seen in palaces and the courts of Kings … They have a way of trifling with us poor soldiers that gives many honest, poor men high disgust' (Wright, 185–6). Horace Walpole characterized him as 'ambitious, greedy, and a dexterous courtier' (Walpole, 2.221).

During the Seven Years' War Albemarle declined offers to command the St Malo and Martinique expeditions. In 1762 he accepted command of the land forces sent to take Havana. The expedition also included his brothers Augustus *Keppel, second in command of the naval forces, and William, a major-general in the army. Albemarle organized a successful landing on 7 June 1762 and forced Havana's surrender on 12 August, though some historians have criticized the slowness that resulted from his reliance on conventional siege warfare. While losing relatively few men to Spanish arms, Albemarle suffered near crippling losses from disease: of 5366 men lost by the army (whose total strength was about 16,000) from 7 June to 9 October 1762, 4708 died from disease. Though Cuba was usefully exchanged for the Floridas in the peace settlement, the losses incurred greatly reduced the manpower available to meet the challenge of Pontiac's rising in North America in 1763–4. This experience probably contributed to the decision to maintain a larger military establishment in the colonies and to seek new sources of revenue to support it. Albemarle's subsequent governorship of Cuba proved controversial. He deported the bishop of Havana for non-co-operation and provoked criticism from merchants who complained (with reason) that he imposed illegal taxes on them. Albemarle himself received more than £122,000 in prize money. In recognition of his triumph George III awarded him the Garter in 1765.

After his return from Cuba, Albemarle became increasingly involved in politics. As Cumberland re-emerged as a figure of importance in the early part of George III's reign, Albemarle frequently acted as his point of contact with the political world and followed his patron into supporting the first Rockingham administration in 1765. After Cumberland's death Albemarle gave his allegiance to the Rockingham whigs and went into opposition with them in 1766. Albemarle was generally regarded as one of the party leaders, though his efforts to foster a union in 1766–7 with the duke of Bedford's followers failed. He never fully recovered his health after his return from Cuba, and his political involvement in his later years was limited by periodic bouts of ill health. Perhaps his greatest contribution to his party was to bring his brother Admiral Augustus Keppel into its ranks. His brother's court martial and acquittal in 1779 made him one of the whig political heroes of the American War of Independence.

Albemarle married relatively late: on 20 April 1770, at Bagshot Park, Windlesham, Surrey, he married Ann (*bap.* 1743, *d.* 1824), youngest daughter of Sir John Miller, baronet, of Chichester and his wife, Susan Combe. They had one child, William Charles Keppel (1772–1849), who succeeded to the earldom. Albemarle also had two children with his mistress, Sarah Stanley. He died ('very rich', according to Lady Mary Coke) of 'the old complaint in his bowels' (*Letters and Journals*, 4.131) on 13 October 1772, and was buried on 22 October at Quidenham, Norfolk, an estate bought with prize money from the capture of Havana. Rockingham mourned him to Burke as 'so honourable, so worthy and so kind a friend' (27 Oct 1772, Burke, *Correspondence*, 2.348).   WILLIAM C. LOWE

Sources S. Keppel, *Three brothers at Havana, 1762* (1981) · R. Whitworth, *William Augustus, duke of Cumberland: a life* (1992) · D. Syrett, ed., *The siege and capture of Havana, 1762*, Navy RS, 114 (1970) · H. Walpole, *Memoirs of the reign of King George the Third*, ed. G. F. R. Barker, 4 vols. (1894) · D. Syrett, 'The British landing at Havana: an example of an eighteenth-century combined operation', *Mariner's Mirror*, 55 (1969), 325–31 · GEC, *Peerage* · P. Watson, 'Keppel, George', HoP, *Commons, 1715–54* · *The letters and journals of Lady Mary Coke*, ed. J. A. Home, 4 vols. (1889–96) · [E. Burke], *The correspondence of Edmund Burke*, 2, ed. L. S. Sutherland (1960) · R. Wright, *The life of Major-General James Wolfe* (1864) · T. R. Keppel, *The life of Augustus, Viscount Keppel*, 2 vols. (1842) · F. O'Gorman, *The rise of party in England: the Rockingham whigs, 1760–1782* (1975) · IGI

Archives BL, corresp. and papers relating to Cuba and Jersey, Add. MS 49528 · CKS, papers relating to Prussian campaigns, U1350/C7/t4 · Suffolk RO, Ipswich, corresp. and papers, incl. those while governor of Jersey and during the attack on Havana | BL, corresp. with duke of Newcastle, Add. MSS 32708–33072 · Hunt. L., letters to Sir George Pocock · Sheff. Arch., Wentworth Woodhouse muniments, letters to Charles, second marquess of Rockingham

Likenesses E. Fisher, mezzotint (after J. Reynolds), BM, NPG · G. Romney, oils, Goodwood, West Sussex

Wealth at death very rich estate; £100,000; £1500 p.a. jointure to wife; £400 p.a. for house: *Letters and journals of Lady Mary Coke*, ed. Home, vol. 4, 131

Keppel, Sir George Olof Roos- [*formerly* George Olof Roos] (1866–1921), army officer and administrator in India, was born at 10 Norfolk Street, Park Lane, London on 7 September 1866, the eldest son of Gustaf Ehrenreich Roos, corn merchant, a Swede who had settled in England, and his wife, Elizabeth Annie, eldest daughter of George Roffey of Twickenham. George Roos was educated at the United Services College, Westward Ho!, Devon, and later at Bonn, Geneva, and the Royal Military College, Sandhurst. In 1890 he changed his name to Roos-Keppel at the request of his Swedish grandmother who was the last remaining member of a branch of the Keppel family which had emigrated from Holland to Sweden generations before.

Roos-Keppel was commissioned second lieutenant in

Sir George Olof Roos-Keppel (1866–1921), by William Robert Colton, 1915

August 1886 in the Royal Scots Fusiliers and saw active service with this regiment during the Third Anglo-Burmese War (1885–6). He then transferred to the north-west frontier of India and served as a transport officer on the Gilgit Road. During this period Roos-Keppel demonstrated great aptitude in dealing with fiercely independent transborder Pathan tribesmen and was seconded to the political department. He served for six years as political officer in the Kurram valley and commandant of the Kurram militia, during which time he developed a detailed knowledge of tribal society and customs and various Pushtu dialects. In 1899 Roos-Keppel was appointed political agent in the Khyber, and over the next eight years he succeeded in winning the respect of, and considerable personal influence over, the powerful Afridi tribe. In January 1900 he was promoted brevet major and gazetted CIE for his successful counter-raid in March 1899 against the Para Chamkanni tribe which removed the need for a much larger punitive military expedition. From October 1903, in addition to his political duties, Roos-Keppel served as commandant of the Khyber rifles, a locally recruited militia raised to police tribal territory; he was later promoted lieutenant-colonel.

Given his lack of experience of civil administration, Roos-Keppel was not the obvious successor to Lieutenant-Colonel Sir Harold Deane, following the latter's death in July 1908, as chief commissioner of the North-West Frontier Province and agent to the governor-general. However, he was given this job over the head of other experienced officers due to his extensive knowledge of tribal affairs. At the same time, in recognition of his role during the February 1908 Bazar valley punitive expedition, he was made a KCIE and awarded the Swedish military order of the sword. Despite lacking knowledge of civil affairs in the settled areas within the administrative border, with his long record of frontier service, Roos-Keppel proved a highly successful chief commissioner. In particular he took a keen interest in education, founding the Islamia

College and school at Peshawar, and took a prominent part in the work of the Indian branch of the Red Cross.

Roos-Keppel played a vital role in keeping order among the trans-border Pathan tribes and maintaining good relations with the amir of Afghanistan throughout the First World War. For his services he was appointed GCSI in 1917. During the Third Anglo-Afghan War Roos-Keppel took immediate action to maintain order within Peshawar city and the settled areas and oversaw the implementation of martial law. Acting on Roos-Keppel's advice the army in India embarked on an immediate offensive that successfully prevented a general tribal rising and quickly ejected the Afghan army from India. Following the end of hostilities in August 1919 Roos-Keppel strongly advocated the reversal of existing British policy by permanently extending direct British control over the independent tribes and forcibly disarming them, building roads throughout their country and establishing and maintaining law and order in the border hills. However, Roos-Keppel was forced to return to England in the autumn of 1919 due to increasing ill health as a result of heart trouble and bronchitis. When he reached London Roos-Keppel was appointed to the council of the secretary of state for India to advise on political affairs. In August 1921 his health broke down completely, however, and after a difficult illness he died, unmarried, on 11 December 1921 at 45 Devonshire Street, London.

Roos-Keppel was an independent, strong-minded, and charismatic man, whose great personal influence over the tribes of the north-west frontier and political skill proved to be of vital importance in securing control of the region during and immediately after the First World War.

T. R. MOREMAN

Sources 'A great warden of the marches: death of Sir George Roos-Keppel', *The Times* (12 March 1921) · *DNB* · L. Baha, *N.-W.F.P. administration under British rule, 1901–1919* (1978) · W. J. Keen, *The North West Frontier Province and the war* (1928) · BL OIOC, Roos-Keppel MSS · T. C. Coen, *The Indian political service* (1971) · *Army List* · *CGPLA Eng. & Wales* (1922) · b. cert. · d. cert.
Archives BL OIOC, corresp. | BL OIOC, letters to Sir Harcourt Butler, MS Eur. F 116 · Bodl. Oxf., corresp. with Sir Aurel Stein · CUL, corresp. with Lord Hardinge
Likenesses W. R. Colton, bronze sculpture, 1915, BL OIOC [*see illus.*]
Wealth at death £20,282 12s. 10d.: probate, 2 March 1922, *CGPLA Eng. & Wales*

Keppel, George Thomas, sixth earl of Albemarle (1799–1891), army officer, second son of William Charles Keppel, fourth earl of Albemarle (1772–1849), and his first wife, the Hon. Elizabeth Southwell (d. 1815), daughter of Lord de Clifford, and grandson of George *Keppel, third earl of Albemarle, was born in Marylebone, Middlesex, on 13 June 1799. His childhood was passed with his grandmother, the Dowager Lady de Clifford, then governess to Princess Charlotte of Wales. The princess, three years his senior, often tipped him liberally. He was at Westminster School from the age of nine until nearly sixteen, but was an indifferent student. When Dr Page, the headmaster, pronounced him unfit for any learned profession, an ensigncy was obtained for him in the 3rd battalion of the

14th regiment. The battalion, consisting chiefly of untried officers and raw recruits, was in the Netherlands, and Keppel, whose commission was dated 4 April 1815, joined it in time to be present at the battle of Waterloo, where he was in the thick of the fighting on the ridge. Footsore and ragged, he marched with the victorious troops to Paris. He returned home with the battalion at the end of the year, and when it was disbanded served with the 2nd battalion of the regiment in the Ionian Islands. This battalion was disbanded at Chichester in 1818, when Keppel was appointed to the 22nd (Cheshire) regiment, with which he served in Mauritius and at the Cape, returning home with the regiment in 1819. For a time he was equerry to the duke of Sussex.

In 1821 Keppel was promoted to a lieutenancy in the 24th regiment, was transferred to the 20th, and ordered to India. There he served as aide-de-camp to the governor-general, the marquess of Hastings, but on Hastings's resignation in 1823 he obtained leave to return home overland. Relying on a slight knowledge of Persian acquired during the long passage out to India, he visited the ruins of Babylon and the court of Tehran, from there journeying to England by way of Baku, Astrakhan, Moscow, and St Petersburg, then a rare feat. His published account is an interesting book. Keppel next served as aide-de-camp to the Marquess Wellesley when lord lieutenant of Ireland. He obtained a company in the 62nd (Wiltshire) regiment in 1825, and after studying at the senior department of the Royal Military College, Sandhurst, obtained a majority on half pay unattached on 20 March 1827. He was not on full pay again, but he rose steadily, finally attaining the honorary rank of general (on half pay of his former commission) on 7 February 1874. In 1829 he visited the theatre of war between the Russians and Turks, was with the English fleet in Turkish waters, visited Constantinople and Adrianople, and travelled in the Balkans. Keppel married on 4 June 1831 Susan (d. 3 Aug 1885), third daughter of Sir Coutts Trotter, bt; they had a son, William Coutts *Keppel, seventh earl of Albemarle, and four daughters, of whom two predeceased their parents.

In 1832 Keppel was returned as a whig MP for East Norfolk in the first reformed parliament, and sat until 1835. In 1837 he unsuccessfully contested Lyme Regis, and in 1841 Lymington. In 1846 he became one of the private secretaries to Lord John Russell, the new premier, and in 1847 was returned for Lymington, for which he sat until 1849, the year of his father's death. On the death of his insane brother, Augustus Frederick, the fifth earl, on 15 March 1851, he succeeded to the title. He was appointed a trustee of Westminster School in 1854, in succession to the first marquess of Anglesey, and was long the 'father of the trust'. He was a familiar and popular figure in London society. He retained his faculties to the end, and held receptions on each anniversary of Waterloo, at his daughter's house in Portman Square.

Albemarle's publications included *Personal Narrative of a Journey from India to England* (2 vols., 1825), *Narrative of a Journey Across the Balkans … and a Visit to … Newly Discovered Ruins in Asia Minor* (1830), and *Fifty Years of my Life* (1876). Some of his speeches in the House of Lords, including those on the Marriage Bill and on torture in the Madras presidency, both in 1856, were printed as pamphlets.

Albemarle died at his London residence, 8 Portman Square, Marylebone, on 21 February 1891, and was buried at Quidenham, Norfolk.

H. M. CHICHESTER, rev. JAMES FALKNER

Sources Army List · Burke, Peerage · Hart's Army List · Broad Arrow (28 Feb 1891) · Broad Arrow (13 June 1891) · G. Thomas, earl of Albemarle, Fifty years of my life, 2 vols. (1876) · GEC, Peerage · WWBMP · The Times (23 Feb 1891) · DNB
Archives Suffolk RO, Ipswich, corresp. and papers
Likenesses Dawson, photograph, repro. in H. O'Donnell, History of the 14th regiment (1883), 332 · wood-engraving (after a daguerreotype by Claudet), NPG; repro. in ILN (1852)
Wealth at death £10,118 0s. 5d.: resworn probate, Aug 1891, CGPLA Eng. & Wales

Keppel, Sir Henry (1809–1904), naval officer, born in Kensington, London, on 14 June 1809, was the sixth surviving son of William Charles Keppel, fourth earl of Albemarle (1772–1849), and his wife, Elizabeth Southwell (d. 1817), daughter of Edward, twentieth Lord de Clifford. His great-uncle was Augustus *Keppel, Viscount Keppel, and his elder brothers, Augustus Frederick and George Thomas, became successively fifth and sixth earls of Albemarle.

Keppel entered the navy on 7 February 1822. After leaving the Royal Naval College, Portsmouth, he was appointed to the *Tweed* and went out to the Cape of Good Hope. He passed his examination in 1828 and was promoted lieutenant on 29 January 1829. Early in 1830 he was appointed to the *Galatea* (Captain Charles Napier) which, after a spell of home service, went to the West Indies. At Barbados Keppel jeopardized his career by breaking an arrest in order to attend a ball. He was next appointed to the *Magicienne* (Captain James H. Plumridge), going out to the East Indies, where he saw active service during the war between the East India Company and the raja of Nanning. His promotion to commander, dated 20 January 1833, recalled him, and in 1834 he was appointed to command the brig *Childers*, in which he served first on the south coast of Spain, co-operating with the forces of the queen regent against the Carlists, and afterwards on the west coast of Africa. On 5 December 1837 he was promoted captain. In 1839 he married Katherine Louisa Crosbie (d. 5 June 1859), daughter of General Sir John Crosbie.

In August 1841 Keppel commissioned the corvette *Dido* for the China station, where he served with distinction during the latter part of the First Opium War under Sir William Parker. When peace was made in August 1842 Keppel was sent to Singapore as senior officer on that part of the station. There he made friends with Sir James Brooke, with whom he returned to Sarawak. For eighteen months he co-operated with Brooke for the suppression of Borneo piracy, and, after many engagements, the *Dido*, together with the East India Company's steamship *Phlegethon*, destroyed the chief stronghold of the pirates, together with some 300 prahus. After two years on half pay he was appointed in 1847 to the frigate *Maeander* and returned to the same station, where his contact with Brooke was resumed. Towards the end of the commission

Sir Henry Keppel (1809–1904), by W. & D. Downey, pubd 1893

he visited Australia, and in 1851 returned to England by the Strait of Magellan.

In 1853 Keppel was appointed by his friend Captain Sir Baldwin Walker, then surveyor of the navy, to the *St Jean d'Acre*, then considered the finest line-of-battle ship in the navy, and he served with distinction in her during the Baltic campaign of 1854, following which the ship was sent to the Black Sea. In July 1855 he moved into the *Rodney* on taking command of the naval brigade ashore before Sevastopol, continuing with it until the fall of the fortress. He received the cross of the Légion d'honneur, the order of the Mejidiye (third class) and, on 4 February 1856, was made a CB, to his considerable annoyance, as he was fully expecting the KCB.

When in the autumn of 1856 Keppel commissioned the frigate *Raleigh*, as commodore and second in command on the China station, his reputation for courage and conduct combined with his family interest to give the ship a certain aristocratic character somewhat uncommon in the service; among the lieutenants were James G. Goodenough, Lord Gillford, and Prince Victor of Hohenlohe, while Lord Charles Scott, Henry F. Stephenson, Arthur Knyvet Wilson, and the Hon. Victor Montagu were midshipmen on board. During the *Raleigh*'s passage war broke out in China, and she was rushed towards Hong Kong. Shortly before reaching there the ship struck an uncharted pinnacle rock and was totally lost. However, there was no loss of life, and Keppel was acquitted by the subsequent court martial. He next hoisted his broad pennant in the chartered river steamer *Hong Kong* and took part in the operations in the Canton River. The attack delivered on the Grand Fleet of war junks in the upper reaches of Fatshan (Foshan) Creek on 1 June 1857 was entrusted to Keppel, under whose personal command practically all of the junks (about seventy) were burnt. The Chinese had obstructed the stream, measured the distances, and made other careful preparations for the defence of their position, and they fought bravely. Keppel's galley was sunk, and five of her crew were killed or wounded. He was warmly complimented by the commander-in-chief, on whose recommendation he was made a KCB. On 22 August 1858 he was promoted to his flag, and he returned home.

In September 1858 Sir Henry was appointed groom-in-waiting to Queen Victoria, a post which he resigned in May 1860 to hoist his flag on the frigate *Forte* as commander-in-chief on the Cape of Good Hope station. While on passage to his station he was accused of having unlawful relations with the wife of the governor at the Cape, who was on board. He was shortly transferred to the Brazilian command, and then recalled. On 31 October 1861 he married Jane Elizabeth West (d. 21 April 1895), daughter of Martin J. West and sister of Sir Algernon West. They had two children: Colin Richard Keppel (b. 3 Dec 1862), who became an admiral, and Maria Walpole Keppel, who married Admiral Frederick Tower Hamilton RN.

Keppel became a vice-admiral on 11 January 1864, and in December 1866 was chosen to be commander-in-chief in China. On 3 July 1869 he was promoted admiral and returned home. In April 1870 he was awarded an admiral's good service pension, and in May 1871 was made a GCB. From November 1872 to 1875 he was commander-in-chief at Devonport; on 5 August 1877 he was promoted admiral of the fleet; and in March 1878 he was appointed first and principal naval aide-de-camp to the queen. By a special order in council his name was retained on the active list of the navy until his death. In 1899 his memoirs, *A Sailor's Life under Four Sovereigns* (3 vols.), was published. Known for his charm, love of sport, and exuberant vitality, he was a close friend of Edward VII, especially when prince of Wales; Alice *Keppel, the king's mistress, was his relative by marriage. He died, aged ninety-four, at his home, 8A The Albany, Piccadilly, London, on 17 January 1904 and was buried at Winkfield church, Berkshire, with naval honours.

An officer of high social rank, great courage, and excellent seamanship, Keppel was too excitable and hasty to be a successful admiral in peacetime. While his diminutive stature only encouraged him to try harder, his social standing made him question those placed in authority over him, most notably Sir Charles Napier in 1854.

L. G. C. LAUGHTON, *rev.* ANDREW LAMBERT

Sources V. Stuart, *The beloved little admiral* (1967) · A. D. Lambert, *The Crimean War: British grand strategy, 1853–56* (1990) · NMM, Keppel MSS · *The Times* (18 Jan 1904) · H. Keppel, *A sailor's life under four sovereigns*, 3 vols. (1899) · *CGPLA Eng. & Wales* (1904)

Archives NMM, diaries, letter-books, logbooks, and papers

Likenesses attrib. A. C. Sterling, three salt prints, c.1845–1853, NPG · J. J. Tissot, watercolour, pencil, and body colour, 1876, NPG · Count Gleichen, marble bust, c.1882, formerly United Service Club, London (c/o the crown commissioners); related marble bust, Royal Collection · Ao, caricature, chromolithograph, NPG; repro. in *VF* (15 Oct 1903) · W. & D. Downey, woodburytype photograph, NPG; repro. in W. Downey and D. Downey, *The cabinet portrait gallery*, 4 (1893) [see illus.] · D. J. Pound, stipple and line engraving (after a photograph by Mayall), BM, NPG; repro. in D. J. Pound, *The drawing room portrait gallery of eminent personages* (1859) · caricature, chromolithograph, NPG; repro. in *VF* (22 April 1876) · portrait, repro. in Stuart, *The beloved little admiral*, 80–81

Wealth at death £3,551 11s. 6d.: probate, 19 Feb 1904, *CGPLA Eng. & Wales*

Keppel, William Anne, second earl of Albemarle (1702–1754), army officer, was born at Whitehall, London, on 5 June 1702, the only son of Arnold Joost van *Keppel, first earl (1669/70–1718), and his wife, Geertruid Johanna Quirina van der Duyn (d. 1741). He was baptized at the Chapel Royal, and Queen Anne, after whom he was named, was his godmother. During his father's lifetime he was styled Viscount Bury. At an early age he travelled to the Netherlands with his father where he was educated. On his return to England he was appointed (25 August 1717) captain and lieutenant-colonel of the grenadier company of the Coldstream Guards; and in 1718 he succeeded to his father's title and estates.

In March 1720 Albemarle accompanied his colonel, William, first Baron Cadogan, upon his diplomatic mission to Berlin and Vienna to negotiate Spain's incorporation in the Quadruple Alliance, at that time including Britain, France, Austria, and Prussia. In 1722, at his family seat in Gelderland, Albemarle entertained the bishop of Munster. He was made lord of the bedchamber to the prince of Wales in October 1722, a position he retained when the prince became George II, and held until 1751. On 21 February 1723 he married, at Caversham, Oxfordshire, Lady Anne Lennox (1703–1789), second daughter of Charles, first duke of Richmond. Albemarle was made a knight of the Bath on 18 May 1725, upon the revival of that order, and in 1727 he was appointed aide-de-camp to the king. On 22 November 1731 he was made colonel of the 29th regiment of foot (later the Worcestershire regiment), then at Gibraltar, which he held until 7 May 1733 when he transferred to the colonelcy of the 3rd troop of Horse Guards.

On 26 September 1737 Albemarle replaced George Hamilton, first earl of Orkney, as governor of Virginia, a post he held until his death though he never visited the colony. As the absentee governor he was vigilant in the exercise of his powers of appointment and patronage, which brought him into conflict with William Gooch, lieutenant-governor of the colony from 1727 to 1749. When Albemarle asserted his right to appoint naval officers of the colony in the late 1730s this drew forth a strong rebuke from Gooch. Gooch was not only angry at this interference in an area he considered his prerogative, but feared the appointment of incompetent placemen to technical

William Anne Keppel, second earl of Albemarle (1702–1754), by John Faber junior, 1751 (after Jean Fournier, 1749)

positions. On this occasion a compromise was achieved in which the lieutenant-governor nominated officers with the agreement of the executive council but Albemarle reserved a right to fill vacancies when they occurred. In the long run this was a one-sided battle. At the end of his term of office Gooch lamented that since Albemarle's appointment nearly every office in the colony had been 'given away in England' (Morton, 2.507).

Albemarle was promoted brigadier-general on 2 July 1739 and major-general on 18 February 1742. He went to Flanders with John Dalrymple, second earl of Stair, in 1742, where he was put in command of the Household Cavalry. In 1743 he was on the staff at the battle of Dettingen, where he led his troop of 'the Blues' against the French household cavalry and had his horse shot from under him. He was transferred to the colonelcy of the Coldstream Guards, his old regiment, in 1744 and was promoted lieutenant-general on 26 February 1745. At Fontenoy he commanded the brigade of guards in the English front line. He was ridden over when facing a French cavalry charge, suffering a severe contusion on the chest. The duke of Cumberland mentioned his conduct in his official dispatch.

In November 1745, following the Jacobite rising, Albemarle joined General George Wade as his second in command at Newcastle, with reinforcements from Flanders. After the fruitless marching of that autumn he was appointed to Cumberland's staff in Scotland in early 1746. On 22 March he was ordered to take command of the advance party of the government army, consisting of two regiments of horse and two brigades of infantry, sent forward to Strathbogie to clear the way for the main army. At Culloden he commanded the first line of the royal army. His appointment to succeed Cumberland as commander-in-chief in Scotland, dated 23 August 1746, was accepted with reluctance. Prebble writes: 'On the whole he behaved with tact and judgement but his views on what should be done to suppress the rebellious spirit of the Scots were conventional and matched his general disapproval of the country' (Prebble, 304). He carried forward Cumberland's plan of pacification with new fortifications and road building. Most of the Culloden battalions were returned to Flanders and the policing of the highlands became a matter for small detachments of mounted troops under the command of junior officers. Albemarle quickly moved his headquarters to Edinburgh, where he set up an espionage network of doubtful quality, which failed to prevent Charles Edward Stuart's eventual escape to France. With the onset of winter and the weak condition of his garrison forces, Albemarle feared a new rising. However, by dint of insistent and repeated petitioning he was released from his command and ordered to join the staff in Flanders in late January 1747. He commanded the British infantry at the battle of Val or Laffeldt later that year and afterwards was appointed commander-in-chief of the British forces in the Low Countries. At the peace of 1748 he was sent as ambassador-extraordinary and minister-plenipotentiary to Paris. During his tenure of office it was believed by Horace Walpole among others that his mistress, Louise Gaucher (d. 1765), sold government instructions to the French court.

On 22 June 1749 Albemarle was made a knight of the Garter. On 12 July 1751 he was appointed groom of the stole and a privy councillor, and in 1752 he was one of the lords justices during the king's absence in Hanover. In 1754 he was sent back to Paris to demand the liberation of some British subjects detained by the French in America, where he died suddenly on 22 December 1754. His remains were brought to England and buried in the chapel in South Audley Street, Grosvenor Square, London, on 21 February 1755.

Albemarle was survived by his wife, Anne, who was lady to the bedchamber to Queen Caroline and a favourite of the king. When in January 1750 she was robbed by nine men in Great Russell Street, London, the king gave her a gold watch and chain the next day. She died on 20 October 1789 at New Street, Spring Gardens, Middlesex. The couple had had eight sons and seven daughters, including George *Keppel, third earl; the admiral Augustus *Keppel, Viscount Keppel; and Frederick *Keppel, bishop of Exeter.

Albemarle left his wife and numerous children nothing on his death. His deserved reputation as the Spendthrift Earl has been established for posterity by the pen of Horace Walpole, who wrote to Sir Horace Mann on 19 May 1750 that at the embassy in Paris he kept

> an immense table there, with sixteen people in his kitchen; his aides-de-camps invite everybody, but he seldom graces the banquet himself, living retired out of town with his old

Columbine—what an extraordinary man! With no fortune at all, and with slight parts, he has £17,000 a year from the government, which he squanders away, though he has great debts, and four or five numerous broods of children of one sort or other! (Walpole, *Corr.*, 20.156)

Upon Albemarle's death Walpole noted that when he married he had £90,000 in the funds, to which his wife brought £25,000 more, most of which he squandered, leaving only £14,000 which was sufficient to cover his debts. George II granted his widow, Anne, a pension of £1200 a year.   JONATHAN SPAIN

Sources GEC, *Peerage*, new edn · C. Dalton, ed., *George the First's army, 1714–1727*, 2 (1912), 336 · G. T. Keppel, *Fifty years of my life* (1876) · E. E. Everard, *The Worcester regiment* (1970), 549 · D. Mackinnon, *Origin and services of the Coldstream guards*, 2 vols. (1833) · G. Arthur, *The story of the household cavalry*, 3 vols. (1909) · K. Tomasson and F. Buist, *Battles of the '45* (1962) · W. A. Speck, *The Butcher: the duke of Cumberland and the suppression of the 45* (1981) · J. Black, *Culloden and the '45* (1990) · C. S. Terry, ed., *The Albemarle papers: the correspondence of William Anne, 2nd earl of Albemarle C in C Scotland, 1746–47*, 2 vols. (1902) · F. H. Skrine, *Fontenoy and Britain's share in the War of the Austrian Succession, 1741–48* (1906) · J. Prebble, *Culloden* (1961) · R. L. Morton, *Colonial Virginia*, 2 (1960) · D. A. Williams, *Political alignments in colonial Virginia politics, 1698–1750* (New York, 1989) · *Report on the manuscripts of Earl Bathurst, preserved at Cirencester Park*, HMC, 76 (1923), 676 · *Report on the manuscripts of Lord Polwarth*, 2, HMC, 67 (1916), 506 · Walpole, *Corr.*

Archives BL, letter-books, Add. MSS 32026–32027 · NL Scot., corresp. relating to Scotland, MSS Rept. MSS 3730–3731, 3736, Adv MS 31.622 · Sheff. Arch., corresp. relating to Scotland and Flanders · Suffolk RO, Ipswich, corresp. and papers · U. Hull, Brynmor Jones L., corresp. | BL, letters to Lord Hardwicke and Robert Keith, Add. MSS 35354–35590 · BL, corresp. with Lord Holdernesse, Egerton MSS 3416, 3455–3457 · BL, corresp. with Sir Benjamin Keene, Add. MSS 43423–43433 · BL, corresp. with duke of Newcastle, Add. MSS 32687–33066 · Hunt. L., letters to Lord London · U. Nott. L., corresp. with Henry Pelham, duke of Newcastle and Lord Holdernesse · W. Sussex RO, letters to duke of Richmond

Likenesses J. Faber junior, mezzotint, 1751 (after J. Fournier, 1749), BM, NPG [*see illus.*] · T. Hudson, portrait, repro. in Tomasson and Buist, *Battles of the '45* · J. Smith, mezzotint (as a child; after G. Kneller), BM, NPG

Wealth at death died in debt

Keppel, William Coutts, seventh earl of Albemarle and Viscount Bury

Keppel, William Coutts, seventh earl of Albemarle and Viscount Bury (1832–1894), politician, was born in London on 15 April 1832, the eldest son of George Thomas *Keppel, sixth earl of Albemarle (1799–1891), and his wife, Susan (*d*. 1885), third daughter of Sir Coutts Trotter, bt. From 1851 to 1891 he was styled Viscount Bury, his father's second title. He was educated at Eton College, and in 1843, when eleven years old, was gazetted ensign and lieutenant in the 43rd regiment. In 1849 he became lieutenant in the Scots guards, and during 1850–51 he was private secretary to Lord John Russell. In 1852 he went to India as aide-de-camp to Lord Frederick Fitzclarence, commander-in-chief at Bombay. In the following year he came home on sick leave, retired from the army, and in December 1854 went to Canada as superintendent of Indian affairs. This experience produced his *Exodus of the Western Nations* (2 vols., 1865), which is really a history of North America, with particular reference to Canada. While in Canada he married, on 15 November 1855, at Dundurn, Sophia Mary, (*d*. 5 April 1917), daughter of Sir Alan Napier MacNab,

speaker of the Canadian parliament, and his second wife, Mary, *née* Stuart. They had three sons and seven daughters.

After his return to England Bury was, on 30 March 1857, elected as a Liberal for Norwich, a notoriously corrupt borough. He was re-elected on 29 April 1859, and again on 28 June following his appointment by Lord Palmerston to the post of treasurer of the household. His election was, however, declared void on petition and on 1 December 1860 he was returned for Wick burghs. He stood for Dover at the general election of 1865, but was defeated, and he ceased to be treasurer of the household in 1866 when the Conservatives came into power. On 17 November 1868 he was returned for Berwick. In 1874 he was defeated for Berwick, and in 1875 for Stroud. He next became a Conservative, and on 6 September 1876 was raised to the peerage during his father's lifetime as Baron Ashford. From March 1878 to April 1880 he was under-secretary for war under Beaconsfield, and in 1885–6 he held the same office under Lord Salisbury. On Easter Sunday 1879 he was received into the Roman Catholic church (his father-in-law's earlier conversion had led to uproar in Canada). He had a public row with W. E. Gladstone in 1880 about the Vatican Council of 1870.

Bury, who was created KCMG in 1870, was an enthusiastic member of the volunteers and in 1860 published a pamphlet on their reform. In the same year he was made lieutenant-colonel of the Civil Service rifle volunteers, and volunteer aide-de-camp to the queen in 1881. He was also author of *The Rinderpest Treated by Homoeopathy in South Holland* (1865) and with G. Lacy Hillier of *Cycling*, in the Badminton Library (1887), a popular work in its day. Bury succeeded his father as seventh earl of Albemarle on 21 February 1891, and died, of paralysis, at Prospect House, Barnes, Surrey, on 28 August 1894, being buried on the 31st at the family seat, Quidenham, Norfolk.

A. F. POLLARD, *rev.* H. C. G. MATTHEW

Sources GEC, *Peerage* · *The Tablet* (1 Sept 1894) · *The Times* (29 Aug 1894) · Gladstone, *Diaries* · P. Baskerville, 'MacNab, Sir Allan Napier', *DCB*, vol. 9

Archives Public Archives of Ontario, Toronto, journal | Bodl. Oxf., MS Eng. lett. 6. 4 · Suffolk RO, Ipswich, letters to Sir Edmund Head

Likenesses J. Edwards, cabinet photograph, 1882?, NPG · D. J. Pound, stipple and line engraving (after a photograph by Mayall), NPG

Wealth at death £20,842 2*s*. 6*d*.: probate, 12 Oct 1894, *CGPLA Eng. & Wales*

Ker. *See also* Kerr.

Ker, Alice Jane Shannan Stewart

Ker, Alice Jane Shannan Stewart (1853–1943), doctor and suffragette, was born on 2 December 1853 at Deskford, Cullen, Banffshire, the eldest child of the Revd William Turnbull Ker (1824–1885), minister of the Free Church of Scotland, and his wife, Margaret Millar, *née* Stevenson (1826–1900), daughter of James Cochran *Stevenson, chemical manufacturer and Liberal MP for South Shields. Her mother's unmarried sisters Elisa, Flora, and Louisa lived in Edinburgh where they were involved in a wide range of social, political, and feminist concerns, their home forming an unofficial centre for the early women's suffrage movement, and, while little is known of Alice's early childhood or her education, she was very close to the Stevenson aunts who, along with her mother, encouraged her to take up a profession.

Through her aunts Alice became acquainted with Sophia Jex-Blake and her student contemporaries at about the time that they were bringing an action against Edinburgh University, attempting to force the institution to permit women to graduate as medical doctors. By 1872 Alice had enrolled at Edinburgh and was taking a variety of classes including anatomy and physiology. In 1873 the university successfully appealed against Jex-Blake's action, effectively closing its doors on women medics. Alice then moved to London to study at the London School of Medicine for Women where she was a strong student, winning prizes in chemistry, materia medica, and practice of medicine. As the school's qualifications were not recognized by the medical register at this time she sat examinations at the King and Queen's College of Physicians in Ireland, the route taken by many female medical pioneers. Alice then spent a further period studying in Boston, USA, and in Bern, Switzerland. She was accepted onto the medical register in 1879, only the thirteenth woman to be so recognized.

Details of Alice's early medical career are sparse, but it is known that she spent some time at the Children's Hospital in Birmingham where she was promoted to senior medical officer in 1881. She also published a book, *Lectures to Women nos. 1–3* (1883), which gave pragmatic advice on a number of medical questions. By 1887 she had returned to Edinburgh and was attempting to establish her own medical practice. This work was interrupted by her marriage, in December 1888, to Edward Stewart Ker (1839–1907), a distant cousin who was sole partner in the firm of Stewart Ker & Son, merchants of Liverpool, and the couple moved to Birkenhead. There, Alice was able to establish a name for herself as one of only two women doctors in the area and was appointed to a variety of positions including honorary medical officer to the Wirral Hospital for Sick Children and honorary medical officer at Birkenhead Lying-In Hospital. She published her second medical book, *Motherhood: a Book for every Woman* (1891), which gave practical and straightforward medical information on confinement and child rearing. She also built up a successful general practice which she ran from the family home at Grange Road. With her husband, she became a well-known figure in local society, enjoying invitations to many of the major parties of the Liverpool 'season'. But she retained an active interest in social questions, especially those relating to women, and became involved in the Women's Local Government Association as well as the RSPCA and the anti-vivisection movement. The couple were also regular attenders at several Anglican churches in Birkenhead.

Alice managed to combine motherhood with her career and voluntary activities. Her first child, Stewart, was born in 1889 but died at the age of sixteen months to the great distress of both parents. Two daughters, Margaret Louise

(*b.* 1892) and Mary Dunlop (*b.* 1896) followed, both of whom survived. Edward took a full part in the upbringing of his daughters, delighting in pram pushing and family walks, and taking the girls to church. Alice continued her busy professional life with the minimum of domestic help, getting up in the middle of the night to feed or soothe her children, and often taking them with her on her rounds.

In 1907 Edward unexpectedly died. He and Alice had been a devoted couple, sharing many interests and delighting in their young family, and his death was a heavy blow. It also left Alice with some spare leisure time, which she filled by increasing her involvement in women's politics. Since her student days she had been a supporter of the idea of women's suffrage, and was a member of the rather sedate Birkenhead Women's Suffrage Society, affiliated to the National Union of Women's Suffrage Societies (NUWSS). She became chairman of this group in 1908 but was increasingly frustrated by their gradualist tactics and in the autumn of 1909 switched her allegiance, joining the Liverpool branch of the militant Women's Social and Political Union (WSPU). Alice supported a number of militant protests in Liverpool and acted as unofficial WSPU doctor to hunger strikers in Walton gaol. As well as participating in demonstrations and selling *Votes for Women* in Liverpool's main shopping streets (which she often did in between visiting patients) Alice was also keen to demonstrate the extent of her commitment through participation in higher levels of militancy. In April 1912 she travelled to London with other members of the Liverpool WSPU to participate in a mass window-smashing raid, smashing windows at Harrods store. Unusually she was offered bail, but declined and was sent to Holloway for two months, where she participated in the hunger strike. During her imprisonment she was emotionally sustained by the support of her WSPU friends, and also by her daughters, who were becoming increasingly involved in 'the cause' themselves. Margaret followed her mother's example in November 1912 and was sent to Walton gaol for setting fire to a pillar box in Liverpool. Alice applauded her actions but privately worried that they threatened Margaret's place at Liverpool University and personally appealed to the vice-chancellor to readmit her daughter.

Alice's fears that her more extreme suffrage activities would lead to the family being forced out of Birkenhead proved unfounded, and she continued her general practice after her release, although by this stage it was diminishing largely owing to a combination of her external commitments and her age. Since her husband's death she had gradually cut her association with the Anglican church in favour of unitarianism and also theosophy which was playing an increasingly important role in her life. In 1914 the family moved from Birkenhead to Wavertree garden suburb, outside Liverpool. Alice became a regular attender at the Liverpool theosophical lodge and was elected to its executive committee. Although she made no real attempt to build up a new medical practice she continued to see some patients, especially attending births. Liverpool WSPU effectively ceased functioning at the outbreak of war, but Alice continued some suffrage activities through the United Suffragists, serving as vice-president of the Liverpool branch. She also briefly worked again with some of her old NUWSS colleagues through the Women's War Service Bureau, for which she ran a series of popular classes in first aid techniques.

In the spring of 1916 the family left Liverpool to live in London. It is unclear exactly why they took this step, although there was some general migration from the city during the First World War. Wartime travel was also difficult, and in London Alice and Margaret were more easily able to visit Mary, now studying at Cambridge. The London base allowed Alice to participate more in theosophy at a national level. She became a familiar figure at the society's national headquarters and a keen attender of several London lodges, becoming chair of the Garden Suburb lodge near Hampstead in 1921. She also reactivated her medical career with great vigour, working long hours at a number of school clinics and infant welfare centres until after the end of the war. In the early 1920s she finally relinquished her medical work and went into retirement. For her this was not synonymous with inactivity and she continued to lecture enthusiastically for the Theosophical Society in London and sometimes further afield in Britain for the next two decades. She also retained links with feminism and was honorary secretary of Hendon women's council. In retirement she lived mainly in north London, first with Mary and a companion of Mary's, Olive Foot, and then with Margaret and her companion Muriel Whiteman. Both of her daughters were schoolteachers, and Alice maintained a lively interest in their careers. In her final years she was increasingly housebound, but paid strong attention to current affairs via the radio. She died on 20 March 1943 in her ninetieth year.

KRISTA COWMAN

Sources B. G. Orchard, *Liverpool's legion of honour* (1893) · C. Blake, *The charge of the parasols* (1990) · priv. coll. · private information (2004) · A. J. S. S. Ker, MSS letters, Women's Library, London · M. Van Helmond, *Votes for women: the events on Merseyside* (1992) [N. B. there are some factual errors and gaps in the above]
Archives priv. coll., personal diaries · Women's Library, London, autograph letter collection
Likenesses photograph, repro. in Van Helmond, *Votes for women* · photograph, repro. in Orchard, *Liverpool's legion of honour*
Wealth at death £876 13s. 9d.: probate, 11 May 1943, CGPLA Eng. & Wales

Ker, Andrew, of Cessford (d. 1526), border chieftain, succeeded his grandfather, Walter Ker of Caverton, as a minor in 1501. His father, Sir Robert Ker of Caverton, a courtier who became warden of the Scottish middle march, was killed by John Heron of Crawley at a border 'day of truce' about 1500. His mother was Christian Rutherford. Andrew Ker was of lawful age to be served heir to his grandfather in 1511. He fought at the battle of Flodden (1513) and became warden of the middle march on 10 August 1515 for a yearly fee of £100 Scots. Also known from his Christian name as Dand, he swore the oath of wardenship promising to keep good rule in the borders. Following in his father's footsteps, he became a cupbearer to

James V at a fee of 20 merks per annum with livery. After 21 September 1507 Ker married Agnes, daughter of Sir Patrick Crichton of Cranstoun Riddel, who had been granted the rights to his marriage by the crown in return for £466 13s. 4d. Scots. Agnes was the widow of George Sinclair, son and heir of Sir Oliver Sinclair of Roslin, who died about 1507. On 20 February 1509 the lands of Auld Roxburgh were confirmed to her in liferent. With Ker she had at least three sons and two daughters, including Mark *Ker, later commendator of Newbattle Abbey.

Cessford was never very far from the tangled politics surrounding the minority of James V. In 1514 he supported the return of the duke of Albany as governor of Scotland, and after the downfall of the third Lord Hume in 1515 Albany rewarded Cessford with the wardenship of the middle march and informed the English warden, Thomas, Lord Dacre, that Cessford was a 'man of gude' who would not avenge his father's murder (*LP Henry VIII*, 2/1, no. 808). Ker was to have been warden of the east march as well, but he refused this as he did not want to 'meddle with the East Marches' (ibid., 870). As warden Ker became the target of English raiders; Lord Dacre regarded him as forgetful and rash, and Cessford Castle was attacked by English soldiers during Anglo-Scottish fighting in 1519. Ker remained in office, however, and was even made a commissioner to treat for an Anglo-Scottish truce in January 1521. The negotiations proved futile as full-scale war broke out in 1523.

By remaining an ally of Albany Cessford incurred the wrath of James V's uncle Henry VIII, leading to the siege of Cessford Castle by Dacre on 21 May 1523, which led to casualties on both sides. Had Cessford not 'surrendered the place on being allowed to depart with bag and baggage' it is doubtful if the English would have taken it as 'the wall was 14 feet thick' (*LP Henry VIII*, 3/2, no. 3039). Cessford's revenge came in July 1524, when 2000 Scots repulsed 1000 English raiders at Smailholm in the Scottish middle march. Although hurt himself, Cessford would have been pleased that his father's murderer, the 'bastard Heron', was killed. Cessford was subsequently warded for disrupting the administration of border justice and for feuding with Scott of Buccleuch. He then allegedly changed his allegiance to England, and was dismissed from his wardenship during March 1525 in favour of Queen Margaret's second husband, the sixth earl of Angus. He nevertheless promised to serve as a deputy to Angus and advise him on border matters.

Cessford's term of office had not been helped by his cousins the Kers of Ferniehirst, who often refused to obey him as warden of the middle march, despite proclamations ordering them to do so. His alliance with Angus exacerbated his difficulties with the Kers of Ferniehirst over the lordship of Jedforest, which had begun before 1520. By 1526 Cessford was supporting Angus against the powerful earl of Arran, whom Sir Andrew Ker of Ferniehirst defended. These two main branches of the Ker kindred could temporarily reconcile their differences to oppose other factions, as when in July 1526 they joined forces to defend the young James V against a threat of kidnap by their territorial rival, Walter Scott of Buccleuch, who had sided with a faction wishing to liberate the king from the control of the Douglases. Ironically it was this action, rather than any internecine border feud, that led to Ker's death at Darnick Moor on 24 July 1526.

Cessford's killer was not Buccleuch, as alleged in some sources, but one of his Elliot servants. Buccleuch was blamed, however, and did not receive a pardon until September 1528. The Ker and Scott families persevered in a blood feud for much of the sixteenth century. Walter *Ker, who was still a minor, succeeded his father and was rewarded by a grateful James V with his family's now-customary office of cupbearer to the king. The Cessford estates and the rights to Walter's marriage were granted to the safekeeping of the latter's uncle, George Ker of Faldonside.   MAUREEN M. MEIKLE

Sources gifts and deposits, NA Scot., GD40/xvi/ad.1, GD135/1136 · NRA Scotland, Roxburghe muniments, 1100 · *The manuscripts of the duke of Roxburghe*, HMC, 34 (1894) · *The manuscripts of the duke of Hamilton*, HMC, 21 (1887) · *APS*, 1424–1567, 312, 330 · J. M. Thomson and others, eds., *Registrum magni sigilli regum Scotorum / The register of the great seal of Scotland*, 11 vols. (1882–1914), vol. 2, nos. 2965, 3307, 3444; vol. 3, no. 1730 · M. Livingstone, D. Hay Fleming, and others, eds., *Registrum secreti sigilli regum Scotorum / The register of the privy seal of Scotland*, 1 (1908), 83, 85, 224, 394–5, 522 · J. B. Paul, ed., *Compota thesaurariorum regum Scotorum / Accounts of the lord high treasurer of Scotland*, 4 (1902), 8; 5 (1903), 33, 98, 160, 308 · R. K. Hannay, ed., *Acts of the lords of council in public affairs, 1501–1554* (1932), 7, 21–2, 53–4, 69, 72, 91–2, 126–7, 132–3, 141, 147, 155, 159, 169–70, 208–10, 214, 217–18, 234, 235 · G. Burnett and others, eds., *The exchequer rolls of Scotland*, 23 vols. (1878–1908), vol. 12, pp.115, 387, 712; vol. 13, pp. 651–2; vol. 15, pp. 203, 590 · J. Lesley, *The history of Scotland*, ed. T. Thomson, Bannatyne Club, 38 (1830), 115, 125, 134–5 · T. Thomson, ed., *A diurnal of remarkable occurrents that have passed within the country of Scotland*, Bannatyne Club, 43 (1833), 10 · *The historie and cronicles of Scotland … by Robert Lindesay of Pitscottie*, ed. A. J. G. Mackay, 1, STS, 42 (1899), 314–15 · *LP Henry VIII*, vols. 1–4 · *Scots peerage*, 7.326–34 · J. Cameron, *James V: the personal rule, 1528–1542*, ed. N. Macdougall (1998), 10, 12, 32 · J. Wormald, *Lords and men in Scotland: bonds of manrent, 1442–1603* (1985), 174, 382–3 · T. I. Rae, *The administration of the Scottish frontier, 1513–1603* (1966) · W. Fraser, *The Scotts of Buccleuch*, 2 (1878), 2.149

Ker, Andrew, of Ferniehirst (d. 1545), border chieftain, was the eldest son of Thomas Ker (d. c.1484), the first Ker laird of Ferniehirst, and his wife, Margaret Ker. He was referred to as Andrew Ker of Crailing in 1491, but had taken his father's designation of Ferniehirst by 1500. By 6 November 1501 he had married Janet Home of Polwarth; they had at least three sons and four daughters including Robert Ker of Ancrum, progenitor of the earls of Lothian. Their eldest son, Thomas, died in 1524, so their second son, John, became heir. Other siblings were well provided for, as this successful branch of the Kers accumulated much property in Jedforest, Jedburgh, Ettrick Forest, and Haddingtonshire, as well as from Kelso Abbey. Ker often resorted to litigation to establish and protect his family's property rights. From the abbreviation of his Christian name he was known as Dand Ker throughout his adult life; he is occasionally confused with Andrew Ker of Cessford during the first decades of the sixteenth century.

Politically the Kers of Ferniehirst were bound to the fifth and sixth earls of Angus until 1528 when the crown took control of the forfeited Angus estates. The Kers benefited financially and socially from the downfall of the house of Angus as the Rutherford lairds of Hundalee and Hunthill then gave bonds of manrent (contracts of mutual obligation) to Ferniehirst instead of to Angus. The Kers were also significant landlords within the town of Jedburgh. Their joint father-and-son office of baillie of Jedforest was confirmed in 1515, as being held from the earl of Angus, and in 1542 from the crown, for £10 Scots per annum. In 1520 the sixth earl and Ferniehirst were in dispute about this office and held rival courts. Ferniehirst and his eldest son were also baillies of Jedburgh Abbey's lands within Roxburghshire for an annual fee of £10 Scots. These bonds and offices undoubtedly made the Kers of Ferniehirst the most powerful family within this part of the Scottish middle march.

Beyond his local influence Ferniehirst was involved with national politics and international affairs connected to the Anglo-Scottish frontier. After the defeat at Flodden in 1513 he attended the Scottish council at Perth. In 1515 he attended parliament for the first time, and he returned again in 1526 to deny charges of treason laid against him by the earl of Angus. Despite being declared 'clene and innocent' he went back to parliament only once more, to condemn the death in 1526 of his kinsman Andrew Ker of Cessford (*APS*, 2.303–4). Ferniehirst began his long service in border administration around 1502 as a deputy warden of the middle march. He was warded in 1516 to keep better rule upon the borders, but he served his country well in time of war. For example, he harried English attackers after Flodden, attacked Wark-on-Tweed in 1522, and burned parts of Norhamshire in 1533. He was badly injured during the Wark attack, but recovered before Ferniehirst and Jedburgh were targeted by English forces in September 1523. There was intermittent friction with the Cessford branch of the Kers over control of the middle march, but their direct blood relationship ensured that this did not erupt into a blood feud. Jointly held wardenships and deputy wardenships were often used as a compromise in this dispute. The killing of Andrew Ker of Cessford provoked a long and bitter feud with the Scotts of Buccleuch; the marriage of Sir Walter Scott to Ferniehirst's daughter Janet in 1530 represented one attempt to settle it, though this ended in divorce.

After Cessford's death in 1526 Ferniehirst continued to serve as a deputy warden, and in 1528 he was elevated to the commission for Anglo-Scottish peace that led to the treaty of Berwick. In 1530 the king recognized Ferniehirst's local power and influence by making him a border commissioner, but he had to swear to a bond of 10,000 merks to enter notorious Liddesdale thieves, hold a justice ayre at Jedburgh, and deliver any of his own men demanded by the opposite warden. It was not until 1538 that Ferniehirst held the middle march wardenship in his own right. He remained in command until 1542, though he reluctantly shared power with Robert, fifth Lord Maxwell, as keeper of Liddesdale in 1541–2. In 1539 Ker was described as 'a shrewd old practitioner of the Border' and was arguably at the peak of his power (*LP Henry VIII*,

14/1, no. 50), having successfully apprehended various troublemakers within his domain and implemented royal justice. In 1540 a grateful James V rewarded his loyalty by making his Jedburgh Forest lands into the free barony of Ferniehirst. Ferniehirst even managed to get a civil court action against him transferred from Edinburgh to Jedburgh, where his son-in-law, Sir James Douglas of Cavers, could be relied upon to give him favourable justice as sheriff of Roxburgh.

This golden age for Ferniehirst was cut short by the renewal of English hostilities in the borders. In 1542 the English respected him as 'a wise and sober man' and clearly wanted him on their side (Bain, 1.347). At first Ferniehirst was loyal and fought off English attacks and bribes, but he was later described as 'so crafty an old fox', for playing one side against the other by simultaneously taking money from both English and Franco-Scottish forces, and he was criticized for being 'superstitious and Popish' in his religion (*LP Henry VIII*, 18/1, no. 592). Nevertheless, persistent and brutal harrying of the Kers and the capture of Ferniehirst and his son in July 1544 led to their assuring to England. Ferniehirst was injured and held captive at Warkworth Castle. He begged to be returned home, but the English privy council mistrusted him. They let him home only in October after he had left his grandson Thomas as a hostage and placed a company of English soldiers in his house. In December he thanked the earl of Shrewsbury for sending 'Thome' to school, but requested that his heir John return as he was himself 'agyt' (*LP Henry VIII*, 19/2, no. 768). He was then forfeited by the Scottish crown for 'tressonabill intercomonyng ... with the auld inymeis of Ingland' (Livingston and others, 3.166).

The assurance of the border lairds remained uncertain, however. They contributed to the Scottish victory at Ancrum Moor on 27 February 1545, but the devastation inflicted by Hertford's invasion in the following September led many lairds to reassure to the English though the house of the 'crasit and secklie' Ferniehirst was spared (BL, Add. MS 32656, fol. 148). John Ferniehirst attended the October parliament on his father's behalf and signed a bond to resist the 'auld Inymis of Ingland and defend the Realm' (*APS*, 2.461–2), but the English garrisoning of southern Scotland forced the Kers to remain in English allegiance until the wars ended in 1549. When Ferniehirst died in October 1545 his grandson was still in English custody, but John Ker's succession was unimpeded.

MAUREEN M. MEIKLE

Sources gifts and deposits, NA Scot., GD6 (Beil MS); GD40 (Lothian MS) · LPL, Talbot MSS, 3192 · *The manuscripts of the duke of Roxburghe*, HMC, 34 (1894) · *The manuscripts of the duke of Hamilton*, HMC, 21 (1887) · C. Jamison, G. R. Batho, and E. G. W. Bill, eds., *A calendar of the Shrewsbury and Talbot papers in the Lambeth Palace Library and the College of Arms*, 2, HMC, JP 7 (1971) · *APS*, 1424–1567, 281, 303–4, 312, 461–2 · J. M. Thomson and others, eds., *Registrum magni sigilli regum Scotorum / The register of the great seal of Scotland*, 11 vols. (1882–1914), vol. 2, nos. 3340, 3674; vol. 3, nos. 249, 366, 577, 639, 2142, 2499 · M. Livingstone, D. Hay Fleming, and others, eds., *Registrum secreti sigilli regum Scotorum / The register of the privy seal of Scotland*, 8 vols. (1908–82), vol. 1, pp. 85, 356, 535–6; vol. 2, pp. 120, 243, 521, 552, 752; vol. 3, pp. 65, 159, 166 · J. B. Paul, ed., *Compota thesaurariorum regum Scotorum / Accounts of the lord high treasurer of Scotland*, 4 (1902), 166; 5 (1903), 47, 234, 386; 6 (1905), 55, 157; 7 (1907), 106; 8 (1908), 103, 344 · R. K. Hannay, ed., *Acts of the lords of council in public affairs, 1501–1554* (1932), 23, 126, 132–3, 142, 169, 218, 286, 298, 311–12, 317, 322, 328, 338–40, 346, 355, 362–3, 367, 388, 405, 492 · A. B. Calderwood, ed., *Acts of the lords of council, 1501–1503*, 3 (1993), 115–16, 119–20, 286, 290, 323 · G. Burnett and others, eds., *The exchequer rolls of Scotland*, 23 vols. (1878–1908), vol. 13, p. 652; vol. 17, pp. 129, 131–2, 261, 263–4, 706 · J. Lesley, *The history of Scotland*, ed. T. Thomson, Bannatyne Club, 38 (1830), 107, 115, 125 · T. Thomson, ed., *A diurnal of remarkable occurrents that have passed within the country of Scotland*, Bannatyne Club, 43 (1833), 6, 14, 34 · *The historie and cronicles of Scotland ... by Robert Lindesay of Pitscottie*, ed. A. J. G. Mackay, 1, STS, 42 (1899), 314 · *LP Henry VIII*, vols. 1–20 · J. Bain, ed., *The Hamilton papers: letters and papers illustrating the political relations of England and Scotland in the XVIth century*, 1, Scottish RO, 12 (1890), 78, 101, 347; 2, Scottish RO, 12 (1892), 455 · *Scots peerage*, 5.50–60 · J. Cameron, *James V: the personal rule, 1528–1542*, ed. N. Macdougall (1998) · J. Wormald, *Lords and men in Scotland: bonds of manrent, 1442–1603* (1985), 174, 323 · T. I. Rae, *The administration of the Scottish frontier, 1513–1603* (1966) · BL, Sadler MSS, Add. MS 32656

Ker, (John) Bellenden [*formerly* John Bellenden Gawler] (**1764–1842**), botanist and man of fashion, was born John Bellenden Gawler, the eldest son of John Gawler (d. 1803) of Ramridge, near Andover, Hampshire, and Caroline (d. 1802), eldest surviving daughter of John Bellenden, third Lord Bellenden (d. 1740). He was baptized on 5 June 1764 at the Temple Church, London. On 5 November 1804 George III, out of regard for Gawler's mother, and at the instance of his second cousin, William Bellenden Ker, seventh Lord Bellenden and fourth duke of Roxburghe, granted him a licence to take the name of Ker Bellenden in lieu of Gawler; he was, however, invariably known as Bellenden Ker. William, fourth duke of Roxburghe, died in 1805 without direct heir. During his lifetime he endeavoured to divert the succession in favour of Ker, and entailed his estates upon him, but both the entail and Ker's claim to the title were ultimately set aside by the House of Lords in favour of James Innes-Ker, fifth duke of Roxburghe, on 11 May 1812.

Bellenden Ker was long known as a wit and man of fashion in London. Many stories were told of the charm of his conversation, and he was the hero of some 'affairs of gallantry'. At an early age he obtained a commission in the 2nd regiment of Life Guards; he was appointed captain on 20 January 1790, and was senior captain in the regiment in 1793, when he was compelled to quit the army owing to his displays of sympathy with the French revolution. His attention must, however, have turned to botany, for in 1801 he brought out, anonymously, his *Recensio plantarum*, a review of all the plants illustrated up to that time in Henry C. Andrews's *Botanist's Repository*. About the same date he began to contribute occasional descriptions of new plants to Samuel Curtis's *Botanical Magazine*, then under the editorship of John Sims, who highly commended Ker in the preface to the fifteenth volume. In 1804 Ker printed an important memoir on a group of plants, the Iridaceae, in *Annals of Botany*. In 1812 the *Botanical Register* was started in opposition to the *Botanical Magazine* and Ker became the first editor. He held the office until about 1823, when John Lindley took sole control. When freed from botanical journalism, Ker revised his memoir on the

Iridaceae of 1804, and brought out *Iridearum genera*, which was published in Brussels in 1828 and was his last important work on botany. On resuming work after a period of illness, he busied himself on *An Essay on the Archaeology of Popular English Phrases and Nursery Rhymes*, which was first published in 1834. He also wrote a number of occasional articles in various gardening papers.

During the later period of his life Ker lived at Ramridge, where he died in June 1842. The genus *Bellendena* commemorates him. With his wife, Ann, about whom nothing more is known, he had one son, Charles Henry Bellenden *Ker.   B. D. JACKSON, *rev.* GILES HUDSON

Sources R. Douglas, *The peerage of Scotland*, 2nd edn, ed. J. P. Wood, 2 (1813), 453–4 · Desmond, *Botanists*, rev. edn · *Scots peerage*, 2.75, 7.353 · *IGI*
Likenesses J. R. Smith, double portrait, mezzotint, pubd 1778 (with his brother; after J. Reynolds), BM, NPG · J. Reynolds, double portrait (with his brother); sold in 1887 [*The Times*, 5 May 1887]

Ker, (Charles) Henry Bellenden [*formerly* Charles Henry Gawler] (*c*.1785–1871), law reformer, was the son of John Bellenden *Ker, formerly Gawler (1764–1842), botanist, and his wife, Ann. He was baptized at St Andrew's, Holborn, London, on 18 February 1787. He joined Lincoln's Inn in London in November 1804, was called to the bar in June 1814, and afterwards practised as a conveyancing barrister. He was eventually appointed a conveyancing counsel to the court of chancery, and for some years was recorder of Andover. He married Elizabeth Anne, daughter of Edward Clarke, a solicitor. They had no children. Ker was a contemporary at Lincoln's Inn of Henry Brougham, who provided the material for Ker's first article in the *Edinburgh Review*, on the education of the poor, in 1819. Ker possibly wrote two further articles at this time on the abuse of charities. He was an energetic member of the Society for the Diffusion of Useful Knowledge and contributed woodcuts, and lives—of Wren and Michelangelo, for instance—to its *Penny Magazine*. He promoted parliamentary reform from 1830 to 1832 and was a member of the Parliamentary Boundary Commission established by the Reform Bill. He stood, unsuccessfully, as a whig for the Norwich constituency in the reformed parliament. He gave evidence before the real property commission in 1828 and sat as a member of the public records commission in 1831.

Ker's most important work as a law reformer was in corporation law, conveyancing, criminal law, and statute law. In 1837 he produced for the Board of Trade a comprehensive report on partnership law and the possible adoption of the French conception of the limited partnership into English law. Ker's suggestion of a system of registration of large partnerships was implemented in the Joint Stock Companies Act (7 & 8 Vict. c. 110) of 1844. These developments were significant in the eventual acceptance of limited liability companies. Ker was an early advocate of a deeds' registration system for conveyancing transactions, and he was a member of the real property commission that recommended such a system in 1850. He was also responsible for drafting the Real Property Amendment Act (8 & 9 Vict. c. 106) of 1844.

In 1833 Lord Brougham, as lord chancellor, appointed Ker a member of the royal commission on the criminal law, which was instructed to digest the criminal law into a single statute. This commission produced eight reports between 1834 and 1845 which culminated in 'An act of crimes and punishments', the first draft code of English criminal law. Lord Brougham attempted to enact this code, but the lord chancellor Lord Lyndhurst decided to appoint another commission to reconsider it. Ker was a member of this commission also, and it produced five reports between 1845 and 1849. It proved impossible to enact their recommendations, though their efforts contributed to the seven criminal-law consolidation acts passed in 1861. Ker was possibly the most important member of these commissions: indeed, it was largely due to his badgering of Brougham that Lyndhurst appointed the second commission.

Ker had a lifelong commitment to the improvement of statute law. His 'great interest and labour' during the first years of the criminal law commission was the preparation of its outline for the reform of statute law (*Parl. papers*, 1835, 35.365). He gave evidence before a select committee of the House of Commons in 1836 on the improvement of statutory drafting, and contributed an article on statute law to the *Edinburgh Review* in 1847. In early 1853 the lord chancellor Lord Cranworth took up the cause of statute law reform, establishing an informal statute revision board of five members and appointing Ker at its head. In August 1854 Lord Cranworth replaced this board with the statute law commission, which included many senior lawyers, judges, and politicians. Ker was its primary working member. He continued to serve on this commission until its demise in 1859.

The 1853 board and the subsequent commission attracted considerable criticism, much of which was personally directed against Ker. The *Law Review* and the *Law Magazine and Review* devoted a series of articles to the failures and defects of the board and the commission, calling attention at one point 'to evidences of the eminent inability and unfitness for his task which are to be found in Mr. Bellenden Ker … Ten thousand years would not produce a result in the present fashion of working' (*Law Review*, 22.93–5). There was criticism in both houses of parliament of the commission's expense and lack of progress. Nevertheless, Ker retained the confidence of Lord Cranworth, who often consulted him on legislative matters, and Lord Brougham paid warm tribute in the House of Lords to his work. Fitzroy Kelly defended the commission in the Commons and referred to the difficulties in translating its work into legislation. Ker retired from practice in 1860 and lived the rest of his life in Cannes, France, where he bought a house with his presumed sister-in-law, the artist Harriet Ludlow *Clarke. He died in Cannes on 2 November 1871. He was survived by his wife.

Ker was interested in art and science, becoming a fellow of the Royal Society in 1819 but resigning in 1830 in protest against the choice of the duke of Sussex as president, and the aristocratic domination of scientific associations which the appointment displayed. He was an original member of the Arundel Society (founded in 1848, for producing printed copies of paintings by old masters), was interested in the foundation of schools of design, and helped to promote the establishment of the Department of Science and Art. He was one of the first private growers of orchids and wrote a series of articles in the *Gardeners' Chronicle*. He had a hasty temper and a sarcastic manner, and he was quick to criticize the work of others; but he was also an energetic and innovative, if sometimes impractical, law reformer. He exemplified the tireless organizer of detail—in the form of data, papers, articles, reports, and draft legislation—whose perseverance and labours provided the foundation for the transformation of the law during his lifetime. He enjoyed strong friendships, as is evidenced by his surviving correspondence with Brougham, Lyndhurst, and Cranworth.

W. R. Cornish and David J. A. Cairns

Sources C. Carr, *A Victorian law reformer's correspondence* (1955) · W. R. Cornish and G. de N. Clark, *Law and society in England, 1750–1950* (1989), 252–7; 598–601 · R. Cross, 'The reports of the criminal law commissioners (1833–1849) and the abortive bills of 1853', *Reshaping the criminal law*, ed. P. R. Glazebrook (1978), 5–20 · J. S. Anderson, *Lawyers and the making of English land law, 1832–1940* (1992) · 'Statute law commission', *Law Review*, 22 (1855), 72–110 · 'The failure and fate of the statute law commission', *Law Magazine*, new ser., 7 (1859), 122–45 · 'The statute law commission', *Law Review*, 18 (1853), 67–76 · *Morning Chronicle* (11 Feb 1854) · *Morning Chronicle* (16 Feb 1854) · Parliamentary debates and papers, various dates · Ker's letters to Lord Brougham, UCL, Brougham MSS · *IGI*
Archives BL, letters to G. Cumberland, Add. MSS 36499–36516 · UCL, Brougham MSS, letters to Society for the Diffusion of Useful Knowledge
Likenesses G. R. Lewis, pencil drawing, BM
Wealth at death under £3000: probate, 18 June 1872?, *CGPLA Eng. & Wales*

Ker, James (*d.* 1768), jeweller and politician, was the son of Thomas Ker of Edinburgh, deacon of the corporation and a magistrate of the city, and his wife, Margaret, daughter and coheir of John Kerr of the Canongate. His grandfather was Sir Thomas Ker of Redden, Roxburghshire, the brother of Robert, first earl of Ancrum. Nothing is known of his early life, but on 8 July 1725 he married Jean (*d.* 1746), daughter of Gavin Thompson, writer to the signet, of Lowget, Edinburgh; the couple had three sons and eleven daughters. In 1734 he was elected deacon of the Incorporation of Goldsmiths, and became engraver to the mint and assay master in 1745.

Ker is reported as having commanded a company of gentleman volunteers, presumably during the Jacobite rising of 1745–6, and if so this probably helped his election on 2 December 1746 to the burgh council of the city of Edinburgh, as deacon of the Goldsmiths. He remained a member until 1754, and was elected convenor of the ordinary council deacons in 1747 and 1750. In 1747 Ker was returned as member of parliament for Edinburgh on the interest of the incorporated trades, of which he was in that year convenor. Although a government supporter himself, he had opposed George Drummond, lord provost of Edinburgh, the candidate supported by the prime minister, Henry Pelham. Ker accordingly called on the third

duke of Argyll and wrote to Pelham the day after his election, to apologize for standing against their candidate and promising his support for the government. Argyll gave him qualified approval; earlier in the year, on 23 July, he had written to Pelham:

> Mr Ker, the Jeweller, is certainly a Whig, but he was too much a Patriot at a certain time to be a favourite of mine, & I am told that he is weak & whymsical, though his professions of zeal for the present Administration is strong enough.
> (U. Nott. L., MS Ne C 1946/2)

On receipt of a friendly reply from Pelham, Ker wrote fulsomely of his loyalty to the administration, and was rewarded with a secret-service pension of £300 per annum. No record remains of Ker's parliamentary activities and it seems likely that he was content to act as a loyal government supporter rather than attempting to make a mark. On the burgh council he appears to have been meddlesome and unco-operative, and to have made many enemies. He was said to have formed an overweening sense of his own status and to have become haughty and vain. By the time of the next election Argyll reported to Pelham that Ker's behaviour and attitude had earned him the hatred and contempt of his fellow citizens. He had apparently highly disobliged many members of the council by bringing in members of the opposite party (who then campaigned against Ker himself), and had made enemies of the merchants by opposing their scheme to improve the harbour of Leith. In addition, a number of traders complained of his high-handed and contemptuous treatment of them, the result being: 'the town will not bear Mr Ker' (Argyll to Pelham, 5 Nov 1753, U. Nott. L., MS Ne C 2215). In 1754 he lost his place on the council and in the same year was not put up for re-election to parliament, and consequently lost his secret-service pension.

Ker's wife, Jean, died on 10 October 1746, and on 6 August 1750 he married for a second time, his bride on this occasion being Elizabeth (Betty) Ker (1713/14–1799), daughter of the late Lord Charles Ker, former director of the chancery and son of the first marquess of Lothian. This marriage resulted in five sons and two daughters. James Ker died on 24 January 1768 at Drumsheugh, near Edinburgh. For much of his life he had held property both in Edinburgh and at Bughtrig, Roxburghshire. His second wife outlived him, and died on 21 February 1799, at the age of eighty-five.

Andrew M. Lang

Sources R. R. Sedgwick, 'Ker, James', HoP, *Commons, 1715–54* · J. Foster, *Members of parliament, Scotland … 1357–1882*, 2nd edn (privately printed, London, 1882) · *Scots Magazine*, 12 (1750), 349 · U. Nott. L., Hallward Library, Newcastle (Clumber) MSS, Ne C 1946/2–3; Ne C 1948; Ne C 1936; Ne C 1937; Ne C 2212/1–2; Ne C 2214; Ne C 2215 · J. Foster, *The peerage, baronetage, and knightage of the British empire for 1881*, [2 pts] [1881] · Anderson, *Scot. nat.* · Irving, *Scots.*
Archives U. Nott. L., Hallward L., Newcastle (Clumber) MSS

Ker, James Innes-, fifth duke of Roxburghe (1736–1823), landowner, was born on 10 January 1736 at Innes House, Morayshire, the second of the three sons of Sir Hary or Henry Innes of Innes, fifth baronet (*d.* 1762), and his wife, Ann, the daughter of Sir James Grant of Grant, sixth baronet, and the sister of Jean Grant, who married the first

Earl Fife. During the rising of 1745 Morayshire was held by the Jacobites, and to avoid falling into their hands Innes was sent across the Moray Firth to Dunrobin Castle, seat of the earls of Sutherland. He was educated at the University of Leiden.

Like many other noblemen of little fortune, Innes took up a military career. He was appointed captain of the 88th foot (the Highland Volunteers) on 7 November 1759, and of the 58th foot in 1779. His elder brother Henry had died by 1759, and so on his father's death on 31 October 1762 he succeeded as sixth baronet. His family claimed to have held Innes since 1160, and at one time possessed the whole territory between the Spey and the Lossie, besides estates in Banffshire; but for a century their fortunes had been ebbing, and in 1767 Innes was obliged to sell his ancient barony of Innes to his first cousin James Duff, second Earl Fife. He did not remain landless for long. On 19 April 1769 he married—at St James's, Westminster—Mary (1730–1807), the eldest daughter of Sir John Wray, twelfth baronet, of Glentworth, Lincolnshire, and his wife, Frances, the daughter of Fairfax Norcliffe of Langton, Yorkshire. His wife inherited the Langton estate soon afterwards, and on 31 May 1769 Innes assumed by royal licence the additional surname of Norcliffe.

Perhaps following the reforming example of his brother-in-law Sir Cecil Wray, Innes-Norcliffe became a member of the Yorkshire Association, and he was one of the delegates who accompanied the movement's leader, Christopher Wyvill, to the meeting of delegates from county associations supporting parliamentary and economic reform in March and April 1781. He does not seem to have been politically active after this time. On his wife's death, on 20 July 1807, the Langton estate passed to her nephew Thomas Dalton.

Innes-Norcliffe, however, was now pursuing a grander inheritance. On 22 October 1805 William Bellenden Ker, fourth duke of Roxburghe, had died, leaving no surviving children. Innes's paternal great-grandfather, Sir James Innes, third baronet, had married in 1666 Margaret Ker, the third daughter of Harry, Lord Ker (d. 1643), himself son of Robert Ker, first earl of Roxburghe. The first earl had secured a regrant of his titles and estates in 1646, favouring first his grandson William Drummond and his descendants in the male line (the last of whom was the fourth duke), then the three younger sons of his daughter Jane, countess of Wigtown, and their descendants in the male line (provided the eldest surviving of the nominated heirs married the eldest surviving daughter of Harry, Lord Ker), and then the daughters of Harry, Lord Ker, in order of seniority, and their descendants in the male line, failing which, the earldom and estates should pass to the earl's nearest heir in the collateral male line. The dukedom of Roxburghe, created in 1707, had been given the same limitation, and, as the great-grandson of the only daughter of Lord Ker to have surviving descendants in the male line, Innes-Norcliffe claimed to have succeeded to the dukedom and estates. He took the surname Innes-Ker, and on 28 July 1807, eight days after his wife's death, married Harriet (bap. 1777, d. 1855), the daughter of Benjamin

Charlewood, of Windlesham, Surrey, and his wife, Mary, who had married as her second husband the engraver Valentine Green. The new Lady Innes-Ker had previously lived 'as a sort of companion' (Farington, Diary, 9.3234) to her husband's daughter.

Innes-Ker's claims were challenged by a number of rivals: Lady Essex Ker, the sister of the third duke; Major-General Walter Ker of Littledean, Roxburghshire, collateral heir male of the first earl; William Drummond of Logiealmond, Perthshire, collateral heir male of the fourth duke; and John Bellenden Ker, in whose favour the fourth duke had entailed the property. It took three days (15, 16, and 20 June 1809) for Lord Chancellor Eldon to state in the House of Lords the grounds on which he preferred Innes-Ker to the other claimants. The litigation continued until 11 May 1812, when the House of Lords finally recognized Innes-Ker as fifth duke of Roxburghe.

Roxburghe thus inherited Floors Castle, near Kelso, Roxburghshire, and the other ducal properties, since the House of Lords overturned the entail settling them on Bellenden Ker. He quickly sold the library of John *Ker, third duke, in order to pay his legal costs. Roxburghe enjoyed his new status by supporting several of his wife's impoverished relatives, some of whom were members of the circle of the diarist Joseph Farington. In 1814 he executed a deed of settlement which placed his estates and property in the hands of trustees, benefiting the heirs of the original entail but protecting the position of his wife and guaranteeing legacies to members of his and his wife's families. At the age of eighty he fathered a son, James Robert Henry (1816–1879), who eventually succeeded him as sixth duke, and the trust deed was amended to provide for his son's minority. Roxburghe died at Floors on 19 July 1823, and was buried in the Ker family vault at Bowden, Roxburghshire. His widow married, at Chelsea on 14 November 1827, Colonel Walter Frederick O'Reilly of the 41st foot. She died on 19 January 1855.

JAMES COOPER, rev. MATTHEW KILBURN

Sources 'Roxburghe', GEC, *Peerage*, new edn · D. Forbes, *An account of the familie of Innes*, ed. C. N. Innes (1864) · Farington, *Diary*, 9.3234; 11.4056, 4129; 14.4897; 16.5708 · *Floors Castle* (1995) · *Scots peerage* · *Reports of cases decided in the House of Lords, upon appeal from Scotland, from 1726 to 1822*, 6 vols. (1849–56), vol. 5 · trust deed and settlement, NA Scot., CC 18/4/6, 267–89
Archives NRA, priv. coll., corresp. and papers
Likenesses V. Green, mezzotint, pubd 1807 (after J. Reynolds), BM · H. Raeburn, portrait, Floors Castle, Borders region · attrib. J. Reynolds, oils, Floors Castle, Borders region · drawing, Floors Castle, Borders region
Wealth at death £32,965 7s. 9d.: will, NA Scot., CC 18/4/6, 267–89

Ker [Kerr; *née* Drummond], **Jane** [Jean], **countess of Roxburghe** (b. in or before **1585**, d. **1643**), courtier, was the third daughter of Patrick, third Lord Drummond (1550–c.1602), and his first wife, Elizabeth Lindsay (d. 1585), eldest daughter of David Lindsay, ninth earl of Crawford, and his second wife, Catherine, daughter of Sir John Campbell of Calder. Her court career spanned more than forty years and two reigns (with a period of enforced retirement between 1617 and 1631). She first appears in connection with royal service in 1602 and in May 1603 was among the few women attendants who accompanied Queen Anne, consort of James VI and I, to Stirling to take custody of Prince Henry. In June 1603 she accompanied the queen to England and remained, as first lady of the bedchamber, in close attendance on the queen and high in her favour until 1616–17.

In 1607–8 Jane Drummond conducted a correspondence with the laird of Glenorchy for a proposed marriage between herself and Archibald Campbell, seventh earl of Argyll. This proposal came to nothing and on 3 February 1614 she married another Scot, Robert *Ker, then Lord Roxburghe (1569/70–1650), a member of the Scottish privy council since 1610. The marriage celebrations, attended by the king and the court, were hosted by the queen at Somerset House, and included the performance of Samuel Daniel's pastoral, *Hymen's Triumph*. Sir John Holles reported a rumour that Roxburghe was to 'be viscounted and a councillor', but did not know whether 'this match or his name', that is Ker (or Carr)—shared with the royal favourite, Somerset—would 'gain him this fleece' (*Portland MSS*, 9.30). Roxburghe was created earl of Roxburghe on 18 September 1616 and the couple had at least three children, two sons (of whom one died in infancy) and a daughter.

From 1603 to 1617 the countess's activities at court were shaped by her Roman Catholicism, her privileged place as the queen's closest attendant and confidante, her support for Spain, and her Scottish kin connections. In 1604, prior to the signing of the Anglo-Spanish peace treaty, the Spanish ambassador, Juan de Taxis, conde de Villa Mediana, argued strongly for keeping her under the protection of Spain 'both to sustain the peace and because of our rivalry with the French' (Loomie, *Toleration*, 54). Besides gifts of money and a jewel she was awarded a secret Spanish pension of approximately £650 (2000 felipes or ducats) which she continued to receive under the code name of Amadis (from the romance 'Amadis de Gaul') until her enforced retirement in 1617. She was also the person on whom the envoys from Catholic states relied, as a confidential informant and conduit to and from the queen, particularly when treating of marriage alliances for the royal offspring. The countess also kept the queen firm in the Roman Catholic faith, being the means by which she was able, covertly, to practise her faith. When a Spanish match for Prince Charles was first mooted in 1614 it was noted that the countess would be the person who, together with the queen, would provide a favourable confessional environment for the infanta.

The countess's surviving letters reveal a witty and politically astute courtier. Active behind the scenes in court and international politics, she kept the queen favourably inclined towards Spain, thereby serving her own interests. In 1614, for example, she sought the assistance of Gondomar, the Spanish ambassador, in obtaining a place for a Ker kinsman in the household of Anne of Austria, working through the duke of Lerma. She was the sister-in-law of Alexander Seton, earl of Dunfermline, chancellor of Scotland, and a kinswoman of James Elphinstone, Lord

Balmerino. Her influence on the queen proved critical in saving the life of Balmerino, when, in 1609, he stood convicted of treason for allegedly falsely obtaining the king's signature on a letter to the pope.

However, in 1617 the queen insisted on the countess's retirement from her service and from court, ostensibly because her husband sought to secure the post of lord chamberlain of Prince Charles's household without either of them informing the queen. Both the Spanish and Venetian ambassadors expressed concern at her departure. Little is known of her activities during her fourteen-year absence from the court. In 1630 Charles I wished to appoint her governess to the prince of Wales but this was objected to on the basis of her religion and Mary, countess of Dorset, was appointed instead. In 1631 however, she was appointed governess to Mary, the princess royal. As Archibald Campbell reported, 'the ladie Roxbrucht hes gottin the upbringing of the kingis young dochter so that now in hir old dayies scho most becum ane new curtier' (NA Scot., MS GD. 112/39/43/22). By 1641 she was governess also to the duke of Gloucester and Princess Elizabeth. In March 1642 the countess accompanied the princess royal to the Netherlands after the princess's marriage to William of Orange. In December 1642, following her return to England, she was asked by parliament to attend on the two younger children 'as formerly' (*Fifth Report*, HMC, appx, 60). She died in London in June 1643 and was probably buried on 7 October 1643, probably in Bowden church, Floors, near Kelso, where her husband was buried on 20 March 1650.   HELEN PAYNE

Sources NA Scot., exchequer accounts, NAS, E21 · W. Fraser, *Memorials of the earls of Haddington*, 2 vols. (1889) · BL, Add. MSS 38138, fol. 186; 27404, fol. 37 · PRO, LS 13/280, fol. 345v; LR 6/154/9; LC 2/4/6, fol. 25v; SC 6/JasI/1656, fol. 16; SC 6/JasI/1648; SC 6/JasI/1650; SC 6/JasI/1653, fol. 21 · rolls series, Duchy of Cornwall Office, London, Box 122A · S. R. Gardiner, 'On certain letters of Diego Sarmiento de Acuna, count of Gondomar, concerning the earl of Somerset', *Archaeologia*, 41 (1867), 151–86 · A. J. Loomie, ed., *Spain and the Jacobean Catholics*, 2 vols., Catholic RS, 64, 68 (1973–8) · A. J. Loomie, *Toleration and diplomacy: the religious issues in Anglo-Spanish relations, 1603–05* (1963) · A. Ballesteros Beretta, ed., *Documentos inéditos para la historia de España: correspondencia oficial de Don Diego Sarmiento de Acuna conde de Gondomar*, 13 vols. (1937–57) · *CSP Venice, 1640–42* · transcripts of state papers, 1603–1625, made by S. R. Gardiner, from original at Simancas and Venice, BL, Add. MS 31111, fol. 45 · *Letters of King James VI & I*, ed. G. P. V. Akrigg (1984) · NA Scot., Breadalbane MSS, GD 112/39/20/2, 3, 5, 13 · *The memoirs of Robert Carey*, ed. F. H. Mares (1972) · *The private correspondence of Jane, Lady Cornwallis, 1613–1644*, ed. Lord Braybrooke (1842) · F. Francisco de Jesus, *El hecho de los tratados del matrimonio pretendido por el principe de Gales con la serenissima infante de España, María / Narrative of the Spanish marriage treaty*, ed. and trans. S. R. Gardiner, CS, 101 (1869) · GEC, *Peerage* · *Scots peerage*, 7.346 · *The manuscripts of his grace the duke of Portland*, 10 vols., HMC, 29 (1891–1931), vol. 9 · *Fifth report*, HMC, 4 (1876) · PRO, PROB 11/197, fol. 140
Likenesses M. Gheeraets, oils, c.1618, repro. in K. Marshall, *Costume in Scottish portraits, 1560–1830* (1986) · oils, Floors Castle
Wealth at death see GEC, *Peerage*, 11.218

Ker, John, of Kersland [*formerly* John Crawfurd] (1673–1726), spy, was born John Crawfurd at Crawfurdland, Ayrshire, on 8 August 1673, the eldest son of Alexander Crawfurd of Fergushill, and grandson of John Crawfurd, laird of Crawfurdland. He assumed the title and arms of Ker of Kersland in 1697 when he acquired Kersland through his wife, Anna, younger daughter of Robert Ker of Kersland. Following Robert Ker's death the estate passed to his son, Daniel Ker of the Cameronians, who was killed at the battle of Steenkerke in 1692, then to his elder daughter, Jean, who sold it to Anna's husband four years later. At the time Crawfurd acquired Kersland he was already in financial trouble, and within a few years his situation worsened so drastically that half of his property was feued and mortgaged to others. In the dedication of his *Memoirs* (published in 1726), Ker denied that money motivated him to carry out intelligence work for the government. Nevertheless his increasing impecuniosity very probably did lead him into espionage and the betrayal of members of the Cameronian sect of Presbyterians, among whom he was accepted as a leader.

During 1706 Scots from a series of social backgrounds and of opposing religious and political persuasions were involved in protests against the treaty of union then under negotiation with English ministers. Even Jacobites in the highlands had hopes of making common cause with the staunch Presbyterian Cameronians of the southwest, and Ker claimed that in order to achieve this the highlanders 'industriously concealed their true Design', namely, the restoration of the Stuart Pretender (Ker, 1.28). On learning that the Cameronians were to meet at Sanquhar in Nithsdale to decide whether to accept the offer to join forces with the highlanders, the duke of Queensberry sent Ker to persuade them to reject the proposal. Ker accepted the commission, explaining afterwards:

> It was then I embarked so heartily in those Measures, which afterwards gave me so much Sorrow; altho' I declare solemnly, that instead of any Mischief in View at that Time, I had rather the Misfortune to believe that I was doing good Service to my own Country, and the Protestant Interest. (ibid., 1.31)

He rode into Nithsdale 'full of unbridled Zeal' (ibid., 1.32), and there persuaded the sect to withhold its support. This, he claimed, was instrumental in blocking the plans of opponents of the union.

Others disputed Ker's role at that time and afterwards. The writer of the preface to the account of Nathaniel Hooke, Louis XIV's agent in Scotland at the time (published in 1760), commented savagely: 'As to the ostentatious offers of the Laird of Kersland, that gentleman's vanity and restless character is too well known in this country, to lay the smallest stress on what he advances' (Hooke, *Secret History*, iii). George Lockhart of Carnwath also despised Ker, asserting that as he

> was known to be a person highly immoral and guilty of several base actions, such as forgery and the like, no person of the least note would have the least intercourse with him, yet he found means to ingratiate himself with several people of no great rank, from whom he picked up stories. (Lockhart, 1.302)

On his return to Edinburgh after persuading the Cameronians to reject the Jacobite overture, Ker was assured that Queen Anne would recognize the service he had rendered her government, and he was granted royal licence to associate with disaffected individuals in order to gather intelligence. By so doing he was 'thereby led into farther Labyrinths, and added to my misfortunes' (Ker, 1.37), being soon, according to his own account, the employer of spies and agents across the country. The first of these 'labyrinths' involved infiltration of Jacobite plotters in the period preceding James Stuart's attempted rising of 1708. With Anne's royal licence in his pocket Ker boldly negotiated with the Jacobites, who referred to him by several code names—Thomas Trustie, Wilks, Wicks, and the Cameronian Mealmonger. Claiming to represent Cameronians of five shires, he held talks with a Roman Catholic named Strachan, offering 13,000 men for the Pretender's service and volunteering to travel to France as a hostage to their loyalty (Hooke, *Correspondence*, 2.308–9). In August 1707 he even urged the French to act soon. 'We are all convinced that the only way to save Scotland is to restore our king,' he wrote. 'The opportunity is excellent; it never was so good; and if you lose it, it will never be found again' (Hooke, *Secret History*, 106–7). Stuart agents revealed much of their plans to Ker, including a plot to seize Edinburgh Castle, and even supplied him with the cipher used in correspondence between Scotland and France. All this was passed to Queensberry, who once again assured him he would be rewarded. 'Truly, I dare say, I was rewarded just as I deserved', he boasted (Ker, 1.47). But before the year was out Ker's duplicity had been discovered, and the duchess of Gordon told Hooke, 'Mr Wicks is turned a knave' (Hooke, *Correspondence*, 2.517). In March 1709 Ker travelled to London, where the lord treasurer, Lord Godolphin, paid him the money he was due. However, according to Lockhart, Ker was paid £500 to £600, which was increased to at least 2000 guineas after he threatened to reveal Godolphin's connections with the Jacobites (Lockhart, 308).

Four years later Ker claimed he was sent to Vienna to promote a scheme for harassing French and Spanish trade. When the emperor rejected his plan, he apparently remained and passed on all the information he could to the Electress Sophia of Hanover. For his trouble he was presented with 'the Emperor's picture in gold, set round with diamonds' (Ker, 1.87). From Vienna Ker moved to Hanover, where he claimed to help secure the Hanoverian succession, and had the pleasure of informing the new British royal family that 'my Joy is so exceeding great, that I think all my Labour and Industry is more than rewarded' (ibid., 1.93). He received a couple of gold medals as a token of his majesty's favour, but wanted more. He asked for the governorship of Bermuda and was refused because, he said, he would not bribe the appropriate officials. He moved on to Holland and then to London, where he offered his services to the government at the start of the 1715 Jacobite rising, but these were rejected, and he was left at the end of the rebellion lamenting the misfortune of so many of his countrymen whose suffering he claimed he might have prevented had he been allowed to intervene. John Ker's life continued on a downhill path, with failure of an attempt to interest the emperor of Austria in the East India Company, and an unsuccessful plan to set up a trading company in the Austrian Netherlands.

During his time abroad Ker's wife, in desperate financial straits, had to make over her furniture and plate to friends in return for money to support herself. In 1718 he sold Fergushill to John Asgill and Robert Hackett for £3600, and half of it was mortgaged back to Ker for £2600. In spite of every effort he ended up in the king's bench debtors' prison in London, where he died on 8 July 1726. He was buried in St George's churchyard, Southwark. His widow soldiered on, producing a forged deed in the name of her elder sister, Jean, through whom Kersland had come to her. However, the estate and barony of Kersland was eventually sold in 1788. The couple were survived by their three daughters: Elizabeth, who married John Campbell of Ellangieg in Argyll, and Anna and Jean, of whom no further details are known. Ker's *Memoirs* was published in three volumes in 1726, the last posthumously. Even so the publisher, Edmund Curll, incurred the wrath of the government for publishing 'a False, Scandalous and Malicious Libel' and was fined 20 marks and forced to stand in the pillory at Charing Cross for a day. Curll, however, had the last word, publishing the government's accusations against him as an appendix to the third volume, reprinted in 1727.   HUGH DOUGLAS

Sources DNB · J. Ker of Kersland, *The memoirs of John Ker*, 3 vols. (1726) [repr. 1727] · G. Lockhart, *The Lockhart papers: containing memoirs and commentaries upon the affairs of Scotland from 1702 to 1715*, 2 vols. (1817) · *Correspondence of Colonel N. Hooke*, ed. W. D. Macray, 2 vols., Roxburghe Club, 92, 95 (1870–71) · N. Hooke, *The secret history of Colonel Hooke's negotiations in Scotland in favour of the Pretender, in 1707* (1760)
Likenesses J. Vandergucht, line engraving, pubd 1726 (after Hammond), BM, NPG; repro. in Ker, *Memoirs* · Hammond, engraving, repro. in Ker, *Memoirs*
Wealth at death in king's bench debtors' prison

Ker, John, first duke of Roxburghe (*c*.1680–1741), politician, was the second of three children of Robert, third earl of Roxburghe (*c*.1658–1682) and his wife, Margaret (1658–1753), eldest daughter of John, first marquess of Tweeddale. On 13 July 1696 Roxburghe's elder brother, Robert, fourth earl of Roxburghe, died, aged eighteen, and Roxburghe was served heir male and of entail to his brother on 22 October.

Roxburghe played a significant part in Scottish politics in the years from 1702 onwards. George Lockhart of Carnwath, who was normally a political opponent of Roxburghe, wrote that Roxburghe:

> was a man of good sense, improven by so much reading and learning that, perhaps, he was the best accomplish'd young man in Europe, and had so charming a way of expressing his thoughts, that he pleased even those 'gainst whom he spoke. (Lockhart, 1.95)

James, second duke of Queensberry, who led Queen Anne's Scottish administration, was keen to discredit his opponents, regardless of whether they were Jacobites or, as in the case of Roxburghe, his fellow whigs. In the winter of 1703–4 Roxburghe, John, ninth earl of Rothes, and

John Ker, first duke of Roxburghe (*c*.1680–1741), by Jonathan Richardson the elder, 1723

George Baillie of Jerviswood went to London to counter the disinformation that Queensberry was spreading about them. They were successful, and Sidney, first earl of Godolphin, head of Anne's English administration, had Queensberry sacked. In 1704 John, second marquess of Tweeddale, formed a new Scottish administration, composed of whigs formerly in opposition: they were known as the 'new party', and subsequently as the squadrone. Roxburghe served as secretary in this administration, from October 1704 to May 1705.

Tweeddale's ministry were discredited by their acquiescing in the judicial lynching at Leith, in March 1705, of the crew of an English ship, the *Worcester*. They were promptly replaced by a ministry made up of Queensberry's cronies under John, second duke of Argyll. None the less the squadrone, once again in opposition, decided to support the Scottish government in the votes that led to the Union of 1707. Recent historians have given much of the credit for this decision to Roxburghe. He believed, or at any rate self-interestedly professed to believe, that the Scottish parliament would vote for union. He phrased this belief succinctly in a letter of 28 November 1705 to George Baillie: 'The motives will be, Trade with most, Hanover with some, ease and security with others' (*Correspondence of George Baillie*, 138).

Under the terms for the Union the Scots were to be compensated for undertaking to help service the pre-Union English national debt. The squadrone were duped into thinking that they would be allowed to help disburse this 'equivalent' money, but this did not happen. As a sop to Roxburghe's pride he was on 25 April 1707 created duke of Roxburghe, marquess of Bowmont and Cessford, earl of Kelso, viscount of Broxmouth, and Lord Ker of Cessford and Caverton, with the same remainder of these dignities as that of the earldom of Roxburghe. This was the last title ever created in the peerage of Scotland. On 1 January 1708 he married Mary (1677–1718), widow of William Savile, second marquess of Halifax, and eldest daughter of Daniel Finch, second earl of Nottingham. Their only child, Robert, was born about 1709, and succeeded his father as second duke of Roxburghe.

Roxburghe continued to play a part in the politics of the newly created British state. He was elected as one of the sixteen representative peers of Scotland in the general elections of 1707, 1708, 1715, and 1727. In March 1709 he was sworn of the privy council. From 1 August to 28 September 1714 he served as one of the lords regent, before the safe arrival in Britain of George I. In November 1715 he served as a volunteer soldier in the Hanoverian army that checked the Jacobite rising at the battle of Sheriffmuir. He was keeper of the privy seal of Scotland from 1714 to 1716, and then became the third (Scottish) secretary of state.

As in the period before 1707 Roxburghe was involved in the competition and jealousies among Scottish whigs. He supported the Peerage Bill of 1719 and, though he was created a knight of the Garter in 1722, he backed John Carteret rather than the rising star, Sir Robert Walpole. Walpole seized the opportunity of the Shawfield riot to dismiss Roxburghe from office in August 1725, following upon a report by Archibald, earl of Ilay, that in Scotland 'by a long series of no-administration, the mere letter of the law had little or no effect with the people' (Coxe, 1.232).

Thereafter Roxburghe, though he acted as deputy high constable (Scotland) at the coronation of George II in 1727, lived largely in political retirement. Floors Castle, Roxburghshire, had been built for him by Sir John Vanbrugh in 1718. He died on 27 February 1741 at Floors, aged about sixty, and was buried at Bowden parish church, also in Roxburghshire. JOHN M. SIMPSON

Sources GEC, *Peerage*, new edn · P. W. J. Riley, *The union of England and Scotland* (1978) · W. Ferguson, *Scotland: 1689 to the present* (1968) · G. Lockhart, *The Lockhart papers: containing memoirs and commentaries upon the affairs of Scotland from 1702 to 1715*, 2 vols. (1817) · *Correspondence of George Baillie of Jerviswood, 1702–1708*, ed. G. E. M. Kynynmond (1842) · W. Coxe, *Memoirs of the life and administration of Sir Robert Walpole, earl of Orford*, 3 vols. (1798) · *Scots peerage*

Archives U. Durham L., notes on coal | NA Scot., letters to Sir William Bennett · NA Scot., corresp. with Lord Leven · NA Scot., letters to duke of Montrose · NRA, priv. coll., letters to his mother

Likenesses J. Richardson the elder, oils, 1723, Floors Castle, Roxburghshire [*see illus.*] · J. Vanderbank, oils, 1738, Inveraray Castle,

Argyll and Bute · oils, Scot. NPG; version, Floors Castle, Roxburghshire

Ker, John (*d*. 1741), Latin poet, was born at Dunblane, Perthshire. He was for a time schoolmaster at Crieff, Perthshire, and about 1710 became a master at the Royal High School, Edinburgh. He composed memorial verses on the death of Archibald Pitcairne (1652–1713), the Latin poet and most important Jacobite literary figure in contemporary Scotland. In 1717 Ker became professor of Greek at King's College, Aberdeen, the first special teacher of the subject there.

In 1725 Ker published in Edinburgh *Donaides, sive, Musarum Aberdonensium de eximia J. Fraseri munificentia carmen eucharisticum*, a poem celebrating the distinguished dons and alumni of Aberdeen University. Further memorial verses include those on the Latin lyricist Sir William Scott of Thirlestane (1624?–1725) and, for the university, *Fraserides, sive, Funebris oratio et elegia in laudem J. Fraserii*, in 1731. In 1727 appeared his paraphrase of the Song of Solomon, *Cantici Solomonis: prior vario carminum genere, altera Sapphicis versibus prescripta … auctore Joanne Kerro*. The volume also contained Arthur Johnson's paraphrase of the same biblical text, dedicated to Charles Edward Stuart as king of Great Britain. Both works were reprinted in 1739, together with a number of original Latin poems, some with similar dedications, by Patrick Adamson, William Barclay, Robert Boyd, George Eglisham, Arthur Johnston, John Johnston, and William Hogg in an anthology, *Poetarum Scotorum musae sacrae*, edited by William Lauder. Ker's strong Jacobite sympathies seem to have been no barrier to higher academic appointments, for on 2 October 1734 he succeeded Adam Watt as professor of Latin at Edinburgh University. Here he studied law and associated again with friends of high school days, enjoying both popularity and the great respect of his students. He also taught the humanity course and was praised by Alexander Carlyle as 'very much master of his business' (*Autobiography*, ed. Burton, 31).

Ker contributed greatly to the growth of antiquarianism so characteristic of the eighteenth century and had a distinct influence in reviving exact Latin scholarship in Scotland. The Latin ballad on the battle of Killiecrankie versified in English by Walter Scott is most probably Ker's. He died in Edinburgh in November 1741.

T. W. BAYNE, *rev.* RICHARD RIDDELL

Sources A. Bower, *The history of the University of Edinburgh*, 2 (1817), 296–314 · L. Bradner, *Musae Anglicanae: a history of Anglo-Latin poetry, 1500–1925* (1940), 291 · *Autobiography of the Rev. Dr. Alexander Carlyle … containing memorials of the men and events of his time*, ed. J. H. Burton (1860), 31 · G. Chalmers, *The life of Thomas Ruddiman* (1794), 98 · R. Chambers, *Songs of Scotland prior to Burns* (1862), 43 · J. Erskine, 'Sermon on the death of [William] Robertson the historian', *Discourses preached on several occasions*, 1 (1798) [see appendix to chapter, p. 271] · A. Grant, *The story of the University of Edinburgh during its first three hundred years*, 2 (1884), 318 · D. K. Money, *The English Horace: Anthony Alsop and the tradition of British Latin verse* (1998), 143

Ker, John, third duke of Roxburghe (1740–1804), book collector, was born on 23 April 1740, at Hanover Square, London, the oldest of four surviving children of Robert Ker, second duke (*c*.1709–1755), and his wife, Essex (*d*.

John Ker, third duke of Roxburghe (1740–1804), by Pompeo
Batoni, 1761–2

1764), daughter of Sir Roger *Mostyn, third baronet. He
succeeded to the dukedom on 20 August 1755, while a
schoolboy at Eton College, which he left in 1758. Later he
travelled in continental Europe, where he became friends
with Christiana Sophia Albertina, eldest daughter of the
duke of Mecklenburg-Strelitz, and intended to marry her.
But in September 1761 Christiana's younger sister, Charlotte, married George III. If Roxburghe had married Christiana, she would have become Charlotte's subject. The
obituary of Roxburghe in the *Gentleman's Magazine* (1st ser.,
74, 1804, 383) says that this problem of etiquette, 'operating with some other reasons, broke off the negociation'.

Whatever the other reasons, Roxburghe never married,
and it is a plausible interpretation that his unlucky
romance changed the character of his life. Certainly, Sir
Walter Scott, who was personally acquainted with Roxburghe, was of this view:

> Youthful misfortunes, of a kind against which neither rank
> nor wealth possess a talisman, had cast an early shade of
> gloom over his prospects, and given to one so splendidly
> endowed with the means of enjoying society that degree of
> reserved melancholy which prefers retirement to the
> splendid scenes of gaiety.   (Scott, 44.446)

Roxburghe did become a lord of the bedchamber (1767),
knight of the Thistle (1768), groom of the stole and first
lord of the bedchamber (1796), privy councillor (1796),
and—being permitted to retain the Thistle, which was

unusual—knight of the Garter (1801). He enjoyed a role at
the court as friend of George III, which would explain why
he lived much of the time in London; he purchased a
house at 13 St James's Square in 1795 and kept his main library there until his death. This friendship with the king
was itself supported by their shared interests in book collecting; George Nicol, bookseller to both George III (since
1781) and the duke, comments on the king's appreciation
of Roxburghe (Nicol and Nicol, 20 [18]). When at Floors
Castle, his Scottish family home, Roxburghe was, as we
know from Scott's description, keen on outdoor pursuits,
but book collecting was his primary interest. In 1807 Nicol
wrote that it was the duke's

> favourite plan to pass through life among his books,
> studiously endeavouring to conceal, from the world, his
> eminent talents, and his extensive knowledge. And so
> successful was he in this endeavour, that neither his
> neighbours in the country, nor his friends in the Capital,
> seem to have been much acquainted with them.   (ibid., 19–
> 20 [17–18])

This passion for book collecting may well have had a
family origin. The Valdarfer Boccaccio (Boccaccio,
Decamerone, 1471), which most sensationally sold in 1812
for £2260, a record price for a single book until 1884, features in a story told by Sir Walter Scott. Two famous collectors, Lord Oxford (either Robert Harley, first earl of
Oxford, or Edward Harley, second earl of Oxford) and Lord
Sunderland (Charles Spencer, third earl of Sunderland),
were dining with Roxburghe's father when they talked
about the 1471 Boccaccio, which the second duke duly
acquired and, on a later occasion, produced for them. 'His
son … who never forgot the little scene upon this occasion, used to ascribe to it the strong passion which he ever
afterwards felt for rare books and editions' (Scott, 44.446–
7). There are serious chronological problems with this
anecdote, but Roxburghe was himself clear about the origins of his interest, and it is likely to contain a kernel of
truth.

It is difficult to judge when Roxburghe's collecting
began in earnest, as it is very poorly documented. The
earliest noteworthy acquisition that can be dated is the
purchase, in 1788, of two volumes of black-letter ballads
previously owned by Thomas Pearson (Nicol and Nicol, 5).
Roxburghe was himself passionately interested in ballad
literature and added a third volume. The three volumes,
now in the British Library, were published by the Ballad
Society as *The Roxburghe Ballads* (ed. W. Chappell and J. W.
Ebsworth, 9 vols., 1869–99). His library grew apace, and at
his death it totalled an estimated 30,000 volumes. The
most significant part was the collection of early English
literature, with twenty-three English incunabula, including fifteen Caxtons, and a large number of rare sixteenth-
century editions; he also owned rare and important early
Scottish books. Analysis suggests that he was driven not so
much by a desire to own early or fine books regardless of
their content (otherwise it would be strange that he
owned no more than about 120 incunabula, and never
acquired a copy of the Gutenberg Bible) as by his subject
interests. Thus, he followed up the romances among his

English literature collection with manuscripts of French Arthurian texts and a wide selection of romances from across mainland Europe. That he collected by theme is also shown by George Nicol, who noted that at the time of his death Roxburghe was 'in full pursuit of collecting our dramatic authors' (Nicol and Nicol, 14).

Roxburghe died at his London house of an inflammation of the liver on 19 March 1804, and was buried at Bowden, near Melrose. He was survived by two sisters, but his younger brother, Robert (b. 1747), had died in 1781, and his successor in the dukedom was the seventh Lord Bellenden. However, the fourth duke died in 1805, leaving a disputed succession. Only when this was resolved in 1812 was the duke's library—in both London and Floors Castle—sent to the sale rooms: in London in two parts, beginning 18 May (forty-two days) and 13 July (four days), totalling £23,341, and in Kelso on 16 September 1813. Roxburghe's fame really stems from the sale of his library, which has gone down in the history of book collecting as the high point of obsessive collecting for which Thomas Frognall Dibdin coined the term 'bibliomania' in his *Bibliomania, or, Book-Madness* (1809). Roxburghe books are today the prized possessions of many of the world's great libraries, and their collector is immortalized by the distinction of having named after him one of the most exclusive and famous of bibliographical societies, the Roxburghe Club, which was formed at a dinner held on 17 June 1812, on the day when the Valdarfer Boccaccio was scheduled for auction. BRIAN HILLYARD

Sources DNB · A catalogue of the library of the late John, duke of Roxburghe, arranged by G. and W. Nicol, booksellers to his majesty, Pall-Mall (1812) · A supplement to the catalogue of the library of the late John, duke of Roxburghe (1812) · A catalogue of the library of the late John, duke of Roxburghe (1813) [sale catalogue, Lauder's Ball-Room, Kelso, 16 Sept 1813] · B. Hillyard, 'John Ker, third duke of Roxburghe', Pre-nineteenth-century British book collectors and bibliographers, ed. W. Baker and K. Womack, DLitB, 213 (1999), 196–206 · G. Nicol and W. Nicol, The preface to a catalogue of the library of the late John, duke of Roxburghe (1807) · W. Scott, review of Pitcairn's Ancient criminal trials of Scotland, QR, 44 (1831), 438–75; repr. in Miscellaneous prose works, 28 vols. (1834–6), vol. 21 · J. A. H. Murray, ed., The complaynt of Scotlande, Early English Text Society, extra ser., no. 17 (1872) · G. N. [G. Nicol], preface, Acts of the Scottish parliament that were cancelled in printed copies bearing the date of Nov. 28, 1566, reprinted from perfect copy of Oct. 12, 1566 [n.d., 1801?] · T. Constable, Archibald Constable and his literary correspondents, 3 vols. (1873) · C. Bigham, The Roxburghe Club: its history and its members, 1812–1927 (1928) · T. F. Dibdin, The bibliographical decameron, 3 vols. (1817) · T. F. Dibdin, The bibliomania, or, Book-madness (1809) · T. F. Dibdin, Reminiscences of a literary life, 2 vols. (1836) · GEC, Peerage, new edn, vol. 11 · Scots peerage · R. A. Austen-Leigh, ed., The Eton College register, 1753–1790 (1921) · A. I. Dasent, The history of St James's Square (1895)

Archives NL Scot., material

Likenesses P. Batoni, oils, 1761–2, Floors Castle [see illus.] · T. Patch, caricature, oils, NPG · W. Say, mezzotint (after W. Beechey), BM, NPG; repro. in J. Ames, Typographical antiquities, ed. T. F. Dibdin, 4 (1819) · C. E. Wagstaff, stipple (after W. Hamilton), BM, NPG; repro. in W. Jerdan, National portrait gallery of illustrious and eminent personages, 3 (1832) · oils, Scot. NPG · oils, Floors Castle · portrait, engraving, repro. in W. Clarke, Repertorium bibliographicum, or, Some account of the most celebrated British libraries (1819)

Ker, John (1819–1886), minister of the United Presbyterian church, was born in the farmhouse of Bield, in the parish of Tweedsmuir, Peeblesshire, on 7 April 1819. His parents moved successively to Fillyside, a farm between Leith and Portobello, and to Abbeyhill, Edinburgh. While his father adhered to the established church, his mother was a seceder, and through that connection young John was exposed to the ministry of John Brown (1784–1858). After education at Edinburgh high school, Ker entered Edinburgh University in 1835 and distinguished himself in Sir William Hamilton's class, where he gained first prize. In 1838 he entered the Divinity Hall of the United Secession church. He also studied French and German, in the latter case committing an entire dictionary to memory, as well as Hebrew and Arabic. In 1842 Ker travelled to Germany, where he studied under Tholuck at Halle for six months.

Licensed in 1844, Ker was called by the congregation of Clayport Street, Alnwick, Northumberland, to which he was ordained on 11 February 1845. He was reluctant to move from there, and it was only at the second attempt that he was translated to East Campbell Street Church, Glasgow, where he was inducted colleague to Dr Kidston and Mr Brash on 19 March 1851. The vigorous young minister soon arrested the decline in the congregation's fortunes and he embarked on an intensive pastoral ministry. He turned down a call to a Bristol charge and similarly declined a request to become his church's first home mission secretary. An expanded church with seating for 1200 was erected in Sydney Place, but Ker's health broke down in 1858 and thereafter he spent much time on the continent. A partial recovery of health allowed him to perform the duties of professor of practical training in the United Presbyterian College from 1876. It was a role to which he was perfectly suited and he was able to discharge his duties up to the time of his sudden death, from heart disease, at The Hermitage, Murrayfield, Edinburgh, where he lived with a married sister, on 4 October 1886. Ker was buried in the new Calton cemetery, Edinburgh, on 7 October.

In spite of the inhibiting influence of poor health and although he lacked the attributes of a conventional leader, Ker was seen by contemporaries as one of the leading figures in his church. As a preacher he bore comparison with William Bruce Robertson (1820–1886), and his published *Sermons* (1869) were hugely popular. His humour, learning, and graciousness endeared him to all he met: 'In the pulpit he was a king, in the class-room a master, in social life lovable, among ripe scholars and grand men the equal of the best' (*Christian Leader*, 2 Dec 1886, 734). The travel and leisure forced on him enabled Ker to be still more cultured, and he was a keen antiquarian with a wide knowledge of Scottish history and an equal interest in current affairs. In 1869 he received the honorary degree of DD from Edinburgh University.

LIONEL ALEXANDER RITCHIE

Sources The Scotsman (5 Oct 1886) · The Scotsman (6 Oct 1886) · The Scotsman (11 Oct 1886) · United Presbyterian Magazine, new ser., 30 (1886), 485–9, 534–40 · Christian Leader, 1 (1882), 449–50, 465–6 · Christian Leader, 5 (1886), 699–700, 715–16, 734 · R. Small, History of the congregations of the United Presbyterian church from 1733 to 1900, 2

(1904), 40–41 • J. Smith, *Our Scottish clergy*, 3rd ser. (1851), 272–80 • *Letters of the Rev John Ker, D.D., 1866–1885* (1890) • *DNB*
Wealth at death £16,944 6s. 1d.: probate, 18 Jan 1887, *CCI*

Ker [Kerr], **Mark** (1517–1584), landowner and administrator, second son of Sir Andrew *Ker (d. 1526) of Cessford, Roxburghshire, and Agnes, daughter of Sir Patrick Crichton of Cranstoun Riddel, Edinburghshire, was born in Edinburgh Castle, of which Sir Patrick was then keeper. After graduating MA from St Andrews University he held several church livings, which he was dispensed to hold although under the canonical age. In 1547 the pope provided him to the abbacy of Newbattle, to be held *in commendam* during the lifetime of the existing abbot James Haswell, and two years later he was dispensed from taking monastic vows. Technically a cleric, he remained the recognized heir to the properties of his powerful border family after the direct heirs of his brother, Sir Walter Ker. In 1555 he was accused of killing a French soldier in a fracas at Newbattle. He gained personal possession of the abbey estates in 1557 on Abbot Haswell's death.

Ker sat in parliament in 1558 and probably in the provincial council of the Scottish church in 1559 (no list of those attending survives). At the same time he associated with the party that favoured religious reform and *rapprochement* with England. He subscribed to the protestant Band of Leith in April 1560, and sat in the so-called Reformation Parliament the following August, voting for the adoption of the protestant confession of faith. Having supported Queen Mary as lawful monarch in the 1560s, he became an extraordinary lord of session and privy councillor in 1569 and sat on several government commissions and inquiries. In 1572 he was a negotiator with Queen Mary's remaining supporters, and he was one of three judges appointed to settle disputes (from the country south of the River Tay) arising from the terms of the pacification of Perth (23 February 1573). In 1575 and 1580 he was appointed to border commissions. Initially a supporter of the regent Morton, he was on the council which carried on the government on the latter's resignation in 1578 and took part in attempts at reconciliation with Morton's representatives. He became a close ally of Esmé Stewart, made duke of Lennox, who arrived from France in 1579, and who some feared might become a focus for a revival of the queen's cause or even of the Roman Catholic faith. Ker, himself a protestant, was sent by Lennox to attempt an accommodation with the ultra-protestant party after the Ruthven raid (1582), in which that party tried to remove the king from Lennox's influence.

Having shed his clerical character for a lay career, and having survived the political storms of the new reign, Ker also exploited the resources of the Newbattle lands which he had acquired on the eve of the Reformation settlement. Through an extensive programme of feuing, which sometimes involved the eviction of long-settled leasehold tenants, the development of coal workings and salt pans, and the sales of wool from huge flocks of sheep, Ker became a wealthy man, possessed at death of an estate valued at just over £16,000 Scots. He treated the surviving monks of Newbattle harshly, turning them out and only

reluctantly paying their maintenance even after they took him to law. He converted the monastic site into a family home which, extended by his descendants, is one of the few Scottish country houses to take its name from the monastery it replaced.

Some time after 1560 Ker married Lady Helen Leslie (d. 1594), daughter of George, fourth earl of Rothes, and widow of Gilbert Seton the younger of Parbroath, with whom he had formed a relationship in the late 1550s. Their eldest son, Mark *Ker, later first earl of Lothian, was born before 20 February 1559, when he and his mother had a charter of abbey lands from the commendator. Their other children were Andrew of Fenton, George, who became a Roman Catholic and was involved in the affair of the so-called Spanish blanks in 1592, William, and Katherine, who married William Maxwell, fourth Lord Herries, from a Roman Catholic recusant family. Ker also had an illegitimate daughter, Margaret, who married John Crawford of Roughsallow, Lanarkshire, while Helen Leslie had a son, David, and a daughter, Janet, from her first marriage. Mark Ker died, at Newbattle, on 19 August 1584, and his wife died on 26 October 1594. They were buried at Newbattle, and both left wills.

MARGARET H. B. SANDERSON

Sources M. H. B. Sanderson, 'Mark Ker, 1517–1584, metamorphosis', *Mary Stewart's people: life in Mary Stewart's Scotland* (1987), 166–78 • NA Scot., Lothian muniments, GD 40 • *Reg. PCS*, 1st ser., vols. 1–2 • registers of testaments, NA Scot., Edinburgh Commissary Court, CC8/8/16, fol. 79 • registers of testaments, NA Scot., Edinburgh Commissary Court, CC8/8/29, fol. 280 • court of session records, registers of acts and decreets, NA Scot., CS6, vol. 18, fol. 273r; vol. 23, fol. 129r; vol. 32, fol. 386v; vol. 43, fol. 38r • R. Pitcairn, ed., *Ancient criminal trials in Scotland*, 7 pts in 3, Bannatyne Club, 42 (1833) • *Scots peerage*, vol. 5
Archives NA Scot., Lothian muniments, records of Newbattle Abbey and the Kers of Cessford
Likenesses attrib. W. Key, oils, 1550–59, Scot. NPG
Wealth at death approx. £16,046 5s. Scots [approx. £1337]: will, NA Scot., CC8/8/16, fol. 79r

Ker [Kerr], **Mark**, **first earl of Lothian** (*b.* in or before **1559**, *d.* **1609**), administrator, was the oldest son of Mark *Ker (1517–1584), commendator of Newbattle, and Lady Helen (d. 1594), daughter of George *Leslie, fourth earl of Rothes. He was born before 20 February 1559, when his father, then technically a cleric, granted a charter of Newbattle Abbey land to him and his mother. His parents married some time soon after 1560. During his lifetime the Newbattle property was steadily transformed into a secular lordship in his favour. On 7 April 1567 Queen Mary made him a grant of the commendatorship for life, to be implemented on the death or demission of his father. In 1581 his father demitted the office in his favour, keeping the liferent, both their names appearing thereafter in charters of abbey land. This transaction was the equivalent of the way in which a secular landowner's son might become *fear* (recognized heir) during his father's lifetime. On 21 August 1584, only two days after his father's death, Mark younger had a ratification from James VI of the 1567 grant. On 28 July 1587 he had a charter from the king granting him and his heirs all the lands belonging to the former abbacy of Newbattle, and on 15 October 1591 he was created Lord Newbattle, all the abbey territories being united into one lordship.

On 10 July 1606 Ker was created earl of Lothian. Concurrently with the transformation of the Newbattle Abbey title and lands into a secular lordship, the monastic buildings were gradually replaced by a private dwelling, of which Sir John Scott of Scotstarvit wrote:

> And the father and son did so metamorphose the buildings that it cannot be known that ever it did belong to the church, by reason of the fair new fabric and stately edifices built thereon ... instead of the old monks has succeeded the deer.
> (J. Scott, *The Staggering State of Scottish Statesmen*, 1754)

Mark Ker followed a career in royal and public service. In 1580, as Mr Mark Ker of Prestongrange, he was made a gentleman of the chamber to James VI. In 1577 he was made master of requests, the appointment being confirmed in 1581. On 18 December 1581 he appears in the privy council record under that title, and thereafter attended many meetings of the council and served on many of its committees. On 8 December 1598 he was among those councillors chosen to sit at Holyroodhouse on Tuesdays and Thursdays to assist the king in the dispatch of business. In September 1599 he was appointed collector of a tax of 20,000 merks levied for certain foreign embassies. In the legal field, he was appointed to succeed his father as an extraordinary lord of session (judge) on 12 November 1584, and in January 1597 he had confirmation of the office of justiciary in the regality of Stow, sold to him by Lord Borthwick. On 28 July 1600 he was commanded to reside at his castle of Neidpath, near Peebles, in order to apply effectively the act of 1567 for the pursuit of thieves. On 19 September 1604 he was made acting chancellor during the absence of the earl of Montrose, then a commissioner in England at the discussions on the proposed Anglo-Scottish parliamentary union. He was also involved in church affairs. In January 1606 he was one of the assessors chosen at Linlithgow for the trial for treason of ministers opposed to the king's ecclesiastical policy, who were imprisoned in Blackness Castle.

Earlier, Ker and other judges had refused to be influenced by the king's attempts to force the court of session to come to an adverse decision against Robert Bruce, minister at Edinburgh, with regard to Bruce's claim to a life pension from the revenues of the abbacy of Arbroath. In 1608 he acted as assessor to the earl of Dunbar, the king's commissioner to the general assembly of the church, and in February 1609 he was on a commission to advise the king on how to bring 'peace and religion' to the isles (*Reg. PCS, 1607–10*, 742).

On being created earl of Lothian, Ker resigned his office of master of requests to his oldest son Robert. Some time before 29 March 1587 he had married Margaret, second daughter of John Maxwell, fourth Lord Herries of Terregles, and Agnes, baroness of Terregles in her own right; she died at Prestongrange on 8 January 1617. Their children were Robert, who became second earl of Lothian, Sir William Ker of Blackhope (who unsuccessfully claimed

the title on his elder brother's death in 1624), James, John, Jean (who married, first, Robert, master of Boyd, second, David Lindsay, twelfth earl of Crawford, and third, Thomas Hamilton of Roberton), Janet (who married William Cunningham, seventh earl of Glencairn), Margaret (who founded Lady Yester's Church in Edinburgh and married, first, James, seventh Lord Hay of Yester, second, Sir Andrew Ker, master of Jedburgh), Isobel (who married William Douglas, first earl of Queensberry), Lilias (who married John, ninth Lord Borthwick), Mary (who married Sir James Richardson of Smeaton), and Elizabeth (who married Sir Alexander Hamilton of Innerwick). The earl himself died on 8 April 1609, having made his will at Newbattle on 1 March 1602 when he was about to leave on a journey through England and France. He left an estate valued at nearly £37,000 Scots.

MARGARET H. B. SANDERSON

Sources *Scots peerage* · *Register of the privy council of Scotland*, 1585–1610, NA Scot. · Edinburgh commissary court, registers of testaments, NA Scot., CC8/8/46, fol. 147v · NA Scot., Lothian MSS, GD 40 · J. M. Thomson and others, eds., *Registrum magni sigilli regum Scotorum / The register of the great seal of Scotland*, 11 vols. (1882–1914), vol. 5

Archives NA Scot., Lothian muniments

Wealth at death approx. £36,992 16s. 6d. Scots [£3000 sterling]

Ker, Neil Ripley (1908–1982), palaeographer, was born on 28 May 1908 in Brompton, London, the only child of Robert Macneil Ker, of Dougalston, Milngavie, later a captain in the 3rd battalion of the Argyll and Sutherland Highlanders, and his second wife, Lucy Winifred, daughter of Henry Strickland-Constable, of Wassand Hall, Yorkshire. Ker was educated at preparatory school in Reigate and at Eton College. He went to Magdalen College, Oxford, in 1927, intending to read philosophy, politics, and economics, but on the advice of C. S. Lewis turned to English language and literature, in which he obtained a second-class honours degree in 1931.

Even as an undergraduate Ker's antiquarian interests and enquiring mind led him to the Bodleian Library to examine the manuscript copies of the texts he was studying. His conviction that firsthand knowledge of the palaeographical and linguistic features of the manuscripts themselves was essential for the study of the texts they contained influenced his choice of BLitt thesis: a study of the manuscripts of Aelfric's homilies (1933). At this time classics, not English, was the traditional breeding ground for palaeographers, but Ker's palaeographical interests were encouraged by another Anglo-Saxon scholar, Kenneth Sisam, whose commendation of the benefits of 'foraging among manuscripts' exercised a strong influence on him.

Ker first began to give classes in palaeography in 1936, and in 1941 he was appointed lecturer in palaeography. He married his second cousin, Jean Frances, daughter of Brigadier Charles Bannatyne Findlay, in 1938. They had four children, a son and three daughters. During the Second World War, as a conscientious objector, he worked as a porter in the Radcliffe Infirmary, Oxford. In 1945 he was elected to a fellowship at Magdalen, and in 1946 was appointed reader in palaeography; he held both posts until his early retirement in 1968. At Magdalen he succeeded C. T. Onions as librarian (1955–68), and was vice-president (1962–3). In 1975 he was elected to an honorary fellowship.

For Ker, palaeography entailed the systematic examination of all aspects of the manuscript book, from the methods of its production, to its owners, past and present. He brought to the subject new standards of observation and description. He was concerned to advance learning by making information available, and to let the information speak for itself, often presenting it in list form. Although he had few pupils in the formal sense, numerous scholars benefited from the information and advice he was always ready to give: his name is ubiquitous in footnotes and acknowledgements.

Ker's acute powers of observation, visual memory, knowledge of manuscripts (especially those of English origin and provenance), and skills of description, are best represented by his many catalogues, among them: *Medieval Libraries of Great Britain* (1941; 2nd edn, 1964); the *Catalogue of Manuscripts Containing Anglo-Saxon* (1957), which was awarded the British Academy's Sir Israel Gollancz memorial prize (1959) for its outstanding contribution to Anglo-Saxon studies; and his largest undertaking, *Medieval Manuscripts of Great Britain* (1969 onwards), in which he intended to catalogue all manuscripts in British institutions which had not yet been described; he was correcting the proofs of the third volume at the time of his death.

Ker's many other publications demonstrate the extent of his contribution to the study of scribal and binding practices, and library history. *English Manuscripts in the Century after the Norman Conquest* (1960), the published version of the lectures given as the first Lyell reader in bibliography (1952–3), is perhaps his finest achievement: a remarkable study of English manuscript production in the twelfth century. A bibliography of his published writings is included in the Festschrift presented to him in 1978, and supplemented in his posthumously collected papers (1985).

Ker won national and international recognition. The honours awarded him include honorary doctorates from the universities of Reading (1964), Leiden (1972), and Cambridge (1975), and fellowships of the British Academy (1958), the Medieval Academy of America (1971), and the Bayerische Akademie der Wissenschaften (1977). He was a gold medallist of the Bibliographical Society (1975), and in 1979 was appointed CBE.

Ker showed astonishing powers of concentration and tireless energy—he was a keen hill walker. To readers in Duke Humfrey's Library his spare figure was a familiar sight, 'proceeding with quick step, all intent on the common pursuit, with a sharp eye … [missing] nothing, the very nose seeming to be on the scent for some recondite fact' (Cheney, xiv). He was always as generous in sharing the fruits of his research with others as he was in giving hospitality at his homes in Kirtlington, near Oxford, and,

after his retirement, at his lochside house at Foss near Pitlochry, and in Edinburgh. He died on 23 August 1982, after a fall on the hillside near his house at Foss.

TERESA WEBBER, rev.

Sources C. R. Cheney, 'Introduction', *Medieval scribes, manuscripts and libraries*, ed. M. B. Parkes and A. G. Watson (1978) · *Magdalen College Record* (autumn 1983), 35–40 · private information (1990) [family] · *The Times* (25 Aug 1982) · A. I. Doyle, 'Neil Ripley Ker, 1908–1982', *PBA*, 80 (1993), 349–59

Archives Bodl. Oxf., working papers on parochial libraries · CUL, notes on Cambridge MSS · LPL, working papers connected with his publications on parochial libraries · LUL, papers relating to the *Lexique polyglotte* · Som. ARS, notes relating to *Book of hours* | Bodl. Oxf., corresp. with R. W. Hunt · Bodl. Oxf., corresp. with Graham Pollard

Likenesses photograph, repro. in N. R. Ker, *Books, collectors and libraries*, ed. A. G. Watson [1985], frontispiece; priv. coll. · photograph, repro. in Doyle, 'Neil Ripley Ker, 1908–1982', facing p. 351; priv. coll. · photograph, Academisch Historisch Museum, Leiden; repro. in Parkes and Watson, eds., *Medieval scribes*, frontispiece

Ker, Patrick (*fl.* **1684–1691**), writer, is generally supposed to have been Scottish, or at least to have had connections with Scotland, though the only evidence of this can be derived from internal witness in his poetry (such as 'An Elegy on Mr John Forbes, Late Sheriff of Aberdeen') and the speculative testimony of a contributor, J. O., to *Notes and Queries* in the late nineteenth century. The latter conjectures that Ker may have been compelled to leave Scotland for the greater tolerance of episcopalianism in England during a period of intense presbyterian conflict.

Ker's cultural production is centred in London, and the period in which his works appeared in print, 1684–91, spans the later reign of Charles II and the ascendancy of James VII and II to the throne. Attribution of his work has been ambiguous, largely owing to the mere inscription of initials in some of his printed works. There is, however, a marked degree of internal textual correspondence and thematic echoes between the ascribed works, and, in one instance, a near identical ornamental illustration of the Trinity facing the frontispiece of two works, *Flosculum poeticum* and *The Map of Man's Misery*.

The most powerful poetic expression of Ker's royalism is found in the collection *Flosculum poeticum: Poems Divine and Humane, Panegyrical, Satyrical, Ironical* (1684). The volume opens with a politically impassioned series of verses on the execution of Charles I, 'Great king and constant martyr', an illustration of Charles in the oak subscribed 'O cruel English nation!' (p. 3), and frequent invocations of 'Loyal hearts'. There are briefer anti-Cromwellian pieces; poetry that celebrates the restoration of Charles II; occasional and dedicatory verse possibly addressed to Ker's London coterie, and a dramatic prologue; religious verse that is frequently subsumed by royalist defence; and a body of amatory and erotic poetry in conventional seventeenth-century anti-platonic, sensualist vein.

Ker's political poetry in two single-sheet broadsides is found in the Luttrell Ballad collection, *An elegy on the deplorable and never enough to be lamented death of the illustrious and serene Charles II* (1685), and *A Mournful Elegy on the Deplorable Death of Charles II* (1685). These elegies proclaim the political renewal augured by the coronation of James

VII and II. Ker is also the probable author of the Latin pan-egyric *In illustrissimum, ac serenissimum, Jacobum II* (1685).

Ker's other major printed work includes a religious almanac, *The Map of Man's Misery* (1690), containing 'spiritual Meditations', and dedicated to Lady Rachel Russell on 24 January 1689; *Logomachia, or, The Conquest of Eloquence* (1690), two rhetorical disputations on classical models; and *Politikos megas: the Grand Politician* (1691), dedicated to the earl of Nottingham on 27 August 1690, a supposed 'translation' of a treatise by (the pseudonymous) Conradus Reinking. Reminiscent of Machiavelli's *Il principe*, it prescribes the most expedient political conduct, reveals 'the Secret Art of State-Policy', describes various duplicitous strategies—'How to speak one's mind freely without any danger'—and even offers military advice to the 'Nobles, Statesmen, Judges, Lawyers, Justices of Peace' to whom the work is addressed.

Ker, a moderately prolific polemicist and political writer, sustained, within the cultural context of late seventeenth-century London, traditions of episcopalian and royalist writing which had particular currency in Scotland. His association with Scotland, however, can only be inferred. S. M. DUNNIGAN

Sources *N&Q*, 2nd ser., 1 (1856), 281 · *N&Q*, 4th ser., 2 (1868), 102–3 · W. C. Hazlitt, *Collections and notes, 1867–1876* (1876)

Ker, Robert, first earl of Roxburghe (1569/70–1650), politician, was the eldest son of Sir William Ker of Cessford (*d.* 1600) and Janet Douglas, daughter of Sir James Douglas of Drumlanrig. Robert was probably born in 1570, being described as fifteen in November 1585 at the time of the fall from power of James Stewart, earl of Arran. He first received lands from the crown in March 1573, including his father's barony of Cessford. He seems to have married relatively young, his wedding to Margaret Maitland taking place on 5 December 1587. She was the only daughter of Sir William *Maitland of Lethington, secretary of state under Mary of Guise and Mary, queen of Scots, and his wife, Jean Fleming, one of the famous 'four Marys', ladies-in-waiting to Mary, queen of Scots. Robert and Margaret had three daughters and one son, William, Lord Ker, who graduated MA from Edinburgh in July 1610 and died in France eight years later. In 1590 Robert Ker murdered William Ker of Ancrum, a member of the rival house of the Kers of Ferniehirst, under cover of darkness in Edinburgh. He was denounced a rebel, his property was escheated to the crown, and he fled to England immediately. He was called back late in the following year by John *Maitland of Thirlestane, his wife's uncle, who was attempting to construct a favourable faction at court. Through Maitland's dealings, Ker received a remission under the great seal in November 1591. The feud between the houses of Cessford and Ferniehirst was not settled until 1607, when Robert Ker of Cessford apologized to the Ferniehirst Kers and paid them 10,000 merks (£6666 13*s.* 4*d.*).

In January 1592 Robert received further lands as a result of the forfeiture of Francis Stewart, first earl of Bothwell. In the autumn of the following year, Maitland of Thirlestane and Ker went to Linlithgow with over 200 horse to

Robert Ker, first earl of Roxburghe (1569/70–1650), by unknown artist

lend support to the royal campaign against Bothwell, who had risen in arms. At this meeting Ker was reconciled with Lord Hume, another border rival. A few weeks later the young laird of Cessford left Edinburgh to go to his wife, accompanied only by one servant. By accident he encountered Bothwell, who also had only one companion, near Humbie and 'meiting twa for twa, they focht allong tyme on horsback'. Cessford's servant was wounded on the cheek but 'at lenthe beathe parteis so wearied with long fechting … they assentit baithe to let utheris depairt and ryd away for that tyme'. Ker returned to Edinburgh 'and tald the Kingis Majestie of that accident' (Moysie, 111). As a result orders were given to raze Bothwell's castle of Crichton. In the spring of 1594 Ker, by now warden depute of the middle march, was appointed, along with Lord Hume and the laird of Buccleuch, to muster troops in the Merse and Teviotdale to resist Bothwell once again.

Ker's aid to the king against Bothwell increased his credit at court. In August he attended the baptism of Prince Henry and was one of four bearers of the 'paile' or canopy of velvet fringed with gold which was held over the infant prince. In October he was promoted warden of the middle march but, in spite of this, he is known to have carried on the border tradition of raiding into England. In February 1598 he was arrested by Sir Robert Carey and handed over to the custody of the archbishop of York, although, probably because of his position, he was released by the beginning of June.

In May 1599 Ker was admitted to the reconstituted privy council and was thereafter a fairly regular attender at meetings of the council, although a number of quite prolonged absences after 1603 suggest sojourns at court in England. He attended his first convention of estates in December 1599, and late in the following year he was raised to the peerage as Lord Roxburghe on the occasion of the baptism of Prince Charles. He subsequently received various lands in the shires of Roxburgh, Dumfries, Peebles, and Berwick. Although licensed 'to depairt and pas furth of' Scotland in August 1602 (*Reg. PCS*, 1st ser., 6.440–41), he does not seem to have taken advantage of this permission but he did accompany his sovereign on his journey south to take up the English throne in April 1603. His absence from the sederunts of the privy council until the beginning of 1606 would suggest that he may have remained at court for a good deal of that time. He did, however, attend parliament at Edinburgh in July 1604, when he was elected one of the lords of the articles, the committee which drafted acts and received petitions. He was also appointed one of the commissioners for negotiating a closer union with England.

A long-standing feud with Sir Robert Ker of Ancrum, resulting from the murder of Ancrum's father, William, was resolved during 1606. After several appearances before the privy council, the parties agreed to be reconciled and 'choppit handis' before the council on 20 November (*Reg. PCS*, 1st ser., 7.272). In 1607 Roxburghe was the commissioner to the synod of Merse and Teviotdale and to the presbyteries within that synod, on behalf of the privy council. In the previous December a packed general assembly at Linlithgow had agreed to have permanent or 'constant' moderators for these ecclesiastical courts but, knowing that there would be opposition within the kirk, prominent local landowners were commissioned by the council in an attempt to ensure their acceptance. In March 1607 Roxburghe sent a messenger to the presbytery of Melrose with a charge from the privy council ordering it to accept their nominated constant moderator within twenty-four hours, 'quhilk was thoucht be the presbiterie to be hard and precipitant deilling' (Melrose presbytery register, NA Scot., CH2/327/1, fol. 2*v*). They refused, and a week later Roxburghe turned up in person, yet still the presbytery stood firm. The matter dragged on through the summer with repeated pressure being applied by Lord Roxburghe yet, in October, the presbytery elected its own moderator in the usual manner. Roxburghe went to the synod in October and urged them to accept a constant moderator and to force their presbyteries to do likewise. According to Calderwood, a member of that synod, 'he got a flatt *Nolumus*' (Calderwood, 6.680).

In that year Roxburghe was granted the properties of the abbacy of Kelso by parliament, in which he was again elected one of the lords of the articles. Throughout the rest of his political career he was very much involved in parliamentary business, attending most meetings of the estates and being appointed to several parliamentary commissions on taxation and ecclesiastical affairs. He was also appointed to several privy council commissions and in 1610 was reappointed to the reconstituted privy council.

Early in 1614, having been widowed, Roxburghe married for a second time, at Somerset House in London, the marriage contract being dated 10 January. His new wife was Jean Drummond (d. 1643) [*see* Ker, Jane, countess of Roxburghe], daughter of Patrick, Lord Drummond, and governess to the children of James VI; they had one child, Harry, born in 1618. On 18 September 1616 Roxburghe became the first earl of Roxburghe, Lord Ker of Cessford and Caverton, and was granted the right to make four knights on the occasion of his elevation. In spite of this he was disappointed at being passed over for the office of chamberlain; his wife fell from favour with Queen Anne and, as a result, they left court for a time. Although apparently initially reluctant to adhere to the five articles of Perth, particularly that which enjoined that communicants receive the sacrament kneeling, he was elected to the lords of the articles in the parliament of 1621 and voted to ratify them. In November of that year he was appointed to the inner 'cabinet' council, a subcommittee of the privy council for dealing with higher affairs of state. Two years later he was appointed to the commission for grievances, intended as a conduit to James VI for Scottish problems and complaints. He was at court at the time of the death of James VI and he attended the king's funeral. Roxburghe had been on a commission responsible for managing the affairs of Prince Charles in Scotland since 1619, and the new king soon confirmed his position as a privy councillor and a member of the grievances commission. He continued to be active in affairs of state, both in England and Scotland, in spite of his advancing years.

In 1637 Roxburghe was made lord privy seal, in spite of his lack of Latin. He was in Edinburgh at the time of the anti-prayer book riot on 23 July and the bishop of Edinburgh used Roxburghe's coach to escape the angry mob after the morning service, the earl's footmen keeping them off with drawn swords. In the autumn the earl attempted to achieve reconciliation by acting as an intermediary between dissident ministers, including Alexander Henderson, and the bishops. In December, having been at court, he was sent by Charles I to Scotland 'to try if he could find aney way to compose bussines' but this did not bear fruit (*Historical Works of Balfour*, 2.237). At the general assembly at Glasgow in November 1638, he was one of six royal nominees to be assessors to the marquess of Hamilton, the king's commissioner. The assembly refused to allow the assessors the right to vote, fearing a precedent which might allow the king to appoint any number of voting commissioner's assessors. In August 1639 he again attended the general assembly, as one of the assessors of the king's commissioner. He attended parliament in the same month but was initially debarred from the parliament house in 1641 because he had not signed the national covenant. After subscribing he was admitted and was soon appointed to a number of committees.

During the 1640s Roxburghe remained prominent in politics, in spite of being in his seventies. He was on the covenanting committees of war for the shire of Roxburgh and the constabularies of Haddington and Lauderdale and he attended parliament regularly. In 1643 his son and his second wife died. He went on to marry Lady Isabel Douglas (d. 1672), daughter of William Douglas, fifth earl of Morton. They had no children. Because of his support for the engagement with Charles I in 1648, he was stripped of all public office by parliament in 1649. He died in the following year, on 18 January, at his house of Floors Castle, near Kelso, and was buried in the family tomb at Bowden kirk on 20 March. His wife lived on until 16 December 1672. According to Roxburghe's direction, his estates and titles passed to his son-in-law Sir William Drummond, husband of his eldest daughter, Jean.   ALAN R. MACDONALD

Sources *Scots peerage*, vol. 7 • *The historical works of Sir James Balfour*, ed. J. Haig, 4 vols. (1824–5) • J. Gordon, *History of Scots affairs from 1637–1641*, ed. J. Robertson and G. Grub, 1, Spalding Club, 1 (1841) • J. Spalding, *Memorialls of the trubles in Scotland and in England, AD 1624 – AD 1645*, ed. J. Stuart, 2 vols., Spalding Club, [21, 23] (1850–51) • *Reg. PCS*, 1st ser. • *Reg. PCS*, 2nd ser. • D. Calderwood, *The history of the Kirk of Scotland*, ed. T. Thomson and D. Laing, 8 vols., Wodrow Society, 7 (1842–9) • [T. Thomson], ed., *The historie and life of King James the Sext*, Bannatyne Club, 13 (1825) • *APS*, 1593–1660 • D. Moysie, *Memoirs of the affairs of Scotland, 1577–1603*, ed. J. Dennistoun, Bannatyne Club, 39 (1830) • register of testaments, NA Scot., Edinburgh commissary court records, CC8/8/66A
Archives Floors Castle, Kelso, Innes Ker family, dukes of Roxburghe • NRA, priv. coll., household accounts and material
Likenesses oils, Floors Castle, Kelso [*see illus.*]
Wealth at death £84,039 Scots: register of testaments, NA Scot., Edinburgh commissary court records, CC8/8/66A, 125–37, 1655

Ker, Robert, first earl of Ancram (1578–1654), courtier and politician, was the eldest son of William Ker of Ancram (d. 1590) and Margaret, daughter of Alexander Dundas of Fingask. His father was assassinated in 1590 and his mother subsequently married Sir George Douglas of Mordington. In 1604 Ker was appointed groom of the bedchamber in the household established for Prince Henry and Princess Elizabeth, and by 1607 he had been knighted, and had married Elizabeth (d. 1620), daughter of Sir John Murray of Blackbarony. Early in 1607 he went abroad 'for doing my lawfull affaires and bissiness' (*Correspondence*, 1.8–9). He was in Paris in March 1608, and after his return to Britain again gained office at court, as a gentleman of the privy chamber and captain of the king's guard in Scotland. Following the death of Prince Henry in November 1612 he became a gentleman of the bedchamber to Prince Charles and resigned his captaincy of the Scottish guard so that he could attend the prince regularly. In 1616 he was granted a pension of £2400 Scots (£200 sterling) from Scottish revenues. A duel with Charles Maxwell of Terregles in February 1620 briefly interrupted his career at court. Ker killed his opponent in the duel, fought near Newmarket, and was banished on being found guilty of manslaughter, but there was agreement that his opponent (who had previously twice killed opponents in duels) had been at fault. He was, therefore, pardoned in October and returned to his duties at court. His first wife having died, in 1621 Ker married Anne Portman, eldest daughter of William Stanley, sixth earl of Derby, and widow of Sir Henry Portman.

In January 1623 Prince Charles set out for Spain, accompanied by the duke of Buckingham, to woo the Spanish infanta, and in April Ker and other courtiers left to join them in Spain, returning with the prince in November. Grants to him by the prince indicate his regard. In December 1622 he was paid £1000 sterling, and in April 1623 King James authorized pensions for him and his wife: the latter, worth £500 sterling a year, brought an agonized comment from the English treasurer about 'the King's favours to his servants being without end' (*Correspondence*, 1.xvi).

Ker's career at court continued to prosper after his master, Charles, acceded to the throne in 1625, and Ker sat in the English parliament for Aylesbury in 1625 and for Preston in 1628–9. The marriage of his eldest son, William *Kerr, to the countess of Lothian led to William's being created earl of Lothian, and Ker busied himself in ensuring that his son could live up to the new rank. Ker was evidently made a baronet in 1631, and was admitted to the Scottish privy council on 23 June 1631, but he saw his future as continuing to lie primarily in England and transferred Ancram and other lands in Scotland to his son. He accompanied King Charles on his visit to Scotland in 1633, as master of the privy purse, and in the coronation honours was created earl of Ancram on 24 June. This was the pinnacle of his career. In 1639 he evidently lost the keepership of the privy purse. Some attributed this to his 'long and evident infirmity', others to retaliation for the support his son Lothian was giving to the Scottish covenanters in resisting the religious policies of Charles I (ibid., 1.xx). Ancram kept his post as a gentleman of the bedchamber until about 1644, but age had probably prevented him remaining with the king after the outbreak of civil war in 1642 and letters in 1643 were addressed to him in London. The pension granted him many years before was now paid irregularly, and by 1647 he was having to seek protection from debtors.

The execution of the king in January 1649 led Ancram to reflect that 'I am creeping down the hill, or rather upp the hill from this world to a better' (*Correspondence*, 1.xxii). The execution and the abolition of monarchy were probably joined by financial considerations, as his pension was no longer paid at all, in persuading him to leave London, and in November 1649 he was staying at his son's house of Newbattle; but he found no safe refuge there, as his arrival at Dordrecht in the Netherlands in September 1650 evidently reflects his reaction to Cromwell's invasion of Scotland. Ancram settled in Amsterdam, and his last years were ones of struggling to subsist. 'I am now leirn'd to be "penny wyse", though I was formerly "pound foole"' (ibid., 1.xxiv). After being visited by two of his grandsons he wrote to Lothian, their father, 'there is nobody more dear than you and yours are to your most loving father' (ibid., 1.xxv). This, written on 9 December 1654, was his last letter, and he died, in Amsterdam, with 'satisfaction to himself' and 'the great content and admiration' of those who were with him, on 18 December (NA Scot., GD40/XII/42). A year before he had been 'striving, by God's assistance, to be ready to die', and had desired a quiet burial, without pomp or fuss (*Correspondence*, 1.xxv). In the event his Dutch creditors prevented his body being buried at all, and even after some of his debts were paid he was still unburied in May 1655, when Cromwell intervened to demand that the funeral be allowed to take place. When he was finally interred is unknown.

Ancram spent his life as a courtier, and showed no sign of trying to gain political influence or use his position to advance any faction except personal and family interests. Beyond family and court, his main interests were literary. He corresponded with the poets William Drummond of Hawthornden and John Donne, and looked after Donne's papers while he was abroad. When Samuel Daniel died in 1619 he left his papers to Ancram. Having heard psalms sung in French and Dutch translations, Ancram himself in the early 1620s translated some of the psalms into English to be sung to the same tunes. Thus three parts of 'the Reformed Church' separated by language through 'the curse which [God] inflicted on mankynd at Babell' could, he hoped, worship God 'with one hart and voice … howsoever they differed in speech' (*Correspondence*, 1.2.488). But Ancram modestly did this work for recreation, and his psalms remained unpublished until 1875. A sonnet in praise of a solitary life was inspired by a sleepless night in the bedchamber at court in 1624, but declaring his poems 'few and evil' he merely sent his 'starved rhime' to his friend Drummond.   DAVID STEVENSON

Sources *Correspondence of Sir Robert Kerr, first earl of Ancram, and his son William, third earl of Lothian*, ed. D. Laing, 2 vols., Roxburghe Club, 100 (1875) · *DNB* · *Scots peerage* · NA Scot., GD40
Archives NA Scot., Lothian muniments, corresp. and papers
Likenesses J. Lievens, oils, *c*.1652, Scot. NPG

Ker, Sir Thomas, of Ferniehirst (*d.* 1586), border chieftain and administrator, was the second son of Sir John Ker (*d.* 1562), laird of Ferniehirst, and his wife, Katherine Ker of Cessford. Thomas inherited the Ferniehirst estates on his father's death in 1562 and married Janet Kirkcaldy of Grange around the same time. They had five surviving children—Andrew, first Lord Jedburgh; William Kirkcaldy of Grange (who succeeded to his mother's lands and took her surname); Mary, who married James Douglas, commendator of Melrose; Julian, married first to Sir Patrick Home of Polwarth and then to Thomas Hamilton, first earl of Haddington; and Margaret, who wed Robert, second Lord Melville. By 1569 Janet had died, and in that year Sir Thomas married Janet Scott, sister of Sir Walter Scott of Buccleuch. The match represented an attempt to pacify a blood feud between the Kers and Scotts, and despite its shaky origins proved a success. Janet bore Sir Thomas three more sons and a daughter—Thomas of Oxnam; Mr James (whose son Robert became second Lord Jedburgh); Robert *Carr or Ker, earl of Somerset, the infamous favourite of James VI and I; and Anne, who in 1583 was noted as a possible bride for the sixth earl of Huntly, but who eventually married John Elphinstone, second Lord Balmerino.

Thomas Ker is first recorded as a hostage for his grandfather, Andrew (Dand) Ker of Ferniehirst, during the 'rough wooing' of the 1540s. In December 1544 Dand thanked the earl of Shrewsbury for sending 'Thome' to school in England. This education perhaps accounts for Thomas's being noted as a protestant when he brought a preacher to Kelso in 1553. In 1560, when the Scottish

Reformation began in earnest, John Knox noted him as 'godly and forward' (*Knox's History*, 1.261). Ferniehirst continued to support the Reformation, but had returned to Roman Catholicism by the mid 1560s through the influence of Mary, queen of Scots. Ker had to run the family estates after his father's death in 1562 and may have had less time for religious activities. His renewed adherence to Roman Catholicism was concrete, rather than *politique*, for in October 1582 the general assembly of the Church of Scotland wanted to 'call before them the Laird of Pharnihirst, his ladie and daughter for going to Mess in France' in order to force them to subscribe the protestant confession of faith (*Booke of the Universall Kirk*, 589).

Ferniehirst continued his family's feud with the Scotts and was consequently summoned before the privy council in November 1562. Nevertheless he was knighted about this time. In 1568 he made a will because he feared an imminent attack by Scott of Buccleuch, but his marriage to Janet Scott calmed these tensions for a while. In the political sphere Ker defended the newly wed Queen Mary against the rebellious forces of the earl of Moray during the 1565 chaseabout raid. Thereafter he never left the queen's cause and after her escape from Lochleven Castle in 1568 he rejoined her forces; he could not, however, prevent their defeat at Langside and Mary's subsequent flight into exile. The queen then corresponded with Ker as if she were still in power, advising him to keep good order and give ready service when it was required. On 26 August 1569 Mary wrote that she hoped to deliver her next message to him in person. The failure of the 1569–70 northern rising must have been a great disappointment to Sir Thomas, who sheltered the rebel earl of Westmorland and his followers at Ferniehirst Castle. The English had their revenge when the forces of the earl of Sussex and Lord Hunsdon launched a two-pronged attack on the houses of those who had abetted the rebels; Ferniehirst Castle was razed to the ground during April 1570.

More disaster followed when Ker gave his support to the 'queen's party', which opposed the 'king's party' during the civil wars of 1570–73. This was a time of confused government, with rival parliaments meeting during 1571. Marians holding Edinburgh Castle elected Ferniehirst provost of Edinburgh on 20 June 1571; he was subsequently forfeited by the king's men on 28 August 1571 at Stirling. Now labelled a firebrand, he took part in the attack by the queen's men on the rival parliament. During this sortie into Stirling, the regent Lennox, grandfather of James VI, was killed, an eventuality which made a restoration of Ferniehirst's estates unlikely. Ker continued to cause trouble in 1572 by leading an attack on Jedburgh because that town had backed his territorial rival, the earl of Angus.

Sir Thomas then joined his father-in-law, Sir William Kirkcaldy of Grange, in defending Edinburgh Castle against the English-backed forces of Regent Morton and the king's men. The Marian defenders surrendered in May 1573, yet just before this capitulation Ferniehirst escaped from the castle and went into England to shelter with his friend Sir John Forster, warden of the English middle march. The English privy council ordered Forster to keep him there to prevent his going to France. After Forster had entered a submission on Ferniehurst's behalf, Morton denounced the latter's character, saying he had 'never heard of any submission of Ferniehurst that in honour or reason could be thought worthy of an answer' (CSP for., 1572–4, 300). Ker returned briefly to Scotland in November 1573 to survey English damage to his properties near Jedburgh. He then complained to Forster that Jedburgh's burghers and Morton's soldiers did 'daily cut and destroy his woods, harass his tenants, and slay his deer' (ibid., 439). Sir Thomas did not mention that he had attacked Morton's lands in 1570–71. By September 1574 he was still in Forster's company as he appeared with other rebels at a border 'day of truce', where they conferred with fellow Scottish borderers.

Morton was furious and by December 1574 had ensured that the forfeiture of Ferniehirst's lands was absolute by granting most of them to the earl of Angus. Ferniehirst travelled to France and remained there until the downfall of Morton in 1581. His debts mounted as he borrowed money from such people as Sir John Forster and Sir Cuthbert Collingwood of Eslington in England, his aunt Dame Isobel Ker of Cessford, John Angus, a Scottish merchant in Paris, and James Beaton, erstwhile archbishop of Glasgow, who was similarly exiled in France. Whether these debts were ever repaid is unclear. Ferniehirst hoped that Queen Mary would repay Beaton, but during 1583–4 Collingwood resorted to demanding his money from Dame Janet Scott as Ferniehirst's factor. Dame Janet was trying to alleviate her husband's debts in France and Scotland by asking Queen Mary to chase up the Spanish pension he had been promised. In an intriguing correspondence Mary sent a ring to Lady Ferniehirst, who reciprocated by sending back political news from Scotland.

Ker had been licensed to return from France in 1580 probably through the influence of the earl of Lennox and an offer of manrent to Regent Morton. That offer was quickly abandoned on the downfall of Morton, at whose execution on 2 June 1581 Ferniehirst 'stood in a shott over against the scaffold, with his large ruffes, delyting in this spectacle' (Calderwood, 3.575). Later that year Ferniehirst was pardoned for all crimes committed between June 1567 and November 1574 and fully restored to his estates; ratification followed in 1583. He was appointed provost of Jedburgh on the king's command in 1581, in order to oust pro-Angus officials in the burgh, while in 1582 the hereditary office of baillie of Jedforest was returned to him upon the forfeiture of the earl of Angus. Ferniehirst was in such great favour in 1582 that he was also granted a five-year protection from all his creditors.

Ferniehirst returned to France in 1582 to avoid the regime of the protestant Ruthven raiders, who had ousted his patron the earl of Lennox. But he returned to Scotland in 1584 and allied himself with the new chancellor of Scotland, the fifth earl of Arran. His first victim was his old rival William Ker of Cessford, whom he unfairly engineered out of the office of warden of the Scottish middle

march. His appointment as warden had disastrous consequences, however, when in July 1585 Lord Francis Russell was killed in mysterious circumstances during a day of truce between Ferniehirst and Sir John Forster. David Hume of Godscroft noted that 'whether by chance or of set purpose is uncertain' (Hume, 402). The blame was nevertheless placed on Ferniehirst, with Arran as his suspected accomplice. As Russell had been Forster's son-in-law, the incident also strained Anglo-Scottish relations.

Ferniehirst had many men with him, but they were not 'ranged in order of battell' as later reports suggested. He was, after all, a pompous man known to like a large garrison around him, and Arran had given him twenty-five hagbutters to carry out his warden duties. Russell was 'slaine in the myddest of his owne men', which suggests a prearranged murder plot. However after the murder both Forster and Ferniehirst 'stood together and made a quietnes', and then took order over pledges and prisoners and 'parted quietly oute of the feeld' (Bain, 1, nos. 330–31). James VI warded both Arran and Ferniehirst and refused to hand Ferniehirst over to the English government. There may have been some enmity between Ferniehirst and Russell as Russell had been intercepting his letters. Russell had called him half lunatic in May 1585, perhaps in response to his arrogance. Ferniehirst swore that he 'would rather the blood of one of his own friends had been shed', but in truth his reputation was shattered by this incident, one that still remains an enigma (PRO, IND1/6887).

Ferniehirst's fall from power caused his wife to return from France in 1585; she lived until the mid-1590s. Meanwhile, on 24 February 1586 Henry Widdrington of the Berwick garrison recorded that 'Sir Thomas Carre the lard of Farnihearst is deceased in the towne of Aberdene' (Bain, 1, no. 417). Still grieving for his son-in-law, Sir John Forster wrote 'I am sorie that he and some betters had not beine hanged' (ibid., 1, no. 421). This was an ignominious end for a man who had once been a powerful border laird and supporter of Queen Mary.   MAUREEN M. MEIKLE

Sources Edinburgh commissary court: testaments, NA Scot., CC8/8 · gifts and deposits, Lothian muniments, NA Scot., GD40 · register of deeds: 1st ser., NA Scot., RD1 · state papers borders, PRO, state paper office, SP59 · indexes to various series, PRO, IND1/6887 · BL, Cotton MS Caligula C VII · royal letters of the marquess of Tweeddale, NL Scot., MS 7103, fol. 1 · Calendar of the manuscripts of the most hon. the marquis of Salisbury, 24 vols., HMC, 9 (1883–1976) · APS, 1424–1592 · CSP Scot. · J. Bain, ed., The border papers: calendar of letters and papers relating to the affairs of the borders of England and Scotland, 2 vols. (1894–6) · APC, 1571–5 · CSP dom., 1547–90 · CSP for., 1558–86 · J. M. Thomson and others, eds., Registrum magni sigilli regum Scotorum / The register of the great seal of Scotland, 11 vols. (1882–1914), vols. 4–5 · Reg. PCS, 1st ser., vols. 1–4 · M. Livingstone, D. Hay Fleming, and others, eds., Registrum secreti sigilli regum Scotorum / The register of the privy seal of Scotland, 4–8 (1952–82) · J. B. Paul and C. T. McInnes, eds., Compota thesaurariorum regum Scotorum / Accounts of the lord high treasurer of Scotland, 8–13 (1908–78) · T. Thomson, ed., Acts and proceedings of the general assemblies of the Kirk of Scotland, 3 pts, Bannatyne Club, 81 (1839–45) · The historie and cronicles of Scotland … by Robert Lindesay of Pitscottie, ed. A. J. G. Mackay, 1, STS, 42 (1899), 220–22, 226–7 · Scots peerage · D. Calderwood, The history of the Kirk of Scotland, ed. T. Thomson and D. Laing, 8 vols., Wodrow Society, 7 (1842–9) · John Knox's History of the Reformation in Scotland, ed. W. C. Dickinson, 2 vols. (1949) · T. Thomson, ed., *A diurnal of remarkable occurrents that have passed within the country of Scotland*, Bannatyne Club, 43 (1833) · M. M. Meikle, 'Lairds and gentlemen: a study of the landed families of the Eastern Anglo-Scottish Borders, *c.*1540–1603', PhD diss., U. Edin., 1989 · *The state papers and letters of Sir Ralph Sadler*, ed. A. Clifford, 2 vols. (1809) · G. Donaldson, *All the queen's men: power and politics in Mary Stewart's Scotland* (1983) · *The Scottish correspondence of Mary of Lorraine*, ed. A. I. Cameron, Scottish History Society, 3rd ser., 10 (1927) · J. Wormald, *Lords and men in Scotland: bonds of manrent, 1442–1603* (1985), 144 · T. I. Rae, *The administration of the Scottish frontier, 1513–1603* (1966) · D. Hume of Godscroft, *The history of the houses of Douglas and Angus* (1644) · R. Grant, 'Politicking Jacobean women: Lady Ferniehirst, the countess of Arran and the countess of Huntly, *c.*1580–1603', *Women in Scotland, c.1100–c.1750*, ed. E. Ewan and M. M. Meikle (1999), 95–104 · W. Fraser, ed., *The Annandale family book of the Johnstones*, 2 vols. (1894) · *LP Henry VIII*, 19/2, no. 768

Ker, Sir Walter, of Cessford (1510–1582), border chieftain and administrator, was the eldest son of Andrew *Ker of Cessford (*d.* 1526) and his wife, Agnes, daughter of Sir Patrick Crichton of Cranstoun Riddel. His father was killed near Melrose in 1526 by a follower of Sir Walter Scott of Branxholm, during an unsuccessful attempt to free James V from the guardianship of the earl of Angus. Sir Andrew's death gave rise to a bitter feud between the Kers and the Scotts. Walter's uncle, George Ker of Faldonside, acted as his tutor until he was served heir on 12 May 1528, aged eighteen. Cessford was cup-bearer to James V from 1528 to 1536 and occupied the office of warden of the Scottish middle march, with a jurisdiction which encompassed Teviotdale, during the years 1535–8, 1542–51, and 1558–70. His position as a border law officer did not, however, prevent his engaging in reiving. The lands of Cessford and Primside in Morebattle parish, Roxburghshire, were created free baronies for him in 1542. He married Isobel (*c.*1515–1585), daughter of Andrew *Ker of Ferniehurst, before 27 September 1543. They had six children: Sir Andrew Ker of Caverton; William Ker of Cessford, who succeeded his father as warden; Thomas; Agnes, who married John Edmonston of that ilk; Isobel, second wife of John Rutherford of Hunthill; and Margaret, who wed Alexander, fifth Lord Home.

During the so-called 'rough wooing' Cessford faced intermittent accusations of collaboration with the English, but on 15 October 1545 he appeared before the council to bind himself to the defence of the nation. Following the Scots defeat at Pinkie on 10 September 1547, however, Cessford submitted to the duke of Somerset at Roxburgh and assured to England. The English exploited his feud with the Scotts to enlist him in raids on Newark Castle and the Buccleuch lands in January 1548. Then in October the Kers burnt Catslack Tower and with it Lady Elizabeth Ker, mother of Walter Scott of Branxholm and also Cessford's own great-aunt. England's grip on the borders was subsequently undermined by French intervention and Cessford was replaced as warden by Scott of Branxholm in 1550, exacerbating the tension between the two men. Knighted by Governor Arran in June 1552, on the evening of 4 October following he avenged his father when with his friends he stabbed Scott of Branxholm to death on Edinburgh High Street, Hume of Cowdenknowes urging Cessford to

'strike for thy father's sake' (Fraser, 2.210). The murderers were outlawed, but on 8 December the crown elected to banish them to France, ordering the Kers to raise 100 horsemen to serve in the continental wars. Their exile was never enforced and a remission was eventually granted on 16 May 1553. On 28 August 1559 Cessford was appointed a commissioner to treat with the English for the ransom of prisoners of war. He joined the protestant lords of the congregation at Leith in April 1560 and sat in the Reformation Parliament. He was frequently censured throughout Queen Mary's reign for his failure as warden to provide adequate redress to people complaining of breaches of the march laws, a failure partly caused by the refusal of his kinsman, Sir Thomas Kerr of Ferniehurst, and his followers to co-operate with him. There was rarely any consistency about relationships among the Ker chiefs, whose long-standing rivalry in the middle march often set them against each other.

In March 1564 a contract arranging marriages between the Kers and the Scotts was made to settle their feud, and Cessford was required to seek the laird of Buccleuch's forgiveness for the murder of the latter's father in St Giles's Kirk, Edinburgh. Significantly, Cessford and Ferniehurst only agreed to stand surety for their own followers, rather than for all of their surname. Like the majority of the realm, Cessford remained loyal to the crown during the chaseabout raid, the revolt by the earl of Moray and duke of Châtelherault in 1565. However, after the queen married the earl of Bothwell in 1567 he opposed her later that year at Carberry Hill, and in 1568 fought valiantly with the king's men at Langside, alongside his son-in-law Lord Home. As a committed protestant Cessford was a natural supporter of Moray's regency, and he assisted the regent's expeditions to suppress Liddesdale in 1569. By contrast Ferniehurst, who had reconverted to Catholicism in the late 1560s, remained loyal to Mary and between 1570 and 1573 acted and was virtually recognized by the English as warden of the middle march. Cessford avoided direct confrontation with him, and in July 1570 pragmatically allowed a Marian raid on Wark, led by Ferniehurst and Buccleuch, to pass and return through that march unchallenged. Despite agreeing to ride against Ferniehurst in February 1571, Cessford made no direct response to his kinsman's attempts to burn Jedburgh, perhaps as a result of his own differences with the Rutherfords among the townsmen. However, he joined with Lord Ruthven's force, which rode from Leith to Jedburgh's rescue in February 1572, and was present at the convention which elected the earl of Morton regent in November.

Four years later Morton antagonized Cessford by seeking to divide the area of the middle march under his jurisdiction, and in August 1578 Sir Walter accompanied the earls of Atholl and Argyll when they rode from Edinburgh to Stirling to secure the regent's deposition before the king. When recommended for an English pension in March 1580 Cessford was noted to be a man 'of great power, constant, stout, valiant' (*CSP Scot.*, 1574–81, 386). Appointed a gentleman of the king's bedchamber in October, he initially favoured the duke of Lennox's regime but evidently grew disenchanted, for he signed the secret band which preceded the Ruthven raid in 1582. He died some time later that year and was probably buried in Bowden parish church.   JOHN SIMMONS

Sources CSP Scot., 1547–83 · Reg. PCS, 1st ser., vols. 1–3 · Scots peerage, 7.332–7 · D. Calderwood, The history of the Kirk of Scotland, ed. T. Thomson and D. Laing, 8 vols., Wodrow Society, 7 (1842–9) · J. M. Thomson and others, eds., Registrum magni sigilli regum Scotorum / The register of the great seal of Scotland, 11 vols. (1882–1914), vols. 3–5 · M. M. Meikle, 'Lairds and gentlemen: a study of the landed families of the Eastern Anglo-Scottish Borders, c.1540–1603', PhD diss., U. Edin., 1989 · J. Knox, The history of the reformation of religion in Scotland, ed. C. Lennox, [rev. edn] (1905) · G. Ridpath, The border history of England and Scotland (1848); repr. (1979) · W. Fraser, The Scotts of Buccleuch, 2 vols. (1878)

Ker, William Paton (1855–1923), literary scholar, was born at Glasgow on 30 August 1855, the eldest son of William Ker, merchant, of that city, and his wife, Caroline Agnes Paton. He passed from Glasgow Academy to Glasgow University, and in 1874 went with a Snell exhibition to Balliol College, Oxford. He obtained a first class in classical moderations (1876) and a second class in literae humaniores (1878). He was awarded the Taylorian scholarship in the latter year, and was elected to a fellowship at All Souls College in November 1879. In 1879 he was appointed assistant to William Young Sellar, professor of humanity in the University of Edinburgh. This assistantship was one of the most valued experiences of his life.

In 1883, at the age of twenty-eight, Ker was appointed professor of English literature and history in the new University College of South Wales, Cardiff. It was hard, pioneering work, and he looked back on it with keen pleasure. Six years later, in 1889, he was appointed as the first holder of the Quain chair of English language and literature in University College, London. Until his resignation of that chair in 1922 he spent most of the long London terms at his house, 95 Gower Street. He gave every week a great number of lectures and classes—in the early years of his professorship as many as a dozen. When the University of London was reorganized in 1900, Ker was appointed chairman of the modern languages board, and later of the English board, and he took the leading part in moulding English studies throughout the university and was instrumental in its development elsewhere, particularly at Oxford. It was not always an easy task. He was inflexible in his hatred of any officialdom which seemed likely to hamper the school and, on the other hand, of any slackness on the part of his colleagues on the board. Ker also threw himself into the general work of the university, as a member of the senate, the academic council, and the faculty of arts, and of the professorial board of his college. He attended meetings assiduously, spoke seldom, and then always very briefly, but with extraordinary effect. He was conservative in politics and in every habit of his daily life, but his conservatism was combined with a readiness for any development upon sound lines. His eagerness for new adventure was shown by the energy with which, even during the distractions of the First World War, he undertook the work of organizing Scandinavian studies in London University. He had been teaching Icelandic to his students

William Paton Ker (1855–1923), by Sir William Rothenstein, 1923

for years, but that was not enough: largely through his initiative and energy a department of Scandinavian studies was founded in 1917, the first in England; he became its director. The establishing of this field as an academic discipline in England must be counted among his achievements.

Such was the 'ubiquitariness' of Ker's mind that he could attend to all the literatures of western Europe, and to the affairs of more than one university, with a thoroughness which made it difficult to believe that each of these interests was not first in his mind. He retained his fellowship at All Souls for forty-four years until his death, for he never married; indeed, the college, quite as much as his house in Gower Street, was his home. His position at All Souls was unique: he was at once a wit, a sage, and an institution; above all, he was the very centre of the college's social life. As a talker he was unequalled; his very silence, frequent enough, breathed sympathy. His kindness to the young fellows was unbounded: the rich stores of his learning, never displayed, were always at their disposal; and many of his happiest hours were spent in taking them for long walks in the country or in sitting with them in the common room in the evening. Almost every weekend in term time was spent in Oxford, and he kept throughout in the closest touch with Oxford affairs. In 1920 he was elected to the chair of poetry at Oxford—a distinction which he retained when he resigned his London chair. His directorship of Scandinavian studies he also retained to the end.

Ker was slow to publish. He was forty-two when Epic and Romance appeared in 1897; until then he had printed hardly anything, except an essay, 'The philosophy of art', which appeared in Essays in Philosophical Criticism in 1883. It was not at once realized how great was the light which Epic and Romance threw on problems which had been puzzling scholars for many years. In 1900 Ker selected and edited *The Essays of John Dryden* (2 vols.), and in 1901–2 he published an edition (with R. W. Chambers) of Lord Berners's translation of Froissart's *Chronicles* (6 vols.) with a characteristic introduction. In *The Dark Ages* (1904) and *English Literature: Medieval* (1912, originally given as the Clark lectures at Trinity College, Cambridge) he compressed into small volumes much of the result of his vast reading. His lectures as professor of poetry were issued in 1923 (*The Art of Poetry: Seven Lectures, 1920–1922*); many of his shorter writings were reprinted in *Essays on Medieval Literature* (1905) and in the two volumes of *Collected Essays of W. P. Ker* (1925) edited by Charles Whibley after Ker's death. *Form and Style in Poetry* (edited by R. W. Chambers, 1928) included lectures delivered in Cambridge and London on the history of poetic forms and the relation of form and substance, subjects which he had made peculiarly his own. He was also an indefatigable reviewer, ranging as widely as he did in his other writings. Throughout his life he composed verse, a collection of which was posthumously published in 1935.

Ker's wide reading in many literatures apart from English and the classics—French, Italian, Spanish, and Scandinavian—and his synthesizing critical intelligence gave to his writings a capacity for shaping generalizations that were of importance particularly in early twentieth-century attempts to historicize medieval literature. He also wrote extensively on writers of later centuries and had a sustained interest in the Scottish literature that was his heritage.

Immense as was the range of Ker's knowledge, he always kept the spirit of an adventurer, wandering far afield when the spirit really prompted, carrying his students with him by his power of mind and temper. Towards the end of his life he gave *Nos manet Oceanus* as his favourite motto; it was in this spirit that in his farewell speech at University College he gave his students the advice of the abbey of Thelema, 'Do what you like'. Few men liked more things, or got more out of life in all its aspects, than Ker. The love of books and the love of nature were the two passions of his life; he loved children also, and animals, climbing, walking, rowing, dancing, good wine, and good fellowship. He had a keen wit and a strong sense of humour, and a firm belief in the virtue of cheerfulness. Above all, he had the instinct for friendship in a most uncommon degree; students and friends alike found him full of generous sympathy and understanding. One noteworthy friendship was with A. E. Housman, in whose appointment at University College he was instrumental. Their relationship is reflected in the fact that Housman gave Ker the manuscript of his *Last Poems* to read and comment on. His personality and achievements were reflected in the affectionate judgement of G. S. Gordon: '[he] is a dear and knows everything' (140).

Ker's vacations were mostly spent walking or climbing, boating or swimming, in Scotland, Switzerland, and elsewhere. During the First World War he was engaged in confidential work for the Admiralty; after the war he returned to the Alps, doing, at the age of sixty-five, strenuous climbs in quick succession, in a way which might have

tried a young and very strong man. His first and last year of complete freedom after the resignation of his London chair in 1922 was passed in this way in the spirit of an explorer, until, on 17 July 1923, he fell dead from heart failure on the Pizzo Bianco, which he had just described as 'the most beautiful spot in the world'. He was buried in the old churchyard at Macugnaga, Italy. Ker began his career at a time when the academic study of English language and literature was still nascent, and comparative literature largely non-existent in England. He had a crucial role in the development of both subjects. His most significant academic relationship was probably with R. W. Chambers, whom he appointed as Quain student at University College in 1899 and who ultimately succeeded him as Quain professor in 1923. Chambers's literary interests were possibly more firmly English than Ker's, but through this appointment in particular, as well as by his own example, Ker did much to institutionalize English as an academic discipline in England.

R. W. CHAMBERS, *rev.* A. S. G. EDWARDS

Sources J. H. P. Pafford, *W. P. Ker, 1855–1923, a bibliography* (1950) · *The letters of G. S. Gordon* (1943), 140 · P. G. Naiditch, *A. E. Housman at University College, London: the election of 1892* (1988), 57–8 [suppl. bibliography] · *The Times* (20 July 1923) · *The Times* (21 July 1923) · *The Times* (23 July 1923) · *The Times* (25 July 1923) · R. W. Chambers, *W. P. Ker, 1855–1923* (1923) · J. MacCunn, *Recollections of W. P. Ker* (1924) · G. Foster, *English Studies*, 5 (1923), 153 · A. D. Godley, 'In memoriam: William Paton Ker', *Alpine Journal*, 35 (1923), 275–7 · *CGPLA Eng. & Wales* (1923)

Archives LUL, corresp. and papers · NL Scot., letters and papers · U. Glas. L., diaries, letters, notebooks, papers, and sketchbooks · UCL, corresp. and papers | All Souls Oxf., letters to Sir William Anston · BL, corresp. with Macmillans, Add. MS 55032 · U. Birm. L., Chambers MSS · U. Leeds, Brotherton L., letters to E. Gosse · U. Oxf., faculty of English language and literature, Icelandic collection · UCL, letters to R. W. Chambers · UCL, letters to Olivia Homer

Likenesses W. Lytton Hannay, oils, 1916, University College, Cardiff · W. Rothenstein, sanguine and white chalk, 1921, All Souls Oxf. · P. W. Steer, oils, 1922, UCL · W. Rothenstein, sanguine and white chalk, 1923, NPG [*see illus.*] · J. Tweed, bronze bust, 1923–4, UCL · J. Tweed, bronze bust, All Souls Oxf.; replica, U. Glas.

Wealth at death £59,426 17s.: confirmation, 19 Oct 1923, *CCI*

Kerans, John Simon (1915–1985), naval officer, was born on 30 June 1915 at Birr, King's county, Ireland, the son of Major Edward Thomas John Kerans DSO, of the Royal Tank Corps and his wife, Eva Wills Hale.

Education and early career Kerans began his formal education in a preparatory school in Gloucester and went on from there to the Royal Naval College at Dartmouth, where he excelled in individual sports, winning caps for both fencing and sprinting and being notable for his exploits at the shooting range, in the swimming pool, and on both the squash and tennis courts. At 5 feet 11 inches in height, fit and blessed with explosive speed, Kerans was an ideal rugby wing three-quarter and represented his college in that position in its competitive fixtures. A lover of classical music and country pursuits, he was a maverick who possessed a strong streak of independence and self-assurance that led him, on occasion, to go to excess socially and bring him almost inevitably into collision with authority. His periodic brushes with the conservative establishment of the Royal Navy hindered his career. There was some consternation in Admiralty circles about how best to exploit his undoubted talents within the service.

After passing out of Dartmouth, Kerans served as both cadet and midshipman on board the battleship HMS *Rodney* in the Home Fleet (1932–3). His next post was as midshipman on the Kent class cruiser HMS *Cornwall* (1933–5), on which he was promoted sub-lieutenant. This led to his spending the next two years at the Royal Naval College, Greenwich, where he did not cover himself with glory in the classroom. Denied promotion and a seagoing appointment, he was sent to serve on the intelligence staff of the China station in Hong Kong and Singapore at a time of increasing Japanese belligerence in the Far East (1937–9). Once the Second World War had begun, however, he was sent as sub-lieutenant to the cruiser HMS *Naiad*, which was being used in the Home Fleet for trade protection duties. In May 1941 *Naiad* was deployed to join force H and become the flagship of 15th cruiser squadron on Malta convoy operations. On 11 March 1942, on return passage to Alexandria from an abortive attempt to intercept a supposedly damaged Italian cruiser in the eastern Mediterranean, *Naiad* was torpedoed and sunk off Mersa Matruh by *U-565*. Kerans was rescued and was rewarded with a shore appointment as staff officer (intelligence) on the staff of the tough, authoritative commander-in-chief Mediterranean and Levant, Admiral Sir John Henry Dacres Cunningham. After being belatedly promoted Kerans was sent to the destroyer minelayer HMS *Icarus* to act as its first lieutenant while it served on the Atlantic convoy route (1943–4).

Brought ashore before operation Overlord to serve on the staff of the commander-in-chief, Portsmouth, Kerans chanced to meet Stephanie Campbell Shires (*b*. 1917/18), at that time a member of the WRNS serving on the staff of combined operations headquarters and someone who helped to plot the D-day invasion. They met once again in Ceylon in 1945 while both were still in the service and decided to get married shortly afterwards, which they did in the parish of Charles, Plymouth, on 7 January 1946. They were married for thirty-nine years and had two daughters.

Transfer to Nanking Making up for lost time Kerans was promoted lieutenant-commander in 1944 and placed in charge of the Hunt type 2 class destroyer HMS *Blackmore*. Remaining with this ship until 1947, he was then transferred by the Admiralty to Hong Kong to serve on the staff of security intelligence. Once the drama of the Malayan emergency began to unfold in the following year, Kerans embarked on a three-month attachment to the Selangor police in Kuala Lumpur. At this point his naval career appeared to be going nowhere and Sir Patrick Brind, the commander-in-chief of the Far East station in Singapore, was evidently almost at a loss to know what to do with him. None the less, just when it appeared that the Royal Navy was giving up on Kerans, an unlikely opportunity presented itself for the mercurial lieutenant-commander

to redeem himself. It came in the shape of an appeal for a competent assistant requested by Captain Vernon Donaldson, the naval attaché at the British embassy in China; he needed help in dealing with the extra workload generated after the British had stationed a warship on the Yangtze (Yangzi) River at Nanking (Nanjing) in November 1948. Brind indicated that Kerans was almost immediately available but that he would be 'under report' status for an indefinite period. Donaldson—a sound, hard-working individual from the Scottish borders—decided to risk having the occasionally disruptive Kerans on his staff. On 3 February 1949 the newly appointed assistant naval attaché arrived in the Chinese nationalist capital to take up his duties just as the government was preparing to withdraw further south to Canton (Guangzhou) in Kwangtung (Guangdong) province. In these tense and fluid circumstances, when a studied calmness was at a premium and much work remained to be done, Kerans's rather brash personality and undisciplined work methods grated on Donaldson's nerves and made him inclined to regret giving his assistant a last chance to save his naval career.

If the Admiralty's policy was to keep Kerans out of harm's way while it decided what to do with him, transferring him from Malaya to China singularly failed to serve this purpose. Instead he was pitched into an extraordinarily controversial situation. Churchill's wartime coalition government had already signed a treaty with the Chinese government of Chiang Kai-shek on 11 January 1943 renouncing all British extraterritorial rights in the country, and Attlee's Labour administration had consolidated this policy by joining with the other major world powers gathered in Moscow in December 1945 in adopting a policy of non-intervention in the civil war that had broken out in China between forces of the nationalist Kuomintang (KMT) and the communist People's Liberation Army (PLA). Yet, contrary to both the spirit and the letter of these two crucial diplomatic accords, the British business community in China and a few leading members of the Commonwealth diplomatic corps in Nanking sought to preserve their economic interests in the country by reviving a British naval presence on the Yangtze. It was a shallow and absurd decision that managed to alienate both communists and nationalists alike and suggests that the British had scant regard for either the tenets of international law or Chinese sovereignty and independence. By February 1949 the Yangtze had become a no man's land between the front lines of the ebullient PLA troops drawn up on the northern bank of the river and the battered KMT forces whose grip on the territory south of the river looked anything but secure. A temporary ceasefire was in place but few expected it to last indefinitely. In the circumstances, therefore, one might have hoped for a suspension of the British guardship scheme until the highly charged political and military situation had settled down. No such enlightened decision was reached in Whitehall and British warships continued to make their scheduled journeys up and down the 200-mile stretch of the lower Yangtze from Shanghai to Nanking as the two armed factions in the Chinese civil war looked on from opposite sides of the river. By mid-April the PLA high command, frustrated by the inconclusive peace negotiations with the KMT, dramatically gave the nationalists a four-day deadline to accept its extremely harsh ultimatum or face the consequences of a resumption of the war.

Amethyst under fire Three days later on 19 April 1949 the frigate HMS *Amethyst* began her latest journey upriver from Shanghai. She was planned to arrive in Nanking to relieve the destroyer HMS *Consort* nine hours before the expiry of the PLA ultimatum at midnight on 20 April. She did not make it. At 9.30 a.m. on 20 April, at a point in the river some 60 miles north-east of Nanking, *Amethyst* came under accurate and withering fire from a communist battery situated at the mouth of the tributary leading to the Kao-yu lakes at San-chiang-ying (Sanjiangying). Within five minutes the frigate had sustained a number of grievous hits that wrecked her bridge, wheelhouse, and low power room, rendered her gyrocompass useless, damaged her electrical, gunnery, lighting, and navigational circuits, and jammed her steering hard to port so that she had driven herself up onto a mudbank just off the western shore of Rose Island. She was stuck, unable to extricate herself and virtually defenceless against the persistent shelling and small arms fire that rained down on her for roughly 90 minutes. Apart from her captain, Lieutenant-Commander B. M. Skinner, who was mortally wounded, the *Amethyst* suffered twenty-two other losses and had thirty-one of its crew wounded in the attack and its immediate aftermath.

When the news of the *Amethyst*'s plight reached the British naval authorities on the Far East station, arrangements were swiftly made for HMS *Consort* to leave Nanking and come to the frigate's assistance. Unfortunately, the British destroyer's arrival on the scene in the early afternoon and her willingness to bombard the shoreline did not overawe the PLA battery crews operating from well-hidden nests of guns along the northern bank of the river. *Consort* was engaged and struck by a number of shells—killing ten of her company and wounding twenty-three others—as she steamed past the forlorn and trapped figure of the *Amethyst*. Later that evening, after a series of running repairs to her engines and steering equipment, the *Amethyst* managed to extricate herself from the mudbank and move to a more sheltered location a short distance upstream of Rose Island. Another abortive attempt to rescue her was mounted on the following day when the 10,000 ton cruiser HMS *London* and the frigate HMS *Black Swan* tried to go to her assistance. Further mayhem resulted with thirteen killed and thirty-two wounded on board the leading ship *London* and seven wounded on her supporting vessel *Black Swan*. In the light of these further incidents no other rescue bids were made or planned by the British naval authorities. As direct action was now ruled out, a resolution of the *Amethyst* crisis would have to be through some form of negotiation with the PLA, but even this possibility was fraught with serious problems since the British government did not have any contact—official or otherwise—with the communist hierarchy and the *Amethyst* had lost her captain and two of her senior

officers were known to be seriously wounded and in urgent need of hospitalization.

In these unfavourable circumstances, Donaldson sent Kerans off to try and establish personal contact with the stricken frigate and her crew. This was easier said than done but eventually, after a number of mishaps, he was able to get on board the *Amethyst* in the mid-afternoon of 22 April. Once he did so he received a call from Vice-Admiral Sir Alexander Madden, the flag officer and second in charge of the Far East station, ordering him to assume acting command of the ship. From then onwards over the next ninety-nine days Kerans became, *de facto*, the Royal Navy's leading figure on the Yangtze and therefore, by extension, the one official seen by the PLA as representing the British government in this crisis. Within a day the communists had crossed the river in force and had established themselves on both banks of the Yangtze. Kerans and the *Amethyst* were trapped. They had become hostages to fortune.

While a political inquest into the background of this crisis opened in the United Kingdom and the British press devoted many column inches to the initial attack on the *Amethyst* and the subsequent rescue attempts, those on board the frigate at the centre of the controversy could only wait with growing impatience upon future developments. Well aware that it might take some time to arrange the release of the *Amethyst* and her crew, Kerans knew that time was not on his side. Every day spent in the fetid heat and humidity of the Yangtze used up precious fuel in the *Amethyst*'s tanks. While shutting down the generators for lengthy periods of the day certainly saved some fuel, it made the business of living on board the frigate more uncomfortable by the hour. In an effort to combat lethargy and restlessness he ensured that everyone on board had a set routine of daily duties to conduct.

Heroic defiance Whatever his past misdemeanours may have been, Kerans was a most resourceful and dashing figure and one who brought an air of self-confidence and individual flair to these proceedings. In fact, the old adage—'cometh the hour, cometh the man'—definitely applies in this instance. Kerans was to perform quite superbly in his new role of acting captain: working closely with the remaining officers and specialists on board and becoming well liked and trusted by the crew who much appreciated both his charismatic personality and his common touch.

Once the PLA had eventually established contact with the *Amethyst* it became obvious that negotiations between the two sides were going to be long and arduous. Clearly, the PLA's case was based on the fact that the British frigate had flagrantly violated Chinese sovereignty by entering the Yangtze in the first place and that it had compounded this grave error by opening fire on the communist battery positions drawn up on the northern bank of the river in the early morning of 20 April. According to the communists' version of the events, the *Amethyst* was engaged by the PLA only in self-defence and that further damage to Chinese property and considerable loss of life on shore among the civilian population was caused by the actions of *Consort*, *London*, and *Black Swan* in their unsuccessful attempts to rescue the beleaguered frigate which had created the incident initially. Kerans's defence tactics rested on saying little about the sovereignty issue and vigorously rejecting the charge that the British warship had been responsible for her own demise by opening fire on the Chinese. Instead he counter-accused the PLA of unleashing a completely unprovoked attack on the *Amethyst*.

Despite the occasional sign of optimism that a breakthrough was imminent, the dreary and contentious negotiations careered on for another three months without resolution. Kerans was instructed by the British government to make some concession on the violation of sovereignty charge, but he had little difficulty in steadfastly refusing to admit any complicity on the question of who fired first on 20 April. Kerans was to demonstrate uncommon tact, patience, and discipline (qualities that he was not especially known for previously) in his role as the Royal Navy's personal intermediary with the PLA in the months to come. His fortitude in adversity and his adroit handling of the often tortuous series of negotiations that ensued could hardly be faulted and were to prove deeply inspirational to the men of the *Amethyst* as the days of their confinement on the Yangtze grew.

Escape By 30 July 1949, however, despairing of an early release of his ship and crew and acutely conscious that the *Amethyst*'s fuel stocks were barely sufficient for her to reach Shanghai under her own steam, Kerans decided to try and escape down the fortified Yangtze at night, without the use of either lights or river pilots, on one of the most difficult stretches of water in the world. After reaching his decision, he informed the officers and crew of the dangers they faced in pursuing this option but the ship's company, cooped up for more than a hundred days in foul conditions, were prepared for anything and enthusiastically supported their captain's bold plan of action. Kerans did not need reminding that if anything went wrong and the *Amethyst* was further disabled and/or sunk by the PLA defence forces on the passage downriver, the Admiralty in London was hardly likely to view his escape bid in a favourable light. None the less, he had sailed metaphorically close to the wind before and he felt he had little choice but to do so again. It was an inspired decision.

Luck was also on Kerans's side. As he debated when to launch his ship's bid for freedom, a fully lit merchant ship, the *Kiang Ling Liberation*, appeared on the scene at 10 p.m. steaming downriver in the direction of Shanghai. Kerans seized the opportunity, gave the order to cut the *Amethyst*'s heavily lagged anchor cable and execute a 180 degree turn in the middle of the river and follow close behind the Chinese ship for as long as possible. Shortly afterwards the ruse was discovered by a PLA battery crew and an intense shelling of the ships began. Unfortunately for the *Kiang Ling Liberation* the PLA inexplicably concentrated its fire on her, reducing the Chinese vessel to a smoking hulk in a few minutes and the *Amethyst*, bearing a charmed life and with only one inconsequential hit, steamed on past the luckless passenger cargo ship downstream as fast as she could go. In the course of the next

seven and a half hours *Amethyst* defied the odds—passing PLA forts and gun posts, going successfully through a defensive boom—and emerged triumphantly to meet the destroyer HMS *Concord* at the mouth of the river estuary. Kerans signalled Brind at the Far East station with a message that would soon be emblazoned across much of the world's press. It read simply: 'Have rejoined the fleet south of Woosung, no damage or casualties. God save the king.' Kerans and the crew of the *Amethyst* now became the toast of a United Kingdom starved of success in the immediate post-war world. Their exploits on the Yangtze made them into instant celebrities at every port of call on their homeward voyage to Plymouth, but no one was accorded more praise than the quintessential *Boy's Own* hero John Simon Kerans.

Awarded the DSO by George VI in a special ceremony at Buckingham Palace on 17 November 1949 and promoted commander in December, Kerans's fame presented the Board of Admiralty with a problem: what was it to do with the new folk hero? Had Kerans really changed or was he still the anti-establishment rebel he had been in the past? In the interim period while the Admiralty waited to see whether Kerans had matured and become totally reliable, he was invited to go on the Royal Navy staff course at Greenwich in the new year. Later in 1950 he was appointed head of the Far East section of the naval intelligence division at the Admiralty in London. He remained in this position for two years before he was sent to take charge of the minesweeper HMS *Rinaldo*, which was serving with NATO forces in Europe (1953–4). Thereafter, he became British naval attaché to Burma, Cambodia, Laos, Thailand, and Vietnam in 1954. This posting ended abruptly in the following year, when he was recalled to London, putting paid to any faint hopes he may have entertained of achieving flag rank before his retirement. Once again the Admiralty was bereft of ideas about what to do with him and so after a year spent essentially marking time he was enlisted on the sea officers' technical course at Portsmouth in 1957. This served as a prelude to his retirement from the service later in the same year at the comparatively young age of forty-two.

Significance Whatever the scale of his misdeeds may have been, Kerans remained a swashbuckling hero for many British people—an individual who had shown great skill, resourcefulness, and tremendous courage in defying both the Yangtze and the communists in order to regain freedom for the *Amethyst* and her crew. As such, he remained much in demand in the public arena for some years to come. Approached by the Conservative Party, he was adopted as its candidate for the north-eastern constituency of the Hartlepools, which he unexpectedly won for the tories by 182 votes in the general election of 1959. Kerans's tenuous hold over this highly marginal constituency faltered as the Conservatives weakened in the early 1960s, and this contributed to his decision not to stand for re-election to parliament in October 1964. Only forty-nine, Kerans still had something to offer the country, but some of the lustre attached to his name had by then worn off—the Yangtze incident had become but a pale memory for many, and the world had moved on. He eventually joined the civil service and served for eleven years on the Pensions Appeal Tribunal until he retired at sixty-five in 1980. He and his wife, Stephanie, continued to live at Oxted, Surrey, but his health steadily deteriorated and he died in the local hospital of cancer on 12 September 1985.

Although John Simon Kerans was a reckless character with an unfortunate tendency to undermine his true potential, he was also an individual who turned his undoubted gifts to great advantage in the most perilous of circumstances. In doing so he achieved a heroic status and gave the British people something to cheer about amid the unrelieved dreariness and austerity of the cold war.

MALCOLM H. MURFETT

Sources M. H. Murfett, *Hostage on the Yangtze: Britain, China and the Amethyst crisis of 1949* (1991) · IWM, John Simon Kerans papers · L. Earl, *Yangtse incident* (1973) · C. E. Lucas Phillips, *Escape of the Amethyst* (1958) · m. cert. · d. cert. · *CGPLA Eng. & Wales* (1985) · *The Times* (13 Sept 1985) · *Daily Telegraph* (14 Sept 1985) · *WWW* · b. cert.

Archives IWM, MSS

Likenesses photograph, 1949, repro. in *The Times* · photograph, NPG · photographs, IWM, John Simon Kerans MSS, photo album

Wealth at death £76,317: probate, 15 Nov 1985, *CGPLA Eng. & Wales*

Kerensky, Oleg Alexander [Oleg Aleksandrovich] (1905–1984), civil engineer, was born in St Petersburg on 16 April 1905, the elder son (there were no daughters) of Aleksandr Fyodorovich Kerensky (1881–1970), barrister, and later briefly the prime minister of the provisional government of Russia prior to the October revolution in 1917, and his wife, Olga Lvovna Baranovskaya. His parents, although not divorced until 1939, did not live together after 1917 and the two sons were brought up solely by their mother. After the Russian revolution they suffered much danger and many privations, including a short term of imprisonment, before escaping via Estonia to London in 1920. Thereafter the sons had regular meetings with their father in London and Paris. Their mother did not marry again.

Oleg and Gleb Kerensky attended Oakfield, a private school in north London, and by 1923 both had obtained the necessary qualifications to gain entry to London University. They studied engineering at the civil and mechanical engineering department of the Northampton Institute (then widely known as Northampton Engineering College and later to become first the Northampton College of Advanced Technology and finally developing into the City University). The brothers passed with honours, Gleb subsequently following a successful career as a mechanical engineer with English Electric, and surviving Oleg.

Following graduation in 1927 and a short period with Oxford city council, Oleg Kerensky joined the bridge department of Dorman Long & Co. Ltd, working first on the tender documents and then on the detailed design and erection scheme for the Sydney harbour bridge. Before leaving Dorman Long in 1937 he also worked on other schemes, including the Bangkok memorial bridge, Lambeth Bridge in London, and the Qasr al-Nil Bridge in Egypt.

From 1937 to 1946 Kerensky worked with the steel construction firm of Holloway Brothers. His work during the Second World War included the construction of units for the prefabricated Mulberry harbours which were used in the Normandy landings. Subsequently, as senior designer, he was in charge of designs for the Baghdad railway bridge and the Lesser Zab and Euphrates bridges. He was naturalized in 1947.

Kerensky's final move was in 1946 to the London consulting firm of Freeman Fox & Partners, where he first worked on the design for a suspension bridge over the River Severn, not at that time proceeded with, although it later formed the basis for the Forth road bridge opened in 1964. He was promoted to partnership in 1955 and assumed responsibility for many major bridges at home and abroad, including Auckland harbour bridge in New Zealand, the Ganges and Brahmaputra bridges in India, the Grosvenor railway bridge in London, the Medway Bridge in Kent, and the Erskine and Friarton bridges in Scotland. In many of these works Kerensky introduced new techniques which he applied with courage and thorough attention to detail, including the use of high tensile rivets as well as bolts and forms of composite action between steel and concrete. In the case of the Medway Bridge he overcame many problems in the construction of the then largest clear-span pre-stressed concrete bridge in the world.

Kerensky also had notable achievements in many highway schemes, such as on the two major motorways M2 and M5, the latter including the technically interesting Almondsbury interchange with the M4, Britain's first four-level interchange.

Throughout his life Kerensky was devoted to the service of his profession. He served as president of, successively, the institutions of Structural Engineers (1970–71) and Highway Engineers (1971–2), and was an active member of the Institution of Civil Engineers (ICE) and of the International Association for Bridge and Structural Engineering. He received many awards from these and other institutions, including the Telford and George Stephenson gold medals of the ICE, the gold medal of the Institution of Structural Engineers, and the gold medal of the Worshipful Company of Carmen, London. He was elected FRS (1970) and was a founder member of the Fellowship of Engineering (1976). He took a lively interest in the education and training of engineers, and had a supportive association with Northampton Engineering College and then with the City University, from which he received an honorary DSc in 1967. He was appointed CBE in 1964.

Kerensky was also very interested in engineering research, and worked in an advisory capacity on various committees, frequently as chairman, for the Welding Institute and the Construction Industry Research and Information Association (CIRIA). After many years serving as chairman of council of CIRIA, he was elected its president in 1979. He also gave advice on investigations into bridge topics carried out at the Transport and Road Research Laboratory. His most continuing, devoted service was probably on the British Standards bridge committee (as chairman from 1958), in particular overseeing for sixteen years the preparation of the comprehensive and innovatory ten-part code which was finally completed in 1984.

Kerensky was a man with a dominating presence, sometimes overwhelming to his juniors, but he showed great kindness and understanding. In 1928 he married Nathalie, daughter of James (Yaxa Moiyitch) Bely, from Russia, a partner in Willis, Faber, Dumas & Partners, insurance brokers. They had one son, Oleg, a journalist and art critic. After his first wife's death in 1969, in 1971 Kerensky married Mrs Dorothy Harvey. She was left disabled following a fall soon after the marriage and was shown the greatest of care and attention by her husband. He was a keen player of bridge, an interest he shared with both his wives. Throughout his life he liked to swim. In early days he was fond of playing rugby and latterly he was a proficient player of croquet. He died at the Cromwell Hospital, Kensington, London, on 25 June 1984, and his wife died the following year. MICHAEL R. HORNE, *rev.*

Sources M. R. Horne, *Memoirs FRS*, 32 (1986), 323–53 · personal knowledge (1990) · 'Oleg Kerensky, British civil engineer', *Annual Obituary* (1984), 325–6 · d. cert.
Likenesses photograph, repro. in Horne, *Memoirs FRS*
Wealth at death £209,610: probate, 13 Sept 1984, *CGPLA Eng. & Wales*

Kermack, William Ogilvy (1898–1970), biochemist and mathematical epidemiologist, was born on 26 April 1898 at Kirriemuir, Forfarshire, the only son of William Kermack, postman, and his wife, Helen, *née* Ogilvy (*d.* 1904). After his mother's death he was mainly brought up by his father's sister. At five he was sent to a local school, Webster's seminary; there he received an excellent education, being taught co-ordinate geometry and geometric conic sections by the headmaster and general science by G. K. Sutherland, later professor of biology at Southampton.

In 1914, aged sixteen, Kermack took thirteenth place in the University of Aberdeen bursary competition: he matriculated in that year. In 1918 he graduated MA with first-class honours in mathematics and natural philosophy and BSc with special distinction in mathematics, natural philosophy, and chemistry, winning four prizes and medals and, in 1919, the Ferguson scholarship in mathematics. After graduation he served six months with the Royal Air Force at the Martlesham Heath Experimental Station. From 1919 until 1921 he worked in a British Dyestuffs Corporation research group under W. H. Perkin and with Robert Robinson at the Dyson Perrins Laboratory, Oxford. This work led to his first publication: it dealt with the synthesis of norharman, the fundamental structural unit of the alkaloids harmaline and harmine.

In 1921 Kermack took charge of the chemistry department at the laboratory of the Royal College of Physicians of Edinburgh. Most of the funding of the laboratory, founded in 1887, came from the Carnegie Trustees for the Universities of Scotland. A. G. McKendrick, director of the

Pasteur Institute at Kasauli, India, had been appointed superintendent in 1920. Like Kermack, he had a deep interest in the mathematical aspects of biology.

While working alone in the chemistry laboratory on 2 June 1924 Kermack was totally and permanently blinded when a preparation exploded, driving caustic alkali into his eyes. He bore his loss with courage and immediately retrained himself. He returned to work before the end of the year, the Board of Scientific and Industrial Research and the Carnegie Trustees providing him with a special assistant. In his subsequent twenty-five years at the college laboratory he published eighty-four papers. In 1925 he married Elsábeletta Raimunda Blásquez, daughter of Raimundo Blásquez of Anguilas, Spain.

Kermack's continued work on the synthesis of indole compounds led to the award of a DSc degree from Aberdeen in 1925, but he also established two new and highly productive collaborative ventures. Work with McKendrick led to the publication in 1927 of the classic paper 'A contribution to the mathematical theory of epidemics' (*PRS*, 115A, 1927, 700–21). This established the threshold theory, a cornerstone of modern theoretical epidemiology. In Kermack and McKendrick's own words, it postulates that:

> for each particular set of infectivity, recovery and death rates, there exists a critical or threshold density of population. If the actual population density be equal to (or below) this threshold value the introduction of one (or more) infected person does not give rise to an epidemic, whereas if the population be only slightly more dense a small epidemic occurs.

In a series of papers published over the next twelve years special cases and dynamics were considered, and the theory was tested against data from the field and from the experiments of Greenwood and others on ectromelia and mouse typhoid.

Kermack's other collaboration was with University of Edinburgh mathematicians. It focused particularly on Whittaker's conjecture on the solution of differential equations by definitive integrals, and the central theorem establishing the existence of a quantity associated with two neighbouring null-geodesics in a Riemannian space that depends on the two geodesics as a whole.

During his lifetime Kermack was best known for his work on the organic chemistry of antimalarials. His work focused on the synthesis of heterocyclic compounds, particularly the creation of quinolone derivatives. He hoped to deduce rules relating structure to chemotherapeutic activity. He collaborated with workers on avian malaria at the Molteno Institute, Cambridge, and chemists in the ICI drystuffs division, receiving support from the Department of Scientific and Industrial Research, the Chemical Society and the Carnegie Trust. His main achievement was to devise a synthetic route to acridines related to atebrine. This facilitated the production of mepacrine, which became the major British antimalarial when the supply of German products was cut off in 1939.

In 1949 Kermack moved to Aberdeen as the first MacLeod-Smith professor of biological chemistry. He built up a department noted for the quality of its teaching and the breadth of its research interests. Active in committee work, he was dean of science from 1961 to 1964, and from 1949 to 1969 an effective governor of the Macaulay Institute for Soil Research and the Rowett Research Institute for Animal Nutrition. During his career he was honoured by election in 1925 to the Royal Society of Edinburgh (council 1946–9) and the Royal Society (1944), and the award of the Freeland Barbour fellowship of the Royal College of Physicians of Edinburgh (1925), the Makdougall Brisbane prize of the Royal Society of Edinburgh (1928), and the LLD (St Andrews) in 1937.

Kermack's wife, Elsábeletta, looked after him devotedly, and he received enormous support from his staff, who read scientific papers to him. Radio was invaluable to him. On the left politically, he was an agnostic. He retired in September 1968, retaining an office in Marischal College, in which he died suddenly on 20 July 1970. His wife survived him.   T. H. PENNINGTON

Sources J. N. Davidson, *Memoirs FRS*, 17 (1971), 399–429 [incl. appendices by F. Yates and W. H. McCrea] · J. Ritchie, *History of the laboratory of the Royal College of Physicians of Edinburgh* (1953) · J. Allen, 'William Ogilvy Kermack', *Aberdeen University Review*, 44 (1971–2), 25–8 · T. Watt, *Roll of graduates of the University of Aberdeen, 1901–1925* (1935) · *DNB*
Likenesses W. Stoneman, photograph, 1946, repro. in Davidson, *Memoirs FRS*
Wealth at death £13,042 13s. 4d.: confirmation, 26 March 1971, *CCI* · £327 3s. 2d.—held in trust: 26 March 1971, *CCI*

Kermode, (Margaret Leotitia) Josephine [*pseud.* Cushag] (1852–1937), author, was born on 18 September 1852 at 73 Parliament Street, Ramsey, Isle of Man. The third daughter of the Revd William Kermode (1814–1890), Anglican priest, and his second wife, Jane Bishop, she was seventh among the fourteen children of William Kermode's two marriages. She was educated at home by a governess, and was encouraged to explore her creative side from an early age. She contributed first to magazines circulated among family and friends, such as the *Ramsey Parsonage Gazette* and *Ny Irey Lhaa*, with her first published poem, 'A Lonan Legend', appearing in 1899. Three volumes of poems appeared between 1907 and 1912, published under the pseudonym Cushag after the then national flower of the Isle of Man, the ragwort. The volume *Poems by Cushag* (1907) was published by G. & L. Johnson, followed by *Ellan Vannin* (1911) and *Manx Melodies* (1922). *Manx Melodies* was a collected edition of her published poems, including those printed in journals such as *Mannin*, the journal of Yn Cheshaght Ghailckagh, the Manx Language Society. Her poetry also appeared in *Ellan Vannin*, the magazine of the World Manx Association, an important link to the homeland for Manx emigrants.

Kermode also wrote plays, the best-known examples of which, *Mylecharaine* (1920) and *The Quaker of Ballafayle* (1926), were published in the *Ramsey Courier* newspaper. Her set of *Peel Plays* was written for the Peel Players, an amateur theatrical company under the wing of Kermode's close friend Sophia Morrison, whose death she commemorated in a poem. A second series, entitled the Glen Auldyn plays, was produced to raise funds for the relief of Belgian refugees during the First World War.

Kermode was heralded by some as a successor to the Manx national poet, T. E. Brown. Indeed, her poetry was highly regarded on the Isle of Man at her time of writing, if not always considered to be as serious in tone as some of Brown's work. An obituary notes that 'she had the key to her people's heart. A sweeter, tenderer soul never lived' (Caine, 'Beloved Manx poet'). Like Brown's, her style was important in that it captured the speech patterns of Manx people and reflected intimate knowledge of their home life. Much of her work was nostalgic for previous generations, with the majority deeply rooted in legends associated with the Isle of Man. Although occasional poems such as 'Cradle Song' are bilingual, Kermode was well known for writing in dialect (Manx English). Together with Brown's her writings were selected as source material for the 1924 volume *A Vocabulary of the Anglo-Manx Dialect*, by Moore, Morrison, and Goodwin.

In republishing a selection of Kermode's poetry as *Them Oul' Times* in 1993, Constance Radcliffe wrote: 'Although imbued with the old certainties of the Christian faith, Cushag had no difficulty in light-heartedly embracing the denizens of the Celtic Other World, a capacity she shared with many of her fellow-countrymen and -women'. She befriended the young Mona Douglas, who in 1962 recalled being told 'tales of Themselves and their dealings with the Glen folk. She was very much at home in the Middle World as the old Gaels called it' (Douglas, 'The good companions'). Alongside the mythical or other world, themes of nature and community are strong in Kermode's work. Although not written in impenetrable dialect, the regional bias of the material has been considered an obstacle to her work being received well outside the island.

'A gentle soul in word and life' was P. W. Caine's description of her in his obituary in the *Isle of Man Weekly Times* (20 February 1937). One of her brothers, Frank Bishop Kermode, also wrote poetry, using the pseudonym Silver Birch. Josephine never married, acting as housekeeper for her brother Philip Moore Callow *Kermode, a noted antiquarian and archaeologist, for most of her life. She moved from the north of the island, where the family grew up, to Douglas on her brother's appointment as first curator at the Manx Museum in 1922. On his death, she returned to Ramsey where she volunteered as a district nurse, before retiring to live with her sister Cherrill in Bournemouth, where she died, at 42 Portchester Road, on 15 February 1937, and where she is buried. A Cushag memorial stands in her home parish of Maughold in the Isle of Man.

                                    BREESHA MADDRELL

Sources C. Radcliffe, ed., *Them oul' times* (privately printed, Maughold, Isle of Man, c.1993) · 'Manx poet dies', *Peel City Guardian* (20 Feb 1937), 5 · 'Death of "Cushag"', *Mona's Herald* (16 Feb 1937), 7 · P. W. Caine, 'Beloved Manx poet dead', *Isle of Man Weekly Times* (20 Feb 1937), 16–17 · 'Passing of "Cushag"', *Isle of Man Examiner* (19 Feb 1937), 17 · 'Death of "Cushag"', *Ramsey Courier* (16 Feb 1937), 2 · M. Douglas, 'The good companions', *Isle of Man Weekly Times* (9 Nov 1962), 7 · d. cert. · *IGI* · A. W. Moore, *Manx worthies* (1901)
Likenesses photograph, c.1875, Manx Museum, Douglas, Isle of Man

Kermode, Philip Moore Callow (1855–1932), archaeologist, was born on 21 March 1855 in Parliament Street, Ramsey, Isle of Man, the second son of fourteen children of William Kermode of Claughbane (1814–1890), chaplain of St Paul's Church, Ramsey, and his second wife, Jane, daughter of W. Bishop of Shelton Hall, Staffordshire. An elder sister was the author (Margaret Leotitia) Josephine *Kermode. Kermode was educated at King William's College and then read for the bar, being admitted a Manx advocate in 1878. Although he was living with some of his siblings at the family house in 1907, Claughbane was sold shortly thereafter, and it seems that for the rest of his life Kermode was short of money (it is not impossible that his family were affected by the collapse of Dumbell's Bank in 1900; according to gossip he would pawn his library when he was short of cash). He had an undemanding job as clerk to the Ramsey justices (1888–1922). He never married. For many years his sister Josephine acted as his housekeeper.

Like many of his generation Kermode had wide amateur interests. A naturalist of more than local reputation (the species *Nassa kermodei* is named after him), his main interest, however, lay in the study of the archaeology of the Isle of Man. Apart from his specialist work on the early sculpture of the Isle of Man, he was adroit at harnessing local energies. He was a founding member of the Isle of Man Natural History and Antiquarian Society (1879) and of the Manx Archaeological Survey (1908) (which recorded the early chapel and cemetery sites in the island), and was deeply involved in setting up the Manx Museum (which, founded in 1886, did not become a reality until 1922, when it moved into permanent premises in Douglas). Kermode, who had fought hard for it, was the first curator.

As a young man Kermode had travelled in Italy and in Scandinavia, where he had studied local antiquities. He excavated widely in the island, particularly with William Herdman at the megalithic monument on Mull Hill and at many chapel sites. Two of his more triumphant finds were the complete skeleton of a giant Irish elk (*Megaceros giganteus*), which he excavated with the British Association in 1897, and the viking boat burial at Knock y Doonee (1930). His excavation technique was rudimentary, but it is largely through his work that we have such a detailed knowledge of Manx archaeology. He was more at ease as a field worker, as is demonstrated by his *List of Manx Antiquities* (1930).

Kermode's claim to fame lies in his detailed study of the corpus of Manx early Christian and viking age funerary sculpture. This is particularly rich in Scandinavian runic inscriptions, ornament, and iconography. Already in the 1880s he began to prepare a corpus of this material, concentrating on the inscriptions and iconography. He was presumably influenced by his friend J. Romilly Allen's corpus of the early Christian monuments of Scotland (1903) and by his contemporary W. G. Collingwood's work on the early sculpture of the north of England. Encouraged by the Norwegian scholars Sophus and Alexander Bugge, by the Swedish runologist Erik Brate, and by Romilly Allen, Kermode (the amateur) published a guide to the sculptures in a small book, *Catalogue of the Manks Crosses with the Runic Inscriptions* (1892). This, with many articles, formed the basis of his *Manx Crosses* (1907, republished with some updated critical apparatus in 1994). Illustrated with his remarkably accurate wash drawings, it remains a standard and much consulted work to this day.

Apart from the honorary degree of MA from Liverpool University, Kermode received few honours in Britain. He was, however, recognized elsewhere. He was a knight grand cross of the Falcon (Iceland), a knight (first class) of St Olaf (Norway), and a corresponding member of the Academy of Sciences of Norway. Kermode died in Ramsey on 5 September 1932 and was buried in Maughold churchyard.   DAVID M. WILSON

Sources J. B. Caine, 'In the beginning', *100 years of heritage: the work of the Manx Museum and National Trust*, ed. S. Harrison (1986), 10–16 · D. M. Wilson, 'Philip Kermode and Manx crosses', in P. M. C. Kermode, *Manx crosses*, 2nd edn (1994), 1–8 · P. G. Rolfe, 'The late P. M. C. Kermode as a naturalist', *Proceedings of the Isle of Man Natural History and Antiquarian Society*, 4/1 (1932–5), 36–9 · W. Cubbon, 'The Kermode family of Ramsey', *Proceedings of the Isle of Man Natural History and Antiquarian Society*, 5/1 (1942–6), 109–21 · [W. Cubbon], 'In memoriam P. M. C. Kermode', *Journal of the Manx Museum*, 2 (1932), 79
Archives Manx Museum, Douglas, Isle of Man, MSS
Likenesses F. Lightowler, plaster bust, 1932, Manx Museum, Douglas, Isle of Man · photographs, Manx Museum, Douglas, Isle of Man

Kéroualle, Louise Renée de Penancoët de, *suo jure* duchess of Portsmouth and *suo jure* duchess of Aubigny in the French nobility (1649–1734), royal mistress, was born in September 1649 at the Manoir de Kéroualle, the family home near Brest, Brittany, France, the second of three children of Guillaume de Penancoët, count de Kéroualle (d. 1690), and his wife, Marie-Anne (d. 1709), daughter of Sebastien de Ploeuc, marquess of Timeur and of Kergolay, and his wife, Marie de Rieux. Kéroualle boasted an ancient lineage but was of relatively minor and apparently somewhat impoverished Breton nobility, while his wife was a connection of the powerful Rieux family. Louise was probably educated at the nearby convent of the Ursulines of Lesneven. Towards the end of 1668 she was appointed a maid of honour to Henriette-Anne, duchess of Orléans and sister of *Charles II ('Madame'), and in June 1670 she was one of her entourage on her visit to England for the signing of the secret treaty of Dover. The death of Madame shortly afterwards proved a turning-point in Louise's life as she was one of Madame's household who were then taken into the service of Charles II's queen, Catherine of Braganza.

The king's mistress The familiar account by Bishop Burnet of de Kéroualle having caught the king's eye at Dover and the duke of Buckingham and Louis XIV then deliberately sending her back in order to ensnare Charles is not supported by other evidence, although the exact circumstances of her new appointment remain unclear. She arrived in September or October 1670 to take up her position as maid of honour and was soon noticed at court, the diarist John Evelyn writing that in November he saw Louise, 'that famed beauty, (but in my opinion of a childish

Louise Renée de Penancoët de Kéroualle, *suo jure* duchess of Portsmouth and *suo jure* duchess of Aubigny in the French nobility (1649–1734), by Sir Peter Lely, *c.*1671–4

simple and baby face)' (Evelyn, 3.564). Contemporary portraits suggest her features and figure were rounded and that she had dark hair and brown eyes. After about a year Louise became the mistress of Charles II (1630–1685), probably during the October 1671 visit of the court to Newmarket when she was invited to stay at Euston, the home of Lord Arlington, expressly with the intent of attracting the king there. The French ambassador colluded in this arrangement and was soon able to report that it had proved successful. Some ten months later, on 29 July 1672, Louise gave birth to her only son by the king, whom she named Charles. She soon became established as the king's main mistress: on 19 August 1673 she was created Baroness Petersfield, countess of Fareham, and duchess of Portsmouth, and was at the same time appointed a lady of the queen's bedchamber. The new duchess's success enabled her to arrange a marriage for her sister, Henriette-Mauricette, who came to England in 1674, was given a pension of £600 a year, and married Philip Herbert, sixth earl of Pembroke. Portsmouth's son was given the last name of Lennox and the young Charles *Lennox was created baron of Settrington, earl of March, and duke of Richmond on 9 August 1675, and on 9 September lord of Torboulton, earl of Darnley, and duke of Lennox in the Scottish peerage.

In October 1676 Portsmouth's main pension from Charles II was established at £8600 a year for life. Her annuities had increased to £11,000 by December 1680 and, with the addition of many payments over and above her pensions, in the last four years of the reign she seems to have collected an average of some £20,000 a year. She was probably the most expensive of Charles's mistresses, but the figure of £136,668 often quoted as having been given to her in 1681 from secret-service money is a mistaken calculation (GEC, *Peerage*, appx M, 130–31). At some point before her son was born Portsmouth was given apartments of her own in Whitehall at the end of the Matted Gallery, which she gradually extended until they consisted of some twenty-four rooms and included about 60 to 70 foot of the gallery. Portsmouth occupied these apartments until the end of the reign, and they became a focal point for her ascendancy at court, where she put on magnificent entertainments and provided the main alternative to meeting the king in his own or the queen's rooms. John Evelyn described them in 1675 as 'luxuriously furnished and with ten times the richness and glory beyond the Queene's' (Evelyn, 4.74). Portsmouth's success was not, however, always assured. In 1674 Charles II contracted a sexually transmitted disease which he passed on to Portsmouth, who reportedly suffered far worse effects from it than he did; this may have been the cause of her recurrent ill health thereafter. Moreover, Nell Gwyn, the king's other mistress at this time, was a constant source of irritation to Portsmouth, and the arrival of Hortense, duchess of Mazarin, in England in December 1675 was potentially an even greater threat. It was soon apparent that the king was attracted to Hortense and this, coupled with Portsmouth's illness in April 1676, gave rise to many rumours that their relationship had become purely platonic and that she would soon be displaced altogether. In August that year Portsmouth, in obvious distress, poured out her troubles to the French ambassador; in December, in the ambassador's presence, she complained to the king of his infidelities, recalling the previous disastrous consequences. However, the king's affair with Mazarin was short-lived, and Portsmouth had regained her position by 1677.

Court politician Portsmouth was careful in her alliances with the king's ministers: in 1673 she fell out with Lord Arlington, whose fortunes were declining, and transferred her allegiance to his rival Thomas Osborne, earl of Danby, the new lord treasurer, in 1674. She assisted Danby's son in gaining a post in the king's bedchamber in 1674, and in April 1676, on reports that Danby and the duke of York had fallen out at Newmarket, she made a hurried journey there in order to support Danby. Portsmouth's progress to the centre of court politics was closely watched and encouraged by Louis XIV, who hoped that she would be useful in promoting French interests. In 1673, however, Portsmouth greatly annoyed the French king by advancing one of the mademoiselles d'Elbeuf as a bride for the duke of York and refusing to desist despite requests conveyed by the French ambassador. The ambassador was not impressed by her apparent ill will towards France, and in his opinion she merited no kindness from Louis XIV. However, at the request of Charles II, in 1674 the estate of Aubigny in France was given to her for life and afterwards to her son. This seems to have encouraged Portsmouth to ask Louis XIV for several positions for her relations in France; although these were refused, an expensive pair of earrings was presented to her in 1675. These gifts saw a significant change in attitude: Portsmouth now frequently expressed gratitude to Louis XIV and began to facilitate access to Charles II for the French ambassador in her apartments, to report useful information to the ambassador, and even, from 1676 onwards, to take part in discussions between the king and the ambassador concerning foreign affairs. In 1677, when it appeared that England was being drawn into war against France, an illness of Portsmouth's in December that year allowed Ambassador Barrillon to enjoy even greater privacy in his meetings with the king, as the rest of the court was shut out of her apartments. Portsmouth was then involved in proposals made in January 1678 to the French concerning a possible exchange of towns in the Spanish Netherlands, discussions in December concerning a secret subsidy for England in return for not calling parliament, and similar discussions in 1679 and 1680. Early in 1680 the ambassador offered inducements of £10,000 each to Portsmouth and her ally the earl of Sunderland to encourage them to facilitate an Anglo-French treaty.

While always assuring the French of her zeal for their interests, Portsmouth kept very much to Charles II's negotiating position, and in fact these discussions did not result in an agreement. However, she certainly appeared to represent French interests and this, her Catholicism, and her association with Danby attracted unfavourable attention. In June 1678 she was indirectly criticized in the House of Commons by Henry Booth, and on 27 April 1679 was named by Thomas Mostyn in a speech that, fortunately for Portsmouth, was not followed up by other MPs. Clearly concerned to maintain her position, she had in fact broken with Danby by March 1679 and was at this point closely associated with Robert, earl of Sunderland, the new secretary of state. She was involved in his secret plans to invite William of Orange over to England in the summer of 1679, William being advised to 'make some application to her' as she had 'more power over him [the king] than can be imagined' (*Diary of … Sidney*, 1.15), and in the autumn of that year they both supported the duke of York against the duke of Monmouth. The opposition kept up the pressure on Portsmouth. In addition to increasingly vitriolic satire, the campaign included the anonymous *Articles of high treason, and other high crimes and misdemeanours against the duchess of Portsmouth*, twenty-two charges accusing her of subverting church and state, which were circulating by 5 January 1680. These were to form the basis of a projected attack on her in the forthcoming parliament, which, however, was soon afterwards prorogued. Then in June 1680, at the Middlesex sessions, the earl of Shaftesbury and his followers entered an information against the duke of York as a recusant and at the same time against the duchess of Portsmouth as a 'common nuisance'. The attack on York and a difference with the duchess of York (who appeared to favour Portsmouth's rival Hortense, duchess of Mazarin) may have persuaded Portsmouth that abandoning her alliance with York was in her own interests. By August she had turned against him and some time afterwards she was reconciled with

the duke of Monmouth. Early in October she arranged meetings between the exclusionist peer Lord Howard of Escrick and the king, and during the following parliamentary session she openly advocated the bill to exclude the duke of York from the throne. When things went badly for the exclusionists, it was reported on 24 October that she was 'crying all day for fear the Parliament should be dissolved' (*Diary of … Sidney*, 2.181). The duke of York wrote in November that Portsmouth 'has play'd me a dog trick' (Emilia, La Marquise Campana de Cavelli, 1.340). Portsmouth also met with exclusionists such as Shaftesbury, and later the 'Southampton Whigs', a group led by such men as Ralph Montagu and William, Lord Russell. When their plans failed, her position at court appeared precarious. However, although Portsmouth had apparently become convinced of the need for exclusion, intriguingly she had acted at least in part with the king's knowledge, as both she and Charles II informed William of Orange when he at last visited England in August 1681. By this time Portsmouth appeared to be recovering her position, and in November 1681 a reconciliation was arranged with the duke of York, Portsmouth later using her influence with the king to allow York to return from Scotland. The king himself arranged a public reconciliation in November between Portsmouth and her inveterate enemy the marquess of Halifax in her apartments. In January 1682 she gave a banquet for the Moroccan ambassador, which was also attended by Nell Gwyn and the daughters of the duchess of Cleveland; 'concubines and catell of that sort … as splendid as jewels, and excess of bravery could make them', wrote John Evelyn disapprovingly (Evelyn, 4.267–8). The instalment of Portsmouth's son as a knight of the Garter in April 1681 and then as master of the horse in January 1682 confirmed her favour with Charles II. She was very much involved in her son's appointment and at least two borough corporations were sufficiently impressed by it to attempt to gain her favour. In 1683 the town of Portsmouth elected the duke of Richmond to the freedom of the borough, which may explain Portsmouth's gift to the town of a pair of silver flagons in that year, and the town of York replaced the duke of Buckingham with Richmond as their high steward, prompting Portsmouth to send a letter of thanks and assure them of her services.

Portsmouth also resumed her role as an intermediary with the French ambassador, and increasingly appears to have pressed Charles to accept French policy. In January 1682 she encouraged him to accept a French conquest of Luxembourg and to resist calls for war with France. She then made a visit to France from March to June 1682. Travelling in great style, she met Louis XIV with messages from Charles II, and was given all the recognition and assurances of kindness that she could wish for. While there she was reported to be 'living at a vast rate … and [is] greatly complimented there; the people flock about her coaches' (*Ormonde MSS*, 6.357). She went from Paris to Brittany, where she bought back the family estates of Kéroualle and Mesnouales which her father had been obliged to sell. This visit visibly raised her status on her return, and she undertook her role in politics with renewed vigour: exchanging letters with Louis XIV, managing the reinstatement of her ally Sunderland as secretary of state in January 1683, supporting the duke of York's and Sidney Godolphin's return to the cabinet council in June and September the same year, and aligning herself with York and his allies against the marquess of Halifax. Persistent rumours of an affair between Portsmouth and the French nobleman Philip de Vendôme in June–November 1683 alarmed the French ambassador, who thought Portsmouth was endangering her position, and he enlisted Louis XIV's support in removing Vendôme from England. Despite these rumours, Charles II's esteem for his mistress showed no sign of decreasing: at his request Louis XIV agreed to create the estate of Aubigny as a duchy for Portsmouth in January 1684, and in November her son was naturalized as a French subject in order that he might inherit her property. She also bought further lands in France, near Brest, at about this time. In September 1684 she accompanied the king on a visit to the town of her title, Portsmouth, and as the king had not taken lodgings in the town (preferring to sleep in his yacht), her lodgings 'was the court in the daytime' (*Hastings MSS*, 2.177). Her illness in October–November 1684 apparently caused a suspension of almost all business. A letter to her from Charles II probably belongs to this period, in which he writes,

> I should do my selfe wrong if I tould you that I love you better then all the world besides, for that were making a comparison where 'tis impossible to express the true passion and kindness I have for my dearest, dearest fubs. (Duchess of Portsmouth's MSS, Goodwood MS 3, unfol.)

On 22 November it was reported that 'since her grace's recovery she is greater and more absolute than ever' (Thomas Wyndham to Viscount Weymouth). Only a few months later, however, on 6 February 1685, Charles II died. According to the French ambassador, it was Portsmouth who on 5 February brought him the news that Charles was at heart a Catholic and pressed him to urge the duke of York to make the necessary arrangements.

Last years After the king's death Portsmouth's influence instantly ceased. Her son was removed as master of the horse and she returned to France in August 1685. In 1686 some incautious remarks concerning Madame de Maintenon almost occasioned an exile from the French court. She visited England in 1686–7 and was present at the marriage of her niece Charlotte to the son of Sir George Jeffreys in July 1688. After the revolution she lost her English pensions but was granted a substantial annuity by Louis XIV. Her apartments in Whitehall were destroyed in the fire of 1691. In the 1690s she lived in Paris, at 3–5 quai Voltaire. Her son Richmond, who had converted to Catholicism at her request in October 1685, secretly went to England in 1692, joined William of Orange, and reconverted. Eventually reconciled with him, she desired to go to England to try to reclaim her pension. She was granted permission in 1698 and visited England from July 1698 to February 1699, but her pension was not reinstated. On her return to France she lived in Paris and at her estate in

Aubigny. The remainder of her life was spent in attempting to regain financial stability, in which she had some success (in 1716 she sold most of her lands in Brittany, and her French pension was greatly increased in 1718 and then converted to a life annuity in 1721), and in good works in the town of Aubigny, where she founded a convent. Her grandson Charles *Lennox, second duke of Richmond, and his wife often visited her at Aubigny, and her last visit to England was in 1732–4. She died in Paris on 14 November 1734 and was buried there on 16 November in the church of the Barefooted Carmelites in the chapel of the Rieux family. Portsmouth's son having predeceased her, her grandson the second duke of Richmond inherited her property.

Unlike Charles II's other mistresses, Portsmouth was not generally accounted a great beauty, nor was she renowned for her wit. On the other hand, her desire and talent for pleasing were noticed. Elizabeth, duchess of Orléans later commented, 'The Duchess of Portsmouth is the finest lady of her kind that I have ever met; she is extremely polite and interesting in her conversation' (Delpech, 193), and indeed in England the hospitality she provided in her magnificent apartments, her unfailing civility to other important courtiers, and her willingness to become an intermediary for Charles II made her a significant and enduring political force at the Restoration court.

S. M. WYNNE

Sources J. Delpech, *The life and times of the duchess of Portsmouth*, trans. A. Lindsay (1953) · S. Wynne, 'The mistresses of Charles II and Restoration court politics, 1660–1685', PhD diss., U. Cam., 1997 · H. Forneron, *Louise de Kéroualle, duchess of Portsmouth, 1649–1734*, ed. and trans. Mrs G. M. Crawford (1887) · W. Sussex RO, duchess of Portsmouth's papers, Goodwood MSS 3–5, 1427 · F.-A. A. de La Chenaye-Desbois, *Dictionnaire de la noblesse: contenant les généalogies, l'histoire et la chronologie des familles nobles de la France*, 3rd edn, 15 (Paris, 1868) · GEC, *Peerage*, new edn, vol. 10 · Baschet transcripts, French diplomatic corresp., 1660–85, PRO, 31/3/107–60 · correspondance politique, Angleterre, Archives du Ministère des Affaires Étrangères, Paris, vols. 79–153 (1663–1685) · Evelyn, *Diary*, vols. 3–4 · *Diary of the times of Charles the Second by the Honourable Henry Sidney (afterwards earl of Romney)*, ed. R. W. Blencowe, 2 vols. (1843) · Marquise Campana de Cavelli, ed., *Les derniers Stuarts à Saint-Germain en Laye*, 2 vols. (Paris, 1871), vol. 1 · *Calendar of the manuscripts of the marquess of Ormonde*, new ser., 8 vols., HMC, 36 (1902–20), vol. 6 · *Report on the manuscripts of the late Reginald Rawdon Hastings*, 4 vols., HMC, 78 (1928–47), vol. 2 · letter of Thomas Wyndham to Viscount Weymouth, Longleat House, Wiltshire, Bath MSS, Thynne MSS, vol. 12, fol. 83

Archives W. Sussex RO, corresp. | U. Nott. L., letters to first earl of Portland

Likenesses S. Verelst, oils, *c.*1670–1672, Parham Park, West Sussex · P. Lely, oils, *c.*1670–1678, Althorp, Northamptonshire · S. Verelst, oils, *c.*1670–1680, Royal Collection · P. Lely, portrait, *c.*1671–1674, John Paul Getty Museum, Los Angeles [*see illus.*] · H. Gascar, oils, *c.*1672–1678, Goodwood House, West Sussex · G. Bower, silver medal, 1673, BM · G. Valck, mezzotint, 1678 (after P. Lely, *c.*1670–1678), BM, NPG · P. Mignard, oils, 1682, NPG · P. Vignon, oils, *c.*1682, Royal Collection · oils, *c.*1682, Goodwood House, West Sussex · G. Kneller, oils, 1684, Goodwood House, West Sussex · G. Kneller, oils, 1687, Sherborne Castle, Dorset · H. Gascar, two portraits, priv. coll. · E. Le Davis, line engraving, BM, NPG · P. Mignard, portrait, NPG · J. Roettier, silver and copper medal, BM · P. van Somer, mezzotint (after P. Lely), BM, NPG · St Baudet, line engraving (after H. Gascar, c.1672–1678), BM · miniature, Berkeley Castle, Gloucestershire

Kerr. *See also* Ker.

Kerr [*née* Bersey; *other married name* Clark], **Anne Patricia** (1925–1973), politician, was born on 24 March 1925 at 20 Hazlewell Road, Putney, south-west London, the daughter of Arnold Leslie Bersey, a chartered accountant, and his wife, Kathleen Isabel, *née* Mitchell. Her family was Methodist. From the mid-1930s she attended St Paul's Girls' School in Hammersmith before being evacuated to Budleigh Salterton in Devon at the start of the Second World War. She attended Exmouth grammar school and Southlands College before volunteering for the Women's Royal Naval Service (WRNS) in 1942. In the WRNS she was stationed at Plymouth, Portsmouth, and Dartmouth. On 6 May 1944 she married James Ewen Doran Clark (*b.* 1923/4), a lieutenant in the Royal Marines, the son of James Thomson Doran Clark, a major in the Royal Army Medical Corps. She left the WRNS before the birth of their son, Patrick, in July 1945.

Anne Clark returned to London at the end of the war and joined the Ealing branch of the Labour Party in the late 1940s. She trained as an actress and joined the actors' union, Equity, in 1951. She was a broadcaster on *Perspective* for BBC television and *Woman's Hour* for BBC radio. Her forays into film work were not very successful. She moved to Roehampton and joined the Putney branch of the Labour Party in 1953, becoming its membership secretary and increasing membership from 2000 to 4000 in three years. Her marriage was dissolved in 1953 and she threw her energy into Labour politics. She stood unsuccessfully for Wandsworth borough council in 1956 but was elected as Labour candidate to the London county council (LCC) in 1958.

From early in her political career Anne Clark combined constituency work with political activism. She was deeply involved in the campaign for the abolition of the death penalty and befriended the family of Derek Bentley, an intellectually disabled epileptic hanged in January 1953 for the murder of a policeman. At the LCC she worked on housing and welfare committees, and when she stood (unsuccessfully) for the seat of Twickenham in the general election of 1959 she campaigned on the housing conditions of the poor. During this campaign she met Russell Whiston Kerr (1921–1983), an Australian air charter executive who stood as Labour candidate for Merton and Morden. They shared political views, and married on 29 April 1960.

In 1962 Anne Kerr became Labour candidate for Rochester and Chatham in Kent and in the general election of 1964 she unseated the Conservative MP. Her energetic local campaigning made her popular with constituents and she was re-elected in 1966. Kerr was a member of the Tribune Group of Labour MPs, which was chaired by her husband, and was a signatory to the charter advocating public ownership and the redistribution of wealth. Her Christian background made her socially conservative as well as deeply committed to a string of national and international causes. She opposed legislation for abortion and easier divorce, and was involved in women's groups as a Christian humanitarian and not a feminist. She chaired the Christian action group for the abolition of capital punishment and successfully lobbied the home secretary over the Christian reburial of Derek Bentley.

In her first speech to the House of Commons Kerr argued that there should be a minister for peace, and her lasting contribution to 1960s British politics was as a peace activist and sponsor of the British peace committee. She was a founding member of the Campaign for Nuclear Disarmament and addressed public demonstrations against the war in Vietnam. She worked with the British council for peace in Vietnam and personally donated large sums to medical aid for Vietnam. She organized petitions for the release of female prisoners in Saigon and chaired a group of women who sent letters of protest about the bombing of Vietnam to the prime ministers of Britain, Australia, and New Zealand, and the president of the United States. In 1965 she and her husband visited Hanoi and she attended conferences on Vietnam held by international peace organizations in Stockholm. In 1968 they visited Chicago to support Eugene McCarthy during his campaign for the presidential nomination on an anti-war ticket; Anne Kerr's arrest during a demonstration, and subsequent detention, received publicity in Britain.

During the 1960s Kerr was a ceaseless international traveller in the dual causes of world peace and equality. She visited Cuba in 1964 and India in 1966. After a trip to Biafra and Nigeria in 1969 she spoke stridently in the House of Commons against the sale of arms during the war in Nigeria. She supported anti-apartheid campaigns and the Movement for Colonial Freedom (later Liberation), and during the Middle East crisis of 1967 refused to support the government's pro-Israeli stand and lobbied on behalf of Palestinian refugees. However, her overseas trips and political campaigns alienated her from those in her constituency who did not share her humanitarian concerns, and she received bigoted hate mail before suffering a heavy defeat in the general election of 1970.

Kerr was devastated by the loss of her parliamentary seat and turned down several alternative offers of Labour candidacy. She threw herself instead into the Amnesty International campaign for the release of women taken prisoner during the military coup in Greece. In November 1970 she formed Women Against the Common Market, a group aiming to muster popular support against the Common Market and lobby parliament. She was motivated by concern about the exclusion of developing countries and chaired this group until her death. She died tragically at her home, 37 Popes Avenue, Twickenham, London, from acute or chronic alcohol poisoning on 29 July 1973.

AMANDA L. CAPERN

Sources U. Hull, Brynmor Jones L., Kerr papers · H. E. Roberts, 'Kerr, Anne Patricia', *DLB*, vol. 10 · *The Times* (30 July 1973) · *The Guardian* (30 July 1973) · b. cert. · m. cert. [James Ewen Doran Clark] · d. cert.

Archives JRL, Labour History Archive and Study Centre, newspaper cuttings · U. Hull, Brynmor Jones L., papers and corresp. relating to constituents of Rochester and Chatham; papers relating to Women Against the Common Market | FILM BBC Film Archives, peace march, 25 April 1962; news item, election campaigning, 24 March 1966; speech at Labour Party conference, 29 Sept 1969 | SOUND BBC Sound Archive, Labour Party conference debate 1960 · BL NSA, Labour Party conference, 1960, C529/14 C1 · BL NSA, Bow dialogues, 18 Oct 1966, C812/15 C11

Likenesses photographs, 1963–72, U. Hull, MSS, DMK/1/1, 30–31, 69, 114, 133–4, 221, 224 · double portrait, photograph, 1970 (with Russell Whiston Kerr), U. Hull, MSS, DMK/1/116 · photograph, repro. in *The Times*

Wealth at death £24,250: probate, 25 Feb 1974, *CGPLA Eng. & Wales*

Kerr, Archibald John Kerr Clark, Baron Inverchapel (1882–1951), diplomatist, was born on 17 March 1882 at Watson's Bay, near Sydney, Australia, the fifth son of John Kerr Clark (1838–1910), sheep station owner, originally from Crossbasket, Hamilton, Lanarkshire, and his wife, Kate Louisa (1846–1926), daughter of Sir John *Robertson, prime minister of New South Wales. Both sides of his family had Scottish roots and Clark Kerr would later acquire land at Inverchapel on Loch Eck, Argyll, where the family had been since the fifteenth century. In March 1911 he took the additional surname of Kerr. In 1889 his parents moved to England, though his father later returned to Australia. He was educated at Bath College, and in France, Germany, and Italy where he studied languages. In March 1906 he passed the examination for the diplomatic service and was posted to Berlin, where he remained from October 1906 to April 1910. He was promoted third secretary in March 1908. He was transferred in April 1910 to Buenos Aires, and in March 1911 to Washington, where he served as British secretary of the British and American claims arbitration tribunal. He was posted to Rome in June 1913, being promoted second secretary in February 1914, and then to Tehran in December 1914, where he served as secretary in charge of commercial matters. He returned to the Foreign Office in November 1916. After an older brother was killed in the First World War he volunteered for service and, despite opposition from the Foreign Office, was finally allowed to enlist as a private in the Scots Guards, though he served only from June to November 1918 before being returned to the Foreign Office at the end of hostilities. In September 1919 he was promoted first secretary and posted to Tangier.

In February 1922 Clark Kerr was posted to Cairo, serving as deputy to Lord Allenby, the high commissioner. He was promoted acting counsellor in November 1923. He favoured support for Egyptian aspirations to end the British protectorate, which he considered inevitable, as the best way of protecting British interests in the future. In November 1924, when Egyptian nationalists shot the sirdar, Sir Lee Stack, it was Clark Kerr who found him, slumped in his car, which had managed to reach the residency. The resultant crisis between Britain and Egypt almost proved fatal for Clark Kerr's career. Allenby acted robustly, but not with the full concurrence of London, which decided to send out a senior diplomat to join Allenby to brief him more fully on London's views. This

Archibald John Kerr Clark Kerr, Baron Inverchapel (1882–1951), by Yousuf Karsh, 1945

new official, Nevile Henderson, would be senior to Clark Kerr, and Allenby, taking umbrage at what he interpreted as an attempt to undermine his authority, proffered his resignation. The Foreign Office felt that Clark Kerr bore some responsibility for the high commissioner's hasty actions and, since he had previously fallen foul of the new permanent under-secretary, Sir William Tyrrell, it was not long before an attempt was made to transfer him to Tokyo.

Clark Kerr, frustrated by the Foreign Office's attitude, considered leaving the service, but supporters in London, most surprisingly Winston Churchill, came to his aid. Churchill's assistance was ironical, since Clark Kerr had previously detested his politics. Churchill, however, approved of Clerk Kerr for maintaining an effective British policy in Egypt, and this goodwill would later be critical in his career. Thus in late 1925 Clark Kerr found himself not only travelling to the Central American republics rather than Tokyo, but with the rank of minister, for which he was still relatively young. The final leg of his journey to Guatemala, where he took up his post in December, was made on a Fyffes banana boat. His time in the region was otherwise uneventful. In February 1928 he was transferred to Chile and in April 1931 he was moved again, this time to be minister at Stockholm. In this as in previous legations he showed diplomatic competence, though there was still a feeling that a shadow hung over him from his time in Egypt which was preventing his appointment to major posts. In January 1935, however, he was appointed KCMG, and in March 1935 he was appointed ambassador to Iraq, one of the least prestigious of the embassy grade posts, but still placing him in the highest rank of the service. The situation in Baghdad was very fluid and Clark Kerr proved adept at dealing with the local complexities. This helped lead to his appointment, after only three years, as ambassador to war-torn China.

It was with his appointment to China, in February 1938, that Clark Kerr embarked upon the greatest phase of his career, serving after Peking (Beijing) as ambassador in Moscow and then in Washington. An opponent of appeasement, he made every effort to pursue policies which would deter Japanese aggression. These views brought him into conflict with those seeking to conciliate Japan, in particular the British ambassador to Tokyo, Sir Robert Craigie. Clark Kerr's views on the rivalry between the Chinese nationalists and the communists were more ambivalent. It appears that in private conversation he predicted the inevitable victory of the forces of Mao Zedong, but his dispatches to London do not convey this view. The truth probably lies in his official dispatches, while his comments in conversation may well have been a product of his diplomatic skill at assessing others' views.

Clark Kerr's success in China was rewarded in January 1942 with promotion to GCMG and in February 1942 with a move to Moscow. His tasks included maintaining serviceable Anglo-Soviet relations, which were being placed under stress by Stalin's demands for a second front. He played a key role in the 1943 Moscow meeting of the foreign ministers of the 'big three' allied powers, which was recognized by his appointment as a privy councillor in January 1944. His three and a half years at Moscow were notable for the skill with which he succeeded in smoothing over the rough places in the wartime relationship between Britain and the USSR. His success was recognized with elevation to the peerage, in April 1946, as Baron Inverchapel of Loch Eck, and appointment, in May 1946, to the post with which he had long wished to cap his career, the Washington embassy. Nevertheless, in many ways Washington was an anticlimax. He thrived best in daunting situations, but in the post-war climate of Washington he faced mostly economic issues, a sphere of diplomatic activity that bored him. He did, however, play a major role in persuading the United States government of the stresses under which Britain was operating, which in turn led to the Truman doctrine and the Marshall plan.

Inverchapel retired from the foreign service in March 1948, but was almost immediately appointed to the new committee on European unity (1948–9). He always affected support for the Labour Party and socialist aspirations. While capable of being a stickler for diplomatic formalities, he insisted that everyone call him Archie. He was eccentric, refusing to write with anything other than goose quill pens. One of the most colourful representatives of an age of notable diplomatists, he was a genuine individual.

Clark Kerr's personal life was complex. He had always enjoyed a close relationship with his mother, who accompanied him to Central America, and he was devastated when she died a few months later. Three years afterwards, while serving in Chile, he married, on 24 April 1929, a Chilean twenty-nine years his junior, Maria Teresa (Tita) Diaz Salas (d. 1987), daughter of Don Javier Diaz Lira, of Santiago. It proved a volatile marriage, with Tita leaving him during the difficult years of his embassy to China. Divorced in 1945, they remarried in 1947, when he held the more salubrious Washington embassy. They had no children. There can be no doubt that Clark Kerr was devoted to his young wife, and that her desertion caused him immense pain, and her subsequent return great joy. He also enjoyed close and emotionally fulfilling relationships with some of his colleagues, among them Harold Nicolson, whom he affectionately dubbed Clarice, and Gerald Villiers. He died at Greenock on 5 July 1951 and was buried at Inverchapel on the 9th.   ERIK GOLDSTEIN

Sources DNB · Bodl. Oxf., MSS Inverchapel · D. Gillies, *Radical diplomat: the life of Archibald Clark Kerr, Lord Inverchapel, 1882–1951* (1999) · W. G. Hayter, *A double life* (1974) · P. Lowe, *Great Britain and the origins of the Pacific war: a study of British policy in east Asia, 1937–1941* (1977) · WWW, 1951–60 · Burke, *Peerage* · FO List
Archives Bodl. Oxf., corresp. and papers · PRO, corresp., FO 800/298–303
Likenesses Y. Karsh, photograph, 1945, NPG [*see illus.*]

Kerr, Cecil Chetwynd [*née* Lady Cecil Chetwynd Chetwynd-Talbot], **marchioness of Lothian** (1808–1877), Roman Catholic convert, was born on 17 April 1808 at Ingestre Hall, Staffordshire, the daughter of Charles Chetwynd-*Talbot, second Earl Talbot of Hensol (1777–1849), and his wife, Frances Thomasine (1782–1819), daughter of Charles Lambart of Beau Parc, co. Meath, Ireland. She was sixth child and younger daughter in a family of twelve children. Her mother died when she was only eleven; her father proved an attentive parent, encouraging her study of Latin and the *Commentaries* of Blackstone. He raised in her his own moderate high-churchmanship to respect the sabbath, the Book of Common Prayer, and the established church. She became a woman whose vitality was combined with a natural reserve, striking rather than beautiful, with a strong sense of moral duty. On 12 July 1831 she married John William Robert Kerr, seventh marquess of Lothian (1794–1841), and they made their home in Scotland, at Newbattle Abbey, Midlothian, although she preferred their house at Monteviot in Roxburghshire. They had five sons and two daughters before the marquess died suddenly at his estate at Bickling, Norfolk, on 14 November 1841. Cecil Lothian never married again and began to devote herself to the care of her children, to the very capable management of the estate, and to a new sense of religion.

Abandoning the religion of her father and husband, with its emphasis on establishment, Lady Lothian became one of the earliest sponsors and financiers of Tractarianism in Scotland. This took the form of her building and endowing a chapel for the Scottish Episcopal church at Jedburgh, near Monteviot. She supervised its construction carefully, building it in the Gothic style approved of by the Camden Ecclesiological Society and Tractarians. It included a stone altar redolent of the Tractarian doctrine of eucharistic sacrifice. She also insisted on the almost unprecedented use of the Scottish communion office, the nonjuring office of eighteenth-century Episcopalians which was preferred by many Tractarians as being more explicitly Catholic than the Book of Common Prayer. The church's consecration on 15 August 1843 was attended by leading high-churchmen and Tractarians, including Walter Farquhar Hook and John Keble. But Lady Lothian became increasingly uncertain about the catholicity of Anglicanism. Her allegiance was gradually undermined by the successive secessions to Rome of John Henry Newman in 1845; the chaplain at Dalkeith who was her spiritual adviser; and, finally, by Henry Manning in 1851, as a consequence of the Gorham judgment. Instructed by Manning, she became a Roman Catholic in June 1851. Her conversion imperilled her guardianship of her sons, as the other guardians appointed by her husband's will sought to have them removed from her custody lest she attempt to convert them to Rome. (They were not concerned about the religion of her daughters.) In a midnight adventure, she escaped from Newbattle Abbey with her younger children, taking them to Edinburgh where they were received into the Roman Catholic church. Her eldest son, William, the eighth marquess, was away at Oxford at the time, and remained a staunch Episcopalian.

Lady Lothian now became a sponsor of Roman Catholicism in Scotland. She built a Roman Catholic church at Dalkeith, began regular visits to Rome, and undertook extensive charitable work in Edinburgh assisted by her friend Charlotte, duchess of Buccleuch, who would eventually convert in 1860. One of Lady Lothian's daughters, Cecil, became a Sacred Heart nun in the convent in Paris in 1859. Having established a connection with the Jesuits in Farm Street, London, Lady Lothian encouraged their opening a church in Edinburgh, and they eventually took over the church at Dalkeith in 1861. She was active in the Refugee Benevolent Fund in London, established as a consequence of the Franco-Prussian War of 1871, but her relief work in England was never as much her own as the missions in Jedburgh and Dalkeith. Her son Lord Walter *Kerr (1839–1927), later admiral of the fleet and senior naval lord, was a companion when his naval life allowed, but his marriage in 1873 brought a new loneliness in her final years. In 1877 Lady Lothian went to Rome for the jubilee of Pius IX and died there on 13 May. Her body was buried at the foot of the altar in the church at Dalkeith.

ROWAN STRONG

Sources C. Kerr, ed., *Cecil marchioness of Lothian: a memoir* (1922) • P. Gallwey, *Salvage from the wreck: a few memories of friends departed, preserved in funeral discourses* (1890) • T. Clarke, 'A display of Tractarian energy: St John's Episcopal Church, Jedburgh', *Records of the Scottish Church History Society*, 27 (1997), 187–219 • W. Perry, *The Oxford Movement in Scotland* (1933) • NA Scot., Buccleuch MSS • GEC, *Peerage*

Archives Bodl. Oxf., Manning MSS • NA Scot., Buccleuch MSS

Likenesses photographs, repro. in Kerr, ed., *Cecil marchioness of Lothian* (1922), frontispiece, 10, 106, 156

Wealth at death under £14,000 in England: probate, 16 June 1877, *CGPLA Eng. & Wales* • £2056 16s. 4d.: inventory, 13 Aug 1877, *CCI*

Kerr, Charles Iain, first Baron Teviot (1874–1968), politician, was born on 3 May 1874, the elder son of Charles Wyndham Rodolph Kerr (1849–1894), grandson of the sixth marquess of Lothian, and his wife, Anna Maria Olivia (d. 1937), daughter of Admiral Sir George Elliot KCB. He was educated at Stephen Hawtrey's School, Windsor. He spent a period (1892–6) as a mining engineer before becoming a stockbroker, and was later senior partner of Kerr, Ware & Co., stockbrokers. On 24 January 1911 he married Muriel Constance, only daughter of William Gordon Canning of Hartpury, Gloucester. On the outbreak of war in 1914 Kerr was commissioned in the machine-gun corps, transferring from the Royal Horse Guards. He served as machine-gun officer with the 3rd cavalry division, was appointed to the DSO in 1919, was awarded the MC, and was mentioned in dispatches.

After the war Kerr entered politics 'in the family tradition' as a Liberal (*The Times*, 8 Jan 1968). He unsuccessfully contested Daventry, Northamptonshire, in 1923 and 1924; Hull Central in 1926; and Swansea West in 1929. On 31 July 1930, after his first marriage ended in divorce, he married Florence Angela (d. 1979), elder daughter of Lieutenant-Colonel Charles Walter Villiers; they had one son. Despite his failures to enter parliament he became 'an outstanding figure' (ibid.) at the Liberal Party headquarters, and chairman of the executive committee of the National Liberal Federation and of the Liberal publicity department. A man of strong anti-socialist views, he risked a promising political career by resigning his Liberal Party offices in 1931 in protest at Lloyd George's support for the Labour government. His talents were soon put to use by Sir John Simon in organizing the secessionist Liberal National (later National Liberal) Party, and at a by-election in June 1932 he was elected for Montrose burghs as a Liberal National.

The close alliance of the Liberal Nationals with the Conservatives suited Kerr's political instincts, which leaned to the right. In his maiden speech in October 1932 he proposed to remedy unemployment by settling the unemployed, with their families, in the dominions. He also appealed to the opposition to drop its motion of censure on the National Government as a 'gesture of good will and cooperation' (*Hansard 5C*, 269, 1932, 861). This mixture of eccentricity with naïvety was typical of Kerr, whose political gift was as an organizer rather than a debater or theorist. He served as chief Liberal National whip (1937–40), and was given minor office as lord commissioner of the Treasury from May 1937 to April 1939, and comptroller of the royal household from April 1939 to May 1940.

On 27 June 1940 Kerr was raised to the peerage as first Baron Teviot. In that year he was elected chairman of the Liberal National Party, a post from which he retired in September 1956. From 1945 he was also chief Liberal National whip in the Lords. During the war he served as chairman of the interdepartmental committee on dentistry, which in 1944 unanimously recommended that a comprehensive dental service should form an integral part of the National Health Service.

In the last years of the war there were abortive talks between the Liberal Nationals and the Liberals about possible reunion. Negotiations broke down over the Liberal National insistence on the continuation after the war of a 'national front' led by Churchill. The general election of 1945 emphasized to Conservatives the importance of Liberal participation in an anti-socialist alliance, but Churchill's overtures to the new Liberal leadership met with stony defiance. This increased the pressure to formalize the long-standing ties with the Liberal Nationals. Teviot was subsequently involved in talks with his opposite number, Lord Woolton, resulting in the Woolton–Teviot agreement of April 1947. This made it possible to merge the two parties at Westminster, although the National Liberals (renamed in 1948) retained some of the symbols of independence, with a party organization, annual conferences, and even (until 1966) their own whip and room in the Commons. In the constituencies the surviving National Liberal associations merged with the local Conservatives. By 1950 there were around sixty 'joint' associations, choosing between them an equal number of Conservative and National Liberal candidates. Teviot was plain about why such a merger was necessary:

> The obvious reason for this cooperation in some 60 constituencies is the menace of Socialism to the British way of life which both Liberals and Conservatives are resolved to preserve. (Teviot to editor, *The Times*, 19 Nov 1949)

He shared Churchill's belief that no major issues divided their two creeds in the post-war era. But to the 'independent liberals', as he disparagingly referred to them, the National Liberals were proponents of a type of Liberalism that stood still between the wars, and was afterwards caught up in the slow forward march of the Conservative Party. Whatever Teviot and his colleagues might argue, the bulk of Liberals preferred independence, much to Lord Woolton's, and indeed Churchill's, regret.

In his frequent contributions to debate in the Lords Teviot revealed himself as a determined opponent of post-war political and social change. He supported the Anglo-French invasion of Suez in 1956; took 'greatest exception' in 1960 (*Hansard 5L*, 227, 1960, 528) to the terms of the Wolfenden report; and in the same year, after the verdict of the jury in the *Lady Chatterley's Lover* case, urged the government to 'take such steps as are possible to ban for all time writings of this nature' (ibid.). A supporter of capital punishment, he called in November 1961 for an inquiry into the deterrent effect of sentencing murderers to death by the same method that they inflicted on their victims. The proposal was greeted with incredulity by Lord Chorley, who spoke next in the debate.

Teviot sat on the boards of numerous companies, including Lloyds Bank, the National Bank of Scotland, and the General Accident, Fire and Life Assurance Corporation. For many years he was a member of St Dunstan's and was on the board of management of its hostel. He was a brigadier, and later ensign, of the Royal Company of Archers, the sovereign's bodyguard in Scotland, and an expert on deer-stalking. He died at his home at 9 North Audley Street, London W1, on 7 January 1968, and was buried three days later at St Mark's, North Audley Street.

MARK POTTLE

Sources WWW · *The Times* (18–19 Nov 1949) · *The Times* (30 Nov 1949) · *The Times* (22 Aug 1950) · *The Times* (9 Oct 1951) · *The Times* (11 Oct 1951) · *The Times* (14 May 1953) · *The Times* (16 May 1953) · *The Times* (22 May 1953) · *The Times* (7 June 1955) · *The Times* (10 June 1955) · *The Times* (15 June 1955) · *The Times* (10 Nov 1961) · *The Times* (8 Jan 1968) · WWBMP · Hansard 5L (1956), 198.717–18; (1960), 227.528–30; (1961), 235.474–5 · Hansard 5C (1932), 269.858–61 · J. Ramsden, *The age of Churchill and Eden, 1940–1957* (1995) · P. Williamson, *National crisis and national government: British politics, the economy and empire, 1926–1932* (1992) · Burke, *Peerage* (1999)
Archives FILM BFI NFTVA, news footage
Wealth at death £3835: probate, 8 May 1968, *CGPLA Eng. & Wales*

Kerr, Sir (John) Graham (1869–1957), zoologist, was born at Rowley Lodge, Arkley, Barnet, Hertfordshire, on 18 September 1869, the only son of James Kerr, a former principal of Hooghly College, Calcutta, and his wife, Sybella Graham, of Hollows, Dumfriesshire. He was third in a family of four, but two of his sisters died in infancy. He was educated at the Royal High School, Edinburgh, and the University of Edinburgh. He first studied mathematics and philosophy, but later joined the medical faculty.

While still a medical student, Kerr interrupted his studies to join an Argentine expedition for the survey of the Pilcomayo from the Paraná to the frontiers of Bolivia, under Captain Juan Page. Kerr's account of this famous expedition (1889–91), *A Naturalist in the Gran Chaco*, was finally published in 1950. During the expedition Kerr was engaged in the study of natural history, especially ornithology, and many new species were collected. However, as the result of an accident, most of the collections were lost. Nevertheless, Kerr's field notes showed that even at this early age he was not only an observer and naturalist of exceptional ability, but also a man of resource, courage, and endurance above the ordinary.

Returning to England in 1891 Kerr entered Christ's College, Cambridge, and obtained first-class honours in both parts of the natural sciences tripos (1894–6). At the same time he was making preparations for a second expedition to Paraguay, primarily to study and collect the lungfish *Lepidosiren*. He was accompanied on this second expedition (1896–7) by J. S. Budgett and their collections (and also those of three subsequent expeditions to the Chaco region) are preserved at the University of Glasgow.

Following his return Kerr was appointed demonstrator in animal morphology (1897–1902) at Cambridge and was a fellow of Christ's (1898–1904). In 1902 he was appointed regius professor of zoology at Glasgow, where he remained until 1935. The following year he married Elizabeth Mary (d. 1934), a first cousin, and daughter of Thomas Kerr, writer to the signet, with whom he had two sons and a daughter.

Throughout Kerr's Glasgow professorship he was specially interested in the teaching of medical students, and his lectures were famous. The approach was largely morphological and embryological and is embodied in his *Zoology for Medical Students* (1921); *Evolution* (1926); and An

Introduction to Zoology (1929). Apart from his heavy teaching and administrative duties, he carried on with research, publishing a whole series of papers, including many on dipnoan embryology. He also wrote the second volume, *Vertebrata*, of the *Textbook of Embryology with the Exception of Mammalia* (1919).

At Glasgow, Kerr took a very active part in university affairs, and was a member of the court from 1913 to 1921. He also served on the governing bodies of various other institutions, and was particularly interested in marine biology. He was chiefly responsible for the foundation of the temporary marine station at Rothesay, Isle of Bute, and was president of the Scottish Marine Biological Association (1942–9). He also devoted much time to the development of the marine biological station at Millport on the Isle of Cumbrae. He was a member of the advisory committee on fishery research from its foundation in 1919, and chairman in 1942–9.

Kerr was also concerned in the development of general scientific activities, and especially natural history, in Scotland. He was elected FRS in 1909; he served on the council of the society (1920–22, 1936–8), and was vice-president (1937–8). He was also president of the Royal Physical Society of Edinburgh (1906–9), and of the Royal Philosophical Society of Glasgow (1925–8); and vice-president and Neill prizewinner (1904) of the Royal Society of Edinburgh. He served for many years on the council of the British Association and was president of the zoology section at the Oxford meeting in 1926. He was knighted in 1939 and other recognitions included the honorary LLD of Edinburgh (1935) and of St Andrews (1950); honorary fellowship of Christ's College, Cambridge (1935); the Linnean gold medal (1955); and associate membership of the Royal Academy of Belgium (1946).

Kerr's own research work was determined mainly by the interests of the Cambridge school of zoology, which at that time were predominantly morphological. Apart from earlier taxonomic work he started with a study of the anatomy of *Nautilus* which was of importance in assessing the relations of the Cephalopoda to other Mollusca. His later work on the lower vertebrates and especially *Lepidosiren* and other Dipnoi led him to abandon the generally accepted view that the legs of land vertebrates had evolved out of the paired fins of fishes. He considered that the methods of movement of vertebrates supported the theory that the simple styliform limb diverged along two lines, one leading to the development of paired fins, the other to the development of jointed limbs. One subject in which he took a special interest was the application of correct biological principles in working out a system of camouflage and on the outbreak of the First World War in 1914 he wrote to the Admiralty advocating the use of obliterative shading and disruption to render ships less conspicuous. This suggestion was eventually adopted and more than 5000 ships were treated by this method, which was used almost universally during the Second World War.

Kerr had a high sense of public duty and was a strong advocate of the value of a biological training. He gradually took a more active interest in politics and in 1935 was elected member of parliament for the Scottish Universities. He then resigned his chair and went to live at Barley, near Royston, Hertfordshire, where he spent the rest of his life. He was a very regular attender at the House of Commons, served on various committees, and for a time was chairman of the parliamentary scientific committee. He remained a member until 1950, when university seats were abolished. Kerr was one of the last survivors of the famous nineteenth-century zoologists, for the most part widely travelled, good naturalists, with an almost encyclopaedic knowledge of their subject. His output of zoological work was very considerable but in later years his many public duties restricted his scientific activities.

In 1936, two years after the death of his first wife, Kerr married Isobel, daughter of A. Dunn Macindoe and widow of Alan Clapperton, solicitor. He died on 21 April 1957 at his home, Dalny Veed, Barley, near Royston.

EDWARD HINDLE, rev.

Sources E. Hindle, *Memoirs FRS*, 4 (1958), 155–66 · Venn, *Alum. Cant.* · personal knowledge (1971) · private information (1971)
Archives RCS Eng., lecture notes · U. Glas. L., Archives and Business Records Centre, corresp. and papers
Likenesses W. Stoneman, portrait, 1917, NPG · B. Adams, portrait (posthumous), priv. coll. · L. A. Bell, charcoal drawing, priv. coll. · oils, U. Glas., department of zoology · photograph, repro. in Hindle, *Memoirs FRS*

Kerr, Jane. *See* Ker, Jane, countess of Roxburghe (*b.* in or before 1585, *d.* 1643).

Kerr, John (1824–1907), physicist, was born on 17 December 1824 at Ardrossan, Ayrshire, the second son of Thomas Kerr, fish dealer, who soon afterwards moved to Skye. Kerr was educated there in a village school, and attended the University of Glasgow, matriculating in 1841. From 1846 he studied under William Thomson, later Lord Kelvin, with whom he remained a friend and collaborator. Although a divinity student, he was one of the earliest to engage in research work in the converted wine cellar where Thomson set up the first physical laboratory in a British university. He graduated in 1849, with Lord Eglinton's prize as the most distinguished student in mathematics and natural philosophy. At Reay, Caithness, on 20 September 1849 he married Marion, daughter of Colonel Balfour of Orkney. They had three sons and four daughters.

After some time spent teaching Kerr was ordained a minister of the Free Church, but he did not take clerical duty. In 1857 he was appointed lecturer in mathematics at the Glasgow Free Church Training College for Teachers. He held this post for forty-four years until his retirement in 1901. Here he set up a small laboratory, equipped mostly at his own expense, and passed his spare time in research.

Kerr's name is associated with two important discoveries concerning the nature of light—the birefringence caused in glass and other insulators when placed in an intense electric field, and what became known as the Kerr effect. In one aspect, the electro-optical effect, the plane of polarization of a beam of light, when passed through glass or certain transparent liquids to which a potential difference is applied, rotates through an angle which depends upon the magnitude of the applied potential difference. Kerr's first paper on this effect was delivered to the British Association meeting at Glasgow in 1876, causing intense excitement among the physicists gathered there. The following year he described the related magneto-optical effect which causes plane polarized light, when reflected from a highly polished pole of an electromagnet, to become elliptically polarized. The mathematical theory of the Kerr effect was first worked out by Professor George Francis Fitzgerald of Dublin. The original Kerr cell consisted of a drilled slab of glass into which electrodes were led; later Kerr preferred liquid-in-glass cells. Examples of his apparatus were preserved at Glasgow University.

Apart from his papers in *Philosophical Transactions* Kerr's only publications were *The Metric System* (1863) and *An Elementary Treatise on Rational Mechanics* (1867). For the latter Glasgow University awarded him the honorary degree of LLD. He was elected FRS in 1890 and received the society's royal medal in 1898. He was awarded in 1902 a civil-list pension of £100 a year. Kerr died at Glasgow on 15 August 1907.

The electro-optical effect was utilized in early television apparatus as a means of modulating beams of light, and Kerr cells were afterwards employed as shutters for high-speed photography, giving speeds as short as 100 nanoseconds. ROBERT STEELE, *rev.* ANITA McCONNELL

Sources A. G., *PRS*, 82A (1909), i-v · *The Times* (19 Aug 1907), 12c · *Nature*, 76 (1907), 575–6 · *WWW* · G. Green and J. T. Lloyd, *Kelvin's instruments and the Kelvin Museum* (1970), 55–6
Archives U. Glas., apparatus
Wealth at death £506 19s. 7d.: confirmation, 22 Jan 1908, *CCI*

Kerr, John (1885–1972), cricketer, was born on 8 April 1885 at Heywood, 1 Margaret Street, Greenock, the son of Daniel Kerr, shipowner, and his wife, Margaret McKirdy. At collegiate school, Greenock, he had a worthy mentor in A. R. Graham, one of the best all-rounders ever to play for the Greenock club, and it was while still at school that Kerr first played for Greenock in 1901, when he headed the batting averages for good measure. After a brief spell in Stafford in 1905–6 and at the Carlton club in Edinburgh in 1907, he returned to Greenock in 1908 and continued to represent them until his retirement in 1940. During his time for Greenock he scored 21,558 runs for the club, averaging over 40, and scoring at least one century against every side in the western union, while amassing over 40,000 runs in club cricket.

Between 1908 and 1933 Kerr represented Scotland, making thirty-nine appearances ranked as first-class. Sir Jack Hobbs reckoned him among the world's best batsmen. Endowed with the technical expertise of an opener and equipped with great concentration and courage, Kerr was originally an off-side player with a ferocious square-cut; when the opposition got used to this, he became a great hooker and puller, thanks in part to his nimble footwork. His highest score in first-class cricket was 178 not out

against Ireland in Dublin in 1923, but he is chiefly remembered for his exploits against Australia. In 1919 he scored 45 not out and 40 (the only man to reach double figures in the second innings) against the Australian Imperial Force at Raeburn Place, Edinburgh, when Scotland just managed to salvage a draw. Then two years later, against Warwick Armstrong's all-powerful 1921 team, he scored 15 and 60 not out at Perth and 147 at Raeburn Place, the only century to be scored that season against the Australians' formidable bowling attack. Only one other Scot in history, the Revd James Aitchinson, has scored a century against Australia. In all Kerr batted fifty-nine times for Scotland in first-class matches, scoring 1975 runs with an average of 37.26. In addition to his batting he was a useful slow bowler and a brilliant slip fielder.

Kerr, whose father and brother and cousin J. Reid Kerr, the Scottish cricket and rugby international, all played for Greenock, became the club's first honorary president in 1956, an office he held until his death. He was an engineer by profession. In his retirement he took up bowls and was an elder in Greenock presbytery, and served on committees of the general assembly of the Church of Scotland, as well as having a long association with the Boys' Brigade. He died, unmarried, at Larkfield Hospital, Greenock, on 27 December 1972. MARK PEEL

Sources *Wisden* (1922) · *Wisden* (1925) · *Wisden* (1973) · C. Martin-Jenkins, *World cricketers: a biographical dictionary* (1996) · P. Bailey, P. Thorn, and P. Wynne-Thomas, *Who's who of cricketers* (1984) · N. L. Stephenson, *'Play!': The story of the Carlton C. C. and a personal record of over fifty years' Scottish cricket* (1949) · T. C. Riddell, *Greenock Cricket Club records, 1887–1937* (1938) · b. cert. · d. cert. · *CCI* (1973)
Likenesses photographs, repro. in Stephenson, *'Play!'*, pp. 86, 255
Wealth at death £29,477.04: corrective inventory, 16 Aug 1973, *CCI*

Kerr, Mark. *See* Ker, Mark (1517–1584); Ker, Mark, first earl of Lothian (*b.* in or before 1559, *d.* 1609).

Kerr, Lord Mark (1676–1752). *See under* Kerr, Robert, first marquess of Lothian (1636–1703).

Kerr, (John Martin) Munro (1868–1960), obstetrician and gynaecologist, was born in Glasgow on 5 December 1868, the son of George Munro Kerr, a ship and insurance broker, and his wife, Jessie Elizabeth Martin. He was educated first at Glasgow Academy and then at Glasgow University where he graduated MB CM in 1890 and MD in 1909. He studied in Berlin, Jena, and Dublin, and on his return in 1894 was appointed assistant to Murdoch Cameron, the regius professor of midwifery and diseases of women in the University of Glasgow. Munro Kerr was appointed to the staff of the Glasgow Maternity Hospital in 1896, becoming visiting surgeon in 1900 and chief of the second gynaecological unit at the Western Infirmary in 1907. In 1910 he was elected to a professorship in the Andersonian College of Medicine, and the following year was appointed to the Muirhead chair of obstetrics and gynaecology in the University of Glasgow. Later (1927) he was translated to the regius chair in those subjects, in which he continued until his retirement in 1934. During this period he held many important positions in Glasgow hospitals and was for a time a member of the board of governors of the Royal Samaritan Hospital for Women, Glasgow. In 1899 he married Emelia Andrewina Elizabeth (d. 1957), daughter of August Johanson of Göteborg; they had one son and three daughters.

Munro Kerr was a foundation fellow and vice-president of the British (later Royal) College of Obstetricians and Gynaecologists. Among other important offices, he served as one-time president of the Faculty of Physicians and Surgeons of Glasgow, and president of the section of obstetrics and gynaecology of the Royal Society of Medicine. Among honours bestowed on him were the honorary LLD of Glasgow (1935) and the first Blair-Bell medal to be awarded by the Royal Society of Medicine (1950). Many medical societies in this and other countries, including the American Gynaecological Society, elected him to their honorary fellowship.

Munro Kerr's early training gave him fluency in many languages, and throughout his long life he acquired an almost encyclopaedic knowledge of medical literature. His natural charm of manner combined with strength of character made him a most persuasive teacher: his 'manner was often informal, sometimes a little dramatic, but always fascinating' (Peel, 25). His easy, conversational style gave his written words added interest and force. Chief among his many publications were *Operative Midwifery* (1908); *Clinical and Operative Gynaecology* (1922); *Maternal Mortality and Morbidity* (1933); and, with colleagues in Glasgow and Edinburgh, the *Combined Textbook of Obstetrics and Gynaecology* (1923). Together with R. W. Johnstone and M. H. Phillips he edited a *Historical Review of British Obstetrics and Gynaecology, 1800–1950* (1954). He was an acknowledged leader of British obstetrics during the first half of the twentieth century, bridging the days when obstetrical practice was relatively primitive to more modern times with a maternal mortality rate reduced to less than one-tenth of its previous figure. He initiated or sponsored many of the innovations during this period: in particular, his name is associated with the lower segment caesarean section whereby that operation became decidedly safer; in the United States it is often referred to as the Kerr operation. Munro Kerr is described as being 'tall, slim and erect; graceful in carriage and in his movements; perfectly dressed and well groomed, tending sometimes to a degree of foppishness, particularly when he sported a monocle, as he often did' (Peel, 25). He died in Canterbury on 7 October 1960.   CHASSAR MOIR, *rev.*

Sources *Journal of Obstetrics and Gynaecology of the British Commonwealth*, 68 (1961) · personal knowledge (1971) · private information (1971) · J. Peel, *The lives of the fellows of the Royal College of Obstetricians and Gynaecologists, 1929–1969* (1976) · *BMJ* (15 Oct 1960) · *BMJ* (24 Oct 1960)
Archives Royal College of Obstetricians and Gynaecologists, London, papers
Likenesses S. Elwes, oils, *c.*1954, Royal College of Obstetricians and Gynaecologists, London · photograph, repro. in *BMJ* (15 Oct 1960)
Wealth at death £20,392 1*s.* 11*d.*: confirmation, 7 Dec 1960, CCI

Kerr, Norman Shanks (1834–1899), physician and temperance advocate, the eldest son of Alexander Kerr, a merchant and shipowner, was born at Glasgow on 17 May 1834. He was educated at Glasgow high school and matriculated in 1852 from Glasgow University, where he supported himself by working on the staff of Glasgow newspapers until he graduated MD and CM in 1861. After a period as resident surgeon to the Lock Hospital, Glasgow, he sailed as surgeon on Canadian mail steamers.

In 1871 Kerr began to practise medicine at Dunstable, where he was the public vaccinator. Three years later he settled at St John's Wood in London and was appointed a parochial medical officer for St Marylebone, a post he retained for twenty-four years. He was twice married: first, in 1871, to Eleanor Georgina, daughter of Edward Gibson of Ballinderry, Ireland; she died in 1892, leaving four daughters and a son, Arthur (d. 1933), a rector in the Church of England. Kerr's second marriage, in 1894, was to Edith Jane (d. 1922), daughter of James Henderson of Belvidere Lodge, Newry, co. Down, Ireland. She served as a vice-president of the British Women's Total Abstinence Union.

The advancement of temperance was a life's work for Kerr. Although he may have consumed alcohol during his time as a ship's doctor and at Dunstable, he was otherwise a life abstainer. He joined the United Kingdom Alliance in 1858, having, at the age of nineteen, already become a founder and secretary of the Glasgow Abstainer's Union. In Glasgow he promoted counter-attractions to discourage the drinking of alcoholic beverages, such as the Coffee Tavern Company and Saturday evening concerts at City Hall. He was also an active member of the Total Abstinence Society, which operated in connection with the University of Glasgow. Later he was vice-president of the Marylebone Temperance and Band of Hope Union, and honorary secretary of a local branch of the Church of England Temperance Society.

Kerr sought to organize medical opinion behind legislation for the compulsory treatment of drunkenness. He argued that drunkenness was a disease rather than a crime or a social problem. However, he did not completely break with the older moralistic condemnation of drunkenness, and stigmatized drunkards as suffering from a type of degeneration that left them morally weak. Despite the conclusions that could be made from his efforts in Glasgow, as a physician he argued for the importance of heredity in creating drunkards against those who stressed the effect of social environment.

Kerr promoted his views through a number of organizations and publications. For many years he was a member and sometimes chairman of the inebriates legislation committee of the British Medical Association. He was elected president of the Society for Promoting Legislation for the Control and Cure of Habitual Drunkards, which he had helped found in 1876. Most important, in 1884 he founded a successor organization, the Society for the Study and Cure of Inebriety. Until his death Kerr served as president of the new society and edited its *Proceedings*. In addition he was vice-president (and from 1881 honorary secretary) of the Homes for Inebriates Association and senior consulting physician to the Dalrymple Home for Inebriates, at Rickmansworth, Hertfordshire. He was corresponding secretary to an American organization, the Association for the Cure of Inebriates, and vice-president of the International Council of Medical Jurisprudence. He wrote several books and many articles, including *Inebriety, its Etiology, Pathology, Treatment, and Jurisprudence* (1888). The Habitual Drunkards Act of 1878 and the Inebriates Act of 1898 resulted in large part from Kerr's labours.

In his 1905 memorial lecture T. D. Crothers characterized Kerr as 'calm' and 'optimistic', a tactful speaker and writer who won over temperance reformers predisposed to reject the disease theory, and a masterful organizer who secured the active co-operation of people with discordant views.

Kerr was an Anglican and a Liberal. Retiring for reasons of ill health, he moved to Hastings in Sussex, where he died at his home, 46 Wellington Square, on 30 May 1899. He was buried in the following month at Paddington cemetery in London.

DAVID M. FAHEY

Philip Henry Kerr, eleventh marquess of Lothian (1882–1940), by Howard Coster, 1935

Sources V. Berridge, 'The Society for the Study of Addiction, 1884–1988', *British Journal of Addiction*, 85/5 (1990), whole issue · V. Berridge and G. Edwards, *Opium and the people* (1981) · B. Harrison, *Dictionary of British temperance biography* (1973) · E. H. Cherrington and others, eds., *Standard encyclopedia of the alcohol problem*, 6 vols. (1924–30) · *The Times* (1 June 1899) · *BMJ* (10 June 1899), 1442 · T. D. Crothers, 'The Norman Kerr memorial lecture', *British Journal of Inebriety*, 3 (1906), 105–26 · H. Rolleston, 'The jubilee of the society and the centenary of the birth of its founder', *British Journal of Inebriety*, 32 (1934), 1–13 · W. I. Addison, ed., *The matriculation albums of the University of Glasgow from 1728 to 1858* (1913) · R. M. MacLeod, 'The edge of hope: social policy and chronic alcoholism, 1870–1900', *Journal of the History of Medicine and Allied Sciences*, 22 (1967), 215–45 · *DNB* · *CGPLA Eng. & Wales* (1899)

Archives Society for the Study of Addiction to Alcohol and Other Drugs, London

Likenesses photograph?, repro. in Berridge, 'Society for the Study of Addiction' · photograph?, repro. in Cherrington, *Standard encyclopedia of the alcohol problem*

Wealth at death £5957 12s. 7d.: probate, 3 July 1899, *CGPLA Eng. & Wales*

Kerr, Philip Henry, eleventh marquess of Lothian (1882–1940)

Kerr, Philip Henry, eleventh marquess of Lothian (1882–1940), writer and politician, was born in London on 18 April 1882, the eldest of five surviving children (an elder sister, *b.* 1880, died in infancy) of Lord Ralph Drury Kerr (1837–1916), army officer, and his wife, Lady Anne (*c.*1857–1931), youngest daughter of Henry Granville Fitzalan-*Howard, fourteenth duke of Norfolk. Kerr's father, the third son of the seventh marquess of Lothian, enjoyed a distinguished army career, mainly in India, but also, from 1891 to 1896, as major-general commanding the Curragh. After his retirement, in 1898, the family settled at Woodburn, a dower house on the Lothian family estate of Newbattle, near Edinburgh. Kerr enjoyed a happy childhood with his three younger sisters, Cecil (1883–1941), Margaret (1884–1962), and Minna (1887–1963), and his brother, David (1893–1914). He was closer to his mother, who was twenty years younger than his father, but the latter deserved as well as demanded his children's respect.

Both Kerr's parents were devout Roman Catholics. It was therefore natural that in September 1892, after private education, he should be sent to Cardinal Newman's foundation, the Oratory School, at Edgbaston. The headmaster, the Revd Dr John Norris, a portly figure 'with a round beaming countenance and the infectious gurgling laughter of a happy child' (Butler, 3), was a frequent visitor to Woodburn. For many years Kerr believed he had a vocation to be a priest, but religious doubts had already surfaced by the time he entered New College, Oxford, in October 1900. They were exacerbated by his conversation and reading (particularly of George Bernard Shaw) there. At one point he thought of joining the army (the Second South African War was then at its height), but he was persuaded otherwise by his parents. His tutors at New College, R. S. Rait and H. A. L. Fisher, were a keen influence on him; with Fisher he maintained a lifelong correspondence and friendship. In 1904 he gained a first-class degree in modern history, but he was an unsuccessful candidate for a fellowship at All Souls College later that year.

South Africa and the *Round Table* South Africa was still very much on Kerr's mind when he came to consider what to do after leaving Oxford, although his thoughts had now turned from joining the army to securing some civilian post in the reconstruction of the former Boer republics. He was undeterred by John Buchan's advice, through Rait, that 'an appointment to the new colonies will be valuable as an apprenticeship in the work of administration, but that it does not offer, in itself, any brilliant future' (R. S. Rait to Lord Ralph Kerr, 26 June 1903, Lothian MSS, GD 40/17/453, fol. 3). Fortuitously, Sir Arthur Lawley, lieutenant-governor of the Transvaal, had served under Lord Ralph Kerr in the 10th hussars, and readily agreed to offer Kerr a post as his assistant private secretary and aide-de-camp. Kerr arrived in Pretoria in February 1905. He remained on Lawley's staff for only two months before Robert Brand, whom Kerr had known at Oxford, took him on as assistant secretary to the inter-colonial council and railway committee of the four South African colonies in

April 1905. He was also secretary to the standing committee on the South African constabulary from December 1905, and secretary to the indigency commission from September 1906. Kerr served directly under Milner for only a week before the latter returned to England, to be succeeded by Lord Selborne. Nevertheless, he became a central figure in Milner's 'Kindergarten', which took on a new life after the departure of Milner himself.

Kerr took part in all the discussions that led to Lionel Curtis's drafting of the 'Selborne memorandum', and he wrote a long appendix, 'South African railway unification', which was published with it as a state paper (*Parl. papers*, 1907, 57, Cd 3564) in 1907. After the publication of the memorandum, Kerr was persuaded by Curtis to leave the inter-colonial council to edit a new monthly journal, *The State*, which was to be published in both English and Dutch, and which was to support the Closer Union societies in their campaign for the unification of the South African colonies. The first issue appeared in December 1908, by which time a national convention was already at work devising a constitution with the support of the four governments. Under Kerr's editorship, *The State* applauded the speed of South African unification and attempted to convey the idea of a distinctive white South African identity. It carried articles by W. Westhofen on the artist Gwelo Goodman, Herbert Baker on Cape Dutch architecture, and Lord Selborne on 'the native problem'. Kerr resigned the editorship in June 1909, handing over to B. K. Long and returning to England on the same boat as the delegates carrying the Bill of Union to Westminster.

Kerr's initial inclination was to attempt to stand for parliament, and in April 1909 he wrote to his father asking him to see Balfour and 'remind him of Uncle Schomberg [Schomberg Henry Kerr, ninth marquess of Lothian, secretary of state for Scotland, 1887–92] and the family connections' (Kerr to Lord Ralph Kerr, 4 April 1909, Lothian MSS, GD 40/17/458, fol. 18). Nevertheless, he was once again overborne by Curtis, who persuaded him to become the editor of a new quarterly journal of imperial and international affairs, the *Round Table*. (Kerr was in fact offered the Unionist candidacy at Midlothian in April 1910, but turned it down.) The *Round Table* was to accompany the creation by Curtis of a network of 'discussion groups' throughout the self-governing parts of the empire. Curtis, Kerr, and their associates were at this stage all convinced of the need for imperial federation—the reconstruction of the imperial government as a body representative of the dominions (as they were called after 1907) as well as of Britain—but it was agreed that the journal in particular should not at first 'come out flat-footed' in favour of federation (May, 77). The details of the plan were agreed in September 1909, and Kerr was appointed editor at £1000 p.a. Soon after, he, Curtis, and William Marris were sent on a fact-finding tour of Canada. The experience had opposite effects on Curtis and Kerr. Curtis was more than ever convinced of the need for immediate federation; Kerr was impressed by the need for caution.

The first issue of the *Round Table* appeared in November 1910, with a long article by Kerr entitled 'Anglo-German rivalry' and contributions from other members of the Round Table network. Kerr was to remain editor, with interruptions, until December 1916, but he continued thereafter to contribute anonymous articles (all *Round Table* articles were anonymous until 1966) on a variety of imperial and international questions. Most were lucid and persuasive, although many were sometimes also long-winded. During his time as editor his views changed significantly, both on the need for and practicability of imperial federation, and on what, following the terminology of the time, he described as the relations between 'advanced' and 'backward' peoples. Southern and eastern Africa were always for him (as for other members of the Round Table) a blind spot. Nevertheless, Kerr soon came to recognize the need for the gradual extension of representative government in Britain's other imperial dependencies. It was he who, in 1912, initiated the Round Table discussions on India which resulted in Curtis's 'principle of the Commonwealth'.

Kerr's advocacy of more rapid moves towards Indian self-government was prompted by discussions with Marris and other progressive officials in India itself, which he visited as part of a lengthy world tour designed to broaden his understanding of international affairs. He returned in August 1912, exhausted, depressed, and suffering from a painful crisis of religious belief. His friends Robert Brand, F. S. Oliver, and Edward Grigg agreed to look after the *Round Table* while he sought a cure from Sir Bertrand Dawson. The latter recommended that Kerr rest at a variety of sanatoria and resorts in Europe. At one, St Moritz, he renewed an acquaintance with Waldorf and Nancy Astor, whom he had met at Hatfield through Lady Selborne. The friendship thus kindled was profoundly to affect the course of his life. Nancy Astor converted to Christian Science towards the end of 1913; she was followed by Kerr and her husband. Kerr did not officially become a member of a Christian Science church until 1923: partly because he knew his apostasy would be painful for his mother, but partly also because he was not yet himself entirely convinced.

Kerr returned to the editorship of the *Round Table* in July 1914, a month before the outbreak of the First World War. His immediate instinct was to enlist. He was persuaded otherwise by Curtis and his colleagues. The death in action of his younger brother, David (a lieutenant in the Royal Scots), in October 1914 affected him badly, and increased the pressure from his parents not to serve. He was eventually called up after the introduction of national service in January 1916, but his Round Table colleagues persuaded the tribunal to exempt him on the grounds that editing the *Round Table* was a vital contribution to the war effort. In later years, Kerr's opponents on the right wing of British politics (notably Violet, Lady Milner, editor of the *National Review*, 1932–48) portrayed him as a shirker. This charge he found deeply wounding. Under his wartime editorship, the *Round Table* reached the apogee of its circulation (some 13,000 in September 1914); many articles were reprinted as pamphlets for distribution in the United States and other neutral countries.

Kerr's were among those most frequently reprinted, providing a cogent analysis of the war's origins, but also a credible set of war aims.

Lloyd George's secretary Kerr was a frequent attender of meetings of the 'Ginger Group' or 'Monday Night Cabal' instituted by Leo Amery in January 1916 to co-ordinate Unionist opposition to the Asquith government and build links with potential Liberal rebels. The Ginger Group brought together Milner and Lloyd George. It was largely through Milner's influence that in December 1916 Kerr was appointed an additional private secretary to the prime minister, Lloyd George, and a member of his 'Garden Suburb'. This latter bureaucratic innovation was by no means universally welcomed. H. W. Massingham criticized the appointment of 'a little body of *illuminati*, whose residence is in the Prime Minister's garden, and their business to cultivate the Prime Minister's mind'. He attacked Kerr in particular, as 'Narcissus', charged with 'rapidly assimilating the popular ideas or tendencies of the day, and presenting them to his chief, as it were, in concentrated pellets' (*The Nation*, 24 Feb 1917). Kerr's initial responsibility was for labour questions, but he was soon given responsibility for imperial and foreign affairs. His primary duty was to summarize and advise on the large quantity of documents submitted to the prime minister by other parts of the government machine, but he was increasingly called upon to act as Lloyd George's adviser and intermediary. His influence on Lloyd George's policy on such matters as war aims, relations with the dominions, and the development of schemes for a League of Nations was considerable. His activities gave rise to considerable resentment—notably from Winston Churchill, whose schemes for larger-scale allied intervention against Bolshevik Russia Kerr indignantly scotched, and from Balfour and Curzon, who felt that their authority as foreign secretaries was undermined by Kerr's role as a 'second Foreign Office'. Kerr, Curzon later noted, 'was a most unsafe and insidious intermediary, being full both of ability and guile. He was the chosen agent of most of his master's intrigues' (Turner, *Larger Idea*, 55).

Kerr remained Lloyd George's private secretary (his sole private secretary after December 1918) until March 1921. As such, he was well placed to help his friend Curtis to influence the Montagu–Chelmsford reforms in India, and himself to influence Lloyd George's European policy in the series of international conferences which followed Versailles. He resigned as Lloyd George's secretary (to be succeeded by Grigg) in order to become managing editor of the *Daily Chronicle* and a director of United Newspapers Ltd, which Lloyd George controlled. He remained in that position only until February 1922, when he resigned in order to concentrate on other activities. Nevertheless, he remained a Lloyd George Liberal until 1931 and a Liberal for the rest of his life. He was made a Companion of Honour in 1920, one of the first of the order. He liked to say that he had been present 'when the idea was contrived by George Nathaniel Curzon, who used to say that one of the

principal ways of winning the war was to satisfy the insatiable appetite of the British public for Honours' (Butler, 248).

One of Kerr's reasons for departing from Lloyd George's service was to devote more time to religious study. By 1922 he was 'convinced that Christian Science is the real key to all our problems, political and economic, no less than personal' (Kerr to Curtis, 28 May 1922, Lothian MSS, GD 40/17/18, fol. 190). In September 1923 he formally applied for membership of the First Church of Christ, Scientist, in London; from that point on his faith in the teachings of Mrs Eddy rarely wavered.

Liberal and federalist After leaving the *Daily Chronicle*, Kerr supported himself by journalism (for the *Christian Science Monitor* and other papers) and by lecture tours of the United States. He turned down the offer of the Unionist candidacy for Roxburghshire—'I don't think the old associations would approve of my views at all' (Kerr to Lady Anne Kerr, 3 Oct 1922, Lothian MSS, GD 40/17/467, fol. 26)—and of the foreign editorship of *The Times*, but in July 1925 he was persuaded to take on the secretaryship of the Rhodes Trust. He remained in this post until April 1939, at a salary of £2000 p.a. and with a large office at Seymour House, Waterloo Place, London. His appointment resulted in Rudyard Kipling's resignation as a trustee: the latter, like many others on the right wing of British politics, held Kerr personally culpable for the empire's retreat in India, and later Ireland and Egypt. With an Oxford secretary (Sir Francis Wylie until 1931, Sir Carleton Allen thereafter) to look after the welfare of Rhodes scholars, Kerr's responsibilities were for the general management of the trust; relations with universities, selection committees, and alumni throughout the empire/Commonwealth and the United States; and the disbursement of funds other than those allocated to the Rhodes scholarships.

Kerr's work enabled him to travel widely, and particularly in the United States, which he enjoyed. He liked the informality of America—when staying with friends it was 'certainly the simple life—no servants and we all eat in the kitchen!' (Kerr to Lady Anne Kerr, 12 April 1922, Lothian MSS, GD 40/17/467, fol. 7)—but he was also convinced that Anglo-American co-operation held the key to the future of the empire/Commonwealth and the stability of international relations. As he told Curtis in 1927, he had not forgotten their earlier vision of imperial federation; but he believed that the First World War 'has brought a much larger idea, the integration of the English-speaking world, also on an organic basis, within the realm of practical possibilities' (Kerr to Curtis, 26 May 1927, Lothian MSS, GD 40/17/227, fols. 156–7).

Kerr devoted much of his time between the wars to developing and expounding an analysis of international relations illustrating federalist principles—most eloquently in his Burge memorial lecture, published as *Pacifism is not Enough, nor Patriotism either* (1935). At the heart of his analysis was a theory of the state which owed more to Hobbes than to Proudhon. In his view the only remedy for

international anarchy was an international commonwealth, just as in the Wild West the only remedy for disorder was the law. Kerr believed that an international
commonwealth would only come about slowly, via the
division of the world into a few great blocs. He further
believed that an Anglo-American bloc would prove to be
the cornerstone of an eventual world commonwealth.
Throughout the inter-war years he was a fervent advocate
of greater understanding and closer co-operation
between Britain and America; but even on this more pro-
saic level he was, for many of those years, a voice crying in
the wilderness.

Kerr was also prominent, although again without any
real success, in the industrial fellowship movement of the
1920s, advocating a diluted form of guild socialism, a partnership between employers and trade unions in the management of industry. He was a member of the Liberal
industrial inquiry which produced Lloyd George's 'yellow
book' of 1928; but it was Keynes's rather than Kerr's ideas
which were dominant. The fundamental implausibility of
Kerr's ideas was exposed by Keynes: 'My real difficulty lies
in the impracticability, or uselessness, of inscribing pious
ideals on a political banner of a kind which could not possibly be embodied in legislation' (Keynes to Kerr, 31 Aug
1927, Lothian MSS, GD 40/17/229, fol. 320).

On 16 March 1930 Kerr succeeded his cousin Robert
Schomberg Kerr as marquess of Lothian, earl of Ancram,
earl of Lothian, viscount of Briene, Lord Ker of Newbattle,
Lord Jedburgh, and Baron Ker of Kersheugh. He inherited
four magnificent houses: Ferniehirst Castle, near Jedburgh, Roxburghshire; Monteviot, the other side of Jedburgh; Newbattle Abbey, on the banks of the Esk, near
Dalkeith; and Blickling Hall, Aylsham, Norfolk. His title
and the wealth associated with it were useful for Lothian.
Nevertheless, he wore his nobility lightly. He was popularly remembered for arriving for the coronation of
George VI in a battered Austin Seven. Most of his estates
were dilapidated when he inherited them, but he was able
to sell enough treasures from the Blickling library and the
Newbattle house both to cover death duties and to initiate
an extensive programme of renovation at Blickling and
(after the death of his aunt Victoria, widow of the ninth
marquess of Lothian, in 1938) Monteviot. Ferniehirst
Castle was loaned to the Youth Hostels Association, while
(with funds from the Carnegie Foundation) Newbattle
Abbey was turned into an adult education college, managed by a trust representing the universities of Glasgow
and Edinburgh. He was remembered at Blickling and
Monteviot as a fair employer and a generous patron,
although he was sometimes also criticized for his aloofness.

In November 1930 Lothian was one of the four Liberal
delegates to the first Round Table Conference on India. In
August 1931 he was brought into the National Government, first as chancellor of the duchy of Lancaster, then,
from November 1931, as under-secretary of state at the
India Office. He played an important role in the genesis of
what would become the Government of India Act of 1935.

As chairman of the franchise committee, he recommended the franchise which, with slight modifications,
was introduced in 1935, increasing the Indian electorate
from 7 to 37 million. He remained committed to free
trade, and in September 1932 followed Herbert Samuel
and other Liberal colleagues out of government in protest
at the Ottawa agreements which introduced imperial
preference. Nevertheless, he remained closely involved in
matters relating to the Indian reforms, as a member of the
second and third Round Table Conferences and the joint
select committee on the Government of India Bill. After
the passage of the reforms he undertook a number of missions to India to seek ways of accommodating the nationalist movement; he stayed with Gandhi in his ashram, and
Nehru and his daughter Indira Gandhi were his guests at
Blickling.

Appeaser Lothian's vision was firmly set on the 'English-
speaking peoples': the empire, gradually evolving into a
Commonwealth of equal and self-governing nations, and
the United States, which had shown by its withdrawal
from the League of Nations how reluctant it was to be
drawn into the disputes of the 'Old World'. He believed
that Britain was not a part of Europe: she had a distinct
history and a separate destiny. He thought that Europe
should be united, but without Britain. 'I venture to proph-
esy that within a decade or two mankind will be organised
in four or five great entities', he wrote in April 1935. 'The
real question is whether that is going to be done by conquest and empire or by voluntary federation' (Lothian to
J. A. Spender, 30 April 1935, Lothian MSS, GD 40/17/296,
fols. 728–9). Lothian's detachment from Europe was
increased by his belief that Germany had been treated
unnecessarily harshly by the treaty of Versailles. A number of contemporaries believed that he was later motivated by 'guilt', since he had drafted many of the Versailles
clauses; but he tried on many occasions during the Versailles conference to persuade Lloyd George to insist on
more moderate terms. His sympathy for Germany was
enlarged by the belief that France had acted unreasonably
both during and after the conference.

After 1919, Lothian was a consistent advocate of the revision of the treaty of Versailles. In the 1920s he was largely
ignored. In the 1930s he was prominent and eventually
notorious as an 'appeaser', who suggested that Hitler
would only start to behave more reasonably—later, that
Hitler would only begin to lose the support of the German
people—if his reasonable demands were met. For
Lothian, those that were reasonable were the ending of
the punitive clauses of the treaty; the assimilation of
German-speaking areas into Germany where plebiscites
showed themselves in favour; and the creation of 'a sort of
Ottawa economic *mitteleuropa*' (Lothian to J. Smuts, 16
March 1937, Lothian MSS, GD 40/17/333, fol. 880). He was
not in favour of the restitution of Germany's forfeited colonies. In January 1935 (and again in May 1937) he met Hitler in Germany and returned to pronounce himself convinced that 'Germany does not want war and is prepared
to renounce it absolutely … provided she is given real
equality' (*The Times*, 31 Jan 1935). When Hitler reoccupied

the Rhineland in March 1936, Lothian was widely reported as saying that the Germans were only occupying 'their own back garden' (Butler, 213). At the time of the Imperial Conference in May 1937, Lothian was particularly active in encouraging the dominion premiers to state their support for a policy of British disengagement from Europe. Popularly, Lothian was closely associated with the policy of appeasement. David Low portrayed him as one of the 'Shiver Sisters' dancing to Hitler's tune (the others being Nancy Astor, Geoffrey Dawson, and J. L. Garvin), and Claud Cockburn identified him as a key member of the Cliveden set. Lothian was increasingly uneasy with the policy. During the Sudeten crisis he wrote to Halifax to urge him to make clear that Britain would side with Czechoslovakia if Germany resorted to force; at the time of Munich he feared another 'Hoare–Laval Plan' (ibid., 225). Nevertheless, it was only after the invasion of the rump Czech state in March 1939 that he finally realized 'that Hitler is in effect a fanatical gangster who will stop at nothing to beat down all possibility of resistance anywhere to his will' (ibid., 227). Following his family motto, *Sero sed serio* ('Late but in earnest'), he then set about energetically calling for a 'grand alliance' against aggression.

Ambassador to Washington By the summer of 1938 Sir Ronald Lindsay had been British ambassador in Washington for more than eight years, and Halifax's thoughts turned to replacing him with someone more 'of the Bryce type' (Turner, *Larger Idea*, 93). In August he approached Lothian, who readily agreed; the appointment was announced in April 1939. 'When I read the announcement yesterday', the veteran American journalist Walter Lippmann wrote, 'it suddenly seemed as if it could not have been anyone else' (ibid., 93). Lothian had aristocratic charm, but democratic ideals; he loved America, and had travelled through it extensively; he had a wide range of contacts, in government, the universities, and journalism; and he was adept at the art of presentation. His appointment was criticized by Americans who identified him with appeasement; by others who suspected that he would use his guile to induce Americans to fight for the preservation of the British empire; and by many Foreign Office officials who suspected, rightly, that Lothian would be difficult to control.

Lothian arrived in Washington on 29 August 1939, and presented his credentials at the White House on 30 August. Four days later, Britain was at war. Lothian maintained a dignified silence only for a short while, before embarking on a series of speeches, broadcasts, and interviews, in which he set out Britain's case. Behind the scenes he played an important role in negotiating the destroyers-for-bases deal of September 1940. In October he returned to Britain for talks, to be invested as a knight of the Thistle, and to persuade Churchill to set out candidly Britain's war needs. At a press conference held on his return to La Guardia airport on 23 November he forced Churchill's hand by admitting, as reported by Sir John Wheeler-Bennett, 'Well, boys, Britain's broke; it's your money we want' (Butler, 307). Lothian's indiscretion caused a sharp fall in international confidence in sterling and played into the hands of German propaganda, but it had its desired effect. On 8 December Churchill wrote to Roosevelt listing Britain's needs. Lothian did not live to see Lend-Lease come into existence, as it did in March 1941. On 7 December he was taken ill, with toxic poisoning arising from a uraemic infection. Following his Christian Science beliefs, he refused ordinary medicine and was attended by a Christian Science practitioner. He died at the British embassy on the morning of 12 December 1940. He was accorded a state funeral in Washington Cathedral the following Sunday, 15 December. His ashes were deposited at the national cemetery, Arlington, for the duration of the war, and were finally laid to rest at Jedburgh Abbey, Roxburghshire, in December 1945. In his will, Lothian left Newbattle Abbey to the Scottish universities and Blickling Hall, with 4500 acres, to the National Trust (having instigated a change in the law in 1938 to enable a reluctant trust to accept large country estates as well as houses: a stimulant to an important development of National Trust objectives). He was succeeded as twelfth marquess by his cousin, Peter Francis Walter Kerr (*b.* 1922), who also inherited the Monteviot estate.

Tall, fair-haired, always rumpled but never dishevelled, Lothian was an attractive figure. 'Most women fall in love with him sooner or later, as far as my experience goes', Brand wrote (p. 236). He never married. Muriel O'Sullivan, his secretary at Blickling, observed that

women had an unusual place in his life … The religion in which he was brought up makes of a woman the Queen of Heaven and the refuge of sinners. In later life he became a convert to a religion founded by a woman.

In her view, 'he did not seem dependent on the companionship of men in the way that the society of women seemed essential to his well-being' (O'Sullivan). He was close to his mother until her death, and to his sisters until his own. Among his many friendships, that with Nancy Astor was perhaps the strongest. He was a keen tennis player and an expert golfer. (He built a golf course for the villagers of Aylsham in the grounds of Blickling Hall, but it was dug up for vegetables during the Second World War.) Despite his inner uncertainties, he exuded charm and self-confidence. Thomas Jones remarked that he conveyed 'a fallacious lucidity of one who had done the thinking and resolved the difficulties for you'; Sir Robert Vansittart described him as 'an incurably superficial Johnny-know-all' (May, 56). A trait which was remarked upon by many of those who knew him best was his fundamental impressionability. It was said of talking to him that one had the strange sensation of talking to the last person he had talked to. His posthumous reputation was severely damaged by his association with the policy of appeasement, and many works published in the 1950s and 1960s made scathing references to him. Later historians have tended on this question to be more charitable, but also to emphasize the significance of his contribution in other areas. Curiously, perhaps, his federalist writings have tended to attract most interest in Italy, after a consignment of his books and pamphlets was smuggled into the prison-island of Ventotene during the Second World War.

Largely through the efforts of Altiero Spinelli and his fellow prisoners, Lothian's writings on international relations have been reinterpreted as founding texts of the European federalist movement. ALEX MAY

Sources NA Scot., Lothian MSS · *DNB* · *WWW* · Burke, *Peerage* · *The Times* (13 Dec 1940) · *The Times* (14 Dec 1940) · *The Times* (16 Dec 1940) · *The Times* (18 Dec 1940) · *The Times* (20 Dec 1940) · *The Times* (24 Dec 1940) · *The Times* (27 Dec 1940) · *The Times* (10 Jan 1941) · [E. Grigg], 'Philip Kerr, marquess of Lothian', *Round Table*, 31 (1941), 197–221 · [Lord Brand], 'Philip Kerr: some personal memories', *Round Table*, 50 (1960), 234–43 · M. O'Sullivan, notes on the late Lord Lothian, typescript, 1949, Bodl. Oxf. · J. R. M. Butler, *Lord Lothian* (1960) · J. Turner, ed., *The larger idea: Lord Lothian and the problem of national sovereignty* (1988) · G. Guderzo, ed., *Lord Lothian: una vita per la pace* (1986) · A. Bosco, *Lord Lothian, un pioniere del federalismo* (1989) · D. Reynolds, *Lord Lothian and Anglo-American relations, 1939–1940* (1983) · P. A. Smith, 'Lord Lothian and British foreign policy, 1918–39', MA diss., Carleton University, 1968 · J. Pinder, 'Prophet not without honour: Lothian and the federal idea', *Round Table*, 72 (1983), 207–20 · J. Pinder and A. Bosco, 'Introduction: Lothian's contribution to the federal idea', in *Pacifism is not enough: collected lectures and speeches of Lord Lothian* (1990), 5–36 · J. E. Kendle, *The Round Table movement and imperial union* (1975) · W. Nimocks, *Milner's young men: the kindergarten in Edwardian imperial affairs* (1968) · H. V. Hodson, 'The Round Table, 1910–81', *Round Table*, 71 (1981), 308–33 · A. C. May, 'The Round Table, 1910–1966', DPhil diss., U. Oxf., 1995 · A. Bosco and A. May, eds., *The Round Table movement, the empire/Commonwealth and British foreign policy* (1997) · C. Quigley, *The Anglo-American establishment from Rhodes to Cliveden* (1981) · R. Symonds, *Oxford and empire: the last lost cause?* (1986) · J. Turner, *Lloyd George's secretariat* (1980) · D. Reynolds, *The creation of the Anglo-American alliance, 1937–41* (1981) · P. B. Rich, *Race and empire in British politics* (1986)

Archives Bodl. Oxf., Round Table corresp. · JRL, *Manchester Guardian* archives, letters to the *Manchester Guardian* · NA Scot., corresp. and papers, 6D 40/17 · PRO, papers relating to visit to Berlin 1937, CAB 21/543 | BL, corresp. with Arthur James Balfour, Add. MS 49797, *passim* · BL, corresp. with Albert Mansbridge, Add. MS 65253 · BL OIOC, memorandum and letters from J. S. Meston, MSS Eur. F 77 · BL OIOC, letters to John, first Viscount Simon, MSS Eur. F 77 · Bodl. Oxf., corresp. with Lionel Curtis · Bodl. Oxf., Geoffrey Dawson MSS · Bodl. Oxf., corresp. with H. A. L. Fisher · Bodl. Oxf., Lionel Hichens MSS · Bodl. Oxf., Gilbert Murray MSS · Bodl. Oxf., corresp. with Sir Horace Rumbold · Bodl. Oxf., corresp. with John, first Viscount Simon · Bodl. Oxf., letters to E. J. Thompson · Bodl. Oxf., Alfred Zimmern MSS · Bodl. RH, Baron Brand MSS · Bodl. RH, corresp. with J. H. Oldham · Bodl. RH, corresp. with Margery Perham and related papers · CUL, corresp. with Sir Samuel Hoare · HLRO, corresp. with David, first Earl Lloyd-George · HLRO, corresp. with Herbert Samuel · NA Scot., corresp. with A. J. Balfour · NL Scot., F. S. Oliver MSS · NL Wales, corresp. with Thomas Jones · PRO NIre., corresp. with Lord Dufferin · Queen's University, Kingston, Ontario, Edward Grigg MSS · U. Reading L., corresp. with Nancy Astor · U. Reading L., corresp. with Waldorf, second Viscount Astor · University of Cape Town Library, corresp. with Patrick Duncan · University of Cape Town Library, corresp. with C. J. Sibbett · Women's Library, London, corresp. with Eleanor Rathbone | FILM BFI NFTVA, documentary footage · BFI NFTVA, news footage

Likenesses W. Stoneman, photograph, 1921, NPG · H. Coster, photograph, 1935, NPG [*see illus.*] · death-mask, 1940, NPG · J. Gunn, oils, 1943, Bodl. RH · F. de B. Footner, watercolour, Blickling Hall, Norfolk · photograph, repro. in *The Times* (13 Dec 1940) · photograph, repro. in *Sunday Times* (22 Dec 1940) · portraits, repro. in Butler, *Lord Lothian* · portraits, Blickling Hall, Norfolk

Wealth at death £464,199 17s. 6d.: confirmation, 12 Dec 1941, *CCI* · gave Blickling Hall to National Trust, and Newbattle Abbey to Combined Scottish Universities

Kerr [Ker], **Robert**, first marquess of Lothian (1636–1703), nobleman, was born at Newbattle House, Edinburghshire, on 8 March 1636, the son of William *Kerr, third earl of Lothian (*c.*1605–1675), and Anne Kerr (*d.* 1677), daughter of Robert Ker, second earl of Lothian, and countess of Lothian in her own right. Styled Lord Kerr of Newbattle, he was educated at the University of Leiden (1651–3), and at Saumur, Angers, and Paris (1654–7). In January or February 1660 he married Lady Jean (*d.* 1700), daughter of Archibald Campbell, marquess of Argyll. His father resigned the estates in his favour in 1665. He helped to keep law and order in the borders, commanding a troop of horse from 1668 to 1676, and perhaps volunteered in the Third Anglo-Dutch War before a secret visit to Paris in September 1673. He succeeded to his father's titles in October 1675.

Poor health took Lothian to Paris and Montpellier from autumn 1679 until summer 1680. Taking the test in 1681, he was briefly a privy councillor from 4 January 1686 until purged with other opponents of the repeal of the penal laws on 16 September. He supported the revolution of 1688 and was appointed a privy councillor on 18 May 1689, and justice-general and sheriff-principal of the shire of Edinburgh on 3 August, as well as serving as a Treasury auditor and in other minor posts until his death. In 1690 he succeeded his uncle Charles as earl of Ancram.

A moderate presbyterian, perhaps influenced by Bishop Robert Leighton, a former minister of Newbattle, Lothian was appointed high commissioner to the general assembly sitting in January 1692, charged with implementing the king's recommendation that the assembly admit episcopal ministers into the kirk who were prepared to accept the confession of faith and submit to the authority of the presbyterian church courts. The presbyterians accepted reports that the king would not press the matter against their unanimous opposition, a belief strengthened by Lothian's moderate tone and his faithfulness in keeping the king's instructions secret. For a month the assembly stalled by attending to routine business, and considered a few episcopalian addresses only at the commissioner's request. Lothian astounded the clergy when on 13 February 1692 he admonished them for failing to unite with their brethren, and as instructed suddenly dissolved the assembly without the usual appointment of another date. Despite Lothian's protests the moderator appointed a date in August 1693, but a constitutional crisis was avoided because an assembly was not held on that date. Partly blamed for the failure of the king's policy, and again beset by ill health, which drove him to Bath in 1693, Lothian consoled himself with his stringed instruments and by improving his house at Newbattle. Having long struggled to maintain the precedence of his title, in 1695 he was humiliated by a parliamentary vote ranking him below other earls, but on 23 June 1701 his support for the court was rewarded with the title of marquess of Lothian. Appointed a commissioner for the Union with England on 25 August 1702, and a privy councillor and commissioner of exchequer on 4–5 February 1703, he died suddenly at London on 15 February, aged sixty-six. A post-mortem examination revealed a diseased gall bladder and the

Robert Kerr, first marquess of Lothian (1636–1703), by Peter Cross, 1667

effects of 'whooring and the clap' (Walter Scott to Robert Scott, 26 Feb 1703, NL Scot., MS 594, no. 2174). He was buried in the family vault at Newbattle parish church.

Lothian's movable estate, including unpaid salary and his investments in the Darien Company, amounted to £15,213 13s. Scots. Of his six sons and five daughters, William *Kerr, second marquess of Lothian, became a soldier. A younger son, **Lord Mark Kerr** (1676–1752), also an army officer, became a captain on 8 June 1693, and was wounded at Almanza on 25 April 1707. A brigadier-general at the capture of Vigo in 1719, he was appointed governor of Guernsey in 1740 and promoted general in 1743. When governor of Berwick upon Tweed in 1745, his reported quip to Sir John Cope, fleeing the Jacobite forces at Prestonpans, that he was the first general to have broken the news of his own defeat, was recorded in the contemporary ballad 'Johnnie Cope'. That year he became governor of Edinburgh Castle. He died, unmarried, in London, on 2 February 1752, and was buried four days later in Kensington.   TRISTRAM CLARKE

Sources *Scots peerage* · M. F. Moore, 'The education of a Scottish nobleman's sons in the seventeenth century', *SHR*, 31 (1952), 1–15, 101–15 · *Correspondence of Sir Robert Kerr, first earl of Ancram, and his son William, third earl of Lothian*, ed. D. Laing, 2 vols., Roxburghe Club, 100 (1875) · *Reg. PCS*, 3rd ser., vols. 2–16 · NA Scot., letters and papers of the Lothian family, c.1650–1703, GD40 · inventory and latter will and testament of the marquess of Lothian, 1707, NA Scot., CC8/8/83 · J. H. Burton, *The history of Scotland*, new edn, 7 (1897) · R. Kerr, marquess of Lothian, letter to the master of Stair, 1 March 1692, NL Scot., MS 599, fols. 13–14 · W. Scott, letter to R. Scott, 26 Feb 1703, NL Scot., MS 594, no. 2174 · *DNB* · P. W. J. Riley, *King William and the Scottish politicians* (1979) · D. Thomson, *A virtuous and noble education* (1971) · *GEC, Peerage* · C. Dalton, *George the First's army, 1714–1727*, 1 (1910) [Lord Mark Kerr] · M. Hook and W. Ross, *The 'forty-five: the last Jacobite rebellion* (1995) [Lord Mark Kerr]
Archives NA Scot., Lothian MSS · NL Scot., papers | NA Scot., Lothian MSS, papers relating to Lord Mark Kerr
Likenesses J. Rutgers Van Niwael, oils, 1653 · attrib. D. Scougall, oils, 1654, Scot. NPG · oil on panel, 1659, Scot. NPG · P. Cross, miniature, oils, 1667, V&A [*see illus.*] · attrib. S. Bombelli, oils, Scot. NPG · C. Lutyens, oils, priv. coll. · style of J. Medina, oils, U. Edin. · J. Medina or W. Aikman, portrait, priv. coll. · attrib. A. Raguineau, oils, priv. coll. · Scottish school, oils, priv. coll. · S. Verelst, oils, Scot. NPG · oils, U. Edin.

Wealth at death £15,213 13s. 0d. Scots—moveable estate; excl. silver plate bequeathed to spouse and heirs: inventory, NA Scot., CC 8/8/83; NA Scot., GD 40/5/64/6

Kerr, Robert (1757–1813), scientific writer and translator, was born on 20 October 1757 at Drumsheugh, Edinburgh, the son of James Kerr (d. 1768), jeweller and goldsmith and MP for Edinburgh city from 1747 to 1754, and his second wife, Elizabeth (1713/14–1799), daughter of Lord Charles Kerr of Cramond, director of chancery in Scotland. Kerr was educated at Edinburgh high school and at the University of Edinburgh and became surgeon to Edinburgh Foundling Hospital, but relinquished a successful medical career to manage a paper mill at Ayton, Berwickshire, which eventually proved a failure. He married at St Cuthbert's Church, Edinburgh, on 27 June 1778, Julia Wardrope. They raised two sons and two daughters. Kerr returned to Edinburgh about 1810.

In later life Kerr occupied himself with historical writing and with translating a broad range of scientific works. His *Elements of Chemistry* (1790), drawing on the text of A. L. Lavoisier, and his *Animal Kingdom, or, Zoological System of Linnaeus* (1792), a translation of part one of Linnaeus's *Systema naturae*, gained him election as fellow of the Royal Society of Edinburgh in 1805. Kerr's works were largely derivative, and his translations were often only extracts or parts of the originals. His *Essay of the Theory of the Earth* (1813) was criticized in the *Edinburgh Review* for its misleading title; it was in fact the introductory essay to Georges Cuvier's four-volume *Recherches sur les ossements fossiles*, researches on the fossil bones found in a specific geological setting. Kerr's biographical *Memoirs of the Life, Writings and Correspondence of the Late Mr William Smellie* (1811) related to the Edinburgh printer, naturalist, and antiquary, who died in 1795, not his medical namesake. He also compiled the first ten of the eighteen volumes of *A General History and Collection of Voyages and Travels* (1811–24). He died at Edinburgh on 11 October 1813 and was buried in Greyfriars churchyard. His son David Wardrope Kerr, a medical student, died in 1815 aged nineteen; he was survived by another son, then a captain in the navy, and two married daughters.

THOMAS SECCOMBE, rev. ANITA McCONNELL

Sources Irving, *Scots.* · J. Foster, *Members of parliament, Scotland … 1357–1882*, 2nd edn (privately printed, London, 1882) · *Edinburgh Evening Courant* (21 Oct 1813), 3c · J. Brown, *The epitaphs and monumental inscriptions in Greyfriars churchyard, Edinburgh* (1867) · *EdinR*, 22 (1813–14), 454–75 · Anderson, *Scot. nat.* · b. cert.

Kerr, Robert (1823–1904), architect, was born at Aberdeen on 17 January 1823, the son of Robert Kerr and his wife, Elizabeth, daughter of Thomas McGowan, yeoman, of Peterhead, and cousin of Joseph Hume. His only brother, Thomas, who settled at Rockford, Illinois, was a doctor of both medicine and divinity. After education in Aberdeen, Kerr was articled to John Smith, the city architect. In 1844 he moved to London, where he was introduced to T. L. Donaldson, professor of architecture at University College. He then spent a year in New York, and returned 'full of liberty and equality and go-aheadism' and believing that the authority of the ancients was 'a most extravagant conception' (*The Builder*, 8, 1850, 542). On 9 March 1848 he married Charlotte Mary Ann, *née* Fox, with whom he had nine children. Three of his four sons later became architects.

Kerr's first book, *The Newleafe Discourses* (1846), attacked both the classicism of the architectural establishment and the romantic medievalism of the ecclesiologists, and in 1847 he was involved, with Charles Gray, in the foundation of the Architectural Association (AA) in London as a vehicle for promoting an improved system of architectural education by means of mutual instruction. He became the first president of the AA and in 1852 he put forward a scheme for architectural training, which came to nothing, but he was later appointed examiner in the voluntary examination established by the Royal Institute of British Architects in 1862; he subsequently became a member of the statutory board of examiners. He was elected a fellow of the institute in 1857, served on the council in 1861–2 and again in 1870–2, and set up the standing committees on art, science, and practice, on the last of which he served himself. He also contributed numerous papers to the institute over a period of forty years from 1860 to 1900, on topics ranging from artificial stone, the competition system, and the housing of the poor to 'Ruskin and emotional architecture' (*Journal of the Royal Institute of British Architects*, 7, 1900, 181–8).

In 1861 Kerr succeeded William Hosking as professor of the arts of construction at King's College, London, a position which he held until 1890. He continued lecturing to the AA, and in 1892–6 he gave a series of lectures, 'Materials: their nature and application'. From 1860 to 1902 he was district surveyor (under the Metropolitan Board of Works and later the London county council) for the parish of St James's, Westminster.

Kerr's architectural practice was relatively small, but in the late 1850s and the 1860s he designed a number of buildings which exemplified his belief in the need for what he called a 'latitudinarian' or eclectic approach to architectural style (cf. 'The Battle of the Styles', *The Builder*, 18, 1860, 292–4). They included Forest Gate Congregational Church, Essex (1856), the National Provident Institution, Gracechurch Street, London (1863; dem.), and a group of houses including: Dunsdale, Westerham, Kent; Ascot Heath House, Berkshire (1868); Ford House, Lingfield, Surrey (1868; now called Greathed Manor); and, most important, Bearwood, Berkshire, a vast neo-Jacobean-style pile for John Walter, proprietor of *The Times* (1865–70; now Bearwood College). The commission for Bearwood came as a result of Kerr's *The Gentleman's House* (1864; 3rd edn, 1871), in which he drew upon the buildings of William Burn and others to provide the most lucid and encyclopaedic account available of mid-Victorian domestic planning. Kerr also put in competition designs for the government offices, Whitehall (1857), and for the Natural History Museum at South Kensington (1864), for which he was awarded the second premium, and he exhibited designs for the Palais de Justice in Brussels and the Reichstag in Berlin at the Royal Academy in 1862 and 1873 respectively.

Kerr's forcible personality was perhaps better displayed in his writings, lectures, and trenchant speeches than in his architecture, though Bearwood is one of the largest and most impressive of all Victorian country houses. He designed very little after 1870 but continued lecturing and writing: he brought out *The Consulting Architect* in 1886, and contributed the chapters 'Plan' and 'Thoroughfare' to *The Principles and Practice of Modern House Construction* (ed. L. Sutcliffe, 1900). He edited (with introduction and enlargement) the third edition of James Fergusson's *History of the Modern Styles of Architecture* in 1891, and for many years he was the main leader writer for *The Architect*. Kerr died on 21 October 1904 at his home, 31 Cathcart Road, London, and was buried at the church of the Annunciation, Chislehurst, Kent.

PAUL WATERHOUSE, *rev.* GEOFFREY TYACK

Sources *RIBA Journal*, 12 (1904–5), 14–15 · *The Builder*, 87 (1904), 435 · J. M. Crook, 'Architecture and history', *Architectural History*, 27 (1984), 555–78, esp. 563–6 · J. Summerson, *The Architectural Association, 1847–1947* (1947) · M. Girouard, *The Victorian country house* (1971) · m. cert.
Likenesses portrait, repro. in *The Builder*, 27 (1869), 846
Wealth at death £8375 7s. 1d.: probate, 29 Nov 1904, CGPLA Eng. & Wales

Kerr, Schomberg Henry, ninth marquess of Lothian (1833–1900), diplomatist and politician, second son of John William Robert Kerr, seventh marquess of Lothian, and his wife, Lady Cecil Chetwynd Talbot, only daughter of Charles Chetwynd *Talbot, second Earl Talbot, was born at Newbattle Abbey, near Dalkeith, on 2 December 1833. His elder brother, William Schomberg Robert Kerr, born on 12 August 1832, succeeded as eighth marquess of Lothian on his father's death on 14 November 1841, but himself died without issue on 4 July 1870. A noted bibliophile, he bequeathed to Oxford University money for the foundation of the marquess of Lothian's prize, awarded annually to a historian.

Schomberg Henry Kerr was educated at Trinity College, Glenalmond, and at Oxford, where he matriculated from New College on 20 October 1851. He left the university without a degree, entered the diplomatic service, and was appointed attaché at Lisbon. He was transferred in 1854 to Tehran, and thence in 1855 to Baghdad. During the Anglo-Persian War of 1856–7 he served as a volunteer on the staff of Sir James Outram, by whom he was publicly thanked at the close of the campaign. He was afterwards attaché at Athens, and in 1862 was appointed second secretary at Frankfurt. He served in the same capacity briefly at Madrid in 1865, then was moved to Vienna.

On 23 February 1865 Kerr married Lady Victoria Alexandrina Montagu-Douglas-Scott, second daughter of Walter Francis Montagu-Douglas-*Scott, the fifth duke of Buccleuch, and his wife, Lady Charlotte Anne; they had three sons and five daughters. Kerr succeeded his elder brother, William Schomberg Robert, as ninth marquess of Lothian and fourth Baron Ker of Kersheugh, Roxburghshire, on 4 July 1870, and in right of the latter peerage took his seat in the House of Lords on 30 March 1871. He moved, on 19

Schomberg Henry Kerr, ninth marquess of Lothian (1833–1900), by Sir William Quiller Orchardson, 1898

March 1874, the address in answer to the queen's speech, and on 5 August following took the oaths for the subordinate office of lord privy seal of Scotland, which he held until his death. He was sworn of the privy council on 6 February 1886, and in Lord Salisbury's second administration succeeded A. J. Balfour as secretary for Scotland, and, as such, *ex officio* keeper of the great seal of Scotland and vice-president of the committee of council for education in Scotland (11 March 1887). The sphere of his administrative duties was further enlarged by a statute of the same year (50 & 51 Vict. c. 52). He held office until the fall of the administration in August 1892, during which period he had charge of the measures of 1889 for the reform and re-endowment of the Scottish universities and the reform of Scottish local government, and several other measures closely affecting Scottish interests.

Kerr was a member of the Historical Manuscripts Commission, was elected in 1877 president of the Royal Society of Antiquaries of Scotland, and received in 1882 the degree of LLD from the University of Edinburgh, of which he was lord rector in 1887–90. He was also vice-president of the Royal Scottish Geographical Society and a member of the governing body of the Imperial Institute. In 1878 he was elected KT and in 1899 a knight of grace of the order of St John of Jerusalem. He was colonel from 1878 to 1889, and afterwards honorary colonel, of the 3rd battalion of the Royal Scots regiment, and captain-general of the Royal Company of Archers from 1884 until his death on 17 January 1900. He died at 39 Grosvenor Square, London,

and was buried at Newbattle Abbey. He was succeeded by his third son, Robert Schomberg Kerr. His widow married Bertram Talbot, and died on 19 June 1938.

J. M. RIGG, *rev.* H. C. G. MATTHEW

Sources GEC, *Peerage* · Irving, *Scots.*
Archives NA Scot., corresp. and papers · NL Scot., diaries, corresp., and papers | Beaulieu Archive, Hampshire, letters to first Baron Montagu of Beaulieu · BL, corresp. with W. E. Gladstone, Add. MSS 44427–44520, *passim* · NA Scot., letters to agent relating to Roxburghshire election · NRA Scotland, priv. coll., letters to R. W. Cochran–Patrick · NRA Scotland, priv. coll., corresp. with Lord Campbell · U. Edin. L., letters to David Laing
Likenesses W. Q. Orchardson, portrait, 1898, Royal Bank of Scotland [*see illus.*] · W. G. Boss, pencil drawing, Scot. NPG · R. T., wood-engraving, NPG; repro. in *ILN* (19 March 1887) · Russell & Sons, photograph, NPG; repro. in *Our conservative and unionist statesmen*, 1 (1896)
Wealth at death £84,531 9s.: confirmation, 17 April 1900, *CCI* · £3553: additional estate, 18 Nov 1905, *CCI* · £88,000: GEC, *Peerage*

Kerr, Sir Thomas (*d.* in or before **1611**), soldier, is first recorded in 1571 as captain to Adam Gordon of Auchindoun, brother to the fifth earl of Huntly, in one of the recurrent outbreaks of the bitter feud between the Gordon and Forbes families. After Auchindoun was victorious at Crabstane on 20 November, he sent Kerr to take possession of Corgarffe, the stronghold of Black Arthour Forbes in Towy; when Forbes's wife, Margaret, refused to surrender, Auchindoun authorized his captain to fire the building, leading to the deaths of the lady and her daughters. His action understandably gave Kerr a reputation for ruthlessness, preserved in the earliest versions of the ballad 'Edom o' Gordon', in which he appears as 'traitour Captaine Care' (Child, 3.430). In February 1573 Kerr was ordered to appear before Regent Morton as one of Auchindoun's agents, but on the 23rd he was comprehended, with the rank of captain, in the pacification of Perth. His relations with the Morton regime remained uneasy, and he was imprisoned in 1578.

Kerr's luck had improved by February 1583, when he was granted a remission as one of the sixth earl of Huntly's household servants. In the following year he served as a commissioner of parliament for Aberdeen. His increasing influence in local government was confirmed on 11 October 1585, when he held court in Inverness as lieutenant-depute, punishing all 'slayris of blak fische' in Loch Ness (Mackay and Boyd, 1.304). In May 1587 he joined the laird of Fentry and Mr David Maxwell in trying to persuade Chancellor Maitland to allow the eighth Lord Maxwell, recently sentenced to banishment, to remain in Scotland. Kerr also served as Huntly's intelligencer, intriguing with the Kerrs in the borders to obtain measurements for the walls of Berwick, ahead of a proposed attack upon them. Writing in September, William Ker of Ford in Northumberland described Kerr as having 'the chefe rule and credit about the Erle Huntlie' and one who stood 'in good favour with the Kinge him selfe' (Bain, 1.270). Thomas Kerr forewarned the earl of two imminent attacks, one by a group of royal councillors (including Maitland) on 1 March 1589, and the other by the master of Glamis on 22 May.

As a burgess of Aberdeen Kerr was less well regarded, being among those complained of in 1591 during a civic dispute over the burgh's black and white friars' crofts. By April 1592 he and his brother James had been assigned to protect the countess of Huntly, the two men being her 'kinsmen and such as she greatly trusted' (*CSP Scot.*, 1589–93, 669). Then in 1594 Kerr reappeared in a military guise, with a reactive strike against the seventh earl of Argyll, who had been authorized by the king to take the Gordon stronghold of Strathbogie; Kerr's stance led to his being declared a traitor, having compounded his offence by refusing to appear before the privy council on 4 November. Kerr subsequently avoided controversy for a while, and on 20 November 1600 he was knighted and promised the isle of St Kilda (Hirtha) in the Western Isles.

Kerr's apparent rehabilitation did not last long, for on 2 June 1601 the council ordered the marquess of Huntly (as the sixth earl had now become) to apprehend him for coining. After receiving a remission alongside his master in April 1603, he served as justiciar for Lewis on 18 July 1605 and was also one of four commissioners of fire and sword ordered to pursue and punish those inhabitants of the northern isles who had refused to surrender their castles and boats to royal officers. In 1610 Kerr received a formal charter for St Kilda, but he was unable to make the grant effective in the face of resistance by the Macleods of Dunvegan. Meanwhile he was still noted as Huntly's factor in the records of the Aberdeen sheriff court, and on 2 October 1610 he served as witness when the marquess transferred his ancestral lands in Berwickshire to the earl of Home. Kerr's personal life remains obscure though he is known to have married one Isobel Buk, mentioned in a sasine of 22 December 1604. He had died by 1 October 1611, when his son John was served as his heir.

J. R. M. SIZER

Sources T. Thomson, ed., *A diurnal of remarkable occurrents that have passed within the country of Scotland*, Bannatyne Club, 43 (1833) • *CSP Scot.*, 1581–3; 1589–93; 1597–1603 • F. J. Child, ed., *The English and Scottish popular ballads*, 5 vols. (1956), 3.423–38 • D. Littlejohn, ed., *Records of the sheriff court of Aberdeenshire*, New Spalding Club, 2: 1598–1649 (1906); 31 • W. Mackay and H. C. Boyd, eds., *Records of Inverness*, New Spalding Club, 1: 1556–86 (1911); 38 • *Reg. PCS*, 1st ser., vols. 3, 4, 5, 7 • G. Donaldson, ed., *Registrum secreti sigilli regum Scotorum* (1982), 1581–4 • J. Bain, ed., *The border papers: calendar of letters and papers relating to the affairs of the borders of England and Scotland*, 2 vols. (1894–6), vol. 1 • J. Anderson, ed., *Calendar of the Laing charters* (1899), 854–1837 • J. Stuart, ed., *Miscellany of the Spalding Club*, 3 (1846), vols. 15, 20 • W. D. Simpson, ed., *Miscellany of the Third Spalding Club*, 2 (1940), vol. 10 • NA Scot., RS 4/3/452v • J. M. Thomson and others, eds., *Registrum magni sigilli regum Scotorum / The register of the great seal of Scotland*, 11 vols. (1882–1914), vol. 5; vol. 7 • [T. Thomson], ed., *The historie and life of King James the Sext*, Bannatyne Club, 13 (1825) • M. D. Young, ed., *The parliaments of Scotland: burgh and shire commissioners*, 2 vols. (1992–3)

Kerr, Lord Walter Talbot (1839–1927), naval officer, was born at Newbattle Abbey, Midlothian, on 28 September 1839, the fourth son of John William Robert Kerr, seventh marquess of Lothian (1794–1841), and his wife, Lady Cecil Chetwynd Talbot (1808–1877) [see Kerr, Cecil Chetwynd], daughter of Charles Chetwynd, second Earl Talbot. Their second son was Schomberg Henry *Kerr, ninth marquess of Lothian. Kerr was educated at Radley College from 1851 to 1853, when he joined the *Prince Regent* as a naval cadet. During the Baltic operations of the Crimean War (1854–5) he served in the *Neptune* and *Cornwallis* and was promoted midshipman in August 1855. The next year he was appointed to the steam frigate *Shannon* (50 guns, Captain William Peel) on the China station. On the outbreak of the Indian mutiny in 1857 the *Shannon* was ordered to Calcutta, and Peel landed with most of his ship's company as a naval brigade. Kerr served with it throughout the mutiny, was wounded in an action near Cawnpore, and was given an independent command at the siege and capture of Lucknow. For this service he was specially rated mate for the rest of the *Shannon*'s commission, and in the following year served for a few months in the same rank in the royal yacht *Victoria and Albert*, and was promoted lieutenant in September 1859. In 1860 he was appointed to the *Emerald* for three years' service in the channel, and in 1864 he went to the *Princess Royal*, flagship on the East Indies and Cape station, for another three years. He was promoted commander in 1868 and served in the *Hercules*, channel squadron, until 1871, and afterwards in the *Lord Warden*, Mediterranean flagship—an appointment John Fisher wanted—until promotion to captain in November 1872. While in the *Hercules* he was awarded the Royal Humane Society's silver medal for jumping overboard from a height of 30 feet into the Tagus to rescue a man who had fallen from the rigging.

Kerr married in 1873 Lady Amabel Cowper (d. 15 Oct 1906), the youngest daughter of George Augustus Frederick, sixth Earl Cowper, and sister of Francis Thomas De Grey, seventh Earl Cowper. They had four sons and two daughters. On the seventh earl's death in 1905 Lady Amabel succeeded to the properties of Brocket Hall, Hertfordshire, and Melbourne Hall, Derbyshire, and became coheir, with Lady Desborough and Lord Lucas, of the barony of Butler.

During his first eleven years on the captains' list, four of them on half pay, Kerr's principal commands were as flag-captain to Sir Beauchamp Seymour (afterwards Lord Alcester) in the channel squadron (1874–7), and in the Mediterranean (1880–81). In September 1880 he was sent by Seymour (who commanded the combined fleet of the five naval powers assembled to enforce, under the terms of the treaty of Berlin, the surrender of Dulcigno to Montenegro by Turkey) on a special mission to Rıza Pasha, the Turkish governor of Albania. He then had a shore appointment as captain of the Medway steam reserve until 1885, when Lord George Hamilton, on becoming first lord of the Admiralty in Lord Salisbury's Conservative government, appointed him his naval private secretary.

Kerr retained this appointment at the Admiralty until nearly a year after his promotion to rear-admiral in January 1889. He then hoisted his flag in the *Trafalgar*, as second in command in the Mediterranean until 1892, when he returned to the Admiralty as junior naval lord: the fifth Earl Spencer (first lord of the Admiralty in Gladstone's fourth government), on taking office, included him in his board for the duties of fourth naval lord, although he was senior to John Fisher, third naval lord and controller. In November 1893 Kerr became second naval lord. The naval lords, led by Sir Frederick Richards (first lord, 1893–9), pressed for a large shipbuilding programme to counter the Franco-Russian threat. Spencer agreed, but Gladstone and Harcourt opposed it. Late in 1893 the naval lords threatened resignation; as Fisher wrote, 'We got the ships and Mr. Gladstone went' (Mackay, 210). Promoted vice-admiral in February 1894, in May 1895 Kerr was appointed vice-admiral commanding the channel squadron, with his flag in the *Majestic*, for two years. In June 1895 he took part with his squadron in the celebration of the opening of the Kiel Canal. In May 1899 G. J. Goschen (Unionist first lord, 1895–1900) brought him back to his former post on the Board of Admiralty, preparatory to succeeding Sir Frederick Richards as first naval lord the following August: Fisher was bitterly disappointed not to be chosen. In 1901 Custance (director of naval intelligence) and in 1902 H. O. Arnold-Forster warned against the German naval threat but Lord Selborne (Unionist first lord, 1900–05) and Kerr considered the Franco-Russian threat the more important, and rejected any immediate anti-German naval redistribution. Kerr continued as first naval lord and was promoted admiral in March 1900; by a special order in council he was then promoted admiral of the fleet in June 1904, until Trafalgar day (21 October) of that year, when Selborne brought Fisher back from Portsmouth to succeed him. He remained on half pay until he retired on account of age in September 1909.

Kerr's early promotions made him a senior captain when he came to the Admiralty as private secretary, but although some naval members of the board were his juniors, he did not presume on his seniority to take a too prominent part in the administration, while his high rank enabled him to be of good service to the first lord in difficulties with members of the board, notably with the disagreement between Lord Charles Beresford, junior or fourth naval lord, and Sir Arthur Hood, senior or first naval lord. By temperament Kerr was unassuming and not opinionative and therefore got on well with his colleagues, naval and civilian, while his moderation and judgement ensured respect for his opinions. He was a thorough seaman with a great love of the service, and was conservative and resistant to change. He was not a man to initiate reform, but when he recognized its necessity he adopted and supported it. His sound common sense and knowledge of the service were of great help to Lord George Hamilton in carrying out the programme of the Naval Defence Act of 1889. Again, as fourth naval lord and second naval lord from 1892 to 1895, his moderation and firmness were of much help to Lord Spencer, when confronted with cabinet difficulties in the carrying out of the second shipbuilding programme. Finally, in his last period of service at the Admiralty as senior naval lord from 1899 to 1904, under lords Goschen and Selborne, he was able to give wise advice in the carrying out of the far-reaching changes in the training and organization of the personnel of the navy, for which Fisher was primarily responsible. Nevertheless, he is known to have regarded Fisher's claims when the latter commanded the Mediterranean Fleet as exaggerated and lacking in proportion. He probably disliked many of Fisher's ideas and certainly his methods.

The relationship between Kerr and Fisher was inherently difficult. Fisher at first feared that Kerr's elevation to senior naval lord doomed his own chances, as he might be too old to succeed Kerr when the latter stepped down. Fisher 'unceasingly harassed' (Boyce, 108) and irritated Kerr by his correspondence demanding strengthening of the Mediterranean Fleet, and Kerr rightly believed that Fisher fed information to 'Navy Leaguers and kindred spirits' (ibid., 138). Kerr was scathing in some of his minutes on Fisher's proposals, describing them as based on impulse rather than calm and deliberate judgement. Kerr asserted they 'had a right to expect something better than a demand for impossibilities from an officer holding the position of the C. in C. in the Mediterranean' (Marder, 400). Kerr advised Selborne against appointing Fisher second and first naval lord, alleging the latter appointment would be 'universally condemned' (Boyce, 137). Fisher, in turn, worked to undermine Kerr's reputation, suggesting that the Board of Admiralty was more concerned with the details of uniforms—'Kerr is humbugging about the oak leaves on the admirals' full-dress coat, etc' (Bennett, 243)—than what he regarded as the dangerous situation in the Mediterranean. Kerr, however, could be equally critical of Fisher's future rival Beresford, then second in command in the Mediterranean, remarking that Beresford's 'impetuosity leads him to launch forth reckless condemnations on insufficient and ill-thought out grounds' (Bennett, 237). Kerr was described as 'politely neutral' in 1903 on the Fisher question and in 1904 he welcomed the prospect of freedom from 'this unpleasant job' (Mackay, 211, 308). During Fisher's absence as commander-in-chief at Portsmouth (1903–4) the implementation of the new scheme rested largely with Kerr, and it was owing to his firmness that things proceeded well until Fisher returned as first sea lord. Kerr had no share in the changes made in the organization of the fleet in 1905. His was not a creative mind, but his character was esteemed by some of his fellow officers, including Selborne. In Lord George Hamilton's words, he might well be termed the *preux chevalier* of the navy. He was created KCB in 1896 and GCB in 1902.

Soon after Kerr entered the navy his widowed mother became, with her younger children, Roman Catholic, and Kerr was thenceforth a devoted Catholic. His religion made him widely suspect in the navy. Fisher wrote in 1901 that Kerr was 'a slave to the Roman Catholic hierarchy … he is a pervert and has all the antagonism of the pervert to the faith he has left' (Hough, 132). He was president of the Catholic Union of Great Britain from 1917 to 1921. After his retirement Kerr resided at Melbourne Hall, Derby, and died there on 12 May 1927. A funeral service was held on 17 May at St David's, Dalkeith.

V. W. BADDELEY, rev. PAUL G. HALPERN

Sources The Times (13 May 1927) • The Times (18 May 1927) • admiralty records • personal knowledge (1937) • private information (1937) • R. F. MacKay, *Fisher of Kilverstone* (1973) • A. J. Marder, The *anatomy of British sea power*, American edn (1940) • G. M. Bennett, *Charlie B: a biography of Admiral Lord Beresford of Metemmeh and Curraghmore* (1968) • *WWW* • Burke, *Peerage* • J. T. Sumida, *In defence of naval supremacy: finance, technology and British naval policy, 1889–1914*, new edn (1993) • *The crisis of British power: the imperial and naval papers of the second earl of Selborne, 1895–1910*, ed. D. G. Boyce (1990) • R. Hough, *First sea lord: an authorised biography of Admiral Lord Fisher* (1969) • H. C. G. Matthew, *Gladstone, 1875–1898* (1995) • R. Gardiner and A. Lambert, eds., *Steam, steel and shellfire: the steam warship, 1815–1905* (1992)

Archives Bodl. Oxf., corresp. with Lord Selborne
Likenesses A. J. Challin, oils, Melbourne Hall, Derbyshire • C. Silvy, carte-de-visite, NPG • Spy [L. Ward], chromolithograph, NPG; repro. in *VF* (8 Nov 1900) • photograph, repro. in *The Times* (13 May 1927)
Wealth at death £79,988 0s. 11d.: probate, 22 Oct 1927, *CGPLA Eng. & Wales*

Kerr, William, third earl of Lothian (*c*.1605–1675), politician, was the eldest son of Robert *Ker, first earl of Ancram (1578–1654), and his first wife, Elizabeth (*d*. 1620), daughter of Sir John Murray of Blackbarony. Soon after James VI's accession to the throne of England, Robert Ker was appointed to the bedchamber of Prince Henry, and in 1613 he became gentleman of the bedchamber to Prince Charles. Thus William Kerr grew up around the court at St James's. He matriculated as a fellow-commoner from Queens' College, Cambridge, in Lent 1621. In March 1621 William's 'first chamber fellow', Patrick Curwen (future MP for Cumberland), left the college to get married, and Robert Ker wrote to console his son, and tell him that 'Your present business is your booke, and the place Cambridge' (*Correspondence*, 1.16). However, William does not seem to have graduated at the university, and we next hear of him in Paris, in April 1624, where he seems to have gone to complete his education. In November he left Paris to begin his grand tour and, after travelling through a number of French towns, visited Turin, Milan, Modena, Bologna, Florence, Siena, Rome, and Venice, and then returned to Paris via Switzerland. His journal of the tour is preserved in the Newbattle collection (NL Scot., MS 5785). As a document of the Renaissance rather than the Reformation, the journal contains admiring descriptions of Italian cities and no disparaging remarks whatsoever about popery. He mentioned his visit to the Sistine Chapel, where 'Michaell Angelo' had painted the last judgement, 'counted the best peace in the world' (*Correspondence*, 1.xlvii).

On completing his education Kerr became a soldier, and raised a company of troops to take part in the duke of Buckingham's ill-fated expedition to the Île de Ré in 1627, during the war with France. In 1628 he participated in the equally unsuccessful attempt to relieve La Rochelle, sailing with the earl of Morton and the earl of Lindsay. In 1629 he fought for the Dutch against the Spanish when 's-Hertogenbosch was besieged by Henry, prince of Orange, and was present when the Spanish troops surrendered the town on 14 September after five months of resistance. In 1630 Kerr returned to Scotland, and on 9 December married Lady Anne (*d*. 1667), eldest daughter of

William Kerr, third earl of Lothian (*c*.1605–1675), by David Scougall

the late Robert Ker, earl of Lothian and heir to the earldom, apparently to be inherited upon her marriage to one of the name of Kerr. Her father had left the Newbattle estates, to which she was heir, heavily in debt, but Sir Robert Ker, father of William, drew from his own estate to cancel the debts, and the lands were granted to William and his new wife. On 31 October 1631 William Kerr was created earl of Lothian and Lord Kerr of Newbattle. He received the patent from the privy council in January 1632. Over the next few years he lived a quiet domestic life. Between 1631 and 1654 his wife gave birth to nine daughters and five sons. Their eldest son, Robert *Kerr, was born in 1636, eventually succeeded his father as the fourth earl of Lothian, and was created marquess of Lothian in 1701.

In the mid-1630s Lothian maintained contact with disaffected noblemen such as Argyll, Rothes, and Balmerino, and on 20 September 1637 he signed the supplication against the service book. On 18 October Lothian and Rothes had to escort Bishop Sydserf through the streets of Edinburgh to protect him from anti-prayer book rioters. His father had urged him to 'carie my self warily in these bryles', and Lothian insisted that he had no intention of being 'mutinous'. He prayed that 'God Almighty move the

King's harte to gentlenes, and that he urge not on this church that that there is sutch a generall aversion to' (*Correspondence*, 1.96). In February 1638 he signed the national covenant, and in November he was chosen as a ruling elder for the presbytery of Dalkeith in the Glasgow general assembly. In March 1639 he was with the covenanting forces who captured Dalkeith House. He also raised a regiment of about 600 horse from Haddington and Jedburgh, and in June he was with the covenanting army at Duns. Following the treaty of Berwick, Lothian and five other covenanters were invited to meet the king at Berwick. Although he accepted the invitation, many were opposed to Lothian and Montrose visiting the king, since both were regarded as lukewarm covenanters whom the king might persuade to desert the cause. Lothian sat as a member of the Edinburgh general assembly in August, and in 1640 he played a full part in the second bishops' war, raising a regiment of 1200 men from Teviotdale. He was a colonel in the covenanting army that crossed the Tweed on 21 August, and on 31 August was appointed governor of Newcastle upon Tyne. He was later reported to be the author of *A true representation of the proceedings of the kingdome of Scotland since the late pacification* (1640). In letters to his father, he insisted that the covenanters were not acting in opposition to the king, and had 'noe thoughts of prejudice towards this Kingdome where we are'. They had simply acted out of 'necessitie', and would 'never returne but with assurance to injoy our religion in puritie, and our nationall liberties'. Although the covenanters would like England to 'gett a reformation like ours', they had not come south 'to reforme Church and State'. 'We shall never refuse the King civill and temporall obedience; if more be demanded we can not give it, and in our lawful defence WE DARE DIE' (*Correspondence*, 1.104–5).

Lothian remained at Newcastle until August 1641, when he returned to Edinburgh to attend parliament. Appointed to the privy council he was, in November, appointed one of parliament's commissioners to continue treaty negotiations with their English counterparts. In the wake of the Irish rising his remit, like that of his colleagues, was expanded to include Scottish military intervention in Ireland. He was appointed lieutenant-general of the Scottish army designed for Ireland, and colonel of a foot regiment which sailed on 24 April 1642 and remained there until February 1644. However, instead of accompanying his men to Ulster, Lothian was selected by the privy council in December 1642 to go on an embassy to France, with royal approval, with regard to France's Scots guard. He set sail on 21 January 1643, and though the mission was delayed at first, it went successfully. By 27 September he was back in London. When he returned to the king at Oxford to report on his embassy, he was arrested for suspected treachery and eventually imprisoned in Bristol Castle, where he almost died from illness. On 3 January 1644 the committee of estates in Edinburgh passed an act approving his mission to France, and the English House of Commons also passed resolutions calling for his release. He was finally released in exchange for Sir Charles Goring in March 1644. The earl of Clarendon claimed that from this day forwards

Lothian 'continued amongst those who upon all occasions, carried the rebellion highest, and shewed the most implacable malice to the person of the King' (Clarendon, *Hist. rebellion*, 4.383). Burnet added that despite his father's loyal service, Lothian was 'ever much hated by the king' (*Burnet's History*, 1.28).

Lothian was present at the Edinburgh parliament in June, and on 17 July an act was passed ordering compensation for his expenses and losses incurred during his diplomatic mission. On 4 September he left Edinburgh to rejoin his regiment, now engaged in the pursuit of Montrose, but he refused to take command of the covenanter expedition after Argyll's resignation. His regiment lost at least 375 men at the battle of Auldearn on 9 May, contributing little to the war effort thereafter. In July and August Lothian took an active part in the sessions of parliament. In early 1646 he was named to that section of the committee of estates assigned to attend the Scottish army in England, and he was with General Leslie's forces when Charles I arrived at Newark in May. Later he received an order to go to treat with the king at Newcastle, and when Charles was given up to the English, Lothian attended him to Holmby House in February 1647. He opposed the engagement of December 1647, and became a key figure in the kirk party government after the defeat of the engagers in August 1648. In December 1648 he and two others were sent to London to uphold Scottish interests. They protested against the trial of Charles I and wrote to the Commons and to Fairfax and Cromwell in a futile attempt to halt proceedings against the king. On 24 February they presented a paper to the English parliament condemning the regicide and the alteration of government, and upholding Charles II. Clarendon condemned this as a 'very calm protestation', and claimed that they were under orders from Argyll not to offend the English regime or give 'a ground of a new war' (Clarendon, *Hist. rebellion*, 5.7–11). However, the Commons placed guards on their lodgings, and when they tried to follow the orders of the Scottish parliament and sail to the Netherlands to see Charles II, they were arrested and imprisoned at Gravesend, then taken to Berwick and detained there, before finally being allowed to return to Scotland.

On 10 March 1649 Lothian was made secretary of state, a position he nominally held until the Restoration. He was also among the commissioners sent to Charles II at The Hague in March 1650. Another commissioner, the minister John Livingstone, later complained that Lothian had been too conciliatory towards Charles because he was worried that the king would not come to Scotland if he heard all the covenanters' demands. The conciliatory approach succeeded in that Charles landed at Aberdeen on 23 June 1650, but in the wake of the covenanters' defeat at Dunbar, Lothian and others were condemned by a remonstrance of the synod of Fife for their 'crooked ways' in the negotiations with the king in the Netherlands (*Correspondence*, 1.xcv). Lothian and Argyll were now caught between those who wanted more purging of persons considered unworthy allies in the cause of the covenants, and those who wanted to readmit engagers to the army. On 1

January 1651 two of Lothian's sons were among the train bearers as Charles II was crowned at Scone. In March, with other covenanter nobles, Lothian argued for four hours with the king against readmitting the Hamiltons and other engagers to the army. With the final defeat of Charles and the Scots at Worcester, Lothian's days as a high-profile politician came to a close. Throughout the 1650s he resided at Newbattle, apart from a number of months between June 1655 and May 1656 in London, where he tried in vain to gain compensation for the expenses he had incurred on public business. Although there were rumours that he was inclined 'to take employment' under the protectorate (*Diary*, ed. Laing, 150), this did not happen. In 1660 he travelled to London, where he had an interview with the king and presented a paper defending his conduct since 1637. He was forced to resign as secretary of state, and though he was given a pension of £1000, this does not seem to have been paid in full. On 27 July 1661 he accompanied Argyll to the scaffold, along with his eldest son, who had married Argyll's daughter. Lothian refused to abjure the covenants and was fined £6000 in 1662. Despite the efforts of friends, the fines were not reduced, and he insisted that he could not afford to pay. On 5 August 1665 he assigned his estates to his son Robert, Lord Kerr of Newbattle, retaining only 'a mean portion' of life-rent. Because of his dire financial situation he was also forced to sell Ancram House. His wife died on 25 March 1667, and from this point little information about Lothian survives. He himself died in October 1675 at Newbattle Abbey.

Lothian's letters and personal manuscripts provide us with privileged access to his mentality. In contrast to Wariston, Lothian was no fervent militant, though his Calvinist piety was genuine. He reflected on approaching communion with 'true fayth in the promyse of salvation through the alone meryts of Jesus Chryst' (NL Scot., 'Miscellanies, or, Commonplace book', Newbattle MS 5788, fol. 9), and referred occasionally to election, 'the covenant of grace', and the necessity of divine revelation (NL Scot., 'Maxims', Newbattle MS 5787, fols. 3–4, 60–60r). When his wife died, he looked forward to her resurrection, and wrote, 'I kisse the rodde. I stoope and lay my selfe loue under His mighty hand, whoe doth every thing well' (*Correspondence*, 480). He wrote enthusiastically of the 'excellent sermons' of the fiery puritan Stephen Marshall (*Correspondence*, 192–3), though his favourite preacher was the eirenic minister of Newbattle, Robert Leighton, who became a bishop after the Restoration. When Leighton resigned his charge in 1652 Lothian wrote that this would be 'a great griefe to me, for never did I gett soe mutch good by any that stoode in a pulpitt' (*Correspondence*, 373). Although Lothian refused to abjure the covenants after 1660, he did not oppose the established church, and continued to act as patron of parish churches.

Lothian was also a sophisticated connoisseur of Renaissance culture. He collected many paintings for Newbattle Abbey and made impressive alterations to the property. In 1666 he listed 1361 books in his library catalogue, the vast majority of which he had collected himself (NL Scot.,

Newbattle MS 5818). The largest proportion were in French, and many others were in Latin or Italian, with only a few in English. The catalogue lists only a very small number of theological books, such as Bayly's *Practice of Piety* and Owen's *Communion with God*. Instead, the collection was rich in humanist works of history, philosophy, geography, politics, and even science. Besides classical works by Homer, Virgil, Cicero, Seneca, and Tacitus, Lothian had also acquired the writings of Machiavelli, Lipsius, Montaigne, Bacon, and Rabelais. His unpublished maxims reflect the influence of such authors, for they reveal his love of history and revolve around the key humanist concepts of virtue, honour, prudence, moderation, public good, and peace (NL Scot., Newbattle MS 5787). Lothian does not fit the stereotype of the covenanter as bigoted presbyterian zealot. His allegiance to the covenanters reminds us of the diversity of the movement which the ineptitude of Charles I's Scottish policies in the 1630s had produced.   JOHN COFFEY

Sources *Correspondence of Sir Robert Kerr, first earl of Ancram, and his son William, third earl of Lothian*, ed. D. Laing, 2 vols., Roxburghe Club, 100 (1875) · *The historical works of Sir James Balfour*, ed. J. Haig, 4 vols. (1824–5) · *The letters and journals of Robert Baillie*, ed. D. Laing, 3 vols. (1841–2) · Clarendon, *Hist. rebellion* · *Scots peerage* · GEC, *Peerage*, new edn · J. R. Young, *The Scottish parliament, 1639–1661: a political and constitutional analysis* (1996) · E. M. Furgol, *A regimental history of the covenanting armies, 1639–1651* (1990) · Venn, *Alum. Cant.*, 1/1; 1/3 · NL Scot., Newbattle MSS 5785, 5787, 5788, 5818 · *The diary of Alexander Brodie of Brodie … and of his son James Brodie*, ed. D. Laing, Spalding Club, 33 (1863) · *DNB* · *Burnet's History of my own time*, ed. O. Airy, new edn, 2 vols. (1897–1900)
Archives NA Scot., corresp. and papers · NL Scot., journal of tour of Italy | NA Scot., Lothian muniments, GD 40 · NL Scot., Newbattle collection, MSS 5730–5841
Likenesses H. Meyer, stipple, 1819 (after G. Jamesone), BM; repro. in E. Lodge, *Portraits of illustrious personages of Great Britain* (1819) · W. N. Gardiner, wash drawing, AM Oxf. · Jamieson, portrait, repro. in Laing, ed., *Correspondence of Sir Robert Kerr*, 2 vols. · H. Meyer, wash drawing, AM Oxf. · D. Scougall, portrait, priv. coll. [*see illus.*]
Wealth at death estates to son; Ancram House sold to pay debts

Kerr, William, second marquess of Lothian (*bap.* 1661, *d.* 1722), army officer and politician, was baptized at Newbattle, Edinburghshire, on 27 March 1661, the eldest son of Robert *Kerr, fourth earl and first marquess of Lothian (1636–1703), and his wife, Lady Jean Campbell (*d.* 1700), daughter of Archibald Campbell, marquess of Argyll. Nothing is known of his early years and education, but on 30 June 1685 he was contracted to marry his cousin Lady Jean Campbell (*c.*1661–1712), daughter of Archibald *Campbell, ninth earl of Argyll. They had a son and four daughters. Not surprisingly given his Campbell connection, Kerr was a zealous promoter of the revolution of 1688. In 1692 he succeeded as fifth Lord Jedburgh by virtue of a contract made in 1669 between his grandfather William Kerr, third earl of Lothian, and Robert Kerr, second Lord Jedburgh. In the Scottish parliament he was an adherent of the court, as was his brother-in-law Archibald *Campbell, tenth earl and first duke of Argyll. He combined politics with a military career, becoming colonel of the 7th dragoons on 1 October 1696. He became a brigadier-general in 1702. He succeeded his father on 15

February 1703, and was promoted major-general on 1 January 1704.

Lothian was now a political associate of his nephew John Campbell, second duke of Argyll, who was appointed commissioner for the session of the Scottish parliament in 1705. It was owing to Argyll's influence that Lothian received a promise from Queen Anne to be made a knight of the Thistle. Lothian proposed on 31 July 1705 a first reading for the bill setting in motion a treaty of union. After the session on 30 October 1705 he received his 'green ribbon'. Thereafter his fortunes tended to follow those of Argyll, and when Argyll was outmanoeuvred by James Douglas, second duke of Queensberry, Lothian was left out of the commission to negotiate a union with England. He was also disappointed in his attempt to succeed General George Ramsay as commander-in-chief in Scotland and had to wait until 25 April 1707 for the colonelcy of the foot guards which he had coveted for over a year. However, with Argyll back in favour by October 1706 and James Ogilvy, earl of Seafield, writing on 7 November 1706 that 'the Duke of Argyll influences the M. of Lothian and his own friends' (*Letters Relating to Scotland*, 101), Lothian supported the union in 1706, voting for the first article on 4 November 1706 and for ratification on 16 January 1707. He was promoted lieutenant-general on 1 January 1707. At Argyll's behest Lothian was chosen a Scottish representative peer in 1707 and again in 1708, but was unseated in February 1709 following a series of petitions objecting to the votes of some peers. John Macky described Lothian when aged about forty-five as 'very handsome; black, with a fine eye', and having 'abundance of fire and may prove a man of business when he applies himself that way; laughs at all revealed religion, yet sets up for a pillar of presbytery' (GEC, *Peerage*). A few years later Daniel Defoe thought Lothian had 'made himself odious by scandalous vices and immoralities, and sordid covetousness' (ibid.).

Following Argyll's decision to switch to the tories in 1710, Lothian appears to have assisted the tories in the 1710 election. He certainly felt able to solicit a British peerage from Robert Harley, first earl of Oxford, in June 1711 and was still asking for instructions on elections from Oxford in 1713. He ceased to be colonel of the Scots guards in 1713, and no doubt followed Argyll into opposition in early 1714. The ineligibility of Scottish peers to sit in the Lords under new British titles clearly rankled and he signed a petition to George I on the subject in November 1714. Back in favour under the new dynasty, in 1715 Lothian was elected a Scottish representative peer. He died in London on 28 February 1722 and was buried on 6 March in Westminster Abbey. His wife had died on 31 July 1712. He was succeeded by his son, William.

STUART HANDLEY

Sources Scots peerage, 5.475–8 · J. L. Chester, ed., *The marriage, baptismal, and burial registers of the collegiate church or abbey of St Peter, Westminster*, Harleian Society, 10 (1876), 305 · P. W. J. Riley, *The union of England and Scotland* (1978), 177, 300 · *Letters relating to Scotland in the reign of Queen Anne by James Ogilvy, first earl of Seafield and others*, ed. P. Hume Brown, Scottish History Society, 2nd ser., 11 (1915), 10, 52, 62, 101, 166 · *Report on the manuscripts of the earl of Mar and Kellie*, HMC, 60 (1904), 254, 318, 373–5 · *The manuscripts of his grace the duke of Portland*, 10 vols., HMC, 29 (1891–1931), vol. 4, pp. 232, 390; vol. 5, p. 5; vol. 10, pp. 184, 210 · P. W. J. Riley, *King William and the Scottish politicians* (1979), 167 · P. W. J. Riley, *The English ministers and Scotland, 1707–1727* (1964), 109, 115, 262 · C. Dalton, ed., *English army lists and commission registers, 1661–1714*, 4 (1898), 3, 120; 5 (1902), 159, 207, 226 · BL, Add. MS 61136, fols. 29–30, 35, 49–50 · *The manuscripts of J. J. Hope Johnstone*, HMC, 46 (1897), 126–7 · N. Luttrell, *A brief historical relation of state affairs from September 1678 to April 1714*, 6 (1857), 151, 377, 403 · IGI

Likenesses W. N. Gardiner, wash drawing (after J. B. Medina), AM Oxf. · Scougal(?), portrait, Newbattle Abbey, Lothian

Kerr, William Henry, fourth marquess of Lothian (*c.*1712–1775), army officer, was the eldest son of William, third marquess (*c.*1690–1767), and Margaret (*d.* 1759), daughter and coheir of Sir Thomas Nicholson of Kemney, first baronet. Until his father's accession to the marquessate in 1722 he was known as Lord Jedburgh; afterwards, as earl of Ancrum. He was appointed a cornet in his granduncle Lord Mark Kerr's regiment (the 11th dragoons) on 20 June 1735. On 6 November of that year, at St James's, Westminster, he married Lady Caroline D'Arcy (*d.* 1778), only daughter of Robert, third earl of Holdernesse; she brought him £20,000. On 9 January 1739 he was made captain in Cornwallis's regiment of foot (the 11th) and in 1741 he was promoted captain and lieutenant-colonel in the 1st regiment of foot guards (the Grenadier Guards).

Ancrum acted as aide-de-camp to William, duke of Cumberland, at Fontenoy (30 April 1745), where he was wounded by a shot in the head. On 4 June 1745 he was promoted to the brevet rank of colonel in the army and on 22 June returned to the 11th dragoons with the rank of lieutenant-colonel. Together with his regiment he joined Cumberland's forces in England in the summer and autumn of 1745, in pursuit of the Jacobite army. In early 1746, after the battle of Falkirk, he joined the government army in Scotland, now under Cumberland's command. In March Cumberland placed him in command of a small force of 100 troopers and 300 foot, dispatched from Aberdeen to take a quantity of Spanish arms and powder stored at Castle Corgaff, at the head of the River Don. Upon his approach the Jacobites quitted the castle, having destroyed the munitions. He returned safely without loss, causing Cumberland to report, 'during the whole expedition he has behaved with the greatest prudence and caution, and much like an officer' (Williams, 39).

At the battle of Culloden, Ancrum was placed in command of the cavalry on the extreme left wing. His orders were to move forward on the flank in readiness for a general pursuit of the highland army, once it was broken and in retreat. Cumberland noted that he carried the pursuit, 'with so good an effect that a very considerable number were killed' (Brett-Smith, 18). Indeed the royal cavalry inflicted terrible casualties across Culloden Moor, and Ancrum, although 'a chivalrous and compassionate man' (Prebble, 115), was ineffectual in preventing the slaughter. His brother Robert, a captain in the grenadier company of Barrel's regiment, which met the full onslaught of the highland charge before it was turned and broken, 'was the person of greatest distinction who was killed there' (Scots peerage, 5.480).

Immediately after the battle Ancrum was sent to the east coast of Scotland to suppress any continuing signs of revolt and to prevent Charles Edward Stuart's escape. After Cumberland's departure he was placed in command of the royal cavalry in Scotland. He rejoined Cumberland on the continent in August 1747 and on 1 December that year was made colonel of the 24th foot, later the South Wales Borderers.

Ancrum represented Richmond in parliament between 1747 and 1763 in the interest of his brother-in-law, Robert D'Arcy, fourth earl of Holdernesse. In the Commons he followed Cumberland's political lead. On the death of his grand-uncle in 1752 he became colonel of the 11th dragoons (8 February) and on 5 November 1755 he was promoted major-general. He served as lieutenant-general under the command of Charles Spencer, third duke of Marlborough, in the expedition to St Malo in 1758. He left his Commons seat in March 1763 after Holdernesse sold Richmond to Sir Lawrence Dundas.

Ancrum succeeded as fourth marquess of Lothian on his father's death on 28 July 1767. On 26 October 1768 he was chosen one of the sixteen representative peers in Scotland, and invested a knight of the Thistle at St James's Palace. He was promoted to the rank of general in 1770, and died at Bath on 12 April 1775. The marchioness died on 15 November 1778. They had three children: William John, fifth marquess; Louisa, who married Lord George Henry Lennox; and Willielmina, who married John Macleod, colonel in the Royal Artillery.   JONATHAN SPAIN

Sources GEC, *Peerage*, new edn · *Scots peerage* · R. R. Sedgwick, 'Kerr, William', HoP, *Commons, 1715–54* · M. M. Drummond, 'Kerr, William', HoP, *Commons, 1754–90* · Burke, *Peerage* (1999) · G. T. Williams, *Historical records of the 11th hussars* (1908) · G. Paton, F. Glennie, and W. P. Symons, eds., *Historical records of the 24th regiment, from its formation, in 1689* (1892) · C. T. Atkinson, *The south Wales borderers, 24th foot, 1689–1937* (1937) · R. Brett-Smith, *The 11th hussars* (1969) · J. Prebble, *Culloden* (1961) · W. A. Speck, *The Butcher: the duke of Cumberland and the suppression of the 45* (1981)
Archives BL, corresp. with earl of Holdernesse · BL, corresp. with duke of Newcastle
Likenesses oils, *c.*1735, Gov. Art Coll. · D. Morier, oils, Scot. NPG · attrib. D. Morier, oils; on loan to Gov. Art Coll.

Kerrich, Thomas (1748–1828), artist and antiquary, was born at the vicarage, Dersingham, Norfolk, on 4 February 1748, the only son of Samuel Kerrich (1696–1768), vicar of Dersingham and rector of Wolferton and West Newton, Norfolk, and his second wife, Barbara (1706–1762), elder daughter of Matthew Postlethwayte, archdeacon of Norwich. Educated at Dersingham school, he soon demonstrated his precocious artistic talents. In 1766, following in his father's footsteps, he had begun a series of studies of the early fourteenth-century knight's effigy in his father's church of Banham, carefully recording evidence of colour and patterning on the monument. His parents had applied to William Hogarth for advice but he, in praising a 'pretty performance', dissuaded them from letting their son take up art for a living on the grounds that the profession was overcrowded. Accordingly Kerrich was educated at Magdalene College, Cambridge, whence he graduated

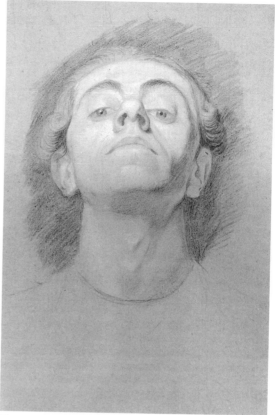

Thomas Kerrich (1748–1828), self-portrait, 1774

BA in 1771 as second senior optime. He was elected to a Wort's travelling scholarship and set out for a four-year tour of the continent in the company of his pupil, Daniel Pettiward, of Trinity College, Cambridge. Throughout his grand tour Kerrich drew medieval monuments. He travelled first to the Netherlands where he fell in love with the work of Rubens and Heemskerk. He was awarded a silver medal for his drawing by the Academy of Painting at Antwerp. He travelled to France, where he spent much of 1772–3 in Paris. Either on this visit, or on his next visit in 1784, he drew in Le Mans, in Cambrai, and the monument to Philippe le Hardi then still reposing in the Chartreuse at Dijon. He spent a year in Rome where he drew classical antiquities as well recording the monuments of medieval knights in Modena, Milan, Siena, Florence, Pisa, Lucca, Bologna, and Civita Castellana; he also gained a deep understanding of Italian medieval architecture.

By 1775 Kerrich had returned to Cambridge where he gained his MA and was elected a fellow of Magdalene. In spite of William Cole's attempt to persuade him to become a portrait painter Kerrich entered the Church of England and was ordained priest at Peterborough on 20 May 1784. He returned to France that year where he gained access to the Cabinet des Dessins and recorded medieval tombs later destroyed in the Revolution. From 1789 to 1796 he served as president of Magdalene, then dominated by the evangelical party. Kerrich was no friend to the evangelicals, whose influence waned during his presidency. In 1793 he acted as taxor of the university and in 1796 he resigned as president. Two years later, on 13 September 1798, he married Sophia (1762–1835), the fourth daughter of the Cambridge physician Richard Hayles, at St Botolph's, Cambridge. They had one son, Richard (1801–1872), and two daughters, the younger of whom, Frances Margaretta, married the Revd Charles Henry *Hartshorne, an antiquary. In 1798 Kerrich became a prebendary of Lincoln Cathedral and in 1812 of Wells.

On 21 September 1797 Kerrich became Cambridge's protobibliothecarius and in the same year was elected a fellow of the Society of Antiquaries. His record as principal librarian of the university has not always been admired. He inherited a position where the problems of copyright were largely resolved and where four cataloguers had been recently appointed. A proper author and subject catalogue was put in hand in 1818. Edward Clarke was a sympathetic sub-librarian and under his influence Kerrich concentrated on acquiring, like his predecessor Richard Farmer, older European publications to complement works of art then in the library.

Kerrich, who was a keen but discerning collector, was involved in many of the great projects of the infant discipline of art history: Horace Walpole's and James Essex's outline for a history of English architecture; Richard Gough's *Sepulchral Monuments*; William Ottley's proposed history of early English painting; John Boydell's Shakspeare Gallery; Sir John Fenn's edition of the Paston letters, which he illustrated with his own lithographs of his portraits; and Sir William Musgrave's undertaking to acquire a complete list of all the pictures in country houses. A skilled and diligent recorder of ancient monuments, he was admired by Charles Stothard, who attributed his achievements to Kerrich's guidance.

Kerrich published four scholarly papers on Gothic buildings and monuments in *Archaeologia*, which were accompanied by his own illustrations. The last of these, 'Observations on the use of the mysterious figure called Vesica Piscis in the architecture of the Middle Ages, and in Gothic architecture', expresses a correct interpretation of the proportions of the ground-plan of Old St Peter's, Rome, although it did not convince all its readers at the time. Kerrich's *Catalogue of the prints which have been engraved after Martin Heemskerk, or, rather, An essay towards such a catalogue*, which was published posthumously in 1829, stands today as the best study of its subject. It is disputed whether he or Robert Masters was the author of an anonymous 'Catalogue of portraits in Cambridge colleges' printed about 1790. William Musgrave's copy, in the British Library, is inscribed in his hand 'Masters', yet most scholars believe it to be Kerrich's work. His own copy is heavily annotated.

Kerrich saw himself as unpopular but he was a friend to most of the antiquaries and artists of his time. He knew well John Flaxman, Joseph Nollekins, Henry Fuseli, Francis Douce, Samuel Lysons, and many of his father's generation, such as Thomas Martin of Palgrave. In 1778 he exchanged portrait prints with Horace Walpole. The brothers Facius engraved Kerrich's portrait drawings of numerous contemporaries. Kerrich was painted in turn in 1815 by Henry Perronet Briggs at the behest of his close friend, Edward Balme. In 1823 he became coheir, with Francis Douce, of the bulk of Nollekins's estate.

Kerrich died at his house in Free School Lane, Cambridge, on 10 May 1828 and was buried in the chancel of Dersingham church. To the university he gave the twelfth-century leper chapel at Barnwell, near Cambridge, which he had bought and restored in 1816. To the university library he gave the portrait of the Lucasian professor, Nicholas Saunderson, by John Vanderbank, and to the Society of Antiquaries he bequeathed his remarkable collection of fifteenth- and early sixteenth-century English and European paintings. After his son's death the Fitzwilliam Museum acquired the best of his sixteenth- and seventeenth-century Netherlandish pictures, notably Rubens's sketches for a set of tapestries depicting the Triumph of the Eucharist, commissioned in 1623 by the Infanta Isabella for the convent of Descalzas Reales in Madrid, and Rubens's design for a title-page, published in 1641.

PAMELA TUDOR-CRAIG

Sources T. Kerrich, correspondence, CCC Cam., MSS 584–611 · BL, Add. MSS 4221, 5726, 5824, 5855, 5874, 6728–6759 · D. McKitterick, *Cambridge University Library, a history: the eighteenth and nineteenth centuries* (1986), chaps. 9, 10 · W. Cole, 'Glass paintings after Heemskerk in England', *Antiquaries Journal*, 60/2 (1980), esp. 248–9 · Walpole, *Corr.* · *GM*, 1st ser., 98/2 (1828), 185 · *GM*, 2nd ser., 4 (1835), 332 · G. W. Owst, 'Iconomania in eighteenth-century Cambridge', *Proceedings of the Cambridge Antiquarian Society*, 42 (1948), 67–91 · P. Cunich and others, *A history of Magdalene College, Cambridge, 1428–1988* (1994), 185, 193 · C. Brooke, *A history of Gonville and Caius College* (1985), 179–82 · T. Cocke, *The ingenious Mr. Essex, architect: a bicentenary exhibition*, nos. 3, 6, 8, 16, 26, pp. 43, 45 [exhibition catalogue, Fitzwilliam Museum, Cambridge] · A. L. Munby, *Connoisseurs and medieval miniatures, 1750–1850* (1972), 42 · Farington, *Diary*, 3.864, 1209; 8.2971, 3146 · J. Goodison, *Catalogue of Cambridge portraits* (1955), XXIII, 26 (30) 85 (119) · Nichols, *Illustrations*, 6.308, 807, 817, 821–8 · C. H. Cooper and J. W. Cooper, *Annals of Cambridge*, 5 vols. (1842–1908), vol. 4, p. 557 · will, PRO, PROB 11/1742/1366 · monument, Dersingham church

Archives BL, Add. MSS 4221, 5726, 5824, 5855, 5874 · BL, drawings, notes, plans, Add. MSS 6728–6776 · CCC Cam., corresp., MSS 584–611 · CUL, family corresp. · Norfolk RO, corresp. and papers · Northants. RO, notebooks, sketches · priv. coll., sketchbooks · S. Antiquaries, Lond., sketches | Bodl. Oxf., corresp. with Francis Douce

Likenesses T. Kerrich, self-portrait, chalk drawing, 1774, NPG [see illus.] · oils, 1795, Magd. Cam. · H. P. Briggs, portrait, 1815, priv. coll. · G. S. Facius, stipple, pubd 1815 (after H. P. Briggs), BM, NPG · chalk portrait, priv. coll.

Wealth at death wealthy: will

Kerrigan, Peter (1899–1977), political organizer, was born on 26 June 1899, at 171 Sandyfaulds Street, Hutchesontown, Glasgow, the son of Peter Kerrigan, a hammerman and later a tramway car driver, and his wife, Mary Ingram Rice (or Ryce), a weaver. He left school in 1914 and was apprenticed at the North British Loco Company in Springburn. From June 1918 to May 1920 he saw service in the Middle East with the Royal Scots. In April 1921 he joined the Communist Party of Great Britain (CPGB). Like many others in Glasgow he disagreed with the party's decision, taken as part of the united front tactic, not to stand candidates against Labour in the 1922 general election. He quit the party, returning in 1924.

Kerrigan was heir to the traditions of Clydeside militancy and from 1923 to 1925 worked as an iron-turner in one of its centres, Beardmore's Parkhead Forge, where he became convenor. Intermittently unemployed, he was a pillar of Glasgow labour in the Amalgamated Engineering Union (AEU) and on the trades council, and played a prominent role in the general strike as chair of the central strike co-ordinating committee. He attended the Third Congress of the Red International of Labour Unions and the Fifth Congress of the Communist International (Comintern) in Moscow in 1924, the beginning of lifelong links with the USSR. On Christmas eve 1926 he married Rose Klasko (1903–1995), a union activist in the clothing trades and foundation member of the CPGB, daughter of Benjamin Klasko, a tailor. The following year he was elected to the executive of the party, a position he retained—with one year's absence—until 1965.

In 1929 Kerrigan was chosen to study at the Lenin School in Moscow. He was appointed the CPGB's Scottish organizer in 1930. Over 6 feet tall, Big Peter was, for most of his life, a teetotaller with a reputation as a political conformist, an austere disciplinarian with a flickering sense of humour. His organizational skills were displayed in the Scotland to London unemployed marches of 1934 and 1936, and his success marked by the election of Willie Gallacher as MP for West Fife in 1935 and the trebling of Scottish membership by 1939. In 1935 he was appointed CPGB representative to the Comintern. In this capacity he had dealings with the South African Communist Party and participated in the Seventh Congress of the Comintern, which formalized the turn of policy from 'class against class' to the popular front.

With the outbreak of the Spanish Civil War, Kerrigan served from December 1937 to April 1938 as a member of the Comintern political commission in Spain. Working under Comintern leader André Marty, Kerrigan was commissar for English-speaking International Brigaders at the Albacete base. He reaffirmed his reputation for discipline and won a new one for courage under fire. After brief spells in Moscow and Britain, he returned to Spain as *Daily Worker* correspondent from May to November 1938. Home once more, he presided over the CPGB's campaign for a Scottish parliament (see his pamphlet *Scotland's March to Peace and Progress*, 1939), made overtures to the Scottish nationalists, and organized a broad-based Scottish convention, though this was aborted by the outbreak of war.

The CPGB's switch from supporting to opposing the Second World War in October 1939 was a test of Kerrigan's Stalinism. He was carried through by his 'sense of loyalty and discipline … we were members of a world communist movement that had an executive with executive powers in Moscow' (Kerrigan, 'British involvement in the Spanish Civil War', 51). He was soon asserting that it was a war by Britain 'to enslave the German people' (P. Kerrigan, *The*

New Stage of the War, 1940, 11). He accepted the further somersault to supporting the war as equably as he did the Hitler–Stalin pact. He was CPGB industrial organizer during 1939–42, national organizer in 1943–51, and national industrial organizer in 1951–65. He stood unsuccessfully for parliament in Shettleston in 1945 and for the Gorbals in a by-election in 1948 and subsequent general elections to 1959.

Kerrigan deserves credit for holding the party's industrial base together during the cold war. Members who encountered him in the 1950s found him 'hard' and 'inflexible'. The events of 1956 shook his faith in Stalin but not in the USSR. A year later he was front-page news. Amid concern over electoral malpractice in the Electrical Trades Union (ETU), it was discovered that the returning officer in a disputed election in the AEU involving a CPGB member was the party's industrial organizer. The best that can be said about Kerrigan's involvement with the ETU ballot-rigging which culminated in the 1961 High Court findings of conspiracy and fraud against party members is that he was incompetent. It is difficult to avoid the judgement that if he didn't know, he should have. The allegations were common knowledge, former party members claimed they raised them, and from 1951 he attended the party's ETU national advisory committee. A further incident in 1964 when a Kerrigan circular paved the way for a ban on communists holding office in the union led to his censure by the party. He stepped down from the executive the following year.

For thirty-five years Kerrigan held key positions in the CPGB. He made a particular contribution to establishing communism in Scotland. His career personifies the manner in which a section of militant workers came to accept Stalinism and the policy imperatives of the USSR. Peter Kerrigan died suddenly at Lewisham Hospital of a heart attack on 15 December 1977 after a life of struggle devoted to the Soviet Union's conception of working-class emancipation. His remains were cremated at the South London crematorium on 22 December. 　　　　JOHN MCILROY

Sources Kerrigan MSS, People's History Museum, Manchester, Communist Party archive, CP/IND/MISC/7, 11, 18, 19, 21, 22 · P. Kerrigan, 'British involvement in the Spanish Civil War, 1936–1939', interview, tape, and transcript, 1976, IWM SA, Acc. 00810/06 · P. Kerrigan, *The road to Spain: anti-fascists at war, 1936–1939*, ed. D. Corkhill and S. Rawnsley (1981), 55–62 · P. Kerrigan, 'From Glasgow', *The general strike 1926*, ed. J. Skelley (1976), 315–29 · P. Kerrigan, in R. A. Leeson, *Strike: a live history, 1887–1971* (1973), 80–81, 90, 114–16 [interview] · *The Times* (17 Dec 1977) · *Morning Star* (17 Dec 1977) · *Morning Star* (23 Dec 1977) · b. cert. · d. cert. · S. Russell, 'Great hearted Kerrigan', *Morning Star* (17 Dec 1977) · J. Lloyd, *Light and liberty: a history of the EETPU* (1990) · F. Copeman, *Reason in revolt* (1948) · B. Alexander, *British volunteers for liberty: Spain, 1936–39* (1982) · B. Darke, *The communist technique in Britain* (1952) · private information (2004) [G. Anthony; R. Frow; K. Halpin; B. Moore; K. Morgan] · I. McDougall, *Voices from the hunger marches*, 2 vols. (1990–91)
Archives Marx Memorial Library, London, corresp. and papers relating to war in Spain · People's History Museum, Manchester, Communist Party archive · Russian Centre for the Preservation and Study of Documents of Recent History, Moscow |FILM BFI NFTVA, documentary footage |SOUND IWM SA, 'British civilian

in England, 1912–1936', IWM, 1976, 810 • IWM SA, oral history interview

Likenesses photograph, 1936, repro. in Copeman, *Reason in revolt*, facing p. 96 • photograph, Jan 1948, repro. in H. Pelling, *The British Communist Party: a historical profile* (1958), facing p. 136 • double portrait, photograph (in youth; with Rose), repro. in *The Guardian* (19 July 1995) • photographs, repro. in *Morning Star* (17 Dec 1977)

Kerrison, Sir Edward, first baronet (1776–1853), army officer, was the only son of Matthias Kerrison (1742–1827), who, from 'an inferior station in life' (*GM*, 1827, 477), had accumulated a fortune through trade, and his wife, Mary, daughter of Edward Barnes of Barnham, Suffolk; he was born at his father's seat, Hexne Hall, near Bungay, Suffolk, on 30 July 1776. He entered the army as cornet in the 6th (Inniskilling) dragoons on 23 June 1796, was promoted captain in October 1798, and was transferred to the 7th hussars that year. With the 7th he served in the Helder expedition of 1799, taking part in the actions of 19 September and 2 and 6 October. He was promoted major in 1803, and lieutenant-colonel in 1805. In October 1808 he embarked with the 7th for Spain, and the following December was severely wounded on the plains of León. He commanded the 7th at the passage of the Oleron, in the action of Sauveterne, and at the battles of Orthez and Toulouse. At the battle of Orthez, the charge headed by Lord Edward Somerset, in which Kerrison with the 7th hussars took the chief part, was highly commended by Wellington. In 1813 he was promoted brevet colonel.

Kerrison served in the 1815 campaign, and was slightly wounded at Waterloo, where his horse was shot under him; but he continued with his regiment, and took part in the occupation of Paris. He was knighted on 5 January 1815; was made CB on 22 June 1815 and KCH in 1821, and created a baronet by patent dated on 27 July 1821; he was made GCH in 1831 and KCB on 18 July 1840. He was tory MP for Shaftesbury from 1812 to 1818, for Northampton from 1818 to 1824, and for Eye, which he had purchased, from 1824 to 1852. He voted against Roman Catholic relief in 1813, 1816, and 1817. Promoted lieutenant-general in 1837, he became a general in 1851.

Kerrison married, on 20 October 1813, Mary Martha (d. 19 April 1860), daughter of Alexander Ellice of Pittencrieff, Fife. They had one son, Edward Clarence Kerrison, second baronet (1821–1886), MP, at whose death the baronetcy became extinct, and three daughters, the second of whom, Emily Harriet (d. 1873), married in 1834 Philip Henry, Viscount Mahon, the historian, afterwards fifth Earl Stanhope. Kerrison died at his house, 13 Great Stanhope Street, London, on 9 March 1853.

THOMAS SECCOMBE, *rev.* ROGER T. STEARN

Sources *GM*, 1st ser., 97/1 (1827), 477 • *GM*, 2nd ser., 39 (1853), 542 • *Annual Register* (1853) • *United Service Gazette* (1853) • J. Foster, *The peerage, baronetage, and knightage of the British empire for 1883*, 2 [1883] • R. Cannon, ed., *Historical record of the seventh, or the queen's own regiment of hussars* (1842) • HoP, *Commons* • R. Muir, *Britain and the defeat of Napoleon, 1807–1815* (1996) • Boase, *Mod. Eng. biog.* • Burke, *Peerage* (1907)

Likenesses W. C. Edwards, line engraving, pubd 1818 (after M. A. Shee), BM; NPG • T. H. Maguire, lithograph, 1851, BM, NPG • J. Brown, stipple (after a photograph by J. E. Mayall), NPG •

G. Hayter, group portrait, oils (*The House of Commons, 1833*), NPG • W. Salter, group portrait, oils (*Waterloo banquet at Apsley House*), Wellington Museum, Apsley House, London • W. Salter, oils, study (*Waterloo banquet*), NPG

Kerry. For this title name *see* Fitzgerald, Maurice, eighteenth knight of Kerry (1774–1849); Fitzgerald, Sir Peter George, nineteenth knight of Kerry (1808–1880).

Kerry and Lixnaw. For this title name *see* Fitzmaurice, Thomas, sixteenth baron of Kerry and Lixnaw (*c*.1502–1590); Fitzmaurice, Patrick, seventeenth baron of Kerry and Lixnaw (*c*.1551–1600); Fitzmaurice, Thomas, eighteenth baron of Kerry and Lixnaw (1574–1630).

Kerseboom, Frederick (1632–1693), painter, was born in Solingen in Germany. His family name was Casaubon according to Samuel Pepys, who described him in a letter of 30 August 1689 to John Evelyn as 'one of much less name than Kneller's, and a stranger' (*Letters and the Second Diary*, 204–5). Kerseboom trained in Amsterdam before studying with Charles le Brun in Paris in the 1650s. He then spent fourteen years in Rome, two of them in Poussin's studio.

In the 1680s Kerseboom moved to London with his nephew Johann Kerseboom [*see below*]. There he executed a few Poussin-influenced history paintings, which are now known only from engravings. According to George Vertue, Kerseboom turned to portrait painting out of economic necessity (Vertue, *Note books*, 5.50). Few of his portraits have been identified. In *Theophilus Leigh* (signed and dated 1685; Trustees of Stoneleigh Abbey Ltd, Warwickshire) Kerseboom presented his sitter with a somewhat rigid dignity, but his pendant portrait *The Hon. Mary Leigh* demonstrates that the painter could depict a female sitter with elegance, and that he was familiar with the fashionable style of Willem Wissing in ladies' portraiture. Kerseboom also produced a half-length self-portrait and worked on glass (according to Buckeridge, 361–2). Frederick Kerseboom died in London and was buried in London at St Andrew's Church, Holborn, on 30 March 1693.

Johann [John] **Kerseboom** (d. 1708), painter, initially worked in Germany before coming to England in the 1680s with his uncle. Johann's early portrait of *Lady Grace Carteret* (Petworth House, Sussex) was engraved by John Smith. His portrait of the *Electress Sophia Dorothea* is known from an engraving by William Faithorne (impression, BM), who also executed six mezzotints after Johann Kerseboom's works.

While Johann Kerseboom's early works reveal the influence of Wissing, he developed his own stylistic idiosyncrasies, including a tendency to elongate the faces of his sitters. He is best-known for his portrait *Robert Boyle*, which became the standard image of the scientist. Several versions exist in the Royal Collection, at the Royal Society, the National Portrait Gallery, and elsewhere, and the portrait was engraved by, among others, John Smith in 1689.

Johann Kerseboom sometimes collaborated with his friend the Dutch painter–engraver Jan Vander Vaart, as in the portrait *Gilbert, Fourth Earl of Coventry* (Antony, Cornwall). Dated 1704, it was signed by Kerseboom and Vander

Vaart. The friends may also have worked together on the full-length portrait *Thomas Osborne, First Duke of Leeds* (1704; NPG). Johann Kerseboom died in London, where he was buried on 26 October 1708. In his will, dated 20 March 1694, Kerseboom stated:

> I stand indebted and doe owe unto my very loveing Friend John Vander Vaart of the parish of St. Paul Covent Garden in the county of Middlesex Painter a considerable sume of money which I am not at present able to pay … Therefore in Satisfaction I give and bequeath unto the said John Vander Vaart All my Estate.

One of his witnesses was the limner Bernard Lens.

ANNE THACKRAY

Sources R. Jeffree, 'Kerseboom', *The dictionary of art*, ed. J. Turner (1996), vol. 17, pp. 915–16 • [B. Buckeridge], 'An essay towards an English school', in R. de Piles, *The art of painting, with the lives and characters of above 300 of the most eminent painters*, 3rd edn (1754), 354–439; facs. edn (1969), 361–2 • C. H. C. Baker, *Lely and the Stuart portrait painters: a study of English portraiture before and after van Dyck*, 2 (1912), 49ff. • Vertue, *Note books*, vols. 4, 5 • E. Waterhouse, *Painting in Britain, 1530–1790* (1953); 4th edn (1978) • M. K. Whinney and O. Millar, *English art, 1625–1714* (1957), 192, n. 3 • O. Millar, *The Tudor, Stuart and early Georgian pictures in the collection of her majesty the queen*, 2 vols. (1963), vol. 1, p. 141 and pl. 145 • O. Millar, 'Gilbert Coventry and his sporting and other paintings', *Burlington Magazine*, 133 (1991), 537–41 • *Letters and the second diary of Samuel Pepys*, ed. R. G. Howarth (1932), 204–5 • will of J. Kerseboom, PRO, PROB 11/505, sig. 263 • inventory, 1996, Stoneleigh Abbey Ltd

Kerseboom, Johann (*d.* 1708). *See under* Kerseboom, Frederick (1632–1693).

Kersey, John, the elder (*bap.* 1616, *d.* 1677), mathematician, son of Anthony Carsaye or Kersey and Alice Fenimore, was baptized at Bodicote, near Banbury, Oxfordshire, on 23 November 1616. He was employed, probably in the 1630s, as tutor to Alexander and Edmund Denton, grandsons of the royalist Sir Alexander Denton, kt (1596–1645) of Hillesden House, Buckinghamshire. In the 1673 dedication of his *Elements of … Algebra* to his former pupils, Kersey expressed gratitude to the family which 'gave both birth and nourishment to his mathematical studies'; his reference to Charles I as 'of ever-blessed memory' might or might not have been from conviction.

By 1650 Kersey was established in London, in Charles Street, near the Covent Garden piazza, as teacher of mathematics and surveyor, and had made the acquaintance of Edmund Wingate, author of *Natural and Artificiall Arithmetique* (2 vols., 1630). Wingate's stock of his *Arithmetique* was becoming exhausted, and he had sufficient confidence in Kersey's ability to ask him to revise and augment the first part of this work for reprinting as a self-contained volume. In this second edition of over 480 pages, published as *Arithmetique Made Easie* (1650), Kersey added a seven-chapter appendix. He 'framed totally anew, the Rules of Division, Reduction … delivered the Doctrine of Fractions … newly framed the Extraction of … roots'. There were eleven further editions by the end of the century, and from 1704 the work was edited by George Shelley (1666–1736) and continued to appear until 1760.

This success encouraged Kersey to embark on his major work, the two-volume *Elements of that Mathematical Art Commonly called Algebra* (1673–4). It was ready in 1667, and his friend John Collins (1626–1683) made strenuous efforts to persuade booksellers to undertake the printing, but times were hard and paper dear. A prospectus was issued early in 1672. In the May Isaac Newton (1642–1727) promised to subscribe, and by July had procured three other subscriptions from Cambridge. Richard Towneley (1629–1707) of Towneley, near Burnley, Lancashire, likewise subscribed and canvassed support.

Kersey based his work mainly on English authors, including Harriot, Oughtred, John Wallis, and Isaac Barrow. Since the subject had only recently attracted attention, his list of all signs and abbreviations is especially interesting. Negative numbers he regarded as fictitious. By 1676 Collins reported that sales were good, and the book became a standard authority used by later authors, such as Edward Cocker. According to one writer, it was judged 'to be the clearest, and most comprehensive system … in any language' (Granger, 2.363–4).

Kersey had been living at the sign of The Globe, Shandoise (Chandos) Street, off St Martin's Lane, Covent Garden, since at least 1670. He died there in mid-May 1677, having long suffered from a stone in the bladder, and was buried at St Paul, Covent Garden, on 23 May. Another John Kersey, presumably his son although nothing is known of a marriage, was a teacher of mathematics in Chandos Street in 1697 and probably died about 1698. The Wingate series had no reference to Kersey the elder's 1677 death, but in 1699 new publishers described the author as 'late teacher of the Mathematicks'; possibly confused themselves, they confused posterity as well.

John Kersey the younger (*b. c.*1660, *d.* in or after 1721), lexicographer, was born about 1660, the son of John, citizen and stationer of St Paul's, Covent Garden, London, who was probably the second John Kersey aforesaid. This third man of the same name was apprenticed in the Stationers' Company on 6 October 1673 to John Martyn and freed on 11 October 1680. In the fourteenth edition (1720) of Wingate's *Arithmetique* there appeared the claim that it was 'now exactly corrected by John Kersey, the last author's son', and the *Dictionary of National Biography*, following this source, also made Kersey the younger a son of Kersey the elder.

Kersey the younger was in a publishing partnership with Henry Faithorne at The Rose in St Paul's Churchyard in 1681–6. Their *Weekly Memorials for the Ingenious*, an abstracting journal, appeared for a year from January 1682; after a quarrel with the anonymous editor, Kersey may have edited the latter issues. He was probably the translator of Plutarch's *Discourse to an Unlearned Prince* (1685), reprinted in 1870 in *Plutarch's Morals*, vol. 4. In 1687 he took as apprentice his brother Alexander, who may have died before completing. He called himself 'Philobibl.' when revising and augmenting the folio sixth edition of E. Phillips's *New World of Words, or, Universal English Dictionary* (1706; 3rd edn, 1721); he had added '20,000 hard words in arts and sciences', while stating that it was 'no part of our design to teach liberal or mechanical arts and sciences as a late learned author has attempted to do', referring to the 1704 *Lexicon technicum* by John Harris. In 1708 he published the octavo *Dictionarium Anglo-Britannicum*, a condensed 'portable' version of the 'voluminous' 1706 work. He was ostensibly still alive when a third, corrected and enlarged, edition appeared in 1721.

RUTH WALLIS

Sources S. P. Rigaud and S. J. Rigaud, eds., *Correspondence of scientific men of the seventeenth century*, 2 vols. (1841) · E. G. R. Taylor, *The mathematical practitioners of Tudor and Stuart England* (1954), 219 · *DNB* · J. Granger, *A biographical history of England, from Egbert the Great to the revolution*, 2 (1769), 363–4 · D. F. McKenzie, ed., *Stationers' Company apprentices*, [2]: *1641–1700* (1974), nos. 2496, 2903 · H. R. Plomer and others, *A dictionary of the printers and booksellers who were at work in England, Scotland, and Ireland from 1668 to 1725* (1922), 114–15, 178

Likenesses W. Faithorne, line engraving (after a painting by Soust, 1672), BM, NPG; repro. in J. Kersey, *Elements of … algebra* (1673), frontispiece

Kersey, John, the younger (*b. c.*1660, *d.* in or after **1721**). *See under* Kersey, John, the elder (*bap.* 1616, *d.* 1677).

Kershaw, Arthur (*fl.* **1800**). *See under* Kershaw, James (*bap.* 1730?, *d.* 1797).

Kershaw, James (*bap.* 1730?, *d.* **1797**), Methodist preacher, was born in Halifax, and may be the individual of that name, son of another James Kershaw, who was baptized in the town on 8 September 1730. Details of his upbringing are unknown. He joined a Socinian club in Halifax, whose members deputed him and another, in 1761, to attend a sermon to be delivered by the evangelical Henry Venn at Huddersfield, in order 'to furnish matter of merriment for the next meeting'. But Kershaw left the church after the sermon exclaiming, 'Surely God is in this place; there is no matter for laughter here.' He subsequently called on the preacher, was converted, and became one of Venn's constant correspondents. Kershaw soon afterwards became known as an itinerant Methodist preacher; he accompanied John Wesley on some of his journeys in the north of England, and was with him in Scotland in 1764 and 1765.

Kershaw settled at Gainsborough, Lincolnshire, about 1770, and was famous in the neighbourhood for his quack medicines. He continued to preach occasionally for the Methodists, and Wesley visited him at Tealby in 1786. Thomas Jackson remembered hearing him preach in a Yorkshire farmhouse: 'He was a fine-looking man, and was known in Yorkshire by the name of "Dr Kershaw". He travelled through the country in his own vehicle, preaching in the villages and giving medical advice to the labouring classes' (Jackson, 220). Charles Atmore described him as talented but unstable, a judgement borne out by James Everett's account of how he was so eager to impress the marquess of Rockingham when given an opportunity of preaching before him that he overshot the mark and brought ridicule and dishonour on the Methodism he represented. Similarly, his well-intentioned intervention in the dispute over the publication of James Hervey's letters to Wesley in 1764 only served to exacerbate the controversy.

Much of Kershaw's leisure after leaving the itinerancy was devoted to writing. In 1780 he published *An Essay on the Principal Parts of the Book of the Revelations*. The same year his epic poem *The Methodist Attempted in Plain Metre* was published in Nottingham. Wesley's disapproval was less on the grounds of its lack of literary merit than for fear that it brought reproach on the Methodists and would hinder the sale and reading of more profitable literature. As a result, the Methodist conference of 1781 decreed that in future no preacher should publish until the text had been seen and edited by Wesley, and that any profits from such publications should be paid into a common fund. An even more ambitious work, *The grand and extensive plan of human redemption from the ruins of the fall … in twelve familiar dialogues*, appeared in 1797, the year of his death at Ashby-de-la-Zouch.

No details exist of Kershaw's marriage, though he did have at least one son, John (*d.* 1855), who entered the Wesleyan ministry in 1788 and was for four years (1823–7) the Methodist book steward, but found the administrative burden too great for him. Thomas Jackson found him 'a most amiable, friendly and upright man' whose acquaintances were struck by his striking resemblance to the duke of Kent. **Arthur Kershaw** (*fl.* 1800), journalist, may also have been James Kershaw's son. Educated at Wesley's Kingswood School near Bristol, he later contributed to the *Monthly Magazine*, and was employed by London booksellers in the enlargement of, among other titles, John Walker's *Universal Gazetteer*.

THOMAS SECCOMBE, *rev.* JOHN A. VICKERS

Sources C. Atmore, *The Methodist memorial* (1801) · L. Tyerman, *The life and times of the Rev. John Wesley*, 3 vols. (1870–71) · T. Jackson, *Recollections of my own life and times*, ed. B. Frankland (1873) · T. E. Brigden, *Proceedings of the Wesley Historical Society*, 3 (1902), 23–4 · *The journal of the Rev. John Wesley*, ed. N. Curnock and others, 8 vols. (1909–16) · F. Cumbers, *The book room* (1956) · J. Everett, *Historical sketches of Wesleyan Methodism in Sheffield* (1823) · *IGI*

Archives JRL, Methodist Archives and Research Centre, letters of John Kershaw and papers

Likenesses plaster medallion, 1795 (after James Tassie), Scot. NPG · engraving, repro. in *Methodist Magazine* (1802)

Kerslake, Thomas (1812–1891), bookseller, was born in July 1812 in Exeter, the son of William Kerslake. He was educated in Exeter and married Catherine Morgan of Bath. In 1828 he moved to Bristol, and with his brother-in-law Samuel Cornish of London began business as a secondhand bookseller in Barton Alley. In 1839 the partnership was dissolved and Kerslake moved to a shop at the bottom of Park Street, Bristol. In 1860 a disastrous fire in the premises resulted in the loss of many rare and valuable books and manuscripts (Kerslake had amassed a valuable collection of antiquarian and archaeological works before the fire). He continued at the same premises, but in 1870 he moved to Queen's Road, retiring shortly after this.

Following his retirement Kerslake devoted himself to antiquarian studies and although self-taught he had a good command of Latin and modern languages. His main interests were in the hagiology and the Anglo-Saxon period of the south-west. He published a number of articles on these subjects, usually at his own expense, as well as contributing papers to national and local archaeological societies. His writings often contained original theories and complex and sometimes controversial arguments.

One controversy in which Kerslake became involved was in the origin of the Pen Pits near Penselwood in Somerset. He believed that this group of amorphous surface undulations were the remains of an old British city and he published two papers on the subject: *A primaeval British Metropolis* (1877) and *Caer Pensauelcoit: a Re-Assertion* (1882). Others claimed that they were merely quarries. Under the auspices of the Somerset Archaeological and Natural History Society a Pen Pits Exploration Committee was set up; rather belatedly Kerslake was invited to join, but he refused. An excavation in 1884 by General Pitt Rivers in his role as inspector of ancient monuments concluded that the pits were quarries for quernstones and should not be scheduled, evoking from Kerslake a scathing paper: *The Liberty of Independent Historical Research* (1885).

Kerslake died at his home, Wynfrid, Clevedon, on 5 January 1891; his wife predeceased him in 1887. They had no children. J. A. MARCHAND

Sources DNB · *Proceedings of the Somerset Archaeological and Natural History Society*, 37 (1891), 131–3 · 'The Anglican invasion of Devon', *Transactions of the Devonshire Association*, 46 (1914), 390 · 'When the Saxons came to Devon', *Transactions of the Devonshire Association*, 51 (1919), 154–5 · d. cert. · IGI

Archives Bodl. Oxf., bills and corresp. with Sir T. Phillipps

Wealth at death £35,455 3s. 3d.: probate, 15 April 1891, *CGPLA Eng. & Wales*

Kersley, George Durant (1906–1993), physician and rheumatologist, was born on 27 December 1906 at 3 Park Lane, Bath, and baptized in Bath Abbey, the elder of two sons of Henry George Kersley (1863–1927), of independent means, and his wife, Edith, *née* Durant (1871–1958). He was educated at Malvern School and in 1925 went to Gonville and Caius College, Cambridge. From 1928 he studied medicine at St Bartholomew's Hospital medical school, qualifying MB, BCh (Cambridge) and MRCP, LRCS (London) in 1931. In 1934 he won a prize for his Cambridge MD thesis. He was elected fellow of the Royal College of Physicians of London in 1943. He married on 1 February 1933 Mary Ada Roper Yeomans (1910–1992), nurse, and daughter of Robert Roper Yeomans, schoolmaster. They had a daughter, Gillian, and a son, Henry Jonathan. This marriage having ended in divorce, on 8 May 1948 Kersley married Lilian May (Mickie) Davis (b. 1920), the daughter of Richard Mark Vernon, motor mechanic, and former wife of Major Kenneth Davis. They had one daughter, Diana Alison Durant, and Kersley became stepfather to Christopher, Mickie's son by her previous marriage.

In 1934 Kersley took up the appointments in Bath as consultant physician (general medicine) at the Royal United Hospital and consultant in rheumatology at the Mineral Water Hospital (later renamed the Royal National Hospital for Rheumatic Diseases). This hospital and the city of Bath became two of the dominant passions of his life. On moving to Bath he joined the Territorial Army in the North Somerset yeomanry as captain. In 1939 he was called up as medical specialist with rank of major, later colonel. He set up the army school of occupational therapy at Taunton and reorganized the army school of physiotherapy at Netley. As adviser in physical medicine to the army he was concerned with training schedules and the rehabilitation of military casualties. After the war he gave up his general medicine commitment in order to concentrate on the rheumatic diseases, running specialist clinics in Bath and Bristol. This was at a time when there was an apparent conflict between science-based academic rheumatology and physical medicine, the latter having strong links with physiotherapy departments and less science-minded army specialists who had been concerned with getting recruits back to active service after injury. As a founder member of the Empire Rheumatism Council (later the Arthritis Research Campaign) and of the British Association for Physical Medicine, Kersley had a foot in both camps. Throughout his life he worked to resolve the apparent antithesis.

The Royal National Hospital for Rheumatic Diseases had been badly damaged in the 'Baedeker' air raids launched in response to the allied bombing of Dresden. Kersley raised money not only to fund repairs to the hospital but also to modernize the interior and add a new research floor. This was a critical time. When the patients were moved into temporary hutted accommodation elsewhere, Kersley found himself up against the regional medical board, the professor of medicine in Bristol, and five successive ministers of health, who all wanted to close the hospital and put the money to other uses. It was greatly to Kersley's credit that he fought off the predators and cynics, taking his case to the House of Lords. The repairs and upgrading were completed in 1965. Under Kersley's guidance, the annual reports of the hospital reflected the increasing volume and quality of research carried out and numbers of patients treated. Younger doctors came to Bath as trainees, many from abroad. Five of the country's professors of rheumatology at Kersley's death had part of their training in Bath. In 1983 he retired, but he continued to give full support to the hospital and the Bath Institute for Rheumatic Diseases, which took over its research and teaching functions and became part of the postgraduate medical school at Bath. In 1986 he saw the celebrations of the quarter-millennium of the hospital, the oldest specialist rheumatology hospital in the world.

Kersley lived and practised at 6 The Circus, Bath, leaving it temporarily to move nearer to the university. But his love for things Georgian took him back to 20 Royal Crescent, where he lived for the rest of his life. He became a city councillor in 1968 and mayor in 1979. He was active in local Conservative politics, a discerning collector of antique glass, and instigator and chairman of the Bath tattoo, which was held from 1954 to 1964 and for which he was appointed OBE. He wrote on the history of medicine in Bath. His practitioner's manual, *The Rheumatic Diseases* (1934), was four times updated; he also wrote *The three 'Rs': rheumatology, rehabilitation and research as viewed from Bath* (1981) and a number of research and historical papers. He made the first complete description of the disease *polymyalgia rheumatica*. His book *A Concise International History of Rheumatology and Rehabilitation* (1991, co-authored with John Glyn), was published by the Royal Society of Medicine, London. He was president of the Heberden Society (1961), vice-chairman of the International League against Rheumatism (1967), and president of the European League against Rheumatism (1969). He was also an honorary member of the American and most European rheumatological associations. In 1971 he was awarded an honorary DSc by the University of Bath. He also served as a deputy lieutenant of Somerset (later Avon), and as colonel (later honorary colonel) of the 19th Southern General Hospital (Territorial Army), which he helped to set up.

Kersley's sixty years of professional life saw signal changes in rheumatology. When his career began, rheumatic fever, rheumatic heart disease, and tuberculosis of bones and joints were rife. By the time he retired they had virtually disappeared, gout had become curable, and surgeons had devised ways to replace damaged joints. Research had switched to osteoporosis and back pain with promising results. The problems of preventing and curing rheumatoid arthritis and other auto-immune diseases of joints had not been solved, although with advances in treatment the outlook for sufferers had vastly improved. He died on 1 September 1993 at the Royal United Hospital, Bath. After cremation, his ashes were buried in the family grave at Bath Abbey cemetery on 29 April 1994. He was survived by his second wife, Mickie, his three children, and his stepson.   ALLAN ST JOHN DIXON

Sources *The Independent* (15 Sept 1993) · *The Times* (28 Sept 1993) · personal knowledge (2004) · private information (2004) [Mrs Gillian Ryan] · b. cert. · m. cert. · d. cert.
Likenesses photograph, RCP Lond. · photograph, repro. in *The Independent*
Wealth at death £56,602—net: *The Times* (5 March 1994)

Kervile [Carvell], **Nicholas** (1527/8–1566), Church of England clergyman, was born in Stour Provost, Dorset. After entering King's College, Cambridge, on 14 August 1545 at the age of seventeen as a scholar from Eton College, he became a fellow in 1548 and graduated BA early in 1550. In 1551 he was one of thirty-seven Oxford and Cambridge scholars who contributed *epigrammata* in Latin and/or Greek to the memorial volume in honour of Martin Bucer, *De obitu doctissimi … Martini Buceri … epistolae duae*. This circumstance perhaps prompted tentative identification with the Cavil (Cavyll, Cauyll) who contributed one, possibly two, verse legends to *A Myrroure for Magistrates*, compiled during Edward VI's reign but first published in 1559.

Who precisely made this identification remains uncertain. In the preface to his edition of the *Mirror* (1815) Joseph Haslewood observed that no particulars were known of Master Cavyll. 'How the two Rogers, surnamed Mortimers, for their sundry vices ended their lives unfortunately, the one An. 1329, the other, 1387' was first attributed to Ca. only in the edition of 1571. The attribution was altered to T. Ch. (Thomas Churchyard?) in that of 1578 (Haslewood, 2.23–31 and note). 'The wilfull fall of the

blacke Smith, and the foolishe ende of the Lorde Awdeley, in June, anno 1496' was likewise not attributed to Maister Cauyll until the edition of 1571 (Haslewood, 2.396–414 and note).

That Nicholas Kervile was the author of either of these two narratives must obviously be open to serious doubt. There is no evidence that he wrote English verse while his claims must face those of a 'rival poet' whose Latin productions were more extensive: James Calfhill, later archdeacon of Colchester, who contributed verses to the memorial volume which quickly followed that to Bucer, *Vita et obitus duorum fratrum Suffolciensium, Henrici et Caroli Brandoni … duabus epistolis explicata* (1551). Clearly Cauyll is as likely to be a rendering of Calfhill as of Kervile and its variants.

Kervile, who proceeded MA in 1553, went abroad after Mary's accession and by October 1554 was living in Zürich with a group of distinguished Oxford and Cambridge scholars in the house of the printer Christopher Froschover. He later migrated to Frankfurt where in the tax-list of 1556 he was stated to be without property and in 1557 to be living in the house of Robert Harrington.

Kervile's fellow exile in Frankfurt, Robert Horne, restored as dean of Durham in 1559 and in urgent need of protestant evangelists, suggested 'Mr Carvile' for one of Durham's vacant prebends. Kervile evidently preferred to remain in the south, becoming chaplain to another Frankfurt exile, Edmund Grindal, newly elevated bishop of London. On 29 July 1560 Grindal collated him to the vicarage of South Weald, Essex, and on 7 November to the nearby rectory of Laindon. He held both livings in plurality until his death. Since the London merchant Nicholas Culverwell stood surety at the exchequer for Laindon's first fruits the two men were undoubtedly related, Kervile using a contracted form of the family name.

On 20 March 1565 Kervile was one of twenty leading nonconformists, including Thomas Sampson, dean of Christ Church, and Laurence Humphrey, president of Magdalen, who petitioned the ecclesiastical commissioners for exemption from wearing the prescribed vestments. According to the endorsement Kervile was one of the five who formally presented it to Matthew Parker, archbishop of Canterbury.

Kervile died at South Weald, and was buried there on 7 August 1566. John Parkhurst, bishop of Norwich, later reported his death to Heinrich Bullinger of Zürich. Nothing is known of his family except that a daughter, Elizabeth, was baptized at South Weald in July 1565 and buried there in September 1567. In October 1566 his (unnamed) widow was cited before Grindal's vicar-general as his executrix but on failing to appear was pronounced contumacious. No will was subsequently registered in the consistory court and there is no record either of probate or of letters of administration.   BRETT USHER

Sources Venn, *Alum. Cant.* · C. H. Garrett, *The Marian exiles: a study in the origins of Elizabethan puritanism* (1938) · *CSP for.*, 1559–60 · register of Edmund Grindal, bishop of London, GL, MS 9531/13, pt 1 · petition of 1565, LPL, Fairhurst MS 2019 · South Weald parish registers, Essex RO, D/P 128/1/2 · H. Robinson, ed. and trans., *The Zurich* *letters, comprising the correspondence of several English bishops and others with some of the Helvetian reformers, during the early part of the reign of Queen Elizabeth*, 2 vols., Parker Society, 7–8 (1842–5) · J. Haslewood, ed., *Mirror for magistrates*, 3 vols. (1815) · LMA, DL/C/332, fol. 146*v* [citation of widow as executrix]

Kessack, James O'Connor (1879–1916), trade unionist, was born on 19 October 1879 at 1 Castle Terrace, Aberdeen, the second of nine children of James O'Connor Kessack, a baker, and his wife, Isabella *née* Davidson, a farmer's daughter. An unskilled labourer, he moved to Glasgow after his mother's death to seek more regular work. Following his father's death he supported the younger members of the family in Glasgow. A religious man and regular churchgoer, Kessack began to embrace socialism in the early 1900s, having hitherto rejected it. Thereafter his conversion to socialism was swift, as was his rise within the labour movement.

As a committed socialist, Kessack regularly addressed political meetings on behalf of the Independent Labour Party. He wrote various articles and in 1907 published his lecture to the Glasgow Clarion Scouts as *The Early Struggles for Political Freedom in Scotland*. Under pressure of work he developed a serious throat infection in 1908 and the ILP financed his visit to Arizona in search of a cure. On return he was adopted as a Labour candidate in various municipal and parliamentary divisions in the Glasgow area between 1909 and 1911. Political success eluded him, however, and thereafter he concentrated on trade union activities.

Kessack became national organizer for the National Union of Dock Labourers (NUDL) in 1909, following James Larkin's dismissal the previous year. He enjoyed some success along the east coast of Scotland, but failed to win over the Clyde dockers and the Glasgow dockers in particular. The reasons behind these failures may have had more to do with his close connections with James Sexton, leader of the NUDL, than any lack of commitment to dock trade unionism on his part. He never laboured as a docker, however, and this could have worked against him as Glasgow had in the past rejected men who had no practical knowledge of dock work.

It would seem more likely that it was Sexton's quarrels with James Larkin that hampered Kessack's work at Glasgow. The conflict between Sexton and Larkin sent shock waves through trade union circles after Larkin was arrested, tried, and found guilty of attempting to defraud the NUDL. Indeed, Sexton gave evidence against Larkin. The Glasgow Trades Council backed a resolution, moved by Joseph Houghton, 'denouncing the attempt to crush Mr Jim Larkin' (Glasgow Trades Council minutes, 29 June 1910), and pronounced him innocent, which echoed the sentiments of the Glasgow dockers. Kessack had in his own words 'nursed the Glasgow branch like a tender baby' (Taplin, 78), but despite his undoubted popularity he could not win over a Glasgow dock labour force which actively protested against Sexton's authoritarian style of leadership.

Kessack initially resigned over the issue, but reconsidered after Sexton's personal intervention. In late December 1910 he sought the assistance of Glasgow Trades Council in his attempt to reorganize the Glasgow dockers. The trades council agreed and assigned a ten-man committee to this task. It was to no avail. In January 1911 Sexton officially closed down the Glasgow branch. Six months later the Glasgow dockers were reorganized under the auspices of the recently formed Scottish Union of Dock Labourers (SUDL). Joseph Houghton was elected the first general secretary of the SUDL.

Kessack continued with the NUDL up to 1914 and saw some considerable success, despite losing the dockers of the Clyde ports of west Scotland and Dundee and Bo'ness on the east coast to the SUDL. He reorganized the Aberdeen branch of the NUDL and set up branches in England where Ben Tillett's Dock, Wharf, Riverside and General Labourers' Union had failed to attract support. His greatest contribution was in setting up NUDL branches at Hull, which hitherto had been the headquarters of William Collison's National Association of Free Labour and considered the epicentre of 'blacklegism' within the port transport industry.

Kessack enlisted in 1914 and rose swiftly to the rank of captain by March 1916, but he died in France at the battle of the Ancre on 13 November of that year leaving a widow and two children resident in Glasgow. Despite his earlier problems with the Glasgow dockers, and for a time the SUDL leadership, he never wavered from his commitment to socialism or dock trade unionism.

WILLIAM KENEFICK

Sources K. Coates and T. Topham, *The making of the Transport and General Workers Union: the emergence of the labour movement, 1870–1922*, 1 (1991), pts 1–2 · E. L. Taplin, *The dockers' union: a study of the National Union of Dock Labourers, 1889–1922*, [another edn] (1986), 78 · W. Kenefick, 'The struggle for control: the importance of the great unrest at Glasgow harbour, 1911–1912', *The roots of red Clydeside? Labour unrest in the west of Scotland, 1910–1914*, ed. W. Kenefick and A. McIvor (1996), 129–52 · W. Kenefick, 'The impact of the past upon the present: the experience of the Clydeside dock labour force, *c.*1850–1914', PhD diss., University of Strathclyde, 1995 · *DLB*, vols. 1–7 · *Forward* (1910–32) · *Glasgow Herald* (1889–1939) · *Daily Record and Mail* (1910–32) · Glasgow Trades Council annual reports and executive minutes, Mitchell L., Glas. · National Union of Dock Labourers (occasional) annual reports, 1889–1923, Mitchell L., Glas., S. F. 331. 8811 3871 SCO · *Annual Report* [Scottish Trades Union Congress] (1897–1945) · *Eastern Morning News* (22 Nov 1916) · CCI (1917)
Archives Mitchell L., Glas., pamphlets
Wealth at death £246 4*s.*: confirmation, 27 March 1917, CCI

Kesson [*née* MacDonald], **Jessie Grant** (1916–1994), writer, was born on 29 October 1916 at the workhouse at Inverness, the second illegitimate daughter of Elizabeth MacDonald (1885–1949), domestic servant. No acknowledgement of paternity was ever made, but she latterly believed her father had been John Foster (1868–1946), sheriff clerk of Elgin and story-writer.

Mother and child lived in the corporation lodging house in Elgin, and then in an attic room. Elizabeth MacDonald's father Robert, a forester, cast her off at her second pregnancy, having quietly accepted the first child into the family. Jessie lived closely with her mother, a pauper, prone to drink and small-time prostitution. She also loved poetry and taught Jessie reams of it orally, as they roamed the countryside together barefoot. For a time they evaded 'the Cruelty Man', but on 19 April 1927 Jessie was removed from her mother's care on grounds of neglect, and was plunged into an entirely new environment: Proctors Kirkville Orphan Training Home, near Skene, Aberdeenshire, where she stayed until she was sixteen, showing great academic promise, and adapting to the new life. The talented girl wanted to go to university, but she was sent to farm service instead, and after two years of failure in yet another institution she had a breakdown and spent a wretched year in the mental hospital in Aberdeen.

This dramatically divided childhood and adolescence nearly destroyed Jessie, in spite of her great zest for life and love of words. Much of the rest of her life involved a hard process of understanding and coming to terms with her past; she convinced herself of her survival and continuity as a person through the process of writing, constructing a version of her life that was true enough and suitable for publication—in a real sense writing herself. After her release from the mental hospital she was 'boarded out' in a tiny hill village above Inverness. There she met John Kesson (1905–1994), who with his siblings had also been 'boarded out' as a child, because of his mother's alcoholism. Jessie later became a champion of victimized children, writing radio plays which effectively drew attention to their deprivation or exploitation, and giving evidence to a Scottish home department investigation.

Jessie married John Kesson in Inverness on 9 April 1937, and they lived briefly in Aberdeen where their daughter Avril was born in March 1938. For a dozen years they were cottar workers, working long hours on farms, living rent-free with perquisites, but with no job security, liable to move house every year at a farmer's whim. Their son Kenneth was born in 1946. The hard-pressed cottar wife began writing to supplement the family income, and from 1941 to 1946 she contributed vigorously to the *Scots Magazine* and *North-East Review* stories, poems, and articles—mainly reconstructions of significant experiences of her youth. In 1946 she moved on to the BBC; her plays, usually autobiographical and produced by Elizabeth Adair, gained great respect in BBC Scotland. Jessie's mother died of syphilis in an institution in Elgin in August 1949, and after demanding that her alienated family attend the funeral, Jessie began to turn her attention to London, where she hoped to write for the new medium of television.

By 1951 the Kesson family had moved to north London. Jessie had a series of hard jobs which fitted in to the children's schedules—cleaning nurses' homes, and a cinema, doing night-shifts caring for children disabled by polio—but from 1955 to 1960 she was deputy head of Cowley Recreational Institute, looking after underprivileged young people, again engaging herself with youth problems. Her radio plays were successful: *The Childhood* (1951), an early version of her first novel *The White Bird Passes* (1958), was repeated many times and regarded as a classic. She wrote somewhere in the region of forty plays, and many talks and features, for the Home Service and the Third Programme, and she also worked a year for *Woman's Hour* in 1961. Some of her poems and radio scripts were published in *Somewhere Beyond* (2000). She was an original with a gift for friendship, from Scottish novelist Nan Shepherd who first encouraged her to write, to BBC producer Stewart Conn, and most importantly Peter Calvocoressi at Chatto and Windus—a firm that treated her very sympathetically, recognizing her unusual talents.

Johnnie Kesson's health was uncertain at intervals after 1960, but Jessie fought on, working full-time at heavy jobs as well as writing novels, radio plays, and wonderful letters to Peter Calvocoressi, and to several producers at the BBC. She rewrote repeatedly, developing material from first sketch to radio play to eventual novel or short story. She published *Glitter of Mica* in 1963, a novel about the inhumanity of the cottaring system, and in 1978 a brilliant novella centring on adolescence, *Where the Apple Ripens*. She became nationally famous in 1980 when Michael Radford adapted *The White Bird Passes* for television, and the two co-wrote the film of *Another Time, Another Place* while Jessie wrote the novel, published in 1983. Part-autobiographical again, this recorded a young cottar wife caring for Italian POWs in the 1940s, as Jessie herself had done.

By this time, Jessie had, to a degree, left her past behind her, and she was often frustrated by the public fixation on *The White Bird*. She was now writing for radio and television about subjects arising from her later jobs, such as the experiences of elderly people in care, or of girls in probation hostels. She was made an honorary LLD by Dundee University in 1984 and a DLitt by the University of Aberdeen in 1987, and became widely celebrated, especially in Scotland. But from 1990 her husband's health was very poor, and his total deafness was a trial to them both. Jessie nursed him devotedly until he died in August 1994, only then giving in to the lung cancer which had been affecting her for some time. She died in Whittington Hospital six weeks later, on 26 September. Husband and wife were both cremated, and their ashes were scattered at Abriachan, where they had first met. A biography, *Jessie Kesson: Writing her Life*, by Isobel Murray, was published in 2000.   ISOBEL MURRAY

Sources NL Scot., Kesson MSS · U. Reading L., special collections, Chatto and Windus archive · files on Kesson, BBC WAC · files on Kesson, BBC Scotland, Glasgow · personal knowledge (2004) · 'Jessie Kesson: the sma' perfect', *Scottish writers talking*, ed. I. Murray (1996), 55–83 · I. Murray, 'Jessie Kesson', *A history of Scottish women's writing*, ed. D. Gifford and D. McMillan (1997), 481–93 · I. Murray, 'Jessie Kesson: writing herself', *Northern visions*, ed. D. Hewitt (1995), 180–89 · J. Hendry, 'Jessie Kesson country', *Scots Magazine*, 132 (1989–90), 11–22 · J. Hendry, 'Jessie Kesson', *The Scotsman* (27 Sept 1994) · L. St Aubin de Terán, 'Jessie Kesson', *The Independent* (28 Sept 1994) · I. Murray, *Jessie Kesson: writing her life* (2000)

Archives BBC Scotland, Glasgow · BBC WAC · NL Scot., papers and literary papers · U. Glas., Scottish Theatre Archive | U. Reading L., Chatto and Windus archive

Likenesses A. Scott, photographs, repro. in Hendry, 'Jessie Kesson country' · photographs, Scot. NPG · photographs, repro. in Murray, *Jessie Kesson* · photographs, priv. coll.

Wealth at death under £125,000: administration, 1994

Keswick, Sir John Henry (1906–1982), merchant, was born at Cowhill, Dumfries, on 13 July 1906, the youngest of three children (all sons) of Major Henry Keswick, of Cowhill Tower, merchant, and his wife, Winifred (Ida) Johnston, also of Dumfriesshire. His childhood years were spent in Hong Kong, where his father was *taipan* (managing senior partner) of the giant trading firm Jardine, Matheson & Co. Ltd, founded in 1832 by Dr William Jardine and James Matheson. The Keswicks and the Jardines were related by marriage in the generation following the founder, and John Keswick was the great-great-great-nephew of Dr Jardine.

After his education at Eton College and at Trinity College, Cambridge, Keswick joined Jardine, Matheson at London in 1928, and served briefly in its New York and Philadelphia offices. By 1931 he was in Shanghai, where he was to spend the better part of the next twenty years as witness to the turbulent history of China, rent by warlords, conquerors, civil war, and social revolution. While learning Chinese from an old Peking scholar who spoke no English, he was also learning the company's export business in its accounting office. Jardines dealt in teas, furs, skins, silks, and oils, and it was heavily involved in engineering and shipping.

With the outbreak of the Sino-Japanese War in 1937, Keswick moved into the international settlement at Shanghai. Appointed a director of Jardines in 1937, he found himself running the company there while his older brother William *Keswick (Tony) was home on leave. As the hostilities closed in upon Shanghai, his mother cabled from Scotland, 'I am very worried about you', to which he replied with a touch of his characteristic humour, 'I am very worried about myself' (Keswick, 212). Beyond managing the company, he was serving with the Shanghai volunteer corps, and collecting money and goods for refugee relief. 'But otherwise', he wrote later, 'we worked in our offices, played tennis and polo, and danced and dined at night, an exciting, rather unreal life' (ibid.).

When the Second World War began in 1939, Keswick returned to Britain, and was appointed to the Ministry of Economic Warfare, with the job of trying to prevent war supplies from reaching Germany through Asia. Midway through the war he was assigned to Lord Louis Mountbatten's south-east Asia command and served as political liaison officer in the British embassy at Chungking (Chongqing). It was there that he met the communist leader Zhou Enlai, with whom he developed a lasting friendship. In 1940, he married Clare, *née* Elwes, the youngest child of Gervase Henry Cary-*Elwes, singer, and his wife, Lady Winefride Mary Elizabeth Feilding; their marriage was exceptionally happy. Their only child, Maggie, edited the sesquicentennial history of Jardine, Matheson & Co., and was the author of *The Chinese Garden*.

At the end of the Second World War Keswick returned to London for discharge by the Foreign Office, and was soon flying back to China, where he proceeded with rebuilding Jardines's business operations, while civil war raged between the nationalist forces of Chiang Kai-shek and the communist armies of Mao Zedong. Keswick recognized the weaknesses of the nationalist government, but doubted that communism would find favour among the tradition-conscious Chinese. However, once the nationalist government fell in 1949, Keswick and the other British merchants concluded that Chiang Kai-shek could not overturn the communist victory. They advised the British government to come to a working arrangement with the communists.

When the communists overran Shanghai in May 1949 there were moments when life was precarious. A colleague wrote home,

> We had to give up having meals in the flat after a couple of bullets came in through the window, but John Keswick shook some good cocktails in the Correspondence Office and Mrs Keswick presided gracefully over excellent meals on a stenographer's desk. (Keswick, 225)

Although the British government recognized the Central People's government in January 1950, the new government's response was icy. Members of the British chamber of commerce at Shanghai, which Keswick chaired, found themselves trapped, for control of their companies was being supplanted by their workers' unions, yet the Central People's government was intent on delaying the departure of foreign firms, so as to secure more foreign funds and to retain foreign technical skills. After more than two years of negotiations, the communist government took ownership and control of Jardines's operations in China and conceded the release of all foreign staff. John Keswick received his exit permit in September 1951 and went from Shanghai to Hong Kong, where he became *taipan* (1951–3).

After Jardine, Matheson & Co. offered a portion of its shares for public subscription on the Hong Kong stock exchange, in 1961, that firm and its London-based subsidiary, Matheson & Co., continued to be guided principally by members of the Keswick family. Upon returning to England, John Keswick became a director of Matheson & Co. (originally established in 1848 by Sir Alexander Matheson as an independently constituted house of finance and agency), and in 1966 he succeeded his brother Tony as the chairman of that company.

Keswick always described himself as a keen student of China and from 1961 to 1973 he was president of the Sino-British Trade Council. He and his wife paid many visits to the People's Republic and persevered in nurturing British ties with China during the menacing days of the Cultural Revolution in the late 1960s. As tensions eased, he visited China in 1970 for consultations with Chinese trade officials, leading to an agreement for more frequent exchange of trade missions, one factor in the relaxation of Sino-British relations preceding the formal exchange of ambassadors in 1972.

Keswick was instrumental in the staging of two British engineering exhibitions in China. The first, in 1964, afforded an opportunity to renew his friendship with Zhou Enlai; and the second, in 1973, constituted a high point in post-Cultural Revolution relations between the two nations. For his service to British interests in the Far East, he was knighted as KCMG in 1972.

Those who knew Keswick well testified to his wonderful humour and his infectious love of life, whether manifest in entertaining Chinese athletes visiting Scotland, in dancing the highland fling in China at Macao, or as the rare European accomplished at playing the Chinese 'finger game' over the dining-table. Throughout his life he made friends easily and his personal warmth earned their abiding affection. Called 'Uncle John' by many Chinese and Japanese students whom he helped, he was equally generous toward the youth of Scotland. He and Lady Keswick were famous for their good-humoured hospitality. His friend the earl of Perth said of him, 'One knew that in seeing John one was going to have fun and one did' (*The Times*, 28 July 1982, 10).

Sir John died of a heart attack, on 5 July 1982, while fishing near his home, Portrack House, Holywood, Dumfriesshire. He was survived by his wife. One week earlier, at Hong Kong, he had joined with other emeritus *taipans* and senior executives in celebrating the 150th anniversary of the founding of Jardine, Matheson & Co.

RICHARD J. GRACE

Sources M. Keswick, ed., *The thistle and the jade: a celebration of 150 years of Jardine, Matheson & Co.* (1982) · *The Times* (8 July 1982) · *The Times* (16 July 1982) · *The Times* (28 July 1982) · *Dumfries and Galloway Standard* (9 July 1982) · *Thistle* [house magazine of Jardine, Matheson & Co. Ltd], 14/2 (July 1982) · *DNB* · R. Boardman, *Britain and the People's Republic of China, 1949–1974* (1976) · private information (2004)
Archives CUL, Jardine, Matheson archive · priv. coll., private papers
Likenesses photograph, 30 May 1950, repro. in Keswick, *Thistle and the jade*, 220 · photograph, 1964 (with Zhou Enlai), repro. in Keswick, *Thistle and the jade*, 222 · photograph, 1977, Hult. Arch. · D. Hill, double portrait (with Sir W. Keswick), Matheson & Co., London · photograph, repro. in *Thistle*, 2

Keswick, Sir William Johnston (1903–1990), businessman and banker, was born on 6 December 1903 in Yokohama, Japan, the second of three sons (there were no daughters) of Major Henry Keswick, of Cowhill Tower, near Dumfries, and his wife, Winifred (Ida) Johnston. Henry Keswick was a senior partner of Jardine, Matheson & Co. and was directly descended from Jean Jardine, the sister of Dr William Jardine, one of the two founders of the company in 1832. William (Tony) Keswick was thus Jardine's great-great-grandnephew. His younger brother, Sir John Henry *Keswick, also became chairman of Jardine, Matheson. William Keswick went to Winchester College in 1917 and rowed for the school before going on to Trinity College, Cambridge, in 1922 to read economics and law for an ordinary degree (BA, 1925).

On leaving Cambridge, Keswick joined Jardine, Matheson in Harbin, Manchuria, in 1925, with a posting to the engineering department. He recalled Harbin as being a grim place in several respects and he welcomed later transfers to Beijing and Tianjin and subsequent promotion to the management team in Hong Kong, where he was *taipan* (head of the firm) in 1934–5, and in Shanghai, where he became *taipan* in 1935.

The decade of the 1930s was a difficult and dangerous time in China, and the international community in Shanghai was challenged both by the growth of communist ideology and by the aggressive policy of the Japanese government towards China, which led to attacks on Shanghai in 1932 and 1937. The authority of the Shanghai municipal council, of which Keswick had become chairman in 1938 (a post virtually equivalent to mayor), was also under attack, with the Japanese pressing for much greater representation, and he survived an assassination attempt by a Japanese member of the council at a ratepayers' meeting early in 1941.

By now the Second World War had already started in Europe and was about to begin in the Far East. In 1941 Keswick was seconded as political adviser to the staff of Duff Cooper (later first Viscount Norwich), then minister of state for the Far East, in Singapore. He joined the Special Operations Executive and went as a staff officer to Washington, as a member of the British shipping mission under Sir J. Arthur Salter. He then served on the staff of the Twenty-First Army group in north Africa, France, Belgium, and the Netherlands, with the rank of brigadier. He also worked in the war cabinet offices, participating in the planning of the Normandy landings. He returned to London after the war and, in 1947 he became a director of Matheson & Co. Ltd, the London correspondents of Jardine, Matheson, and subsequently served as chairman from 1949 to 1966; when he retired he remained on the board as a non-executive director until 1975. He was always a free-trader, feeling strongly that the market should be allowed to determine the business environment without bureaucratic intervention. His approach was down-to-earth and pragmatic and he was scrupulously fair in all his dealings.

A large and imposing figure and tall of stature, Keswick had a presence and authority which marked his many years as a leading figure in the City of London. He was governor of the Hudson's Bay Company from 1952 to 1965 and a director of the Bank of England (1955–73) and of British Petroleum (1950–73). He served as deputy chairman of Sun Alliance Insurance Ltd and a trustee of the National Gallery (1964–71) and was knighted in 1972. He was a member of the king's (later queen's) bodyguard for Scotland (the Royal Company of Archers) from 1949.

In 1937 Keswick married Mary Etheldreda, daughter of Sir Francis Oswald *Lindley, diplomatist, and his wife, Etheldreda Mary, *née* Fraser; they had three sons and one daughter. They shared a wide variety of interests and pastimes. Both loved gardening (a world in which the name of Lindley was honoured) and they created a much admired garden on the outskirts of Shanghai; later they were to create beautiful gardens at their homes at Theydon Bois in Essex and Glenkiln in south-west Scotland. An early friendship with Henry Moore had resulted in a keen interest in sculpture and it was at Glenkiln that Keswick was to place his remarkable collection of statues by Moore, Jacob Epstein, and others on the Galloway moors, where art and nature complemented each other. The Keswicks also collected furniture and pictures, many of them closely associated with the early days of Jardine, Matheson, and they enjoyed tapestry, music, and even hot-air ballooning. Keswick died on 16 February 1990 at the Lister Hospital, Westminster, London. Two of his sons, Henry Neville Lindley Keswick (*b.* 1938) and Simon Lindley Keswick (*b.* 1942), were prominent in Jardines, the former becoming chairman; the third son was Sir (John) Chippendale Lindley Keswick, chairman of Hambros Bank.

JEREMY BROWN, *rev.*

Sources CUL, Jardine, Matheson & Co. MSS · *The Times* (19 Feb 1990) · *The Independent* (20 Feb 1990) · personal knowledge (1996) · *CGPLA Eng. & Wales* (1990)

Archives CUL, Jardine, Matheson archive

Wealth at death £1,078,991: probate, 29 June 1990, *CGPLA Eng. & Wales*

Ketch [Catch], **John** [Jack] (*d.* 1686), public executioner, is in himself an obscure figure. Neither his parents nor his date of birth are known. Parish and probate records provide a little information. Ketch married a woman named Katherine, who survived him, and he and his wife are probably the John and Katherine Catch whose daughter Susanna was baptized on 1 June 1668 at St James's, Clerkenwell, the parish where he was buried eighteen years later. At the time of his death he was living in Spread Eagle Court, which lay on the east side of Gray's Inn Road.

Squire Ketch Even in his own lifetime Jack Ketch's job as the common hangman of London, a position which he held from some point between October 1666 and November 1678, made him a figure of popular mythology: the presiding figure at the execution days which took place eight times a year at Tyburn. In the surviving record he has come down less as an individual in his own right than as a name deployed for satiric purpose in broadsides and pamphlets and a subject of gossip for newsletter writers. Some writers leapt on striking incidents in his life. However, more generally he was presented as the archetype of the hangman by political satirists in the feverish atmosphere of the late 1670s and early 1680s, as he presided at the executions first of the Catholic victims of the Popish Plot allegations, and then of the whig victims of the tory revenge. In using his name in broadsides and pamphlets, propagandists were attempting to exploit the broader place of the common hangman in the imagination of Londoners.

That place was reflected in the appellation 'squire' that was frequently attached to Ketch's name, a status which went back to 1617 when a herald as a joke had granted the then hangman Gregory Brandon a coat of arms. It was also captured in the ironic grandiloquence of several pamphlets. When the Tyburn gallows was lying on the ground in September 1678, quite possibly through vandalism, *The Tyburn Ghost* imagined 'Squire Ketch's Lamentation for the loss of his Shop' (title-page):

> The Tidings was quickly spread abroad. but when it arrived at Squire Ketch's Ear, twas thought at first he would have Truss'd up himself for grief, that he should thus lose all Patience, and fill the Air with Exclamations against the villainous Authors of the Mischief. (*Tyburn Ghost*, 7)

The following year *The Man of Destiny's Hard Fortune, or, Squire Ketch's Declaration* exploited the opportunity for

humour provided by the hangman finding himself imprisoned in the king's bench and Marshalsea prisons for debt:

> shall the famous, the well-known, the redoubtable Squire Ketch, Death's Harbinger, Pluto's Van-courrier, Vice-roy of Fate, and sole Monarch of the Triple Throne, now tamely be Catch-pol'd, Nabb'd, spirited, Shoulder-dabb'd, Enchanted, Lavendar'd, and laid up in pickle in one of the Devil's Pepperboxes? (p. 4)

The pamphlet presented Ketch as a beleaguered tradesman. Twenty had died in his debt, 'having never a shirt on' (a reference to the hangman's perquisite of his victims' clothes); he had been burgled and 'two of the principal Apartments of that ancient Edifice stoln away' (referring to the collapse of the gallows). However, he was looking forward to an upturn in his trade:

> I hope I shall weather all my troubles, there shortly begins a Grand Mart on the Old Bayly, and other Customers are coming on apace; If things fadge right, I doubt not be before Midsomer to have twenty Guinnies with an Apprentice, and, in a Calesh of my own, wait upon my well-beloved Sons in a Cart or Sledg, when they perform their last Pilgrimage to TYBURN. (pp. 7–8)

The pamphlet also relished the cause of Ketch's debt, starkly contrasting with his reputation for hard drinking that other writers noted: he owed

> two and twenty pounds, and odd Farthings, for Milk, Oh abominable! The World sure will scandalize me for a Milksop, and think I fed like an old Britain, on nothing but Cowsbaubby, drink only Whey like a Swine, or stuff my Guts every day with Fools, White-pot [a kind of milk pudding], and Custard. (p. 6)

The eminent physician Increasingly from the late 1670s Ketch's name was called upon with grim humour as the symbol of the appropriate response to treason. A broadside celebrating the execution of Edward Colman on 3 December 1678 for his alleged part in the Popish Plot, *The plotters ballad, being Jack Ketch's incomparable receipt for the cure of trayterous recusants*, was illustrated with a woodcut showing Colman being drawn to Tyburn on a sled with the pope's pardon in his hand, saying 'I am sick of a trayterous disease', while Ketch stood over him with a hatchet in one hand and a rope in the other, saying, 'Here's your Cure. Sir'. The theme was taken up in another broadside published early in 1680, *The Romanists best doctor, who by one infallible remedy, perfectly cures all popish-diseases whatsoever in a quarter of an hours time, By an approved dose which never yet failed his Patients. Which approved remedy may once a month be had at Tyburn, near Paddington, of that famous physician of long practice, John Ketch, Esq; physician in ordinary to the pope*. It placed Ketch in a long line of such 'physicians' from the 1580s onwards. It assumed that the names of earlier hangmen such as Gregory (the nickname also of Richard Brandon who had succeeded his father) would have a resonance with London readers. The last of Ketch's predecessors, 'my Father Dunn', was credited with executing the Fifth Monarchists of Venner's rising in 1661 and Robert Hubert, the Frenchman hanged on 25 October 1666 for having started the great fire of London. The broadsheet concluded by listing those who had died for treason at

Ketch's own hand—from William Staley, hanged, drawn, and quartered on 26 November 1678, onwards.

With the changing political atmosphere, Ketch became the executioner of whig conspirators such as the London activist Stephen College, whom he executed at Oxford on 31 August 1681. His name was now deployed by tory satirists, generally in passing references which took for granted his role of meting out justice to disloyal whigs. Thus one poem of 1683 had the dying earl of Shaftesbury lamenting 'Now heart, break heart, and baffle Ketch and all' (de Lord and others, 3.408), while another on the suicide of the earl of Essex in the Tower on 13 July 1683 reflected that:

Had'st thou but few days courage to withstand,
Jack Catch had done the business to thy hand.
(ibid., 457)

Langley Curtis his Lamentation in Newgate, responding to the gaoling of the whig printer, had as a running refrain Curtis bemoaning the fate of his party:

There's none can defend us
Till Ketch doth befriend us
And send us a-hunting for Walcot below.
(ibid., 499–504)

The last line was varied with the names of different executed whigs. Other satire placed Ketch centre stage. The ballad *A Dialogue between Jack Ketch and his Journey-Man* (1683) has Ketch enjoining his assistant:

Come prithee Nick,
Look sharp, be quick,
  for now begins our Harvest;
Throw by thy Coat
Thou'st have a Cloak,
  for Charles is now in earnest:
His Friends no more shall hang like dogs to please a bloody
  Faction;
Our damn'd Phanatick Plotting Rogues, shall breed no more
  distraction.

The lengthy verse parody *A Bill and Answer betwixt Jack Catch Plaintiff, and Slingsby Bethel & al. Defendants* (1686) imagined Ketch suing the republican Bethel, sheriff of London and Middlesex in 1680–81, for cheating him of his wages, and Bethel admitting that he was Ketch's father. The satire gained particular force from the story that Bethel had been the man who cut off Charles I's head:

To speak on, tho' a friend to the profession [of hangman],
And would again, upon the same occasion,
Faithfully serve the People of the Nation.
But to my great Content, dear Jack I see
While you survive, there'l be no need of me,
Thou art the Top of Fraternity.
(p. 2)

There was, of course, another way of regarding Jack Ketch. His incompetence at the executions of William, Lord Russell, and James Scott, duke of Monmouth, became notorious—the only two beheadings that Ketch performed and his most politically prominent victims. That notoriety was no doubt a matter of partisan hostility, but incompetence also muddied the sombre public message of execution—only serving to highlight the stoicism of the victim and undercut the lesson of the legitimate power of the state—and appeared unnecessarily cruel.

According to an eyewitness at Russell's execution on 21 July 1683, 'The hangman gave him 3 blows, besides sawing with the ax, before he cut his head off' (Thompson, 2.32). Angry rumours of Ketch's incompetence and possibly deliberate inhumanity in executing the whig martyr were met by *The Apologie of John Ketch, Esq.*, purportedly Ketch's own vindication of himself:

However since it is not fit that so Publick a Person as the Executioner of Justice and the Law's Sentence upon Criminals and Malefactors should lye under the scandal of untrue Reports, and be unjustly Expos'd to popular Clamour, I thought it a matter of highest importance to me to clear and Vindicate myself as to the matter of my Lord Russel's Execution, and the hard usage he is said to have had in the Severing of his Head from his Body.

Ketch denied that he had turned up at the execution drunk; that he had received 20 guineas from Russell the night before (though he had received 10 guineas on the scaffold); that after the first blow the peer had said to him, 'you Dog, did I give you 10 Guennies to use me so Inhumanely'; that his first blow had struck Russell on the shoulder; and that he had been consigned to Newgate for his incompetence. Above all, he denied that he 'had given my Lord more Blows then one out of design to put him to more then Ordinary Pain'. Instead he blamed Russell for the messiness of his own death, who, showing 'more Galantry than Discretion' had adopted an unsuitable posture and, refusing to have his eyes covered or make a signal, had flinched when the blow approached. Besides, Ketch had been disturbed as he was taking aim.

The beheading of the duke of Monmouth on 15 July 1685 was even more botched. On the scaffold Monmouth handed Ketch 6 guineas and ordered his servant to pay the executioner more once he had done his job well. 'Do not serve me as you did my Lord Russel,' he reminded Ketch, 'I have heard, you struck him three or four times … If you strike me twice, I cannot promise you not to stir' (*An Account*, 3). In fact Ketch took five blows and almost gave up halfway through the execution. Edmund Verney reported that after the first blow Monmouth

lookt up, & after the third he putt his Leggs a Cross, & the Hangman flung away his Axe, but being chidd tooke it againe & gave him tother two strokes; and severed not his Head from his body till he cut it off with his Knife.   (Verney, 2.404–5)

John Evelyn thought that Ketch's 'five Chopps … so incens'd the people, that had he not ben guarded & got away they would have torne him in pieces' (Evelyn, 4.456). Whig lampoon linked Ketch's name with that other brutal defender of the crown, George Jeffreys: 'While Jeffreys on the bench, Ketch on the gibbet sits' (Macaulay, 3.618).

Downfall, death, and Mr Punch More work for Ketch followed in the wake of Monmouth's rebellion, among it the execution of the former sheriff Henry Cornish outside his house in Cheapside on 23 October. Early in January Ketch fell out with the current sheriffs, and was turned out of his place and gaoled in Bridewell for a week. His replacement as hangman was Pascha Rose, a butcher with a criminal record who was fined and sentenced to be whipped from Rosemary Lane to the Hermitage within days of his appointment. Rose's offence, like Ketch's, was insubordination. In October 1685 he had been brought before the magistrate Charles Osborne as a disturber of the peace; in December, brought before the same magistrate for bigamy, he was charged with having said, 'God damn Justice Osborne … I am sorry I had not a Rasour for him' (Jeaffreson, 4.300), and duly convicted at the January sessions.

The version of these events recorded by the nonconformist diarist Roger Morrice is at best only partially accurate (he has both Ketch and Rose condemned by the City authorities, whereas in both cases they were punished in Middlesex), but gives some sense of the politicized gossip around Ketch's name. According to Morrice, Ketch had presented a bill 'for extraordinary charges in quartering of traitors, and boyling their bodies &c'. When he refused to pay such an exorbitant sum, 'Ketch told the sheriff if he did not pay it, he would serve him as he did his master Cornish'. Hauled before the lord mayor and aldermen, he tried to excuse himself by claiming that his words meant 'not that he would hang him, but that he should execute the offenders himselfe as he told his master Cornish in the like case' (DWL, Morrice Ent'ring Book P, 517). The parallel between Ketch's and Rose's offences was made even stronger in Morrice's version: 'Rose having executed some … came to the sheriff with a bill (which the sheriff somewhat roughly refused to pay) Rose told him if he had had a pistoll in his pockett he would have shot him thorough' (ibid.). According to Morrice it was Ketch who whipped Rose through the streets.

Both Ketch's gaoling and Rose's flogging produced satirical broadsides. The broadside *Jack Catch his Bridewel Oration* (14 January 1686) imagined him addressing his daughter who had come to view him in prison:

Go, get thee home, thou little staring fool,
When I come out thou shalt to th' Boarding School.

It relished presenting Ketch warning his hearers against the vices which had brought him to prison, an ironic variant on the commonplace theme of the sins which led to the gallows:

Thus haughty *Jack* you see will bate his Pride
Rather than be a Tennant to St Bride.
Then learn by me all you that stomach it
All you that grumble as you thought not fit,
To your superiors freely to submit,
Least *I* put in and nimbly tye the String,
Which may perhaps too late repentance bring
And you a Tune that does not please you Sing.

Pleasant Discourse by Way of Dialogue between the Old and New Jack Catch had Old Catch admitting that he had indeed been 'within a Spit and a Stride' of the same punishment as his successor.

Rose was pardoned his fine in February 1686, and appears to have retained the office until he was himself hanged for housebreaking in April. Ketch was reinstated, but was dead within the year. He was buried in St James's, Clerkenwell, on 29 November 1686. His wife was granted the administration of his estate, the record of the grant recognizing Ketch's status as esquire. The antiquary Matthew Hutton provided an apt epitaph on Ketch's reputation for brutality when he reported to Thomas Comber

that the whig pamphleteer Samuel Johnson 'was whipd on Wednesday but civilly used by the new hangman, Jack Ketch being buried 2 dayes before' (*Autobiographies*, 1.150).

Already by 1699 *A New Dictionary of the … Canting Crew* could define 'Jack Kitch' as 'the Hangman of that Name, but now all his Successors'. And for the next century and more 'Jack Ketch' was the generic name for the common hangman: the name 'vulgarly given to all who have succeeded him in his odious office', as Macaulay noted in 1848 (Macaulay, 3.618). 'Dine with John Wilkes, Sir! I'd as soon dine with Jack Ketch!' Boswell imagined would be Samuel Johnson's reply if he suggested such a meeting (J. Boswell, *Life of Johnson*, ed. R. W. Chapman, 1980, 765). A correspondent of Hannah More, Sir William Weller Pepys, paid testimony to the continuing appeal of Ketch's name when in looking for an example of his enthusiasm for all biography he admitted that 'were I to begin the Life of Jack Ketch, I should never quit him till I saw him hanged on his own gallows, and read his last dying speech' (W. Roberts, *Memoirs of the Life and Correspondence of Mrs Hannah More*, 3rd edn, 4 vols., 1834, 3.370). The nickname attached itself to even as notorious a hangman in his own right as William Calcraft, who was active from 1829 onwards. In the 1830s Edmund Gibbon Wakefield entitled an attack on the use of the death penalty for all but the most serious crimes, *The hangman and the judge, or, A letter from Jack Ketch to Mr. Justice Alderson; revised by the ordinary of Newgate* while Charles Whitehead's *The Autobiography of a Notorious Legal Functionary* (*Jack Ketch*) provided a parody of contemporary moralizing crime literature.

However, the durability of Ketch's name was most strikingly witnessed, and indeed sealed, by his role as a foil to Mr Punch. The character of Punch came to England in the Restoration period and his persona was very much established by the early eighteenth century in the booths of Bartholomew fair and elsewhere. However, the classic Punch and Judy puppet show seems to have been a development of the late eighteenth century, its heyday in the decades around 1800. This was very much the Punch and Judy performed in the streets and back rooms of pubs for an adult audience, the show not yet rendered safe for the Victorian parlour or end of the pier. Judy, Jack Ketch, and Lucifer were the three characters most consistently present in versions of the show which had taken shape by 1820, in which the cheerfully amoral serial killer Punch slaughtered his way through wife and baby, the agents of the law, and finally Lucifer—'the triad of social controls: wife, hangman and devil—marriage, law and morality' (Gatrell, 121). In some versions the show climaxed with Ketch's death rather than the Devil's. Bernard Blackmantle in 1826 described Ketch as 'a greater man than old Lucifer' and the scene where Mr Punch duped Ketch into putting his head in the noose as 'the ne plus ultra of [Punch's] exploits, the cream of all his comicalities … Mr John Ketch hangs suspended in the air—Punch stands in a glorious triumph—[and] all the world backs him in his conquest' (Leach, 53). 'Why were you so cruel as to commit so many murders?' Ketch asks Punch in the performance recorded by John Payne Collier; 'But that's no reason why you should be cruel too, and murder me,' Punch replies (Gatrell, 121). Ketch was the only puppet apart from Punch who needed dummy legs, for the jerking movements as he hanged.

The Punch and Judy show presented a world turned upside down, where the hangman was defeated, and was distinctively plebeian. Yet in its sardonic reflections on the common hangman as the brutal guarantor of the social and political order, its grim acknowledgement of his power and its ironic take on the frail pretensions of the human agent who dispensed death on behalf of the state, it is not so far removed from the versions of Ketch that were deployed in the social satire and political propaganda in his own lifetime which so successfully imprinted his name in popular memory.   TIM WALES

Sources J. Bland, *The common hangman* (1984) · R. Hovenden, ed., *A true register of all the christenings, mariages, and burialles in the parishe of St James, Clarkenwell, from … 1551 (to 1754)*, 6 vols., Harleian Society, register section, 9–10, 13, 17, 19–20 (1884–94), 1.234, 5.120 · archdeaconry court of London act book, 1683–7, GL, MS 9050/14, 206 · R. Morrice, 'Ent'ring book', DWL, P. 407, 517; Q. 27 · N. Luttrell, *A brief historical relation of state affairs from September 1678 to April 1714*, 1 (1857), 353–4, 370, 378 · *The Tyburn ghost, or, The strange downfall of the gallows* (1678) · *The plotters ballad, being Jack Ketch's incomparable receipt for the cure of trayterous recusants* (1678) · *The man of destiny's hard fortune, or, Squire Ketch's declaration* (1679) · *The Romanists best doctor* (1680) · *The apologie of John Ketch, esq.; the executioner of London, in vindication of himself as to the execution of the late Lord Russel* (1683) · *A bill and answer betwixt Jack Catch plaintiff, and Slingsby Bethel, & al., defendants of the year 1681* (1686) · *A dialogue between Jack Ketch and his journey-man* (1683) · *Jack Catch his Bridewel oration, or a word or two of advice to his friends* (1686) · *Pleasant discourse by way of dialogue between the old and new Jack Catch* (1686) · G. de F. Lord and others, eds., *Poems on affairs of state: Augustan satirical verse, 1660–1714*, 7 vols. (1963–75), vols. 3–4 (1682–5, 1685–8) · J. C. Jeaffreson, ed., *Middlesex county records*, 4 vols. (1886–92), vol. 4, p. 300 · E. M. Thompson, ed., *Correspondence of the family of Hatton*, 2, CS, new ser., 23 (1878), 32 · *An account of what passed at the execution of the late duke of Monmouth* (1685) · Evelyn, *Diary*, 4.455–6 · F. P. Verney, ed., *Memoirs of the Verney family*, 2 vols. (1907), 2.404–5 · T. B. Macaulay, *The history of England from the accession of James II*, new edn, ed. C. H. Firth, 6 vols. (1913–15), 3.618 · B. E. Gent, *A new dictionary of the … canting crew* (1699) · R. Leach, *The Punch and Judy: history, tradition and meaning* (1985) · V. A. C. Gatrell, *The hanging tree: execution and the English people, 1770–1868* (1994) · *The autobiographies and letters of Thomas Comber, sometime precentor of York and dean of Durham*, ed. C. E. Whiting, 1, SurtS, 156 (1946), 149–50 · Middlesex sessions rolls, December 1685, January 1686, February 1686, LMA, MJ/SR/1678, 1680, 1683 · A. Marks, *Tyburn tree: its history and annals* (1908)

Ketel, Cornelis Govertszoon (1548–1616), painter and poet, was born in Gouda in the Netherlands on 18 March 1548. He was the illegitimate son of Elysabeth Jacobsdochter Ketel (*d.* 1582) and Govert Janszoon van Proyen (*d.* 1574), who was related to the Gouda glass painter Wouter Pieterszoon Crabeth. Cornelis received some training from his uncle Cornelis Jacobszoon Ketel, who was also a glass painter, and subsequently, about 1565, from the painter Anthonie Blocklandt in Delft. In 1566 he went to France, going to Fontainebleau and living in Paris. He was prevented from travelling on to Italy by an edict that commanded temporary residents to return to the Spanish Netherlands, which he did in 1567.

After practising as a painter in Gouda for six years, in 1573 Ketel moved to London, where he initially resided in Southwark with the Netherlandish sculptor William Cure (Willem Keur), a friend of his uncle. In London in 1574 he married Aeltje Gerritsdochter (*d.* 1606), also from Gouda, and the couple had three children who were baptized in London: Gedeon (1576–1579), Ezechiell (*b.* 1578), and Eve (*b.* 1579). The latter two were dead by 28 February 1595, as was another son, Rafel, who was born in Amsterdam in 1581. A further son, Andries, died before November 1613. The family lived in Bishopsgate, near Crosby Place in the City of London. Many of Ketel's wealthy merchant patrons were based in this area, such as Thomas 'Customer' Smythe (1522–1591), who apparently commissioned from Ketel a set of head-and-shoulders portraits of his large family. Nine of these survive, seven in a single British private collection, one in another private collection, and one in the Yale Center for British Art, New Haven, Connecticut. They are all inscribed 1579, and the capital 'A' of the Latin word 'A[nn]o', also written thereon, is in a distinctive serpentine form frequently found on Ketel's British works.

Ketel's earliest London commissions had come from the German merchants at the Steelyard, the Hanseatic trading base next to the Thames. These included the circular double-sided *Portrait of a Gentleman, Probably Adam Wachendorff* (1574; Rijksmuseum, Amsterdam); the back of the wooden panel is painted with the device of a naked cherub blowing bubbles, with a Greek inscription that translates as 'Man's life is like a bubble'—a meditation on the vanity of human life. In 1577 he depicted *Sir Martin Frobisher* at full length (Bodl. Oxf.), the only surviving work from a commission from the Cathay Company for nineteen pictures, among them ones of the Inuit who had accompanied Frobisher back to England from his expedition in search of a north-west passage to China. Records for this commission show that Ketel was charging £5 for a full-length portrait and £1 for a head.

In 1578, according to his Haarlem-based friend and biographer Karel van Mander (writing in 1604, while Ketel was still alive), Edward Seymour, first earl of Hertford, commissioned him to portray Elizabeth I, for which she sat at 'the house of Hantworth'. This work seems not to have survived. (The 'Sieve' portrait of the queen, now in the Pinacoteca Nazionale, Siena, was long thought to be this, but was found in 1988 to be signed by another Netherlandish painter, Quentin Metsys the younger.) Ketel was also said to have painted a portrait of Aubrey de Vere, twentieth earl of Oxford.

In England, according to van Mander, Ketel received many portrait commissions, but none for the allegorical and historical paintings which he preferred to do. He therefore produced a large allegory, on canvas, 'with more than life-sized figures with the symbolic representation of how Power is overcome by Wisdom and Prudence' (van Mander, 358–9). This was purchased by a 'young … English merchant called Mr Pieter Hachten, who presented it to Sir Christoffel Hatten, who died as Lord Chancellor' (ibid.). A large fragment of this picture, signed by Ketel and dated 1580, was recently discovered (priv. coll., USA).

In 1581 Ketel left for Amsterdam: it has been suggested that his free, painterly style of portraiture was out of tune with the more unshadowed, linear manner favoured by clients in England. He seems to have introduced the use of the full-length portrait for middle-class sitters to the northern Netherlands. In Amsterdam he painted many portraits, notably the large full-length group *The Militia Company of Captain Dirck Jacobszoon Rosecrans and Lieutenant Pauw* (1588; Rijksmuseum). He also produced painted and drawn allegories, accompanied by poetic texts, most of which are now lost. The Danish-born painter Pieter Isaacszoon was his pupil. In 1598 he began making clay figures. From around 1599, so van Mander reported, Ketel experimented with painting without the use of a brush, using his fingers and, in 1600, his feet. These works seem to have been conceived as displays of technical virtuosity. In October 1607 he married, second, Ael Jansdochter (*d.* 1630/31). In 1613 he was partially paralysed by a stroke. Ketel died in Amsterdam on 5 August 1616, and was buried there in the Oude Kerk three days later.   KAREN HEARN

Sources K. van Mander, *The lives of the illustrious Netherlandish and German painters*, ed. H. Miedema, 1 (1994), 357–78 · C. P. Cooper, ed., *Proceedings of his majesty's commissioners on the public records of the kingdom, June 1832–August 1833* (1833), 75, 560 · W. Stechow, 'Cornelis Ketels Einzelbildnisse', *Zeitschrift für Bildende Kunst*, 63 (1929–30), 202 · W. Stechow, 'Notes and reviews: Homo bulla', *Art Bulletin*, 20 (1938), 227–8 · R. Strong, *The English icon* (1969), 11, 13, 49, 151–8 · *All the paintings of the Rijksmuseum*, Rijksmuseum (Amsterdam, 1976), 315–16 · T. Schulting, 'Cornelis Ketel en zijn familie: een revisie', *Oud Holland*, 108 (1994), 171–207 · B. A. Heezen-Stoll, *Cornelis Ketel, uytnemende schilder, van der Goude: een iconografische studie van zijn 'historien'* (Delft, 1987) · T. Schulting, review of B. A. Heezen-Stoll, *Oud Holland*, 103 (1989), 54 · K. Hearn, ed., *Dynasties: painting in Tudor and Jacobean England, 1530–1630* (1995), 108–12 [exhibition catalogue, Tate Gallery, London, 12 Oct 1995 – 7 Jan 1996] · R. Jones, 'The methods and materials of three Tudor artists', *Dynasties: painting in Tudor and Jacobean England, 1530–1630*, ed. K. Hearn (1995), 231–9 [exhibition catalogue, Tate Gallery, London, 12 Oct 1995 – 7 Jan 1996] · R. Ekkart, 'Ketel, Cornelis', *The dictionary of art*, ed. J. Turner (1994) · T. Schulting, 'Cornelis Ketel en de gebroeders Wachendorff: geschiedenis van een identificatie', *De Nederlandische Leeuw*, 114 (April–May 1997), 135–66 · T. Schulting, '"Sterckheyt van wijsheyt en voorsichtichteyt verwonnen": overwegingen bij een allegorie van Cornelis Ketel', *Oud Holland*, 111 (1997), 153–62 · E. Auerbach, *Tudor artists* (1954), 107, 173 · M. Edmond, 'Limners and picturemakers', *Walpole Society*, 47 (1978–80), 60–242
Likenesses H. Bary, line engraving, 1659 (after lost self-portrait by C. Ketel), BM; repro. in F. W. H. Hollstein, *Dutch and Flemish etchings, engravings and woodcuts*, 1 (1949), 128, no. 54 · T. Chambers, line engraving, pubd 1762 (after C. Kete), BM, NPG; repro. in H. Walpole, *Anecdotes of painting in England*, 1, 137 · W. H. Worthington, engraving, 1849, repro. in H. Walpole, *Anecdotes of painting in England*, 1a, p. 159 · H. Hondius, engraving, repro. in H. Hondius, *Pictorum aliquot celebrium praecipuae Germaniae inferioris effigies* (1610)

Ketel, William (*fl. c.*1100), thaumaturgical writer, is mentioned only in a lost manuscript of unknown date which contained hagiographical material concerning St John of Beverley, and which was printed (from a transcript) by the seventeenth-century editors of the *Acta sanctorum*. After the conclusion of Folcard's *Life of St John Beverley*, this manuscript contained a series of miracle stories relating

to that saint and headed: 'Other Miracles Written by William Ketel, Clerk of Beverley'. The ensuing chapter began with a dedication, the Latin of which is evidently corrupt, but which was apparently addressed by 'William, least of the clerks of St John' to two of his superiors, who appear as 'Ethal.' and 'Thur.', and who had respectively the offices of provost and master (Raine, *Historians of the Church of York*, 1.261, n. 1). After the series of stories thus introduced, the manuscript preserved a second series, which began with an expression of astonishment that of all the clerks of Beverley only William, 'who is also called Ketel' (ibid., 292), should have related the miracles of St John. The same miracle stories as in the lost manuscript are largely found in BL, Cotton MS Faustina B.iv (twelfth-century), and there is also a selection in BL, Add. MS 61901 (fifteenth-century); but neither of these manuscripts contains the references to William Ketel.

Allowing for the corruption of the dedication, one of the dedicatees of Ketel's miracle stories may have been Thurstan, provost of Beverley, who appears in charters of *c.*1135–52, and died, according to John of Hexham, in 1152. This would suggest that Ketel worked in the first half of the twelfth century, which would not be inconsistent with the fact that the latest datable events in the miracle stories concern the reign of William the Conqueror (Ketel stated that he was relating miracles of which he had personal knowledge or which he knew on good authority). On the other hand, the dedication may mean that the provost was an otherwise unknown Ethal, and Ketel may have worked as early as the late eleventh century. Verbal similarities to Alfred of Beverley (who was writing about 1143) in Ketel's stories probably result from Alfred's having drawn on them rather than vice versa; and, if it is correct (which is not certain) that the reference in the stories to St John's 'former' tomb was made in relation to the tomb established after the translation of 1197, it is likely that this was a later interpolation. The miracle stories are not of great historical interest, although they do contain clues to the development of the cult of St John and of Beverley Minster as a building; and Ketel's account of the visit of King Æthelstan to Beverley appears to be the earliest version of this alleged event. Ketel was a Scandinavian name, properly spelled Ketill, and was widespread in eastern England.   DAVID ROLLASON

Sources J. Raine, ed., *The historians of the church of York and its archbishops*, 3 vols., Rolls Series, 71 (1879–94) [incl. lost MS printed in *Acta sanctorum*] · A. F. Leach, ed., *Memorials of Beverley Minster*, 1, SurtS, 98 (1898) · W. Farrer and others, eds., *Early Yorkshire charters*, 12 vols. (1914–65) · J. Raine, ed., *The priory of Hexham*, 1, SurtS, 44 (1864) · R. K. Morris and E. Cambridge, 'Beverley Minster before the early 13th century', *Medieval art and architecture in the East Riding of Yorkshire*, ed. C. Wilson, British Archaeological Association Conference Transactions, 9 (1989) · G. Fellows-Jensen, *Scandinavian personal names in Lincolnshire and Yorkshire* (1968)

Ketèlbey, Albert William (1875–1959), composer, was born on 9 August 1875 at 41 Alma Street, Aston, Birmingham, the second of the five children of George Henry Ketelbey (*b.* 1854), engraver, and his wife, Sarah Ann

Aston. Albert added the accent to his surname in his earliest publications, and preferred to sign his name as Albert W. Ketèlbey.

Ketèlbey's early interest in music took the form of piano lessons and the local church choir, and he studied composition with A. R. Gaul at the Midland Institute School of Music. An alleged performance of his own piano sonata at the age of eleven cannot be substantiated, but the surviving manuscript of a similar work dated 1888 shows a precocious mastery of composition which helped him gain a scholarship to Trinity College of Music, London. He won several prizes before receiving his licentiate in 1895, and his studies left him well-equipped for a versatile life in music.

Ketèlbey's early appointments included those of organist at St John's, Wimbledon, examiner for Trinity College, and conductor of musicals at several London theatres. There he met the actress Charlotte (Lottie) Siegenberg (d. 1947), whom he married in 1906. As music editor for the publisher A. Hammond & Co. he became fluent in reworking music for different instrumental combinations, notably preparing an edition of Tchaikovsky's recent *Symphonie pathétique*, which he rearranged for the smaller orchestras that were beginning to appear in town parks and on seaside piers.

In 1906 Ketèlbey joined the Columbia Graphophone Company, and for more than twenty years he served as musical director in the burgeoning record industry. In this post he worked with many of the leading musicians of the day, from opera singers and concert pianists to jazz musicians and music-hall stars. More than 600 recordings were issued with him conducting the Court Symphony Orchestra, the Silver Stars Band, and other ensembles. During the First World War he could once again be found in the orchestra pits of the West End, conducting reviews for André Charlot. Items from these shows inevitably found their way into Columbia's recording studio.

From his student days onwards Ketèlbey had a wide variety of his own compositions published, under both his own name and pseudonyms including Raoul Clifford and Anton Vodorinski—salon and educational pieces for piano, drawing-room ballads with words by Florence Hoare (a friend from student days), and later, many 'characteristic pieces' for orchestra. His first major success was *The Phantom Melody* (1912), written for the cellist Auguste Van Biene. This was followed by the orchestral pieces *In a Monastery Garden* (recorded 1914), *Wedgwood Blue* (1920), *In a Persian Market* (1920), *Bells across the Meadows* (1921), *In a Chinese Temple Garden* (1923), *Sanctuary of the Heart* (1924), *Cockney Suite* (1924, with the uproarious ''Appy 'Ampstead' as its finale), and some fifty other titles, most of which were also published in different arrangements for brass band, military band, and piano. A series of eighteen pieces for the silent cinema, with prescriptive titles such as *Danse diabolique* (*for Savages Scenes and Native War-Dances*, *Hurries and Tumult and Storm*), was particularly lucrative, as the Performing Right Society collected royalties for hundreds of performances each day. From 1928 Ketèlbey was able to devote his career to composition, and in 1929 he was nominated on the basis of income as 'Britain's greatest living composer' (*Performing Right Gazette*, October 1929).

The popularity of Ketèlbey's style with lovers of light music during the inter-war years lay in its memorable expressive melodies combined with its ability to set the scene by enhanced use of different kinds of colour: local colour in the choice of characteristic settings, often with explicit narrative captions printed above the music; musical colour in the form of exotic scales and harmonies; orchestral colour in the novel use of singing by the players and of sound effects executed by the drummer; and even colour in the alluring pictures on the covers of the printed sheet music, which brightened the contents of many a piano stool around the world. Everything has been done to establish the vivid musical identity of the camel-drivers, beggars, jugglers, snake charmer, caliph, and princess who are gathered together 'in a Persian market'. In contrast to the colourful self-advertisement of his compositions, the composer himself kept a low profile and appeared in the public eye only for an annual concert tour promoting his own music. He and Lottie had no children, but when not on extended holidays in Nice they held open house for young nieces and nephews at their home in Hampstead.

After the Second World War, Ketèlbey's music fell out of popularity, and in 1947 he suffered a domestic disaster when a flood at his house not only destroyed his manuscripts but also precipitated the illness which killed Lottie. He subsequently married Mabel Maud (d. c.1985), widow of L. S. Pritchett, on 30 October 1948, and spent his final years living at Rookstone, Egypt Hill, Cowes, Isle of Wight. By the time of his death in Cowes on 26 November 1959 he had slipped into obscurity, and his funeral at Golders Green crematorium was attended by just a handful of mourners.   TOM McCANNA

Sources 'Mr Albert W. Ketelbey', *British Musician*, 9 (1896), 271–2 · Allegro, 'The man behind the records', *Musical Mirror* (June 1921), 9–10 · A. W. Ketelbey, 'In a monastery garden', *Music Masterpieces* (March 1926), 183 · W. Neve, 'Pictures in music', *The Lady* (21 Aug 1975) · K. Gänzl, *The British musical theatre*, 2 vols. (1986) · C. Ehrlich, *Harmonious alliance* (1989) · T. McCanna, ed., *The music of Albert W. Ketelbey: a catalogue* (2000) · J. Sant, *Albert W. Ketèlbey (1875–1959)* (2000) · private information (2004) · H. Saxe-Wyndham and G. L'Epine, *Who's who in music*, 2nd edn (1915), 150 · 'Albert William Ketèlbey', *Radio Times* (4 Sept 1931) · *DNB* · F. Andrews, *Columbia 10″ records, 1904–30* (1985) · A. Badrock and F. Andrews, *The complete Regal catalogue* (1991) · R. Taylor, *Columbia twelve-inch records in the United Kingdom, 1906–1930* (1994) · K. Russell, 'Summoned by bells', BBC Radio 3, 30 July 1995 · P. Martland, *Since records began: EMI, the first 100 years* (1997), 100 · *CGPLA Eng. & Wales* (1960) · b. cert. · m. cert.

Archives BBC WAC, letters · Birm. CL, MS · Library of Light-Orchestral Music, Preston, MS · St Antony's Friary, Forest Gate, London, MS | SOUND BL NSA, documentary recording

Likenesses photograph, repro. in *British Musician* · photograph, repro. in *Musical Mirror* · photograph, repro. in *Musical Opinion*, 52 (1929), 531 · photograph, repro. in *Musical Opinion*, 54 (1930), 86 · photograph, repro. in *Musical Opinion*, 61 (1938), 86 · photograph, repro. in *Sunday Times* (2 Aug 1959), 5 · photograph, repro. in *The Gramophone* (Aug 1975), 308 · photograph, repro. in *The Lady* · photograph, repro. in Martland, *Since records began* · photographs, repro. in Sant, *Albert W. Ketèlbey*

Wealth at death £28,492 8s. 7d.: probate, 22 Jan 1960, *CGPLA Eng. & Wales*

Kethe, William (d. 1594), religious polemicist and translator, probably originated in The Mearns, Scotland. Very little is known about his early life; he may have lived in Exeter. What is certain is that by Edward VI's reign he had become a writer of militantly protestant broadside poems. *A Ballet Declaring the Fal of the Whore of Babylone Intytuled 'Tye thy Mare, Tom Boye'* (1548?) satirized the Roman Catholic church, whereas *Of Misrules Contending with Gods Worde by Name* (1553?) expressed confidence that the Edwardian regime would correct unscriptural practice. Following the succession of Mary I, Kethe exiled himself to Frankfurt am Main, Germany, arriving by December 1554 and entering the lists against the Marian government (particularly Lord Chancellor Stephen Gardiner, a Catholic hardliner) with *William Keth his Seeing Glasse* (c.1555). A liturgical dispute now broke out among the English asylum seekers; a puritan faction led by John Knox and including Kethe, William Whittingham, John Foxe, and Anthony Gilby won the backing of John Calvin for their refusal to use the 1552 prayer book which contained ceremonies regarded as papist superstition. In August 1555 the group seceded from Frankfurt and headed for the protection of Calvin's Geneva; on 5 November 1556 Kethe was received into Knox's congregation there, having perhaps spent the interim with Foxe at Basel. Kethe was by now married to Elizabeth, a widow, who accompanied him; they did not have children.

In 1557 Kethe and John Bodley travelled with another group of English exiles from Wesel in Germany to a Swiss refuge at Aarau. Kethe now espoused the radical political ideas developed by some of his colleagues. Christopher Goodman's *How Superior Powers Oght to be Obeyd of their Subjects* (1558) encouraged the people actively to resist Mary as an idolatrous tyrant and Kethe endorsed this in his introductory poem:

> Whom fury long fosterd by sufferance and awe,
> Have right rule subverted, and made will their lawe,
> Whose pride how to temper, this truth will thee tell,
> So as thou resist mayst, and yet not rebel.
> (Warton, 4.225, n. 3)

Kethe also echoed the demand for violent resistance contained in Knox's *Appellation* (1558) by including with it his metrical translation of Psalm 94 and an incitement to 'up and rise with me against this wicked band' (Ridley, 278).

Kethe's lasting achievement was his translation of the Psalms into English metrical verse. He was the single greatest Geneva-based contributor to the psalter published with the 1561 edition of the émigrés' alternative liturgy, *The Forme of Prayers and Ministration of the Sacraments Approved by J Calvyn*. The core psalms were taken from an earlier work by Thomas Sternhold and John Hopkins with the innovation that accompanying tunes were supplied. Kethe's own contribution of twenty-five psalms exhibited a strong French influence. His best-known psalm was 100 ('Al people that on earth do dwel'), known as the 'Old Hundredth', which he set to an existing tune by Louis Bourgeois. Kethe's Psalms were enormously influential: all were included in the Scottish psalter (1564), fewer in the English psalter (1562).

Mary's death and the succession of Elizabeth I were read as providential signs by the Genevans that the issues dividing them from the other exiles should be resolved. In December 1558 the leadership dispatched Kethe on a tour of the other congregations bearing a letter enjoining unity. He returned in January 1559 and probably assisted in the production of the Geneva Bible (1560), which was as immensely popular with committed protestants over the following century as it was anathematical to conformists who deprecated its acceptance of resistance theory. Kethe received permission to leave Geneva in May 1560 and by 14 October 1561 had been appointed rector of Child Okeford Inferior, Dorset, by Henry Capel. As chaplain to William Whittingham he participated in the abortive attempt led by the puritan courtier Ambrose Dudley, earl of Warwick, to hold Newhaven (Le Havre), Normandy, against the French from October 1562 until July 1563. Thomas Wood's letter to Gilby of October 1565 demonstrates that Kethe retained contact with the Genevan brotherhood now based in London, and in 1569 he volunteered as preacher to Dudley's army which put down the rising of the northern earls. With the support of such a powerful patron, and that of local puritan gentry like Sir George Trenchard of Wolveton and the less unequivocally zealous John Williams of Herringstone, he apparently escaped harassment by the church courts, becoming the most prominent of the first wave of puritan clergy in Dorset.

The printed edition of Kethe's assize sermon of 17 January 1571 preached at Blandford Forum, which was dedicated to Dudley, his 'right honourable very good Lord' (Lupton, 5.93), roundly condemned the Dorset county governors for failing to suppress papist attempts to stir up sedition following the queen's deposition by Pope Pius V the previous February. The lord lieutenant himself (either Lord Mountjoy or Sir William Paulet) was openly criticized for imprisoning rather than rewarding one local man who brought seditious papist literature to his attention. The populace of this conservative downland area persisted in sinful ways, which Kethe now condemned in his call for reformation: 'abuse of the Sabbath daye, bulbeatings, beare-beatings, bowlings, dicying, cardying, daunsynges, drunkeness, whoredome and sturdy vagabondes not looked into' (ibid., 94). Peter Birchet, who in October 1573 stabbed the sea dog Sir John Hawkins mistaking him for Sir Christopher Hatton, a courtier unpopular with the godly, has been linked with radical puritanism. However, the puritan Kethe encountered him shortly before the incident and thought him 'clean out of his wits' (Collinson, 150–51). Kethe signed his will on 24 January 1594 and died at his rectory before 6 June, when it was proved; he was buried at Child Okeford. His wife outlived him.   J. FIELDING

Sources C. H. Garrett, *The Marian exiles: a study in the origins of Elizabethan puritanism* (1938), 204–5 · L. Lupton, *A history of the Geneva Bible* (1973), 5.68–95 · will, PRO, PROB 11/84, sig. 46 · J. F. Kellas Johnstone and A. W. Robertson, *Bibliographia Aberdonensis*, ed. W. D. Simpson, Third Spalding Club, 1 (1929), 44–5, 50, 61 · J. Ridley, *John*

Knox (1968), 198, 211, 278, 280, 306 • T. Warton, *The history of English poetry*, rev. edn, ed. R. Price, 4 vols. (1824), vol. 4, p. 225, n. 3 • J. Hutchins, *The history and antiquities of the county of Dorset*, 3rd edn, ed. W. Shipp and J. W. Hodson, 4 (1874), 77–9, 84 • *DNB* • P. J. Anderson, 'Catalogue of the Taylor collection, prefatory note', *Aberdeen University Library Bulletin*, 1 (1911–13), 263–75 • 'Letters of Thomas Wood, puritan, 1566–1577', ed. P. Collinson, *BIHR*, special suppl., 5 (1960) [whole issue] • P. Collinson, *The Elizabethan puritan movement* (1967), 52, 150–51 • D. Underdown, *Fire from heaven: the life of an English town in the seventeenth century* (1992), 157 • D. Underdown, *Revel, riot and rebellion: popular politics and culture in England, 1603–1660* (1985), 47–8, 88, 91 • Bristol RO, EP/A/3/106 • G. Scott Thomson, *Lord lieutenants in the sixteenth century* (1923), 50

Kett, Francis (*c.*1547–1589), physician and alleged heretic, was born in Wymondham, Norfolk, the son of Thomas Kett (*c.*1500–1553), gentleman, and his wife, Agnes (*d.* 1573), and nephew of Robert *Kett (*c.*1492–1549). After the death of her husband, Agnes married Stephen Verdon, who by his will of 1572/3 contributed to the costs of his stepson's education. Having been admitted as a sizar to Clare College, Cambridge, in Michaelmas 1566, Francis graduated BA from Corpus Christi early in 1570. Proceeding MA in 1573, he was elected a fellow of the college in the same year, and at some point he was ordained. On 27 December 1576 he was one of the signatories of a letter thanking the university chancellor, Lord Burghley, for his arbitration in college disputes. He did not marry.

In 1580 Kett resigned his fellowship. He is unlikely to have influenced Christopher Marlowe, as used to be thought, because he left college soon after Marlowe's arrival there. He graduated MD in 1581, and in 1585 'Francis Kett, doctor of phisick' issued *The Glorious and Beautiful Garland of Mans Glorification*. As its dedication to Queen Elizabeth might suggest, this contained nothing doctrinally untoward. But in 1588 Edmund Scambler, bishop of Norwich, framed 'Articles of heretical pravity' against Kett. Kett's views seem to have included both Arian and millenarian elements: according to the charges, he believed Jesus had suffered 'only as Jesus already, and shall suffer hereafter as Christ' (only then becoming divine); that 'Christ is now in his human nature gathering a church in Erthe in Judea'; and that 'this year of our Lord 1588 divers Jews shall be sent to divers countries to publish the new covenant' (Grosart, appx B1). A second official account reports that he also believed in soul-sleeping (psychopannychism). The Norwich minister William Burton reported his conviction that 'Christ is not God, but a good man as others be', but also noted that 'monstrous as he was in opinions, see how holy he would seem to be in his outward conversation. The sacred Bible almost never out of his hands, himself always in prayer, his tongue never ceased praising of God' (Burton, 125).

On 7 October 1588 Scambler wrote to Burghley, urging that Kett be speedily executed as a dangerous blasphemer. He was burnt in the ditch of Norwich Castle on 14 January 1589. Burton was a witness of his horrific death:

> when he went to the fire he was clothed in sackecloth, he went leaping and dauncing: being in the fire, above twenty times together clapping his hands, he cried nothing but blessed bee God … and so continued until the fire had

> consumed all his nether partes, and untill he was stifled with the smoke. (Burton, 125)

ALEXANDER GORDON, *rev.* STEPHEN WRIGHT

Sources W. Grosart, ed., *The Huth Library: the life and complete works of Robert Greene*, 1 (1881) • W. Burton, *David's evidence* (1592) • G. Kett, *The pedigree of Kett of Wymondham* (1913) • L. Kett, *The Ketts of Norfolk, a yeoman family* (1921) [also prints Edmund Scambler's articles] • J. Strype, *Annals of the Reformation and establishment of religion … during Queen Elizabeth's happy reign*, new edn, 3/2 (1824) • Venn, *Alum. Cant.*

Kett, Henry (1761–1825), college teacher and writer, was born in the parish of St Peter Mancroft, Norwich, on 12 February 1761, the son of Benjamin Kett, cordwainer and freeman of that city, and his wife, Mary. He was educated at Norwich grammar school, and in March 1777 was admitted to Trinity College, Oxford. In June he was elected to a Blount exhibition and, the following year, to a scholarship. In 1784 he was elected to a fellowship at Trinity, in which he remained for almost forty years. He undertook various college offices, was an able and kindly tutor, and an impressive preacher who made no enemies within the college. He was a well-regarded Bampton lecturer in 1790, select preacher in 1801–2, classical examiner in 1803–4, and senior fellow of Trinity from 1803. Yet he never achieved the college presidency or any position of real distinction in university life. This failure may be attributed to an apparent lack of purpose or ambition; his interests were eclectic and he enjoyed the lighter side of life.

Kett's long face and straight, bony nose made him the victim of incessant teasing. His perceived equine features earned a crude nickname, Horse Kett, and a wide range of jokes, both learned and puerile ('an oat'—that is, a note—through his door), which he unfailingly took in very good part. A famous verse was composed about his poetical aspirations by his Trinity colleague Thomas Warton:

> Our Kett not a poet
> Why how can you say so?
> For if he's no Ovid
> I'm sure he's a Naso.

Equally well known was Dighton's caricature of the tall, lean figure published as 'A view from Trinity College' in 1807.

Kett's life had several fresh, or false, starts. His first venture was poetry. In 1793 he stood for the professorship of poetry at Oxford, publishing his *Juvenile Poems* in support of his case, but he was defeated by James Hurdis by twenty votes. In 1799 he published *History the Interpreter of Poetry*, which had appeared in three editions by 1800. His translations of John Jortin's poems were published in Jortin's *Miscellaneous Works*. In 1802 the professorship was again vacant; Kett canvassed but did not stand.

By then Kett was focusing on the theory and practice of education. In 1802 he published *Elements of General Knowledge*, a two-volume work based on his own lectures and including moral guidance and detailed bibliographies for the undergraduate and schoolboy. This work was criticized by John Davison in *A Short Account of Certain Notable Discoveries Contained in a Recent Work* (1804) but was resolutely defended by its author, who published, as 'S Nobody of King's College, Oxford', *The Biter Bit, or, Discoveries in a Pamphlet of Certain Notable Discoveries* (1804); *Elements* ran to an eighth edition in 1815. Kett was more daring to tackle the issue of female education, with *Emily: a Moral Tale* (1809). Emily's exciting romance packs a wide range of moral teaching, natural history, and general knowledge into a simple narrative and epistolary structure. A second undergraduate text, *Logic Made Easy* (1809), was Kett's least successful work. His over-simplification of Aristotle provoked a vicious and personal attack from Edward Copelston, who prefaced *The Examiner Examined, or, Logic Vindicated* with a passage from *The Aeneid* ending 'Equo ne credite, Teucri' ('Do not trust the horse, Trojans'). Crushed, Kett endeavoured to suppress the work.

Kett always had a penchant for the light-hearted. He contributed five papers to Thomas Monro's weekly publication, *Olla Podrida* (1788). He published a pleasant travel journal about the Lake District in 1798 and brought out his favourite bons mots as *The Flowers of Wit* (1814). He was a regular contributor to the *Gentleman's Magazine* and wrote two short biographies: one, of William Benwell, appended to *Poems, Odes, Prologues and Epilogues Spoken at Reading School* (1804), and the other, a memoir of Henry Headley, which appeared in *Select Beauties of Ancient English Poetry* (1810).

A devout Christian, Kett endeavoured to live a godly life. In 1787 he was a major contributor to the fund organized by Samuel Parr for the destitute Dr John Uri, former cataloguer of oriental manuscripts. Kett wrote the preface and notes to *Beauties of Christianity* (1813), Shoberl's translation from the French of Chateaubriand. From the second year of his fellowship until 1804 he held the incumbency of Elsfield, Oxfordshire, from Trinity's president, Joseph Chapman. Between 1812 and 1820 he was vicar of Sutton Benger, Wiltshire, and in 1814 Bishop George Tomline appointed him to the sinecure of the perpetual curacy of Hykeham, Lincolnshire.

On Christmas eve 1823, aged sixty-two, Kett married Maria White at Dowdeswell, Gloucestershire, and left Oxford to live at her native Charlton Kings, in the same county. By all accounts his mental state was by now unstable and he was prone to depression; certainly he had withdrawn from active participation in college life for much of the preceding fifteen years. On 30 June 1825—on a visit to Sir J. Gibbons at Stanwell, Middlesex—he drowned while swimming. As late as 1870 Kett's loyal friends were robustly defending his reputation against allegations of suicide. However, the fact that he left instructions in his will that he be buried in the parish where he died but, were he to die in London, that he should be buried in Stanwell, where the vicar was a personal friend, surely suggests more than an accident. On 28 November 1828 his widow married Thomas Nicholl.

Kett, whose obituarist valued his estate at under £25,000, made generous bequests to relatives in Norwich and Somerset; in addition, after Maria's death half his estate was to be divided between the Norfolk and Norwich Hospital, the Radcliffe Infirmary, Oxford, and the Clergy Orphan's School at Regent's Park. He left meticulous instructions regarding the disposal of his manuscripts and copyrights. He had been generous to Trinity College throughout his life, supporting building projects and donating portraits, and on his death he bequeathed £500 to the college's advowson fund, a final touch of irony from the man who had never wanted a college living.

CLARE HOPKINS

Sources *Annual Biography and Obituary*, 10 (1826) · *GM*, 1st ser. 95/2 (1825), 184–5 · *GM*, 1st ser., 98/2 (1828), 558 · *N&Q*, 4th ser., 9 (1872), 380, 448, 517 · W. Tuckwell, *Reminiscences of Oxford* (1900) · G. V. Cox, *Recollections of Oxford* (1868) · *The works of Samuel Parr … with memoirs of his life and writings*, ed. J. Johnstone, 8 vols. (1828) · E. Copleston, *The examiner examined, or, Logic vindicated* (1809) · H. E. D. Blakiston, *Trinity College* (1898) · Trinity College archives, register C, register D, admissions register B, benefactors book C · parish register, Norwich, St Peter Mancroft, 22 Feb 1761 [baptism] · *DNB* · will, PRO, PROB 11/1701, fols. 246r–247r
Likenesses R. Dighton, caricature, coloured etching, pubd 1807, BM; copy, Trinity College, Oxford
Wealth at death under £25,000: *Annual biography*; will, PRO, PROB 11/1701, fols. 246r–247r

Kett, Robert (c.1492–1549), rebel, was the fourth son of Thomas Kett, of Forncett, Norfolk, butcher and landholder (c.1460–1536), and his wife, Margery. His family was descended from the gentry family of Le Chat or Cat which can be traced back in the county to at least the early fourteenth century. That the Wymondham family from which Robert was descended was known as Kett alias Knight might suggest an earlier episode of illegitimacy.

Little is known of Kett's early life. Although his immediate family was no longer gentle, he was a man of some wealth. He lived in Wymondham as a tanner, the description given him in contemporary accounts of the rising that took his name. Tanning was a trade that could require a significant level of investment; Tudor chroniclers suggested that his moveable property was worth 1000 marks (about £670). Kett also had extensive landholdings, including manorial interests, at Wymondham, in whose manorial court he was prosecuted for enclosing lands, which were said to be worth £50 a year. His tax assessments in the 1540s suggest lower levels of wealth. But in their ranking they confirm that Kett, with his brother William, who combined the trades of mercer and butcher at Wymondham, was among the wealthiest members of his community. Both brothers were members of the local guild of St Thomas Becket. Taken together, these shards of evidence suggest that Kett exercised a role and authority in his immediate surroundings commensurate with his wealth and that known to have been exercised by the middling sort of the period. He married, probably before 1515. His wife, Alice, with whom he had up to five sons and who survived him, has been tentatively identified as the daughter of Sir Nicholas Appleyard of Bracon Ash. If this identification is correct, it would confirm that Kett was a man of rising prosperity.

Kett's rebellion In July 1549 rebellion broke out in Norfolk, to which Kett lent both name and leadership. The rising began with an attack on local enclosers, but swelled to a gathering of many thousands which camped at Mousehold Heath outside the regional capital of Norfolk from 10 July until final defeat by a royal army on 27 August. Although it is clear that there had been several earlier episodes of crowd action, the rising's beginnings have traditionally been dated to the celebrations held at Wymondham from 6 to 8 July to commemorate St Thomas Becket. Among the enclosers attacked there was John Flowerdew of Hethersett. Flowerdew, a successful lawyer, was locally unpopular because at the dissolution he had partially demolished the abbey at Wymondham which served also as the parish church. Tradition has it that Kett, who is known to have named one of his sons after the last abbot, Loye Ferrers, and who was said to have played a leading role in trying to prevent the despoliation of the abbey, became involved in the rising as a direct consequence of the feud with Flowerdew. When Flowerdew paid his attackers to throw down Kett's enclosures, Kett was said to have agreed to their destruction and to have offered himself as leader of the protesters. The protesters then decided to march to Norwich, a decision attributed (without supporting evidence) to Kett, where contemporary estimates put their numbers at anywhere between 16,000 and 20,000.

The scale and discipline of the rising have been attributed to the qualities of Kett's leadership—'the force of personality of a great leader of men' (Bindoff, 3). But there is little direct or independent evidence of Kett's role. A later legal case provides a rare glimpse of Kett proceeding out of the camp to the sound of drums to greet a contingent from the Norfolk village of Tunstead, whose leader Kett appointed one of his captains. Joined (reluctantly, it was claimed) by several of Norwich's leading citizens, Kett issued written warrants, copies of which have survived, for the collection of supplies of food and weapons, and, it was alleged, for the destruction of enclosures and detention of local gentry. In these warrants Kett and the others referred to themselves as the king's 'amici ac delegati' ('friends and deputies') and to their assembly as 'the King's Great Camp' (Russell, 47 and n., 107). The protesters also established a representative council which drew up the famous list of grievances, with at their core concern for the rights of commoners and manorial tenants, to which Kett's name is first signatory. Most famously, Kett was said to have dispensed justice beneath a tree, which came to be called the 'oak of reformation', on both disorderly followers and unpopular local gentleman (who were imprisoned in a mansion on nearby Mount Surrey which later came locally to be called Kett's Castle). As the survival of a 'writ' from Kett to Yarmouth's rulers requesting their assistance in resolving an inheritance dispute suggests, Kett's role at the oak of reformation provided a court for others seeking justice.

Kett's refusal of a royal pardon and the defeat of a royal army at the end of July marked a decisive change in the politics of the revolt. Late in August the arrival of another royal army, under the command of the earl of Warwick, led to his defeat after a fierce and bloody battle and to widespread repression. Kett was said to have abandoned Mousehold Heath for Dussindale in response to a prophecy that was thought to augur good fortune for the forthcoming battle:

the countrie gnuffes, Hob, Dick and Hick
with clubes and clouted shoon,
Shall fill up Dussindale with bloud
of slaughtered bodies soone.
(*Holinshed's Chronicles*, 1038)

In so doing he threw away his previous advantage over Warwick's cavalry. The evidence for the prophecy, like the report of an ill omen presaged by a snake falling from a rotten tree into Kett's wife's bosom, comes from hostile 'histories' of the rebellion; it is more likely that Kett's move was forced by the threat to his supply lines.

Kett was captured the day after the battle. By early September he and his brother William were prisoners in the Tower of London. On 26 November both were found guilty of treason by a special commission of oyer and terminer. By 1 December they had been returned to Norwich for execution. On 7 December 1549 Kett was hanged from the walls of Norwich Castle, while his brother was hanged from the steeple of Wymondham church. Following a post-mortem inquisition, whose panel included his old enemy John Flowerdew, held in January 1550, Kett's lands were seized by the crown and later given in reward to Lord Audley for his part in Kett's capture.

Kett's significance Kett and the rising that took his name are bound together in a way that makes it impossible to discuss the one without the other. But it is important to note that the events in Norfolk were but the largest of a series of protesters' camps both elsewhere in East Anglia and in the south-east. His signature always appeared first on the various commands and articles of the protesters, which makes it clear that Kett played a prominent role. But Kett was not, as he is sometimes portrayed, the only leader of the rebellion. The subsequent labelling of the events first as Kett's camp and later as Kett's rising probably exaggerates Kett's leadership and obscures that of others. In a letter written shortly before the final battle, the duke of Somerset referred to 'ket and the other Archtraitours' (BL, Harley MS 523, fol. 52r). In addition to the known leaders of the other camps in Norfolk and Suffolk, there must have been a hierarchy of command in which Kett was joined by others. One such was John Wythe, a copyholder and headborough of Aylsham in Norfolk, denounced as 'the notablest offender that was in the time of rebellion' (Beer, *Rebellion and Riot*, 205) and sentenced to be hanged on his own door. The terse records of the subsequent judicial repression reveal the names of these other leaders, but not their role in the rebellion.

Nevertheless, writing on 1 September 1549, immediately after the rising's suppression, Somerset could refer to 'One Kett, a tanner, being from the beginning the verie chief doer' (Russell, 214). It was the government's decision to try Kett alone with his brother that identified the man with the movement. Thus in subsequent written accounts Kett was made to lend his name to the rising. Existing studies of Kett's rebellion have perhaps failed adequately to acknowledge that the record of Kett's role throughout the rising rests heavily on (near-) contemporary 'histories' whose provenance deserve more critical interrogation. Authorship of the first of these histories has been attributed to a member of the Sotherton family of Norwich, part of the city's ruling circle, whose purpose was in part to exculpate Norwich's leading citizens from any complicity in the rebellion. The second 'history' was written by Alexander Neville, secretary to Matthew Parker, archbishop of Canterbury, who before his elevation had attempted to pacify the disorders by preaching to the rebels. Kett's role therefore has been written almost entirely from hostile sources.

Given the total absence of any firsthand testimony by Kett, during either the rising or the judicial proceedings against him, it has been Kett's fate to have motives attributed to him that reveal more of successive authors' attitudes and of interrelated shifts in political allegiance and historical interpretation. For Alexander Neville writing in the 1560s, Kett was 'of an impudent boldnesse, an unbridled violence' (Neville, B3r, D3r), while in the Elizabethan Holinshed's chronicle Kett was described as 'a man hardie and forward to anie desperat attempt that should be taken in hand' (*Holinshed's Chronicles*, 1028). These were descriptions interchangeable with those of any who dared to disregard the early modern culture of obedience. They were clearly at considerable variance with the historical record, sketchy though it is. Even Sotherton was prepared to acknowledge that Kett admonished the protesters 'to be ware of their robbinge [and] spoylinge' (Beer, 'The commoyson', 83). But by the time of the English revolution Kett's vilification in print had meant that his was a name that could be invoked, along with those other bogeymen of the English landed classes, Wat Tyler and Jack Cade, to dissuade the English from opposing their king and letting loose again the many-headed monster of the people.

Knowledge of Kett thereafter was kept alive by a curious form of local patriotism. This had seen the translation of Neville's original Latin account by a Norfolk minister and its subsequent reprinting, together with more popular accounts printed locally, a tradition that continues to the present with celebrations of Kett in print and poetry. In the short term, Kett's body, hanged in chains from the castle walls and left to rot, provided an immediate mnemonic; cases of sedition, prosecuted in Norwich in the immediate years after the rebellion, reveal a submerged plebeian tradition among those who had been Kett's supporters which fondly remembered the 'merry world' of Mousehold Heath and held 'Robert Kett … an honest man' (Rye, 22, 25). In the longer term the decision of Norwich's authorities to make 27 August an annual day for the ringing of bells in the city's many churches, and for a religious service commemorating their salvation (the latter continuing into the eighteenth century), helped to preserve a memory of Kett which functioned both as an inspiration for later radical movements within the city and as an object of early genteel tourism.

It was the publication of the Reverend Frederick Russell's 1859 study of *Kett's Rebellion in Norfolk* that marked an important shift in Kett's reputation nationally. In part a product of that tradition of local patriotism—Russell had spent his childhood in Norwich fascinated by local reminders of 'Kett the hero'—the work drew on the accounts of Sotherton and Neville, but added greatly to them from his own original archival work. Russell saw in Kett a man who had led a struggle against the feudal system who, though 'commonly considered a rebel, yet the cause he advocated was so just, that one cannot but feel he deserved a better name and better fate' (Russell, viii). His judgement that Kett's 'great misfortune had been to live before his time' set the tone for much subsequent work that relied heavily on his researches. In their sympathies for Kett subsequent writers reflected both broader political shifts and the ability of the English to celebrate rebels—once dead. Kett, now an 'idealist and visionary' and moved by his 'hatred of mastery and thraldom and his love of equality and brotherhood', was claimed as an early (albeit Fabian) socialist, leader of an uprising 'waged by the peasants, with courage and with characteristic good temper and moderation, against their enemies the landowners' (Clayton, 69, 62, 11). Thus taken up by successive reformulations of the left, Kett achieved his apotheosis at Norwich on the occasion of the four-hundredth anniversary of the rising in the erection of a plaque 'in reparation and honour to a leader in the long struggle of the common people of England to escape from a servile life into the freedom of just conditions'. But the rediscovery of Kett as an ancestor by a late Victorian Tory mayor of Cambridge could result also in the publication of a family genealogy which resurrected Kett as a servant of the people whose 'high traditions' the family continued and which led, in its turn, to the erection in Cambridge of Kett House, an office block built in the 1960s, whose end wall is decorated with a large modernist sculpture depicting Kett at the oak of reformation.

In the translation from traitor to popular hero, Kett himself remains a shadowy figure. His long afterlife has allowed successive writers to fashion him after their own interests, reading out from the blunt fact of rebellion his personal, political, and even physical attributes, for which little or no direct evidence exists. But at the core of the story of Kett lies a profound mystery. Why, in a political culture where rebellion could end on the gallows, should a man, then in his late fifties, himself an encloser, and whose wealth placed him on the borders of gentry status, offer himself as the head of a rising of the commons? A re-evaluation of the politics of the protests of 1549 offers some answer. The leaders of other 'camps' in East Anglia, as well as identifiable names among Kett's delegates, were drawn from a similar background, of some wealth and accustomed to exercise authority locally. Kett may have shared their sense of alienation from a local gentry who, engaged in a vigorous extension of seigneurial rights, threatened the interests of wealthy and poorer tenants alike. Protests in 1549, informed by a belief that popular grievances were shared by a royal government whose policies and pronouncements had encouraged a popular expectation of reform, sought to negotiate with, rather than to challenge, royal government. Kett's description of Mousehold Heath as 'the King's Great Camp', and his concern for justice and good governance in the fashioning of the protest, suggests that he shared both beliefs and objectives. At the first offer of pardon by the royal herald sent to Norwich, Kett was said to have replied, 'kings & princes were accustomed to grant pardons to such as are offendors … he trusted that he needed not anie pardon, sith he had done nothing but that belonged to the dutie of a true subject' (*Holinshed's Chronicles*, 969). The words may well be apocryphal, but they suggest that Kett saw himself not as a rebel but as an ally of royal government in the defence of the commonwealth against oppression by the landed class and in the pursuit of justice and good government. It was this political role that he constructed for himself that perhaps helps to explain the government's otherwise improbable accusation that Kett had 'taken upon hym our royall power and dignitie and calleth himselfe M[aste]r and king of Norfolk and Suffolk' (BL, Cotton MS Vespasian F iii, fol. 46). The judgement of the most recent history of Kett's rebellion that Kett was politically naïve and 'showed not the least comprehension of the realities of national politics' (Cornwall, 240–41) fails to do justice to his political strategy. Kett became a victim of the changed political circumstances that followed from the duke of Somerset's need to secure his own political survival by a demonstration to his fellow nobles of his ability to restore order. Paradoxically, it was Kett's death as a traitor that both preserved his memory and sealed his obscurity.

JOHN WALTER

Sources F. W. Russell, *Kett's rebellion in Norfolk* (1859) · D. MacCulloch, 'Kett's rebellion in context', *Past and Present*, 84 (1979), 36–59 · B. L. Beer, *Rebellion and Riot: popular disorder in England during the reign of Edward VI* (1982) · L. M. Kett, *The Ketts of Norfolk: a yeoman family* (1921) · J. Cornwall, *Revolt of the peasantry, 1549* (1977) · S. T. Bindoff, *Kett's rebellion, 1549* (1949) · W. Rye, ed., *Depositions taken before the mayor and aldermen of Norwich, 1549–1567*, Norfolk and Norwich Archaeological Society (1905) · A. Neville, *Norfolkes furies, or, A view of Ketts campe* (1615) · B. L. Beer, '"The commoyson in Norfolk, 1549": a narrative of popular rebellion in sixteenth-century England', *The Journal of Medieval and Renaissance Studies*, 6 (1976), 73–99 · R. Holinshed and others, eds., *The chronicles of England, Scotland and Ireland*, 2nd edn, ed. J. Hooker, 3 vols. in 2 (1586–7) · BL, Harley MS 523 · BL, Cotton MS Vespasian F iii, fol. 46 · *CPR, 1549–51* · *APC, 1547–58* · J. Clayton, *Robert Kett and the Norfolk rising* (1912) · A. De Salvo, *Kett of Cambridge: an eminent Victorian and his family* (1993) · G. Kett, *The pedigree of Kett of Wymondham, c. Norfolk, AD 1180–1912* (1913) · *Report of the Deputy Keeper of the Public Records*, 4 (1843), appx 2
Likenesses R. Burton?, portrait, repro. in Russell, *Kett's rebellion*
Wealth at death 1000 marks moveable property; 40 marks p.a. land

Kettell, Ralph (1563–1643), college head, was probably born between 4 April and 16 June 1563, the third son of John Kettell, gentleman, of Kings Langley, Hertfordshire, and his wife, Jane. On 3 April 1579, shortly before his sixteenth birthday, he matriculated at Trinity College, Oxford, presumably at the instigation of Elizabeth, Lady Paulet, widow of the college's founder, Sir Thomas Pope, who lived nearby at Tittenhanger and who nominated him to a scholarship four months later. He graduated BA

on 7 July 1582 and was elected to a fellowship the following year. He proceeded MA on 23 April 1586, BTh on 11 June 1594, and DTh on 9 May 1597. Trinity was to be Kettell's home for the whole of his adult life. The family link with the college was strengthened by the subsequent admission of his younger brothers Christopher and George. The young college was by no means secure in its finances or religion, but Ralph Yeldard, then president, was a competent administrator and a good example. Kettell played a full part in college life, and when Yeldard died in 1599 he was a natural successor. He was thirty-six, with a commanding physical presence and a gift for quick-fire repartee.

From the beginning Kettell identified closely with his college and relished the minutiae of institutional life, while never losing sight of the bigger picture. A sound steward with a taste for litigation, he created an extensive archive of many of his activities expressly for the benefit of posterity. His writing was firm and compressed, his ink home-made. His greatest undertaking, the building of a new hall in 1620, was necessitated by the collapse of the original medieval structure, which had been undermined by his previous project, the digging of cellars below. It is tempting to see a direct link to his strategy for controlling drunkenness—brewing good beer in house. But perhaps of even greater importance was his inculcation of an atmosphere of college loyalty, which surely helped Trinity weather the years of the political and religious turbulence that followed his death. In 1602 he drew up, and added to the statutes, a levy on all inherited capital or income from every member of the foundation, which he followed by instituting a very profitable plate fund. Before 1620 he had given his name to a substantial house on Broad Street, which he had built as a private investment.

As president Kettell assumed from 23 January 1604 the rectorship of the college living of Garsington, Oxfordshire, and took his parochial duties equally seriously. He married soon after his election, but little evidence remains of his private life. In 1606 his infant daughter was buried two days after her baptism. In 1624 a wife, perhaps his second, was also buried at Garsington. His wide-ranging personal opinions, however, were noted by all who encountered him, and towards the end of his life his assiduity in such matters as supervising college lectures and his eccentricities, which included spying on the evening activities of undergraduates in their rooms, led to his becoming a figure of fun. John Aubrey, admitted to Trinity in 1642, is the source of many uncorroborated observations, which may be taken with a pinch of salt. But Aubrey saw the wisdom behind the 'sharp gray eies' (*Brief Lives*, 175) and knew that Kettell's 'Hasty-pudding' brain (ibid., 177) should never be underestimated. He noted that in his religion Kettell was 'a right Church of England man' (ibid., 176), disliking extremes, avoiding factions, and actively doing good in secret.

It was Aubrey's opinion that Kettell would have reached his century had not the civil war arrived in Oxford. He used his age to avoid taking the unpalatable protestation oath in 1642 and defied both the soldiers and the court ladies who subsequently invaded the scholarly seclusion of Trinity. Kettell died at his college in July 1643, possibly of typhus, which was prevalent in civil war Oxford, and was buried on 5 August in the chancel at Garsington. One of the fellows painted his picture, from memory, on a small board, which became part of the college's picture collection.   CLARE HOPKINS

Sources *John Aubrey: 'Brief lives'*, ed. J. Buchanan-Brown (2000) · H. E. D. Blakiston, *Trinity College* (1898) · W. Pope, *The life of the right reverend father in God, Seth, lord bishop of Salisbury* (1697) · Kettell's register, Trinity College archives, Oxford · register A, Trinity College archives, Oxford · parish register, Garsington, 19 Feb 1624, Oxon. RO [burial] · parish register, Garsington, 5 Aug 1643, Oxon. RO [burial] · will and inventory, Oxf. UA, chancellor's court wills, hyp. B/28 and 15 · calendar in *The Byble in Englyshe*, Trinity College, Oxford, K.10–10 · Foster, *Alum. Oxon.* · W. J. Oldfield, 'Index to the clergy whose ordination, institution, resignation, licence or death is recorded in the diocesan registers of the diocese of Oxford … 1542–1908', 1915, Bodl. Oxf., MS Top. Oxon. c. 250
Archives Trinity College, Oxford, register · Trinity College, Oxford, *computus* | Bodl. Oxf., MS Wood F.23
Likenesses G. Bathurst, oils, *c.*1645, Trinity College, Oxford
Wealth at death £724: will and inventory, Oxf. UA, chancellor's court wills, hyp. B/28 and 15

Ketterich, John. *See* Catterick, John (*d.* 1419).

Kettle, Alice. *See* Kyteler, Alice (*fl.* 1302–1324).

Kettle, Arnold Charles (1916–1986), university professor, was born in 74 Mayfield Avenue, Ealing, Middlesex, on 17 March 1916, the first of the two sons of Charles Mansfield Kettle (1877–1960), manager of a baker's shop in Finchley Road, South Hampstead, where the family lived, and his wife, Ethel Beatrice, *née* Barry. Both Charles Kettle's sons had remarkably successful academic careers, Arnold in particular. Between 1928 and 1934 he was a pupil at Merchant Taylors' School before becoming an undergraduate at Pembroke College, Cambridge. He took a first in the historical tripos in his second year and a first in the English tripos the following year and then moved on to become a research student. During Kettle's time at Cambridge, F. R. Leavis was one of the strongest influences on undergraduates reading English and Leavis's ideas confirmed and reinforced the direction Kettle had begun to follow. Kettle did not share Leavis's firm anti-Marxist opinions, however: by 1936 he had joined the Communist Party and remained a member for the rest of his life.

Kettle was elected a Commonwealth fellow in 1939 and spent the next two years studying at Yale University. He returned to England and was awarded his PhD in January 1942 for his thesis, 'The relation of political and social ideas in the novel of the English Romantic revival'. Once again the direction of Kettle's interests was set and the effect of social policy and development, together with their expression in the novel, was to occupy him for the rest of his life.

When Kettle returned from America the Second World War was still raging and he joined the Royal Corps of Signals, rising to the rank of captain and seeing service in Yugoslavia, Italy, and India. He was demobilized in 1946 and, on 30 January 1946, married Marguerite Rosabelle Carritt, *née* Gale (1915/16–1995) (who from childhood was always known as Margot). They had two sons. Although he was happily married Kettle was bisexual and throughout his life he never fully came to terms with his situation. Doris Lessing in her autobiography *Walking in the Shade* (1997) claims that one reason for his constant loyalty to the Communist Party was that they stood by him and were not prejudiced by his bisexuality.

In 1946 Kettle was appointed as a supervisor at Cambridge where extra staff were needed to teach the undergraduates arriving in large numbers after service in the forces whose studies had been held back for up to six years by the war. He did not stay long in the post of supervisor and in 1947 he was appointed senior lecturer in the English department at Leeds University where Bonamy Dobrée was head. The school of English at Leeds began to expand and continued to grow during Kettle's time there, especially under Professor A. N. Jeffares, with courses in linguistics, folk life studies, and Commonwealth literature. It began to attract applications from overseas, particularly from Africa and India. Kettle played an important role in teaching these overseas students. He had a profound influence on many, notably Dipak Nandy from India, and Wole Soyinka and Ngugi wa Thiong'o (James Ngugi) from Africa.

At this stage in his career Kettle was not a prolific author of scholarly publications but his most significant book, *An Introduction to the English Novel*, appeared in two volumes in 1951 and 1953, with a paperback issue in 1962 and a second edition in 1967; there were translations into Serbo-Croat (1959), Russian (1966), and Japanese (1974). Angus Calder wrote of the book, '[it] has persuaded generations of readers that what it says is simple common sense' (*The Independent*, 27 Dec 1986). Among his other publications from his time at Leeds were two chapters in the *Pelican History of English Literature* (6, 1958; 7, 1961) and a collection of essays which he edited, *Shakespeare in a Changing World* (1964). Scholarly work and university teaching, though, represented only some of his interests and he taught several courses for the Workers' Educational Association in Yorkshire where he was active in the local Communist Party. His commitment to Marxism was constant but it never obtruded into his teaching. On meeting a new group of students he would simply say, 'I am sure you all know what my politics are', and after that he would leave it to them to deduce why certain interpretations of a work were being stressed, or more likely, why others were not being mentioned at all.

What some have seen as a paradox is that a man so sensitive to the subtleties of literature, who could bring new insights to books which nobody had noticed before, could also accept, or at least remain silent about, Stalinism, the suppression of the Hungarian uprising, and the most unsubtle brutalities taking place in the name of communism. In fact, only Kettle and John Gollan, the general secretary, at a Communist Party executive meeting in 1956 voted against a motion to support the Russians in their invasion of Hungary. Because democratic centralism was the rule, neither of them afterwards ever revealed his true opinion.

It was probably Kettle's view that Marxism was fundamentally correct and even if those in control of communist regimes were corrupt, the truth of communism was not affected. He certainly had absolute loyalty to causes he espoused, commitments which went back to early manhood and remained with him all his life. Such commitment may also in retrospect make him seem cold and heartless, but nothing could be further from the truth and all who knew him spoke of his generosity. He was generous with his time and with praise for students' work, with his hospitality to friends and students, and he was unstinting in helping anyone he saw as disadvantaged.

One example of this occurred in the spring of 1956 when Kettle was visiting Czechoslovakia as a member of a delegation. He had one day free and was asked what he would like to do. He said he would like to visit his old friend Marion Slingova. After a show trial in 1948 Marion Slingova's husband had been executed and by 1956 she had been released from prison but to prolong the humiliation she had been given work in a village factory making bicycle wheels. An official car was provided to take Kettle to the village, Marion Slingova was called out of the factory, and they embraced in the centre of the village. The communist officials and the villagers, some of whom thought Kettle was the British ambassador, were amazed, but Kettle's spontaneous action subsequently brought about some improvement in her conditions.

A member of the national executive committee of the Communist Party, Kettle was never a politician in the public eye but preferred to work quietly in the background. He was on the editorial board of *Marxism Today*, as well as being a regular contributor, from its foundation in October 1957 and he wrote many articles for the Communist Party national newspaper the *Daily Worker*, which later became the *Morning Star*. He also published reviews and articles in other left-wing periodicals such as the *Marxist Quarterly* and *Labour Monthly*. In 1963 probably his most important political publication appeared, *Karl Marx, Founder of Modern Communism*; it generated a second edition in 1968 and translations into Norwegian (1966), Italian (1972), and Swedish (1976).

In 1967 Kettle was seconded by Leeds University to the University of Dar es Salaam as professor of literature to run the new department and to help with the division of the University of East Africa into three separate institutions for Kenya, Uganda, and Tanzania. Three years later he was appointed to the Open University as its first professor of literature. Arnold Kettle's experience and approach to teaching were exactly what was needed to launch the Open University. The Open University in turn undoubtedly satisfied him because it had a clear, practical aim—to educate anybody who enrolled. There were no entry requirements and thus the academics were forced to explain their subjects in everyday terms. Kettle had always adopted this approach and, although he had read the abstruse philosophical and literary theoretical Marxist treatises, he never brought any high-flown theories into his own work. He never saw himself as a literary critic but always as a teacher trying to explain how a novel, play,

or poem was moulded by the historical circumstances in which it was written, and at the same time, if it was a great work, how it could still be relevant to modern life. And if he could explain this to a bus driver or a housewife, if he could bring out the full relevance of the work to them in person and let it change their lives, so much the better.

Because of the multi-disciplinary approach, at least in the undergraduate foundation course, Kettle's contribution to Open University teaching covers a much wider range than his previous concentration on the English novel. For example, there is a unit on Stendhal's *Scarlet and Black*, and one, highly regarded, on Mozart's *Marriage of Figaro*. Nevertheless, Open University courses did not take all his time and other academic publications continued to appear, such as *The Nineteenth Century Novel: Critical Essays and Documents* (1972) and 'W. H. Auden: poetry and politics in the thirties' in *Culture and Crisis in Britain in the Thirties* (1979). Recognition of his abilities and achievements at the Open University came in 1973 when he was appointed academic pro-vice-chancellor.

As his unit on *The Marriage of Figaro* shows Kettle had interests outside literature, especially in music and film. Opera and vocal music were his great loves, with Mozart and Schubert *Lieder* taking pride of place.

At some point in 1980 Kettle contracted Parkinson's disease, and he was forced to retire from the Open University in 1981. He finished working on his last publication, the Open University study unit on *Antony and Cleopatra* published in 1983, but he was already very ill and after many months of gradual decline he died in Milton Keynes on Christmas eve 1986. He was cremated there and his ashes were scattered in the Thames.   JOHN R. TURNER

Sources private information (2004) · *The Times* (29 Dec 1986) · *The Independent* (27 Dec 1986) · *Morning Star* (29 Dec 1986) · *The Guardian* (27 Dec 1986) · A. Kettle, *Literature and liberation: selected essays*, ed. G. Martin and W. R. Owens (1988) · D. Lessing, *Walking in the shade: volume two of my autobiography, 1949–1962* (1997) · D. Jefferson and G. Martin, eds., *The uses of fiction: essays on the modern novel in honour of Arnold Kettle* (1982) · *Contemporary authors*, New Revision Series, 6 (1982) · b. cert. · m. cert.

Likenesses photograph, repro. in Martin and Owens, eds., *Literature and liberation*

Wealth at death £55,492: probate, 27 Feb 1987, *CGPLA Eng. & Wales*

Kettle, Edgar Hartley (1882–1936), pathologist, was born in London on 20 April 1882, the son of Edgar Kettle and his wife, Mary Austin Kettle, daughter of Edward Hartley, from Chipping Norton, Oxfordshire. Kettle was educated at Skipton grammar school, where his uncle, Edward Tomson Hartley, was headmaster. When Kettle was sixteen, a childhood tuberculous infection of the knee led to a surgical excision at St Mary's Hospital, London. During his stay in hospital he decided to become medically qualified, despite being advised not to by the surgeon. Kettle entered St Mary's Hospital medical school in 1902 with an entrance scholarship in natural sciences. He spent every available moment in the pathology laboratory. Before qualifying he acted as temporary house surgeon at the French Hospital and Dispensary, Shaftesbury Avenue, London, where he began a lifelong friendship with James

Alexander Murray, of the Imperial Cancer Research Fund, and acquired an enduring interest in cancer research. Kettle was appointed demonstrator in pathology before graduating MB BS (Lond.) in 1907. In 1908 he was invited by Alexander Paine to work in the new pathology department of the Cancer Hospital, Fulham Road, which later became the Royal Marsden Hospital. In 1910 he obtained the MD and visited the famous pathologist, Karl Albert Ludwig Aschoff, at Freiburg in 1911.

Kettle returned to St Mary's as first assistant pathologist in 1912. He became successively assistant lecturer, joint pathologist (with Bernard Spilsbury), pathologist and lecturer in pathology (1918), and ultimately director of the department of general and special pathology in the Institute of Pathology and Medical Research headed by Sir Almroth Wright.

Kettle was unable to serve in the First World War because of his stiff knee, and took over the work of his colleagues away on military service. In addition to routine diagnostic pathology, he taught students, and even acted as resident obstetric officer. In 1916 he became director of pathology to the 3rd London General Hospital at Wandsworth, which cared for war casualties. During this period he opposed the admission of women, but he welcomed them when they were admitted in 1916. Kettle married Marguerite Henrietta Pam (1887–1939) in 1918. She was the daughter of Leopold Pam MD, and had been taught by Kettle. She was a member of the editorial staff of *The Lancet* from 1919 to 1939. They had no children.

In 1924 Kettle became the first full-time professor of pathology and bacteriology in the Welsh National School of Medicine at Cardiff. He overcame many difficulties in mediating between the University College of South Wales and Monmouthshire and the Cardiff Royal Infirmary to obtain pathology material for teaching and research. In 1927 he succeeded Sir Frederick William Andrewes in the chair of pathology at St Bartholomew's Hospital, London. However, he did not take up this post for a year because of a life-threatening perforated gastric ulcer. While at St Bartholomew's, Kettle tried to bring undergraduate pathology up to the standard in the provincial teaching hospitals. In London, the junior staff in pathology were often clinicians in training; he wanted junior staff who intended to follow a career in pathology. At both St Mary's and St Bartholomew's, Kettle gathered around him young men interested in pathology and enthused them with a research ethos.

In 1935 Kettle moved to the new chair of pathology at the British Postgraduate Medical School at Hammersmith (later the Royal Postgraduate Medical School). He chose staff on the basis that clinicians must be helped to practise the best medicine possible, but that to do this every member of the staff of the department of pathology must be an active investigator.

Kettle was a member of the Medical Research Council's committee on industrial solvents and industrial lung disease and its radiology. He represented the council at the international conference on silicosis held at Johannesburg in 1930. At the invitation of the International Labour

Office, he attended the international committee on pneumoconiosis just two months before his death. Kettle was consulting pathologist to St Bartholomew's Hospital and to Queen Alexandra's Military Hospital, Millbank, a member of the executive committee of the Imperial Cancer Research Fund, and treasurer (1928) of the Pathological Society of Great Britain and Ireland. He was president of the pathology sections of the British Medical Association (1928) and of the Royal Society of Medicine (1930–32). As one of the four representatives nominated by the British universities, he gave evidence on the 'Osteopaths Bill' before a committee of the House of Lords. He was elected a fellow of the Royal College of Physicians in 1931, a considerable honour for a pathologist, and was a member of its council in 1936. He became a fellow of the Royal Society in the same year.

Histopathology was Kettle's special province. His early publications dealt with experimental rheumatism, cancer, splenomegaly with secondary anaemia, and the tissue changes in infection. His classical monograph, *The Pathology of Tumours* (1916), illustrated by his own drawings, reached its third edition in 1945. In 1919 he was the first to describe in detail the lesions of gas gangrene. However, his outstanding contribution was a series of papers between 1922 and 1934 on industrial dust diseases of the lung (pneumoconiosis) and, in particular, silicosis, which is caused by silica, and its association with pulmonary tuberculosis. The first paper was with William Ewart Gye, who made a brief but important foray into this field. Kettle and Gye showed that the inflammation and fibrosis caused by silica did not depend, as generally assumed, on its great hardness and insolubility. They provided evidence that its solubility was important. However, the detailed mechanism whereby silica caused fibrosis remained unclear.

Kettle later explored the role of infection in aggravating the damage caused by silica. On the basis of animal experiments he concluded that serious lung damage in man required the combination of exposure to silica together with tuberculous infection. This was later considered unlikely except in massive pulmonary fibrosis. Kettle observed that tubercle bacilli both localized and grew readily at the site of injection of silica. This increased growth of the tubercle bacillus was corroborated by A. C. Allison and D. Hart in 1968. Together with Reginald Hilton, Kettle used injection of dust suspended in saline into the trachea as a rapid method of assessing its ability to cause lung changes. He emphasized including appropriate controls in his experiments and using an adequate number of animals.

Kettle's mastery of histopathology and experimental pathology, his enthusiasm, and his gift of making friends were important elements of his success. He was also an able organizer. He established close relations with his clinical colleagues and made the pathology departments he ran an integral part of the hospital and medical school. Kettle was excellent at repartee and could be devastatingly sarcastic.

About 1935 Kettle developed carcinoma of the stomach

and underwent palliative surgery (gastroenterostomy). He showed great fortitude and was able to return to work for a short time. He died at home, 44 Lansdowne Road, London, on 1 December 1936. He was survived by his wife. The Kettle memorial lectureship in pathology, held in rotation at the four medical schools in which he worked, was established in 1938. Its administration was later taken over by the Royal College of Pathologists and the lecture given at meetings of the Pathology Society.

W. J. BISHOP, rev. GEOFFREY L. ASHERSON

Sources C. H. Andrewes, *Obits. FRS*, 8 (1952–3), 419–30 [obit. of William Ewart Gye] · *The Lancet* (12 Dec 1936), 1427–9 · *St Mary's Hospital Gazette*, 42 (1936), 187–9 [repr. from obit. in *The Times*] · *Journal of Pathology and Bacteriology*, 44 (1937), 493–504 [bibliography] · 'Marguerite Kettle, assistant editor of *The Lancet*', *The Lancet* (13 May 1939), 1128–31 · Z. Cope, *The history of St Mary's Hospital medical school, or, A century of medical education* (1954) · G. Hadfield, *St Bartholomew's Hospital Reports*, 70 (1937), 1–8 [incl. bibliography] · J. A. Murray, *Obits. FRS*, 2 (1936–8), 301–5 · d. cert.
Likenesses W. Stoneman, photograph, 1936, NPG · J. Russell & Sons, photograph, St Bartholomew's Hospital, archives, X 8/1501 · photograph, repro. in *The Lancet* · photograph, repro. in *Journal of Pathology and Bacteriology*, 280 · photograph, repro. in P. Laidlaw, F. R. Fraser, and E. L. Middleton, *BMJ*, 2 (12 Dec 1936), 1236–8 · photograph, repro. in Hadfield, *St Bartholomew's Hospital Reports* · photograph, repro. in Murray, *Obits. FRS*
Wealth at death £7852 12s. 11d.: probate, 25 June 1937, CGPLA Eng. & Wales

Kettle, Sir Rupert Alfred (1817–1894), industrial arbitrator, was born at Birmingham on 9 January 1817, the fifth son of Thomas F. Kettle of Suffolk Street, Birmingham, a glass-stainer, fancy button and military ornament maker, and gilder. The family was descended from Henri Quitel, a Huguenot of Milhaud or Millau in Languedoc, who emigrated to Birmingham on the revocation of the edict of Nantes, and practised there the trade of glass-stainer. Rupert left Birmingham early in life and, after attending Wolverhampton grammar school, was articled to Richard Fryer, a Wolverhampton attorney. Resolving to qualify as a barrister, he entered the Middle Temple on 2 June 1842, was called to the bar on 6 June 1845, and soon obtained a large practice on the Oxford circuit. On 18 December 1851 he married Mary (d. 13 July 1884), only child and heir of William Cooke of Merridale, Wolverhampton. They had four sons and three daughters. At the general election of 1857 Kettle, who was a Liberal of conservative inclinations, was requisitioned to stand against one of the two sitting Liberal MPs for Wolverhampton, but he decided not to pursue his candidature.

In 1859 Kettle was appointed judge of the Worcestershire county courts, and subsequently he acted as chairman of the standing committee for framing the rules for county courts. His position as a judge and the owner of a substantial establishment in an area much affected by industrial disputes led him to take a particular interest in settling conflicts between employers and workers. In 1865, after a strike in the building trade at Wolverhampton had lasted seventeen weeks, Kettle, on invitation from both sides, succeeded in reaching a settlement based on a set of written working rules for the building trade in the town. The essential principle of the new system was that if

the delegates of the contending parties could not agree, an independent umpire should have power to make a final and legally binding award between the delegates of the contending parties. The scheme found favour with the building employers and with the unions, whom Kettle came to see as helpful in securing workers' adherence to arbitration awards, and was rapidly extended to other towns, eventually including a large part of the English building trade.

Describing his schemes in two pamphlets, *Strikes and Arbitrations* (1866) and *Masters and Men* (1871), Kettle gave evidence on their working to the royal commission on trade unions in July 1867 and publicized them at meetings of the Social Science Association. Boards were set up on these lines in the Staffordshire potteries (1868), and subsequently in the coal and iron industries. Although an innovator, Kettle was not a radical: he insisted on applying commercial principles to wage-bargaining, and in particular sought to link wages to the selling price of commodities. He viewed arbitration as an efficient means of determining the market for skilled labour, and tried to place the awards on a legally enforceable basis: but an act of parliament of 1872, which he drafted with lukewarm endorsement by the Trade Union Congress, proved a dead letter. While his methods were more legalistic than those developed by the other contemporary promoter of collective bargaining, A. J. Mundella, the two shared a belief that participation should be voluntary, a founding principle of British industrial relations over the next century. Kettle was much in demand as an arbitrator, presiding over the midland iron trade wages board, and arbitrating in the Teesside iron industry (1869 and 1873) and in the Northumberland coalfield (1875). He was commonly styled the 'Prince of Arbitrators', and on 1 December 1880 he was knighted on Gladstone's recommendation 'for his public services in establishing a system of arbitration between employers and employed'. In 1890 the postmaster-general, Henry Cecil Raikes, consulted Kettle during the strike of the Post Office workers. By 1892 arbitration work was taking up so much of his time that he resigned his county court judgeship.

On 24 November 1882 Kettle was elected a bencher of the Middle Temple. He was one of the senior magistrates and a deputy lieutenant of Staffordshire, and he was assistant chairman of quarter sessions from 1866 to 1891. A supporter of church schools, in 1870 he was elected a member of the first school board for Wolverhampton. He was a watercolour artist of some ability, and several of his pictures were publicly exhibited. Kettle died at his residence, Merridale Hall, Wolverhampton, on 6 October 1894, and was buried on 9 October in the Wolverhampton cemetery.

E. I. CARLYLE, rev. M. C. CURTHOYS

Sources Boase, *Mod. Eng. biog.* · *Wolverhampton Chronicle* (15 April 1891) · *Wolverhampton Chronicle* (10 Oct 1894) · Burke, *Gen. GB* · R. Simms, ed., *Bibliotheca Staffordiensis* (1894) · J. Foster, *Men-at-the-bar: a biographical hand-list of the members of the various inns of court*, 2nd edn (1885) · *Men of the time* · *Biograph and Review*, 4 (1880), 487–8 · W. H. Fraser, *Trade unions and society* (1974) · R. Price, *Masters, unions and men* (1980) · Wood, *Vic. painters*, 2nd edn · census returns, 1881

Likenesses S. Evans, pen-and-ink drawing, NPG · F. Holl, portrait, repro. in *ILN* (13 Oct 1894)

Wealth at death £31,656 2s. 6d.: probate, 6 Nov 1894, *CGPLA Eng. & Wales*

Kettle, Thomas Michael [Tom] (1880–1916), politician and writer, was born on 9 February 1880 at Artane, co. Dublin, the seventh of the twelve children of Andrew Kettle (1833–1916), farmer, and his wife, Margaret, daughter of Laurence McCourt of St Margaret's, co. Dublin. He was exposed to politics from an early age. His father, who had been active in the Tenant League in the 1850s, presided at the first meeting of the National Land League in 1879 and was instrumental in persuading Charles Stuart Parnell to become involved in the Land League. Andrew Kettle was an exacting man, stern, demanding, and stubborn, but his imprisonment in 1881 for involvement in land agitation and his enduring support for Parnell provided his son Thomas with considerable cachet when he embarked on his own political career.

Tom Kettle was raised in comfortable rural surroundings, and like his brothers he attended the Christian Brothers' O'Connell Schools at Richmond Street, Dublin, where he excelled. In 1894 he was sent as a boarder to the Jesuit-run Clongowes Wood College. Quick-tempered, mischievous, and clever, he became known as a wit and an athlete. He enjoyed cycling and cricket and, true to his upbringing, he was also a keen debater and a devout Catholic. After leaving Clongowes with honours in English and French, in 1897 Kettle entered University College, Dublin, a Jesuit-administered constituent college of the Royal University of Ireland. Surrounded by ambitious and politically minded young men, Kettle quickly established himself both as a leading student politician and as a brilliant scholar. He was elected to the prestigious position of auditor of the college's literary and historical society for the 1898–9 session. He distributed pro-Boer leaflets during the early months of the Second South African War and protested against the Irish Literary Theatre's production of W. B. Yeats's *The Countess Cathleen* in 1899. His studies were marred by a mysterious illness which prevented him from taking his bachelor of arts examinations in 1900. He was prone to colds, but it is likely that the 'nervous condition' he suffered was in fact a nervous breakdown. Irregular but revealing references in his diaries, notebooks, and correspondence disclose a melancholy disposition which was prone to depression. He renewed his spirits, as he often did, by travelling on the continent and improving his French and German. Upon his return to Dublin he resumed his studies and took his BA in mental and moral science in 1902.

Kettle was admitted into the Honourable Society of King's Inns to read law in 1903, but even after qualifying in 1905 he rarely practised and devoted most of his time to political journalism. He also maintained his contacts with University College and his fellow students, continuing to participate in debates, contributing to and becoming editor of the college newspaper, and helping to found the Cui Bono Club, a discussion group for recent graduates. A vocal supporter of the Irish Parliamentary Party, Kettle strengthened his links to the constitutionalists by co-founding and becoming president of the Young Ireland branch of the United Irish League in 1904. He had by this time earned the attention of John Redmond, Irish party leader, who hoped that he would stand for a parliamentary seat. Kettle declined the offer and turned instead to the founding and editing of *The Nationist*, an unconventional weekly journal. *The Nationist* pursued an unashamedly pro-Irish party line, but it also reflected Kettle's liberal and often controversial views on a wide range of topics which included education, women's rights, and the Irish literary revival. He resigned from the editorship over a controversy about an allegedly anti-clerical article in 1905.

Kettle accepted the candidature for the vacant parliamentary seat of East Tyrone at a by-election in July 1906, and secured the seat by the narrow margin of eighteen votes to become one of the very few young men to gain admission to the ageing ranks of the Irish Parliamentary Party in the first two decades of the twentieth century. Lauded as a future party leader, in late 1906 he went to America, where he engaged in a series of successful fundraising and propaganda meetings. An amusing and often caustic speaker in the House of Commons, he remained a staunch supporter of the Irish party and of the constitutional path to home rule, but turned his attention to a number of topical questions, including the provision of higher education for Irish Catholics, and to Ireland's economic condition. Increasingly busy and in demand as a speaker, Kettle began to earn a reputation as a heavy drinker and a frequent visitor of bars and clubs.

On 8 September 1909 Kettle married Mary Sheehy (b. 1884), a fellow graduate of the Royal University, a suffragist, and, like Kettle, a member of a well-known nationalist family (her father, David Sheehy, was a nationalist MP). Their daughter Elizabeth (Betty) was born in 1913. Kettle was appointed professor of national economics at University College, a constituent college of the new National University of Ireland. Critics claimed that Kettle could not combine academic life with his work as an MP, and although he held his East Tyrone seat in January 1910, he did not contest it at the general election held in December 1910. Even after he was out of parliament, he remained an active party member and in 1910 he published a collection of essays which reiterated his dedication to home rule by constitutional means. A popular teacher, he was known at University College as a 'professor of all things', but his genuine interest in economics was reflected in a number of publications on financial matters. He greeted the removal of the Lords' veto and the Home Rule Bill of 1912 with great optimism, but his brusque dismissal of Unionist objections to the bill reflected his misunderstanding of their fears about the bill's possible effects. He also crossed swords with Irish feminists who condemned the bill; although he was a vocal and long-time supporter of women's suffrage, Kettle disapproved both of attacks on private property and of placing any cause before the implementation of home rule.

In contrast to most middle-class commentators, Kettle

refused to condemn striking workers in 1913 and published a series of articles which outlined the living and working conditions of Dublin's poor. He presided over the formation of a peace committee which endeavoured to negotiate an agreement between workers and their employers; this organization enjoyed little success, and Kettle's own reputation was tarnished by his appearance at an important meeting in a less than sober state. His excessive drinking became more obvious to friends and colleagues and his work was affected; he appeared to be depressed and he was sent in 1913 to a private hospital in Kent for treatment for 'dipsomania'. Despite this, he became deeply involved with the nationalist Irish Volunteers, a quasi-military organization established in 1913 in opposition to the militant Ulster Volunteer Force. Sent in 1914 to continental Europe to buy arms for the volunteers, Kettle witnessed at first hand the outbreak of the First World War. He travelled through Belgium and France as war correspondent for the *Daily News*, praising the courage of the Belgians and warning against the dire threat to Europe of Prussian militarism. A firm believer in the rights of small nations, Kettle supported Irish involvement in the British war effort, and volunteered for active service upon returning to Dublin in 1914. He was refused an immediate commission on the grounds of ill health (in reality, because of his heavy drinking); he received the rank of lieutenant, but his activities were restricted to recruiting throughout Ireland and England.

Kettle presented himself as an Irish party candidate for a forthcoming by-election at East Galway in December 1914. He was not selected, but his support for the party did not abate and he continued to publish tracts advocating home rule. By 1916 Kettle had published more than ten books and pamphlets and had contributed numerous articles to journals and newspapers, including the *Fortnightly Review*, the *Irish Ecclesiastical Review*, and the *Freeman's Journal*. Many of his works were concerned with Irish politics, but he also published literary reviews, philosophical treatises, and translations from French and German. A prolific and well-regarded poet and essayist, he is probably best remembered for a poem composed shortly before his death, 'To my Daughter, Betty, the Gift of God', which is often included in anthologies of First World War poetry.

Although disillusioned with the war as it dragged on, and questioning British war aims, Kettle maintained that Irish soldiers had a moral duty to join the allied stand against Germany. He was frequently warned and disciplined for being intoxicated while in uniform, but he none the less continued to apply to be sent on active service. His appeals were refused until 1916, when the commanding officer of the 16th division took a chance on Kettle and commissioned him into the Dublin fusiliers. Kettle's health had evidently improved by this time, but it remained delicate. Appalling conditions in the trenches broke his health and he was given a rear area job shortly before the Somme battles. However, he refused offers of a permanent staff position and sick leave, and insisted on returning to his battalion, the 9th Dublin fusiliers.

Before he finally left Ireland in July 1916, Kettle prophesied that the Easter rebels of 1916 would be remembered as heroes while Irishmen serving in the British army would be deemed traitors. His prediction was remarkably astute. Kettle was killed on 9 September 1916, while taking part in the Irish brigade's capture of Ginchy and he was buried near by. The news of his death provoked a wealth of tributes, testifying to Kettle's brilliance, generosity, and wit; he was widely acknowledged as the leading constitutional nationalist of his generation. But the radicalization of Irish politics and the denunciation of the men and women who had supported home rule and the war effort ensured that his fame faded together with the primacy of the constitutional agenda. An attempt to erect a commemorative portrait bust of Kettle was beset by controversy until it was finally placed—without an official unveiling—in St Stephen's Green, Dublin, in 1937.   S. PAŠETA

Sources J. B. Lyons, *The enigma of Tom Kettle: Irish patriot, essayist, poet, British soldier* (1983) · W. Dawson, 'Tom Kettle: essayist', *Studies: an Irish Quarterly Journal*, 20 (1931), 598–610 · A. E. Clery, 'Thomas Kettle', *Studies: an Irish Quarterly Journal*, 5 (1916), 503–15 · S. Pašeta, *Before the revolution: nationalism, social change and Ireland's Catholic élite, 1879–1922* (1999) · CGPLA Ire. (1916)
Archives University College, Dublin, MSS
Likenesses A. Power, bust, c.1937, St Stephen's Green, Dublin
Wealth at death £195 15s. 9d.: probate, 17 Nov 1916, CGPLA Ire.

Kettle, Tilly (1735–1786), portrait painter, was born on 31 January 1735, at 4 Silver Street, London, the third of six children of Henry Kettle (c.1704–c.1773), a coach-painter, and his wife, Ann. Since 1640 five successive generations of the Kettle family had been freemen of the Brewers' Company, although both Tilly Kettle's father and grandfather worked as painters. Kettle may have received some elementary training from his father, who exhibited a 'cilindrical picture; one side a conversation, the other a sleeping Venus' at the Society of Artists in 1772. The only surviving work by Henry Kettle is an unusual panel painting, 'An Anamorphic Vanitas', signed in mirror writing, and which was sold in America in 1997 (ex Christies, New York, 23 May 1997, lot 34).

Tilly Kettle attended William Shipley's drawing school in the Strand, London, where he was a fellow pupil of the architect James Gandon. From there he may have progressed to the St Martin's Lane Academy and the duke of Richmond's sculpture gallery, although this has not been firmly established. During the early 1750s he was introduced to Joshua Reynolds, whose portrait of his pupil Giuseppe Marchi (RA) Kettle copied with minor alterations to the draperies. According to Gandon, when Kettle returned the original he was complimented on the quality of his copy by Reynolds, 'who, however, excused himself from lending any more pictures' (Gandon and Mulvany, 204).

Kettle's earliest identified portrait, a self-portrait of 1760 (priv. coll.), displays the formative influence of Reynolds on his portrait style. His first exhibited work was an unidentified half-length female portrait, which he showed at the Free Society of Artists in 1761. By 1762 Kettle was busy repairing Robert Streater's allegorical ceiling painting at the Sheldonian Theatre, Oxford, during which time he also painted the portrait of Dr Francis Yarborough, principal of Brasenose College, which is signed and dated 1763. Both commissions were probably secured by his friend and patron Sir Richard Kaye, bt, dean of Lincoln College, who introduced him to new clientele over the next few years. From the end of 1762 until about 1764 Kettle worked between Oxford and the midlands. During this time he painted the poet Anna Seward (NPG) and her elder sister, Sarah, as well as numerous portraits of the family of William Legge, second earl of Dartmouth and Sir John Holte, both of whom were related to Kaye. Through these connections he also painted a series of portraits of the Edwards family, including Gerard Ann Edwards, son of the celebrated heiress Mary Edwards.

In 1764 Kettle was invited to take up the livery of the Brewers' Company, although he seems not to have responded. The following year he exhibited three works at the Society of Artists, including a full-length portrait of the actress Mrs Yates as the Chinese Princess Mandane in Arthur Murphy's adaptation of Voltaire's novel *The Orphan of China* (Tate Collection). In the exhibition catalogue he registered his address as Great Queen Street, Lincoln's Inn Fields, London, although by 1767 he was living in Conduit Street. He continued to exhibit portraits at the Society of Artists until 1776, after which he switched his allegiance to the Royal Academy. In 1767 Kettle exhibited a portrait of Miss Eliot as Juno, in the manner of Reynolds, and the following year showed an ambitious group portrait entitled *An Admiral in his Cabin Issuing his Orders*, a portrait of Vice-Admiral Sir Samuel Cornish with Rear-Admiral Sir Richard Kempenfelt and Cornish's secretary, Thomas Parry.

In August 1768 Kettle, possibly encouraged by Cornish, petitioned the East India Company to travel to Bengal to work as an artist. On 21 September permission was granted, and on 27 September securities of £1000 were given by his father and William Arnold, of Walbrook. Kettle set sail on 24 December 1768, on board the *Nottingham*, carrying letters of recommendation from Admiral Cornish and Laurande Sulivan, a director of the East India Company. Kettle, the first professional British artist to make a career in India, arrived in Madras on 2 May 1769.

Kettle spent two years in Madras, among his first commissions a portrait of Lord Pigot, former governor of Madras (priv. coll.), which he had begun before his departure from England. His clientele at this time consisted of nabobs, merchants, and army officers. He also painted a group portrait of Muhammad Ali Khan, nawab of Arcot, with his five sons, which Kettle exhibited at the Society of Artists in 1771, as well as a single full-length portrait of the same sitter (V&A), which he painted of his own volition. More unusual was a series of genre pictures, including *Dancing Girls (Blacks)* (National Gallery of Modern Art, New Delhi), which he exhibited at the Society of Artists in 1772, and a suttee scene showing a woman preparing for self-immolation on her husband's funeral pyre, which was probably displayed at the Free Society of Artists in 1776 as *The ceremony of a gentoo woman taking leave of her relations and*

distributing her jewels prior to ascending the funeral pyre of her deceased husband.

By late 1771 Kettle was in Calcutta, where he stayed briefly before travelling to Fyzabad, at the invitation of Shuja ud-Daula, nawab of Oudh, whose portrait he painted on several occasions during the following year, including a full length with his son (Musée de Versailles, France). In addition to those surviving works from this period, notably the *Dancing-Girl Holding the Stem of a Hookah* (Yale U. CBA), further pictures are known through copies by local Indian artists. During this time Kettle took an Indian *bibi*, or mistress, who bore him two daughters, Ann and Elizabeth, who were baptized in Calcutta respectively on 22 February 1773 and 30 April 1774.

Kettle presumably returned to Calcutta by early 1773, where he stayed for three years. Among his numerous commissions were a large double portrait of Charles and John Sealy (Courtauld Inst.), Sir Elijah Impey, first chief justice of the supreme court (formerly high court, Dacca, Bangladesh, since des.), and Warren Hastings, whom Kettle painted on at least three separate occasions.

On 30 March 1776 Kettle left Calcutta on board the *Talbot*, arriving in London in mid-November. Following what must have been a whirlwind courtship, he married Mary (1753–1798), younger daughter of the architect James *Paine, on 23 February 1777. In a pre-nuptial settlement, dated 22 February, Paine provided £5000, and Kettle the sum of £3000, towards a trust fund. According to the sculptor Joseph Nollekens, the marriage was not a love-match but the result of Paine's 'shuffling, sordid, and dirty conduct' (Milner, 75). Initially Kettle and his wife lived in Berners Street, London, while a grander house was prepared for the couple in Bond Street. In 1777 Kettle also began to exhibit at the Royal Academy, showing his works there intermittently until 1783. Finding it difficult to attract new clientele, Kettle relied at this time upon the network of patrons established in India. These included Josias Dupré, a former governor of Madras, Rear-Admiral Richard Kempenfelt, and Sir Robert Barker, who commissioned a large picture entitled *Shah Alam, Mughal emperor, reviewing the 3rd brigade of the East India Company's troops at Allahabad* (Victoria Memorial, Calcutta). More successful were his more intimate portraits, notably the double portraits of two girls, Elizabeth and Mary Davidson (Dulwich Picture Gallery, London), whose father Kettle had painted in India when he worked for the East India Company. Following his marriage Kettle had two further children, a daughter, Mary, and a son, James, born in November 1782. By now, however, Kettle was experiencing financial problems, which finally forced him, in 1783, to vacate his house in Bond Street. The precise reasons for Kettle's ruin are unknown, his friend James Gandon stating merely that his marriage had 'proved unfortunate and expensive … difficulties and demands of various kinds interfering with his professional pursuits' (Milner, 78). Pursued by creditors, Kettle travelled to Ireland, where he stayed briefly, before deciding to return to India.

On 9 June 1786 Kettle made a will, in which he gave his address as Brussels, a ruse, it has been suggested, to evade his creditors (Milner, 79). Shortly afterwards he set out over land for India. By July he had reached Aleppo, where he painted what may have been his last portrait, *The Turkish Janissary of the English Factory, Aleppo* (priv. coll.). Kettle is thought to have died some time before the end of 1786, possibly in the desert on his way to Basrah, although the exact date and circumstances of his death are unknown. His will was registered at the British cancellaria in Aleppo on 5 July 1787. Kettle's wife died at her sister's house in Gloucester Place, London, in April 1798, bequeathing £5000 each to her son and daughter. In 1810 Kettle's son enlisted in the British army in India, where he died in 1819. MARTIN POSTLE

Sources J. D. Milner, 'Tilly Kettle, 1735–1786', *Walpole Society*, 15 (1926–7), 47–104 · M. Archer, *India and British portraiture, 1770–1825* (1979) · P. Leach, *James Paine* (1988) · E. Cotton, *Tilly Kettle and his portraits* (1925) · J. Gandon and T. J. Mulvany, eds., *The life of James Gandon* (1846)
Likenesses watercolour drawing, *c.*1815 (after presumed self-portrait by T. Kettle, *c.*1815), V&A · self-portrait, oils, priv. coll.
Wealth at death probably in debt

Kettlewell, (Henry) Bernard Davis (1907–1979), ecological geneticist and entomologist, was born on 24 February 1907 in Howden, Yorkshire, the only son of Henry Kettlewell, a merchant, and his wife, Kate Davis. He received his education at Old College, Windermere, and then at Charterhouse School, in Surrey (1920–24). He read medicine and zoology at Gonville and Caius College, Cambridge (1926–9) and then did clinical training at St Bartholomew's Hospital, London, qualifying as a medical practitioner (MB BChir) in 1935. In the following year he married Hazel Margaret Wiltshire, the daughter of Sir Frank Wiltshire, the town clerk of Birmingham. The marriage was close and affectionate and they had two children.

During the Second World War Kettlewell worked as a doctor and anaesthetist in and around London but in the late 1940s, perhaps with the approach of the National Health Service, he decided to give up the further practice of medicine. The family emigrated to South Africa in 1949, where for three years Kettlewell carried out extensive field research into locust control at Cape Town University while at the same time amassing a large collection of Lepidoptera which he later presented to the British Museum. (In time his contributions would form an essential part of the national Rothschild–Cockayne–Kettlewell Collection, a major resource for the study of natural variation and inheritance.)

Kettlewell's South African experiences marked the beginning of a pattern in his scientific life which seemed to suit both his professional interests and his personality, which was outgoing and full-blooded; this led him to engage in sometimes maddening but good-natured controversy with his peers when he fairly thought a point to be of scientific importance. He undertook early research expeditions to the Belgian Congo, to Mozambique, to the Kalahari, and to South Africa's Knysna Forest, where he continued to assemble vast amounts of information about insects, particularly moths.

From early manhood Kettlewell had an unusual combination of talents and habits which served him well in his chosen profession. He devised and carried out field experiments and collection techniques ('mark–release–recapture') which were admirable for their ingenuity and requirements for diligence. An example of his rare combination of skills occurred when he was able to prove, by means of radioactive testing, that a moth he had caught had been affected by a particular nuclear test explosion. His principal hobbies (shooting, growing hybrids, and devising novel lobster traps) suggest that his different personality traits were intertwined whether at work or at play and that he was constantly seeking to join facts and theories wherever he roamed.

In 1952 Kettlewell returned to England (typically for him, by driving the entire Cape Town to Alexandria part of the journey), in order to accept a Nuffield Foundation research post in the genetics laboratory at Oxford University, working under his friend Edmund Brisco Ford, whom he had met in 1937 while both were at an ecological site. Oxford was to be Kettlewell's base for the rest of his life. From the end of the 1950s until 1974 he maintained close connections with the Oxford department of zoology, while carrying on an extensive scientific correspondence with hundreds of other leading evolutionists and entomologists throughout the world. Between 1965 and 1974 he was also closely involved with the Iffley Graduate Society (from 1966 Wolfson College).

While he continued to work at Oxford with sustained energy Kettlewell also travelled abroad numerous times to give lectures to professionals and to lay persons alike, wrote more than sixty articles for specialist journals (such as *Heredity*) and for those intended for a broader public (such as *Nature* and *Scientific American*), made a number of pioneering films about insects and evolution, and wrote a very readable book about Darwin (with Sir Julian Huxley), in the now familiar format of the scientific illustrated biography, written by experts for the public. Meanwhile he was writing scholarly works which were considered to be classics by his peers, notably a paper in 1959 written around a theme he called 'Darwin's missing evidence', providing elegant proof of the reversal of melanism when pollution in an area became diminished and thus showing the force of natural selection in the presence of inheritable variations.

Kettlewell's fame steadily grew and he obtained medals and awards as diverse as the USSR's Darwin medal (1959), the Czechoslovakian Mendel medal (1965), and a doctoral degree from Oxford. He was tireless in his pursuit of first-hand knowledge, undertaking expeditions to Alaska, Ecuador, Iceland, the South Caspian, Madeira, and St Kitts, as well as visiting Brazil and lecturing frequently in the United States and Canada.

Kettlewell's scientific importance will always rest principally upon his pioneering work in industrial melanism, including aposematic melanism, in which the *Biston betularia* peppered moth was the principal object of his studies and experiments. As early as 1955 (and again in

1965), by a series of painstaking field experiments, involving tens of thousands of observations, he was able to prove that those moths which did not match their ecological backgrounds were much more likely to be taken by birds. He understood that enhanced viability was probably based not just upon natural behavioural selection but upon some underlying genetic, pre-adaptive mechanism. He left unresolved the central question of how dominance modifiers could be maintained in a population in the absence of melanic polymorphism, except by mutation. This question anticipated the later unresolved dialogue between the proponents of neutral molecular random drift evolution (Motoo Kimura, in Japan) and those who still favoured neo-Darwinistic selectionism.

In 1973 Kettlewell's life's work was brought together in his principal published work, *The Evolution of Melanism: the Study of a Recurring Necessity*, in which he meticulously narrates his evidence, his reasoning, and his conclusions, starting with possible biblical references to colouring as a sign of inedibility (and hence likelihood to survive) and ending with his latest experiments done in the field and even with the dietary preferences of his household cat. He was able to carry out the most difficult and extensive experiments under the watchful eyes of his peers and produce stately expositions of his findings, but was also gifted at devising everyday examples of proof, meaningful to anyone.

The Evolution of Melanism's thought-provoking subtitle was a characteristic reminder that nature is constantly evolving and that the search for evidence and understanding requires continuous study, to be approached with the vigour, diligence, partisan commitment, and open imagination exemplified by Bernard Kettlewell. Like that other great truant from medicine, Charles Darwin, Kettlewell's results, as well as his methods, illustrate the related propositions that there need not be a barrier between the gifted amateur and the specialized academic and that important and lasting science is done by those who can combine the best elements of those seemingly opposite approaches. Kettlewell died at his home, the vicarage, Steeple Aston, near Oxford, on 11 May 1979, possibly from an accidental overdose of medication to relieve pain from an injury sustained during an experiment. He was survived by his wife and son.

GEOFFREY V. MORSON

Sources Kettlewell archive, www.wolfson.ox.ac.uk/library/archives/Kettlewell · J. Turner, 'Kettlewell, Henry Bernard Davis', *DSB*, suppl., 17.469–71 · C. A. Clarke, 'H. B. D. Kettlewell', *The Caian* (1979–80), 73–5 · H. B. D. Kettlewell, *The evolution of melanism: the study of a recurring necessity* (1973) · J. Hooper, *Of moths and men: the untold story of science and the peppered moth* (2002) · M. Salmon, *The Aurelian legacy: British butterflies and their collectors* (2000) · H. B. D. Kettlewell and J. Huxley, *Darwin and his world* (1965) · *Daily Telegraph* (25 May 1979), 19 · *WWW*, 1971–80 · S. Jenkins-Jones, 'Henry Bernard Davis Kettlewell', *Hutchinson dictionary of scientists* (1996), 268 · H. B. D. Kettlewell, 'Darwin's missing evidence', *Scientific American*, 200 (1959), 48–53 · R. Lewin, *Patterns in evolution: the new molecular view* (1997), 87–105 · J. Venn and others, eds., *Biographical history of Gonville and Caius College*, 5: *Admissions from 1911 to 1932* (1948) · J. Venn and others, eds., *Biographical history of Gonville and Caius College*, 7: *Admissions from 1957 to 1972* (1978) · *CGPLA Eng. & Wales* (1979) ·

N. Tinbergen, 'Happy moments with Bernard Kettlewell', *Lycidas*, 7 (1978–9), 58–60 [house magazine for Wolfson College, Oxford]
Archives Bodl. Oxf., corresp. and papers · Wolfson College, Oxford | Bodl. Oxf., corresp. with Edmund Brisco Ford · NHM, Rothschild–Cockayne–Kettlewell national collection of lepidoptera · Rice University, Houston, Woodson Research Center, corresp. with Sir Julian Huxley · U. Lpool L., corresp. with Sir Cyril Ashley Clarke | FILM University of York, Shetland work (Granada TV) · Wolfson College, Oxford, Kettlewell archive | SOUND Wolfson College, Oxford, Kettlewell archive
Likenesses photograph, probably Wolfson College, Oxford, Kettlewell archive; repro. in *Lycidas*, 7 (1978–9), 58
Wealth at death £54,618: probate, 13 June 1979, *CGPLA Eng. & Wales*

Kettlewell, John (1653–1695), nonjuring Church of England clergyman and theological writer, was born on 10 March 1653 at Brompton in the North Riding of Yorkshire. He was the second, and eldest surviving, son of the three sons and one daughter of John Kettlewell (*d.* 1659), merchant of Northallerton, Yorkshire, and his wife, Elizabeth Ogle. Kettlewell was educated at Northallerton school under the zealous royalist Thomas Smelt. He matriculated at St Edmund Hall, Oxford, on 11 November 1670 as servitor to the principal, Dr Thomas Tully, and graduated BA on 20 June 1674. Kettlewell was elected to a fellowship at Lincoln College on 28 July 1675, partly through the influence of another alumnus of Smelt's school and future nonjuror, Dr George Hickes. Kettlewell proceeded MA on 3 May 1677. He was ordained deacon by the bishop of Oxford, Dr John Fell, in Christ Church Cathedral, Oxford, on 10 June 1677, and priest on 24 February 1678.

Kettlewell's first book, *The Measures of Christian Obedience*, was written between Christmas 1677 and Easter 1678, but not published until 1681, with a dedication, which Hickes had suggested, to Henry Compton, bishop of London. This work on the subject of a Christian's duty to obey the laws of the gospels went through six editions to 1714. It also attracted the attention of Anne Russell, countess of Bedford, who appointed Kettlewell as her chaplain, and of Simon, Lord Digby. As chaplain to the Russell family Kettlewell attempted to counteract the influence of Samuel Johnson, the radical whig chaplain to Lord William Russell, the countess's son. He failed at this, but shortly before his execution for participation in the Rye House plot in 1683 William Russell sent Kettlewell an affectionate message. Digby, a connection of the countess's by marriage, appointed Kettlewell as vicar of Coleshill, Warwickshire, after his first choice, John Rawlet of St Nicholas, Newcastle, had turned him down and recommended Kettlewell.

Kettlewell read his first service at Coleshill on 10 December 1682. He was an effective vicar, providing poor families with copies of the Bible and *The Whole Duty of Man*, and persuading the pious Digby to restore great tithes to the value of £100 to the living. He resigned his fellowship at Lincoln on 22 November 1683 and devoted his whole effort to his parish, where several charities were founded by his means and through gifts from Lord Digby and others. Part of Kettlewell's pastoral duty was to preach in preparation for the worthy reception of the eucharist. The sacrament was extremely important to Kettlewell's piety, and he wanted to encourage more frequent celebration and reception at Coleshill. His preparatory sermons were published in 1683 as *An Help and Exhortation to Worthy Communicating*, with a dedication to Lord Digby. *An Help and Exhortation* went through ten editions to 1737. During the tory reaction Kettlewell earned a reputation as a very strong advocate of passive obedience and non-resistance. A sermon he preached to the clergy after the suppression of the Monmouth revolt, 'Measures of Christian subjection', was published after his death in his collected works. His sermons on the deaths of his patrons were published as *A Funeral Sermon for the Lady Frances Digby* (1684) and *Sermon on the Occasion of the Death of Simon, Lord Digby* (1686). At Coleshill, Kettlewell was a friend of the future founder of the Society for the Propagation of the Gospel, Thomas Bray, who long after Kettlewell's death would continue to recommend his doctrinal works. Despite his devotion to his parish Kettlewell had not given up hope of rising in the church: in 1684, on the death of the archdeacon of Coventry, George Downing, he petitioned the archbishop of Canterbury, William Sancroft, for two offices left vacant by Downing's death, the archidiaconate itself and the prebend of Alrewas. His petition was unsuccessful.

On 4 October 1685 Kettlewell married Jane (*d.* 1719?), daughter of Anthony Lybb (1607–1674) of Hardwick House in the parish of Whitchurch, Oxfordshire, and his wife, Mary Keate (*d.* 1692). The two had been brought together by the curate of Whitchurch, William Musson, who performed the ceremony there. It included what was at the time the unusual feature of the couple's joint reception of the sacrament. Kettlewell's married life seems to have been happy, although Jane suffered from ill health and the couple had no children. Kettlewell's principal diversions from his work were music and walking. He played the violincello, bass viol, and violin.

During the reign of James II, Kettlewell published a visitation sermon, *The Religious Loyalist* (1686) and a work on Christian doctrine, *The practical believer, or, The articles of the apostle's creed drawn out to form a true Christian's heart and practice* (1688), which developed out of his parish catechizing. *The Practical Believer* went through six editions to 1713, and a Welsh translation by Richard ap Robert was published in 1768. Unlike many Church of England divines Kettlewell did not preach against Roman Catholicism during James's reign. During this time Kettlewell's sacramental and Laudian piety drew some unfavourable attention. After his wife's death Digby donated to Coleshill a set of silver communion plates solemnly consecrated by Sancroft, an act that seemed to many idolatrous.

Kettlewell's life was drastically altered by the revolution of 1688. He followed his high tory principles with absolute consistency, continuing to preach against any form of resistance to James II. He quickly removed the dedication to Compton from *The Measures of Christian Obedience* once he learned that Compton had appeared in arms for William of Orange. After the revolution he was harassed by local dissenters and supporters of William, as well as by

soldiers passing through on their way to the war in Ireland. Kettlewell lost his vicarage in 1690 for refusing to take the oaths to the new sovereigns. He relocated to London, where he became one of the leading nonjuring writers and controversialists. His nonjuring publications include *Of Christian prudence, or religious wisdom, not degenerating into irreligious craftiness in trying times* (1691); *Christianity, a doctrine of the cross, or, Passive obedience under any pretended invasion of legal rights and liberties*, published anonymously in 1691 and with Kettlewell's name in 1695; an anonymous contribution to the controversy over Dr William Sherlock's defence of taking the oaths, *The duty of allegiance settled upon its true grounds, in answer to a late book of Dr. Will. Sherlock, entituled the case of the allegiance due to sovereign powers* (1691); and *Of Christian Communion, to be Kept on in the Unity of Christ's Church* (1693). *Of Christian Communion* was a particularly influential work among the moderate nonjurors who envisioned an eventual return to the national church, as in its conclusion Kettlewell endorsed attendance at the services of the established church for those laity without access to nonjuring services. His controversial writings are marked by an absence of rancour and personal abuse, while adhering firmly to the nonjuring position as the only right one.

In the long run Kettlewell's devotional writings during this period were more influential than his nonjuring polemic. *A Companion for the Penitent, and Persons Troubled in Mind* (1694) went through eight editions to 1794, and its office for the sick was employed and praised by as staunch a defender of the established church as William Wake. Sometimes published with *A Companion for the Penitent* was another work of Kettlewell's, *A Companion for the Persecuted, or, An Office for those who Suffer for Righteousness* (1693). *Death Made Comfortable, or, The Way to Die Well* (1695) was published four times to 1722.

Kettlewell's life as a nonjuror was quiet, and he was not attacked by the government. His extreme scrupulousness can be seen in his dealings with Hickes, who was disguised as a soldier while hiding from the government. Such was Kettlewell's horror of any deceit that he would never address the disguised Hickes by his assumed title of 'Major'. Kettlewell's closest friends in the nonjuring community, including the deprived bishop of Bath and Wells, Thomas Ken, and the layman Robert Nelson were of milder temperament and politics than the fiery Hickes. Kettlewell seems to have replaced John Tillotson as a spiritual guide for Nelson when Nelson abandoned the established church for the nonjuring movement. Kettlewell encouraged him in writing his classic *A Companion for the Festivals and Fasts of the Church of England* (1704).

Kettlewell had inherited a farm at Lowfields, near Brompton, from his father, and did not suffer the poverty of many nonjuring clergy. He was also supported from the great tithes of Coleshill, which the Digby family diverted to supporting nonjurors. Kettlewell's good financial situation enabled him to continue his lifelong habit of paying for all purchases on the spot and also to suggest remedies for the desperate financial situation of many nonjuring clergy without being seen as swayed by his own situation.

Kettlewell interceded with Sir William Boothby for the deprived bishop of Kilmore, Dr William Sheridan, and proposed the establishment of a fund for the relief of deprived nonjuring clergy in a letter to the deprived non-juring bishop of Norwich, William Lloyd, dated 20 December 1694. Circulars were distributed supporting the fund and appealing for donations. The project failed, however, as the government's attention was drawn to it. Prosecutions were launched, but they did not affect Kettlewell directly, as he had died in London after a long wasting illness on 12 April 1695.

Kettlewell's deathbed was attended by his wife, sister, and surviving brother, Robert, the publisher of some of his books, as well as Nelson. Jane Kettlewell was named executor of his estate. Kettlewell had earlier settled the farm at Lowfields in a trust to be devoted to the poor of Northallerton and Brompton on Jane's death, which occurred about 1719. Nelson had been given charge of Kettlewell's books and papers, and published several books from Kettlewell's unpublished manuscripts. *Five Discourses on so many Important Points of Practical Religion* appeared in 1696 with a biographical preface by Nelson. It was followed by *An Office for Prisoners for Crimes* in 1697 and *The Great Evil and Danger of Profuseness and Prodigality* in 1705. Nelson also sponsored the publication of the two-volume *A Compleat Collection of the Works of the Reverend and Learned John Kettlewell* in 1719, prefaced with a biography of Kettlewell by Francis Lee that is the chief source for his life.

John Kettlewell was buried on 15 April 1695 at the church of All Hallows Barking, London, where Archbishop William Laud had been interred. Ken performed the funeral ceremony, the only time after his deprivation that he is recorded as officiating in public. The funeral was quite crowded, with thirty or forty clergy and many laity attending.   WILLIAM E. BURNS

Sources DNB · T. T. Carter, *The life and times of John Kettlewell* (1895) · F. Lee, 'Life', in *A compleat collection of the works of John Kettlewell*, 2 vols. (1719), vol. 1 · R. Nelson, biographical preface, in J. Kettlewell, *Five discourses on so many important points of practical religion* (1696) · C. F. Secretan, *Memoirs of the life and times of the pious Robert Nelson* (1860) · will, PRO, PROB 11/425, sig. 52
Likenesses G. Vandergucht, line engraving (after H. Tilson), BM, NPG; repro. in F. Lee, *Memoirs of the life of Mr John Kettlewell* (1718) · G. Vandergucht, line engraving, NPG · G. Vertue, line engraving, BM, NPG; repro. in *Compleat collection* · portrait, repro. in *Compleat collection* (1719), vol. 1, frontispiece

Kettlewell, Samuel (1822–1893), theological writer, born on 31 March 1822, was the son of the Revd William Kettlewell, rector of Kirkheaton, near Huddersfield, and his wife, Mary Midgeley. He matriculated on 24 October 1846 at Durham University, and graduated as a licentiate of theology in 1848. He was ordained deacon in the same year, and priest in 1849 by the bishop of Ripon. He then became a curate at Leeds under Walter Farquhar Hook, and in 1851 he was appointed vicar of St Mark's, Leeds. This, his only incumbency, he resigned in 1870 to devote himself to literary work. He had already published a *Catechism on Gospel History* (1851; 3rd edn, 1878), and two works suggested by the controversy over Irish disestablishment: *A Short*

Account of the Reformation in Ireland, and *Rights and Liberties of the Church* (both 1869). His energies were now mainly devoted to his work on Thomas à Kempis, and in 1877 he published *The Authorship of the 'De imitatione Christi'*, followed in 1882 by *Thomas à Kempis and the Brothers of Common Life* (2 vols.; 2nd edn, 1884). These two books were the fruit of much research in England, Holland, and Belgium, and remain of importance for à Kempian studies. In 1888 Kettlewell published *The Basis of True Christian Unity* (2 vols.), and in 1892 a translation of the *De imitatione*. He had received the Lambeth MA in 1860, and in 1892, in recognition of his work, he was granted the Lambeth DD, the queen countersigning his diploma. He died on 2 November 1893 at his residence, Kesselville House, Eastbourne, where he had retired in 1870; he was twice married, his second wife, Margaret, surviving him.

A. F. POLLARD, *rev.* H. C. G. MATTHEW

Sources *The Times* (21 Nov 1893) · *The Guardian* (8 Nov 1893) · *Eastbourne Chronicle* (5 Nov 1893) · Crockford (1891) · *CGPLA Eng. & Wales* (1893) · Boase, *Mod. Eng. biog.*
Wealth at death £52,527 1s. 5d.: resworn probate, Feb 1894, *CGPLA Eng. & Wales* (1893)

Ketton, Robert of (*fl.* 1141–1157), astronomer and translator, is almost certainly identifiable with Robert, archdeacon of Pamplona (*fl.* 1145–1157): both are attested in Spain in the middle decades of the twelfth century. He often appears in the sources with the toponym Ketenensis, which is usually identified with Ketton in Rutland. A third Robert, a writer and translator of scientific works, also active in Spain at that time and commonly considered to have been identical with the first two Roberts, was in fact a different man, as indicated by his different toponym, Robert of Chester [see below].

A Rodbertus Ketenensis collaborated with Hermann of Carinthia (*fl.* 1138–43) in translating Arabic texts. Their project, as explained by Robert himself, in the preface to his translation of al-Kindi's *Judicia* ('Astrological judgements'), was to study Euclid's *Elements*, Theodosius's *Spherica*, and 'a book of proportions', as preparation for understanding Ptolemy's *Almagest*—all texts that they would have read in Arabic or in translation from Arabic. Moreover Robert, in a letter to Peter the Venerable, abbot of Cluny, written in 1143, promised:

> a celestial gift which embraces within itself the whole of science … revealing most accurately, according to number, proportion and measure, all the celestial circles and their quantities, orders and conditions, and, finally, all the various movements of the stars, and their effects and natures and everything else of this kind. (*Patrologia Latina*, 189.660)

The form Rodbertus Ketenensis is confirmed by Hermann's naming him in this way in the preface to his translation of Ptolemy's *Planisphere* (1 June 1143), which he addresses to Thierry, chancellor of Chartres, the well-known educator. Elsewhere in his translation of this work Hermann indicates that Robert has made available *Albeteni*, which would be the canons and tables of al-Battani, the tenth-century astronomer from Baghdad. Confirmation that Hermann and Robert were working together comes from Peter the Venerable, who met them on the banks of the Ebro in 1141 (probably at Logroño) and persuaded them to depart from their usual study of 'astronomy and geometry' in order to translate some texts concerning Islam. While two texts dedicated by Hermann to Robert are extant (his translation of Abu Maʿshar's *Maius introductorium* of 1140 and his original cosmological work of 1143, *De essentiis*), both expressing his friendship with, and very close dependence on, Robert, there is only one text of Robert that is clearly the fruit of this collaboration: the *Judicia* of al-Kindi. In his preface to this work Robert expresses his reluctance to translate a work of astrology, when his real interest is in geometry and astronomy, but states that he has undertaken the work on Hermann's request lest their friendship should grow cold. Most of the manuscripts of this work state, erroneously, that the translation was made 'per Robertum Anglicum Anno Domini 1272' (probably out of confusion with *Robert the Englishman (*fl. c.*1271)); however, a thirteenth-century English manuscript in the British Library (BL, Cotton MS Appendix vi, fol. 109*r*) gives the name of the translator as 'Roberus [*sic*] de Ketene'. It is possible that another text arose out of Robert and Hermann's work together: that is the version of Euclid's *Elements*, hitherto known as the 'Adelard II', since its earliest manuscript is the copy included in the *Heptateuchon* of Thierry of Chartres, who, as already mentioned, received the dedication of one of Hermann's translations, and Robert mentions 'Euclid' specifically as a text that Hermann and he had studied.

Robert's translations of Islamic material commissioned by Peter the Venerable (known as the Toledan Collection) are well documented. While Hermann translated texts *Liber generation is Mahumet* ('On the generation of Muhammad') and *Doctrina Mahumet* ('The teaching of Muhammad'), Robert translated *Chronica mendosa Saracenorum*—a brief history of the early caliphs—and the centrepiece of the collection, the Koran itself. Robert's translation of the Koran, apparently made with the assistance of a certain Muhammad, is the earliest translation of the Koran into any language. It is quite a free rendering of the Arabic, and breaks up the *sūrat* ('chapters') in a different way from the original. It was used by Peter the Venerable to compile his *Summa* against the Saracens, and was frequently copied. The entire Toledan Collection was printed in 1543 in Basel by Theodore Bibliander, with a preface by Philip Melanchthon.

That this Rodbertus Ketenensis is the 'magister Rodbertus' who appears as archdeacon of Pamplona in charters at Pamplona in 1145, 1147, 1149, 1151, and at Barcelona in 1152, and as canon of Tudela in 1157, is indicated only by the joint testimonies of Peter the Venerable and his secretary, Pierre de Poitiers. The latter, 'editing' the collection of Islamic texts for the abbot of Cluny in 1143 or 1144, mentions the solution of a problem concerning the Islamic faith in the following terms: 'It is stated thus in the Alcoran, just as I myself heard for certain in Spain, both from Peter of Toledo, whose companion I was in translating [Pseudo-Alkindi's *Apologia*], and from Robert, now archdeacon of Pamplona' (*Patrologia Latina*, 189.661). Peter the Venerable, in a letter accompanying the Islamic

material sent to Bernard of Clairvaux in the spring or summer of 1144, refers to the translator 'Roberto Ketenensi de Anglia, qui nunc Pampilonensis ecclesiae archidiaconus est' ('Robert Ketenensis of England, who is now archdeacon of the church of Pamplona'; Kritzeck, 212). Unless Peter the Venerable, misled by a statement of his secretary, confused two Roberts, it would seem that Robert of Ketton became archdeacon of Pamplona shortly before 1144. Unfortunately, none of the documents from Pamplona or Tudela give Robert the archdeacon any cognomen, though almost all of them describe him as *magister*. It is not implausible that a scholar of the arts (which included geometry and astronomy) would progress to theology and a position in the church, as Alexander Neckam (*d.* 1217) and Robert Grosseteste (*d.* 1253) were destined to do later. Master Robert, archdeacon of Pamplona, had a distinguished, if turbulent, career. His archdeaconry was probably that of Valdonsella, whose chief town was Uncastillo, and which was disputed between Navarre and Aragon. On 1 July 1149 he drew up a peace treaty between the king of Navarre, García V (*r.* 1134–50) and the Aragonese party, lead by Raymond-Berengar (IV), count of Barcelona—this important diplomatic service was acknowledged by the pope, Eugenius III. In 1151 he was the delegate of the bishop of Pamplona in a territorial dispute with the bishop of Saragossa. Closer to home Robert is found leading a rebellion of the clergy against their own bishop, Lope (Lupus), which was patched up temporarily. However, relations between him and Bishop Lope eventually reached such a point that he broke with him altogether and sided with the party of the new king of Navarre, Sancho VI (the Wise) (*r.* 1150–94). Presumably through the king's agency, he acquired in exchange for his lost archdeaconship the canonry in the church of Tudela, in the possession of which he is last recorded (1157). On the one hand, Robert's education would fit him well for the roles of diplomat, royal adviser, and redactor of official documents which he evidently fulfilled. On the other hand, since in the team translating Arabic geometrical and astronomical tables he was clearly the senior partner, with contacts in high places, he may already have been destined for a career in the church (there is no evidence for Hermann's preferment). The partnership between Robert of Ketton and Hermann of Carinthia would be parallel to those between other churchmen and 'professional' translators or scientists in Spain, such as Dominicus Gundissalinus, archdeacon of Segovia, and John of Spain, or Mauritius, archdeacon of Toledo, and Marco de Toledo. **Robert of Chester** (*fl.* 1144–1150), scientific writer and translator, has often been confused with the former. Robert of Ketton's progression from scientist to churchman would be unproblematic were it not for the fact that from 1144 onwards, there are further works in Arabic science attributed to a Robert, who has been assumed to be the same as Robert of Ketton. However, these works are attributed not to a Ketenensis but rather to a Cestrensis (of Chester). These texts are: translations of an alchemical work called *Liber Morieni* with a *Praefatio castrensis* and the date '11 Feb., era 1182' (1144), and of al-Khwarizmi's *Algebra*, made by Robertus Cestrensis in Segovia in 1145; an original treatise on the construction of the universal astrolabe written by Robertus Cestrensis in London in 1147; astronomical tables of 1150 or 1170 for the meridian of London 'composed by Robert of Chester' and allegedly based on the tables of al-Battani, which are the second part of further unattributed astronomical tables based on the meridian of Toledo; an original treatise on the use of the planispheric astrolabe; and a revision of Adelard of Bath's version of the astronomical tables of al-Khwarizmi 'arranged in order by Robert of Chester' of unknown date, but including the corrections required for the displacement of the meridian of reference to London. Given that Robert's English base appears to have been London at the time when this was the centre of King Stephen's power, it is possible that he was also responsible for the set of political horoscopes drawn up mainly for the years 1150 and 1151 by a partisan of the king. He may have written a work on rhythmomachy if he is the Castrensis referred to as a theoretician of the game in C. Buxerius's *Nobilissimus et antiquissimus ludus Pythagoreus* (1556); (fol. 42r)). Finally, he may have translated from Arabic Ptolemy's *Tetrabiblos* ('Four books on astrology') in which the anonymous translator speaks of 'Maior Britannia in qua patria nostra excestria' ('greater Britain in which our fatherland is Chester'; Herzog August Bibliothek, Wolfenbüttel, MS Gud. lat. 147), though the date given to the translation, 29 August 1206 (confirmed by the addition of its Arabic equivalent), argues against the attribution.

The manuscripts, several of which fall within the twelfth century, are unanimous in calling this Robert Cestrensis (or Castrensis). It would seem unlikely, therefore, that a scribal confusion between 'Ketenensis' and 'Cestrensis' is involved, as Charles Homer Haskins suggested (Haskins, 120). Either Robert changed his name after completing his translation of the Islamic material, as Richard Lemay has claimed, or Robert of Ketton and Robert of Chester are two different people, as claimed most recently by Richard Southern. The arguments in favour of their identity are that the translations of both Roberts are characterized by a tendency to abbreviate, to write idiomatic Latin, and to avoid Arabisms. Most specifically, both Roberts had some involvement with astronomical tables attributed to al-Battani. However, grounds for separating the two Roberts are strong. Robert of Chester is never associated with Hermann of Carinthia. In the earliest text attributed to Castrensis—the *Liber Morieni*—the translator apologizes for his immature talent and his lack of Latin, as if this were his first attempt at a translation. The translations of Robert of Chester do not seem to fit the rigorous mathematical programme outlined by Robert of Ketton: they do not include Theodosius's *Spherics*, 'a book of proportions', or the *Almagest*, or, for that matter, any work on geometry as preparatory for the study of astronomy, but, on the other hand, take in alchemy and algebra, which have little bearing on astronomy; the translations of alchemical and algebraic texts are apparently the earliest in those subjects. The places of composition of Robert of Chester's works are not in the north of Spain, but in Segovia and London, and his activity lasts until later in the century (if the tables containing the date 1170 are his). If Robert of Ketton follows an expected career structure, progressing from the liberal arts to theology and the church, Robert of Chester's career too is familiar. Like Adelard of Bath (*fl. c.*1080–1150), Alfred of Shareshill (*fl.* 1214x1222), and Daniel of Morley (*d.* 1210), he went abroad to study, but then returned to England to put the fruits of his research at the disposal of his fellow citizens.

CHARLES BURNETT

Sources C. H. Haskins, *Studies in the history of mediaeval science*, 2nd edn (1927), 44–9, 120–3 · J. G. Gaztambide, *Historia de los obispos de Pamplona*, 1 (Pamplona, 1979), 391–432 · R. W. Southern, *Robert Grosseteste: the growth of an English mind in medieval Europe*, 2nd edn (1992), xlvii–xlix · R. P. Mercier, 'Astronomical tables in the twelfth century', *Adelard of Bath: an English scientist and Arabist of the early twelfth century*, ed. C. Burnett (1987), 87–119 · J. D. North, 'Some Norman horoscopes', *Adelard of Bath: an English scientist and Arabist of the early twelfth century*, ed. C. Burnett (1987), 147–61 [here attributed tentatively to Adelard of Bath] · P. Kunitzsch, *Glossar der arabischen Fachausdrücke in der mittelalterlichen europäischen Astrolabliteratur*, Nachrichten der Akademie der Wissenschaften in Göttingen I. Philologisch-historische Klasse, 1982, 11 (1983), 489–92 · R. Lemay, 'L'authenticité de la préface de Robert de Chester à sa traduction du *Morienus* (1144)', *Chrysopœia*, 4 (1991), 3–32 · *Robert of Chester's (?) redaction of Euclid's 'Elements', the so-called Adelard II version*, ed. H. L. L. Busard and M. Folkerts, 1 (1992), 22–31 · 'Petrus Cluniacensis: epistolarum libri sex', *Patrologia Latina*, 189 (1854) [Peter the Venerable, *Letters*] · J. Kritzeck, *Peter the Venerable and Islam* (1964)
Archives BL, Cotton MS Appendix vi, fol. 109v · Herzog August Bibliothek, Wolfenbüttel, MS Gud. lat. 147

Keugh, Mathew (*c.*1744–1798), army officer and Irish nationalist, was born in co. Wexford. A loyalist acquaintance, Charles Jackson, claimed that Keugh was a drummer in the 33rd regiment during the American war. More certain is that Keugh rose from the ranks and was gazetted as an ensign in the 60th regiment on 31 October 1763. He was promoted lieutenant in the 45th foot on 14 July 1769 and transferred to the 27th Inniskilling regiment on 14 March 1772. He retired on the half pay of a captain-lieutenant in 1774 and returned to George's Street, Wexford, where his upstanding reputation and protestantism led to his appointment as a commissioner of the peace. He later disappointed conservative associates by supporting campaigns to reform the Irish parliament and for Catholic emancipation. Little is known of his marriage other than that it was childless and that his wife had been widowed. She was Beauchamp Bagenal Harvey's first cousin and the aunt of Sir Jonah Barrington's wife.

Keugh was closely associated with socially prominent republicans such as Harvey and John Henry Colclough, who engaged in political agitation as early as 1791–2. His support of the whig viceroy, Earl Fitzwilliam, probably led to the revocation of his civil commission in 1796 although the authorities were clearly unaware of the strength of his radical convictions. Documents recovered from Keugh's house in June 1798 indicate his knowledge of Wexford's paramilitary leadership from late 1797. Although he was probably not a formally appointed officer, the United

Irishmen prized members with military experience and it is very likely that Keugh's advice was sought by leading activists. He dined with high-ranking conspirators at Harvey's home in April 1798 and was one of the guests whose conversation aroused Jonah Barrington's suspicions. His outwardly passive conduct, however, enabled him to evade arrest with the advent of the rising and, crucially, he was not named in the confession extracted from Anthony Perry of Inch on 26 May.

While many of his associates languished in gaol that evening, Keugh busied himself fortifying the county town against a possible rebel attack. Such activity may explain Mrs Brownrigg's claim that Keugh was later denounced, wrongly, as an Orangeman. His stature among United Irishmen was revealed on 30 May when the insurgents arrived and appointed him 'governor' of Wexford town. Keugh, assisted by William Kearney, chaired the eight-man committee which administered the 'Wexford republic' and provided logistic support to rebel forces in the field. His moderation reassured nervous neutrals and he responded as best he could to the appeals of imprisoned loyalists for protection. Only four prisoners were put to death in the town between 4 and 20 June, although matters were frequently chaotic. Keugh was technically superseded by Harvey about 7 June when the former commander-in-chief of the New Ross army was made 'president' of the Wexford-based council. Keugh in fact remained the military commander in Wexford town and took steps to bolster its harbour and land defences. Several contemporaries refuted allegations that Keugh concurred in the mass execution of loyalist captives on 20 June. His authority had evidently waned at this critical period to the point that he was incapable of imposing restraint on the extremists attached to Captain Thomas Dixon.

Preserving lives was foremost in Keugh's mind on 21 June when, after consulting with his colleagues in his home, he decided to place the town in the care of Lord Kingsborough until its surrender had been negotiated. Captain McManus of the Antrim militia and Edward Hay were sent to contact Lieutenant-General Gerard Lake at Enniscorthy, who spurned the 'insolent' proposals on the 22nd. The issue was forced later that day when Major-General John Moore's column recaptured the undefended town. Keugh was one of the few insurgents not to have fled and apparently hoped that Kingsborough and others would intercede on his behalf.

Keugh was court-martialled with eight others on 24 June and made a strong speech in which he denied complicity in atrocities. This plea and Kingsborough's support were insufficient to prevent capital conviction. Barrington sought a reprieve from Under-Secretary Edward Cooke in Dublin Castle and was told that Lake did not wish to diminish the exemplary function of the proceedings. Keugh was sent to the makeshift gallows on Wexford Bridge as planned at 11 a.m. on 25 June, where his call for a protestant clergyman elicited the sympathy of General Moore. He was attended by the Revd John Elgee, rector of Wexford. Keugh's head was removed to be spiked on the court house and his mutilated body thrown into the river as a mark of dishonour.   RUÁN O'DONNELL

Sources R. R. Madden, *The United Irishmen: their lives and times*, 2nd edn, 4 vols. (1857–60) · D. Gahan, *The people's rising: Wexford, 1798* (1995) · C. Dickson, *The Wexford rising in 1798* (1955) · R. Musgrave, *Memoirs of the Irish rebellion of 1798*, ed. S. W. Myers and D. E. McKnight, 4th edn (1995) · J. Barrington, *Rise and fall of the Irish nation* (1843) · E. Hay, *History of the insurrection of Wexford* (1803) · T. Cloney, *A personal narrative of those transactions in the county Wexford … during the awful period of 1798* (1832)

Wealth at death house on George's Street, Wexford

Key. *See also* Caius.

Key, Sir Astley Cooper (1821–1888), naval officer, the son of Charles Aston *Key (1793–1849) and his wife Anne, *née* Cooper, was born at St Thomas Street, London, on 18 January 1821. He entered the navy in August 1833, attending the Royal Naval College at Portsmouth, where he won the annual silver medal competition. He passed his lieutenant's examination in August 1840, and after study on the *Excellent* was commissioned on 22 December 1842. In February 1843 he joined the *Curaçao* for the east coast of South America, where in 1844 he transferred to the steam frigate *Gorgon* (Captain Charles Hotham), a reflection of his decision to specialize in steam. On 10 May the *Gorgon* was driven ashore near Montevideo. Key, using his training at *Excellent*, played a leading part in refloating her. He served at the battle of Obligado (fought against the Argentinians on the Rio Parana on 20 November 1845), in which he was slightly wounded, and he was promoted commander as of 18 November. Between 1847 and 1850 he commanded the steamer *Bulldog* in the Mediterranean, being posted on 11 October 1850. In 1853 he took command of the screw frigate *Amphion*, and served in the Baltic in 1854 and 1855, taking a prominent part at Bomarsund, Sveaborg, and operations in the Gulf of Viborg. On 5 July 1855 he was nominated CB. In 1856 he was appointed to the steam battleship *Sans Pareil*, to command the inshore gunboat division. Shortly after this, in 1856, he married Charlotte Lavinia McNeill. In 1857 he took his ship to China with a detachment of marines, which he took to Calcutta during the early stages of the Indian mutiny, before returning to China to command a battalion of the naval brigade at the capture of Canton (Guangzhou) (28–9 December 1857).

In 1859–60 Key served on the royal commission on national defence, and between 1860 and 1863 as captain of the steam reserve at Devonport. On the commission he demonstrated his expertise in naval technology, but also a glaring misunderstanding of the basis of British strategy. He had been appointed on the strength of his known views in favour of local coast defence to a commission predisposed to recommend forts, although British imperial and national security depended on the ability to use the sea not merely to prevent an invasion. In 1864 he became captain of the *Excellent*, and superintendent of the Royal Naval College. On 20 November 1866 he was promoted rear-admiral and became the first director of naval ordnance, a post he had helped to define. Here he demonstrated a preference for close action and simple muzzle-

Sir Astley Cooper Key (1821–1888), by Lock & Whitfield, pubd 1883

loading guns. In 1869 he served as admiral superintendent at Portsmouth and later Malta, before establishing the new Royal Naval College at Greenwich between 1872 and 1876. In April 1873 he became vice-admiral and in May he was appointed KCB. His wife died on 30 December 1874. In early 1876 he took command of the North American station, where he married Evelyn Bartolucci in October 1877 at Halifax, Nova Scotia. She was the daughter of an Italian dancing master and younger than Key's own eldest daughter. He returned in March 1878 to command the Baltic fleet formed during the Russian war scare. On 15 June 1879 he was appointed principal naval aide-de-camp to the queen, and in August became first naval lord, a post he held until the summer of 1885. When he left office he was granted a special pension of £500 per annum.

Key was an early example of an officer who made his career through the mastery of new technology. Unfortunately for the navy, he never developed an equivalent comprehension of strategic needs. He was an obsessive centralizer, and revelled in the minutiae of administration, to the exclusion of the wider issues of policy. This was particularly problematic during the prolonged absences of the first lord of the Admiralty, Lord Northbrook, in Egypt, when he acted as the entire Board of Admiralty.

Key became first naval lord in breach of a compact he had made with Geoffrey Hornby and Beauchamp Seymour that they would all refuse the post without some reform of the Admiralty. He did so apparently from financial embarrassment resulting from his recent second marriage and the marriage of his eldest daughter. A weak character, Key allowed his wife to become a major channel for influence. She was known as 'the Key to promotion'. Key had his own small group of followers in the service, mainly men of his own technical bent, who were referred to as 'the bunch of Keys'. Notable among them was John Fisher, who distanced himself from his old mentor after Key left office. Key's six years at the Admiralty witnessed steady, if unspectacular, progress in all areas. Northbrook was happy to leave naval administration to Key, who was happy to keep the estimates down to the figures he was given. Key was still committed to coast defence and had little comprehension of the navy's role in commerce protection. Under pressure from increasing French construction, he sanctioned the building of six Admiral class ironclads, ships noted more for the weaknesses caused by insufficient displacement than the success of the new breech-loading guns, which were a feature of the Northbrook board's term of office. The 1884 agitation for increased naval expenditure, which resulted in the 'Northbrook programme', was ill timed; not only was the navy markedly superior to the possible danger, but many of the programme's ships would be obsolete before completion. It was a mark of Key's isolation that in the absence of Northbrook his views were hardly noted by a government anxious to escape censure. When the Panjdeh crisis came in 1885, long signalled by Russian advances, the Admiralty was better prepared than it had been in 1878. Key could call on information from the foreign intelligence committee, set up in 1882, the results of the 1878 mobilization, and a number of new ships.

If the mark of successful administration was to leave things better than before, Key's time in office was well spent. He has been criticized for not doing more, particularly on the strategic front, but this ignores the overriding primacy of the battle fleet in national strategy, and the real naval requirements close to home. Key was not an intellectual, and had no elevated ideas on sea power, but in this he was a man of his times. The navy spent the middle years of the century coming to terms with technology, and in the long peace after 1856 it was unsurprising that men such as Key—and his successor in several posts, Arthur Hood—should reach the highest position. By concentrating on practicalities, they provided the navy with the material that was vital to its strength. It was left to another generation to expound the principles of maritime strategy. The contrast between Key and his two rivals for the post of senior naval lord in 1879, Hornby and Seymour, was striking. Key lacked their experience afloat, and demonstrated little leadership. He had few followers, and evoked no lasting loyalty.

On 24 November 1882 Key was nominated GCB, and on 11 August 1884 he was sworn of the privy council. He was at various times elected FRS and FRGS and was awarded an honorary DCL. After retirement he lived at Laggan House, Maidenhead, where he died on 3 March 1888. His second wife survived him.

                          ANDREW LAMBERT

Sources P. H. Colomb, *Memoirs of Admiral the Right Honble. Sir Astley Cooper Key* (1898) · N. A. M. Rodger, 'The dark ages of the admiralty,

1869–1885: change and decay, 1874–1880', *Mariner's Mirror*, 62 (1976), 33–46 • N. A. M. Rodger, 'The dark ages of the admiralty, 1869–1885: peace, retrenchment and reform, 1880–1885', *Mariner's Mirror*, 62 (1976), 121–8 • B. M. Ranft, *Technical change and British naval policy, 1860–1939* (1977) • A. J. Marder, *The anatomy of British sea power*, American edn (1940) • A. D. Lambert, *The Crimean War: British grand strategy, 1853–56* (1990) • personal knowledge (1892) [*DNB*] • B. Mallett, *Lord Northbrook* (1908) • *CGPLA Eng. & Wales* (1888)

Archives BL, corresp. | NMM, Hornby MSS • NMM, Milne MSS
Likenesses portrait, presented in 1876, Royal Naval College • Lock & Whitfield, photograph, pubd 1883, NPG [*see illus.*] • photograph, repro. in Colomb, *Memoirs*, frontispiece
Wealth at death £16,329 18s. 3d.: probate, 23 April 1888, *CGPLA Eng. & Wales*

Key, Charles Aston (1793–1849), surgeon, born in Southwark, London, on 6 October 1793, was the eldest son of Thomas Key (d. 1837), medical practitioner, and Margaret Barry. Thomas Hewitt *Key was a half-brother by a second marriage. Aston Key was educated at Buntingford grammar school, Hertfordshire, and was apprenticed to his father in 1810. He attended the lectures at the United Borough Hospitals in 1812, and became a pupil at Guy's Hospital in 1814. In 1815 his apprenticeship to his father was cancelled, and he became a pupil of Astley Cooper at a large premium. That summer he travelled to Brussels with several other pupils and helped treat the injured after the battle of Waterloo. In 1817–18 he lived with Cooper, and in 1818 married Cooper's niece, Anne Cooper. Key became demonstrator of anatomy at St Thomas's Hospital, but resigned the post in February 1823, though he gave some of Sir Astley Cooper's surgical lectures for two sessions afterwards. In 1827 he edited the second edition of Cooper's work on hernia, which was little different from the first.

Key had qualified at the Royal College of Surgeons in 1821, and in the autumn of the same year was appointed the first assistant surgeon to Guy's, succeeding to a full surgeoncy in January 1824. In this year he introduced the operation for lithotomy with the straight staff, using only a single knife all through. He also published *A Short Treatise on the Section of the Prostate Gland in Lithotomy*. The success of his operations established his reputation as a surgeon. In 1825, on the separation of Guy's from St Thomas's, Key was appointed lecturer on surgery at Guy's, and his classes were for many years very popular. He resigned the lectureship in 1844. In 1845 he was one of the first elected fellows of the Royal College of Surgeons, and in the same year became a member of its council. In 1847 he was appointed surgeon to Prince Albert. Key died of cholera at his home in St Helen's Place, London, on 23 August 1849, leaving his wife and nine children. He was buried in the churchyard of St Dionis Backchurch. His son Sir Astley Cooper *Key is separately noticed.

Key was a great surgical operator and lecturer, his lectures being derived largely from the results of his own experience. He was not a well-read man nor a scientific pathologist, but he contributed fifteen papers to *Guy's Hospital Reports* describing his varied surgical practice. In 1833 he published *A memoir on the advantages and practicability of*

Charles Aston Key (1793–1849), by Francis Holl, pubd 1851 (after George Richmond, 1849)

dividing the stricture in strangulated hernia on the outside of the sac. He was one of the first surgeons in London to use ether as an anaesthetic and to ligature the subclavian artery successfully for the cure of an axillary aneurysm. His dexterity with the knife was remarkable: he was never known to make a mistake through inattention to details. In person he was of commanding presence, thin, and rather tall, with a slightly aquiline nose. In temperament he was brusque, short-tempered, and overbearing.

G. T. BETTANY, *rev.* J. M. T. FORD

Sources *The Lancet* (15 Sept 1849), 300–01 • *The Lancet* (13 Oct 1849), 411–12 • *British and Foreign Medico-Chirurgical Review*, 4 (1849), 572–7 • S. Wilks and G. T. Bettany, *A biographical history of Guy's Hospital* (1892), 329 • V. G. Plarr, *Plarr's Lives of the fellows of the Royal College of Surgeons of England*, rev. D'A. Power, 2 vols. (1930) • *Provincial Medical and Surgical Journal* (5 Sept 1849), 502
Likenesses R. Cruikshank?, group portrait, coloured lithograph, c.1830 (*Benjamin Harrison, autocratic treasurer of Guy's Hospital, backing the gross nepotism of Sir Astley Cooper*), Wellcome L. • J. Doyle, group portrait, coloured lithograph, 1831 (*John Bull presented as the Chinese labourer Hoo Loo surrounded by surgeons discussing the removal of his tumour, satirizing British political reform*), Wellcome L. • F. Holl, stipple, pubd 1851 (after G. Richmond, 1849), BM, NPG, Sci Mus. [*see illus.*] • Beynon and Co., group portrait, coloured lithograph (*The past surgeons and physicians of Guy's Hospital, Southwark, London, with views of the building*; after M. Hanhart), Wellcome L. • plaster bust, Guy's Hospital, London, United Medical and Dental Schools

Key, Sir John, first baronet (1794–1858), lord mayor of London, the eldest son of John Key of Denmark Hill, Surrey, was born on 16 August 1794. He entered his father's business, that of a wholesale stationer, about 1818. The firm had been established in the last century, and then traded as Key Brothers & Son, at 30 Abchurch Lane, London. After several changes of address the business was finally removed to 97 and 103 Newgate Street. Key was elected alderman for the ward of Langbourn on 8 April 1823, and was sheriff of London and Middlesex in 1824. He served the office of master of the Stationers' Company in 1830, and in the same year was elected lord mayor. He was one of the leading supporters of the Reform Bill in the City, and received the unusual honour of re-election to the mayoralty in the following year.

During his second mayoralty, when William IV and Queen Adelaide had arranged to visit the City in order to open the new London Bridge, Key suffered some loss of popularity by advising the king and his ministers not to come to the City on account of the supposed unpopularity of the duke of Wellington. The visit passed off satisfactorily, and Key was created a baronet by William IV on 17 August 1831. He was elected member of parliament for the City in 1832 but retired in August 1833. He supported the immediate abolition of slavery, the introduction of the ballot and triennial parliaments, and the repeal of the corn laws. He removed in 1851 from Langbourn to the ward of Bridge Without, which he represented until 1853. In that year he was elected chamberlain of London after a poll, his opponent being Benjamin Scott, who afterwards succeeded him in that office.

On 17 August 1814 Key married Charlotte, daughter of Francis Green of Dorking, Surrey; they had two sons and three daughters. He died at Streatham, London, on 14 July 1858.

CHARLES WELCH, rev. H. C. G. MATTHEW

Sources Boase, *Mod. Eng. biog.* · *Parliamentary Pocket Companion* (1832–3) · Burke, *Peerage* · *City Press* (1858) · *London's roll of fame: being complimentary notes and addresses from the city of London, on presentation of the honorary freedom of that city* (1884)
Archives U. Durham L., corresp. with second Earl Grey
Likenesses C. Turner, mezzotint, pubd 1832 (after M. Pearson), BM · C. Pearson, portrait, repro. in *London's roll of fame*, 209 · two caricatures, lithographs, NPG · woodcut, NPG
Wealth at death under £50,000: resworn probate, May 1870, *CGPLA Eng. & Wales* (1858)

Key, Thomas Hewitt (1799–1875), Latin scholar, was born in Southwark on 20 March 1799. He was the youngest son of the physician Thomas Key, a member of an old Staffordshire family, and his second wife, Mary Lux Barry; the surgeon Charles Aston *Key (1793–1849) was his half-brother. Thomas was educated at Buntingford grammar school, Hertfordshire, under the headmaster Samuel Dewe; he recalled that Latin and arithmetic were both well taught. In October 1817 he entered St John's College, Cambridge, and was elected scholar; in the spring of 1819 he migrated to Trinity College, where he also gained a scholarship. After graduating in 1821 (nineteenth wrangler) he hoped to enter the bar, but adhered to his father's wishes by studying medicine in Cambridge and at Guy's Hospital in London (1821–4).

On 26 September 1824 Key married Sarah Troward (d. 1884), daughter of the solicitor for the prosecution in the trial of Warren Hastings. In the same year, in Cambridge, he met Francis W. Gilmer, who had come to England to select founding professors for Jefferson's new University of Virginia. Key accepted the chair of pure mathematics as from 1 April 1825; he resigned in the autumn of 1827, and returned to England. The reason given related to the Virginian climate, but the difficulty of controlling sometimes unruly students may also have been a factor. On 18 July 1828 Key was appointed professor of Roman language, literature, and antiquities in the new London University (in 1836 renamed University College, London). He was recommended by his friend and Cambridge contemporary George Long, who held the chair of Greek, and whose Latin and Greek classes Key had taught at Virginia in 1825 during Long's absence in England. In 1832, jointly with his Cambridge contemporary Henry Malden, the professor of Greek, Key became headmaster of the secondary school which formed part of the university. In 1842 he resigned his chair and became sole headmaster of the school, and retained the post until his death in 1875. His own teaching included both Latin and geography.

The London University School formed an integral part of the university and was housed in its premises. After its foundation in 1830 it had been run by a clerical headmaster: neither he nor his successor lasted long, and the school was near collapse when Key and Malden offered to bear the financial risk themselves. The refounded school of 1832 reflected the ideals of its parent body's founders in being unlike a conventional public school of the period. It had no chapel or religious instruction, neither playing fields nor corporal punishment; all subjects were optional; Latin and Greek verse composition was not taught, but natural science was part of the curriculum. The school (in 1838 renamed University College School) flourished during Key's reign, and grew to accommodate very large numbers: from 249 in 1833 to 623 at Key's death.

On his appointment as sole headmaster Key was given the title of professor of comparative grammar, to which no salary was attached. This title, conferred at his own request, reflected a major interest of Key's. He had worked on Latin etymology while in Virginia, and in 1830 had been one of the founding members of a philological society set up in the London University, to whose meetings he contributed several papers. (The society was refounded in 1842 as the Philological Society of London.) In 1829 he had attended the lectures of his colleague Friedrich Rosen, professor of oriental languages, and from them took the characteristic Sanskrit mode of analysis of words according to their stems ('crude forms'). Rosen's influence can be seen in Key's review of Zumpt's *Latin Grammar* (*Quarterly Journal of Education*, January 1831); he expounded the 'crude-form' system in two articles in the *English Journal of Education* (1850–51). Key's *Latin Grammar on the System of Crude Forms* was first published in 1846; later editions appeared in 1858 and 1862. The book was, however, little adopted outside Key's own school, despite the advocacy of his pupil and colleague John Robson, later secretary to the College of Preceptors. Later in the 1840s Key began a Latin dictionary organized on the same principle. Planned as a short book, it turned into a much larger project. Progress was slow (by August 1852 the letter C had been reached), and in 1856 Key abandoned crude forms as an organizing principle. In 1865 he engaged the immigrant German classical scholar Wilhelm Wagner to work with him on the project. Wagner negotiated a contract on equal terms, but soon decided that Key wanted an assistant rather than a partner and gave up the task. (Wagner, a man of independent mind and unafraid to speak it, had already ruined his career chances in Germany by public criticism of his teacher and academic patron Friedrich Ritschl.) After Key's death the dictionary, still nowhere near completed, was prepared for publication by his pupil James Reid (*A Latin Dictionary*, 1888). This was an act of misjudged devotion: the book was severely handled by reviewers.

Key's Latin grammar reflects his wide reading in the language, and particularly his knowledge of Plautus and Terence, authors little studied in England at that time. As a comparative philologist he was, like many of his contemporaries, enthusiastic but uncontrolled: his was the type exemplified by George Eliot's Mr Casaubon and his search for the 'Key to all mythologies'. Key was, for example, willing to argue that 'bad' and 'better' came from the same root. At the meetings of the Philological Society, of which he was president for several years, he became something of an embarrassment: he gave over sixty papers to the society, many advancing extravagant etymologies. Key contributed articles on language to the *Penny Magazine* (1833–42) of the Society for the Diffusion of Useful Knowledge (SDUK). In 1844 the republication of these articles in a single volume led to a controversy with J. W. Donaldson, author of *The New Cratylus* (1839) and *Varronianus* (1844), who charged him with plagiarism. This developed into a three-cornered battle with George Long, Key's colleague and Donaldson's teacher. The polemical pamphlets which ensued were subsequently collected and published by Key with an introduction (*The Controversy about the Varronianus*, 1845).

A number of campaigns claimed Key's attention and support. He was among the founders of the London Library, and became a member of its committee. He was also active in the recruitment campaigns of the late 1850s amid the perceived threat of an invasion from France. For the SDUK, on whose committee he served, he wrote not only on language but also on ancient geography, and provided maps for its atlas. He was elected a fellow of the Royal Society of Literature in 1860.

Key died of bronchitis at his home, 21 Westbourne Terrace, Paddington, London, on 29 November 1875, and was buried in Highgate cemetery. He was survived by his widow and six of their seven children. Key's career had included chairs in three different subjects as well as his headmastership. To some of his pupils he remained an exemplary figure: tall, impressive, and genial—the Red Queen to the White Queen of his shy colleague Henry Malden. His pupil John Hicks recalled that 'his presence [was] commanding, his voice sonorous' (Hicks, 14). Less than exemplary, however, was his reluctance to acknowledge his intellectual debts to Friedrich Rosen, and to give credit to his collaborator Wilhelm Wagner. A marble bust by Thomas Woolner was presented to University College by Key's pupils and friends, but has since disappeared.

CHRISTOPHER STRAY

Sources J. P. Hicks, *T. Hewitt Key: a short memoir* (1893) · DNB · J. Glucker, 'Professor Key and Doctor Wagner: an episode in the history of Victorian scholarship', *Pegasus: classical essays from the University of Exeter*, ed. H. W. Stubbs (1981), 98–123 · H. J. K. Usher and others, *An angel without wings: the history of University College School, 1830–1980* (1981), 15–27 · P. A. Bruce, 'Professor Key and Professor Long', *University of Virginia Alumni Bulletin*, 3rd ser. 27 (July–Aug 1924), 273–8 · [G. Long], *PRS*, 24 (1875–6), x–xvi · P. A. Bruce, *The history of the University of Virginia, 1819–1919*, 5 vols. (c.1920–1922), vols. 1–2 · 'Our headmaster', *The Gower*, 15/8 (March 1914), 418–21 · d. cert. · CGPLA Eng. & Wales (1875)

Archives UCL, corresp. and lecture notes · University of Virginia, Charlottesville, corresp. | UCL, letters to Society for the Diffusion of Useful Knowledge

Likenesses T. Woolner, marble bust, c.1874 · F. Langlois, oils, UCL · oils · photograph, repro. in Usher and others, *Angel without wings*, 16 · photograph, repro. in Bruce, 'Professor Key and Professor Long', 275 · photograph, repro. in P. Magnus, *Fragments, educational and other* (1933), 11 · wood-engraving, NPG; repro. in *ILN* (1875)

Wealth at death under £14,000: probate, 22 Dec 1875, *CGPLA Eng. & Wales*

Keyes [Keys], **Roger** (d. 1477), college head, was admitted to All Souls College, Oxford, as a legist in 1438 from Exeter diocese, and proceeded to the degree of BCnL. As warden from 1443 to 1445, in succession to the founding warden, Richard Andrewes, he was principally concerned with the building of the college, founded by Archbishop Henry Chichele in 1437, as Andrewes had been with concluding the legal arrangements to secure the college's endowments. Keyes's architectural involvement had begun earlier, in September 1441, when he succeeded the clerk John Druell as surveyor of the building works. In that post he was responsible for managing the workmen, overseeing the purchase of materials, co-ordinating work in the different building sites, and collecting and disbursing the necessary sums from Chichele's financial agents, to whom he had also to render accounts. Keyes accounted for the last quarter of 1441, through the following year, until December 1443. There is no reason to suppose that he would have had any particular say in the design of the college, although he has been described as its 'architect'.

On 6 March 1454 Keyes was appointed rector of St Dunstan-in-the-East, London, and afterwards became also a canon of St Paul's, a canon of Salisbury, archdeacon of Barnstaple, and, by 1456, a canon and prebendary of Exeter. He was also appointed precentor of Exeter, a post he held until his death, and from September 1455 until April 1456 he was one of the keepers of the spiritualities of that see *sede vacante*.

In 1448 Keyes was appointed by Henry VI supervisor of the building of Eton College. For this he received a salary of £50 a year. In 1452 he was appointed chaplain to the king, and for his service in the building of Eton was granted in the same year two stags annually from Dartmoor. In 1454 he and his brother Thomas received a grant of arms and patent of nobility. Keyes died on 11 November 1477 at Exeter and was buried there. He gave books both to All Souls College and to Exeter College (of which he had been appointed visitor in November 1442), and to All Souls vestments and vessels for use at the principal altar in the chapel.   JAMES McCONICA

Sources Emden, *Oxf.* · E. F. Jacob, 'The building of All Souls College, 1438–43', *Historical essays in honour of James Tait*, ed. J. G. Edwards, V. H. Galbraith, and E. F. Jacob (1933), 122–3, 125, 129, 130, 133 · N. R. Ker, *Records of All Souls College Library, 1437–1600* (1971), 114 · S. Bentley, ed., *Excerpta historica, or, Illustrations of English history* (1831) · PRO, chancery warrants series 1, c81/1454/15
Archives All Souls Oxf., building accounts

Keyes, Roger John Brownlow, first Baron Keyes (1872–1945), naval officer, was born on 4 October 1872 at Tundiani Fort, north-west frontier of India, the second son of the commander of the Punjab frontier force, Brigadier Sir Charles Patton Keyes (1822–1896), of Croghan, co. Donegal, and his wife, Katherine Jessie (d. 1916), daughter of James Norman of Calcutta.

Service in Africa and China Keyes entered the navy as a cadet at the Royal Naval College, Dartmouth, in the autumn of 1885, passing out in July 1887 and joining HMS *Raleigh*, flagship of the Cape of Good Hope and west coast of Africa station. Keyes exchanged into the corvette *Turquoise* in 1890 because of the opportunity for work in small boats against slavers on the east coast of Africa. He also served in the naval brigade during the punitive expedition against the sultan of Witu, east Africa, in October 1890, gaining the general Africa medal with clasp. Keyes, confirmed in the rank of sub-lieutenant in 1892, served in the armoured cruiser *Immortalité* in the Channel Fleet, in the royal yacht *Victoria and Albert* (July 1893), and, promoted to lieutenant, in the sloop *Beagle* on the south-east coast of South America (1893–6). Keyes then returned to England and served in the corvette *Curaçoa* until he received his first command, the destroyer *Opossum* in the Devonport instructional flotilla (1897–8). This was followed by command of the destroyer *Hart* on the China station in November 1898, with a transfer to the new destroyer *Fame* in January 1899. Keyes saw action with the Hong Kong regiment in April 1899 against Chinese forces resisting the new British lease on the Kowloon peninsula and the following year after the outbreak of the Boxer uprising, in an action reminiscent of an earlier age, led a cutting-out expedition on the Peiho (Beihe) River in June 1900 that captured four Chinese destroyers by means of boarding-parties. Soon afterwards Keyes led an aggressive reconnaissance up the river that destroyed the guns and blew up the magazine of Hsi-Cheng Fort. Keyes was also with the forces that relieved the besieged legations in Peking (Beijing)—he was one of the first into the city—and ended the campaign with special promotion for his services to the rank of commander in November 1900. He had shown what would be a characteristic taste for action, quick

Roger John Brownlow Keyes, first Baron Keyes (1872–1945), by Philip A. de Laszlo, 1923

thinking, initiative, and a willingness to take responsibility.

Keyes was second in command of the Devonport destroyer flotilla (1901–3) and then served in the naval intelligence department. He was naval attaché to Italy and Austria–Hungary (1905–8), an appointment that also included at this time Athens and Constantinople, and was promoted to captain on 1 July 1905. On 10 April 1906 Keyes married Eva Mary Salvin (1882–1973), the elder daughter of Edward Salvin Bowlby (1830–1902), of Gilston Park, Hertfordshire, and Knoydart, Inverness-shire, and his second wife, Elizabeth Agnew (d. 1937). They had two sons and three daughters.

In command of the Submarine Service Keyes commanded the cruiser *Venus* in the Atlantic Fleet (1908–10) before being appointed inspecting captain of submarines in November 1910 and commodore (S) in charge of the Submarine Service in August 1912. Keyes admitted that he did not have extensive technical knowledge and had to rely on his staff. He wanted to break the monopoly of Vickers on the construction of submarines for the Royal Navy and introduce competition into the design process but the results of his efforts were controversial, especially his decision to use foreign designs. The foreign designs proved unsuccessful and when war broke out, despite a number of new types, relatively few were suitable for overseas service. Keyes was probably most effective in training, selection of officers and men, and demonstrating in manoeuvres the offensive capabilities of submarines, especially in making a traditional close blockade impracticable.

Keyes remained in command of the Submarine Service for approximately the first half-year of the war. He was far too active in temperament to treat his position as essentially shore-bound and went to sea as often as possible in a destroyer to work with the submarines. The speed and visibility of a submarine were then very limited and destroyers or light craft could, it was assumed, be useful in acting as scouts. Keyes as a result of these operations suggested the raid on German patrols in the Heligoland bight that led to the action of 28 August 1914, a confused affair that thanks to the timely intervention of Admiral Beatty's battle cruisers resulted in the sinking of three German cruisers and a destroyer. The recall of Lord Fisher as first sea lord in October eventually undermined Keyes's position for Fisher had been one of those most critical of his handling of the Submarine Service. An apparent truce between the two men did not last but thanks to Keyes's friendship with the first lord Winston Churchill he was named chief of staff to Vice-Admiral Carden commanding the British naval forces off the Dardanelles.

The Dardanelles Carden relinquished his command for reasons of health shortly before the major naval attack in March and his successor, Admiral John M. De Robeck, inherited his staff, including Keyes. Keyes was therefore closely associated with the maritime aspects of the Dardanelles campaign from its early stages to the final evacuation. The naval attack of 18 March was thwarted, largely by an undetected line of newly laid Turkish mines. Keyes was undaunted, for him it was a matter of reorganizing the mine-sweeping services to make them more efficient, particularly by fitting destroyers with sweeping gear and reorganizing the trawler sweepers and manning them with volunteer crews from the two British battleships that had been sunk. De Robeck was at first ready to renew the attack but changed his opinion and elected to wait until the military forces gathering at the nearby island of Lemnos could land and secure the commanding heights dominating the narrows. The landing on 25 April established bridgeheads, at heavy cost, but failed to break through and seize the heights. Another landing at Suvla in August also failed to change the situation. By now specially bulged ships had reached the Dardanelles and Keyes and his staff had elaborated plans for a new attack. To Keyes, an attack was imperative for with autumn and winter would come gales making supply of the army over open beaches very difficult. Furthermore, the entry of Bulgaria into the war on the side of the central powers meant that Serbia was about to be overrun, thereby permitting the Germans to open direct rail communications with Turkey. The government hesitated, but De Robeck opposed a new naval attack for even if the ships broke through he did not think it would necessarily mean the surrender of Turkey. Keyes and De Robeck held irreconcilable views on this subject, but the admiral chivalrously permitted Keyes to return to England to plead his case. Keyes had a certain effect on a wavering government, but he was out of his element in the political world and De Robeck—who had the responsibility—also had the decisive say. The government eventually decided to evacuate, although De Robeck's absence in England for three weeks' leave gave Keyes and Admiral R. E. Wemyss, the senior naval officer at Mudros, a new opportunity to plead for a new attack. They were unsuccessful but Keyes would remain convinced until the end of his life that a renewed naval attack would have succeeded and that an Anglo-French fleet off Constantinople would have meant Turkey's exit from the war with incalculable results.

Keyes continued as De Robeck's chief of staff at Salonika where a new front had been established in an unsuccessful attempt to save Serbia. De Robeck had shown remarkable forbearance towards his chief of staff but their relationship was never what it had been before and Keyes chafed at being in what had become a backwater of the war. In June 1916 he received command of the battleship *Centurion* in the 2nd battle squadron of the Grand Fleet. He was promoted to rear-admiral in April 1917 but waited until an admiral's position became vacant in June before leaving *Centurion* to become second in command in the 4th battle squadron with his flag in *Colossus*. In September 1917 Keyes was appointed director of plans at the Admiralty, thanks largely to Wemyss, who had returned from the Mediterranean and was now deputy first sea lord.

Director of plans for the Admiralty In the plans division Keyes was soon concerned with two major but related subjects, notably how to prevent German submarines from passing freely through the Dover Strait, thereby extending the amount of time they could remain on station, and how to block the exits from their bases in Flanders. A fundamental but irreconcilable difference over how to accomplish this existed between Admiral R. H. S. Bacon, commander of the Dover patrol, and the channel barrage committee of which Keyes was president. The question was resolved after Wemyss replaced J. R. Jellicoe as first sea lord on 27 December. One of his first acts was to dismiss Bacon and make Keyes vice-admiral at Dover. Keyes was free to implement his solution, that of a deep minefield patrolled at night by small craft burning flares and using searchlights to force German submarines attempting to pass on the surface into diving into the minefield. The disadvantage, that the craft burning flares were vulnerable to raids and suffered losses, did not deter the British and over a period of time German losses rose and submarine passages declined. Keyes was also able to win approval for implementing his plans for Operation Z-O, using blockships at Zeebrugge and Ostend to close the entrances to the canals leading to the submarine pens at Bruges. The raid on the night of 23 April 1918 is forever linked with Keyes's name and he was created a KCB immediately afterwards. It was executed with great gallantry—eleven Victoria crosses were awarded—and was partially successful at Zeebrugge, although the Germans were able to work around the obstructions within a short time. The attempt at Ostend was a failure as was a second attempt in May. Nevertheless, the raids, combined with the steady pressure of the Dover patrol's barrage—something often overlooked—resulted in a steady decline in German use of the Dover Strait, reducing the advantage of their Flanders bases. The effect of the raid on morale was at least as important as its actual results. It came at a critical point in the war when Ludendorff's offensive on the western front was making great gains. Zeebrugge finally answered the question of a public oblivious to the silent and slow working of sea power: 'What is the navy doing?' The raid answered that question, the navy had acted offensively with a bold stroke against some of the most heavily defended territory in the world even if post-war investigation might result in scaling down some of the original wartime claims—something naval intelligence had for the most part always known.

Keyes was created a KCVO in December 1918 and subsequently received the thanks of parliament, a grant of £10,000, and was created a baronet in October 1919. He commanded the battle-cruiser squadron (1919–21) and was deputy chief of naval staff (1921–5). In this post he played a leading role in the struggle with the newly created Royal Air Force over control of the Fleet Air Arm and is remembered for the Trenchard–Keyes agreement of 1924, concluded with the chief of air staff, Air Marshal Sir Hugh Trenchard, who was also his brother-in-law. The agreement, however, turned out to be only a truce in a long struggle.

Commander-in-chief and admiral of the fleet From June 1925 until June 1928 Keyes was commander-in-chief of the Mediterranean station. This was Britain's premier naval force and Keyes relished the role although in 1926 he had to prepare for the serious prospect of war with Turkey over the Mosul question. This caused him to consider once again his old problem, that of forcing the Dardanelles.

Keyes's final appointment from November 1929 to June 1931 was that of commander-in-chief, Portsmouth. He was promoted to admiral of the fleet in May 1930 but disappointed when the Labour government chose not to appoint him first sea lord. After retirement Keyes was Conservative member of parliament for Portsmouth North from February 1934 until raised to the peerage in 1943. Although not a particularly effective speaker, he was a champion of naval control of Fleet Air Arm and also one of the minority opposing the Munich settlement. When the Second World War began, Keyes was anxious for some active role and certainly did not feel that he was too old. In the crucial debate in the House of Commons over the fiasco of the Norwegian campaign, Keyes—who had presented a plan for a counter-attack at Trondheim—donned his uniform as an admiral of the fleet and delivered a scathing attack on the Chamberlain government, an important factor in its fall. His friendship with the Belgian royal family, dating back to the First World War, had also resulted in his being used as an unofficial link with King Leopold III during the period of Belgian neutrality, and

after the German attack on Belgium, Churchill sent him to Belgium as liaison officer. Keyes spent a harrowing few weeks and as a result of his experiences was for the remainder of his life a staunch defender of the, in his opinion, unfairly criticized king.

Final years In July 1940 Churchill appointed Keyes director of combined operations. This included control over the special assault units eventually known as commandos. Keyes had little to work with and his relations with the naval staff and chiefs of staff were poor. Nevertheless he laboured furiously to expand the commandos, although raiding operations were restricted by the lack of means to carry them out. Keyes wanted to go beyond mere pin-prick raids and execute larger operations, such as Operation Workshop, the seizure of the island of Pantelleria in the Mediterranean. His proposals were rejected and eventually relations with the chiefs of staff grew so bad that in September 1941, when Keyes refused to accept relegation to a mere advisory position, Churchill replaced him with Lord Mountbatten. This aspect of his career remains controversial although there are many who credit him with establishing what eventually became a successful organization and with the ardour to help instil the famous commando spirit, even if he was unable to accomplish all that he had hoped.

Keyes was created a baron in the new year's honours list for 1943 and undertook a goodwill mission to the United States, Australia, and New Zealand (1944–5). He died at his home, Tingewick House, Tingewick, Buckinghamshire, on 26 December 1945, and was buried, after a funeral service in Westminster Abbey, in Dover cemetery on 4 January 1946 in a section reserved for men who fell at Zeebrugge.

Keyes may have been the quintessential man of action but he also wrote highly readable memoirs of the First World War, *The Naval Memoirs* (2 vols., 1934–5), as well as an account of his early career, *Adventures Ashore and Afloat* (1939), and his Lee Knowles lectures at Cambridge, published as *Amphibious Warfare and Combined Operations* (1943). Keyes's career spanned two world wars and there is much about his life that reads like an adventure novel. In his indomitable spirit and eye for action there is also much to remind one of Nelson.   PAUL G. HALPERN

Sources *The Keyes papers*, ed. P. G. Halpern, 3 vols., Navy RS, 117, 121–2 (1972–81) · R. Keyes, *The naval memoirs of Admiral of the Fleet Sir Roger Keyes*, 2 vols. (1934–5) · R. Keyes, *Adventures ashore and afloat* (1939) · C. Aspinall-Oglander, *Roger Keyes* (1951) · Burke, *Peerage* · Burke, *Gen. GB* (1939) · E. Keyes, *Geoffrey Keyes* (1956) · *The Royal Navy list, or, Who's who in the navy* (1915) · *Navy List* (1921–8) · *DNB* · *The Times* (27 Dec 1945) · *The Times* (5 Jan 1946) · WWW

Archives BL, papers, Deposit 9382 | CAC Cam., corresp. and MSS relating to Sir Dudley Pound · CAC Cam., corresp. with Sir John De Robeck · CAC Cam., Tomkinson MSS · CAC Cam., Wester-Wemyss MSS · King's Lond., Liddell Hart C., Hamilton papers · LUL, corresp. with Emile Cammaerts · NAM, letters to his sister Dorothy Goush · NL Scot., letters to R. K. Dickson · NMM, corresp. with Lord Chatfield · NMM, letters to Sir Julian Corbett · NMM, Richmond papers · PRO, corresp. with Sir Bolton Eyres-Monsell, ADM 230 · PRO, letters to Lord Ismay, CAB 127/15 · Shrops. RRC, letters to first Viscount Bridgeman | FILM BFI NFTVA, documentary footage • BFI NFTVA, news footage • IWM FVA, actuality footage • IWM FVA, documentary footage • IWM FVA, news footage | SOUND IWM SA, oral history interviews

Likenesses photographs, 1914–45, IWM • G. Philpot, oils, 1918, IWM • photograph, c.1918, NPG • W. Stoneman, photographs, 1918–40, NPG • A. S. Cope, group portrait, oils, 1921 (*Naval officers of World War I*), NPG • P. A. de Laszlo, oils, 1923, Royal Marines, Eastney, Portsmouth, officer's mess [*see illus.*] • photograph, 1930–39, repro. in *Keyes papers*, ed. Halpern, vol. 3 • T. Van Oss, oils, c.1935, NMM • F. Dodd, charcoal and watercolour drawing, IWM • Elliott & Fry, photographs, NPG

Wealth at death £6323 18s. 3d.: probate, 5 June 1946, CGPLA Eng. & Wales

Keyes, Sidney Arthur Kilworth (1922–1943), poet, was born on 27 May 1922 at The Homestead, West Hill, Dartford, Kent, the only child of Captain Reginald Keyes of the Queen's Own Royal West Kent regiment, a flour miller by trade, and his second wife, Edith Mary (d. 1922), daughter of the Revd Arthur Blackburn, rector of St Paul's, Bradford. Because his mother died from peritonitis when he was only six weeks old, Keyes was brought up in Dartford by his paternal grandparents, and his grandfather, Sidney Kilworth Keyes, a wealthy farmer, dominated his childhood. On the death of his grandfather in 1938 Keyes was inspired to write his first serious poem, 'Elegy'. Keyes's childhood was lonely and isolated. Because he was frail it was thought unwise to allow him to mix with other children, and in consequence he became an avid reader. At the age of nine he was eventually sent to a preparatory school in Dartford. When he was eleven he attended Dartford grammar school, and three years later he went to Tonbridge School, where his main interests centred on literature and the natural world. By the time he left Tonbridge in July 1940 Keyes had written more than seventy poems, discovered in a manuscript book shortly after the war; many are inevitably juvenilia, but 'Nefertiti', written when he was seventeen, marks an advance towards maturity, and his poem 'The Buzzard', the last to be written at Tonbridge, is probably his most accomplished schoolboy work.

Keyes entered Queen's College, Oxford, in October 1940, on a history scholarship. His poetry from this period displays an 'astonishing fluency' (Press, 273); one of his early Oxford poems, 'Remember your Lovers', was written in an examination hall, after he had finished one of his papers early. (He later came to dislike the poem for its 'lush sensuality' (ibid., 273)). It was during his Oxford years that he embarked on a fruitful friendship with the future winner of the queen's gold medal for poetry, John Heath-Stubbs. Heath-Stubbs, whose own childhood had been marred by insensitivity to his progressive blindness, instinctively responded to the darker images of Keyes's own imagination. He understood very well Keyes's desire to investigate through poetry the subjects of pain and death, and his feeling of being in far closer communion with William Blake, William Wordsworth, and Johann Schiller than with any living contemporaries. Keyes was also influenced by artists such as El Greco, and by masters of the macabre, such as Goya, Beddoes, and Rouault. In particular, Keyes had come to identify with the Romantic movement, and it was Heath-Stubbs who was able to broaden Keyes's base by tracing for him the origins of Romanticism in primitive legends through the medieval to the Augustan poets. It was Heath-Stubbs, too, who helped Keyes to perfect his poetic technique, which had tended to trail behind the complexity and variety of his ideas.

Keyes became editor of *Cherwell*, the Oxford student newspaper. In 1941, with Michael Meyer, he edited *Eight Oxford Poets*. He was awarded a first class in part one of the history examination (1941). He had been writing on average a poem a week, and by the end of 1941 he had enough poems to form a first volume, *The Iron Laurel*, but he withheld publication until 1942 in order to include 'The Foreign Gate', a long poem in which, for the first time in his work, Death appears as a real presence. Keyes joined the army in April 1942, and was sent to the officer cadet training unit at Dunbar. During his time there, he composed some of his finest poetry, including the two linked poems, 'Dido's Lament for Aeneas' and 'Rome Remember'. It was also at this time that he wrote 'North Sea', a heartfelt epitaph on his unreciprocated love for Milein Cosman, a refugee from Düsseldorf, who had come to Oxford when the Slade School moved there from London. In September 1942 Keyes was commissioned as a second lieutenant in his father's old regiment. He sailed for Algiers in March 1943 and during the last days of the Tunisian campaign he saw a mere fortnight's active service. He was killed near Sidi Abdullah, north Africa, on 29 April 1943, and was buried in the military cemetery at Massicault. The military historian James Lucas, who served in Tunisia as Keyes's runner, remembered him as 'a gallant Christian gentleman who sacrificed himself for the men under his command'. He was twenty when he died.

A second, posthumous, collection of Sidney Keyes's poems, *The Cruel Solstice*, was published in 1943 and won the Hawthornden prize. His collected poems were edited in 1945 by Michael Meyer, who has recalled that, although Sidney Keyes was inclined to be taciturn in a large gathering or among strangers, to his friends he was witty and delightful company. Notwithstanding Keyes's extreme youth, his output was prodigious and far-ranging, and, with Keith Douglas and Alun Lewis, he must be regarded as one of the outstanding poets of the Second World War, so much of his work having been inspired, before his brief sortie into battle, by an internal preparation for death.

MICHAEL DE-LA-NOY, rev.

Sources J. Guenther, *Sidney Keyes: a biographical inquiry* (1967) • b. cert. • d. cert. • J. Press, 'Keyes, Sidney (Arthur Kilworth)', *The Oxford companion to twentieth-century poetry in English*, ed. I. Hamilton (1994) • CGPLA Eng. & Wales (1944)

Wealth at death £7000: probate, 19 April 1944, CGPLA Eng. & Wales

Keyl, Frederick William [*formerly* Friedrich Wilhelm] (1823–1871), animal painter, was born at Frankfurt am Main on 17 September 1823, son of a wine merchant, Friedrich Wilhelm Christian Keyl (c.1778–1869), and his wife, Henrietta Steinhäuser (b. c.1791). He grew up with a love of hunting and wildlife, which was later reflected in his art. He studied at the Städelsches Kunstinstitut at Frankfurt, under Jacob Becker. In May 1846 Keyl left Frankfurt to spend three months in England, before visiting Brussels where he carried out some commissions, studied with the landscape and animal painter Eugène Verboeckhoven, and met Thomas Jones and Louis Gallait. In April 1847 Keyl returned to England, where he spent the rest of his life; he was naturalized in March 1858.

At the Royal Academy in 1847 Keyl exhibited *Fidelity* (probably painted in Brussels) and, up to 1872, he showed forty-two pictures there, and, from 1850, thirty-four works at the British Institution. Keyl carried out commissions for patrons around the country, including such groups as *Edward and Dora Studd at Tedworth* (1861; ex Sothebys, 18 November 1992), but he seems to have been of a sensitive and nervous disposition, and averse to exhibiting his pictures. In the 1860s he was deeply upset when some of his paintings were rejected by the Royal Academy.

Keyl became the only pupil of Edwin Landseer, and through his introduction the German artist was received at Buckingham Palace, armed with a portfolio of animal studies which the queen liked. Landseer was delighted that some of the royal commissions for animal paintings could be carried out by Keyl: from 1847 the younger artist painted twenty-six oils for Queen Victoria (fifteen of which remain in the Royal Collection) and fifty-four watercolours and sketches. He was also employed to paint photographs, for instance, of the Sardinian ponies given to the queen by King Victor Emmanuel in 1855. His most prestigious commission was to paint Lootie, the Pekinese lion dog, but he also portrayed many other dogs, cows, and the queen's highland pony, Brechin. Despite the extensive patronage of Queen Victoria and Prince Albert, Keyl received no wide recognition and few of his oils or watercolours are in public galleries. He also undertook book illustrations, drawings of animals for woodengravings, plates for the *Illustrated London News*, and illustrations for the cover of the magazine *Chatterbox*.

Keyl's many friends in London included Francis Grant, Thomas Landseer, Ernst August Becker, and Prince Albert's riding-master, Wilhelm Meister. He taught drawing to Sara Constance Woodin (1830–1892), a niece of C. R. Leslie, whom he married on 25 August 1852 and with whom he had nine children, three of whom died in infancy. The family lived in St John's Wood. Keyl was paid 3 guineas a day for his work for the queen, but was, for some years in England, still financially dependent on his father. In 1865, apparently on the verge of a breakdown, the artist stayed at Reigate with his friend and patron James Nicolson. On 5 December 1871, at his home at 67 Carlton Hill, St John's Wood, Keyl died of congestion of the lungs, probably consumption, from which he had suffered all his life; his niece wrote from Frankfurt to her cousin, 'He deserves to rest for his whole life consisted of work, toil, and sacrifice from love for his family' (Weber, 109). He was buried in Kensal Green cemetery.

DELIA MILLAR

Sources H. Weber, *Friedrich Wilhelm Keyl, 1823–1871* (1989) · D. Millar, *The Victorian watercolours and drawings in the collection of her majesty the queen*, 2 vols. (1995), vol. 1, pp. 488–95; vol. 2, pp. 129–33 · m. cert. · d. cert.
Archives NRA, priv. coll., diaries and letters · Royal Arch.
Likenesses E. Landseer, drawing, repro. in Weber, *Friedrich Wilhelm Keyl*, frontispiece · Lucas & Groom, carte-de-visite, NPG
Wealth at death under £450: administration with will, 20 Feb 1872, CGPLA Eng. & Wales

Keymer, John (*fl.* 1584–1622), vintner and writer on commerce, is first heard of as a vintner in Cambridge. In 1583 Queen Elizabeth had granted Sir Walter Ralegh the farm of wines, each retailer to pay him £1 annually for a licence, and Keymer was Ralegh's nominee for the town of Cambridge. This immediately brought him into conflict with the university, ancient holder of the rights to sell wine in the town. In June 1584 the vice-chancellor and the heads of colleges wrote to Lord Burghley and to the earl of Leicester seeking to influence Ralegh, while members of the university wreaked havoc on Keymer's shop, tearing down his sign and assaulting his wife. When Keymer persisted in his trade he was prosecuted in the vice-chancellor's court and imprisoned in February 1585. He was released in December 1586 and ordered to desist from selling wine in or around Cambridge, after which no more was heard of him in that respect.

It seems that Keymer then travelled in Europe, possibly on behalf of Robert Cecil, for in 1598 he wrote to Cecil claiming that among other services he had proposed various actions against the Spaniard in Flanders and at sea. In 1601 he addressed to Queen Elizabeth a pamphlet 'Observations on Dutch fishing', arguing that there was more wealth raised from herrings and other fish in her seas than the king of Spain had from the Indies in four seas, and that many persons in her kingdom were dependent on fishing; accompanying this tract among Cecil's papers is a note that Keymer had 'spent many yeares … in most paynefull and dangerous travell' (*Salisbury MSS*, 8.275). 'Observations on Dutch fishing' was translated into German and published in 1666, and was reissued in England in collections published in 1707 and 1751. About 1605 Keymer presented James I with similar observations on the Dutch fishing industry, which, with its associated trades of shipbuilding, cooperage, and salt making, was seen to be prospering on the back of the herring taken in British waters, which were salted and exported into Europe. The expansion of the Dutch fishery was remarked on by many writers on commerce, some of whom, like Keymer, advocated free trade as a means to increase employment and prosperity among Britain's fishing communities.

Keymer was corresponding with Sir Dudley Carleton in 1619 and on 17 October 1622 he informed Buckingham that he had presented the king with a proposal that would benefit trade and increase revenue. On 20 December 1622 a commission that included Prince Charles, John Williams, bishop of Lincoln, and Buckingham gathered 'to hear the propositions of John Keymer, and consider whether they will tend to the good of the King and the Commonwealth, as is pretended' (*CSP dom., 1619–23*, 469).

Nothing further seems to have been done in this matter. The original manuscript of this proposal, signed by Keymer and dated 1620, is in the Public Record Office, but it was not recognized until the twentieth century; other signed copies survive elsewhere. The treatise was published anonymously in 1653 as *Sir Walter Ralegh's observations touching trade and commerce with the Hollander and other nations as it was presented to King James, wherein is proved that our sea and land commodities serve to inrich and strengthen other countries against our owne.* This anonymity and the existence of a manuscript copy among Ralegh's own papers led to the supposition that Ralegh was the author. A third discourse by Keymer on trades and fishing is among the De La Warr papers. The circumstances of Keymer's death remain obscure. ANITA McCONNELL

Sources C. H. Cooper and J. W. Cooper, *Annals of Cambridge*, 2 (1843); 5 (1908), 316–17 · T. W. Fulton, *The sovereignty of the sea* (1911), 127–8 · [G. E. Manwaring], 'Sir Walter Ralegh and John Keymer', *TLS* (16 July 1925), 480 · *Calendar of the manuscripts of the most hon. the marquis of Salisbury*, 8, HMC, 9 (1899), 275, 299 · *CSP dom.*, 1619–23, 208–9 · A. R. Beer, *Sir Walter Ralegh and his readers in the seventeenth century: speaking to the people* (1997)

Archives LUL, papers relating to fishing and trade with the Netherlands

Keymis [Kemys], **Lawrence** (1564/5–1618), mariner and explorer, was born in Wiltshire and entered Balliol College, Oxford, in 1581 at the age of sixteen. He graduated BA in 1584 and held a junior bursarship in 1585–6, when his admission of liability for unpaid bills and uncollected battels amounting to over £34 was noted. Part of this was still unpaid when the authorities initiated legal proceedings against him in 1591–2, by which time he had evaded them by taking service with Walter Ralegh and Thomas Harriot, his Oxford contemporaries. Keymis became one of Ralegh's most loyal supporters. He accompanied Ralegh on his first visit to Guiana in 1595, which from local information seemed to offer the prospect of reaching the fabled lake Parima and its source of much gold. Ralegh did discover a source of gold among quartz rocks, but realized that this was too difficult to work, and that he needed to find alluvial gold or some softer deposit.

Ralegh's second expedition to the New World consisted of two ships that sailed under Keymis in January 1596 with orders to explore the rivers north of the Amazon delta. Keymis sailed along the coast of Guiana, noted the sizes of the river mouths and the tribes and languages he encountered, and was attracted by reports of a vast lake at the head of the Essequibo. He then entered the Orinoco and proceeded upstream to the Caroni River, where he found a small Spanish settlement, San Tomé, and an ambush defending the passage upriver where on his previous expedition Ralegh had located gold-bearing quartz. Having no armed force, Keymis was obliged to retreat. The only prospect of success, which he conveyed optimistically to Ralegh on his return, was the story of alluvial gold to be found at the foot of Iconuri, a mountain some 15 miles distant.

A long period then elapsed, during which Ralegh was imprisoned in the Tower. In the search for evidence against him Keymis was also detained for some eighteen weeks, first in the Tower, then in the Fleet. Ralegh urged his own release so that he and Keymis might return to Guiana to locate the sources of gold, but he obtained his liberty only in 1616, and was instructed to behave peaceably to the Spanish settlers. His fleet sailed in 1617, and, while Ralegh remained at the mouth of the Orinoco with most of his ships, Keymis set off upriver in December with 250 soldiers and 150 sailors in five vessels. Three reached San Tomé, which consisted of some thirty houses surrounded by a rampart and moat. On the night of 2–3 January 1618 a party under Ralegh's son Walter marched towards the rampart. Firing broke out, Walter led a charge into the settlement, and was killed in the ensuing conflict. This assault was a violation of Ralegh's instructions, but it is unclear whether Keymis had decided that San Tomé must be destroyed before he could search for the mines, or, perhaps more likely, whether the defending Spaniards suspected treachery and fired first.

Keymis then lost his resolve: he alone knew where the mines were said to be, but more than twenty years had passed since his earlier visit. Afraid to let his men witness his failure, while George Ralegh led a party several hundred miles up the Orinoco, Keymis searched for the supposed mines with a few friends, and one night brought back some ore. This, when tested by a refiner, proved worthless. His excursions upriver were resisted by the Spaniards, and he made no effort to reach the alluvial gold at the foot of Iconuri. Eventually he gave up; the plunder from San Tomé was loaded onto the ship and the settlement fired. The ships hastily made their way downriver, fearful lest a larger Spanish force should pursue them, and reached Ralegh's base on 2 March. Keymis had already sent word to Ralegh informing him of the attack on San Tomé and the death of his son; he now had to admit his failure to locate the sources of gold. Ralegh, fully aware of the implications of these events, confronted him with the bitter statement that Keymis had ruined him by his actions, and refused to support the latter in his report to the English backers. Keymis left Ralegh's cabin, saying that he knew what action to take, and went back to his ship. Ralegh then heard a pistol shot, and sent his servant to enquire what was happening, to which Keymis, lying on his bed, replied that he was just discharging a previously loaded pistol. Half an hour later Keymis's boy entered the cabin and found him dead. The ball had only grazed a rib, and after Ralegh's servant had left he stabbed himself to the heart with a long knife. Keymis was unmarried and left his estate to his younger brother Nathaniel.

ANITA McCONNELL

Sources A. M. C. Latham, 'Sir Walter Raleigh's gold mine', *Essays and Studies by Members of the English Association*, new ser., 4 (1951), 94–111 · W. M. Wallace, *Sir Walter Raleigh* (1959) · E. Thompson, *Sir Walter Ralegh: last of the Elizabethans* (1936), 318–22 · R. Hakluyt, *The principal navigations, voyages, traffiques and discoveries of the English nation*, 10, Hakluyt Society, extra ser., 10 (1904), 441–501 · PRO, PROB 11/133, sig. 36 · V. T. Harlow, *Ralegh's last voyage* (1932) · Foster, *Alum. Oxon.* · *CSP dom.*, 1611–18, 528, 531, 540 · J. Jones, *Balliol College: a history, 1263–1939* (1988) · J. Hemming, *The search for Eldorado* (1978) · C. Hill, *Intellectual origins of the English revolution* (1965) · Wood, *Ath.*

Oxon., new edn, 1.433 • H. W. C. Davis, *A history of Balliol College*, rev. R. H. C. Davis and R. Hunt (1963), 85

Keynes. For this title name *see* individual entries under Keynes; *see also* Lopokova, Lydia Vasilievna [Lydia Vasilievna Keynes, Lady Keynes] (1892–1981).

Keynes [*née* Brown], **Florence Ada** (1861–1958), social and political activist, was born on 10 March 1861 at 76 Elizabeth Street, Cheetham, Manchester, the eldest of the three daughters and three sons of Dr John Brown (1830–1922), Congregationalist minister, and his wife, Ada Haydon, *née* Ford (1837–1929), schoolteacher. Educated at home, she was offered a scholarship at Newnham Hall, Cambridge, when she was seventeen, on the strength of her results in the Cambridge senior local examinations. She began her studies there in 1878 by following the syllabuses originally designed to test the educational standards of schoolteachers. Through mutual family acquaintances in the Congregationalist church, she met (John) Neville *Keynes (1852–1949), logician and economist, and they became engaged in 1880. Having passed several examinations at Newnham, she went home to assist in teaching at her mother's school, but returned to Cambridge on her marriage to Keynes on 15 August 1882. Three children, John Maynard *Keynes, economist, Geoffrey Langdon *Keynes, surgeon, and Margaret Neville, social reformer, were born in quick succession.

With her own financial position secured, Florence Keynes turned her attention to voluntary work, following the ideals of service encouraged both by her religious affiliation and by Newnham. She worked for a number of projects associated with the health care and education of girls and mothers, and in 1895 became secretary of the Cambridge branch of the Charity Organization Society. Her public career began in 1907 when she was elected a local poor-law guardian; she became chairman of the board in 1922. Her brief election manifesto emphasized the view that those parts of the board's work which dealt with women, children, the aged, and the sick, were especially the province of women guardians. Her experience as a guardian left her dissatisfied with the possibilities for effective action by the boards: she felt that she needed the wider powers of the local government politician, but women married to householders had no local franchise, nor power to sit as councillors. When in 1914 married women became eligible to serve as town and county councillors, Florence Keynes became the first woman councillor in Cambridge. She served on the borough council for many years, as alderman from 1930 and as mayor in 1932. In 1920 she was among the first group of women to be made magistrates. During her years on the council she took a particular interest in issues of public and mental health, manifested in the founding of the Papworth colony for tuberculosis victims, and in her work for Fulbourn Mental Hospital. On the national stage she campaigned for the establishment of juvenile courts and urged women to act as jurors and magistrates. She was instrumental in the introduction of women police in 1931 after a campaign lasting seventeen years: this was a typical example of the way women lobbied patiently for reforms through what she later called 'long periods of working and waiting' (*Cambridge Daily News*, 19 Jan 1952).

Working in a private or public capacity, through voluntary or official bodies, Florence Keynes helped to start the country's first juvenile labour exchanges, an open-air school for sick children, a scheme to provide free spectacles and dental treatment for needy Cambridge schoolchildren, surgical aids for the disabled, and respectable lodgings for single women, as well as founding the local folk museum, and setting in motion the scheme to rebuild Cambridge's Guildhall. Much of her voluntary work was performed together with colleagues in the National Council of Women, of which she became national president in 1930. Besides numerous papers on social issues and women's contribution to public life, she published late in life two books of memoirs, one of Cambridge and the other of her large and close-knit family, to whom she always extended generous hospitality. On her ninetieth birthday she described the strategy that she and her women colleagues had adopted in their pursuit of social change: identifying a need, experimenting voluntarily with solutions at a local level, and if successful, seeking to persuade central or local government to carry on with the scheme on a wider scale.

Florence Keynes died on 13 February 1958, shortly before her ninety-seventh birthday, at her home in Cambridge, 6 Harvey Road. A memorial service was held for her in King's College chapel on 22 February, attended by representatives of the university, the town, and the many voluntary organizations and projects in which she had been involved.   RITA McWILLIAMS TULLBERG

Sources [A. B. White and others], eds., *Newnham College register, 1871–1971*, 2nd edn, 1 (1979), 64 • C. D. Rackham, 'Florence Ada Keynes, 1861–1958 (Newnham, 1878–1880)', *Newnham College Roll Letter* (1958), 41–3 • N. Brown, *Dissenting forbears: the maternal ancestors of J. M. Keynes* (1988) • G. L. Keynes, *The gates of memory* (1981); repr. (1983) • 'Mrs Keynes looks back on women's work', *Cambridge Daily News* (19 Jan 1952) • 'Death of Mrs F. A. Keynes: life of public service; former mayor', *Cambridge Evening News* (13 Feb 1958) • *The Times* (14 Feb 1958) • *Cambridge Daily News* (24 Feb 1958)
Archives BLPES, corresp. and papers relating to John Maynard Keynes • Cambridge Central Library, Cambridge collection, newspaper cuttings and printed material • Cambs. AS, records of Cambridge Borough Council; voluntary organizations collection • CUL, corresp. • King's Cam., holiday diary | BL, corresp. with Sir Roy Harrod • King's Cam., letters to John Maynard Keynes • King's Cam., letters to Lydia Lopokova Keynes • King's Cam., corresp. with John Saltmarsh | SOUND BBC WAC
Likenesses J. P. Clarke, photographs (including those as alderman and as mayor), Cambridge Central Library, Cambridge collection • O. Edis, photograph, NPG • Ramsey and Muspratt, negatives, Cambridge Central Library, Cambridge collection • oils (of Keynes?), Cambridge Guildhall • photograph, repro. in *Cambridge Independent Press* (7 Feb 1930) • photograph, repro. in *Cambridge Daily News* • photograph, repro. in *Cambridge Evening News*
Wealth at death £7801 3s. 11d.: probate, 27 March 1958, CGPLA Eng. & Wales

Keynes, Sir Geoffrey Langdon (1887–1982), surgeon and literary scholar, was born in Cambridge on 25 March 1887, the younger son and third and youngest child of (John)

Sir Geoffrey Langdon Keynes (1887–1982), by Ramsey & Muspratt, c.1953

Neville *Keynes (1852–1949), lecturer in moral science and later university registrary, and his wife, Florence Ada (1861–1958) [see Keynes, Florence Ada], daughter of the Revd John Brown, minister of Bunyan's chapel at Bedford. His brother was John Maynard *Keynes and his sister Margaret married the physiologist A. V. *Hill. He was educated from 1901 at Rugby School, before gaining in 1906 an exhibition to Pembroke College, Cambridge (of which he was made an honorary fellow in 1965), to study natural sciences, in which he received a first class (part one, 1909). He graduated MA (1913), BChir (1914), and MD (1918). He also became FRCS (1920), FRCP (1953), FRCOG (1950), and FRCS (Canada, 1956).

Keynes pursued several careers with equal intensity and achieved prominence in each. After Cambridge he trained at St Bartholomew's Hospital, London, where in 1913 he won a Brackenbury scholarship in surgery. At the outbreak of the First World War he joined the Royal Army Medical Corps; he spent the following years in France, principally with the Royal Field Artillery and, after July 1916, with casualty clearing stations. This brought him practice as a surgeon on a vast scale; it also engendered a hatred of unnecessarily spilled blood and a lasting dislike of mutilation. He was mentioned in dispatches in 1918. He was a pioneer in blood transfusion, and after observing an American medical team went on to develop his own mechanism. The Keynes flask, which incorporated a device to regulate flow, became standard equipment after the war. In 1921 he joined P. L. Oliver in founding the London blood transfusion service, and in 1922 he issued *Blood*

Transfusion, the first textbook on the subject to be published in Great Britain. Keynes was married, on 12 May 1917, to Margaret Elizabeth (1890–1974), daughter of Sir George Howard *Darwin; they had four sons.

After the war Keynes joined the surgical team at Bart's headed by George Gask, and so encountered Thomas Dunhill, who with Sir B. G. A. Moynihan remained among his most revered teachers and colleagues. Although he stayed in general surgery, Keynes gradually specialized in thyroid, gastrectomy, hernias, and breast cancer, supporting his work at Bart's with private practice. In 1928 he was appointed assistant surgeon at the hospital. He flouted widely held beliefs by his advocacy, from 1929 onwards, of conservative treatment for cancer of the breast. Some have maintained that pioneering the so-called lumpectomy would not have been feasible in later decades given the necessity for all research to be approved by ethics committees. In fact, however, Keynes based his new practice not only on arguments of characteristically straightforward logic but also on a series of impeccably ethical steps. In 1922 at Bart's, after completing research on chronic mastitis, he had started a trial of using radium chloride contained in hollow platinum needles and inserted around the tumour for about a week. For ethical reasons he could not use radium in patients who could be treated surgically, so for the first two years he treated only those with recurrent cancer. The results, Keynes found, were astonishingly good—so good that, after dismissing the accepted theoretical reasons for extensive surgery, from 1924 he started to use the technique for patients with very advanced disease.

Again, so unexpectedly good were the results in fifty patients that Keynes thought it justifiable to use the method for early cancer. As he pointed out in 1937 in an address to the American Surgical Association in New York, not only did radical surgery have an operative mortality of 3 per cent and radium virtually none, but surgical mutilation often deterred patients from attending for treatment early enough. He abandoned the radical operation in favour of radium and later radiotherapy, together with moderate surgery where unavoidable. The wisdom of this approach was acknowledged more slowly than Keynes hoped. Nevertheless, all over the world it became the usual method of treating this commonest of all tumours in women, and Keynes derived much satisfaction from living to see his work rediscovered fifty years later. Much of his research on the topic was, however, ended by his appointment as consulting surgeon to the RAF during the Second World War, a position from which he drew little satisfaction. He reached the rank of acting air vice-marshal in 1944. His work on the thyroid meanwhile inspired his demonstration in 1942 of the link between the thymus gland and myasthenia gravis, though here too he had to face considerable hostility. He retired from Bart's in 1952, and was knighted in 1955.

At Rugby, Keynes had been a contemporary and close friend of Rupert Brooke, whose letters he edited in 1968. Brooke fostered in him a taste for seventeenth-century poetry, and in 1914 Keynes's first author bibliography, of

John Donne (revised in 1932, 1958, and 1972), was published by the Baskerville Club, a group of Cambridge bibliophiles. Like all his subsequent bibliographies, it was compiled not least from his own library, which was to become one of the finest private collections of the twentieth century. In 1916 Keynes issued a preliminary handlist for John Evelyn, in which he was much helped by A. T. Bartholomew, of Cambridge University Library; he developed it into a full bio-bibliography only in 1937, incorporating his Sandars lectures given at Cambridge in 1934. A revised edition followed in 1968. Another early enthusiasm, for Sir Thomas Browne, was encouraged by Sir William Osler; Keynes's bibliography appeared in 1924 (2nd edn, 1968), and his edition of Browne's works came out in 1928–31 (new edn, 1964).

Keynes's work on William Blake, inspired originally by seeing plates from *Job* in a Cambridge shop window, was instrumental in establishing Blake as a central figure in the history of English art and literature. His bibliography, begun about 1909, and much revised under the eye of John Sampson of Liverpool University, was published by the Grolier Club of New York in 1921. Keynes's own collection was to become formidable, rich particularly in drawings, separate prints, books from Blake's own library, and the work of the Blake circle more generally. His edition of the *Writings* (3 vols., Nonesuch Press, 1925) was succeeded by a series of single-volume editions culminating in that for the Oxford Standard Authors in 1966. These in turn were supplemented by editions of the drawings, studies of plates, a new census of the illuminated books (with Edwin Wolf II, in 1953), an edition of the letters (1956; 3rd edn, 1980), and an iconography of Blake and his wife. Many of Keynes's shorter essays were gathered in *Blake Studies* (1949; 2nd edn, 1971). In 1949, with the help principally of Kerrison Preston, W. Graham Robertson's executor, Keynes established the Blake Trust, with the purpose of printing hand-coloured collotype facsimiles of all Blake's major illuminated books. On his death his collection was divided between a family trust, the Fitzwilliam Museum, and Cambridge University Library.

With the foundation by Francis Meynell of the Nonesuch Press in 1923, Keynes found a congenial publisher for much of his literary work. Apart from the writings of Blake, he also edited volumes by John Donne, John Evelyn, William Harvey, William Hazlitt, and Izaak Walton, besides compiling bibliographies of Jane Austen (1929) and Hazlitt (1931; revised edn, 1981): he became by far the most prolific of the press's authors. After the Second World War the foundation of the firm of Rupert Hart-Davis brought another sympathetic outlet, and for the series of Soho Bibliographies begun in 1951 Keynes published works on Rupert Brooke (1954; revised, 1959) and Siegfried Sassoon (1962): he had first met Sassoon in 1933, and oversaw the production of several volumes of his poetry.

In his library Keynes created not only the foundations for a long series of literary bibliographies (his work on Blake led him naturally to the eighteenth-century philosophers, and a bibliography of George Berkeley appeared in 1976), but also the means for an intensive study of

seventeenth-century medicine and science. His biography of William Harvey (1966) gave him the opportunity, in its combination of medical, political, social, and literary history, to exploit his interests to the full: it gained him the James Tait Black memorial prize. He had already published a bibliography of Harvey (1928; revised, 1953), while his several studies of the iconography helped his appointment in 1942 as trustee of the National Portrait Gallery, where he was chairman from 1958 to 1966. These interests led also to bibliographies of John Ray (1951; revised, 1956), Robert Hooke (1960), Sir William Petty (1971), and Martin Lister (1980). His work on Robert Boyle, of whom he had an outstanding collection, was taken up by John Fulton of Yale, and work on Thomas Willis remained uncompleted at his death. As a bibliographer Keynes's influence was magisterial; as a collector he usually kept shrewdly ahead of others, and so avoided many of the pitfalls associated with collecting the merely fashionable. He was a member of both the Roxburghe Club and the Grolier Club. Most of his library passed by bequest and purchase to Cambridge University Library.

For much of his life Keynes's principal relaxation was the ballet, which he followed avidly, beginning with Serge Diaghilev's productions in the 1920s. Balletomania and admiration for Blake's art coalesced in his own ballet *Job*, with music by Ralph Vaughan Williams, first performed by the Camargo Society in 1931 with sets designed by his sister-in-law Gwendolen Raverat; its success helped to ensure the survival of professional ballet in Britain.

Erect, vigorous, and constantly alert, Keynes could be a formidable figure, though his early shyness never entirely deserted him. Of all his vocations, surgery gave him the most satisfaction, and here his courage and decisiveness were ideal characteristics. In the eyes of many he lacked the patience to be a great hospital teacher; but he more than compensated for this by the lucidity of his writing, and the willingness with which he published his discoveries whether in medicine, bibliography, literature, or art history. As the owner of an important library and art collection he sometimes astonished scholars by his generosity, and here he was an inspiring guide.

Keynes gained honorary degrees from Cambridge (LittD, 1965), Oxford (DLitt, 1965), Edinburgh, Birmingham, Sheffield, and Reading. He was elected honorary FBA in 1980. He won many medals and prizes. He died at Brinkley, Cambridgeshire, near Newmarket, on 5 July 1982.

DAVID McKITTERICK, *rev.* STEPHEN LOCK

Sources *The Times* (6 July 1982) · *Geoffrey Keynes: tributes on the occasion of his seventieth birthday*, Osler Club (1961) · G. Keynes, *The gates of memory* (1981) · personal knowledge (1990) · G. Keynes, 'Address to the American Surgical Association', *BMJ* (2 Oct 1937), 643–7 · *CGPLA Eng. & Wales* (1982)

Archives CUL, corresp. relating to publication of his books · King's Cam., corresp. relating to trusteeship of Rupert Brooke's estate and his biography · RCS Eng., corresp. and papers relating to national blood transfusion service | BL, corresp. with Sydney Cockerell, Add. MS 52729 · BL, corresp. of him and his wife with F. C. Cornford, Add. MS 58400 · BLPES, corresp. relating to J. M. Keynes · City Westm. AC, corresp. with Kerrison Preston · CUL, letters to A. N. L. Munby · King's Cam., Brooke MSS · King's Cam., corresp. with Lydia Lopokova Keynes · King's Cam., letters to

W. J. H. Sprott · U. Lpool, corresp. with Andrew Wilson and papers relating to joint research · U. Sussex, corresp. with Leonard Woolf

Likenesses Hills & Saunders, photograph, 1915, NPG · Ramsey & Muspratt, photograph, *c*.1953, NPG, Wellcome L. [*see illus.*] · N. Boonham, bronze bust, 1976, NPG, RCS Eng. · T. L. Poulton, drawing, CUL · G. Spencer, drawing, CUL · J. Ward, pencil and watercolour drawing, Pembroke Cam. · portrait (after pencil drawing by G. Shaw, 1957), Wellcome L.

Wealth at death £180,768: probate, 19 Oct 1982, *CGPLA Eng. & Wales*

Keynes, George (1628–1658), Jesuit, was born in Somerset, the son of Edward Keynes of Compton Pauncefoot and his wife, Anne Brett, both of old Roman Catholic families resident in Somerset. He studied humanities at the English College, St Omer, between 1644 and 1647 before travelling to Rome. He was admitted to the English College at Rome on 27 October 1647, and entered the Society of Jesus in Rome on 2 January 1649. He was sent to England in 1650 and was ordained in 1654 or 1655. He then set sail for the China mission but died either at sea or at the Philippines on 15 October 1658. He may have been the translator of the second, much enlarged, edition of *The Roman Martyrology* printed at St Omer in 1667.

THOMAS SECCOMBE, *rev.* RUTH JORDAN

Sources T. M. McCoog, *English and Welsh Jesuits, 1555–1650*, 2, Catholic RS, 75 (1995), 222 · D. A. Bellenger, ed., *English and Welsh priests, 1558–1800* (1984) · G. Holt, *St Omers and Bruges colleges, 1593–1773: a biographical dictionary*, Catholic RS, 69 (1979) · W. Kelly, ed., *Liber ruber venerabilis collegii Anglorum de urbe*, 2, Catholic RS, 40 (1943) · A. Kenny, ed., *The responsa scholarum of the English College, Rome*, 2, Catholic RS, 55 (1963), 505–6

Keynes, John (1624–1697), Jesuit and religious controversialist, was born at Compton Pauncefoot, Somerset, son of Edward Keynes and Anne Brett. The Keynes family belonged to the Catholic gentry and the name Keynes occurs frequently in accounts of seventeenth-century members of the Society of Jesus. In line with the family tradition John Keynes was sent to the Jesuit school at St Omer. In 1642 he went to St Alban's, the English College at Valladolid, with the intention of becoming a priest. Although he had taken the usual vow to return to England after the completion of his studies in order to work on the mission, the registers at Valladolid state that he was released from his vow and joined the Spanish province of the Society of Jesus. In July 1645 he entered the noviciate at Villagarcia. In the following years he went through the various stages of higher Jesuit studies which he completed by being professed of the four vows on 15 August 1662. Meanwhile he had become a teacher. In 1660 he was professor of theology at the Jesuit College of St Ambrose's in Valladolid, and later taught philosophy and theology at Compostela, Salamanca, and Pamplona. At the end of the 1660s he decided to transfer to the English Jesuit province. He became prefect of studies at the Jesuit college at Liège and in 1670 was at St Omer, where, according to Southwell, he became seriously ill when he attended to the spiritual needs of English and Irish Catholic soldiers during a plague epidemic.

Keynes was sent to England in order to recover but was soon engaged in a theological controversy with the Anglican theologian Edward Stillingfleet. Stillingfleet's *Discourse Concerning the Idolatry in the Church of Rome* (1671) provoked a number of replies from Catholic writers, but Keynes was Stillingfleet's most persistent opponent. His contributions to the debate were two pamphlets, *Doctor Stillingfleet Against Doctor Stillingfleet* (London, 1671), under the pseudonym John Williams, and *Dr Stillingfleet's Principles of Protestancy* (London?, 1673), and a full-length book, *Dr Stillingfleet Still Against Dr Stillingfleet* (Paris?, 1675), under the pseudonym J. W. Although there is some confusion about Keynes's authorship of these works, the testimony of Keynes's contemporary Southwell seems decisive (Ribadeneira, 466). Keynes's basic approach as a controversialist is captured in the title of his more general work, *A rational, compendious way to convince, without any dispute, all persons whatsoever, dissenting from the true religion* (London, 1674; Latin translation, 1684; French, 1688).

In 1672 Keynes became rector of the London district of the English Jesuits and seven years later his name figures prominently on Titus Oates's lists of accomplices in the Popish Plot (Keynes's uncle, the Jesuit Alexander Keynes, was also named). John Keynes managed to escape to the continent in March 1679 and was appointed rector of the college at Liège in January 1680. During his time as rector he wrote another controversial work answering Bishop William Lloyd's *Papists No Catholics* (1677) under the title *No Catholic No Christian*. He was dissuaded from publishing this work by the Jesuit provincial John Warner (Holt, 'Letter book', 465). Together with Thomas Stapleton SJ he wrote *Florus Anglo-Bavaricus* (Liège, 1685), an account of the college at Liège and of the Jesuit priests who suffered in the Popish Plot. The work was dedicated to the patron of the college, Maximilian, duke of Bavaria. In July 1684 he succeeded John Warner as provincial of the English Jesuits. In the following years he was in London, where he was responsible for the founding of the Catholic schools at the Savoy and Fenchurch Street. These schools, of which James II acted as a patron, provided free education for both Catholic and protestant children and proved to be very popular. Inevitably with the revolution in 1688 this surprisingly modern experiment came to an end and the schools were closed. Keynes returned to the continent, where he remained provincial until July 1689. He died eight years later, on 15 May 1697, at the Jesuit house at Watten, Southern Netherlands.

F. BLOM and J. BLOM

Sources *DNB* · E. Henson, ed., *The registers of the English College at Valladolid, 1589–1862*, Catholic RS, 30 (1930), 159, 161–3, 172 · H. Foley, ed., *Records of the English province of the Society of Jesus*, 5 (1879), 97–146, 466, 965–9; 7 (1882–3), 416–17 · P. de Ribadeneira, *Bibliotheca scriptorum Societatis Jesu opus inchoatum* (Rome, 1676), 761–2 · G. Holt, 'The letter book of Fr John Warner', *Archivum Historicum Societatis Jesu*, 53 (1984), 443–68 · T. H. Clancy, *A literary history of the English Jesuits: a century of books, 1615–1714* (1996) · T. H. Clancy, *English Catholic books, 1641–1700: a bibliography*, rev. edn (1996) · T. A. Birrell, introduction, in *Florus Anglo-Bavaricus*, facs. edn (1970) · Gillow, *Lit. biog. hist.*, 4.31 · A. C. F. Beales, *Education under penalty* (1963) · G. Holt, *St Omers and Bruges colleges, 1593–1773: a biographical dictionary*, Catholic RS, 69 (1979) · G. Oliver, *Collections towards illustrating the biography of the Scotch, English and Irish members, SJ* (1838), 111

Keynes, John Maynard, Baron Keynes (1883–1946), economist, was born on 5 June 1883 at 6 Harvey Road, Cambridge, the eldest of the three children of (John) Neville *Keynes (1852–1949), a Cambridge don, and his wife, Florence Ada Brown (1861–1958) [*see* Keynes, Florence Ada], who had come to Cambridge in 1878 at the age of seventeen as an early student of Newnham College. Keynes's father was a prominent figure in the university and was a friend of Alfred Marshall, Henry Sidgwick, and Henry Fawcett. Keynes's mother, more self-confident than her husband, who had something of an inferiority complex and was a great worrier, took an active interest in social work and was in turn justice of the peace, alderman, and mayor. Her father, the Revd John Brown (1830–1922), was the well-known Congregationalist minister of the Bunyan Chapel in Bedford. Both parents outlived their eldest child. Keynes's younger brother, Sir Geoffrey Langdon *Keynes, became a distinguished surgeon and bibliophile and his sister, Margaret Neville, married Professor Archibald Vivian *Hill CH, secretary (1935–45) of the Royal Society.

Early years The family was comfortably off. Neville started married life with an income of £1000; by the time Maynard was twenty-five his father had accumulated the substantial total of £35,000. The family kept three servants—a cook, a parlour maid, and a nursery maid—and there was a German governess. In his first few years Maynard was a sickly child, suffering to begin with from frequent attacks of diarrhoea and thereafter from feverishness. His physical development was punctuated by sudden spurts of growth that left him exhausted, and from time to time he had to be taken away from school. In the summer of 1889 he had an attack of rheumatic fever and a few months later he had to give up attending his kindergarten for a time, suffering from what was diagnosed as St Vitus's dance. A year later the kindergarten he was attending was given up altogether and throughout 1891 he was taught at home. At the beginning of 1892 he began to attend a preparatory school in Cambridge as a day boy, but again his parents became worried that he was overexerting himself and in the autumn of 1893 he was moved for a term to Bedford, where his grandmother reopened her schoolroom for him. When he returned at the beginning of 1894 his father thought him 'not quite up to the mark', but he soon appeared more robust and began to show outstanding talent as a mathematician. It was observed, however, that although he was quick to grasp the point, he was careless about details.

As a child, Maynard was deeply attached to his mother but from the age of about eight onwards he became increasingly close to his father; he worked with him in his study, and they shared a common interest in hobbies such as stamp-collecting and leisure activities such as golf. When his parents entered him for the Eton College scholarship examination in 1897, Maynard was given special tuition and in spite of his father's constant worries, he attained the tenth out of fifteen places and was first equal in mathematics.

Eton and King's At Eton, Keynes's interests broadened and he resisted the efforts of his mathematics master to get him to concentrate more exclusively on mathematics. He read widely, including a good deal of poetry, and his prose style began to take on some of its later characteristics. He won prizes and scholarships of all kinds, including the Tomline prize in mathematics and in his final year an Eton scholarship to King's College, Cambridge, in mathematics

John Maynard Keynes, Baron Keynes (1883–1946), by Gwen Raverat, *c.*1908

and classics. He was one of the seventy scholarship boys at Eton who enjoyed free board and tuition and lived together in the same house—College—while ten times as many fee-paying Oppidans were accommodated in other houses. He was surrounded by an intellectual élite among boys who were highly intelligent and knew that they would later have to work for their living and would be wise to make a beginning at Eton. Keynes showed many later characteristics: quickness of understanding, facility in grasping facts and getting to the nub of the matter, command of words, 'a decided talent for history', and an outstanding ability in mathematics. He did not shine in classics as a versifier but could write with feeling and imagination on classical drama. Although he won an extraordinary number of prizes and his father set great store by his position in class, he took his success quite casually, won golden opinions from his teachers, and was popular with the other boys. But he did not suffer fools gladly: and his letters to his parents were full of critical comments on the stupidity or dullness of those in authority.

It was a mark of his popularity that Keynes was elected to college Pop, the Eton debating society, in January 1901 and latterly spoke almost every week, often at considerable length and without notes. He also revived and presided over the Eton literary society, to which he contributed a paper on Bernard of Cluny. He was much struck by St Bernard's verse and developed a particular interest in medieval Latin poetry. The next three years, from 1902 to 1905, were spent as an undergraduate at King's, nominally in the study of mathematics, in practice mainly in a host of other pursuits: in debates, moral and political, in meetings of societies, and above all as a member of the Apostles—a small group of gifted undergraduates to which he was elected in his second term after preliminary scrutiny as an 'embryo' or potential recruit by two of its members, Lytton Strachey and Leonard Woolf. At the time he was elected the ideas of G. E. Moore, whose *Principia ethica* appeared at the beginning of Keynes's second year, were highly influential among its active members. Moore's *Principia* treated good states of mind as the ultimate object of moral endeavour.

The older, less active, members of the society included philosophers of great distinction such as Russell, Whitehead, Moore, and McTaggart as well as some whose interests were aesthetic rather than philosophical: for example, Roger Fry, E. M. Forster, and Desmond McCarthy. Both interests were absorbed into a common 'search for truth' carried over by some of them into what became the Bloomsbury group, whose members also included Vanessa Bell (*née* Stephen), Clive Bell, Virginia Woolf (*née* Stephen), and Duncan Grant.

Early beliefs: probability Keynes wrote a number of papers for the society analysing the implications of Moore and in 1938 looked back on his influence on the group in a paper read to the memoir club of his Bloomsbury friends on *My Early Beliefs* (not published until 1949, after his death). The key difference in the attitude of Keynes and his friends was that the basis of the calculus of moral action was seen as exclusively personal, not as rules imposed from without. There could be no objective measure of what was good since, if the good consisted of states of mind, these states could be known and judged only by the minds in question. Duty, action, social need simply did not enter. Intuitive judgements were all one could turn to. In a paper he wrote after his tripos he split ethics into speculative and practical, the first establishing 'the usage and significance of the more fundamental terms' and the second concerning itself with conduct and 'the probable grounds of action'. Goodness would be confined to states of mind alone but it would also be necessary to consider fitness as an attribute of objects inspiring good feelings: 'My goodness and the goodness of the universe may both have claims on me but there is no way in which I can weigh one against the other on a common balance.' 'One's prime objects in life', Keynes wrote, 'were love, the creation and enjoyment of aesthetic experience and the pursuit of knowledge. Of these love came a long way first' (*Collected Writings*, 10.436–7). The emphasis on personal states of mind is curious in an economist whose analysis is so much in terms of social interactions and in efforts to make these interactions work to better effect. As Skidelsky has pointed out, there is something suggestive of a monastic ideal in Moore's religion. There is also something of the academic's neglect of the part the community plays in what occurs to us, to our welfare, and to our states of mind.

Keynes was by no means monastic. His years at Eton in exclusively male company helped to produce a homosexual phase in his life that lasted for many years, in which he had a succession of lovers. This does not appear to have led to acts of sodomy until after he completed his degree. Although he was at pains to keep such acts secret, he left a record of them from which it would seem that they were not confined to university friends but occasionally extended to chance encounters with young boys, picked up almost at random. They persisted for a year or two after the war and then ceased completely once he had fallen in love with his future wife. At this stage Keynes's future career was not settled. He might have taken the moral sciences tripos or the economics tripos; in 1906 he might have taken up law as a student of the Inner Temple. He was given weekly supervisions by Alfred Marshall and found pleasure in reading Jevons. As secretary of the Apostles he also set about finding new members.

What occupied Keynes most after completing his degree in 1905 was the preparation of a fellowship dissertation on probability. It was a subject that had been neglected for a generation by philosophers, and economists seemed content to leave it to the statisticians. Keynes was able to submit his dissertation two years later and when not awarded a fellowship produced a new version in 1908, which proved successful. He continued to work at intervals on the subject for a decade more, developing new lines of thought, and adding several chapters on statistical inference. It was only after a final struggle in 1920 to complete it that he was able to publish it as *A Treatise on Probability* in August 1921. The book was largely ignored by economists and treated as a study of interest to philosophers. By the end of the century, however, the significance of probability to life and economic behaviour in an uncertain world had come to be appreciated. What Keynes sought to do in the book was to extend the principles of valid thought to arguments that were not conclusive and certain but to which it was rational to attach *some* weight: matters of belief and opinion based on limited knowledge and subject to uncertainty. Probability was always relative to the evidence available and changed if the knowledge available changed. It had to do with what it was rational to believe, not with truth. On this basis Keynes examined a succession of issues including induction, statistical inference, and the bearing of probability on conduct.

The India Office, 1906–1908 After a visit to Lytton Strachey in London, Keynes decided to concentrate on the civil service entrance examination. He did his usual six hours a day in preparation for the examination, came second to Otto Niemeyer, and by October was at work in the India Office; his first job, which lasted several months, was to arrange the shipment of ten young Ayrshire bulls to Bombay. The work was light, Keynes was quick in getting through it, and he was able to make progress in office hours on his fellowship dissertation. It was not long, however, before he made up his mind to leave. He was bored, frustrated, and repelled as always by the stupidity with which he had to contend. More and more time went on his dissertation as the means by which he might leave the India Office on a prize fellowship. His father sought to dissuade him without success, but he then learned in March 1908 that two other candidates had been placed ahead of him. He was furious with the examiners (A. N. Whitehead and W. E. Johnson) and the fellowship electors, who had taken into account that he could try again the next year.

A Cambridge economist A fortnight later Marshall suggested that Keynes might take the place of D. H. MacGregor, whom Marshall had employed as a lecturer in economics, paying him £100 a year out of his own stipend, and who had just been appointed to a chair in economics in Leeds. Neville Keynes again advised caution. But Keynes had no hesitation and, once Pigou was elected to succeed Marshall and the offer was renewed, he resigned from the India Office. A year later Keynes's revised dissertation was accepted and he was also awarded the Adam Smith prize for an essay on index numbers—an essay on which he drew twenty years later in *A Treatise on Money*. Until the outbreak of war Keynes remained in Cambridge, combining lecturing in economics with an increasing range of other activities. His two years in the India Office had familiarized him with Whitehall, brought him into contact with senior civil servants, and trained him to look at problems through the eyes of an administrator, so laying the foundation for much of his later work.

In Cambridge, as he extended his knowledge of economics and continued to give thought to the logic of probability, he pursued an interest in Indian finance and published in 1913 his first book, *Indian Currency and Finance*.

This was based on lectures he had delivered at the London School of Economics in the spring of 1911. A contract (with Macmillan) in mid-December 1912 was followed by proofs at the beginning of March and publication in June 1913. Meanwhile the government had decided to set up a royal commission on Indian finance and currency, on which Keynes (by this time on holiday in Egypt) was asked to act full-time as secretary. When he asked for freedom to publish his book the offer was changed to one of a seat on the commission and he took his place on it at just under thirty years of age.

Keynes made a deep impression on the other members of the commission, including the chairman, Sir Austen Chamberlain, the secretary, Basil Blackett, and Sir Robert Chalmers, later permanent secretary to the Treasury, and the recommendations reflected his views. In his book he had traced the history and argued the virtues of the gold exchange standard under which there was neither a gold currency nor dependence on a substantial holding of gold as a reserve against external liabilities but a holding of some key currency such as sterling. This he took to be the way of the future. The commission was almost unanimous in supporting the continuation of India's gold exchange standard but was in doubt about a proposal for a state (central) bank and asked Keynes to take part in drawing up a detailed scheme. His draft proposals were circulated over his sole name but were not accepted and were instead included as an annexe to the report, to the applause of Marshall. Keynes had been unsuccessful in persuading the commission to unite the three presidency banks under a federal system with a federal board, exercising its own professional judgement, in charge of operations, but he managed to secure agreement to some less important amendments to the draft report.

In 1912 Keynes took on the editorship of the *Economic Journal* in succession to F. Y. Edgeworth, a post he held until March 1945 and through which he exercised great influence on the next generation of economists. This post was combined from 1913 with that of secretary of the Royal Economic Society, again for over thirty years. Until almost the last moment Keynes doubted whether a European war would break out. On Sunday 2 August he received a letter from Basil Blackett asking him to call at the Treasury the next day and he set off at once in the sidecar of his brother-in-law's motor cycle. The joint-stock banks had been agitating for a suspension of the Bank Charter Act and so of specie payments and had started refusing their customers' sovereigns, thus forcing them to cash £5 notes at the Bank of England. Lloyd George was inclined to agree with them, with the Bank of England and the Treasury in disagreement. A memorandum by Keynes on 3 August made a strong case against suspension and convinced Lloyd George, who, however, rebuked Blackett for 'consulting an outsider without authority' (Harrod, 107).

The Treasury In January 1915 Keynes was recruited to the Treasury, after pressure from Edwin Montagu. It was through Montagu that he was introduced to Lloyd George, Reginald McKenna, and Margot Asquith and the private gatherings of cabinet secretaries and leading ministers. He was at first an assistant to Sir George Paish, who was Lloyd George's chief adviser. In a short time, however, Paish faded from the scene. Initially Keynes's duties were varied but in May 1915 he joined the finance division, where he was responsible for banking, currency, the exchanges, and inter-allied finance. He thus took a prominent part in the organization of inter-allied finance and in the arrangements for raising the necessary dollars.

As 1915 proceeded, Keynes and his Treasury colleagues became doubtful whether the war effort could be enlarged or even sustained with the resources available. Privately he was strongly in favour of a negotiated peace, which he hoped the United States would engineer. In December a proposal to increase the army to seventy divisions by introducing conscription divided the cabinet and threatened to cause several ministerial resignations—including those of the chancellor of the exchequer, Reginald McKenna, and the president of the Board of Trade, Walter Runciman. Legislation was introduced in January to permit conscription of all single men between the ages of sixteen and forty-one; those claiming conscientious objection were allowed to state their case before a local tribunal. At that stage Keynes appears to have considered resignation: the positions of McKenna and Runciman remained in doubt and Keynes said he would resign if they did. His Bloomsbury friends were also pressing him strongly to resign, since he claimed to hold views similar to theirs, to do as they did and claim conscientious objection. On the other hand, it was Keynes's belief that the war would not last much longer, since President Wilson seemed likely to summon a peace conference. He may have been influenced also by the intellectual pleasure that his work afforded him and his greater power to help his friends when they were called before a tribunal. Whatever the reason, he remained in the Treasury to the end.

On 23 February 1916 Keynes was given a certificate of exemption for the next six months in view of his duties. Nevertheless he applied to the tribunal five days later for exemption on grounds of conscientious objection, possibly because he still had resignation in mind. 'I am not prepared', he said, 'on such an issue as this to surrender my right of decision, as to what is or is not my duty, to any other person, and I should think it morally wrong' (Moggridge, 260). Yet when summoned to a hearing to be held on 28 March he sent a note to say he was too busy to attend, and made no further application in August when his exemption was renewed by the Treasury. Presumably he no longer thought it likely that he would resign. Two years later he expressed his opposition to government policy more decisively, writing to Duncan Grant: 'I work for a government I despise for ends I think criminal' (ibid., 279).

Keynes's part in the First World War is not nearly so well known as his part in the second. But his role was at least as demanding and carried somewhat similar responsibilities, although he was less senior in rank and lacking much of the authority he later acquired. In the first he had to struggle against his conscience and the strong disapproval of his friends, while in the second the company was much more congenial. In both he suffered repeatedly from spells of ill health, and in the second his exertions had often to be rationed in the interests of survival. After the early part of 1915, and until the United States entered the war, there was what amounted to a continuing exchange crisis that became increasingly severe as the war went on and the gold reserves ran down. By the autumn of 1916 the United Kingdom was spending over $200 million a month in the United States, largely on behalf of allied governments. For three weeks at the end of the year gold flowed out of Britain at the startling rate of £5 million a day while the Treasury left ministers in the dark in case they reacted by unpegging the pound. Towards the end of February 1917 Keynes reckoned that the available resources would run out within four weeks. At this point the Germans launched unrestricted submarine attacks to cut off American supplies, and on 6 April America declared war on Germany.

Three months earlier Keynes's experience in managing Britain's external finances led to his appointment as head of the Treasury's newly established A division, responsible for all aspects of external finance and reporting directly to the permanent secretary and the chancellor. In May 1917 he was created CB, an award that was denied him earlier by Lloyd George, who, remembering a disagreement with Keynes, deleted his name from the list at the last moment.

A fresh crisis developed in 1917 as the American treasury released dollar funds 'in weekly dribs and drabs' and US funds were withdrawn from London for investment in a $2 billion liberty loan. Again it fell to Keynes to handle the situation and obtain funds from the US at the very last moment. Friction with the Bank of England, which shared management of the exchange rate through a committee of bankers without responsibility for the borrowing operations this entailed, came to a head in July 1917, just after the exchange crisis was resolved. Lord Cunliffe, the governor, demanded the dismissal of Keynes and Chalmers (the permanent secretary) but was himself forced into submission by the chancellor, Bonar Law.

America's entry into the war confirmed its dominant position in financing it. All that Keynes could achieve was to turn over to the US the direct financing of the war needs of France and Italy instead of meeting them indirectly out of Britain's dollar borrowings. Keynes took an increasingly gloomy view of the future: the Americans were set on reducing Britain 'to a position of complete financial helplessness and dependence' (Collected Writings, 16.287); the prolongation of the war was likely to mean 'the disappearance of the social order we have known hitherto' (ibid., 16.265). Food rationing was the last straw: he feared he would have to take frequent trips abroad to get a square meal.

Reparations and the treaty of Versailles After the armistice on 11 November 1918 Keynes was 'put in principal charge of financial matters for the Peace Conference' and early in

January moved to Paris as the chief Treasury representative, with a wide range of duties and inadequate staff. In the absence of the newly appointed chancellor (Austen Chamberlain) he represented the British government on the supreme economic council with full authority. In practice he had little influence on Lloyd George. As he told Margot Asquith, the British were the best-equipped delegation, but for all the use made of them by the prime minister 'we might have been idiots' (Skidelsky, 1.367).

In the period after the armistice Keynes had worked on a Treasury brief on reparations (a matter not mentioned in Wilson's fourteen points). The brief included an estimate both of Germany's capacity to pay and of reparations if limited to the direct damage done to the civilian population of the allies and their property by German aggression, which might be twice as much. The Treasury's estimates, however, were not circulated before much larger sums were under discussion, thanks partly to the views expressed by a cabinet committee under W. M. Hughes, the prime minister of Australia, and partly to popular feeling whipped up in the December election. The Hughes committee claimed that Germany would pay £24,000 million in reparations at an annual rate of £2000 million—rejected by the cabinet as 'a wild and fantastic chimera', while Keynes regarded a *total* of £2000 million as 'a very satisfactory achievement' (Skidelsky, 1.378).

In Paris, Keynes initially had little to do with the actual terms of the peace treaty. The British government had appointed Hughes, Lord Cunliffe (a member of his committee), and Lord Sumner (a judge) as its representatives on the committee on reparation of damage. Instead, he continued to worry about inter-allied finance and became concerned with post-war relief policy. He was also much engaged in negotiating a limited lifting of the naval blockade so as to allow the import of food and other necessities into Germany, provided the German merchant marine was surrendered to the allies. However, he became increasingly involved with the non-reparations financial clauses of the peace treaty and, from the middle of March, the reparations clauses as well. In the end no agreement was reached on what Germany owed or could pay in reparations. Instead, the issues were referred to a reparations commission, which was to report before 1 May 1921. In the interim Germany would be required to pay £1 billion on account. Central to the arrangements over reparations was article 231 of the treaty, the 'war guilt clause' drafted by Keynes and John Foster Dulles.

In a last attempt to permit the financial rehabilitation of Europe, Keynes put forward a plan, after discussion with the South African defence minister, J. C. Smuts, for the raising of funds through the issue of reparation bonds to the value of £1445 million, by Germany and its defeated allies, and jointly guaranteed by the issuing and allied governments. Interest would be paid at 4 per cent, but only after five years, and the bonds would be divided: £1000 million would be delivered as reparations to the European allies (representing the £1 billion due on account) to assist in their reconstruction and most of the balance of £445 million would be used for purchases of food and raw materials by the ex-enemy governments. The bonds were to be acceptable as collateral and jointly guaranteed by the issuing and allied governments. The plan won the support of Austen Chamberlain and was submitted by Lloyd George to President Wilson. The Americans, however, gave the plan no support. It was unlikely to be given congressional approval; it would give the impression that the European countries were insolvent and would permit of larger payments in reparations than the Americans could approve. Lloyd George's reparations policy had torpedoed any effort to finance German recovery or to induce the United States to forgo part of its European debt. What might have repeated the success of France's borrowing in 1871 to pay an indemnity to Germany came to nothing.

When he saw the complete draft treaty early in May, Keynes, like others, was horrified and sent a hasty note to Bradbury and Austen Chamberlain attacking it as showing 'a high degree of unwisdom in almost every direction' (Skidelsky, 1.453). It was 'a paper settlement which even if it is accepted cannot be expected to last' (ibid., 1.455). He remained for a month briefing the prime minister, who had become thoroughly alarmed at the prospects and asked for 'a thoroughgoing revision of the Reparations Clauses'. But it was too late. Keynes resigned his Treasury post on 19 May. Early in June, three weeks before the treaty was signed, Keynes left Paris after telling the prime minister 'I can do no more good here … The battle is lost' (ibid., 1.469). Before the end of the month he had begun *The Economic Consequences of the Peace*.

Economic Consequences was written at high speed and with passionate conviction and often in extravagant terms. Begun on 23 June 1919, it was written in just over three months and published on 12 December. Never afterwards did Keynes complete and publish a book so swiftly. 'I don't really start until I get my proofs back from the printer', he said in 1935. 'Then I can begin serious writing.' As Macmillan did not expect the book to be a best-seller and were conservative in their proposals, Keynes reversed the normal author–publisher relationship: he put up the costs of production, paid Macmillan 10 per cent on those costs as well as 10 per cent on the sale price, and kept any resulting profits. He would use this arrangement for everything else he would publish with Macmillan other than *How to Pay for the War*. For the American edition he made his own arrangements with Harcourt Brace and received a royalty of 15 per cent.

The book was an international best-seller and brought Keynes instant celebrity. Much of it was written in August and September at Charleston, Vanessa Bell's farmhouse on the Sussex downs, but he found time for a whirlwind ten days in London in July: Diaghilev's ballet, an end of ballet season dinner party of thirty-three which he hosted at 46 Gordon Square (the lease of which he had taken over from Clive Bell in 1917), business appointments, a speech, evidence to a government committee on Indian exchange and currency, a discussion at the Tuesday Club (a dining club of City men, public servants, journalists, and academics), lunching and dining out day after day. Although normally a late riser who got to the Treasury a little before noon, he spent his mornings at Charleston writing from 8 a.m. to 1 p.m. and averaged 1000 words a day fit for the printer.

The early chapters were suffused with a sense of impending catastrophe. Keynes drew a vivid picture of the fragility of Western civilization and laid particular stress on the growth of population, the precariousness of Europe's claims on the resources of America, and the prospect of a slow-down in capital accumulation as social inequality diminished. He drew a wickedly brilliant picture of the deliberations of the council of four. When he turned to the havoc of war and the Carthaginian peace just concluded, he reproduced verbatim passages from the memoranda he had prepared on reparations and the rehabilitation of the European economy. Again he called for a cancellation of inter-allied debts and for a revision of the treaty provisions for reparations once new governments showing 'a profounder wisdom and greater magnanimity' (*Collected Writings*, 3.165) were in power. Reparation payments should be well within Germany's capacity to pay: he proposed a total of $10 billion, less the value of merchant ships surrendered, state property in ceded territory, war material, and so on, which he put at $2.5 billion. This would be payable over thirty years at $250 million a year (with no interest liability), beginning in 1923.

Keynes also proposed a fund of $1 billion to provide credits to all the continental belligerents, allied or ex-enemy, and that discharge of capital should rank ahead of all other governmental obligations. The money would be raised from the neutrals, the United Kingdom, and above all from the United States. A second guarantee fund of $1 billion would contribute to the stabilization of European currencies without needing to be drawn upon extensively. Other proposals included the creation of a European free trade union, comprising the former empires of Germany, Austria-Hungary, Russia, and Turkey, but extending if possible to other European countries and to India and Egypt. This would help to limit the disorganization and inefficiency resulting from 'the innumerable new frontiers created between greedy, jealous ... nationalist states' (*Collected Writings*, 3.169).

Keynes's thinking in 1919 was remarkably similar to the thinking behind the Marshall plan in 1947. Without economic recovery Europe could not prosper and without prosperity the obligations of the treaty would be disregarded and national conflicts would revive. Above all, lasting recovery hung more on the rehabilitation of Germany than on any other single factor. The future of Europe had to be assured, not by concentrating exclusively on the potential struggles between nations but by bringing to light the powerful economic forces holding back recovery and redirecting these forces through co-operative action, backed by magnanimous and imaginative assistance. As Keynes put it, 'the perils of the future lay not in frontiers and in sovereignties but in food, coal and transport': to which, later in life, he might have added jobs.

Economic Consequences was followed by a flood of comment in Britain, France, and America. Comment in Britain was generally very favourable, American critics thought Keynes unjust to President Wilson, and French writers brought a variety of charges. Some readers thought his account of the conference too rhetorical; others have since attacked the book as contributing to the sense of guilt towards Germany that inhibited policy in later years. This line of attack was developed in Étienne Mantoux's *The Carthaginian Peace*, published in 1946, after Keynes's (and the author's) death. Mantoux may have been right in thinking that Keynes's passionate attack on the treaty was still influencing opinion twenty years later, encouraging sympathy for Germany and acceptance of a policy of appeasement. But there were more obvious reasons for shrinking from war in the late 1930s.

Although Mantoux does convict Keynes of repeated overstatement and at times of mis-statement and of doing less than justice to French fears of future German aggression, he assumes too readily a parallel between the scale of rearmament expenditure under Hitler (RM 15 billion per annum) or of what Germany procured in wartime from occupied countries, and what might have been paid in reparations. This is to ignore the problem of transfer across the exchanges: the most that Germany paid in any year—RM 2.5 billion in 1929, close to Keynes's estimate of RM 2 billion—represented 20 per cent of German exports in 1929 (40 per cent of exports in 1925) and was more than offset by net capital inflows, so that no net transfer in fact occurred.

Where Keynes was more open to criticism was in building on the assumption that the United States would take part in a cancellation of inter-allied debts, so that France and Britain would be under less pressure to recoup the means of debt repayment in reparations from Germany. He was more severe on Wilson and Lloyd George than was justified, given the political pressures they were under and the differences in their priorities. Both points were discussed in *The Revision of the Treaty*, published in January 1922. On the first, Keynes argued that the American balance of payments would not be sufficiently adaptable to permit of repayment of European debt and that the choice could be between default and cancellation. On the second, he accepted that politicians had to give weight to public opinion but drew a distinction between the opinion expressed in the newspapers and what ordinary people suspect to be true. He surmised that the average Englishman in 1919 'never really believed in the indemnity' and took it with a grain of salt; 'for the time being there could be little harm in going on the indemnity tack' (*Collected Writings*, 3.4). As for Lloyd George, he could claim to have been 'by devious paths, a faithful servant of the possible' (ibid., 3.2).

Journalism: money and foreign exchange Keynes continued to comment on the problems of the inter-allied debts and reparations, contributing frequently to the press on this and other subjects. In July 1921 he was asked to serve on a royal commission on Indian tariffs and agreed. In October he was invited by C. P. Scott, the editor of the *Manchester Guardian*, to edit a series of supplements discussing the economic and financial problem of European reconstruction. He had intended to leave for India at the end of January, but on 21 January 1922 he resigned from the Indian fiscal commission. Instead he concentrated on finding *Guardian* contributors and himself made three contributions to the first reconstruction supplement in April. There were eventually twelve monthly supplements, to which he contributed thirteen articles, and recruited a highly impressive list of contributors from many different countries, including some of the leading continental economists. In advance of the first issue he published in the *Manchester Guardian* on 6 April a plan for the Genoa conference, which began shortly afterwards and which he attended as the newspaper's special correspondent. His article made proposals that reappeared in later Keynes plans; he suggested stabilizing exchange rates at or near their current level; gold was to be withheld from internal circulation and reserved for international use; and central banks were to be allowed to maintain a gap of 5 per cent between their buying and selling price for gold.

Keynes's interests were increasingly directed towards what would later be called 'the management of the economy'. Two forms of economic instability preoccupied him. Of these the first was instability of prices, inflation, deflation, and all that went with them; the second was unemployment and the fluctuations in economic activity giving rise to it. The two were, of course, interconnected since the movement of prices reacted on the level of activity: but the analytical approach to the problem of inflation, for example, was very different from the analysis necessary for an explanation of unemployment. Broadly speaking, Keynes concentrated on price instability in the 1920s but took instability in output and employment as his point of departure in the 1930s.

Keynes began in 1922 with the articles he published in the reconstruction supplements of the *Manchester Guardian Commercial*. Four of these were drawn upon, much revised, in the first three chapters of his *Tract on Monetary Reform*, published in December 1923, and two additional chapters dealing with aims and proposals for future policy were added. From the point of view of economic theory the *Tract* was not particularly original, but was based on the work of Marshall and Pigou. Keynes accepted the quantity theory of money as beyond question and with it the theory of purchasing power parity. But his analysis did contain some novel ideas, such as estimating the value as 'an inflation tax' of the levy exacted on all other holders of cash by a government inflating the currency, or the theory of interest parity in the market for forward exchange. The proposals he put forward were certainly novel. Keynes developed the case for a managed currency in place of the gold standard, which he dismissed as 'a barbarous relic' (*Collected Writings*, 4.138). To return to the gold standard would mean giving priority to stability in the exchange rate and the external value of the currency over its internal value and forcing inflation or deflation on the economy if prices rose or fell in other countries. The report of the Cunliffe committee in 1918 in favour of an early return to gold at the pre-war parity, adopted as official policy, belonged to 'an extinct and almost forgotten order of ideas' (ibid., 4.153) and spelt inevitable deflation and unemployment. Earlier Keynes had proposed pegging to gold at the current (devalued) rate and allowing the rate to appreciate if, as he expected, there was a gradual fall in the price of gold. The Bank of England, through its control over bank rate and the banking system, would seek to maintain price stability and fix buying and selling prices each week at the same time as it fixed bank rate. The exchange rate would then change at intervals, not float freely, as happened later.

The return to gold In July 1924 Keynes was called to give evidence to the Chamberlain–Bradbury committee, which was considering a return to gold. He made it clear that he favoured indefinite control over gold exports and imports but wanted to abandon the practice of holding gold as backing for the note issue and to free it for use exclusively in helping to steady the exchange rate. He continued to express concern at the steady rise in the exchange rate towards the pre-war parity and to emphasize the danger to Britain's competitive position of what was increasingly an overvalued rate. Since nothing was said, speculators assumed that the rate would shortly be fixed at the pre-war parity, and by moving into sterling at a lower rate to profit from the rise, helped to bring it about. Keynes also argued in 1924 for less foreign and more home investment, drawing attention to the low rate of return on foreign investment in relation to the uncertainties, and its more favourable tax treatment. He did not, however, at this stage attack foreign investment as damaging to employment, but confined his objections to the effect on the exchange rate and income levels.

In the summer of 1924 Keynes began a fuller academic treatment of monetary theory. This took shape slowly over the next six years and ultimately appeared in two volumes in October 1930 as *A Treatise on Money*. During these years Keynes was rethinking his theories of economic fluctuations, writing parts of the book at intervals while occupied in many other directions. In the official deliberations leading up to the announcement of the return to gold on 28 April 1925 Keynes's writings were often discussed. Just before the decision to return, Keynes took part in a dinner discussion with the chancellor (Churchill), an ex-chancellor (McKenna), and the two top Treasury officials on the issues involved. Keynes and McKenna argued that at the pre-war parity sterling would be overvalued by 10 per cent, and that this would result in higher unemployment and labour unrest as employers tried to get back into profit by reducing wages. These arguments were ineffective. After the announcement Keynes developed his arguments in *The Economic Consequences of Mr. Churchill*, a republication of articles rejected by *The Times* and published by Beaverbrook in the *Evening Standard*.

Marriage to Lopokova Less than a week after *The Economic Consequences of Mr. Churchill* appeared, Keynes married, on 4 August 1925, Lydia Barocchi [*see* Lopokova, Lydia Vasilievna (1892–1981)]. Lydia's appearance on the London stage in Diaghilev's Ballets Russes towards the end of the war at first left Keynes unimpressed: 'she's a rotten dancer—she has such a stiff bottom', he commented (Skidelsky, 2.93). When he saw her again towards the end of 1921 in other Diaghilev ballets, including *The Sleeping Princess*, he fell deeply in love with her, much to the astonishment of his Bloomsbury friends, who could not think it possible he would marry her. She was one reason for his resignation from the Indian fiscal commission in January 1922. They did not marry until 1925, in part because of the need to obtain annulment of Lydia's earlier marriage to Diaghilev's former business manager, Barocchi. By then they had secured sole possession of 46 Gordon Square and shortly afterwards Keynes took a long lease of Tilton on the Sussex downs near Lewes, a property that had once belonged to his Jesuit forebears. These became his normal residences when free of duties requiring his presence in Cambridge.

The marriage proved a great success and was a turning point in Keynes's life. Lopokova had gifts to which Bloomsbury was blind and she had a firm hold on his affections. When apart they wrote every day and she took charge of him in his illnesses and in wartime, when his energies had to be carefully husbanded. The couple had no children.

An unorthodox Liberal In the 1920s Keynes's frequent articles in the press made heavy demands on his time: not just the *Manchester Guardian* and *The Times* but a host of other papers. Many of his articles were syndicated and appeared in the foreign press. He wrote regularly in the 1920s for the *Nation and Athenaeum*, which he and a group of Liberals had taken over in 1923 and of which he was chairman from 1923, and in the 1930s rather less regularly for the *New Statesman*, with which the *Nation* was merged in 1931 and of which he remained chairman until his death. He again became active in the Liberal Party, lecturing at their summer schools, speaking on behalf of Liberal candidates at elections, and contributing to the Liberal industrial inquiry which Lloyd George set on foot in 1926. Of the inquiry's report, *Britain's Industrial Future*, popularly referred to as the *Liberal Yellow Book*, a substantial part was drafted by Keynes and contained many important proposals by him. He argued for public corporations as the most suitable form of organization for state-owned industries, a national investment board, regulation of stock exchange issues by overseas public bodies, and the reform of budgetary accounts. Before the 1929 election Keynes and Hubert Henderson, the editor of the *Nation*, prepared the pamphlet *Can Lloyd George do it?*, supporting the Liberal Party's proposals. This pamphlet took issue with the Treasury doctrine that loan-financed government investment would make little net addition to employment and no permanent addition since an equivalent amount of investment would be 'crowded out'. But Keynes was not able to rebut the argument by the reasoning he subsequently developed, that in an underemployed economy additional investment would expand employment and so generate the income and hence the savings necessary to finance the investment.

From the 1920s onwards Keynes put his faith in a mixed economy. Though a Liberal, he was no believer in *laissez-faire*; nor was he ever tempted to extreme reliance on the state, such as was implied in a planned economy. What he kept writing about was 'management'. It is a word that appears again and again in the headings of chapters in Book VII of *A Treatise on Money*: 'Management of money', 'National management', 'International management', 'Supranational management'. Similarly, in *The General Theory* it is the management of demand rather than the planning of supply that Keynes prescribes. He may talk about plans in *How to Pay for the War* in a situation where the state had to take complete control with unmistakable objectives; but in peacetime, with no similar agreed objective, more flexible arrangements were required. Apart from the odd piece of journalism, Liberal speech, or the lecture 'The end of *laissez-faire*' (1926), however, he nowhere provided a systematic analysis of the scope for government action.

Keynes was, *par excellence*, the Treasury man, and believed in financial agencies of control, looking initially to monetary policy to regulate the pressure of demand but coming in the 1930s to see in the budget a more comprehensive, direct, and powerful 'organ of action' able to operate over the whole area of spending and saving, not just selectively like credit control. Monetary policy had proved too weak a stimulant after 1932 and was likely to prove too expensive on the restrictive tack in wartime in terms of the interest burden it would leave behind. But Keynes was never one to rely on a single instrument of control and spurn so indispensable a weapon as monetary policy.

The Macmillan committee and *A Treatise on Money* In November 1929, shortly after the Wall Street crash and the rise in bank rate to 6 per cent, Keynes was appointed a member of the Macmillan committee on finance and industry, set up by the Labour government to report on how the banking system affected the working of the economy. Two months later he was asked to join the Economic Advisory Council, made up of senior ministers and an assorted group of outside experts, with the prime minister (MacDonald) in the chair.

Keynes was the dominant figure on the Macmillan committee; he took a leading part in the examination of witnesses and the drafting of the report. He also addressed the committee on five occasions in February and March 1930 and a further three in November on his own views on how the monetary system worked. These followed the lines developed in the *Treatise on Money*, beginning with an exposition of the operation of bank rate and dwelling on the difficulty of managing an economy so dependent as Britain on foreign trade when wages were too high and had become inflexible. He went on to develop his theory of saving and investment, explaining that if bank rate was put up to protect the balance of payments it would work by lowering investment, upsetting the balance between investment and saving, and producing business losses and falling prices. If this was not carried through into a fall in costs and the losses continued, the economy would jam and unemployment would result. It is doubtful whether the committee understood Keynes's exposition.

Keynes also attempted to shape the thinking of the Economic Advisory Council, both through its regular deliberations and its specialist committees, most notably the committee of economists, which met between August and October 1930. However, even among the economists a consensus proved elusive, so divided were they over the role of public works and Keynes's 1930 conversion to a revenue tariff and export subsidy scheme to make British industry more profitable at the 1925 gold standard exchange rate. The full Economic Advisory Council did not survive the collapse of the second Labour government, but the continued existence of its committee on economic information, which produced regular reports on various issues of economic policy, gave Keynes access to officials until the outbreak of war in 1939.

Simultaneously with the end of the committee of economists, the first of Keynes's two major contributions to economic theory, *A Treatise on Money*, was published on 24 October 1930. The *Treatise* was the product of a long intellectual struggle to escape from the ideas in which he had been reared, later dubbed 'classical economics'; for example, the Ricardian view that supply creates its own demand. The focus of the book was on money and prices rather than on output and employment: it contained a full study of the operation of the monetary system, national and international. Fluctuations in prices were no longer explained in terms of changes in the stock of money as in the quantity theory, but in terms of the pressure of demand on the available supply of resources; and the pressure of demand was represented as varying with the magnitude of any divergence between the volume of investment and the availability of savings to finance it. The significance attached by Keynes to such a divergence reflected the success of Dennis Robertson (on whose ideas Keynes drew heavily in the years of the *Treatise*) in convincing Keynes that the major fluctuations in activity originated in booms in investment and that these could not be accounted for solely in terms of banking policy.

In the *Treatise* Keynes's thinking was still in transition and continued to evolve. The fluctuations he had so far considered were largely cyclical and differed from prolonged periods of underemployment of available resources. Moreover, he had not found a conclusive reply to the Treasury's objection to public works: that borrowing to finance additional capital expenditure would absorb savings already financing an equivalent amount of investment, crowd it out, and leave no net increase in expenditure and employment. It was clearly necessary to explain what governed the level of output and employment as a whole and show what set limits to any increase or decrease.

Keynes started from the idea of effective demand for output as a whole and its interactions with savings and investment under conditions of substantial unused resources. In those circumstances fluctuations in output could serve to equate savings and investment with little change in prices and costs. A given increase in investment would start off a multiple increase in income and output as those who were brought into employment spent their income, bringing others into employment; they, in turn, others; and so it would go on. But since the addition to spending would fall short of the addition to income, the expansionary process would slow down and peter out in the absence of a fresh stimulus. Income and output would be higher and savings would increase to match the original increase in investment. Similarly, an initial fall in expenditure would multiply and bring down income and employment but would be limited by the resulting reduction in savings.

The General Theory of Employment, Interest and Money

Keynes was never afraid to abandon one set of ideas for another of greater explanatory power. Soon after the publication of the *Treatise* he had begun to reconsider what governed the level of output and employment. In this he was assisted by a group of young Cambridge dons, who referred to themselves as the Circus, whose views and suggestions were relayed to him by Richard Kahn. The outcome of his rethinking was the publication in February 1936 of the chief of his major theoretical works, *The General Theory of Employment, Interest and Money*. This contained a new and radical analysis of economic instability.

Keynes asked not what made output fluctuate but what governed the level of output in the aggregate. Why in particular did it fall so persistently short of what existing resources—especially manpower—might be expected to permit, leaving a residue of involuntary unemployment? Keynes's answer was in terms of what he called 'effective demand'. This, like output and employment, had to be looked at in terms of aggregates. As effective demand expanded, output would grow, and as it contracted, output would fall. If output in the aggregate fell short of the potential level at the limit of capacity, this would normally reflect a deficiency of demand. There might be other obstacles to full employment, such as a mismatch between the kind of labour seeking employment and the kind of labour in demand. An increase in effective demand might then do little to increase output; but without effective demand there would be no output at all.

Economic policy should therefore provide for the management of demand as a means of controlling the level of output and seek to ensure the fullest possible use of available resources. This might seem to imply little difficulty in reaching full employment; and indeed there was full employment in nearly all the industrial countries in the 1950s and 1960s. But it would be a mistake to attribute that result to the skill of governments since for most of the time governments were seeking to *restrain* demand. Expanding demand may fail for a variety of reasons to ensure higher employment: by giving rise to inflation, or a balance of payments deficit that cannot be sustained; or because domestic resources are incapable of taking advantage of expanding demand in the direction that it takes.

Keynes had also to answer those who thought that a deficiency of demand would disappear of itself. As he pointed out, while commodity markets can nearly always clear themselves through price adjustments, the labour and capital markets do not. A reduction in money wages throughout the economy would be unlikely to do much to expand employment. It would, of course, lower costs; but competition would soon translate the fall in costs into a fall in prices and this in turn would remove the fall in real wages and leave employers no better off.

If efforts were made to restore profits in a depression by cutting wages, it might be possible after great social upheaval to regain competitiveness with other countries, but a general reduction in wages that was soon followed by a general reduction in prices would do little or nothing to expand domestic demand. It is difficult enough to cut money wages but far more difficult to cut *real* wages: not so much because of trade union resistance as because of the competitive spirit of employers.

With the capital market there are other difficulties. Increased saving does not automatically drive down interest rates: it may have quite the opposite effect if a falling-off in spending produces hesitation over future demand. The act of saving does not by itself add to investment. The saver may simply add to his cash holdings while the diminished flow of spending obliges businessmen to borrow more, not for investment but to meet their obligations. Moreover, if additional saving lowers interest rates, which is far from certain, there will be a limit to the reduction because as bonds rise in price, the risk of a reversal and a consequent capital loss becomes ever greater.

As a way of managing demand, Keynes looked first to the encouragement or discouragement of investment. He was not in favour of adding to the government's current expenditure and deliberately running a budget deficit to meet a deficiency of demand. No doubt, he argued, budgets would become unbalanced in a depression in any event, but he had no wish to tempt chancellors to become more spendthrift. Additional government expenditure should be on capital account and financed from a separate capital budget while the regular budget remained, as far as possible, in balance. Apart from public works financed out of the capital budget, there was also scope for operating on investment through changes in interest rates.

If these were not ruled by thrift on the one hand and the productivity of capital assets on the other, how were they determined? Keynes's answer was that interest rates had to match what he called 'the liquidity preference' of the investing public, or their willingness to part with the liquidity afforded by cash for bonds over a range of maturities. By matching the maturity of bond issues to the liquidity preference of investors, it would be possible to borrow at more stable interest rates; and by operating on the stock of money and the supply of liquidity, the government could push interest rates up or down. This part of Keynes's new doctrine had influenced monetary policy in wartime, when the government was able to borrow heavily at a steady 3 per cent. But the view of liquidity preference as *determining* interest rates to the exclusion of thrift and capital productivity was the subject of long controversy.

In the management of demand there were also difficulties on the side of supply. As employment expanded there was always the risk of wage inflation in major centres of industry, with wages rising faster than productivity as labour became scarcer. Keynes regarded wage inflation as a political problem. But in an overheated labour market wages are unlikely to be easily controllable; and there is the further danger that while skilled labour is very much in demand and earning substantial rises in pay, unskilled labour may remain superabundant, with expanding demand producing inflation rather than additional employment. In those circumstances Keynes accepted that it might be necessary to call a halt to expansion, as he urged in 1937, when unemployment was still in excess of 12 per cent. He never envisaged expanding employment to the point at which unemployment fell below about 5 per cent.

While Keynes provided a framework of thinking about inflation and unemployment, he did not provide prescriptions that would be effective in all circumstances. He was well aware of the difficulties of managing demand successfully after the devastation of a long war and of the problems that a high level of demand would pose for the management of the economy. In the *General Theory* the discussion ran exclusively in terms of a closed economy. This led Keynes to neglect the difficulties of an export economy such as Britain in a world depression (although in fact the United States, a much more self-contained economy, was hit very much harder in the 1930s by depression). He never lost sight of the importance of market opinion, particularly in financial markets, but believed that, suitably handled, it could be made to respond positively to expansionist policies rather than thwart them. He accepted that inflation might take root on the side of costs rather than excess demand and did not profess to know how to keep money wages from rising in a fully employed economy. As he told a correspondent in December 1943, 'The task of keeping efficiency wages reasonably stable (I am sure they will creep up steadily in spite of our best efforts) is a political rather than an economic problem' (Kahn, 361).

The *General Theory* gave rise to intense and prolonged controversy. Older economists tended to be highly critical of Keynes's ideas, and many thought them a recipe for inflation, while younger economists in general accepted them with enthusiasm. In 1936 the committee on economic information of the Economic Advisory Council discussed a report by its subcommittee on the trend of unemployment, which forecast a rise to a peak of 20 per cent in 1940. Keynes, troubled by the apparent exhaustion of investment opportunities except in housing construction, took an even gloomier view. In January 1937, when unemployment stood at 12½ per cent, he published three articles in *The Times* on 'How to avoid a slump', arguing in favour of keeping the long-term rate of interest steady, holding back postponable public investment, and planning to have investment projects ready for adoption in the impending slump. On this occasion the official response was a good deal more favourable than previously, thanks to Sir Frederick Phillips in the Treasury and Humbert

Wolfe in the Ministry of Labour. But if the course of events turned out to be in keeping with Keynes's recommendations it was not to any great extent because the government adopted his views. On the other side of the Atlantic the expansionary policies adopted owed little to Keynes's urgings.

Heart trouble From the summer of 1936 Keynes was affected by a prolonged spell of illness, beginning with chest pains and breathlessness. After a complete collapse in May 1937 heart trouble was diagnosed and a complete rest prescribed. He gradually improved, and was writing occasional letters and even the odd article by July 1937. But when he returned to London and Tilton in late September he still needed Lydia's constant care to prevent overexcitement and overwork, and he continued to need it for the rest of his life.

In the run-up to war in 1939 Keynes by his standards at first said little. In March 1937 he had commented in *The Times* on borrowing for rearmament and entered 'a plea for organised policy'. On 10 July 1937 he argued in the *New Statesman* that it was our duty 'to prolong peace, hour by hour, day by day, for as long as we can! We do not know what the future will bring except that it will be quite different from anything we could predict' (*Collected Writings*, 25.62). Keynes spent much of the autumn of 1938 in Cambridge busying himself with the Arts Theatre, which he opened in February 1936 and which he was to give to the city and university of Cambridge as a tribute to his parents, his books, and bursaring, but he was still tiring easily and suffering set-backs. He continued his long-standing controversy in the *Economic Journal* with Dennis Robertson on the determination of the rate of interest. However, in February 1939 his health suffered a set-back. Under radical treatment by a new physician, Dr Janos Plesch, from the spring of 1939, he began to feel better and was able to take more exercise. He wrote more for the *Economic Journal* and resumed attending meetings of the committee on economic information. In April 1939 he published a two-part article in *The Times* on 'Crisis finance'. In this he developed further the argument for avoiding increases in short-term interest rates and unsettling the long-term rate when it was important to hold it steady. As he continued to argue throughout the war, the interest rate structure should remain fixed while the public decided freely how it should distribute its holdings between different maturities.

Even in August 1939 Keynes did not expect war and was still optimistic as late as 30 August. After the Nazi incorporation of Austria into the German Reich he had argued for a British initiative to conclude a European pact between Britain, France, Russia, and any of the smaller states that wished to join. This was to negotiate an end to the Spanish Civil War and settlement of the Sudeten question. But it was an illusion to imagine that such a pact (if it could be concluded) would restore to the democracies 'the capacity to appear formidable' (*Collected Writings*, 28.104).

Keynes as an investor By 1939 Keynes had become a rich man as a result of successful investment. But he was not always successful and success followed a radical change in investment policy. He had begun on a small scale before the First World War and after the war began speculating in foreign exchange on his own account and that of his friends during the winter of 1919–20. At first there was a handsome profit, but by May 1920 he was wiped out and there were heavy losses on each of the currencies sold forward on behalf of his friends. Undeterred, Keynes borrowed for further speculation in currencies and also in commodities and by the end of 1922 had paid off all his debts and accumulated net assets of over £20,000. From November 1919 he was also investing on behalf of his college as second bursar and held the post of first bursar from 1924 until his death. By that time the initial funds, with no net addition, had multiplied in value twelve-fold.

From 1919 onwards Keynes became increasingly involved in the City, advising prominent figures on financial matters, accepting the chairmanship of the National Mutual Life Assurance Society in 1921, but rejecting the offer of the chairmanship of the foreign-owned British Bank of Northern Commerce. On the other hand, he resigned his Girdlers' lectureship in economics and became a supernumerary fellow of King's. He did a limited amount of supervising at King's and limited himself from 1920 to eight lectures, in the Michaelmas term, on his work in progress.

In the 1920s Keynes was not conspicuously successful in his investments; he lost between 1923 and 1929 on the stock exchange but initially made substantial net gains in currencies and commodities. However, he lost heavily in further commodity speculation at the end of the decade, when his net worth fell to under £8000. In the early 1930s, however, his investment policy was extremely successful, and carried his net worth to a peak of over £500,000 in 1936. In the slump that followed his net assets fell to less than £200,000 before more than doubling again by 1946. In those years he ceased to be an active dealer seeking short-term gains on a prediction of turning points in the credit cycle and preferred to take a long-term view, concentrating his investments on a limited number of enterprises of which he had knowledge and in whose management he had full confidence.

Wartime activities It had been Keynes's intention to limit himself to additional teaching duties so as to release his younger colleagues for essential duties in the event of war. But almost immediately he started drafting memoranda on price policy and exchange control. He and a number of similarly aged administrators from the First World War—Walter Layton, William Beveridge, and Arthur Salter—who had not found niches in Whitehall began to meet at 46 Gordon Square to co-ordinate their attempt to influence the war effort. The deliberations of the 'Old Dogs' resulted in a Keynes memorandum of the blockade and a set of notes for President Roosevelt, including one on the finance of post-war reconstruction. After describing the imposts of the first wartime budget as 'chicken-feed to the dragons of war' (*Collected Writings*, 22.31), he developed his own proposals for a comprehensive system of war finance involving compulsory savings.

These appeared in *The Times* in November and were supplemented by statistical estimates in the *Economic Journal* and by a series of consultations and exchanges before the publication in February of his most successful 'essay in persuasion': *How to Pay for the War*. Apart from suggesting ways of adding greatly to the financial resources of the government, this inaugurated the idea of an iron ration at low, fixed prices of a list of necessities in lower-income budgets, with government subsidies if required. He proposed also to assist families with low incomes by introducing family allowances payable directly to the mother. The net effect of these concessions would have been to effect an actual improvement in the condition of the worst-off compared with pre-war years. It was reassuring that the intense campaign with which all this was accompanied did not tell on his health, although he still had to spend long periods resting.

In June 1940 Keynes accepted appointment to a consultative council to the chancellor and in August moved into an office in the Treasury with access to official papers and government officials. He was then free to take a hand in any problem that interested him and at any level with no formal position in the administrative machine. By the autumn of 1940, as his health improved, he was often working twelve hours a day. After a land-mine exploded near his house in Gordon Square he moved to Tilton, from where he left for London by 8 a.m. and where he returned about 8.30 p.m.

Keynes was soon on the chancellor's budget committee and discussing budget strategy with the chancellor and his top advisers. He supported the preparation by James Meade and Richard Stone of national income estimates as a basis for budget calculations and was deeply involved in the 1941 budget proposals and the drafting of the budget speech. Together with the white paper (*Parl. papers*, 1940–41, 8, Cmd 6261) that accompanied it, it represented in Keynes's words, 'a revolution in public finance' (*Collected Writings*, 22.354), moving away from the criterion of balancing the budget to a policy based on balancing the economy and closing what was estimated as 'the inflationary gap'. Over the next four years the official cost of living rose by no more than 4 per cent and a more comprehensive index of consumer prices by 11 per cent. That there was an intelligible and relatively successful policy was largely attributable to Keynes.

As in the First World War, Keynes's energies were increasingly taken up with the problems of external finance, coupled with his part in shaping the post-war world economy. Late in 1940 after a request from the foreign secretary, he drafted a set of 'Proposals to counter the German "New Order"'. In Washington in the summer of 1941 for talks on lend-lease, he became involved in discussions of the 'consideration' for it required by the Americans. This was likely to take the form of a declaration by the British government binding it after the war to non-discrimination in trade and equal treatment of all countries: something that worried him as it paid no regard to the prospective post-war deficit in Britain's balance of payments. On his return to London, after an enforced rest

at Tilton, he took part in further negotiations over the 'consideration', which finally took shape in February 1942 in article VII of the master lend-lease agreement.

The clearing union and Bretton Woods For two years from the autumn of 1941 Keynes was mainly occupied with proposals for the post-war international monetary system. In the immediate post-war years the existing system of exchange controls and bilateral payments agreements would have to continue, but in the long term these arrangements should be superseded by a multilateral scheme with currencies freely convertible. Keynes prepared a plan for an international clearing union to supersede the gold standard and put forward a set of rules for balance of payments adjustment that required creditor countries to take the main initiative. His plan underwent many revisions before being submitted to the Americans, who had prepared a plan of their own—the White plan—for a stabilization fund and (in the initial version) an international bank for reconstruction and development.

The two plans were published in April 1943 and were the subject of negotiations in Washington between the Americans and a British mission in the autumn of 1943, with Keynes and Richard Law in the lead. The American plan rather than the British formed the basis of discussion. On his return to London, Keynes encountered opposition from several ministers, the Bank of England, and some members of the Treasury, based largely on accepting early convertibility, which carried with it the need to deal with Britain's enormous liquid liabilities in the form of sterling balances which they believed would weaken the international role of sterling. Keynes took the view that Britain faced such a desperate balance of payments problem at the end of the war that a substantial loan or grant from the United States was indispensable and that such prospective dependence made it inevitable that America should call the tune on the key elements in international financial arrangements. His opponents disagreed. Agreement was reached on a number of outstanding points, however, and in April 1944, a joint statement by experts on the establishment of an international monetary fund was issued, six months after the conclusion of the Washington discussions. This set the stage for the final conference, attended by representatives of forty-four governments at Bretton Woods, New Hampshire, in July and August. Again the burden fell heavily on Keynes as leader of the British delegation and chairman of the conference commission on the world bank. As he told the chancellor once it was over:

> The pressure of work has been quite unbelievable. It is as though, in the course of three or four weeks, one had to accomplish the preliminary work of many interdepartmental and Cabinet committees, the job of the Parliamentary draftsman, and the passage through several Houses of Parliament of two intricate measures of major dimensions, all this … (with) up to 200 persons in rooms with bad acoustics, shouting through microphones, many of those present, often including the Chairman, with an imperfect knowledge of English. (*Collected Writings*, 26.106–7)

The strain told on Keynes, who suffered an evening of

prostration at the preliminary conference in Atlantic City, two in the first week at Bretton Woods, and three in the third, together with a mild heart attack running upstairs.

The part played by Keynes in the conference was indicated when, in his concluding speech, he moved acceptance of the Final Act and the delegates paid him tribute 'by rising and applauding again and again' (*Wartime Diaries*, 193). The Final Act might do no more than provide a record of the conference; but in practice it established the articles of agreement for fund and bank.

Although Keynes spent most of the war years on external Treasury policy and after 1941 was never as deeply involved in budget preparations until 1946, he found time to pursue other interests of a domestic nature. He had taken an active interest in the visual arts since 1914 and had bought the works of modern French artists on his own and on the National Gallery's account at the sale of Degas's collection in Paris in March 1918. It was an interest fostered by his Bloomsbury friends and quickened by his marriage to Lopokova. In the 1930s he had conceived, planned, and financed the Arts Theatre in Cambridge. In wartime he was offered one appointment after another in 'the civilising arts of life' (*Collected Writings*, 28.368). First he became a trustee of the National Gallery in November 1941. Two months later he accepted chairmanship of the Council for the Encouragement of Music and the Arts, a body to assist the continued provision of music and drama in wartime out of private funds, with matching grants from the government. Although it took up more of his time than he had bargained for, Keynes put new life into the council, obtained an expanding Treasury grant, got the government to undertake to continue the council after the war, and secured the adoption of his proposal for an arts council, funded by the Ministry of Education, to provide an appropriate administrative framework. In 1944, while at Bretton Woods, he accepted the chairmanship of a committee to transform Covent Garden from a dance-hall into the home of national opera and ballet companies. He was able, shortly before his death, to attend their first production, *The Sleeping Beauty*.

Other concerns of Keynes in wartime were the Beveridge proposals for social security and unemployment policy after the war. The Treasury took a highly pessimistic view of what level of unemployment was likely after the war and hence, given the likely level of national income, of what could be afforded in benefits. Keynes, who was enthusiastic about Beveridge's proposals and much more confident than the Treasury about employment prospects, acted as a go-between, bringing Beveridge into touch with a small committee reporting to the Treasury and negotiating some reduction in the prospective cost of Beveridge's proposals. The Treasury remained fearful of the burden on the exchequer and put pressure on Keynes not to use his maiden speech in the House of Lords in May 1943 (he had been made a peer, Baron Keynes of Tilton, in June 1942) to welcome the Beveridge plan as the cheapest scheme on the map. (He made it instead on his proposals for an international clearing union.)

On unemployment Keynes resisted efforts to set on foot a Keynes plan and left it to James Meade and the economic section of the cabinet to make the running, while he limited himself largely to comments on the papers circulated. In stabilizing employment his emphasis then and later was on relying principally on changes in investment, although he accepted Meade's proposal for variations in national insurance contributions over the business cycle as a means of stimulating or checking consumer spending. He expected that after the war a period of excess demand would last for some five years and would be followed by a second period of five to ten years in which supply and demand could be roughly in balance, given appropriate counter-cyclical policies. Thereafter capital saturation would make it necessary to discourage savings and stimulate spending. But since the later phases were speculative it would be wise to concentrate on the immediate post-war situation in the early stages of policy making.

On deficit financing, with which his name has become associated, Keynes was far from enthusiastic. If there was to be a departure from budget balance it should take the form of increased investment, not consumption: chancellors were only too easily tempted into spendthrift policies. 'If serious unemployment does develop', he wrote, 'deficit financing is absolutely certain to happen, and I should like to keep free to object hereafter to the more objectionable forms of it' (*Collected Writings*, 27.353).

Keynes tried hard to get the Treasury to change the tone of the report it prepared on employment policy, warning them of how it would appear to younger economists as showing the Treasury 'intending to stone-wall on everything to the last' (*Collected Writings*, 27.355). But he was delighted to find it calling in Appendix B for the improvement of statistics that an active employment policy was bound to require. He took little part in the preparation of the white paper on employment policy (*Parl. papers*, 1943–4, 8, Cmd 6527) that appeared in May 1944, since he was either heavily engaged on external policy or ill and not in the office. Its opening statement, accepting government responsibility for 'the maintenance of a high and stable level of employment after the war', seemed to him to concede what mattered most.

Early in 1945 Keynes became involved in a joint study of post-war debt management and monetary policy by a committee of the Treasury, economic section, and Inland Revenue officials. Keynes once more took the view that, for at least as long as physical controls, rationing, and other instruments could be used to limit demand, expectations should not be disturbed by using higher interest rates to curb inflation. The public should be left as in wartime to determine freely how it would distribute its holdings between different maturities at the given structure of interest rates. The Treasury might, however, aim at some reduction in bank rate and Treasury bill rates in the interests on saving on payments on sterling balances; and slightly lower rates might be possible even on five- to ten-year bonds. Meade and Robbins, both members of the committee, were not convinced that the use of higher interest rates against the danger of inflation should be abandoned, and Meade was alarmed at Keynes's insistence that employment policy should operate exclusively through variations in public investment in an annual capital budget while what then became an exclusively revenue budget remained balanced in all circumstances. Even the Treasury allowed that budget deficits resulting from business depression should be allowed to remain. The committee was discontinued after the July 1945 election so that, after a preliminary report in May, these issues went unresolved.

The American and Canadian loans For the rest of 1945 Keynes was absorbed in an effort to obtain from the United States and Canada the financial assistance necessary to cope with the large prospective deficit in the balance of payments. Lend-lease had been brought to an abrupt stop with the end of the Japanese war, exports over the next three years were likely to fall short of imports by £1 billion or more, and invisible income (mainly shipping freights and income from foreign investments), which had covered the trade deficit before the war, was now very much smaller. The cabinet would have liked a grant from the United States; and Keynes, who did not himself think such a grant likely, recommended that the negotiating team should be empowered to agree only to a grant of $4–5 billion. He hoped also for satisfactory terms on outstanding issues of commercial policy to which the Americans attached major importance, and even planned himself to conduct the discussion on the subject. Unfortunately, ministers had not included commercial policy specialists in the negotiating team, although it had been made clear that an understanding on trade would have to precede a request to congress for financial aid. Thus after a series of brilliant expositions by Keynes of the British position in mid-September, the financial talks lost all momentum until the commercial policy experts arrived at the end of the month and by mid-October had reached agreement, deferring some of the more controversial issues to a later international conference.

Keynes now had the problem of persuading the cabinet that a large grant-in-aid was out of the question. While ministers still hoped for a substantial grant, they were reluctant to borrow on any scale and fixed $100 million as a limit to annual commitments in interest and amortization. Keynes thought that a limit of $150 million, beginning in five years, might permit a loan of $5 billion, the amount ultimately lent by the Americans and Canadians together. By mid-October he was already showing signs of strain and he was fearful of a breakdown, while ministers insisted on unrealistic deals and sent telegrams that had Keynes 'white with rage' (*Collected Writings*, 24.568). There were also disagreements on Keynes's proposals for dealing with the sterling balances and his account for the Americans of how the sterling area functioned. When the Treasury, advised by the Bank of England, sought to deny that the sterling area system had been discriminatory, Keynes commented that 'some fig leaves that may pass muster with old ladies in London, wilt in a harsher climate' (ibid., 24.584).

A new set of instructions from the cabinet early in November proved entirely unrealistic. Keynes became more and more exhausted, rude, and difficult for his colleagues to deal with. Again ministers provided fresh instructions, which shocked the Americans but seemed to offer the prospect of agreement until the chancellor sought to retract a promise on sterling convertibility made by Keynes in September with ministerial authority. In the last week of November Keynes was on the verge of collapse and resignation. The Bank of England and senior Treasury officials were opposed to Keynes's ideas and 'felt that they were negotiating with Keynes rather than with the Americans' (Moggridge, 813). Following a suggestion Keynes had made earlier, it was decided to send Sir Edward Bridges out to conduct the final negotiations. He rapidly vindicated the line the mission had taken, and ministers were asked to agree to terms virtually unchanged from those previously offered. Even at that point ministers contemplated a breakdown over three points of disagreement, on one of which—the attempt to postpone convertibility until the end of 1948—the Americans still refused to yield.

The loan agreement was signed on 6 December and Keynes returned to Britain on 17 December, the day when the debate opened in the House of Lords on the loan and the Bretton Woods agreements. He attended on the first day and his speech on the second, after a weak presentation of the government's case, was decisive in securing the passage of a vital measure.

After resting for some weeks at Tilton, Keynes felt 'completely recuperated' (*Collected Writings*, 27.427) and was able to resume work at the Treasury, but with considerable distrust in official policy. He was particularly disturbed by what he considered lavish political and military expenditure overseas and expressed his fears of 'a financial Dunkirk' in the absence of an early and drastic change of policy. He wanted to see British forces outside Europe cut in half and policy towards Germany radically revised so as to free Britain from the burden of feeding the Germans. He attached some urgency to settling the problem of the sterling balances but matters were allowed to drift.

On two issues Keynes is widely thought to have been over-optimistic. While in America he had drafted for his superiors in London a memorandum arguing that there was unlikely to be a dollar shortage in post-war years and indeed that, as America became a high-cost country, a dollar surplus would not be very long in emerging. He later worked it up for publication in the *Economic Journal*. The article did not appear until after his death and the beginning of the dollar shortage was still some months away; but before very long Keynes had been shown to be too optimistic. Keynes also lent encouragement to Dalton's unfortunate attempt to lower long-term interest rates to 2½ per cent, suggesting in March and April 1946 the conversion of 3 per cent local loan stock to a 2½ per cent basis.

Keynes's last public appearance was an unhappy one. He took part, expecting 'something of a holiday' in the inaugural meetings of the governors of fund and bank in

Savannah early in March 1946. He suffered two disappointments. The Americans were unwilling to reconsider their unilateral decision to locate both institutions in Washington, not, as the British much preferred, in New York. They were also insistent on the appointment of full-time executive directors (and, at first, full-time alternates as well) at salaries that in no way corresponded to the burden of work. There were other set-backs. He suffered great physical distress from walking too fast through swaying carriages in a very long train to the restaurant car; and on the very rough voyage back he suffered severely from a stomach bug through travel in a badly cleaned cabin used for the transport of GI brides and their babies.

Keynes returned exhausted. He spent a busy fortnight in London before going down to Tilton and even then continued to work on official papers and draft a post-budget memorandum. He went on walks round the farm, read in the garden, had tea with his Bloomsbury friends. Then on 21 April, after walking down from Firle Beacon the previous day, he had another heart attack from which he died within minutes. His ashes were scattered on the downs above the farm.

Keynes had a commanding presence. He was rather tall and broadly built, with a large head, thick, prominent lips, lively eyes, and a bushy military moustache. He could sit very still in a discussion with his legs stretched out in front of him and his hands tucked into the sleeves of his jacket. His voice had resonance and was carefully modulated. He spoke without gestures in a matter-of-fact way, appealing with deliberation and precision to the intelligence with lucid, orderly reasoning enhanced by wit. Lionel Robbins, not always an admirer, came to think of him at Bretton Woods

> as one of the most remarkable men that ever lived. The quick logic, the bird-like swoop of intuition, the vivid fancy, the wide vision, above all the incomparable sense of the fitness of words, all combine to make something several degrees beyond the limit of ordinary human achievement. (*Wartime Diaries*, 158)

Keynes was always kind and understanding with students, and his lectures to them drew a large audience by no means confined to economists. At meetings of his Monday night club for selected students in his rooms at King's he always had something new to say in his summing-up and provided memorable illustrations of his wit: as when in 1933 a speaker remarked that Professor Rexford G. Tugwell (a member of Roosevelt's brains trust) was on a razor's edge, Keynes interjected quick as a flash: 'then there will soon be two Tugwells'.

The quickness of his mind was coupled with an extraordinary range of interests. He had read widely when young and retained a great deal of what he read. Starting as a philosopher, he had no difficulty in mastering economics, although his major contributions to the subject came well after he had become famous. He was interested in history and archaeology as well as in the arts; he associated with artists almost throughout his adult life and spent much of his time at concerts, ballets, and plays and helping to make fuller provision for their production.

In his lectures Keynes once explained the role of intuition in the emergence of new ideas, pointing out that they never had the precision that later critics assigned to them. Ideas were apt to be like balls of wool, with no sharp edges; and the relations between concepts, when first perceived, were equally woolly. Intellectual rigour of the Ricardian type was apt to get in the way of original thinking. He himself thought intuitively and tended to hit on a conclusion before finding a logical path to it. He was less interested in elaborating a theory than in ensuring that it rested on valid premises and relied heavily on his firm grasp of practicalities and magnitudes.

There were many different sides to Keynes: philosopher, economist, editor, pamphleteer, company chairman, college bursar, patron of the arts and intimate friend of writers and artists, government spokesman and adviser. In each capacity he excelled. More than perhaps any other person of his time, he had the power to arouse and persuade informed opinion to the acceptance of novel ideas and proposals. As a speaker he combined lucidity, eloquence, and wit with a penetrating intelligence that no one else could equal. In personality he had great charm, though he was impatient and often biting in the face of stupidity. It is difficult to convey the brilliance of his conversation, the quickness of his wit, his remarkable powers of intuition, and his inspiring devotion to the public good, which finally killed him.

It is primarily as an economist that Keynes is remembered. He was in the line of great British economists from Adam Smith onwards, and it was he who opened up the whole area of macroeconomics, which seeks to explain what governs the level of output, income, and employment. His name will continue to be associated with what has been a major transformation in economic theory.

The world has changed since Keynes's day and the limitations of his ideas have become more apparent. National governments are often unable to play the role he assigned to them. They have not been able to get rid of inflation and unemployment. They have been unequal to the task of making the movement of domestic wages consistent with stable prices or international capital movements consistent with a stable rate of exchange. Public spending has been an unreliable instrument for expanding demand and has usually left behind an added burden of debt that has narrowed the options of policy. Keynes neither solved all the old problems nor foresaw all the new ones. We do not know what fresh solutions he might have offered to current problems. But at least he has provided us with a better starting point for reviewing the workings of the economy and given us an impressive demonstration of the power of economic ideas to remedy some of its defects.

ALEC CAIRNCROSS

Sources *The collected writings of John Maynard Keynes*, ed. D. Moggridge and E. Johnson, 30 vols. (1971–89) • R. J. A. Skidelsky, *John Maynard Keynes*, 3 vols. (1983–2000) • D. E. Moggridge, *Maynard Keynes: an economist's biography* (1992) • R. F. Harrod, *The life of John Maynard Keynes* (1951) • P. F. Clarke, *The Keynesian revolution in the making* (1988) • D. Patinkin and J. Clark Leith, eds., *Keynes, Cambridge and the general theory* (1977) • W. Eltis and P. Sinclair, eds., *Keynes and economic policy* (1988) • M. Keynes, ed., *Essays on John Maynard Keynes*

(1975) · É. Mantoux, *The Carthaginian peace* (1946) · A. P. Thirlwall, ed., *Keynes and laissez-faire* (1978) · *The wartime diaries of Lionel Robbins and James Meade, 1943–45*, ed. S. Howson and D. E. Moggridge (1990) · R. F. Kahn, 'On re-reading Keynes', *PBA*, 60 (1974), 361–91 · D. E. Moggridge and S. Howson, 'Keynes and monetary policy, 1910–46', *Oxford Economic Papers*, 26 (1974) · personal knowledge (2004)

Archives BLPES, corresp. and papers, mainly of other economists relating to his published works · Bodl. Oxf., memoranda on financial situation · King's AC Cam., corresp. and papers · PRO, official corresp. and papers, T 247 · Trinity Cam., corresp. | BL, letters to O. T. Falk, Add. MS 57923 · BL, corresp. with Duncan Grant, Add. MSS 57930–57931, 58120 · BL, corresp. with Macmillans, Add. MSS 55201–55204 · BLPES, corresp. with Lord Beveridge · BLPES, letters to Edwin Cannan · BLPES, letters to F. A. Hayek · BLPES, corresp. with J. E. Meade · Bodl. Oxf., corresp. relating to Society for Protection of Science and Learning · CAC Cam., corresp. with Paul Einzig · CAC Cam., papers and corresp. with Sir Ralph Hawtrey · CAC Cam., corresp. with A. V. Hill · CUL, letters to G. E. Moore · HLRO, corresp. with John St Loe Strachey · JRL, letters to *Manchester Guardian* · King's AC Cam., corresp. with A. E. Felkin · King's AC Cam., corresp. with Richard Kahn · King's AC Cam., corresp. with Joan Violet Robinson · King's AC Cam., corresp. with John Saltmarsh · King's AC Cam., letters to Sir J. T. Sheppard · King's AC Cam., letters to W. J. H. Sprott · NA Scot., corresp. with Lord Lothian, memorandum, GD40 · PRO, papers relating to Chancellor's consultative committee · PRO NIre., corresp. with Edward Carson, D1507 · Trinity Cam., corresp. relating to Hume's treatise · Trinity Cam., corresp. with Sir D. H. Robertson [copies] · U. Birm. L., corresp. with Austen Chamberlain · U. Sussex, letters to Vanessa Bell [copies] · U. Sussex, corresp. with Kingsley Martin | SOUND BL NSA, 'Maynard Keynes', NP798W&R C1 · BL NSA, documentary footage · BL NSA, performance footage

Likenesses D. Grant, oils, 1908, King's Cam. · G. Raverat, watercolour drawing, *c.*1908, NPG [*see illus.*] · W. Stoneman, photographs, 1930–40, NPG · W. Roberts, oils, exh. 1932, NPG · D. Low, pencil caricatures, 1933, NPG · photograph, 1933 (with Jan Smuts), NPG · B. Elkan, bronze bust (posthumous), King's Cam. · B. Elkan, bronze head, King's Cam. · R. Fry, charcoal drawing, King's Cam. · Ginsberg, charcoal drawing, King's Cam. · Ramsey & Muspratt, photographs, NPG · W. Rothenstein, pencil and chalk drawing, King's Cam.

Wealth at death £479,529 12s.: probate, 19 Sept 1946, *CGPLA Eng. & Wales*

Keynes, (John) Neville (1852–1949), logician, economist, and university administrator, was born on 31 August 1852 at Salisbury, Wiltshire, the only son of John Keynes (1805–1878), floriculturist, and his second wife, Anna Maynard Neville. He was reared in a middle-class, staunchly nonconformist household, which included his half-sister (fourteen years his senior), his paternal grandmother, and his father's unmarried sister. At fifteen Neville went to Amersham Hall, a nonconformist boarding-school, and in 1869 he won a scholarship to University College, London. There he won both the London BA and a Cambridge college scholarship. In October 1872 the bright young nonconformist entered Pembroke, a small, traditionally Anglican college, holding its top entrance scholarship in mathematics and classics.

Keynes's objective was a fellowship that would enable him to pursue an academic career. He despaired of getting any intellectual stimulus from the hired coaches who crammed undergraduates for the two traditionally prestigious honours courses. However, students reading moral sciences, where classes were small, enjoyed direct personal tuition from such charismatic dons as Henry Sidgwick and Alfred Marshall on philosophy, political economy, and logic. Accordingly, he read mathematics until May, when a college examination gave him his chance to win the scholarship enabling him to read moral sciences for the next two and a half years. He also crammed successfully for both parts of the London BSc. Finally, after passing out senior moralist at the 1875 tripos, and after getting the London MA gold medal in June, he was elected a fellow of Pembroke in August 1876.

Over the next six years Keynes gave intercollegiate lectures on logic and political economy to honours men and students from the recently founded women's colleges, Girton and Newnham. He held a minor college office (domestic bursar) but socialized mainly with faculty colleagues and the Cambridge Congregationalist community—among whom he met, and fell in love with, Florence Ada Brown (1861–1958) [*see* Keynes, Florence Ada], the Newnhamite daughter of John Brown, minister of Bunyan Meeting, Bedford. They married in August 1882, the year when a radical reform of Cambridge college and university statutes abolished life fellowships (unless held with a major college office) and financed a redistribution of income to the university through a progressive levy on colleges. As a modern don, concerned to improve the quality of higher education in Cambridge, Keynes now focused his ambitions on the career opportunities offered by a reconstructed university, and vacated his fellowship in August 1882. He looked forward to living (and entertaining his many friends) in the family home he built for Florence and himself at 6 Harvey Road. Henceforth, he dedicated his academic talents to logic and political economy, and his managerial skills (scarce among academics) to an evolving and increasingly influential central administration.

Keynes's first administrative appointment was assistant secretary (1881) to the local examinations and lectures syndicate, of which he later became secretary (1892–1910). Elected member of the council of the senate (1893–1925), he served as its secretary (1893–1925), became registrary in 1910, and remained the university's head administrator until his retirement in 1925. He was secretary to the moral sciences board for more years than any of his colleagues and its chairman from 1906 to 1912. He became chairman of the board of economics and politics (1908–20), a member of Newnham College council, and served various other councils and syndicates—each bringing its own load of subcommittees. In sum, throughout four decades, when the 1882 reforms were gradually transforming a loose federation of privileged clerical communities into an integrated and expanding centre of learning, education, and research, Neville Keynes's clear analytical mind, rare organizational ability, undogmatic approach, unpretentious personality, and absolute moral integrity rendered him indispensable whenever difficult or complex or controversial decisions needed to be taken and implemented at university level.

As logician and economist, Keynes was most productive

from 1884 (when he was one of the first twenty-three lecturers appointed by Cambridge University under the new statutes) until 1911. His first book, *Studies and Exercises in Formal Logic* (1884), was a textbook on deductive logic which became a classic in its field. Written as a students' manual it was revised and enlarged to become a lecturers' bible; the fourth edition (1906) was reprinted in 1930. His second book, *The Scope and Method of Political Economy* (1891), systematically analysed the methodological debates dividing economic theorists and undermining the scientific credentials of their discipline. Writing from the perspective of the new Cambridge school of economics (founded by Marshall), Keynes clarified contentious issues and explained the approach adopted by leading contemporary theorists, in Europe and the USA as well as Britain. This carefully researched monograph attracted favourable reviews and created an international reputation for Keynes as an economist. It drew such an authoritative line under the long-running methodological debates that it soon became superfluous, except for students of the history of economic thought. The last of several revisions and reprints appeared in 1930.

Neville Keynes resided in Cambridge until he died there in the Evelyn Nursing Home on 15 November 1949. He was buried three days later, and a memorial service was held at Pembroke. His happy family life had been marred only by the death in 1946 of his brilliant first-born child, John Maynard *Keynes. His beloved Florence died in 1958, leaving their two other distinguished children: Margaret (wife of A. V. Hill), and Geoffrey Langdon *Keynes.

PHYLLIS DEANE

Sources J. N. Keynes, diaries, 1864–1917, U. Cam., Addison MSS, 7827–7867 · C. D. Broad, *Economic Journal*, 60 (1950), 403–7 · F. A. Keynes, *Gathering up the threads* (1950) · G. L. Keynes, *The gates of memory* (1981) · *Cambridge University Reporter* (1873–1924) · Venn, *Alum. Cant.*
Archives CUL, corresp., diaries, papers · King's AC Cam., lecture notes · Pembroke Cam., notebooks · U. Cam., Marshall Library of Economics, corresp. | BL, corresp. with Macmillans, Add. MS 55207 · CAC Cam., corresp. with A. V. Hill · CUL, letters to Francis Jenkinson · King's AC Cam., letters to Oscar Browning
Likenesses G. Kelly, oils, 1927, U. Cam., registrar's office · double portrait, photograph, 1932 (with his wife), repro. in Keynes, *Gates of memory* · photograph, repro. in N. Brown, *Dissenting forebears* (1988)
Wealth at death £17,890 17s. 10d.: probate, 25 Jan 1950, CGPLA Eng. & Wales

Keys, Edward (*bap.* **1795**). *See under* Keys, Samuel (1771–1850).

Keys, John (*bap.* 1797, *d.* 1825). *See under* Keys, Samuel (1771–1850).

Keys [*née* Grey], **Lady Mary** (1545?–1578), noblewoman, was probably born at Bradgate Hall, Leicestershire, the youngest of the three daughters of Henry *Grey, duke of Suffolk (1517–1554), and Frances *Grey, duchess of Suffolk (1517–1559), the daughter of Charles *Brandon, first duke of Suffolk, and Henry VIII's younger sister *Mary. On 21 May 1553 Mary was betrothed to her cousin Arthur, Lord Grey

of Wilton, whose father was an ally of the duke of Northumberland. The attainder and execution of Suffolk in February 1554, however, ruined Mary's marital prospects. Not only was the match with Wilton set aside, but she also lost the prospect of a large inheritance. On her mother's death she co-inherited several baronies which gave her an income of £20 a year from estates in Warwickshire, Lincolnshire, and Nottinghamshire, but the remainder of Frances's property went to her second husband, Adrian Stokes, until his death. Lady Mary was made maid of honour to Elizabeth and received a pension of £80 a year from the queen.

On 10 or 12 August 1565 Mary secretly married Thomas Keys (or Keyes; *d.* 1571), the queen's sergeant porter. They were an ill-matched pair, for Mary was described as 'little, crook-backed and very ugly' (*CSP Spain, 1558–67*, 468), while her husband was stout and about 6 feet 8 inches tall. He was also more than twice her age and a widower with six or seven children. Finally, he was a minor gentleman from Kent, while she was of royal descent. Her high ancestry made Mary's marriage (like that of her elder sister Lady Katherine *Seymour, in 1560) a matter of close interest to the crown. By 19 August the marriage was discovered and the couple were closely interrogated. Keys was sent to the Fleet, while Mary was committed to the care of Mr William Hawtrey. For the next two years Mary stayed at his house, Chequers, in Buckinghamshire, from where she addressed letters to Cecil and Leicester, begging them to intercede with the queen to secure her pardon. Keys meanwhile prepared a petition offering to renounce his wife, but Bishop Grindal of London refused to annul the marriage and referred the matter to the court of arches. In August 1567 Mary was sent to live at the house of her stepgrandmother Katherine Willoughby, dowager duchess of Suffolk. She stayed there until June 1569, when she was removed to the house of Sir Thomas Gresham, who evidently disliked her presence. From 1570 onwards Gresham kept petitioning for her removal 'for the quyetness of my powre wiffe and my howsses' (PRO, SP 12/85, fol. 1).

After several years Elizabeth's anger at the marriage was spent. Although she refused to allow the couple to cohabit, she allowed Keys to leave prison in 1568 and eventually to return to Kent, where he died in 1571. Mary asked permission to wear mourning clothes, and used her married name for the first time. In 1572 Elizabeth agreed that Mary was 'att free leberty' to live where she pleased, but Mary had nowhere to go. She complained that she was 'destetud of all friends' and had insufficient income to live independently (PRO, SP 12/85, fol. 216). She therefore stayed an unwanted guest with Gresham until she went to live with her stepfather in 1573. Some time afterwards she set up her own household in a house near Aldersgate, London, where she died on 20 April 1578. During the last year of her life she occasionally attended court and exchanged new year's gifts with the queen.

Mary was probably buried in Westminster Abbey alongside her mother. In her will she left her possessions to friends and kinswomen. The lease of her house was to be sold for the benefit of her god-daughter Mary Merrick. An inventory of her books reveals an interest in theology. She possessed not only three bibles (including the Geneva Bible) and John Knox's *Answer to a Great Number of Blasphemous Cavillations* (1560), but also works relating to the Admonition controversy of the early 1570s, concerning the government and further reformation of the Church of England. Less surprisingly, she also owned Foxe's book of martyrs.   SUSAN DORAN

Sources H. Ellis, ed., *Original letters illustrative of English history*, 2nd ser., 2 (1827) · inquisition post mortem, 7 May 1560, Frances, countess of Suffolk, PRO, state papers addenda, Edward VI–James I, SP 15/34, fols. 56–57*b*, 58, 61–64 [*CSP domestic, addenda 1580–1625*, 404–5] · livery of Lady Katherine and Lady Mary Grey, 1554, PRO, state papers, Mary, SP 11/4, fols. 95–96 [*CSP domestic, 1547–80, 64*] · Gresham and Mary to Burghley, PRO, state papers domestic, Elizabeth I, SP 12/83, fol. 50 · Gresham and Mary to Burghley, PRO, state papers domestic, Elizabeth I, SP 12/85, fols. 1, 141, 216 · R. Davey, *The sisters of Lady Jane Grey and their wicked grandfather* (1911) · *CSP Spain*, 1558–67 · J. Strype, *Annals of the Reformation and establishment of religion … during Queen Elizabeth's happy reign*, new edn, 2/2 (1824), 210–11 [will] · *Fourth report*, HMC, 3 (1874), 179 · *Correspondence of Matthew Parker*, ed. J. Bruce and T. T. Perowne, Parker Society, 42 (1853) · *Report on the manuscripts of Lord Middleton*, HMC, 69 (1911) · *Report on the Pepys manuscripts*, HMC, 70 (1911) · W. Murdin, *Burghley's state papers* (1759) · C. Merton, 'The women who served Queen Mary and Queen Elizabeth: ladies, gentlewomen and maids of the privy chamber, 1553–1603', PhD diss., U. Cam., 1992
Likenesses H. Holbein, oils, repro. in P. Ganz, *Die Handzeichnungen Hans Holbeins* (Berlin, 1937), no. 100
Wealth at death manors in Warwickshire, Lincolnshire, and Nottinghamshire; lease on house near Aldersgate Street, London

Keys, Samuel (1771–1850), china painter, is of unknown parentage. He was one of the principal gilders and china painters in the old Derby china factory under William Duesbury the elder, to whom he was articled in 1795. Keys was an excellent workman, and much of the success of the china, especially the figures in the Dresden style, was due to his skill in decoration. On 3 August 1795 he married, at Dronfield, Derbyshire, Hannah Gratton, with whom he had three sons. He left Derby some years before the close of the factory and went to work under Minton at Stoke-on-Trent. Later he returned to Derby, where he died in 1850, in his eightieth year. Keys preserved his delicacy of execution to the last. He collected materials for the history of the Derby china factory, which form the foundation of subsequent accounts, notably that by William Chaffers in *Marks and Monograms* (1863).

Keys's three sons were all apprenticed at the Derby factory. **John Keys** (*bap.* 1797, *d.* 1825), watercolour painter, was baptized on 8 September 1797 at St Alkmund's, Derby. He became a skilled flower painter in watercolour and teacher of that art. Some of his pieces were shown in the Derby exhibition of china in 1870; one fine example of his work entered the collection of Joseph Mayer of Liverpool. His watercolour drawings, which included numerous studies of flowers from nature, were described as 'truthful and masterly' (Haslem, 105). He died at the age of twenty-eight. His *Sketches of Old Derby* was published in 1895. **Edward Keys** (*bap.* 1795), modeller, was baptized on either 21 July or 23 August 1795 (two entries for his baptism in the parish register give variant dates) at All Saints, Derby. He left Derby about 1826 and went to work for

Messrs Minton, Daniell, and others in the Staffordshire potteries. He was noted for his small personages, including a statuette of Dr Syntax which sold well. Among his other modelled figures were George IV and Napoleon and characters from Pierce Egan's *Life in London*. **Samuel Keys the younger** (*bap.* 1804), modeller, excelled in modelling small figures of leading theatrical personages, especially comic actors, which sold for between 6 and 8 shillings. His larger figures (28 inches high) of *Innocence* and *Hebe* are in the Victoria and Albert Museum, London. He left Derby in 1830 and went to the Staffordshire potteries district, where he was employed by several firms. In partnership with John Mountford, described by Haslem as the originator of the medium, he established a manufactory for producing Parian ware. He also designed and modelled ornamental objects in majolica and terracotta from drawings of flowers and foliage made by his brother John.

L. H. CUST, *rev.* ANNETTE PEACH

Sources J. Haslem, *The old Derby china factory: the workmen and their productions* (1876) · Desmond, *Botanists* · *IGI* · Mallalieu, *Watercolour artists* · M. Batkin and P. Atterbury, 'The origin and development of Parian', *The Parian phenomenon*, ed. P. Atterbury (1989), 9–21

Keys, Samuel, the younger (*bap.* **1804**). *See under* Keys, Samuel (1771–1850).

Keys, William Herbert (1923–1990), trade unionist, was born on 1 January 1923 at Elliotts Row, Elephant and Castle, London, the third child and second son in the family of four sons and one daughter of George William Keys, printer, and his wife, Jessie Powell. His elder brother and sister died before he was born. He spent his childhood in the Elephant and Castle and was educated at Archbishop Temple Grammar School there. He joined the army in 1939 and served in the rifle brigade throughout the Second World War, until 1946. He had a distinguished war record, becoming one of the youngest sergeant-majors. At one period in the war, cut off near the Nijmegen Bridge, he was behind enemy lines for several days with a handful of his men. He was among the first allied troops to enter Belsen concentration camp. This and his other wartime experiences confirmed his profound dedication to world peace, his total rejection of fascism, and his passionate support for nuclear disarmament.

Bill Keys started his career in the printing works of the Amalgamated Press, Summer Street, London, but in 1953 he became a full-time official of the National Union of Printing, Bookbinding, and Paperworkers when he was appointed national organizer. From 1961 to 1970 he was the secretary of the union's London central branch, while from 1970 to 1974 he was the general president of the Society of Graphical and Allied Trades (SOGAT). On 1 January 1975 he became general secretary of SOGAT, a post he held until he retired in 1985. He served on the general council of the Trades Union Congress for eleven years from 1974.

Keys was a highly successful general secretary of SOGAT and its constituent unions and became one of the foremost leaders in the wider trade union movement. On becoming general secretary, he changed SOGAT from being an inward-looking organization to one which became involved in mainstream issues. He believed strongly that it had a role and responsibility to be active within the Trades Union Congress, the Labour Party, and society at large. He was always an internationalist and forged links with unions throughout the world, not only in the printing sphere but on a much broader basis. His stamina and tenacity made him a formidable negotiator, with the ability to take apart the most complex wage structure and put forward a solution to disputes. He was especially renowned for his habit of kicking off his shoes during the hard negotiating sessions with employers.

Of Keys's many achievements, two stand out. He won a great victory for the continuation of his union's political fund, threatened by the Trade Union Act of 1984, which enforced periodic ballots on the issue. He spearheaded and co-ordinated the political fund ballots in trade unions—one of the few successes of the trade union movement in the years of the government of Margaret Thatcher. SOGAT was the first union to go to ballot and other unions followed. The other was his commitment to the creation of one union for the printing industry. He achieved a number of steps along this way with the merger in 1975 of the Scottish Graphical Association and SOGAT and then in 1982 of NATSOPA and SOGAT. Although his ultimate goal of one union evaded him before his retirement and death, he had put in place the basis of the SOGAT/NGA amalgamation, which took place in October 1991.

For all his successes, Keys's biggest disappointment was his failure to persuade his old London central branch members in Fleet Street to accept modernization and new technology. If the 'programme of action' which he devised in 1977 had been accepted, the move of newspapers to Wapping and the demise of Fleet Street would not have happened in the brutal way it did. He foresaw what would ensue and wanted to avoid it.

On the wider trade union scene Keys made a significant contribution to TUC policy making at a national level, particularly in the role of chairman of the employment policy committee (1976–85) and of the printing industries committee (1974–85). He also presided over the TUC media committee (1977–85) and the equal rights committee (1974–85), and served on the race relations committee (1974–85) and the finance and general purposes committee (1982–5), which is regarded as the TUC's 'inner cabinet'. As one of the elder statesmen of the TUC, he was the trade union nominee for the committee of inquiry which resolved the national steel strike (1980) and the national water strike (1983). He was one of the seven senior TUC leaders who tried to resolve the miners' strike of 1984–5. He was also the TUC nominee on the Commission for Racial Equality (1977–81), the Manpower Services Commission (1979–85), and the Central Arbitration Committee (from 1972). From 1981 to 1985 he was on the TUC–Labour Party liaison committee, and he was a leading light in the trades unions for a Labour victory organization.

Keys was warm, generous, and compassionate. He was well built, 6 feet in height, and some 13 stone in weight. In 1941 he married Enid, daughter of William Gleadhill, who

travelled all over the world doing many jobs, including work in the oilfields of the Persian Gulf. They had two sons, Ian and Keith. He died of heart trouble on 19 May 1990 at his home, 242 Maplin Way, North Thorpe Bay, Essex.   JOHN GENNARD, *rev.*

Sources *The Times* (21 May 1990) · *The Independent* (21 May 1990) · private information (1996)
Wealth at death £143,906: probate, 17 Dec 1990, *CGPLA Eng. & Wales*

Keyse, Thomas (1721–1800), still-life painter and pleasure garden proprietor, was born in Gloucester. He may have been the Thomas Keyse who was baptized at St Mary-le-Crypt, Gloucester, on 30 April 1721, the son of Thomas Keyse and his wife, Mary. A self-taught artist, he was a member of the Free Society of Artists, exhibiting with them from 1761 to 1764 and again in 1773. He specialized in depictions of flowers and fruit, often signed in bold capitals. From 1765 to 1768 he was an occasional exhibitor at the Society of Artists, and he sent two pictures to the Royal Academy in 1799. In 1768 he obtained a premium from the Society of Arts for a new method of setting crayon drawings.

In the late 1760s Keyse opened a tea-garden in Bermondsey, London, and *c.*1770, a chalybeate spring was found, known as the Bermondsey Spa. Here, among other attractions, Keyse kept a permanent gallery of his own work, including, most notably, a life-size painting of a butcher's shop. Obtaining a music licence in the 1780s, he made the gardens into a resort like Vauxhall Gardens, open in the evening during the summer months, and provided fireworks and transparencies, including a set piece of the siege of Gibraltar which he constructed and designed himself. These gardens were also the location of the annual commemorative dinner of the Free Society of Artists. Keyse died at his gardens on 8 February 1800, in his seventy-ninth year. His obituarist noted that Keyse was 'remarkable for painting legs of mutton and rumps of beef in the true Dutch style' (*GM*, 1st ser., 70/1, 1800, 284). The gardens remained open for about five years longer when they were built over, although their memory is preserved by the Spa Road, Bermondsey.

L. H. CUST, *rev.* KATE RETFORD

Sources M. H. Grant, 'A forgotten English flower painter', *Burlington Magazine*, 59 (1931), 75 · D. Lysons, *The environs of London*, 1 (1792), 558 · W. T. Whitley, *Artists and their friends in England, 1700–1799*, 1 (1928), 185; 2 (1928), 349–50 · H. B. Wheatley and P. Cunningham, *London past and present*, 3 vols. (1891), vol. 1, p. 168 · Graves, *Artists*, 136 · Graves, *RA exhibitors* · Redgrave, *Artists* · Waterhouse, *18c painters* · M. H. Grant, *A dictionary of British landscape painters, from the 16th century to the early 20th century* (1952), 109 · *GM*, 1st ser., 70 (1800), 284 · Bryan, *Painters* (1903–5), 3.131 · Graves, *Artists*, 3rd edn, 159 · Desmond, *Botanists*, rev. edn · *IGI*
Likenesses J. Chapman, stipple, pubd 1797 (after S. Drummond), NPG

Keyser, Sir Polydor de (1832–1898), hotelier and politician, was born on 12 December 1832 in rue de l'Église, Dendermonde, Belgium, the younger son of Joost Constant Fidel Armand de Keyser (*b.* 1801) and his wife, Catharina

Sir Polydor de Keyser (1832–1898), by John Caller

Rosalie, *née* Troch. Constant de Keyser and his family had left Ghent intending to establish themselves at Antwerp but during the troubles of 1832, when Antwerp was under siege, they took refuge at Dendermonde and it was there that Polydor was born. His early schooling was in Ghent; his father then moved to London, where by 1845 he had established the Royal Hotel, located at the corner of Victoria Embankment and New Bridge Street, Blackfriars, and Polydor attended school in Fulham before returning briefly to the continent to polish his linguistic skills. He had intended to follow his maternal grandfather as a surgeon but the death of his elder brother necessitated his joining his father in running what was already a successful hotel. The hotel was rebuilt to five storeys in 1874, decorated in the best French taste, with 230 guest rooms and a vast dining-room to seat 400 people. Another wing was added in 1882, making it the largest in London with a total capacity of 480 guests. It had a second dining-room, seating 250, many recreation rooms, gardens, and accommodation for 150 staff.

Polydor de Keyser soon became active in local affairs and rose from such humble offices as member of the West London Union and, despite his Catholic faith, churchwarden of St Bride's, Fleet Street, to membership of the Spectaclemakers' Company and a seat on common council in 1868. He was elected alderman for the ward of Farringdon Without in 1882, and immediately thereafter sheriff, having overcome objections that, as an alien and holder of an innkeeper's licence, he was ineligible for this office. As president of the Belgian Benevolent Society he promoted the British section at the International Exhibition on Hygiene and Lifesaving, held at Brussels in 1876, for which he was made a knight of the order of St Léopold; he was later raised to commander. He was a founder of the Guildhall School of Music and an early president of its management committee. In the autumn of 1887 he became lord mayor of London, the first Catholic to hold this office since the Reformation.

During his year of office de Keyser, accompanied by his wife, Louise, *née* Pléron (1834/5–1895), the two sheriffs, and a host of lesser dignitaries, paid a state visit to Belgium where they were warmly received by King Leopold and his people. An excursion was made to Dendermonde where, amid rapturous welcome from the townsfolk, de Keyser and his entourage visited the house of his birth. His mayoralty coincided with Queen Victoria's jubilee and the silver wedding of the prince and princess of Wales. His desire to celebrate this latter event was frustrated by the period of court mourning which followed the deaths of Kaiser Wilhelm I and (shortly afterwards) Friedrich III, though he was later able to present the royal couple with a silver model of the Imperial Institute. He was knighted in December 1888.

De Keyser accepted the task of presiding over the organization of the British section at the Paris Universal Exhibition of 1889. His efforts bore fruit; the British exhibitors made a good showing at this very successful event, located close to the brand-new Eiffel Tower, and the French government created him a chevalier of the Légion d'honneur. He was a fellow of the Royal Society of Arts, the Royal Geographical and the Statistical societies, a member of the Loriners', Butchers', Innholders', Poulters', and Wyre-Drawers' companies, and held high masonic office.

A supporter of many charities, de Keyser remained as active as hitherto until increasing deafness obliged him to retire from corporation business in 1892. His wife had been in failing health and was not seen at public events for some years prior to her death in January 1895. De Keyser became a recluse after her death; he was struck by an incurable illness and his last years were beset with pain and suffering. He died at his home, 4 Cornwall Mansions, Cornwall Gardens, London, on 14 January 1898 and was buried next to his wife in the family vault at Nunhead cemetery. The de Keysers, having no natural children, had adopted a nephew, Polydor Welchand de Keyser, and he had taken over as manager of the Royal Hotel when it was reformed as a limited company in 1897.

ANITA McCONNELL

Sources M. van Wesemael, 'Sir Polydoor de Keyser, lord mayor van Londen', *Ghendtsche Tydinghen*, 10 (1981), 28–43 • *City Press* (29 Aug 1888), 4f, 5a–c • *City Press* (19 Jan 1898), 5a–c • *The Times* (20 Jan 1898), 9f • *The Times* (7 Sept 1874), 4f • *The Times* (20 April 1882), 10f • *Journal of the Society of Arts*, 46 (1897–8), 211 • *Exposition internationale*

d'hygiène et de sauvetage de 1876 (Brussels, 1876) • *Official catalogue of the British section* (1889) [exhibition catalogue, Universal Exhibition, Paris, 1889] • *CGPLA Eng. & Wales* (1898)
Likenesses J. Caller, oils, Stedelijke Musea, Dendermonde, Belgium [*see illus.*] • Spy [L. Ward], caricature, watercolour study, NPG; repro. in *VF* (26 Nov 1887) • marble bust, Dendermonde town hall, Belgium • photograph, repro. in *City Press* (19 Jan 1898), 5a–c
Wealth at death £147,419 1s. 6d.: resworn probate, Aug 1898, *CGPLA Eng. & Wales*

Keyser, William de (*c*.1647–*c*.1692), painter, was a native of Antwerp. He was a jeweller by profession, with a large and prosperous business in Antwerp, but occupied his leisure hours:

> early & late constantly studying the Art of Painting. in all kinds. in Water. in Oyl. in Enamel. in large & in Small. from one degree to another. till at lenght [*sic*] he wholly applyd himself to study Painting in Oyl painting as large as Nature. (Vertue, *Note books*, 102)

He executed several altarpieces for churches in Antwerp and one for the English nuns in Dunkirk while he was there 'upon some business relating to Jewelling' (ibid.). It pleased them so much that they persuaded him that he could make his fortune as a painter in England and provided him with an introduction to Lord Melfort, then a favourite at the court of James II. Prompted by this encouragement and his ambition to become a painter rather than a jeweller—a profession that he had never liked, according to Vertue—de Keyser, 'without giving the least notice to his wife & Family at home' (ibid., 103), availed himself of a fair wind and a ship returning to England with a 'Friend or two on board' and was soon in London. There he was well received by Lord Melfort and 'by many people of Quality who had known him a broad' and was introduced to James II, 'who promis'd him encouragement in his Art' (ibid.). He decided to settle in England and concentrate on history painting, and sent for his wife and family with instructions to dispose of his business and effects in Antwerp. His timing was unfortunate, for the revolution of 1688 began soon after their arrival and de Keyser was deprived of his best patrons. He continued to work but his finances were drained by 'hangers on' and his study of the philosopher's stone (ibid.).

De Keyser died in reduced circumstances about 1692, aged forty-five. He left a daughter, whom he had educated as an artist. Her husband, a Mr Humble, 'woud not permitt her' to paint, but after his death she showed 'by her performances to have had a good genius. & paints. in Oyl in small, from the Life, & copys paintings very curiously. & neatly' (Vertue, *Note books*, 103). She died in December 1724. Vertue, who knew her personally, stated that she had several paintings by her father, including a self-portrait and an altarpiece of St Catherine commissioned by the queen for Somerset House chapel, and others that showed him to have studied carefully the style and colouring of the Italian masters. A *St Jerome* after de Keyser is at Nottingham Castle Museum.   ARIANNE BURNETTE

Sources Vertue, *Note books*, vol. 1 • C. Wright, *Old master paintings in Britain* (1976) • *Nottingham Castle Museum and Art Gallery fine art collection handlist* [n.d.] • L. Cust, 'DNB notebooks', NPG, Heinz Archive and Library, Cust papers • *DNB*
Likenesses W. de Keyser, self-portrait

Keyworth, Thomas (1782–1852), Congregational minister, son of Thomas Keyworth, a bookseller of Nottingham, was born in that town. On going to London as a young man, he was converted from Unitarianism by the preaching of Dr Draper, and entered Cheshunt College to prepare himself for the Congregational ministry. Called in the first instance to Sleaford, Lincolnshire, he was afterwards minister successively at Runcorn, Wantage, Faversham, and Nottingham. He also occupied for short periods the pulpits of several London chapels. From 1842 to December 1851 he was in charge of a congregation at Aston Tirrold in Berkshire. He retired at the close of 1851, and died at 8 Hewlett Street, Cheltenham, on 7 November 1852.

Keyworth was distinguished for his modesty and integrity. He was an active advocate of a scheme for garden allotments to the poor, and while in London was active in his support of missionary work. His knowledge of Hebrew is best exemplified by his *Principia Hebraica* (1817, written in conjunction with David Jones), while other works, such as his *Daily Expositor of the New Testament*, illustrate the breadth of his learning.

THOMAS SECCOMBE, *rev.* J. M. V. QUINN

Sources *Congregational Year Book* (1853), 212 • *Liverpool Congregational Magazine* (April 1882), 56 • *Eclectic Review*, new ser., 11 (1819) • private information (1892) • d. cert.
Likenesses R. Woodman, stipple, BM

Keyzer [*née* Mitchell], **Isabella** [Bella] (1922–1992), textile and shipyard worker, and women's activist, was born on 29 August 1922 at 3 Blinshall Street, Dundee, the youngest of three children of Thomas Mitchell (*c*.1880–*c*.1949), a baker, and his second wife, Isabella Campbell (*c*.1897–*c*.1972), a confectionery worker and later a part-time cleaner. She had two stepsisters, from her father's first marriage.

Bella, as she was known, grew up in a two-roomed tenement filled with musical instruments and with books that were mainly political tracts, but included novels by Dickens and poetry by Wordsworth. Her father was an active trade unionist and Labour supporter who named his only son Thomas Lenin, and encouraged political discussion around the house. Bella Mitchell left school in 1936 to train as a weaver and worked in a number of textile factories up to the Second World War. She met her future husband, Dirk Keyzer (*c*.1906–1988), a chief engineer in the Royal Netherlands Navy, during the Second World War, in a local dance-hall, 'where', in her own words, 'many a good woman fell' (interview with Eliz Feeney, DOHP 022). A 'regular Navy man', he was posted to the Dutch West Indies. She was working as a canvas weaver at the time, but left to have her only son. Shortly after his birth in 1941, she became a munitions worker but was dissatisfied with the work, particularly because the night-shift meant she saw little of her son. It was then that she became a welder, 'an individual job that you did with your own skill; it was as individual as hand writing'. About 1942 she left for six weeks' training at Rosyth, and then returned to Dundee to work in the Caledon shipyard. Although this proved a 'very rough environment', she said that the work 'suited my personality, it suited my physique' (interview with Eliz Feeney, DOHP 022). She was made redundant a few months before the end of the war.

After her marriage on 1 November 1949 Bella Keyzer left with her husband and son to live in Holland. In 1957 the family returned to Dundee where her husband worked in the small orders department of Veeder-Root. She was employed in assembly work, but grew disillusioned with labour that lacked the skill, status, and wages of welding. Around 1976, after a refresher course at Dundee Technical College, she successfully applied to re-enter the National Union of General Municipal Workers. She began work in a small factory, but wanted to return to the shipyard. Following a number of rejections she began using the name 'Mr I. Keyser' in her job applications. Eventually she was interviewed and employed by the same firm of shipbuilders she had worked for during the war. According to her, 'They were all expecting this young dolly bird to come doon, and doon comes this fat grey haired wifee' (interview with Eliz Feeney, DOHP 022).

After being interviewed by the Dundee Oral History Project in 1985, Bella Keyzer featured in a number of television programmes, and subsequent publications on women's employment in the twentieth century, including *The World's Ill-Divided* (BBC2, first broadcast in 1987), *Out of the Doll's House* (BBC2, 1988), and *Scotland's War* (for Scottish Television, 1989). Although often presented on television and in publications as the typically assertive Dundonian woman, Bella Keyzer was never at ease with this description, stressing instead her feelings of isolation in her personal battle for equality of opportunity. In 1992 Dundee district council presented her with a special award in recognition of her work to promote women's equality in Dundee. She died at Roxburgh House, a hospice attached to the Royal Victoria Hospital, Dundee, on 18 July 1992, and her remains were cremated on 22 July at Dundee crematorium.   GRAHAM R. SMITH

Sources E. Feeney, Interview with Bella Keyzer, recording and transcript, 14–25 Nov 1985, Dundee Central Library, Wellgate Centre, Dundee, Dundee Oral History Project, DOHP 022 · R. MacAuley, *Bella*, with introduction, 1992 [unpublished, DOHP 022] · *Courier and Advertiser* (16 June 1988) · E. Feeney and C. Ritchie, Interview with Thomas Lenin Mitchell, recording and transcript, 8 Jan–20 Feb 1986, Dundee Central Library, Wellgate Centre, Dundee, Dundee Oral History Project, DOHP 028 · A. Holdsworth, *Out of the doll's house: the story of women in the twentieth century* (1988) · G. R. Smith, '"None can compare": from the oral history of a community', *The Dundee book: an anthology of living in the city*, ed. B. Kay (1990), 169–98 · S. Robertson and L. Wilson, *Scotland's war* (1995) · 'The world's illdivided', Dundee Oral History Project, Open Space film and booklet, 29 July 1987 [first broadcast on BBC 2] · personal knowledge (2004) · b. cert. · m. cert. · d. cert.
Archives SOUND Dundee Central Library, Dundee Oral History Project, tapes and transcriptions, DOHP 022
Likenesses photographs, *c.*1943, repro. in 'The world's illdivided', Dundee Oral History Project · photograph, repro. in *Courier and Advertiser* (10 March 1992)

Khaliquzzaman, Choudhry (1889–1973), politician in India and Pakistan, was born on 25 December 1889 in Chunar, in the district of Mirzapur, of the North-Western Provinces of India. He was the fourth of the eight children of Sheikh Mohammad Zaman, an assistant *tahsildar* in British service, and his second wife, Maqboolunnisa Begum, the youngest daughter of Choudhri Riyasat Ali of Bhilwal. He had five brothers and two sisters. Khaliquzzaman was educated at the Jubilee High School, Lucknow, and the Muhammadan Anglo-Oriental College, Aligarh, from which he graduated finally with a BA and LLB in 1916.

At Aligarh, Khaliquzzaman formed friendships with young Muslims like himself who were to push the All-India Muslim League in a radical direction; he also came under the influence of the charismatic pan-Islamist politician Muhammad Ali. In 1912–13 he joined Dr Ansari's Red Crescent mission to assist the Turkish wounded in the Tripoli war. In 1916 he both joined the Indian National Congress and became joint secretary of the All-India Muslim League. In 1917 he began to practise as junior to Muhammad Nasim, the leader of the Oudh bar. In 1919 he assisted the 'ulama' of Firangi Mahal in setting up the central Khilafat committee to press for the protection of the Turkish caliphate and the holy places of Islam. In the non-co-operation movement which followed, in alliance with the Congress led by Gandhi, Khaliquzzaman was the leading political figure in Lucknow, presiding over its Congress committee and going to gaol from December 1921 to December 1922 for his civil disobedience activities.

From 1922 to 1937 Khaliquzzaman took a nationalist stance. He regarded Motilal Nehru as his leader, supporting Nehru's Swaraj Party. At the same time he was chairman of the Lucknow municipal board, 1923–5 and 1929–32. In 1928 he supported Nehru's proposals for a constitutional future for India (the Nehru report) without separate electorates for minorities. In 1929 he was secretary of Dr Ansari's newly-formed Muslim Nationalist Party, which was to fight for Muslim interests within the Congress; and in 1930 he was nominated president of the Congress at a time when government had declared it illegal. From 1932 he was secretary of the Muslim Unity Board, which won one third of the Muslim seats in the 1934 elections to the central legislative assembly. In 1936 he helped to make a deal with M. A. Jinnah on behalf of the board which permitted anti-landlord elements in Muslim politics to have a major voice on the Muslim League parliamentary board. Through this arrangement on 8 February 1935, Khaliquzzaman rejoined the League.

The events surrounding the 1937 general elections were a defining moment in the life of Khaliquzzaman and also in the fortunes of the All-India Muslim League. After the Congress won a substantial victory in the United Provinces, it refused Khaliquzzaman's offer of a coalition with the League, the talks breaking down in part over the number of places to be found for Leaguers in the cabinet, but in the main because the Congress insisted on completely absorbing the League party in the assembly. From now on Khaliquzzaman was leader of the opposition and devoted his energies to the revival of the All-India Muslim League, seconding its Pakistan Resolution on 23 March 1940. He was a League member of the United Provinces legislative assembly until 1947 and a key figure in the leadership at all-India level. After partition Khaliquzzaman did not immediately go to Pakistan, being elected to the Indian constituent assembly and accepting from Jinnah the leadership of the Muslims of independent India. In October 1947, however, he migrated to Pakistan.

Khaliquzzaman's career in Pakistan was less successful. From 1948 to 1950 he was president of the Muslim League. In 1950 he launched his abortive Islamistan movement to create a confederation of Muslim countries. In 1953 he was made governor of East Pakistan but resigned in 1954 when governor's rule was proclaimed there. He was ambassador to Indonesia in 1954–6 and founded the Convention Muslim League in 1962 to support President Ayub Khan and the new Pakistan constitution.

Khaliquzzaman was married first in 1910 to his cousin Fasih-un-Nisa, daughter of Muhammad Nasim, and second in 1930 to Zahida Khatoon, the niece of Haji Istafa Khan, the owner of the well-known Lucknow perfumers Asghar Ali Muhammad Ali. Both wives migrated to Pakistan, the first living the life of a traditional Muslim housewife in Larkana, Sind, and the second living with her husband in Karachi. After falling into a coma, Khaliquzzaman died in Karachi on 17 May 1973 and was buried in the Mewa Shah graveyard there. He was survived by five sons and four daughters from his marriages; his second wife was a poet and minister in the West Pakistan government. Khaliquzzaman was of medium build, habitually wore a moustache, and was known by his friends as Khaliq. He was widely respected as a shrewd, tough, individualistic and, at times, controversial politician. In his frank autobiography, *Pathway to Pakistan* (1961), in which he was critical of Jinnah, he also declared that 'the greatest sacrifice I made for the Muslim cause was my dissociation with my loving and affectionate Hindu friends' (Khaliquzzaman, 342).

FRANCIS ROBINSON

Sources C. Khaliquzzaman, *Pathway to Pakistan* (1961) · F. Robinson, *Separatism among Indian Muslims: the politics of the United Provinces' Muslims, 1860–1923* (1974) · N. K. Jain, ed., *Muslims in India: a biographical dictionary*, 2 vols. (1979–83) · *Dawn* (19 May 1973)
Archives FILM Television interview 'In Retrospect' on Pakistan Television 1970

Khama the Great (c.1835–1923), chief of the Ngwato, was born at Mashu in Ngwato country, in what later became Botswana. Son and heir of Sekogma I (c.1795–1883), Khama grew up in years of relative peace. In his early twenties, to his father's annoyance, he fell under the influence of an itinerant evangelist and in May 1860 was baptized a Christian. John Mackenzie of the London Missionary Society, missionary at Shoshong from 1862 to 1876, became his mentor. Khama remained a devout Christian and an extreme teetotaller, regarded by many Europeans as the exemplar of an African Christian. On 22 May 1862 he married Mogatsamocwasele, known as Mma-Bessie (d. December 1889). It is possible that he had had an earlier marriage. Fierce internal dissensions were common in the Ngwato chiefdom and in 1872, at a time when the Ngwato were beginning to be exposed to new forces of colonial expansion, Khama briefly seized power before restoring

Khama the Great (c.1835–1923), by Elliott & Fry, pubd 1902

his father as chief. In 1875 he deposed his father and from then until his death ruled the chiefdom.

Khama first appealed to the British to act against the Boer trekkers entering his country from the east in 1876. Although nothing was done immediately, the British came to see him as an ally in keeping open the 'road to the north' or 'missionaries' road'—the corridor which ran west of the Transvaal. Khama was delighted when in 1885 a British expeditionary force arrived in the area to expel Boer 'filibusters' and when its leader, Sir Charles Warren, declared a British protectorate over Bechuanaland, including the lands of the Ngwato. Mackenzie, who accompanied Warren, persuaded Khama to offer the British some frontier farmland for the settlement of white Christians, an offer which was not accepted.

In 1895 Khama heard that the British government proposed to transfer the administration of his country to Rhodes's British South Africa Company. With two other Tswana chiefs, he travelled to England to oppose such a transfer. Queen Victoria presented him with a Bible, in which she wrote that that book was the secret of his greatness. Joseph Chamberlain, the colonial secretary, promised the chiefs that they would remain under the queen's protection, though they did agree to cede a narrow strip of territory for the building of a railway to the north.

Khama returned to Bechuanaland to find his European-educated son and heir, Sekogma, in effective control. Disliking Sekogma and suspecting him of wanting to usurp power, Khama in October 1897 forced his son into exile. Khama then married in 1900 a twenty-one-year-old schoolteacher, Semane Setlhoko (1878/9–1937), who bore him a son, Tshekedi *Khama (1905–1959), when he was seventy (he had earlier been married to Elisabetha, his second known wife). In 1907 he recognized Tshekedi as his heir, disowning Sekogma. However, when Khama had a minor accident in 1916, Sekogma returned to Serowe, beginning a process of reconciliation which led in 1920 to his being made heir in place of Tshekedi. Sekogma married, produced an heir, and succeeded Khama, but Khama's prior recognition of Tshekedi helped to fuel tensions in the chiefdom long after his death. He died of pneumonia in his capital of Serowe, in the Bechuanaland protectorate on 21 February 1923, and was buried at Serowe Hill.

Courteous and athletic, Khama's authoritarianism nevertheless estranged him from many of his senior relatives. A pragmatic ruler of the largest reserve in the British protectorate, he proved himself a shrewd entrepreneur, who launched a trading company which was so successful that rivals persuaded the British to close it down in 1916. He continued to receive strong moral support from Christian nonconformists in Britain, and the regard in which he was held, as a Christian gentleman, helped to ensure that the British did not hand over Bechuanaland to either Southern Rhodesia or South Africa.

CHRISTOPHER SAUNDERS

Sources Q. N. Parsons, 'Khama III, the Bamangwato and the British, 1895–1923', PhD diss., U. Edin., 1973 · A. Sillery, 'Kgama III', *DSAB* · A. Sillery, *Founding a protectorate: history of Bechuanaland, 1885–1895* (1965) · J. Chirenje, *Chief Kgama and his times: the story of a southern African ruler* (1978) · Q. N. Parsons, *The word of Khama* (1972) · A. Sillery, *Botswana: a short political history* (1974) · A. Dachs, *Khama of Botswana* (1971) · D. Wylie, *A little god: the twilight of patriarchy in a southern African chiefdom* (1990) · J. Mockford, *Khama: king of the Bamangwato* (1931) · A. Sillery, *John Mackenzie of Bechuanaland* (1971) · Q. N. Parsons, *King Khama, Emperor Joe and the Great White Queen* (1997)

Archives PRO, CO records · SOAS, London Missionary Society MSS

Likenesses Elliott & Fry, photograph, pubd 1902, NPG [*see illus.*] · photographs, repro. in W. C. Willoughby, *Native life on the Transvaal border* (1900) · photographs, repro. in Dachs, *Khama of Botswana* · photographs, repro. in Parsons, *The word of Khama* · photographs, SOAS, London Missionary Society MSS · portrait, South African Library, Cape Town, South Africa

Khama, Sir Seretse (1921–1980), president of Botswana, was born on 1 July 1921 in the royal household at Serowe in the Bechuanaland protectorate, the son of Sekgoma Khama (*c*.1864–1925) and his wife, Tebogo Kabailele (*c*.1900–1930). He was named Seretse, meaning the clay that binds, because his birth marked the final reconciliation after twenty-three years of strife between his father and his grandfather *Khama the Great, *kgosi* or paramount chief of the Ngwato people from 1875 to 1923. Seretse's mother had been chosen by Khama to be the ageing Sekgoma's new bride. Sekgoma died in 1925 and four-year-old Seretse was proclaimed *kgosi*, with his young uncle Tshekedi *Khama (1905–1959) as regent until he came of age. In 1930, after Tebogo's death, Tshekedi became Seretse's sole guardian. An unhappy and often sickly orphan, Seretse was passed between a series of boarding-schools in South Africa, until he blossomed in adolescence as a sportsman and a prefect. He then entered the South African Native College and took a general BA degree in 1944, after which he sailed to England in August 1945 for a legal education. Precluded from first-year examinations at Balliol College, Oxford, after the belated discovery that he lacked the required Latin, he enrolled at the Inner Temple, London, to train as a barrister.

On 29 September 1948 Seretse married an Englishwoman, Ruth Williams (1923–2002), daughter of a retired army officer. The couple had three sons and a daughter.

Sir Seretse Khama (1921–1980), by unknown photographer, *c*.1970

Reacting badly to news of the marriage, Tshekedi ordered him home to account for himself; but in a series of public meetings at Serowe between November 1948 and June 1949 the obvious sincerity of Seretse turned the Ngwato against the imperious Tshekedi. Seretse was tumultuously proclaimed as *kgosi* and Tshekedi retired to disgruntled self-exile. White settler politicians in South Africa and the Rhodesias sprang into action and intimated to the British government, both privately and publicly, that a black chief with a white wife in a neighbouring colony would undermine the whole basis of white (and male) supremacy in Africa. The Labour government, behoven as it was to South Africa for economic and strategic reasons, particularly for gold and uranium, could not admit to bowing before white racism. Its new Commonwealth relations minister, Patrick Gordon *Walker, uttered untruths before parliament; and Britain's high commissioner in southern Africa, Sir Evelyn Baring, set up a judicial inquiry to prove Seretse's unfitness to rule. However, it rendered the contrary opinion and its report was therefore suppressed for thirty years. Seretse and his wife were then induced or deceived into surrendering themselves into exile in England in 1951—an exile that was declared permanent by a Conservative government in 1952.

The shoddy treatment of the Khamas by successive British governments aroused widespread indignation and support from sections of the British press and from the public, ranging from Liberals through Scottish and colonial nationalists to communists and advocates of the hereditary principle. Seretse Khama's exile was not ended until 1956 when a new Commonwealth relations secretary, Alec Douglas-Home, then the fourteenth earl of Home, began to distance British policy from South African apartheid.

Until 1963 Seretse was barred from chieftainship, by which time he had become a republican nationalist happy to remain a commoner. His moderate Democratic Party swept the polls in the first general election of 1965, and he became the first president of the Republic of Botswana in 1966, soon after he received a knighthood from the queen. The new government inherited the poorest economy in Africa, and was noted for its extreme caution. It was often dismissed as a South African or British pawn. The groundwork was laid for the take-off of beef exports and of diamond and copper-nickel mining. President Khama sought out key foreign friends across the ideological spectrum for a liberal democracy, struggling to be as free as possible from its unstable white-ruled neighbours. He confronted traditionalist chiefs obstructing the growth of local democracy, and promoted the rule of law, regular parliamentary elections, and efficiency in administration. Government policy then was that mineral revenues were to be invested in infrastructure for equitable rural development, though the results may now be seen as having promoted economic inequity and the growth of 'cattle barons' investing in urban rather than rural growth.

Known among statesmen for his integrity, infectious humour, and puncturing of pomposity, Seretse Khama struggled against ill health (he had suffered from diabetes since 1960). In 1976 and 1977 he underwent open-heart surgery eight times. He was kept alive by the devoted attention of his wife, Lady Khama, and by a personal drive to achieve final ends. In 1979 Seretse Khama was made a GCB by Queen Elizabeth during her visit to Botswana, and his eldest son, Seretse Ian, became the first *kgosi* of the Ngwato to be installed since 1925.

While Botswana was buffeted by the effects of insurrection in Rhodesia, South-West Africa, and South Africa, Seretse Khama developed a clear vision of the future beyond colonialism and apartheid. He worked hard to bring the independent states of the region together in what became the Southern African Development Community. But years of shuttle diplomacy by air to negotiate peace and harmony in the region led to final exhaustion. After the satisfaction of seeing Zimbabwe achieve its independence in March 1980, and the formal launching of his organization for regional development in April the same year, Seretse Khama died at State House, Gaborone, the capital of Botswana, on 13 July 1980, and was buried on the 20th in the royal graveyard at Serowe Hill. He was survived by Lady Khama.   Q. N. PARSONS

Sources T. Tlou and others, *Seretse Khama, 1921–1980* (1995) · M. Dutfield, *A marriage of inconvenience: the persecution of Ruth and Seretse Khama* (1990) · M. Benson, *Tshekedi Khama* (1960) · J. Redfern, *Ruth and Seretse: 'A Very Disreputable Transaction'* (1955) · J. Holm and P. Molutsi, eds., *Democracy in Botswana* (1989) · J. Parson, *Botswana: liberal democracy and the labor reserve* (1984) · J. Parson, ed., *Succession to high office in Botswana* (1990) · L. A. Picard, ed., *The evolution of modern Botswana* (1985) · L. A. Picard, *The politics of development in Botswana* (1987) · L. Frank, 'Khama and Jonathan: leadership struggles in contemporary southern Africa', *Journal of Developing Areas*, 15 (1981), 173–98 · London Missionary Society · private information (2004)

Archives Khama Memorial Museum, Serowe, Botswana, family MSS | Botswana National Archives, Gaborone, Office of President Series, etc. · PRO, MSS, marked 'Bamangwato affairs', DO 35 series · U. Lond., Institute of Commonwealth Studies, Michael Crowder MSS | FILM BFI NFTVA, news footage · Radio Botswana, Gaborone, films | SOUND Radio Botswana, Gaborone, recorded talk

Likenesses photograph, *c.*1970, Hult. Arch. [*see illus.*] · bronze statue, National Assembly, Gaborone · bronze statue, Serowe, above Kgotla · bronze statue, Mall, Selebi-Phikwe · photographs, Hult. Arch. · portrait, priv. coll. · portrait, De Beers Botswana, Gaborone

Wealth at death estate to wife

Khama, Tshekedi (1905–1959), political leader in Bechuanaland, was born on 17 September 1905 at Serowe in the Bechuanaland protectorate, the younger child and only son of *Khama the Great (*c.*1835–1923), *kgosi e kgolo* (paramount chief or king) of the Ngwato, and his fourth wife, the young, low-born Semane Setlhoko (1878/9–1937). Tshekedi first went to school at Serowe in 1912 and then in 1916 to Lovedale, the Church of Scotland institution in Cape Province. In 1923 he entered the South African Native College at Fort Hare. Tshekedi's half-brother was Sekgoma, rightful heir to the kingdom. Khama quarrelled with Sekgoma and declared Tshekedi, in a will, as his heir, though this was set aside when Khama and Sekgoma were reconciled from 1916 onwards. The reign of Sekgoma II, following his assumption of power on Khama's death in February 1923, was brief but controversial, and continued the dynastic disputes which had marred Khama's reign. Sekgoma died on the morning of Sunday 15 November 1925. His heir, Seretse *Khama (1921–1980), was a minor. In consequence, Tshekedi was declared regent for the duration of Seretse's minority and a council of advisers was agreed in order to help the weak Gorewan Kgamane, Tshekedi's senior royal relative, during the years of Tshekedi's absence at college.

Tshekedi realized that if the region and its disparate peoples were to be kept united under royal authority, then he needed to act decisively. On 9 January 1926 he was installed as regent, and his first act was to abolish the council. Distrustful of the progressive but unpopular Ratshosa family, who had hoped to maintain their influence, he removed Johnnie Ratshosa from his position as his secretary and subsequently humiliated the family by commanding them to attend a *kgotla*, or tribal assembly, on a day when they ought to have been attending a wedding. When they refused they were brought to the *kgotla* and, despite their status, sentenced to a flogging. Simon and Obeditse Ratshosa, in their fury, attempted to assassinate Tshekedi. This allowed Tshekedi to strengthen his hold on the chieftaincy. He banished those members of the Ratshosa family not in prison, and destroyed their property, and he silenced family criticism from his own half-sisters by banishing them. Then, as later, Tshekedi tended to detect dynastic rivalry rather than political processes influenced by changed economic circumstances.

Although Tshekedi secured the support of the privy council for his traditional right to destroy the property of his enemies, the outcome was that Charles Rey, an energetic but impatient British high commissioner (1930–37), was charged with the development of a proclamation to regulate the powers of the chieftaincy. He and Tshekedi were bound to be in conflict: with great shrewdness, Tshekedi was able to mediate between the tribe and the protectorate authorities in ways which enabled him to manipulate 'tradition', while claiming legitimacy in terms of the settlement achieved between the Bechuana chiefs and Joseph Chamberlain in London in 1895. Thus in 1930 Tshekedi attempted to manipulate the regimental system so as to secure communal labour for the desilting of the Serowe Dam. This led to appeals to the British administration against the brutality with which the call was enforced. Tshekedi nevertheless overreached himself in 1933 when he had a philandering white youth, Phineas McIntosh, flogged in the *kgotla*. Although the issue of legality quickly became confused by notions of racial hierarchy, Tshekedi had support from members of the white community in Serowe. The overreacting Rey suspended Tshekedi from the regency and a detachment of marines was sent from Cape Town, with field guns, in a crude display of imperial authority. At the subsequent inquiry, Admiral E. R. G. R. *Evans, acting high commissioner, described Tshekedi as 'extremely capable' but having the faults of 'selfishness' and as preoccupied with the 'study of [his] own personal rights and privileges' (Wylie, 92). Tshekedi was banished from office and, for political reasons, just as quickly restored.

The concern for chiefly rights and Ngwato custom was a hallmark of Tshekedi's attitude towards the protectorate administration. As regent, he was essentially a steward, but sought to maintain the authority of the chiefs. One of his worries was that a codicil to the act establishing the union of South Africa envisaged the transfer, subject to securing the agreement of the chiefs, of Bechuanaland, along with the other high commission territories, to South African administration. The issue dramatically resurfaced in South Africa during the 1930s, under the political leadership of J. M. B. Hertzog. Tshekedi, who consulted many others on the issue, saw a larger political purpose in the maintenance of chiefly authority, preferably under British supervision. He was to become the main voice of opposition to the South African government's ambitions in the region. Believing in the power of law to constrain social change, he contested Charles Rey's reforms. These would have established tribal councils, demoted the *kgotla*, and given the administration the power to recognize chiefs. Although the special court upheld the legal validity of the proclamations, the Bechuanaland chiefs refused to co-operate. C. Arden-Clarke, who formally replaced Rey (1937–42), eventually worked out a compromise with Tshekedi which restored the power of the *kgotla* and established tribal treasuries. In 1936 Tshekedi married Bagakgametse Moloi, but this marriage speedily ended in divorce. In 1938 he married Ella Moshoela and they had five children.

During the Second World War Tshekedi backed the British. He vigorously encouraged men to enlist but cannily secured an agreement that they would not be associated in any way with the South African army. Nevertheless, his robust methods of calling for enlistment were unpopular, and turned minds to thoughts of Seretse who, by 1944, was nearing graduation. Tshekedi successfully faced down Smuts, who in 1942 called for the transfer of the administration 'if only as a reward' for South African support. Tshekedi was also quick, after the end of the war, to bring the issue of South Africa's ambition to incorporate South-West Africa to the attention of the United Nations. He alerted the Anti-Slavery Society, published a pamphlet entitled *The Case for Bechuanaland*, and commissioned Michael Scott to put the issue of South-West Africa directly to the United Nations.

Tshekedi reacted badly to the news, received during September 1948, that Seretse, then studying in London, intended to marry Ruth Williams, a white Englishwoman. Seretse nevertheless went ahead with the marriage and returned to Serowe to face his disapproving uncle and the rest of the family. Initially, and with the support of traditionalists, Tshekedi, a forceful and persuasive speaker, managed to maintain the upper hand. It was not until a third *kgotla*, held during the week of Monday 20 June 1949, that events began to move against Tshekedi. The latter, who had been busy protecting his own cattle interests and tribute, rapidly lost the support of the *kgotla* when others successfully alleged that he wished to keep the chiefship for himself. On the Thursday of that week, by the will of the *kgotla*, the democratically inclined Seretse was acclaimed *kgosi* (or paramount chief).

Tshekedi prudently removed himself and his followers from Gammangwato to Rametsana, in the Kweneng, where his own father had gone into temporary exile. Because he did not accept the legality of the acclamation, he launched an official dispute. However, by attempting to uphold customary law, Tshekedi looked increasingly like a reactionary, and he unwittingly handed a lever to the South African government. Intent on the institutionalization of apartheid and with an eye on incorporation, the South Africans objected both to Seretse's marriage with a white woman, and also to Seretse's election as chief. The British government acquiesced in this view and Seretse was banished in 1950 to the United Kingdom. Tshekedi was banished from the district at the same time. Not easily put down, Tshekedi, in the face of bitter local opposition which blamed him, unjustly, for Seretse's banishment, secured his own return in August 1952 as an ordinary citizen. The British administration, faced with unrest, were anxious to gain Tshekedi's political support for Rasebolai Kgamane, Tshekedi's ally and relative, whom they appointed 'African Authority' (1953–64) in Serowe. Tshekedi, who also served on protectorate-level consultative institutions, continued to work with energy and vision for an economic future for Bechuanaland on a basis other than that of a South African 'labour reserve'. He was not reconciled with Seretse until the middle of 1956 when he took the initiative to go to London to secure Seretse's return. Tshekedi realized that Seretse's authority was needed if the possibility of a beneficial agreement between a mining company and the Ngwato, who owned the mineral rights, were ever to become a reality. On 15 August they were able to make a joint statement to Alec Douglas-Home, the secretary of state for Commonwealth affairs, in which Seretse renounced the chieftaincy. The family dispute was closed, and on 10 October Seretse Khama returned from exile. Democratic reform was initiated and a tribal council established at last.

A triumvirate consisting of Tshekedi, Seretse, and Rasebolai became the focus of political life. Tshekedi, by nature and experience less democratic than Seretse, nevertheless worked with the others to consolidate local democracy and to push for national constitutional change (which reached fruition in 1966 when Seretse was elected the first president of the republic of Botswana). They were seen by the administration as 'three damned sensible men', although the council was not an immediate democratic showpiece, for the three were undoubtedly the dominant figures (Tlou and others, 159). Tshekedi's much looked-for economic success was to come in 1959 when an agreement for mineral development in the country was signed on 2 June with Rhodesian Selection Trust. Tshekedi's health gave way shortly afterwards. He was rushed, with Ella Khama, to London for urgent medical treatment, but died in the London Clinic from kidney failure on 10 June 1959. His body was returned to Serowe, where he was buried at the Khama burial-ground on 17 June, witnessed by the greatest crowd seen there since the interment of Khama the Great.　　　　　WILLIE HENDERSON

Sources T. Tlou and others, *Seretse Khama, 1921–1980* (1995) · D. Wylie, *A little god: the twilight of patriarchy in a southern African chiefdom* (1990) · J. Parson, ed., *Succession to high office in Botswana: three case studies* (1990) · N. Parsons, 'Shots for a black republic: Simon Ratshosa and Botswana nationalism', *African Affairs*, 73 (1974), 383–408 · M. Crowder, *The flogging of Phineas McIntosh: a tale of colonial folly and injustice, Bechuanaland, 1933* (1988) · A. Sillery, *The Bechuanaland Protectorate* (1952) · M. Benson, *Tshekedi Khama* (1960) · M. Crowder, 'Tshekedi Khama and mining in Botswana, 1925–1951', *Organisation and economic change*, ed. A. Mabin (1989), vol. 5 of *Southern African Studies*, 146–67 · M. Crowder, 'Tshekedi Khama and opposition to the British administration of the Bechuanaland protectorate, 1926–1936', *Journal of African History*, 26 (1985), 193–214 · M. Crowder, 'Tshekedi Khama, Smuts, and South-West Africa', *Journal of Modern African Studies*, 265/1 (1987), 25–42 · J. Ramsay, B. Morton, and F. Morton, eds., *Historical dictionary of Botswana*, 3rd edn (1996) · *DNB*

Archives Bodl. RH, papers | Bodl. RH, V. F. Ellenberger MSS; N. V. Redman MSS; Sillery MSS · Bodl. RH, papers relating to deputation to J. H. Thomas · Botswana National Archives, Bamangwato tribal archives; Ngwato Kgotla records

Likenesses group portrait, photograph, 1947, repro. in Wiley, *Little god* · B. Hardy, photograph, 1950, Hult. Arch. · photograph, 1950, Hult. Arch. · G. Robertson, photograph, 1951, Hutlon Getty · S. Charoux, bust, repro. in *DNB* · photographs, Museum of Africa, Johannesburg, South Africa

Wealth at death substantial cattle holdings

Khan Sahib (1883–1958), politician, was born in the village of Utmanzai in the Peshawar district where his father, Khan Behram Khan, was an influential Muhammadzai landowner. With his younger brother, Abdul Ghaffar *Khan, who later became known as the Frontier Gandhi,

he was educated at the Peshawar municipal board high school, and the Edwardes Memorial Mission School; it is possible that he studied medicine in Bombay before proceeding, with a very promising academic record, to Britain to study medicine. He qualified in 1917, having done part of his training at St Thomas's Hospital, where he continued to work for a time. He married his second wife, Mary, an Englishwoman, then sat successfully for the Indian Medical Service (IMS) and returned to India. In 1920 he resigned, with the rank of captain, and set up in private practice in Nowshera.

The 1919 Government of India Act did not concede a measure of responsible government to the North-West Frontier Province, and this precipitated a new birth of political consciousness among the Pakhtuns. Abdul Ghaffar Khan, who had kept to the traditional ways of the Pakhtun tribesman and had become the most outstanding personality in the province, became the leader of the Khudai Khidmatgar ('Servants of God') organization, better known as the Red Shirts. It was not long before Khan Sahib, who had made friends with Jawaharlal Nehru in London and through him had come under the influence of M. K. Gandhi, decided to abandon medicine and join his brother. The alliance between the Muslim Pakhtuns and the Hindu-dominated Congress Party was a development of the greatest political importance which only the Khan brothers could have brought about.

Frequent clashes between the Red Shirts and the government led to the organization's being declared illegal in December 1931 and to the arrest and imprisonment of both brothers. They were then externed from the province. A considerable part of his exile was spent by Khan Sahib at Gandhi's headquarters in the Central Provinces. The agitation for political advance in the North-West Frontier Province was, however, successful and in 1932 it was raised to the status of a governor's province. Dr Khan Sahib was permitted to return to the frontier in May 1935 as a result of his election to the central legislative assembly. The Congress was still technically illegal, but it was permitted in November 1934 to contest the province's central legislative assembly seat, which was made elective that year. Khan Sahib decisively defeated his two opponents. It was not until 1937 that Congress agreed to accept office in the government of the newly autonomous province under the 1935 Government of India Act, and in that year Khan Sahib became chief minister. His first term of office was marked by economic reforms such as the Agricultural Debtors' Relief Act, but also by controversial legislation such as the abolition of the office of *zaildar*, which alienated the sympathies of the large landowners. Nevertheless, his worth as an incorruptible and conscientious administrator was proved beyond question.

After the outbreak of the Second World War in 1939 Khan Sahib resigned office and was again placed under detention, with his brother. The resignation was against his own inclination, but was dictated by the All-India National Congress. He himself sympathized with the British, although party policy called for campaigns against the war effort in 1940 and 1942. Such campaigns were desultory and spasmodic.

Khan Sahib returned to power as chief minister in 1945 after the fall in March of the Muslim League ministry of Aurangzeb Khan. He remained in office until the transfer of power in 1947. At this period, however, he misjudged the political trend. The end to his hopes of maintaining the Congress alliance and the unity of India came with the referendum of July 1947, when the Pakhtuns opted for Pakistan. The Khan brothers were regarded as hostile to Pakistan and were arrested by the new government of M. A. Jinnah in 1948. Abdul Ghaffar went to gaol for a considerable period while Khan Sahib remained under strict surveillance for three years. While his brother remained irreconcilable, he himself recognized that Pakistan had come to stay and that the cause of Pakhtun advancement would best be served by co-operation. Even so the Muslim League leaders were slow to forgive him and it was not until 1954 that he emerged from obscurity. In that year he was appointed minister of communications in the new coalition government at the centre, led by Muhammad Ali Bogra. In October 1955 he became chief minister of the newly integrated West Pakistan. The split with his brother, who bitterly opposed the merger of its provinces into one unit, was now complete.

In the years of political turmoil which were to lead to the revolution that put President Ayub into power at the end of 1958, Khan Sahib's stature steadily grew. When the Muslim League leaders, some of whom remained inveterate in their hostility to him, defected from his coalition, he formed a new Republican Party which retained a majority, albeit a shaky one, until president's rule was temporarily imposed in West Pakistan in March 1957. In December he formed an anti-Muslim League group in the central assembly, and it was a measure of the general respect in which he was held that the members of all parties in this group, which outnumbered the League, pledged their support to the premiership of any person nominated by him.

In Lahore on 9 May 1958 Khan Sahib was murdered by Ata Mohammad, a petty official with a grievance. The event had no political significance but was a tragedy for Pakistan. Khan Sahib was a man of exceptional qualities. Quiet, patient, and courteous in manner, incorruptible and of deep sincerity, he had the stature of a statesman. He was loved for his warm-heartedness and integrity by his people and indeed by persons of all races with whom he came into contact.

He had two sons from his first marriage—the elder of whom made some mark in politics and was for a short time a minister of the West Pakistan government—and a son and a daughter with his English wife, Mary.

F. M. INNES, *rev.* IAN TALBOT

Sources E. Jansson, *India, Pakistan or Pakhtunistan? the nationalist movements in the North-West Frontier Province, 1937–47* (1981) • N. K. Jain, ed., *Muslims in India: a biographical dictionary*, 2 (1983) • M. Desai, *Two servants of God* (1935) • A. K. Gupta, *North West Frontier Province: legislature and freedom struggle, 1932–47* (1976) • A. Qaiyum, *Gold and guns on the Pathan frontier* (Bombay, 1945) • J. Spain, *The Pathan borderland* (1963) • D. G. Tendulkar, *Abdul Ghaffar Khan* (1967) • private information (1971) • personal knowledge (1971)
Archives BL OIOC, Caroe MSS, Cunningham MSS

Khan, Abdul Ghaffar (1890–1988), Pakhtun nationalist, was born in the village of Utmanzai in the Peshawar district of the North-West Frontier Province. He was the fourth child of Khan Behram Khan, an influential Muhammadzai landlord. Following admission to a mosque school at the age of five, he was educated at the municipal board high school, Peshawar, and the Edwardes Memorial Mission School. He quit before completing his studies, to obtain an army commission. He reportedly abandoned this career because he had witnessed a British subaltern insulting an Indian officer. He then restlessly spent a brief spell in a school at Campbellpur and attended the Muhammadan Anglo-Oriental College, Aligarh. Behram Khan wanted him to follow his elder brother, *Khan Sahib, to England for studies, but this plan also fell through.

Despite his own chequered education, Abdul Ghaffar Khan worked from 1910 onwards to popularize schooling among the unlettered Pakhtun tribesmen of the frontier. The Pakhtun nationalist the Haji of Turangzai encouraged his endeavours. He was also influenced at this time by the Muslim seminary at Deoband which he clandestinely visited, and by the writings of Maulana Abul Kalam Azad, who later became the most prominent Muslim Congressman.

Abdul Ghaffar Khan clashed with the British in April 1919, when he organized a public meeting at Utmanzai to protest against the Rowlatt Act, which curtailed Indian legal rights in case of emergency. He was arrested but was released shortly afterwards. He thus embarked on a life of prolonged spells of imprisonment by both the British and Pakistani authorities. After his release he led a party of *muhajarins* (religious refugees) to Afghanistan in August 1920 during the Khilafat movement of protest against the treatment of the *khilafat*, the sultan of Turkey, after the First World War by the victorious allies. He soon retraced his steps convinced of the futility of *hijrat* (religious flight) and attended the December Nagpur session of the Indian National Congress. This session was dominated by the Gandhians, who adopted the creed of non-violent non-co-operation which became the guiding principle of his own public career. Indeed, in later years he was known as the Frontier Gandhi. He resumed his educational activities in 1921, opening an Azad high school at Utmanzai and forming the Anjuman Islah-ul-Afghania (Society for the Reform of the Afghans) to carry on his work. By this date he had also been elected president of the provincial Khilafat committee. His anti-British activities culminated in arrest on 17 December 1921. The poor diet in the frontier and Punjab gaols in which he served his three-year sentence undermined his health. But his spirit was unvanquished, he mixed freely with Hindu and Sikh prisoners, and for the first time read the Hindu scriptural text, the Gita, and the

Abdul Ghaffar Khan (1890–1988), by Narayan Vinayak Virkar

Sikh scripture, the Granth Sahib. On his release his followers honoured him with the title Fakhr-i-Afghan (the Pride of the Afghans).

Shortly afterwards he proceeded on *haj* to Mecca with his second wife and her elder sister. The pilgrimage ended tragically in Jerusalem, where his wife fell to her death from a staircase leaving a son, Abdul Ali, and a daughter, Mehar Taj. Abdul Ghaffar Khan's first wife, who had borne him two sons, Ghani and Wali Khan, had also died prematurely, during an influenza epidemic. Ghaffar Khan did not remarry after this second tragedy.

In May 1928 Abdul Ghaffar Khan launched the monthly Pashto language journal, the *Pakhtun*, which thereafter served as his mouthpiece. Through its columns he expounded his philosophy of Pakhtun nationalism, moral and social reform, non-violence, and Islam. The following year he embodied these ideals in a new grass-roots party called the Afghan Jirga. Three months later, in November 1929, he launched a parallel organization, the Khudai Khidmatgars ('Servants of God'), which was established on quasi-military lines. This movement soon overshadowed the Afghan Jirga. Its members wore uniforms dyed with red brick dust, since their ordinary white clothing showed the dirt too easily. The British thereafter dubbed them the Red Shirts.

Abdul Ghaffar Khan toured the frontier to enrol Khudai Khidmatgars. He both called on the people to reform their social and religious condition, and articulated the poorer classes' grievances against the pro-British large khans from whom he said 'they could expect nothing' as their

only 'desire was to shake hands with the Sahib Bahadurs and to secure employment for their sons'. Although his organizations proclaimed the goal of complete Indian independence, they only affiliated to the Congress in August 1931. Its leaders at this and other times deferred to him because of his immense authority and mass following. The Khudai Khidmatgars' involvement in the civil disobedience struggles of 1930–32, moreover, strengthened the Congress's national claim to be a secular cross-communal organization. For his part, Abdul Ghaffar Khan allied with them in the Indian freedom struggle and quest for Hindu–Muslim unity, but his first priority remained specifically Pakhtun interests.

The British arrested Abdul Ghaffar Khan in April 1930 at the outset of the civil disobedience movement in the frontier. The unrest continued unabated, however, during his incarceration in Gujrat gaol. While in prison he fasted and observed a day of silence each week. He was released after the Gandhi–Irwin pact of 5 March 1931 which ended civil disobedience, and returned in triumph. Many in the crowds which flocked to hear him speak regarded him as a saint who could cure diseases. It was also from this time that he was called the Frontier Gandhi. Abdul Ghaffar Khan certainly cut an impressive figure, tall, rugged, and bearded, clad in rough *khadi* (hand-spun cloth) which he at times wrapped over his head.

The ensuing truce between the Congress and the raj collapsed with the failure of the second round-table conference early in December 1931. Abdul Ghaffar Khan toured the Peshawar valley in preparation for a civil disobedience campaign. The British, however, struck first, and in a crackdown on 24 December they arrested him and the other top frontier nationalists including his brother Dr Khan Sahib. But the continuing disturbances convinced the British that repression should be tempered by constitutional reform. In 1932 they accordingly extended representative government to the frontier.

The Khan brothers were released in August 1934, but externed from the frontier and the neighbouring Punjab. Undaunted they travelled as far afield as Patna, Allahabad, and Calcutta to address meetings. They also stayed as guests at Gandhi's Wardha *ashram* in central India. Abdul Ghaffar Khan was perfectly at home in its austere and simple surroundings. His children Abdul Ali and Mehar Taj later joined him at the *ashram*. He refused to preside over the 1934 Bombay Congress session, declaring: 'I am a Khudai Khidmatgar, I shall only render service'. He nevertheless consented to inaugurate the *swadeshi* exhibition at Bombay and joined the executive committee of the All-India Village Industries Association, which was devoted to Gandhian economic reconstruction. Abdul Ghaffar Khan was rearrested at Wardha on 7 December 1934 after exactly 100 days' freedom. He was later charged with speaking in a way to 'cause disaffection and bring the Government into hatred and contempt'. He served a two-year sentence in Bombay and United Provinces gaols before being released in August 1936. Another year passed before he could return to the frontier. His homecoming resulted from the formation of a Congress-led coalition ministry headed by his brother Dr Khan Sahib following the 1937 provincial elections. Ghaffar Khan used his unaccustomed freedom to reorganize the Khudai Khidmatgars. He also arranged tours for both J. Nehru and Gandhi. On the occasion of the latter's visit in September 1938 he emphasized the importance of the principles of non-violence.

Dr Khan Sahib's ministry resigned following the outbreak of the Second World War. The subsequent civil disobedience movement initiated by the Congress was, in the frontier, very muted in comparison with other regions. Disturbances were limited to the Mardan district. When he attempted to make his way there in defiance of a government ban, Abdul Ghaffar Khan was arrested once more, on 27 October 1942. He spent the remainder of the war years in prisons at Haripur, Abbottabad, and Risalpur. He ran literacy classes for the Khudai Khidmatgars and encouraged them to read both the Koran and the Gita. Every Sunday the political prisoners assembled to sing Iqbal's national verse, 'Hindustan Hamara'. This was followed by talks, discussion, and story-telling. Such displays of communal amity increasingly contrasted with the polarization outside the prison walls. By the time of his release in 1945 the Muslim League had emerged as a major force in both frontier and all-India politics.

Ghaffar Khan attended the 1945 Simla conference as a Congress delegate. He also campaigned vigorously in the 1946 provincial elections. Although the Congress retained power in the frontier, the Muslim League's advance in the Punjab strengthened its Pakistan demand. The Congress high command reluctantly accepted the idea of partition as the price of independence. In Abdul Ghaffar Khan's eyes, however, this was an act of betrayal which threw the Khudai Khidmatgars 'to the wolves'. He exhorted his followers to boycott the June 1947 referendum on the frontier's future, as it did not include an option for Pakhtunistan along with those for India and Pakistan. The referendum result was a crushing blow for the Khan brothers. More than 99 per cent of the total number of votes were cast for Pakistan, although the turnout at 51 per cent was admittedly low.

Pakistan came into being on 14 August 1947: within a week the frontier Congress ministry of Dr Khan Sahib had been dismissed. Abdul Ghaffar Khan took the oath of allegiance to Pakistan as a member of the constituent assembly. The Khudai Khidmatgars had earlier severed their connections with the Indian Congress and replaced the tricolour with the red flag as their party symbol. But the authorities were inevitably suspicious of his continued championing of Pakhtunistan at a time of tension with neighbouring India and Afghanistan. In May 1948 he attempted to spread the Khudai Khidmatgars movement throughout Pakistan. Within a month he was arrested with his son Wali near Bahadur Khel in Kohat, on the charge of planning and fomenting open sedition against the state. The Khudai Khidmatgars were banned shortly afterwards. Ghaffar Khan was in fact to spend even longer periods of imprisonment in Pakistan than in British India.

He was first released in January 1954, but was again externed from the frontier. He attended the budget session of the constituent assembly in Karachi. The following year he headed the campaign against the merging of the provinces of West Pakistan into 'One Unit'. This caused conflict with the authorities. It also led to a breach with Dr Khan Sahib, who in October 1955 became the chief minister of the newly integrated West Pakistan. After a brief spell in prison Abdul Ghaffar Khan joined Baluchi and Sindhi nationalists and left-leaning Punjabi and Bengali politicians to form the National Awami Party in 1957. It called for the dissolution of the One Unit scheme and demanded federal reorganization which would give greater regional autonomy. The National Awami Party's successful passage of a bill through the West Pakistan assembly which provided for the dissolution of the One Unit precipitated Pakistan's headlong descent to military take-over and the abrogation of the 1956 constitution. Abdul Ghaffar Khan was arrested in October 1958 along with other opposition leaders. He was released the following April on account of his age and poor health. But he was disqualified from being a member of any elected body and placed under restrictive orders. He defied these to tour the frontier and was subsequently rearrested in Dera Ismail Khan on 12 April 1961. His health deteriorated alarmingly as he languished in the familiar surroundings of Haripur prison. Shortly after his release in January 1964 he journeyed to England for medical treatment. During this time he stayed at the Sussex home of a former opponent, Sir Olaf Caroe, the one-time governor of the frontier.

Abdul Ghaffar Khan embarked on a lengthy self-imposed exile in Afghanistan in December 1964. His contention that the Durand line, which demarcated Pakistan's western frontier, was an imperialist legacy which artificially divided the Pakhtuns of Pakistan and Afghanistan assured him a warm welcome from the government, although his championing of the Pakhtuns was not well received by Afghanistan's ethnic minorities. He briefly visited India in November 1969 to receive the Nehru peace award. The formation of a National Awami Party government in the frontier in 1972 enabled him to return to Pakistan. A caravan of 6000 lorries escorted him from the Afghan border. Within two months the Bhutto regime had dismissed the frontier government and arrested Wali Khan and the other top National Awami Party leaders for anti-state activities. Abdul Ghaffar Khan was later arrested to prevent his returning to Afghanistan.

After the fall of Bhutto, General Zia ul Haq reversed the policy of repression. He dropped the Awami leaders' charges and released them. After some hesitation Abdul Ghaffar Khan was permitted to return to Afghanistan. For the next two years he shuttled between there and Pakistan. He again ran foul of the Pakistan authorities because he urged the refugees from the Soviet invasion to return home, and denied that the Afghan conflict was a *jihad* (holy war). In December 1985 he attended the Congress centenary celebrations in India, but was now increasingly frail. On 15 May 1987 he was admitted to hospital in Bombay, but was discharged a month later and travelled to

Delhi, where he suffered a stroke on 4 July 1987. From then until his death he never fully recovered consciousness. He was taken by special plane from Delhi to Peshawar on 16 August 1987. After a bout of pneumonia, he died in Peshawar on the morning of 20 January 1988.

Abdul Ghaffar Khan's remarkable career was reflected in the events which surrounded his funeral. The Indian premier, Rajiv Gandhi, flew hurriedly to Peshawar to pay his respects. The governments of India, Pakistan, and Afghanistan each declared a period of official mourning. In accordance with his wishes, Abdul Ghaffar Khan was buried in war-torn Afghanistan. Around 15,000 mourners accompanied the body from Pakistan to its Jalalabad resting place, where they were joined by the beleaguered Afghan president, Dr Najibullah, and his cabinet colleagues.

Abdul Ghaffar Khan was held in such respect because of his sincerity and devotion to the ideal of non-violence. An intensely religious man who lived an austere life, he nevertheless acted as the secular conscience of the Indian subcontinent.　　　　　　　　　　IAN TALBOT

Sources D. G. Tendulkar, *Abdul Ghaffar Khan* (1967) · A. G. Khan, *My life and struggle* (1969) · M. Desai, *Two servants of God* (1935) · G. L. Zutshi, *Frontier Gandhi: the fighter, the politician, the saint* (1970) · A. Qaiyum, *Gold and guns on the Pathan frontier* (Bombay, 1945) · E. Jansson, *India, Pakistan or Pakhtunistan? the nationalist movements in the North-West Frontier Province, 1937–47* (1981) · N. K. Jain, ed., *Muslims in India: a biographical dictionary*, 2 vols. (1979–83) · P. Yarelal, *Thrown to the wolves* (1966) · J. Spain, *The Pathan borderland* (1963) · A. Chand, *India, Pakistan and Afghanistan* (1989) · J. Bright, *Frontier and its Gandhi* (1944) · E. Easwaran, *A man to match his mountains: Badshah Khan, non-violent soldier of Islam* (1984)
Archives BL OIOC, Caroe, Cunningham MSS | FILM BFI NFTVA, news footage · IWM FVA, documentary footage | SOUND IWM SA, oral history interviews
Likenesses N. V. Virkar, photograph, priv. coll. [*see illus.*]

Khan, Sir (Muhammad) Hamidullah (1894–1960), nawab of Bhopal, was born on 9 September 1894 in the Sadar Manzir palace, Bhopal, the third son of Nawab Sultan Jahan Begum (1858–1930), the third successive woman to rule the princely state of Bhopal, and Ali Ahmad Khan (c.1856–1902), her consort. Founded by Dost Muhammad, an Afghan adventurer in the early eighteenth century, Bhopal state in central India comprised 6902 square miles and had a population of 692,448 in 1931. It was the second largest Indian princely state with a Muslim ruler, Hyderabad being the first, but Muslims were a minority of around 10 per cent of its population.

After employing private tutors, most notably Munshi Liaqat Ali, Muhammad Ali, and C. H. Payne, for Hamidullah's early education and enrolling him briefly at the Alexandria Nobles School in Bhopal, his mother chose to send her third son to the Muhammadan Anglo-Oriental (MAO) College at Aligarh, United Provinces, of which she was a generous patron and sometime chancellor, rather than to a chief's college designed for the education of ruling princes and nobles. Saiyid Ahmad Khan had founded the MAO College in 1875 to provide a synthesis of western-style empirical education with Islamic learning to create a new cadre of Muslims able to provide effective leadership

in the British colonial context. Initially the college instilled a strong loyalty to the British raj, but by the 1910s some of its graduates and students had begun to challenge British policies towards Muslims in India and the Middle East. While a student at Aligarh from 1911 to 1915, Hamidullah developed contacts with emerging Muslim political leaders committed to pan-Islamism and more specifically the movement to preserve the *khilafat* of Islam in Constantinople. They included Muhammad Ali, briefly his tutor; Shuaib Qureshi, Ali's son-in-law; Shaukat Ali, Muhammad's brother and co-leader of the Khilafat movement in India; and M. A. Ansari and Hakim Ajmal Khan, Delhi-based supporters of the Khilafat movement and advocates of a more vocal Muslim participation in Indian politics. In 1914, during his student days, Hamidullah was rumoured to have donated 2000 rupees to provide a security for the *Comrade*, a pro-Turkish newspaper founded by Muhammad Ali.

From his college days onward, Hamidullah also personified the stereotype of the Indian prince as skilled sportsman. He played cricket, hockey, and lawn tennis, hunted, and was particularly known as a polo player, both in India and England. He is also credited with inventing a version of polo played on cycles.

Upon graduating BA in 1915 from Allahabad University, with which MAO College was affiliated until it became an autonomous Muslim university in 1920, Hamidullah acquired administrative experience in Bhopal, first as chief secretary to his mother (1916–21) and then as minister of law and justice (1922–6). He continued to support Muslim educational and political projects, such as the financial appeal of Ansari and Ajmal Khan for a Koranic theological college in Delhi, and employed Muslim activists in Bhopal state government. Still, in the aftermath of the First World War Hamidullah responded positively to British requests for support during the Khilafat agitation. Privately he dampened support at Aligarh for the Gandhian civil disobedience campaign in 1921. Publicly in the same year he accepted a CSI when other Indians, such as Rabindranath Tagore, were returning British honours. Hamidullah Khan also served as an aide-de-camp to the prince of Wales during the latter's visit to India in 1921–2, accompanying the royal heir on horseback while hunting in Bhopal. During this visit in February 1922 he was appointed CVO and met Lord Louis Mountbatten, then an aide-de-camp to the prince. Subsequently Hamidullah Khan was appointed GCIE in 1929 and GCSI in 1931.

After his elder two brothers died in 1924, his mother undertook to ensure that Hamidullah would succeed her rather than the elder son of her eldest son. Initially British officials in India vetoed this proposal. Their decision seemed to be based both on a desire to adhere to primogeniture as well as concern about the nawab's ties to the Ali brothers and the time and resources he spent playing polo in England. Not to be denied so easily, Sultan Jahan Begum went to London in 1925 and effectively lobbied the king-emperor and Lord Birkenhead, the secretary of state for India, to override the negative decision. The begum argued that Muslim law and family custom allowed for succession to pass from brother to brother rather than in strict primogeniture. Lord Reading, the new viceroy, agreed to the succession. Upon returning to India, the begum abdicated on 17 May 1926 and installed her third son upon the throne. As a ruler Hamidullah Khan would build upon his network of contacts to become a significant participant in princely, nationalist, and Muslim politics.

Well-educated, intelligent, ambitious, at home in both Indian and British society, Hamidullah Khan quickly joined those princes, such as Ganga Singh of Bikaner and Bhupinder Singh of Patiala, active in the all-Indian political arena. Elected to the standing committee of the chamber of princes, Hamidullah Khan would preside as its chancellor from 1931 to 1932 and, more crucially, from 1944 to 1947. During both terms he claimed a major role for the princely states in any constitutional reforms. While a delegate to the first and second round-table conferences in London in 1930 and 1931 respectively, he staunchly supported princely entry into a federation with British India as long as there were guarantees of princely rights and autonomy. At the same time he facilitated discussions to reinstate joint electorates in British India, to forge a united front among Muslim representatives, and to launch a centrist party of Indian moderate politicians. The nawab was rebuffed on all fronts. Several Muslim delegates refused to concede separate electorates regardless of the safeguards for minorities attached to joint electorates. The princes were divided by personal rivalries and tensions between larger and smaller states. Consequently a rapprochement between Ganga Singh and Bhupinder Singh forced the nawab out of the chancellorship.

From 1930 to 1935 Hamidullah Khan served as chancellor of Aligarh Muslim University, his alma mater. Upon the declaration of war in 1939, he staunchly supported the British with contributions, loans, and personal visits to battle fronts. His services were recognized by the rank of honorary major-general in the Indian army and by being the first Indian to be named an honorary air vice-marshal in the Indian Air Force.

As the British withdrawal from India after the end of the Second World War became imminent, other princely rivals died, and tensions between the Indian National Congress and the Muslim League heightened, Hamidullah again assumed a salient position in all-Indian politics. He was active in constitutional negotiations with Sir Stafford Cripps in 1942 and became chancellor of the chamber again in 1944. First, he undertook a major reorganization of the chamber to improve its operational effectiveness. Next he tried to cultivate support among the princes for major internal reforms within their states to thwart criticisms of autocratic rule. During the negotiations over the cabinet mission plan in 1946, he was a proponent of the princes as a third force which could join with the Muslim League to protect princely and Muslim interests in negotiations with the Indian National Congress. After the Muslim League declined to enter the constituent assembly in late 1946, Hamidullah Khan attempted to craft a division

of India into three areas: a Hindu majority area, a Muslim majority area, and Rajasthan, a confederation of princely states which would federate with the other two areas regarding defence, foreign policy, and transport. The nawab also argued that the princes should not enter the constituent assembly without obtaining significant concessions from the Indian National Congress. Communal tensions with some Hindu princes who were supporters of the Hindu Mahasaba, and the commitment of several major princes to enter the constituent assembly, led Hamidullah to resign from the chamber on 3 June 1947. The nawab now opposed Lord Mountbatten's campaign to secure a quick accession of the princely states to the Indian Union. But after a brief effort to maintain Bhopal as an independent state, the ruler acceded to India.

In 1905 Hamidullah Khan married Princess Maimuna Sultan, a descendant of Shah Shuja, the amir of Afghanistan. They had three daughters, the first of whom, Princess Abida Sultan Begum (b. 1913), moved to Pakistan in 1950 and ultimately forfeited her claim to inherit the title. Frustrated by political developments in both India and Pakistan, Hamidullah Khan abdicated his title of nawab and moved to the Middle East. He died on 4 February 1960 in Bhopal. Princess Mehr Taj Sultan Begum (b. 1915), his second daughter and by then the widow of Nawab Muhammad Iftikhar Ali Khan of Pataudi (1910–1952), of cricket fame, succeeded her father as the nawab begum of Bhopal.   BARBARA N. RAMUSACK

Sources DNB · I. Copland, *The princes of India in the endgame of empire* (1997) · I. Copland, 'The Quaid-i-Azam and the nawab-chancellor: literary paradigms in the historical construction of Indian Muslim identity', *Comparative Studies of South Asia, Africa and the Middle East*, 17 (1997), 52–62 · B. N. Ramusack, *The princes of India in the twilight of empire: dissolution of a patron–client system, 1914–1930* (1978) · *The Times* (5 Feb 1960) · *New York Times* (5 Feb 1960) · V. P. Menon, *The story of the integration of the Indian states* (1956) · S. A. Ali, *Bhopal – past and present* (1970) · K. M. Panikkar, *An autobiography*, trans. K. Krishnamurthy (1977) [Malayalam orig., *Smaranadarppaam* (1950)] · S. Lambert Hurley, 'Out of India: the journeys of the begam of Bhopal, 1901–1930', *Women's Studies International Forum*, 21 (1998), 263–76 · *Memorandum on the Indian states* (1930), 26 · *India Office lists* · private information (2004) [J. McLeod] · S. Lambert Hurley, 'Contesting seclusion: the political emergence of Muslim women in Bhopal, 1901–1930', PhD diss., U. London, 1998 · S. M. Khan, *The begums of Bhopal: a dynasty of women rulers in raj India* (1999) · K. Mittal, *History of Bhopal state: development of constitution, administration and national awakening, 1901–1949* (1990)

Archives Bhopal RO, Madhya Pradesh, India, Bhopal State Political Department records · BL OIOC, Crown Representative records · Bodl. Oxf., corresp. with Lord Monckton · National Archives of India, New Delhi, Foreign and Political Department records · Punjab Archives, Patiala, Punjab, India, Chamber of Princes archive

Likenesses photograph, c.1950, Hult. Arch.

Wealth at death £457,772 16s. 9d.—in England: probate, 1960, CGPLA Eng. & Wales

Khan, (Mohammed) Masud Raza (1924–1989), psychoanalyst, was born on 21 July 1924 at Jhelum in the Punjab in pre-partition India, the second of the three children of the fourth marriage of his father, Fazaldad Khan (c.1846–1943). Khan's father, a wealthy landowner, was seventy-six years old with several middle-aged children by the time he married Khan's mother, Khursheed Begum (1905–1971), a beautiful, illiterate singing-and-dancing-girl of seventeen, who had already borne a son out of wedlock before she met Fazaldad Khan. Due to his mother's background Khan's nuclear family became an alienated offshoot of a respected family in the established hierarchy of what later became Pakistan.

Masud Khan was brought up as a devout Muslim on his father's vast feudal estates. He had an elder brother, Tahir (1923–1983), and a younger sister, Mahmooda (1926–1942). He was a solitary child, very handsome, but had to contend with a slight deformity, a disfigured right ear. At home the family spoke Punjabi but the household had an Oxford educated governess, possibly in an attempt to lift the status of the children and cleanse them of the putative stigma of their mother's reputation. Masud Khan grew up in an isolated, stigmatized yet privileged world; a world of polarities as to his parents' ages, social class, education, and demarcated sexual roles, a world where his leisure time was spent with horses and playing polo. From about 1942 to 1945 he went to the University of the Punjab at Lyallpur (Faisalabad) and Lahore, where he gained his BA and MA degrees.

In 1946 he went to England and was due to attend Balliol College, Oxford, but was accepted for training at the Institute of Psycho-Analysis. He was a tall young man, remarkable for his good looks and elegant bearing, when he entered a world so different from that of his cultural heritage. At twenty-six, however, he became one of the youngest analysts ever to qualify. His psychoanalysts were Ella Sharpe, John Rickman, and, after each of them had died, Donald Winnicott. He was supervised by both Anna Freud and Melanie Klein. When he undertook the further specialist training in child psychoanalysis his supervisors were Donald Winnicott, Clifford Scott, and Marion Milner.

Khan was a maverick in the analytic world. An omnivorous reader with an impressive library, he had a distinctive style and literary flair. With his concept of cumulative trauma, he established himself as one of the major contributors to psychoanalytic theory. That trauma could operate silently with its effect not becoming manifest until later in adolescence was an arresting thought. He, more than any other clinical writer since Freud, managed to convey the very texture and quality of what a true analytic encounter could achieve, the relief of being understood, of feeling knowable, particularly for those patients who were unable to use the more orthodox analytic situation in a meaningful way. However, this attempt to meet the vulnerability and resourcelessness in his patients by, at times, ignoring the accepted conventions governing the patient–analyst relationship, led Khan into repeated clashes with the psychoanalytic establishment. Increasingly his life aroused much comment and criticism particularly among his English colleagues. He had a more wholehearted following in France, Germany, and the United States.

Despite a contemptuous disregard for many of his colleagues, Khan sponsored several new analysts in his successful term as editor of the International Psychoanalytical Library and also in his role as associate editor of both the *International Journal of Psycho-Analysis* and the *International Review of Psycho-Analysis*. A frequent contributor to the *Nouvelle Revue de Psychanalyse*, he was also its foreign co-editor. He was particularly proud of his active role in editing Winnicott's work and was instrumental in publishing it and making him available to a wider public. Consequently Khan was devastated when he was not made Winnicott's literary executor on his death.

Khan published papers extensively in the United States, France, and England. Concerned with the patient's experience of self, he had four books published on this theme; *The Privacy of the Self* (1974), *Alienation in Perversions* (1979), *Hidden Selves* (1983), and finally and unhappily his controversial book containing some antisemitic passages, *When Spring Comes* (1988), which caused his expulsion from the British Psycho-Analytical Society shortly before his death.

A few months after Winnicott's death in January 1971 Khan's mother died. He had always had a difficult relationship with her. This double death was a repetition of an earlier trauma for Khan when, in his adolescence, his younger sister died, followed soon after by his feared but idealized father. Khan's whole style of being, both private and professional, seemed to be based on his caring and cruel father. Both brilliant and learned, Khan remained in essence an Eastern potentate. More than likely this was the self-same style of feudal rule that Khan's father exerted on his family and retainers.

Since the mid-1970s Khan had been dogged by cancer and severe ill health, which, together with an increasing problem with alcohol, led to his removal from the position of training analyst and gradually forced him to give up his thriving practice and concentrate on writing.

Although Khan had numerous affairs in his lifetime, he married only twice. On 26 July 1952 he married Jane Shore (b. 1928/9), a modern dancer, daughter of Bernard Shore, a well-known viola player, but the marriage did not last long. On 23 January 1959 he married the ballerina Svetlana *Beriosova (1932–1998), daughter of Nicholas Beriozoff, director of a ballet company, a marriage which was dissolved in 1974. There were no children from either marriage. Although Khan was treated mainly at the London Clinic throughout his last years of illness, he died in St Mary's Hospital, Praed Street, London, on 7 June 1989. His body was returned to Faisalabad, Pakistan, for burial in the family graveyard. JUDY COOPER

Sources J. Cooper, *Speak of me as I am: the life and work of Masud Khan* (1993) · private information (2004) · personal knowledge (2004) · m. certs. · d. cert.
Archives International Psychoanalytical Association, Broomhills, Woodside Lane, London, diaries and papers | L. Cong., corresp. with Anna Freud | FILM priv. coll.
Likenesses Giacometti, sculpture
Wealth at death £401,175: probate, 31 July 1989, *CGPLA Eng. & Wales* · large feudal estate in Pakistan

Khan, Muhammad Iftikhar Ali, nawab of Pataudi (1910–1952), cricketer, was born in Pataudi in the Punjab on 16 March 1910, the elder son of Muhammad Ibrahim Ali Khan, the nawab of Pataudi (d. before 1927). The princely area of Pataudi, of which he was formally installed as ruler in December 1931, comprised some 53 square miles near Delhi with a population of nearly 19,000. He was educated at the Aitchison Chiefs' College, Lahore, where he was coached by the Oxford blue M. G. Slater. After arriving in Britain in 1926 as a boy of sixteen, his cricket education was further enriched with coaching by the Kent and England batsman Frank Woolley.

Pataudi went up to Balliol College, Oxford, in 1927 and two years later won his university cricket blue. In the 1931 season he scored 1307 runs for the university at an average of 93 and entered the record books through his batting in that year's match against Cambridge. On the first day A. Ratcliffe of Cambridge set a new record for the fixture by scoring 201. Pataudi assured his exhausted colleagues that it would not last twenty-four hours and kept his word by scoring 238. His record still stands. The innings displayed his splendid eye for a cricket ball, the fluency of his stroke play, and his ability to score all round the wicket.

Pataudi toured Australia in 1932–3 as part of Douglas Jardine's infamous 'bodyline' tour, becoming the third of the remarkable trinity of Indian princes (after Ranjitsinhji and Duleepsinhji) to play for England. On his début in the first test at Sydney in December 1932 he scored 102, a slow but valuable innings that helped England secure a ten-wicket victory. But he found relations with Jardine difficult, and after a poor performance in the second test was dropped. His next, and last, appearance for England was against Australia at Trent Bridge in June 1934. The brevity of his test career was despite the fact that in 1933 and 1934 he scored prodigiously for Worcestershire, hitting three double hundreds in 1933 and achieving an average of 91.33 a year later.

By then in poor health, Pataudi returned to India, where he was already part of a continuing web of intrigue to choose a cricket captain. For fifteen years he was seen in India as the captain across the water, a cricketing version of Banquo's ghost at the Indian captaincy table. He could have led India in 1932, when the country made its test début at Lord's, but after playing in one of the final trials he withdrew his name. More than a year before India's 1936 tour of England he accepted the Indian captaincy, only to change his mind, ostensibly on health grounds. In fact, as he privately disclosed, he could not face leading a side to 'please each community … and the rich patrons of the game' (Bose, *History*, 100). In 1939 he married Sajida Sultan, second daughter of Sir Hamidullah *Khan, the nawab of Bhopal. It was possibly the influence of his father-in-law that caused him suddenly before India's 1946 tour of England to emerge out of virtual retirement to claim the crown of the captaincy; at a time when the future of princes in an independent India was at stake, Bhopal thought it important that the team should be led by a princely figure. But although he scored heavily on the tour, averaging 46.71, Pataudi's highest score in the three

Muhammad Iftikhar Ali Khan, nawab of Pataudi (1910–1952), by unknown photographer, 1937

test matches was 22 and he averaged just 11.00. His captaincy not only failed to live up to extravagant Indian hopes but also attracted well-merited English criticism.

India's independence a few months after the tour saw Pataudi lose his small principality, and thereafter he worked for the Indian foreign office. However, he still hankered after playing cricket and in November 1951 MCC approved his application to play for Worcestershire in 1952, which would have coincided with an Indian tour of England. But on 5 January 1952, while playing polo in Delhi, he had a heart attack and died. He had three daughters and a son, Mansur Ali, an eleven-year-old schoolboy in England at the time of his father's death, who was left to fulfil his father's ambitions and become one of India's best-loved captains.   MIHIR BOSE

Sources *Wisden*, esp. 1932, 1953 • *India cricket* • E. W. Swanton, ed., *Barclays world of cricket*, new edn (1980); rev. edn (1986) • C. Martin-Jenkins, *The complete who's who of test cricketers* (1980) • M. Bose, *A history of Indian cricket* (1990) • M. Bose, *A maidan view: the magic of Indian cricket* (1986) • *The Times* (7 Jan 1952) • G. Bolton, *History of the OUCC* (1962) • I. Elliott, ed., *The Balliol College register, 1900–1950*, 3rd edn (privately printed, Oxford, 1953)

Archives FILM BFI NFTVA, news footage • BFI NFTVA, sports footage

Likenesses photograph, 1932, repro. in *Wisden* (1932), 268 • photograph, 1937, Hult. Arch. [*see illus.*] • photograph, 1946 (with W. R. Hammond, the Oval), Hult. Arch.

Khan, Noor-un-Nisa Inayat (1914–1944), secret operations officer, was born on 2 January 1914 in Moscow, the eldest of four children of Hazrat Inayat Khan (1882–1927), a Sufi religious teacher and musician, and his wife, Ora Ray Baker (1890–1949). Her father was descended from the

Noor-un-Nisa Inayat Khan (1914–1944), by unknown photographer

last Mughal emperor of southern India, and her mother was American, of British descent.

In the 1920s and 1930s the family, including Noor's two brothers, Vilayat and Hidayat, and her sister, Khair-un-Nisa, was settled in Suresne, France. By many accounts a very gentle, generous, and somewhat highly strung young woman, Noor spent the 1930s studying a range of subjects in Paris. In 1939 she published *Twenty Jataka Tales*, a collection of children's stories based on a cycle of legends about the Buddha.

After the family fled to England in 1940, Noor enlisted in the Women's Auxiliary Air Force and trained as a radio operator. In the autumn of 1942, she was discreetly approached by a member of the Special Operations Executive (SOE), a secret body which trained men and women to organize resistance groups and co-ordinate sabotage efforts in axis-occupied territory. Noor's knowledge of France and her fluency in French, along with her radio skills, were seen as highly valuable commodities in this context.

During her SOE training some instructors questioned Noor Inayat Khan's suitability as an undercover agent, fearing that she was too emotional, impulsive, and nervous. However, she did have the support of key officers of the SOE's French (F) section, including Vera Atkins, who paid special attention to the women agents being sent to France.

Now code-named Madeleine, Noor was flown into occupied France in June 1943, before her training as an agent was fully completed, to link up with a vast Paris-based network code-named Prosper, which had been engaged in numerous activities ostensibly designed to prepare for an allied invasion. Unbeknown to Noor, however, the Prosper network had become badly compromised because of problems in both London and France. A deadly combination of carelessness, contradictory priorities, treachery, and sheer misfortune led to the destruction of the network in the spring of 1943.

As the radio operator for an agent co-ordinating sabotage in an area south-west of Paris, Noor began making contacts, unaware of how deeply the Germans had penetrated the network. Soon after she arrived, Prosper began to disintegrate around her. Though hundreds of agents

and resistance members were arrested throughout that summer, Noor managed to stay just ahead of German security services. In spite of the danger she continued to transmit regularly to SOE headquarters. Now the only radio operator left in Paris, she was especially valued, but her superiors in London were increasingly concerned for her safety and pressed her to return. This she refused to do until a replacement could be sent.

Noor did make some serious mistakes over security. For example, she inexplicably saved all transmitted and received messages instead of destroying them. However, while this and other errors may have contributed to her fate, the larger disaster unfolding around her made her continued evasion of the Germans extremely unlikely even if she had been an experienced professional. She was arrested at her flat in October 1943. Interrogated at length, she refused to give any details of her work with SOE F section. In November, after two escape attempts from German security headquarters in Paris, she was sent to Pforzheim prison in Germany. In the meantime, the German security services were able to use Noor's captured radio, codes, and messages to deceive SOE headquarters into thinking she was still free.

On 10 September 1944 Noor was taken from Pforzheim to the prison at Karlsruhe, along with three other women from SOE F section. The following day, the women were put on a train for Dachau. On 12 or 13 September 1944 Noor Inayat Khan and her three colleagues were executed at Dachau. In recognition of her efforts and her sacrifice, Noor was awarded a number of posthumous honours, including the French Croix de Guerre and the MBE and George Cross by the British government.

Noor's sex and her aristocratic Indian background, in combination with her dangerous work and tragic death during the war, have often led to her being portrayed in a highly romanticized manner, as the exotic, martyred 'Indian princess' secret agent. This simplistic rendering does not do justice either to the individual or to the experiences of the women agents of the SOE. Noor was part of a ground-breaking effort to train women as undercover operatives in a range of capacities in enemy-occupied territory. These women willingly abandoned contemporary perceptions about the proper roles for women and accepted the high risks of capture, torture, and death that all undercover agents faced. Through skill and luck many of them were able to make major contributions to local resistance efforts and many survived the war. Others were not as fortunate. Of the thirty-nine women SOE agents who served in France, Noor was one of thirteen who died in the performance of her duty. In spite of the terrifying circumstances she faced—for which she was perhaps not best suited or adequately trained—she acted with great determination and integrity and she courageously protected her colleagues and her organization to the end. Noor Inayat Khan stands as both an impressive example of an unusual and important aspect of women's contribution to the allied war effort, and a necessary reminder of the dark side of the too often glamorized world of espionage and covert action.

DEBORAH E. VAN SETERS

Sources J. O. Fuller, *Noor-un-Nisa Inayat Khan*, rev. edn (1988) · L. Jones, *A quiet courage* (1990) · M. R. D. Foot, *SOE in France: an account of the work of the British Special Operations Executive in France, 1940–1944* (1966) · M. R. D. Foot, *SOE: an outline history of the Special Operations Executive, 1940–46* (1984) · D. Stafford, *Britain and European resistance, 1940–45: a survey of the special operations executive* (1983) · B. E. Escott, *Mission improbable* (1991)
Likenesses photograph, repro. in Overton Fuller, *Noor-un-Nisa Inayat Khan*, facing p. 240 · photograph, repro. in Jones, *Quiet courage*, facing p. 183 · photograph, NPG [*see illus.*]

Khan, Osman Ali. *See* Asaf Jah VII (1886–1967).

Khedhouri, Eliahou Abdallah. *See* Kedourie, Elie (1926–1992).

Khudadad Khan (1888–1971), soldier, the first Indian awarded the Victoria Cross, was born on 26 October 1888, at Dabb Village, Chakwal, Jhelum district, Punjab, India, the son of a Pathan.

He entered the Indian army as a sepoy (private), joining the 129th Duke of Connaught's Own Baluchis, who recruited from Muslims of various tribes within the Indian frontier, and was given the regimental number 4050.

The regiment had fought in Persia in 1856, Afghanistan in 1880, and Egypt in 1882. It was stationed at Ferozepore in the Punjab when the First World War began. It sailed to Europe as part of the 7th Ferozepore brigade, 7th Lahore division, becoming one of the first units of the Indian Corps to go into action on the Western Front, along with the 57th Garhwali Rifles.

The first battle of Ypres began on 30 October 1914. Ypres was a Belgian town in Flanders about 40 kilometres from the important channel port of Ostend. The Germans launched a massive offensive against Ostend and Dunkirk, and allied forces defended these vital objectives with strong counter attacks, and heavy casualties on both sides.

On 31 October the 129th Baluchis were placed in the section of the defence line held by the 5th Lancers at Hollebeke, a village south-east of Ypres. This part of the line was subjected to a very heavy enemy bombardment, and the machine-gun section of the battalion came under especially severe shell-fire. Sepoy Khudadad Khan was in the machine-gun section working one of the two guns. The British officer in charge of the detachment, Captain F. F. Dill, was wounded in the head and the other gun was put out of action by a shell. The team of the remaining gun, however, continued to serve the gun and fire under the command of Colour-Havildar Ghulam Muhammad. Eventually the enemy's superior numbers advanced on them despite the severe losses inflicted, and the gun team, fighting to the last, were bayoneted. Khudadad Khan, although himself wounded, continued working his gun after all the other men of the detachment had been killed. He was left by the enemy for dead, but later rendered the machine-gun useless and managed to crawl away and rejoin his unit. Both officers and men displayed the greatest gallantry.

A royal warrant of 1911 had made soldiers of the Indian army eligible to receive the Victoria Cross, and the *London Gazette* of 7 December 1914 stated that Sepoy Khudadad Khan had become the first Indian soldier to be awarded the medal, for his conspicuous gallantry at Hollebeke on 31 October 1914.

He was not, however, the first to receive it, for he was too ill when King George V visited France. He was eventually presented with the VC by the king on 25 January 1915, while he was recovering from his wounds in the Indian convalescent hospital at New Milton in Hampshire.

Khan remained with the army after the First World War, being promoted to subahdar (sergeant) in December 1929. After leaving the regular forces he settled in the Punjab, but made several visits to Britain in connection with the Victoria Cross, and participated in the Victoria Cross centenary review parade in Hyde Park, London, on 26 June 1956. Subahdar Khudadad Khan died on 8 March 1971, in the military centre near Rawalpindi, Pakistan, aged eighty-two.

JAMES W. BANCROFT

Sources The Military Historical Society, Lummis files · IWM, VC files · NAM, Lummis files · LondG (7 Dec 1914) · *Daily Mirror* (26 Jan 1915) · *The Times* (10 March 1971) · O'M. Creagh and E. M. Humphris, *The V.C. and D.S.O.*, 3 [1924] · *The register of the Victoria cross*, 3rd edn (1997)
Likenesses photograph, NAM · photograph, IWM · photograph, repro. in *Daily Mirror* · photograph, repro. in *The Field* (5 July 1956) · portrait, repro. in *Register of the Victoria cross*, 181

Kiallmark, George (1781–1835), violinist and composer, was born in King's Lynn, Norfolk, the son of John Kiallmark, an officer in the Swedish navy, and his wife, Margaret (or Marggrit as it is written in the parish register) Meggitt, a Yorkshire heiress, who lived at Wakefield and was a relation of Sir Joseph Banks. His parents' marriage took place in St Nicholas's Chapel, Lynn, on 4 October 1775. Shortly after George's birth his father, who had run through his property, disappeared and soon died. His widow married her butler, a man named Pottle, and George was adopted by his mother's family. He began his education under the care of a Dr and Mrs Gardiner (*née* Meggitt). From an early age he enjoyed music, and from 1796 to 1798 he studied with a German music teacher.

For some time after 1798 Kiallmark maintained himself in London by teaching the violin and piano, and took violin lessons from F. H. Barthélémon and Paolo Spagnoletti, and studied composition with Von Esch and J. B. Logier. He held many important posts, was a member of all the principal concert and theatre orchestras, and leader of the music at Sadler's Wells. In 1803 he married Mary Carmichael, a cousin of the countess of Rothes, and settled in Islington. He then gave up performing and devoted himself to teaching the harp, violin, and piano, and to composition, entering into arrangements with Chappell and D'Almaine to supply them annually with a fixed number of compositions. His works for the piano included *Introduction and Variations to 'Roy's Wife'*, *Introduction to 'Last Rose of Summer'*, *Variations on 'Home, Sweet Home'*, and *Les fleurs de printemps* in six books. He also wrote a number of songs, among them 'Maid of Athens'. Kiallmark died in Islington in March 1835, leaving a large family.

His eldest son, **George Frederick Kiallmark** (1804–1887), pianist, was born on 7 November 1804 at Camden Street, Islington. He was educated in Margate and began his musical career at the age of fourteen, helping his father with his teaching. He was later a pupil of Logier and taught his system. At the age of sixteen he went to Rouen and on to Paris to study with P.-J.-G. Zimmermann and Frédéric Kalkbrenner. On his return to England in 1825 he became friendly with Clementi, on whose advice he had lessons from Ignaz Moscheles. In 1829 he married Emma Fripp Bryant, the eldest daughter of Dr Bryant of Edgware Road. He gave his first public concert at the King's Theatre in 1832.

When in Paris, Kiallmark became a close friend of Sigismond Thalberg, on whose style he based his own playing. He had a delicate touch, and was a superb performer of the works of Chopin. On hearing him play, Mendelssohn said it was 'a fine sketch of what piano playing should be, and what he will one day make it'.

In 1842 Kiallmark opened an academy for the study of the piano at his home, 29 Percy Street, Tottenham Court Road. During his life he was associated with every great pianist, from Clementi to Rubinstein, and at the age of seventy-eight he studied the sonatas of Niels Gade and Rubinstein. At eighty he was still daily practising Clementi's *Gradus*. He died on 13 December 1887 at 5 Pembridge Gardens, Bayswater, London, only a week after playing one of Thalberg's transcriptions with much of his old fire and brilliancy. He was a fine extempore player, but his compositions have not survived.

R. H. LEGGE, rev. ANNE PIMLOTT BAKER

Sources [Clarke], *The Georgian era: memoirs of the most eminent persons*, 4 (1834), 549 · *MT*, 29 (1888), 52 · F. Niecks, *The life of Chopin*, 2 (1888), 280–81 · private information (1892)
Likenesses W. Simpson, portrait, 1820; formerly in possession of Kiallmark family, 1892 · H. C. Selous, portrait, 1836 (George Frederick Kiallmark); formerly in possession of Kiallmark family, 1892 · E. H. Baily, bust, 1845 (George Frederick Kiallmark); formerly in possession of Kiallmark family, 1892 · J. P. Knight, portrait, 1845 (George Frederick Kiallmark); formerly in possession of Kiallmark family, 1892 · J. Slater, portrait (George Frederick Kiallmark), repro. in *The musical keepsake for 1834*; formerly in possession of Kiallmark family, 1892
Wealth at death £6588 3s. 1d.—George Frederick Kiallmark: probate, 1887

Kiallmark, George Frederick (1804–1887). *See under* Kiallmark, George (1781–1835).

Kickham, Charles Joseph (1828–1882), Fenian leader, was born in early May 1828 at or near Cashel, co. Tipperary, the eldest of the eight children of John Kickham (d. 1861), shopkeeper, of Mullinahone, co. Tipperary, and his wife, Anne Mahony (d. 1848). Charles received his formal education in a local pay school. When he was thirteen an accidental explosion of powder from a hunting gun scarred his face and left him with impaired hearing and vision. The repeal campaign of the 1840s awoke his interest in national politics, while the early *Nation* newspaper (founded 1842) won him over to the romantic nationalism

Charles Joseph Kickham (1828–1882), by unknown engraver, pubd 1869

of the Young Irelanders. He rang the chapel bell to summon support when William Smith O'Brien and his entourage arrived in Mullinahone on 25 July 1848 in the course of their fruitless attempt to foment a rising.

When two curates in nearby Callan began the tenant protection movement in 1849, Kickham became an enthusiastic supporter. And when the independent opposition movement in which the tenant campaign had been absorbed was betrayed, as he saw it, by Sadleir and Keogh in 1852, Kickham had found reason to become permanently disillusioned with parliamentary politics. Admiration for John O'Mahony outweighed doubts about James Stephens when Kickham adhered to the Fenian organization in 1861. In December 1863 he moved to Dublin to join the editorial team of the Fenian weekly the *Irish People*. Over the next twenty-two months he was a regular contributor of leading articles, and specialized in the rebuttal of clerical attacks on Fenianism.

Following government suppression of the *Irish People*, Kickham was arrested on 11 November 1865. Subsequently convicted on a charge of treason felony and sentenced to fourteen years of penal servitude, he served in Pentonville, Portland, and Woking prisons until released in March 1869. On returning home he began the writing of *Knocknagow, or, The Homes of Tipperary* (1873), his most celebrated work. For half a century and more this unwieldily composed evocation of rural life was to be one of the most popular books in Ireland.

From about 1873 until his death Kickham was president

of the supreme council of the Irish Republican Brotherhood (IRB). He advocated an intransigent 'purist' policy, opposing Fenian participation in the home-rule campaign and the land war. He died at the Blackrock, co. Dublin, family home of James O'Connor, journalist and IRB man, on 22 August 1882 and was buried in Mullinahone.

R. V. COMERFORD

Sources R. V. Comerford, *Charles J. Kickham: a study in Irish nationalism and literature* (1979) · J. Maher, ed., *The valley near Slievenamon: a Kickham anthology* (1942)
Archives NRA, priv. coll., papers, corresp., and literary papers | NL Ire., letters to James Francis Xavier O'Brien
Likenesses engraving, pubd 1869, NPG [*see illus.*] · photograph, 1869?, repro. in *Tipperary Annual* (1912) · plaster death mask, 1882, NG Ire.; repro. in Maher, ed., *The valley near Slievenamon*, 58; plaster cast, NG Ire. · J. Hughes, bronze statue, 1898, Main Street, Tipperary
Wealth at death £1577 7s. 2d.: administration, 24 Nov 1882, CGPLA Ire.

Kidd, Benjamin (1858–1916), sociologist, was born on 9 September 1858 near Bandon, co. Cork, the first of eleven children of Benjamin Kidd (c.1831–1914), constable in the Royal Irish Constabulary, and his wife, Mary Rebecca (1833–1916), daughter of John Dawson, landowner of Farranhavane. The Kidd family was protestant, descended from the Askamore Kidds of co. Wexford, while the well-educated Mary Dawson came from urban bourgeois origins. The young Kidd was educated at a small country school in Ennis, co. Clare. The region around the River Fergus estuary instilled in him a lifelong love of rural beauty and wildlife. He became an enthusiastic naturalist with studious habits, a passion for knowledge, and a determination to succeed by means of the classic Victorian virtues of self-help and abstinence. His was to become a classic 'rags to riches' story. His self-belief and drive were to be offset by a retiring disposition, parsimony in money matters, opinionated views, and a pronounced aversion to criticism.

Kidd left school at seventeen, then read part-time for six years under private tutors, first for the Indian Civil Service, later for the Chinese consular service. Meantime in 1877, aged eighteen, he passed the lower division civil service examination and was appointed clerk to the Board of Inland Revenue, London. He moved to London in 1878, and lived a frugal and solitary life until his family emigrated to London in 1881, spending his sparse resources on evening classes (including science) and reading for the bar (ultimately abandoned). He gained publishing and editorial experience, and modest earnings, by preparing civil service examination textbooks, guides, and journals, and by writing naturalist articles. A great deal of his abundant energy during his twenties and early thirties went into civil service reform. He was prominent in the active lower clerks' association: he became the association's secretary (1883–4) and represented the clerks' cause at the Ridley commission of inquiry (1886–8). In 1887 Kidd married Maud Emma Isabel Perry, a handsome, independent woman of west-country origins. It was a love match that proved successful, and the marriage produced three sons: Franklin (1890–1974), and twins John and Rolf (*b*. 1892)).

Benjamin Kidd (1858–1916), by Elliott & Fry, pubd 1894

Franklin was to study science at Cambridge and to become a pioneer in food preservation and a fellow of the Royal Society.

From 1887 Kidd read voraciously across broad fields in a missionary effort to create a new 'science of society'. In Freiburg in 1890 he interviewed the renowned German zoologist August Weismann, whose germ plasm theory he applied to social theory and human behaviour. Kidd was to become an overnight celebrity and social prophet when his *Social Evolution* was published by Macmillan in 1894, with the help of Kidd's chief at the Inland Revenue, Alfred Milner. The book was to become a global best-seller and was translated into at least ten languages, including Chinese and Arabic. What explains the book's success? At a time of challenge for the churches, Kidd justified religion as a countervailing force against destructive, self-assertive rationalism, helping to validate altruistic human behaviour and social conduct that focused upon race survival. Kidd also touched upon widespread fears that socialistic elimination of competition, combined with overpopulation, would result in degeneration of the human species. However, it is misleading to see Kidd as an aggressive apostle of rugged individualism. His reformist style of social Darwinism was more in tune with British 'new Liberalism' or American progressivism. He argued that the answer to society's deep-seated social problems lay in a 'socialized' liberal capitalism and extended democracy. This system would foster the improvement of the race by bringing the masses into the rivalry of life on a footing of equality of opportunity, by raising competition to new heights of efficiency. *Social Evolution* was written with verve and hyperbole at a time of western revolt against reason and debate about genetics, and it caught the temper of its times. However, it also exasperated many intellectuals with its loose speculation and narrow view of reason as the slave of self-interest. Kidd's critics included W. H. Mallock, D. G. Ritchie, J. A. Hobson, Karl Pearson, John Dewey, and Theodore Roosevelt.

Kidd's success gave him financial security and entry into British intellectual and club life. He was drawn into Liberal political circles by William Clarke, the radical journalist, and made enduring friendships with Grant Allen, W. T. Stead, and John Saxon Mills. In 1898 he was elected to the Athenaeum. Serious eye trouble, occasioned by his work on death duty statistics, led him to resign from the civil service in November 1897. He bought shares and property, and became a full-time writer. Photographs show him to have been a small, balding man, with a heavy moustache and piercing dark eyes.

Although not without influence, none of Kidd's later works achieved the extraordinary impact of *Social Evolution*. In his pamphlet *Control of the Tropics* (1898), originally published as a series of articles in *The Times*, Kidd emphasized the importance of tropical resources for the world's industrial nations. He linked a bio-political defence of empire with a programme of social reform at home and a colonial policy of trusteeship that would deliver 'a higher type of social order', and eventually independence, to indigenous peoples. Kidd regarded racial differences as due to cultural rather than genetic factors, and attributed the hegemony of white peoples to their superior 'social efficiency'. Kidd's imperial ideas influenced a generation of administrators and politicians, including Milner, Lugard, and Joseph Chamberlain. His book seemed supremely opportune to expansionists in the United States, and Kidd was lionized when he made a two-month trip to North America in 1898, shortly after the Spanish-American War. Kidd made a significant impact within 'social gospel' circles, among protestant reformers who wanted to apply the 'social law of service' to empire and world politics—most notably Richard T. Ely, Lyman Abbott, Washington Gladden, and Josiah Strong.

In *Principles of Western Civilisation* (1902) Kidd put forward an un-Darwinian type of evolutionary teleology, which stressed the collective future needs of the human species over the short-term interests of the individual. 'Projected efficiency', not present efficiency, was the ruling concept of evolution, and would be the basis for a futurist world order. Influenced by Henry Demarest Lloyd, Kidd made a slashing attack upon global trusts and big business. The book inspired Mao's early mentor Liang Qichao and made a strong impact on Chinese Marxism, but won neither popular nor scholarly acclaim in the west. Many were alienated by Kidd's overblown style, by his semi-mystical and non-testable doctrines, and his reputation began to decline. However, he infiltrated his ideas into the 1902 edition of the *Encyclopaedia Britannica*, for which he wrote the first separate article on sociology. Kidd was a founding father in 1903 of the British Sociological Society. He kept up a busy role in the society's early activities, although he was soon feuding with eugenists led by Karl Pearson, whom he regarded as authoritarian.

After a trip to South Africa in 1902, Kidd immersed himself in political and journalistic agitation. He closely associated himself with 'Milnerites' and Lord Rosebery's Liberal Imperialist pressure group in a campaign to detach the Liberal Party from outworn dogmas of anti-imperialism and free trade. He was won over by the charisma of the unionist statesman Joseph Chamberlain. Kidd resigned from the Liberal Party in January 1905, and became a significant theorist for Chamberlain's politically disruptive tariff reform movement. The Liberal victory of 1906 spelt the end of Kidd's political career. He buried himself in work at his rural retreat in Tonbridge (having moved from Croydon in 1904), but kept in touch with affairs through his journalist friend J. L. Garvin, an associate of the press baron Lord Northcliffe. Between 1905 and 1908 Kidd wrote over ninety pieces for Garvin's Chamberlainite review *The Outlook*. In 1906 he addressed the Royal Institution on group selection, and reworked the themes in his pamphlets *Two Principal Laws of Sociology* (1907–8) and *Individualism and after* (the Herbert Spencer lecture, 1908). He argued that while lower-order evolution took place under red-toothed laws of conflict, higher-order human evolution was subject to natural laws of co-operation and altruism. Apart from an involvement in the suffragette movement in 1912, Kidd spent the last six years of his life in cloistered study at Ditchling, Sussex, working on his last book *The Science of Power* (1916). His mind became increasingly dominated by a pessimistic economism that prophesied a global conflict for resources. He finished his first draft only days before the outbreak of war. This forced him into renewed study of Prussian militarism and prolonged rewriting, despite grievous ill health. He died at his home, 39 Blenheim Park Road, Croydon, from a heart attack on 2 October 1916, and was buried in Bandon cemetery, only a month after completing his book. It was a searing indictment of western civilization, in which Kidd renounced his belief in Darwinism and imperialism, whose doctrines of pagan force had brought the world to the edge of apocalypse. He rested his hopes upon a collectivist future, achieved through a directive cultural conditioning and crucially involving women to achieve peace and altruism. Kidd's writings had been important documents of their time. They faded into obscurity as circumstances changed after the First World War. If there were potentially authoritarian overtones in his work, he also wanted to liberate the forces of the inner life to make a better human existence. In that respect he heralded the twentieth-century revolt against secular materialism, and the search for a new consciousness.

D. P. CROOK

Sources D. P. Crook, *Benjamin Kidd: portrait of a social Darwinist* (1984)
Archives CUL, corresp. and papers · Llanfair, Wales

Likenesses Elliott & Fry, photograph, pubd 1894 [*see illus.*] · photograph, *c.*1894, Llanfair, Kidd MSS
Wealth at death £3179 17*s.* 8*d.*: probate, 7 Nov 1916, *CGPLA Eng. & Wales*

Kidd, James (1761–1834), Church of Scotland minister, born on 6 November 1761, was the youngest son of poor Presbyterian parents residing near Loughbrickland, co. Down. His father, William Kidd, died soon after his birth, and the family moved to Broughshane, co. Antrim. A friendly farmer sent James to a good classical school, and a Cameronian minister taught him Latin. Soon he was able to open a school of his own at Elginy, a neighbouring town. The school flourished and Kidd went to Belfast to study English. He next set up a school at Kildownie, 20 miles from Belfast. He stayed there for about four years, and married Jane (d. 4 June 1829), second daughter of Robert Boyd, farmer, of Carnlea, near Ballymena. They had two sons and three daughters.

Kidd and his wife emigrated to America in April 1784; he soon joined Little, a fellow countryman, in a school at Philadelphia, and next became usher to Pennsylvania College, where he also studied and worked as a proof-reader for the press. Working on Hebrew text encouraged him to learn the language; he bought a Hebrew Bible and, with the help of a Portuguese Jew and by dint of attending the Jewish synagogue in Philadelphia, acquired some fluency in the language. From that time oriental languages became his favourite study. He returned to Britain and settled at Edinburgh, where he became a student at the university, read chemistry and anatomy, and joined the theological classes of the university, supporting himself by offering extra-collegiate classes in oriental languages. In the autumn of 1793 he was appointed professor of oriental languages in Marischal College, Aberdeen. He there completed his theological courses and obtained formal licence as a preacher from the presbytery of Aberdeen on 3 February 1796; he was appointed evening lecturer in Trinity Chapel in the Shiprow. On 18 June 1801 Kidd became minister of the prestigious Gilcomston Chapel of Ease in the suburbs of Aberdeen, where he preached for more than twenty-five years to one of the largest congregations in Scotland. He was at pains to secure variety and freshness in his preaching, constantly looking out for new illustrations and keeping up his student habit of rising at three o'clock every morning. In October 1818 the College of New Jersey conferred on him the honorary degree of DD.

Kidd's powerful preaching and vigorous character overcame violent opposition, and ultimately gained for him an extraordinary popularity. His use of dialect to attract the poor was deplored by his brother ministers. It became an article of popular belief that no one who ever resisted 'the Doctor' had prospered. Stories of his courage, benevolence, and eccentricity were numerous. On the accession of George IV he prayed in public that he 'might be a better king than he had been a prince regent', and when the local authorities complained, asked, 'And where's the man that can't improve?' Kidd not only advocated vaccination from the pulpit, but employed a medical man to vaccinate his converts, and finally forced hundreds into his own house and vaccinated them himself. He is said to have given a stimulus to the study of Hebrew in the north of Scotland, but was not himself a very profound Hebraist. Kidd was a strenuous supporter of the Anti-Patronage Society, and eagerly advocated the popular election of ministers. He marshalled the forces that, after his death, supported the Disruption (1843) in Aberdeen. He was the author of many volumes of sermons and other works of theology, including *An Essay on the Doctrine of the Trinity* (1813), *A Dissertation on the Eternal Sonship of Christ* (1822, new edn by R. Candlish, 1872), and *Rights and Liberties of the Church Vindicated Against Patronages* (1834). He also wrote the second part of the preface to *Memoirs, Diary, and other Writings of Alexander Wood* (1818). Kidd died on 24 December 1834.

GORDON GOODWIN, rev. H. C. G. MATTHEW

Sources J. Stark, *Dr Kidd of Aberdeen* (1898) · *Fasti Scot.*, 7.375–6 · A. Maclaren, *Religion and social class: the Disruption years in Aberdeen* (1974) · *Evening Gazette* [Aberdeen] (28 March 1892) · D. Masson, 'Dead men whom I have known: Dr James Kidd', *Macmillan's Magazine*, 9 (1863–4), 143–59
Likenesses J. Thomson, stipple, pubd 1826 (after W. Derby), NPG · R. Graves, line engraving, BM
Wealth at death £858 11*s.* 9½*d.*: inventory, 1835, Aberdeen

Kidd, John (1775–1851), physician, was born in St James's, Westminster, on 10 September 1775, one of three sons of John Kidd, captain of a merchant ship, the *Swallow*, and his wife, Beatrice, daughter of Samuel Burslem, vicar of Etwall, near Derby. After attending school at Bury St Edmunds, Kidd obtained a king's scholarship at Westminster School in London in 1789. His abilities both attracted the attention of the headmaster, Dr William Vincent, and earned him a place at Oxford upon the 'golden election': he matriculated at Christ Church on 30 May 1793. He graduated BA in 1797 (MA in 1800), and in the same year embarked upon a four-year course of study in medicine at Guy's Hospital, London, as a pupil of Sir Astley Cooper. In 1801 he returned to Oxford and graduated BM, and took up a lectureship in chemistry. He was to remain in Oxford for the rest of his life.

Kidd's most enduring legacy was his contribution to science education. Appointed first Aldrichian professor of chemistry at Oxford in 1803, he took an active part in defining a role for the natural sciences at a time when they seemed to be further marginalized by the priorities of examination reforms. Convinced that the seventeenth-century 'dawn' of the sciences had returned to Oxford, he vehemently opposed critics who suggested otherwise. When the *Encyclopaedia Britannica* of 1817 suggested that Oxford was deficient in scientific studies, Kidd responded with *An Answer to a Charge Against English Universities Contained in the Supplement to the Edinburgh Encyclopaedia* (1818). This included the 'syllabus of a course of lectures on chemistry' that he had published ten years earlier. Offering twenty-six to thirty lectures on Tuesday, Thursday, and Saturday evenings during the Michaelmas and Lent terms, Kidd asserted that his course in chemistry was one of the most comprehensive in the country. Nevertheless, throughout his career he argued for 'no more than an ancillary role for the physical and experimental sciences' (J. Kidd, *An Answer to a Charge Against English Universities*, 1818, 7–8): they were meant to complement divinity, classics, and mathematics within the rubric of a respectable education in the liberal arts.

Kidd maintained this conciliatory approach to the sciences through an appeal to natural theology. Consequently, when he extended the scope of his chemistry lectures to include mineralogy and geology, he firmly yoked these subjects to theology and history by defining them as the explication of the antediluvian world. His *Outlines of Mineralogy* (1809) and *A Geological Essay on the Imperfect Evidence in Support of a Theory of the Earth* (1815) represented the seeds of an Oxford school of geology driven by diluvial theory. A founder member of the Geological Society of London (1807), Kidd lectured on mineralogy and geology to William Buckland, J. J. and W. B. Conybeare, Charles Daubeny, and W. J. Broderip, among others, in the Ashmolean Museum's 'subterranean classroom'. In addition he contributed numerous rocks and minerals to the museum's collections.

On 13 January 1805 Kidd married Isabella, daughter of the Revd Sewington Savery of St Thomas's, Southwark. They had four 'droll little daughters something like' Kidd (Tuckwell, 61). They settled first in St Michael's Street, Oxford, and later moved to 37 St Giles'. For a brief interval around 1817, Kidd and his family also took up residence in the basement of the Ashmolean Museum. A captain of the Oxford Loyal Volunteers in 1803, Kidd soon became an active member of the community and of the university. He attained his DM on 20 January 1804 and was elected unanimously as physician to the Radcliffe Infirmary in 1808. In 1812 he donated 30 guineas towards the construction of the Radcliffe Lunatic Asylum; and he was present when the foundation stone was laid nine years later. Remembered as a physically small man, he was often spotted about the streets of Oxford wearing a spencer, a tailless greatcoat. 'Dr Kidd … a man in all things straightforward and anti-humbug, was the first Medical Doctor in Oxford who rejected the wig and large-brimmed hat, and never, I believe, carried a gold-headed stick' (Cox, 133).

Enjoying a steady ascent within his chosen career, Kidd was elected Lee's reader of anatomy in 1816. His relatively frequent requests gained him some notoriety within the Lee Trust. At his behest the trustees bought the first two microscopes in the university; and in 1819 he acquired two Florentine wax models for his lectures in human and comparative anatomy. Admitted a candidate on 31 March 1817, he was elected a fellow of the Royal College of Physicians of London on 16 March 1818. Upon the retirement of Sir Christopher Pegge, Kidd next became regius professor of medicine at the University of Oxford and resigned the Aldrichian professorship of chemistry. The Tomlin's praelectorship in anatomy, the Aldrichian professorship in anatomy and physiology, and the mastership of the Ewe Elm Hospital were all attached to the regius chair. This combination of appointments netted Kidd an annual income of £466 18s. 10d.

Published as *An introductory lecture to a course in comparative anatomy, illustrative of Paley's natural theology* (1824), Kidd's inaugural lecture as regius professor continued his campaign to locate science within a liberal education. Ostensibly responding to a request by Charles Lloyd, professor of divinity, Kidd sought to demonstrate that comparative anatomy could be subsumed within religious education. Much of this lecture was recycled when he was asked to be one of the eight authors of the *Bridgewater Treatises on the Power, Wisdom and Goodness of God as Manifested in Creation* (1833–6). Regarded as perhaps the weakest, his contribution, *On the Adaptation of External Nature to the Physical Condition of Man* (1833), was characterized as 'but a moderate thousand pounds' worth' (*The Spectator*, 6, 1830, 360). Responding to the perceived threat of transmutationist theories Kidd sought to demonstrate the natural superiority of man to all other animals. He did not, however, provide a Paleyite, rational argument. 'Professing to address those only who believe in revealed as well as natural religion' (Kidd, *On the Adaptation of External Nature*, x), he preached to the converted.

With the added pressures of his multiple appointments Kidd resigned as physician to the Radcliffe Infirmary on 8 March 1826. Nevertheless, he played a leading role in organizing the official response to the visitation of cholera in Oxford in 1832. In June of the same year he played a major role in the meeting at Oxford of the British Association for the Advancement of Science. The following month he attended the inaugural meeting of the Provincial Medical and Surgical Association at the Worcester Royal Infirmary. In April 1834 Kidd gave evidence before the parliamentary select committee on medical education. The architect of a new statute for medical degrees at Oxford (passed in 1833), he was a notable proponent of medical reform. As his *Observations on Medical Reform* (1841) and *Further Observations on Medical Reform* (1842) demonstrated, however, he espoused a Burkean approach. 'Genuine Reform', he declared, 'is genuine "Conservatism"' (Kidd, *Observations on Medical Reform*, 3). He suggested that Oxford and Cambridge should relinquish their licensing powers so that they could play an active part in any future national licensing body. Similarly he attempted to build bridges between the Oxford medical faculty and provincial general practitioners to ensure the university a role in the profession at large. He delivered this message as president of the third annual meeting of the Provincial Medical and Surgical Association. Held at Oxford in July 1835, the meeting assembled in the Radcliffe Library to which Kidd had been appointed librarian in the previous year. In 1836 he added Harveian orator to his list of distinguished achievements.

Kidd's reputation as a teacher, however, suffered a serious blow at the hands of Carl Gustav Carus, physician to the court of Saxony. In his *England und Schottland im Jahre 1844* (1845; translated into English as *The King of Saxony's Journey through England and Scotland in 1844* in 1846), Carus declared that Kidd had become as antiquated as the objects which surrounded him in his Vesalian anatomy theatre. Kidd resigned the Lee's readership in March 1845.

By this time the novelty and vitality of his teaching was waning. But throughout the 1820s his comparative anatomy lectures had consistently attracted audiences of approximately thirty persons. Within the sciences his lectures were second only in popularity to those delivered by William Buckland. Although many of his publications were underpinned by his pedagogical commitment to natural theology, Kidd produced surprisingly secular scientific publications for non-university contexts. His Royal Society paper 'On the anatomy of the mole-cricket' (1825) was almost entirely shorn of any reference to natural theology. A largely descriptive morphological and physiological study of an insect, it represented an early British contribution to a specialist branch of entomology. In addition Kidd produced papers on saltpetre (1814) and naphthalene (1821) for the *Philosophical Transactions*, and a paper on the quantity of blood in animals for the *Edinburgh Philosophical Journal* (1825). He was elected a fellow of the Royal Society on 28 March 1822, and a fellow of the Linnean Society in 1835.

Although he no longer taught actively in the University of Oxford after 1845, Kidd continued as regius professor of medicine and as Radcliffe librarian until his death. By the time of the royal commission of 1850, however, he had become much less optimistic about Oxford's ability to be an effective medical school. After a long period suffering from heart disease he died in the wake of several hours of an acute illness on 17 September 1851 at his home, 37 St Giles', Oxford, aged seventy-six. He was buried in St Giles' churchyard. He bequeathed his home to Christ Church as the official residence of Lee's reader of anatomy.

J. F. M. CLARK

Sources Foster, *Alum. Oxon.* · Munk, *Roll*, vol. 3 · J. Welch, *The list of the queen's scholars of St Peter's College, Westminster*, ed. [C. B. Phillimore], new edn (1852) · H. M. Vernon and K. D. Vernon, *A history of the Oxford Museum* (1909) · A. G. G. Gibson, *The Radcliffe Infirmary* (1926) · *Hist. U. Oxf. 5: 18th-cent. Oxf.* · *Hist. U. Oxf. 6: 19th-cent. Oxf.* · G. V. Cox, *Recollections of Oxford* (1868) · W. Tuckwell, *Reminiscences of Oxford* (1900) · R. T. Gunther, *Early science in Oxford, 1: Chemistry, mathematics, physics and surveying*, OHS, 77 (1923); 3 (1925); 11 (1937) · J. M. Edmonds, 'Kidd, John', *DSB*, 7.363–6 · N. A. Rupke, *The great chain of history: William Buckland and the English school of geology, 1814–1849* (1983) · J. R. Topham, '"An infinite variety of arguments": the *Bridgewater treatises* and British natural theology in the 1830s', Phd diss., University of Lancaster, 1993 · A. V. Simcock, *Robert T. Gunther and the old Ashmolean* (1985) · I. Loudon, *Medical care and the general practitioner, 1750–1850* (1986) · A. H. T. Robb-Smith, *A short history of the Radcliffe Infirmary* (1970) · 'Select committee on medical education', *Parl. papers* (1834), 13.307–19, no. 602 · *The Times* (18 Sept 1851) · d. cert.

Archives Bodl. Oxf., Radcliffe Science Library, letters and papers as Radcliffe librarian · Bodl. Oxf., notebook relating to the history of Ewelme Hospital | Oxf. U. Mus. NH, letters to F. W. Hope

Likenesses chalk drawing, Christ Church Oxf. · pencil and chalk drawing, Oxf. U. Mus. NH

Kidd, Johnny [*real name* Frederick Alfred Heath] (1935–1966), popular singer and songwriter, was born at 3 Shrewsbury Road, Willesden, London, on 23 November 1935, the third and youngest child of Ernest Harold Heath and his wife, Margaret Louisa Voyce. His father was a builder and a partner in the family firm Heath Brothers. Two of Fred Heath's uncles were amateur musicians with their own dance band. After evacuation during the Second World War he attended Leopold Road primary school, Wesley Road secondary modern school, and Willesden Technical College.

After leaving school in 1951 Fred Heath worked at a variety of jobs, including house painting, in a laundry, and as a bookmaker's runner. His musical interest was sparked by the gift of a banjo for his sixteenth birthday. He soon graduated to guitar and began to write songs. In 1955 he formed a comedy skiffle group, the Five Nutters. It won third prize in a skiffle contest at the Willesden Carnival in 1957 and the talent show impresario Carroll Levis booked them for appearances at several London variety theatres. On 22 May 1956 Heath had married Ada Price (b. 1937/8), a machine operator in a food factory, with whom he had two sons. After that marriage ended in divorce he married, on 18 February 1966, Jean Yvonne (b. 1941/2), a hairdresser and daughter of Edward George Complin; they had a daughter.

Heath sang with the Fabulous Freddie Heath Band and joined the Mike West Group before signing a recording contract with HMV, a subsidiary of the EMI company. It was at EMI that Heath was renamed Johnny Kidd and his backing band became the Pirates. Their first recording, a Kidd composition entitled 'Please don't touch', led to radio and television appearances and a tour of US military bases in late 1959. By 1960 the Pirates had become a trio of guitar, bass guitar, and drums, creating an unusual and highly dynamic sound to accompany Kidd's powerful rock and roll voice. In the same year the group adopted flamboyant 'buccaneer' stage outfits and Kidd himself appeared wearing an eyepatch and carrying a cutlass that he would thrust into the stage at the climax of each performance. Kidd's most famous song and most remarkable recording was 'Shakin' all over', a top ten hit in Britain in June 1960. The dramatic guitar part played by session musician Joe Moretti perfectly complemented the charismatic force of Kidd's singing. The song remained a favourite with subsequent generations of musicians and was recorded by The Who, the Canadian group Guess Who, and numerous others.

Three years elapsed before another Kidd record was as successful. The group was to some extent out of step with the fashion in the early 1960s for softer pop music, but suffered also from the attitude of their HMV recording manager Walter (Wally) Ridley, who was antipathetic to rock and roll. Nevertheless, they remained popular with concert and dance-hall audiences all over the country. They also took part in 'package tours' featuring six or seven acts and headed by a visiting American star such as Gene Vincent, Jerry Lee Lewis, or Brenda Lee. In 1963 another Kidd composition—'I'll never get over you'—became their second and last top ten hit. The Pirates, whose line-up was always fluid, now included guitarist Mick Green, whose rhythm and blues style was to influence many younger musicians. By this time, too, the Merseybeat style of the Beatles and others was growing in popularity. It had much in common with the music of Johnny Kidd and the Pirates, who had been the first London rock group to play at Liverpool's famous Cavern Club and had performed alongside Liverpool groups at the Star Club in Hamburg. The Hamburg club-owner presented the group with a large backdrop of a pirate schooner, which was used to decorate the stage for Kidd's performances in later years.

Despite these favourable circumstances, Kidd's popularity subsequently waned. HMV failed to promote his records actively and withdrew an offer to issue an LP of his music. In 1966 Kidd formed the New Pirates and decided to forsake the rock clubs for week-long bookings at cabaret clubs. Shortly after this change of career strategy he was fatally injured in a car accident near Bury, Lancashire, and was declared dead on arrival at the Royal Infirmary, Bolton, on 8 October 1966. His funeral service was held at Golders Green crematorium in north London. Despite his relative lack of success during his lifetime, Johnny Kidd came to be recognized as an influential pioneer of British rock music, and his stage act in particular has been cited as a key influence on such performers as Tom Jones, Dr Feelgood, and Adam Ant. DAVE LAING

Sources J. Firminger, *Remembering Johnny Kidd and the Pirates* (1993) • P. Hardy and D. Laing, *Faber companion to 20th century popular music* (1995) • K. Hunt, *Shakin' all over: the birth of British R&B. The life and times of Johnny Kidd* (1996) • S. Leigh and J. Firminger, *Halfway to paradise: Britpop 1955–1962* • D. McAleer, *Hit parade heroes: British beat before the Beatles* (1993) • b. cert. • m. certs. • d. cert.

Likenesses photograph, repro. in www.johnnykidd.co.uk, 4 Oct 2002

Wealth at death £1208: administration, 21 March 1967, *CGPLA Eng. & Wales*

Kidd, Joseph Bartholomew (1808–1889), painter, was born in Edinburgh. Little is known of his family background and early life. He was a pupil of the landscape painter John Thomson of Duddingston, and on the foundation of the Royal Scottish Academy in 1826 he was elected as an associate, becoming a full academician in 1829. He exhibited seventy-five works at the academy between 1827 and 1836; he also showed two works in 1826 at the Institution for the Encouragement of the Fine Arts in Scotland and exhibited at the Carlisle Academy from 1826 to 1828. About 1836 he moved to London, later resigning his membership of the Royal Scottish Academy and establishing himself as a teacher of drawing in Greenwich. Kidd painted landscapes (often of his native scenery), genre, and marine subjects, and some of his works were engraved. He illustrated Sir Thomas Dick Lauder's *The Miscellany of Natural History* (1833–4) and *West Indian Scenery* (1838–40); some plates by Kidd in the National Maritime Museum, Greenwich, appear to derive from the latter publication. Shortly before his death at his home, 24 Egerton Road, Greenwich, London, on 7 May 1889, he painted a portrait of Queen Victoria for the Royal Hospital schools in Greenwich. He was survived by at least one son. He is sometimes confused with his near contemporary, the painter William *Kidd (1795/6–1863), and some sources mistakenly refer to him as John rather than Joseph. EMILY M. WEEKS

Sources P. J. M. McEwan, *Dictionary of Scottish art and architecture* (1994) • C. B. de Laperriere, ed., *The Royal Scottish Academy exhibitors,* *1826–1990*, 4 vols. (1991) • *DNB* • Redgrave, *Artists* • Bryan, *Painters* • Boase, *Mod. Eng. biog.* • Thieme & Becker, *Allgemeines Lexikon* • M. H. Grant, *A dictionary of British landscape painters, from the 16th century to the early 20th century* (1952) • 'Catalogue of prints and drawings', www.nmm.ac.uk, 1 Dec 1998 • d. cert. • *CGPLA Eng. & Wales* (1889)

Wealth at death £151 10s.: probate, 22 May 1889, *CGPLA Eng. & Wales*

Kidd [*married name* MacDonald]**, Dame Margaret Henderson** (1900–1989), lawyer, was born on 14 March 1900 at Grange Park, Carriden, Bo'ness, Linlithgowshire, the elder daughter of James Kidd (1872–1928) and his wife, Janet Gardner Turnbull (1872–1930), a teacher. Her parents were both Scottish. Her father was a much respected solicitor and (Unionist) MP for the local seat of West Lothian (Linlithgowshire); and on his death in 1928 she contested the seat in the unionist cause but was defeated by Emanuel Shinwell. She was educated at Linlithgow Academy and thereafter at the University of Edinburgh, where she graduated MA and LLB in 1922. Her early legal training was with Mitchell and Baxter, writers to the signet, in Edinburgh where the young Robert Louis Stevenson had preceded her. She had hoped to pursue a diplomatic career but despite the passing of the Sex Disqualification Act, 1919, it was not considered possible. It was her father's suggestion that she should go to the bar 'and have fun'.

When she passed advocate in July 1923 Kidd became the first female member of the Faculty of Advocates, the Scottish bar; and between 1923 and 1948 she remained the only lady advocate. Then and indeed until very much later, the ladies' robing-room was situated off a lower corridor in Parliament House, opposite the condemned cell. Margaret Kidd recalled that hot water was put in only after the Second World War. Although her practice was wide, it centred on family law, where she was appreciated by her contemporaries as adding a new dimension to old problems. She was later to recommend that a family court at sheriff court level would be more responsive. Kidd was the first lady advocate to appear before the House of Lords and before a parliamentary select committee; and in 1948 she had the distinction of becoming the first woman QC in Britain if only by a few months. By that time she had been standing junior counsel for the Post Office and for the Ministry of Works.

Kidd married Donald Somerled MacDonald (d. 1958) on 22 March 1930. He was a writer to the signet and son of a barrister. They had a daughter, Anne, who married a Cambridge surgeon. Much of Kidd's adult life was spent in India Street, Edinburgh, where she regretted the lack of a proper garden. Her flat was filled with plants as well as legal books, good furniture, and paintings. She was kind, welcoming, and encouraging. Herself one of a large family, she always maintained a strong affection and interest in not only her own family and grandchildren, but also her extended family at the bar. Kidd was tall and, even in later life, retained the clear eyes and complexion that can be seen reflected in her portrait as a young advocate hanging in the advocates' reading-room.

In 1960 Kidd became the first lady sheriff-principal

Dame Margaret Henderson Kidd (1900–1989), by unknown photographer

when she was appointed to Dumfries and Galloway. Appointed to Perth in 1966, then the most prestigious of the sheriff-principaldoms, she held the post until retirement in 1974. As sheriff-principal she exercised both a criminal and a civil jurisdiction, apart from the very wide administrative duties which were part of her appointment. Kidd herself took the view that women made particularly apt administrators. In addition, she was keeper of the Advocates' Library, one of the Faculty of Advocates' main honorary posts, from 1956 to 1969. Her successor, A. J. Mackenzie-Stuart, later became the first United Kingdom judge in Europe. Kidd was also editor of the Court of Session law reports of the *Scots Law Times* from 1942 until 1976. During all that time she never failed to meet her set timetable, and wrote her reporters' reports for them where they had failed. Her editor's strength lay in her ability to marshal facts in an orderly fashion.

Kidd had a very active public role in Scotland. She cared about her Christian faith. An assistant lecturer in public law at Edinburgh University, she was also a founder member of the Stair Society. She became a vice-president of the Federation of University Women and of the Electrical Association for Women. A tireless worker for a number of charities, she acted as chairwoman of the Queen's Nursing Institute in Scotland and for Blind Welfare. In addition, Kidd served as a member of the royal commission on betting, lotteries and gaming in 1950 (and said that she always enjoyed a good point-to-point). In 1975 she was made a DBE. She received an honorary LLD from Dundee University in 1982 and Edinburgh University in 1984.

Kidd was a traditionalist, a Conservative by temperament and training. But she could be both formidable and constructive in her criticism of the legal and university institutions of Scotland and of the Conservative Party. Professionally, she did not consider herself discriminated against. Never impressed by her own success, she said that she 'had a lot of luck to be in the right place at the right time'. Those who knew her well pointed to her remarkable integrity, self-discipline, and sheer hard work. As Lord Hope of Craighead said at her death,

> Her success was won by strength of character, courage and integrity and it is a mark of her true qualities that despite what might seem to be the revolutionary nature of her achievements she always held the affection and respect of others. (Hope)

Dame Margaret Kidd died at 53 Madingley Road, Cambridge, on 22 March 1989. A funeral service was held at the Canongate Kirk, Edinburgh. The Scottish bar, and its lady members in particular, owe her a deep debt for the qualities and standards she brought and maintained as its first lady member.   ISOBEL ANNE POOLE

Sources personal knowledge (2004) · private information (2004) · *The Times* (26 March 1989) · 'The Faculty of Advocates scrapbook', unpublished MS, Faculty of Advocates' Library, Edinburgh · Lord Hope, *Glasgow Herald* (27 March 1989) · *Sunday Post* (21 Aug 1977) · *Edinburgh Tatler*, 25 (1978) · Lord Brand, *An advocate's tale: the memoirs of Lord Brand* (1995) · *The journal of Sir Randall Philip*, ed. F. Craddock (1998) · CCI (1989) · CCI (1997) · Lord Stott, *Lord Advocate's diary, 1961–1966* (1991) · E. Shinwell, *Lead with the left: my first ninety-six years* (1981) · b. cert. · d. cert. · Registers of Scotland
Likenesses photograph, Scot. NPG [*see illus.*] · photographs, Parliament House, Edinburgh, Faculty of Advocates · watercolour drawing, Parliament House, Edinburgh
Wealth at death £135,344.09: confirmation, 12 June 1989, CCI · £10: additional inventory, 23 June 1997, CCI

Kidd, Ronald Hubert (1889–1942), founder of the National Council for Civil Liberties, was born at 6 Montpelier Row, Blackheath, London, on 11 July 1889, the son of Leonard Joseph Kidd (*b.* 1858), surgeon, and his wife, Alice Maud, *née* Peek. He entered University College, London, as a science student but did not take a degree. As a young man he campaigned for women's suffrage and lectured for the Workers' Educational Association before serving in the First World War: he was later discharged on health grounds. Thereafter his career was varied, and included employment as a civil servant, journalist, advertiser, actor, and stage manager. For a time he also ran a small radical bookshop in Villiers Street, off the Strand, where freethinkers could buy an unexpurgated copy of *Lady Chatterley's Lover*. Around 1928, while working as a stage manager in a provincial repertory company, Kidd met Sylvia Crowther-Smith (later Scaffardi), fifteen years his junior, who became his lifelong companion. He was then already married: his estranged wife and their child lived in Bristol, where he once worked as a stage director.

The impetus to Kidd's career as a civil liberties campaigner came in November 1932 when he witnessed unemployed hunger marchers on their way to parliament arrested after being incited by police *agents provocateurs*. His sense of this injustice was lasting and in August 1933 he engaged in a correspondence with A. P. Herbert in the

Week-End Review, which led Herbert to take the matter up with Lord Trenchard, commissioner of the Metropolitan Police. Trenchard denied the use of *agents provocateurs* but was drawn into stating that if such conduct were proved those concerned would be severely dealt with. Encouraged that pressure had successfully been brought to bear, Kidd planned a movement that would bring together lawyers, writers, journalists, and members of parliament to monitor police conduct at mass meetings.

What became the National Council for Civil Liberties (NCCL) began with a small invited gathering in the vestry hall of St Martin-in-the-Fields on 22 February 1934. The hall was lent by the Revd 'Dick' Shepherd, a member of the first executive committee of the council alongside Edith Summerskill, Kingsley Martin, and Claud Cockburn. Kidd became general secretary, with a very modest salary, and E. M. Forster the council's first president. The long list of vice-presidents included Clement Attlee, Aneurin Bevan, Vera Brittain, Dingle Foot, George Lansbury, A. A. Milne, J. B. Priestley, and D. N. Pritt. The NCCL initially operated from a tiny room at 3 Dansey Place, Soho, that Kidd shared with Crowther-Smith. She was a constant support and a central figure in the council in her own right. The council later moved to an office on the Charing Cross Road. The amateurishness of the early organization was compensated for by Kidd's 'undaunted and rather solemn persistence' (*Civil Liberty*, June 1942, 1): by the end of 1934 there were 1500 members and by 1940 there were 3000, with 700 affiliated organizations. From modest beginnings Kidd built a national organization with international contacts.

The NCCL's tactics varied to meet the occasion and 'pamphlets, speeches, interviews with cabinet ministers, visits to police stations and police courts, street watchings—all played their part' (Forster, 60). Effective early campaigns included those against the 1934 incitement to disaffection bill; the use by local authorities of public safety regulations to censor political films; and the sectarian application of the law by the government of Northern Ireland. In 1934 Kidd also challenged the 'Trenchard ban' on political meetings in the proximity of labour exchanges. The ban was upheld in the court case *Duncan v. Jones*, in October 1935, giving the police, in Kidd's eyes, arbitrary control over freedom of speech and assembly. His distrust of the police and the courts was further intensified by the events at Thurloe Square on 22 March 1936 when the police baton-charged a peaceful meeting of anti-fascist protesters. When the government refused an official inquiry the NCCL launched its own inquest, which found the police action unwarranted. In 1937 Kidd investigated police harassment of striking miners in Harworth, Nottinghamshire.

Throughout his period as secretary Kidd struggled to allay the fears of some members that the NCCL was a front for the Communist Party, as indeed many on the outside perceived it to be. Special branch files reported that Kidd was himself a communist, and the council effectively run from Communist Party headquarters. Kidd refuted both charges, but there was no denying the strong left-wing bias of the council, which compromised its position as a defender of civil liberties in the widest sense. E. M. Forster was specially concerned on this count and sought to make the council explicitly non-political. It found its antithesis in the far-right Mosley movement, on which it kept a particularly close watch. The first issue of its journal, *Civil Liberty*, edited by Kidd, detailed scores of cases in which Jews, mostly in the East End, were physically attacked or their property damaged by British fascists.

With the outbreak of war Kidd accepted the need for limitations on personal liberty, but he nevertheless regarded as tyrannical the emergency powers subsequently enacted. The NCCL began a campaign against them, culminating in a conference at Beaver Hall, on 4 November, attended by nearly 800 delegates from industrial, political, religious, and peace societies. Partly as a result the home secretary modified some of the regulations. It was, though, only a partial victory, and Kidd continued to oppose regulation 18B, allowing for detention without trial. In 1941 he joined the protests against the ban by the British Broadcasting Corporation upon those considered politically unsound, which was later revoked by the government. And he used the front page of *Civil Liberty* to protest against the suppression of the *Daily Worker* in February 1941, the most notorious act of press censorship during the war.

In 1940 Kidd published *British Liberty in Danger*, which was described as a temperate, well-documented, and in many ways disquieting survey of the 'gradual whittling away of civil liberties' in Britain during the preceding three decades (*TLS*, 485). The lesson of the First World War, Kidd argued, was that civil liberties, once taken away, were not easily won back: it offered a salutary warning for the present conflict. He believed that if the British people would only 'take their democracy seriously' they might yet save it 'from extinction' (Kidd, 254).

After a recurrence of heart trouble in January 1941 Kidd was succeeded as secretary, in November, by Elizabeth Allen. He took the reduced role of director, but even this proved too much. He died of heart failure on 13 May 1942, at his home, 31 Rosehill Court, Carshalton, Surrey, and was cremated at Golders Green crematorium on 16 May. In his funeral address E. M. Forster suggested that Kidd shared with Schiller the belief that none could be truly free unless all were free—'Und eine Freiheit macht uns alles Frei'. To Forster this explained why so many contradictory judgements were passed on Kidd, whom he had heard variously accused of being 'a Communist, a Gladstonian Liberal, a secret agent, the wrong sort of Irishman and a hopeless John Bull' (Forster, 61). Kidd, though, was 'tethered to no formula' (ibid.). Kingsley Martin regarded him as 'just one of Chesterton's Englishmen who have a quixotic desire to uphold a right because it is a right' (*Civil Liberty*, June 1942, 1). MARK POTTLE

Sources R. Kidd, *British liberty in danger: an introduction to the study of civil rights* (1940) · *Manchester Guardian* (14 May 1942), 3 · *Civil Liberty: Journal of the National Council for Civil Liberties*, 3/3 (June 1942) · *Civil Liberty: Journal of the National Council for Civil Liberties*, 3/4 (July–Aug 1942) · M. Lilly, *National Council for Civil Liberties: the first fifty* *years* (1984) · b. cert. · d. cert. · K. D. Ewing and C. A. Gearty, *The struggle for civil liberties: political freedom and the rule of law in Britain, 1914–1945* (2000) · E. M. Forster, *Two cheers for democracy* (1951) · *TLS* (21 Sept 1940) · B. Dyson, *Liberty in Britain, 1934–1994: a diamond jubilee history of the National Council for Civil Liberties* (1994) · *The Times* (24 Feb 1934) · *The Times* (6 Nov 1939) · *The Times* (14 May 1942) · 'Liberty', www.liberty-human-rights.org.uk · R. Skidelsky, *Oswald Mosley* (1990)

Archives NRA, papers

Likenesses H. Coster, photograph, repro. in *Civil Liberty*, 3/3 (June 1942)

Wealth at death £1007 11s. 1d.: probate, 11 Aug 1942?, CGPLA Eng. & Wales

Kidd, Samuel (1804–1843), missionary in Malacca and university professor, was born on 22 November 1804 at Welton, near Hull, and was educated at the village school in Welton. In 1818 he was sent to Hull, where his thoughts were directed towards a missionary career, and in 1820 he entered the London Missionary Society's training college at Gosport. In April 1824 he married Hannah, second daughter of William Irving of Hull. At the end of the same month he was sent by the London Missionary Society to Madras, and thence to the college at Malacca, where he arrived in November 1824. David Collie, the principal, taught him Chinese and he soon spoke Hokkien and Mandarin. In the course of 1826 he published several small tracts in Chinese, and in the year following he was appointed professor of Chinese at the college. On Collie's death in 1828 Kidd succeed him as principal. He became involved in a row between the East India Company and the *Malacca Observer*, which was printed on the college's press.

Exhausted by this and by epileptic fits, to which he had become prone, Kidd returned to Britain in 1832 (his wife Hannah having returned for reasons of health in 1829). His health did not improve and in 1833 he was appointed pastor of a Congregational church at Manningtree in Essex. In 1837 he was appointed professor of Chinese at University College, London, at £60 p.a. for a term of five years. He wrote a memoir of Robert Morrison in 1838, published his inaugural lecture (also in 1838) and *China, or, Illustrations of the Philosophy, Government and Literature of the Chinese* (1841); he also catalogued the Chinese library of the Royal Asiatic Society. It was understood at the time of his nomination to his chair that his appointment would be renewed at the end of that term, and Kidd requested a further five-year term, pointing out that he suffered 'considerable personal expense' in holding the chair (College correspondence, 1843, UCL Archives). Renewal was not immediately granted, and it was while the matter was in debate that Kidd died suddenly on 12 June 1843, at his house in Camden Town, London.

R. K. Douglas, *rev.* H. C. G. Matthew

Sources 'Memoir of the late professor Kidd', *Evangelical Magazine and Missionary Chronicle*, new ser., 21 (1843), 585–92 · *GM*, 2nd ser., 20 (1843), 209 · B. Harrison, *Waiting for China: the Anglo-Chinese college at Malacca, 1818–1843, and early nineteenth-century missions* (1979) · college correspondence, UCL

Archives UCL

Kidd, Thomas (1770–1850), classical scholar and schoolmaster, was the son of Thomas Kidd of Kidd, Yorkshire. He

was educated at Giggleswick School under William Paley before being entered on 14 December 1789 as a sizar of Trinity College, Cambridge, where he took the degrees of BA (as fifth junior optime) in 1794 and MA in 1797. He was for some time second master of Merchant Taylors' School, and in 1818 was appointed headmaster of King's Lynn School; he next became master of Wymondham School, and lastly of Norwich School. He was ordained deacon in 1798, priest in 1799, and was instituted successively to: the rectory of St James Garlickhythe, London, in 1802; the rectory of Croxton, Cambridgeshire, in 1813; the vicarage of Eltisley, Cambridgeshire, in 1814; the vicarage of Bedingham, Norfolk, in 1831; and, for a second time, both the vicarage of Eltisley and the rectory of Croxton in 1835. In 1801 he married Miss Smith, of Hoxton Square, London.

At Cambridge Kidd became acquainted with Richard Porson, who was considerably his senior, and his affection and reverence for him influenced his whole life. He had one of his sons christened Richard Bentley Porson. Though himself a genuine Greek scholar and steeped in Greek literature, he is chiefly remembered for editing the critical works of others. Thus he edited Ruhnken's minor works (1807), Dawes's *Miscellanea critica* (1817), as well as the very valuable volume of Porson's *Tracts and Miscellaneous Criticisms* (1815). He took especial interest in collecting lists of the works of several of the chief English and Dutch scholars. In his preface to *Opuscula Ruhnkeniana* there is a complete list of Thomas Tyrwhitt's works, while his collation of Tyrwhitt's smaller pieces is in the Dyce collection which was bequeathed to the South Kensington (later the Victoria and Albert) Museum. In his review of Sluiter's *Lectiones andocideae* in the *British Critick* for October 1805 he catalogues Valckenaer's criticisms and classical editions. It was due to him that the collection of Richard Bentley's books, which had lain neglected at James Lackington's bookshop, was in 1807 rescued and obtained for the British Museum. Most of the printed books were annotated by Bentley, and Kidd also found several unfinished works in manuscript. At one time he contemplated an edition of Homer, and wrote a series of lengthy criticisms on the Grenville edition in the *Critical Review* for 1803 and 1804. He contributed a variety of essays and reviews to several journals. His 'Imperfect outline of the life of R. P.' was prefixed to Porson's *Tracts and Miscellaneous Criticisms*. His English style is sometimes confused, and always quaint. Despite his veneration of the scholars whose works he catalogued or edited, his own methods were disorganized and his learning ill-digested. One of his footnotes extends to twenty pages. In 1842 Lord Melbourne gave him a civil-list pension of £100 'in token of his services as a scholar and an instructor of youth for nearly half a century'. He died at Croxton, Cambridgeshire, on 27 August 1850, and was buried in Croxton churchyard.

H. R. Luard, *rev.* Richard Smail

Sources Venn, *Alum. Cant.* · *GM*, 1st ser., 77 (1807), 1047–8 · *GM*, 2nd ser., 34 (1850), 557 · M. L. Clarke, *Greek studies in England, 1700–1830* (1945), 90–91

Archives BL, letters to Lord Spencer · Bodl. Oxf., letters to E. H. Barker

Kidd, William (*c*.1645–1701), pirate and privateer, was a Scot, by tradition born in Greenock, Renfrewshire, into the family of a Church of Scotland minister; however, the names of his parents are not known and his date of birth is derived from his age, about fifty-six, when he died. He does not appear in the historical record until 1689 when he was a member of a pirate crew brought into service by Christopher Codrington, governor of the Leeward Islands, as privateers in his struggle against the French in the West Indies during the Williamite wars. Kidd was made captain of the *Blessed William* and saw action on the island of Marie Galante and in the relief of St Martin. His men disliked such service and stole the ship, leaving for New York city, a known pirate haunt. They had also stolen Kidd's booty, worth £2000, so he determined to follow them—in the event fruitlessly—in a ship presented to him by Governor Codrington.

Kidd arrived in New York in time to join the royal forces sent out to suppress the rebellion of Jacob Leisler. Siding with the forces reimposing authority both brought Kidd into favour with the new regime and into friendship with important politicians in the colony, especially his fellow Scot the merchant and landowner Robert Livingston. He decided to settle in New York, marrying, by licence dated 16 May 1691, the twice widowed Sarah Oort (formerly Cox, *née* Bradley; *d*. 1744), who brought property from her prior marriages and with whom he had two daughters. Until 1695 Kidd remained in New York city, occasionally serving as a privateer while making friends among the merchants and politicians. Eventually he tired of this life and he and Livingston concocted a plot to take advantage of Kidd's special skills. Both men appeared in London in 1695 where Livingston approached Richard Coote, earl of Bellomont, the newly appointed governor of New York and Massachusetts Bay, with a plan. The scheme he presented was that Kidd would sail to the Indian Ocean, where pirates had been wreaking havoc. On arrival he planned to capture the pirates and their treasure and return to Massachusetts Bay or England, where the pirates would be tried, their treasure condemned, and the profits divided among the investors. To obtain the necessary documents and funding Bellomont approached his patrons the whig lords who formed the junto administration in London; after listening to the proposal and meeting Kidd they agreed to fund the scheme and obtain the necessary commissions. Kidd, Livingston, and Bellomont were the openly acknowledged investors and the hidden partners were the earls of Shrewsbury, Orford, and Romney and John Lord Somers. Kidd left England with a more powerful ship, the *Adventure Galley*, with commissions to hunt down pirates, attack French commerce, and keep the cargoes he captured free of interference by the owners, an exceptional combination of privileges made possible only through the intervention of his patrons. By April 1696 he had left London and was preparing to sail to New York to obtain more crewmen and to inform his family of his new venture.

Once in New York Kidd recruited ninety men, many of whom were experienced pirates. They left on 6 September 1696 and arrived at Tulear, Madagascar, in January 1697.

Given that Madagascar was the main base of the pirates in the Indian Ocean Kidd's actions to this point seem normal, but he quickly drew suspicion on his motives when he sailed to the Red Sea, where he attacked the pilgrim fleet. These ships were *en route* for India loaded with cargo and pilgrims returning from Mecca. The most likely explanation for his action is that he may have believed that he could raid the fleet and sail away without leaving a trace and then return with his booty claiming it was seized from pirate ships. Much to his surprise the East India Company vessel *The Sceptre* was sailing with the fleet and it aggressively defended the ships. Kidd then sailed for the west coast of India where he unsuccessfully attacked a number of trading vessels. The men, who were on a 'no prey, no pay' contract, were increasingly unhappy and tensions increased until during an altercation Kidd killed his gunner, William Moore, striking his head with a wooden bucket hooped with iron. After this Kidd's luck changed and he captured six ships, of which only two, carrying French passes, could be considered legitimate prey under his commission. Having done enough the *Adventure Galley*, by now in poor condition, sailed for the pirate base of Ste Marie, just off the coast of Madagascar.

Once there, Kidd openly consorted with the pirates he had been sent out to capture. His ship sank in the harbour at Ste Marie and he proceeded home in one of his captured vessels, the *Quedah Merchant*. Most of the original crew remained on the island to better their fortunes. Meanwhile the East India Company, punished by the Mughal government for the actions of the pirates, raised a campaign in England against the pirates and against Kidd in particular: so much so that by 1698 he was a marked man and orders were shortly sent to Bellomont to seize Kidd.

Kidd's first landfall was the Danish island of St Thomas where he discovered that he was an outlaw and that his patrons were out of power. Prior to sailing to New York he stopped on Hispaniola, where he sold much of his cargo to merchants from Curacao and purchased a smaller ship, the *San Antonio*. Moving toward New York he continued to offload crew and cargo when convenient and acquire intelligence about his status. When near New York he hovered off the coast, meeting his friends such as Livingston, who could provide him with little comfort. The key to his future was Bellomont, who was now in Boston. The two exchanged messages while Kidd disposed of valuables, leaving enough on board to tempt Bellomont to make a deal of some sort to secure his freedom. Bellomont listened to Kidd's entreaties but he could not in the end ignore royal orders; he had Kidd arrested and sent to England along with as much of his cargo and fortune as he could seize.

In England Kidd was approached by the tories, who were now in power, to testify against his patrons the whig lords. Kidd refused to play their game, perhaps because he felt that only the whigs could save him now. However, the whigs, now facing charges of treason, were happy to let matters proceed against Kidd in order to get him out of the way. His trial conformed to contemporary practice in the high court of Admiralty which offered the defendant little protection. The one unusual feature was that the French passes he seized from two of the vessels he captured and which were returned to England with him could not be found for him to use as evidence. Not until the twentieth century were they discovered in the Public Record Office. Would they have saved him? No, he had undoubtedly committed piracy against other ships. Who would have kept them from him? Many had reasons to keep even this slender hope from him. Kidd was sentenced to death for piracy and for the murder of Moore, his gunner. He was hanged at execution dock, Wapping, on 23 May 1701. Two attempts were necessary, as the first time the rope split and had to be rapidly replaced.

Kidd's treasure, said to be as much as £400,000, has led to many treasure hunts from Nova Scotia to the South China Sea. Kidd never captured that much: the manifests of his victims were sent to England and their value is nothing of this order. He had ample opportunity to transfer funds to his wife and Livingston while keeping enough to lure Bellomont and the whig lords into obtaining pardons for him. This money was kept by the government and after various levies it amounted to £6000, which was used to purchase the land where Greenwich Hospital today stands. Kidd was survived by his wife, who remarried after his death, to become Sarah Rousby.

ROBERT C. RITCHIE

Sources R. C. Ritchie, *Captain Kidd and the war against the pirates* (1986) • D. M. Hinrichs, *The fateful voyage of Captain Kidd* (1955) • G. Brooks, ed., *The trial of Captain Kidd* (1930) • H. T. Wilkins, *Captain Kidd and his Skeleton Island* (1935) • R. D. Paine, *The book of buried treasure* (1911) • C. Milligan, *Captain William Kidd, gentleman or buccaneer* (1932) • P. Lorrain, *The ordinary of Newgate: his account of the behaviour, confessions, and dying-words of Captain William Kidd* (1701) • E. B. O'Callaghan and B. Fernow, eds. and trans., *Documents relative to the colonial history of the state of New York*, 15 vols. (1853–87) • E. B. O'Callaghan, ed., *The documentary history of the state of New York*, 4 vols. (1850–51)

Likenesses portrait, priv. coll.

Kidd, William (1795/6–1863), painter, was born in Edinburgh. Of his parents, nothing is known. He was first apprenticed to the naïve animal painter James Howe and exhibited his first painting 'aged 13' at the Associated Society of Artists, Edinburgh, in 1809. He was an enthusiastic admirer of the works of Alexander Carse and of Sir David Wilkie, and most of his subjects were domestic scenes from Scottish life, particularly in the manner of the latter. He first exhibited at the Royal Academy in 1817 and at the British Institution in 1818, and was from that time a frequent contributor to both exhibitions as well as to the Society of British Artists. Kidd was very successful in depicting the pathos and humour of rustic life, and his pictures long maintained their popularity, particularly through the medium of engraving. In 1829 Kidd was elected an honorary member of the Royal Scottish Academy. Never able to manage his own affairs, Kidd fell at the end of his life into hopeless financial embarrassment, and was ultimately supported by his friends and a pension from the Royal Academy. He died in London on Christmas eve 1863. A version of his 1832 picture *Indulging*, now at the National Gallery of Scotland, shows Kidd at his finest,

echoing both the psychological and the technical qualities of early work by Wilkie. A small panel, *John Toole the Actor in a Character Part*, in a private collection in Scotland, also reveals considerable charm and characterization.

L. H. CUST, rev. MUNGO CAMPBELL

Sources D. Macmillan, *Painting in Scotland: the golden age* (1986), 175, pl. 90 • W. D. McKay and F. Rinder, *The Royal Scottish Academy, 1826–1916* (1917); repr. (1975) • Graves, *Artists* • file notes, NG Scot.

Kidd, William (1803–1867), publisher and ornithologist, was apprenticed early in life to Baldwin, Craddock, and Joy, a firm of London booksellers. He afterwards entered business on his own account, and had shops successively in Chandos and Regent streets, London. While at Chandos Street he published a *Guide to Gravesend*, *Popular Little Secrets*, and other short essays written by himself. Between May and October 1835 he published twenty-four numbers of a weekly, *London Journal*, dealing with natural history; from 1852 to 1854 he brought out a similar monthly periodical called *Kidd's Own Journal* (later reissued), and during 1863–4 published ten numbers of *Essays and Sketches* on miscellaneous subjects. By that date he had sold his business, and devoted himself entirely to his favourite studies. He was always a keen student of nature, and possessed an astonishing gift of endearing himself to animals. In the later years of his life he lived in New Road, Hammersmith, and set up a fine aviary, which was burnt down and never rebuilt.

Kidd was an independent and eccentric thinker, and talker on religious and social subjects, and delivered many lectures in various parts of the country, under titles such as 'Genial gossip', 'Fashion and its victims', 'The value of little things', and 'Happiness made comparatively easy' (*Liverpool Mercury*, 8 March 1856). As a naturalist Kidd's chief works were: *The Canary* (1854), *The Aviary and its Occupants* (2 pts, 1856), and a number of small books on the goldfinch, the linnet, and other British song birds. He also wrote an introduction to Westcott's *Autobiography of a Gossamer Spider* (1857) and, with F. Buckland, several papers in *Birds and Bird Life* (1863), besides contributing papers on birds and related subjects to the *Gardeners' Chronicle*, and similar periodicals. Between 1854 and 1856 he published many pamphlets on ephemeral subjects, such as *The Heart's Proper Element* (1854), *The Strange Spirits of the Day* (1855), and *The Charmed Ring* (1856).

Kidd, who was married, died at his home, 3 Talbot Villas, New Road, Hammersmith, London, on 7 January 1867, his wife surviving him.

M. G. WATKINS, rev. H. C. G. MATTHEW

Sources GM, 4th ser., 3 (1867), 247 • *The Athenaeum* (12 Jan 1867), 52 • CGPLA Eng. & Wales (1867)

Wealth at death under £1000: resworn probate, May 1867, CGPLA Eng. & Wales

Kidder, Edward (1665/6–1739), cookery teacher and writer, taught cookery in London between about 1720 and 1734, but little else about his life is known. The evidence for his activities is confined mostly to his one published work, the *Receipts of Pastry and Cookery*. In publication by

1720, this exists in six different versions; they give different addresses for his cooking schools and carry his portrait, but the date of the first edition is unknown. All copies are engraved, unusually for a cookery book at the time.

About 1720 Kidder taught at three London cookery schools, in St Martin's-le-Grand, Norris Street, and Little Lincoln's Inn Fields. After abandoning the two latter in 1721 he divided his time between two schools, teaching three afternoons a week at St Martin's-le-Grand and three afternoons at a school next to Furnival's Inn in Holborn, until in 1722 or 1723 he moved to Queen Street, near St Thomas Apostles. Some of his pupils wrote his recipes in blank books with a printed title page, one of which, inscribed by the owner, shows that Kidder was still teaching in Queen Street in 1734. Having risen socially, he donned a gentlemanly wig for his portrait. Passers-by in Holborn 'must have taken notice of a pastry-cook's shop with the following remarkable inscription over the door; "Kidder's pastry-school"' an 'extraordinary Academy … calculated to instruct young ladies in the art and mystery of tarts and cheese-cakes' (*Connoisseur*, 2.190–91). The 'scholars' were mostly 'lower class' (ibid., 192), but the 1720 title page of *Receipts* announced: 'Ladies may be taught at their own Houses'.

Although Kidder ran a pastry school, his recipes covered the whole range of soups, salads, meat, fish, poultry, sauces, and jellies, as well as pies and tarts. His recipes were repeatedly plagiarized throughout the eighteenth century, yet Kidder seems not to have plagiarized recipes himself. He probably taught his students to make established favourites, so even if his *Receipts* may not be especially inventive, it is a valuable record of 170 standard English dishes of the day, accompanied by attractive designs for pie shapes and decorations. The first recipe for puff pastry (identical to the standard commercial product of today) to appear in print is Kidder's.

Kidder died at his house in Holborn on 23 April 1739, aged seventy-three. One of three almost identical obituaries called him 'the famous Pastry-Master' and claimed that he had 'taught near 6000 Ladies the Art of Pastry' (*London Magazine*, 205). SIMON VAREY

Sources E. Kidder, *E. Kidder's receipts of pastry and cookery, for the use of his scholars* [1720] [see also William Andrews Clark Memorial Library, MS K465 M3.R295; bound in London 1720, 1722, 1734] · Mr Town [G. Colman and B. Thornton], *The connoisseur, by Mr Town, critic and censor-general*, 5th edn, 2 (1767), 191–2 · *London Magazine*, 8 (1739), 205 · A. Boyer, *The political state of Great Britain*, 57 (1739)
Likenesses engraving, William Andrews Clark Memorial Library; repro. in Kidder, *Receipts of pastry and cookery*, frontispiece

Kidder, Richard (*bap.* 1634, *d.* 1703), bishop of Bath and Wells, was born at East Grinstead, Sussex, where he was baptized on 9 February 1634, the eighth of nine children of William Kidder, an impoverished member of the lesser gentry, and his wife, Elsabeth (*d.* c.1648), remembered by her son as a woman of great puritan piety.

Education and early career After receiving a basic early education from a local gentlewoman Kidder went to the local grammar school where he was taught 'without reward' by

a Dutchman, a royalist in Anglican orders, Reyner Herman from Nijmegen (*Life*, 2). Kidder later claimed that he owed much to the education he had received from Herman in Latin, Greek, religious principles, and generosity to the poor. Though sufficiently prepared for entry to university, Kidder had insufficient means, and initially trained as an apothecary at Sevenoaks. Nevertheless friends raised money for him and he entered Emmanuel College, Cambridge, as a sizar in June 1649. Here one of the fellows, Samuel Cradock, a noted presbyterian divine, taught him, encouraged him in the religious life, and supplied him with money to finish the course; Kidder later wrote, "tis hardly possible that one man can owe to another more than I do to him' (*Life*, 4). Kidder graduated BA in 1652, but, still without money, left the university, only to be elected a fellow at Emmanuel three years later. Several men who were fellow bishops with him in the 1690s, including John Tillotson, Thomas Tenison, and Simon Patrick, were then at Cambridge; one, James Gardiner, bishop of Lincoln from 1695 to 1705, was also at Emmanuel. Kidder proceeded MA in 1656.

Despite his presbyterian ambience, and despite Cradock's profound influence, Kidder made a clear decision to reject presbyterian ordination and seek Anglican orders, despite the risk of personal disadvantage. In November 1658 Ralph Brownrigg, the deprived bishop of Exeter, ordained him both deacon and priest in one day at a private house in Bury St Edmunds. In 1659 Kidder was appointed to the college living of Stanground, Huntingdonshire. Despite his later protestations that as far as possible he used prayers agreeable to Anglicanism, he must also have conformed to the Westminster directory. Though he declared he had good orders and title, had never taken the covenant, and was 'entirely satisfied in episcopacy and with a liturgy' (*Life*, 11) he refused to subscribe to the newly amended prayer book of 1662 until he had seen it. It did not appear until three weeks after the date required for his conformity, and he was deprived of his living.

Nevertheless, Kidder stayed in the parish, attending the church and preaching in London and the countryside. Without a living and with a young family, following his marriage to his wife, Elisabeth, he was indigent. By 1664 he had conformed, and Arthur Capel, earl of Essex, appointed him to the rectory of Rayne, Essex. Whereas the people at Stanground were 'modest and teachable', here they were 'factious to the greatest degree … such despisers they were of the Common Prayer' (*Life* 14). In his sermons twice on each Sunday, later published in *Convivium coeleste*, he encouraged them to attend holy communion frequently. Afterwards he called those years the 'lost part of [his] life' (ibid.). Here he published *A Young Man's Duty* (1671), so popular that by 1750 it had run to ten editions, and he contributed an appendix of Hebrew proverbs to a collection by his friend John Ray, the botanist (1670). The plague of 1665, bringing many deaths in the village, added to his troubles. Though his own house was infected and isolated and his wife, Elisabeth, smitten, his whole family, including her, survived, and yet all three of his children died soon afterwards from other causes. In 1674 William Sancroft, then dean of St Paul's, offered him the living of St Helen, Bishopsgate, with its huge church and large congregations of well-to-do people. Though he later recorded, 'I would rather have continued minister of St Helen's than gain an archbishopric' (ibid., 19), he served there only briefly. He refused to be instituted, partly for reasons of health, but mainly because, unlike in his other livings, many 'devout and regular' parishioners of puritan persuasion refused to kneel to receive communion, in breach of canon law. Kidder was unwilling to enforce this demand and thus 'send them to the Nonconformists' (Cassan, 2.123).

St Martin Outwich, London In 1674 Kidder was appointed preacher at the Rolls, which gave him an income, and by the patronage of the Merchant Taylors' Company he was instituted to the small, impoverished parish of St Martin Outwich, next door to the lucrative St Helen's. Despite the poor St Martin's stipend he refused dispensation to hold it in plurality with his rectory at Rayne. This he now resigned. Consequently once his Rolls post unexpectedly ended after only four terms he was again in poverty. This, however, was partly relieved by his acting as tutor to Sir William Dawes, later archbishop of York, and George Harbin, the future nonjuror and friend of Thomas Ken, until they went to university. Kidder now joined London's exceptionally gifted clerical circle; the future archbishops Tillotson, Tenison, Wake, and Sharp were fellow incumbents. Many were part of the moderate group connected with Daniel Finch, later second earl of Nottingham. Their spirituality, scholarship, and pastoral care provided 'a luminous interlude', 'a small awakening' in the church (Rupp, 51). The intense spirituality of Kidder's friend Anthony Horneck had a powerful influence on him. It was in this period that gout first struck Kidder; it was to remain his unwelcome companion for life. So painful was it that he soon had to preach kneeling. In 1680 tragedy struck again; another three of his children, including two favourite sons already at Merchant Taylors' School, died, this time from smallpox, a blow which 'laid [Kidder] very low' (Cassan, 2.131). In the parish he catechized zealously to enable parishioners not just to learn but also to understand. He published a little catechism, held frequent communions, and spent much time visiting the poor. Though work was hard it was for him 'the most comfortable and easy part of my life' (Life, 35).

Kidder was now a popular preacher, and increasingly his sermons were printed. The governors of Christ's Hospital entrusted him with the task of examining its condition, his report revealing serious shortcomings. Furthermore, Heneage Finch, first earl of Nottingham, the lord chancellor, had presented him to a prebend of Norwich (1681), which alleviated his poverty. Yet in the 1680s he declined other income producing appointments, including a lectureship in Ipswich twice, a lucrative living in Kent offered by Archbishop Sancroft, and one in Barnes by John Tillotson, dean of St Paul's. Meanwhile, his writing continued, initially with works of pastoral concern, *Charity Directed* (1676), *Discourse on the Christian Sufferer Supported*

(1680), and a second edition of *Convivium coeleste* with prayers (1684). These were followed by *A Demonstration of the Messias* (1684), a more academic work aimed at Jews and deists. He also participated in a translation into Latin of the works of John Lightfoot, the great Hebraist, which became 'a long and painful employment' (Life, 37).

In James II's reign Kidder entered the controversy provoked by the Catholicizing policies, preaching, for instance, against popery on several occasions before the mayor of London. When he perceived the papist tide seeming to threaten Norwich, Kidder was there working hard distributing his books and leaflets. His writings also reflect the time. In 1687 he contributed *The Thirteenth Note, on the Confession of Adversaries* in a reply, with others, to Bellarmine's century-old fifteen notes of the true church. This he followed with *A Second Dialogue between a New Catholic Convert and a Protestant* (1687). His *Reflections on a French Testament of 1686* was published only in 1690 after the revolution. During the turbulent period after Archbishop Sancroft and six bishops had been imprisoned, tried for seditious libel, acquitted, then released, one of them, William Lloyd of St Asaph, stayed secretly with him for several weeks.

Revolution and preferment In 1689, after the accession of William and Mary, Kidder was appointed royal chaplain. As part of Nottingham's group of moderate clergy, he was appointed to the commission set up by William III to review the liturgy and canons for the possible comprehension of dissenters. His particular role was to examine the translation of the Psalms. His meticulous written analysis of the psalter, comparing the original Hebrew with the current version, displayed both his skill as a Hebraist and his natural scholarly qualities. Unfortunately the commission had no time to examine it and it bore no immediate fruit. Nevertheless preferment was once again on the horizon. Even so, again on health grounds he refused a prestigious and wealthy offer, this time of St Paul's, Covent Garden. In 1689, however, when Nottingham recommended him for the deanery of Peterborough, he immediately accepted. Installed in person he clearly found the role rewarding. He was in residence each summer, presiding at chapter meetings; he ordered an annual chapter inspection of the school, and kept good hospitality, living 'in very great peace with the prebendaries' (Life, 60). In 1690 he was created DD at Cambridge by royal mandate.

In the following year Tillotson, now archbishop of Canterbury, with considerable lack of sensitivity, recommended Kidder for the see of Peterborough in succession to his own bishop, Thomas White, who had been deprived as a nonjuror. Kidder bluntly refused, and further made it known that he would decline all others, especially Bath and Wells where Thomas Ken had been deprived. Meanwhile, however, William Beveridge had refused that see, and in a confusion of messages, Kidder found it offered to himself by royal command. After a few days' delay he accepted and was appointed, but soon regretted it. 'I should not have done it were it to do again. I did not consult my ease' (Life, 63). He knew he had a hard act to follow, for the saintly Ken was popular in the diocese and turned out to be resentful of Kidder's intrusion. Tillotson consecrated Kidder as bishop in St Mary-le-Bow Church on 30 August 1691. He was enthroned in person at Wells in September, but returned to Westminster to take the oaths in the Lords on 31 October.

Bishop of Bath and Wells Kidder entered his episcopate with the best of intentions. Despite his poor health he was stubbornly conscientious, rejected the quiet life, and, in common with other new bishops of the 1690s, set about the reform of the diocese. He returned to Wells in May 1692 for his first ordination, only to be so gout stricken that he had to be carried into the palace chapel. He recovered enough to start his primary visitation at Axbridge on 2 June, but in his charge he was characteristically brusque. He threatened suspension to clergy who failed to fulfil the marriage regulations; he further demanded an end to non-residence. 'An oath', he declared, 'is not to be trifled with' (*Charge*, 28–31). By the end of his visitation his gout struck again, 'so violent that there was little hope of my life' (*Life*, 65). In July he began his visitation of the cathedral and the college of vicars-choral, where he was immediately in conflict over non-residence.

Kidder ordained regularly. After his first ordination at Trinity 1692 he conferred orders at least twice a year, usually at Trinity and Michaelmas, sometimes in Advent. All ordinations except one, at St Alfege, London, were held within the diocese, usually in the palace chapel, occasionally in the cathedral or at Bath. Twice, in 1692 and 1693, much to the cathedral chapter's disgust, he conferred Anglican orders *extra tempora* (i.e. outside the traditional ember seasons), but after strict examination, on the talented former dissenters John Gardiner and Nicholas Malarré. If this appeared lax to some he was, however, ruthless with forged orders, even chasing culprits into northern dioceses. He carried out regular triennial visitations of the diocese and cathedral. On his one recorded confirmation tour (1693) in which he congratulated incumbents for conscientious preparation, there were crowds at Bridgwater. He later joyfully recorded, 'I thought I had never done in my whole life a better day's work; I am sure a more painful and wearisome day I never spent' (*Life*, 82).

Despite these positive aspects Kidder's episcopate is sadly remembered more for his running battles with the clergy, especially the cathedral chapter who were supporters of Ken. The Creightons were dominant. Robert (the elder) had been dean and then bishop. His son, also Robert, was precentor, and indeed the whole body was little more than the Creighton family's 'genteel mafiosi' (Rupp, 501). Kidder immediately set to work. 'Corruptions', he warned, 'do not come in all at once and 'tis time to put a stop to them when they are grown to the height that now they are' (*Life*, 124). But in his honest, vigorous confrontation over chapter elections he misjudged the situation. The cathedral clergy, already hostile to him as Ken's usurper, were increasingly antagonized and uncooperative.

Hence Kidder's ordination of the two former dissenters caused major convulsions. In one case two canons, Robert Creighton, the precentor, and Thomas Cheney, once Ken's chaplain, at first positively refused to assist, one initially threatening to leave the diocese rather than participate. Kidder was also at odds with Edwin Sandys, archdeacon of Wells, still one of Ken's close friends. Kidder even initially suspended him for not attending an ordination in 1697, a suspension Kidder had to lift on appeal. He had further trouble with other clergy, and also with laymen such as Harry Bridges, the Jacobite supporter of Ken. The Bridges affair ended in court at London Guildhall, where Kidder had to appear in person to wring an apology from him. Another antagonist was the local doctor, Claver Morris, who tried to court his daughter. Despite all this, as bishop Kidder continued to write, publishing *A Commentary upon the Five Books of Moses* (1694), designed for families, the brief *Life* (1697) of his friend Anthony Horneck the divine, and his *Messias Part II* (1699). He was Boyle lecturer in 1693. A pamphlet *On the Sins of Infirmity* went to the printers just before his death and was published posthumously (1704).

Not a political bishop, Kidder nevertheless regularly attended the Lords until April 1695, after which, as gout took its hold, his attendances grew increasingly spasmodic. Nevertheless, when the attainder of the Jacobite Sir John Fenwick was debated in the Lords in December 1696 Kidder attended the house. Along with eight other prelates, but unlike Archbishop Tenison, he voted against the attainder, and in January he registered his official protest against the proceedings. He attended frequently in the first year of Anne's reign, 1702, but only occasionally in 1703.

Since the late 1670s Kidder had been wracked by ill health. His gout, first appearing at St Martin's, gradually dominated his activities, especially as bishop. He was carried not only to his first ordination in 1692, but also to the Fenwick debates in the Lords in 1696. Increasingly from 1695 he had to winter in Wells, and in 1698 he was ill for twenty-five weeks. Yet he still continued to write in his clear meticulous hand helpful letters to friends outside the diocese. Despite complaints of mounting weakness in August 1702 it was not gout but the great storm of 26–7 November 1703 that killed him. That night Kidder and his wife, Elisabeth, were tragically crushed to death by a chimney stack collapsing through the roof of the bishop's palace. They were buried in Wells Cathedral on 14 December. His wife, with whom Kidder had spent most of his adult life, and who had survived both plague in 1665 and smallpox in 1680, remains a shadowy figure. Two daughters survived them, one of whom, Anne, through her will of 1728, paid for his monument in the cathedral.

Conclusion A noted Hebraist and Old Testament scholar, vigorously publishing and preaching in the 1670s and 1680s, Kidder was also a fine, dedicated, and caring parish priest in Essex and London. He was also friendly with future nonjurors, including William Sancroft, Robert Nelson, and George Harbin. Once bishop, however, his fortune waned. Plagued by persistent ill health he had the misfortune of following Thomas Ken, the most saintly of the nonjurors, whose aura was still all pervasive. Indeed, living nearby, Ken was himself uncharacteristically bitter, dubbing Kidder 'latitudinarian traditour' and after Kidder's death accusing him of not 'keeping the flock within the fold' but even of encouraging them 'to stray' (Plumptre, 2.138). Furthermore, Ken's supporters permeated the diocese, none more intractable than the corrupt cathedral chapter and the archdeacon of Wells. Kidder himself was well aware of his sticky wicket. Taunted during Lords debates for not toeing the government line with 'Don't you know whose bread you are eating?' he retorted briskly, 'I eat no bread but poor Dr. Ken's' (Noble, 2.101n.). When in 1702 Queen Anne offered Kidder translation to Carlisle to facilitate Ken's return, Kidder readily agreed, only to find that Ken rejected the scheme.

Despite this Kidder lacked the sensitivity, perhaps even the sense of humour, to cope with this unenviable situation. Even if he had been in good health he was perhaps temperamentally unsuited to any bishopric, let alone Ken's. Kidder's autobiographical work, verging on the paranoid in places, obsessively refers to the enemies ranged against him and wearily insists on the blamelessness of his own conduct. It is hard to conceive of either Ken or Kidder's successor, George Hooper, writing as he did. His earlier refusals of prestigious livings reveal perhaps that Kidder tended to shy away from heavier burdens, and that he may have been temperamentally unsuited for them. He clearly felt at ease with the Peterborough deanery with its quieter, more scholarly life. As intruder in Ken's see he faced an impossible situation, but his stubborn conscientiousness, his determination to root out corruption, and his confrontational style lacked the skilled diplomacy Hooper later successfully used to loosen the Creighton grip on the cathedral. Nonjurors might rejoice at Kidder's tragic death, but for him also it was perhaps a merciful release. 'A sad, scholarly man' (Rupp, 39), a tragic figure, having lost six children, dogged for years with agonizing ill health, now embattled and alienated in his diocese, he led a life that was far from happy. The traditional cry *nolo episcopari* ('I do not wish to be made a bishop') was perhaps never more honestly and appropriately made.   WILLIAM MARSHALL

Sources E. G. Rupp, *Religion in England, 1688–1791* (1986) · *The life of Richard Kidder, bishop of Bath and Wells*, ed. A. E. Robinson, Somerset RS, 37 (1924) · *Calamy rev.* · *The charge of Richard Kidder at his primary visitation, 1692* (1693) · R. Kidder, *Convivium coeleste* (1674) · R. Kidder, *The young man's duty* (1671) · Kidder's episcopal register, Som. ARS, D/D/B24 · Kidder's subscription book, 1691–1703, Som. ARS, D/D/Bs 7 · will, PRO, PROB 11/474, sig. 31, fols. 245v–246v · bishop of London's register, 1660–75, GL, MS 9531/16 · chapter act book, Peterborough Cathedral, 1660–1814, CUL · *JHL*, 14–17 (1685–1704) · E. H. Plumptre, *The life of Thomas Ken*, 2 vols. (1888) · W. M. Marshall, *George Hooper* (1976) · *Fasti Angl.* (Hardy) · Venn, *Alum. Cant.*, 1/1–2 · S. H. Cassan, *The lives of the bishops of Bath and Wells*, 2 (1829) · Evelyn, *Diary* · *CSP dom.*, 1689–90 · *A biographical history of England, from the revolution to the end of George I's reign: being a continuation of the Rev. J. Granger's work*, ed. M. Noble, 3 vols. (1806) · *IGI* · A. J. Jewers, *Wells Cathedral: its monumental inscriptions* (1892), 158–9 · G. Hennessy, *Novum repertorium ecclesiasticum parochiale Londinense, or, London diocesan clergy succession from the earliest time to the year 1898* (1898)
Archives BL, letters, Add. MSS · Wells Cathedral, MS life
Likenesses R. Clamp, stipple, pubd 1794 (after M. Beale), BM, NPG; repro. in F. G. Waldron, *The Biographical mirrour*, 3 vols. (1795–1810) · M. Beale, oils, Emmanuel College, Cambridge · oils (after M. Beale), bishop's palace, Wells, Somerset

Kidderminster [Kedermyster, Kydermynstre]**, Richard** (*c*.1461–1533/4), abbot of Winchcombe, was probably born at Kidderminster, Worcestershire. The names of his parents are not known. He entered the Benedictine abbey of Winchcombe in Gloucestershire as a novice at the age of fifteen, was ordained acolyte and subdeacon on 18 September 1479 at Worcester, and deacon on 21 September 1482 at Bromyard. About 1483, under the patronage of Abbot John Twyning, he was sent to study theology at Gloucester College in Oxford, where he stayed for three and a half years. He was later admitted BTh, and incepted as DTh in February 1497. In July 1488, soon after his return from Oxford, he was elected abbot of Winchcombe.

As abbot of Winchcombe Richard Kidderminster insisted on both regular observance and a rigorous regime of study within the cloister. Kidderminster's own description of Winchcombe as a 'new university' was once accepted at face value, but more recent research has emphasized the traditional nature of the studies encouraged by Kidderminster at Winchcombe. Kidderminster believed that monks could be better instructed in the protective environment of their cloisters than in the monastic colleges at the universities. His policy seems to have paid off at Winchcombe. Within a few years the size of the community had increased markedly, and when Cromwell attempted to impose a new system of theological education on the abbey in 1535 the monks resisted vigorously. Kidderminster's system of claustral education was neither a significant departure from accepted English Benedictine practice, nor was it an attempt to introduce the new learning of the universities into his monastic community, but the success of his educational venture does demonstrate what an efficient and determined abbot could achieve with limited resources. Kidderminster was also responsible for improving the fabric of the abbey and the town. It was during his abbacy that the precinct was enclosed on the town side by a great ashlar wall, and his carved initials could still be seen on doorways in the parish church and at The George inn at the end of the twentieth century.

Kidderminster's talents as an administrator were recognized by the provincial chapter of the English Benedictines, and he was called upon to fill several offices during his time as abbot of Winchcombe. His first appointment was as collector-general of triennial contributions; by 1513 he was a visitor to various monasteries within the English province; and at the time of Wolsey's attempt to reform the Benedictines, in 1519–20, Kidderminster was third president of the provincial chapter. It is not known what part he played in the rejection of Wolsey's proposed reforms, but considering his own attempts to improve discipline at Winchcombe, and the fact that his commentary on the rule of St Benedict so impressed Bishop John Longland that he sought to have it distributed to all Benedictine monasteries within the diocese of Lincoln, it is probable that Kidderminster was a supporter of limited reform.

By the beginning of Henry VIII's reign Kidderminster was widely recognized as one of the foremost prelates in England. He preached before the king in March 1511, and was soon thereafter appointed as one of the four representatives of the realm at the Lateran council in 1512. It was probably at this time, or perhaps on an earlier visit to Rome, that he preached before the pope. But it is his bold sermon preached at Paul's Cross in London on 4 February 1515 for which he is most famous. In it he defended the clergy's immunity from secular legal jurisdiction by condemning the statute of 4 Hen. VIII c. 2, which had removed the benefit of clergy from clerics not in major orders. The sermon, coming as it did on the heels of the Richard Hunne case, caused a great commotion in the Commons, and led to such heated debate that the king appointed Henry Standish of the London Franciscans to dispute the question with Kidderminster in public. When the spiritual lords, supporting Kidderminster's stance, summoned Standish before convocation in November 1515 to explain his actions, the king determined that convocation had committed *praemunire*, and Cardinal Wolsey was forced to prostrate himself before the king and beg forgiveness for the clergy. In spite of its political sensitivity this affair does not seem to have harmed Kidderminster's career. He continued to be on good terms with both Wolsey and Thomas Cromwell, and in 1531, when Henry VIII was attempting to have his divorce case transferred from Rome to England, Kidderminster was described by the king as being a man of such remarkable learning and experience that he should be a member of the tribunal judging the case.

The only surviving fragment of the several books written by Kidderminster during a long and active career is a manuscript copy of his unpublished history of Winchcombe Abbey completed in 1523 (Bodl. Oxf., MS Twyne 24, pp. 533–58). The atrocious state of the abbey's muniments initially hampered the progress of this work, but Kidderminster was able to consult documents in Rome, and at the Benedictine abbeys of York, Whitby, and Durham, which eventually allowed him to piece together the history of his own monastery. Kidderminster is also said to have written the tracts *Contra doctrinam M. Lutheri* and *De veniis religionis*, but no copies of these survive.

Kidderminster's long and distinguished rule as abbot of Winchcombe continued until late in 1525, when he resigned on account of old age and ill health. He lived on at the abbey after his resignation, and remained active in the monastery's affairs. He wrote his last surviving letter to Thomas Cromwell on 13 January 1532, and died some time between 9 December 1533, when he was licensed to act as a confessor in the diocese of Worcester, and 25 August 1534, when he was not named among the monks of Winchcombe who took the oath of supremacy.

PETER CUNICH

Sources D. Knowles [M. C. Knowles], *The religious orders in England*, 3 (1959), 53–4, 91–5 · W. A. Pantin, 'Abbot Kidderminster and monastic studies', *Downside Review*, 47 (1929), 1–14 · B. Twyne, 'Excerpt ex libro sive transcripto de fundacione monasterii Wynchilcumbensis', 1523, Bodl. Oxf., MS Twyne 24, 552–3 ·

Emden, *Oxf.*, 2.1047 · W. A. Pantin, ed., *Documents illustrating the activities of … the English black monks, 1215–1540*, 3 vols., CS, 3rd ser., 45, 47, 54 (1931–7), vol. 3, pp. 119, 192–3 · *VCH Gloucestershire*, 2.71 · G. Haigh, *The history of Winchcombe Abbey* (1947), 161–9 · D. Royce, ed., *Landboc, sive, Registrum monasterii beatae Mariae virginis et sancti Cenhelmi de Winchelcumba*, 2 (1903), xviii, xxxii-xxxv, lvii · T. Warton, *The history of English poetry*, 4 vols. (1774–81), vol. 2, pp. 447–8 · *The letter book of Robert Joseph*, ed. H. Aveling and W. A. Pantin, OHS, new ser., 19 (1967), xxvii, xlix, 246–7 · Wood, *Ath. Oxon.*, new edn, 1.61–3 · *LP Henry VIII*, vols. 1–5 · Bodl. Oxf., MS Dodsworth 65, fols. 1–4v · Bishop Ghinucci's register, Worcs. RO, b716.094 – BA. 2648/9(i), p. 140 · Record Commissioners, *7th report*, appx 2, p. 304

Kidgell, John (*bap.* 1722, *d. c.*1780), Church of England clergyman and political writer, was baptized on 28 April 1722 at St Mary Woolnoth, London, the son of John Kidgell of St Mary Woolchurch. He was admitted to Winchester College in 1733, and matriculated at Hertford College, Oxford, on 21 March 1741, graduating BA in 1744 and MA in 1747. He was briefly a fellow of Hertford.

Kidgell was ordained a priest, but paid little attention to his duties. He was chaplain to a fellow Wykehamist, William Douglas, third earl of March and from 1778 fourth duke of Queensberry (1725–1810), a man whose dissoluteness matched his own. He stayed in London with Lord March, living as a man about town. Horace Walpole describes him as a 'dainty, priggish parson, much in vogue among the old ladies for his gossiping and quaint sermons' (Walpole, *Last Journals*, 1.247). Preferment gradually accumulated. In 1756 he was assistant preacher to the bishop of Bangor, in December 1758 he became rector of Woolverston, Suffolk, and by 1761 he was morning preacher at the Berkeley Chapel, London. On 7 May 1762 he was instituted to the rectory of Godstone, Surrey (in the gift of John Garth, esquire, of Devizes, Wiltshire), and on 8 June following to that of Horne in the same county by Sir Kendrick Clayton.

Kidgell's embroilment in the Wilkes affair wrecked his career in the Church of England. How far he acted on his own initiative and how far at March's behest remains hard to determine, for his chronic indebtedness had rendered him financially dependent on the peer, his principal patron. In June 1763 Kidgell obtained proofs of the notorious *Essay on Woman* from one of Wilkes's printers (Michael Curry) and money changed hands. Kidgell insisted to the printers that his plan was merely to answer the *Essay* by a series of letters in the press, but it was at this point that March stepped in, he having been in secret consultation with John Montagu, fourth earl of Sandwich, and probably with other members of the administration. Kidgell was ordered to 'endeavour to discover how much of the work was printed off, and to obtain if possible a copy thereof' (Guildhall Library, MS 214, vol. 2, fol. 104) so that the government could build a watertight case against Wilkes for obscene libel. Sandwich duly moved in the Lords that Wilkes be voted the author of the *Essay*, and Kidgell found himself damned as a sordid informer on all sides.

Ignoring the advice of the Treasury solicitor, Philip Carteret Webb, Kidgell then attempted to justify his conduct (and that of the government) with *A genuine and succinct narrative of a scandalous, obscene, and exceedingly profane libel, entitled 'An essay on woman', etc.* (1763). This text, with its show of righteous indignation, ended any chance he had of securing the wealthy rectory of St James's, Piccadilly, through the good offices of Sandwich. His pleas of innocence were received incredulously. Many pamphlets abused and condemned him as a hypocrite priest and prostitute writer, who had publicly offended 'the cause of Decency' by his conduct (*An Expostulatory Letter*, 9). Walpole, who called him 'that dirty dog' (to Hertford, 22 Jan 1764, Walpole, *Corr.*, 38.294), noted how 'He has been pelted in every newspaper, while the work itself [*An Essay on Woman*] was forgot' (to Sir Horace Mann, 8 Jan 1764, Walpole, *Corr.*, 22.195). John Almon put the case succinctly: 'Can the people of England behold such an act, and however they may detest the *Essay on Woman*, not detest and abhor the means by which it was procured?' (Almon, 14).

Kidgell fled the country, carrying with him the funds of the Godstone turnpike (which he tried subsequently to explain) some time after being publicly abused during the trial of Wilkes for seditious libel. He lived initially in the United Provinces, and kept a school in Utrecht to support his family. Between 1766 and 1768 he was writing regularly to Lord March, adamant that he had crossed the channel to avoid the earl's reputation being ruined and hinting strongly at court action unless March paid off his debts. Kidgell was racked by guilt and anger, talked of a forgery introduced into Wilkes's papers, and even wanted to obtain forgiveness from Wilkes personally. March would not be browbeaten and Kidgell was obliged to entreat his pardon for any intemperate words, and his 'making intercession for the most contemptible of men' (6 May 1768, Guildhall Library, MS 214, vol. 3, fol. 43). Meanwhile, in June 1766 the churchwarden of Horne, spurred on by Sir Kendrick Clayton, unsuccessfully instituted proceedings against him in the court of arches for non-residence. Kidgell died *c*.1780 in poverty, his successor as incumbent at Godstone being presented in May that year. His letter of 3 August 1766 to March explains that he is married and has dependants but nothing more is known about his wife and family.

Kidgell published (anonymously) *The Card* (2 vols., 1755), a series of tales partly in epistolary form, and *Original Fables* (1763), in English and French, both for private circulation. In the *Oxford Sausage* (1764, 119–24) there are some amusing lines by him called 'Table Talk', written in 1745. But Kidgell will always be remembered for his conduct over Wilkes and *An Essay on Woman*. Charles Churchill placed him high among the infamous in his gallery of satiric portraits, assailing Kidgell with deep irony in 'The Author' (391–8):

> Are these the arts which policy supplies?
> Are these the steps by which grave churchmen rise?
> Forbid it, Heaven; or, should it turn out so,
> Let me and mine continue mean and low.
> Such be their arts whom interest controls;
> Kidgell and I have free and modest souls:

> We scorn preferment which is gain'd by sin,
> And will, though poor without, have peace within.
> (Churchill, *Poems*)

Kidgell was essentially a weak man who was, nevertheless, honest enough to admit that want of 'experience and discretion' (to March, n.d., Guildhall Library, MS 214, vol. 3, fol. 11) had been his undoing.   NIGEL ASTON

Sources *GM*, 1st ser., 26 (1756), 151 • *GM*, 1st ser., 38 (1768), 613 • T. F. Kirby, *Winchester scholars: a list of the wardens, fellows, and scholars of … Winchester College* (1888), 238 • Foster, *Alum. Oxon.* • Nichols, *Lit. anecdotes*, 9.659 • *N&Q*, 11th ser., 9 (1914), 121–3 *passim* • O. Manning and W. Bray, *The history and antiquities of the county of Surrey*, 2 (1809), 320–21, 337 • E. W. Brayley, J. Britton, and E. W. Brayley, jun., *A topographical history of Surrey*, 4 (1844), 148 • *The last journals of Horace Walpole*, ed. Dr Doran, rev. A. F. Steuart, 1 (1910), 247 • Walpole, *Corr.*, 22.195; 38.294 • 'A. Layman', *An expostulatory letter to the Reverend Mr Kidgell*, 3rd edn (1763) • J. Almon, *A letter to J. Kidgell* (1763) • [C. Johnstone], *Chrysal, or, The adventures of a guinea*, 4th edn, 4 vols. (1764–5), 201–20 • R. R. Rea, *The English press in politics, 1760–1774* (1963), 72–6 • W. C. Brown, *Charles Churchill: poet, rake, and rebel* (1953), 108–9 • R. Postgate, *That devil Wilkes* (1929) • A. Hamilton, *The infamous essay on woman, or, John Wilkes seated between vice and virtue* (1972) • C. Churchill, *Poems*, 2 vols. (1764)

Archives BL, Add. MS 19105, fol. 250; 22132, fols. 238–9 • GL, MSS relating to *Rex v. Wilkes*, MS 214, vol. 3, fols. 1–44 • GL, account of proceedings against Mr Wilkes for being author, printer, and publisher of the *Essay on woman*, MS 214, vol. 2 • Hants. RO, 21M65/E2, Surrey Pres. Deeds, E2/1415, 1416; E2/1455

Wealth at death died in poverty

Kidley, William (*b.* 1605), poet, was the son of John Kidley of Dartmouth, Devon, and Margery Archer. He matriculated at Oxford, where he gave his name as Kidley, alias Pointer; he entered Exeter College on 16 July 1624, and graduated BA on 12 November 1627. In 1624 he composed, in his leisure, 'Kidley's Hawkins, or, A poetical relation of the voyage of Sir Richard Hawkins, knight, unto Mare del Zur' and 'History of the year 1588, with other historical passages of these tymes'. Hawkins's account of his pioneering voyage to the south sea in 1593 had been published in 1622. Kidley's panegyrical poem, which is now among the manuscripts at the British Library, has not been printed. It was designed to be in eight books but only six were completed. The text was classically inspired and several marginal notes reveal slight biographical information, which confirms Dartmouth as Kidley's birthplace and refers both to earlier poetic endeavours and to his intended return to Exeter College in 1639.

T. B. SAUNDERS, rev. ELIZABETH HARESNAPE

Sources Wood, *Ath. Oxon.*, new edn, 2.367–74 • Foster, *Alum. Oxon.* • catalogue of Sloane MSS, BL, MS 2024 • *IGI*

Kidson, Frank (1855–1926), writer and antiquary, was born on 15 November 1855 at 16 Alexander Street, Leeds, youngest of the nine children of Francis Prince Kidson (1810–1872), butcher turned lamp-rate collector, and his wife, Mary (1812–1890), daughter of Joseph Roberts, factory owner. Kidson received, in his own words, 'a limited education' as a boarder at 'a somewhat rough local school' (Broadwood, iii), which he supplemented by reading voraciously in his father's large library. Later, through helping his brother Joseph, a partner in a Leeds firm of antique dealers, he acquired a wide knowledge of paintings, ceramics, and antiques. He started to paint and also to write; his first articles appeared during the early 1880s in a periodical called *The Artist*. With his brother he published *Notes on the Old Leeds Pottery* (1892), but until perhaps the turn of the century, his bread and butter assured by a modest private income derived from his maternal grandfather, he believed that his métier would be landscape painting.

From his mother's singing of traditional songs Kidson received an early introduction to a subject in which from the mid-1870s he took an increasing interest. His involvement was antiquarian in character, and during the course of what became a lifetime's habit he haunted salerooms, shops, and street stalls in search of books and manuscripts. As early as March 1886 he listed in his collection ballad operas, instrumental music, songsters, garlands, tune and song books, and a hefty batch of street ballads. The most expensive item was the six volumes of *Pills to Purge Melancholy*, for which he paid 30s.

Primed with extensive knowledge culled from such material and from other collections in libraries, Kidson embarked on a series of articles for the *Leeds Mercury*, starting in 1886 and dealing with the antecedents of a wide range of songs. These were the first of many such pieces, on both song and dance, traditional and composed, printed and oral, which he contributed to newspapers and periodicals. He supplied 365 more for *Grove's Dictionary of Music and Musicians* (2nd edn, 1904–10); and his formidable skill in unravelling a song's pedigree caused his friends to dub him 'the musical Sherlock Holmes' (Francmanis, 1997, ii).

As well as working from printed and written sources Kidson realized the importance of oral tradition. It has to be said that some of his material was secondhand, passed on by colleagues and friends from their own contacts, but he sought informants himself wherever he could, among relatives, servants, workpeople, and street performers. He took advantage of holiday trips to Scotland and north Yorkshire to find more. His niece and unofficially adopted daughter, Emma Kidson (whom he called Ethel), went with him, memorized the tunes, and sang them back to him when he reached a piano and could take them down.

Such methods were scarcely scientific but even so Kidson amassed a valuable corpus of material and acquired a deserved reputation as a pioneer in the field. He corresponded with other song-seekers, met some, including Sabine Baring-Gould, and joined the committee of the English Folk Song Society on its inception in 1898. He published as *Traditional Tunes* (1891) one volume of songs he had noted from oral tradition, and others appeared posthumously. He edited or co-edited several other volumes of songs drawn from a variety of sources. His other publications include *British Music Publishers* (1900), which remained a standard work for over sixty years, and '*The Beggar's Opera': its Predecessors and Successors* (1922), an important monograph which earned him an honorary MA from Leeds University.

Kidson died, unmarried, on 7 November 1926 at his home, 5 Hamilton Avenue, Chapeltown, Leeds. His native city turned down the opportunity of acquiring Kidson's enormous and priceless collection of books and manuscripts, scores and ballads, and the bulk of it eventually went to the Mitchell Library, Glasgow. Some twenty years after his death a friend wrote that Kidson had 'lived to be obscured where once he had been considered foremost in authority' ('Portraits', 135), but the eclipse proved to be of limited duration. A new wave of interest in traditional song, starting in the 1960s, led to the rediscovery of his collection, the reprinting of some of his books, performances at concerts and on record of songs he had noted, and the appearance of essays and at least one PhD thesis on the significance of the work of a man who called himself 'a journalist and a bit of an author' (Graham, 49).

ROY PALMER

Sources R. Palmer, 'Kidson's collecting', *Folk Music Journal*, 5 (1985–9), 150–75 · R. Cowell, 'Kidson's informants', *Folk Music Journal*, 5 (1985–9), 482–8 · J. V. Francmanis, 'The musical Sherlock Holmes: Frank Kidson and the English folk music revival, c.1890–1926', PhD diss., Leeds Metropolitan University, 1997 · J. V. Francmanis, 'The roving artist: Frank Kidson, pioneer song collector', *Folk Music Journal*, 8/1 (2001), 41–66 · 'Portraits: Frank Kidson, 1855–1927, by some of his friends', *Journal of the English Folk Dance and Song Society*, 5/3 (1948), 127–35 · J. Graham, 'The late Mr Kidson', *English Folk-Dance Society's Journal*, 2nd ser., 1 (1927), 48–51 · L. Broadwood, foreword, in F. Kidson, *Folk-songs of the north countrie* (1927) · 'Mr Frank Kidson', *Musical Herald* (Aug 1913), 227–30 · b. cert. · d. cert. · *CGPLA Eng. & Wales* (1927)
Archives Mitchell L., Glas. · Mitchell L., Glas., literary MSS, sketchbooks, and corresp. · NL Scot., notes on Scottish songs | Vaughan Williams Memorial Library, London | SOUND BL NSA, documentary recordings · BL NSA, performance recording
Likenesses photograph, repro. in 'Mr Frank Kidson', facing p. 227 · photographs, Vaughan Williams Memorial Library, London
Wealth at death £1601 11s. 11d.: probate, 26 April 1927, *CGPLA Eng. & Wales*

Kielmansegg, Sophia Charlotte von [*formerly* Countess Sophia Charlotte von Platen und Hallermund], *suo jure* countess of Darlington and *suo jure* countess of Leinster

(1675–1725), courtier, was probably born at Osnabrück, Germany, the daughter of Clara Elisabeth, Baroness von Platen, *née* von Meysenbug (1648–1700), and most likely of Duke Ernst August of Brunswick and Lüneburg (1629–1698), the ruling bishop of Osnabrück. She was half-sister to George Lewis, elector of Hanover from 1698 and *George I of Great Britain from 1714. Her mother's husband, Franz Ernst, Baron von Platen (1631–1709), governor to Ernst August's legitimate sons, was officially described as her father, but her status as Ernst August's illegitimate daughter was tacitly acknowledged at his court, which moved to Hanover when he inherited that duchy in 1679. Sophia Charlotte (a countess after Baron von Platen was promoted count in 1689) grew into a vivacious young woman who established a close relationship with her half-brother George Lewis. In 1701 the elector's mother, Sophia, wrote to a correspondent asserting that, 'to her certain knowledge' (Hatton, 135), Sophia Charlotte was not George Lewis's mistress. That year she married Johann Adolf, Baron von Kielmansegg (1668–1717), deputy master of the horse to George Lewis; they had three sons and two daughters, the elder of whom was Mary Sophia Charlotte *Howe, Viscountess Howe (1703–1782).

Sophia Charlotte and her family followed George I to London in 1714, where her husband acted as master of the horse in England, although he was unable to draw the salary. She mixed easily with the king's British courtiers, who recognized her as 'so great a favourite that the whole court began to pay her uncommon Respect' (*Lady Mary Wortley Montagu: Essays*, 87). She competed for influence with George's mistress, Melusine von der Schulenburg, who was less comfortable with entertaining than was Sophia Charlotte. Many British courtiers were left with the impression that Sophia Charlotte was the king's mistress as well. Charles Burroughs, confectioner to the royal household, was dismissed by George I in 1716 for using 'indecent expressions concerning the King and Madam Kielmanseck [Kielmansegg] as are not fit to be inserted' (Beattie, 136). Unlike Melusine, she was disliked by Caroline, princess of Wales, who 'thought her a wicked Woman' (*Diary of Mary, Countess Cowper*, 13). Much of Sophia Charlotte's energy was devoted to parading and maintaining her access to the king. After Melusine was made duchess of Leinster, Sophia Charlotte, too, was said to be campaigning for an Irish or British peerage. Her ambition was taken for granted: a newsletter of 14 November 1717 remarked that she 'came to town some weeks since on pretence to be with her husband, who has been indisposed, but as others say upon a difference with the Duchess of Munster' (*Portland MSS*, 5.538). Her husband died on 15 November, and his illness, not her rivalry with Melusine, was the more likely reason for her return to London. Between 1717 and 1721 she was frequently referred to as Countess von Platen, which caused later historians confusion as this was the title of her sister-in-law, who although in Hanover was also believed to have influence with George I.

Sophia Charlotte benefited from gifts from those seeking patronage; for example, between August 1715 and February 1720 she received £9545 from James Brydges, first duke of Chandos, and in February 1720, like Melusine (by then duchess of Kendal) she was given £15,000 of stock by the South Sea Company, with the bonus that £120 would be paid for every point the stock rose above £154. Perhaps to counter any loss of face at court following the collapse of the South Sea Bubble, on 11 September 1721, following her naturalization as a British subject, she was created countess of Leinster in the Irish peerage; on 6 April 1722 she was also made countess of Darlington in the British peerage. The letters patent for both titles had George I describe her as '*consanguineam nostram* (i.e., of our common blood)' (Hatton, 134), and her coat of arms included the arms of Brunswick with a bar sinister, asserting her status as an illegitimate daughter of an elector of Hanover. She died at her home in St James's on 20 April 1725, and was buried on 24 April 1725 in Westminster Abbey. Her 'purchased dwelling house in London situate near Hanover Square' (will, fol. 353), in Great George Street, was left to her daughter Lady Howe, but her 'universal heir' (ibid.) was her eldest son, George Lewis, Count von Kielmansegg. The estate was subsequently the subject of a chancery case between Lady Howe on one side and her brothers on the other.

Like her rival Melusine, Sophia Charlotte's place at court fascinated British courtiers and succeeding commentators. Horace Walpole reminisced of:

> being terrified at her enormous figure … Two fierce black eyes, large & rolling, beneath two lofty arched eyebrows, two acres of cheeks spread with crimson, an ocean of neck that overflowed & was not distinguished from the lower part of her body, and no part restrained by stays. (*Reminiscences*, 29–30)

She became 'the Elephant' of legend, her greed epitomized by her immense bulk, who competed with Melusine, 'the Maypole', to satisfy the depraved sexual demands attributed to George I. Late twentieth-century writing, especially that of Ragnhild Hatton, has corrected these misapprehensions, and instead rehabilitated her as a valued courtier of George I, even showing that she was not as obese as tradition has suggested.

MATTHEW KILBURN

Sources R. Hatton, *George I, elector and king* (1978) · J. M. Beattie, *The English court in the reign of George I* (1967) · J. Carswell, *The South Sea Bubble*, rev. edn (1993) · *Diary of Mary, Countess Cowper*, ed. [S. Cowper] (1865) · *The manuscripts of his grace the duke of Portland*, 10 vols., HMC, 29 (1891–1931), vol. 5, p. 538 · GEC, *Peerage*, new edn, 4.80–81; 14.236 · M. W. Montagu, [Account of the court of George I], in *Lady Mary Wortley Montagu: essays and poems and 'Simplicity, a comedy'*, ed. R. Halsband and I. Grundy (1977), 82–94 · *Reminiscences written by Mr Horace Walpole in 1788*, ed. P. Toynbee (1924) · E. G. L. W. H. von Kielmansegg and E. F. C. L. von Kielmansegg, *Familien-Chronik der Herren, Freiherren und Grafen von Kielmansegg*, 2nd edn (1910) · will, PRO, PROB 11/607, sig. 44, fol. 353
Archives Niedersächsisches Hauptstaatsarchiv Hannover, Hanover, letters · priv. coll. | BL, letter to duchess of Marlborough, Add. MS 61475, fol. 86 · BL, letter to Robert Walpole, Add. MS 64750, fol. 16 · BL, letter to Sir Hans Sloane, Sloane 4059, fol. 243
Likenesses portrait, priv. coll.
Wealth at death approx. £60,000—legacies: 1725, will: PRO, PROB 11/607, sig. 44, fol. 353

Kiffin, William (1616–1701), Particular Baptist minister and author, was born in London of unknown parents, both of whom died in 1625 during an outbreak of plague. His surname is Welsh, an indication that his ancestors originally hailed from Wales. David Honeyman claims the family came from Conwy and that Kiffin was 'certainly' a cousin of the Quaker Ellis Hookes (Honeyman, 46). Four years after the death of his parents Kiffin was apprenticed, probably to a glover. There seems to be no truth in the common assertion that he served as an apprentice to John Lilburne, later an agitator for radical Leveller concerns, though Kiffin and Lilburne were friends in later years. In 1631, depressed about his future prospects as a glover, Kiffin decided to run away from his master. He happened by St Antholin's Church, where the puritan Thomas Foxley was preaching that day on 'the duty of servants to masters'. Seeing a crowd of people going into the church, Kiffin decided to join them and became convinced that Foxley's sermon was intentionally aimed at him. He decided to go back to his master with the resolve to hear regularly 'some of them they called Puritan Ministers' (Orme, 3).

Early years Over the next couple of years Kiffin heard a number of well-known preachers of the day, including John Davenport, Lewis Du Moulin, and the Arminian puritan John Goodwin. Their preaching not only gave him a firm grounding in the central themes of puritan theology and spirituality, but also helped him realize that 'God has not tied himself to any one way of converting a sinner' (Orme, 11). This later freed him from being tied to one particular method of evangelistic preaching.

Towards the end of 1631 Kiffin joined a small group of fellow apprentices, who were in the habit of meeting together in the early morning for prayer, scripture reading, and mutual encouragement. This experience helped in the preparation of Kiffin as the theological and spiritual guide of a Particular Baptist conventicle. Like most of the early Particular Baptist leaders, Kiffin had no formal theological education. He became skilled in the knowledge and use of the scriptures as he first listened regularly to various preachers, then shared with others its impact on his life, and finally preached himself. In 1638 he married Hanna (1615–1682), with whom he had a number of children.

Joining the Baptists By 1638 Kiffin had come to reject Anglican arguments for the idea of a state church and had joined what he termed an 'Independent congregation' in London (Orme, 14). When Kiffin joined this congregation, later known as Devonshire Square Baptist Church, it was without a pastor. At one time it had been led by a Samuel Eaton, who was now in prison, where he died the following year. Kiffin accepted an invitation to preach to the congregation, and at some point over the course of the next three or four years was chosen as their pastor. The preface of the second edition of John Lilburne's *The Christian Mans Triall* (1641), signed W. K., has been attributed to Kiffin.

During this entire period Kiffin continued to study the Bible for direction with regard to the constitution and form of a local church. When, over forty years later, he recalled this period of his life, what stuck out in his memory was his diligent examination of the Bible to find the 'right way of worship' (Kiffin, *Sober Discourse*, 2). By the autumn of 1642 he, as well as the congregation, had come to a decidedly Baptist position. As he wrote,

> After some time [I] concluded that the safest way was to follow the footsteps of the flock (namely that order laid down by Christ and His Apostles, and practised by the primitive Christians in their times) which I found to be that after conversion they were baptised, added to the church, and continued in the apostles' doctrine, fellowship, breaking of bread, and prayer; according to which I thought myself bound to be conformable. (ibid.)

His commitment to the Particular Baptist cause appears to have been sealed by a public debate with the Anglican apologist Daniel Featley held in Southwark on 17 October 1642.

Two years later Kiffin was a signatory for his church, along with the leadership of six other London congregations, of the first London confession of faith. This confession sought to demonstrate the solidarity of the Particular Baptists with the Calvinistic community throughout western and parts of central Europe. In addition, the first London confession spelt out in some detail a Baptist ecclesiology. Kiffin also appears to have played a significant role in drafting the document. The confession would serve as the theological basis for the Particular Baptists during their rapid advance in the late 1640s and the 1650s—it was reprinted a number of times during this period—and then throughout the years of persecution in the 1660s and 1670s after the Restoration. It was replaced only towards the end of the 1670s, by the second London confession of faith, adopted in 1689.

During the late 1640s and 1650s Kiffin emerged as a skilled spokesman for the fledgeling Baptist movement. A number of texts record public debates, either proposed or actual, with a variety of figures. On 3 December 1645 Kiffin, along with his co-religionists Benjamin Cox and Hanserd Knollys, was supposed to have debated with the London presbyterian Edmund Calamy the elder at his Aldermanbury home on the nature and subjects of baptism. The debate was, however, cancelled by the lord mayor, Thomas Adams, owing to rumours that the Baptists were intending to bring 'Swords, Clubs, and Staves' with them in order to slay Calamy (Coxe, Knollys, and Kiffin, 4–6). The previous year, the Dutch Calvinist minister Cesar Calandrini had debated with Kiffin in an attempt to prevent members of his Dutch congregation, then meeting in Austin Friars, London, from joining the Baptists. In 1646 Kiffin and Knollys were involved in a public debate in Coventry with two paedobaptists, John Bryan and Obadiah Grew. Kiffin was a signatory to the dedication in *Walwins Wiles* (1649), an attack on the Levellers usually attributed to John Price. Another debate was in 1654 with the celebrated court physician Peter Chamberlen, a Seventh Day Baptist, over an aspect of church life (*Discourse between Cap. Kiffin, and Dr Chamberlain, about Imposition of Hands*). Hostile witnesses from this period also point to Kiffin's leadership among the Baptists. The presbyterian merchant Joshua Ricraft attacked him as 'the grand ringleader' of the Baptists, while an anonymous publication in 1659 described him as the 'ordained Mufty of all Hereticks and Sectaries' (*The Life and Approaching Death of William Kiffin*, 2).

Kiffin also played a prominent role in the expansion of the movement beyond London. Extant documents from places as far afield as Wales and Northumberland, Ireland and the Midlands reveal Kiffin's involvement in planning the establishment of new churches and associations, then in giving them advice and counsel, and generally in providing stability to the Baptist cause during these early days of the movement. One critical moment came in May 1658, when, at the meeting of the western association of Baptist churches in Dorchester, some individuals who were sympathetic to the potentially subversive politics of the Fifth Monarchy movement sought to convince the representatives of the churches in the association to espouse publicly the ideals and goals of this party. Kiffin, who was present with other representatives from the churches in London, successfully persuaded the western association not to commit itself in this direction. While some of the Fifth

Monarchy movement appear to have been relatively harmless students of the Bible, others had definite revolutionary tendencies and were convinced that they should take an active, even violent, role in the fulfilment of the prophecies of Daniel 2. Open and widespread adherence to these views by the Particular Baptists would have had harmful and serious repercussions for the Baptist movement.

London merchant and civic figure During these years, which also witnessed the upheaval of the English civil war and the establishment of the Commonwealth, Kiffin was extensively engaged as a merchant. He had in 1638 become a freeman of the Leathersellers' Company of London, which enjoyed a monopoly on the leather trade in the capital. His decision about 1645 to take a member of his church as a partner for a trading venture in the Netherlands turned out to be the launching of an enormously successful business. In Kiffin's own words: 'it pleased God so to bless our endeavours, that, from scores of pounds, he brought it to many hundreds and thousands of pounds: giving me more of this world than ever I could have thought to have enjoyed' (Orme, 23). In his later years it appears that the focus of Kiffin's ventures was the cloth trade.

Kiffin's business ventures also led to his involvement in the civic and political affairs of the capital. In 1642, along with other individual Londoners, Kiffin contributed horse and riders for the parliamentary cause. Documents from the late 1650s speak of Kiffin as a 'captain' (*Discourse between Cap. Kiffin, and Dr Chamberlain*) and 'lieutenant-colonel' (*Life and Approaching Death of William Kiffin*, 5) in the London militia. In Oliver Cromwell's last parliament of 1656–8 Kiffin sat as a member for Middlesex and was on good terms with Cromwell. After the restoration of the monarchy in 1660, however, his involvement in political and civic matters was understandably curtailed.

In February 1660, shortly before the Restoration, Kiffin's house, along with those of several others, was raided by order of General George Monck. Kiffin was arrested and some arms—'2 Drums … 5 Old Pikes, and 6 Swords'—seized (Kiffin and others). Though he was soon released—as a result of a letter he wrote to the lord mayor—he had experienced a foretaste of what the next twenty-eight years were to bring for dissenters in general. Over the next three years he was re-arrested three times, though his stays in prison were brief.

On a number of occasions Kiffin used his position and wealth to intervene on behalf of fellow dissenters. In 1664 he was able to rescue twelve General Baptists from Aylesbury, Buckinghamshire, who had been sentenced to death under an Elizabethan law for participation in an illegal conventicle; he went directly to Charles II and obtained a reprieve for them all. In the following decade Kiffin also used his influence at court to clear some New England Baptists from the false charge of murdering a Boston minister.

A quaint account of Kiffin's influential relationship with the king is found in a story related by the eighteenth-century Baptist historian Thomas Crosby. The king had supposedly asked Kiffin for a loan of £40,000. Kiffin was aware that if he gave the king such a loan there was every likelihood that it would never be repaid, and thus offered to make the king a gift of £10,000, which the king gladly accepted. Afterwards, according to Crosby, Kiffin jocosely remarked that he had thereby saved himself £30,000. This story may well be a recollection of an incident in the summer of 1670, when a financially burdened monarch approached the magistracy of London for a loan of £60,000. The response on the part of the aldermen was half-hearted, raising only a third of the needed loan. Seeing an opportunity to drive a wedge between the king and parliament, London dissenters organized the raising of the remaining two-thirds of the requested loan; Kiffin, who subscribed £3600, was the largest of the contributors.

In 1670 Kiffin was elected sheriff of London and Middlesex, though he was subsequently rejected because of his nonconformity. In recognition of this, in the following year he was elected master of the leathersellers, though he was only a liveryman of the company at this time.

Ardent Baptist When a declaration of indulgence was issued on 15 March 1672, Kiffin secured a licence for himself to preach. Although this declaration was withdrawn the following March, there seems to have been liberty enough in London in the years immediately following for Kiffin to participate in major public debates with the Quakers regarding the divinity of Christ, on 28 August and 9 October 1674 at the Barbican meeting-house, and on 16 October at the Quakers' meeting-house in Spitalfields. The second meeting lasted until dark, while so many attended the final meeting that there were fears that the gallery would collapse.

In October 1676 Kiffin and four other London Baptist leaders travelled to the west country to confront the Baptist evangelist Thomas Collier. Originally a member of Kiffin's church in London, Collier became the leading Particular Baptist evangelist in south-west England during the 1650s. In 1674, however, Collier published *A Body of Divinity*, in which he denied original sin, argued that Christ died for all men, and maintained that Christ's humanity was eternal. Collier's important standing within the Particular Baptist community made it imperative that his views be dealt with. A meeting was accordingly arranged between Collier and Kiffin and the other Baptist pastors from London. At the meeting Kiffin took the lead in urging Collier to renounce views the Baptist leader clearly regarded as heretical. Collier refused to do so, and Kiffin and the London Baptist leadership subsequently refused all association with him. When Nehemiah Cox published his rebuttal of Collier, *Vindicia veritatis*, in the following year, Kiffin signed a brief explanatory statement as to why the work was necessary.

During these years Kiffin was also embroiled in another controversy, this time with the quintessential puritan John Bunyan, over the necessity of believer's baptism. Bunyan's *A Confession of my Faith, and a Reason of my Practice* (1672) and *Differences in Judgment about Water-Baptism, No Bar to Communion* (1673) had rejected the standard Particular

Baptist argument that believer's baptism must precede membership in the local church or any of the privileges of that membership: in particular, participation in the Lord's Supper. While there were other written responses to Bunyan, Kiffin's *A Sober Discourse of Right to Church-Communion* (1681) was the most noteworthy advocacy of the closed membership position in this controversy. Kiffin built his case on the regulative principle of scripture, various key scripture texts, examples from the patristic era, and logical reasoning.

The years following the publication of this major work by Kiffin were difficult ones for him personally. His wife, Hanna, died on 6 October 1682. Their two eldest living sons had predeceased her: William, the eldest, had died on 31 August 1669, aged twenty; the other son had died in Venice, Kiffin believing he had been poisoned by a Roman Catholic priest. A daughter, Priscilla, died on 15 March 1679, aged twenty-four. In October 1684 Kiffin was again arrested, this time in the aftermath of the Rye House plot when various London radicals were incarcerated. One of his sons-in-law, Joseph Hayes, a banker, narrowly escaped being executed after being wrongly implicated in this plot. One of the sharpest blows was yet to come, though, what Kiffin called 'no small affliction' (Orme, 54). Two of his grandsons, William and Benjamin Hewling, were executed in September 1685 for their part in the rebellion of the duke of Monmouth—William at Lyme on 12 September and Benjamin at Taunton on 30 September. Kiffin unsuccessfully sought to obtain their freedom by offering £3000 for their acquittal. In his words, 'We missed the right door; for the Lord Chief Justice [George Jeffreys] finding agreements were made with others and so little to himself, was the more provoked to use all manner of cruelty to the poor prisoners: so that few escaped' (ibid., 54). At the sentencing of William, Jeffreys told him that 'his grandfather did as well deserve that death, which he was likely to suffer, as he did' (ibid., 82).

Two years later, in August 1687, James II, as part of an attempt to undermine the power base of the Anglican establishment, informed Kiffin of his intention that Kiffin serve as an alderman of the City of London. Kiffin sought to avoid this appointment, pleading his age, his retirement from active involvement in business and politics, and the deaths of his grandsons: 'a wound to my heart', Kiffin told the king, 'which is still bleeding, and never will close, but in the grave' (Orme, 159). But at length Kiffin had no choice but to serve as an alderman from October 1687 to October of the following year. By the conclusion of his time in office, though, James's regime had but a few weeks left to run before it crumbled in the revolution of 1688 and a new era dawned for all dissenters like Kiffin.

Final days and significance William III's authorization of the Act of Toleration in 1689 provided Kiffin, along with other Baptist leaders in London, with the opportunity to issue a call in July 1689 for a national assembly of Particular Baptists, the first of its kind. Representatives from over one hundred churches gathered. Among other things,

they approved the adoption of the second London confession of faith, originally drawn up in 1677 by William Collins and Nehemiah Cox, co-pastors of the Petty France Church in London. The unity experienced at this assembly was short-lived. In the 1690s the London Baptist community was rent by controversy over the singing of hymns. Kiffin, ever the debater, found himself drawn into the controversy, in which he opposed the singing of hymns in favour of singing psalms only.

Kiffin continued to be active in his pastorate at Devonshire Square during his final years, though he had the help of assistants. Thomas Patient had been his first co-elder. Three years after Patient's death in 1666, Daniel Dyke had been appointed. He served until his death in 1688, when Richard Adams, who succeeded Kiffin as pastor when the latter died in 1701, was ordained co-elder.

By the 1690s Kiffin had remarried. His second wife, Sarah, ran foul of the Devonshire Square Church; on 2 March 1698 she was charged with a number of misdeeds by the church. Upon examination she was found guilty of, among other things, defrauding her husband of £200 and making false accusations about him. When she refused to appear before the church, Sarah was suspended from communion on 24 April. To add sorrow upon sorrow, a third son, Harry, passed away on 8 December 1698. Although these events must have caused Kiffin deep anguish, he does not appear to have wavered in his commitment to the Christian faith. As he had written in 1693 at the conclusion of his autobiography: 'God is, by his providence, shaking the earth under our feet. There is no sure foundation of rest and peace but only in Jesus Christ' (Orme, 90). He died in London on 29 December 1701 and was buried in Bunhill Fields. In his will, dated 23 March 1700, he asked to be buried alongside his first wife and children. He also noted that he had previously paid an annuity to his second wife but this was now the responsibility of his grandson William Kiffin. He named another grandson, Joseph Kiffin, as executor, but evidently the will was contested, as it was not proved until 14 March 1716.

Since the 1640s Kiffin had been a source of strength and stability to the Particular Baptist movement, and played a vital role in its growth and advance. It was during his years of leadership of the movement that those positions distinctive of the Particular Baptists were hammered out, and Kiffin played no small part in the determination of the future identity of this Christian tradition.

MICHAEL A. G. HAYKIN

Sources W. Orme, *Remarkable passages in the life of William Kiffin* (1823) · B. R. White, 'William Kiffin—Baptist pioneer and citizen of London', *Baptist History and Heritage*, 2 (1967), 91–103, 126 · T. Crosby, *The history of the English Baptists, from the Reformation to the beginning of the reign of King George I*, 4 vols. (1738–40), vol. 3 · J. Ivimey, *The life of Mr William Kiffin* (1833) · W. Kiffin, *A sober discourse of right to church-communion* (1681) · B. Coxe, H. Knollys, and W. Kiffin, *A declaration concerning the publike dispute* (1645) · M. D. MacDonald, 'London Calvinistic Baptists, 1689–1727: tensions within a dissenting community under toleration', DPhil diss., U. Oxf., 1982 · B. A. Ramsbottom, *Stranger than fiction: the life of William Kiffin* (1989) · *The life and approaching death of William Kiffin* (1659) · K. Lindley, *Popular politics and religion in civil war London* (1997) · G. S. De Krey, 'The first Restoration crisis: conscience and coercion in London, 1667–73', *Albion*, 25 (1993), 565–80 • W. Kiffin and others, *A letter sent to the right honourable, the lord mayor of the City of London* (1660) • *A discourse between Cap. Kiffin, and Dr Chamberlain, about imposition of hands* (1654) • B. R. White, 'How did William Kiffin join the Baptists?', *Baptist Quarterly*, 23 (1969–70), 201–7 • B. R. White, *The English Baptists of the seventeenth century*, rev. edn (1996) • O. P. Grell, *Calvinist exiles in Tudor and Stuart England* (1996) • M. Tolmie, *The triumph of the saints: the separate churches of London, 1616–1649* (1977) • will, PRO, PROB 11/551, sig. 51 • D. J. Honeyman, 'Ellis Hookes (1635–1681), first recording clerk of the Society of Friends', *Quaker History*, 72 (1983), 43–54

Archives Devonshire Square Baptist Church, Stoke Newington, Devonshire Square church book, MSS 'A' and 'B'

Likenesses oils, 1667, Regent's Park College, Oxford • engraving, repro. in Orme, *Remarkable passages in the life of William Kiffin*, frontispiece

Kiggell, Sir Launcelot Edward (1862–1954), army officer, was born at Wilton House, Ballingarry, co. Limerick, on 2 October 1862. He was the son of Launcelot John Kiggell (1829–1911), of Cahara, Glin, who became a JP and a major in the South Cork light militia, and his wife, Meliora Emily (*d.* 1903), daughter of Edward Brown of Wilton House. His was an Anglo-Irish background of modest means, and he was educated in Ireland.

Kiggell went to the Royal Military College, Sandhurst, and was commissioned into the Royal Warwickshire regiment in May 1882. He was adjutant of the 2nd battalion from 1886 to 1890. On 10 March 1888 he married Eleanor Rose (*d.* 1948), daughter of Colonel Spencer Field. Their three sons were born in 1890, 1894, and 1903. He chose to advance his career through developing his military education, hindered as he was by lack of connections and family wealth. He entered the Staff College, Camberley, in 1893 and graduated in December 1894. In September 1895 he returned to Sandhurst as an instructor. His first staff job was as deputy assistant adjutant-general to south-eastern district in 1897–9; the rest of his career was to lie entirely in staff appointments.

Kiggell served in South Africa throughout the Second South African War, first on the staff of Sir Redvers Buller in late 1899, then for six months on the staff of headquarters at Pretoria, and finally as assistant adjutant-general, Harrismith district. He held the same post in Natal after the war. He was mentioned in dispatches and made a brevet lieutenant-colonel. Between 1904 and 1907 Kiggell served as deputy assistant adjutant-general at the Staff College, during which time he left his mark, such that he was considered as a replacement for Henry Wilson as commandant in 1910. A paper he read to the Aldershot Military Society in 1905 on the future shape of battle was criticized by his audience on the grounds of its being based on the examples and precepts of commanders from the past, with historical examples drawn from the Napoleonic and Franco-Prussian wars. He ignored the lessons of the most recent conflicts, such as the Second South African War and the Russo-Japanese War, the latter then in progress. His revision of the influential *Operations of War* by Sir Edward Hamley for its sixth edition was considered to show 'his lucid, thoughtful and scholarly mind' (*The Times*, 25 Feb 1954).

Kiggell was modern in his controversial approach to the

Sir Launcelot Edward Kiggell (1862–1954), by Walter Stoneman, 1918

importance of political considerations in determining strategy, views expressed at a conference of general staff officers in January 1908; he also advocated changing the name of the Staff College to 'War School', and thereby creating an institution for middle-ranking staff officers—an idea which, years later, was to come about as the Imperial Defence College. This was a view to which many senior officers subscribed, among them Wilson, Rawlinson, Robertson, and Haig, the last of whom wrote, 'Many officers look upon the Staff College as an institution for training staff officers only, whereas, it is really a school for the training of future commanders and leaders' (Bond, 266).

From Camberley Kiggell went on to a succession of staff appointments. He was general staff officer, grade 1, army headquarters (1907–9); brigadier-general in charge of administration, Scottish command (March–October 1909); and then director of staff duties at the War Office (1909–13). In this last appointment he succeeded Douglas Haig, with whom he continued a friendly and professionally respectful correspondence, looking to develop the innovations at staff level instigated as part of Haldane's reforms of the army during the latter's tenure as secretary of state for war (1905–12).

In 1913 Kiggell was appointed commandant at Camberley, succeeding Robertson; he held the post until the Staff College was closed at the outbreak of the First World War. One of the students at the time was Major-General J. F. C. Fuller, who regarded Kiggell as 'a highly educated soldier, but a doctrinaire'. 'He possessed knowledge, but little vision, and at the Staff College he appeared to me to be a dyspeptic, gloomy and doleful man' (Bond, 288).

For the first sixteen months of the war Kiggell was at the War Office, firstly as director of military training and then (1914–15) director of home defence. When Sir Douglas Haig became commander-in-chief of the British armies in France he selected Kiggell as his chief of the general staff only when Richard Butler was excluded on the grounds that he was too junior. Haig had tried, understandably, to transfer most of his old staff from First Army, and Butler had been his chief of staff. Haig wrote to his wife,

> I took Gen. Kiggell as my CGS because I wished to get him out to the front. We can't afford to lose an officer like him. After he has been with me 3 or 4 months he will be able to take command of a Corps and Butler will then take his place. (Terraine, 176)

In fact Kiggell was to stay until January 1918.

Kiggell took over from 'Wully' Robertson, who was promoted chief of the Imperial General Staff (CIGS) in London. Robertson had set about creating an effective staff system for the British expeditionary force, establishing order after the unhappy tenure of Archibald Murray. Kiggell has been blamed for a range of decisions during his period of office: the succeeding wave tactics on 1 July 1916; the delaying of the Cambrai offensive from 20 September to the unsatisfactory 20 November; and continuing third Ypres into October 1917. These charges do not stand up to close examination: Rawlinson did not lay down a particular method for infantry advance in the Fourth Army tactical notes, suggesting that, 'small columns, which can make full use of the folds of the ground to cover their advance, are preferable during the preliminary stages of the advance' (Prior and Wilson, 160). Kiggell was opposed to an early launch of the Cambrai offensive, though his argument, based on the inadvisability of splitting the available troops, was not necessarily as sterile as some have argued. There can be no doubt that it was Haig's decision (though supported by Kiggell) to continue third Ypres through October 1917; while creating a very difficult salient for the British, the capture of the bulk of Passchendaele Ridge at least ensured that British gains were tenable during the winter of 1917.

Kiggell was dismissed shortly after the failure of third Ypres to produce adequate results. It was one of a number of changes in personnel, brought about under political pressure, at general headquarters. In fact Kiggell was an exhausted man, who had a long history of working excessive hours and not taking that leave which was his due. Two doctors deputed to examine him reported that he was suffering from nervous exhaustion. Haig commented that it made him very sad to have to make this decision, 'especially when I reflect over all I and the whole Army owe to Kiggell' (Blake, 278). Haig helped to ensure Kiggell a good posting, as general officer commanding and lieutenant-governor of Guernsey. He was appointed CB in 1908, KCB in 1916, and KCMG in 1918. After retirement in 1920 Kiggell worked on the official history of the war, but had to give it up on health grounds in 1923. He died at his home,

Camas, Croutel Road, in Felixstowe, on 23 February 1954, after a retirement of more than thirty years.

Much of the criticism of Kiggell is based on the fact that, like several other senior officers, he had held no command in the field. There is no doubt that he was a solid, effective administrator, not one to grab the imagination. But that he was basically sound and capable is surely shown by the fact that he was able to rise from a background that was, for the time, unpromising, and from a regiment that was respectable rather than glamorous, through a series of promotions (themselves at a premium) under a variety of chiefs of the Imperial General Staff. Haig would not have tolerated Kiggell if he had been ineffectual or not run his department as Haig wanted it—examples of Haig's rebukes of his subordinates are well known, such as those administered to Rawlinson in 1915 and Plumer in 1916. Kiggell, while not a great chief of the general staff, was the man for the moment, certainly in 1916, with a vast, inexperienced army, most notably among its staff, arriving in France; though it is questionable whether he should have been allowed to carry on for so long.   N. T. A. CAVE

Sources DNB · WWW · J. Hussey, 'Commanders and staff in the First World War', *Bulletin of the Military Historical Society*, 46/184 (May 1996) · B. Bond, *The Victorian army and the Staff College, 1854–1914* (1972) · *The private papers of Douglas Haig, 1914–1919*, ed. R. Blake (1952) · J. Terraine, *Douglas Haig: the educated soldier* (1963) · P. Griffith, ed., *British fighting methods in the Great War* (1996) · P. Griffith, *Battle tactics of the western front: the British army's art of attack, 1916–1918* (1994) · T. Travers, *How the war was won: command and technology in the British army on the western front, 1917–1918* (1992) · R. Prior and T. Wilson, *Command on the western front* (1992) · E. M. Speirs, *Haldane: an army reformer* (1980) · *The Times* (25 Feb 1954) · Burke, *Peerage* (1939) · *CGPLA Eng. & Wales* (1954)

Archives King's Lond., Liddell Hart C., corresp. and papers | PRO, corresp. with official History Committee | FILM IWM FVA, actuality footage

Likenesses W. Stoneman, photograph, 1918, NPG [*see illus.*] · photograph, Staff College, Camberley · photograph, IWM

Wealth at death £2286 1s. 3d.: probate, 26 April 1954, *CGPLA Eng. & Wales*

Kilbracken. For this title name *see* Godley, (John) Arthur, first Baron Kilbracken (1847–1932).

Kilbrandon. For this title name *see* Shaw, Charles James Dalrymple, Baron Kilbrandon (1906–1989).

Kilburn, William (1745–1818), artist and calico printer, was born on 1 November 1745, at Capel Street, Dublin, the only son of Samuel Kilburn, architect of that city. He showed an early talent for drawing, and was apprenticed to John Lisson, an English calico printer with a large works at Leixlip, near Dublin. The family was in financial difficulties at the father's death, and in 1777 Kilburn moved to London, where he obtained a ready sale for his calico designs. He also became acquainted with William Curtis the botanist, and executed the exquisite plates of flowers, drawn and engraved from nature, for Curtis's celebrated *Flora Londinensis* (1777), during which time he lived with his mother and sister in Bermondsey.

Soon afterwards, in 1779, Kilburn accepted the management of a calico-printing factory at Wallington, Surrey, that had been expanded to a leading position by Ansell, Burton, and Bull in the early 1770s, but which was now owned by Newton of nearby Merton Abbey Works. After seven years he was able to purchase Newton's share of the enterprise, and ran it profitably for the rest of his life, though in later years he was threatened with the piracy of his designs by Lancashire printers.

According to an enthusiastic memoir in the *Gentleman's Magazine*, after the acquisition Kilburn rose rapidly in wealth, and was soon the most eminent calico printer in England, having 'brought the art to a pitch of perfection never since equalled' (*GM*, 223). One of his employees, C. O'Brien, wrote the earliest British text on calico printing, and more than a hundred of Kilburn's chintz designs survive to demonstrate the excellence of his floral prints, but in this 'golden age' of English calico printing the claim that his work was unequalled must be recognized as plausible rather than proven. Kilburn's marriage to the eldest daughter of Thomas Brown, a director of the East India Company, gives substance to the claim of economic success, while his leadership of the parliamentary campaign (1787) to secure copyright of design to calico printers confirms his eminence in this lucrative fashion trade. Most probably Kilburn was a unique instance in the London textile trade of the eighteenth century of an artist and designer becoming a successful entrepreneur.

Kilburn never returned to Ireland, though any Irishman who visited him was assured of a hospitable reception. He was known as a generous employer and a man of the highest moral and Christian principles. He was over 6 feet tall, upright and slender in build. Kilburn enjoyed excellent health until a few months before his death when, feeling indisposed, he went to Brighton, but, failing to improve, returned to Wallington, where he died on 23 December 1818.   S. D. CHAPMAN

Sources *GM*, 1st ser., 102/1 (1832), 222–4 · A. K. Longfield, 'William Kilburn and the earliest copyright acts for cotton printing designs', *Burlington Magazine*, 95 (1953), 230–33 · M. Schoeser and C. Rufey, *English and American textiles from 1790 to the present* (1989), 43, 50, 88 · C. O'Brien, *The British manufacturer's companion and callico printer's assistant* (1790) [author describes himself as 'late Designer to Mr Kilburn'] · A. J. Webb, *A compendium of Irish biography* (1878) · G. Saunders, *Rococo silks* (1985)
Archives V&A, chintz designs | GL, Sun Fire Office insurance policy registers

Kilburne, Richard (1605–1678), lawyer and topographer, was baptized at St Mary Woolchurch, London, on 6 October 1605, the fifth and youngest son of Isaac Kilburne and his wife, Mary, daughter of Thomas Clarke of Saffron Walden, Essex. His father's family originated from Kilburne, Yorkshire, later moving to Cambridgeshire and to Essex. Kilburne entered Staple's Inn, became an eminent chancery lawyer, and on five occasions was chosen to be principal of his inn. Writing in 1798 Edward Hasted described Kilburne as 'a man of some eminence … as a lawyer, being as worthy a character, both as a magistrate and an historian' (Hasted, 7.148).

Success in his legal career brought Kilburne into contact with Kent and Sussex. During the later 1620s he inherited

Fowlers, an estate in the parish of Hawkhurst, Kent. Along with his neighbour William Boys he served as a Kentish magistrate and both men were asked during the Commonwealth to marry couples without sacred rites; but whereas Boys married sixty couples, Kilburne married only two. In his legal work he became a steward of two Sussex manors, Brede and Bodiam, from 1639 onwards. During the 1660s he was writing from Fowlers about land in Peasmarsh and 26 acres overlooking Rye, the latter owned by John Halsey of Lincoln's Inn. In one letter, dated 27 December 1669, he asks 'his much respected Freind, Mr Samuell Jeake, at Rye' (Smart, 303), to investigate that these acres were being well used, before replying to their owner. Kilburne's first marriage, to Elizabeth, daughter of William Davy of Beckley, Sussex, produced a family of six sons and three daughters. After Elizabeth's death he married on 24 January 1653 a widow, Sarah Burchet, formerly Short, who brought several children of her previous marriage.

Kilburne's career was similar to that of William Lambarde (1536–1601), whom he much admired; both men were authors of topographical and legal works. Kilburne's first, *A brief survey of the county of Kent, viz. the names of the parishes in the same, in what bailiwick … and division … every of the said parishes is; … the day on which any market or faire is kept therein; the ancient names of the parish churches, etc* (1657), was followed by *A topographie, or survey of the county of Kent, with some chronological, historicall, and other matters touching the same* (1659), that presented, as his 'Epistle Dedicatory' outlined, 'the Kent of his own day', and depicted 'the county as it was before the Civil War'. Hasted, in 1797, was rather dismissive of this work as being 'little more than a Directory' (Hasted, 1.iii). Kent was not well served by early topographers, and Kilburne's small survey was extensively quoted on sixteen occasions by Robert Furley and, over the years in *Archaeologia Cantiana*, as a first source of reference, and not without some praise. The *Topographie* devoted disproportionate attention to Hawkhurst: 10 pages out of 422, or, in the words of one writer, 'as much space to it as to twenty other average parishes' (*Archaeologia Cantiana*, 5, 1863, 59). Kilburne justified this, however:

In respect I finde not any description of this Parish … it having been the place of my habitation for above twenty eight years last past (God's Providence having also there lent me an inheritance), I thought fit to enlarge my selfe upon this place. (Kilburne, 126)

Kilburne's legal notes were published only after his death, as *Choice presidents upon all acts of parliament, relating to the office and duty of a justice of the peace* (1680). It ran through a series of expanded editions, the eighth and last appearing in 1715.

Kilburne died on 15 November 1678 and was buried in the north chancel of Hawkhurst church. He was generous to his sons, William, Isaac, and Thomas, and to his stepchildren, but Fowlers passed to Anne (Mrs Brewer) his only surviving daughter. Regarding his association with Kent, his *Topographie* records 'my Obligation of Gratitude to that County (wherein I have had a comfortable subsistence for above Thirty five years ... and for some of them had the Honour to serve the same)' (Kilburne, 'Epistle Dedicatory').

JOHN WHYMAN

Sources DNB · R. Kilburne, *A topographie, or survey of the county of Kent* (1659) · E. Hasted, *The history and topographical survey of the county of Kent*, 2nd edn, 1 (1797); 7 (1798) · R. Furley, *A history of the weald of Kent*, 3 vols. (1871–4) · F. Hull, 'Kentish historiography', *Archaeologia Cantiana*, 70 (1956), 224 · *Archaeologia Cantiana*, 5 (1863), 59 · H. A. Jeffreys, 'The church of St Laurence Hawkhurst', *Archaeologia Cantiana*, 9 (1874), 240–65, esp. 245, 263 · *Archaeologia Cantiana*, 22 (1897), 45 · *Archaeologia Cantiana*, 30 (1914), 134–5 · *Archaeologia Cantiana*, 63 (1950), 135 · *Archaeologia Cantiana*, 80 (1965), 92 · *Archaeologia Cantiana*, 84 (1969), 240 · J. Winnifrith, 'The medieval church of St Mary, Ebony, and its successors', *Archaeologia Cantiana*, 100 (1984), 157–70, esp. 158–9, 162–3 · W. D. Cooper, 'Hastings rape, castle and town', *Sussex Archaeological Collections*, 2 (1849), 161–6, 167 · M. A. Lower, 'Bodiam and its lords', *Sussex Archaeological Collections*, 9 (1857), 275–302, esp. 294–5 · E. Austen, 'The old house at Broad Oak, Brede', *Sussex Archaeological Collections*, 66 (1925), 136–47, esp. 143 · L. A. Vidler, 'St Bartholomew's hospital at Rye', *Sussex Archaeological Collections*, 83 (1943), 73–99, esp. 97 · T. W. W. Smart, 'The Frewen manuscripts, letters of Richard Kilburne', *Sussex Archaeological Collections*, 16 (1864), 302–4

Archives E. Sussex RO, Frewen MSS, AMS 5574

Likenesses T. Cross, print, 1659, BM, NPG; repro. in Kilburne, *Topographie* · engraving, repro. in Kilburne, *Topographie* · portrait, repro. in E. Evans, *Catalogue of a collection of engraved portraits*, 1 (1836), 195

Kilbye, Richard (1560/61–1620), Hebraist, was born at Redcliffe in Leicestershire; the identities of his parents are unknown. He matriculated from Lincoln College, Oxford, on 20 December 1577, aged sixteen, and was elected to a fellowship of the college on 18 January in the following year. He took his BA degree on 9 December 1578 and his MA on 2 July 1582. On 10 December 1590 he was appointed to the rectorship of Lincoln College. He took the degrees of bachelor and doctor of theology on 7 July 1596, and on 28 September 1601 was installed as prebendary of Lincoln Cathedral. He took part in the translation of the Bible commissioned by King James I in 1604. From 1610 until his death in 1620 he held the regius professorship of Hebrew in the University of Oxford. Although he acquired a considerable scholarly reputation (his acquaintance Isaac Casaubon described him as 'a man of some reading beyond the common'; Feingold, 455), Kilbye's sole publication was a funeral sermon preached in 1612 for Thomas Holland, the university's regius professor of divinity. His intention to publish a continuation of Jean Mercier's commentary on the book of Genesis remained unfulfilled, although a surviving manuscript commentary on Exodus (in Lincoln College Library) indicates the extent of his learning, employing almost 100 Hebrew sources, many of them rare. Upon his death, probably in Oxford, in 1620, Kilbye bequeathed to Lincoln College a large and valuable collection of Hebrew volumes including dictionaries, Bibles, and commentaries on the Pentateuch. He was buried in the chancel of All Saints' Church, Oxford, on 7 November 1620.

DAVID WILSON

Sources *Fasti Angl., 1541–1857*, [Lincoln], 93 · Wood, *Ath. Oxon.*, new edn, 2.287 · Foster, *Alum. Oxon., 1500–1714*, 1.849 · M. Feingold, 'Oriental studies', *Hist. U. Oxf.* 4: *17th-cent. Oxf.*, 449–503, esp. 454–5 · DNB

Archives Lincoln College, Oxford, theological papers

Kildare. For this title name *see* Fitzgerald, John fitz Thomas, first earl of Kildare (d. 1316); Fitzgerald, Thomas fitz John, second earl of Kildare (d. 1328); Fitzgerald, Maurice fitz Thomas, fourth earl of Kildare (c.1322–1390); Fitzgerald, Thomas, seventh earl of Kildare (d. 1478); Fitzgerald, Gerald, eighth earl of Kildare (1456?–1513); Fitzgerald, Gerald, ninth earl of Kildare (1487–1534); Fitzgerald, Thomas, tenth earl of Kildare (1513–1537); Fitzgerald, Elizabeth, countess of Kildare (fl. 1514–1548); Fitzgerald, Gerald, eleventh earl of Kildare (1525–1585); Fitzgerald, George, sixteenth earl of Kildare (bap. 1612, d. 1660).

Kilgour, Mary Stewart (1851–1955), educationist and feminist, was born on 24 September 1851 in Longford, Tasmania, the daughter of John Stewart Kilgour, a Scottish doctor, and his wife, Susan Ann (née Archer). The family returned to Britain in 1854 and eventually settled in Cheltenham. After attending two small private schools there Mary Kilgour spent a brief period as a pupil at Cheltenham Ladies' College. From 1871 until 1873 she taught on the staff of the college and formed what was to prove a lifelong friendship with the headmistress, Dorothea Beale. After a further, brief period of teaching at the Clergy Daughters' School at Casterton she entered Girton College, Cambridge, with a Clothworkers' Company scholarship, to read mathematics. She moved to London after taking the tripos examinations in 1878.

From 1880 until 1906 Kilgour taught mathematics at Queen's College, Harley Street, London—the pioneering college for women founded by F. D. Maurice, Mary Maurice, and others—where she was much respected for her independence of mind and personal charm. However, she became increasingly frustrated by what she felt was complacency and a refusal to keep abreast of new ideas; she resigned in 1906, before reaching retirement age. She retained a deep interest in education and was largely responsible for the eventual opening of College Hall, a university hall of residence for women in the University of London, in 1932. In 1905 she was awarded the honorary degree of MA by Trinity College, Dublin; the University of Cambridge awarded her an honorary titular MA in 1928.

Meanwhile Kilgour had been involved in work that was to have even greater influence and significance. In 1888 she and her close friend Annie Leigh *Browne (1851–1936) were largely responsible for founding the Society for Promoting Women as County Councillors—a group of influential liberal-minded upper middle-class men and women—soon renamed the Women's Local Government Society (WLGS). Browne was appointed honorary secretary and Kilgour honorary treasurer. There was some ambiguity about whether women were eligible for election to the new county councils created by the County Councils Act of 1888, and the new society tested this by sponsoring the candidatures of Jane Cobden in Bow and Bromley, and Margaret (Lady) Sainsbury in Brixton for the new London county council. Both were elected in January

1889. When Lady Sainsbury's election was challenged and then overturned, on the grounds that the Local Government Act of 1888 had not specifically included women in its provisions, the WLGS campaigned for a change in the law to ensure that women's rights to vote and to stand for election to local authorities were specifically guaranteed. Largely owing to their campaigning an act of 1893 gave all women ratepayers the right to vote and allowed women to stand for election in district council elections.

During the next two decades Kilgour wrote several pamphlets and went around the country, addressing meetings and bringing to public attention the valuable contribution that women could make to local government authorities. In 1895–6 she wrote fifty articles for the *Parish Councillor*, urging women to participate in rural local government. In 1900 she wrote a paper, 'Women as members of local sanitary authorities', for the Royal Institution of Public Health congress in Aberdeen, explaining how constructively women and men had already collaborated on public-health issues and urging their continuing participation after the impending transfer of responsibility for public health from the London vestries (on which women served) to the London borough councils (from which women were as yet specifically excluded). The continued campaigning of the WLGS, chiefly inspired by the persistence of Kilgour and Browne, was eventually rewarded after the Liberal landslide of 1906; an act of 1907 finally gave women the right of election to borough and county councils. The WLGS now sponsored several candidates, in many cases with success.

From this time onwards the WLGS concentrated on supporting women candidates and offering legal advice. Kilgour was herself elected to Paddington borough council in 1912 and served until 1919. She supported the work of the National Union of Women's Suffrage Societies and condemned violence.

In 1920 Kilgour and Browne retired from the WLGS but they continued to live in London and to take an interest in political and educational developments. After Browne's death in 1936 Kilgour moved to Sidmouth, where she found more time for her hobby of gardening but also maintained her political interests. She was elected president of Sid Vale Liberal Association, an office which she held until she was over 100. At the age of ninety-nine she opened a new museum in the town. She died in Sidmouth at her home, Hills, Sid Road, Salcombe Regis, on 31 March 1955, aged 103. A memorial fund to provide books for the library was opened at Queen's College, to which many of her old students contributed.   ELAINE KAYE

Sources K. T. Butler and H. I. McMorran, eds., *Girton College register, 1869–1946* (1948) · P. Hollis, *Ladies elect: women in English local government, 1865–1914* (1987) · Women's Local Government Society, annual reports, LMA · Women's Local Government Society, committee minutes, LMA · letters from M. S. Kilgour and H. W. A. Kilgour, Queen's College Archives, London · *The Times* (21 April 1955) · M. S. Kilgour, 'Women as members of local sanitary authorities' (1900) [pamphlet] · Old Queen's Society report, 1955, Queen's College Archive, London · d. cert. · *CGPLA Eng. & Wales* (1955)

Archives Queen's College, London, archive, MSS | LMA, records of Women's Local Government Society

Wealth at death £17,712 9s. 3d.: probate, 8 Aug 1955, *CGPLA Eng. & Wales*

Kilham, Alexander (1762–1798), a founder of the Methodist New Connexion, was born at Epworth, Lincolnshire, on 10 July 1762, the third son of Simon Kilham (d. 1801/2) and his wife, Elizabeth (d. 1785). His father was a linen weaver who later extended his business to include the making of sacking. His parents were zealous Methodists, but the young Alexander left his parents' faith and was careless for a time until, at the age of eighteen, when working at Owston Ferry, not far from his home, he was converted during a revival at Epworth and joined the local Methodist society, where he helped in prayer meetings and other work, until he became a local preacher in 1782, preaching his first sermon at Luddington, Lincolnshire. He came to the notice of the squire of Raithby, Robert Carr Brackenbury, who had just been accepted by Wesley as one of his travelling preachers. After travelling for a short time in Lincolnshire, he accompanied Brackenbury to Jersey, where they were successful in establishing the first Methodist society in spite of much local opposition. They returned to the mainland in the summer of 1784.

In spite of a natural reluctance to lose his son from the family business, Alexander's father raised no objections to his offering his services to Wesley, whom Alexander had met at Nottingham in 1783. Two years later he was received into full connection and was appointed to Horncastle (1785) and Gainsborough (1786) in Lincolnshire. Then followed some years in the East Riding of Yorkshire, and periods in Scarborough (1787–8), Pocklington (1789), and Whitby (1790). He married Sarah Grey (d. 1797) of Pickering at Easter 1788; they had one daughter, Sarah, who survived to adulthood, and two sons who died in infancy.

Kilham had early shown his independent mind when in Grimsby he had registered as a dissenter under the Toleration Act in order to obtain a preaching licence to protect himself against the opposition of the vicar of Skendleby, Edward Brackenbury, his patron's brother. With the death of Wesley his mind found further scope for expression.

Stationed at Newcastle upon Tyne in 1791, Kilham's superintendent was Joseph Cownley, a supporter of greater freedom for Methodist preachers, who had administered the sacrament of the Lord's Supper to his congregation. This had hitherto been forbidden to travelling preachers who had not been ordained, in the interest of the established church. Other calls for greater freedom were made after Wesley's death. In May 1791 the Hull circuit published a circular advising Methodists not to rank themselves as dissenters, to meet only out of church hours, and to receive the sacrament only in the parish church. Cownley had opposed this plea, for which he was strongly criticized. Kilham rushed to his defence in a pamphlet published under the pseudonym Truman and Freeman, which drew on him the censure of the conference in 1792. He was appointed to the Aberdeen circuit, presumably to remove him from the mainstream of Methodist life, but it only served to strengthen his convictions, for the life of the surrounding presbyterian churches was

Alexander Kilham (1762–1798), by W. Collard, pubd 1838 (after unknown artist, 1797)

strongly anti-episcopal and anti-Church of England. From the conference point of view, it could hardly have been a more unfortunate appointment. Henceforth a steady stream of 'reform' pamphlets issued from his pen under pseudonyms such as Aquila and Priscilla and Martin Luther.

Kilham remained in Aberdeen for three years, during which time he clarified his dissenting principles and called for complete separation from the Church of England if Methodists were to gain their 'Gospel privileges'. In his pamphlets he argued not only for the right of Methodists to receive the sacrament at the hands of their own preachers, in their own chapels, but for the right of lay members to have a share in the running of the circuits, and that lay delegates should represent their circuits in conference. Furthermore, he utterly rejected the idea of making some preachers into Methodist bishops.

The turmoil throughout the connexion was such that in 1795 conference agreed to the 'plan of pacification', which granted some of Kilham's requests, though not those relating to the place of laymen in the life of the church. The plan was accepted by all preachers present except Kilham and four or five others, who saw it as only a temporary remedy, arguing for further reforms. At the end of the year Kilham issued another pamphlet, this time under his own name, *The Progress of Liberty amongst the People called Methodists*. In this he elaborated his proposals for the participation of laymen in the governing of the church, especially in the appointment of preachers, both local and travelling. This gave rise to such hostility that Kilham, now stationed at Alnwick, was arraigned first before the district meeting and then before the conference, which dismissed him as a preacher on 28 July 1796.

Kilham now felt free to act. In that year he started the issue of a magazine, the *Methodist Monitor*, in which he set

forth the need for a root and branch reform of Methodism. At the following conference of 1797 at Leeds a 'people's delegation' met, asking for the reforms Kilham had proposed; conference made some minor concessions, but would not move on the subject of nominations of membership or the possibility of meetings taking place without a travelling preacher. The reformers could not accept this, and at that conference three other preachers seceded or were expelled, and these with others met in the Baptist Ebenezer Chapel, Leeds, which they bought as the first chapel of the 'new itinerancy', or the Methodist New Connexion, as it was soon called. William Thom became its first president and the ever indefatigable Kilham its secretary, this of course in addition to circuit duties in Sheffield, to which circuit he had been appointed by the first Methodist New Connexion conference in that year. The organization of the new connexion, which gained 5000 members in the first year, was completed at the conference of 1798. Kilham was sent to the Nottingham circuit, the connexion's largest.

Immediately Kilham set about seeking to extend and build up the new church, which was particularly strong in south and west Yorkshire, north-east Cheshire, and Tyneside. On 12 April 1798 he married his second wife, Hannah Spurr (1774–1832) of Sheffield, who as Mrs Hannah *Kilham worked as a missionary and scholar of unwritten African languages; they had one daughter, Mary, who died in 1802. Travelling both as reformer and evangelist clearly took up much of Kilham's time, and contributed to his ill health. In the autumn of 1798 he set out, in spite of sickness, on a visit to Wales, but caught a severe chill and returned home to Nottingham. He tried to struggle on with his circuit and other engagements, but his heavy work load had completely exhausted him. He died in Nottingham on 20 December 1798, after expressing his zeal for evangelism in his deathbed plea, 'Tell all the world that Jesus is precious.' He was buried in Hockley chapel, Nottingham.   OLIVER A. BECKERLEGGE

Sources J. Blackwell, *The life of the Revd Alexander Kilham* (1838) • W. Cooke, *Methodist reform and its originator* (1850) • J. Grundell and R. Hall, *The life of Mr Alexander Kilham* (1799) • W. J. Townsend, *Alexander Kilham, the first Methodist reformer* (1890) • S. R. Valentine, 'The first Methodist reformer', *Methodist Recorder* (23 Oct 1997), 16 • O. A. Beckerlegge, *United Methodist ministers and their circuits* (1968) • O. A. Beckerlegge and E. A. Rose, *A bibliography of the Methodist New Connexion* (1988) • E. A. Rose, 'Kilham, Andrew', *The Blackwell dictionary of evangelical biography, 1730–1860*, ed. D. M. Lewis (1995)
Archives JRL, corresp. and papers
Likenesses W. Collard, engraving (after unknown artist, 1797), repro. in Blackwell, *Life of the Revd Alexander Kilham* [see illus.]

Kilham [*née* Spurr], **Hannah** (1774–1832), missionary and student of African languages, born at Sheffield on 12 August 1774, was the seventh child of Peter and Hannah Spurr. Her father, a cutler by trade, was a strict Anglican, but her mother let her attend Wesley's services. After her parents' deaths she spent two years at a boarding-school in Chesterfield, where the schoolmaster felt she overstepped the bounds of the 'female province' by her serious study of grammar. Back in Sheffield in 1790 she broke with the Church of England, and in 1794 she joined the Methodist society. When Alexander *Kilham (1762–1798) founded the Methodist New Connexion in Sheffield she joined his congregation; they were married on 12 April 1798 and moved to Nottingham. He died after eight months, on 20 December 1798, and she opened a school to support herself and her step-daughter, Sarah (later her biographer). Increasingly dissatisfied with the rigidity of Methodism, she joined the Society of Friends in 1803, returned to Sheffield, and opened a girls' boarding-school.

Deeply concerned about the plight of the poor in Sheffield, Hannah Kilham founded the Society for the Bettering of the Condition of the Poor and published religious tracts as teaching aids. She also grew interested in the anti-slavery cause, and became convinced that she should go to Africa as a 'school-missionary'. After discussions with missionaries she decided on the experiment of teaching African children in their own languages, not in English, using images and ideas already familiar to them. She learned Wolof from two African sailors in London, published some lessons in Wolof and English, and persuaded the Society of Friends to found a mission in the Gambia. Meanwhile she visited Ireland to investigate and publicize the appalling condition of the rural poor.

The Gambia mission started in 1823 and Kilham opened a school, and taught in Wolof. But with the death of her colleagues in 1824 the mission ended. Meanwhile she had visited Sierra Leone where the large population of liberated Africans, or 'recaptives' freed from the slave ships and speaking numerous languages, offered her far more scope to put her ideas into practice. After three years in London working among the poor in the parish of St Giles-in-the-Fields, she paid another brief visit to Sierra Leone in 1827 and collected specimens of thirty African languages. They included not only languages spoken in Sierra Leone, such as Temne, Susu, and Mende, but Fante (in what became Ghana) Hausa, Yoruba, Igbo, and Urhobo (in Nigeria), and Kongo, witness to the wide catchment area of the Atlantic slave trade. Kilham's *Specimens of African Languages Spoken in the Colony of Sierra Leone*, published on her return to England in 1828, anticipated Sigismund Koelle's great *Polyglotta Africana* (1854), which was to be based, as hers was, on language specimens collected in Sierra Leone. Kilham also published *African School Tracts*, illustrating her methods, beginning with words in the relevant African language, and then going on to sentences, Bible passages, stories, arithmetic, and grammar.

In 1830 Kilham returned to Sierra Leone to put theory into practice. She was given charge of a school for recaptive girls (some of them were brought, at her particular request, straight from the slave ship), in Charlotte village in the mountains above Freetown, where she taught in Mende and Yoruba. She opened a village bookshop and sold her textbooks, and considered drawing up simplified English vocabularies for children to learn English. But she was always restless: sometimes she would reflect in her journal on whether she should not really

leave, to work for the Chinese. In 1832 she paid a brief visit to Liberia to see what progress the schools were making there. On the way back the ship was struck by lightning and put back to Liberia. Hannah Kilham suddenly fell unexpectedly ill, became unconscious, and died on 31 March 1832. Her body was committed to the sea, off the coast of Liberia.   CHRISTOPHER FYFE

Sources DNB · S. Biller, ed., *Memoir of the late Hannah Kilham* (1837) · M. Dickson, *The powerful bond: Hannah Kilham, 1774–1832* (1980)
Likenesses silhouette, Friends House, Euston Road, London

Kilian [St Kilian, Cilian] (*d.* 689?), missionary in Franconia, is also known as Kilian of Würzburg and alternatively as Cellanus, Killena, Cellach, or Mochellóc. His usual feast day is 8 July, but a St Kilian is also commemorated on 26 March.

Accounts of Kilian's life According to the first life of Kilian (*passio minor*), composed no earlier than the latter part of the eighth century, the Irish bishop Killena, also called Kilian, arrived, together with twelve companions (named are Colonat, Gallo, Arnuval, and the deacon Totnan) at Würzburg in Germany. As both locality and people were agreeable to them, they left for Rome in order to obtain from Pope John V a licence to preach the faith. This pope having died before their arrival, the licence was granted by his successor Conon. On the way back, the companions separated, leaving Kilian, Colonat (Colmán), and Totnan (perhaps Donnán) to convert Gozbert, duke of the Thuringians, and his people. When Kilian and his companions tried to convince the duke to divorce his wife, Geilana, the widow of his brother, she had them killed and secretly buried, together with their clothes and books. Not long after, however, Geilana was attacked by madness and killed herself, Gozbert was slain by his servants, and his son Heden was banished. Many miracles occurred in the coming years, leading to the translation of relics, supposed to be those of Kilian, by Burchard, first bishop of Würzburg, with the consent of Pope Zachary and the Frankish king, Pippin III.

The second life (*passio maior*), probably composed in the ninth century, adds some further details, and introduces links with Columbanus of Luxeuil and Bobbio and also with St Gertrude of Nivelles. An Irish source for some parts of this life is suggested by the writer's knowledge of Kilian's Irish name, Cellach: Geilana is claimed to have asserted that the saint took his name from a chalice (*a calice*, which would be *callech* in Irish).

The earlier life of St Kilian has been shown to have been composed at the Frankish court. Furthermore, it shows similarities with the life of St Corbinian, written by Arbeo of Freising on the behest of his Irish friend Virgilius of Salzburg (*d.* 784) and with the lives of St Boniface by Willibald (*d.* 768) and St Amandus by Gislebert of Noyon (*d.* 782), all of which provide a *terminus post quem*. Connections with the Frankish court are obvious in most of these sources and the vehemence with which they portray the evil doings of Duke Gozbert and his wife fits well with the efforts of the Carolingian royal house to obliterate independent local duchies.

Evidence for Kilian's identity The existence of Kilian is not attested by any reliable historical document. His *floruit* has been reconstructed from the details provided by his first life, which was written, at the earliest, a century after his presumed lifetime. The date of 689, now generally thought to be the year of his martyrdom, first appears in Würzburg historiography of the eleventh century. His translation can be dated to the time of Burchard (*d.* 753), who was provided to the see of Würzburg by Boniface. This bishop of Anglo-Saxon origin was closely connected with Pippin III and was one of the mission sent to Pope Zachary to obtain permission for the coronation of Pippin in 751. It would seem that the translation of Kilian's relics coincided with the consecration of the first cathedral at Würzburg, which is, however, dedicated to St Saviour. The first date at which a church (not the cathedral) dedicated to St Kilian is recorded in Würzburg is 779.

Kilian's liturgical commemoration commences at about the same time, when his name was entered in the calendar that Godescalc wrote for Charlemagne. Although no place is named in connection with the martyrdom of Kilian and his companions, its dating to 8 July connects him closely with Würzburg, since there are indications that this date refers to his translation, which may already have been commemorated by Charlemagne in 787 or 788. This has been taken to show that Charlemagne promoted Kilian to the status of a Carolingian patron saint.

Liturgical commemoration at Würzburg itself is not traceable until the middle of the ninth century, and it seems that the earlier centres of his cult may have been the Rhine–Moselle region and Alemannia. However, the feast day of Kilian in the calendars of Echternach and Trier is given as 26 March, a date which may refer to another Kilian, patron of Aubigny (Pas-de-Calais). Furthermore, at the monastery of St Gall (Switzerland), the saint's name appears in charters as early as 759 and 762. As these documents refer to the local monastery and not to Würzburg, it is possible that the cults of both saints, Kilian (Cellanus or Cellach) of Würzburg and Gall (whose Irish name is given in a genealogy of the ninth century as Callech), together with Kilian of Aubigny, all derive from the same source.

The Irish background to Kilian's cult There are no historical sources concerning Kilian preserved in Ireland. His liturgical commemoration is attested by an entry in the early ninth century martyrology of Tallaght. This, which refers to the 'holy Irish martyr Cilianus and his two brothers Aed and Tadg, together with the queen of the Goths Amarma, who were killed by the royal prefect in the hippodrome of the royal palace', has never been satisfactorily interpreted. Only the date of 8 July connects the entry with Würzburg. Two places in Ireland lay claim to the saint, Mullagh in the diocese of Kilmore, and Kilmickilloge in Kerry, mainly because their patrons' feast days coincide with that of Kilian of Würzburg. There are, however, no historical sources for these saints and their cults are first

attested only in the nineteenth century. There is, however, a St Mochellóc (the hypocoristic form of Cellach) mentioned in Irish liturgical texts at 26 March, a day also attested for Kilian in continental calendars. This saint may be identified with the patron of the church at Kilmallock, Limerick.

In any case, the cult of this Irish saint seems to have reached the continent by the eighth century, where it established itself at various centres. The connection with Würzburg may have come about through the need for patrons of the newly founded dioceses in the eastern part of the Frankish kingdom. Kilian was certainly established as the patron of Würzburg by 784, when his compatriot Virgilius of Salzburg included him in his confraternity book as 'Killach episcopus'.   DAGMAR Ó RIAIN-RAEDEL

Sources J. F. Kenney, *The sources for the early history of Ireland* (1929) · 'Passio sancti Kiliani episcopi', *Passiones vitaeque sanctorum aevi Merovingici*, ed. B. Krusch and W. Levison, MGH Scriptores Rerum Merovingicarum, 5 (Hanover, 1910), 711–28 · A. Bigelmaier, 'Die Passio des heiligen Kilian und seiner Gefährten', *Herbipolis Jubilans* [Würzburger Diözesansgeschichtsblätter], 14/15 (1952) · M. Werner, 'Iren und Angelsachsen in Mitteldeutschland', *Die Iren und Europa im früheren Mittelalter*, ed. H. Löwe, 1 (Stuttgart, 1982), 239–318 · A. Wendehorst, 'Die Iren und die Christianisierung Mainfrankens', *Die Iren und Europa im früheren Mittelalter*, ed. H. Löwe, 1 (Stuttgart, 1982), 319–29 · J. Erichsen and E. Brockhoff, eds., *Kilian: Mönch aus Irland aller Franken Patron*, 2 vols., Veröffentlichungen zur Bayerischen Geschichte und Kultur, 18/89 (1989) · A. Gwynn, 'The continuity of the Irish tradition at Würzburg', *Herbipolis Jubilans: 1200 Jahre bistum Würzburg. Festchrift zur Säkularfeier der Erhebung der Kiliansreliquien* (Würzburg, 1952), 57–82 · A. Gwynn, 'New light on St Kilian', *Irish Ecclesiastical Record*, 5th ser., 88 (1957), 1–16 · R. I. Best and H. J. Lawlor, eds., *The martyrology of Tallaght*, HBS, 68 (1931) · *Das Verbrüderungsbuch von St Peter in Salzburg: vollständige Faksimile-Ausgabe im Originalformat*, ed. K. Forstner (Graz, 1974)

Kilkenny, William of (*d.* 1256), administrator and bishop of Ely, may have been identical with the Master William of Kilkenny who, as chancellor of the church of Kilkenny, was elected bishop of Ossory in 1231, but resigned the office in 1232 before his consecration. It is certain, however, that by mid-1234 Kilkenny was a king's clerk, receiving a yearly fee of 60 marks at the exchequer until at least 1237. Drawing on his knowledge of canon and civil law, Kilkenny served Henry III during these years in a variety of ecclesiastical causes. He went twice to the papal court on royal business, in 1234–5 and again in 1237. He acted as the king's proctor in several disputed elections, most famously in the case involving Simon of Elmham's contested election to the bishopric of Norwich between 1236 and 1239. He also represented the king in negotiations with Bishop Robert Grosseteste of Lincoln (*d.* 1253) arising out of a dispute in 1236 between the town and university of Oxford. In return the king presented him to the churches of Powerstock, Dorset, in 1235, and Worfield, Shropshire, in 1236.

Between 1238 and 1247 Kilkenny disappears from royal records. During these years he served in the household of Nicholas of Farnham (*d.* 1257), bishop of Durham from 1241 to 1249, although his connections with Durham began under Bishop Richard Poore (*d.* 1235). In May 1247 he went abroad on royal service, and by November had become archdeacon of Coventry. Not until the autumn of 1249, however, is there clear evidence that Kilkenny had rejoined the king's household. From 30 September 1249 until at least 27 October 1252 he served as controller of the royal wardrobe; and from 28 May 1250 until 5 January 1255 he was keeper of the great seal in England, exercising the responsibilities of the chancellor, and being sometimes accorded the title, but never receiving the emoluments of the office. Together with Richard, earl of Cornwall (d. 1272), Kilkenny played a key role in governing England during the king's expedition to Gascony in 1253–4, his modesty, fidelity, and learning winning the praise of Matthew Paris and the gratitude of the king.

During these years Kilkenny received a variety of ecclesiastical appointments. In 1251 he was appointed to the prebend of Ipthorne in Chichester Cathedral, and the church of Dungervan in the Irish diocese of Lismore. In 1252 he acquired the church of Walton, Lancashire. By the end of 1253 he had also become rector of St Peter's, Northampton, treasurer of Exeter Cathedral, a prebendary of Dublin, and keeper of the royal hospitals at Ospringe, Kent, and Oxford. Although his appointment in 1253 to the St Paul's prebend of Caddington was annulled by the pope, he was successfully preferred to the next available prebend, Consumpta-per-Mare, between January and September 1254. Finally, in late September or October 1254, he was elected bishop of Ely. Kilkenny received the temporalities of his new see on 25 December, and resigned the seal on 5 January 1255. His consecration as bishop was delayed, however, until 15 August 1255, when he was consecrated at Bellay in Savoy by Archbishop Boniface of Canterbury (d. 1270).

Kilkenny's episcopate lasted only a year. In July 1256 he undertook another embassy on the king's behalf, this time to Spain, where he died on 21 September. His heart was returned for burial at Ely. As bishop, Kilkenny resolved a long-standing dispute with Ramsey Abbey over land boundaries in the fens. He also established a chantry to support two university scholars at Cambridge. It is possible that he issued statutes for his diocese. By his will he appointed two additional chaplains to pray for his soul at Ely, leaving 200 marks for their support.

Master William had some connection, perhaps a familial one, with Master Odo of Kilkenny, one of the king's canon lawyers, and with Master Henry of Kilkenny, canon of Chichester. His only certain relative, however, was his nephew Richard son of Robert, a landowner in Waterford, who in 1254 was knighted, in company with the Lord Edward, by the king of Castile.   ROBERT C. STACEY

Sources *Chancery records* · *CEPR letters*, vol. 1 · *Fasti Angl., 1066–1300*, [St Paul's, London] · *Fasti Angl., 1066–1300*, [Monastic cathedrals] · *Fasti Angl., 1066–1300*, [Salisbury] · *Fasti Angl., 1066–1300*, [Chichester] · C. A. F. Meekings, *Studies in 13th century justice and administration* (1981) · Tout, *Admin. hist.*, vol. 1 · L. B. Dibben, 'Chancellor and keeper of the seal under Henry III', *EngHR*, 27 (1912), 39–51 · *VCH Cambridgeshire and the Isle of Ely*, vol. 2 · *Paris, Chron.* · [H. Wharton], ed., *Anglia sacra*, 1 (1691) · Emden, *Oxf.* · F. M. Powicke and C. R. Cheney, eds., *Councils and synods with other documents relating to the English church, 1205–1313*, 1 (1964), 516

Wealth at death see will, Wharton, *Anglia sacra*, 636

Kilkerran. For this title name *see* Fergusson, Sir James, second baronet, Lord Kilkerran (*bap.* 1688, *d.* 1759).

Killamarsh [Kinwolmarsh]**, William** (*d.* 1422), administrator, came from Killamarsh in Derbyshire. He was first named as a king's servant in January 1405, when he petitioned successfully for the grant of forfeited goods to the value of 10 marks. In 1406 he was a clerk in the wardrobe of the king's household, and was granted a yearly rent of £10 from lands in Somercotes and Saltfleetby in Lincolnshire, together with the wardenship of St Cross Hospital in Colchester. Later he was presented to the church of Keyston in Huntingdonshire, and became warden of St James's Hospital, Westminster. In 1407 he received money from the exchequer as agent of Sir John Tiptoft, then keeper of the wardrobe, and by the early years of the reign of Henry V he had risen to the office of cofferer of the household. In this capacity, and as deputy to Sir Roger Leche, keeper of the wardrobe, he was retained to serve in the Agincourt campaign of 1415 with two men-at-arms and nine archers, but he was invalided home on 6 October, nine days before the battle. Nevertheless, on 20 December of that year he was granted the office of clerk of the treasurer, with a special appointment as deputy to Lord Fitzhugh, the treasurer, when the latter was serving in France, and with the reversion of the office of treasurer, if Fitzhugh should die or surrender it while overseas. This was a remarkable appointment, an early recognition that the clerk was the treasurer's deputy; and it was highly unusual to grant the reversion of so high an office—especially to one who had risen from a humble clerkship. Fitzhugh's other responsibilities kept him from fulfilling his duties as treasurer, and Killamarsh duly succeeded him on 26 February 1421; he was reappointed at the beginning of Henry VI's reign, but he died on 18 December 1422.

By the time of his death Killamarsh had become warden of St Martin's-le-Grand in London and a canon of both St Paul's and Chichester cathedrals, but despite his several church preferments it was not until 20 December 1421 that he was ordained subdeacon in St Paul's by the archbishop of Canterbury, Henry Chichele. He is not known to have held any landed property, but the provisions of his will suggest that he expected to have at least £600 to leave. This will, dated at St Martin's-le-Grand on 14 March 1421, ordered that his body should be buried in that church, and provided for prayers for his soul to be said there, and also at St Paul's, in St James's Hospital, Westminster, and in four parish churches, including that of Killamarsh. The principal legatee was William Killamarsh, his nephew, probably the rector of Castor, Northamptonshire (he had been ordained by Archbishop Chichele on 18 December 1417), to whom Killamarsh left 100 marks, his best bed, silver plate, vestments, a breviary, a missal, and a chalice. He left £40 to his brother Alexander, and similar sums to his sister, to his nephews and nieces, to his other relatives at and around Killamarsh, and for the education of Alexander's sons. He also left money to seven servants and his executors, one of whom, Richard Merfyn, had been one of his men-at-arms in 1415, while another, John Wodehouse, had been his colleague in the exchequer. J. L. KIRBY

Sources Chancery records · Exchequer of Receipt, Issue Rolls, PRO, E 403 · Exchequer, Treasury of Receipt, Council and Privy Seal, PRO, E 28/17 · Exchequer, Queen's Remembrancer, Accounts Various, Wardrobe, PRO, E 101/47/11 · E. F. Jacob, ed., *The register of Henry Chichele, archbishop of Canterbury, 1414–1443*, 2, CYS, 42 (1937), 235–7 [will]; 4, CYS, 47 (1947), 328, 346 [ordinations] · J. L. Kirby, 'The rise of the under-treasurer of the exchequer', *EngHR*, 72 (1957), 666–77 · *Fasti Angl., 1300–1541*, [St Paul's, London] · *Fasti Angl., 1300–1541*, [Chichester] · C. Allmand, *Henry V* (1992), 356
Wealth at death over £600: will, Jacob, ed., *Register of Henry Chichele*, 235–7

Killanin. For this title name *see* Morris, Michael, first Baron Killanin (1827–1901).

Killearn. For this title name *see* Lampson, Miles Wedderburn, first Baron Killearn (1880–1964).

Killen, James Bryce (1845–1916), Irish nationalist and journalist, was born in Kells, co. Antrim, the fourth son of Samuel Killen and Mabel Shaw. He took a BA in 1863 at the Queen's University in Ireland, though it is not clear whether this was at Belfast, Cork, or Galway. He went on to read logic, metaphysics, and political economy at the Queen's University in Ireland at Galway and gained a poor MA in 1868. He was admitted to the King's Inns, Dublin, in 1865, and in 1869 he gained a first-class LLB at the Queen's University in Ireland at Galway.

Killen was on three occasions in trouble with the authorities. In May 1869 he addressed the Queen's College, Belfast, Literary and Scientific Society on 'The spirit of Irish history'. He concluded that England could not rule Ireland because it had no idea of the concept of nationality, and the fact of union divided the two nations even more deeply. His speech precipitated a question in parliament by R. Peel Dawson, Conservative MP for Londonderry County, who accused Killen of 'very questionable expressions' and invited the authorities to prosecute him. There had been fears that the literary and scientific societies at both Belfast and Galway were being used by extremists, but in the case of Killen both the college council and the chief secretary for Ireland, Chichester Fortescue, decided to take no action.

Killen was briefly editor of the *Northern Star*, a short-lived Belfast liberal Catholic newspaper founded in 1868, which was thought to hold 'advanced views'. By the opening of the land war he had become a member of the Irish Republican Brotherhood, and with Michael Davitt and James Daly he was one of the founding members of the Land League. In November 1879 he was arrested with Davitt and Daly for making seditious speeches at a land meeting at Gurteen, co. Sligo. In his speech Killen hoped that those present were armed with rifles and that 'the days of namby-pamby speaking were over'. The prosecution received enormous publicity, both in Ireland and abroad. However, the accused were released and the case was abandoned in January 1880.

Killen was temporarily editor of *United Ireland* after the arrests of William O'Brien and Edward O'Donovan in 1881. Killen himself was arrested in November 1881 and sent to Dundalk gaol on suspicion of inciting refusal to pay rent. Of his arrest *The Nation* commented that the warrants had said that these arbitrary arrests and imprisonment were intended to be used for

> certain 'dissolute ruffians and blackguards' whom it was impossible to make amenable to 'the ordinary law'; but not even by the wildest stretch of imagination can any one consider such a man as … Mr Killen … either a ruffian or a blackguard. (*The Nation*, 3 Dec 1881)

Killen frequently appeared as counsel to defendants prosecuted during the land war. He went to America some time in the 1890s and contributed to nationalist newspapers both in Ireland and America. He died in poverty in a Dublin lodging house on 26 December 1916. His obituary in the *Freeman's Journal* spoke of his knowledge of the early stages of the land agitation as 'unrivalled, and his descriptions of scenes and personages of the time … intensely entertaining'. He wrote a number of pamphlets, including *The Incompatibles: 'Sister' England and the Irish Cinderella* (1882) and *A Sketch of Irish History* (1886), which includes the text of 'The spirit of Irish history'. MARIE-LOUISE LEGG

Sources T. W. Moody and J. C. Beckett, *Queen's, Belfast, 1845–1949: the history of a university*, 2 vols. (1959) · *The Times* (28 Dec 1916) · *Freeman's Journal* [Dublin] (29 Dec 1916) · *Belfast News-Letter* (28 Dec 1916) · *The Nation* (3 Dec 1881) · W. O'Brien, *Recollections* (1905), 379 · *Hansard 3* (1869) · D. J. Hickey and J. E. Doherty, *A dictionary of Irish history* (1980); pbk edn (1987)

Killen, John (d. 1803), Irish nationalist, is of unknown origins and family. During the early 1800s he kept an unlicensed Thomas Street pub in Dublin's plebeian manufacturing quarter. Aided by his wife, who was known as the 'Dirty Cook', Killen's fare was sufficiently well regarded to provide an income in a built-up and populous part of the south city. Killen belonged to the illegal society of United Irishmen, an oath-bound organization committed to establishing an independent Irish republic with French military assistance. They fomented the bloody rising of 1798 in which Killen's role, if any, has not been documented. Killen reputedly played an active part on 23 July 1803 when revolutionaries under the overall direction of Robert Emmet attempted to seize Dublin city. Two witnesses of dubious reliability alleged that Killen was in company with the rebel leader Felix Rourke on Bridgefoot Street when the rising of 1803 commenced. Friends and patrons of the Killen family, however, insisted that he had remained indoors that evening and prevented others from venturing out. Contrary to such claims, evidence was presented implicating Killen in the shooting of a dispatch rider of the sixteenth light dragoons near the Thomas Street Cornmarket. Killen was arrested in the aftermath of the failed insurrection and brought to trial with John McCann at Green Street courthouse on 7 September. Both men were capitally convicted, and were executed on Thomas Street on 12 September 1803. Killen was survived by his wife. RUÁN O'DONNELL

Sources R. R. Madden, *The United Irishmen, their lives and times*, 2nd ser., 4 vols. (1857–60), 2 · *State trials*, 28.995–1040 · R. O'Donnell, *Robert Emmet and the rising of 1803* (Cork, 2002) · H. Landreth, *The*

pursuit of Robert Emmet (Dublin, 1949) · L. O'Broin, *The unfortunate Mr Emmet* (Dublin, 1958) · *DNB*

Archives NA Ire., rebellion/state of the country papers · Sheff. Arch., Hardwicke papers **Wealth at death** modest, unlicensed beer cellar: Howell, ed., *State trials*

Killen, Thomas Young

Killen, Thomas Young (1826–1886), minister of the Presbyterian Church in Ireland, son of Edward Killen, a merchant in Ballymena, co. Antrim, was born at Ballymena on 30 October 1826. His boyhood was spent at Glenwherry, to which his father moved in 1832. He was educated initially by a private tutor, and in 1842 entered the Belfast Academical Institution, where he took several prizes. In 1846 he began his theological studies under the theological faculty of the Irish Presbyterian church. In 1847, during his studies, he spent his summer vacation as a missionary in Camlin, co. Roscommon, despite the prevalence of famine fever.

On 19 May 1848 Killen was licensed to preach by the presbytery of Carrickfergus, and returned to the west of Ireland until 25 September 1850, when he was ordained by the presbytery of Letterkenny as minister of Ramelton Third Presbyterian, co. Donegal, where his pastorate proved very successful. During his ministry there, in 1854 he married Elizabeth, daughter of William Wilson of Raphoe, whose brother, Charles, was MP for Donegal in 1876–9. In 1857 Killen received a call from the congregation of Ballykelly, co. Londonderry, and was installed there on 31 March. He took a leading part in the Ulster revival of 1859. Among the new Presbyterian congregations formed in the wake of the revival was Duncairn in Belfast and Killen was called as its first minister in December 1861. It grew rapidly under his ministry and its church building was enlarged twice. He became one of the leading figures in the Irish general assembly, of which in 1882 he was elected moderator. In 1883 the degree of DD was conferred on him by the Presbyterian Theological Faculty, Ireland. He died suddenly of a heart attack on 21 October 1886, at the Duncairn manse, Belfast, leaving a widow and seven children. He was buried on 25 October in Balmoral cemetery, Belfast.

Killen was the author of *A Sacramental Catechism* (1874), which ran through several editions, and was republished in America. For four years (1869–73), he edited a monthly magazine, the *Evangelical Witness*, and on the establishment of the *Witness* newspaper in Belfast in 1874 he wrote much in its columns. He also published several sermons and tracts. THOMAS HAMILTON, *rev.* FINLAY HOLMES

Sources Presbyterian Historical Society archives, Belfast · personal knowledge (1892) · *The Witness* (29 Oct 1886) · R. Allen, *The Presbyterian College, Belfast, 1853–1953* (1954) · *Fasti of the general assembly of the Presbyterian Church in Ireland, 1840–70* · H. Magee, *Fifty years in 'The Irish mission'* (1905?) · J. R. Fisher and J. H. Robb, *Royal Belfast Academical Institution: centenary volume, 1810–1910* (1913) · *Duncairn Presbyterian Church, 1862–1987* · *Minutes of the General Assembly* (1880–90), 296–7 and 368 · *Presbyterian Missionary Herald* (1 Nov 1886), 334 · *Presbyterian Churchman* (Jan 1887) · *McComb's Almanac* (1884) · baptismal register, Nov 1826, First Ballymena Presbyterian Church, Ballymena, co. Antrim · *The Witness* (14 Nov 1879) · B. M. Walker, *Ulster politics: the formative years, 1868–86* (1989) · *CGPLA Ire.* (1886)

Likenesses photograph, repro. in *McComb's Almanac*, frontispiece

Wealth at death £3744 11*s.*: probate, 29 Nov 1886, *CGPLA Eng. & Wales*

Killen, William Dool

Killen, William Dool (1806–1902), ecclesiastical historian, born at Church Street, Ballymena, co. Antrim, on 5 April 1806, was the third of four sons and nine children of John Killen (1768–1828), grocer and seedsman in Ballymena, and his wife, Martha, daughter of Jesse Dool, a farmer in Duneane, co. Antrim. Through his grandmother, Blanche Brice, who had married his paternal grandfather, James Killen, a farmer of Carnmoney in co. Antrim, he could claim descent from Edward Brice, the first Scottish Presbyterian minister to be installed in an Ulster parish in the early seventeenth century. A brother, James Miller Killen (1815–1879), minister in Comber, co. Down, was author of *Our Friends in Heaven* (1854), which ran through many editions, and *Our Companions in Glory* (1862). Thomas Young Killen was his father's great-nephew.

Killen recounted how, after early education in a school connected with the Presbyterian congregation in Ballymena, he was sent to 'the Ballymena Academy'. The grammar school of that name did not come into existence until 1890, but the school which Killen attended may have been known as 'the Academy'. A contemporary who attended the same school was Samuel Davidson, the distinguished Old Testament scholar. In November 1821 Killen entered the collegiate department of the Belfast Academical Institution, where Professor James Thomson, father of Lord Kelvin, took a special interest in him. He took the general certificate in arts of the institution faculty in 1824. After a year as tutor to two brothers preparing to enter Trinity College, Dublin, he returned to the Belfast Institution to take the General Synod of Ulster's course of training for the ministry and was licensed to preach by the Ballymena presbytery in 1827 and ordained in Raphoe, co. Donegal, on 11 November 1829. On 10 August 1830 he married Anne (*d.* 1886), third daughter of Thomas Young of Ballymena.

Through the good offices of the Church of Ireland bishop of Raphoe, Killen was able to use the diocesan library to continue his studies in church history and polity. Later, he was drawn into a bitter controversy concerning the relative merits of episcopacy and presbyterianism, which was provoked by four sermons preached in 1837 in St Columb's Cathedral, Londonderry, by Archibald Boyd. Killen and three other Presbyterian ministers replied in four sermons preached in Londonderry and published in 1839 as *Presbyterianism Defended*. A reply from Boyd and counter-replies from the four ministers ensued. One of these, *The Plea of Presbytery* (1840), which reached a third edition, earned for its authors a vote of thanks from the General Synod of Ulster, one of its last actions before uniting with the Secession Synod to form the general assembly of the Presbyterian Church in Ireland.

In July 1841 Killen was unanimously appointed by the general assembly professor of church history, ecclesiastical government, and pastoral theology in succession to James Seaton Reid. (There was no college building until 1853.) The remainder of his life was spent in Belfast, where the Presbyterian college was opened in 1853 and in which he taught pastoral theology, church government, and church history. In 1869 he was appointed president of the college in succession to Dr Henry Cooke, and in this capacity helped to raise large sums of money for professorial endowments and new buildings. In 1889 he resigned his chair, owing to his age, but continued in the office of president. He died in his home, 4 College Park, Belfast, on 10 January 1902, and was buried on 13 January in Balmoral cemetery, Belfast, where a monument marks his resting place. His wife, Anne, had predeceased him, as had four of their eight children.

Killen received the degrees of DD (1845) and of LLD (1901) from the University of Glasgow. Robert Allen, author of the centenary history of the Presbyterian college, described Killen as a conservative 'with a great contempt for the new ideas which were becoming increasingly popular throughout his life and he could speak of Robertson Smith, for example, as "a conceited theological knight-errant"' (Allen, 164). As a lecturer Killen was somewhat uninspiring, especially in his later years, but he made a considerable contribution to ecclesiastical historiography through his many publications. Chief among these were his completion of James Seaton Reid's magisterial three volume *History of the Presbyterian Church in Ireland* (1853), his *Memoir of John Edgar* (1867), the father of the Irish Presbyterian temperance movement, the *Ecclesiastical History of Ireland* (2 vols., 1875) and his autobiography, *Reminiscences of a Long Life* (1902).

Killen also edited, with introduction and notes, such valuable seventeenth-century writings as Patrick Adair's *A True Narrative of the Rise and Progress of the Presbyterian Church in Ireland*, and Andrew Stewart's *History of the Church in Ireland since the Scots were Naturalized* (1866), and John Mackenzie's *Siege of Derry* (1861).

The contributor to *Presbyterianism Defended* and *The Plea of Presbytery* remained a vigorous champion of Presbyterianism throughout his life. Here his major publications were his *Ancient church: its history, doctrine, worship and constitution traced for the first three hundred years* (1859), *The old Catholic church: the history, doctrine, worship and polity of Christians traced from the apostolic age to the establishment of the Pope as a temporal sovereign, A.D. 755* (1871), *The Ignatian Epistles Entirely Spurious: a Reply to Bishop Lightfoot* (1886), and *The Framework of the Church: a Treatise on Church Government* (1890).

THOMAS HAMILTON, rev. FINLAY HOLMES

Sources W. D. Killen, *Reminiscences of a long life* (1901) · R. Allen, *The Presbyterian College, Belfast, 1853–1953* (1954) · *The Witness* (17 Jan 1902) · Presbyterian Historical Society archives, Belfast · *CGPLA Ire.* (1902)
Archives Presbyterian Historical Society of Ireland, Belfast
Likenesses photograph, c.1863, Union Theological College, Belfast; repro. in Allen, *The Presbyterian College, Belfast*, 100 · photographs, c.1863, Union Theological College, Belfast · R. Hooke, oils, Union Theological College, Belfast, Gamble Library · photograph, repro. in Allen, *The Presbyterian College, Belfast*, 167 · photograph (in old age), repro. in Killen, *Reminiscences of a long life*
Wealth at death £6022 16s. 7d.: probate, 19 Feb 1902, *CGPLA Ire.*

Killick, Esther Margaret (1902–1960), physiologist, was born on 3 May 1902 at 3 Eastwood Road, Ilford, Essex, the posthumous daughter of Dr Arthur Killick and his wife, Henrietta Fanny, *née* Moulton. Killick was educated at Leeds Girls' High School and the University of Leeds, where she was an outstanding medical student. She gained a first class BSc honours degree in physiology, and was appointed as research assistant in 1924 to May Mellanby in Sheffield, to work on calcification in the rabbit. Returning to clinical studies in Leeds after two years she graduated MB ChB in 1929 with distinction in medicine and won the Hardwicke prize in clinical medicine. She was admitted MRCP (London) in 1931, and received the degrees of MSc (Leeds, 1937) and DSc (Leeds, 1952) for her published research.

In 1929, while attached to the department of physiology at Leeds University, Killick became a physiological investigator to the Safety in Mines Research Board. Carbon monoxide, a colourless, odourless gas found in coal mines, is lethal for miners in unventilated spaces. Her appointment stimulated a lifelong investigation of the effects of carbon monoxide poisoning on blood and respiration. Her first paper concerned a related problem, the effect of increased inspiratory resistance—as would be experienced using a mask or breathing apparatus—on the pattern of breathing. In 1935 she became a lecturer in industrial medicine and hygiene in the University of Birmingham. It was here that 'she gassed herself for science' (*Birmingham Gazette*, 27 Aug 1941) by entering a sealed box for several hours at weekly intervals to expose herself to low levels of carbon monoxide. The results of the blood tests she had continually carried out on herself and one other subject during each experiment were published in papers in 1936 and 1948; they also contained an alarming account of loss of consciousness when the oxygen level in the lungs fell too low. Even when the inhalation of carbon monoxide was less traumatic Killick suffered nausea and persistent headaches, and her major review of carbon monoxide anoxaemia (published in *Physiological Reviews*, 20, 1940, 313–44) shows that she was well aware of the potential danger of sudden death. She demonstrated acclimatization lasting for many months, exemplified by a lessening of unpleasant symptoms and a reduced blood level of carbon monoxide for a given level of that inhaled. She was, however, an incessant cigarette smoker, which may have given her some degree of acclimatization to carbon monoxide before the experiments began. The human experiments were extended by studies on mice and cats to analyse processes accompanying the acclimatization.

On 28 July 1938 Killick married the distinguished physiologist Arthur St George Joseph McCarthy Huggett, (b. 1896/7), a widower, who was professor of physiology at St Mary's Hospital medical school. Killick moved to London and in 1939 became a lecturer in applied physiology at the London School of Hygiene and Tropical Medicine. Their daughters, Margaret and Jean, were born in 1940 and 1945. In 1941 Killick was appointed to the Sophia Jex-Blake chair of physiology at the London School of Medicine for Women (which in 1947 became the Royal Free Hospital school of medicine). She was evacuated to Exeter with the preclinical school from 1941 to 1943, at which time it returned to London, only to be damaged by a V2 bomb in 1945, necessitating a further move to Guy's Hospital medical school in south London for a year. Killick remained at the Royal Free Hospital medical school for the rest of her life, and helped to expand and redevelop the department after the war. She wrote an impassioned article on co-education in medicine in 1946, pointing out that equal opportunities for women involved not only their education, but also their equal claim to jobs, earning capacity, and professional renown.

Killick served on numerous committees and boards, and became known as a stickler for precise interpretation. She sat on the Physiological Society committee (1944 to 1948), the Medical Research Council industrial research board (as the only woman member), the National Coal Board as chairman of the physiological panel, the European Coal and Steel community as a member of the committee on medical research on carbon monoxide poisoning, and the board of management of the Maudsley Hospital. As a member of the University of London committee on higher education in the colonies she acted as university inspector and examiner in Africa and the West Indies, and later worked on two university committees guiding colleges in newly developed and independent countries toward university status. Her integrity, calm, and logic in carrying out administrative roles were much appreciated by her colleagues.

In spite of teaching, examining, and administration, Killick continued her research. In 1959 she extended previous investigations on the treatment of carbon monoxide poisoning. Resuscitation attempts were made on dogs that were unconscious from excess carbon monoxide by ventilating them with different gas mixtures. A mixture of 95 per cent oxygen with 5 per cent carbon dioxide proved the most effective in displacing carbon monoxide from the blood because the carbon dioxide stimulated better ventilation than air or oxygen. Her published work consists of several original research papers, a review, and letters concerning medical education and remuneration of medically qualified teachers.

Killick's hobbies included alpine climbing and gardening. A slim, bird-like woman, she seemed reserved and detached to strangers but her colleagues experienced her warmth and vitality and her many acts of kindness. She died in the National Hospital, Queen Square, London, following a cerebral haemorrhage, on 31 May 1960.

LYNN J. BINDMAN

Sources WWW, 1951–60 · R. Bowden, *Royal Free Hospital Journal* (June 1960) · private information (2004) [N. Joels; R. Bowden] · *Magazine of the London (RFH) School of Medicine for Women*, 8/19 (1946), 1–3 · b. cert. · m. cert. · d. cert. · *Nature*, 188 (1960), 535 · *The Times* (21 June 1960)

Archives Royal Free Hospital, London, archives

Likenesses photograph, repro. in Bowden, *Royal Free Hospital Journal* · portrait, Royal Free Hospital School of Medicine, London, physiology department

Wealth at death £14,966 11s. 1d.: administration, 12 Aug 1960, CGPLA Eng. & Wales

Killigrew, Anne (1660–1685), poet and painter, was born in St Martin's Lane, London, the daughter of Dr Henry *Killigrew (1613–1700), chaplain and almoner to the duke of York, master of the Savoy, and prebendary of Westminster, and his wife, Judith (d. 1683). Her uncles Thomas Killigrew (1612–1683) and Sir William Killigrew (1606–1695) were prominent figures in the Restoration theatre. Her brothers Admiral Henry *Killigrew (d. 1712) and Captain James *Killigrew (c.1664–1695) were both naval officers. Her sister Elizabeth (d. 1701) was married to Dr John Lambe, a clergyman. Anne was born shortly before the Restoration 'and christened in a private chamber, when the offices in the common-prayer were not publicly allowed' (Wood, *Ath. Oxon.*, 4.623). She was 'tenderly educated' and soon 'became most admirable in the arts of poetry and painting' (ibid.).

In 1683 Anne is listed as one of the six maids of honour to Mary of Modena. She never married. Her beauty, piety, and exemplary virtue are stressed in all the early records. In 1685 she succumbed to smallpox 'to the unspeakable reluctancy of her relations, and all others who were acquainted with her great virtues' (Wood, *Ath. Oxon.*, 4.623). The date of her death (which occurred in her father's lodgings in the cloisters of Westminster Abbey) is given as 16 June in Henry Killigrew's epitaph, but according to the Savoy chapel register she was buried there on 15 June. Her monument was destroyed by fire in 1864.

Poems by Mrs Anne Killigrew, a collection of twenty-nine items, with three further poems 'found among Mrs Killigrews Papers … though none of hers' (*Poems*, 84), was licensed on 30 September 1685 (title-page dated 1686). The volume encompasses a variety of genres and metres: pastoral, epigram, an unfinished epic, occasional verse, and poetry of general (and often austerely moral) reflection on the joys and pains of human life. The collection is prefaced by three commendatory poems, most notably John Dryden's celebrated pindaric ode 'To the Pious Memory of the Accomplisht Young Lady, Mrs Anne Killigrew, Excellent in the Two Sister-arts of Poesie and Painting', which affirms Anne Killigrew's saintly character and displays substantial first-hand knowledge of her achievements in both poetry and painting.

Only a handful of Anne Killigrew's paintings (which included portraits, biblical and historical paintings, mythological scenes, and landscapes) appears to have survived. A full-length self-portrait, in an allegorical setting, is housed at Berkeley Castle, Gloucestershire. A smaller self-portrait survives in several engraved copies, one forming the frontispiece to her *Poems*. A portrait of James II (formerly attributed to Lely) is in the Royal Collection at Windsor. In 1915–16 a *Venus Attired by the Graces* was reproduced in the *Burlington Magazine* from an original then in private hands. Titles of further paintings are known from Anne Killigrew's poems and from the notebooks of George Vertue. The archives of the National Portrait Gallery contain a photograph of what is possibly the painting of Mary of Modena referred to in lines 134–41 of Dryden's 'To the Pious Memory of … Anne Killigrew'.

DAVID HOPKINS

Anne Killigrew (1660–1685), self-portrait

Sources *Poems by Mrs Anne Killigrew* (1686); facs. edn with introduction by A. Morton (1967) · Wood, *Ath. Oxon.*, new edn, 4.621–3 · G. Ballard, *Memoirs of several ladies of Great Britain* (1752), 337–45 · R. Shiels, *The lives of the poets of Great Britain and Ireland*, ed. T. Cibber, 2 (1753), 224–6 · H. Walpole, *Anecdotes of painting in England: with some account of the principal artists*, ed. R. N. Wornum, new edn, 3 vols. (1888), vol. 2, pp. 106–7 · *DNB* · L. Cust and C. H. C. Baker, 'Notes', *Burlington Magazine*, 28 (1916), 112–13, 116 [incl. reproductions of Anne Killigrew's portrait of James II, and of her *Venus attired by the Graces*] · S. Gillespie, 'Another pindaric ode "To the pious memory of Mrs. Ann Killigrew"', *Restoration*, 20 (1996), 31–5 · E. Wodehouse, 'Anagram on Mistress Ann Killigrew who wrote one or more divine Poeme. My rare wit killing sin', *c*.1689, U. Leeds, Brotherton L., MS Lt 40, fol. 124*v* · *The poems of Anne, countess of Winchilsea*, ed. M. Reynolds (1903), xxii–xxiv · register of the Chapel of St John the Baptist, the Savoy, duchy of Lancaster office, Lancaster Place, Strand, London, Royal Chapel of the Savoy Archive, 15 June 1685 · Vertue, *Note books*, 2.58 [George Vertue's list of Anne Killigrew's paintings, from a sale catalogue of 1727] · photograph of painting by A. Killigrew(?) of Mary of Modena (Este) when duchess of York, NPG, Heinz Archive and Library · E. C. Clayton, *English female artists*, 1 (1876), 59–70 · J. Granger, *A biographical history of England, from Egbert the Great to the revolution*, 2nd edn, 4 (1775), 129 · Boase & Courtney, *Bibl. Corn.*, 1.286–97

Likenesses I. Beckett, mezzotint (after A. Killigrew), BM, NPG; repro. in *Poems*, ed. Morton · A. Blooteling, mezzotint (after A. Killigrew), BM, NPG · T. Chambars, engraving · A. Killigrew, self-portrait · A. Killigrew, self-portrait, oils, Berkeley Castle, Gloucestershire [*see illus.*]

Killigrew, Charles (1655–1724/5), theatre manager and master of the revels, was born at Maestricht on 29 December 1655. He was the first son of Thomas *Killigrew (1612–1683), dramatist, groom of the bedchamber (1661–83), and

master of the revels (1673–7), and Charlotte (*d.* 1716), his second wife, the daughter of Johan van Hesse of Holland, and keeper of the sweet coffers to Catherine of Braganza. Charles Killigrew's elder half-brother, Henry, was a notorious rake and groom of the bedchamber to Charles II; his younger brother by Thomas's second marriage, Robert Killigrew, was a brigadier-general, killed at Almanza in 1707. Charles and his brothers by this marriage were naturalized by act of parliament in 1662.

Charles Killigrew received a grant of the reversion to the mastership of the revels, after Sir Henry Herbert and his father, Thomas, in 1668. In 1670 Thomas Killigrew set up a trust by which Charles would, at his father's death, receive a double share in the Theatre Royal in Drury Lane and, upon his majority, its government. Throughout this period, the theatre experienced recurrent financial difficulties and labour disputes. Early in 1676 Thomas Killigrew persuaded Charles to act as a mediator with the actors in return for the former's patent and interest in the theatre. After the elder Killigrew failed to relinquish these, Charles sued in chancery. The verdict returned on 22 February 1677 forced Thomas Killigrew to turn the company over to his son. Two days later Charles Killigrew was appointed master of the revels, in which post he served until his death. Since the position paid but £10 per annum, his main source of income from it came from the exclusive right to license stage plays, rope-dancers, ballad singers, and other public shows. He triumphed in a dispute with the comptroller of the revels over this right in 1688, but eventually lost the power to license plays in the grant to Sir Richard Steele of 1715. As master of the revels, Killigrew infuriated Colley Cibber by his overly enthusiastic embrace of Jeremy Collier's view of theatrical reform: [He] 'assisted this Reformation with a more zealous Severity than ever. He would strike out whole Scenes of a vicious or immoral Character, tho' it were visibly shewn to be reform'd or punish'd', most notably deleting the entire first act of Cibber's *Richard the Third* on the grounds that its melancholy portrait of Henry VI 'would put weak People too much in mind of King James then living in France' (Cibber, 1.275, 276).

According to his father's biographer, Charles Killigrew 'became a courtier, a man-about-town, a friend of Dryden, and, in spite of apparent literary interests, a very unsuccessful theatre manager' (Harbage, 124–5). This last was despite his capacity for sharp practice towards both fellow shareholders and actors. Partly as a result of their complaints and his lack of financial success, he was by the mid-1690s less active in management. Though he assisted Christopher Rich's rise to power over the united companies, he eventually became an opponent, trying unsuccessfully to have him removed from control of Drury Lane in 1701–2. Given his apparent capacity to offend, it is perhaps not surprising to learn from Luttrell of a duel in January 1693 between 'one Mr. Chamberlain and Mr. Killigrew of the playhouse' (N. Luttrell, *A Brief Historical Relation of State Affairs*, 6 vols., 1857, 3.25).

Killigrew was named a gentleman of the privy chamber in October 1670, a gentleman usher of the privy chamber to Catherine of Braganza by 1684, a commissioner of prizes in 1707, and comptroller of the receipts and payments of the receiver general of customs in 1716. His political sympathies seem to have been whiggish: this would explain the timing of several of the above appointments; his dismissal from the queen dowager's household by the earl of Feversham in August 1697 for 'show[ing] a zeal for this government' (*CSP dom.*, 1697, 287); and his failed contest of the parliamentary representation of Orford against two tories in 1701.

Killigrew married Jemima, niece of Richard Bokenham, mercer, of London. She survived her husband who was buried in the Savoy on 8 January 1725. They had three sons: the eldest, Guildford, was a lieutenant in Lord Mark Kerr's regiment of dragoons during the War of Spanish Succession and a page of honour to the king from 1714 to 1727. He died childless in 1751. Their second son was the playwright Thomas *Killigrew (*bap.* 1694, *d.* 1719). A third son, Charles, inherited the estate at Thornham Hall and his father's interest in the playhouse at Drury Lane and died childless on 9 March 1756.   R. O. BUCHOLZ

Sources A. Harbage, *Thomas Killigrew, cavalier dramatist, 1612–1683* (1930) • L. Hotson, *The Commonwealth and Restoration stage* (1928) • C. Cibber, *An apology for the life of Mr. Colley Cibber*, new edn, ed. R. W. Lowe, 2 vols. (1889) • J. L. Vivian, ed., *The visitations of Cornwall, comprising the herald's visitations of 1530, 1573, and 1620* (1887), 270 • *CSP dom.*, 1667–68, 257 [for reversion to be master of the revels]; 1697, 287 [for removal from queen dowager's household] • J. C. Sainty and R. Bucholz, eds., *Officials of the royal household, 1660–1837*, 1: *Department of the lord chamberlain and associated offices* (1997), 42–3, 129 [for appointment as master of the revels] • W. A. Shaw, ed., *Calendar of treasury books*, 30/2, PRO (1957), 373 [for appointment as comptroller of receipts of the customs] • *Report on manuscripts in various collections*, 8 vols., HMC, 55 (1901–14), vol. 4, p. 271 [Orford election] • *LondG* (2 Feb 1687–2 Feb 1688) [dispute with comptroller of the revels] • PRO, LC 3/24, LC 3/26

Archives BL, corresp. and papers, Add. MS 20032

Killigrew, Sir Henry (1525x8–1603), diplomat, was the fourth son of John Killigrew (*d.* 1568), landowner of Arwennack, Cornwall, and his wife, Elizabeth, second daughter of James Trewennard. His brothers included the MPs John Killigrew (*d.* 1584) and Sir William *Killigrew (*d.* 1622). Based in Cornwall since the mid-thirteenth century the Killigrews owned land in the parish of St Erme near Truro, although the family seat at Arwennack, where Henry Killigrew was most likely born, was not established until 1385. By the reign of Henry VIII the Killigrews were well placed among the west country gentry, John Killigrew being entrusted by the king with the sensitive office of captain of Pendennis Castle. Henry Killigrew may well have attended Cambridge University, although there is no evidence that he ever obtained a degree. Nevertheless he was certainly educated to a high standard. In addition to a thorough grounding in classical languages and literature and a keen interest in music and painting, he possessed a strong grasp of both Italian and French.

Early career and exile, 1552–1558 Killigrew's career as a public servant began in 1552 with his appointment as

harbourmaster for the duchy of Cornwall, the same year that he received the office of collector of rents for the manor of Helston, Cornwall. On 18 February 1553 he was returned as MP for Launceston. No doubt in part this small but useful collection of offices reflected the natural expectations that even a younger son born to a well connected landowning family might reasonably have. It also demonstrated the value of holding the correct religious sympathies under a particular regime. He was already known to John Dudley, duke of Northumberland, for his service to him as a gentleman usher in the mid-1540s, and the strong protestant faith evinced by Killigrew and his family did much to bolster their popularity with the government.

Killigrew's Dudley association did not extend to support for Northumberland's efforts to alter the succession. Killigrew and his family made no effort to oppose Mary's accession. Only when it became clear that a corner-stone of the Counter-Reformation in England would be the queen's marriage to Philip of Spain did Killigrew and his brothers repudiate their allegiance. By December 1553 Killigrew had travelled to the French court to seek the support of Henri II for a planned rising. When this rising failed the French king swiftly distanced himself from the affair, leaving Killigrew and his co-conspirators adrift and exiled. Killigrew remained in Europe until Elizabeth I's accession. By mid-1554 he had joined the household of the protestant François de Vendôme, vidame de Chartres. It was in this capacity that Killigrew gained his first military experience, fighting with the vidame in Italy, experience that was augmented when he once again fought for the French at St Quentin in August 1557. Ironically, another facet of Killigrew's development largely formed during his exile was a strong distrust of the French. For all that he and his fellow exiles were welcomed into the French army, once their usefulness as rebels was exhausted Henri and his advisers treated them with thinly veiled contempt. This poor treatment cemented in Killigrew an enduring dislike of the French that coloured his attitude towards them during his time as a leading Elizabethan diplomat. Most important, it was during this period that he gained invaluable experience of European courts. In addition to the many contacts he made in France he spent time in Italy, not only as part of the vidame's forces, but also in 1556 on a sensitive mission to Edward Courteney, earl of Devonshire, seeking to gain his commitment to lead yet another rebellion against Mary. When this proved unsuccessful, and no doubt heartily disillusioned with his French hosts, Killigrew travelled to Germany and took up residence in Strasbourg. It was there in November 1557 that Thomas Randolph found him, and on Mary's behalf requested that he perform a reconnaissance mission in France. It was significant that this request was apparently made with the full knowledge of Princess Elizabeth. Having completed the mission Killigrew returned to Strasbourg, where he remained until Mary's death. The earlier suggestion that Elizabeth was aware of both Killigrew and his suitability for diplomatic work was confirmed when shortly after her accession the young queen summoned him back to London as a prelude to dispatching him as her envoy to the protestant princes of Germany.

France and Scotland: diplomat and soldier, 1558–1563 Throughout the thirty-five years that Killigrew served Elizabeth as agent and ambassador the focus of his work was to protect England from the encroachment of Catholic Spain and France. By turns ordered to sow dissent among Catholics and forge consensus between protestants, Killigrew's abiding inspiration and succour was his profound protestant faith. Within months of his return to England he was sent on a low-key mission to Otto-Heinrich, the elector palatine, and Christoph, duke of Württemberg, with the aim of re-establishing friendly relations between Germany's protestant princes and England. When he arrived in Heidelberg in December 1558 Killigrew's enthusiasm was such that he may have given the mistaken impression that Elizabeth was actually seeking an alliance with the princes, much to the queen's irritation. Even so, the mission was not entirely fruitless. In addition to signalling England's readiness to reopen communications with Germany's protestant princes, Killigrew also held useful discussions with the new elector palatine, Friedrich III, and his son John Casimir, about the possibility of supplying Elizabeth with mercenaries.

From Germany Killigrew travelled to France to meet his old master, the vidame, now the governor of Calais. His objective was to discuss with him the possibility of the French reinstating Calais to English rule. Killigrew was gulled by the vidames into believing that Henri might entertain such a proposal. He duly forwarded this misinformation both to Elizabeth at court and to her commissioners at Câteau-Cambrésis before arriving at Câteau-Cambrésis himself. There he was promptly detained by the leader of the French negotiators, Anne de Montmorency, constable of France, who took a decidedly dim view of his interference. Killigrew contributed nothing more to the peace talks. He remained in detention until peace was signed after which the constable, no doubt confident that his charge could do no more damage, released him, allowing Killigrew to return home by late March 1559.

Killigrew's homecoming was brief. In May he was dispatched to Paris to serve as secretary to Elizabeth's resident ambassador in France, Sir Nicholas Throckmorton. After Henri died on 10 July 1559 as a result of a jousting accident, leaving the ultra-Catholic Guise faction in control of the French crown, the central aim of the English ambassador and his attaché was to minimize the ability of France to threaten England through her support of Scotland. To this end they gave what tacit support they could to the Huguenot leaders with the hope of further destabilizing France. Additionally they sought, through the dispatch of reports detailing the dangers of further French involvement in Scotland, to persuade the queen and her advisers of the necessity of lending tangible aid to the lords of the congregation. Given the continued presence of French troops in Scotland and the ongoing efforts to increase their numbers, the reports of Throckmorton and Killigrew were sufficient to convince Elizabeth of the

need for action. In March 1560 she ordered William Grey, thirteenth Baron Grey of Wilton, to lead an army to Berwick where it would ready itself to aid the lords of the congregation in their siege of the French garrison in Leith. Ever cautious, however, Elizabeth also attempted to secure a peaceful resolution, acquiescing to the dispatch of a French envoy, Jean de Monluc, bishop of Valence, to Scotland in the hope that he might yet broker an agreement between the regent, Mary de Guise, and the rebels. Both to act as escort, and to ensure that Monluc did not stray from his remit, Killigrew was appointed to accompany him. The two men arrived in Scotland in April, but due largely to the intransigence of both parties the talks came to nothing. In consequence the Anglo-Scottish force assaulted Leith and was duly repulsed with heavy losses. Arriving in London on the same day as the unfortunate news, Killigrew was one of those to bear the queen's wrath. However, his fall from grace was brief. The treaty of Edinburgh and the withdrawal of French troops from Scotland vindicated the hardline policy that Killigrew had so energetically urged upon Elizabeth and the zealous diplomat was once more restored to favour.

For two years Killigrew remained in England, with Sir Robert Dudley acting as his patron. Then in August 1562 he was once again called upon to travel to France. In the aftermath of Henri's death and with the support of the dowager queen, Catherine de' Medici, the Guise opposition to the Huguenot cause was proving implacable. By autumn 1562 the Huguenots had been confined to a handful of strongholds to which their enemies were consistently and successfully laying siege. In sending Killigrew to Normandy, Elizabeth sought to discover the strength of the Huguenot forces and fortifications, and whether, in return for her military and financial support, their leaders would be prepared to cede Calais to the English. With extreme reluctance the French rebels agreed that, in return for an army of 6000 men and a gift of a million crowns, they would permit the English to garrison Newhaven (Le Havre) and Dieppe until such time as they were in a position to restore Calais. At the beginning of October Sir Adrian Poynings sailed with the 1500 strong vanguard of the expeditionary force to Le Havre, where Killigrew awaited him. Without official sanction, but quite possibly with the tacit approval of the queen, Killigrew, in company with Thomas Leighton, immediately set out from Le Havre at the head of a 400 strong Anglo-French force intent upon bringing aid to the Huguenots besieged at Rouen. Their effort proved to be too little too late. Having gained entry to the city Killigrew and Leighton's force could do nothing but forestall the inevitable. Rouen fell on 26 October, and Killigrew was one of the few Englishmen captured who was not subsequently hanged. He became the captive of Henri d'Anville de Montmorency, son of the constable. After the payment of a considerable ransom, Killigrew returned home in May 1563.

Triumph in Scotland, 1563–1575 In recognition of Killigrew's work in Scotland he was appointed in June 1561 to the lucrative office of teller of the exchequer. In addition to the salary of £33 6s. 8d. Killigrew and his three colleagues were responsible for the receipt and dispersal of nearly all the exchequer's revenue, providing them with the opportunity to make considerable profits from short-term speculation. It was another sixteen years before Killigrew received his next appointment, when, in 1577, he was made receiver of piracy fines. Finally, in 1580 Elizabeth appointed him surveyor of the royal armoury. Undoubtedly these offices provided Killigrew with a healthy income, much needed to subsidize the relatively poor diets he received as an ambassador—on average £2 per day; they did not, however, make him an influential figure within the government. He was MP for Saltash in Cornwall in 1563 but did little in parliament. Throughout Elizabeth's reign Killigrew's best hope of exercising influence rested in his relationships with the queen's great favourites, his long time patron, Dudley (now earl of Leicester), and from the later 1560s Killigrew's brother-in-law, Sir William *Cecil (1520/21–1598). On 4 November 1565 Killigrew married Katherine [see Killigrew, Katherine (c.1542–1583)], fifth daughter of gentleman and scholar Sir Anthony *Cooke (1505/6–1576), royal tutor, of Gidea Hall, Essex, and his wife, Anne. The marriage, for all the advantages it conveyed to the young diplomat, was apparently one of love. The couple had four daughters. Sir Nicholas *Bacon (1510–1579), lord keeper, was an influential brother-in-law, but the most important connection was with Cecil. The link to Cecil, originally little to the principal secretary's liking, ultimately secured for Killigrew the support of the most influential man in England.

Barring two brief missions to Scotland in 1566 and 1567 Killigrew remained in England for more than six years after his ill-starred military escapades in France. His next diplomatic mission, begun in February 1569, took him once again to Heidelberg. In response to an overture made by Friedrich III, Killigrew travelled to Germany to explore the possibility of a defensive alliance and discuss conditions under which the queen might grant a loan of 100,000 crowns in order to finance a protestant military expedition against the Low Countries and France. The mission, to which Killigrew was strongly committed, foundered on the reluctance of Friedrich's German allies to form a confederation with a foreign power, and Elizabeth's fear that too close an association with the protestant princes might well serve simply to draw the wrath of the Catholic powers directly upon her. Killigrew was returned as MP for Truro in 1571 and 1572 and was more active on committees than in previous parliaments, including sitting on one concerned with Mary, queen of Scots (12 May 1572).

On 24 August 1572 thousands of Huguenots were killed in the St Bartholomew's day massacre. This did much to convince Elizabeth and her privy councillors that once free of civil war France might well make a determined effort to restore Catholicism to England, as ever using Scotland to facilitate its efforts. To avoid this it would be vital to ensure that Scotland was united under a strong protestant government. To this end Killigrew, recently returned from France, where for the previous three years

he had been serving as secretary to the resident ambassador, Sir Francis Walsingham, was dispatched to Edinburgh. His instructions were to broker a peace between the regency government of James VI, headed by John Erskine, first earl of Mar, and James Douglas, fourth earl of Morton, and the supporters of Mary, Sir William Kirkcaldy of Grange and William Maitland of Lethington. He was instructed to persuade the regency government to take custody of Mary, who was then a prisoner in England, and then arrange her execution as expeditiously as possible, thus relieving Elizabeth of the unwholesome task.

The mission, probably the most challenging of Killigrew's career, also witnessed his greatest success. The ambassador could only get Mar and Morton to connive at the judicial murder of Mary if Elizabeth openly supported them in the act. However, Killigrew was considerably more successful in other respects. Mar died on 29 October 1572, leaving a power vacuum in the regency government. His natural successor, Morton, was disinclined to accept the role without financial and, preferably also, military support from England. Killigrew tried to convince Morton in mid-December that the demands the latter had made were about to be met by Elizabeth. However, Morton was dubious and refused to give way to Killigrew's persuasions that he declare himself governor without firm support in money and military aid from England, which he got. On 31 December the ten-month truce between the two Scottish factions expired and the possibility of renewed conflict seemed great. The leaders of the Scottish queen's party, Kirkcaldy and Maitland, from their position of relative strength in Edinburgh Castle, resisted all Killigrew's attempts to make peace. However, the ambassador had considerably more success with their allies beyond the city. In February 1573 he met the leaders of the two parties, excluding Kirkcaldy and Maitland, at Leith and successfully negotiated an agreement by which the Marians accepted the rule of the regency government in return for liberal concessions on the part of the king. Having helped both to secure the appointment of Morton as governor and to isolate the opposition leaders it only remained for Killigrew to secure the English military support necessary to reduce Edinburgh Castle. This he finally gained in April when Sir William Drury, captain of Berwick, led a force of 1500 men and thirty-three pieces of artillery to Edinburgh. Finally, on 26 May the garrison surrendered. Maitland died in prison on 9 June and Kirkcaldy was executed on 3 August. Due in no small part to the unrelenting efforts of Killigrew, opponents of the regency were either broken or won over, and the danger of a Franco-Scottish alliance eliminated. Over the next two years Killigrew performed two further embassies to Scotland in which he made every effort to nurture Anglo-Scottish relations and support Morton's regency. Elizabeth recalled him in September 1575, bringing to an end the most productive period of his diplomatic career.

Final years, 1575–1603 Aside from his lucrative work as teller of the exchequer, Killigrew was also called upon to offer advice on diplomatic affairs and to act as interpreter and companion to high-ranking foreign guests. His long service to Elizabeth did not go unrewarded. In recognition of his work in Scotland he was granted the manor of Lanreath, Cornwall, in May 1573. The following year Killigrew added to his Cornish holdings with the purchase of the manor of Bottlet from Henry Hastings, third earl of Huntingdon, for £3600. Additionally, he owned an estate in Hendon in Middlesex and a house next to St Paul's churchyard. His position as a significant landowner was reflected in his involvement in local government. In addition to serving as MP for Truro (elected in 1571 and 1572), between about 1579 and 1587 he served on the quorum of the peace for Cornwall. Much of his personal life seems to have been devoted to the management of his estates and correspondence with his puritan friends such as Elizabeth's resident ambassador to the Netherlands, William Davison, and his patrons Burghley and Leicester. In December 1584 his daughter Anne (d. 1632) married Henry *Neville (1561/2–1615) of Wargrave in Berkshire. He was the first of several sons-in-law with whom Killigrew got on well.

In November 1585 Killigrew was summoned to perform his penultimate foreign mission, as one of Leicester's key advisers in the Netherlands. For all that the earl commanded an English relief force that represented one of the best hopes of the states general to defeat the Spanish, his high-handed manner and divisive policies made bitter opponents of the Dutch leaders. As one of Leicester's most senior advisers Killigrew shared in this odium. His situation became still less comfortable when Leicester appointed him joint head of the new chamber of finance in July 1586. Killigrew's main responsibilities were to investigate corruption among the Dutch leadership and to impede commercial activities between the Provinces and their Spanish enemies. Relief came when in November he followed Leicester back to England. In June 1587 he returned to the Low Countries, but unlike Leicester, who received his final recall in November, Killigrew remained with the Dutch for another year. With Leicester's departure he became the most senior civilian English representative in the Netherlands. This was a somewhat empty honour given the distrust and resentment with which the English were regarded by the Dutch leaders, in particular Paul Buys and Johan Oldenbarnevelt. Much of Killigrew's remaining time in the Netherlands was devoted to undoing Leicester's work and seeking to make peace between the states general and those towns that had rejected its authority. Killigrew's long-sought recall finally came in January 1589, largely the result of his continuing unpopularity with the Dutch leaders; it was also an acknowledgement that one of Elizabeth's longest serving diplomats was now both old and tired.

Killigrew's final foreign mission, begun in July 1591, as part of an English expeditionary force sent to assist Henri of Navarre in his siege of Rouen, saw him serving as adviser to Robert Devereux, second earl of Essex, and in company with his old comrade, Leighton, attempting to restrain the incautious young general. He was also responsible for much of the logistical organization of the 3400 strong army. Despite his age and growing infirmity Killigrew seems to have performed this latter duty with considerable competence. He went to great lengths to ensure that the army was fed and discipline maintained, as well as expending much effort and money in arranging for the sick to be transported home. Neither he nor Leighton were able to stop Essex treating the campaign as something of an adventure, nevertheless, the general made clear his gratitude for Killigrew's efforts when he knighted the old diplomat on 20 November, a week before his return to England.

Killigrew largely retired from public service. He retained the tellership of the exchequer until March 1599, and occasionally returned to court to participate in diplomatic negotiations. Katherine Killigrew died on 27 December 1583, and her widower married a Frenchwoman, Jaël de Peigne (d. 1617×34), on 7 November 1590. The couple had three sons, Joseph, Henry, and Robert, and one daughter. Killigrew intervened on behalf of Neville in early 1601, who had become embroiled in Essex's revolt. Killigrew died on 2 March 1603 and was buried in London at St Margaret, Lothbury. His will, proved on 16 April, provided annuities for his wife and two younger sons totalling £140, as well as further bequests to them with a value of £1700.

LUKE MACMAHON

Sources A. C. Miller, *Sir Henry Killigrew, Elizabethan soldier and diplomat* (1963) • *CSP for.*, 1547–88 • *CSP dom.*, 1547–1603 • R. B. Wernham, *Before the Armada: the growth of English foreign policy, 1485–1588* (1966) • J. Warren, *Elizabeth I, religion and foreign affairs* (1993) • HoP, *Commons, 1509–58*, 2.466–7 • HoP, *Commons, 1558–1603*, 2.394–5 • J. L. Vivian, ed., *The visitations of Cornwall, comprising the herald's visitations of 1530, 1573, and 1620* (1887) • D. Trim, '"The foundation stone of the British army?" The Normandy campaign of 1562', *Journal of the Society for Army Historical Research*, 77 (1999), 77–86 • G. R. Hewitt, *Scotland under Morton, 1572–80* (1982)

Archives PRO, corresp., PRO 30/50 | BL, Cotton MSS, corresp. • BL, Harley MSS, papers

Killigrew, Henry (1613–1700), Church of England clergyman, was born on 11 February 1613 at the manor of Hanworth, near Hampton Court, the fifth son of Sir Robert *Killigrew (1579/80–1633), vice-chamberlain to Queen Henrietta Maria, and Mary, daughter of Sir Henry Woodhouse of Kimberley, Norfolk. The brother of Sir William *Killigrew (bap. 1606, d. 1695) and Thomas *Killigrew (1612–1683), both dramatists, Killigrew was educated at Thomas Farnaby's Grammar School in the parish of Cripplegate, presumably from about 1620. He is first mentioned in the will of his grandmother Margaret Killigrew, dated 22 May 1623: to Henry and his brothers Charles, Robert, and Thomas she left the sum of £5, 'to be paid within three months after my decease' (PRO, PROB 11/146/71). Killigrew entered Christ Church, Oxford, as a commoner in 1628, and soon afterwards became a student. While at Oxford he contributed Latin poems to several collections of occasional verse, including *Britanniae natalis* (1630), celebrating the birth of Prince Charles. After having obtained his BA degree on 5 July 1632, Killigrew became one of the quadragesimal collectors, involved in the determination exercises in Lent. Sir Robert, in his will dated 12 September 1632, bequeathed to him 'the market and fairs within the manor and lordship of Crediton, co. Devons.', with all the rents, issues and profits from the same, for a period of seventy years (PRO, PROB 11/164/69).

Killigrew's literary talent soon manifested itself in *The Conspiracy*, a tragedy intended to be produced at the wedding, on 8 January 1635, of Charles Herbert, son of the earl of Pembroke, and Mary Villiers, daughter of the duke of Buckingham. The play was surreptitiously published in 1638, its text having been printed, as the corrected 1653 edition entitled *Pallantus and Eudora* explained, 'from a false and imperfect transcript, the original copy being then (together with the writer of it) in Italy' ('The publisher to the reader'). In July 1638 Killigrew was created MA, travelled abroad, and, 'entering afterwards into the sacred function', towards the beginning of the civil war became a chaplain in the king's army (Wood, *Ath. Oxon.*, 4.622). Immediately after the battle of Edgehill, in November 1642, he was created doctor of divinity and in the same year he became a chaplain to James, duke of York, and prebendary of Westminster. He was a member of the duke's cabinet council, accompanying him to Paris and Brussels in September 1650. With his wife, Judith (d. 1683), a lady-in-waiting to Queen Catharine of Braganza, Killigrew had four children, only two of whom, Elizabeth (b. 1650?, d. 28 Oct 1701) and Henry *Killigrew (d. 9 Nov 1712), an admiral, were to survive their father. James, a captain in the navy, was killed in action in January 1695. Anne *Killigrew, born in 1660, was a poet and painter, whose untimely death of smallpox in June 1685 was commemorated in Dryden's famous ode, prefixed to her posthumously published *Poems* (1686).

After the Restoration, Killigrew appears to have been actively engaged amassing a variety of appointments and offices. In 1660 he was made almoner to the duke of York, with a salary of £100 per annum, superintendent of the affairs of his chapel, and rector of Wheathamsted in Hertfordshire (a post which in 1673 he resigned in favour of Dr John Lambe, husband of his daughter Elizabeth). After the resignation of Gilbert Sheldon, bishop of London, in early July 1663, the king recommended him for the post of master of the Savoy Hospital. He was elected by the clerks and chaplains on 10 July. Killigrew's petition for the government of St John the Baptist and St John the Evangelist's Hospital in Sherborne, Dorset, was referred to the attorney-general on 10 August 1667. He was granted the mastership, 'with power to recover any lands lately belonging to the hospital', in late 1668 or 1669 (*CSP dom.*, *October 1668–December 1669*, 653).

During the Anglo-Dutch War, in August 1673, Killigrew was ordered to deliver up parts of the Savoy Hospital to the 'Commissioners for the sick and wounded, there being a present necessity of providing conveniences for their reception' (*CSP dom.*, *1 March–31 Oct 1673*, 514). As the chaplains later observed, this arrangement had been detrimental to the master and poorer persons in the hospital. Killigrew, after vainly trying to recover the confiscated premises, 'compensated some of the sufferers by pensions and doles' (*DNB*). The eventual ruin of the Savoy Hospital, dissolved in 1702, has nevertheless been generally blamed on Killigrew's mismanagement. In the course of those years, Killigrew distinguished himself as a preacher, author of *Sermons Preached at Whitehall* (1685), and as the (anonymous) translator of Martial's *Epigrams* (1695). His wife, Judith, reputed an accomplished musician, had been buried at the Savoy on 2 February 1683. It was in response to Anthony Wood's enquiries in late 1691 that Killigrew, then living at Westminster Abbey, provided some of the biographical information contained in the present notice. He died on 14 March 1700. J. P. VANDER MOTTEN

Sources Wood, *Ath. Oxon.*, new edn, 4.621 · *DNB* · A. Harbage, *Thomas Killigrew, cavalier dramatist, 1612–1683* (1930) · A. Pritchard, 'According to Wood: sources of A. Wood's lives of poets and dramatists', *Review of English Studies*, new ser., 28 (1977), 268–89, 407–20 · *CSP dom.*, 1663–4; 1666–9; 1673; 1679–80 · Margaret Killigrew's will, 23 May 1623, PRO, PROB 11/146, sig. 71 · Robert Killigrew's will, 12 Sept 1632, PRO, PROB 11/164, sig. 69 · J. P. Vander Motten, *Sir William Killigrew (1606–1695): his life and dramatic works* (1980) · N. Luttrell, *A brief historical relation of state affairs from September 1678 to April 1714*, 4 (1857) · Evelyn, *Diary*, vols. 3–4 · *The Nicholas papers*, ed. G. F. Warner, 1, CS, new ser., 40 (1886) · *De briefwisseling van Constantijn Huygens (1608–1687)*, ed. J. A. Worp, 6 (The Hague, 1917) · F. Madan, *Oxford literature, 1450–1640, and 1641–1650* (1912), vol. 2 of *Oxford books: a bibliography of printed works* (1895–1931); repr. (1964)

Killigrew, Henry (*c*.1652–1712), naval officer, son of Henry *Killigrew (1613–1700), clergyman, and his wife, Judith (d. 1683), and brother of James *Killigrew (d. 1695), served as a volunteer before becoming lieutenant of the *Cambridge* in July 1666. From her he moved to the *Sapphire*, and in 1669 to the *Constant Warwick*. In January 1672 he became captain of the *Forester*, from which he was moved to the *Bonadventure* (June 1672 to August 1673), and afterwards to the *Monck*. He fought in the battles of Schooneveld and the Texel in 1673. After the peace he was almost continuously employed in the Mediterranean, where he successively commanded the *Swan* prize in 1675, the *Harwich* and the *Henrietta* in 1675–6, the *Bristol* and the *Royal Oak* in 1678, and the *Mary* in 1679, returning to England in her in June 1679. He commanded the *Leopard* briefly in 1680 and the *Foresight* between 1680 and 1682; in 1683–4 he was captain of the *Montagu* in Lord Dartmouth's expedition to Tangier, and in 1684–5 of the *Mordaunt* for a voyage to the Gambia. Pepys, serving as Dartmouth's secretary on the Tangier expedition, found Killigrew to be hard-drinking, keen to make as much money as possible from shipping merchants' goods, and owing his great influence with Dartmouth to the fact that he was sleeping with the king's former mistress, the duchess of Cleveland. Even so, Pepys also found 'his manner of living the neatest, and most like a gentleman that I ever saw of any man, and his civility to me extraordinary' (*Tangier Papers*, 46). In 1686 Killigrew went out to the Mediterranean in the *Dragon* as commodore of a small squadron to suppress the Salé corsairs. A detailed account of this voyage was written by G. Wood, Killigrew's clerk in the *Dragon* (BL, Add. MS 19302).

Killigrew returned to England in May 1689, was promoted to vice-admiral of the blue through the influence of Daniel Finch, earl of Nottingham, and during the summer flew his flag in the *Kent* in the channel. In December he was appointed to command a squadron which sailed for the Mediterranean in the following March to prevent the Toulon fleet sailing to Brest. On 9 May 1690 he was refitting at Cadiz when he learned that Admiral Château-Renault was at sea with ten ships of the line. On the 10th Killigrew, having been joined by some of his ships from Gibraltar, was able to pursue with fifteen ships. However, they were foul and sailed badly, allowing Château-Renault easily to sail away from them. Killigrew returned to Cadiz before sailing for home, but bad weather still opposed him. He took thirty-five days to reach Plymouth, and when he arrived the battle of Beachy Head had been fought, leaving the French masters of the channel. Although Killigrew's failure to catch Château-Renault and alleged dilatoriness in returning home attracted much criticism, and rumours of Jacobitism were already attached to his name, he was appointed one of the joint commanders-in-chief (along with Sir Richard Haddock and Sir John Ashby) to succeed the disgraced earl of Torrington, serving until December 1690 when they were replaced by Edward Russell. Killigrew served under Russell as admiral of the blue in 1691, but their relationship was increasingly strained, and Killigrew had no command in 1692. When Russell's fleet won its great victories at Barfleur and La Hogue, he complained that:

a blessing of so large a spread should import evil to no one of the winning side but to me alone. I see myself rendered by it not only useless at present but perhaps for my whole life … I see my adversary raised to a capacity to insult over me and to cross all my pretences, whose malice will let no opportunity slip by which it can express itself.   (Killigrew to Nottingham, 28 May 1692, *Finch MSS*, 4.192)

Killigrew declined the command of the winter squadron in the Mediterranean, regarding it as inferior to the posts he had held, but in 1693 he was again one of the joint admirals, with Sir Cloudesley Shovell and Sir Ralph Delaval, and was appointed a lord commissioner of the Admiralty on 15 April 1693. After the disaster which befell the Smyrna fleet in June 1693 Killigrew, together with Delaval, was dismissed from command and had to face a hostile inquiry by parliament from November to January. Although the admirals were censured for mismanagement, a charge of high breach of trust was defeated by ten votes. Nevertheless, Killigrew lost his colonelcy of the 2nd marine regiment and governorship of Landguard Fort, and was removed from the Admiralty by a warrant dated 24 April 1694. Killigrew and Delaval were widely suspected of Jacobite sympathies and of planning to keep the fleet out of the way to allow James II to invade; indeed, the earl of Ailesbury had held negotiations to this effect with Killigrew early in 1693. Killigrew never commanded again, and spent his later years unsuccessfully attempting to get full and half pay backdated to 1693, although in 1702 he was granted a pension of £700 per annum. He served as MP for Stockbridge, a seat controlled by his brother-in-law, from 1702 to 1705, and for St Albans from 1705 to 1708, dying at St Julians, his seat near St Albans, on 9 November 1712. His wife, Lucy Jervoise, whom he had married in 1692, is believed to have predeceased him.

J. K. LAUGHTON, rev. J. D. DAVIES

Sources PRO, ADM MSS · HoP, *Commons, 1690–1715* [draft] · *The Tangier papers of Samuel Pepys*, ed. E. Chappell, Navy RS, 73 (1935) · *Report on the manuscripts of Allan George Finch*, 5 vols., HMC, 71 (1913–2003) · *The manuscripts of the House of Lords*, new ser., 12 vols. (1900–77), vol. 1 · *Report on the manuscripts of his grace the duke of Buccleuch and Queensberry … preserved at Montagu House*, 3 vols. in 4, HMC, 45 (1899–1926), vol. 2 · *The manuscripts of his grace the duke of Portland*, 10 vols., HMC, 29 (1891–1931), vol. 8 · BL, Add. MS 19302 · *CSP dom., 1689–95* · H. Horwitz, *Revolution politicks: the career of Daniel Finch, second earl of Nottingham, 1647–1730* (1968) · E. B. Powley, *The naval side of King William's war* (1972) · J. Ehrman, *The navy in the war of William III, 1689–1697* (1953) · R. C. Anderson, 'English flag officers, 1688–1713', *Mariner's Mirror*, 35 (1949), 333–41

Archives CKS, corresp. with Admirals Shovell and Delavall and the admiralty · CKS, letters to Alexander Stanhope · PRO, Admiralty MSS

Wealth at death see administration, PRO, PROB 6/87, fol. 154v

Killigrew, James (c.1664–1695), naval officer, was the second son of Henry *Killigrew (1613–1700), dramatist and master of the Savoy Hospital, and his wife, Judith (d. 1683), and was brother of Admiral Henry *Killigrew. He went to sea with his brother, serving as a captain's servant and then as a midshipman in the *Mordaunt* and the *Dragon*, both commanded by his brother, between 1684 and 1688. He was appointed lieutenant successively of the *Garland* (July 1688), the *Portsmouth* (5 September 1688), and the *St Albans* (October 1688), one of the ships which accompanied Arthur Herbert, earl of Torrington to Holland in February 1689 to bring Queen Mary to England. In August 1689 he was appointed second lieutenant of the *Duke*, the flagship of Edward Russell, admiral of the blue. On Russell's recommendation he was promoted captain on 11 April 1690 and appointed to the *Sapphire*. He did not take part in the battle of Beachy Head but was one of the captains who sat on Torrington's courts martial on 10 December 1690, and who acquitted him. Russell described him in his private list of captains as 'a good man, but young' (Folger Shakespeare Library, MS xd. 451 (98)). A lieutenant in the first regiment of marines commanded by Henry Killigrew in 1691, in 1693 he was a captain in Danby's marine regiment.

In 1691 Killigrew served in the Irish seas and in the English Channel, and in July captured a large French privateer from St Malo, originally an English merchant ship. From 1692 to March 1693 he was cruising off the Channel Islands, taking a French merchant ship near Jersey in January 1692, and then in the Baltic. While at sea on 23 March 1693 he exchanged commands with the captain of the *Crown*, moved to the *York* three months later, and spent June and July cruising in the Mediterranean before moving to the *Plymouth*. He was highly thought of by Russell, who recognized his potential by appointing him to command a small detached force of five ships in December 1694. He drew up his will on 5 December and, not having married, left his pay from the marine regiment to Thomas Balderstone and his pay as captain of the *York* to Kenrick Edisbury, a member of the Navy Board, with his brother Henry as executor. On 18 January 1695 he was cruising to the southward of Sardinia when two French men-of-war were sighted, the 60-gun *Content* and 52-gun *Trident*. About 3 p.m. the *Plymouth*, which was ahead of her consorts, engaged the *Content* and at 3.30 Killigrew, 'after he had been in all places … giving necessary instructions and orders to his lieutenants' and encouraging the seamen, was 'wounded mortally in the pit of his stomach by a short bar of Iron about 6 inches long it lodging in his body' (PRO, ADM 51/3935/1; PRO, SP 42/5, fol. 1). The *Plymouth* suffered severely, having been dismasted as well as having the sails and rigging torn to shreds, but the French ships had been delayed until the other English ships came up and, being unable to escape, were both captured, taken into Messina, and afterwards added to the navy. At Messina on 22 January 1695 the *Plymouth*'s chaplain John Percival preached a funeral sermon over Killigrew, and as his coffin was carried on shore in the *Plymouth*'s barge, 'the ship fired 20 guns by the half minute glass'. Killigrew was buried in a 'very pleasant garden on the north side of Messina' (PRO, ADM 51/3935/1). After his death his brother Henry asked whether his estate was not entitled to a share of the prize money, but Russell advised that the money was payable only to the captains whose vessels actually took the ships. Killigrew was a popular captain who encouraged and inspired his crew and showed 'as much courage, bravery and resolution as could be expected from man' (PRO, SP 42/5, fol. 1).   J. K. LAUGHTON, rev. PETER LE FEVRE

Sources *Mordaunt* log book, 1684, PRO, ADM 33/119 · *Dragon* ticket book, PRO, ADM 106/3540 pt 1 · ships' disposition lists, PRO, ADM 8/1, 8/2 · P. Le Fevre, 'The earl of Torrington's court-martial, 10 December 1690', *Mariner's Mirror*, 76 (1990), 243–9 · journal 1, log of *Plymouth*, PRO, ADM 51/3935 · journal 7, master's log of *Sapphire*, PRO, ADM 52/105 · Folger, MS xd. 451 (98) · PRO, SP 42/5 · PRO, PROB 11/426, fol. 66 · J. L. Vivian, ed., *The visitations of Cornwall, comprising the herald's visitations of 1530, 1573, and 1620* (1887), 271
Archives PRO, Admiralty MSS

Killigrew [née Cooke], **Katherine** (c.1542–1583), gentlewoman and scholar, was the fifth daughter of Sir Anthony *Cooke (1505/6–1576), Edward VI's tutor, of Gidea Hall in Essex, and Anne (d. 1553), daughter of Sir William Fitzwilliam, and widow of Sir John Hawes. Like her sisters Elizabeth, Anne *Bacon, and Mildred *Cecil, Katherine was educated in the classics by her father. She became famous for her knowledge of Hebrew, Greek, and Latin, and for her ability to write poetry, although she left little evidence in writing. There is no confirmation of her skill in Hebrew. Katherine was left her choice of books in her father's will of 1575; two in Latin and one in Greek. She married Henry *Killigrew of Cornwall (d. 1603) on 4 November 1565. Henry was often abroad on diplomatic missions, mainly in France and Scotland, and was knighted in 1591 for his services to his country. Katherine remained in England, using her family connections to the Cecils to make requests on behalf of her husband. She wrote verse in Latin to her sister Mildred, asking her to use her influence with her husband William Cecil to excuse Henry from overseas service. In 1582, shortly before her death, Katherine wrote to Cecil on her husband's behalf asking his aid in obtaining lands for him. Henry Killigrew's concern for his wife can be seen in his purchase of an annuity for her from the crown, and his attempts to return to England for the birth of their children.

Katherine Killigrew was a committed puritan, maintaining a friendship with the preacher Edward Dering; she offered him hospitality even when he was in disgrace with the queen. Some clues to her adult life can be learned from Dering's correspondence. Several letters dating from 1575, which he wrote to her at Hendon where she lived with her three daughters, Nan, Bess, and Mary, were printed in his *Godly Letters* (1614). A fourth daughter, Dorothy, is not mentioned in the Dering letters. Katherine suffered from frequent bouts of ill health. In his writing Dering refers to her physical sufferings, and offers her spiritual support and comfort while telling her of his own illness and his problems with his lungs; he died in 1576 of tuberculosis.

Katherine herself died on 27 December 1583 after having given birth to a stillborn child. She left her own epitaph, a verse mainly in Latin demonstrating her certainty of the resurrection. She was buried in the church of St Thomas the Apostle, London, which was burnt down in the 1666 great fire. Her memorial contained four inscriptions which were printed by Stow: one of these, in both Greek and Latin, was composed by her sister Elizabeth Russell. The verse laments the untimely loss of a virtuous sister, commending her wit, learning and grace, and it looks forward to their reunion in heaven. The three other tributes were written by well-known puritan divines, and commented on her learning, modesty, purity, and religious zeal. Camden also praised her knowledge of Greek and Latin in an epitaph.   CAROLINE M. K. BOWDEN

Sources G. Ballard, *Memoirs of several ladies of Great Britain*, ed. R. Perry (1985) · S. Harvey, 'The Cooke sisters: a study of Tudor gentlewomen', PhD diss., Indiana University, 1981 · E. Dering, *Godly letters* (1614) · C. Miller, *Sir Henry Killigrew* (1963) · BL, Add. MS 36294, fol. 34b [Camden's epitaph] · PRO, SP 12/155, fol. 97 [letter to Cecil]

Killigrew, Sir Robert (1579/80–1633), courtier, was born in Lothbury, London, the son of **Sir William Killigrew** (d. 1622), courtier, and his wife, Margaret (d. in or after 1623), daughter of Thomas Saunders of Uxbridge, Middlesex, and grandson of John Killigrew of Arwennack, Cornwall, and his wife, Elizabeth Trewennard. William Killigrew and his brother, Henry *Killigrew, made their fortunes at Elizabeth I's court. William, though less influential than Henry, acted as a diplomatic courier, became a groom of the privy chamber by 1576, farmed the fees from sealing writs in queen's bench and common pleas (from 1578), and was treasurer of the chamber in 1595. He held various offices in Cornwall and Devon, and sat in parliament for Grantham (1571), Helston (1572), Penryn (1584), Fowey (1593), and the county of Cornwall (1597). Knighted by James I at Theobalds on 7 May 1603, he was MP for Liskeard in 1604 and Penryn in 1614 and chamberlain of the exchequer in 1605–8. In 1594 he was granted an eighty-year lease by the crown for the manors of Hanworth and Kempton in Middlesex. He died at his town house in Lothbury, London, on 23 November 1622, and was buried at St Margaret, Lothbury.

Robert Killigrew matriculated from Christ Church, Oxford, in January 1591, aged eleven, but took no degree.

He entered politics as MP for St Mawes in the 1601 parliament, was knighted by James I in July 1603, and represented Newport in 1604. About this time he married Sir Francis Bacon's niece, Mary Woodhouse (*fl.* 1590–1650), daughter of Sir Henry Woodhouse of Kimberley, Norfolk, and his wife, Ann, daughter of Sir Nicholas Bacon. Their eldest child, William, was baptized in May 1606. They had twelve children in all; nine (five sons and four daughters) lived to maturity.

By 1606 Killigrew was at court and he eventually entered the circle of the royal favourite Robert Carr and his friend Sir Thomas Overbury. In June 1612 John Chamberlain noted that Killigrew was one of Carr's 'next favorites', after Overbury himself (*Letters of John Chamberlain*, 1.358). Early in May 1613, a few days after Overbury was imprisoned in the Tower, Killigrew was committed to the Fleet for talking with Overbury at his prison window. Killigrew was quickly released, however, and in July was one of two friends permitted to speak with the ailing Overbury. Still a prisoner in the Tower, Overbury died two months later.

As MP for Helston in 1614 Killigrew was involved in a serious altercation in the Commons' committee investigating 'undertaking'. On 12 May, Sir William Herbert accused the committee's chairman, Sir Roger Owen, of partiality, and Killigrew, demanding that Owen 'should put no more tricks upon the House', grabbed the chairman and threatened to pull him out of his seat (Jansson, 228–9). The next day the Commons forced Killigrew to make a formal apology. His motives remain mysterious, but his friendships with Overbury and Sir Henry Neville, both of whom were rumoured to have devised schemes to manage parliament, suggest that he had some personal stake in the 'undertaking' investigation.

In July 1614 Killigrew was appointed keeper for life of Pendennis Castle in Cornwall but in the early autumn of 1615 his fortunes at court were jeopardized by the arrest of Carr, now earl of Somerset, his wife, and several accomplices on suspicion of poisoning Overbury. Killigrew himself became entangled in the ensuing investigation. One of Somerset's servants testified that shortly after Overbury's imprisonment the former had obtained from Killigrew a potent emetic. Unbeknown to Killigrew, who thought the powder was for Carr, Carr and Overbury planned to use it to fake an illness they hoped would win royal mercy for Overbury. Though never under direct suspicion Killigrew was questioned by the commissioners investigating Overbury's death, and he spoke at Somerset's trial to counter the favourite's assertion that it was one of his powders that had sickened the imprisoned knight.

Despite Somerset's fall Killigrew had little difficulty maintaining his fortunes. Although he failed to secure a patent for the enrolment of apprentices in 1616 and risked royal wrath by duelling with a Captain Burton early in 1618, Killigrew steadily accumulated the fruits of court favour. In October 1618 he was granted the office of protonotary of chancery for life and in December 1619 the favourite, Buckingham, wrote on his behalf about a suit for 'certain concealed lands', stressing that Killigrew was a 'gentleman whom I love and wish very well unto' (Spedding, 7.69–70).

During the 1620s Killigrew sat in the Commons for Newport (1621), Penryn (1624), the county of Cornwall (1625), Tregony (1626), and Bodmin (1628), and he played an occasional but by no means a major role in the contentious sessions of the decade. He was, however, an active patron on Buckingham's behalf in borough elections across Cornwall, where he had been appointed JP in 1617 and deputy lieutenant in 1623. As early as 1614 Killigrew used his family influence to secure for Sir James Whitelocke control of a seat at Helston, and in 1625 and 1626 he secured a seat at Penryn for Buckingham's client Sir Edwin Sandys.

In September 1625 it was reported that Killigrew was to become resident ambassador to the United Provinces; his appointment was confirmed that December, but he never took up residence, probably because his duties at Pendennis kept him in England during the military mobilization of the mid- and late-1620s. He proved an energetic keeper, constantly petitioning the privy council for more money, men, and ordnance, and was appointed to various commissions concerned with the local war effort, including the 1627 commission for the forced loan. He also continued to accumulate court favour and office. In March 1627 he began farming the fees for sealing writs in king's bench and common pleas, and early in 1630 he became vice-chamberlain to Queen Henrietta Maria. In his last years, he renegotiated the lease on his estates at Hanworth and Kempton, continued his Cornish responsibilities, and embarked on controversial fen drainage schemes in Lincolnshire. His entrepreneurial endeavours in the fens were the last of a string of business activities which included investments in the Virginia and New River Companies. Killigrew died at Hanworth in the spring of 1633 and his will was proved on 12 May 1633.

Killigrew was a cosmopolitan and cultured man. When the Dutch diplomat and poet Constantijn Huygens stayed with Killigrew in 1622 he was introduced by his host to many of London's cultural élite, including John Donne, Sir Francis Bacon, the musician and painter Nicholas Lanier, the lutenist Jacques Gaultier, and the lens-grinder Cornelius Drebbel. Killigrew himself dabbled in lens-grinding and in medicine. His skill with medical concoctions had dragged him into the Overbury plot in 1613, and a manuscript of his 'Experimenta' survives in a contemporary compendium of medical and scientific writings. Evidence of his cultural patronage is scarce, but two works—Thomas Farnaby's 1615 edition of Martial's epigrams and a 1613 religious treatise by Thomas Broad— were dedicated to him. Killigrew's personal religious sympathies are unclear. His uncle Henry had been an early and militant protestant, but it has been suggested, solely on the circumstantial evidence of his friendship with the Arminian Richard Thomson, that Killigrew himself had anti-Calvinist leanings.

His widow married Sir Thomas Stafford, gentleman-usher to Henrietta Maria, and a number of his children enjoyed lengthy court careers. Perhaps nurtured by the intellectual atmosphere of the Killigrew home, Killigrew's sons William and Thomas *Killigrew became playwrights, and his son Henry a noted divine. His daughter Elizabeth was an early mistress of Charles II, with whom she had an illegitimate daughter.   ALASTAIR BELLANY

Sources CSP dom., 1611–33 · APC, 1613–14; 1617–19; 1623–5; 1627–8 · M. Jansson, ed., Proceedings in parliament, 1614 (House of Commons) (1988), 228–9 · 'Relation of Giles Rawlins, earl of Somerset's servant, October 1615', PRO, SP 14/82/24 · letters from T. Overbury to R. Carr and R. Killigrew to R. Carr, May 1613, BL, Harleian MS 7002, fols. 281r–281v · J. P. Vander Motten, Sir William Killigrew (1606–1695): his life and dramatic works (1980), 17, 22–6 · P. W. Hasler, 'Killigrew, William', HoP, Commons, 1558–1603 · N. M. Fuidge, 'Killigrew, Henry', 'Killigrew, John I', 'Killigrew, John II', 'Killigrew, Robert', HoP, Commons, 1558–1603 · The letters of John Chamberlain, ed. N. E. McClure, 1 (1939), 358, 451 · State trials, 2.994 · The letters and life of Francis Bacon, ed. J. Spedding, 7 vols. (1861–74), vol. 6, p. 102; vol. 7, pp. 69–70 · A. Duffin, Faction and faith: politics and religion of the Cornish gentry before the civil war (1996), 77, 80, 111, 117, 126–7, 252, 254 · W. A. Shaw, The knights of England, 2 (1906), 104, 127 · 'Killigrew pedigree', Archaeologia, 18 (1817), 99 · Foster, Alum. Oxon., 1500–1714 [Sir Robert Killegrew] · T. K. Rabb, Enterprise and empire: merchant and gentry investment in the expansion of England, 1575–1630 (1967), 327 · D. Lysons, An historical account of those parishes in the county of Middlesex which are not described in 'The environs of London' (1800), 99–101 · F. Blomefield and C. Parkin, An essay towards a topographical history of the county of Norfolk, [2nd edn], 11 vols. (1805–10), vol. 9, p. 353 · S. A. J. Moorat, Catalogue of Western manuscripts on medicine and science in the Wellcome Historical Medical Library, 1 (1962), 526–7 · T. Broade, A touch-stone for a Christian (1613), sig. A2r–sig. A4v · N. Tyacke, Anti-Calvinists: the rise of English Arminianism, c.1590–1640 (1987), 38 · Liber famelicus of Sir James Whitelocke, a judge of the court of king's bench in the reigns of James I and Charles I, ed. J. Bruce, CS, old ser., 70 (1858), 41 · T. K. Rabb, Jacobean gentleman: Sir Edwin Sandys, 1561–1629 (1998), 306 · A. Harbage, Thomas Killigrew, cavalier dramatist, 1612–1683 (1930); repr. (1967), chap. 1

Killigrew, Thomas (1612–1683), playwright and theatre manager, was born on 7 February 1612 at Lothbury, London, and baptized on 20 February at St Margaret, Lothbury, the fourth son of Sir Robert *Killigrew (1579/80–1633) and Mary Woodhouse; he was brother of Sir William *Killigrew and Henry *Killigrew.

Early years, 1612–1641 Although the seat of the family estate was at Hanworth, near Hampton Court, Killigrew was probably raised in London. His interest in the drama may have been aroused at an early age: in October 1662 Pepys reported the story of how Killigrew as a boy would go to the Red Bull playhouse at Clerkenwell, 'and when the man cried to the boys, "Who will go and be a divell, and he shall see the play for nothing?"—then would he go in and be a devil upon the stage' (Pepys, 3.243–4). The earliest mention of Thomas occurs in his grandmother Margerie Killigrew's will, dated 22 May 1623: to him and his brothers Charles (1609–1629), Robert (1611–1635), and Henry (1613–1700), she bequeathed the sum of £5 (Margerie Killigrew's will).

Unlike that of his brothers William (1606–1695) and Henry, who both studied at Oxford, Thomas's formal education appears to have been rather incidental. Correct spelling was an achievement that, even in later life, he never quite attained. As his brother Henry, in a letter to Anthony Wood, testified in November 1691, Thomas 'wanted some learning to poise his excellent natural wit'

Thomas Killigrew (1612–1683), by Sir Anthony Van Dyck, 1638 [left, with an unidentified man]

(Pritchard, 288). What education he had he obtained at court, to which his father, the queen's vice-chamberlain, must have introduced him. Contrary to what has been maintained, however, Thomas did not become a page at court as early as 1625 but some time later. Of his career at court until 1635 or 1636, not much is known. It has been (somewhat implausibly) suggested, on the authority of William Coventry's story as reported by Pepys in July 1665, that Thomas entered the service of Francis, Lord Cottington, when the latter became ambassador to Spain in the autumn of 1629 (Pepys, 9.256).

By July 1632 at the latest Killigrew was serving as a page of honour to Charles I, and over the next few years he tried to supplement his annual salary of £100 with the proceeds from confiscated properties. In his will, dated 12 September 1632, Sir Robert bequeathed to his sons Thomas and Robert his part and portion of all his real estate in the county of Cornwall and 'the yearlie sum of fiftie pounds apeece … to be issuing and going out of all my Manors, lands, tenements and hereditaments' in the same county (Sir Robert Killigrew's will). To Thomas and his heirs he also left 100 acres of fenland in Lincolnshire. But Sir Robert's heavily encumbered bequest was probably an insufficient financial basis for a young courtier to build a career on. In the scramble for money and favour characteristic of one in his position, Thomas managed to ingratiate himself with Queen Henrietta Maria herself. His first play, The Prisoners, a romantic tragicomedy composed in 1635 and performed at the Phoenix, Drury Lane, by Her Majesty's Servants in 1636, may have been a successful bid for royal favour. In October 1635 he was given the opportunity to accompany Walter Montague, the queen's favourite, on his travels to the continent. Montague and his attendants stayed at Calais, Paris, Tours, Orléans, and Loudun, where Killigrew recorded his experiences at the convent of the possessed Ursuline nuns. Before 17 January 1636 they arrived at Vercelli in Italy, then continued south to Rome and Naples, where Killigrew's next two tragicomedies, *Claricilla* and *The Princess*, were composed, in whole or in part. *Claricilla* was performed at the Phoenix before 1641; *The Princess* was probably acted at Blackfriars by the King's Men.

In the spring Killigrew returned to England and on 29 June he married Cecilia Crofts, a maid of honour to the queen. Thomas Carew, a friend of the Crofts family, celebrated the bride's beauty and the groom's happiness in a poem 'On the Marriage of T. K. and C. C. the Morning Stormie'. Henry, the single son from this wedding, was born on Easter day, 9 April 1637. Cecilia died on 1 January 1638 and was buried in Westminster Abbey. In Van Dyck's famous double portrait of *Killigrew and an Unknown Man*, painted in 1638, Killigrew is shown in mourning for Cecilia, wearing her wedding-ring and a small cross with her intertwined initials. The evidence shows that her memory stayed with him throughout the years of his second marriage.

In the course of 1639 Killigrew set off on his travels again. The sons of the earl of Cork, Francis (who married Thomas's sister Elizabeth in October 1639) and Robert Boyle, recorded meeting him in Paris in November. From their correspondence, Killigrew's itinerary can be accurately reconstructed: in March 1640 he joined them in Geneva and left for Basel three weeks later, intending to cross the Alps. He visited the English College of the Jesuits at Rome twice in March 1641 and on his way back to England stopped at Geneva again in April. The title-page of the 1664 folio edition of Killigrew's best-known play, *The Parson's Wedding*, probably written in 1640–41, describes it as having been composed at Basel. Characterized by the Boyles' tutor as one that loved 'profaine and irreligious discourses' (Stoye, 247), Killigrew had somehow acquired the ill fame that was to haunt him ever after.

Exile, 1641–1660 Like most of his relatives, Killigrew joined the royalist side at the outbreak of the civil war. Already in November 1641 he had been employed as a messenger by both the king and the queen. He was summoned to appear before the Commons in February 1642 on suspicion of treason, but not until several months later was he taken into custody and probably placed under house arrest. He continued to occupy his lodgings at The Piazza, Covent Garden, until July 1643, when he was given a pass to join the royalist forces at Oxford. Soon afterwards he may have left England. By April 1647 he had become admitted to the circle of the exiled Prince Charles and was sent to Italy to borrow money for the support of his young master's cause, a mission that proved a moderate success. Killigrew's romantic tragedy *The Pilgrim* may have been written for the Prince of Wales's Company in Paris in 1646. When James, duke of York, established himself at The Hague in May 1648, Killigrew entered his service as groom of the bedchamber. Shortly after the execution of Charles I in 1649, he transferred his services again to the household of Prince Charles in Paris. As the new king's special envoy, he was entrusted with the task of seeking the recognition of Venice and the northern states of Italy. In

November 1649 he scored some success at Turin, then travelled on to Genoa, Leghorn, Pisa, and Florence, where the reception given him was much cooler and the authorities' attitude to the king's cause noncommittal.

Killigrew reached Venice on 14 February 1650 and remained there as Charles's resident for more than two years. During his Italian stay, he found the time to write two lengthy dramatic romances, *Cecilia and Clorinda*, its first part composed in Turin, its second in Florence, and *Bellamira her Dream*, entirely written in Venice. As of June 1651 Killigrew began to experience difficulties in his relationship with the Venetian senate over his alleged involvement in illegal slaughtering and smuggling practices. The senate's request in June 1652 that the English resident be dismissed was largely inspired by political expediency, as the Venetian republic did not wish to antagonize Cromwell's government.

After leaving Venice, Killigrew stayed briefly at The Hague in attendance on the duke of Gloucester. When the duke removed his household to Paris in May 1653, to join his mother and King Charles, Killigrew accompanied him there. Whether *Thomaso, or, The Wanderer*, probably completed in 1654, was written in Madrid, as the title-page of the 1664 edition indicates, has never been ascertained. Largely autobiographical, Killigrew's two-part comedy is a verbose but often sparkling account of the exiled cavaliers' experiences in Spain, France, and the Low Countries. Soon after the court had departed from Paris in June 1654, Killigrew returned to The Hague, home to a large English community. At The Hague, he enjoyed the protection of Elizabeth, queen of Bohemia, who had been in exile there since 1621. To her intercession with Charles II, her nephew, and to the latter's mediation with Willem Frederik of Nassau-Dietz (1613–1664), stadholder of Friesland, Killigrew owed his appointment, in 1655, as a captain in the service of the states general.

It was possibly on the occasion of his first visit to The Hague in summer 1652 that Killigrew had made the acquaintance of Charlotte van Hesse-Piershil (1629–1715), the eldest and well-to-do daughter of Johan van Hesse (*d.* 1638), gentleman of the prince of Orange. The couple were married in the church of the Walloon Reformed Community, on 28 January 1655. As early as October 1655 the newly-weds contemplated leaving the city, signalling their intention to move to Maastricht, where Killigrew's company was garrisoned. On 29 December 1655, their first son, Charles *Killigrew, the future theatre manager, was born there; and on 19 February 1657 a second son, Thomas (*d.* 3 June 1674), was added to the family. In the meantime, Killigrew had himself assigned to a different company, no doubt within the same city. On 1 May 1656, the council of state, in view of Killigrew's reputation as someone having 'courage and experience in matters of war' (Vander Motten, 'Lost Years', 321), appointed him to replace one John More, who had deserted his company.

While in the pay of the states of Friesland, Killigrew also acted as a kind of liaison officer for Charles II. In a letter from Maastricht (intercepted by the intelligence services of John Thurloe, Cromwell's secretary of state), he provided an astute summary of the doings of the major European powers in spring 1657. The English government went on to monitor closely his movements in Charles's service. On 5 April 1658 Sir George Downing informed Thurloe of Killigrew's intention to seek the appointment to a vacant post of regimental major. The prospect of such promotion may have necessitated the family's temporary return to The Hague, for on 28 March 1658 the church register of the Walloon Reformed Community there recorded the christening of a daughter, Charlotte-Marguerite (who may have died in infancy, before the end of 1660).

As groom of the bedchamber, Killigrew accompanied Charles on his semi-secret tour of the United Provinces in early September 1658, a tour which probably took the king as far north as Friesland, where he visited the Frisian stadholder. On 18 October Downing reported to Thurloe that he had 'had an accompt from one Killigrew of his bedchamber' (Vander Motten, 'Lost Years', 324) of Charles's complete itinerary and the company he kept. It is not clear whether such information, if indeed supplied by Killigrew, amounted to a form of treason or was merely an apology for the king's presence on Dutch soil. From the five letters which Charles wrote to Willem Frederik between March 1659 and April 1662, it is evident that even after 1658 Killigrew continued to enjoy the protection and friendship of the monarch and the stadholder. Both men evidently co-operated in protecting Killigrew's interests, as on the occasion of the request which John Milton, Latin secretary to Cromwell, sent to Killigrew's Frisian paymasters on 27 January 1659, pleading that he be not allowed to escape an outstanding English debt. In the final months of the exile, Killigrew was not exclusively involved in state matters. In a letter from Maastricht dated 11 February 1659 and sent to an unknown friend, he declined the latter's offer to become a Catholic, criticizing at length the idolatrous practices of the church of Rome and its position on transubstantiation (Durham University Library, Cosin MS BI 13).

The theatre manager, 1660–1676 Although Pepys on 24 May 1660 recorded meeting Killigrew, 'a gentleman of great esteem with the King' (Pepys, 1.157), on board the *Charles*, the dramatist's wife, pregnant again, and the three children presumably prolonged their stay in Maastricht. Not until after the birth of Robert (baptized on 4 July 1660) did Charlotte move to London. Before the end of the year, she and her three sons were included in an act of naturalization, which in due course was ratified by the king. In May 1662 Charlotte became keeper of the sweet coffer for the queen, and in June she was made first lady of the privy chamber. Despite his recent re-establishment in London, Killigrew on 12 September 1660 acquired the rights of citizenship of Maastricht. His motives for doing so almost five years after settling down at Maastricht are a matter for speculation. As late as 30 November 1660, the king intervened on his behalf with the Frisian stadholder, asking that Killigrew be allowed to retain his military appointment, which he risked losing as a result of the

council of state's plans to cut the expenditure for defence. In the course of 1660 Killigrew petitioned the king for a variety of offices and commodities, including the keepership of the armory at Greenwich, 'in consideration of his expense in attendance on His Majesty abroad' (*CSP dom.*, 1660–61, 101), and a parcel of white plate worth £1200 that had belonged to Cromwell. But the financial compensations which Charles must have promised him during the exile had by the end of 1660 not yet materialized—hence perhaps the dramatist's request to retain his Dutch commandership. Not until November 1661 was he granted an annual pension of £500 as a groom of the bedchamber. By then he had completely changed his mind about his overseas obligations, for on 31 October 1661 the king once again intervened with the stadholder, asking him to allow Killigrew to transfer his company, supposedly for health reasons. The favour was granted and in January 1662 Killigrew's company was sold to one Jeremy Roper for 14,000 guilders.

The most singular mark of the king's esteem was of course the licence which in July 1660 he gave to Killigrew and Sir William Davenant 'to erect two playhouses … to control the charges to be demanded, and the payments to actors … and absolutely suppressing all other playhouses' (*CSP dom.*, 1660–61, 124). Both men thus obtained a virtual monopoly to form two companies of players, produce all and any dramatic entertainments, and license all plays submitted to them. Killigrew's company, known as the King's Men, began acting at the Red Bull on 5 November 1660; they moved to Gibbons's Tennis Court, Vere Street, on 8 November. Davenant's company, under the patronage of the duke of York, possibly started their operations at Salisbury Court by 15 November; they moved to their Lincoln's Inn Fields theatre, fully equipped with movable scenery, in June 1661. When *Claricilla* was revived at Vere Street, on 4 July 1661, Pepys remarked on how empty Killigrew's theatre was 'since the opera begun' (Pepys, 2.132).

On 7 May 1663 the King's Company began acting at the new Theatre Royal, Bridges Street, Killigrew holding both acting and building shares in the company. Killigrew boasted a group of experienced actors and actresses drawn from various earlier troupes, including Michael Mohun, Nicholas Burt, Charles Hart, John Lacy, Anne Marshall, and Elizabeth Weaver. Davenant had to compete with a less seasoned troupe but managed to secure the services of Thomas Betterton, who had briefly been a member of the King's Company. Killigrew also had the exclusive rights to a large repertory of pre-Restoration plays, which included nearly all of Ben Jonson's works and many of Shakespeare's. Despite the heavy preponderance of old plays in the repertory of the Theatre Royal in the 1660s, there were few practising playwrights from the earlier period, but several new gentlemen dramatists attached themselves to Killigrew's company. Sir Robert Howard, holder of one quarter of the shares at Bridges Street, and James and Edward Howard wrote for his company in the early 1660s; so did Roger Boyle, earl of Orrery, and possibly Sir George Etherege. Of the professional playwrights Killigrew went on to recruit, none was more important that

John Dryden. After negotiations with both companies, he became in April 1668 a playwright-sharer with the King's Company, agreeing to provide them with three plays annually in return for one and one-quarter shares. (Dryden broke the agreement in 1678.) Apparently Nathaniel Lee had a similar agreement, and so did Thomas D'Urfey during part of his career. Elkanah Settle also allied himself with the company in 1673.

As Killigrew's annotated copy of his *Comedies and Tragedies* (1664) preserved in the library of Worcester College, Oxford, demonstrates, he was ambitious enough to prepare his own plays for production on the new, scenic stage. *The Princess* was revived at Vere Street on 29 November 1661, 'the first time ... since before the troubles' in Pepys's words (Pepys, 2.223). *Claricilla* and *The Parson's Wedding* proved the most successful of Killigrew's plays. Clandestinely performed at Gibbons's Tennis Court in 1653, *Claricilla* (one of the stock plays of Mohun's troupe at the Red Bull in 1660) was successively revived at Vere Street on 1 December 1660 and 4 July 1661, at court in January 1663, and at Bridges Street in March 1669. A performance of *The Parson's Wedding*, 'acted all by women' according to Pepys (ibid., 5.289), was scheduled at Bridges Street on 5 or 6 October 1664; it was given again at Lincoln's Inn Fields in June 1672. Much more popular, however, than any of his plays was Aphra Behn's *The Rover*, a lively adaptation of *Thomaso*, first produced at Dorset Gardens in March 1677. (As groom of the bedchamber, Killigrew had probably introduced Behn to Charles's intelligence service in 1666.) Despite the manifest advantages Killigrew enjoyed as the manager of the King's Company, he appears to have had insufficient practical sense of the theatre to compete successfully with Davenant, a professional playwright and theatrical innovator. Nevertheless, his theatrical initiatives were by no means despicable. Before the end of 1660, Killigrew beat Davenant in the race to introduce actresses on the stage, a novelty made official in the April 1662 patent issued to him, decreeing that all female parts were to be played by women. On 2 August 1664 he told Pepys of his plans to set up a nursery theatre at Moorfields, 'were we shall have the best Scenes and Machines, the best Musique ... and to that end hath sent for voices and painters and other persons from Italy' (Pepys, 5.230). And in February and September 1667 he boasted to the same interlocutor of the many improvements at his theatre, including the importation of distinguished Italian musicians.

Killigrew's company shared of course in the misfortunes that befell the London stage. In June 1665 the theatres were closed down on account of the plague and on 25 January 1672 a fire destroyed the Theatre Royal, forcing Killigrew's company to move to the playhouse at Lincoln's Inn Fields, recently vacated by the Duke's Men. It is undeniable, however, that the King's Company's problems must be attributed to Killigrew's dubious handling of his theatrical holdings, resulting in conflicts with the disgruntled sharing actors, and, indeed, his own son Charles. As early as 1663, Killigrew had made over his building shares to his brother-in-law Sir John Sayers, to be

held in trust for him; he also temporarily delegated the direction of the company to Hart, Mohun, and Lacy. After the death of Sir Henry Herbert, who in 1661–2 had sued the patent-holders for usurping some of his powers, Killigrew was appointed master of the revels on 1 May 1673 but in February 1677 he resigned the post to his son Charles. Only three weeks later, he was forced by law to turn over to Charles his patent and governorship of the company (in 1682 it was discovered that his theatrical property had not been his to control).

Trying to cope with his expensive habits of getting and spending, including his theatrical investments, Killigrew had to borrow money from his wife, whose interests in the Piershil inheritance had been safeguarded by a 1655 contract. Throughout his term as a patentee he petitioned the king for diverse gifts and licences. In December 1663 he requested the grant of a lease of nineteen messuages 'in Collier Row, Stepney, and Shoreditch, the manor of Puriton-cum-Crandon, and a house in Bridgewater', worth £88 a year (*CSP dom.*, *1660–70*, 686). In March 1670, in consideration of his 'long and faithful services' (ibid., *1670*, 133), he was given the benefit of a bond worth £500, due to the king from one Thomas Pritchard. And the state papers for the years 1671 to 1676 show that he obtained a patent to license 'pedlars and petty chapmen' (ibid., *1671*, 216) and claimed the right to grant licences for lotteries. After 1676 his interest in the theatre business gradually dwindled.

Final years, 1676–1683 According to Pepys, writing on 13 February 1668, Killigrew had been given the title of 'King's fool or jester ... and may with privilege revile or jeere any body ... without offence' (Pepys, 9.66–7). Countless anecdotes survive to prove that it was during his years at Charles's court that Killigrew established his reputation as a flippant conversationalist endowed with a caustic wit. Whether or not this is indicative of a fundamental change of mind, in his declining years he took a fancy to having himself portrayed in a very different guise, first, in the 1670s, as a pilgrim of St James, and after 1680, bearded as St Paul, carrying a sword, the emblem of martyrdom. Financial worries, however, must have weighed the family down, as is suggested by his petition, dated 16 January 1680, for payment of arrears on his pension in the amount of £850.

In 1683 Pier Maria Mazzantini, an Italian physician, asked the king for leave to practise the antidote Orvietan, claiming that it had saved Killigrew's life. 'Weak and indisposed in body', on 15 March 1683 the dramatist drew up his will. He requested to be buried at Westminster Abbey, together with his first wife and his sister Elizabeth (d. 1681). The largest part of his estate, both 'real and personal', and the arrears on his pension went to his son Henry, who was also made the sole executor. Charlotte and her children were left unmentioned. Killigrew died at Whitehall on 19 March 1683. Within days after her husband's death Charlotte petitioned the king for relief, arguing that she had brought 'a considerable fortune to her husband ... though of late by the insinuation of ill people his affections were withdrawn from her so that he has left her and her two youngest sons in a very necessitous condition' (*CSP dom.*, 1683, 220). The king obliged by granting her an annual pension of £200; he also contributed £50 to the funeral. Charlotte was buried on 22 April 1715, having survived her children by several years. Roger, born on 17 September 1663, had died prior to July 1694; Robert, a brigadier-general, was killed at the battle of Almanzor on 14 April 1707; and Elizabeth, born on 3 July 1666, may have been buried at St Martin's on 21 April 1690.

J. P. VANDER MOTTEN

Sources A. Harbage, *Thomas Killigrew, cavalier dramatist, 1612–1683* (1930) · J. P. Vander Motten, 'Thomas Killigrew's "lost courts", 1655-1660', *Neophilologus*, 82 (1998), 311–34 · J. P. Vander Motten, 'Unpublished letters of Charles II', *Restoration: Studies in English Literary Culture, 1660–1700*, 18/1 (1994), 17–26 · J. W. Stoye, 'The whereabouts of Thomas Killigrew, 1639–41', *Review of English Studies*, 25 (1949), 245-8 · Pepys, *Diary*, vols. 1–9 · J. Lough and D. E. L. Crane, 'Thomas Killigrew and the possessed nuns of Loudun: the text of a letter of 1635', *Durham University Journal*, 78 (1985–6), 259–68 · M. W. Walsh, 'Thomas Killigrew's cap and bells', *Theatre Notebook*, 38 (1984), 99-105 · J. P. Vander Motten, 'Thomas Killigrew: a biographical note', *Revue Belge de Philologie et d'Histoire*, 53/3 (1975), 769–75 · M. Rogers, '"Golden houses for shadows": some portraits of Thomas Killigrew and his family', *Art and patronage in the Caroline courts: essays in honour of Sir Oliver Millar*, ed. D. Howarth (1993), 220–42 · Margerie Killigrew's will, 22 May 1623, PRO, PROB 11/146, sig. 71 · Sir Robert Killigrew's will, 12 Sept 1633, PRO, PROB 11/164, sig. 69 · will, 15 March 1683, PRO, PROB 11/372, sig. 36 · *CSP dom.*, 1660–85 · A. Pritchard, 'According to Wood: sources of A. Wood's lives of poets and dramatists', *Review of English Studies*, new ser., 28 (1977), 268–89, 407–20

Archives BL, papers, Add. MS 20032 | Bodl. Oxf., Clarendon MSS · TCD, Trinity College MSS

Likenesses A. Van Dyck, double portrait, oils, 1638, Royal Collection [*see illus.*] · A. Van Dyck, oils, 1638, Weston Park Foundation, Shropshire; copy, NPG · W. Sheppard, oils, 1650, NPG · J. J. Van den Berghe, stipple, 1650 (after W. Sheppard), BM, NPG · pencil drawing, 1650 (after W. Sheppard), NPG · W. Faithorne, line engraving, 1664 (after W. Sheppard), BM, NPG; repro. in T. Killigrew, *Comedies and tragedies* (1664) · mezzotint, 1670?–1679, BM · J. vander Vaart, mezzotint, c.1680 (after W. Wissing), BM · mezzotint, BM, NPG

Wealth at death two houses in Scotland Yard: will, PRO, PROB 11/372, sig. 36, 15 March 1683

Killigrew, Thomas (*bap.* 1694, *d.* 1719), playwright, was baptized on 23 February 1694, the second son of Charles *Killigrew (1655–1724/5), theatre manager, and Jemima, niece of Richard Bokenham, mercer, of London, and the grandson of Thomas *Killigrew the elder (1612–1683), with whose son Thomas (1657–1674) he has sometimes been confused. He was probably the author of *Chit-Chat*, a comedy, first performed at the Theatre Royal, Drury Lane, on 14 February 1719, and published in two separate editions in the same year. Its strong cast included Barton Booth as Worthy, Robert Wilks as Bellamar, Colley Cibber as Alamode, and Anne Oldfield as Florinda. Described in the prologue as the author's 'first Coup d'Essay', *Chit-Chat* proved one of the most popular plays of the 1718–19 season. It was given eleven performances at Drury Lane between its première and 19 March, and another two at Richmond on 6 and 20 June, the former, 'by his Royal Highness's Command' (Avery, 542), celebrating the opening of William Pinkethman's new theatre. *Chit-Chat* was also a financial success: in addition to two author benefits

and a sum of 150 guineas presented him by the prince and the princess of Wales, Killigrew secured the patronage of John Campbell, second duke of Argyll, 'whose interest was so powerfully supported, that it was said the profits of his play amounted to above a thousand pounds', according to Thomas Whincop (Nicoll, 18). In letters addressed to Booth and Steele, the critic John Dennis expressed his indignation at the success of such trivia as *Chit-Chat* and other comedies, when his own tragedy *The Invader of his Country* had never even reached the stage. Killigrew contributed 'The Fable of Aumilius and the Statue of Venus' to *Miscellanea aurea, or, The Golden Medley*, a collection of 'epistolary essays in prose and verse' (1720). He was buried at Kensington on 21 July 1719.   J. P. VANDER MOTTEN

Sources Highfill, Burnim & Langhans, *BDA*, vols. 9, 11 · E. L. Avery, ed., *The London stage, 1660–1800*, pt 2: *1700–1729* (1960) · A. Harbage, *Thomas Killigrew, cavalier dramatist, 1612–1683* (1930) · A. Nicoll, *A history of early eighteenth-century drama, 1700–1750*, 2nd edn (1929) · *The critical works of John Dennis*, ed. E. N. Hooker, 2 (1943) · *DNB*

Killigrew, Sir William (*d.* 1622). *See under* Killigrew, Sir Robert (1579/80–1633).

Killigrew, Sir William (*bap.* 1606, *d.* 1695), courtier and playwright, was baptized on 28 May 1606 at Hanworth, near Hampton Court, Middlesex, the eldest child of Sir Robert *Killigrew (1579/80–1633) and Mary, daughter of Sir Henry Woodhouse of Kimberley, Norfolk; he was brother to Henry *Killigrew (1613–1700) and Thomas *Killigrew (1612–1683).

Early years, 1606–1628 Killigrew was probably educated, from about 1616, at the grammar school in Cripplegate, London, of Thomas Farnaby, the classical scholar, who enjoyed Sir Robert's patronage. About 1619 he may have been sent to the continent to serve as a page at the court of the princes of Orange. As the eldest son, in 1623 William inherited from his paternal grandmother Margerie Killigrew 'tenn pounds of lawfull englishe moneye' (Margerie Killigrew's will), twice the amount left to his brothers Charles (1609–1629), Robert (1611–1635), Thomas, and Henry but substantially less than the enamelled chain plus £50 left to his eldest sister Anne (1607–1641).

On 4 July 1623 Killigrew entered St John's College, Oxford, as a gentleman commoner, taking up the study of civil law. While at Oxford he contributed a poem to *Carolus redux* (1623), a collection celebrating Prince Charles's return from Spain after his wooing of the Infanta. It is doubtful whether William completed the full course of his studies, for on 9 April 1624 the privy council issued a pass for William Killigrew and Maurice Berkeley, a cousin, 'esquires, to travell into the partes beyond the seas for the terme of three yeares and to take with them three servantes, their trunks, and other necessary provisions' (*APC*, 202). Within one or two years at most, William must have been back in England. In 1625 or 1626 he married Mary Hill, daughter of John Hill of Honiley, Warwickshire; and in May 1626 he was knighted. They had seven children, only two of whom, Captain William and Sir Robert (both living in 1701), were to survive their father. Shortly after his return from his travels, Killigrew

Even before his father's death on 22 November 1633, Killigrew had launched out on an adventure that was to preoccupy him in decades to come, the draining of the fenlands in Lincolnshire. On 30 April 1633 Killigrew, his father (involved in draining activities since 1629), and other 'adventurers' were appointed as drainers of the Eight Hundred Fen in Lincolnshire. As stipulated in the various grants, the drainers were to be repaid for their expenses with portions of the drained lands: in 1635, the earl of Lindsey, the main undertaker, Sir William, and others were given 24,000 acres to be divided into 20 lots. A major shareholder, Killigrew from 1634 onwards found it increasingly difficult to keep up with the huge expenses, as is perhaps suggested by his continuous sale of property in Devon bequeathed him by his father. There was also fierce opposition from the commoners, who complained of the drainers' high-handed policy, aimed at the enclosing and dividing of their lands. Riots intensified between 1630 and 1640, the fen people playing havoc with the drainers' possessions, their crops, drains, and fences.

Despite such pressing problems, Killigrew never abandoned his belief in the 'family grandeur' (Harbage, 26). Like his sister Anne in 1636–7 and his brother Thomas in 1636 and again in 1638, Killigrew in 1638 had his portrait painted by Anthony Van Dyck, who in the same year also painted a companion portrait of his wife Mary. In early 1642 Killigrew figured prominently in the events leading up to King Charles's attempt to arrest the five MPs. He was sent to the inns of court to publicize the accusations and seek support for the king, thus making himself guilty of a 'high breach of privilege of Parliament' (Vander Motten, *Killigrew*, 60). The heavy fine he incurred always remained unpaid.

The civil war and the Commonwealth, 1642–1660 At the outbreak of the civil war, Sir William was given the command, under Lord Bernard Stuart, of a troop of horse, the members of which by all accounts distinguished themselves in battle. As a reward for Killigrew's good services at the battle of Edgehill, where he led the charge on 23 October 1642, King Charles created him doctor of civil law at Oxford on 1 or 2 November. That Killigrew enjoyed the king's confidence is also suggested by the various missions with which he was entrusted, including that of a go-between in the peace negotiations of March 1643. In the eyes of many parliamentarian MPs, he had become identified as 'a great and principall Factor for the Cavaliers in this Rebellion and Designe' (Vander Motten, *Killigrew*, 67). Contributions to the war effort, in Cornwall and elsewhere, would have constituted a heavy drain on Sir William's dwindling means. Writing from Exeter on 17 March 1644, he asked Edward Seymour, governor of Dartmouth, to provide him with 'pistolls and carrabins', ensuring him that he would be paid 'soe soone as my purse is a little replenished' (Devon RO 1392M/L16/44/19). His precarious financial situation impelled him to consider seeking a foreign appointment, for in May 1645 he applied for the position of English ambassador in Turkey, a post eventually given to Sir Thomas Bendish. In accordance with the Oxford articles signed by the royalists after the taking of

Sir William Killigrew (*bap.* 1606, *d.* 1695), by Sir Anthony Van Dyck, 1638

obtained a 'firm foothold' at Whitehall (Dasent, 128), being appointed gentleman usher of the privy chamber to Charles I. From now on, he was to hold several major offices of a very diverse character. On 3 March 1628 he was elected by double returns to Charles's third parliament as a member for Newport and Penryn, Cornwall, but he sat only for the latter; and on 21 March following he and his father were jointly granted the governorship, for life, of Pendennis Castle, in the same county.

Soldier and businessman, 1628–1642 Entrusted with the task of guarding the safety of the south-west coast of England, Killigrew was faced at Pendennis with a twofold problem: the poor condition of the stronghold, inadequately garrisoned and in need of urgent repairs; and the quarrels with the fort of St Mawes, trying to usurp the prerogatives of Pendennis with respect to ships entering Falmouth Bay. Killigrew showed himself tenacious of his privileges as governor. As one captain testified in November 1631, Killigrew 'is at peace with neither King's ships nor others; both the Admiral and the writer have been twice shot at by him, going in and coming out'. Sir William was reprimanded by the admiralty and instructed 'never more to offend in that kind' (Vander Motten, *Killigrew*, 40–41). In the course of 1632 and 1633, there were new charges of mismanagement. A Dutch vessel, after causing £2000 worth of damage to an English ship, had been allowed to escape the harbour. Sir William, held personally responsible, was ordered to find compensation for the English captain's losses, all to no avail. This incident may have precipitated his resignation of the governorship, which he surrendered to Sir Nicholas Slanning in April 1635.

the city on 20 June 1646, Killigrew on 5 November 1646 requested permission to compound for his estate (the practice by which royalists were fined for their 'delinquency'). The investigation of his guilt was dragged out until 4 March 1651, when Killigrew's fine was set at one-sixth part of £20.

Between 1647 and the Restoration, Killigrew in a series of 'fen pamphlets', all controversial in tone, gave expression to the drainers' viewpoints and called for a confirmation by law of their interests, meanwhile calling attention to what in 1648 he described as 'the poor estate of himself, his wife, and family, who do beg their bread' (Vander Motten, *Killigrew*, 75). Unhampered by ethical principles, Killigrew was evidently prepared to resort to any means in order to remedy this situation, as appears from the testimony left by Richard Lygon, in a pamphlet dated 18 March 1654. At some time between 1647 and 1652, Sir William had connived with his cousin Jane Berkeley to defraud Lygon of an estate left him by their great-uncle Henry Killigrew (d. 1646) for the payment of his debts. From Lygon's meticulous (but presumably biased) account of the cousins' machinations, Sir William emerges as a smooth-talking and cunning schemer, whose prodigality may at least partly account for his family's destitution.

The most touching testimony as to the Killigrews' impoverished condition during the years of the Commonwealth is provided by the thirteen letters Killigrew addressed to Captain Adam Baynes (1622–1670) between 19 April 1653 and 1 November 1659. A commissioner for the excise, the customs, and sequestered estates, Baynes was a parliamentarian sympathetic to the draining projects. Using Baynes as an intermediary, Killigrew petitioned the council of state on many occasions. His petition of 24 January 1654 was presented to the committee for the fens by Major-General Lambert himself. On 27 July 1654, the council ordered that the drainers be put in possession of the 24,000 acres allotted to them by the commissioners of sewers many years before. This ordinance was never enacted. Finding himself devoid of all manner of subsistence, Killigrew in his letter of 29 March 1655 contemplated leaving 'this Towne' and seeking 'some remote place for a service where I am unknowne, and maye pass by a wronge Name' (Vander Motten, *Killigrew*, 337). In so doing, he may have wanted to follow the example of those of his children who had already left the country. His eldest daughter, Mary (b. 1627?) had become a maid of honour to the princess royal in Holland in 1644 and married Baron Frederik van Nassau-Zuylestein in October 1648; Susan (bap. 1 April 1629) had joined Queen Henrietta Maria on the continent towards 1649; his sons Sir Robert and Captain William both served as soldiers of fortune in the Low Countries, the former from about 1650 until 1659, the latter some time before May 1660, when he married Helena Van der Maa, daughter of a prosperous citizen of The Hague. Judging from Sir William's letter of 15 November 1655, his wife too was living separated from him, the precariousness of their situation accentuated by the latent fear of anti-royalist persecution.

In the service of Charles II Even before the king's official Restoration in May 1660, Killigrew sent him a long letter of diplomatic advice, urging the monarch to accept the conditions on which his return was assumed to depend. As too many of the old royalists and the suffering clergy would expect compensation for their losses, he argued that it would be better for the king not to have the entire revenue at his disposal. Reminding Charles how at Oxford he had used to entertain the king his father with such considerations, Killigrew offered these reflections 'without any designe for myself' (Vander Motten, *Killigrew*, 244). The letter served its purpose, for by July or August 1660 Killigrew was again appointed gentleman usher of the privy chamber and took up lodgings at Whitehall. Shortly afterwards, by February 1664 at the latest, he was made the queen's vice-chamberlain, a position worth £500 a year.

Killigrew evidently used his position at court to acquire various grants and offices for himself and his family. Together with Dorothy Spencer, countess of Sunderland, he was granted parts of 'the profits of certain concealed waste lands in several counties' in June 1661; and in February 1662, both he and Thomas Chiffinch, keeper of the king's jewels, were granted a share of 'certain bonds for sequestration moneys in Lancashire', in the amount of £786. (Vander Motten, *Killigrew*, 106). In January 1664, Killigrew was involved in the contract made by the king with the Company of Pinmakers. His role as an intermediary in raising £5000 for the purchase of wire for the company's use was to have yielded him £100. (As late as 10 March 1676, the pinmakers' plan to reinvigorate their trade was again submitted to the king in a petition signed by Killigrew.) Before 1665, his wife Mary became a dresser to the queen, with an annual pension of £300. In the same year, Killigrew and some co-petitioners requested a grant of the forfeited houses in the town of New Ross, co. Wexford, Ireland.

Killigrew also remained active in the political arena. On 9 April 1664, he was returned to parliament for Richmond, to succeed Sir John Yorke, deceased. He served on several committees in this Long Parliament, which sat from 8 May 1661 until 24 January 1679. And he distinguished himself, as John Milward noted in his parliamentary diary for the years 1666 to 1668, for his unflagging zeal as a defender of the works of draining in Lindsey Level, 'stoutly maintaining ... the ancient bill' brought in twice in November 1667 (Vander Motten, *Killigrew*, 120). When this issue had been brought up for discussion in 1660 and 1661, the drainers and the landowners in the fens had angrily exchanged pamphlets that recapitulated the arguments formulated throughout the 1640s and 1650s. In the debates surrounding the Test Act of 1673, stipulating that all persons holding office in the service of the king or the duke of York were to take an oath of allegiance, Killigrew on 21 March spoke in favour of the amendment excusing the queen's servants from the oath. His loyalty, however, was never a matter of doubt: from 1669 until 1678, his name occurs in several lists of members of the court party, one of these drawn up by the lord treasurer, the earl of Danby, himself.

From letters sent to Danby in 1674, it appears that Killigrew had been closely involved in the king's financial policy. Charles had promised him a pension of £2000 if he were able to increase the two main branches of the revenue, the customs and the excise, both collected by means of the farming system. But Killigrew's proposals had been largely neglected and the pension which he had obtained towards the end of 1665 had amounted to only £500. He now submitted new proposals to the treasurer designed to secure a larger return from the excise. Although his views largely coincided with Danby's own policy, Killigrew's attempts to obtain a (profitable) lease of the excise farm remained unsuccessful. Plans to raise the 'Hearth money', a taxation on fireplaces, which he broached in a letter dated 16 December 1675, went unnoticed as well. Sir William and his wife probably lived in straitened circumstances, as is suggested by the monthly advances made on their pensions from July 1676 on. Sir William continued at Whitehall as vice-chamberlain to the queen until 27 July 1682, when he transferred his office to George Sawyer. But he held on to the annual profits of £516 and was allowed to move his lodgings to Hampton Court.

The final years, 1682–1695 That Sir William's spiritual retirement from the world commenced even before he relinquished his office at court is amply illustrated by the various collections of pious cogitations which he brought out in late 1681. The tone was set by *Midnight Thoughts* (1681), with its lengthy subtitle hinting at the author's lifelong exertions in the fens as well as his new found confidence in the grace of God. *Artless Mid-Night Thoughts* (dated 1684 but probably published in 1690) was partly a reissue of the 1681 collection. While most of the reflections on the frailty of human nature and the idea of imminent death were biblically inspired, Killigrew's self-examinations were indebted to contemporary meditative practices, Jesuit and Quaker as well as puritan and Anglican. The tranquillity of mind that professedly came with the search for a religious anchorage could not shield the old courtier from all worldly anxieties. Late in 1691 he brought an action of covenant against George Sawyer, requesting six years' arrears of salary, dating from 1682. By October 1691, he was living at Westminster Abbey, with his brother Henry. In response to Anthony Wood's enquiries about the Killigrew brothers, Sir William on 28 October and 4 November 1691 provided the biographical information that served as a basis for the account in *Athenae Oxonienses*. On 3 October 1695 he drafted his last will. To his sons Sir Robert and Captain William he bequeathed 2000 acres of fenland; 2500 acres more were to be used for repaying his creditors. Sir William Killigrew died a few days later and was buried in the Savoy chapel on 17 October. Mary, his wife, left unmentioned in the will, may have predeceased him a few years earlier.

Like many other gentleman amateurs, Sir William after 1660 had provided the recently re-opened theatres with a number of moderately successful plays. The first three of these, the tragicomedies *Selindra* and *Ormasdes* and the comedy *Pandora*, were published in *Three Playes* (1664). Together with another tragicomedy, *The Siege of Urbin*,

they were reissued in 1666 as *Four New Playes*. *Selindra*, performed by the King's Company at Gibbons's Tennis Court, Vere Street, on 3 March 1662, was one of the first new plays to be given after the Restoration. According to the prompter John Downes, it was revived at the Theatre Royal, Bridges Street, some time between 1663 and 1682 (Downes, 15). *Ormasdes* was Killigrew's attempt to join the short-lived post-Restoration vogue for plays in decasyllabic couplets initiated by Roger Boyle's *The Generall*. Whether it was ever performed remains uncertain. Entered in the Stationers' register as a comedy in May 1664, *Pandora* had apparently failed on the stage as a tragedy. John Downes included it in a list of plays 'both Old and Modern' staged at the Duke's Theatre, Lincoln's Inn Fields, between 1662 and May 1664 (ibid., 26). Designed for the new, scenic stage, *The Siege of Urbin*, Killigrew's best play, was probably performed in 1665, at the Theatre Royal, as is suggested by the cast of actors contained in the manuscript copy of the play preserved in the Bodleian Library. *The Imperial Tragedy*, an adaptation from *Zeno, sive, Ambitio infelix*, a Latin blood-and-horror play by the English Jesuit Joseph Simons (1593–1671), was Killigrew's last play. Published in 1669, it may have been acted at the Barbican Nursery after 1671 (Langbaine, 535).

Apart from their exploration of the conflicting claims of love, honour, and friendship, *Selindra*, *Ormasdes* (renamed *Love and Friendship* in the 1666 edition) and *The Siege of Urbin*, no less than Killigrew's only tragedy, share with Restoration tragicomedy a marked concern with political issues of current interest, focusing as they do on matters of succession, usurpation, and royal and paternal authority. In its confrontation of old-fashioned Platonic ideals and modern libertine views, *Pandora* reflects the author's commonsensical approach to such issues as love, marriage, and the battle of the sexes. Although of limited literary value, Killigrew's plays are of historical importance for the evidence of authorial revisions some of the printed editions contain, shedding light on a Restoration dramatist's efforts in bringing his plays to final form.

J. P. VANDER MOTTEN

Sources J. P. Vander Motten, *Sir William Killigrew (1606–1695): his life and dramatic works* (1980) · J. P. Vander Motten, 'Some problems of attribution in the canon of Sir William Killigrew's works', *Studies in Bibliography*, 33 (1980), 161–8 · Wood, *Ath. Oxon.*, new edn · A. Harbage, *Thomas Killigrew, cavalier dramatist, 1612–1683* (1930) · J. Y. Akerman, ed., *Proceedings of the Society of Antiquaries of London*, 3 (1853–6) [edn of some Killigrew letters] · letter from Killigrew, 17/3/1643 [1644], Devon RO, 1392 M/L16/44/19 · *APC, 1623–5* · M. Rogers, '"Golden houses for shadows": some portraits of Thomas Killigrew and his family', *Art and patronage in the Caroline courts: essays in honour of Sir Oliver Millar*, ed. D. Howarth (1993), 220–42 · Marjerie Killigrew's will, 22 May 1623, PRO, PROB 11/146, sig. 71 · H. P. Fölting, *De Vroedschap van 's-Gravenhage, 1572–1795* (1985) · A. I. Dasent, *Nell Gwynne, 1600–1687: her life's story from St Giles's to St James's* (1924) · J. Downes, *Roscius Anglicanus, or, An historical review of the stage* (1708) · G. Langbaine, *An account of the English dramatick poets* (1691) · D. Lysons, *An historical account of those parishes in the county of Middlesex which are not described in 'The environs of London'* (1800)
Archives BL, letters to Captain Baynes, Add. MSS 21422–21426
Likenesses A. Van Dyck, oils, 1638, priv. coll. [*see illus.*] · M. Gauci, lithograph (after A. Van Dyck), BM · E. Harding junior, stipple

(after A. Van Dyck), BM, NPG; repro. in F. G. Waldron, *The biographical mirror* (1796) · A. Van Dyck, chalks, BM · portrait, repro. in Vander Motten, *Sir William Killigrew*

Wealth at death 2000 acres of drained fenland and another 2500 acres of undrained fenland: will, PRO, PROB 11/427, sig. 152

Killingworth, Grantham (*bap.* **1698**, *d.* **1778**), religious controversialist, was born in Norwich and baptized on 17 August 1698 at St Gregory's Church there, the son of Daniel Killingworth and his wife, whose father was the General Baptist preacher Thomas *Grantham (1633/4–1692). Killingworth married Elizabeth Cox at All Hallows, London Wall, on 13 October 1730. A layman, Killingworth published widely on behalf of the General Baptists and entered into the controversies over popery and infant baptism. He argued against Thomas Emlyn, John Taylor, Michajah Towgood, James Foster, John Wiche, and Charles Bulkley on baptism, grace, and communion. Killingworth also defended women's right to receive communion. He was a personal friend of William Whiston, to whom he addressed *A Letter … being a Full Answer to his Friendly Address to the Baptists* of 1757. In this work he offered evidence of the cures effected through 'prayer, fasting, and annointing with oyl' by the antitrinitarian Baptist minister William Barron (1679/80–1731).

Killingworth died in 1778, leaving a considerable endowment to the Priory Yard General Baptist Chapel, in Norwich.   ALEXANDER GORDON, *rev.* EMMA MAJOR

Sources ESTC · G. Killingworth, *A supplement to the sermons lately preached at Salters–hall against popery* (1738) · H. Davies, *Worship and theology in England*, 3 (1961) · IGI · W. Whiston, *Memoirs of the life and writings of Mr William Whiston: containing memoirs of several of his friends also*, 2nd edn, 2 vols. (1753), vol. [1], pp. 297, 306, 372 · C. Bulkley, *Notes on the Bible*, ed. J. Toulmin, 3 vols. (1802), 3.xv ff. · J. Toulmin, *An historical view of the state of the protestant dissenters in England* (1814), 353 · D. Neal, *The history of the puritans or protestant nonconformists*, ed. J. Toulmin, new edn, 1 (1822), xxvii

Wealth at death 'considerable endowment' to Priory Yard General Baptist chapel, Norwich: DNB

Killingworth, John (*fl.* 1381–1384). *See under* Killingworth, John (*d.* 1445).

Killingworth [Chillingworth], **John** (*d.* 1445), astronomer and mathematician, was a native of Northumberland who was sent from the Durham diocese to study at Durham College—a Benedictine college at Oxford, where he was however a secular scholar—before finally migrating to Merton College, Oxford, before June 1432. He became a bachelor fellow of Merton perhaps a year later and a fellow in 1436; he held that fellowship until his death. Killingworth occupied various college offices (first bursar, 1439–40, third bursar, 1444–5) and he was junior (northern) proctor of the university from 1441 to 1442. He was principal of two Oxford halls for uncertain periods of time, Corner Hall (he was there in September 1436) and Olifant Hall (there in September 1438). He has been confused with two other Oxford scholars of the same name. The first such **John Killingworth** (*fl.* 1381–1384) was also a fellow of Merton and the works of his later namesake used often to be attributed to him. The second was a monk

of St Albans who became prior of the students of Gloucester College—a Benedictine foundation at Oxford—in 1492.

The *Catalogus vetus* of Merton College describes John Killingworth as a 'noble astronomer who drew up numerous tables' (Emden, *Oxf.*, 2.1050), and while his expertise no doubt spanned the whole of the astronomy of his time, his extant writings are chiefly directed to the improvement of the Alfonsine tables by which the positions and motions of the sun, moon, planets, and stars were to be calculated. In some respects his work represents a high point in medieval mathematical astronomy. It continues in a tradition established in northern Europe by Parisian astronomers about 1320 and by the author of some Oxford tables of 1348 (probably William Batecombe). The aim of all was to lighten the heavy burden of calculation, and here Killingworth achieved more than any other astronomer before him. He solved various difficult technical problems, as evidenced by the tables, but the thought processes leading to his solutions are in some instances a matter for speculation. He seems to have solved a problem of second-order variation for which the differential calculus would now be invoked, but presumably he simply possessed strong intuitive powers, strengthened by long practice in routine computation.

Killingworth wrote an *Algorismus*, a title suggesting an algebra in the tradition established by Latin translations of the work of al-Khwarizmi (*d.* 846)—his name supplied the title and the word 'algorithm'. Such works had not been popular in the Latin West and did not make great inroads into the European university curriculum until after Killingworth's time. In fact Killingworth concentrated only on those parts of the tradition that related to arithmetical calculation, with an eye to astronomical applications (it is noteworthy that he introduces an example for the continued addition of the mean motion of Saturn for eight-day intervals, precisely as required at one stage in the production of his great astronomical work). He explains at length rules for addition, subtraction, multiplication, division, and the extraction of roots, first for decimal and then for sexagesimal numbers. He gives careful and lengthy instructions on how to check computations without repeating the original work in full. The treatise also contains extensive arithmetical tables, reminiscent of modern multiplication tables, except that they run to 60 times 60 and are repeated in sexagesimal form. This was by no means a novelty, but here it was truly an astronomer's working tool.

Killingworth's great compendium of astronomical tables goes under no grand title, but is merely referred to as *Tabulae Kelyngworth* or by the opening words of the accompanying text (canons) explaining how to use them ('Multum conferre dinoscitur non solum astronomis …'). One copy, heavily interlined with gold, must qualify as the most sumptuous set of astronomical tables ever penned. Now in the British Library, Arundel MS 66, it was originally associated with Humphrey, duke of Gloucester. The canons end with the comment that they relate to the easy production of an almanac 'in the manner of the University of Oxford'. They can indeed best be regarded as tables to produce other tables, namely daily ephemerides, or 'almanacs' in one sense of that word. It is possible that the associated canons were completed only after Killingworth died, by Master Thomas Pray of University College, who might also have collaborated in the massive programme of calculation. Half a century after the work was done (the date of an example in the canons is 1444) Lewis Caerleon copied it out and added supplementary material.

There is no doubt that the astronomical tables were primarily intended for astrological use, and according to John Bale, Killingworth wrote a work entitled *Astronomiae judicia*, a plainly astrological title. Bale also mentions an *Arithmeticum opus* (almost certainly a reference to the *Algorismus*), a *De crepusculis* ('On twilight'), and a *De ascensionibus nubium* ('On the heights of clouds'). The last two titles suggest a confusion: *De ascensionibus nubium* is said to have opened with the words 'Ostendere quid sit crepusculum et que causa' ('To show what twilight is and what is its cause'), but these are words identical to the opening of the Latin translation of Ibn al-Haytham (Alhazen; *d.* 1039) on the theme of twilight. The chances are that the last two titles ascribed to Killingworth are one and the same and that they were not his at all. The opening words given for the *De crepusculis* do however look suspiciously like a fragment from canons to astronomical tables. Whatever the truth of the matter, Killingworth was indeed well remembered in the Merton records as a producer of tables, and those of the most advanced sort.

Little is known of other aspects of Killingworth's personal life, beyond an isolated letter to him from the prior of Durham. He died at Merton College on 17 May 1445, and his will was proved six days later. He was buried in the college chapel where a memorial brass with portrait is still to be seen in the transept. His best memorial is his work; and in this he was not only the best of the Merton astronomers, he had few peers in Western mathematical astronomy before Copernicus, who died almost a century after him.

J. D. NORTH

Sources Emden, *Oxf.* · J. D. North, *Stars, minds and fate: essays in ancient and medieval cosmology* (1989), chap. 21 · L. C. Karpinski, 'The algorism of John Killingworth', *EngHR*, 29 (1914), 707–17 · H. E. Salter, ed., *Registrum cancellarii Oxoniensis, 1434–1469*, 1, OHS, 93 (1932), xliv, 21, 113–14 · G. C. Brodrick, *Memorials of Merton College*, OHS, 4 (1885), 232–3 · Bale, *Cat.*
Archives BL, Arundel MS 66
Likenesses effigy on memorial brass, 1445, Merton Oxf.

Killultagh. For this title name *see* Conway, Edward, first Viscount Conway and first Viscount Killultagh (*c.*1564–1631); Conway, Edward, second Viscount Conway and second Viscount Killultagh (*bap.* 1594, *d.* 1655); Conway, Anne, Viscountess Conway and Killultagh (1631–1679).

Kilmaine. For this title name *see* O'Hara, James, second Baron Tyrawley and Baron Kilmaine (1681/2–1773); Browne, John Francis Archibald, sixth Baron Kilmaine (1902–1978).

Kilmaine, Charles Edward Saul Jennings de (1751–1799), army officer in the French service, the son of Theobald Edward Jennings, styled baron of Kilmaine, a physician, and his wife, Eleanor Saul, the daughter of Laurence Saul of Dublin, a distiller, was born on 19 October 1751 in Dublin. Ten years later he went with his family to France. After seven years' service as a junior officer in Austria, he entered the French army in 1774 and in September 1778 became adjutant in a legion owned and commanded by the duc de Lauzun. He served with this unit in Senegal in 1779 and in America under Rochambeau (1780–83), and remained after it was reorganized as a hussar regiment; he attained the grade of captain on 24 May 1788.

With the outbreak of war in April 1792 came rapid promotion. While serving with distinction in the armies of the north and the Ardennes, Kilmaine was named lieutenant-colonel on 1 October 1792, colonel on 9 November 1792, general of brigade on 8 March 1793, and general of division on 15 May 1793. But with the Jacobin government came growing suspicion of the political reliability of *ancien régime* officers. Despite his exemplary service, Kilmaine was suspended on 4 August 1793 and imprisoned on 29 December 1793; his wife, Susanne Kirchmeyer (*b.* 1764/5), was also imprisoned. After his release fifteen months later he participated in the repression of the insurrection of Prairial (20 May 1795) against the Convention. He was restored to his rank on 13 June 1795 and given a command in the army of Italy under Napoleon. During 1796 and 1797 he served in various capacities and participated in numerous engagements: the passage of the Mincio, Castiglione, Mantua, Valeggio, and Verona; he even served as the army's interim commander between 17 November and 21 December 1797. He was then recalled to Paris, where his Irish background, which had been a serious disadvantage during the xenophobia of 1793–4 now made him a valued adviser in French plans for a descent on Ireland. In the spring of 1798 he was briefly appointed commander-in-chief of the so-called army of England. Declining health forced him to resign from the service on 30 December 1798. Kilmaine, who was divorced from his wife, died of chronic dysentery at Paris a year later, on 11 December 1799.

SAMUEL F. SCOTT

Sources R. F. Hayes, *Irish swordsmen of France* (1934) · G. Bodinier, *Dictionnaire des officiers de l'armée royale qui ont combattu aux États-Unis pendant la guerre d'indépendance, 1776–1783* (Vincennes, 1982) · R. F. Hayes, *Ireland and Irishmen in the French Revolution* (1932) · G. Six, *Dictionnaire biographique des généraux et amiraux français de la Révolution et de l'Empire, 1792–1814*, 2 vols. (1934) · *DNB*
Likenesses stipple, 1807, NPG · Bourgeois, stipple (after H. le Dru), NPG · portrait, Tonnay-Charente town hall; repro. in Hayes, *Ireland and Irishmen*, facing p. 141

Kilmany. For this title name *see* Gray, William John St Clair Anstruther-, Baron Kilmany (1905–1985).

Kilmarnock. For this title name *see* Boyd, William, fourth earl of Kilmarnock (1705–1746).

Kilmorey. For this title name *see* Needham, Charles, fourth Viscount Kilmorey (*c.*1637–1660); Needham, Francis Jack, first earl of Kilmorey (1748–1832).

Kilmuir. For this title name *see* Fyfe, David Patrick Maxwell, earl of Kilmuir (1900–1967).

Kilner, Dorothy (1755–1836), children's writer, was born on 17 February 1755, probably at Woodford, Essex, the youngest among the five children of Thomas Kilner (1719–1804), public servant and landowner, and his wife, Frances, *née* Ayscough (1718–1768). Thomas moved in 1759 to Maryland Point, then a rural Essex hamlet, now in London.

On the death of Frances Kilner, Dorothy's sister Eliza (1747–1817) became her 'Mother, Sister, friend' (private information). Dorothy 'possessed unusual strength of mind and much originality of character' (ibid.). By the 1770s Dorothy was exchanging verse epistles on religious, moral, and personal subjects with her childhood friend Mary Ann Maze [**Mary Ann Kilner** (1753–1831)], who was born on 14 December 1753 at Spittal Square, London, the youngest of the three children of James Maze (*d*. 1794), a Huguenot immigrant and prosperous silk throwster and trader, and his wife, Marianne, *née* de Burmann (*d*. in or before 1774). The bilingual Mary Ann was 'highly intellectual, [with] a fertile imagination and a feeling heart' (ibid.). The Maze family lived near the Kilners and shared their cultivated tastes. Mary Ann and Dorothy learned, played, and wrote together. They used the personae of Dorinda and Anna and kept up a verse-epistle soap opera about the lives and matrimonial problems of an imaginary titled family. On 18 September 1774 Dorothy's favourite brother, Thomas (1750–1812), married Mary Ann. Their move to Tom's home and silk-throwing business at 33 Spittal Square affected Dorothy's spirits profoundly. Her struggles (expressed in verse) to cultivate Christian contentment were rewarded with the birth in 1775 of Mary Ann's and Tom's daughter Mary Ann. Four more children followed, of whom Eliza (*b.* 1776) and Frances (*b.* 1783) survived. Thus began Dorothy's career as 'Aunt Do' and as a writer.

Dorothy shared the objections of other contemporary women writers to fantasy and to romances of gallantry, love, and marriage—a state she could afford to forgo from choice, preferring 'darling liberty'. She never married. However, it was as a devoted aunt that she began writing herself and, under an alias, she sought advice about publication from the educationist Sarah Trimmer, who recommended her to the publisher John Marshall, later a family friend. In the decade from 1779 Dorothy produced over a dozen works, published at first anonymously, then as M. P. (Maryland Point), and finally as Mary Pelham. Her *Dialogues and Letters on Morality, Economy and Politeness* (1783?) and *Dialogues on the first principles of religion* (*c.*1787) were didactic and pious works for children. Her *Little Stories for Little Folks*, aimed at the very young, had short episodes and short words.

Mary Ann had by this time produced some half-dozen books, also published by Marshall, under the initials S. S. (Spittal Square). In *The Adventures of a Pincushion* (*c.*1780), a pincushion made by two girls, Martha and Charlotte Airy, is accidentally taken by a visitor. It is variously kept and lost by a number of characters, and its 'adventures' highlight the different virtues and vices of those with whom it comes in contact. Mary Ann wanted her readers to 'avoid the failings, and practise those virtues or accomplishments, which render the contrary examples more worthy of imitation' (*The Adventures of a Pincushion*, 13).

Mary Ann's talking pincushion may have influenced Dorothy's best-known book, *Life and Perambulation of a Mouse* (*c.*1790), in which a visitor to a country house, charged with providing an original story for a winter gathering, relates the life story of a mouse called Nimble. It was the first children's book to give its animal characters distinct personalities, but Dorothy made a rational disclaimer for her talking mouse in a prefix to her tale: 'I must beg leave to assure my readers, that, in *earnest*, I never heard a Mouse speak in all my life; and only wrote the following narrative as being far more entertaining, and not less instructive than my own life would have been' (*Life and Perambulation of a Mouse*, xii). Dorothy's other books included *The Rochfords, or, The Friendly Counsellor* (*c.*1800), *The village school, or, A collection of entertaining histories for the instruction and amusement of all good children* (*c.*1795), *First Going to School, or, The Story of Tom Brown, and his Sisters* (1806), and *Edward the Orphan* (1824). All took the opportunity to show the rewards of goodness and honesty and the punishments of selfishness and misconduct. Mary Ann's books, such as *Jemima Placid, or, The Advantages of a Good-Nature* (*c.*1783), *William Sedley, or, The Evil Day Deferred* (*c.*1783), *The Happy Family, or, Memoirs of Mr and Mrs Norton* (*c.*1790), did likewise. *Memoirs of a Peg-Top* (*c.*1794) was written 'to promote the cause of virtue … with incidents of an amusing nature' (p. vi).

A decline in the silk trade due to a fashion-switch to muslins, plus his wife's ill health, led Tom to sell his business in 1787 and to live off his properties. The family took lodgings at Margate, where the girls attended a day school. About 1789, 'at his father's earnest desire' (private information), Tom and his family moved back to share the Maryland Point house with his father and sisters. A son, George, who was somewhat indulged, was born in 1791. From then on Mary Ann Kilner's life was overshadowed by bereavements and ill health. Her father James Maze died in 1794; her devoted brother James (Gig; he called her Pig) died in 1804, as did Thomas Kilner, Dorothy's father. The year 1812 saw the death of Mary Ann's husband and the birth of her first grandchild, Maria, to young George Kilner, who had set up as a miller in Suffolk where his father had property, and married Maria Garrett of Woodbridge in 1811, before he could afford to support a family. He received financial help from his relatives (notably Dorothy) after he suffered a breakdown in physical health. Mary Ann's eldest child, also Mary Ann, died while visiting George in 1816. In 1817 a fall and resulting back injury made her a chronic invalid, and she was nursed by her daughter Frances. Mary Ann Kilner died on 1 December 1831 and was buried on 8 December at All Saints', West Ham, Essex.

After the death of her sister Eliza in 1817, Dorothy's mind became impaired in her last years. Her eccentricities and trenchant outspokenness intimidated even her beloved nephew George. Devotedly nursed by her niece Frances and great-niece Maria, she died on 5 February 1836 and was buried at All Saints', West Ham.

Years later a trunk was found in the loft at Maryland Point. Left there by Dorothy and Mary Ann and labelled 'For Posterity', it contained copies of their books, which had been in print over forty years, some published in Ireland and the USA. The name Pelham was appropriated by other writers, notably the flamboyant Richard Phillips, and Beatrix Potter may have derived inspiration from *Life and Perambulation of a Mouse* through Charlotte M. Yonge's *A Storehouse of Stories*, in which Dorothy Kilner's tale was reprinted in 1870. The books, prized by collectors for their attractive bindings and illustrations rather than by juvenile readers, still offer, among the exhortations, sympathetic descriptions of children's behaviour and feelings, and lively recreations of their preferred toys and occupations—and not always those approved by their elders.

PATRICIA WRIGHT

Sources private information (2004) [family] · IGI · H. Carpenter and M. Prichard, *The Oxford companion to children's literature*, pbk edn (1999) · family records, Essex RO, Chelmsford · parish register, West Ham, Essex, All Saints', Essex RO, Chelmsford, 5 Feb 1836 [burial] · parish register, West Ham, Essex, All Saints', Essex RO, Chelmsford, 8 Dec 1831 [burial: Mary Ann Kilner]
Likenesses miniature, priv. coll.

Kilner, Mary Ann (1753–1831). *See under* Kilner, Dorothy (1755–1836).

Kilroy, Alix Hester Marie. *See* Meynell, Dame Alix Hester Marie, Lady Meynell (1903–1999).

Kilsby, William (d. 1346), administrator, probably came from the village of Kilsby, Northamptonshire, though his parentage and early history are unknown. He first appears as the recipient of several livings in the king's gift soon after Edward III came to the throne in 1327. He was receiver of the chamber from January 1335 to July 1338, during which time he developed a chamber administration that could respond quickly to the financial needs of war, and allow Edward to field armies in Scotland and France. He himself participated in the campaign of 1335 in Scotland with ten men-at-arms.

Kilsby was promoted to be keeper of the privy seal on 6 July 1338, and was probably responsible for drafting the ordinances of Walton issued six days later, when Edward was about to embark for Flanders for his war against France. The ordinances arranged for co-ordination between the administration that accompanied Edward overseas and the regency government in England, to ensure a steady flow of cash to finance the king's military ambitions. From 1338 to 1340 Kilsby had custody of both the privy seal and the great seal, and was Edward's closest adviser in Flanders. Edward called him his chancellor, even though Richard Bintworth held the office of chancellor in England. With his staff of six clerks, Kilsby engaged in diplomacy as well as the duties of the privy seal, and

was also described as a banneret with a large force of men-at-arms and archers. Throughout these years Kilsby proved to be indispensable to Edward, not only through the offices he filled, but also through his energetic work in raising loans, standing as surety for royal debts, arranging transport, raising troops, witnessing charters, and even investigating royal officials.

1340 marked a critical turning point in Kilsby's career as well as in the politics of Edward's reign. William Melton, archbishop of York, died on 5 April. At first Edward promoted his treasurer, William Zouche, a former keeper of the privy seal and a colleague of Kilsby, for the post, but then switched his support to Kilsby. Nevertheless, the chapter elected Zouche on 2 May. Edward then wrote to the pope on Kilsby's behalf, delaying any appointment for two years. At the same time, Edward's ambitious campaign in France began to founder for want of sufficient funds. On 28 April he had appointed John Stratford, archbishop of Canterbury, to be chancellor and head of the regency government in England, with the specific responsibility of raising enough money for the war. But the effort failed, Stratford resigned, and Edward stormed back to England in November, determined to punish the ministers whom he blamed for his financial failure. Various officials were summarily arrested, but Edward's anger focused primarily on Stratford.

Kilsby accompanied Edward on his return and then led the attack on the archbishop. In April 1341 he and John Darcy arraigned Stratford before the Londoners at the Guildhall and then before the Commons. A vituperative pamphlet war followed between the court and Stratford. The lords in parliament turned against the royal counsellors, forcing Kilsby and his companions to withdraw, and giving Stratford a hearing. But the storm passed quickly. Kilsby did not lose his office, and was reconciled with Stratford in the autumn of 1341. In the winter campaign in Scotland in 1341–2, Kilsby served as a banneret with seven knights and fifty-three esquires.

Kilsby's hopes for high ecclesiastical office ended in April 1342, when Zouche was finally installed as archbishop of York. Then on 4 June he was replaced as keeper of the privy seal, ending his administrative career. He did not, however, lose favour with Edward, and pursued a military career for the rest of his life. He served as a banneret with a large retinue in the Brittany campaign in 1342. Afterwards, he went on pilgrimage to the holy sepulchre, and then to the shrine of St Catherine in Sinai. In 1345 he embarked with the king on the Crécy campaign with a contingent which included 1 banneret, 7 knights, 73 esquires, 68 mounted archers, and 11 archers. He captured a French prisoner, Henri de Verny at Caen, and proceeded to the siege of Calais, where he died, some time between 7 and 30 September 1346. Because of his highly visible role in the controversial finances and policy making of the initial stages of what would become the Hundred Years' War, Kilsby attracted the opposition of some lords during the crisis of 1340–41, and the suspicion of historians afterwards. But his influence on Edward cannot be doubted, nor can Edward's trust in him, as one of a group of servants, lay and clerical, who fashioned royal policy in these years.   Scott L. Waugh

Sources F. Palgrave, ed., *The parliamentary writs and writs of military summons*, 2 vols. in 4 (1827–34) · *Chancery records* · Rymer, *Foedera*, new edn, 2/2; 3/1 · *Adae Murimuth continuatio chronicarum. Robertus de Avesbury de gestis mirabilibus regis Edwardi tertii*, ed. E. M. Thompson, Rolls Series, 93 (1889) · *Chronicon Galfridi le Baker de Swynebroke*, ed. E. M. Thompson (1889), 72, 76, 79, 248, 250 · G. Wrottesley, *Crécy and Calais* (1897); repr. (1898), 7, 35, 133, 153, 158, 202, 205–6 · *The wardrobe book of William de Norwell*, ed. M. Lyon and others (1983) · R. Nicholson, *Edward III and the Scots: the formative years of a military career, 1327–1335* (1965), 249 · Tout, *Admin. hist.*, 3.52, 84–8, 99–102, 114–15, 117–18, 120–26, 131–2, 161–3, 225–6; 4.8, 102, 239, 257, 261, 277, 286–7, 293, 447; 5.11, 14–19, 21–2, 34, 39–40, 53, 77, 81–2, 84, 189 · G. L. Harriss, *King, parliament and public finance in medieval England to 1369* (1975), 246, 284, 295, 303, 306–8, 350, 520–2 · R. M. Haines, *Archbishop John Stratford: political revolutionary and champion of the liberties of the English church*, Pontifical Institute of Medieval Studies: Texts and Studies, 76 (1986), 258, 268, 274–5, 279, 281, 305, 317, 319, 323, 327, 339, 498, 500

Kilsyth. For this title name *see* Livingston, James, of Barncloich, first Viscount Kilsyth (1616–1661).

Kilvert, Francis (1793–1863), Church of England clergyman and writer, was born at 7 Caroline Buildings, Westgate Street, Bath, on 29 March 1793. He was the eldest of the seven sons and one daughter of Francis Kilvert (1757–1817), a coach builder, and his wife, Anna Falkner (1764–1817/18). His uncle the Revd Richard Kilvert was examining chaplain to Bishop Richard Hurd. His grandfather Robert Kilvert, yeoman, of Candover, Shropshire, was first cousin to the bishop; the Kilverts had lived in Shropshire since the twelfth century.

Around 1802 Kilvert's father and grandmother Elizabeth lost money in a bank failure which blighted the family fortunes. He received, however, a good education: he was tutored by Dr Rowlandson at Hungerford, and then attended King Edward's Grammar School, Bath, where he became an assistant master before leaving in 1816. He entered Worcester College, Oxford, on 6 November 1811, graduated BA in 1819, and proceeded MA in 1824. He was ordained deacon by Bishop Richard Beadon in 1816 and priest in 1817. From 1816 until his death Kilvert tutored students, initially in 5 Caroline Buildings, the home of Elizabeth Kilvert, his grandmother, to whom he was much attached and for whom he later composed a long memorial. His father died in 1817, followed by his uncle the Revd Robert Kilvert, then by his mother, and in 1821 by his grandmother. Francis Kilvert, according to his brother Robert, 'well discharged a parent's duty, and was the mainstay of us all' (R. Kilvert, 44).

In 1817 Kilvert became curate at Claverton, near which his cousins William and Frederick Falkner were farmers. He also became minister of St Mary Magdalen's Chapel, Bath, chaplain of Bath Hospital, and evening lecturer at St Mary's, Bathwick. His students—'a sacred trust' (F. Kilvert, xix)—followed him to Claverton; in the mid-1850s these included his nephew (Robert) Francis *Kilvert (1840–1879), whose diary was to become a classic a century later. Initially shy and sensitive, the boy flourished under his uncle's kind and learned guidance. In 1822 Francis Kilvert married Eleonora Adelaide Sophia Leopoldina de Chièvre (c.1791–1870). Serious-minded and well-read, she was French and noble by birth; as a child she had escaped to Britain from the revolution, and had lived with a Quaker family. The couple had three daughters: Anna Sophia (b. 1828), Elizabeth Frances Maria (b. 1829), and Adelaide Mary (b. 1830). In 1842 Mrs Kilvert published a book, *Home Discipline*, which she dedicated to her husband and children, 'the chief joy and happiness of my life'. Kilvert himself had several publications to his name by this date: sermons preached at Christ Church before the national schools had appeared in 1827, and his sermons at St Mary's Church were published in 1837, in which year he became rector of Claverton.

Also in 1837 Kilvert moved into Claverton Lodge, an old and commodious house, with a library lined with glass-fronted bookcases, and with distant views across the hills. His life was filled by tutorial work, clerical duties, his family, and frequent attendances at the Bath Literary Club. Nothing ever tempted him to leave Bath. He wrote and lectured on its history, and after the publication of his *Ralph Allen and Prior Park* (1857), Joseph Hunter of the Record Office described him as 'the Bath biographer' (F. Kilvert, 179). His biography of *Richard Graves of Claverton* followed in 1858. Kilvert's local histories were pleasantly nostalgic descriptions of late eighteenth-century Bath of no lasting value. His literary and learned interests ranged widely. A lover of Latin poetry, especially that of Horace, in 1848 he published *Pinacothecae historicae specimen*, sprightly Latin verses on famous people, starting with the patriarch Abraham and ending with the hymn writer Isaac Watts; he included, among others, Salome, Lord Byron, Joan of Arc, and Horace Walpole. His *Selections from Unpublished Papers of Bishop Warburton* (1841) and *Memoirs of the Life and Writings of Bishop Hurd* (1860) reflected his fascination with eighteenth-century scholarly bishops; Hurd had died in 1808, and Kilvert's book was the first to commemorate him. From time to time Kilvert's literary queries appeared in *Notes and Queries*. After the posthumous publication in 1866 of his *Remains in Verse and Prose*, he was recalled in that journal as 'an accomplished scholar and pious and enlightened clergyman' (Markland, 188). Kilvert died at Claverton Lodge on 16 September 1863 and was buried in the old Widcombe churchyard, Bath. His widow moved to Bath, where she died on 10 January 1870.

Brenda Colloms

Sources R. Kilvert, *More chapters from the Kilvert saga: memoir of the Rev. Robert Kilvert* (1971) · E. Kilvert, *More chapters from the Kilvert saga: rambling recollections* (1971) · F. Kilvert, *Remains in verse and prose* (1866) [with 'Memoir' by W. L. Nichols] · *GM*, 3rd ser., 15 (1863), 652–6 · J. H. Markland, review of F. Kilvert, *Remains in verse and prose*, *N&Q*, 3rd ser., 11 (1867), 188

Archives Bodl. Oxf., corresp. | Bath Central Library, letters incl. to Charles Godwin, collection of epitaphs, and commonplace books · Bodl. Oxf., letters to Nichols family

Likenesses sepia photograph (in old age), repro. in Kilvert, *Remains in verse and prose*, frontispiece

Wealth at death under £3000: probate, 17 Nov 1863, *CGPLA Eng. & Wales*

Kilvert, (Robert) Francis (1840–1879), diarist, was born in Hardenhuish, Wiltshire, on 3 December 1840, the second child and elder son in a family of four daughters and two sons of the Revd Robert Kilvert, rector of Hardenhuish, and his wife, Thermuthis Coleman. He was educated privately at a small school run by his father at Hardenhuish rectory, and latterly at Claverton Lodge School, Bath, run by his uncle Francis *Kilvert. He went up as a commoner to Wadham College, Oxford, in 1858, and took fourth-class honours in law and modern history in 1862. He was ordained deacon in 1863 and priest in 1864, served for two years as his father's curate in Langley Burrell, Wiltshire, and then went as curate to the Revd R. L. Venables in Clyro, Radnorshire. He stayed in Clyro until 1872, then returned to a further curacy under his father in Langley Burrell until 1876, when he was appointed vicar of St Harmon, Radnorshire. There he stayed for little more than a year, being appointed vicar of Bredwardine, Herefordshire, at the end of 1877. He was a popular and energetic country clergyman who wrote conventional verse and made a collection of Radnorshire folklore, some of which was published in local newspapers.

Kilvert kept diaries from the beginning of 1870 until his death, but he remained totally unknown to the general public until the publication of a selection from these diaries in a three-volume edition, edited by William Plomer, in 1938–40. Some of the manuscript diaries had already been destroyed by his widow. They appear to have dealt with the courtship of Kilvert and his wife, and with two previous romantic attachments of Kilvert's. In the 1950s the Kilvert descendants agreed that Mrs Essex Hope, Kilvert's niece, who had custody of the diaries, should burn all except three early ones. She told Jeremy Sandford, who had written radio talks and a radio play about Kilvert, that the family was not happy with some of the matter in the diaries. The surviving three diaries have been published in their entirety, two by the National Library of Wales (1982 and 1989) and one by Alison Hodge (1989). Only a few small fragments survive of the rest of the text.

The diary quickly achieved remarkable popularity, and has been republished in numerous editions. It depicts the periods of Kilvert's life as a curate in Clyro and Langley Burrell, and is a picture of the life of mid-Victorian rural society seen by a sensitive member of the gentry. Kilvert, who was very conscientious in the discharge of his pastoral duties, was acquainted with an unusually broad spectrum of village society, and proved himself a sharp, compassionate, and sometimes humorous observer.

Although Kilvert's judgements are generally conventional and his tastes often sentimental, there are many passages where the prose rises to poetic heights of description. A great lover of the works of William Wordsworth and of his sister, Dorothy Wordsworth, who also kept a journal, Kilvert was keenly aware of the beauties of nature, and some of his descriptions of the Wye valley and the Welsh border are classics of landscape writing. There are some memorable set pieces, such as the climb up Cadair Idris, when a shaken Kilvert thought of Moses on

(Robert) Francis Kilvert (1840–1879), by unknown photographer

Sinai. A week later he wrote of an angel satyr walking the Clyro hills. He loved the Greek classics, and on his walks he believed that he witnessed the Christian and mythic tales blend in a harmonious whole. In a ruined church near Garth, for instance, he thought of owls roosting and satyrs dancing. He walked miles in all weathers, visiting schools and parishioners, and places or people who took his fancy. In 1874 he paid a memorable visit to the Revd William Barnes, whom he called the 'great idyllic poet of England'. He described him as 'half-hermit, half-enchanter', and although he laughed at the humorous poems, he really preferred the pathetic ones.

The diary reflected the two aspects of Kilvert's character, displaying the sociable, well-liked, responsible young curate, always welcome at parties, and the poet who needed his solitary walks to admire and wonder at the power and splendour of the world God had made.

The public events of Kilvert's time left little mark on the border country, and, apart from accounts of occasional visits to London and Oxford and of a holiday in Cornwall, which is one of the diary's *tours de force*, Kilvert's record hardly strays beyond rural Radnorshire and Wiltshire. He paid at least two visits to France and Switzerland, but neither of these is covered by the diary. In 1878 he was offered the English chaplaincy at Cannes, but refused it (against his doctor's advice, for Kilvert was often ill). The more intimate details of his personal life are, however, fully exhibited in the diary. He had no gift for self-analysis, but recorded his propensity for falling in love, just as he recorded in voluptuous detail the sight of the young girls whom he taught in school. Nor was his widow embarrassed by his frankness, for she did not remove those passages. It took readers of a later century to recognize their fundamentally erotic nature. The diary, both a record and a release for Kilvert, took perseverance to complete after a day's work. But he succeeded in turning his diary's limitations—its narrow range of vision and the naïvety of his own judgements—into advantages, to give it a vividness and a simplicity shared by few similar journals, making it both a major document of Victorian rural life and a minor but moving work of literature.

Kilvert's closest friend was Anthony Mayhew, a fellow of Wadham College. They spent holidays together, and Kilvert stayed with Mayhew when he revisited Oxford. Mayhew was the only person permitted to read Kilvert's diary, and he enjoyed the character studies of unusual personages. When the pair were on holiday in Paris, Mayhew introduced to Kilvert Elizabeth Anne Rowland, the daughter of John Rowland of Wootton, near Woodstock. Three years later, on 26 August 1879, she became Kilvert's wife. He had long wished to be married and have children of his own, but as an impoverished curate had been forced to wait until his late thirties. Tragically Kilvert died at Bredwardine vicarage of peritonitis on 23 September 1879, ten days after returning from the honeymoon. The marriage was childless; his widow survived him until 1911, but did not remarry. She returned to Wootton and pursued a life of charitable work in the village.

In 1948 the Kilvert Society was formed in Hereford on the initiative of William Plomer and a Hereford businessman who was a great admirer of Kilvert. Its aims were 'to foster an interest in the Rev. Francis Kilvert, his work, his diary, and the country he loved'. The society has issued a number of publications.

On 16 March 1870, prompted by the sound of a bird singing unseen, Kilvert had written that the words of a good man might live long after he was silent and out of sight, and he quoted: 'He being dead yet speaketh.' Those five words were carved above his grave at Bredwardine, and, for the modern reader, reflect his justified hope that his diary would be read after his death.

A. L. LE QUESNE, rev. BRENDA COLLOMS

Sources W. Plomer, *Kilvert's diary: selections*, 3 vols. (1938–40) · K. Hughes and D. Ifans, *Diary of Francis Kilvert, April–June 1870* (1982) · D. Ifans, *Diary of Francis Kilvert, June–July 1870* (1989) · R. Maber and A. Tregoning, *Kilvert's Cornish diary, July–Aug 1870* (1989) · F. Grice, *Francis Kilvert and his world* (1982) · D. Wordsworth, *Recollections of a tour made in Scotland, 1803*, ed. J. C. Shairp (1874) · D. Lockwood, *Francis Kilvert* (1990) · D. Lockwood, *Kilvert the Victorian* (1992) · B. Colloms, *Victorian country parsons* (1977) · A. L. Le Quesne, *After Kilvert* (1978)

Archives NL Wales, diaries · U. Durham L., diary | Bodl. Oxf., letters to John Nichols

Likenesses photograph, Kilvert Society [*see illus.*] · photographs, repro. in Lockwood, *Francis Kilvert*, following p. 72

Wealth at death under £450: administration, 18 Nov 1879, CGPLA Eng. & Wales

Kilvert, Richard (*c*.1588–1650), lawyer, was the brother of Roger Kilvert, a wine-importing Spanish merchant, but their parents are unknown. Kilvert married Margaret Duppa on 20 February 1614 at St Christopher-le-Stocks, London. They had a son, Robert Richard Kilvert, who was born in 1615. In 1639 Kilvert was said to be living in his brother's house in St Martin's Lane, London.

Kilvert's education is unknown, but by the 1630s he was a lawyer soliciting cases in the Star Chamber and the court of high commission. Throughout his career Kilvert was exposed to attempted bribery and was confronted with allegations of corruption. In the eyes of contemporaries he was bold and without scruples. With reference to his past role in the court of high commission a pamphlet of 1642 claimed: 'Yet even in that Court he was found too corrupt, too libidinous, too treacherous; many Articles were exhibited against him and at last he was reiected as a person infamous and scandalous to Ecclesiastical Jurisdiction' (*The Vintners Answer to some Scandalous Pamphlets Published (as is Supposed) by Richard Kilvert*, 1642). On the other hand Kilvert enjoyed the trust of those in power. He was in contact with the secretary of state, Sir Francis Windebank, the lawyer Sir John Lambe, and James Hamilton, third marquess of Hamilton. Among his closest acquaintances was Archbishop Laud.

Kilvert was involved in several significant cases. In April 1621 he informed the House of Lords of the 'many corruptions' of Sir John Bennet, MP for Oxford University, and promised further evidence (PRO, SP 16/120.107). The Lord Chancellor, who was accused along with Bennet, made large offers to Kilvert to desist from his charges, but Kilvert informed the House of Lords about the attempted bribery. In the proceedings against John Williams, bishop of Lincoln, in 1636 Kilvert played an important role as informer. He petitioned the king to impose a great fine on the bishop on the grounds of evidence brought against him in the court of Star Chamber and collected evidence which aimed at casting doubt on the bishop's religious and political loyalty, and his personal integrity with allegations of fraud and corruption (ibid., 16/362.11). Williams counter-attacked resurrecting an old accusation of perjury against Kilvert and accusing him of living in adultery. In an earlier letter to Secretary Sir John Coke he had voiced his distrust of Kilvert, who 'appears' to have drawn 'the petition and manageth all this business against me, which I pray God may receive such a determination as that his Majesty's service in these parts do not suffer by the favour this felon hath found' (Cowper MSS, 2.153). In 1638 Charles I employed Kilvert as solicitor in endeavouring to levy a fine of £10,000 on the bishop, with £1500 of the fine to go to Kilvert, and Williams was further accused of having tried to corrupt Kilvert and procuring several witnesses to swear falsely in depositions against him.

In 1637, at a time when the vintners were under increasing pressure from the crown for a new imposition of duty on imported wine, Kilvert and the marquess of Hamilton contacted William Abell, alderman and master of the Vintners' Company. Threatening legal action against the vintners, Kilvert and Hamilton pressured Abell into persuading the company to agree to the new tax in return for the farm of the issuing of wine licences for taverns throughout England and Wales at £7000 a year, which increased its obligations to the crown to £37,000 a year. Kilvert received £1000 for his services and a grant of £500 a year out of the farm. Part of the arrangement with the Vintners' Company was the so called 'medium', which obliged the vintners to take from the merchants a set quantity of wines at set prices. Kilvert, however, obtained an order from the king to discharge the vintners from the medium for the future. He also accompanied those company members who rode about to settle the imposition in the country. According to one account he 'as from the King's mouth took the Boldnesse to treat with all men, and in very imperious terms'. When 'all his intimation from the King' failed he threatened Star Chamber action (*Vintners Answer*).

When the wine project began to fail, as many would not pay the new duties, recriminations were voiced from many sides. Parliament, hostile to monopolies, resolved in March 1641 that the new duty was illegal and that Abell and Kilvert were responsible both for its creation and execution. In September 1641 Kilvert was bailed. A number of pamphlets gave derisive accounts of Abell and Kilvert plotting to obtain the monopoly for their own benefit. In 1641 Kilvert defended his role in a pamphlet entitled *A reply to a most untrue relation made and set forth in print by certaine vintners in excuse of their wine project*. His key argument was that the vintners had contrived the wine project out of a desire to enrich themselves and that he was not present when they agreed the project in November 1637. Responding to the testimonies of those involved in the wine project before a committee for the House of Commons, which were printed in *Die Mercurii* on 21 July 1641, Kilvert wrote,

> So that now this whole business being found to be the work of the Company, both in the creation and execution, Master Kilvert is most confident of the justice of the Honorable House of Commons that they will not punish him for the Vintners offence, there being no Petitioner or complaint against him, other then the recrimination of the Counsell of Alderman, Abell, and the Vintners. (Kilvert, *Reply*)

In the end the main punishment fell on Abell, and Kilvert managed to escape scot-free. He was at liberty in December 1643 and seems to have lived comfortably in his house in St Martin's Lane until his death on 3 July 1650.

DAGMAR FREIST

Sources PRO, PROB 6/24, fol. 148r • PRO, PC2, privy council registers, vols. 44–52 • *state papers domestic*, Charles I, PRO, SP 16, 1620–21; 1636–37; 1638–43 • JHC, 2 (1640–42), 26–279 • JHL, 3 (1620–28), 153 • *The manuscripts of the Earl Cowper*, 3 vols., HMC, 23 (1888–9), vol. 2 • Bodl. Oxf., MSS Bankes 41, 44, 50, 52 • A. Crawford, *History of the Vintners Company* (1977) • R. Kilvert, *A reply to a most untrue relation made and set forth in print by certaine vintners in excuse of their wine project* (1641) • [W. Abell?], *A true discovery of the projectors of the wine project, out of the Vintners' owne orders made at their commonhall* (1641) • *Die Mercurii* (26 May 1641) • *Die Mercurii* (21 July 1641) • *A dialogue or accidental discourse betwixt Mr Aldermann Abell and Richard Kilvert, the two maine projectors for wine, and also Alderman Abels wife* (1641) • *The last discourse betwixt Master Abel and Mr Richard Kilvert, interrupted at the*

first by an ancient and angry gentlewoman, who being her selfe unknowne unto the observer of this conference it was conceived by him afterwards to be a certraine friend of Mr Abels (1641) • *The retailing vintners their answer* (1641) • *The copie of a letter sent from the roaring boyes in Elizium: to … Alderman Abel and M. Kilvert* (1641) • DNB • *A true relation of the proposing, threatening and persuading the vintners* (1641)

Archives Bodl. Oxf., Bankes MSS

Likenesses print, pubd 1798 (with W. Abell; after early woodcut), NPG • woodcut, pubd 1810 (facsimile of title to *The copie of a letter sent from the roaring boyes in Elizium*, 1641), BM, NPG

Kilvington [Kylmington], **Richard** (*c*.1305–1361), philosopher and theologian, was the son of a priest from the diocese of York, and was probably born in Kilvington in Yorkshire. He studied and taught at Oxford and must have matriculated no later than 1319. MA by 26 September 1331, when he was included in a list of Oxford graduates sent to Pope John XXII requesting the reservation of benefices, he was BTh by 28 August 1335, when he was granted papal reservation of a benefice in the gift of the abbey of St Albans, and DTh by 1339. During his years at Oxford the controversies surrounding the views of William Ockham (*d*. 1349) dominated the intellectual life of the university, but Kilvington should be counted among those opposed, or at least uncommitted to Ockhamism, with an outlook closer to that of his other near contemporary Walter Burley (*d*. 1345).

Kilvington was one of the philosophers commonly known as the 'Oxford calculators', but—unlike the majority of these—he was not a fellow of Merton College. He was probably a member of Oriel College, as he bequeathed a substantial number of books to its library. The works composed during his Oxford career include: *Sophismata*; *Quaestiones super librum de generatione et corruptione*; *Quaestiones morales super libros ethicorum*; commentary on the *Sentences* of Peter Lombard (described in some manuscripts as *Quaestiones theologicales*); *De intentionibus et remissionibus potentiarum*; and *Quaestiones super libros physicorum*. The *Tractatus de intentionibus et remissionibus potentiarum* previously attributed to him is now known to be a work of his contemporary Richard Swineshead. A sermon he preached, *De adventu domini*, survives (Bodl. Oxf., MS Auct. F.inf.1.2). Kilvington enjoyed the patronage of Richard Bury (*d*. 1345), bishop of Durham, and lived in his household, presumably in the bishop's London palace near St Paul's. Both men accompanied Edward III and his queen to Antwerp in the summer of 1338, and Kilvington was one of the ambassadors appointed to negotiate with the French king Philippe VI in July 1339. After Bury's death he continued in royal service, and is mentioned in 1350 as a king's clerk and as going with royal 'protection and safe conduct' on necessary business to the papal curia in Avignon, where he made useful contacts. By 18 March 1350 he was archdeacon of London. On 5 April 1354 he was provided to the deanery of St Paul's on the petition of Cardinal Pierre du Cros, who described Kilvington as his chaplain.

The principal English supporter of Richard Fitzralph, archbishop of Armagh (*d*. 1360), in his campaign against the pastoral privileges of the friars, in 1356 Kilvington invited Fitzralph to preach at St Paul's Cross in the courtyard of the cathedral. Their quarrel with the mendicants gave rise to sermons, treatises, lawsuits (including one at the papal curia involving Kilvington's former master, Cardinal Pierre du Cros), and papal bulls. It also provoked polemical poetry, in Latin and English, on both sides of the controversy. The anonymous author of one of these works laments the plight of the mendicants: the two Richards, who are described as the lion and the leopard, the worst of wild beasts, are trying to turn London against the friars by their preaching. As the son of a priest, Kilvington is regarded as particularly reprobate. He is almost certainly the author of the defence of Fitzralph, *In causa domini Ardmachani allegationes magistri Ricardi devoti viri contra fratres* ('Allegations on behalf of the lord [archbishop] of Armagh by the devoted master Richard against the friars', Paris, Bibliothèque Nationale, cod. lat. 3222, fols. 111v–116v), and probably also of the *Replicaciones ... contra opusculum ffratris Rogeri Conewey* ('Replies to the little work of Brother Roger Conway', Paris, Bibliothèque Nationale, cod. lat. 3222, fols. 159–194v). In this case he must have followed Fitzralph to Avignon, participated in the hearing before the commission of cardinals, and returned home after the archbishop's death in November 1360. He was dead by 9 September 1361, possibly a victim of the plague, and was buried in St Paul's Cathedral.

KATHERINE WALSH

Sources Emden, *Oxf.*, 2.1050–51 [esp. for his benefices] · *CEPR letters*, 2.364, 520; 3.394, 483, 516, 519 · W. H. Bliss, ed., *Calendar of entries in the papal registers relating to Great Britain and Ireland: petitions to the pope* (1896), 236 · Rymer, *Foedera*, 3rd edn, 2/4.49 · 'Registrum palatinum Dunelmense': the register of Richard de Kellawe, lord palatine and bishop of Durham, ed. T. D. Hardy, 4 vols., Rolls Series, 62 (1873–8), vol. 3, pp. 229, 233, 287, 309 · *The Sophismata of Richard Kilvington*, ed. N. Kretzmann and B. E. Kretzmann (1990) · N. Kretzmann and B. E. Kretzman, introduction and commentary, in *The Sophismata of Richard Kilvington*, ed. N. Kretzmann and B. E. Kretzmann (1990) · N. Kretzmann, 'Richard Kilvington and the logic of instantaneous speed', *Studi sul secolo XIV in memoria di Anneliese Maier*, ed. A. Maierù and A. P. Bagliani (1981), 142–75 · N. Kretzmann, '"Tu scis hoc esse omne quod est hoc": Richard Kilvington and the logic of knowledge', *Meaning and inference in medieval philosophy: studies in memory of Jan Pinborg* (1988), 225–45 · F. Bottin, 'Analisi linguistica e fisica Aristotelica nei Sophysmata di Richard Kilmyngton', *Filosofia e politica, e altri saggi*, ed. C. Giacon (1973), 125–45 · 'L'Opinio de insolubilibus di Richard Kilmyngton', ed. F. Bottin, *Rivista Critica di Storia della Filosofia*, 28 (1973), 409–22 · F. Bottin, 'Un testo fondamentale nell'ambito della *nuova fisica* di Oxford: i Sophismata di Richard Kilmyngton', *Antiqui und moderni: Traditionsbewußtsein und Fortschrittsbewußtsein im späten Mittelalter*, ed. A. Zimmermann (Berlin, 1974), 201–15 · J. B. Schneyer, *Repertorium der lateinischen Sermones des Mittelalters: für die Zeit von 1150–1350*, 5 (Münster, 1974), 158–9 · A. Maierù, *English logic in Italy in the 14th and 15th centuries* (1982) · W. J. Courtenay, *Schools and scholars in fourteenth-century England* (1987) · A. G. Rigg, 'Two Latin poems against the friars', *Mediaeval Studies*, 30 (1968), 106–18 · K. Walsh, *A fourteenth-century scholar and primate: Richard FitzRalph in Oxford, Avignon and Armagh* (1981), esp. 441–54, ad indicem · C. H. Lohr, 'Richard de Kilvington', *Lexikon des Mittelalters*, 7 (1995), fasc. 4, 828
Archives Bibliothèque Nationale, Paris, Cod. lat. 3222 · Bodl. Oxf., MS Auct. F.inf.1.2 (S.C. 1926) | Bibliothèque Nationale, Paris, MS fonds latin 14576, 15564, 16134, 17841 · Bibliotheca Amploniana, Erfurt, MSS 0.74; 0.76; F.313

Kilwardby, Robert (*c*.1215–1279), Dominican philosopher, theologian, and archbishop of Canterbury, is of unknown origins. Study of his writings has allowed approximate dates to be attached to the earlier stages of his career. He studied arts at the University of Paris after the resumption of normal teaching there in 1231 and graduated MA *c*.1237. Bonaventure may have been among his students. He taught in the arts faculty until *c*.1245, then joined the Dominicans, probably in England. At his superiors' request he composed a general introduction to philosophy, *De ortu scientiarum*, *c*.1250. In the early 1250s he lectured on the *Sentences* and the Bible as BTh in Oxford, and became DTh *c*.1256. His *Quaestiones* on the four books of the *Sentences*, written while he was regent master in Oxford, were probably not completed until about 1260, and *De tempore* and *De spiritu phantastico* seem to have been composed even later.

Philosophical and theological writings Kilwardby's writings show that he was well acquainted with the corpus of Aristotelian writings, including, in his Oxford works, all ten books of the *Nicomachean Ethics*, most of which had only recently become available in Latin. His lectures on logic, grammar, and ethics form the most complete collection of works to have survived from the faculty of arts in Paris in the first half of the thirteenth century, but his own main interest and most important influence was in logic and philosophical grammar. Both Roger Bacon (d. 1294) and Albertus Magnus, for instance, were much indebted to him in these fields, and some of his logical works circulated for centuries. His commentary on the *Prior Analytics* ran to seven printed editions between 1499 and 1598, though it was ascribed to Giles of Rome. *De ortu scientiarum* also circulated widely; it was used by Remigio de' Girolami in Florence, for instance, in his *Divisio scientiae*, and as late as 1531 a copy of it was acquired in Valladolid by Christopher Columbus's son, Don Fernando Colón.

In Oxford Kilwardby turned his mind more to theology and especially to the Bible and the fathers, though he did not entirely abandon his earlier philosophical concerns. He applied himself to a study of 'original texts' of the fathers, that is, complete texts rather than florilegia. In his *Quaestiones* on the *Sentences* he shows an awareness of Bonaventure's Parisian commentary and that of his Dominican forerunner in Oxford, Richard Fishacre (d. 1248). In this and other works produced in this period he shows a sometimes quite explicit concern to harmonize traditional Augustinian theology with modern Aristotelian philosophy.

As an aid to his own study and that of his students Kilwardby compiled elaborate indices and guides to a considerable number of texts. These include detailed summaries of at least thirty-five works by or ascribed to Augustine, Peter Lombard's *Sentences*, and one work by John Chrysostom; each text is broken down into small sections and a résumé given of each section. He also prepared alphabetical subject indices of individual treatises by Augustine and Anselm, Damascene's *De fide orthodoxa*, and the *Sentences*, and a comprehensive single concordance of Augustine, Ambrose, Boethius, Isidore, and Anselm, together with the *Sentences* and Comestor's *Historia scholastica*. All these works of reference attest both the conscientiousness and the competence of their author. Possibly more of them remain to be discovered or identified.

The liveliness of Kilwardby's mind and his readiness to take an interest in other people's ideas is shown by the only scholarly writing known to come from the period of his provincialate. In 1271 he, like Albertus Magnus and Thomas Aquinas, was asked by the master of the Dominican order, Giovanni of Vercelli, to comment on forty-three rather odd questions arising from the teaching of some lector whose views had been found disturbing. Aquinas complained politely about the interruption to his own work, but replied concisely and benignly. Albertus wrote at greater length and much less benignly; most of the questions struck him as idiotic, if not completely insane. Kilwardby, by contrast, shows evident interest in some of the questions: in one reply he offers a detailed interpretation of a passage from Aristotle, which he insists must be taken in context; elsewhere he provides short treatises on the nature of infinity and the way to calculate the distance from the surface of the earth to its centre.

Dominican provincial In 1261 Simon of Hinton was dismissed as provincial of England by the Dominican general chapter; Kilwardby was elected to succeed him. In 1272, for unknown reasons, he and several other priors and provincials were absolved by the general chapter, with the rider that they were not to be immediately re-elected to the same positions. Since the chapter of 1272 was particularly concerned with improving discipline in the order, it is likely that the absolved superiors were considered to have failed in some way in this domain. However, the English provincial chapter disregarded the general chapter's ban and re-elected Kilwardby, though he was appointed archbishop of Canterbury soon afterwards. As provincial, one of Kilwardby's first tasks was to implement the decree of the general chapter of 1261, that Oxford should be a *studium generale* for the whole order, in spite of the province's long-standing refusal to co-operate. It may be significant that the Dominican church in Oxford was finally consecrated in 1262, and Lambrick has suggested that the royal alms of £50 per annum, instituted by Henry III, may have been granted at this time to help meet the financial burden of a *studium generale*.

Assuming he attended all the chapters he should have done, Kilwardby had more than his fair share. Normally provincials went to one general chapter in three, but they also had to attend both those that occurred in their own province and those which coincided with the election of a master of the order. So Kilwardby in principle should have been at Bologna (1262), London (1263), Paris (1264, when Giovanni of Vercelli was elected master), Montpellier (1265), Viterbo (1268), and Montpellier again (1271). In addition, he would have presided annually over the provincial chapter, but no trace of the provincial *acta* has survived and even the location of most of the chapters is unknown. The English province at this time still included Scotland and Ireland as well as England and Wales, but there is no way of knowing how actively Kilwardby interested himself in the remoter parts of his territory.

The general chapters while Kilwardby was provincial give the impression that the province was pursuing an unusually enthusiastic policy of expansion: permission was granted for thirteen new foundations, two of them to be in Ireland; no such permissions are recorded between 1250 and 1261, only seven between 1273 and 1282, and then none until 1320. But this evidence must be interpreted with caution. In fact thirteen houses appear to have been founded in England and Wales in the decade before Kilwardby's provincialate and four in Ireland, and other foundations were made between 1282 and 1320. The general chapters of 1262–82 certainly show that the province intended to expand, but chiefly they indicate that Kilwardby and his two immediate successors followed proper constitutional procedures, unlike his two predecessors and William of Hotham (elected 1282) and his successors. Perhaps the absence of permissions between 1250 and 1261, when the province was actually rich in new foundations, indicates pique that the general chapter, meeting in London in 1250, should have imposed a penance on the provincial and told him to be less interested in building. Remarkable too is the almost exact tally between the number of foundations for which the province asked permission during Kilwardby's provincialate and the number of houses founded; he evidently had a taste for realism as well as legal propriety. There is evidence of his personal involvement in the development of the priories in Ilchester and Ipswich. As provincial, Kilwardby commissioned the Dominican Ralph Bocking to compose the life of St Richard of Wyche after the latter's canonization.

Public affairs During the early years of Kilwardby's provincialate the dispute between Henry III and the barons came to its climax, but it is not known what role, if any, he played in these affairs. Some Dominicans perhaps sympathized with Simon de Montfort, whose father had been a friend and benefactor of Dominic, but there is no evidence of Dominican complicity in Montfort's moves against the king. One of the king's most trusted councillors was his Dominican confessor, John of Darlington (d. 1284); after the battle of Evesham Henry wrote an impassioned letter to Kilwardby asking for John to be returned to his service, as being one of the few people trusted by both sides.

There is an equal lack of information about contacts between Kilwardby and Cardinal Ottobuono Fieschi during the latter's important legation in England (1265–8), or with Tedaldo Visconti, who was in his entourage and later, as Gregory X (r. 1271–6), appointed Kilwardby archbishop of Canterbury. In his personal letter Gregory X shows no sign of having been acquainted with his nominee, but Kilwardby must have had some dealings with the legate. The Dominican and Franciscan provincials were responsible for collecting the crusade tax in this period, and members of both orders were active as crusade preachers. The legate had authority to compel friars of either order to assist him in any way he wanted, which he can hardly have used without any reference to the two provincials. At least it must be presumed that Kilwardby assisted at the legate's final and most solemn council, held at St Paul's, London, in April 1268.

Further hints of Kilwardby's involvement in public affairs are furnished by later letters which reveal a warm friendship with Walter of Merton (d. 1277), whose origins must antedate Kilwardby's elevation to Canterbury; his letters to Edward I also suggest previous friendly contacts. Two letters written to support a Jewish leader, Master Elias, who was being calumniated by a fellow Jew whom he had tried to excommunicate, show both Kilwardby's intimacy with Edward's protégé, Robert Burnell (d. 1292), and his involvement with the Jewish community. He claims to have known Elias for a long time, even before becoming archbishop, and has found in him 'more signs of truth and goodness' than in any other Jew. Scattered evidence suggests that Dominicans in England had long been concerned not just with the mission to Jews, but also with protecting them from injustice in an increasingly hostile and paranoid world, in line with papal policy (in 1272 Gregory X announced extra measures to protect Jews from false accusation). Kilwardby had presumably played some part in all this and thereby won the confidence of Master Elias.

Relations with the Franciscans One dispute which Kilwardby was not able to escape was that between the Dominicans and the Franciscans. The basic problem was that, by now, both orders were trying to fill the same slot and there was not room for both of them; they were, not least, trying to attract the same recruits and in 1267–8 Clement IV intervened to try to stop them stealing each other's members. In Oxford a major row broke out in 1269. As the Dominicans saw it, the poverty on which the Franciscans based their claim to superiority was a mere legal fiction. The Dominican Solomon of Ingham precipitated the crisis by telling the Franciscans they would all be damned because they owned things contrary to their profession. Kilwardby was drawn in, as provincial; he refused to move Solomon from Oxford, as the Franciscans wanted, and he admitted that he too was unconvinced that the rival order really owned nothing. The arguments reveal the two orders' different outlooks: the Dominicans took a realistic line (if you have something, you have it), whereas the Franciscans insisted on their claim to own nothing in law. After the intervention of the university a compromise formula was found, allowing the Franciscans to claim that they owned nothing, as their profession required, and the Dominicans to believe in *de facto* Franciscan ownership.

Soon afterwards Kilwardby composed a letter to stop Dominican novices being seduced by Franciscan claims to a higher state of perfection, arguing that the Dominicans' more realistic poverty was better and that their usefulness as preachers was particularly meritorious. John Pecham (d. 1292), on his return to Oxford c.1271, recognized the anti-Franciscan import of the letter (in which Franciscans are never named) and wrote a vicious reply, in which he argued, *inter alia*, that the Dominicans had no right to be preachers at all. Kilwardby's letter still rankled with him in 1280.

Archbishop of Canterbury On 18 July 1270 Archbishop Boniface of Canterbury died. The monks of Christ Church elected their prior, Adam Chillenden, to succeed him, in spite of pressure from Prince Edward to elect Robert Burnell. Chillenden set off to secure confirmation of his election by the Holy See; but the papacy was still vacant and the cardinals at odds with one another. Only on 1 September 1271 was Gregory X elected. On the grounds of royal opposition to his candidacy he persuaded Chillenden to renounce his claim, on condition, apparently, that all the expenses of his trip would be refunded by the new archbishop, a condition that later led to temporary unpleasantness between Kilwardby and the monks. On 11 October 1272 the pope nominated Kilwardby to the see, sending him a personal letter as well as the official appointment. Nicholas Trevet (d. in or after 1334) ascribes to Kilwardby a primary role in the steps taken to ensure an orderly succession after Henry III's death on 16 November 1272, but this is not supported by other chroniclers and is probably untrue, as he had not yet taken possession of his see, whose spiritualities he received on 12 December and the temporalities two days later. He was consecrated by Bishop William Button of Bath and Wells on 26 February 1273, received the pallium on 8 May, and was enthroned in September (17 September according to the Osney chronicle).

On 16 September 1274 Kilwardby presided at the coronation of Edward I. The archbishop seems to have enjoyed generally cordial relations with the new king, but did not play a major role in the public affairs of the realm. He was a solid upholder of royal authority and in 1276 he tried to mediate between Edward and the prince of Wales, Llywelyn, who apparently trusted Kilwardby's impartiality; but his efforts came to nothing and he finally supported military action against Llywelyn. He became involved again at the pope's behest after Llywelyn's defeat in 1277. The prince's intended bride, Simon de Montfort's daughter, Eleanor, had been captured while trying to join him; in January 1277 the pope asked the king to free her. At the same time he ordered Kilwardby and his suffragans to try to get her brother, Amaury, a papal chaplain, who had been captured with her, transferred to Kilwardby's custody. Kilwardby's personal contribution to the outcome is not known, but early in 1278 Amaury de Montfort was handed over to him and later in the year Eleanor was married to Llywelyn in the king's presence.

Archiepiscopal activities As archbishop, Kilwardby clearly took his responsibilities seriously. He conducted visitations of his province, as he was required to do; apart from a complaint about the cost of his stay at Osney in 1276, the chronicles give the impression that his visits were conducted with tact and discretion. He also held a number of provincial councils. He was regarded as a strict enforcer of church discipline; until he was told to desist by the pope, he even tried to impose ordination and residence on a nephew of Cardinal Ottobuono, who held a benefice in

Kent. It appears to have been his mediation that defused and eventually resolved a dispute between the bishop and citizens of Norwich, and in other cases too, as far as one can judge, he acted firmly and fairly. When the need arose he defended the rights of the church even against royal agents.

In his new office Kilwardby did not forget the Dominicans. From 1275 onwards he played a key role in the acquisition and exploitation of a new site for them in London; even after his removal to the papal curia he took an active interest in the progress of the new building. He was also probably involved in the founding of a priory in Salisbury.

Kilwardby also maintained his interest in the University of Oxford. In June 1273 he presided over the inception of his friend Thomas of Hereford (d. 1282) as DTh, at the latter's request; later in the year he supported the king's ban on the bearing of arms by students, expressing the hope that it would secure a better and more attractive environment for the pursuit of learning. He was particularly involved in the college founded by his friend Walter of Merton, who transferred its visitorship from Winchester to Canterbury. Thus it was Kilwardby who confirmed the Merton statutes in 1275 and, during his visitation in 1276, with the support of the founder, he issued some supplementary regulations; after the founder's death, he intervened to protect the college's property. On 18 March 1277, in union with the regent and non-regent masters of the university, he banned the teaching of a series of propositions in grammar, logic, and natural philosophy, on pain of forfeiture of academic position. Since the Oxford condemnation occurred only eleven days after Bishop Tempier's condemnation of 219 propositions current in the arts faculty in Paris, there was presumably some connection between them, though the two lists have little in common; at least they reflect a shared worry over recent developments in philosophy. It is not clear where the initiative came from for the Oxford censure, but it bears the stamp of Kilwardby's own interests. The biggest storm was caused by the censure of propositions related to the doctrine of unicity of form espoused by Thomas Aquinas. The Oxford Dominicans clearly concurred in Kilwardby's censure; in response the general chapter of 1278 sent special visitators to England with authority to punish anyone found guilty of 'scandalizing the whole order' by disrespect towards Aquinas's writings. Kilwardby himself received a stern letter from the Dominican archbishop of Corinth, Pierre de Conflans, to which he replied with a lengthy justification of his hostility to unicity of form.

A persistently troublesome issue was the collection of crusade taxes from the clergy. Kilwardby recognized the pope's right to levy such taxes, and he is reported to have said as much at the Second Council of Lyons in 1274, where he was head of the English delegation. At the same time he was certainly aware that the clergy found them an intolerable financial burden, and he was willing to take action against unfair collecting practices. One of his last major acts as archbishop was to hold a provincial council

in January 1278 to arrange a petition against infringements of the local church's rights by one of the pope's local agents.

Cardinalate and death On 12 March Nicholas III (r. 1277–1280) created Kilwardby cardinal-bishop of Porto, issuing the formal bill of nomination on 4 April. The news was well known in England some time before the official letter arrived, leaving his successor, John Pecham, in doubt about the validity of Kilwardby's episcopal acts in the interim. Towards the end of July Kilwardby took solemn leave of his suffragans and soon afterwards set off for Italy. He took with him a large sum of money and other valuables belonging to the diocese, as well as his official registers, possibly because he was hoping to pursue the interests of Canterbury in the curia. Pecham, who was uncertain whether Kilwardby had intended to return the diocese's property or not, was subsequently unable to recover it.

It has been suggested that Kilwardby's elevation to the cardinalate implies some kind of dissatisfaction with his performance as archbishop. The truth is probably simpler. After the election of Nicholas III there were only six cardinals left, and all seven suburbicarian sees were vacant; the pope was surely just trying to restock the Sacred College with experienced churchmen. Portugal as well as England lost its primate and the Franciscans lost their minister-general, Girolamo da Ascoli, already a seasoned papal diplomat.

It is not known when Kilwardby reached the curia, but he no doubt spent the winter in Rome, where the curia stayed until early July 1279. The pope then went to Monterosi and Soriano, only reaching Viterbo in mid-September, but Kilwardby went straight to Viterbo, from where he wrote to the king on 11 July. He died there on 11 September and was buried in the Dominican church of Santa Maria in Gradi. The date ('III id. Sept.', that is, 11 September, not 10 or 12 as found in many modern works) is given in the Canterbury obits and also in the Osney annals (printed wrongly in the Rolls Series edition). The Dominicans of the Roman province liked to recall the old man's humility in walking around in his plain Dominican mantle (*cappa*) and travelling with only a small retinue of two servants and two friars. His contemporary, the southern French Dominican historian Étienne Salanhac, who probably met Kilwardby during an official visit to Britain in 1261, and perhaps also at the Council of Lyons in 1274, summed him up as *scientia perfectus, moribus ornatus* ('perfect in knowledge, excellent in character'; Salanhac, 186).

SIMON TUGWELL

Sources E. M. F. Sommer-Seckendorff, *Studies in the life of Robert Kilwardby O.P.* (1937) · D. Callus, 'The *Tabulae super originalia patrum* of Robert Kilwardby O.P.', *Studia Mediaevalia R. J. Martin OP* (1948), 243–70 · *Robert Kilwardby O.P. 'De ortu scientiarum'*, ed. A. G. Judy, Auctores Britannici Medii Aevi, 4 (1976) · *Robert Kilwardby O.P. 'On time and imagination'*, ed. P. O. Lewry, Auctores Britannici Medii Aevi, 9 (1987) · R. Kilwardby, *Quaestiones in librum primum sententiarum*, ed. J. Schneider (Munich, 1986) · R. Kilwardby, *Quaestiones in librum secundum sententiarum*, ed. G. Leibold (Munich, 1992) · R. Kilwardby, *Quaestiones in librum tertium sententiarum*, 1: *Christologie*, ed. G. Grössmann (Munich, 1982) · R. Kilwardby,

Quaestiones in librum tertium sententiarum, 2: *Tugendlehre*, ed. G. Leibold (Munich, 1985) · R. Kilwardby, *Quaestiones in librum quartum senteniarum*, ed. R. Schenk (Munich, 1993) · T. Kaeppeli, *Scriptores ordinis praedicatorum medii aevi*, 3 (Rome, 1980), 320–25 · E. Panella, *Scriptores ordinis praedicatorum medii aevi*, 4 (Rome, 1993), 267–9 · P. O. Lewry, 'Robert Kilwardby', *Medieval philosophers*, ed. J. Hackett, DLitB, 115 (1992), 258–61 · J. Bougerol, 'Dossier pour l'étude des rapports entre Saint Bonaventure et Aristotle', *Archives d'Histoire Doctrinale et Littéraire du Moyen Âge*, 40 (1973), 135–222, esp. 137 · J.-G. Bougerol, 'Saint Thomas D'Aquin et Saint Bonaventure frères amis', *1274: année charnière, mutations et continuités* [Lyon, Paris 1974] (Paris, 1977), 741–50 · E. Panella, 'Un'introduzione alla filosofia in uno "Studium" dei Frati Predicatori del XIII secolo', *Cultura e istituzioni nell'ordine domenicano: studi e testi*, Memorie Domenicane, new ser., 12 (1981), 27–126, esp. 74–5 · G. Lambrick and H. Woods, 'Excavations on the second site of the Dominican priory, Oxford', *Oxoniensia*, 41 (1976), 168–231, esp. 208 · *Hist. U. Oxf.* 1: *Early Oxf. schools*, 419–26, 467–8, 498–9 · F. M. Powicke, *The thirteenth century* (1953), vol. 4 of *The Oxford history of England*, ed. G. N. Clarke, 470–71 · F. Godwin, *De praesulibus Angliae commentarius* (1616), 137–9 · N. Trevet, *Annales sex regum Angliae, 1135–1307*, ed. T. Hog, EHS, 6 (1845), 278–9, 283, 291–2, 298, 300, 306 · *Ann. mon.*, 4.256, 270–71, 277, 282 · O. Lewry, 'Robertus Anglicus and the Italian Kilwardby', *English logic in Italy in the 14th and 15th centuries*, ed. A. Maierù (1982), 33–51 · H.-F. Dondaine, 'Le *De 43 questionibus* de Robert Kilwardby', *Archivum Fratrum Praedicatorum*, 47 (1977), 5–50 · A. G. Little, *The Grey friars in Oxford*, OHS, 20 (1892), 320–35 · *Fratris Johannis Pecham Tractatus tres de paupertate*, ed. C. L. Kingsford, A. G. Little, and F. Tocco, British Society for Franciscan Studies, 2 (1910), 121–47 [see also Eng. trans. of Kilwardby's letter in S. Tugwell, *Early Dominicans* (1982), 149–152] · *Registrum epistolarum fratris Johannis Peckham, archiepiscopi Cantuariensis*, ed. C. T. Martin, 1, Rolls Series, 77 (1882), 48, 118, 227; 2, Rolls Series, 77 (1884), 550 · A. Maierelli, ed., *La cronaca di S. Domenico di Perugia* (Spoleto, 1995), 27–8 · Étienne Salanhac (Stephanus de Salaniaco), *De quatuor in quibus Deus Praedicatorum ordinem insignivit*, ed. T. Kaeppeli, Monumenta Ordinis Fratrum Praedicatorum Historica, 22 (1949), 58–9, 186 · [H. Wharton], ed., *Anglia sacra*, 1 (1691), 58 · BL, Arundel MS 68, fol. 41r · S. Tugwell, 'The date of Kilwardby's death', *Dominican History Newsletter*, 6 (1997), 118–20 · BL, Cotton MS Tiberius A.ix, fol. 79 · B. M. Reichert, ed., *Acta capitulorum generalium ordinis praedicatorum*, 3 (Rome, 1898)

Kilwarden. For this title name *see* Wolfe, Arthur, first Viscount Kilwarden (1739–1803).

Kimathi, Dedan Waciuri (1920–1957), Mau Mau leader in Kenya, was born on 31 October 1920 in Thegenge village, Tetu location, Nyeri, the northernmost district of the Kikuyu reserve, to a wealthy peasant household. His mother's name was Waibuthi. He was, reportedly, a clever, headstrong youth who excelled during the few years of schooling he could afford, reliant on earnings from his seed-collecting in the Aberdare (Nyandarwa) mountain forests, and from other odd jobs. Baptized Dedan in his teens, he chose to be circumcised privately, at a dispensary, not in public with his contemporaries. He joined the army in 1941 but was soon discharged, allegedly for drunkenly intimidating fellow recruits. He then worked as a dairy clerk for white settlers, failed as a trader, and took up teaching, to be dismissed by the school's Kikuyu governors for sexual misconduct. After the Second World War he subscribed to the newly formed Kenya African Union (KAU) and became a youth-wing organizer, although he was now married to Mukami, a cultivator.

Rewarded in 1952 by appointment as KAU branch secretary in the 'white highlands' area of Thomson's Falls, he also recruited for the secret Mau Mau movement. The British thought this the KAU's militant wing. African memoirs have since suggested it actually aimed to subvert the constitutional approach of the KAU and its president, Kenyatta, to the problem of white-settler supremacy and colonial rule.

Views differ on whether Kimathi entered the Aberdare forest—soon after the British declared a state of emergency on 20 October 1952—on his own or as emissary of Mau Mau's Nairobi central committee. His ruthless organizing skill won him recognition as a leader in the six months it took for the growing numbers of poorly armed insurgents, perhaps 20,000 at their peak, to group their bands into regional armies. Kimathi took little part in the heavy fighting of mid-1953, when Mau Mau held the initiative against settlers, loyalist Kikuyu guard, and the British troops flown in to support the local forces. In August 1953 Kimathi, now field marshal and head of the Kenya defence council, offered peace to the governor, Sir Evelyn Baring, on impossible terms. Nor could Kimathi speak for Mau Mau. His authority did not run in the other Kikuyu districts, Kiambu and Fort Hall (Murang'a), and was disputed by Stanley Mathenge, another Nyeri man and unlettered champion of local guerrilla self-sufficiency against what many saw as Kimathi's bureaucratic autocracy. Their quarrel about the nature of authority over Kikuyu, stateless people in the past, came to a head in 1954. Kimathi supplanted the unwieldy defence council with the smaller (and almost entirely Nyeri) 'Kenya parliament'. Mathenge responded with his 'Kenya *riigi*', named after the wattle compound gate that was, by tradition, the individual householder's sole right and duty to guard.

Mau Mau aimed, as the KAU's *itungati* or rearguard, to prolong the war until Britain was forced to come to terms with the KAU leaders then imprisoned or detained. By mid-1955, however, the insurgents counted for little. Heavy casualties had shattered them, with 11,000 killed and 5000 captured or surrendered. No longer capable of attacking white farms, they focused on getting supplies from—and thus dividing—their home areas. Few fighters accepted a central authority; some tried to negotiate peace. The British had constricted Mau Mau manoeuvrability by destroying its logistical base in the Nairobi slums, by mass detentions, by 'villagization' of the Kikuyu countryside, and, more positively, by peasant smallholder reform and the promise of a limited enfranchisement of Kenya's Africans. Seemingly in desperation, Kimathi, now styled Sir Dedan, early in 1955 declared himself prime minister, and his forest lover, Wanjiru, his wife and queen—possibly, now, in conscious usurpation of the absent Kenyatta's authority. But the British military task had narrowed into a manhunt. This was guided by pseudo-gangs of turned ex-Mau Mau, some of them motivated by personal resentment against Kimathi. He became increasingly unpredictable and brutal to his followers. The pseudo-gangs helped to eliminate his bodyguard and forced him to keep on the move. Clad in leopard skins and unwashed, he moved fast along game tracks. On 21 October 1956 he was wounded in the thigh and captured by tribal police and Home Guard. The government, exultant, rewarded his captors with 10,000 shillings (£500) to share, and distributed throughout Kenya thousands of leaflets with a photograph of him manacled on a stretcher. He was tried on a charge of possessing a revolver and six rounds of ammunition, a capital offence, and at his trial was defiant. He expected the death sentence but believed he would survive. Reportedly a devout Catholic, he was hanged on 18 February 1957 at Kamiti prison, near Nairobi, and buried either there or, more probably, at Langata cemetery, Nairobi. Following independence a main street in Nairobi was renamed after him.

Kimathi is remembered by many as the champion of true independence, against the neo-colonial venality of politicians whose electoral rise to power Mau Mau had, arguably, made possible. JOHN LONSDALE

Sources D. L. Barnett and K. Njama, *Mau Mau from within* (1966) • M. wa Kinyatti, ed., *Kenya's freedom struggle: the Dedan Kimathi papers* (1987) • P. Maina, *Six Mau Mau generals* (1977) • B. A. Ogot, *Historical dictionary of Kenya* (1981) • R. B. Edgerton, *Mau Mau: an African crucible* (1990) • P. Swan, 'The death of Dedan Kimathi', www.crosswinds. net/~bluegecko, 29 Jan 2002 • J. Karimi, 'Dedan Kimathi was buried at Lang'ata', *East African* [Nairobi] (10 Dec 2001)
Archives PRO, CO.822 and W.O.236 series
Likenesses photograph, 1956, UPI / Bettman archive

Kimber, Cecil (1888–1945), motor car designer, was born at 51 Park Road, West Dulwich, on 12 April 1888, the son of Henry Francis Kimber, an engineer with Kimber Brothers, Manchester, printing ink manufacturers, and his wife, Frances (Fanny) Newhouse, *née* Matthewman, a talented watercolourist. After education at Stockport grammar school he became a salesman for the family firm, but a motor cycle accident provided the occasion for a decisive change of direction in the course of his life. He was lamed by the accident, and so freed from the future obligation of military service, and with £700 compensation he was sufficiently independent to break from the family firm and enter the engineering industry.

In the First World War Kimber worked for Sheffield-Simplex as a design engineer on airships and as a buyer for AC Cars. There he met his first wife, Evelyn Irene Phyllis, daughter of Charles William Hunt, an engineer, of Withington, whom he married in 1915; they had two daughters. Kimber joined E. G. Wrigley of Birmingham, component suppliers, in 1918 and from there made a move in 1921 which brought him into the ambit of William Morris, with whom the longest and best-known phase of his career was associated. It is important to stress that Kimber was never an independent entrepreneur, but a brilliant designer, works organizer, and motivator, who did not own the means of production for his designs. In 1921 he became sales manager of Morris Garages in Oxford and was therefore well placed to succeed E. Armstead as general manager on the latter's suicide in the following year. Kimber's interest in car design resulted in sporting bodies fitted at first to standard then, by 1924, modified Morris chassis, with the acronym of MG (Morris Garages) appearing in an octagonal frame to signal the arrival of MG as an evolving, though not yet separate, marque.

MGs were constructed at Morris Garages's premises in Oxford until 1927, when a new factory was built at Cowley, to be superseded in 1929 by the famous Abingdon works. In the following year the MG Car Company Ltd was registered, with Kimber as managing director under William Morris's control. Abingdon was necessary for the production of the M-type Midget (1928–32), based on the Morris Minor but with the distinctive character associated with MG cars during Kimber's leadership, for which he, above all, was responsible.

Record-breaking and racing successes marked the early 1930s and enhanced the image of the new marque, but as the J-type Midget and the Magnette series took over from the M-type and the effects of the depression were felt, MG production slumped from 2400 per annum in 1932 to 1300 in 1935 with the production of better, but more expensive, cars. Morris reacted by imposing a greater use of Nuffield corporate resources for MG; for example, Morris Bodies replaced the independent Carbodies as coachwork suppliers. Production then increased to 2850 in 1937, the best year of the decade. The difficulties of the mid-1930s underlined the fact that Kimber relied on Morris's goodwill for the survival of MG. In 1938 Kimber's wife died after a long illness which had led to their separation. He then married, in 1938, Muriel Lillian Dewar, a widow, daughter of Frank Reeves Greenwood, a musician.

With the outbreak of the Second World War events moved towards the breakup of Kimber's working relationship with Morris: civilian car production ceased in September 1939 and Kimber had to seek for war contracts for Abingdon. Following the appointment of Miles Thomas as Nuffield vice-chairman in 1941 there was greater insistence on centralized war production within the Nuffield Group and Kimber left MG and went first to Charlesworth Bodies, then to Specialloid Piston Rings as works director. The MG T-series, introduced in 1936, was to carry on the Kimber line when production resumed in 1945, a testimony to what has been described as his 'lovely flair for line'. His daughter's appraisal of her father's 'brilliance as a designer, innovator, works organizer, and manager of men', confirmed by others, is a fitting tribute to a motor industry original. Kimber died on 4 February 1945 at University College Hospital, London, after he was in a railway accident while travelling on Specialloid business. RICHARD A. STOREY

Sources F. W. McComb, *MG by McComb* (1978) • R. Storey, 'Kimber, Cecil', *DBB* • K. Brazendale, ed., *The encyclopedia of supercars* (1992), nos. 82–4 [entry on MG] • J. Cook, 'The man who lived his dream', *The MG log*, ed. P. Haining (1997), 25–42 • M. Thomas, *Out on a wing: an autobiography* (1964) • private information (2004) • b. cert. • d. cert.
Wealth at death £20,382 18s. 10d.: probate, 23 June 1945, *CGPLA Eng. & Wales*

Kimber, Edward (1719–1769), journal editor and writer, was the son of Isaac *Kimber (1692–1755), a General Baptist minister. There is no evidence that Kimber had any formal education. However, it is likely that he gained editorial experience and training as a youth after his father took up the editorship of the *London Magazine* in 1732 (Hayes, 11). In September 1742 Kimber left England for the American colonies, where he spent two years travelling. He recorded his observations on his travels in America, which were later published and would be reflected in his novels. Kimber returned to England in July 1744 and shortly thereafter married Susanna Anne Lunn, of East Kiel, with whom he had two sons, Edward and Richard, and one daughter, Margaretta Maria, who died in infancy.

Kimber worked on a wide range of literary projects and was extremely prolific. He began contributing poetry to the *London Magazine* in 1734, ultimately taking over its editorship in 1755. A significant portion of his travel writing was also printed in the *London Magazine*. Much of his work, however, was published anonymously or pseudonymously. Kimber later explicitly identified himself as the author of numerous poems and essays in his *General Index to … the 'London Magazine'* (1760). He also compiled an index for the *Gentleman's Magazine* (1754) and contributed to the *Universal Magazine* (1750) and to the *Westminster Journal* (1751).

Kimber's seven novels, all anonymously published, enjoyed considerable success in the eighteenth century. Almost all of them went through two editions. His most famous novel, *The Life and Adventures of Joe Thompson* (1750), went through six editions, was translated into French (1762) and German (1765), and was abridged for children by Richard Johnson, with whom he revised Thomas Wotton's *Baronetage*, in 1788. In 1759 he published a translation of C. P. J. de Crebillon's novel, *Heureux orphelins*. Kimber also made indexes for law books and histories, wrote manuals, and compiled several peerages. He has also been credited with *The Ladies Complete Letter-Writer* (1763). He died in 1769, 'a victim, in the Meridian of his Life, to his indefatigable Toils in the Republic of Letters' (Johnson, viii). JEFFREY HERRLE

Sources S. A. Kimber, 'The *Relation of a late expedition to St Augustine* with biographical notes on Isaac and Edward Kimber', *Papers of the Bibliographical Society of America*, 28 (1934), 81–96 · F. G. Black, 'Edward Kimber: anonymous novelist of the mid-eighteenth century', *Harvard Studies and Notes in Philology and Literature*, 17 (1935), 27–42 · K. J. Hayes, 'Introduction', in E. Kimber, *Itinerant observations in America* (1998), 11–24 · R. Johnson, preface, in T. Wotton, *The baronetage of England*, ed. E. Kimber and R. Johnson, 1 (1771), iii–viii · J. J. Tepaske, 'Introduction', in E. Kimber, *Relation of a late expedition* (1976), xi–xliv · A. Chalmers, ed., *The general biographical dictionary*, new edn, 19 (1815), 348–9
Archives BL, assignments of copyright, *Peerages and baronets*, Add. MS 38728 · Bodl. Oxf., receipt for assignment of copyright

Kimber, Isaac (1692–1755), General Baptist minister and historian, was born at Wantage, Berkshire, on 1 December 1692, the son of Isaac and Mary Kimber. He attended the private grammar school in Wantage run by the Revd Mr Slopes and then continued his classical studies under John Ward at Gresham College. Believing his vocation to be in the ministry he undertook a course of ministerial training at Moorfields Academy. Shortly after he had completed his course Kimber married Anna Roberts, on 28 March 1717 in Westminster, and a son, Edward *Kimber, was born in 1719.

Isaac Kimber received his first ministerial appointment in 1722, as assistant to Joseph Burroughs at the chapel in Paul's Alley, Barbican, London. As a preacher, however, he proved uninspiring and unpopular and was replaced by James Foster in June 1724, whereupon he accepted the invitation of Samuel Acton to become his assistant at Baker Street Chapel in Nantwich, Cheshire. There he is reputed to have preached in 1727 the funeral sermon for John Milton's third wife, Elizabeth, but there is some doubt over the validity of this claim. Kimber proved a disappointment to many of the members of his congregation, who had looked upon him as Acton's successor, but when this seemed unlikely they resented the additional subscription for his salary and Kimber was obliged to resign at the end of 1727. He returned to London, where for a short time he was assistant to John Kinch at the chapel in Old Artillery Lane, but when the congregation amalgamated with a neighbouring one his services were no longer required and he left the active ministry. Henceforth, apart from a two-year period (1734–6) when he helped to run John Ward's grammar school in Moorfields, he devoted most of his time to writing and working in various capacities for printers and publishers in London.

Kimber is probably more renowned for his literary efforts, and especially his historical works, than he is for his ministerial labours. For some years after being admitted into the ministry, and having a wife and child to support, he found it necessary to supplement his meagre stipend by writing. One of his first publications was *The Life of Oliver Cromwell* (1724), which ran to six editions and a French translation. He also collaborated on writing a four-volume *History of England*, which he later abridged. His account of the reign of George II was added to the 1740 edition of William Howell's *Medulla historiae Anglicanae*. In addition to his historical publications he compiled a periodical pamphlet, the *Morning Chronicle*, which appeared regularly between January 1728 and May 1732.

Kimber suffered a number of personal misfortunes in his life; he lost the sight of one eye and for over twenty years his wife was afflicted with mental illness. He died, in London, as a result of a stroke in January 1755 and his funeral sermon was preached by his former colleague Joseph Burroughs at Paul's Alley on 9 February.

ALEXANDER GORDON, rev. M. J. MERCER

Sources W. Wilson, *The history and antiquities of the dissenting churches and meeting houses in London, Westminster and Southwark*, 4 vols. (1808–14), vol. 3 · W. Urwick, ed., *Historical sketches of nonconformity in the county palatine of Cheshire, by various ministers and laymen* (1864) · W. T. Whitley, ed., *A Baptist bibliography*, 1 (1916) · W. T. Whitley, ed., *Minutes of the general assembly of the General Baptist churches in England*, 1: *1654–1728* (1909) · A. Chalmers, ed., *The general biographical dictionary*, new edn, 32 vols. (1812–17) · C. Surman, index, DWL · I. Kimber, letter to John Finch, Bodl. Oxf., MS Rawl. letters 43, fol. 141r · IGI
Archives Bodl. Oxf., letter to Dr John Finch
Likenesses T. Kitchin, line engraving (after Smith), BM, NPG; repro. in I. Kimber, *Sermons* (1756)

Kimber, William (1872–1961), morris dancer and musician, was born on 8 September 1872 at Huggett's Cottage, Old Road, Headington Quarry, Oxford, eldest of the four sons and two daughters of William Kimber (1849–1931), builder, and his wife, Sophia Ann (1850–1931), *née* Kimber, smocker, of The Manor, Horspath, Oxfordshire. His father had been a member of the Headington Quarry morris dancers until the team became inactive shortly after the jubilee fête in Oxford in 1887; this was also when Kimber had first danced. About the same time Kimber, who had left school in 1882 to work as a bird-scarer, was apprenticed to the building trade.

Kimber might have remained simply a builder had it not been for two events. The first was that the antiquary Percy Manning persuaded the Headington Quarry team to re-form for a display in Oxford in March 1899. Kimber was not a member of that team, but it continued to perform thereafter, sometimes with him. One performance was at Sandfield Cottage, Headington. Kimber had done building work there at Easter, and had mentioned the morris to Mrs Birch, the owner, promising that the team would call. On seeing the dancing, Mrs Birch enjoined them to visit whenever they danced. That winter, Kimber and his fellows were laid off work because of the poor weather, and decided to dance, unseasonally, to earn money. On Boxing day 1899, they danced at Sandfield Cottage, where Mrs Birch's son-in-law, Cecil Sharp, saw them. Intrigued, he asked Kimber, who was playing concertina (learned by ear from his father) for the dancers, to return the next day. Sharp noted down five tunes from Kimber, who was amazed to hear Sharp play them back to him immediately. This key moment marked the start of Sharp's folk-music collecting, but Kimber was not affected until Mary Neal asked Sharp in 1905 about folk-dances for her Espérance Girls' Club. He gave her Kimber's address; she sought him out and brought him to London to teach the dances. A public performance by the girls in April 1906 initiated a great wave of enthusiasm for morris dancing. Sharp, together with Espérance's musical director Herbert MacIlwaine, published the first collection of dances in 1907, and began lecturing on the subject, using Kimber as demonstrator. As Neal unearthed more former dancers, disputes about authenticity and authority arose. Neal found other dancers from Headington Quarry, and claimed Kimber was inaccurate. In a tense meeting in Headington in 1910, Sharp interrogated Kimber's father and other old dancers to satisfy himself on the authenticity of Kimber's dancing. In all the disputes Kimber promised to 'stick to [Sharp] like a leech'. In later years he always insisted that no matter what he might say, do, or play, if it contradicted Sharp's books then Sharp was right and he wrong. The two relied on each other; as Kimber put it, Sharp could not dance and Kimber could not lecture. While most morris-dancing informants were old men, Kimber was in his athletic prime, 'like a Greek statue … his grace and movements are absolutely classic' (*Musical Times*, March 1911). His dancing for Sharp often resulted in his losing his job, but he always found fresh employment. After Sharp's death in 1924 Kimber said that he had never failed Sharp,

William Kimber (1872–1961), by unknown photographer, 1912

not only at demonstrations, but also in collecting, where he often accompanied Sharp and helped him to reconstruct dances described by former dancers.

Kimber used his skills to train several morris teams around Oxford, including the Oxford police in 1923. He also introduced generations of Headington Quarry children to morris dancing at the local school. He started fresh teams in Headington Quarry itself in 1911–14, again in 1921 (lasting until the mid-1930s), and in 1948 (which side had had an unbroken existence more than half a century later). Kimber's son Fred was a member of the two last; Kimber had married Florence (1869–1917), daughter of Thomas Henry Cripps, railway labourer, in 1894, with whom he had two sons and six daughters. She died in 1917, and on 5 June 1920 he married Bessie Clark (*b.* 1882/3), widow, daughter of William Joseph Kethro, stonemason of Oxford, thereby acquiring a stepdaughter. In his later years he lived in the house he had built, Merryville (from his nickname, Merry), in St Anne's Road, Headington. Though arthritis took its toll—his last dance was at the Royal Albert Hall in 1930—he continued to play the concertina for dancing until his death, using the instrument given to him after a performance before the Worshipful Company of Musicians in 1909. His style of playing was ideal for dancing: bright, brisk, with full chords where necessary for emphasis in the dance. After he stopped dancing, his playing became increasingly fast, sometimes to the frustration of his dancers. Most of the extant recordings were made in this period, and do not show him at his peak.

William Kimber died on 26 December 1961 at his Headington home, exactly sixty-two years after his encounter with Sharp, collapsing from heart failure on going outside to fetch coal. He was buried on 30 December at Headington Quarry parish church, his coffin borne by six of his morris dancers in full regalia. Because of his early and enduring relationship with Sharp, dances from Headington Quarry formed the backbone of morris teaching for half a century, and the fact that so many performed, or enjoyed watching, morris dances throughout the twentieth century was in no small measure due to him.

MICHAEL HEANEY

Sources T. W. Chaundy, 'William Kimber, a portrait', *Journal of the English Folk Dance and Song Society*, 8/4 (1959), 203–11 · *Journal of the English Folk Dance and Song Society*, 9/3 (1962), 115–19 · K. Loveless, disc notes, *William Kimber* (1963) [LP recording] · R. W. Grant, 'Headington Quarry and its morris dancers: a brief chronology up to 1961', *Morris Dancer*, 2/10 (1990), 153–62 · Cecil Sharp corresp., Vaughan Williams Memorial Library, London · 'Death at 89 of William Kimber', *Oxford Times* (29 Dec 1961) · 'Funeral of Mr William Kimber', *Oxford Times* (5 Jan 1962) · K. Chandler, *Morris dancing in the south midlands, 1660–1900* (1993) · private information (2004) · b. cert. · m. cert. · d. cert. · *DNB* · *CGPLA Eng. & Wales* (1962)
Archives FILM Morris Ring Archive, performance footage, film 6 | SOUND BL NSA, 2CDR0001572–2CDR0001577 · BL NSA, documentary recording
Likenesses photograph, 1912, Vaughan Williams Memorial Library, no. 358 [*see illus.*] · J. Gay, photograph, *c.*1950, repro. in *Journal of the English Folk Dance and Song Society* [frontispiece] · A. Morris, painting, Vaughan Williams Memorial Library · photograph (possibly 19 August 1926), Vaughan Williams Memorial Library, no. 2043
Wealth at death £2328 14s. 0d.: administration, 16 March 1962, *CGPLA Eng. & Wales*

Kimber, William (*fl.* 1900–1930). *See under* Sabini, (Charles) Darby (1889–1950).

Kimberley. For this title name *see* Wodehouse, John, first earl of Kimberley (1826–1902).

Kimmins [*née* Hannam], **Dame Grace Thyrza** (1870–1954), child welfare reformer, was born at Lewes, Sussex, on 6 May 1870, the eldest of the family of four of James Hannam, cloth merchant, and his wife, Thyrza Rogers. After leaving Wilton House School, Reading, she embarked upon her philanthropic career as a Wesleyan sister at the West London Mission where, under the name Sister Grace, she founded the first Guild of the Poor Things (later amended to Guild of the Brave Poor Things). She borrowed the guild's name and its motto—'Laetus sorte mea' ('Happy in my lot')—from Juliana Horatio Ewing's popular sentimental fiction *Story of a Short Life*. At the outset the guild merely provided a weekly venue for physically disabled people to gather together for farthing teas, games, and fanciful costumes, but it launched Sister Grace's career as one of the most innovative and forceful advocates for the disabled in twentieth-century Britain.

In December 1895 Grace Hannam joined the women's branch of the Bermondsey settlement in a poor section of south London, under the leadership of the Methodist minister and reformer John Scott Lidgett and the social worker Mary Simmons; she lived in a spartanly furnished working-class flat in Rotherhithe. She soon established a Guild of Play for which she wrote a series of patriotic books detailing songs and dances drawn from the English and imperial past. Influenced by John Ruskin's ideas about the redemptive power of beauty, Sister Grace viewed children's play as a vital moral agent in the transformation of individuals and society, and as a way to examine the history and ethnography of nation, race, and empire. She explored these themes as well as the conditions of child life in the slums in her only published novel, *Polly of Parker's Rents* (1899).

The child psychologist Charles William Kimmins (1856–1948), a London county council inspector of education, and resident at the men's branch of the Bermondsey settlement, served as honorary treasurer of Sister Grace's Guild of Play and thereby initiated their lifelong partnership. His 'retiring' and 'happy go lucky' manner—he researched the therapeutic benefits of child laughter—contrasted markedly with her 'colossal drive' and determination (A. Kimmins, 8). On 28 July 1898, at the Southwark Park Wesleyan Chapel, Lidgett officiated at their wedding before galleries overflowing with disabled children and their families from the nearby slums. The Kimmins's marriage and the subsequent birth of their two sons only deepened their joint commitment to continuing their work on behalf of poor children. In the years before the First World War Grace supervised the growth of a network of guilds of the Brave Poor Things throughout England, though during the inter-war years several local branches insisted on the right to change their name.

A year after moving out of the lodge at the Bermondsey settlement in 1902 Grace Kimmins launched the scheme that dominated the last five decades of her life: the Chailey Heritage Craft School and Hospital, in the Sussex countryside near her birthplace. Sharing with her contemporaries the conviction that slum dwellers needed the benefits of the countryside, she rented a derelict workhouse in Chailey and brought down seven disabled boys from London as its first residents. From the outset she was assisted not only by her husband but by her closest friend and companion, Alice Rennie. Though lacking personal wealth and formal qualifications (neither woman was trained in the medical or educational components of the work), Kimmins and Rennie dreamed of making their fledgeling experiment into the great public school of 'crippledom'. And, to a remarkable extent, they succeeded. With Lidgett's assistance they soon took over a disused industrial school and expanded not only their facilities but the services they provided boys and, after 1908, girls. By training boys in skilled crafts (caning, leatherwork, woodwork) and girls in sewing, fine needlework, and housewifery, Kimmins aimed to transform 'maimed' children into self-respecting and economically independent adults.

The growth of Kimmins's work at Chailey corresponded with a dramatic increase in public interest in the care and treatment of 'physically defective' children in the aftermath of the Second South African War, with its revelation of the supposed 'degeneration' of the working class, and the diffusion of eugenic racial theories. Chailey Heritage's expansion further benefited from the partnership between private voluntary and public municipal bodies encouraged by the Elementary Education (Defective and

Epileptic Children) Act of 1899. Grace effectively used her husband's close ties to the London county council to make Chailey Heritage a major centre for the reception of poor disabled London schoolchildren whose costs were subsidized by municipal rates.

Kimmins seized the opportunities presented by the First World War to apply to the pressing needs of disabled soldiers and sailors the lessons she and her staff had learned in serving children. In addition to offering wounded men advanced orthopaedic and prosthetic rehabilitation programmes and vocational training, Kimmins also attended to the psychology of disablement by pairing each limbless soldier with a similarly disabled boy already familiar with Chailey's therapeutic regime. Kimmins circulated widely the images produced by Chailey Heritage's wartime services to solidify its international reputation and increase public sympathy for its work. During the inter-war period, she devoted herself with tireless energy to raising funds for the expansion of Chailey Heritage's Craft School and Hospital, as titled and wealthy visitors from around the world came to view the work and offer donations. Chailey Heritage's supporters included the Princess Louise, duchess of Argyll, and A. F. Winnington-Ingram, bishop of London, along with members of the royal family who visited Kimmins at Chailey several times. Kimmins retained firm—some felt almost dictatorial—control over all aspects of Chailey Heritage's management while collaborating with leading figures in a variety of fields to ensure it offered the most advanced treatments. For example, Robert Jones, the eminent orthopaedic surgeon, served as head of the executive committee overseeing the medical work, and Margaret Morris developed new forms of dance therapy for the disabled. The renowned child psychologist Cyril Burt described Chailey Heritage in 1931 as 'a great demonstration laboratory where the best that can be done for the crippled child is at once put into practice and tested' (Chailey Heritage, Craft School archives).

While the Second World War marked the zenith of Kimmins's work on behalf of disabled people and the nation, it also set in motion changes to which she found it difficult to adapt. The impending creation of the National Health Service not only accentuated tensions between the school and the hospital, but called for the government to incorporate the hospital as part of the public regional health system. Confronted with growing resentment by hospital personnel at the meddling of non-medical staff, Kimmins resigned her position of leadership of the Chailey Heritage in September 1946. Her husband died in January 1948 and in the summer of 1948, as Chailey Heritage's absorption into the National Health Service approached, Kimmins confessed to the duke of Norfolk that she was 'heartbroken' as 'we all fade out of existence' (Grace Kimmins to duke of Norfolk, 9 June 1948, archives of Chailey Heritage, HB 134/9, E. Sussex RO). She was appointed CBE in 1927 and DBE in 1950, and was also a dame of grace of the order of St John of Jerusalem. She continued to live at Chailey Heritage until her death at the King Edward VII Memorial Hospital, Haywards Heath, Sussex, on 3 March 1954. She was survived by her sons,

Sir Brian Charles Hannam Kimmins (1899–1979), a lieutenant-general in the army, and Anthony Martin Kimmins (1901–1964), film producer, director, and playwright.   SETH KOVEN

Sources collection of newspaper clippings, Chailey Heritage, Sussex, archives (manuscript and printed) of Chailey Heritage Craft School · E. Sussex RO, Chailey Heritage Hospital archive · G. T. Kimmins, *Heritage craft school and hospital* (1948) · *Annual reports* and *Monthly Record* of the Bermondsey Settlement · J. S. Lidgett, *My guided life* (1936) · A. Kimmins, *Half time* (1947) · S. Koven, 'Remembering and dismemberment: crippled children, wounded soldiers and the Great War in Great Britain', *American Historical Review*, 99 (1994), 1167–202
Archives Chailey Heritage, Sussex, Chailey Heritage MSS · E. Sussex RO, Chailey Heritage MSS
Likenesses H. Glock, oils, 1944, Chailey Heritage Hospital and School, East Sussex · photographs, Chailey Heritage Hospital and School, East Sussex
Wealth at death £7458 4s. 6d.: probate, 1 May 1954, CGPLA Eng. & Wales

Kinahan, George Henry (1829–1908), geologist, was born in Dublin on 19 December 1829, the third son among the fifteen children of Daniel Kinahan (1797–1859), barrister, and his wife, Louisa Anne Stuart (*née* Millar). He entered the school of engineering in Trinity College, Dublin, and received the diploma in engineering in 1853 but never graduated in the university. He found employment on the construction of the railway viaduct over the Boyne at Drogheda, but on 21 August 1854 he joined the Geological Survey of Ireland under Joseph Beete Jukes (1811–1869), the local director. On 12 November 1855 he married Harriette Anne Gerrard (*d.* 18 May 1892), from co. Westmeath, and they had several children, at least two of whom predeceased their father. He became senior geologist on 23 March 1861 and district surveyor on 1 March 1869. His survey career began in west Cork and co. Kerry. Later he was stationed at Recess, co. Galway, Wexford town, Avoca, co. Wicklow, and then in co. Donegal at Letterkenny and Rathmelton. He was retired on 31 August 1890 following the completion of the survey's primary mapping of Ireland.

Kinahan had vast experience of Ireland's geology and an unrivalled knowledge of the country's economic geology, but his was a turbulent life in science. He was a massive, bearded man of violent temper. His earlier survey work is excellent, but much of his later work is slovenly and idiosyncratic. In both Wicklow and Donegal much of his mapping was dismissed as erroneous following inspections by his superiors and he became insufferable within the survey. In 1869 he deeply resented the refusal of Sir Roderick Impey Murchison to appoint him Irish director in succession to Jukes, and he regarded the man sent over to the post—Edward *Hull—as an ignorant, intrusive incubus. The feud between the two men poisoned the air of Irish science for more than twenty years.

The most durable of Kinahan's many publications is his *Economic Geology of Ireland* which was originally a series of papers read to the Royal Geological Society of Ireland between 1886 and 1888. He also published in archaeology and natural history. He was elected a member of the Royal Irish Academy on 13 January 1868, and was the president of the Royal Geological Society of Ireland in 1879–81.

Kinahan died at his home, Woodlands, in Clontarf, co. Dublin, on 5 December 1908 and was buried in the Church of Ireland graveyard at Avoca, co. Wicklow. One of his elder brothers was John Robert Kinahan (1828–1863), sometime professor of natural history in the government school attached to the Museum of Irish Industry.

GORDON L. HERRIES DAVIES

Sources TCD, archives of the Geological Survey of Ireland · G. L. Herries Davies, *North from the Hook: 150 years of the Geological Survey of Ireland* (1995) · H. Leonard and R. Clark, 'George Henry Kinahan', *Geological Magazine*, new ser., 5th decade, 6 (1909), 142–3 · *Irish Naturalist*, 18 (1909), 29 · Royal Irish Acad., Kinahan MSS

Archives Royal Irish Acad., corresp. and papers

Likenesses photograph, repro. in Leonard and Clark, *George Henry Kinahan*, 142 · photograph, repro. in *Irish Naturalist* · photograph, repro. in Herries Davies, *North from the Hook*

Wealth at death £314 10s. 4d.: administration with will, 27 June 1909, CGPLA Ire.

Kinahan, Sir Robert George Caldwell [Robin] (1916–1997), businessman and politician, was born on 24 September 1916 in Belfast, the younger son and second child in the family of two sons and three daughters of Henry Kinahan, wine merchant, of Low Wood, Belfast, and his wife (Blanche) Ulaleni (Ula), daughter of Charles Grierson, dean of Belfast and later bishop of Down, Connor, and Dromore. The family came originally from co. Cork and became whiskey distillers in Dublin, where Robert's great-great-grandfather was lord mayor in 1853. His grandfather, Frederick Kinahan, founded the firm Lyle and Kinahan, wine merchants, in Belfast. After attending Stowe School (1929–33) Kinahan joined the family business and won a Vintners' Company scholarship in 1937 to study the wine trade abroad for a year. He worked in Portugal, France, and Germany, learning about wine and visiting famous wine companies. Before the outbreak of the Second World War he joined an Ulster territorial regiment of the Royal Artillery, the 8th Belfast anti-aircraft regiment. He served with the British expeditionary force in France, took part in the air defence of Coventry and London, and fought in India and Burma under General Slim, ending the war as a captain. He was awarded the emergency reserve decoration in 1946. Kinahan returned to the wine business, visiting Spain for three months in 1946 to work in the cellars of Domecq and other sherry producers: this was the final stage of his Vintners' scholarship, postponed because of the Spanish Civil War. On 8 September 1950 he married Coralie Isabel (b. 1924), a painter, daughter of Captain Charles de Burgh of The Lodge, Seaforde, co. Down, a naval officer from an old Anglo-Irish family; they had two sons and three daughters.

Kinahan joined the Ulster Unionist Party after the war, and was asked to stand for election to the council of Belfast corporation. He was elected a councillor for Oldpark, a protestant working-class district, in north Belfast, in 1948. His two main achievements as a city councillor were

the building of a crematorium in Belfast, the first in Ireland, opened (despite the opposition of all the main churches) in 1961, and the banning of pigsties from the backyards of inner-city Belfast. He was high sheriff of Belfast and co. Antrim in 1955. An enthusiastic member of the Orange order, marching every 12 July in the Orange parades, he was a member of Eldon Lodge no. 7, a political lodge, whose members included many Unionist politicians, including John Miller Andrews, prime minister of Northern Ireland from 1940 to 1943, and Bryan Faulkner, prime minister from 1971 to 1972. He was elected to Stormont, the Northern Ireland parliament, as MP for Clifton ward, in 1958, but resigned after a few months to become lord mayor of Belfast in 1959, a position he held for two years. He was knighted in 1961, and left local politics in 1963 to devote himself to his business interests.

A shrewd businessman, Kinahan became chairman of a number of Ulster firms in the 1960s, including Inglis Bakery, a subsidiary of Rank, Hovis, McDougall, from 1962 to 1982; E. T. Green Animal Feeding Stuffs, from 1964 to 1982; and Old Bushmills Whiskey Distillery. After Lyle and Kinahan was sold to Bass Charrington, the brewery group, in 1963, Kinahan remained as chairman until 1978. He was also chairman of the Ulster Bank, a subsidiary of National Westminster Bank, from 1970 to 1982, with a seat on the board of National Westminster Bank in London, and a director of Gallahers Cigarettes, Standard Telephone and Cable, Abbey Life, and Eagle Star Insurance. In the early 1970s he was named the top businessman in Ulster, which made him an IRA target. He was chairman of the Ulster Confederation of British Industry. He also undertook a large amount of charitable and voluntary work. He was treasurer of the friends of Belfast Cathedral for many years, and supported the Ulster Defence Regiment widows fund and the Orange widows and orphans fund. He served on the advisory council of the Ulster Defence Regiment, and was lord lieutenant of Belfast from 1985 to 1991.

When the 'troubles' started in 1969 Kinahan remained committed to the union, continuing to believe that the Orange order's loyalty to the crown was vital to the future of Ulster. Unlike many Unionists he agreed, reluctantly, to serve on the short-lived Northern Ireland Advisory Commission, set up with seven protestant and four Catholic members by William Whitelaw, secretary of state for Northern Ireland, after the suspension of Stormont in 1972 and the imposition of direct rule. Although passionate about Ulster at a time when many were leaving Northern Ireland for an easier life in England, he was not an extremist. A protestant, he tried to create links both with the Catholic population of Belfast, and with the Republic of Ireland. As lord mayor he visited other mayors south of the border, and entertained Catholic cardinals. As chairman of Ulster Bank he made a point of visiting every branch in Northern and southern Ireland. He was popular with the Catholic employees of Lyle and Kinahan, many of whom cheered him when he walked with his lodge in the Orange order parades. He angered the more extreme members of the order in 1968 when he gave away his wife's cousin, a protestant, in marriage to a Catholic, in a Catholic chapel, and also attended a Catholic funeral, and was nearly expelled from the order. Tall and elegantly dressed, he had a courteous and affable manner. He was an excellent tennis player, and a skilful dancer, but in later years he developed severe back problems.

In 1963 Kinahan bought Castle Upton, Templepatrick, a medieval house built by the knights hospitaller and redesigned by Robert Adam in the eighteenth century, the only Robert Adam house in Ireland. He and his wife restored the dilapidated mansion and 300 acres of grounds. He died on 2 May 1997 at the Studio House, 1 The Adam Yard, the small house in the grounds of Castle Upton which they had built and moved into during the last years of his life. He was cremated; a small memorial service was held for him at St Anne's Cathedral, Belfast, on 1 June. Kinahan was survived by his wife, two sons, and two daughters, one daughter having predeceased him. His wife published their joint autobiography, *Behind Every Great Man …?*, in 1992.   ANNE PIMLOTT BAKER

Sources C. Kinahan and R. Kinahan, *Behind every great man …?* (1992) • J. F. Harbinson, *The Ulster unionist party, 1882–1973* (1973) • *The Times* (5 May 1997) • *The Times* (21 May 1997) • *The Independent* (27 May 1997) • *Daily Telegraph* (19 May 1997) • *WWW* • Burke, *Peerage* • *CGPLA Eng. & Wales* (1997)

Likenesses C. de Burgh, portrait, 1961, repro. in Kinahan and Kinahan, *Behind every great man*, cover • photograph, repro. in *The Times* (21 May 1997) • photograph, repro. in *Daily Telegraph* • photograph, repro. in *The Independent*

Wealth at death £180,000: probate, 1997, *CGPLA Eng. & Wales*

Kincaid, Alexander (1710–1777), bookseller and printer, was born in Falkirk on 17 March 1710, the son of James Kincaid, of the Kincaids of Bantaskine, and Isabell Russall. He was apprenticed to the bookseller James M'Euen or McEwen and eventually succeeded to his master's well-situated bookshop at the east end of the Luckenbooths, in the centre of Edinburgh High Street, which he supplemented at various times with a printing office, a warehouse, and an auction room. Upon completion of his apprenticeship, he was made a burgess and guild brother on 20 March 1734, and three years later was elected to the town council, where he would later serve as a bailie on six occasions (1738, 1746, 1747, 1748, 1750, and 1751; elected but declined in 1772), and briefly as provost in 1776-7.

Kincaid launched his career in 1735 by co-publishing and printing, with Robert Fleming, a successful newspaper, the *Edinburgh Evening Courant*, which had been founded by M'Euen in 1718. During the 1740s he was involved in the successful legal defence of the right of Scots to reprint English publications no longer protected by statutory copyright. The few new books he published at that time included the first popular work by David Hume, *Essays, Moral and Political* (1741–2), and an important early book published by Henry Home, later Lord Kames, *Essays upon Several Subjects Concerning British Antiquities* (1747). He also continued M'Euen's tradition of managing large book auctions, and at least six of his printed auction catalogues have survived from the period 1736–49. He was successful enough to obtain the reversion of the office of his majesty's printer and stationer for Scotland, the patent

for which passed the great seal on 21 June 1749 and was in effect, for Kincaid and his heirs, for forty-one years from 6 July 1757. Among other things, this office gave him the lucrative monopoly on the printing of Scottish bibles, catechisms, and psalters.

On 13 October 1751 Kincaid married Caroline Kerr (*d.* 1774), daughter of the late Lord Charles Kerr and Janet Murray; she was the granddaughter of the first marquess of Lothian and, after 1760, the sister-in-law of the third marquess. She was a woman of sufficient culture and intellect to maintain a separate library and to merit an obituary in the *London Chronicle* in August 1774. In the same year as his marriage, Kincaid took as his business partner Alexander Donaldson, with whom he continued publishing occasional new work while increasing his business as a reprinter of English classics, producing, for example, multi-volume editions of Milton (1755) and Swift (1756).

After the breakup of the partnership in May 1758, Kincaid and his new partner, his former apprentice John Bell, did not rival Donaldson as literary reprinters, but they displayed a much deeper commitment to publishing new works by Scottish authors. From 1758 until the dissolution of the firm in May 1771, Kincaid and Bell, in association with the firm of another of M'Euen's former apprentices, Andrew Millar of London, and Millar's junior partner and successor Thomas Cadell, issued the first editions of Adam Smith's *Theory of Moral Sentiments* (1759), Lord Kames's *Elements of Criticism* (1762), Thomas Reid's *Inquiry into the Human Mind* (1764), Adam Ferguson's *Essay on the History of Civil Society* (1767), and other key texts of the Scottish Enlightenment. Some of these works were printed by William Strahan, who may also have been one of M'Euen's former apprentices, and who once remarked that Kincaid was 'open-hearted and generous to a very great degree' and 'the oldest Friend I had in the World' (Strahan to William Creech, 30 Jan 1777, NA Scot., RH 4/26).

By the 1760s, if not earlier, Kincaid was leaving most of his firm's work to his junior partner. In 1764 he admitted to his household William Creech, a newly orphaned nineteen-year-old whose parents had been the recipients of patronage from the noble house of Lothian to which Kincaid's wife belonged. Mrs Kincaid hoped that Creech would provide a role model for their son, Alexander, who would later make his way on the fringes of the book trade, and would write a *History of Edinburgh* (1787), but who was not cut out to take over his father's multifaceted business. That opportunity fell to Creech, who replaced Bell as Kincaid's partner in May 1771 on the strong recommendation of Strahan, and took over the business two years later, when Kincaid withdrew. After 1773 few new books bore his imprint, though in 1776 he was principally responsible for contracting to publish a volume of sermons by Hugh Blair, who told Strahan on 29 October that 'Mr Kincaid, our present Lord Provost, who is my old acquaintance & Friend was very desirous of being concerned in this publication and offered me £100 for the Property, which I have accepted' (NL Scot., MS 1707, fols. 4–5). However, Kincaid had died by the time the book appeared in early February

1777, and the enormous profits and prestige of Blair's extraordinarily successful five volumes of *Sermons* (1777–1801) fell to Creech and his London partners, Strahan, Cadell, and their heirs.

Kincaid was a member of the freemason lodge Canongate Kilwinning no. 2 from 5 December 1771, and of the Society of Captains of the Trained Bands from 3 November 1775. Elected lord provost of Edinburgh in September 1776, he served only four months before his sudden death on 21 January 1777. While in office he was elected praeses of the annual committee of the convention of royal burghs on 20 November 1776, and presided at its next meeting on 9 December. His funeral on 23 January 1777 was attended by large crowds and featured one of the grandest processions in the history of Edinburgh. A year later the *Edinburgh Evening Courant* announced the sale of his 'large and convenient house in the Cowgate', with a coach house and stable for six horses, and soon afterwards his library was put up for sale. RICHARD B. SHER

Sources C. B. Boog-Watson, ed., *Register of Edinburgh apprentices, 1701–1755* (1929) • W. J. Couper, *The Edinburgh periodical press*, 2 vols. (1908) • R. Fleming, 'An account of the life of the late Mr William Creech', in W. Creech, *Edinburgh fugitive pieces* (1815), xi–xli • *The lord provosts of Edinburgh, 1296 to 1932* (1932) [annotated copy in Edinburgh city chambers] • J. Lee, *Memorial for the Bible societies in Scotland* (1824) • W. McDougall, 'Copyright litigation in the court of session, 1738–1749', *Edinburgh Bibliographical Society Transactions*, 5/5 (1971–87), 2–31 • J. Morris, 'Scottish book trade index', www.nls.uk/catalogues/resources/sbti/ • J. D. Pridie, *An historical sketch of the municipal constitution of the city of Edinburgh* (1826) • *Edinburgh Evening Courant* (14 Jan 1778) • NA Scot., RH 4/26 • NL Scot., MS 1707, fols. 4–5 • *Edinburgh Weekly Magazine* (23 Jan 1777)
Wealth at death substantial property

Kincaid, Sir John (1787–1862), army officer, was born at Dalheath House, near Falkirk, Stirlingshire, in January 1787, the second son of John Kincaid of Dalheath and his wife, daughter of John Gaff. Kincaid's father, a 'small lowland Scotch laird … was unfortunately cut off in early life', leaving a 'young family' (Kincaid, *Random Shots*, 3). Having been educated at Polmont School, Polmont, Stirlingshire, John Kincaid grew into 'a lean lank fellow' over 6 feet tall (Kincaid, *Adventures*, 9) and served as a lieutenant in the North York militia. On 27 April 1809, with a draft of volunteers from this militia, he joined the 95th foot (which was to be restyled the Rifle brigade on 16 February 1816) at Hythe, Kent, as a second lieutenant, in time to sail for Walcheren 'where we remained about three weeks, playing at soldiers, smoking *mynheer's* long clay pipes, and drinking his *vrow's* butter-milk, for which I paid liberally with my precious blood to their infernal musquittos [sic]' (ibid., 2).

Kincaid was weakened by 'a horrible ague', but after convalescing in Scotland he returned to Hythe in spring 1810 and went with the 95th's 1st battalion to reinforce Wellington in Spain following the battle of Busaco as his allied troops retreated towards the lines of Torres Vedras, the Anglo-Portuguese fortification defending Lisbon. With the 95th 'Johnny' Kincaid pursued the French when they withdrew from outside the lines in March 1811; he took part in actions at Santarem, Pombal, Redinha, Casal Nova, Foz d'Arouce (where he was concussed and believed

dead), Sabugal, Fuentes d'Oñnoro, Fuente Guinaldo, and Aldea de Ponte. After promotion to first lieutenant on 23 May 1811 Kincaid commanded the battalion's highland company and led a detachment of the storming party at the siege of Ciudad Rodrigo in January 1812; at Badajoz he was adjutant of four companies, 'who were to line the crest of the glacis, and to fire at the ramparts and the top of the left breach' (Kincaid, *Adventures*, 130). He fought at Salamanca and entered Madrid with Wellington in August.

During the withdrawal to winter quarters near Ciudad Rodrigo after three months, Kincaid acted as brigade-major to the 1st brigade of the light division, taking part in the skirmish at Sanmunoz. When Wellington launched another offensive into Spain in 1813, Kincaid was in action at Munos and San Milan, Vitoria, in the Pyrenees, on the Nivelle and Nive rivers, near Bayonne in December 1813, and at the final battle of Toulouse (April 1814). On 21 July 1814 he became adjutant of the 1st battalion, and was recalled from a shooting leave in Scotland to fight at Quatre Bras and Waterloo, where his horse was killed under him. Of Waterloo he wrote: 'The smoke hung so thick about us that, although not more than eighty yards asunder, we could only distinguish each other by the flashes of the pieces … [we were] so many hours enveloped in darkness' (Kincaid, *Adventures*, 254, 256). Having been posted with the 95th immediately east of the Brussels–Charleroi Road, Kincaid became heavily involved in fighting for the knoll and sand-pit opposite La Haye-Sainte.

Kincaid, who was promoted captain in the rifle brigade on 25 November 1826, sold out and retired in June 1831. He was appointed exon of the yeomen of the guard on 25 October 1844, and was knighted on 30 June 1852 on becoming senior exon. In 1847 he was appointed inspector of prisons for Scotland and in 1850 also inspector of factories for Scotland and the north of England. He resigned both appointments through ill health shortly before his death.

In 1830 Kincaid published *Adventures in the Rifle Brigade*, an account of his military life, 1809–15, dedicated to Major-General Sir Andrew Barnard KCB. The book has been reprinted frequently, and in the introduction to the 1929 edition Sir John Fortescue praised Kincaid's descriptions of individuals and 'the daily routine of the campaign, which are of real historical value'. He concluded: 'so long as the Rifle Brigade lasts his *Adventures* will be a text-book for all good riflemen' (Kincaid, *Adventures*, v). Fortescue was, however, led to condemn 'a certain flippancy and Jacosity in his narrative' of the war (ibid.): 'we found their whole army drawn out on the plain, near Redhina, and instantly quarreled with them on a large scale'; the French General Loison's captured Portuguese aide-de-camp 'looked very like a man who would be hanged', his 'handsome' Spanish wife 'very like a woman who would get married again' (ibid., 35, 46). But descriptions of camp life were vivid: lying at night with only a coat or blanket as inadequate protection against the dew and 'a green sod or a smooth stone for a pillow' (ibid., 34). And Kincaid graphically illustrated other privations, such as lack of money through arrears of pay, hunger on the march, and the need to cut the boots off his swollen feet after six days in action. Kincaid's second book, *Random Shots of a Rifleman* (1835), essentially a collection of anecdotes, dedicated to Major-General Lord Fitzroy Somerset KCB, was in Fortescue's estimation 'of not quite equal merit' (ibid., v).

Kincaid was awarded the military general service medal (or Peninsular silver medal) with nine clasps and the Waterloo medal. Curiously, entries in editions of the *Army List*, 1810–17, name him 'Kincaird'. Kincaid died of liver disease on 22 April 1862 at 7 Cambridge Terrace, Hastings, Sussex, survived by his wife, Louisa.

H. M. CHICHESTER, rev. ROGER T. STEARN

Sources *Dod's Peerage* (1852) · *Dod's Peerage* (1858) · C. W. Cope, *History of the rifle brigade* (1880) · *GM*, 3rd ser., 12 (1862), 658 · *Army List* · J. Kincaid, *Adventures in the rifle brigade in the Peninsula, France, and the Netherlands, from 1809 to 1815*, ed. J. W. Fortescue (1929) · J. Kincaid, *Random shots of a rifleman* (1835) · Boase, *Mod. Eng. biog.* · *CGPLA Eng. & Wales* (1862)

Archives W. Sussex RO, letters to duke of Richmond

Wealth at death under £450: probate, 7 May 1862, *CGPLA Eng. & Wales*

Kincairney. For this title name *see* Gloag, William Ellis, Lord Kincairney (1828–1909).

Kincardine. For this title name *see* Bruce, Alexander, second earl of Kincardine (*c*.1629–1680); Bruce, Thomas, seventh earl of Elgin and eleventh earl of Kincardine (1766–1841); Bruce, James, eighth earl of Elgin and twelfth earl of Kincardine (1811–1863); Bruce, Victor Alexander, ninth earl of Elgin and thirteenth earl of Kincardine (1849–1917).

Kincraigie, Thomas (*d*. 1564). *See under* College of justice, procurators of the (*act*. 1532).

Kinder, Philip (*b*. 1597, *d*. in or after 1665), writer and physician, was born on 12 April 1597, the second son of William Kinder (*c*.1540–1623), of Sneinton, Nottinghamshire, and Katherine, daughter of William Dunn of Nottingham. His father had graduated from Brasenose College, Oxford, with a degree in medicine, and Philip chose the same profession, graduating from Pembroke College, Cambridge, in 1616 with a licence to practise medicine, which he was doing 'from his chamber by the East gates in Leicester' by 1620, apparently following Paracelsian principles (MS Ashmole 788, fol. 48; MS Ashmole 429, fol. 43). At some point he married Elizabeth, daughter of John Barkley of Warwickshire, but there were no children.

After his father's death in 1623, Kinder moved back to Sneinton, and by 1629 he was receiving an annuity of £20 p.a. from the Pierrepoints, a powerful family of that town. For reasons probably arising from Kinder's lack of deference, this relationship turned to mutual hostility which eventually caused Henry Pierrepoint and three of his servants to attack Kinder in the cloister of Westminster Abbey in the year 1630. According to Kinder, who took his case to the Star Chamber, they had meant to kill him. Pierrepoint received a royal pardon, and, despite further suits, Kinder was unable to receive satisfactory compensation for his injuries.

In 1640 Kinder was at York with the king's army, probably in the service of the Hastings family of Ashby-de-la-Zouch. He completed a detailed survey of the monuments in York Minster, but the manuscript was lost at Nottingham in 1643 (MS Ashmole 788, fol. 188). After the outbreak of the civil war, the royalist cavalry commander Henry Hastings appointed Kinder to be his agent at the Oxford court, but Kinder complained of being ill rewarded for his services. In 1649 he contributed a Latin memorial inscription and a short English poem to *Lachrymae musarum* (1649), the memorial volume for Hastings's nephew. Kinder was in the garrison of Ashby Castle when it fell to the parliament in 1646. In the period 1650–54 Kinder was at Aston upon Trent; his fortunes were at a low ebb, and he had to remind various influential acquaintances of their promises of money and help.

Kinder wrote Latin, studied Greek and Hebrew, and understood Spanish and Italian. His own writings in verse and prose, Latin and English, include some unusually accomplished verses as well as drama, topography, genealogy, astrology, and literary criticism. Throughout his life he composed Latin epitaphs for his friends, family, and acquaintances.

While at university Kinder had written a Latin comedy, 'Silvia', and a theological treatise which survives in his miscellany. He also composed 'The Ball', a text for a revel or series of danced entries representing the ancient and modern poets (MS Ashmole 788, fols. 205, 103, 3). In 1629 he contributed a Latin elegiac verse to a posthumous volume of verse by his friend and correspondent Sir John Beaumont of Grace Dieu (J. Beaumont, *Bosworth-Field*, 1629). In 1628 he began to develop his 'Trismegeticall Invention', a 'Universal Character' consisting of a system of number-symbols with which, he claimed, any document could be translated into at least ten languages within two hours. In this he anticipated the 1653 *Logopandecteision* of Sir Thomas Urquhart, and like Urquhart he composed a pedigree for himself beginning with Adam and continuing 'without intermission of Centurie or name' (Kinder, *Surfeit*, 28–30; MS Ashmole 788, fols. 50–51, 162).

Probably in the 1630s, and as a bid for royal patronage, Kinder composed 'Eugenia', a Latin treatise that purports to trace the descent from the protoplast Adam, 'of all the Emperors, Kings and Princes of the universal world' (Kinder, *Surfeit*, 23–4). His royalism also expressed itself in the hagiographic tone of his Latin life of Charles I and his fine verses 'The Antiparode' which end 'Honour and Beautie are but Dreames / Since Charles and Mary lost theire Beames' (MS Ashmole 788, fol. 22*v*). In his 'Terminalia' he prophetically interprets the writings of Esdras, John the Divine, Merlin, Ambrose, and St Malachias the Primate as histories of the world, the church, England, and the papacy (MS Ashmole 788, fols. 64–102). In 1636 he provided prefatory verses for William Sampson's *Virtus post funera vivit*. He may have translated Boethius's *De consolatione philosophiae* (MS Ashmole 788, fol. 171).

In the 1650s he composed a pair of treatises, the first upholding papism from the church fathers, the second protestantism. Kinder's purpose was to show the irrelevance of the patristic authors to modern religious controversy (Kinder, *Surfeit*, 10–13). At about the same time, he also wrote 'The Court of Astraea with the Arraignment of Romances', which looks back to the bonfire of the romances in *Don Quixote*, and forwards to Boileau's 'Les héros de roman' (written in 1666). In 1656 there appeared his only published work, *The Surfeit to ABC*, a series of meditations on books and ideas, including the observation that historians of classical antiquity are too naïve in their use of literature as evidence:

> As if one in future ages should make all *England* in ages past to be a *Bartholomew*-Faire, because *Ben. Johnson* hath writ it. Or that the condition of all our *English* women may be drawn out of *Shackespeers* merry wifes of *Windsor*. (Kinder, *Surfeit*, 58)

As well as being an astronomer, Kinder was an expert in the 'art of *shadowes*': he produced logarithmic calculations for 'sun-dialls' and an *ad hoc* method for calculating the time by measuring shadows (Kinder, *Surfeit*, 60–61; MS Ashmole 788, fols. 206, 210). His miscellany manuscript contains not only literary and antiquarian material but also accounts of prophecies and of a vision seen on the night of 16 November 1658 (MS Ashmole 788, fol. 102).

In 1658–60 Kinder was living at Wilson, near Melbourne in Derbyshire. By 1661 he was living at Walton-on-Trent where he consolidated his epistolary friendship with Charles Cotton, who encouraged him to write his best-known work, the project for a 'History of Darby-shire' (1663). About 1662 he moved back to Nottingham, whence he wrote his last dated letters in 1665.

PETER DAVIDSON and IAN WILLIAM McLELLAN

Sources P. Kinder, miscellany, Bodl. Oxf., MS Ashmole 788 · P. Kinder, *The surfeit to ABC* (1656) · E. B. Thomas, 'Philip Kinder: author of "History of Derbyshire"', *Derbyshire Miscellany*, 4/2 (1967), 99–109 · Bodl. Oxf., MS Ashmole 429 · *CSP dom.*, 1637–9
Archives Bodl. Oxf., collections and *Prolusion*

Kindersley, David Guy Barnabas (1915–1995), letter-cutter and alphabet designer, was born at Codicote, Hertfordshire, on 11 June 1915, the fifth and youngest child of Major Guy Molesworth Kindersley (1877–1956), stockbroker and MP, and his wife, Kathleen Agnes Rhoda (1871–1950), eldest daughter of Sir Edmund Harry Elton, arts and crafts potter and eighth baronet of Clevedon Court, Somerset, and his wife, Agnes Mary.

Two childhood homes in Hertfordshire—one with an archaeological site in its garden and the second adjacent to a churchyard—ensured that Kindersley's earliest childhood games took place surrounded by stone carvings and inscriptions. After four years at St Cyprian's, a preparatory school in Eastbourne, he was educated at Marlborough College, Wiltshire. He left school at fifteen through ill health and began to experiment with carving when convalescing at home. He later took drawing classes at the Académie Julian in Paris and worked for a firm of Italian marble carvers, carving in stone the clay forms modelled by established sculptors. Reading Eric Gill's *Art Nonsense*

and Other Essays (1929) led him to despise copying, believing instead that the individual who conceived an idea should be responsible for making their vision in its final three-dimensional form.

In 1934 Kindersley made contact with Eric Gill and secured himself a position at Gill's Pigotts workshop, near High Wycombe, Buckinghamshire. There was no official apprenticeship but the word apprentice was generally used to describe his role. He was introduced to the craft of letter carving in stone for the first time—learning to design and cut unique inscriptions with a hammer and chisel. Gill was preoccupied writing *The Necessity of Belief* (1936). Its call for social unity and a 'brotherhood' of men fuelled Kindersley's interest in the integration of work, family, and social life. He was never a Roman Catholic but he developed a lifelong interest in philosophy and faith as the driving forces behind man as a sincere, creative maker.

Kindersley left Pigotts on 16 June 1936. Still intent on becoming a sculptor he rented a remote cottage near Oakhurst in Sussex. Disappointed in his efforts he apparently buried many of his works in the garden. Gill was still sending him lettering commissions and the proximity of Horsham Art School, headed by the painter Vincent Lines, enabled him to teach a lettering class. Kindersley developed an interest in progressive education, the Bruderhof communities, and the writings of P. D. Ouspensky.

In 1939 Kindersley took on the tenancy of the smallest pub in England, the Smiths' Arms, near his new home in Godmanstone, Dorset. He tried to run his home as a self-sufficient community, while he continued to cut inscriptions. Even in his early twenties his distinctive physical appearance was remarked upon—hair worn long at the sides, oiled Russian wool roll-neck jumpers, and crisp blue linen shirts stood out in a rural community. In later years he was remembered for his wiry white beard and grand collection of ties.

With the outbreak of the Second World War, Kindersley registered as a conscientious objector and received a complete exemption from national service. On 14 September 1939 he married Christine Sharpe and in 1942, with a young family, Kindersley returned to Pigotts to work in Eric Gill's former lettering workshop. Since Gill's death in 1940 it had urgently required skilled craftsmen.

In 1946 Kindersley set up his own letter-cutting workshop at Dales Barn, next to his cottage in Barton, near Cambridge. He began cutting letters into slate, a material he had rarely used before, and created some subtly flourished italics with, for instance, his 'Edward Lively & Richard Thompson' inscription in St Edmund's Church, Cambridge (1947). In later years he was best known for such letter-forms with their increasingly exuberant flourishes.

Commissions in the post-war period included the cut lettering for the Trinity College war memorial, Cambridge (1951) and for the fascia of the Wellcome Building, London (1956). Extensive work on maps, inscriptions, and carvings was undertaken at the American military cemetery, Cambridgeshire (1951–6). His work on heraldry displayed a gift for reducing elaborate designs to unfussy, modern forms—see for instance his carvings for the Fairhaven family at Anglesey Abbey, Cambridgeshire (1952–6). Lettering commissions for glass-engraving and book jackets were also undertaken. Bookplates included a design for the Albert Sperison collection of Eric Gill material at the Richard A. Gleeson Library, University of San Francisco (1977).

The workshop took on a number of apprentices and assistants. Kindersley did not believe that a pupil could learn by hasty cramming: 'those god given periods of boredom should not be denied. These are periods of digestion and relating of knowledge and experience … as he grows in mastery so can his craft like a cup receive more and more stimulus poured into it' (D. Kindersley, 'Education in the workshop', Cardozo-Kindersley Workshop, Cambridge). In the late 1940s, he also set up a school at Dales Barn for his own young children, inspired by Herbert Read's *Education through Art* (1943).

The university printer at Cambridge University Press, Brooke Crutchley, was an influential figure in Kindersley's emerging career. Among other projects, he encouraged his designs for a new street name alphabet which was purchased by the Ministry of Transport (1950). Kindersley became passionately interested in the spacing of letters to ensure maximum legibility and this led in the 1960s to the development of an optical spacing machine. He explained the process in *Optical Letter Spacing for New Printing Systems* (1976). In the 1980s this spacing method developed into a computer program, Logos (Cambridge Supervision Ltd). He was also an adviser to the Shell film unit from 1949 to 1958 and consultant to Letraset International from 1964 until 1988. He designed Octavian typeface with Will Carter for which matrices were issued by Monotype in 1962. Kindersley's other typefaces include Itec Bookface.

Kindersley believed that the responsibility for the conception, design, and craftsmanship of an object belonged under one workshop roof among people who understood each other and the materials with which they worked. With this aim in mind he did his best to ensure that discussions with clients, designing, drawing out on to stone, cutting letters with hand tools, painting, gilding, and sometimes masoning were all part of everyday workshop life. His concern for public recognition of well-made objects was the driving force behind the Designer Craftsman Society and Shop, Cambridge, in the early 1950s. He briefly held the post of president of the Crafts Council of Great Britain in 1963.

Kindersley's first marriage ended in divorce in 1954. Three years later, on 21 June 1957, he married Barbara Pym Eyre Petrie, an artist. In 1967, the year the workshop moved to Chesterton Tower, Cambridge, Kindersley was also appointed senior research fellow at the William Andrews Clark Memorial Library at the University of California, Los Angeles, helping to compile their Eric Gill collection. His recollections of his early training were first published as *Mr Eric Gill* (1967). Subsequently he drew a number of experimental designs for alphabets which culminated in limited edition book collaborations with the printer Christopher Skelton: *Variations on the Theme of 26 Letters* (1969) and *Graphic Sayings* (1971) in addition to an exhibition of hand-coloured lithographs and vacuum formed plastic and perspex alphabets at The Folio Society, London, 1969.

In 1977 the workshop moved to Victoria Road, Cambridge. Lydia Helena (Lida) Lopes-Cardozo had joined the workshop in 1976 and became a business partner in 1981. After a divorce from his second wife Kindersley married Lida in 1986 and they continued to work together and bring up three young sons until Kindersley's death, at the workshop where he lived at 152 Victoria Road, Cambridge, on 2 February 1995. He was buried at St Luke's Church, Cambridge. His later commissions included Barbara Hepworth's tombstone (1979); a relief carving of Sir Philip Sidney, St Paul's Cathedral (1986); a range of inscriptions at St Albans Abbey, Ampleforth Abbey, and Ruskin Gallery, Sheffield (between 1979 and 1994); in addition to stations of the cross for the Oratory School, London (1994) and the design for the British Library gates (1994). Original examples of lettering in public collections include those in Glasgow Gallery of Modern Art; the Victoria and Albert Museum, London; Museum of Modern Art (New York); University of Texas at Austin; and University of California (Los Angeles).   LOTTIE HOARE

Sources L. Hoare, 'David Kindersley's early years, 1915–1956', priv. coll. · M. Shaw, *David Kindersley: his work and workshop* (1989) [Cardozo Kindersley Editions] · D. Kindersley and L. L. Cardozo, *Letters slate cut: workshop practice and the making of letters* (1981) · P. W. Nash and S. Bradbury, *Folio 50: a bibliography of the Folio Society, 1947–1996* (1997) · *CGPLA Eng. & Wales* (1995) · private information (2004) **Archives** Cardozo Kindersley Workshop, Cambridge, MSS | Tate collection, Vincent Lines MSS **Wealth at death** under £125,000: probate, 18 Sept 1995, *CGPLA Eng. & Wales*

Kindersley, Hugh Kenyon Molesworth, second Baron Kindersley (1899–1976), merchant banker and soldier, was born at 20 Egerton Terrace, London, on 7 May 1899, the second son and second child in the family of four sons and two daughters of Robert Molesworth *Kindersley, first Baron Kindersley (1871–1954), merchant banker, and his wife, Gladys Margaret (1875–1968), daughter of Major-General J. P. Beadle. He was educated at Eton College. He succeeded his father as second baron in 1954, his older brother having been killed in action in 1917.

In 1919, after war service Kindersley joined Lazard Brothers & Co., the leading merchant bank, where his father was chairman and where he received a favoured apprenticeship. He was sent out to work in Lazards' businesses in Paris, New York, and Madrid, and with correspondents in Toronto and Berlin. In 1921 he married Nancy Farnsworth (d. 1977), daughter of Dr Geoffrey Boyd of Toronto; they had one son and two daughters.

Kindersley's early specialization was acceptance finance, in which Lazards was carving an important business. He would also have played a role, subsidiary to that of his father and Robert Brand, in Lazards' important bond-issuing business, largely for overseas sovereign clients, and, in the 1930s, in its corporate finance work for British businesses. In 1927 he was appointed a managing director, and in 1932 he spent seven months in Stockholm sorting out the chaos left by the crash of Kreuger and Toll, makers of matches and the Swedish finance empire of Ivar Kreuger, an old connection of Lazards.

In 1953 Kindersley succeeded his father as chairman, when his co-senior was Brand, then aged seventy-five. 'I am the head and looked upon I think as the head of Lazards everywhere, which indeed I am', he said in 1957, 'but in the firm [of seven managing directors] I am *primus inter pares*' (*The Times*, 12 Dec 1957). 'His eminence in the City came not so much from creative financial ability', wrote a biographer, 'but from qualities such as leadership, integrity, loyalty to his colleagues and willingness to accept responsibility for the acts ... of his subordinates' (*DNB*).

In the 1950s and for much of the 1960s Lazards, along with most City merchant banks, rested on its laurels, producing few outstanding entrepreneurs. During the highly controversial 'aluminium war' (1958–9), when Lazards unsuccessfully defended British Aluminium against a ferocious bid orchestrated by Siegmund Warburg, who contemptuously swept aside City practice and decorum, Kindersley was as wrong-footed and as outraged as any of the old school. He gave up the chairmanship in 1964 but continued as a director until 1971.

Kindersley was a major and influential City figure. On his return from war, in 1947 he joined the Bank of England's court, and he remained a director until 1967; for the bank he proved to be a reliable source of City opinion. In 1928 the old and prestigious Royal Exchange Assurance appointed him to its court; he was its governor (1955–68) and the first chairman (1968–70) of the Guardian Royal Exchange. He was also on the boards of, *inter alia*, the British Match Corporation Ltd (1946–69, chairman 1953–9), the British Bank of London and South America (1938–60), Rolls-Royce Ltd (1951–71, chairman 1957–68), and S. H. Pearson & Son Ltd (1953–64). In 1971 he described himself as 'practically entirely out of business' (Bank of England archives, G24/9).

Kindersley's career was marred on two occasions. In 1957, with two other bank directors, he was advised confidentially of a forthcoming change in bank rate. When suspicions were aroused that market transactions, especially in gilt-edged securities, had been effected as a result of inside knowledge, the Parker tribunal investigated. Kindersley appeared before it to explain large gilt-edged transactions at no less than three companies he chaired—Lazards, Royal Exchange, and British Match—immediately ahead of the change and his position was not eased by allegations made privately to the bank by an ex-Lazards' employee. Kindersley was entirely exonerated but undoubtedly he had been humiliated.

Perhaps more damaging to his business reputation was the collapse of Rolls-Royce in 1971. During Kindersley's chairmanship, which ended in 1968, the company had set out to develop the RB211 aircraft engine for the first generation of wide-bodied jets, but it had massively underestimated the challenge. 'The whole future of the Company was hazarded on one contract', inspectors later wrote:

'Once the contract was signed no system of financial control could have significantly influenced the course of events' (McGrindle and Godfrey, 357). Rolls-Royce was rescued by being taken into public ownership; its final deficiency was £61 million. Kindersley, along with the rest of the board, accepted collective responsibility and resigned.

Kindersley fought bravely in two world wars. In 1917–19 he served with the Scots Guards and was awarded an MC. In 1939, notwithstanding his forty years, he rejoined his old regiment as a lieutenant and in 1944, as a brigadier, he commanded the 6th air landing brigade during the Normandy landings, when he received severe leg injuries which forced his retirement and left him with a permanent limp. He was appointed MBE in 1941 and CBE in 1945.

His wartime experiences left Kindersley keenly interested in the well-being of the medical profession. In 1959 he raised, through an appeal, over £3 million on behalf of the Royal College of Surgeons to finance the construction of new buildings and research and postgraduate education. From 1962 he chaired the independent review body on doctors' and dentists' pay, but he resigned in 1970, along with the entire panel, when the government rejected its recommendations. From 1966 he was chairman, and from 1971 president, of the Arthritis and Rheumatism Council and he chaired the Officers' Association from 1946 to 1956.

Kindersley died on 6 October 1976 at his country home, Ramhurst Manor, Leigh, near Tonbridge, Kent. He was succeeded in the barony by his son, Robert Hugh Molesworth Kindersley.   JOHN ORBELL

Sources *DNB* · *The Times* (8 Oct 1976) · *The Times* (12 Dec 1957), 4f [evidence at bank rate enquiry] · *WWW* · Burke, *Peerage* · will, proved, London, 22 March 1977 · R. A. McGrindle and P. Godfrey, *Rolls-Royce Limited: investigation under Section 165 (a)(i) of the Companies Act 1948* (1973) · J. Fforde, *The Bank of England and public policy, 1941–1958* (1992) · P. Beaver, *The match makers: the story of Bryant and May* (1985) · Bank of England archives, London, G24/9 · *CGPLA Eng. & Wales* (1977) · d. cert.

Archives Bank of England archives, London, G24/9 · IWM, letters from the western front

Wealth at death £106,109: probate, 22 March 1977, *CGPLA Eng. & Wales*

Kindersley [*née* Wicksteed], **Jemima** (1741–1809), travel writer, was born into the modest Wicksteed family on 2 October 1741 in Great Yarmouth, Norfolk, where on 19 April 1762 she married Lieutenant Nathaniel Kindersley (1732–1769) of the Royal Artillery. They met at a local ball, where he was doubtless struck by her beauty, for she became known as Pulcherrima. Their only son, Nathaniel (1763–1831), was born on 2 February 1763.

In 1764 Kindersley transferred as captain to the East India Company's Bengal artillery, and sailed for Calcutta with his wife and son. Despite her humble background and initial lack of education, Jemima Kindersley responded to the opportunities of her elevation in society. She acquired a fluent prose style, a knowledge of French, and an acquaintance with the ideas of leading philosophers such as Montesquieu, and historians of South America and Asia, which enabled her to write a confident account of her journey to India and life there, mainly in Calcutta and Allahabad, from 1764 to 1768, *Letters from the Island of Teneriffe, Brazil, the Cape of Good Hope and the East Indies*. Her work gives an interesting account of the early period of British consolidation in north India. It is also important as one of the first travel books by a woman, a field in which there were soon to be many female contributors.

The *Letters*, which contain no personal information and omit her shipwreck in Bengal, record her wide-ranging observations of local life, religion, and culture, and consider more generally the prevailing characteristics of Indian society. She approached India within the framework of Enlightenment thought and concerns elaborated particularly by Montesquieu, believing that climate shaped character, and that presumed 'oriental despotism' undermined politics, society, and military achievement, and controlled the lives of Indian women. She was particularly interested in the latter, and sought to investigate suttee. As a woman she was able to visit a zenana in Allahabad, and gives one of the earliest Western accounts of the appearance and life of Muslim women. Her careful description avoids overdramatization, but stresses the restrictions imposed on them.

Jemima Kindersley returned to England with her son in 1769 because of ill health, and her husband died in Calcutta the same year. The *Letters* were published in 1777, possibly to earn money, since she was left with only a small pension, from which she helped support her mother. Her work met with a warm response; several periodical journals published excerpts, while the *Monthly Review*, though noting that much of her information was not new, praised the narration of 'a variety of amusing particulars with much ease and simplicity, and with every mark of fidelity' (57, 1777, 243). She thus helped set the pattern for women travel writers, who were welcomed for their style and ability to popularize subject-matter which was often dry or difficult of access.

Her interest in the status and treatment of Indian women led her to give wider consideration to the role of women. However, she found that her intended work had been pre-empted by the publication in French of a book by Antoine Thomas, which she translated in 1781 as *Essay on the Character, Manners and Understanding of Women, in Different Ages*. Appended to it were two of her own essays. One incorporated ideas suggested by her experience in India and argued that women were controlled by men in direct relation to the power they possessed over them: thus Indian men, who were highly susceptible to the sexual attractions of women, curtailed their rights and freedom, while Dutchmen, 'unacquainted with that jealousy which torments a Mussulman', granted their women considerable liberty (essay 1, 225). Her second essay called for improved education for women.

She lived in Southampton and later Bath, mixing in cultivated circles. Her son joined the East India Company as a civilian; he shared his mother's literary tastes and interest in India, publishing *Specimens of Hindoo Literature* (1794).

The care of his growing family while he was in India provided an interest in her later years, though she had a reputation for irritability, the result perhaps of loneliness and the ill health from which she never fully recovered. She died in Beaumont Street, Marylebone, Middlesex, probably in April 1809, and was buried on 25 April at St Marylebone.   ROSEMARY CARGILL RAZA

Sources A. F. Kindersley, *A history of the Kindersley family* (1938), 89–100, 177–80 · Burke, *Gen. GB* (1921) · V. C. P. Hodson, *List of officers of the Bengal army, 1758–1834*, 2 (1928), 595–6 · H. D. Love, *Vestiges of old Madras, 1640–1800*, 4 vols. (1913), vol. 2, pp. 616–18 · *Monthly Review*, 57 (1777), 243 · PRO, PROB 11/1497, sig. 382
Likenesses miniature (of Kindersley?), priv. coll.
Wealth at death estate left to son Nathaniel Edward Kindersley, except for minor bequests to friends, relatives, and servants and £4500 divided among her seven grandchildren (£1000 each to the two older granddaughters, and £500 each to the remaining five grandchildren): will, PRO, PROB 11/1497, sig. 382

Kindersley, Sir Richard Torin (1792–1879), judge, eldest son of Nathaniel Edward Kindersley of Sunninghill, Berkshire, was born on 5 October 1792 at Madras, where his father was in the civil service of the East India Company. He was educated first at the East India College, Haileybury, with the intention of entering the Indian Civil Service, but afterwards went to Trinity College, Cambridge, where he was fourth wrangler, graduating BA in January 1814. In October 1815 he was elected a fellow of his college, and proceeded MA in July 1817. He was called to the bar at Lincoln's Inn on 10 February 1818, and had a considerable junior practice. In 1824 he married Mary Anne, only daughter of the Revd James Leigh Bennett of Thorpe Place, Surrey; they had four children.

Appointed king's counsel in January 1835, Kindersley took a leading position in the rolls court. In 1847 he became chancellor of the county palatine of Durham, and in March 1848 a master in chancery. On 20 October 1851 he was appointed a vice-chancellor and knighted. His judgments are mainly reported in Drewry's *Reports*, Drewry and Smale's *Reports*, and the *Law Reports* (Equity Series, 1 and 2). He retired from the bench in 1866, when he became a member of the privy council, and received a pension of £3500 a year. He died at his residence, Clyffe, near Dorchester, Dorset, on 22 October 1879.

J. A. HAMILTON, *rev.* HUGH MOONEY

Sources *The Times* (25 Oct 1879) · *Law Times* (8 Nov 1879), 32 · *Law Journal* (6 Dec 1879), 657, 723
Likenesses G. Richmond, drawing, Lincoln's Inn, London
Wealth at death under £70,000: probate, 15 Nov 1879, *CGPLA Eng. & Wales*

Kindersley, Robert Molesworth, first Baron Kindersley (1871–1954), merchant banker and organizer of the National Savings movement, was born at the Clock House, Wanstead, Essex, on 20 November 1871, the third of eight children and second son of Captain Edward Nassau Molesworth Kindersley (1836–1907), an army officer, and his wife, Ada Good (d. 1908), daughter of John Murray, solicitor, of London, who married in 1868.

Childhood and early life Kindersley's childhood was passed in genteel poverty despite a prosperous family background. Sir Richard Torin Kindersley was his great-uncle and his father had been educated at Eton College and at Oxford before serving for fifteen years with the 19th regiment of foot in the Crimea and India. In 1870, when his wife's doctors forbade her to live in India, Captain Kindersley resigned his commission and became a manufacturing chemist in east London, a task for which he was inexperienced and at which he was unsuccessful. In reduced circumstances, he lived at Wanstead, Essex, where he was a JP, and in 1907 he died, leaving estate of just £155.

Kindersley was educated at Repton School but left in 1887 when his father could no longer afford to keep him there. He then went to work as a clerk at London's Millbank Dock Company before moving on to the important Thames Iron Works and Shipbuilding Company, where he was assistant secretary and private secretary to the chairman, A. F. Hills. In the 1890s the fortunes of Thames Iron Works revived under Hills's leadership; its interests, which had diversified far from shipbuilding, then included the construction of railways in South Africa and Syria, doubtless financed through the City of London. Hills was also a philanthropist and social reformer, introducing at his company a 48 hour week and profit-sharing, and he may have influenced Kindersley's later concern for the self-help of poor people through thrift.

About 1894 Kindersley entered the City and was a clerk with the well-known stockbrokers, David A. Bevan & Co.; in 1901 he was admitted a member of the stock exchange and in 1902 he became a partner in the firm. On 3 November 1896 he had married Gladys Margaret (1875–1968), daughter of Major-General J. P. Beadle; they had four sons and two daughters. This entry into a prosperous middle-class family—his father-in-law in 1902 left an estate of £42,000—together with his advancement in the City meant that his lifestyle was already comfortable. By 1899 he lived at 20 Egerton Terrace, an elegant four-storey terrace house in a desirable part of London's South Kensington.

Merchant banker In 1905 Kindersley moved on to Lazard Brothers & Co., a London merchant bank formed in 1870 by three French brothers who already had houses in Paris and San Francisco and who were later to open one in New York. Although by the 1890s Lazards in London was reckoned very able and had access to large means, it was largely controlled from Paris and had yet to make an impact. Kindersley changed this. As dominant partner he transformed Lazards into one of London's most innovative, aggressive, and successful merchant banks, aided by Robert Brand, a kindred spirit, who joined him in 1909. How this was achieved is not known but its basis lay in the traditional merchant-banking activities of acceptance finance and bond issuance. In the 1920s sterling bonds were issued largely for European sovereign or quasi-sovereign clients, whereas in the 1930s, following the closure of the market to foreign borrowers, Lazards turned increasingly to the provision of advice on corporate finance to British businesses.

At the end of 1919 Kindersley presided over a reconstruction of Lazards when its ownership passed equally to Lord Cowdray's international construction company, S. Pearson & Son Ltd, and to Lazard Frères of Paris. At the same time Lazards converted to a limited company when Kindersley became its chairman; he was also chairman of Whitehall Trust Ltd, the vehicle which held Pearsons' banking interests, from 1922 until 1933, when he joined the main board of Pearsons, which by then had assumed the characteristics of an investment trust. The background to this reconstruction and to the curious arrangement whereby a construction company diversified into merchant banking remains obscure.

Recognition as a major City figure grew after Kindersley was admitted to Lazards. He was on the boards of the Marine Insurance Company from 1909 and the Mercantile Investment and General Trust Company from 1912 to 1948. In 1910 the old and prestigious Hudson's Bay Company made him a director; he was its governor from 1915 until 1925. After the stultifying governorship of Lord Strathcona he breathed new life into this ailing institution, not least by winning for it large and immensely lucrative First World War contracts for the supply and transportation of war materials to the French government.

The Bank of England and international negotiations The source of much of Kindersley's City influence was his directorship of the Bank of England (1914–46) and his membership of the bank's influential committee of Treasury between 1924 and 1926. Kindersley was reckoned an 'active' director (Sayers, 368), and came to the fore at critical times. In 1917 he sat as a junior member of the so-called Revelstoke committee appointed to review the bank's senior management structure. Another early appointment, from 1921 to 1925, was his chairmanship of the advisory committee formed under the Trades Facilities Act; it considered applications for government guarantees in support of loans for capital projects which would reduce unemployment. In 1929 he gave 'substantial and important' evidence (Sayers, 365), very much in line with the bank's own thinking, to the committee on finance and industry—the so-called Macmillan committee; here he coined the phrase 'rules of the game', which subsequently passed into common parlance.

In 1924, seconded by Josiah Stamp, Kindersley was appointed to the important Dawes committee, formed to establish a realistic plan for German reparation payments. The hard and aggressive negotiations which characterized the work of this committee took their toll; the press reported that Kindersley took to his bed because of overwork. General Dawes, in a public statement, later drew attention to Kindersley's 'influential and effective' participation resulting from 'his wide experience as a banker and practical businessman as well as because of his sound economic judgement' (The Times, 11 April 1924). It was a flattering assessment of a formidable negotiator. 'Here at a glance', wrote an obituarist, 'was a man with whom it would be safe to go tiger hunting and whom it would probably be unprofitable to oppose' (The Times, 21 July 1954).

As with several City bankers, 1931 tested Kindersley's

mettle. In June he was sent to Vienna as representative of the Credit Anstalt's foreign creditors to assert their interests before the Austrian government and to negotiate a basis for the bank's reconstruction. In February 1933 he wrote how 'for 15 months I have been very much occupied with Austria, have visited Vienna four times, occupying nearly three months, and [have had] almost daily meetings in London' (Kindersley to Montagu Norman, 1 Feb 1933, Bank of England archives, G24/2). During the preliminary stages of the 1931 financial crisis, which drove Britain from gold, Kindersley was sent to Paris to negotiate support from the Bank of France. Just before the crisis broke in September, he was appointed chairman of the bank's newly formed special committee of foreign exchange, which took day-to-day decisions concerning the management of the sterling exchange; in the aftermath of the crisis it established the bank's widely acknowledged expertise in the foreign-exchange markets.

Yet while Kindersley was active in the Bank of England's affairs and was friendly with Montagu Norman, he was kept from the centre of its power. With the exception of membership between 1924 and 1926, he was kept off the influential committee of Treasury. 'For reasons which you and a few others know', he wrote to Norman in obscure yet pointed fashion in 1933, 'it seems to me that I am precluded from serving on the Treasury Committee even if my colleagues wish it' (Kindersley to Norman, 1 Feb 1933, Bank of England archives, G24/2). In 1933 Norman forbade him to join the 'traffic board', fearing a conflict of interest with the bank and his other business activities.

Kindersley's prominent role in national economic affairs in mid-1931 masked profound crisis and management shortcomings at Lazards. While in July 1931 Kindersley was in Paris seeking vital support from the Bank of France, Lazards was on the brink of collapse, the result of maladministration in the firm's Brussels office, which caused a £6 million loss and obliterated its capital. The need to conceal the precarious position of a leading London house at a moment of national crisis led to the resuscitation of Lazards through Bank of England support; and £3 million was made available, followed by additional support in 1932 when Lazard Frères of Paris ran into difficulties.

From 1926 until 1939, when the Bank of England assumed the task, Kindersley sponsored the collection and publication in the *Economic Journal* of statistics of British overseas investment and its contribution to the balance of payments.

National savings In July 1914 the lord chancellor invited Kindersley with three other City representatives to form a committee to advise on investment policy with regard to the £50 million in funds held by the public trustee department. This marked Kindersley out in 1916 for the vastly more important role of introducing the concept of national savings as a means of financing a very substantial part of the nation's war effort. For this he was remarkably well suited on both business and ideological grounds, as both the efficacy of thrift and the efficiency of voluntary saving rather than imposed taxation appealed to him

greatly. It extended to his absolute rejection of premium bonds which he saw as a lottery and 'the very negation of the spirit of steady and persistent individual effort' (*The Times*, 11 Jan 1918).

In February 1916 the government's campaign was launched, *inter alia*, with the formation of the central advisory committee for war savings, which Kindersley chaired, charged with the task of 'advising upon and approving the financial details of schemes for investment societies and to supervise their working' (*The Times*, 9 Feb 1916). The energy, determination, and imagination which he brought to this task were Olympian. In 1920, when he retired as chairman of what had come to be known as the National Savings Committee, he told the chancellor of the exchequer that since 1916 he had devoted the greater part of his time to its development.

For Kindersley the key to success was volunteer-based organization propelled by a sense that saving was both the proper and the patriotic thing to do. At the end of the war this success was reflected in an organization of 1830 local 'war savings committees', 41,500 'war savings associations', and 14,000 official sales agencies, all administered by 200,000 volunteers; the number of investors in British government securities had risen from 345,000 in 1914 to 17 million by 1918. The achievement, which had brought Kindersley widespread public notice through his addresses from public platforms, was rewarded when he became KBE in 1917 and GBE in 1920. He also received numerous decorations from foreign governments.

In 1920 Kindersley resigned as chairman of the National Savings Committee and became its president; by 1933 he was devoting to it just six days a year. He returned to the charge in 1939 when savings of £9000 million were achieved. In the war years he added radio broadcasts to his means of exhorting the public to save more. 'We must look upon our money as a weapon to be used for the one great purpose of defeating the enemy', he told them in 1940. 'The lustre of that wonderful impression [of fortitude and courage] must not be dimmed by timidity and selfishness on the financial front' (BBC radio broadcast, 3 Oct 1940). He finally resigned as president in 1946; in 1941 he had been created Baron Kindersley of West Hoathly, on account of this war work.

Kindersley adopted his own reasoned position on matters pertaining to economy and society and spoke up for it. From 1937, with Sir Josiah Stamp, he was vice-president of the Industrial Co-partnership Association and on its platform, while applauding 'a remarkable redistribution of wealth since the war', held strongly that 'prosperity must be short-lived unless the results of prosperity are widespread and shared reasonably and fairly between capital and labour' (*The Times*, 18 Feb 1937).

Other activities and final years Kindersley's charitable activities largely supported those of his wife. Between the wars she was charged with fund-raising for London's Elizabeth Garrett Anderson Hospital for Women, in particular for the construction of a new wing; she arranged fund-raising dinners to which Kindersley invited his friends. More ambitiously, in 1936 the two participated fully in raising £30,000 to build a new hospital at East Grinstead, Sussex, close to their country home at Plaw Hatch Hall. His financial expertise was sought by the Church of England, and in 1921 he was appointed to its new central board of finance. His other offices included prime warden of the Fishmongers' Company (1933) and high sheriff of Sussex (1928–9).

Kindersley's appearance was striking and powerful. 'In winning … success he was certainly helped by his personality and presence', wrote an obituarist in 1954; 'his tall figure topped by a countenance expressing bulldog determination in every line, and made more impressive by a pair of bushy black eyebrows drawn straight across it, commanded immediate success' (*The Times*, 21 July 1954).

Kindersley suffered from poor health and from the mid-1920s underwent several major operations, followed by lengthy periods of convalescence. But he made few concessions to this, remaining a director at Lazards until his death, though he gave up the chairmanship in 1953. He died at Queen Victoria Hospital, East Grinstead, on 20 July 1954, aged eighty-two. He was succeeded in the barony by his second son, Hugh Kenyon Molesworth *Kindersley (1899–1976), his eldest son having been killed in action in 1917.   JOHN ORBELL

Sources DNB · D. E. Moggridge, 'Kindersley, Robert Molesworth', DBB · A. F. Kindersley, *A history of the Kindersley family* (1938) · *The Times* (21 July 1954) · *The Times* (1916–37) · *Directory of Directors* · WWW · Burke, *Peerage* · R. S. Sayers, *The Bank of England, 1891–1944*, 3 vols. (1976) · P. C. Newman, *Company of adventurers* (1985) · Bank of England archives, London · CGPLA Eng. & Wales (1954) · d. cert. · b. cert. · m. cert.
Archives Bank of England archives, London, G24/2 | SOUND possibly BBC WAC, Second World War broadcasts
Likenesses Elliott & Fry, photograph, c.1912, NPG · W. Stoneman, two photographs, 1918–45, NPG · W. Orpen, oils, 1919; at National Savings Association, London in 1971 · W. Orpen, oils; at Hudson Bay's Company in 1971
Wealth at death £388,885 18s. 1d.: probate, 25 Sept 1954, CGPLA Eng. & Wales

King, Albert [Bertie] (1912–1981), jazz saxophonist, was born in Colón, Panama, on 19 June 1912, of Jamaican parentage. His father, Fitzgerald King, was a hairdresser. He was brought up in Jamaica, where he studied music at Alpha Cottage School, Kingston. He learned to play the flute, but changed to the clarinet and alto saxophone, mainly playing the latter. By 1934 he was leading one of Jamaica's foremost dance bands, whose members included Leslie 'Jiver' Hutchinson and the pianist Yorke de Sousa.

King moved to London in November 1935; he joined the band of George Lionel 'Happy' Blake at the Cuba Club and worked in 1936–7 with the Emperors of Jazz, led by Leslie Thompson and fronted by Ken Johnson. In May 1937 the African-American alto saxophonist Benny Carter recruited him for the band he was forming for a summer season at Scheveningen Kursaal, Netherlands, and the following winter season at the Bœuf sur le Toit, Paris. In this band, which made records in both countries, King played the tenor saxophone rather than his more usual alto saxophone. Carter, who worked in Europe for some years in the 1930s, became a major influence on King's playing. Back in London, he worked further with Ken Johnson and recorded again in a band led by the visiting African-American pianist Una Mae Carlisle. From December 1938 he was a member of the band led by the Nigerian pianist Fela Sowande at the Old Florida Club. This band appeared under Ken Johnson's name and the direction of its trumpeter, Leslie 'Jiver' Hutchinson, in the film *Traitor Spy* (1939). In 1938–40 King recorded and broadcast regularly with Johnson's own band.

From 1941 King was a stoker in the Royal Navy and played occasionally in a navy band as well as during leave. He was released on medical grounds early in 1943 and on his return to civilian life joined the dance band of Joe Loss. Among other short-lived associations at this time, he was a member of the band formed by the Trinidadian double bass player Clarry (Clarence) Wears to appear in a Ministry of Information propaganda film entitled *Hello! West Indies*. In August 1943 he formed his own band—known as the West Indian Swingtette—to appear at Slavins Club, Granville Place. This band made at least one broadcast, but he disbanded it early in 1944 and in May joined the new band being formed by Leslie Hutchinson. He remained with Hutchinson until the end of 1946, taking part in tours to India (October 1945), the Netherlands (January–February 1946), and Belgium (May–July 1946). In early 1947 he played with the Blue Rockets dance band. He married Kathleen King, otherwise Riley (b. 1909/10), the divorced wife of Leslie Riley and the daughter of John Pritchett, railway locomotive driver, at St Pancras register office on 22 August 1947.

In May 1948 King launched his own dance band at the Empress Ballroom, Dundee, for an extended engagement which ended in October 1950, after which he freelanced in London, playing an engagement with Harry Parry in early 1951. At this time he took part in several recording sessions of African-Caribbean music. In November 1951 he returned to Jamaica to lead the band at the Hotel Casablanca, Montego Bay. He went back to Britain in spring 1952 and during that year was notably associated with the Grant–Lyttelton Paseo Band, an experiment by Humphrey Lyttelton and the Guianese clarinettist Freddy Grant in fusing traditional jazz and Caribbean music. In September 1952 he again went back to the Hotel Casablanca in Jamaica.

After returning to Britain in May 1954 King worked in Cecil Black's dance band at Butlin's, Skegness, during that summer and then with Vic Abbott's band at the Edinburgh Palais until October, when he resumed his career as a jazz musician in London. After some years of eclipse, his swing style was again prominent under the new name 'mainstream' and he was able to participate in several significant recording sessions under his own name and under the leadership of Kenny Baker. He also appeared at the Royal Festival Hall in October 1954 at a concert with Chris Barber's band, playing in a style reflecting Caribbean influences more strongly than did most of his jazz work. From April to July 1956 he led a touring band in India, Singapore, and New Zealand. Once back in Britain, he freelanced, his engagements including a tour with Dill Jones's Trio later in 1956.

From 1958 to 1963 King was based in Jamaica, where his activities included record production. In London in 1964–5 he played in Frank Deniz's band at the Talk of the Town. Later he emigrated to the USA. He was living in Redwood City, San Mateo county, California, working as an apartment manager, when on 2 September 1981 he was murdered during an attempted robbery at his apartment at 770 Ninth Avenue. He was survived by his wife, Kathleen.

HOWARD RYE

Sources J. Chilton, *Who's who of British jazz* (1997) · L. Feather, *Encyclopedia of jazz in the 60s* (New York, 1966) · 'People in the news: under his baton', *Evening Telegraph* [Dundee] (2 June 1948), 2 · 'Bertie King's West Indians on stage', *Melody Maker* (11 Dec 1943), 1 · m. cert.

Archives SOUND BL NSA

Likenesses portrait, repro. in *Melody Maker* (3 Nov 1951), 7

King, Bolton (1860–1937), educational administrator and historian, was born at Chadshunt, Gaydon, near Kineton in Warwickshire, on 8 May 1860, the only son of the second marriage of his father, Edward Bolton King (1801–1878), to Louisa Palmer (1825–1920), descendant of the fourth earl of Aylesford. His father, a landowner, had been Liberal MP for Warwick (1832–7) and for South Warwickshire (1857–9).

King was educated at Eton College from 1872 to 1879, in which year he went up to Balliol College, Oxford, where he obtained first-class honours in modern history in 1883. The master of Balliol, Benjamin Jowett, of whom he was a protégé, noted his seriousness of character and enthusiasm for progressive causes. King abandoned his intention to enter the church through scruples about subscribing to the articles of faith (Jowett, 283), but found an alternative vocation through the influence of Arnold Toynbee and his ideals of social reform. He was closely involved in the foundation of Toynbee Hall Settlement in the East End of London, where he lived and taught until 1892. He was a friend of A. H. D. Acland and belonged to Acland's 'inner ring'. He founded the Toynbee Travellers' Club, which organized educational tours to the continent. Dame Henrietta Barnett referred to his gracious personality, princely generosity, and dreadful clothes (Barnett, 26). He married on 8 May 1895 Lydia (*c.*1869–1965), daughter of George Arnold of Gaydon; they had three sons and one daughter.

King left Toynbee Hall to complete *A History of Italian Unity* (1899) and *Mazzini* (1902). These studies were influential; the first was for long standard and the second is still quoted. *Italy Today* (1901), an account of contemporary Italian history, written in collaboration with Thomas Okey, the master basket maker and self-taught Italian scholar whom he met at Toynbee Hall, is more dated.

Though his stepbrother inherited Chadshunt, King did not lose touch with Warwickshire's labouring community. He set up two experiments in co-operative farming at Radbourne Manor and Ufton Hill. These were well thought out, but ultimately unsuccessful. In Gaydon he built a hall and reading room and houses with allotments for agricultural labourers. He occupied one himself with his wife, Lydia, but later moved to Warwick. With Joseph Ashby of Tysoe, who did most of the fieldwork, he published 'Statistics of some midland villages' in the *Economic Journal* (March and June 1893), setting out the problems that the agricultural working class faced.

King's radical views prevented his election to the newly created Warwickshire county council in 1892, when he stood at Kineton against Lord Willoughby de Broke, but he was chosen as a county alderman. He opposed the Second South African War and stood unsuccessfully for parliament as Liberal candidate for the Stratford upon Avon division of Warwickshire at a by-election in June 1901. Experience as chairman of the Warwickshire technical education committee between 1893 and 1903 led to his appointment in 1904 as Warwickshire's director of education under the 1902 Education Act.

Armed with resources, and supported by the chairman of the county council's education committee, James Broughton Dugdale, King was able to set up a workable administrative structure, build new elementary schools in the populous areas, create new secondary places as at Nuneaton Girls' High School, and provide the educational ladder of minor and major scholarships. Two central intermediate schools in rural areas allowed abler children to stay on if they wished and share the opportunities provided for rural pupil teachers. He strongly supported the 1918 act, which raised the school leaving age to fourteen, and drew up the county's plans to implement the act; these are to be found in his third printed report, *Education in Warwickshire* (1919). This envisaged the setting up of non-selective secondary schools, ten of which were to be created each year until the planned target of sixty schools to cover the whole county was reached. But this ambitious scheme was thwarted for lack of funds. Warwickshire was the only county to set up a successful day continuation school, offering day release up to the age of sixteen, which was enthusiastically adopted by employers in the skilled industries of Rugby. But King was disappointed that day continuation schools were not established elsewhere. His faith in the teaching profession led him to set up a teachers' consultative committee to advise on books and scholarship examinations. He encouraged secondary teachers to write on their teaching subjects and elementary school teachers to expect responsibility from quite young children.

Clashes with his former opponents recurred when, on the outbreak of war in 1914, the education committee circulated a leaflet prepared by King, *Why We Are at War*, containing the passage 'this then is a righteous war. Many of the wars we have fought have not been righteous. We have sometimes done unjust and cruel things'. Asked by the committee to withdraw the latter words, King refused 'as a historian', but offered to resign. His chairman, who had given permission for the publication, took the blame for the issue and the matter was dropped. A later leaflet, *The Schools and the War* (1916), detailing the schools' war effort, was well reviewed in *The Spectator* (22 April 1916) and met with general approval.

When he retired in 1928 King made a moving tribute to the teachers:

> It is upon you that it depends whether Education shall be lifeless or life-giving, whether the children shall go into life just with more or less undigested knowledge, or with character and mind so formed that they grow to be thinking men and women and giving citizens. (King, Browne, and Ibbotson, 28)

In retirement he wrote *Schools of Today* (1929), describing recent changes in education, and supporting the recommendations of the Hadow report, notably that for raising the school leaving age to fifteen. His suspicions of Mussolini's regime were confirmed by Professor Gaetano Salvemini, who had fled from Florence after imprisonment and with whom he spoke on Mazzini at the King's High School, Warwick. A miniature edition of King's study *Fascism in Italy* (1931), translated into Italian, was dropped on Rome by a young airman, Lauro di Bosis. King died on 15 May 1937 at Redholme, Great Missenden, Buckinghamshire, where he lived in his advanced years, and his ashes were interred in the family vault at Chadshunt. The blessing at the interment was pronounced by Bishop Barnes of Birmingham, like King a Christian of advanced opinions.   JOAN D. BROWNE

Sources J. A. R. Pimlott, *Toynbee Hall: fifty years of social progress, 1884–1934* (1935) · T. Okey, *A basketful of memories: an autobiographical sketch* (1930) · M. K. Ashby, *Joseph Ashby of Tysoe, 1859–1919: a study of English village life* (1961) · R. B. King, J. D. Browne, and E. M. H. Ibbotson, *Bolton King: practical idealist*, Warwickshire Local History Society (1978) [incl. full bibliography] · J. D. Browne, 'Toynbee Travellers' Club', *History of Education*, 15 (1986), 11–17 · *Warwick Advertiser* · priv. coll., Bolton King MSS · D. Mack Smith, *Mazzini* (1994) · I. Origo, *A need to testify* (1984) · [H. Barnett], *Canon Barnett: his life, work, and friends*, 2 vols. (1918) · D. J. Mitchell, *A history of Warwickshire county council* (1989) · M. Sturt, *The education of the people* (1967) · *Dear Miss Nightingale: a selection of Benjamin Jowett's letters to Florence Nightingale, 1860–1893*, ed. V. Quinn and J. Prest (1987)

Archives priv. coll., family papers

Likenesses S. Anderson, crayon, 1928, priv. coll. · S. Anderson, crayon, 1928, Warwick Education Office

Wealth at death £14,917 3s. 0d.: probate, 28 June 1937, CGPLA Eng. & Wales

---

King, Boston (1760?–1802), Methodist preacher and writer, was born into slavery on a plantation owned by Richard Waring near Charles Town, South Carolina. King's African-born father, a slave-driver and later mill cutter, and his mother, a seamstress and practitioner of folk medicine, were both favoured by their owner. King's father was also a lay preacher to his fellow slaves. At sixteen Boston King was apprenticed by his owner to a brutal carpenter and severely punished for the misdeeds of other workers. To escape further punishment he sought refuge and freedom with the British forces that had been occupying Charles Town since 1780. He soon contracted smallpox and was quarantined and left behind with the militia when the British regular forces withdrew from their position. Having recovered, King rejoined the regular forces as the servant to the commander and as a carrier of dispatches through enemy lines. He soon sailed from Charles Town to New York city, also under British control.

Shortly afterwards he married a former slave named Violet, twelve years his senior. While at sea he was captured by an American whaler, and taken to New Jersey, but he soon escaped, returning to New York city.

At the end of the war, in 1783, the Kings were among the three thousand former slaves evacuated from New York by the British and resettled in Birchtown, Nova Scotia. There, first Violet and then Boston King had their Christian conversion experiences, and King began preaching in 1785. Faced with general famine and the resentment of competing white workers, their life was extremely difficult until King found regular employment as a carpenter. Conditions improved even further in 1791, when King was appointed Wesleyan Methodist preacher to the black settlement at Preston, near Halifax.

Despite his comfortable situation King felt the call to participate in the Sierra Leone Company's project to establish a colony of free black people in Africa at Freetown, Sierra Leone. He, Violet, and 1200 other free black people sailed to Sierra Leone in 1792. Like many of the new settlers Violet soon died of fever. By 1793 King had remarried. His very limited success as a schoolteacher and missionary to the native Africans prompted the company to send him to England in 1794 for several years of education at the Methodist Kingswood School, near Bristol. His reception in England and his experience of preaching there enabled him to overcome his acknowledged prejudices towards white people. While in England he wrote 'Memoirs of the life of Boston King', which was published in the *Methodist Magazine* for 1798. King had returned to Freetown in 1796 as a somewhat more successful teacher, but he soon left that position to continue his ministry 100 miles south of Freetown, among the Sherbro people, where he died in 1802.   VINCENT CARRETTA

Sources 'Memoirs of the life of Boston King, a black preacher: written by himself, during his residence at Kingswood-School', *Methodist Magazine*, 21 (1798), 105–10, 157–61, 209–13, 261–5 · V. Carretta, ed., *Unchained voices: an anthology of black authors in the English-speaking world of the eighteenth century* (1996) · C. Fyfe, ed., *Our children free and happy: letters from black settlers in Africa in the 1790s* (1991) · C. Fyfe, *A history of Sierra Leone* (1962) · J. W. St G. Walker, *The black loyalists: the search for a promised land in Nova Scotia and Sierra Leone, 1783–1870* (1976) · E. G. Wilson, *The loyal blacks* (1976) · J. W. St G. Walker, 'King, Boston', *DCB*, vol. 5

Archives BL, Add. MSS 41262A, 41262B, 41263, 41264 · Hunt. L., Zachary Macaulay MSS · PRO, AO 12/54, 12/99, 12/102; AO 13, bundle 79; CO 217/63, 217/68, 267/91; 30/8, bundle 344, 30/55, nos. 1215, 4331, 6480, 7419, 7448, 8668, 8800, 8886, 9130, 9304, 9955; WO/1/352 · Public Archives of Nova Scotia, Halifax, MG 1, 219, 948, docs. 196, 340; MG4, 140–41, 143; MG100, 169, #27a; RG 1, 47, doc. 13, 137, 213, 5 Aug 1784; 302, doc. 11, 346, doc. 89, 371, 419–422

King, Bryan (1811–1895), Church of England clergyman, was born in Liverpool on 28 December 1811, the second son of George King, merchant, and his wife, Catherine. He was educated at Shrewsbury School from 1826 to 1831. In 1831 he entered Brasenose College, Oxford, taking a third class in *literae humaniores* in 1834, becoming a fellow of the college, and holding a Hulme exhibition. At Oxford his theological views changed from evangelicalism to Tractarianism. He was deaconed in 1836 and priested in 1837.

King was perpetual curate of St John's, Bethnal Green,

from 1837 to 1842, a Brasenose College living, and played a leading role in the building of new churches in the area. On 28 September 1842 he married Mary Martha Fardell (*d.* 1895), second daughter of Thomas Fardell, rector of Boothby Pagnell. In the same year he was appointed rector to another Brasenose living in the East End, St George-in-the-East. His determination to introduce high-church liturgical practices prompted fierce and sustained opposition from his parishioners and from the dissenters who composed the parish vestry. Matters came to a head in May 1859 when the parishioners elected the Revd Hugh Allen, a virulent anti-Tractarian clergyman, to a lectureship at St George's, provoking a cycle of rioting at the church and half-hearted action by the police which lasted for eighteen months. King's health broke down, and in 1860 he took his family abroad to Bruges for three years. In his absence the parish was run by a succession of clergy who managed to reimpose some order. In 1863 Bishop Tait of London secured an exchange of livings for King, and he became vicar of Avebury in Wiltshire, staying until 1894 and enjoying a quiet semi-retirement.

King's historical significance rests largely on the events surrounding the riots at St George-in-the-East. In the 1840s and 1850s he was regarded as an important Tractarian parish clergyman, being active in the formation of the Society of the Holy Cross, an association for Anglo-Catholic clergy, in 1855. But his energy was sapped by long years in a struggling East End ministry, and then broken by his experience at St George's.

King was described as a handsome man, stubborn and reserved, but sociable and possessing a strong sense of humour. He died on 30 January 1895 in Weston-super-Mare, where he and his wife had settled some months after his retirement. His wife died in October 1895. He was buried on 2 February 1895 at All Saints' Church, Weston-super-Mare. JEREMY MORRIS

Sources W. Crouch, *Bryan King and the riots at St George's-in-the-East* (1904) · *Church Times* (8 Feb 1895) · *The Guardian* (6 Feb 1895) · W. Fong, 'The ritualist crisis: Anglo-Catholics and authority, with special reference to the English Church Union, 1859–82', PhD diss., University of Toronto, 1977 · M. Reynolds, *Martyr of ritualism: Father Mackonochie of St Alban's, Holborn* (1965)
Archives LPL, Tait MSS
Likenesses photograph, repro. in Crouch, *Bryan King and the riots*, frontispiece
Wealth at death £10,197 9s. 1d.: probate, 25 March 1895, *CGPLA Eng. & Wales*

King, Cecil Harmsworth (1901–1987), publisher, was born on 20 February 1901 at Poynter's Hall, Totteridge, Hertfordshire, the fourth child in the family of three sons and three daughters of Sir Lucas White King, professor of oriental languages at Dublin University, and formerly of the Indian Civil Service, and his wife, Geraldine, daughter of Alfred Harmsworth, barrister, and sister of the first viscounts Rothermere [see Harmsworth, Harold Sidney] and Northcliffe [see Harmsworth, Alfred Charles William]. Cecil King's boyhood was unhappy. A brother was killed at Ypres, another when the ship taking him to school was

Cecil Harmsworth King (1901–1987), by Graham Sutherland, 1969

torpedoed. 'Life has always been difficult for me because this is not my world', he wrote in his candid autobiography, *Strictly Personal*, published in 1969. 'Until recently I have hated myself and always wanted to commit suicide'. He remembered his father as 'an irascible old gentleman' and his mother as violent and selfish. He hated his school, Winchester College, and liked Oxford because at Christ Church (he gained a second class in modern history in 1922) he could always be alone. There he fell in love with Agnes Margaret (*d.* 1985), daughter of George Albert *Cooke, canon of Christ Church, Oxford, and regius professor of Hebrew, and his wife, Frances Helen (*d.* 1932), *née* Anderson. He married her in 1923, and there were three sons and a daughter of the marriage (two sons were to die in his old age). King also adopted his deceased nephew's three children.

After Oxford, King's uncle Viscount Rothermere arranged for him to begin work on two of his newspapers, the *Glasgow Record* and *Sunday Mail*. While in Glasgow he developed the skin disease psoriasis, which troubled him for the rest of his life and which precluded him from being called up in the Second World War. King then returned to the south and joined the staff of the *Daily Mail* in 1923, in the advertisement department. In 1926 he transferred to the *Daily Mirror*, of which he became a director in 1929. In its heyday the *Mirror* was not a comfortable habitat for a withdrawn Wykehamist, but when he joined the paper, it was Conservative, middle-class, and failing. With King's support, Guy Bartholomew, editorial director for many years, set about transforming it into an

American-style tabloid, seeking a big working-class audience and willing to sympathize with Labour. King kept 'Bart's' extravagances at bay.

King was made editorial director of the *Sunday Pictorial* in 1937 and wisely appointed the 24-year-old Hugh Cudlipp as editor. He was self-educated, had been brought up in socialist south Wales, was full of passion, and had the journalistic flair that King lacked. After the war, Bartholomew fired Cudlipp, but King ousted Bartholomew in 1951 and brought back Cudlipp as editorial director of Mirror Newspapers. King himself became chairman of the Mirror Group in 1951, a post he held until 1963.

King, Cudlipp, and the papers prospered. King built a vast world publishing empire on this small, rich base. In England, they acquired in 1958 the Amalgamated Press from the Berry family and then took over the Odhams group in order to rationalize the women's magazines. In so doing, they acquired 'Labour's own (and only) paper', the *Daily Herald*. The Labour Party's opposition to this was stifled when King promised to maintain the failing *Herald* for seven years. Halfway through this term the Trades Union Congress parted with their interest in the *Herald* and King changed its title to *The Sun*.

King and Cudlipp were now deeply involved in politics. The Mirror Group was almost a wing of the labour movement. King had greater hopes of Harold Wilson than he had had of his predecessor, Hugh Gaitskell, and believed that without the brilliant campaign conducted by Cudlipp, Wilson would not have won his marginal victory in 1964. Although King hoped to be Wilson's *éminence grise*, Wilson was unable to take his advice. Consequently when he offered to make King a peer and minister of state, King scornfully rejected the opportunity. As the government got into deeper economic difficulties, King became more hostile to Wilson and encouraged ministers to be disloyal to him.

In 1963 the Mirror Group was renamed the International Printing Corporation (IPC), with King as chairman. In 1965 he became a part-time director of the Bank of England. He was also a part-time member of the National Coal Board (1966–9) and a member of the National Parks Commission (1966–9). King felt that what he believed to be his special gifts as an administrator might be put at the service of the nation when the inevitable catastrophe came. He tried, at the dinner parties he gave in his ninth-floor suite in the *Mirror*'s glass building, to persuade other business leaders that there would have to be an emergency government containing men like themselves. King feared there would be hyperinflation and even bloodshed in the streets. Cudlipp and his political executives had a hard time keeping this nonsense out of the paper. They tried in vain to convince King that, though the government deserved criticism, his fears were wildly excessive.

King got Cudlipp to take him to see Earl Mountbatten of Burma in May 1968. He outlined his fears and asked Mountbatten if he would be titular head of an emergency government. Mountbatten had taken care to be accompanied by Sir Solly Zuckerman, the government's scientific adviser, who said at once that this was rank treachery and Mountbatten should have nothing to do with it. Mountbatten agreed with Zuckerman.

Two days later, King published an article in the *Mirror* under his own name entitled 'Enough is enough'. It read:

> Mr Wilson and his government have lost all credit and we are now threatened with the greatest financial crisis in history. It is not to be resolved by lies about our reserves but only by a fresh start under a fresh leader.

The City was appalled. King had resigned the previous night from his directorship of the Bank of England. The pound had a bad day. The Labour Party's reaction was to give stronger support to Wilson. Three weeks later the directors of IPC unanimously dismissed King.

King had served Fleet Street well as chairman of the Newspaper Publishers Association from 1961 to 1968. He put a stop for a year or two to cheque-book journalism and made the Press Council more credible. In his retirement he wrote articles for *The Times*, and produced his autobiography and diaries. The diaries further injured his name because many people felt he had betrayed their confidences.

To lift his low spirits, King required stimulating company and people found him a likeable host at luncheons and dinners. The whole of his professional life was spent in newspapers. He shared his uncle Rothermere's gift for finance but lacked his uncle Northcliffe's genius for popular journalism. King was 6 feet 4 inches tall, a commanding, burly figure with penetrating blue eyes, a quick smile, and, in later life, abundant grey hair.

King retired eventually to Ireland with Dame Ruth Railton, musician and founder and musical director of the National Youth Orchestra. They had married in 1962, after King and his first wife were divorced in the same year. She was the daughter of David Railton, army chaplain and rector of Liverpool. Her lively personality brought him prolonged happiness for the first time. King died on 17 April 1987 at his home, The Pavilion, 23 Greenfield Park, Dublin, where he had lived for the last part of his life.

JOHN BEAVAN, *rev.*

Sources C. H. King, *The Cecil King diary, 1965–1970* (1972) · C. H. King, *The Cecil King diary, 1970–1974* (1975) · C. King, *Strictly personal* (1969) · H. Cudlipp, *Walking on the water* (1976) · *The Times* (20 May 1987) · *The Independent* (20 May 1987) · CGPLA Eng. & Wales (1987)
Archives University of Massachusetts, Boston, papers | HLRO, corresp. with Lord Beaverbrook
Likenesses photograph, 7 March 1961, Hult. Arch. · G. Sutherland, portrait, 1969, priv. coll. [*see illus.*]
Wealth at death £1,062,407: probate, 7 Sept 1987, CGPLA Éire · £329,947 in England and Wales: administration with will, 17 Dec 1987, CGPLA Eng. & Wales

King, Charles (1687–1748), organist and composer, the son of Charles and Mary King, was born at Bury St Edmunds in 1687; since the boy was not baptized until 5 June 1693 it may perhaps be assumed that his parents were nonconformists. If so, the baptism probably took place simply to secure his admission, as a treble, to the choir of St Paul's Cathedral, London, where he would have been trained initially by John Blow and later by Jeremiah Clarke, to whom he was subsequently apprenticed. When his voice broke King evidently stayed on as a supernumerary singer, at a salary of £14 per annum. On 12 July 1707 he took the degree of BMus at Oxford, and three months later (on 14 October) he married Clarke's sister, Ann, in the cathedral, the service being taken by the Revd Sampson Estwick, one of the minor canons and himself a very respectable musician. On 1 December his brother-in-law put a pistol to his head, and very shortly afterwards King succeeded him as almoner and master of the choristers, but not as organist. Curiously, however, he was not formally admitted a vicar-choral until 1730. Meanwhile he had also (in 1715) become organist of St Benet Fink, which post he continued to hold until 1747 when he was dismissed (for dereliction of duties, it may be supposed). When Clarke died it fell to King to see his book of *Choice Lessons for the Harpsichord or Spinett* (1711) through the press.

King himself produced almost no instrumental music, but he was a considerable composer of services and anthems; indeed, he wrote more service settings than any other composer of the period, which fact apparently gave rise to his colleague Maurice Greene's witty description of him as 'a very serviceable man' (Bumpus, *Organists*, 81). Autograph copies of most of these, many of them dated, are now in the library of the Royal Academy of Music, London. But 'featureless competence', as Ian Spink nicely puts it, 'is the level of King's achievement' (Spink, 302). As almoner and master of the choristers of St Paul's, he had many promising chorister pupils, the most distinguished of whom were Maurice Greene, John Alcock, and William Boyce. Why then he should have wished to become music master of Christ's Hospital in 1720 is something of a mystery. In 1725 King served as master of a short-lived lodge of freemasons which met at the Ship without Temple Bar; in January of the following year he was (with Estwick) one of the thirteen original members of the Academy of Vocal (later Ancient) Music, and it may possibly have been for this body that his two surviving secular vocal works were written. One is a setting of part of Dryden's ode for St Cecilia's day ('Twas at the royal feast') first set by Jeremiah Clarke in 1697, the other a *Dialogue between Oliver Cromwell and Charon* dated 1731.

It is not known when his wife died, but King later contracted a second marriage which is said (by Bumpus) to have brought him a fortune of £7000 and a villa at Hampton Court later owned by David Garrick. His second wife predeceased him. King died in London on 17 March 1748 and was buried in the church of St Benet Paul's Wharf on the 25th (and not in Hampton parish church as Bumpus, in his book on the organists of St Paul's, earlier maintained). H. DIACK JOHNSTONE

Sources J. S. Bumpus, *A history of English cathedral music, 1549–1889*, 2 vols. [1908]; repr. with an introduction by W. Shaw (1972), vol. 1, pp. 232–40 · J. S. Bumpus, *The organists and composers of S. Paul's Cathedral* (1891) · D. Dawe, *Organists of the City of London, 1666–1850* (1983) · Highfill, Burnim & Langhans, *BDA*, vol. 9 · I. Spink, *Restoration cathedral music, 1660–1714* (1995) · S. Jeans, 'The Easter psalms of Christ's Hospital', *Proceedings of the Royal Musical Association*, 88 (1961–2), 45–60, esp. 57 · *New Grove* · W. Bingley, *Musical biography*, 1 (1814); repr. (1971), 389–90 · [J. S. Sainsbury], ed., *A dictionary of musicians*, 2 vols. (1825); repr. (New York, 1966) · [Clarke], *The Georgian era: memoirs of the most eminent persons*, 4 vols. (1832–4)

Archives Royal Academy of Music, London, MSS 96–98
Wealth at death money from second marriage: will summarized in Highfill, Burnim & Langhans, *BDA*

King, Charles (*fl.* 1713–1721), merchant and writer on economics, was a significant contributor to the *British Merchant*, a periodical which appeared twice weekly during the hotly debated negotiations towards a commercial treaty with France following the close of the War of the Spanish Succession in summer 1713. The details of his background, family life, and later career are unknown, and nor is it known if he married or had children.

The *British Merchant* was one of a number of periodicals and a rash of pamphlets that followed news of the eighth and ninth, commercial, articles of the treaty of Utrecht, which opened the possibility of a new, less restrictive, trading agreement with France. A consequence of the treaty, if passed by parliament, would be the repeal of a number of laws laying high duties on French imports. Tory sentiment in favour of the eighth and ninth articles was effectively propagandized by the *Mercator*, a paper funded by Viscount Bolingbroke and largely written by Daniel Defoe. It argued that a ready market existed for British goods in France, despite legal prohibitions on trade that had been established in wartime, and that Britain would be a net gainer from any trade with France. The Dutch and Italians, it was argued, imported British goods, then re-exported these to France at a considerable gain, and a net loss to British producers and shipping.

The opponents of the commercial articles of the treaty, drawn mainly from the ranks of the whigs, were convinced that a more open trade with France would be fatal for some infant industries, such as silk manufacturing, and detrimental to Britain's comparative advantage in general. The *British Merchant* concocted statistics to show the treaty would result in an adverse trading balance of £1.4 million. Woollen and linen makers were to the fore in the campaign against the treaty. It was also felt that the new treaty would endanger the Portugal trade established by the Methuen treaty (1703). The earl of Halifax was the major supporter of the *British Merchant*, and King was taken on, alongside Joshua Gee, Henry Martyn, and other leading figures of the merchant community, to rally opposition. The paper ceased publication after parliament voted down the disputed articles, prompting the collapse of that part of the treaty. Some of the most important numbers, however, had a prolonged life and influence, being collected by King in three volumes as *The British Merchant, or, Commerce Preserv'd* in 1721. By this date King had been appointed as chamber-keeper to the Treasury, and the exchequer provided funds for the printing and circulation of the work to each of the corporate towns and boroughs of the nation. The collection enjoyed an authoritative status lasting until mid-century; the last edition was published in 1743. Rather than containing any advances in the theory of trade, the work represented a compilation of contemporary merchant opinion. The writers, King included, had been especially concerned to refute what they saw as the fallacious doctrine of reciprocity as advocated by Bolingbroke and Defoe. Most held fast to mercantilist nostrums of maximizing exports of manufactured goods and minimizing the import of foreign wares. An unregulated overseas trade was held to be an unreliable basis for national prosperity. King sought to preserve the home market for British-made goods, and argued that the 'first and best market of England are the natives and inhabitants of England' (King, 1.165–6). Such ideas would prevail in commercial policy debates until the later part of the eighteenth century.

R. D. SHELDON

Sources DNB · C. King, *The British merchant, or, Commerce preserv'd*, 3 vols. (1721) · D. A. E. Harkness, 'The opposition to the eighth and ninth articles of the commercial treaty of Utrecht', *SHR*, 21 (1923–4), 219–26

King, Charles William (1818–1888), writer on gemstones, was born on 5 September 1818 at Newport, Monmouthshire, the son of Charles King, a shipping agent in the iron trade, and his wife, Anne. He was educated at a private school in Bristol and entered Trinity College, Cambridge, as a sizar, in October 1836; he became a scholar of the college in 1839, and graduated in 1840 as sixth in the first class of the classical tripos. He was elected a fellow in 1842 and ordained deacon in 1845. In May of that year he was granted permission by the master of the college to travel abroad and went to Italy, where he resided at Rome and Florence (1845–50). He studied Italian language and literature, and collected antique gems, which he purchased at moderate prices. King later increased his collection by buying gems from Eastwood, a London dealer, and also at auction in London, where several important collections, including the Mertens-Schaafhausen (Praun), the Hertz, and the Uzielli were put on the market. By 1877 he owned 331 engraved stones, more than two-thirds of which were Greek and Roman; the remainder consisted of Sasanian and oriental gems and magical ('gnostic') amulets. In 1878, when his eyesight was seriously failing, King sold his collection to John Taylor Johnston, president of the Metropolitan Museum of Art at New York, who gave it to that institution in October 1881. A catalogue was printed in 1890, without alterations, from King's own manuscript of 28 February 1878, with the title *The Johnston Collection of Engraved Gems* (Metropolitan Museum, New York, handbook no. 9), which was replaced in the twentieth century by Gisela Richter's more scholarly work.

After his return from Italy, King's life was chiefly spent at Trinity College, Cambridge, where from 1857 he was senior fellow. He was in holy orders, but had no cure. At Cambridge, King took no part in the educational life of the college, but devoted himself to writing books about glyptics, the most widely valued at the time being his two-volume *Antique Gems and Rings* (1872) and a shorter *Handbook of Engraved Gems* (1866; 2nd edn, 1885). He also produced a study of Graeco-Egyptian amulets in *The Gnostics and their Remains, Ancient and Medieval* (1864; 2nd edn, 1887). However, despite his sensitivity to the art of gem-engraving, all his work is marred by a dilettante approach, more typical of the neo-classical age than of later nineteenth-century scholarship. W. Aldis Wright wrote that his works 'may appear to be wanting in familiarity with what is called the literature of the subjects of which they treat' (*The Athenaeum*, 7 April 1888, 441); indeed, he knew little of archaeology in general, although he was widely consulted by contemporaries about ancient gemstones. In the words of a commemorative brass in Trinity College chapel, his friends and colleagues thought him 'a straightforward, witty and eloquent man in his conversation, his writing, and his behaviour' ('Simplex lepidus facundus sermone scriptis moribus'), but he was capable of ungenerous remarks about fellow collectors such as Bram Hertz, whose collection surpassed his own in size and quality (*Antique Gems and Rings*, 282–3, 461). His writings stimulated an interest in glyptics at the time and until the second half of the twentieth century remained the only works in English on a subject in which considerable advances were made abroad, especially by Adolph Furtwängler in Germany, whose *Die antiken Gemmen* (Leipzig, 1900), with its critical scholarship and fine photographs, eclipsed the style of writing exemplified by King. King died, apparently unmarried, at 6 Stratford Place, near Camden Square, Kentish Town, London, after a brief illness, of a bronchial cold, on 25 March 1888, and was buried in Highgate cemetery.

W. W. WROTH, *rev.* MARTIN HENIG

Sources G. M. A. Richter, *The Metropolitan Museum of Art catalogue of engraved gems of the classical style* (1920) · G. M. A. Richter, *Metropolitan Museum of Art, New York, catalogue of engraved gems: Greek, Etruscan and Roman* (1956) · *The Academy* (7 April 1888), 247 · Venn, *Alum. Cant.* · *The Athenaeum* (31 March 1888), 412 · W. Aldis Wright, *The Athenaeum* (7 April 1888), 441 · private information (2004) · d. cert.
Archives Trinity Cam., accounts, corresp., journals, and photographs; MS of works on the gnostics, notes on early gemstones, and archaeological corresp.
Likenesses G. Mason, oils, 1846, Trinity Cam. · Morosini, drawing (reproduction), Trinity Cam. · photograph, Trinity Cam.
Wealth at death £7752 16s. 11d.: probate, 18 Sept 1888, *CGPLA Eng. & Wales*

King, Daniel (c.1616–c.1661), engraver, the son of William King, a baker of Chester, was apprenticed to Randle Holme in September 1630 and admitted to the Painters' Company in Chester in August 1639. He made an annual payment to the company from 1639 to 1642, during which years he employed a number of journeymen. But thereafter he ceased to make payments and evidently left the city, although he remained a member of the company.

Nothing is known about King's movements during the civil war, and he next appears in London in the 1650s, when he was closely associated with the antiquary Sir William Dugdale in making etchings for the first volume of the latter's *Monasticon Anglicanum* in 1665. King's etchings reappeared the following year without any letterpress text and with extra plates under a new title-plate, *The Cathedrall and Conventuall Churches of England and Wales*. This publication bears King's name and has no mention of Dugdale. The 1666 series is known in different forms and with variant title-plates; the plates come in different states, some of which precede those found in some copies of the *Monasticon*—so the two publications must have proceeded in parallel. King evidently kept control of the plates, for the bookseller George Thomason entered the work in the Stationers' register on 14 February 1657, listing fifty-seven plates and stating that they had been drawn 'at the great charge of Daniel King' (Eyre). In 1658 Dugdale prepared a long denunciation should King publish any part of his proposed translation of the *Monasticon*.

In 1656 King published in London *The Vale-Royall of England, or, The County Palatine of Chester Illustrated*, for which he wrote the preface. In it he printed for the first time two essays on Chester written by William Smith and William Webb more than forty years earlier, as well as an essay on the Isle of Man by James Chaloner. This book was illustrated with etchings mostly by Wenceslaus Hollar, which were unsigned and for this reason have often been attributed to King himself; the same is true of the one-sheet etching *An Orthographical Designe of Severall Viewes upon the Road in England and Wales* (c.1660), which, although published by King, is also by Hollar. This mistake has led to a gross overestimation of King's abilities as an etcher, which were decidedly modest. King also wrote a manuscript, 'Miniatura, or, The art of limning' (BL, Add. MS 12461), and translated Gerard Desargues's *Universal Way of Dyaling*, published in 1659.

King reappears in the books of the Chester company in 1659–60, but is there recorded as dead in 1661. Anthony Wood recorded Dugdale's opinion that King was 'a most ignorant silly fellow' who 'was not able to write one line of true English' (Wood, 3.503), and that after King had been robbed and deserted by his wife he had died heart-broken near York House in the Strand about 1664. His plates passed into the stock of John Overton.

ANTONY GRIFFITHS

Sources records of the Painters, Glaziers, Embroiderers and Stationers' Company of Chester, Ches. & Chester ALSS · Wood, *Ath. Oxon.*, new edn, 3.503 · G. Cobb, 'Daniel King: a lesser known seventeenth-century etcher', *Antiquarian Journal*, 54 (1975), 299–301 · A. Griffiths and R. A. Gerard, *The print in Stuart Britain, 1603–1689* (1998), 190–92 [exhibition catalogue, BM, 8 May – 20 Sept 1998] · G. E. B. Eyre, ed., *A transcript of the registers of the Worshipful Company of Stationers from 1640 to 1708*, 3 vols. (1913–14) · *The life, diary, and correspondence of Sir William Dugdale*, ed. W. Hamper (1827), 103

King, David (1806–1883), minister of the United Presbyterian church, was born on 20 May 1806 in Montrose, Forfarshire, the second son of John King (1762–1827), minister of Second United Secession church, Montrose, and his wife, Eliza Young, daughter of a Montrose merchant.

King received his early education at primary and high schools in Montrose and entered Aberdeen University in 1820. After one year there, he transferred to the University of Edinburgh where he completed his arts course, displaying distinction in the classics and science. Preparing for the ministry of the United Secession church, he studied theology in Glasgow under Professor John Dick. On 10 February 1829, he was licensed by the presbytery of Forfar and ordained as minister of First United Secession Church, Dalkeith, on 13 January 1830. In the late summer of 1833 he was called to the large and influential congregation of Greyfriars Secession Church, Glasgow, in succession to Dick, his former tutor, and inducted on 15 October 1833. It was here, over a period of more than twenty years, that

King exercised his most distinguished and effective ministry as a preacher and church leader in Glasgow. He married, on 27 December 1842, Elizabeth (1818–1896), elder daughter of James *Thomson (1786–1849) and Margaret (d. 1830), daughter of William Gardner of Glasgow. They had at least two sons and two daughters.

King was renowned as one of the most outstanding church orators in Scotland during the middle years of the century, both in the pulpit and on the public platform. A biographer asserted that he inaugurated a new era in the preaching of seceders: 'He was eloquent, imaginative, polished, classic in style, and beyond all question intense. He was among the first of our preachers of any note who had the modern attraction of shortness' (Joseph Leckie, *Life of Dr. King*, 45, cited in Woodside, 155). His preaching drew people from all over the city, including university students of all denominations, to fill his 1500-seat sanctuary. Under his dynamic ministry, Greyfriars established numerous mission and educational projects in the city and beyond. It financed a missionary station in Oban; began the first foreign mission to Trinidad of the Secession church; set up educational classes for young people in both religious and secular subjects, and was the first church in Glasgow to establish homes for poor boys.

In these years the great public platform in Scotland for the advocacy of political and social reforms was the city hall of Glasgow. King, along with other leading dissenting ministers of the time, was a popular speaker at public rallies in support of movements for progressive change. He was a strong supporter of the Reform Bill of 1832 and the anti-corn law agitation (Woodside, 217). He was a national leader in the anti-slavery movement, and was accepted as the representative speaker from Scotland at a meeting in Exeter Hall, London, in March 1838, held to press for the abolition of 'negro apprenticeship', a covert form of slavery (Woodside, 216). In recognition of his great services to his church, the city, and the nation, the University of Glasgow awarded him the LLD in 1841.

The demands of ministering to a large congregation eventually undermined King's health, which was never robust. Suffering from nervous strain, he resigned from Greyfriars in March 1855, and went into semi-retirement in Kilcreggan, Dunbartonshire, a resort on the Firth of Clyde. However, his occasional preaching there soon resulted in the establishment of a new preaching point for his denomination. To accommodate the large numbers of summer visitors who flocked to hear him, a church sanctuary was erected in 1858, seating 440. Towards the end of 1861, King left this charge to lay the foundations of a new Presbyterian congregation in London in Westbourne Grove, Bayswater. On 26 January 1862 a new building with accommodation for 1000 worshippers was opened. At the 1863 synod of the United Presbyterian church he was chosen as moderator, and he spoke in favour of the union of English and Scottish presbyterian churches: he was a co-founder of the Evangelical Alliance. Once again, the heavy responsibility of ministering to a growing congregation took its toll on his health, and in April 1869 he returned to Scotland to take on the small charge of Morningside, then a quiet suburb of Edinburgh. It was hoped that with few duties beyond preaching, he could continue to exercise his still considerable gifts. But even with the assistance of many minister colleagues who often supplied the pulpit for him, his strength was unequal to the task. In February 1873 he resigned his charge and ceased all ministerial activity. After extensive travels in search of renewed health, chiefly in Italy, King returned to London, where he died on 20 December 1883.

King wrote several books, among them *The Ruling Eldership* (1845), *The Lord's Supper* (1846), *Geology and Religion* (1849), and the *State and Prospects of Jamaica* (1850), which he had visited in 1848–9; he went to the United States and Canada in the same trip. However, his great gifts as a preacher overshadowed his reputation as an author: a volume of his sermons was published posthumously in 1885.

DONALD C. SMITH

Sources DNB · R. Small, *History of the congregations of the United Presbyterian church from 1733 to 1900*, 2 vols. (1904) · E. King, *Memoir of the late Revd. David King* (1885) · D. Woodside, *The soul of a Scottish church, or, The contribution of the United Presbyterian church to Scottish life and religion* (1918) · W. Mackelvie, *Annals and statistics of the United Presbyterian church*, ed. W. Blair and D. Young (1873) · D. M. Lewis, ed., *The Blackwell dictionary of evangelical biography, 1730–1860*, 2 vols. (1995)

Likenesses E. King, pencil drawing, 1842, NPG · photograph, 1859, repro. in King, *Memoir*, frontispiece · W. H. Egleton, stipple (after H. Anelay), BM, NPG

Wealth at death £4756 7s. 6d.: probate, 16 May 1884, CGPLA Eng. & Wales

King, Dorothea. *See* Johnson, Dorothea (1732–1817).

King, Earl Judson (1901–1962), clinical biochemist, was born on 19 May 1901 in Toronto, Canada, the elder son of the Revd Charles W. King, Baptist minister, and his wife, Charlotte Stark. He was educated at Brandon College and McMaster University, Ontario, graduating in 1921 in chemistry and biology and then continuing to a master's degree in chemistry and, at Toronto University, to a doctorate of philosophy in 1926. In 1927 he married Hazel Marion Keith, biochemist, of Lethbridge, Alberta, who had been a fellow student at Brandon College; they had two daughters.

King was offered a research post in the newly founded Banting Institute in Toronto, where he engaged in the study of the biochemistry of silicosis, an occupational lung disease caused by the inhalation of siliceous dust by miners and others employed in various dusty trades. In 1928 he went to London to work in the Lister Institute, where he became interested in organic phosphate compounds and the phosphatase enzymes which were his second lifelong research subject. He then worked for a short period in the Kaiser Wilhelm Institute at Munich before returning in 1929 to the Banting Institute, where he was promoted to associate professor and in 1931 became head of the biochemical section.

In 1934 King returned to London on being invited to take charge of the chemical pathology department of the new British Postgraduate Medical School at Hammersmith Hospital, a post he retained for the rest of his life. He was appointed reader in chemical pathology in the University of London in 1935 and made professor in 1945.

At Hammersmith, E. H. Kettle, the first professor of pathology, was building up an outstanding academic department with research and teaching based on the best modern hospital practice. The influence of the Hammersmith school came to be felt in all English-speaking countries and King played a full part in this development. He realized the growing importance of accurate biochemical data for the diagnosis and treatment of disease and he pioneered the quantitative analysis of blood constituents which came to replace the somewhat empirical tests of the previous generation. In particular King was dissatisfied with the relatively large volumes of blood required by current methods, and he showed a great deal of ingenuity in refining the analyses so that they could be performed on the amount of blood available from a finger prick. The successive editions of his book, *Microanalysis in Medical Biochemistry* (1946), just one of his many books and articles, were used worldwide in clinical laboratories.

In the meantime King continued his main research interests in the biochemistry of silicosis and the properties of the phosphatase enzymes. His reputation was such that a constant stream of scientists came to work with him before returning to their own laboratories; many were from overseas and King's methods and ideas became known internationally. An indication of his influence was the almost universal use of the eponymous King–Armstrong unit for alkaline phosphatase measurements, which made his name familiar in every clinical laboratory in the world.

The lung damage of silicosis was widely believed to be caused by trauma from the sharp-edged crystals of silica inhaled into the pulmonary tissue. Silica was believed to be almost completely insoluble in body fluids. King rapidly disproved both of these assumptions. He demonstrated that silica slowly and continuously dissolved to produce a toxic action on nearby cells and that the damage was linked to the fineness and number of dust particles. This solubility theory of silicosis opened a large programme of research, into the normal physiology of silica in animals, the effect of other compounds in enhancing or reducing the silica effect, and the complications which resulted from the frequent coexisting tuberculous infection in human cases. In 1937 there arose public interest in the closely related coalminers' pneumoconiosis, and King began experimental work to elucidate the great differences in morbidity from lung disease between different coalfields in the United Kingdom. He became a self-taught and accomplished experimental pathologist and extended his interest to the effects of inhaled asbestos fibres, foreshadowing the widespread concern about the use of asbestos which followed some twenty-five years later.

At the outbreak of the Second World War, King accepted responsibility for pathology laboratories in a number of hospitals in the Middlesex sector. His talents were soon required on a wider scale and he developed methods for the estimation in blood of some new anti-malarial drugs and chemicals, whose introduction had important consequences for the troops in tropical climates. King also headed an investigation into methods for determining haemoglobin; the methods he recommended were adopted in everyday use. He visited India as an adviser to the armed forces on laboratory methods, and was made consultant in medical biochemistry, with the rank of brigadier, to the Royal and Indian Army Medical Corps. From 1950 he was consultant in biochemistry to the Royal Army Medical Corps.

After the war King became progressively involved in scientific administration for the British Postgraduate Medical School, the University of London, and various scientific societies. He was chairman of the Biochemical Society (1957–9) and editor of the *Biochemical Journal*. Shortly after the war he founded the Association of Clinical Biochemists, the first scientific society devoted entirely to the relatively new speciality of clinical biochemistry which King had done so much to establish. He then turned his attention to international scientific matters, helping to found the International Federation of Clinical Chemists, of which he was first chairman (1952–60). He became an honorary MD of the universities of Oslo and Iceland, and was an honorary member of many societies. He was Chadwick lecturer in 1955.

In 1955 a public appeal was launched to fund new buildings for the postgraduate school. King took a prominent part in this work. On an exhausting fund-raising trip to the United States he was taken ill; he recovered but remained in ill health for the next two years. He died suddenly on 31 October 1962, at his home at 2 Sunnydene, Bridgewater Road, Wembley, after a characteristically busy day spent at London University Senate House.

In appearance King was stocky and compact. He moved briskly and spoke abruptly. He had a prodigious appetite for work and a fine talent for spotting promising scientific discoveries or individual scientists. His interests outside his work were few, but he derived a never-ending pleasure from contact with people of every nationality. His main recreation during the summer was touring and camping on the continent, often combined with attendance at a scientific congress. Clinical biochemistry was one of the fastest-developing new medical sciences during the second and third quarters of the twentieth century. King's contribution to it was second to none.

I. D. P. WOOTTON, *rev.*

Sources *Biochemical Journal*, 89 (1963) · *Enzymologia*, 25 (1963) · *Annals of Occupational Hygiene*, 6 (1963) · personal knowledge (1981) · private information (1981) · *CGPLA Eng. & Wales* (1963)
Archives Wellcome L., corresp. with Ernst Chain
Likenesses A. Gray, bust, priv. coll.
Wealth at death £4090 16s.: administration with will, 16 Aug 1963, *CGPLA Eng. & Wales*

King [*alias* Freeman], **Sir Edmund** (*bap.* 1630, *d.* 1709), physician and surgeon, the eldest son of the five sons and four daughters of Edmond King (*d.* 1651) of Northampton, physician, and Alice, was baptized as Edmond on 22 August 1630 in All Saints' Church, Northampton. As Edmund Freeman, alias Kinge, his father received on 9

Sir Edmund King (*bap.* 1630, *d.* 1709), by R. Williams (after Sir Peter Lely, *c.*1678–80)

May 1612 an archbishop's licence to practise medicine and surgery in the dioceses of Peterborough, Lincoln, Norwich, Coventry, and Oxford. His mother was named as the wife of Edmond King in the baptisms of three children at All Saints, Northampton, but no marriage of Edmond and Alice was recorded in Northampton, nor is there an extant licence.

King went to London after his father's death in July 1651 and practised surgery; it is not known if he underwent any apprenticeship. He attended the surgeons at St Bartholomew's Hospital between 1651 and 1660, and as Edmund Freeman, alias King, he received a licence on 1 June 1663 from Archbishop Juxon to practise medicine in England, with the exception of London and 5 miles around. On 12 May 1663 he was given a Lambeth degree of MB, as Edmund Freeman, alias King. He was incorporated MD at Cambridge on 5 October 1671 on his Lambeth degree. Initially King lived in Little Britain, London, in a house which had a museum of anatomical specimens, such as a dried ileocaecal valve pressed in a large paper book. In 1665 he moved to a house in Hatton Garden, where he remained for the rest of his life. On 20 December 1666 he married Rebecca Polsted (*b.* 1631/2), the widow of John Polsted and third daughter of Sir Nicholas *Crisp (*c.*1599–1666), and his wife, Anne Prescott. On 23 February 1666 King witnessed the will of Crisp, who died three days later, at which time King performed an autopsy on him. Rebecca was buried on 27 October 1698 at St Mildred's Church, Bread Street, in her father's vault, where her child, Martha, had been buried on 27 February 1684.

In addition to cultivating an extensive surgical practice

King was active as an experimental anatomist of humans and other animals. On 11 July 1666 John Wilkins, the mathematician and Anglican divine who sponsored an experimental club in natural philosophy while warden of Wadham College, Oxford, proposed King as a member of the Royal Society, and he was admitted as Mr Edmond King on 25 July 1666. On 28 November 1666 he presented a dissected foetus at a meeting. King's notable society activities included his participation in early blood transfusion experiments. Following a protocol for animal-to-animal blood transfusions developed by physician and anatomist Richard Lower, with the assistance of Christopher Wren and others, in Oxford during late 1665 and early 1666, on 14 November 1666 King led in London a group that duplicated Lower's experiment. On 5 December 1666 King collaborated with Lower on bleeding a sheep into a dog at a society meeting. In 1667 he published in the society's *Philosophical Transactions* a detailed account of an experiment that used an apparatus of pipes and quills to transfuse the blood of a calf into a sheep. Samuel Pepys, an onlooker, reflected in his diary that a discussion with friends about the experiment 'did give occasion to many pretty wishes, as of the blood of a Quaker to be let into an Archbishop, and such like' (Pepys, 370–71). King's most notable transfusion work occurred on 23 November 1667, when he undertook a private trial with Lower, who then lived in London, to transfuse blood from a sheep into an Oxford student, Arthur Coga, who was paid 20s. The three participated in a public demonstration before members and guests of the Royal Society a few weeks later, and results were soon published in *Philosophical Transactions*. King and Lower stopped transfusion experiments after a human participant in a French trial died from the effects in February 1668.

From 1666 until 1668 King used his surgical skills in a number of collaborative experiments on respiration with Robert Hooke and Peter Balle. At issue was whether respiration depended on a chemical component in the air entering the blood as it circulated through the lungs (Hooke's, Lower's, and Robert Boyle's position), or a mechanical mixing of blood and air dependent on pulmonary motion (Walter Needham's argument). King also studied insects, primarily ants, and published papers in *Philosophical Transactions* in 1667 and 1670 on ants and leaf-cutter bees. His case notes on post-mortem examinations of patients, as well as his published microscopic researches on reproductive glands in men, guinea pigs, and bulls (*Philosophical Transactions*, 1668), recorded his belief that animal tissues, including human, are primarily composed of fibres, tubes, and liquors.

King's surgical practice expanded greatly in the late 1660s and early 1670s, when he became the preferred surgeon for Thomas Willis, then London's leading physician, and Richard Lower, another collaborator of Willis. King also worked with Willis on autopsies of their patients and in the preparation of part one of Willis's *De anima brutorum* (1672) and *Pharmaceutice rationalis* (1674). Unlike Willis, however, King eschewed making broad hypotheses based on anatomical findings. In addition to referring

patients to him, Willis may have facilitated King's professional success through introducing him to his patron, Gilbert Sheldon, archbishop of Canterbury, and a powerful figure at court. By the mid-1670s King was attending Charles II, who knighted him in 1676, and in a letter of 20 January 1677 recommended him to the Royal College of Physicians for admission as an honorary fellow. The college refused; however, he was admitted as a fellow on 12 April 1687 by the renewed college charter of James II. King attended Charles II during his final illness, which involved seizures. The king's initial revival from a fit after a bleeding administered by King caused the privy council to recommend a fee of £1000, but Charles II's death soon after caused the matter to drop.

In 1693 King was the subject of a complaint made by a Mr Lynn, an apothecary, who stated that King had turned himself and a Dr Biggs out from attending Sir John Heron, claiming that if he (King) had been called in earlier he could have done more, thereby implying that Biggs was less than competent. King asserted his innocence and the charge was dropped.

King retired from practice at the age of seventy-two and died in Hatton Garden on 29 May 1709; he was buried with his wife at St Mildred's, Bread Street, on 3 June. King's will, dated 24 March 1709, refers to portraits of himself by Godfrey Kneller and Peter Lely. The latter work was bequeathed to the Royal College of Physicians while the Kneller seems lost.　ROBERT L. MARTENSEN

Sources DNB · BL, King MSS · Munk, *Roll* · R. G. Frank, *Harvey and the Oxford physiologists* (1994) · LPL, MS FI/C, fols. 121v, 126v · private information (2004) · *Bishop Burnet's History of his own time*, 1, ed. G. Burnet and T. Burnet (1724) · Pepys, *Diary*, 7.370–71 · A. Kippis and others, eds., *Biographia Britannica, or, The lives of the most eminent persons who have flourished in Great Britain and Ireland*, 2nd edn, 5 vols. (1778–93)
Archives BL, collections and medical papers, Sloane MSS 1586–1598, 1640, 4038, 4078 | BL, letters to Lord and Lady Hatton, Add. MS 29585 · NL Scot., corresp. with the first and second marquesses of Tweeddale
Likenesses R. White, line engraving, 1684 (after G. Kneller), BM · W. Faithorne, chalk and watercolour drawing (after a bust), BM · G. Kneller, portrait · P. Lely, oils, RCP Lond. · R. Williams, mezzotint (after P. Lely, c.1678–1680), BM, NPG [*see illus.*] · oils, RCP Lond.

King, Edward (c.1576–1639), Church of Ireland bishop of Elphin, was born in Huntingdonshire; his exact date of birth and the names of his parents are not known. He was admitted as a sizar to St John's College, Cambridge, matriculating about 1594, and graduated BA in 1598 and proceeded MA in 1601. There he was taught by Henry Alvey, who was appointed provost of Trinity College, Dublin, in 1601. Subsequently King became a fellow of that college, and on 18 August 1614 he was awarded the degree of doctor of divinity. In 1604 letters patent were issued to King appointing to him the deanery of Elphin, co. Roscommon. He was appointed vicar of St Catherine's, Dublin, in 1606. On 15 November 1611 he was promoted to the bishopric of Elphin, and he was consecrated the following month.

King was a resident bishop and actively promoted the protestant reformation in his diocese. He did this by improving the finances of the local church. By 1615 he had augmented the value of the bishopric to £300. But it was not until the arrival of Viscount Wentworth as lord deputy of Ireland that the principal gains were made. In 1638 King wrote to the archbishop of Canterbury, William Laud, describing how Wentworth aided him in recovering alienated church lands. In 1637, sure of Wentworth's support, he refused to renew his tenants' leases without a good increase of rent. This brought the bishop's income to £700. The following year, as a result of the breaking of long leases and fee farms, it rose to £1340. With the establishment of the bishopric on a secure financial footing, King sought to improve the financial state of the parochial system in his diocese. He did this by voluntarily surrendering the *quarta pars episcopalis*, the bishop's quarter portion of the parochial tithes, to his clergy. In addition he sought to create unions of parishes, which would create larger congregations better able to support their ministers.

King used his augmented income to re-edify the cathedral church at Elphin. He also constructed a small but strong castle as his episcopal residence on his own lands. Furthermore, he promoted the creation of an English society in his diocese; in 1635 Wentworth noted the transformation of Elphin from an Irish township to a 'handsome' English village. This programme was to be achieved through the appointment of English clergymen to parochial positions. In 1615 diocesan clergy with New English surnames accounted for about half of the parochial incumbents in Elphin. By 1634 most ministers possessed New English surnames.

As a result of King's stewardship, Elphin was seen as one of the most desirable bishoprics in the country, and in 1638 Wentworth proposed to promote King to the vacant archbishopric of Tuam. The lord deputy had planned to reward one of his protégés, William Chappell, with this living. King refused this promotion not only because of the poverty of Tuam but also because of his investment of time and money in Elphin.

Although the name of King's wife is unknown, those of some of his children are: Charles, James, and Susanna. In his final years he complained about his ill health. He died on 8 March 1639 at Elphin and was buried at the cathedral there. Part of his epitaph read: 'This bishop much augmented the revenue of that See, was a constant preacher of God's Word, and a man of great sanctity of Life' (Cotton, 4.125).

CIARAN DIAMOND

Sources 'Canon Leslie's typescript succession list, Elphin', Representative Church Body Library, Dublin, MS 61.2.5 · *The whole works of Sir James Ware concerning Ireland*, ed. and trans. W. Harris, rev. edn, 1 (1764) · A. Ford, *The protestant Reformation in Ireland, 1590–1641*, 2nd edn (1997) · J. D. McCafferty, 'John Bramhall and the reconstruction of the Church of Ireland, 1633–1641', PhD diss., U. Cam., 1996 · Burtchaell & Sadleir, *Alum. Dubl.*, 2nd edn · *Calendar of the Irish patent rolls of James I* (before 1830); facs. edn as *Irish patent rolls of James I* (1966) · R. Lascelles, ed., *Liber munerum publicorum Hiberniae … or, The establishments of Ireland*, 2 vols. [1824–30] · H. Cotton, *Fasti ecclesiae Hibernicae*, 4 (1850) · E. P. Shirley, *Papers relating to the Church of Ireland, 1631–9* (1874) · Strafford papers, Sheff. Arch., Wentworth Woodhouse muniments, vols. 6, 20 · Venn, *Alum. Cant.*, 1/3 · visitation report, 1615, TCD, MS 1066 · visitation report, 1634, TCD, MS 1067 · F. Burke, *Loch Ce and its annals* (1895)

Archives Sheffield Arch., Wentworth Woodhouse muniments, Strafford papers, vol. 20

King, Edward (1611/12–1637), friend of John Milton, was born at Boyle Abbey, Boyle, in Connaught, Ireland. His date of birth is not known, but the fact that he was fourteen when he entered Cambridge in June 1626 and twenty-five when he died in August 1637 means that he must have been born in 1611 or 1612. Edward King was one of the nine children of Sir John *King (d. 1637), a Yorkshireman who had served in Ireland in various administrative capacities since 1585, and his wife, Catherine, *née* Drury (d. 1617), whose father, Robert, was the nephew of Sir William Drury, lord deputy of Ireland. Edward's godfather was his uncle (and namesake) Edward King, bishop of Elphin. Of his brothers and sisters the most prominent were Robert *King (who became a member of Cromwell's council of state), John (who became clerk of the hanaper), Mary (later Lady Charlemont), Margaret (later wife of Sir Gerald Lowther, chief justice of common pleas in Ireland), and Dorothy *Dury (whose second husband was the protestant divine John Dury, a friend of Milton).

Edward was educated at Thomas Farnaby's school in Goldsmiths' Alley, Cripplegate, London; Farnaby was later to contribute a Latin poem to the memorial collection for King. On 9 June 1626 Edward and his brother Roger were admitted as lesser pensioners to Christ's College, Cambridge, and were assigned to William Chappell, who had recently rusticated Milton. Edward proceeded BA in 1630 and MA in 1633. Soon after his MA he would have taken holy orders.

King's final term as an undergraduate began on 7 April 1630 but teaching was soon discontinued because of plague. As the fellows and undergraduates were preparing to leave it became known that Andrew Sandelands intended to resign his fellowship. On 10 June, while most of the fellows were still absent, the vacant fellowship was filled by royal mandate; King Charles appointed King to replace Sandelands. The myth that Milton had hoped to secure the fellowship was first recorded in 1736 and has often been repeated. In fact Milton was not eligible for election, because the statutes of the college prohibited the election of more than one fellow from any county. As long as Michael Honywood (who came from London) remained in post, Milton remained ineligible for election. King was also ineligible, because he was deemed, despite his Irish birth, to be a Yorkshireman, on the grounds that the family seat was Feathercock Hall, near Northallerton, and the college already had a Yorkshireman in the fellowship (William Power). The royal mandate, however, stipulated that King should be appointed 'notwithstanding any statute'. He was appointed to the fellowship as an act of royal patronage, which he enjoyed simply because his family was of the requisite social standing; Milton's was not. The disputes that arose out of King's appointment were not resolved until 1696, when it was decided that eligibility must depend on actual place of birth.

King held his fellowship for the remaining seven years

of his life. During that period he took only thirteen undergraduates because he was not dependent on undergraduate fees for his income. Of these, four were pupils of Thomas Whitehead (at Repton), who had taught Edward's younger brothers; two were pupils of Thomas Lovering at the Perse School in Cambridge; one was the son of the antiquary Roger Dodsworth; one was Edward's nephew Toby Caulfeild (later third Baron Caulfeild of Charlemont), the son of his sister Mary. Of the thirteen, one died as an undergraduate and only six went on to take degrees. As a fellow King was obliged to take his turn at college duties. He was appointed praelector in 1633, and in the academic year 1633/4 the entries in the college admissions book are written in his small and elegant hand; in 1636 he was appointed 'Graecus lector'. Fellows were obliged to preach in chapel in vacations as well as in term-time, and the master of Christ's, Thomas Bainbrigg, deducted up to 16*s*. from the quarterly stipends (£1) of fellows who failed to fulfil this obligation; in 1634 King was fined for this offence.

Sir John King died in Lichfield on 4 January 1637 and was buried at Boyle Abbey on 30 March. King decided to travel to Ireland that summer with a view to seeing his relatives (his brother Robert, his sisters Mary and Margaret, and his uncle Bishop King) and his former tutor William Chappell, who was provost of Trinity College, Dublin; he may also have intended to visit his father's grave in Roscommon. Piracy and the threat of storms made travelling across the Irish Sea a perilous undertaking so King drew up a will (dated 30 July, with a codicil dated two days later) before he left for Chester, where his ship sailed on the spring tide of 10 August. The ship struck a rock off the coast of Anglesey and quickly sank. King was drowned, and his body was carried out to sea and never recovered.

King's friends and colleagues commemorated him in a small volume of poetry which was published in Cambridge in 1638. This slim quarto, of which some thirty-three copies survive (including Izaak Walton's) consists of two parts: the first part, which is entitled *Justa Edovardo King naufrago*, contains twenty poems in Latin and three in Greek; the second part, entitled *Obsequies to the Memory of Mr Edward King*, contains thirteen poems in English, of which the last is Milton's 'Lycidas'. A draft of this poem survives in Milton's poetical notebook, now in Trinity College, Cambridge, and at least two copies of the printed volume (one in the British Library and one in Cambridge University Library) contain corrections to the text of 'Lycidas' in a hand that seems to be Milton's. The contributors to the memorial volume included Edward's brother Henry King (who is often confused with his namesake, the bishop of Chichester), Joseph Beaumont, John Cleveland, Michael Honywood, Henry More, Thomas Farnaby, and Ralph Widdrington. In addition to the thirty-six poems published in *Justa* there are at least four surviving unpublished memorial poems, including two by Clement Paman.

Commemorative poetry accommodates a measure of exaggeration in the praise of the deceased but the repeated and extravagant praise of King's knowledge of Greek and Latin suggests that his learning was exceptional, even by the high standards of that learned age. John Pullen of Magdalene College, for example, describes King (in Latin) as the great glory of Cambridge's men of letters, and Henry More eulogizes him (in Greek) as the light of the lamp of Athens. Such assertions help to explain why the erudite young Milton would describe King as 'a learned friend' in the headnote to 'Lycidas'.

King was the author of ten published Latin poems, seven of which were written to mark the birth of royal children; of the other three, one celebrates the recovery of King Charles from smallpox in the winter of 1632 and another gives thanks for Charles's safe return from his coronation in Scotland in 1633. King's only poem to be free of the constraints of royal encomium was written to welcome the publication of Peter Hausted's comedy *Odium senile*. These ten occasional poems may not achieve the greatness of Milton's best Latin poetry but they are none the less wholly competent and they display a marked independence of expression as well as a firm grasp of the classical tradition. The fact that the poems are largely devoted to the praise of royalty does not point to a partisan political position because King's life ended just as England was beginning to divide into rival supporters of king and parliament; nevertheless the supportive reference to the royal fleet in a poem published in 1637, the year in which John Hampden was tried for refusing to pay ship-money, could not have been politically neutral. Similarly the assertion in a poem written in 1636 that 'sancta maiestas Cathedræ / Dat placidam Italiæ quietem' ('the holy sovereignty of the church grants Italy its calm serenity') may have been appropriate in a poem addressed to a Catholic queen but it is indicative of an unusual degree of tolerance for Roman Catholicism.

Apart from the poems written by King and the poems written in his memory the only other documents that give any hint of his personality and circumstances are his will and the probate inventory of his rooms in Christ's College. In his will he left his books (which were valued at £90) to his colleague John Alsop and his sizar John Potts, and he requested Alsop to burn his papers without reading them or allowing them to be read by anyone else. The inventory is unremarkable, save that £512 (out of a total valuation of nearly £642) consists of 'debts owing unto him by bonds in his book'; these debts, which are described as 'sperate et desperate' ('hopeful and hopeless'), imply that King enjoyed considerable wealth during his brief life. Milton does not name King in 'Lycidas' but the fact that he is remembered in one of the greatest poems in the English language confers on him a degree of immortality that he would not have enjoyed had he not been the learned friend of Milton.

GORDON CAMPBELL

Sources N. Postlethwaite and G. Campbell, *Edward King, Milton's 'Lycidas': poems and documents*, *Milton Quarterly* [special issue], 28/4 (Dec 1994) · N. Postlethwaite and G. Campbell, 'Addenda et corrigenda', *Milton Quarterly*, 29/3 (1995), 93 · *Justa Edovardo King*, ed. E. Le Comte (1978) · admissions book, Christ's College, Cambridge ·

probate inventory, 1637, CUL, vice-chancellor's probate collection • *DNB*

Wealth at death £641 17*s*. 10*d*.: probate inventory, vice-chancellor's probate collection, 1637, CUL

King, Edward (1734/5–1807), writer and antiquary, was baptized at St Peter Mancroft, Norwich, on 22 January 1735, the only son of Edward King (*d*. 1775) of Norwich, and his wife, Sarah. He was educated at Harrow School and at Clare College, Cambridge, where he graduated in 1752. He was admitted a member of Lincoln's Inn on 18 September 1758 and was called to the bar in 1763. His uncle, a linen-draper of Exeter, left him an ample fortune; nevertheless he practised for a number of years on the Norwich circuit before becoming recorder at Kings Lynn. In the course of his duties he 'defended a lady from a faithless lover' and afterwards married her; all that is known of her is that her name was Susanna. He was elected FRS on 14 May 1767 and FSA on 3 May 1770, and became a member of the council of the Society of Antiquaries in 1774.

King's first publication was *An Essay on the English Constitution* (1767), a highly derivative piece of political journalism drawing heavily on Dalrymple and Hume. A number of his papers were published in *Archaeologia* during the 1770s, including 'Remarks on the abbey church of Bury St Edmunds in Suffolk' and two papers on ancient castles. The director of the Society of Antiquaries, Richard Gough, who was responsible for the publication of *Archaeologia*, complained to Jeremiah Milles, the society's president, of King's vanity in insisting on seeing his own papers published. Following the death of Milles in February 1784, King was elected his successor as president of the society on the understanding that Lord De Ferrars (afterwards earl of Leicester) would assume office the following 23 April. During his short presidency King drew up a set of regulations for meetings and initiated a number of administrative reforms, including the appointment of two regular secretaries and a draughtsman, as well as making efforts to increase the revenues of the society by enforcing the collection of membership fees. When April came he sought re-election; he was, however, defeated by an overwhelming majority and was accused of underhand methods in attempting to secure his own election. His speech on quitting the society was printed in 1784, as was his letter vindicating his own conduct. His actions aroused little sympathy within the society (most of whom could see the advantage of having a peer of the realm as president) and prompted Samuel Pegge to comment that 'Edwd. King is a troublesome man, & the Society will do full as well without his Company at their meetings as with it' (letter, 16 Aug 1784, minute books of the Society of Antiquaries). Although he did not contribute any further papers to *Archaeologia* his name appears in the record of council meetings during 1785–6.

This rift with the society did not herald the end of King's antiquarian interests. A paper, 'Vestiges of Oxford Castle', was published in 1796, anticipating the publication of his much larger study on the same subject: *Munimenta antiqua, or, Observations on ancient castles, including remarks on the … progress of architecture … in Great Britain, and on the … change*

in … *laws and customs*, 4 vols. (1799–1806). The book is typical of King's somewhat idiosyncratic approach to antiquarian studies but nevertheless makes a strong case for architectural history and the close analysis of form and style (if less successfully effected). King argued that antiquarianism was a science and that antiquarian research should therefore be conducted in accordance with scientific models of measurement and comparison rather than being concerned with picturesque views. Though many of his contemporaries were contemptuous of his 'foolish theories' (the *Monthly Review* was particularly critical of his obsession with concealed entrances and secret passages) his work was widely cited, and influenced, for example, George Chalmer's *Caledonia* (1810); the plans and plates are generally recognized to have had some lasting value. Louis Dutens disputed King's theories on the invention of the arch, and King responded in a typically vigorous fashion in the final volume of *Munimenta antiqua*, in 1806. The controversy was not ended until King's death, in the following year. King also displayed his scientific learning in the pamphlet *Remarks concerning stones said to have fallen from the clouds, both in these days and in antient times* (1796), which was prompted by a shower of stones that had supposedly fallen in Tuscany in the previous year and been investigated by Abbate Soldani, professor of mathematics at the University of Siena.

King's interests had always been eclectic and he published on a number of other subjects in addition to that of antiquity. In 1785 he circulated anonymously *Proposals for Establishing at Sea a Marine School, or Seminary for Seamen*, which pointed out objections to Jonas Hanway's proposals for a large marine school on land and suggested fitting up a man-of-war instead. Hanway responded with *Observations on a Proposal* (1785). King's *Considerations on the utility of the national debt: and on the present alarming crisis; with a short plan of a mode or relief* was published in 1793; he challenged the widespread anxiety surrounding the inexorable increase of the national debt and argued that rather than being a cause for concern its size should be positively welcomed as an indication of the country's prosperity; furthermore he suggested that the debt should be increased to maximize the amount of wealth in circulation. His pamphlet drew only one response, from Joseph Acland.

King's antiquarian publications had always had a strong providentialist streak but towards the end of his life his theological and mystical interests became increasingly prominent. His theology represents an interesting mixture of eschatology, virulent anti-Catholicism, and a vigorous assertion of the compatibility of scientific truth with revealed religion. In 1788 his *Morsels of Criticism* attempted to show that John the Baptist was an angel from heaven who had formerly appeared in the person of Elijah, and that there would be a second appearance of Christ upon earth. In the same publication he also argued that the earth was a kind of comet on a trajectory towards the sun, by which it would eventually be ignited, while at its centre the earth consisted of a bottomless pit in which the wicked were punished. Though King received sixty copies for personal distribution there was little demand for the remaining texts; a few years later it was mentioned in Mathias's *The Pursuits of Literature* and as a result was reissued, in 1800, with 'a supplemental part designed to show, still more fully, the perfect consistency of philosophical discoveries, and of historical facts, with the revealed Will of God'.

The popular success of *Morsels of Criticism* did nothing to enhance King's reputation as a philosophical commentator on the scriptures, however. In 1793 he had published 'An imitation of the prayer of Abel'; a rather more extraordinary pamphlet, *Remarks on the Signs of the Times*, was published in 1798, in which he claimed that the second coming was imminent, in fulfilment of the prophecy of the second book of Esdras, whose questionable authenticity he vigorously upheld. He also tried to trace the history and progress of the French Revolution to the scriptures. Irritated by Richard Gough's critique in the *Gentleman's Magazine* (*GM*, 68/2, 591–3), he wrote a violent letter to the printer, John Nichols. King added a 'Supplement' in 1799 but this was demolished by Bishop Horsley in the same periodical in his 'Critical disquisitions on the eighteenth chapter of Isaiah, in a letter to E. King'. King's next (anonymous) publication was *Honest Apprehensions, or, The Unbiassed … Confession of Faith of Plain Honest Lay-Man*, which contained an orthodox statement of Trinitarian theology.

King prided himself on the breadth of his reading and his learning, was exceedingly tenacious of his opinions, impervious to criticism, and very defensive of his views. His obituary in the *Gentleman's Magazine* described him as a considerable eccentric, but pious and well-meaning. Little is known of his wife, Susanna; her niece Miss Ann Copson, described as 'an accomplished young lady with a large fortune', completed a number of the drawings for *Munimenta antiqua* and married Henry Windsor, younger brother to the earl of Plymouth, from King's house in Beckenham, Kent (*GM*, 71/1, 390).

King died at his home in Mansfield Street, London, on 16 April 1807, aged seventy-two, and was buried in the churchyard at Beckenham, near to his country seat, The Oakery, on Clay Hill. He was survived by his wife. His extensive collection of prints and drawings was sold by auction in 1808.   R. H. SWEET

Sources A. Chalmers, ed., *The general biographical dictionary*, new edn, 32 vols. (1812–17) • Venn, *Alum. Cant.* • J. Evans, *A history of the Society of Antiquaries* (1956) • *GM*, 1st ser., 45 (1775) • *GM*, 1st ser., 49 (1779), 498–503 • *GM*, 1st ser., 68 (1798), 591–3 • *GM*, 1st ser., 77 (1807), 388–90 • minute books, S. Antiquaries, Lond. • *DNB* • will, PRO, PROB 11/1461, fols. 238v–240r • IGI
Archives CUL, notebook • Norfolk RO, personal accounts • priv. coll., essay on the character of King David • Trinity Cam., corresp. and papers • U. Cam., Sedgwick Museum of Earth Sciences, catalogue of fossil collection

King, Edward, Viscount Kingsborough (1795–1837), antiquary, born on 16 November 1795, was the eldest son of the family of three sons and two daughters of George King, third earl of Kingston in the peerage of Ireland (1771–1839), and Lady Helena Moore (1773–1847), only daughter of Stephen Moore, first Earl Mountcashell. After his father succeeded to the earldom in 1799 he was known by the courtesy title of Viscount Kingsborough. He matriculated at Oxford from Exeter College on 25 June 1814, and in Michaelmas term 1818 gained a second class in classics, but did not graduate. In 1818 and again in 1820 he was elected MP for Cork county, but resigned his seat in 1826 in favour of his younger brother Robert.

Kingsborough was introduced by the bibliophile Sir Thomas Phillipps to Bodley's librarian Bulkeley Bandinel, who showed him the great Mexican manuscript the Codex Mendoza in the Bodleian Library. This determined Kingsborough to devote his life to the study of the antiquities of Mexico. Again with Phillipps's encouragement, Kingsborough promoted and edited, with copious notes, a magnificent work entitled *Antiquities of Mexico, Comprising Facsimiles of Ancient Mexican Paintings and Hieroglyphics* (9 vols., 1830–48). Seven volumes were published during his lifetime. Four copies were printed on vellum, with the plates coloured. The drift of Kingsborough's speculations is to establish the colonization of Mexico by the Israelites. The enterprise cost him more than £32,000. He incurred heavy debts in the preparation of his book, to paper makers and others. He was arrested, apparently in connection with having stood security for a debt of his father's, and was lodged in the sheriff's prison, Dublin, where he caught typhus fever and died within a few days, on 27 February 1837. Kingsborough, who was unmarried, was buried at Mitchelstown. Had he lived, he would have succeeded to the earldom of Kingston and to a substantial income.

Sales of Kingsborough's manuscripts and of the remaining stock of the *Antiquities* were conducted by Charles Sharpe in Dublin on 1 November 1842 and 14 March 1843. On 24 May 1854 further manuscripts were included in a mixed sale in Dublin. Sir Thomas Phillipps was a substantial purchaser at the sales.

GORDON GOODWIN, rev. ALAN BELL

Sources GEC, *Peerage* • A. N. L. Munby, *The formation of the Phillipps library from 1841 to 1872* (1956), vol. 4 of *Phillipps Studies* (1951–60) • HoP, *Commons* • *GM*, 2nd ser., 7 (1837), 537–8 • *Annual Register* (1837) • Foster, *Alum. Oxon.*
Archives Bodl. Oxf., corresp. with Sir Thomas Phillipps
Wealth at death died in debtors' prison

King, Edward (1829–1910), bishop of Lincoln, was born on 29 December 1829 at 8 St James's Place, Piccadilly, the third child and second son of Walker King (1797–1859), rector of Stone, Kent, and canon and archdeacon of Rochester, and his wife, Anne (*d.* 1883), daughter of William Heberden the younger, a distinguished London physician. He grew up in rural Kent and all his life relished the countryside, its people and pursuits—fishing, riding, swimming. Because of indifferent health he was not sent away to school, but educated at home by his father and the curate of St Mary's, Stone, John Day (1813–1864). Day graduated from Brasenose College, Oxford, in 1834 and spent ten years at Stone, where he helped to imbue the young King with his own high-church convictions. When Day became vicar of St Mary's, Ellesmere, Shropshire, in 1846 the young King accompanied him and served as his lay assistant until he went up to Oriel College, Oxford, in 1848.

Education and early career At Oriel, where E. B. Pusey, Hurrell Froude, and J. H. Newman had all been fellows, the Tractarian tradition was still upheld by J. W. Burgon and Charles Marriott. The provost, Edward Hawkins (1789–1882), was fiercely anti-Tractarian and determined to eradicate from his college all trace of the movement. In the formal interview ('collection') at the end of King's first term Hawkins, scenting a whiff of 'Newmania' in the young high-churchman, commented, 'I observe, Mr. King, that you have never missed a single chapel morning or evening, during the whole term. I must warn you, Mr. King, that even too regular attendance at chapel may degenerate into formalism' (Russell, 5). King, however, was confirmed in his Tractarian piety by the example of Charles Marriott, disciple of Newman and embodiment of unselfishness. Years later King acknowledged, 'If I have any good in me, I owe it to Charles Marriott. He was the most Gospel-like man I have ever met' (ibid., 5).

King graduated BA in 1851, and for the rest of his life would draw on the key texts he studied at Oriel, most notably Aristotle's *Ethics* and Joseph Butler's *Analogy of Religion*. After graduation he made a pilgrimage to Palestine in June 1852, and acted as tutor to Lord Lothian's brothers. In March 1854 he saw Samuel Wilberforce, bishop of Oxford, with a view to ordination. Wilberforce ordained him deacon on 11 June 1854 and he served as curate to Edward Elton, vicar of Wheatley, near Oxford. Lord Elton, Edward's grandson, in his memoir *Edward King and our Times* (1958), gives a vivid account of King's four-year curacy: Elton, a recent widower with four young children, found King 'a messenger of peace and consolation', who gave him 'the most constant and affectionate help' (Elton, 32). King discovered at Wheatley a vocation to the country poor: his pastoral sympathy and outgoing happiness—'brightness' was one of his favourite words—drew his people, especially the young men and boys, to the Christian life.

At Michaelmas 1858 Bishop Wilberforce appointed King chaplain of Cuddesdon College, his recently founded (1854) seminary for clergy training. The college had already come under attack for its alleged romanizing tendencies, thanks largely to the uncompromising high-churchmanship of its vice-principal, Henry Parry Liddon. In 1859 Wilberforce dismissed Liddon, and in 1863 appointed King as principal, a post which carried with it the incumbency of the parish of Cuddesdon. The dual role of principal and parish priest suited King to perfection, and his nephew G. F. Wilgress later wrote of him: 'He was at the beck and call of anyone in sickness or in trouble' (Wilgress, 9). During an attack of smallpox he assiduously visited the sick, and when no one else dared put the dead into their coffins he did it himself. He carried this pastoral concern into the life of the college, where Liddon's rigorism was replaced by a more relaxed, though disciplined, community life—in King's words, 'a Christian higgledy-piggledy' (King, 111), with a minimum of rules without stiff formality, a true fellowship of staff and students. As parish priest, teacher, and spiritual guide he gave his students a lasting vision of Christian priesthood. Robert Milman, later bishop of Calcutta, and no sentimentalist, described Cuddesdon under King as, 'like a breath from the Garden of Eden before the door was shut' (ibid., 183). For Scott Holland, 'The whole place was alive with him. His look, his voice, his gaiety, his beauty, his charm, his holiness, filled it and possessed it' (Holland, 51).

Professor of pastoral theology In 1873 W. E. Gladstone appointed King regius professor of pastoral theology at Oxford, a post carrying with it a canonry of Christ Church Cathedral. Archbishop Tait, W. E. Jelf, and others opposed the appointment of a high-churchman lacking scholarly distinction, and King himself was surprised, seeing himself as 'socially unknown, academically nothing' (E. King, *The Love and Wisdom of God*, 1910, 134). Yet he was well-read and impressively equipped, by both gifts and experience, to teach his subject. As professor, he determined to improve his scholarly equipment. He spent the 1875 long vacation in Germany, learning the language as a theological tool to add to the French and Italian in which he was already fluent. F. E. Brightman, the distinguished liturgiologist and King's Oxford colleague, spoke of his 'singularly alert mind' which was 'really alive to the intellectual difficulties of his day' (Brightman, 308). In Oxford, Comte's 'religion of humanity' was gaining ground, and the secularist challenge to Christianity was increasingly powerful. In this intellectual milieu King found the writings of some leading continental Roman Catholics highly pertinent. He read Lacordaire, Doupanloup, Döllinger, and above all J. M. Sailer (1751–1832). Sailer, a professor of theology and bishop of Regensburg, had seen the Enlightenment as a profound challenge to the church, and responded to it, both critically and creatively, in terms of pastoral and theological renewal. King drew on Sailer's great three-volume *Pastoraltheologie* for his Oxford lectures, and found him a kindred spirit. (Twentieth-century Roman Catholic theologians have hailed Sailer both as a proto-ecumenist and as a herald of the more biblical and dynamic doctrine of the church espoused by the Second Vatican Council.) Through lectures, sermons, and his work as spiritual guide and confessor, King exerted, on the wider stage of the university, the same powerful influence as he had at Cuddesdon. His *Pastoral Lectures*, published in 1932 from a student's notebook of 1874, reveal the wide range of sources he drew on: the Bible and prayer book; patristic literature and the works of medieval schoolmen; classic Anglican and Roman Catholic divines; Wesley's Methodism; and even modern novels.

King's Friday evening addresses, given in the Bethel, a large converted wash-house at the bottom of his garden, drew crowds of undergraduates of all types. Scott Holland met a young clergyman in 1883—'intelligent, thoughtful, charming … rowed in his boat at Oxford; and then got wholly snared by King' (H. S. Holland, *A Forty Years' Friendship: Letters from the Late Henry Scott Holland to Mrs Drew*, ed. S. L. Ollard, 1919, 37). Among those King influenced as undergraduates were W. H. Hutton, the historian; G. W. E. Russell, the parliamentarian and author; Francis Paget, later bishop of Oxford; and Winnington-Ingram, later bishop of London. Senior members of the university included Scott Holland and J. R. Illingworth, who made King his regular confessor.

King's Oxford ministry included a commitment to the universal mission of the church, which, he confessed, 'always stirs me up to the very bottom' (Russell, 96). He was a founder of St Stephen's House, Oxford, a missionary training college for priests. The Oxford Mission to Calcutta was first mooted in 1879 in King's rooms at Christ Church. Nearer home, he keenly supported both the Christ Church Mission to Poplar and the Oxford House settlement in Bethnal Green.

Bishop of Lincoln In 1885 Gladstone again overlooked King's rooted political Conservatism and appointed him to the see of Lincoln. King's regret at leaving Oxford was tempered by the prospect of a return to pastoral work among country people. In 1877 he had written: 'I should not choose the University to work in if I had my choice. I would rather be with the simplest agricultural poor, but it is not so arranged' (King, 54). Scott Holland rejoiced to anticipate a 'S. Francis de Sales at Lincoln!' (H. S. Holland, *A Forty Years' Friendship: Letters from the Late Henry Scott Holland to Mrs Drew*, ed. S. L. Ollard, 1919, 86). Yet by no means all approved: the militant Church Association saw him as a Romanizer, and as at Oriel, Cuddesdon, and Christ Church he drew the fire of those who mistrusted the Tractarians. At King's consecration in St Paul's, Liddon extolled the new bishop's 'great grace of sympathy' which had achieved 'so much among so many young men' at Cuddesdon and Oxford. He looked forward to 'an episcopate, which … will rank hereafter with those which in point of moral beauty stand highest on the roll of the later English Church—with Andrewes, with Ken, with Wilson, with Hamilton' (Russell, 104–5).

For all his pastoral gifts, King faced strong challenges in Lincolnshire. The diocese was a Methodist heartland and also had a significant low-church presence. But the new bishop never downplayed his high-church convictions. He wore eucharistic vestments and—arguably the first bishop to do so since the Reformation—the mitre which friends had given him. The work of a large diocese also taxed his health, for which, as well as for recreation, he needed an annual break in the mountains of Switzerland or Italy. He walked with a stoop, and looked older than his fifty-five years. Yet contemporary portraits show his eyes keen and lively, his face open and eager. He had a firm, well-set mouth, resolved without being grim, and a strong chin. His features endorsed his own conviction that 'Gentleness is not weakness, but restrained strength'.

The quality of the Lincolnshire clergy also concerned King. Proverbially they were divisible into those going out of their minds, those who had gone out of their minds, and those with no minds to go out of. He took a keen interest in Bishop's Hostel, the diocesan theological college, encouraged clerical reading societies, and arranged annual retreats for serious clerical study. He responded to the challenge of nonconformity with typical eirenicism: 'I need hardly say that I have never had any harsh feelings against Nonconformists, and, I might add, especially not towards Wesleyans and Primitive Methodists, because I have always felt that it was the want of spiritual life in the Church and brotherly love which led them to separate. The more we can draw near to Christ ourselves and fill ourselves with His Spirit, the greater power we shall have for unity. What we want is more Christlike Christians' (King, 108). This penitent ecumenism did not bring Methodists flooding back into the church, but it drew them to his preaching and sweetened church relations. The Lincolnshire oral tradition suggests that the popular verdict on his simple, direct, evangelical preaching was: 'He's nowt but an owd Methody'.

King's pastoral ideal at Lincoln was expressed in his initial reaction to his appointment: 'I am glad it is John Wesley's diocese. I shall try to be the Bishop of the Poor' (Russell, 86). He moved from the great rambling palace of Riseholme, well out of the city, to the smaller, medieval Old Palace, hard by the cathedral and accessible to his clergy and people. At his consecration he looked forward to becoming 'a big curate in the diocese of Lincoln' (ibid., 108). He lived simply, and his old clothes and worn boots were the despair of well-meaning friends. He used the railways to visit remote parts of the diocese, and delighted in confirming country people, young and old. If a confirmand missed the service from illness, he was known to go to the house and confirm at the bedside.

King was no great administrator, and was prone to fall lamentably behind with correspondence. On the other hand, he made time for individuals of all kinds, and had an extraordinary way of empathizing with them in their needs. In 1887 a young fisherman was condemned to death at Lincoln assizes for killing his sweetheart; he seemed to have no moral sense and appeared simply 'a powerful animal' (Russell, 124). King spent hours with him in the death cell, told him the story of the prodigal son, and held out the promise of forgiveness and new life. The young man was profoundly converted, and King heard his confession, confirmed him, and went with him to the scaffold. King wrote to George Russell, 'his last (and first) Communion … put me to shame. I felt quite unworthy of him. How little the world knows of the inner life' (ibid., 125–6). From then on King regularly ministered to prisoners under sentence of death, and spent long periods with them in prayer and counselling.

The Lincoln judgment Having in 1887 begun to minister to those who had fallen foul of the law, King soon came to trial—in the ecclesiastical courts—himself. In June 1888 the Church Association petitioned the archbishop of Canterbury, Edward White Benson, to try King for alleged ritual acts contrary to the prayer book. Benson convoked a special court to hear the charges, which were that at Lincoln Cathedral and St Peter-at-Gowts parish church King, as celebrant at the eucharist, had: consecrated in the eastward position; allowed lighted candles on the altar in daylight; mixed water and wine in the chalice; had the Agnus Dei sung after the consecration; made the sign of the cross at both absolution and blessing; and conducted the ablutions of the communion vessels. The court found largely in King's favour, but insisted that the chalice should be mixed, if at all, before, not during, the service; that the manual acts—obscured by the eastward position—must be visible to the people; and the sign of the cross must not be used. King was not a rabid ritualist himself, and deprecated 'extravagances'. He saw ritual as a way of giving greater glory to God, who 'has surrounded us with all forms of beauty in nature', and also as a teaching aid 'to bring the people to God, to clothe the dogma in such a way as will lead them to Him' (E. King, *Ezra and Nehemiah …: Two Sermons Preached at S. Barnabas' Church, Oxford*, 1872, 14–15). Yet he was clear that the ritual used must conform to the teaching and discipline of the Church of England. King loyally accepted the 'Lincoln judgment', which effectively put an end to a bitter series of ritual trials. The Church Association appealed to the judicial committee of the privy council, which in 1892 upheld the archbishop's verdict. The four years' controversy involved King in much unwelcome publicity, and aged him to a degree.

During this difficult period King tried to follow the pastoral advice he gave to others—not to let trouble take the heart out of you, but to go quietly and bravely on. The 'quietly' was typical of King's Tractarian spirituality, which emphasized disciplined devotion and deprecated pious verbosity. He was not only thoroughly Anglican, but quintessentially English in his spirituality. Like Julian of Norwich, George Herbert, and Nicholas Ferrar, he sought to unite doctrine and devotion, the holy and the homely, in Christian living. 'I do value so highly a natural growth in holiness, a humble grateful acceptance of the circumstances God has provided for each of us, and I dread the unnatural, forced, cramped ecclesiastical holiness, which is so much more quickly produced, but is so human and so poor' (King, 35). What struck others about King was, in Scott Holland's words, his 'rounded normality' (Holland, 49), in which nature and grace strikingly cohered.

King's Catholic Anglicanism embraced eucharistic devotions, auricular confession, monastic vows, and the renewal of the religious life in the Church of England. At the same time his preaching was Christ-centred, his characteristic way of speaking of Jesus was as 'the Saviour', and he might well be described as an evangelical Catholic. He had none of the gloom that sometimes disfigured early Tractarianism. His vivid, deep-blue eyes radiated hope and joy. Scott Holland recalled that 'It was light that he carried with him, light that shone through him, light that flowed from him. … Those eyes of his were an illumination' (Holland, 48). He had an almost Franciscan delight in nature, and loved birds, trees, and flowers. Yet his greatest love was for people, and in all his pastoral dealings he exemplified von Hügel's claim that Christianity means asceticism without rigorism, and love without sentimentality. King was theologically conservative, yet not narrowly so. In 1891, when the furore over the publication of *Lux mundi* still raged, he invited Charles Gore, the leader of the younger Anglo-Catholics who produced the volume, to take his annual three-day clergy retreat in Lincoln Cathedral. He was also politically Conservative, though strongly in favour of the vote for agricultural labourers as,

among other things, an excellent preparation for heaven. On the other hand, he voted against old age pensions as he feared they would discourage thrift. His experience of working-class life and poverty came mainly from the countryside. Yet he had knowledge of the urban poor, both in Oxford, in the parish of St Barnabas, Jericho, and in Lincoln, where he knew the railwaymen and regularly visited the great engineering works.

King's writings, published after his death, consist mainly of letters, sermons, and addresses. The most significant were *Spiritual Letters of Edward King, D.D.* (1910); *The Love and Wisdom of God* (1910), containing some of his best sermons; *Duty and Conscience* (1911); *Counsels to Nurses* (1911); *Sermons and Addresses* (1911); and *Easter Sermons* (1914). Eric Graham published *Pastoral Lectures of Bishop Edward King* in 1932.

King was unmarried, but showed a genuine appreciation of married life. He died peacefully on 10 March 1910 at the Old Palace, Lincoln, after a short illness, in his eighty-first year. He was buried on 11 March in the cloister garth of his cathedral. Widely acknowledged as a saint in his lifetime, he was formally recognized as one by his church on 24 May 1935. Archbishop Cosmo Gordon Lang preached in Lincoln Cathedral, at a service to commemorate the fiftieth anniversary of King's consecration to Lincoln, on 'Edward King, bishop and saint'. Collect, epistle, and gospel were specially prepared for the commemoration, and have been used in the diocese ever since. He is included in the 'Kalendar of saints' in the 1980 *Alternative Service Book* of the Church of England, under 8 March, as 'Edward King, Bishop of Lincoln, Teacher, Pastor'.

JOHN A. NEWTON

Sources G. W. E. Russell, *Edward King* (1912) · B. W. Randolph and J. W. Townroe, *The mind and work of Bishop King* (1918) · G. F. Wilgress, *Edward King, bishop of Lincoln* [n.d., 1930?] · O. Chadwick, *The founding of Cuddesdon* (1954) · Lord Elton [G. Elton], *Edward King and our times* (1958) · H. S. Holland, *A bundle of memories* (1915) · F. E. Brightman, 'King, Edward', *A dictionary of English church history*, ed. S. L. Ollard and G. Crosse (1912) · J. A. Newton, *Search for a saint: Edward King* (1977) · E. King, *Spiritual letters of Edward King, D.D.* (1910)

Archives Cuddesdon College, Oxford, letters · Lincs. Arch., corresp., dissertations, sermons, and papers · Pusey Oxf., letters | BL, letters to W. E. Gladstone, Add. MSS 44437–44526, *passim* · Bodl. Oxf., letters to Samuel Wilberforce · CKS, letters to Edward Stanhope · Lincs. Arch., letters to Canon Bramley and Revd Larken · LPL, corresp. with Archbishop Benson · LPL, evidence and minutes relating to Lincoln judgment · LPL, corresp. with Frederick Temple · Pusey Oxf., corresp. with J. L. Gibbs

Likenesses G. Richmond, oils, 1873, Cuddesdon College, Oxford · W. W. Ouless, oils, exh. RA 1899, bishop's house, Lincoln · W. B. Richmond, bronze statue, 1914, Lincoln Cathedral · Spy [L. Ward], chromolithograph, caricature, NPG; repro. in *VF* (13 Sept 1890) · group portrait, cabinet photograph, NPG · photograph, NPG · rotary photograph, postcard, NPG · stone effigy, Edward King House, Lincoln

Wealth at death £24,069 3s. 8d.: probate, 4 July 1910, CGPLA Eng. & Wales

King [*née* Gore-Browne], **Dame Ethel Locke** (1864–1956), motor-racing promoter and hospital patron, was born on 3 June 1864 at Government House, Hobart, Tasmania, the younger daughter of Colonel Sir Thomas Gore-Browne

(1807–1887), governor of Tasmania, and his wife, Harriet Louisa, daughter of James Campbell of Craigie House, Ayrshire. She had at least one brother. Ethel left Tasmania in 1868 and spent 1870 and 1871 in Bermuda during her father's term as governor of the colony. The family subsequently returned to England.

On 3 January 1884, at St Mary Abbots, Kensington, at the age of nineteen, Ethel married Hugh Fortescue Locke King (d. 1926), then a barrister. They were married by her uncle, the bishop of Winchester. Her husband was the eldest surviving son of Peter John Locke *King (1811–1885), MP. After their wedding Ethel and her husband travelled to Cairo in Egypt where they spent the remainder of the winter. There were no children from the marriage. Wintering abroad became a regular practice, and after Hugh's father died in 1885 the couple acquired the Mena House, once a royal lodge used by the khedive Isma'il, as a home for themselves. The house was near the pyramids and they turned it into a hotel, enlarging and furnishing it with the proceeds from the sale of parts of the Portmore estate which Hugh had inherited. Because of the couple's extravagance the hotel ran at a loss and was eventually sold at some point after 1900.

Back in England, Ethel played an important part in her husband's management of his property and in farming his estates in Surrey and elsewhere. She was also involved in his decision in 1906 to build the world's first banked motor-racing course in a 'swampy, rabbit infested corner of Surrey' (Gardner, 14). According to his own account the idea had come to Locke King at Brescia, in northern Italy, after the Coppa Floria motor race meeting in 1905, when he had spoken to some of the owners and drivers of the French, German, and Italian cars which had been competing. In reply to his question about why no English car was entered, he was told that the English had no practice in racing cars at speed. A month later, hearing it suggested that a circular track was needed where the cars could be watched over the whole course, Locke King realized that a suitable site lay on his own land.

Motor racing on roads was against the law and, in conjunction with the Royal Automobile Club, Hugh and Ethel Locke King founded the British Automobile Racing Club. The cost of the enterprise escalated and Hugh's health suffered under the strain of meeting demands for more and more money to pay for the project. When they were faced with bankruptcy in 1907 the task was largely taken over by Ethel, who was supported by her brother Francis, their long-standing friend Baron de Rodakowski, and other members of the family. It is doubtful if the circuit ever made a profit, but an industrial estate was later developed on adjacent land.

The Brooklands track was officially opened on 17 June 1907 and a celebratory circuit of the track was headed by Ethel driving her Itala car 'Bambo', which she subsequently raced, notably in the Ladies' Bracelet Handicap of 1908. It was felt that women drivers should not wear smocks like the men, so they sported coloured scarves instead. Ethel was also interested in flying, and Brooklands became one of the pioneering centres for powered flight. On 29 October 1909 she made a flight of ten minutes' duration and reached a height of 200 feet in the Gnome-engined pusher-biplane 'la Gypaete', piloted by the French aviator Louis Paulhan.

In November 1912 Ethel became vice-president of the north Surrey division of the British Red Cross, and she commenced her war service with that organization on the outbreak of the First World War. A spectacular field day was held by the army, at Brooklands in June 1914, to publicize voluntary aid detachments. The event was organized by Ethel and attended by Queen Alexandra and her sister the empress Maria Feodrovna of Russia. Subsequently, Ethel received a letter of thanks and congratulations from the queen.

During the course of the First World War, Ethel Locke King established fourteen auxiliary hospitals in the county, some of which were in houses owned by her husband. One of these, Vigo House, was given to Weybridge in 1923 for use as its cottage hospital. Ethel became assistant county director of the British Red Cross for Surrey, and later she was honorary commandant for Surrey (Weybridge). For her war service she was made DBE on 1 January 1918, and she also received the order of St John.

The War Office took over Brooklands in 1914 and the Royal Flying Corps established its headquarters there. Having started a flying school at Brooklands in 1912, Vickers began building aeroplanes at the site three years later. It was not until 1920 that the motor track reopened. During the following two decades the circuit at Brooklands became renowned, especially for its steeped, banked turn. Motor-racing events at Brooklands became not only great social events, but the circuit also played a key role in British motor-racing history. A number of leading drivers, including Malcolm Campbell, George Eyston, Raymond Mays, Kay Petre, and John Cobb, first came to prominence by winning races at Brooklands.

Hugh Locke King died in 1926, leaving his entire estate to his widow, who was then sixty-one years old. As well as becoming managing director and chief shareholder of the Brooklands Estate Company, Dame Ethel also ran the motor track and the aerodrome. In 1936 she transferred the undertaking to a new company, Byfleet Estates Ltd; and later that year Brooklands (Weybridge) Ltd was formed to acquire the track and aerodrome. Ethel subsequently moved to a house at Caen's Hill on the right of the 'Shell Way' entrance road. Motor racing finally ceased in 1939, and most of the site was sold off for development purposes after the Second World War. Part of the track survived, however, including the famous banked turn, and a Brooklands Museum was opened there.

Dame Ethel died at her home, Caen's Hill, Weybridge, Surrey, on 5 August 1956, at the age of ninety-two. In an obituary in *The Times* the earl of Portsmouth paid tribute to her trenchant wit and courageous nature, adding that 'She had a carriage that had no need of pride yet added inches to her slight, gallant figure' (*The Times*, 14 August 1956).   COLIN J. PARRY

Sources *The Times* (6 Aug 1956) · G. V. Wallop, appreciation, *The Times* (14 Aug 1956) · G. R. D., appreciation, *The Times* (14 Aug 1956) ·

J. S. L. Pulford, 'Hugh Locke King', *The Brookland Greats*, 1 (1995) • C. J. T. Gardner, *Fifty years of Brooklands* (1956) • W. C. Boddy, *The history of Brooklands Motor Course* (1957) • British Red Cross archives, Wonersh, Surrey • Burke, *Peerage* • Burke, *Gen. GB* • Brooklands Museum, Weybridge, Surrey • J. S. L. Pulford, 'The Locke Kings, Brooklands, Weybridge', *Walton and Weybridge Local History Society*, 31 (1996) • d. cert. • m. cert.

Archives Brooklands Museum, Weybridge, Surrey
Likenesses two photographs, 1885–1930, Brooklands Museum
Wealth at death £110,645 7s. 3d.: probate, 2 Nov 1956, *CGPLA Eng. & Wales*

King [*née* Bernard], **Frances Elizabeth** [Fanny] (1757–1821), philanthropist and author, was born on 25 July 1757 at Lincoln, the third daughter and eighth child of Sir Francis *Bernard, baronet (1712–1779), provincial lawyer and later governor of New Jersey and Massachusetts, and Amelia, *née* Offley (*c.*1719–1778), daughter of Stephen Offley of Norton Hall, Derbyshire. Her nine brothers and sisters included the philanthropist Sir Thomas *Bernard, founder of the Society for Bettering the Condition and Improving the Comforts of the Poor.

In 1758 Francis Bernard was appointed governor of the colony of New Jersey in North America, and departed with his wife and four of their children. Frances, described by her great-niece Sophia Higgins, the family biographer, as 'unusually delicate' (Higgins, 1.221), was left under the care of Mrs Beresford, a near relative of her father's, who lived at the Manor House, Nether Winchendon, Buckinghamshire. Sophia Higgins described Frances's education, conducted by her elder sister Jane (*b.* 1748) and Mrs Beresford, as consisting of solid reading, French, music, and needlework, as well as household duties. According to her anonymous memoirist, who may have been her future son-in-law, John Collinson (*c.*1791–1857): 'Here those good principles of religion and active and succouring charity were instilled, which influenced her future life and led her to co-operate with her family in assisting the poor' (*Female Scripture Characters*, v). King later acknowledged her debt to Jane, dedicating her *Female Scripture Characters* 'To a beloved sister, as a grateful memorial of the early instruction and pious example from whence her best blessings have sprung'.

On Sir Francis's return from America in 1769 Frances Elizabeth joined her family, first in Lincoln and subsequently at Nether Winchendon (from May 1772) and Aylesbury (from September of the same year). In her study of the family, Sophia Higgins argues that Frances, known as Fanny to her friends, aged seventeen, was a 'remarkable' and 'self-reliant' girl, due to her almost total separation from her near relatives for her first eleven years (Higgins, 2.274). Her first literary work, *The Rector's Memorandum Book, being Memoirs of a Family in the North*, was written in 1774, the year of her sister Jane's marriage to Charles White, although the text was not published until 1814 and 1819. Her exemplary Christian heroine was represented as educating all the children in the village and nursing the sick. Forced to make an unhappy marriage, she nevertheless demonstrated her spiritual superiority over her unkind husband by her Christian submissiveness, and died a pious and early death.

Frances Elizabeth King (1757–1821), by Edward Scriven, pubd 1822 (after Edward Hastings)

After her mother's death in May 1778 King often stayed with friends and relatives, for example, in Wendover and Yorkshire. She may also have continued a school superintended by her mother in Nether Winchendon. Family letters cited by Higgins suggest she became engaged to the Revd Richard *King (1748–1810), a friend of her brother Scrope, at Nether Winchendon about 1780. According to Higgins this was against the wishes of her brothers, due to King's lack of income, offhand manner, and political views. Nevertheless, Frances affirmed that 'It must rest solely within myself to guide my own conduct' (Higgins, 3.36, citing a letter then at Nether Winchendon). On 17 August 1782 they were married in London. The couple resided at King's livings of Steeple Morden, Cambridgeshire, and at Worthin, Shropshire, which he was granted about 1782, finally settling at Steeple Morden in 1809. The marriage was described as very happy, as the dedication to *The Beneficial Effects of the Christian Temper on Domestic Happiness* (2nd edn, 1807) suggests.

In 1783 Frances Elizabeth King gave birth to twins, Henry and Amelia. Henry died, aged one. Julia Priscilla was born in 1786, and Elizabeth in 1792. King frequently cared for children besides her own offspring, for example fostering her orphaned nephew between 1791 and 1793, and later looking after her grandchildren. Several young girls came to live with King, including the daughters of Lady Ingilby (and at one time Ingilby's son) and a Miss Richardson about 1794. In April 1802 her elder daughter, Amelia, married John Collinson, and in 1808 Julia married her cousin, Thomas Baker.

The Kings' daughter Elizabeth died in 1801, after which

Frances's health, already affected by rheumatism, deteriorated. Following the peace of Amiens, Richard and Frances King stayed in Paris for eight months in 1802, after which Mrs King published *A Tour in France* (1803), based on her journal. This describes philanthropic institutions, the dress and customs of the peasantry, and the author's being shocked by French Sunday rituals.

On their return the Kings stayed in Phillimore Place, Kensington, London. Mrs King supported her brother Thomas in establishing the work of the Society for Bettering the Condition and Improving the Comforts of the Poor (SBCP) in Clapham, particularly among women. The area was divided into districts, each with a female sub-treasurer, in which women established and supervised numerous schools. Higgins cites the manuscript SBCP minutes of the ladies' committee meetings which show Mrs King's involvement: for example, on 17 December 1802 at the second meeting, held at her house in Kensington, money was collected to relieve a poor woman. Further activity included a circular, the result of Thomas and Frances's consultations, which was printed in 1803 as the appendix to the fourth volume of the reports of the SBCP, and a copy of the address sent to female subscribers which, though unsigned, is attributed to King by Higgins.

Frances King was also active in her husband's parishes in the establishment of schools for children of the poor and in other philanthropic societies. Her conduct of the parish library which she founded at Steeple Morden—reading aloud to parents and children, then discussing the books and lending them to children—was described by her sister-in-law in the third volume of the *Reports of the Society for Bettering the Condition and Improving the Comforts of the Poor* (cited in Higgins, 3.291). Her comments on the work of other teachers appear in an article in the fortieth report of the SBCP (1817) in which King wrote approvingly of Mrs Gray's reading, writing, and needlework school in Bishopwearmouth, drawing particular attention to the way the girls were taught and the strict segregation of the sexes. Two surviving letters indicate that King knew Hannah More, and was still subscribing to More's Shipham sickness club in 1810.

On her husband's death in 1810 King went to live near her two married daughters, whose husbands—John Collinson and Thomas Baker—held livings at Gateshead and at Whitburn, co. Durham, respectively. Her memoirist claimed that

> for a period of more than ten years [she] was there also a mother to the poor, a 'Dorcas full of good works and almsdeeds which she did'. She not only established a large Sunday school, a Sick Fund and Clothing Society, but was constant in her superintendance of these institutions, and in visiting the poor at their own houses. (*Female Scripture Characters*, vii)

All this, it was claimed, was without losing the retiring aspect of the female character.

In her published work Mrs King made clear her intention to remedy important omissions made by divines. In *The Beneficial Effects of the Christian Temper on Domestic Happiness*, King lamented how Bishop Beilby Porteous's treatise *The Beneficial Effects of Christianity on the Temporal Concerns of Mankind* had noted only its public benefits, and had not carried the precepts of Christianity into domestic life. As support for her argument she cited William Paley's *Evidences of Christianity*. In her *Female Scripture Characters*, first published in 1811, she points out that the Revd Thomas Robinson, author of *Scripture Characters* (1793), had omitted all but two female figures. King's 'characters' included both 'good' and 'bad' women from the Old and New Testament: Eve, Jezebel, Susanna, Martha and Mary, and Dorcas. Her description of Dorcas, for example, was followed by a homily about the value of learning to nurse the sick, instruct the ignorant, and teach the young. King recommended that a day a week should be set aside (including for children and servants) for work for the poor, but did not regard visiting prisoners as part of female charity. Another recommendation was that women should take the lead in family prayers for the entire household. King's study 'Martha and Mary' included her views on female education, with a description of Andrew Bell's monitorial system and a critique of a model of education based on 'accomplishments' for middle-class girls which neglected the mind. Higgins claimed that this book was intended for middle- or upper-class girls; her memoirist, that it was widely used in schools.

King's writings illustrate the contrasting 'feminist' elements in the writings of early nineteenth-century evangelical philanthropic women, including Hannah More. On the one hand, King insisted on the absolute differences between the functions and capabilities of the sexes. Thus, the proper place of women was within the home, subordinate to their husbands in everything not inconsistent with their duty to God. However, she unequivocally asserted that men were far more likely to be deficient in their domestic duties than women, and that men often treated women as if they existed only for their convenience. She argued that there was no reason to suppose that 'Religion is of any sex' (King, *Beneficial Effects*, 36), and urged men to appreciate their wives and to be mindful of their domestic duties. King's memoirist also points out the contrasting aspects of her personality: 'affectionate and indulgent, she could be strict upon occasion, and know how to enforce authority: possessing a disinterested and almost romantic generosity, she managed with cleverness and scrupulous accuracy all details of business' (*Female Scripture Characters*, vii). An engraving by Edward Scriven after a portrait by Edward Hastings, which shows King wearing a widow's veil, suggests she was a formidable character.

Frances King died at Gateshead on 23 December 1821. She left £1018, which included legacies of £50 each to her sisters Mrs White and Mrs Smith and the three other single women, and the residue of £768 to her grandson, the naval officer and explorer Richard *Collinson; her other grandchildren were General Thomas Bernard Collinson and Julia Stretton, author of *Margaret and her Bridesmaids* and other popular novels.

King represents the exemplar of the godly parson's

wife, a vocation she advised her female readers to recommend to their daughters and which she saw as mirroring that of the ministry for men. Her life story illustrates how early nineteenth-century women could hold what are now regarded as conservative views on the position of women in society, yet exercise considerable power within their own communities through their interpretation of the proper sphere of female responsibility, while commanding respect from the wider audience who read her books. She received a glowing obituary in the *Gentleman's Magazine* (1822) and occupies a place among the pantheon of 'exemplary' religious and philanthropic women of the 1770s–1820s, which includes Sarah Trimmer, Hannah More, and Mary Bosanquet.   MARY CLARE MARTIN

Sources S. E. Higgins, *The Bernards of Abington and Nether Winchendon: a family history*, 4 vols. [1903] · *Female scripture characters exemplifying female virtues by Mrs King with a memoir of the author*, 12th edn (1833) · F. E. King, *The beneficial effects of the Christian temper on domestic happiness*, 2nd edn (1807) · T. Bernard, *The life of Sir Francis Bernard, bart, late governor of Massachusetts Bay* (1790) · [F. E. King], *The rector's memorandum book, being memoirs of a family in the north* (1819) · will, PRO, PROB 11/1653 · *GM*, 1st ser., 92/1 (1822), 90–91
Likenesses E. Scriven, stipple, pubd 1822 (after E. Hastings), NPG [*see illus.*] · T. Woolnoth, stipple (after E. Hastings), BM, NPG; repro. in *Ladies' Monthly Museum* (1824)
Wealth at death £1018: will, PRO, PROB 11/1653

King, Sir George (1840–1909), botanist, was born on 12 April 1840 at Peterhead, Aberdeenshire, the only son of Robert King (1809–1845), bookseller, and his wife, Cecilia, *née* Anderson (1810–1850), daughter of a collector of Inland Revenue. King's father soon moved to Aberdeen, and with an older brother, George, founded the publishing firm of G. and R. King. Both brothers possessed literary aptitudes, the elder writing much on social and religious subjects and the younger compiling a history entitled *The Covenanters in the North* (1846). King's father died in 1845 and his mother five years later, whereupon King became his uncle George's ward. King was educated first at a preparatory school and from autumn 1850 at Aberdeen grammar school, where William Geddes (later principal of Aberdeen University) was his form master. In 1854 King joined his uncle's publishing business. However, at school King had shown a marked predilection for natural history, and in 1861 he left his uncle's service for the University of Aberdeen in order to study medicine as an avenue to a scientific career. There King attended the botany classes of Professor George Dickie and after becoming his assistant, devoted all his spare time to botanical work. Having graduated MB in 1865, King on 2 October entered the Indian Medical Service (IMS), and following a winter's training course at the Army Medical School, Netley, Hampshire, reached Calcutta on 11 April 1866. Although initially employed at hospitals in Calcutta, ill health prompted him to apply for duties in what was considered to be the healthier climate of upper India. From 29 August 1866 he held a series of military–medical positions in central India and Rajputana, but devoted his leisure to quality work as a field naturalist. He subsequently attained the rank of lieutenant-colonel. In September 1868 he was temporarily appointed superintendent to the Saharanpur

Botanic Garden, and next year joined the Indian forest service, being placed in charge of the Dehra Dun forests on 3 December 1869. His efficiency in these positions led the secretary of state for India to promote him in March 1871 to the post of superintendent of the Royal Botanic Garden, Calcutta, and of cinchona cultivation in Bengal. The Calcutta garden had been seriously damaged by two great cyclones in 1864 and 1867, but King completely renovated it, formed an adequate herbarium collection to replace that dispersed by the East India Company in 1828, and later organized the botanical survey of India, of which in 1891 he became the first director. King married, in 1868, Jane (Jeanie) Anne, daughter of Dr G. J. Nicol, of Aberdeen; she died in 1898. Of their two sons the elder, Robert, became an officer in the Royal Engineers.

As manager of the cinchona department King substituted quinine-yielding cinchonas for the poorer kinds previously grown, inaugurated in 1887 an economic method of separating quinine, and established in 1893 a self-supporting method of distributing the drug at a low price. The governments of both Bengal and India recognized King's administrative capacity. On their behalf he acted as a visitor of the Bengal Engineering College, as a manager of the Calcutta Zoological Gardens, and as a trustee of the Indian Museum. He was also professor of botany at the Medical College of Bengal, Calcutta, from 1871 to 1895. He was created CIE in 1890 and KCIE in 1898. The humane services which he rendered in connection with quinine were acknowledged by the grade of officier de l'Instruction publique, and by the gift of a ring of honour from Tsar Alexander III.

King's early writings, although relatively few, were sufficiently valuable to lead Aberdeen University to confer on him the degree of LLD in 1884. He was elected FRS in 1887. In the same year he founded the *Annals of the Royal Botanic Garden, Calcutta*, to which, during the next eleven years, he contributed a series of monographs which placed him among the foremost systematic writers of his time. In 1889 he further undertook a sustained study of the flora of the Malayan peninsula; ten parts of his 'Materials for a flora' of that region were issued before 1898 in the *Journal of the Asiatic Society of Bengal*, of which society he was an active member.

King retired from India on 28 February 1898. Failing health thenceforth reduced his public activity, although in 1899 he was president of the botanical section of the British Association for the Advancement of Science at Dover. Under medical advice he mainly resided at San Remo on the Italian riviera, where he continued his Malayan studies, but each summer he worked at the Royal Botanic Gardens, Kew. With the co-operation of various botanists he carried his Malayan research to the end of the twenty-first part, the revision of which had just been completed when he died of an apoplectic seizure at San Remo on 12 February 1909. A memorial tablet marks his burial place there and records his philanthropic labours. King's services to botanical science and landscape gardening were recognized by the award of medals by the University of Uppsala, the Linnean Society, and the Royal Horticultural Society (Victoria medal). Several plants were named after him, including a genus of orchids, *Kingiella*. King was the author of over sixty publications in addition to those mentioned above. His main recreations were literature and art. DAVID PRAIN, *rev.* ANDREW GROUT

Sources D. P. [D. Prain], *PRS*, 81B (1909), xi–xxviii · *Gardeners' Chronicle*, 3rd ser., 45 (1909), 138 · *Nature*, 79 (1908–9), 493–4 · F. A. Stafleu and R. S. Cowan, *Taxonomic literature: a selective guide*, 2nd edn, 2, Regnum Vegetabile, 98 (1979) · *Bulletin of Miscellaneous Information* [RBG Kew] (1909), 193–7 [bibliography] · *WW* (1908) · private information (1912)

Archives Botanic Garden, Calcutta, herbarium · RBG Kew, herbarium

Likenesses photograph, *c.*1879, RBG Kew; repro. in E. Nelmes and W. Cuthbertson, *'Curtis's Botanical Magazine' dedications, 1827–1927* (1932), frontispiece, 207 · F. Bowcher, bronze medallion, 1899, Zoological Garden, Calcutta; replica, Calcutta Botanic Garden; copy, Scot. NPG

Wealth at death £5582 9s. 1d.: probate, 20 March 1909, CGPLA Eng. & Wales

King, Sir George St Vincent Duckworth, fourth baronet (1809–1891). *See under* King, Sir Richard, second baronet (1774–1834).

King, Gregory (1648–1712), herald and political economist, was born at Lichfield, Staffordshire, on 15 December 1648, the eldest son of Gregory King (*fl.* 1648–1668), who was originally from Leicester, and his first wife, Elizabeth Andrews (*d.* 1668) of Sandwich in Kent. King's later criticisms of his father, who was a mathematician and surveyor, might cast doubt on the statement that 'he was packt away to school at two years of age' (King, 'Miscellaneous notes', xxvi) but certainly he was a student at Lichfield Free School (the grammar school) between the ages of five and fourteen, though in his last two years there he began to help his father with work. At school King excelled, becoming skilled in Greek, Hebrew, and Latin, and he was about to go to university when his father agreed to a suggestion that he become a clerk to the herald William Dugdale.

Cartography and herald's office What might be called King's apprenticeship decisively influenced his life's course. On Dugdale's visitations to scrutinize pedigrees of the élite he acquired a detailed knowledge of local and family circumstances, of the nature of communities, and of the increasingly uncertain interplay of wealth and status. He spent five years criss-crossing the northern counties of England, finding the time to learn French and develop some skills as an artist. In 1667, with Dugdale's visitations complete, King was recommended to Lord Hatton, whom for two years he helped with his antiquarian interests. Between 1669 and 1670 King was back in Lichfield, doing odd jobs, before he secured a position as steward, auditor, and secretary to Dowager Lady Gerard at Sandon in Staffordshire.

In 1672 King left provincial England and the service of the well-to-do for London. There he renewed his acquaintances among the heralds, securing a recommendation to John Ogilby, the printer and cartographer. For Ogilby he initially undertook some minor engravings, including for

Sir Peter Leycester's *Historical Antiquities* (1673). But Ogilby, who in 1671 had obtained a royal warrant for a survey of Britain with a view to publishing a book of maps, soon came to make much greater use of King. King helped to map Essex, digested the notes of the other surveyors, and, critically, in 1672 and 1673 joined Christopher Wren, John Aubrey, and Robert Hooke on a small committee with links to the Royal Society to draw up a questionnaire to be circulated to elicit information for Ogilby's planned *Britannia*. Though shelved, the twenty-two queries were used later in structuring King's exercises in political arithmetic. Indeed, cartography played as important a role in forming King's view of English society as his interest in heraldry. Detailed maps he produced of London and Westminster at this time added considerably to his knowledge of town life (the capital then accounted for about ten per cent of England's population) and he was involved in much other map making besides. He also worked with John Adams, whose *Index villaris*, first published in 1680, listed villages, towns, and cities as well as country seats, and depended in part upon an analysis of hearth tax materials.

Between 1675 and 1680 King spent much of his time as an engraver, often of maps, and was involved in a major survey of the new development of Soho in London—Soho Square initially took his name as King Square. But he remained in touch with his connections at the heralds' office. In ill health Francis Sandford, Rouge Dragon pursuivant, often turned to King for help, notably for his *Genealogical history of the kings of England, and monarchs of Great Britain, &c. from the conquest to the year 1677* (1677). And Thomas Lee, Chester herald, began to make use of King. Through Lee's patronage in May 1677 King took over Sandford's office when Sandford became Lancaster herald, and until 1694 was very active in heraldic matters, becoming registrar of the College of Arms in 1684 and Lancaster herald himself when Sandford resigned, unable to accept the accession of William and Mary in 1689. Consequently King went on further visitations to the midland counties and to London, helped organize the coronations of James II and William III and Mary II, and produced with Sandford the luxurious *History of the Coronation of … James II* (1687). He also undertook three trips to Europe, taking part in the investitures of the Garter of the elector of Brandenburg in 1689, the duke of Celle in 1691, and the elector of Saxony in 1692–3.

Political arithmetic In 1694 King was a leading keeper of the flame of ceremony, hierarchy, and of form, but a dispute with the earl marshal over arrangements for Queen Mary's lavish funeral in 1695 put a stop to his heraldic career. It was also at this point that his autobiography ends (it was perhaps written then). It is a sad irony that from then until his death, a period when he produced the works for which he is now best-known, his pioneering exercises in political arithmetic, details of his life are scanty and highly fragmentary. What is clear is that between 1694 and his death in 1712 King was much involved in producing and analysing statistics for various areas of central government. Along with Blathwayt, Lowndes, and Davenant, King was one of a small band of dedicated public servants at the forefront of expanding and overhauling the institutions of the state as it waged two terrible wars against France, the greatest European power of the period. King's contribution, however, was wholly distinctive, for he developed political arithmetic, 'the art of reasoning by figures, upon things relating to government', in important new ways (C. Davenant, *The Political and Commercial Works of that Celebrated Writer Charles D'Avenant*, ed. C. Whitworth, 5 vols., 1771, 1.128).

King's political arithmetic was notably wide-ranging. For the newly formed Board of Trade he produced an analysis of the population of Gloucester in 1696 and in the following year a valuable survey of almshouses and 'hospitals' that contributed to their analysis of poor relief; in 1697 he compiled an account 'Of the naval trade of England' for 1688; he was secretary to the commissioners for public accounts, probably in 1702–6 and 1708–12; in 1705–6 and 1710 he was secretary to the comptroller of the army accounts (with an annual salary of £300); in 1708 he became a commissioner to state William III's debts; and in 1710 he produced a paper detailing income inequality among the clergy for the governors for Queen Anne's bounty. Whatever the many merits of these efforts King is undoubtedly best known for his 'Natural and political observations upon the state and condition of England, 1696', probably produced for Robert Harley, then a leading figure in the country 'party' that was so critical of William III's financial administration. This is an invaluable document, mainly an exercise in demography, that attempted to estimate population size, its distribution between town and countryside, household size, age distribution, marriage patterns, and birth and death rates. Further guesses are provided of the housing stock, agricultural land use, livestock, and output, various tax revenues, and wealth.

At the heart of the 'Observations' is King's famous social table, 'A scheme of the income and expense of the several families of England calculated for the year 1688'. Here he estimated patterns of household size and income and expenses per head for twenty-six social groups, from temporal peers to vagrants. Historians have long valued the picture this provides of late seventeenth-century society, even though it has obvious inaccuracies (despite being rooted in tax data derived from poll taxes and assessments of marriages, births, and burials). It shows one well-informed view of hierarchy, of the relationship between income and status, and of the extraordinary degree of inequality which then existed. It also betrays a number of common assumptions of the propertied. The poor are judged to be decreasing the wealth of the nation, eminent merchants are placed lower in the pecking order than less prosperous gentlemen, poor clergy are superior to richer freeholders, and, most notably, the poorer half of society is encapsulated in only five categories: common seamen, labouring people and outservants, cottagers and paupers, common soldiers, and vagrants.

King's political arithmetic was highly original and he had no peer until the flowering of the nineteenth-century statistical movement. In the first place he was distinguished by tying his calculations closely to detailed available evidence, often by imaginative use of tax records, though his earlier work as a herald and cartographer was also vital. If King's political arithmetic was more ambitious than that of any other contemporary it was also more securely based and, in that sense, he is better seen as a successor to John Graunt than to Sir William Petty, aspiring to work within the methodological framework championed in the early seventeenth century by Francis Bacon. Second, if he frequently sought to depict the nation as a whole, and sought after generalizations, he well knew that a country was but a collection of individuals, families, and parishes—he made detailed studies of his own family and over a dozen particular communities, including London, a point often overlooked because of the innovative modes of categorization King developed in order to produce generalizations. Third, the breadth of his estimates, and a sense of the interrelationships within society, was distinctive; he attempted to see the nation as an integrated whole and worked hard, if not always successfully, to ensure the internal consistency of his estimates. One particular aspect of this which has proved particularly durable was the so-called 'King–Davenant law of demand', which related grain prices to harvest yields. Finally, he was notable for considering how populations changed over time and attempting crude comparisons between the fortunes of England, France, and Holland. Despite his ambitions there is little doubt that King appreciated the limitations of his approach. His meticulous notebooks show a high degree of speculation and a search for the credible. His close, neat hand suggests to those of a graphological bent a precise, fastidious, not to say obsessive man. Yet his final calculations are often heavily rounded, for anything more detailed would be illusory.

Assessing the importance of King's political arithmetic to contemporaries is very difficult, not least because of the suspicion that only a fraction of his calculations has survived. Moreover, if Harley and Sir Stephen Fox at the Treasury saw some of these, his calculations were very largely unpublished at the time, save some extracts in Davenant's *Essay upon the Probable Methods of Making a People Gainers in the Ballance of Trade* (1699). Rather, King's influence is glimpsed by the various offices he held, by the stimulating effect he clearly had upon the likes of Davenant, through odd references of esteem such as that by Leibniz, and his salary. Consequently, with his death and the passing of the generation of politicians he had worked for his name rapidly faded. It was rediscovered at the end of the eighteenth century when political arithmetic was once again consciously and enthusiastically championed. In 1793 James Dallaway's survey of the history of heraldry in England printed King's autobiography and nine years later George Chalmers first published King's 'Natural and political observations'. Since then King's importance as an acute observer of England has been widely acknowledged, though modern research has sometimes revised his estimates.

As a person King is largely anonymous (very little private correspondence survives) though his public work suggests much about the private man: careful, painstaking, cautious, conservative. In religion he was for the Church of England and, though against James II's religious policies, was, because of his 'great respect to the succession of the Crown by legal descent' (King, 'Miscellaneous notes', xxxviii), unenthusiastic about the succession of William III and Mary II in 1689—it is notable that he held office mostly during the years of tory supremacy under Queen Anne. He was a man of some substance, a property owner, stockholder in the East India Company, and governor of St Bartholomew's Hospital. He was twice married, first on 20 July 1674 to Anne, daughter of John Powel of Tirley in Gloucestershire, and then in 1701 to Frances Grattam, with whom he had three children who all died young. King died in London on 29 December 1712 and was buried in the chancel of St Benet Paul's Wharf, London, the parish where he had lived for some years. An epitaph there by his second wife justly celebrated him as 'a skilful herald, a good accomptant, surveyor, and mathematician, a curious penman, and well versed in political arithmetic' (ibid., xlviii). JULIAN HOPPIT

Sources G. King, 'Some miscellaneous notes of the birth, education, and advancement of Gregory King', in J. Dallaway, *Inquiries into the origin and progress of the science of heraldry in England* (1793), xxv–xlviii • J. Graunt and G. King, *The earliest classics* (1973) [facs. edn with introduction by P. Laslett] • *Two tracts by Gregory King*, ed. G. E. Barnett (1936) • G. Chalmers, 'Notice of the life of Gregory King', *An estimate of the comparative strength of Great Britain*, new edn (1804) • J. Thirsk and J. P. Cooper, eds., *Seventeenth-century economic documents* (1972), 790–98 • J. A. Taylor, 'Gregory King's analysis of clerical livings for John Chamberlayne and the governors of Queen Anne's Bounty', *HJ*, 39 (1996), 241–8 • D. V. Glass, 'Two papers on Gregory King', *Population in history: essays in historical demography*, ed. D. V. Glass and D. E. C. Eversley (1965), 159–220 • R. Stone, *Some British empiricists in the social sciences, 1650–1900* (1997), chaps. 3, 7 • J. Creedy, 'On the King–Davenant "law" of demand', *Scottish Journal of Political Economy*, 33 (1986), 193–212 • G. S. Holmes, 'Gregory King and the social structure of pre-industrial England', *TRHS*, 5th ser., 27 (1977), 41–68 • C. Brooks, 'Projecting, political arithmetic and the act of 1695', *EngHR*, 97 (1982), 31–53

Archives BL, genealogical, heraldic, and other collections, Add. MSS 6591, 6821, 6832–6833, 14024–14026, 34712, 35823, 47189 • Leics. RO, genealogical notes • PRO, papers, T64/302 • S. Antiquaries, Lond., heraldic papers • Samuel Johnson Birthplace Museum, Lichfield, papers • William Salt Library, Stafford, almanack and memoranda book | BL, Harley MSS 6815, 6821, 6837, 6944, 7525 • Bodl. Oxf., heraldic papers • Coll. Arms, notes relating to royal ceremonial and catalogue of Vincent MSS • Warks. CRO, corresp., incl. letters to Sir Richard Newdigate

Likenesses group portrait, repro. in Stone, *Some British empiricists in the social sciences*

King, Harold (1887–1956), organic chemist, was born on 24 February 1887 at Llanengan, Caernarvonshire, the eldest of the four children of Herbert King, and his wife, Ellen Elizabeth Hill. Both parents came from Lancashire farming families and were schoolteachers by profession; in 1891 they moved to Bangor where Harold King received his education, first in St James's church school where his parents were headteachers, then in Friar's grammar school, and finally in the University College at Bangor.

There he was a pupil of K. J. P. Orton, who inspired King with a love of chemistry.

After graduating with first-class honours in 1908, and after a period of research, King had a brief experience of analytical work with the Gas Light and Coke Company at Beckton (1911–12) as the holder of an industrial bursary awarded by the Royal Commission for the Exhibition of 1851. In 1912 he moved to the Wellcome Physiological Research Laboratories. This appointment brought him into contact with H. H. Dale and George Barger and showed him how fruitful collaboration between biologists and chemists could be in medical research. After six months King moved again, to the Wellcome Chemical Works at Dartford. There he received further training in organic chemical research under F. L. Pyman and also made several contributions to problems of pharmaceutical chemistry which arose as a matter of urgency during the war.

In 1919 King was appointed chemist on the staff of the Medical Research Council, with special responsibility for the study of drugs. This post took him to the National Institute for Medical Research, Hampstead, where he again came under Dale's direction. He served the Medical Research Council until his retirement in 1950, and in that time acquired an international reputation as a research worker in applications of organic chemistry to therapy. Apart from his own experimental work he did much to keep the subject of chemotherapy at the forefront of scientific investigation. In 1923 he married Elsie Maud, daughter of Joseph Croft, master tailor. They had one son.

When King began research in chemotherapy the only chemotherapeutic agent really established in medical practice was salvarsan; it was natural therefore that he should direct his first effort to the attempt to find other arsenical drugs with useful therapeutic properties. Although he had no direct success he found out much about the mode of action of these compounds and his observations were a pointer to the later discovery by others of British Antilewisite (BAL) an antidote to arsenical and heavy metal poisoning. He also attempted to produce more effective antimalarial drugs by modifications of the structure of the cinchona alkaloids; here again no immediate success was forthcoming but the work bore fruit later in the influence exercised on the programme of antimalarial research undertaken in the United States during the Second World War. A third chemotherapeutic research, resulting in the discovery of antitrypanosomal activity in a number of diamidines (and related compounds) led to the development by A. J. Ewins of stilbamidine, the most effective drug for the treatment of the tropical disease kala-azar.

If King had his full share of the disappointments which are only too common in chemotherapeutic research, he derived great satisfaction from work which led to the discovery of the methonium drugs, which provided the first effective drug treatment of hypertension. This work was a model of medical research. It began with King's classical study of tube curare from which he isolated the active principle (the alkaloid tubocurarine) and determined its constitution. He then deduced the chemical features responsible for its muscle-relaxing properties and planned the synthesis of a series of simple compounds likely to possess similar activity. He enlisted the collaboration of his physiological colleagues, who confirmed his prediction and, in addition, discovered unexpected properties of some of the compounds that were of value in treating hypertension.

Although King was essentially an experimentalist he worked with Otto Rosenheim to revise the formulation of cholesterol and related compounds which had long been accepted on the authority of eminent German chemists. This brought a clearer understanding of the chemistry of many biologically important compounds including sex hormones, adrenocortical hormones, and heart poisons, and was a scientific achievement of the first magnitude. King was elected FRS in 1933 and was awarded the Hanbury medal of the Pharmaceutical Society (1941) and the Addingham gold medal of the William Hoffman Wood Trust (1952); he was appointed CBE in 1950.

Quiet and retiring in disposition, and unashamedly insular in general outlook, King enjoyed the sheltered environment which a research institute could offer and in which he could spend his days at the laboratory bench; he had no interest in teaching or administration. By nature cool and reserved in personal relationships, he was nevertheless always ready to help a colleague from his own store of knowledge; he in turn drew inspiration from his contacts with others and from his interest in their researches, even in fields far removed from his own.

King retired before he needed to, going to live at Birchwood, Brierley Avenue, Parley Cross, Dorset, where he spent the last years of his life happily absorbed in amateur entomology. He died at home on 20 February 1956, being survived by his widow and son.

C. R. HARINGTON, rev.

Sources C. R. Harington, *Memoirs FRS*, 2 (1956), 157–71 · personal knowledge (1971)
Likenesses photograph, repro. in Harrington, *Memoirs FRS* · photographs, National Institute for Medical Research, London
Wealth at death £17,317 19s. 11d.: administration, 27 June 1956, *CGPLA Eng. & Wales*

King, Haynes (1831–1904), landscape and genre painter, was born in December 1831 in Barbados, the son of Robert Morgan King and his wife, Maria. He went to London in 1854 and studied at Leigh's academy (afterwards Heatherley's) in Newman Street. He first exhibited in 1857 at the Society of British Artists and was elected a member in 1864; many of his works were exhibited there, and forty-eight were shown at the Royal Academy between 1860 and 1904. He also exhibited at the New Watercolour Society and the British Institution. He lived for a time with Thomas Faed, the Scottish painter of sentimental scenes of peasant life, who influenced his style. On 14 August 1866 he married Annie Elizabeth Willson, the widowed daughter of William Preston.

King painted genre subjects, interiors, landscapes, and coast scenes with figures. His works include *The Anxious*

Look-Out (exh. Society of British Artists, 1860), *The Lace Maker* (exh. RA, 1866), *A Water-Carrier, Rome* (exh. Society of British Artists, 1868), *Homeless* (exh. RA, 1872), *News from the Cape* (exh. RA, 1879), *Approaching Footsteps* (exh. RA, 1883), *Getting Granny's Advice* (exh. RA, 1890), *The New Gown* (exh. RA, 1892), and *Latest Intelligence*, which was shown at the Royal Academy in 1904. *Flirtation and Jealousy* (1874) is in the collection of the Bethnal Green Museum of Childhood, London, and *An Interesting Paragraph* is at Leeds City Art Gallery.

King spent the last fourteen years of his life living in the house of the painter Henry Yeend King in Finchley Road, London. He committed suicide on 17 May 1904 by jumping in front of a train at Swiss Cottage Station. He had been ill for some time and was about to move to a nursing home.

B. S. LONG, rev. ANNE PIMLOTT BAKER

Sources Wood, *Vic. painters*, 3rd edn · J. Johnson, ed., *Works exhibited at the Royal Society of British Artists, 1824–1893, and the New English Art Club, 1888–1917*, 2 vols. (1975) · Graves, *RA exhibitors* · *The Times* (18 May 1904) · *The Times* (21 May 1904) · m. cert. · private information (1912) [H. Y. King] · Graves, *Artists* · *Art Journal*, new ser., 24 (1904), 272
Wealth at death £2199 8s.: probate, 14 June 1904, *CGPLA Eng. & Wales*

King, Henry (1592–1669), poet and bishop of Chichester, was the eldest of the five sons and four daughters of John *King (d. 1621), archdeacon of Nottingham and later bishop of London, and his wife, Joan, daughter of Henry Freeman of Henley, Buckinghamshire. He was baptized on 16 January 1592 at Worminghall, near Oxford, home of his grandfather Philip. He was educated as founder's kin at Lord Williams' School, Thame, then from about 1600 at Westminster School with his next brother, John (1595–1639), who shared all his subsequent education. They both matriculated from Christ Church, Oxford (of which their father had become dean in 1605), on 20 January 1609, were tutored by Samuel Fell, and were admitted BA and MA on 19 June 1611, the year their father was made bishop of London. Both contributed to university collections of Latin epitaphs and congratulatory poems from 1612 to 1625.

King left Oxford on 10 July 1616, probably because he married Anne Berkeley (c.1600–1624), eldest daughter and heir of Sir Robert Berkeley of Boycourt in Kent, who had died in 1614. She then lived in Oxford with her great-aunt Lloyd, widow of the second principal of Jesus College (her family evidently fought for a better marriage). In 1619 the Kings leased part of Vicaridge House at the west end of St Paul's in London. Of their seven children two, John and Henry, survived infancy. Anne herself died in 1624, aged only twenty-four, and was buried in Bishop John King's tomb in St Paul's on 24 January. Her husband's moving *Exequy* on her death is the poem by which he is chiefly remembered.

King must have been ordained by 24 January 1616, when he was collated to the prebend of St Pancras in St Paul's Cathedral, which carried with it the office of confessor, and was given the rectory and patronage of Chigwell, Essex. He was made archdeacon of Colchester on 10 April 1617, sinecure rector of Fulham on 18 November 1618, and

Henry King (1592–1669), by unknown artist

soon after became an honorary member of Lincoln's Inn and a royal chaplain-in-ordinary. He preached his first public sermon at Paul's Cross on 5 November 1617, criticized by John Chamberlain as overbold, being 'so young man in such a place and at such a time' (*Letters of John Chamberlain*, 2.44).

King's first printed sermon, preached at James I's request at Paul's Cross on 25 November 1621, was a vindication of his father's loyalty to the English church 'Upon Occasion of that False and Scandalous Report' that he had converted to Roman Catholicism before his death. It sets the tone of Henry King's wry, often humorous and temperate comments (unusual at that time) on extremes in religion. That same year John Donne was appointed dean of St Paul's: he and King remained close friends until Donne's death in 1631, and several of King's sermons show his familiarity with Donne's sermons, then still in manuscript. As an executor, Henry commissioned the statue of Donne in St Paul's which survived the great fire, and probably, to judge by the idiosyncratic rhetorical punctuation, he was the careful editor of his *Poems* (1633).

King became canon of Christ Church by proxy on 3 March 1624, his only preferment for fifteen years. He and his brother John, made canon in August, were admitted BD and DD on 19 May 1625, and on 10 July, Act Sunday, preached at St Mary's: Henry in the morning and John in the afternoon, the sermons being printed together. Henry's sermon closely resembles Donne's on the same text, Psalm 32: 5, not through plagiarism, but by way of answer to Donne; other implicit dialogues with Donne occur in King's 1626 Lent sermon and in the third section of *An Exposition upon the Lord's Prayer*.

Most of King's lyrics belong to the early 1620s; another group can be dated 1630 to 1633; he also wrote satires and elegies on friends and public figures. All the early lyrics were set to music by John Wilson and are included in his song manuscript (Bodl. Oxf., MS Mus.b.1). King was a keen musician, bequeathing a 'cabinett organ made by Craddocke' in his will. Until the interregnum the poems circulated in carefully copied quarto manuscript volumes commissioned by King (apparently a unique situation); one of his scribes can be identified as Thomas Manne, student of Christ Church and later rector of St Olave, Silver Street, London. King revised and augmented the collections regularly so that wrong attributions of his poems can be dismissed.

As a royal chaplain King preached at Whitehall, delivering the prestigious Lent sermons. King's most lyrical of these, for 1626 and 1627, were printed, as was his Easter Spittle sermon before the lord mayor of London and the common councillors in 1626, with descriptions of the recent devastating plague visitation. His *Exposition upon the Lord's Prayer* (1628) is based on afternoon sermons at St Paul's. They begin about 1623 (as a reference to Prince Charles's recently abandoned Spanish marriage shows); the 1625 plague evidently caused a gap in the series, and each section looks gracefully towards James I's own commentary on the prayer. King's moderate Calvinist theology, his dislike of extremes, his keen sense of loss after his young wife's death, his firmly expressed pastoral teaching, his learning, and views on his times and life in general are best seen in these eleven sermons.

There are no lyric poems or printed sermons from the period subsequent to 1634 which coincides with Laud's archbishopric. In 1633, after eight years' service, King ceased to sit on the court of high commission. On 6 February 1639, however, King was installed as dean of Rochester, where in 1640 he built a new deanery. That same year he preached a significant Accession day sermon at Paul's Cross on 27 March emphasizing the importance of obedience to Charles I's sacred authority in language which anticipated parts of the ecclesiastical canons passed by convocation in the following weeks.

King was appointed bishop of Chichester on 12 October 1641, and consecrated on 6 February 1642, the day after parliament passed a bill excluding bishops from the Lords. Like his two predecessors he held the rectory of Petworth to compensate for the poverty of the bishopric. He lived in the palace at Chichester until the siege of December 1642, when he fled (not, as reported, taken prisoner) first to Petworth, then to Albury. He lived with his widowed sister, Elizabeth Holt, and her family, presumably in the house he had rented from George Aungier since 1634, close to his second cousin George Duncombe, with whom he was frequently involved in financial transactions (he also held bonds with the earls of Northumberland and Arundel).

In 1643 King was harshly sequestered, but managed to transfer the St Paul's Churchyard house to his son Henry. William Oughtred, at Shere, near Albury, coached King's son John, who seduced his daughter. After this difficult episode King moved, in 1645, to live with his nephew, John King's son, at Blakesware, Hertfordshire, and by 1647 was at Richings, near Slough, home of Lady Salter, niece of Brian Duppa, where he set up a small praying community with family and friends. On 11 March 1649 he wrote an elegy 'from my sad retirement' on Charles I, buried at nearby Windsor. That year John Hales, on losing his Eton fellowship, became their chaplain until 1655. In 1651 King published *The Psalmes of David … to be Sung after the Old Tunes used in the Churches* (some were later set to music by Playford in *Psalms and Hymns*, 1671); King's letter to Bishop Ussher in October with a presentation copy explains his reasons. About this time King also wrote to Izaak Walton, an old friend through John Donne, although later omitted from King's will.

Thereafter King stayed sometimes with his sister, Dorothy Hubert, and her husband, Sir Richard, at Langley, or with his brother Philip at Hitcham. King drew up his will in 1653 when he was engaged with Duppa in travelling the country ordaining men according to the rite of the forbidden Book of Common Prayer. About 1655, when few bishops remained alive, it was proposed that he should cross with one other to the continent for fresh consecrations, but none would accompany him. His *Poems, Elegies and Paradoxes* was first printed by Richard Marriott and Henry Herringman in 1657 from authoritative manuscripts, ostensibly without his permission; a second edition, published in 1664, was augmented by the elegy on Charles I and four others.

Named for the archbishopric of York at the Restoration (as his disgruntled prospective successor at Chichester, Edward Burton, reported), King lost it by going down to settle affairs in his diocese. His visitation sermon, 8 October 1662, shows how sensitively he dealt with the jarring factions among his clergy, 'laying controversies asleep and silencing disputes' (Hobbs, *Sermons*, 37). He was active in the House of Lords.

Two of King's Whitehall sermons were published, that for Charles II's Accession day anniversary in 1661, first of the new reign (reprinted 1713, when another civil war seemed to threaten), and that for Charles I's execution, published in January 1665. 'A good and eloquent' sermon heard on 8 March 1663 by Samuel Pepys, one listed for Lent 1666, and one heard by John Evelyn on 28 February 1669 have not survived, nor has a visitation sermon reported by Giles Moore, rector of Horsted Keynes, on 8 September 1669 (*The Journal of Giles Moore*, ed. R. Bird, Sussex RS, 68, 1971, 232). King's preaching was much esteemed and imitated in his own day. Bishop Brian Duppa's funeral sermon, preached in Westminster Abbey on 24 April 1662, is an excellent example of his style, and a valuable source for Duppa's life and the interregnum. It reveals that King had also preached the Garter day sermon at Windsor in 1661.

King died on 30 September 1669 at the bishop's palace, and was buried on 8 October in the south choir aisle of Chichester Cathedral. As his will requested he received a simple ledger stone like his father's, with the words 'Deposita redditurae animae', but the family then ordered the ornate memorial later placed in the north transept. His second son, Henry, a gentleman of the royal chamber, had predeceased him on 21 February, and his heir, John, died on 10 March 1671, leaving his father's books, described in Henry's will as 'a small remainder of a large Library taken from me at Chichester contrary to the condicon and contracte of the Generall and Counsell of Warre' (PRO, PROB 11/133, sig. 136, 16 Nov 1669), to recreate the cathedral library. About 300 of 2000 books survive there, among them some twenty titles from John Donne's library. The York gospels, lost during the civil wars, were also mysteriously returned by King's executors.

MARY HOBBS

Sources J. Hannah, ed., *Poems and psalms of Henry King D.D., bishop of Chichester* (1843), introductory material · M. Crum, introduction, in *The poems of Henry King, bishop of Chichester*, ed. M. Crum (1965) · M. Hobbs, ed., *The sermons of Henry King, bishop of Chichester* (1992), introduction, bibliography · M. Hobbs, 'The Restoration correspondence of Bishop Henry King', *Sussex Archaeological Collections*, 125 (1987), 139–53 · G. L. Keynes, *A bibliography of Henry King D.D., bishop of Chichester* (1977) · R. Berman, *Henry King and the seventeenth century* (1965) · Pepys, *Diary*, 4.69 · Evelyn, *Diary*, 3.524 · Wood, *Ath. Oxon.*, new edn, 3.839 · *The letters of John Chamberlain*, ed. N. E. McClure, 2 (1939), 44 · will, 16 Nov 1669, PRO, PROB 11/133, sig. 136

Archives BL, Add. MS 62134 | Bodl. Oxf., Fell papers, Rawl. MSS D 317, 398, 912 · CUL, Keynes collection, Phillipps MS 9325

Likenesses oils, 1642, city council chamber, Chichester · oils, Christ Church Oxf. [*see illus.*]

Wealth at death £4340 in named moneys 'of that which is not in my possession' (that is, loans and bonds to be recovered by executors); also plate and books: will, PRO, PROB 11/133, sig. 136, 16 Nov 1669

King, Horace Maybray, Baron Maybray-King (1901–1986), politician and speaker of the House of Commons, was born on 25 May 1901 at 91 Stapylton Street, Grangetown, near Middlesbrough, the second child in the family of two sons and two daughters of John William King, insurance agent (previously steelworker), and his wife, Margaret Ann Maybray. He was educated at Norton council school and Stockton secondary school. He obtained first-class honours in English at King's College, London University, in 1922 and in the same year was appointed to a teaching post at Taunton's School in Southampton. He became head of English in 1930, and remained there until 1947, when he became headmaster of Regent's Park secondary school in Southampton. He was an inspiring teacher, able to secure respect in a formal environment without heavy use of sanctions. A duodenal ulcer meant that he was not liable for military service in the Second World War. For several years he studied part-time for a PhD on Shakespeare, and his thesis was accepted by King's College in 1940. He published widely on subjects as diverse as Homer, Macaulay, parliament, and Sherlock Holmes.

On 21 December 1924 King married Victoria Florence (1896/7–1966), daughter of George Harris, bookseller. Born in Southwark, prior to her marriage she was a schoolteacher. Once in Southampton she became a significant political figure. A Labour councillor in 1928–31

Horace Maybray King, Baron Maybray-King (1901–1986), by
Walter Bird, 1966

and from 1933, she was coronation mayor in 1953 and
played a leading role in hospital administration. In political circles Horace King initially tended to be viewed as
Mrs King's husband. They had one daughter.

King joined the socialist society at university and was a
Labour Party member from his arrival in Southampton. By
the mid-1930s his concern over British foreign policy led
to support for a united front. He narrowly escaped expulsion from the Southampton Labour Party after sharing a
platform with communists.

In the Labour landslide of 1945 King unsuccessfully
fought the safe Conservative constituency of New Forest
and Christchurch. The following year he was elected to
Hampshire county council, serving with one three-year
break until 1965, and eventually becoming Labour Party
group leader. He was elected to the House of Commons in
February 1950 as member for the extremely marginal
Southampton Test constituency. Prior to the 1955 election
King succeeded in transferring his candidacy to the adjacent and much safer Itchen constituency.

King quickly demonstrated a flair for publicity. He
arrived at the House of Commons for the first time wearing a cloth cap in memory of James Keir Hardie, and made
the first maiden speech of all the 1950 entrants. He was a
very active back-bencher; within the Parliamentary
Labour Party he stood with the right. He was a keen supporter of the Anglo-American alliance, making frequent
visits to the United States, and he backed Hugh Gaitskell
against unilateralism, but he was never a factionalist and

attempted to remain on good terms with all sections of
the party.

As early as 1953 King joined the speaker's panel. In
November 1964, following Labour's return to office, he
became chairman of ways and means and deputy speaker.
Almost a year later, with the death of Sir Harry Hylton-Foster in September 1965, he became the first speaker
from the Labour benches. At the same time he was sworn
of the privy council.

King assumed the speakership in a context of increasing
demands for parliamentary reform. While no procedural
die-hard, he was a traditionalist with a generally rosy view
of established practices. One innovation, the speeding up
of question time, probably reduced further the influence
of the back-bencher. His speakership saw changes in parliamentary procedure that could seem significant by comparison with earlier inertia, but in real terms they were
modest. Unlike many of his predecessors, he had no legal
training but his headmasterly and avuncular style soon
established his authority.

King retired as speaker at the end of 1970. He became a
life peer, as Baron Maybray-King, in 1971 and attended the
House of Lords regularly for several years, serving as deputy speaker there. His career contained much that was
characteristic of Labour politics of the first half of the
twentieth century. He was self-improving, cautiously
reformist, and respectful of many venerable British practices. Yet there were paradoxes. The traditionalist was a
showman; as speaker he turned on the Blackpool illuminations. In Southampton he seemed a proper, somewhat
puritanical, figure; at Westminster he was highly clubbable and well known in the bars. He was an accomplished player of the piano and piano accordion and loved
entertaining children. The bonhomie masked a more
complex and elusive character. Maybray-King had honorary degrees from Southampton (1967), London (1967), Durham (1968), Bath (1969), Ottawa (1969), and Loughborough
(1971), and was honorary FRCP.

King's first wife died in 1966. He then married on 22 July
1967 Una (1906/7–1978), daughter of William Herbert Porter, industrial manager. His second wife was a retired
Southampton headmistress and had been King's honorary chauffeur in the last years of his political career. She
died in 1978 and Maybray-King married on 30 January 1981
Mrs Ivy Duncan Forster (b. 1914/15), a widow from co. Durham. She was the daughter of John Edward Davison,
miner. The marriage was dissolved in 1985, and finally, on
29 March 1986, Maybray-King married Sheila Catherine (b.
1923/4), retired secretary and daughter of John Atkinson,
dental mechanic. There were no children of the last three
marriages. Maybray-King died in the Royal Hampshire
Hospital, Southampton, on 3 September 1986.

DAVID HOWELL, rev.

Sources files, *Southampton Evening Echo* · *The Times* (4 Sept 1986) ·
Daily Telegraph (4 Sept 1986) · private information (1996) · m. certs ·
CGPLA Eng. & Wales (1986)
Likenesses W. Bird, photograph, 1966, NPG [*see illus.*] · photograph, Hult. Arch.
Wealth at death £128,345: probate, 22 Oct 1986, *CGPLA Eng. &
Wales*

King, Humphrey (*fl.* **1595–1613**), poet, was the author of *An halfe-penny-worth of wit, in a pennyworth of paper, or, The hermites tale, the third impression* (1613). No earlier edition is known but it must have been printed some years previously. *Robin the Devil his two penniworth of wit in half a penniworth of paper, by Robert Lee, a famous fencer of London, alias Robin the Devil* (1607) is mentioned in West's sale catalogue of 1773 and may have been an earlier edition but it is not now known to be extant. A jocular, mock dedicatory epistle to the countess of Sussex is prefixed to King's poem. He acknowledges that his work is 'a course homespun linsey woolsey webbe of wit' but, seeing his 'inferiours in the gifts of learning, wisedome, and understanding, torment the Print daily', he is 'the bolder to shoulder in amongst them' (King). This is followed by an address to the reader, three short copies of verses, and three anonymous sonnets; the second of which Thomas Corser cautiously attributed to either Thomas Nashe or Robert Greene. *The Hermites Tale* takes the form of a dialogue between a disillusioned hermit and a young man, concerning the vices and follies of the age, the growth of luxury, and the decay of hospitality. Puritan sensibilities are attacked in one part, and allusions are made to the legend of Robin Hood, to the works of Skelton, and to the activities of Richard Tarton (sigs. D2v, Er).

King was the dedicatee of Anthony Chute's panegyrical tract *Tabacco*, printed posthumously in 1595. The author was a friend of Gabriel Harvey and this text, the first English work on the subject, testifies to King's exalted reputation among London smokers: 'What your experience is in this divine hearbe, al men do know, and acknowledge you to bee The Sovereigne of Tabacco' (Nicholl, 227).

Four years later Thomas Nashe dedicated his *Lenten Stuffe* to

> his worthie good patron, Lustie Humfrey, according as the townsmen doo christen him, little Numps as the Nobilitie and Courtiers do name him, and Honest Humfrey, as all his friendes and acquaintance esteeme him, king of the Tobacconists *hic & ubique*, and a singular Mecaenas to the Pipe and the Tabour.

At the end of the dedicatory epistle Nashe refers to the forthcoming 'sacred Poeme of the Hermites Tale, that will restore the golden age amongst us'. This address reveals a burlesque and boisterous relationship between the two men—'A King thou art by name and a King of good fellowshippe' (*Nashes Lenten Stuff*, sig. A3r)—and emphasizes that although King himself was a poet he was an 'unlearned lover of poetry' (ibid., sig. A2r). In 1600 Nicholas Breton, under the guise of the imperfect anagram Salohein Treboun, dedicated his rare *Pasquils Mistresse, or, The Worthie and Unworthie Woman* to 'Lustie Humfrey, honest wagge' (Breton, sig. A2r), having been motivated by the desire to advise his good friend, who was evidently at that time considering the prospect of marriage.

Little is known of King's biographical details but it is possible that he could claim kinship with the King family of Halstead, Essex. Lusty Humfrey recurs as a frequent form of address, and several colleagues, as well as King himself, make reference to his uneducated state. His circle appears to have favoured punning uses of the poet's surname, a tendency adopted by King in an unpublished plea for unity to James I, entitled 'H. King to a King' (Corser, 339).

A. H. BULLEN, rev. ELIZABETH HARESNAPE

Sources R. J. Kane, 'Anthony Chute, Thomas Nashe, and the first English work on tobacco', *Review of English Studies*, 7 (1931), 151–9 · N. Breton, *Pasquils mistresse, or, The worthie and unworthie woman: with his description and passion of that furie, jealousie* (1600), sig. A2r–v · *Nashes Lenten stuffe* (1599), sigs. A2r–A3v · C. Nicholl, *A cup of news: the life of Thomas Nashe* (1984), 227–8 · H. King, *An halfe-penny-worth of wit, in a penny-worth of paper, or, The hermites tale* (1613) · T. Corser, *Collectanea Anglo-poetica, or, A … catalogue of a … collection of early English poetry*, 8, Chetham Society, 102 (1878), 334–9 · *BL cat.* · M. Crum, ed., *First-line index of English poetry, 1500–1800, in manuscripts of the Bodleian Library, Oxford*, 2 vols. (1969)

King, James, Lord Eythin (**1589–1652**), royalist army officer, was the son of David King of Warbester in Orkney and his wife, Mary, daughter of Adam Stewart, Carthusian prior of Perth and illegitimate son of James V.

Swedish service King entered Swedish service at the age of twenty, and was eventually joined by his brothers David (who rose to the rank of major) and John King of Warbester and his cousin James King of the Barra family, who became a colonel. Little is known of the first ten years of his service; by 1619 he was serving in the Småland regiment commanded by his fellow Scot Alexander Leslie. King was eventually promoted and in 1622 served as a captain in the Scottish regiment of Patrick Ruthven, the future earl of Forth and of Brentford and lord general of Charles I's armies during the early years of the civil war. About 1623 King had his portrait painted directly onto the wall of Skokloster Castle, where it survives.

In 1624 King became a major in Otto von Scheiding's regiment. From 1626 to 1630 he was back with the Scottish regiments, where he served as lieutenant-colonel to David Drummond and Patrick Ruthven, but he did not stay with his countrymen for long. The Scottish military diarist Robert Monro listed King as general-major and colonel of the Dutch cavalry and infantry in service by 1632. Following the death of Gustavus Adolphus in November, King departed from purely military affairs when he was appointed governor of Vlotho, a garrison town on the banks of the Weser. The following year, while stationed as a colonel in the city of Thuw in the bishopric of Bremen, he joined the German political and literary society *Fruchtbringenden Gesellschaft* (the Fruitful Society) under the name of *Der Verbleibende* (the one who remains). King had married a Pomeranian woman, Dilliana Van der Borchens. She probably died in 1634; her will was proved on 10 November of that year.

King continued as a prominent field commander. In 1636 he was lieutenant-general in Leslie's army in Westphalia. The following year he joined forces with the landgrave of Hesse in his attempts to push the imperial forces out of his territories; initial success turned into a forced retreat into Westphalia, and when the landgrave broke up his army King was forced to withdraw his small command into garrisons. In 1638 he was ordered by Marshal Johan Banér to join his army, then at Münster, with that of

Charles Lewis, the elector palatine, and his brother Prince Rupert, the nephews of Charles I. The combined forces were decisively defeated at the battle of Lemgo (also known as the battle of Vlotho), near Minden in October; Rupert was captured. King was credited with orchestrating the orderly withdrawal of the only part of the army not to be routed. He managed to evade both capture and serious injury, and received a Swedish knighthood for his services. Recriminations over Lemgo were to poison relations between King and Prince Rupert at a crucial juncture for the royalist cause six years later.

Charles I's agent News of the troubled situation in Scotland led King to retire from Swedish service. He explained to the Swedish Riksråd that he did not wish to serve in the Swedish army without his former field commander, Alexander Leslie, who had returned to Scotland to uphold the covenant. King sought, as did many Scottish officers, compensation for the wage arrears due to him. The Riksråd agreed that in view of his twenty-six years' service to the Swedish crown he should receive the outstanding money and a pension of 1200 riksdaler. They also argued that this gesture would ensure the continued support of the Scots for Sweden and its designs against Denmark–Norway and the Habsburg empire—suggesting that they saw King as sympathetic to his native country at this time of conflict between Scotland and its king. After all, the Scottish covenanters were pressing a protestant ideal far closer to King's heart than the ecclesiastical reforms pressed by Charles I.

On leaving Sweden King took up residence in Hamburg, choosing to sit out the war there rather than return to Britain to fight against his old commander Leslie. He certainly helped the king's cause there, even if the degree to which he wished for a Scottish defeat is uncertain. On 28 June 1639 he signed a testimonial with his kinsman Colonel James King confirming that arms bought by Sir Thomas Roe were serviceable and fit for the king's service: in fact they were found to be in such poor condition that they had to be returned to Hamburg.

King returned briefly to Britain and was awarded a pension of £1000 per annum by Charles I. He was soon dispatched back to Hamburg with orders to build up an army of trained officers and soldiers that he was expected to lead home against the covenanters. Rumours circulated that the English lord treasurer had been instructed to issue King with £50,000 to purchase arms from Christian IV of Denmark–Norway, but apparently no merchant could be found to make up this money. Undaunted by his lack of funds, King pressured Christian to provide 3000 Danish cavalry for use against the covenanters: his attempts were ultimately unavailing, though Christian did order that horses intended for Spanish service be diverted to England.

Christian declared his willingness to help Charles but asked for a written proposal for the transfer of the Orkney and Shetland islands to the Danish crown as the price of his assistance to the Stuart crown. King demurred: putting the business in writing would threaten its secrecy. In truth it is difficult to see King, as the son of an Orkneyman and a member of the Swedish nobility, being happy about seeing his family's home islands given away to the enemy of the country he had served most of his life. King's father had been sheriff depute for his wife's cousin, Patrick Stewart, earl of Orkney, who had conducted what amounted to a private war against Christian IV over Danish attacks on Orcadian shipping. The plan fell through when Christian rejected Charles's offer to pawn the islands for 50,000 gold guilders, a sum which in his opinion overvalued them. Meanwhile King successfully wooed Sir John Cochrane, the Scottish emissary to Denmark and Hamburg, and played an important part in detaching him for the covenanting cause.

On his return to Scotland in 1641 King faced charges concerning his alleged unpatriotic behaviour in Denmark during the bishops' wars. However, in November the Scottish parliament dismissed the charges as groundless and declared that King had been a good patriot. While in Scotland, King maintained his Scandinavian connections, writing to the Swedish chancellor, Axel Oxenstierna, expressing his hope of continued good relations between the Swedish and British monarchies. He also published a declaration about Danish negotiations with the empire which were suspected by both the Swedish and Scottish governments.

The northern army After his short spell at home King returned to Hamburg to raise money for Charles I in preparation for the approaching war in England. On 28 March 1642 he was created by the king at York Lord Eythin, the title taken from the River Ythan in Aberdeenshire, where King had property at Birness and Dudwick. When he attended Henrietta Maria at The Hague in mid-November, there were those who doubted whether King would accept the command in England that she was urging him to take on; he had already responded to a previous request by demanding from Secretary Vane a recognized position and the regular payment of his pension. It was only on 18 December (NS) that the queen could write to her husband that King was willing to accept a command, though she did emphasize that it was advisable 'not to employ him under any one whom he might command'. However, he had made clear that he would have no problems serving under the king's commander in the north: 'he has testified to me that whoever submits to serve under my lord Newcastle has simply to obey, and also that he has a particular esteem for my lord Newcastle' (*Letters of Queen Henrietta Maria*, 150).

Eythin landed in Yorkshire in January or February 1643, and *en route* to the king's northern army mauled a force of Sir Hugh Cholmley's. He joined the marquess of Newcastle at York, where he was appointed lieutenant-general and commander of the infantry in the king's northern army and became Newcastle's principal military adviser in the campaigns of 1643 in Yorkshire and the east midlands and in the north the following year. According to Clarendon, Eythin, 'notwithstanding the unavoidable prejudice of being a Scotchman, ordered his foot with great wisdom and dexterity' (Clarendon, *Hist. rebellion*,

2.466). The alliance between Scotland and the English parliament in September 1643 inevitably put Eythin in an invidious position: he faced an invasion by his fellow countrymen commanded by his old chief Alexander Leslie, now earl of Leven. In February 1644 King held Newcastle upon Tyne against Leven's forces; the Scottish soldier of fortune James Turner, who had served under King in Germany, later recorded that:

> I admired then nor could I wonder enough since, that he never endeavourd to give his countrymen a visite. He was a person of great honor; bot what he had savd of it at Vlotho in Germanie, where he made shipwracke of much of it, he losd in England.   (Turner, 31)

Turner may also have been reflecting on the fact that Newcastle's experienced army let Leven's raw troops outmanoeuvre them and march south. Suspicions about Eythin's reliability were evident in the English camp. Late in 1643 a packet of letters washed up at Scarborough included a letter from King to his agent at Hamburg, asking him to send him his horses with all speed, 'and in caise hee could not gett saife passage to England, hee should send them to Scotland, where Generall Leshley would give them a saife conduct'. Newcastle had dismissed the suspicions of (the now royalist) Cholmley: 'hee had soe great assurance of Generall Kings fidelity that hee interpreted the great acquaintance and friendshipp formerly between Leshley and King might give him confidence to write such a letter' (*Memoirs and Memorials*, 147). Nevertheless such suspicions continued and led King to threaten to throw up his command and return to Germany. On 5 April the queen wrote to Newcastle urging him to appeal to his lieutenant's loyalty and silence those who spoke against him.

From 22 April Newcastle's army was besieged in York by the combined forces of Leven's Scots and the northern army led by the Fairfaxes, later reinforced by the army of the eastern association. Even Sir Philip Warwick, who in his memoirs regarded Eythin as no better than a traitor who had deliberately misadvised Newcastle to leave the north exposed to the Scottish invasion at the beginning of the year, grudgingly conceded that at York 'in this compact place Lieutenant-General King so demeaned himself, that as he shewed eminency in soldiery and personal stoutness, so there appeared no want of loyalty, for now he fought not singly against his own nation' (Warwick, 308).

Marston Moor   On 30 June the Scottish and parliamentarian army withdrew at the approach of the royalist relieving force under Prince Rupert, who, believing in Charles's positive command to attack the larger enemy army ordered Newcastle to draw his army out of York on 2 July. Eythin was opposed to the move and advised against Newcastle committing all his forces in such a risky business, but he was left to bring up the infantry. The foot, which had orders to march out of York at 4 a.m., did not reach Marston Moor until between two and four in the afternoon. Various reasons were given for this delay: that part of the infantry was too busy looting the abandoned enemy trenches, that it was pay day and the men would not march until they had been paid and—according to the

hostile Cholmley—that Eythin had given an order for them to stand down. Modern historians of the battle, while acquitting Eythin of disloyalty, have concluded that he did indeed drag his feet in bringing the northern infantry to the battlefield and then only brought 3000 out of the 4000 foot in the city, perhaps in hope of preventing a risky battle that day. When he reached the field he was relentlessly negative when he spoke with the prince. According to Cholmley:

> The Prince demanded of King how hee liked the marshelling of his army, whoe replide hee did not approve of itt being drawne too neare the enemy, and in a place of disadvantage. Then said the Prince, 'They may be drawne a further disstance.' 'Noe sir,' said King, 'it is too laite.' It is s[ai]d King dissuaded the Prince from fighting, saying, 'Sir, your forwardness lost us the day in Germany, where yourself was taken prisoner'. Upon the disswasions of the Marquess and King, and that it was so neare night, The Prince was resolved not to ioyne battle that day.   (*Memoirs and Memorials*, 136)

The delay in King's infantry coming onto the field, with men still filing into position and the army relaxing from the preparedness of the day, gave the advantage and initiative to the enemy. In the ensuing battle Eythin commanded the second line of the royalist infantry, with about 1500 of the York foot in their allotted position and the rest strung out across the moor. The battle shattered the northern army. The following day Eythin's advice, that Newcastle should go into exile, 'conceiving the Kings affairs absolutely destroyed by loss of this battle', overbore that of the marquess's other advisers to head north to raise more troops (*Memoirs and Memorials*, 139). Newcastle, Eythin, and their party went to Scarborough and from there sailed to Hamburg where they arrived on 8 July. Eythin later learnt that a furious Rupert had considered recalling him and charging him with treason; in January 1645 he wrote to the prince protesting his innocence. In July 1644 the Scottish parliament forfaulted King for his service at Marston Moor.

Last years   In 1645 Eythin returned to Sweden where he was created Baron Sandshult in Kalmar, with a pension of 1800 riksdaler per annum. When the moderate engager party gained control of the Scottish government in 1647 his forfaulture was rescinded, and the Scottish parliament sent letters in his favour to both Queen Christina and the city of Hamburg.

In 1649 the new king, Charles II, sent orders to Eythin and Patrick Ruthven, to petition Queen Christina for military aid in support of the campaign being prepared by the marquess of Montrose. Eythin was commissioned lieutenant-general under Montrose in 1650 and was expected to command the major force destined for Scotland from Scandinavia; it was hoped that the two men would use their family connections in the Orkneys to raise support there. Only a small advance party ever sailed, and Eythin never left Sweden, as the king struck a deal with the new hardline regime in Scotland which left Montrose as the sacrificial lamb to be slaughtered as the price of Charles II's kingdom. Although alienated from the king by the betrayal of Montrose, Eythin did undertake negotiations to bring Charles to Sweden, but in the event the king did not come. In 1651 the Scottish parliament passed an act in favour of Eythin. He died a few months later in Stockholm on 9 June 1652 and was publicly buried on 18 June in Stockholm's Riddarholm Church, burial place of the Swedish kings. With his first wife Eythin had no children; with his second, whose name is unknown, he had a daughter who predeceased him.

Eythin's nephews, the sons of John King, both remained in Swedish service. James served as a page to King Charles X and he and his brother became naturalized Swedish noblemen in 1672. In his will, made in 1646, Eythin had earmarked his estates for his brother John and his family. However, his heavy investment in Montrose's campaign left him penniless. Over the years he had paid for royalist weapons out of his own pocket and lent the crown £40,000. Neither this money nor his £1000 pension was ever paid him. In Scotland a creditor took over the administration of his estate. In Sweden his property had to be sold to the Scottish commander Field Marshal Robert Douglas to pay some of his debts; the family never recovered from this burden. In 1684 Henry King and his mother received money from Charles XI to relieve their destitution: a Swedish king was left compensating for debts that should have been repaid by an ungrateful house of Stuart. STEVE MURDOCH and TIM WALES

Sources Scots peerage · GEC, Peerage · K. Connermann, Die Mitglieder der Fruchtbringenden Gesellschaft, 1617–1650 (1985), 239–40 · S. Murdoch and A. Grosjean, 'Scotland, Scandinavia and Northern Europe, 1580–1707', www.abdn.ac.uk/ssne/ · King's creditive to Christian IV from Charles I, July 1640, Danish Rigsarkiv, Copenhagen, TKUA England A13 · letter to the marquis of Hamilton, NA Scot., GD 406/1/1146, 1147 · letter to Charles I, 24 Oct 1640, PRO, SP 75/15, fol. 475 · Averie to Vane, 10/20 and 17/27, Sept 1641, PRO, SP 75/16, fols. 87, 89 · PRO, SP 81/43–50 · certificate of General King upon arms sent to England, 28 June 1639, PRO, SP 81/47, fol. 102 · PRO, SP 81/47, fol. 107 · military muster rolls, Krigsarkivet, Stockholm, 1619/11; 1622/2, 4; 1623/4; 1624/6; 1626/1, 11; 1627/8, 9, 11, 12, 14; 1628/4, 10; 1629/10, 12, 13, 15, 17; 1630/9, 14; 1631/6, 23–27; 1632/24; 1636/1, 2; 1638/4 · letter of Charles II to Queen Christina, 28 May 1649, Riksarkivet, Stockholm, Anglica 517 · APS, 1661–9, 606 · C. F. Bricka and J. A. Fridericia, eds., Kong Christian den fjerdes egenhaendige breve, 4: 1636–1640 (Copenhagen, 1882), 300–01, 358, 361, 368, 378, 395; 5.256–7, 398–9; 8.219 · CSP dom., 1639–41; 1650 · N. A. Kullberg, S. Bergh, and P. Sondén, eds., Svenska riksrådets protokoll, 18 vols. (Stockholm, 1878–1959), vol. 8, p. 551 · S. R. Gardiner, ed., Letters and papers illustrating the relations between Charles the Second and Scotland in 1650, Scottish History Society, 17 (1894), 10 · The letters and journals of Robert Baillie, ed. D. Laing, 3 vols. (1841–2), vol. 1, pp. 269–70; vol. 2, pp. 80, 105 · Rikskansleren Axel Oxenstiernas skrifter och brefvexling, 15 vols. (Stockholm, 1888–1977), 9.958–9 · J. Spalding, Memorialls of the trubles in Scotland and in England, AD 1624 – AD 1645, ed. J. Stuart, 2, Spalding Club, [23] (1851), 99, 108, 168–9 · Declaration of the committee of estates of the parliament of Scotland in vindication of their proceedings from the aspersions of a scandelous pamphlet published by that excommunicate traytor James Grahame (January 1650), BL, Thomason Tract E.549 (22) · G. Wishart, The memoirs of James Marquis of Montrose, 1639–1650, ed. and trans. A. Murdoch and H. F. Morland Simpson (1893), 273 · A. Baker, A battlefield atlas of the English civil war (1986), 60–67 · G. Elgenstierna, Den introducerade svenska adelns ättartavlor, med tillägg och rättelser, 9 vols. (Stockholm, 1925–36), 5.126 · J. A. Fridericia, Danmarks ydre politiske historie i tider fra freden i Prag till freden i Brömsebro, 1629–1645, 2 vols. (Copenhagen, 1972), 2.316 · H. Marryat, One year in Sweden including a visit to the Isle of Gotland, 2 vols. (1862), 490 · DNB · The memoirs and memorials of Sir Hugh Cholmley of Whitby, 1600–1657, ed. J. Binns, Yorkshire Archaeological Society, 153 (2000) · P. R. Newman, Royalist officers in England and Wales, 1642–1660: a biographical dictionary (1981) · P. Newman, The battle of Marston Moor, 1644 (1981) · P. Young, Marston Moor, 1644: the campaign and the battle (1970) · W. A. Day, ed., The Pythouse papers (1879) · Letters of Queen Henrietta Maria, ed. M. A. E. Green (1857) · P. Warwick, Memoirs of the reign of King Charles I (1813) · J. Turner, Memoirs of his own life and times, 1632–1670, ed. T. Thomson, Bannatyne Club, 28 (1829) · Clarendon, Hist. rebellion
Archives U. Aberdeen L., corresp. and papers
Likenesses portrait, c.1623, Skokloster Castle, Sweden; repro. in Old-lore miscellany of Orkney, Shetland, Caithness and Sutherland, ed. A. W. Johnston and A. Johnston (1907–46), vol. 5, p. 166
Wealth at death in debt: all biographical articles cited

King, James (bap. 1750, d. 1784), naval officer, was baptized on 13 July 1750, at Clitheroe, Lancashire, the second son of James King (1714–1795), curate of Clitheroe (afterwards dean of Raphoe), and his wife, Anne, née Walker (1713–1794). Walker King, bishop of Rochester, was his younger brother. At an early age he entered Clitheroe grammar school where he remained until he was twelve years old; and on 19 November 1762 he entered the navy under the patronage of his kinsman, Captain William Norton, brother of the first Lord Grantley, serving under him in the Assistance. He afterwards served in the Guernsey (Captain James Chads) under Commodore Hugh Palliser on the Newfoundland station.

King was promoted lieutenant on 10 January 1771, and appointed to the Cambridge followed by several other ships before being placed on half pay in May 1773. He was then granted leave to go abroad and spent some time in Paris, devoting himself principally to scientific study; on his return he settled at Oxford with his brother Walker, then a fellow of Corpus Christi College, where James may have studied. Here he made the acquaintance of Thomas Hornsby who in 1776 recommended him as a competent astronomer to accompany James Cook's third voyage. He was accordingly appointed to the Resolution as second-lieutenant. At the time of Cook's death at Hawaii (14 February 1779) King was on shore in charge of the observatory. He had with him only a few men, but was reinforced by some of a boat's crew who had been rowing off the mouth of the bay before the disturbance with the Hawaiians began. This brought the number of the party up to twenty-four, and fortifying themselves in a neighbouring heiau, or open-air temple, they succeeded in repelling the attack of the Hawaiians until they were relieved, two hours later, by the ships' boats. On the death of Captain Charles Clerke (22 August 1779) King succeeded to the command of the Discovery, and on arriving in England he was advanced to post rank (3 October 1780).

In 1781 King was appointed to the frigate Crocodile, attached to the Channel Fleet, and towards the end of the year he was moved to the Resistance (40 guns), in which he went out to the West Indies in charge of a convoy of 500 merchant ships; these he succeeded in conducting safely to their destination, but the intense anxiety of the duty is said to have turned his hair grey. King's constitution was never strong, and he came back to England with his health impaired. It was under this disadvantage, while living

James King (*bap.* 1750, *d.* 1784), by John Webber, 1782

with his brother Thomas, rector of St Mary Magdalene, Woodstock, near Oxford, that he assisted in preparing Cook's journal of the third voyage for the press, and wrote the narrative of the final part of the voyage, which formed the third volume. King's astronomical observations, together with those of Cook and William Bayly, were published by order of the commissioners of longitude in 1782; for this work he was elected FRS. He was also made an honorary LLD at Oxford University. In 1783 the state of his health compelled him to go to Nice, where he died, unmarried, of tuberculosis on 16 November 1784. He was buried at Nice, but there is a memorial tablet to him and his parents in St Mary Magdalene Church, Woodstock. The narrative of Cook's third voyage was issued in 1784.

J. K. LAUGHTON, *rev.* ANDREW C. F. DAVID

Sources A. David, 'James King', *The charts and coastal views of Captain Cook's voyages*, ed. A. David, R. Joppien, and B. Smith, 3 (1997), lxxvii–lxxviii · J. C. Beaglehole, *The life of Captain James Cook*, Hakluyt Society, 37 (1974) · *The journals of Captain James Cook*, ed. J. C. Beaglehole, 3/1–2, Hakluyt Society, 36a–b (1967) · G. Gilbert, *Captain Cook's final voyage: the journal of midshipman George Gilbert*, ed. C. Holmes (1982) · BL, Egerton MS 2185, fol. 111 · memorial tablet, church of St Mary Magdalene, Woodstock, Oxfordshire
Archives Hydrographic Office, Taunton, running journal, OD 279 · PRO, Admiralty papers, Log and Proceedings, Adm 55/116 and 112 | BL, letters to Douglas, Egerton MS 2180 · NL Aus., letters to John Montagu, fourth earl of Sandwich
Likenesses J. Webber, oils, 1782, NL Aus. [*see illus.*] · F. Bartolozzi, stipple, pubd 1784 (after J. Webber), BM, NPG · J. Hogg, medallion engraving (after S. Shelley), BM; repro. in Beaglehole, ed., *Journals*, title-page
Wealth at death see will, PRO, PROB 11/1135, sig. 559

King [*married name* Taylor], **Jessie Marion** (1875–1949), illustrator and designer, was born on 20 March 1875 at the manse, New Kilpatrick, Dunbartonshire, the third daughter of the Revd James Waters King (1836–1898), Church of Scotland minister, and his wife, Mary Ann (1846–1896), daughter of James(?) Anderson, baker and miller, of Lanark; a younger brother was born a year later. Educated at the parish school in New Kilpatrick until 1891, she took a course at Queen Margaret College, Glasgow, before studying at Glasgow School of Art from 1892 to 1899, under F. H. (Fra) Newbery, who led the school into a golden era. Fellow students included Helen Paxton Brown, Annie French, Ann Macbeth, and Katherine Cameron as well as Margaret and Frances Macdonald, who in 1896 with Charles Rennie Mackintosh and Herbert MacNair launched the influential 'Glasgow style' allied to European art nouveau. As a student King developed her mannered mode of outline drawing, combining delicately patterned surfaces with nervous, elongated lines and arabesque forms within grid-like frames often containing lettering, influenced by Aubrey Beardsley, Jan Toorop, and the late graphic style of Burne-Jones. Early successes included a national silver medal (1898) for illustrations to Edwin Arnold's *The Light of Asia* (1879), despite the 'excessive attenuation' of her figures, a gold medal at the international exhibition of 'Modern decorative art' in Turin (1902), and a commission from the Berlin publishing firm Globus Verlag. Work for British publishers established her as a leading illustrator alongside Arthur Rackham, Kate Greenaway, and Laurence Housman. A checklist of items reveals nearly 300 design projects in sixty years, ranging from art books to advertising cards. Her preferred medium was pen and ink, with watercolour, on vellum, and favourite motifs included ships with billowing sails, fairy maidens with billowing skirts, and intricate skeins of petals or birds composed of tiny dots, like a dew-drenched spider's web. Influenced by a Gaelic-speaking nursemaid with a fund of folklore, Jessie believed herself gifted with 'second sight' and her art was inspired by fantasy, while its minuteness derived from close, myopic vision. From 1899 to 1907 she taught book design at the Glasgow School of Art and from about 1905 she also designed fabrics and jewellery. Solo shows included ones at the Bruton Street Gallery, London (1905), and the Annans' Gallery, Glasgow (1907). From 1905 she was an active member of the Glasgow Society of Lady Artists. On 29 September 1908, after a ten-year engagement, she married Ernest Archibald Taylor (1874–1951), furniture designer and artist. The couple lived briefly in Salford, where their only child, Merle Elspeth, was born in 1909, before moving in 1910 to Paris, where Taylor ran a teaching atelier and King continued with illustration, also exhibiting at the Salon and the 1914 'Arts décoratifs' exhibition. Friends and acquaintances included Henri Matisse, Marie Laurencin, T.-A. Steinlen, J. D. Fergusson, and S. J. Peploe, and King's graphic style was subtly influenced by post-impressionist colour and Leon Bakst's Ballets Russes designs, becoming simpler and bolder. Later landscapes in coloured inks were particularly successful. She also learned the technique of batik printing, which became her forte. Each summer, the Taylors ran painting

Jessie Marion King (1875–1949), by James Craig Annan

courses at High Corrie, Isle of Arran, and applied arts courses in Kirkcudbright, an artistic colony, where they settled in 1915. According to Robert Burns, of Edinburgh College of Art, no student's training was complete without a stay in one of the cottages at their home, Greengate. Wearing wide-brimmed hats and buckled shoes like a nursery-rhyme character, King (familiarly known as Jake) became a notable figure in Kirkcudbright, where she organized and designed community pageants. She decorated ceramic ware, designed wooden toys, and with Taylor produced murals for several Lanarkshire schools—a public art commission cut short by economic depression. An encouraging mentor to younger artists like Marion Harvey, Anna Hotchkis, and Cecile Walton, King's whimsical illustrative style attracted no followers, however, with the exception of Ronald Searle, whose angular figures recall King's. When she died at home on 3 August 1949, her work was not highly regarded, and the first retrospective shows only took place in the 1970s including one at the National Library of Scotland, Edinburgh, since when her idiosyncratic art has steadily risen in critical and commercial favour. She was cremated at Kirkcudbright and her ashes were scattered at the church of Minard, Argyll, where her devoted nurse and housekeeper, Mary McNab (d. 1938), was buried.   JAN MARSH

Sources C. White, *The enchanted world of Jessie M. King* (1989) · J. Burkhauser, ed., *The Glasgow girls: women in art and design, 1880–1920* (1990) · information from Barclay Lennie Fine Art Ltd, Glasgow · C. Oliver, introduction, in *Jessie M. King, 1875–1949*, Scottish Arts Council (1971) [exhibition catalogue, Edinburgh and London] · D. Gaze, ed., *Dictionary of women artists*, 2 vols. (1997) · M. Tidcombe, *Women bookbinders, 1880–1920* (1996) · J. Halsby and P. Harris, *The dictionary of Scottish painters, 1600–1960* (1990) · D. Macmillan, *Scottish art in the 20th century* (1994)

Archives Barclay Lennie Fine Art, Glasgow, MSS and art works · NL Scot., corresp. and papers · Stewartry Museum, Kirkcudbright, art notes and MSS · U. Glas. L., corresp. and papers

Likenesses photograph, c.1920, NPG · L. Alexander, oils, 1949, Tolbooth Art Centre, Kirkcudbright · J. C. Annan, photograph, Scot. NPG [*see illus.*] · portraits, Barclay Lennie Fine Art, Glasgow · portraits, Glasgow Museums and Art Gallery · portraits, Stewartry Museum, Kirkcudbright

Wealth at death £111 1s. 11d.: confirmation, 8 Jan 1951, CCI

King, John (d. 1621), bishop of London, was one of twelve children of Philip King (d. 1592) and his wife, Elizabeth, daughter of Edmund Conquest. According to Thomas Fuller his birth took place in the ancestral home at Worminghall, Buckinghamshire, in the same chamber as his father had been born. A brass erected in Worminghall church by Elizabeth King records that her husband was educated at the expense of his uncle Robert *King (d. 1557), abbot of Oseney and Thame and first bishop of Oxford, and of his kinsman John Williams, Lord Williams of Thame (c.1500–1559). John King was sent to Westminster School, whence in 1577 he was elected a student of Christ Church, Oxford. He graduated BA on 26 January 1580, at which time he was presented to the London parish of St Anne and St Agnes, and to a prebend at Windsor. He proceeded MA on 15 February 1583.

King served as domestic chaplain to John Piers, a former dean of Christ Church and now bishop of Salisbury, and followed his household north upon his translation to York in 1588. In that year King became preacher to the city of York. Piers preferred him to the archdeaconry of Nottingham in 1590 and on 2 July 1591 he proceeded BD. King established a reputation as a powerful evangelical preacher, and delivered Piers's funeral sermon at York on 17 November 1594 (printed in 1597). Probably during his time in York, King married Joan, daughter of Henry Freeman of Staffordshire; their eldest son, Henry *King (d. 1669), was born at Worminghall in January 1592, and their second, John King [*see below*] at York in 1595.

Shortly afterwards King joined the household of the newly appointed lord keeper Thomas Egerton, a noted patron of evangelical clergy, as his domestic chaplain. Another appointee in Egerton's household was John Donne, who was to remain intimate with the King family. In May 1597 King was instituted rector of St Andrew's, Holborn, London, and in October 1599 prebend of Sneating in St Paul's, both by royal prerogative following the consecrations of Richard Bancroft to London and William Cotton to Exeter respectively. From these pulpits King established himself as one of London's foremost preachers, noted for Calvinist orthodoxy, moral rectitude, and strident anti-Catholicism. In December 1601 he was created DD at Oxford. It has often been stated that King was a chaplain to Elizabeth but at the accession of James in 1603 Archbishop John Whitgift listed him among nineteen prominent preachers who were 'no chapleins' yet 'fitt to

John King (*d.* 1621), attrib. Nicholas Lockey, *c.*1620

preach' before the new sovereign (Westminster Abbey muniment book 15, fol. 6). King's eminence and reliability in the pulpit received official endorsement when Whitgift appointed him to deliver the first Sunday sermon at court after Elizabeth's death, and it would seem that Whitgift's faith in him was not misplaced. King's discourse evidently made a deep impression on John Manningham, who transcribed his notes from the sermon at unprecedented length. Deftly but forcefully addressing concerns about Roman Catholic agitation at the succession, King warned against 'intestine discord', eulogizing Elizabeth, and welcoming James as a new Solomon (*Diary of John Manningham*, 211–17).

Upon his arrival in London, James made King one of his chaplains in ordinary. He was to remain one of the most popular court preachers of the reign, praised by James in one of his predictable puns as 'the king of preachers' (Wood, *Ath. Oxon.*, 2.295). He was also held in particular regard by Queen Anne. With the enthusiastic endorsement by petition of thirty-two students (that is, fellows) of the college, James appointed King dean of Christ Church in August 1605. Thus King became the latest of the college's unbroken succession of evangelical Calvinist heads, who had dominated theology and churchmanship in Oxford since the beginning of Elizabeth's reign. He served as vice-chancellor of Oxford University from 1607 until 1610.

In September 1605 King was one of four chaplains selected by James to instruct leaders of Scottish presbyterianism in sermons at Hampton Court (an appointment which led to the later assumption that he was chosen to preach at the Hampton Court Conference in 1604, which

King did not in fact attend). King's contribution, printed by royal command, asserted the royal prerogative over ecclesiastical causes, as well as episcopacy instituted by divine right. Although he accepted the possibility of other forms of church government as legitimate abroad, he held presbyterianism to be inherently anti-monarchical and therefore illegitimate in the kingdoms of England and Scotland. The sermon's prime target, James Melvill, called the performance 'a most violent invective againes the Presbyteries' (*Autobiography and Diary*, 667).

In December 1610 King was collated to the prebend of Milton Manor in Lincoln Cathedral but he resigned this and all his other preferments after his consecration at Lambeth as bishop of London on 8 September 1611. Fuller praised him as 'full fraught with episcopal qualities' (Fuller, *Worthies*, 1.138). Like his friend and most recent patron, George Abbot—his predecessor in London and now promoted archbishop of Canterbury—King exemplified the evangelical Calvinistic model of the preaching chief pastor, in contrast to the disciplinarian and ceremonialist style emerging among proto-Arminians such as Lancelot Andrewes and Richard Neile. Distinctive was King's commitment to continuing to preach himself, and not only in élite pulpits such as the court and Paul's Cross; King took pride in preaching a parochial sermon somewhere in his diocese every Sunday during his episcopate. He also assiduously appointed like-minded men to livings in his diocese, and the huge number of dedications to him of sermons printed by aspiring young evangelicals attests to his position as an evangelical patron, perhaps second only to Abbot. King and Abbot, sometimes with the dean of the Chapel Royal, James Montagu, formed the nexus of evangelical interests at court, as they also did on the court of high commission. King's visitation articles (in 1612 and 1615) show similar evangelical priorities in their insistence on catechizing, and their comparative lack of concern for strict ceremonial conformity. In 1613 King and Abbot were joint dedicatees of the fourth edition of Andrew Willet's seminal statement of English Calvinistic church polity, *Synopsis papismi*, where both were praised for standing firm against the encroachment of the 'semi-popish errors' encouraged by Richard Hooker's anti-puritanism (Milton, 22). King figured prominently in the protestant triumphalism surrounding the marriage of Princess Elizabeth to the elector palatine on 14 February 1613. On the Tuesday after the wedding, King preached at court on a text chosen by James I ('Thy wife shall be as the fruitfull vine' (Psalm 28: 3), a sermon notable not only for King's trademark anti-Catholicism, but also for its celebration of women and the equality between partners in marriage. This may inform an understanding of the bishop's own conjugal and domestic happiness, remarked upon by Donne and others. Describing his participation in a sociable family dinner that year in their house at St Paul's, Donne referred jocularly to the couple as 'the King' and 'the Queen' (Bald, 282). Later in 1613 King and Abbot led the godly opposition on the commission hearing the divorce suit brought against the earl of Essex by his countess, Frances Howard.

In his last years as bishop King presided over a campaign for the restoration of St Paul's Cathedral, marked by James's only visit there on 26 March 1620 to hear King preach from Paul's Cross. Also in 1620 King presided at the festival consecration of the earl of Bridgewater's private chapel at Bridgewater House in the Barbican. King's appeal for the cathedral epitomizes the lesser-known fact that concern for the maintenance and beautification of church fabrics throughout his diocese was a particular achievement of his episcopate. Upon his elevation to the see, King commissioned Anthony Munday to compile a parish-by-parish survey of church refurbishments in the City of London; although Munday did not complete his task until the 1630s, King received the dedication of Munday's 1618 edition of his expansion of Stow's *Survey of London*.

King's health failed within a year of James's visit to St Paul's. Suffering from gall and bladder stones, on 4 March 1621 he wrote his will 'weake in body and full of payne', and six days later John Chamberlain reported that his family hoped only 'to kepe him alive … till our Lady day [25 March] be past, for the goode of his children' (who would benefit from the episcopal revenues due then), after which time he would consent to surgical removal of the stones (*Letters of John Chamberlain*, 2.352). He died on 30 March 1621. King's will directed that he be buried 'in the Cathedrall church of St Paule without any pompe or solempnities onlie with a Tombestone with this Inscription (*Resurgam*)' (PRO, PROB 11/137, fols. 285r–286r). Accordingly the day after his death 'at night he was buried privatly in Paules' (*Letters of John Chamberlain*, 2.360). Fuller transcribes the fine elegy on the humility of King and the modesty of his burial that was inscribed on a brass plaque placed on the wall adjacent to the tomb. King was survived by his wife, five sons—Henry *King, John, Philip, William, and Robert—and four unmarried daughters, Elizabeth, Mary, Dorothy, and Anne. All received significant cash bequests from an estate Chamberlain estimated at more than £12,000 in value. Dorothy and Anne were bequeathed King's gifts of plate from Queen Anne; Henry was given the first choice of forty books from his father's library, with the remainder to be divided between the younger sons. King appointed as overseers Archbishop Abbot and Sir Henry Martin, chancellor of London diocese. False rumours of a deathbed conversion to Roman Catholicism by King were fully exploited by Catholic presses at home and abroad; these claims were sharply refuted by his eldest son, Henry, residentiary canon of St Paul's, in a sermon at Paul's Cross on 25 November, printed immediately.

King's second son, **John King** (1595–1639), Church of England clergyman, was born in York and educated with his elder brother Henry at Westminster School, London. He matriculated from Christ Church, Oxford, on 20 January 1609, aged fourteen, and graduated BA on 19 June 1611; he proceeded MA on 7 July 1614, and published poems in the university collections of 1613 and 1619. He became a prebendary of St Paul's in 1616. Rector of Remenham, Berkshire, and (for three years) public orator to Oxford University from 1622, he became a canon of Christ Church in 1624 and proceeded BD and DD on 19 May 1625. That year he became a canon of Windsor and published a sermon preached at Oxford. He died on 3 January 1639 and was buried in Christ Church Cathedral.

P. E. McCullough

Sources Foster, *Alum. Oxon.* · Wood, *Ath. Oxon.* · will, PRO, PROB 11/137, fols. 285r–286v · *VCH Buckinghamshire* · Fuller, *Worthies* · K. Fincham, *Prelate as pastor: the episcopate of James I* (1990) · A. Milton, *Catholic and Reformed: the Roman and protestant churches in English protestant thought, 1600–1640* (1995) · P. E. McCullough, *Sermons at court: politics and religion in Elizabethan and Jacobean preaching* (1998) [incl. CD-ROM] · *Hist. U. Oxf.* 4: *17th-cent. Oxf.* · *The diary of John Manningham of the Middle Temple, 1602–1603*, ed. R. P. Sorlien (Hanover, NH, 1976) · J. F. Merritt, 'Puritans, Laudians and the phenomenon of church building in Jacobean London', *HJ*, 41 (1998), 935–60 · R. C. Bald, *John Donne: a life*, ed. W. Milgate (1970) · *The autobiography and diary of Mr James Melvill*, ed. R. Pitcairn, Wodrow Society (1842) · *The letters of John Chamberlain*, ed. N. E. McClure, 2 vols. (1939)
Archives Folger, theological commonplace book
Likenesses attrib. N. Lockey, oils, *c*.1620, Fulham Palace, London [*see illus.*] · F. Delaram, line engraving, BM, NPG · attrib. N. Lockey, oils, version, NPG · S. de Passe, line engraving (after N. Lockey), BM, NPG · line engraving, BM, NPG; repro. in J. J. Boissard, *Bibliotheca chalcographica* (Frankfurt, 1664) · oils, Christ Church Oxf.
Wealth at death '12 thousand pounds': *The letters of John Chamberlain*, ed. McClure, 2.360

King, Sir John (*d.* 1637), politician and landowner, was born of a Yorkshire family, although the name of his parents and details of his early years remain unknown. He is first recorded in Ireland in July 1585 as secretary to Richard Bingham, governor of Connaught. By early 1601 he was deputy vice-treasurer of Ireland, a post of considerable practical importance, and went on to become clerk of the crown in chancery and clerk of the hanaper (12 July 1603), muster master-general and clerk of the cheque (11 May 1609), and a member of both the Irish privy council (June 1609) and the council of Munster (20 May 1615). He was knighted on 7 July 1610. At an unknown date he married Catherine, daughter of Robert Drury, nephew to Sir William Drury, lord deputy of Ireland. They had six sons and three daughters, including Dorothy *Dury.

Following the completion of the conquest of Ireland in 1603 King was able to use his government connections to benefit massively. A poor system of record keeping and ignorance of geography allowed well-placed officials to use royal grants to claim lands far in excess of what was intended. Between 1603 and 1607 he received lands in twenty-one different counties. He probably sold most of this and concentrated his holdings in co. Roscommon, having a residence at Boyle. He invested heavily in developing Boyle and appears as constable of Boyle Castle from September 1606. In 1613–15 he sat as MP for Roscommon county but only after Oliver St John, governor of Connaught, had manipulated electoral proceedings. He was joint caretaker governor of Connaught in 1615.

Despite his land interests in co. Roscommon, King continued to pursue an administrative career and based himself in Dublin, living at Baggotrath. With his vast experience, particularly in financial affairs, he would have exerted considerable influence behind the scenes, being a regular attender of council meetings and a member of many government land commissions. He was also commissioner for the plantations of Wexford (1614) and Leitrim and Ely O'Carroll (1619). For obscure reasons in June 1615 he insinuated that Lord Deputy Chichester was mismanaging royal finances, thereby precipitating the governor's removal from office. Political motives aside he always showed great concern for the health of the Irish exchequer. He died on 4 January 1637 at Lichfield, Staffordshire, and was buried in Boyle on 30 March. He was succeeded by his second son, Sir Robert *King. His eldest son, Edward *King, drowned in 1637; an early John Milton poem, 'Lycidas' (1638), lamented his death.

GORDON GOODWIN, rev. TERRY CLAVIN

Sources R. Lascelles, ed., *Liber munerum publicorum Hiberniae … or, The establishments of Ireland*, 2 vols. [1824–30], 2.24, 99, 189 · *Calendar of the Irish patent rolls of James I* (before 1830); facs. edn as *Irish patent rolls of James I* (1966) · *CSP Ire.*, 1574–85; 1588–92; 1600–01; 1603–25; 1633–47 · J. Lodge, *The peerage of Ireland*, 3 (1754), 218–22 · J. McCavitt, *Sir Arthur Chichester* (1998), 216–17 · B. McGrath, 'The membership of the Irish House of Commons, 1613–15', MLitt diss., TCD, 1985, 91–2

King, John (1595–1639). *See under* King, John (d. 1621).

King, John (*bap.* 1614, *d.* 1681), physician, was baptized Joannes Regius in the Dutch church at Austin Friars, London, on 11 September 1614, the first of six children of the Revd Joannes Regius (1574–1627), a minister of that church, and his second wife, Johanna. His father's family were pillars of the Flemish Reformed church, his grandfather Jacobus Regius having been a minister of the London Dutch church from 1572 until 1601. King's father studied divinity at Leiden and Heidelberg, where he took his degree in theology in 1595. He was a staunch defender of orthodox Calvinism against the heresies of Servetus and Arminius. Persecuted for their religion in the Netherlands, the Regius family took refuge in London. In 1601 Joannes Regius succeeded his father as a minister of the Dutch church at Austin Friars, where he remained until his death in 1627. Between 1604 and 1625 he had eleven children, of whom four survived him. Among these was John King, the only one of six children of the Revd Regius's second wife to survive infancy. At least some of these children died in the London plague of 1625. King's father died of the stone in 1627 and under his father's will he received £360.

In 1633 King began his medical education at Leiden. After five years he earned his MD, his thesis being on the subject of fevers, and returned to London. He incorporated on his Leiden degree at the University of Oxford on 14 January 1641. King was proposed by the president of the College of Physicians, Othowell Meverell, for election to the college on 22 December 1643 and was approved 'by a majority of the votes' (annals, RCP Lond., bk 3.4). It was not until 1648, however, that he was able to fill a vacant fellowship.

On 6 April 1643 King married, in the London Dutch church, Joanna Marolois, the widow of Jacob de Backer. On 13 December 1643 King was nominated for a deaconship in the Dutch church. He was not elected. In the same year he and his wife were to be found in the parish of St Olave Jewry, where, of seventy-one ratepayers King was assessed as the tenth wealthiest. A parliamentary assessment of April 1643 rated King's household seventeenth out of a total of sixty-four assessed. King aligned himself with the parliamentary cause when he signed the solemn league and covenant on 2 October 1643. In 1644 he was assessed by a parliamentary committee raising money to fight Charles I at £100, indicating that he was not among the top rank of physicians, who were assessed at £250.

King had three daughters and two sons. At least two of his daughters were baptized in both the English and the Dutch church, showing that King was concerned about maintaining good relations with both communities. King was formally elected to the long-awaited fellowship in the College of Physicians on 9 August 1648. On 25 September 1648 King subscribed to the relief of the Dutch church in Colchester, where civil war still raged. He was an unsuccessful candidate for the eldership of the Dutch church on five separate occasions between 1652 and 1659. As a fellow of the College of Physicians, King attended at least one college meeting a year from 1648 to 1674. He was elected a censor of the college in 1651, 1659, and 1661. From 25 June 1651 to 1654 King and George Ent had charge of the college library. To mark the end of his stewardship, King presented the college with the four volumes of the *Historiae naturalis* by the Polish physician Joannes Jonstonus. Between 1675 and 1679 he was absent from college proceedings. None the less, in 1680, he was made an elect.

King died from jaundice at his house in Austin Friars on 28 October 1681. He was buried six days later in the parish church of St Peter-le-Poer, where his father was also buried. In his will King left 'all my East Indian Actions in the Chambre of Amsterdam', £100 sterling, 'and also my Studie of Books' to his eldest son, John King [see below]. To his other son, James King ('who is now at Surat in the East Indies, and well settled there'), he left another £100. The rest of his estate was to be shared by his surviving daughters, Mary Philipps and Hester King, but with a special provision for Hester who 'is verie weak impotent and infirme by reason of a melancholick Distemp[er] upon her, and thereby is disabled to helpe or mainteyne herself' (PRO, PROB 11/368, sig. 166). John King left no publications beyond his Leiden thesis of 1638. He does, however, represent the presence of London's Anglo-Dutch community in the seventeenth-century medical profession.

King has in the past been confused with other individuals. Among these was another physician, John King (1604–1688), who also took an MD at Leiden and was also the father of a John King, in this instance the lawyer Sir John King (1639–1677). Munk's *Roll of the Royal College of Physicians* conflates the lives of these two John Kings.

John King (*b.* 1648, *d.* in or after 1686), the eldest son of John King, was born in London on 5 June 1648 and was educated at the Merchant Taylors' School. He was admitted a pensioner at Gonville and Caius College, Cambridge, on 21 June 1666. From 1667 to 1671 he was a scholar at Caius. He received an MB from the university on 26 November 1670, and was admitted to Leiden, probably on 20 May 1671.

Through the influence of Sir Andrew King he became university professor at Gresham College, London, on 2 October 1676. In the following month, on 30 November 1676, he also became a fellow of the Royal Society, proposed by Abraham Hill, a founding member of that society. King remained professor at Gresham until his resignation on 20 August 1686.   WILLIAM BIRKEN

Sources W. Birken, 'Dr John King (1614–1681) and Dr Assuerus Regemorter (1615–1650)', *Medical History*, 20 (1976), 276–95 · R. W. Innes Smith, *English-speaking students of medicine at the University of Leyden* (1932) · Venn, *Alum. Cant.* · J. Ward, *The lives of the professors of Gresham College* (1740); repr. (1967) · M. Hunter, *The Royal Society and its fellows, 1660–1700: the morphology of an early scientific institution* (1982) · O. P. Grell and A. Cunningham, eds., *Medicine and the Reformation* (1993) · W. J. C. Moens, ed., *The marriage, baptismal, and burial registers, 1571 to 1874, and monumental inscriptions of the Dutch Reformed church, Austin Friars, London* (privately printed, Lymington, 1884), 61 · Munk, *Roll* · parish register, St Peter-le-Poer, GL, MS 4093/1

Wealth at death left 'Studie of Books' plus £100 to eldest son; £100 to other son; remainder shared by two surviving daughters: will, PRO, PROB 11/368, sig. 166

King, John (*d.* 1679), covenanter field preacher and martyr, of whose early life nothing is known, first appears among that group of ministers who refused to acquiesce in the re-establishment of the prelacy in the Scottish church after 1662. Unable to secure the tenure of a parish, he was protected from the authorities by his patron Henry Erskine, third Lord Cardross, whom he served as chaplain. He married, and had at least one child.

King's wider preaching commitments to the lowland congregations driven out of doors by the legislation of 1661–2 did not go unnoticed by central government. In 1674 he was arrested for leading the worship at local conventicles and was brought before the Scottish privy council. Lord Cardross was fined heavily for allowing him to minister to his family, while King was released from custody pending further questioning only upon the payment of a bond of 5000 merks. However, King continued his activities and ignored all subsequent summonses to the courts in Edinburgh. In May 1675 a party of soldiers commanded by Sir Mungo Murray took the law into their own hands and raided Cardross's home during his absence. Under the cover of darkness they dragged King's pregnant wife from her bed, rifled through his personal papers, and placed King under close arrest. Before they could spirit their prisoner away, a mob of 'country people who had profited by Mr. King's ministry assembled together' on the road out of Cardross, surrounded the soldiers, and prised the minister away from their grasp (Crookshank, 1.373).

On 12 June 1675 Charles II ordered an investigation into the circumstances of King's escape and on 6 August King was pronounced an outlaw by the Scottish privy council. Over the next four years he criss-crossed the lowland shires, preaching to congregations in the fields and to individuals in their private houses. He was reported as active in Fife, Perth, Stirling, and in the city of Glasgow, in summer 1677, solemnizing weddings and baptisms and preaching before crowds which included many affluent tradesmen. His luck ran out on 31 May 1679, when he and

fourteen companions were taken on the road from Falkirk to Rutherglen by government troops commanded by John Graham of Claverhouse. However, the tables were turned the next day at Drumclog when Claverhouse encountered unexpected resistance from those attending a great conventicle, strengthened by several of King's friends who had eluded capture. The covenanter host surged forward, scattering the government troopers and liberating the prisoners, and as Claverhouse rode headlong in flight past King, the preacher called after his persecutor, inviting him to stay behind and benefit from hearing the sermon which he would now be able to preach in the afternoon.

The victory at Drumclog bought King three more precious weeks of freedom, which he spent with the rebel army. Although he afterwards denied that he had been present at the covenanters' abortive assault upon Glasgow and had worn a sword only in order to disguise himself from being took for a preacher', it seems likely that he was influential in the army's councils and fought at the battle of Bothwell Bridge on 22 June 1679 (Crookshank, 2.58). Following the rout of the covenanter forces he fled to Dalry parish, seeking sanctuary with the laird of Blair. However, he was surprised *en route* by a party of Chrichton's dragoons, captured, and promptly escorted to Edinburgh, where the accidental death of one of his guards, who had boasted that he was carrying 'King to Hell', was attributed by successive generations of presbyterian hagiographers to an act of divine providence.

Faced with the prospect of torture, King confessed that he had been in arms with the rebels, and on 22 July was indicted for high treason. At his trial on 28 July he argued that he had been forced against his will to join the rebel host after the battle of Drumclog, but in view of his earlier confession this counted for little with the judge and verdicts of guilty were duly brought in against him and his co-accused, John Kid. Well-meaning attempts by a fellow prisoner at the Edinburgh Tolbooth, Robert Fleming, to persuade King and Kid to accept the duke of Lauderdale's new offer of indulgences and thereby save their lives, were briskly rejected. The two ministers went to the scaffold together at the Mercat Cross on 14 August 1679, and in his final speech King launched a fresh attack upon the errors of popery, episcopacy, and Erastianism, before taking leave of his 'poor wife and child' (Tutchin, 178–82) and looking forward to an 'everlasting life [and] glory' (Crookshank, 2.64–5). After his body was cut down from the gibbet, it was dismembered on an adjacent scaffold in full view of the crowd. His head and right hand were subsequently displayed on the Netherbow gate of Edinburgh, while his corpse was thrown into an unmarked grave within the precincts of Greyfriars churchyard. Although he was undoubtedly an accomplished preacher, only one of King's sermons—delivered at Kilmarnock on 22 August 1678—survives (collected by John Howie). In it King laments the sorrows heaped upon the Scottish nation by the 'dreadful formality of many' in their daily religious practices and by the 'breach and violation of the covenants' by people from all social ranks. He chooses, however, to return to his biblical text in order to appeal to God to 'remember mercy' even in the midst of his wrath, and to deliver his chosen people from the clutches of their enemies (Howie, *Faithful Contendings*, 30–44).

JOHN CALLOW

Sources W. Crookshank, *The history of the state and sufferings of the Church of Scotland*, 2 vols. (1749) • *Reg. PCS*, 3rd ser., vols. 5–6 • R. Wodrow, *The history of the sufferings of the Church of Scotland from the Restauration to the revolution*, 2 vols. (1721–2) • J. Howie, ed., *Faithful contendings displayed* (1780) • W. H. Carslaw, preface, in J. Howie, *The Scots worthies*, ed. W. H. Carslaw, [new edn] (1870), ix–xv • R. C. Paterson, *A land afflicted: Scotland and the covenanter wars* (1998) • P. Walker and A. Shields, *Biographia Presbyteriana*, ed. J. Stevenson, 1 (1827) • J. Tutchin, *The western martyrology, or, The bloody assizes*, 5th edn (1873) • *The manuscripts of the duke of Hamilton*, HMC, 21 (1887), 159 • A. Smellie, *Men of the covenant* (1903) • J. K. Hewison, *The covenanters: a history of the church in Scotland from the Reformation to the revolution*, 2nd edn, 2 vols. (1913) • *A cloud of witnesses* (1730)

King, John, first Baron Kingston (*c*.1620–1676), army officer, was the eldest son of Sir Robert *King (*d*. 1657) and his first wife, Frances (*d*. 1638), daughter of Sir Henry Folliott, first baron of Ballyshannon, and his wife, Anne Strode. When Sir Robert went to England in 1642 after the outbreak of the Irish rising he left John in command of Boyle Castle, co. Roscommon. In the late 1640s King joined his father in London, where he sought to recruit a regiment, but it was as major in Richard Coote's horse regiment that he was active in the last years of the war in Ireland. He gained fame for his capture of the general of the Ormondist army, Heber Macmahon, the Roman Catholic bishop of Clogher, after its defeat at Scarrifhollis on 21 June 1650; he was present at the siege of Charlemont two months later, and served as parliamentary commissioner in the conclusion of both the articles of Galway on 5 April 1652 and the articles with Clanricarde on 28 June 1652. After the war he served as commissioner for setting out lands to the soldiers in Sligo. During the 1650s King and his father bought a large number of transplantation certificates and soldiers' debentures. King himself purchased substantial estates in co. Dublin from the adventurer John Blackwell, while his marriage, in 1657, to Catherine (*d*. 1669), daughter of Sir William Fenton, brought him the Munster lands of the white knights, including Mitchelstown Castle, to which she was heir. Henry Cromwell knighted him on 7 June 1658 and two days later recommended that he be appointed to succeed his father as muster master general, observing that 'he is a person of no less meritt than his father, being grown a very serious, and, I hope, religious man' (Thurloe, 7.162).

After the fall of the protectorate King became deeply involved in the moves towards the restoration of Charles II. He had taken up a regimental command in the remodelled Irish army by February 1660, represented Boyle in the general convention which assembled in March, and was one of the four men in Ireland to be favoured with a personal letter of encouragement from Charles. He was chosen to present General Monck with the humble address of 8 May in which the army in Ireland welcomed the Restoration and was appointed one of the convention's commissioners to attend King Charles. He was

knighted on 5 June 1660 and on 4 September both ennobled as Baron Kingston and sworn of the Irish privy council. He was appointed a member of the presidency council of Connaught on 17 March 1661 and nominated two days later to the commission which was intended to execute the provisions of the king's 'gracious declaration' of November 1660. Though the commission proved abortive, Kingston's interests were carefully protected in the parliamentary arrangements which replaced it. He benefited from a proviso in the Act of Settlement in 1662, was one of twenty-two individuals who were declared exempt from the obligation to retrench a third of their estates in the Act of Explanation in 1665, and secured recognition of his claim as a '49 officer (one owed payment for services prior to 1649). He was appointed commissary-general on 11 May 1661, given the captaincy of a troop on 15 November, and made colonel of a horse regiment on 20 April 1667. On 2 April 1666, on Ormond's urging, he was joined with John, Lord Berkeley, as president of Connaught, an arrangement which lasted until the abolition of the office in 1672 when both men were allowed to retain the fees and profits of the post and Berkeley was granted a pension with reversion to Kingston.

Kingston's last years were occupied in securing ratification of the complex arrangements he had made to acquire reprisal lands (property surrendered to compensate other claimants) to make up his full entitlement under the settlement. A favourable recommendation by arbiters was approved by Ormond and accepted by Kingston, and on 9 March 1676 the king ordered that he should be excepted from the stop recently placed on the disposal of reprisal lands and that the transaction should be completed. Kingston died within days, in March 1676, and the instruction was renewed for his heir, Robert *King, second Baron Kingston (*c*.1660–1693), on 10 April. Kingston's younger son John succeeded as third baron in 1693.

AIDAN CLARKE

Sources *CSP Ire.*, 1660–70 • *CSP dom.*, 1671–6 • J. Lodge, *The peerage of Ireland*, rev. M. Archdall, rev. edn, 3 (1789) • R. D. King-Harman, *The Kings: earls of Kingston* (1959) • Thurloe, *State papers*, vol. 7 • A. Clarke, *Prelude to Restoration in Ireland* (1999) • Bodl. Oxf., MS Clarendon 70 • Bodl. Oxf., MS Carte 213 • B. McGrath, 'Biographical dictionary of the membership of the Irish House of Commons, 1640–1641', PhD diss., University of Dublin, 1997
Archives BL, corresp. relating to sale of land, MS 46951

King, Sir John (1639–1677), lawyer, was born at St Albans, Hertfordshire, on 5 February 1639, the eldest son of John King (1604–1681), physician, of Aldersgate Street, London, and his second wife, Elizabeth (1611–1661/2), youngest daughter of Barne Roberts of Willesden, Middlesex. His grandfather, John Le Roy, had moved to England from France in 1572, and then changed his name to King. King was educated at St Albans Free School and Eton College (*c*.1652–1655) before matriculating in 1655 at Queens' College, Cambridge. Although originally intended for the church, King chose the law instead. In November 1660 he entered the Inner Temple, being called to the bar on 9 February 1668. By this date he had married, on 20 February 1666 or 1667, Joyce (*d*. 1688), daughter and heir of William

Bennett of High Rothing, Essex. They had two sons and five daughters (four of whom died young).

King made his initial impact as a lawyer in the fire court set up following the fire of London, but soon progressed to chancery cases. He was knighted on 10 December 1674 and became a king's counsel on 23 January 1675, saving for his office as solicitor-general of the duke of York. In 1676 he was the top practiser in chancery, earning £4700,

> for he was cut out by nature and formed by education for that business. He had the most of an orator and was withal the most polite and affable gentleman that I ever knew wear a gown. His principal care was to be instructed and then his performance was easy.   (North, 1.380)

North felt that King was overworked, and that an unhappy marriage kept him out late in the taverns of the town. Burnet hinted at other pressures, believing that King was being groomed by the court as a successor to Sir William Jones, the attorney-general. At any event King died relatively young.

King made his will on 27 June 1677, 'sick in body', and died on the 29th at his house in Salisbury Court, London. He was buried on 4 July 1677 at the Temple Church, Inner Temple, where there is an inscription in the triforium and a stone in the churchyard to his memory. His wife, in her will of 1 July 1684, remembered her husband as 'the most tenderly affectionate husband that ever woman was blessed withal', and following her death was buried on 20 April 1688, also in the Inner Temple.

STUART HANDLEY

Sources G. H. Sawtell, *A brief and true narrative of the life and death of Sir John King* (1855) · Venn, *Alum. Cant.* · Sainty, *King's counsel* · W. Sterry, ed., *The Eton College register, 1441–1698* (1943), 198–9 · *Register of burials at the Temple Church, 1628–1853* (1905), 22, 26 [with introduction by H. G. Woods] · R. North, *The lives of … Francis North … Dudley North … and … John North*, ed. A. Jessopp, 1 (1890), 380–81 · *GM*, 1st ser., 52 (1782), 110–12 · will, PRO, PROB 11/354, sig. 75 · will, PRO, PROB 11/391, sig. 62 · *IGI* · *Bishop Burnet's History*, 2.98 · Munk, *Roll*
Likenesses oils, *c.*1674 (of King?), NPG · W. Sherwin, print, BM, NPG · miniature, Royal Collection

King, John (*b.* 1648, *d.* in or after **1686**). *See under* King, John (*bap.* 1614, *d.* 1681).

King, John (1652–1732), Church of England clergyman, was born at St Columb, Cornwall, on 1 May 1652, the son of John King of Manaccan, Cornwall. He matriculated at Exeter College, Oxford, as a poor scholar on 7 July 1674. He graduated BA in 1678 and proceeded MA in 1681; in 1698, when his friend Sir William Dawes was master of St Catharine's College, Cambridge, he was created DD there.

King's first position after ordination was as curate of Bray, Berkshire, when he evidently met Ann, youngest daughter of William Durham, whom he married on 9 September 1685. They had no children and Ann died within five years of their wedding. On 3 June 1690 King married, as his second wife, Elizabeth (1665/6–1727), daughter of Joseph Aris of Adstone, Northamptonshire, and widow of the Revd John Eston, through whom he acquired the living of Pertenhall, Bedfordshire, to which he was immediately instituted on 7 June 1690. He vacated this benefice for institution by exchange to Chelsea on 22 November

1694, the two preferments being worth about £150 a year each, but the stipend of the new living was greatly increased by letting the glebe for building in consequence of Chelsea's growing population. King stated in 1717 that the parish contained about 350 houses and that fifty years before there had been fewer than 40. The gravel soil, elevated position, and clear air of the place were thought particularly healthy, and many people, including Jonathan Swift in 1711, went there to benefit. King wrote, 'No village in the vicinity of London contributes more to the ease and recovery of asthmatical and consumptive persons' (Beaver, 49). King inherited the rectory in such a ruinous state that he had to buy a house in Church Lane (now Old Church Street). He may also have held the livings of West Wycombe (between 1684 and 1695) and of Harrold, Bedfordshire, from 1697 to at least 1710. He was collated to the prebendal stall of Weighton in York Minster by Dawes, now archbishop of York.

King was one of the earliest subscribers to the Society for Promoting Christian Knowledge. As well as two sermons, King published anonymously against the nonconformist Increase Mather (*Animadversions on a Pamphlet Intituled a Letter of Advice to the Nonconformists*, which appeared in a second edition under his own name the following year) and the deist John Toland (*Tolando-pseudologo-mastix*, 1721). In 1710 he published *The Case of John Atherton*, a defence of the bishop of Waterford executed for buggery in 1640, which sought to clear his name and align his cause with that of other clerical victims of charges trumped up by enemies of the church. King's antiquarian interests were reflected in his manuscript account of Chelsea, from which extracts were drawn by later antiquarians, and the notes he prepared for Thomas Hearne on Sir Thomas More's house there.

King died at Church Lane, Chelsea, on 30 May 1732, and was buried in the chancel of Pertenhall church on 13 June; a large mural monument was erected to his memory. His wife died at Chelsea on 22 June 1727, aged sixty-one, and was also buried at Pertenhall. King was survived by three sons, among them the classical scholar and physician John *King (1696–1728), and three daughters.

W. P. COURTNEY, *rev.* LEONARD W. COWIE

Sources T. Faulkner, *An historical and topographical description of Chelsea and its environments* (1810) · A. Beaver, *Memories of old Chelsea* (1892); repr. 1971 · D. Lysons, *The environs of London*, 4 (1796) · B. Denny, *Chelsea past* (1996) · S. Halkett and J. Laing, *A dictionary of the anonymous and pseudonymous literature of Great Britain*, 1 (1882) · Nichols, *Lit. anecdotes* · W. Gaunt, *Kensington and Chelsea* (1975) · R. W. Blunt, *An illustrated handbook to the parish of Chelsea* (1900) · E. McClure, ed., *A chapter in English church history: being the minutes of the Society for Promoting Christian Knowledge for … 1698–1704* (1888) · Foster, *Alum. Oxon.* · Venn, *Alum. Cant.* · will, PRO, PROB 11/652, sig. 168 · *Fasti Angl., 1541–1857*, [York]
Archives BL, Sloane MS 4055
Wealth at death copyhold farm in Tilbrook, Bedfordshire; copyhold closes in Kimbolton, Huntingdonshire; leases, land, and tenements in Pertenhall, Bedfordshire; freehold estate in Elmhurst, Staffordshire: will, PRO, PROB 11/652, sig. 168

King, John (1696–1728), classical scholar and physician, was born at Adstone, Northamptonshire, on 5 August

1696, the eldest son of John *King (1652–1732), Church of England clergyman, and his second wife, Elizabeth, *née* Aris (1665/6–1727), widow of the Revd John Eston. He was educated at Eton College and King's College, Cambridge, where he was elected a fellow, graduating BA (1719) and MA (1722). Although he did not take a medical degree, King established himself as a physician in St George's parish, Stamford, Lincolnshire. He soon acquired a great reputation and on 12 August 1724 he was elected to the scholarly and conversational Spalding Gentlemen's Society. Three years later he married Lucy, daughter of Thomas Morice, paymaster of the British forces at Lisbon, his intention then being to settle in London under the direction of his brother-in-law, the physician John Freind.

In 1722 King published an *Epistola ad Johannem Freind*, an attack on the remarks of Daniel Wilhelm Triller on Hippocrates' treatises on epidemics. King's edition of *Euripidis Hecuba, Orestes et Phoenissae* in the original Greek with Latin translation appeared in 1726, the product of nearly five years' work. In 1748 Thomas Morrell published for use at Eton the same three plays, together with *Alcestis*, in which he gave nearly the whole of King's translation and notes. Morrell's contemporary, the antiquary Roger Gale, took a less generous view of King's ability which he thought more that 'of a trader than a scholar' (Gale, 3.80). King intended to move to London but before this could be accomplished he died at Stamford from fever on 12 October 1728. He was buried at Pertenhall, Bedfordshire, his father's former living. He was survived by his wife and their only son, also John, who became rector of Pertenhall (1752–1800) and a fellow of King's College, Cambridge, before his death, aged eighty-five, on 6 October 1812.

W. P. COURTNEY, rev. PHILIP CARTER

Sources Nichols, *Lit. anecdotes*, 3.752, 6.13, 93 · Venn, *Alum. Cant.* · R. Gale, *Reliquiae Galeanae, or, Miscellaneous pieces by Roger and Samuel Gale*, 3 parts (1790) · will, PRO, PROB 11/625, fol. 92r–v · *GM*, 1st ser., 82/2 (1812), 450

King, John [*formerly* Jacob Rey] (*c.*1753–1824), moneylender and radical, was born in London, the son of Moses Rey, a Jewish street trader of Gibraltarian or north African origin; he was named Jacob. He was educated at the charity school of the Spanish and Portuguese Jews and then, in 1771, apprenticed by the school to a Jewish merchant house in the City of London. After leaving school he Anglicized his name to John King; later, when famous, he was known as Jew King. After completing his apprenticeship he served in an attorney's office for a short period; soon thereafter he ventured forth as a moneylender, a trade at which he was an almost immediate success, as witnessed by the fact that in 1775 he donated £100 to the charity school, in gratitude for his education, and by his marriage the following year to Sara, the daughter of Benjamin Nunes Lara, a City merchant.

Although usually described as a moneylender King was, more precisely, a money broker—a middleman who negotiated loans with funds supplied by persons who desired a high return on their money but wished to avoid the notoriety associated with moneylending. His clients included noble gamblers and profligates (Lord Byron among them) as well as more humble persons unable to live within their means. In 1806 he raised money for the millenarian prophetess Joanna Southcott, who, it was revealed in court proceedings the following year, had no intention of repaying him since she expected the millennium to arrive first. In the pursuit of well-born clients King entertained lavishly and frequently. In cultivating these contacts his long-term liaison with Jane Isabella Butler, the widowed countess of Lanesborough (1737–1828), was of great assistance. They met in 1783 and a year later King divorced his wife before a rabbinical court in Leghorn, Italy, where he had fled to escape imprisonment. Although they lived as husband and wife for forty years it does not appear that they married. In addition to his loan activities, to which there was often a criminal dimension, King was linked to various other frauds and swindles and was frequently before the courts. From 1805 to 1811, for example, he headed a group of former Jacobins who extorted money from members of the royal family, the prime minister, government officials, and other notables.

While pursuing these unsavoury activities King also took part in the anti-ministerial reform agitation of the late eighteenth and early nineteenth centuries. Indeed he was one of the first Jews anywhere in Europe to participate in politics in pursuit of goals unrelated to matters of Jewish status. As a youth he met and was influenced by Tom Paine, and from the early 1780s (except for a brief period in the 1790s) championed reform causes. In 1783 he published an indictment of ministerial policy, *Thoughts on the difficulties and distresses in which the peace of 1783 has involved the people of England*. In the 1790s he was close to leaders of the London Corresponding Society and contributed to their defence when they were tried for high treason in 1794. He edited or wrote for several radical newspapers, including *The Argus* and the *British Guardian*, and participated in most of the radical campaigns of 1802–15, especially the 1808–9 attack on the duke of York for allowing his mistress, Mary Anne Clarke, to sell military preferments.

For most of his adult life King was alienated from Judaism, even claiming in court in 1795 that he had been a member of the Church of England all his adult life. But there is no evidence that he converted to Christianity, even though he lived almost exclusively among Christians and not Jews. Then in the late 1790s he reversed course and began to re-embrace his Jewish identity, eventually becoming a spirited defender of his ancestral faith. He capped his return to Judaism with the publication, in 1817, of a new edition of David Levi's apologia *Dissertations on the Prophecies of the Old Testament*, which was first published between 1793 and 1800; in his introduction King offered a surprisingly traditional defence of rabbinic Judaism. In August 1824 he died and was buried in Florence, where he and Lady Lanesborough had lived since about 1817.

TODD M. ENDELMAN

Sources T. M. Endelman, 'The checkered career of "Jew" King: a study in Anglo-Jewish social history', *AJS Review*, 7–8 (1982–3), 69–100 · I. McCalman, *Radical underworld: prophets, revolutionaries, and pornographers in London, 1795–1840* (1988) · *Byron's letters and journals*, ed. L. A. Marchand, 1 (1973) · M. Thale, ed., *Selections from the papers of the London Corresponding Society, 1792–1799* (1983)
Likenesses caricature, repro. in *Town and Country Magazine*, 19 (1787), 298

King, John (1759–1830), Home Office official and politician, was baptized on 23 May 1759 at Clitheroe, Lancashire, the fifth son of the Revd James King, curate of Clitheroe and later chaplain to the House of Commons and dean of Raphoe, and his wife, Anne, daughter and coheir of John Walker of Hungrill, Yorkshire. After studying at Christ Church, Oxford, where he matriculated in 1777 and graduated BA (1781) and MA (1784), he went on to study law at both Lincoln's Inn and Gray's Inn, before being called to the bar in 1790.

King's first governmental post came in January 1791 when he was appointed as a law clerk at the Home Office, on a salary of £300 a year. In December 1791 he was made an under-secretary of state in the Home Office, his salary rising fivefold to £1500 a year. Thus began a career which saw King become one of a group of talented young civil servants that was to be responsible for the administration of government under William Pitt the younger in the 1790s during the war against the French Revolution and the struggle against domestic radicals and reformers: a group which included men such as Francis Freeling, William Wickham, William Huskisson, and Evan Nepean. King was also intimately connected at this time with Edmund Burke and his circle of relatives and admirers, Burke stating that King's 'promotion to so honourable and advantageous a situation made us the happiest people in the world' (*Correspondence*, 6.454). George Canning, too, thought highly of King, describing him as 'one of the worthiest and friendliest and best sort of men in the world' (*Letter-Journal*, 36); King was clearly part of a set of young Pittites who both worked and socialized together.

On 9 April 1792 King married Harriot Margaret, daughter of the Rt Revd Charles *Moss, bishop of Bath and Wells; they had four sons and a daughter. In December 1794 King took on further duties when he became responsible for much of the correspondence of the alien office, which, as well as monitoring French *émigrés* in Britain under the provisions of the Alien Act of 1793, rapidly became the hub of an intelligence operation which involved counter-revolutionary activity and intelligence gathering at home, in Ireland, and on the continent. King's contribution to this effort was recognized in 1798 when he became one of the joint superintendents of aliens, along with William Wickham and Charles William Flint. In 1806, upon Lord Grenville's assumption of the premiership at the head of the ministry of all the talents, King was promoted to the post of joint secretary to the Treasury, where he superintended ministerial patronage. This position necessitated a seat in parliament and in March 1806 he was returned for the Irish pocket borough of Enniskillen, co. Fermanagh. His parliamentary career was a short one: he gave up his seat in July 1806, having found regular attendance at the House of Commons detrimental to his health. Thereupon King became comptroller of army accounts, a post he held until his death. He died on 30 March 1830 in Grosvenor Place, London, having gone into the office the previous day.

STEPHEN M. LEE

Sources R. G. Thorne, 'King, John', HoP, *Commons, 1790–1820* · *The letter-journal of George Canning, 1793–1795*, ed. P. Jupp, CS, 4th ser., 41 (1991) · *The correspondence of Edmund Burke*, ed. T. W. Copeland and others, 10 vols. (1958–78) · E. Sparrow, 'The alien office, 1792–1806', *HJ*, 33 (1990), 361–84 · E. Sparrow, 'Secret service under Pitt's administration, 1792–1806', *History*, new ser., 83 (1998), 280–94 · *GM*, 1st ser., 100/1 (1830), 282 · J. Ehrman, *The younger Pitt*, 3: *The consuming struggle* (1996) · C. Emsley, 'The home office and its source of information and investigation, 1791–1801', *EngHR*, 94 (1979), 532–61 · Foster, *Alum. Oxon.* · IGI
Archives BL, notes on the army, Add. MS 69079 | BL, corresp. with Lord Liverpool, Evan Nepean, Lord Grenville, Add. MSS 58972, 69038 · Lincs. Arch., corresp. with Sir Joseph Banks · PRO NIre., corresp. with Lord Castlereagh · Sheff. Arch., corresp. with Edmund Burke · U. Nott. L., letters to duke of Portland

King, John (1788–1847), history and portrait painter, was born in Dartmouth, Devon, and at twenty entered the Royal Academy Schools. He first exhibited at the Royal Academy in 1814 and from 1817 showed there almost annually until 1845. The majority of his subjects were drawn from the Bible or from Shakespeare. From 1821 he was also a fairly regular exhibitor at the British Institution, but from 1824 at least half the works he showed there were portraits. King had moved to Bristol by early 1824, for in June a local newspaper reported that his painting of Jeremiah, for whom he had used a Bristol sitter, had sold on the opening day of the British Institution exhibition to Earl Fitzwilliam.

In October 1825 King lectured at the Bristol Institution on his recollections of the fine arts of Flanders, implying an earlier visit to the continent. There is, however, little evidence of King entering into the social life of the Bristol artists. He has been confused with the Bristol surgeon and friend of so many Bristol artists, Dr John King (born Johann Koenig, (1766–1846)). Dr King was to review King's work, finding it singularly unoriginal and conventional. King may have moved back to London as early as 1826, but he maintained close contacts with Bristol and exhibited there until at least 1839. He completed an enormous and now lost painting, *The Incredulity of St Thomas*, for St Thomas's Church in Bristol in 1828 and in 1830 his altarpiece for St Mark's Chapel on College Green, Bristol, was installed (later high in the north transept). In 1828 King exhibited a portrait of the Plymouth-born artist James Northcote RA whose grandiose Shakespearian subjects King may well have striven to emulate, and in the following year he exhibited a portrait of Francis Danby ARA (City Museum and Art Gallery, Bristol), whom King claimed as a friend. He died, presumably unmarried, of apoplexy at Dartmouth on 12 July 1847. Samuel Redgrave noted that his paintings, 'most of which remained on his hands, were sold by auction the same year, and produced only small sums' (Redgrave, *Artists*, 251). King bequeathed all his estate to his niece Sarah Elizabeth King of Brixham, Devon.   FRANCIS GREENACRE

Sources Redgrave, *Artists* · DNB · Graves, *RA exhibitors* · Graves, *Brit. Inst.* · Bristol Institution, its origin and progress, vol. 1, bound MS volume, Bristol Reference Library · John King's exhibition reviews, bound vol. of proofs, City Museum and Art Gallery, Bristol, MG 3742 · folder of notes etc., Bristol Artists 'A', Bristol Reference Library, G. W. Braikenridge collection, B23779 · letters to G. W. Braikenridge, Bristol Reference Library, 22329 · Bristol Institution, minute book, Bristol Reference Library · will, PRO, PROB 11/2061, sig. 654
Archives City Museum and Art Gallery, Bristol, papers

King, John Duncan (1788–1863), army officer and landscape painter, was born in the city of Waterford, Ireland, on 4 November 1788 and entered the army as an ensign in the 71st regiment in August 1806. He purchased a lieutenancy on 18 February 1808, before exchanging into the 3rd battalion, 1st (or Royal) regiment, with which he saw active service from July 1809 in the Walcheren expedition, and later that year in the Peninsular War. He was present at the battle of Busaco on 27 September 1810. On 13 June 1811 he transferred to the 7th Royal Fusiliers, engaging in various skirmishes that autumn. In 1813 he fought at the battles of Vitoria and the Pyrenees, receiving a severe wound in the right shoulder on 28 July 1813. For this he received additional pay and an eighteen-month pension. On 18 January 1815 he married Sally Tindal, with whom he had four sons, and who predeceased him. He returned to overseas duty in May 1815, was present at the capture of Paris, and remained with the army of occupation until 1818. On 20 April 1820 he exchanged to the 8th foot on half pay. Influenced by Claude Lorrain, he pursued his interest in landscape painting, exhibiting views of Spain and Portugal at the Royal Academy in 1824. He studied under Horace Vernet in Paris in 1825. On 14 May 1829 he returned briefly to regimental duty with the 75th foot, purchasing a captaincy on 16 March 1830. However, he soon retired, going on half pay on 28 December 1830; he then travelled, painting views of India, Tahiti, France, Ireland, and England. Between 1824 and 1858 he exhibited eighteen paintings at the Royal Academy, thirty-nine at the British Institution, and two at the Society of British Artists, Suffolk Street. In March 1851 King was made a military knight of Windsor, and he lived at 17 Lower Ward, Windsor Castle, until his death there on 21 August 1863. Since then his work has been largely forgotten and he is not represented in any major British collection.

JENNY SPENCER-SMITH

Sources DNB · 'Statement of the services of John Duncan King of the 75th regiment with a record of such other particulars as may be useful in case of his death', PRO, WO 25/799, fol. 341 · 'Statement of service for retired officers, 1829', PRO, WO 25/764, fol. 101 · *Army List* · *Art Journal*, 25 (1863), 198–9 · J. Emile, 'Horace Vernet', *Art Journal*, 25 (1863), 52–3 · Graves, *RA exhibitors* · J. P. Groves, ed., *Historical records of the 7th or royal regiment of fusiliers* (1903) · CGPLA Eng. & Wales (1863)
Wealth at death under £1000: administration, 16 Sept 1863, CGPLA Eng. & Wales

King, John Glen (1731/2–1787), Church of England clergyman, was born in Stowmarket, in Suffolk, the son of George King (*d.* 1756), rector of Nowton, Suffolk. Having attended a school at Swaffham he matriculated at Gonville and Caius College, Cambridge, on 9 October 1747, at the age of fifteen; he graduated BA in 1752 and MA in 1763. He was ordained deacon at Norwich on 22 December 1754 and priest at Ely on 19 September 1756. In 1760 he was presented by the crown to the vicarage of Berwick Parva, Norfolk.

In July 1763 King was appointed chaplain to the English factory in St Petersburg. Though he was appointed medallist to Catherine II he failed to enter court circles and consequently left no impression of himself in Russia. This was due partly to the dislike conceived of him by Princess Dashkova, one of the most influential society ladies of the time, but primarily to his lack of social graces. King devoted much of his time to the study of the history and liturgical rites of the Orthodox church. He was encouraged to write a book about this by Sir George Macartney, English ambassador to the court of Catherine II, whom King met in St Petersburg in 1765. The first short version of King's book, entitled *The Present State of the Church of Russia*, appeared as an appendix to Macartney's own work on Russia in 1767. Between 1770 and 1772 King was in England, trying to publish his book on the Russian church and seeking a church preferment. On 10 January 1771 he was made a fellow of the Society of Antiquaries of London, and on 12 February he was elected a fellow of the Royal Society. He was incorporated MA at Oxford on 19 March 1771, as a member of Christ Church, and on 23 March he took the Oxford degrees of BD and DD.

After the publication of his book *The Rites and Ceremonies of the Greek Church* in 1772 King's scholarly reputation was established; the work was highly acclaimed and became a standard text on the subject. However, he failed to find a position in England and had to return to the English factory in St Petersburg, where he spent some eleven years altogether, returning to England in the spring of 1774. He was living in Greenwich when he wrote his will on 2 November 1780, while leasing Tavistock Chapel, St Martin-in-the-Fields, from the duke of Bedford. In July 1783 he was presented to the rectory of Wormley, Hertfordshire, by Sir Abraham Hume, bt. In the summer of 1786 he purchased the chapelry of Spring Gardens, Charing Cross, London; he also purchased, though precisely when is unknown, Dr Warner's chapel in Long Acre. Apart from the two versions of *The Rites and Ceremonies of the Greek Church* his works include: *Verses*, in the Cambridge University collection on the death of Frederick, prince of Wales (1752); 'A letter to the bishop of Durham, containing some observations on the climate of Russia, and the northern countries, with a view of the flying Mountains at Zarsko Sello, near St Petersburg', written in 1778 and published in the *Westminster Magazine* (vol. 8, 1780); and *Nummi familiarum et imperatorum Romanorum*. This substantial catalogue of Roman coinage was probably published in 1787 and includes 102 plates without letterpress.

King was married, first, to Ann Magdalen (1743/4–1767),

daughter of Michael Combrune; she died in Russia, aged twenty-three, leaving King a seventeen-month-old baby, Anna Henrietta. King's second wife, whom he married on 1 August 1776, was Jane, daughter of John Hyde of Blackheath. She is said by Nichols to have died in August 1789 but she may still have been alive in June 1790.

King had few friends. He had hoped that George Macartney, whom he had known in Russia, would be his patron but their correspondence shows that Macartney was unwilling to continue the acquaintance. King's only known close friend was the musician and music historian Charles Burney, whose daughter Fanny regarded King as a ridiculous man and commented that he 'spouted Shakespeare, Pope and others' (*Early Diary*, 134), imitated Garrick, and that her father had observed that he could talk 'three hours upon any given subject, without saying any thing' (ibid., 154). His social popularity was probably also undermined by his financial advice to Elizabeth Allen, later the second wife of Charles Burney, whom King recommended to invest in the merchant banker William Gomm's timber concession in northern Russia; Gomm was declared bankrupt in 1767, after Mrs Allen had invested £5000 in his enterprise. King's last years were devoted to archaeological and numismatic research. He died at his house on Edward Street, Berwick Street, Soho, after a few hours' illness, on 3 November 1787, and was buried on 7 November in Wormley churchyard.

M. UNKOVSKAYA

Sources A. G. Cross, introduction, *A Russian almanack for the year 1767*, 2nd edn [offprint] · BL, Add. MS 5874, fol. 45; Add. MSS 33733–33791 · *GM*, 1st ser., 57 (1787), 1030 · *GM*, 1st ser., 59 (1789), 916 · Nichols, *Lit. anecdotes*, 3.623, 4.760 · *A catalogue of all graduates … in the University of Oxford, between … 1659 and … 1850* (1851), 385 · W. Hustler, ed., *Graduati Cantabrigienses* (1823), 275 · W. T. Lowndes, *The bibliographer's manual of English literature*, ed. H. G. Bohn, [new edn], 3 (1864), 1274 · H. H. Robbins, *Our first ambassador to China* (1908) · A. G. Cross, 'Chaplains to the British factory in St Petersburg, 1723–1813', *European Studies Review*, 2/2 (1972), 125–42 · P. A. Scholes, *The great Dr Burney: his life, his travels, his works, his family and his friends*, 2 vols. (1948) · private information (2004) [L. Bettany] · *The early diary of Frances Burney, 1768–1778*, ed. A. R. Ellis, another edn, 1 (1913), 134–5, 149–60, 199 · *Critical Review*, 33 (1772), 265–74 · M. Ledkovsky, 'A linguistic bridge to orthodoxy', www.roca.org/OA/157/157f.htm, 2 Oct 2000 · *Engraved Brit. ports.*, 2.697 · *DNB* · will, PRO, PROB 11/1160, sig. 558

Archives BL, letters to Sir George Macartney, Add. MSS 5874, fol. 45, 33764–33791 · Yale U., Beinecke L., letters to Sir George Macartney, Osborn (MSS) manuscript files K, nos 8230–8487f.

Likenesses P. Falconet, engraving, 1771, BM · P. Fourdrinier?, engraving · G. Smith, stipple (after P. Falconet, 1771), BM, NPG

Wealth at death see will, PRO, PROB 11/1160, sig. 558

King, Leonard William (1869–1919), Assyriologist and archaeologist, was born on 8 December 1869 at Fern House, 20 The Common, Upper Clapton, London, the fifth of six sons, and eleventh of twelve children, of Robert King (1825–1886), timber merchant, and his wife, Mary Jane (1830–1890), eldest daughter of John Henry Scarborough.

Influenced by William Parker Brooke at Rugby School, where he 'got his cap at football' (Thompson, 'Leonard William King', 625), King matriculated at King's College, Cambridge, on 29 January 1889. He displayed linguistic ability, was exhibitioner in 1890 and 1891, and graduated BA with a first class in part one of the theological tripos in 1891. He studied Syriac until appointed assistant of the second class in the department of Egyptian and Assyrian antiquities, British Museum, on 15 August 1892, at a salary of £120 plus annual increment of £10, under its newly designated keeper, E. A. Wallis Budge. 'No chief ever had a more loyal or faithful subordinate' (Rogers, 91). On 6 November 1905 he was promoted, exceptionally, to assistant of the first class, in recognition of excavating Nineveh, and to the rank of assistant keeper on 21 July 1913, at a salary of £520. In appearance King was 'no frail creature, but broad of shoulders, stocky' (ibid., 89), with heavy moustache and thinning hair.

With respect to cuneiform studies King was self-taught, learning the difficult scripts and their various usages by preparing his own editions of major inscriptions already published. Recognition came early with election as fellow of the Society of Antiquaries (1898) and of the Royal Geographical Society (1905), and to the Society of Biblical Archaeologists (1903). His Assyriological successor, Sidney Smith, noted that 'as a copyist he was final; the endless queries one received from academics who had never handled a tablet about this sign or that were a waste of time' (letter to Clyde Curry Smith, 24 Feb 1964). In the first decades of the twentieth century, King became, as variously described by contemporaries, 'the master Assyriologist' (D. D. Luckenbill, in *American Journal of Semitic Languages and Literature*, 36, 1919–20, 167), 'the outstanding British Assyriologist' (G. R. Driver, in *PBA*, 30, 1944, 5), 'easily the foremost of the younger generation of cuneiform scholars in England' (notice of death, King's, Lond., 1919), whose 'cuneiform handwriting was a joy to behold' (Budge, 174).

Besides carrying out routine museum duties, King published officially for the British Museum trustees. Of thirty-four parts of *Cuneiform Texts* issued between 1896 and 1914, he prepared sixteen, assisted or provided the index for three others, and corrected two more. He transcribed *Hittite Texts in the Cuneiform Character* (posthumously published in 1920). These remain indispensable to scholars. While assisting Budge in the preparation of *A Guide to the Babylonian and Assyrian Antiquities* (1900; 2nd edn, 1908) and *Annals of the Kings of Assyria* (1902), and Reginald Campbell Thompson in preparing *The Sculptures and Inscriptions of Darius the Great on the Rock of Behistun in Persia* (1907), King was responsible for *Babylonian Boundary Stones and Memorial Tablets* (1912), the supplement (1914) to the *Catalogue of Cuneiform Tablets in the Kouyunjik Collection*, and *Bronze Reliefs from the Gates of Shalmaneser* (1915).

On 3 September 1901 King went, initially at his own expense, to survey ancient Mesopotamia, observe sites previously excavated, ascertain archaeological work in progress, and recommend renewal of excavations by the museum trustees. Between his return (3 January 1902) and departure for excavation (15 November 1902), he combined museum duties with intensive preparation. He left Constantinople on 22 December and used the intervening time before official permission from the Ottoman government reached him at Mosul / Nineveh on 2 March 1903 to complete an elaborate survey of the ancient mound. King suspended work in the heat of summer and travelled to the area around Lake Van, collating inscriptions on mountainous sites.

Despite bouts of malaria and dysentery, King continued with the excavations. A brief respite at Christmas 1903 allowed him to inspect German excavations at Assur and learn their newer surveying techniques. His colleague Reginald Campbell Thompson brought a tachymeter to Nineveh, where they performed comprehensive topographical survey mapping of the entire site, before shutting down excavations on 18 April 1904 to go east into Persia and copy anew the great trilingual inscription at Behistan. On 21 June King left Thompson excavating and travelled to London, where he arrived on 1 August after making inscriptional discoveries en route. All this work is well documented in personal weekly letters to Budge, formal reports to the trustees, and private correspondence.

In October 1904 King suffered a severe recurrence of tropical illnesses. He was treated and brought back to health by Sir James Cantlie and professionally nursed by Anna Maria Burke (1867–1958), third daughter of Henry Anthony Burke of Tully, co. Galway. King's inability to return to Mesopotamia meant that Thompson closed the excavation, on 11 February 1905. In renewed health King married his nurse, on 21 February 1906, in Ballinamallard church, Drumkeen, Ireland; they had one son, Leonard Nevill (b. 5 December 1907, killed in an RAF accident on 28 July 1955), and one daughter, Audrey Helen (b. 1 Feb 1910).

In addition to his publications for the British Museum, King wrote fifteen volumes, including the first twentieth-century history of Babylonia and Assyria in English (*A History of Sumer and Akkad*, 1910, and *A History of Babylon*, 1915), wherein appeared detailed translations, commentaries, notes, vocabularies, and indices; forty-five articles or review articles in learned journals; and twenty-eight entries in major encyclopaedias—many standing the test of time. He was joint author, with H. R. H. Hall, of *Egypt and Western Asia in the Light of Recent Discoveries* (1907) and editor of *Paganism and Christianity in Egypt* by P. D. Scott-Moncrieff (1913, posthumously with Hall) as well as of *The Spoken Arabic of Mesopotamia* by John Van Ess (1916).

On 11 June 1912 King's name was added to the general committee of the Palestine Exploration Fund, of which he later became chairman. From 23 April to 17 June 1914 he took a 'study vacation' to examine seals and sealed tablets in the Assyriological museums of Paris, Berlin, Vienna, and Constantinople. In 1914 he received his LittD from Cambridge. In 1915 he was named professor of Assyrian and Babylonian archaeology at King's College, London, where he had been lecturer in Assyrian since 1910. He was elected fellow of the Royal Asiatic Society in 1916 and gave the prestigious Schweich lectures of the British Academy in that year. From 15 January 1916 King's services were lent to the Admiralty where he prepared anonymously maps and intelligence handbooks of inestimable value to the

war effort. In 1918 as British forces liberated Mesopotamia, King was inoculated against tropical diseases in preparation to join Thompson in renewed excavations at the sites of Ur and Eridu. However, before he could set out he succumbed to influenza, followed by bronchitis, from which he died at Brooke House Nursing Home, Clapton, London, on 20 August 1919, his productive career thereby being truncated at midlife. His funeral service was held at St Mary's Church, Bryanston Square, London, and the interment took place at Abney Park cemetery, Stoke Newington on 25 August.   CLYDE CURRY SMITH

Sources C. C. Smith, 'The impact of Assyriology upon Old Testament study with special reference to the publications of Leonard William King', PhD diss., University of Chicago, 1968 · M. M. D'Andrea, 'Letters of Leonard William King, 1902–1904; introduced, edited and annotated with special reference to the excavations of Nineveh', MA diss., University of Wisconsin, River Falls, 1981 · C. C. Smith, 'The comprehensive bibliography of Leonard William King (1869–1919)', 1974, University of Wisconsin, River Falls, Chalmer Davies Library [report filed with Committee on Research and Studies] · R. C. Thompson, 'Mosul, 1904', *A pilgrim's scrip* (1915), 18–92 · R. C. Thompson, 'From Mosul to Behistun', *A pilgrim's scrip* (1915), 93–126 · R. C. Thompson and R. W. Hutchinson, 'The re-opening of the Kouyunjik excavations', *A century of exploration at Nineveh* (1929), 57–71 · R. W. Rogers, 'Leonard William King, Assyriologist, 1869–1919', *American Journal of Semitic Languages and Literatures*, 36 (1920), 89–94 · E. A. W. Budge, *The rise and progress of Assyriology* (1925) · R. C. Thompson, 'Leonard William King', *Journal of the Royal Asiatic Society of Great Britain and Ireland* (1919), 625–6 · C. C. Smith, 'Leonard William King, 1869–1919', *Read more about it*, ed. C. J. Kohoyda-Inglis (1989), 3.373–5 · *WWW*, 1961–70 · private information (2004) [family] · *The Times* (23 Aug 1919) · *The Times* (25–6 Aug 1919) · H. R. Hall, 'Prof. L. W. King', *Nature*, 104 (1919–20) · *Palestine Exploration Fund Quarterly Statement* (Oct 1919) · *Annual Report of the Council* [King's College, Cambridge] (1919) · *Proceedings of the Society of Antiquaries of London*, 2nd ser., 32 (1919–20), 165–6 · *Journal of the American Oriental Society*, 39 (1919) · *Annual Register* (1919) · *Orientalische Literaturzeitung* (1920) · *Journal of Egyptian Archaeology*, 6 (1920) · d. cert. · CGPLA Eng. & Wales (1919)

Archives BM, corresp. | BM, Trustees' archives

Likenesses photograph, 1903, repro. in J. M. Russell, *The final sack of Nineveh* (1998) · Elliott and Fry, photograph, repro. in Budge, *Rise and progress of Assyriology*

Wealth at death £2550 4s. 6d.: probate, 6 Nov 1919, CGPLA Eng. & Wales

King, (William Lyon) Mackenzie (1874–1950), prime minister of Canada, was born on 17 December 1874 at Berlin (later renamed Kitchener), Ontario, the first son and second child of John King (1843–1916), a law lecturer and author, and his wife, Isabel Grace (1843–1917), daughter of the Upper Canadian rebel of 1837 William Lyon *Mackenzie. King's mother, who was born in exile in the United States, was the dominant personality in the household and she raised her son with a powerful need to vindicate her father's cause. In a long political life King fought his grandfather's battles against toryism, imperialism, and privilege, and in his own mind, if not necessarily those of all his compatriots or of historians, he was both consistent and successful.

Early life Mackenzie King was a bright and able student. After attending local schools in his home town, he went to the University of Toronto in 1891. Short, stocky, moon-

(William Lyon) Mackenzie King (1874–1950), by unknown photographer

faced, there he none the less became the archetypal 'big man on campus', a powerful figure in student politics and one of the leaders in a major student strike occasioned by the dismissal of a popular professor in 1895. Having graduated BA he turned to law, gaining his degree the next year and writing in Toronto newspapers. Then it was off to Chicago, where, with a fellowship of $320, he intended to do graduate work in sociology. But it was his social work at Hull House, a famous settlement house run by Jane Addams, that attracted him most, and his studies languished until he left Addams's employ to try to concentrate on his classwork. He contracted typhoid fever in early 1897 but this led to an improvement in his social life. In Toronto, King had had many girlfriends but few attachments, and his nights had been preoccupied with rescue work with fallen women, with 'strolls' and 'wasted time'—phrases from King's diary that Charles Stacey interpreted as sessions with prostitutes, though they might just as easily have been voyeurism or simple time-wasting. But in Chicago, King became strongly attracted to one of his nurses, Mathilde Grossert, a relationship fated to be doomed by the expectations of his mother that he marry someone befitting the station that she imagined for her son. King tried to keep up the budding relationship when he went off to Harvard University in 1897 but the family pressure was too strong. In fact King could never shake off his mother's hold over him, even after her death in 1917, and he remained a lifelong bachelor. He was a lonely man with very few friends, and he suffered in his private solitude. None the less he completed his master of

arts degree in 1898 and his oral examination for the doctorate the next year. Eleven years later, utilizing government reports that he had prepared in lieu of a dissertation, King received his PhD from Harvard.

In the interim King laid the groundwork of his subsequent career. A promising young scholar interested in sociology and social work—relatively new fields of study in a North America that was only beginning to think seriously about the conditions of workers and the poor—he wrote a series of muckraking articles on sweatshops in the late summer of 1897 for the *Toronto Mail and Empire*. That turned into a government research job, thanks to his family connections with Sir William Mulock, postmaster-general in Sir Wilfrid Laurier's government. Mulock was quick to put some of King's ideas into practice in his own department and King submitted a formal report on sweatshops in 1898. In 1900 Mulock offered him the post of editor of the *Labour Gazette* and a salary of C$1500 a year in the newly created department of labour, and King, who had been considering a teaching post at Harvard, accepted. At the age of twenty-five he now had a good position; a few months later he was made deputy minister of labour.

Civil servant to politician For the next eight years King studied labour questions, used the government's good offices (and its weak legislation) to try to settle labour disputes (he resolved eleven of fifteen strikes in which he intervened between 1900 and 1902), served as editor of the *Labour Gazette*, and built up a formidable reputation as a young man on the rise. He knew everyone worth knowing, not least the prime minister. He undertook missions in Canada—serving as a royal commissioner to investigate an anti-Japanese riot in Vancouver and, on another occasion, to study how Japanese and other labourers were induced to immigrate to Canada. He also went abroad, travelling to the Far East, Britain, and the United States to conduct investigations into the opium trade and to negotiate a 'gentleman's agreement' (with the support and encouragement of President Theodore Roosevelt) with Japan to control immigration to North America. In 1906 he received the CMG—apparently on the personal recommendation of the governor-general, Earl Grey.

As implied by that honour, in everything that King did he showed that he had the knack of winning the support of the influential and, at the same time, an uncanny ability to capture the public mood. When a close friend from university, Henry Albert Harper, drowned while trying to rescue a woman from the Ottawa River in 1901 King organized the erection of a statue of Sir Galahad in his memory and published *The Secret of Heroism* (1908) as a tribute. This was a genuine human response but it also served King's purposes in establishing his high profile. No one was surprised, therefore, when in 1908 he ran for election as a Liberal in his home town, Berlin, won, and a year later was named labour minister by Laurier.

King was a good, tireless cabinet minister and, in his own mind, the all but designated successor to Laurier. His preferred tactic was conciliation—in light of the powers given to the provinces to deal with labour questions in the British North America Act, King had few real weapons;

conciliation was the course he had followed as deputy minister and the course he preached to management and labour. Labour largely scorned his method, as did management, but that suggested that King was characteristically in the middle and just slightly ahead of his time. This did not save him in 1911, when the Laurier government, campaigning in support of a reciprocity or free trade agreement negotiated with the United States, went down to defeat at the hands of Robert Borden and the Conservative Party. King himself lost his seat.

The next eight years were difficult for King. He had to find work, and he became a labour expert in the employ of John D. Rockefeller jun. and the Rockefeller Foundation, most especially in dealing with labour troubles that had begun in 1913 in the Colorado coalfields. Conciliation and company unions were his watchwords and there can be little doubt that he served the interests of capital first while ameliorating the conditions of labour second. The salary paid him by the Rockefellers was good and the connections he established were lifelong.

The outbreak of war in 1914 made King's work in the United States look almost unpatriotic. Why was he not in the army? In King's mind there was no difficulty in dealing with this question. He was forty in 1914, his parents were old and ill—both would die during the course of the war and King would continue to venerate his mother for the rest of his life—and he had to help to support his siblings. Critics then and later dismissed such arguments as self-serving but they had cogency. Perhaps it was his concern about appearances that none the less led King to a near breakdown in 1916, a crisis that he treated sensibly by seeking psychological assistance at Johns Hopkins University Hospital in Baltimore, Maryland. Recovered and trying to keep his name forward in Canadian politics, King ran in the 1917 election but lost, in North York. The issue was conscription for overseas service, and King philosophically supported compulsory service (and even wrote an anonymous article in the *New York Outlook* (25 July 1917) in favour of it). But when the Liberal Party split on the issue and when a Union government of conscriptionists was formed under Sir Robert Borden, King decided to remain with Laurier and to oppose the Union. Despite his and the Liberal Party's election defeat that loyalty would pay off handsomely.

The end of the First World War, with all its terrible casualties and dislocation, produced terrific and unprecedented labour unrest in Canada. Rising prices, the return of the armies, government disorganization—all combined to create a climate that, to some, seemed at times to verge on revolution. King was a genuine expert on labour questions—had the Rockefellers not employed him?—and in 1918 he published a long book, *Industry and Humanity*, that wrestled the questions of the day to the ground. Industrialists had the duty to deal humanely with workers, he argued, and the book, with incomprehensible fold-out charts and prose dripping with near-religious intensity, sold well but remained largely unread.

Party leader and prime minister That mattered little. When Sir Wilfrid Laurier died in February 1919 and when the

Winnipeg general strike erupted in May, King seemed to be the man of the hour, as Liberals gathered in convention to select a new party leader. There were other, better-known candidates—the aged W. S. Fielding, George Graham of Ontario, and D. D. McKenzie of Nova Scotia, who had been the party's house leader after Laurier's death. King was the youngest and easily the ablest, the candidate who had remained loyal to Laurier in 1917 and, most importantly, had written a book on the great issue of the day—the relations between labour and capital. The party platform drafted at the convention (with King's fingerprints all over it) was reformist as well. And King himself helped his cause immeasurably with a superb speech that brought the audience, cheering, to its feet. The issue of the leadership was sealed when the Quebec delegates, marshalled in King's support by Ernest Lapointe, voted for him *en bloc*, though it took three ballots to determine the outcome. King was now what he had long believed himself to be, the successor to Laurier.

King's task as Liberal leader was multifaceted. He had to reunite the Liberals' conscriptionist and anti-conscriptionist wings—in effect its English-Canadian and Quebec members. He had to try to keep a light in the window of the Liberal Party so that it could remain the ultimate home for restive farmers, then beginning to organize themselves into a separate, if loosely constructed, Progressive Party. He had to develop a tariff policy that had an appeal to the farmers yet did not alienate the industrial interests of central Canada. He had to put forward a reformist policy to show workers that his party could deal with their needs. He had to defeat the Union government, still led by Borden but with Arthur Meighen in the wings. And above all he had to demonstrate that he was a leader, a man with the capacity to inspire his caucus and the country.

From his selection as leader until the general election in December 1921 King worked tirelessly to rebuild his party, his image as a vigorous reformer generally going over well. Not with the farmers, however, although the efforts of Borden and his successor, Arthur Meighen, to hold the unpopular wartime coalition together did nothing to help them with the Progressives. Prime Minister Meighen campaigned in the general election in favour of a high tariff but King ran against the Union government and on the Liberals' reformist 1919 platform and on his reputation as a conciliator, the man to bring French and English Canadians, east and west, farmer, worker, and industrialist together. King's message worked, the Liberals capturing 116 seats (including all 65 in Quebec, which then and later played a key role in keeping him in power), the Progressives 64, and poor Meighen's tattered coalition only 50. King had won but, as his was the first minority government in Canadian history, he would be forced to rely on the Progressives to govern and his conciliatory skills would be tested to the limit.

Again King was helped by Meighen. Though a great orator Meighen was so blinkered as to think every compromise a betrayal; the farmers' views were simply wrong and dangerous to boot, so he attacked and attacked again, sarcasm dripping off his every word. King on the other hand held out an olive branch, trying to bring the Progressives into his cabinet from the outset. This effort failing, he began offering small concessions on tariffs—he could not offer major ones because the government's industrial supporters in central Canada were certain to object—and modifications to railway freight rates to seduce the farmers back to Liberalism. The Progressive leader, T. A. Crerar, a former Liberal and Unionist, left his fractious colleagues and eventually entered King's cabinet in 1929. Political seduction, it was obvious now, was King's stock in trade, and pragmatism and compromise his weapons. The *laissez-faire* legislative record of his first government was far from impressive but King had again made the Liberal Party into an agency of French–English reconciliation, and he had gone a substantial distance in bringing farmers back to his side.

Where King had real success was on the international stage. He was a soft nationalist, a supporter of British ideals and the monarchy, but a bristling opponent of arrogant Whitehall interference in Canada's autonomy. In 1922 Lloyd George had publicly asked for Canadian support for British intervention at Chanak before any official request even reached Ottawa. King was outraged at this assertion of a common imperial foreign policy but in public he said only that parliament would decide. Parliament was not in session, of course, so no decision was forthcoming and no Canadian contingent went off to Turkey. Angered by the assumptions of London, King went to the Imperial Conference of 1923, intending to get autonomy recognized—as a self-governing dominion Canada had to make its own policy. The British foreign secretary, Lord Curzon, found the Canadian leader 'obstinate, tiresome and stupid' but King prevailed and the conference communiqué recognized that the diplomatic unity of the empire was a relic of the past. Indeed as Canada and the United States had earlier that year negotiated and signed a halibut treaty the Imperial Conference had merely caught up to the reality. And at the 1926 Imperial Conference the new relationship was recognized formally with the statement that the dominions were:

> autonomous Communities within the British Empire, equal in status, in no way subordinate to one another in any aspect of their domestic or external affairs, though united by a common allegiance to the Crown, and freely associated as members of the British Commonwealth of Nations.

King's stubbornness and insistence on making foreign policy decisions in Canada had greatly accelerated the process of turning the empire into the Commonwealth.

At home, however, King's government was in difficulty with westerners, maritimers, and imperialist Ontarians. In the 1925 election the issues had been much the same as those of four years earlier. Meighen still called for a high tariff but now he had King's record to denounce. For his part King seemed satisfied with the stability that he had brought to the country, and his campaign was as uninspired as the 'common-sense' tariff that he called for. The results shocked the Liberals; Meighen won 116 seats, the

Progressives were reduced to 24, there were a few independents, and King took only 99. There were rumblings within the Liberal Party about King's leadership and he lost his own seat. To almost everyone's astonishment he decided to try to govern on the assumption that he could get the support of the Progressives. This was his constitutional right but the governor-general, Viscount Byng, was clearly unhappy, a factor that soon became critical.

The cause of the government's concern was a major scandal in the customs department that threatened to blow up into a government-wrecking affair. King tried to keep the Progressives and Labour MPs on side by supporting the establishment of old age pensions and by lowering taxes but the scandal, investigated by a parliamentary committee, directly implicated two successive customs ministers. Facing defeat on a motion of censure King went to Byng to seek a dissolution. He had governed successfully for nine months, he told the governor-general, and believed that he was entitled to get what he asked; Byng disagreed, refused King a dissolution, and properly decided that Conservative leader Meighen must get a chance to govern. King promptly resigned and told parliament of this. There was no longer a prime minister, he said, violating every convention of parliamentary government, and the next day Meighen held the reins. Under the rules of that era ministers, once named, had to resign their seats and be re-elected in a by-election. Instead of adjourning the House of Commons the too eager Meighen played just as fast and loose with the rules as King had—he resigned his own seat but appointed acting ministers. The Liberals, with Meighen fuming in the public galleries, argued that if the acting ministers were legally running their departments they must vacate their seats; if they did not hold office legally they had no right to govern. The clever argument did the trick with the Progressive MPs, and Meighen lost a critical vote by one—when a Progressive MP broke an agreement to pair. Meighen quickly received the dissolution that Byng had refused King.

The election of 1926 decided whether King or Meighen, the Liberals or the Conservatives, would make the century theirs. Meighen attacked the King record brilliantly, his speeches excoriating the corruption that the former prime minister had allowed to flourish. For his part King attacked Byng's refusal to grant him a dissolution: what right did a British-appointed official have to interfere in the operations of Canada's democracy? The King–Byng affair was muddy enough to confuse most voters but the nationalism of King struck a chord, even with unhappy Progressives and supporters of Maritime rights. More to the point, perhaps, Meighen's Ulster rectitude and rigour did not, and the election was a Liberal cakewalk. Meighen won 91 seats, the Progressives dropped to 20, and King had a comfortable majority with 128. It was to be Mackenzie King's Canada.

Even so King's second administration was as lacklustre as his first. The role of government was to do as little as possible and King presided over a country that was happily enjoying the booming twenties. The diamond jubilee of confederation was celebrated in 1927, radio became popular, and King's slight Scottish burr now could be heard across the land. But when depression hit in the autumn of 1929 King seemingly missed its significance, seeing the downturn as a normal cyclical event. He thus opened the door to Richard Bedford Bennett, the new Conservative leader, who promised to blast his way into the markets of the world with a retaliatory tariff policy, and thus create jobs. King himself made a rare political error when he said that he would not give 5 cents to any province with a Conservative government. The unemployed, those on relief, and the press in the seven provinces that did not have Liberal governments did not appreciate that, and in the election of 1930 King suffered a defeat that surprised him. Bennett had 138 seats, King only 90.

Perhaps King had been lucky to lose when he did. The depression's effects were devastating in Canada, and Bennett, despite spending unprecedented sums on relief, made scarcely a dent in unemployment. Worse, the prime minister projected the image of the tycoon that he was and not even the revelations of a huge scandal over hydroelectric power contracts that plunged King and his party fund-raisers into the 'Valley of Humiliation' did much to make the Conservative government look good. King had a difficult time personally in opposition, fretting over his legacy and worrying about his own solitary life, and he began dabbling seriously in spiritualism. There were frequent sessions with mediums, all carefully recorded in his diaries, as he sought word from his relatives and friends in the after-life, table-rapping sessions, and a near-fixation on coincidental junctures of the hands of the clock or the formation of tea leaves in the bottom of a cup. Like many of his age and time King was grasping for certainty in a world whose economy had collapsed and whose beliefs had been shattered by the First World War. While he could not find this certainty he never lost his grasp on reality nor did he ever seriously seek political advice from his spiritualist guides.

Fortunately for King it was simply a matter of waiting for the next election, as Bennett floundered, seeking to craft a reformist new deal that alienated many of his business supporters. It was 'King or Chaos', the Liberals thus cried, offering no policies of any substance, and although there were new parties on the left and the right in the 1935 balloting King won a huge majority, taking 178 seats.

King was now in his sixty-first year and he remained vigorous and alert. His record as party leader throughout sixteen years had been superb, if measured by building and holding together a disparate coalition. As prime minister his record—aside from his successes in strengthening Canada's autonomous place within the Commonwealth—was weak. There had been no great achievements, no attempt—the insubstantial old age pensions legislation notwithstanding—to put into law the great reform platform of 1919 to which King's party had committed itself. But as fate had it King would have thirteen more years in power and his achievements in those years were legion.

There was relatively little to cheer about in domestic policy in the second half of the 1930s. King's government took the Bank of Canada, created as a quasi-governmental agency by Bennett, and made it a nationally-owned central bank. It established a massive royal commission on dominion–provincial relations to investigate the fiscal plight of the provinces, given many powers and few monetary resources, and it began to move toward a national system of unemployment insurance. There were initiatives in housing, and in 1939, under the influence of Keynesian economics, the first stimulative deficit budget. This was better than King's previous administrations but he had done very little to deal with the economic problems afflicting the country.

Nor was King's record stellar on foreign policy questions. Bennett had seemed willing to see Canada play a vigorous role at the League of Nations in the Italo-Ethiopian conflict but King was not. Nor did King lend any support to tepid British or French efforts to rein in Germany. In his view Canada had no stake in eastern Europe, and the tensions at home between French and English Canadians, always exacerbated by the prospect of involvement in a 'British' war, demanded that Canada speak softly. Nor did Canada have a big stick. The regular army, navy, and air force had only 10,000, all ranks, the reserves were weak, and there was no modern equipment. But King did tell Adolf Hitler in 1937 that Canadians would swim the ocean to fight if Germany went to war with Britain and he did work assiduously to cultivate President Franklin Roosevelt.

King and Roosevelt were not close friends and the disparity in their nations' power was substantial. But they respected each other as political leaders and they understood that geography obliged them to work together. King worried about the gulf between the USA and Britain and he believed strongly that trade made good friends. Within days of taking office in 1935 he was pressing forward trade negotiations with Washington that, though begun by Bennett, had become stalled. The resulting agreement, the first since the defeat of reciprocity in 1911, was a signal that trade relations were going to become closer. Two years later there was a second agreement, and in 1938 Canada, the USA, and the UK, after an intricate negotiation complicated by imperial preferences, signed yet another trade pact. Simultaneously King and Roosevelt were beginning to bring their countries toward co-operation in defence. Secret staff talks took place and in 1938 Roosevelt, speaking in Canada, put Canada under the American defence umbrella. When war came in 1939 the good relations established between the two leaders mattered.

Wartime leader The Second World War was a testing time for King and Canada. By skilful backing and filling King kept the country united. Hardline imperialists regularly jeered at King as the 'American', and French Canadian isolationists pronounced him 'ready, aye ready' anytime Britain called. In fact King had desperately hoped to stay out of the war—like most Canadians he had cheered the Munich agreement of 1938—but he and his cabinet, including the justice minister, Ernest Lapointe, and the other Quebec ministers, had agreed that Canada had to join in if Britain went to war; English Canadian public opinion would demand nothing less. But King could decide the scope of involvement and his instincts were for a war of limited liability and, as he declared in March 1939, a war without conscription for overseas service. And when Britain went to war on 3 September King delayed Canada's declaration of war for a week, time enough for parliament to decide to enter. Soon after King began the negotiations with Britain that led to the British Commonwealth air training plan, a scheme that he had London declare to be Canada's major contribution to the war. For a time it seemed doubtful that a division of infantry would proceed overseas but again opinion demanded that. Canada was in the war—reluctantly in Quebec, with limited enthusiasm in English Canada—but in; and united. This was a huge achievement.

King soon faced attacks from both the reluctant and the enthusiastic. In September Premier Maurice Duplessis of Quebec used the war as an excuse for a snap election, charging that the federal government was centralizing power with wartime emergency orders. In effect Ottawa viewed this election as an attack on the war and unity, and King's Quebec ministers, promising no conscription, entered the fray. Duplessis was smashed and a Liberal government under Adelard Godbout took power. Early in the new year of 1940, however, Premier Mitchell Hepburn of Ontario, a Liberal but no supporter of King, charged that the federal government was doing nothing in the war and had his legislature condemn the war effort. King used this extraordinary action to justify his own election call, catching the opposition completely unready. Again the government pledged itself against conscription, and it scored a second successive huge victory. King was in power with a fresh mandate when the fortunes of war turned against the allies in the spring of 1940.

That change in fortune had huge impact on Canada's war. From being a war of limited liability, with the major Canadian effort directed to air training, it was now a struggle for survival with all stops pulled. There would be a vastly expanded air training plan (that eventually produced 131,000 aircrew), a very large navy that played an increasingly important role in the convoy war, and a larger army than in the First World War. Britain's peril also emboldened the conscriptionists in the country and cabinet, and King fought a long rearguard action to stave off the inevitable. The first bite at the cherry came in June 1940, when the National Resources Mobilization Act authorized home defence conscription for thirty days; over time this term was stretched to cover the war's duration. In November 1941 a slightly irregular Conservative meeting made Arthur Meighen party leader once again, and the conscription tom-toms began to beat insistently. King countered with a plebiscite that, without mentioning the word conscription, asked for release from the government's pledges of 1939-40. The government won but French Canadians voted heavily 'no', although Lapointe's replacement, Louis St Laurent, made an impressive beginning in campaigning for the 'yes' side. The National Resources Mobilization Act was duly amended, but with King's pledge that the change meant 'not necessarily conscription, but conscription if necessary'. That classic King

formulation in fact described his manpower policy with precision. Defence minister J. L. Ralston none the less almost resigned and one Quebec minister actually did so.

King held the party together for two more years until heavy infantry casualties in Italy and Normandy created a reinforcement crisis in the autumn of 1944. Desperate to keep the country together and aware that sending home defence conscripts could jeopardize unity at a time when the war was all but won, King sacked the conscriptionist Ralston and appointed General A. G. L. McNaughton, former commander of the First Canadian Army overseas, in his place. McNaughton tried and failed to persuade home defence conscripts to volunteer for the front and, after an agonizing three weeks and in the face of threatened resignations of senior army commanders, King reversed course and decided to dispatch 16,000 conscripts overseas. Quebec was restive but King prevailed in the House of Commons and, helped by St Laurent's calm acceptance of the necessity of a measure of conscription, Québecois eventually concluded that King had done his very best to hold off compulsory service.

King was similarly successful in his relations with Roosevelt. The defeats on the continent in 1940 for the first time put Canada's safety in peril, not least if a defeated Britain had to surrender the Royal Navy. At the president's request King found himself uncomfortably in the middle, conveying American demands on the future of the British fleet to Winston Churchill. He also found Roosevelt pressing for a defence alliance in August 1940, and King agreed, first because he had no choice and, secondly, because the alliance let Canada do its utmost to get men and machines overseas without worrying about home defence. The change in imperial masters none the less proved fateful. So too did the shift in economic dependence to the USA. The war greatly expanded Canadian industry—and hence the import of metals, munitions components, and weapons from the south. By early 1941 Canada was all but bereft of American dollars, and King went to Roosevelt's home at Hyde Park, New York, in April 1941 to plead his case. The result in effect was an agreement that the Americans would buy as much in Canada as Canada was buying in the USA; at a stroke that resolved the dollar crisis and let Canadian industry work flat out. The results, directed by the powerful minister of munitions and supply, C. D. Howe, were hugely impressive and Canada gave Britain and the allies billions of dollars in goods and supplies under mutual aid.

Relations between Canada and the USA were generally very good indeed and featured few of the battles that troubled relations with the British. Those tended to revolve around Canada's assertion of its new-found strength. Though King never sought any role in strategic decisions, which he left to Winston Churchill and President Roosevelt, he was determined that Canada's role in key areas where it had power be recognized. Arguing the functional principle King claimed a special place for Canada in food production, in resources, and in relief. Aided by a brilliant team in the department of external affairs (of which he was minister) he had substantial success in getting Canada a special place on the Anglo-American combined food board and the combined production and resources board; Canada did not succeed, however, in getting its claims recognized on the United Nations Relief and Rehabilitation Administration, although that did not stop the country from contributing heavily to European relief efforts.

At the same time King at last began to implement the 1919 Liberal Party platform. It was evident that Canadians feared the return of depression at the war's end and equally evident that the socialist Co-operative Commonwealth Federation was making gains. In 1940 King pushed unemployment insurance into law, knowing full well that wartime employment would allow a large insurance fund to be built up to meet the expected post-war dislocations. In 1943 the Liberal Party renewed its pledges of social welfare, and in the next two years the government put in place family allowances (this single programme cost almost half the total pre-war federal budget), allocated large sums for housing, created a department of health and welfare, and in the veterans' charter created what was probably the best package of benefits for demobilized servicemen and women anywhere. At the same time the Keynesian mood that had taken hold in 1939 led the government to create a shelf of large public works projects to soak up the expected post-war unemployment and, in a 1945 white paper, to promise full employment.

The government's war record was superb, Canada putting more than a million men into the field and generating a huge industrial and agricultural effort—and all without inflation or a cut in living standards; in fact, the war saw Canadians with more money in their pockets and much better fed than in the depression years. For once King deserved an election sweep but the 1945 election was a tough fight. He prevailed by stressing the government's war record and the splendid veterans' benefits offered to returning servicemen and women, the social welfare policies already put into effect, the plans that the government had put in place for post-war reconstruction, and by denouncing the socialists and Conservatives for their disruptive schemes. King was as always firmly in the middle and his cautious conscription policies had won him the support of Quebec; that was sufficient to give him 127 seats in a house of 245, the tories garnering 67 and the Co-operative Commonwealth Federation 28. It was a victory, but a narrow one.

Last years King was now almost seventy-one years old and he was perceptibly failing. He had his good days, when he was as sharp and forceful as ever, but increasingly his small office staff found his moods difficult to anticipate or deal with. He had always expected his officials to be available at all hours but now the petulance and inconsiderateness spiralled out of control. Still, there was no sign of his preparing to step down, though when he persuaded St Laurent to remain in politics in 1945 and then, in 1946, made him secretary of state for external affairs, the first non-prime minister to hold the post, that was almost certainly an indication of King's choice of successor.

There was no shortage of concerns and issues. The expected economic downturn at war's end did not occur, something in part at least attributable to government preparations, planning, and spending. The gross national product had doubled during six years of war and, after a brief pause, it continued to grow. The new Canada would be prosperous, unlike the old. But the federal government's attempts to re-order confederation and to entrench the powers that Ottawa had exercised during the war foundered in the face of opposition from Ontario and Quebec. And the push toward a social welfare state all but ceased. Even so the government established Canadian citizenship under the law and for a time looked as if it might put a Canadian flag in place. King also put into train the entry of Newfoundland into confederation, a long-sought Canadian goal that came to fruition in April 1949, a few months after his departure from office.

What preoccupied King's last years however was less domestic questions than the international stage. He had been the *de facto* creator of the Commonwealth, the man who sought greater autonomy for Canada. But he followed Britain's lead wherever possible in the post-war world, and his government loaned the United Kingdom C$1.25 billion in 1946, fully one-third of that provided by the much bigger, much richer United States. He mistrusted the United Nations that he had helped to create, fearing that it was both a talking shop and an international body that might involve Canada in conflict. He admired the United States but he had no doubt that it had long-term designs on Canada. King was a bundle of contradictions, to be sure, but his nationalism, internationalism, Anglophilia, and anti-Americanism all reflected long-lived streams in the Canadian consciousness.

The Soviet Union in particular troubled this deeply anti-communist leader. In September 1945 a Soviet cipher officer, Igor Gouzenko, defected from the embassy in Ottawa, carrying documents proving that the USSR had run spy rings in Canada during the war. There were indications too in Gouzenko's material of espionage in high places in Washington and London. This affair, quickly communicated to the USA and the UK, demonstrated that public servants could violate their oaths for ideological reasons and showed that the Soviet Union remained an implacable foe of the democracies. The cold war was in formation and by 1948, with King's support, Canada was in secret discussions with London and Washington about the need for a north Atlantic alliance.

At the same time Canada and the United States had begun to discuss a free-trade arrangement, motivated in part at least by security concerns. King had agreed to the initiation of these discussions but, when a draft treaty was produced, he suddenly developed cold feet. How would he be perceived by history if he tied Canada forever to its neighbour? That was not an unreasonable response, given the then still powerful force of British sentiment in Canada and the attacks that had been levelled against King for years that he was a continentalist. To the fury of his officials King killed the deal, and the idea of free trade was not to be revived for forty years.

But at last it was time to go. In January 1948 King

announced that he would retire after a party leadership convention in August and, though he was ostensibly neutral, he clearly gave his support to St Laurent. The Quebecker duly won and King went off to Europe, still prime minister. It proved difficult for him to give up power and the handover did not finally take place until 15 November.

King, as an old man, intended to write his memoirs, utilizing his astonishing diary and vast collection of papers, but he could never get organized enough to begin. Always lonely he was left with only a few friends, servants, and his dog. His health was breaking down, and he died, at his country retreat, Kingsmere, near Ottawa, on 22 July 1950. Crowds turned out to walk past his bier but there was little emotion. King had never been loved by his people or his colleagues, though many of the latter feared him and some admired him as a leader of skill. He was buried in Toronto on 27 July.

King's legacy after twenty-one years in office was a Liberal Party that had become Canada's 'government party'. The Liberals had held the centre of the road so skilfully and for so long with a politics based on nationalism, national unity, and a degree of social welfare that the opposition on the left and right had been disarmed. This was King's doing, for he made his party the master of reconciliatory politics. Thanks to King, Canada's twentieth century belonged to the Liberal Party.

Historians then and since were ordinarily less kind in their judgements. King's peculiarities, his attachment to his dead mother and to his dogs, his spiritualist yearnings, and his alleged sexual encounters with prostitutes fed an unhealthy interest in the more bizarre aspects of his life. Most of these revelations had been discovered when his diaries were opened to public scrutiny, documents that King's will had ordered to be destroyed but that his literary executors had decided to preserve. Historians will be eternally grateful for the executors' decision but certainly King's reputation suffered, as the diaries fed the fires stoked by sensationalists. King's shrewd judgement, his constant attention to French Canada, his great steps forward in Canadian nationhood were, while not forgotten, routinely downplayed by writers and the media. And his cautious weighing of options and alternatives—do nothing by halves that can be done by quarters, poet F. R. Scott put it—generally was viewed as reflecting a flaw in his and the Canadian character.

More seriously historians were deeply divided on King's legacy. Quebec *nationaliste* historians tended to see him as a prime minister who paid little serious attention to Quebec concerns—had he not imposed conscription despite his promises? Conservative English-speaking historians contrarily saw King as slavishly following the dictates of Quebec opinion, even to the point of killing the British empire and denying the army overseas the reinforcements that it needed, in order to continue in office. Left-wing scholars viewed King as a hypocritical politician who doled out carefully timed dollops of social welfare in order to gut social democracy, while right-wingers

objected to the way that his baby bonus, for example, had weakened the country's moral fibre.

King's policies remained firmly in the centre of the road, however, despite attacks from the political left and right, and so on balance has most historical opinion. In 1997 *Maclean's* magazine commissioned a ranking of Canadian prime ministers. In their selection, based on region, age, and gender as well as academic distinction, twenty-five historians and political scientists ranked Mackenzie King first, ahead of Sir John A. Macdonald and Sir Wilfrid Laurier. The scholars expressed little admiration for King the man but offered unbounded admiration for his political skills and attention to Canadian unity. There was justice in this, for no one can rule a nation as disparate as Canada for so long without talents of a high order. The pendulum of opinion had swung, perhaps to Canadians' surprise.

J. L. GRANATSTEIN

Sources R. M. Dawson, *William Lyon Mackenzie King*, 1 (Toronto, 1958) · H. B. Neatby, *William Lyon Mackenzie King*, 2–3 (Toronto, 1963–76) · J. W. Pickersgill, *The Mackenzie King record*, 1–4 (Toronto, 1960–70) · C. P. Stacey, *A very double life* (Toronto, 1976) · J. English and J. O. Stubbs, eds., *Mackenzie King: widening the debate* (Toronto, 1978) · C. Gray, *Mrs. King* (Toronto, 1997) · J. L. Granatstein, *Canada's war: the politics of the Mackenzie King government, 1939–1945* (1975) · J. L. Granatstein and J. M. Hitsman, *Broken promises: a history of conscription in Canada* (1977) · R. Cuff and J. L. Granatstein, *Canadian–American relations in wartime* (1975) · R. D. Cuff and J. L. Granatstein, *American dollars—Canadian prosperity: Canadian–American economic relations, 1945-1950* (1978) · J. L. Granatstein, *The Ottawa men: the civil service mandarins, 1935–1957* (1982) · R. Whitaker, *The government party: organizing and financing the liberal party of Canada, 1930–1958* (Toronto, 1977) · H. S. Ferns and B. Ostry, *The age of Mackenzie King* (1955) · D. Creighton, *The forked road: Canada, 1939–1957* (Toronto, 1976) · J. Esberey, *Knight of the holy spirit: a study of William Lyon Mackenzie King* (Toronto, 1980) · J. Eayrs, *In defence of Canada*, 1–4 (Toronto, 1964–80) · C. P. Stacey, *Canada and the age of conflict: a history of Canadian external policies*, 2 (1981) · C. P. Stacey, *Arms, men and governments: the war policies of Canada, 1939–45* (Ottawa, 1970)

Archives NA Canada, MSS | BL, letters to J. A. Spender and Mrs. Spender, Add. MS 46388 · Bodl. Oxf., corresp. with Viscount Addison · Bodl. Oxf., corresp. with Herbert Samuel · Bodl. Oxf., letters to Sir Alfred Zimmern · CKS, corresp. with Lord Stanhope · Cumbria AS, Carlisle, letters to Lord Howard of Penrith · HLRO, corresp. with Lord Beaverbrook, and extracts of his diaries and letters · JRL, Methodist Archives and Research Centre, corresp. with Frank O. Salisbury · NA Canada, Department of External Affairs records · NA Scot., corresp. with Arthur Balfour | FILM BFI NFTVA, current affairs footage · BFI NFTVA, documentary footage · BFI NFTVA, news footage

Likenesses F. Salisbury, portrait, 1945, House of Commons, Ottawa · J. W. L. Foster, portrait, Laurier House, Ottawa · Y. Karsh, portrait · W. Orpen, portrait, Laurier House, Ottawa · photograph, NPG [*see illus.*]

Wealth at death C$681,252 and land at Kingsmere, Quebec: Stacey, *A very double life*

King, Mary [Moll] (1696–1747), businesswoman, was born on Vine Street in the parish of St Giles-in-the-Fields, London. Her father, Crispin, was a cobbler, and her mother peddled fruit, greens, and fish. At a young age Moll began to sell fruit from a barrow and earned a reputation for industry and good temper. She married Thomas King (1694–1739), who had been educated at Eton College and admitted to King's College, Cambridge, in 1717, and the two of them saved enough money to open a stall in Covent

Garden. After a few years they bought a house in Covent Garden market in which she sold coffee, tea, and chocolate. Soon they owned three adjoining shacks, and the business flourished; it became, in fact, 'a feature of the Piazza itself' (Chancellor, 62). They catered to the early morning market crowd, daytime shoppers and idlers, and, in a tavern atmosphere, to the evening pleasure-seekers, who ranged from actors from the nearby theatres and fashionable couples seeking slightly risqué experiences to ladies of pleasure and their clients. Among the services she offered was sending a servant bearing a light with her customers to the bagnios she recommended.

The Kings benefited from upper-class acquaintances, Tom from his time at school and Moll from her brief affair with William Murray, first earl of Mansfield. A common legend is that George II once came with Viscount Gage and was almost drawn into a fight. 'Noblemen and the first *beaux* ... after leaving Court would go to her house in full dress, with swords ... and in rich brocaded silk coats, and ... conversed with ... chimney-sweepers, gardeners, and the market-people' (Chancellor, 63). Visitors described playing fashionable card-games and enjoying 'the best of conversation' (Shelley, 208).

Moll and Tom bought land at Haverstock Hill near Hampstead and built a large, comfortable country house. They had a son born on 30 August 1730 and named for his father, whom they sent to Westminster School. For over twenty years King's was the most notorious and successful meeting-place in Covent Garden. William Hogarth depicted Moll's coffee house in his *Morning*; her building and sign are clearly visible, and a fight is going on inside. Ronald Paulson points out that Hogarth places it to the other side of the square from its actual location so that it partially obscures Inigo Jones's St Paul's and forms the juxtaposition he wanted. Henry Fielding refers to it in *Pasquin*, and the prologue to his *Covent Garden Tragedy* asks 'What rake is ignorant of King's Coffee House?'.

Throughout her career, King was prosecuted for keeping a disorderly house. *The Life and Character of Moll King* says she was indicted nearly twenty times but very rarely convicted. For example, in May 1736 she was censured for allowing the men who disrupted a mass to get drunk at her house, and in November 1737 she was fined for keeping a 'Disorderly House at which sexual offences were committed' (Burford, 58). She was in king's bench prison briefly in June 1739 for refusing to pay a £200 fine for beating a young man in her coffee house; she insisted she was keeping order and said 'if she was to pay Two Hundred Pounds to all the insolent Boys she had thrash'd for their Impudence, the Bank of *England* would be unable to furnish her with the Cash' (*Life and Character*, 15).

King retired to Hampstead in 1745, rented a pew in a church, and lived her last years quietly. She died at Hampstead on 17 September 1747. Some time afterwards, possibly that year, an anonymous account of her life and character was published. PAULA R. BACKSCHEIDER

Sources *The life and character of Moll King* (1747?) · E. J. Burford, *Wits, wenches, and wantons* (1986) · R. Paulson, *Hogarth's graphic works*, 3rd edn (1989) · E. B. Chancellor, *The annals of Covent Garden*

(1930) · J. Timbs, *Clubs and club life in London: with anecdotes of its famous coffee houses, hostelries, and taverns, from the seventeenth century to the present time* (1872); repr. (1967) · J. Barber, *Tom King's: or, the Paphian grove* (1738) · H. Shelley, *Inns and taverns of old London* (1909)
Likenesses portraits, June 1739, repro. in Burford, *Wits, wenches, and wantons*, 54 · portrait, repro. in J. Caulfield, *Portraits, memoirs, and characters of remarkable persons from the revolution ... to the end of the reign of George II* (1819)

King, Matthew Peter (*c*.1773–1823), composer, was born in London. Very little is known of him beyond a catalogue of his works. Apparently he studied composition with Charles Frederick Horn, and the appearance of his earliest compositions under the name of 'Master King' could mean, as suggested by Cudworth (1980), that he was a child prodigy. He seems to have spent most of his life in London.

Early works, before 1800, include a series of piano sonatas and other pieces for keyboard; some theoretical treatises dating from around the turn of the century concentrate on the practice of thoroughbass and challenge the theories of A. F. C. Kollmann. King then turned his efforts to vocal music, especially for the stage, and in this area he enjoyed some success. Between 1804 and 1819 he produced several stage works, sometimes in collaboration with Michael Kelly, John Braham, or John Davy, to librettos generally by James Kenney or S. J. Arnold. These were performed at Covent Garden, Drury Lane, and the English Opera at the Lyceum Theatre, and include the comic opera *Matrimony* (with Kenney; Drury Lane, 20 November 1804); the melodrama *Timour the Tartar* (with M. G. Lewis; Covent Garden, 29 April 1811); and the musical farce *Turn out!* (with Kenney; Lyceum, 7 March 1812). Among other compositions are a number of glees, ballads, madrigals, and piano pieces, and an oratorio, *The Intercession*, which was produced at Covent Garden on 1 June 1816. An aria from this work, 'Eve's Lamentation', became very popular for a time.

King was a gifted musician and his operas enjoyed considerable vogue. He died in London in January 1823. His son, C. M. King, composed and published some songs and piano pieces. R. F. SHARP, *rev.* DAVID J. GOLBY

Sources C. Cudworth, 'King, Matthew Peter', *New Grove* · R. Clarence [H. J. Eldredge], *'The Stage' cyclopaedia: a bibliography of plays* (1909)

King, Oliver (*d.* 1503), bishop of Bath and Wells, was born in London. He became a king's scholar at Eton College (*c*.1445–9) and a scholar and fellow of King's College, Cambridge, from 1449 to 1460–65, graduating MA by 1456–7. He then studied civil law at Orléans and Cambridge, gaining a doctorate by 1481. Meanwhile he served as junior proctor of the University of Cambridge (1459–60), was ordained subdeacon (1467) and deacon (1473), and began to collect benefices, starting with the rectory of Broughton, Hampshire, in 1466 and the wardenship of St John's Hospital, Dorchester, Dorset, in 1473. His preferments multiplied thereafter as he advanced in the royal service. King may have been secretary to Edward, prince of Wales, son of Henry VI, during the prince's French exile, but success came in the service of the prince's nemesis, Edward

IV. From the clerkship of the signet in 1473 King advanced to the post of principal secretary for the French tongue in 1476. In 1475 he went as ambassador to the duke of Brittany, and in 1479 to the king of France. In 1480 he became the king's secretary; that year alone brought him three prebends and two successive rectories, and on 17 April 1482 he added the archdeaconry of Oxford.

At Edward's death King became secretary to Edward V, but the protector, Richard of Gloucester, dispensed with his services and had him arrested on 13 June 1483. His movements thereafter are obscure, but by December 1485 he was sufficiently in the confidence of Henry VII to be sent on embassy to France. Early in 1486 he was named as a commissioner to survey the king's rights in Calais, and in 1487 he accompanied French ambassadors from London to Dover. The spiral of promotions recommenced in 1487 with another prebend and the archdeaconry of Berkshire, and in August of that year he regained the secretaryship. In July 1488 he was granted a papal licence to visit the churches of his archdeaconries by deputy because he was constantly engaged in the king's business. By that year he was also registrar of the Order of the Garter. The flow of benefices culminated in his provision to the bishopric of Exeter on 1 October 1492 (he was probably consecrated early in February 1493). His promotion was accompanied by a dispensation to retain his other benefices. Three years later he was translated to Bath and Wells, by bull of 6 November 1495. On this final promotion he relinquished the secretaryship, although he continued to sit in the king's council and to take part in great occasions at court.

At Exeter, King appears to have been completely non-resident, but he visited Wells with the king in September 1497, and began to spend more time in his diocese from 1499, staying mostly at Bath. A visitation in that year brought a number of suspected heretics to light, and King heard one case in person, but he never ordained in either of his sees. Dr Thomas Gilbert as vicar-general and Thomas Cornish, bishop of Tenos, as suffragan deputized for him in both dioceses. At Bath and Wells he apparently promised the king the nomination to the major livings in his gift, but became distressed when this resulted in the appointment of a non-resident precentor of Wells—the future archbishop William Warham (d. 1532)—and a consequent decay in the conduct of cathedral services. The other exception he made to this arrangement was in the promotion of his own nephew William Cousin to the deanship of Wells in 1498. In this as in other instances he used the see's resources to provide for his relations, but in his last years he also became a benefactor to his see. He left generous quantities of plate and images to Wells Cathedral and Bath Abbey, and rebuilt the abbey's church with a vault of which his masons promised him that 'ther shal be noone so goodely neither in England nor in France' (Robinson, 4). He claimed that the rebuilding was inspired by a dream, in which he saw the Trinity with angels ascending and descending on a ladder and an olive tree supporting a crown, and heard a voice bidding 'Let an olive establish the crowne, and let a king restore the church' ('Letter to Prince Henry', 1.9).

King paid attention not only to rebuilding the monks' church, but also to reforming the irregularities in their conduct revealed at visitation. In his will he asked to be buried in the newly built choir, rather than in the chantry chapel he had constructed between 1492 and 1496 in St George's Chapel, Windsor, but it is unclear which site was chosen when he died on 29 August 1503. At Windsor his chapel contains oak panels painted with the pictures of his four royal masters—Prince Edward, Edward IV, Edward V, and Henry VII; at Bath carved ladders and angels alluding to his dream survive on the west front, but the inscription derived from the book of Judges (9: 8) recorded by Sir John Harington in the reign of James I, and by Thomas Dingley half a century later,

> The trees going to chuse their king
> Sayd bee to us that Oliver King

is now lost.   S. J. GUNN

Sources Emden, *Cam.* · H. Maxwell-Lyte, ed., *Registers of Oliver King, bishop of Bath and Wells, 1496–1503, and Hadrian de Castello, bishop of Bath and Wells, 1503–1518*, Somerset RS, 54 (1939) · J. A. Robinson, 'Correspondence of Bishop Oliver King and Sir Reginald Bray', *Proceedings of the Somersetshire Archaeological and Natural History Society*, 60/2 (1914), 1–10 · F. W. Weaver, ed., *Somerset medieval wills*, 2, Somerset RS, 19 (1903), 44–6 · 'Letter to Prince Henry from Sir John Harington: of the bishops of Bath and Wells, and first of Dr Oliver King', in J. Harington, *Nugae antiquae*, 1 (1769), 5–27, esp. 8–10 · Devon RO, Chanter XII 2 · R. Horrox, *Richard III, a study of service*, Cambridge Studies in Medieval Life and Thought, 4th ser., 11 (1989), 104, 117 · *History from marble, compiled in the reign of Charles II by Thomas Dingley*, ed. J. G. Nichols, 1, CS, 94 (1867), xxii · W. Campbell, ed., *Materials for a history of the reign of Henry VII*, 2 vols., Rolls Series, 60 (1873–7) · C. G. Bayne and W. H. Dunham, eds., *Select cases in the council of Henry VII*, SeldS, 75 (1958) · *CEPR letters*, 14.226–7 · J. A. F. Thomson, *The later Lollards, 1414–1520* (1965) · J. A. F. Thomson, *The early Tudor church and society, 1485–1529* (1993)
Archives Wells, register | Devon RO, Chanter XII 2
Wealth at death see will, Weaver, ed., *Somerset medieval wills*

King, Paul [*name in religion* Paulus a Sancto Spiritu] (*d.* 1655), Franciscan friar, supposedly baptized David, was the son of Cornelius King, who was employed by one of the barons of Upper Ossory as a clerk or secretary. His uncle, Murtagh King, was a convert to protestantism and beneficed by William Bedell, bishop of Kilmore, who employed him to translate the Old Testament into Irish. King was a native of Leinster, but in early life appears to have fallen victim to piracy, and was imprisoned for a time 'among the Moors' (*DNB*). He owed his liberation to the Franciscan friar Luke Wadding. This may have marked the beginning of King's religious life, and he was eventually to take the name in religion Paulus a Sancto Spiritu.

By 1641 King was teaching moral theology at Brindisi in Italy, and in 1644 he was doing similar work at Kilkenny. He probably spent time in Rome in 1646–7. In September 1647 King was appointed lector of theology at Kilkenny friary. There he became a staunch supporter of the papal nuncio Giovanni Battista Rinuccini, who had arrived in Ireland in November 1645, espousing his cause against the supreme council of the confederate Catholics. In May 1648 the nuncio passed his second censure on the confederates in reaction to the perceived implications of their dealings with Lord Inchiquin—the recall of the marquess of Ormond to resume his authority as lord lieutenant. Two months later King, then acting as Rinuccini's confidential agent, was arrested by order of the supreme council. This prompted him to write to Heber Macmahon, bishop of Clogher, inviting Owen Roe O'Neill and his Ulster army, which had always held more aloof from the confederate leadership, to seize Kilkenny and all the nuncio's enemies before Lord Lieutenant Ormond's anticipated arrival in Ireland. The letter was intercepted and King fled to the continent.

In February 1649 King was chosen by the middle chapter of the Franciscan order to rule as guardian of the friary of Kilkenny, but was then replaced by the pseudo-chapter of 1649, which installed the maverick Peter Walsh instead. At Louvain, King wrote a bitter diatribe against Rinuccini's opponents and the Anglo-Irish party generally. This pamphlet, *Epistola nobilis Hiberni*, was widely circulated in Catholic Europe, largely by the hands of Franciscan monks in France, Spain, and Italy, in order, so it was said, 'to instigate those powers against the English and protestant interest in Ireland' (Ohlmeyer, 4). But its primary purpose was to distance the supporters of the nuncio from the collapse of the Kilkenny confederacy and lay the blame elsewhere. Offering an extremely partisan view of developments in Ireland, it drew a sharp response from a 'controversial and none too scrupulous' Ormondist priest from Cork, John Callaghan, or MacCallaghan, who wrote under the pseudonym Philopater Iranaeus (*DNB*). His *Vindiciarum Catholicorum Hiberniae*, published at Paris in 1650, which defended the Inchiquin truce, was mistakenly attributed to Richard Bellings, secretary to the Catholic confederacy, under whose name it was entered on the papal index of forbidden books in 1654. Callaghan alleged that King was guilty of numerous crimes, but the attempted betrayal of Kilkenny was the only one he cited. The controversy rumbled on for several years, continuing in the pages of the *Commentarius Rinuccinianus* and in a pamphlet written by John Ponce (Punch), who defended his fellow Franciscan against the Ormondists.

At the time of his appointment *in absentia* as guardian of the Kilkenny friary, King had also received his instructions to set out for Rome on urgent provincial business. He had arrived by the time the Franciscans celebrated the feast of their patron saint in 1649. The support of the order helped King overcome some of the inconvenience of his connection with Rinuccini. Pope Innocent X was said to have lost sympathy with his nuncio after the débâcle of 1648, while his successor, Alexander VII, was also disparaging of the 1648 censure, having himself resisted treating signatories to the distasteful Westphalian peace in similar fashion while nuncio to the German negotiations. On 21 November 1649 King was nominated guardian of St Isidore's College at Rome in succession to its founder, and King's personal saviour, Luke Wadding, towards whom King later behaved less than graciously. The theologian and historian John Colgan recommended King for the post of commissary responsible for the continental Franciscan colleges, and although he did not receive the appointment King was for some years

procurator-general of the order. In his *Vindiciarum* Callaghan regretted having had no opportunity to show King's patrons that punishment would have been more fitting than such promotions as these. Ponce, on the other hand, averred that King was worthy of much greater honours. In 1651 King attended the general chapter of the Franciscan order in place of the custos of the Irish province, Patrick Brenan. In 1652 he published a Latin elegy on Cardinal Ximenes. While at Rome, King projected a book in ten volumes in honour of his order, but lived to publish only a kind of syllabus, written in Latin in an 'easy style … with vigour, but incorrectly', which was licensed in 1654 as an 'earnest of a great work' (*DNB*). It is believed that King died at Rome the following year.

RICHARD BAGWELL, rev. SEAN KELSEY

Sources G. Cleary, *Father Luke Wadding and St Isidore's College, Rome* (1925) · B. Millett, *The Irish Franciscans, 1651–1665* (1964) · T. W. Moody and others, eds., *A new history of Ireland*, 3: *Early modern Ireland, 1534–1691* (1976) · P. J. Corish, 'John Callaghan and the controversies amongst the Irish in Paris, 1648–1654', *Irish Theological Quarterly*, 21 (1954), 32–50 · J. H. Ohlmeyer, ed., *Political thought in seventeenth-century Ireland* (2000)

King, Peter, first Baron King (1669–1734), lord chancellor, was born in Exeter, the son of Jerome King, a prosperous grocer and drysalter, and Anne, daughter of Peter Locke and first cousin of John *Locke, the philosopher.

Origins and early career, 1669–1701 King was educated among the dissenters in Exeter, probably by Joseph Hallett (*bap.* 1620, *d.* 1689), who founded the dissenting academy there. Certainly he read deeply in theology and religious history, under the influence of the Exeter presbyterians, and he may have been intended for the nonconformist ministry. In 1691 he published anonymously *An Enquiry into the Constitution, Discipline, Unity & Worship of the Primitive Church*, an intervention in the debates arising out of the Toleration Act and the dissenters' desire for a full measure of comprehension, undertaken to show that in its organization and discipline the primitive church involved elements of presbyterianism as well as episcopacy. It attracted considerable attention, and continued to represent dissenting views into the early eighteenth century. A second part, dealing with the forms of worship of the early fathers, was completed within a few years, but was not published until 1713.

Such an early demonstration of learning and reasoned argument seems to have persuaded King's family that he should follow a legal career; he was admitted to the Middle Temple on 23 October 1694, and may have studied civil law at Leiden, although his name does not appear in the published list of students for the period. He was called to the bar on 3 June 1698, on the recommendation of Sir George Treby, lord chief justice, whom Locke had urged to befriend him. Locke subsequently became a second father to King, sending a constant stream of advice and providing him with an entrée into his London circle of acquaintances, which included whig grandees, judges, Isaac Newton, and Somers, the lord chancellor. In return King carried out Locke's business in the capital, especially the management of his financial affairs. His practice on the published *The History of the Apostles Creed: with Critical Observations on its Several Articles*. At first this attracted greater attention in Europe than in England, but ultimately it became a foundational text for further research, and generated several editions over the next forty years, one in Latin translation. His energies were now principally given over to his legal practice and attendance in parliament, wherein his nonconformist conscience inclined him to country measures as well as whiggism. He distinguished himself in January 1704 by making an able speech in the great debate over the Aylesbury election case, maintaining the right of electors to have a remedy at common law for denial of their votes, against tory insistence on the privileges of the Commons. In September 1704 Locke congratulated him on his marriage to Anne (1688/9–1767), the daughter of Richard Seyes of Boverton in Glamorgan, who had a fortune of at least £4000; but he lost his mentor the following month, acquiring half of his landholdings and many of his books. During the next few years the focus of his life shifted with increasing success: while he became recorder of Glastonbury in July 1705, his prospects centred on the capital, and when he came to purchase a major estate in 1710 he settled on the manor of Ockham in Surrey, within easy carriage distance of London.

In parliament between 1705 and 1708 King was prominent among an important group of independent whigs which maintained a broadly 'country' programme of measures. He sponsored a moderate place bill in January 1705; he was one of the leaders in the unsuccessful campaign for the 'whimsical' place clause added to the Regency Bill in January and February 1706; and in December 1707 he took a prominent part in the whig attack on the administration of the Admiralty. Indeed, although he was normally inclined to act with the junto whigs in party issues, his enthusiasm for eliminating 'interest' and exposing administrative mismanagement induced him to support the tory-inspired inquiry into the conduct of the war in Spain in late 1707 and 1708. By this time he had made an impression, and in the spring of 1708 the whigs in the government were keen to appease him with office: 'if he were engag'd, the Whymsical Whigs … wou'd have no Head to govern them, and having generally very indifferent ones of their own, cou'd do no great mischief' (A. Mainwaring to duchess of Marlborough, 9 April 1708, BL, Add. MS 61459, fols. 24–5). Unfortunately his speeches against the Admiralty had offended Queen Anne, who believed they were aimed at her husband, Prince George, the lord high admiral. She therefore vetoed a proposal that he should be appointed solicitor-general, and would not even countenance his becoming one of her counsel. In the event the administration arranged for him to be elected recorder of London on 27 July, and he was knighted on 12 September. The whig junto also nominated him as their preferred candidate for speaker after the general election of 1708, although he eventually gave way to the court candidate, Sir Richard Onslow.

As recorder of London, King was present at the commemorative service held in St Paul's Cathedral on 5 November 1709, when Dr Henry Sacheverell preached on

Peter King, first Baron King (1669–1734), by Daniel de Coning, 1720

western circuit and at Westminster expanded rapidly: the reports show that by 1702 he was appearing regularly as a junior in king's bench, both on behalf of private individuals and in pleas of the crown. He also benefited from the patronage of the Devon gentry, and in February 1701 he was brought into parliament for Bere Alston, a Devon borough partly controlled by Sir Francis Drake of Buckland Abbey, one of the leaders of the west country whigs. He arrived in parliament at a critical juncture, and Locke urged him to put attendance in the Commons before his practice on circuit, although at first, he recommended, he should prompt more experienced members rather than speak himself: 'hereby you will recommend your self when people shall observe soe much modesty joyned with your parts and judgment' (Locke to King, 31 Jan 1701, Bodl. Oxf., MS Locke c. 40, fol. 100). But he made his first speech within a month of his election, and was a partisan in the bitter struggles over the impeachment of the whig lords and the Kentish petition.

Lawyer–parliamentarian, 1702–1714 King was a man of strong moral principles, informed by his faith, which he carried into his public life as well as his writings. He was an early member of the Society for the Propagation of the Gospel in Foreign Parts, founded in 1701, and in 1702 he the text 'in peril among False Brethren', and he subsequently objected to the explosive sermon in the court of aldermen. In December 1709 he took a leading role in censuring Sacheverell's high-flying doctrines in the Commons, and in January he was one of the committee that drew up articles of impeachment. At the trial he naturally took principal responsibility for the second article, which accused Sacheverell of condemning the Toleration Act of 1689. In a closely reasoned but temperate speech on 28 February he effectively demolished the defendant's disingenuous answer, to the effect that he did not intend his criticisms to refer to the act, and showed that his words could be construed only as an argument that liberty of conscience tended ultimately to treason, and that such indulgence should be suppressed, rather than encouraged. Indeed, he cleverly contended that Sacheverell had denied the queen's supremacy over the church, in so far as Sacheverell maintained that the clergy's censures against the dissenters were beyond earthly power to reverse. He also deployed all his deep historical learning to praise Archbishop Edmund Grindal, whom Sacheverell had condemned for recommending toleration to Queen Elizabeth, as 'a man universally esteemed for his virtue, piety, and learning' (*State trials*, 15.149). He reiterated this last point nine days later, on 9 March, when he replied to the defence on the second article. This was the high point of King's parliamentary career: his performance could have left no one in doubt of his forensic ability, and by taking a prominent part in such a party set piece he publicly declared his political allegiances.

Certainly King's instinct for independence and scrupulous governance survived—in December 1711 he brought in a hopeless motion for balloting at elections, which was duly lost by a large majority, and in 1713 he supported another place clause—but for the remainder of Anne's reign he was clearly identified as one of the whig leaders in the Commons, especially in their resistance to the tory peace and concern for the Hanoverian succession. In June 1712 he spoke up for William Fleetwood, bishop of St Asaph, an opponent of the peace, who was attacked by the tories on the pretext of objecting to the preface of his recently published collection of sermons. And in February 1713 he was counsel for the whig journalist George Ridpath, prosecuted by the government for attacking the peace in his *Flying Post*. In July of that year he also defended William Whiston before the court of delegates upon Whiston's prosecution for denying the Trinity. Naturally, in March 1714 he spoke against concurring in the address of thanks for the treaty of Utrecht, concentrating on the need for further safeguards to protect the protestant succession. And of course, as a whig and dissenter, he resisted the Schism Bill in May, deploying his reputation as a patristic scholar to compare it to the Roman persecution of the early Christians.

Chief justice, 1714–1725 When George I arrived in London, King gave a gracious speech of welcome on behalf of the corporation. With the death of Queen Anne the veto on his further promotion was removed, and upon the nomination of Lord Chancellor Cowper he became lord chief justice of common pleas on 27 October 1714, in place of Thomas Trevor, first Baron Trevor, who was removed on political grounds. As such, he shared in the augmentation of all the judges' salaries obtained via the petition of Sir Thomas Parker, chief justice of king's bench. King had now left the Commons and was now effectively removed from the front line of party strife, and during his decade on the common law bench was only occasionally called upon to try state prosecutions. But he continued to influence elections in Devon, and managed the parliamentary borough of Bere Alston for his former patron Sir Francis Drake, thereby obliging Robert Walpole, whose brother was returned to one of the seats in the parliament of 1715. After the Jacobite rising of 1715 he presided at the special commission which tried the commoners accused of taking part. His report to the secretary of state on the proceedings is remarkable for its fairness and humanity towards the prisoners, several of whom he recommended to the king's mercy. With the majority of the judges, in 1718 he gave his opinion for the king when they were tendered questions about his legal right to supervise the education and marriages of the children of the prince of Wales. And in October 1719 he presided at the Old Bailey trial of John Matthews for treason in publishing a tract alleging the right of the Pretender, James Stuart, to the throne. Matthews was only nineteen years of age, and one of the crown counsel admitted he was merely 'an obstinate instrument in the hands of some greater person' (*State trials*, 15.1338), but King summed up clinically and the jury brought in a guilty verdict.

The only other significant criminal trial for which King was responsible was *R. v. Woodburne and Coke*, for a murderous attack on Edward Crispe, Coke's brother-in-law, which was held at Bury St Edmunds in March 1722. Crispe had survived the assault, and since attempted murder was only a misdemeanour at common law, the defendants were prosecuted under a capital clause in an obscure statute of 1670 (22 & 23 Chas. II c. 1) directed against malicious maiming and wounding. Although not represented by counsel, Coke attempted to take advantage of his confessed intention to kill, rather than maim, but King would not accept this as a point of law for argument, and insisted the intention was a matter of fact for the jury, who found both men guilty. His severe speech on giving judgment in this case suggests that his decision may have been influenced by personal abhorrence at the callousness of the crime, from which Coke hoped to inherit Crispe's estate. Some later authorities believed that he allowed the statute to be extended too far (*State trials*, 16.54–94).

Lord chancellor, 1725–1733 In 1725, when Lord Chancellor Macclesfield (previously Sir Thomas Parker) was impeached, King was chosen to conduct his trial. The proceedings were conducted at the bar of the House of Lords, wherein he was commissioned to preside as their speaker. Although the trial took thirteen days in May, his role was largely a formal one, since he was not a peer and had no voice but as the mouthpiece of the Lords. Four days after pronouncing sentence, on 29 May, he was created Baron

King, of Ockham, and on 1 June he was appointed lord chancellor himself, with an additional salary of £1200 in consideration of loss of profits from sales of masterships in chancery. But although he had given great satisfaction in common pleas, and his reputation for integrity made the appointment popular, expectations of his performance were greatly disappointed. He was not experienced in chancery practice, and his lack of equity learning destroyed his confidence, thereby enervating his dispatch. Lord Hervey said of his practice on the bench:

> He had such a diffidence of himself that he did not dare to do right, for fear of doing wrong; decrees were always extorted from him; and had he been let alone he would never have given any suitor his due, for fear of giving him what was not so. (Hervey, 1.280–81)

Several of his decisions were reversed on appeal to the Lords, but he was able to settle some important points of doctrine. In *Coppin* v. *Coppin* (1725) he ruled that a will settling land in England must conform to the rules of English law, even when made abroad. And in *Croft* v. *Pyke* (1733) he determined that a partner's joint estate was liable first to the debts of the partnership, before payment of legacies to his heirs. He was generally reluctant to interpose against the common law, although in cases of married women's separate property he accepted that the practice of the court was to compel a husband to make a settlement on the wife before recovering his wife's portion by equity (*Milner* v. *Colmer*, 1731, and *Brown et Uxor* v. *Elton*, 1733).

King's impact on the administration of the court was more significant than his contribution to doctrine, however. The circumstances of his predecessor's disgrace meant that his inclination for honest management was encouraged, and he achieved some important reforms. Steps were taken to ensure that the suitors who were liable to lose by the insolvency of the delinquent masters in chancery were indemnified, and he sponsored legislation which required that suitors' money should in future be paid into the Bank of England. The office of accountant-general was established to oversee the funds and securities brought into the court. Indeed, his reforming efforts may have extended beyond the court of chancery; for during his period in office the legislature was attentive to contemporary complaints about the mysterious nature and crippling expense of litigation proceedings generally. Although not recorded as a speaker at the relevant debate in the Lords, he is said to have been the author of the 1731 statute which required all legal documents and processes to use English, rather than Latin or law French. It may be no coincidence that in 1732 a committee of the House of Commons criticized the increase in the number of chancery officers since the sixteenth century; and in 1733, following its recommendation, a royal commission was established to report on the fees taken in all the courts of England and Wales. King also resisted the extension of royal patronage in the church. He had been reappointed by George II in June 1727, but in July the king told him that henceforth he intended to nominate to all the ecclesiastical offices previously within the chancellor's patronage. King thereupon replied 'that this was a right belonging to the office, annexed to it by act of parliament and immemorial usage, and I hoped he would not put things out of their ancient course' (King's diary, 8 July 1727, in Campbell, 6.108). The king subsequently gave up the point, although Walpole reported that he was 'disobliged' by the lord chancellor's 'peremptory manner' (Ryder's diary, 18 Oct 1739).

Death and significance King ruined his health by his efforts to become competent in equity, and by sitting late to deal with the increasing arrears in his court. It is said that towards the end he dozed on the bench, while the proceedings of the court were substantially controlled by Sir Philip Yorke and Charles Talbot, the leaders of the chancery bar. After a paralytic stroke he was forced to resign on 19 November 1733, accepting a gratuity of £20,000. He died of a further stroke at Ockham on 22 July 1734, and was buried in the church there, being survived by his wife, who lived until 1 July 1767, and six children, including four sons, John (*bap.* 1706, *d.* 1740), Peter (*bap.* 1709, *d.* 1754), William (1711–1767), and Thomas (1712–1779), each successively Baron King of Ockham, and two daughters, Elizabeth and Anne, who died unmarried. By his will, in addition to his principal estate at Ockham he left separate estates in land to his two eldest sons and £8000 each to his younger children. But he desired to be buried 'with as little funeral show as possible', and commended his wife and children 'to the protection and providence of Almighty God, which will be their best Defence'. A monument by Rysbrack memorialized him as 'a friend to true religion and liberty' (HoP, *Commons, 1690–1715*).

Although he had been an important politician during the party warfare under Anne, and he presided as president of the regency council during the monarch's absence in Hanover, King had little influence over major policy decisions as lord chancellor. Indeed in his later years some old acquaintances and political allies were alienated by what they discerned as a departure from his disinterested principles. William Whiston relates his disappointment on approaching King for a prebend on behalf of a friend:

> I found so prodigious a Change in him, such strange Coldness in the Matters that concerned Religion, and such an earnest Inclination to Money and Power, that I gave up my Hopes quickly. Nay, indeed, I soon perceived that he disposed of his Preferments almost wholly at the Request of such Men as could best support him in his high Station, without Regard to Christianity. (*Memoirs of … William Whiston*, 1.35)

These comments on King are qualified by Whiston's self-righteousness, but Walpole also said that he became excessively avaricious after becoming a peer, insisting on having a tellership of the exchequer for his eldest son and claiming a service of plate as speaker of the House of Lords (Ryder's diary, 18 Oct 1739). While these accusations of worldly materialism sit uneasily with his public behaviour, there is no doubt that King was unwise to accept an office for which he was manifestly unsuited, and his reputation suffered accordingly. He was a man whose virtues provoked unusual expectations, however, and it is unfortunate that his successors in office did not follow his lead in reforming the administration of justice.

DAVID LEMMINGS

Sources State trials · Cobbett, Parl. hist., vol. 6 · W. N. Welsby, Lives of eminent English judges of the seventeenth and eighteenth centuries (1846) · DNB · E. Foss, Biographia juridica: a biographical dictionary of the judges of England … 1066–1870 (1870) · Bodl. Oxf., MSS Locke c. 12, c. 38, c. 40 · J. Campbell, Lives of the lord chancellors, 4th edn, 10 vols. (1856–7) · will, PRO, PROB 11/666, fols. 263–4 · M. J. K., 'King, Peter', HoP, Commons, 1690–1715 [draft] · ER, vols. 2, 24, 88, 91–2 · Holdsworth, Eng. law, vol. 12 · G. S. Holmes, British politics in the age of Anne (1967) · G. Holmes, The trial of Doctor Sacheverell (1973) · Mainwaring letters, BL, Add. MS 61459 · D. Hayton, 'The country interest and the party system, 1689–c.1720', Party and management in parliament, 1660–1784, ed. C. Jones (1984), 37–85 · D. Hayton, 'Moral reform and country politics in the late seventeenth-century House of Commons', Past and Present, 128 (1990), 48–91 · J. Hervey, Memoirs of the reign of George the Second, ed. J. W. Croker, 2 vols. (1848) · Memoirs of the life and writings of Mr. William Whiston. Containing memoirs of several of his friends also. Written by himself. (1749) · Lord King, The life of John Locke, with extracts from his correspondence, journals, and commonplace books, 2nd edn, 2 vols. (1830), vol. 2 appx, 'Notes of domestic and foreign affairs, during the last years of the reign of George I and the early part of the reign of George II' · D. Lemmings, Gentlemen and barristers: the inns of court and the English bar, 1680–1730 (1990) · G. Holmes, Augustan England (1982) · diary of Dudley Ryder, 18 Oct 1739, Sandon Hall, Staffordshire, Harrowby MSS, vol. 430, doc. 24, pt 1, p.3 · GEC, Peerage, 7.275–6 · Sainty, Judges

Archives Bodl. Oxf., corresp. · Bodl. Oxf., papers, incl. extracts from the House of Commons journals · Lincoln's Inn, London, case reports · Surrey HC, official papers | Bodl. Oxf., corresp. with John Locke

Likenesses J. Simon, mezzotint, 1718 (after M. Dahl), BM, NPG · D. de Coning, oils, 1720, NPG [see illus.] · G. Vertue, line engraving, 1724, BM, NPG · J. Faber junior, mezzotint, 1730 (after M. Dahl), BM, NPG · Rysbrack, memorial, Ockham parish church, Surrey

Wealth at death manor of Ockham, Surrey; also owned manor and advowson of East Clandon, Surrey, and further land in the parishes of Send, Surrey, and Long Ditton, Surrey; house in Norfolk Street, St Clements Danes, Middlesex; large personal estate in money and securities

King, Peter, seventh Baron King

King, Peter, seventh Baron King (1775–1833), politician, was born on 31 August 1775, the eldest son of Peter, the sixth baron, and Charlotte, daughter of Edward Tredcroft of Horsham, and great-grandson of Peter King, first Baron King, lord chancellor. He was educated at Eton College and Trinity College, Cambridge, and succeeded to the title in 1793. After a short tour on the continent he returned to England on coming of age, and took his seat in the House of Lords. True to the whig traditions of his family, he acted with Lord Holland, whose motion for an inquiry into the causes of the failure of the expedition to the Low Countries he supported in his maiden speech on 12 February 1800.

Except to oppose a Habeas Corpus Suspension Bill, or a bill to prolong the suspension of cash payments by the Banks of England and Ireland, begun in 1797, King at first rarely intervened in debate. He made a profound study of the currency question, and published his findings in a pamphlet entitled *Thoughts on the Restriction of Payments in Specie at the Banks of England and Ireland* (2nd edn, 1803). Much enlarged, it was reissued as *Thoughts on the Effects of the Bank Restrictions* (1804). In this classic tract King argued

Peter King, seventh Baron King (1775–1833), by John Linnell, 1832

that the suspension had caused an excessive issue of notes, particularly by the Bank of Ireland, and a consequent depreciation of the paper and appreciation of bullion, and he advocated a gradual return to the system of specie payment. It was reviewed by Horner in the *Edinburgh Review* (2.402), and attracted much attention, but produced no practical result. As the depreciation increased, King in 1811 gave notice to his leasehold tenantry that he could no longer accept notes in payment of rent, except at a discount varying according to the date of the lease. Ministers, alarmed lest his example should be followed generally, hastily introduced a measure making notes of the Banks of England and Ireland payable on demand legal tender in payment of rent out of court, and prohibiting the acceptance or payment of more than 21s. for a guinea. King opposed the bill, and justified his own conduct in an able and spirited speech (afterwards published as a pamphlet), but it passed into law, and was followed in 1812 by a measure making the notes legal tender in all cases (51 Geo. III, c. 127; 52 Geo. III, c. 50). He sat in the Lords' committee on cash payments in 1819 and took part in the debates on it in 1820, describing an internal failure of consumption, largely due to cash payments coupled with high taxation.

King was from the first, and as long as he lived, a determined opponent of the corn laws, which he denounced as a 'job of jobs'. He supported Catholic emancipation and the commutation of tithes, and opposed grants in aid of the Society for the Propagation of the Gospel in Foreign Parts, pluralities, and other abuses, and was suspected of a leaning to Presbyterianism (see Antischismaticus, *Hierarchia versus Anarchiam*, 1831; and J. T. Law, *A letter to Lord King controverting the sentiments lately delivered in parliament by his lordship, Mr. O'Connell, and Mr. Sheil, as to the fourfold division of tithes*, 1832). His long-standing interest in Locke was embodied in his *Life of John Locke*, published in 1829 and reissued with extra material in 1830; his hatred of the corn laws and of corruption prompted his *Short History of the Job of Jobs* (1825).

King married, on 26 May 1804, Lady Hester Fortescue, daughter of Hugh, first Earl Fortescue and his wife, Hester; they had two sons, William, created Lord Lovelace in 1838, and Peter John Locke *King. King died suddenly on 4 June 1833 at his house in Dover Street, London, and his widow died aged eighty-nine in 1873 at their home, Brooklands, in Weybridge, Surrey. As Henry Brougham's praise of his capacity and character testifies, King's unexpected death ended a career of increasing distinction.

J. M. RIGG, rev. H. C. G. MATTHEW

Sources *A selection from the speeches and writings of the late Lord King with a short introductory memoir by Earl Fortescue* (1844) · H. Brougham, *Historical sketches of statesmen who flourished in the time of George III*, 2nd ser. (1839) · B. Hilton, *Corn, cash, commerce: the economic policies of the tory governments, 1815–1830* (1977) · GEC, *Peerage*
Archives BL, corresp. with Lord Holland, Add. MS 51572
Likenesses J. Faber junior, mezzotint, 1830 (after M. Dahl), BM, NPG · J. Simon, mezzotint, 1830 (after M. Dahl), BM, NPG · J. Linnell, oils, 1832, NPG [*see illus.*] · E. U. Eddis, engraving · M. Gauci, lithograph (after E. U. Eddis), BM, NPG · G. Hayter, group portrait, oils (*The trial of Queen Caroline, 1820*)), NPG · R. Westmacott junior, bust, All Saints Church, Ockham, Surrey

King, Peter John Locke (1811–1885), politician, second son of Peter *King, seventh Baron King (1775–1833), and brother of William King-Noel, first earl of Lovelace, was born at Ockham, Surrey, on 25 January 1811. He was educated at Harrow School and at Trinity College, Cambridge, where he graduated BA 1831, and MA 1833.

In 1837 King unsuccessfully contested East Surrey, but he was elected for the same constituency on 11 August 1847, and retained his seat until the conservative reaction at the general election in February 1874. He supported an alteration in the law of primogeniture for many sessions, various of his speeches being published as pamphlets. On 11 August 1854 his Real Estate Charges Act was passed, according to which mortgaged estates descend with and bear their own burdens; it became known as Locke King's Act. In the session of 1856 he was successful in obtaining the repeal of 120 sleeping statutes which were liable to be put into force from time to time. He also waged war against the statute law commission, and more than once denounced it as a job. His letters to *The Times* on chancery reform were reprinted in *A Bleak House Narrative of Real Life* (1856). King introduced a bill for abolishing the property qualification of members, which passed the House of Lords on 28 June 1858, and in eight successive sessions he brought forward a County Franchise Bill, on one occasion, 20 February 1851, defeating and causing the resignation of the Russell ministry. He succeeded in carrying through the House of Commons a bill for extending the £10 franchise to the county constituencies, so as to include every

Peter John Locke King (1811–1885), by John & Charles Watkins

adult male who came within the conditions of the borough suffrage. He was also well known for his advocacy of the ballot and of the abolition of church rates, and for his strenuous opposition to the principle and practice alike of endowments for religious purposes. He was distinguished by the legislative effectiveness of his moderate radicalism.

King married, on 22 March 1836, Louisa Elizabeth, daughter of William Henry Hoare of Mitcham Grove, Surrey. She died in 1884, leaving two sons and four daughters. King died at his home, Brooklands, Weybridge, on 12 November 1885. G. C. BOASE, rev. H. C. G. MATTHEW

Sources Boase, *Mod. Eng. biog.* · *The Times* (14 Nov 1885)
Archives Bodl. Oxf., letters to Lord Lovelace · Bodl. Oxf., corresp. with Sir J. G. Wilkinson and papers
Likenesses John & Charles Watkins, photograph, NPG [*see illus.*] · D. J. Pound, stipple and line engraving (after a photograph by Mayall), NPG; repro. in D. J. Pound, *Drawing room portrait gallery of eminent persons* (1859) · portrait, repro. in *Statesmen of England* (1862), no. 46 · woodcut, NPG; repro. in *Illustrated Times* (12 June 1858)
Wealth at death £266,860 11s. 11d.—in UK: probate, July 1886, *CGPLA Eng. & Wales*

King, Philip Gidley (1758–1808), naval officer and colonial governor, was born at Launceston, Cornwall, on 23 April 1758, the only son of Philip King, a local draper, and his wife, daughter of John Gidley, an Exeter attorney. Educated at Mr Bailey's school, Yarmouth, he joined the navy on 22 December 1770 as captain's servant in the *Swallow*, and served for five years in the East Indies. In July 1775, on moving to American waters, he became a midshipman in the *Liverpool*, and after two more changes he was commissioned lieutenant in the *Renown* in December 1778, according to one of his examiners, 'one of the most promising young men I have ever met'. Next year he returned home to serve in the Channel Fleet, coming under Captain Arthur Phillip in November 1781. Two years later he was in Indian waters, still under Phillip, but he was paid off in 1784, when war ended, and was on half pay for two years.

In October 1786, when the expedition to establish a penal colony in New South Wales was being fitted out, Phillip, its commander, appointed King second lieutenant of the *Sirius* (20 guns), which was convoying the transports. After many delays in sailing the expedition reached Port Jackson (Sydney) on 26 January 1788, and within three weeks Phillip sent King, 'an officer of merit, whose perseverance may be depended on' (A. Phillip to Lord Sydney, 15 May 1788; *Historical Records of Australia*, ser. 1, 1.20), with seventeen men and six women to occupy Norfolk Island, to 'anticipate' any foreign power, and, he hoped, to prepare its prolific flax-plant for use in the navy. Unfortunately he could not do this, having no flax-dressers; he also found that the island had no timber good for naval masts and no good harbour. However, by January 1790 King had 50 acres under cultivation with wheat and maize and a plentiful supply of fruit and vegetables, so Phillip was able to send two companies of marines and 183 convicts with 27 children to the island to relieve the pressure on provisions in Sydney. In April he sent King to England to report on the settlement, and strongly recommended his promotion.

Upon reaching London in December King learned that he had been appointed lieutenant-governor of Norfolk Island, and on 2 March 1791 he was promoted commander. Nine days later, at St Martin-in-the-Fields, he married his cousin, Anna Josepha Coombe (1764/5–1844) of Hattersleigh, Devon, according to marine-officer Ralph Clarke's journal 'a genteel woman' but 'not very pretty', though Elizabeth Macarthur thought her 'possessed of a great share of good nature' and King's friend, the future commissary W. N. Chapman, described her as 'almost an angel' (Bassett, 16, 20–21). They sailed in the *Gorgon* on 15 March, reaching Sydney on 21 September and Norfolk Island on 4 November. There, on 13 December, their first child, the future Captain Phillip Parker *King RN (1791–1856), was born, to join King's two illegitimate sons, the future naval officers Norfolk (1789–1839) and Sydney (1790–1840), whose mother, Ann Inett (*b.* 1757), a mantua maker of Grimley, Worcestershire, had been found guilty on 11 March 1786 of stealing clothing and linen, and transported for seven years (in 1792 she married another convict).

On Norfolk Island, Anna Josepha had to live with only one female companion of her own class, Mrs Paterson, wife of Captain William Paterson, bring up her family (increased by two girls), and nurse her husband, as he suffered increasingly from gout, inflammation of the lungs,

difficulty in breathing, and stomach pain. However, despite his ill health, trouble associated with the ill discipline of the New South Wales Corps, and shortage of officials King was a success. After a visit the colony's chaplain, the Revd Samuel Marsden, reported to the Society for the Propagation of the Gospel in Foreign Parts that King's 'whole attention seems occupied in promoting the real interest' of the islanders (2 Jan 1796; *Historical Records of New South Wales*, 3.1). By 1796 King had built a girls' school and an orphanage, funded from customs duties. He had not been able to promote flax production, for two young Maori brought from New Zealand, said to be flax-dressers, told him that flax-dressing was 'woman's work', and they knew nothing about it. However, he restored the economy, which had deteriorated while he was away, and encouraged former marines and former convicts to cultivate land. By 1796 240 people occupied Norfolk Island, with 1500 acres cleared; there were nearly 5000 livestock, mainly swine, five-sixths of these privately owned, and nearly 350 people working as labourers. Although there was a shortage of labour for public works King had built a strong wharf, a large storehouse, barracks, a water-mill, and a government house. But his health had not improved, and he had to ask for sick leave. The Kings departed in October, reaching London next May, with another daughter, Elizabeth, born in February.

In England, King, now in better health, sent to Sir Joseph Banks and Lord Sydney the native plants he had brought with him, and set about obtaining another appointment. Supported by Arthur Phillip, Banks, and officials at both the Admiralty and the Home Office, King was given, in May 1798, a dormant commission to succeed John Hunter as governor of New South Wales at a salary of £1000 per annum. Although he had been given his sailing orders, lengthy discussions about the design of a ship that would carry Banks's plants for the colony and two false starts delayed his departure and strained his finances. He was promoted post captain in December but did not sail until November 1799 in the 300-ton whaler *Speedy*, with his wife and his daughter Elizabeth, leaving behind his three sons and his other surviving daughter.

King arrived in April 1800, but Hunter did not leave, much to the new governor's irritation. He could do little more than criticize Hunter, deplore the misbehaviour allegedly prevailing in Sydney, and reiterate his plans for reform, which included establishing a convict outstation, controlling the liquor trade more effectively, and encouraging sheep- and cattle-breeding, cloth manufacture, coalmining, wine-growing, and the budding whale and seal fisheries—and incidentally send Banks a pickled platypus (*Ornithorhynchus paradox*) to prove to the sceptics that such a creature existed. But on 28 September he assumed command.

The thriving fisheries were stimulated by the discoveries in Bass Strait in 1801–2 by lieutenants Grant and Murray, whom King had sent out from Sydney, and by Matthew Flinders on his voyage to circumnavigate Australia. Following their reports in May 1802, King wrote to London strongly recommending that a settlement be established at the newly discovered Port Phillip. This project (carried out by Captain David Collins but quickly abandoned), he argued, would reduce the number of convicts in Sydney, where he was worried by the arrival of so many Irish rebels, and would anticipate possible French designs in the area, of which the appearance of Nicolas Baudin's allegedly scientific expedition (political according to its hydrographer, François Peron) had made him suspicious. These fears led him in November 1802 to send a ship to King Island and examine Port Phillip again. In the following year he ordered the foundation of a settlement under Lieutenant Bowen on the River Derwent in Van Diemen's Land, which, founded in September 1803 and reinforced by Collins's party leaving Port Phillip in January 1804, quickly became an important whaling station. In 1804 King sent a party to Port Dalrymple, on the south side of Bass Strait, to investigate Port Phillip further while checking the appearance of Americans whaling and sealing there. King also continued exploration and expansion elsewhere. He helped to develop the pork and sandalwood trades in the Pacific. In 1801 he had sent a party to examine the Hunter River and establish a penal settlement there to exploit the coal, timber, and shells for lime—temporarily in 1801–2 and permanently in April 1804. Unfortunately expeditions of exploration to the west were less successful, as the Blue Mountains appeared an impossible barrier.

This was less important as long as the colony was regarded primarily as a penal settlement, though during King's term only about 2500 convicts arrived, nearly half in 1800–1. Of these about 500 were Irish rebels whom King feared might rebel again in the colony, as indeed about 300 did do in 1804, so he was relieved to ship off the most dangerous to either Newcastle or Norfolk Island. The low numbers of convicts meant fewer public works, with only about 200 men working on them; the majority were assigned to private employment. King reduced the number of government supported servants for military officers and officials from 250 to 58 and tightened the regulations controlling employers' treatment of their convicts. He also laid the foundation of the ticket-of-leave system for the well-behaved, believing that offenders were not consigned 'to Oblivion and disgrace for ever', but when emancipated became 'as Free and Susceptible to every Right as Free Born Britons as any Soul in the Territory' (*Historical Records of Australia*, 4.276).

Mindful of the need for economy in public expenditure and for more reliable food supplies, King encouraged agriculture by increasing land grants to private farmers and the assignment of convicts to private service. He insisted on licences for liquor imports and sent away two-fifths of the 170,000 gallons of spirits brought to Sydney while he was governor. He was also active in importing livestock for food, distributing 60 per cent to deserving settlers, and by the end of his term the area under wheat, maize, and barley had risen from 7000 to 11,000 acres—all under private (not government) cultivation—and virtually no farmer remained 'on the stores'. These measures, together with the fact that only a small number of convicts were arriving and others were completing their sentences, meant that he was able to reduce the proportion of people drawing government rations from about three-quarters to one-third, and despite an increase of 30 per cent in the total population, he drew 20 per cent less in treasury bills for stores than his predecessor John Hunter had done in 1796–8. He also encouraged the colony's infant industries—flour milling, salt extraction, tanneries and leather, woollen and cloth manufacture, agricultural implements, boat building, timber working, and brick making, though all these were necessarily on a small scale; King showed less interest in wool, though on instructions from London he granted more than 60,000 acres for the first time to assist pastoralists, especially John Macarthur and Samuel Marsden. On the debit side, he was in constant trouble with the officers of the New South Wales Corps and local liquor traders. The opening of an orphanage, financed by the (unauthorized) imposition of a 5 per cent import duty on spirits and all non-British goods, his convict policy, his permission for transported Irish priests to celebrate mass, and his establishment of the *Sydney Gazette* (censored though it was) to provide information though not 'political discussion' all show a progressive attitude to social policy.

King was a capable and conscientious administrator, and, though occasionally profiting from his position, did little unusual by eighteenth-century standards, and was a pillar of rectitude compared with almost all his subordinates—and many of his superiors in London. Sickness accentuated his hot temper, but he was plagued by incapable officials and an arrogant, insolent, and often disobedient military force, though his life in Sydney was greatly helped by the presence of Anna Josepha, a tower of strength in the management of 'Mrs King's Orphanage' and in many personal relationships; she was a very friendly hostess to both Matthew Flinders and Nicolas Baudin (later receiving a dessert service of Sèvres china) and a devoted nurse to her husband as his gout worsened and his general health declined while he waited two years for his successor, William Bligh, to arrive after King had submitted his resignation in 1804. When he did, King was unfit to travel, and could not sail before the *Buffalo* departed on 10 February 1807; he settled in Tooting, Surrey, and died in London on 3 September 1808, aged fifty, within a year of his arrival. He was buried in St Nicholas's churchyard, Lower Tooting. He was survived by his wife, his two natural sons, and four of his five legitimate children; his elder surviving daughter, Maria, married Hannibal Macarthur, cousin of his erstwhile opponent John, in 1812.

In May 1809 the Treasury granted Mrs King a pension—£265 per annum, reduced to £200 in 1810—and for some time she and the younger children lived in some poverty in Edgware Road, London, but in time her land and cattle in New South Wales, granted to her by Bligh when he assumed office, improved her financial situation. She longed to go back, but not until 1832 did she overcome the opposition of her children and return with her son Phillip to live with the Hannibal Macarthurs (and her eight grand-children) at Parramatta—a stately matriarch, as before caring for the local children and the sick and a pillar of the church. A very sensible woman, and one of the more useful and courageous pioneers of the colony, she died on 26 July 1844, aged seventy-nine.   A. G. L. SHAW

Sources DNB · [F. Watson], ed., *Historical records of Australia*, 1st ser., 1–7 (1914–16) · [F. Watson], ed., *Historical records of Australia*, 3rd ser., 1 (1921) · F. M. Bladen, ed., *Historical records of New South Wales*, 7 vols. (1892–1901) · A. G. L. Shaw, 'King, Philip Gidley', *AusDB*, vol. 5 · M. Bassett, *The governor's lady* (1956) · D. R. Hainsworth, *The Sydney traders* (1972) · F. Crowley, ed., *A new history of Australia* (1974) · F. Horner, *The French reconnaissance* (1987)
Archives Mitchell L., NSW, corresp. and papers · NL Aus., journal · State Library of New South Wales, Dixson Wing, corresp. · State Library of New South Wales, Dixson Wing, notes on Norfolk Island and naval signals | NL Aus., Banks MSS · NRA, priv. coll., corresp. with Sir Joseph Banks · State Library of New South Wales, Sydney, Mitchell Collection, corresp. with Sir Joseph Banks
Likenesses W. Skelton, line engraving, 1789 (after J. Wright), BM; repro. in A. Phillip, *Voyage of Governor Phillip to Botany Bay* (1789) · miniature, c.1800, Mitchell L., NSW
Wealth at death £2000: *Historical records of New South Wales*, vol. 6, p. 642

King, Phillip Parker (1791–1856), naval officer and hydrographer, born at Government House, Norfolk Island on 13 December 1791, was the third, but only legitimate, son of Captain Philip Gidley *King (1758–1808), naval officer and colonial governor. His mother was Captain King's wife, Anna Josepha, *née* Coombe (1764/5–1844). Arthur Phillips, governor of New South Wales, was his godfather. He went to England with his parents in 1796, and was educated there at the Revd Peter Thomas Burford's boarding school at Stratford Grove in Essex. Although granted a place at the Royal Naval Academy, Portsmouth, he failed to be admitted there. He entered the navy in November 1807, on the frigate *Diana*, and after six years of active service in the Bay of Biscay, the North Sea, and the Mediterranean, was promoted by Sir Edward Pellew to lieutenant of the *Trident* on 28 February 1814. On 29 January 1817 he married Harriet (d. 1874), one of the six daughters of Christopher Lethbridge of Madford, Launceston, Cornwall, deputy recorder of Launceston. They had eight children.

Early in 1817 King was appointed to survey the coast of Australia, and was sent out to take command of the *Mermaid*, a cutter of 84 tons, with eighteen officers and men. He arrived in Port Jackson in September 1817, and for the next five years was engaged, almost without intermission, on the survey. He examined and delineated the greater part of the west, north, and north-east coasts, and laid down a new route from Sydney to Torres Strait, inside the Barrier Reef. In December 1820 the *Mermaid* was found to be no longer seaworthy, and King was transferred to a newly purchased ship, which was renamed the *Bathurst*. This was about double the size of the *Mermaid*, and carried twice the number of men, but the work on which she was employed was essentially the same. King was promoted commander on 17 July 1821, but continued the survey

until April 1822. In September the *Bathurst* sailed for England, arriving in April 1823. King's voyages had made significant contributions to Australian exploration. For the next two years he was occupied with the narrative and the charts of his survey. The charts were published by the hydrographic office, and formed the basis of those used for the rest of the century. His *Narrative of the Survey of the Intertropical and Western Coasts of Australia* was published in 1827.

On 26 February 1824, King was elected FRS; he was also FLS. In September 1825 he was appointed to the *Adventure*, with instructions to survey 'the southern coast of South America from the Rio Plata round to Chiloe, and of Tierra del Fuego'. The *Adventure* was accompanied by the *Beagle*, commanded by Captain Stokes, and, after Stokes's death, by Captain Robert FitzRoy. During the four years from 1826 to 1830 the work was carried on with diligence and an exactness which established the reputations of both King and FitzRoy in the very first rank of hydrographers. King was advanced to post rank on 25 February 1830, and in the following November the two ships returned to England. In April and May 1831 King read an account of the results of his voyage before the Royal Geographical Society, and in 1832 published a volume of *Sailing directions to the coasts of eastern and western Patagonia, including the Straits of Magalhaen and the sea-coast of Tierra del Fuego*. In 1839 a more popular account of his and FitzRoy's voyage was published in the first volume of the *Voyages of the Adventure and Beagle*, edited by Captain FitzRoy.

King had no further service in the navy, but returned to New South Wales, where he had already been granted land, settled in Sydney, and entered busily into the sometimes dubious affairs of the colony; he was for many years commissioner of the Australian Agricultural Company, and a member of the legislative council. In September 1855 he became a rear-admiral on the retired list. Following an apoplectic fit he died at his home, Grantham Villa, North Sydney, on 26 February 1856.

J. K. LAUGHTON, *rev.* ANDREW LAMBERT

Sources G. S. Ritchie, *The Admiralty chart: British naval hydrography in the nineteenth century* (1967) · M. Gillen, *The founders of Australia* (1989) · O'Byrne, *Naval biog. dict.* · J. Marshall, *Royal naval biography*, 3/2 (1832), 200–26 · *GM*, 3rd ser., 1 (1856), 246–7 · *AusDB* · M. Hordern, *King of the Australian coast: the work of Phillip Parker King in the Mermaid and Bathurst 1817–1822* (1997)
Archives Admiralty Library, logbooks · Mitchell L., NSW, corresp. and papers · Naval Library, London · RBG Kew, chart · State Library of New South Wales, Sydney, Dixson Wing, letters and map | NL Aus., corresp. relating to Parramatta observatory · RBG Kew, letters to Sir William Hooker
Likenesses portrait, oils, c.1816, priv. coll.; repro. in M. Hordern, *King of the Australian coast* (1997), facing p. 10 · T. Woolner, plaster relief, 1825–9, Art Gallery of New South Wales, Sydney, Australia · miniature, c.1826, priv. coll.; repro. in M. Hordern, *King of the Australian coast* (1997), facing p. 394

King, (Hubert) Raymond (1897–1983), head teacher, was born at 72 Jarratt Street, Doncaster, Yorkshire, on 25 December 1897, the son of Harry King, a railway clerk, and his wife, Emily Howard. He attended King Edward VI School in East Retford, Nottinghamshire, until the age of eighteen, when he left to join the army. He served with distinction on the western front, where he was awarded the Military Medal, the Belgian Croix de Guerre, and the Distinguished Conduct Medal. He refused to be commissioned as an officer, preferring to remain among the men, but accepted the rank of temporary company sergeant-major.

In 1919 King entered Magdalene College, Cambridge, where he took a first class in part one of the historical tripos and studied English during his third year, gaining a second. After graduating in 1922 he completed a one-year teacher training course based at the Cambridge University education department and successfully submitted a thesis for the university diploma in education. He completed his teaching practice at Westminster School and, in 1923, was appointed to the staff of Portsmouth grammar school. Just three years later, at the age of twenty-eight, he was appointed headmaster of Scarborough high school, a selective grammar school, where he introduced a system of regular 'diligence' assessments, based upon pupils' effort and improvement rather than attainment. In 1932 he moved to London to become headmaster of Wandsworth Boys' Grammar School. He was to remain at the school until his retirement in 1963. During this period, however, the character of the school dramatically changed from that of a three-form selective entry institution to one of the largest comprehensive schools in England.

During the 1920s and 1930s King became aware of arguments for widening access to secondary education, such as those set out in R. H. Tawney's pamphlet for the Labour Party, *Secondary Education for All* (1922), and in the 1926 Hadow report, *The Education of the Adolescent*. A number of teacher unions, including King's own association, the Incorporated Association of Head Masters, went further by challenging the principle of eleven-plus selection and supporting the establishment of secondary 'multilateral' or 'comprehensive' schools. For a period King kept an open mind about these questions, but during the Second World War, when the staff and boys of the Wandsworth school were evacuated to several scattered centres in the Surrey countryside, he became an active participant in many debates concerning post-war educational reconstruction. In 1942 King and three other London county council (LCC) grammar school head teachers published *A Democratic Reconstruction of Education*, a 15,000-word pamphlet, which directly led to the founding of the Conference for the Democratic Reconstruction of Education. King was the first chairman of this organization, which called for the absorption of public schools into local systems of education and the introduction of comprehensive education. The enthusiasm of the conference for comprehensive schooling was shared by another organization chaired by King, the English New Education Fellowship (ENEF). In 1950 King was the unattributed author of a widely circulated ENEF pamphlet, simply entitled *The Comprehensive School*.

Although in 1947 the LCC committed itself, in the London school plan, to the long-term development of a fully comprehensive system, early progress depended upon the co-operation of liberal-minded grammar school heads such as King. Acting largely on his own initiative, rather than following instructions from County Hall, King modified Wandsworth's pupil intake to include boys who had not originally been selected for a grammar school education from age eleven. After successfully absorbing a group of boys from the junior technical branch of the Brixton School of Building in 1947, a further non-grammar form was introduced in the following year. By 1955 there were three such non-selective first-year groups in addition to the cohort of boys who had entered the school as a result of passing the eleven-plus examination. In order to advance along the lines indicated in the London school plan, the LCC then announced that Wandsworth would become one of five showpiece comprehensives which had formerly been grammar schools. King relished the challenges associated with the transition to a comprehensive school and, with the support of his staff and governors, prepared for the amalgamation with a local technical school in the autumn of 1956.

Wandsworth comprehensive school was a vast, fifteen-form entry institution, attended by some 2130 boys. In terms of organization, like many large urban comprehensives, the lower and upper schools were located in separate buildings and a 'house' grouping system, for which King was a great enthusiast, operated throughout the school. Predictably, after 1956 he was in great demand as a public speaker and commentator. In 1958 he joined the editorial board of *Forum*, a journal founded by Robin Pedley, Brian Simon, and Jack Walton for the purpose of promoting comprehensive education. King wrote regularly for *Forum* and in 1964, having retired from Wandsworth, he became chair of the editorial board.

King was also active at an international level. Before the Second World War he was an enthusiastic youth hosteller and arranged exchanges with schools in Germany and Sweden. In 1945 he represented Rotary International at a conference of UNESCO. Later he served as education adviser to the United Kingdom National Commission for UNESCO, and from 1947 to 1961 he chaired its textbooks sub-committee. He continued to attend European conferences into his eighties. Latterly he lived at New Malden, Surrey. King died at Kingston Hospital, Kingston upon Thames, Surrey, on 21 March 1983, leaving a widow, Mary, herself an active member of the ENEF, and a son, Lionel.

DAVID CROOK

Sources B. Simon, *Does education matter?* (1985), chap. 7, 152–72 • R. Waters, 'Raymond King: a personal appreciation', *Forum*, 26/1 (1983), 24–5 • *The Times* (7 April 1983) • b. cert. • d. cert.
Wealth at death £97,118: probate, 20 July 1983, *CGPLA Eng. & Wales*

King, Sir Richard, first baronet (1730–1806), naval officer, was born at Gosport, Hampshire, on 10 August 1730, the third but first surviving son of Curtis King (d. 1745), master in the navy and afterwards master-attendant at Woolwich Dockyard, and Mary (fl. c.1700–c.1750), daughter of Lieutenant Benjamin Barnett RN (d. 1703), and sister of Commodore Curtis *Barnett.

King entered the navy in 1738 on the *Berwick* (70 guns), of

Sir Richard King, first baronet (1730–1806), by William Grimaldi, 1792

which his father was master, but he was soon moved to the *Dragon* (60 guns), commanded by his uncle, Barnett, whom he accompanied to the Mediterranean. He returned to England in the summer of 1742. In March 1744 he joined Barnett in the *Deptford* (60 guns), and in January 1745 took part in the capture of three French East-Indiamen in the Strait of Banca, which the governor of Batavia bought for £92,000. Probably as a result of this action King was promoted lieutenant on 1 February 1745. Other prizes followed before Barnett reached Madras where he died in April 1746. King returned to England at the end of the war, but in 1754 he again went to the East Indies, as lieutenant of the *Tiger* (60 guns), from which he was moved by the commander-in-chief, Rear-Admiral Charles Watson into the flagship *Kent* (70 guns) as first lieutenant. King was thus at the taking and destruction of the pirate stronghold of Gheria in February 1756, capturing stores, money and valuables to the value of approximately £130,000; and on 23 July 1756 he was promoted commander of the fireship *Blaze*, bought by the admiral the previous day. Unfortunately the *Blaze* sprang a leak and was sent to Bombay for repairs so that King was merely a volunteer, though an active one, in the capture of Calcutta Fort in December 1756.

King took an equally active part and commanded the boats and landing party at the capture of the city of Hooghly, 30 miles north of Calcutta, on 10 January 1757. His courage and promptitude pleased Watson who, in February, as a mark of favour, sent him home with dispatches, in the sloop *Pilot*, with a strong recommendation to Earl Temple, the first lord of the Admiralty. King made an exceptionally swift passage, never stopping until he reached England in July 1757. The first lord, now Lord Anson, appreciative of zeal and activity in an officer, immediately ordered King to the West Indies in the sloop *Bonetta*, from which he was posted, by Commodore John Moore, to the frigate *Rye* (24 guns) on 29 January 1759. Moore's squadron, reinforced in January 1759 for an attack on the French islands, made an unsuccessful attack on Martinique but captured Guadeloupe in May. In that month King was moved to the *Ludlow Castle* (40 guns) and

sent home with a convoy; and in the following January he was appointed to the frigate *Argo* (28 guns), in which he cruised with some success on the coast of France and in the North Sea.

On the outbreak of war with Spain in 1762 an attack on the Philippines was planned and King was chosen to convey General Draper to the East Indies, where he arrived in June. He took part in the expedition to Manila, which set sail on 6 October, and on 31 October, with Captain Hyde Parker, he captured the *Santissima Trinidad*, an immensely rich galleon from Manila. Parker and King had hoped to take the annual Acapulco galleon, the *Santa Philippina*, but, missing her, had chanced on an almost equally golden prize. The total prize money was estimated at $3 million (more than £600,000), and King's personal share was more than £30,000. In 1763 he returned, with the galleon, to England, commanding the *Grafton* (68 guns). It was this fortune and the consequent rise in status which enabled him, on 30 November 1769, to marry Susannah Margaretta Coker (d. 1794), daughter of William Coker of Mappowder, Dorset. The couple had three daughters and a son, Richard *King, naval officer.

During the Falklands crisis with Spain in 1770 King commanded the *Northumberland* (68 guns). Following a series of short-term commands in early 1778 he was appointed to the *Pallas* (36 guns) in which he convoyed the Quebec trade to Canada; he then formed part of a successful expedition, with Commodore John Evans, against the French islands of St Pierre and Miquelon, before returning to England in command of the *Europe* (64 guns). In January 1779 he was appointed to the *Exeter* (64 guns), part of Sir Edward Hughes's squadron which sailed in March for the East Indies and captured the French west African trading station of Goree *en route*. On arrival King was ordered to wear a broad pennant as an established commodore and second in command. Thereafter he was at the taking of Negapatam in November 1781 and of Trincomalee from the Dutch in January 1782, and in all Hughes's actions with the French commander Suffren. In that off Sadras, 17 February 1782, the *Exeter* was the rearmost ship of the English line. For some time she was attacked by four French ships and severely mauled, being almost entirely dismasted, receiving several shot below the waterline, and having ten men killed and 47 wounded. As the flag captain, Reynolds, was killed, his brains were dashed in King's face, temporarily blinding him. The master, seeing two more enemy ships bearing down on the *Exeter*, asked what they should do. Wiping his face with his handkerchief, King replied, 'There is nothing to be done but to fight her till she sinks' (*DNB*). A lucky shift of wind, however, allowed the British van to tack to the assistance of their rear, the *Exeter* was rescued by the *Hero*, and the French withdrew. The other actions between Hughes and Suffren were on 12 April, 6 July, and 3 September 1782—in this last the *Exeter* was again engaged by four French ships—and 20 June 1783. The *Exeter* played a distinguished part in all these naval battles, having a total of 178 men killed and wounded. King himself was unhurt, though in the action of 20 June a shot struck the speaking trumpet out of his hand. So badly damaged was the *Exeter* that, on the passage home with nine sail of the line, she was condemned at the Cape of Good Hope as unseaworthy, and King moved to the *Hero* for the remainder of the passage. He arrived in England in May 1784, and was knighted on 2 June.

Peace brought unemployment, but on 24 September 1787 he was promoted rear-admiral of the white. In September 1789 he applied to William Pitt for a baronetcy, 'in consideration of long and faithful service at sea and a firm attachment to his Majesty's person and government' (HoP, *Commons*, 4.337). On 24 June 1790 he wrote again, urging his attachment to the present government, in the recent election. King had gone to Portsmouth to vote for the government candidate, despite a fever. Ignoring both comfort and dignity he made the journey from the Downs in the sloop *Wasp* 'because the captain had a vote for the county, that he might be in a convenient situation to attend the election' (ibid.).

Whether this was decisive or not, King was promoted rear-admiral of the red on 21 September 1790 and commander-in-chief at the Downs. In the mobilization of the fleet at Spithead in 1791 he was given a junior command in the *St George*. He was made a baronet on 18 July 1792 and appointed governor and commander-in-chief at Newfoundland until 1794. In the same year he was returned unopposed as MP for Rochester. King is reputed to have spent about £5000 in these elections, and on standing again in May 1796, when he won handsomely, he referred to his exertions on behalf of his constituents, but he made no impact in the Commons and retired in 1802.

King had repeatedly applied to Pitt for promotion and in 1796 he made an unsuccessful application for the governorship of Greenwich Hospital. Having become vice-admiral of the red in July 1793, he was promoted admiral of the blue on 1 June 1795, admiral of the white on 14 February 1799, and finally admiral of the red on 9 November 1805. This was a considerable achievement for someone of King's social background, and illustrates how connections, courage, and luck could make a naval career the path to professional and social advancement. King's naval career had been distinguished and lucrative. He invested in East India Company stock and at his death was worth approximately £35,000. He died on 27 November 1806 at his London house, 39 Devonshire Place, Marylebone, and was buried at Marylebone church on 4 December.

P. K. CRIMMIN

Sources J. Charnock, ed., *Biographia navalis*, 6 (1798), 369–73 · J. Ralfe, *The naval biography of Great Britain*, 1 (1828), 225–30 · D. Syrett and R. L. DiNardo, *The commissioned sea officers of the Royal Navy, 1660–1815*, rev. edn, Occasional Publications of the Navy RS, 1 (1994) · P. A. Symonds, 'King, Richard', HoP, *Commons, 1790–1820* · W. L. Clowes, *The Royal Navy: a history from the earliest times to the present*, 7 vols. (1897–1903), vols. 3–4 · H. Richmond, *The war in India, 1763–83* (1931) · GEC, *Baronetage*, 5.279 · J. Hutchins, *The history and antiquities of the county of Dorset*, 3rd edn, ed. W. Shipp and J. W. Hodson, 3 (1868), 723 · D. Lyon, *The sailing navy list: all the ships of the Royal Navy, built, purchased and captured, 1688–1860* (1993)
Archives Yale U., letter and order books
Likenesses W. Grimaldi, miniature, 1792, NPG [*see illus.*] · plaster medallion, 1804 (after W. Tassie), Scot. NPG · W. Beechey, portrait; formerly in possession of the family, 1892 · Ridley, lithograph (after a miniature), repro. in Clowes, *The Royal Navy*, vol. 3, p. 240
Wealth at death approx. £35,000 through East India stock: Symonds, 'King, Richard'

King, Richard (1748–1810), Church of England clergyman, was born in the parish of St Augustine, Bristol, on 30 November 1748, the son of Henry King, who lived in that parish. He was admitted scholar of Winchester College in 1762, matriculated at Oxford University from Queen's College on 4 April 1767, and was elected fellow of New College in 1768; he graduated BA in 1772, and proceeded MA in 1776. In 1782 he resigned his fellowship, and received the college livings of Worthen, Shropshire, and Steeple Morden, Cambridgeshire. On 17 August 1782 he married Frances Elizabeth Bernard (1757–1821) [*see* King, Frances Elizabeth], third daughter of Sir Francis Bernard, governor of Massachusetts Bay. His wife was a philanthropist and devotional writer. According to an obituary, King was 'eminently orthodox and loyal: he was a strenuous assertor of the rights of the establishment of which he was a member' (*GM*, 80/2, 1810, 589).

King wrote *A Discourse on the Inspiration of the Scriptures* (1805). Two years later *Remarks on the Alliance between Church and State, and on the Test Laws* appeared. Another work, *Brother Abraham's Answer to Peter Plymley* (1808), was a reply to Sydney Smith's book of letters on the subject of Catholics, addressed to a brother (Abraham), who lived in the country. King died at Steeple Morden, Cambridgeshire, on 30 October 1810.

GORDON GOODWIN, rev. ROBERT BROWN

Sources *GM*, 1st ser., 80 (1810), 589 · *GM*, 1st ser., 92/1 (1822), 90 · Foster, *Alum. Oxon.*
Archives Bucks. RLSS, letters to Bernard Scrope

King, Sir Richard, second baronet (1774–1834), naval officer, was born on 28 November 1774, the only son of Admiral Sir Richard *King, first baronet (1730–1806), and his wife, Susannah Margaretta (*d.* 1794), daughter of William Coker, of Mappowder, Dorset. He entered the navy in 1788 on the *Crown* in the East Indies with Commodore Cornwallis, by whom he was made lieutenant on 14 November 1791, commander in 1793, and captain on 14 May 1794. On his return to England he was appointed in November 1794 to the *Aurora* (28 guns), for cruising service in the channel. He commanded different ships with credit in the channel and the North Sea. King married, in 1803, Sarah Anne (*d.* 1819), only daughter of Vice-Admiral Sir John Thomas Duckworth; they had four sons and one daughter. In April 1804 he was appointed to the *Achille* (74 guns), in which, on 21 October 1805, he served at Trafalgar.

On the death of his father in November 1806, King succeeded to the baronetcy, but continued in the *Achille*, employed on the west coast of France and Spain until 1811, when he was appointed captain of the fleet to Sir Charles Cotton in the Mediterranean, and afterwards in the channel. He was promoted rear-admiral on 12 August 1812, and for the rest of the war had his flag in the *San Josef* (110 guns), in the Mediterranean, as second in command to Sir Edward Pellew. He was made a KCB on 2 January 1815, was commander-in-chief in the East Indies from 1816 to 1820, and became vice-admiral on 19 July 1821. In 1822, he married Maria Susanna (*d.* 8 January 1871), daughter of Admiral Sir Charles Cotton; they had four sons and three daughters. In July 1833 he was appointed commander-in-chief at the Nore. He died of cholera at Admiralty House, Sheerness, on 5 August 1834.

King's second son from his first marriage, Admiral **Sir George St Vincent Duckworth King**, fourth baronet (1809–1891), naval officer, was born at Stonehouse, Devon, on 15 July 1809, entered the Royal Naval College in February 1822, served in the Mediterranean, East Indies, and West Indies, and was promoted captain in 1841. He married on 16 December 1847 Lady Caroline Mary Dawson-Damer (*d.* 5 December 1851), sister of the third earl of Portarlington; they had a son and a daughter. He was captain of the *Leander*, and afterwards of the *Rodney*, in the Black Sea during the Crimean War in 1854–5, and was second in command of the naval brigade at the siege of Sevastopol. He became rear-admiral in 1863, was commander-in-chief in China from 1863 to 1867, and was made vice-admiral in 1867, KCB in May 1873, and admiral in 1875. He succeeded to the baronetcy on the death of his elder brother on 2 November 1887. He died at Wear House, Exeter, on 18 August 1891.   J. K. LAUGHTON, rev. ANDREW LAMBERT

Sources D. Syrett and R. L. DiNardo, *The commissioned sea officers of the Royal Navy, 1660–1815*, rev. edn, Occasional Publications of the Navy RS, 1 (1994) • O'Byrne, *Naval biog. dict.* • *United Service Journal*, 3 (1834), 232 • J. Marshall, *Royal naval biography*, 1/2 (1823), 545 • J. Ralfe, *The naval biography of Great Britain*, 3 (1828) • Boase, *Mod. Eng. biog.* • Burke, *Peerage* (1894) • *GM*, 2nd ser., 2 (1834)
Archives BL, letters to Lord Bridport, Add. MSS 35196–35198 • NMM, corresp. with Sir Evan Nepean
Likenesses C. Turner, mezzotint, pubd 1835 (after Saunders), BM; NPG • W. Ridley, stipple (after a miniature), BM; repro. in *Naval Chronicle* (1803)

King, Richard (1810/11–1876), Arctic traveller and ethnologist, was born in London, the son of Richard King. He was educated at St Paul's School, London, and in 1824 began a seven-year apprenticeship to an apothecary. In 1832 he was made licentiate of the Society of Apothecaries and member of the Royal College of Surgeons. He was appointed surgeon and naturalist to the expedition led by George Back to look for John Ross, who had been gone four years on a search for the north-west passage. Although only second in command, King had a much more arduous share of the work than Back and was largely responsible for the success of the expedition. Back's *Narrative* (2 vols., 1836) contains meteorological and botanical appendices by King who also wrote his own *Narrative* (2 vols., 1836). King's is in many respects the better book, since he showed a far deeper understanding of the indigenous peoples of the Arctic and did not indulge in dramatic exaggeration. His narrative made clear that, had the journey been better organized, more could have been accomplished. He resolved to return and complete his discoveries, a resolution which remained unfulfilled, not least because Back prevented his gaining the support of potential sponsors. In 1836 King proposed an expedition to clear up the uncertainty surrounding the Boothia isthmus, which he rightly

suspected was the extreme north-eastern point of the continent. After the colonial secretary rejected his proposal, King took the highly unusual step of opening a public subscription for the £1000 he needed. The subscription went well until the Admiralty and the Hudson's Bay Company each decided to send an expedition to the area, neither under King's command but both, as he thought, inspired by him. The Admiralty expedition was a failure but the company, using the methods and even some of the personnel that King had suggested, achieved complete success. In 1842 King again proposed an expedition and was again rebuffed.

King took great interest in Franklin's expedition and was one of the first to raise the alarm when he failed to return. He insisted, at first on very slender evidence, that Franklin's party would be found near the mouth of the Great Fish River. His opinion was discounted and in 1847 and 1856 his offer to lead a search party was refused. His loud and continued insistence on the need to search his favoured site increased the animosity of the Admiralty, the Hudson's Bay Company, and the Royal Geographical Society, who were also irritated by popular journals which took up King's point of view. Matters were not helped by King's *Franklin Search from First to Last* (1855) which set out his own convictions and dwelt on the obduracy of those who would not listen to him. Franklin's party was finally found by M'Clintock in 1859 in the spot King had suggested eleven years earlier. The delay, however, probably made no material difference since, even if his advice been taken immediately, it would probably have come too late to save any of Franklin's men.

King took no further part in Arctic affairs but was active in his profession and in learned societies, notably the Ethnological Society (later the Royal Anthropological Society), which he helped found in 1842. He served on the council and contributed several valuable works on the Inuit (1844), North American Indians (1869), Manxmen (1870), and the Sami (1871). His medical works on the cause of death in stillborn babies and on cholera were much respected at the time and he received several medical honours. In 1857 he married Elizabeth Lumley and they had at least one son, Richard. He died at his home at 1 Blandford Street, Manchester Square, London, of cerebral congestion on 4 February 1876.   ELIZABETH BAIGENT

Sources H. N. Wallace, *The navy, the company and Richard King: British exploration in the Canadian Arctic, 1829–1860* (1980) • *DCB*, vol. 10 • Boase, *Mod. Eng. biog.* • *Medical Times and Gazette* (12 Feb 1876), 240 • *The Athenaeum* (12 Feb 1876), 236 • d. cert.

King, Richard John (1818–1879), antiquary, eldest son of Richard King (*d.* 1829) and his wife, Mary Grace Windeatt (1798–1884), was born on 18 January 1818 at Montpelier, Pennycross, a chapelry attached to St Andrew, Plymouth. He matriculated at Exeter College, Oxford, on 17 November 1836, and graduated BA in 1841. On his father's death he inherited considerable property, including the estate of Bigadon in Buckfastleigh, Devon, where he lived until 1854. However, the lands were heavily mortgaged, and in that year King was forced by financial pressures to sell them, as well as his father's collection of pictures and the magnificent library which he himself had built up. He then moved to The Limes, Crediton, where he supported himself by writing. King's literary career had started early. While still an undergraduate, he printed in 1840, for private distribution, thirty-three copies of two lectures read before the Essay Society of Exeter College. Their subjects were 'The supernatural beings of the Middle Ages' and 'The origin of the romance literature of the twelfth and thirteenth centuries'. To the *Oxford Essays* for 1856 he contributed a paper on 'Carlovingian romance'. His first separate publication was *Selections from Early Ballad Poetry* (1842), with many notes and preliminary observations. In 1850 he published an anonymous novel entitled *Anschar: a Story of the North*: set in the viking period, it met with no great success. In 1856 he published the first two chapters of an intended history of Devon, under the title of *The Forest of Dartmoor and its Borders: an Historical Sketch*.

King was elected a member of the Devonshire Association in 1874, and served as president in 1875, when his address dealt with the early history of the county. He contributed several papers to the association's *Transactions*, and at the time of his death was on no fewer than eight of its special committees. With several other members he was involved in translating and editing the *Devonshire Domesday*.

King was a large contributor to Murray's series of handbooks to the English counties. He prepared handbooks on Kent and Sussex (1858), on Surrey and Hampshire and the Isle of Wight (1858), and on Essex, Suffolk, Norfolk, and Cambridgeshire (1870). He also worked on Yorkshire (1866–8), Northamptonshire (1872–7), Warwickshire and Hertfordshire (1872–5), and the fifth and later editions of Devon and Cornwall. He was the leading writer in the same publisher's series of Handbooks to the Cathedrals of England (1861–9) and in the subsequent volume on the *Cathedrals of Wales* (1873). Sections of both the county and cathedral handbooks were also issued separately. For many years King was a regular contributor to the *Saturday Review*, the *Quarterly Review*, and *Fraser's Magazine*. A selection from his articles, including his early paper on 'Carlovingian romance', was published in 1874 under the title of *Sketches and Studies*. King also frequently wrote for *The Academy* and *Notes and Queries*, and contributed to the ninth edition of the *Encyclopaedia Britannica*. The first five parts of *Our Own Country* (1878–83) were written by him for Cassel & Co., and he assisted in the compilation of *Picturesque Europe* (1876–9). His paper on 'Bristol Cathedral' appeared in volume 3 of the *Transactions of the Bristol and Gloucestershire Archaeological Society*, and a letter by him, 'On the family and parentage of Judhael de Totnais', is in W. Cotton's *A Graphic and Historical Sketch of the Antiquities of Totnes* (1850).

King died at his home, The Limes, Crediton, on 10 February 1879, and was buried in Crediton churchyard. The stained-glass east window of the lady chapel was dedicated to his memory. The east window and four smaller windows in Buckfastleigh church were given by him while he was living at Bigadon.

W. P. COURTNEY, *rev.* IAN MAXTED

Sources *Report and Transactions of the Devonshire Association*, 11 (1879), 58–60 · W. P. Courtney, *The Academy* (22 Feb 1879), 165 · *N&Q*, 5th ser., 11 (1879), 180 · W. H. K. Wright, *West-country poets* (1896), 292–5 · H. Starkey, 'Richard John King, 1818–1879', *Dartmoor Magazine*, 15 (1989), 26–7 · B. Mann, 'Introduction', in R. J. King, *The hill farm: a Dartmoor idyll* (1993) · private information (1892) · *CGPLA Eng. & Wales* (1879)

Archives Devon RO, drawings and notes

Wealth at death under £300: probate, 22 March 1879, *CGPLA Eng. & Wales*

King, Robert (*d.* 1557), abbot of Thame and bishop of Oxford, was the second son of William King of Thame, yeoman, who was still living in 1508. He became a monk at the Cistercian abbey of Rewley, near Oxford, spending some of his time studying at St Bernard's College before obtaining his bachelor degree in theology in February 1507. He was university preacher on Passion Sunday 1512. In May 1515 he was appointed abbot of Bruern, also in Oxfordshire, and he became doctor of theology in March 1519. John Longland, bishop of Lincoln between 1521 and 1547, was a patron of King, and it was due to the bishop that he became abbot of Thame, probably in 1527 (the year in which he resigned from Bruern), following serious complaints about the previous abbot. On 7 January 1527 King was made a suffragan to the bishop of Lincoln with the title Reonensis (from the diocese of Rheon in the province of Constantinople), while on 15 April 1535 he received the prebend of Crackpole St Mary in Lincoln Cathedral, exchanging it in November 1536 for that of Biggleswade; he held the latter until 1542. In 1530 he is also recorded as vicar of Charlbury in Oxfordshire.

On 22 December 1537, although he was a Cistercian, King was elected abbot of the Augustinian house of Osney, an appointment organized by John London and John Tregonwell, themselves acting on the instructions of Thomas Cromwell, to whom King was connected by the marriage of his brother William to Anne Williams, a relative of Cromwell's. This election was made simply to facilitate the abbey's surrender, which took place on 17 November 1539, the day after that of Thame.

King's reward was the new bishopric of Osney and Thame founded on 1 September 1542. He surrendered his office on 20 May 1545, but had his diocesan status renewed on 26 January 1546, when the new diocese of Oxford was established, with the former priory church of St Frideswide (part of the new college of Christ Church) replacing Osney as its cathedral. As bishop of Osney and Thame King lived both at Gloucester Hall in Oxford and at Thame Park (as his former monastery became known). Gloucester Hall did not, however, form part of the endowment of the bishopric of Oxford, and after Thame Park was conveyed to Sir John (later Lord) Williams of Thame, the brother of Anne Williams and an associate of King's, in July 1547, it is not clear where the bishop lived.

King remained bishop of Oxford throughout the reigns of Edward VI and Mary, apparently adjusting his religious convictions to suit the climate of the times, although his attendance at the trial of Thomas Cranmer in 1555 as one of the 'persecuting bishops that died before Queen Mary' (*Acts and Monuments*, 8.636) is at least consistent with his having preached a sermon at Stamford some seventeen years previously denouncing those who read the New Testament in English.

Whatever King's doctrinal beliefs, his status as a patron of architecture is demonstrated by his work at Thame Park, probably of *c*.1530, where his three-storey tower completed the abbot's lodging range begun by his predecessor, John Warren; the most notable feature of the tower is the parlour, in which Renaissance panels of arabesques, roundels, mermaids, putti, and the like constitute a splendid sight above the rich linenfold panelling below. A heraldic frieze displays King's connections, with the arms of Norreys, Fermor, Longland, and others, as well as those of the crown, being represented alongside his own initials. Given this Italianate taste it is perhaps surprising that after King died, on 4 December 1557, he should have been interred in a tomb in Oxford Cathedral which is entirely Gothic in character, comprising an elaborately traceried tomb chest with vaulted canopy. It now stands in the south transept. NICHOLAS DOGGETT

Sources VCH Oxfordshire, 2.81, 85–6; 7.169, 177 · LP Henry VIII, 4/3, no. 5189; 12/1, no. 360; 12/2, no. 1246; 17, no. 881 (p. 490) · Wood, *Ath. Oxon.*, new edn, 2.774–5 · F. G. Lee, *The history, description and antiquities of the prebendal church of the Blessed Virgin Mary of Thame* (1883) · G. G. Perry, 'The visitation of the monastery of Thame, 1526', *EngHR*, 3 (1888), 704–22 · W. Godfrey, 'The abbot's parlour, Thame Park', *Archaeological Journal*, 86 (1929), 59–68 · W. H. Stevenson and H. E. Salter, *The early history of St John's College, Oxford*, OHS, new ser., 1 (1939), 30, 46 · *Oxfordshire*, Pevsner (1974), 80, 121, 809–11 · J. Strype, *Memorials of the most reverend father in God, Thomas Cranmer* (1694), 52, 481, 1649 · C. Platt, *The abbeys and priories of medieval England* (1984), 214, 217–18 · *The acts and monuments of John Foxe*, new edn, ed. G. Townsend, 8 (1849), 636 · J. E. Thorold Rogers, ed., *Oxford city documents, financial and judicial, 1268–1665*, OHS, 18 (1891), 133 · Emden, *Oxf.*, 2.1072 · will, PRO, PROB 11/42B, sig. 13 · monument, Oxford Cathedral
Likenesses attrib. B. Van Linge, stained-glass window, Christ Church Oxf.
Wealth at death see will, 1557, PRO, PROB 11/42B, sig. 13

King, Sir Robert (*d.* 1657), politician, was the eldest son of Sir John *King (*d.* 1637) of Boyle Abbey, co. Roscommon, and his wife, Catherine Drury. He succeeded his father as muster-master-general of Ireland in 1618, was knighted in 1621, and served in the administration of Ireland throughout the 1620s and 1630s. King married twice. His first wife, Frances Folliott, the daughter of Henry Folliott, first Baron Folliott, of Ballyshannon, died on 13 March 1638. His second wife, Sophia Cecil (*c*.1618–1691), the daughter of Sir Edward Zouch of Woking, Surrey, had married Edward *Cecil, Viscount Wimbledon, in 1635 and was left a rich young widow on Wimbledon's death in November 1638. Cecil (or Wimbledon) House on the Strand was to be King's residence in London in the 1640s and 1650s and the place where he was to die.

Elected for the borough of Boyle in the Irish parliaments of 1634 and 1640, King played no part in the initial attack on the earl of Strafford, and gave evidence against his old master only once he had been called to London as a witness. In the event, his account of Strafford's tyrannical intentions, and his support of Sir Henry Vane's evidence 'that the army in Ireland should be employed against England' (BL, Harleian MS 164, fol. 153), was an important factor in bringing about the lord lieutenant's execution.

King was still in London at the outbreak of the Irish rising in October 1641, but in 1642 he returned to Roscommon, where he fought in the battle of Ballintobber. In April 1643 he travelled to Oxford with William Jephson and Arthur Hill, hoping to persuade Charles I to allow parliament to raise more money for the Irish war. Their failure confirmed King in his support of parliament, and in the summer of 1643 he was appointed to a council of war for Ireland, and he continued to give advice to the various Irish committees. He had taken the solemn league and covenant by late 1644, and in January 1645 Charles I finally dismissed him as muster-master-general, saying that he was 'a person disaffected to us, having taken the Covenant and adhering to the rebels' (Bodl. Oxf., MS Carte 13, fol. 528r). In April 1645 King was appointed one of parliament's Ulster commissioners, with orders to direct the war effort and liaise with the Scottish commanders in the province. From November 1645 the Ulster commissioners were involved in attempts to persuade the king's lord lieutenant, the marquess of Ormond (James Butler), to join the parliamentarians. Ormond's decision to make peace with the Irish confederates in the summer of 1646 was a set-back, but the collapse of the 'Ormond peace' soon afterwards gave King and his colleagues another chance. In September King was named one of the five commissioners who would reopen peace talks with Ormond. In June 1647 an agreement was finally concluded, and the lord lieutenant surrendered Dublin to parliament. King's position during these negotiations was ambiguous. He was loyal to parliament but was also considered to be one of Ormond's friends, and he corresponded privately with the lord lieutenant during the negotiations. King also remained aloof from the factionalism of Westminster, and his primary concern seems to have been the survival of the protestant interest in Ireland.

This overriding concern for the fate of Ireland also characterized King's reaction to the 'revolution' of the late 1640s and early 1650s. He was apparently happy to serve parliament after the execution of the king, and he advised Oliver Cromwell in his invasion of Ireland in August 1649. He was reappointed muster-master-general in November 1649, and returned in early 1651 to Ireland, where he helped to organize the pay and supply the army. During this period he cemented his ties with the Irish protestant community with a series of marriages for his children with leading families such as the Cootes, Merediths, and Fentons. His strong ties with the regime and the Irish protestants made him an influential figure in the early Cromwellian parliaments: he was chosen to represent Ireland in the nominated assembly of 1653, and sat for Sligo, Leitrim, and Roscommon in the parliament of 1654. He was elected for the same seat in 1656, and was expected to play an important part in the forthcoming parliament. King duly travelled to England, but fell ill in the winter of 1656–7 and died in June 1657. He was succeeded by his son, Sir John *King, who became Lord Kingston in 1660.

PATRICK LITTLE

Sources HoP, *Commons, 1640–60* [draft] · Bodl. Oxf., MSS Carte · *CSP Ire.*, 1625–57 · *CSP dom.*, 1644–56 · *Report on the manuscripts of the earl of Egmont*, 2 vols. in 3, HMC, 63 (1905–9), vol. 1 · R. Dunlop, ed., *Ireland under the Commonwealth*, 2 vols. (1913) · *JHC*, 2–7 (1640–59) · Sheffield University Library, Hartlib MSS · *Report on the manuscripts of the late Reginald Rawdon Hastings*, 4 vols., HMC, 78 (1928–47) · G. Radcliffe, *The earl of Strafforde's letters and dispatches, with an essay towards his life*, ed. W. Knowler, 2 vols. (1739) · PRO, PROB 11/265, fols. 120–21 · J. Lodge, *The peerage of Ireland*, 4 (1754) · 'Kingston', GEC, *Peerage* · 'Wimbledon', GEC, *Peerage*
Archives Bodl. Oxf., Carte MSS

King, Robert (1599/1600–1676), college head, was born in Kent. He matriculated pensioner of Christ's College, Cambridge, on 5 July 1617, graduating BA in 1621 and proceeding MA in 1624. From 1625 he was a fellow of his college. On 16 January 1628 (or 1629) he was admitted proctor in the consistory court of the bishop of Ely. During academic year 1629–30 he was junior proctor of the university. In 1636 he received the degree of LLD. That year King resigned his fellowship, and by 1637 he had married Frances (d. 1684), daughter of Jasper Wareyn of Great Thurlow, Suffolk. The Jasper Wareyn who matriculated at Christ's five years before King, in 1612, was probably her brother.

On 10 October 1641 King was admitted advocate in the court of arches. From 1641 to 1664 he was official to the archdeacon of Suffolk, and from 1642 to 1645 held the additional office of commissary in that archdeaconry. In 1645 he became commissary in the neighbouring archdeaconry of Sudbury; this post he resigned in the same year, but he remained official of Sudbury from 1645 to 1674. On 28 October 1645 he was elected master of Trinity Hall, following the refusal of the place by the fellows' first choice, John Selden. King's election was approved by the House of Lords on 6 November, but the Commons were disinclined to endorse the promotion of a man so closely involved in the machinery of the Laudian church. The fellows of Trinity Hall were told to try again, and in March 1646 they elected John Bond.

King's sympathies were clearly with the royalist cause, and following the Restoration he was re-elected to the mastership on 20 August 1660. By the end of that year he had also been appointed chancellor, commissary, and vicar-general to Bishop Matthew Wren of Ely, retaining all three posts to his death. He was confirmed in office by the bishop's patent of 20 December 1662, and the diocesan records give ample evidence of the work he did there.

As master of Trinity Hall, King was involved in a running controversy over the appointment of clergymen to fellowships designated for laymen. The younger dons objected in particular to the crown's nomination of Robert Eade, who was in orders and who owed his MA to the king's mandate. In February 1666 the master of Corpus, Francis Wilford, sent the earl of Manchester an account of the disputes at Trinity Hall, observing that King was 'soe quiet and peaceable a person' that he could not understand the fellows' behaviour. This (thought Wilford) must be because of King's 'great mildness … in government', since as an LLD he might be thought to know his own college's statutes (Malden, 154). In March the matter was referred to a royal commission, which unsurprisingly upheld and extended the crown's right to nominate.

King died at Trinity Hall lodge on 6 November 1676 aged seventy-six, and was buried in the college chapel; a marble tomb slab displays his arms: sable, a lion rampant a la queue furchée argent. His daughter Anne was buried at Great Thurlow in 1660, aged twenty-two. His only son, also Robert, entered St John's College, Cambridge, in 1657 and trained for the law. He is said to have become vicar of Witcham, Cambridgeshire, in 1673; yet he is not mentioned in King's will of 17 April 1672. This left to his grandsons Robert, Henry, and Thomas a property at Sowley Green (near Great Thurlow) which King had bought. The interest in another landholding nearby at Great Bradley, which King had leased from St John's College, was passed to his widow. She was buried at Great Thurlow on 18 April 1684.

C. S. KNIGHTON

Sources Venn, *Alum. Cant.* · J. Peile, *Biographical register of Christ's College, 1505–1905, and of the earlier foundation, God's House, 1448–1505*, ed. [J. A. Venn], 1 (1910), 318 · H. E. Malden, *Trinity Hall* (1902), 145, 152–3 · W. Stevenson, *A supplement to the first edition of Mr Bentham's history and antiquities of the cathedral and conventual church of Ely* (1817), 11, 21, 28 · F. Blomefield and C. Parkin, *An essay towards a topographical history of the county of Norfolk*, [2nd edn], 11 vols. (1805–10), vol. 3, pp. 657–8, 661 · *JHC*, 4 (1644–6), 228, 308, 489 · *JHL*, 7 (1644–5), 600–01, 630, 678 · BL, Add. MSS 5808, fols. 218–19; 19138, fols. 211v–212; Harleian MS 7043, 22, 23, 25–6, 30 · will, PRO, PROB 11/352, fols. 251–251v · monument, Trinity Hall chapel, Cambridge
Archives CUL, Ely diocesan archives, act book as vicar-general, D/2/52 · CUL, Ely diocesan archives, administration book, G/2/2, fols. 1–52 · CUL, Ely diocesan archives, recommendation following visitation by subject as vicar-general of three Cambridgeshire deaneries, 7/1665, B/2/59
Wealth at death house and ground near Sowley Green, Suffolk; leased another property (at Great Bradley); no significant bequests: will, PRO, PROB 11/352, fols. 251–251v

King, Robert, second Baron Kingston (c.1660–1693), army officer, was the eldest son of John *King, first Baron Kingston (d. 1676), parliamentarian soldier and owner of large estates in Ireland, and his wife, Catharine (d. 1669), daughter of Sir William Fenton of Mitchelstown, co. Cork. He was trained to a military career, receiving a cornet's commission in his father's cavalry regiment in 1663, while still an infant. Brought up on the family estate at Boyle Abbey, co. Roscommon, he was educated by a private tutor.

Kingston purchased a captain's commission in the duke of Ormond's cavalry regiment in 1684 and within two years was the regiment's colonel. He was deprived of his post in 1687 during Tyrconnell's purge of protestant officers from the Irish army. On the eve of civil war he left his estate in Boyle and travelled to Sligo, where on 4 January 1689 he and Captain Chidley Coote were elected joint commanders of the forces in the county by the protestant association of Sligo. Kingston garrisoned the town, improved its defences, and garrisoned posts on the borders with Mayo and Roscommon to prevent incursions by Irish raiders, against whom he was active in a series of

Robert King, second Baron Kingston (c.1660–1693), by John Michael Wright, c.1676

skirmishes. On 7 March, Tyrconnell issued a proclamation in Dublin offering a free pardon to all those who laid down their arms, but specifically excluded Kingston and nine others as being 'principal actors in the rebellion' who were 'not deserving of His Majesty's mercy or favour' (Leslie, 22).

Kingston received several messages from Robert Lundy, the governor of Londonderry, urging him to leave Sligo so that the protestant forces might be consolidated. He abandoned Sligo to the Irish on 22 March and led his troops and the whole protestant population to Ballyshannon, which was then held and fortified by his cousin Henry Folliot. On 14 April, Kingston received an order from Lundy to join forces with him, by which time King James's Irish army had got between him and Londonderry. Unable either to return to Sligo, which was then occupied by the Irish, or to reach Lundy, Kingston instructed his men to join the garrisons at Enniskillen, Ballyshannon, and Donegal. With some of his officers he seized two French smacks at Killybegs, from where he sailed to get help. He arrived in Scotland after a hazardous seven-day crossing, having left all his possessions behind 'but some plate'.

While in England, Kingston was attainted by the Dublin parliament and his lands were sequestered. In October 1689 he was chosen by other Irish exiles to sit on a committee to address the king in parliament and make proposals for the settlement of Ireland. On 17 February 1690 he married Margaret Harbord (d. 1698), a daughter of William *Harbord (d. 1692), the vice-treasurer of Ireland. In London he wrote an account of his actions in Sligo, which was published in Mackenzie's *Narrative of the Siege of London-Derry* (1690). After the war his property was restored to him and he took his seat in the Irish parliament of 1692. He died in December 1693 leaving no children. By his will he demised all his property either to charitable purposes or to his cousins in an attempt to prevent his lands from passing to his brother John, the third baron (1664–1728), who had married Margaret O'Cahan, a Catholic who had been a servant in his father's house. After fifteen years of litigation, his brother succeeded to most of the estates in 1708.   PIERS WAUCHOPE

Sources J. MacKenzie, *A narrative of the siege of London-Derry* (1690) · W. King, *The state of the protestants of Ireland under the late King James's government* (1691) · [C. Leslie], *An answer to a book, intituled, the state of the protestants of Ireland under the late King James's government* (1692) · *A vindication of Sir Robert King's designs and actions in relation to the late and present Lord Kingston* (1699) · J. Lodge, *The peerage of Ireland*, rev. M. Archdall, rev. edn, 3 (1789) · *Journal of the Very Rev. Rowland Davies*, ed. R. Caulfield, CS, 68 (1857) · W. G. Wood-Martin, *History of Sligo*, 3 vols. (1882–92) · *Calendar of the manuscripts of the marquess of Ormonde*, new ser., 8 vols., HMC, 36 (1902–20), vol. 7, p. 291 · C. Dalton, ed., *Irish army lists, 1661–1685* (privately printed, London, 1907) · J. Redington, ed., *Calendar of Treasury papers*, 1, PRO (1868), 55 · GEC, *Peerage*, new edn, vol. 7

Likenesses J. M. Wright, portrait, *c.*1676, Ulster Museum, Belfast [*see illus.*]

Wealth at death left large estates in Ireland

King, Robert (d. 1726?), composer and concert promoter, was admitted to the royal private musick as a violinist on 6 February 1680. In December 1689 he was granted a royal licence to promote concerts and apparently did so with the composer Johann Franck, first at the Two Golden Balls in Bow Street, London, and from January 1691 at Charles Street, Covent Garden, in a purpose-built room soon to be used also for auctions of paintings and called The Vendu. In September 1691 it was 'inlarging to a far greater Dimension for the Convenience of Mr. FRANK's and Mr. KING's Musick' (*LondG*, 14–17 Sept 1691). King graduated MusB at Cambridge in 1696. James Brydges, later duke of Chandos, wrote in his diary of visits by King in 1697 'to play with me on the flute [recorder]' (Baker and Baker, 37). By January 1698 King was organizing concerts with John Banister at York Buildings, Villiers Street, and in June 1699 the music publisher John Walsh advertised 'a choice Collection of new Musick, made for Mr. *Banister's* and Mr. *King's* Consort, performed by Gentlemen at Exeter Exchange' (*Flying Post*, 8–10 June 1699). In July 1700 King and Banister were selling 'The New Sonata's of the famous Signior Archangelo Corelli' (*LondG*, 8–11 July 1700) and they advertised sonatas by Nicola Cosimi in November 1702.

King composed songs and instrumental music for the theatre, concerts, and amateur performers. His songs appeared in numerous collections, including *Choice Ayres and Songs* (1684), *The Theater of Music* (1685–7), *Comes Amoris*

(1687–93), *The Banquet of Music* (1688–90), and *Thesaurus musicus* (1693–5), in issues of the *Gentleman's Journal* (1692–4), and in *Mercurius Musicus* (1699). Many of these songs were republished in editions of *Wit and Mirth* between 1700 and 1720. The manuscripts of some of his songs and incidental music from the 1690s are in the British Library. About 1690 King, displeased by incorrect and badly printed versions of his songs 'in the Common Printed Books about Town', published his *Songs for One Two and Three Voices*, writing in his preface that he had 'imitated the Italians in their manner of Ariettas; who for there Excellence in Vocal Musick are (in my Judgment) the best Paterns' (Smith, 6). He published another thirty-three pieces in *A Second Booke of Songs Together with a Pastorall Elegy, on … Queen Mary* (1698?). Instrumental music by him appeared in *Tripla concordia* (1677), *Thesaurus musicus*, *The Theater of Music*, and other publications up to 1705. He was replaced in the private musick on 6 November 1726, but details of his death are not known. Manuscripts of his songs and other compositions are in the British Library; the Bodleian Library, Oxford; Christ Church, Oxford; the Royal College of Music, London; and the University of Pittsburgh, Pennsylvania.

OLIVE BALDWIN and THELMA WILSON

Sources A. Ashbee, ed., *Records of English court music*, 1 (1986) · A. Ashbee, ed., *Records of English court music*, 2 (1987) · A. Ashbee, ed., *Records of English court music*, 5 (1991) · A. Ashbee, ed., *Records of English court music*, 8 (1995) · A. Ashbee and D. Lasocki, eds., *A biographical dictionary of English court musicians, 1485–1714*, 2 vols. (1998) · C. L. Day and E. B. Murrie, *English song-books, 1651–1702: a bibliography with a first-line index of songs* (1940) · M. Tilmouth, 'A calendar of references to music in newspapers published in London and the provinces (1660–1719)', *Royal Musical Association Research Chronicle*, 1 (1961), esp. 10–11, 22, 34, 44–5, 52 · *Flying Post* (8–10 June 1699) · *Flying Post* (20–23 Jan 1705) · *LondG* (26–30 March 1691) · *LondG* (16–20 April 1691) · *LondG* (14–17 Sept 1691) · *LondG* (3–7 March 1692) · *LondG* (6–10 Jan 1698) · *LondG* (8–11 July 1700) · *LondG* (2–5 Nov 1702) · *Post Man* (15–18 Aug 1702) · W. Van Lennep and others, eds., *The London stage, 1660–1800*, pt 1: *1660–1700* (1965) · C. A. Price, *Music in the Restoration theatre* (1979) · W. C. Smith, *A bibliography of the musical works published by John Walsh … 1695–1720* (1948); repr. (1968) · R. Elkin, *The old concert rooms of London* (1955) · C. H. C. Baker and M. I. Baker, *The life and circumstances of James Brydges* (1949) · Venn, *Alum. Cant.* · P. Holman, 'King, Robert', *New Grove*, 2nd edn

King, Robert, second earl of Kingston (1754–1799), accused murderer and property developer, was the eldest son of Edward King, first earl of Kingston (1726–1797), then MP for Boyle and later for co. Sligo, and his wife, Jane (d. 1784), illegitimate daughter of Thomas Caulfield of Donamon, co. Roscommon. After schooling at Eton College, King assumed the title Viscount Kingsborough in 1768. On 5 December of the following year at St Michael's, Dublin, he married his cousin, Caroline (1755–1823), only daughter of Richard FitzGerald of Mount Ophaly in co. Kildare and Margaret King, heir to the estate of Mitchelstown, co. Cork, from her father, the fourth and last Baron Kingston.

The couple's first child, George, was born in 1771, by which time Kingsborough was in London on the first stage of a European tour which took him to Paris before his return to Mitchelstown in 1776. Lord and Lady Kingsborough had a further five sons and five daughters, who were brought up alongside one Henry Gerald FitzGerald, the illegitimate son of Caroline's brother. FitzGerald appears to have been a dashing and spirited young man who rose to the rank of colonel in the army. Though married, in 1797 he eloped with the Kingsboroughs' third daughter, Mary Elizabeth, who was soon after reunited with the family following the viscount's offer of a reward of 100 guineas for information.

This, however, was not sufficient for Kingsborough's son Colonel Robert Edward King, who challenged FitzGerald to a duel in Hyde Park, London, on 1 October 1797. Plans for a rematch after an inconclusive first exchange were prevented when both men were arrested on the instruction of George III (*GM*, 67, 1797, 1120–21). Now disguised, FitzGerald returned to Kilworth, near Mitchelstown, to where Mary had been taken. His presence came to the attention of Robert Edward King and his father, who, following the first earl of Kingston's death (8 November 1797), had assumed the earldom. Father and son confronted FitzGerald at his lodgings in Kilworth, and a struggle ensued between King and his sister's seducer. In the course of the fight Kingston produced a pistol, fired, and killed FitzGerald. On his arrest the newly ennobled earl demanded his right to be tried in the Irish House of Lords, where he was represented by John Philpot Curran. The trial, the third of its kind in the Irish house, began on 18 May 1798. Faced with a press sympathetic to the actions of an honourable and protective father, the crown offered no evidence against Kingston, who was subsequently acquitted, as was his son at the Cork assizes.

There remains a second, somewhat less sensational, side to Kingston's career. Before his ennoblement he was three times elected MP for co. Cork. Prior to his confrontation with Colonel FitzGerald, Kingston had also earned recognition for his redevelopment of the Mitchelstown estate, which he had inherited at his marriage. Among his more notable improvements were the building of Kingston College, the construction of a new town on a 138 acre site, and the modernization of Mitchelstown Castle along neo-Palladian lines. In this Kingston was assisted and advised by the agrarian improver Arthur Young, who worked on the estate between 1777 and 1778. A decade later Lord and Lady Kingston employed, briefly and unhappily, the young Mary Wollstonecraft as governess to their three eldest daughters. Wollstonecraft's principal dealings were with Caroline, whom she found more engrossed in her lapdogs than in her children; Lord Kingston, though a lesser presence, was thought a scarcely more edifying role model, his countenance suggesting no 'more than good humour, and a little *fun* not refined' (Wollstonecraft to Eliza Bishop, 5 Nov 1786, *Collected Letters*, 123).

Kingston died at Mitchelstown Castle on 17 April 1799, whereupon the title passed to his eldest son, George. He was survived by his wife, from whom he had long been separated; she lived until 13 January 1823 and was buried in Putney, Surrey. Lady Mary Elizabeth King, the object of

FitzGerald's intemperate passions, moved to Wales, where, under a false name, she lodged with a clergyman's family until her marriage in April 1805 to George Galbraith Meares of co. Sligo. She died at Shirehampton, Gloucestershire, in summer 1819. The erstwhile defender of her honour, Robert Edward, later first Viscount Lorton, subsequently travelled and wrote on the Italian states before his death in 1854.　　　　　　　　PHILIP CARTER

Sources *DNB* · GEC, *Peerage* · *GM*, 1st ser., 69 (1799), 350–51 · *GM*, 1st ser., 89/1 (1819), 587 · *Annual Register* (1797), 55–7 · B. Power, *From the Danes to Dairygold: a history of Mitchelstown* (Mitchelstown, 1996) · J. Kelly, *That damn'd thing called honour: duelling in Ireland, 1570–1860* (1995) · *Public Register, or, Freeman's Journal* (28 Dec 1797) · *Public Register, or, Freeman's Journal* (28 May 1798) · C. Tomalin, *The life and death of Mary Wollstonecraft* (1974) · C. Tomalin, *The life and death of Mary Wollstonecraft*, new edn (1985) · *Collected letters of Mary Wollstonecraft*, ed. R. M. Wardle (1979)

King, Rufus (1755–1827), revolutionary and politician in the United States of America, was born on 25 March 1755 in Scarborough, Massachusetts, the first of the three children of Richard King (1718–1775), merchant, and Isabella, *née* Bragdon (1731–1759). After six years at Governor Dummer Academy in Byfield, Massachusetts, he entered Harvard College in 1773. In 1775 his father petitioned that he be allowed to attend Church of England rather than Congregational services while at college. After graduating first in his class in 1777, King studied law for three years with Theophilus Parsons of Newburyport, Massachusetts. During the summer of 1778 he served briefly as a volunteer staff officer in the abortive Franco-American campaign to recover Newport, Rhode Island.

King began practising law in 1780. His eloquence quickly made him Parsons's rival in court. In 1783 Newburyport elected him to the lower house of the legislature; in November 1784 the legislature chose him as a delegate to congress. There King supported the exclusion of slavery from the Northwest Territories and John Jay's efforts to win commercial concessions in the Spanish Caribbean by temporarily abandoning free navigation of the Mississippi. On 30 March 1786 he married Mary Alsop (1769–1819), the daughter of a wealthy New York merchant, with whom he had seven children.

With other Massachusetts delegates in congress, King initially opposed attempts to revise the articles of confederation. Shays's rebellion (1786), however, changed his mind. Named as a delegate to the Philadelphia convention (1787), he pressed for a strong central government while opposing equal representation of the states in the senate. Returning to Massachusetts after the convention, he was influential in the state's eventual ratification of the new constitution.

In 1788 King moved to New York city so that his wife could be near her family. Factional divisions within New York's leadership led to his selection as senator in the first congress where he became a firm supporter of Alexander Hamilton's policies to fund the revolutionary debt and establish the Bank of the United States.

Unsympathetic to the French Revolution even in its earliest phases, King joined Jay in humiliating the French ambassador Edmund Genêt in 1793 by accusing him of threatening an appeal to the people against George Washington's policy of neutrality. When the British seizure of American ships inflamed war sentiment against Britain, King supported Jay's appointment as special ambassador to London. Subsequently he joined Hamilton and Jay in defending the Jay treaty, writing ten of the influential Camillus essays that appeared in the newspapers.

King refused Washington's invitation to become secretary of state in 1795, but accepted appointment as ambassador to Britain, serving in London from July 1796 to 1803. During his ambassadorship Anglo-American relations improved dramatically despite the increasing number of American seamen impressed by the Royal Navy. After his return to the United States he was the unsuccessful federalist vice-presidential candidate in 1804, receiving only 14 of 190 possible electoral votes.

Following the election of 1804 King's public career went into temporary eclipse. He bought an estate at Jamaica on Long Island and took up the life of a gentleman farmer. Although his electoral vote for the vice-presidency increased in 1808 because of Thomas Jefferson's Embargo Act, he did not actively re-enter politics until the Madison administration declared war on Britain in 1812. Factional divisions among New York's republicans again led to his selection as senator after the presidential election later that year. While he opposed many of the administration's war policies, King was considered a moderate federalist because of his willingness to support republican defence measures in 1814. This distanced him from the Hartford convention (1814), which many felt had flirted with treason.

King emerged from the war as one of the few federalist leaders whose loyalty to the republic remained unquestioned. Though he garnered only 34 out of 221 possible votes as the federalist presidential candidate in 1816, he continued to serve in the senate until 1825. He was the principal author of the Navigation Act of 1818 that retaliated against continued British exclusions of American shipping. He also opposed the admission of Missouri as a slave state in 1820, proposed that revenues arising from the sale of public lands be dedicated to the emancipation and colonization of enslaved Africans once the funded debt had been retired, and pressed for the abandonment of the congressional caucus. In 1821 he was a member of the convention that revised New York's constitution. After retiring from the senate in 1825, he served briefly but ineffectually as ambassador to Britain before returning to Jamaica, Long Island, to die on 29 April 1827. He was buried there on 2 May in the churchyard of the Grace Episcopal Church.　　　　　　　　RICHARD BUEL JUN.

Sources R. Ernst, *Rufus King, American federalist* (1968) · S. E. Siry, 'King, Rufus', *ANB* · C. R. King, *The life and correspondence of Rufus King*, 6 vols. (1894–1900) · C. M. Fuess, 'King, Rufus', *DAB* · M. Farrand, ed., *The records of the federal conventions of 1787*, rev. edn, 1–3 (1937)

Archives Hunt. L. | BL, corresp. with Lord Grenville, Add. MS 59049 · New York Historical Society, letters to Sir Evan Nepean · Boconnoc, Lostwithiel, Cornwall, Grenville MSS

Likenesses J. Turnbull, miniature, oils, 1792, Yale U., Art Gallery • engraving, 1792 (after a miniature by J. Turnbull), repro. in *Harpers*, 68 (1884), 943 • G. Stuart, oils?, *c*.1819, priv. coll. • W. S. Leney, engraving (after a watercolour by J. S. Wood), repro. in *Delaplaine's repository* (1815)

Wealth at death $140,000: Ernst, *Rufus King*, 404

King, Samuel William (1821–1868), traveller and scientist, was born on 20 September 1821 at Gainsborough, Lincolnshire, the eldest son of William Hutchinson King of Manchester, vicar of Nuneaton, Warwickshire, and Eliza Sanders of Morton House, Lincolnshire. He was admitted to St Catharine's College, Cambridge, in 1841, graduated BA in 1845, and proceeded MA in 1853. He was ordained deacon at Chester in 1846 and priest at Manchester in 1848, and was curate at Walley, Lancashire, before becoming rector of Saxlingham Nethergate, Norfolk, in 1851. In 1849 he married Emma, daughter of John Fort MP.

King was from boyhood an enthusiastic entomologist and geologist, and helped his friend Charles Lyell in his investigations in England and abroad. In 1860 they explored the deposits at Hoxne, Suffolk, and in 1865 King investigated the cave at Aurignac, which had been described by Lyell in his *Antiquity of Man* (1863) as containing human remains interred in the palaeolithic age. King's findings, published by William Boyd Dawkins in 1871, suggested a far later date for the human remains. He travelled frequently in continental Europe, and was an enthusiastic mountain climber. His wife usually accompanied him, and the records of a long expedition in northern Piedmont made about 1855 are contained in King's only book, *The Italian Valleys of the Pennine Alps* (1858), illustrated from drawings made by the author. He was a fellow of the Royal Geographical Society (1858), the Geological Society (1860), and of the Society of Antiquaries.

Worsening health put an end to King's geological work and led him to travel abroad. He died at Pontresina, Switzerland, on 8 July 1868, and was buried there. His collection of fossil mammalia from the Norfolk forest beds he bequeathed to the Museum of Practical Geology, Jermyn Street, London. Its main importance derives from the careful notes on the stratigraphical position of each specimen. He published a number of articles on zoology and archaeology, of minor but not lasting interest.

W. A. J. ARCHBOLD, *rev.* ELIZABETH BAIGENT

Sources Probate • Venn, *Alum. Cant.* • Boase, *Mod. Eng. biog.* • T. H. Huxley, *Quarterly Journal of the Geological Society*, 25 (1869), xxix–xxx • W. B. Dawkins, 'The date of the interment in the Aurignac cave', *Nature*, 4 (1871), 208–9 • C. Lyell, *Antiquity of man* (1863) • private information (1892)

Archives U. Edin. L., letters to Sir Charles Lyell

Wealth at death under £8000: probate, 6 Aug 1868, *CGPLA Eng. & Wales*

King, Thomas (*d. c.*1769), portrait painter, was a pupil of George Knapton. Although he was an artist of ability, he was eccentric and thriftless in his habits. Four of his portraits have been engraved in mezzotint: Anthony Maddox the rope-dancer and Matthew Skeggs the actor (as Signor Bumbasto, playing on a broomstick as if it were a cello), both by R. Houston; John Keeling JP, by J. McArdell; and John Harrison the chronometer maker, by P. J. Tassaert.

Prints after his portraits are held in the British Museum. He died in the Bull and Axe public house in John Street, Oxford Road, London, about 1769, and was buried in St Marylebone churchyard.

F. M. O'DONOGHUE, *rev.* SARAH HERRING

Sources Thieme & Becker, *Allgemeines Lexikon* • Waterhouse, *18c painters* • Bénézit, *Dict.* • E. Edwards, *Anecdotes of painters* (1808); facs. edn (1970) • Redgrave, *Artists* • *Engraved Brit. ports.* • J. C. Smith, *British mezzotinto portraits*, 4 vols. in 5 (1878–84), vol. 2, pp. 673, 687, 876; vol. 3, pp. 1354–5

King, Thomas (1730–1805), actor and theatre manager, was born on 20 August 1730 in the parish of St George, Hanover Square, the son of a London merchant. He entered Westminster School at the age of six, and is probably the Thomas King on the school list in 1736. At the age of fourteen he was articled to a solicitor, but, having gained a taste for the stage as an amateur, he ran away to join a company of strolling players when he was seventeen, in the company of Ned Shuter. In later life he would say that his first company was playing at Yarmouth, and that after a very short time he transferred to one in Tonbridge, having had two days at sea in between. In summer 1748 he was performing small parts in a booth theatre at Windsor, set up by Richard Yates, a London actor, when David Garrick saw him, recognized his potential, and engaged him for Drury Lane. King stayed there, however, for two years only, playing minor roles. In summer 1749 he went with other London actors for a season at the Jacob's Wells Theatre in Bristol, where he did rather better: Hannah Pritchard was in the company, and chose him to play Benedick to her Beatrice and Rover to her Clarinda. He also had a chance at Romeo. Back in London for the winter he had slightly better parts: the Younger Brother in John Dalton's and Thomas Arne's *Comus*, and Claudio in *Much Ado about Nothing*, for instance. But following another summer in Bristol, in the autumn of 1750 he left Drury Lane for Ireland. It was nine years before he returned.

Ireland Why King should have taken himself away from the centre of the London stage at this early point in his career is uncertain, but it turned out well. Thomas Sheridan was having a sparkling success as manager of the Smock Alley Theatre in Dublin, and under his guidance King developed his strengths as a comedian. He became a popular favourite of audiences in Dublin as well as in Cork, where he played two summers. It was in Dublin also that he developed a particular specialism in delivering prologues and epilogues—a more important craft in his day than it has ever been since.

Although he had gone to Dublin in the company of a Miss Cole, a dancer, King transferred his affections at some stage to Mary Baker (1730–1813), another dancer, who, after experience at Covent Garden and Drury Lane, also arrived on the Dublin stage in 1750.

In the summer closure of 1751 King returned to England to play at Simpson's Theatre in Bath; he went there a second time, in 1755 after Simpson himself had died, to act and to manage the theatre in what was to be its last season. This was his first experience of management, but there was to be a good deal more. Mary Baker came with

Thomas King (1730–1805), by John Young, pubd 1803 (after Johan Zoffany, c.1780) [as Puff in *The Critic* by Richard Brinsley Sheridan]

him, and from this time they were partners for life, marrying in 1760. *The Secret History of the Green Rooms* (1790) claimed that Frances Barton, a young actress in the company, gave Mary grounds for jealousy during that summer. If so, it would have been for the last time. Although King was to play opposite her many times in future, when she was better known as Frances Abington—most notably as Sir Peter to her Lady Teazle—he found her a troublesome colleague at Drury Lane and shared Garrick's dislike of her.

Drury Lane: the Garrick years King was brought back to Drury Lane in October 1759, after Garrick had lost the services of his principal comedian, Henry Woodward, who had gone to Ireland with Spranger Barry to set up a new theatre. By the time of Garrick's retirement in 1776 he had become his most loyal lieutenant, as well as his closest friend within the profession. He advanced in skill and reputation, and came to be regarded as the supreme comic actor of his age. He wrote his first plays in the period: *Love at First Sight* (1763) and *Wit's Last Stake* (1768). Neither is more than run-of-the-mill.

King's creation of the part of Lord Ogleby, in *The Clandestine Marriage*, by Garrick and George Colman the elder, put the seal on his pre-eminence. The part had been intended for Garrick himself, and his passing it on to King (who undertook it reluctantly) caused a breach between the authors, with serious consequences, but it gave King a huge success.

Garrick capitalized on the public affection felt for King by sending him before the curtain when audiences were unruly, for instance when William O'Brien's *The Duel*, after a poor start, was announced to be repeated, in December 1772; and when Samuel Reddish failed to turn up to play on 3 March 1773. He made frequent use of his talents as a speaker of prologues and epilogues: *The Picture of a Playhouse; or, Bucks have at ye All* (1760), probably written by James Love, became the most celebrated, all-purpose epilogue of the age. Garrick also gave King a huge range of parts, both classical and new. In Shakespeare he played Parolles, Pistol, Speed, Osric, Shylock, Touchstone, Malvolio, and Cloten, as well as others after Garrick had retired. He appeared in revivals of Jonson and Wycherley. The many new parts he created for Garrick have not lasted as well as those which Sheridan later gave him: Vandercrab in Henry Lee's *The New Peerage* now means little; and it is merely a curiosity that he had, in his first years with Garrick, a small part in Johnson's *Irene*, and that at the end of his career he played the Fool in Samuel Ireland's Shakespeare forgery *Vortigern*.

In 1769 Garrick staged his three-day jubilee in Stratford upon Avon, a celebration of Shakespeare in the town of his birth, which included spectacular processions, masquerades, dinners, and fireworks, but no Shakespeare play. The climax was Garrick's reciting of a jubilee ode in a specially built rotunda before a thousand spectators. King was cast as devil's advocate, rising up to voice a mean-spirited condemnation of Shakespeare and to repeat all Garrick's enemies' criticisms of the festival, so that the ode could triumphantly refute them. Boswell, who was present, thought that this detracted from the dignity of the occasion. Others misunderstood the event entirely, believing King to be a genuine protester; but it did perhaps contribute to the rapture with which the ode was received.

Because of the Stratford rain Garrick incurred losses. However, he recouped these in a stage version of the jubilee at Drury Lane in that and the following season, with great success. King had a large but different role in it. Garrick and King had one of their few differences in 1772. King, sensitive for his wife's position in the company, had noticed that his opposite number at Covent Garden, Woodward (now returned from Ireland), was paid at a higher rate than he was, and interpreted it as a want of esteem. 'You have been for years my chief and shall be my last theatrical connection', wrote Garrick; but he went on to reproach him, with the suspicion and sensitivity to gossip that was one of his faults, with having 'whisper'd about in hints and ambiguities your uneasiness, all which by circulation have partly crept into the public prints' (*Letters*, 2.823, 6 November 1772). In the hothouse atmosphere of the theatre, others saw King as one of the channels by which Garrick's suspicions of others were fed, but this was perhaps no more than the price of intimacy with him. But the affection between them was real. When Garrick retired in 1776 he sent King a gift:

Accept a small token of our long and constant attachment to each other—I flatter myself that this sword, as it is a theatrical one, will not cut love between us, and that it will not be less valuable to you for having dangled at my side some part of last winter. (*Letters*, 3.1112, 25 June 1776)

In the last decade of his career Garrick was frequently absent through sickness or on travels, and King would be left in charge of productions, as acting manager (a role similar to but without the powers of the modern director). He was also one of Garrick's talent scouts. Most notably, Garrick sent him to Cheltenham to see the young Sarah Siddons in Nicholas Rowe's *The Fair Penitent*, and on his favourable report gave her a trial at Drury Lane in 1775. She played Portia to King's Shylock, billed as 'a young lady, her first appearance', but neither played well, and it was seven years before Siddons came back.

Bristol and Sadler's Wells The London theatres were closed each summer from June until the middle of September, and the actors normally continued their profession elsewhere. King had had experience in management at Bath, in the 1750s, and he returned to it in Bristol in 1770. The King Street Theatre (which operated only during the summers, like other provincial theatres) had had mixed fortunes since its opening in 1766. William Powell, its first manager, died suddenly in 1769, in the height of the summer season, and his partner Charles Holland died the following December. King bought a share of the theatre and managed it during the next two seasons, bringing to it actors such as Charles Bannister and John Moody. He had problems holding the company together, however, and suffered financial losses, and in June 1771 he had a serious coach accident on the way from London. He sold his share to James Dodd the following winter.

Since 1769 King had had a role in the management of the Sadler's Wells Theatre, and on giving up Bristol he bought a major share in it. Sadler's Wells, described in 1744 as a place 'of great extravagance, luxury, idleness and ill-fame' (Mander and Mitchenson, 246), was a resort where a wooden music house had been replaced by an unlicensed stone theatre in 1765. A summer programme of music, pantomime, acrobatic displays, and illegitimate drama had been successfully managed by Thomas Rosoman, a builder. Rosoman retired in 1772. King assumed full control and held it for ten years. He made no change of policy; he was as accomplished a showman as an actor. But under his reign the music improved, through the work of Charles Dibdin; the hazards on the roads from central London were reduced, through better policing; and audiences became more fashionable, drinking tea and good wine during the shows rather than porter. The theatre developed a taste for patriotic spectacle. King had begun to reduce his participation in Sadler's Wells in 1779, and from 1782 he was fully engaged in the management of Drury Lane, on behalf of Richard Brinsley Sheridan.

Drury Lane under Sheridan Garrick retired in 1776 and passed over the control of the theatre to Sheridan, having sold a half share to him, his father-in-law Thomas Linley, and a certain Dr Gray. Sheridan started brilliantly, with *The School for Scandal* (1777), which gave King one of his greatest roles in Sir Peter Teazle. *The Critic* followed in August 1779, with King playing Puff, the writer of the pretentious tragedy 'The Spanish Armada'. (There was a sly joke here, for King himself had two months previously presented at Sadler's Wells a stirring pageant about Queen Elizabeth, which had spectacularly depicted the defeat of the Armada.) In succeeding years, while becoming increasingly occupied in national politics, Sheridan was to provide two or three further scripts for the Drury Lane company, but his interest in management grew less, and his control of the theatre deteriorated. In September 1782 King agreed to take over the stage management of the theatre for him. Essentially a kind, agreeable man, he found the quarrelling of his actors and their lack of discipline very troubling—and he was losing money by it. After one season he had had enough; he refused to sign on again either as actor or manager, and spent the next twelve months away from London, touring Scotland, Wales, and Ireland. His London celebrity had preceded him, and guaranteed success.

King returned in 1783 and yielded again to Sheridan's charm, resuming the burden for another five years. This period was no easier than the earlier one, and ended spectacularly in 1788 with a series of public statements which expose both the general difficulties of theatre management in the period and specific failings in Sheridan as theatre licensee. The management of Drury Lane passed to John Philip Kemble, a much sterner operator. King went on tour again in 1788–9. Tate Wilkinson remembers his generosity in refusing payment after a dismal house in York and playing a whole week in Leeds the following month without payment, in further recompense. On his return to London, King took the extreme step of signing for Covent Garden, and he played there during the 1789–90 season. In summer 1790 he was on tour again, and was appearing in Edinburgh when John Jackson, the manager, went into hiding to escape debtors; King, with his usual goodwill, took over the management for a month.

The call back to Drury Lane was strong. King returned in September 1790 and remained there until he retired. He was growing fat and suffering from gout, but he was still able to hold audiences with his old parts and still ventured on new; and he still (according to his diary) lived perpetually on the edge of exasperation with Sheridan. He gave up the stage on 22 May 1802, with a final performance of Sir Peter Teazle. A lavish presentation was made to him in the green room by Dorothy Jordan on behalf of the whole company.

In his prime King was a tall, handsome man, although his nose was thought rather too long. He was at home and respected in all company; Boswell found him 'a genteel, agreeable man' during the Stratford jubilee and was glad to breakfast with him in London a month later, and in 1783 he was elected to the Sublime Society of Beefsteaks. He was the master of the Drury Lane Theatrical Fund for a few years in succession to Garrick, though he gave this up when he took on the management of Drury Lane. He had, however, one disastrous failing: he was a heavy gambler. His wife and Garrick prevailed on him to give up the habit on one occasion, and he remained free of it for a number of years, but relapsed.

Although it was his destiny to play the lieutenant to two

of the geniuses of the eighteenth-century theatre, Garrick and Sheridan, King had outstanding personal qualities of his own. In an age of great actors he was among the greatest, and he created at least two roles which have remained in the permanent repertory. At a time when the theatre in various forms was the dominant mode of popular culture, he was one of the essential organizers and managers of it. In a profession where rivalries and jealousy were endemic, he comes down as a kindly reconciler.

King and his wife had an ideally supportive marriage, in spite of the heavy debts his habit incurred. When he was on tour they wrote to each other almost every day. He died at his home in New Store Street, Bedford Square, London, on 11 December 1805. The whole Drury Lane company attended his funeral in St Paul's, Covent Garden, where he was buried on 20 December. His wife survived him until 30 November 1813, in some poverty because of his gambling, but relieved a little by a benefit given for her in 1806. There is no record of any children. JOHN LEVITT

Sources T. King, 'Diaries', BL, Add. MSS 45136–7 · G. W. Stone, ed., *The London stage, 1660–1800*, pt 4: *1747–1776* (1962) · C. B. Hogan, ed., *The London stage, 1660–1800*, pt 5: *1776–1800* (1968) · Highfill, Burnim & Langhans, *BDA* · *The letters of David Garrick*, ed. D. M. Little and G. M. Kahrl, 3 vols. (1963) · [J. Haslewood], *The secret history of the green rooms: containing authentic and entertaining memoirs of the actors and actresses in the three theatres royal*, 2 vols. (1790) · *Theatrical biography, or, Memoirs of the principal performers of the three Theatre Royals*, 2 vols. (1772) · T. Wilkinson, *The wandering patentee, or, A history of the Yorkshire theatres from 1770 to the present time*, 4 vols. (1795) · R. Jenkins, *Memoirs of the Bristol stage* (1826) · *IGI* · J. Cradock, *Literary and miscellaneous memoirs*, ed. J. B. Nichols, 2nd edn, 4 vols. (1826–8) · R. Hitchcock, *An historical view of the Irish stage from the earliest period down to the close of the season 1788*, 2 vols. (1788–94) · D. Macmillan, *Catalogue of the Larpent plays in the Huntington Library* (1939) · R. Mander and J. Mitchenson, *The theatres of London*, 2nd edn (1963) **Archives** BL, diaries and papers, Add. MSS 45136–45138 | V&A NAL, corresp. with David Garrick **Likenesses** J. Zoffany, double portrait, oils, c.1769–1770 (with Mrs Baddeley), Garr. Club · J. R. Smith, mezzotint, pubd 1772 (after H. D. Hamilton), BM, NPG · J. Roberts, group portrait, oils, exh. RA 1779, Garr. Club · J. Young, engraving, pubd 1803 (after J. Zoffany, c.1780), NPG [see illus.] · W. Daniell, soft-ground etching, pubd 1809 (after G. Dance), BM, NPG · S. De Wilde, portrait, Garr. Club · B. Wilson, oils, Garr. Club · attrib. B. Wilson, oils, Garr. Club · J. Zoffany, oils (as Touchstone), Garr. Club · portraits, Harvard TC · prints, BM, NPG **Wealth at death** very little: J. Doran, *Their majesties servants* (1860)

King, Thomas (1835–1888), pugilist, was born in Silver Street, Stepney, on 14 August 1835, and as a youth served before the mast both in the navy and in a trading vessel. About 1858 he obtained a position as foreman of labourers at the Victoria docks. His courage in disposing of a dock bully known as Brighton Bill commended him to the notice of the ex-champion Jem Ward, who coached him with gloves at The George in Ratcliffe Highway. On 27 November 1860, on the Kentish marshes, King beat Tommy Truckle of Portsmouth in forty-nine rounds (sixty-two minutes). He was now taken in hand and trained by Nat Langham at The Feathers, Wandsworth, for a contest with William Evans (Young Broome). The betting of two to one on King was justified by the event on 21 October 1861,

after a long fight interrupted by the police at the seventeenth round, but then resumed until the forty-third.

The fight between the Young Sailor, as King was called, and the 'scientific' Jem Mace of Norwich, the national champion, had a different outcome: King was outclassed after displaying the utmost pluck in a contest of sixty-eight minutes (28 January 1862). A return match, which excited much greater interest, took place at Aldershot (26 November 1862). The betting was seven to four on Mace, who had the best of the fighting, but was knocked out by a single blow, a 'terrific cross-counter on the left cheek', in the nineteenth round. In this battle of thirty-eight minutes King had shown himself a glutton for punishment, of a 'bottom' and endurance worthy of the best traditions of the ring.

King now married and announced his intention of leaving the ring, thus acquiescing in the resumption of the championship by Mace. But he was yet to champion England against America in the great fight with the Benicia Boy, John Camel Heenan, the adversary of Tom Sayers. The ring was pitched at Wadhurst, near Tunbridge Wells, at an early hour on 10 December 1863. King weighed a little below 13 stone, Heenan (much the favourite) just over 14; both were over 6 feet in height. Heenan's game was to close in and wrestle his antagonist to the ground. King's consisted of dealing his adversary a series of sledge-hammer blows on his nose. Both were extremely successful in their respective tactics, and in the absence of the orthodox feinting, sparring, and 'science', the result came to be mainly a question of sheer endurance. At the eighteenth round the tide of victory turned in King's favour. At the close of the twenty-fourth round, after nearly forty minutes' fighting, Heenan lay unconscious and his seconds threw up the sponge. Public anxiety as to his condition was allayed by a medical report in *The Times* (12 December). Both combatants appeared in person at Wadhurst, in answer to a summons, on 22 December, when they were bound over to keep the peace, and both King and Heenan agreed never to fight again in Britain. King, having won about £4000 in stakes and presents, fulfilled his promise to the letter. He subsequently set up as a bookmaker in Tulse Hill and Hastings and became a wealthy man. He also invested in barge property.

In 1867 King won a couple of sculling races on the Thames, but in later years was best-known for his success in metropolitan flower shows. He died of bronchitis at Clarence House, Clarence Road, Clapham, on 4 October 1888, and was buried in Norwood cemetery. He was survived by his wife, Jane Elizabeth, and at least one daughter. After 1863 the vigilance of the police confined bare-knuckle pugilism in England more and more to the disreputable and dangerous classes, and Tom King is thus not incorrectly termed by the historian of the English prize-ring as Ultimus Romanorum.

THOMAS SECCOMBE, rev. JULIAN LOCK

Sources H. D. Miles, *Pugilistica: being one hundred and forty-four years of the history of British boxing*, 3 vols. (1880–81), vol. 3, pp. 490–518 · Boase, *Mod. Eng. biog.* · H. Cleveland, *Fisticuffs and personalities of the prize ring* (1923) · N. S. Fleischer, *The heavyweight championship, 1719–*

1949 (1949) • [F. Dowling], *Fistiana* (1868) • W. E. Harding, ed., *The champions of the American prize ring* (New York, 1881) • *The Times* (11 Dec 1863) • *The Times* (12 Dec 1863) • R. Flanagan, *West Norwood cemetery's sportsmen* (1995) • *CGPLA Eng. & Wales* (1889)
Likenesses engraving (after a photograph), repro. in Miles, *Pugilistica*, vol. 3. facing p. 490 • engraving (after a photograph), repro. in Harding, *Champions of the American prize ring*
Wealth at death £49,718 13s.: resworn probate, April 1889, *CGPLA Eng. & Wales*

King, Thomas Chiswell (1818–1893), actor, was born at Twyning, near Tewkesbury, Gloucestershire, on 24 April 1818. He adopted his wife's maiden name of Chiswell in addition to his own name on his marriage, which took place shortly after he joined the theatrical profession. He was apprenticed in his youth to a painting and paper-hanging business in Cheltenham, and acquired a taste for the stage through acting with amateurs. About 1840 he joined the company of the ballad composer Alexander Lee to support Harriett Waylett in one-act dramas and operettas in Cheltenham, Worcester, Warwick, and Leamington Spa. In 1843 he became attached in a subordinate capacity to the Simpson–Munro company at Birmingham, playing Conrade in *Much Ado about Nothing* and Sir Thomas Fairfax in *The Field of the Forty Footsteps*. The following year he was seen as Young Scrooge in *A Christmas Carol*, in which his wife played Fezziwig.

King made rapid progress in his profession, and by August 1847 was playing leading business on the York circuit under J. L. Pritchard. He went on to Gourlay's Victoria Theatre, Edinburgh, in June 1848, and remained there for four months. In November 1848 he joined W. H. Murray's company at the Theatre Royal in the same city, where he appeared as Sir Richard Wroughton in *The Jacobite*. In April 1850 he supported Charles Kean during the latter's visit to Edinburgh, and was engaged by him to play secondary tragic parts during the opening season of his management in London.

King made his début at the Princess's in October 1850, as Bassanio in *The Merchant of Venice*, and subsequently played the King in 1 *Henry IV*. In January 1851 he was seen as the exiled Duke when *As You Like It* was performed before the queen at Windsor. Late in the year he was engaged by John Harris of Dublin as leading actor at the Theatre Royal there. He opened under the new management as Colonel Buckthorne in Boucicault's *Love in a Maze*, and soon became an abiding favourite with Dublin playgoers. He remained in the city for five seasons and appeared in no fewer than fifteen notable Shakespearian productions: his Macbeth, Master Ford, Hotspur, and Leontes met with much approbation. During 1855 he was in leading support to Helen Faucit, Samuel Phelps, and Isabella Glyn during their visits to Dublin. In March 1856 he abruptly left the Theatre Royal, and in April began a three-week engagement in *Hamlet* at the Queen's Theatre, Dublin. In October 1856 he opened at Birmingham with Isabella Glyn. King remained there after her departure, and was seen as John Mildmay in Tom Taylor's comedy *Still Waters Run Deep* and as Quasimodo in *Esmeralda*. In July 1857 he made his first

appearance in Manchester. After returning to Birmingham he appeared as Mephistopheles in Boucicault's version of *Faust and Marguerite*, which ran for forty-eight nights at a great profit. During 1859 he fulfilled several engagements at the Queen's Theatre, Dublin, and also played at the City of London Theatre as Hamlet.

From 1861 to 1868 King's record was one of splendid strolling. In March 1869 he was given a trial engagement at Drury Lane by F. C. Chatterton, and opened there as Richelieu to the Julie de Mortemar of his daughter Bessie, who was making her London début. He was favourably received, and subsequently played Hamlet and Julian St Pierre, besides alternating Othello and Iago with Charles Dillon. At the same house in 1870 he was the original Varney in Andrew Halliday's *Amy Robsart*. At Easter 1871 he moved to the Adelphi, where he originated the role of Quasimodo in Halliday's version of *Notre Dame*, which ran for most of the year.

King made his American début on 11 September 1873 at the Lyceum Theatre, New York, as Quasimodo. The play did not repeat its Adelphi success, although it was performed for six weeks. Afterwards he made a successful tour of Canada, exclusively in Shakespearian plays, and returned to New York and the Lyceum in March 1874.

From 1878 to 1880 King leased the Worcester theatre, an unprofitable speculation. In 1883 he made a short provincial tour under J. Pitt Hardacre's management, but he had outlived his popularity. He was the last exponent of an increasingly unpopular school of acting which subordinated intelligence to precept and tradition. Later appearances were infrequent, but in July 1890 he performed for six nights to good houses at the Queen's Theatre, Manchester, and was much admired as Ingomar, one of his most characteristic roles. He retired finally to King's Heath, Worcestershire, where he died on 21 October 1893. He was buried at Claines, near Worcester. He had a son and two daughters, all of whom took to the stage, his elder daughter, Bessie King, being the most successful.

A sound second-rank tragedian, King had a tall and shapely figure, with dark expressive features and well-set eyes. His rich bass voice was flexible and resonant. A temperate, graceful actor, he had more individuality and fewer vices of style than most conventional tragedians. He never established his hold in London, but in one or two sizeable provincial centres, notably Dublin and Birmingham, his following was large and affectionate.

W. J. LAWRENCE, rev. NILANJANA BANERJI

Sources C. E. Pascoe, ed., *The dramatic list* (1879) • C. E. Pascoe, ed., *The dramatic list*, 2nd edn (1880) • J. C. Dibdin, *The annals of the Edinburgh stage* (1888) • R. M. Levey and J. O'Rorke, *Annals of the Theatre Royal, Dublin* (1880) • J. W. Cole, *The life and theatrical times of Charles Kean … including a summary of the English stage for the last fifty years*, 2nd edn, 2 vols. (1860) • M. Williams, *Some London theatres past and present* (1883) • *Birmingham Faces and Places*, 5 (1893), 188–90 • *Freeman's Journal* [Dublin] • Hall, *Dramatic ports.* • *DNB*
Likenesses J. Draycott, photograph, repro. in *Birmingham Faces and Places*, facing p. 187 • print, Harvard TC

King, Sir (Frederic) Truby (1858–1938), promoter of the child welfare movement, was born on 1 April 1858 at Mangorei farmstead, near New Plymouth, New Zealand, the

fifth of the seven children of Thomas King, a bank manager and member of parliament, and his wife, Mary
Chilman. A sickly child, he was educated at home by a
tutor who encouraged him in the habit of single-minded
concentration which characterized his career. King followed his father into banking but, at the age of twenty-
two, opted for medicine. He left New Zealand in August
1880 to study at the University of Edinburgh, where, in
1886, he graduated MB CM (first class) and was awarded
the Ettles scholarship as the top medical student; in 1888
he completed Edinburgh's new BSc degree in public
health. One crucial influence on him at Edinburgh was the
writings of Herbert Spencer, whose thought infused
King's subsequent output; another influence was the lecturer in mental diseases T. S. Clouston, who taught the
moral therapy that King later extended from the mentally
ill in New Zealand to babies and mothers in his campaign
of 'practical eugenics' (Smith, *Mothers and King Baby*, 91).

On 26 October 1887 King married Isabella Cockburn
Millar (1860–1927), daughter of Adam Millar, a jeweller.
Bella was a former dux of the Edinburgh Educational Institution for Young Ladies, and an honours winner in the
examinations set by the Edinburgh Association for the
University Education of Women. In professional terms
her linguistic and literary skills provided a fund of
strength for her husband. After their return to New Zealand in 1888 she was his personal secretary. In 1905 the
couple adopted a daughter, the child of a widowed nurse.
While Bella wrote weekly newspaper articles for her husband, entitled 'Our babies', from 1929 their adopted
daughter, Mary Truby King, helped to make her father's
name as an authority on baby care in Australia, as did imperial devotees from the First World War, nurses, and supporters along the trade routes of the British empire.

King had dual careers in mental and infant health. His
work with the insane began in 1889 with his appointment
as medical superintendent of Seacliff Asylum, New
Zealand's largest mental asylum, near Dunedin, a post he
held for thirty years. He became famous, however, for his
work in infant welfare, which grew from his preoccupation with racial betterment. In 1907 he and a group of
wealthy women founded the Royal New Zealand Society
for the Health of Women and Children, which became
known as the Plunket Society, while his rules of mothercraft became the Plunket system; both were named for
Lady Plunket, wife of the New Zealand governor-general,
who was patron of this women's voluntary organization
in her role as leader of colonial society.

The Plunket Society sought to 'inculcate a lofty view of
the responsibilities of maternity and the duty of every
mother to fit herself for … the natural calls of motherhood', to promote breastfeeding, to educate mothers, and
to employ and train nurses (Plunket Society records). King
also began the first of a series of Karitane baby hospitals in
his beach house at Karitane, near Dunedin; these provided a model for infant welfare nurse training schools
and for mothercraft homes, and were run along the lines
of tuberculosis sanatoriums (King himself suffered from
tuberculosis). His books, *Feeding and Care of Baby* (1908,

1910; 1st British edn, 1913) and *The Expectant Mother, and
Baby's First Month* (1916), together with numerous pamphlets, publicized the twelve essentials of infant care and
feeding, with an emphasis on 'regularity of habits',
'mothering', and 'management'. One influence on King's
routines was his experiments with the feeding of plants
and animals on the Seacliff Asylum's farm. It became part
of the King mythology that he wiped out mortality from
diarrhoea among bucket-fed calves before turning his
attention to the bottle-fed infant. In New Zealand, King
lectured to farmers on scientific feeding, in 1905, before
offering lectures on mothercraft. He considered that suck-
ling was the 'only perfect method of feeding any young
mammal'; consequently 'Nature's milk recipes' set the
standard for the bottle-fed. Scientific mothers, and farmers, shared a moral duty to prepare the best substitute for
the milk 'specially designed … by the Creator' (Smith,
Mothers and King Baby, 93). For the human baby this was
humanized milk, that is to say, cow's milk modified to
resemble breast milk as closely as possible. King's infant
feeding formulas, which he and his nurses insisted conformed to the laws of nature, were unoriginal; the idea
came from the American advocates of percentage feeding, professors T. M. Rotch and L. Emmett Holt.

King also adapted Holt's catechismal method of dos and
don'ts to make his message clear and simple. Mothers
who followed his twelve rules, with their emphasis on
regular habits, would produce a healthy baby, sound in
character and pure in thought; in short a baby reared to
King's rules would follow the ten commandments. 'Power
to obey the "Ten Commandments", or to conform to the
temporal laws and usages of Society', he warned, 'is not to
be expected of "SPOILED" babies when they reach adult
life' (F. T. King, 135–6). By the 1920s King's name had
become synonymous with the prescription of feeding by
the clock, three- or four-hourly, which reached its apogee
between the wars. 'Perfect regularity of habits, initiated
by "Feeding and Sleeping by the Clock", [was] the ultimate
foundation of all-round obedience' (Smith, *Mothers and
King Baby*, 95). King's code embodied active puritanism,
fusing post-Darwinian science with traditional moral
edicts. The rigidity of his routines and his emphasis on
the moral duties of motherhood weighed heavily on
women, whether he was proclaiming that mothercraft
would be the saving of the race, or copying Holt in
instructing mothers that, if their babies' bowels would
not move before 10 a.m., they had to 'MAKE them move'
(Smith, *Mothers and King Baby*, 96, 98–9).

In reality King's rules were complicated and unnatural.
Screaming babies testified that mothering could not be
ordered by the clock, yet the routines advocated by King
and his matrons still have their devotees. While he
demanded obedience and discipline from mothers and
babies, however, he failed to meet his own high standards.
His behaviour was erratic and, because of the missionary
zeal which drove him to pursue his latest obsession and
potential converts at the expense of other commitments,
his habits were nocturnal. In 1917 he was appointed CMG;

in 1925 he was knighted for his services to women and children in New Zealand.

In an imperial world King's connections worked to his advantage. Lady Plunket and Winifride Wrench invited him to London during the First World War, to establish a Karitane hospital, and accordingly, in 1918, he organized a mothercraft training centre for the Babies of the Empire Society, to train infant welfare nurses for the empire; Lady Plunket's sister, Lady Munro Ferguson, wife of the Australian governor-general, invited King to Australia in 1919. By then King was an imperial authority in the campaign to save baby life and had served on the executive of the National Baby Week council. The nurses who trained with King in London spread his version of the infant welfare message. One was Matron Mabel Liddiard, who perpetuated her mentor's reputation through the Mothercraft Training Society and through her book for British middle-class mothers, *The Mothercraft Manual* (1924). The royal seal of approval, provided by the duchess of York and her little daughters, was important; to many a young mother the regimen patronized and advertised as used by royalty had to be worth a try.

Appointed New Zealand's first director of child welfare under the department of health in 1921, King's significance was as a proselytizer at home and overseas. He inspired and irritated with his conviction of rightness, goading supporters and opponents to establish their own programmes. In Australia, the United Kingdom, and Canada, King invited controversy as a visiting infant welfare authority who polarized opinions; in turn this helped raise his profile in the public domain. On a trip to England, in 1913, he strove to expose a discrepancy between his feeding tables and those of Eric Pritchard in order to show that his own were right. Australia became a battleground over infant feeding in the 1920s; the Australian medical profession and infant welfare experts resented being preached at, asserting that they knew what was best for the Australian baby. The debate was fiercest over the protein component of infant feeding formulas. King insisted on low protein in humanized milk because 'God put 1.4 per cent protein into breast milk' (Smith, *Mothers and King Baby*, 124). However, leading paediatricians in the white dominions and in London profoundly disagreed with him, and opted for strong, high protein feeds to assist babies' growth.

King's changing historiographical reputation is indicated by challenges to the *Dictionary of National Biography*'s judgement, in 1949, that: 'Thanks mainly to King and the adoption of his methods … the rate of infant mortality has fallen in a marked manner'. Such claims were exaggerated. King insisted that Plunket methods were the one essential cause of New Zealand's record in white infant mortality, which, until his death in 1938, was the lowest in the world and made New Zealand a model for infant welfare when circumstances varied in other countries. The fact that many believed him demonstrates the force of his rhetoric and charisma. Without his power to mesmerize nurses and mothers as the paternalistic figurehead of what was essentially a women's movement, and without

his dogmatism, his advertisements, and his musical delivery, the Plunket system would not have gained its international reputation in infant welfare. King affected infant mortality, not by his methods but by stirring up anxieties about standards of motherhood. He helped to put mothers and babies on the agenda with his claim that 'perfect motherhood is perfect patriotism' (Smith, *Mothers and King Baby*, 91).

In the 1920s King built a bungalow on a spectacular hilltop at Wellington; this was followed, in 1927, by a Karitane mothercraft home, and a model factory where the Karitane Products Society manufactured the emulsion and sugar, Kariol and Karilac, deemed essential for King's bottle-feeding formulas and exported to the faithful in other countries. King died at Melrose, Wellington, on 9 February 1938. In a funeral eulogy the bishop of Wellington said that King had the eyes 'of a visionary, almost of the fanatic' (Smith, *Mothers and King Baby*, 88). He was the first New Zealand private citizen to receive a state funeral and possibly the only bankrupt to be so honoured, his assets having been spent on his idealism. In 1957 he became the first New Zealander to have his image replace the monarch's on a postage stamp. Sir Frederic and Lady Truby King lie buried on their hilltop, the Plunket Society's motto, 'to help the mothers and save the babies', cemented on their grave.

PHILIPPA MEIN SMITH

Sources M. T. King, *Truby King: the man* (1948) · P. L. M. Smith, *Mothers and King baby* (1997) · B. Brookes, 'King, Frederic Truby', *DNZB*, vol. 2 · R. M. Burdon, *New Zealand notables*, series 2 (1945) · P. M. Smith, 'Isabella Truby King', *The book of New Zealand women*, ed. C. Macdonald, B. Williams, and M. Penfold (1991), 354–6 · Hocken Library, Dunedin, New Zealand, Plunket Society records, AG7 · Hocken Library, Dunedin, New Zealand, Karitane Hospital records, AG38 · NL NZ, Turnbull L., King family MSS, MS 1004 · F. T. King, *Feeding and care of baby* (1913) · *DNB* · private information (2004)

Archives NL NZ, Turnbull L., family papers · NL NZ, Turnbull L., pamphlets · University of Otago, Dunedin, Hocken Library, Plunket Society records | University of Otago, Dunedin, Hocken Library, Karitane Hospital records · University of Otago, Dunedin, Hocken Library, Seacliff Archives

Likenesses photograph, Hocken Library, Dunedin · photograph, NL NZ Turnbull L.

King, William (1624–1680), musician, was the son of George King (d. 1665), organist of Winchester Cathedral. He was admitted a lay clerk of Magdalen College, Oxford, on 18 October 1648 and graduated BA on 5 June 1649. He gained in 1652 a chaplaincy at Magdalen, which he left in 1654. He was appointed organist at New College on 10 December 1664.

King composed songs and sacred vocal music. Eighteen anthems and three services are in the New College part-books (Bodl. Oxf., MS Mus. C.48). His anthems 'O be joyful in God' and 'The Lord is King' enjoyed wide circulation. His old-fashioned syllabic style sometimes produced inelegant homophony with little harmonic interest. His verse anthems often used two trebles and had weak concluding alleluias. As a composer of songs King was an isolated figure. The examples in his *Songs and Ayres* (Oxford, 1668) reject the tuneful influence of the dance but are marked by a suppleness of line. This anticipates younger composers and brings freedom to what would otherwise be a rigid declamatory pattern. King died at New College on 7 November 1680. He was buried there in the cloisters beneath the epitaph 'his singular eminence in music made him a partaker of the consort of angels'.

DAVID S. KNIGHT

Sources M. Tilmouth, 'King, William', *New Grove* • H. W. Shaw, *The succession of organists of the Chapel Royal and the cathedrals of England and Wales from c.1538* (1991) • I. Spink, *English song: Dowland to Purcell* (1974) • Foster, *Alum. Oxon.* • DNB

King, William (1650–1729), Church of Ireland archbishop of Dublin, was born in Antrim town on 1 May 1650, the son of James King (still alive in 1701), who had emigrated to Ulster from Barra in Aberdeenshire and who was later said to have been a miller or a merchant. In 1658 he moved with his household from Antrim to co. Tyrone.

Early life, 1650–1691 King's later reference to the family's inability to support him while a student at Trinity College, Dublin, suggests that by that time at least it was not prosperous. A fragmentary autobiography, written some time after 1697, describes a succession of unsatisfactory early schooling experiences, with sudden breakthroughs in reading, mathematics, and later Latin being attributed primarily to the young King's own efforts. He entered the Royal School at Dungannon in 1662, and was admitted to Trinity College, Dublin, on 7 April 1667.

James King was, according to his son, 'a most rigid adherent of the Presbyterian sect' (King, *A Great Archbishop*, 2), although at the time of William's birth he was under excommunication for having refused to accept the solemn league and covenant. William King presents himself in his autobiography as having been poorly instructed in, and largely indifferent to, religion of any kind until his arrival at Trinity College. There the influence of his tutor John Christian led him to undergo a period of spiritual crisis and anxious enquiry, by the end of which he had become a convinced member of the established church. He graduated BA on 23 February 1670, and on 25 October 1671 was admitted to deacon's orders as chaplain to John Parker, archbishop of Tuam, who appointed him to the prebend of Kilmainmore, co. Mayo, on 14 July 1673. King received his MA in 1673 and was ordained on 12 April 1674, taking up residence in Parker's household. He resigned Kilmainmore on becoming provost of the cathedral of St Mary, Tuam, on 26 October 1676 and took up residence in the town of Tuam. On 27 October 1679 Parker, now archbishop of Dublin, had him appointed chancellor of St Patrick's and minister of St Werburgh's parish in the city. King later presented this demanding assignment, plunging him into a round of intense pastoral effort combined with diligent study, as having rescued him from the life of provincial inactivity into which he had been preparing to settle. During this period at St Werburgh's he engaged in his first public controversy. In response to the former dean of Derry's apologia for his conversion to Catholicism, King published *An answer to the considerations which obliged Peter Manby … to embrace, what he calls the Catholick*

William King (1650–1729), by John Faber junior, 1729 (after Charles Jervas)

religion (1687). Manby's reply led King to publish *A Vindication of the Answer* (1688), to which, after a further paper by Manby, he added *A Vindication of the Christian Religion and Reformation* (1688).

King was appointed chaplain to the lord deputy, the earl of Arran, on 20 October 1683, and on 25 November 1684 chaplain to the lord lieutenant, the duke of Ormond. He received his BD and DD degrees from Trinity College on 11 July 1688. He was installed as dean of St Patrick's on 1 February 1689. In the same month the archbishop of Dublin, Francis Marsh, withdrew to England, having appointed King and Samuel Foley (King's successor as chancellor of St Patrick's) as commissaries to manage the diocese in his absence. When Foley, too, fled to England King was left in sole charge. He later had Anthony Dopping, bishop of Meath, elected guardian of the diocese by the city's two cathedral chapters. According to his own account this was because he feared the authority he had been given was insufficient. However it has been suggested (*Diary*, 10) that he may have believed that his commission lapsed following Marsh's attainder for treason by the Jacobite parliament. King and Dopping worked closely together to maintain ecclesiastical discipline and sustain protestant morale in Jacobite-dominated Dublin. King was arrested in July 1689 and imprisoned in Dublin Castle until December. He was again detained, along with other prominent protestants, in June 1690, and was held until the occupation of the city by Williamite forces following the battle of the Boyne.

King's conduct in 1689–91 subsequently became the subject of controversy, especially in his exchanges with the nonjuror Charles Leslie, who accused him of having abandoned his earlier principles of passive resistance by providing military intelligence to the Williamites. His own version was that he had taken no direct action and had advised no one else to take up arms; the furthest he had gone was to accept that it was lawful to accept the deliverance that providence had sent in the person of William of Orange. His arrest by the Jacobite authorities he blamed on the indiscreet publication of letters that others had sent to correspondents in England and Ulster. However, he seems to have admitted privately to James Bonnell that he had, in fact, transmitted intelligence both to the duke of Schomberg, William's commander in Ulster, and directly to England, and even to have boasted of the ingenuity with which he ensured that these letters could not be traced back to him (Bonnell to John Strype, 21 Feb 1691, 24 April 1691, CUL, Baumgartner Papers, Strype MSS I, fols. 87, 93). In 1691 he published a detailed defence of his own and others' conduct, *The State of the Protestants of Ireland under the Late King James's Government* (1691), which established him as the leading Irish defender of the revolution. His central argument was that Irish protestants were justified in withdrawing their allegiance from James II because a ruler who sought the destruction of his subjects, as James had done when he placed them in the power of their Catholic enemies, abdicated his government over them. Even here, however, he held back from justifying direct resistance. He insisted that those who had taken up arms at Derry and Enniskillen had done so only in self-defence, and presented Irish protestants in general as having passively accepted the deliverance sent by providence or, alternatively, as having acquiesced in the *de facto* transfer of power in England, as Ireland's dependent status required them to do. The argument that James's removal had been the work of providence was stated even more clearly in *Europe's Deliverance from France and Slavery* (1691), a sermon preached at St Patrick's before the lords justices on 30 November 1690, which concluded bluntly that ''twas manifestly God rather than the people set our king and queen on the throne' (p. 21).

Bishop of Derry, 1691–1703 In summer 1690 King used contacts in England to urge on the new monarchs his claims for a bishopric. He was appointed bishop of Derry on 7 December 1690 and consecrated on 25 January 1691. He took up residence in March and began a vigorous campaign to restore regular pastoral services in a diocese ravaged by war and which had been without a resident bishop for two years. His autobiography records a sharp initial conflict with clergy who were using post-war economic dislocation as an excuse not to live on their benefices. By 1693 there were twenty-eight beneficed clergy living in the diocese, compared with only ten in May 1691, as well as eleven curates. King also lobbied the government for funds for church repair and the provision of glebes and houses. He paid close attention to the provision of schools, established a library at Derry for the use of the clergy and gentry, and sought to make schoolmasters and clergy the agents of a revived system of parish-based

moral discipline. When a colony of episcopalian highlanders settled at Clonmany in co. Donegal, King provided a minister able to preach and conduct services in Gaelic.

In addition to these efforts to improve pastoral standards in his own diocese, King joined with other reform-minded bishops, notably Nathaniel Foy of Waterford and Lismore and Dopping, to lobby the English government for a programme of church reform in Ireland, concentrating particularly on the issue of ecclesiastical appointments. In 1693–4 he was one of the commissioners appointed to investigate the outstanding clerical scandal of the period when Thomas Hacket, bishop of Down and Connor, was removed, along with several of his clergy, following complaints of long-term absenteeism, neglect, and mismanagement.

In Derry, King came into conflict with the Presbyterians, who outnumbered conformists in the diocese and dominated urban government in Derry city and other centres. In 1694 he published *A Discourse Concerning the Inventions of Men in the Worship of God*, which sought to show that the practice of the Church of Ireland in relation to music, forms of prayer, the celebration of the eucharist, and other matters was in closer conformity with scripture than that of the Presbyterians. The pamphlet was attacked by Joseph Boyse, who had earlier clashed with King over comments made during his controversy with Manby, and by the Presbyterian minister of Derry itself, Robert Craighead. King replied to Boyse in *An Admonition to the Dissenting Inhabitants of Derry* (1694), followed by *A Second Admonition* (1695). Alarm at the threat from dissent, as well as an acute concern to protect the church's legal entitlements, also played a part in King's prolonged controversy with the Irish Society of London. This began as a dispute over terms for the renewal of the society's sixty-year lease on church lands, which expired in 1694, but broadened into a conflict over the ownership of other lands and fishing rights. King was concerned to curb the power of the society, which he saw as supporting the dissenting interest, and to generate revenue for an Anglican college at Derry that would combat Presbyterian influence in the region. The society, on the other hand, had the backing of the Presbyterian-dominated corporation of the city. In November 1697 the Irish House of Lords, reversing an earlier decision of chancery, granted King possession of the disputed lands. The society, however, appealed to the English House of Lords, which overturned the Irish decision in May 1698. When King continued to assert his right, the English House of Lords tried unsuccessfully to have him brought to England to face charges of contempt. In the end the Irish executive helped to negotiate a compromise solution. The episode did not turn King into an Irish patriot. As early as 1695 he had told Bonnell that he had no hopes for the forthcoming parliament because 'England doth not intend we should do ourselves good, and will look to it, lest we should' (28 June 1695, TCD, MS 1995–2008, no. 445). But the sense of personal grievance almost certainly contributed to his vehement response to later constitutional conflicts.

The State of the Protestants, with its remorseless catalogue of the abuses endured under Tyrconnell's government, has given King an undeserved reputation as an anti-Catholic polemicist. In fact he was a strong critic of much of the anti-Catholic legislation proposed or introduced during the 1690s. He accepted without question that Catholics, on account of their dangerous principles, should be excluded from civil office. However, he regarded the promises made to them in the treaty of Limerick as an agreement binding in honour, and signed the formal protest against what he considered the fraudulently incomplete bill to ratify the treaty passed in 1697. He also condemned the draconian bill to preserve the king's person, complaining that 'men of no religion, nay that scoffed at all religion … should impose on men that had some, though an ill one'. Specifically, he considered that the arbitrary power it was proposed to vest in magistrates was a breach of Magna Carta, while to take away men's lives or liberties for refusing to renounce an article of faith, the authority of the pope, amounted to religious persecution (TCD, MS 750/1, pp. 134, 147–50).

In 1702 King published his most important philosophical work, *De origine male* (The origin of evil). Conceived as a reply to the scepticism of Pierre Bayle and his followers, this took as its starting point the argument that we can achieve a pragmatic if necessarily incomplete knowledge of God, as a unitary, omnipotent and perfect first cause, by analogy from His works. Although God had created the best possible world, evil existed owing to the necessary imperfection of created things, the natural evil created by the movement of matter according to physical laws, and the moral evil arising from the existence of human free will. The book attracted comment from Bayle as well as from Leibnitz and others. An English translation by Edmund Law appeared in 1731 and went through five editions by 1781. King's other major philosophical work, his published sermon *Divine Predestination and Foreknowledge, Consistent with the Freedom of Man's will* (1709), sought to reconcile divine omniscience and human freedom by arguing that God's foreknowledge of events, which we know only by analogy, should not be assumed to be identical with that of humankind. Although King is often described as drawing on Lockean epistemology, Kelly (in *The Dictionary of Eighteenth-Century British Philosophers*) emphasizes instead his debt to older scholastic concepts. Berman (in his introduction to Carpenter's edition of the sermon) has characterized his overall philosophical outlook as 'theological representationalism', noting the debt to his fellow Irish bishop Peter Browne.

Archbishop of Dublin, 1703–1729 On 11 March 1703 King was appointed archbishop of Dublin. He approached his duties with the same scrupulous concern for propriety, attention to administrative detail, and rigorous disciplinary zeal that he had shown in Derry. Writing to Francis Annesley on 24 March 1713, he admitted that he was not surprised by claims that he was excessively strict:

> … on recollection I remember I have degraded four from their orders. I have laid in jail two excommunicated clergymen who died there. I have writs or warrants out against three more. I have discovered six or seven with counterfeit letters of orders and some in good places turned out on that account. I have deprived of their living six or seven and have suspended or otherwise censured about 30. Add to these many that I have rejected from orders, several to whom I have refused benefices or institution for want of qualifications and the many I have chid or reproved, both publicly and privately.   (TCD, MS 750/4/1, pp. 133–4)

In addition to measures against unsatisfactory clergy King was particularly insistent on refusing to ordain those who seemed to him unprepared or unsuited for the clerical life, or for whom there was no realistic prospect of employment. There were also more positive achievements. During King's episcopate the number of churches in repair in the diocese rose from 27 to 69, while he claimed in 1727 that he had built eleven glebe houses. As in Derry he fiercely defended the legal rights of the see. In 1704 he began what was to be a twenty-year struggle to establish his jurisdiction over Christ Church Cathedral. The dean and chapter accused King of invading their liberties as a royal foundation. He insisted that the issue was a matter of ecclesiastical discipline, alleging that the chapter had failed to supply clergymen or provide for the repair of churches in the twenty-seven parishes appropriated to it. A first legal battle, over rights of visitation, commenced in 1711; a second, arising from the chapter's refusal to admit King's nephew, Robert Dougat, whom he had appointed archdeacon of Dublin, began in 1715. Both dragged on until 1724, when the British House of Lords gave final judgment in King's favour.

At national level King was by now a leading spokesman for the established church. He took a leading part in the attempt to persuade Queen Anne to redirect for ecclesiastical purposes the former papal dues known as the first fruits and twentieth parts, and vigorously opposed attempts in 1707–8 to secure the removal of the sacramental test. He also joined in the campaign which eventually secured a meeting of convocation in 1703. He initially saw this revival of the representative body of the clergy as the best means of tackling the church's institutional weaknesses, and on 16 January 1705 supplied the prolocutor of convocation, Samuel Synge, with a long list of proposed reforms, covering pluralities, non-residence, the qualifications of candidates of ordination, and the supply of curates in large or appropriated livings (TCD, MS 750/3/1, pp. 67–72). In 1709 the chief secretary paid tribute to his success in damping down an unproductive debate on the issue of dissent, reporting that 'the archbishop is looked upon as the oracle of the church party in this kingdom' (*The Letters of Joseph Addison*, ed. W. Graham, 1941, 144). However King became increasingly disillusioned at the failure of convocation to implement the sort of practical reforms he had advocated, although he placed the blame for this failure mainly on his fellow bishops, who had repeatedly failed to respond to initiatives sent up from the lower house.

As conflict between whig and tory intensified during Anne's reign King wrote critically of what he saw as the unnecessary importation into Ireland of the factional divisions of English politics. The only issue that concerned the protestants of Ireland, he insisted, was the maintenance of the protestant succession. His own political principles remained conservative. In 1701, for example, he complained to Bishop Thomas Lindsay of Killaloe that the powers to be given to the English privy council under the Act of Succession made the monarch 'a princeps concilii', adding that 'I cannot but with concern think to what a pass the king has brought the monarchy by a republican ministry' (21 March 1701, TCD, MS 750/2/2, p. 88). In December 1710 he observed that if the new tory ministry 'go on as they begin … they will confound whiggism' (King to Francis Annesley, 16 Dec 1710, TCD, MS 2531, p. 238). As late as January 1714 he sought to dissuade leading whigs from taking what he considered the extreme step of voting against the crown's choice of speaker.

The new whig ministry's choice of King as one of the three lords justices appointed on 4 September 1714 can thus be seen as reflecting his status as a known supporter of the protestant interest in its two great crises of 1688–90 and 1710–14, rather than any strong party affiliation. King himself supported the impeachment of the English tory leaders, but argued that the majority of the rank and file had been unaware of their Jacobite intrigues and that all well-affected men should be fairly treated. Later, however, he sought to minimize and defend as reasonable the extensive purge of tory office holders of all levels that had in fact taken place (TCD, MS 2533, pp. 116–17). Lord Coningsby, in a confidential report to George I, described him as 'a perfectly honest man, truly zealous for your Majesty and your service but entirely a stranger to the business he is engaged in' (PRO NIre., D638/145). However King's own correspondence suggests that he approached his duties confidently and systematically, dealing firmly but without undue panic with the Irish repercussions of the Jacobite rising in England and Scotland in 1715. He continued as lord justice until 6 September 1715, and was to serve again from 22 February to 27 April 1717, and from 25 November 1717 to 31 May 1719.

Despite this political prominence King's relationship with the new whig establishment was an uneasy one. One major reason was his continued commitment to the defence of the established church and the containment of dissent. As before, he saw the main threat as coming from the Presbyterians of Ulster. He maintained a watchful opposition to further attempts in 1715–16 to secure the repeal of the test. Writing to Archbishop Wake of Canterbury on 24 March 1716 he insisted that the Ulster Presbyterians were wholly different from English nonconformists: 'they are a people embodied under their lay elders, presbyteries and synods, … and will be just so far the king's subjects as their lay elders and presbyteries will allow them' (TCD, MS 2533, p. 165). However, he also opposed legal concessions to Quakers on the grounds that they did not subscribe to what he considered fundamental Christian doctrines, and joined with Bishop Moreton of Kildare in attempts to force French protestant refugees to conform to the liturgy of the Church of Ireland. In the same way his vigorous opposition to the Irish Toleration Act of 1719 was motivated less by the negligible improvement it brought to the status of Presbyterians than by the

absence of any requirement that those claiming its protection should make even the most basic profession of Christian faith, so that 'Jews, Turks, deists, pagans, &c. may all set up for teachers' (Mant, 2.342).

Where Catholics were concerned King remained critical of existing policy. He supported the proposals of the Revd John Richardson in 1712 to promote a new missionary effort by producing bibles and prayer books in Irish, and criticized the lukewarm response of his fellow bishops, although he also privately suggested that Richardson had been precipitate in launching his scheme without proper backing. Shortly after the accession of George I, in January 1715, he addressed two long letters to the new lord lieutenant, the earl of Sunderland, condemning what he saw as the ruinous policy of subjecting Catholics to excessively severe penal laws that were not then enforced, and calling for a more consistent approach. He opposed bills in 1719 and 1723 which sought to impose new and harsher penalties on unregistered priests. By 1727, on the other hand, he had come to feel that policy had moved too far in the opposite direction, complaining that he did not 'remember Popery so rampant, or so much encouraged, as at present, except in King James's time' (Mant, 2.487).

When new lords justices were appointed in October 1719 King was not included, explaining to Archbishop Wake that, by his opposition to the Toleration Act and other measures, 'I have quite lost the favour of the government here' (Mant, 2.337). He was, however, reappointed to the lord justiceship between 31 January 1722 and 13 August 1723, although this was only, according to his own account, to facilitate the exclusion of Lord Chancellor Midleton (TCD, MS 750/7, p. 88). Henry Downes, bishop of Killala, one of the English-born bishops who had repeatedly been made aware of King's hostility, believed that his show of indifference at being excluded in 1719 merely concealed his mortification at the implied loss of consequence. Downes was likewise sceptical of King's claims in 1722 that his reappointment to the office would kill him, suggesting that 'perhaps he would have been as uneasy had he been left out of the government'. He also reported that King had made his fellow lords justices 'sick of him', because he left such 'invidious work' as the signing of patents for pensions to them, 'and serves himself at the expense of their and some other greater person's honour' (Nichols, 2.497, 536, 556).

By this time King had emerged not only as a critic of whig laxity in religious policy but as an intransigent defender of Ireland's constitutional rights. The insistence of the British House of Lords on its entitlement to deliver final judgment in the case of Sherlock v. Annesley in 1719 revived the issue of legislative and judicial autonomy that had arisen in his own dispute with the Irish Society. King led the Irish lords in having the Irish barons of the exchequer taken into custody for implementing the decision of the British house, and in drawing up a 'Representation' reasserting their status as the court of final appeal. William Nicolson, the English-born bishop of Derry, reported that he had become the 'darling' of the mob, and that 'The Angel of St Patrick's is now the Guardian of the

Kingdom' (McNally, 159). In 1720–21 he opposed the proposal for an Irish bank, and in 1722–5 he was a prominent opponent of Wood's halfpence. On 19 December 1723 the lord lieutenant, the duke of Grafton, reported to Walpole that King

> is very indiscreet in his actions and expressions, pretty ungovernable, and has some wild notions, which sometimes make him impracticable in business, and he is to a ridiculous extravagance, national. Upon some points (of which the jurisdiction of the house of lords is a principal one) he loses both his temper and his reason.   (Coxe, 2.357)

Even after the ministry had capitulated King sought to drive home the victory by adding to the Lords' resolution of thanks a reference characterizing the surrender of the patent as an instance not just of the king's 'goodness' and 'condescension' but also of his 'great wisdom' (Letters … Boulter, 1.41–2).

King was also largely responsible for the sharp divide that emerged in the years after 1714 between bishops of Irish and English origin. In the immediate aftermath of the change of government in August 1714 the new whig ministry had taken King's advice in filling three vacant bishoprics. However the appointment of the Welshman John Evans to Meath in 1716 and of the Englishman William Nicolson to Derry in 1718 caused outrage in Irish church circles. King complained bitterly that English churchmen, having squandered the resources of their own church for short-term profit, were now beginning to invade the better managed Irish establishment, and that the disposal of the best dioceses to outsiders left native clergy with little incentive to diligence or self-improvement. In the case of Nicolson he took his revenge by insisting that he should take the most junior place on the episcopal bench in the House of Lords, despite having held an English bishopric for sixteen years. Tensions were further exacerbated when five recently appointed outsiders broke ranks to support the Toleration Bill, leaving King to complain to an English correspondent that the measure could have been defeated 'if your brethren that came from your side the water had not deserted us' (King to Annesley, 10 Nov 1719, TCD, MS 750/5, p. 200). Later, in 1722, he refused to consecrate Josiah Hort as bishop of Ferns and Leighlin, objecting to his dissenting background and claiming that he had not been properly ordained; instead Hort had to be consecrated by a specially constituted commission composed of three English bishops.

Following the death of Thomas Lindsay, archbishop of Armagh, on 13 July 1724 there was speculation that King might succeed him as primate. In the event the see went to Hugh Boulter. King's attitude to thus being passed over remains unclear. A well-known anecdote, first recorded by Orrery in 1752, presented him as greeting Boulter on their first meeting, from a chair in his parlour, with the sarcastic comment that he was too old to rise. King himself insisted that he had resisted pressure from friends to press his claims on the grounds that 'a crazy, lame and superannuated primate' could be of no service to either the church or the kingdom (King, A Great Archbishop, 248 n.

4). However this was precisely the sort of self-denial that Bishop Downes had earlier dismissed as spurious. What is clear is that Boulter from the start regarded King as the leader of a rival 'Irish' faction within the church, whose influence should be systematically curbed by further appointments of Englishmen as sees became vacant. By contrast one of the executive's leading parliamentary managers, Marmaduke Coghill, reporting in September 1727 on attempts by Midleton, now openly in opposition, to woo King, believed that the archbishop could be kept in good humour for the coming session by a kind message from the king ('it would captivate the old gentleman, who is highly pleased with such compliments') and possibly the bestowal of a living that he sought for his nephew (BL, Add. MSS 21122, fol. 32).

Reputation   William King was the single most important Irish protestant churchman of his era. He was also a central figure in Irish intellectual life for four decades. In addition to his theological writings and his *State of the Protestants* he was an early member of the Dublin Philosophical Society, to which he presented papers on a range of scientific topics. Two of these, on the origin of Irish bogs (1684) and on the use of sea shells as manure (1708), were published in the *Philosophical Transactions*. However a mock speech printed at the time he received his DD (1688) derided his bad Latin, and a modern editor has likewise commented on the 'curious Latin' of his autobiography (*Diary*, 19). His extensive personal correspondence, mainly preserved in Trinity College, Dublin, makes him almost certainly the most thoroughly documented figure in late seventeenth- and early eighteenth-century Ireland, and provides a vivid if often opinionated depiction of political and ecclesiastical affairs. Richard Mant in 1840 and Sir Charles King in 1906 presented uniformly favourable accounts of a dedicated churchman and great reforming bishop and archbishop. Contemporary opponents such as Downes and Boulter suspected that his declarations of disinterested principle could also mask personal ambition, malice, and resentment. Yet even Grafton, while deploring his political volatility, described him as 'charitable, hospitable, a despiser of riches, and an excellent bishop' (Coxe, 2.357). Patrick Kelly has suggested plausibly that King's childhood experiences in an Ulster devastated by civil war, and what he saw as his providential survival during the crisis of 1688–90, provided the basis for his unwavering commitment to the constitution in church and state as the only guarantees against anarchy.

Portraits of King in middle life suggest a man of average build with broad, regular features. An anonymous contemporary account stated that he had acquired from his schoolmaster at Dungannon 'an habit of speaking in the Scotch dialect that he lamented all his days after, … which, with a kind of lisping and stammering natural to him, render his voice and manner of speaking very ungraceful' (G. T. Stokes, *Some Worthies of the Irish Church*, 1900, 149 n. 1). He suffered from gout from the early age of twenty-five. His autobiography records how his labours in St Werburgh's led to a collapse in his health, forcing him to go to England to take the waters at Tunbridge Wells.

Complaints of illness recur throughout his later correspondence, but his survival until the age of seventy-nine suggests a strong constitution. He never married. A funeral sermon claimed that he had chosen 'a single life' so as to be able to devote as much as possible of his resources to charity, but he himself admitted to Swift in 1712 that he had 'an awkward way of address to ladies' (*Correspondence of Jonathan Swift*, 1.290). He died at the episcopal palace of St Sepulchre on 8 May 1729 and was buried in St Mary's Church, Donnybrook, on 10 May. He left his property, valued at £17,000, to public purposes, including the Archbishop King's lecturership in divinity at Trinity College, Dublin, which he had founded in 1718.

S. J. CONNOLLY

Sources C. S. King, ed., *A great archbishop of Dublin: William King D.D., 1650–1729* (1906) · R. Mant, *History of the Church of Ireland*, 2 vols. (1840) · *The diary of William King, D.D. kept during his imprisonment in Dublin Castle, 1689*, ed. H. J. Lawlor (1903) · D. Berman, introduction, in *Archbishop King's sermon on predestination*, ed. A. Carpenter (1976), vol. 4 of *Irish writings from the age of Swift* (1972–9) · J. C. Beckett, 'William King's administration of the diocese of Derry, 1691–1703', *Irish Historical Studies*, 4 (1944–5), 164–80 · P. Kelly, 'Archbishop William King and colonial nationalism', *Worsted in the game: losers in Irish history*, ed. C. Brady (1989), 84–98 · R. T. C. Kennedy, 'The administration of the diocese of Dublin and Glendalough in the eighteenth century', MLitt diss., University of Dublin, 1968 · A. Carpenter, 'William King and the threats to the Church of Ireland during the reign of James II', *Irish Historical Studies*, 18 (1972–3), 22–8 · *The correspondence of Jonathan Swift*, ed. H. Williams, 5 vols. (1963–5) · J. Nichols, ed., *Letters on various subjects ... to and from William Nicolson*, 2 vols. (1809) · *Letters written by his excellency Hugh Boulter D.D. lord primate of all Ireland*, 2 vols. (1769–70) · P. McNally, *Parties, patriots and undertakers: parliamentary politics in early Hanoverian Ireland* (1997) · K. T. Hoppen, *The common scientist in the seventeenth century: a study of the Dublin Philosophical Society, 1683–1708* (1970) · DNB · W. Coxe, *Memoirs of the life and administration of Sir Robert Walpole, earl of Orford*, 3 vols. (1798) · P. Kelly, 'King, William', *The dictionary of eighteenth-century British philosophers*, ed. J. W. Yolton, J. V. Price, and J. Stephens (1999) · P. O'Regan, *Archbishop William King (1650–1729) and the constitution in church and state* (2000)
Archives Armagh Public Library, collection, H.II.19 · BL, collections for monastic history of Dublin, Egerton MS 1776 · NL Ire., MSS 2055–2056 · TCD, corresp. and letter-books, MSS 750, 1995–2000, 2531–2537 · U. Aberdeen L., diary, papers, and sermons | Bodl. Oxf., letters to Henry Dodwell · LPL, corresp. with Society for the Propagation of the Gospel
Likenesses T. Beard, mezzotint, pubd 1729 (after M. Dahl), NG Ire. · J. Faber junior, mezzotint, 1729 (after C. Jervas), BM [*see illus.*] · R. Purcell, mezzotint, pubd 1753 (after C. Jervas), NG Ire. · R. Home, oils, *c.*1783–1788 (after C. Jervas), TCD · A. Miller, mezzotint (after C. Jervas), BM · portrait, TCD; repro. in King, ed., *Great archbishop of Dublin*
Wealth at death £17,000: DNB

King, William (1663–1712), writer, was born in London, the son of Ezekias King (*b.* 1637, *d.* in or after 1672), gentleman. His forebears included merchants and a clergyman grandparent, Ezekias King, who turned presbyterian and was silenced in 1662. William King was a king's scholar at Westminster School, from 1678 to 1681, under Richard Busby's headmastership. He was admitted to Christ Church, Oxford, as a king's student in Michaelmas term 1681, matriculated on 16 December, and graduated BA on 8 December 1685, as a grand compounder—this higher fee indicating an estate worth at least £300 per annum. After

proceeding MA (6 July 1688) he embarked on the study of civil law, becoming BCL and DCL (7 July 1692) and a member of Doctors' Commons (12 November)—a more prestigious than lucrative branch of advocacy. At Oxford he read widely but, as Dr Johnson calculated, could hardly have dispatched in eight years the twenty-two thousand books and manuscripts alleged, from his *Adversaria*, by Joseph Browne (Johnson, *Poets*, 26; Browne, 16).

King had already embarked on a writer's life: *Reflections upon Mons Varillas's History of Heresy*, written with Edward Hannes (1688), defended Wycliffe; *An Answer to a Book* (1693) attacked William Sherlock, accused of tritheism; *Animadversions on a Pretended Account of Danmark* (1694) disputed Robert Molesworth's exposure of Danish absolutism, earning him Prince George of Denmark's gratitude and the post—which seems not to have involved much— of secretary to his wife, Princess Anne. King also wrote poetry in Dryden's *Examen poeticum* (1693) and translations for the bookseller Thomas Bennet. A letter from King recalling, from spring 1694, Richard Bentley's 'Pride and Insolence' in a conversation, overheard by King, between Bentley and Bennet, was printed in the collaborative attack on Bentley by the so-called Christ Church wits (C. Boyle, *Dr Bentley's Dissertations ... Examin'd*, 1698, 8). King supposedly contributed their mock-proof that Bentley had not written his own dissertation; also a satirical index; if so, he wrote the *Examination*'s best parts. Bentley, in his revised *Dissertation*, poured scorn on King's letter, quoting Horace's 'The filth and venom of Rupilius King' (R. Bentley, *A Dissertation upon the Epistles of Phalaris*, 1699, xxix). King then ridiculed 'Bentivoglio' in his anonymous *Dialogues of the Dead* (1699); he may also have written the appendix *A Short Account of Dr Bentley's Humanity* (1699).

King was making fun of other people too: *A Journey to London* (1698) parodied Martin Lister's recent *Journey to Paris*, with its triviality and muddle; *The Transactioneer* (1700), two dialogues reminiscent of Shadwell's *Virtuoso*, caricatured the Royal Society's secretary, Hans Sloane. Perhaps King was lazy and preferred being a littérateur to a lawyer (Nichols, 1.xiv); but he looks conscientious enough in two business letters to under-secretary John Ellis (Engel, 39–40). His most famous case was lost: defending the earl of Anglesey in the House of Lords (February–April 1701) against his wife's action for separation. Soon after that King gave up Doctors' Commons to become a judge of the Admiralty court in Dublin. His reasons are unclear, but the move must owe something to the earl of Rochester, who arrived in Ireland as lord lieutenant on 16 September 1701: King had some family connection with the Hydes and had been active in tory politics (Engel, 36–7). He arrived in Dublin before Rochester, only to find his patent delayed and the Admiralty court defunct. The city regarded King's appointment as an infringement of its rights: although he was appointed agent for prizes at Dublin on 29 August 1702, he was still waiting for his Admiralty court commission when he wrote to Ellis on 16 January 1703 and complained, *inter alia*, of the Irish people's being 'insolent, & proud as they are poor' (BL, Add. MS 28890, fol. 17).

King found an English friend in Anthony Upton, judge of common pleas, who entertained him on his estate at Mountown outside Dublin. King's poem about the red cow 'Mully of Mountown' was pirated, as was a parody of Orpheus and Eurydice, and attributed to 'the author of the Tale of a tub'. King published authorized versions of both poems in *Some Remarks on the 'Tale of a Tub'* (1704), where he denied writing *A Tale*. He was replaced as agent for prizes on 13 May 1706 but secured the vicar-generalship of Armagh. On 19 June 1707, helped perhaps by the new lord lieutenant, the earl of Pembroke, he was made keeper of the records in Dublin Castle. The post was poorly paid and required more of an antiquary than King was; he resigned on 28 November 1707 and returned to England.

King was now dependent on his income as a writer: Bernard Lintott paid him 30 guineas each for *The Art of Cookery, in Imitation of Horace's Art of Poetry* ([1708]) and *The Art of Love: in Imitation of Ovid De arte amandi* ([1708]). The poems' popularity prompted Lintott to print a two-volume collection of King's *Miscellanies* ([1708–9]); also his *Historical Account of the Heathen Gods and Heroes*, much used in schools, for which he subsequently received £50. King returned to his attack on Sloane with the mock-proceedings *Useful Transactions in Philosophy*, which ran for three issues (January–September 1709). In May 1711 Gay noted its demise and added that the 'Author deserves a much better Fate, than to Languish out the small remainder of his Life in the *Fleet Prison*' (*Poetry and Prose*, 2.449). On 19 December 1711 Swift described King, whose Irish footman had just died, as 'a poor starving wit' (Swift, 2.442). But King commended himself to Swift as a high-church tory, publishing five pro-Sacheverell pamphlets (1710–11) and early in 1712 satirizing Marlborough in *Rufinus, or, An Historical Essay*.

On 8 January 1712 Swift wrote to Archbishop King in Dublin, 'I have got poor Dr. *King* … to be Gazetteer, which will be worth 250 *l*. to him, if he be diligent and sober, for which I am engaged.' In his reply the archbishop fears that 'poor Dr. King' will 'forfeit your recognisance' (J. Swift, *Correspondence*, vol. 1, ed. H. Williams, 1963, 286, 290). His apprehension was justified: on 1 July 1712 the *Gazette's* editorship was taken over by Charles Ford; according to Thomas Hearne, King 'did not hold it above two Months' (Swift, 2.543; *Remarks*, 4.45).

Although King's health was now poor, he wrote *Useful Miscellanies* (1712), worked on translations, and celebrated Bolingbroke's return from France (August 1712) with a poem, *Britain's Palladium*. Living with a friend at Lambeth, he made another tory gesture: when Archbishop Tenison did not celebrate the surrender of Dunkirk, King 'invited the watermen and his poor neighbours … to partake of some barrels of ale' (Nichols, xxv). On 24 December 1712 Lord Clarendon learned that King was seriously ill and had him brought to a lodging in the Strand opposite Somerset House. That night he made his will (PRO, PROB 11/531), leaving everything to his sister Elizabeth, and about noon on Christmas day he died. He had never married. He was buried in the north cloister of Westminster Abbey on 27 December 1712. Hearne commented, 'he was so addicted to the Buffooning way, that he neglected his proper Business'; Gay, however, had allowed King 'a World of Wit, yet as it lies in one particular way of Raillery, the Town soon grew weary of his Writings' (*Remarks*, 4.45; *Poetry and Prose*, 2.449).

HUGH DE QUEHEN

Sources D. Engel, 'The ingenious Dr King', PhD diss., U. Edin., 1989 · W. King, 'Memoirs', *The original works of William King*, ed. J. Nichols, 1 (1776), ix–xxix · J. Browne, 'Life', in *Remains of … Dr William King* (1732), 1–168 · S. Johnson, *Lives of the English poets*, ed. G. B. Hill, [new edn], 3 vols. (1905) · J. Swift, *Journal to Stella*, ed. H. Williams, 2 (1948) · *John Gay: poetry and prose*, ed. V. A. Dearing and C. E. Beckwith, 2 (1974) · *Remarks and collections of Thomas Hearne*, ed. C. E. Doble and others, 4, OHS, 34 (1898) · D. F. Foxon, ed., *English verse, 1701–1750: a catalogue of separately printed poems with notes on contemporary collected editions*, 2 vols. (1975) · Bénézit, *Dict.*, 4th edn · *CSP dom.*, 1671–2 · *Calamy rev.* · W. A. Shaw, ed., *Calendar of treasury books*, 17/1, PRO (1947), 345
Likenesses T. Cook, engraving (after R. Dellow, or J. Vandergucht), repro. in Nichols, ed., *Original works* · J. Vandergucht, line engraving (after R. Dellow), BM; repro. in Browne, ed., *Remains*
Wealth at death see will, PRO, PROB 11/531, sig. 14

King, William (1685–1763), college head and Jacobite sympathizer, was born at Stepney, Middlesex, on 5 March 1685 and baptized there six days later, the son of Peregrine King (1649–1714), a Church of England clergyman, and his wife, Margaret (*c*.1651–1692/3), daughter of Sir William Smyth, first baronet, of Radclive, Buckinghamshire. His mother died when he was seven. Having attended the free school in Salisbury he entered Balliol College, Oxford, on 9 July 1701. At the end of an interrupted undergraduate career he was admitted a fellow commoner in June 1709, and proceeded BCL on 12 July 1709 and DCL on 8 July 1715. In late autumn 1709 he married his cousin Henrietta Maria Wither at St Anne's, Westminster; a son, Charles (1711–1759), vicar of Great Bedwyn from 1748 until his death, and a daughter, Dorothy (*d*. 1761), who married William *Melmoth (*bap*. 1710, *d*. 1799), were the only children of the marriage.

Though called to the bar at Gray's Inn on 12 July 1712 King never sought practice, but he retained rights of residence in the Temple until 1747. Instead, supported by a modest patrimony he devoted himself to scholarship, literature, and politics. From about 1714 until 1722 he acted as secretary successively to James Butler, second duke of Ormond, and Ormond's brother Charles Butler, second earl of Arran—who both served as chancellor of Oxford University and whose Jacobite loyalties he shared. His *Political and Literary Anecdotes* contains reminiscences of a dinner at Ormond's house in Richmond at the time of the Jacobite rising of 1715 that was attended by Jacobite leaders, including the earl of Mar, Bishop Francis Atterbury, and Sir William Wyndham. In Oxford he was on friendly terms with Thomas Hearne, the Jacobite antiquary and diarist, who recorded in 1718 that King's rooms in Balliol contained portraits of Charles I, James II, and Prince Rupert, and in 1720 that King had been proud to show him a newly struck medallion of the exiled Stuart queen Clementina. In the parliamentary election of 1722 King was chosen by the high tories of Oxford to stand for the second university seat against a sitting moderate tory, George Clarke. He

William King (1685–1763), by John Faber junior, 1751 (after John Michael Williams, 1750)

resigned his post as secretary to the chancellor before contesting the election, which he eventually lost heavily, despite securing majorities over Clarke in five colleges (Corpus Christi, Exeter, Jesus, St John's, and Lincoln).

On 9 December 1719, following the death of Dr John Hudson, King was installed as principal of St Mary Hall, Oxford. This small institution had no fellows and no corporate body to govern it, and King, who remained principal for the next forty-four years, came to refer to it as 'my monastery' (Greenwood, 19). During his time as principal the east side of the quadrangle was rebuilt and a new room added to the principal's lodgings.

King's earliest, and longest, work—a mock-heroic poem called *The Toast*—appeared first in octavo in Dublin in 1732 and then, complete in four books, in a handsome quarto London edition in 1736. It has been justly described as 'one of the strangest and most vituperative pieces of writing which eighteenth-century England produced … an original and ingenious conception … spoilt by its author's prurience and lack of reticence' (Greenwood, 40, 357). Although he reissued the work in 1747 King later professed regret at its tone, and remaining copies were burnt at his death. It was written to relieve the frustrations of his attempt to secure the restitution of a loan of several thousand pounds to his uncle Sir Thomas Smyth, of Dublin, and his elderly and extravagant wife, Myra, the former countess of Newburgh. This lawsuit, which obliged King to make frequent and protracted visits to Ireland over a period of nearly twenty years, eventually cost King more in legal fees than the sum that he was seeking to recover, and when the matter was finally concluded, in 1746, he

was only partly successful. However, it proved the instrument for establishing contact between King and Jonathan Swift—to whom, as 'Cadenus', King dedicated the complete version of *The Toast*, in nine pages of Latin dactylic hexameters containing 'some of the most elegant tributes ever paid to Swift' (ibid., 57), who was equally complimentary in return. They corresponded for about five years, and Swift sought King's assistance over the publication of some of his own work. In the summer of 1737 King received a manuscript of Swift's *History of the Four Last Years of the Queen*. Concluding rapidly that the authentic text could not safely be printed, he worked effectively to postpone publication. Holding similar views about *Verses on the Death of Dr Swift*, a manuscript of which he received early in 1738, King was principally responsible for the fact that the text published by Charles Bathurst in January 1739 suffered from extensive excisions and interpolations. King's attempts to assuage Swift's displeasure failed, and their association ended. During this period King also wrote regularly for the opposition paper *Common Sense, or, The Englishman's Journal*. A satirical piece, published on 28 May 1737, was particularly notable: King proposing that the people of Britain ('Corsica') should 'have such a King as *Jupiter* first gave to the Frogs' (ibid., 79).

At the same time King began to compose his first political satires in Latin verse. *Miltonis epistola ad Pollionem*, which appeared in two separate folio editions in 1738, was an extended poem in Latin hexameter dedicated to Alexander Pope and attacking the corruption of the whig government and the venality of the times. Reprinted in Edward Popham's *Selecta poemata Anglorum Latina* (1774), it was widely read. A sequel, *Sermo pedestris*, with two separate folio editions in 1739, was more academic in tone and included a striking attack on the political subservience of the contemporary episcopal bench. *Scamnum, ecloga* (1740), dedicated to George Keith, Earl Marischal, who had been attainted and exiled after commanding troops during the 1715 rising, was a grand eclogue on the preoccupations of the tory opposition. *Templum libertatis* (2 vols., 1742–3), an unfinished allegorical epic in dactylic hexameter inspired by *Paradise Lost*, was a celebration of British liberty under threat, and included a fine apostrophe to Oxford—'one of the most superb passages in Anglo-Latin poetry' (Greenwood, 131)—and a notable description of Stowe.

By delivering Latin speeches on major university occasions King soon established a reputation for oratory as well as for writing. His success derived from elegance of composition, a confident delivery, and—very frequently—an aggressive political message. *Tres oratiunculae habitae in domo convocationis Oxon* (1743), marking the granting of honorary DCL degrees to the sixth duke of Hamilton, the third earl of Lichfield, and John Boyle, fifth earl of Orrery, contrasted the virtues and patriotic independence of the honorands with the general corruption and servility of the times. Orrery was King's literary and political associate for many years, and his notable translation of Pliny's *Epistles* owed much to King's encouragement. King's most influential speech was undoubtedly that given on 13 April 1749 at the opening of the new Radcliffe

Library, designed by King's friend James Gibbs. In this speech, printed in 1749 as *Oratio in Theatro Sheldoniano habita idibus Aprilis, MDCCXLIX: die dedicationis Bibliothecae Radclivianae* and reprinted in 1750, King praised the high-tory Radcliffe trustees, among whom were three Jacobites (the fourth duke of Beaufort, Sir Walter Wagstaffe Bagot, and Sir Watkin Williams-Wynn). He went on to expound familiar themes, condemning modern luxury and invoking nostalgia for ancient virtue, and rising to an enthusiastically received peroration in which six prayers for the delivery of the nation, all commencing '*REDEAT*', were generally understood to signify the restoration of the exiled Stuart family. Thomas Warton's description evokes the scene:

> See, on yon Sage how all attentive stand,
> To catch his darting eye, and waving hand.
> Hark! he begins, with all a Tully's art,
> To pour the dictates of a Cato's heart:
> Skill'd to pronounce what noblest thoughts inspire,
> He blends the speaker's with the patriot's fire;
> Bold to conceive, nor timorous to conceal,
> What Britons dare to think, he dares to tell.
> (T. Warton, *The Triumphs of Isis*; Greenwood, 200)

Ten years later, at the installation of the seventh earl of Westmorland as chancellor in July 1759, following the death of the earl of Arran, Samuel Johnson (whose MA diploma had been brought to him by King in February 1755) clapped his hands until they were sore at another virtuoso speech, which lasted fifty minutes but whose text has not been preserved.

Unsurprisingly St Mary Hall in King's time acquired a reputation for Jacobitism. A nonjuring clergyman, John Leake, lodged there with his wife for at least three years after 1725, by special leave of the principal, and the leader of a notorious Jacobite disturbance in Oxford on the night of 23 February 1748 was an undergraduate of the college, James Dawes. Though it is unlikely that King had any direct connection with this disturbance his Jacobite convictions remained strong at the time. In 1746, after the battle of Culloden, he had described the duke of Cumberland as a man 'qui timet omnia praeter Deum' ('who is afraid of everything except God'), and in September 1749 he attended the important Jacobite gathering at Lichfield races and prepared a list of 275 loyal gentlemen who were present. In September 1750 he was introduced to Prince Charles Edward Stuart at the house of Lady Primrose in Essex Street, London, although he later became disillusioned by the prince's avarice and religious duplicity. Oxford whigs—such as Richard Blacow of Exeter College, John Gilbert, canon of Christ Church, Edward Bentham of Oriel, John Burton of Corpus Christi, and Robert Jenner of Trinity, all of whom were engaged in controversy with King about this time—were slow to detect the waning enthusiasm for the Stuart cause that King chronicled in his *Political and Literary Anecdotes of his Own Times*, composed about 1760 but not published until 1818. King's final reconciliation with the court came in 1761, when he accompanied a university deputation to present an address of congratulation on the royal marriage and was personally introduced to George III by Lord Shelburne.

Despite his abjuration of Jacobitism King remained an active Anglo-Latin writer and scholar. His collected writings, *Opera Guilielmi King*, were published in 1760, and a new composition of the same date, *Aviti epistola ad Perillam, virginem Scotam*, contained significant praise for the condition of Britain under the house of Hanover. Two further short Latin works were published in 1761: *Elogium*, on Dr John Taylor, an eccentric oculist, and *Epitaphium Richardi Nash*, a long and elaborate tribute that 'excelled in grandeur many which had been composed in memory of sovereign rulers' (Greenwood, 311). On 8 July 1763 King made his last encaenia speech; a witness, Charles Godwyn, commented that 'his strength and memory, and the applause he received, were just the same as usual' (Nichols, *Lit. anecdotes*, 8.236).

King died at Bath on 30 December 1763 and was buried on 5 January 1764 at Ealing, where he had succeeded his father as lessee of the rectory. His heart, enclosed in a silver urn, was deposited in the chapel of St Mary Hall, with a monument to his memory and a Latin epitaph of his own composition; it was subsequently moved to Oriel College chapel. A brief obituary in *Jackson's Oxford Journal* of January 1764 noted that King was 'the oldest Head of a House in Oxford' and 'a gentleman whose Character in the polite and literary World is too well known to need any Encomium, and who was universally allowed to be the most celebrated Orator in all Europe'. RICHARD SHARP

Sources D. Greenwood, *William King: tory and Jacobite* (1969) · W. King, *Political and literary anecdotes of his own times* (1818), 2nd edn (1819) · J. C. D. Clark, *Samuel Johnson* (1994) · *DNB* · P. K. Monod, *Jacobitism and the English people, 1688–1788* (1989) · *Remarks and collections of Thomas Hearne*, ed. C. E. Doble and others, 11 vols., OHS, 2, 7, 13, 34, 42–3, 48, 50, 65, 67, 72 (1885–1921) · E. Cruickshanks, *Political untouchables: the tories and the '45* (1979) · *Hist. U. Oxf.* 5: *18th-cent. Oxf.* · D. K. Money, *The English Horace: Anthony Alsop and the tradition of British Latin verse* (1998)
Archives Bodl. Oxf., letters to John Boyle, earl of Cork, MS Eng. hist. d. 103
Likenesses J. M. Williams, oils, 1750, Bodl. Oxf. · J. Faber junior, mezzotint, 1751 (after J. M. Williams, 1750), BM, NPG [*see illus.*] · T. Hudson, oils · J. Macardell, mezzotint (after T. Hudson), BM, NPG · T. Worlidge, etching · T. Worlidge, oils, Oriel College, Oxford

King, William (1701–1769), Independent minister, was born in Wiltshire on 9 June 1701. He was educated at a local school, and in 1721 entered the University of Utrecht. He studied successfully there, and on returning to England in 1724 became minister at the Independent church at Chesham, Buckinghamshire, where he also ran a school. He was ordained on 25 April 1725.

King moved to London in 1740, and in February of that year became pastor of the Independent church in Hare Court, Aldersgate Street, as successor to Samuel Bruce. Shortly afterwards he received from a Scottish university a diploma creating him DD. From 1748 until his death he was merchant's lecturer at Pinners' Hall, where he delivered 192 lectures (sermons) in total. He was engaged also for many years in Sunday evening lectures at Silver Street and Lime Street chapels, but according to Walter Wilson he was not a popular preacher and never distinguished himself as an author.

During the last four years of his life King suffered great pain from a gallstone. He preached for the last time at Hare Court on 26 February 1769 and died at Pinners' Hall on 4 March. He was buried in Bunhill Fields. He was survived by two children, William and Ann, but not by his wife, who appears to have died before October 1768, when he made his will.

THOMAS SECCOMBE, rev. M. J. MERCER

Sources C. Surman, index of dissenting ministers, DWL · W. Wilson, *The history and antiquities of the dissenting churches and meeting houses in London, Westminster and Southwark*, 4 vols. (1808–14), vol. 3, pp. 299–301 · J. A. Jones, ed., *Bunhill memorials* (1849), 135–6 · W. H. Summers, *History of the Wiltshire and the East Somerset Congregational Union* (1849), 39 · T. S. Jones, *Presbyterian chapels and charities in England* (1869), 652, 687 · A. Mearns, ed., *London Congregational directory and church guide* (1885), 53 · will, PRO, PROB 11/946 · *GM*, 1st ser., 39 (1769), 168 · *Album studiosorum academiae Rheno-Traiectinae MDCXXXVI–MDCCCLXXXVI: accedunt nomina curatorum et professorum per eadem secula* (Utrecht, 1886), 122
Likenesses Hopwood, stipple (after an oil painting), NPG; repro. in Wilson, *History and antiquities of dissenting churches*, 229 · oils, probably Hare Court Chapel, Aldersgate Street, London
Wealth at death see will, PRO, PROB 11/946

King, William (1786–1865), physician and promoter of co-operative principles, was born on 17 April 1786 at Ipswich, one of ten children of the Revd John King (1738–1822) and his wife, Elizabeth Sarah, *née* Bishop. King was educated at Ipswich grammar school, where his father had been master. Aged fifteen he entered Westminster School, subsequently going up to Peterhouse, Cambridge. He graduated BA in 1809 and MA in 1812. Originally intended for the church, King studied medicine at St Bartholomew's Hospital, London, and in France, at Montpellier and Paris. He returned to Cambridge in 1817, graduating MD in 1819. In 1820 he became a fellow of the Royal College of Physicians. On 17 January 1821 he married Mary Hooker of Rottingdean, and the following December settled in Brighton.

King supported initiatives promoting working-class self-help and charitable organization in Brighton, associating with philanthropists including Elizabeth Fry and Lady Noel Byron. Educational interests led him to sponsor the establishment of a mechanics' institute in 1825. Speaking engagements at the institute initiated his involvement with co-operation. Many of the workmen who fostered co-operation locally, including their leader William Bryan, were institute members. 1827 saw the establishment of the Brighton Co-operative Benevolent Fund Association to amass capital in support of Owenite communitarianism, and an extension of fund-raising through the foundation of a co-operative trading association.

King's contribution to co-operation was educational, leaving a legacy of national importance. *The Co-Operator*, a monthly periodical started by him in May 1828, outlined the potential for societal transformation through the extension of co-operative activity from retailing to manufacture and self-employment, and eventual full community. Publication of such ideas in an intelligible form contributed greatly to the upsurge of co-operative society

foundations in the late 1820s and early 1830s. However, King's willingness to publish advocacy of élite patronage for co-operation and his unease about Owenite radicalism and anti-clericalism led to attacks on him in other co-operative journals. These contributed to his decision to cease publication in August 1830. Requests that he republish essays from *The Co-Operator*, and an invitation to the 1833 Co-operative Congress, were declined. He was aware, too, that advocacy of progressive causes, also including Catholic emancipation, was damaging his professional prospects.

King's subsequent career was chiefly of local significance. In 1842 he was elected physician to the Sussex County Hospital. He was also physician to the Brighton Provident Dispensary from 1849. As one of the commissioners responsible for urban government in Brighton, he played a leading role in the town's acquisition of the Royal Pavilion in 1850.

Although few copies of *The Co-Operator* survived, its advocacy of association was rediscovered by later co-operators, including the Rochdale Society of Equitable Pioneers in the 1840s. King's ideas anticipated aspects of Christian socialism, which itself sponsored co-operatives during the 1850s. King expressed support for such initiatives and maintained a continuing faith in co-operation's redemptive power. He retired as physician to the Sussex Hospital in 1861. In his latter years he suffered from a heart condition, which led to his death on 19 October 1865, at his home, 23 Montpelier Road, Brighton. He was buried in Hove parish church on 25 October. King was survived by his wife and at least two children, a daughter, Catherine, and a son, George. MARTIN PURVIS

Sources T. W. Mercer, *Co-operation's prophet: the life and letters of Dr. William King of Brighton* (1947) · S. Pollard, 'Dr. William King: a co-operative pioneer', *Co-operative College Papers*, 6 (1959), 17–33 · H. F. Bing and J. Saville, 'King, William', *DLB*, vol. 1 · d. cert. · *Annual Register* (1822), 267–8 [obit. of John King] · A. Dale, *Brighton town and Brighton people* (1976) · W. King, letter, *Christian Socialist* (11 Oct 1851) · *CGPLA Eng. & Wales* (1865)
Archives BL OIOC, corresp., MSS Eur. B 295 · Brighton Public Library, papers incl. MS book of notes, chiefly relating to the Royal Pavilion · E. Sussex RO, records of the Brighton Improvement Commissioners, DB/B 58 60–73 series · E. Sussex RO, records of the Royal Sussex County Hospital, Brighton, DB 28–54, 61–2, 64, 95–5 series | Bodl. Oxf., corresp. with Byron and Lovelace families
Likenesses portraits, c.1830–1855, repro. in Mercer, *Co-operation's prophet* · L. Leuliette, photograph, c.1860, repro. in Mercer, *Co-operation's prophet* · bust, Royal Pavilion, Brighton
Wealth at death under £5000: probate, 24 Nov 1865, *CGPLA Eng. & Wales*

King, William (1809–1886), geologist, was born in Low Row, Sunderland, co. Durham on 22 April 1809, the son of William King, coal caster, and his wife, Eleanor (*née* Armstrong), confectioner and shopkeeper. He was educated at Mr Finlay's school in Moor Street, Sunderland, and during short careers, as an apprentice ironmonger and as a bookshop owner and librarian, he established a reputation as an avid collector of fossils. He married Jane Nicholson in 1839, and in 1841 was appointed to the curatorship of the

Newcastle Museum (later the Hancock Museum), Newcastle upon Tyne, leaving the post in 1847 following a disagreement with his employers.

In October 1849 King was appointed to the foundation chair of mineralogy and geology of Queen's College, Galway. During a distinguished career he published more than seventy scientific papers, established the geology and natural history museum in the college, and developed a teaching programme in geology for the arts, agriculture, and engineering faculties. In 1859 King was appointed examiner in geology, mineralogy, and physical geology for the Queen's University of Ireland. His research programme ranged from the shell structure of brachiopods to the development of cleavage in metamorphic rocks and the uplift of the Burren. His *Monograph of the Permian Fossils of England*, published in 1850 by the Palaeontographical Society, formed the basis for the description of the Permian system; his many taxonomic papers helped set the agenda for animal and plant classifications. He recognized the antiquity of Neanderthal man, gave modified support to Darwin's *Origin of Species* and with Thomas Henry Rowney, professor of chemistry at Queen's College, Galway, established the non-organic nature of the dawn animal *Eozoon*. His son, William King jun. studied geology at the college and was later director of the geological survey of India.

King was elected to the Geological Society of France and the Natural History and Medical Society of Dresden, lectured in Bandon and Galway for the committee of lectures, Dublin Castle, and organized all-Ireland field excursions. In 1870 he was awarded the first honorary DSc by the Queen's University. King was appointed to the new chair in natural history, geology, and mineralogy in 1882, but resigned following a stroke in 1883 and was appointed emeritus professor. He died at home in Glenoir, Taylor's Hill, Galway on 24 June 1886.   DAVID A. T. HARPER

Sources D. A. T. Harper, '"The king of Queen's College", William King D.Sc., first professor of geology at Galway', *William King D.Sc., a palaeontological tribute*, ed. D. A. T. Harper (1988), 1–24 • W. Brockie, 'Sunderland worthies, no. 8, Professor William King', *Sunderland Public Library Circular*, 10 (1910), 206–10 • T. Pettigrew, 'William King (?1808–1886): biographical note', *GCG: Newsletter of the Geological Curators Group*, 3 (1980), 327–9 • G. L. H. Davies, 'William King and the Irish geological community', *William King D.Sc., a palaeontological tribute*, ed. D. A. T. Harper (1988), 25–32 • D. A. T. Harper, 'The James Mitchell Museum: a museum of a museum in University College, Galway', *Geological Curator*, 5 (1988–94), 292–7 • S. Turner, 'Collections and collectors of note: William King, 1808–1886', *GCG: Newsletter of the Geological Curators Group*, 3 (1980), 323–6 • R. J. Anderson, 'The Natural History Museum, Queen's College Galway', *Irish Naturalists' Journal*, 8 (1899), 125–31 • M. D. Fewtrell, 'The James Mitchell Geology Museum, University College, Galway', *Irish Naturalists' Journal*, 19 (1979), 309–10 • M. D. Fewtrell and P. D. Ryan, 'Queen's College Museum, Galway', *GCG: Newsletter of the Geological Curators Group*, 2 (1979), 173–81 • *Nature*, 34 (1886), 200–01
Archives GS Lond. • National University of Ireland, Galway, James Mitchell Museum, archive • U. Cam., Sedgwick Museum of Earth Sciences, archive | NMG Wales, De la Beche corresp.
Likenesses photograph, 1870–79, University College, Galway, Ireland

King, William Bernard Robinson (1889–1963), geologist, was born on 12 November 1889 at West Burton, near Aysgarth, Yorkshire, the younger son of William Robinson King (1854–1921), solicitor, and his wife, Florence Muriel, *née* Theed (1865–1943). Bill, as he became widely known, was very much a Yorkshireman: records of the Kings as yeoman farmers in Wensleydale date back to 1640. Educated at Mr Houfe's school in Aysgarth and then at Uppingham School, Rutland, in 1908 he followed his father and elder brother to Jesus College, Cambridge. He gained first-class honours in part two (geology) of the natural sciences tripos in 1912 and won the Harkness scholarship.

Appointed to the Geological Survey of Great Britain in October 1912, King undertook field surveys for its Flint and Oswestry memoirs but following the outbreak of the First World War he was commissioned on 21 September 1914 as a second lieutenant in the Royal Welch Fusiliers. From June 1915 he served in France as a staff lieutenant to the chief engineer, British expeditionary force. The British forces put down over 400 borings for water behind the western front during the war, and King supervised and interpreted many of these. He also developed specialist water-supply maps, and from 1916 collaborated with T. W. Edgeworth David on the siting of mines and dugouts. On leave, on 7 June 1916 he married Margaret Amy Passingham (1885–1972) at Eastnor, Herefordshire. Promoted lieutenant on 1 June 1916 and captain on 27 April 1918, King was twice mentioned in dispatches, and finally appointed OBE (military division).

Demobilized in 1919, King returned to the survey before appointment in 1920 as a demonstrator and professorial assistant at Cambridge. He became a fellow of Jesus College in 1920 and of Magdalene College in 1922, coincidentally the years in which his daughters Margaret and Cuchlaine were born. At Cambridge he published fourteen papers, based on his war work in France and his survey work in Wales, and on Palaeozoic stratigraphy and palaeontology and Pleistocene sedimentary geology. In 1931 he was appointed Yates-Goldsmid professor of geology at University College, London. Another thirteen papers followed, mostly on Palaeozoic or Pleistocene themes.

Following the outbreak of the Second World War, King was appointed to a regular army emergency commission in the Royal Engineers: second lieutenant on 13 September 1939, war substantive captain on 13 December 1939, and temporary major on 26 August 1940. Serving in France with the British expeditionary force he earned a Military Cross for bravery in convoying high explosive from Boulogne to Bailleul, and Kassel, before being evacuated from Dunkirk. On his return to England, he was attached to northern command, and then from 1941 to 1943 to general headquarters home forces, from which developed Twenty-First Army group. He assisted planning for the 1944 invasion of Normandy by initiating studies into potential water supply, the ability of ground conditions to support traffic, the availability of stone and gravel as construction materials, and the nature of beach sediments. Most importantly, he influenced the decision to invade via the Calvados coast rather than the Cotentin peninsula because the geological conditions were more favourable for the rapid construction of temporary airfields. He also initiated studies of the floor of the English Channel to facilitate laying of piped fuel supplies to sustain military operations. Promoted lieutenant-colonel on 22 October 1943, King was soon afterwards released from the army to become Woodwardian professor of geology at Cambridge.

After the war King edited, and largely wrote, volume 15, *Application of Geology*, of the Royal Engineers' textbook *Military Engineering*, and helped to establish a pool of geologist officers within the reserve army. Papers on Palaeozoic and Pleistocene geology, on hydrogeology, military geology, and on the geology of the English Channel brought his total publications to over fifty. He was a fellow of the Geological Society of London from 1912 (secretary, 1937–40 and 1944–6; president, 1953–5; and a council member for seventeen years in total), a fellow of the Royal Society from 1949 (council member, 1954–6), an active member of several other British learned societies, and a foreign correspondent of the Palaeontological Society of India, the Geological Society of America, and the Geological Society of France. In 1949 and 1950 he was president of the Yorkshire Geological Society, and in 1951 was president of section C of the British Association for the Advancement of Science. The Geological Society of London awarded him its Wollaston fund in 1920 and Murchison medal in 1951, the Société Géologique du Nord its Gosselet medal in 1923, and the Geological Society of France its Prestwich medal in 1945. He was made a DSc of Cambridge University in 1937, and received honorary doctorates from two French universities: Lille in 1947, for his military geological work in the two world wars, and Rennes in 1952, largely for his work on the geology of the English Channel. Yet he was also a committed teacher of undergraduates, at his best during fieldwork, noted for his enthusiasm, informality, and hospitality.

In 1955, King retired to Worton near Askrigg, in his native North Riding of Yorkshire. He died on 23 January 1963 in Friarage Hospital at Northallerton, from thrombosis following a minor operation. After a funeral service at Askrigg, he was cremated at Darlington on 28 January 1963. His ashes were later scattered on Worton Edges, on pasture belonging to a farm inherited from his father.

E. P. F. ROSE

Sources F. W. Shotton, *Memoirs FRS*, 9 (1963), 171–82 · E. P. F. Rose and M. S. Rosenbaum, 'British military geologists', *Proceedings of the Geologists' Association*, 104 (1993), 41–9, 95–108 · E. P. F. Rose and N. F. Hughes, 'Sapper geology [pts. 1-2]', *Royal Engineers Journal*, new ser., 107 (1993), 27–33, 173–81 · F. McD. C. T., 'In memoriam: D. K. and W. B. R. K.', *Magdalene College Magazine and Record*, new ser., 7 (1962–3), 13–16 · *The Times* (25 Jan 1963) · *Proceedings of the Geological Society of London*, 1611 (1962–3), 150–53 · *Nature*, 198 (1963), 244 · *The historical register of the University of Cambridge, supplement, 1911–20* (1922) · L. J. Chubb, 'Geology at University College London, 1826–1941', UCL, department of geological sciences · admissions register and 'Conclusion Book', Jesus College, Cambridge, Archives, col. 4.7 · E. P. F. Rose and M. S. Rosenbaum, 'British military geologists through war and peace in the 19th and 20th centuries', *Military geology in war and peace*, ed. J. R. Underwood and P. L. Guth (1998) · E. P. F. Rose and C. Pareyn, 'Geology and the liberation of Normandy, France, 1944', *Geology Today*, 11 (1995), 58–63 · *The work of the royal engineers in the European war, 1914–19*, Royal Engineers' Institute (1921) · P. A. Sabine, 'Geologists at war: a forensic investigation in the field of war-time diplomacy', *Proceedings of the Geologists' Association*, 102 (1991), 139–43 · O. T. Jones, 'Address to Murchison medallist', *Proceedings of the Geological Society of London*, 1475 (1951), xxx · private information (2004) [daughters] · m. cert. · b. cert. · d. cert.

Likenesses photograph, *c*.1914, repro. in Rose and Hughes, 'Sapper geology', 28 · photograph, Sept 1915, repro. in Rose and Rosenbaum, 'British military geologists', 44 · photograph, *c*.1940, repro. in Rose and Rosenbaum, 'British military geologists', 96 · photograph, *c*.1943, repro. in Rose and Hughes, 'Sapper geology', 180 · J. Hookham, pencil, Magd. Cam. · photograph, repro. in *Memoirs FRS*, frontispiece · photograph (after a drawing), repro. in F. McD. C. T., 'In memoriam: D. K. and W. B. R. K.', frontispiece · portraits, GS Lond.

Wealth at death £57,445 8s. 4d.: probate, 30 Aug 1963, *CGPLA Eng. & Wales*

Kingdon, Emmeline Maria (1817–1890), headmistress, was probably born at Bridgerule, Devon, the youngest daughter of the Revd Thomas Hockin Kingdon (1775–1853), rector of Pyworthy and vicar of Bridgerule, and his wife, Caroline, eldest daughter of Samuel Nicholson of Ham Common, Surrey. The couple also had three sons, two of whom, Samuel Nicholson and George Thomas, became clerics, eventually succeeding their father at Bridgerule and Pyworthy respectively. The youngest son, Paul Augustine, became a barrister.

Following her mother's death Kingdon kept house for her father, assisted him with his business affairs and with parish duties, and devoted considerable time to the village school. After her father's death in 1853 Kingdon made a number of visits to friends and relatives. As did many unmarried females of her time and class, she provided support to the households in which she stayed when required, though it is not known whether she pursued her educational interests during this time.

In the autumn of 1864 Kingdon answered an advertisement for the post of lady superintendent for a new school to be opened in Bath in the following year. The Royal School for Daughters of Officers of the Army was the brainchild of the philanthropist Alfred Douglas Hamilton, who knew of an existing institution of a similar nature, the Royal Female Naval School at Richmond, established in 1840. The advertisement attracted a total of seventy-six applications; according to an obituary notice in the *Bath Chronicle*, Kingdon's success in securing the post was in part due to a testimonial from Florence Nightingale, whom she appears to have met at some point during her travels following the death of her father.

The Royal School occupied an imposing, and domestically inconvenient, neo-Gothic building on Lansdown, Bath, and much time during Kingdon's early months as lady superintendent was spent overseeing its conversion into accommodation suitable for girls and governesses. The school officially opened on 24 August 1865. It had thirty pupils, over half of whom, from needy families, had been 'elected' at reduced fees, and three governesses, though the number of pupils expanded rapidly both during and after Kingdon's time. Discipline in the new school was strict; Kingdon imposed a rigorous routine on her charges.

The Royal School's educational aims were twofold: to imbue its pupils with the habits and attitudes of 'gentlewomen', while also giving them, as the school's founding committee expressed it, 'sound and useful knowledge together with such accomplishments and such practice in domestic economy as might qualify them for a useful situation in life' (Osborne and Manisty, 26). The curriculum, devised by Kingdon, included vocational subjects such as English, arithmetic, and French, as well as 'aesthetic subjects' such as music, drawing, and deportment, and was thus typical of the curricula to be found in girls' schools by the 1870s. It reflected wider contemporary debates about the education of middle-class girls and women which attempted to reconcile the conflicting demands of the philosophy of a liberal education and the need for increasing numbers of middle-class women to earn a livelihood with Victorian conceptions of femininity.

Kingdon remained as lady superintendent until her retirement in July 1874. She returned only a year later, however, after the school had encountered problems with Miss Rosa Adams, her replacement. Kingdon remained with the school in her resumed post for a further six years, until ill health—a stroke, resulting in paralysis—led to permanent retirement in July 1882. During this time she continued to consolidate the school's academic credentials, with considerable success: in 1876 pupils from the Royal School were entered for the Cambridge University local examinations.

In appearance Kingdon was 'a dear little stately lady in a lace cap' (Osborne and Manisty, 31); one photograph suggests a likeness to the school's patron, Queen Victoria. Like her more famous contemporary, Miss Buss, Kingdon was described as possessing a maternal and sympathetic nature. Past pupils recalled her kindness, self-control, and 'an indescribable air of distinction' (ibid.). The emphasis of these testimonies on their subject's womanly qualities is typical, but Kingdon's formidable administrative and managerial skills—which drew praise from the educationist Joshua Fitch whom the committee invited to inspect the school in 1875—and her role in attaining a high reputation for the school should also be noted. Emmeline Maria Kingdon, who was unmarried, died at her home, 1 Dynham Road, West Hampstead, London, on 25 March 1890, and was buried on 29 March at Paddington cemetery.   ELIZABETH A. McCARTY

Sources H. Osborne and P. Manisty, *A history of the Royal School for Daughters of Officers of the Army, 1864–1965* (1966) · Boase, *Mod. Eng. biog.*

Likenesses photograph, repro. in Osborne and Manisty, *History of the Royal School for Daughters of Officers of the Army*, 104

Wealth at death £6156 10s. 5d.: probate, 9 May 1890, *CGPLA Eng. & Wales*

King-Hall. For this title name *see* Hall, (William) Stephen Richard King-, Baron King-Hall (1893–1966).

Kinghorn, Alexander (*fl.* 1513–1529), diplomat, appears to have originated at Kinghorn in Fife. Nothing is known of his family except that he had a brother, and that he was related to Archbishop James Beaton of St Andrews. He may have been identical with 'the lang Doctor of Denmark' who was granted an annual pension of £40 Scots in 1511 (*Compota*, 1507–13, 267–8). This would show both that he was *persona grata* at the court of James IV, and that he had obtained his MD by this date. He is not recorded as attending any Scottish university, however, and may have studied abroad. This would be in keeping with the first certain reference to him, when in 1513 he was appointed professor of medicine in the University of Copenhagen and physician in ordinary to King Christian II of Denmark and Norway. Rector of the university in 1517, he is recorded as dean of the faculty of medicine on 19 January 1523. His career also had an ecclesiastical strand, though nothing is known of his orders. On 30 December 1517 he obtained royal letters of presentation to the parish of Nr Kirkeby (Falster) with its annex of Nr Alslev. However, this probably meant only that he received part of the income, while having to pay a resident vicar. Elected dean of Roskilde Cathedral in 1521 or 1522, by 1523 he had become chaplain and councillor to King Christian.

According to a dispatch sent to Wolsey from the Low Countries in 1522, Kinghorn had been a Danish envoy to Scotland in 1515, but this cannot be confirmed. In the spring of 1519 he was sent to Scotland to raise mercenaries for service against Sweden. Successful in that mission, in the summer of 1521 he accompanied Christian to the Low Countries, and in the last months of that king's reign was sent to England and Scotland to try to obtain their support against the Danish revolt that broke out in 1523. Neither country would provide aid, but in April 1523 Christian was offered asylum in Scotland. By the time Kinghorn returned to Denmark Christian was in exile and his uncle Frederik, duke of Holstein, elected king as Frederik I, controlled much of the country. But Kinghorn remained loyal to Christian, and in June 1523 the latter again sent him as his envoy to Scotland.

Kinghorn's chances of success depended very largely on the stance of the Scottish government. The regent, Albany, stood for alliance with France, whereas Christian II was allied to France's Habsburg enemy. Moreover, at a time when Scotland needed men and money for her war against England, Frederik I had much more to offer than his exiled nephew. In May 1524 Albany informed Frederik that he had prevented Kinghorn from negotiating in Scotland on Christian's behalf; later in the year Frederik asked Albany to have Kinghorn arrested. By then the regent had left Scotland, however, and Kinghorn's position was correspondingly improved. So far in favour with the new regency government that on 24 October 1524 he was granted the usufruct of land by Kinghorn in Fife, once held by his niece Elizabeth Kinghorn, for his 'gud and thankfull service done to the king', he was able to stay in Scotland as resident ambassador for Christian II (Livingstone, 498). When he went to see his employer in the Low Countries, probably in June 1525, Kinghorn was able to report that the Scottish government had decided to maintain its alliance with Christian, despite his exile. Consequently the latter's servants were allowed to sell prizes, trade, and levy mercenaries in Scotland, his men-of-war could operate from Scottish ports, and he himself was again offered asylum in Scotland.

By September 1525 Kinghorn was back in Scotland. James V's government confirmed its support for Christian II and urged him to act more energetically in order to recover power. In the early spring of 1527 Kinghorn again travelled to the Low Countries, but the recurrence of an earlier sickness prevented his joining his master. The Scottish government declared itself ready to send up to 5000 men in Christian's support, transported in Scottish ships but victualled and paid by him. No doubt it was in response that during that summer Frederik I sent another native Scot, John Elgin, as his own envoy to Scotland, to renew the alliance between the two countries, but the Scots declared that no such renewal was necessary, and so avoided having to choose openly between the rival kings. Kinghorn reported to Christian that Elgin had won support for Frederik's cause through bribery, but that he and Christian's chancellor had won back most of those so persuaded.

Kinghorn may have visited Christian once more during the winter of 1528–9, but by April 1529 he was certainly in Scotland. At this point he disappears from the records, and it is not known when or where he died. That Christian II continued to enjoy Scottish support as he prepared for his attempted return to Denmark in 1531 must be counted among the achievements of his ambassador. Alexander Kinghorn is a good representative of the early sixteenth-century Scots who obtained employment in Denmark, many of them as diplomats. His perceived trustworthiness, together with his family links in Scotland and his political connections in Denmark, made him a man to whom delicate missions could be entrusted by the governments of both countries. THOMAS RIIS

Sources T. Riis, *Should auld acquaintance be forgot … Scottish–Danish relations, c.1450–1707*, 2 vols. (1988) • *Diplomatarium Norvegicum*, 10–11, 13, 15 (Christiania, 1878–1900) • C. F. Allen, *Breve og Aktstykker til Oplysming af Christian den Andens og Frederik den Føstes Historie*, 1 (Copenhagen, 1854) • J. B. Paul, ed., *Compota thesaurariorum regum Scotorum / Accounts of the lord high treasurer of Scotland*, 4 (1902) • M. Livingstone, D. Hay Fleming, and others, eds., *Registrum secreti sigilli regum Scotorum / The register of the privy seal of Scotland*, 1 (1908) **Archives** Riksarkivet, Copenhagen, Münchenersamlingen C bundle 17

Kinghorn, Joseph (1766–1832), Particular Baptist minister, was born at Gateshead on 17 January 1766. His father, David Kinghorn (1737–1822), was a shoemaker and Baptist preacher at Newcastle upon Tyne; he was ordained on 1 May 1771 as minister of a Baptist congregation at Bishop Burton in the East Riding of Yorkshire, serving until July 1799, when he retired to Norwich. Joseph was the eldest son of David and his second wife, Elizabeth (1737/8–1810), second daughter of Joseph Jopling of Satley. After four years' classical schooling, Kinghorn was taken on trial as an apprentice to a watch- and clockmaker in Hull in 1779, but in March 1781 became a clerk in Richard Fishwick's white-lead works at Elswick, Northumberland. In April 1783 he was baptized by his father at Bishop Burton and looked forward to entering the ministry. He made the

acquaintance of Robert Hall (1764–1831) and had thoughts of joining him at the University of Aberdeen, but on 20 August 1784 he entered the Bristol Baptist college, under Caleb Evans. Among his fellow students his most intimate friend was James Hinton, father of John Howard Hinton. On leaving the college he ministered for several months (from May 1788) at Fairford, where some found his Calvinism not high enough: he was always in favour of a robust call to the unconverted to turn to God. His former employer, Richard Fishwick, introduced his name to the Baptist congregation at St Mary's Chapel, Norwich, located in the parish of St Mary-in-Coslany. On 27 March 1789 he settled in Norwich, and he was ordained on 20 May 1790. One of his closest friends there was William Wilkin of Costessy, a farmer and miller of both fortune and culture. Wilkin died in 1799 leaving his eight-year old son, Simon, to the care of the bachelor Kinghorn, who soon began a school for his ward and other pupils.

Kinghorn's ministry at Norwich, which lasted until his death, was unusually distinguished. He was famed for his pulpit rhetoric, which was at once scriptural, systematic, and practical; his power of apt illustration was noted by Edward Irving. In 1804 he was invited to preside over the new Horton College, about to be established in Bradford, and six years later was invited to take a similar position at the new college established by the London Particular Baptists at Stepney. Kinghorn had an extremely high view of his local pastorate and therefore refused to move from Norwich, though he did prepare in his own home a number of candidates for ministerial training for work both in Britain and overseas. His old chapel was replaced in 1811 by a very handsome structure on the same site.

Like many dissenters Kinghorn welcomed the French Revolution, and the fall of the Bastille in particular, but he was not a political preacher, though he was active in seeking the removal of dissenting disabilities. He also worked for the opening up of British India to dissenting missionaries through the revision of the East India Company charter in 1813, by persuading Bishop Bathurst of Norwich to present the case in the Lords and William Smith (MP for Norwich and a Unitarian associate of the Clapham Sect) to present it in the Commons. In the communion controversy which much occupied Baptists in the years following the end of the French wars, Kinghorn, after some initial hesitation, became the chief spokesman of the closed-communion position, against the open-communion position of his friend, Robert Hall. Kinghorn believed that baptism as a believer was clearly required by the New Testament as a prerequisite for participation in holy communion, and that unless this position were protected, Baptist insights into the restriction of baptism to believers would be lost. Kinghorn served on the committee of the infant Baptist Missionary Society and journeyed to Scotland in 1818 and 1822 on its behalf. In every enterprise connected with the Baptist denomination he played a prominent part, and has been called 'the de facto Bishop of the Baptists in Norfolk' (Jewson, 73).

Norwich at this time enjoyed a lively intellectual life. From 1790 Kinghorn was a member of the Speculative

Society, of which William Taylor, the German scholar, was the leading spirit; the society welcomed cultured Roman Catholics to its discussions, alongside representatives of all protestant churches. Kinghorn gave considerable time to linguistic and critical studies, not only mastering Greek, Hebrew, and Syriac, but also becoming an authority on rabbinical writings. He was much involved in the work of the London Society for Promoting Christianity among the Jews. In 1828 he was awarded the honorary degree of MA by Brown University in Providence, Rhode Island, but never advertised the honour.

Kinghorn died, unmarried, on 1 September 1832, and was buried on 7 September in the vestibule of St Mary's Chapel. Joseph John Gurney, the Quaker philanthropist, spoke at his funeral; the sermon was preached by John Alexander, minister of Prince's Street Congregational Church.

A list of twenty of Kinghorn's publications is given in Wilkin's biography; they include controversial works on the nature of the church, Christian baptism, the terms of communion, and the training of Christian ministers, as well as treatises in opposition to the beliefs of Unitarians and Roman Catholics. He wrote on Christian worship and edited several collections of hymns. A number of his sermons were published, and he was a frequent contributor to the *Baptist Magazine*, the *Eclectic Review*, and the *Evangelical Magazine*. Wilkin also enumerates twelve of his unpublished manuscripts, chiefly controversial. The catalogue of his extensive library was published at Norwich in 1833.

ALEXANDER GORDON, *rev.* J. H. Y. BRIGGS

Sources M. H. Wilkin, *Joseph Kinghorn of Norwich* (1855) · *Baptist Magazine*, 47 (1855), 333–9 · M. Walker, *Baptists at the table* (1992) · C. B. Jewson, *The Baptists in Norfolk* (1957)
Archives Regent's Park College, Oxford, Angus Library, corresp. | Norfolk RO, Wilkin MSS
Likenesses portrait, 1813?, repro. in *Baptist Magazine* (1835) · W. Bond, stipple, pubd 1833 (after A. Robertson, 1813), NPG · J. M. Johnson, lithograph, NPG · portrait, repro. in Wilkin, *Joseph Kinghorn of Norwich*

Kinglake, Alexander William (1809–1891), historian and travel writer, was born on 5 August 1809, in Taunton, Somerset, the eldest son of William Kinglake (*d.* 1852), banker and solicitor, and his wife, Mary (*d.* 1853), daughter of Thomas Woodforde from Castle Cary. He was one of four sons and two daughters who survived to adulthood. The Kinglakes were descended from the Scottish Kinlochs, who had migrated to England under James I and Anglicized their name. Alexander William, known as Alec to his family, did not grow tall, had a pallid complexion and was short-sighted. Taught to read by his mother, he developed a lasting love of Homer, and in childhood also became a proficient horseman. Through his grandfather, the family inherited Saltmoor, in Somerset, where Kinglake became lord of the manor on his father's death. At the age of twelve, he went to board with the Revd George Coleridge at Ottery St Mary in Devon, which Kinglake considered 'a sad intellectual fall' from his mother's tuition. Between April 1823 and July 1828, he happily attended Eton College, where he became a good oarsman and swimmer. His

Alexander William Kinglake (1809–1891), by Elliott & Fry

one regret was that myopia denied him a military career. After Eton, he went to Trinity College, Cambridge, where Alfred Tennyson, Arthur Hallam, and William Makepeace Thackeray were contemporaries. He spoke in union debates and seemed perpetually short of money, but secured a BA in 1832, and an MA four years later. After Cambridge, he entered Lincoln's Inn on 14 April 1832 and studied law under Bryan Procter (whose wife Anne's literary circle included Thomas Carlyle) and visited Wales and France to reveal an early taste for travel.

In August 1834, Kinglake set out on an eighteen-month odyssey through Europe and the Ottoman empire. After encountering plague in Constantinople, he travelled to Smyrna, Cyprus, Beirut, the Holy Land, and Jerusalem, before crossing the Sinai Desert to Cairo. Following three weeks in Egypt, he returned north through Damascus and Asia Minor then via Athens, Corfu, Rome, and Turin to London. On 5 May 1837, Kinglake was called to the bar but did not enjoy a distinguished legal career. He continued to travel, visiting Switzerland in 1843, and the following year *Eothen*, his account of the 1834–5 Turkish adventures, was published and included two of his own watercolours. Leslie Stephen wrote of *Eothen* in the *Dictionary of National Biography*: 'though the book was rather absurdly compared with the ordinary records of travel, it is more akin to

Sterne's *Sentimental Journey*, and is a delightful record of personal impressions rather than outward facts'. Soon after *Eothen*, two articles appeared in *Quarterly Review*: 'Rights of women' (December 1844) and 'The Mediterranean a French lake' (March 1845). Kinglake became a member of the Travellers' Club in 1845 and, eight years later, of the Athenaeum.

From August until October 1845, Kinglake travelled in Algeria, where he met Colonel A. J. L. de St Arnaud and heard about Colonel A. J. J. Pélissier, who would each command the French forces in the Crimea and were currently suppressing rebel tribesmen. Back in London, Kinglake resumed a busy social life. The writer Mrs M. C. M. Simpson recorded that 'he was exceedingly courteous to women and very generous to all who needed help' (de Gaury, 88). Although not musical he entertained Caroline Norton at the opera, and allegedly vied with the exiled Louis Napoleon (later Napoleon III) for the same mistress, the wealthy courtesan and self-styled Miss Howard (Elizabeth Ann Maryett). In February 1846, he crossed to Calais for a duel with Edward Marlborough FitzGerald, which failed to take place. The high point of his many travels occurred in 1854. Kinglake went with John Delane, editor of *The Times*, and A. H. Layard MP to Constantinople and on to join the invasion fleet off the Crimean coast on 10 September 1854. After the military landing, he went ashore, witnessed the battle of the Alma from close hand, dined that night with Lord Raglan (commander of the British army, whom he had met riding with the duke of Beaufort's hounds in 1853), helped the wounded, sketched and recorded the scenes in his diary. Kinglake rode with the allies towards Sevastopol and watched them take up siege positions on upland to the south. From there, he saw the charges of the heavy and light brigades on 25 October near Balaklava, though soon afterwards he was invalided back to England.

In 1852 Kinglake had failed to enter parliament, but five years later he secured election for Bridgwater, as a Liberal. He spoke frequently in the house, but made little impact due to his weak voice and unimpressive demeanour, although he successfully took up the case of British engineers unjustly gaoled in Naples, gaining for them release and compensation. In 1869 he was unseated after bribery involving his election agent. He then concentrated on his massive work *The Invasion of the Crimea*, which would cover eight volumes, the first published in 1863, the last in 1887. Kinglake had been granted unlimited access to Lord Raglan's papers by his widow, consulted French, Russian, and Turkish sources, and corresponded and interviewed exhaustively. He returned to the Crimea, hosted by the Russian engineer Todleben, who had so ably defended Sevastopol. But Kinglake's diligence, which delayed completion of the story until a generation after the war, frustrated readers and subjected him to repeated and tiresome letters from individuals like Lord Cardigan, who were determined to see their version of events in print. Inevitably, there were criticisms, not least because Kinglake's anti-French bias showed through. Nevertheless, W. G. Romaine, judge-advocate in the Crimea, wrote: 'For once the world is agreed and welcomes your work with a chorus of praise'; and Sir Robert Morier whimsically observed: 'It is a noble monument ... one singularly typical of the imbecility and heroism which make up the British character' (de Gaury, 131–2).

During the work's gestation, Kinglake published, anonymously, in *Blackwood's Magazine* (September 1872) 'The life of Madame de La Fayette'. He still rode frequently in Rotten Row when over seventy. Towards the end of his life, he engaged in prolonged correspondence with Olga Novikov, god-daughter of the tsar, and also the Turkish playwright, Augusta Persee, wife of Sir William Gregory, under whose influence he subscribed to the defence of the Egyptian nationalist leader, Arabi Pasha. Kinglake dined regularly at the Travellers' and Athenaeum, despite increasing deafness, which made conversation difficult. In his eightieth year, on doctor's advice, he forsook the clubs, as gout and throat cancer took their toll. He died on 1 January 1891 at his home, 17 Bayswater Terrace, London, and was cremated at Woking, following a service in Christ Church, Lancaster Gate. His ashes were placed near family graves at Pitminster church, Somerset. Although Kinglake lived in rented rooms, he owned the manorial lands at Saltmoor, which were left to two nieces, as he had remained unmarried. The rents were allocated as annuities to certain friends and retainers, and provision was made for the nurse, Alice Dumper, who cared for him during his last days. His collection of books, oriental swords, and other artefacts was distributed among friends.

Janet Ross, daughter of a long-standing acquaintance, wrote about 'that marvellous mixture of pride, of humility, of daring and intense shyness', and Kinglake himself admitted that, 'I have all my life suffered from constitutional shyness' (de Gaury, 146, 128). He also chided Olga Novikov, 'pray remember that I am a heathen' (ibid., 135), reinforcing Thackeray's post-Cambridge conclusion that Kinglake was an atheist. JOHN SWEETMAN

Sources G. de Gaury, *Travelling gent: the life of Alexander Kinglake (1809–1891)* (1972) · W. Tuckwell, *A. W. Kinglake: a biographical and literary study* (1902) · A. W. Kinglake, *Eothen* (1844) · A. W. Kinglake, *The invasion of the Crimea*, 8 vols. (1863–87) · M. C. M. Simpson, *Many memories of many people* (1898) · J. Sweetman, *Raglan: from the Peninsula to the Crimea* (1993) · C. Hibbert, *The destruction of Lord Raglan* [1961] · *The Times* (3 Jan 1891) · *CGPLA Eng. & Wales* (1892)

Archives Bodl. Oxf., letters · CUL, corresp. and papers · CUL, corresp. and papers collected for his history of the Crimean War | BL, letters to T. H. S. Escott, Add. MS 58783 · BL, letters to Sir M. E. Grant Duff · Bodl. Oxf., letters to Richard Bentley and George Bentley · CUL, letters to Edward Herries · Essex RO, corresp. with G. D. Warburton · FM Cam., letters to Mrs Wynne Finch and her son Guy Le Strange · Gwent RO, letters to Somerset family · Mitchell L., Glas., Glasgow City Archives, letters to Sir William Stirling-Maxwell · NL Scot., corresp. with Blackwoods, MS of *The invasion of the Crimea* · NRA, priv. coll., letters to John Swinton · NRA, priv. coll., corresp. with Lord Wemyss · TCD, letters to William Edward Hartpole Leckey and Mrs Leckey · Trinity Cam., letters to Lord Houghton · U. Newcastle, Robinson L., letters to Madame de Bury · U. Nott., Pelham MSS

Likenesses H. M. Haviland, oils, *c.*1863, NPG · Elliott & Fry, photograph, NPG [*see illus.*] · London Stereoscopic Co., carte-de-visite · J. Watkins, carte-de-visite, NPG · Webber & Blizard, carte-de-visite,

NPG · caricature, chromolithograph, NPG; repro. in *VF* (2 March 1872)

Wealth at death £16,296 17s. 3d.: resworn probate, June 1892, *CGPLA Eng. & Wales* (1891)

Kinglake, Robert (1765–1842), physician, graduated MD at Göttingen, and also studied at Edinburgh. After practising for some years as a surgeon at Chipping Norton, Oxfordshire, he moved to Somerset, first to Chilton upon Polden and then in 1802 to Taunton. At Taunton he frequently attended public meetings and made a number of speeches in support of the first Reform Bill. He was a member of the Royal Medical Society of Edinburgh, the Physical Society of Göttingen, and other learned societies. He married Joanna, daughter of Anthony Apperlay, of Herefordshire. They had at least two sons.

Kinglake attracted considerable attention through his writings on gout, in which he advocated the cooling treatment. His first papers on the subject appeared in 1801 and 1803 in the *Medical and Physical Journal* (nos. 33 and 48). His views were opposed by William Wadd, W. Perry, John Hunt, J. King, and others. He replied to his antagonists in: *A Dissertation on Gout* (1804, with appendix), and in a *Reply to Mr Edlin's Two Cases of Gout* (1804). He also published in 1820 his 'Observations on the medical effects of digitalis' in the *Medical and Physical Journal*. In Robert Macnish's *Anatomy of Drunkenness* (1827) there is a short article by the author on Kinglake's experiment with ether.

Kinglake died on 26 September 1842 at West Monkton rectory, near Taunton, the home of his son, the Revd W. C. Kinglake. [ANON.], *rev.* CLAIRE L. NUTT

Sources Watt, *Bibl. Brit.* · *GM*, 2nd ser., 18 (1842), 556 · *WWBMP*

Kings Norton. For this title name *see* Cox, (Harold) Roxbee, Baron Kings Norton (1902–1997).

Kingsborough. For this title name *see* King, Edward, Viscount Kingsborough (1795–1837).

Kingsburgh. For this title name *see* Macdonald, Sir John Hay Athole, Lord Kingsburgh (1836–1919).

Kingsbury, William (1744–1818), Independent minister, was born on 12 July 1744 in Bishopsgate Street, London, one of five children of Thomas Kingsbury. In 1753 his father died, and William was placed at Merchant Taylors' School; later, under the patronage of Sir John Barnard, he was sent to Christ's Hospital school. In October 1758, through the interest of Dr Thomas Gibbons, he became a boarder at the Congregational academy, Mile End, under Gibbons himself, Dr John Conder, and Dr John Walker. Walker's free instruction included Hebrew, mathematics, geography, astronomy, and experimental philosophy. In 1760 Kingsbury became a divinity student, mainly because of Conder's persuasiveness and a conversion experience on Tuesday 7 October. In February 1762 he joined the Independent congregation at Haberdashers' Hall, where Gibbons was pastor. In August 1763, the year his mother died, Kingsbury preached his first sermon at Bethnal Green. In September, having preached at Lower Tooting, he was invited to be pastor. Until mid-1764, when he left the academy, he travelled weekly to Tooting.

In the autumn, Kingsbury preached at Above Bar Congregational Church in Southampton. On 28 December 1764 he was appointed pastor and ordained there on 8 October 1765. In 1767 the University of Aberdeen awarded him the degree of master of arts. On 23 November 1768 he married at Holy Trinity, Gosport, Mary Andrews (1744/5–1789), daughter of Independent minister Mordecai Andrews. They had four sons and four daughters. In 1787 he was invited to be resident tutor at Homerton Academy. He declined, but, advised by his friend John Howard, opened an academy in Southampton. Kingsbury describes their first meeting in 1772 in James Baldwin Brown's *Memoirs of Howard*. Another friend was the evangelical divine John Newton. Other educational interests of his included Sunday schools, which he helped form in Southampton in 1786, charity schools, and the Revd David Bogue's seminary in Gosport for training missionaries. In 1793 Kingsbury became a founder contributor and trustee of the *Evangelical Magazine*.

Following the death of his wife on 2 January 1789, aged forty-four, Kingsbury married in spring 1790 Miss Redfearne. The following year Kingsbury's eldest son suffered a breakdown from which he never recovered. About the same time, Mrs Kingsbury developed a progressive mental disorder. By 1809 the condition was severe, and she was institutionalized. From 1776 onwards Kingsbury himself experienced periods of illness and depression. His extensive diaries present a 'picture of persevering piety, … strict habit of severe self-observation … a practice of viewing all … events with reference to the over-ruling providence, … and the merciful designs of the Almighty God' (Bullar, 23).

Kingsbury's ministry was dominated by popular evangelical preaching: 'Thousands of manuscript sermons attest the diligence with which he … prepared' (Bullar, 179). Some, often funeral sermons, were published. He habitually preached special sermons. One, on the recovery of George III (1789), was subsequently preached in at least two Anglican churches. Kingsbury, however, vociferously defended nonconformist beliefs and practices. A sermon in which the Revd Richard Mant criticized extemporary prayer led to the publication of *The manner in which the protestant dissenters perform prayer in public worship, represented and vindicated* (1796). He was also passionate about evangelical mission. In 1798 he published *An Apology for Village Preachers*. A founder member of the London Missionary Society, on 22 September 1795 he presided at two of the inaugural meetings. For a time he was a director of the society.

In 1802 George Clayton was appointed Kingsbury's assistant at Above Bar. Despite good relations, Clayton moved in 1804. On 8 October 1805 Henry Lacey became co-pastor. Relations were less harmonious and Lacey resigned in 1807. On resigning the pastorate of Above Bar in 1809, an annuity of £200 was agreed, but in a letter dated 9 August Kingsbury declared, 'I *cannot* be prevailed upon to receive more than £120'. Kingsbury moved to

Caversham, near Reading, where he opened a small place of worship. He died in Caversham on 18 February 1818 after a paralytic stroke. His daughter, Sarah Jameson, and son, Walter, were present. He was buried in Reading, and George Clayton delivered the funeral sermon. The Revd David Bogue preached a memorial sermon in Southampton.   DIANA K. JONES

Sources J. Bullar, *Memoirs of the late Rev William Kingsbury MA* (1819) · S. Stainer, *History of the Above Bar Congregational Church, Southampton, from 1662 to 1908* (1909) · *DNB* · church book, 1726–1798, Above Bar Congregational Church, Southampton, Civic Centre, Southampton, Archives Office, D/ABC 1/2 · church book, 1798–1809, Above Bar Congregational Church, Southampton, Civic Centre, Southampton, Archives Office, D/ABC 1/3 · LMS board minutes and annual reports, 1795–8, SOAS, Archives of the Council for World Mission (incorporating the London Missionary Society) · [J. Watkins and F. Shoberl], *A biographical dictionary of the living authors of Great Britain and Ireland* (1816) · Allibone, *Dict.* · J. B. Brown, *Memoirs of the public and private life of John Howard, the philanthropist* (1818) · E. F. Hatfield, *The poets of the church: a series of biographical sketches of hymn writers* (1884) · J. Morison, *The fathers and founders of the London Missionary Society*, 1 [1840] · D. M. Sale, *The hymn writers of Hampshire* (1975) · J. H. Taylor, 'A tale of Taylors. A family and their church: Above Bar, Southampton', *Journal of the United Reformed Church History Society*, 5 (1992–7) · W. Wilson, *The history and antiquities of the dissenting churches and meeting houses in London, Westminster and Southwark*, 4 vols. (1808–14) · *Above Bar Congregational Church, 1662–1912: 250th anniversary celebrations* (1912) · *Evangelical Magazine and Missionary Chronicle*, 26 (1818), 161 · W. Kingsbury, letter to J. Eyre, Aug 1795, SOAS, Archives of the Council for World Mission (incorporating the London Missionary Society), home office extra box 1 · H. Lacey, letter to the church and congregation at Above Bar Congregational Church, June 1807, Civic Centre, Southampton, Archives Office, D/ABC 20/2 · W. Kingsbury, letter to Walter Wilson, June 1809, DWL, MS 12.64(34) · W. Kingsbury to Above Bar Congregational church, July 1809, Civic Centre, Southampton, Archives Office, D/ABS 20/3 and 4

Likenesses H. Dawe, mezzotint (after M. Spilsbury), BM · photograph (after an engraving?), Avenue St Andrews United Reformed Church, Southampton · portrait, repro. in Stainer, *History of the Above Bar Congregational Church* · portrait, repro. in *Above Bar Congregational Church, 1662–1912* · stipple, NPG; repro. in *Evangelical Magazine* (1795)

Wealth at death £120 p.a. in annuity

Kingscote [*née* Wolff], **Adeline Georgiana Isabella** [*pseuds.* Lucas Cleeve, Mary Walpole] (**1860–1908**), novelist and travel writer, was the daughter of Adeline Douglas (1826/7–1916) and Sir Henry Drummond Charles *Wolff (1830–1908), diplomatist and MP. Her paternal grandfather was the Revd Joseph *Wolff, co-founder of the Irvingite Church, and her maternal grandfather was Walter Sholto Douglas. An accomplished linguist, Kingscote was among the first women to attend Oxford University, and on 25 June 1885 in St Paul's, Wilton Place, London, she married Howard Kingscote (*b.* 1844/5), a lieutenant-colonel in the Oxfordshire light infantry. While living in India with her husband she wrote *Tales of the Sun, or, Folklore of Southern India* (1890) and *The English Baby in India and how to Rear it* (1893), both published under the name Mrs H. Kingscote. The latter offers sensible advice but demonstrates contemporary prejudice in arguing against the use of Indian nurses.

The Kingscotes returned to England in 1895 when Howard Kingscote was appointed commander of Cowley barracks. They moved into Bury Knowle House in Headington, Oxfordshire, where Kingscote began her prolific career as a novelist. She wrote *The Love Seeker* (1908) as Mary Walpole, and under the pseudonym Lucas Cleeve she published more than sixty novels, including *The Woman who Wouldn't* (1895), her response to Grant Allen's *The Woman who Did* (1895). Feminist concerns figure in the novels: in her posthumously published novel *The Love Letters of a Faithless Wife* (1911), for example, the heroine, Hertha Atherton, feels so unfulfilled by her marriage to a cold and neglectful husband that she contemplates embarking upon a series of extramarital liaisons. Hertha argues that there are two kinds of husbands: 'The men who love again anywhere and everywhere, and who are unfaithful; and the men who, when they have married a wife, don't want to love or be loved any more'. Her husband falls into the latter camp; none the less Hertha remains faithful—but the very fact of her temptation serves as a warning to unappreciative husbands.

Though Kingscote continued to write until her death, at times producing as many as eight books a year, she is remembered more for her charm and financial irresponsibility than for her works of fiction. Her powers of persuasion enabled her to extract large sums of money from male admirers, while her 'consuming brown eyes' (Jenkins) captivated the future MP for Oxford, Frank Gray. Working as a solicitor's clerk in 1898, he met Kingscote when he went to Bury Knowle House to serve writs on her. She was described by Gray as 'the finest adventuress I ever met' (ibid.), but her extravagance caught up with her in 1899 when she was forced to declare bankruptcy for the astonishing sum of £100,000. The entire contents of Bury Knowle House, down to the bottles of Moët et Chandon in the cellar, were auctioned in June 1899. Undaunted by financial disaster, she continued to write until her death at Château d'Oex in Switzerland on 13 September 1908.

EMMA PLASKITT

Sources Blain, Clements & Grundy, *Feminist comp.*, 214 · S. Jenkins, users.ox.ac.uk/~uzdh0149/he…history/famouspeople/kingscote.htm · www.headington.org.uk · J. Sutherland, *The Longman companion to Victorian fiction* (1988)

Kingscote, Henry Robert (**1802–1882**), philanthropist, was born on 25 May 1802, the second son of Thomas Kingscote (*d.* 1811), the brother of Robert Kingscote of Kingscote, Gloucestershire; his mother was Harriet, the third daughter of Sir Henry Peyton of Doddington in the same county. He was educated at Harrow School, and early became a cricketer and rider to hounds. Six feet five inches tall, he played his first match at Lord's on 21 May 1823. President of the MCC for 1827, he initiated a three-match series between Sussex—whose bowlers used the controversial round-arm style denounced by its opponents as 'throwing'—and 'All England', which aroused much interest.

A narrow escape from drowning, probably in the late 1820s, apparently led to his conversion. An evangelical, he became a friend of Bishop Charles Blomfield, and with him was instrumental in founding the Church of England Scripture Readers' Association and the Metropolitan Visiting and Relief Association, of which he was a trustee all his life. He munificently assisted St Matthias, Bethnal Green. In 1846 he published *A Letter to … the Archbishop of Canterbury on the Present Wants of the Church*, which ran through several editions. In it he urged the extension of lay agency and the foundation of new bishoprics.

A leading and generous London evangelical, in 1846 Kingscote helped to found the Southwark Fund for schools and churches, and in 1847 he assisted in alleviating the distress of the famine in Ireland. He sent out supplies to the troops during the Crimean War. In 1868 he was one of the founders of the British and Colonial Emigration Society; he was also the founder of the scheme for establishing workshops for the indigent blind, which was not very successful, and of the National Orphan Asylum at Ham Common, Surrey, in 1849.

Kingscote married, on 11 July 1833, Harriet Elizabeth Tower of Weald Hall, Essex; they had three sons and five daughters. Harriet died on 10 March 1875. Kingscote died on 13 July 1882 at his home, 10 Seville Street, Lowndes Square, London.

W. A. J. ARCHBOLD, *rev.* MARK CLEMENT

Sources *The Times* (14 July 1882), 8 · Boase, *Mod. Eng. biog.* · Burke, *Gen. GB* · D. M. Lewis, ed., *The Blackwell dictionary of evangelical biography, 1730–1860*, 2 vols. (1995) · T. Lewis, *Double century: the story of MCC and cricket* (1987)
Archives LPL, corresp. with Charles Blomfield · LUL, letters to Lord Overstone
Wealth at death £2708 10s. 3d.: probate, 29 July 1882, *CGPLA Eng. & Wales*

Kingscote, Sir Robert Nigel Fitzhardinge (1830–1908), courtier and agriculturist, born at Kingscote Park, Gloucestershire, on 28 February 1830, was the only son of Thomas Henry Kingscote (1799–1861), and his first wife, Lady Isabella (1809–1831), sixth daughter of Henry Somerset, sixth duke of Beaufort. He was educated at a school at Weymouth before going abroad with a tutor until the age of sixteen, when he obtained a commission in the Scots Fusilier Guards through the influence of his maternal great-uncle, Lord Fitzroy Somerset (afterwards Lord Raglan). In 1854 he went out to the Crimea as aide-de-camp to Lord Raglan, whose body he escorted back to England in 1855. He was made brevet major on 12 December 1854, and subsequently lieutenant-colonel and CB.

Kingscote sold out of the guards in 1856, and thereafter lived a retired life in the country. On the death of his father on 19 December 1861 he inherited the Kingscote estate, and he kept up the family traditions as a squire, breeder of pedigree livestock, and follower of the hounds. He was Liberal MP for West Gloucestershire from 1852 to 1885, and in 1885 was made a commissioner of woods and forests by Gladstone, which post he retained until 1895.

Kingscote married first, on 13 March 1851, the Hon. Caroline Sophia Wyndham, daughter of George, first Baron Leconfield; she died on 19 March 1852. He married second, on 5 February 1856 Lady Emily Marie Curzon

(1836–1910), daughter of Richard, first Earl Howe. They had one son and two daughters.

From 1859 to 1866 Kingscote was parliamentary groom in waiting to Queen Victoria, and thus began a lifelong intimacy with the royal family, especially with the prince of Wales. In May 1864 he was appointed superintendent of the prince of Wales's stables, a post which he held until 1885. He was a member of council of the prince of Wales from 1886, and receiver-general of the duchy of Cornwall from 1888. In 1867 he was appointed extra equerry to the prince, and was made extra equerry to the king and paymaster-general of the royal household on Edward VII's accession. His wife, Lady Emily, also served in the royal household, as lady of the bedchamber to Queen Alexandra. He was made KCB (civil) in 1889 and GCVO in 1902. Kingscote died at Worth Park, Sussex, on 22 September 1908.

Kingscote was a recognized authority on agriculture and an active member of the Royal Agricultural Society from 1854 to 1906. He was chairman of the finance committee for thirty-one years (1875–1906), and was president of the society at Bristol in 1878. He was chairman of the governors of the Royal Veterinary College, and an active member of the council of the Royal Agricultural College at Cirencester, of the Smithfield Club, Shorthorn Society, Hunters' Improvement Society, and numerous other agricultural organizations. He was also a member of the two royal commissions on agriculture of 1879 and 1893.

ERNEST CLARKE, *rev.* K. D. REYNOLDS

Sources E. Clarke, *Journal of the Royal Agricultural Society of England*, 69 (1908) · W. A. Lindsay, *The royal household* (1898) · *WWW* · Burke, *Gen. GB*
Archives Glos. RO, corresp. and papers, incl. his Crimean journal, and family papers | Gwent RO, corresp. with Lord Raglan
Likenesses A. de Brie, photogravure, 1908 (after a portrait in oils), priv. coll.; repro. in Clarke, *Journal of the Royal Agricultural Society* · W. Roffe, stipple (after a photograph by Barraud), NPG; repro. in *Baily's Magazine* (1891) · Spy [L. Ward], caricature, watercolour study, NPG; repro. in *VF* (14 Feb 1880) · oils, priv. coll.
Wealth at death £21,729 5s. 9d.: probate, 30 Oct 1908, *CGPLA Eng. & Wales*

Kingsdown. For this title name *see* Leigh, Thomas Pemberton, Baron Kingsdown (1793–1867).

Kingsford [*née* Bonus], **Anna** [Annie] (1846–1888), physician and spiritualist, was born on 16 September 1846 at Maryland Point, Stratford, Essex. She was a sickly child, the youngest daughter of twelve children born to Elizabeth Ann Schröder and her husband, John Bonus (*d.* 1865), a London merchant and shipowner. According to Kingsford's spiritual soulmate and biographer Edward Maitland (1824–1897), who believed Kingsford to be a 'special instrument of the Gods' (Maitland, 1.114), the Bonuses were descended from 'a great Italian family' (ibid., 1), one of whom was a cardinal 'of strong mystical tendencies' (ibid.). If this is true, then it might explain where the origins of Kingsford's own clairvoyant talents lay. As a child she would converse with flowers and believed herself to be a fairy, and at an early age displayed mystical 'powers' of premonition. As an adult she functioned within two fringe movements: theosophy, which sought a mystical and intuitive understanding of and contact with the divine, and spiritualism, which supported the idea of the existence of the human character after death and the ability of the dead to communicate with the living via a medium. Kingsford often attended seances with Maitland, received religious information by means of dreams (many of which were published in *Dreams and Dream Stories*, 1888), and discovered a strong spiritual affinity with, among others, Anne Boleyn and Joan of Arc. As an adolescent she also demonstrated her talents as an author: at thirteen she wrote her first book, *Beatrice: a Tale of the Early Christians* (1863), and received 2 guineas from the publishers for her efforts. Thereafter followed a series of poems for the *Churchman's Companion*. She continued writing throughout her life, expounding her (radical) views on spiritualism, vegetarianism, and anti-vivisection. She wrote stories under the name of Ninon Kingsford for the *Penny Post* from 1868 to 1872 and a series of weekly articles for the *Ladies Pictorial* between 1884 and 1887.

On new year's eve 1867 Annie Bonus married her 22-year-old cousin Algernon Godfrey Kingsford (1845–1913), the son of Godfrey Kingsford, a priest, and then moved to Lichfield where Algernon Kingsford trained to enter the ministry. Kingsford soon gave birth to her only child, a daughter named Eadith, an event which did little to improve her poor health. She often lapsed into trance-like states and suffered from severe asthma, epilepsy, neuralgia, and nervous panics which often prevented physical exertion. In 1870 she experienced a religious reawakening after receiving three nocturnal visits from Mary Magdalen. She converted to Catholicism and adopted, alongside her other identities, the names Mary Magdalen Maria Johanna. Kingsford later became somewhat dissatisfied with what she discerned as the materialism and idolatry of Catholicism, and she criticised the Roman Catholic church's avoidance of the vivisection question. Kingsford never seems to have acquired a secure sense of who she was; she was tormented rather than contented by life, and believed that her karma would allow her neither rest nor a peaceful existence.

By the time Kingsford converted to Catholicism her husband had accepted a curacy at Atcham near Shrewsbury which proved detrimental to his wife's health. She decided to remove herself from these deleterious surroundings and also make a life for herself outside her marriage. In 1872 she purchased *The Lady's Own Paper*, and divided her time between Shrewsbury and the journal's offices in London. It was at about this time that she made the acquaintance of Edward Maitland. While acting as editor Kingsford was made aware of vivisection after she published a letter by the anti-vivisectionist Frances Power Cobbe, and in 1874 she decided to train for a medical career in order to find out more about medical research. She undertook her training, without her husband and daughter, in France, and received her medical degree in 1880. The topic of her dissertation, 'De l'alimentation végétale chez l'homme', reflected her growing animal welfare and vegetarian sentiments, and was eventually published in London in 1881 as *The Perfect Way in Diet*. She believed that only with a vegetarian diet would body and soul be united and feed off each other: 'his [the vegetarian's] sensuous enjoyments will be keener, his perceptions clearer, his brain stronger, his whole person lighter, purer, and more healthful' (Kingsford, 504). While studying in France Kingsford apparently suffered a stroke which paralysed her left side, although she seems to have recovered. Kingsford compensated for corporeal weakness by honing her spiritual powers. In 1877 Kingsford and Maitland were 'visited' by Sir William Fergusson (1808–1877) who encouraged the pair to work for the abolition of vivisection; she brought to the public's attention the physical damage done to animals and the moral damage done to man in works such as 'The uselessness of vivisection' (1882) and *Notes by a Medical Student*. In 1880 she sat on the board of the International Society for the Suppression of Vivisection until a conflict among board members over Kingsford's presence and Maitland's pamphlet, *The Woman and the Age*, prompted her and Maitland to resign. In 1883 she organized anti-vivisection societies in France and Geneva, and was also, for a brief spell in 1883 and 1884, president of the London lodges of both the Theosophical Society and the Hermetic Society, which she founded. Her spiritualism fed into her anti-vivisection activities, and she considered her talents an asset to the cause, especially after she convinced herself that she had willed the French vivisector Claude Bernard's death in 1878. 'Oh! I will make it dangerous, nay, deadly, to be a vivisector,' she told Maitland (Maitland, 1.252).

Alongside her spiritual and anti-vivisection work Kingsford also supported the English women's movement. As early as 1867 she canvassed for signatures for a petition supporting married women's property rights, and her move to London in 1872 facilitated greater participation in women's rights activities by bringing her into contact with many of the feminists of her day, Frances Power Cobbe, Barbara Bodichon, and Elizabeth Wolstenholme. Kingsford contributed to debate by writing in 1868 *An Essay on the Admission of Women to the Parliamentary Franchise* wherein she argued for suffrage on the grounds that it would allow women to fulfil their God given functions as responsible citizens. Her active role in the women's rights movement lasted only a short time; she became increasingly frustrated and dissatisfied with what she detected as the denigration of women as wives and mothers and an unnecessary antagonism between the sexes. She herself seems to have lived an unconventional married life; she spent more time with Maitland than with her husband and daughter, although there is no indication that Algernon stood in the way of his wife's activities. She divided her time, with Maitland in tow, between London, the continent, and Atcham, and was plagued by extreme ill health and pain which was relieved by increasingly liberal doses of chloroform and morphine. Kingsford died in Maitland's arms from consumption at 15 Wynnstay Gardens, Kensington, London, on 22 February 1888. Algernon was not present. She was buried at Atcham a week later.

LORI WILLIAMSON

Sources E. Maitland, *Anna Kingsford: her life, letters, diary, and work*, 3rd edn, ed. S. H. Hart, 2 vols. (1913) • N. Kingsford [A. Kingsford], 'The best food for man', *Westminster Review*, 102 (1874), 500–14 • *Nature*, 25 (1881–2), 482 • R. D. French, *Antivivisection and medical science in Victorian society* (1975) • DNB • b. cert. • m. cert. • d. cert.
Likenesses photograph (aged thirty-eight), repro. in Maitland, *Anna Kingsford*, vol. 1, frontispiece • photograph (aged twenty-three), repro. in Maitland, *Anna Kingsford*, facing p. 15
Wealth at death £887 11s.: resworn probate, July 1889, *CGPLA Eng. & Wales* (1888)

Kingsford, Charles Lethbridge

Kingsford, Charles Lethbridge (1862–1926), historian, was born at Ludlow, Shropshire, on Christmas day 1862, third son of the Revd Sampson Kingsford (1825–1890), headmaster of Ludlow grammar school, and his wife, Helen, daughter of William Lethbridge of Tavistock. From Rossall School he won a scholarship to St John's College, Oxford, where he gained a first in *literae humaniores* (1885) and a second in modern history (1886), and received the Arnold prize for an essay on 'The Reformation in France' (1888). In 1889 he joined the editorial staff of the *Dictionary of National Biography*, but he left in 1890 to become an examiner for the education department, an administrative post which was not regarded as particularly demanding. Between 1889 and 1899 he contributed over 300 biographies of medieval politicians, clerics, and men of letters to the dictionary. In 1892 he married Alys, daughter of Charles Thomas *Hudson. The marriage was childless.

Kingsford was promoted to assistant secretary at the education department in 1905 but resigned from the civil service in 1912, finding the changes in his department, which had been at the centre of a public row in 1911, made it no longer congenial. Apart from serving as private secretary to Sir Arthur Boscawen at the Ministry of Pensions in 1917 and 1918, he devoted the rest of his life to historical research as an independent scholar.

Although Kingsford's historical reputation is based mainly on a substantial corpus of works on fifteenth-century England and its sources, his earliest books were a scholarly edition of the thirteenth-century political poem *The Song of Lewes* (1890) and, with T. A. Archer, *The Crusades: the Story of the Latin Kingdom of Jerusalem* (1894). An article for the *Dictionary of National Biography* on Henry V (1891) probably first fired his interest in the fifteenth century and, in 1901, came his biography *Henry V: the Typical Medieval Hero*, a book firmly founded on the study of original sources. This was followed, in 1911, by an edition of *The First English Life of Henry V*, a valuable contribution to the debate on the king's life and times. His discovery of the importance of city chronicles for Henry V's reign resulted, in 1905, in the publication of three *Chronicles of London*, prefaced by a scholarly introduction surveying all the different manuscripts of London chronicles then known, their dates, contents, and the complex interrelation of their texts. His enthusiasm for London history and topography found expression, too, in a masterly new edition of John Stow's *Survey of London* (1908): the introduction is both learned and entertaining; the text, freed from the accretions of earlier editors, is treated as a 'venerable original'; and over a hundred pages of notes reveal his deep knowledge of topography, records, and letters. Further work on London and its sources followed: in 1910 he edited two sixteenth-century London chronicles for the Camden Society; in 1915 he wrote *The Grey Friars of London* for the British Society of Franciscan Studies, while his *Collectanea Franciscana* (1922) provided information about many London citizens who died between 1374 and 1537; and *The Early History of Piccadilly, Leicester Square, Soho and their Neighbourhood*, published by the London Topographical Society in 1926 and inspired by a plan of the region drawn in 1585, is the last of many debts London owes to Kingsford's insight and industry.

Kingsford's two-volume edition of *The Stonor Letters and Papers, 1290–1483* (1919) demonstrated both his thoroughness as an editor and his recognition of the importance of the Stonor archive; his Stonor materials were further published in 1996 (edited and introduced by Christine Carpenter). He undertook work for the Historical Manuscripts Commission on the manuscripts of Lord De L'Isle and Dudley (1925); and he wrote on 'The kingdom of Jerusalem 1099–1291' for the *Cambridge Medieval History*, contributed more than thirty biographies to the *Encyclopaedia Britannica* (among them six English kings, 1377–1485), and published articles in a range of learned journals including the *English Historical Review*, *Archaeologia*, and the *London Topographical Record*. His range of interests found expression in histories of the Middlesex regiment (1916) and the Royal Warwickshire regiment (1921). No less impressive was his service, as committee member and officer, for the Royal Historical Society, Historical Association, Society of Antiquaries, London Topographical Society, British Society of Franciscan Studies, and Canterbury and York Society. In 1924 he was elected a fellow of the British Academy.

Kingsford's most important books originated in lecture series for Oxford University in 1910 and 1923: *English Historical Literature in the Fifteenth Century* (1913), a critical exposition and analysis of literary sources ranging from chronicles, biographies, and histories to letters, ballads, and poems, and *Prejudice and Promise in Fifteenth Century England* (1925), the text of his Ford lectures, where he exposed the 'prejudice' of Tudor historians of the era culminating in William Shakespeare's cycle of history plays and highlighted the 'promise' evident in the spirit of adventure, commercial enterprise, social growth, and intellectual ferment of the age. For Kingsford the seeds of Tudor greatness lay in the fifteenth century: his deep knowledge of its historical sources enabled him to demonstrate that, despite political crises, periodic social disorder and the Wars of the Roses, there was much in the epoch to merit respect, even admiration.

As a man, Kingsford was rather reserved and solitary but he exhibited a strong sense of duty and of justice, proved an able administrator and a conscientious colleague, and possessed a sense of humour that occasionally found expression even in his writings; as a historian his range of interests was impressive, his scholarship and research conscientious and methodical, and he not only displayed real insight into the past but also communicated an infectious enthusiasm and excitement about historical discovery. His immense industry and insatiable curiosity about history remained undiminished until, as a result of a sudden seizure, he died at his home, 15 Argyll Road, Kensington, London, on 27 November 1926. He was buried at South Tawton, Devon. His wife survived him.

KEITH DOCKRAY

Sources DNB · A. G. Little, 'Charles Lethbridge Kingsford, 1862–1926', PBA, 12 (1926), 348–56 · E. Jeffries Davis, 'The work of C. L. Kingsford in London history and topography', London Topographical Record, 14 (1928) · The Times (29 Nov 1926) · G. Sutherland, 'Administrators in education after 1870', Studies in the growth of nineteenth-century government, ed. G. Sutherland (1972)
Archives LUL, papers relating to Dictionary of National Biography · S. Antiquaries, Lond., index of published references to London parishes | Bodl. Oxf., letters to Francis Marvin
Likenesses Bassano, photograph, c.1924, British Academy, London · Elliott & Fry, photograph, NPG
Wealth at death £29,980 4s. 2d.: probate, 2 Feb 1927, CGPLA Eng. & Wales

Kingsford, William (1819–1898), civil engineer and historian, born on 23 December 1819 in the parish of St Lawrence Jewry, London, was the son of William Kingsford, innkeeper of Lad Lane, London, and his wife, Elizabeth. Educated at Nicholas Wanostrocht's Alfred House Academy in Camberwell, he shared his teacher's preference for physical pursuits over book learning. He was articled at an early age to an architect, but disliked the life and enlisted in the 1st dragoon guards at the age of seventeen. He went with his regiment to Canada in 1837, became sergeant, and in 1840 obtained his discharge, despite the fact that his colonel, Sir George Cathcart, offered to procure a commission for him.

Kingsford had learned some rudimentary surveying with his regiment and on the strength of this entered the office of the city surveyor of Montreal in 1841, and in 1842 was promoted to deputy city surveyor, a post which he held until July 1845. Meanwhile, in 1844, with Murdo McIver, he founded the Montreal Times. He vigorously supported the constitutional party in the paper and during the election riots of 1844 in which he was a prominent vigilante. His reform opponents took revenge two years later, nearly killing him and leaving him with two scars to the head.

In 1846 Kingsford returned to surveying and took temporary positions across Lower Canada, acquiring as he did so the skills of civil engineering. On 29 March 1848 he married Maria Margaret, daughter of William Burns Lindsay, clerk of the legislative assembly of the province of Canada; they had two children. In 1849 he moved to the United States, laying out building lots in Brooklyn, NY, and then in 1850 becoming assistant engineer on the Hudson River railroad, New York. In 1851 he went to Panama to work on the railway and then on the water supply for Panama City. He returned to Canada in 1852 and surveyed several stretches of track for the Grand Trunk, especially around Montreal, and helped construct Victoria Bridge across the St Lawrence at Montreal. He was chief engineer of the city of Toronto for a few months during 1855, but,

when he found that his assistants' salaries were to be paid from his own, he returned to work for the Grand Trunk around Toronto until 1864. After undertaking freelance work in Canada, he went to England in 1865, where his experience and his mastery of French, German, Italian, and Spanish led to his being engaged by some English firms, including Thomas Brassey, to advise on railway construction and other commercial projects in Europe.

In 1867, at the instigation of English capitalists who hoped to build the Canadian Intercolonial Railway, Kingsford returned to Canada, where he remained for the rest of his life. As the dominion resolved to build the line as a government work, he reverted to freelance civil engineering, while continuing his journalism. As a vocal Conservative he benefited when, from 1870, the department of public works was in the hands of the Liberal-Conservative ministry. He was appointed engineer in charge of the harbours of the Great Lakes and the St Lawrence. He continued in this post until 31 December 1879 when he was dismissed by Sir Hector Louis Langevin, minister of public works, ostensibly because reorganization in the department had made the post redundant. Kingsford argued that his was a professional post which should be unaffected by party politics, and the Canadian House of Commons debated the case which tested the incompatibility of the old patronage and the new professionalism. Kingsford argued his point in Kingsford and Sir Hector Langevin (1882) but achieved no redress beyond six months' salary.

Thus, at the age of sixty, Kingsford found himself cut off from the public civil-engineering projects which gave his profession a unique standing in the new country. He turned instead to history, using material he had collected himself and that in government offices. He had already published several works on Canadian history and geography and his professional life had given him good knowledge of Canadian topography and of military matters. He set to work, following a strict daily routine which allowed him to complete the ten volumes of his History of Canada between 1887 and 1898. To raise the $1200 needed to produce each volume he mortgaged his house and furniture, and he and the project were saved from ruin only through the intervention of friends. The History was warmly received in both England and Canada: Queen's University at Kingston and Dalhousie in Nova Scotia conferred on him the degree of LLD and McGill University gave his name to a recently endowed chair of history. However, the work was criticized by academic historians in Canada, then just beginning to assert professional control over the writing of history, and a more recent judgement is that his History was 'a generally uncoordinated recapitulation of commonplaces, interrupted by irrelevant digressions and delivered in a pedestrian prose of interminable length' (DCB).

Kingsford was a fellow of the Royal Society of Canada, to which he contributed several papers, and in 1887 helped found the Canadian Society of Civil Engineers. He died on 29 September 1898, just a few months after completing his history: his widow was granted a civil-list pension of £100. As Taylor remarks in the *Dictionary of Canadian Biography*, it is a pity that Kingsford is remembered primarily as an amateur historian, when his real contribution was as a professional civil engineer.   ELIZABETH BAIGENT

Sources M. B. Taylor, 'Kingsford, William', *DCB*, vol. 12 • C. C. Berger, *The writing of Canadian history* (1986) • J. K. McConica, 'Kingsford and whiggery in Canadian history', *Canadian History Review*, 40 (1959), 108–20 • J. G. Bourinot, 'Bibliography of the members of the Royal Society of Canada', *Proceedings and Transactions of the Royal Society of Canada*, 12 (1894), 1–79 • *DNB*
Likenesses photograph, repro. in *Transactions of the Royal Society of Canada*, 2nd ser., 5 (1899)

Kingsley, Charles (1781–1860), Church of England clergyman, was born near Lymington in Hampshire. His family included some distinguished soldiers, notably General William Kingsley. Brought up as a country gentleman, he was educated at Harrow School and, for two months, at Brasenose College, Oxford. He then retired to Battramsley House near Lymington in the New Forest, where he devoted himself to the pursuits of a country gentleman before discovering, at the age of twenty-six, that all his money had gone. He married Mary (1787–1873), the daughter of Nathan Lucas of Barbados and Rushford Lodge, Norfolk. Mary's organizing ability was a great asset to Kingsley after his funds ran out; when, almost certainly following her advice, he eventually made his career in the church it was Mary who did most of the parish visiting.

In 1807 Kingsley entered Trinity Hall, Cambridge, to study divinity, and nine years later, at the age of thirty-five, graduated from Sidney Sussex College, Cambridge with an LLB degree. While at Trinity Hall he had established a friendship with Herbert Marsh, then Lady Margaret professor of divinity, who became bishop of Peterborough in 1819. The two men shared an interest in the scientific approach to biblical criticism which Marsh had studied in Germany.

After a curacy at Clifton in Nottinghamshire Kingsley became curate at Holne in Devon, where his son Charles *Kingsley, the author, was born in June 1819. So great was Mary Kingsley's love of the Devon countryside that she walked about it constantly during her pregnancy, hoping to communicate this passion to her unborn child. After Holne, the family moved to Burton upon Trent, where Kingsley had been offered the position of curate-in-charge. Then, on 23 January 1824, he was appointed by his old friend the bishop of Peterborough to the rectory of Barnack, near Stamford, in Lincolnshire. In 1830, in accordance with a previous arrangement, Kingsley was succeeded at Barnack by Bishop Marsh's son.

At Barnack Kingsley was able to enjoy field sports and natural history. He now received an income of £1200 a year (to which was added the living of North Clifton, where he had installed a friend as curate). When he was old enough, Charles junior was allowed to accompany his father on shooting expeditions in the fens. Having caught malaria, then prevalent in the fens, Kingsley was advised to return to Devon, where he was presented to the living

at Clovelly (worth £350 a year) and encouraged his son's interest in courageous exploits at sea. His younger son George Henry *Kingsley became a notable traveller.

In 1836 Kingsley accepted the living of St Luke's, Chelsea, a large and wealthy church, recently built in the neo-Gothic style (which Kingsley hated) to serve the newly built Cadogan estates. His parishioners now numbered thousands, not hundreds. Describing life as a youth in Chelsea, the younger Charles Kingsley wrote of his boredom with the busy parish work in which his parents were absorbed. Charles junior described visitors to the rectory as ugly and splay-footed beings, 'three-fourths of whom can't sing, and the other quarter sing miles out of tune, with voices like love-sick parrots' (Chitty, 48). He recalled seeing 'silly women blown about with every wind, falling in love with the preacher instead of his sermon, and with his sermon instead of the Bible' (Kingsley, 9).

During the 1830s, when the Oxford Movement was at its height, Kingsley was known to *The Times* as a significant evangelical, and was one of the earliest Anglican evangelical rectors to work with the London City Mission. He died on 29 February 1860 at the Chelsea rectory, survived by his wife, with his now famous son at his side. He was buried in Brompton cemetery under an epitaph composed by Charles junior which described him as: 'endowed by God with many noble gifts of mind and body. He preserved through all vicissitudes of fortune a loving heart and stainless honour, and having won in all his various Cures the respect and affection of his people, [he] ruled the Parish of Chelsea well and wisely for more than twenty years.'   ROGER STEER

Sources S. Chitty, *The beast and the monk: a life of Charles Kingsley* (1974) • *Charles Kingsley: his letters and memories of his life*, ed. F. E. Kingsley, abridged edn (1885) • R. Steer, 'Kingsley, Charles', *The Blackwell dictionary of evangelical biography, 1730–1860*, ed. D. M. Lewis (1995)
Wealth at death under £2000: probate, 20 March 1860, *CGPLA Eng. & Wales*

Kingsley, Charles (1819–1875), novelist, Church of England clergyman, and controversialist, was born on 12 June 1819 at Holne vicarage, Devon, on the eastern edge of Dartmoor. He was the eldest of the six surviving children of Revd Charles *Kingsley (1781–1860), then (briefly) curate of Holne, a Hampshire country gentleman from an old family, including soldiers who had fought at Naseby and at Minden, who had taken orders only at the age of thirty-five, three years previously, after his mismanaged inheritance was exhausted. His mother, Mary Lucas (1787–1873), was born in Barbados, the daughter of a judge who had inherited slave-run sugar plantations. But any prospect of substantial wealth from this source eventually passing to the Kingsley family vanished with the decline of the West Indian sugar trade and the abolition of slavery in 1833. His father's subsequent career in the church took the family to Nottinghamshire, to Barnack, near Stamford (1824–30), close to the fen country which later supplied background for his historical novel *Hereward the Wake*, to Clovelly on

Charles Kingsley (1819–1875), by Lowes Cato Dickinson, 1862

the north Devon coast (1830–36), which inspired an enduring fascination with sea and shore later reflected in *Westward Ho!* and *The Water-Babies*, and, finally, in 1836, to St Luke's rectory, Chelsea (1836–60).

Education A delicate, nervous, imaginative child afflicted with a stutter which persisted into adult life, Kingsley nevertheless shared his father's passion for country sports and natural history. His education started at home, where he showed a precocious interest in writing sermons and poems. In 1831 he and his brother Herbert were sent to a preparatory school at Clifton, where he was a horrified and fascinated witness to the Bristol riots associated with the Reform Bill agitation, an experience which influenced his ambivalent attitude towards popular politics in later years. The following year the boys went to Helston grammar school in Cornwall, a small school run by Revd Derwent Coleridge, second son of the poet. Kingsley had an attack of cholera at the school (English cholera rather than the more virulent Asiatic cholera then ravaging Cornwall), which left him with a lifelong intestinal weakness but also stimulated his passion for sanitary reform as a way of containing and preventing disease. He seems to have learnt a great deal from informal botanizing expeditions with one of the masters, C. A. Johns, later a distinguished naturalist, and from browsing in the headmaster's library, where he encountered arcane treasures such as Iamblichus and Porphyry, but his formal instruction in classics and mathematics was rather neglected until he and his family moved to London in 1836. He studied at King's College, London (1836–8), where he worked hard and engaged in extensive private reading. Living at home, he became increasingly bored and irritated with the puritanical restrictions of rectory life and the endless fuss of church business and district visiting in his father's large and active evangelical parish.

In October 1838 Kingsley went up to Magdalene College, Cambridge. Lonely, intensely shy, and physically restless,

he gradually found companionship through rowing and riding to hounds, and acquired a close friend in the brilliantly eccentric athlete and amateur scientist Charles Mansfield, another clergyman's son. He discovered the calming effects of tobacco and was soon addicted, though he had already suffered from lung disease. More significantly, he developed religious doubts. He managed to win a scholarship in the May examinations at the end of his first year, and during the long vacation of 1839 met his future wife, Frances Eliza Grenfell, known as Fanny [see Kingsley, Frances Eliza (1814–1891)], devout daughter of Pascoe Grenfell (1761–1838) MP, a wealthy industrialist who had married (as his second wife) Georgiana St Leger, daughter of the first Viscount Doneraile. Kingsley gradually shared his religious difficulties with her. A prolonged period of feverish restlessness, dissipation, and depression, interspersed with fishing trips, boxing lessons, and geologizing expeditions with Professor Sedgwick, came to an end in 1841 when he and Fanny came to an understanding and he resolved to become a clergyman. Six months of desperate work to make up lost time secured him a first class in classics in 1842, and he was ordained to the curacy of Eversley in Hampshire, where he immediately proved himself an energetic pastor deeply concerned with the poor.

Marriage and writing Despite Fanny's predilection for a celibate life associated with one of the Anglican sisterhoods springing up under the influence of the Oxford Movement, and despite opposition from her family mainly because of Kingsley's lack of funds, they eventually married on 10 January 1844. One of Fanny's sisters had married the well-connected Revd Sidney Godolphin Osborne, and it was through Osborne's influence that Kingsley was appointed to the curacy of Pimperne in Dorset and turned his mind increasingly to the problems of agrarian poverty, on which Osborne had published pamphlets. He had spent the difficult years just before his marriage in a bizarre religiously erotic correspondence with Fanny, and in reading Coleridge, F. D. Maurice, and Carlyle under her guidance to develop some kind of intellectual framework to reconcile his poetic, almost pantheistic love of the physical world, his developing social concern, and his powerful awakened sexuality with traditional religious belief. He also began to write and illustrate a prose life of St Elizabeth of Hungary, a conspicuously married saint, as a wedding present for Fanny; it was an early instalment in his lifelong crusade against the celibate ideal of the religious life which had threatened to keep Fanny from him. The material was eventually reworked as a rather uneven quasi-Shakespearian verse tragedy, *The Saint's Tragedy*, and published in 1848 with an aggressively protestant preface. It seemed to attract little attention at the time except among critics of the Oxford Movement in Oxford itself, but Baron von Bunsen, the Prussian ambassador, and Prince Albert greatly admired it, as did Daniel Macmillan, later Kingsley's publisher. In May 1844 Kingsley was invited to return to Eversley as rector, and proceeded to transform a badly neglected parish in what was then a wild country district. A daughter, Rose, was born in 1846. He corresponded with F. D. Maurice, then professor of English and history at King's College, London, on parish and theological matters, and came increasingly under his influence. In 1847 Maurice stood godfather to the Kingsleys' second child, a son who was named after him. In 1848, on Maurice's recommendation, Kingsley obtained a part-time appointment as professor of English at the newly formed Queen's College for Women in London, where he gave lectures on Anglo-Saxon literature and history, among other topics.

Christian socialism Like Maurice and Maurice's friends the London barristers J. M. Ludlow and Thomas Hughes, Kingsley was affected by the growing social unrest of the 'hungry forties'. When the Chartist movement organized a major demonstration at Kennington Common for 10 April 1848, he and Ludlow were present in person. He sat up late that night drafting a poster addressed to Chartists and signed 'A Working Parson', being deeply sympathetic to the hunger and poverty which had prompted the demonstration but claiming the constitutional reforms demanded by the Charter would not go far enough to secure genuine freedom and reform: that depended on developing moral independence from demagogues and from electoral bribery and corruption, and on reuniting politics with religion.

In company with Maurice and his friends Kingsley threw himself into a controversial new Christian socialist movement devoted to spreading this gospel and to setting up co-operative workshops for tailors and other oppressed trades. Kingsley and Ludlow co-edited the short-lived Christian socialist journal *Politics for the People*, launched on 6 May 1848. Writing as Parson Lot, Kingsley supplied much of the copy for the paper himself, as well as contributing to its successors the *Christian Socialist* and the *Journal of Association*. At a time when the Church of England had remained conspicuously aloof from working-class political movements, he caused consternation by declaring himself a Chartist as well as a Church of England parson. But he was a moralist and a reformer rather than a revolutionary, an upholder of the House of Lords who abhorred the 'physical force' strand in Chartism and dreaded any recurrence of the mob violence he had witnessed as a schoolboy at the Bristol riots. Even so, he was briefly banned from preaching in the diocese of London. His first novel, *Yeast*, characteristically vivid and chaotic, responding to the ferment of the times, attacked celibacy and bad landlords and drew on his experience of rural poverty; it began to appear serially in *Fraser's Magazine* in July 1848, though it was brought to a hurried conclusion as the publisher, John Parker, became alarmed by its radical tendency.

Financial worries and the prolonged strain and excitement of all these activities alongside Kingsley's regular parish work brought about the first of several episodes of complete nervous exhaustion. He resigned his position at Queen's College and retreated to Devon for a period of complete rest. But he soon recovered sufficiently to write *Cheap Clothes and Nasty* (1850), an indignant Christian socialist pamphlet about the clothing industry, and to

start work on *Alton Locke* (1850), a propagandist novel about a working tailor and poet (partly modelled on his Chartist friend Thomas Cooper) who becomes an active Chartist and eventually a Christian. This incorporates some of Kingsley's other recurring concerns, such as sanitary reform, and his conviction that science and religion needed to learn from each other. The novel was harshly reviewed, though Thomas Carlyle liked it—perhaps because the sympathetic portrait of the radical bookseller Sandy Mackaye was clearly modelled on himself.

Historical novels Kingsley's direct involvement with Christian socialism gradually slackened, and he played little part in the movement's most enduring achievement, the Working Men's College, founded in 1852, but his natural combativeness and his vision of a manly and socially committed Christianity, comprehensive and democratic, found alternative expression, notably in his first historical novel, *Hypatia* (1853), subtitled *New Foes with an Old Face*. The new foes were J. H. Newman, now a Roman Catholic, and the other leaders of the Oxford Movement, such as E. B. Pusey; the old face imputed to them was that of the fanatical (and of course celibate) monks of fifth-century Alexandria who murdered the Neoplatonist philosopher Hypatia, and who Kingsley viewed as extreme and discreditable examples of the asceticism of the early church from which contemporary Catholic spirituality had drawn inspiration. By way of contrast Kingsley introduces the ostrich-hunting married bishop Synesius and, a little improbably, a crew of cheerfully brutal proto-British Goths who embody Kingsleyan virtues of rough, unconventional decency, courage, physical sturdiness, and a saving respect for women.

Kingsley had already introduced the type in Lancelot Smith, the hero of *Yeast*, and it was to recur in later work—in the bluff sea dogs of *Westward Ho!* and the fierce Saxon warriors in *Hereward the Wake*, and even in the presentation of Greek heroes such as Perseus in *The Heroes* (1856), written for children. T. C. Sandars, reviewing *Two Years Ago* in the *Saturday Review* (February 1857), insisted that he preached a gospel of 'muscular Christianity' (Feb 1857, 176), a gibe taken up by other critics, but Kingsley preferred to call it 'Christian manliness', exemplified by biblical heroes such as David, on whom he delivered a series of sermons published in 1865. Contemporary evidence suggests Kingsley's aggressive masculinity in print was balanced by vulnerability, quick sympathy, and a feminine sensitivity in private. He was far from being the hearty muscular giant he seemed to idolize: nervously active, tall, thin, with piercing eyes and beaky features, he had had more than his share of physical illness since childhood.

Kingsley's greatest popular success, the historical novel *Westward Ho!* (1855), was originally planned as a patriotic anti-Catholic tale about the defeat of the Spanish Armada which he hoped would strike a sympathetic note amid contemporary anxieties about 'the Pope and the French invasion', triggered by the restoration of the papal hierarchy in England in 1850 and the aggressive anti-English posturing of Emperor Napoleon III. By the time the novel was finished patriotic feeling had been redirected, as England was fighting Russia in the Crimean War, of which Kingsley was an enthusiastic supporter, but this made the novel seem even more timely. His pamphlet *Brave Words for Brave Soldiers and Sailors* (1855) was published the same month as *Westward Ho!* and distributed among the troops at Sevastopol. The Crimean War and the outbreak of cholera in 1853–4 were the principal events of the recent past invoked by the title of his next novel *Two Years Ago* (1857), his most successful and coherent novel of contemporary life. Kingsley's continuing concern with sanitary reform, which had led him to join a deputation to the prime minister on the subject in 1854, was dramatized in the efforts of his doctor hero to combat cholera and unhealthy housing conditions.

Regius professor at Cambridge The prince consort had admired the protestant and Germanic emphasis of Kingsley's *Saint's Tragedy* and *Hypatia*, and shared his scientific and sanitary enthusiasms, and this led to his appointment as chaplain to the queen in 1859. In 1860, again on the recommendation of the prince consort, Kingsley succeeded Sir James Stephen as regius professor of modern history at Cambridge, then a part-time appointment. He was not the first choice, and he lacked some of the critical and technical skills of later professional historians, but he had published historical lectures on *Alexandria and her Schools* (1854) as a scholarly offshoot of his background research for *Hypatia* and he was a popular historical novelist and public figure. Despite his own misgivings his inaugural lecture, 'The limits of exact science applied to history', was a conspicuous success, and in subsequent lectures he was able to hold steady audiences of 100 or more undergraduates, far more than his predecessors had managed. He stimulated interest in his subject and was an effective and tactful private tutor to the prince of Wales during his brief period at Cambridge. But he encountered stern if not entirely disinterested criticism. His Romantic fascination with manly Goths and other early Germanic peoples was rather undiscriminating. The lectures published as *The Roman and the Teuton* (1864) and his imaginative rather than critical use of sources in *Hereward the Wake* (1866) were savagely attacked by the historian of Anglo-Saxon and Norman England, E. A. Freeman, who was eager to establish historical studies on a more rigorously professional footing and wanted professors of history to be severe scholars. Professional diffidence, exacerbated by Freeman's criticism, continuing ill health, renewed money worries since there were now four children to educate and launch into adult life (Mary [see Harrison, Mary St Leger] had been born in 1852 and Grenville in 1858), and the strain of preparing lectures, induced him to resign his professorship in 1869, hoping for preferment in the church. A few months later the queen appointed him to a vacant canonry at Chester which was better paid and less demanding. He showed some interest in becoming dean of Winchester in 1872, but this came to nothing. The following year Gladstone proposed, with the approval of the queen, that he should exchange his Chester canonry for a much more lucrative one at Westminster Abbey, and he

accepted. Despite his habitual nervousness in public he was a popular and effective preacher when he was in residence and worked particularly well with the dean, A. P. Stanley, with whose broad-church religious views he was substantially in agreement.

Success and royal favour have been blamed for silencing the radical in Kingsley, but this overstates the case. It is true that he modified the criticism of Cambridge in the revised edition of *Alton Locke* published in 1862. But even in his Christian socialist heyday his democratic sympathies had been modified by distrust of constitutional reform without moral improvement and by admiration for benignly autocratic Carlylean heroes such as the mysterious Barnakill in *Yeast*. Early in the 1850s, before royal patronage had been extended to him, he sensed that there were different battles to be fought. The increased prosperity of the 1850s and 1860s seemed to have alleviated the worst economic injustices which he had attacked in *Yeast* and *Alton Locke*, but he continued to be controversially outspoken on other social and religious issues, supporting sanitary reform, women's education, medical degrees for women, and Darwinian evolution. A proposal to award him an honorary DCL at Oxford in 1863 was successfully blocked by Pusey and his followers, who never forgave him for *Hypatia*.

Dispute with J. H. Newman The most damaging controversy of Kingsley's career began with an article in *Macmillan's Magazine* (January 1864), in which he reviewed volumes 7 and 8 of the new *History of England* by J. A. Froude, an old friend who had married one of Fanny's sisters. In discussing Froude's treatment of Catholic intrigue in the reign of Elizabeth I, matter he had already dramatized in *Westward Ho!*, Kingsley bluntly opined that 'Truth for its own sake has never been a virtue of the Roman clergy. Father Newman informs us that it need not, and on the whole ought not, to be' (*Charles Kingsley: his Letters*, 216), a contention he supported, rather inadequately, by citing Newman's (Anglican) sermon 'Wisdom and innocence' (1844). An exchange of letters and a pamphlet war ensued, culminating in Newman's celebrated *Apologia pro vita sua* written to vindicate his integrity. Newman had little difficulty in making fun of Kingsley's protestant prejudices and scored easy debating points against his hasty opponent, whose reputation suffered accordingly, but commentators at the time and subsequently disagreed about the merits of the case. Kingsley was in a sense renewing a long-standing debate in moral theology: casuists such as St Alphonsus Liguori had controversially justified equivocation and evasions in particular situations for the greater good of the church. But this was hardly the real issue. Kingsley, the embattled activist, sensed that Catholic spirituality exemplified by Newman could sanction serene, even disdainful, withdrawal from the everyday problems and responsibilities of secular life and from ordinary moral accountability, and he resented and felt threatened by it, especially because it had encouraged Fanny's original sense of a special celibate vocation. Newman chose to respond to his gibes in largely personal terms which did not fully address the more general questions.

Later publications, politics, and poetry Kingsley's continuing fascination with natural history, particularly marine biology, was less controversial. He gave popular lectures on the subject even when he was in residence at Chester and published enthusiastic works such as *Glaucus, or, The Wonders of the Shore* (1855) and *Madam How and Lady Why* (1869). He welcomed the publication of Darwin's *Origin of Species* in 1859 because it seemed consistent with his own idiosyncratic theory of related moral and physical evolution which he had already illustrated in an evolutionary dream sequence at the end of *Alton Locke*. His most enduringly popular book, *The Water-Babies* (1863), began as a story for his own children and an attack on the continuing employment of climbing boys to sweep chimneys. But the story sends little Tom on an evolutionary moral journey and includes incidental satiric commentary on education, fashion, and current affairs, as well as mockery of post-Darwinian controversies about human descent and distinctiveness and the nature of scientific evidence. His main target was the agnostic scientist and polemicist T. H. Huxley, with whom he was, however, on friendly terms.

Kingsley's last novel, *Hereward the Wake* (1866), was perhaps his least successful. It set out to be a patriotic narrative of romantically unavailing resistance to William the Conqueror and the Norman yoke, but this was unhelpfully complicated by attacks on degenerate Anglo-Saxon monks and priests and the presence of Danish and Anglo-Danish warriors. The Kingsleys had been guests at the wedding of the prince of Wales to Princess Alexandra of Denmark in 1863, and the Schleswig-Holstein crisis of 1863–4 had briefly kindled interest in Danish affairs, but the Danish elements in the novel only added to the confusions endemic in the sources. The narrative was a grim saga with an unattractive hero redeemed only by strength, savage cunning, and military prowess.

Kingsley, like Carlyle before him, had always rather admired strong men, however bloodthirsty, and had embarrassed his more liberal friends such as J. M. Ludlow by hero-worshipping Raja Brooke of Sarawak, to whom *Westward Ho!* was dedicated. John Eyre, Australian explorer and subsequently governor of Jamaica, was another of his slightly dubious heroes. Kingsley had been impressed by Harriet Beecher Stowe and the moral fervour of New England abolitionism, but unlike most of his associates from his Christian socialist days he was lukewarm about Abraham Lincoln, sympathetic to the gentlemanly American south during the civil war, and a little distrustful of black people. Descended on his mother's side from West Indian plantation owners, his first sympathies were with the white community in the West Indies. Though he largely avoided the racist hysteria of Carlyle, he joined with him in 1866 to defend Governor Eyre from charges of excessive severity in suppressing an alleged uprising, while friends such as J. M. Ludlow and Thomas Hughes had joined J. S. Mill's Jamaica committee to press for Eyre's prosecution for murder.

Financial worries until the last few years of his life drove Kingsley to write too much. Though there are some fine essays, such as his introductions to Susan Winkworth's translations from the German of *Theologia Germanica* (1854) and *Tauler* (1857), he rushed into print too quickly, attacking Emerson in his quasi-Platonic dialogue *Phaethon, or, Loose Thoughts for Loose Thinkers* (1852), dashing off rather unsympathetic sketches of *The Hermits* for Macmillan's Sunday Library (1868), and freely airing his religious and aesthetic prejudices in often opinionated essays and reviews injudiciously collected as *Miscellanies* (1859) and *Plays and Puritans* (1873). But Kingsley's love of outdoor life, his eye for landscape, and his fascination with the natural and human history of particular places gave rise to vivid, quirky occasional essays such as 'North Devon' and 'Chalk stream studies', originally written for *Fraser's Magazine*, which he collected as *Prose Idylls* (1873). He had written poetry all his life and, while his output was very uneven, the best poems have worn well. These range from songs and ballads such as 'The Sands of Dee' and 'The Last Buccanier' to more ambitious narrative poems such as 'Andromeda', one of the few more or less successful English experiments in quantitative hexameters. In poems such as 'Elegiacs' there is a strong melancholy strain at odds with the boisterous vigour of much of his prose. He kept faith with his Christian socialist past to the extent of reprinting various poems 'connected with 1848–9' in a collected volume, *Poems* (1871). His sense of poetry as essentially musical attracted composers, and there are song settings of some of his lyrics by Charles Gounod, John Hullah, and the young Gustav Holst. He collaborated very successfully and amicably with Sterndale Bennett, composer and professor of music at Cambridge, in a light-hearted formal ode performed at the installation of the duke of Devonshire as chancellor of the university in 1862.

Death and reputation In his later years, dogged by ill health and recurring periods of exhaustion and depression, Kingsley seems to have seen himself as a spent force. A lifelong ambition was realized in the winter of 1869–70 when he had the opportunity to visit the West Indies, described enthusiastically in *At Last* (1871). A lecture tour in the United States in 1874, which took him as far west as Colorado Springs, was undertaken as much to consolidate his improved finances as to see the country, and it proved not only exhilarating but exhausting and ultimately fatal. He was seriously ill in Colorado, and ill again with a liver complaint soon after his return. Fanny fell dangerously ill in December 1874 and he neglected his own health to look after her until he had to take to bed himself with inflammation of the right lung. Fanny recovered, but Kingsley died at Eversley on 23 January 1875. Dean Stanley offered Westminster Abbey, but he was buried in Eversley churchyard. The Bramshill hunt servants and the Gypsies of the common, as well as Dean Stanley and a representative of the prince of Wales, attended the funeral.

The sheer variousness of Kingsley's career affected his reputation in his own time and subsequently. He did many interesting things in a short lifetime, but few of them supremely well and almost none without controversy. His Christian socialism attracted notice in France and Germany as well as in Britain, though his politics have satisfied neither radicals nor conservatives. He was outstanding as a parish clergyman, though increasingly absent from his parish. The popular preacher, the historian, and the scientific popularizer were soon forgotten. The churchman was recalled, rather unfairly, only as Newman's luckless antagonist. Kingsley the novelist has fared better: he is still remembered as a children's writer, mainly for *The Water-Babies*. *Westward Ho!* and *Hereward the Wake*, like *The Water-Babies*, have been frequently reprinted and adapted, and have survived, a little precariously, as juvenile classics. *Alton Locke* has retained a more specialised academic readership as a Victorian 'social-problem' novel. Literary criticism has become more tolerant of Kingsley's eccentricities of form and vivid incoherence, if not of his outlook on race, class, and gender. Historians of literature, sexuality, and social movements continue to be interested in his work.

Norman Vance

Sources *Charles Kingsley: his letters and memories of his life*, ed. F. E. Kingsley, 5th edn, 2 vols. (1877) • R. B. Martin, *The dust of combat: a life of Charles Kingsley* (1959) • S. Chitty, *The beast and the monk: a life of Charles Kingsley* (1974) • O. Chadwick, 'Kingsley's chair', *Theology*, 78 (1975), 2–8 • N. Vance, *The sinews of the spirit: the ideal of Christian manliness in Victorian literature and religious thought* (1985) • M. F. Thorp, *Charles Kingsley, 1819–1875* (1937) • L. K. Uffelman, *Charles Kingsley* (1979), 151–7 • T. Byrom, 'The novels of Charles Kingsley, 1848–1857', BLitt diss., U. Oxf., 1967 • N. Vance, 'The ideal of Christian manliness', DPhil diss., U. Oxf., 1975 • *The Times* (25 Jan 1875), 9–10 • E. R. Norman, *The Victorian Christian socialists* (1987) • J. Maynard, *Victorian discourses on sexuality and religion* (1993)
Archives BL, corresp. and papers, literary MSS, and travel notes, Add. MSS 41296–41299 • BL, letters to his wife and family, Add. MSS 62552–62557 • Bodl. Oxf., sermons • Charterhouse School, papers and literary MSS • Harvard U., Houghton L., papers • Hunt. L., letters • Magd. Cam., sermons • McGill University, Montreal, McLennan Library, sermons • Morgan L., papers • NYPL, papers • Princeton University Library, New Jersey, sermons and letters • Wellcome L., sermons and papers | BL, corresp. with W. E. Gladstone, Add. MSS 44392–44438 • BL, letters to James Hunt, RP500 [microfilm] • BL, corresp. with Macmillans, Add. MS 54911 • BL, corresp. with Lord Stanmore, Add. MS 49272 • Bodl. Oxf., letters to John Ludlow • Bodl. Oxf., corresp. with Friedrich Max Muller • Bodl. Oxf., letters to Sir Henry Taylor • Bucks. RLSS, letters to C. P. Grenfell • Castle Howard, letters to ninth earl of Carlisle • CUL, letters to Philip Henry Gosse • CUL, corresp. with John Ludlow • ICL, corresp. with Thomas Huxley • NL Scot., letters to Alexander Campbell Fraser • Royal Institution of Great Britain, London, letters to Henry Bence Jones • Trinity Cam., letters to Lord Houghton • U. Leeds, Brotherton L., corresp. with Philip Henry Gosse
Likenesses line engraving, pubd 1861 (after a photograph by D. J. Pound; after J. J. E. Mayall), NPG • L. C. Dickinson, oils, 1862, NPG [*see illus.*] • C. H. Jeens, stipple and line engraving, 1874 (after a photograph), BM, NPG • T. Woolner, marble bust, 1875, Westminster Abbey, London; related plaster cast, 1875, NPG; related medallion, St Mary's Church, Eversley, Hampshire • stipple and line engraving, pubd 1876 (after a photograph by C. H. Jeens), BM, NPG • R. C. Belt, marble bust, Chester Cathedral • A. Cecioni, caricature, watercolour, NPG; repro. in *VF* (30 March 1872) • Cundall & Downes, photograph, NPG • L. Dickinson, oils, Magd. Cam. • Elliott & Fry, photograph, NPG • W. S. Hunt, pen and ink drawing (after photograph, 1874), NPG • London Stereoscopic Co., photograph, NPG • Mayall, photograph, NPG • R. W. Thrupp, photograph, NPG • J. & C. Watkins, photograph, NPG • photographs, NPG • statue, Victoria Park, Bideford, Devon

Kingsley [*née* Grenfell], **Frances Eliza** [Fanny] (1814–1891), biographer, was born at Taplow House, near Maidenhead, the eleventh child, and seventh and youngest daughter, of Pascoe *Grenfell (*bap.* 1761, *d.* 1838) [*see under* Grenfell family], MP for Great Marlow, and his second wife, Georgiana St Leger, youngest daughter of Viscount Doneraile. The Grenfell family was originally Cornish and claimed a connection with Sir Richard Grenville. Pascoe Grenfell had amassed a substantial fortune through Welsh and Cornish mining interests, and his own second marriage into the aristocracy set the pattern for future alliances in the family which enhanced its growing prominence in finance, politics, and the army and navy. Fanny's nephews included a governor of the Bank of England (H. R. *Grenfell) and a field marshal (F. W. *Grenfell); Julian *Grenfell, the poet, was a great-great-nephew.

As was common in well-to-do families, the Grenfell sons were sent to public schools but the daughters were educated privately. Fanny had opportunities to read widely in modern literatures and in history and theology. By the mid-1830s she was living at home with three devout, unmarried sisters. All were attracted to the Catholic spirituality revived within the Church of England under Tractarian influences, and considered forming or joining some kind of Anglican sisterhood similar to the Puseyite Park Village community established some years later, in 1845.

However, on 6 July 1839, when the family was staying at Braziers Park near Ipsden, Oxfordshire, Fanny met Charles *Kingsley (1819–1875), five years her junior, then a rather wild Cambridge undergraduate. This encounter was fictionalized as the meeting of the lovely and learned Argemone with Lancelot Smith in Kingsley's first novel *Yeast* (1848), which was always Fanny's favourite. From this moment, later acclaimed as their true wedding day, the sisterhood project was doomed. Fanny's mother had died in 1818 and her father in 1838, so her ambitious half-brother Charles Pascoe had just become head of the family. In the course of a protracted courtship, carried on mainly by letter in the face of the stern disapproval of her brother and most of the Grenfell family, Fanny turned Kingsley's thoughts to ordination, introducing him to the writings of Coleridge, Carlyle, and F. D. Maurice, which became central to his religious outlook. It is clear from the startling mixture of religion and frank sexuality in Kingsley's sometimes vividly illustrated letters to Fanny from this period that almost from the outset the relationship involved powerful physical attraction and a corresponding defiance of celibate religious idealism. Despite all difficulties they were finally married by special licence in Bath on 10 January 1844.

Even then they could not live together until Kingsley was able to move from his Dorset curacy, held through the good offices of Fanny's brother-in-law, to become rector of Eversley in Hampshire. They moved into the damp and inconvenient rectory in May 1844. Here Fanny stayed for most of her married life. She played little part in Kingsley's public life in London and elsewhere, though they both attended the first women's suffrage meeting in 1869. Four children were born, Rose (1846), Maurice (1847), Mary (1852), and Grenville (1858), amid miscarriages and repeated periods of ill health. Holidays for convalescence added to constant financial worries. But Fanny was usually a cheerful and supportive wife and mother, energetically involved with parish work and amanuensis for many of her husband's books. Dark-haired, heavy-featured but with beautiful eyes, almost Spanish in appearance, she was a good manager, kind and hospitable if sometimes daunting, regarded as the original of the redoubtable Eleanor in Kingsley's *Alton Locke* (1850).

In later life Fanny suffered from angina and was unable to accompany Kingsley on his travels to the West Indies and the United States. She was seriously ill after a heart attack in 1875, when her husband was also ill; though she recovered, he did not. Semi-invalid, she spent her widowhood at Tachbrook Mallory, near Leamington Spa. Almost immediately she began work on *Charles Kingsley: his Letters and Memoirs of his Life* (1877), which was frequently reprinted. A popular abridged edition appeared in 1879. She also edited four volumes of pious selections from Kingsley's writings. Subsequent biographers have complained of her uncritical attitude and her reticences and suppressions, including the omission of all reference to Kingsley's spendthrift brother Henry, whom she disliked, but she made available a great deal of interesting unpublished material and wrote with intelligent sympathy, insisting that her argumentative husband was a prophetic teacher. She continued to take an informed interest in theological controversy, and her compilation *From Death to Life* (1887) convincingly demonstrated that Kingsley had anticipated contemporary liberal discussion of life after death. Fanny died on 12 December 1891 at Tachbrook Mallory.   NORMAN VANCE

Sources B. Colloms, *Charles Kingsley: the lion of Eversley* (1975) • M. F. Thorp, *Charles Kingsley, 1819–1875* (1937) • *Memoirs of Field-Marshal Lord Grenfell* (1925) • Burke, *Peerage* • m. cert.
Archives CUL, corresp. with John Ludlow
Likenesses A. Covey-Crump, painting or drawing, repro. in S. Chitty, *The beast and the monk: a life of Charles Kingsley* (1975), facing p. 128 • photograph, repro. in Thorp, *Charles Kingsley*, facing p. 35
Wealth at death £3940 13s. 4d.: probate, 25 Jan 1892, *CGPLA Eng. & Wales*

Kingsley, George Henry (1826–1892), physician and traveller, the fourth of the five children of the Revd Charles *Kingsley (1781–1860) of Battramsley House in the New Forest, and his wife, Mary (1787–1873), daughter of Nathan Lucas, was born at Barnack rectory, Barnack, Northamptonshire, on 14 February 1826. Charles *Kingsley and Henry *Kingsley were his brothers. He was educated in London at King's College School and at St George's Hospital, and in Paris, where he was slightly wounded on the barricades of 1848. His work in combating an outbreak of cholera in Flintshire was commemorated by his brother Charles in the portrait of Tom Thurnall in *Two Years Ago*. He completed his medical education at Heidelberg, and returned to England about 1850.

Kingsley then became private physician to the marquess of Ailesbury, the duke of Norfolk, the duke of Sutherland, and the first and second earls of Ellesmere. Kingsley also had a keen interest in literature. He produced a translation of Heyse's *Four Phases of Love* (1857) and *A Gossip on the Sutherland Hillside* (1861). During his time as physician to the earl of Ellesmere he compiled a catalogue of the Elizabethan drama quartos held in the library at Bridgewater House, and he edited Francis Thynne's *Animadversions upon the Annotacions and Corrections of the Impressions of Chaucer's Workes … Reprinted in 1598* (1865).

Kingsley married Mary Bailey (*d.* 1892) in 1860; they had a daughter, Mary Henrietta *Kingsley, and a son, Charles. In 1862 ill health had forced Kingsley to take a cruise on HMS *St George*; this seems to have been the beginning of more than twenty years' almost continuous travel. He made several trips to the Mediterranean, and one to Egypt with the duke of Rutland. Indeed most of his journeys were undertaken as the medical adviser or travelling companion of members of the aristocracy. In 1866 he accompanied Lady Herbert of Lea and her children on a tour of Spain, and in the following year he travelled with Lady Herbert's eldest son, the earl of Pembroke, to the south seas. A book describing their experiences, *South Sea Bubbles by the Earl and the Doctor* (1872), proved extremely popular.

In 1870 Kingsley set off with Lord Dunraven on a visit to the USA and Canada which was to last five years. During this visit Kingsley, who was a fellow of both the Linnean Society and the Royal Microscopical Society, made many contributions as a naturalist to *The Field* magazine under the pseudonym of 'the Doctor'. Natural history apart, he still found time to shoot 'not only moose in the forest of Arcadia, but almost every other kind of living thing' (Kingsley, 99). During his visit Kingsley met Buffalo Bill, described as belonging 'to the school of Charles I, pale, large eyed and dreamy' (ibid., 135), and treated Rocky Mountain Jim. It seems that only bad weather prevented Kingsley from being with General Custer at the Little Bighorn. After visits to Florida and the southern states in 1888 Kingsley went on to travel even more extensively, with journeys to Newfoundland, Cape Cod, Japan, New Zealand, and Australia.

Kingsley hated town life and noise. He also possessed a temper which his daughter described as 'volcanic but never vindictive' (Kingsley, 195). This combination made his return to domestic life in England somewhat trying for Kingsley, who 'loved the bright eyes of danger' (ibid., 202), and the rest of the household; his daughter had to remove her fighting cocks out of range of his hearing; the maid had to grease the bearing of the kitchen pump and could never sing more than a line and a half of a hymn. His greatest anger was reserved for 'Mr Gladstone, or any Roman Catholic Priest … the sight of printed reports of Mr Gladstone's observations or any priestly form would rouse [him] from any depths of study or contemplation into a very pretty temper' (ibid., 200). Newspapers reporting Gladstone's speeches would regularly be torn to shreds or thrust into the fire.

Kingsley moved from his London house in Southwood

Lane, Highgate, to Bexleyheath, Kent, in 1879, and from there to Cambridge, where, after suffering from a bout of rheumatic fever, he died peacefully at his home, 7 Mortimer Road, on 5 February 1892. He was buried at Highgate cemetery in London; his wife died six weeks later.

THOMAS SECCOMBE, rev. MICHAEL BEVAN

Sources G. H. Kingsley, *Notes on sport and travel, with a memoir by Mary H. Kingsley* (1900) · *The Athenaeum* (13 Feb 1892), 214 · *Cambridge Chronicle* (12 Feb 1892) · *Cambridge Chronicle* (19 Feb 1892) · *Manchester Guardian* (8 Feb 1892) · private information (1892)
Archives BL, letters to Macmillans, Add. MSS 55253–55258
Likenesses photograph, repro. in Kingsley, *Notes on sport and travel*, frontispiece
Wealth at death £8618 11s. 7d.: administration with will, 9 Aug 1892, *CGPLA Eng. & Wales*

Kingsley, Henry (1830–1876), novelist and essayist, was born on 2 January 1830 at Barnack, Northamptonshire, near Stamford, the youngest of the eight children of the Revd Charles *Kingsley (1781–1860) and his wife, Mary Lucas (1785–1873), daughter of Nathan Lucas of Rushford Lodge, Norfolk, and Farley Hall, Barbados. He was the brother of Charles *Kingsley (1819–1875), the Anglican clergyman and novelist, and George Henry *Kingsley (1826–1892), a physician and scholar, and the uncle of Mary St Leger Harrison (1852–1931), who wrote novels under the name of Lucas Malet, and Mary Henrietta Kingsley (1862–1900), the African explorer and writer.

Reared in Clovelly, Devon, which later would become the setting for several of his novels, and then in 1836 in Chelsea, Kingsley attended King's College School, London, from 1844, and then King's College in 1847. After a two-year stint at Colebrook, studying under the Revd Thomas Drosier, he matriculated at Worcester College, Oxford, on 6 March 1850. According to contemporaneous accounts, his Oxford years were noted more for his addiction to athletics and exuberant social pleasures than to academic pursuits. He won a wager that he could run a mile, row a mile, and trot a mile within fifteen minutes, and he later won the Diamond Sculls at Henley-on-Thames. As to his other overindulgences, he engaged in wine-drinking breakfasts and suppers, pipe-smoking contests, and numerous rags and riots. Along with Edwin Arnold (1833–1904), the future poet and orientalist, he was co-founder of the Fez Club, a short-lived nonsensical secret society of fifty undergraduate men dedicated to misogamy, misogyny, and 'celibate freedom' who donned fezzes and other special accessories and met for breakfast at Dickenson's Hotel and Coffee House in the Turl in Oxford to eat, to smoke oriental tobacco in oriental pipes, and to defend male superiority over 'the gentler sex'.

Without sitting for a degree and with the benefit of a timely legacy, Kingsley left Oxford in 1853 to seek his fortune in the Australian goldfields. For slightly more than four years (December 1853 to February 1858) and without any communication with his parents, he drifted and struggled in Australia with little financial success, labouring in the goldfields, being employed as an agricultural worker and stock driver, and wandering as a 'sundowner',

arriving at outstations at sunset, seeking food and lodging. He made no fortune, but he would later use his experiences and his first-hand information about Australia in several of his novels and some of his essays. A series of nine watercolours that he painted of Australian landscapes that interested him is on record at the Mitchell Library, State Library of New South Wales, Sydney.

Just as abruptly as he had left England, Kingsley returned to it. In May 1858 he arrived in England and went first to London to his parents' former home at St Luke's in Chelsea. It is said that he was afraid that they might have died during his long absence, and so he paced up and down outside the rectory for over an hour, dreading the news that he might hear. Finally, taking heart, he knocked on the door and was relieved to learn that his parents were living at Eversley, Hampshire. He settled with them and finished a novel begun in Australia, the critically and commercially successful *Recollections of Geoffry Hamlyn* (1859), a romance set mainly in early nineteenth-century Australia. The nineteenth-century critic Desmond Byrne, writing an appreciative account of Kingsley from an Australian point of view, remarked that he

> was the first to describe in fiction the rural life of the country, to recognize the beginning of an aristocracy of landholders, and to commemorate the pervading spirit of cheerful confidence to which so much of the rapid development of Australia was due.   (Byrne, 107)

Kingsley continued his success by publishing his acknowledged masterpiece among his seventeen novels, *Ravenshoe* (1862), a work this time set mainly in England. Although the novel pits Roman Catholicism against protestantism, the story centres on Charles Ravenshoe, a young, irresponsible man whose character is reminiscent of Kingsley during his Oxford and Australian days. Charles develops from impetuous boyhood to a sobered manhood, through circumstances that include his involvement in the Crimean War, specifically the charge of the light brigade. Like most of Kingsley's romances, *Ravenshoe* depicts the adventures of heroic-tinged gentry with noble spirits who have difficulties adjusting to the changing Victorian age. As Michael Sadleir has stated, 'No writer of the mid-Victorian age had so delicate a sympathy for splendour in decay, so sensitive an admiration for the forlorn present of a noble past. He is the prose-laureate of wasted beauty' (*EdinR*, 330). Kingsley's third novel, *Austin Elliot* (1863), did not achieve the success of the first two novels.

On 19 July 1864, at St Luke's Church, Chelsea, London, Kingsley married his second cousin, Sarah Maria Kingsley Hazelwood (1842–1922), a governess, and moved to Hillside House, Wargrave, near Henley-on-Thames, where they lived until late 1869. There he published extensively: numerous essays and reviews in such periodicals as *Macmillan's Magazine*, *North British Review*, and the *Fortnightly Review*; an edition of *Robinson Crusoe* with a biographical introduction of Daniel Defoe (1868); *Tales of Old Travel* (1869), a collection of well-researched essays which retold fourteen different ancient and modern exploration narratives; and five novels, four of which were published in both serialization and volume formats. His major novels during this time include his second Australian one, *The Hillyars and the Burtons: a Story of Two Families* (1865), an involved saga about two families, one high-born and rich and the other low-born and poor, combining his memories of Chelsea with the fictionalization of some of his Australian experiences. He also wrote *Leighton Court* (1866), a slight but rather charming tale of country life, and one of his own favourite novels, *Mademoiselle Mathilde* (1868), a work dealing with the French Revolution which, like Dickens's *A Tale of Two Cities* (1859), ends with an impersonation at the guillotine.

During his years at Wargrave, Kingsley unintentionally became involved in the intense Governor Edward Eyre controversy which rocked and bitterly divided Britain's intellectual world. Prior to his becoming governor of Jamaica and being involved in the native rebellion against him, Eyre had been a well-known and respected Australian explorer. Coincidentally, Kingsley had written a very favourable two-part article on Eyre's Australian travels for *Macmillan's Magazine* (October and November 1865), the first of which had appeared a few weeks before the rebellion. Some of his comments regarding Eyre were reprinted in *The Times* and set up a public correspondence between Kingsley and a reader who took exception to some of his remarks. Merely on the periphery of the controversy, Kingsley never publicly defended Governor Eyre; rather, he was exalting Eyre in his role as an Australian explorer.

In the late 1860s Kingsley found himself burdened with debt caused in part by his wife's chronic illness (exacerbated by frequent miscarriages) and in part by poor financial management and extravagance. Suffering from the consequent debilitating pressure of producing one novel after another, on 1 October 1869 he accepted the editorship of the Edinburgh *Daily Review*, a daily penny journal that was the organ of the Free Presbyterian church, and with Sarah moved to Goshen Back, Morningside, in Edinburgh. Kingsley's lack of the journalistic acumen necessary to be an effective editor, combined with tension between him and the Free Church party management on ecclesiastical and civil matters, soon proved that he was not suited to the position. The outbreak of the Franco-Prussian War gave him an opportunity to separate himself from his editorial desk, and on 5 August 1870 he left Edinburgh for Luxembourg. A much better war correspondent than editor, he vividly and at times poetically described the destruction and inhumanity of war as he witnessed the battle of Sedan and visited hospitals with the Red Cross Society. His coverage was published in the *Daily Review* during September 1870, and he also used his experiences as a basis for his novel *Valentin: a French Boy's Story of Sedan* (1872), which was also serialized in *Every Boy's Annual* (1873). Towards the end of his eight weeks as a correspondent he was weakened by an attack of bronchitis and returned to Edinburgh. He resigned as editor of the *Daily Review* in April 1871.

The Kingsleys left Edinburgh for London and lived first at 24 Bernard Square, near Russell Square, Bloomsbury, and then at 29 Fortress Terrace, in semi-rural Kentish Town. Desperate for money and at odds with his brother Charles and his wife because of constant pleas for financial assistance, Kingsley feverishly produced one poorly received novel after another, such as *The Harveys* (1872) and *Oakshott Castle* (1873), the latter called by the *Saturday Review* almost the 'worst novel ever written' (26 April 1873, 563). Both the quality of his work and his health deteriorated. In the summer of 1875 the Kingsleys made their final move, to Cuckfield, Sussex, where they lived in an old timbered and gabled cottage called The Attress. Kingsley published the novels *Number Seventeen* (1875) and *The Grange Garden* (1876), a few short stories, and *Fireside Studies* (1876), a collection of seven essays on literary figures such as Addison and Steele, Beaumont and Fletcher, and Ben Jonson, five of which had been published previously in *Temple Bar* and the *New Quarterly Magazine*. However, he was seriously ill from cancer of the tongue and trachea. He died at The Attress on 24 May 1876 and was buried on the 29th at Cuckfield; his wife survived him. His last work, *The Mystery of the Island* (1877), a children's novella, was published posthumously.

In appearance Kingsley was short and had a plain, undistinguished face. In later years he grew a full, bushy beard. John Cordy Jeaffreson, his friend and fellow student at Worcester College, described him as having a

> weedy frame and curious visage. ... Resembling Charles Kingsley (who was far from well looking) in the straight mouth, and deep line, descending on either side of the face from the unshapely nose to the corner of the graceless lips, which distinguished the clergyman's visage. (Jeaffreson, 1.79)

Although overshadowed as a novelist by his brother, Henry Kingsley has always entertained a dedicated coterie. In 1895 Sir Arthur Quiller-Couch, for example, wrote:

> I worshipped his books as a boy; today I find them full of faults—often preposterous, usually ill-constructed, at times unnatural beyond belief. ... And yet each time I read *Ravenshoe*—and I must be close upon 'double figures'—I like it better. Henry did my green unknowing youth engage, and I find it next to impossible to give him up and quite impossible to choose the venerated Charles as a substitute in my riper age. (Quiller-Couch, 67)

Other admirers, such as Clement Shorter, Justin McCarthy, Michael Sadleir, and Angela Thirkell, would agree with the assessment that Kingsley was

> a gifted and spirited storyteller, whose prose at its best has a quiet force and a felicity that make it worthy to be placed beside that of the finest literary craftsmen. ... [H]e had the ability to create fresh descriptions of manly and noble action and beautiful Australian and English sea and landscape scenes. And, above all, his own enjoyment of life infuses his best romances with a vigor and joviality that still captivate readers. (Scheuerle, 1)

WILLIAM H. SCHEUERLE

Sources W. H. Scheuerle, *The neglected brother: a study of Henry Kingsley* (1971) · J. S. D. Mellick, *The passing guest: a life of Henry Kingsley* (1983) · S. M. Ellis, *Henry Kingsley, 1830–1876: towards a vindication* (1931) · E. Huxley, *The Kingsleys* (1973) · M. Sadleir, 'Henry Kingsley: a portrait', *EdinR*, 240 (1924), 330–48; repr. in rev. form as 'Henry Kingsley', *TLS* (2 Jan 1930) · R. L. Wolff, 'Henry Kingsley', *Harvard Library Bulletin*, 13 (1959), 195–226 · A. Thirkell, 'Henry Kingsley',

Nineteenth-Century Fiction, 5 (Dec 1950), 175–87 · A. Thirkell, 'Henry Kingsley', *Nineteenth-Century Fiction* (March 1951), 273–93 · D. Byrne, *Australian writers* (1896) · A. Quiller-Couch, *Adventures in criticism* (1925) · J. C. Jeaffreson, *A book of recollections*, 2 vols. (1894) · *DNB* · *CGPLA Eng. & Wales* (1876)

Archives Harvard U., Houghton L., letters | BL, letters to Macmillans, Add. MS 54916 · NYPL, letters to Alexander Macmillan · University of Illinois, letters to George Bentley

Likenesses attrib. J. Jacques, watercolour drawing, 1834, Worcester College, Oxford · W. S. Hunt, pen drawing, *c.*1874 (after a photograph, *c.*1874), NPG · Mason & Co., carte-de-visite, NPG · wood-engraving (after a photograph by London Stereoscopic Co.), NPG; repro. in *ILN* (3 June 1876)

Wealth at death under £450: administration with will, 4 Aug 1876, *CGPLA Eng. & Wales*

Kingsley, Mary Henrietta (1862–1900), traveller and writer, born in Islington, London, on 13 October 1862, was the eldest child of George Henry *Kingsley (1826–1892), a physician and traveller, and his wife and former housekeeper, Mary Bailey (*d.* 1892). The novelists Charles Kingsley and Henry Kingsley were her uncles. Her parents married only four days before her birth, but she managed to keep this a secret throughout her life, and indeed it remained undisclosed until long after her death.

Early life at home In 1863, soon after Mary Kingsley's birth, her parents moved to Highgate, where her only sibling, Charles, was born in 1866. Her father, an enthusiastic traveller, attached himself as private physician to titled families on their world tours, using the opportunity to collect ethnographical information; he was rarely at home. The remaining family led a private, even secluded life, and Mary grew up a rather silent girl, shirking social gatherings. Describing herself as a 'doer of odd jobs' (letter to Matthew Nathan, 12 March 1899, Nathan MSS), as a young woman she supported her mother in household duties and assisted in her father's amateur anthropological work, for which she learned German. She was not sent to school, but read omnivorously, and created a world of her own among the travel, natural history, and science books in her father's library.

In 1879 the family moved to Bexleyheath in Kent, and in the spring of 1886 to Cambridge, where Mary's brother had entered Christ's College to study law. This change had a great effect on her; she made friends among the academic community, including Francis Burkitt and Agnes Smith Lewis, and began to develop her own academic and social skills. About the spring of 1888, Lucy Toulmin Smith, an old family friend, gave her her first taste of foreign travel when she took her to Paris for a week.

During the four years that followed, Mary Kingsley devoted herself to nursing her mother, whose health deteriorated to such an extent that she lost the power of speech and was, eventually, paralysed. During the latter part of this period she also had care of her father, who had returned home broken in health after rheumatic fever. Dr Kingsley died in February 1892, and his wife in April. The heavy sense of responsibility which had weighed on Mary was lightened, and after a trip to the Canary Islands in August she returned restored in health and refreshed in mind, full of new possibilities awakened by all she had

Mary Henrietta Kingsley (1862–1900), by unknown photographer

seen, especially the people and goods from the African continent about which she had so avidly read.

Mary Kingsley moved with her brother to an attic flat in Addison Road, Kensington. Filled with a passion for travel and bolstered by a desire to further her anthropological studies, she thought first of going to India, but decided eventually on a voyage to west Africa. She acquired a collector's outfit and posted letters of introduction to missionaries, traders, and government officials on the west African coast. With a new-found sense of freedom, she drew up her will and set out alone in August 1893.

Mary Kingsley in Africa Mary Kingsley first touched African soil in Freetown, Sierra Leone, on 17 August, then headed slowly south to Luanda. After making her way north again, in October she visited Richard Dennett's trading station at Cabinda. Information gathered on this two-week visit was later utilized in an introduction to Dennett's *Notes on the Folk Lore of the Fjort—French Congo* (1898). She also collected or purchased scientific specimens along her route. She reached Liverpool again in December 1893.

The collections which Mary Kingsley brought home were considered valuable by the scientific community, and the voyage had been a foretaste of what she might do with more definite aims and better preparation. Determined to undertake a more definite research project in west Africa, she contacted Dr Albert Günther, keeper of zoology at the British Museum, who gave her a large range of collectors' materials. By the end of the year she had secured a commission from the publisher George Macmillan for a book on west Africa. With increased expertise, resources, and confidence, she sailed from Liverpool on 23 December 1894 in the company of Lady Ethel Macdonald, the wife of the commissioner-general of the Oil Rivers Protectorate, whom she had met in Calabar in 1893.

Mary Kingsley stayed four months with the Macdonalds at the Calabar residency, nursing the European residents through a smallpox outbreak and, despite the Brass uprising, making brief trips inland, and accompanied the Macdonalds on an official visit to the Spanish governor on Fernando Po. In April she travelled upriver to Ekene to visit the maverick Scottish missionary Mary Slessor, with whom she formed a strong bond of friendship.

At the beginning of May, Mary Kingsley began her journey south to Gabon, before ascending the Ogooué River and passing through the dangerous rapids above N'Djolé. A short though daring journey through a part of the Fang country which had never been reached by a European before, leading her own two-canoe expedition from Lambarene on the Ogooué River to Agonjo on the upper waters of the Ramboë River, established her reputation as an explorer. In August she visited Corisco Island. The last feat of this second African journey was the ascent of Mount Cameroun (13,760 ft) by a route previously unattempted by a European.

In order to pay her way and make contact with African peoples, Mary Kingsley learned to trade in rubber, ivory, tobacco, and other common trading goods. She brought home a collection of insects, shells, and plants; eighteen species of reptiles; and sixty-five species of fish, of which three were entirely new and were named after her. Careful notes and observations on the spot, combined with the writings of earlier travellers, were afterwards used as the foundation for her lectures, articles, and books.

Return to England Mary Kingsley landed in England on 30 November 1895. There was immediate press interest in her 'surprising and courageous adventures' (*Daily Telegraph*, 3 Dec 1895, 3). Angered by the inevitable focus on her achievements as a lone woman, her first venture into print was a letter to the *Daily Telegraph*, countering a report that she was a 'New Woman'. News of her travels was quickly followed by a flood of invitations to write articles and give talks. In February her first lecture, delivered before the Scottish Geographical Society, was read out by a male fellow while she was present on the platform; the following month her paper to the Liverpool Geographical Society was read by the trader James Irvine. Although the Liverpool talk was similar in content to that delivered in Scotland, she added an outline of her proposals for a system of informal economic imperialism in Africa, knowing that her audience would contain members of Liverpool's commercial community.

In January 1897 Mary Kingsley's first book, *Travels in West Africa, Congo Français, Corisco and Cameroons*, was published, reflecting her own eclectic interests, as a collection of 'facts, good healthy facts … all hopelessly adrift and mixed up pretty nearly as much as the cargo in a palm oil trader—missionary intelligence entangled in the

Lippoums Genera of beetles—trade statistics with the habits of fish' (letter to George Macmillan, 18 Dec 1894, Macmillan MSS). Nevertheless, the publicity surrounding publication put her in contact with yet more influential people, including the Liverpool businessman John Holt, the Indian expert Sir Alfred Lyall, and the anthropologist James Frazer. By June 1897 she had engaged a lecture agent, Gerald Christy.

Mary Kingsley's article in *The Spectator* of 19 March 1898 on the imposition of a 'hut-tax' in Sierra Leone drew her into another political controversy, and led to her being approached by the colonial secretary, Joseph Chamberlain, who clandestinely courted her advice. With huge work demands and an unfulfilled longing to return to the African continent, that same year she suffered a breakdown.

Mary Kingsley's vision for Africa During the next two years Mary Kingsley lectured on west Africa throughout the country, speaking to divergent audiences, including nurses, working men, scientists, scholars, and both the Liverpool and Manchester chambers of commerce, where she was the first woman to address the members. Her great desire was that the general public should know the conditions of life and government in the west African colonies. She drew attention to the injustices of the crown colony system of British rule and spoke out in favour of British trading interests in the area, defending the 'liquor traffic' which had been condemned by the missionary societies.

In private, Mary Kingsley claimed that her understanding of and sympathy for African societies arose from an ability to 'think in black' ('West Africa', 59), owing particularly to the fact that she was a woman. From this position she defended polygamy and even the slave trade. The missionary societies' attempts to Europeanize Africans, she said, was misguided and harmful, immersing Africans in a 'second hand rubbishy white culture' (*Travels in West Africa*, 20). In her own writing, she focused on the Fang, Africans who were still 'in the raw state' (letter to E. S. Hartland, 5 Jan 1897, Hartland MSS).

With such controversial views, and wary of claims that her lone travels and public work were inappropriate activities for a woman, Mary Kingsley always took pains to dress conservatively, usually in black, and to tie back her long hay-coloured hair in a tight bun secured with plenty of pins, giving the impression of a far older woman. She was not conventionally attractive; Lucy Toulmin Smith wrote that 'her fine square brow was her chief beauty' (*DNB*). But this hard appearance was softened by a keen sense of humour, displayed in both her talks and her writing.

Although publicly denying any political ambitions, in private Mary Kingsley rigorously networked behind the scenes, firing off letters to those in positions of influence, including John Strachey, editor of *The Spectator*, and Sir George Goldie of the Royal Niger Company, cultivating their friendship with what she called 'feminine artfulness' (letter to John Holt, 1 Jan 1898, Holt MSS).

In February 1899 *West African Studies* appeared. Mary

Kingsley's second book was far more ambitious than her first, outlining an 'alternative plan' for west Africa. This would put administrative control in the hands of European trading interests and incorporate African opinion. An arrangement of economic ties under British merchants rather than administrative control through 'pen-pushers and ostrich feathers' was her aim. Only such a system, she claimed, would leave African cultural, legal, and social organizations intact.

In February 1899, at a dinner party, Mary Kingsley was introduced to Matthew Nathan, the recently appointed acting governor of Sierra Leone, for whom she developed an unrequited attachment. Her relationships with other professional women were often competitive and confrontational; in particular she clashed with Flora Shaw, colonial editor of *The Times*, who refused to review her books. In August 1899 she withheld her support from a petition requesting women's admission to the learned societies. 'These androgynes [*sic*] I have no time for', she complained (letter to John Scott Keltie, 1 Dec 1899, Royal Geographical Society correspondence, 1881–1910).

Death in Africa Mary Kingsley's health continued to suffer under the strain of being a 'bushman *and* a drawing-roomer' (letter to Hatty Johnson, 27 Jan 1898, South African Library), and she longed to get away. The Second South African War of 1899 turned her thoughts to South Africa, from where she hoped to return to her own west coast. She sailed on 11 March 1900. On her arrival at Cape Town she offered her services as a nurse and was posted to the Simon's Town Palace Hospital to tend to Boer prisoners of war. Within two months the typhoid that was killing her patients struck her, and on 3 June 1900 she died. According to her own wishes, she was buried at sea. The coffin was conveyed from Simon's Town harbour on a torpedo boat with full military honours.

Commentators on Mary Kingsley's life and work have often accredited her with laying the political foundation for the introduction of indirect rule in Northern Nigeria. But it is in the informal sector of political life that she left her legacy. Her appeal for an understanding of African social and legal systems and the importance of commercial interests forged a new pressure group in colonial politics called the Fair Commerce Party, Third Party, or simply 'Kingsleyism' (*Glasgow Herald*, 27 Dec 1902). The journalist E. D. Morel, the businessman John Holt, and the historian Alice Stopford Green were central in this movement, and the Congo Reform Association and African Society, founded in Mary Kingsley's memory, were the new forums through which they operated.

Mary Kingsley's lone travels, her sympathy for African societies, and her unorthodox views suggest a woman with radical opinions on both race and gender. In this spirit her work has been republished (*Travels in West Africa*, Virago, 1982), and biographies have portrayed her as a pioneer (Katherine Frank, *A Voyager Out*, 1987). The Mary Kingsley medal of the Liverpool School of Tropical Medicine was founded in her honour. But her social conservatism, and in particular her declarations against the widening of women's rights, dog attempts to reclaim her as a proto-feminist. At the same time the seriousness of her political programme and the tragedy of her death make it impossible for her to be recast successfully as one of the wearisomely sprightly lady travellers discovered in the 1980s and 1990s. Enigmatic and impossible to stereotype, Mary Kingsley established in her lifetime and has retained after her death the reputation as one of the most celebrated of all women travellers and travel writers. Her courage, skill, and adaptability in little-known and difficult terrain were remarkable; her insight into African culture was penetrating, especially in one whose direct contact with the continent stretched over only two years; the skill with which she advanced her ideas in Britain was formidable; her literary talent, despite her self-deprecating description, was conspicuous; and the scope of her intellect was wide. But, unlike other women travellers, even Isabella Bishop, Mary Kingsley's engagement with and her often prescient if idiosyncratic views on social and political questions have ensured that her reputation extends well beyond the confines of travel and travel writing.

D. J. BIRKETT

Sources D. Birkett, *Mary Kingsley (1862–1900): a biographical bibliography* (1993) · D. Birkett, *Mary Kingsley: imperial adventuress* (1992) · K. Frank, *A voyager out* (1987) · S. Gwynn, *The life of Mary Kinglsey* (1932) · R. Kipling, *Mary Kingsley* (1932) · E. D. Morel, *Affairs of west Africa* (1902) · E. W. Blyden, *The African Society and Miss Mary H. Kingsley* (1901) · M. Kingsley, 'West Africa from an ethnologist's point of view', *Transactions of the Liverpool Geographical Society* (1897)
Archives CUL, Royal Commonwealth Society collection, corresp. and articles · Royal African Society, London | BL, corresp. with Macmillans, Add. MSS 54914–54915 · BL, letters to B. C. Skeat, Add. MS 68892 · BLPES, letters to E. D. Morel · Bodl. Oxf., letters to Sir Matthew Nathan · Bodl. RH, corresp. with John Holt and others · Bodl. RH, letters to Professor E. B. Taylor and his wife · HLRO, letters to John St Loe Strachey · NHM, letters to A. C. L. G. Günther and R. W. T. Günther · NL Ire., Gwynn, Stopford Green MSS · NL Wales, Hartland MSS · RGS, letters to Royal Geographical Society and others · South Africa Library, Hatty Johnson MSS · U. Birm. L., Chamberlain MSS · U. Leeds, Brotherton L., Clodd MSS · U. Lpool L., corresp. with George Macmillan and related papers
Likenesses B. De Cardi, miniature, *c.*1870–1875 · A. Covey-Crump, two photographs, *c.*1893–1898 · group portrait, photograph, 1895, CUL, Royal Commonwealth Society collection · photogravure, *c.*1896, NPG · two caricatures, 1899, Trinity Cam. · Ibo?, bust?, *c.*1902–1905, Liverpool Museum · photograph, Liverpool Library · photograph, CUL, Royal Commonwealth Society collection [*see illus.*]
Wealth at death £3439 12*s.* 0*d.*: probate, 7 Nov 1900, *CGPLA Eng. & Wales*

Kingsley, William (1698/9–1769), army officer, was the son of William Kingsley (1669–1705), army officer and landowner, of St Anne's parish, Westminster, and his wife, Alice, daughter and heir of William Randolph of Maidstone, Kent. He was a direct descendant from William Kingsley, archdeacon of Canterbury (1584–1647), who established the Kingsleys, who were of Lancashire origin, as a Kentish landed family in the mid-seventeenth century; from him Charles Kingsley the novelist also traced his descent.

Kingsley's father, William, was an ensign in Sir Edward Dering's regiment of foot (later the 24th foot) which was raised in Kent in March 1689 for service in William III's

Irish campaign. He remained in service in Ireland and Flanders, latterly in Colonel William Selwyn's regiment of foot, until he retired on half-pay in 1697. Kingsley's mother had brought her husband considerable property in Maidstone including a residence thenceforward known as Kingsley House, as well as an estate in the parish of Kennington, near Ashford, in Kent.

Kingsley matriculated at St John's, Oxford, on 19 November 1717, aged eighteen, but he did not take a degree. On 24 June 1721 he was commissioned lieutenant and captain in the 3rd foot guards (later the Scots Guards) in the company commanded by Lieutenant-Colonel Wolfe, father of General James Wolfe. He was promoted captain-lieutenant in the same regiment in 1743; captain and lieutenant-colonel in 1745; brevet colonel in 1750; and regimental major, with the rank of colonel of foot, on 29 January 1751. He was aide-de-camp to his colonel, John Murray, second earl of Dunmore, at Dettingen, and was present with the 1st battalion of his regiment at the battle of Fontenoy, where a cannon-ball passed between his legs and killed four men behind him, on 11 May 1745. When the collected grenadier companies of the several regiments of guards marched from London for the north in the following December (the 'march to Finchley'), he was one of the officers sent ahead into Northamptonshire by the duke of Cumberland to obtain information of the enemy's movements. He was appointed lieutenant-colonel of the Scots guards in 1752. On 22 May 1756 Kingsley was made colonel of the Lancashire Fusiliers. James Wolfe, then lieutenant-colonel of the regiment at Devizes, wrote of him: 'Our new colonel is a sensible man, and very sociable and polite' (Smyth, 37n.).

Kingsley was with his regiment in the Rochefort expedition of 1757, and afterwards went to Germany as major-general (commission dated 20 January 1758). He greatly distinguished himself at the battle of Minden on 1 August 1759, at the head of a brigade composed of the 20th (Kingsley's), 25th (Home's), and 51st (Brudenell's) foot, which was very prominently engaged. 'Kingsley's grenadiers', as the 20th was popularly called, is said to have marched through some gardens or hedges where the men put roses in their buttonholes, a circumstance subsequently commemorated by the regimental custom of wearing 'Minden roses' in the caps on each anniversary of the day. The successful advance of the 'Minden battalions' is still regarded as a feat of bravery and endurance without parallel in the campaigns of the British army in the eighteenth century. The regiment had six officers and eighty men killed and eleven officers and 224 men wounded, and was excused from all further duty on account of its losses. In his general order of 2 August, Prince Ferdinand complimented both Kingsley and Waldegrave, his fellow commander, 'for their great courage, and the good order in which they conducted their brigades' (Smyth, 57). On 4 August a countermanding order announced: 'Kingsley's regiment of the British line will resume its share of the duty at its own request'. Kingsley was afterwards engaged at Ziezenberg and elsewhere. He was appointed governor of Fort William on 22 March 1760 but did not reside there.

He became a lieutenant-general in December 1760, and was appointed to the command of a secret expedition, with William Draper as his quartermaster-general. The force was at first destined for eastward of the Cape, but was afterwards ordered to rendezvous at Quiberon for an attempt on Belle Île on the coast of Brittany. The death of George II and other circumstances delayed the expedition, and Kingsley's orders were eventually countermanded. He was not actively employed again.

Kingsley was an outspoken, independent Englishman, extremely popular with his soldiers, and an active freemason. He was over seventy years of age and unmarried at the time of his death at Kingsley House, Stone Street, Maidstone, on 9 October 1769. He was buried in the family vault at St Mary's Church, Kennington, near Ashford, Kent. Upon inheriting the family estates he had bequeathed most of the property, for life, to his sister, Alicia, who married Stephen Otway, of Maidstone. However, she died before him in 1761. His other sister, Caroline, a spinster, died in 1756. By his will of 16 March 1764 (proven on 26 October 1769) Kingsley House and his estates in Kennington, Patricksbourne, and elsewhere, passed to his first cousin, Charles Kingsley, of London. The mansion remained in the family's possession until sold for building sites in the mid-nineteenth century. It was demolished in 1855.   H. M. CHICHESTER, rev. JONATHAN SPAIN

Sources C. Dalton, ed., *George the First's army, 1714–1727*, 2 (1912), 272 · B. Smyth, *History of the XXth regiment, 1688–1888* (1889) · C. Ray, *Regiment of the line* (1963) · W. Berry, *Pedigrees of the families of the county of Kent* (1830), 306 · E. Hasted, *The history and topographical survey of the county of Kent*, 2 (1782), 263–9, 453–5, 482, 722 · J. M. Russell, *The history of Maidstone* (1881), 340 · W. D. Pink, 'Kingsley of Sarratt, Canterbury and London', *The Genealogist*, new ser., 29 (1912–13), 21–4 · *N&Q*, 10th ser., 8 (1907), 109, 158, 294, 378 · *Scots Magazine*, 31 (1769) · Foster, *Alum. Oxon.* · P. Mackesy, *The coward of Minden: the affair of Lord George Sackville* (1979)
Archives Lancashire Fusiliers Museum, Bury, diary | BL, corresp. with duke of Newcastle, Add. MSS 32732, 32896, 32918
Likenesses J. Reynolds, oils, 1760 · R. Houston, print (after J. Reynolds, 1760), BM, NPG

Kingsmill family (*per. c.*1480–1698), gentry, had before the last decades of the fifteenth century developed interests principally in Berkshire. They acted as bailiffs of Basingstoke, Hampshire, and established a residence at Barkham, some 12 miles away. Their situation began to change when Richard Kingsmill (*d.* 1511) married Amy, daughter of Richard Ingpen of Longparish, Hampshire. In 1501 he received Katherine of Aragon and her entourage on their way to her marriage with Prince Arthur. More important he worked hard to get his son **John** [i] **Kingsmill** (*c.*1460–1509) a good start in life. John attended Winchester College from 1470 to 1474 and went on to New College, Oxford, in the latter year. He was a full fellow of New College from 1476 to 1479. Between 1487 and 1489 he provided legal counsel to Magdalen College, Oxford. The Middle Temple admitted him in 1489. From 1492 to 1504 he served as steward of Winchester College. Returned to parliament for Heytesbury, Wiltshire, in 1491, he became a JP for Hampshire in 1493, a position he retained until his death, and in the same year began to try cases in the court of requests. By 1494 he was a bencher of the Middle Temple and on 12 November 1495 he became a serjeant-at-law. In 1497 he became a king's serjeant. By 1499 he had gained a national reputation for his 'authority and worship' as a fine but expensive lawyer. Henry VII appointed him a justice of common pleas on 2 July 1504, and chief justice for Lancaster on 9 January 1507.

Richard Kingsmill established another important connection for his son by arranging his marriage with Jane, daughter of John Gifford of Ichell, Hampshire, under a contract of 10 August 1490. While the Giffords were not among the most prominent of Hampshire's gentry, they occupied a more prestigious position than the Kingsmills, and John Gifford rightly saw John [i] Kingsmill as a young man of potential. John Kingsmill's marriage to Jane Gifford produced four children: John; Alice, who married Thomas Bullock of Arborfield, Berkshire; Mary, who married Richard Waller of Oldstoke, Hampshire; and Morpheta, a nun who became prioress and then abbess of Wherwell Abbey, Hampshire. Their father died on 11 May 1509, having lived long enough to leave his family with good local and national connections.

Sir John [ii] **Kingsmill** (c.1497–1556) maintained the upward social momentum established by his father, whom he followed into a legal career. He entered Lincoln's Inn in October 1516 and was called to the bar on 9 May 1521. It was also in 1521 that he took the momentous step of marrying Constance (d. 1580/81), the daughter of John Goring of Burton, Sussex, and the sister of William Goring. Although the Gorings were only a modest family of Sussex gentry, the connection had important long-term results. First, another Goring daughter, Anne, married Richard Gifford, strengthening the Kingsmill–Gifford family alliance. Second, the Gorings were early protestants, and the influence of Constance and Anne helped bring both the Kingsmill and Gifford families into the reforming movement. Third, William Goring became an ally of Thomas Cromwell and helped to introduce his Kingsmill brother-in-law into that important political connection by the early 1530s. Fourth, by 1537 Kingsmill acquired the manor of Litchfield from the Gorings, his first substantial property in Hampshire.

By 1530 John Kingsmill's career was starting to blossom. Knighted in that year by Henry VIII, he became steward of Mottisfont Priory in Hampshire. In 1533 he became involved in local government, serving as commissioner to inquire about wastes committed in various forests. He was appointed a JP in 1537, continuing to hold that office until his death, and served as sheriff of Hampshire in 1538–9 and 1543–4. During the late 1530s he worked closely with Cromwell's protégé Thomas Wriothesley, and both men greatly benefited from the dissolution of the monasteries. Kingsmill's acquisitions included the manors of Sandford and Woodcott and also, in 1540, the rich manor of Sidmonton, which replaced Barkham as the family's principal residence.

During 1539 Kingsmill worked hard as sheriff to assure the election of Cromwell's candidates as Hampshire's representatives in parliament. As a result he earned the enmity of the conservative Stephen Gardiner, bishop of Winchester. Nevertheless after the fall of Cromwell in 1540 Kingsmill remained active in local government and was sheriff again in 1543–4. Under Edward VI he was a commissioner for the dissolution of chantries in 1548. Queen Mary pardoned him for offences committed prior to 1 October 1553, and thereafter he was inactive in local government and politics.

Sir John [ii] Kingsmill left a large, successful, and staunchly protestant family when he died on 11 August 1556, although the significance of his legacy was not immediately apparent in the unfavourable atmosphere of the Marian restoration of Catholicism. During summer 1558 Hampshire experienced its only burning of a heretic, a gentleman named Thomas Bembridge, who happened to be a relative of both Anne Gifford and Constance Kingsmill. Bembridge recanted at the first attempt to burn him and his relatives illegally saved him from the fire. The privy council ordered a second and successful execution shortly afterwards, which created lasting bitterness among the Kingsmills and Giffords, especially toward the sheriff, Sir Richard Pexsall.

Elizabeth I's accession immediately revived the Kingsmills' prospects and her reign can largely be considered the zenith of the family's fortunes. Sir John and Constance Kingsmill had seventeen children. Their eldest son, and heir, **Sir William** [i] **Kingsmill** (c.1526–1593), is not recorded as attending any university or inn of court. On 17 January 1553 his father had contracted for William's marriage to Bridget, the daughter of Simon Ralegh of Farnborough, Warwickshire. A JP for Hampshire from 1558 he remained in that office until shortly before his death. He was appointed sheriff of the county in 1563, and in 1564 Bishop Robert Horne of Winchester identified him as a favourer of protestantism. He was knighted in 1569, and in that year supported Horne in a dispute with religious conservatives over local office-holding. He was also active in local musters and enforcing laws against recusants. In 1571 he added to the family estates by purchasing Malshanger and Wootton manors. He died on 10 November 1593.

The other Kingsmills of Sir William's generation also did well for themselves and were determined supporters of the protestant religion. The second son, **Richard Kingsmill** (c.1528–1600), followed the family tradition of a legal career and became more prominent politically than his older brother. Admitted to Lincoln's Inn on 6 June 1543 he was called to the bar in 1548. In 1555 Sir John Thynne recommended him for a position in Princess Elizabeth's household. He served Lincoln's Inn as a reader in 1558, 1559, 1566, and 1567; as treasurer in 1563; and as governor in 1568. A Hampshire JP from 1558 until his death, he was elected MP for Calne, Wiltshire, in 1559 and for Heytesbury, Wiltshire, in 1563. Appointed a commissioner for the establishment of true religion in the north of England in 1559, he was also identified as a favourer of the protestant religion in 1564 by Bishop Horne. During the 1560s he attempted to use his protestant and family connections to obtain the attorneyship of the court of wards, but did not succeed until 1573. He became surveyor of the court in 1590. Meanwhile in 1584 and 1586 he was elected a knight of the shire for Hampshire. He also built up his estate, acquiring the manors of Shoddesden, Hurstborne Fauconers, Tangley, Highclere, and Burghclere. He married Alice, the daughter of Richard Fauconer of Hurstborne, Hampshire, after 1557. Their daughter and heir, Constance, married Sir Thomas Lucy of Charlecote, Warwickshire. Alice had died by about 1574, when her husband married Elizabeth Stonehouse (*née* Woodrofe). Richard Kingsmill's death on 24 September 1600 without a male heir resulted in the breaking up of his estate. He was buried at Highclere, Hampshire.

Sir John [ii] Kingsmill's other sons included Henry Kingsmill (*c*.1534–1577), who studied civil law in Paris and Padua, and under Mary went into exile at Venice in the household of the earl of Bedford. By 1560 he was a member of the royal household and in 1563 sat in parliament for Downton, Wiltshire, through the patronage of Bishop Horne. A firm protestant in the Genevan style, he died young. John [iii] Kingsmill (*c*.1536–1590) was a member of Magdalen College, Oxford, graduating BA in 1553 and MA in 1562. A fellow of Magdalen between 1556 and 1572, he became that college's bursar in 1563. At Oxford he displayed strongly protestant sympathies and opposed vestments. Appointed chancellor of Winchester diocese in 1570, he sat in parliament for Ludgershall, Wiltshire, in 1584 and 1586. During his last years he lived at the Magdalen College manor of King's Enham, where he died in 1590 apparently unmarried. Andrew *Kingsmill (1537/8–1569) studied civil law at Oxford but became more interested in Calvinist theology and biblical studies. He travelled to Geneva in 1566, became a minister there, and died at Lausanne leaving several devotional writings that were published posthumously. George Kingsmill (*c*.1539–1606) began his legal studies at Lincoln's Inn in 1560 and was called to the bar in 1567. A highly regarded lawyer, who was made a queen's serjeant in 1595, in 1579 he purchased the stewardship of King's Somborne hundred which probably accounts for his election in 1584 and 1586 as MP for Stockbridge in that hundred. After 1595 he married Sarah, the widow of Francis, Lord Hastings. In 1599 George Kingsmill became a judge in the court of common pleas like his grandfather. Dying without children in April 1606, he left to his widow an estate which included lands inherited from his brother Richard. **Thomas Kingsmill** (*d.* in or after 1605?) was a demy of Magdalen College, Oxford, in 1558. A strong protestant, he and his brother John were disciplined on 2 May 1559 for expressing heretical views and for shaving their heads in mockery of the tonsure. Nevertheless he became a fellow of Magdalen in that year, and graduated BA on 27 November. Reader in natural philosophy 1563–5 and public orator 1565–9, he proceeded MA in 1564. In 1569 he resigned his fellowship and became the university's first regius professor of Hebrew on the recommendation of Robert Dudley, earl of Leicester. Unlike his immediate successors he was appointed for life, but mental illness blighted his career; in the words of Anthony Wood, he became 'distempered in brain with too

much lucubration' (Wood, *Ath. Oxon.*, 1.758). In 1579 Richard Hooker began serving as his deputy, but Kingsmill later recovered and retained his chair until 1591. Whether he died in that year or later is unclear, as books by him were published in 1602 and 1605, the latter dedicated to James I.

Sir John and Constance Kingsmill also had five daughters, four of whom married well. The eldest daughter, Catherine, married Sir Richard Norton of Hampshire, so bringing the head of a hitherto strongly Catholic family into the protestant camp; Margaret married John Thornborough of Shotesden, Hampshire; Jane married John Cupper, whose premature death in 1566 furnished the inspiration for some of Andrew Kingsmill's devotional writing; Alice married James *Pilkington (1520–1576), a Marian exile and the first protestant bishop of Durham—a relationship which her brother Richard exploited to advance his career.

By the time Constance Kingsmill died, between April 1580 and June 1581, the fortunes of her late husband's family were starting to go into decline. Her sons Andrew and Henry had predeceased her; Thomas was insane, at least intermittently. Her eldest son Sir William [i] was not the man his father and grandfather had been, while the achievements of Richard, George, and John would be stillborn owing to their failure to produce male heirs. The fortunes of the Kingsmill family lay in the hands of her grandson William.

Sir William [ii] **Kingsmill** (*c*.1557–1618) showed himself a respected member of the magisterial gentry of Hampshire. Besides being a JP he served as sheriff of Hampshire in 1601–2 and 1612–13. He was knighted in 1606. He also maintained his family's long-standing political alliances, for instance by siding with Sir Henry Wallop, a kinsman through the Giffords, during a disputed parliamentary election for Hampshire in 1614. Before about 1588 he married Ann, the daughter of William Wilks of Hadnell, Warwickshire, and the widow of Anthony Dryden. His marriage, like that of his parents and grandparents, was fertile, producing five sons and seven daughters, although not all survived to adulthood. But unlike most of his forebears Sir William was not longlived, and unfortunately for the family neither were his son and his grandson. His heir, **Sir Henry Kingsmill** (*c*.1588–1624), was his father's eldest surviving son, though his second by birth. In 1610 he married the formidable Bridget (*d.* 1672), daughter of John White of Hampshire. Knighted in 1611, Sir Henry died prematurely in 1624, leaving as his son and heir the eleven-year-old **Sir William** [iii] **Kingsmill** (1613–1661). Bridget inherited two thirds of her husband's estates and also purchased the wardship of her son. The latter attained his majority in 1634, but because his mother outlived him he never gained full control of the Kingsmill lands.

The relationship between mother and son was sometimes stormy. Even stormier was the political situation of England in 1640 when William [iii] Kingsmill first became a JP in Hampshire. Charles I appointed him sheriff of

Hampshire at Reading about November 1642, but the parliamentary general Sir William Waller removed him from that office during October 1643. The king also knighted him, possibly on his appointment as sheriff and no later than October 1644. Although Sir William was a thoroughgoing royalist in his sentiments he never fought against parliament, and Charles I did not particularly trust him. In his actions as opposed to his words Kingsmill appears to have been a neutralist. His estates suffered during the civil war as there was considerable military activity in northern Hampshire. He had submitted to the local parliamentary committee for compounding by 1645, and from 1646 to 1650 was again a JP for Hampshire. He may have participated in royalist plotting during 1649 or 1650, after the king's execution, but thereafter he lived in outward quiet and acceptance of the regimes of the Commonwealth and protectorate. Privately he produced poetry that was deeply critical of the political situation. On 21 February 1654, at the comparatively late age of forty-one, he married Ann, daughter of Sir Anthony Haslewood. They had a son and two daughters, Bridget and Anne.

Sir William died on 3 September 1661 leaving as his heir the six-year-old **Sir William [iv] Kingsmill** (c.1655–1698), who from 1664 was raised by his uncle Sir William Haslewood. William Kingsmill was knighted in 1680. His relationship with his former guardian clearly deteriorated badly, for on 3 November 1683 he killed his uncle after a quarrel in which, Kingsmill claimed, Haslewood gave him great provocation and drew his sword on him. He was pardoned the manslaughter on 14 June 1684, in spite of the opposition of the dead man's family. He was married twice, first to Frances Calwell, with whom he had four children, including his heir, another William, and second to a woman named Rebecca, who bore him two daughters. He died on 26 November 1698. His son and heir William [v] Kingsmill (1685–1766) never married and suffered from insanity during the last thirty years of his life. The family's lands and arms passed by act of parliament in 1766 to the Brice family, who also adopted the Kingsmill name.

RONALD H. FRITZE

Sources R. H. Fritze, '"A rare example of godlynesse amongst gentlemen": the role of the Kingsmill and Gifford families in promoting the Reformation in Hampshire', *Protestantism and the national church in sixteenth century England*, ed. P. Lake and M. Dowling (1987), 144–61 · J. Eames, 'The poems of Sir William Kingsmill (1613–1661): a critical edition', PhD diss., U. Birm., 1982 · HoP, *Commons, 1558–1603* · R. H. Fritze, 'Faith and faction: religious changes, national politics, and the development of local factionalism in Hampshire, 1485–1570', PhD diss., U. Cam., 1981 · R. H. Fritze, 'The role of family and religion in the local politics of early Elizabethan England: the case of Hampshire in the 1560s', *HJ*, 25 (1982), 267–87 · *VCH Hampshire and the Isle of Wight*, 2.1074 · R. Fritze, 'The justices of the peace in Hampshire, 1529–1564: a social, political, and economic study', MA diss., Louisiana State University, 1976 · B. Richmond, 'The work of the justices of the peace in Hampshire, 1603–1642', MPhil diss., U. Southampton, 1969 · D. Heifetz, 'The justices of the peace in Hampshire, 1625 to 1675', PhD diss., U. Cal., Irvine, 1978 · *Hampshire and the Isle of Wight*, Pevsner (1967) · HoP, *Commons, 1509–58* · Foster, *Alum. Oxon.* · Wood, *Ath. Oxon.*, new edn · G. D. Duncan, 'Public lectures and professorial chairs', *Hist. U. Oxf.* 3: *Colleg. univ.*, 335–61 · E. W. Ives, *The common lawyers of pre-Reformation England* (1983) · chancery, examiners' office, town depositions, PRO, C24/10 · chancery, inquisitions post mortem, PRO, C142/110/142, C142/246/107 · wills, PRO, PROB 11/16 · W. A. Shaw, *The knights of England*, 2 vols. (1906) · W. P. Baildon, ed., *The records of the Honorable Society of Lincoln's Inn: admissions*, 2 vols. (1896)

Archives NRA, priv. coll., papers [microfilm at Institute of Historical Research, London]

Likenesses double portrait, effigy (Sir Henry Kingsmill with his wife Bridget), St Mary's Church, Kingsclere, Hampshire · effigy (Richard Kingsmill), St Michael and All Angels Church, Highclere, Hampshire

Kingsmill, Andrew (1537/8–1569), civil lawyer and religious activist, was the second son of Sir John *Kingsmill (c.1497–1556) [see under Kingsmill family (per. c.1480–1698)] of Sidmonton, Hampshire, and Constance Goring (d. 1580/81) of Burton, Sussex; he was the fourth of their thirteen children. The Kingsmills were a family of common lawyers that had been prominent in the local politics of Hampshire only since the later 1530s. Both the Kingsmill and Goring families had supported Thomas Cromwell and his policies during the 1530s, along with the incipient cause of protestantism.

Andrew Kingsmill shared his parents' commitment to protestantism and followed his father in studying the law, although in his case it was the civil law. On 23 August 1553 he matriculated at Corpus Christi College, Oxford, and in 1558 All Souls College elected him a fellow. At the beginning of 1562 he earned the degree of BCL, and with it a reputation for great legal learning which propelled him into the position of dean of law at All Souls College. But during that same time his interests shifted to studying the Bible and theology. Francis Mills, his friend and contemporary at All Souls, reported that Kingsmill wrote his *A View of Man's Estate; wherein the Great Mercy of God in Man's Free Justification is Showed* (posthumously published in London, 1574; reprinted 1576 and 1577) when he was twenty-two years old. According to that statement composition would have taken place some time between 1559 and 1561, but a printed note at the end of the book reads 'By M. A. K. The yeare of our Lorde 1562'. It was also said that Kingsmill could recite from memory in Greek the epistles to the Romans and Galatians, the first epistle of St John, various other chapters from the Old and New testaments, and certain psalms.

According to Wood, at the beginning of Elizabeth's reign Kingsmill was sometimes engaged in preaching protestantism, albeit informally, in an Oxford still dominated by Marian Catholics. During the vestiarian controversy he took up a position opposed to the use of vestments, and wrote to Archbishop Matthew Parker urging tolerance of nonconformity in that matter, which he defined as an indifferent practice. He discussed the same issue with his brother-in-law, Bishop James Pilkington of Durham. In 1566 an anti-vestiarian delegation, including Kingsmill, was sent to Theodore Beza of Geneva but failed to obtain his full support. Kingsmill never returned to England. Instead he remained in Geneva, where he was well regarded. After studying Greek, Hebrew, and theology there for three years as preparation for becoming a minister of religion, he moved on to Lausanne, where he died during September 1569, aged only thirty-one. In his will he left £5 to All Souls to buy the works of Calvin and Peter Martyr for the college library; they were purchased in 1576. Kingsmill published nothing during his short life, but two of his writings were posthumously seen through to publication by Francis Mills, his literary executor and a fellow protestant. Like *A View of Man's Estate*, his other work, *A most excellent and comfortable treatise, for all such as are any maner of way either troubled in minde or afflicted in bodie* (1577; repr. 1578, 1585), was theological and devotional in nature. Mills assessed Andrew Kingsmill as 'a Phoenix among Lawyers, a rare example of godlynesse amongst gentlemen' (*A View of Man's Estate*, preface, sig. A iii).

RONALD H. FRITZE

Sources DNB · F. Mills, 'Preface', in A. Kingsmill, *A view of man's estate* (1574) · Wood, *Ath. Oxon.*, new edn, 1.373–4 · R. H. Fritze, '"A rare example of godlynesse amongst gentlemen": the role of the Kingsmill and Gifford families in promoting the Reformation in Hampshire', *Protestantism and the national church in sixteenth century England*, ed. P. Lake and M. Dowling (1987), 144–61 · C. M. Dent, *Protestant reformers in Elizabethan Oxford* (1983) · N. R. Ker, 'The provision of books', *Hist. U. Oxf.* 3: *Colleg. univ.*, 441–77 · J. K. McConica and C. S. Knighton, 'Some sixteenth-century Corpus families: Kingsmills, Nappers, Lancasters, and others', *The Pelican* (1978–9), 6–9 [magazine of Corpus Christi College, Oxford] · Foster, *Alum. Oxon.* · will, PRO, PROB 11/63, fol. 24 · PRO, chancery, inquisitions post mortem, series II, C142/110/142 · PRO, chancery, town depositions, C24/10/Dale v Rumbold

Wealth at death £5 to All Souls College, Oxford: Ker, 'Provision of books'; will, PRO, PROB 11/63, fol. 24

Kingsmill, Sir Henry (*c*.1588–1624). *See under* Kingsmill family (*per. c*.1480–1698).

Kingsmill, Hugh. *See* Lunn, Hugh Kingsmill (1889–1949).

Kingsmill, John (*c*.1460–1509). *See under* Kingsmill family (*per. c*.1480–1698).

Kingsmill, Sir John (*c*.1497–1556). *See under* Kingsmill family (*per. c*.1480–1698).

Kingsmill, Joseph (1805/6–1865), penologist and prison chaplain, was born in co. Kilkenny, Ireland, the son of Thomas Kingsmill. He entered Trinity College, Dublin, in 1826, was prizeman in classics and divinity, and proceeded to his BA in 1831 and MA in 1836. He was ordained deacon in 1831 by the bishop of Dromore and presented by the bishop of Chester in 1832. His historical significance is in his role as chaplain to Pentonville prison.

Pentonville 'model prison' received its first intake on 21 December 1842 and was fêted as the most important breakthrough in penal discipline of the age. Constructed in tiered lines of cells radiating from a central block it aimed to ensure the perfect operation of the separate system. In this system prisoners were isolated in individual cells, even attending chapel in separate cubicles, and were subjected to a battery of reforming influences in cell education, catechization, admonition, trade training, and so forth. The theory was that, with psychological defences broken down and mutual corruption ended by cellular isolation, prisoners would emerge from Pentonville at least reformed and at best converted to a sense of personal redemption and relationship with Christ. Pentonville was set up as the model for others to admire and emulate. It held a daily average of 500 men all sentenced to transportation and sent to Australasia on completion of the first eighteen months (subsequently reduced to nine) in Pentonville. In the late 1850s this nine months' separation formed the initial phase of penal servitude, which replaced transportation, and the prisoners went on to associated labour in Portland thereafter.

Kingsmill was appointed assistant chaplain to the Revd J. Ralph when the prison opened, but a year later was promoted to chaplain, with his assistant between 1844 and 1855 another noted protagonist of separation, John Burt. Kingsmill served in this office until 1859 and his governor throughout was Robert Hosking. The prison was at first superintended by a committee including designers of the Victorian cellular prison, Joshua Jebb, William Crawford, and Whitworth Russell, and subsequently became one of the convict prisons supervised by Jebb, now chairman of the directors of convict prisons and a staunch supporter of Kingsmill. Initially in Kingsmill's department were the assistant chaplain, principal schoolmaster, and his three assistant schoolmasters. He was responsible for ensuring three Sunday services, each with sermon, visiting all prisoners in their cells or hospital to instruct, persuade, and comfort them, supervising the library, and advising as to the reformatory impact of the prison on individuals and collectively. Between 1845 and 1855 he carried out over 100,000 cell visits and spent between ten and twelve hours daily at the prison.

Kingsmill was a significant figure in the spread of the separate system throughout the country, for Pentonville, alongside Reading, was lauded as a demonstration of the system. He ardently publicized his work and views in annual reports published by parliament and in books and pamphlets, of which *Chapters on Prisons and Prisoners* (three editions after 1849) was best known. He also gave evidence to the 1847 House of Lords committee on criminal law, transportation, and reformatories for juvenile offenders. Kingsmill theorized that recidivist criminality was progressive and thrived in overcrowded, miserable homes with criminal or vicious parents and in criminogenic neighbourhoods with numerous temptations to vice, such as dance-halls, taverns, and concert rooms, with individuals descending into street or lodging-house dwelling, sexual licence, generalized addiction to drink, and ultimately recidivism. However his distinctive contribution was the notion that the first link in the progressive chain was a choice made by the individual to reject Christ. This first step was the necessary precursor of the rest.

The aim of Kingsmill's approach was therefore at best to reconcile the prisoner with God through Christ, or at least to achieve moral change. Arguing that technical education merely made a thief a better-educated thief, he insisted on a moral and spiritual base for all parts of the regime. He wanted basic education in prison to ensure understanding of Christian and moral truths and competence in the workplace outside, and distrusted more advanced education of prisoners as harmful diversion. He insisted that congregate prison discipline, no matter how regulated, resulted in corruption, and that only separation could make possible inner reformation. He was well aware that prison conversions could be feigned or short-lived, but was sure that Christian prison officers, the reverse of the stereotype of the earlier dissolute, foul-mouthed turnkeys, had huge potential for influence in the separate system. Indeed his *Address to Officers in Charge of Prisoners* (1853) was distributed by the directors of convict prisons to every officer in the service. He opposed reduction of the separation part of the transportation or penal servitude sentence from eighteen to nine months, and did battle with those who argued that separation caused insanity. He also strongly supported the new reformatories for juvenile offenders.

Towards the end of his ministry Kingsmill realized that the potential of separation for conversion had been exaggerated, but he continued to extol it on grounds of its general moral, penal, and deterrent value. In addition, with some reservations, he welcomed the end of transportation in favour of penal servitude, for he distrusted the former disposal as tending to undo the moral gains made in separation. In addition he was one of that group of prison chaplains who, like John Clay of Preston, established a body of empirical criminological knowledge. Kingsmill surveyed cohorts of prisoners in order to measure their education, knowledge, and recidivism using case description and quantitative analysis.

Kingsmill retired from Pentonville in 1860 and was replaced by his assistant Ambrose Sherwin, who had recently succeeded John Burt, who had taken a full prison chaplaincy in Birmingham. In that year also retired his governor, Hosking. Kingsmill had suffered considerable ill health. Almost at once the stalled cubicles in the chapel at Pentonville were demolished, for the era of severe moralistic evangelicalism in prisons, of which Kingsmill was an important representative, was passing in favour of a much more pessimistic approach to prison discipline.

Kingsmill feared the expansion of the Roman Catholic church (see his *On the Idolatry of the Church of Rome*, 1836) and resisted attempts to establish Catholic ministry to prisons, although he facilitated access to a Roman Catholic priest if a Catholic prisoner specifically pressed for this (see his *Roman Catholic Chaplains to Gaols*, 1854). He also advocated strong protestant missionary activity, and his *British Rule and British Christianity in India* (1859), *Missions and Missionaries Historically Viewed* (1853), and *Ojibura Indians … of British America* (1855) reflected this. In conventional evangelical style he vigorously demanded the keeping of the sabbath in *The Sabbath: the Working Man's True Charter* (1856). Kingsmill's wife was named as Margaret Thomas Kingsmill at the swearing of his probate: it is not known when they married. He held no living after his retirement, and died aged fifty-nine of 'bronchitis, after a long illness' on 25 December 1865 at his home, 142 Marina, St Leonards, Sussex (*GM*). As his widow was his universal legatee, it seems likely that they had no children.

BILL FORSYTHE

Sources S. McConville, *A history of English prison administration*, 1: *1750–1877* (1981) · L. Radzinowicz and R. Hood, *A history of English criminal law and its administration from 1750*, rev. edn, 5: *The emergence of penal policy in Victorian and Edwardian England* (1990) · annual reports, Pentonville prison, *Parl. papers* (1842–52) · 'Directors of convict prisons', *Parl. papers* (1852–60) [annual reports] · 'Select committee of the House of Lords on … criminal law', *Parl. papers* (1847), vol. 7, nos. 447, 534 [juvenile offenders and transportation] · Crockford (1865) · *Clergy List* (1848) · *National union catalog*, Library of Congress · *GM*, 4th ser., 1 (1866), 290 · Burtchaell & Sadleir, *Alum. Dubl.* · *CGPLA Eng. & Wales* (1866) · d. cert.

Wealth at death under £800: administration with will, 18 Jan 1866, *CGPLA Eng. & Wales*

Kingsmill, Richard (*c.*1528–1600). *See under* Kingsmill family (*per. c.*1480–1698).

Kingsmill, Sir Robert Brice, first baronet (1730–1805), naval officer, was the second of the two sons of Charles Brice (1683/4–1748) of Castle Chichester, Island Magee, co. Antrim, a captain in the army, and Jane, daughter of William Robinson of Newtonards, co. Down. Robert Brice was made a lieutenant on 29 April 1756, appointed commander of the sloop *Swallow* in February 1761, and confirmed in the rank on 3 July as a result of his capture of the French privateer *Sultan* (10 guns). In 1762 he commanded the bomb-vessel *Basilisk* at Sir George Rodney's capture of Martinique and St Lucia, where he was wounded. On 26 May he was posted to the *Crescent* (28 guns), and in 1764 returned to England. Some time between 1762 and 1764 he married Elizabeth (1716–1783), only surviving daughter of Hugh Corry of Newtonards, co. Down, and his wife, Frances Kingsmill (1682–1721), of Sydmonton, Hampshire. On the death, on 8 January 1766, of her last surviving maternal uncle, William Kingsmill, a bachelor, Elizabeth Brice succeeded to the Kingsmill estates and her husband assumed the surname Kingsmill by act of parliament.

Kingsmill commanded the *Vigilant* (64 guns) in the battle of Ushant on 27 July 1778. In November of that year Lord Sandwich thought Kingsmill 'a good officer but rather discontented and complaining' though he had not 'shewn any violence' (HoP, *Commons*, 3.12) in the controversy which followed the battle. Yet after the courts martial Kingsmill resigned his command. He sat as the MP for Yarmouth, Isle of Wight, between 1779 and 1780, and he considered standing for the county in 1780, but withdrew before the poll. He voted consistently against Lord North's administration and, unsurprisingly, was not employed at sea again until the change of ministry in 1782, when he was appointed to the *Elizabeth* (74 guns), part of a small squadron ordered to the East Indies. Violent storms in the Bay of Biscay forced the dismasted *Elizabeth* to return to Portsmouth where she remained as a guardship after the peace in 1783. Kingsmill commanded her until 1786, and the *Duke* (90 guns) in the Spanish armament of 1790. From 5 April 1784 to 1790 he represented Tregony, Cornwall, in the government interest. Though there is no record of his having spoken in the Commons, Kingsmill voted for Pitt's parliamentary reform bill in 1785, but against Richmond's fortification plans in 1786 and against Pitt in the Regency crisis of 1788/89.

On 1 February 1793 he was promoted rear-admiral of the white and on 31 August he was appointed commander-in-chief on the Irish station. Further promotions were to rear-admiral of the red on 12 April 1794, vice-admiral of the white (4 July), and vice-admiral of the red (1 June 1795). Such rapid promotion perhaps compensated for the difficulties of an admiral who was required, with limited means, to protect the Irish trade and counter the potential threat to Ireland of a French invasion. In 1795 Kingsmill commanded two ships of the line, seven frigates, and four smaller vessels. Such numbers prevented him from confronting French invasion forces at Bantry Bay in December 1796. In the autumn of 1797 his force was increased to between twenty and twenty-five ships, but thereafter it was again reduced to twelve ships.

Kingsmill's post was arduous. In February 1798 he wished to retire but Lord Spencer hoped he would not think 'of quitting a situation in which he had been of such essential service' (Kingsmill MSS, 19M61/4203), and in October that year his ships defeated a French invasion force at Lough Swilly. For this Kingsmill received the freedom and thanks of the cities of Cork, Dublin, Bristol, Liverpool, and London and was made admiral of the blue on 14 February 1799. On 9 September 1800, just before he left Ireland, he gave 'a splendid entertainment' (*Naval Chronicle*, 4.247) for the merchants, mayor, and corporation of the city of Cork. Numerous toasts praised Kingsmill's attention to their interests and his ability and vigilance in protecting trade. Kingsmill struck his flag on 23 November and was created a baronet on 24 November 1800. Having been promoted admiral of the white on 23 April 1804 and admiral of the red on 9 November 1805, he saw no further service and died at his home, Sydmonton House, Hampshire, on 23 November 1805; he was buried at St Mary's, Kingsclere, Hampshire. His brother Edward (d. 1796), principal surveyor of revenue at Belfast, assumed the surname Kingsmill in January 1788. Edward's son, Major Robert Kingsmill (1772–1825), succeeded his uncle as second baronet. On his death the title became extinct.

J. K. LAUGHTON, rev. P. K. CRIMMIN

Sources Hants. RO, Kingsmill MSS · J. Charnock, ed., *Biographia navalis*, 6 (1798), 485–8 · D. Syrett and R. L. DiNardo, *The commissioned sea officers of the Royal Navy, 1660–1815*, rev. edn, Occasional Publications of the Navy RS, 1 (1994) · M. M. Drummond, 'Kingsmill, Robert', HoP, *Commons* · *Naval Chronicle*, 4 (1801), 247 · *Naval Chronicle*, 5 (1801), 189–212 · GEC, *Baronetage* · Burke, *Gen. GB* (1871) · *VCH Hampshire and the Isle of Wight*, 4.254, 327
Archives Hants. RO, corresp. and papers · NMM, letters and binder books, and log of HMS *Elizabeth* | BL, Althorp MSS, Add. MS G. 178 · BL, Bridport MSS, Add. MS 35199 · Sheff. Arch., corresp. with Earl Fitzwilliam · Yale U., Beinecke L., letters to Sir John Duckworth
Likenesses J. Reynolds, portrait, 1764–6, Tate collection · P. Roberts, group portrait, stipple, pubd 1800 (*British admirals*), BM · W. Ridley, stipple (after L. F. Abbott), BM, NPG; repro. in *Naval Chronicle*, 4 · photographs (after portraits), Hants. RO, Kingsmill MSS, 19M61/2914–2916 · portrait, repro. in *Naval Chronicle*, facing p. 189
Wealth at death approx. £6000–£7000: Kingsmill MSS, Hants. RO

Kingsmill, Thomas (*d.* in or after 1605?). *See under* Kingsmill family (*per. c.*1480–1698).

Kingsmill, Sir William (*c.*1526–1593). *See under* Kingsmill family (*per. c.*1480–1698).

Kingsmill, Sir William (*c.*1557–1618). *See under* Kingsmill family (*per. c.*1480–1698).

Kingsmill, Sir William (1613–1661). *See under* Kingsmill family (*per. c.*1480–1698).

Kingsmill, Sir William (*c.*1655–1698). *See under* Kingsmill family (*per. c.*1480–1698).

Kingsnorth, Richard (*d.* 1677), General Baptist minister, was almost certainly born in Kent. No details survive of his birth, parents, or indeed his career before 1640, although it has been suggested that he was either a mercer or a farmer (*DNB*). Indeed, the home where he spent his adult life has been described as a 'farm house' (Ivimey, 2.233).

By 1640 Kingsnorth was apparently living at Spilshill House in Staplehurst, Kent, and seems to have held pastoral responsibilities extending to outlying villages including, according to a local chapel book, Smarden, Frittenden, and Headcorn. In 1640 he was a founding elder of a congregation in Smarden—a gathered church which seems to have met in one or more private houses. This gathering was almost certainly connected with a congregational centre in Staplehurst; its precise denomination at this time is unclear.

In 1644 Kingsnorth was among a number of 'churchmen' before whom Francis Cornwell, a Baptist minister from Marden, preached a controversial and influential visitation sermon in Cranbrook. Won over by Cornwell's doctrine of believers' baptism, Kingsnorth was subsequently baptized by William Jeffery, a Sevenoaks minister who had defended Cornwell in the dispute arising from his sermon. Having undertaken to publish a confutation of Cornwell's views, Christopher Blackwood, vicar of Staplehurst, similarly became converted; he and Kingsnorth then proceeded to gather together a Baptist congregation in the latter's home, Spilshill House. In common with the majority of the congregation, Kingsnorth subscribed to the doctrine of universal atonement, and was thereupon elected and ordained pastor; Blackwood, doctrinally isolated in his belief in particular election, occupied an ancillary position and subsequently left the church. Around 1656 the congregation, by now 100 strong, expanded to adjacent villages including Headcorn and Smarden. In 1672 Kingsnorth and three of his sons were granted licences to preach at private houses in Charing and Frittenden in addition to Staplehurst and Smarden. Kingsnorth remained the church's pastor until his death at Spilshill House in 1677.

Author of *The True Tything of the Gospel Ministers* (1657), Kingsnorth is also credited with the authorship of two other works which are no longer extant. In *The Pearl of Truth, Found out between Two Rocks of Error* (1670) and *Gospel Certainty of Everlasting Felicity* (date unknown), he appears to have consolidated his spiritual and pastoral position by attacking directly the doctrine of particular election.

Nothing is known about Kingsnorth's personal life. We can infer, however, that he married, since five sons followed him into the ministry. In the absence of either information or anecdote about his character, it nevertheless appears that latent doctrinal differences within the church were neutralized by a collective attitude of forbearance under Kingsnorth's leadership. The church continued to expand widely during his lifetime, and it was not until after Kingsnorth's death in 1677 that a definitive secession occurred—a division reflected in the factionalized leadership of his sons. BETH LYNCH

Sources F. Haslewood, *Memorials of Smarden, Kent* (1886) · E. Balley, *Struggles for conscience, or, Religious annals at Staplehurst: a memorial* (1862) · J. Ivimey, *A history of the English Baptists*, 4 vols. (1811–30) · A. Taylor, *The history of the English General Baptists*, 2 vols. (1818) · *CSP dom.*, 1660–85 · W. T. Whitley, ed., *A Baptist bibliography*, 2 vols. (1916–22) · private information (2004) [M. Ballard, Centre for Kentish Studies, Maidstone, Kent]

Kingston. For this title name *see* King, John, first Baron Kingston (*c.*1620–1676); Seton, Alexander, first Viscount Kingston (1621–1691); King, Robert, second Baron Kingston (*c.*1660–1693); King, Robert, second earl of Kingston (1754–1799).

Kingston, Sir Anthony (*c.*1508–1556), landowner and conspirator, was the only son of Sir William Kingston (*d.* 1540) of Elmore and Painswick, Gloucestershire. Since he began to acquire stewardships and other minor offices in Gloucestershire in 1528, Anthony was probably born about 1508, or perhaps a little earlier. Nothing is known of his upbringing, but the conventional education of the son of a substantial gentleman and courtier can be assumed. His first significant preferment was as keeper of Berkeley Castle and steward of the lordship, in 1531, an appointment that must be attributable to his father's influence at court. He was also sheriff of Gloucestershire for the first time in 1533–4, three years before he was appointed to the commission of the peace. In 1536 he secured the relatively minor court position of sergeant of the hawks, and by 1539 had been promoted to esquire of the body. Since the rise of the privy chamber this was no longer an influential position close to the king's person, but it indicated a promising career. He had accompanied the court to Calais as early as 1532, attended Prince Edward's baptism in 1537, and assisted at the reception of Anne of Cleves in 1540. Apart from his father's influence, part of the secret of his success seems to have been that he was a skilled jouster, a quality that always appealed to Henry, even after he had given up the lists himself. In 1536 he raised 100 of his own men against the Pilgrimage of Grace, and was placed in command of the whole Gloucestershire contingent, numbering about 1000. He is alleged to have been involved in a skirmish at Louth in October 1536, but there was no serious fighting, and this experience can hardly count as a campaign. He served in France in 1544, along with many other members of the royal household, but was in no sense a professional soldier.

Kingston was knighted on 2 May 1540, which was an acknowledgement of his service at court rather than in the field, and probably a recognition of his standing in Gloucestershire; he sat in the Commons for the county in 1539, 1542, and 1545. His father died on 14 September 1540, and Sir Anthony succeeded to his substantial estates. By 1546 he was *custos rotulorum* and thereafter he served on numerous local commissions, for musters, chantries, and church goods. He sympathized with the protestant policies adopted after 1547. In 1549 he served as provost marshal under Lord Russell in the suppression of the southwestern rebellion, a position in which he behaved with considerable brutality, and in 1551 became a member of the council in the marches of Wales. He sat again in the Commons for Gloucestershire in 1547 and in March 1553. He received a number of minor grants of monastic land, and was sheriff for a second time in 1550–51, and also a vice-admiral.

Kingston married twice. His first wife was Dorothy, the daughter of Robert Harpur. As he had married her before October 1524, this match had probably been arranged by his father to cement a connection with the Staffords, of whom Harpur had been a retainer. The marriage was not a success, and by 1533 Anthony was petitioning Cranmer to arrange a divorce. However, subjects did not have the benefit of the king's options, and he was unsuccessful. Within two years Dorothy was dead, but if there were any suspicious circumstances, they were never alluded to. His second wife, whom he had married by 1537, was Mary, daughter of Sir John Gainsford of Crowhurst, Surrey, and widow of Sir William Courtenay (*d.* 1535) of Powderham, Devon. Again a business arrangement may be suspected, and the marriage was a personal failure. By 1552 Kingston was estranged from his wife, and openly keeping a mistress. When John Hooper, the bishop of Gloucester, upbraided him for this adultery, he abused the bishop and struck him a blow, an offence for which he was fined the large sum of £500.

When Edward VI died in July 1553, Kingston was ordered, like many others, to raise men to support Jane Grey's claim. He did not do so, but whether because of lack of sympathy or shortness of time is not apparent. He was regarded with suspicion by Mary's council, and in spite of his position did not sit in the parliaments of October 1553, March 1554, or November 1554. However, in February 1555 he was named to the commission that was established to carry out the death sentence against Hooper for heresy. According to Foxe, Sir Anthony claimed that the bishop had converted him from his sins: 'God did appoynt you to call me beyng a lost child' (Foxe, 1509), presumably as a result of their clash in 1552. He took a tearful farewell of Hooper, but felt constrained to do his duty as a commissioner, and perhaps as a result resumed his county seat in parliament in October 1555, a session for which he was also named knight marshal.

There Kingston played a leading role in frustrating the council's attempt to confiscate the property of the religious exiles, forcing a division at a favourable moment by locking the doors of the house. For this he was briefly in the Tower after the session closed, but was released upon his humble submission. At the same time, however, he was deeply involved in a conspiracy initiated by Henry

Dudley and supported by the French ambassador, to launch an invasion by English exiles from France, backed by French arms and money. His plan appears to have been to raise a force in the south-west to support the invasion, and one of the ambassador's agents wrote that he could 'assuredly raise more than six thousand men in his district' (Harbison, 280). This was probably a major exaggeration, but it was never put to the test. The plot was broken up in February and March 1556. Kingston was arrested at the beginning of April, and questioned in Gloucestershire on the 8th and 9th. There was little hard evidence against him, but it was decided to bring him to London. He died on the way, at Cirencester, on 14 April 1556. There is no reason to suppose that the causes were other than natural. He had settled part of his estate on his illegitimate sons, Anthony and Edmund, by a deed of feoffment in 1547, and seems to have left no will. His estranged wife appears to have predeceased him, because, after an inquisition post mortem in October 1556, the residue of his estate passed to a niece, Frances, the wife of Sir Henry Jerningham.

DAVID LOADES

Sources HoP, Commons, 1509–58, 2.468–70 · CSP dom., 1547–58 · E. H. Harbison, *Rival ambassadors at the court of Queen Mary* (1940) · F. Rose-Troup, *The western rebellion of 1549* (1913) · CPR, 1547–53 · C. Wriothesley, *A chronicle of England during the reigns of the Tudors from AD 1485 to 1559*, ed. W. D. Hamilton, 2 vols., CS, new ser., 11, 20 (1875–7) · J. G. Nichols, ed., *The chronicle of Queen Jane, and of two years of Queen Mary*, CS, old ser., 48 (1850) · D. M. Loades, *Two Tudor conspiracies* (1965) · A. L. Rowse, *Tudor Cornwall: portrait of a society* (1941) · J. Foxe, *Actes and monuments*, 4th edn, 2 vols. (1583)
Archives Archives du Ministère des Affaires Étrangères, Paris

Kingston, Charles Cameron (1850–1908), politician in Australia, was born in Grote Street, Adelaide, South Australia, on 22 October 1850, the youngest of six children (five of whom survived infancy) of Sir George Strickland Kingston (1807–1880), architect and civil engineer, and his wife, Ludovina daSilva, *née* Cameron (1824–1851). His father arrived in South Australia in 1836 to be deputy surveyor-general of the newly founded colony; in 1857, following the granting of self-government, he became South Australia's first speaker, a position he held until his death in November 1880. His mother was born in Van Diemen's Land (now Tasmania), the daughter of Colonel Charles Cameron, a distinguished, highly respected soldier who was commandant at Port Dalrymple, and his second wife, Ludovina Rosa daSilva, a member of a noble Portuguese family. Charles Kingston was just twelve months old when his mother died in October 1851.

Kingston was educated at the Adelaide Educational Institution which was run by John Lorenzo Young. According to Young, Kingston was the most gifted student he ever taught. Kingston, who was big for his age and very strong, was a mischievous bully who was given to practical joking. He was not beyond making his schoolmaster the butt of these jokes.

When he was seventeen, Kingston was articled to Samuel James Way, who would go on to become South Australia's chief justice, lieutenant-governor, and chancellor of Adelaide University. Kingston's admission to the bar in March 1873 was not without incident, for Bartholomew

Joseph McCarthy turned up at the supreme court to lodge an objection, claiming that Kingston had seduced his young sister Lucy May McCarthy (d. 1919) and was not a fit candidate. Three months later Kingston and Lucy eloped and were married on 25 June 1873 in St George's Church of England, Woodforde. Kingston continued to work in Way's office until Way was appointed chief justice in 1876. He then went into business on his own.

Kingston was never a man to do things by halves. He worked hard, his business flourished, and he gained a reputation for fighting for the less fortunate. Three months after his father's death, in March 1881, he announced his intention to stand for the strong working-class house of assembly seat of West Adelaide. At his public meeting he stressed his friendship for the working man, criticized the taxation system which favoured the wealthy, and indicated his opposition to Chinese immigration. To a question on free trade versus protection he replied that, in his opinion, free trade would only work when it was adopted by the entire world and South Australia had a much larger population 'or, better still, when there was a united Australia numbering many millions of inhabitants' (*Adelaide Register*, 25 March 1881). Clearly, at this early stage, he favoured Australian federation. He never wavered from this conviction.

A Kingston contemporary described him as 'Virile and Great, but Faulty'. The assessment was accurate. As a politician he proved himself to be intelligent, committed, and hard-working. He certainly did not gain financially from his position as he neglected his legal practice in favour of politics. Paradoxically, he was at once kind-hearted and a bully with a short fuse and a vicious tongue. He cared nothing for society's rules and had no religion. His private life was far from moral and at times his behaviour was quite eccentric. By mid-1884, when he was appointed attorney-general to John Colton's government (June 1884–June 1885), his ability had been noted and he had gained a well-deserved reputation as an expert parliamentary draftsman. Late in 1885 this reputation was tarnished when he was named as co-respondent in a divorce case brought by Richard Watson against his wife, Elizabeth. This was not Kingston's only extramarital affair but the long-suffering Lucy, herself childless, remained a loyal wife and even adopted Mrs Watson's son, Kevin, fathered by Kingston. The young man died of tuberculosis in 1902 at the age of eighteen.

In spite of the scandal Kingston was re-elected for West Adelaide in 1887 and named as attorney-general in the government of Thomas Playford (June 1887–June 1889). When Playford was replaced by John Colton, Kingston played a leading, often vitriolic, role in opposition. Early in 1892 he accepted the position of chief secretary in Playford's second ministry. During Playford's absence overseas he was acting premier. In late 1892 Kingston challenged a political opponent, Richard Chaffey Baker, to a duel and was bound over to keep the peace for twelve months. The order still had six months to run when, in June 1893, Kingston became South Australia's premier.

With the support of the newly formed Labor Party

Kingston remained in power for a then record six years (June 1893–December 1899). He introduced much progressive legislation—votes for women, conciliation and arbitration legislation, trade and tariff reforms, and the floating of the State Bank of South Australia. But his aggressive manner and vicious tongue caused difficulties. The dispute at the Adelaide Hospital, which dragged on for six years, divided the community and damaged health care and the training of medical students. He engaged in wars of words with fellow premiers and noted South Australians. On two occasions he was attacked in the street, once with a horsewhip, once with a stick, by individuals who took exception to his arrogance. He resigned from the house of assembly on 7 February 1900 and in late September won the Upper house seat of Central District at a by-election. He resigned in December to join the federal parliament. On a visit to London for Queen Victoria's diamond jubilee in 1897, Kingston was sworn of the privy council and given an honorary doctor of laws degree by Oxford University. He refused a knighthood.

Kingston's commitment to Australian unity was second to none and he was a delegate to all but one of the conferences on federation. In 1891 he joined Edmund Barton, Inglis Clark, and Samuel Griffith to prepare a draft federal constitution. He was president of the Adelaide session of the Federation Convention (March 1897) and of subsequent sessions in Sydney (September) and Melbourne (February–March 1898). He represented South Australia in London for the proclamation of the Commonwealth Bill and, with Barton and Alfred Deakin, led a spirited battle against the secretary of state for colonies, Joseph Chamberlain, who attempted to alter the federation document.

When the commonwealth of Australia came into being on 1 January 1901, Prime Minister Barton appointed Kingston minister of trade and customs. In this capacity he introduced the Customs Machinery Bill which was not universally popular. The hostility rebounded on Kingston but he ruthlessly enforced its provisions. Kingston was widely tipped to be Australia's second prime minister but on 13 July 1903 he resigned his portfolio ostensibly because he disagreed with sections of the Conciliation and Arbitration Bill. In fact his health had deteriorated to such an extent that he was no longer well enough to carry out his ministerial duties. He remained a member of parliament but after the beginning of 1904 was seldom seen in the House. He died in his rooms at Eagle Chambers, King William Street, Adelaide, on 11 May 1908 of a cerebral thrombosis. Following a state funeral his remains were interred on 13 May in the Kingston family vault in the Adelaide cemetery. Kingston, who had neglected his private affairs, left a net estate of just £50. MARGARET GLASS

Sources M. Glass, *Charles Cameron Kingston* (1997) · L. F. Crisp, *Federation fathers*, ed. J. Hart (1990) · A. Deakin, *The federal story: the inner history of the federal cause*, ed. H. Brookes (1944) · A. Deakin, *Federated Australia* (1968) · NL Aus., Barton MSS · NL Aus., Deakin MSS · State Library of South Australia, Adelaide, Mortlock Library of South Australiana, Bonython MSS · MSS, 1893–1900, South Australia's premier's department · Parliamentary Debates, 1881–1900, government of South Australia · Parliamentary Debates, 1901–8, commonwealth of Australia · official reports, National Australasian Convention debates · *South Australian Register* (1873–1908) · *South Australian Advertiser* (1873–1908)

Archives Mortlock Library, Adelaide, Bonython MSS · NL Aus., Barton MSS · NL Aus., Deakin MSS · NL Aus., Sumon MSS

Likenesses A. Drury, statue, Victoria Square, Adelaide, Australia · A. Patterson, portrait, Parliament House, Canberra, Australia · bust, Parliament House, Adelaide, Australia

Wealth at death £50 after debts paid: letter written 10 Aug 1908 by Frederick Holder to prime minister Alfred Deakin, asking for financial help for Mrs Kingston, Deakin MSS, NL Aus.

Kingston, Gertrude [*real name* Gertrude Angela Kohnstamm] (1862–1937), actress, was born at Durham House, Highbury New Park, Islington, London, on 24 September 1862, the daughter of Heiman Kohnstamm, merchant, and his wife, Teresina, *née* Friedmann. Edwin Max Kohnstamm (later Konstam; 1870–1956), a county court judge, was her brother. She was educated at home for the first years of her life, and travelled widely with her mother and governess. When her artistic talents became obvious, she was sent abroad to study painting in Berlin and Paris, under Carolus-Duran, Henner, and Goussot, afterwards publishing three illustrated books. She began her stage career as an amateur while still a child, imitating popular actors such as Irving and Berhardt. At the age of fifteen she was chosen by W. S. Gilbert to play the lead in an amateur production of his *Broken Hearts*. However, painting remained her first love, and it was not until her marriage that she considered pursuing a career as an actress.

On 31 July 1889, in the parish of St George, Hanover Square, she married George Silver (1858/9–1899), a captain in the East Surrey regiment and the son of James Silver of the Madras civil service. She decided to take to the stage as a means of supporting them both, Silver's income being insufficient. At the recommendation of Ellen Terry she became a pupil of Miss Sarah Thorne at Margate, adopting the name Kingston for stage purposes, and appearing in a number of roles including Ophelia in *Hamlet* and Emilia in *Othello*. Shortly afterwards she was invited by Beerbohm Tree to appear as Mrs Harkaway in *Partners*, although she later regretted accepting the role, feeling that she was unable to return to tragic acting, having become typecast as 'clever' at comedy. Yet after this first appearance she achieved considerable success on the London stage. She became well known and in demand for a variety of roles, including that of Clara Dexter in *The Woodbarrow*, which she also produced, and that of Mrs Graves in *A Matchmaker*, which she co-wrote with Clotilde Graves and which was criticized for its equation of marriage with prostitution.

In 1899 Kingston was widowed, her husband dying of heart failure just as war broke out in South Africa. By then she was sufficiently influential to raise subscriptions for the actors' and actresses' hospital hut to be set up in Cape Town for soldiers fighting in the Second South African War. In her autobiography she wrote of her regret that she was dissuaded from volunteering to nurse there herself, feeling that this would have been a valuable opportunity to gain medical training to be put to use in the First World

War. However, several accounts of her life suggest that she did serve there, and was mentioned in dispatches. For the next ten years she remained active on the stage, most notably appearing in Euripides' *The Trojan Women* as Helen, at the suggestion of George Bernard Shaw. Many felt that this was her finest performance.

In 1910 Kingston became the lessee of the Little Theatre in the Adelphi, London, which was built largely to her specification and was the first British theatre to adopt certain lighting techniques, including 'dimmer' lights, which had been invented in the United States. Her season at the Little was inspired by the Royal Court's introduction of highbrow and classical drama to a commercial audience, and thus opened with Aristophanes' *Lysistrata*, in which she played the title role. Lillah Macarthy took over the management of the Little Theatre in 1911, yet in 1912 Kingston returned to play Madame Arcadina in *The Seagull*. Later that year she appeared as Lady Cecily Waynflete in *Captain Brassbound's Conversion*. She then took the leading role in the opening run of *Queen Catherine*; this part was written for her by George Bernard Shaw, who regarded her as 'the only Queen who could do justice to our combined talents' (Shaw, 901).

Throughout much of the First World War Kingston was in the United States, speaking about the war effort in Britain and appearing in Boston in a triple bill consisting of *Queen Catherine* and two other Shaw plays. She also appeared, in 1916, as Ermyntrude in *The Inca of Perusalem* with the Pioneer Players, the suffragist theatre company. Kingston had long been active as a speaker within the suffrage movement, having realized the injustice of her own position as a voteless taxpayer. During the war she also experienced the recurrence of an interest in spiritualism which she had acquired after an experiment in 1905. She felt that she was able to communicate with those who had been killed, and to receive messages from them for their loved ones. Later in life, she also gained comfort from spiritualist communication with her late sister, and through the same means received messages from Oscar Wilde.

After the war Kingston continued to act, and was also much in demand as a public speaker for the Conservative Party, even considering standing for parliament herself in 1924. She also taught public speaking, and wrote numerous articles on a wide range of subjects. In 1927 an exhibition of her work in lacquer was staged in New York, her technique becoming known as Kingston lacquer, and the same year she produced and appeared in *Nevertheless* in London. Her final performance was as Queen Elizabeth in *When Essex Died* in 1932. She died at the Empire Nursing Home, Vincent Square, Westminster, London, on 7 November 1937. Her own assessment of her career, that it was 'a tale of high endeavour and of short results; of big beginnings and little ends; of vital movements railroaded by signals of "blocked line"' (Kingston, 9) seems modest when set against the record of her achievements in acting, producing, art, politics, and journalism.

KATE STEEDMAN

Sources G. Kingston, *Curtsey while you're thinking* (1937) · G. B. Shaw, preface, *Queen Catherine* (1972) · *Who was who in the theatre,* *1912–1976*, 4 vols. (1978) · *The Times* (9 Nov 1937) · *WWW* · K. Powell, *Women and Victorian theatre* (1997) · K. Cockin, *Women and the theatre in the age of suffrage: the Pioneer Players, 1911–25* (2000) · b. cert. · m. cert. · d. cert. · *CGPLA Eng. & Wales* (1938)

Likenesses J. Sargent, portrait, repro. in Kingston, *Curtsey while you're thinking* · Yevonde, photograph, repro. in Kingston, *Curtsey while you're thinking*

Wealth at death £9802 9s. 6d.: probate, 1938, *CGPLA Eng. & Wales*

Kingston, Richard (b. *c*.1635, d. 1710?), political writer, was, according to his own statements, an MA graduate from an unknown university, and was ordained by the bishop of Galloway on 17 July 1662 at Westminster. In 1665 he became minister at St James's, Clerkenwell, and was resident there during the plague, though he had resigned this preferment by 17 September 1667. Kingston is thought to have been married first to Elizabeth Webb at St James's, Clerkenwell, on 28 January 1668; after separating from his first wife, in 1671 he married a daughter of the rector of Boughton, about whom no further details are known. In 1699 he claimed to be the father of nine children, though details of parentage are unknown. After his move from Clerkenwell Kingston may have been curate of Irthlingborough in Northamptonshire from about 1669 through the patronage of the earl of Banbury. In 1678 he received the living of Henbury in Gloucestershire, and on 6 February 1682 was made chaplain-in-ordinary to Charles II. He asserts that a prebend and a rectory were added to Henbury, and in 1688 he seems to have been rector of Raydon in Suffolk. Kingston also states that he suffered for preaching against Roman Catholics. He remained at Henbury, where he had a small estate, until the revolution of 1688, when he sold his property and moved to London.

In the 1690s Kingston became a trusted and valued government spy, corresponding frequently with Lord Nottingham and Sir William Trumbull. He passed on information about Jacobite activities, noting journeys and correspondence between Jacobites in England and France, and the plans of the Jacobite press in London. He was awarded a government pension that fell into arrears and he suffered extreme poverty. A petition from him dated 1699 states that £600 was due to him, that he had assisted as a witness at the conviction of three traitors, had brought £1225 into the Treasury by the seizure of French silks, and that he had printed thirteen books on behalf of the government at his own expense.

In his *Modest Answer to Captain Smith's Immodest Memorial of Secret Service* (1700) Kingston attacked Matthew Smith, a notorious rogue and spy, who had just published his *Memoirs of Secret Service* (1699), and a violent controversy ensued. Kingston attributed Smith's work to the satirist Tom Brown (1663–1704), whom he described as 'a rank prostituted Jacobite' (*Memoirs of Secret Service*, 7). Smith responded by charging Kingston with having forged his letters of orders and with various immoral activities. Kingston countered these allegations in a rejoinder by publishing an account of his life, *Impudence, Lying and Forgery Detected and Chastiz'd* (1700), with letters of support and testimonials and a certificate signed by one Thomas Beesly, asserting that he had been ordained with Kingston. However, his testimony was not wholly plausible on account of there being a discrepancy over the name of the ordaining bishop, and the fact that by 1700 Beesly had been dead for three years.

Kingston also intervened in the controversy which raged in 1707–9 about the so-called French Prophets, a millenarian group, complaining in his book *Enthusiastic Imposters No Divinely Inspired Prophets* that, like hell, the French Prophets sect refused no one. In 1707 his attack on John Freind's vindication of the earl of Peterborough's conduct in Spain appeared, and he was promptly arrested by an order of the House of Lords. He was, however, released on 19 January 1708, and the attorney-general was instructed to prosecute him. Kingston published three sermons, one on the plague, and several other religious and political works. He may have been the Richard Kingston 'late of Chelsea College', who died in 1710 (PRO, PROB 6/86).

W. A. J. ARCHBOLD, *rev.* M. E. CLAYTON

Sources *Report on the manuscripts of the marquis of Downshire*, 6 vols. in 7, HMC, 75 (1924–95), vol. 1 · *Report on the manuscripts of Allan George George Finch*, 5 vols., HMC, 71 (1913–2003), vol. 4 · P. A. Hopkins, 'Sham plots and real plots in the 1690s', *Ideology and conspiracy: aspects of Jacobitism, 1689–1759*, ed. E. Cruickshanks (1982), 89–110 · W. J. Pinks, *The history of Clerkenwell*, ed. E. J. Wood (1865) · H. Schwartz, *The French prophets: the history of a millenarian group in eighteenth-century England* (1980)
Archives BL, corresp. with Sir William Trumbull · Leics. RO, letters to Lord Nottingham
Likenesses line engraving, 1665, BM; repro. in R. Kingston, *Pillulae Pestilentiales, or, A spiritual receipt for cure of the plague* (1665)

Kingston, Sir William (*c.*1476–1540), courtier and administrator, is of uncertain origins, but was probably a member of a Gloucestershire family related to the barons Berkeley of Berkeley Castle; he also had some connection with the third duke of Buckingham. His marriages are uncertain as well: his first two wives (the order is unclear) were Anne, widow of Sir John Guise (*d.* 1501), and Elizabeth (surname unknown). By 1534 he had wed Mary, daughter of Richard Scrope and widow of Edward Jerningham (*d.* 1515) of Somerleighton, Suffolk. He had one son, Anthony *Kingston, and one or two daughters. A brother, George, was left £40 in Sir William's will.

William's career as a courtier probably began in his early twenties. He was a yeoman of the chamber from 1497 to 1509 and was present at Henry VII's funeral as a gentleman usher. He served in Henry VIII's early military campaigns: in 1511 he received ordnance for the army and in 1512 he was named under-marshal. He travelled to Spain with Dr William Knight but had to report that their embassy to Charles V was not going well and that the English forces led by Thomas Grey, second marquess of Dorset, were disheartened. At the end of the year he was paid for his expenses after returning to England with a small entourage. In 1513 he fought at Flodden on 9 September, was knighted in October, and received conduct money for his men when the army was disbanded in November.

In 1510 Kingston and Arthur Plantagenet, Viscount Lisle, were licensed to export 2000 woollen kerseys without paying duty. A JP for Gloucestershire since 1506, in 1514 he was named one of the king's sewers with a stipend of 40

marks a year and was also pricked sheriff of Gloucestershire, in which capacity he was instructed to assist in apprehending heretics and Lollards. During these years he often took part in jousts, tournaments, and other courtly entertainments, in some of which the king himself participated. He was also sufficiently in favour with Cardinal Wolsey to be chosen one of the four 'knights of the body in the privy chamber', with a salary of £100, when in May 1519 Henry was persuaded to dismiss his younger 'minions' and replace them with more sober middle-aged knights. The minions were soon back at court, but Kingston's career did not suffer. Subsequent memoranda frequently list him among the king's attendants and as keeper of jewels and plate. In 1521 he was named one of the king's carvers.

On 20 April 1520 the English ambassador Sir Richard Wingfield reported from Blois how the three-year-old dauphin had taken 'a marvellous pleasure in young Kyngston, whom, after he had seen once, he called him *beau fils*' (*LP Henry VIII*, vol. 3, pt 1, no. 752). Probably this was Sir William's son, Anthony, who was then about twelve; it is not recorded whether Sir William was present, but he certainly attended Henry VIII at the Field of Cloth of Gold in June and at his meeting with Charles V in July. Evidently in appreciation of his services, the king gave him a costly bay horse with cut ears, purchased from a French courtier.

Kingston was a member of the grand jury which indicted the third duke of Buckingham for treason in 1521 and subsequently profited from the duke's fall; Henry made him steward and bailiff of Buckingham's possessions in Gloucestershire as well as constable of Thornbury Castle and master of all the hunts in the county. At about the same time Kingston, who together with several other courtiers had lodgings in the Blackfriars, was granted three tenements with shops, cellars, and gardens in the parish of St Martin near Ludgate, to be held for the annual rent of a red rose.

In 1521 Henry VIII wished Kingston to attend him regularly in the privy chamber, as he had few other companions. Nevertheless in the following year he was charged with raising 300 'pioneers' in the Forest of Dean for service in France, and in 1523 he served in the army sent into Scotland, leading thirty men in the rearguard during a short campaign in which the earl of Surrey captured and burnt Kelso. Later in the year he left to serve in France under the duke of Suffolk, to Surrey's regret.

Kingston was a knight of the shire for Gloucestershire in the parliaments of 1529 and 1536. Between sessions he accompanied the king and Anne Boleyn to Calais in October 1532. Since he was a friend of the lord deputy, Viscount Lisle, he took a close interest in affairs there. In 1536 he wrote to Lisle concerning a book of ordinances for Calais that would shortly pass the Commons, 'but at the reading there was one that would have had it committed (as the manner is)', thereby providing interesting evidence for the growing use of parliamentary committees; Kingston assured Lisle that it would shortly pass and was 'a good book' (*LP Henry VIII*, vol. 10, no. 336). In the parliament of 1536 Kingston frequently acted as a liaison between the two houses. He spoke on the conservative side in the debate about the Act of Six Articles in 1539, rebuking the position taken on the eucharist by the evangelical Thomas Broke and even saying that if Broke repeated his arguments before the council after the act had passed, 'I will bring a fagot to help to burn you withal' (*Acts and Monuments*, 5.504–5). Sir Nicholas Hare, the speaker, said that he found Kingston's remarks more offensive than Broke's.

As constable of the Tower from 28 May 1524 Kingston was responsible for the custody of a number of state prisoners. In November 1529 he was sent from London to Yorkshire to take charge of Wolsey and, according to the cardinal's biographer George Cavendish, treated his prisoner with consideration. He had several conversations with the dying minister, in one of which the latter advised him how to deal with the king if he ever became a privy councillor. Kingston, who subsequently told Henry how his mission had fared, was a councillor by 1533. In 1536 he similarly treated Anne Boleyn with respect during her imprisonment in the Tower, assuring her that she would be taken to the royal lodgings she had occupied before her coronation rather than to a dungeon, as she feared. It is possible, however, that his reports were the basis for some of the charges against Anne at her trial. His wife Mary was one of the queen's attendants before her execution, to which Kingston escorted her. In 1540 it was his duty to inform Thomas Cromwell of the charges against him, and presumably to carry the fallen minister's response to the king.

During the last years of his life Kingston received additional offices and lands. In 1539 he was named comptroller of the king's household and was installed as a knight of the Garter. He profited from the dissolution of the monasteries, in March 1537 receiving the site and possessions of the Cistercian abbey of Flaxley, Gloucestershire. He was granted a number of wardships, including that of Edmund Jerningham, his wife's son from her first marriage. After Cromwell's fall he acquired, for £1000, the manors of Painswick and Morton Valence, both in Gloucestershire, which Cromwell had purchased from the Lisles for £1400.

Kingston died at Painswick on 14 September 1540 and was buried there. In his will, drawn up on 26 June 1539, he made a traditional bequest of his soul to God, the Virgin, and the heavenly host. Among numerous bequests of money, plate, and clothes, he left to his son and heir, Anthony, six great silver-gilt bowls given him by the king of France. His wife, William Fitzwilliam, earl of Southampton, and Sir Anthony Browne were named as his executors.   STANFORD LEHMBERG

Sources LP Henry VIII, vols. 1–16 · HoP, Commons, 1509–58, 2.470–71 · M. St C. Byrne, ed., *The Lisle letters*, 6 vols. (1981) · S. Lehmberg, *The Reformation Parliament, 1529–1536* (1970) · S. Lehmberg, *The later parliaments of Henry VIII, 1539–1547* (1977) · E. W. Ives, *Anne Boleyn* (1986) · R. M. Warnicke, *The rise and fall of Anne Boleyn* (1989) · *The acts and monuments of John Foxe*, ed. S. R. Cattley, 8 vols. (1837–41) · G. Cavendish, 'Life and death of Cardinal Wolsey', *Two early Tudor lives*, ed. R. S. Sylvester and D. P. Harding (1962) · will, PRO, PROB 11/28, fols. 252r–252v · DNB · D. Starkey, *The reign of Henry VIII: personalities and politics* (1985)
Archives PRO, state papers, Henry VIII · PRO, Lisle letters
Wealth at death paid £1000 for Painswick and Morton Valence, Gloucestershire; property in London

Kingston, William Henry Giles (1814–1880), children's writer, born in Harley Street, London, on 28 February 1814, was eldest son of Lucy Henry Kingston and Frances Sophia Rooke. His maternal grandfather was Sir Giles *Rooke, justice of the common pleas. He was educated at Eagle House, Hammersmith, Middlesex, and by private tutors. As a child he frequently travelled to the family residence in Portugal, thereby developing a lifelong affection for the sea. Unable to follow a career in the navy, he entered his father's wine business in Oporto in 1833, and soon began writing newspaper articles on Portugal, which were translated into Portuguese. He was instrumental in the successful conclusion of the 1842 trade treaty with Portugal, for which he was awarded the honour of knight of the military order of Christ and a pension from the queen of Portugal.

Kingston's first book, *The Circassian Chief*, was published in 1843, and while still living in Oporto he wrote *The Prime Minister* (1845), a historical novel, and *Lusitanian Sketches* (1845), descriptions of travels in Portugal. After settling in England, he interested himself in the emigration movement. He became organizing secretary of the Colonisation Society, lectured on colonization in 1849, and visited the western highlands on behalf of the emigration commissioners. He edited two journals: *The Colonist* (1844), and the *Colonial Magazine and East India Review* (1849–52), as well as writing a number of pamphlets on emigration and emigrants' welfare. These included *Some Suggestions for a System of General Emigration* (1848); *The Emigrant Voyagers' Manual* (1850), and *How to Emigrate, or, The British Colonists: a Tale* (1850). A man of strong evangelical convictions, he became a founding member and organizing secretary of the Society for Promoting Missions to Seamen. He afterwards took an active part in the volunteer movement, recalling some of his experiences in *Our Soldiers* (1863).

From 1850 Kingston's chief occupation was writing books for boys, and editing boys' annuals and weekly periodicals. His best-known stories, are: *Peter the Whaler* (1851); *The Three Midshipmen* (1873); and its sequels *The Three Lieutenants* (1875), *The Three Commanders* (1876), and *The Three Admirals* (1878). In all, he wrote over 130 stories for boys, many of which had a nautical theme, as for example, *Blue Jackets* (1854), *The Cruise of the Frolic* (1860), and *Our Sailors* (1863), which were based on his own cruising and yachting experiences.

Kingston travelled widely and described his experiences in *My Travels in Many Lands* (1862), *The Western World* (1874), and *A Yacht Voyage Round England* (1879). Following his marriage in 1853 to Agnes Kinloch (d. 1913), his honeymoon was spent in Canada. *Western Wanderings, or, A Pleasure Tour in Canada* (1856) recounts his journey. He wrote popular records of travel and adventure in America, Africa, India, and Australia; a biography of Captain Cook; and a history of the navy. He also wrote many historical tales dealing with almost all periods and countries, from *Eldol the Druid* (1874) and *Jovinian: a Tale of Early Papal Rome* (1877) onwards, and undertook some popular historical compilations like *Half-Hours with the Kings and Queens of England* (1876). At the time his stories were very popular; his tales were quite innocuous, but most of them proved ephemeral. In addition to writing books, Kingston founded two boys' periodicals: *Kingston's Magazine for Boys* (1859–62) and *Union Jack*, which he started only a few months before his death in 1880. The former was a didactic journal full of instructional articles, most of which were written by Kingston himself. It also contained a number of translations, and although these bore Kingston's name, they were actually the work of his wife, Agnes, a competent linguist. She translated *The Swiss Family Robinson* from the German and a number of separately published stories by Jules Verne, all of which cite her husband as the translator.

Despite his prolific literary output of some five or six books a year, Kingston suffered serious financial difficulties with a family of eight children to support. In 1868 he applied for, and was awarded, grants of £50 and £100, from the Royal Literary Fund. His poor health and reduced circumstances caused him to become a recluse in later life. Realizing he had not long to live, he wrote a touching valedictory letter to *Union Jack* readers on 2 August 1880. He died three days later at his home, Stormont Lodge, 3 Brondesbury Park Villas, Willesden Lane, London.

J. A. HAMILTON, *rev.* DIANA DIXON

Sources M. R. Kingsford, *The life, work and influence of William Henry Giles Kingston* (1947) · *Boy's Own Paper* (11 Sept 1880), 796–7 · *The Times* (10 Aug 1880), 10 · W. H. G. Kingston, introduction, in W. H. G. Kingston, *James Braithwaite, the supercargo* (1882), v–ix · *Union Jack* (25 Aug 1880) · *The Athenaeum* (14 Aug 1880), 211–12 · *CGPLA Eng. & Wales* (1880) · *The Times* (6 Aug 1853)
Archives Essex RO, corresp. with G. D. Warburton
Likenesses photograph, repro. in Kingsford, *Life, work and influence* · photograph, repro. in Kingston, *James Braithwaite* · photograph, repro. in *Boy's Own Paper*
Wealth at death under £4000: probate, 18 Sept 1880, *CGPLA Eng. & Wales*

Kingston upon Hull. For this title name *see* Pierrepont, Robert, first earl of Kingston upon Hull (1584–1643); Pierrepont, Evelyn, first duke of Kingston upon Hull (*bap.* 1667, *d.* 1726); Pierrepont, Evelyn, second duke of Kingston upon Hull (1712–1773); Chudleigh, Elizabeth [Elizabeth Pierrepont, duchess of Kingston upon Hull] (*c.*1720–1788).

Kinloch. For this title name *see* Penney, William, Lord Kinloch (1801–1872).

Kinloch, George, of Kinloch (1775–1833), politician, was born on 30 April 1775 in Dundee, the younger son (there were no daughters) of Captain George Oliphant Kinloch of the 53rd regiment of foot, and his wife, Anne, daughter of Colonel John Balneavis. Captain Kinloch had inherited the estate of Kinloch in Strathmore from his younger brother, John, who had purchased it from the proceeds of a fortune made as a sugar planter in Jamaica, and had died in 1770. Captain Kinloch himself died in 1775 and his widow in 1782.

George Kinloch of Kinloch (1775–1833), by William Sharp (after Miss M. Saunders)

John, their elder son, was a permanent invalid, and for the sake of his health the boys were sent abroad to France and Italy. John died in Nice in 1789, and George returned to Scotland in 1791. He studied at Edinburgh University during 1791–2 but did not graduate. He became laird of the Kinloch estate on his twenty-first birthday in 1796. In the same year he married his cousin Helen, daughter of John and Joanna Smyth, and between 1797 and 1805 they had six daughters and two sons.

In 1797, as part of his duties as a young laird, Kinloch was appointed to command the Coupar Angus company of the volunteers, territorials who were recruited to meet the danger of a possible French invasion, but in Scotland confined their activities to suppressing riots aroused by the Militia Acts and the press-gangs. Eleven years later, in 1808, Kinloch decided that he was opposed to the maintenance of a standing army in time of peace and resigned his commission. In 1812 he attacked the war in Spain: 'we have been fighting for a worthless king, an insolent nobility and a useless clergy'. In addition to his burgeoning radicalism, he was a progressive landlord, and the only landlord of consequence in Scotland who supported the radical reform movement in the early nineteenth century. He took his part in local politics as a JP and was active in working for the development of Dundee harbour as a member of the Dundee Harbour Board. In 1817 he spoke in Dundee in support of annual parliaments and universal suffrage.

As a result of the Peterloo massacre in Manchester in August 1819, Kinloch, who from his youth in France had held liberal views, became actively opposed to the oppressive measures enforced by the authorities acting under the orders of the tory government. He agreed to preside over a public meeting of the people of Dundee to be held on 10 November 1819 to protest against 'the unprovoked, cruel and cowardly attack made on the people of Manchester' and 'to suggest the means most likely to lead to a reform of abuses'. The meeting was held as advertised and Kinloch addressed it in a wordy speech in which, after pleading with his audience to keep the peace, he criticized the government for excessive taxation, and declaimed: 'In short, the whole of our misfortune as a nation, the whole of our misery, the whole of our distress, can be clearly traced to the circumstances of the people being deprived of their share of the British Constitution by not having a voice in the election of persons to represent them in the House of Commons.' The speech was reported in the *Dundee Advertiser*.

Two weeks after the meeting Kinloch was astounded to be confronted with a warrant for his arrest on a charge of sedition, issued on the authority of the Home Office in London. He was allowed bail, but after consulting his lawyers, Henry Cockburn and Francis Jeffrey, he was convinced that it was highly probable that he would be convicted for sedition and sent to Botany Bay. He decided that he had no alternative but to flee abroad. He reached Paris on 24 December, two days after having been declared an outlaw in the High Court.

For the next three years (1820–22) Kinloch lived in exile in France. In January 1822 Robert Peel became home secretary and in October the leader of the Peterloo riot was released from prison. Hoping that, in the changed climate of opinion in England, he would soon be granted a pardon, Kinloch returned secretly to London, where for some time he remained under cover until early in 1823, when he made a clandestine return to Scotland. Then, in May 1823, the hoped-for pardon arrived and he was able to resume a normal life at Kinloch.

Dundee was one of the new constituencies created by the 1832 Reform Act. Kinloch stood as the whig candidate in the election that followed, and in December of that year was elected the first MP for the borough. He took his seat in the house in February 1833, but did not enjoy his position for long as, in the following month, he caught a chill and died in London on 28 March 1833.

CHARLES TENNANT, rev. H. C. G. MATTHEW

Sources C. Tennant, *The radical laird* (1970) · W. H. Roach, 'Kinloch, George', *BDMBR*, vol. 1
Archives NRA, priv. coll., corresp. and papers
Likenesses statue, 1872, Albert Square, Dundee · W. Sharp, lithograph (after M. Saunders), BM, NPG [*see illus.*]

Kinloch, George Ritchie (1797/8–1877), lawyer and antiquary, was born probably in Jamaica, one of at least seven children of George Kinloch (1741–1802), deputy judge advocate and master in chancery in Jamaica, and his wife, Susannah, *née* Wigglesworth (1759–1841), of Edinburgh. Named after his father and in memory of a dead elder brother, Kinloch returned from Jamaica as a young boy and was educated in Edinburgh, where he qualified as a writer to the signet. His early and not unsuccessful career as a clerk to several advocates depute must have been somewhat blighted by the death of his first wife, Mary Stewart. They married on 8 September 1817, and their only

child, Susan Janet, was born on 6 August 1819. Mary Stewart evidently died not long afterwards, because on 29 July 1822 he married Helen Tod (1799–1879).

A successful professional of wide literary interests, Kinloch is best known for his genuine and informed interest in Scottish song, particularly in that from his family's ancestral homelands in the north east of Scotland. Between 1827 and 1848 he edited or contributed to nine works. These ranged from his *Ballad Book* (1827), recounting the life and songs of 'Mussel mou'd Charlie … a celebrated peripatetick ballad singer in the town and county of Aberdeen', to *Nugea Scoticae*, a jointly edited work preserving 'fugitive pieces' illustrative of Scottish affairs from 1535 to 1781. His most important work, however, was his studious, informative, and original *Ancient Scottish Ballads* (1827), intended to redress the preponderance of such text as Scott's *Border Minstrelsy*, drawn from southern Scotland. The glowing acknowledgement paid to Kinloch by Dr John Jamieson in his preface to the supplement to the Scottish dictionary of 1824 also bears testimony to his enthusiasm for and knowledge of the Scots language; it is a pity that his projected work on Scottish proverbs never appeared.

Between 1842 and 1869 Kinloch held the office of principal keeper of the register of deeds and probative writs. During this time he was a member of the Maitland and other literary societies, and 'devoted much time to the work that fell to him as treasurer and one of the trustees, of the Paterson and Pape fund for the relief of decayed old men and women' (*The Scotsman*). Kinloch died at his family home, West Coates Villa, Edinburgh, on 21 April 1877.

RICHARD IAN HUNTER

Sources *The Scotsman* (24 April 1877), 4 · private information (2004) · *Calendar of testaments and inventories* · IGI · will, proved, Edinburgh, 30 April 1877 · *Catalogue of the … library and collection of manuscripts of the late George R. Kinloch* (1877) [sale catalogue, Mr Dowell, Edinburgh, 3–4 Dec 1877] · d. cert.
Archives NL Scot., catalogue of the library; pasquils of the nineteenth century | Edinburgh City Archives, letters and town clerk's letter-books
Wealth at death £24,616 6s. 6d.: confirmation, 28 June 1877, *CCI*

Kinloch, John Parlane (1885–1932), medical officer of health, was born on 2 November 1885 at Back Street, Renton, Dunbartonshire, the son of James Kinloch, grocer and farmer, and his wife, Margaret Ewing Parlane. After an early education at Glasgow high school, he graduated MB ChB from the University of Glasgow in 1909. Through the same institution he gained his diploma in public health (Cambridge) with distinction in 1910, and in 1913 was awarded the degree of MD with commendation.

Kinloch's first appointments were as pupil assistant in the Glasgow public health department (1909–10), as house surgeon and later house physician at the Victoria Infirmary, Glasgow (1910–11), and as external resident medical officer, Queen Charlotte's Lying In Hospital, London (1911–12). In 1912 he became resident medical officer at Glasgow's Ruchill Fever Hospital, managing the phthisis wards of Scotland's second largest infectious diseases institution. He was appointed deputy medical officer of health for the city of Aberdeen and lecturer in public health at the University of Aberdeen in 1914. With the outbreak of war he joined the Royal Army Medical Corps as captain, and in 1918 commanded a mobile hygienic field laboratory in France. The war years also saw his first publications. The findings of his MD thesis on the excretion of urinary solids in the nephritis of scarlet fever and diphtheria appeared in the *Journal of Pathology and Bacteriology* (1914), and he established himself in preventive medicine with articles on the extermination of lice in the *British Medical Journal* (1915, 1916) and the effect of vaccinia on the health of children in *The Lancet* (1917). His research interest then turned to the impact of diet on health and the measurement of the energy value of food consumed. Publications on the subject included an article in the *British Medical Journal* (1921) co-authored with John Boyd Orr, of the Rowett Research Institute.

In 1923 Kinloch became reader in public health at the University of Aberdeen and then succeeded Matthew Hay as head of the university's public health department and medical officer of health for Aberdeen. In this post he also acted as physician superintendent of Aberdeen's City Fever Hospital, and, from 1926, of Woodend Hospital. His success was founded first upon the application of advances in bacteriology and immunology to public health work. Working with a small team on outbreaks of food poisoning, he broke new ground in identifying bacteria responsible for epidemics of paratyphoid fever, dysentery, and other enteric diseases. These findings were regularly presented to the wider academic audience, most notably in 1926, when his team published three articles in the *Journal of Hygiene*. Other innovations included the certification by the public health department of milk from the city's dairies, based on bacteriological counts. Aberdeen also pioneered the immunization of children against diphtheria and scarlet fever, devising a combined diphtheria and scarlet fever prophylactic, establishing the appropriate doses of serum, and using the newly developed Dick Test for susceptibility to scarlet fever to immunize against return cases in adults. Again the work was noticed by public health professionals, following articles on the 'newer knowledge of diphtheria and scarlet fever' in the *Journal of Hygiene* (1927) and the *Journal of the Royal Sanitary Institute* (1928). Finally a study of maternal mortality in the city in 1918–27 demonstrated the danger of doctors as streptococcal carriers, leading to recommendations in the *British Medical Journal* (1929) for the reorganization of the midwifery service.

Equally significant were Kinloch's innovations in public health administration. He persuaded the town council to take over the poor law institution from the inept management of Aberdeen parish council and adapt it for use as a municipal hospital for both general and infectious cases. This caused considerable friction with both the leadership of the main voluntary hospital, Aberdeen Royal Infirmary, and the university medical faculty. Not only did it trespass on the province of the voluntary sector by providing rate-aided care for acute patients, it also threatened long-heralded plans for a new joint hospital and medical

school on a greenfield site outside the city. Other than Bradford, Aberdeen was the only British town to municipalize its poor law infirmary in advance of the Local Government Acts of 1929, which made statutory provision for the 'appropriation' of such hospitals and effectively removed the stigma of pauperism from public medical relief. The acts also aimed to promote the co-ordination of health services, both between different arms of local government and between voluntary and public institutions. Here again Kinloch's Aberdeen foreshadowed later developments. When the joint hospital scheme eventually began, public money was used alongside philanthropy and university funds. Also the city developed a series of agreements with county councils in north-east Scotland to integrate regional administration of infectious disease hospitals and laboratory work. These developments were discussed in his article 'The future of local authority hospital services', in *Transactions of the Royal Sanitary Association of Scotland* (1927).

In 1928 Kinloch was appointed to the newly created post of chief medical officer at the Department of Health for Scotland, which in 1929 took over the responsibilities of the Scottish board of health. Effectively he was the successor of Sir Leslie Mackenzie, who had been the medical member of the board. His appointment was intended to further the implementation of the Local Government Act, and he began to proselytize actively in speeches and articles for municipal appropriation of poor law hospitals and for regional integration of voluntary and public health provision. Examples include his lecture 'The meaning of an adequate health service', published in the *Transactions of the Royal Sanitary Association of Scotland* in 1929, and the article 'Reform of hospital services in Great Britain', in the *Journal of State Medicine* (1930). He also advocated closer ties between general practitioners and the statutory medical service with a view to elevating the preventive role of the family doctor. In 1930 he established and chaired a scientific advisory committee with the brief of advising the department and promoting medical research in support of public health goals. He became a member of the Royal College of Physicians (Edinburgh) in 1929, and was elected vice-president of the Royal Sanitary Association of Scotland in 1930, becoming its president the following year. His presidential address evoked the Greek ideal of the healthy citizen: 'One of the fundamental aims of Statecraft … should be the promotion of the health of the individual to the end that as a race we may grow in health and vigour' (J. Parlane Kinloch, 'Health services in the modern state', *Journal of the Royal Sanitary Institute*, 52, 1931–2, 38).

During this period Kinloch resided at 15 Montpelier Park, Edinburgh. He was divorced; the name of his wife and dates of his marriage are not known. He died of heart failure on 31 January 1932, while walking at Laurieston, Oxhill, Dunbartonshire, and was buried at Millburn churchyard, Renton, on 3 February 1932. His early death cut short a growing reputation: indeed he appears in the historical record chiefly as an ideologue who blocked the progress of Aberdeen's hospital scheme (Logie, 166–71).

Kinloch's significance lies first in his efforts to yoke medical science to public health work in a period when research into infectious diseases suffered from official neglect (Bryder, 80). He combined his role of medical officer of health in Aberdeen with a university position that allowed him both to apply biomedical research in his civic duties and also to exert a broader influence through publication of findings. His reputation also rests on his early and active support for a state health service; the Aberdeen experiment in municipalization helped shape the Local Government Acts, while his enthusiasm for regional integration presaged later thinking about the structure of the National Health Service. Kinloch's speeches and writing were infused with idealism and urgency, conjuring images of a 'threshold of a new era', characterized by 'the impending expansion of the statutory health services to embrace every requirement for preserving the health of the people' (*Report by the Medical Officer of Health, J. Parlane Kinloch M.D., for the Year 1924*, city of Aberdeen, 1925, 7). In this sense he may be regarded as a progenitor of the British NHS.   MARTIN GORSKY

Sources *BMJ* (13 Feb 1932), 311–13 [incl. appreciation by Sir Walter Fletcher, secretary to the Medical Research Council] · *The Lancet* (6 Feb 1932), 319–20 · *Public Health* (March 1932), 164–5 · applications for university posts, Kinloch, J. P., U. Aberdeen L., special libraries and archives, MSU912 · minutes of the faculty of medicine, 1925–6, U. Aberdeen L., special libraries and archives, U647/2 · N. J. Logie, 'History of the Aberdeen joint hospital scheme and site', *Aberdeen Medico-Chirurgical Society: a bicentennial history, 1789–1989*, ed. G. P. Milne (1989), 155–78 · A. Newsholme, *International studies on the relation between the private and official practice of medicine with special reference to the prevention of disease*, 3 (1931), 481–98 · L. Bryder, 'Public health research and the MRC', *Historical perspectives on the role of the MRC*, ed. J. Austoker and L. Bryder (1989), 59–81 · D. F. Smith, 'The early institutional and scientific development of the Rowett Research Institute', *To the greit support and advancement of helth*, ed. A. Adam, D. Smith, and F. Watson (1996), 45–53 · b. cert. · d. cert. · *CCI* (1932)
Archives U. Aberdeen, applications for university posts, MSU912 | Aberdeen Central Library, minutes of the town council of Aberdeen · U. Aberdeen L., minutes of the faculty of medicine, U647/2
Likenesses photograph, repro. in *Transactions of the Royal Sanitary Association of Scotland* (1931), frontispiece
Wealth at death £80: confirmation, 8 March 1932, *CCI*

Kinloch, William (*fl.* 1582), composer, is of unknown parentage. Nothing certain is known of his life, although he has been plausibly identified as a musician within the circle of James Lauder, himself a musician in the service of Mary, queen of Scots, and later of James VI. Lauder retained a pension from the imprisoned queen, for whom his son John also worked. In a letter dated 2 October 1582 Lauder reports to his son that his daggers and knives will be sent by 'Mr. William Kynlowgch' on his next journey from Scotland to London. None of Kinloch's extant music, all of which is for keyboard instruments, bears any indication of Catholic sympathies, but the letter conveniently documents a pattern of life that would explain its preservation in an English as well as in a Scottish manuscript.

The Scottish manuscript is that known as Duncan Burnett's manuscript (NL Scot., MS 9447, formerly Panmure 10 in the collection of the earl of Dalhousie), copied about 1600–10. Five out of twenty-three keyboard pieces are here attributed to Kinloch (or Kinloche, with the first name variously spelt), though it seems certain that he wrote several of the others as well. It is clear from these that Kinloch was something of a virtuoso player. 'The Batell of Pavie' is a technically demanding setting of a tune long popular on the continent. The 'fantassie', which is mainly an exercise in complex rhythms in the manner of some of William Byrd's fantasias, opens with a lengthy passage for crossed hands.

The English source of Kinloch's music is BL, Add. MS 30485 (*c*.1600), a manuscript associated with and partly written by the composer Thomas Weelkes. Here he is identified simply as 'kinloughe', the composer of a pavan and galliard. There can be no doubt that this is the work of the same composer: the general style is very similar, and, moreover, there exists in the London manuscript an anonymous 'Quadran' pavan and galliard which bears a close musical relationship with 'the quadrant paven' and its associated 'gaillart' in the Duncan Burnett manuscript.

Unfortunately Kinloch's music has none of the distinctive features that might otherwise identify it as Scottish: its principles of composition are those of the Elizabethan and Jacobean virginalists, several of whom wrote music of equal or greater difficulty. It has been conjectured that he also composed some of the anonymous secular vocal music that survives in Scottish sources of the time, but this remains to be demonstrated convincingly.

JOHN CALDWELL

Sources H. M. Shire, 'Musical servitors to Queen Mary Stuart', *Music and Letters*, 40 (1959), 15–18 · H. M. Shire, *Song, dance and poetry at the court of Scotland under King James VI*, ed. K. Elliott (1969) · T. Dart, 'New sources of virginal music', *Music and Letters*, 35 (1954), 93–106 · H. G. Farmer, *A history of music in Scotland* (1947) · G. J. Munro, 'Scottish church music and musicians, 1500–1700', PhD diss., Glasgow, 2000 · *CSP Scot.*, 1581–3, 6, no. 187

Kinloss. For this title name *see* Bruce, Edward, first Lord Kinloss and first Baron Bruce of Kinloss (1548/9–1611).

Kinnaird, Agneta Olivia (1850–1940). *See under* Kinnaird, Mary Jane, Lady Kinnaird (1816–1888).

Kinnaird, Arthur Fitzgerald, tenth Lord Kinnaird of Inchture and second Baron Kinnaird of Rossie (1814–1887), philanthropist, the third son of Charles *Kinnaird, eighth Lord Kinnaird of Inchture (1780–1826), and his wife, Lady Olivia Letitia Catherine Fitzgerald (1787–1858), the youngest daughter of William Robert *Fitzgerald, second duke of Leinster, was born at Rossie Priory, Inchture, Perthshire, on 8 July 1814. He was educated at Eton College (1829–35) and afterwards received an appointment in the Foreign Office. From July 1835 to September 1837 he was posted to St Petersburg, where he served for a time as private secretary to the ambassador, the earl of Durham. In 1837 he became a partner in the banking house of Ransom & Co., Pall Mall East, in succession to his uncle the Hon. Douglas James William Kinnaird. Eventually he became head of the firm, which took the name Ransom, Bouverie & Co.

Arthur Fitzgerald Kinnaird, tenth Lord Kinnaird of Inchture and second Baron Kinnaird of Rossie (1814–1887), by W. E. Debenham

Kinnaird sat in the House of Commons for Perth as a Liberal (1837–9), was re-elected for that city in 1852, and continued to represent it until January 1878, when he succeeded his brother George William Fox *Kinnaird as Lord Kinnaird. In the House of Commons he supported free trade and spoke frequently on Indian questions. In 1857, in response to information given to him by protestant missionaries, he called for an inquiry into social conditions in Bengal. A devout evangelical (he underwent a conversion experience in Paris as a young man), he had an abiding interest in measures affecting religion and was a strong opponent of the bill for legalizing marriage with a deceased wife's sister. Like Lord Shaftesbury, with whom he worked on several charitable campaigns (including the education of ragged children), he also took a keen interest in all matters concerning the well-being of the working classes.

Kinnaird married Mary Jane (d. 1888), the daughter of the London banker William Henry Hoare, on 28 June 1843 at Hornsey [see Kinnaird, Mary Jane]. Well matched, they worked in fruitful religious and social partnership. Their home at 2 Pall Mall East was a meeting place for social reformers and served as a clearing house of information for a host of evangelical causes, from district nursing and female education to foreign missions and temperance. As a leading light of the Gospel temperance movement, Kinnaird was instrumental in setting up coffee houses in working-class neighbourhoods. He was a man of considerable wealth, and contributed large sums of money to his favoured charities.

A familiar figure at the May meetings of the evangelical societies at Exeter Hall, Kinnaird sat on innumerable charitable committees. Among the public institutions with which he was more especially connected were the Church Missionary Society, the London City Mission, the Ragged School Union, the Ranyard Mission, the Destitute Children's Dinner Society, the Lock Hospital, Dr Barnardo's, the National Temperance League, and the Royal Society for Discharged Prisoners. Meanwhile, on his Scottish estates, he took a paternal interest in his tenants. He was, as one of his contemporaries put it, an example of 'the preserving salt of the British aristocracy' (Fraser, 141), a high-minded paternalist who helped to give Victorian Britain its reputation for moral seriousness. He died, after a long illness, at his London home on 26 April 1887, leaving one son, Arthur Fitzgerald *Kinnaird, the eleventh Lord Kinnaird of Inchture, and five daughters. He was buried in the churchyard at Rossie, Perthshire.   FRANK PROCHASKA

Sources D. Fraser, *Mary Jane Kinnaird* (1890) · K. Heasman, *Evangelicals in action: an appraisal of their social work in the Victorian era* (1962) · *The Times* (27 April 1887) · *Hansard 3* (1857), 145.1587–1603 · GEC, *Peerage*

Archives LPL, corresp. · Perth and Kinross Council Archive, estate corresp., and papers | BL, corresp. with W. E. Gladstone and others · Bodl. Oxf., corresp. with Lord Kimberley · University of Dundee, corresp. with the bishop of Brechin and Lord Strathmore

Likenesses Ape [C. Pellegrini], caricature, chromolithograph, NPG; repro. in *VF* (15 Jan 1876) · W. E. Debenham, photograph, NPG [see illus.] · photograph, repro. in Fraser, *Mary Jane Kinnaird*

Wealth at death £255,166 0s. 4d.: probate, 1 July 1887, *CGPLA Eng. & Wales*

Kinnaird, Arthur Fitzgerald, eleventh Lord Kinnaird of Inchture and third Baron Kinnaird of Rossie (1847–1923), footballer and philanthropist, was born in London on 16 February 1847, the only son of Arthur Fitzgerald *Kinnaird, tenth Lord Kinnaird of Inchture and second Baron Kinnaird of Rossie (1814–1887), and his wife, Mary Jane, née Hoare, Lady *Kinnaird (1816–1888). Emily *Kinnaird [see under Kinnaird, Mary Jane] was the youngest of his six sisters. After preparatory school at Cheam, Kinnaird went to Eton College in October 1861, precisely when football was first being developed as an organized sport in the leading schools. He clearly had an aptitude for several sports—he was a fine runner, swimmer, and cricketer, and later represented Cambridge University at tennis—but it was on the football field that he truly excelled. By the time he went up to Trinity College, Cambridge, in 1865 he had acquired a zeal both to play and to spread the game. Before he graduated in 1869 he had already been elected as the Old Etonians' representative on the Football Association (FA) committee.

On going down from Cambridge in 1869, Kinnaird began his banking career, becoming a partner in the West End firm Ransom, Bouverie & Co., in which the Kinnaird family had been involved since the eighteenth century. He

Arthur Fitzgerald Kinnaird, eleventh Lord Kinnaird of Inchture and third Baron Kinnaird of Rossie (1847–1923), by Bassano, c.1905

remained a partner when the bank became part of Barclay, Bevan, Tritton & Co. in 1888. When further amalgamations led to the establishment of Barclays Bank Ltd in 1896, Kinnaird became a director, as well as principal director of the local head office in Pall Mall, which was later named in his honour. He retained these banking appointments until his death.

While in London Kinnaird began his work for voluntary associations, inspired by the example of his parents and of his father's friend Lord Shaftesbury. He taught in ragged schools in the poorer parts of London and visited India, principally to see the hospitals and missions that his mother, a founder of the Foreign Evangelisation Society, had helped to establish. He was a founder of the Boys' Brigade in 1870 and in the same year, with his Etonian friend Quintin Hogg, he established Homes for Working Boys. His work for Christian youth organizations continued a family concern: in 1887 he succeeded his father as president of the YWCA, founded by his mother, and in the same year joined the council of the YMCA, of which he became president in succession to George Williams in 1905. The YMCA's object, he proclaimed in 1908, was 'to win young men for Christ' (Yapp, 27). It was estimated that in total he held some twenty presidencies of voluntary organizations and over forty vice-presidencies and thirty treasurerships. Among the associations enjoying his support were the Church Missionary Society, the London City Mission, the National Rifle Association, the Boy Scouts, and the London Lock Hospital.

On 19 August 1875 Kinnaird married Mary Alma Victoria, daughter of Sir Andrew Agnew, eighth baronet, a Scottish landowner, Liberal MP for Wigtownshire, and a promoter of sabbatarianism. In 1887 Kinnaird succeeded his father to the barony and to the family seat at Rossie Priory, Inchture, Perthshire, with estates amounting to over 17,000 acres. As a Scottish peer of Liberal inclinations and strong evangelical convictions, Kinnaird occasionally spoke in the House of Lords on religious questions, complaining in 1899 of the failure of bishops to halt the spread of ritualism. In 1907 he was appointed by the Liberal government as lord high commissioner to the general assembly of the Church of Scotland.

Kinnaird is best remembered, however, for his key role in the development of association football. As one of the most brilliant of the first generation of public-school footballers, he made his début for Scotland in 1873 and captained Wanderers to victory over Oxford University in the second FA cup final, scoring 'a very well-obtained goal' after 'a splendid run, outpacing the opposite backs'. His record of FA cup final appearances will probably never be equalled: he played in a total of eleven finals (if two replayed matches are included) and captained the Old Etonians five times and the Wanderers twice. He gained five winners' medals. Known for his skill, stamina, kicking, tackling, and speed, Kinnaird was an easily recognizable and popular figure on the pitch, with his white breeches, quartered cricket cap, and long red beard. He was a noted exponent of 'hacking'—the deliberate kicking of an opponent's shins—which was extolled by Kinnaird and some others as crucial to the 'manly' character of football. But it was not for the faint-hearted. His mother once told the FA secretary, C. W. Alcock, of her fear that Arthur would one day return with a broken leg. 'If he does, it won't be his own', Alcock replied (Gibson and Pickford, 3.131).

In the early 1880s Kinnaird played a historic role as player and official (he was elected FA treasurer in 1878) in the transition of the game from a public-school, amateur sport into a popular, professional one. In February 1882 he backed a tough resolution against professionalism. The following month he captained the Old Etonians to FA cup victory over a quasi-professional, northern working-class team, Blackburn Rovers. Kinnaird celebrated by doing a headstand in front of the Kennington Oval pavilion. But in 1883 another Blackburn team finally overcame the Old Etonians, despite another valiant performance by Kinnaird. The age of the public-school team in first-class football was over. With his old Harrovian friend Alcock, Kinnaird was quick to recognize that professionalism could not be wiped out by FA resolutions, and the two men persuaded the FA in 1885 'under stringent conditions' to legalize professionalism. They thus gave English football that distinctive character of professionalism under amateur control which lasted until the 1960s. They also saved football from the social and ethical rupture that rugby was to suffer in 1895.

In 1890 Kinnaird became president of the FA, in succession to Sir Francis Marindin. Although real power on the

FA council had shifted towards more bourgeois types, Kinnaird's position as a nobleman, his presence, and his personality helped to develop the game's ties both with the leaders of the political parties and with the monarchy. Lord Rosebery, A. J. Balfour, and the king himself were all guests of honour with Kinnaird at cup finals before the First World War. Such connections did much to protect the game when it came under attack for continuing during the first year of the war. He was justly celebrated for keeping together the aristocratic traditions, and the popular basis, of the national game.

However, the war brought great personal suffering to Kinnaird. His eldest son, Douglas Arthur, was killed in action in the third month of the conflict and another of his sons was killed in 1917. Then, on 20 January 1923, his wife died. She had been guest of honour at the 1895 cup final (whether from personal interest or conjugal duty is not known), and her own active involvement in voluntary concerns shared with her husband suggests that here was a practical as well as emotional partnership. For Kinnaird there was little in life without her: he died at their London home, 10 St James's Square, on 30 January 1923, ten days later.

For Kinnaird, apart from being sheer fun, football had great moral and physical benefits: 'I believe that all right-minded people have good reason to thank God for the great progress of this popular national game', he said late in life (Young, 155–6). It was simply of a piece with his overall mission in life, his devotion to evangelizing Christianity, to youth, to physical fitness and ideals of manliness and sportsmanship, to the poor, and to his country. His funeral on 2 February 1923 at the Kinnaird family burial-ground at Rossie Priory was attended by bankers, old football colleagues, and representatives of the legion voluntary organizations that owed so much to him. They were perhaps surprised at how much they had in common.

NICHOLAS FISHWICK

Sources 'Arthur Fitzgerald, eleventh Baron Kinnaird', *Spread Eagle*, 37 (1962), 4–6 · A. Gibson and W. Pickford, *Association football and the men who made it*, 4 vols. [1905–6], vol. 3, pp. 129–31 · *The Times* (31 Jan 1923) · *The Times* (3 Feb 1923) · E. Kinnaird, *Reminiscences* (1925) · A. Yapp, *In the service of youth* (1927) · M. Tyler, *Cup final extra!* (1981) · P. M. Young, *A history of British football* (1973) · Burke, *Peerage* · Venn, *Alum. Cant.*
Archives NRA Scotland | BL, letters to Lord Gladstone, Add. MSS 46082–46084, *passim*
Likenesses Bassano, photograph, c.1905, NPG [*see illus.*] · J. Lafayette, photograph, repro. in Gibson and Pickford, *Association football and the men who made it*, vol. 1, frontispiece · caricature, Federation of International Football Associations, museum collection
Wealth at death £250,000: probate, 24 Feb 1923, *CGPLA Eng. & Wales*

Kinnaird, Charles, eighth Lord Kinnaird of Inchture (1780–1826), politician and art collector, was the eldest surviving son of George, seventh Lord Kinnaird of Inchture (*d.* 1805), and his wife, Elizabeth, only daughter of Griffin Ransom, banker, of Westminster, and his wife, Elizabeth, daughter of Andrew Jelf, architect. He was born on 12 April 1780, and was copiously educated at Eton College and at the universities of Edinburgh (where he was

president of the Speculative Society), Cambridge (Trinity College, 1798–1800), and Glasgow. He was admitted to Lincoln's Inn in 1799. He also studied at Geneva in 1800–02. His father's connection with the whigs enabled him to obtain a seat in the House of Commons, as member for Leominster in 1802. From that time until the death of his father in 1805 he voted consistently with the Foxite whigs, and rendered valuable aid to the party in the repeated attacks made upon the Addington ministry. On his reluctant succession to the title he was a Scottish representative peer from December 1806 to June 1807. Despite his usefulness as an adviser on Scottish affairs, he failed to persuade his friends to obtain a British title for him and he was reduced to 'whispering, gesticulating and prophecizing' (HoP, *Commons*). On 8 May 1806 he married Lady Olivia Letitia Catherine Fitzgerald (1787–1858), youngest daughter of the second duke of Leinster and his wife, Emilia, *née* Usher. They had three sons, including George William Fox *Kinnaird, and two daughters. In 1807 he began the construction of Rossie Priory in the Carse of Gowrie, Perthshire.

Kinnaird travelled much on the continent and was an avaricious buyer of works of art dispersed during the Napoleonic wars; in particular he bought much of the collection of Philippe Égalité, duke of Orléans, and important Greek, Roman, and Egyptian sculptures. He was said to have given extravagant sums for what he regarded as his best pictures (which included works by Titian, Poussin, Teniers, and Rubens), with the result that in 1813 he was forced to sell his London possessions (Whitley, 2.212–13). Some of the remnant of the collection he sold to the National Gallery and the rest were brought together at Rossie Priory. Kinnaird died on 12 December 1826 in Regency Square, Brighton.

A. H. MILLAR, *rev.* H. C. G. MATTHEW

Sources GEC, *Peerage* · L. Melville, *The fair land of Gowrie* (1939) · HoP, *Commons* · A. H. Millar, *The historical castles and mansions of Scotland: Perthshire and Forfarshire* (1890) · W. T. Whitley, *Artists and their friends in England, 1700–1799*, 2 vols. (1928)
Archives BL, corresp. with Lord Holland, Add. MS 51590
Likenesses W. Bone, pencil drawing (after J. Northcote, 1809), NPG · Northcote, portrait, Rossie Priory, Perthshire · marble bust, Rossie church, Perthshire

Kinnaird, Douglas James William (1788–1830), writer and politician, was born on 26 February 1788, the fourth surviving son of George, seventh Lord Kinnaird (1754–1805), of Inchture, Perthshire, and Elizabeth (*d.* 1805), sole heir to Griffin Ransom, banker, of Westminster. He was educated briefly at Eton College (1799–1802), then at Göttingen University, where he acquired fluent French and German. He graduated MA from Trinity College, Cambridge, in 1811. In July 1813, with John Cam Hobhouse, he visited the Russian Emperor Alexander I's headquarters at Peterswaldau. Kinnaird then witnessed the Russo-Prussian victory over the French at Kulm, on 30 August. Travelling via Prague to Paris, he was present at Louis XVIII's first entry, on 28 April 1814, before returning to England with the journalist William Jerdan.

Although Kinnaird had been acquainted with Byron at

Douglas James William Kinnaird (1788–1830), by unknown artist

Cambridge, their friendship began in earnest in the winter of 1814 when Thomas Moore recalls 'those evenings we passed together at the house of … Douglas Kinnaird, where music,—followed by its accustomed sequel of supper, brandy and water, and not a little laughter,—kept us together, usually till rather a late hour' (Moore, 3.136–7). These parties were presided over by Kinnaird's mistress, the minor actor and singer Maria Keppel, mother to a son born in April 1814. Their relationship, which lasted from 1809 to 1818, was extremely volatile, with frequent separations. Neither she, nor the illegitimate child, was remembered in his will. In May 1815 Kinnaird was elected to the management subcommittee of Drury Lane Theatre, boasting to Hobhouse of 'drawing our friend Byron into the same situation'. He continued 'the Lord is delighted with his office, & will, I think fill it nobly' (BL, Add. MS 47224, fol. 3). Not surprisingly, he wrote a letter dated 26 March 1816, denying all Lady Byron's charges against her husband (Broughton, 2.320–21); but the sharing of Kinnaird's bachelor lifestyle and his close involvement with the stage undoubtedly hastened the collapse of Byron's marriage. Kinnaird introduced the poet to both Edmund Kean and Isaac Nathan, for the latter of whom Byron wrote the *Hebrew Melodies*, 'at the request of my friend, the Hon. Douglas Kinnaird' ('Advertisement' to *Hebrew Melodies*, January 1815).

On 22 April 1816 Kinnaird and Maria Keppel went to Dover to say goodbye to Byron before he left England for ever, taking two bottles of champagne and a cake as parting gifts. Byron had awarded him power of attorney, so that thereafter, as well as handling all of his English

finances, Kinnaird was the chief recipient of his correspondence from Italy. He commissioned Byron's 'Monody on the Death of the Right Hon. R. B. Sheridan', written at Villa Diodati in July 1816, spoken by Mrs Davison at Drury Lane on 7 September that year. Effectively running that playhouse after the suicide of Sir Samuel Whitbread, Kinnaird's greatest theatrical coup was to persuade Junius Brutus Booth to leave Covent Garden and act Iago to Kean's Othello on 20 February 1817. 'It was made the more dramatic by the fact that Kinnaird had got Kean to convey the invitation to Booth and invite his own antagonist to do battle with him' (Macqueen Pope, 250). Thus the 'greatest histrionic battle of the century was arranged' (Playfair, 170); but Booth was obliged to concede that Kean 'had won a signal victory' (ibid., 173).

In 1817, in Munich with his brother Charles *Kinnaird (1780–1826), Kinnaird dined with Maximilian I of Bavaria and his son-in-law Eugène de Beauharnais, later meeting Princess Hortense of Holland at Augsberg. The brothers travelled on to Venice where they saw Byron. The significance of this visit (19 September–1 October) is that Kinnaird brought a copy of John Hookham Frere's recently published 'Whistlecraft'. Seeing *ottava rima* successfully applied to comic English poetry immediately inspired Byron to write *Beppo*, and subsequently influenced *Don Juan* itself.

Politically on the radical left, Kinnaird was a member of the 'Rota' dining club, and first attempted to enter parliament in the general election of 1818. Although nominated as a candidate for the Westminster seat, he stood down in favour of Sir Francis Burdett. Kinnaird was however elected MP for Bishops Castle, Shropshire, at a by-election in July the following year. This enabled him to speak defending his friend in the debate on Hobhouse's notorious *Trifling Mistake* pamphlet in December 1819, when the latter was imprisoned for breach of parliamentary privilege. On 16 December from Newgate Hobhouse wrote 'D. Kinnaird … has made a failure in the H. of Commons & is ashamed—or his partners wish to keep him from public meetings' (BL, Add. MS 56540), alluding to his avoidance of mass reform rallies and increased involvement with the family bank. On the dissolution of the partnership with Sir F. B. Morland that year, Kinnaird became sole managing director. In the general election of March 1820 he was re-elected by only four votes in the double return for Bishops Castle, but declared 'not duly elected' in July when he stood down from parliament never to return. Yet his political activism continued; in January 1821 he was again in Paris, 'staying with Lord Rancliffe' and meeting liberal members of the chamber of deputies (BL, Add. MS 47224, fol. 17). He also remained a speaker at East India House debates and published *Remarks on the Volume of Hyderabad Papers, etc* in 1825. His only other publication was a free adaptation of John Fletcher's *Merchant of Bruges* (1815), which enjoyed some success at Drury Lane in that year.

As well as handling Byron's English finances, Kinnaird was also deeply involved in the publication of all his works after 1816, being sent manuscripts and instructed to '*correct* the *proofs* and arrange with [John] Murray for me' (*Byron's Letters and Journals*, 5.83). When the first canto of 'Don Juan' arrived in London in December 1818, alone among Byron's friends Kinnaird 'did not *then* [according to Hobhouse] see the objection to publishing' (Graham, 257); though Hobhouse and Scrope Berdmore Davies later 'changed his opinion' (ibid., 260). It was Kinnaird who, on 14 May 1824, was the first in England to learn of Byron's fate at Missolonghi, immediately writing from his own sickbed to Hobhouse: 'delay is absurd & I know not how to soften what your own fortitude alone can make you bear like a man—Byron is no more' (BL, Add. MS 47224, fol. 26). To Hobhouse's relief, Kinnaird then volunteered to break the news of her brother's death to Augusta Leigh. Soon afterwards he was involved with Byron's funeral arrangements, including applying to Dr Ireland, dean of Westminster, to request interment in the Abbey. This annoyed Hobhouse because it had 'given [Ireland] an opportunity to refuse burial' there (Marchand, 468). On 16 May 1824 Kinnaird was 'obliged to depart immediately for Scotland' (Broughton, 3.336), so he was not present at the destruction, the following day, of Byron's 'Memoirs'. This was diplomatic, but he must have been against the burning.

Despite describing that lady as 'I think half = witted' (BL, Add. MS 47224, fol. 40), Kinnaird was anxious to help Augusta Leigh when he realized her to be 'in great difficulty' financially in 1829. Before he could do so, however, he succumbed to a cancer which he had bravely suffered for several years. He died at his Pall Mall home, aged forty-two, on Friday 12 March 1830, less than a fortnight after writing his will, and was buried at St Martin-in-the-Fields, London, on 19 March. John Cam Hobhouse was being modest when he told Samuel Rogers, 'I am sure Kinnaird is the best friend Byron ever had in the world' (BL, Add. MS 56548), but he certainly came a close second to Hobhouse.   RALPH LLOYD-JONES

Sources Kinnaird's letters to J. C. Hobhouse, BL, Add. MS 47224 · diary of J. C. Hobhouse, BL, Add. MS 56540 · Baron Broughton [J. C. Hobhouse], *Recollections of a long life*, ed. Lady Dorchester [C. Carleton], 6 vols. (1909–11), vols. 2–3 · L. A. Marchand, *Byron: a portrait* (1971) · *Letters and journals of Lord Byron, with notices of his life*, ed. T. Moore, 3 (1832) · *Byron's letters and journals*, ed. L. A. Marchand, 5 (1976) · *Byron's bulldog: the letters of John Cam Hobhouse to Lord Byron*, ed. P. W. Graham (1984) · W. J. Macqueen Pope, *Theatre Royal, Drury Lane* (1945) · G. Playfair, *Kean: the life and paradox of the great actor* (1950) · *GM*, 1st ser., 100/1 (1830), 465 · H. E. C. Stapylton, *The Eton school lists, from 1791 to 1850*, 2nd edn (1864)
Archives Bodl. Oxf., corresp. | BL, corresp. with J. C. Hobhouse, Add. MSS 36456–36471 · BL, letters to J. C. Hobhouse, Add. MS 47224 · John Murray, London, letters to Lord Byron
Likenesses G. Hayter, group portrait, oils (*The trial of Queen Caroline, 1820*), NPG · pastel, priv. coll. [*see illus.*]
Wealth at death over £20,000 mostly left to nephew: will, 1830, PRO, PROB 11/1768, fols. 263–4

Kinnaird, Emily Cecilia (1855–1947). *See under* Kinnaird, Mary Jane, Lady Kinnaird (1816–1888).

Kinnaird, George, first Lord Kinnaird of Inchture (*d.* 1689), nobleman, was the second son of Patrick Kinnaird (*c.*1590–*c.*1658) of Inchture, Perthshire, and his wife, Euphemia (*fl.* 1609), daughter of Gilbert Gray of Bandirran. He gained the reputation of being an ardent royalist. On 10 October 1659 the noblemen, gentlemen, and heritors of Perthshire appointed him and John Nairne of Muckersie to meet General George Monck in Edinburgh to discuss the affairs of the county. He appears to have pointed to the prospects for disorder if English troops were withdrawn and to have put the idea of authorizing local notables to keep order. On 3 December he had a further commission to go to Berwick, again to discuss Perthshire concerns with Monck. According to a tradition in the Carse of Gowrie, Perthshire, Monck was at this time particularly grateful to Kinnaird for arranging the provisions for his forces.

After the Restoration Charles II personally knighted Kinnaird in gratitude for his services to the royalist cause, creating him Sir George Kinnaird of Rossie, in Perthshire. According to John Lamont he was one of the first Scots upon whom Charles II conferred that honour. Also in 1661 he apparently received all the family properties from his elder brother, John. On 19 November 1650 he had married Margaret (*d.* 1704), daughter of James Crichton of Ruthven, Perthshire, and they settled at Rossie, Perthshire, with their six sons.

Business frequently took Kinnaird to Edinburgh, however. He sat for Perthshire in the first Scottish parliament of the new reign and was a commissioner to visit the universities of Aberdeen and for the plantation of kirks. He became a member of the Scottish privy council (1661) and on 28 December 1682 was further rewarded with the title of first Lord Kinnaird of Inchture. When at home on his estate he had frequently been involved in arguments with his minister and local kirk session and appears to have ceased attending church during the covenanting period of the late 1660s and 1670s. In 1685 he voted for the execution by hanging rather than beheading of the leading covenanter Archibald, ninth earl of Argyll. Kinnaird died on 29 December 1689.

A. H. MILLAR, *rev.* ROSALIND K. MARSHALL

Sources *Scots peerage*, 5.209 · M. D. Young, ed., *The parliaments of Scotland: burgh and shire commissioners*, 1 (1992), 398 · *APS* · *The book of record: a diary written by Patrick first earl of Strathmore and other documents relating to Glamis Castle, 1684–9*, ed. A. H. Millar, Scottish History Society, 9 (1890), 149 · *Fifth report*, HMC, 4 (1876), 621 [Rossie Priory MSS] · *The diary of Mr John Lamont of Newton, 1649–1671*, ed. G. R. Kinloch, Maitland Club, 7 (1830), 128, 184 · F. D. Dow, *Cromwellian Scotland, 1651–1660* (1979)
Archives Perth and Kinross Council Archive, Perth, corresp. · Rossie Priory, Perthshire, MSS | BL, letters to Charles II and duke of Lauderdale, Add. MSS 23114–23122; 23243–23247

Kinnaird, George William Fox, ninth Lord Kinnaird of Inchture, Baron Rossie, and first Baron Kinnaird of Rossie (1807–1878), landowner, eldest son of Charles *Kinnaird, eighth Lord Kinnaird of Inchture (1780–1826), and his wife, Lady Olivia Letitia Catherine (1787–1858), daughter of William Robert *Fitzgerald, second duke of Leinster, was born on 14 April 1807 at Drimmie House, Perthshire—the family mansion before the erection of Rossie Priory. He was educated at Eton College, and then

George William Fox Kinnaird, ninth Lord Kinnaird of
Inchture, Baron Rossie, and first Baron Kinnaird of Rossie
(1807–1878), by James Valentine

entered the army as an officer of the guards; he afterwards
transferred to the Connaught Rangers. He succeeded to
the Scottish peerage on the death of his father, on 11
December 1826, having resigned his commission. In recognition of his father's and grandfather's support for the
Liberal Party, in 1831 Kinnaird was, on the recommendation of Earl Grey, raised to the rank of a peer of the United
Kingdom, with the title of Baron Rossie of Rossie, the
name of a portion of the family estates at Inchture, Perthshire. In 1860 a further title was added—that of Baron Kinnaird of Rossie, which could be inherited by his brother
and his heirs male. On 14 December 1837 Kinnaird married the Hon. Frances Anna Georgiana Ponsonby (1817–
1910), daughter of Lord de Mauley; they had two sons and
one daughter, all of whom predeceased him.

A considerable part of Kinnaird's youth was spent in
Italy. Like his father he was very interested in archaeology,
and he conducted important excavations near Rome
which resulted in the discovery of a number of Roman
antiquities; these were later preserved at Rossie Priory. On
15 January 1840 Kinnaird was made a privy councillor; he
was chosen a knight of the Order of the Thistle on 6 July

1857. He was appointed lord lieutenant of Perthshire on
28 February 1866, a position he held until his death.

As a large landowner Kinnaird, unlike many of his contemporaries, insisted on becoming personally involved in
agricultural issues. Acknowledging the need for modernization he was one of the earliest reformers of the old
style of husbandry prevailing in the Carse of Gowrie. His
interest in farm mechanization led to the introduction of
steam ploughs, threshing machines, and other agricultural implements on his estate in Scotland. He sought
energetically to improve the condition of the labouring
classes, organizing evening schools for the ploughmen
and establishing free reading-rooms and libraries about
his estate. It was largely through his exertions that the
railway system in the east of Scotland was developed, and
the line connecting Perth and Dundee, which ran through
part of his property, was constructed with his guidance.
He helped to found and maintain industrial schools
throughout the country, and his philanthropic aims
extended to the reform of criminals, especially young
offenders.

Kinnaird's principal legislative work was the drafting of
the important measure for the closing of public houses on
Sunday, known as the Forbes Mackenzie Act from the
name of William Forbes Mackenzie, MP for Peeblesshire,
who introduced it in the House of Commons. It received
the royal assent in 1853. Kinnaird was particularly interested in the issue of smoke pollution, the reform of the
Royal Mint (on which subject he wrote several pamphlets), and the regulation of mines. He was chairman of the
mining commission. As a Liberal politician he took a
prominent part in the agitation for free trade, and was
personally associated with David Ricardo, Richard Cobden, and John Bright; he took the role of chairman at an
important meeting of the Anti-Corn Law League at Covent
Garden Theatre. Kinnaird's liberal views were also shown
by his aid to Polish refugees, and his friendship with
Giuseppe Mazzini and with Garibaldi.

Kinnaird also had a wide-ranging interest in science. He
spent some time in developing photography with Fox Talbot, and in forming an extensive geological collection,
with the aid of Sir Charles Lyell. Kinnaird died at Rossie
Priory on 6 January 1878, in his seventy-first year, and was
buried four days later at Old Rossie. The titles and estates
fell at his death to his eldest surviving brother, Arthur Fitzgerald *Kinnaird.   A. H. MILLAR, rev. JOHN MARTIN

Sources *The Times* (8 Jan 1878) · A. H. Millar, *The historical castles and
mansions of Scotland: Perthshire and Forfarshire* (1890) · *Dundee Advertiser* (9 Jan 1878) · *Dundee Courier and Argus* (7 Jan 1878), 3 · GEC, *Peerage* · d. cert.
Archives BL, corresp. with W. E. Gladstone and others · University of Dundee, corresp. with Lord Shaftesbury · W. Sussex RO, letters to duke of Richmond
Likenesses S. Bellin, group portrait, mixed engraving, pubd 1850
(after *Meeting of the council of the Anti-Corn Law League* by J. R. Herbert,
pubd 1850), BM, NPG · J. Archer, oils, Dundee City Art Gallery ·
W. Brodie, marble bust, Dundee City Art Gallery · attrib. J. R. Swinton, oils, Winton House, Lothian region · J. Valentine, carte-de-
visite, NPG [*see illus.*]
Wealth at death £79,629 19s. 8d.: confirmation, 9 July 1878, CCI ·
£58 5s. 7d.: additional estate, 11 Aug 1879, CCI

Kinnaird, Gertrude Mary (1853–1931). *See under* Kinnaird, Mary Jane, Lady Kinnaird (1816–1888).

Kinnaird, Louisa Elizabeth (1848–1926). *See under* Kinnaird, Mary Jane, Lady Kinnaird (1816–1888).

Kinnaird [*née* Hoare], **Mary Jane**, Lady Kinnaird (1816–1888), philanthropist and a founder of the Young Women's Christian Association (YWCA), was born on 14 March 1816 at Blatherwick Park, Northamptonshire, the youngest of the six children of William Henry Hoare (1776–1819), of Broomfield House, Battersea, Surrey, and of Louisa Elizabeth (*d.* 1816), daughter of Sir Gerard Noel and Diana, Baroness Barham. Both her parents died in her infancy and she spent her childhood at the Surrey house of her grandfather, Henry Hoare, and, after his death in 1828, at the house of one of her uncles or of her brother Henry, who was her guardian. She was educated by a governess, who did not offer much intellectual stimulus. She was musical, and became a good pianist. Like her future husband, though in her case from a high-church background, she read William Romaine and turned to evangelicalism. She formed the habit of careful Bible study and of morning prayers, which she was to build upon in later life. When she came of age in 1837 she chose to live with her maternal uncle, the Hon. and Revd Baptist *Noel (1799–1873), then incumbent of St John's Chapel, Bedford Row, London, and was effectively his private secretary. She became very involved with the poor of the area, and worked especially to help women and girls. In 1841 she set up the St John's Training School for Domestic Servants (later moved to the site of Westbourne Day Schools, built by her husband). Through travel with Baptist Noel she acquired a lifelong interest in the development of protestantism on the continent. Merle d'Aubigné and Frédéric Monod were to visit her frequently in London (and she later helped to raise money to erect a Calvin memorial hall in Geneva, as well as supporting the protestant cause in Italy and Bohemia). At this time she was said to be quiet and to have little small talk, but to be keen on debate and to be animated when a subject arose which interested her. She was to become the driving force behind a formidable range of evangelical initiatives, and to acquire a reputation for forcefulness.

On 28 June 1843 in Hornsey church, Mary Jane Hoare married Arthur Fitzgerald *Kinnaird, tenth Lord Kinnaird of Inchture and second Baron Kinnaird of Rossie (1814–1887). They were to work closely together on projects of common concern, and drew upon a wide range of powerful family connections. They settled in London, and the house to which they moved soon after their marriage, 35 Hyde Park Gardens, became a great philanthropic centre. On Wednesday evenings the couple held salons to discuss missionary, educational, and reforming activities at home and abroad. Mary Jane Kinnaird worked on the editing of a volume of family prayers, for which she solicited contributions from nearly all of the most famous evangelical clergy of the day, with the aim of raising money to build a chapel for the Lock Hospital and Asylum in which both

Mary Jane Kinnaird, Lady Kinnaird (1816–1888), by Byrne & Co.

she and her husband were interested. In 1856 the Kinnairds moved to 2 Pall Mall East, above the bank where Arthur Kinnaird worked. There they were to continue to provide the focus of evangelical campaigning initiatives. Mrs Ranyard's council to run the Bible women met there, with both Arthur and Mary Jane Kinnaird serving on it, and other meetings were convened during the debates over India in the 1850s and the American Civil War. A campaign was launched there in 1871 against the slave trade on the east coast of Africa, and the house was also a centre for the revival movements of 1859–60 and 1873–5. Mary Jane Kinnaird was subsequently much involved in the Mildmay conferences.

Mary Jane Kinnaird would not address public meetings on principle, believing that this was not a woman's role, but she seems to have provided the impetus behind many of the projects which she and her husband sponsored. She may even have written his speeches. The one major issue on which they seem to have differed was that of female suffrage: while he supported it, she opposed it. She organized Thursday afternoon Bible reading meetings for women and mothers' meetings at her home, and she was active in local causes. She was one of the founders of the British Ladies' Female Emigration Society, and she encouraged the foundation of the Christian Colportage Association. She became particularly well-informed about India and said that when she died India would be found written on her heart. Although the evangelical impulse was uppermost, she recognized the importance of taking the widest possible view of the situation there; she emphasized the urgent need both for public works and for developing civil administration on lines which would limit the racial tensions which she could see increasing in the 1860s. She took a special interest in the condition of women in India, promoting in the 1850s the Indian Female Normal School and Instruction Society, to which was joined a female medical mission in 1872. In 1888 the society had sixty-six schools in India, and its visitors had access to 1353 zenanas. In 1906–7 a school in Lahore which she had worked to support, and which was to become the first women's college in the Punjab, changed its name to the Kinnaird Christian Girls' High School (later Kinnaird College) in her honour.

Mary Jane Kinnaird achieved most in her role in the YWCA. During the Crimean War she was involved with Florence Nightingale (1820–1910) in preparing nurses to be sent out to the field. In 1855 she established a more permanent nurses' home—the North London Home—for girls coming to London. A lending library and other amenities were attached, and it was the first institution of its kind in the capital. In 1861 she proposed the establishment of the United Association for the Christian and Domestic Improvement of Young Women, and by 1871 she had set up two homes and four institutes. Simultaneously Emma Robarts was organizing a very successful women's prayer union. In 1877, the year of Emma Robarts's death, it was decided to merge the two movements under the title of the Young Women's Christian Association. Lord Shaftesbury became president, and Arthur Kinnaird treasurer. On the model of the YMCA it became a national (and subsequently international) movement to establish under Christian auspices institutes, libraries, and educational classes for young women working away from home. A monthly magazine, *Our Own Gazette*, was produced at the cover price of 1d., and was owned jointly by Arthur Kinnaird (by then tenth Lord Kinnaird) and Mrs Stephen Menzies of Liverpool, who edited it. It reached a circulation of nearly 100,000. While she was not involved in the active management, Mary Jane Kinnaird remained a pivotal force in the development of the organization. At her death she was president of the YWCA and of the related Factory Helpers' Union. Her husband died on 26 April 1887, and she died on 1 December 1888, at Plaistow Lodge, Plaistow, Kent. She was buried beside her husband in the churchyard at Rossie, Perthshire, the family seat.

The Kinnairds' children were brought up to be as committed philanthropists as their parents. Six survived to adulthood (the first child having died very young): Frederica Georgina (1845–1929), Arthur Fitzgerald *Kinnaird (1847–1923), **Louisa Elizabeth Kinnaird** (1848–1926), **Agneta Olivia Kinnaird** (1850–1940), **Gertrude Mary Kinnaird** (1853–1931), and **Emily Cecilia Kinnaird** (1855–1947). The daughters were all educated at home and started taking Bible classes and mothers' meetings when they were very young, and they acted as secretaries to their parents. They became especially involved with their mother's principal concerns, and the three sisters who did not marry—Louisa, Gertrude, and Emily—were frequent

collaborators. Louisa worked alongside her mother in the London Bible and Domestic Mission. Louisa and Emily lived together throughout their lives, and, although Louisa was less dynamic, in the 1880s she represented the YWCA in Plaistow, south-east London. Emily and Gertrude acted as representatives for Rossie Priory. Gertrude worked for the Zenana Bible and Medical Mission, both in London and in India.

Emily Kinnaird, who took on the role of family memoirist, devoted her considerable energies to several causes. She went on a mission to India with Gertrude in 1889, and returned frequently, in 1905–6 again with her sister. She became vice-president of the Scottish branch of the Zenana Bible and Medical Mission. In 1944 she published in Lucknow *My Adopted Country, 1889–1944*, an account of her commitment to India. In Britain she was initially inspired to philanthropic work by the work of Catherine Marsh and Elizabeth Garnett among railway navvies, and she maintained this interest, spending one out of every four Sundays in a navvy mission station. She was an elder of Regent Square Presbyterian Church in London. Her main commitment was to the YWCA, on whose behalf she exploited every connection she had. It was reported that she arrived at her friends' houses before breakfast and refused to allow them to eat until she had extracted a cheque from them. She was for twenty-five years (from 1881) honorary secretary of the London division of the YWCA, and in 1906 she became honorary finance secretary of the British organization as a whole. She was also district referee for Forfarshire and Kincardineshire, and vice-president of the Scottish council. As honorary secretary for London she took a leading role in creating the Council of Women Workers (later the National Council of Women), on whose committee she sat for many years. She travelled extensively in representing the YWCA and became a member of the committee of the international YWCA. During the First World War she established more than 300 centres under the aegis of the YWCA to cater for WAACs and for munition and other war workers. She also set up a training home to provide an effective secretariat for the YWCA. As well as teaching the Bible, she lectured on business methods and public speaking, thus developing her mother's work in a fundamentally new idiom. She made an important contribution towards expanding the YWCA into a larger-scale organization, catering for young women entering a wider range of professions and developing new expectations. In 1918 she was appointed OBE, and in 1920 CBE. She was a lively and tough-minded person, sympathetic to the Labour Party. The only recreation she listed in *Who's Who* was bicycling, which clearly helped to maintain her vigour through a long life. She died in September 1947.   JANE GARNETT

Sources D. Fraser, *Mary Jane Kinnaird* (1890) • E. Kinnaird, *Reminiscences* (1925) • J. Duguid, *The blue triangle* (1955) • *Our Own Gazette* (1889–1928) • *WWW* • C. Binfield, *George Williams and the YMCA: a study in Victorian social attitudes* (1973) • G. M. Kinnaird, *All about the Girls' Zenana Missionary Union of the Zenana Bible and Medical Mission* [n.d.] • *IGI* • *The Times* (11 Sept 1947) • Burke, *Peerage* (1939)

Likenesses Byrne & Co., photograph, Women's Library, London [see illus.] • photograph, repro. in Fraser, *Kinnaird*, frontispiece •

photograph (with a student of Kinnaird School and Kinnaird College, Lahore), repro. in Kinnaird, *Reminiscences*, frontispiece **Wealth at death** £14,019 6s. 5d.: probate, 14 Feb 1889, *CGPLA Eng. & Wales*

Kinnear, Alexander Smith, Baron Kinnear (1833–1917), judge, was born in Edinburgh on 3 November 1833, the second son of John Gardiner Kinnear, merchant, and his wife, Mary, daughter of Alexander Smith, banker. After studying at the universities of Glasgow and Edinburgh he was called to the Scots bar in 1856, where he took time to establish a practice. In his career as a pleader the decisive moment came with the celebrated and disastrous failure of the City of Glasgow Bank in 1878. A mass of litigation ensued in which Kinnear was retained for the liquidator. His appointment was a success. The abstruse issues of insolvency and ranking, on which the cases often turned, had a special attraction for him. Thereafter professional advancement followed rapidly. In 1881 he was elected dean of the Faculty of Advocates and took silk, and a year later he was promoted to the Court of Session bench, taking the judicial title of Lord Kinnear. He was not yet fifty, and was to remain on the bench for more than thirty years, first as a lord ordinary and later, from 1890 onwards, as a member of the first division of the inner house (which exercises appellate jurisdiction).

As a judge Kinnear enjoyed a high reputation among his contemporaries, especially in the recondite area of feudal law. Lord Macmillan, who must have appeared before him many times, described him as 'possessed of one of the most perfect of legal minds' and as 'a paragon of dignified learning and courtesy' (Macmillan, 45). His beacon may have shone all the brighter in what was generally rather a weak period on the Court of Session bench. Later his reputation fell back a little. To modern eyes the Court of Session of the period was dominated by Lord McLaren, an almost exact contemporary of Kinnear's, and by Lord Dunedin, some sixteen years his junior but who, as lord president from 1905, chaired the first division. Kinnear had neither the deep learning of McLaren nor the showmanship of Dunedin. Like both, however, he was an exponent of British (or imperial) law and had little interest in Scottish law's civilian roots. This tended to impair his grasp of property law and hence to undermine his claims to feudal scholarship. In summary, his judicial legacy was one of solid achievement rather than of sparkling insight; but even decades later an *obiter dictum* by Lord Kinnear remains a useful weapon in the advocate's armoury.

Kinnear attracted numerous professional honours. Both of his former universities awarded him the honorary degree of LLD (Edinburgh in 1878 and Glasgow in 1894). He was elevated to the peerage, as Baron Kinnear of Spurness, on 5 February 1897, and he was made a privy councillor in 1911.

Little is known of Kinnear's life off the bench. He was chairman of the Scottish Universities Commission from 1889 to 1897, and in 1904–5 he served on the royal commission appointed following the judgment of the House of Lords in the Free Church case. He took no part in politics. He did not contribute to the literature of the law, though

there is early published work on Catullus (*North British Review*, 36.204) and on Shelley (*Quarterly Review*, 110.289). He did not publish memoirs and is barely mentioned in those of his contemporaries who did. Surviving photographs suggest a rather austere man of slight build and with angular features. Like many Scottish judges both before and since, he lived in the Edinburgh 'new town', at 2 Moray Place. He was unmarried.

Kinnear did not retire from the bench until 23 October 1913, shortly before his eightieth birthday. In the four years that remained to him he sat from time to time as an appellate judge in the House of Lords. He died in Edinburgh on 20 December 1917. KENNETH G. C. REID

Sources *Scots Law Times* (20 Jan 1894), 439 · *Scots Law Times: News* (12 Jan 1918) · *Scottish Law Review*, 34 (1918) · *Journal of Jurisprudence*, 26 (1882) · F. J. Grant, ed., *The Faculty of Advocates in Scotland, 1532–1943*, Scottish RS, 145 (1944) · H. Macmillan, *A man of law's tale* (1952) · H. F. Andorsen, ed., *Memoirs of Lord Salvesen* (1949) · DNB
Likenesses photograph, repro. in *Judicial Review* (1901), frontispiece · photograph, repro. in *Scots Law Times* (1894), 439 · photograph, repro. in *Scots Law Times* (1918)
Wealth at death £49,260 13s. 7d.: confirmation, 21 Jan 1918, CCI · £8 8s.: additional estate, 29 April 1918, CCI

Kinnear, Georgina (1826/1828–1914), headmistress, was born in Edinburgh, the second of the seven children of John Gardiner Kinnear and his wife, Mary, the daughter of banker Alexander Smith. About 1832 the family moved to Glasgow, where John Kinnear became the partner in a firm of commission merchants and power-loom manufacturers. The only one of their children to marry was the eldest sister, Marion, who married Robert Lockhart, a brother of Sir Walter Scott's son-in-law. The younger brother, Alexander Smith *Kinnear, became Baron Kinnear of Spurness and senator of the college of justice. Aptly, he chaired the Scottish universities commission of 1889 that passed the ordinance admitting women to degrees and university classes.

Georgina Kinnear never went to school, receiving the usual superficial education of girls of her time. But she was a natural student. While quite a young child she developed the habit of getting up about 5 a.m. to sit wrapped in a shawl reading, and it was a habit she retained to within a few years of her death. She learned languages from her brothers' tutors, but owed most to her own efforts and industry and instinctive knowledge of how to learn. As was the convention of the time, when older she travelled widely in Europe and became fluent in French and German and later Russian.

In 1860 Miss Kinnear, by then in her thirties, was 'permitted' by her parents to travel with family friends, Lord and Lady Napier, to The Hague to assist with the education of their sons. The following year Napier was appointed ambassador at St Petersburg. Miss Kinnear accompanied his family there and immediately began to study the Russian language and culture. When the Napier's sons went to school she transferred herself to the family of Nikolay Milyutin, a reforming minister under Tsar Alexander II. According to Miss Kinnear's cousin, Marion Murray, Milyutin frequently consulted Miss Kinnear, particularly about British political methods. She later returned to Russia after his death, spending several summers with Mme Milyutin and her daughters in the interior of Russia or in the Crimea. She saw and learned much about the life of the peasants, for whom she had a high esteem: 'They are a fine people and only need education' (Murray, 529).

It was, however, the secondary and higher education of women and girls that was of particular interest to Miss Kinnear. Alice Younger believed that during a visit to London in the 1860s Miss Kinnear assisted in some of the inquiries on which the women's evidence to the schools inquiry commission was based (*The Park School, Glasgow, 1880–1930*, 23). Wishing to become acquainted with the practical organization of a large school, she joined the staff of Cheltenham Ladies' College under Dorothea Beale in 1874. There she made such an impact that, when Louisa Lumsden (also a teacher there) was appointed headmistress of the new St Andrews School for Girls (later St Leonards School) in 1877, at her strong recommendation Miss Kinnear was made the fourth founder member of the staff.

In 1880 Miss Kinnear was selected from fifty candidates to be the first headmistress of the Park School, Glasgow, founded by the newly established Glasgow Girls' School Company. Appointed at a salary of £400, she remained in the post for twenty years. She was left without interference by the directors to manage the school as she wished, and pupils, staff, and inspectors alike agreed that her inexhaustible questing spirit permeated the whole atmosphere of the school. Having taken up schoolteaching late in a life much involved in thinking about educational matters, and after experiencing other cultures and conventions, she had her own decided views on educational methods and aims, in many of which she differed from the conventional wisdom of even the reformers of the day.

Miss Kinnear herself taught English and history in a style more appropriate for a university and often above the understanding of most of her pupils. Nevertheless they found her lessons immensely stimulating. Her battle cry was 'think for yourself', and her 'Whys?', thrown into lessons on the most taken for granted of subjects, encouraged pupils to do just that. She disapproved of examinations on intellectual grounds, but reluctantly accepted them as practical means of forwarding girls' educational standards, and Park pupils who entered public examinations did well. Pupils went on to enter the Oxbridge women's colleges or Queen Margaret College, Glasgow, before the opening of the Scottish universities to women in 1892. Miss Kinnear believed in keeping school and play hours separate and disliked homework as she felt this encouraged desultory habits of work. Like many Scots she preferred day schools to boarding-schools. She also held strong views on adequate pay and refused part of her salary so that no member of staff should be underpaid.

Miss Kinnear was an ardent Liberal and reformer. She only once attended the headmistresses' conference, and then said nothing because she disagreed with so much, particularly the complacency of the participants as to the

progress of women's education. 'Compare the number of men and women students in the Universities; when there are more women than men, as there ought to be, we may begin to speak of progress' (Murray, 529). She was described by an early Park pupil as 'a charming but formidable woman, full of new ideas of a woman's place in the world' (Lightwood, 29).

Miss Kinnear was small, with a dignified but rather old-fashioned appearance. She had dark, piercing eyes and a wonderful smile which occasionally lit her face. She always dressed in black, with a fine lace collar held in place by a flashing diamond and a lace cap over thick braids of dark hair. She would rustle into the classroom in full silk skirt with a swinging step and hoist herself onto the high chair at the desk, giving a little kick to get into position. She had great tolerance and a high sense of justice. She was concerned with overall schemes, not petty matters: 'It is of no significance, my dear' was an often-used phrase. She treated the girls as equals, though they in turn regarded her with a mixture of awe and fear. She aimed at instilling religious and moral principles, a love of study, and habits of diligence, concentration, and self-control in her pupils. She was kind, always willing to help, insightful about character, and unselfconscious about herself.

A natural, self-taught intellectual, Miss Kinnear loved history, especially the Elizabethan period, Russian politics, the Old Testament (which she interpreted as a dramatic picture of human life), and the growth and structure of a language (she published privately in 1904 a grammar book quite incomprehensible to most of her pupils, *The Use of Words*). She was a fine needlewoman and loved walking, which was her only exercise. Above all she was a brilliant talker, combining graphic description with keen analysis and illustrating her remarks with shrewd and humorous comments, the words flowing so rapidly listeners had difficulty keeping up with her.

When Miss Kinnear retired she drew up an elaborate scheme of study for herself, but could not pursue it, for her health broke down shortly after she moved back to Edinburgh to live with her remaining family. For the next fourteen years she lived a restricted and latterly invalid life, reverting in her final illness to speaking much of the time in Russian. She died on 26 April 1914 at her home, 11 Darnaway Street, Edinburgh, and was buried three days later at the city's St George's Church.   LINDY MOORE

Sources [M. Murray], *Journal of Education*, new ser., 36 (1914), 529–30 · J. Lightwood, *The Park School, 1880–1980* (1980) · *The Park School, Glasgow, 1880–1930* (1930) · R. Phillips, 'Seventy-five years ago', *The Park School Chronicle* (1955), 52–4 · J. Grant and others, *St Leonards School, 1877–1927* (1928) · Scotch Education Department, 'Inspection of higher schools: Park School, Glasgow', 1887, NA Scot., MS ED.17/97 · *CGPLA Eng. & Wales* (1914)
Archives U. Leeds, Brotherton L., Special Collections, MS 851
Likenesses J. Guthrie, oils, 1900, Laurel Park School, 4 Lilybank Terrace, Glasgow
Wealth at death £2435 5s. 6d.: confirmation, 1 July 1914, *CCI*

Kinnear, John Boyd (1828–1920), politician and agriculturist, was born in Edinburgh on 15 March 1828, the eldest son of Charles Kinnear (*b.* 1795?), of Kinloch, Fife, and

Christiana Boyd Greenshields. He was educated at home and then at the universities of St Andrews and Edinburgh, where he was a member of the Speculative Society. He was admitted a member of the Faculty of Advocates in March 1850 and to the English bar at the Inner Temple, London, some six years later, but did not practise. On 12 August 1852 he married Sarah Harriet Frith (1824–1866), the only daughter of George Frith, of Worksop, Nottinghamshire.

From 1852 to 1856 Kinnear acted as political secretary to the lord advocate, his most noticeable achievement in this office being his drafting of the Scottish Bankruptcy Bill. In the 1860s he turned to journalism and acted as leader writer to several journals, including the *Daily News*, the *Morning Star*, the *London Review*, and the *Pall Mall Gazette*. He was also active in this period in the volunteer movement and apparently attached himself at one point to a guards' battalion to improve his drill technique. What was described as 'his public spirit and enthusiasm in the cause of freedom, combined with an independent and virile temperament' (*The Scotsman*, 11 Nov 1920), led him, furthermore, to volunteer to help in Italy in the struggle against Austria. Kinnear served as a private in the forces commanded by Giuseppe Garibaldi in the Trentino Mountains in the war of 1866. A similar commitment to national self-determination in Europe is evident from his involvement with, among others, John Stuart Mill and Giuseppe Mazzini, in efforts to set up the Balkan Liberation Society, the aim of which was to create a confederation of Christian Balkan states liberated from Turkish rule.

On 19 March 1868, after the death of his first wife in 1866, Kinnear married Theresa Bassano (1828–1929), the fourth daughter of Clemente Bassano, a Venetian lawyer, active also in London. There appear to have been no children from either marriage. Later that same year Kinnear stood for Fife as an advanced Liberal against the sitting moderate Liberal MP, Sir Robert Anstruther of Balcaskie. He was defeated, in part because his opponent received the votes of Conservatives in the county.

Kinnear's return thereafter to London, and to the editorial staff of the *Pall Mall Gazette*, was to be short-lived. In 1870, following a breakdown in his health caused by the strain of work, he moved to Guernsey on medical advice. The subsequent period, until his permanent return to the Kinloch estate in 1884, was marked by more journalistic activity, on reform issues in general and on Irish and land issues in particular. Kinnear wrote, for example, the article entitled 'Land' for the ninth edition of the *Encyclopaedia Britannica*. In 1881 he travelled to Ireland and returned convinced that the solution to the Irish question lay in a settlement of the land-reform issue, a position he publicized in his pamphlet *Facts about Ireland* (1883).

Kinnear was elected to parliament as a Liberal for the new East Fife constituency in 1885 and began a parliamentary career that was cut short by his refusal to support W. E. Gladstone's Irish Home Rule Bill. Standing as a Liberal Unionist in 1886, he lost his seat to the Gladstonian Liberal H. H. Asquith. However, he had been involved in farming in Fife since 1882, and his election defeat,

together with the prevailing agricultural depression, led him to become still more actively engaged on his estate, taking the management of several of his farms into his own hands. As an agricultural innovator he experimented with new scientific ideas in dairying, imported livestock from Guernsey, ran a profit-sharing scheme for his employees, and opened direct sales outlets for his estate's milk in Edinburgh and St Andrews, all with reported success. He ran the estate business until 1905, when he relinquished control due to advancing age.

In retirement Kinnear remained true to a nineteenth-century concept of personal freedom and of social responsibility based on voluntaryism. He was well known in Fife for his charity, for addresses on religious subjects, and as the first chairman of the Cupar Educational Trust. In his pamphlet *Reform Questions in 1884* he had put forward ideas advanced for the time, such as the enfranchisement of women and the abolition of the House of Lords—in his view, the enfranchisement of peers. From 1911 he took his resistance to the reforms of the new Liberalism so far as to face prosecution for non-compliance with the National Insurance Act. As a leader of the opposition in Scotland to this measure, Kinnear objected especially to its compulsory elements as an interference with individual liberty, a position which led him to refuse to pay the required premiums.

Kinnear died at Kinloch on 10 November 1920 and was buried on 13 November in Collessie churchyard. His widow died in 1929, by then a centenarian. Kinnear's political fortunes reflected the developments of his time. He remained true to the nineteenth-century old Liberal tradition of individualism and voluntaryism and lived long enough to be clearly out of step with the more collectivist, state-oriented new Liberalism of the early twentieth century. His defeat in 1886 by Asquith, later leader of the new Liberal government whose policy he so much opposed, adds some poignancy to the contrast.

GORDON F. MILLAR

Sources *The Scotsman* (11 Nov 1920) · *Glasgow Herald* (11 Nov 1920) · *The Times* (11 Nov 1920) · *Fifeshire Advertiser* (13 Nov 1920) · 'Collessie Loon', 'In and around our parish days of yore', *Fife Free Press* (2 Dec 1939) · *Fife Free Press* (20 Nov 1920) · S. P. Walker, *The Faculty of Advocates, 1800–1986* (1987), 93 · F. J. Grant, ed., *The Faculty of Advocates in Scotland, 1532–1943*, Scottish RS, 145 (1944), 118 · WWW · WWBMP · *Scots Law Times: News* (20 Nov 1920) · J. B. Kinnear, *Reform questions in 1884* (1884) · J. B. Kinnear, *Facts about Ireland* (1883) · *Dundee Advertiser* (24 Nov 1868) · *The Scotsman* (2 Nov 1868) · *Daily Record and Mail* (11 Nov 1920) · IGI · GM, 2nd ser., 38 (1852), 412 · GM, 4th ser., 3 (1866), 119 · GM, 4th ser., 5 (1868), 674

Wealth at death £2473 11s. 10d.: confirmation, 28 Jan 1921, CCI · £707 4s. 7d.: additional estate, 26 Aug 1921, CCI

Kinnear, Sir Norman Boyd (1882–1957), ornithologist, was born in Edinburgh, on 11 August 1882, the younger son of Charles George Hood Kinnear, of Drum, Aberdeenshire, architect, and colonel of the Midlothian volunteer artillery, and his wife, Jessie Jane, daughter of Wellwood Herries Maxwell, of Munches, Kirkcudbrightshire, formerly MP for the stewartry of Kirkcudbright; she was a granddaughter of Sir William Jardine. He was educated at the Edinburgh Academy and Trinity College, Glenalmond;

Sir Norman Boyd Kinnear (1882–1957), by Walter Stoneman, 1950

he subsequently went to the duke of Richmond and Gordon's estate office as a pupil, and later acted as assistant in an estate office in Lanarkshire. Keenly interested in natural history, in 1905 he became a voluntary assistant at the Royal Scottish Museum under W. Eagle Clarke, where he was engaged in identifying the skin collections of birds. Kinnear accompanied Clarke on his expeditions to Fair Isle, where they made observations on bird migration. In the spring of 1907 he made a voyage on a whaler to the Greenland seas and collected natural history specimens, chiefly birds, which he presented to the Royal Scottish Museum.

In November 1907 Kinnear was appointed officer-in-charge of the museum of the Bombay Natural History Society, and shortly after became one of the editors of its journal. In 1911 he organized and directed a systematic survey of the mammals of India, Burma, and Ceylon. Kinnear himself assembled the large collections obtained and provisionally identified and catalogued them before dispatch to the British Museum in London.

In 1913 Kinnear married Gwendolin Beatrice Langford, daughter of William Wright Millard, medical practitioner in Edinburgh; they had two daughters.

On the outbreak of the First World War Kinnear made several unsuccessful attempts to join the Indian army. He did, however, serve in the Bombay volunteer rifles and in 1915–19 acted as intelligence officer for the Bombay defended port. He was twice mentioned in dispatches.

In 1920 Kinnear returned to Britain to become an assistant in the department of zoology of the British Museum (Natural History); he was appointed assistant keeper in 1928, deputy keeper in charge of birds in 1936, and keeper of zoology in 1945. In 1947, on the day after he had reached the age of retirement, it was announced that he had been appointed director of the museum, an exceptional step, and a great tribute to him. He was the first ornithologist to assume this position, which he held for three years. He was appointed CB in 1948 and knighted in 1950.

Kinnear joined the British Ornithologists' Union at the age of twenty and rendered notable service for fifty-five years. He was its president in 1943–8 and after the Second World War did much to re-establish cordial relations with ornithologists in other countries. He was editor of the *Bulletin of the British Ornithologists' Club* from 1925 to 1930; in 1935 he was appointed a member of the British section of the International Council for Bird Preservation, and was chairman from 1947 until his death. He also helped to draw up the proposals for the Protection of Birds Act of 1954.

An active supporter of the National Trust, Kinnear joined its estates committee in 1935 and the executive committee in 1942, remaining a member of both until his death. He was a vice-president of the Society for the Promotion of Nature Reserves and was on the committees that led to the formation of the Nature Conservancy, of which he was a member from its establishment in 1949 until 1955. He was a fellow of the Zoological Society of London, served on its council, and was elected a vice-president. He was also a fellow of the Linnean Society of London.

Most of Kinnear's published work, which appeared chiefly in *The Ibis* and the *Journal of the Bombay Natural History Society*, dealt with birds, especially those of the east, including central and south Arabia, Indo-China, north-east Burma, and south-east Tibet. He described a number of new forms in the *Bulletin* and was responsible for the zoological notes in the publications of the Hakluyt Society. He was particularly interested in early ornithologists and did much work on James Cook's voyages and the records made by his naturalists.

Kinnear's memory was phenomenal and he could quote statements and references with the greatest accuracy and detail. He also made copious notes, mostly on small pieces of paper, but writing did not come easily to him and he was far more inclined to help the work of others to reach publication. His retiring nature sometimes resulted in an apparent gruffness; he did not care for committees and certainly disliked taking the chair. Although specializing in birds, Kinnear was a good general naturalist and was equally interested in mammals, insects, and plants. He enjoyed shooting and fishing, but gardening was his greatest hobby. Kinnear died at his home, 2 Burghley Road, Wimbledon, on his seventy-fifth birthday, 11 August 1957; his wife survived him.

PHYLLIS BARCLAY-SMITH, *rev.* V. M. QUIRKE

Sources *Journal of the Bombay Natural History Society* (Dec 1957) · W. T. Stearn, *The Natural History Museum at South Kensington: a history of the British Museum (Natural History), 1753–1980* (1981) · personal knowledge (1971) · private information (1971) · *CGPLA Eng. & Wales* (1957)
Archives NHM, letter-books, journal of whaling voyage, notes · U. Edin. L., corresp. and papers
Likenesses W. Stoneman, photograph, 1950, NPG [*see illus.*]
Wealth at death £38,019 0s. 9d.: probate, 27 Nov 1957, *CGPLA Eng. & Wales*

Kinneder. For this title name *see* Erskine, William, Lord Kinneder (*bap.* 1768, *d.* 1822).

Kinneir, Sir John Macdonald (1782–1830), army officer, traveller, and diplomatist, born at Carnden, Linlithgow, on 3 February 1782, was the illegitimate son of John Macdonald, comptroller of customs at Bo'ness, and Mrs Cecilia Maria Kinneir. In 1802 he was nominated to a cadetship by Sir William Bensley, under the name of Macdonald, which he retained in the Indian army lists up to his death. On 21 September 1804 he was appointed ensign in the Madras native infantry, but was not posted until the formation of the 24th (out of the 1st) Madras native infantry on 1 January 1807, when he joined the new regiment as lieutenant. He became captain in the same regiment on 14 April 1818, and afterwards attained the army rank of brevet lieutenant-colonel. For some time he was secretary to the officer commanding in Malabar and Kanara. He was attached to Sir John Malcolm's mission in Persia in 1808–9, during part of which time he was supernumerary agent at Bushehr, and made numerous journeys in Persia. On the breaking up of the mission in 1810 Macdonald travelled from Baghdad, by way of Mosul and Diyarbakır, to Constantinople, visited Manisa and Smyrna, and returned to England through Spain and Portugal.

Ordered to rejoin his regiment, Macdonald started for Stockholm in January 1813 with Colonel Neil Campbell, one of the military commissioners sent to northern Europe, intending to reach India through Russia and Persia. The French retreat from Moscow having left open a more southerly route, he accompanied Campbell from Stockholm to the tsar's headquarters at Kilisch in Poland, and went through Austria and Hungary to Constantinople. After visiting Asia Minor and Cyprus he returned to Constantinople, and from there travelled to Baghdad and Bombay. He published a *Narrative of travels in Asia Minor, Armenia, and Kurdistan in 1813–14, with remarks on the marches of Alexander the Great and of the ten thousand Greeks* (1818). From the title-page it appears that he had at that time taken his mother's surname of Kinneir, although there is no record in the India Office of his change of name. After 1813 he was for some years town-major of Fort St George, Madras, and resident to the nawab of the Carnatic.

In 1823–4 it was proposed to withdraw the chargé d'affaires who had represented British interests at Tehran since 1815, and to replace him as before by an East India Company's envoy. The shah, Futteh Ali, consented reluctantly, and Kinneir was appointed envoy in 1824. He arrived at the shah's camp at Ahar in September 1826 to find the Persians engaged in active hostilities with the

Russians. Futteh Ali claimed the British subsidy to which, by treaty, Persia was entitled if attacked by a European power. Kinneir would not agree to this, as Persia had been the aggressor. Extensive military operations followed, during which Kinneir was present with the Persian army. On 19 October 1827 the frontier fortress of Erivan was stormed by Prince Paskevich's troops and a Russian division was pushed on to Tabriz. The shah's chief minister, Ali Yar Khan, deserted him on the approach of the Russians, and fled with Kinneir, who ably did his utmost to bring about a peace. The Russians, though declining to admit his official character, gratefully accepted his mediation in a private capacity. A treaty of peace was signed at Turkmanchai on 23 February 1828, involving loss of territory to Persia and the loss of the influence previously enjoyed by the British mission. No blame has been attributed to Kinneir, who won the respect of both Persians and Russians. He received the Persian order of the Sun and Lion, and on 17 November 1829 was knighted (as Sir John Macdonald).

In 1825 Kinneir had married Amelia Harriet (*d.* 1860), third daughter, with his first wife, of Lieutenant-General Sir Alexander *Campbell, first baronet, who died commander-in-chief at Madras in 1824. Kinneir remained as envoy in Persia until his death at Tabriz on 11 June 1830, when a three months' mourning was observed by the shah and the inhabitants.

H. M. CHICHESTER, *rev.* JAMES FALKNER

Sources *Indian Army List* · *GM*, 1st ser., 100/2 (1830), 190, 649
Archives U. Edin., letter-book, corresp., and papers relating to Persia | BL OIOC, letters to Lord Amherst, MS Eur. F 140

Kinnemond, Thomas (*d.* 1657), army officer in the Swedish service, was born in Scotland at a place noted in the Swedish peerage lists as Calensk or Calensh. Although it is uncertain who his parents were, it is known that he and his brother Patrick emigrated to Sweden in the 1620s, before entire Scottish regiments began to take service in Sweden, and so the brothers served with Swedish troops. Little information survives on Patrick, who joined the Swedish army in 1624, and rose to the rank of colonel before he died in 1645.

Thomas Kinnemond served first as an ensign in Johan Baner's Östergötland infantry regiment in 1628, where he subsequently became a lieutenant under Erik Hand's command in 1629. He became major of the city militia in Augsburg in 1633. Not much is known of Kinnemond's movements after this until 1637 when he was appointed master of court at the castle in Koporie in Ingermanland; and in 1640 he was a lieutenant-colonel of a squadron of Viborg men. He became a full colonel in 1649 and was the colonel-in-chief of the Viborg regiment by 1651. During this time he also served as the commandant at Nyenmünde Fort.

In 1650 Kinnemond was naturalized and ennobled, as was his brother, posthumously, in a wave of ennoblements authorized by Queen Kristina of Sweden. His social standing was further enhanced by the land in Livonia which he inherited through his uncle John, who had also entered the Swedish service. In 1651 Kinnemond became a colonel and commandant at Dünamünde Fort, which he himself had constructed. It is not known when he married Christina Scott, the daughter of Colonel James Scott and his wife, Margaret Gibson, although his choice of a Scottish wife implies that his ties to Scotland were still strong. They had seven children, of whom only two survived. He died in 1657. His son Patrick also entered Swedish service.   A. N. L. GROSJEAN

Sources military muster rolls, Krigsarkivet, Stockholm, *MR* 1628/13, 14, 1629/9, 10, 12, 13, 15, 17, 1630/7, 8, 1631/5, 1633/7, 1640/11, 1641/10, 16, 1642/9, 1643/14, 1645/19, 1647/11, 12, 1648/15, 1649/9, 1650/6, 1651/4, 10, 1654/5, 1655/7 · G. Elgenstierna, *Den introducerade svenska adelns ättartavlor med tillägg och rättelser*, 9 vols. (1925–36), vol. 4 · H. Marryat, *One year in Sweden: including a visit to the isle of Gotland*, 2 vols. (1862) · O. Donner, *A brief sketch of the Scottish families in Finland and Sweden* (Helsingfors, 1884) · N. A. Kullberg, S. Bergh, and P. Sondén, eds., *Svenska riksrådets protokoll*, 18 vols. (Stockholm, 1878–1959), vol. 5, pp. 11–12
Wealth at death inherited land from uncle: Elgenstierna, *Svenska adelns ättartavlor*, vol. 4

Kinnoull. For this title name *see* Hay, George, first earl of Kinnoull (*bap*. 1570, *d*. 1634); Hay, George, eighth earl of Kinnoull (1689–1758); Hay, Thomas, ninth earl of Kinnoull (1710–1787).

Kinns, Samuel (1826–1903), Christian apologist, was born in Colchester, the son of J. O. Kinns, of Great Totham, Essex, a Congregationalist minister. He was educated at Colchester grammar school and then privately.

In 1856 Kinns founded a boys' school, The College, Highbury New Park, of which he remained proprietor and principal until 1885. In 1859 he became a fellow of the Royal Astronomical Society and received a PhD from the University of Jena. In 1885 he was ordained deacon in the Church of England and served a year's curacy at All Souls, Langham Place. Ordained priest in 1886, he was vicar of Holy Trinity, Minories, from 29 March 1889, retiring upon the closure of the church on 1 January 1899.

Kinns came to public notice in 1882, when he published *Moses and Geology*, a detailed attempt to harmonize the creation account of Genesis 1 with the latest scientific theories of discovered fossil remains. This proved highly popular, and was acclaimed by Lord Shaftesbury and leading clergy, although it evoked criticism from scientific and biblical experts; Kinns gave public lectures in its defence. Since 1878 he had also been lecturing in the British Museum on the support given to biblical history by the Egyptian and Assyrian monuments. This became the subject of a second popular book, *Graven in the Rock* (1891). He died at his home, 182 Haverstock Hill, London, on 14 July 1903.   R. S. SIMPSON

Sources *The Times* (17 July 1903), 8 · A. T. C. Pratt, ed., *People of the period: being a collection of the biographies of upwards of six thousand living celebrities*, 2 vols. (1897) · Crockford (1903) · 'Assyrian antiquities', *The Times* (9 July 1878), 4 · d. cert.
Likenesses group portrait, photograph, repro. in S. Kinns, *Six hundred years* (1898), 473
Wealth at death £207 8*s*. 6*d*.: probate, 25 Jan 1904, *CGPLA Eng. & Wales*

Kinross. For this title name *see* Balfour, John Blair, first Baron Kinross (1837–1905).

Kinross, John (1855–1931), architect, was born on 3 July 1855 at Shore Road, Stirling, the second of four sons of William Kinross (1810–1874), carriage builder, and his second wife, Ann (1821–1899), *née* Marshall. Kinross attended Stirling high school from 1865 to 1870. He took an architectural apprenticeship with John Hutchison IA (1841–1908) in Glasgow from 1870 to about 1875, and then moved to the Edinburgh office of Wardrop and Reid, architects. In 1880–81 he toured Italy studying, publishing *Details from Italian Buildings Chiefly Renaissance* (1882) on his return. In this year he joined Henry Seymour (1857–1912) in partnership in Edinburgh, undertaking predominantly ecclesiastical work. On 13 August 1889 Kinross married (Mary Louisa) Margaret (1863–1935), teacher, daughter of George Blythe Hall, a banker in York: they had two children, Eveleen Mary (1894–1969) and John Blythe (1904–1989). After leaving Seymour, Kinross began independent practice in 1890, enjoying major restoration projects such as the Carmelite friary church, South Queensferry, Midlothian (1889–90), and the Augustinian priory, St Andrews, Fife (1893–8), and the patronage of the third marquess of Bute. He was active in the Edinburgh Architectural Association, serving as president in 1898–9, and was committed to the Royal Scottish Academy, becoming associate in 1893 and full academician in 1905.

Work for Kinross's other leading patron, Sir James Percy Miller, bt, of Manderston, Berwickshire, began in 1890, including extensive work across the estate and to the mansion. By 1897 the large volume of work in which he was engaged led to partnership with Harold Ogle Tarbolton (1869–1947), though Kinross reverted to independent practice in 1905. During the following years he took an active role in the development of the architectural education in Scotland through continued involvement with academic bodies. He pursued his earlier search for a school of design, creating a new college of art in Edinburgh on whose board of management he sat (1908–11 and 1919–21), constantly insisting upon the study of historic fabric and the link with craftsmanship in design education. Kinross joined J. Inch Morrison (*d*. 1944) in practice in 1920. His other major works include the restorations of Falkland Palace, Fife (1890–98), Greyfriars convent (1896–1900), and the Michaelkirk, Moray (1900–01), new work at St Mary's, Chapeltown, Moray (1896–7), stables at Altyre, Moray (1902), and Ingliston, near Edinburgh (*c*.1900–02), houses at Carlekemp, Haddington (1898–1900), and The Peel, Selkirk (1904–6). He worked particularly with Gothic, Renaissance, and Scottish seventeenth-century styles. Kinross was regarded highly by his colleagues in the profession. He died on 7 January 1931 at his home, 2 Abercromby Place, Edinburgh; after a funeral at St Paul's episcopal church he was buried at Grange cemetery, Grange Road, Edinburgh.   DEBORAH MAYS

Sources D. Mays, 'John Kinross: his life and work, 1855–1931', PhD diss., St Andrew's University, 1988 · private information (2004) [J. B. Kinross, son] · Scott Morton archive, Royal Commission on the Ancient and Historical Monuments of Scotland, Edinburgh, National Monuments Record of Scotland · Royal Scot. Acad. · Mount Stuart Trust, Isle of Bute, Bute MSS · NRA Scotland

[Manderston, Berwickshire records] · archive, Royal Incorporation of Architects in Scotland, Edinburgh, Edinburgh Architectural Association archive

Archives NL Scot., papers · Royal Incorporation of Architects in Scotland, Edinburgh, Edinburgh Architectural Association papers · Royal Scot. Acad., papers | Mount Stuart Trust, Isle of Bute, Bute archive · Royal Commission on the Ancient and Historical Monuments of Scotland, Edinburgh, National Monuments Record of Scotland, Italian sketches by Kinross and Scott Morton archive

Likenesses photograph, 1904, priv. coll. · W. B. Rhind, bronze bust, 1922, Scot. NPG · photograph, 1928, priv. coll.

Wealth at death £5562 15s. 9d.: confirmation, 13 Feb 1931, CCI

Kinsey, John (1693–1750), politician and lawyer, was born in Philadelphia, the son of John Kinsey, politician and Quaker minister, and Sarah, née Stevens. Kinsey probably attended Philadelphia's Friends' public school until the family moved to Woodbridge, New Jersey, about 1703. Kinsey then began an apprenticeship with a joiner in New York. However, his 'Inquisitive disposition, and a Genius for something above his then employ' prompted him to study law, probably in Philadelphia with David Lloyd. He was admitted to the bar there in 1724 and to that at New Jersey in 1725, before settling in Woodbridge to practise law. On 9 September 1725 he married Mary Kearney, daughter of Philp Kearney of Philadelphia. During the 1720s and early 1730s he served as a legislator in the New Jersey assembly. He was named speaker of the house in 1730, a position formerly held by his father. In addition, he is often credited with preparing the first compilation of New Jersey laws in the year 1732.

Kinsey moved to Philadelphia in 1730 and was immediately elected to the Pennsylvania legislature. He held seats concurrently in the Pennsylvania and New Jersey assemblies during the 1730s. In 1739 he obtained the position of speaker in the Pennsylvania house, which he retained, bar a short interlude, for the remainder of his life. Between 1738 and 1741 Kinsey also served as attorney-general and as chief justice of the supreme court of Pennsylvania (1743–50). In addition, he was named acting trustee of the Pennsylvania general loan office in 1739, another position which he held until his death. Named in 1737 as a commissioner to settle the boundary dispute between Maryland and Pennsylvania, he also served as a representative to the Albany Convention with the Six Nations in 1745.

Alongside these offices, Kinsey was also a prominent member of the Philadelphia Quaker community. Between 1730 and 1750 he was the presiding clerk of the Philadelphia yearly meeting, the most important position within the Quaker denomination. As both chief clerk of the Friends' meeting and speaker of the Pennsylvania house, Kinsey had attained the highest leadership role in both of these institutions. He further served the Quakers as correspondent to the London meeting and overseer of the press.

On 11 May 1750, while trying a case in Burlington before the New Jersey supreme court, Kinsey suffered what may have been a stroke. He died that evening and was buried two days later. It was later discovered that his estate owed £3000 to the general loan office, a sum—fifteen times his salary as chief justice—that he had taken for his own use. Disclosure of Kinsey's misappropriation of government finances came as a severe blow to the Quaker denomination, coming as it did after Friends had been warned in 1746 not to dishonour the community through corrupt business practices. Kinsey's posthumous reputation means that he has been invariably overlooked in histories of Quakerism in Philadelphia. More recently the work of Edwin B. Bronner and others has focused attention on Kinsey's contribution as one of the most significant Quaker political and religious leaders in colonial America.   SUSAN A. HOFFMAN

Sources E. B. Bronner, 'The disgrace of John Kinsey, Quaker politician, 1739–1750', *Pennsylvania Magazine of History and Biography*, 75 (1951), 400–15 · T. Wendel, 'The speaker of the house, Pennsylvania, 1701–1776', *Pennsylvania Magazine of History and Biography*, 97 (1973), 3–21 · J. R. Soderlund, *Quakers and slavery: a divided spirit* (1985) · A. Tully, *William Penn's legacy: politics and social structure in provincial Pennsylvania, 1726–1755* (1977) · F. B. Tolles, *Meeting house and counting house: the Quaker merchants of colonial Philadelphia, 1682–1763* (1948) · I. Sharpless, *Political leaders of provincial Pennsylvania* (1919); repr. (1971) · E. B. Bronner, 'Kinsey, John', *ANB*

Archives Hist. Soc. Penn., Pemberton papers · Hist. Soc. Penn., corresp. of John Smith · New Jersey State Archives, Newark, New Jersey laws

Wealth at death £3000 in debt to government

Kinsey, William Morgan (1788–1851), Church of England clergyman and traveller, born at Abergavenny, Monmouthshire, was son of Robert Morgan Kinsey, solicitor and banker at Abergavenny, and Caroline Hannah, his wife, daughter of Sir James Harington, bt. He matriculated at Oxford on 28 November 1805, became a scholar of Trinity College, graduated BA in 1809, and proceeded MA in 1813. In 1815 he was elected a fellow of his college, dean in 1822, vice-president in 1823, and bursar in 1824. In 1822 he graduated BD.

In 1827 Kinsey made a tour in Portugal with the intention of making the country better known to the English people. From his journals and a series of letters written to his friend Thomas Haynes Bayly, as well as from historical and other sources, Kinsey published *Portugal Illustrated* (1828), an interesting account of the country, and well illustrated with engravings by G. Cooke and Skelton from drawings chiefly made by a companion during his tour. It was dedicated to Lord Auckland, to whom Kinsey was chaplain, and a second edition appeared in 1829. In 1830 Kinsey was travelling with Viscount Alford in Belgium, and, happening to be at Brussels at the outbreak of the revolution in August of that year, was an eye-witness. About 1832 he was appointed minister of St John's Church, Cheltenham, where he made a reputation as a preacher and published a few sermons. In 1843 he was appointed rector of Rotherfield Greys, Oxfordshire, where he lived until his death on 6 April 1851. He was the author of a few other pamphlets, and in January 1848 contributed a paper to the *Gentleman's Magazine* entitled 'Random recollections of a visit to Walton Hall'.

L. H. CUST, *rev.* H. C. G. MATTHEW

Sources *GM*, 2nd ser., 36 (1851), 95 · Foster, *Alum. Oxon.* · I. O. Martins, *William Morgan Kinsey, uma ilustração de Portugal* (1987)

Kinsman, Andrew (*bap.* **1724**, *d.* **1793**), Methodist preacher, was baptized at Tavistock parish church, Devon, on 11 November 1724, the son of John Kinsman and Mary, his wife. He was converted to Methodism about 1740 by reading the sermons of George Whitefield, whom he met locally in 1744. Though he maintained contact with local Wesleyan Methodists, and knew both John and Charles Wesley, Kinsman held to the Calvinistic Methodism learned from Whitefield. He moved to Plymouth in 1745 and joined a Methodist society of Whitefield's converts. Ann Tiley (*d.* 1774) had given a site in Bretonside in the town for a tabernacle (or chapel) in 1744, and on 28 October of the following year she and Kinsman were married. This gave him a controlling position in the tabernacle, for many years the leading centre of Methodism in Plymouth. In 1753 he strengthened his position by opening a chapel in Devonport called the Upper Room. His wife died in July 1774 and in October 1776 he married Mrs Joanna Webber of London, who survived him.

At first the tabernacle was supplied by a series of itinerant Calvinistic Methodist preachers, but by 1748 Kinsman took over the leadership and from 1750 preached regularly. He was ordained a minister at Broadmead Baptist chapel in Bristol on 4 August 1763 by five nonconformist and Methodist preachers. After this he was much in request to preach in other churches each summer, when he employed students (usually connected with the countess of Huntingdon) as temporary ministers for his two chapels. He had continued his grocery business, but in 1771 he gave it to his son and went to live at Devonport. For a year before his death at Devonport on 28 February 1793 he suffered from dropsy. He was buried in Stoke Damerel parish churchyard in Devonport after a service in his Upper Room. In his lifetime Kinsman maintained the Methodist character of his two Calvinistic congregations, but after his death both embraced dissent.

ROGER F. S. THORNE

Sources 'The Rev. Andrew Kinsman, late minister of the gospel at Plymouth-Dock, in the county of Devon', *Evangelical Magazine*, 1 (1793), 45–60 · C. E. Welch, 'Andrew Kinsman's churches at Plymouth', *Report and Transactions of the Devonshire Association*, 97 (1965), 212–36 · Tavistock baptisms, 1993, Devon RO [transcript]
Likenesses engraving, repro. in 'The Rev. Andrew Kinsman', *Evangelical Magazine*, facing p. 45

Kintore. For this title name *see* Keith, John, first earl of Kintore (*d.* 1715).

Kinwelmersh [Kinwelmershe, Kindlemarsh], **Francis** (*bap.* **1538**), poet, was baptized on 18 October 1538, the son of Richard Kinwelmersh or Kyndelmershe of All Hallows, Bread Street, London. The poet entered Gray's Inn in 1557. Two students of the same surname, Anthony and Robert, were admitted in 1561 and 1563 respectively and were probably his brothers. At least one of them was the son of the man who built lodgings at Gray's Inn known as 'Kyndelmarshes buyldings', so the Kinwelmershes would have been a substantial presence there in the 1560s. Francis and Anthony were probably part of a literary clique at Gray's

Inn which included Alexander Neville; in 1565 the poet George Gascoigne wrote his 'Memories' in response to a challenge set by their 'felowship'.

The following year Kinwelmersh collaborated with Gascoigne on *Jocasta*, a translation of Dolce's *Giocasta*, itself based on Euripides' *Phoenissae*, which was performed in the hall of their inn in the course of 1566 and first published in Gascoigne's anonymous *A Hundreth Sundrie Flowres* in 1573. Kinwelmersh was responsible for acts I and IV. The play has been noted as the first Greek tragedy on the English stage. Gabriel Harvey called it a 'statelie tragedie' in his copy (Bodl. Oxf., MS Mal. 792, sig. 2B) and Roger, Lord North, kept a manuscript of the play (BL, Add. MS 34063). *STC, 1475–1640*, attributes to Francis Kinwelmersh the translation of Adrien le Roy's *A Briefe and Plaine Instruction … for the Lute* (1574).

Kinwelmersh was a contributor to *The Paradyse of Dainty Devises* (1576), and his initials, F. K., and, in later editions, F. Kindlemarsh, appear on the title-page. In all the editions, several poems carry his initials and one ('For Whitsunday') is signed M. Kindlemarsh.

F. K. is mentioned in complimentary terms by William Webbe in *A Discourse of English Poetrie* (1586); and in Bodenham's preface to *Bel-vedere, or, The Garden of the Muses* (1600), Francis Kindlemarsh, esquire, is listed with Norton, Gascoigne, Atchelow, and Whetstone among deceased authors to whose published and unpublished writings 'due right' is given by the compiler.

The poet is probably the Francis Kinwelmersh of Charlton, Shropshire, whose will was proved on 21 October 1589; he died in financial difficulties, leaving his lease of Charlton mortgaged for £100 to his wife, Cicely. This Kinwelmersh administered his brother Thomas's estate in May 1575 and died before 16 May 1580, when a new administrator was appointed. The History of Parliament also identifies the poet as the Francis Kinwelmershe, esquire, elected MP for Droitwich, Worcestershire, in 1571 and then for Bossiney, Cornwall, on 27 April 1572 (probably by the patronage of Francis Russell, second earl of Bedford, who controlled the borough; Russell's name had appeared next to Kinwelmersh's in the admission register of Gray's Inn). GILLIAN AUSTEN

Sources *The complete works of George Gascoigne*, ed. J. W. Cunliffe, 1 (1907), 62 · *STC, 1475–1640* · C. C. Stopes, *Shakespeare's industry* (1916) · G. Goodwin, 'Kinwelmersh family', *N&Q*, 8th ser., 12 (1897), 423–4 · J. Foster, *The register of admissions to Gray's Inn, 1521–1889, together with the register of marriages in Gray's Inn chapel, 1695–1754* (privately printed, London, 1889) · R. J. Fletcher, ed., *The pension book of Gray's Inn*, 1 (1901) · S. M. Thorpe, 'Kinwelmersh, Francis', HoP, *Commons, 1558–1603* · will, PRO, PROB 11/74, sig. 79 · J. Bodenham, *Bel-vedere, or, The garden of the Muses* (1600) · *DNB*
Wealth at death his only visible asset, the lease of Charlton, was mortgaged for £100: will, PRO, PROB 11/74, sig. 79

Kip, Johannes (*b.* before **1653**, *d.* **1721?**), draughtsman and engraver, was born in Amsterdam. He trained there under the engraver Bastiaen Stopendael from May 1668, probably for two years, and lived in Stopendael's house on the Angeliersgracht. His marriage to Elisabeth Breda in

Amsterdam on 5 April 1680 resulted in at least one daughter, whose name is unknown. Kip's earliest dated engraving is from 1672, and he provided many plates for books published from this date onwards. In 1686 he made six plates of *William of Orange, his Wife and Attendants Near The Hague*. Shortly after William's usurpation of the English throne in 1689 Kip travelled to England, although it is not known if this was motivated by connections with William's court.

The majority of Kip's work consists of topography, which has been called 'the most dynamic area of publishing … in the first quarter of the century' (Clayton, *The English Print*, 75). It was possibly for William's court that he began to develop and produce the bird's-eye prospect views of country houses on which his reputation rests. The first view was of the Chelsea Hospital—in which William had quickly taken a personal interest on becoming king—which Kip drew and engraved in 1690. About 1698 he began producing drawings and plates for his best-known work, *Britannia illustrata, or, Views of several of the queen's palaces, as also of the principal seats of the nobility and gentry of Great Britain*, a collection of high-quality engraved bird's-eye prospects sold on single sheets from about 1700 and issued together in 1707. For the first volume of this work, which achieved 'immediate success' (Harris, 140), Kip engraved the views drawn by Leonard Knyff, but for the second volume he drew and engraved the views himself. He probably sold out his interests in the work before or shortly after its publication, and it was expanded by booksellers with contributions from other artists from 1709. Kip also drew and engraved the sixty-five plates for Robert Atkyn's *The Ancient and Present State of Gloucestershire* (1712) and engraved Thomas Bladeslade's drawings for John Harris's *The History of Kent* (1719).

During his career in Britain Kip produced engraved portraits, frontispieces, and architectural miscellany, and for an unknown period lived in and sold prints from his house on St John's Street, Westminster. His contemporary reputation as a fashionable engraver probably peaked in 1708 with the appearance of *Britannia illustrata*, but he found himself superseded by the engraver Henry Hulsburgh, who introduced a more up-to-date architectural survey into the expanded work of 1715. Kip retained a persuasive reputation as a draughtsman and engraver. He published a 12-sheet view of St James's Park from Buckingham House in 1710, and was chosen by Godfrey Kneller to survey his new house about 1715.

Kip can probably be identified with the John Kipp who was buried in St Margaret's Church, Westminster, on 12 August 1721. It is not known when his wife died, but his daughter outlived him and, having reputedly been taught by him, seems to have been known as an artist of some merit. Since his death Kip's reputation has suffered, with the credit for much of the draughtsmanship in his work going to Knyff. NICHOLAS GRINDLE

Sources F. D. O. Obreen, ed., *Archief voor Nederlandsche kunstgeschiedenis*, 7 vols. (Rotterdam, 1877–90), vol. 7 · J. Harris, *The artist and the country house: a history of country house and garden view painting in Britain, 1540–1870* (1979) · parish register, St Margaret's,

Westminster, City Westm. AC · T. Clayton, *The English print, 1688–1802* (1997) · E. Harris and N. Savage, *British architectural books and writers, 1556–1785* (1990) · T. Clayton, 'Publishing houses', *The Georgian country house*, ed. D. Arnold (1998) · J. Turner, ed., *The dictionary of art*, 34 vols. (1996) · Bénézit, *Dict.*, 4th edn

Kip, William (*fl. c.*1585–1618), engraver, born in Utrecht, arrived in England about 1585. He was perhaps primarily a goldsmith and jeweller and is so described on the various returns of aliens which provide almost the sole extant biographical record. While no known examples of his work as a goldsmith or jeweller survive, his output of printed work is notable for a number of important maps. The most significant of these is the four-sheet wall-map of the British Isles, *A Description of the Kingdoms of England, Scotland & Ireland with al the Ilands Adiacent*, engraved for Hans Woutneel in 1603, a handsome production known only in a single surviving copy, with a pictorial genealogical table celebrating the union of the crowns of England and Scotland. More widely known is the important sequence of thirty-four county maps after John Norden and Christopher Saxton engraved by Kip for the 1607 edition of William Camden's *Britannia*. Other examples include the map of Hertfordshire for Norden's *Speculi Britanniae* (1598), two miniature maps in roundels of England and the world of about 1602, also engraved for Woutneel, and Edward Wright's important untitled two-sheet map of the world of about 1610.

Beyond maps, Kip was responsible for engraving a portrait of Queen Elizabeth, probably dating from the 1590s but known only in a later state, as well as Stephen Harrison's magnificent series *The Arch's of Triumph Erected in Honor of James* (1604)—the earliest English set of plates to show the lavish temporary architecture erected for ceremonial events.

Kip had a son, Immanuel, baptized in 1597, and daughters Debora (*bap.* 1601) and Rebecca (*bap.* 1603). Debora married Balthazar Gerbier in or before 1618 and appears, with her children, in a well-known portrait by Rubens apparently dating from early in 1629 and now in the National Gallery of Art, Washington, DC. Kip is recorded living in Coleman Street, London, with his wife and an English-born child in 1617 (when he was said to have been in England for thirty-two years) and living in the Candlewick ward of the City with a daughter and her Dutch husband, presumably Gerbier, in 1618. The household also included a young painter from Amsterdam and a young merchant from Hamburg. It is not known when or where he died. LAURENCE WORMS

Sources A. M. Hind, *Engraving in England in the sixteenth and seventeenth centuries*, 1 (1952), 192, 210–11; 2 (1955), 17–34 · A. Griffiths and R. A. Gerard, *The print in Stuart Britain, 1603–1689* (1998), 41–5 [exhibition catalogue, BM, 8 May – 20 Sept 1998] · R. E. G. Kirk and E. F. Kirk, eds., *Returns of aliens dwelling in the city and suburbs of London, from the reign of Henry VIII to that of James I*, Huguenot Society of London, 10/3 (1907) · W. J. C. Moens, ed., *The marriage, baptismal, and burial registers, 1571 to 1874, and monumental inscriptions of the Dutch Reformed church, Austin Friars, London* (privately printed, Lymington, 1884) · R. W. Shirley, *The mapping of the world: early printed world maps, 1472–1700* (1983) · R. W. Shirley, *Early printed maps of the British Isles*, rev. edn (1991) · E. Lynam, 'Woutneel's map of the British Isles, 1603', *GJ*, 82 (1933), 536–8 · [E. Lynam], 'A Woutneel map of

1602', *GJ*, 89 (1937), 573–4 · *IGI* · B. Adams, *London illustrated, 1604–1851* (1983)

Kipling, Alice (1837–1910). *See under* Macdonald sisters (*act.* 1837–1925).

Kipling, (Joseph) Rudyard (1865–1936), writer and poet, was born in Bombay, India, on 30 December 1865, the son of John Lockwood Kipling (1837–1911), professor of architectural sculpture in the Sir Jamsetjee Jejeebhoy School of Art in Bombay, and his wife, Alice *Kipling [*see under* Macdonald sisters]. The name Joseph (never used) was family tradition, elder sons being named Joseph or John in alternation; 'Rudyard' came from Lake Rudyard in Staffordshire, where his parents had first met. Both his father and his mother were the children of Methodist ministers, and both quietly rebelled against their evangelical origins. Kipling was brought up in indifference to organized religion; although he always believed in the reality of the spiritual, he never held any religious doctrine. His childish impressions of Muslim, Hindu, and Parsi—he recalled 'little Hindu temples' with 'dimly-seen, friendly Gods' (Kipling, *Something of Myself*, chap. 1)—made him more sympathetic to those forms than to the charmless protestantism he afterwards encountered in England.

Early years and education In 1871 the Kipling family, now including his younger sister Alice (always called Trix), Rudyard's only sibling, returned to England on leave. On their return to India the parents left their children with people in Southsea, now part of Portsmouth, who had advertised their services in caring for the children of English parents in India. It was a usual practice for the children of the English in India to be thus separated from their parents, but Rudyard and his sister were not prepared for the event. 'We had had no preparation or explanation', Kipling's sister wrote; 'it was like a double death, or rather, like an avalanche that had swept away everything happy and familiar' (Fleming, 171). Nor is it known why the parents chose to put them in the hands of paid guardians rather than with one or more members of Alice Kipling's family. One sister was married to Alfred Baldwin, a prosperous manufacturer: their child, about the same age as Rudyard, was Stanley *Baldwin, afterwards prime minister; another sister had married Sir Edward Burne-*Jones, the painter; a third sister had married Sir Edward *Poynter, who became president of the Royal Academy. By 1871 all of these families would have been able and willing to receive the Kipling children.

Instead they went to Southsea, to a house now notorious as the House of Desolation (so-called in Kipling's 'Baa baa, black sheep'). Kipling was not yet six years old; Trix was three. Here he attended 'a terrible little day-school' (Kipling, *Something of Myself*, chap. 1). The woman who cared for them, Mrs Pryse Agar Holloway, is, in Kipling's account of her as Aunty Rosa, a monster. Deliberately cruel and unjust, she tries to set sister against brother, systematically humiliates the young Kipling, allows her son to terrorize him mentally and physically, and denies him simple pleasures. She also introduces a Calvinistic protestantism into Kipling's experience: 'I had never heard of Hell, so I

(Joseph) Rudyard Kipling (1865–1936), by Sir Philip Burne-Jones, 1899

was introduced to it in all its terrors' (ibid.). He took refuge in reading. One of his punishments was to be compelled to read devotional literature: in this way he acquired a mastery of biblical phrase and image. The Kipling children remained with Mrs Holloway for five and a half years: towards the end of that time, Kipling's eyesight began to fail, and to his other miseries were added 'the nameless terrors of broad daylight that were only coats on pegs after all' (ibid.). Kipling's mother returned from India in April 1877, and for the rest of the year her children lived with her. At the beginning of the next year Kipling went off to public school; Trix returned to the care of Mrs Holloway.

The truth of Kipling's description of his childhood has been doubted: Mrs Holloway was not cruel but misunderstood by a spoiled, preternaturally imaginative child; 'Baa baa, black sheep' is fiction, not autobiography; or, if autobiography, then shamelessly self-indulgent. And how can one explain Trix's return to Southsea? We cannot now know the facts. The effects of Kipling's abandonment in the House of Desolation upon his psyche, and, in turn, upon his works, continues to be at the centre of biographical and interpretive arguments. Kipling's own judgement was that his sufferings 'drained me of any capacity for real, personal hate for the rest of my days', a conclusion not generally agreed with. He also thought that the experience contributed to the growth of the artist: 'it demanded constant wariness, the habit of observation, and attendance on moods and tempers' (Kipling, *Something of Myself*, chap. 1). If he blamed his parents, that did not appear in his behaviour towards them; he was not merely dutiful and loving but seems genuinely to have admired them both.

Kipling believed that what 'saved' him during his South-sea ordeal was an annual visit to his aunt, Georgiana Burne-Jones, at The Grange, in Fulham, London, where he 'possessed a paradise' of 'love and affection' (Kipling, *Something of Myself*, chap. 1). He was also much interested at The Grange in the example of his uncle at work and by Burne-Jones's conversations with such friends as William Morris, interests that Kipling's own artist father must have helped to encourage. We know little about Kipling's imaginative development until rather late in his school-days, but the impact of Burne-Jones and of the group to which he belonged, devoted to the highest standards of craftsmanship and to an unembarrassed worship of beauty, must be allowed to have had an important part in forming Kipling.

At the beginning of 1878 Kipling was sent to the United Services College at Westward Ho!, Bideford, north Devon, founded in 1874 by army officers in order to provide an affordable public school for their sons. Most of the students had the army as their goal. The headmaster, Cormell Price, an Oxford graduate, was a friend from early days of both Burne-Jones and of Kipling's mother. The new, raw, impoverished school was an unlikely place, but, after a long period of unhappiness following his entry, Kipling thrived there. For this happy result he always credited Price, whose virtues he magnified in the figure of the Head in *Stalky & Co.*; more practically, he remained devoted to Price to the end of his days, helping him financially in his retirement and, after Price's death, acting as a trustee for Price's son. It is now impossible to see Kipling's school-days uncoloured by *Stalky & Co.* (1899), Kipling's fictional version of his life at Westward Ho! The bare facts that we have are often mildly at variance with *Stalky*, but the energy of the *Stalky* version overwhelms all attempts to correct the record. One may safely say that Kipling did make friends with Lionel *Dunsterville (Stalky), with G. C. Beresford (M'Turk), was himself a recognizable original for Beetle, and was impressed more than he knew by the example of William Carr Crofts (King) and his passion for Latin literature. He admired Price, was given the run of Price's library, and edited the school paper, revived by Price for the express purpose of allowing Kipling to edit it. He also began to experiment in poetry, the form of literature he loved first and best. The extent and variety of Kipling's precocious exercises in poetry have been made clear in Andrew Rutherford's edition, *Early Verse by Rudyard Kipling* (1986), which includes fluent imitations of popular ballads, Pope, Keats, Browning, and Swinburne, among many others. In 1881 his parents privately printed a selection of this work under the title *Schoolboy Lyrics*. Though it was produced without Kipling's knowledge, and though he was embarrassed by it then and afterwards, the book is technically Kipling's first and is now one of the *rarissima* in his bibliography.

Despite the army flavour of the United Services College, Kipling's interests at the time seem to have been almost wholly literary. His school-days ended in May 1882; an indifferent school record and his parents' lack of means put Oxford and Cambridge out of the question. For a brief time Kipling flirted with the idea of medicine (an admiration for doctors and an interest in the art of healing always remained with him). Kipling's parents were both occasional contributors to the *Civil and Military Gazette* (*CMG*), published in Lahore, where, in 1875, John Lockwood Kipling had been appointed head of both the newly founded Mayo School of Art and of the Lahore Museum. Through his parents' influence with the proprietors of the paper Kipling was offered a position as sub-editor and went to India in September 1882, arriving in Lahore towards the end of October. For the next six years and four months Kipling was to work uninterruptedly on newspapers in India.

Journalist in India Though he was at first kept to routine editorial work, gradually Kipling began to write more, and more variously, for the paper—verse, an irregular column of local gossip, summaries of official reports, news paragraphs, and the like. In March 1884 he was sent to Patiala to report a state visit of the viceroy, and his success in this trial was such that from that point on the flow of his writing in the *CMG* is unchecked. The overflow found other outlets. In 1884 he and his sister published a collection of verses titled *Echoes*, exhibiting English life in India in the form of parodies of standard poets: Kipling's knowledge of American literature appears in his parodies of Emerson, Longfellow, and Joaquin Miller. For Christmas 1885 all four Kiplings published an annual called *Quartette*, containing such distinguished early work as 'The Strange Ride of Morrowbie Jukes' and 'The Phantom 'Rickshaw'. These exhibit the remarkably precocious maturity—Kipling was not yet twenty when they were written—that prompted Henry James to write of Kipling as a youth who 'has stolen the formidable mask of maturity and rushes about making people jump with the deep sounds, the sportive exaggerations of tone, that issue from its painted lips' (James).

In 1886 Kipling published *Departmental Ditties*, lightly satirical verses about official life in India reprinted from the *CMG*. This, which Kipling always regarded as his first book, had a great success among the community it satirized. It also drew a brief, friendly notice from Andrew Lang in London, Kipling's first recognition in England.

As a journalist, Kipling was neither a civil servant nor a military officer, but could move freely among the different levels of Lahore society. The capital of the Punjab, Lahore abounded in high officials. It was also an army post, and Kipling discovered a new pleasure in observing and making friends with the officers and men of the British troops stationed at Fort Lahore and at Mian Mir, the nearby barracks. He wandered through the streets of Lahore at night, and though he claimed afterwards to have seen perhaps more of native life than in fact he did, he certainly paid that life more sympathetic attention than usually allowed to the English in India. In 1886, while still under age, he joined the masonic lodge Hope and Perseverance of Lahore, and was active in its affairs while he remained in Lahore. The prominence of masonic lore and masonic symbolism in Kipling's work from this time on is a recognized critical topic, as is the attraction to fraternal or exclusive organizations (for example Stalky & Co., Soldiers Three, the Seonee Pack, the Janeites) witnessed by his membership in the freemasons.

In November 1887 Kipling, now recognized as one of the best journalists in India, was transferred by his proprietors to their other, larger paper, *The Pioneer*, of Allahabad. Lahore had been Muslim; Allahabad, on the banks of the Ganges, was Hindu. Kipling made no secret of his preference for the Muslim element in India, a preference only reinforced by his residence in Allahabad. His work now mostly consisted in providing verse or fiction for his paper, or in carrying out special assignments. Kipling now travelled round India to produce the articles collected in *From Sea to Sea* (1900) as 'Letters of marque', 'The city of dreadful night', 'Among the railway folk', and 'The Giridh coal-fields', articles that combined the oldest India with the newest one of railways, factories, and other works of the raj. Before he went to Allahabad Kipling had been publishing a series of stories in the *CMG* under the title 'Plain Tales from the Hills', the hills being the high foothills of the Himalayas at Simla, the summer capital of British India where Kipling had spent several of his summer leaves. Simla society, with its gossip, jealousies, amours, and other amusements, gave Kipling his material; the 'Plain Tales' were a sort of 'Departmental Ditties' converted to prose and somewhat more serious. In book form *Plain Tales from the Hills* (1888) was an immediate hit.

Early in 1888 Kipling's proprietors, confident of their star young employee's productive power, made him editor of a new weekly supplement to *The Pioneer* called the *Week's News*, which provided a page to be filled each week with a new fiction. Kipling now began to pour out the stories that, collected and reprinted in the series of paperbacks called the Railway Library, made his name in India and, soon enough, in England and America as well. Carrying modestly anonymous illustrated covers drawn by John Lockwood Kipling, the series of volumes—the product of a single year—included *Soldiers Three* (1888), *The Story of the Gadsbys* (1888), *In Black and White* (1889), *Under the Deodars* (1889), *The Phantom 'Rickshaw* (1889), and *Wee Willie Winkie* (1889). This prodigality was no fluke. Kipling, throughout his career, always found more opportunities for fiction and poetry bidding for his attention than he could possibly respond to. As he wrote to his sister late in life, the ideas kept 'rising in the head … one behind the other' (Kipling, letter, 8–10 March 1931). And so it always was.

Return to England and early fame India was now too small for Kipling. Before the end of 1888 he had determined to return to England to try his fortunes as a writer, and early in March 1889 he sailed from Calcutta for London. He reversed the usual route and travelled to Singapore, China, and Japan, before crossing the north Pacific to San Francisco and then across the United States. He sent back stories at every stage of his journey to *The Pioneer*, later collected in *From Sea to Sea*. His companions on the voyage were Professor and Mrs Alex Hill, friends from Allahabad.

Mrs Hill, an American, was more than an ordinary friend; she had been confidante and muse to Kipling and had exercised a strong attraction upon him during the entire period of his life in Allahabad. While staying with her family in Pennsylvania towards the end of his journey Kipling became engaged to her sister, Caroline Taylor. The engagement did not long survive Kipling's return to England, but it is a curious episode in his emotional life, apparently having more to do with his feelings towards Mrs Hill than towards her sister. The articles that Kipling sent back to India during his travels across the Pacific and the Atlantic were typical of his youthful manner—enthusiastic, unrestrained, sometimes tactless, but always striking and vivid. One of them reports his pilgrimage to the greatly admired Mark Twain in upstate New York. On his travels across the American continent Kipling saw reason to confirm his already formed opinion of the United States as an attractive but violent and lawless community. Did he in fact see a man shot dead in a Chinese gambling-hell in San Francisco? No matter. He wrote as though he had. Americans were a people 'without the Law'.

Kipling at last arrived in England early in October 1889, took chambers in London, and almost at once entered into his fame. Some editors already knew his work, or had heard of it; others needed only to see some of it to bid eagerly for it. He had no interval of starving in a garret (nor did he ever have to worry about money) but rather had to defend himself against demands he could not possibly meet. He encountered this sudden success warily: publishers were rascals; editors wanted only to skim one's brains; the public cared only for the latest celebrity, no sooner exalted than cast aside. Kipling was determined that he would have nothing to do with this. He put his literary affairs in the hands of an agent and for the rest of his life had no direct dealings with publishers. He would be identified with no literary clique, and he sought to avoid publicity. He did join the Savile Club, and was gratified by the friendship of such men as Andrew Lang, H. Rider Haggard, Edmund Gosse, Thomas Hardy, and Sir Walter Besant. In the course of his life Kipling would have many other literary and artistic acquaintances—Henry James, for example, whose achievement Kipling fully appreciated—but he did not seek them out, and always seemed to prefer public men or men of action, Theodore Roosevelt or Dr Jameson, for example. A more agreeable side of this stand-offishness was Kipling's resolve never to criticize or to comment in print on the work of his fellow authors, a resolve strictly maintained throughout his life, despite the fact that his private comments and indirect published remarks show him to have been an extremely shrewd judge.

Kipling's return to London at the end of 1889 began a quarter-century of unbroken production of literary work of the highest originality, distinction, and popularity: three novels, four volumes of poems, twelve volumes of stories, including such unclassifiable inventions as the *Jungle Books* and *Puck of Pook's Hill*, four volumes of essays and sketches, and much miscellaneous writing, some of it uncollected, came from his pen between 1890 and 1914. It would be difficult to match this record for sustained quantity, variety, and quality in the whole of English literature. Kipling's fame grew immense, and was matched by his sales, which were measured in the millions world-wide and which were never much affected by the chops and changes in his critical reputation.

Kipling's first impact upon a wide public was as the poet of British India, including the British tommy, a subject quite new to most readers. It is likely that, despite all Kipling's varied later work, the Indian association will always come first whenever his name is mentioned. Kipling's 'imperialism' did not crystallize until after his return to England, when he saw that the realities of the empire at work were unknown to the people at home; thereafter it was a part of his artistic purpose to give a voice to the administrators, the soldiers, and their women who made the empire function. Two ideas running through his work arise in connection with his imagination of India but are not confined to it: the notion of a 'law' that must be obeyed as the condition of human society, and the notion that what we do is set for us by the conditions of our situation—by 'history'. Thus Kipling's 'imperialists' are not swashbuckling conquistadores but men whose work has been laid upon them: in this sense they do not differ from the English at home or from any other historical community. Another theme, not yet much apparent but always present, was that of the occult—of things beyond the grasp of reason but nevertheless powerful. Kipling the man, as opposed to the artist, was hostile to such ideas: he held that his sister's long periods of mental disturbance were partly caused by the 'soul-destroying business of "spiritualism"' (Kipling, letter, 3 June 1927). Nevertheless, many stories, from the early 'Phantom 'Rickshaw' to the late 'Wish House', show how strongly Kipling the artist was drawn in that direction. Another marked interest was in giving to every kind of creature a voice—from the dialect of *Soldiers Three* to the canine speech of *Thy Servant a Dog* (1930): in doing this, Kipling displays one of the largest vocabularies in English literature.

When Kipling burst upon the public in 1889 he was just about to turn twenty-four. A short, slight man, his notable features were bushy dark eyebrows, penetrating bright blue eyes behind thick spectacles, a full, bristling moustache, and a prominent cleft chin. These made him an easy mark for the caricaturists, the most formidable of them Max Beerbohm, upon whom Kipling long exercised the fascination of abomination. Kipling was beginning to lose his hair at the time he left India, and by the end of the 1890s he was bald on top, a strong contrast to the bushy eyebrows and moustache. He was inordinately fond of tobacco, as was his father, and enjoyed it in cigarettes, cigars, and pipes. Otherwise he was temperate in his habits, though he knew and enjoyed good food and wine until illness denied it to him (George Saintsbury's *Notes on a Cellar-Book* is dedicated to Kipling). Drunkenness he abhorred. His defective eyesight is supposed to have adversely affected his athletic ability, but he at least attempted to play polo and tennis in India. Fishing especially appealed to him, and he seems to have been at least a competent fly-fisherman. His daughter remembered him as 'compact of neatness and energy. He never fumbled, and his gestures were alway expressive' (Carrington, 517).

Kipling was no ordinary reader, but consumed books of every kind, rapidly and in large numbers. His years of journalism had taught him that no subject was without interest, and he enjoyed forms of print not usually regarded as attractive, including blue books (official government reports). Although a literary traditionalist, who knew English literature thoroughly and French literature well, and who delighted in the Latin of Horace, Kipling read widely in current literature as a matter of course. He claimed to be unmusical, though he was acutely sensitive to metrical form. Painting interested him, as one would expect in a man whose father and two of whose uncles were professional artists, and his own work in illustrating the *Just So Stories* shows that he had a distinct gift. But he does not seem to have paid any special attention to the graphic arts.

Within the first two years of his entering the London literary life, Kipling produced *The Light that Failed* (1890), *Life's Handicap* (1891), *The Naulahka* (1892, in collaboration with Wolcott Balestier), *Barrack-Room Ballads* (1892), and most of the stories collected in *Many Inventions* (1893); to this one may add *Plain Tales from the Hills* and the six volumes of the Railway Library, now reprinted from the Indian editions for the British and American public. Readers who had not heard of Kipling at the beginning of 1890 could have a whole shelf of Kipling by the end of 1892. Kipling several times broke down under the strain of his work, a strain complicated by the confusions of his personal life. The engagement to Caroline Taylor ended early in 1890; at the same time he encountered again a woman named Flo Garrard, to whom he had imagined himself engaged when he left England for India and who contributed to the figure of Maisie in *The Light that Failed*. Kipling renewed his pursuit of Flo Garrard for a time, unsuccessfully.

Marriage and residence in the United States In August 1891 Kipling set out on a voyage around the southern hemisphere, making his first visit to South Africa and his only visits to New Zealand and Australia. In December he reached Lahore, where he learned of the sudden death of his friend, the American Wolcott Balestier, with whom he had collaborated on the romance called *The Naulahka*, and to whom *Barrack-Room Ballads* was dedicated. Kipling immediately left Lahore (he was never to return to India), arrived in London early in January, and at once married Balestier's sister, Caroline (1862–1939), by special licence on 18 January 1892. This curious story has never been elucidated, and hardly any record survives of the early history of the Balestier–Kipling relation. It has been suggested that the attraction between Wolcott Balestier and Kipling was homosexual, but, if so, it is hard to see how that explains Kipling's marriage to the sister. Kipling and Caroline Balestier had been known to each other since 1890 and there is some reason to think that there had been an understanding between them before Kipling set off on his voyage. Many, but by no means all, of those who knew the Kiplings did not like Mrs Kipling, finding her dictatorial, selfish, and ill-spirited. Whatever others thought, Rudyard and Caroline appear to have been happy in each other and maintained a steady mutual respect and affection through forty-four years of marriage.

They travelled as far as Japan on their wedding-journey, when the failure of Kipling's bank drove them back to Vermont, where Mrs Kipling's family then lived. There they bought property near Brattleboro, built a house, and began a family: Josephine, their first child, was born in 1893, Elsie, their second, in 1896. Kipling flourished in the isolation of Vermont in the citadel of his own house: here he wrote *The Jungle Book* (1894), *The Second Jungle Book* (1895), *Captains Courageous* (1897), and most of the stories collected in *The Day's Work* (1898); he also published the second collection of his poems, *The Seven Seas* (1896), mostly written between 1892 and 1896. He hoped in time to write stories about America (*Captains Courageous* is a very restricted venture); in the meantime, the subject of India grew steadily less prominent in his work. On his fairly frequent expeditions out of Vermont, Kipling made the acquaintance of a wide range of distinguished Americans, including Charles Eliot Norton, Theodore Roosevelt, Samuel Langley, Henry Adams, and Brander Matthews. Nevertheless, the American episode ended badly. Kipling was much troubled by the anti-English spirit aroused by a border dispute between Britain and Venezuela at the end of 1895. In 1896 he quarrelled with his brother-in-law, Beatty Balestier, had him arrested for threatened violence, and was humiliated in a courtroom hearing. In September the Kiplings left Vermont for England.

After a false start in Devon they settled at The Elms, Rottingdean, Sussex, where the Burne-Joneses also had a house. Here, in August 1897, the Kiplings' last child and only son, John, was born. Early in 1899 Kipling, with some idea of repairing his American relations, took his family to New York; there he and the children fell ill. Josephine and Kipling developed pneumonia, and for many days in February and March Kipling's struggle against death was headline news across the United States. At the crisis of Kipling's illness, Josephine died, unknown to him. Not until June was Kipling strong enough to return to England, never to visit the United States again.

While recuperating Kipling put together the articles in *From Sea to Sea* (2 vols., 1900), compelled by pirated American editions thus to reprint early work that he would otherwise have left in obscurity. About this time Kipling fought several cases in the American courts, always unsuccessfully, against what he regarded as piratical publishing. *Stalky & Co.* appeared at the end of 1899; *Kim*, which Kipling had matured for nearly a decade, in 1901; the *Just So Stories*, begun as stories for Josephine, were published serially from 1897 and collected in 1902. Kipling called *Kim* 'a labour of great love' and thought it 'a bit more wise and temperate than much of my stuff' (15 Jan 1900, *Letters*, 3.11). It is, effectively, his farewell to India, in the form of a romance that has pleased even many of those not disposed to like Kipling's work.

South Africa and England After his serious illness Kipling was advised to spend his winters out of England. In the winter of 1898 he had taken his family to South Africa, where he had met Rhodes and Milner and had travelled as far as Bulawayo. He now determined to make South Africa his regular winter home, a decision that coincided with the outbreak of the Second South African War.

From this time until he abandoned it in 1908, South Africa played a large part in Kipling's life. His admiration for Rhodes, Milner, and Jameson was unqualified. In South Africa in the spring of 1900 he was delighted to serve briefly, at Lord Roberts's invitation, on the staff of a paper called *The Friend*, got out for the troops at Bloemfontein. Two of the journalists he met on the staff, Perceval Landon and H. A. Gwynne, remained lifelong friends. Kipling's one experience of live battle was outside Bloemfontein in March 1900.

South Africa and the war reinvigorated Kipling: 'I'm glad I didn't die last year', he wrote from Cape Town (7 April 1900, *Letters*, 2.14). The experience did him no good with his public, however. The British unpreparedness exposed by the early Boer successes persuaded Kipling and many others that the country needed fresh discipline. Kipling now took up the theme of preparedness through compulsory military service, and his hectoring of the British public on this subject (for example in 'The Islanders') alienated many readers. The poems of *The Five Nations* (1903) and the stories of *Traffics and Discoveries* (1904) are the main literary memorials of Kipling's South African adventure, but they are not only that. Two stories in the collection—'They' and 'Mrs. Bathurst'—embody a delicacy of suggestion and a richness of allusion greater, perhaps, than what had been seen in Kipling's work before. They mark out the line of development leading to the great stories of Kipling's last decade. The contrast from this point on in Kipling's life between the stridency of his political views and the wide sympathy of his work shows how little we understand the relations of politics to literature. Unfortunately, much of Kipling's work continues to be judged through a simple connection of the two.

When Kipling and his family returned to Cape Town at the end of 1900 they lived in a house called The Woolsack, built for them by Rhodes in the grounds of his Cape Town estate. Here Kipling and his wife consulted with Rhodes about his scheme for international scholarships at Oxford (Kipling was later a Rhodes trustee), and here Kipling dreamed about a South African future after Rhodes's ideas, in which a dominant English population would create a golden peace and prosperity. The dreams were shattered by the great Liberal victory in Britain in 1906, followed by the return to responsible government of the Boers. Kipling saw this as the destruction of all that Rhodes had worked for; after a last stay in the winter of 1908 he left, bitterly disappointed, never to return to South Africa.

Kipling now turned to English history on the widest possible basis. In 1902 he bought a seventeenth-century house called Bateman's, Burwash, Sussex, where he spent the rest of his life, and where he made himself master of the traditions and topography of the region (the house is now a Kipling memorial owned by the National Trust). He was helped in this by the advent of automobile travel, of which he was an early and enthusiastic champion. As he wrote in April 1904,

> The chief end of my car is the discovery of England. To me it is a land full of stupefying marvels and mysteries; and a day in the car in an English county is a day in some fairy museum where all the exhibits are alive and real and yet none the less delightfully mixed up with books.

Locomotion always fascinated Kipling, and to stories about ships ('The Ship that Found Itself') or trains ('.007') or airships in the future ('With the Night Mail') were now added car stories ('Steam Tactics'). The 'discovery of England' was embodied in *Puck of Pook's Hill* (1906) and *Rewards and Fairies* (1910), supplemented by the poems that Kipling contributed to the *History of England* (1911), written as a school text by the Oxford historian C. R. L. Fletcher. *Actions and Reactions* (1909), a very miscellaneous collection, includes stories from 1899 to 1909. *Songs from Books* (1912) brings together the many poems contained within or accompanying Kipling's stories.

In the first decade of the twentieth century Kipling was at the height of his fame and prestige, notwithstanding the discordant notes that began to be heard during the Second South African War. In 1907 he toured Canada, preaching the gospel of empire all the more emphatically now that South Africa was lost; his reception was not that of a private person but of a state dignitary, as he crossed and re-crossed the continent in a private rail car. His observations on this occasion appear in *Letters to the Family* (1908). In 1907 he was awarded honorary degrees by the University of Durham and by Oxford, and at the end of the year he received the Nobel prize for literature, the first English writer to be so distinguished. In the next year Cambridge gave him an honorary degree. Kipling refused all the official honours offered him, including the Order of Merit, because he did not wish to be identified with any government. He was never formally offered the Laureate-ship, but he would have refused it on the same grounds.

Deeply out of sympathy with the Liberal government, whose 'corruption' he attacked in the savage verses in 'Gehazi', and distressed by the social tensions expressed in the great strikes of 1910–12, Kipling saw the struggle over home rule as a test of strength between the forces of preservation and dissolution. When civil war and a rebellion of the army threatened over the fate of Ulster in 1914, Kipling joined the League of the British Covenant, helped to form refugee committees, made an inflammatory speech against the government, and published such passionate verses as 'Ulster' and 'The Covenant'.

The war years All this was swept away in a moment by the outbreak of the First World War in August. Kipling put his writing entirely at the service of the war effort, as the record of his publication in these years shows: *The New Army in Training* (1915); *France at War* (1915), from Kipling's tour as a correspondent in France; *The Fringes of the Fleet* (1915), on the naval auxiliaries, submarines, and patrols; *Sea Warfare* (1916), partly written from reports furnished

by the Admiralty; *The Eyes of Asia* (1918), written from the letters of Indian troops in England; and the series of articles from the Italian front called 'The war in the mountains' (1917), never published separately by Kipling. *A Diversity of Creatures* (1917) had been planned for publication in October 1914, but postponed: Kipling was careful to date the stories so that they could be seen to be pre-war compositions. The last two stories in the collection—'Swept and Garnished' and the much-misunderstood 'Mary Postgate'—had obviously been written after the outbreak of the war and needed no dating.

John Kipling, who had been commissioned in the Irish Guards at the outset of the war, had gone to France in August 1915; in September, a month after his eighteenth birthday, he was reported wounded and missing in the battle of Loos. His body was never found in Kipling's lifetime: the grave was identified in 1992. John's death coincided with the onset of Kipling's suffering from the undiagnosed duodenal ulcer that tormented the last twenty years of his life and that at last killed him. Under these afflictions, as the war dragged on, Kipling grew more bitter, his hatred of the Germans more violent. The exhilaration he had felt in the early days of the Second South African War was now replaced by a melancholy weariness in the face of the war's great destruction. When the armistice came at last he fled to Bateman's from the rejoicing in London: 'I … had my dark hour alone' (18 Nov 1918, *Letters*, 4.520). To the end, Kipling regarded the peace settlement as a betrayal; the conduct of the United States in remaining for so long neutral was an irredeemable dishonour. Kipling's first book to be published after his years in the service of the war were ended was the volume of poems called *The Years Between* (1919); some of these, from before the war, reflected the turbulent political conflicts of those days; others, recording the experiences of the war, varied from savage to desolate. It is by far the darkest of all Kipling's collections.

After the war The war remained constantly present to Kipling through two of his activities. He was made a member of the Imperial War Graves Commission in 1917, and served conscientiously until his death. He attended committees, wrote publicity for the commission, chose or composed inscriptions for its memorials, and visited its cemeteries in his travels on the continent and the Near East. In 1917 he also accepted an invitation to write the war history of his son's regiment, the Irish Guards. This work occupied him until 1923, when *The Irish Guards in the Great War* appeared in two volumes. His only other book in the first years after the war was *Letters of Travel (1892–1913)* (1920), a collection of travel articles from Kipling's wedding journey in 1892, his Canadian tour of 1907, and his first visit to Egypt in 1913. This, like *A Diversity of Creatures*, had been planned for publication in 1914 but was deferred by the war.

Kipling worked despite increasing illness, marked by frequent and unpredictable bouts of violent pain. Different doctors made different diagnoses, all of them wrong. In 1921 the diagnosis was 'septic foci of the teeth', and all of his teeth were removed. In 1922 (he then weighed under 9 stone) he was operated on for a 'twisted bowel'. Not until 1933 was a duodenal ulcer diagnosed by doctors in Paris, too late to provide any relief. His wife's health was also deteriorating in ways that put much strain on Kipling too: she was rheumatic, diabetic, and depressive. Even before the war she had sought hydropathic treatment in the south of France; from 1915 on they were frequently in Bath for the same purpose. Their travels after the war were largely quests for the warmth that would relieve her pains: Algeria, Spain, Sicily, Egypt, Brazil, the Caribbean, and, especially, the south of France. France was, of all countries, the one that Kipling most enjoyed, and for many years he explored it by car with undiminished pleasure in its people and places.

The Kiplings continued to entertain regularly at Bateman's and to visit London often, where their headquarters were at Brown's Hotel. They were faithful to old friends; by this time, perhaps inevitably, a larger proportion of them were titled, official, or wealthy than had been the case before the war. Many among Kipling's young friends were those he made in his son's regiment, the Irish Guards: one of these, Captain George Bambridge MC, married Kipling's surviving child, Elsie, in 1924. The marriage was childless.

Owing mostly to his ill health, Kipling's production sank in the years between the end of the war and his death. Some of what he published now was not new but a gathering-up of existing work: *Land and Sea Tales for Scouts and Guides* (1923) includes stories from 1893 to 1923; *A Book of Words* (1928) collects Kipling's speeches from 1906 to 1927. Some of the speeches, in effect brief essays to be spoken, are highly characteristic and interesting. Most important of the retrospective publications is *Verse: Inclusive Edition*, in three volumes (1919): this was Kipling's effort to arrange his poetical work, and was followed by one-volume editions in 1927 and 1933. He also began work on the great collected edition of his work published posthumously (though signed by Kipling) as the Sussex Edition (1937–9). This was planned by Macmillan as a monument to the author who had been a pillar of the firm's prosperity and is one of the most splendid of modern editions.

Kipling, who always liked to give speech to the speechless, and who had always been a dog-lover, combined these inclinations in a series of stories collected as *Thy Servant a Dog, Told by Boots* (1930). Kipling also took a professional interest in the film adaptations of his work, which went back at least to 1911. In 1921 he worked on scripts from 'The Gate of the Hundred Sorrows', 'Soldiers Three', and 'Without Benefit of Clergy': only the last of these was filmed. He helped develop the script for the unsuccessful *One Family* produced by the Empire Marketing Board in 1930, and he reviewed the scripts for *Captains Courageous* and *Wee Willie Winkie*, both released in 1937, after Kipling's death. If Kipling's production diminished through illness, what he managed to produce was nevertheless of the highest distinction. *Debits and Credits* (1926) and *Limits and Renewals* (1932) show Kipling's art in its richest maturity in such stories as 'The Wish House', 'The Eye of Allah', 'The Gardener', 'Dayspring Mishandled', and 'The Church that was at Antioch', to name no more. The themes of self-sacrifice, of healing, and of indestructible love are prominent in these.

On 12 January 1936, two weeks after his seventieth birthday, Kipling and his wife were at Brown's Hotel, *en route* for the south of France, when he was stricken by haemorrhage from a perforated ulcer. Taken to the Middlesex Hospital, he was operated on the next day and died there on 18 January, his wedding anniversary. He was cremated at Golders Green, Middlesex, and the ashes were buried in Poets' Corner, Westminster Abbey, on 23 January. It was noted that the pallbearers included no literary men but, as his biographer C. E. Carrington put it, 'the Prime Minister, an Admiral, a General, the Master of a Cambridge College, Professor Mackail from Oxford, Sir Fabian Ware, and two old friends H. A. Gwynne and A. P. Watt' (p. 506). Some months before his death Kipling had begun work on an autobiography. This incomplete work was published posthumously as *Something of Myself: for my Friends Known and Unknown* (1937).

Reputation Kipling's critical reputation—as distinguished from his popularity among readers—has never been very firmly fixed. Even when the novelty and brilliance of his work had dazzled the public at the beginning of the 1890s, there had been doubting and hesitant voices, troubled by the excesses, the 'hooliganism', the 'vulgarity' of Kipling's work. His enthusiasm for the English cause in the Second South African War alienated many, and his constant urging of preparedness grew tedious and offensive, as did his accusations of corruption against the government. Others never reconciled themselves to the disappearance of India from Kipling's stories and poems. And there was certainly some reaction against the mere fact of his prominence: he had begun so early and had become so famous that, in time, a certain weariness of response was inevitable. He was so quotable (more than eighty entries in the *Oxford Dictionary of Quotations*) that he dwindled into cliché. After the war, when formal experiment was demanded as a necessary sign of belonging to the present, the apparent conventionality of Kipling's stories and poems made him easy to disregard. Among the young, Kipling could be—and was—thought of as a dead author, belonging to a dead order of faith in the empire. When, after the next war, the parts of the empire became independent countries and everything associated with the colonial became anathema, it was remembered that Kipling had admired the colonial idea. To a generation whose critical guides had not led them to read Kipling, this seemed enough to know. The censorship of political correctness habitually barred Kipling from a place among school texts in the United States in the late twentieth century.

The labels that are conventionally attached to Kipling—'imperialist', 'racist', 'jingoist'—express a very superficial knowledge of his work, which eludes all labels in its range and variety. There has yet been no writer of short stories in English to challenge his achievement, which ranges through space from India to the home counties, and through time from Stone Age man to the contemporary world of football matches and motor cars. These stories, moreover, exhibit every kind of treatment, from the farcical to the tragic, and their structures vary from the simplest anecdote to the most complex and allusive philosophical fiction, dense enough to support endless exegesis and commentary. He excelled in stories of adventure ('The Man who would be King'), as well as in stories of obscure English life ('The Wish House'). He excelled in historical fiction ('The Eye of Allah'). He excelled in stories for children (*Just So Stories*) and in that kind of story that appeals both to child and adult (*Puck of Pook's Hill*) according, as he said, 'to the shifting light of sex, youth, and experience' (Kipling, *Something of Myself*). He created a great picaresque romance in *Kim*. His stories touch the occult at one extreme ('A Madonna of the Trenches') and the technicalities of modern machinery at the other ('The Devil and the Deep Sea'). No list can begin to exhaust the possibilities. And what may be said of his prose work may apply even more strongly to his poetry, whose extraordinary variety of form and content is only now beginning to be appreciated. Among modern writers in English, only Thomas Hardy can be compared to Kipling for high achievement in both poetry and prose. Kipling's work is not only of the highest artistic excellence, it is deeply humane and fully expresses the sense of one of his favourite texts: 'Praised be Allah for the diversity of his creatures.' THOMAS PINNEY

Sources R. Kipling, *Something of myself and other autobiographical writings*, ed. T. Pinney (1990) · *The letters of Rudyard Kipling*, ed. T. Pinney, 4 vols. (1990–99) · C. E. Carrington, *Rudyard Kipling: his life and work*, rev. edn (1978) · Lord Birkenhead, *Rudyard Kipling* (1978) · DNB · R. E. Harbord, ed., *The readers' guide to Rudyard Kipling's work*, 8 vols. (1961–9) · R. Kipling, *Early verse*, ed. A. Rutherford (1986) · A. K. Fleming, 'Some childhood memories of Rudyard Kipling', *Chambers's Journal* (March 1939), 168–72 · A. K. Fleming, 'Some childhood memories of Rudyard Kipling', *Chambers's Journal* (July 1939), 506–11 · R. Kipling, letters, 8–10 March 1931, U. Sussex, Kipling MSS · H. James, 'Introduction', *Mine own people* (1891) · J. M. S. Tompkins, *The art of Rudyard Kipling* (1959) · R. Kipling, letter to Edith Macdonald, 3 June 1927, U. Sussex, Kipling MSS

Archives Bodl. Oxf., corresp. · Col. U., Butler Library, corresp. and literary papers · Cornell University, Ithaca, New York, corresp., family corresp., and literary papers · Dalhousie University, Halifax, Nova Scotia, corresp. and literary papers · Harvard U., Houghton L., corresp. and papers · Hunt. L., corresp. and literary papers · L. Cong., corresp. and papers · NL Aus., corresp. · NRA, corresp. and literary MSS · Princeton University, New Jersey, papers · Ransom HRC, corresp. and literary papers · Syracuse University, New York, George Arents Research Library, corresp. and literary papers · U. Cal., Berkeley, Bancroft Library, corresp. · U. Sussex Library, corresp. and literary papers · University of Rochester, New York, Rush Rhees Library, corresp. and papers · Yale U., papers | BL, corresp. with Macmillans and corrected proofs, Add. MSS 54940, 55846–55875 · BL, corresp. with Society of Authors, Add. MS 56734 · Bodl. Oxf., corresp. with Lady Milner · CKS, corresp. with Lady Milner · Commonwealth War Graves Commission, corresp. and papers relating to Imperial War Graves Commission · Hagley Hall, Hagley, Worcestershire, letters to the Leonard family · HLRO, corresp. with Lord Beaverbrook · HLRO, corresp. with John St Loe Strachey · Kipling Society, London, letters to J. H. C. Brooking · McGill University, Montreal, McLennan Library, family corresp. with Lockwood and Meta de Forest · Metropolitan Toronto Reference Library, corresp. with James Watson Barry · NMM, letters to Sir Percy Bates · NMM, letters to Leslie Cope-Cornford · Norfolk RO, letters to Sir Henry Rider Haggard · PRO NIre., corresp. with Edward Carson · Richmond Local Studies Library, London, corresp. with Douglas Sladen · U. Sussex Library, corresp. and papers relating to school life and friends, in particular George Beresford · U. Sussex Library, letters to L. C. Dunsterville · U. Sussex Library, letters to Harry Lewin · U. Sussex Library, corresp. and literary MSS kept by Miss Parker, his secretary · University of Essex Library, Colchester, letters to Samuel Levi Bensusan · Wisconsin State Historical Society, Madison, corresp. with F. N. Finney | FILM BFI NFTVA, home footage | SOUND BL NSA, recorded talks; performance recordings; documentary recording

Likenesses Bourne and Shepherd (Simla), photograph, 1887–8, U. Sussex, Kipling papers; repro. in Kipling, *Early verse* (1986), frontispiece · J. Collier, oils, 1891, Bateman's, Burwash, Sussex · Violet, duchess of Rutland, lithograph, 1891, NPG · D. Strang, etching, 1898 (after W. Strang, c.1898), NPG · W. Strang, pencil drawing, c.1898, NPG · P. Burne-Jones, oils, 1899, NPG; copy?, Johannesburg Art Gallery [*see illus.*] · W. Nicholson, coloured woodcut, 1899, NPG · W. Cushing Loring, pencil drawing, 1901, Athenaeum, London · W. Strang, oils, 1913, Magd. Cam. · photograph, 1913, repro. in *The Bookman* [NY], 38 (1913) · E. Kapp, chalk drawing, 1914, Barber Institute of Fine Arts, Birmingham · H. Manuel, photograph, c.1915 · W. Stoneman, photograph, 1924, NPG · F. Dodd, chalk drawing, 1929, FM Cam. · F. Dodd, charcoal drawing, 1929, FM Cam. · photograph, c.1930, repro. in *War writings and poems*, Outward bound edition, vol. 34, frontispiece · W. Rothenstein, chalk drawing, c.1932, NPG; related drawing, FM Cam. · W. Stoneman, photograph, 1934?, NPG · G. Bingguely-Lejeune, bronze cast of bust, c.1936–1937, NPG · M. Beerbohm, caricature, repro. in *The poets' corner* (1904) · M. Beerbohm, caricature, AM Oxf. · M. Beerbohm, caricature, U. Cal., Berkeley, Bancroft Library · M. Beerbohm, caricature, Harvard TC · M. Beerbohm, caricature, NYPL · M. Beerbohm, caricature, oils (*Edwardian Parade*), U. Texas · H. Furniss, pen-and-ink drawing, NPG · A. P. F. Ritchie, cigarette card, NPG · Spy [L. Ward], lithograph, NPG; repro. in *VF* (7 June 1894) · photograph, NPG

Wealth at death £121,470 4s. 0d.: probate, 6 April 1936, CGPLA Eng. & Wales

Kipling, Thomas (*bap.* 1745, *d.* 1822), dean of Peterborough, born at Bowes, Yorkshire, was the son of William Kipling, a cattle salesman, and Margaret, his wife. He was baptized at Bowes on 20 October 1745. He received his early education at Scorton and Sedbergh schools, and was admitted a sizar of St John's College, Cambridge, on 28 June 1764. He graduated BA in 1768, and proceeded MA in 1771, BD in 1779, and DD in 1784. He was ordained deacon on 29 May 1768 and priest on 10 June 1770. He was admitted as a fellow of St John's in 1769, removed on a mandate of the bishop of Ely, as visitor, and readmitted in 1771. In 1773 he was elected one of the taxors of the university. In 1782 he was elected Lady Margaret's preacher, on the resignation of Dr Richard Farmer. In 1787 he was appointed deputy regius professor of divinity, as the professor, Dr Richard Watson, was in ill health. In 1792 he preached the Boyle lectures, but, as was often the case, these were not published. In 1784 he became vicar of Holme-on-Spalding Moor in Yorkshire, a living, in the gift of his college, which he held until his death. In 1798 he was appointed dean of Peterborough and rector of Fiskerton in Lincolnshire.

In 1778 Kipling published a work on optics which Gunning accurately described as 'little read and soon forgotten' (Gunning, 2.49). His major publication was the *Codex*

Theodori Bezae Cantabrigiensis, evangelia et apostolorum acta complectens, quadratis literis, Graeco-Latinus (1793), printed at the Cambridge University press. The impression was limited to 250 copies. This edition of the Codex Bezae was a splendid specimen of typography, the types resembling the uncial characters of the original manuscript, and the *British Critic* described it as 'a facsimile edition' (*British Critic*, Feb 1794, 140). This work was, however, marred by a Latin preface which Kipling wrote, littered with linguistic errors for which he was gently reprimanded by his few friends and savagely lampooned by his many enemies. Dr Thomas Edwards described it as 'disgraceful to a literary society' and coined the term 'a Kiplingism' to mean a grammatical error (Edwards, iv, 28). This term was repeated with glee in the humorous undergraduate handbook *Gradus ad Cantabrigiam* (1824, 64–5). Gunning suggests that Kipling was something of a laughing stock in the university as a pretentious eccentric, but he was also cantankerous and vindictive. He engaged in three major controversies. In 1793 he played a leading part in the prosecution of William Frend of Jesus College for his Unitarian views. Although he was an inefficient prosecutor, by his conduct and manner 'he rendered himself obnoxious to an independent party in the University' (*Annual Biography*, 449). In 1802 his *The Articles of the Church of England Proved not to be Calvinistic* attacked his opponents so bitterly that a Calvinist critic justly reflected, 'a controversial writer must be strangely blinded by passion … or puffed up with a vain conceit of his own superiority who flatters himself that his notions cannot be opposed without dishonest intentions' (Academicus, 1). In 1809 he turned on the Roman Catholics. Some Irish Catholics had reprinted Thomas Ward's 1688 *Errata of the Protestant Bible* and Kipling denounced them in *Certain accusations brought recently by Irish papists against British and Irish protestants of every denomination* (1809), insisting that Linus, not St Peter, was the first bishop of Rome (p. 66). In 1815 he attacked the Roman Catholic John Lingard's *Strictures* on Herbert Marsh's *Comparative View of the Churches of England and Rome*, first threatening him with prosecution for using the term 'modern church of England', but later withdrawing.

Kipling's unpopularity at Cambridge was evidenced by his failure in elections for the rectory of Bedale, Yorkshire, in 1775 and for the Lady Margaret professor of divinity in 1788. A contemporary obituary suggested his appointment as dean of Peterborough in 1798 was 'as a reward for his political services and as some consolation for the mortifications he had experienced' (*Annual Biography*, 449). Thomas Kipling died on 28 January 1822 at the vicarage of Holme-on-Spalding Moor. He never married.

ROBERT HOLE

Sources Venn, *Alum. Cant.* · H. Gunning, *Reminiscences of the university, town, and county of Cambridge, from the year 1780*, 2 vols. (1854) · F. Knight, *University rebel: the life of William Frend, 1757–1841* (1971) · T. Edwards, *Remarks on Dr. Kipling's preface to Beza* (1793) · Academicus, *Remarks on a pamphlet by Thomas Kipling* (1802) · *Annual Biography and Obituary*, 7 (1823), 449 · *British Critic*, 3 (1794), 139–47, 361–73 · *Fasti Angl.* (Hardy) · *Gradus ad Cantabrigiam, or, The new university guide* (1824) · C. H. Cooper, *Annals of Cambridge*, 4 (1852) · Nichols, *Lit. anecdotes* · parish register, Bowes, Durham RO, EP/Bow 1/1 · private information (2004)

Kippenberger, Sir Howard Karl (1897–1957), army officer, was born on 28 January 1897 at Ladbrooks, near Christchurch, New Zealand, the eldest son of Karl Kippenberger (1872–1952), a schoolteacher, and his wife, Annie Elizabeth Howard (1870?–1952). He was educated first at Ladbrooks School and Prebbleton School. His parents gave up teaching for dairy farming in 1911 and sent him to Christchurch Boys' High School, but he was expelled in 1912 for persistent misconduct.

After three years of reluctantly milking the family cows Kippenberger volunteered for active military service in December 1915 and left New Zealand with the 12th reinforcement in May 1916; he reached the Somme front in September. While reading *The Times* on 10 November 1916 he was wounded in the right arm by shrapnel from a 'friendly' artillery shell and in March 1917 was invalided home.

By 1920 Kippenberger had qualified in Christchurch as a lawyer, and on 28 September 1922 he married a law office typist, Ruth Isabel (1897–1967), the daughter of Joseph Henry Flynn of Lyttelton, Christchurch's port, and his wife, Adelaide Jane Gray. They had two sons and one daughter. He practised as a lawyer and served as a borough councillor (until 1936) in and around Rangiora, north of Christchurch.

Kippenberger joined the Territorial Force in 1924 and was promoted lieutenant-colonel in command of the 1st battalion, Canterbury regiment, in August 1936. He gradually acquired an excellent military history library (now housed in the Army Museum's Kippenberger Pavilion at Waiouru, central North Island) and constructed several model battlefields, but he had no opportunity either for staff college study or for participation in realistic exercises with professional soldiers. On 5 January 1940 he sailed from Lyttelton with the 1st echelon in command of 20th battalion, a force of 800 men raised from the South Island, and on 12 February arrived in Egypt. Keenly recalling the mindless miseries inflicted on him during the First World War, he insisted on practical training and sensible discipline and took a constant interest in matters of welfare and morale.

Early in March 1941 the New Zealand division, commanded by General Freyberg, was sent to Greece. From then until the end of the war in Europe, as Kippenberger's obituary in *The Times* recorded, 'active service [was] rather too mild a word to describe the bitter fighting, the gruelling soldiering which the New Zealanders experienced in one campaign after another' (*The Times*, 6 May 1957). For example, of the forty officers in Kippenberger's battalion in March 1941, only eight were not killed, seriously wounded, or captured during the next four years.

The ill-conceived Greek campaign gave Kippenberger every opportunity to begin learning a difficult skill: how to conduct a fighting retreat—in this case, of 300 miles in three weeks over rugged terrain, opposed by more experienced and better-equipped German troops enjoying air superiority. But he kept his head amid much confusion

Sir Howard Karl Kippenberger (1897–1957), by unknown photographer, 1952

and panic before embarking most of his men for Crete on 28 April. Promoted colonel and appointed to command 10th brigade, he began to make a name for himself by leading a briefly successful counter-attack at Galatos on 25 May. In Crete, however, even more so than in Greece, his chief task—for which he earned a DSO (gazetted on 4 November 1941)—was to salvage as many men as possible from another defeat. In the western desert, Tunisia, and Italy, he became a most inspiring commander, often close to the action. After being wounded and captured at Belhamed Ridge on 26 November 1941, he escaped within a week and a delighted Freyberg promptly gave him command as a brigadier of 5th brigade, a force of 5000 men, one-third of the division's total strength. His highly visible leadership throughout the rest of the North African campaign was recognized by the award of a bar to his DSO (gazetted 23 February 1943).

Kippenberger won the respect, the trust, and even the love of many who served with him, despite the fact—as he recorded then and later—that his own mistakes contributed to the heavy casualties suffered: mistakes in planning, navigation, management of reserves, communications, supplies, and choice of battlefield objectives. He was equally frank in his criticism of other commanders (of tanks in particular, believing that they often failed to support infantry with either enthusiasm or skill). He even

criticized Freyberg, New Zealand's military icon, a man whom he regarded highly, especially for excessive caution during the pursuit of axis forces following the battle of El Alamein in October 1942.

After four months' leave in New Zealand Kippenberger resumed command of 5th brigade in Italy on 25 November 1943 and endured yet more hard fighting, with men untrained in mountain warfare, in that defender's paradise. On 14 February 1944 he took command (as a temporary major-general) of the New Zealand division at Monte Cassino. While observing artillery fire from Mount Trocchio on 2 March 1944 he stepped on an anti-personnel mine. Prompt medical attention saved his life, but not his feet, and a steady stream of honours—promotion in May to permanent major-general, CBE in August, CB in December, and the ultimate accolade of knighthood in June 1948—were small consolations in the rest of his life for constant pain, manfully borne.

Kippenberger proved an inspired choice in 1946 as editor-in-chief of the official war histories—still the largest publishing effort in New Zealand's history, producing forty-eight volumes and twenty-four booklets—because his reputation with everyone who mattered in government and military circles was so high. He commissioned able writers and researchers, demanded high standards of factual accuracy and clear prose, and rejected censorship other than his own discretion. He had intended to write a final overview volume, a task for which his lively account of his own wartime career, *Infantry Brigadier* (1949, repr. 1961, and translated into seven languages), showed him perfectly capable.

Having been elected president of the Returned Services' Association in 1948, Kippenberger soon angered a majority of its members and his fellow citizens by vehemently—though unsuccessfully—opposing a proposed rugby tour of South Africa in 1949 that excluded, as the hosts demanded, Maori players. His opinion that race relations in New Zealand mattered more than rugby was far ahead of its time; even so, he remained president of the association until 1955.

Kippenberger was a slim, dark man of medium height and impressive presence. Often grim-faced (even when free of pain) and reluctant to smile without reason, he was quietly spoken, contemptuous of blather, and a poor public speaker. 'New Zealand's most distinguished civilian soldier, a practical man of letters, able administrator and gentleman' (*Evening Post* [Wellington], 6 May 1957) suffered a cerebral haemorrhage at his home in Thorndon, Wellington, on 4 May 1957 and died early the next morning in Wellington Hospital. He was buried in Wellington on 7 May. VINCENT ORANGE

Sources G. Harper, *Kippenberger: an inspired New Zealand commander* (1997) • H. Kippenberger, *Infantry brigadier* (1949) • D. J. C. Pringle and W. A. Glue, *20 battalion and armoured regiment* (1957) • A. Ross, *23 battalion* (1959) • J. L. Scoullar, *Battle for Egypt: the summer of 1942* (1955) • R. Walker, *Alam Halfa and Alamein* (1967) • W. G. Stevens, *Bardia to Enfidaville* (1962) • N. C. Phillips, *The Sangro to Cassino* (1957), vol. 1 of *Italy* • I. McGibbon, '"Something of them is here recorded": official war history in New Zealand', unpublished paper, Canberra, 1 Oct 1998 • R. Walker, 'The New Zealand Second

World War history project', *Military Affairs*, 22 (1969), 173–81 · J. McLeod, *Myth and reality: the New Zealand soldier in World War II* (1986) · H. Kippenberger, 'The New Zealand army', *Journal of the Royal United Service Institution*, 102 (1957), 66–74 · W. A. Glue, 'Working for Kip', *RSA Review*, 73 (1998), 19 · private information (2004) [Dictionary of New Zealand Biography] · ministry of defence, Wellington

Archives Archives New Zealand, Wellington, papers · Canterbury Museum, Christchurch, papers · NL NZ, Turnbull L., papers · Queen Elizabeth II Army Memorial Museum and Military Studies Centre, Waiouru, New Zealand, book collection · Rangiora Museum and Early Records Society, papers | SOUND Radio New Zealand, Timaru, sound archives

Likenesses photograph, 1952, NL NZ, Turnbull L. [*see illus.*] · A. Deans, portrait (after his portrait by A. Deans, 1940), repro. in Harper, *Kippenberger*, jacket · photograph, repro. in Harper, *Kippenberger*, following p. 216 · sketch, repro. in *Evening Post* [Wellington] (6 May 1957)

Kipping, Frederic Stanley (1863–1949), chemist, was born at Higher Broughton, Manchester, on 16 August 1863, the eldest son of James Stanley Kipping, an official in the Manchester branch of the Bank of England, and his wife, Julia, daughter of the Manchester painter Charles Allen *Duval. In 1874 he entered Manchester grammar school, having already acquired an interest in chemistry through a family friend, J. Carter Bell, the public analyst for Cheshire. After a year at the *lycée* at Caen, he matriculated in the University of London and entered Owens College, Manchester, in 1879. Kipping studied mathematics, physics, botany, chemistry, and zoology and graduated London external BSc in 1882. He then became chemist to the Manchester Gas Department, but in 1886 he entered Baeyer's laboratory at Munich, where he met W. H. *Perkin. His first research, on the synthesis of closed carbon chains, commenced under Perkin's guidance. Thus began an association which continued until Perkin died in 1929.

In 1887 Kipping received a PhD at Munich, obtained the DSc of London University, and was appointed demonstrator in chemistry under Perkin at Heriot-Watt College, Edinburgh, later becoming assistant professor of chemistry and lecturer in agricultural chemistry. During the Edinburgh period he and Perkin began writing a textbook of organic chemistry, which ran through many editions and became famous as 'Perkin and Kipping'. He continued his research on cyclic compounds during this time.

On 3 March 1888 Kipping married his cousin Lilian, daughter of William Thomas Holland JP, a merchant, of Bridgwater, Somerset. They had two sons, one of whom, Frederick Barry Kipping, also became a chemist, and two daughters. His wife survived him. In 1900 Kipping moved to London as chief demonstrator in the chemistry department of the Central Technical College under H. E. Armstrong, where he was also associated with W. J. Pope, M. O. Forster, and Arthur *Lapworth (Both Lapworth and Perkin married sisters of Lilian Holland.) During this period he published several joint papers with Pope and Lapworth, chiefly on derivatives of camphor. His collaboration with Pope continued for many years, and together they introduced *d*-bromocamphorsulphonic acid as an agent for resolving optical isomers.

In 1897 Kipping was elected a fellow of the Royal Society and appointed to the chair of chemistry at University College, Nottingham, which he held until 1936. Here, at first unaided, then in collaboration with his staff and students, he initiated various lines of research. A notable collaborator was Robert Robison (1883–1941), who worked with Kipping both as a student and as a postdoctoral researcher. After 1901 Kipping was mainly concerned with organic compounds of silicon, on which he published over fifty papers. He showed that the asymmetric silicon atom can give rise to optical isomerism and he resolved three compounds containing such atoms into their enantiomorphs. For this work he was awarded the Longstaff medal of the Chemical Society in 1909. In the course of his pioneering work on organo-silicon compounds, he produced many polymeric materials which he called silicones. Many years later these silicones found important applications as inert, water-repellent, polymers, though he himself had failed to foresee their practical importance. He also worked on the stereochemistry of nitrogen, and during the First World War was involved in the scheme for preparing some scarce synthetic drugs. He received the Davy medal of the Royal Society in 1918.

Kipping was one of the foremost among those professors of chemistry in the UK who, in the early years of the twentieth century, with few students and very slender resources, upheld a high standard of research. Through his work the department of chemistry at Nottingham became known throughout the world. His severe scientific standards were both the despair and the inspiration of research students. His dry, humorous remarks, his caustic comments, and rather gruff encouragements, long remained in the memories of his pupils. To those who gave of their best he offered his friendly interest and readiness to help throughout the years. He was an athlete and a sportsman, and it was said that he owed his perennial youthfulness to an expert manipulation of cyclic compounds on the golf course, the tennis court, and the billiard table. Kipping served two terms as a vice-president of the Chemical Society and a term on its council.

In 1921 Sir Jesse Boot donated a site later known as University Park, defraying the cost of the building and equipment of a new University College, and endowed the chair of chemistry at Nottingham. Kipping moved into the new department in 1928. Eight years later he retired, but continued to work in his old laboratory and to direct a few research students. In 1936 he received the honorary degree of DSc from the University of Leeds, and delivered the Bakerian lecture of the Royal Society on organic derivatives of silicon.

In September 1939 he moved to 11 Marine Terrace, Cricieth, where he and his younger son, Frederic Barry, rewrote Perkin and Kipping; this version appeared after the Second World War, the first edition having been published in 1894. Kipping died at his home in Cricieth on 30 April 1949 following a short illness, shortly after his old college at Nottingham had acquired university status.

FREDERICK CHALLENGER, *rev.* JOHN SHORTER

Sources *JCS* (1951), 849–62 · F. Challenger, *Obits. FRS*, 7 (1950–51), 183–219 · personal knowledge (1959) · m. cert. · d. cert.
Likenesses W. Stoneman, photograph, 1917, NPG · Lafayette Ltd, photograph, RS · Maull & Fox, photograph, RS · photograph, RS
Wealth at death £24,309 10s. 9d.: probate, 25 Aug 1949, *CGPLA Eng. & Wales*

Kipping, Sir Norman Victor (1901–1979), electrical engineer and industrialist, was born at 40 Allerton Road, Stoke Newington, London, on 11 May 1901, the younger son and second of three children of Percival Philip Kipping, electrical engineer and owner of the Universal Telephone Company, and his wife, Rose Eleanor Allam. Educated at University College School and Birkbeck College, London University (he did not take a degree), he joined the General Post Office in 1920 as a junior engineer. Over the next twenty years he worked his way up the electrical engineering industry, finally becoming works manager of Standard Telephones and Cables, in charge of a staff of 10,000. He married in June 1928 Eileen, daughter of Thomas Rose, produce company secretary, and had two sons and a daughter to whom, with his grandchildren, he was deeply devoted.

In May 1942 Kipping was called in to the Ministry of Production and put in charge of its regional organization, which he set up and led; and at the end of the war he was appointed under-secretary in the Board of Trade. For these services he was knighted in 1946. His wartime knowledge of industry stood him in good stead when appointed director-general of the Federation of British Industries (FBI) in the same year, and there too he created a structure of regional councils for consultations and representation with member companies across the land. For the next nineteen years he led the FBI until it became a major voice for industry.

An early initiative was the setting up in 1948 (with the Trades Union Congress and the British Employers' Confederation) of the Anglo-American Council on Productivity (AACP). Consisting of leading industrialists and trade unionists on both sides of the Atlantic and financed by Marshall aid, the AACP set out to raise productivity standards in British industry by drawing on American experiences; and to this end some sixty-six teams made study visits to the USA and reported back to their industries. Kipping served as joint secretary both of the AACP and of the British Productivity Council which succeeded it in 1952.

A great believer in joint endeavour between unions and management to national ends, Kipping was a leading founder member in 1949 of the Dollar Exports Board (later Council) and from 1960 of the Western Hemisphere Export Council and the Export Council for Europe; and, with government, of the tripartite National Production Advisory Council, the precursor of the National Economic Development Council. In this work he won the confidence and respect of ministers and civil servants under successive governments and of successive general secretaries of the TUC, who became personal friends.

A major strand in Kipping's FBI career was the promotion of British trade; and in a series of British trade exhibitions overseas he developed a flair for showmanship coupled with a meticulous attention to organizational detail. After successful exhibitions in Copenhagen and Baghdad, he persuaded the FBI to set up in 1953 for such enterprises as British Overseas Fairs Ltd, which he led. Successful fairs were mounted each year, successively in Copenhagen, Damascus, Helsinki, Brussels, Lisbon, New York, Moscow, Stockholm, Sydney, Barcelona, Tokyo, and Oslo—in all of which Kipping and his wife played a leading role with grace and zest.

No linguist, Kipping was nevertheless a convinced internationalist. He revived in post-war Europe an annual gathering of his counterparts around the continent and their wives, which made him many devoted friends. He was also diligent in the Council of European Industrial Federations; and became a convinced supporter first of the European Free Trade Association and later of the European Economic Community.

Outside Europe Kipping regularly quartered the globe on behalf of British industry, promoting investment as well as trade; and led, for example, a major trade mission to Nigeria (1961) and a voyage of rediscovery to Japan in the same year. India became a special love: he visited it often and invented what the Indians affectionately dubbed 'Kipping aid', whereby vital supplies were financed by UK aid for British companies producing there, to the mutual benefit of them and of the Indian economy.

After doubling the membership of the FBI during his term, perhaps the achievement of which Kipping was most proud was his role as co-author of the merger which in 1965 brought into being the Confederation of British Industry. That done, he retired happy and spent his still unflagging energies as a director of Joseph Lucas and of Pilkingtons; president of the Anglo-Finnish Society; chairman of the governing council of University College School; and vice-chairman of the Fulton committee on the civil service (1966–8), to name only a few. In 1966 he was appointed GCMG, having been created KBE in 1962. He also held honours from Denmark, Finland, Italy, and Sweden. He was an honorary fellow of the British Institute of Management and an honorary DSc of Loughborough (1966). To the *Dictionary of National Biography* he contributed the notices of Sir Hugh Beaver, Sir Richard Costain, and Sir John Woods.

A big man, in physique and personality, Kipping was also genial and kindly to friends and colleagues, and, although no intellectual, a shrewd judge of people, ideas, and the issues that mattered. From his often arduous day he would return to his home in Barnet (where he was also a JP) for solace and for what the family knew as 'father's SLITS' (something light in the study). Kipping once observed: 'You can find many who will push a rock up a hill, and a few who will push it across the top: but if you find one who will push it down the other side, you have found a winner' (personal knowledge). He was such a one. Kipping died at his home, 36 Barrydene, Oakleigh Road, North Whetstone, Barnet, London, on 29 June 1979.

JOHN WHITEHORN, *rev.*

Sources N. Kipping, *Summing up* (1972) · N. Kipping, *The Suez contractors* (1969) · *Daily Telegraph* (30 June 1979) · 'Sir Norman Kipping: task of organizing industrialists', *The Times* (23 Nov 1979), obituaries suppl., 3a · private information (1986) · personal knowledge (1986) · *CGPLA Eng. & Wales* (1979)
Archives U. Warwick Mod. RC, papers to director-general
Wealth at death £56,042: probate, 3 Sept 1979, *CGPLA Eng. & Wales*

Kippis, Andrew (1725–1795), Presbyterian minister and biographer, was born in Nottingham on 28 March 1725, the second son of Robert Kippis (*c*.1698–1730), silk hosier of the city, and his wife, Anne Ryther. His parents were loyal dissenters of Calvinist background, his mother being the granddaughter of John *Ryther (1631x5–1681), the ejected vicar of Frodingham, Lincolnshire. Following the death of his father Kippis was placed in the care of his paternal grandfather, Andrew Kippis, at Sleaford, Lincolnshire, where his early education took place. Living in a dissenting environment he was encouraged to prepare for the ministry. He had already given up the Calvinism in which he had been instructed: 'The agent employed in effecting this important change was the *Treatise on God's Law* by Elisha Coles', Kippis wrote later; 'it was put into my hands when 13 or 14 by some zealous friends, to instruct and confirm me in the doctrine it contained. The reading of it, however produced the contrary effect' (Wilson, 4.105).

Kippis entered Philip Doddridge's academy at Northampton in 1741, and after five years' study he was appointed pastor of an Independent congregation at Sleaford in September 1746.

> In his youth he was an assiduous student … he once read for three years at the rate of 16 hours *per* day; and one of the works … which he read entirely through, was the General Dictionary, in 10 volumes; this he added laid the foundation of his taste and skill in biographical composition. (*GM*, 803)

He moved to Dorking, Surrey, in November 1750, in the place of John Mason. Kippis held rather advanced views for many of the dissenters of his day, which arose out of his wide reading; 'he was the first of the Dorking ministers to fall into the Arian errors' (Cleal, 358).

In June 1753 Kippis was appointed minister of the Presbyterian congregation meeting in Princes Street, Westminster, where he remained for the rest of his life. He was a competent speaker, but nothing more than this and not noted for originality. It was the area of his work in which he least excelled, although he was in regular demand as a preacher. On 21 September 1753 he married Elizabeth (*c*.1723–1796), daughter of Isaac Bott, a merchant of Boston, Lincolnshire, and his wife, Hannah. All their children died in infancy; 'In the early part of their marriage, they lost two sons within a week, the eldest not quite three years' (*GM*, 913–14).

Kippis built up his early literary reputation by writing for the *Gentleman's Magazine* and for the *Monthly Review*, in which he took a leading part from its inception. He also wrote extensively for *The Library and Moral and Critical Magazine*, which he edited in 1761–2, and for the *New Annual Register*. The *History of Ancient Literature* and the *Review of Modern Books* contained much of his input until

Andrew Kippis (1725–1795), by Francesco Bartolozzi, pubd 1792 (after William Artaud)

1784. Most of his contributions were historical or theological. His style, while not exciting, was clear and reflected his wide classical, historical, and biographical knowledge; he was constantly with his books at home in Westminster. He also cultivated acquaintanceship with the leading literary figures of his day and became widely known not only among dissenters but also in London intellectual circles. 'No man was more cheerful in company than Dr Kippis. He had a strong taste for ridicule, and enjoyed lively and pleasant sallies' (*GM*, 804).

Kippis was a strong promoter of the dissenting cause and was highly respected as a representative by both the Presbyterians and the Independents. He sat lightly in this denominational divide and did not express controversial theology in public. However, his slow shift in theology and his association with the unitarian position led some Baptists to suspect him; 'Robert Hall once said that Kippis laid so many books upon his head that his brains could not move' (Cleal, 358). In 1763 his orthodoxy was sufficiently respected for him to be appointed to succeed David Jennings as classical tutor at the Coward Trust's Hoxton Academy. He withdrew from this office in 1784, before the dissolution of the academy in the following year. In June 1767 he was made DD of the University of Edinburgh, and was further honoured by being made fellow of the Society of Antiquaries in 1788 and of the Royal Society in 1779. He subsequently served on the council of both bodies and published a book on the controversies within the Royal Society in 1784.

Kippis helped to organize petitions to parliament aimed at securing the rights of dissenters. He played a large part in the campaign for relief from subscription to the Thirty-

Nine Articles for dissenting ministers in 1772 and 1773. Bills in each year designed to achieve relief passed the Commons but were rejected by the Lords. He published, in both 1772 and 1773, *A Vindication of the Protestant Dissenting Ministers … in the Matter of Subscription*, which achieved wide circulation. In 1779 a similar bill, which substituted a general declaration of belief in place of subscription, became law. In that year Kippis chaired the committee appointed by the dissenters to agitate for relief. The act was essentially a compromise that, while it completely satisfied no one, strengthened the legal position of dissent generally. He sat on the committees organized by the dissenting deputies to agitate for the repeal of the Test and Corporation Acts between 1787 and 1790. Early in 1787 he led a deputation of leading dissenters to William Pitt, the prime minister, to press their case. It was of no avail, for it was many years after Kippis's death before the acts were repealed. He was motivated in the parliamentary campaign by his strong affirmation of individual liberty, equal religious rights, and the reform of parliament. However, his belief in reform rather than revolution meant that he took a conservative rather than a radical position; he was no republican and was firmly against insurrection. 'The principles of the British Constitution he had diligently studied. To these he was zealously attached; and he ably defended them, though he was not unappraized of the corruption' (Rees, 40).

In 1786 Kippis was appointed one of the tutors, with Richard Price, Joseph Priestley, and Gilbert Wakefield, at the new dissenting college formed at Hackney; this in many minds confirmed his gradual movement towards unitarianism. He resigned after a few years but continued to give the college his loyal support. Among his pupils were William Godwin and the poet Samuel Rogers, who later recalled his teachers in the first part of *The Pleasures of Memory*:

> Guides of my life, instructors of my youth,
> Who first unveiled the hallowed form of truth;
> Whose every word enlightened and endeared.
> (Clayden, 1.418)

Kippis produced several biographies besides his extensive output in magazines. Lives of Anthony Ashley Cooper, first earl of Shaftesbury (1790; republished, 1836), Captain Cook (1778), Philip Doddridge (1792), and Job Orton (1822) are among the most notable. His posthumous fame among Unitarians arose from his joint editorship, with Abraham Rees, Thomas Jervis, and Thomas Morgan, of *A Collection of Hymns and Psalms for Public and Private Worship* (1795). This work passed through many editions in the nineteenth century, reaching a ninth edition in 1823, and was known as Kippis's or Rees's Collection. It was widely used among Presbyterian congregations that became Unitarian, and was in regular use as late as the 1850s; a new, enlarged edition, edited by Edmund Kell, appeared in 1852. 'It was the first of the Unitarian books to attain any very extended circulation' (Julian, 1193). Kippis in his youth wrote poetry, and two of his hymns appear in *A Collection*. 'Great God, in vain man's narrow view' was widely

adopted in later collections and appears in James Martineau's *Hymns* (1840 and 1873); 'How rich thy gifts, almighty God', written in 1759, appeared in several collections and parts of it found a place in editions of the *Congregational Hymn Book* in 1836 and 1859.

It is for his *Biographia Britannica*, of which he was editor and prime mover, that Kippis is mainly known. He was recognized, for good or ill, depending on the view of the reader, as the leading biographer of his day. While the *Biographia* was partial in coverage and the selection of those included was open to criticism the five volumes that did appear mark a significant development in biographical literature that was built upon in the following century. It was a monumental achievement of scholarship, not only on Kippis's part but also on that of the contributors whom he employed. The first volume appeared in 1778, the second in 1780, the third in 1784, the fourth in 1789, and the fifth in 1793, ending with Fastolf. A few copies of the first part of the sixth volume, ending with Foster, appeared in 1795 but the remainder were lost in a disastrous fire at the printers' office on 8 February 1808, and no other editor was found to complete the work. The entries in the *Biographia* are not always consistent in the information that they contain. Kippis often added extensive notes, printed in smaller typeface, to the entries prepared by his contributors. On occasion these notes are longer than the entry itself and do not make for easy reading of the whole. To his credit some of his notes constitute original material that is not to be found elsewhere. It is generally accepted that Kippis was too laudatory in his evaluations but this is probably reflective of the time and of his caution in expressing controversial views. He was one of the few people of sufficient breadth of learning and personal contact with many of his subjects to have prepared the volumes; Dr Johnson was another, but he states that he had declined the task. Kippis's attention to detail meant that he could not complete the *Biographia*, and his style is best summarized in a contemporary statement as 'without animation yet clear, perspicuous … and always suited to the subject' (*Protestant Dissenter's Magazine*, 1795, 5).

The importance of the *Biographia* was clear at the time, and the volumes elicited strong opinions when they appeared. According to James Boswell in the first edition of his *Life of Dr Johnson*, Johnson criticized Kippis for including proportionately more dissenting ministers than Anglican clergymen; Boswell withdrew the statement from his next edition. In the period 1776–80 the correspondence between Horace Walpole and the Revd William Cole shows how eagerly members of the intelligentsia waited for the volumes to appear to see what was said about whom. They cannot have been alone in this eagerness. 'Shall I beg you to transcribe the passage in which Dr Kippis abuses my father [Sir Robert Walpole] and me, for I shall not buy the new edition, only to purchase abuse on me and mine' (Walpole to Cole, 10 June 1778, Walpole, *Corr.*, 90). Cole, writing to Walpole on 1 March 1780, says:

> I received the volume on February 24 and ran over it as to the new articles and additions by the 27th at night, and have

made a perfect book of remarks and censures upon it … matters of doctrine only I took notice of, which are all tending to what offends my orthodoxy, viz., Arianism, Socinianism, Deism and Independency. (ibid., 196)

Kippis was attacked for being partisan, inaccurate, and too laudatory, but most recognized his achievement.

Much of the dispute and the fame came towards the end of Kippis's life. Personally he lamented the decline of the Presbyterian interest and of his own congregation in particular. As a result of his long pastorate of forty-three years his congregation was small. He continued to preach to them to within weeks of his death, on 8 October 1795 at his home in Crown Street, Westminster. 'He is said to have had a cough these 30 years and to have often predicted that, when that ceased, he should depart' (GM, 884). He was buried alongside his dissenting friends in Bunhill Fields burial-ground on 15 October, an event followed by possibly the most numerous, lengthy, and laudatory obituaries to appear in the national press and journals for a dissenting minister in the late eighteenth century.

ALAN RUSTON

Sources A. Rees, *A sermon preached at the meetinghouse in Prince's street, Westminster, on the eighteenth of October, 1795, upon … the much lamented death of the Rev. Andrew Kippis* (1795), 23–55 · *Protestant Dissenter's Magazine*, 3 (1796), 1–6 · W. Wilson, *The history and antiquities of the dissenting churches and meeting houses in London, Westminster and Southwark*, 4 vols. (1808–14), vol. 4, pp. 103–17 · *GM*, 1st ser., 65 (1795), 803–5, 882–4, 913–14 · J. Julian, ed., *A dictionary of hymnology*, rev. edn (1907), 624, 1193 · P. W. Clayden, *Rogers and his contemporaries* (1889), vol. 1, p. 418 · *IGI* · C. Surman, index, DWL · E. E. Cleal, *The story of congregationalism in Surrey* (1868), 357–8 · *DNB* · Walpole, *Corr.*, 11.90, 196 · D. Davie, *Essays in dissent* (1995), 191–202 · T. Davis, ed., *Committees for repeal of the Test and Corporation Acts minutes, 1786–90, 1827–28* (1978), 9–10, 47, 97, 106, 115, 129 · I. Rivers, *Books and their readers in eighteenth-century England* (2001), 135–69

Archives DWL, letters · Harris Man. Oxf., letters | BL, letters to second Lord Hardwicke, Add. MSS 35614–35625, *passim* · NRA, priv. coll., letters to Lord Shelburne · Yale U., Beinecke L., corresp. with James Boswell

Likenesses J. Sayers, caricature, etching, pubd 1790 (*The repeal of the Test Act*), NPG · F. Bartolozzi, stipple, pubd 1792 (after W. Artaud), BM, NPG [*see illus.*] · J. Baker, line engraving, pubd 1796 (after J. Hazlitt), NPG; repro. in *Universal Magazine* (1796) · Chapman, engraving, 1798, repro. in Wilson, *History and antiquities*, facing p. 114 · Ridley, engraving, pubd 1799 (after unknown artist), repro. in Wilson, *History and antiquities*, facing p. 103 · W. Artaud, oils, DWL

Wealth at death see will, 16 July 1757, PRO, PROB 11/1267, fol. 258

Kippist, Richard (1812–1882), librarian and botanist, was born on 11 June 1812 in Stoke Newington, Middlesex. Nothing is known of his parents or his early education, but it seems that he gained his first botanical knowledge by working and travelling with the botanist Joseph Woods, author of *Tourist's Flora*. In 1830 Kippist became an assistant to David Don (1800–1841), the librarian of the Linnean Society, and was paid 7s. 6d. a week; there he helped Nathaniel Wallich with the distribution of his East Indian herbarium, which he had presented to the society. Following the death of Don, Kippist became the society's librarian in 1842, after a fiercely contested election; he remained in this post for nearly forty years, specializing in Australian plants, at rare intervals publishing articles,

and always displaying an outstanding devotion to the society. According to his obituary in the society's *Proceedings*, 'his love of accuracy excused his seemingly rigid punctiliousness'. He belonged to the Royal Botanical Society and the Microscopical Society and frequently judged at flower shows. A genus, *Kippistia*, was twice dedicated to him, but the name was subsequently changed. Finally, in 1880, the Linnean Society persuaded its by now physically and mentally exhausted librarian to retire, on a full salary pension. However, Kippist lived to enjoy his pension for only a short time; he died at his home, 10 Burnaby Street, Ashburnham Road, King's Road, Chelsea, on 14 January 1882 and was buried at Brompton cemetery a week later on 21 January.

MARGOT WALKER

Sources A. T. Gage and W. T. Stearn, *A bicentenary history of the Linnean Society of London* (1988) · J. Miers, 'On the hippocrateaceae of South America', *Transactions of the Linnean Society of London*, 28 (1873), 319–432, esp. 416–19 · *Gardeners' Chronicle*, new ser., 17 (1882), 91 · *Journal of Botany, British and Foreign*, 20 (1882), 63–4 · *Nature*, 25 (1881–2), 275 · *Proceedings of the Linnean Society of London* (1880–82), 64–5 · *CGPLA Eng. & Wales* (1882) · Desmond, *Botanists*, rev. edn

Likenesses Maull & Polyblank, albumen print photograph, c.1854, Linn. Soc. · Maull & Co., albumen print carte-de-visite, Linn. Soc.

Wealth at death £1949 19s. 3d.: probate, 6 March 1882, *CGPLA Eng. & Wales*

Kiralfy [*formerly* Königsbaum], **Imre** (1845–1919), dancer and impresario, was born in Pest in the Austro-Hungarian empire, the first of the seven children of Jacob Königsbaum, a clothing manufacturer, and his wife, Anna (Rosa) Weisberger. The Königsbaums were a prosperous family of Jewish descent. However, their family business was ruined in the Hungarian revolution of 1848, after which they suffered temporary poverty and Imre's nationalist father narrowly escaped imprisonment by the Austrians.

As a boy Kiralfy showed a precocious talent for music, art, and especially dance, making his stage début when four years old, as a Hungarian folk dancer. He appeared under the name Kiralfy, which shortly became the family's new name. His brother, Bolossy (1848–1932), soon joined him on stage. Their parents, in particular their mother, managed their careers as they toured the cities of the empire. When they were no longer *wunderkinder* their careers declined to provincial theatres until they were joined by their sister Haniola (1851–1889).

The family moved first to Berlin and then to Paris, where the critic Théophile Gautier praised Imre and Bolossy for their 'agility, quickness, lack of affectation, strength, and musicality' (Barker, xxvii). Eventually five of Kiralfy's six siblings joined him on stage and they performed in variety theatres in Britain, France, and the Low Countries. They were in Paris during the 1867 Universal Exhibition which was the first of many exhibitions Imre visited. In Brussels Imre and Bolossy organized the pageantry and sports of a royal summer fête in 1868. In New York, in 1872, Kiralfy married an English woman, Marie Graham (1851–1942), who was one of the extra dancers who had sailed to the USA with the Kiralfy family troupe two years earlier. They had nine children, of whom three died in childhood.

The USA was the Kiralfy brothers' land of opportunity. They became famous producers of increasingly grandiose, dance-based spectacles. Their shows, such as their long-running version of Verne's *Around the World in Eighty Days*, featured large female chorus lines, high quality sets and costumes, usually made in Europe, and innovative special effects. The family lived on Washington Square, New York. Professional and personal differences led to the dissolution of the brothers' partnership in 1887, leading to estrangement and subsequent rivalry.

In 1887 Imre Kiralfy took *The Fall of Babylon*, which was originally a non-commercial spectacle in Cincinnati, to an open-air arena on Staten Island. He next produced *Nero, or, The Fall of Rome*, in association with Barnum and Bailey's *Greatest Show on Earth*, in New York and then in London's Olympia. At Olympia in 1891 he created *Venice in London*, a combined spectacular play and exhibition; the exhibition replicated Venice's bridges, canals, and a glass factory.

Assisted by his son Charles, Kiralfy created the spectacle *America* for the vast Auditorium Theatre in Chicago to coincide with the 1893 World's Columbian Exposition. *America* was a critical and box office success, grossing $900,000 in its seven-month run. He returned to London and rebuilt the Earls Court exhibition grounds as a small-scale version of Chicago's 'White City' of 1893, with a ferris wheel, amusement park, and palatial exhibition halls in a Mughal Indian style. At night it was an electrically illuminated wonderland.

The Empire of India Exhibition of 1895 reopened Earls Court and prestigious international exhibitions followed annually. In the late 1890s Kiralfy developed close links with the British Empire League and became a senior freemason. By 1905 his vision had outgrown Earls Court and he was planning, with his sons' assistance, the vast Great White City at Shepherd's Bush. Built in a palatial oriental style, it opened in 1908 with the Franco-British Exhibition which 8 million people visited, including Edward VII and the president of France. The Olympic Games were also held there in 1908, in the purpose-built stadium. This was the zenith of Kiralfy's long career and he was acknowledged as an impresario and exhibition director of genius. The Anglo-American Exhibition of 1914 was the last international exhibition to be held at the White City, although the sports stadium remained in use.

Kiralfy died at the Bedford Hotel, Brighton, on 27 April 1919, aged seventy-four; his ashes were interred at Kensal Green but transferred to the Kiralfy mausoleum, Greenwood cemetery, New York city, in 1924. He died wealthy, leaving £136,000 in his will, and famous on both sides of the Atlantic. Kiralfy was a cosmopolitan Hungarian who became British—he was naturalized in 1901. He created two state-of-the-art 'white cities' which achieved social respectability, popularity, and profitability by combining culture, technology, pleasure, and the exotic.

JAVIER PES

Sources B. Gregory, 'The spectacle plays and exhibitions of Imre Kiralfy, 1887–1914', PhD diss., Manchester University, 1988 · *Bolossy Kiralfy, creator of great musical spectacles: an autobiography*, ed. B. M. Barker (1988) · I. Kiralfy, autobiography and notes, Museum of London, Kiralfy collection · I. Kiralfy, 'My reminiscences', *Strand Magazine*, 37 (1909) · J. M. Mackenzie, *Propaganda and empire: the manipulation of British public opinion, 1880–1960* (1984), 97–120 · H. T. Hartley, *Eighty-eight not out* (1939) · *The Times* (29 April 1919) · *New York Times* (29 April 1919) · d. cert. · m. cert., USA

Archives Museum of London, autobiographical notes, programmes, blueprints, family information

Likenesses photograph, *c*.1908, Museum of London, Kiralfy collection

Wealth at death £136,680 7*s*. 3*d*.: probate, 19 June 1919, *CGPLA Eng. & Wales*

Kirby, Elizabeth (1823–1873). *See under* Kirby, Mary (1817–1893).

Kirby, John (*c*.1690–1753), surveyor and topographer, was, according to his grandson William Kirby (1759–1850), the well-known entomologist, descended from a north-country royalist who, suffering for his loyalty, took his family to Halesworth, Suffolk. This ancestry is supported by the fact that William and his father used the arms of the Lancashire family of Kirby, a visitation family with royalist sympathies. However, the only John Kirby in the Halesworth registers was born to a shoemaker, Stephen, in 1682 and died in 1736.

Apparently, Kirby at first kept a school at Orford, but was certainly 'of Erwarton' and occupied 'a small overshot mill at the bottom of the park [of the Hall]' when he married Alice Brown (1685/6–1766) at St Nicholas's Church, Ipswich, on 10 October 1714. The couple moved to Wickham Market, where Kirby also kept a mill, probably Glevering watermill, which was where their five sons and six daughters were born; all the children were christened there or at Hacheston. The best-known are three of the four eldest: John (1715–1750), under-treasurer at the Middle Temple, Joshua *Kirby (1716–1774), artist and friend of Gainsborough, and William, attorney of Witnesham Hall. Family letters published by his granddaughter Sarah Trimmer show that John Kirby brought up the family to be devout and god-fearing; in his Gainsborough portrait he looks stern.

By 1725 Kirby was practising land surveying to support his growing family, and during the next twenty years he drew up plans of estates in more than twenty east Suffolk parishes. His last plans were dated 1745, by which time he was also selling books. In 1732 he set out with Nathaniel Bacon junior (whose own plans are dated 1736–44) to survey the whole county for a small octavo gazetteer and road book entitled *The Suffolk Traveller*, which was published in Ipswich in 1735. A careful manuscript draft of part of the book is in the Suffolk Record Office. John Tanner of Lowestoft was the 'reverend gentleman' thanked for the forty-page table of parishes, patrons, and impropriations printed at the end of the book. Subscribers were also offered the survey in map form in two editions. R. Collins engraved the more lavish edition of 1736, priced 10*s*., at one inch to the mile and dedicated to the duke of Grafton, with the arms of 126 noblemen and gentlemen who had paid an extra half a guinea towards engraving. A cheaper version, engraved by James Basire at half the scale and without arms, followed in 1737. In 1763 Joshua and William Kirby advertised an enlarged edition of the *Traveller*,

John Kirby (c.1690–1753), by Thomas Gainsborough, before 1750

with frontispiece map (four miles to the inch) and four road maps all prepared for the engraver by Andrew Baldrey, Joshua Kirby's partner in business as house and herald painters. A plan of Ipswich, reduced from Ogilby (1674), and maps of separate hundreds which Baldrey had drawn exist only as originals. Although Thomas Martin and John Tanner (d. 1759) made additions to an interleaved copy of the first edition, all incorporated by the editor, the Revd Richard Canning of Ipswich, the title-page still proclaims John Kirby as the author, albeit posthumously. Joshua and William Kirby also republished the two wall maps, the larger re-engraved by John Ryland with twelve views and the arms and estate owners' names revised, and dated 1766. The half-scale map reappeared still dated 1737, but bearing the imprint of John Shave, an Ipswich publisher and bookseller of the 1760s. Most extant prints from the 1766 plates were made in 1825, when Stephen Piper of Ipswich, claiming to have revised them, merely added his name as publisher. Of later attempts to bring the book up to date (Woodbridge, c.1817 and 1829) the second is more useful; also useful is Augustine Page's supplement published in Ipswich in 1844.

By 1751 Kirby was living in Ipswich; he died of 'a mortification of the leg which came on very suddenly' (W. Kirby to W. Layton, 17 Oct 1807, Kirby MSS) at William's Ipswich house on 13 December 1753 and he was buried three days later in St Mary-le-Tower churchyard. His wife, Alice, survived to the age of eighty and after her death was laid beside him, on 30 October 1766.   J. M. BLATCHLY

Sources Nichols, *Illustrations*, 6.541–4 · Suffolk RO, Ipswich, Kirby MSS · W. Dugdale, *The visitation of the county palatine of Lancaster,* made in the year 1664–5, ed. F. R. Raines, 3 vols., Chetham Society, 84–5, 88 (1872–3) · parish register, Ipswich, St Nicholas, 1714 [marriage] · parish register (burial), Ipswich, St Mary-le-Tower, 1753 · *DNB*

Archives Suffolk RO, Ipswich, partial MS of his *Suffolk traveller*, HD376/1

Likenesses T. Gainsborough, oils, before 1750, FM Cam. [*see illus.*]

Kirby, Joshua (1716–1774), artist and architect, was born at Parham, Suffolk, the second of eleven children of John *Kirby (c.1690–1753), former schoolmaster and surveyor, and Alice Brown (1685/6–1766). Educated at home, Glevering Mill, Joshua helped to collect material for his father's road-book, *The Suffolk Traveller* (1735) and a map of Suffolk (1736). Two of his drawings of Scole Inn, Norfolk, were engraved by John Fessey in 1739. In that year he married Sarah Bull (c.1718–1775) of Framlingham and lived at Ipswich, where he had already joined a house- and coach-painting business: he also became active in St Mary-le-Tower church affairs.

Commissioned to design an altarpiece for St Mary's, Hadleigh, Suffolk, in 1744, in 1748 Kirby published *An historical account of the twelve prints of monasteries, castles, antient churches and monuments, in … Suffolk … drawn by J. Kirby,* which had been preceded by the twelve prints to which the publication referred. The views, engraved in London by Joseph Wood, were commended by George Vertue (*Note Books*, 6.203), and Kirby's experience enabled him to assist his new friend Thomas Gainsborough with the painting of *St Mary's, Hadleigh* (c.1748; priv. coll.).

In London in 1751 Kirby, with William Hogarth, enjoyed the discomfiture of Thomas Hudson (whom he disliked), who was deceived by a pastiche Rembrandt etching which had been faked by their dinner host, Benjamin Wilson. That spring he also advertised Hogarth's prints for sale in the *Ipswich Journal* and invited subscriptions for his own *Dr. Brook Taylor's Method of Perspective Made Easy, both in Theory and Practice* that was published in February 1754 and dedicated to Hogarth, who contributed a comic frontispiece. In the previous month the Academy of Painting and Sculpture had approved Kirby's three lectures on perspective and his book, and elected him a member. Reprinted immediately (1755) with additions and again in 1765 and 1768, Kirby's book became the standard exposition of perspective for British artists until superseded by Thomas Malton's treatise in 1775. Maintaining an empiric approach, Hogarth stood firm with Kirby on disputed points, an association which led to Kirby's being featured in two of Paul Sandby's satirical prints on Hogarth's *Analysis of Beauty* in 1754. In June 1757 he responded to Isaac Ware's redundant translation in 1756 of L. Sirigatti's *Practice of Perspective* (1596) with a furious pamphlet, *Sirigatti Analys'd*. As this merely exposed his own limitations and conceit it was hastily withdrawn (J. Highmore, *Monthly Review*, January 1758, 66).

Meanwhile, through the intercession of the earl of Bute, Kirby had become teacher of perspective and fortifications to the prince of Wales in 1756, having moved with his family to Great Queen Street, London, the previous September when he left the Ipswich business in the hands of Andrew Baldrey (d. 1802). Baldrey then acquired it in 1759 when the Kirbys moved to Kew Green, Richmond, Surrey. In 1761 Kirby published the handsome *Perspective of Architecture Deduced from the Principles of Dr. Brook Taylor* which included as plate 44 *House with a Colonnade* (drawing; Royal Collection) by the prince, who was closely involved with the publication and paid for the many illustrations. On his accession as George III in 1761, the king rewarded his jovial and devoted preceptor by appointing Kirby and his son William Kirby (1743–1771) joint clerks of the works at Kew and Richmond (PRO, Works, Accounts, 5/69). The post was no sinecure and William, a promising artist, went with his wife to study architecture in Italy at the king's expense in 1768–9. On their return William Kirby was given a house at Kew, where he died in 1771. Of Kirby's brothers who became lawyers, the elder brother John (b. 1715) died in 1750 while under-treasurer at the Middle Temple, and Stephen (b. 1717) was training under him but died in 1741. Kirby designed an extension to Kew chapel (never implemented, BL, Kings Maps, xl 46 h), having in 1762 built St George's Chapel in Brentford, Middlesex, where his daughter, Sarah [see Trimmer, Sarah (1741–1810)], the religious writer, married James Trimmer. With his younger brother, William, Kirby published revised editions of *The Suffolk Traveller* (1764) and his father's map (1766), embellished with more of his Suffolk views. In 1767 he was elected a fellow of the Royal Society and a fellow of the Society of Antiquaries.

Kirby contributed three drawings (Metropolitan Museum of Art, New York) to *Gardens and Buildings at Kew* (1763) by Sir William Chambers, who gave Kirby his many orders for works on the royal estates. Overwork was exacerbated by his presidency (1768–71) of the Incorporated Society of Artists, assumed after dissensions had caused the resignation of most eminent directors. After assuming this position Kirby was soon humiliated by his chance discovery that the king with Benjamin West and Chambers was planning a royal academy, formed in December 1768. Although proposed as the academy's professor of perspective, Kirby stayed loyal to his society, struggling to retain the king's interest until ill health forced his resignation. From 1761 he had exhibited mainly drawings including *St Albans Abbey* (1767; department of prints and drawings, British Museum) but the oils *Kew Ferry* (1767) and *Ockham Mill* (1769) were attributed by Horace Walpole to the king. The only known landscape in oil signed by Kirby, dated 1761, is at Gainsborough's House, Sudbury, Suffolk.

Kirby died peacefully at Kew Green on 20 June 1774, and was buried in Kew chapel (now St Anne's, Kew). He had owned many works by Gainsborough (which appeared in the Trimmer sale, Christies, 17 March 1860), who had painted Kirby with his wife (c.1750; National Portrait Gallery, London) and separately in two further portraits (V&A; Fitzwilliam Museum, Cambridge). Such was Gainsborough's confidence in his 'old friend pudging Josh' (Grant, 1.63), whose faith in Heaven was proverbial, that he was buried alongside him at St Anne's, Kew.

FELICITY OWEN

Sources F. Owen, 'Joshua Kirby, 1716–74', *Gainsborough's House Review* (1995–6), 61–76 • Colvin, *Archs.* • R. Paulson, *Hogarth: his life, art and times*, 2 (1971), 151, 158–60, 206, 286 • J. Hayes, *The landscape paintings of Thomas Gainsborough*, 2 vols. (1982) • J. Roberts, *Royal artists: from Mary queen of Scots to the present day* (1987) • W. T. Whitley, *Artists and their friends in England, 1700–1799*, 1 (1928), 221–42 • *Ipswich Journal* (1751–74) • E. Harris and N. Savage, *British architectural books and writers, 1556–1785* (1990) • M. Kitson, ed., 'Hogarth's "Apology for painters"', *Walpole Society*, 41 (1966–8), 46–111, esp. 109 • *Some account of the life and writings of Mrs. Trimmer*, 1 (1814), 1–19 • A. P. Oppé, *English drawings … at Windsor Castle* (1950), 19–20 • Graves, *Soc. Artists* • J. Ingamells, ed., *A dictionary of British and Irish travellers in Italy, 1701–1800* (1997) • M. H. Grant, *A chronological history of the old English landscape painters*, 1 (1926), 63–4

Archives RA, papers • Wellcome L., papers | PRO, Office of Works records, minutes, 14/1 • PRO, Office of Works records, accounts, 5/69

Likenesses T. Gainsborough, double portrait, oils, c.1750 (with his wife), NPG • T. Gainsborough, oils, c.1757–1778, V&A; unfinished • T. Gainsborough, oils, 1760–1769?, FM Cam. • P. Falconet, pencil, 1768; Christies, 12 Nov 1968, lot 50 • J. Scott, mezzotint, pubd 1879 (after T. Gainsborough), BM, NPG • J. Dixon, mezzotint (after T. Gainsborough), BM, NPG • W. Maddocks, stipple (after P. Falconet), Gainsborough's House, Sudbury • D. Pariset, engraving (after P. Falconet), BM

Wealth at death £300 to wife, further £300 if needed; rest to Mr and Mrs Trimmer: wills, 7 Aug 1772, and 11 July 1774

Kirby [married name Gregg], **Mary** (1817–1893), writer on natural history, was the second of five children of John Kirby (d. 1848), a prosperous Leicester hosiery manufacturer, and Sarah Bentley, an invalid whose death in 1835 left Mary and her elder sister in charge of the household. Religion and education were family priorities; Mrs Kirby took the children to Robert Hall's Baptist chapel and Mary was sent to schools in Market Harborough and Leicester. Mary also received instruction in languages from a family friend and went to lectures at the local mechanics' institute.

Seaside holidays at Ramsgate first shaped Mary Kirby's interest in collecting and studying plants, and local flora later became her focus. In 1840, recuperating from an injury, she spent time in Charnwood Forest near Loughborough, and botany was both an occupation and a resource. She became caught up in the mid-century 'botanical mania'. Aided by clergyman–naturalist Andrew Bloxam she compiled and edited the first *Flora of Leicestershire*, issued as a preliminary list in 1848 with blank pages for local botanists to enter records and observations. The definitive issue in 1850 groups more than 900 flowering plants and ferns according to the orders of the natural system, and cites localities and details about habitats. Notes of general and medical interest were prepared by Mary Kirby's youngest sister, **Elizabeth Kirby** (1823–1873), to 'enlist the sympathies of some readers who feel little or no interest in botanical science'.

After the death of John Kirby in 1848 the unmarried Kirby sisters were able to stay for two years rent-free in the family home in Friar Lane, Leicester, and later obtained the freehold. Long-term economic planning was necessary, however, and Mary and Elizabeth began to 'plot and plan for book-writing' (M. Kirby, 70). With Mary's botanical knowledge and Elizabeth's writing skills, they embarked on a career as joint authors of juvenile and natural history books.

Mary and Elizabeth Kirby worked as a sisterly writing team for twenty-five years, and produced a steady stream of more than twenty-five publications that included illustrated books, serial tales for magazines, school books, and fiction of an improving kind. In *The Discontented Children, and how they were Cured* (1854), their first original story book, the children of a gentleman and a gamekeeper are given the opportunity to experience each other's lives; the rustic children, restored to their parents after adventures and hardships, were 'only too happy to find themselves once more among their equals and in their proper station'. The second edition, in 1859, contains illustrations by Phiz. Their natural history books, written principally for young readers, were informational rather than moralizing. *Plants of the Land and Water* (1857), one of two of their books issued in the Observing Eye series, presents botanical information and 'curious facts' about the uses of plants, in the form of 'Short and Entertaining Chapters on the Vegetable World'. Their books on insects were *Caterpillars, Butterflies, and Moths* (1857) and *Sketches of Insect Life* (1874). *The Sea and its Wonders* (1873), with short informational chapters on topics such as the Gulf Stream and the turtle, aimed to 'allure' the young reader to study 'the great book of Nature, rather than to perplex him with a strictly scientific arrangement'. *Chapters on Trees* (1873), a 'Popular Account of Their Nature and Uses', aims for a general rather than juvenile readership, and is well stocked with botanical information as well as history and folklore about trees from around the world.

During their long and successful joint career as Victorian professional women writers, the Kirby sisters published with Thomas Jarrold, Griffith and Farran, Thomas Nelson, and Routledge. Mary Kirby wrote that 'Earned money seems always the sweetest and best of any; and we were glad to find a ready sale for our manuscripts, and also to put the profits into our pockets' (M. Kirby, 165). She recalls in her autobiography that they once wrote:

> a humourous piece of what would happen a hundred years hence; how the men would be thrust out from all the professions by the women, and even the government of the country would be carried on by women, and in the houses of parliament there would not be a man to be seen.   (ibid., 126)

Mary and Elizabeth Kirby lived in Norwich and Great Yarmouth after 1855. Elizabeth was in delicate mental health, but they maintained a regular writing schedule. On 1 August 1860 Mary, aged forty-three, married Henry Gregg (d. 1881), curate of a church in Norwich, with Elizabeth as a witness. The sisters bought the living of Brooksby, Leicestershire, for Gregg, and they all lived together in Melton Mowbray in Six Elms, a house built for them. Mary and Elizabeth continued writing their books together, and the latter also issued four titles separately: *Steps Up the Ladder, or, The Will and the Way* (1862), *Dame Buckle and her Pet Johnny* (1867), *Lost Cities Brought to Light* (1871), and *Margaret's Choice* (1872). She died on 23 June 1873, at Six Elms.

Mary Kirby was widowed in 1881, and money troubles ensued. Her autobiography, *Leaflets from my Life: a Narrative Biography* (1887), a rich source book of local history and mid-nineteenth-century social history, is filled with detail about family connections and social routines in the middle-class household of her youth and adult life. She died on 15 October 1893 at her home in Melton Mowbray, aged seventy-six, and was buried in the same grave as her husband and her sister near the wall of the Brooksby church. Her will, dated 27 January 1891, left an estate of £730 to her only surviving sister, Mme Katharine Coulin.

ANN B. SHTEIR

Sources M. Kirby, *Leaflets from my life* (1887) · J. D. Bennett, 'Mary Kirby: a biographical note' (typescript), 1965, Leics. RO, pamphlet box 24A · J. Kirby, diary, 1813–48, Leics. RO, DE619 · A. R. Horwood and C. W. F. Noel, *The flora of Leicestershire and Rutland … with biographies of former botanists (1620–1933)* (1933) · 'Kirby, Elizabeth', *DNB* · m. cert. · d. cert. · d. cert. [Elizabeth Kirby]
Wealth at death £730; estate left to only surviving sister: will, 1891; Bennett, 'Mary Kirby'

Kirby, Richard (1649–1693?), astrologer and medical practitioner, was born on 13 July 1649 of unknown parentage. In an early work he apologized for his mean education. Henry Coley (1633–1704), a close friend, was probably his astrological teacher. His early works, ephemerides for 1681 and 1682 and an almanac for 1684, were uncontroversial but Kirby became notorious in the mid-1680s when he responded to the threat from popery and absolutism at home and the French and Ottomans abroad by predicting sensational changes throughout Europe. His *Vates astrologicus* (1683) promised the death of Louis XIV, the devastation of France, Italy, and Spain and the overthrow of the papacy, before the rise of a great conqueror in 1699 who would bring peace to the whole world. Many of these prophecies were drawn from John Holwell's *Catastrophe mundi*, or from the astrological works of Richard Edlin and William Lilly. Kirby found it expedient to withdraw from London in 1687–8, and was denounced by the tory astrologer John Gadbury in 1688. He was able to speak out freely once more after the revolution of 1688, and published *Catastrophe Galliae* in 1690, in which he promised the conquest of France and Ireland and a golden age of freedom for Britain, and mocked Gadbury for predicting that the year 1688 would pass uneventfully.

In 1681 Kirby was living in Fulham, but he worked from an address in London, advertising his services as teacher and consultant at the sign of the Iron-Jack, a smith's shop in Fetter Lane. Kirby attended from Monday to Wednesday, his partner Philip Mayle on the other days. Like several whig astrologers, Kirby wished to reform astrology by restoring its original purity, a cause championed by the Italian Ptolemaist, Placidus de Titis. In 1687 he and his friend John Bishop published *The Marrow of Astrology*, offering a Ptolemaic account of the zodiacal signs and the planets based on Placidus's work. Kirby's section was dedicated to Elias Ashmole, Bishop's to Robert Boyle. Their partnership foundered when Bishop tried to claim sole credit for the work. By this date Kirby had moved to King Street, Soho, at the sign of the Figura Mundi, complaining that the Fulham rabble had abused him as a witch or athe-ist. It is possible but unproven that he was the Mr Richard Kirby tried for murder at the Old Bailey in 1687 after a brawl at a gambling house in St Bride's, and acquitted on a plea of self-defence. He was still lodging in King Street when he published his last work in 1693, an account of a fourteen-year-old hysteric or epileptic, Sarah Bower of Wapping. She claimed to be possessed by the devil and the case attracted widespread interest. Kirby saw her on 19 November 1693 and used his account to advertise his suc-cess in curing bewitched patients in Norfolk and Suffolk (possibly during his retreat from London in 1687–8). He promised further details in a book then almost complete; as no such work is known, he probably did not live to fin-ish it. The exact date of his death is unknown, but nothing is heard of him after 1693.   BERNARD CAPP

Sources B. S. Capp, *Astrology and the popular press: English almanacs, 1500–1800* (1979) · Bodl. Oxf., MS Ashmole 436 · *The proceedings … the Old-Bayly, the 7th, 8th, and 9th days of December* (1687) · J. Gadbury, *A diary of the celestial motions for 1690* (1690)
Likenesses engraving, repro. in R. Kirby, *Vates astrologicus* (1683)

Kirby, William (1759–1850), entomologist and naturalist, was born at Witnesham, near Ipswich, Suffolk, on 18 Sep-tember 1759, the son of William Kirby (d. 1791), a solicitor, and his wife, Lucy Meadows. He had four sisters.

Kirby's initial interest in natural history was fostered by his mother, who had a conchological collection from which she taught him the names of shells. In 1770 mother and son made a small herbarium at Witnesham. His mother died in 1776 and Kirby was subsequently educated at Ipswich grammar school and Gonville and Caius Col-lege, Cambridge. He graduated in 1781 and was ordained deacon in June 1782. He was later appointed rector of Barham, Suffolk, and vicar of Coddenham and was given the permanent living of Barham in 1796. He returned to natural history studies after receiving his appointment, although these appear not to have interfered with his pas-toral duties.

In the summer of 1797 Kirby went on a natural history excursion to Ely, Northampton, Huntingdon, and Cam-bridge with the naturalist Thomas Marsham (d. 1819). His natural history interest at this time seems to have been largely botanical and he had a particular interest in cryptogamic plants. He is known to have had a copy of James Edward Smith's *English Botany*. He served as secre-tary to the local militia during the invasion scare of 1803–5, his job being to look after the women and children. By 1805 Kirby was acquainted with William Spence (1783–1860) of Hull, and by 1809 he knew William Hooker. The three are known to have had natural history rambles together.

Kirby wrote on mycological and zoological topics but turned his attention to entomology in the 1790s with the finding of a 'very beautiful golden bug' on his window sill. He communicated his natural history findings to the Linnean Society of London, on whose first list of fellows (1798) his name appears. He wrote his first paper in 1793, but his first major entomological work, on the bees col-lected in his parish—*Monographia apium Angliae*—

appeared in 1802 and was illustrated with colour plates. In this he described some 200 types, many of which are still recognized as species. Kirby is said to have learned the techniques of engraving in order better to understand natural history illustration. In 1808 Spence suggested a collaboration to produce a basic work on entomology. This was begun in 1809 and resulted in their pioneering illustrated volumes *Introduction to Entomology* (1815–26); editions appeared throughout the early nineteenth cen-tury, the last being the sixth (1843).

Kirby's first wife, Sarah Ripper, died in 1814. The follow-ing year he took his MA. He married again in early 1817, and in the June went with his second wife, Charlotte Rod-well (d. 1844), for a short trip to Paris. Kirby took an active part in the Zoological Club of the Linnean Society which provided the key management for the new Zoological Society in 1826. His work was both economically and taxo-nomically orientated, and in addition to bees he wrote on insect spoilage of wheat, timber, and, in 1808, on *Apion*, or weevils. Among his better-known entomological works is his paper on the insect parasites of bees, the Strepsiptera, an entirely new order described by him in 1815. In his 'Century of insects' (*Transactions of the Linnean Society*, 12, 1818, 375–453) he described new species from specimens in English natural history cabinets. He was elected FRS in 1818 and shortly afterwards described some of the insects brought back from Australia by Robert Brown on the *Inves-tigator* expedition of 1801–5. The theme of overseas ento-mology was taken up again when he wrote on the insects brought back from the Canadian Arctic by John Richard-son from the expedition of 1825–7. This was his entomo-logical contribution to the illustrated *Fauna boreali Ameri-cana* (1837). He became honorary president of the Entomo-logical Society of London in 1837 and gave his insect collection to that society. (It was later, in 1863, given to the British Museum and much of it survives in the Natural History Museum, London.) The *History of the Collections* (vol. 2) noted that Kirby's specimens from his 'Century of insects', Robert Brown's Australian material, Richard-son's Canadian insects, and some of Kirby's beetles and his bees from the *Monographia apium Angliae* were extant in 1906.

Kirby lived in the closing years of pre-Darwinian natural history. It was a time when the foundations of entomol-ogy were being laid and he corresponded widely with nat-uralists at home and abroad, including Sir Joseph Banks, Alexander Macleay (1767–1848), J. C. Dale (1792–1872), Edward Sabine, the Oxford-based naturalist the Revd F. W. Hope, N. A. Vigors, J. C. Fabricius (1745–1808) of Kiel, Adam Afzelius (1750–1837) in Sweden, Ludwig Imhoff (1801–1868) in Switzerland, and the French entomologist P. A. Latreille (1762–1833), among many others. Kirby's corres-pondents are of interest because their names appear in some of his insect names.

In later years Kirby seems to have lived the life of a quiet country parson and his portraits show him as a well-built man of medium height with blue eyes. He seems to have been a believer in the non-Calvinistic Anglican tradition. His meditations in 1829 on the temptations and passion of

Our Lord were based on those of the early seventeenth-century Bishop Andrews. In the autumn of 1830 he was approached by J. G. Children of the British Museum, the archbishop of Canterbury, and the bishop of London acting for the trustees of the eighth duke of Bridgewater through the Royal Society to begin work on a contribution for what became known as the *Bridgewater Treatise*. In 1835 he contributed to this work 'The habitats and instincts of animals'.

Kirby died at Barham on 4 July 1850. He appears to have been a much-loved pastor to his country congregation and was buried in the chancel of his parish church. The Revd William Kirby is not to be confused with the later entomologist, William F. Kirby (1844–1912) of Leicester.

D. T. Moore

Sources J. Freeman, *Life of the Rev. William Kirby, M.A.* (1852) · *Abstracts of the Papers Communicated to the Royal Society of London*, 5 (1843–50), 1023–6 · W. Spence, *Proceedings of the Linnean Society of London*, 2 (1848–55), 133–5 · P. Gilbert, *A compendium of the biographical literature on deceased entomologists* (1977) · Desmond, *Botanists*, rev. edn · *DNB*
Archives Linn. Soc., corresp. and papers · NHM, catalogues of insects · NHM, notebook · Suffolk RO, Ipswich, diaries of journeys in Norfolk and Suffolk | Oxf. U. Mus. NH, letters to J. C. Dale · Oxf. U. Mus. NH, letters to F. W. Hope · Oxf. U. Mus. NH, letters to J. O. Wedwood · Scott Polar RI, corresp. with John Richardson · Suffolk RO, Ipswich, notitia villaris for Barham
Likenesses T. H. Maguire, lithograph, 1851 (after photograph by F. H. Bischoff), BM, NPG; repro. in T. H. Maguire, *Portraits of honorary members of the Ipswich Museum* (1852) · R. J. Lane, lithograph (aged eighty-nine; after W. B. Spence), NPG · T. Lupton, mezzotint (after H. Howard), BM, NPG · W. B. Spence, two lithographs (after his portrait), BM, NPG · engraving, repro. in W. Kirby and W. Spence, *An introduction to entomology*, 4 vols. (1815–26) · engraving, repro. in Freeman, *Life of the Rev. William Kirby* · oils, Gon. & Caius Cam. · oils, Linn. Soc. · portrait, Hunt Library, Kew · print, Linn. Soc. · watercolour drawing, Linn. Soc.

Kirbye, George (*d.* 1634), composer, first emerges in 1592 as a major contributor to Thomas East's psalter. By 1597 he was a domestic musician in the service of Sir Robert Jermyn of Rushbrooke Hall, near Bury St Edmunds, and in that year he published his *First Set of English Madrigalls, to 4, 5, and 6 Voyces*, which comprised twenty-four pieces dedicated to two of Sir Robert's daughters, for whose 'delight & contentments' Kirbye had originally composed them. Rushbrooke was close to Hengrave Hall where one of the greatest of the English madrigalists, John Wilbye, was also in service, and the two men must have been acquainted; significantly, perhaps, Wilbye provided one of only two instances of another composer setting a text already used by Kirbye. In 1601 Kirbye contributed a madrigal to *The Triumphs of Oriana*, the collection of madrigals in honour of the ageing Queen Elizabeth, but he published no further volume of his own, though eighteen more madrigals by him survive in manuscript sources. On 16 February 1598 he had married Anne Saxye (*d.* 1626) at nearby Bradfield St George. There seem to have been no children from the marriage. Nothing more is known of Kirbye until 1626, when he was living in Whiting Street in Bury St Edmunds, where he was evidently churchwarden

at St Mary's Church; during the next two years his name appears in the parish registers.

Though Kirbye's date of birth remains unknown, it was probably some time before 1570, for clearly eight of his works surviving in manuscript sources were in fact viol-accompanied solo songs more typical of the earlier years of Elizabeth's reign, though with words subsequently fitted to the string parts to make them resemble madrigals, and this points to a date of composition no later than the 1580s, and very probably earlier. Even the contents of Kirbye's single published madrigal volume hint at a composer no longer in his first youth, for these are little marked by the bright, lively manner newly paraded in Thomas Morley's volumes of the earlier 1590s, and they set no light verse; instead they favour a generally more serious aesthetic and all are in a minor mode. But Kirbye had certainly become familiar with Italian madrigals, and for his published collection the madrigals (and especially those of Luca Marenzio) which had been printed with English words in the anthologies of Nicholas Yonge (*Musica transalpina*, 1588) and Thomas Watson (*Italian Madrigals Englished*, 1590) seem to have been his prime models. Kirbye's own examples reveal an admirable and inventive artisan, fluent and tasteful, who employed word-painting and chromaticism judiciously and who, while lacking those broader imaginative insights that marked the greatest of his contemporaries such as Wilbye, was able on occasions to produce moments that are truly memorable. Moreover, his *Oriana* contribution, 'With Angel's Face' (published in the first edition with a different text: 'Bright Phoebus Greets'), shows that he could also confidently command a more brilliant, extravert style.

Kirbye was buried in St Mary's, Bury St Edmunds, on 6 October 1634 and his will reveals that he was by then a man of some substance. Three of his madrigals survive as 'contrafacta' (that is, with sacred texts substituted). In addition, a small quantity of church music by him is extant, as is a single instrumental pavan, though most of these pieces survive incomplete.

David Brown

Sources G. Kirbye, preface, *The first set of English madrigalls, to 4, 5, and 6 voyces* (1597) · Grove, *Dict. mus.* (1954), 4.761 · *New Grove*, 2nd edn · C. Monson, 'George Kirbye and the English madrigal', *Music and Letters*, 59 (1978), 290–315 · E. H. Fellowes, *The English madrigal composers*, 2nd edn (1950)
Wealth at death property, goods, and chattels: Grove, *Dict. mus.*

Kirk, John (1724?–1778?), medallist, probably became a pupil of the medallist James Anthony Dassier about 1740. It is difficult to be certain of his life because of the profusion of medallists and engravers named John Kirk. From about 1740 until 1778 he produced a large number of medals signed KIRK or I. KIRK. In 1745 he was probably living in St Paul's Churchyard, and in 1745–6 several medals were struck by John Kirk and A. Kirk. The *Gentleman's Magazine* reported the death on 19 November 1761 of a 'Mr Kirk senior' of that address, which may have been his father or brother. In 1762–3 he received premiums from the Society of Artists and in 1773 and 1775–6 exhibited medals of the royal family and others. Many of his medals commemorate the victories of the War of the Austrian

Succession and the Seven Years' War, though others are for royalty, politicians, and civic associations such as the British Fishery Society (1751).

Although some authorities list Kirk's death as 27 November 1776, this appears unlikely, as he probably produced several medals in 1778, including a commemoration of the earl of Chatham. He may have been the John Kirk, 'engraver', of St James's, who made his will on 13 November 1778, and which was proved by his widow, Catherine, on 5 December 1778. A further confusion may arise from the report in the *Gentleman's Magazine* on 31 March 1791 of the death of 'Mr Kirk, seal-engraver, in St Paul's Churchyard'.   STUART HANDLEY

Sources Redgrave, *Artists*, 251 · L. Forrer, *Biographical dictionary of medallists*, 8 vols. (1904–30), 3 (1907), 162–5 · E. Hawkins, *Medallic illustrations of the history of Great Britain and Ireland to the death of George II*, ed. A. W. Franks and H. A. Grueber, 2 (1885), 729 · *GM*, 1st ser., 31 (1761), 539; 61 (1791), 383 · *European Magazine and London Review*, 19 (1791), 319 · H. A. Grueber, 'English personal medals from 1760', *Numismatic Chronicle*, 3rd ser., 10 (1890), 51–98, esp. 54 · will, PRO, PROB 11/1048, fol. 186r

Kirk, John (1760–1851), Roman Catholic priest and antiquary, was born at Acton Burnell, Shropshire, on 13 April 1760, the son of William Kirk and his wife, Mary Fielding, both of whom were Catholics. He was educated at Sedgley Park School from 1770 to 1773. On 5 June 1773 he was admitted to the English College, Rome, where he was the last scholar received there by the Jesuits before they were replaced by Italian secular clerics. Kirk's diary for the period 1773 to 1779, now in the college archives, is the main source for internal college politics in these years. The young Kirk, disliking the new administration (which he represented as harsh and oppressive), portrayed the Jesuit period as a golden age. However, since he spent only three months at the college before the new administration was established, his complaints must be treated with caution. Although the new authorities tightened up the discipline of the college, they did not introduce any regulations which were not common in Italian seminaries.

Kirk was ordained priest on 18 December 1784 and returned to England in August 1785. His first mission was at Aldenham Hall, Shropshire, the home of Sir Richard Acton, but he soon left to become chaplain at Sedgley Park, where he became vice-president in 1786 and president on 27 April 1793. Before this appointment he had served at the small mission of Pipe Hall, near Lichfield, where he was also in charge of the congregation of Tamworth. In July 1797 he left Sedgley Park to become chaplain and private secretary to Charles Berington, vicar apostolic of the Midland district. He lived with Berington at Longbirch, where he had charge of the mission. He assisted Berington's cousin, the controversial cisalpine historian Joseph Berington, with his *History of the Rise, Progress and Decline of the Papal Power*, and became one of the Staffordshire Squadron, a group of liberal clergy advocating a form of ecclesiastical democracy in opposition to Walmesley, the vicar apostolic of the western district. Charles Berington's sudden death in June 1798, in Kirk's arms, led to the disintegration of this liberal party. Kirk remained at Longbirch until Gregory Stapleton was appointed to succeed Berington in 1801, when he moved to Lichfield to serve three local congregations. His involvement with the Staffordshire Squadron may account for his subsequent lack of promotion.

At Lichfield he built a chapel which was opened on 11 November 1803. He enjoyed cordial relations with his protestant neighbours; on his arrival in Lichfield he met with a more than metaphorically warm reception from the cathedral dignitaries, who found him lodgings above a bakery. When he converted his chapel into the church of St Cross in 1834, members of the municipal corporation subscribed to his funds to mark their respect. Although he was hooted at during the 1826 general election, and an effigy of Wiseman was displayed outside his windows during the 'papal aggression' crisis of 1850, he was influential in Lichfield society. He built chapels at Hopwas and Tamworth.

However, Kirk's main labours during the fifty years he spent in Lichfield lay in 'the cabinet rather than the field, in the study rather than the pulpit' (*Tablet*, 52). As a young man he had read Charles Dodd's *Church History of England* (1737–42), and had decided to write a continuation of the work, covering the history of eighteenth-century English Catholicism. His extensive collection of materials for this work was described in a *Letter to the Rev. Joseph Berington* (1826). The continuation of the *History*, however, remained unwritten, and Kirk handed over most of his materials to Mark Aloysius Tierney, who brought out a new, but incomplete, edition of Dodd between 1839 and 1843. The manuscripts subsequently passed to the Westminster Diocesan Archives, and in 1908 one of the manuscripts was edited by J. H. Pollen and E. Burton and published as *Biographies of English Catholics in the Eighteenth Century*. It remains an essential (if not always accurate) source for historians of eighteenth-century English Catholicism. Kirk helped to prepare for publication the papers of Sir Ralph Sadler, Elizabeth I's ambassador to Scotland, which appeared in 1809 with an introduction by Walter Scott. He also collaborated with the Coventry antiquary Thomas Sharp. To his contemporaries, however, he was best known for his work *The Faith of Catholics* (1813), which was written in collaboration with Joseph Berington. Later described as one of the nineteenth-century's most enduring controversial works, it was republished in 1830 and 1846, and a Latin translation was published in Bonn in 1844. It provoked replies from John Graham, who criticized it in a review included in his *Annals of Ireland* (1819), and from R. T. P. Pope in his *Roman Misquotation* (1840). Kirk also published an edition of a Roman Catholic tract of 1680, *Roman Catholic Principles in Reference to God and the King* (1815), with an introduction identifying the author as the Benedictine abbot of Lamspringe, James Corker.

In 1841 Pope Gregory XVI conferred a DD upon Kirk. Kirk died at Lichfield on 21 December 1851 and was buried at St Cross Church. In his obituary by Henry Weedall, president of Oscott College, he was described as 'a living chronicle of persons, places and facts … a perfect specimen of the olden times, a type of the fine old English Priest; methodical, dignified, devout' (*The Tablet*, 52).

ROSEMARY MITCHELL

Sources *The Tablet* (24 Jan 1852), 52–3 · *The Rambler*, 9 (1852), 44–9 · *Catholic Directory* (1852), 129–36 · *GM*, 2nd ser., 37 (1852), 304–6 · A. Laird, 'The English College, Rome, under Italian secular administration, 1773–1798', *Recusant History*, 14 (1977–8), 127–47 · E. Duffy, 'Ecclesiastical democracy detected [pts 1–2]', *Recusant History*, 10 (1969–70), 193–209, 309–31 · E. Duffy, 'Ecclesiastical democracy detected [pt 3]', *Recusant History*, 13 (1975–6), 123–48 · *DNB* · J. H. Pollen and E. Burton, introduction, in J. Kirk, *Biographies of English Catholics in the eighteenth century*, ed. J. H. Pollen and E. Burton (1909), vii–xvi · J. C. H. Aveling, *The handle and the axe: the Catholic recusants in England from Reformation to emancipation* (1976), 332–5
Archives Roman Catholic archdiocesan archives, Birmingham, corresp. and papers · Southwark Roman Catholic diocesan archives, notes relating to Stapleton · Venerable English College, Rome, diary · Westm. DA, corresp. and papers
Likenesses Deere?, engraving (after Mackey?), repro. in *Catholic Directory* (1853), frontispiece

Kirk, Sir John (1832–1922), naturalist and political agent, was born on 19 December 1832 at Barry, Forfarshire, the second of the four children of the Revd John Kirk, minister of Barry, and his wife, Christian Carnegie, who was descended from a cadet branch of the Carnegie family of Southesk. He was educated at Arbroath high school until 1845, then at Madras College, St Andrews, whence he matriculated at Edinburgh University in 1847. After two years in the faculty of arts, he moved to medicine, graduating MD in 1854 with a thesis on the structure of the kidney. While still an undergraduate Kirk was elected fellow of the Edinburgh Botanical Society.

Kirk worked for a year as a doctor in the Edinburgh Royal Infirmary before volunteering for the Crimean War. In 1855 he was posted to the Yerenkevy Hospital on the Dardanelles, where he spent his spare time studying the botany of Asia Minor and the Turkish language. He would often go out hunting and Beddoe, his colleague, wrote, 'Kirk was the only genuine sportsman or hunter among us, and he generally secured a big bustard or a wild swan or two, and some smaller game' (Coupland, 60). He returned to England in 1857 with the intention of teaching natural history at Queen's University, Kingston, Canada, but soon gave up this idea when he was appointed to accompany David Livingstone on his second Zambezi expedition, as doctor and naturalist.

From 1858 to 1863 Kirk was Livingstone's chief assistant and proved a valuable member of the expedition. He was an enthusiastic amateur photographer and although Charles Livingstone was the official photographer, almost all the surviving photographs were made by Kirk. The party explored the Shire valley and highlands, and made the earliest investigation of Lake Nyasa and its surroundings (although this claim has been disputed by the Portuguese). They then ascended the Zambezi as far as Sasheke, and made a thorough examination of the Victoria Falls. As the expedition was making its return journey, in November 1860, Kirk was nearly drowned in the Kebra-basa

rapids. Three years later he suffered a severe attack of dysentery and was made to return to Britain. There he met and became engaged to Helen (*d.* 1914), daughter of Charles Cooke of Ledbury, Herefordshire.

Kirk's botanical collections were considerable and laid the foundations of the *Flora of Tropical Africa* (1868–1917), which was published under the auspices of the government. He was offered a high post at the Royal Botanic Gardens, Kew, but, desiring to return to Africa, he accepted instead the post of medical officer to the Zanzibar Agency, which he took up in January 1866. That same year he was appointed vice-consul and in the following year, in Zanzibar, he married Helen Cooke. They had one son and five daughters.

Kirk so helped many European nations to develop their trade with Zanzibar that he acted as consul for the Hamburg Republic, and consul-general for Portugal and Italy, subsequently receiving decorations from the latter two countries. In 1873 he persuaded the sultan of Zanzibar to sign an anti-slavery treaty, closing the island's slave markets, and providing protection for all liberated slaves. The adverse effects on the coastal towns Kirk offset by establishing the east African rubber trade in 1878, the fruit of his discovery of the rubber-yielding vine (*Landolphia*). In time, Kirk became virtual ruler of Zanzibar.

The German East Africa Company was founded in 1885. By 1887 it had twelve stations in east Africa and was seeking to acquire from native chiefs land over which the sultan of Zanzibar claimed nominal authority. In 1886 Kirk began the negotiations that led to the sultan's making great concessions from his mainland territories to the East African Association (later the Imperial British East Africa Company) in the following year.

Following his retirement from the consular service in July 1886, Kirk continued to serve the state in several capacities in African affairs. He was British plenipotentiary to the African slave-trade conference at Brussels (1889–90). In 1895, he was sent to Nigeria to inquire into a dispute, which had resulted in considerable fighting and loss of life, between the Brass natives and the Royal Niger Company. From 1895 he was chairman of the government committee for the construction of the Uganda Railway, and in the following year he was appointed to the Royal Society's tsetse fly committee.

In 1882, Kirk was awarded the Royal Geographical Society's patron's medal, later serving as the society's vice-president (1891–4) and foreign secretary (1894–1911). In 1882 Kirk also became vice-president of the Linnean Society. In 1887 he was elected a fellow of the Royal Society and in 1894 became its vice-president. He was appointed CMG in 1879 and was created KCMG in 1881, GCMG in 1886, and KCB in 1890. He was honoured with the degrees of LLD from Edinburgh in 1890, ScD from Cambridge in 1897, and DCL from Oxford in 1898. His name was attached to several of the animals and plants that he identified, notably Kirk's red colobus monkey, Kirk's dik-dik, and Kirkia, a species of Acacia.

From 1887 Kirk lived in Sevenoaks with his wife and children, though he still made a number of foreign visits.

These ended in 1907, owing to the impairment of his sight. He died on 15 January 1922, at Wavertree, his home in Sevenoaks.   MICHAEL D. MCMULLEN

Sources W. G. Blaikie, *Personal life of David Livingstone* (1880) · R. Coupland, *Kirk on the Zambesi* (1928) · H. H. Johnston, 'Sir John Kirk', *GJ*, 59 (1922), 225–8 · R. W. Beachy, *A history of east Africa, 1592–1902* (1996) · A. Sheriff, *Slaves, spices, and ivory in Zanzibar* (1987) · R. Foskett, ed., *The Zambesi journal and letters of Dr. John Kirk, 1858–63*, 2 vols. (1965) · R. Foskett, ed., *The Zambesi doctors: David Livingstone's letters to John Kirk, 1858, 1872* (1964) · D. Liebowitz, *The physician and the slave trade: John Kirk, the Livingstone expeditions and the crusade against slavery in east Africa* (1999) · *CGPLA Eng. & Wales* (1922)
Archives NL Scot., corresp. and papers · NRA, priv. coll., corresp. and papers | BL OIOC, corresp. with Sir Alfred Lyall, MSS Eur. F 132 · Bodl. RH, corresp. with F. D. Lugard · NL Scot., letters to J. A. Grant · NL Scot., corresp. with David Livingstone, incl. maps and sketches · RGS, corresp. with Royal Geographical Society · SOAS, letters to Sir William Mackinnon
Likenesses A. H. Kirk, watercolour drawing, 1915, NPG; repro. in Coupland, *Kirk on the Zambesi* · Maull & Fox, photograph, RS
Wealth at death £44,234 7s. 4d.: probate, 20 April 1922, *CGPLA Eng. & Wales*

Kirk, Sir John (1847–1922), philanthropist, the second son of Alfred Kirk, tinsmith and brazier, of Kegworth, Leicestershire, and his wife, Mary, daughter of Harry Wilkins, was born at Kegworth on 10 June 1847. He was educated at Castle Donington grammar school, Leicestershire. Part of his boyhood was spent in France, but at the age of sixteen, after his father's death, he went to London and was appointed | clerk to the Pure Literature Society.

In 1867 Kirk began work for the Ragged School Union, then housed in 'two rooms and a cupboard' in Exeter Hall, Strand. He acted as evening schools visitor from 1873 to 1879, during which period he was secretary of the Open Air Mission, but in 1879 he was appointed secretary of the Ragged School Union. He thus became closely associated with Anthony Ashley Cooper, seventh earl of Shaftesbury, president of the union from 1844 until his death in 1885. It was largely owing to Kirk's power of adaptation, his gift of seizing opportunities, and his determination that the union survived the critical years following the passage of the Elementary Education Act of 1870. Thereafter ragged schools were transformed into mission Sunday schools with multiplying activities: country holiday homes, the 'cripple' mission, and clothing guilds were developed.

Kirk married in 1872 Elizabeth (*d.* 1934), daughter of George Ayris of Witney, Oxfordshire; they had four sons and three daughters. He was knighted in 1907 and a public testimonial was presented to him at the Mansion House; his title was altered from secretary to director. His jubilee of service was celebrated in 1917, also at the Mansion House, when he took the opportunity of presenting a cheque for £1000, which he had raised privately, for the establishment of a Shaftesbury Foundation Fund. The same year he delivered the first Shaftesbury lecture, a notable review and forecast of child welfare.

During Kirk's period of service the annual income of the union increased from £6000 to £60,000. In 1914 its title, as an incorporated body, was changed to the Shaftesbury Society and Ragged School Union. Kirk resigned the position of director in 1919, but accepted the post of honorary

treasurer, which he held until his death, which took place at his home, Tanglewood, Westcott, Dorking, Surrey, on 3 April 1922. The freehold quarters of the society in John Street, Bloomsbury, used to bear Kirk's name, and he was late remembered (until the 1990s) by John Kirk House, 25 Pearl Close, London; but the best tribute to his philanthropic career is the great expansion of the work of the society which he guided for fifty years.

In 1892 Kirk helped Cyril Arthur Pearson to start the Pearson 'fresh air fund' for enabling poor city children to have rural holidays, and in 1909 he founded the National Federation of Christian Workers among Poor Children. Kirk travelled widely. He visited the United States and Canada four times, also South Africa, and in 1911 went on a world tour which included America, Australia, and New Zealand. He was a modest man, open-minded, observant, and possessed of a great capacity for the service of others. In religion he was a devout evangelical.

A. BLACK, *rev.* H. C. G. MATTHEW

Sources *The Times* (5 April 1922) · J. Smart, *Mr John Kirk, the children's friend* (1907) · D. Williamson, *Sir John Kirk* (1922) · D. Williamson, *Lord Shaftesbury's legacy* (1924) · D. Williamson, *Ninety—not out* (1934) · E. A. G. Clark, 'The last of the voluntaryists: the Ragged School Union in the school board era', *History of education*, 11 (1982), 23–34 · *CGPLA Eng. & Wales* (1922)
Archives Shaftesbury Society Library, 16 Kingston Road, London, notebooks
Likenesses F. Statton, portrait; last known at John Kirk House, 1937
Wealth at death £2104 18s. 8d.: probate, 24 June 1922, *CGPLA Eng. & Wales*

Kirk, Kenneth Escott (1886–1954), bishop of Oxford, was born on 21 February 1886 in Sheffield, the eldest child of Frank Herbert Kirk, secretary and director of Samuel Osborn & Co. of the Clyde Steel and Iron Works, Sheffield, and his wife, Edith Escott. His grandfather John Kirk was a well-known Wesleyan Methodist minister in the neighbourhood and Kirk was baptized at the Wesley Chapel, Fulwood Road, Sheffield. When he was about twelve years old his family joined the Church of England and he was subsequently brought up as an Anglican.

Kirk was educated at the Royal Grammar School, Sheffield, and at St John's College, Oxford, where he was a Casberd scholar. He took first classes in honour moderations (1906) and in *literae humaniores* (1908). In 1909 he was appointed secretary of the student union's organization for looking after oriental students in London. From 1910 to 1912 he was warden of the University College Hall at Ealing, and assistant to the professor of philosophy at University College, London. He was ordained deacon in 1912 and priest in 1913 and was curate of Denaby Main, Yorkshire, from 1912 to 1914. In 1913 he was awarded the senior Denyer and Johnson scholarship and in the following year was made tutor of Keble College, Oxford, although the outbreak of the First World War prevented him from coming into residence until 1919. During the war he served as a chaplain to the forces in France and Flanders, and his experiences led to the publication of his first book, *A Study*

Kenneth Escott Kirk (1886–1954), by Howard Coster, 1937

of Silent Minds, in 1918 and directed his thoughts to the subject of moral theology.

After the war Kirk returned to Oxford, and in 1919 was elected a prize fellow of Magdalen, which office he held, together with his tutorship at Keble, until he was appointed fellow and chaplain of Trinity in 1922. In 1920 he published *Some Principles of Moral Theology*, to be followed in 1925 and 1927 by its two sequels, *Ignorance, Faith and Conformity*, and *Conscience and its Problems*. The study of moral theology which had flourished in England in the seventeenth century had in the two succeeding centuries been much neglected, and Kirk's three books were pioneer works which did much to revive interest in the subject in the Church of England. He became reader in moral theology in 1927 and was the obvious successor to R. L. Ottley as regius professor of moral and pastoral theology and canon of Christ Church, to which titles he was appointed in 1933.

In 1928 Kirk delivered the Bampton lectures which were published in 1931 under the title *The Vision of God*. This is generally considered his greatest book and is a work of immensely wide learning and insight. He also contributed essays on subjects of dogmatic theology to the volumes *Essays Catholic and Critical* (1926) and *Essays on the Trinity and the Incarnation* (1928), and in 1935 published a volume of

highly characteristic sermons under the title of *The Fourth River*. He took the degrees of BD in 1922 and DD in 1926.

In 1921 Kirk married Beatrice Caynton Yonge (*d.* 1934), daughter of Francis Reynolds Yonge Radcliffe, county court judge of the Oxfordshire circuit. They had three daughters and two sons; their elder son was Sir Peter Michael *Kirk (1928–1977), a Conservative politician.

In addition to his academic distinctions Kirk was an active and influential tutor and college chaplain, and also played an important part in university administration. In 1921 he was appointed controller of lodgings in the university and in the course of the next few years he built up this office into a system of supervising and licensing lodgings which was of great benefit to the undergraduates.

Kirk's distinction and many-sided abilities made him an obvious candidate for a bishopric, and on the resignation of T. B. Strong in 1937 he was appointed bishop of Oxford. He was consecrated in St Paul's Cathedral on 30 November and enthroned at Christ Church on 8 December. The exceptionally large diocese taxed his powers of administration to the full. He decided that it ought to be worked on the basis of the three counties of Oxfordshire, Buckinghamshire, and Berkshire which composed it. Each of these counties already constituted an archdeaconry, and the archdeacon of Buckingham was bishop-suffragan of Buckingham, while the archdeacon of Oxford was also in episcopal orders. So that permanent episcopal care might be provided for each of the three counties Kirk secured the revival of the suffragan bishopric of Reading for Berkshire and the creation of a new suffragan see of Dorchester for Oxfordshire. Kirk had inherited to the full his father's business ability and he gave particular attention to the finances of the diocese. He transferred the whole administration of the diocese to Oxford from Cuddesdon and never himself took up residence there.

As bishop of Oxford, Kirk managed to retain a much closer touch with the life of the university than had any of his recent predecessors. He was a delegate of Oxford University Press, honorary fellow of St John's and Trinity colleges, president of the Oxford University Church Union and a much sought-after preacher in the university church, college chapels, and other churches frequented by undergraduates. During the latter part of his episcopate he held every term a simple and informal confirmation service for members of the university, at which his characteristically original and carefully thought-out addresses always made a deep impression. Shortly before becoming a bishop he published a valuable *Commentary on the Epistle to the Romans* (1937); in 1939 he edited and contributed to the volume called *The Study of Theology*; and in 1946 he published a small book on the *Church Dedications of the Oxford Diocese*.

As well as being an administrator and a figure in academic life Kirk was very much a pastoral bishop. He had a singular gift for adapting his style of preaching to widely differing congregations; at parochial gatherings he made a point of speaking individually to as many as he could, and all to whom he spoke felt that he was interested in them as persons. He liked to attend clerical gatherings not as bishop of Oxford but as Dr Kirk who had come to discuss common problems with fellow priests. No bishop was more free of pompousness and yet he was never without great personal dignity. Throughout the whole diocese he inspired a deep affection which manifested itself to a remarkable degree after his death.

In the church at large Kirk's episcopate was remarkable in a number of ways. In 1938 he became chairman of the advisory council on religious communities in the Church of England which had been set up a few years before to help the bishops and the communities in a variety of problems which arose in their relationships. In addition he was visitor of thirteen communities and gained an intimate knowledge of their life. He was trusted by the communities as probably no bishop before him, and he was able to perform a unique work of quietly integrating them into the general life of the Church of England. The *Directory of the Religious Life* which was first published in 1943 was compiled under his immediate supervision.

Kirk's connection with the Woodard schools dated from 1924, and he had shown his usefulness to such an extent that early in 1937, before his nomination as bishop of Oxford, he was elected provost of the southern division. He felt obliged, on account of other work, to resign this office in 1944, but two years later he became the first president of the entire Woodard corporation (the Corporation of SS Mary and Nicholas). His knowledge of the schools was close and intimate and he did much to place the finances of the corporation on a sound basis. In 1937 he wrote *The Story of the Woodard Schools* (new edn, 1952).

Theologically Kirk had always been associated with the Anglo-Catholic wing of the church and, although his administration of the diocese was wholly free from partisanship and he was trusted and served by Anglo-Catholics and evangelicals alike, it was inevitable that in the church at large he should be regarded by high-churchmen as their natural leader. Current schemes of reunion (particularly the south India scheme) led him into the position of spokesman for Anglo-Catholics in convocation and at the 1948 Lambeth conference. The volume *The Apostolic Ministry*, edited and contributed to by him in 1946, was concerned very much with this subject. He took a strict view in matters relating to divorce and his position was expounded in a book *Marriage and Divorce*, originally published in 1933, but completely revised in 1948 in the light of developments in church and state and of his own experience as a bishop.

Kirk died in Oxford on 8 June 1954 on the way to the Radcliffe Infirmary.   E. W. KEMP, *rev.*

Sources The Times (11 June 1954) · E. W. Kemp, ed., *The life and letters of Kenneth Escott Kirk* (1959) · private information (1971) · personal knowledge (1971) · *CGPLA Eng. & Wales* (1954)
Archives Bodl. Oxf., papers · LPL, corresp. and papers | BL, letters to Albert Mansbridge, Add. MSS 652553–652556 · LPL, corresp. with George Bell · LPL, corresp. with Edwin James Palmer
Likenesses H. Coster, photograph, 1937, NPG [*see illus.*] · W. Stoneman, photograph, 1945, NPG · H. Coster, photographs, NPG · H. Knight, portrait, diocesan church house, Oxford
Wealth at death £48,816 17s. 5d.: probate, 29 Sept 1954, *CGPLA Eng. & Wales*

Kirk, Norman Eric (1923–1974), prime minister of New Zealand, was born at Nathan Home at Waimate, a small farming centre in South Canterbury, New Zealand, on 6 January 1923, the eldest of the three children of Norman Kirk (1902–1968) and his wife, Vera Janet Jury (1901–1972), both devout members of the Salvation Army. His father, a cabinet-maker by trade, found little work in Waimate; the family moved to Christchurch, but, as the effects of depression deepened, Kirk's childhood experience was of a father often unemployed and unjustly treated. He attended the Linwood Avenue primary school, where he did not shine academically but developed a lifelong passion for books. He left school at the age of twelve; a number of short-lived jobs followed, and when he was sixteen he moved away from home to the North Island and a job with the railways at Frankton. While working in Auckland as a ferry engineer Kirk married, on 17 July 1943, (Lucy) Ruth (1921/2–1999), the daughter of George Frederick Miller, who worked in the post office at Paeroa. The same year he joined the Labour Party. There followed five lean years as an engineer boilerman in a dairy factory at Katikati, near Tauranga. In 1949 the growing family—three sons and a daughter, with a second daughter yet to arrive—moved to Kaiapoi, just out of Christchurch, where the Jurys had lived. Having built his own house from concrete blocks he made himself, Kirk turned to politics. He revived the moribund local branch of the Labour Party and in 1953, at the age of thirty, was elected mayor of Kaiapoi—the youngest mayor in the country. An effective administrator, he was re-elected in 1956 but resigned the following year to enter parliament after winning the marginal seat of Lyttelton. He held this until 1969, when he won the safe Sydenham seat with a record majority.

Kirk was a hard worker for his constituency—establishing a particularly close bond with the off-shore Chatham Islands, which were attached to the Lyttelton electorate—and an able parliamentarian. He also moved steadily to strengthen his position in the Labour Party hierarchy. He was elected vice-president of the party in 1963, and twelve months later he became its president. In 1965, when he was forty-two, he successfully challenged Arnold Nordmeyer for the leadership of the parliamentary Labour Party, and he was re-elected in 1968. Kirk's impatience for power, stemming in part from his conviction that he was destined to die young, found a response in the party's preoccupation with finding a leader who could convince the voters of Labour's relevance to New Zealand in the second half of the twentieth century. The goal of socialism gave way to that of social justice. The party's traditional ties with the industrial movement, if not severed, were greatly reduced. With little sympathy for theoretical or doctrinaire lines of action, and a suspicion of those with an education better than his own, Kirk was a practical man with a tender heart, a politician largely motivated by his own experience. That experience, paradoxically, was more characteristic of the Labour leadership of an earlier generation than of Kirk's contemporaries. His remarkable rise to leadership in the party was not, at first, matched by a comparable impact on the country. The

Norman Eric Kirk (1923–1974), by Morrie Hill, *c.*1971

party was defeated at the general election of 1966 and again, more narrowly, in 1969. Kirk knew he would almost certainly be given only one more chance. This vulnerability strengthened his feeling of being a loner, his distrust of his colleagues, his authoritarian streak. It also led to a change of style: expert help transformed clumsy obesity into a suave and commanding presence; television revealed a quietly persuasive manner. Moreover, at a time when the United States was disengaging in south-east Asia and British entry to the European Common Market was imminent, Kirk's bold call for greater New Zealand self-reliance, for independence of judgement and action, carried conviction. In December 1972 he led the Labour Party to a sweeping victory.

In his short period of office Kirk proved to be a vigorous prime minister and an innovative foreign minister ready to probe accepted assumptions about the nature of international political relations and especially New Zealand's role within them. New Zealand foreign policy reflected Kirk's firm adherence to moral principles in foreign relations. Its successful implementation, he believed, rested on understanding and acceptance by the New Zealand public, and he worked tirelessly to achieve this. He told New Zealanders they were decent and humane people; many rose to his description. In 1973, braving the political

peril, he finally called on the New Zealand Rugby Football Union to abandon the tour by an all-white South African side for the sake of the country's wider interests. In the case of French nuclear testing in the Pacific he sought to mobilize opinion more widely by sending a New Zealand naval vessel into the Mururoa testing zone. Subsequently, by taking New Zealand's case against testing to the International Court of Justice he (along with Australia) drove France to end nuclear testing in the south Pacific atmosphere. Both intellectual conviction and warm humanity strengthened a particular concern with the problems of the neighbouring Pacific and Asian areas, where Kirk sought to encourage regional co-operation and the more effective use of increased New Zealand aid. He established close personal relations with leaders of developing countries such as Julius Nyerere of Tanzania and Sheikh Mujibur Rahman of Bangladesh, and in particular with the leaders of Commonwealth countries, with whom he developed a strong rapport at the Commonwealth heads of government meeting in Ottawa in 1973.

Kirk's broad humanitarian philosophy, his formidable intellect, and his strong sense of New Zealand identity came together brilliantly in his conduct of foreign policy. His government was notably less successful in its domestic policies. Kirk himself was conservative on many social questions, his practical experience often an inadequate basis for grappling with problems of social and economic change. Convinced that the answer to social injustice lay in central government planning and spending, he was, to his intense frustration, blocked by the impact on New Zealand of the downturn in the world economy and the unprecedented world rise in oil prices. In his last year of office ill health activated a suspicious streak, and this, along with his aggressive determination to have his own way, stretched the loyalty of colleagues, while Kirk himself was increasingly less able to provide effective leadership. An operation in April 1974 that would have been minor for a healthy man led to a series of complications. Kirk resisted proper treatment and, with obstinate courage, struggled to carry on. On 31 August, three days after finally agreeing to enter hospital in Wellington, he died of heart failure. He was buried on 5 September in Waimate cemetery.

In his brief twenty-one months as prime minister Kirk captured the imagination and the affection of many New Zealanders. In intellect, as in physical stature, he was a big man. He possessed a tremendous drive for self-improvement and a capacity to listen, to reflect, and to judge that, in the months before his health began to fail, was unmatched in prime ministers since Peter Fraser. Seizing the brief opportunity given him he, more than anyone, changed the thinking of New Zealanders about their place in the Pacific, their right to make their independent decisions on foreign affairs, and their duties as responsible members of the world community.

T. H. BEAGLEHOLE

Sources M. Hayward, *Diary of the Kirk years* (1981) · J. Dunmore, *Norman Kirk: a portrait* (1972) · T. Garnier, B. Kohn, and P. Booth, *The* *hunter and the hill: New Zealand politics and the Kirk years* (1978) · J. Eagles and C. James, *The making of a New Zealand prime minister* (1973) · M. Bassett, *The third labour government: a personal history* (1976) · private information (1986) [*Dictionary of New Zealand Biography*]

Archives Archives New Zealand, Wellington, papers
Likenesses M. Hill, photograph, *c.*1971, NL NZ, Turnbull L. [*see illus.*] · double portrait, photograph, 20 April 1971 (with Harold Wilson), Hult. Arch.

Kirk, Sir Peter Michael (1928–1977), politician, was born on 18 May 1928 at 10 Norham Road, Oxford, the fourth of five children of Kenneth Escott *Kirk (1886–1954), bishop of Oxford, and his wife, Beatrice Caynton Yonge Radcliffe (*d.* 1934). It was a high-church household, and his sister Patricia married Eric Kemp, bishop of Chichester. He was educated at Marlborough College and at Trinity College, Oxford, where he obtained a degree in history and became president of the union in 1949, and at Zürich University. Kirk started his working life in Glasgow as a journalist with Kemsley Newspapers Ltd, and then moved to London as their diplomatic correspondent; in 1953–4 he was seconded for a period to the United States to work on the *Trenton Times*. Throughout his career, except when holding ministerial office, he continued to act as a freelance press commentator on domestic and international affairs. He first entered Conservative politics as a councillor in Carshalton. On 26 August 1950 he married Elizabeth Mary Graham (*b.* 1927/8), daughter of Richard Brockbank Graham, headmaster of Bradford grammar school; they had three sons.

At the general election of April 1955 Kirk was elected Conservative MP for Gravesend. In the 1964 general election he was defeated but his absence from parliament was short: he succeeded R. A. Butler as MP for Saffron Walden at a by-election in March 1965, and held that seat until his death. He made his mark as an independent-minded MP, with a robust approach to matters of conscience, particularly through his support (as unofficial whip) for Sydney Silverman's bill in favour of abolishing capital punishment. In 1958 he published *One Army Strong* and went as a delegate to the World Council of Churches in Delhi.

During the years 1955 to 1972 Britain was a spectator of the early years of European integration, at first through her own choice, and subsequently, in 1963 and 1967, because of the French veto on Britain's application to join the European Economic Community (EEC). Kirk accumulated ministerial experience as parliamentary undersecretary for the army (April–October 1964) and for the navy (1970–72). But he was also an internationalist, an inveterate traveller, and an excellent linguist, and when out of office he played an important part in those European bodies where the United Kingdom was represented. He was a delegate to the Council of Europe (1956–63; 1966–70) and to the Western European Union (1959–70). In 1964, in a report published by the Western European Union assembly, he emphasized the inevitability of the resumption of Britain's attempt to join the EEC (following De Gaulle's veto in 1963) and argued that this should involve the promotion in Britain of the idea of Europe's collective political and military responsibilities, as well as the details of economic integration ('The British questionmark to Europe', *Ten Years of Seven-Power Europe*, 1964).

This background made Kirk the natural choice for Edward Heath to ask to lead the British delegation to the European parliament when Britain joined the EEC in January 1973. Until the first direct European elections in June 1979, the thirty-six British MEPs (as they came to be known) were nominated by their parties, roughly in proportion to party strength, from the House of Commons and House of Lords. Kirk found himself personally responsible for creating from scratch an eighteen-strong European team of MPs and peers which had to represent the full spectrum of opinion on Europe in the Conservative Party, while also respecting the need for expertise on key subjects, and geographical spread. His next task was to fit the Conservatives into the political structure of the parliament itself. They eventually formed a separate party 'group' with the two Danish conservatives. Kirk found the relationship with the Conservatives' nearest political allies, the Christian Democrats, a difficult one, since their goodwill varied according to their nationality.

Kirk's aim when he led the first Conservative delegation to the European parliament in January 1973 was to make the parliament a more obviously effective instrument. He believed that it was not using to the full its powers to assert itself over the European Commission, and also, particularly in budgetary matters, to make its presence felt in the Council of Ministers. He built his opening speech, which was widely admired, on the theme of 'power to the parliament' ('European parliament debates', 16 Jan 1973, *Official Journal of the European Community*, annex 157, 14). He followed this up by tabling a memorandum outlining possible procedural changes, and ways of enhancing the role of the parliament by using powers already in the treaty but so far unexploited. A year earlier the parliament had received the report of a working party under Professor Georges Vedel on its powers, so it had already begun to push its role forward. The Conservatives, however, supplied not only additional ideas, but also the energy and determination to make parliamentary procedures work. By September 1976 Kirk could justifiably claim that most of his proposals had survived and been incorporated in the practice of the parliament, most notably a question time on the Westminster model ('Britain's imprint on Europe', *The Spectator*, 4 Sept 1976). He was working on further proposals for institutional reform at the time of his death, and although these were not necessarily welcome to the very conservative parliament of his day, most of them too came to pass over the next twenty years. In 1976 he received a knighthood for his political services.

Kirk himself served in the parliament as a member of the political affairs committee and in 1974 oversaw the production of a European Conservative group policy document, *Our Common Cause*, which looked to the ultimate goal of a European union. Some of its ideas for more majority voting, a common currency, and harmonization of value added tax (VAT) were already far from the Conservative mainstream, but the national political focus had turned away from the parliament, and it was little noticed.

Kirk was a lucid speaker on complex issues, and played a very active part in the campaign for a 'Yes' vote in the British referendum on membership of the EEC in May–June 1975. But the limits on his enthusiasm for European integration were well illustrated in July 1975, when the parliament debated the future of European union. He opposed the idea that Europe should have a single decision-making body, and warned that the movement to European union must be gradual and have the full support 'not just of the governments and the parliaments but of public opinion in the whole of our nine countries' ('European parliament debates', 9 July 1975, *Official Journal of the European Community*, annex 193, 117).

In 1976 Kirk took the chance to move the first motion of censure against the European Commission ever to be pressed to a vote in the European parliament. The issue was unpromisingly obscure—that of the commission's failure to deal with the milk surplus. But it was the first time that key members of the commission, the president and agricultural commissioner, were publicly called to account, and to explain their policy to the parliament. The Conservatives failed to secure the votes of the farmer-dominated Christian Democrat group and the actual result of the vote was disappointing, with 109 against censure and only 18 for the motion. Not for the first time, the Conservatives found that their fellow MEPs preferred to work with the commission rather than attack it.

Kirk's hard work in the parliament won him considerable praise and respect. But at home the relationship with the Conservative leadership, after the initial euphoria, deteriorated: Margaret Thatcher's succession to the leadership in 1975 caused him particular despair because of her ignorance of European issues. He loved music, but found little time to relax from the round of politics and travelling. He suffered from heart problems, and the 'dual mandate', with the constant need to attend votes in Strasbourg and Westminster, and his own determination to continue as a very active local MP in a large rural constituency, finally exacted the heaviest price on him personally. His last speech in the House of Commons was on the subject of the imminent change to direct elections for the European parliament: Kirk himself felt that 'the case for some form of proportional representation is pretty strong' (*Hansard 5C*, 928, 25 March 1977, 1665).

Kirk died of heart failure at his home, Coote's Farm, Steeple Bumpstead, Essex, on 17 April 1977 and was buried at Saffron Walden. He was survived by his wife. The Conservative Party lost an important leader of the post-war generation of those politicians who saw a wholehearted British commitment to European integration as a natural response to the need to avoid future European conflicts. It also lost one of its most enlightened advocates and assiduous practitioners of European unity at a very crucial time in the party's relationship to European issues.

CAROLINE JACKSON

Sources C. Jackson, 'The first British MEPs', *Contemporary European History*, 2 (1993) • *The Times* (18 April 1977) • Hansard • *European parliament debates* • *'Times' guide to the House of Commons* (1955–70) • b. cert. • m. cert. • d. cert.
Archives SOUND BL NSA, documentary recordings • BL NSA, news recordings
Likenesses photograph, 3 June 1975, Hult. Arch.
Wealth at death £41,619: probate, 21 July 1977, *CGPLA Eng. & Wales*

Kirk, Robert (1644–1692), Gaelic scholar, was born on 9 December 1644, probably at Aberfoyle, Perthshire, the seventh and youngest son of James Kirk (1608/1609?–1658), minister there, and his wife, Elizabeth Carkettle (d. 1679). He studied at Edinburgh University (where he graduated MA on 19 July 1661), and afterwards at St Andrews. On 8 November 1664 he became the minister of Balquhidder, Perthshire, and from 23 October 1667 to 3 April 1688 he was clerk to the synod of Dunblane, a position in which he earned considerable respect from his colleagues. On 14 January 1678 he married Isabel, daughter of Sir Colin Campbell of Mochaster (1616–1668) and Margaret Menzies (d. 1681). They had two sons, Colin (d. 1725), who eventually became a writer to the signet in Edinburgh, and William, who died an infant. Isabel died on 25 December 1680, aged twenty-five, and was buried at Balquhidder; Kirk himself cut the epitaph on her gravestone. A firm episcopalian, he took the oath imposed by the Test Act of 1681.

Kirk's parish was then entirely Gaelic speaking, and the minister was the scholarly author of the first complete metrical psalter in Gaelic, for ten years the only version in the language, *Psalma Dhaibhidh an meadrachd*, of which 221 copies were published in 1684. He had learned that the synod of Argyll intended to publish a rival version, and he resorted to curious expedients to keep himself awake while working night and day to forestall them. The following year, on 9 June 1685, he was appointed to his father's old charge at Aberfoyle. Over the next few years he became involved in two projects financed by the scientist Robert Boyle. Following the appearance in 1685 of a version of the Bible in Irish type, comprising the Old Testament (by Bedell) and the New Testament (by O'Donnell), James Kirkwood (1650?–1708), a deprived Scottish minister living in Bedfordshire, persuaded Kirk, and his lawyer-relative Colin Campbell of Carwhin, agent to the earl of Breadalbane, to take responsibility for its distribution in the highlands. There were 200 copies, sufficient to provide one for each parish, but Kirk regarded the number of bibles as ridiculous, perhaps because some were 'alienated to private use'. The Irish characters were unfamiliar to highlanders, and he proposed that more copies should be made available transliterated into roman characters. Boyle agreed to subsidise the cost as he had that of a Gaelic version of Charteris's *Catechism* (1688), to which Kirk had contributed. During the time of considerable uncertainty in the Scottish church that succeeded the political events of 1688, the intrepid Kirk, who had been permitted to continue in the ministry despite his unrepentant episcopalianism, went to London for eight months to supervise the printing of what came to be known as Kirk's Bible, completed by April 1690. He also produced a small vocabulary of 464 difficult words, which foreshadowed future Gaelic dictionaries; this was later revised and republished in 1702 by Edward Lhuyd (d. 1709).

While in London, Kirk, who had a keen interest in fairy superstitions, met Bishop Edward Stillingfleet and his wife, Elizabeth. The bishop was a seventh son, and the couple, who were themselves to have seven sons, intrigued by what this might imply, asked Kirk for further information. In response he wrote, and addressed to Elizabeth Stillingfleet, the curious *The secret commonwealth, or, An essay on the nature and actions of the subterranean (and for the most part) invisible people heretofore going under the name of faunes and fairies, or the lyke, among the low country Scots, as they are described by those who have the second sight* (1691), a work later published in several different versions.

Kirk married again, a son, Robert (d. 1758), being born about 1690. His second wife, Margaret Campbell of Fordie, was a cousin of his first wife. Margaret was pregnant with their second child, Marjorie, when Kirk died, at Aberfoyle, on 14 May 1692. He was buried in the old kirkyard there. Kirkwood continued the task of distributing the bibles after Kirk's death, in spite of opposition in England because it might encourage Gaelic. Interest in Kirk has persisted, partly because a successor at Aberfoyle, Patrick Graham (1750–1835), drew him to the attention of Sir Walter Scott who mentioned him in *Rob Roy* (1818). In his *Sketches of Perthshire* (1812), Graham related that Kirk did not die, but was 'taken' by the fairies whose secrets he had betrayed. According to Graham, Kirk reappeared at the baptism of his posthumous child. Manifesting himself to a 'mutual relation', the minister had asked that his brother-in-law, Thomas Graham of Duchray, cast a dagger above his head, to release him, but, 'in his astonishment', Duchray failed, leaving Kirk captive in fairyland. Since then many distinguished folklorists have investigated the Fairy Minister, but this has meant that the importance of Kirk's work, as the scholar who was among the first to record highland folk-beliefs as well as to make the Bible accessible to highlanders, has sometimes been underestimated.   LOUIS STOTT

Sources M. Hunter, ed., *The occult laboratory: magic, science and second sight in late seventeenth century Scotland* (2001) • R. Kirk, *The secret commonwealth*, ed. S. Sanderson (1975) • M. M. Rossi, 'Text criticism of Robert Kirk's secret commonwealth', *Edinburgh Bibliographical Society Transactions*, 3 (1948–55), 253–68 • D. Maclean, 'Life and literary labours of Rev. Robert Kirk of Aberfoyle', *Transactions of the Gaelic Society of Inverness*, 31 (1922–4), 328–66 • P. Graham, *Sketches descriptive of picturesque scenery on the southern confines of Perthshire*, 2nd edn (1812) • J. Wilson, *Register of the diocesan synod of Dunblane* (1877) • J. Reid, *Bibliotheca Scoto-Celtica, or, An account of all the books which have been printed in the Gaelic language* (1832), 20–22 • D. MacKinnon, *The Gaelic Bible and psalter: being the story of the translation of the scriptures into Scottish Gaelic* (1930) • A. Nisbet, *Heraldry* (1722–4), 1.429 • C. Rodger, *Monuments and monumental inscriptions in Scotland* (1871–2) • W. A. Gillies, *In famed Breadalbane* (1938) • D. S. Thomson, ed., *The companion to Gaelic Scotland* (1983) • D. B. Smith, 'Mr Robert Kirk's notebook', *SHR*, 18 (1920–21), 237–48 • J. L. Campbell, 'An early Scottish Gaelic vocabulary', *Scottish Gaelic Studies*, 5/1 (1938), 76–93 • *Fasti Scot.*, new edn, 4.334–5, 337

Archives NA Scot., letters and papers, GD 50 • U. Edin. L., commonplace books and sermons

Kirk, Thomas (*c.*1765–1797), painter and engraver, was a pupil of Richard Cosway. He won a silver palette at the Society of Arts for a history piece in 1785, and first exhibited the same year at the Royal Academy, showing *Venus Presenting Love to Calypso*. He continued to exhibit there in alternate years until 1791; in 1794 he showed mainly miniatures and in 1795 a number of drawings illustrating popular works of fiction. He last exhibited in 1796, when he sent *Evening* and *A Dream*. Kirk's drawings for Charles Cooke's series of *Poets* were praised by connoisseurs such as Edward Dayes and Samuel Redgrave. He painted miniatures in the style of Cosway and also engraved in stipple, contributing to both Thomas Macklin's exhibition of biblical paintings and Boydell's *Shakspeare Gallery*. For the gallery, he was the only artist to engrave one of his own pictures; this painting, from *Titus Andronicus*, act IV, scene i, is now in the collection of the Royal Shakespeare Theatre in Stratford upon Avon. Kirk also designed an admission ticket for a concert of the Choral Fund of the Haymarket Theatre in 1796. He died in London of lung tuberculosis on 18 November 1797, and was buried later that month in St Pancras Old Church. According to Redgrave, he was working on a proof on the day he died.

L. H. CUST, rev. ANNE PUETZ

Sources Thieme & Becker, *Allgemeines Lexikon* • W. H. Friedman, *Boydell's Shakespeare Gallery* (1976), 196–7, 264 • Redgrave, *Artists* • Bryan, *Painters* (1886–9) • Bénézit, *Dict.* • *The works of the late Edward Dayes*, ed. E. W. Brayley (privately printed, London, 1805)

Kirk, Thomas (1781–1845), sculptor, was born in Cork, the son of William Kirk, a native of Edinburgh, and his wife, Elizabeth, *née* Bible. His parents moved to Cork from Newry, co. Down, but Kirk settled in Dublin in early life and studied in the drawing schools of the Royal Dublin Society where he won medals in 1797 and 1800. He was then employed as an ornamental stonecarver by Henry Darley, a stonecutter. He established himself as a sculptor at 21 Jervis Street and became noted for his fine work in relief on mantelpieces and monuments. His busts also gained him a rapid reputation, and they were considered remarkable for the delicate handling of the marble and for distinctness of detail. Seventy of these have been recorded; many are described in W. G. Strickland's *Dictionary of Irish Artists*. In March 1808 he married Eliza Robinson (1788–1869), daughter of Joseph Robinson, a builder, of Golden Lane, Dublin; they had twelve children. One son, Joseph Robinson Kirk (1821–1894), became a sculptor and a member of the Royal Hibernian Academy; others were the Revd William Boyton Kirk DD, and the Very Revd Francis J. Kirk of St Mary of the Angels, Bayswater, London. Of their four daughters—Mary, Anne, Elizabeth (Eliza), and Margaret (or Catherine)—Eliza Kirk (b. 1812) became a sculptor.

In 1810 Kirk exhibited *Piety and Chastity* (Dublin Pro-Cathedral) at the Society of Artists in Dublin—the first time he had shown at that institution. On the foundation of the Royal Hibernian Academy in 1823 he was chosen as one of the founder members, and he exhibited there for the rest of his life. He was successful in the competition for the Nelson monument in Dublin, and executed the 13 foot high statue of the admiral in Portland stone on the memorial column in Sackville Street (O'Connell Street; 1808, destr. 1966), which established his reputation. Another major public monument was the colossal statue of Thomas Spring-Rice, Lord Monteagle, at Limerick, exhibited at the Royal Hibernian Academy (RHA) in 1821. He also executed a marble statue of George IV in the Linen Hall, Dublin (exh. RHA 1827) and one of the duke of Wellington (exh. RHA 1829); and a model for that of George III for the Bank of Ireland in Dublin, which was carried out in marble by John Bacon the younger. Possibly his most important work was the statue of the political reformer Sir Sidney Smith (exh. RA, 1839), commissioned by parliament and placed in the Royal Naval Hospital in Greenwich. Many of his busts, which were esteemed for their accurate and expressive modelling and their faithfulness as likenesses, are in the premises of the Royal College of Surgeons in Ireland, the Royal Dublin Society, the library of Trinity College, and elsewhere in Dublin. Among them are busts of Thomas Moore (exh. RHA 1829 and other versions), J. Wilson Croker (1819, Hawkins Street, Dublin), Angelica Catalani (exh. RHA 1826), Francis Johnson (exh. RHA 1827, destr.), and Bartholomew Lloyd, provost of Trinity College, Dublin. Among his groups were *The Young Champion* and *The Young Suppliant* (both exh. RHA 1843), executed for Lord de Grey when lord lieutenant, and *The Orphan Girl* (1832, Thomas Abbot memorial) and the Nathaniel Sneyd memorial—both in Christ Church, Dublin; in his funerary memorials he favoured reliefs on the theme of the good Samaritan. Other works were *The Young Dogstealer* for Viscount Powerscourt (1840) and figures of Hibernia, Mercury, and Fidelity (1817) on the pediment of the General Post Office in Dublin. One of his finest was *The Parting Glance*, the memorial to Lady Rossmore (exh. RHA 1843) in Monaghan—a neo-classical deathbed scene tempered with Victorian sentiment. He also made the figure of a sailor (1817), 12 feet high and cast in metal, as a navigational aid at the entrance to Sligo harbour. Kirk died in Dublin on 19 April 1845 and was buried in Mount Jerome cemetery in Dublin. On his tomb is a life-size female figure, the work of his son, Joseph Robinson Kirk.

L. H. CUST, rev. JOHN TURPIN

Sources W. G. Strickland, *A dictionary of Irish artists*, 1 (1913); repr. with introduction by T. J. Snoddy (1989), 587–92 [incl. catalogue of his works] · Graves, *Artists* · *Bolster's Quarterly Magazine*, 2 (1827), 263 · W. B. S. Taylor, *The origin, progress and present condition of the fine arts in England and Ireland*, 2 vols. (1841) · private information (1892)

Likenesses portrait, repro. in Strickland, *Dictionary of Irish artists*, vol. 1, pl. xxxvi

Kirkaldy, David (1820–1897), engineer, was born on 4 April 1820 at Mayfield, near Dundee, the second among three children of William Kirkaldy (1786–1858), merchant and shipper, and his wife, Susannah (1796–1824), daughter of George Davidson of Dunoon and his wife, Margaret. His parents were both Scottish.

Kirkaldy was educated under Dr Low of Dundee and then at Merchiston School, Edinburgh, where he also attended lectures at the university. Having returned home, he worked briefly in his father's office but in August 1843 began a belated apprenticeship at Robert Napier's Vulcan Foundry in Glasgow. Following a period in the workshops he moved, in 1847, to the drawing office and soon became 'Chief Draughtsman and Calculator'. He early demonstrated two important characteristics: the meticulous collection of data, and his delight in engineering drawing as both a technical language and an aesthetic end in itself. His engineering drawings were exhibited in Paris, and his sectional drawing of the RMS *Persia* was hung at the summer exhibition at the Royal Academy in 1861. On 2 June 1858 Kirkaldy married Annamelia Yates Miller (1836–1866); they had a son and a daughter.

In April 1858 Kirkaldy had begun his first tests on wrought-iron and steel specimens for Napier, and designed the tensile testing machine. This important series of tests ended in September 1861 and gained a wider circulation on the publication of his book *Experiments of Wrought-Iron and Steel* (1862). This book was the springboard for Kirkaldy's subsequent lifelong career as an independent tester of constructional materials. He left the Napier firm in 1861 and spent two and a half years designing his own testing machine at home in Corunna Street, Glasgow. The enormous testing machine weighed 116 tons, had an overall length of 47 feet 6 inches, and could apply a maximum load of 446 tons. Kirkaldy said it was designed 'for the purpose of testing all kinds of constructive materials, and that under the various stresses, namely Pulling, Thrusting, Bending, Twisting, Shearing, Punching, and Bulging' (Kirkaldy to Sir Thomas Bouch, 16 Jan 1880; repr. in Kirkaldy, appendix, p. xxiv). The machine was built by Greenwood and Batley in Leeds, at Kirkaldy's expense, and was installed in an existing building in The Grove, Southwark.

Kirkaldy opened his works here on 1 January 1866, and Joseph Cubitt almost immediately engaged him to test materials for Blackfriars Bridge, then under construction. Kirkaldy never advertised for work, yet it arrived from clients all over the world; within a fortnight of his opening, Krupps of Essen sent material for testing. After a few years Kirkaldy leased a plot in the newly constructed Southwark Street and erected a new building for the testing works which opened in January 1874. The address, 99 Southwark Street, became very well known and attracted visiting eminent engineers and clients worldwide. In April 1869 steel specimens from the St Louis Bridge were sent to Kirkaldy for testing (by the American engineer J. B. Eads), and likewise metal recovered from the bed of the Tay after the bridge disaster of 1879. In addition Kirkaldy undertook research work for the steel committee of the Institution of Civil Engineers and on riveted joints for the Institution of Mechanical Engineers. He made significant contributions to the techniques, and standardization, of testing materials. In 1886 Professor Alexander Kennedy of University College, London, said:

Mr Kirkaldy … was the first man to set up and work in a systematic manner a testing-machine powerful enough to deal with the largest specimens … and at the same time of such a high degree of accuracy that its results have from the first been accepted as of real scientific value. (*PICE*, 73; quoted in Smith, 49)

With more levity a commentator in the *American Engineer* wrote that the testing apparatus was 'strangely like Mr Kirkaldy himself in some of its features. It is wonderfully fine and accurate … as well as a strong piece of mechanism, like him it is very *sensitive*' (14 July 1882; quoted in Smith, 60).

Kirkaldy was elected a member of the Institution of Civil Engineers in 1885, and in 1888 was made an honorary freeman of the Company of Turners. He died of heart disease on 25 January 1897 at his home, 45 Carleton Road, Islington, London. His obituary in *The Engineer* (5 February 1897, 147) described him as:

Cautious to a degree; enthusiastic past belief; honest as the sun; outspoken and fearless as a Viking, he laboured in a field previously untilled … Kirkaldy was the terror of so many persons, that it is probable that at one time he was the best hated man in London.

He was buried in Highgate cemetery. His son, William George Kirkaldy (1862–1914), author of a book on his father's innovatory testing system, succeeded him at the works, and his grandson David W. H. Kirkaldy (1910–1992) carried on there until April 1965. The works became a museum of materials testing, with Kirkaldy's motto—'Facts not opinion'—carved above the main entrance.

DENIS SMITH

Sources family papers, Kirkaldy Testing Museum, 99 Southwark Street, London SE1 · D. Smith, 'David Kirkaldy (1820–1897) and engineering materials testing', *Transactions of the Newcomen Society*, 52 (1980–81), 49–65 · W. G. Kirkaldy, *Illustrations of David Kirkaldy's system of mechanical testing* (1891) · *PICE*, 88 (1886–7), 1–152; 128 (1896–7), 351–6 · order books, Leeds Library, Greenwood and Batley archives · *Engineering* (9 Feb 1866), 90; (20 Jan 1871), 51; (29 Jan 1897), 148 · *The Engineer* (14 Nov 1965), 341; (27 Jan 1871), 61; (5 Feb 1897), 147 · *Mechanic's Magazine* (9 March 1866), 152–3; (27 Jan 1871), 56 · *The Merchistonian* [Merchiston School], 6/2 (April 1879), 68 · Captain Seddon, 'Our present knowledge of building materials and how to improve it', *Professional Papers of the Royal Corps of Engineers*, new ser., 22 (1874), 19–37 · *Transactions of the Institution of Engineers in Scotland*, 4, 171 [report of meeting held on 4 Sept 1861]; 6, 50–51 [report of meeting held on 24 Dec 1862] · *Dundee Advertiser* (9 May 1891) · J. Holland, 'Facts not opinions', *Australian Metrologist*, 17 (June 1999), 9–12 · d. cert. · private information (2004) [grandson]
Archives Kirkaldy Testing Museum, London, letters, reports, photographs · Sci. Mus., original drawings of Testing Machine | SOUND taped interviews with David W. H. Kirkaldy (grandson of subject)
Likenesses engraving, repro. in Kirkaldy, *Illustrations* · photograph (in old age), repro. in Smith, p. 62
Wealth at death £8453 8s. 3d.: probate, 23 July 1897, *CGPLA Eng. & Wales*

Kirkall, Elisha (1681/2–1742), engraver, was born at Sheffield in Yorkshire in 1681 or 1682 (Vertue gave his age as forty in 1722) and became one of the most enterprising and engaging engraver–publishers of his generation. According to George Vertue his father was a locksmith and in Sheffield he 'had some small beginnings to

Engrave' (Vertue, *Note books*, 3.6). He arrived in London about 1702 and an early trade card advertises him as a jobbing engraver, undertaking 'All sorts of engraving as Steel & Silver Seals with Flat Stitch upon Copper Plates large or small, & coats of arms according to true Heraldry' (trade card, British Museum). But Kirkall soon made or exploited one very marketable discovery: 'an Invention of engraving on the same sort of Metal which Types are cast with' (Jackson, 26). He was the first to produce a design cut in relief in metal so that it could be set with ordinary type. This innovation proved extremely popular with the book trade, and Kirkall produced a very large number of headpieces, tailpieces, and capitals. It would appear that he married soon after he arrived in London: another trade card, cut in relief on metal and advertising the names of Elisha and Elizabeth Kirkall, is dated 31 August 1707. The card possibly implies that Elizabeth Kirkall shared her husband's work. His output was certainly prodigious. Vertue, who was not habitually generous to his rivals, referred to Kirkall as 'an Industrious man' (Vertue, *Note books*, 6.188) and over the following decades he produced a very large number of book illustrations in etching or in metalcut sometimes, as with Samuel Croxall's *Fables* (1722), cut in white line. They include a set of tiny prayer-book illustrations after Le Fage for Lintott (1714) and plates to illustrate Terence (1713), Ovid (1717), Dryden (1717), Lucan (1718), and Pope's *Iliad* (1715–20) as well as a wide variety of other works including Richard Bradley's *The Gentleman and Gardener's Kalendar* (1718).

Kirkall was a member of the Great Queen Street Academy and benefited both from Louis Chéron's lessons in life drawing and from the network of professional contacts that radiated from the academy and its convivial counterpart, the Rose and Crown Club. Kirkall's career suddenly blossomed as a result of a scheme to imitate sixteenth-century drawings in the collections of leading virtuosi in a 'chiaroscuro' technique superficially resembling that of the Renaissance artist Ugo da Carpi. To judge from the subscription ticket the scheme was launched in 1722, and prints were delivered in late 1724. Kirkall printed in relief from metal plates using rocker-work for tone and, although Jackson stated that 'the Curious complained, that the ancient manner of Hugo di Carpi was not found in this Performance' (Jackson, 31), Kirkall's achievement was widely admired. The project promoted Kirkall as a serious artist and prompted similar schemes to publish paintings in noble collections. In 1727 he issued sixteen seascapes by the van de Velde printed in sea-green ink from which Vertue gathered that Kirkall made almost £1000. Kirkall went on to scrape numerous other decorative 'chiaroscuro' mezzotints including copies of William Hogarth's *Harlot's Progress* (1732) and maritime subjects including a set after Peter Monamy, twelve prints of the whale fishery, and six of the East India Company's settlements.

Meanwhile Kirkall continued his prolific and versatile output of commissioned work, engraving eight plates for Thomas Baston's *Twenty-Two Ships of his Majesty's Navy*

(1726), seventy-three plates for James Gibbs's *A Book of Architecture* (1728), and a large number of antiquarian subjects, chiefly for William Stukeley. He engraved innovative colour-printed plates for John Martyn's *Historia plantarum rariorum* (1728) and for the *Catalogus plantarum* (1730) published by London's leading gardeners. From at least 1724 he lived around Fleet Street, first in Wine-Office Court and then in Dogwell Court. In 1731 his son Charles was apprenticed to the portrait painter Gawen Hamilton. By the time of Kirkall's death his wife, Elizabeth, had died and he had married a second woman, named Deborah. According to Vertue he died in December 1742 at Whitefriars, Fleet Street, having lived in London 'near 40 years' (Vertue, *Note books*, 3.113). His son Charles proved his will on 26 January 1743. Most of his copperplates were bought by the Bowles family. An album in the British Museum contains fine examples of many of his prints. Other examples can be found in the Bodleian Library and Ashmolean Museum, Oxford, and the National Maritime Museum, London.   TIMOTHY CLAYTON

Sources Vertue, *Note books*, vols. 3, 6 · administration, PRO, PROB 6/119, fol. 11v · *A catalogue of maps, prints, copy-books &c. from off copper plates, printed for John Bowles and Son* [1753] · 'Catalogue of prints and drawings', www.nmm.ac.uk · 'George Clarke print collection', www.prints.worc.ox.ac.uk · J. B. Jackson, *An enquiry into the origin of printing in Europe: by a lover of art* (1752) · E. Hodnet, 'Elisha Kirkall', *Book Collector*, 25 (1976), 195–209 · I. Bignamini, 'George Vertue, art historian, and art institutions in London, 1689–1768', *Walpole Society*, 54 (1988), 1–148 · T. Clayton, *The English print, 1688–1802* (1997) · F. Russell, 'The Derby collection (1721–1735)', *Walpole Society*, 53 (1987), 143–80 · I. Maxted, ed., *The British book trades, 1710–1777: an index of the masters and their apprentices* (1983) · R. Godfrey, *Printmaking in Britain* (1978)

Kirkbride, Sir Alec Seath (1897–1978), colonial official and diplomatist, was born on 28 August 1897 at Mansfield, Nottinghamshire, the elder son of Joseph Kirkbride, lithographer, of Clacton-on-Sea, Essex, and his wife, Isabel, *née* Bradley. In 1906 his father took up a post in the Egyptian customs service. Though a protestant, he sent his two sons to a Jesuit college where the teaching was in French, and where they learned fluent Arabic from schoolfellows.

In January 1916 Kirkbride enlisted in the Royal Engineers. After six months spent recruiting for the Egyptian labour corps, he was posted to Beersheba, Palestine, to prospect the possibility of a motorable track from there to Tafilah on the escarpment across the Jordan. He proved this impossible, but during the posting he met T. E. Lawrence in a snowstorm on the heights: 'A taciturn, enduring fellow, only a boy in years, but ruthless in action, who messed for eight months with the Arab officers, their silent companion', Lawrence described him in *Seven Pillars of Wisdom* (Lawrence, 511). Lawrence later offered him a post in the Arab army of regulars. This gave him his first contact with educated Arab nationalists. With them he took part in the successful destruction of the railways near Deraa, and with Nuri al-Said he watched the British cavalry streaming north towards Damascus. He himself was one of the first Englishmen into Damascus. For his part in the Arab revolt he was awarded the Military Cross.

As long as Faisal was king of Syria, Transjordan was part of his kingdom; but in July 1920 he was banished by the French from Damascus, and Britain was granted a mandate over Palestine, including Transjordan. Kirkbride was chosen as one of six Arabic-speaking British officers to represent the Palestine government in Transjordan. Each had his own 'little kingdom'. Kirkbride was sent to Kerak, 50 miles south of Amman; his younger brother, Alan, was appointed to administer Amman. In Kerak, he ran what he called 'the National Government of Moab'. 'I was, in fact, truly my own master' (Kirkbride, *Crackle of Thorns*, 20). But this changed when, in January 1921, the Amir Abdullah arrived from Hejaz bent on avenging his brother and taking Syria. From their first meeting, the two men took a liking to each other. Abdullah particularly appreciated Kirkbride's full acknowledgement of his right to the land, at a time when not every one either in the British empire or in the Arab world shared this attitude. In March 1921 Winston Churchill, in Jerusalem, confirmed Abdullah as amir of Transjordan; this he remained until Transjordan became a kingdom in 1946.

Kirkbride was posted to Jerusalem in 1922, where he served the Palestine government as junior assistant secretary and, from 1926, assistant secretary. In 1927, to his pleasure, he returned to Amman as assistant British resident. While there, his friendship with Abdullah developed into close co-operation. In 1937, his friend L. Y. Andrews was murdered at Nazareth by Palestinian rebels, and Kirkbride was chosen to replace him as commissioner for Galilee. He succeeded in calming the tensions temporarily, and left in 1939 a popular figure. In the latter year he returned to Transjordan as British resident—chief British representative—in Amman. He remained there as British minister after the emirate became a kingdom in 1946, and was knighted in that year.

Already during the Second World War, the first signs of friction between Kirkbride and Abdullah emerged. While they were in total agreement on the need for Transjordanian troops to help Britain in its struggle against Iraqi nationalists in the summer of 1941, on other issues they failed to agree. In particular, Kirkbride regarded Abdullah's scheme for Greater Syria (a plan for the unification of Palestine, Transjordan, Syria, and Lebanon under his own rule) as wildly ambitious. In 1947 it was Kirkbride who, at the last moment, foiled Abdullah's plan to annex part of southern Syria. Nevertheless, Kirkbride regarded Abdullah as Britain's most loyal ally in the Middle East, and it was largely through his good services that Abdullah was able to convince London to base its Palestine policy, towards the end of the mandatory era, on a strong Anglo-Transjordanian alliance.

Abdullah's main aim was to enlarge his kingdom by annexing parts of mandatory Palestine to Transjordan. In November 1947 he negotiated an understanding with the Jewish Agency, based on dividing post-mandatory Palestine between the Hashemites and the Jews. In January 1948 he secured the approval of the foreign secretary,

Ernest Bevin, for the scheme, provided the Transjordanian army did not transgress into the areas designated as a Jewish state by the United Nations partition resolution of November 1947. Nevertheless, Kirkbride was apprehensive of the extent to which Abdullah had gone in his negotiations with the Jews, and feared that the king was unnecessarily antagonizing the rest of the Arab world, which had declared its total objection to any solution of the Palestine problem based on partition or recognition of a Jewish state. Kirkbride's apprehensions were increased when, after the Arab-Israeli War of 1948 had ended with a relative success for Transjordan, which had gained new territory, the West Bank and east Jerusalem, Abdullah sought to conclude a formal peace treaty with the Israelis. The Arab world, leaders and public alike, accused the Transjordanians of betraying the general Arab cause by occupying parts of Palestine without giving them to the Palestinian national movement, and by not keeping their promise to assist the other Arab armies during the fighting.

A second area of disagreement was Abdullah's policy vis-à-vis the West Bank. Transjordan, at the end of the war, had incorporated a large Palestinian population, consisting both of refugees and of permanent residents. Indeed, the majority of the population of the newly enlarged kingdom was now Palestinian. The king was confident of his popularity among the Palestinians and wished to allow them a high level of participation in the making of a new Jordan. Kirkbride suspected that the democratization of politics in Transjordan would bring anti-Hashemite Palestinians into power. He warned London in his dispatches that this could bring about the downfall of Abdullah's regime. He also opposed Abdullah's wish to settle most of the Palestinian refugees in Transjordan itself—Abdullah again banking on his unwarranted conviction that he was highly popular among the Palestinians.

In the last year of Abdullah's reign, Kirkbride's main worry was the connection between ill wishers outside and inside the kingdom. He was fully aware that both in Syria and in Egypt important political forces wanted to see Abdullah's downfall. Together with Glubb Pasha, the British commander of the Arab Legion, he tried hard to thwart Egyptian and Syrian attempts to collude with anti-Hashemite Palestinians against the king. These attempts culminated in July 1951 in the assassination of the king by a Palestinian. Kirkbride was on leave the day the king was assassinated. When he returned, he sent a very pessimistic note to London, predicting the end of Hashemite rule in Jordan. He was wrong, but he was right to fear that, after Abdullah's death, Jordan's politics would become more anti-British and more pan-Arabist. He was unhappy with the choice of Abdullah's heir, Talal, a choice which was made contrary to his advice and indicated just how much his influence in the kingdom had diminished. He asked for a new position in the Arab world and was offered the post of British minister in Libya.

In Libya Kirkbride encountered familiar problems, finding himself at once preoccupied with shoring up the position of a traditional ruler whose throne was threatened

by pro-Egyptian army officers. But, unlike in Transjordan, he was careful not to involve the British too much in domestic matters, and in 1952 he successfully advised against a request by Idris to allow British troops in Libya to help him against rebellious officers. A year later Kirkbride negotiated an Anglo-Libyan treaty, the main point of which was the consent of Idris to the occupation by Britain of several bases on his territory for nearly twenty more years. He became ambassador in 1954, and retired from the foreign service the same year.

After his retirement Kirkbride was a director of the British Bank of the Middle East (1956–72) and wrote three books of memoirs. His recreations were amateur archaeology, coin collecting, and shooting, usually alone. He married on 19 February 1921 Edith Florence, daughter of William James, of North Finchley, Middlesex. They had three sons; she died on 21 June 1966. On 23 March 1967 he married Ethel Mary James, his first wife's niece, who nursed him through the long illness of which he died at Worthing on 22 November 1978.   ILAN PAPPÉ

Sources A. Kirkbride, *A crackle of thorns: experiences in the Middle East* (1956) · A. Kirkbride, *An awakening: the Arab campaign, 1917–18* (1971) · A. Kirkbride, *From the wings: Amman memoirs, 1947–1951* (1976) · T. E. Lawrence, *Seven pillars of wisdom: a triumph* (1935) · J. B. Glubb, *A soldier with the Arabs* (1958) · I. Pappé, 'Sir Alec Kirkbride and the making of Greater Transjordan', *Asian and African Studies*, 23 (1989), 43–70 · St Ant. Oxf., Middle East Centre, Monroe MSS · *DNB* · *CGPLA Eng. & Wales* (1979)

Archives St Ant. Oxf., Middle East Centre, Monroe MSS | FILM BFI NFTVA, news footage · IWM FVA, documentary footage

Wealth at death £33,437: probate, 8 Jan 1979, *CGPLA Eng. & Wales*

Kirkbride [*married name* Kirkbride-Helbaek], **Diana Victoria Warcup** (1915–1997), archaeologist, was born on 22 October 1915 at Peyton Hall, Boxford, Suffolk, the second daughter of Major Thomas Warcup Kirkbride (1875–1957), soldier, and his wife, Dorothea Desirée Wollerson (1890–1970), music critic. She was educated at Wycombe Abbey School, High Wycombe (1935–9). Her life in archaeology was inspired by discovering J. H. Breasted's *History of Egypt* (1906) in her Women's Royal Naval Service quarters during the Second World War. She read Egyptology at University College, London (1946–50), gaining an academic postgraduate diploma in 1950. Simultaneous studies at the Institute of Archaeology, London (then independent), under her future mentors Dame Kathleen Kenyon and Sir Max Mallowan led her into Palestinian and Mesopotamian archaeology, to which her professional life was principally devoted.

Early experience as site supervisor for Mallowan at Nimrud (1951) and for Kenyon at Jericho (1952), where Diana Kirkbride was in charge of excavating Bronze Age tombs, led to her employment as a field assistant (1953) by Gerald Lankester Harding, director of antiquities for Jordan. She never forgot her 'wonderful lift' of spirits on first crossing the Jordanian frontier (personal knowledge); thereafter she invested those spirits in that country above all others. Nevertheless she was hardly prepared by Harding for the first job that he gave her, a venture into Roman archaeology. This was the excavation and restoration of the ruined south theatre at Jerash (1953–7), a vast but ultimately triumphant undertaking. Her assignment by Harding (1956) to southern Jordan, then archaeologically largely unknown apart from the legendary Nabatean city of Petra, began the most fruitful time of her life. Initially she excavated the paved and colonnaded *cardo*, the main street at Petra, correctly concluding that it postdated Roman annexation in AD 106. While at Petra, but tiring of Roman and Nabatean remains, she taught her Bedouin workmen (largely her sole—and perennially devoted—companions for the first three years) to recognize older sites and artefacts. She was rewarded when they brought her finely worked flint blades from a rock shelter in the nearby Wadi Madamagh. Her excavation (1956) showed that this had been a late palaeolithic hunter-gatherers' camp. The Bedouin later showed her an area called Beidha, an hour's walk north from Petra, where worked flints were scattered among ruined stone walls. She concluded that there a small Natufian settlement (*c.*10,000 BC) had been later reoccupied and enlarged by neolithic villagers, in the eighth–seventh millennia BC.

Following Diana Kirkbride's excavation at Beidha (1958–67) the site remains associated with her name. It became, she later wrote, 'peculiarly a part of myself' (Kirkbride, 7). In Beidha's relatively shallow deposits she pioneered a technique of broad horizontal exposure (some 75 per cent of the clustered village houses and workshops) in contrast to Kenyon's narrow trench method in excavating Jericho's enormous depth. Thus Beidha's architectural sequence was revealed together with its domestic life—sustained by cultivated cereals and goat-herding combined with specialist craft-working and trading activities. As Beidha's significance became apparent she gathered a larger team of specialists around her. Among them was the Danish palaeobotanist Hans Helbaek (1907–1981), whom she married in 1964.

During these years Diana Kirkbride excavated elsewhere in Jordan, notably in the Wadi Rumm (1959), but declined further opportunities in favour of working at Adlun, in Lebanon (1958 and 1963) as site supervisor for Professor Dorothy Garrod, then in failing health. There she sublimated her relative disinterest in this important site and its lower palaeolithic remains out of respect and affection for Garrod.

Shortly after the 1967 Six Day War the directorships of two British schools of archaeology, in Jerusalem (sponsor of Beidha) and Iraq, fell vacant. Kathleen Kenyon (in the Levant) and Max Mallowan (in Mesopotamia) each wanted Kirkbride in their archaeological domains. Disconcerted and unhappy with the changed status of Jerusalem she chose Iraq (1969–75). Despite her apprehensions that administration and bureaucracy there would prevail over her fieldwork she nevertheless determinedly surveyed (with Lankester Harding) the northern Jezirah desert. She identified her chosen site, Umm Dabaghiyah, by a late neolithic groundstone axe lying on its small mound. After four seasons' work she interpreted this then unique site as

a pre-Hassuna settlement, probably specializing in hunting the local onager (wild ass) herds, and processing, storing, and trading the skins. Her excavation thus revealed the hitherto unknown importance of this area of northern Iraq during the earliest phase of the ceramic neolithic.

Diana Kirkbride left Iraq without regret. Thereafter her fieldwork was occasional, most notably a final season at Beidha (1983). She settled in Denmark, and remained there after Hans Helbaek's death, in 1981, until her own, on 13 August 1997 at her home, Augustenborggade 21 A 8, Aarhus, of heart failure. After her cremation in England her ashes were blown out to sea towards Denmark from Scolt Head, in Norfolk.

Diana Kirkbride belonged to the last generation of English women archaeologists who fell, in Walter de la Mare's words, under 'the spell of far Arabia', although her approach was more practical than romantic. A strong, forthright, and independent-minded woman who preferred to work alone, she won and was afforded the courtesy accorded in Arab countries to male guests. Her principal and enduring contribution was to reveal the Jordanian desert neolithic, thus changing perspectives of Near Eastern prehistoric archaeology. She published prolifically (over fifty papers), albeit often only briefly, in the principal journals concerned with her subject. Exceptionally her achievements were not backed by an independent income but she was supported by many distinguished organizations—notably, as Wainwright fellow in Near Eastern archaeology, by Oxford University (1962). She was elected fellow of the Society of Antiquaries in 1963.

JANE CALLANDER

Sources personal knowledge (2004) · private information (2004) [J. Ashby, nephew; K. I. Wright; J. Oates; P. Parr] · *The Independent* (5 Oct 1997) · *Levant*, 30 (1998), iii–v · D. Kirkbride, foreword, in B. F. Byrd, 'The Natufian encampment at Beidha', *Excavations at Beidha*, Jutland Archaeological Society Publications, 1 (1989) · b. cert.
Archives University of Copenhagen, Carsten Niebuhr Institute of Near Eastern Studies, professional and personal papers, photographs
Likenesses photograph (at Beidha) · photographs, University of Copenhagen, Carsten Niebuhr Institute · photographs, priv. coll.

Kirkby, John (*d.* 1290), administrator and bishop of Ely, began his career as a clerk in Henry III's chancery. He may have been related to the John Kirkby who acted as justice in 1227 and 1236, and who was perhaps parson of Kirkby Lonsdale, Westmorland, but the name was a common one, and such identification is conjectural. He was keeper of the rolls of chancery in 1269, and received custody of the great seal on 7 August 1272 on the death of the chancellor, Richard Middleton. On Henry III's death on 16 November, Kirkby handed the seal to Walter Giffard, archbishop of York, and the other councillors of the new king. He remained in the chancery under Edward I, and when the chancellor, Robert Burnell, was absent, it was Kirkby who always had custody of the seal, notably in February 1278, May 1279, February 1281, and March 1283. He was vice-chancellor in fact, if not in title, and was so termed by the author of the Dunstable annals. He was a member of the royal council from at least as early as 1276.

In 1282 Edward I was in urgent need of money to pay for the Welsh war. On 19 June he informed the sheriffs from Chester that he had appointed Kirkby as his commissioner for announcing certain important matters to all the shires (except Cornwall). Walter of Amundsham was associated with him, and he was to be given all assistance. Similar writs went to the boroughs, religious houses, and other authorities. The aim of Kirkby's mission was to obtain voluntary gifts and loans, and in the course of his travels in the autumn he collected about £16,500, and aroused considerable hostility, reflected in the comments of chroniclers. The money raised, however, was insufficient for the king's purposes. Meetings were summoned at York and Northampton early in 1283; Kirkby was sent to the latter as the king's representative, together with Edmund, earl of Cornwall, and the treasurer, Richard Ware, the abbot of Westminster. A grant of a thirtieth was duly obtained; the sums previously collected by Kirkby were set against the tax.

On 6 January 1284 Kirkby was appointed treasurer, on the death of the abbot of Westminster. He was almost certainly responsible for the major overhaul of the exchequer which took place in the aftermath of the Welsh war, a process which began with the statute of Rhuddlan in 1284. This dealt with the problems of debts owed to the crown, and attempted to speed up exchequer procedure. In the next year the treasurer instigated the survey known as Kirkby's Quest, a detailed investigation into debts owed to the crown, and into various dues and rents, including feudal resources. This was undertaken in the context of recent reforms in exchequer administration, and was very wide-ranging. Regrettably few full returns survive.

Kirkby's interests were not confined to financial matters. He also played a significant role in the king's dispute with London. In 1285 he was appointed to head a special commission to investigate the state of public order in the city, following the scandal of the murder of the goldsmith Lawrence Duket by the followers of Ralph Crepyn, a city alderman. In order to avoid appearing before Kirkby at an inquest held in the Tower, the mayor resigned his office. Kirkby immediately seized the city into the king's hands, and ordered the citizens to appear before the king at Westminster. Two officials were appointed by Kirkby to perform the sheriffs' task of collecting the customary farm of the city. The city was then put under a warden appointed by the king, and did not recover its liberties until 1298. Kirkby's action was extremely unpopular.

Kirkby's services to the crown were rewarded by the grant of so many benefices that he was widely regarded as a scandalous pluralist. The process of acquisition began in 1271, when he received a grant from Henry III of rents worth 47s. 9d. yearly in Medbourne, Leicestershire, along with the advowson of the church there. Although he was only in deacon's orders, he became rector of St Buryan, Cornwall, dean of Wimborne, canon of Wells and York, and, after 1272, archdeacon of Coventry. In 1283 he was elected bishop of Rochester, but Archbishop Pecham was resolutely hostile to rewarding officials in this way, and he exerted so much pressure that Kirkby resigned his claims

to the see. Pecham then ordered a fresh election, on the grounds that Kirkby's pluralism had made him an impossible candidate.

On 26 July 1286 Kirkby was elected bishop of Ely, and on 7 August he was presented to the king, who was at Melun in France. This time Pecham made no objections, and confirmed the election on 17 August. On 21 September the archbishop in person ordained Kirkby a priest at Faversham, consecrating him bishop the next day at Canterbury. Election to a bishopric did not distract Kirkby from affairs of state. In 1287 he went to south Wales to assist in putting down the rebellion of Rhys ap Maredudd. He attempted to negotiate a tax at a gathering in London in February 1289, but the magnates refused to make a grant in the absence of the king. According to the Osney annals, he then initiated a tallage, which did not require consent, but nothing was collected. Edward supported him in his actions; he was not one of those officials who lost office in the purge that followed the king's return to England in August 1289.

Kirkby was a generous benefactor to his see. He gave The Bell inn in London to provide for celebrating his anniversary, and in his will left his successors a house, later called Ely Place, and nine cottages in Holborn. He died at Ely on 26 March 1290. His health was affected by an operation to bleed him, and he suffered a recurrence of a fever which had affected him earlier in the year. He was buried in his cathedral, on the north side of the choir. The chroniclers' verdict on him was for the most part unfavourable: Bartholomew Cotton quoted some Latin lines describing him as greedy, loquacious, self-assertive, and quarrelsome. The Dunstable annalist, however, admitted that he was just and truthful. He left as heir his brother, William; he also had four married sisters. At the time of his death all were in their thirties; he cannot himself have been of any great age.

MICHAEL PRESTWICH

Sources Ann. mon. · Bartholomaei de Cotton … Historia Anglicana, ed. H. R. Luard, Rolls Series, 16 (1859) · Chancery records · Inquisitions and assessments relating to feudal aids, 6 vols., PRO (1899–1921) · Registrum epistolarum fratris Johannis Peckham, archiepiscopi Cantuariensis, ed. C. T. Martin, 3 vols., Rolls Series, 77 (1882–5) · The survey of the county of York, taken by John de Kirkby, ed. R. H. Scaife, SurtS, 49 (1867) · Tout, Admin. hist. · M. Prestwich, Edward I (1988)
Archives PRO, E 368 · PRO, SC/1

Kirkby, John (d. 1352), bishop of Carlisle, is first recorded in 1312, as a canon of the Augustinian priory of Carlisle. Like most of his fellows, he was probably a native of north-west England. Nothing is known of his education, though he is recorded as lending books on canon and civil law. He was ordained priest on 23 March 1314, suggesting that he was at least twenty-five by then. No later than 1330, and probably in 1325, he was elected prior. His priorate was marked by a series of disputes with Bishop John Ross, during which both he and the canons of Carlisle Cathedral were excommunicated. However, when Ross died in 1332, Kirkby was elected to succeed him. Royal assent was granted on 18 May, Archbishop Melton of York confirmed the election on 2 July, and the temporalities were restored a week later. He was consecrated by Melton on 19 July. The see had been reserved to the pope, but on 4 December 1333 John XXII confirmed Kirkby as bishop. Kirkby had already, on 9 October 1333, undertaken to revoke his predecessor's sentences of excommunication, and at the same time he confirmed the priory in its rights and tithes.

Throughout his episcopate Kirkby was closely involved in border affairs. He may have accompanied Sir Anthony Lucy on a raid into the Scottish west march in March 1333—the two were subsequently in dispute with Ranulf Dacre, sheriff of Cumberland, over the ransom of two prisoners. At Newcastle on 12 June 1334 he witnessed Edward Balliol's homage to Edward III for the Scottish crown. In July 1335, with a retinue of forty men-at-arms, he joined the army with which Edward III invaded Scotland from Carlisle. For the campaign of 1337, having contracted to serve under Thomas Beauchamp, eleventh earl of Warwick, he took part in an attack upon Teviotdale, Moffatdale, and Nithsdale in September, and then in an unsuccessful attempt to intercept a Scottish force raiding Redesdale and Coquetdale. Such activities, according to the Lanercost chronicle, earned for Kirkby the particular hatred of the Scots, and when they raided Cumberland in October that year, they singled out his manor of Rose (which he had received licence to crenellate in April 1336) for destruction. In November he joined the force relieving Edinburgh Castle, but excused himself from further participation in that year's campaigning, on the grounds of the harm he had suffered at the hands of the Scots, and of his lack of a retinue. For the same reason he petitioned the king in the following spring for a life grant of the keepership of Carlisle Castle. The custody was granted during pleasure in June 1339, and Kirkby held it only intermittently until 1345. He also contracted to supply soldiers to Edward Balliol's command, and in 1343 was appointed a keeper of the truce with Scotland.

Although he attended a number of parliaments in the early 1340s, for much of his episcopate Kirkby resided in his diocese, where he made at least two visitations, and was assiduous in conducting ordinations. Even so, he would appear at first sight to have been hardly more popular with his flock than he was with the Scots. Attacks on the bishop and his men were reported in 1333 and 1337, while on 31 July 1345 a violent disturbance broke out in Carlisle between the citizens and the castle garrison, during which the soldiers, allegedly with Kirkby's connivance, set upon the townsfolk and killed four of them, including one of the city bailiffs. Kirkby lost his custody of Carlisle Castle as a result of this riot. He also engaged in a prolonged dispute with his archdeacon, while a visitation of his diocese in 1338 led to altercations with a number of monastic houses over their claims to advowsons. It is possible that some, at least, of this apparent quarrelsomeness was the result of Kirkby's efforts to recover ground lost under his two predecessors, bishops Halton and Ross, through either their ill health or the disorder arising from Scottish attacks. Not all of it proved disadvantageous to his see; indeed, a lawsuit with Ross's executors led in 1347 to a judgment which stands to this day, laying down that

the ornaments of a deceased bishop's chapel belong to his diocese, and not to his personal estate.

By then Kirkby had resumed his career as a soldier. About Easter 1345, having joined forces with Sir Thomas Lucy and Sir Robert Ogle to confront a Scottish invasion led by Sir William Douglas, he was unhorsed and nearly captured in a conflict that ended in the rout of the Scots. In March 1346 he was appointed a warden of the west march. However, it is unclear whether he fought at Nevilles Cross on 17 October following—the chronicler Geoffrey Baker's claim that he was present is not confirmed by other sources. Early in 1348 he was commissioned to accompany the king's daughter Joan to Spain, for her marriage to the future Pedro I of Castile, but she died of plague at Bordeaux in September. Kirkby himself was presumed to be back in his diocese by April 1349, when Archbishop Zouche of York sent him instructions concerning the spiritual precautions he was to take there against the black death. But his register contains no entries after 2 June 1347, and his whereabouts when he died, on 23 November 1352, went unrecorded.

RICHARD K. ROSE

Sources *The register of John Kirkby, bishop of Carlisle, 1332–1352, and the register of John Ross, bishop of Carlisle, 1325–1332*, ed. R. L. Storey, 2 vols., CYS, 79, 81 (1993–5) · *The register of William Melton, archbishop of York, 1317–1340*, 1, ed. R. M. T. Hill, CYS, 70 (1970), nos. 308, 310, 350, 359 · J. Raine, ed., *Historical papers and letters from the northern registers*, Rolls Series, 61 (1873), 364–8 · J. Stevenson, ed., *Chronicon de Lanercost, 1201–1346*, Bannatyne Club, 65 (1839), 253–4, 276, 291–3 · *Thomae Walsingham, quondam monachi S. Albani, historia Anglicana*, ed. H. T. Riley, 2 vols., pt 1 of *Chronica monasterii S. Albani*, Rolls Series, 28 (1863–4), vol. 1 · *Chancery records* · *CEPR letters*, vol. 2 · R. K. Rose, 'The bishops and diocese of Carlisle: church and society on the Anglo-Scottish border, 1292–1395', PhD diss., U. Edin., 1983 · H. Summerson, *Medieval Carlisle: the city and the borders from the late eleventh to the mid-sixteenth century*, 1, Cumberland and Westmorland Antiquarian and Archaeological Society, extra ser., 25 (1993), 274–8 · C. M. L. Bouch, *Prelates and people of the lake counties: a history of the diocese of Carlisle, 1133–1933* (1948) · *The register of John de Halton, bishop of Carlisle, AD 1292–1324*, ed. W. N. Thompson, 2 vols., CYS, 12–13 (1913) · PRO, exchequer, lord treasurer's remembrancer, pipe rolls, E372/198 m 38d · PRO, special collections, ministers' accounts, SC6/1144/14 · *Fasti Angl., 1300–1541*, [York], 97
Archives Cumbria AS, Carlisle, register

Kirkby, John (c.1705–1754), Church of England clergyman and grammarian, claimed to have been born in Cumberland, though in the register of St John's College, Cambridge, from where he appears to have graduated BA in 1726, and proceeded MA in 1745, his birthplace is noted as Londesborough, Yorkshire. Like his father, the Revd Thomas Kirkby, he intended to make a career in the church, but in this, as in his other major ventures in life, he was not very successful. According to his own account, quoted by Edward Gibbon in his *Memoirs*, he began life as a poor curate in Cumberland. On 13 June 1725 he married Ann Stable of Egremont; they had several children, of whom only one appears to have outlived her father. In 1739 Kirkby was appointed vicar of Waldershare, Kent, and four years later in 1743 rector of Blackmanstone in Romney Marsh, but a publication of his that same year on behalf of the poorer clergy at Canterbury is believed to have excluded him from further preferment. Kirkby was equally unlucky in his tutorship of Edward Gibbon, who was only seven at the time. Unluckily omitting one morning in November 1745 the name of George II in prayer, he was dismissed by Gibbon's father after only eighteen months of service (E. Gibbon, *Memoirs*). While with the Gibbons, Kirkby wrote a grammar of English which, together with a Latin grammar, was published as *A New English Grammar* (1746). The grammar partly plagiarized Anne Fisher's *New Grammar*, which had been published a year earlier in Newcastle. This makes Fisher, not Kirkby, the ancestor of the rule for the use of sex-indefinite 'he'. But unlike Fisher's grammar, Kirkby's was not very popular, for it was never reprinted. Nor does the dedication of the grammar to Gibbon's father appear to have had its desired effect.

Kirkby's plagiarism of Fisher's grammar has gone undetected until very recently; another act of plagiarism was, however, soon discovered. In 1745 he published a novel called *Automathes*, a second edition of which appeared in Dublin a year later. Gibbon describes it as a poor performance, and as a plagiarism of well-known romances. It seems largely borrowed from the *History of Autonous* (1736). The publication of the grammar and Kirkby's attempt at a novel indicate that he was looking for a career outside the church. Another direction he appears to have considered is that of natural philosophy. In 1748 he published a book called *The Doctrine of Ultimators*, of which he presented two copies to the Royal Society in January 1752. In the letter accompanying the gift he suggests that he might like to 'establish Weekly Lectures of different Sorts in some Part of London' (RS archives, L&P 2.251), adding that 'it wou d be no small Advantage to these Purposes, to have the Honour of Subscribing my self one of your Society' (ibid.). Kirkby's gift was duly acknowledged and entered in the minute-books of the society, but the unlucky Kirkby was dismissed in a letter by Thomas Birch with the words 'I sincerely wish you Success in all your Studies & Labours for the public' (BL, Add. MS 4312, fol. 455).

Before reaching the age of fifty Kirkby died, a widower, living either in Peter Street, Canterbury, from where he had addressed the Royal Society two years earlier, or in the precinct of Norwich Cathedral, which was his last address according to the grant of probate on 10 December 1754 (PRO, PROB 6/130, fol. 148r). His 'Goods Chattels & Credits', whatever they may have been, went to his daughter Anne, who was married to a clergyman called John Jeffery the younger. INGRID TIEKEN-BOON VAN OSTADE

Sources I. Tieken-Boon van Ostade, 'John Kirkby and *The practice of speaking and writing in English*: identification of a manuscript', *Leeds Studies in English*, new ser., 23 (1992), 157–79 • [J. S. V. Kirkby], *Lexicon grammaticorum*, ed. H. Stammerjohann (1996) • F. Bergström, 'John Kirkby (1746) on English pronunciation', *Studia Neophilologica*, 27 (1995), 65–104 • R. V. Wallis and P. J. Wallis, eds., *Biobibliography of British mathematics and its applications*, 2 (1986), 205–6 • *N&Q*, 6th ser., 12 (1885), 68, 177 • Venn, *Alum. Cant.*

Archives BL, corresp. with T. Birch, Add. MS 4312, fols. 24, 26 • RS, corresp. with T. Birch, L&P 2.251

Kirkby, Margaret (*d.* 1391x4), anchoress, of Richmondshire, was a disciple of the hermit Richard Rolle (*d.* 1349).

Information about her comes from a biographical office of Rolle written between 1381 and 1383, when Margaret returned to the nunnery at Hampole some thirty-four years after Rolle's death. Her recollections were used to provide a biography of the hermit celebrating his sanctity. Miracles reported by pilgrims from all over the north were also recorded to encourage an unofficial cult. Margaret was also instrumental in the composition of a liturgical commemoration of the gift of *canor*, the mystical ecstasy that Rolle celebrated in his writings. Additional information is provided in a brief life of Rolle written before 1405.

From a gentry family in Kirkby Ravensworth, Margaret probably first became interested in the solitary life as a young nun of Hampole guided by the convent's spiritual director, Richard Rolle. It was for her that he wrote his English translation and commentary on the Psalms which linked the growth in intensity of religious experience of *canor* with an understanding of the Psalms. Margaret became an anchoress in East Layton in Richmondshire (possibly in 1348) and Rolle wrote for her *The Form of Living*, the first vernacular guide for recluses since the *Ancrene Riwle*. Rolle addressed Margaret personally, discussing the problems she would face as a recluse far from his guidance, such as excessive abstinence and the high expectations placed on her by others; and he encouraged her in the attainment of ecstasy by creating for her the verbal equivalent of *canor* in English. He also presented her with a collection of his works made into a single treatise including: *The Form of Living*, *The Commandment of Love*, *Ego dormio*, prose pieces and lyrics beginning with a rubric reading 'a tract of Richard hermit to Margaret Kirkby recluse on the contemplative life'. The volume, copied *c.*1430, survives as Longleat MS 27. In *The Form of Living* and the compilation *On the Contemplative Life* Rolle showed that his whole mystical system, which celebrated the pre-eminence of *canor* and the solitary life, was of pastoral relevance to his outstanding disciple and that he attempted to initiate Margaret into thoughts and spiritual experiences previously available only in his Latin works.

What Rolle's letters of direction omit are the personal tensions Margaret felt when leaving Hampole, which are recounted in the biographical office. She suffered seizures that could be cured only by Rolle who would sit with her at her anchorage window until she slept on his shoulder. After one attack Rolle confessed that even if she were the devil (who had once taken the form of a beautiful woman who had loved him) he would still have held her. After Rolle's death her illness never returned, and the biographical office gives, through the symbol of the anchorage window, a romantic unity to a platonic Yorkshire love story that anticipates *Wuthering Heights*.

However, Margaret's career was of wider historical significance. In 1357 she obtained the unusual concession of being allowed to change cells and was enclosed in Ainderby so that she could observe the celebration of mass in the parish church. Thirteenth-century episcopal registers had emphasized the recluse's service to God through a penitential, ascetic life, and the achievement of a mystic union with God was mentioned if at all only in passing. The register of John Thoresby, archbishop of York, confirming the enclosure, offers, in common with the epistles of Rolle, a more celebratory tone saying Margaret desired an eremitic life in order that she might fashion herself as a servant of God more freely and more quietly with pious prayers and vigils. Such language indicates how she and Rolle were pioneering a change in the conception of the eremitic vocation.

The enclosure at Ainderby churchyard brought her to the attention of Richard Scrope, the rector from 1368 and later archbishop of York. He was probably the medium through which Rolle's writings came to the attention of the Cambridge-educated northerners in the service of Thomas Arundel, archbishop of Canterbury, including Walter Hilton; this led to a pastoral response to Rolle's teachings that provided contemplative instructions for layfolk. Other members of the Scrope family showed an interest in Margaret's servant, Elizabeth. In 1405 Stephen, second Lord Scrope of Masham, left legacies to Elizabeth and the anchoress of Kirkby Wiske. Henry, third Lord Scrope, and patron of many anchoresses, owned an autograph volume of Rolle's writings and this may well have come into the possession of the family through Margaret Kirkby; it is through Henry Scrope, the king's treasurer, that the teachings of Rolle and Margaret's example inspired Henry V and Henry, Baron Fitzhugh of Tanfield, to establish the eremitic communities of Sheen and Syon.

Although she did not write anything herself, Margaret may have influenced Julian of Norwich, author of *Revelations of Divine Love*. Among Margaret's patrons were Sir Brian Stapleton of Bedale, lord of the manor of East Layton (where Margaret was first enclosed), who bequeathed in 1394 a silver ewer once belonging to her. His brother, Sir Miles Stapleton, moved to Ingham in East Anglia and his son, also Sir Miles, whose daughter became an anchoress, was a patron of Julian of Norwich.

Having returned some time between 1381 and 1383, Margaret lived at Hampole until her death ten years later. To judge from Stapleton's bequest, this occurred in or before 1394. She was buried in the cemetery of Hampole near her master and her remains are presumably in the garden of the old schoolhouse of Hampole on the site of the convent.   JONATHAN HUGHES

Sources J. Hughes, *Pastors and visionaries: religion and secular life in late medieval Yorkshire* (1988) • N. Watson, *Richard Rolle and the invention of authority* (1991) • *The 'Officium et miracula' of Richard Rolle of Hampole*, ed. R. M. Woolley (1919) • H. E. Allen, *Writings ascribed to Richard Rolle, hermit at Hampole, and materials for his biography* (1927) • A. K. Warren, *Anchorites and their patrons in medieval England* (1985) • R. M. Clay, *The hermits and anchorites of England* (1914) • Österreichische Nationalbibliothek, Vienna, MS 4485

Kirkby, Richard (*c*.1658–1703), naval officer, was the fourth child and second son of Richard Kirkby (*c*.1625–1681) of Kirkby, Lancashire, and his second wife, Isabel, daughter of Sir William Hudleston of Cumbria. He passed his naval lieutenant's examination on 28 March 1689 and

was appointed second lieutenant of the *Advice*. On 12 February 1690 he was appointed captain of the *Success* hired ship, a commission he owed to Arthur Herbert and to his cousin Sir John Lowther, one of the Admiralty commissioners. His ship was part of the fleet sent to capture St Kitts, but he was not employed as a captain for the fourteen months after the *Success* returned to England in April 1692. In 1694 he was appointed to the *Southampton* and served under Edward Russell in the Mediterranean. In a fight with two French vessels on 18–19 January 1695 it was noticed that he 'kept as far off' the heavily armed *Content* 'as his guns could reach reasonably firing now and then 2 or 3 guns at him' (PRO, ADM 51/3935/1), and he was excluded from a share in the prize money. Apparently the *Southampton* was not a well-disciplined ship; its chaplain, Ellis Cooper, left after some unpleasantness with Kirkby, the boatswain was broken and flogged for disobedience and insolence, and a seaman was sentenced to be flogged and 'towed ashore' for 'scandalous actions'.

In 1696 the *Southampton* was sent to the West Indies and was one of the ships which burned Petit Guave on 28 June 1697. On its return in 1698 Kirkby was tried by court martial on charges of embezzlement and cruelty, accused of punishing a seaman for straggling by ordering him to be 'tied up by the right arm and left leg for several hours' (PRO, ADM 1/5260). Though cleared, he spent the next two years unemployed and on half-pay. He blamed 'the great power and interest of my Lord of Orford' (Edward Russell) for his being overlooked (PRO, ADM 1/2004).

In February 1701 Kirkby was appointed to the *Ruby*, probably due to Lowther, and was sent to the West Indies. By March he had moved to the *Defiance*, and was 'eldest officer under the flag' from the death of Rear-Admiral Henry Martin until the arrival of Rear-Admiral William Whetstone in May 1702. Second in command of the squadron under Vice-Admiral John Benbow which met a French squadron off St Mary on 19 August, he, like most of the captains, ignored Benbow's signals to close the enemy and engage. After a five-day running skirmish the English were beaten off and Benbow mortally wounded. On return to Jamaica Kirkby and his fellow mutineers were tried by court martial. Evidence against him came from over two dozen officers, and it was reported that he had not encouraged his men to fight but dodged behind the mizzenmast 'falling down on the deck at the sound of a shot'. Though heard, he was condemned to be shot for cowardice and disobedience. In a long letter to the Admiralty secretary Josiah Burchett he alleged that Benbow's injudicious and ignorant conduct was the cause of the defeat, that his evidence was falsified, that members of his crew who wanted to defend him were browbeaten by the dying Benbow, and that the court was adjourned when he sought to present evidence. Captain Edward Acton carried him to England, where sentence was to be carried out, arriving in Plymouth on 15 April the day before the executions were to take place. In the evening Kirkby was 'very calm and easy, not railing or reviling, but forgiving all the world and praying, for the Queen's health and prosperity', a stance retained the following day also (PRO, ADM

1/1436). He wrote an account of his actions which he hoped would be published, and drew up his will, leaving everything to his sister Elizabeth. During the day 'land and sea officers with others' came on board the *Bristol* to see the execution, as did two parsons 'to pray and give the sacrament' to Kirkby and Captain Cooper Wade (ibid.). At 6 p.m. Kirkby, 'kneeling on the larboard side of the forecastle' facing the six musketeers appointed to shoot him, was executed, having lifted his hand as 'a signal to be shot'. After the execution Kirkby's body was placed in his coffin, 'being by him', which was carried on shore and buried under the communion table in Plymouth church (PRO, ADM 52/7/8). Kirkby seems to have been a bully, resentful that his merits had not got him a flag rank, and a coward, a trait which led to his undoing and death.

J. K. LAUGHTON, *rev.* PETER LE FEVRE

Sources W. Dugdale, *The visitation of the county palatine of Lancaster, made in the year 1664–5*, ed. F. R. Raines, 3 vols., Chetham Society, 84–5, 88 (1872–3) · paybook of *Advice*, PRO, ADM 33/139 · Lt. Richard Kirkby's log, *Advice*, PRO, ADM 51/13, pt 2 · Capt. Richard Kirkby's log, *Success*, PRO, ADM 51/938, pt 9 · first lieutenant's log, *Plymouth*, PRO, ADM 51/3935, pt 1 · list of captains, May 1692, PRO, ADM 8/2 · Richard Kirkby's letters, 1698–1703, PRO, ADM 1/2004 · Edward Acton's letter, 16 April 1703, PRO, ADM 1/1436 · journal 8, master's log, *Bristol*, PRO, ADM 52/7 · PRO, PROB 11/470, fol. 67 · list of captains, 1688–1715, NMM, Sergison MS SER/136 · court martial records, PRO, ADM 1/5620

Kirkcaldy, Sir James, of Grange (*d.* 1556), administrator, was the eldest son of William Kirkcaldy of Grange (Fife). Although less well-known than his son, Sir William *Kirkcaldy (*c.*1520–1573), who was hanged for his championship of Queen Mary's cause, Sir James played an important part in the public affairs of mid-sixteenth-century Scotland. He was a prominent Fife laird, with lands and castles at Grange, near Burntisland, and Hallyards in Auchtertool parish. The latter was held from the bishop of Dunkeld and included the settlement of Newbigging which the king created a burgh of barony, with its market revenues, in 1541. Important land acquisitions had also come to Kirkcaldy on the forfeiture of Lord Glamis in 1537, including land in the barony of Kinghorn, Fife, which he transferred to his son William. In March 1538 the king granted him, jointly with the royal favourite Oliver Sinclair of Pitcairns, the wardship of the extensive lands of the earldom of Caithness.

Kirkcaldy had a long career in the king's service. In the 1520s he took part with those who tried to detach the young James V from the power of the Douglases, and in August 1527 he had to pay for a remission for assisting the earl of Lennox in an attempt to do so. Described by Sir James Melville of Halhill (his brother-in-law) as 'a stout bold man' (Melville, 11) who was always prepared to back up his words with action, he frequently gave personal advice to the king and appears to have enjoyed the royal confidence. From the early 1530s he received livery clothes and fees as a gentleman of the king's chamber and trusted servant. He was among those who accompanied James to France in the autumn of 1536 for an extended visit during which the king married Princess Madeleine

de Valois. In 1538 he was referred to as steward and in 1542 as a sewar (server at table) in the royal household.

Kirkcaldy was made lord treasurer in 1538, entering office on 24 March. In September and December of that year he was an auditor of the accounts rendered by David Beaton, then abbot of Arbroath (later cardinal), who had handled the king's expenses in France in 1536–7, though Kirkcaldy also appears to have had some financial responsibility during the king's time in France. As treasurer he was a regular witness of royal charters and other important state transactions. He frequently acted as an auditor of the exchequer accounts rendered by his financial colleague the comptroller. His responsibilities for the king's finances overlapped with those of the royal pursemaster, but he is recorded as personally supervising and handling the transfer of money to and from the king's coffers; in 1542 he gave £2520 to John Barton to buy munitions in Denmark. Like other officers of state he found that his salary often fell into arrears. On 21 February 1540 he and the comptroller were awarded the sum of £333 6s. 8d. arrears of fees. Kirkcaldy retained his post of treasurer for some months after James's death (on 14 December 1542), and rendered his final account on 13 August 1543.

Kirkcaldy's identification with those who wished both closer alliance with England and serious reform of the church had already made him a particular target for the resentment of Cardinal David Beaton and his fellow prelates, especially since his close relationship with the king made it difficult for them to apprehend him on a charge of heresy. Both Melville and John Knox recounted that in 1540, when the clergy presented James with a long list of suspected heretics whom he might prosecute and forfeit, the king declined to act on the allegations because of Kirkcaldy's counsel. Kirkcaldy is said to have encouraged James to meet Henry VIII at York in 1541, a plan that was undermined by the cardinal, and after the king's death Kirkcaldy was one of those who encouraged James Hamilton, earl of Arran, to assume the sole governorship, 'when as he appeared to be a true gospeller' (Melville, 20).

Even before the act of parliament of 1543 (passed during the cardinal's detention) which sanctioned the use of the Bible in English, Kirkcaldy was said to have carried an English New Testament in his pouch. He associated with some of those who most strongly advocated religious reform, such as his father-in-law, Sir John Melville, and Henry Balnaves, author of a theological treatise on the doctrine of justification, who became his colleague as treasurer's clerk. In July 1544 Kirkcaldy was one of the associates of the Earl Marischal (soon to give public support to the reformer George Wishart) who were given letters of protection during the Earl Marischal's absence in France; others included the lairds of Fyvie, Philorth, and Pittarrow, and Henry Balnaves, all at one time or another suspected or accused of heresy. The clergy took their revenge on Kirkcaldy by persuading Governor Arran to deprive him of the treasurership (before 13 August 1543, when the office was said to be vacant), and it was granted instead to Arran's kinsman John Hamilton, abbot of Paisley and later archbishop of St Andrews. Balnaves was likewise deprived of the clerkship to the treasury. However, in summer 1543 Cardinal Beaton used Kirkcaldy as a mediator with the latter's allies, the earl of Rothes, Lord Gray, and Balnaves, when they were accused of obstructing the governor's journey to Dundee; and Arran himself continued to communicate with Kirkcaldy over the backlog of business from his time as treasurer and as late as 22 April 1545 sent him more than £900—owed as 'superexpenses' on his final account.

With his son William and others, Kirkcaldy was involved in the plot against Cardinal Beaton, and he joined the *castilians in St Andrews the day after the assassination, carried out on 29 May 1546. For this he was forfeited and his property granted to various persons, including the now reinstated Lord Glamis, from whose forfeiture Kirkcaldy had earlier benefited. On 4 September 1546 his tenants at Grange and Hallyards were warned to hand over any of his goods in their possession or be reckoned participants in his crimes. On the fall of St Andrews Castle in summer 1547 Kirkcaldy was among those Scots taken prisoner to France, first to Cherbourg, where he and his fellow captives refused to attend mass, and then to Mont-St Michel, from where some of them escaped. Kirkcaldy had advised against the escape attempt, fearing that those left behind would be more severely treated. He served for a time in the French galleys before being released with other Scots, partly on the intercession of Mary of Guise, queen dowager of Scotland, in July 1550. Kirkcaldy died in 1556. According to Knox, the family's forfeiture was reduced by parliament in 1563 (there is no official record of this), and his son Sir William was 'retoured' (recognized as successor) on 4 May 1564.

Kirkcaldy married Janet, daughter of Sir John Melville of Raith, by about 1520. They had five recorded sons: Sir William *Kirkcaldy, the heir; James (who was hanged with William after the surrender of Edinburgh Castle in 1573); David; Thomas; and George. Their four recorded daughters were Marjory, who about 1540 was contracted to marry Sir Henry Ramsay of Colluthie; Agnes, by 1542 married, as his first wife, to Sir Robert Drummond of Carnock; Marion, married by 10 January 1541 to William, son of Gabriel Semple of Cathcart; and Elizabeth, married to Sir John Mowbray of Barnbougle. Janet Melville, who survived her husband, petitioned parliament in 1546 to be allowed to keep her terce lands despite his forfeiture. The lady of Grange who gave hospitality to James V at Hallyards on his last journey to Falkland at the end of 1542, and who was described by Knox as 'an ancient godly matron' (Knox's History, 1.38), may have been Kirkcaldy's mother, as Janet Melville could hardly have been elderly when, after her husband's forfeiture in 1546, she and 'sevin of hir bairnis' were dependent on the charity of her father, who was alive until December 1548 (Fraser, 3.89).

MARGARET H. B. SANDERSON

Sources J. M. Thomson and others, eds., *Registrum magni sigilli regum Scotorum / The register of the great seal of Scotland*, 11 vols. (1882–1914), vol. 3 · M. Livingstone and others, eds., *Registrum secreti sigilli regum Scotorum / The register of the privy seal of Scotland*, 2–4 (1921–52) · J. B. Paul, ed., *Compota thesaurariorum regum Scotorum / Accounts of the lord high treasurer of Scotland*, 6–8 (1905–8) · G. Burnett and others, eds., *The exchequer rolls of Scotland*, 23 vols. (1878–1908), vols. 17–18 · *Memoirs of his own life by Sir James Melville of Halhill*, ed. T. Thomson, Bannatyne Club, 18 (1827) · *John Knox's History of the Reformation in Scotland*, ed. W. C. Dickinson, 1 (1949) · W. Fraser, ed., *The Melvilles, earls of Melville, and the Leslies, earls of Leven*, 3 vols. (1890) · G. Neilson and H. Paton, eds., *Acts of the lords of council in civil causes, 1496–1501*, 2 (1918) · *APS*, 1424–1567
Archives NA Scot.

Kirkcaldy, Sir William, of Grange (c.1520–1573), soldier and politician, was the eldest son of Sir James *Kirkcaldy (d. 1556) and Janet Melville, daughter of Sir John Melville of Raith. He was listed with his father, then treasurer of Scotland, following James V's death on 14 December 1542, as a witness of a purported statement of the king's will. His father probably arranged his presence in order to promote his prospects under the new regime during the minority of Mary, queen of Scots.

St Andrews and France William Kirkcaldy and his father seem to have been early converts to protestantism, and Sir James lost his post as treasurer in 1543 when Cardinal David Beaton, archbishop of St Andrews, orchestrated a move away from reforming policies. The two Kirkcaldys participated in the audacious capture and murder of Beaton on 29 May 1546; and William Kirkcaldy was the first man to enter St Andrews Castle, after which it was occupied by the murderers. Kirkcaldy was sent to London to seek English aid and was rewarded on 3 September with £50 sterling as the first instalment of an irregularly paid pension. He had evidently returned by the time the castle was besieged by a French force under Leone Strozzi. On 30 July 1547, after bombardment, the castle surrendered to Strozzi, and Kirkcaldy and the other 'castilians' were taken as prisoners to France. According to John Knox, another of the prisoners,

> they arrived first at Fécamp and thereafter passed up the water of Seine and lay before Rouen; where the principal gentlemen, who looked for freedom, were dispersed and put in sundry prisons. The rest were left in the galleys, and were miserably treated. (*Knox's History*, 1.96–7)

Kirkcaldy's lands were forfeited on 27 November 1547. The escape of three Scots, including Kirkcaldy, from Mont-St Michel was reported to Henri II on 25 June 1550; Knox dated it to the previous Epiphany (6 January). On 26 February 1551 the English ambassador in France, Sir John Mason, reported that he had accepted Kirkcaldy's offer of his services as a spy, with the alias of Coraxe. However, there is no further evidence of Kirkcaldy's action in this role, perhaps because of the downfall of the duke of Somerset.

It appears that Kirkcaldy next joined the French army, probably for Henri II's spring offensive of 1552 into Lorraine. Henri Cleutin, seigneur d'Oysel, Henri II's lieutenant-general in Scotland, wrote to Mary of Guise from France on 19 August 1553, informing her that the French king and the constable, Anne de Montmorency, intended to make use of Kirkcaldy's talents in their dealings with Scotland. Sir James Melville, who served in

Montmorency's train from 1553 to 1557, mentions Kirkcaldy in connection with the death of Norman Leslie, master of Rothes (another of the former castilians), at the battle of Renty in August 1554: 'no man made more dull [i.e. mourning] nor the laird of Grange, who came to the camp the next day after, from a quiet raid where he had been directed' (Melville, 26). By 30 November 1556 the English ambassador in France, Nicholas Wotton, reported:

> [Kirkcaldy] offers to serve her Majesty [Mary Tudor] for the like pension he had formerly in England, wherever she pleases and whether in England, the Low Countries, or here, says he shall have good intelligence of the affairs of Scotland and of France by his intimacy with both those nations. (PRO, SP 69/9/146v–149r, in cipher; cf. *CSP for.*, 1553–8, 277)

On 1 March 1557 Wotton reported that Kirkcaldy desired to see Scotland delivered from the yoke of the French, commenting: 'either he must be a very great and crafty dissembler or else he bears no good will at all to the French men and next to his own country he bears a good minde to England' (PRO, SP 69/10/43r). Meanwhile, Kirkcaldy petitioned the French king for restoration to his and his father's lands and titles, which was granted by Mary, queen of Scots at Henri II's special desire at Paris on 17 February 1557 (see original charter, NA Scot., GD 26/1/4/86), and on 28 May he was at Dieppe waiting for a ship to Scotland. In September 1558 he was arrested by the English at Berwick as a spy, but was apparently released.

Problems of identity   The problems involved in determining Kirkcaldy's activities in the 1550s are compounded by the eulogy of him written by Sir James Melville, which has been a key source for his biographers. Melville asserts that during Kirkcaldy's sojourn in France from 1547 to 1557 he was captain of 100 light horse and was extolled by the dukes of Vendôme and Aumale and the prince of Condé. Whereas Montmorency would only speak to him 'on couerit', Henri II called him a 'valliant man' and chose him as a sporting companion; Henri also gave him a pension which Kirkcaldy chose to ignore. Kirkcaldy's biographers have assumed that he commanded one of the regular companies that formed the core of the French standing army; these originated from the fifteen ancient *companies des ordonnances*, of which the Scots were considered the 'premier company'. Unfortunately it is impossible to substantiate any of Melville's assertions in the French archives, and if Kirkcaldy really had been a captain of one of the *companies des ordonnances* it would have been recorded. Foreign mercenaries were often employed as temporary 'extraordinary' troops in addition to the regular French army, and Kirkcaldy was probably captain of 100 Scots in this category. Melville's stories about Kirkcaldy would apply much more closely to James Hamilton, third earl of Arran, who served the French crown with distinction as a soldier in the 1550s. When writing his memoirs in the 1590s, Melville could hardly laud Arran, who had been insane since 1562, but may have borrowed some of the incidents of Arran's career in order to construct his eulogy of Kirkcaldy.

Relations with Queen Mary   From early 1559 Kirkcaldy was often at the forefront of political events in Scotland. He may well have joined Mary of Guise's service in or soon after 1557, and in early 1559 was closely associated with William Maitland of Lethington, who had been appointed royal secretary by Mary in 1558; both participated in the protestant and anti-French uprising against her. Sir James Croft, the English governor of Berwick, reported on 20 July 1559:

> Money is owing [to Kirkcaldy] for serving in the late wars, in the hope whereof he drives time. The man is poor and cannot travail in these matters without charges, wherein he must be relieved by the Queen [Elizabeth] if these proceedings go forwards.   (*CSP for.*, 1558–9, 1.401)

A few days later Kirkcaldy openly declared himself with the protestants.

Kirkcaldy took a leading part in the fighting that followed, conducting numerous skirmishes and ambushes and helping to besiege Sempill Castle. The English ambassador, Thomas Randolph, praised Kirkcaldy in February 1561: 'of any other besides this man, Grange deserveth most for his earnest affection to the Queen's [Elizabeth's] service; and his credit and means thereto are as good as many a greater name' (*CSP Scot.*, 1547–63, 515). In October 1561 Kirkcaldy was again called to serve when fighting erupted on the borders. His military skills were also used in the campaign against the fourth earl of Huntly that culminated in the battle of Corrichie on 28 October 1562. On 1 November following he was rewarded with the barony of Nauchtane, in a grant that shows he was now a knight.

Kirkcaldy joined the uprising of the earl of Moray and other lords against Mary's marriage to Darnley in August 1565. He was forced to relinquish his house of Hallyards, and when the uprising collapsed he fled with the others to England. He returned with Moray at the time of the murder of David Riccio on 9 March 1566, and was pardoned on the 25th. After the murder of Darnley and the acquittal of the leading suspect, the fourth earl of Bothwell, the latter began moves to marry the queen. On 20 April 1567, when a number of nobles were signing the so-called Ainslie bond supporting the marriage, Kirkcaldy wrote a frank letter to the second earl of Bedford expressing his view that Bothwell had been responsible for Darnley's death. He initially suggested how Mary could retrieve the situation: having 'lost the favour we bore to her, yet if she will pursue revenge for the murder, she will win the hearts of all honest Scotsmen again'. However, he added:

> she intends to take the prince out of Mar's hands and put him in Bothwell's keeping, who murdered his father ... for she has said she cares not to lose France, England and her own country for him, and shall go with him to the world's end in a white petticoat.   (*CSP Scot.*, 1563–9, 2.322–3)

It appears that there was a long-standing mutual dislike between Kirkcaldy and Bothwell, and Kirkcaldy now felt committed 'to enterprise the revenge' of Darnley's murder: 'I must either take it in hand or leave the country, which I am determined to do, if I get licence; but Bothwell minds to cut me off when I obtain it'. He urged Bedford, 'I pray you let know what your mistress will do, for if we seek France, we may find favour: but I would rather persuade to lean to England' (ibid., 2.325).

Kirkcaldy was requested to write again to Bedford on 8

May following a meeting of the earls of Argyll, Morton, Atholl, and Mar, at Stirling, where they decided to seek Mary's liberation from Bothwell (who had abducted her on 24 April). Kirkcaldy was in the lords' army against Mary and Bothwell at Carberry on 15 June, and it was to him that Mary surrendered. On 10 August, after the queen's deposition, Kirkcaldy and Sir William Murray of Tullibardine were commissioned to pursue the fugitive Bothwell. They sailed to Orkney but Bothwell escaped. On their return in September Kirkcaldy was appointed captain of Edinburgh Castle by Regent Moray.

Mary escaped from Lochleven Castle on 2 May 1568. On 8 May Kirkcaldy signed a bond with the provost of Edinburgh, Sir Simon Preston of Craigmillar. In Moray's force at Langside on 13 May, Kirkcaldy commanded the horsemen and was rewarded with the escheat of the laird of Bass. Thereafter he moved slowly away from supporting the regent, apparently influenced by Maitland, but the progress of his defection is hard to chart. In February 1569 he was still a loyal supporter of Moray when Maitland clearly was not. Maitland's escape to Edinburgh Castle on 9 September, however, was arranged by Kirkcaldy. On 16 September Maitland wrote to the duke of Norfolk that Kirkcaldy 'will be good in all her [Mary's] causes so far as with honour he may. He mislikes altogether my lord regent's proceedings in as much as he doth see him run a direct course to his own overthrow' (Cameron, 1.69). Kirkcaldy, however, was still receiving gifts from the king's party in October, and in that month he was also elected provost of Edinburgh. Sir William Drury reported on 9 December that Kirkcaldy was loyal to the king's party. After Moray's murder on 10 January 1570, Kirkcaldy carried the standard at his funeral on 14 February. Randolph wrote in April that he did not doubt Kirkcaldy's sincerity, 'except Lethington enchant him' (CSP Scot., 1569–71, 125).

Taking sides Further English doubts soon emerged. The earl of Sussex reported to Elizabeth on 4 May 1570: 'understanding the Laird of Grange might be alienated from his former good affection towards your majesty, I wrote a very plain letter to him'; to which Kirkcaldy had replied on 29 April:

> [the] whole matter rests on two heads: the one, that I have declined from my old friends in this realm who heretofor have desired the amity of England; the other that I have given countenance to others who have capitulated to the French.

Kirkcaldy claimed that:

> all my friends, so far as I know, are yet desirous of the amity of England ... particularly towards the Queen's majesty, as well for benefits received of her father and brother by me and my friends, as for religion's sake, and her honourable dealings with this realm in the beginning of her reign. (CSP Scot., 1569–71, 149, 151–2)

He refused to march on Glasgow with Sussex and the king's party in June, and refused them entry to Edinburgh Castle. He seems to have resented the domineering attitude of the English towards Scotland and their preference for Lennox as regent. Kirkcaldy refused to co-operate in Lennox's appointment, and would not even shoot off any ordnance from the castle to mark the occasion.

On 6 December 1570 Kirkcaldy wrote to Sir William Cecil with an assessment of his own position in Anglo-Scottish affairs. He reminded Cecil of 'the lamentable estate of this country', of 'the unnatural division of the noblemen and "whole body" of this realm', which in his own small way he had tried to 'extinguish'. He had also offered his services to Queen Elizabeth as he believed it was within her power 'to bring these two realms to their former amity', because 'if either of the parties should be "forced" to seek remedy by foreign forces, the end thereof will be miserable' (CSP Scot., 1569–71, 440). Cecil replied on 10 January 1571 that he could not 'promise any more than his former doings declare' (ibid., 462), to which Kirkcaldy responded with barely concealed hostility on 29 January. In March he was entering into confrontation with the burgh of Edinburgh, and his men took and fortified the steeple of St Giles. In the castle he had the royal regalia, the principal store of ordnance, and the state papers of the kingdom. By 13 April he was openly refusing to recognize Lennox as regent. His public position was that he had always been loyal to Moray but that the cause he and Moray represented had been betrayed by Moray's successors.

In the meantime Kirkcaldy and Maitland were negotiating with France for assistance. Monsieur Verac was sent as French ambassador, officially with instructions to seek a reconciliation between the Scottish factions, but as soon as Verac arrived at Leith on 5 July he was detained by the king's party. In his coffers was found correspondence with Maitland and Kirkcaldy concerning Mary's restoration.

At the end of August 1571 the regent held a parliament at Stirling. Kirkcaldy, the fifth earl of Huntly, and the lairds of Ferniehurst and Buccleuch along with 280 horsemen and sixty harquebusiers made a surprise attack on the town on 4 September. They captured many prisoners, including the regent, but were forced to release them when a relieving force issued from Stirling Castle. During the affray Lennox was killed and the Marians retreated. In the aftermath Kirkcaldy was forfeited for the third time in his life, on 30 September, and on 5 September a full-scale siege of Edinburgh Castle began.

Castilian in Edinburgh Kirkcaldy sent his brother James to the French court to seek aid, his arrival there being reported on 5 January 1572. Although there are a number of notices of James Kirkcaldy's imminent departure from the French court from 31 January 1572 onwards, he did not return to Scotland until January 1573. A truce was agreed between the queen's and king's parties on 1 August 1572 for two months, and it was later extended to the end of the year. The new regent, Morton, offered Kirkcaldy and the castilians the same terms as Mar had proposed when he was regent. But Kirkcaldy insisted on a universal amnesty, which Morton would not accept. He therefore invested the castle, and on 1 January 1573 Kirkcaldy signalled the resumption of hostilities by a bombardment of the town. When James Kirkcaldy finally returned to Scotland bearing the long-awaited money and munitions from France for the queen's party, he was captured and his precious cargo and ship confiscated on Morton's instructions.

At the urging of Elizabeth's representatives Morton's government made a final attempt at conciliation with the castilians. On 27 March 1573 Henry Killigrew sent Kirkcaldy and Maitland the pacification of Perth by which the conditional surrender of the remaining nobles of the queen's party had recently been agreed (23 February). On 6 April the fifth earl of Rothes, an old friend of Kirkcaldy, entered the castle as mediator, but he was no more successful than others had been. Kirkcaldy now stipulated that all his personal debts were to be paid, that he should retain Blackness Castle, and that the English should guarantee his life. As regards Queen Mary's jewels, 'the said laird of Grange shall not be [ac]countable therefore nor charged in any sort to make reckoning or deliverance of the same or any part thereof to any person but only to herself'; and finally, all properties should be returned to him and his supporters (Cameron, 1.120–25). After the king's party rejected these terms, Sir William Drury and an English army crossed the border in April while siege guns were sent by sea to Leith. On 28 May, after eleven days of bombardment, the castle surrendered. Kirkcaldy, Maitland, and nine other leaders were imprisoned.

On 29 May Maitland and Kirkcaldy wrote to Lord Burghley, begging that they might be allowed to go to live in England. On 31 May Morton told Burghley that the fate of the prisoners 'rests now in her majesty' (CSP Scot., 1571–4, 575). Maitland died on 9 June. At some stage after the fall of the castle a bond of manrent was offered to Morton in return for Kirkcaldy's life, by which 100 gentlemen promised Kirkcaldy's loyalty and their own to Morton if Kirkcaldy were spared. The offer was refused. At the end of July, Morton finally received advice from Queen Elizabeth that she would leave 'the judgment and ordering of those matters to him' (ibid., 582). Kirkcaldy was tried for treason on 3 August 1573 and executed in Edinburgh the same day, fulfilling John Knox's prophecy that he would 'hang from a gallows in the face of the sun' (Hewitt, 27). Kirkcaldy was survived by his wife, Margaret Learmonth (daughter of Sir James Learmonth of Dairsie, provost of St Andrews), whom he had married between 1557 and 1564, by their daughter Janet, and by an illegitimate daughter whose recent birth was mentioned in 1573. His lands were eventually restored to his nephew William in 1581.

In the end Kirkcaldy emerges as a Scottish martyr along the lines of, but not to the same degree as, William Wallace, who also had been a laird, soldier, and charismatic leader of men, and who also was hanged, drawn, and quartered for his adherence to his honour, principles, and ideals. The English ambassadors Killigrew and Randolph 'boisted planly to bring down that proud gyantis pryd, wha presumed to be a nother Wallace, as they allegit' (Melville, 257). Kirkcaldy wanted the peaceful union of Scotland with England, with two independent equal kingdoms, united by the protestant religion, each having its own hereditary monarch. This desire was naive, as no Tudor monarch would have countenanced it.

Melville's assessment of Kirkcaldy's personal character is credible: he was 'a lusty, stark and well-proportioned personnage, hardy and of a magnanimous courage'; in all his enterprises he was 'secret and prudent' and when he was 'victorious, he was very mercifull, and naturally liberal', a friend to all men in adversity and an enemy to greed and ambition. Some loved him for 'his religion, uprightness and manliness', others 'depended upon him for his good fortune and apparent promotion, whereby divers of them hoped to be advanced and rewarded'. But Melville goes too far when he claims that Kirkcaldy 'refused sundry great offices, even the office of Regent, and benefices and great pensions' (Melville, 257–8). Kirkcaldy was granted and accepted appointments, benefices, and pensions befitting his status of laird. His character has been over-romanticized, but does contain much to admire. His importance before 1559 has been exaggerated, but from that date onwards he was often a consequential figure.   ELIZABETH BONNER

Sources state papers foreign, PRO, Edward VI, SP 68, Mary SP 69 · correspondance politique, Angleterre, Archives du Ministère des Affaires Étrangères, Paris, IX, fols. 99–100 · original charter of Mary, queen of Scots, signed in Paris 17 February 1557, NA Scot., GD 26/1/4/86 · CSP Scot., 1547–74 · CSP for., 1547–74 · APC, 1556–8 · M. Livingstone, D. Hay Fleming, and others, eds., Registrum secreti sigilli regum Scotorum / The register of the privy seal of Scotland, 4–6 (1952–63), 1556–67, 1567–74 · Reg. PCS, 1st ser., vol. 1 · J. B. Paul, ed., Compota thesaurariorum regum Scotorum / Accounts of the lord high treasurer of Scotland, 11 (1916) · John Knox's History of the Reformation in Scotland, ed. W. C. Dickinson, 2 vols. (1949) · Memoirs of his own life by Sir James Melville of Halhill, ed. T. Thomson, Bannatyne Club, 18 (1827) · D. Calderwood, The history of the Kirk of Scotland, ed. T. Thomson and D. Laing, Wodrow Society, 7 (1842–9) · T. Thomson, ed., A diurnal of remarkable occurrents that have passed within the country of Scotland, Bannatyne Club, 43 (1833) · E. Bonner, ed., The Scots and the French army, 1547–1559: French military and financial documents concerning Scotland during the reign of Henri II, Scottish History Society, 5th ser. [forthcoming] · The Warrender papers, ed. A. I. Cameron, 2 vols., Scottish History Society, 3rd ser., 18–19 (1931–2) · J. Grant, Memoirs and adventures of Sir William Kirkaldy of Grange (1849) · G. Donaldson, Scotland: James V to James VII (1965) · G. Donaldson, All the queen's men (1983) · G. Donaldson and J. Morpeth, eds., A dictionary of Scottish history (1977) · M. Lynch, Scotland and the Reformation (1981) · G. R. Hewitt, Scotland under Morton, 1572–80 (1982) · J. Wormald, Lords and men in Scotland: bonds of manrent, 1442–1603 (1985) · D. B. Smith, 'La Belle Écossaise', SHR, 14 (1916–17), 398–400 · E. Bonner, 'The recovery of St Andrews Castle in 1547: French naval policy and diplomacy in the British Isles', EngHR, 111 (1996), 578–97 · E. Bonner, 'Scotland's "auld alliance" with France, 1295–1560', History, 84 (1999), 5–30 · M. Loughlin, 'The career of Maitland of Lethington, c.1526–1573', PhD diss., U. Edin., 1991

Likenesses attrib. Clouet, portrait (Kirkcaldy?), repro. in Donaldson, All the queen's men; priv. coll.

Kirkcudbright. For this title name see Maclellan, Robert, first Lord Kirkcudbright (d. 1639).

Kirke, Edward (1553–1613), Church of England clergyman, was born in London, where he attended St Anthony's School. He was a sizar at Pembroke College, Cambridge, matriculating in 1571 (Spenser matriculated in 1569; Gabriel Harvey was made a fellow in 1570). He transferred to Gonville and Caius College about 1574/5 and was awarded BA in 1574/5 and MA in 1578. He was ordained rector of Risby, Suffolk, on 26 May 1580, on the institution of Sir Thomas Kytson, a post which he held until his death. Kytson was the uncle of the Spenser sisters of Althorp—Elizabeth, Anne, and Alice—to whom Spenser referred in

Colin Clouts Come Home Againe (1591). One of Kirke's account books shows that he bought 'a shepard's Calendar' for 2s. in 1583, possibly Spenser's poem. Kirke was made rector of Lackford, the adjoining parish, on 21 August 1587 and chaplain to Lord Darcy in 1603. He died at Risby on 10 November 1613, at the age of sixty, and was buried in the parish churchyard; his grave remains, with an epitaph. Kirke made a will on 7 November, in which he left various small sums to his relatives and friends. He mentions a wife, Helen; a daughter, Margaret, married to George Whiter; and another son-in-law, Richard Buckle.

Kirke is notable because he may have been the E. K. who wrote the notes to Edmund Spenser's *The Shepheardes Calender* (1579). On this basis, and one or two other tantalising references in Spenser's letters to Gabriel Harvey, Kirke is conjectured to have been a close friend of his university contemporary. However, the evidence that Kirke was the author of the glosses and notes to Spenser's *Shepheardes Calender* is inconclusive. Spenser must have known Kirke, given their proximity at Pembroke College. In his letter of 16 October 1579 to Gabriel Harvey from Leicester House, published as one of the *Three Proper and Wittie, Familiar Letters* (1580), Spenser states that 'Maister E. K. hartily desireth to be commended unto your Worshippe' and refers to 'hys paynefull and dutifull Verses of your selfe'. In the next paragraph Spenser states that he has received a letter from Harvey at 'Mystresse *Kerkes*' and later writes that Harvey can always send him letters 'safely to me by *Mistresse Kerke*, and by none other'. In another of the letters Spenser refers to the gloss to *The Shepheardes Calender*, in which 'be some things excellently, and many things wittily, discoursed of E. K.' Furthermore in a note to the May eclogue in the calendar E. K. translates the epitaph to the Greek king Sardanaplus in exactly the same way that Spenser himself does in his three letters.

This last detail indicates either that E. K. may have been Spenser himself, as some scholars argue, or that he was indeed a close friend of Spenser's, making Edward Kirke a prime candidate. It is also possible that the Mistress Kerke referred to in the published letters is Edward's widowed mother, as Alexander Grossart suggested. But, given the bantering and iconoclastic style and tone of the letters, it is equally possible that Mistress Kerke is a fictional character, a literary device, or even a lost joke. Certainly the reader does not have to take everything in the published letters on trust.

The same is true of *The Shepheardes Calender*. E. K. may well have been a genuine commentator on the poem, in which case Kirke is once again a plausible candidate. However, it should not be overlooked that it is extremely unlikely that Spenser simply wrote the poem and passed it on to a publisher, who decided to include a commentary with or without the poet's permission; some scholars have argued that Spenser generally saw his works through the press with painstaking attention to detail. The text of *The Shepheardes Calender* is designed to imitate a classical work with commentary, of the type that European humanists were publishing throughout the second half of the sixteenth century. In doing so the young poet announces his arrival on the literary scene by comparing his work to that of established ancient writers. No English writer had attempted anything so audacious before. The commentary provided by E. K. is full of odd readings and some judgements that neither Spenser nor their author was likely to have believed. As David R. Shore notes, though E. K. claims that 'by meanes of some familiar acquaintance I was made privie to his [Spenser's] counsell and secret meaning in them', 'in fact, he solves few of the mysteries that have intrigued those attracted to the *Calender*'s historical allegory' (Hamilton and others, 231). It is likely that the author of the poem intended such secrecy. If E. K. was Edward Kirke it is probable, as Alexander Judson suggested (Judson, 40), that he composed the commentary and glossary as a riddle, sometimes telling the truth, sometimes misleading the reader and hiding information, probably in collaboration with Spenser and Harvey.　ANDREW HADFIELD

Sources Venn, *Alum. Cant.*, 1/3.24 · Cooper, *Ath. Cantab.*, 2.244–5 · *DNB* · *The complete works in verse and prose of Edmund Spenser*, ed. A. B. Grosart, 9 vols. (1882–4) · A. C. Hamilton and others, eds., *The Spenser encyclopedia* (1990), 231 · *The poetical works of Edmund Spenser*, ed. J. C. Smith and E. De Selincourt (1912) · A. C. Judson, *The life of Edmund Spenser* (1945), 39–40 · D. Hamer, 'Some Spenser problems', *N&Q*, 180 (1941), 183–4, 220–24, 238–41

Kirke, George (c.1600–1675), courtier, was probably born in Scotland, the son of George Kirke (possibly MP in 1626 for Clitheroe, Lancashire) who was groom of the bedchamber and gentleman of the robes to both James I and Charles I and was succeeded in 1630 by his son who had been appointed groom of the bedchamber to Prince Charles in 1621. In 1632 complaints were made after Kirke claimed £5000 expenditure on the king's robes but refused to present the bills.

Kirke's first wife was Anne (*bap.* 1607, *d.* 1641), the eldest daughter of Sir Robert *Killigrew and sister of William *Killigrew, Thomas *Killigrew, and Henry *Killigrew. As a wedding present, Charles gave them the manor of Sheriff Hutton, in Yorkshire, which Kirke sold in 1650. A son, Charles, was born in 1633, and it is likely that the George Kirke born 27 January 1635 at Sunbury (2 miles from Hampton Court) was also their child. An unnamed daughter was buried in Westminster Abbey in 1640. Anne, who was painted by Van Dyck, was appointed dresser to Queen Henrietta Maria in 1637. Anne was drowned under London Bridge on 8 July 1641 when her barge overturned. She was buried in Westminster Abbey.

Kirke took every opportunity to make money. From about 1629 he became involved in projects to drain marshes. Together with Sir Robert Killigrew and Sir John Heydon, he organized marshland drainage in Norfolk, Lincoln, Kent, Sussex, and Carmarthen. Kirke took particular responsibility for the Holland Fen project near Swineshead in Lincolnshire, which was first proposed in 1635. The draining of the fens provoked disturbances among the fenmen who were intent on defending their traditional economy. In 1636 there were riots at West Fen. The leaders were imprisoned at Lincoln, where Kirke believed they should remain as 'by which means the rest of the rioters will be found out these being the ringleaders of all the rest' (Lindley, 89). Further unrest occurred at Holland Fen in 1640 and in August the following year rioters expropriated large amounts of grain from Kirke's tenants. Kirke lost these lands during the Commonwealth but tried, unsuccessfully, to regain them in 1661.

Kirke was also a lessee of Gillingham Forest, Dorset, part of the crown's disafforestation scheme, a device used to raise revenue. At some point he obtained rights over clay used for manufacturing tobacco pipes and in 1631 was involved in a precursor of the Royal African Company. In 1634 he failed to obtain the post of sayer (of threads) in Ireland; however, the lord deputy, Wentworth, promised to advance Kirke's other Irish projects.

In 1642 Kirke, who four years earlier had described himself as 'his Majesty's ancientest servant' (CSP dom., 1638, 144), was additionally appointed keeper of Whitehall Palace at £186 per annum. At Oxford on 26 February 1646 Kirke married Mary (d. 1701?), daughter of Aurelian *Townshend. Mary was given away by Charles I. While imprisoned in Hampton Court Charles borrowed from her a painting of the queen. Edmund Ludlow refers to a Mrs Kirk's enjoying a splendid, and lavish, entertainment by Lord Francis Villiers the night before he was killed in the earl of Holland's abortive rising in 1648. The children of the second marriage were Percy *Kirke, Diana (b. c.1648), Mary (b. 1649/50), and Philip.

Kirke House, 'next le Timberyard' adjoining Spring Garden, was acquired in 1632 and is described in the Survey of London (16.82–6). During the Commonwealth Kirke stayed in obscurity. He was assessed in 1643 at £500, being described in the Calendar ... of the Committee for Compounding for October 1645 as 'Kirke, of Nonsuch, Surrey, and Charing Cross' in a list of notables 'who are all Papists'. Kirke lost the post of keeper of Whitehall Palace, his house and goods were sequestered and demised to Lord Sheffield and Mr Lisle at £50 a year but the sequestration was discharged two years later. Kirke rebuilt the house on a grand scale between 1648 and 1652, living temporarily at 5 Chandos Street.

In 1664 Kirke regained the post of keeper of Whitehall Palace:

> Grant to George Kirke of the office of keeping the King's palace called York Place with the great garden and orchards, bowling alleys and coney yard near the Cockpit, with the jewels and robes in the palace; and a further grant of all the tenements etc. in Westminster belonging to his place, except three houses (called Paradise, Hell and Purgatory) near the Exchequer, in lieu of which he is to have an annuity of £12.3.4. (CSP dom., 1664, 498)

In 1674 the post passed to the younger son Philip. Kirke's wife, Mary, who claimed a place as volary keeper in 1663 and who clearly enjoyed royal protection, was then granted several rooms in Whitehall, on condition that her husband surrendered some of his rooms. When Kirke's daughter Diana was born, Charles I promised her £2000, which was given later, probably on her sixteenth birthday, in 1664. Diana married Aubrey de Vere, earl of Oxford,

in 1673. Her sister Mary, who was reputedly simultaneously the mistress of the duke of York, the duke of Monmouth, and the earl of Mulgrave, married Sir Thomas Vernon in 1677. Kirke's family was severely lambasted in Charles Sackville's poem 'A Faithfull Catalogue of our most Eminent Ninnies' (Poems on Affairs of State, 4.191–211), where Mary was 'Vernon, the glory of that lustful tribe'.

George Kirke was buried on 26 May 1675 at St Margaret's, Westminster, unlike most of his family who were buried in the abbey. He died intestate but a limited administration, involving a sum of £2000, was granted to Henry Killigrew in 1680. Philip Kirke's appointment as keeper (worth £500 in 1685) was confirmed on his father's death, but Philip died two years later so the position went to his brother Piercy, and then to his son, also Piercy (d. 1741).

PHILIP LEWIN

Sources CSP dom., 1625–74 · Sheffield, Strafford MSS 8/156–7 · G. E. Aylmer, The king's servants: the civil service of Charles I, 1625–1642 (1961) · Calendar of the Clarendon state papers preserved in the Bodleian Library, 5: 1660–1726, ed. F. J. Routledge (1970), 3 · M. A. E. Green, ed., Calendar of the proceedings of the committee for advance of money, 1642–1656, 3 vols., PRO (1888) · M. A. E. Green, ed., Calendar of the proceedings of the committee for compounding ... 1643–1660, 2, PRO (1890), Oct 1645 · JHL, 9 (1646–7), 520 [letter from Charles I to Colonel Whaley] · The memoirs of Edmund Ludlow, ed. C. H. Firth, 2 vols. (1894), vol. 1, p. 198 · Poems on affairs of state, 4 vols. (1704), vol. 4, pp. 191–211 · J. L. Chester, ed., The marriage, baptismal, and burial registers of the collegiate church or abbey of St Peter, Westminster, Harleian Society, 10 (1876) · K. Lindley, Fenland riots and the English revolution (1982) · parish register, St Margaret's, Westminster, 26 May 1675 [burial] · will of Mary Kirke, PRO, PROB 11/463 · administration of George Kirke, PRO, PROB 6/55

Kirke, John (fl. 1629–1643), actor and playwright, first appears in a patent for the travelling Red Bull company at Reading in 1629. In 1634 he was a member of the same company in London (now playing at the Fortune) and the following year he became a groom of the chamber as a member of Prince Charles's men, again at the Red Bull. Kirke and his wife, Elizabeth, lived in the parish of St James's, Clerkenwell, Middlesex, where they had three children between 1633 and 1643 (Marie, Parry, and John), all of whom died in infancy.

Kirke was author of a popular tragicomedy, The Seven Champions of Christendome, licensed for the press on 13 July 1638 at the same time as The Life and Death of Jack Straw and Watt Tyler by John Kirke, of which nothing is known. The Seven Champions was printed the same year, with a title-page declaring that it had been 'Acted at the Cocke-pit, and at the Red-Bull in St. Johns Streete, with a generall liking'. The dedication is addressed to the author's 'much respected and worthy friend, Master John Waite', possibly the travelling actor of the same name. The play is based on Richard Johnson's very popular chivalric romance of the same name, also showing the influence of Shakespeare's Tempest and Winter's Tale. In June 1642 Kirke paid master of the revels Sir Henry Herbert for two plays, one of which Herbert burnt 'for the ribaldry and offense that was in it', but he was not necessarily the author (Lawrence, 591). Kirke was author of the dedication to Sir Kenelm Digby prefixed to Shirley's *Martyred Soldier* (1638) and he may have been the subject of Thomas Jordan's *Epitaph on my Worthy Friend, Mr. John Kirk*, first printed in 1643.

DAVID KATHMAN

Sources G. E. Bentley, *The Jacobean and Caroline stage*, 7 vols. (1941–68), vol. 2, pp. 492–3, vol. 4, pp. 710–15 • W. J. Lawrence, 'John Kirke, the Caroline actor-dramatist', *Studies in Philology*, 21 (1924), 586–93 • G. E. Dawson, introduction, in *The seven champions of Christendome by John Kirke* (1929), vii–xxii • J. Freehafer, 'Shakespeare's *Tempest* and *The seven champions*', *Studies in Philology*, 66 (1969), 87–103 • *DNB*

Kirke, Percy (d. **1691**), army officer, was the son of George *Kirke (d. 1675), groom of the bedchamber and keeper of Whitehall Palace to Charles II, and Mary Townshend (1626–1701), a daughter of the poet Aurelian *Townshend. While a teenager Kirke joined the Admiralty regiment as an ensign in 1666, and in 1670 the earl of Oxford, who had married one of Kirke's sisters, made him cornet of his own troop in his regiment of horse. In 1673 he took a temporary commission in the duke of Monmouth's regiment, then serving as part of the French army under Marshal Turenne in Flanders. He fought at the victory over the imperialists at Enzheim (4 October 1674), in which he was wounded in three places. After the battle Louis Duras wrote to Monmouth that Kirke 'is certainly one of the bravest lads in the world and is much esteemed as is also his brother' (Atkinson, 43). His younger brother Charles also fought at Enzheim, but received a fatal wound. In July the next year Kirke challenged and wounded Lord Mulgrave in a duel 'for having debauch'd and abus'd his sister' (Morrison, 304).

Kirke married Lady Mary Howard (d. 1707), a daughter of the fourth earl of Suffolk, with whom he had at least one son and two daughters. Lord Oxford promoted Kirke to captain-lieutenant in 1675 and Duras, impressed with him since Enzheim, promoted him to lieutenant-colonel of his regiment of dragoons in 1678. Two years later he took over the command of Lord Plymouth's regiment of foot, which was posted to Tangier in the summer of 1680. He took part in the last and most successful battle against the Moors (27 October 1680), in which he and Thomas Tollemache were praised for having 'behaved themselves like brave and gallant men' (*A Particular Relation*). In January 1681 he undertook a three-month mission to the court of the Moroccan sultan Mawlay Isma'il at Meknes, where he was promised a four-year peace. Later that year he succeeded Edward Sackville as governor of Tangier and remained so until relieved by George Legge, Lord Dartmouth, in August 1683.

Samuel Pepys stayed in Tangier between August and December 1683 during the last months of the garrison. He was disgusted by Kirke's fast and violent temper, his high-handedness, his bawdy table talk, his boasts of his sexual conquests, his keeping of a mistress in a bathhouse (notwithstanding his wife being in Tangier), his 'damns and curses', his placing himself above the law, his expulsion of the Jews from Tangier, his flagrant corruption ('nothing being sold in the town without his licence'), and his intimidation of all who crossed him. It was even rumoured that Kirke had arranged the murder of two of his creditors. 'The tyranny and vice of Kirke in his way is stupendous.' He was 'a very brute' (*Tangier Papers*).

After the evacuation of Tangier, Kirke arrived in England in early 1684, where his Tangier regiment was renamed the Queen's regiment of foot. The regiment retained its colours depicting a paschal lamb, from which it was nicknamed Kirke's Lambs. During Monmouth's western rebellion of 1685 he commanded his regiment at the battle of Sedgemoor on 6 July 1685, in which the Lambs were one of the four infantry regiments present in the royal army. Three days after the battle, in which Monmouth's men were scattered, Kirke:

> ordered several prisoners at Taunton to be hanged up; and being then at an entertainment, as every new health was drunk he had a fresh man turned off; and observing how they shaked their legs in the agonies of death, he called it dancing, and ordered music to play to them.   (Stackhouse, 234)

This signalled the start of a six-week campaign of pacification that has since become notorious, although at the time he was censured by the government not so much for brutality but for selling pardons to suspected rebels before they could be brought to the assizes. In August that year he was promoted to brigadier. According to Bishop Burnet, Kirke gave 'as smart a reply as any' when it was suggested that he change his religion by embracing Catholicism. 'He told them that he was unhappily pre-engaged, for that if ever he changed he had promised the King of Morocco to turn Mahometam' (Stackhouse, 249). In the autumn of 1688 he was one of the chief plotters in the army against King James, but was nevertheless sent on ahead of the main forces to Warminster to block the advance of the prince of Orange's invading army. On 19 November 1688 he sent Patrick Sarsfield off towards the enemy, which resulted in the bloody skirmish at Wincanton, but shortly afterwards was himself arrested in Salisbury for attempting to desert to William. He was sent back to London, but was released by the privy council, who claimed to find no evidence against him.

After the revolution Kirke was promoted by William III to major-general, and on 29 April 1689 was placed in charge of the Londonderry relief force. Delays and bad weather prevented him from arriving in Lough Foyle until 11 June. Having seen that there was a boom across the river below the city, he called a council of war and made the much criticized decision to wait for reinforcements so that Londonderry might be relieved from the land. He detached 600 men from the fleet to set up a fort on the Isle of Inch on Lough Swilly, which had the effect of dividing the Jacobite forces then threatening Enniskillen. On 14 July he sent a message to Londonderry advising the defenders to 'be good husbands to your victuals and by God's help we shall overcome these barbarous people' (Milligan, 324), and then sailed to Inch. He arrived to find a message from the city that the garrison was down to its last provisions, and another from Schomberg ordering him to attempt the relief. He sailed back to Lough Foyle and ordered three ships to sail up to the city. On 28 July the boom across the river was broken and all three vessels reached the quayside in Londonderry. On 31 July the Irish army raised the siege and marched away.

On 4 August Kirke processed through Londonderry with Walker and Michelburne and was feted as the city's deliverer. Three days later he re-formed the forces in Londonderry by halving the number of regiments and officers, an act which was greatly resented in the city. His response was to erect a new gallows, on which he threatened to hang those who complained, and to issue orders to the sentries to disarm everyone leaving the city. Writing of Kirke at this time, Sir James Caldwell asked 'whether profest atheism and debauchery are fit weapons to beat down popery?' (Cunningham and Whalley, 211). From Londonderry Kirke marched to Coleraine, which was abandoned by the Irish on his approach, and then to Dundalk, where he joined Schomberg's army in early September. He took an active part in the battle of the Boyne (1 July 1690), where he 'went from one place to another, as the posture of affairs required' (Story, 82). After the fall of Dublin he was sent on ahead to summon Waterford, which surrendered to him on 25 July.

Kirke took part in the unsuccessful siege of Limerick in August 1690, where he was involved in directing the fighting in which the outlying forts were captured. After the raising of the siege he led a relief force in September 1690 to Birr, which was being attacked by the duke of Berwick. Kirke had most of the town pulled down for firewood, garrisoned and fortified the castle, and ordered that all houses between Birr and Banagher be burnt. He spent the following winter based in Mullingar, from where he led a raid towards Athlone in March 1691.

In April 1691 Kirke was one of three generals relieved of their commands in Ireland and posted to the continent. He arrived in England on 30 May 1691, was promoted to lieutenant-general, and joined King William's army in Flanders. He served under the prince of Waldeck for the rest of that year's campaign against the French, but fell ill while in the camp at Ninove. He was taken to Brussels to recuperate but died there on 31 October 1691. According to Bishop Wilson (*Works of Thomas Wilson*, 7 vols., 1847–63, 6.372) Kirke's final sufferings were the same as those of King Antiochus: 'Whiles he lived in sorrow and pain, his flesh fell away, and the filthiness of his smell was noisome to all his army' (2 Maccabees 9:9). His successor as colonel of the Queen's regiment in 1696 petitioned the Treasury for £1000 because Kirke 'had received the pay of the regiment and applied it to his own use' (Redington, 524).

His eldest surviving son, **Percy Kirke** (1683–1741), was commissioned as an ensign at the age of one, a lieutenant in his father's regiment at the age of five, and a captain when he was six (and was placed on the sick list by his father when the regiment was reviewed in Dundalk in October 1689). At the age of nineteen he took part in the raid on Vigo (1702) and at twenty-four commanded his father's old regiment at the battle of Almanza (1707), where he was captured. He purchased the colonelcy in 1710 and commanded his regiment in the disastrous Canadian expedition of 1711. From 1730 his regiment was stationed in Gibraltar. He was promoted to lieutenant-

general in 1739. He died a bachelor and was buried in Westminster Abbey, where his niece raised an elaborate monument to him.   PIERS WAUCHOPE

Sources C. T. Atkinson, 'Feversham's account of the battle of Enzheim, 1674', *Journal of the Society for Army Historical Research*, 1 (1922) · A. Morrison, ed., *The Bulstrode papers* (1897) · *An abridgement of Bishop Burnet's History of his own times*, ed. T. Stackhouse (1906) · *A particular relation of the late success of his majesties forces at Tangier against the Moors* (1680) · *The Tangier papers of Samuel Pepys*, ed. E. Chappell, Navy RS, 73 (1935) · E. M. G. Routh, *Tangier: England's lost Atlantic outpost, 1661–1684* (1912) · N. Luttrell, *A brief historical relation of state affairs from September 1678 to April 1714*, 6 vols. (1857) · J. Cunningham and M. Whalley, 'Queries against Major General Kirke', *Irish Sword*, 16 (1985–6), 208–16 · J. Hempton, ed., *The siege and history of Londonderry* (1861) · C. Dalton, ed., *English army lists and commission registers, 1661–1714*, 6 vols. (1892–1904) · C. Dalton, 'Child commissions in the army, 1661–1714', *N&Q*, 8th ser., 8 (1895), 421–3 · E. D'Auvergne, *The history of the Campagne in Flanders for the year 1691* (1735) · J. L. Chester, ed., *The marriage, baptismal, and burial registers of the collegiate church or abbey of St Peter, Westminster*, Harleian Society, 10 (1876) · J. Davis, *The history of the second queen's royal regiment*, 1–3 (1887–95) · J. Redington, ed., *Calendar of Treasury papers*, 1, PRO (1868) · T. L. Cooke, *The picture of Parsonstown* (1826) · G. Story, *An impartial history of the wars of Ireland* (1693) · C. D. Milligan, *History of the siege of Londonderry, 1689* (1951)
Archives Yale U., Farmington, Lewis Walpole Library, letter-book
Likenesses G. Kneller, oils, c.1690, repro. in A. J. Guy and J. Spencer-Smith, eds., *1688: glorious revolution?* (1988) · P. Scheemakers, bust, after 1743, Westminster Abbey

Kirke, Percy (1683–1741). *See under* Kirke, Percy (d. 1691).

Kirke, Thomas (1650–1706), antiquary and topographer, born on 22 December 1650, was the eldest son of Gilbert Kirke (1624–1663) of Cookridge, near Leeds, and his wife, Margaret Layton (d. 1688), daughter of Francis Layton of Rawden, Yorkshire. On 28 May 1668 Kirke matriculated at Trinity College, Cambridge, where his tutor was the Yorkshire antiquary and cleric Miles Gale, but he did not graduate.

Kirke was also a distant relative and close acquaintance of another Yorkshire scholar and topographer Ralph Thoresby, who acknowledged that 'my dear friend', or 'mon cher ami, Mr. Kirk' had often accompanied him on his antiquarian rambles (*Diary of Ralph Thoresby*, 1.380, 390). At Cookridge Kirke, a virtuoso engaging in a wide range of intellectual and practical activities, himself designed a 'most surprizing Labyrinth', or maze, with over 300 separate vistas which attracted admiring visits from 'almost all Foreigners and Gentlemen of Curiosity of our own Nation' (Thoresby, *Ducatus Leodiensis*, 159). In May 1677 Kirke undertook a three-month tour of Scotland, covering nearly 1000 miles and incorporating visits to Edinburgh, St Andrews, Aberdeen, Inverness, the Orkney Islands, Perth, Stirling, and Glasgow. From his observations he anonymously published a polemical pamphlet in 1679 entitled *A Modern Account of Scotland … Written from Thence by an English Gentleman*. According to Kirke's splenetic and caustic narrative, the Scots were not only 'Proud, Arrogant, Vain-glorious boasters, Bloody, Barbarous and Inhuman Butchers', but also perfect 'English-haters', who 'shew their pride in exalting themselves and depressing their Neighbours' (Kirke, 11). During his travels Kirke had however also kept a detailed topographical journal which Thoresby subsequently transcribed and which was later included as an appendix to Thoresby's own posthumously published diary and correspondence.

On 11 July 1678 Kirke had married Rosamund (1661–1688), daughter and coheir of Robert Abbott of Purston Jacklin, with whom he had two sons and two daughters. She died on 30 August 1688.

On 30 November 1693 Kirke was elected a fellow of the Royal Society and contributed an account of an orphaned lamb being successfully suckled by a castrated ram to the society's *Philosophical Transactions* the following year.

After Kirke's death on 24 April 1706 Thoresby claimed to have composed a memoir of Kirke for inclusion in his projected topography of Leeds. Although Thoresby's work was never completed, there survives an anonymous poetical dialogue between Kirke's ghost and his former Cambridge tutor, Gale, which includes a description of various curiosities contained in Kirke's antiquarian museum at Cookridge (BL, Add. MS 4459). The collection was, however, sold by auction in 1710, following the death of Kirke's surviving son, Thomas, the previous year.

CLARE JACKSON

Sources R. Thoresby, *Ducatus Leodiensis, or, The topography of … Leedes*, ed. T. D. Whitaker, 2nd edn (1816) · *The diary of Ralph Thoresby*, ed. J. Hunter, 2 vols. (1830) · [J. Hunter], ed., *Letters of eminent men, addressed to Ralph Thoresby*, 2 vols. (1832) · [T. Kirke], *A modern account of Scotland … written from thence by an English gentleman* (1679) · P. H. Brown, ed., *Tours in Scotland, 1677 and 1681* (1892) · T. Thomson, *History of the Royal Society from its institution to the end of the eighteenth century* (1812) · W. T. Lancaster, ed., *Letters addressed to Ralph Thoresby FRS*, Thoresby Society, 21 (1912) · T. Kirke, 'An account of a lamb suckled by a weather sheep', *PTRS*, 18 (1694), 263–4 · W. W. Rouse Ball and J. A. Venn, eds., *Admissions to Trinity College, Cambridge*, 2 (1913) · Venn, *Alum. Cant.* · 'A dialogue betwixt ye Ghost of Tho: Kirke de Cookridge esq. and Milo Gale, Rector de Keighley, D. July 8. 1706', BL, Add. MS 4459, fols. 45–8
Archives BL, letters to William Blathwayt, Add. MS 21486 · BL, Sloane MS 4036 · BL, corresp., Stowe MSS 748–749 · Yale U., Beinecke L., letters to William Blathwayt

Kirkes, William Senhouse (1823–1864), physician, was born in 1823 at Holker in north Lancashire. After education at Cartmel grammar school he was, at the age of thirteen, apprenticed to a partnership of surgeons in Lancaster, and from there went in 1841 to St Bartholomew's Hospital, London. He was distinguished in the medical school's examinations, and in 1846 graduated MD in Berlin. In 1855 he was elected a fellow of the Royal College of Physicians, and in 1856 delivered the Goulstonian lectures there. James Paget was then warden of the college of St Bartholomew's Hospital, and in 1848 he and Kirkes published a *Handbook of Physiology*, which soon became popular among students of medicine. Further editions by Kirkes appeared, and after his death there were further editions by William Morrant Baker and Vincent Dormer Harris.

In 1848 Kirkes was appointed demonstrator of morbid anatomy at St Bartholomew's Hospital, and in 1854 defeated John William Hue in a contest for the office of assistant physician. He became lecturer on botany and then on medicine, and in 1864, when George Burrows

resigned, he was elected physician to the hospital. He died at his house, 2 Lower Seymour Street, London, on 8 December 1864, of double pneumonia with pericarditis, after five days' illness. He left a widow, Caroline. His most original work was a paper in the *Medico-Chirurgical Transactions* (35, 1852, 281–324), 'On some of the principal effects resulting from the detachment of fibririous deposits from the interior of the heart, and their mixture with the circulating blood'—a classic description of embolism. After Kirkes's death friends and students at St Bartholomew's Hospital contributed to produce a gold medal awarded annually to the student with the best examination in the diagnosis and treatment of patients.

NORMAN MOORE, *rev.* RACHEL E. DAVIES

Sources *BMJ* (24 Dec 1864) · *GM*, 3rd ser., 18 (1865), 124 · H. H. Hussey, ed., 'W. S. Kirkes, 1823–1864, physician to St Bartholomew's Hospital', *Journal of the American Medical Association*, 211/12 (1970), 2010–11 [editorial] · Boase, *Mod. Eng. biog.* · Munk, *Roll* · *CGPLA Eng. & Wales* (1865)
Archives St Bartholomew's Hospital, London, MSS records
Wealth at death under £4000: probate, 13 Jan 1865, *CGPLA Eng. & Wales*

Kirkestede, Henry (*b. c.*1314, *d.* in or after 1378), prior of Bury St Edmunds and bibliographer, was known to early modern biographers as Bostonus Buriensis or John Boston of Bury. Kirkestede came from the Bury dependency of Kirstead ('Kirkestede' and 'Kerkestede' in Bury documents) in Norfolk, not from Kirkstead in Lincolnshire as was previously believed. He was ordained priest at Ely in 1338. If he was then twenty-four, the earliest age canonically permitted, he would have been born in 1314. Ordination normally took place seven years after the completion of the novitiate. Kirkestede would have entered the abbey at Bury as a novice monk between the ages of seventeen and twenty-one (*c.*1331–*c.*1335). His activities at Bury can be reconstructed from the numerous notes, some of them signed, that he wrote in Bury manuscripts.

Kirkestede's life can be divided roughly into two parts. The first was a relatively peaceful period between 1338 and 1361, in which should be situated his work as novice master and librarian as well as most of his written work relating to these occupations, the *Speculum* and the *Catalogus*. The second part, a turbulent period from 1361, when he became prior, until his death in or after 1378, was dominated by the effects on the abbey of the black death, which visited Bury in 1349, 1361, and 1368.

By 1346 Kirkestede was one of the abbot's chaplains, doubtless involved in defending the abbey against accusations of corruption by Bishop Bateman of Norwich. He was also one of the monks who served as novice master, to judge from his annotations in treatises concerning the novitiate, the education of monks, and the life and miracles of St Edmund. From an early date Kirkestede was responsible for the abbey's books, an occupation that he continued throughout his life. Bury's library had grown rapidly in the thirteenth century and amounted to approximately 1500 manuscripts by 1338. Kirkestede reorganized the library. He gave each codex an ex-libris, a pressmark (consisting of a letter of the alphabet for the author or subject and an arabic number), and a table of contents. He drew up an inventory of the books, the first since the late twelfth century. The inventory does not survive but there are contemporary references to it. He also rehoused the books, because of the destruction caused by the uprising of 1327.

Kirkestede became prior of Bury in 1361, after the deaths from plague of his predecessor Edmund Brundish and the abbot-elect Henry Hunstanton. He records that, in addition, eighteen monks died of plague in that year alone. He remained prior until some time before 1374. During his tenure he presided over the rebuilding of the great bell-tower which had collapsed in a storm in 1362. He was present at the visitation of the abbey *c.*1368 by Thomas de la Mare, abbot of St Albans, to inquire into the murder of a monk. Despite his administrative burdens and the difficulties of the times, Kirkestede pursued his interests in the novices and the library. The latest datable note in his hand is an annotation at the death of Gregory XI in 1378.

Kirkestede probably wrote two works, both biobibliographies. He was evidently responsible for the enlargement of the *Speculum coenobitarum*, with its list of monastic writers and their works. This compilation represents the earliest known use of the Franciscan *Registrum*; it is presumably the treatise on the history of monks and monasticism attributed to Bostonus Buriensis by John Bale.

Kirkestede's main work, the *Catalogus scriptorum ecclesie*, compiled for the use of Bury novices, was a substantial bibliography of ecclesiastical writers and their works in the tradition of the patristic *De viris illustribus*. The catalogue was assembled from early medieval works of this type by Jerome, Gennadius, and Isidore, from Cassiodorus's *Institutes*, from Dominican lists of their writers, and from the mine of biobibliographic information in Vincent of Beauvais's *Speculum historiale*. Kirkestede supplied each author with a brief biographical notice and a list of their works. To the lists of titles he added the opening and closing words, most often taken from Bury manuscripts. In addition he absorbed virtually the whole of the early fourteenth-century English Franciscan location list of books known as the *Registrum Anglie de libris doctorum et auctorum veterum*, including its system of noting the location of copies of texts by means of arabic numerals which correspond to a numbered list of 189 libraries. He used a manuscript of the *Registrum* that is no longer extant. Kirkestede also visited a number of libraries in East Anglia, among them St John's and St Botulph's, Colchester, Ramsey, St Albans, St Benet of Hulme, Holy Trinity, Aldgate, Peterborough, Crowland, and Pipewell. For these and other houses and for Bury itself, the *Catalogus* provides a valuable record of their books. Drafts of the biobibliographic entries for Bede, Boethius, Cassian, Chrysostom, Petrus Tripolitanus, and Raoul de Flaix survive in his hand on the flyleaves of Bury manuscripts. Kirkestede's entries for many writers, Englishmen among them, preserve the earliest efforts to compile a list of what

that author wrote, forming the origin of a bibliographic tradition that descends to early modern times through Bale and Thomas Tanner. The *Catalogus* affords modern scholars a view of the legacy of ancient, patristic, and medieval Latin writing that was known in fourteenth-century East Anglia.

Bale acquired a copy of Kirkestede's manuscript of the *Catalogus* from a pensioned Bury monk soon after the dissolution of the abbey, and made extensive extracts from it for his *Scriptorum illustrium maioris Britanniae ... catalogus* (Basel, 1557, 1559). Bale created the identity of Bostonus Buriensis from references in the prologue and the colophon in this manuscript. Bale's manuscript passed through James Ussher and Thomas Gale to Tanner before it vanished. It was the source of Tanner's transcript, now CUL, Add. MS 3470. The entries pertaining to English authors were published in 1748 in the preface of Tanner's *Bibliotheca Britannico-Hibernica*. R. H. ROUSE

Sources R. H. Rouse, 'Bostonus Buriensis and the author of the *Catalogus scriptorum ecclesiae*', *Speculum*, 41 (1966), 471–99 · R. H. Rouse and others, eds., *Registrum Anglie de libris doctorum et auctorum veterum* (1991) · R. H. Rouse and M. A. Rouse, eds., *The Catalogus scriptorum ecclesiae of Henry of Kirkestede* [forthcoming] · Tanner, *Bibl. Brit.-Hib.* · R. Hunt, 'Tanner's Bibliotheca Britannico-Hibernica', *Bodleian Library Record*, 2 (1949), 249–58 · R. Sharpe, 'Reconstructing the medieval library of Bury St Edmunds: the lost catalogue of Henry of Kirkstead', *Bury St Edmunds: medieval art, architecture, archaeology and economy*, ed. A. Gransden (1998), 204–18 · A. Gransden, 'Some manuscripts from Bury St Edmunds Abbey: exhibition catalogue', *Bury St Edmunds: medieval art, architecture, archaeology and economy*, ed. A. Gransden (1998), 228–85 · R. M. Thomson, *The archives of the abbey of Bury St Edmunds*, Suffolk RS, 21 (1980) · R. Thomson, 'Obedientaries of St Edmund's Abbey', *Proceedings of the Suffolk Institute of Archaeology and History*, 35 (1982), 91–103
Archives CUL, Add. MS 3470

Kirkham, Walter of (*d.* 1260), administrator and bishop of Durham, may have come from Kirkham in Yorkshire. It was perhaps as a protégé of Hubert de Burgh that he emerged early in 1224 as one of two accountants of the principal financial department of the royal household, the wardrobe. In August 1231, with de Burgh's star waning, he apparently left royal service, but he returned to office, and once more accounted for the wardrobe, between May 1234 and October 1236, at a time of important administrative reforms. His government career was supported by the normal accumulation of ecclesiastical benefices. In 1226 he was briefly dean of the royal free chapel of Penkridge, Staffordshire, moving on to that of St Mary's, Shrewsbury. In 1227 he became parson of Rudby, Yorkshire, and during the latter part of 1229 dean of St Martin's-le-Grand in London, another royal chapel, often bestowed on leading royal servants; the royal manor of Newport in Essex, where the church formed a major part of the dean's endowment, was granted to him for life shortly afterwards. By 1232 he held a canonry at York, to which was added a canonry at Lincoln in 1235, and another at Chichester within a year.

In 1244 Kirkham became dean of York. Then, following the resignation of Nicholas of Farnham he was elected bishop of Durham on 21 April 1249, despite Henry III's efforts on behalf of his own half-brother, Aymer de Valence (*d.* 1260). Temporalities were restored on 20 October, and Kirkham was consecrated in York by Archbishop Walter de Gray on 5 December. He connived with the prior of Durham in raising with the pope the generous provision that diverted almost a third of the bishopric's endowments to the support of Farnham throughout the eight years of his retirement; their application was unsuccessful. He confirmed Farnham's gifts to the Durham monks, and himself granted them a tract of wood and waste in the Pennine foothills at Muggleswick, with licence to enclose it. When the see of Carlisle fell vacant in 1254 he claimed the sequestration fruits arising during vacancies from churches in his diocese that belonged to the bishopric of Carlisle; he pursued the claim tenaciously and it was finally accepted shortly after his death, following a payment of 1000 marks by the bishop of Durham. An increasingly violent dispute with John de Balliol over knights' fees in the wapentake of Sadberge (co. Durham), in the course of which the bishop was ambushed and four of his servants taken prisoner, was probably ended by Kirkham's imposing on Balliol the penance of assigning money in perpetuity to support poor scholars at Oxford—the first steps towards the foundation of Balliol College. It is not known whether he issued any diocesan statutes; those formerly attributed to him are now believed to be those of Bishop Farnham.

Accounts differ as to whether it was Kirkham, or Peter d'Aigueblanche, bishop of Hereford, who was sent by the king to Rome in 1255 with a blank sealed schedule which was used to pledge the English church to Sienese merchants for 9000 marks. Kirkham was certainly appointed to commissions on affairs relating to Scotland, and took part in the major embassy sent in 1257 in response to problems arising during Alexander III's minority. He may have given tacit support to the provisions of Oxford in 1258, for in that year he quarrelled with the king and refused to come to court. Moreover it was in Kirkham's London palace that Simon de Montfort set up his household in 1258; here, on the riverside landing stage, took place the oft-quoted exchange between Montfort and Henry III, when the king admitted that his fear of thunder and lightning was outweighed by his fear of Simon. Kirkham died, full of days, at the episcopal manor of Howden in Yorkshire on 9 August 1260, and was buried in Durham Cathedral chapter house eight days later.   A. J. PIPER

Sources *Chancery records* · C. T. Clay, ed., *York Minster fasti*, 1, Yorkshire Archaeological Society, 123 (1958), 4–6 · Tout, *Admin. hist.*, vol. 1 · *Historiae Dunelmensis scriptores tres: Gaufridus de Coldingham, Robertus de Graystanes, et Willielmus de Chambre*, ed. J. Raine, SurtS, 9 (1839) · F. Barlow, ed., *Durham annals and documents of the thirteenth century*, SurtS, 155 (1945) · Paris, *Chron.* · J. Stevenson, ed., *Chronicon de Lanercost, 1201–1346*, Bannatyne Club, 65 (1839) · *Ann. mon.* · W. E. Lunt, *Financial relations of the papacy with England to 1327* (1939), 266–7 · [J. Raine], ed., *Wills and inventories*, 1, SurtS, 2 (1835), 11

Likenesses engraving, 1838 (after seal), repro. in R. Surtees, *The history and antiquities of the county palatinate of Durham*, 4 (1840) · seal (principal seal and *secretum* as bishop of Durham), repro. in

W. Greenwell, *Catalogue of the seals in the treasury of the dean and chapter of Durham*, ed. C. H. H. Blair (1911–21), pl. 49

Kirkhoven, Catherine. *See* Stanhope, Katherine, *suo jure* countess of Chesterfield, and Lady Stanhope (*bap.* 1609, *d.* 1667).

Kirkhoven, Charles Henry, Baron Wotton and earl of Bellamont (1643–1682/3). *See under* Stanhope, Katherine, *suo jure* countess of Chesterfield, and Lady Stanhope (*bap.* 1609, *d.* 1667).

Kirkland, Sarah. *See* Bembridge, Sarah (*c.*1794–1880).

Kirkland, Thomas (*bap.* 1722, *d.* 1798), physician, the son of Thomas Kirkland (*d.* 1751), attorney-at-law, and his second wife, Mary, daughter of Colonel Allsop, was born at Ashbourne, Derbyshire, and baptized there on 14 October 1722. He attended Ashbourne and Tamworth grammar schools and was apprenticed to Mr Holbrooke, a surgeon of Loughborough. After leaving Loughborough Kirkland travelled to London, where he attended the lectures of Thomas Lawrence, before returning to set up practice in Ashby-de-la-Zouch, Leicestershire, some time before 1747. He married Dorothy Palmer (*d.* 1785), daughter of a barrister-at-law, and his wife, Elizabeth (*née* Bate), on 3 August 1747. They had twelve children, six of whom died in infancy. In 1754 he published *A Treatise on the Gangrenes*.

On Friday 18 January 1760 Kirkland, who was treating a patient at nearby Coleorton, received a message asking him to attend at Staunton Harold Hall, the home of Laurence Shirley, fourth Earl Ferrers (1720–1760). Before arriving at the hall Kirkland was told that Lord Ferrers had shot and wounded James Johnson, his steward. Ferrers believed that Johnson had been conspiring against him in business matters, and after luring him to Staunton Harold Hall, shot Johnson, who was kneeling, from no more than 3 yards. Kirkland was aware that he was entering a potentially dangerous situation, as Ferrers was notorious for his violent behaviour and uncontrollable temper. He used violence towards both his mistress and his wife and was 'always carrying pistols to bed and threatening to kill her, and being jealous without provocation' (Crane, 7). Kirkland treated the injured Johnson in the presence of a clearly agitated and unstable Ferrers, and did all he could to calm Ferrers, who was still making threats against Johnson's life. Kirkland assured him that Johnson would live, in the hope that this would dissuade Ferrers from escaping and prevent him from causing any further bloodshed. Ferrers however warned him, 'Be sure Kirkland you don't tell me any lies, for by God, I shall break your head if you do' (Crane, 14). In a calmer interlude Ferrers offered to pay Kirkland for his services, an offer to which Kirkland wisely responded that he 'did not desire it but when it was most convenient for his Lordship' (Crane, 15). Later that evening Ferrers insisted that Kirkland should stay the night, and he offered Kirkland money if he would set the affair in a 'favourable light' (Crane, 14–15).

After Ferrers had gone to bed that night, Kirkland left

the hall, returning later with a group of seven or eight colliers, some of them armed, who collected the ailing Johnson and returned him to his home, where Kirkland stayed until 7 a.m. He then left to consult with a Mr Piddocke and a Mr Pestell, two local legal men, who advised that Ferrers should be arrested at once. John Johnson died at 9 a.m. Ferrers was arrested shortly afterwards, following a struggle with a group of local men, and was held at the White Hart public house in Ashby. 'I glory in his death' was his response after being told of Johnson's fate (Crane, 18).

Kirkland conducted the autopsy on Johnson's body before the inquest and

> found a wound made by a leaden bullet immediately under the lowest rib on his left side, which bullet passing obliquely downward had made another wound thro' the gut called Colon and going under the Psoas Muscle and thro' the Os Inominatium at its junction with the spine rested in the Os Sacrum, from which place I extracted it.   (Crane, 19)

Ferrers was found guilty of murder and hanged at Tyburn on 5 May 1760, his defence of 'occasional insanity of mind' having been rejected (Crane, 23). Kirkland later supplied a curious postscript to these events, which was published in the *Gentleman's Magazine* only after his death. On the day of Johnson's shooting Kirkland had a premonition in which he was in the House of Lords giving evidence in a murder trial; this, he said, caused him to be on his guard after receiving the message, later that day, which asked him to go to Staunton Harold Hall.

Kirkland led a less dramatic existence after these events. He published *An Essay on the Methods of Suppressing Haemorrhages from Divided Arteries* (1763), and *An Essay towards an Improvement in the Cure of those Diseases which are the Cause of Fevers* (1767). With the help of a testimonial from Erasmus Darwin, he was awarded an MD by St Andrews on 27 December 1769. He was a member of the Royal Medical societies of Edinburgh and London. Among his other publications were *A Treatise on Childbed Fevers with Two Dissertations, the one on the Brain, the other on the Sympathy of the Nerves* (1774), and *An Inquiry into the Present State of Medical Surgery* (2 vols., 1783–6).

Kirkland had a wide range of interests outside medicine; he took a keen interest in music, claiming to be the 'first Hoboy player in Ashby, and the worst in all England' (Crane, 54), subscribed to the foundation of an agricultural society for Leicestershire, and took pleasure from his garden, which he 'adorned with numerous statues and heathen deities' (Crane, 54). Kirkland died in Ashby-de-la-Zouch on 17 January 1798 and was buried on 22 January in St Helen's Church. He was survived by his sons and daughters.   MICHAEL BEVAN

Sources *GM*, 1st ser., 68 (1798), 88–9, 254 • P. J. Wallis and R. V. Wallis, *Eighteenth century medics*, 2nd edn (1988) • A. Crane, *The Kirkland papers, 1753–1869* (1990)
Likenesses J. R. Smith, mezzotint, 1794, BM; repro. in Crane, *Kirkland papers* • J. R. Smith, sketch, 1794, repro. in Crane, *Kirkland papers*

Kirkley, Sir (Howard) Leslie (1911–1989), charity director, was born on 13 March 1911 in Manchester, the youngest in the family of two sons and one daughter of Albert Kirkley,

a Manchester schoolmaster, and his wife, Elizabeth Winifred Harris. He matriculated from Manchester Central High School, qualified in Manchester's local government examinations, and became an associate of the Chartered Institute of Secretaries. His early career in local government stirred a growing interest in politics which was reinforced by his staunchly Liberal father and by visits to the Rhondda, which was then suffering from the depression. His consequent involvement with social welfare issues at home was matched by concern for peace abroad. An active organizer for the Peace Pledge Union, he registered as a conscientious objector with unconditional exemption. In 1940 Manchester council decided to sack registered conscientious objectors and Kirkley lost his job. It was a moment of truth which revealed his commitment, courage, and unyielding refusal to compromise on matters of principle.

A number of jobs followed before Kirkley's appointment in 1942 as regional secretary for the Fellowship of Reconciliation based in Leeds. Here he became a founder member and honorary secretary to the Leeds European relief committee, sending food to war-torn Greece and, following the war, clothing to Germany and Austria. After the war came his first direct and successful experience of running a business, for the Quaker painting and decorating firm of Harry Seel. A secure future seemed assured when, in 1951, recruited by Cecil Jackson-Cole, he moved to Oxford to become general secretary to the Oxford Committee for Famine Relief, one of whose founders was T. R. *Milford. Over the next twenty-four years he transformed this small local committee into a leading national and international organization.

The transformation began with the committee's involvement in disaster relief after the Greek earthquake in 1953. There followed help to refugees: victims of the Korean war, the Chinese civil war, the Hungarian uprising, and the Algerian war, and displaced Palestinians. Kirkley's personal visits to disaster areas, and the committee's high-profile role, together with the pioneering use of professional fund-raising methods, achieved rapid growth. As chairman of the World Refugee Year's public relations and publicity committee, Kirkley visited Congo (1961), and the huge public response which the plight of the starving refugees invoked catapulted his organization—which in 1961 became Oxfam, with Kirkley as its first director—into the role of a major medium for prompt disaster relief.

The 1960s saw Oxfam move into long-term development work with a network of field staff. Kirkley played a key role within the freedom from hunger campaign (1960–65) and consequently became interested in the causes of poverty. He began to campaign for a new interpretation of charity to include the examination of the causes of hunger and poverty as well as their relief. This soon brought complaints from the Charity Commission. Kirkley doggedly stood firm and successfully moved the frontier forward with his skilful and non-confrontational approach. His leadership also achieved a growing network of Oxfam shops, establishment of Oxfam Trading, encouragement of independent Oxfams overseas, provision of development education for schools, and establishment of the World Development Movement to campaign on issues which charity law prevented Oxfam from pursuing. Kirkley had succeeded handsomely in his aim 'to professionalize the whole business of charity without losing its soul in the process'. When he left Oxfam in 1974 it was a high-profile and flourishing organization of international renown and in the United Kingdom the antiquated concept of charity had been challenged.

Departure from Oxfam did not mean retirement. A further decade of involvement with voluntary and public organizations was to follow: as a member of the Board of Crown Agents (1974–80), chairman of the standing conference on refugees and the British Refugee Council (1974–81), chairman of the disasters' emergency committee (1977–81), and chief executive of the Voluntary and Christian Service Trust, the parent body of Help the Aged and Action Aid (1979–84). Here Kirkley's organizational talents provided a cost-effective management structure which enabled Help the Aged to become a mainstream charity and to encourage an international network of similar indigenous organizations: Help the Aged International.

Colleagues from all stages of his working life remembered Kirkley for his particular blend of warmth, optimism, energy, obstinacy, grit, and practical business sense. His efficient administrative skills were self-evident, but he was never a bureaucrat, disliking committees and preferring to work through personal contact. His were political skills. His management strengths lay in his ability to pick people of talent and commitment and motivate them to give of their best, allowing them freedom to operate creatively while, with his quiet style of leadership, he retained ultimate control.

Kirkley became a knight commander of the order of St Sylvester in 1963, and in 1974 was given the Victor Gollancz humanity award. He was appointed CBE in 1966 and knighted in 1977. Honorary MAs came from the universities of Oxford (1969), Leeds (1970), and Bradford (1974), and an honorary fellowship from Manchester Polytechnic (1971). He was also head shepherd of the Greek village of Livaderon.

Stocky in build, informal in dress and manner, with straightforward northern bluntness and a quizzical smile, Kirkley was outwardly easy-going, with a Quaker preference for compromise over confrontation. But the relaxed manner masked a steely determination, and his courage and tenacity could appear as obstinacy to frustrated colleagues. He had been raised an Anglican but his pacifism during the war led him to join the Quakers, and the deep sense of service which motivated him sprang from his Christian socialist commitment.

A lover of music, theatre, and country walks, Kirkley drew rich pleasure from life. Devoted to his dogs and to his family—who had none the less to take their place—he was twice married, first in 1936 to Elsie May (d. 1956), daughter of John Rothwell, accountant, and second to (Constance Nina) Mary, daughter of Thomas Bannister-

Jones, clergyman. His family comprised three sons and two daughters, one daughter and one son being from the first marriage. Despite a serious heart attack in 1986 he continued to work for the things in which he believed. He died in the John Radcliffe Hospital, Oxford, on 9 January 1989.   FRANK JUDD, *rev.*

Sources *The Times* (10 Jan 1989) · *The Independent* (11 Jan 1989) · Oxfam, Oxford, archives · personal knowledge (1996) · private information (1996) · *CGPLA Eng. & Wales* (1989)
Archives Oxfam, Oxford, archives
Wealth at death under £70,000: probate, 1 Sept 1989, *CGPLA Eng. & Wales*

Kirkman [Kirckman, Kirchman], **Abraham** (1737–1794), harpsichord maker, was born on 2 June 1737 at Bischweiler, near Strasbourg, the second of numerous children born to his father, Abraham Kirchmann (1704–1792), of Bischweiler, and Suzanna Saucourt (formerly Omphalius). His paternal grandparents were Abraham Kirkman (1673–1754), of Bischweiler, and his second wife, Margaret Prevot (d. 1706). In the same year as his wife's death, that Abraham married Suzanna M. Burckhard, his third wife; their eldest child being the celebrated Jacob *Kirkman, founder of the Kirkman firm of harpsichord builders.

The young Abraham Kirkman had moved to London by 13 August 1758, when he married Charlotte Neubauer (d. 1798), second daughter of a London harpsichord maker, Frederic Neubauer, at St James's, Westminster. It may have been as early as 1771 that Jacob Kirkman took his nephew Abraham into partnership with him, for a harpsichord is noted in the workbooks of Thomas Green of Hertford (*fl.* 1718–1791), as belonging to Sir Abraham and Lady Hume, of Wormley, Bury, and signed 'Jacobus and Abraham Kirckman 1771 fecit'. The atypical use of the English word 'and' plus the singular verb 'fecit' must give rise to caution when considering the accuracy of Green's reportage. What is certain is that in 1772 several Kirkman harpsichords were signed by the partners 'Jacobus et Abraham Kirckman Londini Fecerunt 1772'. It seems that the harpsichord making business was highly successful, and both partners used their money wisely, particularly investing it in property. Unlike his uncle, Abraham appears not to have become a moneylender and, as Jacob grew older and more interested in his other financial activities, Abraham probably became the effective 'director' of the firm. By 1790 Jacob had retired to Greenwich, and Abraham most probably took his own son, Joseph, into the firm. A very few harpsichords are signed by Abraham and Joseph, the latest known being dated 1791.

By 1772 Abraham Kirkman had moved, with his family, into 18 Broad Street, Soho, where he was close to his uncle Jacob, who from 1750 had lived at no. 19, while his kinsman, the organist and composer Jacob *Kirkman (d. 1812?), lived at no. 20 from 1780. This row of typical London upper working-class houses still exists, though there has been much reparation of bomb damage caused in the Second World War.

Abraham Kirkman died in 1794 at one of his properties at Hammersmith, though probably because he owned a substantial house (called the White House) at Greenwich he was buried at St Alfege, Greenwich, like his uncle Jacob. The church registers record the event simply as '16 April 1794, Abraham Kirkman a Gent'.

The rise of piano making among all the London harpsichord makers in the last quarter of the eighteenth century saw harpsichord building in sharp decline; nevertheless, two harpsichords signed by Abraham's son Joseph dated 1798 and one dated 1800 still exist.

An examination of the 1792 will of Abraham Kirkman shows that at his death his wife was still alive. Three sons are mentioned: Jacob, Joseph, and George Frederick; and five daughters: Charlotte Susannah, who was married to William Wheatley, organist at Greenwich, Harriet, Frances, Ann, and Maria—the last four were under twenty-one at that date. He also owned a copyhold house at Hammersmith (presumably the house where he died), which had outhouses, buildings, a garden, and land near the River Thames. This is probably the building now called Kent House which still stands, and two more houses near to it. His Greenwich property in Crooms Hill (probably the White House) was leased to a Mrs Farr for £150 per annum. In addition there was a further house at Crooms Hill, a leasehold house in Upper Brook Street, another in Compton Street, two in Kennington, Vauxhall, one in King's Row, Grosvenor Street, and others in John Street, Tottenham Court Road, and Peter Street, and an estate in Carmarthen. Despite the amount of property owned by Abraham at his death, it was probably less than half that of his uncle Jacob.

Abraham's wife, Charlotte, died intestate in 1798 at Upper Berkeley Street. The administration of her goods, credits, and chattels was granted to her two sons, named as Joseph and Abraham, on 16 November 1798, by which time the effects were valued at less than £1000.

CHARLES MOULD

Sources C. Mould, 'The development of the English harpsichord with particular reference to the work of Kirkman', DPhil diss., U. Oxf., 1976 • D. H. Boalch, *Makers of the harpsichord and clavichord, 1440–1840*, ed. C. Mould, 3rd edn (1995) • IGI

Wealth at death approx. twelve properties: Mould, 'Development of the English harpsichord'

Kirkman, Francis (*b.* 1632, *d.* in or after 1680), bookseller and writer, was born on 23 August 1632, the eldest son of Francis Kirkman (1602–1661), a citizen of London and member of the Blacksmiths' Company, and his wife, Ellen. Many details of his biography are drawn from his *The Unlucky Citizen* (1673), a picaresque tale that has been taken as autobiographical. Kirkman was inflamed from an early age with dreams of adventure, which were indirectly fulfilled by his career in the book trade. He had little interest in school, but began collecting chivalric romances and taught himself French in order to translate the sixth book of *Amadis de Gaul*. His parents forbade his seeking his fortune abroad or training as a bookseller; apprenticed to a scrivener, he ran away. His next master, a disreputable scrivener, allowed Kirkman to furnish the office with his impressive-looking library of romances. In 1652, while still an apprentice, he sacrificed most of his library

to finance the publication of his schoolboy translation of *Amadis*. Also in 1652 he published *The Loves and Adventures of Clerio & Lozia*, claiming it too as a translation from French. In 1653 Kirkman set up a tiny shop near the Tower, practising the trades of scrivener and bookseller, and became a freeman of the Blacksmiths' (he was never a member of the Stationers' Company). In May 1654 he presented Ann Phillips with an inscribed copy of his *Amadis* (Bodl. Oxf., Vet.A.3.e.559). They were married in June 1654 in St Olave, Hart Street, where their daughter, Elizabeth, was baptized in May 1655. On his father's death in 1661 Kirkman quickly squandered a sizeable inheritance.

Although a poor manager of money, Kirkman applied sound entrepreneurial instincts to meeting new demands for leisure reading. By the later 1650s he had become a theatre lover, and soon after the Restoration, he fell into reissuing pre-interregnum plays with Henry Marsh, Nathaniel Brook, and Thomas Johnson. The collaborators were accused of piracy, probably for their edition of Fletcher's *Scornfull Lady*. Kirkman later charged that Marsh swindled him extensively, but he took over Marsh's business on his death from the plague in 1666. Kirkman republished Marsh's 1662 *The Wits, or, Sport upon Sport* in 1672, and published a second part in 1673, preserving more of the drolls and farces performed clandestinely during the interregnum. By the end of his career Kirkman had published some twenty-five plays, including his own satire *The Presbyterian Lash* (1661), a satire on the presbyterian clergyman Zachary Clofton who was accused of whipping his maidservant, a number of republished titles, and a few plays previously extant only in manuscript, including Webster and Rowley's *Cure for a Cuckold* (1661) and *The Thracian Wonder* (1661). His most significant accomplishment, however, was his authoritative collection of English printed drama. The preface to *Tom Tyler and his Wife* (1661) listed Kirkman's collection of 690 plays, including almost every English play published to date, all available at his shop for sale or reading 'for a reasonable consideration'. Ten years later, a preface to Danter's translation of Corneille's *Nicomède* catalogued 806 plays. Kirkman's catalogue (incorporating the research of previous booksellers) was expanded by Gerard Langbaine the younger into the formative document of English dramatic bibliography.

Less widely recognized is Kirkman's similar influence on the canon of English prose romance: his preface to *The Famous and Delectable History of Don Bellianis of Greece* (1673, a loosely translated chivalric romance) surveys the available chivalric, Elizabethan, and heroic romances, its recommendations perhaps sustaining these titles' long popular success. Kirkman himself wrote fictional works in nearly every subgenre of the period. The two works published in 1652 span chivalric and heroic tastes in romance; *The Unlucky Citizen* exemplifies picaresque autobiography (and details abuses in the book trade). Kirkman's repeated publication of *The English Rogue* made a valuable commodity of that sprawling, bawdy tale. In 1666 he reissued and expanded the first part (first published in 1665) by Richard Head; he published a second part (probably of his own writing) in 1668, and third and fourth parts (claiming Head as co-author) in 1671. Kirkman also wrote what is arguably the best-developed of the fictionalized autobiographies of the famous impostor Mary Carleton, *The Counterfeit Lady Unveiled* (1673).

Despite recurrent financial difficulties, Kirkman had a long career in the book trade, keeping shops bearing (from 1661) the sign of John Fletcher's Head in various locations including Thames Street, Fenchurch Street, and St Paul's Churchyard. His last imprint is dated 1680.

L. H. NEWCOMB

Sources R. C. Bald, 'Francis Kirkman, bookseller and author', *Modern Philology*, 41 (1943–4), 17–32 · S. Gibson, *Bibliography of Francis Kirkman*, Oxford Bibliographical Society Publications, new ser., 1/2 (1947) [imprint 1949] · *DNB* · H. R. Plomer and others, *A dictionary of the printers and booksellers who were at work in England, Scotland, and Ireland from 1668 to 1725* (1922) · F. Kirkman, *The unlucky citizen* (1673) · P. Salzman, *English prose fiction, 1558–1700: a critical history* (1985) · E. Bernbaum, *The Mary Carleton narratives, 1663–1673* (1914) · J. J. Elson, ed., 'Introduction', *The wits, or, Sport upon sport* (1932) · W. W. Greg, 'Essay introductory', *A list of masques, pageants, &c., supplementary to a list of English plays* (1902), i–xxi · C. F. Main, 'The German princess, or, Mary Carleton in fact and fiction', *Harvard Library Bulletin*, 10 (1956), 166–85 · [F. Kirkman], *The counterfeit lady unveiled*, ed. S. Peterson (1961) · P. Salzman, 'Alterations to *The English rogue*', *The Library*, 6th ser., 4 (1982), 49–56 · A. Johns, *The nature of the book: print and knowledge in the making* (1998)

Likenesses line engraving, BM; repro. in Kirkman, *Unlucky citizen*

Kirkman [Kirckman, Kirchmann], **Jacob** (1710–1792), harpsichord maker, was born on 4 March 1710 at Bischweiler (or Bischwiller), near Strasbourg, the first of seven children of Abraham Kirchmann (1673–1754) of Bischweiler and his wife, Suzanna M. Burckhard (whom he had married in 1706). Jacob, though born in Alsace, could also claim Swiss ancestry, for his great-grandfather Conrad lived at Burgdorf, in the canton of Bern. The archives of Bischweiler describe Jacob as *ébeniste* ('cabinet-maker').

At some point in the early 1730s Kirkman moved to London to work for Hermann Tabel,

> a Fleming, who had learned his business [of harpsichord making] in the house of the successor of Ruckers at Antwerp, [and] was, it is believed, the first person who made Harpsichords in London, where he resided between 1680 and 1720. (J. S. Broadwood, ed., *Some Notes Made … in 1838 with Observations and Elucidations by H. F. Broadwood*, 1862)

Little of substance is known about Tabel, but the often quoted remarks above now seem to have gained universal acceptance. Certainly his one surviving harpsichord, a two-manual instrument signed and dated 1721, shows much affinity with the instruments from the Ruckers' workshops. Thus, it is not surprising that the young Kirkman learned to emulate his master's instruments and eventually, when free of his apprenticeship, probably on Tabel's death, built harpsichords which were very similar to the 1721 Tabel, with many of the characteristics of the Flemish school, whose instruments were prized throughout Europe and beyond.

Tabel was married to Susanna (*née* Virgoe), and Charles Burney, writing in Rees's *Cyclopaedia*, relates that:

> Kirchmann worked with the celebrated Tabel as his foreman and finisher till the time of his death [in 1738]. Soon after

which … Kirchmann married his master's widow, by which prudent measure he became possessed of all Tabel's seasoned wood, tools and stock in trade.

Certainly there is no doubt that Kirkman benefited considerably by his marriage to Susanna Tabel, for the *Daily Gazetteer* of 8 May 1739 carried the following advertisement:

> Whereas Mr. Hermann Tabel late of Swallow Street, the famous Harpsichord maker, dead, hath left several fine Harpsichords to be disposed of by Mr. Kirkman, his late Foreman; this is to acquaint the Curious, that the said Harpsichords, which are the finest he ever made, are to be seen at the said Mr. Kirckmann's the corner of Pulteney Court in Cambridge Street, over against Silver Street, near Golden Square.

Susanna, however, was dead by 1740 at the latest, and Kirkman never remarried. Exactly when he started to build instruments of his own is not clear, for though the firm of Kirkman & Sons dated their foundation from 1730 (advertisement in the *Daily Graphic*, 31 July 1893, and in the first issue of the *Evening News*, 26 July 1881), the earliest surviving signed and dated Kirkman harpsichord is a two-manual instrument with the inscription 'Jacobus Kirkman Londini fecit 1744'.

The spelling of Kirkman's name has caused some confusion. It can be seen from the above quotations that the German form Kirchmann was adopted by Burney and others, while the more Anglicized Kirkman is first found when Jacob's signature appears in Tabel's will, to which he was a witness in 1738. This form continued to be used on the nameboards of the harpsichords made throughout his life, though from at least 1755 (when he was naturalized) he customarily signed his name Kirkman in legal documents, several of which still survive.

By the end of 1739, probably on the death of Susanna, Kirkman had moved to new premises at 17 Great Pulteney Street, in close proximity to his rival Burkat Shudi, but by 1750 he was established at 19 Broad Street in a house which, despite some damage in the Second World War, was still standing at the close of the twentieth century in substantially its original form. In due course other members of the family came to live in the range of houses. Abraham *Kirkman, Jacob's nephew, was at no. 18 from 1772, when Jacob, having no children, took him into partnership, while Abraham's brother, Jacob *Kirkman, the organist and composer, occupied no. 20 in 1780.

Kirkman, like his rival Shudi, made a number of standard instruments, of which the simplest is a single-manual harpsichord with two 8 foot registers, while a more versatile single had two 8 foot and one 4 foot. Two-manual instruments include a dogleg 8 foot register available from both manuals, a second 8 foot and a 4 foot on the lower manual, and an 8 foot lute stop on the upper manual. The surviving instruments are without exception in heavy oak cases with veneered and cross-banded external decoration. There is similar decoration in the keywell, though several with richly marquetried keywells in a variety of woods survive. These instruments are signed 'Jacobus Kirckman fecit Londini [date]' until 1760 when the form is 'Jacobus Kirckman Londini fecit [date]'. Then in 1772, when Abraham joined his uncle, the signature becomes 'Jacobus et Abraham Kirckman Londini fecerunt [date]'. It seems that from 1789 Jacob ceased to take much active part in the business, for the instruments are then signed jointly by Abraham and his son Joseph, Jacob having retired to his house at Greenwich, probably the one now named Park Hall, at the top of Crooms Hill. Like several other harpsichord makers, he became very wealthy, partly from harpsichord making, but more from wise investment in property, and also moneylending.

Kirkman died in May 1792 and, despite his request to be interred in the German church in the Savoy, was buried in the church of St Alfege, Greenwich on 9 June, being described in the registers simply as 'Jacob Kirkman a Gent'. CHARLES MOULD

Sources D. H. Boalch, *Makers of the harpsichord and clavichord, 1440–1840*, ed. C. Mould, 3rd edn (1995) · C. Mould, 'The development of the English harpsichord with particular reference to the work of Kirkman', DPhil diss., U. Oxf., 1976
Likenesses attrib. L. F. Abbott, oils, *c.*1775–1800 (of Kirkman?), repro. in Mould, 'The development of the English harpsichord', 290
Wealth at death £200,000, probaby an overest.: Dr Charles Burney, Rees's *Cyclopaedia* · seventeen properties; was owed annuities and money: Mould, 'Development of the English harpsichord', 181–2

Kirkman, Jacob (*d.* 1812?), composer, was a nephew of the Jacob *Kirkman who had a harpsichord-making business in Broad Street, Golden Square, London, about 1770. The family was of Alsatian origin. The younger Kirkman built up a reputation in London before the end of the eighteenth century as a pianist and composer of works for the piano. He may have been the Jacob Kirkman who was organist of St George's Church, Hanover Square, and he may also have been the Jacob Kirkman who died in Upper Guilford Street on 29 April 1812, at the age of sixty-seven.

Kirkman's published works included piano duets, sonatas for harpsichord and violin, eight ballads dedicated to the marchioness of Salisbury, and a collection of six voluntaries for the organ, harpsichord, or piano. With John Keeble he published *Forty Interludes to be Played between the Verses of the Psalms*.

R. H. LEGGE, rev. ANNE PIMLOTT BAKER

Sources *New Grove* · [J. S. Sainsbury], ed., *A dictionary of musicians*, 2 vols. (1824) · *GM*, 1st ser., 82/1 (1812), 596

Kirkman, James Spedding (1906–1989), archaeologist, was born at 91 Thurlestone Road, West Norwood, south London, on 22 December 1906, the son of Benjamin Spedding Francis Henry Kirkman and his wife, Ada Eleanor Hope (*née* Wright). His father was described as a colonial broker; subsequently he took up rubber planting in Ceylon. The son's upbringing was, nevertheless, mainly in England; he was educated at Clifton College and Cambridge (Gonville and Caius College, 1925–8), where he read history (part one) and English, gaining respectable but not distinguished grades. He followed, at first, close to his father's steps in the Far East, as administrative officer in British North Borneo (1929–32) and tea planter in Ceylon.

But Kirkman yearned for a more creative career and to develop his enthusiasm for history. Accordingly, on returning to England in 1934–5, he volunteered on archaeological excavations, notably the celebrated campaign of Mortimer Wheeler at the Iron Age hill fort of Maiden Castle. With the experience thus gained, he assisted C. A. Ralegh Radford at Castle Dore in Cornwall in 1937 and J. Leslie Starkey on the British Museum's excavations at Lachish in Palestine. He was developing a personal interest in late Roman archaeology, only to be interrupted by the Second World War and his being commissioned in the Royal Air Force. He served as a rear gunner, but, because of his knowledge of Arabic, was soon posted to the Middle East command (with assignments as far as Iraq). In Cairo he met and married on 9 April 1942 Dorothy Constance (*b.* 1901/2), the daughter of John Frederick Layton; she was a secretary with general headquarters Middle East.

After the war Kirkman worked with the Iraqi embassy in London and the Arabic service of the BBC. But he was looking for an opportunity in archaeology, and in 1948 he was recommended to Dr Louis S. B. Leakey in east Africa for the wardenship of Gedi Royal National Park on the Kenya coast. Gedi, being a complex of medieval stone ruins, one of the so-called 'Arab' settlements on the Swahili coast, lay outside Leakey's own Stone Age interest; it required an archaeologist competent to record and conserve the site, which was densely overgrown at that time. Kirkman's appointment set a precedent in the region because, despite some official concern for historic monuments, there had been no professional archaeologists in the colonial services of eastern Africa, except for rare museum curatorships. He exceeded expectations with his systematic recording and excavating, not only at Gedi but along the whole of the Kenya coast. As his expertise in the subject increased in the 1950s, his services were sought by neighbouring governments to probe the ruins of the trading town of Kilwa on the Tanganyikan coast and others on Pemba and Zanzibar islands.

James Kirkman was thus the pioneer of Swahili archaeology, as one would now define it—although, being cautious by inclination, he did not call it that. In keeping with the received wisdom of the colonial period, he saw the medieval stone towns of the coast as the work of Arab immigrants and traders (in ivory and other products), and regarded these ruins as more relevant to the history and culture of the Indian Ocean than to that of Africa. By this view, the indigenous population of the African coast, the Swahili, played a subservient role as labourers, porters, and slaves. Later, in the changing intellectual climate following the independence of east African countries and the new lines of research which that generated, this conservative historical outlook was increasingly questioned. But that did not diminish Kirkman's achievement in opening up virtually single-handedly the archaeological dimension to Swahili culture and history, and in setting out the cultural, architectural, and chronological evidence which subsequent scholars could use and, if need be, reinterpret.

Kirkman's contributions included special studies of ruined mosques and their coral architecture as well as of the styles of Islamic tombs, using the evolution of these alongside imported ceramics, from Arabia and the Persian Gulf and also China, to date the sites and their successive stages of occupation. The Gedi excavations were published in two hardback volumes, *The Arab City of Gedi: Excavations at the Great Mosque* (1954) and *Gedi: the Palace* (1963), as well as a pamphlet of the Royal Anthropological Institute (1960); another book reported his excavations at Ungwana (1966). Other sites and surveys were covered by a series of articles in several journals, notably *Ars Orientalis*, *Antiquaries Journal*, and *Tanganyika Notes and Records*. He also wrote a more general and popular account, *Men and Monuments on the East African Coast* (1964), which was noted for its individual, if not idiosyncratic, manner of historical and archaeological presentation, as well as its penchant for unexpected asides and opinions.

Although he maintained contact with colleagues in Britain and elsewhere, through constant correspondence and the occasional lecture at the Society of Antiquaries when on leave, James Kirkman worked in virtual academic isolation in Kenya. His archaeological fieldwork was noted for its integrity and meticulous factual reporting, barely influenced by changing fashions or novel theories. Until 1957, when Neville Chittick was appointed government archaeologist in neighbouring Tanganyika and began investigating Kilwa and other coastal sites, there was no one qualified to discuss Kirkman's findings or conclusions (especially since the archaeology of the interior was dominated by Leakey and Stone Age research, and interest in the African Iron Age and the history of the existing populations had barely begun). Chittick quickly realized that Kirkman was too modest in his conclusions, and that his dating of coastal sites, their buildings and levels, could be pushed back a century or more. Moreover, by concentrating on masonry remains and relying on identifiable imports, Kirkman had failed to appreciate the length of occupation of many of the harbour and seaside settlements. As Chittick demonstrated at Kilwa and other sites in the 1960s, and Mark Horton at Shanga and on Pemba and Zanzibar in the 1980s, this Swahili civilization, which Kirkman imagined as flourishing from the twelfth to the sixteenth centuries, stretches back in fact to the early Islamic era, to the ninth if not eighth century.

The other, and more spectacular, achievement of James Kirkman was the restoration of Fort Jesus, the Portuguese fortress built in Mombasa in the 1590s to control the town, its harbour, and the shipping of the region. Over the next 300 years this massive fort experienced a colourful history of siege, capture, massacre, and bombardment, and was eventually turned into a prison in the British colonial period. In 1958 it was declared a historical monument and, through Kirkman's initiative and the financial support of the Calouste Gulbenkian Foundation in Lisbon, work began on restoration, archaeological investigation, and a museum display. As a result, Fort Jesus became the most visited historical site in the whole of east Africa; it is in a real sense a monument to James Kirkman's years of devoted service on the coast of Kenya. His research on the fort was published in 1974 by Oxford University Press as *Fort Jesus* (Memoir 4 of the British Institute in Eastern Africa).

In 1972 Kirkman retired to Cambridge. He then served until his death on the council of the British Institute in Eastern Africa, an organization devoted to historical and archaeological research whose foundation in 1960 he had helped encourage. At Mombasa he had become expert in the history of ships and of naval guns, and the evidence obtainable from wrecks. Appropriately he lent his services to the *International Journal of Nautical and Underwater Archaeology* as assistant editor from 1975 and as editor from 1982. Furthermore, he helped to prepare a short pictorial volume to accompany an exhibition at the Museum of Mankind on the city of San'aʾ in Yemen (as part of the World of Islam Festival in London in 1976). He was noted for his humorous story-telling—all the more effective because of his combination of elegant diction with a distinctive stutter—especially when guiding visitors around Fort Jesus or other historical monuments.

Kirkman was a fellow of the Society of Antiquaries of London (elected 1957) and, in recognition of his achievements, received the Portuguese honour of officer of the order of Dom Henrique in 1960, and was appointed OBE in 1967. He died in Addenbrooke's Hospital, Cambridge, on 26 April 1989, and was buried at Fen Ditton cemetery, Cambridge; he was survived by his wife and their one son.   J. E. G. SUTTON

Sources *The Times* (3 May 1989) · *The Guardian* (9 May 1989) · *The Independent* (9 May 1989) · *Antiquaries Journal*, 70 (1990), 522 · *Azania* [journal of the British Institute in Eastern Africa], 25 (1990), 106–8 · *International Journal of Nautical Archaeology*, 18 (1989), 189–90 · E. B. Martin, *Kenya Past and Present* [Kenya Museum Society], 2/1 (1973), 40–41 · *Paideuma* [Frobenius-Institut, Frankfurt am Main], 28 (1982) [James Kirkman issue, inc. contributions of J. de V. Allen and T. H. Wilson, and bibliography] · Gon. & Caius Cam. · b. cert. · m. cert. · d. cert. · personal knowledge (2004)
Archives Fort Jesus Museum, Mombasa, archaeological field notes · priv. coll., collection of colour photograph transparencies
Likenesses photograph, c.1970, Fort Jesus Museum, Mombasa · photograph, c.1981, repro. in *Paideuma*
Wealth at death £50,256: probate, 27 July 1989, *CGPLA Eng. & Wales*

Kirkman, Sir Sidney Chevalier (1895–1982), army officer, was born on 29 July 1895 at Bedford, the elder son (there were no daughters) of John Parke Kirkman, schoolmaster, of Bedford, and his wife, Eva Anchoretta, daughter of Captain Henry Whyte of the 14th Madras native infantry. Kirkman was educated at Bedford School, where he was a boarder in his father's house (Glanyrafon). After attending the Royal Military Academy, Woolwich, he was commissioned in the Royal Artillery (RA) in February 1915, and served on the western front and in Italy during the First World War. He was wounded twice, at Loos and when commanding his battery near Cambrai. He was twice mentioned in dispatches and awarded the MC in 1918.

Between the wars he served, at staff and regimental duty, in Egypt, Palestine, Malta, and India and attended the Staff College at Camberley in 1931–2. In 1932 he married Amy Caroline, second daughter of the Revd Charles Erskine Clarke, vicar of Reigate; they had two sons. A skilled horseman, Kirkman excelled at polo, but as a serious professional soldier he chafed at the virtual standstill in promotion of those years. The Second World War introduced a dramatic change of tempo and from being a major with twenty-four years' service he was to reach full general's rank in eight years.

Kirkman returned home from India in 1940 to command the 65th medium regiment RA (TA) and within six months was appointed commander RA (brigadier, 1941) of the 56th division. At an artillery exercise soon after this he was asked by his corps commander, General B. L. Montgomery, what he thought of the latter's summing-up speech. His forthright reply was that the general had omitted two most important lessons; this was to prove the start of a long and close association between the two men, so that Montgomery described Kirkman in his memoirs as the best artilleryman in the British army. Within eighteen months Kirkman was successively appointed Montgomery's artillery commander in 12th corps, south eastern command, and Eighth Army in the western desert.

At El Alamein and throughout the subsequent advance Kirkman displayed the techniques of artillery employment and fire planning in which he so fervently believed. He continued these methods as brigadier (1942) RA, Eighteenth Army group in Tunisia, but with the ending of the north African campaign he was promoted to command the 50th Northumbrian division in time to prepare it for the invasion of Sicily. His insistence on thorough training, as much as his own calm but forceful leadership, was reflected in the division's impressive performance throughout the island campaign, particularly at the hard-fought battle of Primasole Bridge. After Sicily the 50th division returned to England to prepare for the Normandy landings, but in January 1944 Kirkman returned to Italy to command 13th corps.

In the ensuing year he played a leading part in the offensive led by Sir H. R. L. G. Alexander which finally broke the Cassino line and carried the allied armies into the mountains south of Bologna. It was in these rocky heights that during the last winter of the war he spent the most demanding months of his whole career, serving under the American General Mark Clark; to him, high-minded, courteous, and imperturbable British officers like Kirkman were an enigma. In February 1945 Kirkman was invalided home, but he was soon appointed in swift succession to southern command and 1st corps in Germany. In September he went to the War Office as deputy chief of the Imperial General Staff and two years later, on promotion, to quartermaster-general. In both appointments he proved a wise and energetic member of the army council, as Emanuel Shinwell, the secretary of state, later testified.

On retirement in 1950 Kirkman was appointed special government representative to investigate British military expenditure in Germany and subsequently to look for economies in the home forces. In 1954 he was made director-general of civil defence, charged with creating a tenable basic doctrine and a functional organization to implement it. For six years he toured Britain, lecturing, and striving to animate national and local government

planning—a difficult task in the prevailing political climate.

He was appointed OBE (1941), CBE (1943), CB (1944), KBE (1945), KCB (1949), and GCB (1951). He became commander of the American Legion of Merit, was an officer of the Légion d'honneur and was awarded the Croix de Guerre. From 1947 to 1957 he was the RA colonel-commandant.

Kirkman, known as Kirkie, was a tall, handsome man, charming and amusing to his friends and considered a hard but fair taskmaster by those who worked with him. He had a clear, incisive mind, and as a practising Christian regarded integrity and honesty as paramount virtues. In his later years, despite worsening arthritis, he enjoyed the company of his grandchildren, his garden, and winter visits to southern France. Kirkman died at Southampton on 5 November 1982, shortly after his fiftieth wedding anniversary.   TOM DAVIS, *rev.*

Sources King's Lond., Liddell Hart C., S. C. Kirkman MSS · N. Hamilton and S. C. Kirkman, interview, IWM · *The Times* (6 Nov 1982) · *Gunner Magazine*, 146 (Jan 1983) · *Ousel* [Bedford School Magazine] (March 1983) · D. Graham and S. Bidwell, *Tug of war* (1986) · personal knowledge (1990) · private information (1990) · *CGPLA Eng. & Wales* (1983)

Archives King's Lond., Liddell Hart C., corresp., diaries, and reports

Wealth at death £277,774: probate, 10 Jan 1983, *CGPLA Eng. & Wales*

Kirkman, Thomas Penyngton (1806–1895), mathematician and philosopher, was born on 31 March 1806 in Bolton, Lancashire, the only son of John Kirkman (d. 1839), cotton dealer, and his wife, Elizabeth. Baptized Pennington, he adopted the spelling Penyngton in later life. He was educated at Bolton grammar school, where he was the best scholar in the school, but in spite of protestations by the headmaster was removed at the age of fourteen to work in his father's business. During his years in the cotton trade he studied the classics and taught himself French and German. At the age of twenty-three he broke away and enrolled as a student at Trinity College, Dublin, supporting himself financially by private tutoring. He studied the required subjects of philosophy, classics, mathematics, and science, and graduated BA in 1833.

After a year as private tutor to an Irish baronet Kirkman returned to England and took holy orders in 1835. Following curacies in Bury, Lancashire, and Lymm, Cheshire, he moved in 1839 to a curacy in Croft, near Warrington, and in 1845 became rector of the newly created parish of Croft-with-Southworth, where he remained for over fifty years. At the Croft rectory:

> with an expenditure of mental labour that only the finest of physical constitutions could have sustained, he devoted, practically, the whole of his time (for the parochial work was small) to the study of pure mathematics, the higher criticism of the Old Testament, and questions of first principles. (W. W. Kirkman, 238)

On 8 June 1841 he married Eliza Ann Wright of Runcorn, Cheshire, with whom he had seven children. To support his family he supplemented his parish income by private tutoring, later augmented by the income from some property inherited by his wife.

It is not known when Kirkman's interests in mathematics developed, but in 1844 he was inspired by a combinatorial prize question in the *Lady's and Gentleman's Diary*, set by the editor, the Revd William Woolhouse. This led to a pioneering paper in 1847 on the arrangements of objects into groups of three with each pair of objects appearing just once; such arrangements are now called 'Steiner triple systems', after the Swiss mathematician Jakob Steiner, even though Kirkman had priority and contributed much more than Steiner to the subject. In 1850 Kirkman presented the problem for which he is best remembered, the 'fifteen schoolgirls problem', of arranging fifteen young ladies in groups of three on each of seven days so that each young lady walks with every other one just once. He continued to write in this area for a further twelve years, and is now recognized as the founding father of design theory.

Kirkman's next area of mathematical interest was hypercomplex numbers, or 'pluquaternions', as he named them, following Sir William Rowan Hamilton's 1840s work on quaternions; Kirkman's election as a fellow of the Royal Society on 11 June 1857 arose partly from his studies in this area. About 1850 he also wrote on geometry—in particular, the sixty points of concurrence that arise from Pascal's six-points-on-a-hexagon theorem when the six points are permuted in all possible ways; this work did much to establish his reputation in British mathematical circles.

From 1853 Kirkman made pioneering contributions to the classification and enumeration of polyhedra (or 'polyedra', as he called them), and to the emerging theory of groups. Unfortunately his writings were couched in such obscure terminology that a substantial memoir on polyhedra was turned down by the Royal Society as being unreadable. Later, when the Paris Académie des Sciences proposed a *grand prix de mathématiques* for advances in these areas, Kirkman's entry for the 1860 groups prize was unsuccessful; in consequence he chose not to submit for the 1861 polyhedron prize. The resentments he felt against the Royal Society and the Paris Académie made him increasingly embittered, and his disillusionment spilled over into his relationships with leading mathematicians of the day. In spite of this he collaborated with Tait on the classification of knots with up to eleven crossings, and regularly contributed difficult mathematical questions to the *Educational Times* until he was well into his eighties.

Kirkman's contributions in other areas have barely survived. He wrote a book, *Philosophy without Assumptions* (1876), and became embroiled in theological controversies, such as his support for the rebel Bishop Colenso, who asserted that the early books of the Bible need not be taken literally. Kirkman also wrote pamphlets supporting free enquiry and free expression, but criticized the materialistic and evolutional philosophy espoused by such as Tyndall, Huxley, and Spencer. In his *Philosophy* he memorably paraphrased Spencer's description of evolution as 'a change from an indefinite, incoherent, homogeneity to a definite, coherent, heterogeneity; through continuous differentiations and integrations' (H. Spencer, *First Principles*, 1863, 216), as 'a change from a nohowish untalkaboutable all-likeness, to a somehowish and in-general-talkaboutable not-all-likeness, by continuous somethingelse-ifications and sticktogetherations' (T. P. Kirkman, 292).

Thomas Kirkman died at his home, Fernroyd, St Margaret's Road, Bowdon, near Altrincham, on 3 February 1895. In a letter he summarized his career: 'What I have done [is] not likely to be talked about intelligently by people so long as I live. But it is a faint pleasure to think it will one day win a little praise' (Macfarlane). His wife survived him by less than a fortnight.   ROBIN J. WILSON

Sources N. L. Biggs, 'T. P. Kirkman, mathematician', *Bulletin of the London Mathematical Society*, 13 (1981), 97–120 · S. Mills, 'Thomas Kirkman—the mathematical cleric of Croft', *Memoirs of the Literary and Philosophical Society of Manchester*, 120 (1977–80), 100–09 · A. Macfarlane, *Lectures on ten British mathematicians of the nineteenth century* (1916), 122–33 · H. Perfect, 'The Revd Thomas Penyngton Kirkman FRS, 1806–1895: schoolgirl parades—but much more!', *Mathematical Spectrum*, 28/1 (1955–6), 1–6 · *DSB* · W. W. Kirkman, 'Thomas Penyngton Kirkman', *Memoirs of the Literary and Philosophical Society of Manchester*, 4th ser., 9 (1895), 238–43 · T. P. Kirkman, *Philosophy without assumptions* (1876) · m. cert. · *CGPLA Eng. & Wales* (1895)

Archives CUL, letters to Sir George Stokes

Likenesses photograph, repro. in Macfarlane, *Lectures*

Wealth at death £10,983 9s. 1d.: probate, 20 April 1895, *CGPLA Eng. & Wales*

Kirkpatrick, **Sir Ivone Augustine** (1897–1964), diplomatist, was born on 3 February 1897 in Wellington, India, the elder son of Colonel Ivone Kirkpatrick (1860–1936) of the South Staffordshire regiment, and his wife, Mary (d. 1931), daughter of General Sir Arthur Edward *Hardinge, later commander-in-chief, Bombay army, and governor of Gibraltar. His father was a descendant of a Scottish family which settled in Ireland during the eighteenth century. His mother was former maid of honour to Queen Victoria, and her grandfather Henry Hardinge, first Viscount Hardinge of Lahore, served in the cabinets of Wellington and Peel, and was later governor-general of India in 1844–8. Her first cousin, Charles Hardinge, Baron Hardinge of Penshurst, was permanent under-secretary of the Foreign Office in 1906–10 and 1916–20, and viceroy of India in 1910–16.

A Roman Catholic, Kirkpatrick was educated at Downside School from 1907 to 1914. On the outbreak of the First World War he volunteered for active service and was commissioned in November 1914 in the Royal Inniskilling Fusiliers. Severely wounded in action against the Turks in August 1915, he was accepted by Balliol College, Oxford, in October, but chose to resume his war service early in 1916 when he was employed in propaganda and intelligence activities. During the last year of the war he was stationed in the Netherlands from where he ran a network of British agents operating in German-occupied territory.

In July 1919 Kirkpatrick entered the foreign service and was posted to Brazil for one year, returning to London in August 1920 to take up a post in the western department of the Foreign Office. In appearance and manner Kirkpatrick was small, dapper, and decisive. Possessed of an

Sir Ivone Augustine Kirkpatrick (1897–1964), by Walter Stoneman, 1948

incisive mind, he soon established a reputation as a quick thinker and rapid worker who took pride in officemanship. He was promoted second secretary in December 1920 and first secretary in October 1928. On 10 January 1929 he married Violet Caulfield, daughter of Colonel Reginald James Cope Cottell, army surgeon, of 7 Phillimore Terrace, London; they had one son, Ivone Peter (*b.* 1930), and one daughter, Cecilia Sybil (*b.* 1932).

During the 1930s his postings gave Kirkpatrick firsthand experience of dealing with the emerging European dictatorships: three years in Rome, from 1930 to 1933, were followed by a transfer to Berlin in August 1933 as head of Chancery, where he remained until December 1938. Through skilful cultivation of personal contacts and a dedication to duty, Kirkpatrick achieved a position of real stature and influence during this period. Indeed, these years proved the most formative part of his career, imbuing him with a deep loathing for totalitarian dictatorships of both the Nazi and communist variants. Remembered by his friend and contemporary Gladwyn Jebb (later Lord Gladwyn) as a 'very brave and forthright man' who was unafraid of 'speaking his mind to his own superiors' (Jebb, 269), his views frequently conflicted with those of Sir Nevile Henderson, ambassador to Germany from April 1937, who took a more sanguine view of Hitler's ambitions. Kirkpatrick's memoirs are notable for their equivocation about the Munich settlement of the Czech crisis of

1938, but he returned to London convinced of the necessity of resisting the Nazis; his contempt for the Chamberlain government's appeasement of Hitler's demands informed his judgement for the remainder of his career.

During the Second World War Kirkpatrick was once again employed in the propaganda and information work which he had so relished twenty-five years earlier. Appointed director of the foreign division of the Ministry of Information in April 1940, he became controller of the European services of the BBC in October 1941. Here he made a major contribution which included the task of interviewing Hitler's deputy, Rudolf Hess, following Hess's flight to Scotland in May 1941. In September 1944 Kirkpatrick was appointed to organize the British element of the Allied Control Commission for Germany, and following the end of the war he served at supreme allied headquarters as British political adviser to General Eisenhower until that organization's disbandment. By the time he returned to the Foreign Office he had become convinced not only that the USSR was aggressively expansionist, but that Britain's post-war difficulties overseas were being 'deliberately aggravated by a savage Soviet campaign of anti-British propaganda' and that Britain should make a reply 'by all means at our disposal' (Yasamee and Hamilton, 159, 206). Appointed assistant under-secretary responsible for information work in August 1945, Kirkpatrick was instrumental in the creation of the information policy machinery which served the Foreign Office during the cold war. Promoted deputy under-secretary in April 1948, he oversaw policy administration for western Europe and then in February 1949 became permanent under-secretary overseeing the German section of the Foreign Office, the former 'Control Office for Germany and Austria'. Both postings brought him into close contact with the foreign secretary, Ernest Bevin, for whom he had the greatest respect and affection.

Between June 1950 and November 1953 Kirkpatrick was British high commissioner in Germany and, as one of the three joint sovereigns of western Germany, carried immense responsibility particularly with respect to the negotiation of the Bonn conventions during 1951–2, which terminated the occupation regime and (in parallel) prepared the way for the rearmament of West Germany. During this period he established cordial relations with Chancellor Adenauer, although he was unable to cement the close relationship his predecessor General Sir Brian Robertson had enjoyed with the West German leader.

Kirkpatrick returned to London in November 1953 to succeed Sir William Strang as permanent under-secretary in the Foreign Office. It was to be his last post since he was due to retire on his sixtieth birthday in February 1957. During these years he served under three foreign secretaries, Eden, Macmillan, and Selwyn Lloyd, but the episode for which this period is remembered is the Suez crisis which occupied him for his final six months in office and, rightly or wrongly, did much to tarnish his reputation. Kirkpatrick's role in this episode, and in particular his unwavering support for the use of force to recover the Suez Canal, has been a subject of the severest criticism both by his contemporaries, who were dismayed by his connivance at the exclusion of the Foreign Office from the decision-making process during the crucial weeks in October and early November 1956, and by historians. Undoubtedly, his judgement was overly influenced by his experiences in Germany during the 1930s and in particular his contempt for any policy which could be described as appeasement, and he obliquely acknowledged as much in the few sentences he devoted to the Suez crisis in his memoirs (Kirkpatrick, 262–3). However, the indictment of him both for his views and for his loyalty to the prime minister may have been unduly harsh. Many shared his suspicion of Nasser's long-term intentions, and his respect for higher authority had been inculcated through an Edwardian education when a more rigorous observance of duty and deference to hierarchy pertained.

Nevertheless, it is difficult to escape the conclusion that Kirkpatrick was unsuited by temperament or training to fill this post during a period of rapid decline in British power. During his formative years Britain was a great power and he, along with many others, was slow to accept either the fact or the implications of its diminution. This in itself is unremarkable. However, the lack of a formal education after the age of seventeen may have reinforced his predisposition towards rigidity of thought: he had little time either for research and analysis or prolonged discussion. A quick thinker with an authoritative manner, his combative nature and perfunctory style of decision making would have precluded the process of reflection and detached judgement which are generally accepted as the diplomatist's province and are especially important during moments of international crisis.

After retiring from the Foreign Office in February 1957 Kirkpatrick served for five years as chairman of the Independent Television Authority. In addition to his memoirs he wrote *Mussolini: Study of a Demagogue* (published posthumously in 1964). He was appointed CMG in 1939, KCMG in 1948, KCB in 1951, GCMG in 1953, and GCB in 1956. He died at his home, Donacomper, Celbridge, co. Kildare, Ireland, on 25 May 1964. He was survived by his wife and two children.   ANN LANE

Sources I. Kirkpatrick, *The inner circle: memoirs of Ivone Kirkpatrick* (1959) · *DNB* · *The Times* (26 May 1964) · *WWW* · *FO List* (1956) · P. Gore-Booth, *With great truth and respect* (1974) · H. M. G. Jebb [Lord Gladwyn], *The memoirs of Lord Gladwyn* (1972) · E. Shuckburgh, *Descent to Suez: diaries, 1951–56*, ed. J. Charmley (1986) · H. J. Yasamee and K. A. Hamilton, eds., *Documents on British policy overseas*, 1st ser., 7: *United Nations: Iran, cold war and world organisation, 2 January 1946 – 13 January 1947* (1995) · Burke, *Peerage* · *CGPLA Eng. & Wales* (1964)
Archives IWM, papers relating to work in Germany | Bodl. Oxf., corresp. with Lord Monckton · PRO, Foreign Office MSS, FO371 and FO800
Likenesses W. Stoneman, photograph, 1948, NPG [*see illus.*] · photograph, repro. in Kirkpatrick, *Inner circle*
Wealth at death £21,500 effects in England: probate, 2 Dec 1964, *CGPLA Eng. & Wales*

Kirkpatrick, James (*c*.1676–1743), non-subscribing Presbyterian minister, was probably born in Scotland, and was the son of Hugh Kirkpatrick (*d*. 1712), who was minister successively at Lurgan, co. Armagh, at Dalry and at Old Cumnock in Scotland, and finally at Ballymoney, co. Antrim. He matriculated at Glasgow University on 10 February 1691, being described as *Scoto-Hibernus*. Fellow students at Glasgow included John Simson and John Abernethy. On returning to Ireland he was licensed by the presbytery of Route in 1697. In 1699 he received a call from the congregation at Antrim but did not take this up, instead accepting a call to Templepatrick, co. Antrim, where he was ordained on 7 August 1699. Although he did marry, the name of his wife has not been recorded. While at Templepatrick he published *A Sermon Occasioned by the King's Death* (1702) and in 1703 he was appointed one of the trustees for the distribution of *regium donum*.

On 24 September 1706 Kirkpatrick resigned his charge at Templepatrick and accepted a call to Belfast as colleague to John McBride. Here he became a powerful defender of Presbyterian rights and a leading exponent of non-subscription. McBride had fled to Scotland to avoid arrest because of his refusal to take the oath abjuring the claims to the throne of James II's son. The Belfast congregation was growing rapidly, and in June 1706 McBride had written from Stranraer that if there were 3000 members there should be two meeting-houses and two distinct congregations. This was agreed and after some complicated negotiations the synod approved on 1 June 1708 the division of the Belfast congregation, McBride becoming minister of the congregation meeting in the old meeting-house and Kirkpatrick becoming minister of the Second Congregation in their new meeting-house, which had been built immediately behind the first. In 1712 Kirkpatrick was appointed moderator of the synod of Ulster and in the following year he published one of his major works, *An Historical Essay upon the Loyalty of Presbyterians* (1713). This is a substantial work, thought to have been published by James Blow of Belfast, which was produced as a response to the attacks on the Presbyterians by William Tisdall, vicar of Belfast. It was designed to account for the conduct of dissenters in recent history and to demonstrate the loyalty of Presbyterians.

From 1705 Kirkpatrick had been an early and influential member of the Belfast Society, an association of ministers which met to discuss theology. In the same year the synod introduced compulsory subscription to the Westminster confession and the Belfast Society provided the leadership of the campaign against subscription. In 1721 Kirkpatrick published an able plea for non-subscription in *A Vindication of the Presbyterian Ministers in the North of Ireland*. As the subscription controversy grew more heated the subscribing minority in both the First and Second congregations left to form the Third Congregation. When they held their first communion in February 1724 they refused to admit Kirkpatrick and Samuel Haliday (McBride's successor at the first congregation), which led Kirkpatrick to go into print with *A Scripture Plea Against a Fatal Rupture and Breach of Christian Communion* (1724). Matters came to a head in 1725, when all the non-subscribers were placed in the presbytery of Antrim; in 1726 they were finally excluded from the synod.

In 1732 Kirkpatrick received the degrees of MD and DD

from Glasgow University. His later publications included not only theological works but a medical treatise, combining, as he did, the work of a physician with a pastoral office. His final work, *A Defence of Christian Liberty*, was published posthumously by James Blow in 1743. Kirkpatrick died in 1743, in Dublin, and was survived by his wife. The date and place of his burial are unknown.

A. D. G. STEERS

Sources [A. Gordon], 'Congregational memoirs: Templepatrick', *The Disciple*, 2 (1882), 170–75 • T. Witherow, *Historical and literary memorials of presbyterianism in Ireland, 1623–1731* (1879) • S. S. Millin, *History of the second congregation of protestant dissenters in Belfast … 1708–1896* (1900), 19–24 • *Records of the General Synod of Ulster, from 1691 to 1820*, 1 (1890) • C. Innes, ed., *Munimenta alme Universitatis Glasguensis / Records of the University of Glasgow from its foundation till 1727*, 3, Maitland Club, 72 (1854), 149 • W. I. Addison, *A roll of graduates of the University of Glasgow from 31st December 1727 to 31st December 1897* (1898), 314 • J. McConnell and others, eds., *Fasti of the Irish Presbyterian church, 1613–1840*, rev. S. G. McConnell, 2 vols. in 12 pts (1935–51) • *Fasti Scot.*, new edn, 3.25, 85; 7.531 • P. Brooke, *Ulster Presbyterianism* (1987) • J. S. Reid and W. D. Killen, *History of the Presbyterian church in Ireland*, new edn, 3 (1867) • J. Anderson, ed., *Catalogue of early Belfast printed books, 1694 to 1830*, new edn (1890) • R. F. G. Holmes, *Our Irish Presbyterian heritage* (1985) • *DNB*

Likenesses watercolour, First Presbyterian Church, Rosemary Street, Belfast; repro. in S. S. Millin, *History of the second congregation of protestant dissenters in Belfast* (1900)

Kirkpatrick [Kilpatrick], **James** (1696–1770), physician, was born in Carlow in Ireland. Few details of his life survive. As a young man he sailed to America and practised in Charlestown, South Carolina. In 1739 he was involved in a dispute with a fellow practitioner, Dr Thomas Dale, regarding the treatment of inoculated patients. By the early 1740s Kirkpatrick had travelled back to Britain with his sons and settled in London. About this time he began to style himself MD.

Kirkpatrick was a respected authority on inoculation— the practice of deliberately infecting a susceptible person with smallpox in the hope of inducing a mild case and thus immunity to further attack—a procedure introduced to Britain in 1722 and to America shortly thereafter. Kirkpatrick's *Essay on Inoculation* (1753) discussed the principles of the practice, speculated as to why inoculated smallpox was less dangerous than the natural disease, and considered the best times and ages at which to inoculate. It concluded with case histories of deaths attributed to inoculation, drawn from his experience in Charlestown. His *Analysis of Inoculation*, published the following year, was effectively a textbook of the practice and was widely cited. Kirkpatrick offered no new insights into the procedure. His practice was based on the commonly held belief that during smallpox some specific material separated out from the bloodstream, passed into the pocks and out of the body—hence leaving its victims immune to further attack. He therefore recommended practitioners to inoculate at the age and season when there was the minimum amount of this 'pabulum' in the body and to further reduce it prior to the operation through a 'lowering', mainly vegetarian, diet and a series of purges. The work described the therapeutic regimen in exhaustive detail: for example, Kirkpatrick spent several pages debating

whether asparagus should be allowed in the preparatory diet. His emphasis on individualized therapy, tailored to the circumstances and constitution of each patient, rationalized the role of physicians in supervising inoculation at a time when their original monopoly of the practice was being challenged by surgeons and apothecaries.

Kirkpatrick also engaged in pamphlet debates over inoculation, in which his style became tediously long-winded and his hypersensitivity to any slight meant that the medical arguments were secondary to personal invective and defence of his own character. *A Full and Clear Reply to Dr. Thomas Dale* (1739) vehemently criticized his target for his dangerously bad management of cases of inoculation. *A Letter to the Real and Genuine Pierce Dod, MD* (1746) published under the pseudonym Dod Pierce, but attributed to Kirkpatrick and his fellow physicians William Barrowby and Isaac Schomberg, satirized a pamphlet by Peirce *Dod dealing with cases of smallpox after inoculation.

Kirkpatrick also published a short pamphlet on a medical curiosity—a corpse disinterred from a church vault in Staverton, near Totnes, after almost eighty years yet showing no signs of decomposition—and he translated S. A. D. Tissot's popular health text, *Advice to the People in General with Regard to their Health* (1765).

Kirkpatrick had literary aspirations. He published *The Sea-Piece* (1750), a volume of extremely bad poetry (with his usual long preface and dedication) written during his original voyage to America, and translated some verses of Pope into Latin. He died in 1770.

DEBORAH BRUNTON

Sources D. J. O'Donoghue, *The poets of Ireland: a biographical dictionary with bibliographical particulars*, 1 vol. in 3 pts (1892–3) • J. Kirkpatrick, *The sea-piece* (1750) • P. J. Wallis and R. V. Wallis, *Eighteenth century medics*, 2nd edn (1988)

Kirkpatrick, John (bap. 1687, d. 1728), antiquary and draughtsman, was baptized on 7 March 1687 at Haveringland, Norfolk, the eldest of seven children of Thomas Kirkpatrick (d. 1710?), probably a grazier, and his wife, Anne Sendall (d. 1742). His father was from Closeburn, Dumfriesshire, and apparently was related to the baronetcy of Kirkpatrick. Nothing is known of his mother's family. His parents married at Haveringland on 6 May 1686, and the family moved to the parish of St Stephen, Norwich, about 1691. There is no record of his education, but he was apprenticed to Thomas Andrew, merchant, of St Clement's parish, and became a freeman as linen draper on 24 February 1711. He is so described in the 1714 Norwich poll in St George Tombland. He later entered the service of John Custance, alderman, whom he subsequently joined in partnership, and with whose family he shared a house in St Andrew's parish until his death. Kirkpatrick served as a common councillor and auditor from 1719 to 1727, and in 1726 was appointed treasurer of the great hospital in St Helen's parish. He married Ann Harvey, the youngest daughter of John Harvey, a Norwich merchant, who seems to have predeceased him; there were no children.

Throughout his adult life Kirkpatrick was a member of 'a little Society of Icenian Antiquaries' (Nichols, 3.433)

John Kirkpatrick (*bap.* 1687, *d.* 1728), by John Theodore Heins

that included Thomas Tanner, Benjamin Mackerell, and Peter Le Neve, with whom he exchanged notes. It was through Le Neve's influence that he was elected fellow of the Society of Antiquaries on 18 February 1719. He compiled extensive and valuable notes relating to the history of Norwich and built up noteworthy collections of manuscript and printed books and ancient coins, all of which he left to the city. He was also a fine artist and his views of the ancient city gates of Norwich (1720) were copied and etched by Henry Ninham in 1864. His notes were also used in Robert Fitch's introduction to John Ninham's views of Norwich gates in 1861. Other drawings are listed by Johnson and in Gough's *British Topography*. His draughtsmanship is sometimes confused with that of his younger brother Thomas Kirkpatrick (*c.*1690–1755), chamberlain of Norwich 1732–44. It was Thomas who drew the large north-east prospect of Norwich, which was published by John in 1723.

Kirkpatrick published nothing else during his lifetime. He died on 20 August 1728 and was buried in St Helen's Church, Norwich, on 27 August 1728. In 1741 Thomas Kirkpatrick attempted to forestall the publication of Francis Blomefield's *History of Norwich* by announcing the imminent publication of a specimen of his brother's work. Blomefield had advertised his own access to Kirkpatrick's materials, although he possessed only the original rough notes exchanged with Le Neve, but this specimen was not published. Kirkpatrick's *Notes Concerning Norwich Castle* were, however, published in 1836 and 1847, and his *History of the Religious Orders and Communities … of Norwich* in 1845, with a preface by Dawson Turner. *The Streets and Lanes of the City of Norwich* was edited from Kirkpatrick's notes by William Hudson in 1889, but other valuable manuscript works listed in the 1845 preface appear to have been lost.

Kirkpatrick's substantial bequest of early printed and manuscript books may be identified from Mackerell's catalogue of the Norwich City Library in 1732, but a proposed catalogue of his coin collection was never published. The bulk of the coin collection was subsequently lost through neglect and pilfering. Kirkpatrick's historical manuscripts were left to his brother Thomas during his lifetime and to the city thereafter, but were also subsequently dispersed.   DAVID STOKER

Sources F. Johnson, 'John Kirkpatrick, antiquary', *Norfolk Archaeology*, 23 (1927–9), 285–304 · D. Turner, 'Preface', in J. Kirkpatrick, *History of the religious orders and communities … of Norwich*, ed. D. Turner (1845) · *The correspondence of the Reverend Francis Blomefield, 1705–52*, ed. D. Stoker, Norfolk RS, 55 (1992), 234–5 · D. Stoker, 'Benjamin Mackerell, antiquary, librarian, and plagiarist', *Norfolk Archaeology*, 42 (1994–7), 1–12 · G. Stephen, 'A descriptive list of Norwich plans', in T. Chubb, *A descriptive list of printed maps of Norfolk* (1928), 204–6 · [J. Chambers], *A general history of the county of Norfolk*, 2 (1829), 1181, 1208 · P. Millican, *The register of the freemen of Norwich, 1548–1713* (1934), 95 · Nichols, *Illustrations*, 3.418, 421, 433–4 · R. G. [R. Gough], *British topography*, [new edn], 2 (1780), 4–34 *passim*, 252 · R. Gough, *A chronological list of the Society of Antiquaries* (1798), 3 · H. Ninham, *Views of the ancient city gates of Norwich as they appeared in 1722* (1864) · R. Fitch, *Views of the gates of Norwich* (1861) · F. I. Dunn, 'The Norwich grocers' play and the Kirkpatrick papers at Norwich', *N&Q*, 217 (1972), 202–3 · R. Frostick, *The printed plans of Norwich, 1558–1840* (2002), 29–33

Archives Bodl. Oxf., Norfolk notes · Norfolk RO, drawings and notes · Norfolk RO, index to a collection made by Anthony Norris · Norfolk RO, transcript of Norwich Cathedral's cellarer's roll · NRA, priv. coll., historical notes

Likenesses oils, *c.*1750, Norwich corporation; repro. in Johnson, 'John Kirkpatrick, antiquary' · W. C. Edwards, etching (after D. Heins), BM · J. T. Heins, portrait, Norwich Castle Museum and Art Gallery [*see illus.*]

Wealth at death legacies to Norwich Corporation

Kirkpatrick, John Simpson (1892–1915), war hero, was born at South Shields, co. Durham, on 6 July 1892, the son of Robert Kirkpatrick and his wife, Sarah Simpson. Robert Kirkpatrick was a merchant captain until in 1904 an accident ended his working life. His surviving children, one son baptized John Simpson and three daughters, were still young. Three other sons had died of scarlet fever. The boy attended two local state schools, Barnes Road School and Mortimer Road School in South Shields, but his surviving letters demonstrate that his education was severely limited. From the age of ten or eleven, John made some contribution to the family's small income. A surviving letter to his mother recalled an early escapade in which he had stolen a duck to add to the family's diet. He soon showed a gift for working with animals, first in helping with the riding donkeys on the local beach, and then with a horse-drawn milk cart.

In 1909, aged seventeen, Kirkpatrick joined a local Territorial Army unit, but when his father died in October the same year he decided to emigrate to Australia. Unable to afford a passage, he joined a Tyne-based coaster and then enlisted on another ship at Leith, intending to desert when she reached Australia. In July 1910 he jumped ship at

John Simpson Kirkpatrick (1892–1915), by unknown photographer, c.1915 [in Shrapnel Gully, Gallipoli, with a wounded soldier on his donkey]

Newcastle, New South Wales. To avoid legal consequences he dropped his surname and took the name John Simpson. For the next few years he had various jobs, working in a colliery and a cane field, but mostly employed in local shipping. Whenever he could he sent money home to support his mother and sisters. By 1914 he was homesick and when the First World War began he enlisted in the Australian Army Medical Corps in the belief that this would lead to his being posted to Britain. Instead, the 3rd Australian field ambulance was sent to Egypt and then, in April 1915, to Gallipoli. While his transport was moored at Mudros, Simpson broke into the ship's stores to obtain extra food.

As a medical orderly during the Gallipoli campaign, Simpson's main duty was to convey wounded soldiers (principally those suffering from leg wounds) from the immediate fighting area down to the field hospital in the area of the disembarkation beaches, often under enemy fire, along a route that included Sniper's Alley and Shrapnel Gully. Shortly after the landings he found a stray donkey in a nearby gully and appropriated it. For the next three weeks he continued his rescue work with the donkey, careless of danger and usually whistling cheerfully *en route*. On 19 May 1915 he was shot by a Turkish sniper, the donkey continuing on its way to the field hospital with its mortally wounded patient. He was buried on the beach at Hell Spit, Gallipoli.

Subsequently John Simpson Kirkpatrick became an important symbol of Anzac heroism at Gallipoli, his story much exploited for propaganda purposes during the First World War and even revived for similar purposes during the Vietnam war. He is much better known in Australia than in Britain, and Australian pride in his heroism is associated with resentment that it received such inadequate recognition—only a mention in dispatches—from the British military authorities. A modern monograph has discussed the mechanism whereby his last weeks acquired such significant and widespread symbolic importance in

Australia. Attempts to argue that he was a convinced political radical and an enemy of imperialism, using some unsophisticated expressions attacking wealth and privilege in surviving letters, are less convincing (Cochrane). In Australia monuments to 'the Man with the Donkey' include a full-size bronze statue in the shrine of remembrance at Australia's national war memorial and other statues in at least five cities. A similar statue was erected in South Shields only in 1988, financed by public subscription after the local council refused any subsidy from public funds. Kirkpatrick also appears prominently in a memorial frieze at Gallipoli. In 1965 he was the centrepiece of three Australian postage stamps celebrating the fiftieth anniversary of the Gallipoli landings. Annual celebrations in Australia still commemorate his last heroic weeks.   NORMAN MCCORD

Sources I. Benson, *The Man with the Donkey: John Simpson Kirkpatrick, the good Samaritan of Gallipoli* (1965) • P. Cochrane, *Simpson and the donkey: the making of a legend* (1992) • T. Curran, *Across the bar: the story of 'Simpson', the Man with the Donkey: Australia and Tyneside's great military hero* (1994) • *AusDB* • *Sunday Telegraph* (12 Nov 2000) **Archives** Australian War Memorial, Canberra, letters **Likenesses** photograph, c.1915, Australian War Memorial, Canberra [*see illus.*] • photographs, repro. in Benson, *Man with the Donkey* • photographs, repro. in Curran, *Across the bar* • statue, South Shields • statue, Australian War Memorial, Canberra

Kirkpatrick, Thomas Percy Claude (1869–1954), physician and medical historian, the second son of John Rutheroford Kirkpatrick (d. 1889), king's professor of midwifery in the University of Dublin, and his wife, Catherine Drury, was born at 32 Rutland Square, Dublin, on 10 September 1869. The family later moved locally, to 4 Upper Merrion Street. Educated in Foyle College, Londonderry, and at Trinity College, Dublin, Kirkpatrick took a first in history in 1891, before reading medicine. He graduated MB and then MD in 1895, was admitted a member of the Royal College of Physicians of Ireland in 1903, was elected FRCPI in 1904, and became honorary FRCP, London, in 1942.

Kirkpatrick was registrar of the Royal College of Physicians of Ireland for forty-four years (1910–54), and general secretary of the Royal Academy of Medicine in Ireland for an almost equal period. Informally known to his colleagues as Percy or Kirk, he was anaesthetist to Dr Steevens' Hospital, Dublin, before his appointment there as honorary visiting physician. He took a particular interest in what were then termed venereal diseases; to facilitate his patients (many of whom were prostitutes) he held a clinic for women at a discreet hour in the early morning in order to foster anonymity. Syphilis was rife and Paul Erlich's '606'—the drug known as Salvarsan—was an important development; Kirkpatrick reported its benefits in the *Dublin Journal of Medical Science* in May 1918.

A member of the Bibliographical Society, Kirkpatrick was a prolific author. His articles on anaesthesia and clinical subjects, published in the *Medical Press and Circular* and the *Dublin Journal of Medical Science*, were ephemeral; his contributions to medical history are of a different calibre.

He was an inspiration and source of information to successive generations of Irish medical historians. His major works are his *History of the Medical Teaching in Trinity College, Dublin* (1912), for which he was awarded the honorary LittD degree of his own university; *The Book of the Rotunda Hospital* (1913); and *History of Dr Steevens' Hospital, 1720–1920* (1924). His biographical essays deal with Sir William Petty, Oliver Goldsmith, Edward Hill, Abraham Colles, and others too numerous to identify; many other aspects of Dublin medicine attracted his attention and his indices to the biographical notices and historical papers in the *Dublin Journal of Medical Science* are extremely useful. A chronological hand-list of Kirkpatrick's publications was compiled by his friend and colleague, Dr F. S. Bourke; a further bibliographical essay has been contributed to a Trinity College publication, *Longroom*, by Ms Mary O'Doherty (1998). The quality of Kirkpatrick's work earned the respect of the general historians. He was president of the Irish Historical Society from 1948 to 1951 and honorary DLitt of the National University of Ireland.

For many years it was Kirkpatrick's practice to collect printed information about Irish doctors from a wide range of newspapers and periodicals. Placed in envelopes, these cuttings, some thousands in number, are filed in the Royal College of Physicians of Ireland, and the Kirkpatrick archive is an invaluable source for biographers.

Kirkpatrick enjoyed good health and his attendance at Dr Steevens' Hospital was rarely interrupted; as he grew older he was inclined to boast that he had not spent a night away from Dublin for forty years. He was almost certain to be found there on Sundays, too, not on the wards but in the Worth Library, a bookman's dream that had existed in Dr Steevens' Hospital from 1733, the gift of Dr Edward Worth (1678–1733), who had assembled a remarkable collection of superbly bound books. Percy Kirkpatrick's great pleasure was to dust and polish these volumes, which to this day remain in mint condition. Kirkpatrick's article 'The Worth Library and Steevens' Hospital' appeared in the *Dublin Journal of Medical Science* in March 1919 and was followed by a similar account of Sir Patrick Dun's Library. Kirkpatrick himself amassed a large private collection of books and manuscripts; those of medical interest—1100 printed volumes, 3500 pamphlets, and 126 manuscripts, with author and subject card catalogue—were bequeathed to the Royal College of Physicians of Ireland; the remainder were auctioned by Sothebys.

Elected a member of the Royal Irish Academy in 1906, Kirkpatrick served on the council and held office as vice-president (1941–5 and 1949–54) and president (1946–9). He contributed an article on Charles Willoughby to the academy's *Proceedings* in 1923. A gregarious, clubbable man, Kirkpatrick remained a bachelor of an old-fashioned kind, his residence at 11 Fitzwilliam Place cared for by his unmarried sister, Sibyl. He was ten minutes' walking distance from the Friendly Brothers' Club, where he could be sure of company. After dinner he liked to make punch for his friends, or act as marker in the billiard room, while his lively conversation entertained fellow members.

In his younger days Kirkpatrick cycled daily to the hospital, smoking a pipe as he rolled along, and then mounting his bicycle by the back step. Later, one or other of his younger colleagues picked him up in the mornings and drove him to work, to be rewarded *en route* by the historian's comments on little-known aspects of the city.

During Kirkpatrick's tenure of the office of registrar in the Royal College of Physicians, he saw many presidents come and go. The college acknowledged his long service by presenting him his portrait, by Leo Whelan, which now hangs in the library. The governors of Dr Steevens' Hospital, likewise inspired, commissioned Brigid Ganly (at Kirkpatrick's express wish) to paint the portrait that has a prominent place in the hospital, now the headquarters of the Eastern Regional Health Authority.

Kirkpatrick died in Dr Steevens' Hospital from hypostatic pneumonia and chronic uraemia on 9 July 1954, and was buried in Mount Jerome cemetery. His admirable qualities are summarized in an obituary written by his friend William Doolin:

> Kirk was that rare and lovely being, a humanist in his outlook and in his interests, his humanism lighted by compassion. In his specialised field of clinical work, he often brought to mind Savonarola's axiom: 'The physician that bringeth love and charity to the sick, if he be good and learned and skilful, none can be better than he.' In his written work he had three notable gifts: solid learning, so lightly borne, a sense of style, and a deep integrity of craftsmanship. (Doolin, 364–5)

J. B. LYONS

Sources W. Doolin, *Irish Journal of Medical Science*, 344 (1954), 364–5 · M. O'Doherty, 'T. Percy Kirkpatrick, physician, bibliophile', *Longroom*, 43 (1998), 38–43 · F. S. Bourke, 'Chronological handlist of Dr Kirkpatrick's published work', *Irish Journal of Medical Science*, 344 (1954), 371–4 · T. P. C. Kirkpatrick, *History of the medical teaching in Trinity College, Dublin, and of the School of Physic in Ireland* (1912) · b. cert. · d. cert.
Archives Royal College of Physicians of Ireland, Dublin, archive
Likenesses B. Ganly, oils, Dr Steevens' Hospital, Dublin, Ireland · S. Murphy, relief roundel on memorial tablet, Dr Steevens' Hospital, Dublin, Ireland · S. O'Sullivan, drawing, Dr Steevens' Hospital, Dublin, Ireland · J. Sleator, oils, Friendly Brothers' Club, Dublin · L. Whelan, oils, Royal College of Physicians of Ireland, Dublin
Wealth at death £10,204: probate, 16 Aug 1954, *CGPLA Éire*

Kirkpatrick, William (1754–1812), army officer in the East India Company and diplomatist, was the illegitimate son of James Kirkpatrick (1730–1818), a colonel in the East India Company's army, and Mrs Booth, wife of a London solicitor. Born in Ireland, Kirkpatrick was raised at boarding-school, supported but unacknowledged by his father. In 1771 his father, 'the Handsome Colonel', purchased Kirkpatrick an East India Company military cadetship and the young man sailed for Bengal. He had a half-sister from the Booths's marriage whom he probably never met, and two younger half-brothers, his father's legitimate children, George and James Achilles, whom he met in India after their father placed them in the company's service and told them of their half-sibling. Ambitious for promotion, Kirkpatrick learned Indian languages and gained access to Indian information networks.

William Kirkpatrick (1754–1812), by Thomas Hickey, c.1799–1800 [with his assistants]

Known as Kirk to his friends, he was regarded as a generous if sometimes profligate companion. He suffered from rheumatism, gambled, drank, and told John Kennaway of a melancholia, the 'kind of shadow or image of a calm sorrow or grief', he often experienced (Kirkpatrick to Kennaway, 13 June 1779, Devon RO, Kennaway MS 961 M add F2 1/3).

In 1779 Kirkpatrick became interpreter for Lieutenant-Colonel Stibbert, commander-in-chief of the Bengal army, and in 1781 was made a captain. He purchased and had compilations made of Indian texts, establishing a useful network of Indian contacts. Poona's representative at Hyderabad said Kirkpatrick was 'expert in everything', having 'wonderful intelligence and mastery of Persian speech, is equally careful in writing, understands accounts, and is well informed in public business and is versed in astronomy' (G. R. Kale to Nana Fadnis, 20 Feb 1794, in Sarkar, 1.ix).

In 1782 rheumatism and the Indian climate caused Kirkpatrick to resign from the East India Company service. With the two children he had with his Indian mistress, he sailed for England, and *en route* for Europe wrote his *Grammar of the Hindoo Dialect and an Arabic and Persian Vocabulary*, which was published in the same year under the company's patronage. In London he published translations of Persian works and promoted the Bengal Orphan Fund (later the Bengal Military Fund), a trust providing charity for soldiers' orphans which he had founded before his reluctant departure from India. Failing to support himself, he resumed his commission in 1784 and, leaving his

children under his father's care, returned to India. In Calcutta, on 26 September 1785, he married Maria Rawson. Although the couple had four daughters, it was an unhappy union. On 21 November 1786 he began his brief tenure as resident to Mahadji Sindhia. Kirkpatrick wrote to Governor-General Cornwallis of how Sindhia and his court were insulting and inattentive. The maharaja in turn complained of the resident's haughty attitude. In October 1787 Kirkpatrick was replaced and he returned to regimental duties.

Kirkpatrick's career languished until 1790, when he joined Cornwallis's staff as interpreter during the Third Anglo-Mysore War. In 1792 he headed a diplomatic mission to Nepal, leading the first Britons into that kingdom. Kirkpatrick told Cornwallis's secretary, Colonel Ross, on 27 October 1792, that the mission went to settle a dispute between Nepal and Tibet and 'to advance useful knowledge' (BL OIOC, Kirkpatrick MSS, MS Eur. F/228/1, fol. 41). Arriving after the dispute ended, he spent three weeks in Nepal, and though he returned to India without concrete benefit, the mission was regarded as a successful foray into an unknown land.

In January 1794 Kirkpatrick replaced Sir John Kennaway as resident to the nizam of Hyderabad. He followed Governor-General Sir John Shore's non-interventionist policy: despite the nizam's pleas and his own sentiments, he refused to involve the company in the Maratha–Hyderabad war of 1795; and in 1796, during the Poona succession crisis, he did not attempt to restrain the nizam from interceding in Maratha affairs. Meanwhile, he continued to pursue local knowledge. A network of Indian informants supplied him with news and gossip both from Hyderabad and from across the subcontinent, and his hired scribes copied books from Mughal archives. This enabled him to produce road-maps and to assist James Rennell with an atlas of northern India.

Kirkpatrick's rheumatism persisted, forcing his resignation from the residency and a second departure from India, in 1797. At Cape Town he met Richard Wellesley, earl of Mornington, who was *en route* for Bengal to take office as governor-general. Wellesley interviewed those at the Cape with Indian experience. At Wellesley's request Kirkpatrick wrote essays on Indian affairs. After their meetings Kirkpatrick believed Wellesley intended to follow Shore's non-interventionist policy toward the Indian princes, while Wellesley held that Kirkpatrick had supplied information necessary to pursue the forward policy instructed by London. Wellesley accordingly offered Kirkpatrick a job in Calcutta and, despite his health, he accepted. Working closely with Wellesley as secretary to the secret and political department, he acted as adviser to his half-brother James Achilles Kirkpatrick, the Hyderabad resident, when the nizam signed the treaty of Hyderabad, by which Hyderabad became a British protectorate. In the spring of 1799, during the Fourth Anglo-Mysore War, William Kirkpatrick accompanied Wellesley to Madras. After the death of Tipu Sultan and Seringapatam's fall in May 1799, Kirkpatrick sat on the Mysore settlement commission. In 1801 he was unable to take up his appointment as Poona resident owing to rheumatism, which was causing him to keep bandages wrapped tightly around his knees and forehead.

Kirkpatrick left India in 1802, and settled in Exeter, where he lived at Southernhay House. He continued to pursue his Indian interests, and helped select the East India Company's library, a collection now part of the British Library. In 1804 he published translations of documents said to have been discovered at Seringapatam, and in 1811 an account of Nepal. He also studied the Indian calendar, endeavouring to detail Tipu Sultan's horoscope and understand that ruler's fate. By 1809 rheumatism confined Kirkpatrick to his chair. In the summer of 1812 he auctioned his possessions and on 22 August 1812 he overdosed on laudanum near London, an apparent suicide.

BRENDAN CARNDUFF

Sources BL OIOC, Kirkpatrick MSS, MS Eur F 228 · BL, Wellesley MSS · BL OIOC, Strachey MSS, MS Eur. F 127 · Devon RO, Kennaway MS 961 M · J. Sarkar and others, eds., *English records of Maratha history: Poona residency correspondence*, 1–4 (1936–53), vols. 1–4 · R. H. Phillimore, ed., *Historical records of the survey of India*, 1 (1945) · J. Philippart, *East India military calendar*, 2 (1824) · *Kirkpatrick of Closeburn* (1858) · R. Newton, *Eighteenth-century Exeter* (1984)

Archives BL, corresp. and papers, Add. MSS 13584–13586; 13526–13527 · BL OIOC, home misc. series, corresp. and papers relating to India, MS Eur. F 128 · BL OIOC, MS Eur. F 228 | BL, corresp. with Lord Wellesley, Add. MSS 37279, 37282 · BL OIOC, Malet MSS, MS Eur. F 149 · Devon RO, Kennaway MSS · PRO, corresp. with Lord Cornwallis, PRO30/11

Likenesses T. Hickey, group portrait, c.1799–1800 (*Colonel William Kirkpatrick with attendants*), NG Ire. [*see illus.*] · W. Hickey, portrait, Victoria Memorial Hall, Calcutta, India · portrait, repro. in A. Buddle, ed., *The tiger and the thistle: Tipu Sultan and the Scots in India* (1999), 21

Kirkpatrick, William Baillie (1802–1882), minister of the Presbyterian Church in Ireland, was born near Ballynahinch, co. Down, in March 1802. After spending some time at a local classical school conducted by the Revd Arthur Neilson of Rademon, he went to the Royal Belfast Academical Institution. He later graduated from Glasgow College with the degree of MA. Kirkpatrick studied theology in the collegiate department of the Royal Belfast Academical Institution, under the divinity professor of the synod of Ulster. He had been brought up under Unitarian influences but these were soon rejected in favour of evangelical doctrines. In 1827 he was licensed by the presbytery of Armagh, and on 29 July 1829 ordained one of the ministers of Mary's Abbey church, Dublin. He soon acquired an outstanding reputation as a good preacher and a caring pastor.

In 1850 Kirkpatrick was moderator of the general assembly, and for many years convener of the home mission scheme and of the committee on the state of religion. He was appointed by the government to be a commissioner of charitable donations and bequests, and a commissioner of endowed schools. During his ministry in Dublin a fine new church was built in Rutland Square, at a cost of £14,000, for the Mary's Abbey congregation, by Alexander Findlater JP. Kirkpatrick died on 23 September 1882 at Bray, co. Wicklow, and was buried on 27 September in Mount Jerome cemetery, Dublin, leaving a widow, Bessie, two sons, and six daughters. His main publication was *Chapters in Irish History* (n.d. [1875]), which reached a second edition. He was regarded as one of the leading presbyterian ministers of Dublin and the entire south of Ireland during this period.

THOMAS HAMILTON, *rev.* DAVID HUDDLESTON

Sources *McComb's Presbyterian Almanac* (1883), 87–8 · C. H. Irwin, *A history of presbyterianism in Dublin and the south and west of Ireland* (1892) · W. T. Latimer, *A history of the Irish Presbyterians*, 2nd edn (1902) · *A history of congregations in the Presbyterian Church in Ireland, 1610–1982*, Presbyterian Church in Ireland (1982) · *CGPLA Ire.* (1882) · *Belfast Witness* (29 Sept 1882), 4

Wealth at death £461 17s. 10d. in England: Irish probate resealed in England, 10 Nov 1882, *CGPLA Eng. & Wales* · £2884 10s. 3d.: probate, 20 Oct 1882, *CGPLA Ire.*

Kirkstall, Hugh of (c.1165–c.1227), Cistercian monk and chronicler, was the author of the *Narratio de fundatione* of Fountains Abbey, and probable author of the foundation history of Kirkstall Abbey. Both these Cistercian houses were in Yorkshire. The *Narratio* contains two references to Hugh; he names himself in his address to Abbot John of Fountains (1203–11), and states that he received the habit at the hands of Abbot Ralph Haget of Kirkstall in the third year of his abbacy, and lived under his rule for seven years. This places Hugh's entry into the monastic life c.1184, and implies his birth not later than c.1165. Although he is not named as the author of the Kirkstall history, which was completed shortly after c.1204 and which survives in Bodl. Oxf., MS Laud misc. 722, similarities between portions of this and the *Narratio* make it likely; and it may have been on the basis of his earlier work that Abbot John commissioned Hugh to write an account of the origins of Fountains. The *Narratio*, begun c.1205–6 and completed c.1227, is a much longer and more ambitious work. It purports to be the reminiscences, committed to writing by Hugh, of the aged monk Serlo, who had been educated at St Mary's Abbey, York, had entered religion at Fountains c.1137, and been one of the party that colonized Kirkstall in 1147. Certainly the description of events up to 1147, especially the career of Abbot Richard (II) and the fire at Fountains Abbey, is vivid. However, after 1190–91 when Ralph Haget moved from Kirkstall to become abbot of Fountains, it was Hugh himself who became the eyewitness.

But Hugh's *Narratio* was much more than personal testimony. In addition to Serlo's and his own recollections, Hugh had access to, and used, archival material—charters, possibly an early register of the abbey, and letters, including those of St Bernard and Archbishop Thurstan—and also literary models. The latter appear to have been mostly Cistercian—the Byland foundation history, which predated that of Kirkstall by just a few years, and more especially the *Exordium parvum*. A Cistercian audience would not have failed to recognize the similarities that Hugh conveys between the foundation of Fountains and that of Cîteaux itself. The *Narratio* survives in only one medieval manuscript (Trinity College, Cambridge, Gale MS O.I.79), evidently an incomplete copy of the original, and the text was revised in the last half of the fifteenth century to produce a different recension. The literary merits of the *Narratio* are generally considered to be few. However, in it Hugh of Kirkstall vividly evokes the spirit and spirituality of the great age of Cistercian monasticism in the north of England.   JANET BURTON

Sources J. R. Walbran, ed., *Memorials of the abbey of St Mary of Fountains*, 1, SurtS, 42 (1863) · Dugdale, *Monasticon*, new edn, 5.292–306 · E. K. Clark, ed. and trans., 'The foundation of Kirkstall Abbey', *Miscellanea*, Thoresby Society, 4 (1895), 169–208 · D. Baker, 'The genesis of English Cistercian chronicles: the foundation history of Fountains Abbey, pt 1', *Analecta Cisterciensia*, 25 (1969), 14–41 · L. G. D. Baker, 'The foundation of Fountains Abbey', *Northern History*, 4 (1969), 29–43 · D. Bethell, 'The foundation of Fountains Abbey and the state of St Mary's York in 1132', *Journal of Ecclesiastical History*, 17 (1966), 11–27

Archives Bodl. Oxf., MS Laud misc 722, fols. 129r–198v · Trinity Cam., Gale MS O.I.79

Kirkton, James (*d.* 1699), Church of Scotland minister and historian, was born most probably in south-east Scotland; his parents are unknown. He graduated MA at Edinburgh in 1647, and became minister of Lanark (second charge) in 1655 and of Mertoun in Berwickshire in 1657. On 31 December 1657 he married Elizabeth Baillie (*c.*1640–1697); they had five children who reached maturity.

At Mertoun, Kirkton excommunicated a local landowner, Anthony Haig, for being a Quaker, and afterwards had difficulty collecting his stipend. He was expelled in 1662 with about 270 other presbyterian ministers who refused to conform to episcopacy. Kirkton moved to Edinburgh, became a noted illegal preacher there, and was a leading opponent of the second indulgence of 1672, which would have allowed most presbyterian ministers to function officially again though under strict conditions. He also conducted a long debate by letters against Gideon Scott on the tenets of Quakers. In 1674 Kirkton was declared rebel, but seems to have lived openly for two more years until arrested by Captain Carstairs. He was rescued by his brother-in-law, Robert *Baillie of Jerviswood (*d.* 1684), but Baillie and his companions were imprisoned and fined, and Kirkton and the other rebel ministers 'intercommuned', which meant that anyone conversing with them could be held equally guilty of their crimes. He then lived mainly in England and the Netherlands.

With the Toleration Act of 1687 Kirkton returned to Scotland and was minister of Edinburgh's Tolbooth parish from 1691. In his last years he was again a famous preacher, and financially prosperous. One source records that Kirkton had a weak voice, and that his dark periwig disguised hair of a different colour. All agree that he had a marked Scots accent, and that his speech was terse, idiomatic, and often sardonic. The most famous anti-presbyterian tract, *The Scotch Presbyterian Eloquence* (1692), describes Kirkton as 'the Everlasting Comedian of their Party' (20), and ridicules him more than any other minister. He appears somewhat more favourably in Pitcairn's satirical play, *The Assembly* (written 1692), as Mr Covenant Plain-Dealer.

Kirkton wrote a short biography of John Welsh (1703), and *The Secret and True History of the Church of Scotland*, from 1660 to 1679, which also covers many secular issues. It was

completed in 1693, apparently in reaction to *Scotch Presbyterian Eloquence*, and circulated in manuscripts in the eighteenth century. Much of his evidence is included in Robert Wodrow's *The History of the Sufferings of the Church of Scotland* (1721–2), but Kirkton's history remains an important historical source: he was well informed (his contacts included the duchess of Lauderdale, whose husband controlled Scotland), usually temperate in judgements, and apparently reliable. Indeed Sir Walter Scott (relative of Gideon Scott, the Quaker) says in his review of the history that Kirkton was 'incapable of perverting the truth so far as it was known to him' (Scott, 506).

Kirkton's wife died in April 1697; he himself died on 17 September 1699. He was buried on 20 September 1699 in Greyfriars churchyard, Edinburgh, where most of his family were interred.   RALPH STEWART

Sources J. Curate [G. Crokatt], *The Scotch Presbyterian eloquence* (1692) · [A. Pitcairn], *The assembly* (1722) · J. Kirkton, *The secret and true history of the Church of Scotland*, ed. C. K. Sharpe (1817), biographical notice · *Fasti Scot.*, new edn · [W. Scott], review of *Secret and true history*, *QR*, 18 (1817–18), 502–41 · R. Scott-Moncrieff, 'Note on the arrest of Mr Robert Baillie', *Proceedings of the Society of Antiquaries of Scotland*, 44 (1909–10), 286–301 · J. Kirkton, *A history of the Church of Scotland, 1660–1679*, ed. R. Stewart (1992), i–xvii · J. Russell, *The Haigs of Bemersyde* (1881), 267–70 · legal deeds, 1680–1700, NA Scot. · H. Paton, ed., *Register of interments in the Greyfriars burying-ground, Edinburgh, 1658–1700*, Scottish RS, 26 (1902) · G. Rule, *A just and modest reproof of a pamphlet called the Scotch Presbyterian eloquence* (1693) · W. H. L. Melville, ed., *Leven and Melville papers: letters and state papers chiefly addressed to George, earl of Melville … 1689–1691*, Bannatyne Club, 77 (1843) · m. reg. Scot. · *The household book of Lady Grisell Baillie, 1692–1733*, ed. R. Scott-Moncrieff, Scottish History Society, new ser., 1 (1911)

Archives NL Scot., Wodrow MSS

Kirkup, Seymour Stocker (1788–1880), painter and antiquary, was born in London, the eldest child of Joseph Kirkup, jeweller and diamond merchant. In 1809, after a period of study under John Flaxman, he entered the Royal Academy Schools, where, in 1811, he won a medal for his drawing of Apollo in Raphael's *Parnassus*. He admired Flaxman, Henry Fuseli, and J. M. W. Turner as teachers and credited Sir Thomas Lawrence with encouraging him to paint portraits. Through one fellow student, Charles Eastlake, he met B. R. Haydon; through another, he met William Blake. He learned early to value association with remarkable personages, preferably not tories.

In 1816, troubled by signs of pulmonary weakness, Kirkup travelled to Italy, planning to stay six months. He lived there for the rest of his long life. At Rome he joined his friend Eastlake in drawing at the English Academy. In November 1820 Joseph Severn and John Keats arrived, bearing a letter to Kirkup from Charles Armitage Brown. In bed with a fever, Kirkup missed Keats's funeral in February 1821 but showed unremitting kindness to Severn. The generous Kirkup, Severn understood, had a small fortune. Kirkup made a good appearance, though just over 5 feet tall (Keats's size, Severn remarked); and he talked engagingly about all the arts. At the interment of Shelley's ashes in January 1823, he met the adventurer E. J. Trelawny, whom he later painted against a background showing the entrance to a cave on Mount Parnassus wearing

Suliote dress, including a turban and large red sash, into the top of which an ataghan and knife are thrust.

In 1824, after a severe illness, Kirkup visited Florence. Captivated, he lived there for forty-eight years. For a time he shared quarters near the duomo with Charles Brown, who became acquainted with Kirkup's three successive mistresses; but then he settled in spacious apartments near the south-west corner of the Ponte Vecchio. His circle of Anglo-Florentine friends included W. S. Landor, Robert and Elizabeth Browning, and T. A. Trollope. Among visiting acquaintances were William Hazlitt and Nathaniel Hawthorne. According to Leigh Hunt, Kirkup had too much money and not enough accomplishment to succeed as a painter; but he sent a *Cassio* to the Royal Academy (exh. 1833) and painted portraits of Rose Aylmer's half-sister, A. H. Layard's mother, and A. C. Swinburne's mother.

Work on illustrations for Lord Vernon's edition of Dante's works made Kirkup an ardent Dantophile. He became a disciple of Professor Gabriele Rossetti, the leading Dantean in London; and in 1840, with G. A. Bezzi, a Piedmontese, and R. H. Wilde, an American, he employed a restorer to search for Giotto's portrait of Dante in the chapel of the Palazzo del Podestà, or Bargello. The portrait, known to Vasari, had been covered with whitewash; it was uncovered on 21 July 1840. Not without difficulty, Kirkup made a tracing and, in his copy of the *Convivio*, a coloured sketch. He sent a copy of the tracing and a small watercolour sketch to Professor Rossetti, whose elder son, Dante Gabriel Rossetti, painted a watercolour, *Giotto Painting Dante's Portrait* (1852). For Vernon, Kirkup made, from the tracing and the coloured sketch in the *Convivio*, the drawing on which Vincent Brooks based the chromolithograph published by the Arundel Society in 1859.

Kirkup, who believed in spirits, convinced himself in 1854 that his housekeeper's beautiful daughter, Regina Ronti, possessed mediumistic talents: she saw Dante in the room, looking like a life-mask prized by Kirkup but subsequently discredited. Only seventeen in 1854, Regina bore a daughter, Imogen or Bibi. Though mystified by this event, Kirkup accepted in 1856 Regina's deathbed asseveration that the child was his. Bibi at two, according to Kirkup, manifested her own ability to call up spirits, including Dante's. On the occasion of Dante's 600th birthday in 1865, when Kirkup received a knighthood in the order of Santi Maurizio e Lazzaro, Victor Emmanuel addressed him (inadvertently, it was said) not as *cavaliere* but as *barone*—which title Kirkup adopted. He owed the honour, he informed Swinburne, to Dante; and in 1866 Bibi reported confirmation by Dante himself. Even loyal friends deplored Kirkup's over-credulousness.

Kirkup at eighty, pallid, white-bearded, slovenly, very deaf, seldom emerged from his litter of manuscripts, early printed books, and miscellaneous treasures—his life-mask of Dante, a portrait of Savonarola, a carved chest once owned by Machiavelli, a crystal ball, a faded puppet show enjoyed by Bibi and her playmate Paolina Carboni. Then *gli spiriti* advised the *barone* to sell all his possessions and move to Leghorn. The sale at Sothebys in December 1871 fetched only £2555 for 4194 lots. At Leghorn, Bibi had a suitor; she married him and died at twenty-five. At eighty-seven, on 16 February 1875, Kirkup married Paolina Carboni, then twenty-two. They resided at via Scali del Ponte Nuovo 4, Leghorn, where he died on 3 January 1880. He was buried on 5 January in the British cemetery, Leghorn.

L. H. CUST, *rev.* DAVID ROBERTSON

Sources D. Robertson, 'Weave a circle: Baron Kirkup and his greatest friends', *From Smollett to James*, ed. S. I. Mintz and others (1981), 237–60 • Lady Eastlake [E. Eastlake], 'Memoir of Sir Charles Eastlake', in C. L. Eastlake, *Contributions to the literature of the fine arts*, 2nd ser. (1870) • *The diary of Benjamin Robert Haydon*, ed. W. B. Pope, 5 vols. (1960–63) • *The letters of Charles Armitage Brown*, ed. J. Stillinger (1966) • W. Sharp, *Life and letters of Joseph Severn* (1892) • *Letters of Edward John Trelawny*, ed. H. B. Forman (1910) • D. Crane, *Lord Byron's jackal: the life of Edward John Trelawny*, new edn (1999), 144 and pl. 20 • L. Hunt, *Lord Byron and some of his contemporaries* (1828) • J. Forster, *Walter Savage Landor*, 2 vols. (1869) • E. B. Browning, *Letters to her sister, 1846–1859*, ed. L. Huxley (1930) • W. M. Rossetti, *Gabriele Rossetti* (1901) • W. M. Rossetti, ed., *Rossetti papers* (1903) • H. C. Marillier, *Dante Gabriel Rossetti* (1899) • R. T. Holbrook, *Portraits of Dante* (1921) • E. Gosse, 'Swinburne and Kirkup', *London Mercury*, 3 (1920–21), 156–65 • CGPLA Eng. & Wales (1880) • Eastlake, correspondence in Lawrence letter-books, RA • Severn, correspondence to his sister Maria, Keats Memorial Library, Hampstead • N. Hawthorne, Italian journal, Morgan L.

Archives BL, letters to Sir Austen Layard, Add. MSS 38986–38999, *passim* • Bodl. Oxf., letters to F. C. Brooke • Istituto per la Storia del Risorgimento, Rome, letters to G. Rossetti • priv. coll., letters to Lady Westmorland • UCL, letters to H. C. Barlow

Likenesses S. Kirkup, self-portrait, 1844; formerly in possession of Thomas Marchant at Lewisham • G. Hayter, pencil and wash, BM

Wealth at death under £200—effects in England: probate, 6 Oct 1880, CGPLA Eng. & Wales

Kirkwood, David, first Baron Kirkwood (1872–1955),

trade unionist and politician, was born at Parkhead, Glasgow, on 8 July 1872, the son of John Kirkwood and his wife, Jean, daughter of William Brown. An older brother had died as an infant, and his parents also had an adopted daughter. His father was a labourer who rose to be winding-master in a weaving mill at a wage of 28s. a week and was a descendant of a family of farmworkers who had migrated a century earlier from the hamlet of Gartmore in Perthshire on the ancestral estate of R. B. Cunninghame Graham.

From 1877 Kirkwood attended Parkhead public school (where he won a prize for Bible knowledge), but left at the age of twelve to take employment as a message boy at a weekly wage of 3s. 6d. He lost this job when a visiting factory inspector discovered his age, but he continued in similar work until the age of fourteen, when he was apprenticed as an engineer, working from 6 a.m. to 5.30 p.m. for a weekly wage of 5s. At twenty he became a member of the Amalgamated Society of Engineers. Three years later, when working at Parkhead Forge, he took part in a strike resulting from unskilled men, paid at labourers' rates, being put on to skilled engineers' work. The engineers were defeated, and at the end of the strike Kirkwood and one other were dismissed and told that they would never again work at the forge. (However, he did return there in 1910.) He was employed at other places, at John

Brown's on Clydebank, and at the Mount Vernon Steel Works where he became engineer foreman. In his spare time he attended evening classes, temperance society meetings, and was a keen reader of romantic Scottish history and ballad literature. On 30 June 1899 Kirkwood married Elizabeth (d. 1956), daughter of Robert Smith, of Parkhead; they had four sons and two daughters.

By 1910 Kirkwood was taking a prominent part in trade union affairs, and after returning to Parkhead Forge became convener of shop stewards. He joined the Socialist Labour Party, but in 1914 left it for the Independent Labour Party and the Union of Democratic Control, coming decisively under the influence of Ramsay MacDonald and John Wheatley.

In 1915 Kirkwood led an agitation to gain the Clyde engineers an increase of 2d. per hour, but quickly accepted the compromise offer of 1d., so as not to affect the war effort. But Kirkwood began to agitate against the restrictions of the Munitions Act, and discontent among the engineers was also growing because of the widespread raising of house rents. Property owners were taking advantage of the competition for accommodation for munition workers, and there were also dramatic instances of soldiers' wives being evicted for inability to pay the increased rents. Kirkwood became heavily involved in these protests. He always denied that he had ever urged a strike of munition workers, but the government used its powers under the Defence of the Realm Act in March 1916 to deport him to Edinburgh as a troublemaker. He remained there for fourteen months, consistently refusing to sign any document promising 'good behaviour' as a condition of his return to the Clyde. Finally the order was revoked without this condition, and through the intervention of Winston Churchill, Kirkwood was employed as a manager at Beardmore's Mile End shell factory in Glasgow. There he operated a bonus for production system, and doubled the output of his department.

At the general election of 1918 Kirkwood stood for the Dumbarton burghs constituency but was defeated. In January 1919 he was knocked unconscious by a police baton outside the Glasgow municipal offices while attempting to calm a demonstration that was becoming violent. A press photograph of the incident ensured his acquittal on the charge of complicity in a sedition trial resulting from the demonstration. Later in 1919 he was elected to the Glasgow corporation representing the Mile End ward. On the corporation he was concerned chiefly with housing problems and was a keen advocate of municipal housing schemes, to be financed by interest-free loans from the national government.

In 1922 Kirkwood was elected MP for Dumbarton burghs, which he represented until a change of boundaries in 1950, after which he represented East Dunbartonshire. He was described in his obituary in *The Times* as a 'fiery man', and was twice suspended from parliament. After one suspension in March 1925, the entire opposition, led by Ramsay MacDonald, walked out in protest; a few days later the suspension was withdrawn on the

motion of Stanley Baldwin. Kirkwood was a keen member of the Empire Parliamentary Association and in 1928 was a member of its delegation which toured Canada. He promoted a bill in July 1924 to have the stone of destiny restored to Scotland, but it made little progress in the house.

Always the sentimental and romantic Scot, ready with quotations from the Bible, Robert Burns, and Scottish proverbs, and with a fine sense of humour and a powerful voice, Kirkwood toured the country as a propagandist for socialism. Although a tough political fighter, he made friends in all the political parties, and a major achievement of his public career was the success of his personal effort to secure resumption of work on Cunard's liner the *Queen Mary*, which had stood half-finished on the stocks, a gaunt reminder of the great depression on Clydeside. He became a privy councillor in 1948, was given the freedom of Clydebank in 1951, and on 22 December 1951 was created a baron. In the House of Lords the following year he made the plea that working people should be given wise, enthusiastic leadership, and be set an unselfish example by their employers. Kirkwood's autobiography, *My Life of Revolt*, was published in 1935. He died in hospital in Glasgow on 16 April 1955 and was succeeded in his title by his third and elder surviving son, David (1903–1970).

THOMAS JOHNSTON, rev. MARC BRODIE

Sources D. Kirkwood, *My life of revolt* (1935) · *The Times* (22 April 1955) · *Glasgow Herald* (18 April 1955) · Burke, *Peerage* · personal knowledge (1971)
Archives NRA, priv. coll., papers
Likenesses photograph, 1919, Scot. NPG; *see illus. in* Maclean, John (1879–1923) · D. Low, pencil caricature, NPG · caricature, repro. in Kirkwood, *My life of revolt*, 246 · photograph, repro. in *The Times*, 15d · photographs, repro. in Kirkwood, *My life of revolt*, frontispiece, 52, 110
Wealth at death £9757 11s. 9d.: confirmation, 30 Sept 1955, CCI

Kirkwood, James (b. c.1650, d. in or after 1709), clergyman and advocate of parochial libraries, was born in or near Dunbar. His schooling took place there, and from 1666 he studied at Edinburgh University, where he graduated MA in 1670. Scott's *Fasti ecclesiae Scoticanae* (Fasti Scot., 2.132) states that he was chaplain to Sir John Campbell of Glenorchy, later earl of Caithness and earl of Breadalbane. This period of service must have occurred between 1670 and 1676 and coincided with theological study. It is to these years that should be attributed Kirkwood's great interest in the highlands, although there is no evidence that he himself knew Gaelic.

On 13 July 1676 Kirkwood was licensed as a probationer by the presbytery of Haddington, and he thereafter preached in various parishes. In particular he assisted at the Fife parish of Wemyss in 1677–8 during the terminal illness of the minister, James Nairn. Presented to the borders parish of Minto in February 1679, he was collated by the bishop and installed in May. However, he was deprived after 1 November 1681 for refusing to take the test. In 1683 he was probably allowed to preach at Colmonell, Ayrshire, but soon moved to England, becoming on 1 March 1685 rector of Astwick in Bedfordshire. This appointment was possibly the result of an acquaintance with Gilbert Burnet, a protégé of Nairn, who after 1688 became bishop of Salisbury. Burnet was intimate with Robert Boyle the chemist; another close friend of Boyle was Thomas Barlow, bishop of Lincoln, in whose diocese Astwick lay. Kirkwood remained at Astwick until January 1702, when he was outed as a nonjuror. His means of earning a living thereafter is unknown. Elected on 4 March 1703 a corresponding member for Scotland of the Society for Promoting Christian Knowledge (SPCK), he seems to have moved back north by the end of 1704. His last known places of residence were Alderston and Ferrygate, both in his native Haddingtonshire.

Kirkwood is remembered for involvement in two enterprises: the distribution of the Bible in Gaelic to highland parishes; and the advocacy of parish libraries throughout Scotland, particularly the highlands. During his employment with Glenorchy, Kirkwood would have become aware of the highlanders' ignorance of the Bible through the lack of printed editions in Gaelic. Coming into contact with Boyle in the mid-1680s, he learned of Boyle's sponsorship of an edition of the new Testament in classical Gaelic in 1681 for distribution in Ireland. In 1685 Boyle financed the first printed edition of the Old Testament in classical Gaelic for similar distribution. Kirkwood prevailed upon Boyle to allow some 200 of these to be diverted to Scotland, along with any undistributed copies of the 1681 New Testament. Unfortunately classical Gaelic differed considerably from spoken Scottish Gaelic, and the texts were printed in a fount using Irish letter-forms. It took many years for copies to be distributed: communications were difficult and the times troubled; and after the triumph of presbyterianism in 1688 many Scottish clerics viewed the episcopalian (and future nonjuror) Kirkwood with suspicion. The promotion of Gaelic itself was also contentious, but Kirkwood was convinced of the merit of his actions, producing a justificatory printed broadside (*An Answer to the Objection Against Printing the Bible in Irish*), probably about 1689.

Kirkwood prevailed upon Boyle and others to finance a version of the Gaelic Bible in a Roman fount, printed in an edition of 3000 in London in 1690, along with a separate issue of 1000 New Testaments. The work was edited by Robert Kirk, minister of Aberfoyle, who also provided a Scottish Gaelic glossary and made textual alterations to conform with Scottish usage. Kirk also about this time probably supplied Boyle, via Kirkwood, with information about highland rites and customs. Although the general assembly of the Church of Scotland had encouraged distribution of these copies in an act of 11 November 1690, no doubt more closely to supervise the scheme, it took until the end of the decade for distribution to start, following further agitation by Kirkwood. About 1000 bibles went to Argyll alone, with hundreds going to other parts of the highlands. With these bibles often went a catechism, with prayers and creed, in Gaelic, printed in London in 1688, a publication initiated by Kirkwood and again subsidized by Boyle.

In 1698 the SPCK was founded, with its main interest the formation of parochial libraries, particularly in the colonies, and charity schools. Kirkwood wholeheartedly endorsed the society's aims and placed them in a Scottish context. In 1699 he anonymously had a tract printed (most probably in Edinburgh) entitled *An overture for founding and maintaining of bibliothecks in every paroch throughout this kingdom*. Under this ambitious and radical scheme the parish minister's private books were to form the nucleus of each library, the parish schoolmaster was to act as librarian, and a uniform system of cataloguing was to be adopted throughout the country, with a union catalogue kept in Edinburgh. Nothing came of this proposal, but he modified his ideas in a second anonymous tract of 1702, *A copy of a letter anent a project, for erecting a library, in every presbytry, or at least county in the highlands*. This had been anticipated by a printed broadside probably of 1701 (*An Account of a Design to Erect Libraries in the Highlands*). Money was raised, and by the end of 1705 about 100 boxes of books, some designed for presbyteries and some for parishes, had been assembled and shipped to Edinburgh, complete with catalogues. Upwards of 4000 books and 2000 pamphlets were involved. By then Kirkwood was a member of the SPCK, and although the English and Anglican overtones of the society made presbyterian Scots wary, the general assembly felt it best, as it did with Bible distribution, to supervise the scheme by ensuring its own direct involvement: acts of support were passed in 1703, 1704, 1705, 1706, and 1709. Boxes were distributed but, as with bibles, the difficult political and religious situation and the remoteness of the region created many setbacks. Most libraries lasted only a short time.

Even within the SPCK criticism of the scheme was recorded in May 1704. However, Kirkwood defended himself to the society's satisfaction. He had been interested in the society's other main interest, charity schools, since the late 1690s. The promotion of schools, particularly in the highlands, grew in importance for him in his last years. He was possibly the author of *Proposals concerning the propagation of Christian knowledge in the highlands and islands of Scotland* (1707?), and the Society in Scotland for the Propagation of Christian Knowledge was established in July 1709, with Kirkwood a founder member. This is the last contemporary record of Kirkwood; it is assumed he died soon afterwards. As there is no reference in any source to a wife, it also has to be assumed that Kirkwood was unmarried. Besides the tracts and broadsides already mentioned he wrote: *An account of the design of printing about 3000 bibles in Irish, with the Psalms of David in metre, for the use of the highlanders* (1689?); *A memorial concerning the disorders of the highlands. Especially the northern parts thereof, and the isles of Scotland. With an account of some means by which the same may be redressed and prevented* (1703); and *The true interest of families, or, Directions how parents may be happy in their children … To which is annexed a discourse about the right way of improving our time* (1692). This went into a second edition the following year, entitled *A New Family Book*. All his works except the last were issued anonymously.

MURRAY C. T. SIMPSON

Sources G. P. Johnston, 'Notices of a collection of MSS relating to the circulation of the Irish bibles in 1685 and 1690 in the highlands and the association of the Rev. James Kirkwood therewith', *Publications of the Edinburgh Bibliographical Society*, 6 (1901), 1–18 [also privately printed in an edn of 18 copies, 1904] · W. R. Aitken, *A history of the public library movement in Scotland to 1955* (1971), 6–13 · *Fasti Scot.*, new edn, 2.132, 334 · T. Birch, *The life of the Honourable Robert Boyle* (1744), 396–430 · D. Maclean, 'Life and literary labours of Rev. Robert Kirk of Aberfoyle', *Transactions of the Gaelic Society of Inverness*, 31 (1922–4), 328–66 · E. McClure, ed., *A chapter in English church history: being the minutes of the Society for Promoting Christian Knowledge for … 1698–1704* (1888), 214, 217, 243, 246–7, 274 · R. E. W. Maddison, 'Robert Boyle and the Irish Bible', *Bulletin of the John Rylands Library*, 41 (1958), 81–101
Archives NL Scot., corresp. · NL Scot., nineteenth-century transcripts of documents by Kirkwood, MS 821 · U. Edin., New Coll. L., collection | NL Scot., Lee papers, MSS 3430, fols. 123, 130–32, 3450, fols. 13–19

Kirkwood, James (*d.* 1711x20), schoolmaster and grammarian, was a native of Dunbar. At the time that he was first approached to be schoolmaster in Linlithgow, in May 1674, he was acting as tutor, or 'governour', to Lord Bruce at the Old College, Glasgow, where he lodged with Gilbert Burnet, then professor of divinity. Kirkwood accepted the offer from Sir Robert Milne of Barntoun, the provost of Linlithgow, in January 1675 on terms that he maintained involved a fixed annual salary of 400 merks and tenure *ad vitam aut culpam*. On 1 August of that year he married Gelecina van Beest, with whom he had at least seven children. His school enjoyed a considerable reputation and it was attended by John Dalrymple, second earl of Stair, who also boarded with Kirkwood, presumably after the accident in 1682 in which he shot his brother.

In 1689 Kirkwood found himself at odds with the new town council, apparently because of his continuing adherence to episcopalianism. In taking up the post he had replaced a schoolmaster, David Skeoch, who had been removed for attending presbyterian conventicles. As Kirkwood showed little willingness to adapt to the changed political circumstances his salary was reduced to 300 merks in October 1689 and he lived under the threat of further sanctions. In the following February he, his pregnant wife, and their children were forcibly ejected from their home. Having withdrawn temporarily to Edinburgh, Kirkwood exacted a twin revenge, pursuing his cause against the town council through the courts while at the same time publishing an extensive account of his sufferings; *A short information of the plea betwixt the town council of Lithgow and Mr James Kirkwood, schoolmaster there, whereof a more full account may perhaps come out hereafter* appeared in 1690. Kirkwood redeemed his promise in an extended version, *The History of the Twenty Seven Gods of Linlithgow* (1711). The title referred to the council's charge that he was a reviler of the gods of the people; Kirkwood interpreted 'gods' to mean the twenty-seven members of the town council. The council was fined 4000 merks in 1692 but as late as 1711 Kirkwood complained that he had received nothing by way of reparation.

Initially without employment Kirkwood then set up a private school in Edinburgh before becoming schoolmaster at Kelso at the invitation of the countess of Roxburghe.

Kirkwood maintained that he had accepted the offer in preference to other positions, including the professorship of humanity in St Andrews University and a similar post in Virginia. This increased his displeasure when conflicts arose. The position of schoolmaster would normally have been held jointly with the offices of precentor and session clerk; Kirkwood was unacceptable to the kirk session in these roles but without the conjunction of offices his salary was naturally diminished. His dispute with the local minister, William Jack (or Jacque), and the kirk session were chronicled in *Mr Kirkwood's Plea before the Kirk, and Civil Judicatures of Scotland* (1698). Wild allegations were made: among other things Kirkwood was accused of trying to force his attentions on a woman servant of Sir John Home of Blackadder and using obscene expressions in explaining Latin words to his scholars. Once again the root of the issue was suspicion of Kirkwood's episcopalian sympathies, although even here the truth remains elusive and Kirkwood denied, for example, that he had served the episcopalian meeting-house as session clerk. Unsuccessful in pursuit of the offices to which he felt himself entitled, he appears to have continued in his role as schoolmaster until succeeded by David Chrystie in 1708.

As a grammarian Kirkwood based his reputation on his *Grammatica facilis* (1674). In 1678 he published a *Rhetoricae compendium*. Just after his ejection from Linlithgow, and at the suggestion of Lord Stair, he was consulted by the commissioners for colleges and schools as to the best Latin grammar to be used in Scottish schools. When asked his opinion of Despauter's grammar he opined that 'if its superfluities were rescinded, the defects supply'd, the intricacies cleared, the errors rectified, and the method amended, it might well pass for an excellent Grammar' (J. Kirkwood, *The History of the Twenty Seven Gods of Linlithgow*, 1711, iii). At the commissioners' direction he published *Grammatica Despauteriana, cum nova novi generis glossa: cui subjunguntur singula primae partis exempla vernacula reddita* (1695). This went to further editions in 1700, 1711, and 1720, though by that time it had been superseded by Thomas Ruddiman's *Rudiments of the Latin Tongue* (1714). Kirkwood had died by the time of the fourth edition, in 1720, although details of the exact date and place of his death are unknown.　　　LIONEL ALEXANDER RITCHIE

Sources J. Smith, *History of Kelso grammar school* (1909), 21–4 · G. Waldie, *A history of the town and palace of Linlithgow* (1879), 85–8 · J. Penney, *Historical account of Linlithgowshire* (1831), 78–9, 215–17 · J. Miller, *The history of Dunbar* (1830), 213–14 · Chambers, *Scots.* (1855), 3.325 · *DNB* · *IGI*

Kirton, Edmund (*d.* 1466), abbot of Westminster, was born into the Coppledike family of Lincolnshire, and his surname derives from one or other of the two villages named Kirton in that county. Joan Barton, of 'Cotes' (Hertfordshire), who bequeathed to him a silver chalice in 1437, was a cousin, and Edward Kirton, described as a canon, who is also mentioned in her will, may have been a brother. Kirton entered the Benedictine monastery in 1403–4 and was sent to Gloucester College, Oxford, in 1407, two years before his ordination to the priesthood: intellectually, he was outstanding. His long residence at Oxford, during which he proceeded DTh, culminated in his appointment as *prior studentium* in 1426. In the course of his Oxford years, he was employed several times on business for the provincial chapter of English black monks, and it may also have been in this period that he preached before Pope Martin V (*r.* 1417–31), presumably at Rome, an event recorded in his epitaph.

After Kirton's return to Westminster, he served as sacrist (1433–40) and so had the opportunity of proving himself in a major office. Anthony Wood's belief that he was summoned to Basel in 1437 to answer a charge of heresy is without foundation. In the abbatial election of 1440, which was conducted by scrutiny, he obtained fewer votes than Prior Nicholas Ashby, but, assisted by a letter of recommendation from the University of Oxford, was provided to the abbacy by Pope Eugenius IV (*r.* 1431–47) later in the year. The demands of office, manageable to the sacrist, quickly proved too much for the abbot, and in 1444 visitors appointed by the provincial chapter suspended Kirton. His offence on this occasion was, it appears, maladministration. Moral charges, including fornication, followed two years later, and, in respect of these, Kirton underwent at least the first stages of a trial before papal judges. He survived both these crises and later allegations by Ralph Aleyn, a monk of Westminster, that he had committed Aleyn to prison on a trumped-up charge of theft. The debts that he left to his successor, George Norwych (*d.* 1469), were occasioned at least in part by circumstances beyond his control: the need for expensive repairs to the monks' dormitory and to the rose window in the south transept of the abbey church. Yet Kirton lacked the businesslike qualities needed to take the monastery through a difficult financial period. He resigned in 1462, probably on the grounds of old age, and was granted a generous pension of £166 13s. 4d. per annum. It is not known where he spent his retirement. He died on 3 October 1466 and was buried in St Andrew's Chapel, in the north transept of the abbey church. The brass on his altar-tomb, which bore his family arms, survived into the eighteenth century. An engraving is reproduced in Dart's *Westmonasterium, or, The history and antiquities of the abbey church of St. Peter's, Westminster* (Dart, 2, facing p. 2).   BARBARA F. HARVEY

Sources E. H. Pearce, *The monks of Westminster* (1916), 128–9 · Emden, *Oxf.*, 2.1080 · private information (2004) [Revd Norman Tanner SJ] · V. H. Galbraith, 'A visitation of Westminster in 1444', *EngHR*, 37 (1922), 83–8 · G. Whitteridge, 'A note on some of the medieval wills in the possession of Saint Bartholomew's Hospital', *St. Bartholomew's Hospital Journal*, 46 (1938–9), 183–6 · T. Trowles, ed., *Westminster Abbey official guide*, new edn (1997), 54–5 · R. Widmore, *An enquiry into the time of the first foundation of Westminster Abbey* (1743), 114–15 [incl. epitaph] · Westminster Abbey Muniment Room, WAM, 64270 [the allegations of Br R. Aleyn] · B. Harvey, *Living and dying in England, 1100–1540: the monastic experience* (1993), 206–7 · J. Dart, *Westmonasterium, or, The history and antiquities of the abbey church of St. Peter's, Westminster* (1723), 2 · Bodl. Oxf., MS Arch. Selden B.23, fol. 103v

Archives Bodl. Oxf., MS Arch. Selden B.23, fol. 103v [copy]

Likenesses brass tomb effigy, repro. in Dart, *Westmonasterium*

Kirwan, Francis (1589–1661), Roman Catholic bishop of Killala, was born in Galway, the son of Matthew Kirwan, merchant, and Julia Lynch, both from long-established and wealthy merchant families of the city. He was educated there by his mother's uncle, a priest named Arthur Lynch. He then went to Lisbon, Portugal, to study at the Irish College founded there for the education of students for the priesthood in 1593. Poor health forced a premature return, but he completed his studies in Galway and was ordained priest there in 1614. In 1615 he went to France for further studies, and for a short time taught philosophy in the schools of the Congregation of the Oratory at Dieppe. In 1620 he returned to Ireland as vicar-general of Archbishop Conry of Tuam, who remained in exile for political reasons.

When the Wars of Religion ended in France in 1598 the ideals of the Counter-Reformation began to flourish there, and it was clear when he returned to Ireland that Kirwan had absorbed them to a considerable degree. Society in the west of Ireland was now so solidly Roman Catholic that he was in practice free to function. He based himself in his native Galway, where his social position would also have helped him. From there he carried out regular visitation of the extensive diocese, including the wild and trackless western parts and even the islands. Here especially he found much to reform, ignorance of even basic truths of religion among the laity, and a clergy not well equipped to instruct them or in some other respects to give them example.

Kirwan made great efforts to build up an educated and devoted priesthood. Before candidates were sent to seminaries in Europe they spent some time in his household in Galway, where they received training as envisaged by the reforms of the Council of Trent and as put in practice by such figures as St Charles Borromeo, archbishop of Milan, for whom Kirwan had a particular reverence. In a deeply traditional society he also had a wide-ranging social function, settling not only religious but also secular disputes with the approval of Roman Catholic magistrates. He combined his attachment to the new reforms with a native austerity, as was shown by his devotion to the traditional pilgrimages of Croagh Patrick and Lough Derg. A real shrewdness went with a thorough asceticism, exemplified in the reported case of the man he had ordered to take back the wife he had put away. It is said that the man claimed he would rather suffer the pains of hell than his wife's company, but changed his mind very quickly when invited to put his finger in a candle flame.

Archbishop Conry died in 1629 and was succeeded by Malachy O'Queely. O'Queely, though resident, asked Kirwan to continue as his vicar, and he agreed. But about 1636 Kirwan set out again for France, where he worked to develop the continental base so vital to the religious reorganization in Ireland. In Paris, however, despite his friendship with so influential a figure as St Vincent de Paul, he failed in his efforts to set up what would have been a second Irish seminary in the city.

Meanwhile, the archbishop of Tuam and others had procured Kirwan's appointment to the see of Killala. He accepted with real reluctance, and was consecrated bishop at St Vincent de Paul's headquarters, St Lazare, on 7 May 1645. He took possession of his see on 5 October

1646. In fact, much of his time was to be taken up with the political affairs of the Irish Confederate Catholics. He sided against the papal nuncio Rinuccini in the dispute which finally tore the Confederates apart in 1648 and arguably incurred excommunication, a fact which weighed very much on his conscience until he secured what he considered satisfactory absolution.

Oliver Cromwell landed in Ireland on 15 August 1649 and his military campaign ended with the surrender of Galway on 12 April 1652. After this Kirwan was a fugitive, dependent on what was inevitably the diminishing power of the Roman Catholic gentry to protect him. He made his way to Galway, where he finally gave himself up in 1654. For a time he was allowed to live under house arrest, but he was later imprisoned and then deported in the summer of 1655.

Kirwan arrived in Nantes in August, and two years later he went to Rennes, where he remained until his death. Many Irish exiles found refuge in Brittany, but most had to live in great poverty. Kirwan was fortunate to find a generous benefactor at Rennes, where he also helped the local bishop. He died there, deeply revered, on 27 August 1661. On his deathbed he was received into the Society of Jesus, whom he had always highly regarded, and on 29 August he was buried in their church in Rennes. A bronze plaque with a brief inscription was placed on his tomb.

RICHARD BAGWELL, *rev.* PATRICK J. CORISH

Sources J. Lynch, *Pii Antistitis icon, sive, De vita et morte … Francisci Kirovani* (1669); facs. edn (1951) • J. Linchaeo [J. Lynch], *De praesulibus Hiberniae*, ed. J. F. O'Doherty, IMC, 2 (1944), 328–34 • B. O'Ferrall and D. O'Connell, *Commentarius Rinuccinianus de sedis apostolicae legatione ad foederatos Hiberniae Catholicos per annos 1645–1649*, ed. J. Kavanagh, IMC, 3 (1939); 4 (1941); 5 (1944) • C. Eubel and others, eds., *Hierarchia Catholica medii et recentioris aevi*, 4, ed. C. Eubel and P. Gauchat (Passau, 1935) • D. F. Cregan, 'The social and cultural background of a Counter-Reformation episcopate, 1618–60', *Studies in Irish history presented to R. Dudley Edwards*, ed. A. Cosgrove and D. McCartney (1979), 85–117 • [J. Lynch], *The portrait of a pious bishop*, ed. C. P. Meehan (1884)

Likenesses attrib. C. Hisam, engraving, 1661, repro. in Lynch, *Pii Antistitis icon*, frontispiece

Kirwan, Sir (Archibald) Laurence Patrick [Larry] (1907–1999), archaeologist and geographer, was born on 13 May 1907 in Cork, the second son of Patrick John Kirwan and his wife, Mabel, *née* Norton. His father came from an old Galway family, the Kirwans of Cregg, and was a Shakespearian actor and producer as well as an author and novelist.

Larry Kirwan (as he was invariably known) was educated at Wimbledon College and then at Merton College, Oxford (from 1925 to 1926), which he left without having taken a degree, an omission that he rectified in 1935 by graduating BLitt from Oxford for a thesis on Lower Nubia in the Byzantine period. His early interest in archaeology was largely inspired by early contact with Sir Flinders Petrie, the professor of Egyptology at London University. After a season of working in Egypt for the British Museum, he was appointed in 1929 as assistant director of the archaeological survey of Nubia sponsored by the Egyptian department of antiquities. This was a necessary prelude to the

Sir (Archibald) Laurence Patrick Kirwan (1907–1999), by Bassano, *c.*1962

raising of the Aswan Dam in 1935 and a valuable first experience of responsible fieldwork. It was during this period that he met, and in 1932 married, Joan Elizabeth (Victoria) Chetwynd, with whom he had one daughter. In 1934 he was appointed director of Oxford University expeditions to the Sudan, and from 1937 to 1939 he was Tweedie fellow in archaeology at Edinburgh University, which extended his opportunities of fieldwork in the Sudan.

A year before the outbreak of the Second World War Kirwan joined the Territorial Army on the reserve of officers and was quickly drafted into staff work after the start of the war. From 1942 to 1945 he was on the joint staffs in the Ministry of Defence and Cabinet Office. He ended the war as a lieutenant-colonel, with experience of working with government departments which stood him in good stead in his next job.

By the end of the war the Royal Geographical Society (RGS) had been run for the past thirty years by the distinguished mathematician A. J. Hinks. The society needed revitalizing, and its president Lord Rennell—the explorer, diplomat, and banker—approached Kirwan about taking it on as director and secretary. Kirwan was not a geographer, his primary interests being in archaeology and history, and prominent people in the society (notably the polar explorer Sir James Wordie, who was its honorary secretary at the time) opposed the appointment. However, Kirwan was accepted, and remained in the post for the next thirty years. He also edited the society's *Geographical*

Journal for the whole of this time—and indeed for three years after his retirement.

During his tenure at the RGS Kirwan was a driving force behind a large number of notable expeditions. These included the Norwegian-British-Swedish expedition to Queen Maud Land led by John Giaver from 1949 to 1952, the ecological survey of south Turkana from 1960 to 1962, and the joint expedition with the Royal Society to Mato Grosso led by Iain Bishop from 1967 to 1969. But by far the most celebrated of the RGS expeditions with which he was associated were John Hunt's first successful assault on Everest in 1953, and the first trans-Antarctica expedition led by Vivian Fuchs from 1955 to 1957. These events brought the RGS into a national prominence which it had not enjoyed since the days of Livingstone and Stanley in the mid-nineteenth century.

In all his activities at the RGS Kirwan strove successfully to keep a balance between the various strands that made up the society's membership and character. He fostered close and good relations with geography departments in British and foreign universities, becoming a member of the University of London's board of geographical studies, and of the national committee for geography of the Royal Society; he also presided in 1961–2 over section E of the British Association for the Advancement of Science. At the same time he also gave much close and sympathetic attention to applications for the society's support from individuals or young groups of explorers who sought encouragement, finance, and often scientific motivation from the society.

Kirwan was a well-known figure on the international geographical circuit. The 24th International Geographical Congress was held at the RGS building in Kensington Gore in 1964 and in the nearby buildings of Imperial College. The congress, consisting of over 2000 geographers, was opened by the queen and involved Kirwan in a great deal of administrative work. He also travelled widely and kept up his connections and interests in Nubia and the Sudan; in both Egypt and the Sudan he held honorary posts in academic and geographical organizations. He was an official adviser on the Aswan High Dam project, and often appeared to be happiest when he could get away from his office to the wilder regions he had known in his youth.

Kirwan's most substantial international achievement was probably his leadership of the field mission in the court of arbitration in the Argentine–Chilean frontier dispute in the extreme south of those countries in 1966. He characteristically surveyed the ground in person, riding on horseback over large distances. He was also, from 1968 to 1981, a member (and from 1970 to 1980 deputy chairman) of the committee for the landscape development of trunk roads in the United Kingdom. These and other public-spirited activities drew Kirwan to the attention of the British government, and he was appointed CMG in 1958 and knighted KCMG in 1972.

Kirwan's historical bent led him to take a close interest in the archives and map room of the RGS as well as in its journal. He developed a particular interest in polar exploration following Fuchs's Antarctica expedition and he wrote a history of the subject, entitled *The White Road*, in 1959. On retiring as director of the RGS in 1975 he was awarded the society's founder's medal. After retirement he held a visiting professorship at Cairo University and several other honorary academic appointments.

Kirwan's first marriage ended in divorce, and on 19 July 1949 he married Stella Mary Monck, the daughter of Roger Buchanan, an antique furniture dealer, and the former wife of Bosworth Edwin Monk Monck, from whom she had obtained a divorce. Although there were no children of this second marriage, it was happy and long-lasting. Stella Kirwan died in 1997 only two years before they would have celebrated their golden wedding. Kirwan's last years were saddened by this bereavement and by the increasing loss of his eyesight. He continued to live in Rosenau Crescent, south-west London, and died of oesophageal cancer in the Trinity Hospice on Clapham Common on 16 April 1999. He was survived by the daughter of his first marriage.

Larry Kirwan was a survivor from the age of heroic and magisterial archaeologists in the mould of Sir Mortimer Wheeler. He left the RGS as a thriving and respected institution—a memorial to the greater part of his life's work, which spanned the period of the winding up of the British empire. He was an imposing figure, 6 feet 6 inches tall, with a commanding presence which could be daunting, particularly on first acquaintance. He had none of the paternalistic manner of his predecessor at the RGS and could be demanding in his standards and requirements of his staff. But he was always accessible and considerate towards younger fellows of the society, especially to those attempting rigorous and daring expeditions. Explorers such as Robin Hanbury-Tenison and John Hemming (his successor as director of the RGS) owed much to his encouragement. While he directed the RGS, no country in the world could match the British activity in young scientific expeditions. Above all he made the RGS a congenial meeting place for different age-groups, different academic disciplines, and those with widely different approaches to the practice and development of geography.

JOHN URE

Sources L. Kirwan, *The white road* (1959) · *The Guardian* (21 April 1999) · *The Times* (22 April 1999) · *Daily Telegraph* (24 April 1999) · *The Independent* (7 May 1999) · *WWW* · personal knowledge (2004) · private information (2004) · b. cert. · d. cert.
Archives National University of Ireland, Galway · RGS, personal papers, archaeological papers relating to Nubia, papers relating to visits to Sudan · SOAS, papers on archaeology in Ethiopia, Sudan, and the Arabian peninsula | Bodl. Oxf., letters to O. G. S. Crawford
Likenesses photograph, 1950–59, repro. in *The Independent* · photograph, 1952, repro. in *Daily Telegraph* · Bassano, photograph, *c.*1962, RGS [*see illus.*] · photograph, 1966, repro. in *The Guardian* · photograph, repro. in *The Times*
Wealth at death £196,786: probate, 12 July 1999, *CGPLA Eng. & Wales*

Kirwan, Owen (*d.* 1803), Irish nationalist, is of unknown origins and family. Sometimes described as a tailor, he was a dealer in secondhand clothes and living at 64 Plunket Street, Dublin, in early 1803 when contacted by the agents of the United Irish leader Robert Emmet. While there is no evidence that Kirwan participated in the rising of 1798, his early initiation into the plot of 1803 strongly indicates that he was none the less a respected United Irishman in the south city. He belonged to the same revolutionary cell as Patrick Street publican Thomas Maguaran and was related to Patrick McCabe, both of whom played significant roles in the rising.

Kirwan worked in an illegal arms depot run by Scottish republican John McIntosh in June and July 1803 at 26 Patrick Street. Hinged pikes, signal rockets, and other munitions were manufactured and concealed behind false partition walls. An explosion of loose powder wrecked the building on 16 July 1803 and killed one of Kirwan's co-workers. This setback persuaded the leadership coterie attached to Emmet to attempt a coup in the capital the following week without awaiting the arrival of their French allies. Upon sighting a rocket in the sky on 23 July Kirwan donned a green jacket presented to him by his wife and led about ten associates to a rallying point on Thomas Street. They were present when skirmishing broke out and Chief Justice Kilwarden was killed. Dismayed by this and other unexpected reverses, Emmet went into hiding in the Dublin mountains leaving the city men under the control of secondary commanders. Kirwan's greatly augmented force returned briefly to his home for refreshments before assisting in the attack on the Coombe barracks of the 21st regiment. The eventual dispersal of the lightly armed rebels brought the abortive rising to a close.

Kirwan was arrested at home on 25 July and tried on 1 September by a special commission convened at Green Street courthouse. Given the quality and quantity of eyewitness testimony against Kirwan, the capital sentence imposed by Judge Baron George on the 2nd was almost inevitable, notwithstanding the characteristically robust defence mounted by John Philpot Curran. Kirwan was executed on Thomas Street on 3 September 1803. He was survived by his wife, about whom nothing further is known.

RUÁN O'DONNELL

Sources R. R. Madden, *The United Irishmen, their lives and times*, 2nd ser., 4 vols. (1857–60), 3 · *State trials*, 28.799–84 · R. O'Donnell, *Robert Emmet and the rising of 1803* (Cork, 2002) · H. Landreth, *The pursuit of Robert Emmet* (Dublin, 1949) · L. O'Broin, *The unfortunate Mr Emmet* (Dublin, 1958) · *DNB*
Archives BL, Hardwicke papers · NA Ire., rebellion / state of the country papers

Kirwan, Richard (1733–1812), chemist and mineralogist, was born at Cloghballymore House, near Kinvara, co. Galway, Ireland, the second son of Martin Kirwan (*d.* 1741) of Cregg Castle, near Corrundulla, and his wife, Mary, daughter of Patrick French. After the death of his father he was placed in the care of his maternal grandparents at Cloghballymore House. He was educated by the family chaplain until sent (together with his brothers Andrew and Hyacinth) to Erasmus Smith School in Galway.

Though Kirwan's father had been brought up a Roman Catholic, he had conformed to the tenets of the established church in order to avoid the restrictions of the penal laws. However, he wanted his second son, who would not inherit the family estates, to become a Catholic priest. Accordingly Kirwan was sent to Poitiers, where Jesuits had established a college for Irish clerical students, and subsequently to the novitiate at St Omer. Preparations for a priesthood were, however, abandoned after the death, as a result of a duel in Dublin about 1755, of his elder brother, Patrick.

In February 1757 Kirwan married Anne Blake (*d.* 1765), the daughter of Sir Thomas and Lady Blake of Menlough Castle, on the southern shores of Lough Corrib. They had two daughters. The couple lived at Menlough, where Kirwan equipped a chemical laboratory, in which he apparently spent most of his time, earning his mother-in-law's disapproval. A surviving letter sent to him by his mother in 1750 shows that at Poitiers too he had initially neglected his legitimate studies in order to read books on chemistry.

When his wife died in 1765, Kirwan was in London studying law. In 1764 he had renounced Catholicism as a prerequisite of being called to the Irish bar in 1766. He practised in Dublin for two years and developed an intense dislike of the profession. After a further period in London, he returned to Ireland, about 1772, and went to live about 10 miles north-east of Galway at Cregg Castle, which had been built by his great-great-grandfather. He made some alterations and built a laboratory in the grounds.

Kirwan returned to London in 1777. Early in 1780, the year of his election to the Royal Society, he began to reside at 11 Newman Street, off Oxford Street, which became a rendezvous for scientists and members of society. Initially he was greatly influenced by Joseph Priestley, who persuaded him to become a Unitarian. He began to correspond with scientists in Europe, notably Torbern Bergman and Guyton de Morveau. Letters between Kirwan and Guyton in the period 1782–1802 chart the course of their close friendship and gradual divergence of their views on the phlogiston theory and Lavoisier's new theory of combustion.

Kirwan is known to historians for his ambiguous involvement in the chemical revolution. His *Essay on Phlogiston and the Constitution of Acids*, in which he sought to reconcile the established phlogistic chemistry with Lavoisier's new theory, was published in 1787, the year he left London. Priestley had recently discovered that 'inflammable air' (hydrogen) could, like charcoal, revive a metal from its calx, and (like Priestley himself) Kirwan believed that the revival of a metal from its calx took place through the addition of phlogiston. He therefore used Priestley's discovery to suggest that inflammable air was simply phlogiston in its gaseous state. However, he had to contend with Lavoisier's apparently contradictory finding that the process of reviving a calx resulted in a loss of weight, whereas the addition of phlogiston should have increased it; while calcination, believed to involve loss of phlogiston, resulted in an increase in weight. He therefore partially accepted Lavoisier's suggestion that the weight changes should be attributed to the addition of oxygen in calcination and its removal when the process was reversed, but he sought to make this consistent with the theory of phlogiston by postulating that in calcination the oxygen united with the metal's phlogiston to form 'fixed air' (carbon dioxide).

Kirwan's ideas on phlogiston were initially published as the second part of a paper which was mainly devoted to the experiments on chemical affinity for which he won the Royal Society's Copley medal in 1782. This experimental programme was continued in his later years, after he returned to Ireland. Meanwhile his *Essay on Phlogiston* was rapidly translated into French by Lavoisier's wife, Marie-Anne, and brought out in 1788 with critical notes by six French savants, including her husband. Kirwan's subsequent abandonment of the phlogistic cause may have been brought about by this publication. Alternatively it is possible that he was converted by his fellow countryman William Higgins's *A Comparative View of the Phlogistic and Antiphlogistic Theories* (1789), which was sharply critical of his attempt to reconcile the two systems. Be that as it may, his only known comment when he relinquished the phlogiston theory in 1791 was that it was impossible to prove that fixed air was ever formed from the combination of phlogiston and oxygen.

Kirwan's *An Estimate of the Temperature at Different Latitudes*, an early work on comparative climatology, was also published in 1787. Much of his work published in the *Transactions* of the Royal Irish Academy, of which he was the second president in 1799, was on meteorology. It included synopses of the weather in Dublin from 1788 to 1808, which he compiled from daily records using instruments set up behind his house at 6 Cavendish Row, Dublin. His most important paper, 'On the variations of the atmosphere' (*Transactions of the Royal Irish Academy*, 8, 1802, 269–507), showed an early understanding of air masses.

Kirwan's most important work however was his *Elements of Mineralogy*, published in 1784 and revised in 1794–6. The revised edition was aided by his negotiated purchase, for the Royal Dublin Society, of the Leskean collections (about 7000 specimens assembled by N. G. Leske, professor of natural history at Leipzig). His *Essay on the Analysis of Mineral Waters* (1799) is a good account of the qualitative and quantitative methods of analysis then available. He also wrote informatively on subjects related to Ireland's economy, notably on coal and coalmining. His writings on geology included *Geological Essays* (1799) and various papers, and are largely a defence of the Mosaic account of the creation against James Hutton's theory of the earth, which Kirwan believed was atheistic and therefore subversive. Towards the end of his life Kirwan turned to philosophical writing, publishing a lengthy critique of Hume's philosophy in *Transactions of the Royal Irish Academy* (vol. 8, 1801); a two-volume *Logick* (1807), concerned particularly with practical applications in metaphysics and religion and with probability theory; and *Metaphysical Essays* (1811), a staunch defence of Berkeley's immaterialism.

In his later life Kirwan developed a morbid fear of catching a cold, and Lady Morgan (formerly the author Sydney Owenson) described how, one fine spring evening, she was received by Kirwan clad in a cloak, shawl, and slouch hat, sitting on a sofa completely surrounded by a large screen, while a huge fire blazed on the hearth. He died at his home on 1 June 1812, and was buried a week later in the yard of the old St George's Church in Dublin. His library was bequeathed to the Royal Irish Academy. An earlier collection of his books came to be housed in the Athenaeum Library in Salem, Massachusetts, after the ship carrying it from Galway to London was captured by a privateer, and eventually sold at Salem.   E. L. SCOTT

Sources M. Donovan, 'Biographical account of the late Richard Kirwan', *Proceedings of the Royal Irish Academy*, 4 (1847–50), 81–118 [list of papers] · P. J. McLaughlin, 'Richard Kirwan, 1733–1812', *Studies*, 28 (1939), 461–74, 593–605 · P. J. McLaughlin, 'Richard Kirwan, 1733–1812', *Studies*, 29 (1940), 71–83, 281–300 · F. E. Dixon, 'Richard Kirwan, the Dublin philosopher', *Dublin Historical Record*, 24/3 (1970–71), 53–64 · E. Grison, M. Goupil, and P. Bret, eds., *A scientific correspondence during the chemical revolution* (1994) · Lady Morgan, *Book of the boudoir*, 1 (1829) · J. O'Reardon, 'The life and work of Richard Kirwan', *National Magazine* [Dublin], 1 (1830), 330–42, 469–75 · J. R. O'Flanagan, 'Richard Kirwan', *Dublin Saturday Magazine*, 2 (1865), 242–4, 254–6, 266–9 · W. H. Brock, *The Fontana history of chemistry* (1992) · C. Mollan, W. Davis, and B. Finucane, eds., *Some people and places in Irish science and technology* (1985)

Archives Royal Irish Acad.

Likenesses Broca, engraving, repro. in *Dublin Magazine, or Monthly Memorialist*, 1 (1812), 64 · H. D. Hamilton, oils, Royal Dublin Society · drawing, NL Ire. · oils, Royal Irish Acad.

Kirwan, Stephen (*d.* 1601), Church of Ireland bishop of Clonfert, was born in Galway and came from a prominent Anglo-Norman family. He was typical of the transitional generation of native Irish clergy in Elizabeth's reign who accepted appointments within the established (though hardly protestant) church, but whose own religious convictions were ambiguous, and whose children were Roman Catholic. He was educated at Oxford *c.*1566, and in Paris and Louvain, where, according to a hostile source, 'he both heard and said many a mass' (Cunningham, 19). During his studies he held the archdeaconry of Annaghdown and the rectory of Killmacryan (both Tuam). In 1572 he was nominated by the queen to the see of Kilmacduagh in the province of Tuam; letters patent for his consecration were issued on 13 April 1573. On 30 March 1582 he was nominated to Clonfert, and letters patent for his consecration were issued on 24 May. Active in local government in Connaught, he served as a justice and commissioner for the province, 1580–1601.

The strongly protestant Sir Turlough O'Brien claimed *c.*1591 that though at the time of his appointment to Clonfert, Kirwan 'professed and swore to reformed disposition', he was in fact a lukewarm evangelist, more interested in the 'glutted security of corporate ease' than preaching. Kirwan could, O'Brien thought, best be termed 'the English-Romish bishop O'Kirovan of Clonfert'. Kirwan's eldest son, according to O'Brien, had run away to Spain and become an 'Antichristian rebel, a Spanish subject', while his other two sons, who remained in Ireland, were 'papish recusants' (Cunningham, 19). Kirwan died before 4 November 1601, when the see was said to be vacant following his death; at the time of his death he also held the deanery of Clonfert.   ALAN FORD

Sources Wood, *Ath. Oxon.*, new edn, 2.846 · B. Cunningham, ed., 'A view of religious affiliation and practice in Thomond, 1591', *Archivium Hibernicum*, 48 (1994), 13–24 · K. W. Nicholls, ed., 'Visitation of the dioceses of Clonfert, Tuam, and Kilmacduagh, c.1565–67', *Analecta Hibernica*, 26 (1970), 144–58 · *The Irish fiants of the Tudor sovereigns*, 4 vols. (1994) · *CSP Ire.*, 1601–3, 149 · PRO, SP 63/209/172, 4 Nov 1601 · E. B. Fryde and others, eds., *Handbook of British chronology*, 3rd edn, Royal Historical Society Guides and Handbooks, 2 (1986)

Kirwan, Walter Blake (1754–1805), Church of Ireland dean of Killala, was born at Gortha, co. Galway, into a Roman Catholic family. He was the elder son of Patrick Fitz Thomas Kirwan of Galway and Mary, second daughter of Walter Blake of Carrowbrowne. He was educated at the English College at St Omer. At the age of seventeen he accompanied a relative to St Croix in the West Indies. Much affected by the climate and by the cruelty of that society he left after six years and went to the University of Louvain, where he took holy orders and was appointed professor of natural and moral philosophy. In 1778 he became chaplain to the Neapolitan ambassador at the British court, and the eloquence of the sermons which he preached in London in this capacity attracted marked attention.

In 1787 Kirwan left the Roman Catholic church, and on 24 June preached his first sermon to a protestant congregation in St Peter's Church, Dublin. He continued to officiate at St Peter's, where he proved to be an immensely popular speaker, for several years. His services were eagerly sought for charity sermons, and churches where he preached were often overrun by crowds eager to attend. It was not uncommon for collections of up to £1200 to be taken on such occasions. In 1789 Kirwan was collated by the archbishop of Dublin to the prebend of Howth, co. Dublin; in the same year he was preferred to the living of St Nicholas Without in the city of Dublin. On 22 September 1798 Kirwan married Wilhelmina, the youngest daughter of Goddard Richards of Grange, co. Wexford; the couple had two daughters and two sons, one of whom, Antony la Touche Kirwan, later became dean of Limerick.

In 1800 Kirwan was appointed dean of Killala. He died at his house, Mount Pleasant, near Dublin, on 27 October 1805. He was survived by his wife, who was granted a crown pension of £300 per annum for life, with reversion to her daughters. A volume of Kirwan's sermons was published posthumously in 1816, reaching a second edition later that year.

THOMAS HAMILTON, *rev.* PHILIP CARTER

Sources [W. Kirwan ?], 'Sketch of his life', in W. B. Kirwan, *Sermons*, 2nd edn (1816) · H. Cotton, *Fasti ecclesiae Hibernicae*, 1–2 (1845–8) · M. J. Blake, *Blake family records, 1300 to 1600* (1902), 191–2 · M. J. Blake, *Blake family records, 1600 to 1700* (1905), 211
Likenesses W. Ward, mezzotint, pubd 1806 (after H. D. Hamilton), BM · M. A. Shee, oils, NPG, NG Ire.

Kissin, Harry Aaron, Baron Kissin (1912–1997), businessman and financier, was born on 23 August 1912 in Danzig, Germany, the son of Russian Jewish parents, Israel Kissin, grain merchant, and his wife, Reusi, *née* Model. He was brought up in Danzig and studied law at Basel University, Switzerland, where he afterwards practised as a lawyer until 1933 when he moved to London. His parents subsequently lived in Paris; after his father's death, his mother moved to London. On 1 June 1935 Kissin married Ruth Deborah Samuel (*b.* 1911), daughter of Siegmund Samuel. They had a son and a daughter.

In London Kissin initially worked for P. Winn's Produce Company Ltd, drug merchants and shellac and general importers and exporters, which had recently been established by Paul Winn & Co. Ltd, general merchants. At this time he was especially friendly with Siegmund Warburg, Henry Grunfeld, and Eric Korner, then developing their financing and commodity broking business, New Trading Co., which in the post-war years emerged as the merchant bank of S. G. Warburg & Co. During the Second World War Kissin was especially concerned with Barking Brassware Co., manufacturers of sanitary fittings and a connection of Winns, whose output he converted to shell production.

About 1947 Kissin established his own firm of G. H. Kay (Overseas), general import and export merchants, of Drapers Gardens, London, although he sustained his link with Winns as it shared the same address. His new firm quickly developed an important trading business with eastern Europe (especially Poland and Yugoslavia) and Latin America; it specialized in rubber. He was managing director and the largest single shareholder. Clement Davies, leader of the Liberal Party, and T. L. (Tom) Horabin, a Labour MP and business consultant, sat with him on the board.

At this time G. H. Kay developed business links with the well known and long established yet somewhat moribund commodity brokers, Lewis and Peat, of Mincing Lane. Soon Kissin acquired a controlling interest in this public company through another of his companies, Kay Finance Co. Boardroom conflict arose and in 1955 Kay orchestrated the resignation of several Lewis and Peat directors and obtained executive control. As major shareholder and as non-executive deputy chairman from 1954, managing director from 1958, and chairman from 1961, Kissin revived and expanded Lewis and Peat by diversifying it from broking into dealing and broadening the range of commodities and goods in which it dealt, often through the timely acquisition of ailing businesses. He was recognized as particularly adept at this and employed as his adviser S. G. Warburg & Co. He also diversified Lewis and Peat into service provision to the commodity industry—for example through insurance and ship broking—and into processing commodities such as rubber and cocoa through the establishment of plant overseas. Profits grew from £231,000 in 1961 to £2.15 million a decade later. Under Kissin, Lewis and Peat emerged as a dynamic force amid the decaying commodity firms of Mincing Lane and Mark Lane which in the 1950s and 1960s for the most part failed to adapt to rapid structural change in their industry.

Kissin's management style was certainly energetic, hands-on, and at times ruthless. As with firms such as Warburgs, it marked him out as an outsider not above suspicion in the closed world of the City at that time. This did not, however, stand in his way in 1972 when he diversified

Peats into financial services through its takeover of the privately owned and patrician merchant bank Guinness Mahon, although at the time the transaction was referred to as a merger. The acquisition of this business, with its membership of the prestigious Accepting Houses Committee, brought the Guinness Peat Group, as Kissin's firm was now known, into the mainstream of City business life.

In 1974 Kissin was created a life peer as Baron Kissin of Camden by Harold Wilson. He had known Wilson since the late 1940s when Wilson was president of the Board of Trade and when Kissin acted as the board's consultant on trade with China and the Far East. They became close friends. In the early 1950s Lewis and Peat appears to have employed Wilson as a consultant, although Kissin was always quite clear that he made no payments of any kind to him. Kissin supported the Labour Party—for example, arranging the funding for vital private opinion polls during the 1974 election campaigns—and joined the group of eastern European émigré supporters and friends who gathered around Wilson. His elevation to a peerage coincided with the high point of his business career. In the 1970s Guinness Peat continued to prosper and when Kissin retired in 1979 his company was reckoned to be the 112th largest UK public company; he owned about 9 per cent of its equity.

After 1979 Kissin continued as life president of Guinness Peat and as a major shareholder, a combination which enabled him to exercise considerable influence and he did not flinch from doing so; the *Daily Telegraph* labelled him 'the ghost in the Guinness Peat boardroom' (*Daily Telegraph*). His autocratic style had frequently brought him into conflict with colleagues and this was vividly underlined in 1982 in a power struggle with Edmund Dell, a former Labour secretary of state for trade and Kissin's successor as chairman and chief executive. Without Kissin's hands-on management, Guinness Peat soon lost its way, and in 1981–2 chalked up losses of over £30 million; a dispute between the two over a recovery programme led to a bitter and highly public power struggle which resulted in Dell being ousted. With the encouragement of the Bank of England, anxious to protect Guinness Mahon from the problems of the wider group, Alastair Morton was brought in as Dell's successor. His ruthless restructuring of the group became a cause of further public strife for Kissin, who sought to preserve the value of his still-considerable shareholding. The surviving parts, in which Kissin maintained shareholdings, were soon subject to hostile takeover or ran into difficulties in the recession of the early 1990s. As part of this restructuring, Kissin and his son led a management buy-out of the commodities division which subsequently traded as Lewis and Peat Holdings Ltd; Kissin was its chairman until 1987.

Away from business Kissin's charitable work reflected his informed interest in music. This led him to a directorship of the Royal Opera House from 1973 to 1984; he established and was first chairman, until 1980, of the Royal Opera House Trust, which raised funds for the first major

extension to the house, completed in 1982. He was an amateur painter and chaired the council of the Institute of Contemporary Art from 1968 to 1975. He collected seventeenth-century Dutch and Flemish pictures. He supported Jewish causes and Israel, where he was a governor of the Bezalel Academy of Arts and Design from 1975 to 1987, and of the Hebrew University of Jerusalem in 1980. He was active in the House of Lords from the mid-1980s, sitting as a cross-bencher. He died of heart failure at 38 Hereford House, 66 North Row, Westminster, on 22 November 1997 and was buried at Bushey cemetery, Hertfordshire five days later. His wife survived him. A concert to celebrate his life was held at the Wigmore Hall, London, at which his relative, the leading Russian pianist Yevgeny Kissin, played.   JOHN ORBELL

Sources *The Times* (12 Dec 1997) · *Daily Telegraph* (21 Dec 1997) · L. McGrandle, *Two centuries of Lewis and Peat, 1775–1975* (privately printed, 1975) · P. Ziegler, *Wilson: the authorised life of Lord Wilson of Rievaulx* (1993) · *Debrett's Peerage* · *WWW* · *The Guardian* (16 Dec 1997) · M. Falkender, *Downing St in perspective* (1983) · private information (2004) · m. cert. · d. cert.

Likenesses photograph, repro. in *The Guardian* · photograph, repro. in *The Times* · photograph, repro. in *Daily Telegraph*

Kitcat, Dick. *See* Doyle, Richard (1824–1883).

Kitchen, (William) Frederick [Fred] (**1890–1969**), author, was born at Edwinstowe, Nottinghamshire, on 28 December 1890; his name was registered as William James Noel Kitchen, the son of William Hodgson Kitchen, a farm labourer, and his wife, Elizabeth Alice Alsop. Soon afterwards the family moved to Sandbeck, near Maltby in Yorkshire, where William Kitchen senior took up the post of cowman on a nobleman's estate. He died in 1903. Fred Kitchen left elementary school the following year to start work (initially at 1s. 3d. a day) on the first of a succession of farms, punctuated by a spell as a railway navvy. In 1912 he became a miner. Having courted a doctor's maid called Helen (1893/4–1920) for five years, during which time they saved money to set up house, he married her on 3 February 1915; in fact named Frances (according to their marriage certificate), she was the daughter of Willie Hanslock, a groom. Five years later she was dead, leaving him with small children to bring up. After the miners' strike of 1921 he went back to the land; and in 1925, by then married again, to Elizabeth, he took work as a cowman on a dairy farm near Sheffield. Two years later he moved back to Nottinghamshire, and in 1930 transferred with his employer to Kilton Forest Farm at Worksop.

Kitchen was a keen reader (the high point of the first year of his marriage to Helen was their joint purchase of the Dickens Library) who also began writing, and had poems published by a local newspaper as early as 1924. In 1933 he enrolled for evening classes run by the Workers' Educational Association at Worksop, where his tutor encouraged him to publish more. The result was his autobiographical book, *Brother to the Ox*; brought out by Dent in 1940, it won a Foyles literary prize. Its success (with reprints following in 1941, 1944, 1945, and 1947) led to radio talks, a series of articles in the *Daily Mirror*, and a string of further commissions from Dent, including *Life on* the Land (1941), *The Farming Front* (1943), and *Jesse and his Friends* (1945), all of which drew on Kitchen's own experience.

Kitchen continued to work as a cowman (on £2 a week, with a tied cottage, a quart of milk a day, and free potatoes), but he was sacked for taking new year's day off in 1941. Drawing on his earnings from *Brother to the Ox* he bought a smallholding on the Oxcroft estate near Worksop, through a scheme run by the Land Settlement Association, even though to work it he had to adapt his agricultural skills to horticulture. In 1946 he moved to Pleasant View, a bungalow with half an acre of ground in Moor Lane at Bolsover, Derbyshire. He continued to work until his seventies as a school gardener for the local education authority.

He was a member of the Town End Methodist Church at Bolsover, and became a local preacher. He joined Toc H, and also the North-east Derbyshire Field Club. He gave talks, including on his native Maltby, which he revisited for the purpose—the return of the hireling, he reflected. He carried on writing, invariably for Dent, save for a slim volume of verse published elsewhere. Most of his books were factually based: *Settlers in England* (1947), *What the Countryman wants to Know* (1948), *Foxendale Farm* (1959) and its two sequels (1961 and 1964), *Goslington: Portrait of a Village* (1965), and *Nettleworth Parva* (1968). *Songs of Sherwood* (1948) is a collection of essays and poems, and there were two novels, *Commoners* (1950) and *The Ploughman Homeward Plods* (1960). In addition, *Brother to the Ox* was reprinted in 1963, with an epilogue by Kitchen, and again in 1982 and 1984 after a television adaptation was shown in 1981. Though *Commoners* has its partisans, *Brother to the Ox* was undoubtedly his best book; Raymond Williams characterized it as 'one of the very few direct and unmediated accounts of a rural labourer's life … the true voice of the surviving countryman' (Williams, 263).

Kitchen was a man of great natural courtesy, whose habit of going to thank the engine driver after any train journey was remembered by his children. They recalled a happy father, always singing. After an illness of two weeks he died at the Royal Hospital, Chesterfield, on 16 September 1969; he was cremated at Brimington, Derbyshire. He left a son, four daughters, seven grandchildren—and a minor classic.   ROY PALMER

Sources R. Redfern, 'Fred Kitchen—man of country life and letters', *Derbyshire Countryside*, 36/5 (May 1971), 56 · R. Palmer, 'The voice of a working man', *Birmingham Post* (13 Nov 1981) · private information (2004) [W. Kitchen, son] · F. Kitchen, epilogue, *Brother to the ox*, repr. (1963) · R. Williams, *The city and the country* (1973) · b. cert. · m. cert. [Frances Hanslock] · d. cert.
Archives FILM Yorkshire television?
Likenesses photographs, priv. coll.
Wealth at death £3805: administration, 29 Oct 1969, *CGPLA Eng. & Wales*

Kitchen, Jane (*d.* 1658), farmer and parish constable, lived in Upton by Southwell in Nottinghamshire. Nothing is known of her early life. In 1619 she married John Kitchen (*d.* 1643), yeoman and churchwarden, son of John Kitchen of Upton, outside the parish of Upton; together they had

three children who survived, Thomas, Elizabeth, and William. At the time of John's death in October 1643 all lived in Upton and the two younger children were still in the family home, which appears to have had two parlours, a chamber over, a cellar, a kitchen, and a yard. John left £56 in moveable goods, the bulk of which passed to Elizabeth; the farm was left to Jane.

The Kitchen family was part of the network of householders in Upton that provided the village's officeholders: churchwarden, constables, and overseers of the poor. In Upton these posts were held by house row; the substantial householders held them in a rotation system based on the position of their properties in the village. It fell to the Kitchen property to provide a constable at Epiphany 1644, and because of John's death the post went to Jane. This was perhaps not unusual in Upton; in 1643 widow Jane Parlethorpe served as churchwarden. In common with other women of means who came into the post Jane Kitchen hired a male substitute constable, William Chappell, to act as the public figure and to do the 'legwork' but the constables' accounts make it clear that, within the village, Jane was recognized as the responsible party.

When Jane came into office there were two rival garrisons established in Nottinghamshire. Upton was close to the royalist garrison at Newark, and most of the wartime business that year concerned it and the commission of array based there, but the parliamentarian garrison at Nottingham also began to make increasing demands on the parish. Additionally from late February 1644 until 22 March Sir John Meldrum besieged Newark, and Jane had to provide him with hens and calves from her own farm as well as administer similar levies from others. After the siege was raised Lord Loughborough's forces remained in the area collecting provisions. Jane's accounts are some of the longest in the Upton constables' book; taking up fifteen pages they record the minutiae of wartime administration and reflect the burden of work placed on constables. They also throw a perhaps unique light on the practicalities of being a woman constable during the early modern period. Jane did not serve as constable again before her death and does not appear to have held any other parish office. She died in Upton in 1658, having left no surviving will.   MARTYN BENNETT

Sources account book of the constables of Upton, Notts. Arch., PR 1710 · M. Bennett, *A Nottinghamshire village in war and peace* (1995) · will, Notts. Arch., PRSW 20/19a [John Kitchen]
Archives Notts. Arch., papers from Upton parish

Kitchener, Lord. *See* Roberts, Aldwyn (1922–2000).

Kitchener, Horatio Herbert, **Earl Kitchener of Khartoum** (1850–1916), army officer, was born on 24 June 1850 at Gunsborough Villa (now Coolbeha House), near Listowel, co. Kerry, the third child and second son of Lieutenant-Colonel Henry Horatio Kitchener (1805–1894) and his first wife, Frances Ann (*d.* 1864), daughter of the Revd John *Chevallier and his third wife, Elizabeth, *née* Cole. Kitchener's family were English not Anglo-Irish: his father had only recently bought land in Ireland.

Horatio Herbert Kitchener, Earl Kitchener of Khartoum (1850–1916), by Sir Hubert von Herkomer and Frederick Goodall, 1890

Early life Henry Kitchener was a retired officer—an unpopular, tenant-evicting, improving landowner, a domestic martinet, and an eccentric who used newspapers instead of blankets in bed. As Frances Kitchener suffered from tuberculosis, the family moved to Switzerland in 1864. He attended an English boarding-school at the Château du Grand Clos at Renaz, where his Irish accent and country ways led to his being teased and unhappy. He devoted himself to his books, and became fluent in French and German. His health broke down in the spring of 1867, and he moved to Cambridge to stay with a cousin, Francis Kitchener. He prepared with a crammer for the entrance examination for the Royal Military Academy, Woolwich. He took the examination in January 1868, passing twenty-eighth out of fifty-six. After an undistinguished two years, he passed out in December 1870. He spent his Christmas holidays in France with his father. During the Franco-Prussian War Kitchener, pro-French and eager to see action, joined a field ambulance unit of the French Second Army of the Loire. The rout at the battle of Le Mans (January 1871) of ill-trained French levies apparently later influenced his attitude to the Territorial Force. Kitchener's first military experience was cut short when he caught pneumonia as the result of catching chill during a balloon ascent, and was taken back to England by his father. Meanwhile, he was commissioned into the Royal Engineers on 4 January 1871. His service in France had violated British neutrality, and he was reprimanded by the duke of Cambridge, the commander-in-chief.

Early career, 1871–1882 From 1871 to 1873 Kitchener was at the School of Military Engineering, Chatham. His superior performance there attracted the attention of Brigadier-General George Richards Graves of the War Office staff. Kitchener was appointed his aide-de-camp in 1873 and attended the Austro-Hungarian military manoeuvres, where he favourably impressed the Austrian emperor. Kitchener was posted to Aldershot, but did not enjoy his time there—he longed for action rather than military routine—as much as he had his experiences at Chatham; however, he did perfect his surveying skills which, together with his high-church religious enthusiasm, then led to his being seconded to the Palestine Exploration Fund (PEF) in November 1874.

For the next four years Kitchener surveyed in Palestine. He learned passable Arabic and became familiar with Arabic culture and mores. Further, he learned to work with minimal supervision. During the Russo-Turkish War the position of the PEF's expedition was awkward, and, in dealing with local authorities, he developed negotiating skills that were to be of great value to him.

Kitchener's work earned him a minor reputation as both a surveyor and a man who knew the Near East. In 1878 he was seconded to the Foreign Office and charged with the mapping of Cyprus. An outsider to the Wolseley 'ring' of military reformers, his desire to prepare a thorough and scientific map ran foul of the desires of Wolseley, the high commissioner, who wanted only a rough guide for the purpose of local taxation. Kitchener's attempts to appeal over Wolseley's head failed, and he was saved only by Wolseley's transfer and his own new posting, as military vice-consul, to Kastamonu in northern Turkey. From June 1879, when he took up the post, he spent nine months gaining an acquaintance with Ottoman brutality. In March 1880 he returned to Cyprus at the request of the new high commissioner, Sir Robert Biddulph, and for the next two years continued his survey. At this time he began to cultivate two things which were to distinguish him for the rest of his life: his swooping moustaches and his collection of pottery and porcelain.

Egypt and Sudan, 1882–1899 Kitchener still craved action, with its opportunity of advancement. He took leave in July 1882 and went to Egypt, where he served unofficially with the British force that bombarded Alexandria, reconnoitring ashore disguised as a Levantine. He was reprimanded, but secured a posting to Egypt early in 1883, at the same time as being promoted captain. In 1884 he acted as an intelligence officer for the relief expedition sent to the Sudan to rescue Charles George Gordon; he continually pressed Wolseley, the commander of the expedition, to push forward more rapidly. Despite the expedition's failure to save Gordon, Kitchener emerged with credit and some fame. Promoted brevet lieutenant-colonel in June 1885, he resigned his Egyptian commission and returned to England, where his fame had been spread by the press and his father. The press had a crucial role in creating the Kitchener legend. Kitchener used his new status as a social lion to make many connections which later proved useful.

Late in 1885 Kitchener was appointed the British member of the Zanzibar boundary commission. There he got a taste of international rivalries as he and the French and German commissioners wrangled over the limits of the sultan of Zanzibar's territory; he was created CMG in 1886. From 1886 to 1888 Kitchener was governor-general of the eastern Sudan and the Red sea littoral, and much of his time was spent fighting Osman Digna, a ruthless slave trader. During a skirmish in January 1888 Kitchener was shot in the jaw, and required several months' convalescence. That summer he returned to England on leave, where Lord Salisbury, the prime minister, arranged for him to be adjutant-general of the Egyptian army (Egyptian appointments were Foreign Office not War Office responsibility), a post he took up in September 1888. His promotion was resented, and he was unpopular with British officers and the British community in Egypt. In 1889 he had an important role in the battle of Toski on 3 August, for which he was created CB. After a brief leave in India he was given the additional position of inspector-general of police in the autumn of 1889. For the next two and half years Kitchener held this dual power, achieving a substantial reduction in crime.

On 13 April 1892 Kitchener was made sirdar (commander-in-chief) of the Egyptian army. This offended many who believed he owed his appointment more to his assiduous cultivation of the powerful than to his abilities. Such a view was reinforced by his tour of country houses when on leave in England, and by the prominent persons, including the prince of Wales, who stayed with him in Egypt. Kitchener however immediately set about reforming the Egyptian army, gathering around him a cadre of eager young officers nicknamed 'Kitchener's band of boys'. The fact that Kitchener surrounded himself with similar groups throughout his career, and never married, led to speculations that he was a homosexual. There is no evidence that this was so. Early in his career Kitchener had several flirtations with women. He was apparently in love with, and may have been engaged to, Hermione Baker, the beautiful young daughter of Valentine Baker, commander of the Egyptian gendarmarie, but she died from typhoid in January 1885, aged eighteen. In 1902 he unsuccessfully courted Lord Londonderry's daughter, Helen Mary Theresa. He was friendly, in her old age, with the courtesan Catherine Walters ('Skittles').

With a limited budget, Kitchener developed in Egypt a reputation for efficiency, ruthlessness, and penny-pinching. He was created KCMG in 1894. Most of his army reform had been undertaken with the aim of reconquering Sudan. In 1896 the opportunity to secure this objective arose when the Italian government appealed for aid, worried that the disaster of Adowa would lead to the collapse of Italy's position in eastern Africa. Salisbury's government authorized Kitchener to begin the reconquest of Sudan. The first stage was to take the province of Dongola, which Kitchener began in June. The campaign consisted of a series of advances up the Nile, with Kitchener attending assiduously to logistics. Victory at Firket on 7 June was followed by methodical preparations and the occupation of Dongola on 24 September. Kitchener was made major-general and KCB. He wished to follow up his victories, but financial considerations enforced delay, and he went to England in the autumn to lobby for increased finance. His efforts were aided by fears of a French occupation of the upper Nile—Captain Marchand had begun a French expedition from west Africa towards the Nile watershed—and when Kitchener returned to Egypt in December he did so with financial backing for a further advance.

In 1897 Kitchener began a campaign noted as much for its impressive railway construction, organized by Percy Girouard, as for its battles. On 7 August Kitchener's army took Abu Hamed and then occupied Berber on 31 August. Here matters paused, as the Egyptian government, under the British agent, Lord Cromer, was reluctant to provide further funds. An open clash between Kitchener and Cromer was averted, but the sirdar insisted that his army would be perilously exposed unless a further advance were permitted. By the beginning of 1898 Kitchener had received more money and British reinforcements. The first battle of the renewed campaign was fought at the Atbara on 8 April. Kitchener's victory was followed by an advance towards the Mahdist capital, Omdurman, which the Anglo-Egyptian forces reached on 1 September. On 2 September the Madhists attacked the Anglo-Egyptian position, and were mown down by Anglo-Egyptian firepower. The result was a decisive victory and the occupation of Omdurman, accompanied by vigorous repression. Gordon had been avenged. This triumph did not end Kitchener's duties, for he was immediately ordered up the Nile to Fashoda, where Captain Marchand had claimed much of upper Sudan for France. Kitchener met Marchand on 19 September in what was quickly dubbed 'the Fashoda incident'. Kitchener's cautious, correct, and considerate treatment of Marchand ensured that, in fact, no incident occurred at Fashoda that might have precipitated war between Britain and France. Even before France had decided that Marchand must withdraw, Kitchener had returned home to England to a hero's welcome.

As he rose Kitchener provoked continued resentment and criticism. Anti-imperialists hated his imperial victories and triumphs. Some British officers were jealous of his success, and for varied reasons there was among senior officers much suspicion of him. His relations with the press were largely poor: calling correspondents 'drunken swabs' may have been accurate, but was resented. However, he helped favoured journalists, and one of them, G. W. Steevens of the *Daily Mail*—through his popular *With Kitchener to Khartum* (1898), with its dramatic portrayal of Kitchener as the cold, dedicated, powerful 'Sudan Machine' and 'man of destiny'—particularly helped to form the popular image of Kitchener.

Despite radicals' and others' criticism of Kitchener's behaviour, particularly his desecration of the Mahdi's tomb at Omdurman and his taking of the latter's skull, the British public lionized the sirdar. Awarded many honours—including an Oxford DCL in 1899—he was frequently mobbed when he appeared in public. A grateful government gave him a reward of £30,000, and he was created Baron Kitchener of Khartoum and Aspall in 1898. While being fêted throughout Britain he began to display the avarice that characterized him the rest of his life. Offered gifts, he requested gold plate, and he made a habit of asking for objects that he admired. He sometimes stole attractive objects from his hosts, and at Simla he took plants from his neighbour's garden.

Kitchener served as governor-general of Sudan from 19 January to 18 December 1899; then, at the height of the emergency in South Africa, was appointed chief of staff to the commander-in-chief, Lord Roberts, who was dispatched to restore the reputation of British arms. Kitchener's governor-generalship had not been particularly successful, despite his military achievement in pacifying Sudan and his rebuilding of Khartoum, for his style of governance—a lack of system, with power concentrated in his own hands—did not prove as effective in civil affairs as it had in war.

The Second South African War, 1900–1902 South Africa increased Kitchener's reputation as a soldier. Officially chief of staff, in fact he was Roberts's deputy, right-hand man, and troubleshooter: he and Roberts worked well and harmoniously together. The war suited his experience and abilities: it required both logistical expertise and the ability to operate over difficult terrain, and Kitchener had proved himself master of these in Sudan. On arriving in Cape Town on 10 January 1900 Kitchener and Roberts faced a difficult situation; from the beginning of the war the Boers had enjoyed almost unbroken success, culminating with their triumphs in 'black week' in December 1899.

Kitchener's initial task was to reorganize the transportation system. He utilized the methods—the creation of a pool of transport under centralized control—effective in Sudan. This policy proved inefficient. Its implementation, despite officers' protests, was typical of Kitchener: he showed no respect for what he believed to be a foolish adherence to outmoded methods and organization. The British army moved swiftly in early February to raise the siege of Kimberley, but it was at Paardeberg on 18 February that Kitchener saw his first action. This battle was one of the most controversial of his career. Overruling, with Roberts's authorization, officers of senior rank and greater experience, he ordered an assault on the Boer position. His attempt to command his dispersed force by galloping from position to position led to confusion. The entrenched Boers, armed with the modern weapons the Sudanese had wholly lacked, defeated his attack, inflicting heavy casualties. When Roberts arrived on the 19th the British settled down to besiege the Boers, the action that Kitchener's critics had suggested.

While Paardeberg was besieged Roberts sent Kitchener to repair the railway system in the Orange Free State. At the end of March he rejoined Roberts at Bloemfontein, where the two spent April planning the next phase of the war—the advance on Pretoria. This began in May, and on 5 June Roberts entered Pretoria. With the Boers in disarray it appeared the war might soon end. That it did not was

largely due to the action of Christian De Wet, one of the most intrepid of the Boer commanders. De Wet's forces had evaded Roberts's drive from Bloemfontein to Pretoria, and, after most of the British force had moved forward, on 7 June De Wet struck at its lines of communication. Kitchener was sent southward from Pretoria to deal with this new menace. For the next two months Kitchener pursued the Boer guerrillas, De Wet finally eluding his pursuer by mid-August. However, Kitchener had secured Roberts's supply lines, and the British successes against the Boers continued unabated. By November President Kruger had fled to Europe, and Roberts returned to Britain on the 29th, leaving Kitchener in command.

Kitchener was left with the task of ending the war, and his efforts to do so belied his reputation as a man interested only in fighting and complete victory. In February 1901 he opened peace negotiations with General Louis Botha. Kitchener offered generous terms: an amnesty for all rebels (although they would be temporarily disfranchised), the status of a crown colony with a clear timetable for a transition to self-government, a promise of no new taxes to pay for the war, assistance to re-establish farmers, and £1 million compensation for war loss of property. The Boers rejected the terms and fighting resumed.

To deal with the Boers' guerrilla tactics, Kitchener used two complementary methods. The first was to divide the country up into a grid by building a series of blockhouses and barbed-wire fences, and by instituting drives along these grids using columns of mounted troops. It was owing to the rugged terrain and the Boers' familiarity with the countryside that this policy was not initially successful. Kitchener's second method was resource denial, achieved by destroying Boer farms and—continuing and intensifying the process begun under Roberts—gathering the occupants, mostly women and children, into forty-six 'refugee' or 'concentration' camps where they could not aid the commandos. However, the hastily improvised and initially under-supplied camps were insanitary, and as many as 26,000 (the figure is uncertain) died of disease. Emily Hobhouse, whom Kitchener called 'that bloody woman' and whom he deported, revealed the extent of what Sir Henry Campbell-Bannerman called 'methods of barbarism', and a War Office inquiry was held. This found that the disease and mortality were largely the result of administrative incompetence rather than of Kitchener's policy. His priorities were elsewhere, and he agreed to the transfer of the camps to the Colonial Office (March 1901), and to reforms. Reforms were implemented, and the death rate had been greatly reduced by the beginning of 1902.

By April 1902, harried by Kitchener's drives and tired of war, the Boer leadership put out peace feelers. During the negotiations Kitchener played an important role. He wanted the war to end, partly so that he could move on to India. He displayed the same tact and sensitivity to the *amour propre* of the Boers that he had in dealing with Marchand earlier. He acted as a conciliatory middleman between the Boers and the British high commissioner, Lord Milner, the latter pushing for a more severe peace than the former were willing to accept. The result was the moderate treaty of Vereeniging, signed on 31 May 1902.

When Kitchener returned to Britain in July 1902, to another hero's welcome, he was given the thanks of parliament and a grant of £50,000, and Edward VII made him both one of the inaugural members of the Order of Merit and a viscount. He was also promoted full general, preliminary to his taking command of the Indian army. In the tradition of imperial conquest, he had returned with Boer statues looted from their capitals, which he intended to erect in his private park, when acquired; but in 1909, at government insistence, they were secretly returned to South Africa. Kitchener used his time in England to further his social ties, particularly to Lady Cranborne—wife of Viscount Cranborne (from 1903 fourth marquess of Salisbury), first cousin of A. J. Balfour—whose widespread web of political influence made her a particularly valuable confidante. He also gave evidence to the royal commission on the Second South African War, scathingly condemning regular army methods. Many, including the secretary of state for war, St John Brodrick, wanted him to go to the War Office to implement reforms, but he was adamant that he wished to go to India.

India, 1902–1909 The new commander-in-chief left for India on 17 October 1902. On 28 November he landed in Bombay and, three days later, met the viceroy, Lord Curzon. Their relationship was to be difficult. Although from different backgrounds—Curzon an aristocrat and Kitchener gentry—they were of similar temperament: each was imperious, sensitive to the merest slight, and convinced that his opinion was the only possible correct one. Although Curzon had pushed hard for Kitchener's appointment—he was convinced that only a man of Kitchener's drive could carry out the necessary army reforms—he did not expect that Kitchener would prove unmalleable and, more surprisingly, able to better him in intrigue.

Kitchener's initial aim in India was to reorganize the army and to make it an effective force. Beginning in April 1903 Kitchener explored the reaches of India, particularly the north-west frontier, where he expected a Russian advance in the near future. By the end of August he had travelled thousands of miles over rugged terrain and had obtained a first-hand knowledge of the country. He believed that the Indian army was backward technically and organizationally. He reorganized it, and increased the number of troops available to fight against Russia at the expense of those dedicated to maintaining internal security. Further, he wished to build an extensive series of military railways to transport troops to the north-west frontier. This plan was deemed too expensive and too likely to offend the amir of Afghanistan, whose friendship the British government courted. These were the kinds of reform that Curzon had hoped for when he had lobbied for Kitchener's appointment, and there was no particular friction between the two men on these issues.

Instead, the centre of contention was civil–military relations. The existing military system in India had a dual nature, as it comprised, in addition to the commander-in-

chief, the military member of the viceroy's council. The commander-in-chief was the executive head of the army, responsible for its training and direction; the military member was in charge of non-combatant matters, including supply and transport, and prepared the army's budget. Thus the military member acted in some ways as a military officer but in other ways as a civilian minister in the viceroy's council. While the military member was an army officer (normally a major-general), he was responsible to the viceroy, and therefore outside the military line of command. With competent, co-operative men—such as Roberts and G. T. Chesney—the system could work adequately, but it had potential for conflict. Roberts continued to favour it, claiming that nobody could satisfactorily carry out the duties of both officials, and that the Indian government needed the advice of an officer expert on India and the Indian army. However, the situation was unacceptable to Kitchener, who was used to having full authority and near-complete autonomy. Curzon argued that the military member was necessary in order that the viceroy could be kept informed on military matters.

Several clashes between the two men over this issue early in 1903 led to an uneasy truce. But in June 1904 Curzon, on leave in London, attended a meeting of the committee of imperial defence. There he found that Kitchener had submitted an analysis of Indian defence in which all defects were blamed on the existence of the military member. Curzon reacted sharply, and argued that the issue was constitutional, involving the principle of whether the military should be subordinated to civilian authority. Roberts, Kitchener's predecessor in India, concurred with Curzon's arguments, as initially did Balfour, the prime minister. However, the matter was not easily decided. Kitchener had his own adherents in the cabinet, and his threat (on 24 September) to resign was viewed with dismay. The Unionist government was unpopular and politically vulnerable, and the resignation of Britain's most popular serving soldier would have exposed it to further attack. The result was that Balfour persuaded Curzon to re-examine dual control when he returned to India. Kitchener continued to intrigue against Curzon, using Lady Salisbury particularly as a channel to Balfour, as well as St John Brodrick (war minister, 1900–03, and secretary of state for India, 1903–5), who was apparently jealous of Curzon, Repington (*The Times* military correspondent), H. A. Gwynne (editor of *The Standard*), and others.

The reconsideration took place in early 1905. By March it was clear that no compromise was possible. At a key meeting of the viceroy's council on 10 March Kitchener refused to defend his position orally, fearing that Curzon, a master of debate, would out-argue him. Such unwillingness to engage in discussion was typical of Kitchener: he was to behave similarly during the First World War. However, the result of the meeting was that the dispute was referred to London. Curzon and Kitchener began intense lobbying. The cabinet reached an uneasy compromise: the military member would be retained, but would have a new title (military supply member), a restricted purview, and would wear civilian clothes. This was a victory for Kitchener, although not a complete one. However, Curzon refused to give up. In June he denounced the settlement, and in August threatened to resign unless the British cabinet accepted his nominee (whom Kitchener opposed) as the new military supply member. The cabinet accepted Curzon's resignation: Kitchener had triumphed.

Kitchener spent just over four more years in India. In the period until September 1907 he spent much of his time demanding a greater allocation of forces to India in order to defend against any possible Russian invasion. He also bitterly opposed the Anglo-Russian convention, with its implication that the defence of India would rely on détente with Russia rather than on military strength. Throughout the negotiation of the convention, and even after its signing, Kitchener attempted, as the foreign editor of *The Times* wrote, to 'wirepull the press against it' (Chirol to Nicolson, 27 Oct 1907, PRO, Nicolson papers, FO 800/340). However, he was not successful, and earned the dislike of the Liberal secretary of state for India, Lord Morley.

Egypt again, 1909–1914 Morley's hostility was of particular significance when Kitchener left India in September 1909. While Kitchener was promoted field marshal, his future employment was in doubt. Earlier in the year he had turned down the offer of the Mediterranean command, based on Malta, then had reluctantly agreed to it when pressed by Edward VII. But he was not pleased with the appointment. Before taking up the post Kitchener made a seven-month tour, visiting Singapore, Hong Kong, the Manchurian battlefields, Japan, Australia, and New Zealand before returning home via the United States. When he arrived in Britain on 26 April 1910 the king released him from his promise on the Mediterranean command. He coveted two posts: the viceroyalty of India and the ambassadorship at Constantinople. However, Morley threatened resignation if Kitchener were sent to India, and Sir Edward Grey, the foreign secretary, wished to reserve ambassadorial posts for career diplomats. Kitchener's attempts to utilize his social connections were weakened by the death on 6 May of Edward VII (though George V was to support him during the First World War), and the prime minister, Asquith, was not inclined to risk political difficulties by overruling one of his own cabinet members during the constitutional crisis.

For the next year Kitchener was at loose ends, concentrating on private matters, including the purchase and renovation of Broome Park, near Canterbury. He gutted and redecorated it, ornamenting the walls with a 'K. K.' monogram, and intending it as the stately home of an enduring Kitchener landed dynasty. In July 1911 the death of the British agent and consul-general in Egypt, Eldon Gorst, cleared the way for Kitchener's appointment to that office. He arrived in Egypt on 29 September 1911, and for the next three years governed the country. He maintained Egypt's neutrality during the war between Turkey and Italy. Despite hostility from nationalists—some of whom tried to assassinate him—and from Khedive Abbas Hilmi II, whom he described as 'this wicked little Khedive'

(Magnus, 272) and wanted to depose—Kitchener introduced important reforms, including those to protect fellahin from usurers and lawyers, and promote large-scale land reclamation. He also implemented constitutional change: the organic law of 1913. He lived longer in Egypt than anywhere else and apparently regarded it as his spiritual home. Introduced by the duke of Connaught, Kitchener became a keen freemason. He was grand master of Egypt and Sudan, and also held important office in India and England. His personal politics were tory, and he disliked the Liberal social reforms.

Secretary of state for war, 1914–1916 Kitchener's time in Egypt was considered a success and in June 1914 he was granted an earldom. He travelled to England to receive it, but before he could return to Egypt Asquith requested that he stay in England, pending the outcome of the July crisis. At the outbreak of war in August 1914 the secretaryship of state for war was—since J. E. B. Seely had resigned over the Curragh incident earlier in 1914—being held on an interim basis by the prime minister. Asquith initially wanted Haldane back at the War Office, but Repington in *The Times* and others in the press demanded Kitchener. Asquith had misgivings, considering it 'a hazardous experiment', but invited Kitchener. Kitchener was reluctant, but agreed: he told Girouard, 'May God preserve me from the politicians' (Simkins, 35). On 6 August he became secretary of state for war: a popular appointment which strengthened the government and increased public confidence. Kitchener brought to his new office both strengths and weaknesses. He had waged two wars in which he had dealt with all aspects of warfare, including both command and logistics. He was used to being in charge of large enterprises, he was not afraid to take responsibility and make decisions, and he enjoyed public confidence. However, he had no experience of modern European war, almost no knowledge of the British army at home, and a limited understanding of the War Office. Perhaps most importantly, he had no experience of working in a cabinet. Nevertheless in the opening stage of the war he, Asquith, and Churchill formed a dominant triumvirate in the cabinet.

Kitchener's initial response to the war was prescient. The British government had entered it expecting to fight in a limited fashion and to make a primarily naval and financial contribution, otherwise carrying on with 'business as usual'. Further, the general military consensus was that the war would be short, decided by early decisive battles, and 'over by Christmas'. Kitchener, though accepting the continental strategy, rejected all these assumptions. He believed the war would be long—three years—and that Britain would have to raise a continental-scale army; the cabinet accepted. Thus Kitchener, as David French has written, 'was responsible for one of the most complete and far-reaching reversals of policy of the whole war … one of the most important and far-reaching decisions taken by the British throughout the war' (French, *Economic and Strategic Planning*, 124, 127). Agreeing with his cabinet colleagues that conscription was then impractical and unnecessary, he appealed for volunteers. The response was massive.

Controversially, instead of utilizing the existing structure of the Territorial Force (TF), Kitchener chose to create a new mass volunteer force (known as the 'new' or 'Kitchener' armies), essentially by expanding the regular army through the normal recruiting channels under the adjutant-general's department of the War Office. While Kitchener had a professional prejudice against the TF, viewing it as an army of amateurs, he had solid military reasons for his decision. First, he was concerned that the TF might not be available for service overseas, since the terms of enrolment in the TF did not oblige its members to serve abroad and some actually refused to do so. Second, Kitchener feared a possible German invasion of Britain; he saw the TF as a home defence force against invasion or raids, and believed that the use of the TF to expand the army would disorganize the TF for its home defence role.

Kitchener was also aware that Britain was fighting in an alliance. He therefore attempted to ensure cordial Anglo-French relations, notably by making a dramatic trip to France in early September 1914 to order the commander of the British expeditionary force (BEF), Sir John French, not to withdraw the BEF, and assure the French that it would remain in the field. In an effort to reinforce his authority he wore his field marshal's uniform on this mission, which angered French. Kitchener kept a close eye on the eastern front, believing Russian success necessary to keep the German forces divided and so prevent their defeating the French—of whose military strength he held an unfavourable opinion—and attempting an invasion of Britain. Kitchener also began a massive programme of producing munitions for his New Armies. Peter Simkins has written: 'it was in providing the vital impetus for the mobilisation of national resources that he made his most significant contribution to the war effort' (Simkins, 39).

While Kitchener's predictions were accurate and his actions sound, his methods of carrying out his ideas and his ability to explain them were not. At the War Office he found himself with an inadequate staff, for most of the most competent officers had accompanied the BEF to France. This only accentuated his own inclination to run a one-man show, in his usual style. However, the war was too complex for any one person to deal with adequately, and the nickname 'K of Chaos', coined by General Neville Lyttelton during the Second South African War, soon resurfaced. Nevertheless, it was no small feat to create a large-scale armaments industry, capable of supplying a multi-million man army. Kitchener was severely criticized, notably by *The Times* and other Northcliffe papers, for not providing sufficient shells for the BEF, particularly in May 1915 during the 'shell scandal'. The 'scandal' was fomented both by French, who needed a scapegoat for his western front failure and who intensely disliked Kitchener and wanted him removed, and by that 'deceitful fellow' Repington, the *Times* correspondent and French's personal guest. Yet munition shortages were common to all the belligerents. Subsequent scholarship has shown that the great increases in production of armaments that took place in 1916, and for which Lloyd George took credit as the first minister of munitions, were largely the result of Kitchener's earlier initiatives. Kitchener was generally in favour of the creation of new ministries to help wage the war more efficiently; however, he did not wish to lose his overall direction of affairs.

Kitchener's aim in the war stemmed from his assumptions about its long duration. He wanted Britain to play the decisive role. He reckoned that by about the end of 1916 the other belligerents would have exhausted their forces, while Britain's newly created armies would make her the dominant partner in the entente. Therefore he wished to retain in Britain as much of the New Armies as possible, rather than send them to the continent piecemeal. He did, not, however, explain his policies well to his cabinet colleagues. Kitchener rightly believed them too indiscreet, and mostly ignorant of military matters; in any case, he did not wish to argue with them. As a result, and because changing news from the eastern front influenced him, his views often seemed erratic to the other members of the government, and they soon became disenchanted with his advice.

This was particularly noticeable over the Dardanelles campaign of 1915. Kitchener himself had agreed to the attack only as a naval venture, believing that, if it were not successful, the Royal Navy could withdraw without a further British commitment. However, once events had led to the sending of British troops to the Dardanelles, Kitchener seemed to vacillate between advocating the retention of the British forces there and arguing that they should be evacuated. This seeming irresolution was based on his attempt to balance both the effect of withdrawal on British prestige among Muslims and its impact on French government stability against the need to end a failed and costly operation, wasting troops and resources needed elsewhere. But the subtlety of his reasoning was not evident to others. In December 1915 one of Kitchener's admirers, George V's private secretary, wrote: 'K.'s position at present is untenable. He is discredited with all his 21 colleagues in the Cabinet. Even his colleagues on the War Commttee think he is a positive danger. He has been so unstable in his advice on military affairs' (Wigram to Robertson, Dec 1915, King's Lond., Liddell Hart C., I/12/28). Nevertheless the king, 'a strong Kitchenerite' (who in June 1915 made him a KG), continued to support him; his reputation with the public continued high, and thus he remained an asset to the government which, L. S. Amery wrote in 1916, 'largely rested (as far as the opinion of the masses was concerned) upon K.'s reputation' (*Amery Diaries*, 1.130). His image aided recruiting: the 'Your Country needs You' poster, designed by Alfred Leete in 1914 and depicting Kitchener pointing vigorously at the viewer, became perhaps the best-known poster in the world.

Concern about Kitchener's ability to carry on the war led, in mid-December 1915, to the appointment of Major-General Sir William Robertson as chief of the Imperial General Staff. Robertson was charged with bringing improved administrative methods to the War Office, while providing the cabinet with military information and advice. While Kitchener might well have resented this diminution in his own powers, he and Robertson worked closely and effectively together. To some extent Kitchener became a figurehead in the government, more valuable for his public presence than for his actual contributions, but was still able to do useful service, particularly during the Anglo-French Sykes–Picot discussions on the post-war Near East.

On 5 June 1916 Kitchener sailed from Scapa Flow for Russia on the armoured cruiser HMS *Hampshire*. His ostensibly secret mission was to discuss with the Russian government co-ordination between the western and eastern fronts. That evening, in heavy seas off Orkney, the *Hampshire* struck a German mine and sank with the loss of nearly all aboard, including Kitchener. His body was never found. His death shocked the public and was followed by enormous public mourning. The available evidence suggests the loss of the *Hampshire* resulted not, as some alleged, from conspiracy, treachery, sabotage, or deliberate German intent, but from British naval bungling, and from a refusal to consider intelligence of U-boat activity and the weather forecast. Strange rumours circulated that Kitchener was not really dead, but a German prisoner, or sleeping in a cave in some remote island of the Hebrides.

Personality and reputation Kitchener was a dominating figure. He was tall (6 feet 2 inches, then well above average height), powerfully built, straight, and soldierly, with a suntanned florid complexion, the well-known moustaches, and 'an expression made all the more inscrutable by a strong cast in his bright blue eyes' (Amery, *Political Life*, 1.124). A 'Herculean personality', intensely ambitious, proud, autocratic, determined, tough-minded, obsessional, acquisitive, secretive, devious, contradictory, enigmatic, and, perhaps necessarily, callous, he was regarded by some of his contemporaries as 'oriental' and 'un-Europeanized'. Responses to him varied. Lord Esher wrote in 1899, 'Kitchener is not attractive … it is the coarseness of his fibre, which appears in his face to a marked degree' (Magnus, 152). Lord Cromer said he was 'not a very likeable fellow' (Pakenham, 315). Amery considered 'he was essentially an improviser and hustler, one who could achieve results by force of will-power and dominating personality' (Amery, *Political Life*, 1.124). Yet he could be charming, and he attracted ladies. Despite some hostility among politicians and officers, from the Sudan until his death Kitchener was to the British public a popular imperial hero—'the Paladin of the War' (Reginald, Viscount Esher, 120)—though apparently, unlike Roberts, admired but not loved. Arguably Gordon was a hero for an age of evangelicalism, Kitchener for an age of social Darwinism. After his death Kitchener was often dismissed, in Margot Asquith's phrase, as a great poster but not a great man. Much of the credit for his successes during the war was appropriated by Lloyd George and others, while his early death made him a convenient scapegoat for governmental mistakes. His secretive methods and unwillingness to explain his actions to his colleagues facilitated the reduction of his reputation. For years historians followed Lloyd George's *War Memoirs* in criticizing Kitchener as a

strategist and administrator and minimizing his achievement in munitions production, and he was regarded as one of the bunglers who mismanaged the First World War. Since the 1970s, and with the availability of more First World War primary documents, scholarship has largely rehabilitated Kitchener's reputation. George Cassar, David French, and Keith Neilson have gone far to vindicate Kitchener's strategic vision in the First World War, while Peter Simkins has shown his role in the raising of the British army in 1914 and 1915. Historians have agreed that his greatest achievement was, having inherited a continental commitment, to provide an army capable of meeting it. Trevor Royle's 1985 biography of Kitchener showed that many of the earlier criticisms of Kitchener were based on personal animosities rather than on historical evidence. While his faults—a lack of organization and a tendency to attempt to do too much on his own—are still acknowledged, Kitchener's strengths—his foresight, his industry, and his strength of character—have been re-emphasized. Kitchener, with his many warts, has been recognized as among the greatest of Victorian imperial soldiers, and as the architect of Britain's victory in the First World War.   KEITH NEILSON

Sources G. H. Cassar, *Kitchener: architect of victory* (1977) • T. Royle, *The Kitchener enigma* (1985) • D. French, *British strategy and war aims* (1986) • D. French, *British economic and strategic planning, 1905–1915* (1982) • K. Neilson, 'Kitchener: a reputation refurbished?', *Canadian Journal of History*, 15 (1980), 207–27 • P. Magnus, *Kitchener: portrait of an imperialist* (1958) • PRO, Kitchener MSS • PRO, Haig MSS • BL OIOC, Curzon MSS • CUL, Hardinge MSS • King's Lond., Liddell Hart C., Robertson MSS • L. S. Amery, *My political life*, 1 (1953) • P. Simkins, *Kitchener's army* (1988) • A. Hunter, *Kitchener's sword arm* (1996) • T. Pakenham, *The Boer War* (1979) • S. B. Spies, *Methods of barbarism* (Cape Town, 1977) • I. F. W. Beckett and K. Simpson, eds., *A nation in arms* (1985) • D. Gilmour, *Curzon* (1994) • G. W. Steevens, *With Kitchener to Khartum* (1898) • N. Goradia, *Lord Curzon* (1993) • Reginald, Viscount Esher [R. B. Brett], *The tragedy of Lord Kitchener* (1921) • R. Holmes, *The little field-marshal: Sir John French* (1981) • B. Bond, ed., *The First World War and British military history* (1991) • *The Leo Amery diaries*, ed. J. Barnes and D. Nicholson, 1 (1980)

Archives BL, corresp. and papers, Add. MSS 52276–52278 • BL, working papers relating to survey of Palestine, Add. MS 69848 • CKS, estate corresp. • Palestine Exploration Fund, corresp. and papers relating to Palestine Exploration Fund • PRO, corresp. and papers, WO 159; 30/57 • Royal Engineers Museum | BL, corresp. with Arthur James Balfour, Add. MS 49726 • BL, letters to Lady Ilchester, Add. MS 51370 • BL OIOC, corresp. with Lord Ampthill, MS Eur. E 233 • BL OIOC, corresp. with Edmund Barrow, MS Eur. E 420 • BL OIOC, letters to Lord Birdwood, MS Eur. D 556 • BL OIOC, letters to Harcourt Butler, MS Eur. F 116 • BL OIOC, Curzon MSS • BL OIOC, corresp. and papers relating to India, MS Eur. D 686 • BL OIOC, letters to Lord Morley, MS Eur. D 573 • BL OIOC, corresp. with Henry Richards, MS Eur. F 122 • BL OIOC, letters to James Dunlop Smith, MS Eur. D 686 • Bodl. Oxf., corresp. with Herbert Asquith • Bodl. Oxf., letters to Lord and Lady Edward Cecil • Bodl. Oxf., corresp. with H. A. Gwynne • Bodl. Oxf., corresp. with Lewis Harcourt • Bodl. Oxf., corresp. with Lord Milner • CUL, corresp. with Lord Hardinge • Glos. RO, corresp. with Michael Hicks Beach • HLRO, corresp. with Andrew Bonar Law • HLRO, letters to David Lloyd George • King's Lond., Liddell Hart C., Robertson MSS • Lpool RO, corresp. with Lord Derby • NAM, letters to Earl Roberts • NAM, letters to Evelyn Wood • NL Aus., corresp. with Alfred Deakin • NL Scot., corresp. with Lord Haldane • NL Scot., corresp. with Lord Rosebery • PRO, corresp. with Lord Cromer, vols. 5, 7, 8,

22 • PRO, Haig MSS • U. Birm. L., corresp. with Joseph Chamberlain • U. Newcastle, Robinson L., corresp. with Walter Runciman | FILM BFI NFTVA, *Reputations*, Channel 4, 8 June 1998 • BFI NFTVA, documentary footage • BFI NFTVA, news footage

Likenesses H. von Herkomer and F. Goodall, oils, 1890, NPG [*see illus.*] • photographs, 1898, NPG • H. von Angeli, oils, 1899, Royal Engineers, Chattenden barracks • C. M. Horsfall, pastel drawing, 1899, NPG • A. S. Cope, oils, 1900, Royal Engineers, Brompton • Duffus Bros., platinum print, 1901, NPG • W. Strang, chalk drawing, 1910, Royal Collection • R. C. Belt, bronze bust, 1916, Gov. Art Coll. • J. Collier, oils, 1916 (replica of portrait of 1910), Oriental Club, London • W. G. John, bronze bust, exh. RA 1917, Gordon Memorial College, Khartoum • W. R. Dick, marble effigy, 1923, St Paul's Cathedral, London • J. Guthrie, group portrait, oils, 1924–30 (*Statesmen of World War I, 1914–18*), NPG • J. Tweed, bronze statue, 1926, Horse Guards Parade, London • H. von Angeli, oils, Royal Collection • W. G. John, plaster bust, IWM • A. Leete, recruiting poster, IWM; repro. in *London Opinion* (15 Sept 1914), cover • Spy [L. Ward], caricature, watercolour study, NPG; repro. in *VF* (23 Feb 1899) • Spy [L. Ward], chromolithograph caricature (*A general group*), NPG; repro. in *VF* (29 Nov 1900) • chalk and wash drawing, NPG • photographs, IWM, NAM

Wealth at death £171,421 14s. 8d.: probate, 28 June 1916, *CGPLA Eng. & Wales*

Kitchin, Anthony [*name in religion* Dunstan] (1477–1563), bishop of Llandaff, was of unknown parentage and origins. He entered Westminster Abbey as a mature vocation in 1511 and celebrated his first mass in 1517, by when he was studying at Gloucester College, Oxford. He was admitted BTh in 1525 and the following year was appointed prior of students, a post that involved supervising Benedictine students outside as well as within the loose federation of 'staircases' which made up the Benedictine Gloucester College. In 1532 he became abbot of Eynsham, near Oxford, and in 1538, shortly before the dissolution of his abbey, he proceeded DTh. He does not appear to have been a very active abbot. In September 1535 the king's visitor, John Tregonwell, reported of Eynsham that 'The abbot is chaste in his living; looks well to the reparation of the house; but he is negligent in overseeing his brethren, which he excuses by his daily infirmity' (*LP Henry VIII*, 9, no. 457). He took the line of least resistance in the political and theological controversies of the 1530s, subscribing the royal supremacy in 1534 and the articles of religion in 1536. About the beginning of 1537 John Perkins, an Oxford lawyer who seems to have become mentally disturbed, brought a series of vague accusations of treason against Kitchin and the abbot of Osney, but these were speedily dismissed. Kitchin surrendered his abbey on 4 December 1538, receiving a pension of £133 6s. 8d. and an appointment as royal chaplain-in-ordinary. In 1545 he replaced Robert Holgate as bishop of Llandaff: he was to be the first resident bishop the diocese had had for over a century.

The diocese was not (as a later bishop, Francis Godwin, claimed) one of the wealthiest in the land; it was in fact the second poorest. Kitchin thus gave up his pension for a diocese whose total income was only a little larger: and he was virtually unique among bishops of Llandaff before the nineteenth century in that he held no other preferments. The accusations (notably by Godwin) that he ruined the diocese by incompetent management also

need to be treated with scepticism. In spite of considerable pressure, in effect he alienated no land outright, though he was forced to make several long leases and grants in perpetuity, including one of the manor of Llandaff to the Matthews family in 1553. His lease of the episcopal palace and manor of Matharn to William Lewis of St Pierre is best interpreted as a collusive grant to keep the lands out of other hands. Even so, in the early 1590s he was criticized by Gervase Babington with rueful humour in the comment that he was now bishop only of 'Aff', for all the land had gone.

A more serious criticism is Kitchin's compliance in accepting a series of radical religious changes. He was prepared to oppose government policy, notably in his opposition to clerical marriage in 1549, but he never pushed his arguments so far that he could be removed from office. In 1554, again, he took his own line when, on the reconciliation of the kingdom with Rome, he was the only bishop not to seek absolution from the sin of schism. If he did not consider himself a schismatic, he may also have felt that he had protected his diocese from sin. Clearly a most reluctant persecutor, he showed his compassion in his efforts to persuade Rawlins White, presented by John Foxe as no more than a Cardiff fisherman but probably the leader of a group of local heretics, to save his life by recanting, and persevered in them up to the moment when White went to the stake in March 1555.

In 1559, along with the other Marian bishops, Kitchin voted in the Lords against the restoration of the royal supremacy and the Act of Uniformity. Elizabeth succeeded in removing the other intransigents. Kitchin could not be removed, but he was eventually outnumbered. Characteristically, he backed down rather than fight and be defeated. His refusal to take the oath of supremacy nearly cost him his diocese in 1559, but he eventually accepted a curiously worded compromise. He was also allowed to refuse Elizabeth's mandate to consecrate Matthew Parker as archbishop of Canterbury, a refusal that has subsequently called into question the validity of all Anglican orders. J. C. Whitebrook's theory that Kitchin did in fact consecrate Parker in a private ceremony is almost certainly fantasy.

The extent of Kitchin's success as a pastoral bishop, and the justification for his sacrifice of principle, is seen in the condition of his diocese at the time of his death. The survey of the clergy in the winter of 1560–61 showed many gaps in the parochial ministry, caused partly by the slump in clerical recruitment and the devastating effects of the influenza epidemics of the late 1550s and partly by absenteeism. By 1563, however, the situation had improved considerably. Few parishes were without incumbents, though there was still much pluralism; several absentees had been persuaded to return; and there had been a marked upturn in recruitment.

Kitchin was now eighty-six. He had been blind for some years and was too ill to attend the parliament of 1562. He died at his palace at Matharn on 31 October 1563 and was buried in the parish church: no monument survives. Nor has his will survived, though there are references to it in other documents. An inventory of the contents of his palace lists property worth £109. It makes pathetic reading: some old clothes and furnishings (possibly bought when he left the religious life); a little silver and gilt plate; forty books (alas, no details); and a well-equipped kitchen, suggesting that he was fulfilling another pastoral obligation, that of hospitality.   MADELEINE GRAY

Sources Emden, *Oxf.*, 4.330 · M. Gray, 'The cloister and the hearth: two Reformation bishops of Llandaff', *Journal of Welsh Religious History*, 3 (1995), 15–34 · *LP Henry VIII*, vol. 9 · J. Gwynfor Jones, 'The Reformation bishops of Llandaff', *Morgannwg*, 32 (1988), 38–43 · E. H. Pearce, *The monks of Westminster* (1916) · F. J. Shirley, *Elizabeth's first archbishop* (1948) · J. C. Whitebrook, *The consecration of Matthew Parker* (1945) · G. Williams, 'The ecclesiastical history of Glamorgan, 1527–1642', *Glamorgan county history*, 4 (1974) · exchequer, king's remembrancer, special commissions of inquiry, PRO, E178/3451 · G. R. Elton, *Star chamber stories* (1958)
Wealth at death £109: PRO, E178/3451

Kitchin, George William (1827–1912), scholar and dean of Durham, was born at Naughton, Suffolk, on 7 December 1827, the fifth child of the Revd Isaac Kitchin, rector from 1833 of St Stephen's, Ipswich, and his wife, Mary, daughter of the Revd J. Bardgett, rector of Melmerby, Cumberland. Kitchin's father, who came from a family of west Cumberland 'statesmen' (small proprietors), was one of the non-graduate clergy educated at St Bees College. Kitchin himself went to Ipswich grammar school and King's College, London, and in 1846 he was elected to a studentship at Christ Church, Oxford, where he was a contemporary of William Stubbs. He graduated with first classes in classics and mathematics in 1850. In 1852 he took orders and was appointed a tutor of Christ Church; he published an edition of Bacon's *Novum organum* in 1855. In the same year he became headmaster of a preparatory school at Twyford, Hampshire.

Kitchin returned to Oxford in 1861 on his appointment as censor of Christ Church, a post which he held until 1863, when he vacated his studentship on his marriage to Alice Maud (*c*.1844–1930), daughter of Bridges Taylor, British consul for Denmark. Kitchin was in 1863 tutor to Frederick, prince of Denmark; his wife was a friend of Queen Alexandra. The Kitchins had a family of three sons and two daughters, the eldest of whom, Alexandra ('Xie'), was a frequent photographic subject for Kitchin's Christ Church colleague C. L. Dodgson.

From 1863 to 1883 Kitchin was a lecturer for several Oxford colleges, and was an important figure in the development of teaching in modern humanities subjects. An early participant, from 1870, in the scheme to provide intercollegiate lectures in modern history, he was one of those who established that subject as an undergraduate discipline at Oxford. With C. W. Boase he edited an English translation (1875) of Ranke's *Englische Geschichte*, and he wrote *A History of France* (3 vols., 1873–7), both of which were intended for the use of students. A university examiner in mathematics (1854), classics (1869–70), and modern history (1874–6, 1879–80), he was also a promoter of the teaching of modern languages, giving evidence in 1877 on behalf of the Taylor Institution to the statutory

George William Kitchin (1827–1912), by Lewis Carroll (Charles Lutwidge Dodgson), 1859

commission on Oxford chaired by Lord Selborne. His translations of A. Brachet's works on French grammar and etymology were regarded as pioneering contributions to the study of French philology. He was secretary to the delegates of Oxford University Press from 1866 to 1868. As secretary to the school-books committee (1865–74) he organized the first Clarendon Press editions of the English classics, 'which did much to promote the serious study, if not the sympathetic appreciation, of English literature in schools' (*DNB*). He contributed to the series an edition of Spenser's *Faerie queene*.

Kitchin's most significant achievement at Oxford was to organize the scheme for admitting students living in lodgings and not belonging to any college or hall. This idea was especially favoured by radical supporters of university extension, who believed that the adoption of this Scottish university practice would bring an Oxford education within the reach of students of limited means. As the first censor of non-collegiate students (as they came to be known) from their admission in 1868, he was particularly energetic in carrying out the new scheme. Not educated at a public school himself, he had a strong personal sentiment in favour of broadening Oxford's social base. At his suggestion, Gladstone presented the nucleus of a library, now in the library of St Catherine's College, Oxford (Gladstone, *Diaries*, 9 Feb 1874). By 1883, when Kitchin relinquished the censorship, the experiment of admitting such students had proved successful, though without effecting the transformation in the character of the university for which many of the scheme's original proponents had hoped.

In April 1883 Gladstone appointed Kitchin to the deanery of Winchester in recognition of his 'great services in Oxford to the cause of education' (Gladstone). His income at Winchester was severely reduced by the pension paid to his predecessor and as a result of the agricultural depression. In 1894 on Lord Rosebery's recommendation he transferred to the deanery of Durham. As *ex officio* warden of Durham University, he was immediately active in bringing about the supplementary charter of 1895, which permitted the admission of women students to the university. Chairman of the council of Cheltenham Ladies' College, he had been among the first supporters of the women's higher education at Oxford; at the opening of St Hilda's Hall (later College), Oxford, in 1893, he spoke of the 'unmixed benefit' which had resulted from the foundation of women's colleges. At Durham, he also helped the smooth passage of a change in the constitution of the university, in 1908, by which the dean and chapter ceased to be the governing body, their powers being assumed by the university senate. He had been familiar with a similar transfer of authority at Christ Church, Oxford, in 1867. Under the new statutes for Durham, he was expressly named as the first chancellor of the university.

Kitchin was known as a broad-churchman, but was not regarded as a profound theologian. His scholarly activities at Winchester and Durham were principally works of local history and archaeology. Among his later writing were a history of Winchester (1890) and a biography of Harold Browne, bishop of Winchester (1895). He edited several volumes of records for the Hampshire Record Society and the Surtees Society, and he was elected FSA in 1889. For all his pioneering work in the teaching of history, and his considerable number of publications, the result of extensive use of manuscript authorities, he never produced a work of sufficient originality to gain him a wider reputation as a historian. His most frequently cited publication has proved to be the essay *Ruskin at Oxford* (1903).

A strong Liberal in politics, Kitchin had been one of the secretaries to Gladstone's election committee at Oxford in 1865, and remained a loyal Gladstonian after the home-rule split. His pulpit utterances in support of the Boers during the Second South African War of 1899–1902 were not well received, and coloured contemporary assessments of his career; his successor at Durham commented, 'Kitchin to the outer world was mainly a rather obstinate "little Englander"' (H. H. Henson, *Retrospect of an Unimportant Life*, 1, 1942, 151). A supporter of temperance, peasant proprietorship (he farmed 36 acres near Wadhurst, Sussex), and Ruskinian economics, Kitchin welcomed the rise of Labour as an independent political force, contributing an introduction to the autobiography (1910) of John Wilson, leader of the Durham miners. His *Letter to the Labour Party* (1905), while maintaining a slightly dated view of social politics—he regarded state old-age pensions as

bribes to the electorate—put forward a far-sighted scheme of education in citizenship.

Kitchin died at the deanery, Durham, on 13 October 1912. In accordance with his will, which requested a simple funeral, no biography of him was written.

M. C. CURTHOYS

Sources *The Times* (14 Oct 1912) • *The Times* (15 Oct 1912) • *The Times* (16 Oct 1912) • *The Times* (14 Dec 1912) • *Oxford Magazine* (24 Oct 1912) • A. T. C. Pratt, ed., *People of the period: being a collection of the biographies of upwards of six thousand living celebrities*, 2 vols. (1897) • *Men and women of the time* (1899) • Foster, *Alum. Oxon.* • P. Sutcliffe, *The Oxford University Press: an informal history* (1978) • C. E. Whiting, *The University of Durham, 1832–1932* (1932) • M. E. Rayner, *The centenary history of St Hilda's College, Oxford* (1993) • *The letters of Lewis Carroll*, ed. M. N. Cohen and R. L. Green, 2 vols. (1979) • Gladstone, *Diaries*

Archives BL, corresp. with W. E. Gladstone, Add. MSS 44406–44526 *passim* • BL, corresp. with Macmillans, Add. MS 55054 • CUL, letters to B. F. Westcott • King's AC Cam., letters to Oscar Browning

Likenesses L. Carroll [C. L. Dodgson], photograph, 1859, NPG [*see illus.*] • H. M. Paget, oils, Non-collegiate Building, Oxford • J. W. Schofield, oils, U. Durham • oils, Christ Church Oxf.

Wealth at death £7579 8s. 4d.: resworn probate, 10 Dec 1912, CGPLA Eng. & Wales

Kitchin, John (d. in or before **1588**), legal writer, was admitted to Gray's Inn in 1544 and called to the bar there in 1547, but nothing is known of his date of birth or parentage. A reading he gave at the inn in 1564 on the Henrican Statute of Leases (32 Hen. VIII c. 28), which survives in more than one manuscript copy, contains an interesting discussion of the elements required to enact a statute, as well as a lengthy exposition of how to make a good lease. Appointed reader again in 1572 and treasurer in 1575, Kitchin regularly attended pension meetings at the inn during his lifetime. Little else is known of his career except that he practised in the city of London courts. Kitchin was buried at Islington; his son John was granted administration of his estate in 1588.

In 1580 and 1581 Kitchin published two works of some professional importance, *Le court leete et court baron* and *Retourna brevium novelment corrigee*. Both were built on content and formats that had previously been available in manuscript as well as print, but Kitchin reconstituted them with exposition under alphabetical headings that gathered together a great deal of learning from the year-books and later case law. Addressing *Le court leete* to students at the inns of chancery, and claiming that his intention was to improve their knowledge, he expressed the hope that professionally trained lawyers would soon completely replace those stewards of manorial courts who were merely the 'servants' of the lords and 'ignorant in the law' (Kytchin, preface). Indeed, he went so far as to suggest that any manorial court not kept by a properly trained lawyer should be subject to forfeiture under *quo warranto* proceedings. Quoting from a range of legal authorities stretching from Bracton and Britton to Fortescue, St German, and Staunford, Kitchin acknowledged that one purpose of manorial courts was to maintain the interests of the lords, but he also placed them within a broader framework of royal, as opposed to seigneurial, justice that had been ordained for the punishment of enormities and nuisances to the 'publique' within the precinct of the courts. *Le court leete* was republished many times in the 1580s, the 1590s, and during the course of the seventeenth century, often along with *Retourna brevium*.

CHRISTOPHER W. BROOKS

Sources R. J. Fletcher, ed., *The pension book of Gray's Inn*, 1 (1901) · J. Kytchin, *Le court leete et court baron* (1580) · BL, Lansdowne MS 1134, fols. 46v ff. [reading, Sept 1564] · administration, PRO, PROB 6/4, fol. 65v

Kitchin, Thomas (1719–1784), cartographer and engraver, was born in the parish of St Olave, Southwark, most probably on 4 August 1719, apparently the eldest of several children of Thomas Kitchin, hat dyer, and his wife, Mary Birr, whom he married in 1716.

Kitchin was apprenticed to the map engraver Emanuel Bowen on 6 December 1732. He finished his time in 1739 and on 25 December that year married his master's daughter, Sarah. Despite the family connection with his former master Kitchin was at work independently from at least 1741. From 1746, when he was made free of the Merchant Taylors' Company, he took on apprentices in his expanding firm. His early production includes John Elphinstone's map of Scotland (1746), used before Culloden, the first pocket atlas of Scotland, *Geographia Scotiae* (1748–9), and *The Small English Atlas* (1749), co-published with Thomas Jefferys, another of Bowen's apprentices. The *Large English Atlas* (serially produced with Bowen between 1749 and 1760) was the most important county atlas since Elizabethan times and the first real attempt to cover the whole country at large scale. In 1755 Kitchin engraved the great John Mitchell map of North America, used at the peace treaties of Paris and Versailles, and the standard map until the end of the century.

Originally based in Clerkenwell, by late 1755 Kitchin was established at The Star (no. 59), Holborn Hill, opposite Ely House, running a substantial business producing all kinds of engraved material, even including portraits and caricatures. Further county atlases appeared in the 1760s. Larger individual works were Andrew Armstrong's survey of Northumberland (1769), awarded a 50 guinea prize by the Society of Arts, the twelve-sheet road map *England and Wales* (1770), and Bernhard Ratzer's elegant plans of New York (1769–70). From 1773 Kitchin appears in the *Royal Kalendar* as hydrographer to the king. Eventually retiring from Holborn to St Albans, Kitchin continued map making to the end of his life. Prolific and reliable, he produced countless maps for travel books and geographies, and the 170 maps he produced for the *London Magazine* alone (1747–83) would prove sufficient companion for the entire history of his time.

As an engraver, Kitchin showed a fine technical facility, the lettering clean and assured and the etched decoration from his workshop among the most impressive of all English rococo work. He is also known as an amateur painter. Clues to his personal life are meagre. An early publication, *The English Orpheus*, a collection of drinking songs of about 1743, is light-hearted, especially where it appears to poke fun at Kitchin's Welsh master. The well-written *Traveller's Guide* (1783) has both wry humour and relaxed confidence. He was extremely active in the Baptist community and served as deacon of his chapel. His will, which requests burial 'with as little expense as may be', shows a more than conventional piety.

Kitchin married his second wife, Jane (1719/20–1789), daughter of the Baptist minister Joseph Burroughs, on 27 May 1762. To the latter he left a comfortable estate. His son of the first marriage, Thomas Bowen Kitchin, apprenticed to his father in 1754 and also hydrographer to the king, had already inherited the stock-in-trade. Kitchin died in St Albans on 23 June 1784 and was buried in St Albans Abbey on 29 June. A memorial inscription in St Albans Abbey has not survived.

LAURENCE WORMS, *rev.*

Sources *British Library map library catalogue* (1998) [CD-ROM] · Merchant Taylors' Company, apprenticeship books 19, 20, GL, 19/171 et seq. · parish register, 1719, St Olave, Southwark · parish register, Hart Street, St Olave, 1762 [marriage] · parish register, Clerkenwell, St John, 1739 [marriage] · will, LMA, consistory court DL/C/367, fols. 288–9 · I. Maxted, *The London book trades, 1775–1800: a preliminary checklist of members* (1977) · L. Worms, 'Thomas Kitchin's "journey of life": hydrographer to George III, mapmaker and engraver', *Map Collector*, 62 (1993), 2–8; 63 (1993), 14–20 · L. J. Maguire, ed., *The church book of the church meeting at Paul's Alley, Barbican … 1739 to 1768* (1990) [occasional paper 10 of the General Baptist Assembly; DWL, MSS 38.73, 38.74] · 'Barbican church minute book, 1699–1739', Angus Library · 'A list of members of the church at Barbican', Angus Library · 'Minute book of Glasshouse Yard Chapel', Angus Library · R. Clutterbuck, ed., *The history and antiquities of the county of Hertford*, 1 (1815), 80 · W. W. Ristow, *American maps and mapmakers* (1985), 244

Wealth at death total unknown; incl. approximately £750 in Bank of England annuities

Kitchiner, William (1778–1827), epicure and writer, was baptized at St Clement Danes, Westminster, in May 1778, the son of William Kitchiner (d. 1794), and his wife, Mary, *née* Grave. Both parents were originally from Hertfordshire; Kitchiner senior had built up a prosperous business as a coal merchant, operating from a Thames-side wharf below Fountain Court, the Strand, and achieved local eminence as 'Justice Kitchner' (Diprose, 2.28). At his death he left his wife adequately provided for, and his estate (which included property along the Strand at Beaufort Buildings and Fountain Court) in trust for his son.

In later life Kitchiner let it be understood that he had been schooled at Eton and held a medical degree from Glasgow; in fact he had not attended either establishment but by claiming a Scottish medical degree, which barred him from practice in England, he could style himself Dr Kitchiner MD, and as he possessed an extensive library of medical books, this title was not challenged. Being financially independent he was able to marry early. On 3 August 1799 he married Elizabeth Oram, also of St Clement Danes parish, but the couple soon parted, and a subsequent liaison with Elizabeth Gifford led to the birth of a son, William Brown Kitchiner, on 23 June 1804. He was acknowledged by his father, educated at Charterhouse (1818–22), then at St John's College, Cambridge (1824–6), which he left without a degree. In later years Kitchiner lived with Elizabeth Friend, to whom he left his house and a comfortable bequest.

William Kitchiner (1778–1827), by Charles Turner, pubd 1827

Kitchiner's inheritance permitted him to enjoy, and to write extensively on, those three arts which most pleased him: music, gastronomy, and optics, and these interests were also represented in his library. He composed an operetta entitled *Love among the Roses, or, The Master Key*, was author of *Observations on Vocal Music* (1821), and a prolific writer of patriotic and sea songs. His interest in culinary matters was wide-ranging. His friend William Jerdan commented: 'His medical and gastronomical practices were wonderfully combined, insomuch that his guests could not tell whether what was set before them was a meal or a prescription' (Jerdan, 282–7). Around 1812 Kitchiner was living near the observatory at Camden Town, but he later settled at 43 Warren Street, Marylebone, Middlesex, where the weekly meetings of his 'committee of taste' were attended by the most eminent members of society. They arrived to be greeted by Kitchiner at the piano; their meal might have been prepared with the assistance of Henry Osborne, chef to Sir Joseph Banks; after a stimulating discussion, they were expected to depart promptly at eleven. The most famous of Kitchiner's numerous cookery books, *The Cook's Oracle*, first appeared in 1817 and went through many editions, even after his death. It was written in a down-to-earth style, and demonstrated Kitchiner's familiarity with the entire process, from shopping, through preparing and serving the dishes, to cleaning up. It was an acknowledged source of inspiration for Mrs Beeton, and was mined by the writers of other household guides. The related subject of digestion and medical treatment of a more or less purgative nature were subsumed in his *Peptic Precepts* (1821), a subject itself included in his exhaustive *The Traveller's Oracle* (1827), which covered all conceivable aspects of travel, although Kitchiner himself had never been abroad.

In 1819 Kitchiner was elected a fellow of the Royal Society. A considerable portion of his income was spent on his optical interests. At his death he possessed eighty-nine telescopes—of which several, by the best makers, had been bought at auction from the estates of deceased astronomers—besides numerous opera glasses and several microscopes. Kitchiner frequented opticians' shops, discussing improvements to instruments. He devised about 1820 the 'pancratic eye-tube', which allowed continuous adjustment of focus on the common refracting telescope. His *Practical Observations on Telescopes* (1815) went through several editions, and was later expanded into *The Economy of the Eyes*, in two volumes (1824). Kitchiner was often accused of plagiarism in his books, and it is true that not all his 'borrowings' were acknowledged.

Kitchiner's end was unexpected and in some degree suspect. On 26 February 1827 he dined with his friend John Braham at 69 Baker Street, overstayed his own preferred hour of departure, and on reaching his house suffered a heart attack, from which he shortly died. He was buried at St Clement Danes on 6 March; his son erected a memorial to him in St Pancras New Church. Sothebys auctioned his library and scientific instruments in July 1827. It transpired that Kitchiner had intended to alter his will on the day following his death, because he had come to the conclusion that his son did not deserve to inherit. His timely demise meant that William Brown Kitchiner did inherit; he married in 1828 Georgiana Macdonell, daughter of Major Edgworth of London, and died impoverished at Ostend, Belgium, in 1861. ANITA McCONNELL

Sources F. Schiller, 'Haslam of "Bedlam", Kitchiner of the "oracles": two doctors under mad King George III and their friendship', *Medical History*, 28 (1984), 189–201 · T. Bridge and C. C. English, *William Kitchiner, regency eccentric* (1992) · W. Jerdan, *Men I have known* (1866), 282–7 · *GM*, 1st ser., 69 (1799), 1190 · *GM*, 1st ser., 97/1 (1827), 470–72 · W. Kitchiner, *The economy of the eyes* (1824) · J. Diprose, *Some account of the parish of Saint Clement Danes*, 2 (1876), 28 · W. Kitchiner, 'On the size best adapted for achromatic glasses', *Philosophical Magazine*, 46 (1815), 122–9 · 'Practical observations on telescopes', *Philosophical Magazine*, 44 (1814), 461–5 [review] · Grove, *Dict. mus.* (1927) · parish registers, St Clement Danes, City Westm. AC · sale catalogues (1827) [Sothebys, July 1827; annotated copies, BL, SCS 155(5), 155(6)]

Archives NL Scot., corresp. with Archibald Constable

Likenesses W. Brockedon, pencil and chalk drawing, *c.*1826, NPG · C. Turner, mezzotint, pubd 1827, BM, NPG [*see illus.*] · E. Finden, stipple, pubd 1829 (after bust by J. Kendrick; after W. H. Brooke), NPG

Kitching, John Alwyne (1908–1996), cell physiologist and marine ecologist, was born on 24 October 1908 in York, the younger child of John Nainby Kitching (1845–1914), joint managing director of an engineering firm in Leeds, and his wife, Alice Edith, daughter of the Revd George Yeats, vicar of Heworth church in York. His elder sister died in infancy, and his father died of a heart attack when Alwyne, as he was known as a child, was five. His mother moved to Bournemouth, where Kitching attended preparatory school before moving on to Cheltenham College in 1922. During his early life he travelled widely in Europe with his mother, who was a watercolour artist and described her travels in a series of radio broadcasts in 1924. In these years Kitching developed strong interests in natural history and entered Trinity College, Cambridge, in 1927 to study zoology, botany, and geology in the natural sciences tripos, graduating with a degree in zoology in 1931.

As a Cambridge undergraduate Kitching encountered the two principal topics which dominated his later career. An interest in cell physiology was aroused principally by Carl Pantin, and in marine ecology by G. A. Steven at Easter classes at the Marine Biological Association in Plymouth. These interests were consolidated during his appointment as lecturer at Birkbeck College, London. There he gained his PhD in 1933 through studies of the physiology of contractile vacuoles of protozoa. He also pioneered research in sublittoral marine ecology, with H. C. Gilson and T. T. Macan, as probably the first biological researcher to use a diving helmet. Kitching married Evelyn Mary Oliver, of Hendon, Middlesex, a biology graduate from Birkbeck, on 24 March 1934, and one son and three daughters were born over subsequent years.

After a brief lecturing appointment at Edinburgh, Kitching, now known to all as Jack, moved in 1937 to lecture at the University of Bristol. During a Rockefeller fellowship at Princeton University in 1938–9 he collaborated with Daniel Pease in research on the effects of high pressure and modified gas concentrations on cells. He was to return to this interest after the war, but more immediately it may have led to his wartime work at the University of Toronto on problems associated with lack of oxygen at high altitudes and exposure of ditched aircrew to cold water. In 1947 he was appointed OBE for services to the RAF.

Kitching returned to his lectureship in Bristol in 1945, was promoted to a readership in 1949, and was elected to fellowship of the Royal Society in 1960. In 1963 he was appointed to a chair in biology at the newly established University of East Anglia, where he acted as dean of the school of biological sciences from 1967 to 1970, and remained active there well after formal retirement in 1974. At both universities he pursued productive research in cell physiology. Using ingenious techniques, described in fourteen papers, he demonstrated the role of contractile vacuoles in removing excess water and controlling cell volume of protozoa. He and his students also performed studies on the effects of high hydrostatic pressures on protozoan cells, and especially on structures formed from microtubules, as well as studying the mechanism of suctorial feeding in suctorian ciliate protozoa and the effects of anaesthetic gases upon cell structures.

Kitching's summer vacations throughout were devoted to marine ecology, with support from numerous colleagues, most consistently F. John Ebling. They formed an effective pair, Kitching a shy but single-minded scientist and Ebling a gregarious organizer. Together they led annual expeditions, largely manned by students, to study the ecology of Lough Ine (or Hyne) in co. Cork. Sea water flows into and out of the fully saline lough through a narrow rapids channel, exposing marine organisms to strong currents. In earlier years many techniques including diving were used to investigate the physico-chemical features and the distribution of littoral and sublittoral organisms in the rapids, the lough, and the nearby coast. Later experimental work examined the dependence of the distribution of organisms on physico-chemical factors and predation. The results of this ground breaking research were described in thirty-four papers over more than forty years, earlier work being summarized by Kitching and Ebling in *Advances in Ecological Research* in 1967, and later work by Kitching in the same journal in 1987.

Kitching was a tall, impressive man, somewhat aloof, but most conscientious. He was interested in all aspects of the natural world, an enthusiastic gardener, an energetic traveller, and prolific photographer. He saw a pre-publication copy of his final work, *The Biology of Rocky Shores* (1996), jointly written with Colin Little, shortly before he died in Norwich on 1 April 1996. He was survived by his wife and four children.　　MICHAEL A. SLEIGH

Sources T. Norton, 'Jack A. Kitching, OBE, FRS (1908–1996): the forgotten pioneer', *Historical Diving Times*, 17 (1996), 10–11 · M. A. Sleigh, *Memoirs FRS*, 43 (1997), 267–84 · *The Times* (17 April 1996) · *The Guardian* (25 April 1996) · *Journal of Eukaryotic Microbiology*, 43 (1996) · *WWW* · personal knowledge (2004) · private information (2004) · *CGPLA Eng. & Wales* (1996)

Archives RS, papers

Likenesses photograph, repro. in *Memoirs FRS*, 268 · photograph, repro. in Norton, 'Jack A. Kitching'

Wealth at death £638,194: probate, 12 July 1996, *CGPLA Eng. & Wales*

Kitchingman, John (1740?–1781), painter, was a pupil at Shipley's drawing academy and afterwards at the Royal Academy Schools, which he entered on 4 April 1769, gaining that year the academy's silver medal. His name is entered in the schools' register as Kitchenman. Of his parents, nothing is known. He married when young, on 20 March 1764 at St Martin-in-the-Fields, Westminster, London, Christian Gibson. They had a daughter, Jane (baptized in 1768 at St Paul's, Covent Garden), and a son, Charles (baptized in 1770 at St Paul's, Covent Garden). He was awarded several premiums by the Society of Arts; he exhibited miniatures with the Free Society from 1766 to 1768, and from 1770 was a constant contributor to the Royal Academy exhibitions, sending, besides portraits, figure subjects and sea pieces. An example of his work, dated 1766, is in the Victoria and Albert Museum, London. His *Beggar and Dog*, a subject from Henry Mackenzie's *Man of Feeling*, exhibited in 1775, was mezzotinted on a large scale by H. Kingsbury, and a set of four pictures representing the building, chase, unlading, and dissolution of a cutter, which appeared at the Royal Academy in the last year of his life, was well engraved by B. T. Pouncy; his portraits *Mrs Elizabeth Carter*, *Mr Macklin as Shylock*, and *Mrs Yates as Alicia in Nicholas Rowe's 'Jane Shore'* were also engraved. Kitchingman was fond of boating, and in 1777 won the duke of Cumberland's cup in the annual sailing contest on the Thames. Kitchingman separated from his wife and fell into intemperate habits. He died 'immediately after suffering the amputation of his leg, the bone of which was, in consequence of a strain, so much disordered as to baffle the attempts of the most eminent of the faculty' (*GM*) in King Street, Covent Garden, London, on 28 December 1781. According to an affidavit by one Humphrey Tomkinson (a jeweller) and Thomas Simmonds (a tailor) made during a successful lawsuit by Kitchingman's sister, Beata Moore, to obtain administration of her brother's estate, Christian Kitchingman was a 'person of bad character and for several years last past hath been of a very loose and unsettled turn of mind' (Prob 29/42).

F. M. O'DONOGHUE, rev. J. DESMARAIS

Sources E. Edwards, *Anecdotes of painters* (1808); facs. edn (1970) · Redgrave, *Artists* · Graves, *RA exhibitors* · *The exhibition of the Royal Academy* (1770–81) [exhibition catalogues] · J. Gould, *Biographical dictionary of painters, sculptors, engravers and architects*, new edn, 2 vols. (1839) · M. Pilkington, *A general dictionary of painters: containing memoirs of the lives and works*, ed. A. Cunningham and R. A. Davenport, new edn (1857) · Bryan, *Painters* (1886–9) · Waterhouse, *18c painters* · *Checklist of British artists in the Witt Library*, Courtauld Institute, Witt Library (1991) · admon., PRO, PROB 6/158, fol. 108r [by decree] · S. C. Hutchison, 'The Royal Academy Schools, 1768–1830', *Walpole Society*, 38 (1960–62), 123–91, esp. 133 · D. Foskett, *Miniatures: dictionary and guide* (1987) · *GM*, 1st ser., 52 (1782), 46

Wealth at death under £100: administration, PRO, PROB 6/158, fol. 108r

Kite, Charles (*bap.* 1760?, *d.* 1811), surgeon, may have been the son of Samuel Kite baptized at Gravesend, Kent, on 1 October 1760. Kite was a member of the Company of Surgeons in London, and practised at Gravesend, Kent. Little else is known about his life. Besides contributing to the *Memoirs of the London Medical Society* and other medical journals, he wrote: *An Essay on the Recovery of the Apparently Dead* (1788), for which he was awarded the silver medal of the Humane Society, and *Essays and observations, physiological and medical, on the submersion of animals, and on the resin of the aeoroides resinifera, or yellow resin of Botany Bay* (1795). He died in Gravesend in 1811.

GORDON GOODWIN, rev. PATRICK WALLIS

Sources Watt, *Bibl. Brit.* · P. J. Wallis and R. V. Wallis, *Eighteenth century medics*, 2nd edn (1988) · IGI

Kite, John (*d.* 1537), archbishop of Armagh and bishop of Carlisle, was born in London to unknown parents. He was admitted a king's scholar at Eton College about 1476, and then went to King's College, Cambridge, also as a scholar, in 1480. His graduation is not recorded, but in 1494/5 he proceeded BCnL. For unspecified reasons he was excused lecturing in the following academic year. By then he had already started to acquire ecclesiastical benefices, starting in 1493, when he became a canon of Tamworth with the prebend of Wilmercote. He became rector of Wolferton, Norfolk, in 1496, and of Boscombe, Wiltshire, in 1499. Subsequent preferments included prebends in Chichester Cathedral (1507), Salisbury Cathedral (1510), and Crediton collegiate church (1513). A royal chaplain by 1509, in that capacity he took part in the funeral of Henry VII and the coronation of Henry VIII; by February 1510 he had become subdean of the Chapel Royal. In the latter capacity he took part in court revels. Although his presence seems to have been partly associated with the music provided by the chapel's children, there is evidence that he had a fine singing voice, which enabled him to appear as a performer in his own right; hence his being provided with 16 yards of blue damask in February 1511, 'for a garment of strange fashion, and a rolled cap like that of a Baron of the Exchequer' (*LP Henry VIII*, vol. 2/2, p. 1496).

Throughout his career Kite was friendly with Thomas Wolsey, to whom he owed his provision to the archbishopric of Armagh on 24 October 1513. The appointment seems to have been intended as a reward, but Kite regarded it as more of an 'honourable exile' (Ellis, 115), and returned to England at regular intervals. He was present when Wolsey received his cardinal's hat on 15 November 1515, and he also attended the baptism of Princess Mary on 21 February 1516. At the end of February 1518 he was sent with John Bourchier, second Baron Bourchier, on an embassy to Charles I of Castile (later Emperor Charles V). Delays and diplomatic manoeuvring plagued their mission, as Kite's letters to Henry VIII and Wolsey amply record. Henry shared their frustration, and in a letter of 4 November 1518 he rebuked Kite, complaining that his reports were brief and contained little of importance, and suggesting that he had not discussed matters as fully with Charles as the king desired. Clearly troubled by Henry's loss of confidence in him, Kite responded by complaining of delays that were beyond his control, while allowing that his lack of diplomatic experience could have contributed to his difficulties. Subsequent letters were more detailed, and Kite reported on Charles's preparations against the Turks and on tensions between the Flemish and the Spaniards. By 8 January 1519 Kite had taken his leave of the Spanish king and set off for England. No doubt his experience abroad lay behind his being included among those who attended Henry VIII in 1520, both at the Field of Cloth of Gold in June and at his meeting with Charles at Gravelines in July.

Kite was never comfortable with his position as archbishop of Armagh. He may have savoured his status as primate of Ireland, but he quite obviously did not like either the country or its inhabitants, as he showed in plaintive letters to Wolsey. No sooner had he arrived than he was writing of being 'far from your heaven, from the sight of our most gracious King and Queen ... from the wealth of all the joys of England' (*LP Henry VIII*, vol. 1/1, no. 2907), and described with horror his coming to Drogheda, where his ship was attacked by two Breton pirates, who were driven off only with difficulty. He urged the king to come to Ireland to restore order, and in his early letters to Wolsey anticipated some kind of royal intervention, but as it became clear that Henry's priorities lay elsewhere, so Kite himself lost interest in Irish affairs. In 1515 he formed part of a mission which reported to the council at Greenwich and complained of Ireland's parlous state. Its complaints were dismissed, and thereafter Kite spent little if any time in Ireland.

Kite secured a formal release from involvement with Ireland on 12 July 1521 when he was translated to the see of

Carlisle, at a cost of 1790 ducats in papal fees. The temporalities were restored on 12 November. To preserve his status he was also made archbishop of Thebes *in partibus infidelium*, while perhaps because Carlisle was a poor diocese he was by 1522 holding the rectory of St Stephen Walbrook, London, *in commendam*. Wolsey sent him north to help maintain order on the borders and to assist Thomas, second Baron Dacre, the warden of the marches, as councillor and treasurer in conflicts with the Scots. His letters to Wolsey reveal an appalling situation, though he did not attribute it to Scottish raids. He reported in June 1523 that there was 'more theft, more extortion, by English thieves, than there is by all the Scots of Scotland' (*LP Henry VIII*, vol. 3/2, no. 2328), and a year later complained that in travelling from Newcastle to Carlisle he would be forced to ride some 60 miles out of his way to avoid bandits. Other royal agents, notably the earl of Surrey, echoed his views.

Kite was more energetic in the north than he ever was in Ireland. He continued the work of his predecessors in rebuilding his palace, Rose Castle, and in October 1523 begged Wolsey's mercy for the people of Newcastle, presumably under sentence of excommunication as they had been unable to receive the sacraments since before Easter. He seems to have been one of the bishops whose estate management involved the granting of longer leases, for his successor Robert Aldridge commented in 1537 that Kite had 'left nothing unlet for more years than he or his successor will probably see' (*LP Henry VIII*, vol. 12/2, no. 848). Kite's epitaph (now lost) was apparently referring to his episcopate when it described him as 'Kepyng nobyl Houshold wyth grete Hospitality' (Cooper, *Ath. Cantab.*, 63). But he still longed to return to court. His letters to Wolsey, in one of which he apologized to the cardinal for detaining his own archdeacon (who was also Wolsey's secretary) in the north, and in another even claimed to have dreamed of the cardinal, help to explain why the sixth earl of Northumberland dubbed him 'the flatteryng Byshope of Carel' (Bouch, 187). He remained loyal to Wolsey, however, and after the latter's fall from power lent him 'dysshes to eate hys meate in And plate to drynke in and also lynnyn clothes to occupie' (Cavendish, 104).

Kite was probably conservative in his religious views, as might have been expected of a friend of Viscount Lisle, but he supported the king in his pursuit of a divorce from Katherine of Aragon, and in 1534 subscribed the oath of supremacy. By the 1530s he seems to have been living mainly in London, where in 1536 he was recorded as playing cards with Sir William Kingston. He died there on 19 June 1537 and was buried in Stepney parish church three days later.   D. G. NEWCOMBE

Sources Emden, *Cam.*, 339 · W. Sterry, ed., *The Eton College register, 1441–1698* (1943) · *LP Henry VIII*, vols. 1–12 · Cooper, *Ath. Cantab.*, 1.62–3 · *Fasti Angl., 1066–1300*, [York] · M. Bateson, ed., *Grace book B*, 2 (1905) · S. G. Ellis, *Ireland in the age of the Tudors, 1447–1603*, 2nd edn (1998) · G. Hennessy, *Novum repertorium ecclesiasticum parochiale Londinense, or, London diocesan clergy succession from the earliest time to the year 1898* (1898) · A. Gwyn, *The medieval province of Armagh, 1470–1545* (1946) · P. Gwyn, *The king's cardinal* (1990) · C. M. L. Bouch, *Prelates and people of the lake counties: a history of the diocese of Carlisle, 1133–1933* (1948) · *New Grove*, vol. 4, p. 795 · G. Cavendish, *The life and death of Cardinal Wolsey*, ed. R. S. Sylvester, EETS, original ser., 243 (1959)

Kitson family (*per. c.*1520–*c.*1660), gentry, owed its great house, Hengrave Hall, near Bury St Edmunds, Suffolk, and supporting estates both in that county and in the west country to the fortune amassed by Sir Thomas *Kitson (1485–1540), a merchant adventurer who was knighted in 1533 upon becoming sheriff of London. He acquired first, in 1521–3, the Suffolk estates of the attainted duke of Buckingham, including Hengrave, and then in 1538 and 1539 contiguous lands formerly the property of Bury St Edmunds Abbey. The remarkable archive of personal and estate papers preserved largely intact in the Suffolk Record Office and Cambridge University Library makes possible an account of the stability of the family fortunes and the integrity of the Hengrave estate in spite of the vicissitudes of family descent and of national religious and political upheavals. No less remarkable is the transmission of recognizable traits of character descending through four generations of heiresses.

Rising towards nobility In spite of the care spent in building his fortune, Sir Thomas Kitson avoided taking action over the final settlement of his affairs. As he lay dying in September 1540 he had to be prompted by his man of business, in the presence of witnesses, to reaffirm his previously expressed intention to settle the manor of Hengrave and his personal fortune on his wife, Margaret [*see below*]. He also intended that she should enjoy during her lifetime all the revenues of his Suffolk and west country estates. This nuncupative will made the provision for his daughters dependent on their mother but acknowledged that the unborn child carried by his wife might well be a son, and receive his estates in tail, if he should survive until his majority. Within four hours of expressing these testamentary wishes Sir Thomas died and his modest funeral rites took place under the supervision of Bluemantle Pursuivant at a cost of £257 7*s*. 2*d*., mourning cloth being provided from his London warehouse and augmented by purchases from fellow mercers.

Margaret Kitson [**Margaret Bourchier** [*née* Donnington], countess of Bath (1510–1562)], was Sir Thomas's second wife (the identity of his first is unknown). She was the daughter and sole heir of John Donnington (*d.* 1544) of Stoke Newington, member of the Salters' Company and citizen of London. As the inheritor of two fortunes she was an extremely wealthy woman in her own right and, as such, became the architect of her family's rising social status, building on her husband's influence as a major landholder in west Suffolk. She presided over her growing household with a keen eye to expenditure and exercised the same sharp eye in seeking out advantageous marriages for her four Kitson daughters and for herself. Her own second marriage, to Sir Richard *Long (*d.* 1546) [*see under* Henry VIII, privy chamber of (*act.* 1509–1547)], gentleman of the privy chamber and master of the royal buckhounds and hawks, introduced her into court circles. The king stood godfather to their son, Henry, in March 1543; the marriage also produced three daughters. By Sir

Richard's will Margaret Long received her jointure from his revenues in Cambridgeshire, Bedfordshire, and Essex and was appointed his sole executor. She had already purchased the wardship and marriage of her only son from her first marriage, another Thomas Kitson [see below], and presumably had him educated at home—there is no evidence of his attending a university or inn of court. Margaret's attention was fixed upon securing a marriage for her remaining Kitson daughter, Frances, and this she achieved during her courtship by John Bourchier, third earl of Bath (1489–1561). The marriage articles drawn up between the earl and Margaret Long also provided for the marriage of Frances Kitson and Lord Fitzwarine, the earl's son from his second marriage; if the latter did not survive to consummate the marriage, Frances was to marry the earl's next heir.

The two couples were married just before Christmas 1548; two daughters were born to the earl and countess and a son, William, to the Fitzwarines. Lord Fitzwarine died in 1557, leaving his son to succeed as earl of Bath upon his grandfather's death in 1561. Thus Margaret Bourchier found herself arranging the funeral of her third husband. The sombre magnificence of the rites proper to an earl's rank could not be managed in the same economical style that had marked Sir Thomas Kitson's burial. When it became known to the College of Arms that the countess intended to employ local craftsmen to fashion the accoutrements, the matter was raised with the earl marshal, while Sir Thomas Cornwallis warned the countess of the bad impression given by her penny-pinching ways. The heralds 'have much complained … that your ladyship hath putt the doing and making of arms … unto country paynters' (Gage, 134). In the event, the Clarencieux Herald undertook the supervision and the earl was interred with all appropriate state. The countess died on 20 December 1562. The grand table tomb erected by her direction in Hengrave church bears effigies of the earl and countess of Bath, coronetted and in full ceremonial robes, lying together, Sir Thomas Kitson in full armour below the table. Sir Richard Long is commemorated by his arms, quartering Kitson, on a plaque mounted on an elaborate superstructure, bearing also all the heraldic achievements of the Kitson, Donnington, Long, and Bourchier connections.

Maintaining a position Sir Thomas Kitson (1540–1603) was born on 9 October 1540. In 1557 he married Jane, daughter of William, first Baron Paget, but she died in the following year. Thomas was thus barely twenty at the time of his second marriage, which took place at Kenninghall Palace in December 1560 under the auspices of the duchess of Norfolk. His second wife, **Elizabeth Kitson**, Lady Kitson (1546/7–1628), was the eldest daughter of Sir Thomas Cornwallis of Brome, and came to her marriage handsomely dowered with a portion of £600 and a training in the duchess's household which fitted her to preside over large households in Suffolk and London, where players and musicians were welcomed and splendour was tempered with elegance. The Kitsons were notable patrons of music in the late sixteenth and early seventeenth centuries, forming an excellent collection of instruments and music books, and employing first Edward Johnson and later the celebrated madrigalist John Wilbye, who acted as their resident musician in both Suffolk and London from about 1598 until Elizabeth Kitson's death. At a more mundane level, Thomas Kitson was piloted through the intricacies of county politics by his father-in-law, Sir Thomas Cornwallis, learning to hold his tongue and keep his temper, even in the face of deliberate provocation. He was introduced to Lord Keeper Nicholas Bacon, whose country house at Redgrave was some 20 miles away, and into the fourth duke of Norfolk's circle of young protégés. But the winds of religious change were beginning to blow coldly. Himself Catholic by sympathy, and married into a staunchly recusant family, Kitson found he had been maliciously accused to Lord Keeper Bacon of remarking that:

> touching the religion now observed, it was such as pleased my L. Keeper, and Mr Secretary Cecyll, tappoint, and not to procede of any devise of the Queens Majestie to continewe it, wherof herself was very indifferent in matters of religion. (Gage, 177)

Kitson was able to convince Bacon that he had been misreported. He was less fortunate when in October 1569 he was arrested with other members of the Norfolk circle and questioned by privy councillors about his knowledge of the duke's plans to marry Mary, queen of Scots. The interrogation included 'matters of religion' to which Kitson replied that he 'did not receive the Communion these 4 or 5 years but sometimes came to sermons with the Lord Chief Justice', presumably the assize sermons (*Salisbury MSS*, 1.431). Eventually he decided that the right course for him was to submit: 'I am rightly resolved, without any scrupelouse conceite … to repaire to such service, both myself and my familie, as by your Majesties procedings is now in use' (Gage, 178). In August 1578 he received his reward. The queen, on progress through East Anglia, knighted him at Bury St Edmunds and on her return journey through Suffolk:

> to Sir Thomas Kytson's, where, in very deede, the fare and banquet did so exceede a number of other places, that it is worthy the mention. A show representing the fayries, as well as might be, was there seene, in the which show a riche jewell was presented to the Queen's Highness. (Gage, 180)

Kitson's efforts were not always crowned with success. In 1577 he had taken advantage of a visit from his young nephew William, fourth earl of Bath, then an undergraduate at Trinity College, Cambridge, to engineer his marriage to Mary Cornwallis, his wife's youngest sister. The marriage ceremony was performed late at night and the couple duly bedded. All seemed well until the young man returned to Cambridge and declared his delight in his new bride to his tutor. His mother was summoned to Cambridge, shut the bridegroom with her in her chamber, and, after what was evidently a scene worthy of her own mother, Margaret, dispatched him far from Hengrave. Although the marriage was judged to be valid, it appears eventually to have been set aside on grounds of disparagement, arising from Mary Cornwallis's Catholicism. Nevertheless, to her family and especially to Kitson, who acknowledged that the marriage had been of his contriving, she remained the rightful countess of Bath, receiving a handsome bequest of £300 under Sir Thomas Kitson's will and an annuity of £20 from her sister in 1626, which she was able to enjoy until her own death in 1627.

Material property, personal crisis During the last two decades of the sixteenth century the Kitson estates continued to prosper under experienced officials. Life at Hengrave and in the London house in Austin Friars was only clouded by anxiety over the religious tensions that affected the family. Lady Kitson used her old court acquaintances in 1581 to intercede for her father, in close confinement for recusancy, and in 1599 to have her own presentment for recusancy removed from the Bury St Edmunds petty sessions to London, by means of a writ of *certiorari*. Thomas Kitson's name appeared on a list of known recusants in 1588 but without any untoward consequences. When his will was drawn up in 1601, eighteen months before his death, the preamble was as ambiguously phrased as his religious commitment had been. His funeral, which took place on 2 March 1603 in Hengrave church following his death on 28 January, was conducted by a clergyman likely to have been sympathetic to traditionalist practice. During her widowhood Lady Kitson divided her time between a new house built in Clerkenwell by her husband *c*.1601, and Hengrave Hall. Much time was devoted to charitable works, in supervising the building of almshouses, endowed under Sir Thomas Kitson's will, for the poor in and around the Hengrave and Bury St Edmunds estate. Her grandchildren and great-grandchildren found a ready welcome at Hengrave, and in the last weeks of her life the household accounts note '18d paid for cakes for my mistress and the Lady Gage's children' (Suffolk RO (W), Hengrave MSS, HA528/38). Lady Kitson died on 2 August 1628; her will ordered that her funeral should take place without any pomp, either early in the morning or late at night. She was buried in the tomb erected by her for her husband in 1608, in the south chapel of Hengrave church. The effigies of Sir Thomas, of Jane Paget, his wife for less than a year, and of Elizabeth Cornwallis, his wife for forty-three years, lie side by side.

Sir Thomas and Lady Kitson had three children. Their son, John, lived for only a few days. The elder of their two daughters, Margaret, who was born in 1563, was married in 1582 to Sir Charles Cavendish of Welbeck, son of Bess of Hardwick, the redoubtable countess of Shrewsbury. Their marriage articles confirmed the inheritance of all the Kitson estates in Suffolk and the west country to Margaret Cavendish and her heirs, after the deaths of her parents. But while her father and his father-in-law were investigating malpractices by Sir Thomas's steward in Devon, late in the summer of 1582, Margaret died in childbirth, and Kitson and Cornwallis, who had been planning a visit to Derbyshire, instead 'toke their jorney presentlie home to comfort the Lady Kitson whom they found very much dismayed and sorrowful for the death of her said daughter' (Suffolk RO (E), Cornwallis MSS, Box 1.2). The sole survivor of Thomas's and Elizabeth's children, and the heir to their estates, was thus Margaret's younger sister Mary Kitson

[**Mary Darcy**, Lady Darcy of Chiche (1565/6–1644)], who in 1583 married Thomas Darcy, third Baron Darcy of Chiche. They had a son and four daughters, of whom the son and two daughters predeceased their parents.

Although both had been brought up as Catholics, Lord and Lady Darcy were familiar figures at court, although Lord Darcy's duty of inspecting the east coast defences took him away from time to time. Mary Darcy's beauty and vivacity brought her jealous enemies at court who lost no time in repeating to her husband some cutting remarks she had made about him in his absence. To compound the injury, Lord Darcy suspected her of unbecoming flirtations, if not of outright adultery. The marriage broke down in 1594 and a deed of separation was executed whereby Lady Darcy received a settlement of £350 per annum and the eventual reversion of the Kitson estates. A portrait of Lady Darcy shows her at full length, the deed of separation grasped in her hand, inscribed 'If not, I care not', presumably dismissing any suggestion of reconciliation. Elizabeth, the eldest daughter, was married to Lord Savage and after the death of her father, who had been created successively Viscount Colchester and Earl Rivers, in 1640 became heir to his estates. The youngest daughter, **Penelope Darcy** (*d*. 1660/61), spent time at Hengrave Hall with her grandmother, and it was there that according to family tradition she promised to marry each of three quarrelling suitors in turn, Sir George Trenchard, Sir John Gage, baronet, and Sir William Hervey. Her short marriage in 1610 to Sir George Trenchard was followed in 1611 by her marriage to Sir John Gage of Firle, Sussex. He died in 1633, leaving five sons and five daughters. As heir to the Kitson estates Penelope Gage was often at Hengrave, staying with her grandmother whom in appearance and temperament she greatly resembled. After Lady Kitson's death in 1628 all the furnishings, books, and musical instruments in the house were settled by her will upon the owners of Hengrave Hall, first on her daughter Mary and then upon her granddaughter Penelope.

The impact of recusancy The Gages were burdened with the standard recusancy fine of £20 per month for not attending church in Sussex from 1625 to 1644, and in Middlesex, where Penelope had spent much time in her family's Clerkenwell house, between 1629 and 1641. The anti-Catholic climate of London in 1641 and a lengthy period of ill health made withdrawal to Hengrave Hall attractive but once there, Lady Gage found herself again under threat. During the Stour Valley anti-popery riots of 1642 a mob attacked and sacked the Essex and Suffolk houses owned by her sister, Elizabeth, Countess Rivers, and the sheriff of Suffolk and magistrates who included Penelope's cousin Sir William Spring were ordered by parliament to search Hengrave Hall and seize any arms found there. Lady Gage wrote to her mother, Lady Darcy:

> I told them the armes had been 100 yeares in Catholicke's hands, and never yet hurt a finger of anybody, and I wished they never might … we are daily threatened by the common sort of people, and for our defence have nothing left us. (Gage, 220)

Lady Darcy died in 1644, having settled Hengrave Hall

and the Suffolk estates on Penelope, who in 1642 had married the last of her suitors, Sir William Hervey of Ickworth. Hengrave Hall became home to a large household, largely composed of recusants and related to one another by marriages within the Gage and Hervey families. As her eldest son, John Gage, had inherited his father's Sussex estates in 1633, Lady Hervey settled Hengrave Hall and her Suffolk estates on her third son, Edward Gage:

> an earnest desire to raise another branch of my family, hath moved me to settle and assure my manors and heritaments on my said son Edward, wherat I desire my other sons to be in no ways displeased with their said brother Edward, this being done without any solicitation of his. (Gage, 241)

Thereafter the Suffolk estates of the first Sir Thomas Kitson, having descended through the female line for three generations, remained in the hands of the Gage family until 1820. JOY ROWE

Sources J. Gage, *The history and antiquities of Hengrave in Suffolk* (1822) · D. MacCulloch, *Suffolk and the Tudors: politics and religion in an English county, 1500–1600* (1986) · A. Simpson, *The wealth of the gentry* (1961) · R. Strong, *The English icon* (1969) · D. McGrath and J. Rowe, 'The recusancy of Sir Thomas Cornwallis', *Proceedings of the Suffolk Institute of Archaeology*, 28/3 (1961), 226–69 · B. J. Harris, *English aristocratic women* (2002) · J. Walter, 'The Stour Valley riots', *Religious dissent in East Anglia* [Norwich 1996], ed. E. Chadd (1996), 121–40 · *Calendar of the manuscripts of the most hon. the marquis of Salisbury*, 24 vols., HMC, 9 (1883–1976), vols. 1–2 · *Miscellanea, XII*, Catholic RS, 22 (1921), 120 · P. Morant, *The history and antiquities of the county of Essex*, 2 vols. (1768) · E. Farrer, *Portraits in Suffolk houses (west)* (1908) · GEC, *Peerage*, new edn, vols. 4, 11 · Coll. Arms, MS 442 · CUL, Hengrave MSS · Suffolk RO, Bury St Edmunds, Hengrave MSS · Suffolk RO, Ipswich, Cornwallis MSS · BL, Add. MS 30267 · *New Grove*, 9.676; 20.410–12

Archives CUL, Hengrave MSS · Suffolk RO, Bury St Edmunds, Hengrave MSS | BL, Add. MS 30267 · Suffolk RO, Ipswich, Cornwallis MSS

Likenesses J. Gage, portrait, 1617 (Mary Darcy, engr. Cooper) · E. Farrer, portrait (Lady Penelope Hervey, Sir William Hervey), Suffolk Houses (West) · J. Gage, portrait (Penelope Gage, engr. Cooper) · G. Gower, group of portraits, oils (Sir Thomas Kitson II, Lady Kitson, Lady Mary Darcy, Mary Cornwallis) · Le Keux, effigies and monuments, engravings (Sir T. Kitson, Earl and Countess of Bath, Thomas Kitson II, Jane Paget, Elizabeth Kitson)

Wealth at death Suffolk estates remained intact 1540–1660: wills, inventories, estate papers 1540–?

Kitson, Alexander Harper (1921–1997), trade unionist, was born on 21 October 1921 at Kirknewton, Midlothian, the son of Alexander Harper Kitson and his wife, Mary Lockhart, *née* Greig. His father, a lifelong trade unionist, had been a shale miner until, in the year Kitson was born, he was victimized after a lockout; he then found a job in the coalmines but again, after the 1926 general strike, was blacklisted and hounded out of the industry. His mother's father, David Greig, was a railwayman and active in the National Union of Railwaymen at local and national level until he retired in 1937. With that family background the young Kitson grew up in a home that was dedicated to trade unionism and socialism—and with the experience of economic deprivation and struggle.

Kitson went to the local elementary school at Kirknewton and left at fourteen to become a van boy with St Cuthbert's Co-operative Society in Edinburgh. The year was 1935, when high unemployment throughout Scotland

meant that times were hard. Young Kitson had to cycle 15 miles to work every day, but there were few options. Two years later the Co-op moved him to a milk delivery round—work that was organized by the Shop Assistants' Union, which Kitson joined immediately and in which, in the family tradition, he quickly became a shop steward. It was while he worked that milk round that Kitson met Tommy (later Sean) Connery (Big Tam, as he was known) who became his mate on the milk round. It was the beginning of a lifelong friendship between Kitson and Sean Connery, who later went on to a job as a scene-shifter at Edinburgh's King's Theatre, the first step on the ladder to Hollywood and fame as 007. Connery's father was then a member of the Scottish Horse and Motormen's Union, the organization Kitson was later to lead. Kitson moved from his job with the Co-op to take up work as a road haulage driver and joined the Horse and Motormen's Union. At the age of twenty-five he became a full-time official of the union—the youngest the union had ever had. During the war he rose rapidly in the hierarchy of the Horse and Motormen. He wanted to join the navy but was rejected on medical grounds and was then conscripted under the wartime regulations of the Ministry of Labour to drive trucks carrying war supplies across the country. On 21 March 1942 he married Annie Brown (1921/2–1997), a baker's confectioner and daughter of George Sutherland McLeod, a mason's labourer. There were two daughters of the marriage, Joyce and Irene.

By the early 1950s Kitson was a well-known figure at his union conferences, and in 1956 he was appointed national organizer. He was elected general secretary of the union three years later, in 1959. Six years after that he agreed to merge his union, with its 20,000 members, with the Transport and General Workers' Union (TGWU), then under the leadership of Jack Jones. The two men established a firm friendship and Jones appointed Kitson a senior executive officer of the TGWU in 1971. Effectively this placed Kitson as number three to Jones, with Harry Urwin as the deputy general secretary. Many observers then began to regard Kitson as a possible successor to Jones. But that did not happen. When Jones retired in 1977 Kitson fought Moss Evans for the succession but was heavily defeated by Evans. Yet that did not mar their relationship, and when Evans took over as general secretary he appointed Kitson as his deputy on the retirement of Urwin. Indeed when Evans became seriously ill in 1981 Kitson took over control of the TGWU and remained acting general secretary for a full year, holding the post during a critical biennial delegate conference of the union in that year.

Perhaps the most testing time for Kitson as number two in the TGWU was during the 'winter of discontent' in 1978–79, which eventually led to the fall of the Callaghan government and to Margaret Thatcher's premiership. Kitson worked closely with Evans, who later recalled Kitson's valiant attempt to avoid the worst impact of that period of intense industrial conflict. After weeks of the toughest negotiation with the road haulage employers at the end of December 1978, Kitson reached a compromise in the pay deal for the union's truck-drivers. He was convinced the deal would not only end the strike but much of the surrounding conflict as well. But the transport secretary, Bill Rodgers, vetoed the pay settlement. Kitson exploded and almost came to physical blows with the minister. To the end of his life Kitson held the view that had the Callaghan government allowed him to ratify that pay deal the industrial and political climate could have been transformed and the Callaghan government saved. Yet in some ways Kitson reached the high peak of his career in 1981, when he was acting general secretary of the TGWU and his union's representative on Labour's executive as well as chairman of the Labour Party that year. It was the year of the battle between Denis Healey and Tony Benn for the deputy leadership of the party. Unexpectedly Kitson steered his union vote away from Benn because, though well to the left, he had become persuaded that Benn and his followers might well destroy the Labour Party. With great political courage he led the union away from a vote for Benn—probably the decisive factor in clearing the way for Healey.

By the time Kitson retired in 1986 he had completed an exceptional record of posts in the labour movement: twenty-one years a member of the Scottish TUC general council and its chairman in 1966, and seventeen years as a member of Labour's national executive and latterly head of its international committee. He was also a pioneering campaigner for Scottish devolution—though not independence—bolstered by his own claim that he had personally persuaded Harold Wilson to change course in the 1970s and support devolution, so launching the Labour Party in that direction. There was one serious blip on Kitson's record of delicate diplomatic balance between his left-wing politics and his pragmatism as a union leader. During a visit to Moscow in 1977 as a fraternal delegate from the Scottish TUC to celebrate the sixtieth anniversary of the Soviet revolution, he was quoted in *Pravda* as declaring that the Soviets had done more to provide jobs for British workers than any British government that century. It was a declaration that landed Kitson in great trouble, not only with the British media but with his own party leaders in London. He was summoned back from Moscow on the orders of the Callaghan government. Somehow he managed to extricate himself from his troubles, though it always remained something of a mystery as to precisely how he escaped still greater embarrassment.

Outside trade unionism and politics Kitson's great love was the Heart of Midlothian Football Club, where he was chairman in 1993–4. He became a justice of the peace and ended his life as chairman of the Lothian Region Transport Board, of which he had been a director since 1986. He died at the Western General Hospital, Edinburgh, on 2 August 1997, after a long battle against cancer. He was survived by his two daughters, his wife having predeceased him by a few weeks. His funeral was held at Warriston crematorium, Edinburgh, on 7 August 1997, and was attended by a host of Scottish Labour Party and trade union leaders.   GEOFFREY GOODMAN

Sources *TGWU Record* · TUC and Scottish TUC, Annual Reports · A. Tuckett, *The Scottish carter* (1967) · *WWW* · b. cert. · m. cert. · d. cert. · *The Times* (4 Aug 1997) · *Daily Telegraph* (4 Aug 1997) · *The Independent* (4 Aug 1997) · *The Guardian* (5 Aug 1997) · *The Scotsman* (8 Aug 1997) · private information (2004) · personal knowledge (2004)
Likenesses photograph, repro. in *The Times* · photograph, repro. in *Daily Telegraph* · photograph, repro. in *The Independent* · photograph, repro. in *The Guardian*
Wealth at death £189,783.62: confirmation, 4 Dec 1997, NA Scot., SC/CO 1052/59

Kitson, Elizabeth, Lady Kitson (1546/7–1628). *See under* Kitson family (*per. c.*1520–*c.*1660).

Kitson, James (1807–1885), ironmaster and locomotive builder, was born in Leeds on 27 October 1807, the eldest of six children of a licensed victualler and his wife. He may be the James Kitson who was baptized in Leeds on 3 January 1808, the son of William Kitson. He was educated at local schools and at the Leeds Mechanics' Institution and Literary Society, where he was a diligent student in drawing and mathematics. On 20 September 1828 he married Ann, daughter of John Newton, owner of a painting and decorating firm. They had four sons and two daughters.

Encouraged by his studies of *A Practical Treatise on Rail-Roads*, by Nicholas Wood, Kitson quickly realized the great potential future of steam locomotive traction and in 1837 he joined Charles Todd, who had been apprenticed to James Fenton of the locomotive builders Fenton, Murray, and Jackson, and David Laird, a farmer and financier, in establishing Todd, Kitson, and Laird at the Railway foundry in Leeds, manufacturers of machinery and locomotives.

In 1838 six locomotives were built for the Liverpool and Manchester Railway. In 1839 Kitson and Laird withdrew from this partnership and established the Airedale foundry, also in Leeds, whose first locomotives were built for the North Midland Railway in 1840. David Laird withdrew in 1842 and the firm was reconstituted as Kitson, Thompson, and Hewitson. Large numbers of locomotives were built for home and overseas railways. Among these was the 0-6-0 type (1849) with inside cylinders and frames, for the Leeds and Thirsk Railway, a design which established the standard for freight locomotives in Britain over many decades. The first export locomotives (for the Orléans–Bordeaux railway) were built in 1846, followed by those for the Kiel–Altona line in 1848, and many more for India, Australia, South Africa, South America, and elsewhere.

Kitson's great organizing ability, technical ingenuity, and grasp of industrial developments formed the mainspring of these activities. In 1854 he felt it desirable to acquire a source of good Yorkshire iron for the Airedale foundry and established the Monk Bridge ironworks nearby, which was managed by his sons Frederick William and James *Kitson (later first Baron Airedale), the former having previously been principal locomotive designer at Airedale. After the retirement of Isaac Thompson in 1858 and the death of William Hewitson in 1863 the Kitson family took complete control of the firm, and later James Kitson, junior, and the third son, John Hawthorn, who managed the Airedale foundry from 1863, became partners with their father.

Kitson's first wife died and on 24 January 1868 he married Elizabeth, daughter of the Revd John E. Scroope Hutchinson, vicar of East Stoke, Nottinghamshire. They had two sons and two daughters. Kitson retired from the business in 1876, but was a man of wide interests and many activities outside his industrial work. Very musical and with a fine voice, in his youth he had built an organ in an outhouse of his father's premises. Later he became chairman of the orchestral committee for the Leeds music festival. He was also chairman of the Leeds Northern Railway and later a director of the North Eastern Railway. He was vice-chairman and later chairman of the Yorkshire Banking Company. An alderman of Leeds in 1858–68, he was mayor in 1860–61, as well as being a magistrate for Leeds borough and for the West Riding of Yorkshire. Kitson died at Elmet Hall, Roundhay, Leeds, on 30 June 1885.   GEORGE W. CARPENTER, rev.

Sources Engineering (3 July 1885) · E. Kitson Clark, Kitsons of Leeds, 1837–1937 (1938) · E. L. Ahrons, The British steam railway locomotive, 1825–1925 (1927) · CGPLA Eng. & Wales (1885)
Likenesses bust, Institution of Mechanical Engineers, London
Wealth at death £100: probate, 1885

Kitson, James, first Baron Airedale (1835–1911), locomotive manufacturer and politician, was born on 22 September 1835 at Leeds, the second of four sons of James *Kitson (1807–1885) of Elmet Hall, Leeds, and his wife, Ann, daughter of John Newton of Leeds. The elder James Kitson, a man of modest origins, went into partnership as a locomotive manufacturer at the Airedale foundry, Hunslet, at about the time of his second son's birth. This business flourished, so that the younger James was able to attend the Wakefield proprietary school and University College, London, where he studied chemistry and natural sciences.

In 1854, at the age of nineteen, Kitson and his elder brother, Frederick William (1829–1877), were put in charge of a recently established ironworks at Monk Bridge, Leeds, which their father had bought for them. They built Monkbridge into a vast concern. In 1858 it was amalgamated with Airedale foundry, and the business became a limited liability company with a £250,000 capital in 1886, though still exclusively under family control. Frederick withdrew through ill health several years before his death in 1877, and James Kitson was effectively head of the firm from 1862, though his father did not retire until 1876. Kitson married Emily Christiana, daughter of Joseph Cliff of Wortley, Leeds, on 20 June 1860. They had three sons and two daughters. After her death in 1873, he married Mary Laura, daughter of Edward Fisher Smith, of Dudley, on 1 June 1881, with whom he had a son and a daughter. Kitson was assisted in running the firm by his younger brother John Hawthorn Kitson (1843–1899), and later by sons and nephews.

The Airedale foundry principally made railway locomotives, producing, from the time of its inception until the end of the nineteenth century, almost 6000 engines for the home market and for export to twenty-eight other countries. There was also diversification into stationary engines for agricultural machinery, and steam engines for tramways. From the 1880s, the Monkbridge works made steel on the Siemens–Martin open-hearth process. Airedale and Monkbridge each employed about 2000 workers at the time of Kitson's death in 1911. Kitson was prominent in business circles: he was president of the Leeds chamber of commerce (1880–81), president of the Iron and Steel Institute (1889–91), and recipient of its Bessemer gold medal in 1903; he served as a member of the council of the Institution of Civil Engineers (1899–1901), and was a member of the Institution of Mechanical Engineers from 1859; he was also president of the Iron Trade Association. Other business interests included chairmanships of the Yorkshire Banking Company, the London and Northern Steamship Company, and the Baku Russian Petroleum Company, and directorships of the London City and Midland Bank and the North Eastern Railway Company.

Kitson had been a member of the Mill Hill Unitarian Chapel since childhood, from the time his family left the Church of England. He was devoted to the Unitarians for the rest of his life; he taught in Sunday school, and served as superintendent and later as chairman of the chapel's trustees. A memorial window to him was unveiled there in 1916. His interests included social and educational work, and at an early age he became prominent in the mechanics' institute movement, helping to establish a branch in Holbeck, and acting as secretary of the Yorkshire Union of Mechanics' Institutes for seven years. Kitson was involved in launching a self-help model dwelling scheme in 1862, designed to enable working men to buy houses on easy terms, though run as a business rather than a charity. He was also a governor of the Leeds General Infirmary and contributed to organizations involved in treating tuberculosis and in training nurses. He supported the Yorkshire College, later the University of Leeds, from its inception in the 1870s. He was a member of the Leeds rifle volunteer corps shortly after its foundation in 1859, rising from the ranks to become a captain, and remained honorary colonel until 1905.

It was Kitson's long-standing interest in education which brought an introduction to national politics during the controversy following the passage of W. E. Forster's Education Act in 1870. He was instrumental in forming a branch of the National Education League in Leeds, becoming secretary and a member of its national council. In 1880 he was president of the Leeds Liberal Association, running the campaign for W. E. Gladstone's election as member of parliament, with great success. Gladstone was also elected for Midlothian, and at a by-election the Leeds seat passed to his son, Herbert. Kitson retained a cordial relationship with Gladstone, and organized his notable visit to Leeds in October 1881, during which the prime minister stayed at Kitson's house, Spring Bank in Headingley. Kitson supported Gladstone over Irish home rule. As president of the National Liberal Federation from 1883 until 1890, he kept it out of the hands of the Liberal Unionists. Standing as a Gladstonian Liberal, Kitson became member of parliament for the Colne Valley in 1892, holding the seat until

1907. During his parliamentary career he was a prominent campaigner for old-age pensions. He also served as the first lord mayor of Leeds, in 1896–7, although never a member of the council. He was created a baronet in 1886, was sworn of the privy council in 1906, and became Baron Airedale of Gledhow in 1907. Other honours included an honorary degree of DSc from the University of Leeds in 1904, and the freedom of his home city in 1906.

Airedale died at the Hotel Meurice in Paris on 16 March 1911, after suffering a heart attack while returning by train from the south of France. After a funeral service at Mill Hill, his body was taken on 22 March to Roundhay church for burial, along a route lined by 4000 workpeople. A memorial service attended by a hundred MPs was held at St Margaret's Church, Westminster.

GILLIAN COOKSON

Sources *Leeds Mercury* (17 March 1911) · *Yorkshire Post* (17 March 1911) · *Yorkshire Observer* (17 March 1911) · *The Times* (17 March 1911) · *The Guardian* (17 March 1911) · *Institution of Mechanical Engineers: Proceedings* (1911), 409 · W. G. Rimmer, 'Kitson, James', *DBB* · GEC, *Peerage* · W. H. Scott, *The West Riding of Yorkshire at the opening of the twentieth century: contemporary biographies*, ed. W. T. Pike (1902), 109 · C. Hargrove, *In memory of James Kitson, 1st Baron Airedale* (1911) · *Institution of Mechanical Engineers: Proceedings* (1878), 11 [obit. of Frederick William Kitson] · *Institution of Mechanical Engineers: Proceedings* (1899), 269 [obit. of John Hawthorn Kitson] · E. K. Clark, *Kitsons of Leeds, 1837–1937* (1938) · Gladstone, *Diaries*
Archives W. Yorks. AS, Leeds, letters and photographs | BL, corresp. with Lord Gladstone, Add. MSS 46027–46028 · BL, corresp. with W. E. Gladstone, Add. MSS 44472–44789 *passim*, 46044, fols. 8–23
Likenesses J. S. Sargent, portrait, 1905; in possession of the family, Gledhow Hall, Leeds, 1912 · Spruce, bust, 1911; formerly, Leeds town hall · B. Stone, photograph, NPG · photograph, repro. in Rimmer, 'Kitson, James' · photograph, repro. in Pike, ed., *The West Riding of Yorkshire* · photograph, repro. in *Yorkshire Observer* · photograph, repro. in Hargrove, *In memory of James Kitson*
Wealth at death £1,000,000: probate, 31 March 1911, *CGPLA Eng. & Wales*

Kitson, Michael William Lely (1926–1998), art historian, was born on 30 January 1926 at 10 Grange Park, Ealing, Middlesex, one of the sons of Bernard Meredith Kitson, a Church of England clergyman, and his wife, Helen May Lely. His ancestors included the novelist Anthony Trollope and the painter Sir Peter Lely. Kitson attended Gresham's School at Holt, Norfolk, whence he would readily cycle 20 miles to see the paintings at Holkham Hall. In 1944 he went to read English at King's College, Cambridge, but national service intervened, and the years 1945–8 saw him commissioned into the Royal Engineers and attached to security intelligence Middle East in Egypt. His degree course completed (BA 1950), he married Annabella Leslie (b. 1923/4), daughter of John Leslie Cloudsley, a civil engineer, on 8 July 1950 and began to study art history at the Courtauld Institute of Art, University of London.

Kitson became an assistant lecturer in the history of art at the Slade School of Fine Art, University College, London, in 1952. Most of his career, however, was spent at the Courtauld Institute, based in Portman Square, where he was first a lecturer (1955–67), then a reader (1967–78). In the 1950s the Courtauld took the lead in establishing art history as a serious academic discipline in Britain, and

Kitson shared an interest in seventeenth-century French painting with Anthony Blunt, its director, whose memoir he subsequently contributed to the *Dictionary of National Biography*. Kitson made a stimulating and sympathetic tutor, generous with his time and free of self-importance, though students had to grow used to his arriving slightly late and flustered, collapsing in a chair, and appearing to fall asleep while they read their essays. Quiet and fastidious, he insisted on clarity of expression.

The extreme pains which Kitson took over his own scholarship and prose resulted in many esteemed articles, exhibition catalogues, and shorter monographs—all produced by burning quantities of midnight oil and tobacco, usually long after the publisher's deadline. Probably influenced in his approach by his earlier literary studies, his preference was to reassess the finest works of the masters; his central concern was to try to explain what made such pictures truly great. Few authors could have equalled his introductory essays for illustrated volumes about the art of Frans Hals (1965), Rembrandt (1969), and Caravaggio (1969).

At a time when the Courtauld was often accused of undervaluing British art, Kitson wrote a study of J. M. W. Turner (1964) and catalogued an exhibition of his watercolours (1974). Hogarth and Constable also received his close attention, and he was involved in presenting British painting to European viewers at major exhibitions held in Paris in 1972 and Munich in 1979.

The international art world respected Michael Kitson as an authority on Claude Lorrain, celebrated French painter of ideal landscapes. He planned and organized the first exhibition devoted to Claude at the Hayward Gallery, London, for the Arts Council in 1969 and catalogued the *Liber veritatis*, the artist's own drawings of his paintings, for the British Museum in 1978.

Kitson's marriage, which produced two sons, was dissolved in 1971. He was appointed professor in 1978 and two years later became deputy director of the Courtauld Institute. A mild, courteous man, high-browed and bespectacled, his ability to generate harmony between historians of diverse views was based upon his own broad-church conception of the history of art; his own artistic sympathies were themselves wide-ranging. Kitson relinquished his post at the Courtauld in 1985 to go as director of studies to the Paul Mellon Centre for Studies in British Art. Located at 20 Bloomsbury Square, London, the centre was affiliated to Yale University, which he often visited as a deputy adjunct professor. There he met Judith Colton (b. 1943), an American scholar of seventeenth-century French art, who became his close companion.

Kitson continued to write after retirement in 1992, contributing the masterly entry on Claude Lorrain for the multi-volume Macmillan *Dictionary of Art* (1996) and an essay on Sir Denis Mahon for *Discovering the Italian Baroque* (1997), the catalogue of the Mahon collection on show at the National Gallery. He died of lung cancer at his home, 72 Halton Road, Islington, London, on 7 August 1998.

JASON TOMES

Sources *The Independent* (11 Aug 1998) · *Daily Telegraph* (12 Aug 1998) · *The Times* (11 Aug 1998) · *The Guardian* (11 Aug 1998) · N. Macgregor, 'Michael Kitson address at memorial service, St Clement Dane's, 23 October 1998', *Courtauld Institute of Art Newsletter*, 7 (spring 1999) · b. cert. · m. cert. · d. cert.

Kitson, Sir Thomas (1485–1540), merchant and local politician, was born in Warton, Lancashire, the son of Robert Kitson. He was apprenticed to Richard Glasyer, a mercer and merchant adventurer of London, and became free of the City in 1507. He was already trading on his own account on a substantial scale in 1509, and his accounts show that he remained active as a merchant adventurer until his death. In 1534–5, when he exported 625 cloths, only ten merchants exported larger quantities. He dealt mainly in the broadcloths of Hampshire, Wiltshire, and Somerset, but also traded on a more limited scale in the coarser Lancashire cottons, Welsh frises, and coarse woollen Kendal penistones, and he cultivated close connections with clothiers in these areas, among them John Clyfflide of Beckington, Thomas Davy of Warminster, Richard Earl of Melksham, and Gilbert Sariscold of Manchester. His imports of fustians, velvets, linens, and spices were typical of the merchant adventurers, although in the 1530s most of the profits of his cloth sales were repatriated by bills of exchange, his exports in that decade being valued at £44,416 compared with imports of only £10,906. His profits on the export of cloth have been calculated as being of the order of 15 to 20 per cent, and, although the profit margins on imports were probably much lower, he accumulated a substantial fortune.

Kitson's wealth was such that it was rumoured in the City that he had been responsible for the scale of Cardinal Wolsey's fiscal demands in 1522: 'it was mych long of me that the cete prest so grete a sum at this tyme' (CUL, Hengrave Hall deposit, MS 88(1), no. 1). The citizens seem to have retaliated by assessing him harshly, for his assessment was altered from 1000 marks to 4000 marks. Perhaps the assessment of 1535 that his goods were worth 4000 marks (£2666) was near the truth, for the inventory taken on his death valued his net estate at £3142 17s. 1d. His rising prosperity was marked by his acquisition of properties in Suffolk, Devon, Dorset, Somerset, and Nottinghamshire. His most important purchase was the manor of Hengrave in Suffolk, bought from the duke of Buckingham, together with the manor of Colston Basset in Nottinghamshire, for £2340 in 1521, shortly before the duke's attainder. It was at Hengrave that Kitson built the splendid mansion which still survives. More than £3500 was spent on building works there between 1525 and 1539; the house was graced with an avant-garde oriel window incorporating several Renaissance features, and its chapel was decorated with stained glass probably imported from France. Kitson retained a house in London in the parish of St Mary Magdalen, Milk Street, as well as a suburban residence at Stoke Newington, Middlesex.

As a young man Kitson had shown a reluctance to participate in the affairs of his livery company, being forced to spend a night in prison in 1509 for his refusal to serve among the bachelors and attend on the presentation of the new mayor at the exchequer, but his civic career was otherwise conventional. He served as sheriff of London in 1533–4, and on 28 July 1534 was elected alderman of Castle Baynard ward, where he remained until his death. He was a warden of the Mercers' Company in 1525–6 and 1533–4, and served as master in 1534–5. He was knighted in 1533.

The identity of Kitson's first wife is unknown, although there was a daughter, Elizabeth, who married Edmund Crofts of Westowe in Suffolk. His second wife was Margaret, the only child of John Donnington of Stoke Newington, a member of the Salters' Company of London, and his wife, Elizabeth Pye. From this marriage he had a posthumous son, Thomas, and four daughters. His widow, Dame Margaret (d. 1561), was an attractive catch for Sir Richard Long (d. 1546), a gentleman of the privy chamber, and she remarried within two months of her husband's death. In 1548 she took as her third husband John Bourchier, earl of Bath (d. 1560). She commissioned the lavish tomb with effigies of herself and her husbands which can still be seen in Hengrave church. Kitson's four daughters all seem to have made advantageous marriages: Catherine to Sir John Spencer of Wormleighton in Warwickshire, Dorothy [see Tasburgh, Dorothy] to Sir Thomas Packington of Aylesbury, Frances to John Bourchier, Lord Fitzwarine, and Anne to Sir William Spring of Pakenham in Suffolk. His son, Sir Thomas Kitson (1540–1603), was briefly (1557–8) married to Jane, the daughter of William, Lord Paget, but acquired a firm ally in Sir Thomas Cornwallis by marrying his daughter Elizabeth in 1560. Although conforming to the Elizabethan settlement, he was associated with the conservatives among the Suffolk gentry.

Kitson died at Hengrave on 11 September 1540 and was buried in Hengrave church. The brevity of his will makes it difficult to determine his religious inclinations, but he seems to have been aligned with the more conservative clergy. He had numerous business dealings with John Kite, bishop of Carlisle, to whose will he was overseer, and his funeral sermon was preached by Dr Nicholas Wilson, the arch-conservative rector of St Thomas the Apostle in London. CHARLES WELCH, *rev.* IAN W. ARCHER

Sources J. Gage, *The history and antiquities of Hengrave, in Suffolk* (1822) · P. H. Ramsey, 'The merchant adventurers in the first half of the sixteenth century', DPhil diss., U. Oxf., 1958 · A. B. Beaven, ed., *The aldermen of the City of London, temp. Henry III–[1912]*, 2 vols. (1908–13) · LP Henry VIII · PRO, customs accounts · repertories of court of aldermen; journals of court of common council, CLRO · Mercers' Hall, London, acts of court · H. Wayment, 'The stained glass in the oratory', Hengrave Hall, Suffolk · L. Lyell and F. D. Watney, eds., *Acts of court of the Mercers' Company, 1453–1527* (1936) · CUL, Hengrave Hall deposit · will, PRO, PROB 11/29, sig. 30
Archives CUL, Hengrave Hall deposit
Likenesses portrait, 16th cent.; formerly at Hengrave Hall, Suffolk · R. W. Siever, engraving, repro. in J. Gage, *The history and antiquities of Suffolk: Thingoe hundred* (1838) · effigy, church of St John Lateran, Hengrave, Suffolk
Wealth at death £3142 17s. 1d.—goods only: inventory, CUL, Hengrave Hall deposit, MS 88(1), no. 166

Kitson, Sir Thomas (1540–1603). *See under* Kitson family (*per. c.*1520–*c.*1660).

Kitto, John (1804–1854), writer and missionary, son of John Kitto, a Cornish stonemason, and Elizabeth Picken, was born at Plymouth on 4 December 1804. He was a sickly lad, caring for nothing but books. Between his eighth and eleventh years he was at four different Plymouth schools, and had no other schooling. In 1814 he was taken by his father to assist him at his trade. On 13 February 1817, while carrying slates up a high ladder, he fell 35 feet, as a result of which he became stone-deaf. Unable to work, he was left to spend his time as he pleased, and devoted himself to reading, selling scraps of old iron, and painting children's pictures and shop labels to make money to buy books. On 15 November 1819 he was sent to the workhouse, where he was set to learn shoemaking. In November 1821 he was apprenticed to a Plymouth shoemaker named Bowden, who treated him badly, and in May 1822 he was taken back into the workhouse. In July 1823 some gentlemen became interested in his case, made provision for his support, and got permission for him to read in the public library. In 1824 Anthony Norris *Groves, an Exeter dentist and one of the early Plymouth Brethren, took him as a pupil, giving him board, lodging, and a small salary. Soon after he underwent a religious conversion and in July 1825 went, at the suggestion of Groves, to the Missionary College at Islington, to be trained for employment by the Church Missionary Society as a printer at one of their foreign presses. In June 1827 he was sent by the society to Malta, but his interest in writing seems to have prevented his giving his whole attention to his duties, and in January 1829 he returned to England.

In June of that year Kitto became a member of a private mission party organized by Groves, and in company with him and others sailed for Persia; an interesting account of the journey appears in his journals. The party reached Baghdad in December, and Kitto, besides acting as tutor to Groves's children, opened an Armenian school. A terrible plague destroyed some 50,000 of the inhabitants of Baghdad in little more than a month, and carried off five out of thirteen inmates of Groves's house. A flood and a siege by Ali Pasha of Aleppo followed; the schools were broken up, and in September 1832 Kitto left Baghdad. On reaching England, after a journey of nine months, he obtained an introduction to the Society for the Diffusion of Useful Knowledge, and was engaged to write for the *Penny Magazine*, in which the 'Deaf traveller' and other papers of his appeared. He also at this time contributed to the *Companion to the Almanack*, the *Companion to the Newspaper*, the *Printing Machine*, and Charles Knight's *Cyclopaedia*. On 21 September 1833 he married a Miss Fenwick; she and seven of their children survived him.

At the suggestion of Charles Knight Kitto began in 1834 a series of narratives illustrative of the life of blind, deaf, and mute people, later collected as *The Lost Senses* (1845); in 1835 he wrote a 'Biblical commentary', which resulted in *The Pictorial Bible*, originally published anonymously in monthly parts. It was completed in May 1838, and was well received (3 vols. octavo, and 4 vols. quarto, 1835–8). The notes were afterwards published separately under the title *The Illustrated Commentary* (5 vols., 1840). He next

John Kitto (1804–1854), by Edward Burton, pubd 1856 (after John Samuelson Templeton)

agreed with Knight to write a *Pictorial History of Palestine and the Holy Land, Including a Complete History of the Jews*, which he completed after nearly three years of hard work (1840). *The Christian Traveller* was then planned, a work intended to give some account of missionary activities; but Knight ran out of money and only three parts of it appeared (1841). These were the most notable of the many illustrated biblical works which made Kitto a prominent, but never financially successful, author. Following Knight's failure, Kitto suffered much hardship. He had to sell his house at Islington and move to Woking. He wrote for Messrs A. and C. Black, Edinburgh, who published his *History of Palestine* (1843). He also began the *Cyclopaedia of Biblical Literature*, on which he was at work until 1845 (2 vols., 1845). In 1844, though a layman, he received the degree of DD from the University of Giessen, and in 1845 was made a fellow of the Society of Antiquaries. In 1848 he began the *Journal of Sacred Literature*, which he edited until 1853. Financial difficulties continued to press upon him. The *Journal of Sacred Literature* did not pay the cost of printing, and he was obliged to leave Woking for a cheaper house at Camden Town. In 1849 he began the preparation of the *Daily Bible Illustrations* for Messrs Oliphant of Edinburgh, to be published in quarterly parts. Volume 1 appeared in December of that year, and the concluding volume in January 1854. He was given a civil-list pension of £100 per annum in 1850 in recognition of his 'useful and meritorious literary works'. His health, never robust, began seriously to fail in 1851. In August 1854 he went to Germany to try the effect of mineral waters, but on 25

November 1854 died at Cannstadt, where he had settled. His remains were buried in the cemetery there, a tombstone being erected over them by Mr Oliphant, his publisher.

THOMAS HAMILTON, *rev.* H. C. G. MATTHEW

Sources J. Kitto, *The lost senses*, 2 vols. (1845) • *Memoirs of John Kitto*, ed. J. E. Ryland (1856)
Likenesses E. Burton, engraving (after J. S. Templeton), repro. in Ryland, ed., *Memoirs of John Kitto* [see illus.]

Kitton, Frederic George (1856–1904), illustrator and writer, was born at Golding Street, Heigham, Norwich, on 5 May 1856, the son of Frederic Kitton, tobacconist, and Mary Spence. His father, who had some reputation as an amateur biologist and microscopist, appears to have prompted his interest in the disciplines of research. It was, however, as a draughtsman that the young Kitton excelled. At the age of seventeen he was apprenticed as a wood-engraver, serving under W. L. Thomas on the staff of *The Graphic* in London. He contributed illustrations to the magazine in the years 1874–85 and later worked for the *Illustrated London News* (1889–90) and for the *English Illustrated Magazine*. He was noted as an etcher and as a prolific drawer of landscapes and buildings. His developing interest in the life, fiction, circumstances, and circle of Dickens became evident in his short studies of the work of Hablot K. Brown (1882) and John Leech (1883) and in his contribution of illustrations to W. R. Hughes's *A Week's Tramp in Dickens-Land* (1891). Kitton had accompanied Hughes as a 'fellow-tramp' on the original excursion through Kent in the summer of 1888 which formed the basis of the book. Kitton's studies of Dickens include *Dickensiana: a Bibliography of the Literature Relating to Charles Dickens and his Writings* (1886), the copiously illustrated and highly informative *Charles Dickens by Pen and Pencil* (1890), *The Novels of Charles Dickens: a Bibliography and Sketch* (1897), *Dickens and his Illustrators* (1899), and the posthumously published *The Dickens Country* (1905). He annotated the Rochester edition of Dickens's works (1900) and in 1903 had published a prospectus for the Autograph or Millionaire's edition on which he was working at the time of his death. Kitton was a very competent annotator and a lively and knowledgeable writer on Dickens, if one prone, as Arthur Waugh put it, to see life and literature 'like a mosaic' with 'his eye … on the pieces, not upon the piece' (Waugh, 6).

Kitton was one of the founders, and an enthusiastic vice-president, of the Dickens Fellowship (1902). It was he who organized and compiled the catalogue of the fellowship's 1903 Dickens exhibition, and he who in the same year was the moving spirit behind the public campaign for the purchase by Portsmouth corporation of Dickens's birthplace.

From 1888 Kitton lived at Pré Mill House, St Albans. His loyalty to his adopted city and county was manifested not simply in his campaigns to save historic buildings in Hertfordshire and in his occasional writings on St Albans but also in his helping to procure the purchase for the Hertfordshire County Museum of the Sir John Evans collection of books, manuscripts, drawings, and ephemera; these he later catalogued and arranged. He married Emily Clara,

second daughter of H. A. Lawford, in 1889. There were no children. Kitton died at 49 Beaumont Street in London on 10 September 1904 of complications following an operation in March.

Kitton's Dickens library was purchased from his widow by a subscription organized by the Dickens Fellowship as the nucleus for the proposed national Dickens library. It was formally presented to the Guildhall Library by Lord James of Hereford on 7 February 1908 but was transferred to the Dickens House, 48 Doughty Street, London, in January 1926.

ANDREW SANDERS

Sources A. Waugh, 'Introduction', in F. G. Kitton, *The Dickens country* (1905), v–x • *The Athenaeum* (17 Sept 1904), 385 • W. Jerrold, *The Academy* (17 Sept 1904), 192–3 • W. Jerrold, *The Academy* (24 Sept 1904), 225 • *Hertfordshire Standard* (16 Sept 1904) • J. W. T. Ley, 'The Dickens Fellowship, 1902–1923: a retrospect', *The Dickensian*, 19 (1923), 178–95 • S. Houfe, *The dictionary of British book illustrators and caricaturists, 1800–1914* (1978) • catalogue [The Dickens House] • b. cert. • d. cert.
Archives Dickens House Museum and Library, London, papers
Likenesses double portrait, photograph (with W. R. Hughes), repro. in *The Dickensian*, 81 (1952), 2
Wealth at death £583: administration, 20 May 1905, *CGPLA Eng. & Wales*

Kiwanuka, Joseph (1899–1966), Roman Catholic archbishop of Rubaga, Uganda, was born on 11 June 1899 at Nakirebe, Mawokota, Uganda, the son of Victoro Katumba Munduekanika, peasant farmer, and his wife, Felisita (Félicité) Nankya Namukasa Sabawebwa, Roman Catholics related to four of the martyrs who had died during the reign of Kabaka (king) Mwanga (c.1866–1903) of Buganda in 1886/7. Soon after Kiwanuka's birth the White Fathers (Société des Missionaires d'Afrique) established a mission they named Mitala Maria (Hills of Mary) near Kiwanuka's home, and he began his education there in 1909. His intelligence and his diligence in religion were noted, and in 1913, the year that the first Ugandan Catholic priests were ordained, he started on the road to priesthood. For the next six years he attended Bukalasa junior seminary before spending ten years at Katigondo major seminary where he was thoroughly schooled in Latin as well as theology. Both institutions were at Villa Maria, the heart of a deeply Catholic area of south-western Buganda.

Immediately after ordination Kiwanuka was sent to the Angelicum, the Dominican university in Rome, where in 1932 he obtained a doctorate in canon law, the first African to do so. He then spent a year at Maison-Carrée in Algiers, Algeria, at the White Fathers' noviciate, being accepted as the first African member of the society in 1933. He then returned to parish work in Uganda. In 1939 the parishes in and around Masaka were formed into an apostolic vicariate, the equivalent, in a mission territory, of a bishopric, and Pope Pius XII consecrated Kiwanuka titular bishop of Thibica in St Peter's on 29 October 1939, the first black African bishop of modern times, and placed him in charge of Masaka which was staffed entirely by Ugandan priests. The establishment of a vicariate wholly staffed by Ugandans was seen by many at the time as dangerously innovative, but the Catholics of the area, and indeed of

Uganda, were immensely proud of this achievement, and under Kiwanuka Masaka thrived, a close-knit, fiercely loyal community. In 1953, when the Catholic hierarchy was erected in Uganda, Masaka became a residential episcopal see with Kiwanuka as its bishop.

1953 was a year of crisis in Buganda when the kabaka, Mutesa II (1924–1969), was deported by the British for refusing to comply with demands made of him by the governor, Sir Andrew Benjamin Cohen (1909–1968), and was therefore deemed to have broken the terms of the Uganda agreement (1900). Kiwanuka's considerable authority helped to keep a measure of calm. He was appointed a member of the Hancock committee which was set up to find a way of enabling the kabaka to return while saving face for the British authorities.

On the retirement of Archbishop Cabana of Rubaga in 1960, Kiwanuka was appointed to succeed him as metropolitan archbishop for Uganda, and was installed in Rubaga Cathedral on 5 March 1961. During the next few years as independence approached he wrote a series of pastoral letters on educational and social as well as spiritual topics, leading up to the letter of November 1961 in which he warned the Buganda separatist party, Kabaka Yekka (the Kabaka Only), that refusal to accept that the kabaka must become a constitutional monarch would undermine the monarchy. This caused great controversy, but its truth was apparently demonstrated soon after Kiwanuka's death when President Obote overthrew the kabaka, driving him into exile, and abolishing all the Ugandan monarchies. At independence in 1962 Kiwanuka issued a statement jointly with the Anglican archbishop, Leslie Wilfrid Brown (1912–1999), an almost unprecedented ecumenical action.

Kiwanuka attended the Second Vatican Council in Rome, and was present in St Peter's when, on Sunday 18 October 1964, during the third session of the council, the Pope canonized the twenty-two Catholic Uganda martyrs. In 1965, during the fourth session of the council, his failing health led to his hospitalization. He recovered sufficiently to be flown back to Uganda where he was welcomed back in Rubaga Cathedral, but soon after he died at Rubaga, on 22 February 1966. Immense crowds attended the requiem mass in the cathedral, and his body was placed in a glass coffin in the south transept near the martyrs' altar and remained there for some years before being finally buried. In the spirit of the Second Vatican Council and in token of their friendship, Kiwanuka gave instructions that his personal ring be given to the Anglican bishop of Namirembe, Bishop Dunstan Nsubuga.

M. LOUISE PIROUET

Sources 'Notes biographiques: Archbishop Joseph Kiwanuka', *Petit Echo* [White Fathers] (July–Aug 1966), 370–78 • J. M. Waliggo, *A history of African priests: Katigondo major seminary, 1911–1986* (1988) • Y. Tourigny, *So abundant a harvest: the Catholic church in Uganda, 1879–1979* (1979) • A. Hastings, *The church in Africa, 1450–1950* (1994) • A. Hastings, *A history of African Christianity, 1950–1975* (1979) • A. Hastings, *Church and mission in modern Africa* (1967) • A. Hastings, *African Catholicism: essays in discovery* (1989) • L. Brown, *Three worlds: one word* (1981) • D. A. Low, *The mind of Buganda: documents of the modern history of an African kingdom* (1971) • D. A. Low, *Buganda in modern history*

(1971) • P. Kavuma, *Crisis in Buganda, 1953: the story of the exile and return of the kabaka, Mutesa II* (1979) • *The Times* (25 Feb 1966) • *The Times* (1 March 1966)
Archives Archivio Generale, Rome, Missionari d'Africa • Archdiocese of Rubaga, Uganda, archives of Masaka diocese, letters and diocesan/pastoral letters
Likenesses photograph, repro. in 'Notes biographiques'

Kiwanuka, Mugumba Benedicto (1922–1972), lawyer and prime minister of Uganda, was born on 8 May 1922 at Kisabwa in Masaka district, Buganda, the third son of Fulgensio Musoke (d. 1940), a Catholic minor chief whose extravagant lifestyle caused difficulties for his family, and his wife, Eularia, *née* Nalubowa. Kiwanuka was educated at Catholic primary schools and St Peter's junior secondary school, Nsambya, where his abilities were noted, but lack of money for fees interrupted his studies and in 1941 he joined the King's African rifles. He served in the Second World War in Egypt and Palestine. In 1946 he was demobilized and became a court clerk and interpreter, which kindled his interest in law, and on 18 February 1947 he married Maxcencia Zalwango, aged eighteen. Determined to study further he went to Pius XII Catholic University in Basutoland (Lesotho) and then to London University from 1952 to 1956 where he gained his LLB and was called to the bar. In London he involved himself in student politics as secretary of the Uganda Students' Association, and in Ugandan politics, during the period when Kabaka Mutesa II of Buganda was exiled to Britain.

After returning to Uganda Kiwanuka quickly built up a prosperous law practice, while remaining active in politics. A devout Catholic, he joined the Catholic-dominated Democratic Party (DP) rather than the protestant-dominated groups which coalesced into the Uganda People's Congress (UPC). He was elected president of the DP in 1958, and in 1959 gave up his legal practice to concentrate on politics, working to make the DP into a party which represented all Ugandans, not only Catholics. Although a member of the *lukiiko* (assembly of Ganda chiefs) he found himself at loggerheads with the kabaka's government, which wanted Uganda to become a federal rather than a unitary state, and concentrated on his work as a member of legislative council, the body which became Uganda's parliament at independence in 1962. In 1961 he became minister without portfolio and leader of the house and of government business.

Buganda boycotted the 1961 pre-independence elections, enabling the DP to win power under Kiwanuka's leadership, and from 1961 to 1962 he was Uganda's first prime minister. In the 1962 elections the UPC, led by Milton Obote, formed a tactical alliance with Kabaka Yekka, the Buganda royalist party, in order to win power, and the DP lost to this alliance. Under Kiwanuka the DP became the focus of opposition to Obote, and in September 1969 their headquarters was raided by police. Kiwanuka was arrested, charged with treason, and tried, but acquitted for lack of evidence. At the end of 1969, after an attempt was made to assassinate Obote, Kiwanuka was arrested again and detained without trial, and the DP was banned. He spent just over a year in a cell measuring 8 feet square, only being released in 1971 when General Idi Amin overthrew Obote in a coup. Understandably Kiwanuka welcomed the coup and accepted appointment as chief justice. He tried to bring in much-needed reforms, but soon realized the brutality and lawlessness of Amin's rule. He protested against the expulsion of the Asians decreed by Amin in August 1972, and argued for them to be allowed to retain their property. Then, at the request of the British high commissioner, he agreed to intervene in the case of Daniel Stewart, who had been arrested and detained without trial. He issued a writ of habeas corpus on Stewart's behalf, said that the army had no powers of arrest, and when Stewart came before the court dismissed the case against him and ordered his release, to Amin's fury. Although Kiwanuka knew that he was in danger, he refused to flee the country. After attending mass on Sunday 21 September 1972 he went to his office. There he was abducted by soldiers and taken to Luzira prison where he was murdered and his body secretly disposed of. He is remembered by many Ugandans as a martyr for justice.

M. LOUISE PIROUET

Sources A. Bade, *Benedicto Kiwanuka: the man and his politics* (Kampala, 1996) · *Uganda and human rights: reports of the international commission of jurists to the United Nations* (1977) · E. G. Wilson, *Who's who in east Africa, 1963–64* (1964) · E. G. Wilson, *Who's who in east Africa, 1965–66* (1966) · E. G. Wilson, *Who's who in east Africa, 1967–68* (1968) · P. Mutibwa, *Uganda since independence: a story of unfulfilled hopes* (1992) · F. A. W. Bwengye, *The agony of Uganda from Idi Amin to Obote: an analysis of the 1980 controversial general election and its aftermath* (1985) · H. Kyemba, *State of blood: the inside story of Idi Amin's reign of terror* (1977) · D. Martin, *General Amin* (1974)

Likenesses photograph, repro. in Bade, *Benedicto Kiwanuka*, cover

Klein, Alfred Leopold Charles de Beaumont. *See* Beaumont, Charles-Louis Leopold Alfred de (1902–1972).

Klein, Edward Emanuel (1844–1925), histologist and bacteriologist, was born on 31 October 1844 in Osijek (Essek), Slavonia, the son of Michael Klein, a tanner of Austrian-Jewish extraction. He obtained his medical degree from the University of Vienna and then worked in the laboratories of the physiologist Ernst von Brücke and the pathologist Salomon Stricker. Klein specialized in histology and first visited Britain briefly in 1869 to arrange terms for the translation of Stricker's famous *Handbook of Human and Comparative Histology*. In 1871 he was invited to return by John Simon and John Burdon Sanderson to help with the pioneering pathological research supported by the medical department of the privy council at the Brown Animal Sanatory Institute, London. He came to Britain as Emanuel Klein, but soon acquired the additional forename of Edward and was widely known as E. E. Klein.

Klein worked at the 'Brown' from 1871 to 1897, largely on contract research for the medical department. He also lectured at St Bartholomew's Hospital, London, on histology and bacteriology, and undertook private consultancies. Between 1889 and 1891 he held the post of professor of bacteriology at the newly inaugurated College of State Medicine, London. He was elected a fellow of the Royal Society in 1875 and was a founder of the Medical Research Club in 1891. He retired from St Bartholomew's in 1911.

Klein quickly established his reputation in Britain writing the histology section for the famous *Handbook for the Physiological Laboratory* (1873), which he edited jointly with John Burdon Sanderson, Michael Foster, and Laudner Brunton. He gained some notoriety in his evidence to the royal commission on vivisection in 1876, when, allegedly owing to his poor command of English, he was led to say that he had 'no regard at all for the suffering of animals'. Initially Klein continued to work on histology, publishing the two-volume *Anatomy of the Lymphatic System* (1873, 1875), followed by his co-authored *Atlas of Histology* (with Noble Smith in 1879) and *Elements of Histology* (with J. S. Edkins in 1889). He was editor of the *Quarterly Journal of Microscopy* between 1877 and 1892.

From the time of his arrival Klein found his skills in microscopy and tissue preparation in demand in the study of the role of micro-organisms in disease. His career gradually moved to the new science of bacteriology, not least because microscopy seemed to hold the key to identifying the germs causing contagious and infectious diseases. Klein was well placed to be a pioneer in the subject and in 1874 it was announced that he had discovered the germs of two diseases—sheep pox and typhoid fever. However, in both cases his claims were refuted. Klein's reputation suffered from these and later misjudgements, such as his opposition to Robert Koch's identification of the cholera bacillus and his belief that cows and cats could be sources of diphtheria in humans. However, Klein played a crucial role in diffusing Koch's bacteriological methods and new techniques in microscopy. He incorporated modern approaches into his work in the 1880s, though he was not destined to make a major discovery of a pathogenic germ.

None the less Klein influenced the development of bacteriology in Britain, not least by demonstrating its utility. The great bulk of his bacteriological work, almost one hundred reports, was published in government blue books rather than in scientific or medical journals. These investigations, often commissioned by medical officers of health or local government agencies, covered all manner of disease problems: smallpox, typhoid fever, scarlet fever, swine fever, tuberculosis, meat poisoning, anthrax, ophthalmia, cholera, foot-and-mouth disease, pneumonia, disinfection, fowl diarrhoea, grouse disease, pheasant disease, diphtheria, immunity defects, oyster infections, psorosperms, plague, enteritis, milk-borne infections, trypanosomes, and problems of food preservation. Klein was the author of the first successful British textbook on bacteriology, *Micro-Organisms and Disease: an Introduction to the Study of Specific Micro-Organisms* (1884), and he taught some of the next generation of bacteriological researchers, including Frederick Treves, Ronald Ross, and Mervyn Gordon. However, he never established a school and did not play a major role in the institutionalization of bacteriology in Britain: hence the title of 'father of British bacteriology' would be a misnomer.

Klein married Mrs Sophia Amelia Mawley (1842/3–1919),

a widow and the daughter of William Metcalfe, on 25 July 1877. They had two daughters and a son, and were a close family. Klein enjoyed music and was a keen chess player, taking on leading players with the smallest of handicaps. He was naturalized British in 1887, but never lost his mid-European accent. After his retirement he moved to Chislehurst in Kent, and then back to Earls Court in London when he began to suffer chronic bronchitis. After his wife's death Klein spent his final days in Hove, Sussex, where he died of chronic bronchitis at his home, 13 Wilbury Villas, on 9 February 1925. He was buried at Hove cemetery.   MICHAEL WORBOYS

Sources W. Bulloch, 'Emanuel Klein', *Journal of Pathology and Bacteriology*, 28 (1925), 684–99 · F. W. A. [F. W. Andrewes], *PRS*, 98B (1925), xxv–xxix · *BMJ* (21 Feb 1925), 388 · *The Lancet* (21 Feb 1925), 411–12 · *The Times* (12 Feb 1925) · m. cert. · *CGPLA Eng. & Wales* (1925) · d. cert.
Archives PRO, medical department files
Likenesses photograph, repro. in *Journal of Pathology and Bacteriology*, 28 (1925), 394, pl. 36
Wealth at death £14,598 12s. 9d.: probate, 26 March 1925, *CGPLA Eng. & Wales*

Klein [*née* Reizes], **Melanie** (1882–1960), psychoanalyst, was born on 30 March 1882 at Tiefer Gruben 8, Vienna, the daughter of Moritz Reizes (1828–1900), doctor and dentist, and a Jewish scholar from a rigidly Orthodox Polish family, and Libussa Deutsch (1852–1914), the granddaughter of a liberal rabbi. The youngest of four children, she idolized an older sister who died when Melanie was four. Subsequently she was devoted to her brother Emmanuel and his intellectual interests, but he also died, when she was twenty. The family was not wealthy and she became engaged at the age of seventeen to Arthur Stephan Klein (1878–1939), a second cousin and the son of Jacob Klein, a successful businessman, whom she married in 1903, after her father's death. This thwarted her education, and her initial ambition to study medicine. Arthur Klein, an engineer, worked for a number of companies in different parts of Europe, while Melanie Klein gave birth to her daughter, Melitta, in 1904 and to two sons (born in 1907 and 1914). The family moved repeatedly and she missed the lively intellectual life of Vienna a great deal. This, together with her marriage no longer being supportive, led her to periods of depression in which her mother intervened, looking after the children while sending Klein away for recuperative tours on her own.

The death of Klein's mother, just four months after the birth of the youngest child, precipitated a crisis. Now in Budapest, she discovered Freud's *On Dreams*, probably in 1914, and shortly afterwards started in analysis with Sandor Ferenczi, an early and important follower of Freud. She may have gained the contact through her husband, who was a work colleague of Ferenczi's brother. Her analysis with Ferenczi was intermittent due to his absences on war service. By 1919 however, Ferenczi had convinced her that she might contribute to psychoanalytic discoveries herself by making observations on children, which she did, initially with her own children. These observations resulted in her first paper, 'The development

Melanie Klein (1882–1960), by Jane Bown, 1959

of a child', in 1921 (*Imago*, 7, 251–309; *International Journal of Psycho-Analysis*, 4, 1923, 419–74). At this time psychoanalysts were attempting to confirm Freud's theories of child development, which he had sketched out from his work largely with adults. There was considerable incentive therefore for direct observation of children, and a number of analysts were doing this. Klein however went one step further than research: she was the first to work therapeutically with young children. Up to this point a form of therapeutic pedagogy had evolved in Vienna with older children and adolescents. To reach the younger child's own private world Klein needed a method not based wholly on words, and she turned to the child's natural means of expression, play. She gave each child in her practice a set of their own small toys, and watched and sometimes engaged in the play of the child, while from time to time making interpretations of the unconscious significance of the play. With this play technique she was able to analyse children in the third year of life.

After the family left Hungary in 1919, during the political upheavals, Melanie Klein went with her children to stay with her parents-in-law in Czechoslovakia, while Arthur found work in Sweden, thus beginning a separation which ended in divorce in 1923. In 1920 she met Karl Abraham at a psychoanalytic congress and he persuaded her to move to Berlin, which she did in 1921. He was the leading analyst in the Berlin Psychoanalytical Society, and a leading proponent of a formal training for new psycho-analysts. Klein had a further analysis herself with Abraham during 1924–5. He encouraged her to work with children, and to develop her play technique. With the end of her marriage she seems, despite having three children with her, to have enjoyed Berlin life with great gusto. Alix Strachey, the wife of Freud's translator James Strachey, who was also in Berlin for an analysis with Abraham, remarked of Klein one evening:

> She was frightfully excited and determined to have a thousand adventures, and soon infected me with some of her spirits ... she's really a very good sort and makes no secret of her hopes, fears and pleasures, which are of the simplest sort. Only she's got a damned sharp eye for neurotics. (Strachey and Strachey, 193)

Alix Strachey was nevertheless very impressed with her work and arranged for Klein to come to London to present a series of papers on her work with children. These lectures were held in the home of Adrian Stephen at 50 Gordon Square over a period of three weeks in July 1925. She aroused great interest in a number of the members of the British Psycho-Analytical Society who were working with children. Ernest Jones, the leading proponent of Freud's work in Britain, invited Klein to come to London for a year principally to analyse the children of several analysts, including his own two children. Abraham died late in 1925, and Melanie Klein decided to accept the offer in 1926; she eventually decided to stay permanently, settling for most of her life at 42 Clifton Hill, in St John's Wood, London. She immediately joined the British Psycho-Analytical Society and with the mixture of her strong personal presence, her gift for clinical observation, the rigorous training experience in Berlin, and her new research on children she quickly became a leading figure.

Psychoanalysis during the 1920s was attracting very considerable attention both in the medical world (particularly military medicine as psychoanalysis had proved to be effective in treating shell-shock victims in the First World War) and also within intellectual circles. Klein's series of publications during the 1920s attracted attention across the psychoanalytic world of Europe. Also at this time another method of working with children was developed in Vienna. Anna Freud, the youngest daughter of Sigmund Freud, advanced the psychoanalytically oriented pedagogy under her father's guidance. She and other psychoanalysts in Vienna took a diverging position from Klein and the many British psychoanalysts who followed her. The two camps disagreed over the depth of interpretation of the unconscious, and the presence, or absence, of transference in children. Anna Freud's book of lectures on child analysis appeared in 1926, in German (but not in England). Klein published her major work *The Psychoanalysis of Children* in 1932. This detailed many theoretical views from her clinical research findings on the minds of young children, which Klein believed amplified Freud's theories of child development. Viennese analysts believed that Klein's new ideas were sufficiently discrepant with Freud's to cast doubt on whether she could be considered a psychoanalyst at all.

Delayed by the war, a collection of her earlier papers which included many on child analysis appeared in 1948 (*Contributions to Psycho-Analysis*). These defined her view of the infant as experiencing itself in relation to others at the outset of life, despite the immaturity of the infant's perceptions. Hence she became aware of the central importance of phantasies, arising from internal states, and their powerful and distorting effects on the earliest relations with other people.

Freud had used his work with adults to extrapolate back to the development of the child, and Klein extended this by claiming that her work with children allowed her to extrapolate back with the same validity to the earliest stages of infancy. Her work at this time also involved an increasing number of adult patients in which she could discover the later results of the early stages she had found in children.

Although she was deeply occupied with her work, her zest for meeting people led Virginia Woolf on one occasion, an anniversary of the Psycho-Analytical Society in 1939, to complain that she felt pressed by Melanie Klein for an invitation to dinner. Nevertheless, Woolf found Klein a 'woman of character and force and some submerged—how shall I say—not craft, but subtlety: something working underground. A pull, a twist, like an undertow: menacing. A bluff grey-haired lady, with large bright imaginative eyes' (*Diary of Virginia Woolf*).

Psychoanalysis dominated Klein's family: her oldest child, Melitta, had become an analyst at an early age. She was promoted, but maybe dominated, by her mother, and in the mid-1930s family rows between them spilled out into professional disagreements in the meetings of the Psycho-Analytical Society.

In 1934 Klein became a British subject, and seemed to be installed as the leading psychoanalytic researcher in Britain. She evolved new ideas which were published in a major paper in 1935, 'A contribution to the psychogenesis of manic-depressive states' (*International Journal of Psycho-Analysis*, 16, 145–74). Here she introduced the notion of the depressive position as a crucial maturational step in the early stages of infancy. This expanded on Freud's work which he had published in 'Mourning and melancholia' in 1917. It drew attention to internalized phantasy figures such as the 'super ego' which Klein elaborated as 'internal objects'. A further major paper on the depressive position appeared in 1940, 'Mourning and its relation to manic-depressive states' (*International Journal of Psycho-Analysis*, 21, 125–53).

The disagreement over the technique and findings of child analysis was passionate and became an institutional opposition between the Viennese Psychoanalytical Society and the British. Ernest Jones was active, though unsuccessful, in resolving these differences during the 1930s, and the tide of political change in Europe brought this to a head. After the Nazi *Anschluss* in Austria the Freud family were forced into exile, and moved to London in June 1938. Sigmund Freud died in September 1939 leaving Anna Freud to preserve the exactness of his work. Klein was dismayed that the detractors of her work were in London, and was concerned that her ideas would be lost under the patronage that the Freud prestige would now exert against her.

Klein began from then on to consolidate a group of exceptional loyalty, her closest colleagues being Joan Riviere, Susan Isaacs, and Paula Heimann. The blitzkrieg on London in 1941–2 rendered serious intellectual life virtually in abeyance, but afterwards the psychoanalysts began to reform the society, and had to address the problem of the feverish disagreements between the two camps. The means of doing this was a series of committee discussions leading to eighteen months of scientific meetings to which Kleinians presented their ideas for discussion by the whole society. The very detailed archival documentation of these 'Controversial Discussions' has been published in *The Freud–Klein Controversies, 1940–1945* (1991), edited by Pearl King and Riccardo Steiner. These exposed the differences between the two groups with great clarity, but failed to resolve any.

Eventually Melanie Klein, Anna Freud, and Sylvia Payne (now president of the society following Jones's retirement) formed a 'gentleman's agreement' that allowed the business of the society to continue despite the disagreements. This included offering two streams in the training programme to students who would be aligned with one or the other group. Klein no longer had the general support of the society and devoted herself to co-ordinating her group of supporters and attracting new students. Despite this she retained her primary interest in clinical work and psychoanalytic research, reporting, in 1946, yet another important theoretical advance, the notion of the paranoid-schizoid position ('Notes on some schizoid mechanisms', *International Journal of Psycho-Analysis*, 27, 99–110). She was now working with quite disturbed children and adults, and was pushing her research into the field of psychosis, which, she argued, allowed her to formulate the very earliest weeks and months of infant development. Many of her followers subsequently made major advances in understanding psychosis. These new ideas created even sharper divisions between her group and other analysts. The latter either aligned themselves with Anna Freud in preserving Freud's classic texts, or with an emerging middle group who sought a creative balance of ideas.

A further step in driving the Kleinian group apart from others in the British Psycho-Analytical Society occurred with the publication in 1957 of Klein's short book *Envy and Gratitude*, which elaborated the inherent bipolar relationships of the infant at the outset of life. By this time she had consolidated her group and many of them contributed papers to a special edition of the *International Journal of Psycho-Analysis* in 1952 for her seventieth birthday (later published as *New Directions in Psycho-Analysis* in 1955).

In 1960 Klein fell ill from a cancer, and died postoperatively at University College Hospital, London, on 22 September 1960. Her body was cremated at Golders Green. The attractiveness of her open and sometimes astringent personality made her many extraordinarily loyal friends, and also enemies who seemingly felt no inhibition about reviling her work publicly. But as her obituary in *The Times* remarked: 'The power and acuity of her intellect had strength and integrity, her originality and creativeness left one in no doubt that one was in touch with an outstanding personality'.

It still remains an effort to approach Klein's work in a balanced way, as the passions of the controversy remain within the psychoanalytic world. Despite this, her play technique has strongly influenced all child psychotherapists and child analysts, and it remains a standard method. Her ideas are now seriously considered in academic disciplines far removed from the clinical situation including film and cultural studies, social science, history, and philosophy. Klein's focus on the early relationship of the infant with the mother balanced Freud's emphasis on the importance of the father, and this has given Klein an importance in gender studies. A definitive collection of all her published written work appeared in 1975—*The Writings of Melanie Klein*; they include two books, thirty-seven papers, and five short contributions. A biography was undertaken by Phyllis Grosskurth and published in 1987, and a play by Nicholas Wright adapted part of the biography for the stage. Several portraits, drawings, and a bust exist. The British Psycho-Analytical Society has a small collection of toys similar to those she originally used. A large archive of her letters, unpublished notes and fragments, and case notes, together with photographs from all periods of her life, is kept in the library of the Wellcome Institute for the History of Medicine.

Melanie Klein's influence on psychoanalysis developed steadily after 1960, notably in South America, and latterly in Europe and the United States. Many psychoanalytic ideas developed on the back of her clinical formulations, and the research analyses of schizophrenic patients from the 1950s contributed especially to the understanding of symbol formation, and to the exploration of emotional containment. These revolutionized object relations theory and later infiltrated most schools of psychoanalysis and psychotherapy. Her developments in technique permanently influenced the technical practice of psychoanalysis and the understanding of the scope of the transference.

R. D. HINSHELWOOD

Sources H. Segal, *Klein* (1979) · *The Times* (23 Sept 1960) · *The Guardian* (23 Sept 1960) · W. R. Bion, H. Rosenfeld, and H. Segal, *International Journal of Psycho-Analysis*, 42 (1961), 4–8 · P. Grosskurth, *Melanie Klein: her world and her work* (1985) · private information (2004) [Hanna Segal, Betty Joseph] · *Bloomsbury/Freud: the letters of James and Alix Strachey, 1924–1928*, ed. P. Meisel and W. Kendrick (1986) · *The diary of Virginia Woolf*, ed. A. O. Bell and A. McNeillie, 5 (1984) · *CGPLA Eng. & Wales* (1960)

Archives Wellcome L., corresp., diaries, and papers

Likenesses O. Neman, bust, 1939 · F. Topolski, drawing, 1957, priv. coll. · J. Bown, photograph, 1959, priv. coll. [*see illus.*] · I. McWhirter, pencil drawing, NPG · bronze bust, British Psychoanalytical Society, London · photographs, Wellcome L. · photographs, Wellcome L. · photographs, British Psychoanalytical Society, London

Wealth at death £34,264 5s. 4d.: probate, 24 Nov 1960, *CGPLA Eng. & Wales*

Kleinwort, Sir Alexander Drake, first baronet (1858–1935), merchant banker, was born on 17 October 1858 at

The Avenue, Grove Hill, in Camberwell, London, the second son and fourth child of Alexander Frederick Henry *Kleinwort (1815–1886), founder of the family bank, Kleinwort, Sons & Co., and his wife, Sophie Charlotte, *née* Greverus (1820–1860). It was his father's intention from Kleinwort's birth that he should enter the family business, and no concession was made to try to assimilate him into his father's adopted country. While his contemporaries and in economic terms his peers were being dispatched first to preparatory and then to public schools, he was educated at home until the age of twelve and taken once a week to his father's office to learn about banking. In 1870 he was sent to boarding-school at the *Real Gymnasium* in Karlsruhe, Germany, and he then attended the Institut Supérieur de Commerce in Antwerp, Belgium, where he obtained the *licence en sciences commerciales*.

In 1878 Kleinwort entered the family firm as a salaried clerk earning £8 per month. Two years later, in order to meet and become familiar with the bank's agents and clients abroad, he embarked on a world tour during which he spent one year in the United States. On his return to London in 1883 he was appointed first manager and then partner in the bank, and on the death of his father in 1886 he assumed the direction of the family bank with the new senior partner, his elder brother Herman.

The bank that Herman and Alexander Kleinwort inherited was primarily an accepting house, capitalized at £600,000, with a coveted credit-rating. By 1913, however, its capitalization had risen to £4.4 million and acceptances, which had been £5 million in 1890, were now £14.2 million, making Kleinworts one of the two leading London houses, the other being Rothschilds. Alexander Kleinwort's particular and decisive contribution was to develop a joint operation with Goldman Sachs of New York, which led to the formation of a highly profitable issuing partnership with them and another American house, Lehman Brothers. Together they helped to raise capital for newly emergent manufacturing and retail companies, including Sears Roebuck in 1906 and F. W. Woolworth in 1911. This was at a time when the Wall Street market leader J. P. Morgan would not have anything to do with them, as helping such firms to go public was thought unworthy of consideration. Kleinwort also followed a successful high-risk policy of increasing the number of bills of exchange accepted from the 1890 norm, of three to four times capital, to five times by 1908, thereby enabling the bank to undertake a much greater volume of business.

Kleinwort had inherited his father's ambition and single-mindedness in his approach to business. Disregarding the latter's instruction, however, to remember that Herman was his elder brother, in 1915 he brought about Herman's retirement, thereafter acting as *de facto* senior partner until his death. None the less, the years of the First World War were to prove unhappy, as he felt both personally and professionally the force of the prevailing anti-German feeling. The bank too was adversely affected as, with the bulk of its banking business centred in Germany, it faced the defaults of many German and Austrian clients.

Kleinwort was one of the leading bankers who initiated the negotiations for a moratorium on outstanding bills with the chancellor of the exchequer on 1 August 1914. Given the nature and degree of its exposure, Kleinwort did well to ensure that the bank emerged after the war remarkably unscathed, though inevitably business was much diminished. As he drifted into old age his favourite nephew, Herman Andreae, increasingly took on partnership responsibilities.

Kleinwort was elected an underwriting member of Lloyd's in 1886. In 1884 he had succeeded his father's former partner, Edward Cohen, as a director of the North British and Mercantile Insurance Company, and he became its chairman in 1928. In addition he was on the boards of the Railway Passenger Assurance Company and the Ocean Marine Insurance Company, on both of which he was to assume the chair in 1928. However, Kleinwort deliberately chose to have few other outside interests, in marked contrast to the vast majority of his peers in the City, because he believed that such involvements would allow him less time to devote to his bank's business and could produce a conflict of interest. His only concession to a public persona was membership of the Liberal Party, to which he once responded to a request for funds by immediately writing out a cheque for £20,000. During Asquith's premiership he subsequently accepted a baronetcy, in 1909.

Of medium height, with a long flowing beard, curly hair, and blue eyes, in later life this appearance gave Kleinwort something of the air of an Old Testament prophet as imagined in Victorian schoolbooks after the model of Michaelangelo's *David*. He was equally forbidding: a man of extreme punctuality, he ordered his life with absolute precision. He loved fast cars from their introduction at the turn of the century, and the villagers of Cuckfield in Sussex where he lived could regulate their lives by his clockwork departure every morning for London, as could the policeman on London Bridge as Kleinwort's Bentley roared past him at a quarter past three every afternoon on his return journey.

Kleinwort married in 1889 Étiennette (d. 1946), daughter of Étienne Girard, a French merchant who had settled in Belgium and America. They had five sons and two daughters, of whom the two younger sons, Ernest Greverus *Kleinwort and Cyril, succeeded him in the family bank.

Kleinwort died on 8 June 1935 at his country home, Bolnore House, Cuckfield, Sussex, after being knocked down by a cyclist, while on his daily 3 mile walk round his estate and the nearby lanes. He was buried in the village churchyard at Cuckfield.   JEHANNE WAKE

Sources J. Wake, *Kleinwort Benson: a history of two families in banking* (1997) · b. cert. · d. cert. · G. R. Searle, *Corruption in British politics, 1895–1930* (1987) · *CGPLA Eng. & Wales* (1935) · S. Diaper, 'Kleinwort, Sir Alexander Drake', *DBB*
Archives GL, Kleinwort, Sons & Co. MSS · Kleinwort Benson plc, London, Kleinwort Benson MSS · priv. coll.
Likenesses W. Orpen, portrait, Kleinwort Benson plc
Wealth at death £607,017 12s. 1d.: probate, 20 Aug 1935, *CGPLA Eng. & Wales*

Kleinwort, Alexander Frederick Henry [*formerly* Alexander Friedrich Heinrich] (**1815–1886**), merchant and merchant banker, was born on 18 November 1815, at Schloss Gerdeshagen, Satow, duchy of Mecklenburg, the fifth of eight children of Heinrich Kleinwort (1762–1831), a merchant of Altona, and his second wife, Wilhelmine (1783–1846), daughter of Gotthard von Hövell of Lübeck. He had two half-brothers and three half-sisters from his father's first marriage.

In 1819 a downturn in Heinrich Kleinwort's fortunes entailed the sale of the Gerdeshagen estate, and his family rejoined other Kleinwort relatives based at the Rosenhof in Altona, where Alexander was educated at home. On 18 March 1831 he was apprenticed to the Hamburg firm of Anderson and Höber, a leading house in the English trade, and by Easter 1835 he was given a clerkship in the storage and warehouse department. Determined to improve his position he put some of his small capital towards lessons in English, a language then considered essential for promotion. The Kleinwort tradition was centred in proprietorship, and as there were Höber sons Kleinwort formed the ambition of making his fortune in Cuba, where he could find employment and act as correspondent for Anderson and Höber. Thus on 15 June 1838 he arrived in Havana to take up a position as a copy clerk in H. Rottman & Co., a small import-export firm, where he was paid 178 Reichsthaler per month, considerably more than he had earned in Hamburg.

To build up his own capital Kleinwort lived extremely frugally—his single concession to a preference for fine clothes being a partiality for yellow trousers, which led him to be dubbed El Canario—and he exercised the strictest thrift by, for instance, hiding letters in newspapers to avoid incurring any charge when letter postal rates were increased. As part of this strategy he set about trading on his own account with various friends, in cigars, guns, currency, and clothes, which he smuggled to avoid the hefty customs duty of 30 per cent; every shilling saved on costs was 'a rung on the ladder which I climb from nothing to something' (Kleinwort to Herr Höber, 18 March 1842, Kleinwort MSS).

On 1 January 1840 Kleinwort joined as a copyist Drake Brothers & Co., one of the largest and most important merchant houses in Cuba, specializing in sugar. In May 1840 he was promoted to chief clerk, and since the Drake family did not directly involve themselves in the business he rapidly rose under the wing of the all-powerful general manager José Morales; he soon became first accountant, and then manager in 1845. Throughout this period he continued to earn money on his own account, but his great opportunity came when Morales decided to expand Drakes's European business and, having long nurtured the German business at a junior level, Kleinwort was given this responsibility. On 1 November 1848 he was able to purchase for $50,000 a partnership that entitled him to 12.5 per cent of the profits.

Kleinwort now had to undertake some travelling to London, where he met and in 1852 married Sophie Charlotte (1820–1860), the only child of Drakes's London agent Herman Diderich Greverus, and his wife, Frederike Kuhlmann, both of whom had come originally from Oldenburg in Germany. The couple had two sons and two daughters. When Greverus retired and handed over his business interests to him, Kleinwort founded his own company, Kleinwort and Cohen, on 1 January 1855, at 3 White Hart Court, Lombard Street, London, with his former colleague and his father-in-law's protégé and partner, Edward Cohen. In 1858 the partnership was dissolved and reformed as Drake, Kleinwort, and Cohen, with a broadened capital of £200,000; the majority of this was injected by James Drake, who remained a sleeping partner, and the firm had offices at 7 Mincing Lane. By 1865 Kleinwort, the senior executive partner, had increased the firm's capital to £651,000, and when in 1870 James Drake retired it had acquired the coveted description of 'first class'. The name of the business now reverted to Kleinwort, Cohen & Co., with Kleinwort as senior partner. His strategy was to concentrate on the finance of trade rather than the purchase and transport of goods, and the firm benefited from the expanding American economy. In consequence, by 1883, when Edward Cohen retired and Kleinwort's two sons, Herman Greverus and Alexander Drake *Kleinwort, entered the business, the firm was counted one of the leading accepting houses in the City.

Kleinwort was from the beginning very ambitious, single-minded, and quick to identify and exploit any opportunity. Denied the education and wealth that his family's social standing might have led him to expect, he made his own way in life and expressed his business philosophy thus: 'Whenever I see that I can do something even if it brings me only a small profit, I do not fear any effort or privation' (Kleinwort to F. Karck, 21 June 1839, Kleinwort MSS). His life was dedicated to his business and his family, who were inculcated with the idea that the affairs of the bank came first, to the exclusion of all other interests. Alexander Kleinwort died on 7 January 1886, from a throat infection that had led to pneumonia, in the home given to him as a wedding present by his father-in-law, The Glebe, Champion Hill, Camberwell. He was buried at Norwood cemetery.   JEHANNE WAKE

Sources J. Wake, *Kleinwort Benson: a history of two families in banking* (1997) • *CGPLA Eng. & Wales* (1886) • d. cert. • London, Kleinwort Benson MSS, A. Kleinwort to Herr Höber (18/3/1842) • Kleinwort letter book, Mainz MSS, A. Kleinwort to F. Karck (21/6/1839) • b. cert. • b. cert. [Alexander Drake Kleinwort]
Archives Kleinwort Benson plc, London, Kleinwort Benson MSS
Likenesses two portraits, 1855–85, Kleinwort Benson plc, London
Wealth at death £701,334 12s. 1d.: probate, 5 Feb 1886, *CGPLA Eng. & Wales*

Kleinwort, Ernest Greverus (**1901–1977**), merchant banker, was born on 13 September 1901 at Bolnore House, Cuckfield, Sussex, the sixth of the seven children of Sir Alexander Drake *Kleinwort, first baronet (1858–1935), merchant banker, and his wife, Étiennette (d. 1946), daughter of Étienne Girard, a Frenchman who had settled in Kentucky. He had four brothers, two of whom died young, and two sisters. In 1909 he was sent to a preparatory school, but the unhappiness of his elder brother Henry after a few terms caused his father to remove them both. Thereafter he and his brothers were educated at home by their sister Henrietta and a tutor, Evan McColl; they were never sent to public school, owing to the Germanophobia engendered by the First World War. This reclusive upbringing, with its absence of friends and outside influences, had the effect of binding Ernest closely to his younger brother Cyril (1905–1980) and to their father, whom they worshipped. He was their link with the outside world, and he remained the dominating influence in their lives even after Ernest went in 1920 to Jesus College, Cambridge. He gained an upper-second class in part one, French and German, and the only first class of his year in part two, economics.

In 1923 Ernest Kleinwort joined the family bank, Kleinwort, Sons & Co., as a trainee clerk. He worked for six months in the English department and then moved through every other department. He always felt that he and his brother Cyril had had a head start in learning about the business, as 'Father talked nothing but merchant banking, so we couldn't help absorbing it' (Chapman and Diaper, 220, n. 15). Mealtimes had long provided a regular opportunity for instruction in the basic principles of banking as well as in the need for self-discipline: 'Moderation in all things' and 'Never become emotionally involved in any business problem' were two dicta handed down by their father from their grandfather. On 1 January 1927 Ernest, aged twenty-five, and Cyril, aged twenty-one, became partners in the firm, each with initial participations of £50,000. Their partnership of nearly forty years was remarkable for its complementarity and the complete absence of rivalry or acrimony between them. They were the first partners whom the staff knew as colleagues and also the first to take an active interest in staff conditions. Kleinwort married on 29 December 1932 Joan Nightingale, daughter of Arthur W. Crossley. They had one daughter and one son.

The early years of the brothers' partnership proved to be extremely challenging. Although in 1927 the bank had a capital of £3.78 million and maintained a leading position among accepting houses, trading conditions rapidly deteriorated. The stockmarket crashed in 1929 and this was followed two years later by the German banking crisis. With almost half of its acceptances on German account Kleinworts faced insolvency for the first time in its history. Kleinwort represented his firm on the nine-member joint committee appointed to represent the Accepting Houses Committee and the British Bankers' Association in discussions with the Bank of England and the Treasury to consider the 'standstill agreement' of 1931. This agreement and its subsequent renewals during the 1930s meant that credits to Germany were frozen but that interest was guaranteed. Kleinwort was also involved in similar negotiations to reschedule the commercial debts of Austria, Hungary, Czechoslovakia, and Romania. Some $12 million of Kleinworts' outstanding debt, nearly four times the partners' capital, was thus frozen at a time

when international accepting business was shrinking, and facing further disruption by war.

As most of the continent fell under the jurisdiction of the Trading with the Enemy Act during the Second World War, it was, Kleinwort recalled, 'a case of putting the firm's business once again on a "care and maintenance" basis, a task that fell to my lot' (Kleinwort to Elbra, 30 Jan 1963, Kleinwort Benson archives). Kleinwort was the partner in charge of the holding operation at the bank's City office and at Bolnore in Sussex, to which the main staff were evacuated in 1939. Although he enlisted in the ranks of the Royal Air Force, in 1942, and obtained his commission, unofficially he joined the team of ultra-secret codebreakers at Bletchley, and lived in spartan lodgings nearby.

After the war Kleinworts, like other City houses, stumbled along among the rubble of its devastated business as it tried to revive its pre-war client relations. Ernest realized that the recovery of outstanding German debts was vital to the security of the firm, and despite the war he continued to have faith in German honour, even coining the phrase 'the courageous banker' to describe someone who believed that German claims would be validated. He served as a leading member of the British Bankers' Association committee for German affairs under the chairmanship of Sir Edward Reid of Baring Brothers, who later said that 'Kleinwort proved absolutely brilliant at the debt negotiations' (interview with Hermann Abs, Kleinwort Benson archives). Kleinwort also sat on the creditors' committee appointed by the tripartite commission on German debt to negotiate a settlement between Britain, France, America, and Germany, and he represented the British Bankers' Association committee for German affairs at the talks at Lancaster House, which lasted from 1951 to 1954, when agreement was reached on German debt repayment.

Progress in rebuilding the business of the bank was protracted, owing to unfavourable trade conditions and the weight of exchange control regulations. Ernest Kleinwort supported his brother's view that they must diversify away from acceptance business and become involved in corporate finance, which promised to be an area of expansion and was far less capital intensive than wholesale banking. This was not an easy task, however, as corporate clients remained loyal to their traditional advisers. Kleinworts therefore merged with the investment banking firm of Robert Benson Lonsdale and in 1961 Ernest Kleinwort became chairman of the new group, Kleinwort Benson Lonsdale, and of its banking subsidiary, Kleinwort Benson Ltd. The combined assets of £60 million then made Kleinwort Benson one of the largest banks in the City. Kleinwort retired as chairman of Kleinwort Benson in 1966 but continued as chairman of the group until 1968.

Of above average height, slim, and with fair hair and the family's blue eyes, Kleinwort was a firm believer in personal fitness. Encouraged by his father to take plenty of exercise through sporting interests as an antidote to desk work at the bank, his love of horsemanship and hunting was abiding; he hunted at least once a week and when he could not be on a horse he rode a bicycle, becoming known in the City as 'the bicycling chairman'. He enjoyed skiing and the company of beautiful women, and was an immensely knowledgeable gardener. At Heaselands, the Victorian farmhouse at Haywards Heath that he altered and then in 1932 entirely rebuilt, he created a nationally renowned garden of quite exceptional beauty and interest.

Kleinwort was above all a perfectionist who relentlessly pursued excellence through a combination of integrity and a meticulous attention to detail. When invited by Peter Scott to become a trustee of the British national appeal for the World Wildlife Fund in 1962 and to help him build the fund into a leading organization for nature conservation, Kleinwort immediately made it a prime objective. The fund's in-house phrase soon became 'the importance of seeing Ernest' (Scott, 2–3), such was his contribution to the financial and administrative strength of the World Wildlife Fund, and he served on the international board of trustees of the fund between 1967 and 1976. His untiring efforts for international conservation were recognized when he received the insignia of the commander of the Netherlands order of the Golden Ark in 1974. He was also a member of the council of the Wildfowl Trust from 1967 to 1977, and he became vice-president in 1970. As well as encouraging others he himself gave most generously, but much of his philanthropy was performed anonymously; its recipients ranged from hospitals to family planning projects in Jamaica, and from schemes concerned with medical ethics to Cheshire Homes.

Kleinwort died suddenly, from heart failure, seated in an armchair opposite his wife, at Heaselands House on 3 November 1977. He was buried near his father in the village churchyard at Cuckfield, Sussex. Kleinwort's son Kenneth succeeded his uncle in the baronetcy in 1983.

JEHANNE WAKE

Sources J. Wake, *Kleinwort Benson: a history of two families in banking* (1997) · S. Chapman and S. Diaper, 'The history of Kleinwort Benson Ltd', unpublished typescript, 1984, Kleinwort Benson archives, London · H. Abs, interview with Ernest Kleinwort, May 1990, Kleinwort Benson archives, London · A. G. L. Hellyer, 'Landscape of an individualist', *Country Life*, 140 (1966), 536–8 · P. Scott, 'Ernest Kleinwort', *Kleinwort Benson Magazine*, 25 (spring 1978), 2–3 · Kleinwort Benson archives, London, Elbra MSS · *CGPLA Eng. & Wales* (1977) · b. cert. · m. cert. · d. cert.
Archives Kleinwort Benson plc, London, archives | Kleinwort Benson plc, London, Elbra MSS
Likenesses E. I. Halliday, portrait, 1964, Kleinwort Benson Group, 20 Fenchurch Street, London
Wealth at death £730,666: probate, 23 Nov 1977, *CGPLA Eng. & Wales*

Klickmann [*married name* Henderson-Smith], **(Emily) Flora** (1867–1958), journal editor and author, was born at 18 Millbrook Road, Brixton, London, on 26 January 1867, the second of the six children of Rudolph Friedrich August Klickmann (1842–1928), administrator in a timber company, and his wife, Frances Emma (Fanny) Warne

(1837–1904). She was educated at Trinity College of Music and the Royal College of Organists, London, aspiring to a career as a recitalist. She was among the first women instrumentalists to play the massive American organ at the Crystal Palace—'still in her pigtails', as she observed—and enjoyed the friendship of Sir George Grove and August Manns, who later unsuccessfully proposed marriage to her.

Flora Klickmann's musical aspirations ended when she suffered a breakdown in health, physicians advising a less strenuous lifestyle. Her entry into journalism might have seemed unlikely following this advice, though from her first job, on *Sylvia's Home Journal*, she wrote on musical topics, later pioneering a new style of interview journalism in her 'Moments with modern musicians' series in the *Windsor Magazine*, which she joined in 1895. This grounding in editorial responsibility, involving meetings with writers and illustrators from both sides of the Atlantic, enabled her to take on major roles. Her editorial assignments included reshaping the journal of the Wesleyan Methodist Missionary Society, the *Foreign Field*, into an attractive format, and doing similar work for the British and Foreign Bible Society. A devout Christian, she did not however consider herself 'slotted into any religious niche', and was not committed to any single denomination. Her mentor in journalism was James Bowden, who had been a member of the Ward Lock and Bowden company, publishers of the *Windsor Magazine*, before becoming the general manager of the Religious Tract Society, one of the best-known juvenile and magazine publishers of the time.

In 1908 Flora Klickmann herself joined the Religious Tract Society as editor of the *Girls' Own Paper and Woman's Magazine*, following the death of Charles Peters, editor since the paper's foundation in 1880. Under Peters, who invited his friends from the art and musical worlds to write for it, the *Girls' Own Paper* departed from the tried and trusted religious formulae of the Religious Tract Society titles, and thrived in an increasingly competitive market. Flora Klickmann had little need to change the editorial mix, though she slowly upgraded the layout and typography, using more inset illustrations: by the 1920s her use of colour printing showered the pages with floral images. During her first decade as editor she also placed more emphasis on embroidery and needlework, or 'stitchcraft', to borrow the title of a quarterly launched in 1913. There was also additional material on 'home art' (or domestic science, as it was later called), including cookery. One of her missions was to make school work more practical, and to help children discover the pleasures they could derive from good needlework, and even from making their own clothes, the latter being an example of the self-sufficiency which she promoted. The more religious copy was confined in the main to her own editorial column of replies to readers' questions.

On 9 June 1913 Flora Klickmann married Ebenezer Henderson-Smith (1854–1937), a widower with children, though she continued to publish under her former name.

An avuncular figure identified as 'the head of affairs' in her own writings, he was advertising manager for the Religious Tract Society and in 1879 was one of the editorial team who put together the first issue of the *Boy's Own Paper*, the success of which prompted the launch of the paper for girls. They lived at Sydenham Hill, London, where for many years she was organist and music arranger of the Crystal Palace co-operative festivals initiated by Edward Owen Greening. In 1923 they moved to Brockweir in Gloucestershire. In 1930 she left the *Girls' Own Paper*, not entirely voluntarily. Long-distance editorial control of the magazine inevitably created problems. The fundamental reason for her departure, however, was the Religious Tract Society management's need to shape its magazine titles in the face of new monthly women's magazines, with an emphasis on home furnishing, modern living, and style in dress as well as décor in the home.

Flora Klickmann's reputation as a writer was secured by her series of Flower Patch books, much of the material for which had first appeared in the *Girls' Own Paper*. Blending character stories with evocative descriptions of the rural scene, the books also offered a reflection on religion, largely Christian, but going beyond the 'meeting centredness' of formal religion. Hers was a 'green spirituality', which found a receptive readership long after her death; in the tradition of Victorian naturalists she sought to reawaken a sense of wonder in her readers and to arouse their interest in the flora and fauna of the countryside. The Flower Patch books reached a wide market, consisting largely though not exclusively of her magazine buyers. The first in the series, *The Flower Patch among the Hills*, published by the Religious Tract Society in 1916, was quickly reprinted, and along with the second title, *Between the Larch Woods and the Weir* (1917), remains her best-known work. *The Flower Patch Garden Book* (1933) contains practical advice reflecting her commitment to wholesome food grown without the use of chemicals. The final title, *Weeding the Flower Patch*, appeared in 1947.

Although suffering bouts of exhaustion, Flora Klickmann kept up a flow of works: on crochet, on countering anxiety (*Mending your Nerves*), advice for aspiring writers (*The Lure of the Pen*), discussions of religious issues raised by correspondents to *Girls' Own Paper* (*Many Questions*), as well as children's books (such as *The Lady with the Crumbs*). She destroyed the material for a planned autobiographical memoir after it was rejected by a publisher in the 1940s. She died at her home, Flower Patch, Brockweir, Gloucestershire, on 20 November 1958, and was buried at the Moravian church at Brockweir on 27 November 1958.

DAVID LAZELL

Sources D. Lazell, *Flora Klickmann and her flower patch: the story of the Girls' Own Paper and the flower patch among the hills* (1976) [repr. 1993] • private information (2004) [family, B. Kingslake] • F. Klickmann, family tree book, 1953 • *WWW* • Crystal Palace festivals, Co-operative College archives, Holyoake House, Manchester • H. Simonis, *The street of ink: an intimate history of journalism* (1917) • chapter on Flora Klickmann, *The storytellers: a glimpse into the lives of 12 English writers* (1985) • S. G. Green, *The story of the Religious Tract Society for one hundred years* (1899) • E. Honor Ward, *Girls' Own Guide* (1992) • *Girls' Own Paper* [web page], Oct 2000 • b. cert. • m. cert. • d. cert.
Wealth at death £8763 13s. 0d.: probate, 6 Feb 1959, *CGPLA Eng. & Wales*

Klitz, Philip (1805–1854), composer, was born on 7 January 1805 at Lymington, Hampshire, the eldest of the six sons of George Philip Klitz (1777–1839), of Biebrich, Germany, a composer and drum-major in the Royal Flintshire militia, and his wife, Elizabeth Lane of Boldre (1775–1838). All six sons became musicians.

Philip Klitz moved to Southampton about 1828, and in 1831 conducted Paganini's concert there. A brilliant pianist and violinist, he was also a popular lecturer and a successful proponent of the Hullah system of sight-singing. He became organist of St Lawrence and St Joseph's Church, Southampton, and from 1845 to his death was organist of All Saints' Church. On 20 June 1834 or 1835 he married Charlotte Lyte, half-sister of Henry F. Lyte, the hymn writer. They had one son, George, who also became a composer.

Among Klitz's compositions were *Songs of the mid-watch, the poetry by Captain Willes Johnson, the music composed for and dedicated to the British navy* (1838). These six songs were, by order of the Admiralty, reprinted in *Songs of Charles Dibdin, arranged by T. Dibdin* (1850). Klitz was one of the first to write songs for the concerts of 'black-face minstrels': both 'Miss Ginger' and 'Dinah Dear' (1847) became very popular. He was an active freemason, and his 'Faith, Hope, and Charity' was performed at the Hampshire lodges. As well as his musical works, he also published *Sketches of life, character, and scenery in the New Forest: a series of tales, rural, domestic, legendary, and humorous* (1850). He died at 24 Portland Place, Southampton, on 13 January 1854.

G. C. BOASE, rev. ANNE PIMLOTT BAKER

Sources Boase, *Mod. Eng. biog.* • *GM*, 2nd ser., 41 (1854), 328 • *Hampshire Independent* (14 Jan 1854), 5 • private information (1892)

Klose, Francis Joseph (1784–1830), composer and piano teacher, was born in London, the son of a professor of music. His first teacher was his father, and he later studied the piano and composition with Franz Tomich, a pupil of Haydn. He was an excellent violinist, and was a member both of the orchestra of the King's Theatre and of the Concerts of Ancient Music. But he became so successful as a piano teacher that he gave up most of his public engagements and devoted himself almost entirely to teaching. He was also a prolific composer, and his sentimental ballads were especially popular. He set ballads by the leading poets of the day, notably Byron's 'Adieu! adieu! my native land', Lady Caroline Lamb's 'Can'st thou bid my heart forget', and 'The rose had been washed' by William Cowper. His other published works included a ballet, *Les déguisemens amoureux*, for the King's Theatre, sonatinas for the piano, a grand sonata for piano, violin, and flute, and *Practical Hints for Acquiring Thoroughbass* (1822). His piano music was popular with teachers. Klose died in Beaumont Street, Marylebone, on 8 March 1830.

R. H. LEGGE, rev. ANNE PIMLOTT BAKER

Sources [J. S. Sainsbury], ed., *A dictionary of musicians*, 2nd edn, 2 vols. (1827) · [Clarke], *The Georgian era: memoirs of the most eminent persons*, 4 (1834), 532 · *GM*, 1st ser., 100/1 (1830), 472–3

Klugmann, Norman John [James] (**1912–1977**), political activist and writer, was born in Hampstead, London, on 27 February 1912, the third son and fourth child of Samuel Klugmann, a wealthy Jewish rope and twine merchant, and his wife, Anna Rosenheim. He entered Gresham's School, Holt, in 1926, and left in 1931 with a modern languages scholarship to Trinity College, Cambridge. A contemporary schoolfellow was the future defector Donald Maclean. At Cambridge Klugmann gained a first in French and an upper second in German in part one of the tripos (1932) and a first in part two (1934). He was researching during the academic year 1934/5, but was already deeply immersed in what was to become his lifelong work for the Communist Party. He was to prove one of the most effective and durable activists of the Cambridge far left, then at its zenith. Prominent among a slightly older generation of his comrades were David Haden-Guest, Anthony Blunt, and Maurice Cornforth, who married Klugmann's sister Kitty. Outstanding undergraduate contemporaries included Maclean, Guy Burgess, and the spectacular John Cornford, killed in Spain in 1936. Cornford, a tireless zealot, and Klugmann, amiable, assiduous, and gently persuasive, worked outwards from the growing communist cell in Trinity to expand successfully the Cambridge Socialist Society and similar student groups in other universities—ensuring that, in the popular front mode of the day, they were all Marxist dominated.

Norman John Klugmann (1912–1977), by unknown photographer

Klugmann's outstanding linguistic ability and missionary zeal soon impelled him to work for the party abroad. From 1935 to 1939 he was secretary of the World Student Association against War and Fascism in Paris, visiting the Balkans, the Middle East, India, and China, where he led a student delegation to meet Mao Zedong. Conscripted into the Royal Army Service Corps, he transferred to the intelligence corps and by 1942 was a corporal clerk in the Cairo headquarters of the Special Operations Executive. Within a year he was commissioned and by the spring of 1943 was promoted captain. His pre-war knowledge of Yugoslavia and of its youthful anti-Fascists enabled him to make a widely praised contribution to the briefing and organization of Special Operations Executive agents. During his wartime career in Cairo, which culminated in his promotion to the rank of major, he was much respected and liked for his intelligence and warm, good-humoured manner.

Between April 1945 and July 1946 Klugmann worked with the United Nations Relief and Rehabilitation Administration mission to Yugoslavia. Returning then to England, he lived in Clapham, at times almost submerged physically in his vast library of communist texts. He was head of the party's education department from 1950 to 1960, and a member of its executive committee from 1952 and later of its political committee, until compelled to resign in 1963 owing to chronic asthma. At the inception of the monthly *Marxism Today* in 1957 he became assistant editor to John Gollan, succeeding in 1963 to the editorship, which he retained until 1977.

An undeviating adherence to party orthodoxy contrasted oddly with Klugmann's general reputation for civilized enlightenment. Thus in his *From Trotsky to Tito* (1951) he roundly condemned the Yugoslav leaders, once his heroes, observing that 'their treachery had been long and carefully concealed'. Commenting on Stalin's death in *Labour Monthly* (April 1953), he described him as 'the world's greatest working class leader' and as 'the man of peace, of international fraternity'. He worked for many years on his *History of the Communist Party of Great Britain*. Volume 1, dealing with the early years 1920–24, was published in 1968; volume 2, covering 1925 and the general strike, in 1969. He was also prominent in the activity known as Christian–Marxist dialogue. In 1968 he collaborated in *What Kind of a Revolution?* with the Anglican priest Paul Oestreicher, who in that work described Marxists as part of the latent church. In the same year Klugmann edited *Dialogue of Christianity and Marxism*, essays originally published in *Marxism Today*. Without deviating an inch from his Marxist orthodoxy, he managed to convey in this area of his work for the party a general impression of bridge-building benevolence.

A revealing aspect of Klugmann's mind and character is to be found in *A Reader's Guide to the Study of Marxism*, an undated pamphlet, in which his advice to tutors and leaders of discussion groups is a model exposition of how to teach cogently and attractively and goes a long way to explain the affection and respect he commanded among the young faithful of the party. He died of a heart attack in Stockwell Hospital, London, on 14 September 1977. He was unmarried.   T. E. B. HOWARTH, *rev.*

Sources *The Times* (26 Sept 1977) · *Morning Star* (16 Sept 1977) · A. Boyle, *The climate of treason: five who spied for Russia* (1979) · *CGPLA Eng. & Wales* (1977)
Archives SOUND IWM SA, oral history interviews
Likenesses photograph, People's History Museum, Manchester [*see illus.*]
Wealth at death £20,492: probate, 7 Dec 1977, *CGPLA Eng. & Wales*

Klumpke, Dorothea (1861–1942). *See under* Roberts, Isaac (1829–1904).

Klux, Sir Hartung von [Sir Hartung van Clux] (*d.* **1445**), diplomat and soldier, was from central Europe, but there is uncertainty about his precise origins (whether a Dane or a German); his family seems to have been settled at Gröditz, near Bautzen, and von Klux described himself (1413) as a knight from Tzschocha in Silesia. He was in England by November 1399, a month after the accession of Henry IV, whom he may have met when Henry was crusading in eastern Europe (1390–93). He was a king's esquire by 4 November, when Henry granted him an annuity of £40 for life; a further annual grant of 40 marks for life on 3 December 1400 was to support his new dignity of king's knight, conferred during the Scottish campaign. By this stage, he seems to have been a member of Henry IV's household. He served against the Welsh rebels, and on 13 November 1409 was granted a life annuity of £50 drawn on the alien priory of Pembroke (replacing the grant of 1399). Henry V and Henry VI confirmed these rewards, and von Klux enjoyed them until his death; Henry V even added, in 1413, £20 per annum from the alien priory of Llangennydd, in Gower, in recognition of his loyal service.

Von Klux's years in England made him bilingual, and his loyalty to Emperor Sigismund (*d.* 1437) qualified him as an envoy between 1411 and 1444, at a time when the great schism and church councils, and the Anglo-French and Hussite wars, gave England's relations with Germany, Hungary, Poland, and Bohemia great importance. With the encouragement of Prince Henry, Henry IV sent him to Sigismund's court in 1411 to conclude an alliance and commercial agreement, and to intervene on behalf of the Teutonic knights; when the master of their order came to England in 1415, von Klux escorted him to the king. Henry V again dispatched him in July 1414 to negotiate a German alliance which (von Klux reported) Sigismund favoured. During the following eight years his 'prudence and circumspection' (Rymer, *Foedera*, 2nd edn, 4/2.183–4) made him a regular figure in Henry's plans to secure allies on France's eastern border among German princes and the Hanse, as well as with the Genoese and the king of Aragon. Diplomacy was interspersed with military service in Henry V's expeditions to France between 1415 and 1417. He was rewarded with captured Norman estates north of Caen in May 1418—Creully, Courseulles, Villers, and Domfront. Sigismund also valued him as an adviser and diplomat in the years 1411–37, and in 1419–20 von Klux mediated between the Teutonic knights and the Polish king on behalf of both Sigismund and Henry V. On returning to England in 1421 he was elected knight of the Garter (3 May), but soon afterwards returned to Sigismund's court until Henry V's death brought him back to attend his patron's funeral in 1422. After Henry's death he spent fifteen years in Sigismund's service, partly advancing Anglo-German discussions, including arrangements for Cardinal Beaufort's crusade against the Hussites (1427–9). Sigismund sent him on missions to Poland (1424), the Council of Basel (1433), Austria (1436), and elsewhere, and he was present at the siege of unreconciled Hussites at Tabor (1438). Sigismund's successors, Albrecht II and Friedrich III, retained him as a counsellor, and in May 1440 Henry VI engaged the 'noble and faithful' von Klux as envoy to renew treaties with Emperor Friedrich and with Bohemian lords who had captured the English heretic, Peter Payne (Williams, 1.13). His last visit to England, in 1444, was on behalf of Friedrich, who was anxious to be elected a Garter knight. Von Klux was dead by 12 May 1445, when his own stall at Windsor was declared vacant. He was buried, a 'noble warrior' (Stow, 1.243), in St Michael Paternoster Royal, London, a popular burial place with prominent Londoners.   R. A. GRIFFITHS

Sources PRO · *Chancery records* · Rymer, *Foedera*, 2nd edn, vols. 4–5 · *Deutsche Reichstagsakten unter Kaiser Sigmund*, 2–5, ed. G. Kerler and others (Gotha, 1883–98) · F. B. Fahlbusch, 'Hartung von Klux', *Studia Luxemburgensia: Festschrift Heinz Stoob*, ed. F. B. Fahlbusch and P. Johanek (1989), 353–403 · J. Anstis, ed., *The register of the most noble order of the Garter*, 1 (1724) · P. Chaplais, *English medieval diplomatic practice*, 1, PRO (1982) · J. H. Wylie, *History of England under Henry the Fourth*, 4 vols. (1884–98) · J. H. Wylie and W. T. Waugh, eds., *The reign of Henry the Fifth*, 3 vols. (1914–29) · *Memorials of the reign of Henry VI: official correspondence of Thomas Bekynton, secretary to King Henry VI and bishop of Bath and Wells*, ed. G. Williams, 2 vols., Rolls Series, 56 (1872) · J. Stow, *A survay of London*, rev. edn (1603); repr. with introduction by C. L. Kingsford as *A survey of London*, 2 vols. (1908); repr. with addns (1971) · *Report of the Deputy Keeper of the Public Records*, 41 (1880) [Norman rolls]

Knapp, John Leonard (1767–1845), botanist, was born on 9 May 1767 at Shenley, Buckinghamshire, the youngest son of the Revd Primatt Knapp, rector of Shenley, and Keturah, third daughter of Nathaniel French of Antigua. After attending school at Thame in Oxfordshire he went at an early age into the navy. He was present at an engagement with John Paul Jones (1747–1792) the pirate, and sailed under Captain Philip Carteret (*d.* 1796), but ill health caused him to leave the navy while he was still young. He had joined the Herefordshire militia by September 1792 (when he became a lieutenant) and was present with that regiment during the riots at Bristol Bridge in September 1793. In 1795 he became a captain in the Northamptonshire militia, but resigned later that year. Until about 1805 he lived mainly at Powick, near Worcester.

From an early age Knapp took an interest in natural history. Later, for a number of years he took long summer botanical excursions. On one of these he visited Scotland with George Don and collected several of the rarest species of British grasses. He published *The Gramina Britannica* in 1804 using many of the specimens from his botanical tour of Scotland; it contained 119 coloured plates of grasses drawn by Knapp. Unfortunately a fire at the printing works of T. Bensley at Bolt Court destroyed all of the impressions except for a hundred copies that were with the binder. It was reprinted by Mr Strong of Bristol in 1842 with little alteration of the original text and no addition of species.

In October 1804 at Walcot, Bath, Knapp married Lydia Frances (1772/3–1838), youngest daughter of Arthur Freeman, a plantation owner in Antigua. They had seven children, of whom three lived to survive Knapp. In 1805 he went to live at Llan-ffwyst, near Abergavenny, Monmouthshire, and from there during the spring of 1813 he made his last move, to Alveston near Bristol, Gloucestershire, where he owned some farmland.

In 1818 Knapp published anonymously a poem, *Arthur, or, The Pastor of the Village*, also printed by Bensley. Between 1820 and 1830 he wrote a series of articles for the *Time's Telescope* under the title of 'The naturalist's diary'. These formed the germ of his most successful work, also anonymous, *The Journal of a Naturalist* (1829), which reached a fourth edition. The book is an account of the natural history, country life, and agriculture along the escarpment from Alveston to Thornbury in Gloucestershire and was inspired by Gilbert White's *Natural History of Selborne* (1789).

Knapp's last years were spent at Alveston where he was a churchwarden. His time was now spent almost entirely in the pursuit of natural history and the cultivation of his garden, even up to the day before his death, at his home, Old Alveston House, on 29 April 1845. He was buried six days later at the old St Helen's Church, Ridgeway, Alveston (now disused). Knapp was a fellow of the Linnean Society (from 1796) and a fellow of the Society of Antiquaries. He was elected an honorary member of the Bristol Philosophical and Literary Society in 1824. J. W. White described Knapp as 'a charming botanist and traveller through the inexhaustible regions of nature' (White, 85). The genus of grasses previously named *Milbora* by Adanson was called *Knappia* by Smith.   ROGER F. VAUGHAN

Sources *GM*, 2nd ser., 23 (1845), 653 · *Annals and Magazine of Natural History*, 16 (1845), 419–20 · H. J. Riddelsdell and others, eds., *Flora of Gloucestershire* (privately printed, Cheltenham, 1948), cxvii–cxviii · J. W. White, *The flora of Bristol* (1912), 85–6 · burial records for St Helen's Church, Alveston, Bristol RO, FYSH FCP/ALV/R/4(9) · P. J. M. Nethercott, 'J. L. Knapp's *Gramina Britannica*', *Proceedings of the Bristol Naturalists' Society*, 36 (1976), 113–17 · *Gloucestershire Notes and Queries*, 1 (1881), 374 · Alveston Women's Institute, *Alveston our village within living memory*, ed. C. Cunningham (privately printed, 1959) [Bristol RO] · probate will, Bucks. RLSS, D/KN 13 · *Proceedings of the Linnean Society of London*, 1 (1838–48), 244–5 · *The Athenaeum* (10 May 1845), 463 · G. S. Boulger, 'Nature's famous disciples. John Leonard Knapp', *Life-lore*, 1 (May 1889), 257
Archives BM, drawings of fungi · Bristol City Museum and Art Gallery, herbarium of British grasses · Bucks. RLSS, notebooks and papers · NHM, plant collections · Edinburgh, plant collections | Linn. Soc., letters to Sir James Smith

Likenesses Parker, wax bust, RBG Kew · portrait, Hunt Library, Kew

Knapp, William (1698–1768), composer, was born at Wareham, Dorset. A glover and property owner, he became one of the burgesses of Poole, and was parish clerk at St James's, Poole, for thirty-nine years. Knapp was apparently a 'difficult personality' (*New Grove*), and trained the choirs of several Dorset churches. He published two popular collections of church music, *A Sett of New Psalm Tunes and Anthems* (1738; 8th edn, 1770) and *New Church Melody* (1753; 5th edn, 1764). Both works contained music from earlier collections, as well as original compositions by Knapp. One of his psalm tunes, 'Wareham', appeared in both volumes: it continued in use throughout the twentieth century. Knapp's tunes and anthems were widely collected in Britain and the American colonies, and reveal his 'undoubted flair for effective melody' (*New Grove*). Knapp died in Poole and was buried there on 26 September 1768.

J. C. HADDEN, *rev.* K. D. REYNOLDS

Sources N. Temperley, 'Knapp, William', *New Grove* · 'Knapp, William', Grove, *Dict. mus.* (1927) · J. Hutchins, *The history and antiquities of the county of Dorset*, 3rd edn, ed. W. Shipp and J. W. Hodson, 4 vols. (1861–74)

Knapton, Charles (*d.* 1742). *See under* Knapton, George (1698–1778).

Knapton, George (1698–1778), painter and art connoisseur, was born in London, the son or nephew of the bookseller and publisher James Knapton (*d.* 1736). Between 1715 and 1722 he studied under Jonathan Richardson the elder, whose writings on art were published by James Knapton, and in 1720 he was a subscriber to the St Martin's Lane Academy in London. In 1723, with Arthur Pond, he became a founder member of the Roman Club. Two years later they went to Rome, where they engaged in the business of sending back to England plaster casts from the antique. Pond returned to England in 1727 but Knapton stayed seven years in Italy. In a letter to his brother Charles Knapton [*see below*] he described the new excavations at Herculaneum (and his account was later published by the Royal Society, in 1740), and he visited Venice before returning home in 1732. While in Italy he would have met many British travellers, among them Sir Francis Dashwood (second baronet) and Lord Middlesex (later second duke of Dorset) who became the principal movers of the Society of Dilettanti in London. At the first meeting of the society in 1736 Knapton was made its painter, thereby becoming the only dilettante not distinguished by rank or wealth.

Italy had 'opend the eyes of his understanding' and 'finding he coud not make any extraordinary matter' of painting in oil (Vertue, *Note books*, 3.62, 109), Knapton, together with Pond and William Hoare, turned to pastel. They had doubtless been inspired in Venice by the pastels of Rosalba Carriera, whose influence is much apparent in Knapton's surviving pastels at Chatsworth, Derbyshire. By 1736 he had drawn the young Horace Walpole (work untraced). In 1741 Francis Cotes became his pupil and by the end of the decade he had received several commissions from Frederick, prince of Wales, for pastels of his children, sometimes emblematically portrayed according to the prince's 'directions & commands' (Millar, 1.189); three examples remain in the Royal Collection at Windsor and Buckingham Palace. Knapton may also have been involved, with his brother Charles, Pond, and Gravelot, in finding and copying older portraits to be engraved by Jacobus Houbraken in Amsterdam and published by Knapton's kinsmen, the brothers John and Paul Knapton, between 1743 and 1752 as illustrations for Thomas Birch's *Lives and Characters of Eighty Illustrious Persons of Great Britain*.

Knapton meanwhile had maintained his ambition to practise in oils. In 1741 the Society of Dilettanti decreed that members should each sit to him in fancy dress and by 1749 he had painted twenty-one competent but curiously irreverent half-lengths (Society of Dilettanti, London). In 1743 Vertue placed him 'in the first class' of painters (Vertue, *Note books*, 3.117) and the following year Walpole found him painting Lady Carteret (work untraced) 'with corn like the Goddess of Plenty, and a mild dove in her arms like Mrs Venus' (Walpole, *Corr.*, 18.467). Most of his surviving portraits in oil date between 1741 and 1751. They include *The 3rd Earl of Burlington* (1743, Chatsworth, Derbyshire), *John Spencer and his Son* (1745, Althorp, Northamptonshire), the attractive *Lucy Ebberton* (c.1750, Dulwich Picture Gallery, London; engraved by J. McArdell), and the very large *Family of Frederick, Prince of Wales* (1751, Marlborough House, London). In 1750 Vertue commented on Knapton's 'great improvement in oyl paintings' (Vertue, *Note books*, 3.154), mentioning with particular approval a large group (untraced) of the duke of Bedford and his family. Two full-size copies by Knapton after Van Dyck remain at Woburn Abbey, Bedfordshire. Further portraits are known only through engravings, the earliest dated plates being those of the Italian singers John Carestini (1735) and Lisabetta Du Parc (1737), and the last Sir George Vandeput (1750).

By 1750 Knapton was also recognized as 'the most skillfull judge or Connoiesseur of Pictures' (Vertue, *Note books*, 3.154). In 1746 he had made an inventory of the pictures at Althorp for Lord Spencer and in 1750 the prince of Wales asked him, together with George Vertue, to inspect the pictures in the Royal Collection. In May 1765, on the death of Stephen Slaughter, Knapton succeeded as surveyor and keeper of the king's pictures. Connoisseurship had replaced painting; his last dated painting is from 1755 (*Dr Samuel Wathen and his Family*, City of Birmingham Museum and Art Gallery) and he resigned as painter to the Dilettanti in 1763.

Knapton died, apparently unmarried, in 1778; Walpole thought he was dying in January, but he lived on until December, when he was buried in Kensington. Throughout his life he had maintained a professional dignity, according to the ideals of his master Richardson, as both gentleman painter and connoisseur. His technical ability as an artist was not outstanding, but his success was always facilitated by social connection. In 1732 Vertue had

suggested that his association with the Knapton publishing house brought him both 'acquaintance & employment' (Vertue, *Note books*, 3.62) and in 1736 membership of the Dilettanti considerably enlarged his circle. He was much favoured by Lord Spencer and the dukes of Bedford and Devonshire before finally attracting royal patronage.

George Knapton's brother **Charles Knapton** (d. 1742) was a landscape painter and engraver whose work was closely associated with the Knapton publishing business. He copied portraits (see above) and old master drawings (particularly those of Guercino), assisting Arthur Pond in preparing *Prints in Imitation of Drawings*, published in 1735–6. With his wife, Elizabeth, whom he had married before 1728, he marketed a series of caricature heads etched by Pond and engravings of Italian landscapes chosen by Pond. After his death in the autumn of 1742 his wife became the mistress and business associate of Pond (d. 1758), whom she survived.   JOHN INGAMELLS

Sources Vertue, *Note books*, 3.12–14, 62, 109, 117, 154; 6.170, 192 · L. Lippincott, *Selling art in Georgian London* (1983), 14 ff. · J. Ingamells, ed., *A dictionary of British and Irish travellers in Italy, 1701–1800* (1997), 580–81 · H. Walpole, *Anecdotes of painting in England ... collected by the late George Vertue, and now digested and published*, 4th edn, 4 (1786), 127 · L. Cust and S. Colvin, eds., *History of the Society of Dilettanti* (1898), 8, 64, 77, 216–19 · Walpole, *Corr.*, 18.467; 23.342 · K. J. Garlick, 'A catalogue of paintings at Althorp', *Walpole Society*, 45 (1974–6), esp. 42–3, 94–105 [whole issue] · O. Millar, *The Tudor, Stuart and early Georgian pictures in the collection of her majesty the queen*, 2 vols. (1963), vol. 1, pp. 30, 189–90 · J. C. Smith, *British mezzotinto portraits*, 1 (1878), 321, 342; 2 (1879), 845, 857, 873 · G. Scharf, *Catalogue of the collection of pictures at Woburn Abbey* (1890), 148, 171, 267 · H. M. Hake, 'Pond and Knapton's imitations of drawings', *Print Collector's Quarterly*, 9 (1922), 324–49 · L. Lippincott, 'Arthur Pond's journal ... 1734–1750', *Walpole Society*, 54 (1988), 220–333

Likenesses J. Reynolds, group portrait, oils, c.1777–1779 (*The Society of Dilettanti*), Brooks's Club, London, Society of Dilettanti

Knapton, John (*bap.* 1696, *d.* 1767×70), bookseller, was baptized at St Faith's under St Paul's, London, on 23 April 1696, the third of twelve children of James Knapton (d. 1736) and his wife, Hester. His father opened his first bookshop at the Queen's Head in St Paul's Churchyard in 1688, moving it two years later to the nearby Crown, and became a leading London bookseller. John's younger brother **Paul Knapton** (*bap.* 1703, *d.* 1755), the Knaptons' eighth child, was baptized in the same parish as his brother on 20 January 1703.

John served his apprenticeship with his father during 1712–19; Paul, however, was apprenticed to the bookseller Arthur Bettesworth between 1721 and 1728 where his term overlapped with that of Charles Hitch, who would later collaborate with the brothers in publishing ventures. John's name appeared on title-pages with his father's from 1722, most notably in the publication of the successful multi-volume translation of Paul de Rapin, *History of England* (1728–33); his brother's name first appears on a joint imprint in 1730. On 3 January 1735 the Knaptons opened new premises at the Crown in Ludgate Street, London; eighteen months later, on 21 November 1736, James Knapton died, leaving his two sons to carry on the business. Paul married Elizabeth Chalwell (d. in or after 1765) in Stevenage on 14 February 1741 but had no children; he probably played only a small role in the day-to-day running of the shop. Like his father before him, John served as master of the Stationers' Company, holding the office three times between 1742 and 1745.

The Knapton family had had an association with Alexander Pope since at least 1725, when James Knapton had subscribed to Pope's six-volume edition of Shakespeare's works. In 1737 John Knapton co-published the authorized text of Pope's letters, his first direct venture with the poet; in the same year he mediated in Pope's dispute with the printer James Watson. Pope was evidently pleased with Knapton's handling of his publishing affairs as in 1741 he recommended William Warburton to Knapton, initiating an alliance which would result in Warburton's successful edition of Pope's *Works* a decade later. A cousin of the Knapton brothers, George Knapton, who studied under Pope's friend Jonathan Richardson, made an oil painting of Pope after Sir Godfrey Kneller. Another cousin and artist, Charles Knapton, collaborated with Arthur Pond on the *Essay on Man* medallion. The Knaptons thus played an integral part not only in publishing Pope's works but also in perpetuating his visual image.

As substantial copyright owners, the Knaptons joined the long struggle by the London book trade to protect literary property. In 1744 John Knapton and Andrew Millar made an unsuccessful attempt in the Edinburgh court of session to control the Scottish reprints of London editions; and three years later the Knaptons published Warburton's *Letter to a Member of Parliament Concerning Literary Property*. However, John Knapton seems to have become pragmatic over this issue; he was instrumental in persuading Warburton to drop a court action against the Glasgow printer Robert Foulis over a Scottish edition of Pope's *Letters*.

As part of the group of booksellers who agreed to publish Samuel Johnson's *Dictionary* in 1746, the names of the Knaptons appear on the imprint to the first edition some nine years later. However, Paul Knapton died in the same year, on 12 June 1755, and within days John was facing bankruptcy from debts that had been building since the early 1750s. Most of Knapton's stock and copyrights were auctioned off at the Queen's Head tavern on 25 September 1755, two days after the administration of Paul's estate was granted to his widow, Elizabeth. The sale of copyrights alone realized more than £4600, enough to pay off the two largest creditors, William Bowyer (the Knaptons' long-standing printer) and Warburton. Andrew Millar acquired the Knapton share in Pope's *Works*, much to the disappointment of the bookseller Robert Dodsley, who had fallen out of favour with Warburton. Knapton's debts were fully paid off within three years, but in 1761 he auctioned off more of his stock and continued in a limited capacity to publish new authors like William Mason and the occasional play such as *Hamlet* and *The Alchemist*.

From about 1757 Knapton had lived at Marsh-gate (now Sheen Road), Richmond, Surrey, and after his retirement continued to live in Richmond, where he drew up his will on 24 September 1765. He died at some point between 23 June 1767, when he added a codicil and was still a resident of Richmond, and 6 October 1770 when the will was proved, leaving £4000 in trust and almost £2500 in bequests. A lifelong bachelor, he had no direct heirs and the business was continued by Robert Horsfield.

DONALD W. NICHOL

Sources *Pope's literary legacy: the book-trade correspondence of William Warburton and John Knapton*, ed. D. W. Nichol (1992) · DNB · ESTC · M. Mack, *Collected in himself* (1982) · administration, PRO, PROB 6/131, fol. 203r [Paul Knapton] · will, PRO, PROB 11/961, sig. 367 · D. W. Nichol, 'J. J. and P. Knapton', *The British literary book trade, 1700–1820*, ed. J. K. Bracken and J. Silver, DLitB, 154 (1995), 170–75 · GM, 1st ser., 6 (1736), 685
Archives BL, Egerton MSS 1954, 1959
Wealth at death £4000 in trusts; approx. £2500 in bequests: will, PRO, PROB 11/961, sig. 367

Knapton, Paul (*bap.* 1703, *d.* 1755). *See under* Knapton, John (*bap.* 1696, *d.* 1767x70).

Knapton, Philip (1788–1833), composer and music publisher, was born in York on 20 October 1788, the son of Samuel Knapton, a music publisher and instrument maker who took over Thomas Haxby's business in York about 1796. He received his musical education at Cambridge, under Charles Hague, but did not graduate from the university. After returning to York, he joined his father's business about 1820, and remained in the city until his death. He was active in local musical life, and served as one of the assistant conductors at the York festivals of 1823, 1825, and 1828.

Knapton composed several overtures, piano concertos, and other orchestral works, and arranged a number of fantasias on popular airs for piano and harp. His piano arrangement of Lady Nairne's song 'Caller Herrin' and his music for the song 'There be none of Beauty's Daughter' (*c.*1818) enjoyed considerable popularity. He also produced a *Collection of tunes for psalms and hymns, selected as a supplement to those now used … in York* (1810). The publishing business was taken over in 1829 by William Hardman and later by Henry Banks; it was still in existence as Banks & Son in the late twentieth century. Knapton died in York on 20 June 1833.

R. F. SHARP, *rev.* DAVID J. GOLBY

Sources P. W. Jones, 'Knapton, Philip', *New Grove* · C. Humphries and W. C. Smith, *Music publishing in the British Isles, from the beginning until the middle of the nineteenth century: a dictionary of engravers, printers, publishers, and music sellers*, 2nd edn (1970)
Likenesses attrib. A. Mayer, oils, York City Art Gallery

Knapwell [Clapwell], **Richard** (*fl.* 1284–1286), Dominican friar and theologian, is of unknown origins. He is known almost exclusively for his role in the bitter conflict over some of the teachings of Thomas Aquinas that followed the latter's death in 1277. The opposition to Aquinas was led chiefly by Franciscans, who officially adopted the Parisian master William de la Mare as their anti-Thomist spokesman. The Dominicans formally rallied round Aquinas. One of the most contentious issues was Aquinas's espousal of the Aristotelian doctrine that the soul is the form of the body, and his consequent denial that the body, as such, owes its identity to any other form. In the eyes of his critics, this principle of unicity of form made it impossible to identify the body that hung dead on the cross as the body of Christ, which would have dangerous implications for Christian doctrine.

When the Dominican archbishop of Canterbury, Robert Kilwardby (d. 1279), condemned some Thomistic propositions, including unicity of form, in 1277, his English brethren scandalized their order by their failure to defend Thomas. Yet by 1284 the Oxford priory had produced three substantial retorts to de la Mare, including the *Correctorium quare*, the most substantial of them all; Knapwell has been shown to be the author of this *correctorium*, on the basis of other writings securely attributed to him. His authorship of another pro-Thomist work, an *impugnatio* against Giles of Rome, has also been plausibly suggested. It is not known when he went to Oxford, but his lectures on the *Sentences* have been dated between 1269 and 1277, and he incepted as a DD in 1284.

It looks as if the appointment of the Franciscan John Pecham (d. 1292) as archbishop of Canterbury in 1279 generated a partisan reaction among the Dominicans; Pecham was not only a leader of theological opposition to Aquinas, he also adopted a generally polemical stance towards the Dominicans, exemplified in his attack on that order in *Contra Kilwardby*. Knapwell admits he had once been convinced by the arguments against unicity of form, and in the *Notabilia* on the *Sentences*, from his time as bachelor of the *Sentences* in Oxford, he is clearly struggling to combine some of Aquinas's teaching with traditional Augustinianism. But by 1284 he was a fearless, if not always intelligent, champion of Aquinas and of unicity of form in particular. 1284 was an alarming year for the Oxford Dominicans: it was known that Pecham was planning to visit Oxford and the Dominicans several times wrote to their provincial, William of Hotham (d. 1298), expressing their fear that Pecham was planning something dreadful against them. After repeated delays Pecham finally arrived in October, and he renewed the condemnations of 1277, making particularly clear his detestation of the doctrine of unicity of form. The university was unwilling to co-operate and the Dominicans did their best to undermine Pecham's position.

Pecham tried to involve the pope, Martin IV (r. 1281–5), who had earlier been active, as legate in Paris, in Bishop Tempier's moves against Aquinas from 1270 onwards, but Martin died without doing anything. Knapwell, in defiance of Pecham, held a disputation on unicity of form, in which he tried to defuse opposition to the doctrine. Pecham was furious, and his temper was not improved by an anonymous pamphlet, possibly by Knapwell, in which the archbishop was himself advised to observe the *unica forma* of silence. In 1286 he drafted an explicit condemnation of Knapwell, but Hotham indicated that he was going to appeal to the pope against such an infringement of his order's privileges, so Pecham made do with a vaguer condemnation, in which Knapwell was not named. What happened after that is not clear. Godefroi de Fontaines mentions a conversation he had in Paris in 1286 with someone he calls Valens, who may be Knapwell. According to the annals of Dunstable, Knapwell appealed to the pope in person, only to have perpetual silence imposed on him by

Nicholas IV (r. 1288–92), after which he went to Bologna, continued to propagate his 'heretical' doctrines, and finally went mad, tore his eyes out, and died wretchedly. The Dunstable annalist did not like Dominicans, and Pecham had already referred to the unnamed 'inventors' of unicity of form as perishing miserably in Italy (presumably a generalization based on the fate of the contemporary Paris theologian Siger of Brabant); probably no more credence should be given to the Dunstable story than to the discreditable tales about Pecham that were current in Dominican circles by the mid-1290s.

SIMON TUGWELL

Sources M. D. Chenu, 'La première diffusion du Thomisme à Oxford: Knapwell et ses *Notes* sur les "*Sentences*"', *Archives d'Histoire Doctrinale et Littéraire du Moyen Âge*, 3 (1928), 185–200 · [R. Knapwell], *Le 'Correctorium corruptorii quare'*, ed. P. Glorieux (Paris, 1927) · *Richard Knapwell. 'Quaestio disputata de unitate formae'*, ed. F. E. Kelley (1982) · *Registrum epistolarum fratris Johannis Peckham, archiepiscopi Cantuariensis*, ed. C. T. Martin, 3, Rolls Series, 77 (1885), 840–43, 852–3, 862–72, 896–902, 921–3 · *Ann. mon.*, 3.323–5; 4.297–9, 306–7 · A. G. Little and F. Pelster, *Oxford theology and theologians*, OHS, 96 (1934), 89–91 · T. Kaeppeli, *Scriptores ordinis praedicatorum medii aevi*, 3 (Rome, 1980), 306–7 · E. Panella, *Scriptores ordinis praedicatorum medii aevi*, 4 (Rome, 1993), 262 · Thomas von Sutton, *Quaestiones ordinariae*, ed. J. Schneider (Munich, 1977), *66–7, *85–9 · Emden, *Oxf.*, 2.1058 · D. L. Douie, *Archbishop Pecham* (1952), 280–99 · S. Tugwell, *Albert and Thomas* (1988), 238–42 · W. A. Hinnebusch, *The early English Friars Preachers* (1951), 348–56 · F. Pelster, 'Die Sätze der Londoner Verurteilung von 1286 und die Schriften des Magister Richard von Knapwell O.P.', *Archivum Fratrum Praedicatorum*, 16 (1946), 83–106 · F. Pelster, 'Richard von Knapwell O.P. Seine *Quaestiones disputatae* und sein *Quodlibet*', *Zeitschrift für Katholische Theologie*, 52 (1928), 473–91 · M. de Wulf and A. Pelzer, eds., *Les quatre premiers quodlibets de Godefroid de Fontaines* (1904), 198

Knaresborough, Robert of. *See* Robert of Knaresborough (d. 1218?).

Knatchbull, Sir Edward, fourth baronet (c.1674–1730), politician, was born about 1674, the first son of Sir Thomas Knatchbull, third baronet (d. 1712/13), of Mersham Hatch, Kent, and his wife, Mary (1654–1724?), the daughter of Sir Edward *Dering, second baronet, of Surrenden Dering, Kent. His father was a younger son who inherited his elder brother's baronetcy in 1696, thereby transforming his own son's prospects. Before this Edward seemed set for a diplomatic career, as in March 1694 he received a pass to travel to Hamburg, no doubt to facilitate his employment as secretary to the envoy to Brunswick-Luneburg, James Cresset. Following his return home, as the heir to a baronetcy, he no longer had to seek employment. On 22 December 1698 he made a favourable marriage to Alice (bap. 1676, d. 1723), the daughter of John Wyndham of Norrington, Wiltshire, and the sister of Thomas, Lord Wyndham, lord chancellor of Ireland from 1726 to 1739, receiving thereby a portion of £6000.

His father's connection to the Finches (he had served as secretary to Lord Chancellor Heneage Finch) stood Knatchbull in good stead when the opportunity arose to enter parliament for Rochester in 1702. Although a tory, he seems to have gravitated towards the more moderate toryism espoused by Robert Harley rather than the more rigid variety propounded by the Finches. Thus he was named muster-master of the marines in February 1704 (a post formerly held by his father). He opposed the tack of the Occasional Conformity Bill to the Land Tax Bill in November 1704, but was defeated at Rochester in the election the following year. He remained out of the Commons until 1713. His father handed Mersham over to him in 1706 and Knatchbull busied himself with local office. Indeed, his lower political profile perhaps helped him to retain his office as muster-master until 1709.

Despite Harley's leading role in the new ministry of 1710, no post was found for Knatchbull. However, his father's death (between July 1712 and September 1713) allowed him to take advantage of the family's prestige within the county to become knight of the shire at the 1713 election. In the 1714 session (during which Knatchbull kept a diary) he was regarded as important enough in the Commons to be called to meetings at which the leaders of the tory ministry sought to improve their parliamentary management. He moved the resolution in the committee of the whole house on 15 April that the protestant succession was not in danger and he played an important role in the passage of the Schism Bill. Although courted by Viscount Bolingbroke, he probably did not abandon Lord Oxford during the power struggle of the summer of 1714. Knatchbull was defeated at the 1715 election, but was elected for Kent in 1722. His diary for this parliament provides a wealth of information on debates. His own conduct evinced a moderate toryism which gradually shaded into support for Sir Robert Walpole and ended with his voting against his party on the address in the last session. He later voted against a motion attacking Walpole personally. As a consequence he found a sharp diminution of his support in Kent and eventually had to stand down in his native shire, but he was able to return to the Commons for the Cornish borough of Lostwithiel in a by-election in 1728 after securing government support. Thereafter he consistently supported the whig ministry, except for one vote on a place matter.

Knatchbull died on 3 April 1730 at his London house in Golden Square of a fever occasioned by a long sitting a few days earlier on the inquiry in Dunkirk. His will directed that he be buried with his ancestors in the family vault in Mersham church. He was survived by four sons and two daughters, one son and one daughter having predeceased him.   STUART HANDLEY

Sources R. R. Sedgwick, 'Knatchbull, Sir Edward', HoP, *Commons* · *The parliamentary diary of Sir Edward Knatchbull, 1722–1730*, ed. A. N. Newman, CS, 3rd ser., 94 (1963), 211–18 · A. N. Newman, ed., 'Proceedings in the House of Commons, March–June 1714', *BIHR*, 34 (1961), 211–17 · H. M. Knatchbull-Hugessen, *Kentish family* (1960) · will, PRO, PROB 11/637, sig. 100 · *Manuscripts of the earl of Egmont: diary of Viscount Percival, afterwards first earl of Egmont*, 3 vols., HMC, 63 (1920–23), vol. 1, pp. 90–91 · D. B. Horn, ed., *British diplomatic representatives, 1689–1789*, CS, 3rd ser., 46 (1932), 49 · Cobbett, *Parl. hist.*, 6.1346 · A. Boyer, *The political state of Great Britain*, 39 (1730) · *The diaries and papers of Sir Edward Dering, second baronet, 1644 to 1684*, ed. M. F. Bond (1976), 112, pedigree · *IGI*
Archives CKS, corresp., notebook, and diary
Likenesses M. Dahl, portrait, repro. in Knatchbull-Hugessen, *Kentish family*, following p. 96

Knatchbull, Sir Edward, ninth baronet (1781–1849), politician, eldest son of Sir Edward Knatchbull of Mersham Hatch, Kent, eighth baronet, and Mary, daughter and coheir of William Westom Hugessen of Provender in the same county, was born on 20 December 1781. He was educated at Winchester College 1794–9, matriculated from Christ Church, Oxford, in 1800, and enrolled at Lincoln's Inn in 1803. He was receiver-general for Kent 1814–19, resigning, following his father's death and his succession to the baronetcy on 21 September 1819, so as to occupy his father's seat as member for Kent. He held the seat from November 1819 until 1830, when he did not stand for re-election. He was a strong opponent of corn-law reform and of Catholic emancipation, on 12 February 1829 stinging Peel to ill temper in the Commons by his taunts of inconsistency on the Catholic question. He became a prominent figure among the ultra-tories. His amendment on distress in February 1830 was only defeated by whigs coming to the aid of Wellington's government. In November 1830 Knatchbull and Sir Richard Vyvyan engineered the downfall of Wellington's government by giving the ultra vote in support of Sir Henry Parnell's retrenchment motion. Like other ultras, Knatchbull favoured moderate political reform, especially if it stopped the rick burning caused by the Swing riots in Kent. But, unlike some of his ultra colleagues, he refused Lord Grey's offer of office when the whig government was formed. He subsequently promoted, without success, a resolution in favour of moderate reform if the Reform Bill of 1831 was defeated on second reading (on which Knatchbull paired).

In 1832 Knatchbull was elected for East Kent, representing it until 1845, when he retired. Much though he distrusted Peel, he was his paymaster-general, in the cabinet, in 1834 and again in 1841. His opposition in cabinet to the 1842 budget was unsuccessful and he had little enthusiasm for the political direction of Peel's government. The death of his favourite child, Fanny Elizabeth, in February 1845 confirmed a decision to retire adumbrated earlier; he resigned office on 15 February.

Knatchbull's domestic life was no happier than his political. He married, on 25 August 1806, Annabella Christiana, daughter of Sir John Honywood, bt. She died on 4 April 1814 after bearing at least four sons and a daughter, Mary. He married, secondly, on 24 October 1820, Fanny Catherine, eldest daughter of Edward Knight of Godmersham Park, Kent. They had four sons and at least one daughter. Three of his sons from his first marriage died young, his daughter Mary eloped, and he disinherited his eldest son, Norton Joseph, because of the extravagant behaviour of his wife, Mary. He altered his will in favour of Edward Knatchbull [see Hugessen, Edward, first Baron Brabourne], his eldest son from his second marriage, with the proviso that he take the name Hugessen on inheriting, which he did.

Knatchbull was neither as ultra-protestant nor as protectionist as his record suggests. He had a knack of muddling into political crises and finding himself leader of a following he did not wholeheartedly represent. He died on 24 May 1849.   H. C. G. MATTHEW

Sources H. Knatchbull-Hugessen, *Kentish family* (1960) • N. Gash, *Sir Robert Peel: the life of Sir Robert Peel after 1830* (1972) • M. Brock, *The Great Reform Act* (1973) • *GM*, 2nd ser., 32 (1849), 89
Archives CKS, corresp., journal, and papers | BL, corresp. with Sir Robert Peel, Add. MSS 40308–40557 • Cornwall RO, Vyvyan MSS • U. Southampton L., letters to first duke of Wellington
Likenesses J. S. Copley, pencil and chalk study, 1800–02, University of Nebraska Art Galleries, Lincoln • J. S. Copley, double portrait, oils (with his brother), County Hall, Maidstone, Kent • G. Hayter, group portrait, oils (*The House of Commons, 1833*), NPG • T. Phillips, oils, County Hall, Maidstone, Kent

Knatchbull, Elizabeth [*name in religion* Lucy] (1584–1629), abbess of the Convent of the Immaculate Conception, Ghent, was the daughter of Reginald Knatchbull of Saltwood Castle and his wife, Ann Elizabeth Crispe, of Kent. She entered the English Benedictine convent in Brussels in 1604 and was professed in January 1611, taking the name in religion Lucy. She was described as having a very attractive appearance, with a gentle nature and sense of humour, bringing pleasure to those with whom she lived. In her writings she confessed that leaving the world had led to agonizing self-examination and she had suffered torments, but ultimately the darkness had gone and she had embraced her noviciate with joy. The soul-searching continued throughout the rest of her life, with recurring dark periods where she saw herself beset by devils. In the depths of her despair she said that she was redeemed by a sense of God's love, which ultimately brought her peace.

Lucy Knatchbull was the centre of the group of sisters who wished to have Jesuit confessors, her resolution perhaps being strengthened by the arrival in Brussels of John, her eldest brother, who had become a Jesuit. Lucy Knatchbull approached the archbishop of Malines, the convent's visitor, explaining that the convent was overcrowded and asking permission to leave. In 1624 she led a small and impoverished group of four choir sisters and a lay sister to Ghent where they established a small Benedictine house dedicated to the Immaculate Conception. She was elected abbess and her reputation soon attracted new recruits from England. The new convent established a small school from the beginning, educating both potential postulants and lay girls. The rules of the convent were based on the constitutions of the Brussels foundation and, like Brussels, Ghent observed the rules strictly, the abbess setting the example personally. In her papers after her death were found details of the austerities she practised, including wearing hair girdles and iron chains, and standing in a tub of cold water. By the end of the first year they had twenty-two members and new premises had to be sought. Lucy Knatchbull organized the purchase of land and the construction of a new monastery, paying for it out of the dowries of postulants. The community moved to the new premises on the bank of the Scheldt in 1628.

Much of what we know about Abbess Lucy Knatchbull derives from Toby Matthew, who became her spiritual adviser, kept a few of her papers, and subsequently wrote a biography which remained unpublished until the twentieth century. Although Lucy Knatchbull wrote extensively for the benefit of the nuns in her convent, according to convent records out of humility she insisted that her manuscripts should be burnt after her death, and she published nothing in her lifetime. She wrote spiritual exercises and meditations and she copied out an inspirational work written by the abbess of Elpidia in Saxony for the benefit of the nuns in her care. In his biography Matthew particularly admired Lucy Knatchbull's charity and humility and the way she made a total sacrifice of herself for God. He recognized the favours and privileges she received from God through her visions and mystical experiences, while acknowledging her acceptance of God as the source of such favours rather than her own merit. In her own words:

> I do here from the bottom of my heart, for his greater glory, renounce all manner of mine own Satisfaction; only this I beseech and beg at his merciful hand … that I may serve him truly, humbly, and faithfully, and that my whole Soule may every moment of my Life and in all eternity love him. (Matthew, 49)

She died at the convent on 5 August 1629, after a long and painful illness; the convent annals record that after only five years it had thirty members, including choir nuns, lay sisters, and scholars. CAROLINE M. K. BOWDEN

Sources T. Matthew, *The life of Lady Lucy Knatchbull*, ed. D. Knowles (1931) • *Annals of the English Benedictines at Ghent, now at St Mary's Abbey, Oulton in Staffordshire* (privately printed, [1894]) • P. Guilday, *The English Catholic refugees on the continent, 1558–1795* (1914) • C. Dodd [H. Tootell], *The church history of England, from the year 1500, to the year 1688*, 3 vols. (1737–42) • 'Obituary notices of the nuns of the English Benedictine abbey of Ghent in Flanders, 1627–1811', *Miscellanea, XI*, Catholic RS, 19 (1917), 1–92

Knatchbull, Mary (1610–1696), abbess of the Convent of the Immaculate Conception, Ghent, was the daughter of Reginald Knatchbull the younger of Kent. With her sister Margaret she was among the first novices of the Benedictine Convent of the Immaculate Conception established in Ghent in 1624; their aunt Lucy Knatchbull was first abbess. Before being elected abbess in 1650 Mary Knatchbull filled a number of official positions in the monastery including novice mistress and prioress. The new abbess inherited a serious debt of some £6000 resulting from a building programme undertaken by her predecessors, but also an otherwise flourishing community of eighty members. She established a regime of strict economies to try to resolve the financial problems and arranged the restructuring of the debt, significantly reducing the interest paid. At the same time she led the spiritual life of the convent, instituting a series of measures to improve the practice of the liturgy and spiritual exercises for the sisters.

As well as directing the convent, during the 1650s Mary Knatchbull developed close relations with Charles II's court in exile in Flanders, even providing hospitality for the royal entourage itself. She acted as a regular clearing house for the mail of key royalist advisers, including Edward Hyde, later earl of Clarendon, and the earl of Ormond, particularly in the period 1658–60. The abbess had a wide network of contacts, both religious and secular, who sent her information which she passed on. In addition, she lent Charles substantial sums of money which would otherwise have served the convent. The centrality of the abbess's role in the royalist court in exile in this

Mary Knatchbull (1610–1696), attrib. Samuel van Hoogstraten

period was recognized by contemporaries in that she was approached to act as an intermediary by both male and female petitioners seeking favours from senior royalists. By 1659 she was sufficiently confident in her knowledge of the political situation to offer advice to be passed on to the king about organizing his Restoration using disguised female names for the king and key figures to avoid discovery. Charles called at the convent to say goodbye in May 1660 before leaving for England, repaying only a small part of his debt and promising full repayment once he reached London. The nuns joined in part of the celebrations of Charles's Restoration; however, once he was crowned the promises of recompense turned out to be hollow. Mary Knatchbull herself twice led a deputation to London to try to recover the debt, but she was only partly successful, recovering £1000, about a third of the total, with a promise of more to come.

On her return from London Mary Knatchbull appears to have put all her energies into her role as abbess. She had founded two new houses from Ghent, the first at Boulogne (1653, moving to Pontoise in 1658), the other at Dunkirk (1662), and was to start a third at Ypres (1665), making both practical arrangements and advising on spiritual and pastoral care in the initial stages. Her aristocratic and royal connections facilitated the negotiations, although there were problems with the bishop of Boulogne which necessitated tactful handling before he eventually agreed to her plans. The foundation of Dunkirk was complicated by the sale of the town by Charles II to France, although the convent survived. Ypres, however, intended by the founder to be an Irish house, suffered financial problems.

According to convent annals Mary Knatchbull's golden jubilee in 1678 was celebrated with as much solemnity as their limited means would allow. As she grew older she was much venerated within the order, being described by its chronicler, Abbess Anne Neville, as having great virtue and wisdom and being widely renowned for the eloquence of her pen. Certainly this can be seen in her letters to the royal courtiers, the bishop of Boulogne, and the English royal family, with whom she maintained contact until virtually the end of her life. In addition she wrote an account of the founding of the convent at Boulogne and recorded her advice to the sisters. In it she displayed her understanding of the difficulties involved in establishing a successful new house and the temptations to cut corners regarding the observance of disciplined monastic ritual. She advised them to 'imagine yourselves to become againe novices and together with those you admitt assume for yeare att least the exact practice of the novitiate' ('Foundation of Boulogne', fols. 84–5).

Mary Knatchbull's skills as a financial manager were admired, but she was never able to restore the financial security of the Ghent convent, and the annals note that on her death, on 6 March 1696, the debts were almost greater than when she became abbess. A number of the English convents experienced similar problems towards the end of the seventeenth century as fewer recruits joined and income was reduced, but her generosity to the king and his failure to repay in full undoubtedly contributed to the severity of the problems. However, the annals also emphasize the significance of her spiritual leadership and the success of two out of the three foundations she organized. Most of the documents the abbess left relate to the practical and managerial side of her activities; little remains to illustrate her spirituality apart from the opinions of the sisters. Mary Knatchbull was a remarkable woman who gained respect from contemporaries in two discrete worlds: the cloister and a political world outside the cloister walls.

CAROLINE M. K. BOWDEN

Sources *Annals of the English Benedictines at Ghent, now at St Mary's Abbey, Oulton in Staffordshire* (privately printed, [1894]) · H. Knatchbull-Hugessen, *Kentish family* (1960) · 'Registers of the English Benedictine nuns at Pontoise, now at Teignmouth, 1680', *Miscellanea, X*, Catholic RS, 17 (1915), 248–326 · A. Neville, 'English Benedictine nuns in Flanders, 1598–1687', ed. M. J. Rumsey, *Miscellanea, V*, Catholic RS, 6 (1909), 1–72 · B. Whelan, *Historic English convents of to-day* (1936) · 'The foundation of Boulogne written by my Lady Mary Knatchbull', St Mary's Abbey, Buckfastleigh, Devon
Archives Bodl. Oxf., corresp. · St Mary's Convent, Oulton, Staffordshire · St Mary's Convent, Buckfastleigh, Devon · Westminster Archdiocesan Archives
Likenesses attrib. S. van Hoogstraten, portrait, County Hall, Maidstone, Knatchbull collection [*see illus.*] · oils, priv. coll.

Knatchbull, Sir Norton, first baronet (1602–1685), politician and biblical scholar, was born on 26 December 1602, the eldest surviving son of Thomas Knatchbull (1572–1623) of Maidstone and his wife, Eleanor (1574–1638), daughter of John Astley, master of the revels. He was educated at Eton College from 1615 to 1618, matriculated at Cambridge as a fellow-commoner of St John's College on 20 March 1619, and graduated BA in 1620. In 1624, as his father and uncles had done, he entered the Middle Temple, London. On 22 October 1630 he married Dorothy, daughter of Thomas Westrowe, member of the Grocers' Company and alderman of London. They had thirteen children. His uncle Sir Norton Knatchbull of Mersham Hatch, Kent, sheriff of that county in 1608 and MP for Hythe in 1609, had founded the free school at Ashford. The younger Norton succeeded to the family estate on the death of his uncle in 1636. He confirmed the deed of endowment for the school of £30 per annum and subsequently added to the buildings.

In 1639 Knatchbull was elected member of parliament for New Romney, Kent, and was knighted at Whitehall in London by Charles I. He was made a baronet on 4 August 1641. Although originally inclined towards the opposition to Charles I, he was summoned in November 1642 with twenty-seven others to appear before the House of Commons as a delinquent, and in the following year he was fined 1000 marks for neglecting his services to the house and the county committee. His considerable delay in taking the covenant reflected his distaste for the militant presbyterianism it represented. Knatchbull did not sit in the house after Pride's Purge, and occupied himself instead with his Hebrew studies.

In 1659 Knatchbull published *Animadversiones in libros novi testamenti*. The work demonstrates a considerable breadth of learning, reflecting the author's use of his large library. It is also intrepid in its arguments for considering historical circumstances and contemporary idiom, and for suggesting the existence of scribal errors in the transmission of the sacred text. A second edition with appendix was published in 1672 and a third, emended, at Oxford in 1677; a fourth edition, in English, appeared in 1692, entitled *Annotations upon some Difficult Texts in All the Books of the New Testament* (Cambridge, 1693). The preface states that Knatchbull undertook the translation, probably shortly before his death. It is preceded by an 'Encomiastick upon the most Learned and Judicious Author', by Thomas Walker of Sidney Sussex College. The work was well received in England and abroad, was reprinted on the continent, and was held in high regard well into the eighteenth century.

At the general election of 1660 Knatchbull's New Romney constituency honoured him by electing him together with his son on condition that they both took out their freedom. Knatchbull sat on only five committees in the Convention, and probably voted with the court. Re-elected in 1661, he participated more actively in the Cavalier Parliament, but he did not take part in formulating the Clarendon code or in later measures against its deviser. By now a widower, he married on 27 November 1662 Dorothy, daughter of Sir Robert Honeywood of Charing, Kent, widow of Sir Edward Steward of Barking, Essex, who survived him. They had no children. In 1669 Sir Thomas Osborne identified him as one of the members to be engaged by the duke of Buckingham. Owing to advancing years he probably did not attend any sessions after 1673. In December 1675 Sir Richard Wiseman listed him as a probable government supporter, recording his recent absence, and in 1677 Lord Shaftesbury marked him

'doubly vile', probably because his younger son was secretary to Lord Chancellor Finch (HoP, *Commons, 1660–90*, 692).

In 1680 Pierre du Moulin the younger dedicated to Knatchbull his *Short view of the chief points in controversy between the reformed churches and the church of Rome*, a translation from an unprinted manuscript by his father, Pierre du Moulin the elder. Knatchbull had acquired the manuscript for his collection and handed it over for the purposes of publication. Du Moulin praised Knatchbull's combination of piety and learning well known to the world.

Knatchbull died at Mersham Hatch on 3 February 1685 and was buried in the family vault under the chancel of Mersham church, where a Latin epitaph styled him *Criticorum coryphaeus et oraculum*, comparing his eloquence with that of Cicero and Chrysostom and his judgement with that of Varro and Jerome. In his will he left considerable sums to the poor around his estate, and the sum of £40 to his servant Francis. The estate passed to his eldest son, John.   NICHOLAS KEENE

Sources M. W. Helms and B. D. Henning, 'Knatchbull, Sir Norton', HoP, *Commons, 1660–90*, 2.692 • W. L. Alexander, *A cyclopaedia of biblical literature, originally edited by John Kilto*, 3rd edn (1864) • J. Bullord, *The library of Sir Norton Knatchbull* (1698) • Keeler, *Long Parliament* • P. du Moulin the younger, *A short view of the chief points in controversy between the reformed churches and the church of Rome* (1680) • *Hasted's history of Kent: corrected, enlarged, and continued to the present time*, ed. H. H. Drake (1886) • T. Wotton, *The English baronets: being a genealogical and historical account of their families* (1727) • will, PRO, PROB 11/381, sig. 110 • J. Cave-Brown, *The history of the parish church of All Saints', Maidstone* [n.d.], 159–60
Archives CKS, corresp.
Likenesses S. van Hoogstraten, portrait, oils, 1667, Maidstone County Hall
Wealth at death see will, PRO, PROB 11/381, sig. 110

Kneale, William Calvert (1906–1990), philosopher, was born on 22 June 1906 in Liverpool, the youngest of the three children of William Kneale (1860–1933), a superintendent in a large building firm, and his wife, Hannah Calvert (1869–1941). He was educated at the Liverpool Institute before going with a classical scholarship to Brasenose College, Oxford, where he got first-class honours in mods (1925) and Greats (1927). After postgraduate study at Paris and Freiburg (where he attended Husserl's lectures), and lecturing posts at Aberdeen (1929–31) and Newcastle (1931–2), he returned to Oxford in 1932. Apart from a wartime stint as a civil servant in the Ministry of Shipping, he taught there until 1966, first as a tutorial fellow of Exeter College and from 1960 as White's professor of moral philosophy. He was elected a fellow of the British Academy in 1950 and was its vice-president for 1971–2. Unflappable and a good judge of people, he was senior tutor of his college for the five unsettled years immediately after the war. In 1964 he chaired an influential committee of inquiry set up by the university to look at the undergraduate curriculum. At that time nearly all courses were in a single subject (with Greats and philosophy, politics, and economics as rare exceptions), and the Kneale committee opened the way for the creation of numerous bipartite honours schools.

Kneale was one of the group of young turks who transformed philosophy at Oxford in the thirties. The leader was his close friend Gilbert Ryle, but Kneale, though sharing its ideals of rigour and clarity, kept his distance from the particular programme associated with Ryle and J. L. Austin that came to be popularly known as 'Oxford philosophy'.

Kneale saw his primary vocation as that of a teacher, and believed in philosophy as a training for public life. In his 1967 Marett memorial lecture entitled *The Responsibility of Criminals*, he said:

> the first step toward the reform of penal law must be an effort to get rid of confused thinking. So long as we are muddled and uncertain about our aims it is always possible that we may fall into injustice or inefficiency—or, what is more likely, both at once.

A subsequent head of the Central Intelligence Agency attributed his own success to having learned from his tutorials with Kneale how to use logic to find out what really were the determining issues in a problematic subject matter.

Kneale wrote two books as well as forty articles on metaphysics, philosophy of mind, theory of knowledge, philosophy of science, and philosophical logic. The first book, *Probability and Induction* (1949), argued for an uncompromisingly realist account of probability and—in the teeth of the dominant Humean identification of laws of nature with mere conjunctions of events—for the thesis that they involve principles of necessity on a par with the necessity of laws of logic. If his arguments here had less influence than they deserved, the article 'The province of logic', published in *Contemporary British Philosophy: Personal Statements, Third Series* (1956), edited by H. D. Lewis, had an impact out of proportion to its length. Inspired by the project of defining the logical constants in terms of the rules of inference with which they are correlated, it generalized the notion of deduction to cover rules of inference with several conclusions as well as several premises. This innovation was to make Kneale one of the two founding fathers (Rudolf Carnap being the other) of a new subject, multiple-conclusion logic.

Kneale's monument, however, is undoubtedly *The Development of Logic* (1962), a classic among histories of the subject. 'Logic' here means formal logic, the study of valid principles of inference applicable to all kinds of topic, and the book narrates its development from its beginnings in ancient Greece down to the late twentieth century. Kneale held that philosophical problems cannot be properly appreciated without an understanding of their history, and the book is written in this spirit. That is to say, his concern is as much to throw light on the subject of logic and its problems as to write history for history's sake. So he scrutinizes each work on logic for its interest as a contribution to the subject, goes on to ask 'is it true?', and takes as long as he thinks necessary to clear matters up. Renowned for his judgement (and hence much in demand as an examiner and assessor), he brought to the task his marvellous sense of relative size and worth in the intellectual realm. Reminding his readers that 'matters which are now perfectly plain were very difficult when they were first thought of', he succeeded in bringing order and sense into an extraordinarily complex mass of material, much of which (for example from medieval logic) might well seem to resist both. His phenomenal erudition was deployed with the lightest of touches, though American reviewers were startled to find that while Greek authors were quoted in English, Latin passages were left in the original without even an accompanying translation. It seems that in 1962 a not unworldly Oxford don might simply take it for granted that any educated person would have a basic knowledge of Latin.

Kneale was brought up as a Methodist. As an undergraduate he was attracted to Catholicism by the works of G. K. Chesterton, but remained—rather regretfully—a sympathetic agnostic all his adult life. In politics he was a strong supporter of the Liberal Party. Inveterately curious, facts of every kind always interested him and his house was full of reference books. A kind, conscientious, upright man, he lived a hospitable, simple, and industrious life. In 1938 he married an Oxford colleague, Martha Hurst, tutor in philosophy at Lady Margaret Hall. Each had to obtain permission from their governing body to live together out of college. She was, among other things, a scholar of ancient philosophy, and is duly credited as joint author of *The Development of Logic*, having taken charge of the chapters on ancient logic in the latter part of its lengthy evolution. The couple had a son, George, a statistician, and a daughter, Jane Heal FBA, who became herself a distinguished philosopher. By 1966 he was beginning to be troubled by arthritis and back trouble, and retired early from his Oxford chair to be freer to work on a projected third book, 'The instrument of thought'. This was a study of how languages came to have the structure found in the languages of civilization, but he never quite got the text to a state with which he was satisfied. He and his wife both had roots in the Yorkshire dales, and on his retirement settled in Wharfedale, at Burnsall and then Grassington, where he died at a concert in the town hall of a sudden heart attack on 24 June 1990. He was survived by his wife.

TIMOTHY SMILEY

Sources T. Smiley, 'William Calvert Kneale, 1906–1990', *PBA*, 87 (1995), 385–97 · private information (2004) [family; former pupils] · personal knowledge (2004) · d. cert. · *CGPLA Eng. & Wales* (1990)

Likenesses W. Stoneman, photograph, repro. in Smiley, 'William Calvert Kneale'

Wealth at death £134,904: probate, 21 Aug 1990, *CGPLA Eng. & Wales*

Knell, Paul (*d.* 1666), Church of England clergyman, was the son of Barnabas Knell (*d.* 1646), minister of Reculver in Kent from 1602, who was sequestered from the living by parliament in the year of his death. Paul Knell was admitted as sizar at Clare College, Cambridge, on 18 June 1632, graduating BA in 1636. Upon the outbreak of civil war he joined the royalist cause as chaplain to a regiment of cuirassiers, to whom he preached a sermon, 'The convoy of a

Christian', in August 1643, during the siege of Gloucester. He later joined the king at Oxford, where he was incorporated DD at Oxford University on 21 January 1644 and where he preached 'A severe sentence against secure citizens' at St Mary's on 17 March 1644.

After the end of the civil war in England, Knell lived a peripatetic and insecure life. He was cited for intrusion at the parish of St Dunstan's, Canterbury, in July 1647, and spent much of 1648 in London, where he was able to preach and publish. A sermon at Gray's Inn in April was published as *Israel and England Paralelled*, in which Knell defended both church and king, and attacked the 'silly schismaticall assembly' (Knell, *Israel and England*, 17). Another sermon, at St Peter Cornhill, was published as *The Life-Guard of a Loyall Christian*, in which he cast the king's opponents as the 'Devil's darlings' (Knell, *Life-Guard*, 2) and claimed that the institutions of neither church nor monarchy could be destroyed by the deaths of particular incumbents. His most famous sermon, however, was preached at St Peter Paul's Wharf in September 1648 and published as *A Looking-Glasse for Levellers*, in which Knell attacked the 'conspiracy of Levellers against our sovereign', and claimed that 'destruction is in their way, they are still opposing of treaties, the way of peace have they not known, like horse leaches, they never think they have blood enough' (Knell, *Looking-Glasse*, 13–14). Thereafter, Knell may have been forced into exile. He later claimed to have preached a sermon, 'The Assumption of the Messiah', before Charles II at The Hague in May 1649. However, he soon returned to England, and helped to raise money for royalist ministers in Essex in 1650.

During the late 1650s Knell, like other Anglican divines, appears to have been able to minister unmolested in London. He settled in the parish of St Peter Paul's Wharf, where he had married one Anne Powell on 3 August 1648, and where he was styled 'minister' from 1657. In June 1660 he petitioned for a prebend at either Windsor or Worcester, claiming to have suffered greatly by plunder, sequestration, and imprisonment in the troubles, and to have been reduced to destitution. He republished some of his earlier works as *Five Seasonable Sermons*, perhaps in order to remind the new king of his service to the royal cause. Knell's request was not granted, but he was made vicar of Newchurch in Kent, in May 1662, and vicar of St Dunstan's, Canterbury, in 1664, although he continued to live in London with his second wife, Elizabeth, whom he married some time before July 1663. Knell was buried at St Dunstan's, Canterbury, on 24 August 1666.

J. T. PEACEY

Sources Walker rev. · P. Knell, *Israel and England paralelled* (1648) · P. Knell, *The life-guard of a loyall Christian* (1648) · P. Knell, *A looking-glasse for Levellers* (1648) · P. Knell, *Five seasonable sermons* (1660) · W. A. Littledale, ed., *The registers of St Bene't and St Peter, Paul's Wharf, London*, 4 vols., Harleian Society, register section, 38–41 (1909–12) · J. M. Cowper, ed., *The register booke of christeninges, marriages and burialls in Saint Dunstan's, Canterbury, 1559–1800* (1887) · CSP dom., 1660–61 · Venn, *Alum. Cant.* · Foster, *Alum. Oxon.* · archdeaconry wills, Canterbury City and Cathedral Archives, A793 · E. Hasted, *The history and topographical survey of the county of Kent*, 2nd edn, 12 vols. (1797–1801)

Knell, Thomas, the elder (*d.* 1576/7), religious writer and Church of England clergyman, was most likely a native of Kent. Many of the details of his life are uncertain, and he has suffered from confusion with another Thomas *Knell, probably his son. The elder of the two men first appears in the years around 1550 as the author of a broadsheet entitled *An ABC to the Christen Congregacion, or, A Pathe Way to the Heavenly Habitacion* (ESTC 15029). Written in verse it has a perceptibly evangelical character, not least in its rejection of salvation by works and its emphasis on the primacy of scripture, while its many references to the plight of the poor suggest an affinity to the 'commonwealth' literature of Edward VI's reign.

The elder Thomas Knell may have been identical with the man of that name who was minister at Ashford, Kent, in 1552, who may in turn have been the Thomas Knell, described as a *quondam* minister, who was enrolled as a resident of Geneva on 14 October 1557 and was received into John Knox's congregation there in the following month. It is also possible, however, that he was the Thomas Knolle recorded in 1557 as subscribing the 'new discipline' at Frankfurt-am-Main, and that he there came to know Alexander Nowell, who later secured ecclesiastical preferment for the elder Thomas Knell. But no certain identification is possible. By contrast it is clear that in January 1560 the elder Thomas Knell was collated by Archbishop Matthew Parker to the rectory of Warehorne, near Romney Marsh, worth £19 per annum. He also appears to have served the neighbouring parish of Snave.

A survey of the Canterbury diocesan clergy of 1562 shows that Thomas Knell, rector of Warehorne, was a married BA who was learned but who had been forbidden to preach. He was allegedly resident and hospitable at Warehorne, his only benefice. In September 1569, again described as a BA, he was dispensed to hold a second benefice within 30 miles of Warehorne, a dispensation doubtless necessitated by his collation, that same month and again at Parker's hands, to the vicarage of Lyminge, near Folkestone, valued at £10 18s. 8d. per annum. He was inducted there in December. Shortly afterwards, now resident at Lyminge, he was recorded as a licensed preacher. The presentation in March 1570 to the vicarage of Dartford of a Thomas Knell, who may also have been the incumbent of Warehorne and Lyminge, seems not to have taken effect.

By 16 October 1570 Knell had resigned his vicarage of Lyminge. From this point it becomes increasingly difficult to distinguish him from his younger namesake, but it is certain that it was the older man who, on the petition of Alexander Nowell, dean of St Paul's, was presented by the queen to the rectory of St Nicholas Acon, London, on 2 March 1571, and was instituted four days later. The living was valued at £13 per annum. His daughter Zephora was baptized there in October. It was probably the same man who in May 1571 was instituted to the Middlesex vicarage of Hackney (valued at £20 per annum) on the presentation of the rector. Knell resigned St Nicholas Acon and Hackney by 30 March and in April 1573 respectively, and in May was presented by the queen to another London vicarage, that of St Bride, Fleet Street, valued at £16 per annum. This presentation, too, was made on the petition of Dean Nowell. But he does not seem to have severed all connections with Kent, since Barnaby Knell, the son of Thomas Knell, clerk, was baptized at Warehorne in October 1574.

By 23 March 1574 Knell had resigned the vicarage of St Bride, probably as a result of his appointment, at an unknown date, as chaplain to Walter Devereux, earl of Essex. With royal support Essex had set out to conquer and colonize Antrim in summer 1573, and was later appointed governor of Ulster. Having returned to England in November 1575 he went back to Ireland in July 1576, and a month later began to display symptoms of either dysentery or typhoid. A contemporary account of his steady physical decline (perhaps by Thomas Churchyard) records that among the clergymen who ministered to Essex in Dublin Castle was Thomas Knell, described as both preacher and chaplain. Essex is reported as continually desiring his chaplain to say prayers, and when he hoped to extract a promise from his attendants that they would not seek to prolong his life, and so his torments, Knell and another clerical ministrant, John Brown, counselled patience, with Knell declaring, of the earl's death, that 'for you it ys expedient but not for us neither for the Church of God' (Folger Shakespeare Library, MS V.b.317, unfoliated). Essex finally died on 22 September 1576.

There were rumours that Essex had been poisoned, the finger of suspicion being pointed at Robert Dudley, earl of Leicester, who had enjoyed a probably adulterous relationship with the dead man's wife (they married in 1578). To scotch these damaging allegations Sir Henry Sidney, the lord deputy of Ireland, required Knell to divulge all he knew. In a report which provides incidental evidence of his knowledge of Latin, Knell confirmed that he had been continually present throughout Essex's last illness, and that he had even administered 'a glister' to the sick man. After the earl had declared his own suspicions of poison he had been sent 'a peece of unicornes horne' which Knell 'rased' and then gave to him, making Essex vomit. Admitting that others of the household had fallen sick at the same time as their master, Knell described in vivid terms the unwholesome symptoms of the earl's malady and the distressing findings of the *post mortem* examination (BL, Add. MS 32092, fol. 5r–5v). None of this could either confirm or disprove the charges of poisoning, but Sidney certainly felt that Knell had erred on the side of credulity. In February 1577, after the chaplain's account had been circulated, Sidney told Leicester that he hoped that his investigations had satisfied him and others 'touching the false bruit of the Earl of Essex's poisoning', and declared that he would have 'made Knell retract his foolish speech', had not 'God prevented me, he dying of the same disease as the Earl, which was most certainly a mere flux' (*De L'Isle and Dudley MSS*, 2.51). No will has been found and it is not known exactly when Knell died or where he was buried, though it was probably in Dublin. A Margaret Knell, widow, who was buried at Warehorne on 3 May 1577, may have been his wife.

Two books by the elder Thomas Knell were published in 1581. *A Godlie and Necesserie Treatise, Touching the Use and Abuse of Praier* (ESTC 15033.3), is a work of straightforward divinity, notable only for its expression of support for bishops as 'publike persons' who receive 'their authoritie from their naturall prince' (sig. C2v). Internal evidence suggests that *Certain True Marks wherby to Knowe a Papist* (ESTC 15031), a warning against militant Catholicism, was probably written in the late 1560s. Perhaps it was the younger Thomas Knell who secured the posthumous publication of the older man's writings.

DAVID J. CRANKSHAW

Sources Folger, MS V.b.317 · BL, Add. MS 32092 · *Report on the manuscripts of Lord De L'Isle and Dudley*, 6 vols., HMC, 77 (1925–66) · CCC Cam., Parker Library, MS 580 · office of first fruits and tenths, composition books, PRO, E 334/8 · CPR, 1563–6; 1569–75 · *Registrum Matthei Parker, diocesis Cantuariensis, AD 1559–1575*, ed. W. H. Frere and E. M. Thompson, 2, CYS, 36 (1928) · G. Hennessy, *Novum repertorium ecclesiasticum parochiale Londinense, or, London diocesan clergy succession from the earliest time to the year 1898* (1898) · A. J. Willis, ed., *Canterbury licences (general), 1568–1646* (1972) · C. H. Garrett, *The Marian exiles: a study in the origins of Elizabethan puritanism* (1938) · M. A. Simpson, *John Knox and the troubles begun at Frankfurt* (1975) · T. Watt, *Cheap print and popular piety, 1550–1640* (1991) · W. B. Devereux, *Lives and letters of the Devereux, earls of Essex … 1540–1646*, 1 (1853) · Canterbury Cathedral Archives, MS Dca/BT/205/14

Archives BL, Add. MS 32092, fols. 5r–6r [copy]

Knell, Thomas, the younger (1543/4–*c*.1592), Church of England clergyman and pamphleteer, was presumably the son of Thomas *Knell the elder (d. 1576/7). When ordained deacon on 24 June 1567 by Edmund Grindal, bishop of London, he was living at Great Stambridge, Essex, stated that he had been born in Canterbury, and gave his age as twenty-three. Grindal ordained him priest on 17 April 1568, merely as 'of London'. He was probably, therefore, the 'Mr' Thomas Knell who was paid £4 per quarter for serving (presumably as curate) in the London parish of St James Garlickhithe between Easter and Christmas 1568 and again for the quarter ending at Lady day 1570. Meanwhile he appears to have served as curate in St Giles Cripplegate during 1569.

Failing to find higher preferment Knell seems to have plunged into the Elizabethan equivalent of tabloid journalism. In the will of an obscure London curate, Henry Holtbie, proved on 4 August 1568, he was bequeathed a copy of *The palace of pleasure* on condition that he restore to Holtbie's wife all the other books that he had borrowed. In 1569 he published, in verse, *An epitaph, or rather a short discourse made upon the life & death of D. [Edmund] Boner, Bisshop of London*. Probably in response to the northern rising of 1569–70 there followed a flurry of anti-Catholic verse tracts. These effusions were undoubtedly intended to win him promotion but in the event they were unsuccessful.

It is not clear whether it was he or Thomas Knell the elder who on 21 March 1570 received letters patent for the vicarage of Dartford, Kent, from the lord keeper, Sir Nicholas Bacon. The presentation was made at the petition of Lord Mountjoy and at the commendation of James Pilkington, bishop of Durham, but no institution is subsequently recorded. Knell the younger was present on 8 August 1570 at the execution of John Felton, condemned for setting up in the churchyard of St Paul's Cathedral Pius V's bull excommunicating Elizabeth, and accordingly published *A piththy note to papists all and some that joy in Feltons martirdome*. The anonymous title-page states that the tract, which enshrines a blow-by-blow account of the execution, was 'set forth by one that knew his life, and was with him at the hour of his death'. Only on the final page did he reveal himself as 'T. Knel Juni.' This was followed in early 1571 by *A declaration of such tempestious, and outragious fluddes, as hath been in England*, previously attributed to Knell senior, and *An historicall discource of the life and death of doctor Story*, a diatribe against Bonner's hated chancellor, John Story, executed for treason on 1 June 1571.

Since the composition record for St Nicholas Acon, London (15 March 1571), clearly states that the new incumbent was Thomas Knell 'senior' (PRO, E 334/8, fol. 236*v*), both logic and chronology suggest that it was the elder Thomas who also subsequently held, but quickly relinquished, the vicarages of Hackney, Middlesex, and of St Bride, London, between early 1571 and early 1574. In that case nothing further is known of the younger man's activities until the latter months of 1573 when, in the wake of the *Admonition to the parliament* (1572) many Londoners suspected of nonconformity, both men and women, were required to sign a form of subscription to the English prayer book. Since Knell was one of them—his signature is preserved among the Petyt MSS as 'Thomas Knell Jnr'—his nonconformity may have prompted him to retire from the capital.

Thus the younger Thomas Knell may have been the 'Mr Knell clerke' who, along with his wife, was presented during Archbishop Parker's episcopal visitation of 1573 for not receiving communion in the parish of St Alphege, Canterbury, at Easter or since. Of two tracts published in 1581, *Certain true marks wherby to knowe a papist* is signed only 'Thomas Knell' but *A Godlie and Necesserie Treatise, Touching the Use and Abuse of Praier* is clearly by Thomas Knell the elder. It seems likely that the younger Knell died about 1592 since a probate record exists for one Thomas Knell, clerk, of the parish of Kenardington, Kent.

BRETT USHER

Sources G. Hennessy, *Novum repertorium ecclesiasticum parochiale Londinense, or, London diocesan clergy succession from the earliest time to the year 1898* (1898) • GL, MS 9535/1, fols. 132*r*, 136*v* [ordination] • BL, Lansdowne MS 443, fols. 182*v*, 192*v*, 208*v* [letters patent for Dartford, St Nicholas Acon, St Bride's] • will, LMA, DL/C/358, fol. 110*r–v* [of Henry Holtbie] • Inner Temple Library, London, Petyt MS 538, vol. 47, fol. 519 [subscription 1573] • office of first fruits and tenths, composition books, PRO, E 334/8, fol. 236*v*
Archives Inner Temple, London, Petyt MSS

Knell, William (*d.* 1587), actor, may have been the son of Henry Knell, an immigrant from Bremen whose will was proved on 17 September 1585, though there is nothing more than an uncommon name to link them. The details of Knell's early career as a player are not known, but he was prominent enough by 1583, or at the latest by 1585, to be selected by Edmund Tilney, under commission from Sir Francis Walsingham, as one in the new company of Queen's Men. The selection is significant because it was expected of Tilney that the Queen's Men would outshine

all rival companies, then operating under the patronage of such Tudor grandees as the earls of Sussex, Leicester, and Warwick. In a group rich in clowns, Knell's specialism was probably in heroic parts: he is described as 'playing Henry the fift' in the book of *Tarlton's Jests* (*Shakespeare Jest-Books*, ed. W. C. Hazlitt, 1864, 2.218), presumably in *The Famous Victories of Henry V*, which is known to have been in the repertory of the Queen's Men. It is the only role to which Knell's name can be confidently attached.

The Queen's Men, whether or not the members individually shared Walsingham's concerns, were expected to tour the provinces during the summer and early autumn with a broadly protestant and insistently patriotic repertory. Travelling conditions were rough and the schedule often gruelling. In such circumstances, friendships are tested. On the evening of 13 June 1587, for reasons unknown, Knell drew his sword and attacked his fellow actor John Towne. It was in self-defence, a coroner's inquest concluded, that Towne stuck his own sword through his assailant's neck. Knell was dead within half an hour. The skirmish took place in White Hound Close, Thame, near Oxford. Because the Queen's Men visited Stratford upon Avon during this same tour, speculative biographers have mentioned Shakespeare as a possible replacement for Knell, but there is no evidence to sustain the theory.

Administration of Knell's estate was granted to his widow, Rebecca (*d.* 1619), by the commissary court of London on 12 December 1587. In that ruling, Knell is referred to as 'of St Mary Aldermanbury', but his place of burial is unknown. On 10 March 1588 Rebecca married the actor John Heminges, famous as Shakespeare's colleague and editor; they had several children. She died in the late summer of 1619, and was buried at St Mary Aldermanbury on 2 September. Heminges's will makes no mention of children by her first husband.

PETER THOMSON

Sources M. Eccles, *Shakespeare in Warwickshire* (1961) • E. A. J. Honigmann and S. Brock, eds., *Playhouse wills, 1558–1642: an edition of wills by Shakespeare and his contemporaries in the London theatre* (1993) • S. McMillin and S.-B. MacLean, *The Queen's Men and their plays* (1998) • A. Gurr, *The Shakespearian playing companies* (1996) • E. Nungezer, *A dictionary of actors* (1929)
Wealth at death see administration: Commissary Court of London, 12 December 1587

Knell, William Adolphus (1801–1875), marine painter, was born in Carisbrooke, Hampshire, in 1801, the son of William Knell and Jane Richardson. He lived in London and first exhibited at the Royal Academy of Arts in 1825 with *The Royal Squadron at Spithead*. Initially adopting the popular Dutch seventeenth-century marine style, in mid-career he shifted to an English manner to maintain his share of the market. The results were lighter and less heavy-handed pictures marked by translucent seas and broader handling in the skies. He specialized in inshore scenes of England, France, and the Low Countries, but many of his major works depicted naval action. Eight drawings by Knell, reproduced in coloured aquatint by Newton Smith Fielding, illustrated the *Epitome, Historical* and Statistical, Descriptive of the Royal Naval Services of England by E. Miles and Lieutenant L. Miles, published in 1841.

Knell contributed twenty-nine pictures to the Royal Academy from 1825 to 1866, forty-four to the British Institution from 1825 until 1867, and twenty to the Society of British Artists. He entered *The Destruction of Toulon by the British, 18 June 1793* and *The Battle off Cape St. Vincent, 14 February 1797* to the Westminster Hall competition of 1847. The latter, described as 'another masterly naval battle, treated with a spirit of effect worthy of praise' (*Art Union*, 272), was one of only four pictures purchased by the Westminster commissioners for the nation that year, for £200. He painted at Queen Victoria's 'special command' (Millar, 133) *The Naval Review at Spithead, 11 August 1853* (1854; Royal Collection) for £150 and *The Arrival of Prince Albert, 6 February 1840* (1840; Royal Collection), which was engraved by William Miller (1796–1882) for the *Art Journal* (1 June 1857, p. 188) and the *Royal Gallery of Art* (2.25). Other major works include *Pilot Boats off Dover* (exh. RA, 1847; Victoria Art Gallery, Bath), and *The Arrival of the Princess Alexandra at Gravesend, 1863* (Danish Royal Collection).

Knell married Susannah Williams (*née* Cross), a widow, on 22 August 1846, when he was described as a widower. Their eldest son, William Callcott Knell (*fl.* 1848–1879), produced more vigorous and heavily worked marine scenes than his father and another son, Adolphus Knell (1855–1880), similarly turned away from the Dutch marine manner to produce oils likened to Turner sketches. John Henry Knell, who exhibited four pictures at the Royal Academy in 1833 and 1834, was probably Knell's brother. Knell died at his London home, 329 Kentish Town Road, on 9 July 1875, and was buried in the Abney Park cemetery, Stoke Newington.

A number of Knell's pictures are in public collections in Derby, Edinburgh, Hull, Newcastle, York, and the National Maritime Museum, Greenwich, which owns twelve oils.   JASON ROSENFELD

Sources D. Brook-Hart, *British 19th century marine painting* (1974) · Wood, *Vic. painters*, 3rd edn · *Art Union*, 9 (1847), 269, 272, 311 · review, *Art Journal*, 19 (1857), 188 · O. Millar, *The Victorian pictures in the collection of her majesty the queen*, 2 vols. (1992) · S. C. Hall, ed., *The Royal Gallery of Art, ancient and modern*, 2 (1858) · *Catalogue of works of art sent in … for exhibition in Westminster Hall* (1847) [exhibition catalogue, Westminster Hall] · J. Johnson, ed., *Works exhibited at the Royal Society of British Artists, 1824–1893, and the New English Art Club, 1888–1917*, 2 vols. (1975) · Graves, *RA exhibitors* · Graves, *Artists* · *DNB* · Redgrave, *Artists* · C. Hemming, *British painters of the coast and sea* (1988) · S. T. Prideaux, *Aquatint engraving* (1909), 152, 376 · A. Wilson, *A dictionary of British marine painters* (1967) · *Concise catalogue of oil paintings in the National Maritime Museum* (1988) · A. Graves, *A century of loan exhibitions, 1813–1912*, 5 vols. (1913–15), vol. 4 · m. cert. · d. cert. · IGI

Kneller, Sir Godfrey [*formerly* Gottfried Kniller], **baronet** (1646–1723), history and portrait painter, was born Gottfried Kniller (which name he used, together with Kneller, until well into his thirties) at Lübeck, north Germany, on 8 August 1646, the third son of Zacharias Kniller (1611–1675) and Lucia Beuten (*d.* in or after 1676). Zacharias's father owned an estate near Halle in Saxony and served Count Mansfelt as surveyor-general of mines

Sir Godfrey Kneller, baronet (1646–1723), self-portrait, 1685

and inspector of revenues. Zacharias attended the University of Leipzig, was an official at Queen Eleanor of Sweden's court, and settled in Lübeck as chief surveyor.

The continental years, 1646–1676 Kneller was intended for the army and after a grounding in Latin went to the University of Leiden to study mathematics. But his inclination turned 'strongly to drawing figures after the historical manner' (Buckeridge, 393). He moved to Amsterdam where his father placed him 'under the care of Rembrandt', a fact also attested to by Marshall Smith (Smith, 23). J. C. Weyerman, a Dutch painter who became Kneller's assistant in 1709, said that he studied under Rembrandt and Ferdinand Bol (Weyerman, 3.68) as did the engraver and historian George Vertue (Vertue, *Note books*, 1.58, 2.119). Kneller's early work shows the influence of both artists, stylistically and in the emphasis on large-scale 'history' paintings, that is figure paintings with a didactic purpose, whose subjects were drawn from the Bible, or antiquity, including mythologies and allegories. From the time of Alberti, in the fifteenth century, *istoria* (history) was regarded as 'the greatest work of the painter' (Alberti, 70), a theory which was still accepted in seventeenth-century Holland (Blankert and others, 18).

Kneller's earliest dated painting is actually a portrait, the three-quarter-length *Johann Philipp von Schönborn, Prince-Bishop of Würzburg and Elector of Mainz* (1666; Kunsthistorischesmuseum, Vienna). Its high quality indicates that less mature works must have preceded it. A commission from this exalted sitter was doubtless due to the painter's nationality, aristocratic family connections, and his membership of the Rembrandt school.

Kneller's first dated history painting is his *Isaac Blessing Jacob* (1668; St Annenmuseum, Lübeck), whose composition recalls Rembrandt's *Danaë* (Hermitage Museum, St Petersburg), but the shadowed, profiled, hunched Jacob creates tension in this more compressed composition. Also of 1668 are the *Old Student* and *Young Student*, allegories of the contemplative and active life, painted for the Lübeck Stadtbibliothek (now St Annenmuseum). (The latter, much inferior in quality, is by **John Zacharias** [Zachary] **Kneller** (1642–1702), Kneller's elder brother, who was born in Lübeck on 15 December 1642.) Kneller's next dated painting, *Elijah and the Angel* (1672; Tate collection), is a bold, dramatic work.

Until 1986 the Vienna, Lübeck, and London works were the only known paintings from Kneller's Amsterdam period. In that year, in a remarkable scholarly breakthrough, Sumowski identified nine more early works by Kneller, including a large *Self-Portrait* (c.1670; priv. coll.) in which Kneller proclaims his allegiance to neo-stoicism, a popular philosophy in the period which attracted artists such as Poussin, Rubens, and Van Dyck. Kneller shows himself copying an engraving (probably of Andromeda, as a symbol of patience) below which is a skull. Behind are an archer *écorché*, and a bust of Seneca against a column, symbolizing the Stoic virtue of fortitude.

Kneller's composition appears to be inspired by the *Duet*, by the Antwerp painter Theodor Rombouts (1597–1637), perhaps via the engraving by Schelte à Bolswert. However, Kneller may have seen the original painting (now lost) in Antwerp, since we know that he visited that city 'when he was young' (Vertue, *Note books*, 5.26). His journey probably took place c.1669, and influenced Kneller to adopt bolder, more dynamic forms, including plunging diagonals and dramatic foreshortening.

The largest Kneller identified by Sumowski is the 8.5 by 6 feet *Dismissal of Hagar* (c.1670; Alte Pinakothek, Munich) whose composition derives from a Rembrandt etching. But Kneller's figures are grander and more dynamic, with expansive, poignant gestures and poses. The picture, formerly at the Würzburg Residenz, was probably commissioned by Prince-Bishop Schönborn. Another work attributed by Sumowski to Kneller is *Joseph Interpreting the Dreams of the Butler and the Baker* (Staatliches Museum, Schwerin), for which Kneller's composition drawing survives, wrongly attributed to Bol (Kunsthalle, Hamburg). The model for the baker also appears in the 'Rest on the Flight' (actually *St Joseph's Dream in the Stable at Bethlehem* Malerisamling, Nivaagaards), attributed by Sumowski to Cornelis Bisschop. That model is seen yet again in *Scholar in an Interior* (ex Sothebys, New York, 4 June 1987, lot 37; priv. coll.) described in the catalogue as by a follower of Carel van der Pluym, which is closely related stylistically to the Lübeck *Old Student*. Hence *St Joseph's Dream* and *Scholar in an Interior* should also be attributed to Kneller (Stewart, *Wisdom*, 44). All these paintings have a gravity characteristic of many of his best mature works.

A remarkable recent early Kneller discovery by Wolff-Thomsen is the *Sacrifice of Manoah*, until 1945 in the St Katherinenkirche, Lübeck, and since then in the depot of the St Annenmuseum there, wrongly ascribed to an amateur. The *Manoah* dates from the mid- to late 1660s and is almost as large as the *Dismissal of Hagar* but the figures are less dynamic. Manoah's head derives from one by Bol in his *Descent of Moses from Mount Sinai* (Town Hall, Amsterdam) and Manoah's wife is based on the same model as Sarah in Kneller's 1668 *Isaac Blessing Jacob*. A standing angel lights the sacrificial fire with his staff; normally he flies upwards from the fire. Kneller's inventive iconography derives from the story of Gideon and the Angel, which like Manoah's appears in the Book of Judges.

In 1672 Kneller went with his brother to Italy. He studied in Rome with Bernini and Carlo Maratta, and 'began to acquire fame in history-painting, having first studied architecture and anatomy; the latter aptly disposing him to relish the antique statues, and to improve by them' (Buckeridge, 394). He also 'Copied very much after Raphael' (Smith, 23). In Venice he 'studied Titians Works, especially his Portraits' and painted members of the Donado, Mocenigo, Garzoni, and Basadonna families (ibid.). His portrait of Cardinal Basadonna was engraved. The pastellist Rosalba Carriera later admired one of Kneller's portraits of a member of the Mocenigo family. Two oval bust paintings survive, one of the Nuremberg sculptor Georg Schweigger (1674; Herzog Anton Ulrich-Museum, Brunswick), and the other of the most prominent contemporary Venetian painter, Sebastiano Bombelli (1675; Museo Civico, Udine).

Kneller's Titianesque *Herr von Copet* (1675; Kurpfälzisches Museum, Heidelberg) was painted in Nuremberg, where Kneller impressed Joachim von Sandrart. The return of the Kneller brothers to Lübeck in 1675 was prompted by the illness of their father, who died in April of that year. The following year they erected a painted wooden monument to their father in the St Katherinenkirche. From nearby Hamburg, they went to England because of Kneller's 'longing to see Sir Anthony Van Dyck's Works, being most ambitious of imitating that great Master' (Smith, 24).

England: rise to ascendancy, 1676–1688 In London Kneller lodged with the Hamburg merchant John Banckes, whose portrait he painted in 1676 (Tate collection). By April 1677 Kneller had moved to rooms in Durham Yard procured for him by the duke of Monmouth's secretary, James Vernon. Kneller's Marattesque *James Vernon* is now in the National Portrait Gallery, London. His early portrait of Anne Scott, duchess of Monmouth, is known from its engraving in mezzotint. The painter obtained commissions from her Scottish relations, the Hamiltons and the Tweeddales, who continued to be staunch patrons throughout his career.

In 1678 Kneller painted the armoured three-quarter-length *Duke of Monmouth* (priv. coll.). He used a Titian pose, but stylistically the painting was influenced by the work of such French émigrés as Henri Gascars. The next year Kneller painted a portrait of Charles II for Monmouth, competing with the king's principal painter, Sir Peter Lely. Kneller's portrait is known from Robert White's engraving after it of 1679. After painting the king Kneller's 'reputation daily increased so that most noblemen & Ladies would have their picture done by him' (Vertue, *Note books*, 1.28).

After his brief flirtation with the French style, Kneller mainly allied himself to the quieter colour and more painterly handling of the Lely–Van Dyck tradition. He borrowed a Lely design for his *Duchess of Hamilton* (1679; priv. coll.) and his full-lengths *Henry Somerset, 1st Duke of Beaufort* (priv. coll.) and *James Cecil, 3rd Earl of Salisbury* (priv. coll.) of about 1680–82 are variations of a pattern used by Lely for portraying sitters in garter robes.

In 1682 Kneller (and probably his brother John) moved to the Piazza, Covent Garden, where Lely had lived until his death in 1680. In 1683 the Kneller brothers were granted letters of denization. John Kneller painted small-scale portraits 'about a foot square' (Yale Center for British Art, New Haven, Connecticut, Kingsweston MS, fol. 14), miniatures, copies of Godfrey Kneller's work, and 'several Pieces in still-life exceeding well' (Vertue, *Note books*, 2.146). A panel, *Dead Partridge and Implements of the Chase*, signed 'J. Z. Kneller' was at Christies on 4 July 1952 (lot 11). John Kneller was buried in St Paul's, Covent Garden, on 31 August 1702.

Godfrey Kneller's *Duke of York as Lord High Admiral* (1684; NPG) for the Scottish privy council, Edinburgh, is more assured than earlier full-lengths and employs a swagger design. As a type, the full-length *Duchess of Portsmouth* (1684; priv. coll.) derives from Lely's *Duchess of Norfolk* (1677; priv. coll.), itself indebted to Van Dyck, but Kneller's figure has more thrust and energy and is more solidly planted on the ground. She is portrayed as Bathsheba (from Dryden's *Absolom and Achitophel*).

In 1684 Kneller painted a splendid life-size equestrian portrait (rare in England since those painted by Van Dyck) of Mohammed Ohadu, the Moroccan ambassador (Chiswick House, London). Ohadu and his retinue rode in Hyde Park 'very short, & could stand upright in full speede, managing their spears with incredible agility' (Evelyn, 4.269). The swirling forms and diagonals capture that verve. The subject recalls Rembrandt's copies of Mughal miniature equestrian portraits, while the rich colour and the detailed metal trappings are reminiscent of Kneller's own Amsterdam history paintings.

In late 1684 Charles II sent Kneller to paint Louis XIV in France, where he took the opportunity to make a large drawing of the antique *Diane de Versailles* (British Museum). On his return, the painter produced his most memorable image of Charles himself (Walker Art Gallery, Liverpool). Also of 1685 is the full-length *Philip, Lord Wharton* (priv. coll.), a challenging commission, since Wharton had sat to Van Dyck, and possessed the largest private collection of that artist's portraits. The formal peer's robes are softened by Wharton's amiable expression and lolling posture. Their cool scarlet contrasts with austere greys and browns.

Kneller's portrait of Michael Alphonsus Shen Fu-Tsung (1687; Royal Collection) was painted for James II. The conical figure points to a crucifix in his left hand and looks to the light at the upper left. It is a picture of serene simplicity, whose numinous feeling is enhanced by the concave, apsidal space of the back wall. Kneller also worked for members of James's opposition such as the fifth earl (later first duke) of Bedford, for example the double full-length *Ladies Catherine and Rachel Russell* (1686; priv. coll.). The orphaned children of the whig 'martyr' Lord William Russell are shown below an urn on which one putto frightens another with a mask (symbolizing death), while at the right is a dog (symbolizing faith). Behind is a fountain of dolphins supporting a shell basin (adapted from Bernini's piazza Barberini *Triton Fountain*) on which Cupid subdues a lion, the Christian-antique consolatory theme of *omnia vincit amor* (love conquers all).

Kneller created further sympathetic portraits of fellow artists, for example *Antonio Verrio* (priv. coll.), and three of the medallist Abraham Simon. One of the latter is a remarkable reclining full-length (Agnes Etherington Art Centre, Queen's University, Kingston, Ontario) showing Simon in pilgrim dress looking towards heavenly light, but chained to a globe. Simon was a Cynic, despising material things, including personal hygiene. Perhaps common philosophy drew the Stoic and the Cynic together. It is to Kneller's credit that he could see beyond Simon's squalid appearance. Moreover he risked his reputation by association with one whose aggressively independent behaviour had alienated James II and members of the nobility.

By the mid-1680s Kneller was the most important portrait painter in England. His wide experience and the range of his work, especially in full-lengths, was unparalleled since Van Dyck. In his *Self-Portrait* (1685; NPG) he looks confidently over his shoulder, a pose derived from a *Self-Portrait* by Van Dyck (priv. coll.). Kneller had 'a pleasant conversation finely entertaining when a Painting' (Vertue, *Note books*, 2.122). His ability to capture a likeness was also recognized by contemporaries, whose familiarity with his work was assisted by mezzotint engravings. Kneller took considerable interest in prints made after his work and formed a close relationship with John Smith, the greatest mezzotinter of his age.

William and Mary, 1688–1702: principal painter During the reign of William and Mary, Kneller's position as court and society painter was unrivalled. Antonio Verrio, successor to Sir Peter Lely as principal painter to the king, refused to work for the new regime. John Riley, who was made principal painter jointly with Kneller on 24 July 1689, died in 1691 leaving him in sole possession of the post. Kneller was knighted in 1692, given a sword as a special mark of favour, and made a gentleman of the privy chamber. Perhaps at the king's instance, Kneller received an honorary doctorate from the University of Oxford in 1695. Four years later William III gave him a large gold medal with the royal image and a gold chain, like those given to Van Dyck by Charles I. Honours also came from abroad. In 1700 Kneller was ennobled and made a knight of the Holy Roman empire by Emperor Leopold.

In 1690 Kneller painted full-length state portraits of the new sovereigns (Royal Collection). They recall Van Dyck's portraits of Charles I and Henrietta Maria, thus emulating Kneller's great Flemish predecessor and alluding to William and Mary's common ancestors. Copies were distributed at home and abroad, more widely than any royal images until Allan Ramsay's portraits of George III and Queen Charlotte.

Kneller's earliest large-scale work for William III was the equestrian *Duke of Schomberg* (*c*.1689; apparently formerly at Hampton Court, now priv. coll.), a powerful reinterpretation of Van Dyck's *Duc d'Arenberg*. In 1697 Kneller, having accompanied the king to Ryswick, Holland, for the signing of a treaty, was sent to Brussels to paint an equestrian portrait (now lost) of Maximilian II Emanuel, elector of Bavaria.

In 1697 William III commissioned his own allegorical equestrian portrait from Kneller. In an oil sketch (formerly Gatschina Palace), the king is depicted in battle; his stallion is engaged in a levade, a battle movement whereby the horse rears up in order to trample down the enemy; the composition is based on Bernini's *Louis XIV*. Another oil sketch (Het Loo Palace, Apeldoorn) became the final model for the equestrian portrait of the king (1701) at Hampton Court Palace. Here the king is mounted on a horse which is seen pacing by the seashore, trampling only emblems of war, with Neptune behind at the left. The king is welcomed by Ceres and Flora at the right, while above Peace, Cupid, and Mercury look down. In the new composition William III is not just a victorious warrior, but a bringer of peace and prosperity. It is a joyful celebration of his deliverance of England from James II's despotism and foreign domination, and alludes to the imperial Roman *adventus*. William is conceived as a modern Hercules, inaugurating a new golden age, affirming thereby his 'British Trojan' descent from Aeneas.

In June 1689 Queen Mary told Goodwin Wharton that she would have sixteen of the most beautiful Dutch and English court ladies painted; he persuaded her 'for the credit of the nation' to select only English women (Wharton, 255–6). Kneller began with the duchess of Grafton in January 1690; by Michaelmas 1691 he had received £400 for eight full-length portraits. The Hampton Court Beauties were painted in emulation of those painted by Lely for Queen Mary's mother, Anne Hyde, duchess of York. Kneller's Beauties are much less sensual than those painted by Lely, but like his include Neoplatonic allusions. As part of the same rhetoric, the 'Prologue' to Purcell's 1689 *Dido and Aeneas* eulogized the king as Apollo and Queen Mary as Venus and 'the Sovereign Queen of Beauty' (Stewart, *Sir Godfrey Kneller and the English Baroque Portrait*, 44). Kneller personally commemorated Queen Mary's death in 1694 by a design, engraved by Smith, showing Cupid with a discarded broken bow and arrows by the queen's tomb, wistfully regarding the inscription 'Pastora is no more'. Both imagery and text derive in part from William Congreve's memorial poem to the queen.

Kneller had a large private practice: an anonymous account of 1693 says that he received up to fourteen sitters in one day, but made some sit ten to twelve times (Ozias Humphry, memorandum book, 1777–95, vol. 2, fol. 39v,

BL, Add. MS 22950). His range is wide and includes the elegiac *Arabella Hunt* (Gov. Art Coll.), inspired by Tobias Stimmer's engraving *The Lutenist*; the *Lady Lempster* (ex Christies, 22 November 1935, lot 45) crouching by a stream in a pose adapted from an antique *Venus with a Shell*, now in the Louvre, but then in the Villa Borghese; and the *Lady Howard* (known through Smith's mezzotint), reclining by a stream in a pose inspired by the celebrated antique *The Sleeping Ariadne* (Vatican, Rome). Both the latter portraits also follow the English 'melancholy' portrait tradition which had developed in Elizabethan and Jacobean times, and derived from the Renaissance interpretation of the theory of the humours, in which the melancholy humour indicated a retiring, contemplative nature.

An outstanding male portrait is Kneller's *Isaac Newton* (1689; priv. coll.), whose fervent pose recalls Bernini's *Gabriele Fonseca*. His *Grinling Gibbons* (*c*.1690; Hermitage, St Petersburg) is an allegory of prudence, showing the sculptor aggressively confronting Bernini's *Proserpina* with the compasses of wisdom, like Aeneas with the golden bough in his descent to Hades. The posthumous *Sir Thomas Wharton* (1694; priv. coll.), ancient in breastplate and buff jerkin, is *hommage à* Van Dyck, a tough, earthy translation of Van Dyck's elegant full-length of the same sitter painted sixty years before. By contrast, his portraits of the five youthful sons of the duchess of Hamilton (priv. coll.) are all glamorous in black armour.

John Dryden (1697; Trinity College, Cambridge) with its varied texture (including primed canvas left visible) and cool lilac and warm brown tones, shows the impact of Rubens's late work on Kneller at Brussels. This impact is also evident in his drawings and can be seen in the dashing handling of chalk in the life-size head study (Courtauld Inst.)—a practice not seen in England since Holbein, which Kneller revived in the early 1680s—for his *Jean Baptiste Monnoyer* (lost). This 'Rubenisme' was part of a European trend away from 'Poussinisme'.

To the standard portrait sizes—bust, 30 by 25 inches; three-quarter length, 50 by 40 inches; and full-length, about 90 by 60 inches—Kneller added the 'kit-cat' (36 × 28 inches) named after the famous whig dining club. The earliest are *John Dryden* (1697) and the *6th Earl of Dorset* (only the latter being a Kit-Cat member). Both were first owned by the publisher and secretary of the club, Jacob Tonson, to whom some forty members presented their portraits by Kneller over the next quarter of a century. All now belong to the National Portrait Gallery, London.

The kit-cat format allows the life-size depiction of the head and shoulders plus one or both hands. Kneller had portrayed this view of sitters in the 30 by 25 inches (bust) format, but under life-size, in, for example, *John Smith* (1696; Tate collection). The kit-cat scale heightens the sense of realism. The format was used by Raphael in the *Castiglione* (Musée du Louvre, Paris), which Rembrandt copied in 1640. Subsequently Rembrandt and members of his school occasionally used the format.

Peter the Great (Royal Collection) was painted for King William in 1698. Quieter in pose, but rich in colour and handling of paint are *Nathaniel, Lord Crewe* (1698) and *Dr.*

John Wallis (1701) (both Bodl. Oxf.), the former in peer's robes, the latter in academic dress. Wallis was a famous elderly mathematician. Kneller claimed that he had 'never done a better picture, nor one so good' as that of this 'great man' (*Letters … of Samuel Pepys*, 310). The three-quarter-length *Matthew Prior* (1700; Trinity College, Cambridge) with its dramatic lighting, thin, angular forms, and the bravura handling of paint creates a memorable image. The absence of a wig gives Prior a fortuitously modern look—what the artist aimed at was the appearance of an ancient Roman. Another powerful example, of about 1696, is his head-and-shoulders portrait of Ishack Pereyra (Bevis Marks Synagogue, London).

Augustan prose, 1702–1723 Following the death of William III, Kneller continued as principal painter to Queen Anne. After the victory of Ramillies (1706), he planned an allegorical equestrian portrait of the duke of Marlborough in a brilliant Rubensian oil sketch (NPG). Its design emulates the early Christian *Barberini Ivory* (Musée du Louvre, Paris; then in Rome), a Roman emperor's gift to a consul, and was, perhaps, a royal commission. In 1708 he planned a large work, *Queen Anne Presenting the Plans of Blenheim to Military Merit* (priv. coll.) for Blenheim Palace Library. The central figures and the eagle derive from those of the emperor Constantine and his architect in Rubens's tapestry *The Building of Constantinople*, appropriately, since Constantine (then thought to be half-British) had been acclaimed emperor in Britain. A further witty touch is that, adjacent to a sun-king standard trophy, Apollo, the sun god, proclaims Marlborough's fame. Kneller was 'much commended for his skill' in designing this oil sketch, a commission from Queen Anne (Vertue, *Note books*, 3.23). Because of Marlborough's dismissal from office in 1712 neither of these projects was completed.

Another commission from Queen Anne was for a series of fourteen Admirals (NMM) painted in emulation of those done by Lely for her father, the duke of York. The series was divided between Kneller and Michael Dahl, a Swede who had been much patronized before her accession by the queen's husband, Prince George of Denmark. As principal painter Kneller may perhaps have regarded the division of the commission as a slight; but his admirals have a dash and martial spirit lacking in the Dahls. A serious challenger to Kneller's position was John Closterman who in 1702 defeated Kneller in a competition for the London Guildhall *Queen Anne* (lost) and acquired important patrons such as the duke of Marlborough. Closterman's early death in May 1711 left Kneller supreme again. In 1712 Lady Wentworth called him unequivocally 'the best painter we have' (Cartwright, 279n.).

Kneller's only surviving religious picture of this period is the *Conversion of St. Paul* (*c*.1705–10; Agnes Etherington Art Centre, Queen's University, Kingston, Ontario), a modello whose purpose is unknown. Its sources lie in works by Rubens and Raphael. The unusually prominent javelin in the foreground refers to Saul, from whom Paul derived his Jewish name. King Saul had infamously flung a javelin at David (Christ's ancestor), a prefiguration of the later Saul's persecution of Christians.

At this time Kneller painted several charming small-scale works (priv. coll.), complete in themselves, for Lady Elizabeth Southwell (*née* Cromwell). Of these, *St. Cecilia* (1703) may have been inspired by Congreve's *Hymn to Harmony Written in Honour of St. Cecilia's Day*, since a version was given to the poet. The unfinished *Lady Elizabeth and her Family* of *c*.1706 is perhaps an allegory on marriage or the education of a prince. The scale and intimacy of these works anticipates the vogue for the conversation piece of the 1730s.

In 1712 Kneller painted a portrait of the duke of Marlborough for the duke of Chandos (priv. coll.), signing with the imperfect 'faciebat'. Kneller signed two other paintings 'faciebat': *William III* (Royal Collection), *Dr John Wallis* (Bodl. Oxf.), and one drawing, *Cupids Struggling for the Palm* (the combat of earthly and celestial love) (*c*.1715–20; E. B. Crocker Art Gallery, Sacramento, California). In antiquity this was a 'provisional signature … the artist … having intended to improve' wherein Pliny saw 'a wealth of diffidence' (Pliny, 1.17). Kneller's diffidence about his ability to complete images of these three great figures and of the Neoplatonic doctrine of the triumph of celestial love says much about his choice of heroes, and his idealism.

William III defended European liberty against what Kneller called France's 'Slavish Government' (*Letters … of Samuel Pepys*, 204). The duke of Marlborough became Louis XIV's nemesis. Kneller had planned to be a soldier, and as an old man jocularly told John Gay: 'I should have been a general of an army; for when I was in *Venice*, there was a *Girandole*, and all the *Place St. Mark* was in a smoke of gunpowder, and I did like the smell' (Richardson, 204). In his youth Kneller also studied mathematics which may explain his great admiration for Wallis.

Despite his development of the kit-cat portrait, Kneller continued to use the 30 by 25 inches format for busts (head-and-shoulders views), often with brilliant results, for example the bewigged *Newton* (1702; NPG); *John Locke* (1704; Virginia Museum of Fine Arts, Richmond), time-ravaged, in his own hair; and *Anthony Henley* (1705; priv. coll.) in a cap. Interestingly, Kneller had earlier painted fine portraits of all three sitters.

About 1710 Kneller's style became more classical, as can be seen by comparing the kit-cats *William Congreve* (1709), for which there is a fine head study in the Courtauld Institute, and *Jacob Tonson* (1717). Congreve is tall, twisting, and lit by flickering light; the handling is painterly. The Tonson portrait is quiet and broader in proportion; although there are still painterly passages in the sleeve, the other forms are more solidly and carefully rendered.

In 1703 Kneller moved to Great Queen Street, Lincoln's Inn Fields. (At his death he owned numbers 57 and 58, and also numbers 55 and 56, having purchased the latter from Thomas Stonor in March 1718.) In 1709 Kneller built a villa at Whitton, Middlesex, about 8 miles from London, where he lived in the summer 'visited & courted by all People of Honour & distinction' (Vertue, *Note books*, 2.121). The unusual design of Kneller's villa (whose staircase was decorated by Louis Laguerre and Kneller) was attributed first to Christopher Wren and then to William Talman.

On 23 January 1704 Kneller married Susanna Grave (d. 1729), widow, daughter of the Revd John Cawley, archdeacon of London and rector of Henley-on-Thames. The marriage was childless. Kneller had had a mistress, Mrs Voss, with whom he had a daughter, Catherine (b. c.1685x90), whom he used as model for St Catherine (known from Smith's mezzotint) and as St Agnes (Yale U. CBA). Catherine married James Huckle about 1706–7, had a son, Godfrey (who later changed his name to Kneller and became the painter's heir), and died in February 1714.

Of himself and possibly his son-in-law, Kneller painted a small-scale portrait (Marquette University Collection of Fine Arts, Milwaukee, Wisconsin), whose design recalls Van Dyck's Earl of Newport and Lord George Goring (Petworth House, Sussex). Another small self-portrait of c.1706–11, with the kit-cat collection, is a version of the three-quarter-length (Uffizi Gallery, Florence) that the artist presented to Grand Duke Cosimo III at his request. In these works and in his Self-Portrait (1721; priv. coll.) Kneller's gestures are expansive, and his expression confident. In all Kneller wears a wig, and the medal, chain, and sword presented to him by William III.

The Self-Portrait of 1710 (priv. coll.) depicts Kneller at the age of sixty-four, then an advanced age. His father and his master Bol both died at this age, and Rembrandt a year younger. Kneller wears a cap and plain grey coat, into which he tucks his right hand. There are no accessories except for what appears be the tip of the painter's brush under his right arm. There is grave, stoic resignation in the pose and expression, but also vulnerability.

In 1711 'an Accademy for Drawing and Painting was contrived and established in London' (Vertue, Note books, 1.2). At the first meeting 'Sir Godfrey Kneller was agreed unanimously to be the Governor' (ibid., 6.168–9); he was re-elected annually until 1718, when factions developed and after two years the academy collapsed.

George I's accession in 1714 brought final honours for Kneller. The king retained him as principal painter and created him a baronet in 1715. This rank was not surpassed by any artist until Frederic Leighton received a peerage in 1896. In 1717 the seventy-one-year-old Kneller wrote that he was 'Living altogether heer [Whitton] … Except extraordinary occassions in his Majesties and the Royal family Servis, and Sume particular good frinds' (MSS L.1678. 6.VI.1957, V&A). Of the king Kneller painted a fine profile bust for the coinage (Neuhaus bei Schliersee) and for the Guildhall, London, a full-length (destroyed in the Second World War) in state robes, crowned, holding the regalia, like van Somer's James I (Royal Collection). This was a dynastic statement: George I's claim to the throne was through James I's daughter.

Kneller remained creative throughout his last decade. He painted group portraits, the finest being the Duke of Chandos and Family (1713; National Gallery of Canada, Ottawa), showing the duke, his recently deceased duchess, and their two boys in a design inspired by a famous relief (thought to be antique), The Image of Faith. Some of the colour and handling are influenced by Antonio Pellegrini, a Venetian painter then a director of the London academy.

Kneller painted splendid full-length female dismounted hunting portraits. The finest is the Countess of Mar (c.1715; on loan to the Scottish National Portrait Gallery, Edinburgh), ravishing in colour and handling; the cool lilac and silver of the dress set off by pink ribbons; the featheriness of the trees foreshadowing those in late works by Gainsborough. His brilliant indoor female full-length Henrietta Howard, Countess of Suffolk (c.1719; Blickling Hall, Norfolk; mis-attributed to Dahl, and Thomas Gibson) shows the sitter in a masquerade dress of warm pink and cool silver against a severe architectural setting. In the statuesque 'Beauties' tradition are Elizabeth, Lady Middleton (1713; priv. coll.) and the Marchioness of Rockingham (1720; Aston Hall, Birmingham City Art Gallery), both featuring cupid–dolphin fountains. The former also includes a fine grisaille relief of Pan overcome by cupids ('omnia vincit amor'). Perhaps the finest late male full-length is Thomas Pitt, 1st Earl of Londonderry (c.1720; Chevening, Kent), austere in design (the architecture recalling the Countess of Suffolk) yet rich in colour.

Of 1721 is Kneller's bust-length portrait of Alexander Pope (priv. coll.). The poet is ivy-crowned, in profile, looking upwards. The pose derives from a coin of Alexander the Great as Jupiter Ammon (reversed, like a succeeding monarch on coinage), the silhouette framed by a serpent biting its tail, the classical symbol of eternity. That this witty assemblage of numismatic motifs was the work of a seventy-five-year-old is not the least remarkable feature about it.

Also of 1721 is Kneller's bold profile pen-and-ink drawing of the antiquary William Stukeley, wigless (NPG), perhaps a study for an engraving. His free sketch in the same medium of the mezzotinter John Smith (priv. coll.) shows the sitter informally, in a cap. Its squiggly calligraphy recalls the Rembrandt school in which Kneller had been trained.

An outstanding three-quarter-length known as William Cheselden (1722; RCS Eng.), probably represents Dr Richard Mead, who saved Kneller from a violent fever in May that year. Beside the sitter is Hygeia (Health), a child of Aesculapius (implying that Mead is another). The design emulates Rubens's Sir Theodore de Mayerne (North Carolina Museum of Arts, Raleigh, North Carolina) then owned by Mead. Kneller entirely repainted Hygeia, probably to harmonize with the scale of the Aesculapius statue in the Rubens portrait, for which the Mead portrait may have been designed as a pendant.

Kneller's equestrian portrait King Henry IV as Duke of Hereford at the Coventry Duel (1723; priv. coll.) was painted for Earl Coningsby's Hampton Court, Herefordshire. Kneller reused the design and colour of the horse in his painting of William III in 1701 at Hampton Court, thus making Henry IV's sufferings under, and eventual triumph over, the despotic Richard II a type that prefigures the history of William III and James II.

Kneller died on 26 October 1723 and was:

> laid in state at his [London] house ... over his Coffin his Arms
> Crest Sur coat. gold spurrs &c. ecocheon & penants & he was
> carryd out of Town in a herse thursday November 7 ... many
> coaches 6 horses & men in Cloaks on horse back in a grand
> manner.   (Vertue, *Note books*, 2.123)

He was buried in St Mary's Church, Twickenham, on 7 November.

Kneller 'lost 20 thousand pounds in the South Sea [Company]. yet has [1722] clear 2 thousand a Year income' (Vertue, *Note books*, 3.15). In his will of 27 April 1723 Kneller left his wife a life interest in his estate, which was then to go to his godson, Godfrey Kneller Huckle, which led to chancery suits (1725–33). Along with Whitton and the London houses, Kneller owned another property, the famous tavern, Pontack's, in Abchurch Lane, and shares in mining machinery, Becker's Engine. Kneller left £300 and a design (British Museum) for his monument, which he wanted to be erected in Twickenham. But this would have involved moving the memorial to Pope's father, at which Pope demurred, although he did write Kneller's epitaph. The monument to Kneller, by Rysbrack, was set up in Westminster Abbey in 1730.

Reputation and achievement   Vertue characterized 'Ho[garth as] a man whose high conceit of himself & of all his operations, puts all the painters at defiance not excepting the late famous Sr. Godf. Kneller—& Vandyke amongst them' (Vertue, *Note books*, 3.111). This puts Kneller in fine company, but seems to clash with Marshall Smith's comment in 1692 that Kneller was 'a gentleman of good *Morals*, True to his *Friends*, *Affable* and free from ... *Affectation* or *Pride*' (Smith, 23). Both assessments may be correct. To his friends and contemporaries Kneller may have been as Smith described him. For some of the younger generation, impatient with authority and what they saw as pomposity, Kneller became an object of derision. In 1760 Hogarth recalled that the London academy had been started:

> by some gentlemen painters of the first rank, who, in their
> forms imitated the Academy in France, but conducted their
> business with less fuss and solemnity; yet the little that there
> was of it soon became the object of ridicule ... and [Kneller]
> and his adherents ... found themselves comically
> represented marching in ridiculous procession round the
> walls of their room.   (Pye, 20)

But it is unlikely that the caricaturists included George Vertue, a younger academy member, despite his belief in the Governor's 'high conceit'. In 1721 he extolled Kneller as 'This great & Admirable Genius', 'this great man', and 'the Morning Star for all other Portrait Painters in his Time' (Vertue, *Note books*, 2.119, 122, 121).

Kneller's reputation remained high long after his death. In Henry Fielding's *Tom Jones* the heroine, Sophia Western, is 'most like the picture of Lady Ranelagh', a Hampton Court Beauty (1749, bk 4, chap. 2). The painters Joseph Highmore, John Vanderbank, Allan Ramsay, and Joseph Wright of Derby paid homage by making copies of Kneller's works or reusing his designs. Gainsborough wrote enthusiastically of Kneller's 'pencil or touch' (Gainsborough, 63), and Reynolds, who owned a Kneller self-portrait, 'admired and studied' (Dallaway, 73) his *Lord Crewe* (Bodl. Oxf.). Abroad, he had at least one German pupil, J. L. Hirschmann of Nuremberg. Dutch artists employed Kneller's designs through mezzotints and in Russia the Dane Virgilius Eriksen 'borrowed' the horse from the *William III* at Hampton Court for the equestrian portraits of Catherine the Great he painted in 1762. American colonial painters also availed themselves of Kneller's patterns, like the Dutch, through mezzotints.

Change came with Horace Walpole's enormously influential *Anecdotes of Painting in England* (1762–80), reprinted by J. Dallaway with additional notes in 1826. Walpole crassly condemned Kneller's patron William III: 'This prince, like most in our annals, contributed nothing to the advancement of the arts. He was born in a country [Holland] where taste never flourished' (Walpole, 2.201). Walpole also castigated Kneller's 'master Rembrandt's unnatural chiaroscuro' (ibid., 2.205).

Although Walpole admired Kneller's equestrian oil sketch of William III (then at Houghton Hall, Norfolk), and praised the Kit-Cat Club series and the *Grinling Gibbons* (also then at Houghton), he thought the Hampton Court picture a 'tame and poor performance' (Walpole, 2.203). Walpole also wrote that Kneller's 'draperies are [usually] so carelessly finished, that they resemble no silk or stuff the world ever saw' (ibid., 2.204 n. 3). On this Dallaway enlarged: 'He, sometimes, in the haste of finishing, left part of the primed cloth uncovered. This fault ... proceeded from haste and rapaciousness'. With the latter Dallaway expanded on Walpole's baseless charge that 'where [Kneller] offered one picture to fame, he sacrificed twenty to lucre [because] he met with customers of so little judgment' (ibid., 2.201–13).

In their criticism of Kneller's technique Walpole and Dallaway reflected neoclassical prejudice against baroque 'visible' brushwork, in favour of smooth 'finished' surfaces. But in response to their writings, Kneller's reputation plummeted. In 1848 his monument at Westminster Abbey was moved from the nave to the south aisle, truncated, and the remaining portion was placed too high to be properly noticed. Whitton became the Royal School of Military Music and was entirely rebuilt, thus destroying its unusual design.

Xenophobia in England increased prejudice against Kneller. In 1845 the engraver John Pye dismissed Kneller as 'a German' (Pye, 19). 'British art', as recorded in Pye's *Patronage of British Art* (1845), only began with Hogarth, a view which is still encountered. By the early twentieth century Kneller's continental achievements were almost forgotten. The estimate of his level of intelligence also fell. 'The matter [of being a Rembrandt pupil] is not very important as regards Kneller's formation ... the revelation of [Rembrandt's] deep communings with life was no doubt beyond the puzzled Godfrey' (Baker, *Lely and the Stuart Portrait Painters*, 76–7). In his *In Good King Charles's Golden Days* (1939) Bernard Shaw wanted to include Hogarth but for chronological reasons had instead to use Kneller: 'Kneller had not Hogarth's brains; but I have had to endow him with them to provide Newton with a victorious antagonist' (*Bodley Head Bernard Shaw*, 205).

Ironically Kneller was admired by Hogarth, who told Archbishop Herring that 'some of our chief Dignitaries in the Church have had the best luck in their portraits. The most excellent heads painted by Van Dyck and Kneller were those of Laud and Tillotson' (Antal, 225). The design of the chauvinist portrait signed 'W. Hogarth Anglus' (Dulwich Picture Gallery, London) derives from Kneller's *Sir Richard Steele* (1711), a Kit-Cat Club portrait the engravings of which Hogarth owned. Indeed Hogarth's directness owes much to works by Kneller such as *Ishack Pereyra* and *Jacob Tonson*. Kneller's *Self-Portrait* (1710) was long attributed to Hogarth.

The later twentieth century saw a reassessment of Kneller. Collins Baker, reversing the judgements of Walpole and Dallaway (and his own earlier opinion), lauded Kneller 'as a technician … not unworthy of … [the] company [of Hals, Rembrandt and Velázquez] … in England no predecessor [of Kneller's] had practised his particular use of open, fluent brushwork, interplaying broken colour' (Baker, 'Craftsmanship', 29). Sir Ellis Waterhouse and Sir Oliver Millar stressed the high quality of many of Kneller's English works and his unusual range in full-length and equestrian portraits. Sumowski brilliantly recovered some of Kneller's Amsterdam works.

In Amsterdam Kneller was a history painter of distinction. In England he painted a few (fine) histories, and created a remarkable portrait gallery including virtually everyone of importance from the time of Charles II to George I. He developed the Van Dyck–Lely tradition along simpler, more direct lines, especially after the experience of seeing works by Rubens in Brussels in 1697. Kneller ran a studio, which produced much routine work, as had Lely, Van Dyck, Rubens, and Titian. But Kneller's own works are always soundly drawn and painted—at their best they are inspired. His grasp of the character and mind of his sitters, and his ability to express them in design and colour, is often brilliant. With a Newton, a Locke, a Dryden, a Prior, or a Pope he almost always rose to the occasion and produced a masterpiece. His intense, virtually religious, dedication to his art is attested to by Pope in a letter to Jonathan Richardson (13 January 1731): 'Sir Godfrey Kneller call'd imploying the pencil [paint-brush], the prayer of the painter, and affirm'd it to be his proper way of serving God, by the talent he gave him' (Wimsatt, 139). Kneller's strong sense of duty to his profession is shown by his acceptance of the governorship of the London academy at the age of sixty-five, and remaining in that office, a thankless task, for seven years.

Nevertheless, Kneller's teaching at the London academy and the legacy of his works had a powerful impact on succeeding generations. Thanks to renewed interest in the seventeenth century, Kneller's technical qualities as a painter and designer are now once more appreciated. But the intellectual side of his art, including his invention, imaginative use of allegory, and wit, are still inadequately recognized. Nor is sufficient account taken of Kneller's influence on later English painters, including Hogarth,

Gainsborough, and Reynolds. Because of his industry and longevity Kneller has long been known as Britain's most prolific portraitist. He should also be acknowledged as one of her greatest and most important.

J. DOUGLAS STEWART

Sources J. D. Stewart, *Sir Godfrey Kneller* (1971) [exhibition catalogue, NPG, London] · J. D. Stewart, *Sir Godfrey Kneller and the English baroque portrait* (1983) · J. D. Stewart, 'Sir Godfrey Kneller as painter of histories and *portraits historiés*', *Art and patronage in the Caroline courts: essays in honour of Sir Oliver Millar*, ed. D. Howarth (1993), 243–63 · J. D. Stewart, 'King William the "Deliverer" and Shakespeare's "Hopeful" Harry of Hereford: a Kneller drawing discovered and elucidated', *Apollo*, 142 (Nov 1995), 25–32 · V. Manuth and others, eds., *Wisdom, knowledge and magic: the image of the scholar in seventeenth-century Dutch art* (1996), nos. 9, 29 [exhibition catalogue, Agnes Etherington Arts Centre, Queen's University, Kingston, ON, 15 Oct 1996 – 13 April 1997] · E. K. Waterhouse, *The dictionary of British 16th and 17th century painters* (1988), 154–8 · O. Millar, 'Stuart painting', *The connoisseur new guide to English painting and sculpture*, ed. L. G. G. Ramsay (1962), 27–44 · Vertue, *Note books* · [B. Buckeridge], 'An essay towards an English school of painting', in R. de Piles, *The art of painting, with the lives and characters of above 300 of the most eminent painters*, 3rd edn (1754), 354–439 [John Zachary Kneller and Sir Godfrey Kneller] · M. S. [M. Smith], *The art of painting according to the theory and practice of the best Italian, French and German painters* (1692), 23–4 · Joachim von Sandrarts Academie der Bau-, Bild-, und Mahlerey-Künste von 1675, ed. A. R. Peltzer (Munich, 1925), 350–52 · rate books, Westminster Public Library · W. H. Hunt, ed., *The registers of St Paul's Church, Covent Garden, London*, 4, Harleian Society, register section, 36 (1908), 184 · H. Walpole, *Anecdotes of painting in England: with some account of the principal artists*, ed. R. N. Wornum, new edn, 3 vols. (1849); repr. (1876); repr. in 4 vols. (New York, 1969) · J. C. Weyerman, *De levens-beschryvingen der Nederlandsche konst-schilders en konst-schilderessen*, 4 vols. (The Hague, 1729–69) · L. B. Alberti, *On painting*, ed. and trans. J. R. Spencer (1966) · A. Blankert and others, *Gods, saints and heroes: Dutch painting in the age of Rembrandt* (1980) [exhibition catalogue, National Gallery of Art, Washington, DC] · W. K. Wimsatt, *The portraits of Alexander Pope* (1965) · *The Wentworth papers, 1705–1739*, ed. J. J. Cartwright (1883) · W. A. Ackermann, *Der Porträtmaler Sir G. Kneller* (1845) · W. Sumowski, *Gemälde der Rembrandt-Schüler*, 3 (Landau, 1983), nos. 970–77 · Evelyn, *Diary* · *Letters and the second diary of Samuel Pepys*, ed. R. G. Howarth (1932) · Pliny the elder, *Natural history, praef. 26*, 1 (1938) · J. Richardson, jun., *Richardsoniana* (1776) · T. Gainsborough, *Letters*, ed. M. Woodall (1963) · C. H. C. Baker, *Lely and the Stuart portrait painters: a study of English portraiture before and after van Dyck*, 2 vols. (1912) · C. H. Collins Baker, *Lely and Kneller* (1922) · C. H. Collins Baker, 'The craftsmanship of Kneller', *The Connoisseur*, 127 (1951), 29–32 · J. Pye, *Patronage of British art: an historical sketch* (1845) · J. Dallaway, *Anecdotes of the arts in England, or, Comparative remarks on architecture, sculpture and painting* (1800) · D. Lysons, *The environs of London*, 3 (1795), 595 · W. E. Riley, *The parish of St Giles-in-the-Fields*, ed. L. Gomme, 2, Survey of London, 5 (1914), 55 · GEC, *Baronetage*, 5.27–8 · W. A. Shaw, *The knights of England*, 2 (1906), 267 · *The Bodley Head Bernard Shaw: collected plays with their prefaces*, 7 (1974) · F. Antal, *Hogarth and his place in European art* (1962) · E. Croft-Murray, *Decorative painting in England, 1537–1837*, 1 (1962) · 'A list of pictures at Kingsweston taken July 1695', Yale U. CBA · G. Kneller, letter in Italian to his brother, John Zachary, then at York, 12 April 1677, BL, Add. MS 4277, fol. 104 · G. Wharton, 'Autobiography', BL, Add. MSS 20006–20007 [quoted in J. Kent Clark, *Goodwin Wharton* (1984)] · G. Kneller, three letters to H. Masters, 1717–18, V&A NAL, L.1678 (A & B) 6. VI. 1957 · PRO, PROB 11/594, fols. 281r–286r · U. Wolff-Thomsen, 'Magdalena Hedwig Röder und Gottfried Kneller: eine Neuentdeckung', *Nordlinglen; Beiträge zur Kunst- und Kulturgeschichte Schleswig-Holstein*, 69 (2000), 7–13 · K. Gibson, '"Best Belov'd of Kings": the iconography of King Charles II', PhD diss., Courtauld Inst., 1997

Archives V&A NAL, letters to lord mayor of London and miscellanea
Likenesses G. Kneller, self-portrait, oils, c.1680, V&A · A. Verrio, oils, 1680–84 · R. Collin, line engraving, 1684 (after G. Kneller), BM · G. Kneller, self-portrait, oils, 1685, NPG [see illus.] · G. Kneller, self-portrait, oils, c.1688–1690, priv. coll. · attrib. J. Cavalier, ivory medallion, c.1690, NPG · G. Kneller, self-portrait, oils, 1706–11, NPG · G. Kneller, self-portrait, oils, 1710, priv. coll. · J. M. Rysbrack, bust, Westminster Abbey · R. White, engraving (after G. Kneller, c.1680), repro. in *Joachim von Sandrarts Academie*
Wealth at death wealthy: will, PRO, PROB 11/584, fols. 281r–286r

Kneller, John Zacharias (1642–1702). *See under* Kneller, Sir Godfrey, baronet (1646–1723).

Knevet, Ralph (*bap.* 1602, *d.* 1672), poet and Church of England clergyman, was baptized at St Margaret's, Hardwick, Norfolk, on 19 February 1602, the seventh child and second son of 'Raphe Nevett and Alis', relatives of the great Norfolk family of Knyvett. Admitted pensioner at Peterhouse, Cambridge, on 3 September 1616, Knevet seems not to have resided after December 1618. He was probably tutor in the Oxnead household of his patron William Paston in Norfolk (Paston's maternal grandfather was Sir Thomas Knyvett of Ashwell Thorpe). When Paston's wife, Lady Katherine Bute, died after childbirth on 30 December 1636, Knevet wrote *Funerall Elegies* (1637) as well as an inscription for the monument by Nicholas Stone, the celebrated master mason. In 1638 Knevet and Nicholas Stone jun. accompanied Paston on a tour to Florence and to Rome, where they then waited for Paston's return from Egypt in March 1639. The cautious Paston may have designed the journey 'to avoid employment' and involvement during an unstable period; he was readily discharged from sequestration on 3 June 1644.

Knevet's first published work is *Stratiōtikon, or, A Discourse of Militarie Discipline* (1628), which is prefaced by thirty-seven dedicatory poems addressed in hierarchic order to Norfolk gentry active in militia organization or public affairs. It partly resembles instructional treatises like Roger Ascham's *Toxophilus* (1545), Barnaby Riche's *Alarme to England* (1578), and Sir Henry Knyvett's *The Defence of the Realme*, a manuscript presented to Queen Elizabeth in 1596. But *Stratiōtikon* also belongs with the verse georgic, fashionable in the 1620s. Knevet expresses forthrightly (if in allegorical guise) his concern about the papacy's secular power, and advances Spartan arguments for military training to promote discipline and preparedness. He concludes with a dark threnody on two Norfolk military men who had died on the Île de Ré expedition (1627).

On 3 May 1631 a masque by Knevet, *Rhodon and Iris*, was presented at Norwich to the Society of Florists, for whom William Strode (c.1632–1635) and Matthew Stevenson (1645) were later to write. Again allegory licenses bold speech—this time satire of hypocritical puritans, besides two local individuals, an ambitious lawyer, and a military coxcomb. It provoked protests, which in turn elicited a published version (entered 12 November 1631 and printed in both Norwich and London). Its verse is sometimes rough, as if prose has been set as verse.

Knevet's *Funerall Elegies* (1637), written within three months, argue for cessation of grief in the exalted vein of mid-century elegies. Some have compared it to Donne's panegyrics on Elizabeth Drury but Knevet's praise is less wildly excessive: Lady Katherine actually was 'patronesse Of all [his] hopes' (*Shorter Poems*, 265). Otherwise Knevet's work remained in manuscript until the twentieth century. *A Supplement of 'The Faery Queene' in Three Bookes*, dated 1635, continues Spenser's poem through books VII–IX with a *mise en scène* in Norfolk and continental Europe. The manuscript (CUL, MS Ee.3.53) is a fair copy in Knevet's hand, which he had prepared for publication; for some reason, however, he changed his mind and later purged it of almost all evidence of his authorship. *A Supplement* shows Knevet's interest in contemporary affairs (Albanio figures James I; Callimachus, Gustavus Adolphus) but inevitably disappoints any reader expecting Spenser's larger reach.

A Gallery to the Temple (BL, Add. MS 27447) contains Knevet's best poems. It remained in manuscript until careful editions by G. Pellegrini (R. Knevet, *A Gallery to the Temple*, Studi e Testi, 6, 1954) and A. M. Charles (1966). Probably written in the 1640s, it was subsequently inscribed for 'Sir Robert Paston's Lady' (*Shorter Poems*, 277). Unlike such other homages to George Herbert as Christopher Harvey's, Knevet only occasionally imitates *The Temple* closely. As his title, from Giambattista Marino's *La galeria* (1619) suggests, Knevet means to present foreign spoils. Rejecting Italian superstition and English coldness ('The Extremes'), his devotional warmth, like Crashaw's, is capable of surprise ('Truth'; 'The Feast'). A preface expounds Knevet's critical opinions, which include admiration of the Italian poets Vittoria Colonna and Marino, and dislike of secular Italian academies.

In 1652 Knevet was presented by William Paston to the living of St Michael's, Lyng, Norfolk, valued at £66 per annum. He officiated as preaching minister until 21 September 1662, when he was ordained by the moderate presbyterian bishop Edward Reynolds. Knevet kept the parish register in his own hand until 9 August 1671. On 22 January 1672 he made a will, leaving all to his wife, Anne, his executor; he died probably before 25 March, and certainly before 16 July, when the will was entered for probate. Knevet was buried in the chancel at St Michael's, Lyng.

ALASTAIR FOWLER

Sources *The shorter poems of Ralph Knevet: a critical edition*, ed. A. M. Charles (1966) · W. M. Merchant, 'Ralph Knevet of Norfolk, poet of civill warre', *Essays and Studies by Members of the English Association*, new ser., 13 (1960), 21–35 · C. B. Millican, 'Ralph Knevet, author of the "Supplement" to Spenser's *Faerie Queene*', *Review of English Studies*, 14 (1938), 44–52 · A. M. Charles, 'Touching David's harp: George Herbert and Ralph Knevet', *George Herbert Journal*, 2 (1978), 54–69 · K.-J. Höltgen, 'Ralph Knevet's ordination', *N&Q*, 212 (1967), 311 · K.-J. Höltgen, 'Ralph Knevet under the Commonwealth', *N&Q*, 215 (1970), 407–8 · S. El-Gabalawy, 'Two obscure disciples of George Herbert', *N&Q*, 222 (1977), 541–2

Knewstub [Knewstubs], John (1544–1624), Church of England clergyman, was born in Kirkby Stephen in Westmorland in 1544. Nothing is known of his youth until his attendance at St John's College, Cambridge, from which

he graduated BA in 1564. In 1567 he was admitted to a fellowship at St John's, where he soon emerged as a member of the puritan faction in the university, being among those who petitioned against the wearing of clerical vestments. He was one of a group—along with Ezekiel Culverwell, John Carter, and others—that met with Lawrence Chaderton to expound and discuss the scriptures, and he developed lifelong friendships with John Still, Adam Winthrop, Henry Sandes, Roger Goad, and others. His *Lectures … upon the Twentieth Chapter of Exodus*, first published in 1577, went through four printings between then and 1584. Delivered while he was at Cambridge, they set forth the developing English Calvinist theology which expounded God's determination of those who were elect and thus in covenant with him.

Shortly before that work appeared Knewstub had emerged as an important figure in the church when in 1576 he preached the Good Friday sermon at Paul's Cross against the Family of Love. Opposition to the Familists preoccupied him over the next five years. In 1580 he was engaged to investigate the influence of the Family of Love at the royal court and was then chosen to deliver letters from the privy council to five bishops ordering the investigation of the sect in their dioceses. He was himself appointed to the investigating commission in the diocese of Norwich. In 1581 he helped to prepare and promote a bill against the Familists which was introduced into the parliament that met in the early months of that year. His prominence in the attack upon these heterodox opinions helped to mask his own reservations concerning church practices, and the prominent connections that he made during this campaign were useful in protecting him from episcopal attacks on nonconformity in the 1580s.

Meanwhile, in 1579 he was presented to the living of Cockfield, Suffolk, by Sir William Spring. In 1582 he hosted a gathering of mostly East Anglian clergy to discuss the observance of the Book of Common Prayer. The following year a group of Suffolk ministers, including Knewstub and others who had attended the Cockfield meeting, appealed to the bishop of Norwich in protest against Archbishop Whitgift's three articles, which intended to enforce clerical conformity. The ministers took the occasion to express their concerns about such matters as the rite of baptism and burial practices. Along with other signatories Knewstub was suspended from his ministry for his nonconformity, but through the intervention of Lord Burghley and others this proved temporary. In 1585–6 Knewstub served as a chaplain to the earl of Leicester on the latter's expedition to the Netherlands, another reflection of his connections with prominent puritans at court.

In Suffolk Knewstub had emerged as leader of the combination lecture that functioned at Bury St Edmunds, and in 1589 he became engaged in a dispute with Thomas Rogers, who had been excluded from the lecture after preaching a sermon perceived to be critical of Chaderton. Throughout the latter part of Elizabeth's reign Knewstub was one of the dominant figures in the puritan movement in the Stour valley borderland of Suffolk and Essex. He travelled throughout the region, preaching and visiting such clerical colleagues as Richard Rogers, Ezekiel Culverwell, and Stephen Egerton, as well as lay supporters of the movement. His advice was sought on ecclesiastical appointments. Along with John Still he was consulted by the townsmen of Bury St Edmunds over the choice of town preachers. In 1592 he joined with Chaderton, Roger Goad, and Still, among others, in recommending John Ward of Haverhill to be town preacher of Ipswich. Though he continued to be cited in visitations for refusal either to wear the surplice or to sign with the cross in baptism, no action was taken against him. He was also noted for his advocacy of fasts and strict sabbath observance. No record of Knewstub's subscription to Whitgift's three articles has been found, and it is likely that, in common with many other clergymen, he offered only a qualified conformity.

In 1595 Knewstub was proposed by Goad and others as master of St John's after the death of William Whitaker, but he was not elected. In 1596 he was named as an overseer of the Boxford grammar school chartered by the queen. Fellow overseers included Adam Winthrop, Thomas Lovell, Henry Sandes, and members of the Waldegrave and Gurdon families.

In 1603 Knewstub was chosen to be one of the puritan spokesmen at the following year's Hampton Court conference. When the sought-for reforms were denied he pleaded with the king for tolerance of those in Suffolk who desired to avoid use of the surplice and signing with the cross in baptism, but his plea was rejected. Correspondence between his friends William Bedell and Samuel Ward indicates that at this time Knewstub was concerned with the possible consequences of continuing nonconformity and was seeking a curate who would conduct services while wearing a surplice. This stratagem failed, and in 1606 he was presented for not using the sign of the cross in baptism and for not wearing the surplice. In 1611 he was again cited for not wearing the surplice. Yet he escaped deprivation.

Knewstub continued to play a prominent role in efforts to foster the piety of the godly in the Stour valley, and he preached strongly on the need to exercise Christian love to all members of the community. In 1605 he preached the funeral sermon for Robert Welche of Little Waldingfield and with his fellow clergymen carried the coffin to the graveyard. He joined Richard Rogers of Wethersfield, Essex, in acting as spiritual physician to an Essex youth. In September 1613, along with John Winthrop Groton, Henry Sandes (the lecturer of Boxford), and others, he formed a covenanted spiritual association whose members were pledged to remember each other in their prayers every Friday and to meet annually to renew their communion. In 1618 he preached the funeral sermon for Richard Rogers.

Knewstub died at Cockfield and was buried there on 31 May 1624. In his will (drawn up on the 20th) he left gifts to Henry Sandes of Boxford, Ezekiel Culverwell, Samuel Ward of Ipswich, John Wilson of Sudbury, and others. He left £20 to buy a house or land whose revenue should be yearly distributed to the poor of Cockfield; if that annual income was not disposed of as directed, the money could be claimed by St John's College to supplement the two exhibitions which Knewstub had founded in 1620 to enable both a native of Kirkby Stephen and a youth of Cockfield to study there. Knewstub was not married, but left money to three nephews and several other relatives. The supervisors of his will were headed by his 'worshipfull good friend' John Winthrop of Groton, the son of Knewstub's ally Adam Winthrop and himself the future governor of the Massachusetts Bay Colony.

Knewstub often preached what might be called a social gospel, urging his listeners to exercise charity towards their neighbours, and contemporary testimony indicates that he practised what he preached. Richard Rogers in his diary referred to his friend Knewstub as 'in prayer unwearyed', and a man of 'rare humility, joined with great knowledge and wisdom' who was noted for 'his bearing of wrongs' and 'bountiful liberality with mercifulness' (Knappen, 95–6). In *The Real Christian* Giles Firmin records an episode that bears this out. Rogers and Knewstub were travelling together when they encountered a noted reprobate. Rogers moved to pass on, but Knewstub conversed with the man courteously and then reproved Rogers, saying that his friend's indifference 'is not the way to win wicked men to a liking of the Gospel and the way of God, but rather to beat them off' (Firmin, 67–8).

FRANCIS J. BREMER

Sources *Two Elizabethan puritan diaries, by Richard Rogers and Samuel Ward*, ed. M. M. Knappen, SCH, 2 [1933] · I. Morgan, *Godly preachers of the Elizabethan church* (1965) · C. W. Marsh, *The Family of Love in English society, 1550–1630*, another edn (1994) · L. Trinterud, ed., *Elizabethan puritanism* (1971) · P. Collinson, *The Elizabethan puritan movement* (1967) · G. Firmin, *The real Christian, or, A treatise of effectual calling* (1670) · *DNB* · *The Winthrop papers*, ed. W. C. Ford and others, 1 (1929) · J. Craig, 'The "Cambridge Boies": Thomas Rogers and the "brethren" in Bury St Edmunds', *Belief and practice in Reformation England: a tribute to Patrick Collinson from his students*, ed. S. Wabuda and C. Litzenberger (1998), 154–76 · T. Webster, *Godly clergy in early Stuart England: the Caroline puritan movement, c.1620–1643* (1997) · D. MacCulloch, *The later reformation in England, 1547–1603* (1990) · F. J. Bremer, *Congregational communion: clerical friendship in the Anglo-American puritan community, 1610–1692* (1994) · will, PRO, PROB 11/143, sig. 53

Wealth at death see will, PRO, PROB 11/143, sig. 53, fols. 428v–429r

Knibb, William (1803–1845), missionary and abolitionist, was born in Kettering, Northamptonshire, on 7 September 1803; one of twins, he was the fifth of eight children of Thomas Knibb, a tailor who subsequently became bankrupt, and Mary, *née* Dexter. William attended the Kettering Free School, and at the age of twelve joined his brother Thomas as an apprentice in a firm of printers which had moved to Bristol. Their employer was the son of the Baptist minister in Kettering, who was also secretary of the Baptist Missionary Society. Through this connection, William and Thomas Knibb both became Baptists.

In 1822 Thomas Knibb began work as a teacher in a Baptist school in Kingston, Jamaica. William, who also saw himself as a missionary, taught in a Sunday school for poor children and preached in a district in Bristol known as the Beggar's Opera or Beggars' Uproars. When Thomas

William Knibb (1803–1845), by George Baxter, 1847

Knibb died after only fifteen months in Jamaica, William volunteered to take his place and was accepted. He spent three months training as a teacher at the Borough Road school of the British and Foreign School Society; there, his teachers described him as a strapping young man, bounding with energy; they also saw him as impulsive but hoped that his personality would be balanced by the calming influence of his new wife, Mary Watkins, whom he married about October 1824, a month before sailing to Jamaica on 5 November.

The situation for nonconformist missionaries in Jamaica in the 1820s was very difficult. When Knibb arrived in the colony in 1825, the dissenting missionaries were barely tolerated. The planters distrusted the missionaries' involvement with the slaves, and this situation was made worse by the British government's decision to ameliorate slavery, beginning in 1823. At first Knibb taught at a school in Kingston and, as was to be the case so often in the future, was instrumental in the construction of a new building for the school (he never seemed to hesitate in undertaking heavy expenditures for building and buying land and was frequently personally encumbered as a result). He also preached at a chapel in Port Royal, near Kingston, before starting a new mission in 1829 in Savanna la Mar, in south-western Jamaica. Although he was to remain at this mission station only briefly before moving to Falmouth on Jamaica's north coast a year later, it was in Savanna la Mar that he ran into his first serious difficulties with the planters.

While Knibb was in Falmouth during the Easter period in 1830, some of his church members used his house in Savanna la Mar for prayer meetings. During one of these meetings, a group of people headed by a free coloured carpenter interrupted the prayers and reported them to the magistrates. The complaint was that slaves and free coloureds were preaching and teaching without permission, which was a violation of the slave code. Their leader, Sam Swiney, the slave deacon of the Baptist church, was found guilty and sentenced to two weeks' hard labour and twenty lashes. On the day of the punishment, Knibb accompanied Swiney at the flogging, and, as he was taken away to begin hard labour, Knibb shouted, 'Sam, whatever you want, send to me and you shall have it' (Wright, 46). The case generated considerable publicity and eventually reached the Colonial Office, where the judgment against Swiney was declared illegal.

Tension in Jamaica rose dramatically in 1831, when the British government sought to have the Jamaican colonists pass an order in council further ameliorating the condition of the slaves. A massive slave rebellion broke out in western Jamaica just after Christmas 1831, and in scenes of confusion and disarray Knibb, along with several other missionaries, was arrested and threatened with death. The white people blamed the missionaries, and especially the Baptists, for the slave rebellion and destroyed most of the Baptist and Methodist chapels in the western part of the island. Although Knibb was indicted, the case was thrown out of court. The missionaries then dispatched Knibb to England to defend themselves against the slanders of the planters.

On landing in England and on hearing that the Reform Bill had been passed, Knibb was reputed to have said, 'Thank God. Now I'll have slavery down. I will never rest, day or night, till I see it destroyed, root and branch' (Wright, 112). He spoke at a large meeting of the representatives of the dissenting bodies at Exeter Hall in London, and was a witness before select committees of both houses of parliament. In his views on slavery Knibb was considerably ahead of the committee of the Baptist Missionary Society. When the secretary of the committee, John Dyer, urged Knibb to be prudent and to pursue a temperate policy, Knibb refused to remain silent and threatened to resign from the society. Knibb subsequently toured all over Britain speaking against slavery to much acclaim. In August 1833 parliament passed the bill to abolish slavery; it became effective a year later, on 1 August 1834. When Knibb returned to Jamaica that October, slavery had ended.

The period after the formal abolition of slavery was to see significant growth in the Baptist church in Jamaica. In the ten years after 1831 membership in the church grew from 11,000 to 30,000, and the number of ministers grew from sixteen to twenty-seven. Knibb had an important role in this increase; within a year of his return to Jamaica he received 400 new members into his church at Falmouth. By 1837 he had established three new country stations, each with a chapel and school. Knibb's own family grew as well; he and his wife had four sons and five daughters. Four of the children died in infancy and the only boy to survive, William, died in 1837 at the age of twelve. There were suggestions that Knibb lived well; his congregation built him and his family a substantial house in Kettering, near Falmouth, worth £1000. But Knibb's comfortable lifestyle did not affect his concern for black people in Jamaica.

Knibb opposed the apprenticeship system, the period between the abolition of slavery and full freedom. But full freedom in 1838 brought a new dimension to Knibb's work: he actively sought to negotiate fair wages for the ex-slaves. He published a weekly newspaper for the freedmen, the *Baptist Herald and Friend of Africa*, and he was also involved in buying land for the freedmen and establishing free villages for them. He frequently proclaimed his identity with black people and attended the Anti-Slavery Convention in England in 1840, speaking again on behalf of the freedmen. He returned to England in 1842 and 1845, to raise money for the mission in Jamaica and to highlight the plight of the former slaves. Knibb not only sought to protect the freedmen from exploitation by the planters; he also hoped to influence the elections to the Jamaican house of assembly and return candidates committed to disestablishment. Although Knibb founded the Anti-State Church Convention for this purpose, the governor, Lord Elgin, managed to outmanoeuvre Knibb and called an election in 1844 before the new voters, most of whom were freedmen, were eligible to take part in it.

Late in 1845 Knibb was stricken with yellow fever, and he died at Kettering on 15 November. Nearly 8000 people joined the funeral procession in Falmouth, where he was buried. The funeral orations did not omit to point out some of Knibb's flaws: among them his egotism and love of power. But they also highlighted his enormous contribution to ending slavery and his commitment to freedom for the mass of Jamaicans.   GAD HEUMAN

Sources P. Wright, *Knibb, 'the notorious' slaves' missionary, 1803–1845* (1973) · M. Turner, *Slaves and missionaries: the disintegration of Jamaican slave society, 1787–1834* (1982) · P. D. Curtin, *Two Jamaicas: the role of ideas in a tropical colony, 1830–1865* (1955) · R. J. Stewart, *Religion and society in post-emancipation Jamaica* (1992) · *DNB* · B. Stanley, *The history of the Baptist Missionary Society, 1792–1992* (1992)
Archives Regent's Park College, Oxford, Angus Library, Baptist Missionary Society archives, corresp. and papers
Likenesses lithograph, 1838, NPG · medallion, 1838, Falmouth church, Jamaica · B. Smith, lithograph, pubd 1845, NPG · G. Baxter, colour print, 1847, NPG [*see illus.*] · J. Cochran, stipple and line engraving (after daguerreotype), NPG · B. R. Haydon, group portrait, oils (*The Anti-slavery Convention, 1840*), NPG · A. Zobel, engraving, repro. in Wright, *Knibb*

Knight family (*per. c.*1680–1897), ironmasters, came to prominence with the activities of **Richard Knight** (1659–1745). He was the son of Richard Knight of Madeley, Shropshire, and he learned his trade while working at the Lower Coalbrookdale forge. He then moved to take over the Morton forge on the River Roden, also in Shropshire. Here he met and married Elizabeth (1671–1754), the daughter of Andrew Payne of Shawbury, a member of a prominent Shropshire family involved in the iron industry. They had four sons, two of whom followed their father into the iron trade. At various times Richard Knight held furnaces at Flaxley in the Forest of Dean, Willey in Shropshire, and Ruabon in north Wales. He also owned several forges in Shropshire and the Stour valley.

Richard Knight's interests in the iron industry of the midlands were further expanded when he entered the 'Ironworks in Partnership', which was dominated by the

*Foley family (*per. c.*1620–1716). The group comprised several ironmasters who brought their ironmaking properties together to form an important company, which was a major force within the British charcoal iron industry. Also from about 1698 Richard Knight operated the Bringewood furnace and forge and these were later linked with the Charlcotte furnace.

By 1725 Richard Knight had left the Ironworks in Partnership in order to expand his ironmaking interests in the Stour valley. This he achieved with the help of his son **Edward Knight** (1699–1780) when they entered into a partnership with Sir Thomas Lyttleton of Hagley Hall. Lyttleton brought Hales furnace into the partnership while the Knights contributed forges at Cookley and Whittington, both situated on the River Stour. The pig iron from Hales could be refined at the Stour forges to make wrought iron. This iron then found a ready market among the smiths and nailers of the midlands.

Richard Knight seems to have exhibited much drive and enthusiasm in building up his ironmaking empire. He was certainly not afraid of switching his resources from area to area and managed to build up a large personal fortune through his activities in the iron trade. He died in 1745, five years after his retirement from the active management of the family's ironworks.

The Knight family's interest in the iron trade now lay in two distinct and separate partnerships. The Bringewood partnership held furnaces at Bringewood and Charlcotte in Shropshire and the forge at Bringewood. The Stour partnership held Hales furnace and a series of forges along the River Stour; it was dominated by the Knights and from the late 1730s was totally in the hands of the family. From the retirement of Richard Knight the iron business had been managed by his sons Edward and **Ralph Knight** (1703–1754), who married Mary Dupa. Edward Knight was the innovator and in the late 1730s and early 1740s he built a plating mill at Bringewood to produce plate to be tinned at one of the family's Stour forges. This was one of the earliest tin-plate making concerns in Britain. In 1726 Edward married Elizabeth James, heir of Olton End, Warwickshire. The marriage produced three sons and three daughters.

Ralph Knight died in 1754 and Edward Knight was then later helped in the management of the works by his sons, **James Knight** (1735–1808) and **John** [i] **Knight** (1740–1795). James was unmarried, but John [i] married Henrietta Cunyngham. The successful operation of all the Knight family's ironworks allowed a period of expansion in the 1740s and 1750s, when Aston furnace and a forge at Bromford, near Birmingham, were purchased. The four furnaces owned by the family gave it an important position in the British iron industry and in the late 1750s the Knights produced about 8 per cent of Britain's total pig iron output.

Edward Knight had the foresight to adapt to the changing conditions in the iron industry during the 1750s. Charcoal iron was now competing with coke iron, whose manufacture was spreading quickly. Edward Knight used his home at Wolverley House, Worcestershire, as the centre of his operations and Wolverley forge was one of the most important parts of his ironmaking empire. It was here during the 1750s that Edward Knight introduced the manufacture of wrought iron using coke iron from Shropshire. Edward Knight was one of the first ironmasters to use coke iron at a forge, so demonstrating the acceptability of coke iron and heralding its dominance over charcoal iron.

Edward Knight retired from his business interests in 1771 leaving the furnaces and forges to be managed by James Knight, John [i] Knight, and their uncle Abraham Spooner. This took place during a period of great uncertainty as the charcoal iron industry came under increasing pressure from the spread of the manufacture of iron using coke as a fuel. The activities of the Bringewood partnership ended in 1779 and by 1785 all the family's charcoal-fired furnaces had been finally blown out. Edward Knight died in 1780.

The death of John [i] Knight in 1795 allowed his son **John** [ii] **Knight** (1765–1850) to take a prominent position in the Stour partnership. He had a most dynamic disposition for he immediately drew up plans to modernize the family's forges. John [ii] Knight applied the new methods of making wrought iron with coke to the forges. However, the death of James Knight in 1808 prompted a dismemberment of the partnership. The Spooner family took over the ownership of the properties around Birmingham, leaving John [ii] Knight with a reduced number of forges along the River Stour. Knight now concentrated his resources at one site on the Stour. This was the Cookley ironworks, where the manufacture of wire and tin plate was introduced alongside the production of wrought iron. After successfully modernizing Cookley John [ii] Knight seems to have searched for further challenges using money generated by the sale of shares in the Cookley concern. This took the form of purchases of land on Exmoor and in 1830 Knight took up residence in the area at Simonsbath House. His first wife was Helen Charlotte Weir. John [ii] Knight's considerable talents and energies were now being channelled away from the iron trade and into a scheme for taming and farming parts of Exmoor's wild lands. This interest in Exmoor was financed by selling some of his holdings in the family business to outsiders. However, Knight did not realize all his schemes for Exmoor since the health of his second wife, Jane Elizabeth Winn, daughter of the first Baron Headley, began to fail, which prompted a move to Jersey and then, later, another to Rome, where she died in 1841.

The sale of shares in the Cookley ironworks left the Knight family as a minority holder in the partnership. However, deaths among the partners in the late 1870s and early 1880s forced **Sir Frederic Winn Knight** (1812–1897), John [ii] Knight's eldest son, to become managing partner. At the age of sixty-nine Frederic Winn Knight became the manager of the Cookley Iron and Tinplate Works, although he acknowledged that previously he had taken no interest in its management. He was educated at Charterhouse School (*c.*1823–1828) and at the age of twenty-nine took over the management of the Knight estates on Exmoor. Frederic Winn Knight married Maria Louisa Couling Gibbs in 1850 and they had one son. He was a man of great determination and almost boundless energy. In the same year that he took over the running of the Knight estates he was elected MP for West Worcestershire. Frederic Winn Knight represented the constituency for forty-four years and while an MP he was parliamentary secretary to the Poor Law Board in 1852 under Lord Derby's administration and again in 1858–9 under Lord Palmerston. His only commercial experience before the management of Cookley was gained as a director of the Bank of London and the National Provincial Insurance Association. Frederic Winn Knight was knighted in 1886 for public services as a member of parliament and a justice of the peace. He seems to have inherited the family trait of making bold decisions, for in 1886 he moved the iron business from Cookley to Brockmoor at Brierley Hill in the Black Country. He died at 19 Marlborough Buildings, Bath, on 3 May 1897. He was survived by his wife. The new works was operated by a new limited company with Knight involvement into the early years of the twentieth century.

The Knights are a unique family within the story of the British iron industry. Although other midland families, such as the Foleys and the Darbys, had a long involvement in the iron trade, not one can match the activities of the Knights, which stretch from the seventeenth century to the twentieth.   LAURENCE INCE

Sources L. Ince, *The Knight family and the British iron industry, 1695–1902* (1991) • C. S. Orwin and R. J. Sellick, *The reclamation of Exmoor forest* (1970) • Burke, *Gen. GB* • *WWW*, 1897–1915 [Sir Frederic Winn Knight] • *CGPLA Eng. & Wales* (1897) [Sir Frederic Winn Knight]
Archives Worcs. RO, MSS | Herefs. RO, Downton Castle papers
Wealth at death £107,681 17s. 1d.—Sir Frederic Winn Knight: probate, 12 July 1897, *CGPLA Eng. & Wales*

Knight, Alfred Edward (1898–1974), piano manufacturer, was born at 99 Camberwell Road, south London, on 26 December 1898, the son of Alfred Edward Knight, journeyman piano maker, and his wife, Florence Jane, *née* Liversage. His family had been involved with piano making for the previous four generations, his great-great-grandfather having worked in the Broadwood workshop when it was at Westminster. Knight attended the West Square Central Boys' School, Southwark, where he showed a talent for wood- and metalwork. He spent part of his spare time while at school helping in the factory of the Hicks company in the New Kent Road, entering an apprenticeship there in 1913 at the age of fourteen. Having successfully completed his training, by 1919 he had started to work for the piano manufacturers Squire and Longson of Medlar Street, Camberwell. In 1923 he married Florence Jenny, daughter of Alfred George Slodden, a machinist; they had two daughters.

British piano makers in the years following the First World War were confronted by turbulent industrial relations, changing economic circumstances, and in some cases, fundamental weaknesses in management, which led, for example, to the collapse of the Brinsmead firm in 1920. Nevertheless, Squire and Longson survived the period, making good quality instruments under the brand name of Cremona, and also under the name Welmar for Whelpdale, Maxwell, and Codd until 1929 when their premises were destroyed by fire—a fate suffered so often by instrument makers. The factory was rebuilt, but Knight left in 1931 to set up a new business, Booker and Knight, at a factory in Carysfort Road, Stoke Newington. This bold step in the most severe years of the depression was rewarded with success, for by 1935 Knight was able to buy out Booker and set up his own Knight Piano Company. By 1939 the firm was making 1000 instruments a year.

Alfie, as he was known, was 'a bustling cheerful Londoner, with a brisk line in chat, a consummate salesman, as well as a fine craftsman. He was gregarious and loved meeting people' (Wainwright). Among the honours bestowed on Knight were the freedom and honorary citizenship of the city of Santiago, as well as a knighthood of the honorable order of Kentucky colonels. Knight was also appointed OBE in 1966 for his services to music and to musical education. In both areas he was an active participant, having been president of the Association of Blind Piano Tuners, a competent pianist, and a devoted educator. He toured schools, lecturing and expounding the philosophy that:

> Music is something you can do and appreciate for the whole of a lifetime … When parents give their children a musical education they are giving them the greatest gift possible. The playing of a musical instrument and appreciation of music is about the only thing left that can be done from nine to ninety. (ibid.)

Knight is noted chiefly for his innovation in the use of plastics in place of wood in piano construction, and it is significant that in a number of reference books on the piano it is almost only in this connection that he is mentioned. By personal research he developed a nylon impregnated with glass fibre and graphite as the main material which could give stability in a wide range of hostile environments. His lead in the development of piano actions was significant, and the world dominance of actions by Herrburger Brooks and other American firms was successfully challenged by the setting up of British Piano Actions (BPA) at Llanelli in south Wales, a company of which Knight was a director. In 1958 BPA found itself under threat from American rivals, and though Knight did much to keep the company alive, it went into liquidation in 1983.

The Knight Piano Company moved in 1955 to a new factory at Loughton in Essex, and there the firm concentrated on a range of standard upright models. A small grand piano was made for a short time by the firm, but it was unsuccessful and was withdrawn. The uprights however were of good quality and many hundreds survived in the demanding environment of schools, and even troops' canteens, testifying to their durability. They also continued to satisfy a considerable demand from the domestic market.

Knight died at his home, 26 Wellfields, Loughton, Essex, on 3 September 1974. His three children were all involved in the company. Sylvia Florence married John York, a director of Alfred Knight Ltd, and succeeded to the chairmanship of the company on her father's death. Gillian, his second daughter, worked for the company until her marriage, and after taking charge of the technical side of the firm his son Michael became the company's general manager.   CHARLES MOULD

Sources D. H. E. Wainwright, 'Knight, Alfred Edward', *DBB* · C. Ehrlich, *The piano: a history* (1976) · b. cert. · d. cert.
Likenesses photograph, repro. in Wainwright, 'Knight, Alfred Edward', 610
Wealth at death £35,612: probate, 15 April 1975, *CGPLA Eng. & Wales*

Knight, Anne (1786–1862), slavery abolitionist and campaigner for women's rights, was born on 2 November 1786 at Chelmsford, Essex, the third of the eight children of William Knight (1756–1814), wholesale grocer, and his wife, Priscilla, *née* Allen (1753–1829). Her mother was first cousin to the philanthropist William Allen, while she herself was first cousin to the chemist William Allen Miller. Her younger sister Maria (1791–1870) married in 1814 the abolitionist John Candler (1787–1869) and with him travelled to the West Indies and United States in the anti-slavery cause; they were for some years (1842–6) superintendents of The Retreat, York, the Quaker mental hospital founded by William Tuke.

In 1824, having by then a good knowledge of French and German, Anne Knight travelled on the continent with a group of fellow Quakers, combining sightseeing with religious and philanthropic concerns. From her base in the Chelmsford Ladies' Anti-Slavery Society she was deeply involved with the anti-slavery movement, travelling frequently to London and working with Thomas Clarkson, Joseph Sturge, Richard and Hannah Webb, and Elizabeth Pease (later Nichol). During the 1830s she returned several times to France in the same cause, in 1834 undertaking a speaking tour. The 1840 World's Anti-Slavery Convention in London gave her the opportunity to meet such American abolitionists as William Lloyd Garrison, Wendell Phillips, and Lucretia Mott. The movement for women's suffrage in Britain has been dated from the exclusion of women from the floor of this conference, for it drew women's attention to their marginal status within the movement, and highlighted the limitations placed on their capacity to act in the public sphere. In July 1848 the first women's rights convention in the United States was held at Seneca Falls, New York. The previous year an anonymous leaflet was issued in Britain claiming that 'Never will the nations of the earth be well governed, until both sexes, as well as all parties, are fully represented and have an influence, a voice, and a hand in the enactment and administration of the laws'. It has been persuasively argued that the author was Anne Knight. Certainly from the 1840s she had been writing frequent letters (she was a voluminous correspondent) to American abolitionists, including Angelina Grimké, and she was capable of sharp rejoinders to Chartists who suggested that the class struggle took precedence over that for women's rights.

Anne Knight (1786–1862), by unknown photographer, *c.*1855

Although Knight was in many ways typical of nonconformist women abolitionists, her views were more radical than many: a sympathizer with Chartism, she was interested in the British and French utopian socialist movements, maintained links with the White Quakers in Ireland, and in the 1840s supported the radical Garrisonian wing of the American abolition movement. Her support for women's rights led her in 1851 to be involved in forming the first organization for women's suffrage in Britain, the Sheffield Female Reform Association. In 1847 or 1848 Anne Knight left Chelmsford for Paris and, after living there enthusiastically (despite her Quaker upbringing) through the year of revolutions, she was at the international peace conference in Paris in 1849. Lucretia Mott described her in the 1840s as 'a singular looking woman—very pleasant and polite' (F. B. Tolles, ed., *Slavery and 'the Woman Question'*, 1952, 29).

In the late 1850s Anne Knight moved to Waldersbach, a village in the Vosges, south-west of Strasbourg. This had been the home of the pastor Jean-Frédéric Oberlin (1740–1820), whose philanthropic work she revered. Here she lived for the last few years of her life, lodging with Oberlin's grandson, and died there after a short illness on 4 November 1862.

Researches into Anne Knight's life have been hindered

by persistent confusion of her with another **Anne Knight** [*née* Waspe] (1792–1860), children's writer. This Anne Knight was born at Woodbridge, Suffolk, on 28 October 1792, the eldest of the eight children of Jonathan Waspe (1756?–1818), a leather-cutter, and his wife, Phebe, *née* Gibbs (1761–1851). She married in 1818 her first cousin and fellow Quaker James Knight (1794–1820) of Southwark. After her husband's early death, she returned to Woodbridge, where by 1826 she was keeping a school. She was a close friend of the poet Bernard Barton, and is frequently mentioned in Charles Lamb's letters to him. She was the author of a number of books for children, certainly *School-Room Lyrics* (1846), and most probably of *Poetic Gleanings* (1827), *Mornings in the Library* (1828), with a prefatory poem by Barton, and *Mary Gray* (1831), works which were previously ascribed to Anne Knight the social campaigner. Anne Knight the author died at her home in Woodbridge on 11 December 1860, and was buried in the Quaker burial-ground there.   EDWARD H. MILLIGAN

Sources *Annual Monitor* (1864) · G. Malmgreen, 'Anne Knight and the radical subculture', *Quaker History*, 71 (1982), 100–13 · J. Smith, ed., *A descriptive catalogue of Friends' books*, 2 (1867), 70–71 · 'Dictionary of Quaker biography', RS Friends, Lond. [card index] · O. Banks, *The biographical dictionary of British feminists*, 2 vols. (1985–90) · C. Midgley, *Women against slavery: the British campaigns, 1780–1870* (1992)
Archives Boston PL, letters to American abolitionists · RS Friends, Lond., memorandum book
Likenesses photograph, *c*.1855, RS Friends, Lond. [*see illus.*]
Wealth at death under £450: probate, 22 Jan 1863, *CGPLA Eng. & Wales* · under £200—Anne Knight, *née* Waspe: probate, 21 Dec 1860, *CGPLA Eng. & Wales*

Knight, Anne (1792–1860). *See under* Knight, Anne (1786–1862).

Knight, Bert Cyril James Gabriel (1904–1981), microbiologist, was born on 4 February 1904 at Glebe Cottage, Chart Lane, Reigate, Surrey, the son of Cyril Fennel Knight (1877–1944), furniture merchant, and his wife, Kate Gabriel (1872/3–1954). Educated at Reigate grammar school and University College, London, he took a BSc (1925) and MSc (1927) in chemistry. Originally biased towards physical chemistry he was appointed a demonstrator in University College's biochemistry department, where he first became interested in microbes. In 1929, the year in which, on 17 August, he married Doris Kemp, he joined the bacteriology team working under Paul Fildes at the London Hospital, moving with them in 1934 to the Middlesex Hospital.

Realizing that little could be learned about the biochemistry of microbes when they were grown in the ill-defined broths then customary, Knight set about devising culture media containing only known chemicals. He showed that some bacteria would multiply in such media only if trace amounts of vitamins or amino acids were made available. In a 1936 review of the topic he proposed that all bacteria need such essential metabolites, but that some had lost the ability to manufacture their own supplies. This concept underpinned much of later chemical microbiology,

for example, the microbiological assay of such metabolites, the elucidation of their pathways of biosynthesis, and the design of anti-bacterial drugs which act by interfering with their metabolism. Knight became an international authority on bacterial nutrition, research for which he received the degree of DSc (London) in 1938.

During the Second World War Knight worked at the Lister Institute and the Wellcome laboratories principally on the chemical nature and action of toxins formed by Clostridia, specialized bacteria which often infect war wounds. He also became interested in a then neglected group of tiny bacteria known as Mycoplasmas (later Mollicutes), which cause diseases in plants and cattle. In 1944 Knight and Kemp divorced and on 27 December in that year he married Frideswide Stewart [*see below*], a political activist and writer. They had three sons (one died in infancy) and two daughters.

By the end of the war Knight was very conscious that, though microbiology was a distinctive discipline, no learned society nor any educational centre dedicated to it existed. He joined several like-minded biologists to found the Society for General Microbiology in 1945, served on its original committee, and, when post-war paper shortages eased, became the first and longest-serving editor of its *Journal of General Microbiology*. As editor he revealed a deep concern for clarity of language and brevity of expression, and the *Journal* rapidly gained an international reputation for carefully written papers of the highest scientific quality. Much laborious editing, not always welcomed by authors, was required to sustain that quality, but the society, and the international reputation of British microbiology, benefited enormously. In 1951 Knight became professor in charge of Britain's first ever department of microbiology, at the University of Reading. There he remained until his retirement in 1969, teaching, building up his department, and developing his research on Mollicutes.

Knight loved France and French literature. He visited France often and, initially pseudonymously as Jonathan Kemp, published translations of French classics; he was a noted authority on the works of Stendhal. He was a left-wing socialist; brought up to the Church of England he abandoned Christianity about 1931 in favour of Marxism. He was a man of imposing appearance, often gruff and forthright in manner, and intolerant of affectation and humbug. Yet he was humorous, kind, and at times unexpectedly diffident. He inspired great affection among his friends and colleagues. On retirement he moved to Cambridge, where he died on 29 October 1981. He was cremated at Cambridge on 9 November.

Knight's second wife, **Frideswide Frances Emma** [Frida] **Knight** [*née* Stewart] (1910–1996), communist activist, was born on 11 November 1910, one of four daughters (there was one son) of the Revd Dr Hugh Fraser Stewart (1863–1948), theologian and scholar of French literature and fellow and dean of St John's College, Cambridge, and his wife, Jessie Graham, *née* Crum (*d*. 1966), an early Newnham student and the first to gain a first-class degree there. Frida enjoyed a liberal Cambridge childhood, but her schooling was curtailed at the age of fourteen by a rare heart condition. Sent to Italy to recuperate, she became an active anti-fascist, and soon joined the Communist Party. In 1937 she went to Spain under the auspices of the national joint committe for Spanish relief, helping to establish a children's hospital at Malaga, then working in Madrid as a typist and translator for the republican press agency. After the Francoist victory she assisted republicans held in camps in France; in 1940 she was interned by the Germans but escaped, taking to England to de Gaulle a message hidden in a cigarette. For the next two years she worked in London for the Free French. She remained a member of the Communist Party until it formally ended in 1991. At her home in Reading she was also active in the Campaign for Nuclear Disarmament, and when back in Cambridge she founded Cambridge Against the Missile Bases, arranged concerts by Soviet performers, and chaired the Cambridge–Cuba solidarity campaign. Her several publications included books on her escape from France, the French resistance, William Frend (1757–1841), reformer and scientific writer, and Cambridge music from the middle ages onwards. She also contributed articles to the communist *Daily Worker*, later the *Morning Star*. She died on 2 October 1996.　　　　JOHN R. POSTGATE

Sources L. J. Zatman, *Journal of General Microbiology*, 129 (1983), 1261–8 · private information (2004) [family] · personal knowledge (2004) · [L. J. Zatman], *The Times* (10 Nov 1981) · *WWW*, 1981–90 · *The Times* (1 Nov 1996) · m. cert. · d. cert. · *The Guardian* (15 Oct 1996) · *CGPLA Eng. & Wales* (1981) · *CGPLA Eng. & Wales* (1997)
Archives Trinity Cam., corresp. with R. L. M. Synge · Wellcome L., corresp. with Henry McIlwain
Likenesses photograph, 1950–59, repro. in Zatman, *Journal of General Microbiology*, 1263
Wealth at death £81,527: probate, 16 Dec 1981, *CGPLA Eng. & Wales* · £205,269—Frideswide Frances Emma Knight: probate, 1997, *CGPLA Eng. & Wales*

Knight, Charles (1791–1873), publisher and writer, was born on 15 March 1791 in Windsor, the son of Charles Knight (d. 1824), bookseller and stationer, and his wife, Mary (d. 1792), daughter of John Binfield, a farmer in Iver, Buckinghamshire.

Early life and education Knight's childhood and early adulthood were spent in Windsor, a conservative provincial town whose meagre amusements he experienced to the full: he read unrestrictedly in the bookshop; he rambled in the Great Park and he visited the castle's state apartments and paintings; he was moved by the beauty and the solemnity of the service in St George's Chapel (although, after his confirmation, he told his father that his religious scepticism was such that he would become either a Quaker or a Unitarian); he attended the tiny Theatre Royal, to which he had free admission from the age of eight.

Knight went to a day school in Windsor in the late 1790s, where his education was 'altogether rotework' (Knight, 1.23). In 1803, however, he was sent to Dr Nicholas's school in Ealing, a more stimulating environment where he learned to read for 'solid improvement' (ibid., 1.54). However, in 1805 he left the school to become his father's

Charles Knight (1791–1873), by Antoine Claudet

apprentice, and spent the next three years learning the print trade. Clearly disappointed at the abrupt termination of his formal education, he gave himself up to 'desultory reading to the neglect of all systematic acquirement' (ibid., 1.69); this thorough grounding in contemporary popular literature later stood him in good stead as a publisher. Deciding to make literature his profession, he embarked on a course of more serious reading, mainly history and law, and in 1810 founded an unsuccessful reading club for young men in Windsor. He also began to write poetry, essays, and plays and in 1813 published a play, *Arminius*.

Knight's interest in books extended beyond their educative uses: by the age of seventeen, he was a confirmed bibliophile, and a buyer and seller of second-hand books and a collector of rare books. A client gave him an imperfect first folio edition of Shakespeare, which he made complete by printing the missing pages from a facsimile edition. At the completion of his apprenticeship in 1812, however, his interests were directed away from the more staid side of his father's business to the expanding press industry. Staying for some weeks with the newspaper editor George Lane, he sampled the London journalistic world, sitting in the Commons gallery with reporters. On his return to Windsor, on 1 August 1812 he became the joint proprietor with his father and the sole editor (until 1827) of the *Windsor and Eton Express*, the borough's first newspaper. The cost of stamp tax and paper duty and the difficulties of the subscription system made the initial outlay great and the price of the paper was consequently high. However, it throve and in the first weeks of its establishment, the paper had the exciting news of the July battle of Salamanca to report.

Early career in Windsor As a journalist, Knight was resolved to be 'the temperate advocate of everything that thinking men will support—Toleration, Education of the Poor, Diffusion of Religious Knowledge, Public Economy' (Knight, 1.124). Accordingly he supported Catholic emancipation, advocated low taxation, and favoured only moderate protectionism and limited parliamentary reform. His social conscience had first been awakened in his adolescence, when the heavy taxation, high prices, miserable housing, and poor sanitary conditions endured by the poor of Windsor had made him 'a sort of Communist' (ibid., 1.75). During the next decade, his social concerns deepened: in the post-war period of economic distress and political protest, he became convinced that enclosure and mechanical innovations were depriving people of their livelihoods.

This Cobbett-like humour was tempered by some practical experience of local government. In 1818 Knight was appointed as an overseer of the poor. Appalled by the wasteful expenditure of the committee and the number of fraudulent claimants, he attempted to reform the administration of poor relief, calling for visitations of the out-poor in their homes to ensure a fairer and more economical system. Believing that the state should assist the less fortunate in so far as it was able, he also tried to promote vaccination and to provide employment on public works for able-bodied paupers. His social philosophy was also influenced by John Sumner Bird, then a fellow at Eton College and later archbishop of Canterbury: Bird's dovetailing of Christian theology with Malthusian social and economic views fitted with Knight's growing belief that the poor must be encouraged to better their own condition through prudential financial planning and, significantly, autodidacticism. Complex as he believed the causes of poverty to be, he recalled that he 'never had any doubt of the advantages of educating [the poor]' (Knight, 1.191).

In December 1819 Knight wrote an article in the *Express* denouncing cheap publications as irreligious and anti-government, and calling for the provision of more 'healthful' literature. He now attempted to publish an example of the latter: with Edward Hawke Locker as joint editor, Knight decided to publish a monthly serial entitled the *Plain Englishman*, of which the first number appeared in January 1820. Lasting nearly three years (until December 1822), the journal advocated moderate social reforms, avoiding contentious political issues such as the Queen Caroline affair. It was the first of a series of short-lived journals in which Knight was involved. In October 1820 he published the first number of *The Etonian*, which perished after only ten months; it was succeeded in 1823 by *Knight's Quarterly Magazine*, which survived until late 1824. The contributors for both publications were largely Etonians, including W. M. Praed, John Moultrie, and T. B. Macaulay, but the *Quarterly* also brought Knight into contact with such London literati as Thomas De Quincey and Barry St Leger. With St Leger he published for two months in 1826 a 'smart weekly sheet' (Knight, 1.342), entitled the *Brazen Head*. His connections to the metropolitan literary and journalistic world were also strengthened by his position as editor and part-proprietor (from 1820) of the London weekly, *The Guardian*, where he continued to promote tepidly progressive but largely non-partisan views. The paper necessitated constant visits to London, a relief to Knight who felt stifled in Windsor. On the advice of J. W. Croker, he decided to enter London publishing, and in 1822–3 he sold *The Guardian* and took premises in Pall Mall East; he moved his family—in late 1814 he had married Sarah (1791/2–1879), daughter of William Vinicombe, an architect, and they had, eventually, two sons and five daughters—into a cottage in Brompton.

Publisher of the Society for the Diffusion of Useful Knowledge Knight's career as a London publisher began rather shakily. One of his earliest and most promising publications, R. C. Dallas's *Correspondence of Lord Byron*, provoked a court case in 1824; the work appeared only in a paraphrased version under a different title. Then his grand scheme for publishing a 'national library' of cheap and informative abridgements of important works was stifled by the financial panic of 1825–6. In autumn 1826, a close friend, Matthew Davenport Hill, had introduced Knight to Lord Brougham, who was then establishing the Society for the Diffusion of Useful Knowledge (SDUK) and had expressed interest in the publisher's scheme. Negotiations were opened with John Murray, who offered to merge Knight's business with his firm and to publish the 'national library'. The collapse of this arrangement forced Knight to put his business in the hands of trustees in spring 1827.

Knight now supported himself by literary hack work, writing for J. S. Buckingham's *The Sphinx* and editing an annual, *Friendship's Offering* (1828). From July 1827 he also acted as reader and superintendent for the publications of the SDUK, a far more promising employment. Under the aegis of the society, with Baldwin and Cradock as publishers, he produced in 1828 *The British Almanac*; 10,000 copies sold in a week, according to its proud progenitor, and *A Companion to the Almanac* followed. Knight added to the society's Library of Useful Knowledge a Library of Entertaining Knowledge (1829–37), publishing the first volume in the series from his own regained premises in Pall Mall East. Until the dissolution of the society, he remained its principal publisher (and its creditor), forming important connections with such men as Henry Hallam, James Stuart Mill, Isaac Goldsmid, and James Allen.

In 1828 Knight had undertaken a tour of the midlands industrial towns to organize local committees for the SDUK: it produced a revolution in his understanding of industrialization and capitalism which completed the transformation of his social and political philosophy from his teenage tory radicalism to the whiggish utilitarianism which characterized his mature outlook. In addition to meeting a range of literary and antiquarian figures, Knight visited factories and finally appreciated the role of machinery in the industrial revolution. He also became convinced of the necessity of low taxation and free trade to safeguard industry, and still more of the importance of harmonious relations between industrialists and workforce, whose interests he believed to be too interdependent to allow any separation. Knight was opposed to trade unions, as indeed to most organizations with entirely working-class leadership and membership, and viewed popular demonstrations with no sympathy (as his reaction to the Bristol riots of 1831 and, later, the Chartist meeting of 1848 displayed). These views, strongly reliant on the economics of Adam Smith, were expressed in *The Results of Machinery* and *The Rights of Industry* (both 1831).

The *Penny Magazine* and other publications Knight's publications for the SDUK were astonishingly diverse. In addition to volumes in the Library of Entertaining Knowledge, he started the *Working Man's Companion* (1830–32) and the *Quarterly Journal of Education* (1831–5). The best-known and most significant of his publications, however, was the *Penny Magazine* (1832–45), the first issue of which appeared on 31 March 1832, 'the most successful experiment in popular literature that England had seen' (Knight, 2.179). The joint idea of Matthew Davenport Hill and Knight, it was aimed primarily at a working-class readership and served up a wholesome diet of informative articles on art, literature, natural history, science, history, and biography (but not politics or religion), intended to encourage thrift, self-discipline, self-education, and other social and moral desiderata. Although undoubtedly read by the self-improving artisan, it probably enjoyed a much larger audience among the middle classes, particularly among adolescents with a thirst for knowledge or didactic parents. It was the first lavishly illustrated publication to be offered to the working classes at an affordable price, and according to Knight by the end of 1832 it was enjoying sales of nearly 200,000 in weekly numbers and monthly parts. Its sales easily outstripped rivals such as *Chambers's Edinburgh Journal* and the *Saturday Magazine*.

Its lack of controversial material and its pragmatic attempt to explain an increasingly complex society to itself were probably important factors in the *Penny Magazine*'s appeal to a mass audience. But its success owed even more to Knight's copious use of illustrations, his wholesale mechanization and improvement of his printing equipment, and his well-developed system of distribution. Knight had early decided that illustrations were the key to attractive popular publications, and he aimed to capitalize on the development of the new reproductive medium of wood-engraving, which by the 1830s was overtaking the more expensive method of steel-engraving and even recently discovered lithography. Based in London, Knight had access to a growing ghetto of skilled designers and engravers, including William Harvey, Thomas Williams, John Orrin Smith, Ebenezer Landells, the Whympers, the Dalziel brothers, and Edmund Evans. However,

the availability of engravers was not in itself sufficient. Experiencing difficulties in the production of cheap images for *The Menageries*, Knight worked with the printer and inventor Edward Cowper to adapt his printing machinery to produce more illustrations by stereotype castings and steam printing. Casts of Knight's best cuts were later sent all over the world for insertion in popular publications. The mechanization of his plant was combined with the use of a nationwide network of wholesalers and retailers, which he had built up during his first four years with the SDUK.

The *Penny Magazine* was joined, in January 1833, by the *Penny Cyclopedia*, at a penny for a weekly sheet. This immense project tested Knight's commitment to the cause of popular education: costs soon forced the price up to 4*d*., and sales flagged. Over the eleven years of its publication, Knight suffered chronic financial loss, with the profits of his other more successful enterprises being entirely swallowed up. Nevertheless, he saw the project through, employing a distinguished band of contributors including Southwood Smith, Andrew Ure, and Charles Eastlake, and ensuring a fully contemporary ethos by covering new inventions such as photography and including the biographies of living statesmen. The *Cyclopedia* was a highly influential work in its day, and represented a remarkable achievement for the hard-pressed Knight.

Other publications by Knight—some published under the auspices of the SDUK, some independently—included the *Gallery of Portraits* (1832–4); *The Pictorial Bible* (1836–8), with commentaries by John Kitto; *The Thousand and One Nights* (1838–41) in a new translation by Edward Lane; *The Pictorial History of England* (1837?–1844), by G. L. Craik and Charles Macfarlane; *London* (1841–4); *Old England* (1845–6); and *The Land We Live in* (1847–50). He also published from 1844 Knight's Weekly Volumes, which began with Knight's own biography of William Caxton.

Social life and character During the 1830s and 1840s Knight became a well-known and respected figure in London literary, publishing, and political circles. He moved his business into the heart of the City, 22 Ludgate Street, in 1833; from 1833 he lived at Hampstead, moving in 1835 to Highgate. In 1837 he played a part in the establishment of the penny post. He became an early member of the Reform Club in 1834 (although his admission to the Garrick Club was delayed by rumours about his 1827 near bankruptcy). In the same year, he was appointed publisher to the poor-law commission (he was a hearty supporter of the new poor law, and became a close friend of Edwin Chadwick). In 1850 he was publisher to the General Board of Health and he himself wrote a pamphlet of advice during the cholera epidemic of 1853. Impressed by the Great Exhibition of 1851, Knight agreed to act as a juror at the Paris Universal Exhibition of 1855, writing the part of the report dealing with drawing, modelling, printing, and other related media.

Despite his almost heroic industriousness, Knight was a sociable soul: although he had a quick temper, his contemporaries remembered him as a generous employer and a popular companion. According to one of his contributors, Charles Macfarlane, he put up Thomas De Quincey in his own house for three months while waiting for him to produce a sketch of Milton for the *Gallery of Portraits*; he also let Leigh Hunt stay rent-free in his Brompton cottage for two years. One overworked contributor, Harriet Martineau, was invited to join his family for a month's holiday in St Leonards. His altruistic character may well explain Knight's lack of financial success as a publisher, as he was no mean statistician and clearly knew how to balance his books. He was, however, incurably kind, essentially idealistic, and—according to Macfarlane—'about the worst man of business that has ever belonged to the "Trade"' (Macfarlane, 96).

In 1845 Knight met Douglas Jerrold, the playwright and *Punch* contributor, with whom he visited Dublin and Killarney in 1849, to view the effects of the Irish potato famine; he also came to know such younger literary lights as W. M. Thackeray and Charles Dickens. He contributed to the first two volumes of Dickens's *Household Words* and joined the novelist's Amateur Company of the Guild, which toured the provinces in 1850–51; the two men differed amicably on the issue of the working-class thirst for fiction, which Knight inevitably viewed as unimproving. In a letter to Knight of 17 March 1854 Dickens argued that:

> The English are, so far as I know, the hardest worked people on whom the sun shines. Be content if in their wretched intervals of leisure they read for amusement and do no worse. They are born to the oar and live and die at it. (*The Letters of Charles Dickens*, 12 vols., 1965–2002, 7.294)

His position was vindicated by the collapse of the readership for the *Penny Magazine*, which was no doubt caused by the exclusion of fiction from its pages.

Knight as author: Shakespeare scholar and historian Throughout his career, Knight had always been an author as well as editor and publisher. However, his first major project as an author took shape in 1837, when he resolved to produce a pictorial edition of Shakespeare's works. He started searching for 'authentic' visual materials and began a critical reading of the texts. His edition was based substantially—indeed, too substantially—on the first folio edition, although he made comparisons with other quartos and, in some cases, with originals in the British Museum. His background reading led to a deep interest in Shakespeare's life and the edition, published between 1838 and 1841 (he published six later editions of the works of Shakespeare), was prefaced with a one-volume biography. Knight succeeded in contextualizing Shakespeare's life as no biographer except Nathan Drake had done, and in dismissing a couple of the more absurd legends surrounding the playwright's early life. But he was prone to speculation—even suggesting that Shakespeare had visited Italy and Scotland—and all too dependent on J. P. Collier's forgeries, the traces of which were visible even in the last revised edition.

Knight's retreat from publishing grew more pronounced in the late 1840s. In 1844 the last volume of the *Penny Cyclopedia* appeared and in 1846 the SDUK itself was dissolved; from 1855 he withdrew from his publishing business, his own works appearing with Bradbury and Evans, and Murray (the firm of Charles Knight & Co.—based from 1848 at 90 Fleet Street—continued to publish long after his death). Knight's fascination with Shakespeare was but one aspect of his wider enthusiasm for English history and culture; it was this field of scholarship which he now explored more fully. In the 1840s—in addition to writing the first sixteen chapters of *A History of the Thirty Years' Peace* (1849–50)—he had contributed as author as well as editor to such works as *Old England* and *The Land we Live in*, early illustrated examples of the tourist and heritage literature which is now a staple of British publishing. These heavily illustrated but essentially lightweight works were succeeded by a more serious historical enterprise, Knight's *Popular History of England* (1855–62)—'perhaps the most arduous work of his life, and in some respects the most successful' (Clowes, 84). Knight aimed to write a social and cultural history of the English people but, in an era which was only just beginning to see the professionalization of history as a discipline, he lacked the appropriate critical training and apparatus to achieve this ambition. The *History* was instead an essentially constitutional history, a whiggish narrative of national progress, based on protestantism, economic prosperity, and harmonious co-operation between different social classes. Separate chapters covered the social, economic, and cultural history of the country—a compartmentalization which Knight had objected to in *The Pictorial History* and had hoped to avoid—but the *History* was a largely conventional interpretation of English history within the context of later Victorian historiography, a partial forerunner of J. R. Green's infinitely more popular *History of the English People*. Knight's illustrations, judiciously selected and recycled from his historical publications of the 1840s, enjoy a higher profile, still appearing occasionally in history textbooks and popular historical works.

A veteran campaigner against paper tax and excessive stamp duties (fearful of cheap radical political journals, he held that some duty should be charged), Knight was the author from the 1830s onwards of a variety of pamphlets, including *The Struggles of a Book Against Excessive Taxation* (1850). He also took an interest in the history of publishing, producing *The Old Printer and the Modern Press* (1854) and *Shadows of Old Booksellers* (1867).

Later years and assessment The elderly Knight looked like a benign patriarch, with an 'ample brow, long white locks, and slightly bowed figure' (*The Athenaeum*, 343). In 1864–5 he published his rather long-winded autobiography, *Passages of a Working Life*. With *The Old Printer and the Modern Press*, it provides a unique insight into the world of nineteenth-century popular publishing; unlike many other publishers, Knight analysed supply and demand in detail, giving print runs and sales figures for some of his publications. Four other works followed the autobiography in 1867–8, but by this time Knight was losing his eyesight. He spent his later years at various addresses in London, Surrey, and Ventnor on the Isle of Wight, before moving to Addlestone in Surrey, where he died at his home at

Grove End on 9 March 1873. He was buried in the old burial-ground, Bachelor's Acre, Windsor, on 14 March.

Knight was, in the words of his *Athenaeum* obituarist, 'a highly useful man' (*The Athenaeum*, 343). With the Chambers brothers and John Cassell, he stands as a key figure in the development of the popular press and literature. Neither a great writer, nor a commercially successful publisher, nor an outstanding journalist, he is nevertheless significant in all these areas. He at once recorded and participated in the most remarkable events of the nineteenth-century newspaper and publishing worlds: the development of the provincial press, the mechanization of the printing press, the introduction of cheap illustrations, the expansion of popular publications to include educational works, and the abolition of 'taxes on knowledge'. Publisher to the 'Schoolmaster Abroad', this popular educator—as he saw himself—influenced the minds of thousands of Victorian men, women, and children (some working-class but still more middle-class). Yet he still awaits a full-scale modern biography.

Rosemary Mitchell

Sources C. Knight, *Passages of a working life during half a century*, 3 vols. (1864–5) • A. C. Cherry, 'A life of Charles Knight (1791–1873), with special reference to his political and educational activities', MA diss., U. Lond., 1943 • A. A. Clowes, *Charles Knight: a sketch* (1892) • C. C. Morbey, *Charles Knight: an appreciation and bibliography of a great Victorian publisher* (1979) • *The Athenaeum* (15 March 1873), 343–4 • *ILN* (22 March 1873) • S. Schoenbaum, *Shakespeare's lives*, new edn (1991); pbk edn (1993) • P. Anderson, *The printed image and the transformation of popular culture, 1790–1860* (1991) • R. A. Mitchell, *Picturing the past: English history in text and image, 1830–1870* (2000) • S. Bennett, 'Revolutions in thought: serial publication and the mass market for reading', *The Victorian periodical press: samplings and soundings*, ed. J. Shattock and M. Wolff (1982), 225–57 • S. Bennett, 'The editorial character and readership of the *Penny Magazine*', *Victorian Periodicals Review*, 17 (1984), 127–41 • W. F. Kennedy, 'Lord Brougham, Charles Knight, and *The rights of industry*', *Economica*, new ser., 29 (1962), 58–71 • H. Smith, *The Society for the Diffusion of Useful Knowledge* (1974) • J. H. Weiner, *The war of the unstamped: the movement to repeal the British newspaper tax, 1830–36* (1969) • C. Macfarlane, *Reminiscences of a literary life* (1917) • D. Stow, *Charles Knight's London* (1990) • R. Davenport-Hill and F. Davenport-Hill, *The recorder of Birmingham: a memoir of Matthew Davenport Hill* (1878) • *Harriet Martineau's autobiography*, ed. M. W. Chapman, 3 vols. (1877) • S. Smiles, *A publisher and his friends: memoir and correspondence of the late John Murray*, 2 vols. (1891) • *CGPLA Eng. & Wales* (1873)

Archives U. Birm. L., letters to Harriet Martineau • UCL, letters to the Society for the Diffusion of Useful Knowledge

Likenesses photograph, *c*.1870, *Windsor and Eton Express*; repro. in Clowes, *Charles Knight* • J. Durham, marble bust, 1874, NPG • woodcut, 1875 (after photograph by Edwards & Bult), NPG; repro. in *Family Friend*, 69 (1875) • A. Claudet, photograph, NPG [*see illus.*] • C. H. Kerr, oils (after W. C. Dobson), Corporation of London • woodcut, NPG; repro. in *Illustrated Review* (1873)

Wealth at death under £3000: probate, 29 April 1873, *CGPLA Eng. & Wales*

Knight, Charles Parsons (*b.* 1742/3, *d.* in or after 1826), stipple engraver, emerged as an artistic personality in the 1780s, at which time he was working for the engraver–publisher William Dickinson. Nothing is known about his upbringing or training, but he may have come late to printmaking. His marriage to Catherine brought them two children: a daughter, Martha, born on 14 December 1770, who also became an engraver, and a son, Charles, who entered the Royal Academy Schools in March 1788 shortly before his seventeenth birthday, and may have been the C. Knight who exhibited four miniatures at the Royal Academy between 1793 and 1816.

In 1781 Knight was living in Berwick Street, Westminster, but he had moved west to Queen's Row, Brompton, by 1785 when he published on his own account two drawings by John Raphael Smith. As a book illustrator Knight produced rather indifferent prints for Edward and Sylvester Harding's *Shakespeare Illustrated* (1793) and the *Memoirs of Count Grammont* (1794), and he stippled a large number of small portraits for books and magazines as well as for separate publication. But ultimately he gained a good reputation for his numerous larger prints after contemporary artists. In the mid-1780s his name began to appear on dotted prints published by William Dickinson, notably on a series of plates after Bunbury, and between 1784 and Dickinson's bankruptcy in 1793 Knight worked chiefly but by no means exclusively for Dickinson. It is plausible that he may have been largely responsible for similar prints that appeared in the early 1780s under Dickinson's name. He is said to have been the engraver of *Of such is the Kingdom of God* (1784), the first of three prints forming a triptych after Matthew William Peters. Similarly, the fine full-length portrait of Elizabeth Farren, later countess of Derby, published under Bartolozzi's name in 1792, is said to have been largely engraved by Knight. Knight's work included a large number of separately published stipples of literary and genre scenes by such artists as Thomas Stothard, Henry Singleton, and Francis Wheatley. Among the relatively few prints that he published himself were *Scarcity in India* and *British Plenty* (1794) after Singleton. He was one of the original governors of the short-lived Society of Engravers, founded in 1803. By 1826 he was living in Hammersmith, Middlesex, where at eighty-three he published a portrait of the Revd Thomas Stephen Attwood, minister of Hammersmith. The date of his death is unknown, but it probably occurred soon afterwards.

Timothy Clayton and Anita McConnell

Sources C. Le Blanc, *Manuel de l'amateur d'estampes*, 2 (Paris, 1855–6), 463 • D. Alexander, 'Knight, Charles (Parsons)', *The dictionary of art*, ed. J. Turner (1996) • Dodd's manuscript history of English engravers, BL, Add. MS 33402 • Redgrave, *Artists*

Knight, (Ellis) Cornelia (1757–1837), author and courtier, was the only child of Sir Joseph Knight (*d.* 1775), rear-admiral of the white, and his second wife, Phillipina Deane (1726–1799). From the age of five she was educated for three days a week as a day pupil at the boarding-school kept by four Swiss sisters, the Misses Thomassets, in London. On the other three days of the week she was instructed in French, Latin, the elements of Greek, mathematics, geography, and history by a visiting master, M. Petitpierre, who had formerly been pastor at Neuchâtel; she was taught to dance by Mr Novere, a highly fashionable dancing-master. Her mother was a great friend of Frances Reynolds, the sister of Sir Joshua Reynolds, and Knight thus came to know Dr Johnson and his

(Ellis) **Cornelia Knight** (1757–1837), by Angelica Kauffman, 1793

circle. When her mother failed to obtain a widow's pension after the death of Joseph Knight in 1775, mother and daughter were forced to move abroad in order to economize.

Initially intending to remain abroad for three years, Cornelia and Lady Knight travelled first to Paris and Toulouse, and then on to Rome, where they settled for eight years and mingled with the best society. Lady Knight was proud of her achievement in maintaining their social connections and propriety despite their frugal style of life and wrote in March 1793: 'I am sure few persons in the world have preserved independence upon so small a pittance, or are more clear of pecuniary obligations' (Ingamells, 581). During the late 1780s and early 1790s they toured northern Italy and France, and briefly visited Naples before returning again to Rome, where they remained from 1791 to 1798. Cornelia had acquired a reputation for her learning—in May 1790 her mother wrote that she was busy learning Swedish, her tenth language—and devoted much of her time to drawing and writing; she had amassed some 1800 drawings, 'some with the pen, but mostly coloured ones, the former from imagination, the latter from nature' (ibid., 582–3), and in 1790 she published her first work, *Dinarbas: a Tale*. *Dinarbas* was a continuation of Samuel Johnson's moral adventure *Rasselas*, and is interesting principally as a record of Knight's views on education and conduct. She drew on her classical education for her next work, *Flaminius: a View of the Military, Social, and Political Life of the Romans* (1792); she announced in the preface that 'To bring history to life, is the chief intention of this publication' (p. vii). They spent the last year of Lady Knight's life in Naples and, during the Jacobin

revolution there, in Palermo, in the company of Sir William and Emma Hamilton and Lord Nelson. Cornelia obtained the title of Nelson's poet laureate through her verses celebrating his victories, and dedicated her ode *The Battle of the Nile* to Sir William Hamilton 'as a tribute of gratitude from a daughter of the waves for the distinguished attentions confer'd on the British Navy' by him and his wife. On her mother's death, on 20 July 1799, she complied with the latter's wishes and placed herself under the protection of Lady Hamilton.

On her return to England in November 1800 with the now notorious *ménage à trois* of the Hamiltons and Nelson, Knight was advised by her friends that she was damaging her reputation by remaining in their company. She immediately left and severed her connections with her erstwhile patrons, much to their disgust. Emma gave vent to her feelings by writing in a copy of Molière she had been given by Knight: 'Altho she is clever and learned She is dirty illbred ungrateful bad mannered false and deceitful But my Heart takes a noble vengeance I forgive her' (Constantine, 254). Little is known of Knight in the years before she was appointed companion to Queen Charlotte in 1805, and thereafter her autobiography again falls silent until 1813, when she became companion to the queen's granddaughter Princess Charlotte. She incurred the queen's lasting enmity for abandoning her service, but she was desperate to escape the dull and monotonous court life at Windsor. Her new employment certainly proved a complete contrast, as she found herself entangled in the intrigues, quarrels, misunderstandings, and recriminations that were the daily staple of Charlotte's court, and she fell out disastrously with the princess's closest confidante, Mercer Elphinstone. The princess's refusal in July 1814 to marry her father's intended match for her, the prince of Orange, caused the prince regent to dismiss all her attendants, including Knight. Knight afterwards wrote revealingly about her influence on the young princess:

> either I ought to have remained with the queen, or I ought to have carried things with a higher hand to be really useful while I was with Princess Charlotte … I had the romantic desire that Princess Charlotte should think for herself, and think wisely. Was that to be expected from a girl of seventeen, and from one who had never had proper care taken of her since early childhood? (*Autobiography*, 213)

In spring 1817 Knight returned abroad. She thereafter spent most of her life on the continent, where her connection with the British court admitted her to the highest social circles and enabled her to collect the anecdotes that appear in her autobiography. In 1833 she published *Sir Guy de Lusignan*, a romance from the time of the crusades. Although she frequently revisited Britain, she died in Paris on 17 December 1837. An edited version of her autobiography, with selections from her diaries, was published in two volumes by Sir John William Kaye in 1861, with the help of James Hutton, and ran to three editions. Its popular success was dented by a stinging review in the *Quarterly Review*, possibly influenced by her old enemy Mercer Elphinstone, who was still alive. The reviewer criticized Knight for constantly 'imputing, often by such quiet insinuation as is not readily detected, low or crooked motives to almost every person concerned in the Princess Charlotte's affairs', and went on to comment:

> It is therefore one of those books of scandal of which it is impossible not to regret the publication; such as so but cause unnecessary annoyance, if not to the living, to those who cherish the memories of their dead, while they add absolutely nothing to our knowledge of any fraction of history worth knowing. (QR, 140, Jan 1862)

It is precisely because of her frank account of the chaos and unhappiness of Princess Charlotte's court that Knight's autobiography is valued today.

RICHARD GARNETT, rev. S. J. SKEDD

Sources *The autobiography of Miss Knight, companion to Princess Charlotte*, ed. R. Fulford (1960) · *Lady Knight's letters from France and Italy, 1776–1795*, ed. Lady Elliott-Drake (1905) · J. Ingamells, ed., *A dictionary of British and Irish travellers in Italy, 1701–1800* (1997) · *Letters of the Princess Charlotte, 1811–1817*, ed. A. Aspinall (1949) · *QR*, 140 (Jan 1862) · D. Constantine, *Fields of fire: a life of Sir William Hamilton* (2001)
Archives Niedersächsisches Hauptstaatsarchiv Hannover, Hannover, letters to duke of Cumberland · U. Nott. L., letters to countess of Charleville
Likenesses A. Kauffman, oils, 1793, Man. City Gall. [*see illus.*]

Knight, Edward (1699–1780). *See under* Knight family (*per.* c.1680–1897).

Knight, Edward (1774–1826), actor, commonly known as Little Knight and spoken of as a Yorkshireman, was born in Birmingham. While training as an artist and practising as a sign-painter, he was stirred to emulation by the performance of a provincial theatrical company. He appeared accordingly at Newcastle under Lyme, Staffordshire, as Hob in *Hob in the Well*, and was so complete a victim to stage fright that, despite the encouragement of a friendly audience, he ran off the stage and quitted the town. A year later at Raither in north Wales, with a salary of 5s. per week, he was fortunate enough to get through the same part in safety. While playing Frank Oatland in Thomas Morton's *A Cure for the Heartache* he was seen and engaged by Nunns, the manager of the Stafford theatre. He stayed in Stafford for some years, increasing in reputation by playing such parts as Arno, Sylvester Daggerwood, and Lingo. About 1801 he married Sarah Clews (c.1781–1806), the daughter of a local wine merchant.

Tate Wilkinson, to whom Knight introduced himself, engaged the actor for the York circuit about 1803. He began as Frank Oatland, played in *The Jew and the Doctor*, and was Davy in *Bon Ton*, in all of which roles he was favourably received. After a time he was gratified by the present from Wilkinson of a chest containing all the appliances of an actor's wardrobe, with the compliment: 'I have been long looking for some one who knew how to value them; you are the very man.' While at Leeds in 1806 Knight's wife died at the early age of twenty-four, only five years after their marriage. Left with a young family, he married in 1807 Susan Smith (1788–1859), who had succeeded her sister, Sarah Bartley, as leading lady of the York company in 1805, and, though an actress of no great power, was a remarkable favourite.

Engaged by Wroughton, on the report of Bannister, for Drury Lane for three years, at a salary rising from £7 to £9, Knight arrived with his new wife and children in London to find the theatre burnt down. However, the company moved to the Lyceum, where Knight made his first London appearance on 14 October 1809, as Timothy Quaint in *The Soldier's Daughter* and Robin Roughhead in *Fortune's Frolic*. The favourable impression he made in these characters, and as Label in *The Prize*, was reinforced by his creation of Jerry Blossom in Pocock's *Hit or Miss* (February 1810), Scrub in Farquhar's *The Beaux' Stratagem*, and Zekiel Homespun in Colman's *The Heir-at-Law*. He was also the original Diego in *The Kiss*, an adaptation of Fletcher's *The Spanish Curate*. With the company he went to the new theatre in Drury Lane, where he remained until his death. Simple in *The Merry Wives of Windsor* (23 October 1812) is the first part in which he can be traced at this house. The Clown in *Twelfth Night* and Little John in *Robin Hood* were given during his first season. Knight played many parts, chiefly domestics, rustics, farm labourers, and similar roles, and was the representative of scores of characters in minor pieces by Thomas Dibdin, Isaac Pocock, James Kenney, and other writers. Francis in *Henry IV*, Sim in *Wild Oats*, Stephen Harrowby in *The Poor Gentleman*, David in *The Rivals*, Silky in *The Road to Ruin*, Peter in *Romeo and Juliet*, Isaac in *The Duenna*, Nym in *Henry V*, and Crabtree represent the range of his abilities.

During the season of 1825–6 Knight retired from the stage in consequence of illness. He died on 21 February 1826 at his house in Great Queen Street, Lincoln's Inn Fields, and was buried on 27 February in a vault in St Pancras New Church. His son from his first marriage, John Prescott *Knight, became a renowned portrait painter.

Knight was a shy, careful, benevolent, and retiring man, who shrank from social intimacies, and was wholly domestic in habits. His figure was small and pliable, his height being 5 feet 2 inches, his hair and eyes were dark, and his voice was shrill but not unmusical. He sang well and made up well, and in various lines of pert servants was unequalled. He was the author of a musical farce in two acts entitled *The Sailor and Soldier, or, Fashionable Amusement*, which was produced for his benefit in Hull in 1805. It is without merit.

JOSEPH KNIGHT, rev. NILANJANA BANERJI

Sources *Oxberry's Dramatic Biography*, 2/23 (1825), 106–18 · *The biography of the British stage, being correct narratives of the lives of all the principal actors and actresses* (1824) · *Era Almanack and Annual* (1892) · Hall, *Dramatic ports.* · D. E. Baker, *Biographia dramatica, or, A companion to the playhouse*, rev. I. Reed, new edn, rev. S. Jones, 3 vols. in 4 (1812) · Genest, *Eng. stage* · D. Terry, *British theatrical gallery* (1822), no. 2 · W. C. Russell, *Representative actors* (1872), 300–02 [taken from Genest, *New Monthly Magazine*, 1826]
Likenesses S. De Wilde, watercolour drawing, 1810, Garr. Club · T. Wright, stipple, pubd 1820 (after G. Clint), BM, NPG · G. Clint, group portrait, oils, exh. RA 1821, Garr. Club · T. Woolnoth, stipple, pubd 1821 (after G. Clint), Harvard TC, NPG · F. Waldeck, lithograph, pubd 1822 (after W. Foster), Harvard TC, NPG · H. E. Dawe, mezzotint, pubd 1825 (after J. P. Knight), BM, NPG · G. Clint, engraving, Garr. Club · H. R. Cook, stipple (as Jerry Blossom in *Hit or miss*; after W. Foster), Harvard TC, NPG · R. Cooper, coloured print (after G. Clint; after portrait, pubd 8 April 1822), repro. in

Terry, *British theatrical gallery* · W. Foster, two watercolour drawings, Garr. Club, NPG · M. Gauci, coloured lithograph (as Jerry Blossom in *Hit or miss*; after W. Foster), Harvard TC, NPG · J. Wiche, pencil and watercolour drawing, BM · coloured etchings, Harvard TC, NPG · plate, repro. in *Theatrical Inquisitor* (1812) · plate, repro. in *The Theatre* (1 May 1819) · plate, repro. in *British Stage* (May 1819) · plate, repro. in *The Drama* (1821) · plate, repro. in *Oxberry's Dramatic Biography* · portrait, repro. in *Era Almanack and Annual* · prints, BM, Harvard TC, NPG

Knight, Elizabeth (1869–1933), doctor and campaigner for women's suffrage, was born on 31 August 1869 at Hive House, Northfleet, Kent, the third child and only daughter of John Messer Knight (1813/14–1880), a cement manufacturer, and his wife, Hannah, *née* Lucas. The family was Quaker; the firm of Knight, Bevan, and Sturge was eventually amalgamated with others in Associated Portland Cement Manufacturers Ltd. Elizabeth Knight was educated at Kensington high school and at Newnham College, Cambridge (1888–91), where she read classics but did not take a degree. She trained at the London School of Medicine for Women, qualifying in 1904, and then practised as a general practitioner in London until her death, with a brief interlude in 1912–13 when she returned to Cambridge to study for the diploma in public health.

Elizabeth Knight joined the Women's Freedom League, one of the main societies campaigning for women's suffrage, and in 1908 was imprisoned after attempting to interview the prime minister, H. H. Asquith, at 10 Downing Street. She turned her prison experience to good use by writing a pamphlet, *Social and Sanitary Conditions of Prison Life*. She was a stalwart of the tax resistance campaign, by which women refused to pay taxes while unrepresented in parliament, was prosecuted on several occasions, and received two further prison sentences. Elizabeth Knight was a wealthy woman, having inherited a share of her father's estate, and a generous benefactor to the suffrage cause. By 1913 she was treasurer of the Women's Freedom League, holding this position until her death, and during her lifetime she subsidized the league's paper, *The Vote*. During the First World War Elizabeth Knight actively opposed the 40D regulation, which involved the compulsory examination of women suspected of having transmitted venereal disease to a member of the armed forces. In 1920 she helped to found the Minerva Club, which was open to men and women in sympathy with progressive thought and which attracted members from all branches of the erstwhile militant suffrage movement. A very long lease on its premises in Bloomsbury, on the west side of Brunswick Square, was paid for by Dr Knight, who also furnished the club and supported it financially during her lifetime. In the years before women achieved full enfranchisement in 1928, she ran the press and publicity campaign for the equal political rights campaign. Elizabeth Knight never married, but adopted a daughter, Elsie Glover Knight. She died at 13 Victoria Road, Brighton, on 29 October 1933, after being injured there in a road accident.

ELIZABETH CRAWFORD

Sources S. Newsome, *Women's Freedom League, 1907–1957* (1957) · A. J. Francis, *The cement industry, 1796–1914: a history* (1977) · will of Elizabeth Knight · b. cert. · d. cert. · O. Banks, *The biographical dictionary of British feminists*, 2 (1990) · [A. B. White and others], eds., *Newnham College register, 1871–1971*, 2nd edn, 1 (1979), 97

Wealth at death £248,621 4s. od.: resworn probate, 16 Dec 1933, CGPLA Eng. & Wales

Knight, Eric Mowbray [*pseud.* Richard Hallas] (1897–1943), author and journalist, was born on 10 April 1897 in Menston, near Leeds, the third of the four sons of Frederick Harrison Knight, a prosperous but profligate Quaker wholesale jeweller, and his wife, Hilda Marion Creasser (1876?–1919?). The elder Knight disappeared in 1899, reputedly killed in the Second South African War but suspected of having absconded to Australia, leaving his family in penury. Hilda Knight secured a post as governess in a noble household in St Petersburg, remaining there for some years before emigrating to the United States, where she remarried. Eric was sent to live with relatives in Leeds and later in Skircoat Green. A pupil at the Bewerley Street School in Leeds until the age of thirteen, he had become a 'half-timer' the previous year while working as a bobbin-setter in a worsted mill, and later worked in an engineering works, a glass-blowing factory, and a spinning mill. In 1912 the family was reunited in Philadelphia, but Knight soon left home to work in a lumber yard and carpet mill before attending the Cambridge (Massachusetts) Latin school and the Boston Museum of Fine Arts School.

Shortly after marrying Dorothy Noyes Hall of Boston on 28 July 1917, Knight enlisted in Princess Patricia's Canadian light infantry, later seeing action as a signaller in Flanders and in France. After the war Knight, by now the father of three daughters, tried unsuccessfully to establish himself as a painter and as a journalist. In the 1920s he served as an artillery specialist with the US army reserve at Fort Sill, Oklahoma, subsequently settling in Philadelphia, where he found employment as a film critic on the *Public Ledger* between 1928 and 1934. Estranged from his first wife by 1929, Knight married the writer and editor Jere Brylawski (1907–1996) on 2 December 1932.

A six-month stint in Hollywood as a screenwriter whose scripts were never adopted left Knight with a distaste for the American film industry. The Knights then cultivated an alfalfa ranch in southern California before returning to the east, where they eventually bought and renovated Springhouse Farm, a ramshackle stone house attached to a working farm in Pleasant Valley, Pennsylvania. On the basis of a handful of published stories and an unimpressive first novel, *Invitation to Life* (1934), Knight resolved to devote himself fully to writing. His first short story had been published in 1930, and for the next twelve years his fiction appeared regularly in American magazines, especially the *Saturday Evening Post* and *Esquire*. Many of these stories were reminiscences of Yorkshire village life, usually laced with local dialect and frequently involving a whimsical character named Sam Small, the protagonist of his novella *The Flying Yorkshireman* (1938).

Knight's *Song on your Bugles* (1937) was a quasi-autobiographical proletarian novel recounting the struggles of a gifted young Yorkshireman to reconcile artistic fulfilment with working-class solidarity; though favourably reviewed, it was a commercial failure. The next year he published a contemporary thriller set in Los Angeles, *You Play the Black and the Red Comes Up*, under the pseudonym Richard Hallas. In 1938 the *Saturday Evening Post* commissioned Knight to report on industrial conditions in distressed areas of Yorkshire. His first-hand account, expressing outrage at the closing of mines and factories, also inspired his fourth novel, *The Happy Land* (1940), published in England as *Now we Pray for our Country*. In 1940 he agreed to expand a previously published short story into a juvenile novel, the enduringly popular *Lassie Come Home*, the story of a resourceful and loyal sheep dog. The original film, starring Roddy McDowall and Elizabeth Taylor (1943), was followed by six sequels, six television series, and was updated and remade in 1994.

Despite disenchantment with British industrial and diplomatic policies and his assimilation to American life, Knight responded to the advent of war as a patriotic Yorkshireman. His last and most successful novel, *This above All* (1941), acclaimed as one of the finest novels of the war, was both a realistic love story that transcended class boundaries and a debate about whether Britain, weakened by social stratification and deficient leadership, deserved to win. During the second half of 1941 *This above All* was the best-selling novel in America and was quickly adapted into a popular Hollywood film starring Tyrone Power and Joan Fontaine.

For the first time Knight achieved literary fame and financial security. He lectured extensively on behalf of the British war effort and was interviewed in the media. He travelled to England late in 1941 to report on conditions in wartime London, to broadcast about America to British audiences, and to collaborate with Paul Rotha on the documentary film *World of Plenty* for the Ministry of Information. Knight was commissioned in the American army after being recruited by Frank Capra to provide scripts for the military propaganda series *Why we Fight* and for *Know your Ally—Britain*, among the most significant documentary films ever produced. In addition he wrote *A Short Guide to Great Britain*, an orientation manual distributed to American soldiers before embarkation.

Although Knight always regarded himself as a British expatriate, his accent retaining traces of his Yorkshire background, his personal and professional identity was increasingly American, and at the end of 1942 he became a citizen. On 15 January 1943 Knight, recently promoted to the rank of major in the army special services division, was killed when a transport plane on which he was travelling to Cairo crashed in the Surinam jungle. In 1944 he was posthumously awarded the Legion of Merit for his role in explaining the war to American soldiers. Although his only lasting monument is *Lassie Come Home*, its name immortalized as his never was, Knight merits recognition for his contribution to greater Anglo-American understanding.   F. M. Leventhal

Sources Yale U., Beinecke L., Knight papers · P. Rotha, ed., *Portrait of a flying Yorkshireman* (1952) · J. Knight, biographical information, Yale U., Borland papers · M. Block, ed., 'Knight, Eric (Mowbray)',

Current Biography Yearbook (1942), 462–5 · 'Knight, Eric (Mowbray)', *Contemporary Authors: Permanent Series*, 137 (1992), 252–4 · S. J. Kunitz and H. Haycraft, eds., *Twentieth century authors: a biographical dictionary of modern literature* (1942) · S. J. Kunitz and V. Colby, eds., *Twentieth-century authors: a biographical dictionary of modern literature, first supplement* (1955) · *Who's who in America*, 22nd edn (1942–3) · *New York Times* (22 Jan 1943) · b. cert.

Archives Yale U. | Princeton University, New Haven, Story Magazine archive · U. Cal., Los Angeles, Paul Rotha collection · Wesleyan University, Middletown, Connecticut, cinema archives, Frank Capra MSS · Yale U., Borland MSS

Likenesses P. Hurd, egg tempera, 1941, Springhouse Farm, Pleasant Valley, Pennsylvania · Oggiano, photograph, repro. in *New York Times Book Review* (5 April 1942) · photograph, repro. in Rotha, ed., *Portrait of a flying Yorkshireman*, frontispiece

Knight, Sir Frederic Winn (1812–1897). *See under* Knight family (*per. c.*1680–1897).

Knight, Frideswide Frances Emma (1910–1996). *See under* Knight, Bert Cyril James Gabriel (1904–1981).

Knight, Gilfred Norman (1891–1978), indexer, was born on 12 September 1891 at Ridgewood, Sylvan Road, Upper Norwood, Croydon, the only son of William Frederick Knight, solicitor, and his wife, Annie Louisa Adams. He was educated at Bradfield College and Balliol College, Oxford (1910–13), where he graduated with second-class honours in jurisprudence. He joined Lincoln's Inn as a Tancred scholar in 1914, but obtained a commission and served with the East Surrey regiment. After being badly wounded at the battle of Loos (1915), Knight returned home and was appointed adjutant of 16 officer cadet battalion. He never practised as a solicitor, owing to a Zeppelin bomb attack which caused considerable damage to Lincoln's Inn just at the time when he was called to the bar. He did, however, set himself up as a tutor, advertising himself as a barrister and offering tuition for matriculation, Sandhurst and Woolwich entrance, civil service, responsions, police college, and so on. Surprisingly, many of the advertisements appeared in theatre programmes, including those for the pier at Hastings, when Knight lived at 5 Edmund Road, Clive Vale, Hastings, during the 1930s.

G. Norman Knight, or GNK as he was affectionately known, was a solitary man who never married. As assistant to the West India committee (1919–26, 1938–9), he spent the first few years after the First World War travelling to and living in the West Indies. In 1930 he joined the civil service and in the following year went to India as guardian to the only son of his highness the nawab of Ranpur. During the Second World War he worked first in the censorship department (1940–42) and finally in the War Office, from which department he retired in 1956. Life for a bachelor civil servant between the wars was pleasant and not too demanding. In between travelling Knight rented a studio flat in Chelsea, where he attempted to break out from his stifling middle-class background:

> No longer am I bound down by the stale conventions, the tyranny of fixed hours, and all the trivialities and tediousnesses of the ordinary, middle-class home. No longer am I expected to do certain things at stated hours, or pretend

that I have done them, for the sole reason that anything else 'is not done'. (*West London Press*, 3 Oct 1930)

But despite this seeming quest for bohemianism, Knight was a conventional man who enjoyed the company of men, visits to his local pub, smoking his pipe, and playing chess. One of his chess companions was Quentin Crisp. For a period of ten years he would regularly meet Crisp either in Chelsea, when Knight would visit one of his two sisters in Fulham, or at Western Mansions in Barnet, where Knight lived during the 1960s.

> I received the impression that, like me, he lived entirely in one room; the place was dim and infested with books. When we were together, I never felt that he was withholding from me any part of his life; I formed the opinion that his past really had been uneventful and that, when middle age set in, he had become, if not lonely, solitary. (Q. Crisp, letter to the Society of Indexers, 1979)

Knight was an inveterate writer of letters, articles, books, and poetry on subjects as diverse as the origin of the mysterious 'Gordouli' of Balliol's bawdy song (one Arthur Galletti di Cadilhac, a startlingly handsome Italian student who was at Trinity 1895–9), how to cook a marrow, the stopping of grog by the Admiralty, anthologies on chess, and *The Pocket History of Freemasonry* (1953), which he co-authored with Fred L. Pick and, after the latter's death, revised with Frederick Smyth in 1969. All this stood Knight in good stead when, in 1925, he took up indexing, presumably to help fill his leisure hours, slack time in the office, and the journey from home to work. Soon after retiring Knight decided to do something about this interest. In the thirty years he had been practising he had never met another indexer and he could not believe that he was the only one doing such a necessary job. As a result of writing letters to national papers and several discreet luncheons at the Civil Service Club, the inaugural meeting of the Society of Indexers (SI) took place in March 1957 at the National Book League.

> There are far too many societies. But plenty of people will readily supply a list of half a dozen that can be dispensed with in order to make room for the newly formed Society of Indexers. Here is a necessary body if ever there was one,

wrote the leader writer in *The Times* on 8 May 1957.

G. Norman Knight continued to index books for the rest of his long life, winning the Wheatley medal (instituted by the Library Association in 1961) for his index to Randolph S. Churchill's *Winston S. Churchill*, vol. 2, 1901–1919 (1967) and the first Society of Indexers' Carey award in 1977 for outstanding services to indexing. He also found the time to produce the British standards BS3700: *Recommendations for the Preparation of Indexes* (1965), which won a commendation from the Library Association, and at the time of his death he had just completed writing the definitive text on indexing: *Indexing, the Art of*, which was published posthumously in 1979.

GNK died peacefully on 17 August 1978 at Scio House, Roehampton, and in accordance with his wishes he was buried with his mother in Nunhead cemetery, on 31 August. Later that year the Society of Indexers opened a fund in his name 'to further some practical aspect of indexing'. A fitting memorial to a man who for thirty years

indexed alone but who finally found a 'family' of several hundred like-minded individuals, all passionate about indexing. GERALDINE BEARE

Sources *WW* (1975) · *The Indexer*, 10/4 (Oct 1977) · *The Indexer*, 2/3 (April 1979) · *The Times* (8 May 1957) · *The Times* (21 Aug 1978) · newspaper cuttings held by the Society of Indexers in Sheffield · private information (2004) [F. Smyth] · *West London Press* (3 Oct 1930) · b. cert. · *CGPLA Eng. & Wales* (1979)
Archives Society of Indexers, Sheffield, archives
Likenesses photograph, 1970–79, repro. in *The Indexer*, 11/3 (1979) · photographs, Society of Indexers, Sheffield
Wealth at death £2163: probate, 31 Jan 1979, *CGPLA Eng. & Wales*

Knight, Gowin (*bap.* 1713, *d.* 1772), physician and inventor of geomagnetic instruments, was baptized at Corringham, Lincolnshire, on 10 September 1713, the son of the local vicar Robert Knight and his wife, Elizabeth. In 1724 the family moved to Leeds, where Knight was educated at the grammar school. In 1731 and 1735 he won scholarships to Magdalen Hall and then to Magdalen College; he studied natural philosophy and medicine at Oxford until 1741. Soon afterwards he went to London, where he spent the rest of his life. In 1750 he moved from Lincoln's Inn Fields to Crane Court, Fleet Street; from 1756 he lived at the British Museum.

By 1744 Knight was practising as a physician in London, and had embarked on the research that won him world renown for his magnets and compasses. He developed techniques for magnetizing steel bars by a repetitive process of stroking them with other magnets to build up their strength. Cheaper and more reliable than natural lodestone, these artificial magnets vitally affected subsequent experimental investigations into magnetic phenomena, popular and educational performances, and navigational practices. Knight also transformed traditional maritime compasses into precise instruments. He thus contributed to the introduction of natural philosophical techniques into navigation, and helped consolidate the increasingly influential role of the Royal Society on mercantile voyages of imperial exploration.

Between 1744 and 1750 Knight gave several spectacular demonstrations of his magnetic bars and compasses at the society, and was rapidly acclaimed as an international expert. He published several papers in the *Philosophical Transactions*, which he later edited into a discreet advertising brochure (1758). Made a fellow in 1745, he was awarded the prestigious Copley medal in 1747 for—as the president expressed it—helping the British people 'to increase and promote greatly our foreign trade and commerce, whereby we are provided at home with the fruits, the conveniences, the curiosities and the riches of the most distant climates' (M. Folkes, presidential address, Royal Society journal book, 19.366). Largely because of the commercial significance of navigation, Knight gained social prestige as well as financial reward by promoting his bars, compasses, and other inventions. He exemplified contemporary upwardly mobile entrepreneurs who carved out new types of career in a commercializing society.

Adopting discreet, gentlemanly techniques of self-advertisement, and protecting his methods by secrecy,

Gowin Knight (*bap.* 1713, *d.* 1772), by Benjamin Wilson

Knight sold his magnetic inventions privately and also through the instrument dealers George Adams and Jean Magellan. He targeted the quality end of the market for instruments of natural philosophy, warding off cheaper imitations by a signed certificate. He sold three sizes of expensive steel magnetic bars, ranging in price from 2½ guineas a pair to 10 guineas for a pair 15 inches long. He also invented portable cases for storing his bars to prevent the loss of their strength, exceptionally powerful magnets made from iron and linseed oil, and a variation compass for natural philosophers to measure the patterns of terrestrial magnetism. He constructed an impressive wheeled device made from two magazines, each comprising 240 magnetic bars, for magnetizing steel bars more easily than with the laborious stroking procedure. Displayed to eminent visitors at the British Museum, this machine was subsequently used by Michael Faraday. Knight also patented a mechanical window blind and invented a naval sounding device.

After examining a compass damaged during a freak storm, Knight emphasized the benefits a philosophical approach could bring to navigational problems. Following extensive experimentation, he introduced two greatly modified maritime instruments: a steering compass for indicating a ship's course and an azimuth compass, designed in collaboration with John Smeaton, for measuring the angle of variation (the angle at a particular place between geographical north and the direction in which a compass needle is pointing). Knight mounted his compasses in durable non-magnetic brass instead of the usual casings made from perishable wood and iron nails, and he

made slender rectangular needles from hard, permanently magnetized steel, which would not rust. His other numerous innovations designed to increase accuracy included revolutionizing the needle's suspension and incorporating a finely divided brass scale. His high-quality instruments were expensive, but could yield far more precise measurements than older models. However, they were more suitable for a philosopher's private study than the rolling deck of an ocean-going ship: bad weather curtailed his own trials at sea.

Knight negotiated lucrative contracts to supply the Royal Navy with magnets and compasses. Benefiting from contacts made through the Royal Society, he convinced naval experts of the value of his inventions, and the board of longitude awarded him £300 in 1752. Later that year, after a perfunctory testing programme, the Admiralty board ordered all ships being fitted for foreign service to be supplied with one of Knight's compasses. Navigators agreed that Knight's bars were greatly superior to natural lodestone for remagnetizing compass needles. They were initially enthusiastic about his compasses: fitting out the *Endeavour*, James Cook wrote to the Admiralty, 'Doctor Knight hath got an Azimuth Compass of an Improv'd con-[s]truction which may prove to be of more general use than the old ones' (*The Journals of Captain James Cook*, ed. J. C. Beaglehole, 1955, 1.clxix). But experienced mariners increasingly accused Knight of designing an instrument that performed badly at sea, particularly in stormy weather. Knight constantly implemented modifications, and, in the face of increasing competition from rival compass makers, became the first to seek protection by patenting a revised model of his azimuth compass in 1766. Despite continued criticism from seafarers, Knight's compasses remained official issue for all the ships in the Royal Navy until well into the nineteenth century.

In 1748 Knight produced a theoretical treatise on natural philosophy, republished by John Nourse six years later, entitled *Two Simple Active Principles, Attraction and Repulsion*. Using Newton's suggestions in the *Opticks*, Knight sought to explain all natural phenomena—light, heat, and gravity as well as magnetism—by aethers made up of elementary attractive and repulsive particles. Knight claimed that these particles cluster round one another to build up larger corpuscles of varying size and net force, which combine to produce fluids and solids of different characteristics. For this Newtonian text he also drew on his own experiments and on continental research into metallurgy and mining. Knight's densely written book was little referred to by his contemporaries, though some Victorian scientists revived interest in his ideas. Benjamin Franklin judged Knight 'the greatest Master of Practical Magnetics that has appear'd in any Age' (*The Papers of Benjamin Franklin*, ed. L. W. Labaree, 1963, 6.103), but never quite found the 'Leisure to peruse his Writings with the Attention necessary to become Master of his Doctrine' (ibid., 1961, 4.256).

Knight was elected a member of the Royal Society council in 1751. He achieved an increasingly influential position in the society, though he was defeated by seventy-six votes to ninety-one when he competed with Thomas Birch for the post of secretary. For a few years, Knight was active at the Society for the Encouragement of Arts, Manufactures, and Commerce. In 1756 he successfully applied for the post of principal librarian at the newly founded British Museum, which was largely controlled by fellows of the Royal Society. Knight remained at the museum until his death, sixteen years later. For £200 a year, he acted as live-in caretaker, responsible for displaying the exhibits and supervising public access. He played a key role in the adoption of the Linnaean system of classification, and participated in international correspondence networks to enlarge the collections.

Knight became publicly recognized in polite society as a man of importance. Participating in élite circles, he contributed to John Fothergill's reforming medical club and journal, and invested with him in a financially disastrous Cornish mining venture. Also close to Birch, Benjamin Wilson, Henry Baker, and John Pringle, Knight dined with influential statesmen and aristocrats, and was discussed by the king. Wilson, a schoolfriend from Leeds, portrayed him in an etching and an oil painting. Knight was increasingly reputed to be reclusive and ill-tempered, antagonizing visitors, staff, and trustees at the museum, where he very probably lived alone. Critics—including Samuel Johnson and Edmund Stone—deplored his marketing strategies and his secretiveness, and he became involved in a bitter priority dispute with John Canton. Knight persistently refused to divulge his magnetizing techniques, although partial accounts were published after his death. He died in his rooms in the museum on 8 June 1772, and was buried in London at either St George's, Bloomsbury, or the parochial cemetery near the Foundling Hospital.

PATRICIA FARA

Sources P. Fara, *Sympathetic attractions: magnetic practices, beliefs, and symbolism in eighteenth-century England* (1996) · DNB · G. Knight, *A collection of some pages ... relating to the use of Dr Knight's magnetical bars* (1758) · A. de Morgan, 'Dr Gowin Knight', *N&Q*, 2nd ser., 10 (1860), 281–2 · BM, Add. MS 45871a, fol. 83

Archives Sci. Mus.

Likenesses B. Wilson, etching (after his oil painting), BM, NPG, RS · B. Wilson, oils, BM [*see illus.*]

Knight, Harold (1874–1961). *See under* Knight, Dame Laura (1877–1970).

Knight [*née* St John], **Henrietta, Lady Luxborough** (1699–1756), poet and letter writer, was born at Lydiard Park, Wiltshire, on 15 July 1699, the only daughter of Henry, first Viscount St John (1652–1742), and his second wife, Angelica Magdalene Pellisary (*c*.1666–1736), a French widow. Henrietta's half-brother was Henry *St John, first Viscount Bolingbroke (1678–1751), with whom she remained in contact even in her most difficult years. She spent her early life at the St Johns' house at Battersea after Bolingbroke's attainder and flight to France in 1715. Scandal touched her name for the first time in 1719, but on 10 June 1727 she married Robert Knight (1702–1772), later Baron Luxborough. They travelled regularly to France, where Robert Knight senior had fled at the collapse of the

South Sea Company from which, as cashier, he made a huge illegal fortune.

Immediately after her marriage Henrietta was suspected of having an affair with her London physician, Dr Charles Peters (1695–1746). She and Robert Knight had two children, Henry (*b.* 1728) and Henrietta (*b.* 1729). She was accused by her husband of having also become pregnant by a young cleric, John *Dalton (*bap.* 1709, *d.* 1763), tutor in the household of her friend Frances Seymour, countess of Hertford. She appears to have given birth late in 1736. In that year Knight arranged a separation order from his wife, having found her love letters to Dalton. She was obliged to live on £500 a year at Barrells, Ullenhall, a Knight estate in a remote part of Warwickshire, never to see her children, or to visit London and Bath. A remarkable monument in a local parish church, set up by Knight, commemorated Henry and Henrietta as her only offspring with her husband. His bitterness towards his wife never diminished.

Isolated in Warwickshire, Henrietta relied on correspondents to keep in touch with contemporary affairs. Her attempts to be reconciled with Knight failed and, for some time, she was ostracized by the best local society. However, she became friendly with the poet William Shenstone (1714–1763) of The Leasowes, Worcestershire, and with others, including Richard Jago (1715–1781) and William Somervile (1675–1742). They formed the 'Warwickshire coterie'; she was known in their literary circle as Asteria. Much of her correspondence with Shenstone (1742–55) discussed garden design, literature, decor, and architecture, and they exchanged several visits. At Barrells she created a *ferme ornée*, with many rare plants, exotic birds, and fowl. She was slowly accepted into midland society as visitors came to view the gardens at Barrells. She continued to correspond regularly with Bolingbroke until his death. Her married daughter was also involved in a scandal, eloping and being divorced in 1753.

Lady Luxborough's portraits show her to be a strikingly beautiful woman, although an unfashionable brunette, and Walpole's description of her as 'lusty' and high-coloured, with a 'great black bush of hair' is both accurate and spiteful (Walpole, *Corr.*, 32.243–4). Some of her poems, given to the publisher Robert Dodsley by Shenstone, were published in the 1775 edition of Dodsley's *Collection of Poems by Several Hands*, and much of her correspondence with Shenstone was published in 1775 and with the duchess of Somerset in 1778. In the last years of her life when she was ill, she finally visited Bath in 1752, and was also attended by Dr John Wall (1708–1766) of Worcester. From about 1750 she was in severe financial difficulties, and her friendship with Shenstone appears to have cooled shortly before her death at Barrells on 26 March 1756. She was buried at St Peter's, Wootton Wawen, Warwickshire.

JOAN LANE

Sources *The letters of William Shenstone*, ed. M. Williams (1939) · W. Sichel, *Bolingbroke and his times: the sequel* (1902) · M. Williams, *Lady Luxborough goes to Bath* (1945) · M. R. Hopkinson, *Married to Mercury* (1936) · C. G. Hey, *The Warwickshire coterie* (1991) · A. M. W. Stirling, *The merry wives of Battersea* (1956) · A. E. Carden, *The Knights of*

Barrells (privately printed, 1993) · F. L. Colvile, *The worthies of War-wickshire who lived between 1500 and 1800* [1870] · *Report on the manu-scripts of the earl of Denbigh, part V,* HMC, 68 (1911) · *Select letters between the late duchess of Somerset … and others,* ed. T. Hull, 2 vols. (1778) · Walpole, *Corr.,* vols. 11, 17, 32, 43 · GEC, *Peerage*
Archives BL, family corresp., Add. MS 45889 | BL, corresp. with William Shenstone, the duchess of Somerset, and Lady Smithson, Add. MSS 23728, 28958, 34196
Likenesses oils, *c.*1720, Lydiard Park, Wiltshire · oils, *c.*1730, priv. coll. · engraving, repro. in J. Merridew, *Catalogue of engraved por-traits of nobility, gentry, clergymen … in the county of Warwick* (1848) · oils (as a young child)

Knight, Henry Gally (1786–1846), architectural writer and antiquary, was born on 2 December 1786, the only son of Henry Gally Knight of Langold Hall, Yorkshire, barrister, and his wife, Selina, daughter of William Fitzherbert of Tissington, Derbyshire. His grandfather John Gally (who assumed the additional name of Knight) was MP for Ald-borough and Boroughbridge, and a son of Henry *Gally DD, the classical scholar. Knight was educated at Eton Col-lege, and entered Trinity College, Cambridge, in 1805. He was a founder member of Grilion's Club in 1812, and joined Brooks's Club in 1816. Between 1816 and 1830 he published a number of poems, including 'Ilderim, a Syr-ian Tale' (1816), which often drew inspiration from his earlier travels through Spain, Sicily, Greece, Egypt, and Palestine. Knight's poetry received mixed reviews from Byron, and in 1831 he turned his attention to the study of architecture. He had married in 1828 Henrietta, third daughter of Anthony Hardolphe Eyre of Grove, Notting-hamshire, but had no children. In May 1831 Knight, accompanied by the architect Richard Hussey, travelled to France to study the buildings and libraries of Normandy. After his return to England he published *An Architectural Tour in Normandy* (1836), which was translated into French by M. A. Campion and published in Caen in 1838. This work had a significant influence upon the French anti-quarian Arcisse de Caumont, and in recognition of his work Knight was made a foreign member of the Société Française. In August 1836 he travelled to Messina with the architect George Moore, a pupil of Edward Blore. Knight produced two books relating to this expedition: *The Nor-mans in Sicily* (1838; French translation by M. A. Campion, 1839; German translation, ed. C. R. Lepsius, 1841) and *Sara-cenic and Norman Remains to Illustrate the 'Normans in Sicily'* (1840). In 1842–4 he published the two-volume *The Ecclesias-tical Architecture of Italy from … Constantine to the 15th Century,* with eighty-one litho-chromatic plates, some by Owen Jones. Although Knight's work was that of an amateur antiquarian and lacked acute stylistic analysis, his books did influence some early Victorian architects. *The Ecclesias-tical Architecture of Italy* in particular provided accurate, vis-ual documentation relating to Italian medieval architec-ture. Of great interest were the details of the various char-acteristic forms of polychromy.

Knight, who had succeeded to the family estates on his father's death in 1808, was MP for Aldborough (1814–15), for Malton (1831–2), and for North Nottinghamshire (1835–46). As an MP he was regarded by his contempor-aries as a fluent but infrequent speaker. In 1841 he was a member of the select committee on the fine arts, which initiated the historical fresco paintings in the houses of parliament. He was also deputy lieutenant of Notting-hamshire. He died in Lower Grosvenor Street, London, where he lived, on 9 February 1846, and was buried in Fir-beck church, Yorkshire, on 17 February. His will directed that his Langold estate should be sold for the benefit of some friends. His other estates at Firbeck, Kirton, and Warsop were left to his widow during her lifetime. After her death the Firbeck estate and mansion were to go to the ecclesiastical commissioners for charitable uses. Some manuscripts relating to Knight's tour in 1810–11 remained in the hands of his family.

W. W. WROTH, *rev.* JANE HARDING

Sources N. Pevsner, *Some architectural writers of the nineteenth cen-tury* (1972), 37–40, 42 n. 53, 48 n. 16, 60, 67–8, 95, 113, 248 n. 57 · H. R. Hitchcock, *Early Victorian architecture in Britain,* 2 vols. (1954) · Colvin, *Archs.* · M. Crinson, *Empire building: orientalism and Victorian architecture* (1996) · Venn, *Alum. Cant.* · HoP, *Commons, 1790–1820*
Archives Derbys. RO, corresp. and papers | BL, corresp. with Sir Robert Peel, Add. MSS 40424–40565, *passim* · JRL, letters to Edward Davies Davenport · Lpool RO, letters to Lord Stanley · U. Nott. L., letters to duke of Newcastle · U. Nott. L., corresp. with duke of Portland
Likenesses J. Partridge, group portrait, oils (*The fine arts commis-sioners, 1846*), NPG

Knight, James (*c.*1640–1719x24), colonial administrator and merchant, seems to have been born about 1640 (since he was apparently nearly eighty in 1719), possibly in Bisham, Berkshire, described later as his home in his will; his parents are unknown. A lifelong connection to the Hudson's Bay Company began on 16 May 1676 when he was employed as a carpenter. He appears to have spent the next five years building or rebuilding factories at Rupert, Moose, and Albany rivers in James Bay. Passed over in the appointment of deputy governor in Hudson Bay he returned in 1681 to England, where he reported to the company and advised on preparations for a voyage the fol-lowing year. A 'faithfull and true Serveant' and 'able and dexterous in their business', on 11 May 1682 he was made deputy governor at Hudson Bay and chief factor at Albany on a yearly salary of £100 (Kenney, 25). With his brother, Richard, Knight sailed to Hudson Bay and remained there until 1685 when he returned to England. In December that year he faced, and denied, accusations, made by Governor Henry Sergeant, of private trading. The case concluded in November 1687 with the company unsatisfied with Knight's defence.

Knight does not reappear in company records until five years later when he is described as 'of London, merchant', suggesting his occupation and residence in the interven-ing period. In March 1692 the company offered him the command of an expedition to protect York Fort and recover the bottom of the bay from the French. Royal let-ters patent issued on 15 June 1692 made him governor and commander-in-chief of all forts, factories, and territories in Hudson Bay. That month he sailed with the most power-ful expedition the company had yet sent, comprising four ships and 213 men. The following summer the forces attacked and took Albany Fort, which became the only fort in English hands from October 1694 until August 1696, when the English retook York Fort. By this time Knight and his wife, Elizabeth, had a son, Gilpin. By the treaty of Ryswick (20 September 1697) Albany was to be returned to the French and York Fort, recently retaken by the French, to the English. In June 1698 the company employed Knight to oversee the exchange; however, it never took place. He travelled to Hudson Bay and for the following two years was governor of Albany on an annual salary of £400, double the amount he had been receiving since April 1693.

By November 1700 Knight had returned to London, where he obtained £400 of company stock; added to the £200 of stock he had acquired in 1692, this made him eligible to sit on the committee of the general court. He was elected the following week, and every subsequent year until November 1713. In 1710 he travelled to the Netherlands 'to Soliciter the Company's affaires at the treaty of Peace' (Kenney, 47). The articles of the treaty of Utrecht (11 April 1713) provided that the French should return Hudson Bay territories to Britain and pay the company for damages. On 11 September 1714 Knight received the formal French surrender at York Fort, and subsequently became governor there.

To further trade Knight set out to improve relations between Crees and Athapascans, and to establish a post on the Churchill River (the latter is recorded in his published journal). He received a number of reports, particularly from a slave woman, Thanadelthur, of a yellow metal, and on his return to England in 1718 he approached the company with plans for an expedition to discover the mines. In June 1719 the expedition departed, instructed to search for a north-west passage. Knight never returned and evidence collected by explorers in the following years suggested that both expedition ships had been wrecked. Almost fifty years later Samuel Hearne confirmed these reports; his interviews with Inuit suggested that some of Knight's party survived two winters on the Marble Island. In the late twentieth century the Marble Island site was excavated and divers investigated the wrecks; although inconclusive, the evidence suggests that perhaps not all of Knight's party died of starvation or scurvy on Marble Island. Knight's will was probated on 23 September 1724. Given that apparently he was almost eighty in 1719 he had probably died soon after arriving on the island (Robson, appx 1, 37).   NATASHA GLAISYER

Sources J. F. Kenney, ed., *The founding of Churchill* (1932) [incl. Knight's diary 14 July to 13 Sept 1717] · K. G. Davies, ed., *Letters from Hudson Bay* (1965) · E. S. Dodge, 'Knight, James', *DCB*, vol. 2 · J. Robson, *An account of six years residence in Hudson's-bay* (1752) · E. E. Rich, *Hudson's Bay Company, 1670–1870*, 1 (Toronto, 1960) · J. Geiger and O. Beattie, *Dead silence: the greatest mystery in Arctic discovery* (1993) · S. Hearne, *A journey from Prince of Wales's Fort in Hudson's Bay to the northern ocean* (1795) · 'Report from the committee appointed to inquire into … Hudson's Bay', *Reports from Committees of the House of Commons*, 2 (1748–9), 213–86 · W. G. Ross and W. Barr, 'Voyages in northwestern Hudson bay (1720–1772) and discovery of the Knight relics on Marble Island', *Musk-Ox*, 11 (1972), 28–33 · W. Zacharchuk, 'The house that Knight built', *Beaver*, 304/2 (1973), 12–15 · R. Smith and W. Barr, 'Marble Island: a search for the Knight expedition, August 6–15, 1970', *Musk-Ox*, 8 (1971), 40–46

Archives Provincial Archives of Manitoba, Winnipeg, Hudson's Bay Company archives [microfilm at PRO]

Knight, James (1735–1808). *See under* Knight family (*per.* c.1680–1897).

Knight, James (*bap.* 1793, *d.* 1863). *See under* Knight, Samuel (1759–1827).

Knight, John (*d.* 1606?), mariner, was described by Captain James Hall of Hull as 'my Countrie-man'; beyond this, his origins remain obscure. In 1605 he sailed on a voyage of exploration to Greenland. The fleet was commanded by John Cunningham, a Scot employed by Christian IV of Denmark. Cunningham sailed in the admiral *Trost* with James Hall as his pilot. The vice-admiral the *Røde Løve* was captained by a Danish nobleman Godske Lindenov, while Knight was steersman of the pinnace *Katten* or *Marekatten*.

The ships left Copenhagen on 2 May 1605. The *Trost* sighted the coast of Greenland in latitude 59°50' on 30 May, but the fleet's attempts at exploration were hampered by ice and fog. The *Røde Løve* parted company on 11 June and returned to Copenhagen with skins and narwhal ivory. Meanwhile the *Trost* and *Katten* reached an area of coastline without ice, and bartered goods with the Inuit in the Itivdleq Fjord. Hall and Knight sailed away in the pinnace to explore and map the harbours between the latitudes of 66°30' and 68°35', surviving skirmishes with Inuit. The islands at latitude 66°59' were named after Knight. On 11 July the two ships started home through the ice, and arrived in Copenhagen on 10 August.

In 1606 Knight undertook a voyage on behalf of the English East India and Muscovy companies in search of the north-west passage. He commanded the *Hopewell*, a pinnace of 40 tons, which sailed from Gravesend on 18 April making for the Orkney Islands, where bad weather detained the ship until 12 May. The voyage was uneventful until 3 June, when the *Hopewell* met with the ice floes that were to hamper her progress. In his journal Knight describes the daily battle with the ice, and how his men manoeuvred the *Hopewell* through narrow gaps with spars, boat-hooks, and oars. Land was sighted on 13 June, but two days later the ship was nearly crushed, tossed by high winds and stormy seas against the ice. On 19 June the *Hopewell* reached land at latitude 56°48' on the coast of Labrador. Knight managed to steer into a cove where a storm on 24 June broke off the rudder, flooded the ship, and drove her aground.

Knight's journal ends abruptly: 'Thursday the 26th beinge faire wether'. Another hand has added an explanation. On the morning of 26 June 1606 Knight rowed to an island and went ashore with three others, taking instruments for mapping and weapons to defend themselves if necessary. Two sailors left in the shallop waited until eleven o'clock at night but Knight and his men did not return. The remaining eight crew members attempted a search for their colleagues, but were thwarted by the ice. They patched up the *Hopewell* sufficiently to sail to Newfoundland for repairs and arrived in Dartmouth on 24 September 1606. Evidence given by the crew at a high court of admiralty inquiry in November that year satisfied the sponsors of the voyage that the loss of Knight and his men was not the result of desertion or mutiny.

MARGARET MAKEPEACE

Sources S. Purchas, *Hakluytus posthumus, or, Purchas his pilgrimes*, bk 1 (1625); repr. Hakluyt Society, extra ser., 14 (1905), vol. 14, chaps. 14–16 · journal of John Knight in the *Hopewell*, 1606, BL OIOC, L/MAR/A/II · C. R. Markham, ed., *The voyages of Sir James Lancaster kt to the East Indies … and the voyage of Captain John Knight to seek the north-west passage* (1877) · C. C. A. Gosch, ed., *Danish Arctic expeditions, 1605 to 1620*, 1, Hakluyt Society, 1st ser., 96 (1897) · T. Rundall, ed., *Narratives of voyages towards the north-west* (1849), chap. 5 · F. Gad, *The history of Greenland*, 1 (1970) · BL OIOC, B/2, fol. 33*v* [pass to John Knight issued 10 April 1606] · D. B. Quinn, A. M. Quinn, and S. Hillier, eds., *New American world: a documentary history of North America to 1612*, 4 (1979), chap. 82
Archives BL OIOC, journal in the *Hopewell*, L/MAR/A/II

Knight, Sir John (*bap.* 1613, *d.* 1683), merchant and local politician, the third but second surviving son of George Knight (*d.* 1659), a mercer, and his wife, Anne, the daughter of William Deyos, was baptized on 24 November 1613 in Bristol. He inherited his father's business in Temple Street, and became one of the most prosperous merchants in the city and a prominent high-church member of the common council. On 9 April 1640 he married Martha, the daughter of Thomas Cole, a merchant, of Bristol; they had three sons and eight daughters.

Knight was knighted by Charles II on 5 September 1663, on the occasion of the king's visit to Bristol, and elected mayor in the same year. His tenure of office was a year of terror distinguished by his persecution of radical sectarians under the old recusancy laws and the Conventicles Act (1664). A critic of republican ideas who feared radical risings, he had Baptists arrested, disrupted Quaker meetings, paid large sums to have their houses watched, and concerted measures with Guy Carleton, bishop of Bristol, for their punishment. Some 920 persons are said to have suffered for their religion during his mayoralty, and many moderate churchmen were scandalized by the mayor's rushing out of church on Sundays in pursuit of recalcitrant nonconformists.

Knight's intolerance increased with the years, and in 1669 he denounced the other members of the common council, including his cousin and namesake John Knight, who was mayor of Bristol in the following year, as 'fanatics'. In 1680, being infirm, he desired the city to nominate another person to take care of their affairs in the common council, but though he no longer had any official status he still occasionally acted as an informer. His antipathy to Roman Catholics was as strong as that against nonconformists. In 1681 he was fined for assaulting the mayor of Bristol in the course of his duty, and for calling several members of the common council 'papists, popish dogs, jesuits, and popish devils'. In August 1680 he had acted as emissary from William Bedloe to Chief-Justice North before the latter's receiving Bedloe's dying deposition, and it is apropos of this that Roger North sums him up as 'the most perverse, clamorous old party man in the whole city or nation' (North, 253).

Knight became a member of the Bristol Society of Merchant Venturers in 1639 and was master of the society in 1663–4. He represented Bristol during the parliaments of 1661, 1678, and 1679, and was highly indignant at not being re-elected in 1681. He sat on seven committees concerned with ecclesiastical legislation in the Cavalier Parliament and served in the two Exclusion Parliaments. He died in December 1683, and was buried at Temple Church, Bristol. The value of his estate is not mentioned in his will, but it does not seem to have been substantial.

THOMAS SECCOMBE, *rev.* KENNETH MORGAN

Sources M. W. Helms and J. P. Ferris, 'Knight, John', HoP, *Commons* · D. H. Sacks, *The widening gate: Bristol and the Atlantic economy, 1450–1700* (1991) · J. Latimer, *The annals of Bristol in the seventeenth century* (1900) · P. McGrath, ed., *Merchants and merchandise in seventeenth-century Bristol*, Bristol RS, 19 (1955) · R. North, *Examen, or, An enquiry into the credit and veracity of a pretended complete history* (1740) · J. Evans, *A chronological outline of the history of Bristol* (1824) · T. Garrard, *Edward Colston, the philanthropist*, ed. S. G. Tovey (1852) · S. Seyer, *Memoirs historical and topographical of Bristol*, 2 vols. (1821–3) · will, PRO, PROB 11/375, sig. 18
Wealth at death not substantial: calendar of will in McGrath, ed., *Merchants and merchandise*, 64–7

Knight, John (1616?–1679). *See under* Knight, Sir John (*d.* 1718).

Knight, John (*bap.* 1622, *d.* 1680), surgeon, was baptized in St Bride's, Fleet Street, London, on 18 September 1622, the second son of Thomas Knight of Shoe Lane (*d.* 1652) and his wife, Sarah. Thomas was a herald painter and servant to successive Garter kings of arms; it is likely that he was himself the son of Thomas, Chester herald (*d.* 1618), and grandson of Edmund, Norroy king of arms (*d.* 1593), whose heraldic manuscripts were inherited by the surgeon on his elder brother's death in 1662 and were left by him to Gonville and Caius College, Cambridge. The bequest of these and other books suggests that John was a member of Gonville and Caius, but there is no record of his education there. Indeed by the age of seventeen he had begun a medical career by apprenticeship to Edward *Molins, a London surgeon. Molins, and Knight's later master Lawrence Lowe, assisted the royalists during the civil war; Knight did likewise, and was with Prince Rupert's forces at the taking of Leicester in 1645.

On 26 August 1647 Knight married, at St Matthew's, Ipswich, Mary, daughter of William Hawes, sometime town clerk there. For a time he lived at King's Lynn, but by September 1648 he was with the prince of Wales in the Netherlands. He sailed in an abortive mission to seize Scilly, was captured, and escaped to Jersey. For the remainder of the interregnum he stayed with the exiled court, mixing light espionage with medical duties. Lord Chancellor Hyde was among his patients, as presumably was the king himself.

In May 1660 Knight returned to England in the king's suite. It was his particular responsibility to arrange the restoration of royal thaumaturgy for scrofula sufferers seeking Charles II's touch. It also fell to him to embalm the king's youngest brother the duke of Gloucester, who died in September 1660. On 11 July 1661 he was appointed serjeant-surgeon, which confirmed his right to perform state embalmings. Also in 1661 he received from the Garter the rare honour of bearing the cross of St George as an inescutcheon. On 3 October 1662 he was admitted to the Barber-Surgeons' Company, of which he was master in 1663–4 and 1677–8. On 16 December 1664 he was appointed surgeon-general of all forces in England and Wales, and during the Anglo-Dutch wars of 1665–7 and 1672–4 he gave unremitting service to the navy. Many of his extensive dispatches to Secretary Sir Joseph Williamson survive in the state papers.

In 1669 the king recommended Knight to Cambridge for an MD, but it is not clear that he took the degree. He was an eye witness to the battle of Sole Bay (28 May 1672) and subsequently escorted Lord Sandwich's body to his state funeral. On 20 May 1676 he received the licentiate of the Royal College of Physicians by the king's mandate. It was at Knight's urging that in 1678 the skeletons discovered four years earlier at the Tower of London, and assumed to be those of Edward V and his brother, were buried in Westminster Abbey. Examination of the remains in 1933 seemingly confirmed Knight's belief that they were those of the murdered princes.

Knight was a friend of George Monck and his son Christopher, dukes of Albemarle, and lodged at their town house and their Essex seat, New Hall. Samuel Pepys had been known to him since 1662; their navy work brought them together, and they shared a love of books. Knight wrote a history of St George's cross which he presented to Pepys, to whom he bequeathed other books. Apart from the manuscripts given to Gonville and Caius, most of Knight's library was left to the Ipswich Town Library, now at Ipswich School. These arrangements were made because Knight's only son, Thomas, died in 1675. Knight's wife died in 1679, and was buried in St Bride's on 30 June. Knight himself made his will on 20 October 1680 and was buried in St Bride's on 27 November.　　　C. S. KNIGHTON

Sources Munk, *Roll*, 1.388 · E. M. Calvert and R. T. C. Calvert, *Serjeant Surgeon John Knight: surgeon general, 1664–1680* (1939) · M. R. James, *A descriptive catalogue of the manuscripts in the library of Gonville and Caius College, Cambridge*, 3 vols. (1907–14), 1.viii–ix; 2.585–618, 631, 637–8; 3.43 · parish register, St Bride's, Fleet Street, 1587–1653, GL, MS 6536 [baptism] · parish register, St Bride's, Fleet Street, 1587–1653, GL, MS 6537 [marriage] · parish register, St Bride's, Fleet Street, 1598–1653, GL, MS 6538 [burial] · parish register, St Bride's, Fleet Street, 1653–72, GL, MS 6540/1 [burial] · parish register, St Bride's, Fleet Street, 1673–95, GL, MS 6540/2 [burial] · will, PRO, PROB 11/228, fols. 409v–410 [will of Thomas Knight, father] · will, PRO, PROB 11/307, fols. 309v–310 [will of William Knight, brother] · will, PRO, PROB 11/364, fols. 114v–115v, 337–338v; 11/367, fols. 240–41; 11/368, fols. 61–61v · J. M. Blatchly, *The town library of Ipswich provided for the use of the preachers in 1599: a history and catalogue* (1989), 40–41, 195–9, and keyed entries · C. S. Knighton and T. Wilson, 'Serjeant Knight's discourse on the cross and flags of St George (1678)', *Antiquaries Journal*, 81 [2001] · *CSP dom.*, 1660–61, 556; 1661–2, 37, 484–5; 1664–5, 115; 1672, 83–4 · G. D. Squibb, *Reports of heraldic cases in the court of chivalry, 1623–1732* (1956), 67 · W. H. Godfrey, A. Wagner, and H. Stanford London, *The College of Arms, Queen Victoria Street* (1963), 111–12 · S. Young, *The annals of the Barber-Surgeons of London* (1890), 9, 10, 499–500 · private information (2004) [T. Woodcock, Norroy and Ulster king of arms]

Archives BL, medical notes and prescriptions, Sloane MSS 206A, B, 211 · Gon. & Caius Cam., MSS 515–578/328, 598/494, 599/281, 606/513*, 794/799–799/804, 800–805 | Bodl. Oxf., extract from account of order of St Anthony in Ethiopia, from lost MS compiled or owned by him, MS Ashmole 1115, fols. 147–8 · Magd. Cam., 'Discourse containing the history of the cross of St. George, and its becoming the sole distinction-flag, badge or cognizance of England, by sea and land', no. 2877, pp. 402–36
Wealth at death over £2300 in pecuniary bequests: PRO, PROB 11/364, fols. 114v–115v, 337–338v

Knight, Sir John (*d.* 1718), merchant and politician, was the elder son of **John Knight** (1616?–1679) of Bristol, merchant, and his first wife, a Somerset woman whose maiden name was Parsons. The elder John Knight was the grandson of the effective founder of the family's position within the civic and mercantile worlds of Bristol, Francis Knight (*d.* 1616), through Francis's second son, Edward. Another of Francis's grandsons, by his eldest son, was Sir John *Knight (*bap.* 1613, *d.* 1683), often known as 'the elder', another prominent figure in Restoration Bristol whose political and business career intertwined with those of his cousin and nephew.

John Knight, the son of Edward Knight and his wife, Martha Challoner, served as apprentice to his merchant father from 1634 to 1641. He based his fortune, however, on East Anglian fenland purchased during the 1640s. His first wife had died and he had remarried by 1651; his second wife was Mary Latch (*d.* 1681). He returned to Bristol by the early 1650s, where he established a sugar refinery at the Great House, St Augustine's Back, which was supplied by his West Indian plantations. He was warden of the Merchant Venturers three times (1654–5, 1655–6, and 1661–2), and master once (1666–7). In 1664 he was appointed sheriff of Bristol. Unlike his son, he was sympathetic to dissenters and gave them a respite from harassment during his mayoralty of Bristol in 1670–71. His most important foe in this period was his cousin and former business partner, Sir John Knight the elder, with whom he fought numerous lawsuits. In 1675 he gave his fenland and West Indian properties to his younger son, Joseph, while his elder son, John, inherited the Bristol sugar business and lands at Congresbury, Somerset, after his father's death on 29 March 1679, though the will led to legal contests within the family.

The younger John Knight spent several years representing his father's interests in the West Indies, apparently living in Montserrat. He had returned to Bristol by the early 1670s and married Anne Smith, daughter of Thomas Smith of Long Ashton, Somerset; they had one son and two daughters. In June 1674 he was elected to Bristol's common council, though for a while he refused to serve. In November 1675 he joined the Merchant Venturers of Bristol, but it was not until September 1679 that he accepted election to the city's common council. The younger Knight's father had died six months earlier, which henceforth makes it easier to discern which of that name was performing increasingly prominent functions for the Merchant Venturers and the city corporation. He now became a warden of the Merchant Venturers and in

September 1681 was made one of the city's two sheriffs for the year following.

The shrievalty provided Knight with his first major opportunity to exercise leadership, which he did by directing the persecution of protestant dissenters. He quickly came into regular contact with officers of the royal court and convinced them of his zeal for the king's interests. Knight was also one of those leading an attack on Sir Robert Atkyns, the city's recorder and a justice of common pleas recently dismissed for his opposition to the royal court. Knight's campaign to close conventicles and harass dissenters became so extreme that he soon spurred a vigorous opposition within the corporation, which became seriously divided. Despite the conflict in Bristol, Knight was presented to the king at Newmarket in March 1682, where he was knighted. In these years it thus becomes easy to confuse Knight with his uncle, Sir John Knight the elder. This senior Sir John, though also a prominent foe of conventicles, as evidenced by his actions as mayor in 1663–4, opposed his namesake until his death in late 1683. The junior Sir John was sometimes known as 'the younger' or 'of The Hill', after his place of residence in St Michael's parish.

In December 1682 Knight and others wrote to the government recommending the dismissal of four aldermen who allegedly stirred trouble in the corporation. From this arose the suggestion that Bristol, like other corporations in this period, be served with an information in the nature of *quo warranto* to compel them to surrender their charter, thus permitting the issue of a new charter to install Knight's 'loyal' partisans firmly in power. Knight managed the surrender process, keeping Secretary of State Sir Leoline Jenkins informed about shifting local political alignments. Although he expected a favourable outcome, Knight misjudged the situation and failed to convince a majority of the corporation to vote to surrender the charter in March 1683. By now many in the corporation, even his allies, had become suspicious of what a new charter might do to increase Knight's power. But legal process against the city moved forward until a charter surrender was at last obtained in early 1684.

Knight now looked to Whitehall for greater preferment in return for his services, and put himself forward to be governor of the Leeward Islands. Some in England supported his nomination, but many islanders remembered Knight's 'rude behaviour and insolence' (Latimer, 423) while he lived there and petitioned against his appointment, effectively ending his ambitions. Surprisingly, Knight requested the king's permission to resign from Bristol's council in July 1684, only one month after he had gained the city's new charter. Throughout this period, despite his divisive political efforts, Knight was frequently called upon to use his influence to represent Bristol's mercantile interests at court. Hoping to build on this influence, Knight stood unsuccessfully at a parliamentary by-election in December 1685.

By this time Knight's worries were shifting from protestant dissenters to Catholics, whose interests King James now promoted. In April 1686 Knight reported a Catholic

meeting to the mayor and sheriffs, and they arrested a priest and others. News soon arrived at court of Knight's aggressive manner toward Catholics and other citizens in this and other incidents. By late May the 'violent tory in Bristol' (Luttrell, 1.379) had been arrested and brought before the privy council to explain his actions, for which he was now imprisoned. A writ of habeas corpus failed to gain his release, but when tried by a jury in Bristol in November, Knight was acquitted.

Knight rejoined the common council upon the restoration of Bristol's pre-1684 corporation in October 1688. Elected to represent Bristol in the convention of 1689, Knight soon became known as one of those who disagreed that King James's departure had made the throne vacant and thus as one who opposed making William and Mary monarchs. Knight was returned to parliament in 1690; he was elected mayor of Bristol later that year. At Westminster Knight worked to protect Bristol's trading interests in Africa and elsewhere, but he earned greatest fame for his popular attack on foreigners in the debate on a Naturalization Bill. His speech questioned the loyalty and integrity of the measure's supporters; he concluded by moving that 'let us first kick the bill out of the House, and then foreigners out of the kingdom' (Knight, 8). The Commons voted to condemn the speech in its published form and it was burnt by the hangman, though not before Knight had denied all knowledge of how it appeared in print. Knight was in contact with the exiled Jacobite court in these years. After the assassination plot of 1696 Knight was detained on suspicion of his Jacobitism, though he was released for lack of evidence. Knight did not stand for parliament in 1695; when he did so in 1698, he failed to regain his seat.

In 1702 Knight resigned from Bristol's common council once again and later retired to the small estate at Congresbury that he had inherited from his father. He died in apparent poverty in February 1718.

PAUL D. HALLIDAY

Sources HoP, *Commons, 1660–90*, 3.692–7 · CSP dom., 1680–1702 · J. Latimer, *The annals of Bristol in the seventeenth century* (1900) · J. Knight, *The following speech* (1694) · N. Luttrell, *A brief historical relation of state affairs from September 1678 to April 1714*, 6 vols. (1857) · J. Latimer, *The annals of Bristol in the eighteenth century* (1893) · privy council registers, 1683–7, PRO, PC 2/70; PC 2/71 · R. C. Latham, ed., *Bristol charters, 1509–1899*, Bristol RS, 12 (1947) · A. Grey, ed., *Debates of the House of Commons, from the year 1667 to the year 1694*, 10 vols. (1763) · *Report on the manuscripts of the marquis of Downshire*, 6 vols. in 7, HMC, 75 (1924–95), vol. 1 · *Calendar of the manuscripts of the marquess of Ormonde*, new ser., 8 vols., HMC, 36 (1902–20), vol. 7 · R. Hayden, ed., *The records of a church in Christ in Bristol, 1640–1687*, Bristol RS, 27 (1974) · I. V. Hall, 'John Knight, junior, sugar refiner at the great house on St. Augustine's Back, 1654–1679: Bristol's second sugar house', *Transactions of the Bristol and Gloucestershire Archaeological Society*, 68 (1949), 110–64 · King's Bench Rule and Order Books, PRO, KB21/23; KB · A. B. Beaven, 'The Knights of Bristol', *N&Q*, 9th ser., 3 (1899), 321–2 · A. Sabin, ed., *The registers, 1577–1700*, Bristol and Gloucestershire Archaeological Society Publications, 3 (1956) [parish of St Augustine the Less] · E. Ralph and M. E. Williams, eds., *The inhabitants of Bristol in 1696*, Bristol RS, 25 (1968) · P. McGrath, ed., *Merchants and merchandise in seventeenth-century Bristol*, Bristol RS, 19 (1955) · P. McGrath, ed., *Records relating to the Society* *of Merchant Venturers of the city of Bristol in the seventeenth century*, Bristol RS, 17 (1951) · BL, Add. MS 5540

Wealth at death apparently in poverty · between £5000 and £6000, and estate in Westbury-on-Trym; John Knight (1616?–1679): Hall, 'John Knight', 159; HoP, *Commons, 1660–90*

Knight, John (1740–1795). *See under* Knight family (*per. c.*1680–1897).

Knight, Sir John (*bap.* 1747, *d.* 1831), naval officer and surveyor, was baptized on 21 February 1747 at Dundee, the fourth of five known children of Rear-Admiral John Knight (*c.*1710–1788) and his wife, Jean Hay. In 1758 Knight joined the frigate *Tartar*, commanded by his father, in the expedition against St Malo and Cherbourg under Lord Howe. After the peace of 1763 he served in the *Romney*, flagship of the commander of the North American station, under Lord Colville and his successor Sir Samuel Hood, and gained experience of nautical surveying assisting J. F. W. Des Barres. Knight returned to North America as second-lieutenant of the sloop *Falcon* (Captain John Linzee) in April 1775 when war with the colonists threatened. The *Falcon* arrived in Boston three days before the opening skirmish at Lexington and was one of the vessels that covered the attack on Bunker Hill.

Early in 1776 Knight was taken prisoner while attempting to bring off an American schooner which had been driven on shore. After several months on parole in Massachusetts he was exchanged in December 1776, and appointed by Lord Howe to command the *Haerlem*, a hired ship, in which he was active against the enemy's coasting trade and also engaged in hydrographic work for Des Barres's New England charts. He was next moved to Howe's flagship, the *Eagle*, and used his intimate knowledge of the coast to lead the fleet through narrow channels to cut off d'Estaing's squadron from Boston. Knight married Prudence Reynolds (*d.* before 1799) in America on 17 February 1778 and the following autumn returned to England.

In 1780 Knight joined the *Barfleur*, flagship of Sir Samuel Hood, and was her first lieutenant in the actions off Martinique on 29 April and Chesapeake Bay on 5 September 1781. He was posted captain with command of the *Shrewsbury* on 21 September 1781, but in January 1782, at Hood's request, he returned to the *Barfleur* as flag-captain, and commanded her in the action at St Kitts, the skirmish of 9 April, and the battle of the Saints on 12 April. He was personally responsible for the professional education of Prince William Henry, the future William IV and a midshipman in the *Barfleur*. In 1787–8 Knight was again appointed flag-captain to Hood, first in the *Barfleur* at Portsmouth, and then in 1793, when Hood became commander-in-chief in the Mediterranean, in the *Victory*. On his return from the Mediterranean Knight was appointed to the *Montagu* in the North Sea under Admiral Adam Duncan.

When mutiny broke out in 1797 the *Montagu* was one of the first and worst affected ships. She was taken by her crew to the Nore, where her surgeon was tarred and feathered, and rowed through the fleet. After the mutiny was quelled the *Montagu* played a distinguished part in the battle of Camperdown on 11 October 1797. In 1798 Knight commanded a detached squadron on the coast of Ireland, and in 1799–1800 he was in command of the inshore squadron blockading Brest, where he made a chart of the area. On 1 October 1799, after Prudence's death, Knight married Love Pickman Oliver (1754–1839), a widow, and daughter of a New England loyalist and Massachusetts judge, Peter Frye. Knight was promoted rear-admiral on 1 January 1801 and in 1805 succeeded Sir Richard Bickerton at Gibraltar where he performed unspectacular work with great confidence. He became vice-admiral on 9 November 1805, admiral on 4 December 1813, and a KCB on 2 January 1815, but saw no further naval service.

Knight's portrait shows a wiry, bright-eyed man. Sir William Hotham, who served with him, considered him clever, brave, professionally able, and 'remarkably quick and active' (Hotham, 1.53). He was a skilful surveyor and his published charts included several of Corsica, Brest, Portsmouth, Cork, and the North Sea. Hood evidently respected him but Hotham reported that he was not popular in naval circles. He had a poor reputation for maintaining discipline and undeserved doubt was cast on his courage at Camperdown.

Knight and his first wife, Prudence, had eight children and, according to Hotham, he was thought to pay too much attention to domestic affairs and consider his ship 'more a house in which he was residing with his family than a ship of the British fleet!' (Hotham, 1.53). Knight died suddenly on 16 June 1831 at his house, Woodend, at Soberton, Hampshire; he was buried at Soberton on 28 June.   SUSANNA FISHER

Sources 'Biographical memoirs of John Knight, esq., rear-admiral of the white squadron', *Naval Chronicle*, 11 (1804), 425–31 · *Pages and portraits from the past: being the private papers of Sir William Hotham*, ed. A. M. W. Stirling, 2 vols. (1919) · J. Ralfe, *The naval biography of Great Britain*, 2 (1828), 352–6 · J. Marshall, *Royal naval biography*, 1/1 (1823), 154–65 · *British Library map library catalogue* (1998) [CD-ROM] · GM, 1st ser., 101/2 (1831), 81–2 · D. Syrett and R. L. DiNardo, *The commissioned sea officers of the Royal Navy, 1660–1815*, rev. edn, Occasional Publications of the Navy RS, 1 (1994) · parish register, Soberton, Hampshire, 28 June 1831 [burial] · IGI

Archives BL, printed charts from surveys | BL, corresp. with Lord Nelson, Add. MSS 34902–34931

Likenesses G. Noble and J. Parker, group portrait, line engraving, 1803? (*Commemoration of 11th Oct 1797*; after J. Smart), BM, NPG · W. Ridley, stipple, pubd 1804 (after J. Smart), BM, NPG

Wealth at death over £35,000, excl. leasehold properties in Deptford, Torrington Square, Camberwell, Grafton Street, and Soberton: PRO, death duty registers IR 26/1296/214; will, PRO, PROB 11/1800

Knight, John (1765–1850). *See under* Knight family (*per. c.*1680–1897).

Knight, John Baverstock (1785–1859), land surveyor and painter, was born on 3 May 1785 at the rectory, Langton Long Blandford, Dorset, the third of eight children of James Forster Knight (1751–1808), captain, 3rd Dorset militia, and his wife, Sophia (1751/2–1820), daughter of Colonel John Kay. His parents lived at the Down House, Blandford St Mary, which Knight had inherited with Littleton and Langton manors. John was baptized at Langton rectory, home of his aunt (wife of the rector, Dr J. H. Ridout), on 28 May 1786. Knight was educated privately at home, then at

Mr Longman's Commercial School at Child Okeford. He started his career as land surveyor and agent as assistant to his father, a reputed connoisseur of art who encouraged his son's talents in drawing, and lived at his parents' home, the Manor House, Anderson, Dorset. He married Elinor Bulkeley Evans (*fl.* 1809–1824), daughter of the Revd Humphrey Evans of Glanville Wootton, on 20 December 1809; they moved to West Lodge, Piddlehinton, Dorset, in 1812 and had eight children.

Knight followed a strict daily regime, rising at 5 a.m., painting from 6 a.m. to 9 a.m., then embarking on business. He invented a surveying instrument to measure the exact extent of land from a relatively remote location; his expertise as a surveyor and in architectural design led to his arbitrating in property disputes. Knight was employed by many landowners including the duke of Bedford, and Eton and Winchester colleges. Most of his work was in Dorset, but in 1811 he surveyed in Devon for Christ Church, Oxford, and in 1812 he reported on estates in Antrim, Londonderry, and Tipperary. He was an inclosure commissioner in Hampshire and Dorset, and was engaged on tithe work in Dorset (*c.*1839–45) with his son Humphrey Evans Knight and other surveyors, including George Easton, John Martin, and, probably, Levi Luckham.

Knight built a studio at Piddlehinton, decorating it with a mythological painting. He painted portraits in oils of many county families including Josiah Wedgwood of Eastbury Park, Lord Arundell of Wardour, the sixth duke of Bedford and, in 1820 and 1821, James John Farquharson of Langton and his family. His portraits were commended by Sir Thomas Lawrence; his copies of old masters were good enough to deceive experts. He was an honorary exhibitor at the Royal Academy in 1818 and 1819; Benjamin West and Henry Fuseli praised his skill. Knight was versatile and also produced watercolours, etchings, and miniatures. An album containing watercolours and pen and wash drawings of places on the duke of Bedford's estates, together with other works by Knight, is now in Dorset County Museum. His drawings, many of which are of Lake District scenes (such as *Lodore, Derwentwater*; V&A), show the influence of J. R. Cozens, J. S. Cotman, and Thomas Girtin. Many are in monochrome or blue-grey; others use light colour, for example *Axbridge Vale* (Tate collection). Hardie regards them as his best work, with skilful handling of receding planes and a strong feeling for composition. His etchings were mostly topographical and were published in the *Gentleman's Magazine* from 1816 and in the second edition of J. Hutchins's *History of Dorset* (1815). Knight was prolific: he painted throughout the British Isles and on the continent. Particularly large collections of his work are in the Victoria and Albert Museum, London, the Victoria Art Gallery, Bath, the Dorchester Museum, and Dorset County Record Office, with others in many regional museums.

Knight was 'a magnificent specimen of the country squire' (MacColl, 171), tall, handsome, and stately. He owned land at Brockenhurst in Hampshire as well as in Piddlehinton. His interests in the countryside were wide-ranging and included horticulture; he was an excellent sportsman. He was well-loved, a churchwarden, and notable for his charities. He was a wit and wrote poetry.

In 1856 he resigned his membership of the Royal Agricultural Society of England and his health began to fail. He died at his daughter's house at Broadway, Dorset, on 14 May 1859 and was buried there on 19 May.

SARAH BENDALL

Sources F. Knight, *Biography of John Baverstock Knight, 1785–1859* (1908) · M. Hardie, *Water-colour painting in Britain*, ed. D. Snelgrove, J. Mayne, and B. Taylor, 2: *The Romantic period* (1967), 117–18, 125, 129–30 · Dorset RO, Knight family MS D.1271 · D. MacColl, *Burlington Magazine*, 34 (1919), 171–2 · T. Brocklebank, 'A Dorset artist', *Notes and Queries for Somerset and Dorset*, 28 (1963), 134–5 · F. W. Steer and others, *Dictionary of land surveyors and local map-makers of Great Britain and Ireland, 1530–1850*, ed. P. Eden, 2nd edn, ed. S. Bendall, 2 vols. (1997) · *GM*, 3rd ser., 7 (1859), 310–11 · F. Knight, 'John Baverstock Knight', *Dorset yearbook*, 21 (1925), 114–18 · J. Hutchins, *The history and antiquities of the county of Dorset*, 2nd edn, ed. R. Gough and J. B. Nichols, 4 (1815) · D. Fletcher, *The emergence of estate maps: Christ Church, Oxford, 1600 to 1840* (1995) · artist's file, archive material, Courtauld Inst., Witt Library · CGPLA Eng. & Wales (1859)
Archives Dorset RO, family MSS
Likenesses J. B. Knight, self-portrait, pastel?, 1809, priv. coll. · J. B. Knight, self-portrait, oils, 1835, Dorset County Museum, Dorchester · photograph (of portrait), Dorset RO
Wealth at death under £2000: probate, 19 July 1859, CGPLA Eng. & Wales

Knight, John Prescott (1803–1881), portrait painter, was born on 9 March 1803 in Stafford, the second of the three sons of Edward *Knight (1774–1826), the comedian affectionately known as Little Knight, and the actress Sarah Clews (*c.*1781–1806). The Knight family soon moved to London, where Edward and Sarah furthered their acting careers and John began school at a 'classical and commercial academy' (Knight). Knight then went to work as a junior clerk for a West India merchant in Mark Lane, London, a position ending with the firm's bankruptcy. After seeing copies Knight had made of images by Benjamin West contained in the family Bible, Knight's father recognized his son's talent and sent him to study drawing with Henry Sass for six months and colouring with George Clint for another six months. In August 1823 Knight was accepted as a painting student in the Royal Academy Schools. In an attempt to supplement his income, Knight utilized his family connections and occasionally acted on the London stage. Economic pressures worsened in 1826 with the death of his father, and Knight's career as a portrait painter began in earnest.

About 280 oil paintings are attributed to Knight, of which four-fifths are portraits, including such notables as *Sir Walter Scott* (1826; priv. coll.), the architect *Sir Charles Barry* (1851; NPG), and *Sir Charles Eastlake* (1857; priv. coll). Knight was also well known for large group portraits such as *The Heroes of Waterloo* (1842; priv. coll.), depicting the duke of Wellington receiving dinner guests on the anniversary of the victory, and *The Peninsular Heroes* (1848; priv. coll.). Knight also painted a number of religious subjects which reflected his dedication to the Catholic Apostolic church, of which he became a deacon in 1847.

On 1 November 1831 Knight married Clarissa Isabella Hague (*d.* 1869), who was herself an accomplished painter,

John Prescott Knight (1803–1881), by Maull & Polyblank

of still-life and domestic scenes, and they had two sons and a daughter. While he was highly regarded as a portraitist, it was Knight's extraordinarily long and devoted service to the Royal Academy which brought him accolades from his colleagues. Elected an associate of the Royal Academy in 1836 and a full academician in 1844, he served as teacher and then professor of perspective from October 1839 until April 1860. In October 1847 Knight was elected secretary of the Royal Academy, a prestigious office with a yearly salary of £400, which he held until May 1873. He was made a chevalier of the Légion d'honneur in 1878.

Knight died at his home, 24 Maida Hill West, London, on 26 March 1881, and was buried in Kensal Green cemetery.

DOUGLAS FORDHAM

Sources H. Dyson, *John Prescott Knight RA: a catalogue* (1971) · J. P. Knight, 'Autobiographical sketch', *Art Journal*, 11 (1849), 209 · D. Robertson, *Sir Charles Eastlake and the Victorian art world* (1978) · *ILN* (9 April 1881), 349 · D. Millar, *The Victorian watercolours and drawings in the collection of her majesty the queen*, 2 vols. (1995), 133–4 · W. Sandby, *The history of the Royal Academy of Arts*, 2 (1862), 174–5 · Graves, *RA exhibitors*, 4 (1905), 342–5 · *DNB*

Likenesses J. P. Knight, self-portrait, oils, exh. RA 1829?, Stafford Art Gallery · mezzotint, c.1830, Stafford Art Gallery · C. Baugniet, lithograph, 1844, BM · D. Maclise, black chalk drawing, c.1860, V&A · J. Adams-Acton, sculpture, exh. RA 1873 · J. P. Knight, self-portrait, oils, priv. coll. · Maull & Polyblank, carte-de-visite, NPG [see illus.] · R. and E. Taylor, woodcut (as an elderly man; after photograph), BM, NPG; repro. in *John Prescott Knight* · mezzotint, BM · photograph, carte-de-visite, NPG · wood-engraving (*Members of the Royal Academy in 1857*), NPG; repro. in *ILN* (2 May 1857) · woodcut, BM, NPG; repro. in *Art Journal*

Wealth at death under £50: probate, 8 April 1881, *CGPLA Eng. & Wales*

Knight, Joseph (1829–1907), drama critic, born at Leeds on 24 May 1829, was the elder son of Joseph Knight, a cloth merchant, who was from Carlisle. His mother, Marianne, the daughter of Joseph Wheelwright, became blind in middle life but lived to the age of seventy-three. Knight was educated at a private boarding-school, Bramham College, near Tadcaster, and rose to be head of the school. He early showed a taste for poetry, and in 1848 a promising poem by him, 'The Sea by Moonlight', was printed at Sheffield by the headmaster for circulation among his pupils' parents.

At the age of nineteen Knight joined his father in business. He devoted his leisure to literature, collecting and reading books, and took a prominent part in the literary activities of Leeds. He especially enjoyed Elizabethan and early French poetry, and he never lost his admiration for the work of Michael Drayton, George Wither, and Ronsard. With his fellow townsman Alfred Austin, afterwards poet laureate, he helped to found a mechanics' institute at Leeds, at which he lectured on literary subjects. In April 1854 he lectured on 'The Fairies of English Poetry' before the Leeds Philosophical and Literary Society. At Leeds, too, he made the acquaintance of William Edward Forster, who stayed at Knight's house while he was parliamentary candidate for the constituency in 1859. Knight seconded Forster's nomination. On 3 June 1856 Knight married, at the parish church in Leeds, Rachel Wilkinson, the youngest daughter of John Wilkinson of Gledhall Mount, near Leeds. Their first child, Philip Sidney, who later emigrated to Australia, was born on 2 February 1857; they also had two daughters, who became Mrs Ian Forbes Robertson and Mrs Mansel Sympson.

In 1860 Knight adventurously abandoned a business career in Leeds for a journalistic life in London. He was in fact called to the bar at Lincoln's Inn in 1863, but concentrated more on building a literary career for himself. He found early employment in 1861 as drama critic for the *Literary Gazette* through a chance meeting with the editor, John Morley. Thereafter he occupied himself largely with writing about the contemporary stage. In 1869 he succeeded John Abraham Heraud as drama critic of *The Athenaeum*, a post he retained until his death. In 1871, during the siege of Paris, he used his influence to secure an invitation to the Comédie-Française to act at the Gaiety Theatre in London; he also contributed an account of English literature to the French magazine *Le Livre*. He was drama critic for the *Sunday Times* and *The Globe*, and for the *Daily Graphic* from 1894 to 1906. But Knight's dramatic interests always ranged far beyond the contemporary theatre. He was well versed in dramatic history, and from 1883 to the close of the first supplement in 1901 was the chief contributor of articles on actors and actresses to the *Dictionary of National Biography*, writing some 375 entries. On his article on the life of Garrick he later based an independent memoir, which appeared in 1894.

Knight's charm, good looks, courtesy, and fine literary taste made him welcome in literary and dramatic circles from his first arrival in London. His early associates there included John Westland Marston and Sebastian Evans, to both of whom he owed advice and encouragement. At Marston's house he met leading authors and playwrights. Thomas Purnell, a journalist, introduced him to Swinburne and Dante Gabriel Rossetti. One of Rossetti's last letters was addressed to Knight, and in 1887 Knight published a sympathetic and discriminating *Life of Rossetti* in the Great Writers series.

Knight found varied opportunities of proving his literary knowledge. He contributed the *causerie* signed Sylvanus Urban to the *Gentleman's Magazine* from 1887 until near his death, and he was a reviewer of general literature for *The Athenaeum*. In July 1883, on the death of Henry Frederick Turle, he became editor of *Notes and Queries*, and retained that office for life. In that capacity he indulged his versatile antiquarian and literary tastes and formed many new acquaintances. In the same year he edited Downes's *Roscius Anglicanus* with a historical preface. In 1893 he published *Theatrical Notes, 1874–1879*, a collection of articles on drama from *The Athenaeum*. He was also the author of *The History of the Stage during the Victorian Era* and *The Stage in the Year 1900–1901*.

With strong sympathies for the bohemian life, Knight was long a leading member of the Arundel Club. But after 1883, when he was elected to the Garrick Club, his leisure was mainly spent there. In May 1893 he was elected fellow of the Society of Antiquaries. In July 1905 the dramatic profession entertained him, as the oldest living drama critic, to dinner at the Savoy Hotel. Sir Henry Irving took the chair, and the French performers Coquelin and Gabrielle Réjane were among the guests. Knight died at his house, 27 Camden Square, London, on 23 June 1907, and was buried in Highgate cemetery.

SIDNEY LEE, *rev.* NILANJANA BANERJI

Sources J. Foster, *Men-at-the-bar: a biographical hand-list of the members of the various inns of court*, 2nd edn (1885) · *The Times* (24 June 1907) · B. Hunt and J. Parker, eds., *The green room book, or, Who's who on the stage* (1906–9) · WWW · *The life and reminiscences of E. L. Blanchard, with notes from the diary of Wm. Blanchard*, ed. C. W. Scott and C. Howard, 2 vols. (1891) · *The Athenaeum* (29 June 1907), 791–2 · *N&Q*, 10th ser., 7 (1907), 501 · J. C. Francis, *Notes by the way* (1909) · V. Rendall, *Some reminiscences of Joseph Knight* (1911) · d. cert. · personal knowledge (1912)

Archives BL, corresp. and papers, Add. MSS 62694–62698

Likenesses W. B. Scott, bookplate, 1881 · M. W., miniature, 1901, Garr. Club · L. Ward, coloured chalk drawing, June 1905 · M. Grose, oils, 1912, Garr. Club · H. Furniss, two caricatures, pen-and-ink sketches, NPG · Walker & Boutall, photogravure, NPG

Wealth at death £3013 6s. 2d.: probate, 27 July 1907, CGPLA Eng. & Wales

Knight, Joseph (1837–1909), landscape painter and engraver, the son of Joseph and Eliza Knight, was born in London on 27 January 1837. When he was seven an accident made it necessary for his right arm to be amputated, but neither this setback, nor parental disapproval, deterred him from pursuing his chosen profession. In 1845 the family moved to Manchester, where Knight spent the earlier part of his career as an artist, visiting France, Holland, and Italy. On 29 October 1859 he married Elizabeth Radford (*b.* 1837/8) of Manchester, who survived him with a daughter, Clara, later Mrs Beswick (*b.* 1861), a landscape and genre painter, and a member of the Royal Cambrian Academy. Knight was self-taught, and began with figure subjects, but later changed to the landscapes by which he made his name. He became a member of the Manchester Academy of Fine Arts in 1868. In 1871 he moved to London and in 1875 to north Wales, where he settled. He made a reputation both as a painter in oil and in watercolour, and as an engraver and etcher. Rather sombre Welsh landscapes furnished the subjects of many of his pictures and engravings, which bore titles such as *Cloud and Crag* and *Conway Marsh*; and he became a member of the Royal Cambrian Academy.

Knight exhibited from 1861 onward at various London galleries, contributing to the Royal Academy for the first time in 1869. In 1882 he was elected a member of the Institute of Painters in Water Colours and an associate of the Society of Painter Etchers, of which he became a fellow in 1883. From that year to 1908 he sent 104 original mezzotint engravings, varied occasionally by etchings, to the exhibitions of the Painter Etchers. His output was prolific, if rather monotonous and lacking in expression. His painting *Tidal River* (1877) was purchased for the Tate (Chantrey bequest), and *Showery Weather* (1876) by Liverpool corporation for its permanent gallery. The corporations of Manchester, Oldham, Salford, and Blackburn also purchased examples of Knight's work, and some of his engravings are in the British Museum. He was represented at the Paris Universal Exhibition in 1889, where he was awarded a bronze medal, and at the Brussels International Exhibition in 1897.

Knight died at his home, Bryn-glas, Glan-y-môr Road, Llan-rhos, near Conwy, Caernarvonshire, on 2 January 1909. CAMPBELL DODGSON, *rev.* MARK POTTLE

Sources *The Times* (6 Jan 1909) · *The Times* (11 Jan 1909) · J. Johnson and A. Greutzner, *The dictionary of British artists, 1880–1940* (1976), vol. 5 of *Dictionary of British art* · G. M. Waters, *Dictionary of British artists, working 1900–1950* (1975) · Wood, *Vic. painters*, 3rd edn · Mallalieu, *Watercolour artists* · A. T. C. Pratt, ed., *People of the period: being a collection of the biographies of upwards of six thousand living celebrities*, 2 vols. (1897) · *Men and women of the time* (1899) · WWW · private information (1912) · m. cert. · d. cert.

Wealth at death £1468 5s.: probate, 11 March 1909, CGPLA Eng. & Wales

Knight, Joseph Philip (1812–1887), songwriter, was born in Bradford-on-Avon, Wiltshire, on 26 July 1812, the youngest son of Francis Knight DD, vicar of Bradford-on-Avon. At the age of sixteen he studied harmony and thoroughbass with John Davis Corfe, organist of Bristol Cathedral, and began composing. He subsequently published in 1832 a set of six songs under the pseudonym Philip Mortimer. Among these were 'Old Times', later sung by Henry Phillips, and 'Go, Forget Me', which became popular both in England and in Germany. Under his own name, and in collaboration with Haynes Bayly, Knight went on to write numerous songs, the most notable of which were 'The Veteran' and 'She Wore a Wreath of Roses'. After these came, among others, a solo song,

'The Parting', and a duet, 'Let's Take this World as some Wide Scene', both with words by Thomas Moore. In 1839 Knight visited the USA, where he composed his most famous song, 'Rocked in the Cradle of the Deep', which was for a long time associated with John Braham. On his return to England in 1841 he produced 'Beautiful Venice', 'Say, What shall my Song be To-night?' and 'The Dream', with words by the Hon. Mrs Caroline Norton. Some years afterwards he was ordained by the bishop of Exeter, and was appointed to the charge of St Agnes in the Isles of Scilly, where he remained for some years. He then married and moved abroad, but finally returned to England, retired from the ministry, and resumed composition. Knight wrote in all about two hundred songs, duets, and trios, many of which enjoyed great popularity in their time. He was praised for his command of pure English melody. He was also an excellent organist, particularly skilled at improvisation. He died in Great Yarmouth, Norfolk, on 2 June 1887.   J. C. HADDEN, *rev.* DAVID J. GOLBY

Sources G. Grove, 'Knight, Joseph Philip', Grove, *Dict. mus.* · *Clergy List* (1847–50)

Likenesses lithograph, BM

Knight [*née* Johnson], **Dame Laura** (1877–1970), painter, was born on 4 August 1877 at Long Eaton, in Nottinghamshire, the youngest of the three daughters of Charles Johnson, of no settled occupation, and his wife, Charlotte Bates. Johnson left his wife and family when he discovered that the Bates lace manufactory was on the downgrade, leaving Charlotte to bring up her daughters by teaching art in Nottingham schools. She was determined that Laura, who early showed a talent for drawing, should be properly trained. Laura was educated at Brincliffe School and at St Quentin in northern France, where an aunt who lived there promised to get her a place in a Paris atelier. This did not materialize, to Laura's bitter disappointment, and she returned home, entering the Nottingham School of Art when she was fourteen.

While there Laura Johnson met the prize student **Harold Knight** (1874–1961). A painter, he was born at 7 Tennyson Street, Sherwood, Nottingham, on 27 January 1874, the eldest son of William Knight, a local architect, and his wife, Elizabeth Lindsay Symington, whose rigid puritan temperament did not make for a happy home life for the family of three brothers and two sisters. It is probable that Harold's reserve, which was to grow on him, had its roots in those early years, when natural instincts were sternly repressed. He was educated at Nottingham high school, and went on to the Nottingham School of Art, where he soon made his mark as an outstanding student. Wilson Foster was a strong influence, and Harold learnt how to imitate nature faithfully.

Though they were later to marry, Knight was in no way emotionally involved with Laura at art school; the atmosphere at home made him concentrate on his painting, which he determined should be his career. He entered the competitions for provincial students held yearly at the South Kensington College of Art in London, and won gold, silver, and bronze medals. In 1895 he won a British Institute travelling scholarship worth £50 a year for two years.

Dame Laura Knight (1877–1970), self-portrait, 1913

He elected to remain for a year in Nottingham in order to sell his paintings and add to the scholarship. The following year he went to Paris, studying with Jean Paul Laurens and Benjamin Constant, but did not find the French ateliers congenial and returned to Nottingham before the year was up. It is surprising to note that he did not appear to be at all influenced by the new wave in Paris, the artistic centre of Europe, where those painters who succeeded the early impressionists were pushing out the boundaries of art further than they had been before.

Knight had kept up his friendship with Laura Johnson, and when she and her sister were taken by an aunt for a painting holiday at Staithes, a fishing village near Whitby on the Yorkshire coast, Harold was invited to join the party. There was a small artists' colony at Staithes, and Harold decided to remain for a time. He made a modest livelihood selling his work to dealers in Nottingham. Laura, too, remained with her sister, and painted scores of studies of the fisherfolk, selling them when she could, and living on a small allowance from an uncle.

Harold Knight sent pictures to the Royal Academy in London, and had a few small canvases taken. In 1902 his painting of a fishing boat, *The Last Coble*, was bought by the trustees of the Holbrook bequest and presented to the Nottingham Museum and Art Gallery. Laura had a picture, *Mother and Child*, accepted by the Royal Academy, which was sold. Both were at last making a little money.

Marriage and early career On 3 June 1903 Harold Knight, then nearly thirty, and Laura Johnson, then nearly twenty-six, were married. Their long, individual careers from this point onwards were closely connected, and Harold's development is considered alongside that of Laura. Like

Harold, Laura was much influenced by the naturalistic methods taught at Nottingham School of Art, and when she went to live in Staithes her studies and painting were all on firmly traditional lines. Also, like him, she entered regularly for the South Kensington College of Art competitions, and won gold, silver, and bronze medals, as well as a Princess of Wales scholarship.

After their marriage the Knights remained in Yorkshire for a time, but decided if they were going to advance with their work they ought to move. In 1905 they took a number of their canvases to London, and were much encouraged when Ernest Brown, a partner in Brown and Phillips (Oliver Brown), of the Leicester Galleries gave an exhibition of their work. Some pictures were sold, and a substantial cheque from Brown enabled them to sail on a cargo boat to Holland, which they had always wanted to visit. They remained for some weeks in Amsterdam, where Harold was able to study the paintings of the artist he admired most, Vermeer, and Laura was entranced by the picturesque nature of everything. On their return they sold a sufficient number of pictures between them to go to Holland again the following year, staying at Laren, well known to Dutch artists. In 1906 Harold had a picture, *A Cup of Tea*, accepted by the Royal Academy, and Laura had a Dutch interior taken. Harold's picture was hung on the line and bought for the Brisbane Gallery. They were able to go to Holland for a year, and brought back a large number of canvases, some of which they sold, but many had to be burnt or painted over. They decided to leave Staithes and move to Newlyn, in Cornwall.

The colony of artists at Newlyn, led by Stanhope A. Forbes and his wife, Elizabeth Armstrong, rejected the idealized subjects that had made so much Victorian painting dull and lifeless. They insisted on 'the simple truth of nature' in art, with an emphasis on painting out of doors. Laura Knight had always preferred working in the open, and the marvellous quality of the Cornish light was a constant inspiration. Harold also painted out of doors, but he had a feeling for interiors and reflected light. Each had developed a strongly individual style, and both were selling their pictures at the Leicester Galleries, and getting known in London.

Alfred James Munnings, already being talked about as a talented artist, came to Newlyn. Harold Knight did not care for the uninhibited young man in the check suit and yellow neckerchief, but Laura began a friendship with him which was to last. She was attracted by his overwhelming vitality, which matched her own exuberant temperament. She was in her element at Newlyn, painting the effects of sun and light on the naked bodies of bathers. She loved large canvases, and was tireless in making scores of studies. Her painting *Daughters of the Sun*, exhibited at the Royal Academy in 1909, was praised as a stunningly effective painting, but she priced it too highly (at £600) and it did not sell. (This fixation about the monetary value of her work was to grow.)

The temperamental differences in the Knights' work and their divergence of outlook was apparent. In spite of the aims of the Newlyn group, Harold kept to his own

vision, what Norman Garstin called the 'authoritative formulae' of the art establishment of former centuries (Garstin, 186). It was generally agreed that he was not interested in experiment and analysis; lucidity of statement was the dominating factor of his work. He lacked emotional force; his goal, as always, was mastery of his medium, and this he achieved. Laura's paintings showed an opulence of style and a flamboyance which was part of her nature. She painted a huge canvas, *The Green Feather*, in a day, and sent it to the Carnegie Institute of Pittsburgh, Pennsylvania, which had an international exhibition every year. It got an honourable mention and was sold to the National Gallery of Canada for £400—the best price, Laura said, she had ever been paid for a day's work.

In 1912 Harold Knight became seriously ill with infected teeth, and neither he nor Laura began painting again for six months. Harold had begun to get commissions for portraits, and they could now save money. They also made friends with new arrivals at Newlyn, Augustus John and his wife, and Barry Jackson, a wealthy theatre impresario from Birmingham.

After the outbreak of war in 1914, Harold Knight, who was a conscientious objector, was directed to work as a farmer's labourer. Their savings diminished. In 1916 Laura received an unexpected Canadian government commission, through a critic who was an admirer of her excellent technique, to paint soldiers bathing at Witley camp. This turned out to be a non-event; instead, she worked there on studies of boxing, though she had never attempted anything like it before. The finished canvas was one of the most realistic paintings she had ever achieved, and the resulting publicity added to her growing fame.

Major works Soon after the end of the war, the Knights moved to London. Harold was now established as a portrait painter. Laura, always ready to try something new, got permission to work behind the scenes of Diaghilev's ballet company. Through Barry Jackson she was allowed to work backstage in the theatre. In 1922 she was invited to go to America as one of the European representatives on the jury for that year's international exhibition at Pittsburgh. On her return, she and Harold took a long lease of 9 (the number was later changed to 16) Langford Place, St John's Wood, which was to be their permanent home and where each had a studio.

Harold Knight's now established reputation as a meticulous, skilful portrait painter continued to bring him many commissions. In 1926 he was invited to go to Baltimore to paint Dr John Finney of the Johns Hopkins Memorial Hospital; the generous fee enabled him to bring Laura to America and she made many studies in the wards of the famous hospital reserved for black people. An honour which filled her with pride came in 1927, when she was elected associate of the Royal Academy, after A. J. Munnings had put her name forward several times without success. She was the second woman associate of the Royal Academy, the first being Annie Swynnerton, then eighty years old.

Laura Knight had always been interested in the technical problems of drawing movement, and she now began to work in a field that had fascinated her since childhood, the circus. Munnings introduced her to Bertram Mills, the owner of Mills's circus, who gave her permission to go where she liked during rehearsals, and soon she was producing studies of trapeze artists, acrobats, tumblers, jugglers, contortionists, as well as dwarfs, clowns, and the circus animals. She painted a huge canvas, *Charivari*, which brought in nearly everyone in circus life; it was exhibited at the Royal Academy summer exhibition in 1929 and was caricatured in *Punch*, with politicians portrayed as the various circus performers.

Harold Knight was elected an associate of the Royal Academy in 1928. In 1929 Laura was appointed a Dame Commander of the British empire, an honour that she accepted with pride, but that did not prevent her from travelling round with a circus, her friends there puzzled why she should now be officially a dame when she had obviously always been one. From circus life she went on to paint Gypsies at Epsom and Ascot, working in an old Rolls-Royce fitted up as a miniature studio. Her long-standing friendship with Barry Jackson led to her going to the Malvern festival, which he had founded. Harold went with her every year, and they met many celebrities of the time, including G. Bernard Shaw, whom Laura painted. But the portrait was not considered to be successful, either as a likeness or a painting.

Harold Knight's reputation continued to grow in this genre. A portrait of the pianist Ethel Bartlett playing on a grand piano was exhibited at the Royal Academy summer exhibition in 1929 and was highly praised for its charm and beautiful sense of colour. In 1933 a fine portrait of the lord bishop of Truro was exhibited at the Royal Academy summer exhibition and enhanced Harold's reputation as a first-class painter of pictorial realism; it was described as a restrained and dignified piece of work. In fact, Harold could achieve a great deal more than pictorial realism, as is shown in his portrait of the 'supertramp' W. H. Davies, which conveyed the character of the poet through the expression in the eyes. The portrait is in the Merthyr Tudful Art Gallery.

In 1936 Laura Knight was elected Royal Academician, the first woman to become a full member of the Royal Academy. She served on the selection and hanging committee, and was later involved in a row over a portrait of T. S. Eliot by P. Wyndham Lewis, which the academy had rejected. Augustus John resigned from the academy in protest, and Laura tried to act as mediator. It was now well known, however, that she was not sympathetic to new ideas in art, and she took the side of the academy in the dispute.

Harold Knight was elected a Royal Academician in 1937. The Knights were living in Colwall, near Malvern, when war came in 1939. They were hit financially, as several portrait commissions which Harold had accepted were cancelled. Laura was soon working, as the War Artists' Advisory Committee had come into being, and she did a number of paintings for them. Her most notable canvas was for the Ministry of Munitions, of a woman munitions worker called Ruby Loftus screwing the breech ring in a Bofors gun, a delicate operation thought impossible for a woman to do. Laura's photographic eye for detail and command of technique brought an extraordinary reality to the painting, one of the best she had ever achieved. It is in the Imperial War Museum, London.

War correspondent Then came a unique assignment. In 1946, at the age of sixty-eight, Laura Knight went to Nuremberg to paint what was to be a pictorial record of the war criminals' trial; she was rated officially as a war correspondent. Harold had left their home in London and was living in the Park Hotel in Colwall. Laura wrote to him frequently, describing the scenes in court. She made scores of sketches, and her final large picture of the prisoners in the dock was unusual for her, in that it was surrounded by vivid impressions of their crimes. It is now in the Imperial War Museum, London.

Later years Back in England, Laura and Harold Knight returned to Langford Place. Harold's health had long been failing, and he found it difficult to paint because of arthritis. Laura took him to Colwall, which he liked better than any other place in England, and he died at the Park Hotel there on 3 October 1961, at the age of eighty-seven. His work was summed up variously, with the emphasis on its pictorial quality, but there was no question about his great achievements as a superb master of his craft. If he was not the English Vermeer, he brought many of the fine qualities of the Dutch old master into his work. Some critics wondered why he had not attained a higher eminence. Perhaps there is something in the remark that Laura made more than once. 'I stood in his way'. She never tried to explain how.

Harold Knight was an honorary member of the Royal Institute of Oil Painters, the Royal Society of Portrait Painters, and the Royal West of England Academy. He is represented in many public collections, including the Welsh National Gallery, Cardiff; Merthyr Tudful Art Gallery; the Tate collection, London; the Royal Academy; and in the art galleries of Leeds, Rochdale, Preston, Newcastle upon Tyne, Nottingham, and Manchester; abroad in the Municipal Gallery, Perth, Australia; and in Brisbane, Cape Town, and New Zealand.

Laura Knight put on an exhibition of Harold's pictures, and spent her remaining years arranging for exhibitions of her own work. These showed her astounding range in oils, watercolour, etchings, and pencil drawings, with subjects which included landscape, seascape, the Cornish sunlight on nudes, circus scenes, Gypsies, ballet dancers and actors, bomber crews and balloon sites in wartime, and the Nuremberg trial, all executed with incredible facility. A retrospective exhibition in the diploma gallery at the Royal Academy in the summer of 1965 was the accolade of her long career. She went to an exhibition of her work, '75 years of painting', at the Upper Grosvenor Galleries in 1969. This was her swansong. She was unable to go to an exhibition of her work put on at Nottingham Castle during the Nottingham festival, 1970, though she made a gallant attempt to do so. She died at her home in

London on 7 July 1970, in her ninety-third year. There were no children of the marriage.

Laura Knight was an honorary member of the Royal Society of Painters in Water Colours, the Royal Society of Painter-Etchers and Engravers, the Royal West of England Academy, the Society of Women Artists, and the Royal Society of Portrait Painters. Her honours include the gold medal, San Francisco, 1915, and an honorary mention, Paris Salon, 1928. She is represented in many public collections, including the National Portrait Gallery, the Royal Academy, the Victoria and Albert Museum, the Tate collection, the British Museum, and the Imperial War Museum, London, as well as in collections abroad. She wrote the autobiographical *Oil Paint and Grease Paint* (1936), *A Proper Circus Omie* (1962), and *The Magic of a Line* (1965). She was made an honorary LLD by St Andrews University (1931) and an honorary DLitt by Nottingham University (1951).

JANET DUNBAR, rev.

Sources J. Dunbar, *Laura Knight* (1975) · N. Garstin, 'The art of Harold and Laura Knight', *The Studio*, 57 (1912–13), 183–200 · E. A. T., 'Studio-talk', *The Studio*, 69 (1916–17), 144 · H. B. Grimsditch, 'Mr Harold Knight: a quiet painter', *The Studio*, 96 (1928), 14–21 · G. St Bernard, 'Royal Academy 1931: a survey', *The Studio*, 102 (1931), 3–19 · 'The Royal Academy', *The Studio*, 106 (1933), 3–11 · D. Goldring, 'The Royal Academy, 1935', *The Studio*, 110 (1935), 15–21 · b. cert. [Harold Knight] · *CGPLA Eng. & Wales* (1961) [Harold Knight] · private information (1981) · personal knowledge (1981) · *CGPLA Eng. & Wales* (1970)
Archives Notts. Arch., corresp. and papers; Nuremberg diary and engagement diaries | Tate collection, corresp. with Eileen Mayo · U. Birm. L., letters to John Ramsay Allardyce Nicoll and Josephine Nicoll
Likenesses A. Munnings, drawing, *c*.1911, Sir Alfred Munnings Art Museum, Castle House, Dedham, Essex · L. Knight, self-portrait, 1913, NPG [*see illus.*] · W. Stoneman, photograph, 1930, NPG · W. Bird, photograph, 1964, NPG · J. S. Lewinski, photograph, 1967, NPG · N. Vogel, photograph, 1969, NPG · H. Knight, self-portrait, NPG · A. Munnings, two watercolour sketches, Sir Alfred Munnings Art Museum, Castle House, Dedham, Essex · Madame Yevonde, four prints, NPG
Wealth at death £73,134: probate, 11 Aug 1970, *CGPLA Eng. & Wales* · £25,482 5s. 11d.—Harold Knight: probate, 17 Nov 1961, *CGPLA Eng. & Wales*

Knight, Mary (*bap.* 1631, *d.* in or after **1698**), singer, was baptized at St Gregory by Paul's, London, on 7 April 1631, the daughter of Stephen Knight (*d.* 1655) and his wife, Margaret (1596/7–1677), daughter of John Faldo and Anne Gravely of Bedfordshire, and widow of John Birkhead. The poet Henry *Birkhead (1617–1696) was Mary's half-brother. In 1640 he and Stephen Knight were appointed by Archbishop William Laud to the registry of the diocese of Norwich, Knight being dismissed from his post in 1646 for having served as a trooper in the royalist regiment of Sir Edward Waldegrave. On 30 July 1649 Mary married Henry Geery at St Peter Paul's Wharf. They may have had a son but apparently separated soon afterwards as nothing more is heard of Geery and Mary continued to be known as Mary Knight.

Mary studied music under Henry Lawes and sang at the musicales he organized in the 1650s. The royalist circles which congregated around Lawes included Mary's relative the royalist propagandist Sir John Berkenhead and the poet Katherine Philips; all three contributed commendatory poems to Lawes's *Second Book of Ayres and Dialogues*, published in 1655. Mary's poem praised Lawes's teaching—'If I have art it is from thee'—and commented on the transient nature of her art:

Twere weakness to suppose my breath
Could thy rich Ayres preserve from death.
(M. Knight, quoted in Evans, 207–8)

By 1659 Mary was well known; on 19 May that year she dined with the writer John Evelyn who described her as a 'famous singer' (Highfill, Burnim & Langhans, *BDA*, 9.60). After the restoration of Charles II in 1660 Mary became a favourite at court, perhaps helped by Berkenhead who had been appointed master of requests, and there were rumours for a short time in the mid-1660s that she was a mistress of the king, although these cannot be confirmed. She was certainly never an acknowledged royal mistress and continued to earn her living by singing. In September 1667 Mary was apparently giving public performances at Gray's Inn Fields; the diarist Samuel Pepys missed hearing her there on 27 September 1667 but hoped to try again another day. Her status as a professional singer who also had respectable connections, and who performed for both the fashionable and the general public, was probably unique in the period, her fame and position being unrivalled by any other female singer.

In 1672 Charles II granted Mary a pension of £200 for life. In December 1674 she gave a concert at Mr Slingsby's, earning the highest praise from Evelyn who wrote that she 'sung incomparably, & doubtlesse has the greatest reach of any English woman; she had lately ben roming in Italy: and was much improv'd' (Evelyn, quoted in Highfill, Burnim & Langhans, *BDA*, 9.61). She had a leading role in the most important court masque of the decade, *Calisto*, performed in early 1675, singing the parts of Peace and Daphne. She may have had lodgings in Whitehall, since a warrant for £100 to furnish a room for Mistress Knight was written in December 1675. According to the monument erected by Mary on her mother's death in 1677 she was one of eleven children from her mother's two marriages but by that time only two were left alive, herself and Henry Birkhead. Her prominence at court attracted the attention of satirists. 'Madam Nelley's Complaint: a Satyr' of about 1680, suggested that she was a close friend of Nell Gwyn and had even lived with her, but that they had recently become rivals for the favours of William Dutton Colt. As a Roman Catholic Mary was also the subject of political satire during the succession crisis of 1679–81 which suggested she was a 'spy for Rome' (Chappell and Elsworth, 5.131). In 1683 she made a visit to France, prompting suspicions that she had gone there on a secret mission for Charles II, although this seems unlikely.

James II continued Mary's pension and after the revolution of 1688 she followed the exiled king into France, but she had returned by September 1696 when her brother died at her house in Birdcage Walk, St James's Park. Mary's son may also have died by this point as although he had been named in Henry Birkhead's will of 1688, Birkhead's last will, made in 1694, made no mention of him. Birkhead appointed Mary one of his executors. She appears to have lost her Stuart pension but William III had sufficient sympathy for her to grant her £100 a year, which seems to have been paid from January 1697. The last notice of Mary was a warrant for a licence to remain in England, having previously left and returned without leave, on 24 January 1698.

S. M. WYNNE

Sources Highfill, Burnim & Langhans, *BDA* · J. H. Pittock, *Henry Birkhead: founder of the Oxford chair of poetry* (1999) · P. W. Thomas, *Sir John Berkenhead, 1617–1679* (1969) · W. M. Evans, *Henry Lawes: musician and friend of poets* (1941) · BL, Harley MS 6835, fol. 29v · *The collected works of Katherine Philips the matchless Orinda*, ed. P. Thomas, 2 (1992) · PRO, LC 5/141, p. 305 · *IGI* · M. A. E. Green, ed., *Calendar of the proceedings of the committee for compounding ... 1643–1660*, 5 vols., PRO (1889–92) · W. A. Shaw, ed., *Calendar of treasury books*, 7, PRO (1916); 17 (1947) · *CSP dom., 1673–5; 1686–7; 1698* · *Report on the manuscripts of the late Reginald Rawdon Hastings*, 4 vols., HMC, 78 (1928–47), vol. 2, p. 174 · W. Chappell and J. W. Elsworth, eds., *The Roxburghe ballads*, 8 vols. (1869–1901)

Knight, Mary Ann (1776–1851), miniature painter, was born on 7 September 1776 in Birchin Lane, Cornhill, London, and was baptized on 28 October 1776 in the parish church of St Michael Cornhill, the daughter of John Knight, merchant, and his wife, Frances, *née* Woodcock. In order to provide financial assistance to her parents, who later became impoverished, Mary Ann began to receive commissions to paint miniature portraits in 1802, at the age of twenty-six, and continued to paint until 1836. She had been a pupil of the miniaturist Andrew *Plimer, who had married her sister, (Joanna) Louisa in 1801, and later she was to spend much time in the Plimer household, and painted several portraits of her nieces and nephews.

In *Andrew and Nathaniel Plimer* (1903) George Williamson included an account of Mary Ann Knight together with a list of her works 'extracted from her own note-books', then in the possession of Plimer family descendants (Williamson, 73). He noted that 'She kept a very careful account of her earnings, and records that she made the sum of £5,171 9s. 8d. being an average of 150 guineas a year throughout the above period' (ibid., 74). At first she charged between 2 and 4 guineas a portrait; by the end of 1805 she received 9 guineas for a larger- and 7 guineas for a smaller-sized portrait. About 1815 her success at portrait painting is indicated by her fees of between 20 and 30 guineas. She was particularly in demand for portraits of children, her success with whom Williamson attributed to 'her own engaging charm, quiet soft voice, merry vivacious manner, and great kindliness of disposition' (ibid., 77). She told her young sitters many stories and 'was able to represent them as real children, and to capture in her rapid and sketchy portraits excellent likenesses' (ibid.). While not immune to the custom of painting children as angels or in classical costume her most successful portraits of children are naturally posed. Williamson noted that Miss Knight sometimes copied the style of Anthony Stewart, a noted painter of portraits of babies. The fee of £42 that she received for a group portrait of the children of Sir William Rush in 1814 was identical with that which she obtained in 1821 for a picture entitled *Venus and Adonis*. When she ceased work in 1836 she recorded

having painted a total of 696 portraits. Her own list appears to be incomplete, however. Of the thirty portraits she exhibited at the Royal Academy between 1803 and 1830 some do not appear on her own list; in 1805 she exhibited at the academy a portrait, *Captain Norton Teyoninhakarlawen, a chief of the Mohawks, one of the Five Nations in Upper Canada*. One of her signed miniatures, now in the Victoria and Albert Museum, London, is also of interest for the lock of hair intricately plaited in a sheaf design enclosed on the reverse.

Miss Knight lived at St John's Wood and at Wicken, Stony Stratford, the address of her parents. In 1813 her studio was in Old Bond Street, London. In old age she lived at Grove End Road, St John's Wood, London, where she died, unmarried, in 1851 at the age of seventy-five.

Of her miniatures Williamson noted that 'The finest work I have seen by Mary Ann Knight is at Oxford in the University Galleries; it might at first glance be attributed to Andrew Plimer so much does it resemble his work' (Williamson, 76). The miniature, of a young girl (c.1810–1820; AM Oxf.), is well painted and has subsequently been attributed both to Miss Knight and to Andrew Plimer. While her miniatures are generally of 'a large size' and 'pale, even washy in colour' she occasionally used a rich colour scheme and was 'very partial to the use of a rich purple, resembling the bloom of a grape' (ibid., 77). Her miniatures of members of the Manners family are reproduced in Williamson (facing p. 76).

Apart from her miniatures Williamson drew attention to Mary Ann Knight's 'rough sketches made in a wash of sepia ... in which she coloured the faces with the very faintest wash of carmine' (Williamson, 78). One of these was of the dramatist and poet Joanna Baillie. While Miss Baillie would not allow the portrait to be engraved, as she did not want to see it 'all over the place' (ibid., 75), a copy was taken and either this or the original is now in the Scottish National Portrait Gallery, Edinburgh, together with another of the socialist and philanthropist Robert Owen (1771–1858). The original of the Baillie portrait was included in a large sketchbook, subsequently in the possession of Plimer family descendants, containing a variety of 'first sketches' in pencil and watercolour. These also included portraits of the writer Lucy Aikin (or Aitken); Lady Caroline Lamb and Anne Isabella, Lady Byron (both City of Nottingham Museums, Newstead Abbey collection); the artist's mother, Mrs Knight (ibid., facing p. 74); Andrew Plimer's daughters; and a self-portrait. A chalk and watercolour drawing of Prince Hoare by Miss Knight after a portrait by Sir Thomas Lawrence is in the British Museum. According to Williamson 'these portraits deserve much more attention' (ibid., 79). The whereabouts of many of these sketches remains unknown.

ANNETTE PEACH

Sources G. C. Williamson, *Andrew and Nathaniel Plimer: miniature painters* (1903) · R. Walker, *Miniatures: a selection of miniatures in the Ashmolean Museum* (1997) · card catalogue of miniatures, AM Oxf. · C. F. Bell, list of miniature portraits, 1897, AM Oxf. [bequeathed to U. Oxf. by the Revd William Bentinck L. Hawkins and exhibited in the University Picture Gallery] · H. Smailes, *The concise catalogue of the Scottish National Portrait Gallery* (1990) · artist's file, archive material, NPG · B. S. Long, *British miniaturists* (1929) · private information (2004) [Haidée Jackson]

Likenesses M. Knight, self-portrait, miniature, exh. 1865, South Kensington Museum; lent by Miss Carpenter · M. Knight, self-portrait, watercolour and pencil drawing

Knight, (Charles Henry) Maxwell (1900–1968), intelligence officer and naturalist, was born on 9 July 1900 at 199 Selhurst Road, South Norwood, Croydon, one of at least two sons of Hugh Coleraine Knight (*d.* 1914), a solicitor, and his wife, Ada Phyllis Roberts, *née* Handcock (*d.* 1925). His philandering father managed to bankrupt his legal practice. At fourteen Knight was sent to HMS *Worcester* (the Thames Nautical Training College), off Greenhithe, Kent, to be trained as an officer for the merchant navy. After the death of an older brother on the western front in 1916, Knight volunteered for the Royal Navy and served on armed merchantmen. After the war he briefly worked at the Ministry of Shipping, before taking a post as a teacher of Latin at a minor preparatory school in Putney. On 29 December 1925 he married Gwladys Evelyn Amy (*d.* 1934), daughter of Charles Edward Hamilton Poole, a military officer.

Knight was personally recruited for MI5 by Vernon Kell, the director-general, in 1925. Kell saw in Knight someone with a perfect cover: a young gentleman about town, much in demand for débutante parties, whose new career did not interfere with his enthusiasm for the cellar clubs of Soho and Leicester Square, or his enthusiasm for American jazz and new dances like the Charleston.

At MI5, Knight worked with Guy Liddell in B division, charged with the surveillance of extremists of the right and left. Once trained Knight was given the plum job of recruiting and running individual agents. An apartment at 308 Hood House, Dolphin Square, was rented. As Captain King or Mr K. he was able, perhaps even obliged, to maintain a lively social life as professional cover. He spent the early 1930s dining out with journalists, secretaries, and débutantes. At weekends he joined his wife at the Exmoor pub and hotel which she ran, and where the fishing was splendid. Gwladys died on 17 November 1934, and on 28 August 1937 Knight married Lois Mary, a secretary, daughter of William Drave Coplestone; this marriage was ended by divorce in 1943.

Penetration of the headquarters of the Communist Party of Great Britain at King Street had long been an MI5 priority. Knight had the phones tapped and party members working in industry were secretly vetted. Knight recruited agents including Olga Gray, who at nineteen volunteered for office duties with the anti-war movement. Gray's dedication and efficiency won the confidence of the Communist Party leaders at King Street and she was given greater responsibilities, culminating in a request that she set up a safe house for the use of a spy ring operating at the Woolwich arsenal. It was as Miss X that she testified at the trial which sent Percy Glading to prison for six years for espionage. The smashing of the Woolwich arsenal spy ring was a triumph of MI5 methodology, and of Knight's patience.

Knight's agents included Tom Driberg, who was writing

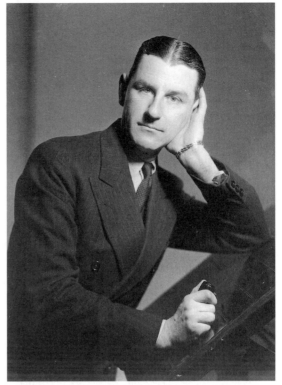

(**Charles Henry) Maxwell Knight** (1900–1968), by Howard Coster, 1934

the William Hickey column for the *Daily Express*. Driberg gave Knight access to the 'Café Communists', whose public school education and experience at Oxford or Cambridge provided them with superb cover for espionage. Knight recruited Bill Younger, stepson of his friends Dennis and Joan Wheatley, to spy on Oxford undergraduates. Known Nazi sympathizers, such as William Joyce, were also used as informants. Knight seems to have preferred attractive young women of respectable backgrounds for the task of penetrating the inner circle of Britain's domestic Nazis.

Knight's greatest success against Nazi espionage came in 1940 with the arrest of Tyler Kent, cipher clerk in the American embassy in London. Kent had made contact with Anna Wolkoff, a member of the Right Club, and gave her copies of the telegrams between Churchill and Roosevelt, which were passed to the Italian embassy. Used with some cleverness, the compromising plans for Lend-Lease could have discredited Roosevelt and possibly driven Churchill from office. With the agreement of the American ambassador, Kent was tried in camera and sentenced to seven years in prison. Wolkoff was given ten years.

In May 1940, five days after the arrest of Tyler Kent, Max Knight's patron, Vernon Kell, was sacked by Churchill. Knight was never again as secure in MI5, and his handling of the case of Ben Greene JP had nearly disastrous consequences for Knight's career. Greene, a cousin of the novelist Graham Greene, was interned after being falsely accused by one of Knight's agents, Harold Kurtz, who had forged letters implicating Greene and had lied about them in court. A member of the Peace Pledge Union and founding member of the British People's Party, Greene was a pacifist who opposed war with Germany. Greene was eventually released. The case weakened confidence in Knight's judgement.

Knight became obsessed with the suspicion that communists had penetrated MI5. After Driberg was expelled from the Communist Party in 1941, Knight suspected that someone in MI5 had passed on information about him to Harry Pollitt. Anthony Blunt was questioned by MI5 about his role in the betrayal of Driberg. In 1941 Knight asked Roger Hollis and Guy Liddell to investigate Soviet penetration of the security services, and sent a secret report, 'The Comintern is not dead', to his friend Desmond Morton, who was Churchill's private secretary. None of those who read the report was persuaded by the evidence Knight had amassed.

With the appointment of Sir Percy Sillitoe as director-general of MI5 in 1946 Knight's position was further weakened. Dolphin Square was closed, and Knight felt himself unheeded and bypassed. The running of agents was largely left to his deputy, John Bingham, whose career as a novelist was just beginning. David Cornwell (later the writer John le Carré) was regarded as one of Knight's protégés in the early 1950s.

On 18 November 1944 Knight married for the third time. His wife, Susan Mary Durell (d. 1983), daughter of Henry Durell Barnes, worked in MI5's registry during the war. In 1945 he made the first of many naturalist talks for the BBC, and become a regular contributor to *The Field* and *Country Life*. The defections of Maclean and Burgess in May 1951 were followed by the replacement of Sillitoe by Dick White as head of MI5. Guy Liddell was shunted off to the Atomic Energy Authority. But it was too late for Knight to reconstruct his career and he retired from MI5 in 1956. He was appointed OBE.

Knight had written two thrillers in the 1930s, *Crime Cargo* (1934) and *Gunmen's Holiday* (1935), attempting without success to recreate in Britain the American hard-boiled novel. He also wrote several books on natural history for young readers: *The Young Naturalist's Field Guide* (1952), and the posthumously published *Pets and their Problems* (1968) and *Be a Nature Detective* (1969).

Maxwell Knight died on 24 January 1968 at the Royal Berkshire Hospital, Reading, following a heart attack. At his memorial service he was remembered as Uncle Max, the genial naturalist of the wireless and early days of television. By the 1980s Knight's hidden career was finally revealed: in the inter-war years he had been the MI5 agent-runner who had penetrated espionage operations on both the right and left. Knight was an eccentric and an amateur naturalist; his conduct as head of counter-espionage was professional and exemplary. ERIC HOMBERGER

Sources A. Masters, *The man who was M: the life of Maxwell Knight* (1984) • E. Homberger, '"Uncle Max" and his thrillers', *Intelligence and National Security*, 3/2 (1988), 312–21 • N. West, *MI5: British security service operations, 1900–1945* (1981) • R. Griffiths, *Patriotism perverted: Captain Ramsay, the Right Club and British anti-Semitism* (1998) • C. Andrew, *Secret service: the making of the British intelligence community* (1985) • J. Miller, *One girl's war: personal exploits in MI5's most secret station* (1986) • *The Times* (27 Jan 1968), 10 • b. cert. • m. certs. • d. cert.

Archives FILM BFI NFTVA, documentary footage

Likenesses H. Coster, photograph, 1934, NPG [*see illus.*] • photograph, 1940, repro. in Masters, *The man who was M*, facing p. 118

Knight, Sir Ralph (1619?–1691), parliamentarian army officer, was the son of William Knight of Newbury, Berkshire, and his wife, Alice Worthington. He gave his age as forty-seven at the herald's visitation of Yorkshire on 10 April 1666 and he was reported as being aged seventy-one when he died on 21 April 1691. His life is obscure until the civil war. In 1643 he served as a commander of a troop of cavalry in the Earl of Manchester's regiment of horse. In 1645 he was appointed to the New Model Army as captain in Mathew Tomlinson's cavalry regiment. Shortly after the regiment formed, the House of Lords, which had suggested that he be appointed to another regiment, apparently in order to exclude a radical officer, showed favour to Knight by ordering that his men be paid 1s. a day each more than other troopers. Knight has left one direct record of his military service in these years, his account of the siege of Winchester in October 1645. By 1647 he had attained the rank of major in the same regiment. In July of that year he put his name to a statement of the army's grievances, the agitators' letter to the masters of Trinity House.

Knight married on 23 June 1646 Faith (1616/17–1671), daughter of William Dickinson, vicar of Rotherham, Yorkshire. They had eight sons and seven daughters (of whom three sons and two daughters died young). Knight settled in Yorkshire. Two of his children were baptized at Rotherham in 1647 and 1648, and in 1650 he purchased Langold on the Yorkshire–Nottinghamshire border and paid £920 for the former crown manor of Taunchelfe, also in Yorkshire. From that date his children were baptized at the local parish church, St John's, Langold. In 1653 Knight was appointed a deputy lieutenant for the West Riding.

Much of Knight's later military service was spent in Scotland. In October 1653, in the absence of its colonel, Major Knight commanded Tomlinson's regiment when it was sent there to suppress Glencairn's rising. The following year the new commander-in-chief in Scotland, George Monck, became the regiment's colonel. In 1656 Knight was stationed at Linlithgow. It was probably owing to Monck's influence that he was returned to parliament for Sutherland, Ross and Cromarty, his election being reported on 25 January 1659. According to Sir Richard Baker, Knight, then at home in Yorkshire, was suspected of complicity with Lord Castleton in the royalist plotting which manifested itself in Sir George Booth's rising in August 1659, and for his own safety returned to his command in Scotland. Knight was certainly a key member of the circle surrounding Monck, when he decided to oppose the new military regime in England which had succeeded the restored Rump Parliament. On 3 November 1659 Knight was named one of three commissioners from

Monck's army to be sent to negotiate with the army leaders in England, following their decision to send John Lambert north to confront Monck's army. In London on 15 November Knight signed an agreement which provided for the dispersal of both armies and for a meeting on 6 December in which a new republican government would be settled upon. These terms were regarded as inadequate by Monck, and Knight, now appointed colonel of a regiment of horse, took part in the Scottish army's march into England on 2 January 1660, leading the advance party which secured Newcastle.

Knight was one of the key agents used by Monck to subdue the radical elements remaining in the army in February–March 1660. He was able to secure a seat in the Convention Parliament, being elected on 9 April 1660 on the Howard interest at Morpeth, following a recommendation by Monck. In the Convention he was able to act as a spokesman for Monck: thus when Monck's chaplain preached before the Commons, it was Knight who was asked on 10 May to convey the thanks of the house. He was given leave by the house to attend Monck at Blackheath on 28 May, and on the following day he presented the king with a declaration from the army. In May or June 1660 he was knighted for 'good service', and on 3 August he was given a pension of £600 p.a. until lands of the equivalent value were settled upon him. In the Commons he was willing to defend the major-generals William Boteler and James Berry, General Charles Fleetwood, and Sir Arthur Hesilrige. He supported episcopacy, but was clearly in favour of a broad-church settlement, not wanting to see the imposition of the Thirty-Nine Articles and consequent deprivation of so many ministers.

With his regiment disbanded, Knight did not stand again for parliament, but he appears to have remained in London for a time as he was exempt from the order of June 1662 removing former army officers from London. He was also in local office as a justice in Yorkshire, Nottinghamshire, and Westminster. In 1662 he purchased the manor of Letwill, Yorkshire. Knight appears to have been known to Sir Thomas Osborne (the future earl of Danby) as early as 1665, and in 1666, when Osborne wanted to raise a troop of horse, it was suggested that Knight be his lieutenant. On 13 June 1667 Knight was made a captain of a company of non-regimental horse which was raised in the military emergency from the Nottinghamshire–Yorkshire border, and which marched to Yarmouth in case of a Dutch invasion, before being disbanded on 16 August 1667. Knight's wife died in 1671, and that year he converted his pension into a lump sum of £8000. On 12 May 1673 he became lieutenant-colonel of the duke of Buckingham's regiment of foot, and in 1675 he bought the manor of Warsop in Nottinghamshire, which opened the way to a deputy lieutenant commission in the county.

In 1678–9 the presbyterian Oliver Heywood preached at Firbeck Chapel, Yorkshire, in front of Knight and his son-in-law Richard Taylor. When parliament was dissolved in January 1679 Knight was seen as a possible election manager should the duke of Newcastle see fit to sponsor Danby's son at East Retford, and in August he was assisting the countess of Danby while her husband was incarcerated in the Tower. On a trip to London in the winter of 1682–3 Knight professed to Heywood the dilemma he would face should his office as justice require him to prosecute dissenters, as he would not 'meddle' with them. By 1684 Sir John Reresby was reporting that Knight was often too ill to attend militia musters. When the 'three questions' testing support for James II's religious policies were tendered in Yorkshire he was described as 'out of the commission of the peace'.

In 1687 Knight married, by licence dated 17 May, Elizabeth Rolleston of Warsop, whose husband, John, had been buried in the local church in 1681. Knight made his will on 25 December 1689. He referred to £1000 owed to him by the king, which he had spent many years trying to recover. He died on 21 April 1691 at Firbeck and was buried there two days later, his funeral sermon referring to him as 'a true lover of the Church of England, and of all her legitimate offspring' (White, 31). He was succeeded in turn by his eldest surviving sons, John (*bap.* 1648, *d.* 1695) and Isaac (1652/3–1721).

STUART HANDLEY

Sources M. W. Helms and J. P. Ferris, 'Knight, Ralph', HoP, *Commons, 1660–90* · *Dugdale's visitation of Yorkshire, with additions*, ed. J. W. Clay, 1 (1899), 9–10 · J. Hunter, *South Yorkshire: the history and topography of the deanery of Doncaster*, 2 vols. (1828), 1.297–302 · C. Dalton, ed., *English army lists and commission registers, 1661–1714*, 1 (1892), 76, 146 · *The manuscripts of Sir William Fitzherbert ... and others*, HMC, 32 (1893), 3–5 · *The Rev. Oliver Heywood ... his autobiography, diaries, anecdote and event books*, ed. J. H. Turner, 4 vols. (1881–5), 2.61, 92, 158; 4.83, 85 · G. Davies, *The restoration of Charles II, 1658–1660* (1955) · R. Hutton, *The Restoration: a political and religious history of England and Wales, 1658–1667* (1985) · R. Baker, *A chronicle of the kings of England* (1679), 665 · Thurloe, *State papers*, 7.600 · C. Holmes, *The eastern association in the English civil war* (1974), 175, 240 · M. H. White, *Memoirs of the house of White of Wallingwells* (1886), 29–32 · F. D. Dow, *Cromwellian Scotland, 1651–1660* (1979), 238, 258 · C. H. Firth and G. Davies, *The regimental history of Cromwell's army*, 2 vols. (1940) · R. K. G. Temple, ed., 'The original officer list of the New Model Army', *BIHR*, 59 (1986), 50–77

Knight, Ralph (1703–1754). *See under* Knight family (*per.* c.1680–1897).

Knight, Richard (1659–1745). *See under* Knight family (*per.* c.1680–1897).

Knight, Richard Payne (1751–1824), art collector and writer, was born at Wormsley Grange, Herefordshire, on 11 February 1751, the eldest son of the four children of Thomas Knight (1697–1764), rector of Bewdley, and his wife, formerly his servant, Ursula Nash (*b.* 1723/4). His two sisters, Barbara (1756–1775) and Ursula (1760–1777), died young but his brother, Thomas Andrew *Knight (1759–1838), became a renowned horticulturist. Knight took his middle name from his grandmother, Elizabeth Payne, whose husband, the ironmaster Richard *Knight (1659–1745) [*see under* Knight family (*per.* c.1680–1897)] had made one of the first great fortunes of the industrial revolution. Knight inherited much of the family fortune on the death of his uncle Richard Knight in 1765.

Richard Payne Knight (1751–1824), by Sir Thomas Lawrence, 1794

Education, travel, and architecture On account of his poor health Knight was educated at home until his father's death in 1764. Thereafter he was taught by a private tutor, Mr Blyth, at Coleshill, Warwickshire, who introduced him to Greek, at which he excelled. He did not go to university but instead went on the grand tour in 1772, when he came of age and gained control of his fortune. He travelled through France to Florence, Rome, and Naples. On his return to England in 1773 he began to design himself a new house on the estates he had inherited at Downton, Herefordshire. The house, which became known as Downton Castle, was built from 1774 to 1778 by Thomas Farnolls Pritchard; the interior was not completed for another few years. Built on an asymmetrical plan that owed much to the designs of John Vanbrugh, and with embattled parapets that echoed the medieval castles of the Welsh borders, the castle was entered through a large, square tower that housed a circular, domed dining-room based on the Pantheon. Knight's personal involvement with the project—he was kept informed about the building works by his uncle and agent Samuel Nash while he was abroad—allowed him to express his highly individual taste in architecture. The integration of landscape (the site overlooked the wooded valley of the River Teme) and buildings, which was inspired by the paintings of Claude Lorrain, enabled Knight to both conceptualize and realize his ideas on the picturesque. The building of Downton Castle, which preoccupied him throughout his life, was a landmark in English eighteenth-century architecture and set the fashion for castellated buildings, such as William Beckford's Fonthill and John Nash's East Cowes Castle, that typify the picturesque movement.

While work at Downton was in progress Knight again travelled south, and in the late summer of 1776 was touring Switzerland with the landscape painter John Robert Cozens. After some months in Rome, Knight undertook an apparently planned expedition to Sicily in April 1777 with the fashionable German landscape painter Jakob Philipp Hackert and the English shipbuilder and amateur artist Charles Gore (1729–1807). Perhaps under the influence of Johann Joachim Winckelmann's ideas on the pre-eminence of Greek art, they aimed to explore the remains of Greek architecture in Italy, most probably with a view to publication. Sailing via the ruined Doric temples at Paestum and the island of Lipari, they visited Patti, Segesta, Selinus and Agrigento, Syracuse and Taormina, and climbed Mount Etna. While Hackert and Gore recorded the various stages of their journey in sketches Knight kept a diary in which he flaunted his knowledge of classical architecture and literature. He also commented on local customs and contemporary political issues, agitating against all forms of 'priestcraft', a favourite topic throughout his life. By July the party was back in Rome, where their sketches were worked up into finished watercolours by Cozens, and Knight reached Paris by the end of the year. The plan of publishing the illustrations seems to have been abandoned a few years later.

MP and dilettante Back in England Knight was returned as MP, first for Leominster, in September 1780, and then for Ludlow, in April 1784. He represented Ludlow until 1806 and aligned himself with the opposition whigs against Pitt's government. Sponsored by Charles James Fox, whom he greatly admired, he became a member of Brooks's Club in 1788 and opposed the administration's conduct of the war with France in the 1790s. Although he took part in Westminster affairs Knight pursued the interests developed on his visits to the continent more vigorously than his political duties.

In 1781 Knight was elected a member of the Society of Dilettanti which in 1786 issued his first publication, *An Account of the Remains of the Worship of Priapus*. This included the account communicated to the society in 1781 by Sir William Hamilton, British diplomatic representative in Naples, of the wax phallic votive offerings made at the Catholic festival at St Cosmo's shrine at Iserno, Abruzzo. In his discourse that ostensibly examined the survival of phallic worship in Christian ceremonies Knight suggested that sexual symbolism lay at the basis of all religions. He went so far as to identify Christ with Priapus and to declare that the Christian cross was a transformation of a phallic symbol. He wrote in the wake of similar contemporary investigations into the symbolical language of antiquity, in particular the *Recherches sur l'origine, l'esprit, et les progrès des arts de la Grèce* (1785) by Hugues, Baron d'Hancarville, a former associate and collaborator of Hamilton's in Naples. In spite of the fact that Knight's *Account* was published privately it became notorious and was condemned as scandalous, irreligious, and obscene by critics such as T. J. Mathias, William Mavor, and the editors of the *British Critic*, Robert Nares and William Beloe.

Aesthetics, civilization, and taste Perhaps as an antidote to this early *faux pas* Knight concentrated on fashioning the landscape surrounding his house at Downton in a new, picturesque mode. In pursuing this interest he published *The Landscape: a Didactic Poem* in 1794. Ostentatiously quoting both Virgil and Lucretius as his literary models, Knight was dismissive of the pleasingly irregular gardens created by Capability Brown. Instead he advocated the rougher and more 'picturesque beauty' of natural landscapes as represented in the paintings of Claude Lorrain, whose works he avidly collected, or those of Dutch and Flemish artists, whom he championed. However, unlike his friend and neighbour Uvedale Price, whose *Essay on the Picturesque* was published in the same year, Knight was not really interested in the practical issues of garden design. In shaping his natural surroundings he was concerned rather with their evocative effect on the spectator. He adopted the argument proposed by Archibald Alison in his *Essay on the Nature and Principles of Taste* (1790) that aesthetic notions are created by the association of sensory impressions with the emotions and ideas in the mind of the spectator. As with his European Romantic contemporaries, landscape and its representation—which had always occupied a lowly position in the academic hierarchy of artistic genres—provided him with an opportunity to experiment with new ideas and associations.

Knight used landscape as a metaphor to pursue the political and moral issues that preoccupied him: the superstition and bigotry of the Christian church, his claims to freedom of expression, and his opposition to any kind of political and personal oppression. He developed these ideas further in a second long, didactic poem, *The Progress of Civil Society* (1796), an encyclopaedic investigation into the history of mankind, progressing from international to national, and personal interrelations between peoples and people. Like Winckelmann, Knight regarded fifth-century Greece as the culmination of civil society and he linked its success to the political and personal freedoms enjoyed by its citizens. In modern times he saw, with Montesquieu, religious superstition, repressive government, and personal bigotry as the cause of mankind's decline. 'Missing the mood of the moment' (Ballantyne, 112), Knight ended his poem with an enthusiastic endorsement of the French Revolution, which, despite his condemnation of the violence of the terror, understandably further antagonized his critics, who attacked him in conservative journals such as the *British Critic* and *The Anti-Jacobin*. Furthermore he was blackballed from the Literary Society in 1795.

Knight's reputation as a national arbiter of taste was confirmed by his most successful publication, *An Analytical Inquiry into the Principles of Taste* (1805), which appeared four years after Uvedale Price's *Dialogue on the Distinct Characters of the Picturesque and the Beautiful*. Sceptical of the notion that taste could be governed by general rules, Knight—as he had done in the second edition of *The Landscape* (1795)—

rejected Price's attempt to define 'picturesque' as an aesthetic category between the 'beautiful' and 'sublime' categories that had been established by Edmund Burke. Instead Knight argued for a diversity of tastes, quoting from David Hume's 'Of the standard of taste': 'Beauty is no quality in things themselves: it exists merely in the mind, which contemplates them, and each mind perceives a different beauty' (R. Knight, *An Analytical Inquiry into the Principles of Taste*, 4th edn, 1808, 16). Guided by Archibald Alison's concept of an 'association of ideas', Knight examined human sensory perception, associations, and emotions, giving priority to the sense of sight. Sight, in response to colour and light, offered the spectator intellectual pleasures through the association of a variety of ideas. These ideas could be evoked either in the contemplation of natural scenery or in works of art, which appealed to the spectator through 'tints, happily broken and blended, and irregular masses of light and shadow harmoniously melted into each other' as well as through their associations with literature, philosophy, and the imagination. The 'correct' response to these stimuli, however, Knight argued, could be achieved only by the educated spectator—in other words by connoisseurs who had the time, money, and energy to cultivate their tastes and educate their minds. Knight's associationism thus remained specialized and élitist, a notion suggested perhaps in the portrait by Thomas Lawrence (1794; Whitworth Art Gallery, Manchester), which shows Knight, the 'arrogant connoisseur', pointedly staring into space while knowingly leafing through a volume of drawings in his lap.

Collector and scholar Throughout the 1790s Knight devoted considerable time and attention to his Greek studies. Two publications resulted: *An Analytical Essay on the Greek Alphabet* (1791) and *Carmina Homerica Ilias et Odyssea* (1808; 1820), which contested that Homer was not the author of *The Odyssey*. He formed an unrivalled collection of small bronzes (mostly bought from Sir William Hamilton in 1794), coins (principally acquired at the sale of Matthew Duane's collection in 1785), gems, and cameos, which were displayed in a purpose-built gallery in his London house, 3 Soho Square. Sketches of Italian scenes dominated his collection of drawings, which boasted over 150 sketches by Claude. A co-founder of the British Institution, which was established in 1805 to encourage British artists, he enthusiastically promoted the talents of the artist Richard Westall, from whom he commissioned paintings on classical and historical subjects. A selection of his antiquities, together with some of his friend and fellow member of the Society of Dilettanti Charles Townley, were superbly illustrated in *Specimens of Ancient Sculpture* (2 vols., 1809–35), to which Knight provided the accompanying commentary and brief history of ancient art. In *An Inquiry into the Symbolical Language of Ancient Art and Mythology* (1818), originally intended as an introduction to the delayed second volume of *Specimens of Ancient Sculpture*, he produced a series of comparative investigations into the sexual symbolism of the art of different religions.

Having stood down from parliament in 1806 Knight

made over Downton Castle to his brother, who was married and had a family, in 1808 and retired to a very modest house on the estate, Stonebrook Cottage. Just as he was gradually withdrawing from public engagements Knight sparked a new controversy, this time over the Elgin marbles. When Thomas Bruce, seventh earl of Elgin, brought to Britain the marble sculptures from the Parthenon, Knight declared, without having seen them, that Elgin had 'lost his labour', as they were 'not Greek … but Roman of the time of Hadrian' (*The Life of B. R. H[aydon] … from his Autobiography and Journals*, ed. T. Taylor, 3 vols., 1853, 1.272). When the sculptures were exhibited in London they were the first major works of classical Greek sculpture to have been put on public display in western Europe. Dilettanti and connoisseurs such as Knight who had acquired their expertise on the grand tour to Rome and other Italian cities were familiar only with Roman and Hellenstic copies of original Greek works that were displayed in Italian galleries. They therefore failed fully to appreciate the aesthetic value of the Elgin marbles. Knight in particular thought that they were Hadrianic copies because they did not meet his expectations of Greek art, which he had always extolled as the epitome of human achievement. His lukewarm appreciation, which was shared by William Wilkins and Lord Aberdeen, was at odds with the ecstatic reaction of John Flaxman, Benjamin Robert Haydon, Thomas Lawrence, and Benjamin West to the marbles. In 1816 Knight was called to give evidence to the parliamentary select committee set up to determine their value and legal status; despite his reservations about the marbles' quality he advised that they should be purchased.

Knight's spectacular error of judgement about the Elgin marbles and the subsequent controversy had a catastrophic effect on his reputation. He endured stinging criticism from John Wilson Croker in the *Quarterly Review* and from Haydon, whose evidence had not been heard before the select committee, in an article, 'On the judgment of connoisseurs being preferred to that of professional men', published in both *The Examiner* and *The Champion*. In a passionate, almost deranged, personal attack, in which he extolled his own piety while labelling his opponent as a demonic fiend, Haydon correctly predicted that the marbles' fame would rise as Knight's sank into oblivion. Knight had already alienated the prince regent by criticizing his architectural taste in the *Edinburgh Review* and by supporting the cause of the prince's estranged wife, and unsurprisingly he was not chosen as the new professor of ancient literature at the Royal Academy in 1818. The following year he attracted more controversy when, in his capacity as a magistrate, he ordered the cavalry to break up a demonstration by the colliers at his mines at Clee Hill, in Shropshire.

Death Despite his damaged reputation Knight was elected vice-president of the Society of Antiquaries in 1819 (his friend and ally Lord Aberdeen was president). His final publication, *Alfred*, a poetic romance, appeared in 1823. He died in London, of an apoplectic stroke, on 23 April 1824 and was buried at Wormsley church, Herefordshire, on 11 May. A trustee of the British Museum since 1814, he bequeathed his collections to the museum so that they could be displayed alongside those of Townley and Clayton Mordaunt Cracherode. Estimated to be worth at least £30,000, his bequest included over 1144 drawings, over 5205 coins, and 800 bronzes.

C. STUMPF-CONDRY and S. J. SKEDD

Sources A. Ballantyne, *Architecture, landscape, and liberty* (1997) · M. Clarke and N. Penny, eds., *The arrogant connoisseur: Richard Payne Knight (1751–1824)* (1982) · R. P. Knight, *Expedition into Sicily, 1777*, ed. C. Stumpf (1986) · 'Tagebuch einer Reise nach Sicilien von Henry Knight', trans. J. W. von Goethe, in P. Hackert, *Biographische Skizze, meist nach dessen eigenen Aufsätzen entworfen, von Goethe* (Tübingen, 1811), [53]–143 · Farington, *Diary* · S. Daniels and C. Watkins, *The picturesque landscape: visions of Georgian Herefordshire* (1994) · I. Jenkins and K. Sloan, *Vases & volcanoes: Sir William Hamilton and his collection* (1996) · C. Hussey, *The picturesque: studies in a point of view* (1927) · J. J. Mayoux, *Richard Payne Knight et le pittoresque* (1932) · F. J. Messman, *Richard Payne Knight: the twilight of virtuosity* (1974) · W. Hipple, *The beautiful, the sublime, and the picturesque in eighteenth century British aesthetic theory* (1957) · DNB · Bodl. Oxf., MS Eng. misc. d. 158

Archives Bodl. Oxf., Knight MS, autobiography, Montagu MS d.3, fols. 124–6 · Goethe–Schiller Archiv, Weimar, Knight MS, Sicilian diary, MS 25/XLIV, 7 | BL, letters to Lord Aberdeen, Add. MSS 43229–43231 · Herefs. RO, Downton Castle papers · S. Antiquaries, Lond., Dilettanti papers, miscellaneous MS material and the society's minutes

Likenesses N. Hone, oils, 1770–79, priv. coll. · T. Lawrence, oils, 1794, Whitworth Art Gallery, Manchester [*see illus.*] · T. Lawrence, oils, 1805, Brooks's Club, London, Society of Dilettanti · J. Bacon, marble bust, c.1811, BM · J. Bacon, marble and bronze bust, 1814, NPG

Wealth at death collections of bronzes, gems, coins, and drawings bequeathed to British Museum, lowest est. £30,000: Clarke and Penny, eds., *Arrogant connoisseur*, 17 · estates and personal wealth consisting principally of pictures, wine, and 'money lent by him at interest to a partner of a country Bank which failed soon after his death': Herefs. RO, Downton Castle papers, T74–525, cited Clarke and Penny, eds., *Arrogant connoisseur*, 18 n. 130

Knight, (George) Richard Wilson (1897–1985), literary scholar, was born in Sutton, Surrey, on 19 September 1897, the younger son and younger child—the elder being W. F. Jackson Knight, the Virgilian scholar—of George Knight (*d.* 1943), of the Northern Insurance Company, and his wife, Caroline Louisa Jackson (*d.* 1950), daughter of Captain John Barclay Jackson, of the West India regiment. Educated at Dulwich College (1909–14), Knight was employed in insurance offices until 1916, when he volunteered for the army. As a motorcycle dispatch rider in the Royal Engineers he served in Mesopotamia, India, and Persia, when chess became a favourite off-duty recreation.

Demobilized in 1920, Knight taught mathematics in preparatory schools until matriculating at St Edmund Hall, Oxford, in 1921. Graduating with second-class honours in English language and literature in 1923, a year in which he represented Oxford against Cambridge at chess, he taught at Hawtreys School, Westgate-on-Sea, Kent, until 1925, when he was appointed English master at Dean Close School, Cheltenham, Gloucestershire. Between 1923 and 1931 he also wrote poems which were published in 1968 under the title of *Gold-Dust*. In an interesting preface the author relates the writing of them to various incidents.

Now started a period of unceasing literary productivity.

After three unpublished novels—though the first, *Klinton Top* (1927), was printed in 1984—Knight began the long series of Shakespeare studies that brought him renown. Rejecting the name of critic, Knight styled himself an 'interpreter'. Characters in the plays, a previous focus of attention, though highly important, were but components in a 'spatio-lineal' design to which symbols, metaphors, images, and poetic evocations contributed. A play of Shakespeare was an 'expanded metaphor', the matrix of its characters.

In *Myth and Miracle: an Essay on the Mystic Symbolism of Shakespeare* (1929) Knight offered an original reading of Shakespeare's intuition of immortality in the last plays. This was followed by *The Wheel of Fire: Essays in Interpretation of Shakespeare's Sombre Tragedies* (1930), with an introduction by T. S. Eliot, which led to Knight's election to the chancellor's chair of English in Trinity College, University of Toronto, in 1931.

In Toronto, besides writing *The Imperial Theme* (1931), which focused on Shakespeare's Roman plays, and *The Shakespearian Tempest* (1932), Knight addressed himself to producing and acting Shakespeare at the Hart House Theatre. He later said that in acting in Shakespeare he found his supreme satisfaction. The results of theory and practice found expression in *Principles of Shakespearian Production* (1936). But he also extended his method of 'interpretation' to other poets with *The Starlit Dome* (1941) on the Romantics, and to religion, with *The Christian Renaissance* (1933), and, in time, to international politics, with *The Olive and the Sword* (1944) and *Hiroshima* (1946).

Knight resigned his chair in 1940 so as not to be distant from his mother and brother in wartime England. He was also a fervent patriot and produced *This Sceptered Isle* at the Westminster Theatre, London, in 1941, with Henry Ainley as the narrator. After teaching geography at Stowe School (1941–6), he was appointed in 1946 reader in English literature at the University of Leeds, where he remained, much loved and admired by colleagues and students, until his retirement in 1962. He was elevated to a personal chair in 1956. Further books on Shakespeare appeared: *The Crown of Life* (1947) and *The Sovereign Flower* (1958) are especially notable. A lecture course at Leeds on British drama was published under the title of *The Golden Labyrinth* (1962). Knight also acted and produced at Leeds, revealing a particular interest in Shakespeare's *Timon of Athens*. At about this time he composed his own play, *The Last of the Incas*. He wrote a series of books on Lord Byron, and a notable work on Alexander Pope. Indeed, no poet, from Spenser to the twentieth century, escaped his invigorating comment. *Neglected Powers* (1971), on recent writers, reveals a special interest in John Cowper Powys.

After his mother's death in 1950 Knight became interested in spiritualism. In 1961 Philip Hobsbaum heard Knight lecture on the Restoration dramatist Nathaniel Lee, when Knight averred that the spirits in Lee's work were probably true. In his biography of his brother Jackson, Knight includes passages showing his firm beliefs, although he never proselytized. On retirement he shared a home in Exeter with his brother until the latter's death.

He published *Jackson Knight: a Biography* (1975), where he relates the story of his subject's family and his own part in that story. In 1974 he assumed by statutory declaration Richard as a second forename, for he had always been called Dick by his closest associates, from childhood onwards. Even in his eighties he made tours of North America to perform his one-man show, *Shakespeare's Dramatic Challenge*, and he continued to publish.

Knight was appointed CBE in 1968, was elected an honorary fellow of St Edmund Hall in 1965, and was made an honorary LittD of Sheffield and DLitt of Exeter in 1966 and 1968 respectively.

Knight relished sympathetic humour, disliked cynicism, and was innocent of malice. His conversation was vitalizing. He had a beautiful speaking voice, and left many tape recordings. He liked the colourful, whether in nature or art. He never married. Knight died from a pulmonary embolism at his home, Caroline House, Streatham Rise, Exeter, on 20 March 1985. His body was cremated in Exeter. FRANCIS BERRY

Sources *The Times* (23 March 1985) · G. W. Knight, *Jackson Knight: a biography* (1975) · personal knowledge (2004) · *CGPLA Eng. & Wales* (1985)

Archives U. Leeds, Brotherton L., corresp. and papers · University of Northern Colorado, Greeley | RS, letters to Royal Society of Literature · U. Leeds, Brotherton L., corresp. with Francis Berry and papers · U. Leeds, Brotherton L., letters to John Van Domelen · U. Leeds, Brotherton L., letters to Gerald Pollinger | S O U N D Yeovil College, Yeovil, Somerset, Department of Educational Resources, 4 tapes of Knight reading from Shakespeare

Likenesses Martyn Bros., photograph, 1926, repro. in G. W. Knight, *Klinton top* (1984), frontispiece · photograph, repro. in G. W. Knight, *Atlantic crossing* (1936), frontispiece

Wealth at death £116,447: probate, 16 April 1985, *CGPLA Eng. & Wales* · £10,000: further grant, 21 June 1985, *CGPLA Eng. & Wales*

Knight, Robert (1825–1890), newspaper editor in India, was born on 13 March 1825 at Vauxhall Walk, Lambeth, London, the fifth of eleven children of William Knight (1785–1855), a banker's clerk, and his second wife, Anna Maria (b. 1795/6), daughter of James Coombs, of Frome, Somerset, and later of London. The details of Robert Knight's upbringing and education are unknown. He was apparently influenced by the climate of reform during the 1830s; his later editorials strongly advocated principles of humane liberalism and classical economics.

Knight left for Bombay in 1847 to act as an agent for an importer of wine and spirits. During his first years there he lived in the home of Major George Wingate, a land settlement officer, who taught him much about Indian economic problems. Knight thought that the answer to India's poverty and misery lay in sensible economics and Christian-inspired social reforms under British guidance. Several other jobs in Bombay's commercial world soon followed. On 2 November 1854 he married Catherine Hannah (1837–1890), the daughter of William Hugh Payne, a local schoolteacher and customs inspector. The marriage was by all accounts successful and produced twelve children.

Knight's first connection with journalism resulted in the freelance articles on economics which he sold to local newspapers. At the end of 1856 he was engaged as interim editor of the *Bombay Times* to replace Dr George Buist, who was going on home leave. Thus Knight was editing Bombay's leading newspaper in May 1857, when the uprising that followed the Sepoy mutiny broke out. Knight's editorials deplored the bloodshed but called for calm and common sense in relations between Britain and India. However, Dr Buist hastened back, resumed charge, and led British denunciations of the Indian character. This angered the Indian businessmen who held a majority of the *Bombay Times* stock. They ousted Buist and gave the permanent editorship to Knight in December 1857 (*Bombay Times and Journal of Commerce*, 6 Jan 1858, special supplement). Knight became increasingly disillusioned by British rule in India and criticized its reform efforts as blundering and futile. He was one of the first Englishmen to call for representative government to defend India's interests. The maturing Indian press spread such views, and Knight's revealing economic statistics fed early Indian nationalist opinion.

In 1860 Knight became the first agent in India of the Reuters news agency. He then formed his own telegraphic agency, selling news dispatches to other papers around India. The *Bombay Times* merged with its rival *The Standard* on 1 January 1860, and on 18 May 1861 the name was changed to *Times of India* to reflect its broader scope in burgeoning Bombay. However, in 1869 Knight left the paper after a bitter quarrel with his partner, Mathias Mull (*Times of India*, Bombay, 3 Feb 1869). In the same year he went on to found a monthly journal, the *Indian Economist*, which allowed full scope for his interest in economic problems. Engaged by the Bengal government to supervise some statistical surveys, he left Bombay for Calcutta as an assistant secretary. The arrangement was disappointing, as Knight chafed at the bureaucratic chores, but the *Indian Economist*, which he took with him to Calcutta, continued to be critical of the imperial government. The Bengal government bought out the paper, but Knight used the money to help found a new daily, *The Statesman*, which merged with a former missionary weekly, the *Friend of India*. This infuriated Bengal officials, who dismissed Knight from his assistant secretaryship for violating regulations against officeholders writing for the press (National Archives of India, India home department, public proceedings, Feb 1875, 260A). Knight had no alternative but to become editor of the *Statesman and Friend of India*.

Once editor, Knight vehemently attacked the Conservatives' imperial policies. The pressures on Afghanistan, leading to a British invasion in 1878, were seen as a costly overreaction to an imaginary threat from Russia. Knight viewed the imperial durbar of 1877, at which Queen Victoria was proclaimed empress of India, as 'cheap and meaningless vanities ... Beaconsfield "fireworks"' (*Statesman and Friend of India*, 6 Jan 1877). The repeal of India's tariff on cotton cloth imports showed the government's subservience to British economic interests. In 1879 Knight took the battle to London, where he produced a weekly edition of *The Statesman*, explaining India's problems and

attacking Conservative policies. The paper had some political influence, but was a financial loss and disappeared in 1881. Meanwhile Knight nearly lost the Calcutta *Statesman* too—it was saved only by the munificence of a wealthy Bengali estate, the Paikpara Raj.

Knight returned to Calcutta in 1883 and sprang to the defence of Lord Ripon, the Liberal viceroy, against attacks by British residents. His exposure of affairs in the princely state of Hyderabad, where he accused British officials of corrupt dealings in connivance with shady court politicians, provoked widespread resentment. A former defender of imperialism, Knight came to believe that British rule had failed as a vehicle for Indian progress and the welfare of its people. In 1886 he supported the year-old Indian National Congress, writing that only the people themselves, and not even well-meaning foreigners, could understand and protect their interests (*Statesman and Friend of India*, 26 Dec 1886).

Robert Knight died in Calcutta on 27 January 1890, apparently from malaria, and was buried nearby on the following day, at Circular Road cemetery. He had given India an aggressively independent press, creating the *Times of India*, the pre-eminent paper of western India, and *The Statesman*, the pre-eminent paper of eastern India, and in so doing he helped to promote political awareness among the indigenous peoples.

EDWIN HIRSCHMANN

Sources public proceedings, Feb 1875, National Archives of India, New Delhi, India, India home dept., 260A · *Statesman and Friend of India* [Calcutta] (6 Jan 1877) · *Statesman and Friend of India* [Calcutta] (26 Dec 1886) · *Times of India* [Bombay] (3 Feb 1869) · S. C. Sanial, 'History of journalism—V', *Calcutta Review*, 127 (1908), 364–96 · S. C. Sanial, 'History of the press in India—IX', *Calcutta Review*, 130 (1910), 116–18, 264–94 · S. C. Sanial, 'History of the press in India—X', *Calcutta Review*, 131 (1910), 352–80 · S. C. Sanial, 'The father of Indian journalism—I', *Calcutta Review*, 3rd ser., 19 (1926), 288–322 · S. C. Sanial, 'The father of Indian journalism—II', *Calcutta Review*, 3rd ser., 20 (1926), 28–63 · S. C. Sanial, 'The father of Indian journalism—III', *Calcutta Review*, 3rd ser., 20 (1926), 302–49 · E. Hirschmann, 'An editor speaks for the natives: Robert Knight in 19th century India', *Journalism Quarterly*, 63 (1986), 260–67 · D. E. Wacha, *Rise and growth of Bombay municipal government* (1913) · Salar Jung MSS, misc. letters, Andhra Pradesh State Archives, Hyderabad, India · private information (2004) [daughter]
Archives Andhra Pradesh State Archives, Hyderabad, India, Salar Jung MSS, letters | BL OIOC, newspapers edited by him
Likenesses marble bust, offices of *The Statesman*, Calcutta · photograph (in middle age), priv. coll.

Knight, Robert (1833–1911), trade unionist, was born on 5 September 1833 in Lifton, Devon, the son of a blacksmith. He attended the village school until the age of twelve when he began his training in metalworking with his father. Following the customary tramp around the country to extend his skills, he settled in 1857 as an angle-iron smith at the Devonport Dockyard in Plymouth where he stayed for the next fourteen years, becoming increasingly involved in the local affairs of the United Society of Boilermakers and Iron and Steel Shipbuilders. Presented by his supporters as a vigorous leader of demarcation disputes against the shipwrights, he was elected as the union's general secretary in 1871, a post he held, first in Liverpool and then in Newcastle, until his retirement in 1899. Robert Knight was of average height with thick dark hair and a full beard; socially he could be charming, but his most notable capacities were for hard work, thorough preparation, and logical argument. He was married twice, his first wife having died in 1879, and had two sons and a daughter.

At first Knight's responsibilities as general secretary were fairly straightforward as, although the Boilermakers' Society like many of the earlier craft unions was in need of improved administration, this was a period of low unemployment and growing union influence. He was therefore able to make an immediate impression on the boilermakers' organizational structure and benefit provisions, as well as to inaugurate unusually thorough and accurate annual reports on membership, finances, and branch activities in a format retained substantially intact by the union until the 1960s. Once again his reputation as an outstanding organizer spread beyond the area of his immediate responsibilities and in 1875 he was elected chairman of the parliamentary committee of the Trades Union Congress (TUC). As this coincided with the peak of the union campaign against the restrictive elements of the trade union legislation of 1871, Knight worked closely with George Howell and subsequently appeared on the platform at the victory celebrations, giving a speech which was notable for its ambitious vision of the role of trade unionists in pressing for further social reforms in the areas of education and housing. However, the fifteen years after 1875 were to be bleak ones for the unions, with persistently high unemployment eroding financial reserves and involvement in ill-timed industrial disputes leading to the collapse of many organizations. In this context Knight began to pursue an increasingly cautious and moderate policy, largely withdrawing from national labour affairs to focus on his own union's survival, and placing the long-term health of its finances above the temptation of short-term local wage increases. This led to friction with some of the branches, particularly in the shipbuilding districts where the bulk of the union's membership was now concentrated. As a result, the union's head office was moved from Liverpool to a special new building in Newcastle upon Tyne in 1890, allowing Knight not only to maintain closer links with his members in the shipyards but also to play a prominent role in the affairs of this highly democratic community: particularly in St James's Congregational Church, in the local Liberal Party, and as a magistrate.

This combination of industrial caution and political Liberalism led the new generation of more militant, frequently socialist-influenced, union leaders who began to emerge after 1889 to see Knight as one of the leading figures of an outdated and unimaginative style of trade unionism. However, even in the 1880s he had been a keen advocate of the incorporation of neighbouring semi-skilled groups to secure the boilermakers' bargaining position, and he adapted rapidly to the improved economic conditions of the 1890s. He initiated co-operation between unions to reduce wasteful demarcation disputes,

leading to the establishment of the Federation of Engineering and Shipbuilding Trades in 1890; he pressed the employers to set up fully recognized local wage-bargaining procedures, beginning on the north-east coast in 1894; and he pioneered trade union initiative over industry-wide agreements, most notably on the number of apprentices in 1893. This ambitious programme of co-ordinated labour action to regulate industrial conditions led the Fabian socialists Sidney and Beatrice Webb to praise Knight's progressive role in their *History of Trade Unionism* (1894).

Politically, however, Knight remained a confirmed radical Liberal and once again began to take a more active role within the TUC, this time as one of the most articulate opponents of the new generation of socialists: he preferred local collective bargaining to the statutory imposition of the eight-hour day, and he preferred constitutional reform to the public ownership of industry. Moreover, when the Conservative victory in the 1895 general election was widely blamed on the disruptive behaviour of the Independent Labour Party, Knight became one of the leading supporters of the rule changes which excluded the most prominent socialist activists from the TUC. This pushed the Webbs into changing their line, and in the opening section of *Industrial Democracy* (1897) they painted an influential portrait of Knight as an autocrat whose power in the wider labour movement was based on the decay of democracy within his own organization. However, this relied on a distorted account of the internal arrangements of the Boilermakers' Society, as was immediately demonstrated by its members' approval of a major reform of its constitution in the face of forceful opposition from Knight. For its part, the Independent Labour Party began to move towards greater co-operation with the older generation of radical-Liberal trade unionists and, as one of this group's senior statesmen, Knight had a major role to play in the response. As a long-standing advocate of union federation he worked closely with 'new unionists' to establish the General Federation of Trade Unions in 1899, and as a long-standing advocate of greater union representation in parliament he worked along with other 'old unionists' such as W. J. Davis and Alexander Wilkie to build a co-operative relationship with Keir Hardie around the conference which founded the Labour Representation Committee in 1900.

Following his retirement, Knight remained active in local affairs; he died from pneumonia on 17 September 1911 at 19 Highbury, his home in Newcastle, and was buried in St Andrew's cemetery, Newcastle. He was survived by his second wife and two sons and a daughter.

ALASTAIR J. REID

Sources *Beehive labour portrait gallery*, 2 (1874), 5–6 · J. E. Mortimer, *History of the Boilermakers' Society*, 1: *1834–1906* (1973) · *DLB* · A. J. Reid, 'Old unionism reconsidered: the radicalism of Robert Knight, 1870–1900', *Currents of radicalism: popular radicalism, organised labour, and party politics in Britain, 1850–1914*, ed. E. F. Biagini and A. Reid (1991), 214–43

Wealth at death £9078 5*s.* 9*d.*: probate, 29 Dec 1911, *CGPLA Eng. & Wales*

Knight, Samuel (1677/8–1746), Church of England clergyman and antiquary, was born in London, the son of John Knight, a freeman of the Mercers' Company. William Cole claimed that Knight was brought up a dissenter. He was educated at St Paul's School and entered Trinity College, Cambridge, as a sizar on 10 April 1697, aged nineteen. He graduated BA during the year 1702–3, MA in 1706, and DD in 1717, and was later incorporated at Oxford in 1740. He was ordained priest by John Moore, bishop of Norwich, on 24 September 1704 and became chaplain to Edward Russell, earl of Orford, who in 1707 presented him to the rectory of Burrough Green, in Cambridgeshire, and the vicarage of Chippenham, in Suffolk. In 1714 John Moore, by then bishop of Ely, collated him to the seventh prebendal stall in Ely Cathedral, and in 1717 to the rectory of Bluntisham, in Huntingdonshire. On 22 August 1717 at St Mary in the Marsh, Norwich, Knight married Hannah (*bap.* 4 May 1681), daughter of Talbot Pepys of Impington, in Cambridgeshire. She died on 14 April 1719, after the birth of their son, Samuel, and was buried at Bluntisham.

Knight was one of the 'revivers' of the Society of Antiquaries in 1717 and a member of the Spalding Gentlemen's Society, whose members included most distinguished antiquarian scholars of the day. He was a friend and correspondent of the majority of these, who included Edmund Gibson, Thomas Tanner, White Kennett, and William Cole. No doubt he had been influenced in this direction by Thomas Gale, master of St Paul's School, whose son Roger was one of Knight's correspondents, and by his patron Bishop Moore. He was encouraged in his antiquarian studies by Thomas Baker, fellow of St John's College, Cambridge. Knight was a collector of manuscripts and used his periods of residence at Ely to investigate the manuscripts there. He also worked on a historical account of the Ely Cathedral manuscripts, which, though apparently not completed, was used by James Bentham in his history of the cathedral. In 1724 Knight published a life of John Colet, dean of St Paul's and founder of St Paul's School. This had been begun by White Kennett, who gave it up when he began to plan the publication of all the important historical documents of Charles II's reign and handed over the materials to Knight for completion; Knight made little public acknowledgement of Kennett's major contribution to the work. He published a life of Erasmus in 1726, of which John Jortin, a subsequent biographer of Erasmus, commented: 'Dr Knight's work is indeed confused and not over elegant, but it contains many good materials' (Jortin, 617). Knight made collections of material for biographies of Archbishop John Peckham, bishops Robert Grosseteste, John Overall, Lancelot Andrewes, George Mountain, and Robert Sanderson, and of John Strype. He also annotated and completed Bishop Simon Patrick's autobiography, the manuscript of which he owned.

Knight appears to have been an 'active and useful' residentiary canon at Ely (Nichols, 5.354). He was involved in a concerted attempt by the dean and chapter to make benefactions to the governors of Queen Anne's bounty, to attract further benefactions of £200 for livings in their gift, so that their endowments were increased by a total of £400 each.

Knight continued to receive ecclesiastical preferment in the later part of his career. On 29 December 1730 he was appointed a chaplain to George II. In 1735 Thomas Sherlock, bishop of Salisbury, collated him to the archdeaconry of Berkshire. Knight was an active archdeacon and made regular diurnal visitations, unusual for a pluralist. When his turn came to preach at Salisbury Cathedral as archdeacon he used his visits to study the manuscripts in the chapter house. In 1742 Richard Reynolds, bishop of Lincoln, collated him to the prebendal stall of Leighton Ecclesia in Lincoln Cathedral.

Knight died on 10 December 1746 and was buried beside his wife in the chancel of Bluntisham church, where the inscription on his monument was composed by his friend Dr Castle, dean of Hereford and master of Corpus Christi College, Cambridge. He left an 'ample fortune' (*GM*) to his son, Samuel, fellow of Trinity, who was ordained priest in 1743 and whose father's interest was remembered when Bishop Sherlock awarded him the valuable sinecure rectory of Fulham in Middlesex. W. M. JACOB

Sources Venn, *Alum. Cant.* · *GM*, 1st ser., 60 (1790), 85 · Nichols, *Lit. anecdotes*, vols. 2, 4–6 · J. Jortin, *Life of Erasmus* (1758) · F. Peck, ed., *Desiderata curiosa*, new edn, 2 vols. in 1 (1779) · G. V. Bennett, *White Kennett, 1660–1728, bishop of Peterborough* (1957) · D. C. Douglas, *English scholars, 1660–1730*, 2nd edn (1951) · *IGI*

Archives BL, corresp., Add. MSS 5847, fol. 23; 32556, fol. 116; 32699, fol. 343; 37700, fol. 72 · CUL, letters, notes, and historical collections | CUL, Baumgartner papers · CUL, letters to John Strype · NA Scot., letters to Sir John Clerk

Knight, Samuel (1759–1827), Church of England clergyman, was born in Halifax on 9 March 1759, the son of Titus Knight (*d.* 1793), Independent minister at Halifax, and his second wife. Influenced by the countess of Huntingdon, Titus Knight became minister of a Methodist chapel in 1763, and regularly assisted George Whitefield at Tottenham Court Chapel and elsewhere.

Samuel Knight attended Hipperholme grammar school and entered Magdalene College, Cambridge, as a sizar in 1779. He graduated BA as seventh wrangler in 1783 and was elected fellow, proceeding MA in 1786. In April 1783 he was appointed curate of Wintringham, Lincolnshire, and took pupils. On 13 July 1789 he married Frances Lawrence at Roxby-cum-Risby, Lincolnshire. They had at least two sons and three daughters. In 1794 he was presented to the vicarage of Humberstone, Lincolnshire, but continued to reside at Wintringham, where he received pupils into his house; he was also curate of Roxby. In 1798 he was the first to obtain the perpetual curacy of Holy Trinity, Halifax, and he moved there with his pupils. In December 1817 he was appointed vicar of Halifax.

Knight was the author of the popular devotional work, *Forms of Prayer* (1791), which passed through sixteen editions in his lifetime. He died in Halifax on 9 January 1827.

The younger of Knight's two sons, **James Knight** (*bap.* 1793, *d.* 1863), religious writer, was baptized on 25 April 1793 at Wintringham. He matriculated from Lincoln College, Oxford, in 1811, and was a scholar there from 1812 to

1815, graduating BA in 1814 and proceeding MA in 1817. He was appointed perpetual curate of St Paul's Church, Sheffield, in 1824, and resigned the living in 1860. He published various commentaries on Christianity, and edited his father's *Sermons and Miscellaneous Works* (2 vols., 1828), which were published together with a memoir by his brother, the Revd William Knight. He died at Barton upon Humber, Lincolnshire, on 30 August 1863.

GORDON GOODWIN, rev. EMMA MAJOR

Sources GM, 1st ser., 97/1 (1827), 282 · Venn, *Alum. Cant.* · W. Knight, 'Memoir', in *Sermons and miscellaneous works of the Rev. Samuel Knight*, ed. J. Knight, 1 (1828), xxi–cxxv · J. Darling, *Cyclopaedia bibliographica: a library manual of theological and general literature*, 2 vols. (1854–9) · Foster, *Alum. Oxon.* [James Knight] · IGI · ESTC
Likenesses stipple, pubd 1837, BM, NPG · W. T. Fry, engraving, repro. in *Sermons and miscellaneous works*, ed. Knight
Wealth at death under £5000—James Knight: will, 19 Sept 1863, CGPLA Eng. & Wales

Knight, Thomas (d. 1820), actor and playwright, was born in Dorset of a family which was of some importance but not wealthy. He was intended for the bar, and received lessons in elocution from the actor Charles Macklin. A favourite with Macklin, he accompanied him to the theatre, and acquired in his visits tastes that led him to adopt the stage as a profession. At an unrecorded date he appeared at the Richmond theatre as Charles Surface, but failed conspicuously. He then joined Austin's company at Lancaster. Before leaving London he tried vainly to force upon Macklin payment for his services as a teacher. Tate Wilkinson saw Knight, it is said, in Edinburgh, and engaged him for the York circuit. His first appearance was made in York in 1782 as Lothario to the Calista of Dorothy Jordan. Wilkinson, who was greatly disappointed with him, advised him to quit the stage, but Knight struggled on, playing Charles Oakley, Spatterdash in John O'Keefe's *The Young Quaker*, and Carbine in *The Fair American*, and gradually grew in public favour. Wilkinson generously acknowledged the error of his former judgement, and during the five years in which Knight remained with the company he took the lead, and had only one quarrel with the management: finding his name as Twineall in *Such Things Are* put third on the list, the customary place for the character, he refused to appear. On 27 October 1787 he played at the Bath theatre as the Copper Captain. Spatterdash, the Duke of Monmouth in *Such Things Were*, and the Marquis in *The Midnight Hour* followed.

In 1787 Knight married at Bath **Margaret Farren** (d. 1804), actress, the sister of the countess of Derby. She was the daughter of George Farren, a surgeon and apothecary in Cork, and his wife, whose father was a Liverpool publican and brewer named Wright. Both George Farren and his wife acted. Margaret Farren had been seen at an early age in London, having played at the Haymarket on 18 June 1777, under the name Peggy Farren, Titania in *The Fairy Tale*, a two-act adaptation of *A Midsummer Night's Dream*. She joined Wilkinson in 1782, left him to act in Scotland and Ireland, and rejoined him in 1786. In that year she appeared with Knight in York, where she was a favourite. Soon after her marriage she made her first

appearance in Bath as Miss Peggy in *The Country Girl* to her husband's Sparkish. In the course of the same season Knight acted thirty characters, among which Touchstone, Trappanti, Claudio in *Measure for Measure*, Trim in *The Funeral*, Sir Charles Racket, and Pendragon may be mentioned. In Bath, as at Bristol, which was under the same management, he played during the nine years of his engagement an endless variety of comic parts—Charles Surface, Antonio in *Follies of a Day*, the Clown in *All's Well that Ends Well*, Mercutio, Duretête, Goldfinch, Dromio of Ephesus, Pistol, and Autolycus being among the most easily recognizable.

Knight's first appearance at Covent Garden took place on 25 September 1795, as Jacob in *The Chapter of Accidents* (when his wife played Bridget) and Skirmish in *The Deserter*. The most important of the huge number of parts he took at the theatre were Sim in *Wild Oats*, Hodge, Bob Acres, Slender in *The Merry Wives of Windsor*, Roderigo, Gratiano, Dick Dowlas, Sir Benjamin Backbite, Tony Lumpkin, Sergeant Kite in *The Recruiting Officer*, Sir Andrew Aguecheek, Touchstone, and Lucio in *Measure for Measure*. His original parts included Young Testy in Holman's *Abroad and at Home*, Count Cassel in Elizabeth Inchbald's adaptation *Lovers' Vows*, Changeable in Thomas Dibdin's *The Jew and the Doctor*, Farmer Ashfield in Morton's *Speed the Plough*, and Corporal Foss in *The Poor Gentleman*. After the couple had remained for three years at Covent Garden, they went together to Edinburgh, where she played on 2 July 1799 Aura in *The Farm House*, and he made what was called, probably in error, his first appearance in the city as Sir Harry Beagle in *The Jealous Wife*. Margaret Knight afterwards performed at Newcastle and elsewhere before returning to Bath, where she died on 28 July 1804.

With well-known artists such as J. G. Holman, H. Johnston, J. S. Munden, and Charles Incledon, Knight signed the significant *Statement of the differences subsisting between the proprietors and performers of the Theatre-Royal, Covent Garden* (3rd edn, London, 1800). The lease of the Liverpool Theatre was taken by Knight in partnership with the actor W. T. Lewis, and the house opened on 6 June 1803 with *No Song, No Supper* and Thomas Morton's *Speed the Plough*, together with an address by Thomas Dibdin, spoken by Knight. During this season Knight remained at Covent Garden, where his last performance took place for his benefit, on 15 May 1804, as Farmer Ashfield in *Speed the Plough*, and, for the first time, Lenitive in *The Prize*. He also spoke an address. In 1802 he was living at 10 Tavistock Street, Covent Garden. While managing the Liverpool theatre he lived first at Norton Hall, Lichfield, and then at Woore, Shropshire. In 1817 a new lease was granted to Knight, Thomas Lewis, a son of his late partner, and Banks, with whom Knight became associated in the management of the Manchester theatre. Knight died, with 'appalling suddenness', at the Manor House, Woore, on 4 February 1820.

Knight wrote many pieces himself. His *Thelyphthora, or, The Blessings of Two Wives at Once*, a farce, was acted at Hull in 1783, but neither printed nor apparently brought to London; *Trudge and Wowski*, a prelude, supposedly from

Inkle and Yarico, was acted by Knight in Bristol in 1790, and *Honest Thieves*, a two-act abridgement of *The Committee*, by Sir Robert Howard, was produced at Covent Garden, with Knight as Abel, on 9 May 1797. On 14 November 1799 he appeared at Covent Garden as Robert Maythorn in his own *The Turnpike Gate*. This farce was printed in 1799, was well received, went through five editions in two years, and was constantly performed. Charles Munden made a noteworthy success in it as Crack. The anonymous author of the 'Managers' note-book', which appeared in the *New Monthly Magazine*, attributes to Knight *The Masked Friend*, an anonymous and unprinted reduction to three acts of Holcroft's *Duplicity*, given at Covent Garden on 6 May 1796, with Knight as Squire Turnbull and his wife as Miss Turnbull. The same author attributes to him *Hints for Painters*, an unprinted farce, given on the same occasion, and *What would the Man be at?* a one-act piece, unprinted, in which Knight played Charles, George, and Will Belford, three brothers. Knight also wrote an *Ode on the Late Naval War and the Siege of Gibraltar* (1784) and some comic songs or recitations.

Although he lived in good style, and consorted with men of science and letters, Knight accumulated considerable savings, which were augmented by a legacy from an uncle. His repertory was not unlike that of his namesake Edward Knight. He had a light and elegant figure, a melodious voice, and much sense and tact. As Watty Cockney in *The Romp*, a version of Isaac Bickerstaff's *Love in the City*, chosen for his second part, he did not create much effect, and his wife's Priscilla Tomboy was a failure, the result being that both were relegated for a time into obscurity. His great parts were Jacob Gawkey, Plethora in Thomas Morton's *Secrets Worth Knowing*, Count Cassel, and Farmer Ashfield, all very distinct characterizations. His Master Stephen in Ben Jonson's *Every Man in his Humour*, which he revived, also won much praise. During the latter part of his life he assumed the position of a country gentleman, and he left a reputation for great liberality.

JOSEPH KNIGHT, rev. KLAUS STIERSTORFER

Sources T. Wilkinson, *The wandering patentee, or, A history of the Yorkshire theatres from 1770 to the present time*, 4 vols. (1795) · *Managers' Notebook* · Genest, *Eng. stage*, vol. 7 · D. E. Baker, *Biographia dramatica, or, A companion to the playhouse*, rev. I. Reed, new edn, rev. S. Jones, 1/2 (1812), 441–2 · *The thespian dictionary, or, Dramatic biography of the present age*, 2nd edn (1805) · J. C. Dibdin, *The annals of the Edinburgh stage* (1888) · Highfill, Burnim & Langhans, *BDA* · J. Johnstone and others, *A statement of the differences subsisting between the proprietors and performers of the Theatre-Royal, Covent-Garden* (1800)
Likenesses J. Zoffany, oils, c.1795–1796, Garr. Club · S. De Wilde, oils (as Jacob Giawkey in *The chapter of accidents*), Garr. Club · T. C. Wageman, pencil drawing, Garr. Club
Wealth at death considerable savings: *DNB*

Knight, Thomas Andrew (1759–1838), horticulturist and plant physiologist, was born on 12 August 1759 at Wormsley Grange, near Ludlow, Herefordshire, the younger son of Thomas Knight (1697–1764), non-resident rector of Ribbesford and Bewdley, Worcestershire, and Ursula Nash (*b.* 1723/4). His father was very wealthy, having inherited a substantial income and land from the mining activities of Richard Knight (1659–1745), and neither Knight nor his elder brother, the antiquary Richard Payne *Knight, had any need to take up a profession.

Knight was educated at Ludlow School and briefly at a school in Chiswick, and matriculated at Balliol College, Oxford, on 13 February 1778. Although he half-heartedly intended to enter the church, he did not take his degree, having spent most of his time as a sportsman. From about 1780 he lived with his widowed mother at Maryknowle, until 1791 when he married Frances Felton, daughter of Humphrey Felton of Woodhall, near Shrewsbury, and moved to a family estate at Elton. There his acute but untrained scientific interests emerged and he began experimenting with new varieties of fruits and vegetables. He became a successful cattle-breeder and was recommended by his brother to Sir Joseph Banks as a suitable man to return information about Herefordshire to the board of agriculture. He met Banks in 1795 and, with his encouragement, began sending articles to the Royal Society. His first papers on grafting and on the diseases of fruit trees were well received and in 1805 he was elected FRS. In 1806 he received the Copley medal for his papers on plant physiology. These early papers set out his ideas about the movement of sap in plants and the effects of gravity, moisture, and sunlight on roots and leaves. To test his ideas he devised an ingenious revolving apparatus which eliminated the effect of gravity, and which was illustrated in Davy's *Elements of Agricultural Chemistry* (1813). He believed the movements within plants to be solely mechanical.

Knight discovered his real vocation in the Horticultural Society. He was not one of the founder members but was brought in by Banks to draft the formal prospectus in 1804 and retrospectively declared one of the twenty-eight original members. From 1811 to his death in 1838 he was president, skilfully orchestrating the society's expansion and consolidation, including the acquisition of gardens in Hammersmith and Chiswick, new offices, a library, the introduction of exhibitions, medals, annual fêtes, and displays, the publication of the *Transactions*, the funding and direction of overseas collectors, and a training programme for up to thirty-six young gardeners in a 'National School for the Propagation of Horticultural Knowledge'. Public controversy over this lavish expenditure marred the end of his presidency and an anonymous pamphlet in 1829, probably by Charles Henry Bellenden Ker, which was loudly taken up by J. C. Loudon in the *Gardeners' Magazine*, forced an inquiry into the society's management. Knight felt his absence from London was partly to blame. Nevertheless, the society struck a medal in his honour in 1836. Knight's numerous papers in the Horticultural Society's *Transactions* included studies on sap, buds, germination, bark, early varieties, forcing-houses, layering, manure, mildew, blight, and greenhouse design.

In 1808 or 1809 Knight moved into Downton Castle, Herefordshire, a castellated house and 10,000 acre estate built and owned by his elder brother, Richard Payne Knight, who, tired of overseeing the property, had moved to a cottage in the grounds. Making the most of this opportunity, Knight threw himself into horticultural and agricultural experiments of the highest calibre, which brought him into contact with continental physiologists such as Dutrochet, who visited Downton in 1827. Sir Humphry Davy, who included some of Knight's results in various editions of his *Elements of Agricultural Chemistry*, also visited, and praised the Downton fishing in his *Salmonia*.

Knight was particularly alarmed by an apparent decline in traditional varieties of fruit, considering it a matter of urgency to breed new varieties as well as to conduct scientific experiments on grafting, hybridity, fecundity, and heredity. Most of these researches were published in the *Philosophical Transactions of the Royal Society*, or the *Transactions of the Royal Horticultural Society*, and were later collected in *A Selection from the Physiological and Horticultural Papers* (1841). Charles Darwin afterwards appreciated many of his observations.

Knight grew and exhibited specialist fruit and vegetables himself, earning several Horticultural Society medals. A variety of garden pea carries his name and his general observations on peas earn him a minor place in the history of genetics for adumbrating some of Mendel's results. His researches included occasional studies into animal instincts and heredity. He investigated meat production in sheep, breeding from a Merino ram given to him by George III. This work provided the basis for several publications about tithes, in which he suggested tithe value should be calculated by meat rather than corn, since the former could be produced more efficiently than the latter.

Knight was a whig of the old school, a lax Christian, and an engaging host. He was able to remember long sections of abstruse text and amused friends by reciting them perfectly, page after page. He had an only son, Thomas Andrew BA, who died in a family shooting accident in November 1827, and three daughters. On the death of his son the inheritance of the estates passed, not without family difficulties, from Richard Payne Knight to Thomas Knight's grandsons. The oldest daughter, Frances (*b.* 1793), shared in Knight's experiments and married Thomas Pendarves Stackhouse Acton; the second married Sir William Rouse Boughton; and the third, Francis Walpole. Knight died on 11 May 1838 in the London house of his daughter Frances, who wrote a short memoir after his death. He was buried at Wormsley on 22 May.　　　　JANET BROWNE

Sources D. M. Simpkins, 'Knight, Thomas Andrew', *DSB* · F. Acton, 'Life', in *A selection from the physiological and horticultural papers published…by the late T. A. Knight, to which is prefixed a sketch of his life.*, ed. G. Bentham and J. Lindley (1841) · *Abstracts of the Papers Printed in the Philosophical Transactions of the Royal Society of London*, 4 (1837–43), 92–3 · H. R. Fletcher, *The story of the Royal Horticultural Society, 1804–1968* (1969) · *DNB* · will, PRO, PROB 11/1902, sig. 651
Archives Linn. Soc., papers · RS, papers | BL, letters to Sir Joseph Banks, Add. MSS 33980–33982 · NHM, letter-book, letters to Sir Joseph Banks · Suffolk RO, Bury St Edmunds, letters to marquess of Bristol
Likenesses S. Cousins, mezzotint, 1836 (after S. Cole), Wellcome L. · S. Cousins, mezzotint, pubd 1836 (after S. Cole), BM · S. Cole, portrait, Kew · R. J. Lane, lithograph (after S. Cole, 1834), NPG ·

drawing, City Art Gallery, Hereford · portrait, repro. in Acton, 'Life'

Knight, William (1475/6–1547), diplomat and bishop of Bath and Wells, was admitted as a scholar to Winchester College in 1487, aged eleven, the son of a college tenant in London. Little is known of his family. In 1514 he referred to John Newington, mercer of London, as his kinsman, and in 1547 left a legacy to Margaret James of London, his cousin. He went up to New College, Oxford, where he was admitted scholar on 12 May 1491 and elected fellow on 12 June 1493. He vacated his fellowship in 1495. Anthony Wood claims he then entered royal service and rose to become secretary to both Henry VII and Henry VIII, but it is more likely that he went to Italy to study. He was in Ferrara studying law in 1501 and was BCL by 1504 and DCL by 28 October 1506, when he visited the English College, Rome, from London. He was incorporated as DCL at Oxford on 12 October 1531. His education overseas so influenced him that in 1516 he was described as a good Italian.

Knight's recorded diplomatic career, which for much of its course was shaped by Henry VIII's anti-French policy, began in June 1512 when he sailed with the marquess of Dorset and an English army to Spain as an ambassador to Ferdinand II of Aragon. His reports back to Wolsey suggest that he was closely associated with him, so much so as to arouse suspicion of him in the army's council and to threaten his personal safety there. After the army's return to England in October 1512, Knight proceeded to Ferdinand's court in the following February to negotiate a new treaty. Ferdinand's determination to maintain his truce with the French resulted in Knight's recall on 29 June 1513.

In February 1514 Knight was sent to the court of the regent of the Netherlands, Margaret of Savoy, to further Henry VIII's alliance with the emperor Maximilian against France and to finalize arrangements for the marriage between Charles, the emperor's heir, and Mary Tudor. The hostility of Charles's counsellors to the match and Maximilian's procrastination alerted Knight to the untrustworthiness of England's allies. In a forthright report sent on 2 May he advised Wolsey to make peace with the French, but during the summer was sent to negotiate with the Swiss to secure their aid against the French before this course was eventually taken. On 7 May 1515 he was appointed to negotiate with Charles about renewing the treaty of Windsor of 1506, and in July attended a conference at Bruges which decided that commercial grievances for the next five years should be adjudicated under the terms of the *intercursus magnus* of 1495. On 2 October he was appointed to conclude a treaty with Charles, a task completed in March 1516.

On 13 December 1516 Knight was appointed to convey the protest of the enemies of France who formed the Holy League to France and Venice, but on 30 December was sent to the Low Countries, instructed to draw the emperor and Charles, now king of Spain, away from French influence. In February 1517, while he was in Brussels, he became convinced of Habsburg duplicity and advised Wolsey to recall him. On 26 August 1517 he was made a commissioner to settle disputes in Calais between English and French merchants. In January 1518 he was sent as ambassador to the court of Margaret of Savoy and, apart from a visit to the ailing Emperor Maximilian (December 1518 to January 1519), remained there until returning to England in February 1519. He was appointed a commissioner to settle disputes between English merchants and the Hanse (10 June 1520) and attended the Field of Cloth of Gold on 24 June 1520.

In October 1521 Knight was chosen ambassador to Charles V, though the emperor demurred on account of Knight's non-noble status, which he deemed a slight to his dignity. He was also designated ambassador to the Swiss in January 1522, and, after an audience with Charles V in Brussels on 9 February, he went on to Zürich (by 13 March), but was unable to induce the Swiss to recall their troops from French service in Milan. He returned to England in April 1522.

After helping to draft a treaty with the imperial commissioners concerning the wool staple in Calais, 17 January 1523, Knight returned to the court of Margaret of Savoy in April. On 22 June in that year he was commissioned to negotiate a treaty with the duc de Bourbon against François I, with orders to leave Margaret on pretence of going to the Swiss and, in disguise, to meet Adrian de Croy, an imperial agent, at Bourg-en-Bresse. But by the time he neared Bourg on 13 July, de Croy had already completed negotiations with Bourbon's envoys. Knight returned to his post at Brussels, taking formal leave of Margaret on 3 May 1525.

In 1526 Knight replaced Richard Pace as royal secretary, receiving the signet on 20 August. He began to complain of illness, and of age and failing eyesight. Even so, Henry decided to send him to the pope, probably to seek a dispensation for him to marry again without an annulment of his first marriage. When Wolsey, then in France, heard of the mission, he urged Henry that Cardinal Ghinucci was better qualified to serve his secret matter as he had more experience than Knight and better access to the pope. Knight, as instructed, met Wolsey, who was confident that he would be recalled, but Henry in further orders told him to leave for Rome immediately. Knight now had a new secret purpose: to obtain a dispensation for Henry to marry any woman, even one related in the first degree of affinity through either licit or illicit intercourse—a clear reference to Anne Boleyn, who as a result of the king's earlier affair with her sister Mary was related to Henry in precisely this way.

Unable to delay him, Wolsey instructed Knight to make for Venice. By 4 November he was at Foligno where he waited for a safe conduct to Rome. Once this was procured, he resumed his journey. Following the sack of Rome in May 1527, Clement VII fled to Orvieto, where Knight followed and had an audience with him. He received the dispensation he requested on 23 December, but without a clause stating Henry's current marriage was invalid. He also obtained a commission for Wolsey to hear the case against Queen Katherine, but not on the terms the cardinal had wanted. Knight then made for home.

Arriving at Asti early in January 1528, he was instructed by Wolsey to persuade the pope to send a second legate to England, but, as Sir Gregory Casale was nearer Orvieto, Knight continued his journey north and arrived in Calais on 3 February. His letter to Henry of 21 April shows he was aware his mission to Rome had failed. By this time he was at the French court.

On 27–8 November 1528 Knight was included in an embassy to François I and the pope about the king's Great Matter. Two envoys were sent on ahead while Knight, because of his age and infirmity, followed with further instructions. By late December he was still at Calais, recovering from a tempestuous crossing, but by 8 January 1529 had reached Paris, concerned that his tardiness would be interpreted as negligence. After an audience with François he proceeded to Lyons, arriving late in January, where he was met by Stephen Gardiner who continued to Rome while Knight returned to the French court. Once it became clear that François I and Charles V were intent on making peace, Knight was included in the English delegation to negotiate with both at Cambrai (30 June). Just before the conclusion of the treaty, on 5 August, Knight was replaced by Stephen Gardiner as the king's principal secretary. Perhaps this owed less to royal displeasure with Knight than to Henry's awareness of his need for a younger, more vigorous servant. In February 1532 Knight was a delegate appointed to negotiate the renewal of the *intercursus magnus* with the emperor's commissioners. This was his last mission.

Knight was one of the best rewarded clerical careerists of his age. A royal chaplain by March 1513 and a protonotary apostolic by February 1514, he was rector of Barton, Bedfordshire, 1504–11, of Sandhurst, Kent, 1508–15, of Stowting, Kent (vacated by 1513), of Chartham, Kent, 1514–15, and of All Hallows, Bread Street, London, 1515–37. He was dean of the hospital and college of the Newarke, Leicester, 1515–17, and prebendary of Farndon, Lincoln Cathedral, 1516–41, of Horton, Salisbury Cathedral, 1517–41, and of Chamberlainwood, St Paul's Cathedral, 1517–41. He was rector of Romaldkirk, Yorkshire, 1518–41, and also prebendary, Bangor Cathedral, 1520–41, archdeacon of Chester, 1522–41, and archdeacon of Huntingdon, 1523–41. In addition he was rector of Bangor Monachorum, Flintshire, 1527–41, prebendary of St Stephen's Chapel, Westminster, 1527–41, archdeacon of Richmond, 1529–41, and prebendary of Haselbere, Wells Cathedral, 1535–41. Finally Knight was elected bishop of Bath and Wells on 23 April 1541, received the royal assent on 19 May, and was consecrated ten days later. He was granted a coat of arms on 14 July 1514.

Knight's slow promotion to the episcopate might be attributed to his religious conservatism. In the 1530s vacant sees often went to reformers. He paid Friar Forrest to pray for the soul of Dean Richard Wolman, and in his will made bequests to endow obits and a temporary chantry for ten years. But when religious reaction set in from 1539, his prospects became more hopeful. Henry VIII planned to include Knight's archdeaconries of Chester and Richmond in a new diocese of Chester; both were highly privileged jurisdictions and to have left them in existence would have rendered the bishop without effective jurisdictional influence in his diocese. Knight's surrender of the two archdeaconries and their appurtenances to the crown soon after his election to the bishopric of Bath and Wells smacks of a quid pro quo.

Knight's career as an ecclesiastic was undistinguished. As archdeacon of Richmond he was in dispute with Archbishop Lee of York by 1533 over jurisdiction. As bishop of Bath and Wells he spent much of his time at his episcopal residence at Wivelscombe, Somerset, and it was probably there that he died, on 29 September 1547. He made several grants of presentations to livings and favourable leases, but only alienated one episcopal manor to the crown, that of Wick, Gloucestershire, on 20 June 1545.

In old age Knight was reputed to be wealthy. In July 1544 Henry VIII assessed him for a forced loan of £3000, £2000 more than the next most highly rated bishops. Knight offered 1000 marks as his 'free and poor gift'. Under pressure another 1000 marks was extracted from him as a loan. Despite his reputed wealth, the most lavish bequest in his will of 12 August 1547 (which disposed of over £500 in cash) was £100 for his own tomb. New College, Oxford, was left £40, and Winchester College £20, while smaller charitable legacies were made to the poor, prisoners, and for the repair of the highways.

Knight played a significant part in the introduction of Renaissance design and architecture into England. His works at Horton Court, Gloucestershire, dated 1521, include a Renaissance-style fireplace and front doorway, and a detached loggia with four stucco roundels of figures from classical antiquity embedded in its back wall. The inscription on the former market cross at Wells, Somerset, asserted that it was built in 1542 at the expense of Knight and Dean Wolman. Within the nave of Wells Cathedral is a stone pulpit bearing Knight's arms, described as 'one of the earliest attempts in England at a serious understanding of the Renaissance' (Pevsner, *Gloucestershire*, 309). He is supposed to have been buried nearby.

RICHARD CLARK

Sources LP Henry VIII · Emden, *Oxf.*, 2.1063–4 · CSP Spain, 1509–25; 1529–33 · CSP Venice, 1509–33 · J. J. Scarisbrick, *Henry VIII* (1968) · Wood, *Ath. Oxon.*, 1st edn · P. M. Hembry, *The bishops of Bath and Wells, 1540–1640: social and economic problems* (1967) · L. B. Smith, *Tudor prelates and politics, 1536–1558* (1953) · J. Gairdner, 'New lights on the divorce of Henry VIII [pt 1]', *EngHR*, 11 (1896), 673–702 · C. Haigh, 'Finance and administration in a new diocese: Chester, 1541–1641', *Continuity and change: personnel and administration of the Church of England, 1500–1642*, ed. R. O'Day and F. Heal (1976), 145–66 · C. Haigh, *Reformation and resistance in Tudor Lancashire* (1975) · F. Heal, *Of prelates and princes: a study of the economic and social position of the Tudor episcopate* (1980) · *Gloucestershire: the Cotswolds*, Pevsner (1970) · *Somerset: north and Bristol*, Pevsner (1958) · *Fasti Angl., 1300–1541*, [St Paul's, London] · *Fasti Angl., 1300–1541*, [Coventry] · *Fasti Angl., 1300–1541*, [Welsh dioceses] · P. Gwyn, *The king's cardinal: the rise and fall of Thomas Wolsey* (1990) · E. W. Ives, *Anne Boleyn* (1986) · R. M. Warnicke, *The rise and fall of Anne Boleyn* (1989) · N. Williams, *The cardinal and the secretary: Thomas Wolsey and Thomas Cromwell* (1975) · T. Scott Holmes, 'Ecclesiastical history', *VCH Somerset*, 2.1–67 · F. M. G. Evans, *The principal secretary of state: a survey of the office from 1558 to 1680* (1923) · G. M. Bell, *A handlist of British diplomatic representatives, 1509–1688*, Royal Historical Society Guides and Handbooks, 16 (1990) · F. W. Weaver, ed., *Somerset medieval wills*, 3, Somerset RS, 21 (1905), 97–8
Archives BL, Cotton MSS, letters to Henry VIII and Thomas Wolsey
Wealth at death bequeathed £523 13s. 4d. in cash; also plate, goods, and a rent: will, Weaver, ed., *Somerset medieval wills*

Knight, William (d. 1615/16), clergyman and religious writer, was probably born at Arlington, Sussex. He was probably the man who matriculated from Christ's College, Cambridge, in November 1575, graduated BA in 1580, and was ordained as a priest in the diocese of Peterborough on 5 September 1583. In 1591 he was admitted as rector of Arlington. Knight became a radical puritan. On 30 April 1605 he was one of ten Sussex preachers deprived for persistent nonconformity by Anthony Watson, bishop of Chichester, and a William Smith was instituted to the vicarage. However, within five years Knight became reconciled to the Church of England. About 1596 he had begun a long work, which he issued in 1610 as *A Concordance Axiomaticall, Containing a Survey of Theological Propositions*. In his prefatory remarks the author criticized himself and other ministers in the area for their earlier tendency 'to minister occasions of discontentment to others' and for 'taking pleasure in rash invectives or calumniations against things established by order among us', recommending that they earn 'contentment to ourselves, according to these rules to preach Jesus Christ … labouring to establish in the hearts of our people, the grounds of faith, and the blessed practise of obedience'. This work is signed from Arlington, Sussex, on 20 July 1610, but if Knight had gained readmission to a benefice locally the fact is not recorded. He may perhaps have held a curacy and lived in the house of his upbringing. Knight died, at Arlington, between signing his will on 20 October 1615 and the grant of probate on 30 March 1616.

A second William Knight (d. 1623), Church of England clergyman, from Derbyshire, may perhaps have been baptized at Egginton, in that county on 20 January 1563. He too attended Christ's College, Cambridge, matriculating as a pensioner in July 1579, graduating BA in 1583 and proceeding MA in 1586. He was admitted as a fellow of the college in 1583, was active on college business from 1586 at its properties in Nottinghamshire, and later in Leicestershire, and was appointed dean in 1588. Following his marriage to Agnes Hobson at Papworth Everard, Cambridgeshire, on 11 June 1595, Knight resigned his fellowship. On 19 April 1598, after the death of Thomas Willet, and on the presentation of Edward Francklin, clerk, he was instituted to the rectory of Barley, Hertfordshire. On 29 January 1599 he was succeeded there by Thomas's famous son Andrew Willet (1562–1621), who resigned his own rectory of Little Grandsen, Cambridgeshire, in favour of Knight. The two men had been contemporaries at Christ's, and Willet wrote of Knight that he was 'vir probens, prudens, doctus, mihique amicissimus' ('a man of honesty, prudence, learning, and a very good friend to me'; *Harmony on*

I Samuel 1, foreword). The demesne lands of Little Gransden had been used to support the heads of Cambridge colleges, and Knight is reported to have been involved in negotiations with parishioners over these impositions. He died in 1573 and was buried at Little Gransden on 25 November.

A third William Knight (*c*.1573–1617?), Church of England clergyman and translator, matriculated as a sizar from St John's College, Cambridge, in 1593, graduating BA in 1596. He proceeded MA in 1599 and was incorporated in that degree at Oxford on 12 July 1603. The following year Knight was presented to the rectory of Hinderclay in the diocese of Norwich but, it seems, he was actually instituted to another Suffolk rectory, Culford, on 7 August 1604. He was there in 1612, at which time the rights of presentation were held by Sir Nathaniel Bacon of Stiffkey. It is likely that this was the William Knight who had translated *Mundus alter et idem sive terrar Australis* by Joseph Hall (1574–1656), later bishop of Exeter and then of Norwich, and who in 1609 confided to Hall his doubts as to his own fitness for the ministry. Hall replied that he was 'sorry to hear of your discontentment' but that 'the cause is from yourself', stressing that divinity was a hard but rewarding taskmaster, and adding that 'We scholars are aptest of all others to make ourselves miserable' (Hall, 3.115–16). Nothing more is certainly known of this man, but in April 1617 a clergyman of his name fell seriously ill and died a week later at Puriton near Bridgwater, Somerset. In a nuncupative will proved on 19 December 1617 he left all his property to his wife, Mabel. STEPHEN WRIGHT

Sources Venn, *Alum. Cant.* · J. Peile, *Biographical register of Christ's College, 1505–1905, and of the earlier foundation, God's House, 1448–1505*, ed. [J. A. Venn], 1 (1910) · *The Registrum vagum of Anthony Harison*, ed. T. F. Barton, 2 vols., Norfolk RS, 32–3 (1963–4) · R. Clutterbuck, ed., *The history and antiquities of the county of Hertford*, 3 vols. (1815–27) · G. Hennessy, *Chichester diocese clergy lists* (1900) · H. I. Longden, *Northamptonshire and Rutland clergy from 1500*, ed. P. I. King and others, 16 vols. in 6, Northamptonshire RS (1938–52) · W. Knight [W. Knight of Arlington], *A concordance* (1610) · *VCH Cambridgeshire and the Isle of Ely*, vol. 5 · J. Hall, *Epistles*, 3 vols. (1608–11), vol. 3 · K. Fincham, *Prelate as pastor: the episcopate of James I* (1990) · will, PRO, PROB 11/142, fols. 654*v* [W. Knight of Little Gransden] · will, PRO, PROB 11/130 fols. 430–31 [W. Knight of Puriton] · *IGI* · Cooper, *Ath. Cantab.*, 3.16 · W. Hall, ed., *Calendar of wills and administrations in the archdeaconary court of Lewes*, British RS, 24 (1901)

Knight, William (1786–1844), natural philosopher, was born in Aberdeen on 17 September 1786, the son of William Knight, a bookseller in that city and his wife, Janet Hoyes. In 1793 he entered the Aberdeen grammar school, where he was a contemporary of Lord Byron (whose disposition he described in later life as most damnable). He entered the Marischal College in 1798, graduated MA there in 1802, and delivered several courses of lectures to the students in natural history and chemistry between 1810 and 1816. He also published, in 1813, his *Outlines of Botany*.

In 1816 Knight was elected to the professorship of natural philosophy in the Belfast Academical Institution. In 1817 he received from Marischal College the degree of LLD, and in the following year he published his chief

work, *Facts and Observations towards Forming a New Theory of the Earth*, a series of papers on geological subjects. This was followed in 1820 by *First Day in Heaven, a Fragment*, a curious book, which Knight himself subsequently suppressed. On 17 September 1821 Knight married Jean, the eldest daughter of George Glennie, professor of moral philosophy at Marischal College. The couple later had two sons and four daughters.

Knight returned to Aberdeen from Belfast in 1822 when he was appointed professor of natural philosophy at the Marischal College. His style of lecturing, according to Professor Masson, was characterized by much pungency, occasionally relieved by a 'sarcastic scurrility which no other lecturer ventured on, and which was far from pleasant' (*Macmillan's Magazine*, 9.331). Though his teaching was varied and interesting, its effect was greatly marred by the shallowness of his mathematical knowledge.

Knight died at Aberdeen on 3 December 1844. He left eight volumes of manuscript collections relating to Marischal College which went to the library of the University of Aberdeen (and formed the basis of the *Fasti academiae Mariscallanae*, edited by P. J. Anderson for the New Spalding Club). He also left relatives some autobiographical material which was said to contain racy criticisms of contemporaries.

THOMAS SECCOMBE, *rev.* PETER OSBORNE

Sources private information (1892) [P. J. Anderson, secretary, New Spalding Club, Aberdeen] · *Alma Mater* [Aberdeen University] (Jan–Feb 1889) · *James Riddell's Aberdeen and its folk: from the 20th to the 50th year of the present century* (1868) · old parochial register (baptism), General Register Office for Scotland, Edinburgh

Archives BL, letters to second Earl Spencer · U. Aberdeen L., lectures

Knight, William Henry (1823–1863), genre painter, was born on 26 September 1823 at Newbury, Berkshire, where his father, John Knight, was a schoolmaster; he was articled to a solicitor named Gray in that town, but after having two pictures accepted by the Society of British Artists in 1844 he decided to pursue an artistic career. In the following year he moved to London and took lodgings in the Kennington Road. He supported himself financially by drawing crayon portraits while studying at the British Museum and in the Royal Academy Schools. In 1846 he sent his first contribution to the academy exhibition, *Boys Playing at Draughts*, which was purchased by Alderman David Salomons. From that year he was a constant exhibitor at the academy, and he also sent many pictures to the British Institution. Among his works were *A Christmas Party Preparing for Blind Man's Buff* (1850), *Boys Snowballing* (1853), *The Village School* (1857), *The Lost Change* (1859), and *An Unexpected Trump* (1861). These titles indicate the character of Knight's art, which was limited to scenes of everyday life, generally small-scale, and usually involved children. Knight died on 31 July 1863 at his home, 15 Godolphin Road, New Road, Hammersmith, leaving a widow, Jane Sarah, and six children.

F. M. O'DONOGHUE, *rev.* SUZANNE FAGENCE COOPER

Sources J. Dafforne, 'William Henry Knight', *Art Journal*, 25 (1863), 133–5 · Bryan, *Painters* · Redgrave, *Artists* · *The exhibition of the Royal*

Academy (1846–62) [exhibition catalogues] · d. cert. · *CGPLA Eng. & Wales* (1863)
Wealth at death £1500: probate, 19 Sept 1863, *CGPLA Eng. & Wales*

Knightbridge, John (1619/20–1677), founder of the Knightbridge professorship in moral theology at Cambridge, was the fourth son of John Knightbridge (*d.* 1640), attorney of Chelmsford, Essex, and his wife, Mary, daughter of Charles Tucker of Lincoln's Inn. He matriculated from Wadham College, Oxford, on 8 December 1637, aged seventeen. His elder brother Richard (*b.* 1611/12) had matriculated from there in 1629. John was a scholar from 1639 to 1647, and graduated BA on 4 December 1641. On 3 May 1645 he migrated to Peterhouse, Cambridge, where five days later he was admitted to a fellowship in place of the ejected Christopher Bankes of Yorkshire. He became lecturer at St Nicholas, Newcastle, in 1657, and after resigning his fellowship in July 1659 he became rector of Spofforth, Yorkshire. He was also rector of Holy Trinity, Dorchester, from 1663 to 1670. In 1673 Knightbridge took the degree of DD, having graduated BD from Peterhouse in 1655.

It is, however, for the bequests of his will rather than the scope of his learning that Knightbridge is most remembered; he died in the parish of St Paul, Covent Garden, London, in December 1677, having made provision for bequests to benefit both his colleges and his home town. He left £40 each to the common funds of Wadham and Peterhouse, and gave to the master and fellows of Peterhouse as feoffees in trust his fee-farm rent of the manor of Heslington near York, a house in the Minories, London, £7 a year from his land in Chelmsford called Little Vinters, and another house and land on condition that they paid £50 annually to a professor of moral theology or casuistical divinity. The first election to the chair, called the Knightbridge professorship, followed in 1683, the first holder of the post being Thomas Smoult of St John's College, who himself further endowed it with a bequest upon his death in 1707. Later Knightbridge professors included Edmund Law, later bishop of Carlisle, and Frederick Denison Maurice; Knightbridge himself was enrolled among the primary benefactors of the university at Cambridge's commemoration services. He also presented a library for the use of the clergy of Chelmsford and the neighbourhood. This was long housed in a chapel on the north side of Chelmsford parish church; since the church's elevation to cathedral status the Knightbridge library has been moved to the cathedral's south porch library.

GORDON GOODWIN, *rev.* T. P. J. EDLIN

Sources J. R. Tanner, ed., *Historical register of the University of Cambridge to 1910* (1917), 84, 166 · Foster, *Alum. Oxon.*, *1500–1714*, 2.863 · W. C. Metcalfe, ed., *The visitations of Essex*, 1, Harleian Society, 13 (1878), pt 1, p. 432 · *Cantabrigienses graduati* (1787), 229 · F. Chancellor, 'Architecture of Chelmsford church', *Transactions of the Essex Archaeological Society*, 2 (1863), 197 · private information (2004) [Chelmsford Cathedral] · Wood, *Ath. Oxon.* · Venn, *Alum. Cant.* · will, PROB 11/357, fol. 16
Archives Chelmsford Cathedral, South Porch Library

Knightley, Sir Edmund (*d.* 1542), lawyer, was the third son of Sir Richard Knightley (*d.* 1534) of Lincoln's Inn and Fawsley, Northamptonshire, and Jane, daughter and heir of Henry Skynnerton (or Skennard) of Alderton. He was admitted to the Middle Temple in 1505, and as a barrister served as reader of Strand Inn in 1519. As early as 1515 he was elected to parliament for Reading, and in 1529 was returned for Wilton, though he had no apparent connection with either Berkshire or Wiltshire. In 1520 he made an impressive match with Ursula de Vere, daughter and coheir of the fourteenth earl of Oxford, the widow of George Windsor, and from 1522 until 1526 he held the lucrative post of attorney-general to the duchy of Lancaster. On becoming a bencher of the Middle Temple in 1523 he gave a reading on the 1484 Statute of Uses (1 Ric. III c. 1). He was added to the Northamptonshire commission of the peace in 1524, served on various *ad hoc* commissions in that county, and was recorder of Coventry in the same period.

Knightley was created serjeant-at-law in November 1531, and became a member of Serjeants' Inn, Fleet Street. The following year he became involved in a dispute with the crown over some property, and after making 'proclamations' slandering the king's title was in September 1532 committed to the Fleet by the 'lord chancellor' (presumably Lord Keeper Audley). His impetuous behaviour probably prevented his rise to office. In October 1537 Audley proposed him for a judgeship, praising his 'great wit and learning' but adding the somewhat qualified recommendation that:

> though he be wilful and full of fond inventions, yet it is to be thought if ever he will be an honest man that now he hath these great possessions and may have the estimation of a judge, he will leave all his own fancies and become a new man. (*LP Henry VIII*, 12/2, no. 805)

Cromwell was not minded to attempt the experiment, and Knightley received no further professional advancement. In 1538 he inherited substantial entailed family properties on the death of his elder brother Sir Richard, and rebuilt the great hall at Fawsley. A window panel from Fawsley, with the arms of Knightley impaling Vere, is now in the Burrell collection at Glasgow. Knightley probably gave up practice at the bar about this time. Indeed, in 1539 he asked Cromwell to obtain for him a discharge from the degree of serjeant. Late in life he was knighted, an unusual distinction for a serjeant who was not a king's serjeant. He died on 12 September 1542 and was buried at Fawsley, where his monumental brass represents him in armour rather than in a serjeant's robes. He left six daughters; his wife survived him.

J. H. BAKER

Sources HoP, *Commons, 1509–58*, 2.476–9 · R. Somerville, *History of the duchy of Lancaster, 1265–1603* (1953), 407 · *LP Henry VIII*, vols. 12–15 · Baker, *Serjeants*, 52, 168, 522 · C. H. Hopwood, ed., *Middle Temple records*, 1: *1501–1603* (1904) · M. D. Harris, ed., *The Coventry leet book*, 3, EETS, 138 (1909), 693 · Bodl. Oxf., MS Rawl. C. 705, fol. 30v · CUL, MS Hh.3.9, fols. 91v–92v · W. C. Metcalfe, *A book of knights banneret, knights of the Bath and knights bachelor* (1885), 70 · inquisition post mortem, PRO, C142/68/27 · monument, Fawsley church, Northamptonshire
Likenesses alabaster effigy, 1534, Fawsley, Northamptonshire · brass effigy on monument, 1542, Fawsley, Northamptonshire

Knightley [*née* Bowater], **Louisa Mary**, **Lady Knightley** (1842–1913), churchwoman and women's activist, was born on 25 April 1842 at 37 Lower Grosvenor Street, London, the only child of Major-General Sir Edward *Bowater (1787–1861) and his wife, Emilia Mary, daughter of Colonel Michael Barne of Sotterley and Dunwich, Suffolk, and his wife, Mary. Her father had been a member of the royal household for more than three decades, first as equerry to William IV when he ascended the throne in 1830, then to the prince consort, and in old age as groom-in-waiting to Queen Victoria. Louisa Bowater, who was a cousin of the women's activist Emilia Jessie Boucherett, was educated at home by a German governess. At the age of fourteen she began to record daily happenings in her journal, a routine which continued for the rest of her life. The family connection with royalty was strengthened when the queen and the prince consort asked Sir Edward Bowater to take their delicate child, Prince Leopold (later duke of Albany), to the south of France for the winter of 1861. When the duke married Princess Helena of Waldeck-Pyrmont in 1882, Lady Knightley was appointed one of her extra ladies-in-waiting.

At the age of twenty-seven, Louisa Bowater met and married, on 20 October 1869, Sir Rainald *Knightley, third baronet (1819–1895), of Fawsley, Northamptonshire. He was then fifty years of age: there were no children of the marriage. Although she was by inclination a Liberal, Lady Knightley transferred her allegiance on marriage and wholeheartedly supported her husband, who had been Conservative member for South Northamptonshire since 1852. She shared Rainald's personal dislike for Disraeli, approving of his refusal to accept the under-secretaryship for foreign affairs in 1866 in the Derby administration after Disraeli had been appointed leader of the House of Commons.

Louisa Knightley was a woman of commanding presence and a fluent public speaker. She espoused many causes, especially those connected with the church. The Girls' Friendly Society, founded in 1874 at a meeting of Anglican ladies and which aimed at training respectable young girls in religion and in domestic service, early attracted her attention. She was president of the Peterborough diocese branch of the society for twenty-five years (1879–1904) and a vice-president of the national organization. She was also a strong supporter of the Working Ladies Guild, established in 1876 by Lady Mary Feilding, and was a member of its committee from the beginning.

In an age when women could play only a minor role on the political stage, Lady Knightley had larger ambitions. Randolph Churchill and other members of the Fourth Party founded the Primrose League in 1883 in order to mobilize opinion and votes for the Conservative Party, and Louisa Knightley became one of its most enthusiastic members. She was enrolled as a dame in May 1885, inaugurated the Knightley (Daventry) Habitation in October of that year, and served on the central Ladies' Grand Council executive committee from 1885 to 1907. She organized vigorous canvassing for her husband in the towns and villages of South Northamptonshire and it was widely acknowledged that Sir Rainald owed his seat to her efforts in the 1885 and 1886 elections (W. R. D. Adkins, *Our County*, 1893, 20–24).

Denied the franchise, Lady Knightley recorded in her journal in 1885 on polling day, 'Then he [Rainald] voted for himself while I waited outside and felt, for the first time personally, the utter anomaly of my not having a vote, while Joe Bull has!' (27 Nov 1885, Knightley MSS, K2902). She took a keen interest in attempts to secure legislation in the Commons to give women the vote, and was one of the first presidents of the Conservative and Unionist Women's Franchise Association, 1908, a constitutional, or non-militant, organization.

It was widely believed that it was at his wife's promptings that Sir Rainald, after almost forty years in the Commons, approached Salisbury for a seat in the House of Lords. In August 1892 he was given the title of Baron Knightley of Fawsley. After his death in December 1895 Lady Knightley devoted much of her time to improving the lot of women in employment. She attended her first conference of the National Union of Women Workers in October 1896 and was a vice-president ten years later. In 1900 she was elected a member of the committee of the Freedom of Labour Defence League, the object of which was to prevent the exploitation of industrial workers, especially women, in their capacity as wage-earners. She was also for some time president of the Northamptonshire branch of the Society for Promoting the Return of Women as Poor Law Guardians.

An enthusiastic supporter of the empire, Lady Knightley was elected president of the South African Colonization Society in 1901, visited South Africa four years later, and was editor of *Imperial Colonist* (1901–13). She was also involved in the work of the British Women's Emigration Association, which promoted the protected emigration of women and children, and especially the 'superior class of women', becoming its president in 1908.

However, Fawsley remained the focus of Louisa Knightley's activities, despite the calls made on her by other organizations. She was prominent in public life in her adopted county, Northamptonshire. After the reorganization of local government in 1888 she was elected chair of her parish council, Badby. She was co-opted onto the Northamptonshire education committee following the Education Act of 1902 and served on its higher education committee from 1903 to 1913. She died on 2 October 1913 at Fawsley, aged seventy-one, shortly after a visit to her by Queen Mary, and was buried in Fawsley churchyard five days later.

PETER GORDON

Sources *The journals of Lady Knightley of Fawsley, 1856–1884*, ed. J. Cartwright (1915) • Northants. RO, Knightley papers • P. Gordon, 'Lady Knightley and the South Northamptonshire election of 1885', *Northamptonshire Past and Present*, 6 (1978–83), 265–73 • *The Times* (3 Oct 1913) • *Northampton Herald* (3 Oct 1913), 6 • *Northampton Mercury* (3 Oct 1913), 5 • b. cert. • m. cert. • d. cert.
Archives BL, Add. MSS 46360–46361 • Northants. RO
Likenesses photograph, *c*.1890, Northants. RO
Wealth at death £4567 7s. 8d.: probate, 3 Feb 1914, CGPLA Eng. & Wales

Knightley, Rainald, Baron Knightley (1819–1895), land-owner and politician, was born at Upper Brook Street, London, on 22 October 1819, the second child and only son of Sir Charles Knightley, second baronet (*d*. 1864), of Fawsley Park, near Daventry, Northamptonshire, and his wife, Selina Mary, daughter of Felton Lionel Hervey of Englefield Green, Surrey. The Knightley family was one of the oldest in Northamptonshire, having occupied the estate of Fawsley continuously since the reign of Henry V. Charles Knightley was an old-fashioned country gentleman, member of parliament for Northamptonshire, and a dashing fox-hunter famed for his jumping feats with the Pytchley hunt; he presided in feudal state at Fawsley, where he brewed his estate beer, bred a famous herd of cattle, and dispensed generous doles of beef and blankets at Christmas. Rainald Knightley was educated at Eton College and with a private tutor. He began to hunt at the age of six and continued to do so until he was seventy-six. One of the best riders across country with the Pytchley hunt, he lacked the geniality and warmth that made his father so popular. He succeeded his father as Conservative member of parliament for Northamptonshire in 1852, representing the county until 1892. In 1864 Sir Charles died and Knightley succeeded as third baronet, inheriting an estate of 8000 acres and the Tudor house at Fawsley. Declaring that he had a duty to his family to marry, and that the old house would be the death of any self-respecting wife, he commissioned the architect Salvin to make lavish additions (1867–8). He then proceeded to find a wife, marrying the formidable Louisa Mary Bowater [*see* Knightley, Louisa Mary (1842–1913)], twenty-three years his junior, on 20 October 1869. They had no children.

Tall and stately with a fine aquiline nose, Knightley was inordinately proud of his lineage.

And [K]nightly to the listening earth
Repeats the story of his birth

quipped Sir William Harcourt (GEC, *Peerage*). Aristocracy was the guiding principle of his politics. Silent and reserved, he distrusted Disraeli and democracy in equal measure. He refused Derby's offer of the post of under-secretary for foreign affairs in 1866 because he would not serve under Disraeli. In 1866 he joined Lord Elcho in opposing the Liberal Reform Bill, working with the Adullamite Robert Lowe to create 'a strong Constitutional party' or anti-Gladstone coalition, only (as his wife wrote) 'to see it all destroyed the following year, and … the country ruined by Mr Disraeli' (*Journals of Lady Knightley*, 230). As a result, Knightley was 'very badly treated' at the 1868 election, when the party wirepullers attempted to replace him, but he managed to keep his seat (ibid., 174). Acting as an independent Conservative, he took his lead from Lord Salisbury, whom he warmly admired. Prompted by his wife, Knightley voted in favour of the 1872 Woman's Franchise Bill; and thanks to Louisa, too, the Knightleys conquered London society. A leading authority on whist, Knightley was in 1863 one of the committee of six members of the Arlington Club (later the Turf), who reformed the rules of the game. For many years he was to be seen playing whist at the Carlton.

After 1878, Knightley's Fawsley estates were severely hit by the agricultural depression. 'Rainald feels deeply the bad spirit shown among the tenants who have been on the estate so many years' noted his wife (*Journals of Lady Knightley*, 346). His constituents grumbled that they rarely saw him, and his attendance at Westminster declined. In the 1884–5 session he voted in only twenty-four of the 266 divisions. He was a reluctant protagonist in the 1885 election ('R. went off groaning', wrote Louisa) and it was largely due to the efforts of Lady Knightley in organizing the local Conservatives that her husband was returned in 1885 and 1886. Augustus Hare, who visited Fawsley in 1884, found Knightley 'a splendid type of an English gentleman, very conservative, very courteous, very clever' (Hare, 404–5). The Revd Charles Clarke depicted him as Peregrine Bayard in his novel *Crumbs from a Sportsman's Table* (1865). Knightley retired in July 1892, when he was rewarded for his years of silent service with a peerage, being created Baron Knightley of Fawsley on 23 August 1892. He died at Fawsley Park on 19 December 1895 and was buried at Fawsley. The peerage became extinct on his death.   JANE RIDLEY

Sources *The journals of Lady Knightley of Fawsley, 1856–1884*, ed. J. Cartwright (1915) · GEC, *Peerage*, new edn, vol. 7 · Boase, *Mod. Eng. biog.* · *VCH Northamptonshire*, 2.359 · *VCH Northamptonshire*, suppl. · A. J. C. Hare, *The story of my life*, 5 (1900), 404–5 · John Clarke, 'History of Blackley', typescript, 1995 · *The Times* (20 Dec 1895) · W. P. Courtney, *English whist and English whist players* (1894)
Archives Northants. RO, bank books; travel journals
Likenesses Count D'Orsay, drawing, 1845, NPG · photograph, 1869, repro. in *Journals of Lady Knightley*, ed. Cartwright, facing p. 160 · Spy [L. Ward], cartoon, 1881, NPG · portrait, repro. in [W. B. Boutton], *The history of White's*, 1 (1892), 226 · portrait, repro. in *ILN* (3 Sept 1892), 300
Wealth at death £23,023 13*s*. 5*d*.: probate, 28 April 1896, CGPLA Eng. & Wales

Knightley, Sir Richard (1533–1615), politician and patron of puritans, was the eldest son of Sir Valentine Knightley of Fawsley, Northamptonshire, and his wife, Anne, the daughter of Edward Ferrers of Warwickshire. The family fortunes were based on sheep farming, for which the lands on their estates were enclosed, and on the death of his father in 1566 Sir Richard inherited an extensive property said to be worth £13,000 a year. By that date he had already moved into the circle of Robert Dudley, earl of Leicester, who knighted him at Kenilworth in 1565 during the royal progress there. Knightley's religious sympathies with the puritans were already apparent, and in 1567 he was among other associates of Leicester granted a patent as governors of the property of ministers of the gospel in Warwickshire, an initiative which created a fund to support preaching clergy. Knightley married first, in 1556, Mary (*d*. 1573), the daughter of Sir Richard Fermor; they had three sons and three daughters. His second wife was Elizabeth (*d*. 1603), daughter of Edward *Seymour, duke of Somerset; they had seven sons and two daughters.

Knightley's social position soon secured for him a central role in the government of his own county; he was a regular member of the bench, and was appointed sheriff in 1568, 1581, and 1589. He was deputy lieutenant of the

Sir Richard Knightley (1533–1615), by unknown artist, 1567

county and heavily involved in militia and musters through into his eighties, disrupted briefly by removal from office following his support for those puritan ministers unwilling to subscribe to the canons of 1604. This was not the first occasion, however, on which his puritan sympathies had brought him into conflict with authority. In 1581 Knightley, in association with Leicester, endowed a lectureship at Towcester for Andrew King, one of the ministers deprived during the vestiarian controversy; King had been active in the town since at least 1574. But it was the radical preaching at nearby Southam five years earlier, in 1576, that had drawn the attention of the privy council. The exercise there was said to attract local justices, and it is certain that Knightley was involved, as some of those attending sermons at Southam were also accused of gadding to sermons at Fawsley. The suppression of the exercises marked a watershed in Elizabethan religious history, but Knightley continued to support puritan clergy in those parishes where he was patron, and to use his influence in the county to secure other livings for godly ministers.

Knightley took these concerns with him when elected to parliament as member for Northampton in 1584, and when he served on committees dealing with church attendance and pluralism. In the parliament of 1586 he was on the committee which drew up the unsuccessful petition for reform of the ministry. Knightley shared the strong anti-papist views of his fellow puritans, being present at the execution of Anthony Babington in 1586 and the

execution and funeral of Mary, queen of Scots the following year, though he remained sympathetic to his Catholic neighbours. By the late 1580s hopes for further reform of the church through parliament had receded and the puritans adopted an alternative strategy of local initiatives, whereby clergy were organized into classes, in order to bring about their aims. Northamptonshire became a noted centre of this movement, and many of Knightley's clerical appointees were involved. Another crisis ensued, with the clerical leadership being tried before Star Chamber in 1591. By then Knightley had himself been arraigned before that body because of his involvement in the publication of the Marprelate tracts. Knightley was actually in London during August 1588, attending to militia business relating to the Armada when the Marprelate press was removed from East Molesey to a building on his estate at Fawsley. He later claimed to have had no knowledge of the printing of *The Epitome*, which took place there over the following months, but several of his servants were implicated in both the printing and distribution of the books. By the end of the year Knightley had arranged for the removal of the Marprelate press to the Coventry house of his nephew, John Hales. While this was taking place Knightley's standing with the council remained high, and with the support of the lord chancellor, Sir Christopher Hatton, who was also lord lieutenant of Northamptonshire, he was elected as MP for the county in autumn 1588. In contrast to previous sessions Knightley played no part in the commissions dealing with religious affairs in this parliament, and after its dissolution he returned to his work as deputy lieutenant. The discovery of copies of the Marprelate tracts in the possession of Knightley's servant, who was carrying them to his master's brother-in-law, the earl of Hertford, resulted in Knightley's imprisonment in the Fleet in November 1589. He was tried before his friend Hatton who, with Archbishop Whitgift, interceded with the queen to procure his release from gaol on payment of a fine of £2000.

By the end of 1591 Knightley had resumed his county responsibilities, sitting on several commissions. By that date the classis movement had been disbanded, and puritan activists subsequently adopted a less overtly political agenda. Along with several other local gentry Knightley continued to support puritan ministers in the area, and his status locally, reflected in his re-election as MP for the county in 1597, offered them protection. By this time the family estates had been diminished, due in part to the extravagance of his elder sons, Valentine and Edward, and this occasioned complicated settlements which were also designed to protect the interests of his second wife, Elizabeth, and her children. This marriage placed Knightley on the fringes of the succession question, and he was given custody of his nephew Viscount Beauchamp following the latter's involvement in the Essex conspiracy, but there was no truth in the rumour that he proclaimed his nephew king on the death of Elizabeth. The accession of James revived the religious debates, and in 1605 Knightley joined other county gentry in a petition supporting those puritan ministers who were being prosecuted for their failure to subscribe to the canons of 1604. With his old friend Sir Edward Montague, and another old campaigner, Sir Francis Hastings, Knightley was fined before Star Chamber and removed from the deputy lieutenancy and the commission of the peace; but he was soon restored to his local offices, maintaining an active presence until his death. His support for puritans also continued, and Fawsley became the home of John Dod, the celebrated preacher and catechist, at this time. Knightley died at Fawsley on 1 September 1615.

WILLIAM JOSEPH SHEILS

Sources L. H. Carlson, *Martin Marprelate, gentleman: Master Job Throkmorton laid open in his colors* (1981) • W. J. Sheils, *The puritans in the diocese of Peterborough, 1558–1610*, Northamptonshire RS, 30 (1979) • J. Goring and J. Wake, eds., *Northamptonshire lieutenancy papers and other documents, 1580–1614*, Northamptonshire RS, 27 (1975) • HoP, *Commons, 1558–1603* • P. Collinson, *The Elizabethan puritan movement* (1967) • J. Bridges, *The history and antiquities of Northamptonshire*, ed. P. Whalley, 2 vols. (1791)
Archives Northants. RO, corresp. and papers
Likenesses portrait, 1567, priv. coll. [*see illus.*] • portrait; formerly at Fawsley, Northamptonshire [not traced]

Knightley, Richard (1593–1639), politician, was born on 2 June 1593, the eldest surviving son of Edward Knightley, esquire (*d.* 1598), of Preston Capes, Northamptonshire, and his wife, Mary Coles (1577–1611), daughter of Peter Coles, gentleman, of Preston Capes. He was admitted to Gray's Inn on 21 October 1612 and on 4 July 1614 married Bridget (*c.*1593–1639×55), daughter of Sir Thomas *Lucy of Charlecote, Warwickshire. The marriage was childless and in the inquest following Knightley's death it was declared that his widow was a lunatic. Knightley sat as knight of the shire for Northamptonshire in the parliaments of 1621, 1624, 1625, and 1628–9.

During the 1620s and 1630s Knightley was an influential figure in Northamptonshire, where he inherited the religious and political connections of his renowned grandfather Sir Richard *Knightley of Fawsley. The family had been established in the county since the early fifteenth century when they acquired a large estate centred on the manor of Fawsley. Richard Knightley succeeded to this in 1618 when his uncle, Sir Valentine, died without leaving a male heir; and Fawsley Hall became his principal residence. His return to parliament at a by-election in November 1621 was a reflection of the family's status among the gentry in the western half of the shire, where they were second only to the Spencers of Althorp. Knightley became a justice of the peace about the same time and was made a deputy lieutenant in the mid-1620s.

Knightley was an active figure in local government, notable particularly for the vigour with which he pursued Roman Catholics. This led to a *cause célèbre* in October 1625 when he was assaulted while leading a search for arms at the house of the Catholic Lord Vaux. Vaux seems to have been provoked by Knightley's insistence that, in accordance with the recent statute, his brother be fined for swearing; but Vaux was summoned before the council and imprisoned. Knightley's anti-popery and determination to punish swearing were symptoms of a Calvinist zeal which lay at the heart of his beliefs and many of his

actions. His will referred to his conviction that he would 'be receaved into everlasting happiness as one of the elect of God' (will) and he was described by a contemporary as 'a great countenancer and protector of the puritans' (Cliffe, 182). He continued the family tradition of promoting a godly preaching ministry. His restoration of the impropriated livings of Fawsley and Preston Capes to the church earned praise in a 1641 survey of the state of the clergy; he was said to be the 'bosom friend' of John Preston, the distinguished court preacher and chaplain to Prince Charles, who retired to Fawsley to die in July 1628 (Morgan, 70); and he supported and protected individual ministers. The main beneficiary of this patronage was John Dod, the eminent puritan divine who had been hounded out of various livings for his failure to conform. Soon after 1625 Knightley procured a licence for him to preach at Fawsley, and he remained there until his death in 1645, shielded from the church authorities in the 1620s and 1630s by Knightley's influence and sustained by a series of trust funds. Knightley's lay friends were also drawn mainly from the ranks of fellow puritans. Among local gentry those he collaborated most closely with were puritans such as Sir Thomas Crewe and his son, John, Christopher Sherland, the recorder of Northampton, and, especially, his near neighbours Erasmus Dryden and his son, Sir John, who also protected Dod. The feoffees Knightley chose to administer Dod's trust were virtually a roll-call of godly allies outside the shire, including Lord Saye and Sele, John Hampden, John Pym, Sir Arthur Hesilrige, and Sir Nathaniel Rich.

Knightley's standing in puritan circles, and his own commitment to the godly cause, ensured that from the mid-1620s he was drawn increasingly into national politics. During the 1624 parliament, when the duke of Buckingham was recruiting puritan allies to support his policy of war against Spain, he became a client of the royal favourite. By late April he was writing to him in familiar terms, lamenting the duke's absence from court and impressing on him the need for urgency in dealing with Spain and the impeachment of Lord Treasurer Cranfield. The relationship continued through 1625 until November, when it was disrupted by Knightley's being pricked as a sheriff to prevent him from sitting in parliament the following year. This was Charles's doing—apparently because he disapproved of Knightley's role in the Vaux case—but he assumed it was the work of Buckingham and loudly protested his 'continual and sole dependence' on him and 'the endeavours he had used in parliament' for his and the king's service (Anstruther, 448). Early in 1626 he appears to have become even more disillusioned with the royal favourite. Preston wrote to him soon after the York House conference in February warning that the duke had disappointed their earlier hopes that he would become a supporter of the godly cause. From this point onwards Knightley was a forceful opponent of court policy.

This became apparent in January 1627 when Knightley led resistance to the forced loan in Northamptonshire. At a meeting with a delegation of privy councillors in Northampton he presented a protest by local gentry and freeholders declaring that they were willing to pay the levy only if it was approved by parliament. He was summoned to London where he refused to kneel before the council table—'lest … he should seem to acknowledge a fault'—and was promptly imprisoned in the Fleet (Cust, 166). However, he remained defiant, continuing to co-ordinate opposition and agitate for the loan refusers to be heard in court which eventually resulted in the *Five Knights* case. He was released from confinement the following January and was again elected knight of the shire for the 1628 parliament.

In spite of his reputation in Northamptonshire as 'a parliament man of much esteem' (Ball, 152), Knightley was never in the front rank of Commons orators; however, he was a diligent attender of committees and would speak out on the issues which concerned him. Foremost among these was religion. He was quick to support any measures to curb Catholics, urging that they be disarmed in February 1624 and warning of the dangers of not enforcing the recusancy statutes in June 1625. He was also very conscious of threats to Calvinist orthodoxy, protesting at the poisonous influence of Arminian sermons in June 1628. His most significant interventions on secular issues were in 1628. He was especially concerned about the dangers of billeting, repeatedly warning that the presence of Catholic Irish soldiers in Northamptonshire was a standing invitation to a papist uprising. He also delivered a fierce attack on Buckingham, whom he described as 'an enemy of all christendom', because of his willingness to grant letters of marque to Catholics and thereby undermine the loyalty of the navy (Johnson, *Proceedings*, 4.120). This last speech—following closely on an attack on Buckingham's religion by his friend Sherland—marked the final stage of Knightley's turning against his former patron.

After the dissolution of parliament in 1629 Knightley's opportunities to intervene in national politics became limited, but he remained a central figure among opponents of Charles's regime. He was 'the most faithful friend and brother' to Sir John Eliot while the latter was incarcerated in the Tower in the early 1630s, supplying him with a stream of advice and support (Forster, 492). In addition he was a leading shareholder in the Providence Island Company, originally established to colonize the West Indies but at the same time providing a forum for covert meetings between leading opponents of royal policy. These were also taking place at Fawsley and at Lord Brooke's residence of Warwick Castle and out of them emerged, among other things, a co-ordinated resistance to the crown's prerogative taxation in which Knightley continued to play his part. According to the earl of Exeter, 'Precise Ric Knightley' was among those who refused to pay knighthood fines in 1630, giving as his reason the fact that he had been sheriff at the time of the king's coronation and could not leave the shire (U. Nott. L., Clifton MSS, 631). He was less openly opposed to ship money than

Saye and Hampden, but he was still reported to the council for stirring up disputes over ratings in Northamptonshire.

The impression which emerges from a study of Knightley's career is of a forceful and principled politician who commanded enormous respect among his contemporaries. His commitment to defending the Calvinist religion and the liberties of the subject was unswerving and, had he survived, he would surely have been an influential member of the parliamentarian leadership during the civil war. He died on 8 November 1639 and was buried at Fawsley on the 11th. His cousin Richard Knightley (1580–1650), son of Thomas Knightley of Burgh Hall, Staffordshire, succeeded him, and was in turn succeeded by his son Sir Richard *Knightley (1609/10–1661).

RICHARD CUST

Sources Greaves & Zaller, *BDBR*, vol. 2, 158–9 · *VCH Northamptonshire*, suppl. 165–8 · I. Morgan, *Prince Charles's puritan chaplain* (1957) · T. Ball, *The life of the renowned Doctor Preston* (1885) · J. T. Cliffe, *The puritan gentry: the great puritan families of early Stuart England* (1984) · will, PRO, PROB 11/181, sig. 186 · A. J. Fielding, 'Conformists, puritans and the church courts: the diocese of Peterborough, 1603–1642', PhD diss., U. Birm., 1989 · R. C. Johnson and others, eds., *Proceedings in parliament, 1628*, 6 vols. (1977–83) · *The Fortescue papers*, ed. S. R. Gardiner, CS, new ser., 1 (1871) · R. P. Cust, *The forced loan and English politics, 1626–1628* (1987) · J. Forster, *Sir John Eliot: a biography*, 2 vols. (1864) · C. Russell, *Parliaments and English politics, 1621–1629* (1979) · R. E. Ruigh, *The parliament of 1624: politics and foreign policy* (1971) · G. Anstruther, *Vaux of Harrowden: a recusant family* (1953) · K. O. Kupperman, *Providence Island, 1630–1641: the other colony* (1993)
Archives Northants. RO, papers | Northants. RO, Montagu of Boughton MSS
Wealth at death see will, PRO, PROB 11/181, sig. 186

Knightley, Sir Richard (1609/10–1661), politician, was the eldest son of Richard Knightley (1580–1650) of Fawsley, Northamptonshire, and Jane (*bap.* 1584, *d.* 1657), daughter of Sir Edward Littleton. The great-nephew of Sir Richard *Knightley (1533–1615), he matriculated from Lincoln College, Oxford, in 1628, aged eighteen. He graduated BA in 1631, proceeded MA in 1633, and entered Gray's Inn later that year. His family had connections with the Eliots of Port Eliot, one of the great parliamentarian affinities of the age. The association was strengthened further when, about 1637, Richard married Elizabeth (*d.* 1643), daughter of John Hampden. They had a son, Richard, who died unmarried in 1665, and a daughter, Elizabeth, who died in infancy. After Elizabeth's death, on 22 July 1647 he married Anne (1615–1703), widow of Essex Devereux, son and heir of Walter Devereux, fifth Viscount Hereford, and daughter of Sir William Courten. They had a son, Essex, and two daughters, Elizabeth and Jane.

Knightley was elected as MP for Northampton in the Short Parliament in April 1640. After its dissolution he invited Hampden, Pym, and other opposition leaders to Fawsley. He was returned for Northampton again in November to the Long Parliament. In 1643 he was one of John Pym's pallbearers. An extremely active parliamentarian throughout the 1640s he eventually reached the higher echelons of the wartime administration when he joined the Derby House committee in May 1648. In explanation of his middle group allegiance during the first war it has been said that Knightley was among those who were able to 'reconcile a desire for primitive episcopacy with support for resolute prosecution of the war' (Underdown, 64–5). However, his allegiance was ductile, and by the time of the 1647 crisis between parliament and the army he was often found making common cause with the political presbyterians, and he remained at Westminster during the apprentices' putsch. In December 1648 he appears to have strongly favoured concluding with the king on the terms agreed at Newport. Despite his middle group credentials he was imprisoned for a fortnight after Pride's Purge.

After the execution of Charles I, Knightley kept out of politics until the fall of the Rump Parliament. In 1651 a licence to go abroad was granted to one Richard Knightley. In 1655 he was described as one of those local governors 'who do not persecute but are loving to Friends' (DNB). He came to accept the protectorate, and represented his native county in Richard Cromwell's parliament (declining a nomination to serve as speaker), remarking that 'A Commonwealth was never for the common weal' (Underdown, 345). When the Rump was restored in May 1659 Knightley joined with William Prynne and others in attempting unsuccessfully to enter the house. Subsequently he was prominent in securing the readmission of the secluded members in February 1660, and soon afterwards he was appointed to the council of state. Rejected at the Northamptonshire election to the Convention later that year on account of an ill-judged remark about the return of the Stuart king to England, Knightley was elected instead, on the Eliot interest, for St Germans, Cornwall. In the Convention, Knightley spoke on the problem of dealing with maimed soldiers, widows, and orphans and sat on committees for instructing messengers to the king and preparing for his reception. Lord Wharton counted Knightley as a friend, and after the restoration of Charles II, Knightley was certainly active in support of indemnity for Wharton's associate Richard Salway. He also opposed an attempt to exclude all those who sat in judgment on Charles I from the Act of Indemnity, and supported lenience in the treatment of those who had supported the interregnum regimes. He appears to have favoured some sort of church settlement which would comprehend non-Anglicans, to have found the Worcester House declaration acceptable, and to have been amenable to the case for modified episcopacy. It has been suggested that 'on religious questions he generally followed the Presbyterian line' (Helms and Watson, 2.700).

Knightley was made a knight of the Bath in the king's 1661 coronation honours, but died shortly afterwards in London on 29 June. He was buried on 9 July at Fawsley.

SEAN KELSEY

Sources DNB · H. I. Longden, The visitation of the county of Northampton in the year 1681, Harleian Society, 87 (1935), 108–9 · Keeler, Long Parliament, 243 · J. Bridges, The history and antiquities of Northamptonshire, ed. P. Whalley, 1 (1791), 66–70 · J. Hexter, The reign of King Pym (1941), 6 · D. Underdown, Pride's Purge: politics in the puritan revolution (1971), 64–5, 84n., 345 · M. W. Helms and P. Watson, 'Knightley, Richard', HoP, Commons, 1660–90, 2.699–700 · IGI · Foster, Alum. Oxon. · will, PRO, PROB 11/321, fols. 306v–307 · will, PRO, PROB 6/37, fol. 90r · will, PRO, PROB 11/215, fols. 42v–43
Wealth at death 'son inherited an estate valued, for matrimonial purposes, at £2000 p.a.': HoP, Commons, 1660–90, 2.700; will, PRO, PROB 11/321, fols. 306v–307

Knighton, Henry (d. c.1396), chronicler and Augustinian canon, of the abbey of St Mary de Pratis, Leicester, most probably took his name from the abbey's own manor of Knighton, on the southern boundary of the borough of Leicester. The date of his birth and his parentage are unrecorded, and all that is known of his life comes from the content of his chronicle, which he wrote between 1379 and 1396, and some references from archival sources. He was apparently a member of the house in 1363, when he saw Edward III at Leicester; his residence is attested in the 1370s, and he was still active in 1389. He probably went blind in his later years, and he wrote nothing later than 1396. He bequeathed three books—two devotional works and an encyclopaedia—to the abbey library. He almost certainly died and was buried at St Mary de Pratis.

Knighton's chronicle survives in two manuscripts in the Cottonian collection in the British Library. The earlier, BL, Cotton MS Tiberius C.vii, is clearly close to the author, though none of its scribes' hands (some six in all) can be confidently attributed to him. It is certainly this copy of the work that was catalogued in the abbey library c.1490 by William Charite. The second manuscript, BL, Cotton MS Claudius E.iii, is wholly derivative, and was probably made in Leicester early in the fifteenth century.

The chronicle is a history of England from the Norman conquest to the last decade of the fourteenth century, with some introductory passages on events before 1066, including the legend of Guy of Warwick. Knighton explains his purpose in the opening chapters, and identifies himself by spelling out his name (as Henricus Cnitthon) in their initial letters, after the style of his model, Ranulf Higden (d. 1364). He planned a text in four books, but feared that he might not be able to complete it, a misgiving that probably refers both to his failing sight and to the unusual structure of the narrative.

The chronicle ends inconsequentially in 1396, but there is a break in the narrative between 1372 and 1376 that has caused much confusion. It appears that Knighton set out to write an account of his own times, beginning soon after the death of Abbot Clowne of Leicester in 1378, and then resolved to expand it into a general history from 1066. To that end he conflated the seventh book of Higden's Polychronicon and the early fourteenth-century chronicle of Walter of Guisborough, which took him as far as 1340. He then launched upon his own composition, from the beginning of the war in 1337. During the 1380s he was therefore engaged in two works, one a history of Richard II's reign as it unfolded, and the other substantially a history of the Hundred Years' War. In the event he was unable to connect the two, though he came very close to doing so: a matter of four years.

J. R. Lumby, who edited the Claudius manuscript for the

Rolls Series, was familiar with the *Polychronicon*, but failed to identify Guisborough, and attributed his oversight to deceit on Knighton's part. He also propounded a theory that Knighton, whom he regarded as a plagiarist and fraud, had written only the first half of the chronicle, and that the section from 1376 onwards was the work of an anonymous continuator. The error, attested by references to '*Cont. Knighton*' in the works of T. F. Tout and others, was finally corrected by V. H. Galbraith in 1957.

The chronicle does nevertheless fall into two parts. In his account of the opening phases of the French war Knighton is writing at some remove in time from his material, though he shows himself a resourceful editor and narrator. His great hero was Henry of Grosmont, first duke of Lancaster (*d.* 1361), and though it is not clear that he knew Lancaster personally, he drew much of his material from the Lancastrian household at Leicester and elsewhere. The second part of the narrative is concerned with contemporary events, running from the onset of the great schism (1378) and the peasants' revolt in 1381 to the rise of Lollardy, and the parliamentary crisis of 1387–8.

There again Knighton enjoyed particular sources of information. He speaks familiarly of John of Gaunt, duke of Lancaster, and his son Henry Bolingbroke, and he quotes the duke's officials when he reports the sack of the Savoy in 1381 and Gaunt's expedition to Spain in 1386–9. His account of the appellants' campaign against the king's friends in 1387–8, and the proceedings of the Merciless Parliament in 1388, reflects quite close connections with Bolingbroke.

When he described the beginnings of Lollardy, Knighton found his privileged position embarrassing. His fellow canon Philip Repyndon (*d.* 1424), who became abbot of Leicester in 1393, had been a distinguished follower of John Wyclif (*d.* 1384) and an enthusiastic preacher of Lollard beliefs to the laity in Leicester and elsewhere. William Swinderby, a formidable popularist and radical, was allowed to live in the abbey at some time before 1382, probably under Repyndon's patronage. Repyndon gave Knighton a variety of Lollard papers, and was evidently better assured of his ultimate justification than Knighton himself could feel.

For Knighton emerges from his work as staunchly orthodox and conservative. He sympathizes with the victims of incompetent and oppressive government, but not with rebellion as a remedy for their wrongs. He accepts Bolingbroke as a warrantor for the appellants' cause, but does not blame Richard for his favourites' failings, and treats the king as intelligent and imposing. Lollardy he condemns wholeheartedly, and does what he can, within the evidence that he deploys, to protect Repyndon from the consequences of past follies.

Beyond those large themes, Knighton tells a zestful story, and shows an informed interest in economic affairs: in wages, prices, and the business of supply. His putative audience liked tales of battle and military enterprise, and so did he, but he knew that campaigns had to be paid for as well as enjoyed. How far his own experience of such matters extended it is impossible now to tell, but it seems likely that at the least he had some firsthand knowledge of administration, in his own house if no farther afield.

G. H. MARTIN

Sources BL, Cotton MS Tiberius C.vii · *Knighton's chronicle, 1337–1396*, ed. and trans. G. H. Martin, OMT (1995) [Lat. orig., *Chronica de eventibus Angliae a tempore regis Edgari usque mortem regis Ricardi Secundi*, with parallel Eng. text] · V. H. Galbraith, 'The chronicle of Henry Knighton', *Fritz Saxl, 1890–1948: a volume of memorial essays from his friends in England*, ed. D. J. Gordon (1957), 136–45
Archives BL, Cotton MS Claudius E.iii · BL, Cotton MS Tiberius C.vii

Knighton, Sir William, first baronet (1776–1836), courtier and physician, son of William Knighton, was born at Bere Ferrers, Devon. His family had an estate at Grenofen, Whitchurch, Devon, but his father was disinherited, and, dying very early, left his widow in poverty. Knighton, after a little schooling at Newton Bushell, Devon, was sent at an early age to study medicine under his uncle, Dr Bredall, a surgeon in Tavistock. He afterwards spent two years at Guy's Hospital, London, where he studied anatomy under Henry Cline and surgery under Sir Astley Cooper, in addition to attending lectures on midwifery and physic. At the age of twenty-one he returned to Devon and obtained an assistant surgeon's post at the Royal Naval Hospital in Plymouth. At the end of 1797 he settled in practice at Devonport.

In 1800 Knighton married Dorothea, youngest daughter of Captain James *Hawker RN, and in 1803 he moved to London. He began practice as an accoucheur, but shortly moved to Edinburgh after learning that his medical education was not yet sufficient to meet the requirements of the Royal College of Physicians. After three years' additional study, he once more returned to London, received a degree from the archbishop of Canterbury, and the degree of MD from the University of Aberdeen (21 April 1806). He was admitted a licentiate of the Royal College of Physicians on 25 June 1806 and began practice in Hanover Square, primarily as an accoucheur. By that time Knighton had already made the acquaintance of the Marquess Wellesley, whom he attended as domestic physician on his embassy to Spain in 1809.

In 1810 Wellesley introduced his protégé to the prince of Wales, with the result that he became one of the prince's physicians, and was shortly afterwards created a baronet (1812). The prince told Sir Walter Farquhar, in explanation of this appointment, that Knighton was the best-mannered doctor he had ever met. Knighton had been a close friend of Sir John Macmahon, and when, on the latter's death in 1817, he came, as executor, into possession of papers compromising to the prince, he immediately delivered them to him. Shortly afterwards the prince appointed Knighton to the auditorship of the duchy of Cornwall and of the duchy of Lancaster, and soon began more and more to consult him on matters of business. 'I was now beginning to be made his Confidential Friend in all those secret concerns which a life of pleasure and sensuality had exposed him to', Knighton later recalled in his

Sir William Knighton, first baronet (1776–1836), by Charles Turner, pubd 1823 (after Sir Thomas Lawrence, 1822–3)

diary (Lawrence MS 51256). By 1821 Knighton was regularly dining tête-à-tête with the regent, now George IV, and was discreetly and efficiently negotiating with the Rothschilds on behalf of the king and scattered members of the royal family.

Knighton's firmness of character appeared in his management of George IV's inextricably confused affairs. In spite of the king's extravagance, Knighton gradually reduced his finances to order, caused the debts to be steadily liquidated, and asserted over the king's weak mind an authority which few of the ministers enjoyed. The king wrote to him as 'dearest friend', signed himself 'most affectionately yours', and gave him written authority to notify the royal tradesmen that no goods were to be supplied or work done on account of the privy purse except upon Knighton's written orders.

In September 1822 Knighton gave up his lucrative medical practice to devote himself fully to the king's service, having been officially appointed keeper of the privy purse in succession to Sir Benjamin Bloomfield, who had fulfilled that office as well as that of private secretary. In securing the resignation of Bloomfield, the latter office had been abolished, and the Liverpool ministry, believing the position to be an unconstitutional one, was unwilling to revive it on Knighton's behalf, or to admit him to the privy council. Nevertheless, Knighton functioned as unofficial private secretary for the duration of the king's reign, a position which kept him in daily contact with the king's ministers.

Knighton was frequently employed on confidential missions for the king both at home and abroad for a variety of purposes, carrying private messages to his majesty's ambassadors, looking after the well-being of the younger members of the Conyngham family, and securing the financial interests of the royal family. He was sent to Paris in 1823, and in 1824 made three journeys in rapid succession to Paris, Spain, and Sardinia. These sudden and toilsome journeys, which continued yearly and often several times a year until 1825 and 1826, probably contributed to bring on the severe illness which overtook him in 1827. He was highly esteemed by the royal family and by the ministry, having taken to heart the duke of Wellington's advice to beware how he interfered in politics; but he became the object of considerable ill will, owing to his undoubted influence with the king who rarely attended to business without Knighton's urging and assistance. The prejudice which then existed against medical men also left Knighton vulnerable to criticism. Liverpool refused to make Knighton a privy councillor because he had been 'accoucheur to all the ladies in London'. This refusal would remain a sore point with both Knighton and the king. 'It is really too bad to reflect that all this intriguing and ill-humour', Mrs Arbuthnot observed in 1823, 'is going on because Lord Liverpool refused to admit into the Privy Council a fellow who, fifteen years ago, carried phials and pill boxes about the town of Plymouth' (*Journal of Mrs Arbuthnot*, 1.186; 2.256). Knighton's profession, as well as the Rothschild connection, provided the basis for an attack upon him in the House of Commons on 18 February 1828; but Peel denied the existence of an invisible power behind the throne. According to Greville, the attack appears to have been got up as a joke by Henry de Ros and himself; but to Knighton, who was then abroad and unable to defend himself, it was very painful.

Knighton attended the king almost night and day during his last illness, was present even at political interviews in the royal closet, and appears to have been sincerely attached to the king. His vigilance prevented Lady Conyngham from profiting by the temporary disorder at Windsor during the king's illness to lay hands on any of the royal jewels, and after the king's death on 26 June 1830 Knighton was busily occupied for several months in winding up his affairs. He subsequently gave up his house in London and retired into the country, which suited his failing health better than town. He died, however, in Stratford Place, Oxford Street, London, on 11 October 1836 of an 'enlargement of the heart', and was buried at Kensal Green cemetery.

Knighton had considerable taste, especially in painting, being a friend of Lawrence and a patron of Wilkie. He also possessed very great social tact, a sound business capacity, and honestly fulfilled the duties of a very delicate position. Although he long held a position where his court interest might have commanded almost any favour, he proved himself greedy neither of money nor honours, and kept aloof from all intrigue. He left a widow, one son, and one daughter.

J. A. HAMILTON, rev. JUDITH SCHNEID LEWIS

Sources A. Aspinall, 'George IV and Sir William Knighton', *EngHR*, 55 (1940), 57–82 · *The letters of King George IV, 1812–1830*, ed.

A. Aspinall, 3 vols. (1938) · Lady Knighton, *Memoirs of Sir William Knighton*, 2 vols. (1838) · *The journal of Mrs Arbuthnot, 1820–1832*, ed. F. Bamford and the duke of Wellington [G. Wellesley], 2 vols. (1950) · Munk, *Roll* · J. Richardson, *George IV: a portrait* (1966) · C. Hibbert, *George IV, 2: Regent and king* (1973) · J. S. Lewis, *In the family way: childbearing in the British aristocracy, 1760–1860* (1986) · I. Butler, *The eldest brother: the Marquess Wellesley, the duke of Wellington's eldest brother* (1973) · *GM*, 2nd ser., 6 (1836), 652–3 · *The Greville memoirs, 1814–1860*, ed. L. Strachey and R. Fulford, 8 vols. (1938)

Archives Royal Arch., papers | BL, corresp. with Lord Aberdeen, Add. MS 43039 · BL, corresp. with Lord Liverpool, Add. MSS 38190–38302, 38564 *passim* · BL, corresp. with Sir Robert Peel, Add. MSS 40299–40300 · BL, Wellesley MSS · Bucks. RLSS, letters to Viscount Goderich · NL Scot., letters to Sir Walter Scott · NRA, Canning MSS · RA, corresp. with Thomas Lawrence · Slane Castle, Meath, Conyngham MSS · W. Yorks. AS, Leeds, corresp. with George Canning

Likenesses T. Lawrence, portrait, 1823, priv. coll. · C. Turner, mezzotint, pubd 1823 (after T. Lawrence, 1822–3), BM, NPG [*see illus.*] · E. H. Baily, bust, 1837, RA · D. Wilkie, portrait, 1837, University of Dundee · Maurin, lithograph, pubd 1838 (after T. Lawrence), NPG · S. Cousins, mezzotint (after T. Lawrence), BM, NPG

Lionel Charles Knights (1906–1997), by unknown photographer

Knights, Lionel Charles (1906–1997), university teacher and literary scholar, was born on 15 May 1906 at Grantham, Lincolnshire, the first child of Charles Edwin Knights (1882–1972), technical draftsman and salesman, and his wife, Lois, *née* Kenney (d. 1947).

L. C. Knights defined his background as that of an uncultured lower middle-class person sensitively aware of social hierarchy. He was educated at grammar schools: Kings' School in Grantham, Hutchinson's in Glasgow, and Cambridgeshire County High School for Boys. He was admitted to Selwyn College, Cambridge, in 1925. Although an exhibitioner, he was unable to afford rooms in college and so lived at home for his first two undergraduate years. An award from the Goldsmiths' Company enabled him to live in college for his third year, alleviating the sense of 'not belonging' which became an underlying psychological motif throughout his life. He distinguished himself in history for two years and in English for one, winning the Charles Oldham Shakespeare prize, shared with Humphrey Jennings. A skilled examinee—he diffidently described himself as a 'pot-hunter'—he graduated in 1928 and was awarded the members' prize for an essay on the current state of literary criticism. During the essay's preparation H. S. Bennett recommended that Knights seek the advice of F. R. Leavis, then an untenured lecturer a dozen years older. An exciting friendship thus began. Leavis and his wife, Queenie, introduced Knights to a circle of ambitious graduate students who worked on cultural studies that combined literary criticism, history, and sociology.

After his graduation Knights supported himself by schoolmastering, teaching adult education classes, and marking examinations until he was elected to a research fellowship at Christ's College (1930–31) which enabled him to work on a doctoral thesis. He helped to organize the English Research Society, a discussion group in the Leavis circle which proved ephemeral, but in 1932 he became founder editor of *Scrutiny: A Quarterly Review*. Published from his parents' home, to which he moved when his fellowship expired, *Scrutiny* dealt with all aspects of modern culture, but had literary criticism at its heart. Knights enjoyed pronouncing the title 'Scrrrutiny', with its suitably rasping sound. He sought contributors and was its roving salesman. After two issues Leavis took on the editorship of *Scrutiny* and remained in the post until 1953, though Knights was fairly active up to and during the war years.

Part-time teaching continued while Knights wrote for journals such as T. S. Eliot's *The Criterion*. A lecture given at King's College, London, was published by Gordon Fraser's Minority Press as *How many Children had Lady Macbeth?* (1933) and had a long-lasting reputation, to Knights's rueful regret. The title satirically alluded to such appendices in A. C. Bradley's *Shakespearean Tragedy* (1904) as 'Where was Hamlet at the time of his father's death?' Knights argued that Shakespeare's plays are works of metaphor and symbolism, not realistic narratives—thereby decisively identifying with Leavis's conception of poetic drama, and with that of G. Wilson Knight's *The Wheel of Fire* (1930). As he said later, the modern critic should see Shakespeare's tragedies 'as imaginative wholes rather than dramatic constructions designed to exhibit "character"' (*Some Shakespearean Themes; an Approach to Hamlet*, 1966, 178).

A one-year post at Manchester University in 1933 was followed by a permanent lectureship there in 1935. On 31 October 1936 Knights married one of his third-year students, Elizabeth Mary Barnes (1911/12–1998), who became for a short while a teacher of the deaf. They had two children. Frank and Queenie Leavis helped them out with £100, the *Shorter Oxford English Dictionary*, and a basket of walnuts from their garden.

Knights's doctoral thesis became his major work, *Drama and Society in the Age of Jonson* (1937), 'an early attempt to find significant relations between economic conditions and what the Marxists called the cultural superstructure' (as he described it in his unpublished autobiography) in which literature was used as data to reveal 'the quality and the minute particulars of experience … forever beyond our reach'. The way in which Knights combined politics, literature, and history anticipated the integrated cultural studies of the literary 'new historicism' fifty years later. He made clear the book's debt to the Leavises and to R. H. Tawney but the even manner of Knights's prose (and sociable personality) has been contrasted with the argumentative dash of Leavis. Yet Knights was equally obdurate in his concern for discriminating quality in culture, unfashionably comparing the lost world of seventeenth-century Britain to that of the twentieth century. He wrote a series of polemics for *Scrutiny* questioning the ascendancy of Restoration comedy ('the reality and the myth') and the practice and principles of teacher education. He also provided criticism of seventeenth-century writing in his *Explorations* (1946).

Exempt from military service on health grounds, Knights remained at Manchester until 1947 when he became professor of English at Sheffield. Here he ran the department on a shoestring, teaching many mature undergraduates returned from the services. In 1953 he became Winterstroke professor at Bristol. The university was apprehensive about the arrival of a 'Leavisite', but Knights was friendly to Anglo-Saxon and had a high regard for Susie Tucker, the leading teacher in Old English and Norse. Knights developed the interdisciplinary courses (with Russian and with French) for which the department became famous. He continued to publish, notably *Some Shakespearean Themes* (1959), *An Approach to Hamlet* (1960), and *Further Explorations: Essays in Criticism* (1965).

Knights could not resist appointment by the crown to the King Edward VII chair of English at Cambridge in 1965, though Elizabeth Knights, whose roots were in the west country, disliked the prospect and the reality—as did, in the event, her husband who was disappointed by the experience of returning to Cambridge University, 'a Borges-like invention' (Knights, 'Viewpoint', 135). He chaired the faculty board only periodically, so had little control over the smooth working of teaching—that is, with arranging and revitalizing undergraduate courses and choosing set books. Life was very different from running a department in a civic university. There was faction on the board, tension between it and the college teachers, and the new phenomenon of student protest. There was no warmth in Knights's relationship with the Leavises. Knights was still hurt that Leavis had closed *Scrutiny* in 1953 without consulting him. Leavis himself was now in angry retirement, embittered by conflicts over the machinations for founding a lectureship in his name and Queenie Leavis was contemptuous—envying, perhaps, Knights's seemingly prosperous career in the provinces away from the literary critical culture wars of Cambridge. Knights disliked the collegiate customs: Elizabeth was not allowed to dine on guest nights at his adoptive college, Queens'. He thought the dons talked only about motoring.

There were visiting chairs abroad, including Pittsburgh in 1961 and 1966, and Berkeley in 1970 where he calmed a student demonstration by leading participants away for discussion in a chapel off the campus. In 1971 he delivered the Clark lectures at Trinity College, Cambridge, called *Public Voices: Literature and Politics with Special Reference to the Seventeenth Century*, in which he tried to explain his admiration for political men who could combine a principled firmness of mind and purpose with flexibility and openness to the other side.

After his retirement in 1973 Knights slowly completed a detailed memoir, 'Middleman: a partial autobiography', which he vainly hoped to see published. He had known D. W. Winnicott and had always been interested in psychoanalysis: he now addressed in writing a deep-seated unease about his accomplishments. In 1991 he moved from Jesus Lane in Cambridge to be near his son and daughter-in-law in Durham, where Benjamin Knights, also a literary scholar and author of a book about the literary intelligentsia of the nineteenth century, was a lecturer in adult education.

Knights was tall and bony with a deceptive air of fragility but, until his last years, he took stairs at a run. He had to wear thick-lensed spectacles, and after an unsuccessful retina operation to his right eye, he wore a black patch which gave him a piratical appearance. He disdained material comfort.

Knights especially valued his relationship with his sister Kathleen who died in 1988. In the 1970s the Knightses had cared for Elizabeth's father; as Elizabeth's own infirmity increased, Knights looked after her at home until she went into residential care in 1993. L. C. Knights died at St Margaret's Nursing Home, St Margaret's Garth, Durham, on 8 March 1997.   IAN MACKILLOP

Sources personal knowledge (2004) · L. C. Knights, 'Middleman: a partial autobiography', MS autobiography, CUL · L. C. Knights, 'Viewpoint', *Cambridge Review* (Oct 1993), 136–8 · *Selwyn College Calendar* (1997–8) · 'Remembering *Scrutiny*', *Sewanee Review* (1981), 560–85 · *WW* (1990) · I. MacKillop, *F. R. Leavis: a life in criticism* (1995) · m. cert. · d. cert.
Archives CUL, MS, 'Middleman: a partial autobiography' · priv. coll., letters
Likenesses photograph, News International Syndication, London [*see illus.*]

Knights, Winifred Margaret (1899–1947). *See under* Monnington, Sir (Walter) Thomas (1902–1976).

Knijff, Leendert [*known as* Leonard Knyff] (1650–1722), painter, was born at Haarlem, Netherlands, on 10 August 1650, where he was baptized four days later. His mother was Lydia Leenderts of Delft, the widow of Jacob Bas of Haarlem; his father was Wouter Knijff (*b. c.*1607, *d.* after 1693), painter, born at Wesel, widower of Gerritje Jans van Houten. Leendert had two elder half-brothers, Jacobus and Johannes. Wouter Knijff specialized exclusively in river scenes, in a manner which owed much to Salomon van Ruysdael and Jan van Goyen. It has been suggested that Leendert studied with his father, but since the son's early speciality was the game piece, in the manner of Jan and Elias Vonck, it is perhaps more likely that he learned his art from a professional still-life painter. By 1681 Leendert was in London, living in the parish of St Martin-in-the-Fields. He returned to Holland in 1693 and again in

1695, when a pass was issued for 'Mr Leonard Knife, a protestant, to go to Harwich or Gravesend for Holland' (Honour, 337). Knijff was one of a number of resident aliens on whose behalf a warrant was sent to the attorney-general, on 8 June 1694, to prepare a bill for the great seal to make them 'free denizens of England' (ibid.). While in London, Knijff extended his repertoire, painting portraits such as the massive (265 × 276 cm) *Viscount Irwin* (1700; Temple Newsam House, Leeds); animal portraits including *The Dog 'Caper'* (Christies, 20 November 1981); animal fancy pieces, for example *Greyhound Catching a Hare* (1697; Temple Newsam House) and *Pugs, Greyhound and Spaniel with Dead Game* (1698, priv. coll.); and topographical landscapes, consisting largely of bird's-eye views of English country estates. Only a few painted landscapes by Knijff have survived; these include *Windsor Castle* and *Hampton Court from the East*, both in the Royal Collection; his topographical work is known largely through drawings and prints. Many of his drawings were engraved by Jan Kip for volume 1 of *Britannia illustrata*, or *Nouveau théâtre de la Grande Bretagne*, published by David Mortier in 1708. A number of drawings connected with this publication are preserved in the British Museum, including works such as *Hampton Court from the South* not used by Kip. Knijff's landscape drawings reveal a diligent eye for detail but a mediocre grasp of perspective, and their main importance lies in their unique documentary value. As an artist his most successful works were always his still lifes of dead game such as *Dead Birds* in the Bredius Museum, The Hague, and the splendid *Dogs, Dead Peacock and Game* (Christies, 24 February 1939). Knijff married rather late in life, on 26 February 1708, Elizabeth Cox; the couple had two children, Leonard and Lyddia. In financial terms he seems to have done quite well for himself; when he came to draw up his will on 16 April 1722 he could boast of 'being now possessed of One Thousand and seven hundred pounds more or less in the stock of the South Sea Company' (will, PROB 11/588, fols. 272v–273r). In his directions for the dispersal of his fortune he showed a precise interest in money which suggests the avid investor. His executors were John Boulter and John Coushmaker; Knijff gave each of them 'Twenty Pounds for Mourning, and two pictures a piece such as they shall choose out of those of mine own paintings' (ibid.). The witnesses included Clara Roestraten, widow of the still-life painter Pieter van Roestraten. The will was not proved until 22 December 1722, an unusually long delay, since Knijff was buried in the New Chapel, Broadway, in the parish of St Margaret's Westminster, on 24 April 1722. In May 1723 his pictures were auctioned off, in accordance with his will, to provide funds for the education of his children. When his widow, Elizabeth, came to draw up her will on 31 July 1742 she made no mention of her son, which perhaps suggests that he was no longer alive, and she said that her daughter was dead. The bulk of her estate was left to Lyddia's son, James Ratcliffe. Elizabeth was buried on 10 July 1747, 'in the Chappell in the Broad Way Westminster as near my late husband deceased as conveniently may'.

PAUL TAYLOR

Sources H. Honour, 'Leonard Knyff', *Burlington Magazine*, 96 (1954), 335–8 · will, PRO, PROB 11/588, sig. 240 · will of Elizabeth Knijff, PRO, PROB 11/755, sig. 184 · parish register, St Margaret's, Westminster, 24 April 1722 [burial] · *IGI* · A. van der Willigen, *Les artistes de Harlem* (1870) · [L. Knyff and J. Kip], *Nouveau théâtre de la Grande Bretagne* (1708); facs edn with a new introduction, notes, and index as *Britannia illustrata: Knyff and Kip*, ed. J. Harris and G. Jackson-Stops (1984) [facs. of *Nouveau théâtre de la Grande Bretagne*, London, 1708] · Thieme & Becker, *Allgemeines Lexikon* · S. A. Sullivan, *The Dutch gamepiece* (1984) · 'Knijff (3) Leaonard Knyff', *The dictionary of art*, ed. J. Turner (1996)

Wealth at death approx. £1700—in South Sea stock; house, goods, and paintings: will, PRO, PROB 11/588, sig. 240

Knill, Richard (1787–1857), missionary, fourth child of Richard Knill, carpenter (d. 15 December 1826), and his wife, Mary Tucker (d. 1826), was born at Braunton, near Barnstaple, Devon, on 14 April 1787. In 1804 he enlisted as a soldier, but was soon afterwards bought out by his friends. He became a student of the Western Academy at Axminster in 1812, and under the influence of a sermon by Dr Alexander Waugh volunteered for missionary work. He was accepted by the London Missionary Society, and embarked for Madras on 20 April 1816. There he took services in English, while studying the native languages. His health soon failed, and he was sent in September 1818 to Nagercoil in Travancore, from where, after suffering from cholera, he returned to England on 30 November 1819. A cold climate was recommended for his health, so he sailed on 18 October 1820 for St Petersburg, intending to go to Siberia as a missionary, but British and American missionaries persuaded him to remain in that city. His mission had some success and obtained the support of the tsar and the royal family. A Protestant Bible Society was formed for supplying the Bible in their own tongues to Germans, Finns, Poles, Livonians, and other persons not belonging to the Greek church. A school was opened for the children of foreigners, and a mission to the sailors at Kronstadt established. On 9 January 1823 he married Sarah, daughter of James and Isabella Notman of St Petersburg, with whom he had five children.

On his return to England in August 1833 to obtain funds for building a larger church in St Petersburg, Knill was so successful a fund-raiser for the London Missionary Society that he was asked to remain at home, and for eight years he travelled widely in the United Kingdom, pleading the claims of the foreign missions. Exhausted by these labours, he on 1 January 1842 settled down as Congregational minister at Wotton under Edge, Gloucestershire, where he remained until he moved to Chester in 1848. His last days were some of the best of his career, and his preaching in the Chester Theatre for twenty Sunday afternoons was most successful. Few men of his time had greater mastery over large groups of people. Knill published a number of works on religion and missions, including *The Happy Death-Bed* (1833) and *A Dialogue between a Romish Priest and R. Knill, Missionary* (1841). He died at 28 Queen Street, Chester, on 2 January 1857.

G. C. BOASE, *rev.* H. C. G. MATTHEW

Sources R. Knill, *The life of the Rev. Richard Knill, of St Petersburg*, ed. C. M. Birrell (1859) · *Congregational Year Book* (1857), 212–14 · 'Memoir of the late Rev. Richard Knill', *Evangelical Magazine and Missionary Chronicle*, new ser., 35 (1857), 137–45 · *The Nonconformist* (7 Jan 1857) · *The Nonconformist* (14 Jan 1857) · *Chester Chronicle* (3 Jan 1857) · *Chester Chronicle* (10 Jan 1857) · Boase, *Mod. Eng. biog.*
Likenesses two portraits, repro. in *The life of the Rev. Richard Knill, of St Petersburg*, new edn, ed. C. M. Birrell and J. A. James (1978)

Knipe, Thomas (1638/9–1711), headmaster, was born in Middlesex, probably in Westminster, the son of Thomas Knipe, a clergyman, whose wife may have been called Anne. He was educated at Westminster School, admitted a scholar on Archbishop John Williams's foundation in 1652 and captain of the king's scholars in 1656. In 1657 he was elected to a scholarship at Christ Church, Oxford, but did not matriculate until 31 July 1658. He graduated BA on 22 February 1661 and proceeded MA on 1 December 1663. From 1661 Knipe was employed as usher at his old school. In 1663 he became second master there under Richard Busby, who is said to have appreciated Knipe's merits. Knipe married twice. His first wife was Anne, daughter of Devereux Wolseley, of Ravenstone, Staffordshire, and sister or sister-in-law of Thomas Sprat, dean of Westminster from 1683 and bishop of Rochester from 1684; she died on 24 August 1685. His second wife, whom he married in 1694 when she was aged thirty-five, was Alice Talbot (*d*. 1723), a widow, of St Margaret's parish. Knipe's son Richard, Busby's godson, became high bailiff of Westminster in 1692, and Knipe himself became head master by patent dated 6 April 1695, the day of Busby's death. He proceeded BD and DD the following 3 July. Although scarcely so formidable as his predecessor, he was respected by his pupils, who included two future prime ministers (Henry Pelham and his brother Thomas Pelham-Holles, duke of Newcastle) and two who almost held that office (William Pulteney and John Carteret, Lord Granville). A letter from Knipe to Lord Herbert of Cherbury, whose son Henry was at Westminster, and 'stood in the yard, crying, and blubbering, and roaring' (Warner, 1.164), shows that he was a strict disciplinarian, but he lacked the dynamism for the major building work then necessary.

Knipe's head mastership saw the revival of the Latin play after a lapse of some years. He also published Greek and Hebrew grammars for the use of Westminsters—an edition of the Greek grammar of Apollodorus Atheniensis (1686) and *Hebraicae grammatiicæ rudimenta* (1708). He had some part in, and is indeed said to have been the author of, *Grammatica Busbeiana auctior et emendatior* (1702). The *Graecae linguae dialecti in usum scholae Westmonasteriensis* (1706) of Michel Maittaire had a commendatory preface by Knipe and he was himself the dedicatee of *An Historical Account of the Heathen Gods and Heroes* (1710) by William King, an Old Westminster.

On 13 October 1707 Knipe was presented to a canonry of Westminster, and installed on 17 October. He died at Hampstead on 5 or 6 August 1711, in his seventy-third year. He was buried beside his first wife and several of his children on 9 August in the north cloister of Westminster Abbey; a monument was put up to him in the south aisle by his widow, Alice, who received by his will a £100 annuity. This and other bequests—£50 annuities to his grandsons Richard and Thomas Knipe and £1500 to his granddaughter Anne Knipe (for which his nephew Thomas Sprat was a trustee)—reveal that he had accumulated a comfortable wealth.   C. S. KNIGHTON

Sources *Old Westminsters*, 1.545 · Foster, *Alum. Oxon.* · J. Sargeaunt, *Annals of Westminster School* (1898), 142, 235–8 · L. E. Tanner, *Westminster School* (1934), 23 · *Fasti Angl., 1541–1857*, [Ely], 87 · *A biographical history of England, from the revolution to the end of George I's reign: being a continuation of the Rev. J. Granger's work*, ed. M. Noble, 2 (1806), 119–20 · R. Warner, ed., *Epistolatory curiosities*, 2 pts in 1 (1818), 1.163–5 · J. L. Chester, ed., *The marriage, baptismal, and burial registers of the collegiate church or abbey of St Peter, Westminster*, Harleian Society, 10 (1876), 69, 185, 213–4, 226, 253–4, 272, 308, 316 · W. King, *An historical account of the heathen gods and heroes* (1710); new edn with introduction by H. R. Williamson (1965), 9–10 · PRO, PROB 11/522, fols. 209*v*–210*r*
Likenesses Michael Dahl, portrait, 1696 · J. Smith, mezzotint, 1712 (after M. Dahl, 1696), BM, NPG; copy, Westminster School
Wealth at death comfortable: will, PRO, PROB 11/522, fols. 209*v*–210*r*

Knipp, Elizabeth [Mary] (*d*. 1680x82), actress and singer, performed with the King's Company in London shortly after the Restoration. Nothing is known of her before then. Her first name may have been either Elizabeth (as she appears on a lord chancellor's warrant of 1672) or Mary (as she is named in a poem by Sir Charles Sedley). Her husband was Christopher Knipp, and they are probably the Christopher Knipp and Elizabeth Carpenter who were married at Knightsbridge Chapel in 1659. Their possible children appear in the parish registers of St Paul's, Covent Garden, St Clement Danes, and St Giles-in-the-Fields: Ursula (*bap*. 26 Dec 1663), 'Samuell Son of Christopher Nepp' (*bur*. 16 July 1666), Catherine (*bur*. 20 July 1667), and Mary (*bap*. 7 June 1672). Mrs Knipp certainly lost an infant son at the time that Samuel was buried; she had a young daughter, 'mighty pretty and witty', alive in February 1667 (Pepys, 8.57).

Mrs Knipp is known primarily through the diary of Samuel *Pepys. His first reference to her is on 6 December 1665, when he sees 'Knipp, who is pretty enough, but the most excellent, mad-hum[ou]red thing; and sings the noblest that ever I heard in my life' (Pepys, 6.321). He often praises her singing: he writes on 2 January 1667 that he saw Fletcher and Massinger's *The Custom of the Country*, 'wherein Knipp does the Widow well; but of all the plays that ever I did see, the worst, having neither plot, language, nor anything in the earth that is acceptable. Only, Knipp sings a little song admirably' (ibid., 8.3). She often danced, sang, or both between acts of plays.

Mrs Knipp's earliest role may have been Lusetta in Thomas Killigrew's *Thomaso*, in November 1664. In tragedy, Mrs Knipp played Alibech in Dryden's *The Indian Emperor* (1665) and Felicia in his *Tyrannic Love* (1669), and Aglave in Nathaniel Lee's *Sophonisba* (1675); in comedy, she played Otrante in Richard Rhodes's *Flora's Vagaries* (1667), and characters in three of Wycherley's comedies: Lady Fidget in *The Country Wife* (1675), Lady Flippant in *Love in a*

Wood (1671), and Eliza in *The Plain Dealer* (1676). She consistently appears in cast lists as secondary, supporting characters.

Her singing and acting were avenues to a greater intimacy between Pepys and Knipp. On 2 January 1666, he writes of 'my dear Mrs. Knipp, with whom I sang; and in perfect pleasure I was to hear her sing, and especially her little Scotch song of *Barbary Allen*' (Pepys, 7.1). Several days later she signs her letter to him as Bab Allen; he responds as Dapper Dicky. The second of January was also their first recorded physical encounter: 'so I got into the coach where Mrs. Knipp was, and got her upon my knee (the coach being full) and played with her breasts and sung' (ibid., 7.2). Their first sexual intercourse may have been in April 1668. That he much admired her beauty is evident from an entry dated 17 August 1667: 'I was pleased to see … her come out in her night-gowne, with no locks on, but her bare face and hair only tied up in a knot behind; which is the comeliest dress that ever I saw her in to her advantage' (Pepys, 8.388–9). He expresses disgust at the mean circumstances in which she lived and wrote that 'she lives a sad life with that ill-natured fellow her husband', who, he states, 'is a kind of Jocky', that is, a horse-trader (ibid., 7.5; 9.391).

In October 1668, after jealousy and irritation, Mrs Pepys finally required Pepys to forgo seeing Mrs Knipp. Pepys promised, but then struggled with his vow and limited his visits to the King's Company theatre to avoid encountering the actress. After this, little is recorded about Mrs Knipp except for her stage performances. She was arrested for unidentified 'misdemeanors' in February 1668 and again in April 1668. Her last recorded performance was as Mrs Dorothy in D'Urfey's *Trick for Trick* in March 1678. She probably joined the group of players who headed to Edinburgh in 1680. Pepys had recorded seeing Knipp with the actor Joseph *Haines (*d.* 1701) in May 1668, and a 1682 manuscript poem in the British Library by Haines states that she had died giving birth to their daughter there: 'To Madam Gwin, a Rhymeing Supplication' states that Knipp is 'In Child birth from mee to Lizeum departed' (Cameron, 'Jo Haynes, *Infamis*', 63). No other evidence exists to indicate that she returned to London or that her acting career continued after 1682.

CHERYL WANKO

Sources Highfill, Burnim & Langhans, *BDA* · W. Van Lennep and others, eds., *The London stage, 1660–1800*, pt 1: *1660–1700* (1965) · Pepys, *Diary* · K. M. Cameron, 'Jo Haynes, *Infamis*', *Theatre Notebook*, 24 (1969–70), 56–67 · J. Milhous and R. D. Hume, eds., *A register of English theatrical documents, 1660–1737*, 1 (1991) · K. M. Cameron, 'The Edinburgh theatre, 1668–1682', *Theatre Notebook*, 18 (1963–4), 18–25

Knobel, Edward Ball (1841–1930), chemist and astronomer, was born on 21 October 1841 at 24 Upper Baker Street, Marylebone, Middlesex, the son of William Edward Knobel, a solicitor at Lincoln's Inn Fields, and his wife, Emily, *née* Roberts. He was educated at La Capelle in France and subsequently at Stockwell grammar school, London. After leaving school Knobel studied law for two years but in 1861 abandoned the subject and entered the Royal School of Mines to study geology. He completed two years of the three-year course with distinction but was then advised by Professor A. W. Hoffman to apply for a post as an analytical chemist with Bass & Co., the brewers at Burton upon Trent. Knobel was employed by the brewery for thirteen years, rising to become manager and head brewer.

In 1869 he married Margaret, daughter of Henry Whitehead, a solicitor, and they enjoyed a happy partnership until her death in 1922. They had two sons and two daughters, who survived both parents.

In 1875 Knobel was appointed manager and chief dye chemist to Courtaulds at Bocking in Essex, a post he occupied with distinction for seventeen years. In 1892 he offered his services as a scientific expert to Alfred Harman, owner of the Britannia Works Company Ltd, a successful photographic materials manufacturer. Knobel joined the company on 23 June 1893. Within a week he was appointed a director and eighteen months later, when Harman retired due to ill health, became managing director. Knobel's rapid advancement may be partly explained by the suggestion that he was distantly related to Harman's wife, but there is no doubt that he was an outstanding man. For five years he was the only scientist on the staff and he made major technical and economic contributions. During this period the company prospered to the extent that in 1897 the profit was 50 per cent higher than in 1892. In 1898 Harman sold the business although he retained shares in the new company, which was renamed Ilford, Limited in 1900. Knobel retained his position as managing director and, with Harman, supported an amalgamation with Kodak suggested by George Eastman in 1902. This move was opposed by the shareholders and, seeking opportunities to develop markets in other ways, Knobel travelled to Japan in 1906 to explore the possibilities of opening a subsidiary company. The venture was a failure and within two months he returned home. In subsequent discussions Knobel complained of the board's lack of co-operation. The board vigorously denied the accusation and in 1907, after failing to secure his resignation, dismissed him, bringing his significant business career to a close.

Knobel made notable contributions to astronomy, although the work was largely carried out in his spare time. He was a keen astronomical observer during his years in Burton and in 1873 published papers illustrated by sketches of Jupiter and Mars. In a minor way he was an inventor, his astrometer and observing seat for reflecting telescopes being shown at the 1876 exhibition. Two of Knobel's astrometers are preserved in the Science Museum astronomy collection. His move to Essex in 1875 prevented further work as an observer. Instead, he began to study astronomical bibliography and concentrated on this area for the remainder of his life, publishing numerous papers. He became an authority on Arabic and Persian manuscripts and produced commentaries on aspects of the star catalogues of Uluǧ Beg, al-Sufi, and al-Achasi. Perhaps his most notable contribution dates from 1915. Continuing work begun by the German-American astronomer, C. H. F. Peters, he produced an edition of Ptolemy's star catalogue which involved collating Greek, Latin, and Arabic manuscripts. An edition of Uluǧ Beg's catalogue followed in 1917, derived from thirty translations of Persian manuscripts. Knobel made a major contribution to the administration of the Royal Astronomical Society. He was elected to the council in 1876 and served continuously until his death, except for one year, 1922–3. He was twice president (1892–3 and 1900–01), served for fifteen years as treasurer (1895–1900 and 1913–22) and ten as secretary (1882–92). He was vice-president at the time of his death. In recognition of his services to astronomy he was awarded the honorary degree of DSc at Oxford in 1927.

Knobel was a man of many interests. As an accomplished musician and violinist, he served on the council of the Queen's Hall Concert Society and played in festival performances at the Crystal Palace for twenty-three years. He was a fellow of the Geological Society for twenty-five years, received the honorary freedom of the Spectacle Makers' Company in 1899, and was a frequent visitor to Lord's cricket ground. For many years he was one of the Admiralty's appointed visitors to Royal Greenwich Observatory.

Knobel died on 25 July 1930 at his home, 32 Tavistock Square, London, at the age of eighty-eight. His funeral took place at Golders Green crematorium on 29 July, when, together with members of the family, the mourners included the astronomer royal, Sir Frank Dyson, and the Admiralty's representative, Admiral Sir Herbert Purey-Cust.   JOHN WARD

Sources R. J. Hercock and G. A. Jones, *Silver by the ton: the history of Ilford Limited, 1879–1979* (1979) · *Monthly Notices of the Royal Astronomical Society*, 91 (1930–31), 318–21 · *The Times* (28 July 1930), 14 · *Nature*, 126 (1930), 249 · R. J. Hercock, 'Knobel, Edward Ball', *DBB* · P. J. T. Morris and C. A. Russell, *Archives of the British chemical industry, 1750–1914: a handlist* (1988) · *History of the Royal Astronomical Society*, [1]: 1820–1920, ed. J. L. E. Dreyer and H. H. Turner (1923) · *Catalogue of the special loan collection of scientific apparatus at the South Kensington Museum*, 3rd edn (1877), 406, 438 · *British Journal of Photography* (1 Aug 1930), 468 · *The Times* (30 July 1930), 15 · *The Times* (25 Sept 1930), 15 · d. cert.
Archives Essex RO, notebooks | Essex RO, Ilford Limited Archives · RAS, letters to Royal Astronomical Society · Sci. Mus., Ilford MSS
Likenesses photograph, RAS
Wealth at death £9,279 11s. 6d.: probate, 4 Sept 1930, *CGPLA Eng. & Wales*

Knoblock [*formerly* Knoblaugh], **Edward** (1874–1945), playwright, was born at 60 West 17th Street, New York, on 7 April 1874, the fourth of the eleven children of Charles Knoblaugh, a wealthy businessman and a descendant of nineteenth-century immigrants from Germany. From the age of four he was given regular piano lessons by his mother: both his parents were accomplished musicians. In 1880 his mother died suddenly; his father remarried in 1885 but he too died in 1887. This drastically affected the

family's financial status and, constrained by real economic hardship, the stepmother took Charles Knoblaugh's children to Germany, where she was able to follow a career as a professional pianist. She was kind, and even indulgent, to the children but was severe with Edward in one particular respect: his penchant for improvisation on the piano. She believed he 'would do much better to play the music as it was written' (DLitB, 10.281). Little by little, Knoblaugh's piano-playing dwindled and diminished. He gradually forgot it and for the next two years pursued a happy enough life as a German schoolboy.

As early as 1886 Knoblaugh began to write plays, which he tried out on his family, using friends and relatives as 'actors'. In 1890 a major bequest from Edward's paternal uncle Henry, who died in that year, improved the family's financial situation. On the strength of this the Knoblaughs returned to the fashionable house in New York. At the age of seventeen Knoblaugh was advised by a professional dramatist to consider seriously the possibility of taking up playwriting as a career. The young man rejected the idea, saying that he had decided to train as an architect (which he viewed as a 'safer' profession). But a year later he changed his mind and announced to his family that he was going to be a playwright. His stepmother supported his decision but made one condition: that he should first obtain a university degree.

Knoblaugh enrolled at Harvard University in 1892 and graduated in 1896, having studied, among other things, playwriting and theatre history under George Pierce Baker. In August 1896, on the advice of Charles Frohman, Knoblaugh went to Paris to learn his trade. In the following year he went on to London, fell in love with the city and its theatres, and decided to make his permanent home there.

During the next dozen or so years Knoblaugh applied himself assiduously to his playwriting. He sent scripts to managers in both London and New York, but without any immediate results. He also made it his business to get to know as many theatre people as possible, not only for the purpose of soliciting their patronage but also in order to learn as much as he could about how theatres worked and, especially, what was required of a playwright. He offered scripts to both Henry Irving and Herbert Beerbohm Tree, but without success. He talked with Bernard Shaw, who, in 1899, gave him the tiny part of Jo in the first production of *You Never can Tell*. He made the acquaintance of Granville Barker, Somerset Maugham, and Lena Ashwell, who in New York in 1906 produced his first play, *The Shulamite*, and repeated its success at the Savoy Theatre in London later the same year. While in America with this production, Knoblaugh wrote *The Faun*, which played briefly in New York in 1909 and was revived in London in 1913. Meanwhile, he had written the one play for which he is now remembered: *Kismet*. Loosely based on *The Arabian Nights*, it was rejected by Tree in 1910 and by almost every manager in New York. Taken up, however, by Oscar Asche, it became an immediate and immense success in London after opening at the Garrick Theatre on 19 April 1911 with Oscar Asche and Lily Brayton, and subsequently in New

York with Otis Skinner and Rita Jolivet. *Kismet* held the stage for many years. In retrospect, however, Knoblock's best work might be judged to be three or four plays on which he collaborated with some other author. Especially notable is *Milestones* (1912). The plot and the organization of the piece were Knoblaugh's; the dialogue Arnold Bennett's.

Knoblaugh became a naturalized British citizen in 1914 and at the same time changed the spelling of his surname to Knoblock. He served in the British army with the intelligence service during the First World War. His volume of verse written on board a hospital ship, *Cot5*, was published in 1915 and he went on writing plays. One of these, *Tiger! Tiger!*, was produced at Ford's Theatre, Baltimore, on 4 November 1918.

After the war Knoblock divided his time between London and Hollywood, writing for the film company of Douglas Fairbanks and Mary Pickford. He adapted *The Three Musketeers* in 1921, wrote the film *Rosita* for Pickford, and was a consultant on Fairbanks's 1923 classic *The Thief of Baghdad*. He is credited with a number of other movie adaptations during the 1920s and 1930s, and *Kismet* was made into a film in 1930. During the 1930s, Knoblock again collaborated with Bennett on a dramatization of Bennett's novel *Mr Prohack* and with J. B. Priestley on a dramatization of *The Good Companions* (1931). Laurence Irving, in a memoir of his father and his grandfather—*The Precarious Crust*—ventures the opinion that Knoblock taught Bennett, Priestley, and others 'the rudiments of play carpentry' (Irving, 122). Other collaborative adaptations of novels were *Grand Hotel* (1931), with Vicki Baum, *Evensong* (1932), with Beverley Nichols, and *The Edwardians* (1937), with Vita Sackville-West.

Altogether, Knoblock wrote some thirty or forty plays, almost all of them performed in either London or New York (or both) between 1911 and 1945. Very few of them enjoyed later revivals. He also published four novels—*The Ant Heap* (1929), *The Man with Two Mirrors* (1931), *The Love Lady* (1933), and *Inexperience* (1941)—and *Round the Room: an Autobiography* (1939).

Always busy, always energetic, a conscientious mediocrity rather than a really distinguished writer, Knoblock nevertheless was always a person of determination and singleness of purpose. For many years he suffered from gradually failing health which in the final stages effectively prevented him from writing for the last six years or so of his life. He died at his sister's home, 21 Ashley Place, London, on 19 July 1945 at the age of seventy-one. He never married.

Kismet continued to be Knoblock's most popular work. In 1944 another film version starred Ronald Colman and Marlene Dietrich, while in the 1950s the play was the basis of a musical with a score adapted from Borodin. It won five Tony awards in 1954. This, too, was filmed in 1955, directed by Vincente Minnelli and starring Howard Keel and Ann Blyth.   ERIC SALMON

Sources J. Vere, ed., *Kismet and other plays by Edward Knoblock* (1957) • F. C. Brown, ed., *My lady's dress: a play by Edward Knoblock* (New York, 1911) • D. H. Laurence, ed., *Collected plays of Bernard Shaw* (Reinhardt, 1970) • S. Weintraub, ed., *Modern British dramatists, 1900–1945*, DLitB, 10 (1982), 279–88 • L. Irving, *The precarious crust* (1971) • E. Knoblock, *Round the room: an autobiography* (1939) • *The Times* (20 July 1945) • d. cert.

Archives Harvard U., Houghton L., corresp. and papers • University of Rochester, New York, Rush Rhees Library, corresp. and papers | BL, letters to Roger Quilter, Add. MS 70598 • JRL, letters to Basil Dean and Alex Rea • TCD, letters to James O'Hannay

Likenesses two photographs, repro. in DLitB

Wealth at death £11,821 1*s*. 5*d*.: probate, 29 Oct 1945, *CGPLA Eng. & Wales*

Knock, visionaries of (*act.* 1879), numbered more than a dozen local people who, about sundown on Thursday 21 August 1879, reported a complex supernatural apparition at the gable of the church at Knock, a poor rural village in co. Mayo in western Ireland. The central figure was the Virgin Mary, crowned and praying; she was flanked by St Joseph and St John the Evangelist. On an altar to these figures' left was a lamb and a cross and the whole scene was surrounded by a brilliant silvery-white light. The vision persisted for several hours, the life-size personages neither moving nor speaking. The first to see it summoned others, and all who came saw it, although not everybody saw all parts of the scene.

On 8 October 1879 fifteen witnesses gave depositions to an investigating commission of priests. Whether there were other seers is not clear. Those interviewed were subjected neither to intense ecclesiastical cross-examination nor to civil prosecution as happened at other apparition sites. Journalists who interviewed them later were generally more sympathetic than sceptical and, equally unusually, the local priest, who chaired the investigation, was an enthusiastic promoter.

Relatively little is known about the individual seers. Up to nine of those giving depositions were connected by ties of kinship. Many considered **Mary Beirne** [Byrne; *married name* O'Connell] (*c*.1850–1936) to have been the chief witness. Single and twenty-nine, the daughter of Dominic Beirne, she was living with her widowed mother, **Margaret Beirne** [*née* Bourke] (*c*.1810–1909), aged sixty-eight; her unmarried siblings **Margaret Beirne** (*c*.1858–1880) and **Dominick Beirne** (*c*.1858–1885), both in their early twenties; and her eight-year-old niece, **Catherine Murray** (1870/71–*c*.1882). All five were seers. Also present were **Dominick Beirne** (*c*.1843–1915), aged thirty-six, one of Mary's cousins; his five-year-old nephew, **John Curry** (*b*. 1873/4, *d*. in or after 1936), who lived with him; and their neighbour **Patrick Beirne** (*c*.1863–1943), aged sixteen, who was also probably a relative. Another Beirne cousin, **Patrick Hill** (*c*.1868–1927), aged eleven, gave the most detailed description of the apparition.

The Beirnes were described as honest, industrious, and respectable people, and Mary Beirne in particular was said to have been intelligent, forthcoming, earnest, and truthful. The main Beirne family were small tenant farmers in an area of small farms, poor soil, and abject poverty. To earn their rent, a majority of the men in the area worked as harvest labourers in England, and one Beirne son was on such a trip when the apparition occurred. Yet the family appeared better off than most of their neighbours:

reporters described their cottage as comfortable with 'substantial' furniture, and they could afford occasional visits to a seaside resort 40 miles away, perhaps visiting a relative who was a priest there.

Apart from a few whose families probably benefited from the pilgrim trade, the witnesses' unspectacular lives were outwardly generally unaffected by the apparition. Mary Beirne married a local man, James O'Connell (*d. c.*1926), on 1 July 1882; they had six children. Throughout her life she often told her story to pilgrims, and like the other surviving witnesses, John Curry and Patrick Beirne, repeated it to a second church inquiry shortly before her death in 1936. Her siblings did not long survive the apparition, Margaret dying in 1880 and Dominick in 1885, both of tuberculosis. Catherine Murray died at age eleven. The widowed Mrs Beirne lived to be ninety-eight, her house later catering to pilgrims. The elder Dominick Beirne continued as a farmer and cattle dealer; he had five children and died in 1915. By 1936 John Curry was living in a New York city home for the aged run by nuns. Patrick Beirne, allegedly drinking to excess and disagreeing with priests, later ran a grocery shop in Knock. Born about 1863, he married Rose Curry on 8 April 1911, was widowed in 1919, and died childless in the County Home, Castlebar, co. Mayo, in 1943. Patrick Hill married a local girl, Annie McNabb, on 16 October 1897; they had five children born between 1898 and 1907. By the time his wife died in 1917, Patrick had emigrated to Boston, Massachusetts, where he died in 1927.

Six people besides the Beirne relatives gave depositions. The priest's housekeeper, **Mary McLoughlin** (*d.* after 1904), was middle-aged and allegedly fond of alcohol. Although she lived in Knock for at least another quarter of a century, when or where she was born or died is not known. The same is true of **John Durkan** (*c.*1855–*c.*1925x35), a 'servant boy' estimated to be about twenty-four in 1879. Apparently he lived into his seventies but never married. **Bridget Trench** (*c.*1804–1886), aged seventy-four, lived seven more years; one sceptical priest alleged that she depended on the charity of neighbours. **Mrs Hugh Flatley** (*c.*1835–1923) outlived two husbands, and **Judith Campbell** (1857–1893) married a local man and had six children. **Patrick Walsh** (*b.* 1813x24), whose age was reported as both fifty-five and sixty-five, was a more substantial farmer than most in the area. Unlike the others he was not at the church gable; he testified that he saw a bright light at the church from his farm half a mile away. He had twelve children; three of his six sons became priests.

Press reports of the apparition began in January 1880 and quickly became extensive. Other visions, sometimes more elaborate, were reported in Knock and several other places in Ireland in the following months. Hundreds of reports were published of people being miraculously cured of various ailments through use of cement from Knock church. The publicity and the miracles brought throngs of pilgrims to Knock in the early 1880s but ever fewer came later. An attempt by Mary Francis Clare

*Cusack, the Nun of Kenmare, to found a convent in Knock in 1882–3 ended in controversy and failure.

A 1930s revival led by lay people and encouraged by the local priest and archbishop again turned Knock into a major pilgrimage site, and Knock became a centre of the pronounced Marianism in Irish Catholicism in the decades after the Second World War. The history of Knock paralleled developments on the European continent where a 1917 apparition at Fatima in Portugal, interpreted as anti-communist, led to numerous Marian apparitions, especially in the Cold War era, along with their associated pilgrimages and devotions. Following the Second Vatican Council in the 1960s, an interpretation of the apparition that had been present but secondary from the beginning was given greater prominence, one highlighting the altar, the cross, and the lamb. In the 1970s and 1980s Knock's position as one of the leading Marian shrines was reinforced and confirmed by a visit by Pope John Paul II in 1979, the building of a major basilica adjacent to the apparition church, and the opening nearby of an international airport.   EUGENE HYNES

Sources C. Rynne, *Knock, 1879–1979* (Dublin, 1979) · J. MacPhilpin, *The apparitions and miracles at Knock, also the official depositions of the eye-witnesses* (1880) · [T. Sexton], *The illustrated record of the apparitions at the church of Knock* (1880) [generally wrongly ascribed to T. D. Sullivan] · Sister Mary Francis Clare [M. A. Cusack], *Three visits to Knock, with the medical certificates of cures and authentic accounts of apparitions* [n.d., 1882?] · L. Ua Cadhain [W. Coyne], *Venerable Archdeacon Cavanagh, pastor of Knock (1867–1897)* (1953) · M. Walsh, *The apparition at Knock: a survey of facts and evidence* (1955) · Father F. Lennon to Father Cavanagh, 16 May 1880?, Archdiocesan archives, Bishop's Residence, Tuam · J. Donnelly, 'The Marian shrine of Knock: the first decade', *Éire–Ireland*, 28/2 (1993), 54–97 · W. Christian, 'Religious apparitions and the Cold War in southern Europe', *Religion, power and protest in local communities*, ed. E. R. Wolf (1984) · d. cert. [Mary Flatley]

Knolles, Richard (late 1540s–1610), historian and translator, was born some time in the late 1540s, probably at Cold Ashby, Northamptonshire, possibly the son of Francis Knolles (or Knowlis) of Cold Ashby. He entered Lincoln College, Oxford, where he graduated BA on 24 January 1565, probably in his late teens, and was elected to a fellowship. Remaining at Lincoln in an increasingly senior capacity, he proceeded MA on 4 July 1570, and from the evidence of his signature on college documents stayed there until at least August 1572. In 1576 he is recorded as returning to the college as a visitor. His post-Oxford career of more than thirty years was probably spent almost entirely as headmaster of the grammar school at Sandwich, Kent, founded by Sir Roger Manwood about 1563. In 1568 Manwood had established four scholarships at Lincoln College, two of which were reserved for pupils of his grammar school; he would have met Knolles during the administration of these scholarships. Documentary evidence shows that Knolles was still headmaster of the school in 1606, though he was then being pressed by the governors to retire on a pension due to a perceived lack of diligence in carrying out his teaching duties.

After Sir Roger Manwood's death in 1592, his son Sir

Peter became Knolles's patron in both a professional and a literary sense. Acquainted with many of the learned scholars of the period, and subsequently himself a member of the Society of Antiquaries, Sir Peter not only encouraged Knolles to write but was also in a position to obtain for him the loan of books, reports, and other source materials from Robert Cotton and others (BL, Cotton MS Julius C.III, fol. 225, records Knolles's acknowledgement to Cotton). Knolles produced three substantial pieces of work. He is best known for *The Generall Historie of the Turkes*, first published in 1603. Compiled from a range of Byzantine and western histories, travellers' reports and letters, together with material from Leunclavius's recent Latin translation of a late fifteenth-century Ottoman chronicle, Knolles's was the first major work on the subject to appear in English, and was quickly recognized as a masterpiece of narrative synthesis. There is no evidence that he had any original personal reason for choosing to write a history of the Ottomans; the suggestion came possibly from Sir Peter Manwood in the light of growing interest in the Ottoman state in London following the chartering in 1581 of the Turkey (subsequently Levant) Company and increased commercial and diplomatic relations with the empire. A second edition appeared in 1610, incorporating both a continuation of the history to 1609 (a total of 1296 folio pages) and, appended to the main narrative, Knolles's fifteen-page 'Discourse on the greatnesse of the Ottoman Turkes', analysing the strengths and weaknesses of the state.

As a compilation Knolles's work is of a piece with the then popular genre of 'generall histories' of various countries. It is, however, distinguished by an elegant and compelling style and by Knolles's underlying presentation of Ottoman success as being in large part 'the just and secret judgement of the Almightie' in the face of 'the smal care the Christian princes … have had of the common state of the Christian commonweale'. He repeatedly draws attention to the need for Christian unity to combat the Turks successfully, contrasting European disunity with 'a rare unitie and agreement' among the Ottomans in both religious and political affairs (introduction, Knolles, 1631 edn, ii). Subsequent editions in 1621, 1631, and 1638 included continuations by other writers: for 1609–20 by the translator and compiler Edward Grimeston; for 1620–28 based on the dispatches of Sir Thomas Roe, English ambassador in Constantinople, and containing translations of Ottoman diplomatic correspondence. The sixth edition of 1687–1700 was brought out by Sir Paul Rycaut, and is particularly valuable for the account of Rycaut's own residency in Constantinople from 1661 to 1667 as secretary to the English ambassador. A two-volume abridgement was issued in 1701 by John Savage. Knolles's literary style was admired by such writers as Johnson, who praises it in no. 122 of *The Rambler*, and Byron, and the work's reputation as an engrossing account survived well into the nineteenth century.

Knolles's second published work was his translation of Jean Bodin's *La république*, which appeared in 1606 as The *Six Bookes of a Commonweale*, dedicated to Sir Peter Manwood. Working critically from both French and Latin originals, Knolles produced not simply a translation but 'a work of independent judgement' (McRae, A38–39) which both illuminated textual difficulties in Bodin's texts and also showed how the latter's work could be understood by a near-contemporary English reader. No doubt it was in aid of such understanding that Knolles chose to translate *république* as 'commonweale', a term with familiar associations in England. Bodin's absolutist treatise was influential in seventeenth-century England, especially among royalists; however, Knolles's translation of it was not reprinted after 1606, which suggests it had only a limited role in circulating the Frenchman's ideas.

Knolles's third major undertaking was an unpublished translation from the Latin original of Camden's *Britannia*. This survives in the Bodleian Library (MS Ashmole 849), but remains little known. Knolles died in Sandwich and was buried there in St Mary's Church on 2 July 1610. He is not known to have married. CHRISTINE WOODHEAD

Sources R. Knolles and [E. Grimstone], *The generall historie of the Turkes*, 4th edn (1631) • K. D. McRae, introduction, in J. Bodin, *The six bookes of a commonweale*, ed. K. D. McRae (1962) • Wood, *Ath. Oxon.*, new edn, 2.79–83 • HoP, *Commons, 1558–1603* • W. Boys, *Collections for an history of Sandwich in Kent* (1792, [1892]) • S. Johnson, *The rambler*, 2, ed. W. J. Bate and A. B. Strauss (1969), 290–91 • *DNB*

Knolles [Knollys], **Sir Robert** (d. 1407), soldier, was probably the son of Richard, who was of burgess or yeoman stock from Tushingham in the parish of Malpas, Cheshire. His mother is frequently named as Eva Calveley, sister of Sir Hugh *Calveley, with whom Robert had a lifelong friendship. But no convincing proof of Eva's existence has ever been found, nor of a family relationship between Robert and Hugh, long professional brothers-in-arms, though their families were associated as early as 1354 when Sir John Wingfield granted Lea manor in Churton Heath, Cheshire, to Mabel Calveley and Henry Newton, chaplain, with remainders in tail to Hugh and David Calveley (both described as 'the elder'), and Robert, son of Richard Knolles.

Early career Knolles and Calveley first appear together in arms in documents relating to the siege of La Roche-Derrien in northern Brittany in 1346, when Knolles may have served as an archer under Calveley, probably his senior by a few years. But Knolles was already a knight when next glimpsed, in one of the most notable chivalric feats of the later middle ages, the battle of the Thirty (26 March 1351). This was fought between two teams representing the Anglo-Breton and Franco-Breton forces then disputing the succession to the Breton throne in a civil war that began after the death of Duke John (III) in 1341 without direct heirs. They agreed to joust à outrance, following a challenge by Jean de Beaumanoir, captain of Josselin, to the English captain of Ploërmel, whom he accused of mercilessly exploiting the local population. Combatants were killed on both sides and the rest wounded in a bitter contest in which the Anglo-Bretons were vanquished and both Calveley and Knolles made prisoner.

Sir Robert Knolles (d. 1407), boss, c.1420 [kneeling, left, with his wife, Constance (right), and the Trinity between]

Released shortly afterwards, Knolles soon amassed a considerable personal landed fortune in south-eastern Brittany and neighbouring Mayenne, while acknowledging allegiance to Edward III and his ward, John de Montfort. In February 1352 Edward III confirmed his possession of Le Grand Fougeray, between Nantes and Rennes, which he had recently captured. He also held Châteaublanc (Ille-et-Vilaine) and La Gravelle (Mayenne) through the 1350s. When Gui de Nesle, marshal of France, brought troops in support of Charles de Blois, Montfort's rival, in the summer of 1352, Knolles fought alongside Sir Walter Bentley, Edward's lieutenant in the duchy. At Mauron (Morbihan) on 14 August 1352, a shattering defeat was inflicted on the French by using a combination of dismounted men-at-arms and archers that had already proved effective in the Breton war and at Crécy (1346). Evidence for the moveable wealth Knolles had already amassed from his career is provided by a schedule of plate and other goods, drawn up at Sutton Vautort, Devon, forfeit when Knolles fell temporarily out of favour in 1354, probably for disobeying Bentley's successor, Thomas Holland. In 1355 Edward III also revoked an earlier grant of the castle of Pestivien (Côtes-d'Armor).

However, in June 1356 Knolles joined Henry, duke of Lancaster, with 300 men-at-arms and 500 archers drawn from Breton garrisons, contributing a third of Lancaster's force, in a *chevauchée* through Normandy in support of Godefroy de Harcourt and Philippe de Navarre that reached as far as Verneuil, before returning to base at the abbey of Montebourg in the Cotentin. Skirmishing around Rouen and a siege of Domfront followed. But Lancaster failed to link up with Edward, prince of Wales, who

had launched his own famous raid from Bordeaux that culminated in the battle of Poitiers, from which Knolles, unable to cross the Loire, was also absent, despite some reports to the contrary.

Knolles's next campaign with Lancaster was an unsuccessful siege of Rennes (October 1356–June 1357). When this was lifted, he led an attack on Honfleur in Normandy with Sir James Pipe, where according to the chronicler Henry Knighton, with some 600 men, they defeated Robert de Clermont, marshal of France, with 800 men-at-arms and 5000 infantry, killing at least 500, while another surprise attack resulted in the slaughter of a further 1000 Frenchmen. Whatever the exact figures or circumstances (much embroidered by chroniclers, who also mention Knolles at a siege of Dinan), it is in these years that he gained his reputation as 'the most able and skilful man of arms in all the companies' (*Chroniques de J. Froissart*, 5.366), cool, calculating, knowing when to retreat but striking with terrible effect.

Knolles in the Orléannais and Auvergne, 1358–1359 Knolles's reputation as 'a true demon of war' (Bridges, 178) was most spectacularly demonstrated in a great raid into the Orléannais and upper Loire region in autumn 1358 when he ostentatiously displayed a banner announcing:

> Qui Robert Canolle prendera,
> Cent mille moutons gagnera.
> (*Chroniques de J. Froissart*, 5.351)

He burnt the suburbs of Orléans, and, establishing himself at Châteauneuf-sur-Loire, ravaged the Auxerrois where numerous other English garrisons were living off the countryside, as they had been doing in Brittany and Normandy for years, and where the charred gables marking his progress became known as 'Knolles's mitres'. A first attack on Auxerre in January 1359 was repulsed, but on 10 March 1359 the town was delivered to him, despite the presence of a garrison under the renowned *routier* Arnaud de Cervole (the Archpriest). Among Knolles's companions on this occasion was Sir Thomas Fogg; he was later joined by Ieuan Wyn, known as the Poursuivant d'Amour, a famous Welsh mercenary, and by Calveley. On 30 April the Auxerrois agreed to pay 40,000 moutons and hand over pearls worth a further 10,000 moutons (approximately £10,000 in total) to be rid of Knolles.

Knolles now turned his attentions to the Auvergne, after apparently abandoning even more ambitious plans to attack the Comtat Venaissin, where Pope Innocent VI and his cardinals became highly alarmed at his progress when he was allegedly within twelve leagues of Avignon. Using Pont-du-Château as he had previously exploited Châteauneuf, Knolles raided widely in the Auvergne, taking Cusset, attacking St Pourçain, and even moving on Le Puy. On 25 June 1359 the townsmen of Millau in the Rouergue received letters warning them of his approach. But a counter-attack led by Thomas de la Marche, deputy of the dauphin, Charles, regent of France during the absence in prison of his father, Jean II, following his capture at Poitiers, forced a retreat after some captains accompanying Knolles went off independently. Burning Montbrison and sacking churches and abbeys around St Étienne, Knolles then began a staged withdrawal in which he was joined by Calveley, who had been fighting with other Anglo-Navarrese forces on the borders of Burgundy. Knolles passed through Limoges, and by the autumn was back in Brittany where he captured the future constable of France, Bertrand du Guesclin, who was establishing his own formidable credentials as a captain by similarly ruthless means.

The treaty of Brétigny–Calais (May–October 1360) brought the first phase of the Hundred Years' War to a close and temporarily restricted opportunities for freebooters like Knolles. He was confirmed in possession of his French estates, visited England, obtained a pardon for any crimes committed abroad, sat in the court of chivalry, and regularized the payments he owed Edward III for his castles in France. But by October 1361 he was clearly tired of inactivity since he is reported fighting in Savoy, *en route* for Italy with Sir John Hawkwood and Annechin de Bongarden, though little appears to be known about his actions there. By 1363 he was back in Brittany, serving at the relief of Bécherel in June, and accompanying John de Montfort to Poitiers in November, when the prince of Wales tried to negotiate a peaceful end to the Breton civil war by bringing the two rivals together. When discussions finally broke down in February 1364, following another meeting at Poitiers attended by Knolles, preparations began for the inevitable military campaign that was to follow. In March 1364, Montfort conferred on him the lordships of Derval and Rougé (Loire-Atlantique), whose rightful owner had been a prisoner since the battle of Poitiers. As the Breton rivals manoeuvred for advantage in the summer, Knolles brought a force of 900 or 1000 men to Montfort's siege of Auray (Morbihan). He then fought, under the overall command of Sir John Chandos, in the vanguard of the Anglo-Breton army, which inflicted a crushing defeat on Charles de Blois as he attempted to lift the siege. Blois himself was killed on the field (29 September 1364) and Knolles took several prisoners, including the count of Auxerre. In April 1365, by the first treaty of Guérande, Charles V finally acknowledged John de Montfort as duke of Brittany.

Middle years With his wife, Constance, to whom he was married by 1355, and who hailed from Yorkshire, though she had spent much of the previous decade in Brittany, whence she sometimes personally led small contingents of English troops, Knolles briefly settled down to enjoy his Breton estates and his prominent position at the ducal court. In 1365 he negotiated the return of La Gravelle, Segré, and Ingrande (Mayenne) to Amaury de Craon for 10,000 livres and arranged an exchange of Châteaublanc and Fougeray with John de Montfort for an annual rent of 2000 livres on the lordships of Conq (Concarneau) and Rosporden (Finistère), though he retained Derval and Rougé, which should have returned to their lord under the peace of Guérande, despite his protests. Knolles was, however, forced to disgorge some profits from the raid of 1358–9, in his search for respectability and social acceptance, by repaying some of the 40,000 moutons Auxerre had agreed to pay, in exchange for a papal pardon. On 4

August 1366 the abbot of St Aubin d'Angers was ordered to return jewels, relics, and other goods which he had deposited at the abbey to St Germain d'Auxerre.

Early in 1367 Edward, the Black Prince, summoned Knolles to join his expedition to Spain in support of Pedro the Cruel of Castile. After crossing the Pyrenees via Roncevalles, he reconnoitred around Navaretta in February and March with Sir William Felton. But he escaped the skirmish in which Felton was killed and fought on the left wing at Nájera (3 April 1367), before returning to Brittany. At Candlemas 1368 he was at Dinan (Côtes-d'Armor) when, in a celebrated incident, John de Montfort's efforts to expunge a painting of his late rival, Blois, from the walls of the Dominican friary resulted in an apparently miraculous occurrence, as drops of blood seeped through whitewash used to obliterate the image. Witnesses later recalled that Knolles (who, according to the Chandos herald, was a man of few words), berated those collecting the liquid for their credulity: 'Countryfolk and villeins, do you believe he was a saint? By St George, you lie, you idiots! He was no saint!' (Plaine and Serent, 283). In March 1368 Knolles had a further protection to come to England with his wife and an entourage of sixty persons. From this period he began acquiring manors in Norfolk where he eventually retired. At the same time, he also cast envious eyes on an even more prestigious lordship, the *vicomté* of Limoges, held by the widow of Charles de Blois, but at the time still under the Black Prince's dominion, which he attempted to purchase.

At the end of 1368 Knolles was again campaigning in the Rouergue. After bringing reinforcements from Brittany in the spring of 1369, he waged war in the Cahorsin between May and July, besieging Domme and attacking Rocamadour and Villefranche, before joining the earls of Cambridge and Pembroke in Poitou. He was at the Black Prince's court at Angoulême in January 1370 and at the relief of Belleperche, before returning once more to Derval, from whence he was summoned to England by Edward III.

The expedition of 1370 Since the reopening of the war with France in 1369, the English had recorded no major successes. It was decided early in 1370 that a large expedition should be launched which for the first time was to be commanded by a captain below the rank of earl. It was for this task that Knolles was chosen. The original intention seems to have been to give him sole charge of a force to invade Normandy in June and link up with Charles II of Navarre, with whom negotiations were in train. But delays and growing criticism of the decision to appoint Knolles to such a high command forced a change of plan. This had disastrous consequences. On 13 June Knolles agreed terms with Sir Alan Buxhull, Sir Thomas Grandison, and Sir John Bourchier, who were now to share command with him, over the division of their expected profits. On 20 June Knolles sealed an indenture to serve with 2000 men-at-arms and 2000 archers for two years, with permission to fight anywhere in France outside Aquitaine. On 5 July he appeared before the king's council to agree these terms, as the other captains did in the next few days.

Ships (under John, Lord Neville, and the admiral, Ralph Ferrers), troops, and supplies had been gathering for some weeks and by 22 July, Knolles, his men, and horses (some 8464 in total), were ready to set out from Calais, having crossed from Winchelsea and Rye.

Spreading out into smaller bands and marching in roughly parallel lines, Knolles's troops pillaged their way through Picardy, Champagne, and the Île-de-France into Normandy, the Chartrain, the Vendômois, and Maine in the next five months, inflicting much superficial damage but avoiding sieges of major strong points, for instance, bypassing Rheims and Paris, though Knolles tried on several occasions to offer battle. By the autumn disagreements among the commanders, all of whom felt socially superior to Knolles, and, in the case of Sir John Minsterworth (who called Knolles 'an old brigand'), even hints of treasonable communication with the enemy, together led to a complete breakdown in discipline and the disintegration of the army. Knolles himself eventually found refuge at his castle of Derval, some men later returning to England from western Breton ports, while another division, under Thomas Grandison, after hot pursuit, was finally defeated by du Guesclin at Pontvallain, 30 kilometres south of Le Mans, on 4 December 1370. For the first time, the French army had effectively employed the Fabian tactics that allowed Charles V in the next few years to regain most of the territory lost before 1360: it had shadowed the invading force, picked off stragglers, and avoided full-scale battle by withdrawing to well-defended towns whenever the English approached.

In the recriminations that followed this disaster (for a time it was believed that Knolles had perished, and his attempt to assuage Edward III with a large sum of money was foiled when most of it was embezzled by William, Lord Latimer), Edward III seized Knolles's properties in England. For several years he was out of favour, serving the Black Prince in Gascony or guarding his interests in Brittany. However, worsening relations between John de Montfort and his nobility placed these in jeopardy and in May 1373 Charles V declared the lordships of Rougé and Derval forfeit after du Guesclin had overrun all the duchy except Brest Castle. Here Knolles was captain for Montfort, who had fled into exile in England. He was besieged in June; terms and hostages for the delivery of Brest to du Guesclin were agreed in July, but aid provided by the earl of Salisbury, cruising in the channel, allowed Knolles to renege. He also disavowed a similar agreement by his lieutenant, Hugh Browe, to deliver Derval to the French in the autumn though, unlike Brest, it did eventually fall in 1374. Knolles also gained more experience of naval warfare: Walsingham reports him attacking Spanish shipping off Sluys in 1374; a ship owned by him was lost off Purbeck while carrying his goods from Plymouth to London in 1371; and in autumn 1377 he was in the fleet sent to the relief of Brest under Thomas of Woodstock, earl of Buckingham.

On land, Knolles campaigned in the Cotentin in June 1374 where the English still held St Sauveur-le-Vicomte,

shortly before it was besieged by the admiral of France, Jean de Vienne, though it resisted for almost a year before falling. Knolles may also have fought around Niort (Deux-Sèvres) in this period, finally receiving a full pardon for the expedition of 1370. He continued to consolidate his English estates, investing not only in rural properties in Norfolk, Kent, and Wiltshire, but establishing strong links with leading citizens of London, where he acquired extensive possessions, including the manor of St Pancras and houses and shops in Islington, Kentish Town, and the parishes of All Hallows, Barking, and St Giles Cripplegate.

During the Anglo-French truces of 1374–7 Knolles acted as a conservator, and was involved both as a defendant and as a commissioner in further court of chivalry cases. But as soon as the truces expired, he was to the fore in military affairs. He was appointed captain of Brest once more in January 1378, from where he attacked John de Montfort's domestic enemies. He continued in office for a short period after the duke agreed to deliver the castle officially into English keeping in April 1378, but was replaced in June 1378, only to raid Harfleur with Richard (III) Fitzalan, earl of Arundel, and then accompany John of Gaunt, duke of Lancaster, in his siege of St Malo in August. If not already one of Gaunt's retainers, Knolles subsequently received an annual fee from him as he had from the Black Prince. A domestic moment is revealed about 1 October 1378, when he dined congenially with John de Montfort at Cheshunt, Hertfordshire, one of the manors that Richard II had delivered in exchange for Brest. In February 1379 Knolles was appointed along with Sir John Cobham, Robert Bealknap, and others, including Sir Thomas Fogg and Sir John Devereux, with whom he had frequently campaigned in France, to guard the coasts of Kent. He went back to Brittany with Montfort in the summer, when the Breton nobility suddenly relented and asked the duke to return to his throne. After returning to England in 1380, he was retained as one of Buckingham's captains for another great *chevauchée*, with a retinue of 140 men-at-arms and 240 archers. They left Calais almost exactly ten years to the day after the expedition of 1370.

Buckingham's army took an almost identical route to that of 1370 through northern-eastern France, before sweeping westwards around Paris, reaching Nantes in October. Here a siege was laid on behalf of John de Montfort against his most stubborn domestic opponent, Olivier, lord of Clisson, who had just succeeded du Guesclin as constable of France, following the latter's death in July 1380. The siege was long and ultimately unsuccessful, with winter weather causing much sickness among the besiegers. There was also growing tension between Montfort and his English allies, as he secretly negotiated terms with the French, finally ratified in the second treaty of Guérande in April 1381. To pacify Buckingham and his lieutenants, who reluctantly agreed to return to England, Montfort had to make substantial payments, though it is not clear what Knolles's share was. He was back in England, however, in time to take a characteristically robust part in suppressing the peasants' revolt. In order to disperse the mob, one chronicler reports that Knolles counselled Richard II to issue a proclamation on 13 June stating that Gaunt (who had been in Scotland on a diplomatic mission) was approaching London with a large force, while on 14 June Knolles was with the king at Mile End, when he met the rebels. On 15 June, after William Walworth killed Wat Tyler in Richard's presence at Smithfield, Knolles brought soldiers whom he had been gathering in the city to surround the leaderless rebels, a move that appears carefully co-ordinated with Walworth's actions, though Richard succeeded in persuading them to disperse without the need for Knolles to exercise force. This timely service earned Knolles the freedom of the city, a title he proudly boasted in his wills, as well as other rewards. There was one final campaign in 1383 with Bishop Despenser to Flanders, though he was appointed to later commissions for the defence of the realm, as in 1385 when he is reported gathering troops at Sandwich. Following his experience of pacifying London in 1381, he helped suppress a riot there in 1384, and at the time of the Merciless Parliament a faction, led by Nicholas Exton, wanted to appoint him captain of the city, but his fighting days were over.

Later years War had made Knolles a wealthy man. Much booty inevitably passed quickly through his hands as larders and cellars were looted, food and wine consumed, and material possessions generously shared with his own men or even, in the case of Auxerre, returned to their owners. But Knolles also proved astute not only in converting some gains into real estate but in lending specie and increasing his liquid assets. It is impossible to draw an exact balance sheet. Most payments to him concern military service, for which confusing pledges and assignments were made by the crown. Many of these could not be honoured. This led to much complex bargaining and rescheduling of debts. But from the early 1370s Knolles increasingly developed mercantile interests and lent money to private individuals as well as to the crown. In 1382, for example, Richard II acknowledged loans totalling £6888; and it may have been through his contacts in the city that a presumed relative, Thomas Knolles (d. 1435), one of Robert's executors, was able to make a highly successful career as a grocer and citizen who was twice mayor of London.

After 1381, with advancing years, Knolles's attentions turned more obviously to charitable and religious foundations. The traditional view (derived from Stow) that he helped establish an English hospital at Rome with Calveley and Hawkwood is now discounted, but he did receive a licence in 1389 to visit 'the Roman court for the quieting of his conscience' (Rymer, *Foedera*, 7.641). His two chief concerns were rebuilding the bridge over the Medway at Rochester, with its associated chapel, an enterprise taken in hand with John, third Lord Cobham by March 1388 and completed in the 1390s, and founding a college at Pontefract, the probable birthplace of his wife. In this he was following a fashion set by other old soldiers—Sir Walter

Mauny's patronage of the London Charterhouse, Sir Nicholas Cantilupe's establishment of Beauvale Priory, Nottinghamshire, or Calveley's own foundation of a collegiate church at Bunbury, Cheshire, under a will which Knolles executed—and reflecting an ascetic piety shared with other members of Gaunt's retinue. In 1385 Richard II confirmed Knolles's plans for a chantry at Pontefract, staffed by a warden and six priests, with an almshouse for thirteen poor persons. After Constance's own death (c.1389), he paid a further fine of £240 for another royal confirmation, and bestowed on it a wealth of vestments and chapel furnishings (some possibly loot) as well as 1000 marks in cash under his second will (1404). The college was dissolved at the Reformation, but Knolles's Almshouses survived until 1881, when their endowments were reinvested with others to fund the still flourishing Pontefract Charities. At Rochester the new bridge served until 1856, before being replaced. But the chapel, dissolved in 1548, was saved. After restoration in the 1930s, it now provides a boardroom for the wardens of the Rochester Bridge Trust, with the arms of Cobham and Knolles displayed in its east window.

Following his death on 15 August 1407 at Sculthorpe, his chief Norfolk manor, Knolles, a small but physically powerful man, was commemorated by Walsingham as 'a most invincible knight, whose arms the kingdom of France had felt against it for many years, the duchy of Brittany feared, and the lands of the Spaniards dreaded' (*St Albans Chronicle*, 22). The most famous English professional soldier of the Hundred Years' War, he was described by the same author as 'a poor and humble valet [who rose to be] a great leader of soldiers, possessed of regal riches' (*Historia Anglicana*, 1.286), yet he was buried with little pomp at the Whitefriars, London, alongside his wife. Knolles left a huge range of bequests to household servants and churches in London and elsewhere, including £5 to Malpas parish church. In earlier years Constance accompanied him with their 'boys' on his expeditions. None survived their parents; a son, who died young, was buried in the abbey of Prières (Morbihan), about 1360. Since there were no direct heirs, the residue of his estate was settled on the college at Pontefract, while Knolles's fame was preserved by the display of his arms in several Norfolk churches (some of which, like Harpley and Sculthorpe, he rebuilt) and on other monuments that reflect family ties and friendships, like the tombs of Calveley at Bunbury and Thomas Knolles at North Mimms, Hertfordshire, or Bodiam Castle, Sussex, the home of Sir Edward Dallingridge, while a boss in the cloisters of Norwich Cathedral portrays Robert and Constance at prayer, flanking a representation of the Trinity.

MICHAEL JONES

Sources Archives Départementales de la Loire Atlantique, Nantes, sér. E · Archives Nationales, Paris, sér. J and JJ · Archbishop Arundel's register, LPL, vol. 1, fols. 245r–246r and 247v–249r (wills of 1404 and 1389) · V. H. Galbraith, ed., *The Anonimalle chronicle, 1333 to 1381* (1927); repr. with corrections (1970) · *Chancery records* · *Chroniques de J. Froissart*, ed. S. Luce and others, 15 vols. (Paris, 1869–1975) · M. Jones, ed., *Recueil des actes de Jean IV, duc de Bretagne*, 3 vols. (Paris, 1980–2001) · Rymer, *Foedera*, new edn · *Thomae Walsingham, quondam monachi S. Albani, historia Anglicana*, ed. H. T. Riley, 2 vols., pt 1 of *Chronica monasterii S. Albani*, Rolls Series, 28 (1863–4) • J. S. C. Bridges, 'Two Cheshire soldiers of fortune of the XIV century: Sir Hugh Calveley and Sir Robert Knolles', *Journal of the Architectural, Archaeological, and Historic Society for the County and City of Chester and North Wales*, new ser., 14 (1908), 112–231 • R. Delachenal, *Histoire de Charles V*, 5 vols. (Paris, 1909–31) • M. Jones, *Ducal Brittany, 1364–1399* (1970) • M. J. Bennett, *Community, class and careerism: Cheshire and Lancashire society in the age of 'Sir Gawain and the Green Knight'* (1983) • K. A. Fowler, 'Les finances et la discipline dans les armées anglaises en France au XIVe siècle', *Actes du colloque international de Cocherel, 16, 17 et 18 mai 1964, Les Cahiers Vernonnais*, 4 (1964), 55–84 • J. Sherborne, 'Indentured retinues and English expeditions to France, 1369–1380', *EngHR*, 79 (1964), 718–46; repr. in J. Sherborne, *War, politics and culture in fourteenth-century England*, ed. A. Tuck (1994), 1–28 • Archives Départementales d'Eure-et-Loir, E 2691 • Archives Départementales d'Ille-et-Vilaine, sér. 1 F 619 • Archives Départementales du Morbihan, Vannes, 45 H 1 • Bibliothèque Nationale, Paris, MS nouv. acq. fr. 3653 • PRO, Gascon rolls, C61 • PRO, treaty rolls, C76 • *A descriptive catalogue of ancient deeds in the Public Record Office*, 6 vols. (1890–1915) • PRO, accounts various, E101 • PRO, warrants for issues, E404 • E. Perroy, ed., 'The Anglo-French negotiations at Bruges, 1374–7', *Camden miscellany, XIX*, CS, 3rd ser., 80 (1952) • J. Artières, 'Documents sur la ville de Millau', *Archives Historiques du Rouergue*, 7 (1930) • H. R. Brush, 'La bataille de trente Anglais et de trente Bretons', *Modern Philology*, 9 (1911–12), 511–44; 10 (1912–13), 82–136 • *CEPR letters*, vols. 3–7 • W. H. Bliss, ed., *Calendar of entries in the papal registers relating to Great Britain and Ireland: petitions to the pope* (1896) • R. R. Sharpe, ed., *Calendar of letter-books preserved in the archives of the corporation of the City of London*, [12 vols.] (1899–1912), vol. H • R. H. Ellis, ed., *Catalogue of seals in the Public Record Office: personal seals*, 1 (1978) • *La vie du Prince Noir by Chandos herald*, ed. D. B. Tyson (1975) • [T. Walsingham], *Chronicon Angliae, ab anno Domini 1328 usque ad annum 1388*, ed. E. M. Thompson, Rolls Series, 64 (1874) • S. Luce, ed., *Chronique des quatre premiers Valois, 1327–1393* (Paris, 1862) • Cuvelier, *La chanson de Bertrand du Guesclin*, ed. J.-C. Faucon, 3 vols. (Toulouse, 1990–91) • F. S. Haydon, ed., *Eulogium historiarum sive temporis*, 3 vols., Rolls Series, 9 (1858) • *Inquisitions and assessments relating to feudal aids*, 3, PRO (1904) • *Chronicon Galfridi le Baker de Swynebroke*, ed. E. M. Thompson (1889) • *Knighton's chronicle, 1337–1396*, ed. and trans. G. H. Martin, OMT (1995) [Lat. orig., *Chronica de eventibus Angliae a tempore regis Edgari usque mortem regis Ricardi Secundi*, with parallel Eng. text] • P. Lecacheux and G. Mollat, eds., *Lettres secrètes et curiales du pape Urbain V, 1362–1370*, 4 vols. (Paris, 1902–55) • P. H. Morice, *Mémoires pour servir de preuves à l'histoire ecclésiastique et civile de Bretagne*, 3 vols. (Paris, 1742–6) • *Œuvres*, ed. K. de Lettenhove and A. Scheler, 28 vols. (Brussels, 1867–77) • F. Plaine and A. de Serent, *Monuments du procès de canonisation du bienheureux Charles de Blois, duc de Bretagne, 1320–1364* (1921) • M. C. B. Dawes, ed., *Register of Edward, the Black Prince*, PRO, 3 (1932) • *Adae Murimuth continuatio chronicarum. Robertus de Avesbury de gestis mirabilibus regis Edwardi tertii*, ed. E. M. Thompson, Rolls Series, 93 (1889) • *Scalacronica: the reigns of Edward I, Edward II and Edward III as recorded by Sir Thomas Gray*, trans. H. Maxwell (1907) • T. Otterbourne, 'Chronica regum Angliae', in *Duo rerum Anglicarum scriptores veteres, Thomas Otterbourne et Joh. Whethamstede*, ed. T. Hearne, 1 (1732), 1–285 • T. Walsingham, *The St Albans chronicle, 1406–1420*, ed. V. H. Galbraith (1937) • I. Atherton and others, eds., *Norwich Cathedral: church, city and diocese, 1096–1996* (1996) • R. Barber, *Edward, prince of Wales and Aquitaine: a biography of the Black Prince* (1978) • M. Boudet, *Thomas de la Marche, Bâtard de France et ses aventures (1318–1361)* (1900) [repr. 1978] • B. de Broussillon, *La maison de Craon, 1050–1480: étude historique accompagnée du cartulaire de Craon*, 2 vols. (1893) • E. L. Cox, *The Green Count of Savoy: Amadeus VI and transalpine Savoy in the fourteenth century* (1967) • H. Denifle, *La désolation des églises, monastères et hôpitaux en France pendant la Guerre de Cent Ans*, 2 vols. (1897–9) • K. Fowler, *The king's lieutenant: Henry of Grosmont, first duke of Lancaster, 1310–1361* (1969) • A. Goodman, *John of Gaunt: the exercise of princely power in fourteenth-century Europe* (1992) • J. B. Henneman, *Olivier de Clisson and political society in France* *under Charles V and Charles VI* (1996) • G. Holmes, *The Good Parliament* (1975) • M. Jones, 'Sir Thomas Dagworth et la guerre civile en Bretagne au XIVe siècle: quelques documents inédits', *Annales de Bretagne*, 87 (1980), 621–39 • M. Jones, 'The fortunes of war: the military career of John, second Lord Bourchier (d. 1400)', *Essex Archaeology and History*, 26 (1995), 145–61 • A. de La Borderie and B. Pocquet, *Histoire de Bretagne*, 3–4 (1896–1906) [continuée par B. Pocquet] • S. Luce, *Histoire de Bertrand du Guesclin et de son époque: la jeunesse de Bertrand (1320–1364)* (1876) • G. Minois, *Du Guesclin* (1993) • P. Morgan, *War and society in medieval Cheshire, 1277–1403*, Chetham Society, 3rd ser., 34 (1987) • P. E. Russell, *The English intervention in Spain and Portugal in the time of Edward III and Richard II* (1955) • N. Saul, *Richard II* (1997) • J. Temple-Leader and G. Marcotti, *Sir John Hawkwood* (1889) • S. Walker, *The Lancastrian affinity, 1361–1399* (1990) • N. Yates and J. M. Gibson, eds., *Traffic and politics: the construction and management of Rochester Bridge, A.D. 43–1993*, Kent History Project (1994) [for the Rochester Bridge Trust]

Archives Archives Départementales d'Eure-et-Loir, E 2691 • Archives Départementales d'Ille-et-Villaine, sér. 1 F 619 • Archives Départementales de la Loire Atlantique, Nantes, sér. E • Archives Départementales du Morbihan, Vannes, 45 H 1 • Archives Nationales, Paris, sér. J and JJ • Bibliothèque Nationale, Paris, MS Nouv. acq. française 3653 • LPL, register of Archbishop Arundel, vol. 1, fols. 245r–246r, 247v–249r • PRO, C 61, 76; E 40, E 101, E 326, E 329, E 404

Likenesses boss, *c.*1420, Norwich Cathedral [*see illus.*]

Wealth at death see wills, Archbishop Arundel's register, LPL, vol. 1, fols. 245r–246r, 247v–249r

Knolles, Thomas (*d.* 1435), merchant and mayor of London, enjoyed an extraordinarily long career and was one of the few Londoners to serve twice as mayor. It has been said that he was an immigrant from Cheshire, but his father could have been the Richard Knolles who left property in Cheapside, while the Alison Knolles who was one of the few women to be a member of the Grocers' Company, and who appears in its list in 1383, could have been either his mother or a kinswoman. However, Thomas's election as warden of the company in 1387, without any previous mention in the city's records, raises the possibility that he purchased citizenship, aided by his connection with Sir Robert Knolles (*d.* 1407), whose executor and likely kinsman he was. In 1393 he was elected alderman for Dowgate, and the following year he served as sheriff. He transferred in 1397 to Cordwainer ward, where his house was in Watling Street, which was part of the grocers' trading quarter in St Antonin's parish. He was one of the leading parishioners who nominated chaplains to one of its chantries.

There is no evidence that Knolles made his fortune, as the richest grocers normally did, by exporting wool or cloth; rather it would appear from two large debts owed to him by a provincial mercer and dyer that he principally distributed raw materials for the cloth trade. In the commercial depression of the early fifteenth century he ventured into tin, and was the partner of a prominent Cornish tin merchant, John Megre, who started manufacturing pewter in London in 1397. Knolles also invested in property in London and, moreover, had an estate at North Mimms in Hertfordshire. By 1412 his rents amounted to £38, making him one of the richest owners of property in the city, but this income was modest compared with the capital he amassed.

Some of his property in Sopers Lane came to him as a

reward for his services to the new Lancastrian dynasty. He may well have advanced in the grocers' ranks because his views coincided with those of the Chichele brothers who were committed Lancastrians. A lack of coin and a contraction of trade turned many Londoners against the government of Richard II, and it seems likely that Knolles was chosen as mayor in 1399 because he had been a leading supporter of the Lancastrian usurpation. At Christmas 1399 he rode out to Windsor to warn Henry IV of a plot by dissentient earls to restore Richard II, and afterwards he supported the new king with loans which helped to obtain the commercial policies Londoners wanted. Knolles's choice as one of the four treasurers appointed by parliament in 1404 to supervise expenditure on war demonstrates the public confidence he enjoyed, as indeed does his re-election as mayor in 1410. But by then the commercial recession was making men unwilling to accept public office, and Knolles's wealth was sorely needed by the city. He was the highest contributor to the city's loan for Henry V's campaign of 1417, lending £200; and he had represented London in parliament the previous year.

Knolles was also a generous benefactor to the city, taking an active part in the rebuilding of the Guildhall in his second mayoralty. His religious orthodoxy is implied by his obtaining a papal indult to use a portable altar, by his appointment in January 1414 as one of the commissioners investigating Lollardy after Oldcastle's rebellion, and by his rebuilding of St Antonin's Church. He also acquired the advowson of the church of All Hallows, Honey Lane. His wealth funded many charitable works. With his son he provided fresh piped water for the prisoners of Newgate and Ludgate, and his wills show a concern for the poor of his mistery and for his estate at North Mimms. He was also a benefactor to the Grocers' Company, and with Robert Chichele he promoted the acquisition of its hall. They were two of the trustees who acquired its site in 1425, and Knolles contributed £62 5s. in 1427 towards the building, while with his son Thomas he secured the company's incorporation in 1428. Among other gifts he paid for its almshouses in 1431.

Knolles's family life and friendships seem to have reflected his generosity of spirit. According to the inscription his son had carved on his memorial in St Antonin's Church, he and his wife, Joan, were married for sixty years and had nineteen children, of whom four sons and three daughters survived their father's death at Watling Street between 29 June and 11 July 1435. His eldest son, Thomas, followed his father in the Grocers' Company, while William became a grocer in Bristol. Knolles's daughter Marjorie married the grocer John Chichele, whom he assisted in repaying a large debt. The quality of Knolles's friendship appears from his joint offer with Robert Chichele in 1413 of 10,000 marks as security for Henry Somer (d. 1450), the chancellor of the exchequer, when he was impeached in parliament. He also brought up in his household, and was the guardian of, the son of a deceased fellow parishioner and grocer, John Oxney, whose widow he remembered in his will. A chantry was established for Knolles and his family in St Antonin's Church, in support of which

Alderman William Gregory, a skinner, bequeathed an annual rent in 1461. Knolles clearly inspired a long-lasting affection. PAMELA NIGHTINGALE

Sources E. F. Jacob, ed., The register of Henry Chichele, archbishop of Canterbury, 1414–1443, 2, CYS, 42 (1937), 661 · P. Nightingale, A medieval mercantile community: the Grocers' Company and the politics and trade of London, 1000–1485 (1995) · S. L. Thrupp, The merchant class of medieval London, 1300–1500 (1948), 230, 351–2 · R. R. Sharpe, ed., Calendar of letter-books preserved in the archives of the corporation of the City of London, [12 vols.] (1899–1912), vol. B · CPR, 1396–1401; 1408–13; 1416–22 · CClR, 1402–13, 1419–29 · CLRO, hustings rolls · J. Stow, A survay of London, rev. edn (1603); repr. with introduction by C. L. Kingsford as A survey of London, 2 vols. (1908); repr. with addns (1971)

Knolles, Thomas. *See* Knollys, Thomas (d. 1546).

Knollys, Charles, styled fourth earl of Banbury (bap. 1662, d. 1740), peerage claimant and duellist, was baptized at Boughton, Northamptonshire, on 3 June 1662, the eldest son of Nicholas *Knollys (1631–1674) [see under Knollys, William, earl of Banbury], who claimed to be third earl of Banbury, and his second wife, Anne Sherard (d. 1680). Nothing is known of his early years and education, but it can be safely assumed that he was drawn into his father's struggle for his title from an early age. Nicholas, whose father may have been William Knollys, the eighty-six-year-old first earl of Banbury, or his mother's lover and eventual second husband, Edward, fourth Baron Vaux, had since 1661 been excluded from the House of Lords, which firmly believed that he was illegitimate.

In June 1685 Knollys petitioned the Lords for a writ of summons. As had happened in his father's case, an order of the house for a full hearing went unfulfilled, and his claim remained undetermined. It was still at issue when on 16 May 1689 he married, at the Nag's Head Coffee House, James Street, Covent Garden, Elizabeth (bap. 1663, d. 1699), daughter of Michael Lister of Burwell, Lincolnshire, and his wife, Ann Burrell. She took the title countess of Banbury. At the same time Knollys seems to have been involved with an actress, Elizabeth Price, with whom he apparently travelled in France and Italy from November 1689 until the spring of 1692. Price, in a claim rejected by the court of arches in 1697, said she married Knollys at Verona in 1692. They were reputedly the parents of Sir Charles *Knowles, first baronet (d. 1777), although a later unknown mistress may well have been Knowles's mother.

The dispute over the Banbury title took on a new urgency in 1692. Abandoning his mistress, who then drifted to the Stuart court at St Germain, Knollys returned to London. His callous behaviour towards his wife probably was behind the duel he then fought with his brother-in-law, Captain Philip Lawson. Knollys killed Lawson, and on 7 December 1692 the Middlesex grand jury indicted him for murder—as Charles Knollys, esquire. His life in the balance, Knollys petitioned the Lords for trial as a peer, a move which provoked the house to resolve that he had no right to the Banbury title—a decision against which twenty peers entered a protest in the Lords' journal. The upper house remained, by a relatively small majority of about eight, unpersuaded by Knollys's claims. Judicial proceedings, however, gave his claim an important boost, and rescued him from his murder charge as well. Knollys successfully had his trial moved from the Middlesex sessions to the king's bench, and at his arraignment in Hilary term 1693 he argued that his indictment was invalid, since he had been charged as Charles Knollys and not earl of Banbury. In Trinity term 1694, after months of argument, the four judges of the king's bench, agreeing unanimously, threw out the indictment on the principle that *pater est quem nuptiae demonstrant*, presuming the legitimacy of children born in wedlock, and freed Knollys.

Reinforced by the judges' unambiguous support for his claim to the earldom, Knollys continued to press ahead, petitioning again in 1698. The Lords, to whom William III referred the petition, reiterated their 1693 resolution and complained about the judges' presumption. His marriage, on 30 April 1702, at St Bride's, London, to Mary (d. 1762), daughter of a London merchant, Thomas Woods, might have eased his financial plight, but was a sign of his declining social position. Yet Knollys saw a new chance for his claim in 1712, as Queen Anne's government desperately sought votes in the Lords for its policies. He petitioned the queen in March, but the privy council, to whom it was referred, had not reported by Anne's death in August 1714. Knollys made a final attempt, in 1727, at the accession of George II. He petitioned once again for a writ of summons, but the attorney-general, Sir Philip Yorke, in 1728 advised that the matter should be taken no further on the grounds that the Lords and king's bench could not agree on the case. From then until his death at Dunkirk on 26 August 1740, Knollys seems to have given up the unequal struggle. He was buried on 28 August. His only surviving son with his first wife, William Knollys (1694–1740), who became MP for Banbury in 1733, always styled himself Viscount Wallingford as the eldest son of the earl of Banbury, but died just under three months before his father, on 6 June 1740, and so was unable to renew the claim. His eldest son with his second wife, Charles Knollys (1703–1771), went into the church, and neither Charles nor his two sons, William Knollys (1726–1776) and Thomas Woods Knollys (1727–1793), laid formal claim to the title.

The son of Thomas and his wife, Mary Porter (d. 1798), **William Knollys**, styled eighth earl of Banbury (bap. 1763, d. 1834), army officer, was baptized at St Thomas's, Winchester, on 2 March 1763. He entered the army as an ensign in the 3rd foot guards in 1778, was promoted lieutenant in 1788, lieutenant-colonel in 1793, and colonel (brevet) in 1795. On 23 June 1795, at St Thomas's, Winchester, he married Charlotte Martha (d. 1818), daughter of Ebenezer Blackwell, a London banker. He was promoted major-general in 1802.

In 1806 Knollys petitioned the crown for a writ of summons to the House of Lords as earl of Banbury. The report of the attorney-general, Sir Vicary Gibbs, on the case took two years to complete, and was ambiguous, declaring that no final decision about the earldom had been reached in the multitude of proceedings in the case since the 1660s, but suggesting that Nicholas Knollys's legitimacy was doubtful. The petition was referred to the committee of privileges of the House of Lords, who reported after a further five years' discussion that Knollys had not made out his claim. On 15 March 1813 the Lords resolved that Knollys was not entitled to the earldom. The decision was controversial, and sparked a formal protest by eleven peers led by the former lord chancellor, Lord Erskine.

Defeated, Knollys abandoned the use of the title earl of Banbury, and returned to his military career. He had been promoted lieutenant-general in 1808, was lieutenant-governor of St John's, Newfoundland, from 1818 to 1827, was promoted general in 1819, and was governor of Limerick from 1826 until his death in Paris on 20 March 1834, from influenza. His descendants never formally claimed the earldom, although his son Sir William Thomas *Knollys (1797–1883) asserted his right to the title in a letter to the *Morning Post* in 1863 and in his will, and his grandson William Wallingford Knollys (1833–1904) did the same in a letter to *The Times* in 1883. Another grandson was Francis *Knollys, private secretary to Edward VII, who was to return the family to the Lords when he was created Baron Knollys in 1902 and Viscount Knollys in 1911.

VICTOR STATER

Sources GEC, *Peerage* · H. Nicolas, *Treatise on the law of adulterine bastardy* (1836) · *The case of Charles, earl of Banbury* (c.1698) · *The arguments of the Lord Chief Justice Holt and Judge H. Powell in the controverted point of peerage in the case of the king and queen against C. Knowles, otherwise earl of Banbury* (1716) · CSP dom., 1673–5 · E. Cruickshanks, 'Knollys, William', HoP, Commons, 1715–54 · Burke, *Peerage* (1999)

Knollys, Edward George William Tyrwhitt, second Viscount Knollys (1895–1966), businessman and public servant, was born at St James's Palace, London, on 16 January 1895, the only son (he had one sister) of Francis *Knollys, first viscount (1837–1924), private secretary from 1870 to 1910 to the prince of Wales who became Edward VII, and from 1910 to 1913 to George V, and his wife, Ardyn Mary (d. 1922), daughter of Sir Henry Thomas Tyrwhitt, baronet. Knollys was educated at Harrow School (1908–12) and New College, Oxford. He served in the First World War, first in the 16th London regiment (Territorial Army) and then in the Royal Flying Corps, where he flew in balloons as an observer. He was awarded the DFC, the order of the crown of Belgium, and the Croix de Guerre, and was appointed MBE. In 1924 he succeeded his father. In 1928 he married Margaret Mary Josephine (d. 1987), daughter of Sir Stuart Auchincloss Coats, baronet. There were a son and daughter of the marriage.

Despite encouragement, then and later, notably from the prince of Wales (later Edward VIII), to follow his father's footsteps in royal service, Knollys decided to break away and make a business career for himself. After studying accountancy, he joined Barclays Bank and spent three years in Cape Town (1929–32) as local director of Barclays (Dominion, Colonial and Overseas). Thence he moved to the insurance business, being appointed in 1932 a director in London of the Employers' Liability Assurance Corporation, of which he became managing director the following year. Most of the Employers' business lay in North America, and it was in the handling of these

American clients and managers that Knollys's remarkable talent for personal relationships, patient negotiation, and hard work first came to light. Overcoming initial difficulties, Knollys soon won wide respect as a leader in his field which after the Second World War was widened by the merger, in 1960, of the Employers' with the larger Northern Assurance. Knollys was the first chairman of the joint company.

In the early years of the war Knollys became deputy commissioner for civil defence, south-eastern region, before, in 1941, being made KCMG and appointed governor and commander-in-chief of Bermuda. This post, traditionally filled by a senior serving general, had become a sensitive one. Under Anglo-American wartime agreements, a naval and air base had been leased to the United States. Considerable problems were created by the arrival on the little British island of large numbers of American servicemen and construction staff. Knollys's sure touch with Americans, his tact and intelligence with all, enabled him to excel in the task he had been sent to perform.

In 1943 Knollys was appointed first full-time chairman of the British Overseas Airways Corporation. BOAC was operating with converted war planes, and Knollys saw that the one special element it could offer was courtesy, kindness, and understanding. These qualities, filtering down from the chairman's office, where a firm polite charm and elegantly good manners prevailed, permeated the staff. During the four years of his chairmanship, the corporation was given new systems of management, new methods of operation, and a development plan which enabled it to compete in the expanding post-war market.

In 1947 Knollys—known to all his friends as Edgey (an abbreviation for Edward and George, the names of his two godfathers Edward VII and George V)—returned to his business career, but four years later was again lent to the government. The outbreak of the Korean War in June 1950 had resulted in scarcity and high prices for many raw materials, thus threatening the economic stability of western Europe, particularly Britain. Knollys's task (with the rank of minister) was to represent Britain at the International Materials Conference in Washington. Once again, his ability to get on with people, especially Americans, equipped him to perform a formidable feat in protecting British interests. For this, he was promoted to GCMG in 1952.

In 1956 Knollys became chairman of Vickers Ltd, the large shipbuilding, engineering, steel, and aircraft concern, on to whose board he had been brought four years earlier. In some respects it was a curious appointment. For all his financial acumen and ability to handle people, Knollys had no knowledge of industry and no technical qualifications. Nevertheless, he brought to Vickers his customary sense of style, epitomized by the decision, taken under his chairmanship, to give the company a new and fitting London headquarters. The result was the Vickers tower at Millbank, which at the time made a welcome contrast to the giant concrete matchboxes obscuring the London skyline. Knollys's influence on Vickers's financial

fortunes was less spectacular. He was only partially successful in steering the company away from its traditional armament-producing role into other, more varied activities. Some of the men chosen, under his chairmanship, for top management posts did not prove to possess the special flair and skill needed for the exceptionally difficult task facing the company. Knollys retired from his post in 1962, but continued as chairman of the English Steel Corporation (which he had become in 1959) until 1965.

Knollys was elected FRSA in 1962. A good shot and golfer, a respectable fly fisherman, a keen gardener, and, in his later years, an amateur painter, Knollys found the best relaxation from hard work in a country setting. Tall, well-dressed, and good-looking, he combined a sense of well-bred self-assurance with a certain diffidence of manner, accentuated by a nervous habit of adding the unnecessary phrase 'in that way' to many of his sentences. Much of his small stock of spare time was given to charitable interests, particularly the RAF Benevolent Fund, of whose council he was chairman for many years. He was a trustee of Churchill College, Cambridge.

Knollys died at 10 Bryanston Square, London on 3 December 1966. He was survived by his wife and children; his son, David Francis Dudley Knollys (b. 1931) succeeded to the viscountcy. FRANK GILES, rev.

Sources The Times (5 Dec 1966), 12d · The Times (7 Dec 1966), 14d · personal knowledge (1981) · private information (1981) · d. cert. **Likenesses** W. Stoneman, photograph, 1949, NPG · R. N. Hepple, group portrait, c.1955 · R. Tollast, drawing, CAC Cam. **Wealth at death** £65,272: probate, 13 Feb 1967, CGPLA Eng. & Wales

Knollys, Sir Francis (1511/12–1596), politician, was the elder son of **Robert Knollys** (d. 1520/21), courtier, and Lettice (d. 1557/8), daughter of Sir Thomas Peniston of Hawridge, Buckinghamshire. Robert was fifth in descent from Sir Thomas Knollys (d. 1435), lord mayor of London in 1399 and 1410, who directed the rebuilding of the Guildhall in 1400 and rebuilt St Antholin's Church in Watling Street. In 1488 Robert Knollys was one of Henry VII's henchmen, and late in that year was appointed to wait on Prince Arthur. He received a reward of £5 for each of the three years 1488 to 1490, and when Henry VII met Archduke Philip in 1500 he accompanied the English king as one of the ushers of the chamber. He continued in the same office under Henry VIII, and received an annuity of £20 on 15 November 1509, and a grant of Rookes Manor in Hampshire—part of the confiscated property of Sir Richard Empson—on 10 February 1511. On 9 July 1514 Robert and his wife were jointly granted the manor of Rotherfield Greys, near Henley-on-Thames, Oxfordshire, in survivorship, at an annual rent of a red rose at midsummer. Other royal gifts followed. Knollys made his will on 13 November 1520, and it was proved on 19 June 1521. He was buried in the London church of St Helen, Bishopsgate. His widow became the second wife of Sir Robert Lee of Burston, Buckinghamshire. He died in 1537, and she became the second wife of Sir Thomas Tresham of Rushton, Northamptonshire, prior (under Mary I) of the knights of St

John of Jerusalem. Her will, dated 28 June 1557, was proved on 11 June 1558.

Robert Knollys's career exhibits an interesting parallel to those of the founders of the Russell and Cecil dynasties. The service of each began under the first Tudor, continuing under his son. Like the Russells and the Cecils, Knollys was able to acquire lands and gentry status. Knollys, of course, died while his son was a child but seems to have established himself so well in the royal favour that Henry VIII extended his patronage to the son. His children included, besides Francis, a son, Henry, and two daughters, Mary and Jane. The latter married Sir Richard Wingfield of Kimbolton Castle. The son Henry (d. 1583) was in some favour with Edward VI and Elizabeth I. He went abroad with his brother Francis during Mary's reign. In 1562 he was sent on a diplomatic mission to Germany to observe the temper of German protestants, and in 1569 was temporarily employed in warding both Mary, queen of Scots, at Tutbury and the duke of Norfolk in the Tower. He was MP for Grampound in 1547, New Shoreham in 1563, Guildford in 1571, and Christchurch in 1572. His will, dated 27 July 1583, was proved on 2 September.

Francis Knollys succeeded his father in 1524, although a contested claim to the inheritance was not settled until he secured an act of parliament in 1545. According to tradition he attended Magdalen College, Oxford, but there is no record of this. He sat in 1533 in the fifth session of the 1529 parliament, the result of a 1532 by-election. He must have found a patron, conceivably Cromwell. He almost certainly sat in the 1536 house and probably in 1539, but the constituency is not known in any of these cases. Before the next parliament he married, about 1540, Katherine (1529/30–1569), the daughter of William Carey of Aldenham, Berkshire, and Mary, sister to Queen Anne Boleyn. Katherine's brother Henry, Lord Hunsdon, was later Knollys's colleague in the privy council. In 1545 he sat in parliament for Horsham as a nominee of his wife's kinsman the third duke of Norfolk. In 1547 he represented the newly enfranchised Cornish borough of Camelford, possibly as a protégé of Protector Somerset. He may have sat in the spring parliament of 1553 but the records are too sparse to make this certain.

Early career Knollys's court career began with his appointment as a gentleman pensioner in that newly founded body in 1539; he served until 1544. He was master of the horse to Prince Edward by 1547. He also launched a military career, campaigning in the Flanders expedition of 1543 and with the king in northern France the following year. His service at Pinkie in 1547 earned him a knighthood. In Edward's reign he became constable of Wallingford Castle and steward of Ewelme. He was a JP for Oxfordshire from 1547 to 1554.

Knollys was moving in advanced protestant circles by 1551, when he attended discussions on the eucharist in Cecil's house. The precise circumstances of his conversion to the new faith are unknown, but the experience was a profound one. It shaped every aspect of his public career to the end of his life. Of the men who became his fellows on the council only Bedford shared his depth of religious conviction. There is doubtful evidence that he went to Lausanne immediately after Mary's accession to arrange for the reception of English exiles. He was certainly in England in 1554, since he was named as JP for Oxfordshire in February of that year and sold land in Cambridge, but by 1555–6 he was a student at Basel. Later he and his family lived at Frankfurt, and it was from there that he returned to England at Elizabeth's accession, possibly even before the event. On 14 January 1559 the queen admitted him to the privy council and at the same time appointed him vice-chamberlain of the household. His wife became a lady of the bedchamber, a post she held until her death on 15 January 1569, aged thirty-nine; the queen was much attached to her, and paid for her funeral in Westminster Abbey.

In the parliament which met in 1559 Knollys and Sir John Cooke were the two most prominent Marian exiles among its members. They had a key role to play: the bill designed to restore the Edwardian religious order was committed to their care. They piloted it successfully through the lower house only to see it emasculated in the upper. What role Knollys may have played in the post-Easter sitting is not known. Over the next four years he was employed in a variety of assignments. In 1560 he was dealing with the special Spanish ambassador, Glajon, sent to mediate between the English government and the Guise regency in Edinburgh, bringing the reassuring message that Spain would not intervene. In the same year Cecil considered him as a possible replacement for Throckmorton as ambassador in Paris, but he was ruled out as lacking adequate private means.

In 1562 Knollys was appointed captain at Portsmouth and placed in charge of sending supplies to the English force at Newhaven (Le Havre). As the enterprise faltered in 1563 he was asked to report on strategies of withdrawal, a move which he was urging, and in June was ordered to cross to Newhaven, but the withdrawal pre-empted a visit to the plague-ridden port. About the same time he was sent on a tour of inspection of defences in the Channel Islands and the Isle of Wight. Then in 1566 he was sent to Ireland for a two-month stint to advise Sir Henry Sidney, the lord deputy, on the O'Neill problem in Ulster. It was while he was there that he heard of the death of the treasurer of the chamber. Quick to apply for the vacant post, citing the burden of a family of twelve children, he won the appointment. He had already in 1565 been named captain of the guard. In 1570, when he was promoted treasurer of the household, he apparently laid down the other offices.

In 1568 a much more onerous responsibility fell on Knollys's shoulders, an assignment which, however, displayed the queen's confidence in her kinsman. On news of Mary Stuart's arrival in England in May 1568, Knollys was sent north to be her guardian. Accompanied by Lord Scrope, the warden of the west marches, he met the Scottish queen at Carlisle at the close of the month. Although impressed by her personality, he saw her from the first as a danger to the realm. In their initial encounter he responded to her invective against Moray by reminding her that there were occasions when the deposition of princes was justified—*inter alia* murder—a reply which reduced her to tears. After further dealings with Mary, Knollys and Scrope urged that she either be allowed to return to Scotland unimpeded by Elizabeth, or remain in England at the pleasure of the queen. Knollys believed she would return home only when French help was available. He warned of the risks of her escape 'with devices of toys or towels at windows' (Wright, 1.276–80) and urged that she be moved further away from the border. In the following months he was forthright in arguing with Cecil that the queen must support Moray and if that meant exposing 'the spots in Mary's coat' (ibid., 1.280–1), the sooner the better. He complained bitterly of Elizabeth's hesitation in making a decision, which, he said, weakened her friends and strengthened her enemies. By July he had persuaded Mary to move to the more secure situation of Bolton, achieving this on his own initiative without royal authority.

Mary remained in Knollys's custody until the end of 1568. In December Elizabeth sought to involve him in her tortuous dealings with Mary. He was to press on her a scheme by which she would abdicate and remain in England at the queen's pleasure. Moray would continue as regent and Prince James be brought to England for his education. In return the charges against her would be consigned to oblivion. All this was to be delivered as of his own devising. This was to be done before the arrival at Bolton of Mary's agent, the bishop of Ross, who was being purposely delayed in London. Knollys carried out his instructions but when Ross arrived he brought a very different proposal—that Mary and James should reign jointly. Sir Francis scolded his mistress roundly for allowing Ross to suggest such an alternative. He went on to lecture the queen:

> Now as Your Majesty's judgement must needs be ruled by such affections and passions of your mind as happen to have dominion over you; so yet the resolutions digested by the deliberate consultations of your most faithful counsellor ought ever to be had in most account in their weighty affairs. (Haynes, 497–8)

He reiterated that she must disgrace Mary and support Moray. This was plain speaking. Within three weeks, in February 1569, Knollys had the pleasure of transferring his charge to the earl of Shrewsbury.

Parliamentary manager Knollys had another role, a major and continuing one, in the first dozen years of the reign, as manager of crown business in the Commons, where he sat in no fewer than eleven sessions. In 1559 he represented Arundel, probably through the good offices of his fellow councillor the earl of Arundel. In the same year he succeeded the late Lord Williams of Thames as *custos rotulorum* for Oxfordshire, and in 1564 he became high steward of the city of Oxford. From 1563 to 1593 without a break he represented the shire in parliament. His position enabled him to place his son Henry (*d.* 1582) as his fellow knight of the shire in 1572, and William (*d.* 1632) in 1584 and 1593. Edward (*d.* 1575) and Francis (*d.* 1648) served as

burgesses for Oxford city between 1571 and 1589. Sir Francis Knollys's parliamentary patronage was large. In 1563 he most probably nominated the Taunton burgesses (he leased the castle and borough); in Oxfordshire he controlled the New Woodstock seat in 1571 and 1572, and at Banbury in 1563 his relative Francis Walsingham sat. From 1563 to 1586 one of the Knollys family always sat for Reading, where Leicester was patron. Indeed no fewer than six of his sons sat in the Elizabethan Commons, the largest family group in the house.

The government's business manager and its voice in the house, Knollys sat on all committees dealing with matters of concern to the government and was responsible for nominating speakers, carrying bills to and from the Lords, reporting on conferences with the upper house, reporting on the work of major committees, and—often a painful task—conveying the queen's will to the Commons. It was his special business to shepherd government measures on their way through the house, ensuring their successful passage. He had also to keep close watch on private initiatives which might cross the government's intentions or arouse the royal displeasure.

In 1559, sharing the leadership of the returned exiles with Sir Anthony Cooke, Knollys was a member of the committee which probably amended the government's Supremacy Bill. He also served in a commission to enforce the Statute of Supremacy. In 1563 he was the head of a committee which amended an anti-Catholic bill so as to make first refusal of the oath of supremacy subject to the penalty of *praemunire* and the second to death—this against the queen's will: in debate he declared 'this business must be settled sword in hand and not by words and that he would be foremost in the struggle' (HoP, *Commons, 1558–1603*, 2.410). In 1566 he played a prominent part in the exchange between the queen and parliament over her marriage. He delivered her message promising marriage, served on the conference with the Lords on the succession, was among the thirty MPs summoned to hear her further words on the subject, and then finally was the bearer of the royal command to cease debate on the issue. His committee appointments were numerous: five in 1563, six in 1566. Their subjects included the queen's revenues, coneys, informers, excess of apparel, drinking and swearing, and the garrison of Berwick.

The restless 1571 parliament loaded Knollys with difficult tasks. The religious radicals, led in the house by Strickland, were pressing for reform of the Book of Common Prayer, a measure with which Knollys probably sympathized. Nevertheless, he did his duty in opposing the move, arguing that matters of ceremony as distinct from those of doctrine were solely for the queen's authority as supreme governor. He sought to sweeten the pill by suggesting that there were secret reasons why the queen did not want the move now. Then on the sequestration and imprisonment of Strickland, Knollys had to defend the royal action, asserting that the MP's offence lay not in his words uttered in the house but in his offering a bill against the queen's prerogative. Strickland, argued Knollys, erred in his zeal, but without malice to the royal dignity. Apart from this Knollys made a long speech on the subsidy and reported the subsequent committee. He spoke twice on the Treason Bill, and also on usury and vagabonds. He served on eleven other committees, chairing some of them; their subjects included coneys once again, along with recusant priests, church attendance, and other matters.

In 1572 Knollys had to deal once more with the problem of the Scottish queen. He had previously, in October 1569, been sent on a sensitive commission to arrest the duke of Norfolk, who had retired to his home ground at Kenninghall and seemed for a moment about to resist. Knollys brought him successfully to the Tower. That event triggered off the northern uprising among the gentry whose loyalty Knollys had questioned in 1568. Now, in the aftermath, parliament met in an agitated mood. On 12 May 1572 a committee was appointed to confer with the Lords on the queen of Scots. After the report on the conference was heard, Knollys urged a further meeting. There followed a move to bring forward the succession question. It was Knollys's business to stifle this move. While declaring his own wish for a settlement of the succession, he warned that it would founder on royal opposition and urged prayer to God to change the queen's heart. When a proposal was made to petition the queen to execute Mary, Knollys argued it was best to approach the queen 'by way of opinion [rather] than request' (HoP, *Commons, 1558–1603*, 2.411). Given his views on the queen of Scots, it must have cost him something to take this line. When the queen rejected a bill of attainder, Knollys saw that the Commons were still unsatisfied and suggested a petition of both houses urging the queen to reconsider. The petition was duly drawn up and presented; the royal response was to forbid discussion of the Scottish queen's matter.

The Commons now turned to the question of Norfolk, in the Tower under sentence of death; the house began to agitate for his execution. Knollys's own view was that were the duke his brother, he would have him dead, but he urged delay in pressing the queen. The house, persuaded by his argument, agreed to postpone action until the following Monday. Before the house sat that morning Norfolk went to the block. In the aftermath of that event the Commons was concerned with the case of Arthur Hall, a dependant of Norfolk's, who was brought before the bar. Knollys again spoke against punishing Hall for his opinions, urging moderation in dealing with a rash head and a fool.

There was ample routine business which involved Knollys, but the largest piece was a bill giving clergy the right to vary the order of service by omissions or additions, with episcopal approval. Knollys heartily approved of the measure, declaring 'that diverse mischiefs grew by the straitness of the statute for uniformity of common prayer', for which the bill offered remedy (HoP, *Commons, 1558–1603*, 2.412). But he was aware that the preamble, critical of the Book of Common Prayer, would offend the queen. Accordingly he managed its removal from the bill as well as eliminating the more extreme changes proposed by the bill's backers. At this juncture Elizabeth asked to see the religious bills before the house. When she declared her dislike for this measure, Knollys defended it, showing her that even in the Chapel Royal the prescribed order of the prayer book was daily broken. The queen responded graciously and asserted that she would take all good protestants to her protection. The bill passed both houses but in spite of her fair words did not receive her assent.

1572 was the last parliament when Knollys bore the burden of responsibility for managing the house. That task was now taken on by Sir Christopher Hatton and Sir Walter Mildmay. Knollys, now sixty, continued to play an active role in parliament. In the first session of 1576 he sat on the committee examining Peter Wentworth, bringing in the report which recommended Wentworth's committal to the Tower. Besides this committee he sat on nearly a dozen others. In the second session he was similarly burdened, and spoke against Paul Wentworth's motion for a public fast. In 1584 he was no less busy, again sitting on a round dozen committees, reporting a bill against seditious words and practices, and attending a conference with the Lords on that subject. He also spoke against the puritans' bold attack on the establishment in the book and bill motion. Not until 1586–7 did his activities begin to diminish, but he did sit on the inter-house conference on the fate of Mary Stuart and moved the subsidy bill to pay for the newly launched war in the Low Countries. Then in 1589 his duties again increased with the chairmanship of half a dozen committees, including that on the vexed question of purveyance. In 1593, at eighty-one, he still chaired at least two committees.

Privy councillor Of Knollys's activities as privy councillor the record is sparse, but a surviving letter of January 1578 to Secretary Wilson is revealing. The queen, it seems, was unwilling to listen to Knollys's advice, so he poured his frustrated anguish into Wilson's ears. According to the letter, Knollys knows the queen is loath to hear him, 'and indeed my speech hath no grave worthie of her Majestie's ears … and therefore I am the more silent, altho when I may be heard … rather than my silence shold be gyltie of her danger, I do utter my unworthy speech unto her Majestie'. He knows the queen must be obeyed in all matters which do not touch the danger of her estate, but if she does 'not supress and subject her own will and her own affections unto sound advice of open cownsayle in matters touching the preventing of her danger, she will be utterly overthrown'. Who will give safe counsel if she will not listen? 'Nay, who will not shrinkingly … play the partes of Richard the Second's men than to enter into the odious office of crossing her Majestie's wylle?' Specifically she must act to prevent a Spanish conquest of the Low Countries, to check the drift of Scotland into French arms, and to halt papist activity. Turning to domestic matters, he bewails the suspension of Archbishop Grindal, which will raise the 'pride and practice' of papists. Thinking on all this leads him to wish for a private life; he is not cut out to be a courtier. He ends by praying Wilson to hide nothing of this letter from the queen (Wright, 2.74–6).

In August of the same year Knollys rejoiced in the

queen's change of mind in agreeing to aid the states general; had she acted sooner—rejecting the advice of those who feared war with Spain—the present crisis might have been avoided. It might be too late now. Fearful of a Spanish victory which might lead to a Franco-Spanish alliance against England, Knollys was equally concerned that French support for the rebels would give them dominance in the Netherlands. Two years later, during the prolonged episode of the Anjou match, Knollys wrote to Leicester outlining his objections. The earl was now his son-in-law; his daughter Lettice Knollys, widowed by the first earl of Essex, had married Leicester. In 1585 Knollys was a member of the council committee to negotiate the treaty of alliance with the Dutch along with Burghley, Leicester, Hatton, Walsingham, Admiral Howard, and his brother-in-law Hunsdon. Later in the year the same body of men (minus Leicester) was busy with instructions for the treasurer at war.

Puritan militant Knollys had always been sympathetic to those who found the 1559 settlement but halfly reformed. He gave voice to these sentiments in his lamentations on Grindal's fate. He was alarmed, however, by the manifestations of the religious left. In 1581 he wrote to the chancellors of the two universities to condemn a recently published English translation of a work by Sebastian Castellio with its freewill doctrines. Knollys blamed the bishop of London, John Aylmer, for failing in his role as clerical censor in prohibiting publication. Such writing would discredit mainstream protestantism, giving a weapon to the papists, who, he feared, were gaining in strength and who were more dangerous than all the sects. In 1584 he would vote against the radical proposals embodied in the bill and the book.

It was the accession of John Whitgift to the primacy and his ensuing programme of enforced clerical conformity that aroused Knollys to active intervention in the affairs of the church. The matter was one of practice rather than doctrine. The new archbishop had required of all clergy unqualified subscription to three articles accepting the royal governorship, the Thirty-Nine Articles, and the Book of Common Prayer. Those refusing the required oath were suspended. When the parliament of 1584 met, members of the lower house initiated a petition to the queen which called for the restoration of the suspended clergy, a bar on proceedings against clergy who omitted any part of the prayer book, and the suspension of unqualified and unlearned clergy. Knollys headed the delegation which sought the Lords' participation in the petition. The upper house, after some hesitation, were persuaded to support the document. It was effectually denied by the queen.

In May some of the councillors wrote to Whitgift in behalf of the suspended clergy. Knollys followed with a letter to the primate in June, urging Whitgift to 'open the mouths' of the zealous preacher non-signers by lifting their suspension. Their preaching was sorely needed in the campaign against the papists, whose words were all too persuasive to a people naturally given to superstition and idolatry. They could be withstood only by preaching. The cause was one not only of religion but of policy, the very maintenance of the queen's personal safety, threatened as it was by a still untamed papistry. Knollys also sent Whitgift a writing which argued the equality of all clerics and impugned episcopal authority as encroaching on the royal supremacy. Whitgift refused Knollys's request, and the latter turned to Burghley for support against a policy which silenced sound preaching while neglecting the popish menace.

In 1589 Knollys returned to the fray. The archbishop had made a visitation of Peterborough diocese. Puritan sources sent a copy of the articles to Knollys, who wrote indignantly to Burghley demanding a public acknowledgement by the bishops that they had no superiority over their brethren except as they were given authority by the queen. He followed this by a denunciation of the covetous ambition of church governors who despised the humble doctrine of Christ's government, citing the Bible as asserting the equality of all ministers. There followed a bombardment of letters to Burghley, denouncing the misuse of episcopal authority on biblical authority. Then, shifting ground, he argued the legal case. Henry VIII had granted the bishops the same authority as their predecessors, but Cranmer had secured a statute conferring legal powers. This, however, had been repealed in the present reign, hence the illegality of ecclesiastical courts. These activities had now won the queen's disapproval. In 1590 or 1591 she banned Knollys from her presence. This was not the first occasion of royal displeasure; some years earlier she had forbidden him to deal with the puritans.

In 1591 Cartwright and Travers had been ordered to appear before Star Chamber. Knollys had not been notified, but soon found out that the chancellor had proposed to afforce the court with a DD and a DCL. Asked his opinion of this man, Knollys responded that since the queen would not allow him to speak his conscience he could answer only with her consent, but he reiterated his argument against episcopal authority and desired it to be debated publicly. He then appealed to Burghley, bemoaning the strait in which he found himself. It was deadly grief to him to offend the queen publicly, yet he would rather die than impugn her safety by a pleasing speech. He asked Burghley to show his letter to the queen so that she might give him leave to speak his conscience publicly—or else, if this denied, to make him a private man.

Knollys's position in these years had moved beyond objection to specific acts of the archbishop to an assault on the episcopal office as exercised by Whitgift. In his view the archbishop was asserting a divine right origin for his authority and hence independence of, if not superiority to, the crown. Knollys was insistent that bishops had no inherent superiority over other clergy, and that whatever powers they exercised derived solely from the queen.

There seems to have been a reconciliation with the queen, since Knollys wrote in January 1592 of a conversation with her in which she declared she feared puritans more than papists, to which he retorted that the former could only act through parliament with her consent. He urged that they be given open and fair trial to defend themselves against charges of treason and sedition. The queen's attitude towards the puritans countered Knollys's repeated assertion that what was at stake was an argument not merely about ecclesiastical matters but about the queen's safety. He had developed an obsessive notion of the link between abuses of episcopal authority and the queen's security. Only through the preaching which Whitgift forbade could the deadly menace of papistry be crushed.

Knollys continued indefatigable in the cause. In his last parliament, that of 1593, he again championed the puritans. Early in the session James Morice brought forward a bill which assailed ecclesiastical jurisdiction and specifically forbade the requirement to subscribe to the contentious articles set out by Whitgift. Knollys spoke out boldly in its favour: the bill was intended to reform abuses. If bishops were indeed acting illegally, they should suffer the penalties of *praemunire*. In a letter to Burghley, Knollys set out what he saw as the larger issue. The clergy sought to have a separate clerical government, exempt from the actions of the temporal government. That was his final word on the subject. He continued in council attendance but in much diminished frequency. He died on 19 July 1596, and was buried at Rotherfield Greys, Oxfordshire.

Knollys was consistent in his deep-rooted loyalty to evangelical protestantism, but in his public career bowed, sometimes reluctantly, to his royal mistress's differing views. He became an articulate champion of the evangelical party and a bold critic of the official ecclesiastical policy only in the last decade of his life. As he saw it, Whitgift's efforts to ensure conformity in worship and doctrine would stifle the preaching of the gospel, halt the progress of renewed reform, and lose the battle against a still unconquered papistry. The queen and the archbishop saw the puritans as a menace to the unity of the church just as dangerous as the papists. Those who would have sympathized with Knollys were fast disappearing. He was virtually the sole survivor of the heady Edwardian years, for him the first stage in what was to be a continuing work of reform. Such a conception was in stark contrast to the royal view, which saw the queen defending a completed and unified order under attack by irresponsible dissidents. Yet although Elizabeth silenced Knollys, he retained her confidence as a councillor. In 1593 she rewarded him with the Order of the Garter.

Knollys had been granted the lordship and manor of Caversham with lands in Berkshire, Oxfordshire, and Reading by Edward VI. In 1563 and 1564 Elizabeth granted Sir Francis and 'our beloved kinswoman', his wife, lands in Buckinghamshire, Somerset (seven manors), Berkshire, and Oxfordshire. Knollys exchanged the Somerset lands for property near Reading. He acquired control of Kimbolton Castle, Huntingdonshire, as guardian (with Walter Mildmay) of the estates of his nephew and great-nephew the Wingfields, Charles and Edward.

Knollys had at least seven sons and four daughters. The eldest son, Henry, predeceased his father, but after a considerable public career. An MP and esquire of the body, he married the daughter of the privy councillor Sir Ambrose

Cave. William *Knollys, the second son, succeeded to his father's offices and won promotion and an earldom. Of the others, all had parliamentary careers. Of the four daughters, Lettice married first Walter Devereux, first earl of Essex, to whom she bore Robert, the famous second earl. Second, she married Robert Dudley, earl of Leicester, and lastly Sir Christopher Blount. Cecilia, maid of honour to the queen, married Sir Thomas Leighton, captain of Guernsey; Anne married Thomas, Lord De La Warr; and Katherine married first Gerald Fitzgerald, Lord Offaly, and second Sir Philip Boteler. WALLACE T. MacCAFFREY

Sources HoP, *Commons, 1509–58* · HoP, *Commons, 1558–1603* · J. Neale, *Elizabeth I and her parliaments, 1559–81* (1953) · J. Neale, *Elizabeth I and her parliaments, 1584–1601* (1957) · *Calendar of the manuscripts of the most hon. the marquis of Salisbury*, 1–2, HMC, 9 (1883–8) · T. Wright, *Queen Elizabeth and her times* (1838), vols. 1 and 2 · H. Ellis, ed., *Original letters illustrative of English history*, 1st ser., 2 (1824), 238–5, 251–4 · J. Strype, *The life and acts of John Whitgift*, new edn, 3 vols. (1822), vols. 1–2 · W. D. J. Cargill Thompson, *Studies in the Reformation* (1980) · P. Collinson, *The Elizabethan puritan movement* (1967) · *CSP dom.*, 1547–90 · *CSP for.*, 1588–1603 · S. Haynes, *A collection of state papers* (1740) · *CPR*, 1547–82
Archives BL, financial tracts, Add. MS 41614 · Hunt. L., 'A booke of exchange of merchants' | BL, Cotton MSS, papers
Likenesses alabaster and marble tomb effigy (with wife), Rotherfield Greys church, Oxfordshire

Knollys, Francis, first Viscount Knollys (1837–1924), courtier, was born in London on 16 July 1837, the second son of General Sir William Thomas *Knollys (1797–1883) and his wife, Elizabeth, *née* St Aubyn (*d.* 1878), the daughter of Sir John *St Aubyn, fifth baronet. The Knollys family had a tradition of serving as royal courtiers which dated back to the sixteenth century, when Sir William Knollys had held the office of treasurer of the household of Queen Elizabeth I. Francis Knollys's father, General Sir William Knollys, was comptroller and treasurer to the household of Albert Edward, prince of Wales, between 1862 and 1877. Francis Knollys's sister, the Hon. Charlotte Knollys (*d.* 1930), was a woman of the bedchamber to Queen Alexandra from 1872 until the queen's death in 1925.

Francis Knollys was educated in Guernsey, where his father was military governor. Between 1851 and 1854 he attended the Royal Military College, Sandhurst, and thereafter he obtained a commission as an ensign in the 23rd regiment of foot. However, he quickly appreciated that he was not best suited to a military career, and entered the civil service as a junior examiner of the commissioners of audit in 1855. He took up the post despite his father's reservations that such a position might not be suitable for a gentleman. In 1862 Francis Knollys became a clerk for his father in the household of the prince of Wales, and in 1870 he was appointed the prince's private secretary in succession to Herbert Fisher.

Queen Victoria opposed Knollys's appointment as the prince of Wales's private secretary because she believed that he had a lecherous nature and disapproved of his support for the Liberal Party. However, the prince strongly resisted her attempts to veto Knollys's appointment, writing to his mother on 2 July 1870, 'He has so much to do for me lately that I am convinced he will suit me in every way'

(Magnus, 110). The judgement proved to be correct. Knollys was a diligent, loyal, and discreet private secretary. He gave the prince advice when his reputation was endangered, as, for example, when Albert Edward was implicated in the Tranby Croft card-cheating scandal of 1891. Knollys also championed the prince's desire to be found useful employment and his right to be given access to government papers. This privilege was granted to the prince only in 1892. Knollys also proved politically neutral. His enthusiasm for Gladstone's election victory in 1880 was a rare instance when he strayed from political impartiality. He became the prince of Wales's most trusted adviser and acted as intermediary between the prince and many of the leading politicians of the day, such as Gladstone, Disraeli, and Rosebery. He accompanied the prince of Wales on his visit to India in the winter of 1875–6, but otherwise he rarely travelled abroad with him. On 11 April 1887 Knollys married Ardyn Mary (d. 1922), elder daughter of Sir Henry Thomas Tyrwhitt and his wife, Emma, Baroness Berners. They had a son and a daughter.

When Albert Edward ascended the throne in January 1901 as Edward VII, Knollys became private secretary to the king. Edward VII bestowed the title of Baron Knollys upon him in July 1902. Knollys continued to act as one of the king's principal advisers in home, foreign, and constitutional affairs. He kept up a regular correspondence with the principal figures in both the Unionist and Liberal parties, such as Balfour, Campbell-Bannerman, Asquith, Grey, and Haldane. His own sympathies continued to lie with the Liberals, a fact which was known and which caused grumblings among the Unionists. However, the king's own instincts were invariably conservative, and thus Knollys's Liberal sympathies became an asset rather than a drawback when the Liberals returned to power in December 1905. Knollys was a Liberal of the old school. Despite the Liberal landslide in the general election of January 1906, he lamented the fact that so few 'gentlemen' had been elected to the House of Commons. He co-operated with Grey, Asquith, and Haldane in the autumn of 1905 in order to persuade these three Liberal Imperialists to participate in the cabinet of the radical Sir Henry Campbell-Bannerman. Knollys was also hostile to both Lloyd-George and Winston Churchill, both of whom he regarded as too extreme on social and constitutional issues, and suspect in their approach towards foreign affairs.

In foreign affairs, Knollys vigorously defended the king's right to be consulted by the government. He advised the king on ambassadorial appointments, one of the areas where the sovereign retained considerable influence. Knollys was also one of those, along with Sir Charles Hardinge, Admiral Sir John Fisher, and Viscount Esher, who awakened Edward VII to the danger posed by imperial Germany to Britain's security. This led Kaiser Wilhelm II, Edward VII's nephew, to conclude that Knollys was one of Germany's principal enemies at the British court. Knollys certainly viewed the Kaiser with distaste. He was also a firm supporter of Fisher's naval reforms because he

saw that it was essential to prevent Germany from obtaining superiority over Britain in battleship construction. However, after Edward VII's death Knollys became disillusioned with a foreign policy which he believed had made Britain the captive of French and Russian interests, and by 1911 he was sceptical as to the merits of the policy of entente with those powers which had been pursued by both Unionist and Liberal governments since 1903.

Knollys was also, along with Viscount Esher, one of the king's principal advisers on constitutional affairs. He jealously guarded what remained of the royal prerogative and tried, largely in vain, to extend it. He asserted, anachronistically, that the king had the right to be consulted by the cabinet before legislation was enacted, and reprimanded the prime minister, A. J. Balfour, when Balfour failed to seek the king's approval in advance for various territorial concessions to France made as a result of the Anglo-French agreement of April 1904. Knollys also felt that neither Campbell-Bannerman nor Asquith sought the king's advice as often as they should have done. The attempt by Knollys and Esher to champion and safeguard the powers of the crown was ultimately counterproductive. Knollys wished to restore the position which had existed in the 1840s and 1850s, when the prince consort had effectively been an informal member of the cabinet and when the monarchy had been more directly involved in government. However it was no longer possible for the crown to exercise the same level of influence over government in the early 1900s as it had done in the mid-Victorian era. By constantly defining the monarch's role with reference to the past rather than the present, Knollys contributed to friction between the king and his ministers.

After Edward VII's death in May 1910 Knollys was invited to serve as joint private secretary to King George V along with Sir Arthur Bigge (created Lord Stamfordham in 1911), who had been the new king's private secretary when he was prince of Wales. George V had great affection for Knollys, whom he had known since childhood. On a professional level, however, the new arrangement proved difficult. Knollys's Liberal sympathies conflicted with Stamfordham's instinctive toryism, which was shared by George V. Knollys's position was undermined during the constitutional crisis of 1910. In November 1910 Knollys persuaded the king to give the Liberal prime minister, H. H. Asquith, a secret guarantee that he would create 500 Liberal peers if the Unionist majority in the House of Lords continued to oppose the passage of the Parliament Bill, which aimed to subordinate the power of the upper house to that of the House of Commons. Knollys's motive was to prevent the king from being dragged into the dispute between the Lords and Commons. In acting as he did, Knollys believed that he was safeguarding the political neutrality of the monarchy. However he did not tell the king that the Unionist leader, A. J. Balfour, would have been prepared to form a government in 1910, thus convincing the king he had no choice but to accept the Liberals' demands. As a result Knollys was later accused by both Balfour and Stamfordham of having tricked the king into making a decision which he did not have to take. They implied that Knollys had done so because his own sympathies lay with the Liberal government rather than with the Unionist opposition. Knollys continued to serve as joint private secretary until February 1913. However, from 1911 onwards Lord Stamfordham was the king's principal adviser, a fact tacitly admitted by Knollys in a letter to Asquith in 1913.

Knollys was an individual with far more positive characteristics than negative ones. He was diligent, discreet, a master of the art of concise letter writing, and a loyal servant of the crown. In general, he maintained an outward appearance of political impartiality, despite his own Liberal convictions. He was a popular figure with the royal family, who nicknamed him Fooks, and he had a gift for friendship. He formed part of a circle of advisers to Edward VII, which included Admiral Fisher, Viscount Esher, and the marqués de Soveral, which dined regularly at Brooks's. He was also noted for his self-deprecating humour. He had an unorthodox approach to the game of golf. Sir Frederick Ponsonby recalled that Knollys 'always played in a square-shaped billycock hat and a London tail-coat, and hit so hard that his hat almost invariably fell off' (Ponsonby, 137). Knollys was also an indifferent linguist and a poor shot. More seriously, he had some professional and character weaknesses. It is evident that during the early years of Edward VII's reign, at least, he ran the sovereign's private office less efficiently than had Sir Henry Ponsonby and Sir Arthur Bigge under Queen Victoria. He was also extremely protective of his position in relation to Edward VII, employing two assistant private secretaries rather than one so that neither could challenge his pre-eminence.

In retirement Knollys continued to take an interest in public affairs and to maintain contact with the royal family. He held the honorary position of lord-in-waiting to Queen Alexandra between 1910 and his death. Despite professing to lack an interest in honours and decorations, he obtained a considerable number during his lifetime. He was created KCMG in 1886, KCB in 1897, GCVO in 1901, ISO in 1903, and was made a viscount by George V on 4 July 1911. He also possessed many foreign orders, including the grand cross of the Portuguese order of Christ and the Prussian order of the Red Eagle. Knollys died at Lockwell, Batchworth Heath, Rickmansworth, on 15 August 1924 and was buried in Highgate cemetery. His son, Edward George William Tyrwhitt *Knollys, succeeded him as second viscount.   RODERICK R. MCLEAN

Sources DNB · G. St Aubyn, *Edward VII, prince and king* (1979) · P. Magnus, *King Edward the Seventh* (1964) · F. Ponsonby, *Recollections of three reigns* (1951) · K. Rose, *King George V* (1983) · H. Nicolson, *King George V: his life and reign* (1952) · F. Hardie, *The political influence of the British monarchy* (1952) · *Journals and letters of Reginald, Viscount Esher*, ed. M. V. Brett and Oliver, Viscount Esher, 4 vols. (1934–8) · P. Fraser, *Lord Esher: a political biography* (1973) · R. R. McLean, 'Monarchy and diplomacy in Europe, 1900–1910', DPhil diss., U. Sussex, 1996 · CAC Cam., Esher MSS · NL Scot., Rosebery MSS · Royal Arch. · NL Scot., Haldane MSS · NL Scot., Murray of Elibank MSS · CUL, Hardinge MSS · Burke, *Peerage* (1939) · *WW* (1922)

Archives Royal Arch., papers · Royal Arch., private and military papers | BL, corresp. with Sir Henry Campbell-Bannerman, Add. MSS 41207–41208 · BL, corresp. with Sir F. L. Bertie, Add. MSS 63011–62012 · BL, corresp. with John Burns, MS 46281, 46303 · BL, corresp. with Sir Charles Dilke, Add. MS 43874 · BL, letters to T. H. S. Escott, Add. MS 58784 · BL, corresp. with Lord Gladstone, Add. MS 45985 · BL, corresp. with W. E. Gladstone, Add. MS 44230 · BL, corresp. with Sir Edward Walter Hamilton, Add. MSS 48604–48606 · BL OIOC, letters to Lord Curzon, no. 292 · Bodl. Oxf., letters to H. W. Acland and S. A. Acland · Bodl. Oxf., corresp. with Herbert Asquith · Bodl. Oxf., corresp. with A. J. Balfour and others · Bodl. Oxf., corresp. with Sir Henry Burdett · Bodl. Oxf., corresp. with Sir William Harcourt and Lewis Harcourt · Bodl. Oxf., corresp. with Lord Kimberley · Bodl. Oxf., corresp. with Arthur Ponsonby · Bodl. Oxf., corresp. with Lord Selborne · Bucks. RLSS, letters to duke of Buckingham · CAC Cam., corresp. with Lord Randolph Churchill · CAC Cam., corresp. with Lord Esher · CAC Cam., letters to Lord Fisher · CAC Cam., letters to W. T. Stead · CKS, letters to Aretas Akers-Douglas · CUL, Crewe MSS · CUL, corresp. with Sir Charles Hardinge · Glos. RO, letters to Sir Michael Hicks Beach · ICL, letters to Lord Playfair · Lambton Park, Chester-le-Street, co. Durham, corresp. with third earl of Durham · NL Scot., corresp. with Lord Haldane · NL Scot., corresp. with Lord Rosebery · NMM, corresp. with Sir Berkeley Milne · NRA, priv. coll., letters to Joseph Levy · PRO, corresp. with Lord Middleton, PRO 30/67 · PRO, letters to Odo Russell, FO 18 · PRO NIre., corresp. with Sir S. K. MacDonnell · PRO NIre., corresp. with Reginald McKenna

Likenesses C. Pellegrini, caricature, gouache, 1870, Royal Collection · Spy [L. Ward], chromolithograph caricature, NPG; repro. in *VF* (14 March 1891) · photographs, Royal Arch. · photographs, priv. coll.

Wealth at death £5223 17s. 9d.: administration, 4 Oct 1924, CGPLA Eng. & Wales

Knollys, Hanserd (1598–1691), Particular Baptist minister and author, was born in Calkwell, near Louth in Lincolnshire, but grew up in Scartho, near Grimsby (also in Lincolnshire). His father, Richard Knollys, was vicar of two churches in Grimsby and Scartho. The first name of his mother is unknown but his maternal grandparents were Richard Hanserd and Christobel Sutcliffe.

Education and early life Hanserd Knollys was educated at home by a private tutor and later at Grimsby grammar school and St Catharine's College, Cambridge. The precise date of his matriculation (as a pensioner) is unclear with the sources being inconsistent on the point. Some authorities, including *Alumni Cantabrigienses* itself, indicate 1629, but it was more probably in 1627. From his own brief account of his days at Cambridge it is plain that Knollys was already greatly concerned with spiritual matters, and it was at Cambridge that he came under the influence of puritans, whose works, he reports, he spent a good deal of time reading. Knollys later taught at Gainsborough grammar school, but after his ordination by the bishop of Peterborough as deacon on 29 June 1629 and then, the following day, his ordination as priest, he was given a small living at Humberstone (Lincolnshire). On 22 May 1632 he married Anne Cheney of Wyberton (d. 1671), near Boston, Lincolnshire, 'a holy, discreet woman, and a help meet for me, in the ways of her household, and also in the way of holiness; who was my companion in all my sufferings, travels, and hardships that we endured for the gospel' (Knollys and Kiffin, 8–9). The marriage lasted almost forty years and produced seven sons and three daughters.

Some time after his marriage, probably about 1636, Knollys came to the view that the wearing of a surplice,

Hanserd Knollys (1598–1691), by unknown engraver

the use of the sign of the cross at baptism, and the admission of those known to be wicked to the eucharist were all improper, and resigned his living. Thinking well of Knollys the bishop of Lincoln, John Williams, was keen that he should not resign and offered him a better living. Knollys refused. However, with the full knowledge of the bishop he did continue to preach. The bishop's toleration is not altogether surprising: he was already well known for his toleration of puritans. Furthermore Knollys's particular objection to practices considered either non-biblical and / or high church, would have gained a sympathetic hearing from the fundamentally anti-Laudian Williams. Knollys's disagreement with established religion, however, deepened to the point where he came to the view, in his words, that 'my ordination received from the Bishop was not right, and though I had preached some years by virtue of that ordination, I had not received any seal from Christ of my ministry'. Knollys therefore renounced not only his living but his ordination itself and determined 'not to preach any more, until I had a clear call and commission from Christ' (Knollys and Kiffin, 9). Such a call came, it seems, after extended discussions with the puritan minister John Wheelwright, who convinced Knollys that he should seek righteousness by grace. It was at this point, Knollys later stated, that he 'began to preach the doctrine of free grace, according to the tenor of the new and everlasting covenant, for three or four years together, whereby very many sinners were converted, and many believers were established in the faith' (ibid., 16).

American sojourn In 1636 Knollys was arrested by order of the court of high commission and taken to the house of the man who served the warrant but, Knollys later wrote, 'God helped me to convince him, and he was so greatly terrified in his conscience that he set open the doors and let me go away' (Knollys and Kiffin, 16). Knollys then fled with his family to London where he spent some considerable time before boarding a ship for Boston, Massachusetts. In the *Life* he describes a hard sea passage lasting fourteen weeks. During the passage, according to Governor Winthrop, one of Knollys's children died.

Knollys's time in Boston was relatively short: he himself indicates that he was in America 'about four years' (Knollys and Kiffin, 17), though it may have been slightly less than this. According to White, Knollys may not have arrived in Boston before the summer of 1638, and he arrived back in London on 24 December 1641. His time in America was not particularly easy. He arrived without means of support and with very little money, living in a house that a friend had loaned him. He became unpopular in Boston itself on account of alleged antinomianism, an unwelcome reputation that did not diminish when, upon moving to Pascataquack (Piscataqua) where he gathered a church, he was charged with, and apparently admitted to, sexual misconduct. (It is worth noting that Wheelwright had also departed for Massachusetts in 1636 and he too quickly became involved in the antinomian controversy there. Though documentary evidence to support the conclusion is lacking, then, it may have been that Knollys's association with his old spiritual adviser continued during this time.)

There were other troubles as well, including a significant dispute with another exile, Thomas Larkham, which resulted in charges of inciting a riot. Knollys got himself into further trouble for criticizing the Massachusetts magistrates and as a result was forced to leave the area and move to Long Island, though here too a protest was filed against him. Perhaps somewhat fortunately Knollys was at this time called home by his ageing father, a call which he answered, and thus ended what must have been a far less than happy sojourn.

England and further dissent On returning to London in December 1641 Knollys once again faced financial hardship from which he was rescued, he later reported, by some Christian friends. One of these was Dr John Bastwick, a determined presbyterian, who like Knollys had previously found himself on the wrong side of the law. Despite this initial act of friendship, however, Knollys and Bastwick were later to engage in bitter doctrinal dispute on the question of church government. These Christian friends provided free lodgings and in addition some money. Preferring, Knollys wrote, to work for a living than to be maintained by such charity he returned to school teaching, at first by taking on some former pupils of a deceased schoolmaster who had lived nearby and then by becoming master of the free school in the parish of St Mary Axe. Times appear to have been happier and he reports considerable success in gathering 140 day scholars and sixteen boarders. Knollys left this employment, however, to become a preacher in the parliamentarian army. As uncompromising as ever, it seems, he felt constrained to leave the army too once he 'did perceive the commanders sought their own things more than the cause of God and his people, breaking their vows and solemn engagements' (Knollys and Kiffin, 20). Again he returned to London and again he was arrested for unlicensed preaching. However, though he was kept several days in gaol, he was released after giving an account of himself to the authorities. About this time he was preaching also in Suffolk, for which again he was arrested and was again, according to his own account, acquitted and indeed given permission by parliament upon the petition of the inhabitants of Ipswich to preach in the region without hindrance. However, following another disturbance, probably near Woodbridge, during which he was 'stoned out of the pulpit', his efforts became once more concentrated in London (ibid., 22). Tensions continued and further arrests followed.

By 1644 it seems that Knollys became a member of Henry Jessey's congregation. Jessey was the minister of an Independent church in London, a church which has a strong claim to being the first Independent church in the capital, the founder of which was Henry Jacob. By the time Knollys joined the group this congregation had already suffered some internal dispute on the question of both the mode and timing of baptism (it was really the latter rather than the former that was the central issue in early Baptist controversies). This controversy quickly touched Knollys and his wife, who both refused to have their newborn son baptized. Jessey himself originally adopted a view in favour of infant baptism (by immersion); however, when the question was revisited, his views changed and he was subsequently himself baptized by Knollys in June 1645, laying himself open to the charge of Anabaptism.

Knollys himself 'gathered' a church in 1645, one of the first Particular Baptist congregations anywhere (Knollys and Kiffin, 25). This met next door to St Helen, Bishopgate, where on 10 August 1645 he was heard to pray for the Leveller leader John Lilburne; he was evicted from the property and moved his activities to Finsbury Fields. From there the church moved to Coleman Street, George Yard, Whitechapel, and finally to Broken Wharf, Thames Street. Knollys maintained his association with this congregation for the rest of his life, though in his own words 'I was absent from the Church sometimes upon just occasions, and with their leave, or forced from them by violent persecution' (ibid., 23). Along with another former Church of England clergyman Benjamin Cox he subscribed to the second edition of the confession of faith issued by the London Baptists in 1646. Also in 1646 came *An Appendix to a Confession of Faith*, written by Cox, but probably expressing the views of the whole London Baptist group. 'The high

Calvinist soteriology and a refusal to admit any to communion who had not been baptised as believers' are evident throughout that document (White, 9).

Throughout this time Knollys continued teaching to provide the means of support for himself and his family, though he took on other posts too. Between 1645 and 1660 he held several offices including examiner at the customs and excise, a post he relinquished on 29 March 1653. He was clerk of the check until 23 May 1655. It was during this time that he studied with Christian Ravis from whom he learned Hebrew. Knollys also returned to Scartho, his home, where, on 12 October 1658 he was installed as vicar of St Giles, a post he held for some time without relinquishing his leadership of the London church. Knollys' ministry in Scartho is a surprising turn of events: he had, after all, resigned from the Church of England a dozen years earlier and was by this time quite clearly in the nonconformist camp. How Knollys himself accommodated two apparently divergent sets of views is unclear, and one can only assume that his father's term in the same church meant that, as a Knollys, he was accepted even if he was known to hold rather different views. (Cheney Knollys, Hanserd's son, was later to serve in the same parish.) Quite how unusual this arrangement was in the late 1640s is not entirely clear; however, we do know that some nineteen Particular Baptists were ejected from other livings during the period from 1660 to 1662.

Thomas Venner's insurrection in April 1657 and the subsequent clampdown it brought once more led to Knollys's arrest. There is no hard evidence that Knollys was in substantial sympathy with the views of Venner or the Fifth Monarchists, but he was nevertheless judged guilty by association on at least two counts. Both have an element of plausibility: first, a number of Venner's followers had previously belonged to Knollys's congregation and some fourteen of them, though not Knollys himself, had signed the Fifth Monarchist manifesto, *A Declaration of Several of the Churches of Christ*; and second, Knollys had visited the Fifth Monarchist visionary Anna Trapnell, though what the purpose of this visit was is unclear. There was hence certainly some smoke, if not an obvious fire, and Knollys was subsequently committed to Newgate prison where he remained for eighteen weeks. The Act of Pardon which accompanied the restored king's coronation gave him his freedom. His continued association (loosely at least) with, and preaching at, All Hallows Church, a focal point of millenarian excitement in London, however, meant that he remained under suspicion, with the result that he fled first to the Netherlands and then to Germany where he remained, he reported, for 'two or three years' (Knollys and Kiffin, 25). During this time he had substantial property confiscated in London, despite, he claimed, winning a legal battle relating to this matter. After this time he returned to London via Rotterdam and once back in London resumed his teaching; by the time of his death he had built up a substantial school.

Final years On 19 May 1670 Knollys was again arrested during a meeting at George Yard and was sent to Bishopsgate compter, but was allowed to preach to the prisoners. He was soon set at liberty again. The last twenty years of his life are left uncharted in his autobiography. But it is plain they were hard for him physically, emotionally, and spiritually. He struggled against illness, the loss of family through sickness and death (his wife died on 30 April 1671), and his own doubts. In his preface to Knollys's *Life*, William Kiffin suggests that Knollys did write more, but that the latter part was lost. From other sources, however, it is plain that Knollys became a central figure in the first steps towards the consolidation and formal organization of the Baptist movement. For example, together with Kiffin, he was among the first London signatories who called for the assembly of churches held in London from 3 to 12 September 1689. It was here that the impetus towards the consolidation of the Baptist movement really took hold. He attended also the assemblies of 1690 and 1691. He died on 19 September 1691 and was buried in Bunhill Fields, London.

As a key figure in the early growth of the Baptist movement, especially the Particular Baptists, Knollys's influence should not be underestimated. Even if, as now seems probable, he did not himself convert Jessey to the Baptist cause, he was at least a partner in the discussions and central to developments. His extended period as minister of an Independent congregation in London brought some stability, as did his drive towards final organization, while his undoubted learning was put to the task of providing some theological undergirding of positions that were emerging.

Knollys was a prolific author. One of the more important of his works is his autobiography, published posthumously as *The life and death of that old disciple of Jesus Christ and eminent minister of the gospel, Mr Hanserd Knollys who died in the ninety third year of his age; written in his own hand to the year 1672 and continued in general, in an epistle by Mr William Kiffin, to which is added his last legacy to the church* (1692). This work provides a firsthand account of the trials and strains, as well as the beliefs, of a seventeenth-century English dissenter and as such provides a window on the turbulent and somewhat unstable political and religious world which he inhabited. The same is true of his several polemical works such as his *A Moderate Answer to Dr Bastwick's Book called 'Independency not God's Ordinance'* (1645), which outlines his views on the nature of the Christian congregation and places the same in the direct context of the seventeenth-century debate regarding episcopacy and church government in general. The following year, 1646, Knollys published *The Shining of a Flaming-Fire in Zion*, another polemical work, this time aimed at a book by 'Mr Saltmarsh'. Knollys's work disputes Saltmarsh's interpretation of a number of New Testament texts relating to baptism and in the course of doing so again both outlines his own views on the issue and places them in the broader context in which they were formed. His writings on the book of Revelation are particularly informative, for they indicate further (and in dramatic form) the extent to which polemics were an important part of the world that Knollys inhabited. This is seen especially in *An Exposition of the Whole Book of the Revelation* (1689) and *An Exposition of the*

Eleventh Chapter of Revelation (1679) which illustrate clearly enough the widespread fears of Catholic plots. Unsurprisingly in both these works Knollys reflects the standard protestant view of his day, namely that the archvillain of Revelation is the pope and that the book as a whole outlines the struggle between the true church and its enemies. He also published a number of grammars of the Greek, Latin, and Hebrew languages.

KENNETH G. C. NEWPORT

Sources H. Knollys, *The life and death of that old disciple of Jesus Christ and eminent minister of the gospel, Mr Hanserd Knollys*, ed. W. Kiffin (1692) · J. Culross, *Hanserd Knollys* (1895) · T. Harrison, *A sermon preached on the decease of Mr. Hanserd Knollis, minister of the gospel, preached at Pinners-Hall, Octob. 4. 1691* (1694) · M. A. G. Haykin, *Kiffin, Knollys and Keach: rediscovering our English Baptist heritage* (1996) · M. James, *Religious liberty on trial: Hanserd Knollys—early Baptist hero* (1997) · K. G. C. Newport, *Apocalypse and millennium: studies in biblical eisegesis* (2000) · A. D. Pope, *Hanserd Knollys: seventeenth century Baptist* (1965) · J. Savage, *Winthrop's history* (1853) · M. Watts, *The dissenters*, 2 vols. (1978–95) · B. R. White, *Hanserd Knollys and radical English dissent* (1977) · A. Laurence, *Parliamentary army chaplains, 1642–1651*, Royal Historical Society Studies in History, 59 (1990), 142–3

Archives DWL

Likenesses F. H. Van Hove, print, BM, NPG; repro. in Knollys and Kiffin, *Life and death* · engraving, repro. in Culross, *Hanserd Knollys* · engraving, repro. in James, *Religious liberty on trial* · line engraving, NPG [see illus.]

Knollys, Lettice. *See* Dudley, Lettice, countess of Essex and countess of Leicester (*b.* after 1540, *d.* 1634).

Knollys, Nicholas, third earl of Banbury (1631–1674). *See under* Knollys, William, first earl of Banbury (*c.*1545–1632).

Knollys, Sir Robert. *See* Knolles, Sir Robert (*d.* 1407).

Knollys, Robert (*d.* 1520/21). *See under* Knollys, Sir Francis (1511/12–1596).

Knollys [Knolles], **Thomas** (*d.* 1546), college head, was probably from Halifax, Yorkshire. In 1495 he was ordained acolyte and admitted to Magdalen College as a bachelor fellow; by 1498/9 he had taken up a fellowship. In 1500/01 he was appointed as an Ingledew chaplain-fellow at Magdalen, taking his MA and becoming second bursar at the college the next year. On 30 June 1502 he was instituted as vicar of Wakefield, a living he retained until his death. Knollys was admitted BTh on 19 April 1515, and was awarded his DTh in June 1518. In January 1528, following Wolsey's legatine visitation which superseded the authority of the bishop of Winchester, Laurence Stubbes, the president of Magdalen, resigned. Thomas Knollys was nominated to the vacancy, probably by Wolsey. In the contest which followed on 6 February 1528 he was chosen in preference to John Higdon, a former president. Knollys was one of those who delivered the university's determination against the validity of the king's divorce in 1531.

On 13 March 1535 the members of the college unanimously pledged their allegiance to the king as head of the established church. But it is clear that Knollys had reservations about the new dispensation, and he spent a large sum on adorning the high altar of the chapel. His staunchly traditional outlook on religious rites and ceremonies sat uncomfortably with government policy now evolving under the direction of Thomas Cromwell. In 1535 Cromwell tried to remove Knollys from the presidency, but his nominee, Thomas Marshall, was rejected by the Magdalen fellows. The following year, however, a more acceptable candidate was found in Owen Oglethorpe, whose candidature the fellows agreed to support in the event of the death of the incumbent president. Pressure, meanwhile, was put on Knollys; on 3 February 1536 he set his signature to a letter of resignation. The fellows proceeded to the installation of Oglethorpe, and Knollys retired to Yorkshire. On 7 May 1536 he was instituted as vicar of South Kirkby; he held the living until his death on 9 May 1546 in Wakefield. He was buried at Wakefield church.   STEPHEN WRIGHT

Sources Emden, *Oxf.* · G. Harriss, 'A loyal but troublesome college, 1458–1672', *Magdalen College and the crown: essays for the tercentenary of the restoration of the college, 1688*, ed. L. Brockliss, G. Harriss, and A. Macintyre (1988), 9–30 · H. A. Wilson, *Magdalen College* (1899) · W. D. Macray, *A register of the members of St Mary Magdalen College, Oxford*, 8 vols. (1894–1915), vol. 1 · J. R. Bloxam, *A register of the presidents, fellows … of Saint Mary Magdalen College*, 8 vols. (1853–85) · Foster, *Alum. Oxon.* · *Fasti Angl., 1300–1541*, [York]

Knollys, William, first earl of Banbury (*c.*1545–1632), courtier, was the second son of Sir Francis *Knollys (1511/12–1596), politician, and his wife, Katherine (1529/30–1569), daughter of William Carey of Aldenham, Hertfordshire, and his wife, Mary. His mother was Anne Boleyn's niece, and so Knollys was cousin to *Elizabeth I, a relationship that did much to advance his career. His brothers included Henry (*c.*1542–1582), Edward (*c.*1546–1575), Robert (*c.*1547–1619), Richard (*c.*1548–1596), and Francis (*c.*1550–1648), who were all MPs. He had four sisters, including Lettice *Dudley (*b.* after 1540, *d.* 1634). He was particularly close to Lettice. The exact date and place of Knollys's birth is unknown. In his youth his parents took great care of his education: he was first tutored by Julius Palmer, who was burnt as a heretic in 1556, and then studied at Eton College (1560). Knollys attended Magdalen College, Oxford, probably as a commoner, in or before 1564 (where he was tutored by Laurence Humphrey), and then the Middle Temple in 1565. He was created MA on 27 September 1592.

In 1569 Knollys commanded a company during the suppression of the northern uprising and in 1570 he became a gentleman pensioner. He served under his father guarding Mary, queen of Scots, at Bolton Castle, Yorkshire, in July and August 1568 and was in both the expeditions into Scotland in 1570 and at the siege of Edinburgh Castle in 1573. Knollys was elected MP for Stafford in 1571 and then, in 1572, for Tregony, Cornwall. Shortly afterwards (probably in 1573), he married Dorothy (1529/30–1605), fifth daughter and coheir of Edmund Braye, first Baron Braye, and his wife, Jane, and widow of Edmund Brydges, second Baron Chandos. The couple had no surviving children. In 1582 Knollys's position in the world changed dramatically after the death of his older brother, Henry. Now his father's heir, he assumed a more prominent political role.

William Knollys, first earl of Banbury (*c.*1545–1632), by Daniel Mytens

He joined Sir Francis Knollys as knight of the shire for Oxfordshire in 1584, and in November 1585 the queen sent him to Scotland as ambassador-extraordinary. In January 1586 he left for the Netherlands, where he served as a captain under his brother-in-law Robert Dudley, earl of Leicester, who knighted him. Knollys's association with Leicester went back to the earl's marriage to his sister in 1578; he was a trustee of her jointure in 1584. He supported his knighthood with the profits from his office as keeper of the Marshalsea prison (1586). Although Knollys did not stay on the continent long, he served briefly as governor of Ostend before he returned to England with Leicester, where his military experience and political prominence earned him command of the Oxfordshire and Gloucestershire regiment raised in the Armada crisis of 1588.

Knollys was re-elected as knight of the shire for Oxfordshire in 1593, 1597, and 1601. He was the senior knight after his father's death in 1596. His succession to his father's position meant a significant increase in his power. Until 1596 his political role centred mostly on the House of Commons and local affairs—he was an active JP and deputy lieutenant, particularly in Oxfordshire and Berkshire. On 30 August 1596, however, the queen appointed him comptroller of the household and a privy councilor, both positions that his father once occupied. She also named him lord lieutenant of Oxfordshire and Berkshire, an office he held for almost forty years. In 1599 Knollys returned to the Netherlands as an envoy to the states of Holland.

Knollys was uncle to Robert *Devereux, second earl of Essex (1565–1601), and sided with his nephew in the factional struggle between the favourite and Sir Robert Cecil. He escaped compromise during Essex's rebellion in 1601, however, and in fact testified for the prosecution during the earl's trial. His timely abandonment of Essex secured him the office of treasurer of the household in 1602, and on 13 May 1603 James I elevated him to the peerage as Baron Knollys of Greys. Still wary of Cecil, Knollys allied himself to the Howards through his second marriage. His first wife died on 31 October 1605 and on 23 December he married Elizabeth (bap. 1586, d. 1658), the nineteen-year-old daughter of Thomas *Howard, first earl of Suffolk (1561–1626), and his second wife, Katherine. Although over forty years separated the couple, Knollys could now hope for an heir and further political advancement. In the end he achieved both, though he discovered that neither blessing was unalloyed. The couple had two sons, including Nicholas [see below], and a daughter. The countess was a well-known Catholic and suspicion fell on both her husband and herself as a result. Over the next ten years Knollys's career flourished, though. In 1606 he became cofferer to Henry, prince of Wales, and in 1614 a treasury commissioner and master of the court of wards. In the same year rumour falsely appointed him lord chamberlain of the household and in 1615 he followed his father as KG, being elected on 24 April and installed on 22 May. On 7 November 1616 the king promoted him Viscount Wallingford. His prominence at court made him a much sought after patron: he was high steward of Reading, Abingdon, Wallingford, Banbury, and Oxford.

Lord Treasurer Suffolk's fall in 1618 brought his son-in-law down as well. In November John Chamberlain reported that Wallingford would be sacked as master of the court of wards for misadministration. After a brief struggle, he resigned—with the king's consolation that his only fault was his poor choice of a wife. Wallingford was also on bad terms with the new favourite, George Villiers, first duke of Buckingham, who coveted his house in the Tiltyard. A reconciliation of sorts came in 1622, when the duke bought the house.

Although he continued his attendance in the House of Lords and was an active lord lieutenant, Wallingford withdrew from the court after 1619. On 18 August 1626 Charles I promoted him first earl of Banbury, possibly as a reward for his effort to drum up loans for the crown in his lieutenancy. The king provoked the ire of the House of Lords by granting Banbury precedence over six other earls created since the coronation. Charles justified this unusual favour by noting Banbury's lack of an heir, and the house grudgingly accepted, stipulating that the title's precedence

would revert to its normal position should there be a second earl. In fact the fears of the house were entirely justified, for on 10 April 1627 the countess of Banbury bore a son, Edward (1627–1645), at Rotherfield Greys, the family's Oxfordshire home. A father at last at eighty-two, it is not surprising that two years later Banbury excused himself from attendance at parliament as 'old and lame and fit for no use, but attends his majesty and his friends with his prayers' (CSP dom., 1629–31, 84). Banbury finally died, aged about eighty-seven, in Paternoster Row, London, on 25 May 1632. He was buried at Rotherfield Greys.

The succession to Banbury's title generated controversy for over two hundred years, a dispute whose origins lay in the mysterious paternity of the countess of Banbury's two sons, Edward and his younger brother, Nicholas, born in 1631. The countess gave birth to a daughter who died as an infant years before Edward was born, but until 1627, when she was over forty, there were no other children. It was unusual, though by no means unprecedented for a woman of her age to give birth. What raised suspicions about Edward and Nicholas was that the countess was openly involved with Edward *Vaux, fourth Baron Vaux (1588–1661) [see under Vaux, Thomas, second Baron Vaux (1509–1556)]. Banbury's will, dated 19 May 1630, left almost all of his estate to his wife, but made no mention of Edward, then three years old. Moreover, the countess married Vaux only about five weeks after her husband's death. Edward, a minor at the earl's death, was called earl of Banbury on 9 February 1641 in a suit in the court of chancery, but he never sat in the Lords; about June, 1645, he was murdered in a dispute while travelling in France, aged eighteen.

Nicholas Knollys, third earl of Banbury (1631–1674), nobleman, was born on 3 January 1631 at Harrowden, Vaux's Northamptonshire home. At fifteen he assumed the title as third earl of Banbury. He is referred to as Lord Banbury in a settlement made by Vaux in 1646, and it was as earl of Banbury that he petitioned Oliver Cromwell for permission to sell lands on 27 February 1655. By this time he was jailed for debts amounting to £10,000. His first wife, Isabella (d. 1655), daughter of Mountjoy Blount, first earl of Newport, and his wife, Anne, died shortly afterwards. On 4 October that year, at Stapleford, Leicestershire, he married Anne (d. 1680), daughter of William Sherard, first Baron Sherard, and his wife, Abigail, thus improving, at least temporarily, his financial position. This was enhanced further, when his mother died on 17 April 1658, freeing up the dower estate.

Banbury took his seat in the Lords during the Convention Parliament in 1660, where his attendance earned him a place on two committees—but in July 1660 someone in the house challenged his legitimacy. Although the house ordered a hearing at the bar, it took no action. Banbury did not receive a summons to the Cavalier Parliament and in 1661 he petitioned Charles II for his writ. The king referred the petition to the Lords' committee of privileges, which in July 1661 resolved that Nicholas Knollys was the legitimate earl of Banbury. However, the full house refused to go along. While it is very probable that Nicholas's father was, in fact, Vaux, the Lords, in refusing to accept his legitimacy, was setting aside a long-honoured principle of the common law, which presumed that children born in wedlock were sired by their mother's husband. Banbury remained excluded from his seat, and in December 1661 a bill bastardizing him was read in the Lords, though it was never passed. The earl continued his efforts to regain his seat, petitioning the Lords and the king regularly. In August 1665 he disrupted the progress of James, duke of York, through Northamptonshire. After York declined an invitation to dine at Banbury's house, the earl stopped the royal carriage and 'laid hold of His Highness's leg and pulled so hard that he had almost drawn off his shoe' (*CSP dom.*, 1664–5, 498). Unfortunately these histrionics failed to advance Banbury's case, and he never again sat in the Lords. He died on 14 March 1674 at Boughton, Northamptonshire, and was buried there, leaving the struggle to his son Charles *Knollys, fourth earl of Banbury (*bap.* 1662, *d.* 1740), and his descendants.   VICTOR STATER

Sources GEC, *Peerage* · HoP, *Commons, 1558–1603*, 2.408–20 · *CSP dom.*, 1603–23; 1625–6; 1629–31; 1655–7; 1664–5 · H. Nicolas, *Treatise on the law of adulterie bastardy* (1836) · Evelyn, *Diary*, 3.99, 490
Archives BL, corresp. and MSS, Add. MS 26886 · CKS, MS · Hants. RO, Knollys MS, corresp., 1814–81 · Warks. CRO, Knollys MS, corresp. · Warks. CRO, letters | NRA, priv. coll., letters to earl of Essex
Likenesses alabaster and marble funeral monument, *c.*1632, Rotherfield Greys church, Oxfordshire · D. Mytens, oils, Ranger's House, London [*see illus.*] · S. de Passe?, line engraving, BL, NPG

Knollys, William, styled eighth earl of Banbury (*bap.* **1763, *d.* 1834).** *See under* Knollys, Charles, styled fourth earl of Banbury (*bap.* 1662, *d.* 1740).

Knollys, Sir William Thomas (1797–1883), army officer and courtier, born on 1 August 1797, was the eldest son of General William *Knollys, styled eighth earl of Banbury [*see under* Knollys, Charles, styled fourth earl of Banbury], and his wife, Charlotte Martha Blackwell. Until 1813 William held the courtesy title of Viscount Wallingford. Educated at Harrow School and the Royal Military College, Sandhurst, Knollys received his first commission in 1813, when little more than sixteen, in the 3rd, later Scots, Guards, and was almost immediately dispatched to the Peninsula. From there he crossed the Bidassoa into France with the victorious British army, and, after the passage of the Adour, was attached to the force that invested Bayonne. Knollys narrowly escaped capture during a French attack at Bayonne on 14 April 1814.

On the signing of peace he returned to England, but directly after the battle of Waterloo he was sent to join the army of occupation in Paris. In 1821 he was appointed adjutant, and from this worked his way through successive grades to become lieutenant-colonel of his battalion in 1844, and then regimental colonel in 1850. His adjutant was Sir Frederick Stephenson, and under their joint efforts the regiment was held to be one of the best drilled, disciplined, and organized in the British army. On 29 September 1830 he married Elizabeth (*d.* 1878), the illegitimate daughter of Sir John *St Aubyn; they had five sons and three daughters.

From 1850 Knollys instructed Prince Albert in the art of soldiering, and won his firm support. In 1854 he was promoted major-general and appointed governor of Guernsey, and in 1855 he went to Paris to study the French system of supplying troops when in action. At the same time the camp at Aldershot was created, with Knollys in command. The army at the time utterly lacked administrative cohesion. It therefore fell to Knollys's lot not only to form his Aldershot staff and to organize the troops into brigades and divisions, but to initiate the diverse departments of commissariat, transport, stores, and even the medical and chaplain's departments. He took it upon himself to instruct some of the first arrivals in camp in how to pitch tents, and by sharing a tent life with them taught them the elementary duties of soldiers in the field. On the death of General Bucknall Estcourt, chief of the staff in the Crimea, in June 1855, Knollys was selected to succeed him; but the appointment was cancelled, on the ground of his seniority, which would have entailed the supersession of many other Crimean generals. Notwithstanding his disappointment, he resumed his labours at Aldershot with undiminished energy. Aldershot was unpopular with the public, but Knollys received undiminished support from Prince Albert, who with the queen visited the camp frequently. Success exceeded expectation. General von Moltke was one of the foreign visitors to the camp, and, on the rare occasions when he broke his habitual silence, he evinced his surprise and approval at the progress made by British troops. When Knollys's command came to an end in 1860 he had established Aldershot on a basis of efficient organization.

In 1861, at the instance of the prince consort, Knollys accepted the post of president of the council of military education. In 1862 he was selected by the queen as treasurer and comptroller of the household of the prince of Wales. For fifteen years he performed the responsible and laborious duties attached to this confidential position, frequently accompanying the prince, especially during the earlier period, in his travels abroad and in his visits to foreign courts. The position was no sinecure. Victoria regarded him as 'a species of Mentor ... who would be responsible to Me to a great extent for what took place', and tried to hold him to account when the prince's actions displeased her, as they did when he visited Garibaldi at Stafford House in 1864. Knollys's reports to the queen convey his constant anxiety over the prince's gambling and morals, and over the intransigent dislike of the Prussians felt by Alexandra, which caused particular difficulties during a visit to Wiesbaden in 1867. He retired from office in 1877, and became gentleman usher of the black rod in the same year.

The honorary distinctions of LLD and DCL were conferred on Knollys by the universities of Oxford and Cambridge (respectively) in 1863 and 1864. In 1867 he was created a KCB, and in 1871 he was made a member of the privy council. In 1872 he once more had a short interlude of military duty, when he was appointed umpire in chief in conjunction with Sir Hope Grant during the Salisbury manoeuvres. On 19 June 1883 Knollys was gazetted to the colonelcy of the Scots Guards, the regiment in which he had begun his career. He died four days later, on 23 June 1883 at his home, Black Rod's House, Westminster Palace, in his eighty-sixth year, and was carried to his grave in Highgate cemetery on 27 June by sergeants of his old regiment. His second son, Francis *Knollys, later Viscount Knollys, inherited the family estates, to the exclusion of his elder brother.

HENRY KNOLLYS, rev. K. D. REYNOLDS

Sources GEC, *Peerage* · private information (1892) · P. Magnus, *King Edward the Seventh* (1964) · C. Hibbert, *Edward VII* (1976) · Boase, *Mod. Eng. biog.*
Archives CKS, papers · Hants. RO, corresp. · NAM, notes relating to history of Scots guards, papers · Royal Arch., corresp. and papers | BL, corresp. with W. E. Gladstone, Add. MSS 44182–44450 *passim* · Lpool RO, letters to fourteenth earl of Derby
Likenesses portrait, Royal Collection · wood-engraving, NPG; repro. in *ILN* (1863) · woodcut, NPG
Wealth at death £32,348 17s. 10d.: probate, 30 Aug 1883, CGPLA Eng. & Wales

Knoop, (Carl) Julius Gerhard von, Baron von Knoop in the Prussian nobility (1822–1893), merchant and banker, was born on 17 November 1822 in Bremen, north Germany, the fifth of the eight children of Gerhard Knoop (1782–1862), a tobacco merchant, and his wife, Anna Rebecca (1793–1878), the daughter of Peter Frerichs (1764–1811), a dyer from Bremen, and his wife, Anna (1775–1853). The Knoop family had lived intermittently in Bremen since the seventeenth century. Gerhard Knoop enjoyed little commercial success, and his business went into liquidation in 1833.

Julius Knoop is believed to have attended local parish schools in Bremen, first in the St Stephan district and then in St Pauli, leaving at the age of fourteen to serve a commercial apprenticeship with a local firm. He went to Manchester around 1840 to work for his uncles Johann Andreas and Johann Hinrich Frerichs, partners in a trading house, De Jersey & Co., which specialized in the export of cotton to Russia. His elder brother, Ludwig, had spent a year with De Jersey from 1838 before representing them in Russia, where he achieved spectacular success, being credited with the establishment of 122 cotton textile mills on behalf of his Russian clients. On 7 May 1847 Julius married Theodora Henrietta Carolina, the daughter of Peter Frerichs, a merchant, at Cheltenham; the couple had a daughter and three sons.

In the 1850s the restless energy of the two Knoop brothers clashed with the more cautious approach of their uncles. The Frerichs brothers progressively withdrew from the business, leaving Julius as the senior partner with effective control of operations in both Manchester and London. Despite his commercial career being overshadowed by that of his celebrated elder brother, Julius made a major contribution to the Knoop family's commercial success. Their essentially collaborative venture may have manifested itself largely in the form of Russian textile mills, owned, controlled, or supplied by his brother's Russian firm, L. Knoop & Co.; however, the important but less visible aspect of the business outside Russia, the handling of their cotton supplies from the

United States and elsewhere, and particularly the supply of textile machinery and the requisite finance, was largely the responsibility of Julius. At some point, before or during the American civil war, Julius established a new house, Knoop, Hanemann & Co., in New York and New Orleans. By the 1870s it had a large business shipping cotton, mainly from Savannah and Charleston.

On the fiftieth anniversary of De Jersey & Co. in 1877 the glowing tributes from such companies as Platt Bros. in Oldham, Hick, Hargreaves in Bolton, John Musgrave & Sons, Bolton, Mather and Platt in Salford, and Edward Green & Son in Wakefield, whose products the Knoops marketed in Russia, make it clear that Julius, through his industry, skill, and perseverance, was seen by them as the driving force behind the company's operations outside Russia. It was reflected too in De Jersey's large shareholdings in Russian textile mills and Russian banks. Whether these were taken into account in the Bank of England's 1882 estimate of De Jersey & Co.'s capital at more than £1 million is uncertain. De Jersey's compensation claim after the Russian Revolution for its sequestrated Russian assets was approximately £6 million, but this excluded the Knoop family's largest textile mill at Krenholm in Estonia, suggesting that Julius on his death would have been worth well over £1 million.

Although he remained the senior partner until his death, Julius Knoop progressively handed over the running of De Jersey & Co. to other partners, including his sons Andreas Wilhelm and Ludwig Carl, partners from 1877 and 1891 respectively. From 1866 his time was increasingly spent in Germany at Wiesbaden, a favourite summer resort of the Prussian nobility. Here he had built an impressive mansion, Knoop-Villa, in extensive grounds on Wiesbaden's western side. With his wife Theodora, he was soon an important figure in Wiesbaden's social and cultural circles. He gave generously towards the construction costs of the city's new kindergarten. He became master of the local hunt and entertained Kaiser Wilhelm I. He was raised to the Prussian nobility in 1877 and was made a hereditary baron in 1888 under the style of Baron (Freiherr) von Knoop. He died in Wiesbaden on 16 April 1893 and was buried at Nordfriedhof, Wiesbaden. Knoop's mansion was demolished in 1907 to allow Wiesbaden's expansion, but he and his wife are commemorated there in the street names Juliusstrasse and Theodorenstrasse.

STUART THOMPSTONE

Sources S. Thompstone, 'Ludwig Knoop: the Arkwright of Russia', *Textile History*, 15 (1984) · A. Wolde, *Ludwig Knoop: Erinnerungsbilder aus seinem Leben* (privately printed, Bremen, 1928) · 'Alt Wiesbaden', *Rhein Main Presse* (27 May 1994) · 'Alt-Wiesbaden', *Rhein Main Presse* (31 May 1994) · *Stammtafel der Familie Knoop* (1897) [see also unpubd suppl.] · commercial circulars, U. Nott., Brandt MSS · *Kontora Knop i yeye znacheniye* (1895) [The house of Knoop and its significance] · Otto, Graf zu Stolberg-Wernigerode, ed., *Neue deutsche Biographie* (Berlin, 1953–) · Harvard U., Baker Library, R. G. Dun registers · m. cert.
Archives Harvard U., Baker Library, R. G. Dun registers
Likenesses photograph, c.1840, repro. in Wolde, *Ludwig Knoop* · K. Kögler, group portrait, oils, 1875, priv. coll.

Knott, Cargill Gilston (1856–1922), physicist and seismologist, was born on 30 June 1856 in Valleyfield, Midlothian, the sixth son in the family of seven sons and one daughter of Pelham Knott (1818–1864), clerk in a paper mill and later paper (commission) agent of Penicuik, and his wife, Helen Macintyre (1817–1894), daughter of Patrick McOmish, writer of Edinburgh, and his wife, Elizabeth Arrott. The family, though originally English, had been settled in Scotland for several generations. Maternally, Knott was descended from the brother of Donald Cargill the Martyr. Following the death of his father Knott was brought up by an aunt and uncle in Edinburgh and he attended Arbroath high school (1864–72). He went on to Edinburgh University in October 1872. After gaining his BSc in 1876 he became a research assistant to P. G. Tait, professor of natural philosophy. Knott worked in his laboratory—an ill-equipped attic—until 1883, after obtaining his DSc with a thesis on researches in contact electricity in 1879.

In 1883 Knott travelled to Japan to succeed J. A. Ewing as professor of physics in the Imperial College of Engineering (later the Imperial University of Japan). In June 1885 at the British legation in Tokyo he married Mary (formerly Jane) Gray Dixon (1860–1934), eldest daughter of the Revd James Main Dixon, minister of Free Martyrs Church, Paisley, and his wife, Jane Gray; they had one son and three daughters. In Tokyo Knott worked closely with J. Milne, T. Gray, and F. Omori to develop the new science of seismology. He applied Fourier analysis to investigate annual periodicity of earthquake shocks (1886) and developed a theory to explain the reflection and refraction of earthquake waves at the boundary between rock and water (1888). In 1887 he and A. Tanakadate conducted the first magnetic survey of Japan, for which Knott had the unusual distinction of being decorated by the emperor in 1891 with the order of the Rising Sun (class 4). On his return to Scotland that same year Knott was appointed lecturer in mathematics and in 1892 reader in applied mathematics at Edinburgh University.

In 1899 Knott extended his earlier theory to wave behaviour at the interface between two different types of rock. This work laid the foundation for the later unravelling of the interior structure of the earth through observation of the behaviour of seismic waves as they are transmitted through it from distant earthquakes.

Knott became a fellow of the Royal Society of Edinburgh in 1880 and its general secretary in 1912, and was a principal founder of the Edinburgh Mathematical Society. He was Thompson lecturer, United Free Church college, Aberdeen, in 1905–6 and 1913–14. His 113 publications include the books: *Electricity and Magnetism* (1893), *The Physics of Earthquake Phenomena* (1908), and the *Life and Scientific Work of Peter Guthrie Tait* (1911). He received the Keith prize of the Royal Society of Edinburgh for work on the magnetic properties of iron and nickel in 1897. He held an honorary LLD of the University of St Andrews (1916) and was elected FRS in 1920.

His contemporaries remembered Knott as kindly, painstaking, cheerful, and imperturbably good-natured. He enjoyed golf and chess and held office in the United Free Church of Scotland. Knott died of aortic heart disease on 26 October 1922 at 42 Upper Gray Street, Edinburgh, where he had lived since 1891. He was buried on 28 October at Newington cemetery, Edinburgh.

RICHARD J. HOWARTH

Sources E. T. Whittaker, *Proceedings of the Royal Society of Edinburgh*, 43 (1922–3), 237–48 · R. A. S., *PRS*, 102A (1922–3), xxvii–xxviii · A. L. Turner, *History of the University of Edinburgh, 1883–1933* (1933) · U. Edin. L., special collections division, university archives · *WW* · Mortonhill crematorium, Edinburgh · b. cert. · m. cert. · d. cert. · m. cert. [Helen McOmish] · d. cert. [Helen Knott] · d. cert. [Pelham Knott] · d. cert. [Mary Gray Knott]
Archives CUL, corresp. with Lord Kelvin · U. Edin. L., letters to Revd Osmond Fisher
Likenesses group portrait, photograph (*Graduates in engineering of 1921*), U. Edin. · photograph, Royal Society of Edinburgh; repro. in Whittaker, *Proceedings of the Royal Society of Edinburgh*, facing p. 237
Wealth at death £4237 17s. 1d.: confirmation, 16 Dec 1922, *CCI*

Knott, Edward [*formerly* Matthew Wilson] (1581–1656), Jesuit, was born Matthew Wilson at Catchburn, Morpeth, Northumberland, on 24 February 1581. His father was Edward Wilson but his mother's name is unknown; he described his parents as 'respectable' (Kenny, 122). His family in the main conformed to the established religion. He received some education in England and then through the offices of a Catholic friend was sent to the English College, Douai, arriving on 24 September 1599. Here he was accepted into the Roman Catholic church. On 20 August 1602 he left for the English College, Rome. He was duly ordained priest on 27 March 1606 and entered the Society of Jesus in October of that year. He completed the rigorous training of a Jesuit, taking the four vows finally on 30 September 1618, and played the while an active part in the work of the English College, Rome.

Then in 1622 the decision was taken to send Knott north, to the English mission. There were to be three strands to his life now: he continued to work as an educationist; this role was combined with the position as one of the leading administrators of the English province; and he became a writer of religious tracts. Much of his time was spent in the Spanish Netherlands in the various educational institutions attached to the English province: as superior of the noviciate at Watten in 1622 and 1637–8; rector and then prefect of the house of studies at Liège in 1627–8 and 1646; and as spiritual prefect at the tertianship in Ghent, 1647–9. The provincial in London required a deputy over the channel to run the fairly considerable English establishment in the Spanish Netherlands. Much of Knott's career was passed in this capacity: a year after he arrived (1623) he was appointed vice-provincial in what would later become Belgium; in 1625–6 and 1632 he was designated substitute for the provincial there. He did, however, work in England, based largely in London, certainly in 1624, 1635–6, 1643–4, 1645–6, 1647, and in the early 1650s. He was captured when returning to England in April 1629 and was imprisoned in the Clink until January 1632, when he was released through the intercession of Marie de' Medici, and banished.

Knott was well regarded by his superiors and colleagues,

and there was little competition for the extremely difficult position of provincial. In November 1630 Richard Blount recommended that Knott succeed him in that post, but the general was reluctant, pointing out that he had worked almost entirely on the continent and was not well known in England; he was also in prison. As a result Knott was passed over in favour of Henry More. When More stood down Knott was eventually appointed, on 3 June 1639. But now a new difficulty faced him. From 1630 Knott had been active as a controversial religious writer; he was to write a total of eight titles, some of which went through more than one edition. Knott was a most effective pamphleteer, generally—and for his age, unusually—concise, writing one book, as he tells us, in one week. He engaged in two great debates: first as part of the internecine Catholic disputes between regulars and seculars over the appointment of a bishop to the English mission, which he opposed. Second, he played a part in a long-running controversy with the protestant Edward Chillingworth. His contribution to this debate was considered sufficiently offensive by Charles I for the king to let it be known that he did not wish Knott to take up his appointment as provincial in 1639. So Knott was ordered by the general to remain in the Netherlands. When, in June 1643, he finally came to England as provincial Knott began a tour of the priests under his command. His stay was again cut short, this time by the need to attend in November 1645 the general congregation called to Rome to elect a general in succession to Vitelleschi. Here he acquitted himself well, always adding, according to report, something new when it came to his turn to speak. By now Knott was certainly the most important English Jesuit; it was he who was given the task by the general of choosing which of two candidates should be the next provincial in 1646; he was nominated in 1649 by the outgoing provincial as his replacement, but not appointed. Finally, in March 1652 he was reappointed provincial. He died in office on 4 January 1656 in London, and was buried next day in the church of St Pancras.   PETER HOLMES

Sources T. M. McCoog, ed., *Monumenta Angliae*, 1–2 (1992) • T. M. McCoog, *English and Welsh Jesuits, 1555–1650*, 2 vols., Catholic RS, 74–5 (1994–5) • H. Foley, ed., *Records of the English province of the Society of Jesus*, 7 vols. in 8 (1875–83) • G. Anstruther, *The seminary priests*, 4 vols. (1969–77) • DNB • A. F. Allison and D. M. Rogers, eds., *The contemporary printed literature of the English Counter-Reformation between 1558 and 1640*, 2 vols. (1989–94) • T. H. Clancy, *English Catholic books, 1641–1700: a bibliography* [1974] • Wood, *Ath. Oxon.*, new edn, 3.91–3, 182, 386, 388, 995 • R. Stanfield, ed., 'The archpriest controversy', *Miscellanea, XII*, Catholic RS, 22 (1921), 132–86, esp. 186 • A. Kenny, ed., *The responsa scholarum of the English College, Rome*, 1, Catholic RS, 54 (1962), 122–3 • W. Kelly, ed., *Liber ruber venerabilis collegii Anglorum de urbe*, 1, Catholic RS, 37 (1940), 129 • A. F. Allison, 'Richard Smith's Gallican backers and Jesuit opponents [pt 1]', *Recusant History*, 18 (1986–7), 329–401 • A. F. Allison, 'Sir Toby Matthew, the author of *Charity mistaken*', *Recusant History*, 5 (1959–60), 128–30

Knott, Ralph (1878–1929), architect, was born in Pont Street, Chelsea, on 3 May 1878, the eighth child and youngest son of Samuel Knott, a prosperous tailor in Pont Street, and his wife, Elizabeth Ann White, from Portland, Dorset. Educated at the City of London School, he served his articles in the architectural practice of Woodd and Ainslie.

During this time he studied at the Architectural Association, and was taught etching by Frank Brangwyn. About 1900 he joined the office of Aston Webb, where he worked on the Admiralty Arch and the Victoria and Albert Museum. A fine draughtsman and watercolourist, he was placed second in the Tite prize of 1901. During his period with Webb, Knott—together with E. Stone Collins—entered competitions for the Bristol Reference Library (1902) and the Malvern Free Library (1904), in both of which they were placed second, and for the Lambeth municipal buildings (1905).

In June 1907 Knott took leave of absence from Webb's office to work on a design for the new county hall for the London county council. The competition for this monumental building was held in two stages; the first, open, stage attracted ninety-nine entries, from which fifteen were selected to join a further eight well-known firms which had been invited directly into the second stage. The assessors for the second stage, Norman Shaw, Aston Webb (elected to the role by the competitors), and the London county council's chief architect, W. E. Riley, unanimously selected Knott as overall winner, a decision ratified by the council in February 1908. Knott was twenty-nine years old, with almost no practical experience of architecture. Although the winning design was Knott's, he had been helped in the draughting work by his friend E. Stone Collins. This gave rise to the first element of friction between Knott and W. E. Riley; for Collins had been, until he left to set up practice with Knott in April 1908, employed in the London county council's architect's department.

After setting up offices in Robert Street, Adelphi, Knott embarked upon a long process of design modifications under both political and aesthetic influences. The Progressive Party had initiated the whole drive towards a new and monumental county hall. In the midst of the competition they were defeated by the Municipal Reform Party, and had the cost not been prohibitive they would have cancelled the project entirely. In the event the budget was reduced, and Knott had no choice but to cut back on some of the grander aspects of his design. The Municipal Reformers also decided they could do without the northern end of the building, in the short term, so that, when County Hall was officially opened by George V in 1922, it consisted of a centrepiece with only one wing, which for a decade presented the Thames with a severely lopsided composition. The northernmost quarter of the building was completed after Knott's death, to designs heavily modified by Collins, and opened in 1933.

Pressure for design modification came also from the assessors themselves, who continued to supervise the development of the project over several years. Shaw guided Knott through the aesthetic perplexities resulting from the altered brief, always encouraging and often astute; however, Riley, the council's man, was autocratic and impatient, and must often have been a thorn in Knott's side. Work on site also proceeded slowly. Difficulties with the foundations were followed by the outbreak of war in 1914. All work was halted in 1915, and Knott designed workshops for the Royal Air Force until 1918.

Both Knott's competition project and the building as completed are part of a neo-classical revival with origins in the urban redevelopment schemes of the previous ten years. The competition design had placed a grand crescent on the land side—facing Belvedere Road—and the council chamber nestled within it. On the Thames front a giant portico came down to the river's edge. That grandeur was soon trimmed, but Knott contrived to shift the semicircular feature onto the riverfront. The most successful sequence of spaces is undoubtedly the members' carriage drive, leading from Westminster Bridge Road to the council chamber. This monumental set piece is one of the finest 'Piranesian' compositions ever realized. It has been described as 'the realisation to full scale and in three dimensions of an Ecole des Beaux-Arts student's drawing' (Gray, 230).

Though Knott's career was almost entirely absorbed by County Hall, he did carry out a number of smaller commissions, and in 1913 he and Collins found the time to enter the Devonport Guildhall competition, in which they gained third place. Among Knott's smaller works were a house in modified County Hall style in Upper Grosvenor Street, Mayfair (1908–9), and Mallord House, Chelsea, completed in 1911. The Chelsea house, designed for the painter Cecil Hunt, shows Knott working entirely successfully in a free-style classical vein, with the plain brick and tile mass of the building containing one or two finely detailed classical elements on an exaggerated scale. In 1923 the British government commissioned Knott to design office buildings and the speaker's house in Belfast as part of the parliament buildings for Northern Ireland. This work was mostly taken over by Arnold Thornely, and Knott's contribution was restricted to the speaker's house (1927–8), a fine building which shares County Hall's grand architectural manner. He also carried on with domestic work, and built a factory in Gravesend, Kent, for W. T. Henley's cable works.

Knott was elected fellow of the Royal Institute of British Architects in 1921. On 21 January 1919 he married Ada (b. 1876/7), widow of Sidney James Longden and daughter of Richard Brown, a church artist. He died quite suddenly on 25 January 1929 at his home, West Lodge, Christchurch Road, Mortlake, leaving no children. His wife survived him.   ANTHONY OSLER MCINTYRE

Sources H. Hobhouse, ed., *County Hall*, 17 (1991) · London county council records of staffing, management, accommodation, and organizational matters, LMA · London county council architect's department: records of council buildings (construction and maintenance), LMA · A. S. Gray, *Edwardian architecture: a biographical dictionary* (1985) · *DNB* · b. cert. · m. cert. · d. cert. · *CGPLA Eng. & Wales* (1929)
Likenesses photograph, 1908, Hult. Arch. · photograph, 1922, repro. in *ILN* (15 July 1922), 105 · G. Bayes, bronze bas relief, 1931; formerly at London County Hall
Wealth at death £160: probate, 14 Feb 1929, *CGPLA Eng. & Wales*

Knowler, William (*bap.* 1699, *d.* 1773), Church of England clergyman, third son of Gilbert Knowler of Stroud House, Herne, in Kent, was born at Herne and baptized there on 9 May 1699. He was educated at school in Canterbury under Mr Smith and then at St John's College, Cambridge, whence he matriculated in 1717. He graduated BA in 1721, MA in 1724, and LLD in 1728. On leaving Cambridge, he was ordained priest on 9 June 1723 and became chaplain to Thomas Watson Wentworth, then Lord Malton, later marquess of Rockingham. Lord Malton had inherited the papers of his great-grandfather, Thomas Wentworth, earl of Strafford, and Knowler was given the task of publishing a selection from them. This appeared in 1739 under the title of *The Earl of Strafford's Letters and Despatches*. In the dedication to Lord Malton, Knowler states that the papers were selected in order to vindicate Strafford's memory from 'the aspersions of acting upon arbitrary principles, and being a friend to the Roman catholics'. It is possible that Knowler obtained some help from William Oldys's *Essay on Epistolary Writings with Respect to the Grand Collection of Thomas, Earl of Strafford* (1729), which was also dedicated to Lord Malton. Knowler was presented by his patron, first, in 1725, to the living of Irthlingborough, Northamptonshire, then, in 1736, to the vicarage of Hutton Buscel, Yorkshire, and afterwards, in 1740, to the living of Boddington, Northamptonshire. On 3 May 1749 he married Mary Dalton at Lincoln's Inn Chapel, Holborn. In 1766 he had prepared for the press a translation of Chrysostom's commentary on St Paul's epistle to the Galatians, which was never printed. He died in December 1773, and was buried at Boddington on 26 January 1774. He was survived by his wife and a son and four daughters.

C. H. FIRTH, *rev.* J. A. MARCHAND

Sources Nichols, *Lit. anecdotes*, 2.129–30 · Venn, *Alum. Cant.* · *GM*, 1st ser., 44 (1774), 46 · *IGI* · *A literary antiquary: memoir of William Oldys … together with his diary*, ed. J. Yeowell (1862), viii · *Curiosities of literature, by I. D'Israeli*, ed. B. Corney (1837), 113 · will, proved, 13 April 1774, PRO, PROB 11/997, fols. 72r–73v
Wealth at death £2000 to wife, to be split between four daughters and son on her death; £20 to William Bowyer: will, PRO, PROB 11/997, fols. 72r–73v

Knowles. *See also* Knollys.

Knowles, Sir Charles, first baronet (*d.* 1777), naval officer, was reputedly the son of Charles *Knollys, styled fourth earl of Banbury (*bap.* 1662, *d.* 1740); the identity of his mother, the date of his birth, and details of his upbringing are all unknown. His abilities as an engineer suggest a sound education. He may have served as a volunteer on the *Bedford* in 1708 and the *Valeur* in 1711, but the muster book of the latter does not record his presence on the ship. In March 1718 he entered the *Buckingham* with Captain Charles Strickland, whom he followed to the *Lennox* in April, with the rating of captain's servant; he continued in the *Lennox* until December 1720. For much of this time the *Lennox* was in the Mediterranean under the orders of Sir George Byng, and from Knowles's own papers it appears that in the battle off Cape Passaro in August 1718 he was serving on the *Barfleur*, Byng's flagship. Between June 1721 and June 1726 he served in the frigate *Lyme* under Lord Vere Beauclerk, rated first captain's servant and later steward and able seaman. Knowles passed his lieutenant's examination on 30 January 1729 and in the following year he was promoted lieutenant of the *Trial*. In March 1731 he was moved to the *Lion*, flagship of Rear-Admiral Charles Stewart in the West Indies.

On 24 November 1731 Knowles was promoted commander of the *Southampton* (40 guns) serving as a hulk at Port Antonio, Jamaica. There Knowles served as an engineer in the development of the port for use by the Royal Navy. He returned to England in 1735 but it was not until February 1737 that he became captain of the *Diamond*. In her he went out to the West Indies and in November 1739 joined Vice-Admiral Edward Vernon at Porto Bello where he was ordered to destroy the settlement's forts. In March 1740 Knowles was involved in the attack on the port of Chagres to the west-south-west of Port Bello. On its surrender he was appointed governor of the castle pending the destruction of the defences. In June he returned to England and on arrival was appointed to the *Weymouth* (60 guns). In October the *Weymouth* was one of the fleet under Rear-Admiral Sir Chaloner Ogle which escorted the expeditionary army under Major-General Lord Cathcart to the West Indies. Knowles took part in the unsuccessful expedition against Cartagena during March and April 1741, and acted throughout as Vernon's principal surveyor and engineer. He was active in examining the approaches to the several points of attack, cutting the boom across the Boca Chica, taking possession of the Castillo Grande, and destroying the captured works before the fleet left. A pamphlet entitled *An Account of the Expedition to Carthagena* (1743), highly critical of the army's conduct in the campaign, is generally attributed to Knowles.

After the failure at Cartagena, Knowles was moved into the *Lichfield*, and in the course of 1742 into the *Suffolk* (70 guns). In her he commanded a squadron which was sent to act against the Spanish settlements on the Caracas coast. The Spaniards were prepared for his arrival and when the squadron attacked La Guayra on 18 February 1743 it was beaten off with very heavy losses. After refitting, it attacked Puerto Cabello on 15 and 24 April with no better fortune. On 28 April it was decided that the squadron was no longer able to engage the enemy, and Knowles returned to Jamaica where, between 1743 and 1745, he continued as second in command under Ogle. Towards the end of 1745 he returned to England, and after a short time in the Downs, as second in command under Vice-Admiral William Martin, he was, early in 1746, sent out as governor of Louisbourg, which had been captured from the French a few months before. There he remained for upwards of two years, but he disliked the place and was eager to return to the West Indies. In the large promotion of 15 July 1747 he was made rear-admiral of the white, and at the same time was appointed commander-in-chief at Jamaica.

In February 1748, with his flag in the *Cornwall*, Knowles took the squadron to the south coast of Cuba. After capturing Port Louis, Hispaniola (St Domingue) on 8 March he arrived off Santiago in April and prepared for an attack. An attack was immediately attempted, but the failure of this assault resulted in a disagreement between Knowles and Captain Dent in the *Plymouth*, the former commander-in-chief, who led in. Dent was sent home to be tried on,

and later cleared of, a charge of not having done his utmost. Meanwhile Knowles, having refitted the ships at Jamaica, took them for a cruise off Havana in hopes of intercepting the Spanish treasure fleet. This occurred on 1 October and heavy fighting ensued between the *Cornwall*, the *Strafford* (Captain David Brodie), and the Spanish ships *Africa* and *Conquistador*. In writing of the engagement to Lord Anson, Knowles spoke of the 'bashfulness' of some of his captains. They in turn accused Knowles of delaying the attack, engaging in a straggling line, and providing a false report to the Admiralty. A court martial on Knowles was accordingly ordered, and sat at Deptford in December 1749. Captain Thomas Innes of the *Warwick* acted as prosecutor, in the name of the captains. The court decided that Knowles was at fault in taking his fleet into action in such a straggling line, and also in not going on board another ship and leading the chase in person. He was sentenced to be reprimanded. The four captains were themselves then put on their trial: Holmes was honourably acquitted, Charles Powlett and Edmund Toll were reprimanded, and Thomas Innes suspended for three months. Many duels followed. Knowles received four challenges and exchanged shots with Holmes on 24 February. A meeting also took place between Innes and Edward Clarke, the principal witness against him, and Innes was mortally wounded. Several more duels were forbidden by the king, who ordered the challengers into custody.

On 28 November 1749 Knowles was elected MP for Gatton in Surrey. His interest in this pocket borough of about twenty-two electors is not clear, but his objective was almost certainly to further his career, and in 1752 he gave it up on being appointed governor of Jamaica. He offended the residents by insisting on the supreme jurisdiction of the English parliament, and by moving the seat of government to Kingston, thus causing a depreciation of property in Spanish Town. A petition for his removal, signed by nineteen members of the assembly, was presented to the king, and charges of 'illegal, cruel, and arbitrary acts' were laid before the House of Commons. After examination by a committee of the whole house, the assembly's action was condemned as 'derogatory to the rights of the crown and people of Great Britain', and Knowles's conduct, by implication, fully justified. But Knowles had already returned to England and resigned the governorship in January 1756.

On 4 February 1755 Knowles had been promoted vice-admiral, and in 1757, with his flag in the *Neptune*, he was second in command under Sir Edward Hawke in the abortive expedition against Rochefort. Knowles was among those reproached for this failure and responded with a pamphlet, *The Conduct of Admiral Knowles on the Late Expedition Set in a True Light* (1758). This met with scant favour, and a notice of it in the *Critical Review* (1758, 5.438) was so extreme that the editor, Tobias Smollett, was tried for libel and sentenced to a £100 fine and three months' imprisonment. Nevertheless Knowles's share in the miscarriage offended the government. He was superseded in his command and, though he retained his flag in the *Royal*

Anne, guardship at Portsmouth, he had no further active service in the English navy.

On 3 December 1760 Knowles was promoted to the rank of admiral of the white. In October 1765 he was created a baronet, and on 5 November 1765 nominated rear-admiral of Great Britain. In October 1770 he accepted an appointment as chief of the surveying branch in the Russian navy and reluctantly resigned as rear-admiral. Knowles carried out surveys of the Baltic yards and ships and made a series of suggestions for administrative and technical improvements, based largely on the British model. He returned to England on the conclusion of peace between Russia and Turkey (1774) and in the following year he published a translation of M. de la Croix's *Abstract on the Mechanism of the Motions of Floating Bodies*. In the preface he claimed to have verified the author's principles by a number of experiments, and to have found them effective in several line-of-battle ships and frigates that he built while in Russia. Knowles was married twice: first in 1740 to Mary Alleyne (d. 1742); they had one son, Edward, who was killed in command of the *Peregrine* (1762). In July 1750 he married Maria-Magdalena Theresa, daughter of the comte de Bouget; they had one daughter and a son, Charles Henry *Knowles, also a naval officer. Knowles died at his home in Bulstrode Street, St Marylebone, Middlesex, on 9 December 1777, reportedly after having suffered a paralytic stroke brought on by bathing in the sea at Weymouth. He was buried next to his first wife in St Nicholas's Church, Guildford.

J. K. LAUGHTON, *rev.* RICHARD HARDING

Sources captains' letters, PRO, ADM 1/2006–2008 · PRO, Louisbourg MSS, CO 5/44 · secretary of state—Jamaica, PRO, CO 137/58 · BL, Anson MSS, MS 15956 · PRO, ADM 6/9, 132; ADM 6/11, 94; ADM 6/14, 92 · examination certificate, PRO, ADM 107/3, 192 · PRO, ADM 36/1898–1900 (*Lyme*); ADM 36/4269 (*Torbay*); ADM 36/1825 (*Lion*); ADM 36/4343 (*Trial*) · PRO, PROB 11/1038 q23 · J. Charnock, ed., *Biographia navalis*, 4 (1796), 343–69
Archives Admiralty Library, naval papers · BL, narrative and remarks on siege of Havana and Isle of Cuba, Add. MS 23678 · priv. coll. | BL, letters to Lord Anson, Add. MS 15956 · BL, corresp. with the duke of Newcastle, Add. MSS 32715–32966, *passim* · NMM, letter-book of corresp. with Catherine, empress of Russia · PRO, Louisbourg MSS, CO 5/44 · PRO, ADM 1/2006–2008 · U. Hull, Brynmor Jones L., letters to Charles Hotham
Likenesses G. Bickham, group portrait, line engraving, *c.*1765 (*Six admirals*), BM · J. Ridley, stipple, pubd 1803, NPG · T. Hudson, mezzotint (after J. Faber junior), BM, NPG · mezzotint, BM

Knowles, Sir Charles Henry, second baronet (1754–1831), naval officer, was born in Kingston, Jamaica, on 24 August 1754, the son of Sir Charles *Knowles, baronet (d. 1777), then governor of the island, and his second wife, Maria-Magdalena Theresa, daughter of the comte de Bouget. Educated at Eton College (*c.*1764–1766) and the University of Glasgow, Charles Henry entered the Royal Navy in 1768 as a captain's servant to the Hon. Samuel Barrington in the *Venus*. He spent the next six and a half years serving in various ships until, on 1 January 1776, he was commissioned lieutenant. He served in the *Boreas* from May 1776 and arrived in New York in August, where he spent the next five months in operations against the American rebels. Knowles returned to Britain briefly in

January 1777 to be with his ailing father but returned to North America that summer, though he left for England again when his father died on 9 December, whereupon he became second baronet.

Knowles returned to active service when he sailed for the Leeward Islands in the summer of 1778. He took part in an action in the Cul-de-Sac off St Lucia on 15 December, while in the *Ceres*. This ship was shortly afterwards captured by a French squadron and Knowles was briefly held prisoner. He was soon exchanged, however, and was then court martialled with the captain and other officers and acquitted for the loss of the ship. In May 1779 he received his first independent command, as acting master and commander of the storeship *Supply*. He fought in an action off Grenada on 6 July 1779, while in the *Prince of Wales*, when he was slightly wounded. At the end of October 1779 he returned to England.

Knowles volunteered for service once more in December, and went with Admiral Sir George Rodney to Gibraltar. Rodney evidently thought highly of him, as Knowles was promoted to substantive commander of the *Minorca* at the end of January 1780 and, just a week later, to post captain of the *Porcupine*. While in the *Porcupine*, Knowles engaged in several actions with Spanish and French privateers as well as escorting several merchant vessels. He was taken ill in Minorca and briefly blockaded there by a French squadron, but in January 1781 he was enabled by their departure to head for Gibraltar where he remained until April 1782. On his return to England he was falsely accused of piracy and murder, but having successfully cleared his name he went back to Gibraltar, where he served as senior naval officer until April 1783. While there he captured and retained possession of the Spanish ship of the line *San Miguel*, and in her he returned to England.

During the peace Knowles prepared several papers on naval matters and in 1788 embarked on a tour of France. When war started in February 1793 he was appointed to the *Daedalus* which he took to North America. In January 1794 a French squadron arrived in American waters, but Knowles was able to evade capture by the French vessels. In the summer of 1794 he left for Britain and took command of the *Edgar*, a poorly manned and dilapidated ship of the line, in which he sailed for Norway and then to the Texel, where the *Edgar* lost masts and had to be towed back to Britain.

Knowles left for the Mediterranean in the *Goliath* in March 1796, and took part in the battle of Cape St Vincent on 14 February 1797. Like many officers he came in for sharp criticism from Admiral Sir John Jervis. By contrast the journal of the seaman John Nicol reveals him as a very popular captain with the lower deck; he also received public thanks for his role in the battle. However, while Knowles was at dinner in Lagos Bay with some other officers his ship received orders and sailed without him. To compensate him for this affront the Admiralty appointed Knowles to command the first rate *Britannia* (100 guns), but ill health apparently prevented him from accepting the post.

Knowles saw no further active service, but he received

steady promotion through the higher ranks of the navy, being made rear-admiral on 14 February 1799, vice admiral on 23 April 1804, and full admiral on 31 July 1810. An innovative thinker, Knowles may have made the earliest suggestion for naval aircraft when he put forward the proposal to use balloons flown from shipboard to observe Brest in 1803. On 10 September 1800 he married Charlotte (d. 1867), daughter of Charles Johnstone. They had four children: one son, Francis Charles; and three daughters, Louisa Charlotte, Georgiana Henrietta, and Maria Louisa Theresa. Knowles continued to produce works on naval affairs, publishing his last edition of his *Observations on Naval Tactics* in 1830. In recognition of his services, on the accession of George IV in 1820, he was made a supplementary knight grand cross in the Order of the Bath. He died on 28 November 1831.

J. K. LAUGHTON, rev. MICHAEL PARTRIDGE

Sources J. Ralfe, 'Knowles, Charles Henry', *The naval biography of Great Britain*, 2 (1828), 227–59 · J. Marshall, *Royal naval biography*, 1 (1823), 113–16 · Burke, *Peerage* (1847) · commission book, PRO, ADM 6/87, (1 Jan 1776) · L. E. Holland, 'The development of signalling in the Royal Navy', *Mariner's Mirror*, 39 (1953), 5–26 · D. Syrett, *The Royal Navy in American waters, 1775–1783* (1989) · B. Tunstall, *Naval warfare in the age of sail: the evolution of fighting tactics, 1650–1815*, ed. N. Tracy (1990) · D. B. Smith, 'Kite balloon ships', *Mariner's Mirror*, 13 (1927), 172–3
Archives BL, letters to the second Earl Spencer
Likenesses Worthington and Parker, group portrait, line engraving, pubd 1803 (*Naval victories, commemoration of the 14th February, 179*; after R. Smirke), BM, NPG

Knowles, Sir **Francis Gerald William**, sixth baronet (1915–1974), biologist, was born on 9 March 1915 at Ottawa, the only child of Sir Francis Howe Seymour Knowles, fifth baronet, prehistorian and sometime physical anthropologist to the geological survey of Canada, and his wife, Kathleen Constance Averina, daughter of William Lennon, county inspector, Royal Irish Constabulary. He was educated in England, at Radley College and at Oriel College, Oxford, graduating BA (second class) in the honour school of zoology in 1936. Awarded the Oxford University Naples scholarship, he visited the Stazione Zoologica in 1937–8. He began investigating the role of hormones in the regulation of colour change in lampreys and crustaceans. He was awarded his MA and PhD in 1939.

When his scholarship ended in 1938 Knowles became senior biology master at Marlborough College. While at Marlborough he published several biological texts, including *Man and other Living Things* (1945) and *Biology and Man* (1950), and also continued his researches on crustacean colour change, working during school holidays at marine biological laboratories with support from the Royal Society and the Nuffield Foundation. These activities gave his pupils an insight into scientific research that could have been found in few other schools at that time. In 1948 Knowles married Ruth Jessie, daughter of the Revd Arthur Brooke-Smith, and widow of Pilot Officer Richard Guy Hulse of the RAF. They had one son, Charles Francis

(b. 1951), and three daughters. (There was also a stepdaughter.) In 1953 Knowles succeeded his father as baronet.

In his later years at Marlborough, Knowles became aware of the new perspectives that had been opened in comparative endocrinology through the discovery of neurosecretion: the process by which certain nerve cells secrete hormones into the bloodstream. He was quick to exploit this concept, making skilful use of a variety of new techniques, including electron microscopy, which retained his special interest. Presentation of his results, delivered at international gatherings with calculated panache, brought him a reputation that led to his appointment in 1958 as lecturer, with special responsibility for electron microscopy, in the department of anatomy at Birmingham University.

Quickly establishing himself as a dynamic biologist, satisfied with nothing less than perfection in technique, Knowles expanded his researches to include the study of neurosecretory pathways in the brain and pituitary gland of the dogfish and, later, of the rhesus monkey. He was promoted reader in 1963, elected FRS in 1966, and was made professor of comparative endocrinology in 1967, in which year, however, he moved to the University of London as professor of anatomy at King's College.

At King's, Knowles soon abandoned primate research and turned once again to fish, despite the obvious difficulties of working on these animals from a London base. He took a full share in administration, serving with distinction as dean, and, at national level, becoming chairman of the biological sciences committee of the Science Research Council and a member of its science board. He organized the sixth international symposium on neurosecretion, which was held in London in September 1973. He took particular pleasure in the task, for this was the twentieth anniversary of the first symposium, where he had presented the results of his pioneering crustacean studies.

Knowles was essentially a solitary researcher. However, he took pleasure in wide-ranging discussions and enjoyed provoking reactions to the sometimes unorthodox views which flowed from his fertile mind with the flamboyance that was a marked feature of his character. This element came to the fore in 1955 with his purchase of Avebury Manor in Wiltshire. Restoration of the Elizabethan residence became an absorbing love, and an outlet for his unerringly elegant taste. The house was first opened to the public in May 1956, but also served as a grand family home. Set against this background, remote from academic biology, he appeared to one of his colleagues as 'a fascinating man who would really have been more at home in the eighteenth century'. To another he gave proof that 'one could be both a distinguished scholar and a warm vibrant person'. Knowles died in London on 13 July 1974.

E. J. W. BARRINGTON, rev.

Sources E. J. W. Barrington, *Memoirs FRS*, 21 (1975), 431–46 · personal knowledge (1986) · private information (1986) · *The Times* (18 July 1974)
Wealth at death £135,331: probate, 21 Aug 1974, *CGPLA Eng. & Wales*

Knowles, Gilbert (1667–1734), Roman Catholic priest and botanist, was born in Hampshire, professed at St Gregory's, Douai, France, and was ordained priest in 1700. He was sent to the Benedictine northern province in 1705, and stationed at Newburgh, Yorkshire, in 1710–19. In that year he was transferred to Wenby, where he remained until 1721. Probably during or soon after that time he composed his *Materia medica botanica* (1723), dedicated to Dr Richard Mead, and consisting of 7355 Latin hexameters. Four hundred plants of the materia medica are described and their uses in medicine explained. Various episodes are interwoven with the subject for the sake of ornament. Knowles alludes to his verses as being written 'rudi Minerva' and he was evidently a close student of both Virgil's style and his matter.

Knowles subsequently returned to Douai, where he died on 8 September 1734.

M. G. WATKINS, *rev.* ANITA MCCONNELL

Sources Gillow, *Lit. biog. hist.* • T. B. Snow, *Obit book of the English Benedictines from 1600 to 1912*, rev. H. N. Birt (privately printed, Edinburgh, 1913), 89 • Nichols, *Illustrations*, 8.442–3 • R. Pulteney, *Historical and biographical sketches of the progress of botany in England*, 1 (1790), 282
Likenesses J. Faber junior, mezzotint (after T. Murray), BM; repro. in G. Knowles, *Materia medica botanica* (1723)

Knowles, Herbert (1798–1817), poet, was born at Gomersal, near Leeds, Yorkshire. His parentage is said to have been very humble, but it is also stated that he was the brother of J. C. Knowles, subsequently QC. He was early orphaned and was about to enter a merchant's office at Liverpool when his talents came to the notice of three benevolent clergymen, who raised £20 a year towards his education on the condition that his friends contributed another £30, and sent him to Richmond grammar school, Yorkshire.

Lacking funds to obtain a sizarship at St John's College, Cambridge, Knowles wrote to Southey, sending him the poem entitled 'The Three Tabernacles', better known as 'Stanzas in Richmond Churchyard', which he had composed on 7 October 1816. Southey, with his usual generosity, promised £10 a year, and obtained a further £20 from Earl Spencer and Samuel Rogers. Knowles's letter to Southey, dated 28 December 1816, shows his modesty, candour, and good sense. He puts aside excessive expectations, but undertakes to 'strive that my passage through the university, if not splendid, shall be respectable'. His verses were printed in the *Literary Gazette* for 1819 and 1824, and the *Literary Souvenir* for 1825 (reprinted in the *Saturday Magazine*, vol. 16); and a correspondent of *Notes and Queries* possessed several unpublished pieces.

Knowles was elected a sizar on 31 January 1817, but was already fatally ill, and died on 17 February 1817 at Gomersal. His precocious talents and early death invite the inevitable comparison with Chatterton.

RICHARD GARNETT, *rev.* JOHN D. HAIGH

Sources *N&Q*, 2nd ser., 8 (1859), 28, 55, 79, 116, 153 • *The life and correspondence of Robert Southey*, ed. C. C. Southey, 6 vols. (1849–50),

vol. 4, pp. 221–7 • N. Carlisle, *A concise description of the endowed grammar schools in England and Wales*, 2 vols. (1818)

Knowles, Horace John (1884–1954). *See under* Knowles, Reginald Lionel (1879–1950).

Knowles, James (1759–1840), schoolmaster and lexicographer, was probably born in Dublin, the youngest of three sons and one daughter of John Knowles of Dublin, and Frances, daughter of the Revd Dr Dennis Sheridan of Quilca; he also had a sister. His father, who worked as treasurer in Sheridan's theatre in Smock Alley, died at an early age, and his mother provided for her young family by opening a girls' school in Dublin which proved a financial success. His mother's brother, Thomas *Sheridan, elocutionist and author of a renowned *Pronouncing Dictionary*, directed his education and intended him for the church. This plan was thwarted when Knowles fell in love on holiday in Cork with a singer, Jane Daunt (*d.* 1800), daughter of Andrew Peace, physician. A great beauty, she was recently widowed and had an infant daughter. They married in 1780 and established a school in Cork in 1780, which soon prospered. Their first two children died in infancy but the birth of a son, James Sheridan *Knowles (1784–1862), was followed by the birth of two daughters. The family's fortunes suffered when Knowles signed a petition for Catholic emancipation, and then went bail for a friend, the editor of a liberal paper, who had been prosecuted for libel by the government. His pupils, who were the sons of the local protestant gentry, deserted him, and in 1783 he and his family left Cork for London. He was helped by his first cousin Richard Brinsley Sheridan to continue his career as a schoolmaster, by setting up a private school in Sidcup.

Following his wife's death in 1800 Knowles married Miss Maxwell, but this remarriage did not please his son, who abruptly left home one day. Relations seemed to improve when James Sheridan Knowles relinquished his appointment as headmaster of the English department in the newly founded Belfast Academical Institution in favour of his father. Knowles gave up his school in Sidcup, which then had forty boarders, and began teaching in the Institution in April 1814, with his son as his assistant. This arrangement proved disastrous, not least because father and son differed fundamentally on the correct method and style of reading and elocution. These differences were exacerbated by Knowles's attitude; according to one historian of the school 'he displayed a mixture of truculence, petulance, tactlessness, bravado and down-right viciousness which made it a general relief when he finally went' (Jamieson, 13). After two and a half years in the post he was asked in 1817 to resign for the sake of the school, which had suffered a decline in pupil numbers, but he refused to go quietly. He published a pamphlet that claimed he was the aggrieved party and obtained a testimonial from some of the leading citizens in Belfast, but after barricading himself in the schoolmaster's house for several days, he was forced to leave. He returned to London, where he appears to have carried on his profession as 'teacher of reading, elocution, grammar, and composition'

(J. Knowles, *Orthoëpy and Elocution*, 1829, title-page) for several years. In 1829 he seems to have joined his son in Glasgow, where he brought out a little book entitled *Orthoëpy and Elocution*. About this time, although he was now seventy and suffering from the stone, he began to compile a dictionary. His grandson recalled how he would rise at four in the morning and plod 'through his dismal labours with all the zest and enthusiasm of youth in the pursuit of some bright fancy' (Knowles, 122). It was published in London in 1835 as *A Pronouncing and Explanatory Dictionary of the English Language* and was dedicated to William IV. A dispute with the printer over the number of copies embroiled him in a protracted lawsuit, which incurred costs of some £3000 that were borne by his long-suffering son.

Knowles died at his son's house, Alfred Place, Bedford Square, London, on 6 February 1840, and was buried at Highgate cemetery.   T. B. SAUNDERS, *rev.* S. J. SKEDD

Sources R. B. Knowles, *The life of James Sheridan Knowles* (1872) · *GM*, 2nd ser., 13 (1840), 440–41 · J. Knowles, 'A brief statement of Mr Knowles's case, in reference to the managers and visitors of the Belfast Academical Institution', in J. Knowles, *Orthoëpy and elocution* (1829) [preface] · J. R. Fisher and J. H. Robb, *Royal Belfast Academical Institution: centenary volume, 1810–1910* (1913) · J. Jamieson, *The history of the Royal Belfast Academical Institution, 1810–1960* (1959, [1960])
Likenesses J. Scott, mezzotint (after G. Lance), BM, NPG

Knowles, James Sheridan (1784–1862), playwright, was born at Cork on 12 May 1784, the son of James *Knowles (1759–1840), lexicographer, and his first wife, Jane (*d.* 1800), daughter of Andrew Peace, medical practitioner of Cork, and widow of a Mr Daunt. Richard Brinsley Sheridan, from whom he derived his second name, was his father's first cousin. At the age of six Knowles was placed in his father's school at Cork, but in 1793 moved with the family to London. There he made early efforts in verse, and at the age of twelve attempted a play, in which he acted with his juvenile companions, as well as the libretto of an opera on the story of the chevalier de Grillon. A few months later he wrote 'The Welch Harper', a ballad which was set to music and became popular. He was befriended by William Hazlitt, an acquaintance of the family, who helped him with advice and introduced him to Samuel Taylor Coleridge and Charles Lamb.

Knowles's mother, from whom he received much encouragement, died in 1800; and on his father's second marriage soon afterwards, to a Miss Maxwell, Knowles, unable to agree with his stepmother, impulsively left home and lived for some time from hand to mouth, helped by his friends. During this period he served as an ensign in the Wiltshire militia, and afterwards (1805) in the Tower Hamlets militia, before studying medicine under Dr Willan, taking the degree of MD from the University of Aberdeen, and becoming resident vaccinator to the Jennerian Society. Meanwhile he was writing small tragedies and 'dabbling in private theatricals'. By 1808 he had abandoned medicine and taken to the provincial stage. He probably made his first appearance at Bath. Subsequently he played Hamlet with little success at the Crow Street Theatre, Dublin. In a company at Wexford he met,

James Sheridan Knowles (1784–1862), by Wilhelm Trautschold, exh. RA 1849

and on 25 October 1809 married, Maria Charteris (*d.* 1841) of Edinburgh. They acted together in Cherry's company at Waterford, and there Knowles made the acquaintance of Edmund Kean, for whom he wrote *Leo, or, The Gipsy* (1810), which was well received at the Waterford Theatre. In the same year he published *Fugitive Pieces*, a small volume of poems. After a season in Swansea, where his eldest son was born, Knowles acted in Belfast. There he wrote and performed in a highly charged drama called *Brian Boroihme, or, The Maid of Erin* (1811), which proved very popular.

But these efforts produced a very small income, and Knowles was driven to seek a living by teaching. He opened a school of his own in Belfast, and assembled for his pupils a series of extracts for declamation under the title of *The Elocutionist*, which ran through many editions. In 1813 he was invited to offer himself for the post of first headmaster in English subjects in the Belfast Academical Institution; but he declined this appointment in favour of his father, contenting himself with the position of assistant. Three years later the dismissal of his father made it necessary for the son to leave Belfast, and Knowles moved to Glasgow, where he established and ran a school for nearly twelve years.

On 13 February 1815 Knowles's tragedy *Caius Gracchus* had been greeted as a work of genius in Belfast. It demonstrated, at least, a sensitive response to Shakespeare's *Coriolanus*. Edmund Kean saw in it the promise of meaty parts in contemporary tragedy, and suggested to Knowles a play on the subject of Virginius. Though at this period he was teaching thirteen hours a day, Knowles wrote the drama in three months; but by the time it was ready Kean had accepted another play on the same theme. Knowles, having waited in hope until 1820, produced *Virginius* in Glasgow, where John Tait, a friend of William Charles Macready, saw it, and urged Macready to read it. This marked the beginning of a tumultuous relationship which would last over twenty years and see the production of seven of Knowles's plays. *Virginius*, performed at Covent Garden on 17 May 1820, with Macready in the title role, was the first. Excited reviewers wrote of a dramatic renaissance, recognizing in Knowles's mixture of Roman grandiloquence and English domesticity a new and distinctive voice. Among the congratulations which Knowles received was one in verse from Charles Lamb. Knowles then remodelled his *Caius Gracchus*, and Macready staged it at Covent Garden on 18 November 1823. A decorous adaptation of Massinger's *The Fatal Dowry* followed, and then, at Macready's suggestion, *William Tell*, which opened at Drury Lane on 11 May 1825. Playwright and actor shared an interest in the portrayal of devoted fathers, and exploited it to their mutual advantage. In *The Spirit of the Age* (1825), Hazlitt pronounced Knowles the finest writer of his time, and there was a chorus of agreement in the theatrical journals. But Knowles made little money by his dramatic successes. In 1823 and 1824 he added to his income by conducting the literary department of the *Free Press*, a Glasgow paper which advocated liberal and social reform. His school did not prosper, and he began lecturing on oratory and drama, earning the praises of John Wilson (Christopher North) in the *Noctes Ambrosianae*.

Knowles's first comedy, *The Beggar's Daughter of Bethnal Green*, was produced at Drury Lane on 22 November 1828. It was based on the well-known ballad, which had already inspired a play by Henry Chettle and John Day (written about 1600, and printed in London, 1659). Though expectation ran high, the play was damned at the first performance, according to Knowles's defenders because of the malicious actions of a claque from the temporarily closed Covent Garden. In a reworked version, it held the stage for a further fifty years. In 1830 Knowles left Glasgow with his wife and their son, and settled in Newhaven, near Edinburgh, and there, while working at a new comedy, he put the last touches to his *Alfred the Great, or, The Patriot King*. This opened at Drury Lane on 28 April 1831 with Macready in the title role and owed its success to the audience's sentimental attachment to the legendary hero-king. It is among the weakest of Knowles's twenty published plays.

The Hunchback, a much better play, was initially accepted by the authorities at Drury Lane, but Macready asked for changes, and his hesitation over the revised text caused a breach between the two men. Knowles demanded the return of his manuscript, and took it to Charles Kemble at Covent Garden. It was produced there on 5 April 1832, with Knowles himself in the part of Master Walter. According to Westland Marston, this was Knowles's favourite among his plays, but even so friendly a critic as Marston could find little beyond fervour and sincerity to praise in Knowles's acting, 'which did not gain in charm

by the addition of a strong Irish brogue' (Marston, 268). *The Hunchback* was a great success, and enjoyed an almost uninterrupted run until the end of the season, but Knowles's acting did not meet with much approval. On taking *The Hunchback* to Glasgow and Edinburgh, he was received with enthusiasm by his former friends and pupils. When his next important play, *The Wife*, was brought out at Covent Garden on 24 April 1833, Charles Lamb wrote both prologue and epilogue. In this, his prime, Knowles was widely recognized as the leading dramatist of the day.

On 10 September 1837 *The Love Chase*, Knowles's second comedy, and perhaps his best play, opened at the Haymarket. Like *Old Maids* (1841), it is an adroitly plotted story of three contrasting courtships, witty enough to merit revival. Those of his friends who found Knowles's moral gravity excessive were quick to celebrate his comic skills.

Knowles, despite much adverse criticism, continued to act until 1843, and by his own account was well paid for it. He acted as Macbeth at the Coburg, and in some of his own plays at Covent Garden, where Macready found him 'raw, energetic, harsh, but with mind and purpose' (*Diaries*, 1.45). After Knowles's successful tour of America in 1834, Macready's attitude to him changed, not least because of Knowles's flagrant parading of his young protégée Emma Marian Maria Elphinstone, who had returned from America with him in 1835, and whom he married on 23 July 1842, the year after the death of his first wife. The relationship was further strained when Knowles was credited with *The Bridal* (1837), an adaptation (and bowdlerization) of Beaumont and Fletcher's *The Maid's Tragedy* (1610–11), which was more Macready's than Knowles's. Literary fame had probably turned Knowles's head. Few of the dozen plays he wrote between 1836 and his abandonment of the theatre in 1844 enhanced his reputation; nor did the publication of two quickly forgotten novels, *Fortescue* (1846) and *George Lovell* (1847).

It is not difficult to detect signs of religious fervour in Knowles's writing, but his contemporaries were startled when, in 1844, he began a new career as a Baptist preacher. His intentions were evangelical, but his style remained histrionic, and he retained a fondness for the theatre. He was on the committee that engineered the purchase of Shakespeare's birthplace, and it was reported in 1848, when the purchase was completed, that the custodianship was offered to him. He never filled the office, but at his death the trustees of the birthplace recorded their belief that he had been in receipt of the dividends of £1500, invested in the names of Forster and Dickens, 'for the ostensible purpose of founding a custodianship of the birthplace', and enquiries were made into the investment and appropriation of the dividends (extract from trustees' minute book, 31 Dec 1862).

Financial anxiety was a familiar demon to Knowles, who had made strenuous efforts to discharge his father's debts. Having rejected the offer of a civil-list pension of £100 in 1847, he accepted one of £200 in 1848. He now entered into religious controversy with the publication, in 1851, of *The idol demolished by its own priest: an answer to Cardinal Newman's lectures on transubstantiation*. Himself a sufferer from rheumatism, he was also an active promoter of the water cure, and an admired itinerant preacher almost until his death. His native city of Cork honoured him at a banquet early in 1862, and on 30 November 1862 he died in Torquay. He was buried in the Glasgow necropolis. He was survived by his son, Richard Brinsley Sheridan *Knowles (1820–1882), who produced a privately printed *Life of James Sheridan Knowles* in 1872. Two volumes of *Lectures on Dramatic Literature* were published posthumously in 1873.

T. B. SAUNDERS, *rev.* PETER THOMSON

Sources R. B. Knowles, *Life of J. S. Knowles* (1872) · L. H. Meeks, *Knowles and the theatre of his time* (1933) · *The diaries of William Charles Macready, 1833–1851*, ed. W. Toynbee, 2 vols. (1912) · J. W. Marston, *Our recent actors*, 2 vols. (1888) · A. S. Downer, *The eminent tragedian William Charles Macready* (1966) · C. H. Shattuck, ed., *Bulwer and Macready: a chronicle of the early Victorian theatre* (1958) · A. Nicoll, *Early nineteenth century drama, 1800–1850*, 2nd edn (1955), vol. 4 of *A history of English drama, 1660–1900* (1952–9) · A. Bunn, *The stage: both before and behind the curtain*, 3 vols. (1840) · J. S. Knowles, *Dramatic works*, 3 vols. (1841) · W. Hazlitt, *The spirit of the age* (1825) · R. H. Horne, ed., *A new spirit of the age* (New York, 1845)
Archives Cork Archives Institute, lectures and plays · Hunt. L., letters | BL, letters to Royal Literary Fund, Loan 96 · King's AC Cam., letters to Elizabeth and T. P. Le Fanu · NL Scot., letters to Oliver & Boyd
Likenesses R. J. Lane, lithograph, pubd 1826 (after C. Harding), NPG · H. S. Sadd, mezzotint, pubd 1840 (after S. S. Osgood), BM · W. Trautschold, oils, exh. RA 1849, NPG [*see illus.*] · D. Maclise, lithograph, 1873, BM · J. Douglas, carte-de-visite, NPG · Finden, engraving (after drawing by T. Wageman, *c.*1830), repro. in *Diaries*, vol. 1, ed. Toynbee · R. J. Lane, lithograph (after Count D'Orsay), NPG

Knowles, James Thomas (1806–1884), architect, was born on 23 September 1806 at 41 Bell Street, Reigate, the premises of his parents, the Surrey glaziers James Knowles (1778–1813) and Maria, *née* Gale (d. 1836). One of six children, Knowles probably attended the local parish school before being apprenticed as a glazier and plumber, possibly in or around London. This London experience, his membership of the freemasons (1834), and local connections probably helped him gain access to his first clients. For example it was probably through his family's association with Reigate landowner the earl of Hardwicke that Knowles met Captain the Hon. George Francis Wyndham, later the fourth earl of Egremont and an important client.

On 18 January 1831 Knowles married Susannah Brown (1810–1876), and in 1836, on the death of his mother, he inherited the family business. But he was already styling himself 'architect', and since around 1833 had been establishing himself as a designer of large classical country houses; for example, he rebuilt Bramley Park, Surrey, for the fourth earl of Egremont in 1837. Following his unbuilt design for a vast country house (Egremont Castle, Somerset, 1838), the smaller, 'Greco-Lilliputian' (*Country Life*, 7 Sept 1945) Silverton Park, Devon (1839–45) achieved its grandeur through architectural treatment rather than dimensions. Knowles also designed country rectories, and churches, for example St John the Evangelist, Redhill, Surrey (1842–3; extensively remodelled by J. L. Pearson, 1889).

The architecturally and socially ambitious Knowles

entered the Houses of Parliament design competition in 1836. In 1840 he severed his links with the glazier's trade, moving to Clapham with his wife, three daughters, and two sons (both of whom were apprenticed to him by 1848). Though practising from 1 Raymond Buildings, Gray's Inn, since 1839 at least, Knowles only became a fellow of the RIBA in 1847. Knowles's own palazzo-style house, Friday Grove, Clapham (1845), marked his social arrival and advertised his architectural style. In 1851 he entered the Great Exhibition competition, and was selected for 'honourable and favourable mention' (*The Builder*, 8 June 1850). His reputation was further enhanced by his houses and business premises for London commercialists, particularly the fashionable palazzo-style warehouses for draper William Cook at St Paul's Churchyard (1853) and for bookseller Hodgson at Chancery Lane (1854). *The Builder* described Cook's as 'more like a Walhalla than a warehouse' (19 Feb 1853), and praised Hodgson's (which exhibited hallmark 'eyelid' window hoods and openwork decoration) as 'a substantially beautiful … business pile' (18 Aug 1885) designed to be both aesthetic and functional.

Knowles's connection with the Cook family led to his only known foreign travel and commission—the rebuilding of Villa Monserrate at Cintra in Portugal (*c.*1858–63), as an elaborate and exotic villa of corridor-linked pavilions, topped with 'oriental' cupolas. An 1870 poem praised this imaginative 'Knowlesian' architecture and, though a later commentator criticized it as 'barbarous orientalism … built in a moorish delerium' (Macaulay, 137), it is now a national monument.

The blending of styles and favourite motifs in an attempt to synthesize a particularly English contemporary style is Knowles's hallmark, and is nowhere better illustrated than in one joint commission with his eldest son, James Thomas *Knowles (1831–1908), the Grosvenor Hotel (1859–63), serving London's Victoria railway station. Here the spatially exciting interior, external 'eyelid' windows, and vigorous applied decoration, beneath the complex curving roof-forms, give the 'Knowlesian' flavour. The 'Grosvenor style' fused Gothic, Moorish, and classical in the elder Knowles's search for what was 'truly grand, and beautiful, and original in design' (*The Builder*, 8 June 1850). His son's biographer describes the Knowleses as 'eclectics and reconcilers both' (Metcalf, ix): the 'rumbustious' decoration (M. Girouard, *The Victorian Country House*, 1979, 294), which earned the Grosvenor the accolade of having 'the largest swags in London' (*Building News*, 20 March 1863, 210–11), perhaps demonstrates the influence of the younger Knowles, as his father's later style was more conservative.

Knowles was evidently a practical man who valued convenience, 'fitness in design … and durability … in construction' (*The Builder*, 15 June 1850). His pragmatic approach and willingness to engage theoretical issues are demonstrated by his 1850 address to the RIBA on 'The propriety of the application of cements … to the exterior of buildings', which was vigorously debated against a background of Ruskinian notions of honesty in architecture.

Knowles, dignified, 'determined', and 'self-reliant' (Metcalf, 19), largely practised alone in the later 1860s, his last commercial work being Tarn's drapers at Elephant and Castle, Southwark (1863), after which he returned to domestic practice, with Hedsor House, Buckinghamshire, for Lord Boston (1865–8). He retired from Raymond Buildings in 1869, but in 1872–3 designed a memorial fountain at Wigton, Cumberland, for long-standing client textile magnate George Moore. In retirement Knowles remained a dedicated and active member of the RIBA council (a record of his activities may be found in RIBA *Transactions*, 47, 1884, 619, and *The Builder*, 3 May 1884, 604). He died on 23 March 1884 at 49 Russell Square, Bloomsbury, where he lived with his younger son, George, after Susannah's death in 1876. He was buried with her at Norwood cemetery.   M. A. GOODALL

Sources Clapham Antiquarian Society [files of miscellany collected by E. Smith and held by the honorary secretary] · P. Metcalf, *James Knowles: Victorian editor and architect* (1980) · J. T. Knowles, 'On the propriety of the application of cements [pt 1]', *The Builder*, 8 (1850), 266–7 · J. T. Knowles, 'On the propriety of the application of cements [pt 2]', *The Builder*, 8 (1850), 278–9 · 'The Grosvenor Hotel [pt 1]', *The Builder*, 18 (1860), 755 · 'The Grosvenor Hotel [pt 2]', *The Builder*, 19 (1861), 374–5 · J. Summerson, 'A vanished house', *Country Life*, 98 (1945), 428 · C. F. R. Ackland, 'A vanished house', *Country Life*, 98 (1945), 516 · S. Angell, 'On the open spaces of our metropolis', *The Builder*, 12 (1854), 287 · *The Builder*, 11 (1853), 113 · R. Macaulay, *They went to Portugal* (1946), 137 · *Fairy life and fairyland: a lyric poem … Thomas the Rhymer* (1870), 196, 202–7 · J. Knowles, 'New building at the junction of Chancery Lane and Fleet Street', *The Builder*, 13 (1855), 389–91 · *The Builder*, 46 (1884), 604 · *Transactions of the Royal Institute of British Architects*, 47 (1884), 619 · M. H. Port, ed., *The Houses of Parliament* (1976), 36, 41, pl. 28 · biography file, RIBA BAL · A. K. Placzek, ed., *Macmillan encyclopedia of architects*, 4 vols. (1982) · *Friday Grove* (1876) [sale catalogue, Clapham] · *CGPLA Eng. & Wales* (1884) · d. cert. · photographs, sales particulars, listed buildings descriptions, Wilts. & Swindon RO · archive file 89425, National Monuments Record Office, Swindon · archive file 88995, National Monuments Record Office, Swindon

Archives City Westm. AC, corresp. and papers · RIBA BAL, drawings collection · RIBA BAL, biographical file · V&A, drawings and papers

Likenesses H. Tidey, double portraits, watercolour, 1852 (with Susannah Knowles), priv. coll. · photograph, 18 Nov 1860, probably priv. coll.; copy, Clapham Antiquarian Society · photograph, c.1871, priv. coll.

Wealth at death £16,522 17s. 8d.: probate, 6 May 1884, *CGPLA Eng. & Wales*

Knowles, Sir James Thomas (1831–1908), journal editor and architect, born at Reigate, Surrey, on 13 October 1831, was the eldest child in the family of two sons and three daughters of James Thomas *Knowles (1806–1884), architect, and his wife, Susannah (1810–1876), daughter of George Brown, surgeon and apothecary in Rotherhithe. About 1839 his father built for himself a large house in Clapham Park, and there or in the near neighbourhood Knowles lived until 1884.

Knowles entered his father's office in 1846 as an apprentice. He also attended the evening lectures on architecture at University College, London, begun by T. L. Donaldson. His early journalistic interests were reflected in the *Clapham Magazine*, which appeared briefly in 1850–51, edited by Knowles and his friend Henry Hewett, who later

Sir James Thomas Knowles (1831–1908), by Arthur James Knowles, c.1903

married Knowles's sister Emmeline. Knowles published a prize essay, 'Architectural education', in 1852, became an associate of the Royal Institute of British Architects in 1853, and a fellow of the institute in 1870. In 1853 and 1854 he travelled abroad with Hewett, especially in Italy. On his return he worked with his father on the latter's chief commission, the Grosvenor Hotel at Victoria, London. Knowles practised his profession with success for some thirty years. He built, according to his own account, 'many hundreds of houses, besides several churches, hospitals, clubs, warehouses, stores, roads, and bridges'. His chief commissions were three churches in Clapham (St Stephen's, St Saviour's, and St Philip's); Albert Mansions, Victoria Street; the Thatched House Club in St James's Street (1865); and Sir Erasmus Wilson's enlargement of the Sea Bathing Hospital at Margate in 1882. Albert Grant (Baron Grant) was at one time a client. In 1873 Knowles designed a palatial residence for Baron Grant, which was erected in Kensington High Street on the site of demolished slums; but the house was never occupied and was pulled down in 1883, when its place was taken by Kensington Court. In 1874, too, when Baron Grant purchased Leicester Square with a view to converting it into a public open space, he entrusted Knowles with the task of laying out the ground, and designing the square.

But Knowles's activity and alertness of mind always ranged beyond the limits of his professional work. A little volume, compiled from the *Morte d'Arthur* of Sir Thomas Malory, *The Story of King Arthur and his Knights of the Round Table*, which he published in 1862, reached an eighth edition in 1895, and met with Tennyson's approval. In 1866 Knowles called on Tennyson at Freshwater and became a close friend for life. He designed for the poet, without charge, his new house at Aldworth in 1869.

Early in the same year, when Knowles was entertaining Tennyson and a neighbour, Charles Pritchard, at his house at Clapham, the possibility was canvassed of forming a representative 'theological society' to discuss the bases of morality. With characteristic energy Knowles communicated with champions of all schools of thought, and obtained their assent to join such a society. A first meeting was held at Willis's Rooms on 21 April 1869 and the Metaphysical Society was then constituted. The original members included A. P. Stanley, H. E. Manning, W. G. Ward, R. H. Hutton, James Martineau, Bishop Ellicott, Walter Bagehot, T. H. Huxley, John Tyndall, W. E. Gladstone, and J. A. Froude. Knowles acted as general secretary. Early anticipations of failure were belied, and under Knowles's direction the society flourished for twelve years. The members dined together month by month at a hotel, and a discussion followed. The society dissolved in 1881 because, said Tennyson, the members failed to define what metaphysics meant. According to Knowles, all possible subjects had then been exhausted, while pressure of other work compelled his withdrawal from the society's direction. The Metaphysical Society was an imaginative and rather improbably successful attempt to maintain unity through discussion at a time when party and intellectual factors implied division.

Knowles's management of the Metaphysical Society brought him into personal touch with the chief intellectual men of the day. His relations with Gladstone were soon as close as those with Tennyson. He turned such relationships to public advantage. In 1870 he became editor of the *Contemporary Review* in succession to Dean Alford, and he persuaded many members of the Metaphysical Society to contribute to the pages of the magazine either papers which they had read at the society's meetings or original articles. In January 1877 the *Contemporary* changed hands, and a disagreement with the new proprietors, who included Samuel Morley, led Knowles to end his connection with it (January 1877 was his last number as editor). Thereupon he founded under his sole proprietorship and editorship a new periodical which he called the *Nineteenth Century*. The first number appeared in March and was introduced by a sonnet by Tennyson. Members of the Metaphysical Society continued to support Knowles, and Gladstone, Manning, Sir John Lubbock, Bishop Ellicott, and Fitzjames Stephen were early contributors to the new venture, whose professed aim was to provide a platform from which men of all parties and persuasions might address the public in their own names. 'Signed writing' was the essential principle of the *Nineteenth Century*, even more so than with the *Contemporary*. With diplomatic skill Knowles induced writers of renown to engage in controversy with one another in his magazine on matters of

moment, at times in symposia, but commonly in independent articles. Gladstone, who contributed fifty-five articles and reviews, complimented Knowles on his success in keeping 'the "Nineteenth Century" pot boiling' (13 May 1888, J. Morley, *Life of Gladstone*, 1903, 3.360). The result was a successful and very profitable journal. In January 1901 he renamed the magazine *The Nineteenth Century and After*; he edited it until his death.

Knowles, who gave up architectural practice in 1883, moved next year from Clapham to Queen Anne's Lodge, by St James's Park, Westminster, where he constantly entertained a distinguished circle of friends and collected pictures and works of art. Tennyson's portrait by Millais in 1881, and Gladstone's portrait by Pierre Troubetzkoy in 1893 were painted for his collection. Although his interests were mainly absorbed by the *Nineteenth Century*, he found time for some other public activities. In 1871 he organized the Paris Food Fund for the relief of the besieged population in Paris, and induced Manning, Huxley, Lubbock, and Ruskin to act with him on the committee. In 1882 he energetically opposed the channel tunnel scheme. When the proposal was revived in 1890, Knowles repeated his denunciation in the *Nineteenth Century*, and in Gladstone's view crushed the plan. Knowles was also active in philanthropy, joining Lord Shaftesbury, Baroness Burdett Coutts, and Octavia Hill in starting the Sanitary Laws Enforcement Society, and originating the first fund for giving toys to children in hospitals and workhouses.

In 1860 Knowles married Jane Emma, daughter of the Revd Abraham Borradaile; they had one son and one daughter before she died in childbirth in 1863. In February 1865 he married Isabel Mary, daughter of Henry William Hewlett, barrister, and sister of his friend. His second wife survived him with one son and two daughters. Knowles was made KCVO when visiting Queen Alexandra and the king at Sandringham in 1903. In his later years he lived in Brighton as well as London, and he died of a heart attack on 13 February 1908 at his home, 3 Percival Terrace, Brighton; his funeral service was at St Peter's, Brighton, and he was buried in the extramural cemetery, Brighton. Knowles's pictures and other works of art were sold at Christies from 26 to 29 May 1908.

SIDNEY LEE, rev. H. C. G. MATTHEW

Sources *The Times* (14 Feb 1908) · *RIBA Journal*, 15 (1907–8), 276 · P. Metcalfe, *James Knowles* (1980) [with list of his buildings] · A. W. Brown, *The metaphysical society* (1947)
Archives City Westm. AC, corresp. and papers | BL, corresp. with W. E. Gladstone, Add. MSS 44231–44282 · BL, corresp. with Florence Nightingale, Add. MS 45806 · ICL, letters to Thomas Huxley and Mrs Huxley and Leonard Huxley · Lincoln Central Library, Tennyson Research Centre, Tennyson MSS · U. Durham L., letters to Henry George, third Earl Grey
Likenesses A. J. Knowles, photograph, *c.*1903, repro. in Metcalfe, *James Knowles*, frontispiece [*see illus.*]
Wealth at death £30,271 12*s.* 3*d.*: probate, 13 March 1908, *CGPLA Eng. & Wales*

Knowles, John (*c.*1606–1685), nonconformist minister, was born in Lincolnshire. A brilliant scholar, he graduated BA from Magdalene College, Cambridge, in 1623 and in

1625 was elected fellow of St Catharine's College, where he proved a successful and popular tutor. In 1627 he proceeded MA and was ordained deacon (18 March) and priest (3 October) at Peterborough. On the advice of the master, Richard Sibbes, he joined in electing to a fellowship at St Catharine's Laud's nominee, John Ellis (1606–1681), an act of compliance which he afterwards bitterly regretted. In 1635 Colchester elected him to the corporation lectureship at St Botolph's. He preached with great fervour and exerted considerable public influence. He delivered the 1636 funeral sermon for his close friend, the great Essex puritan, John Rogers, lecturer of Dedham, and engineered the appointment of his successor, Matthew Newcomen. In 1637 his candidate for the mastership of Colchester grammar school, William Dugard, prevailed over Laud's, but 'the getting in of a schoolmaster proved the outing of a lecturer' (*Calamy rev.*, 605). Knowles's opposition to ceremonies and adamant refusal to communicate at the altar in a mixed multitude led to the revocation of his licence and to his resignation in 1637.

In 1639 Knowles embarked for New England, and in December that year he was called to be co-pastor with George Phillips at Watertown. He married about this time Elizabeth, daughter of Thomas *Willis, the famous schoolmaster of Isleworth, Middlesex, and Lynn, Massachusetts, with whom he had two daughters. In 1642 Knowles joined the Harvard board of overseers and on 7 October was one of three ministers sent to Virginia in response to requests from puritan settlers there. Their nonconformity soon led to their silencing and expulsion by the new governor, Sir William Berkeley. Knowles returned in 1643 to Watertown, where he continued to minister, alone after Phillips's death in 1644, and with John Sherman from 1647. In 1650 he became a freeman and on 31 December was a signatory to a letter congratulating Cromwell on his suppression of the Irish uprising.

In 1651 Knowles returned to England and was appointed lecturer in Bristol Cathedral. He was also rector of St Werburgh and pastor of Castle Green congregationalist church, Bristol. In 1654 he was an assistant to the Somerset commission, and in September 1658 was one of the representatives of the congregationalist churches at the Savoy Assembly in London. He was several times barracked by Quakers: on 6 October 1659 his door was assailed with a chopping knife. He claimed credit for eliciting the Dodderidge bequest for Harvard College from a former Bristol recorder.

Deprived at the Restoration, Knowles went to London where he remained until his death. He was briefly lecturer at All Hallows-the-Great in 1661 and 1662 but was forced underground after the 1662 Act of Uniformity. In August 1664 he was reported to be holding £1000 for the benefit of 'godly men' and continued to solicit funds for Harvard. He was reported as holding conventicles at various places in London in 1664 and 1665, and courageously continued to minister during the great plague. By 27 October 1671, when he received the freedom of Bristol, he had married his second wife, Deborah, daughter of Thomas Barwicke. The next year an invitation to become president of Harvard coincided with the royal declaration of indulgence, and he declined. Though continuing correspondence, the next year he sold his remaining Massachusetts property. Instead, in the new tolerant atmosphere, he became a colleague of Thomas Kentish in ministering to a presbyterian group in St Katharine by the Tower, afterwards in Eastcheap (ultimately at the king's weighhouse). He had many narrow escapes after the cancelling of the Act of Indulgence in 1673 and in 1676 was preaching at Booby Lane, Wapping. He died in London on 10 April 1685. By his will, dated from Shadwell, 10 May 1680, he left bequests to his son, Samuel, and daughters Anne (wife of Benjamin Eyre) and Martha (wife of Thomas Impey).

ROGER THOMPSON

Sources DNB · *New England Historical and Genealogical Register*, 7 (1853), 281, 283 · *New England Historical and Genealogical Register*, 30 (1876), 463 · *Collections of the Massachusetts Historical Society*, 3rd ser., 1 (1825), 65–6 · H. Bond, *Genealogies and history of Watertown* (1861), 329 · S. E. Morison, *The tercentennial history of Harvard College and University, 1636–1936*, 1: *The founding of Harvard College* (1935), 169, 386–7, 407 · S. E. Morison, *The tercentennial history of Harvard College and University, 1636–1936*, 3–4: *Harvard College in the seventeenth century* (1936), 382, 391–2 · C. Francis, *Historical sketch of Watertown* (1830), 29–31 · Venn, *Alum. Cant.* · F. J. Bremer, *Congregational communion: clerical friendship in the Anglo-American puritan community, 1610–1692* (1994) · Greaves & Zaller, *BDBR*, vol. 2, 162–3 · *Calamy rev.*

Knowles, John (*c*.1625–1677), antitrinitarian preacher and religious controversialist, was born at Gloucester, the eldest of the three children of Henry Knowles, a prosperous tradesman in that city, and his wife, Ann (*d*. 1661/2), who appointed her 'Loveing Son John Knowles' (will, 8 April 1661, Glos. RO) sole executor in her will.

Knowles's education is unknown but he was already preaching to Independent congregations as a teenager and he was clearly familiar with both the Greek text of the New Testament and the Latin commentators. Suspected of being an antitrinitarian for his association with the teacher John Biddle, he was requested about 1646 by the parliamentary committee at Gloucester to state his theological views. He sent them a letter confessing that he had denied for a while 'the Godhead of the holy Ghost' but that afterwards he had been convinced that 'the holy ghost is God' (Eaton, 234). In 1646 Knowles found himself in controversy with the minister Giles Workman, who objected to Knowles's manuscript tract defending lay preaching, a document which Knowles then developed in his *A Modest Plea for Private Mens Preaching* (1648). By 1648 he had moved from Gloucester to London where he lodged in Aldersgate Street with Edward Atkinson, an antitrinitarian. He then joined the parliamentary army, belonging to 'the Life-Guard of his Excellency Sir Thomas Fairfax' (Knowles, *Modest Plea*). He succeeded the Independent Samuel Eaton as preacher to the army garrison at Chester in 1650. His preaching at Chester was 'the earliest recorded case of avowed antitrinitarianism in an English pulpit' (Wilbur, 198). During his stay there he secretly distributed Biddle's *Confession of Faith*. Samuel Eaton was ill disposed towards his successor, no doubt because he had heard rumours of his 'unsoundnesse in the Doctrine of the Trinity' (Eaton, 5), and he sent a paper to Knowles's flock in defence of orthodoxy. Knowles replied with *A Friendly Debate on a Weighty Subject* (1650), in which he expressed views which were Arian rather than Socinian, arguing that Christ was truly the son of God but was not himself 'that most high God, whose Being and Actings are originally of himself' (Greaves & Zaller, *BDBR*, 163). Eaton countered with *The Mystery of God Incarnate* (1650) and *A Vindication, or, Further Confirmation of some other Scriptures* (1651).

By the end of 1650 Eaton succeeded in securing Knowles's removal, as is evident from Thomas Porter's pamphlet *A Serious Exercitation*, published on 26 December 1650 and directed against the 'late Preacher at Chester' John Knowles. Knowles came twice to the notice of the council of state for his erroneous opinions, witnesses being questioned about his views on 12 October 1650, when he was still in Chester, and on 19 November 1650, when he was back again in Gloucester. It is unclear whether any further action was taken but he then moved to the small country town of Pershore in Worcestershire, where he lived for some fifteen years as a professed minister. Here he devoted himself to studying, preaching, and collecting money in aid of the Polish exiles. From 5 June 1662 to 1 April 1665 he carried on an interesting correspondence with his Socinian friend Henry Hedworth, who vainly invited him to London to take charge of Biddle's congregation.

On 9 April 1665 Knowles was arrested under suspicion of disaffection towards the government. He was imprisoned first at Worcester and then, at the end of May, committed to the Gatehouse, Westminster. Papers found in his house at Pershore were seized and made the basis of charges of heresy and sedition. On 23 June he petitioned Lord Arlington for a speedy trial. In July he wrote to the king and to the duke of Albemarle protesting his innocence and entreating release, as the plague was then raging in London. These appeals were left unheeded for on 2 February 1666 he petitioned again. Not long after this fourth petition he was released.

Knowles remained in London and it seems that he accepted the invitation to become the leader of a group of Socinians. In 1668 he published his final works, this time on the moral theory of atonement, in opposition to the Calvinist Robert Ferguson, publishing two pamphlets, *The Freeness of Gods Grace in the Forgiveness of Sins by Jesus* (1668) and *An Answer to Mr. Ferguson's Book* (1668), in both of which he argued that the sacrifice on the cross had for ever reconciled man to God. In early 1676 he is said to have preached at a Socinian meeting-house in Coleman Street. He was buried at St Peter Cornhill, London, on 23 November 1677. His will, dated 1 May 1676, named his nephew John Knowles and Henry Hedworth as executors. He owned a significant number of 'Books of value', some of which apparently went to a library in Gloucester, and he left 'a Third of all he had, for the Relief of Men persecuted for Religion, and other Charities' (Nye, 16).

DARIO PFANNER

Sources H. J. McLachlan, *Socinianism in seventeenth-century England* (1951), 255–87 · *DNB* · W. B. Patterson, 'Knowles, John', Greaves & Zaller, *BDBR* · W. H. Burgess, 'John Knowles and Henry Hedworth, seventeenth-century Unitarian pioneers', *Transactions of the Unitarian Historical Society*, 5 (1931), 1–16 · *CSP dom., 1650; 1661–6; 1680–81* · S. Eaton, *The mystery of God incarnate* (1650) · J. Knowles, *A modest plea for private mens preaching* (1648) · will of Ann Knowles, proved 1662, Glos. RO · E. Wilbur, *A history of Unitarianism in Transylvania, England, and America* (1952), 197–8 · [J. Knowles], *A friendly debate on a weighty subject* (1650) · S. Nye, *The grounds and occasions of the controversy concerning the unity of God* (1698), 16 · R. Wallace, *Antitrinitarian biography* (1850), vol. 3, pp. 210–21 · will, PRO, PROB 11/361, sig. 132

Archives PRO, state paper 29, vol. 119, 25.III; vol. 125, 14; vol. 126, 46; vol. 127, 135; vol. 147, 19

Wealth at death see will, PRO, PROB 11/361, sig. 132

Knowles, John (1781–1841), naval surveyor and biographer, was born on 24 March 1781 at 14 Union Street, Deptford, London, the eldest of the three sons of John Knowles (*d.* 1814), shipwright, and his wife, Mary Posgate, and was baptized on 19 April 1781 at St Paul's, Deptford. He was privately educated at Bexleyheath. On 30 March 1798 he was appointed as one of the four clerks to the surveyors in the Navy Office. By 1806 he had risen to chief clerk (salary £500, later £650, p.a.). He was superannuated with a pension of £498 in August 1832, thereafter becoming managing director of the Economic Life Assurance Society until 1835.

Knowles was the author of *An Inquiry into the Means Taken to Preserve the British Navy* (1821), in recognition of which he was elected, in July 1821, fellow of the Royal Society, and *The Principles and Practice of Constructing Ships* (1822). Knowles is best-known, however, for his long friendship with Henry *Fuseli and his biography of the painter. Knowles was introduced to Fuseli by their mutual friend John Bonnycastle in June 1805. Since the Navy Office was only a few steps from the Royal Academy across Somerset Place, Knowles and Fuseli saw each other almost daily for the next twenty years. The *Life and Writings of Henry Fuseli* (3 vols., 1831) was an expanded version of Knowles's anonymous memoir in the *Annual Biography and Obituary for the Year 1826* (232–70). Knowles's biography is notable for its factual accuracy; the accompanying volumes made accessible all of Fuseli's writings on art, including the *Lectures on Painting* (comprising twelve lectures, separately published by Knowles in 1830), the 'Aphorisms on Art', and the unfinished 'History of Art in Italy'. Knowles was executor to both the painter and his widow, Sophia (*d.* 1832). Knowles's collection of paintings included choice works by Giorgione, Titian, Rembrandt, Van Dyck, Gainsborough, and Reynolds, and fourteen paintings by Fuseli.

Knowles died, unmarried, at Ashburton, Devon, on 21 July 1841, having moved from London in 1840 to live with his brother Samuel Posgate Knowles. He was buried in the Whitheare family tomb in Ashburton churchyard. His portrait was painted by S. P. Knowles, Samuel Drummond, and Charles Landseer, and a marble bust was executed by William Behnes (exh. RA, 1836). Photographs of these remain in a private collection. Knowles was one of the original members of the Athenaeum and a lithograph by 'W. D.' after Landseer's portrait was included in Thomas McLean's *Athenaeum Portraits* (no. 25).

D. H. WEINGLASS

Sources T. W. Windeatt, 'John Knowles, FRS', *Report and Transactions of the Devonshire Association*, 28 (1896), 338–41 · J. Knowles, *The life and writings of Henry Fuseli*, 3 vols. (1831) · D. H. Weinglass, introduction, in J. Knowles, *The life and writings of Henry Fuseli*, 1 (1982), 5–12 · *The collected English letters of Henry Fuseli*, ed. D. H. Weinglass (1982), 542–4, 563–4, 580–3 · *Catalogue of the valuable collection of pictures … sold by Christie & Manson* (22 April 1842) [125 lots, priced and annotated copy and letter of acct, DHW/MC] · J. M. Collinge, *Navy Board officials, 1660–1832* (1978), 17, 35, 37–8, 47, 117 · St Paul, Deptford, ratebook for 1781, Lewisham Archives · dockyard officers index, NMM · J. Knowles, 'Letters from various kings' re 'Preservation of the navy' and 'Life of Fuseli', priv. coll. · PRO, PROB 11/1954, fols. 30r–31v · Lpool RO, Roscoe papers, 2276–2281 · Dorset RO, Rackett papers, NV 107 · Fuseli letters, RA, FU/1–5 · Zentralbibliothek, Zürich, to Heinrich Füssli, MS Lindt 73 · letters to Carrick-Moore family, priv. coll. · St Paul, Deptford, parish register, Lewisham Archives, 1781 [baptism] · J. T. Smith, *Nollekens and his times*, 2 (1828), 425–7 · J. T. Smith, *Nollekens and his times*, ed. W. Whitten, new edn, 2 (1920), 344–6 · *GM*, 1st ser., 84/2 (1814), 605 · *GM*, 2nd ser., 16 (1841), 331 · *Catalogue of scientific papers*, Royal Society, 3 (1869), 695 · G. F. von Waagen, *Works of art and artists in England*, 3 vols. (1838), 2.402 · A. Graves, *Summary of and index to Waagen* (1911), 282 · 1827, BL, 46611, fol. 49 (1830); 41395, fol. 183 (1827) · *The Times* (24 Oct 1841), 7e

Archives Dorset RO, letters to Thomas Rackett · Lpool RO, Roscoe papers, 2276–2281 · priv. coll., letters to Carrick-Moore family · Zentralbibliothek, Zürich, letters to Heinrich Füssli

Likenesses W. Drummond, lithograph (after C. Landseer), BM, NPG · photograph (after S. Drummond, 1827), priv. coll.; repro. in Knowles, 'Letters from various kings' · photograph (after marble bust by W. Behnes, 1836), priv. coll.; repro. in Knowles, 'Letters from various kings' · photograph (after S. P. Knowles), priv. coll.; repro. in Knowles, 'Letters from various kings'

Wealth at death pictures sold for £708: prices catalogue and letter from auctioneers, priv. coll.; will, PRO, PROB 11/1954, fols. 30r–31v

Knowles [*née* Tomn], **Lilian Charlotte Anne** (1870–1926), economic historian, was born on 9 October 1870 in a country residence, Rosedale, Killagorden, St Clement, near Truro in Cornwall, the eldest daughter of Philip Sandy Tom (1822–1888), a local landowner and a barrister, and his wife, Mary Anne (d. 1924), daughter of Revd Maurice Yescombe. She attended the Truro High School for Girls from its foundation in 1880 until 1888. Her mother changed the spelling of the family name to Tomn by deed poll in 1888 after her husband's death. Lilian then accompanied her mother and sister on a two-year tour of Europe, where she learned French, German, and Italian. In 1890 she went to Girton College, Cambridge, where she studied history. She read for the paper in English economic history, taught by William Cunningham, a follower of the historical school of economics. Both Cunningham and F. W. Maitland, who were key architects of the Cambridge historical tripos, encouraged students at the new women's colleges to take the economic history paper, and to do research in the subject.

Tomn achieved a first class in the historical tripos in 1893, and in the following year became the first woman to obtain a first class in the law tripos, with only J. C. Smuts ranked above her in the tripos list. But there was little immediate recognition, for Cambridge did not grant degrees to women until 1948, and she expressed her disappointment at the time: 'though the man gets the title [BA], the woman only gets the certificate' (L. Tomn, 'Girton as I

knew it', *Truro High School Newsletter*, 1897, 43). In 1895 she joined the chambers of Sir Hugh Pollock, Gray's Inn, with a view to entering the law, but she left after six months to take up Cunningham's invitation to be a research assistant for the third edition of his *The Growth of English Industry and Commerce in Modern Times*. In 1896 she registered as a research student at the newly founded London School of Economics (LSE), where Cunningham was an external lecturer.

In 1904 Tomn was appointed to a teachership in modern economic history at the LSE, becoming the first full-time teacher of the subject at any British university. In the following year she took the title of DLitt at Trinity College, Dublin, among the 200 Girtonians who took degrees there between 1904 and 1907, when Dublin opened them to qualified women from other universities. She married Charles Matthew Knowles, her former external student and a barrister, in 1907; they had a son.

In 1907 Lilian Knowles was appointed reader in economic history at the University of London, but she had to wait until 1921 before she was promoted to professor. As such she was only the second professor of economic history in the country, and the first of only two female professors appointed in the discipline before the Second World War. Between 1920 and 1924 she was dean to the faculty of economics at London, the first woman dean of faculty in the university. She was a member of the council of the Royal Economic Society and of the Royal Historical Society.

Knowles was a country tory, patriot, and imperialist. She was a product of the historical school of economists not just in her training, but in her interests in the economic and political relations between states, and in the association of that school with the tariff reform movement. She was remembered above all as a great teacher, and her books followed from what she sought to teach. Her teaching was vigorous and wide in scope, but also attentive to original sources. To her the LSE was a place to which people came to be taught, and she threw her soul into teaching: she published little until the last ten years of her life. She had a new conception of her subject and the boundaries of what could be taught. She was, as Beveridge described, 'fascinated by the romance of pioneering, of man's triumph over the wilderness and over disease in the tropics and elsewhere' (Beveridge, 'Professor Lilian Knowles, 1870–1926', 119). But these were new subjects for economic history, and finding the sources was a pioneer venture in itself.

> When I first began to teach Economic History …, No one in England at that time taught the foreign economic history of the nineteenth or any other century … what was usually taught at other places as far as recent Economic History was concerned was Labour, and that only one side of Labour, viz., Trade Unionism. I have endeavoured in my teaching to stress the overwhelming importance of transport, colonial development and agriculture, while allotting the social and labour side a very important place … I think my students realize that English Economic History by itself is one-sided, and that England must be treated as part of a great Western civilization acting on other Powers and being reacted on in turn by them.   (Knowles, xv)

Knowles developed new courses on the economic development of the great powers and of the British overseas empire, and wrote the textbooks to map out the field, 'so there would be a solid foundation on which others could build'. She endorsed Cunningham's view that with a textbook 'my subject will never die' (Knowles, xv). She planned a two-volume survey of the great powers, and a three-volume survey of the empire. Between 1921 and 1924 two of these volumes were published: *The Industrial and Commercial Revolutions in Great Britain during the Nineteenth Century* (1921) and the first volume of *The Economic Development of the British Overseas Empire* (1924). Two further volumes of the empire survey were published after her death, edited by her husband, in 1930, and the volume intended to follow her *Industrial and Commercial Revolutions, Economic Development in the Nineteenth-Century. France, Germany, Russia and the United States*, was published in 1932. Solid narrative accounts of an imperial ethos, they were displaced as the framework for teaching comparative history at the LSE during the later 1920s and 1930s by new emphases on world history and on the application to history of social scientific theory, including theories of economic development and Marxism.

Knowles also supervised many of the theses which later became classics of economic history. Among these were a number by women. Her research students included Alice Clark, Joyce Dunlop, and Ivy Pinchbeck, working on women's and children's labour, Mabel Buer on population, Dorothy George on Stuart finances, Julia Mann on cotton, Alice Radice on Anglo-Irish trade, and Vera Anstey on Indian economic history. She also served on two government committees. The first was appointed in March 1918 by Bonar Law to inquire into and report upon wartime increases in the cost of living to the working classes. She served with W. J. Ashley, A. L. Bowley, and Mrs Pember Reeves. She later served on the royal commission on income tax (1919–20), and was the only woman among its twenty-three members.

Knowles was conscious of her almost unique position as a senior female academic in her field, and was proud that she had managed to combine marriage and motherhood with an academic career, but she did not participate in the suffrage campaigns. Instead, she expressed her uncompromising views on women's paid employment in her writing and in her own practice in her job. She defended equal pay for women, criticizing women prepared to take less who undercut the labour market, and refused herself to take less than a man's pay because she was a woman. This led to a long dispute with the LSE administration over her own working conditions and salary, and was to continue in her defence of the position of her younger colleague Eileen Power. Motherhood did not soften her own views on social policy. When Beveridge introduced a scheme of family allowances for the LSE staff she opposed it, arguing that it was a premium on irresponsibility, for it would make a colleague with five children immensely better off than she, with only one. She addressed issues of the impact of industrialization on women's employment and working conditions in her *Industrial and Commercial Revolutions* (1921), where she showed a familiarity with current international debate on the issue, and she was astute enough to see that women's economic history was a major historical issue, and one that the LSE should support.

Knowles was, in the strictest sense, a pioneer: she was the first full-time lecturer in economic history in Britain, and was later to become the first professor of economic history at the LSE. She wrote the first general textbooks of modern economic history, both British and European, and the first economic histories of the British empire. She contracted cancer in 1924, and resigned her post before retiring to Cornwall, where she worked on her books. She died in a nursing home at 1 Gambier Terrace, Hope Street, Liverpool, on 25 April 1926, and was buried in Renwyn parish church, near Truro. Her husband survived her.

MAXINE L. BERG

Sources W. H. Beveridge, 'Professor Lilian Knowles (1870–1926)', *Economica*, 6 (1926), 119–20 · G. Wallace, 'Lilian Knowles', *Economica*, 6 (1926), 120–22 · T. E. Gregory, 'Professor Lilian Knowles', *Economic Journal*, 36 (1926), 561–72 · C. M. Knowles, 'Professor Lilian Knowles, 1870–1926', in C. M. Knowles and L. C. A. Knowles, *The economic development of the British overseas empire*, 2 (1930), vii–xxii · K. T. Butler and H. I. McMorran, eds., *Girton College register, 1869–1946* (1948) · b. cert. · d. cert. · W. H. Beveridge, *The LSE and its problems* (1960), 49 · T. C. Barker, 'The beginnings of the Economic History Society', *Economic History Review*, 2nd ser., 30 (1977), 1–19 · M. Berg, 'The first women economic historians', *Economic History Review*, 2nd ser., 45 (1992), 308–29 · *The Times* (27 April 1926) · private information (2004) [T. Barker]

Archives BLPES, lecture notes and papers mainly relating to historical interests · London School of Economics, personal file

Likenesses photograph, repro. in Knowles and Knowles, *Economic development of the British overseas empire*, frontispiece

Wealth at death £32,605 8s. 10d.: resworn probate, 29 June 1926, *CGPLA Eng. & Wales*

Knowles, Mabel Winifred [*pseuds.* May Wynne, Lester Lurgan] (1875–1949), popular writer and church worker, was born at Ribblesdene, Leigham Court Road, Streatham, London, on 1 January 1875, the second daughter of William Knowles, a London merchant banker, and his wife, Emma Letitia Paxton. She was educated at home, and she remained single throughout her life.

Knowles's first books were essentially religious and rather old-fashioned. *Life's Object* (1899), a short volume evidently intended as a confirmation gift, recommended that girls exercise influence at home and avoid both athletics and the reading of 'foolish mawkish love stories'. *In the Shadows* (1900) had consoling thoughts for mourners, and early children's books such as *Mollie's Adventures* (1903) imitated the 'city arab' tales of the 1860s and 1870s.

During the next decade, however, Knowles became skilled in two genres that proved widely popular with girls and women, eventually publishing more than 200 books as well as stories for *Cassell's Family Magazine*, *Lady's Realm*, *Pall Mall Magazine*, and other periodicals. Under the penname May Wynne she became known as a writer of safe but thrilling historical romances. Most of them featured young women on their own in some exciting era when they could become servants of an endangered queen. As in a 1917 title, *A Spy for Napoleon*, the heroine often encountered 'real' characters from history (especially Charles Stuart or Henri of Navarre). The story might eventually be resolved in orthodox Christian domesticity—but not until after several hundred pages of intrigue and melodrama.

May Wynne also produced more than a hundred children's books. The most interesting gave contemporary girls their own opportunities for peril and bravery. *An English Girl in Serbia* (1916), among others, used the First World War as a setting. Dozens of school and guide adventures also emphasized courage. In *Peggy's First Term* (1922), for example, a Canadian girl in an English school wins friends through an act of heroism, and in *Lost in the Jungle* (1921) two shipwrecked daughters of an officer save themselves and a boy companion with the skills they have learned as girl guides.

Between 1910 and 1913, before perfecting the formulas that made May Wynne popular, Knowles published under the name Lester Lurgan six science-fiction or detective novels, including *Bohemian Blood* (1910) and *A Message from Mars* (1912). In addition, some of her historical novels were made into films.

For the last twenty-five years of her life, while continuing to write popular fiction, Mabel Knowles was in charge of the St Luke's Mission Church in London's Victoria Docks and lived nearby at Tyne House, 93 Maplin Road. She died of heart failure at 124 Butchers Road, Victoria Docks, London, on 29 November 1949 while preparing to lead a mission service for women.   SALLY MITCHELL

Sources M. Cadogan, 'Wynne, May', *Twentieth-century romance and historical writers*, ed. L. Henderson, 2nd edn (1990), 712–15 • *The Times* (30 Nov 1949) • *The Times* (5 Dec 1949) • b. cert. • d. cert. • *CGPLA Eng. & Wales* (1950) • *WWW*
Likenesses photograph, repro. in *The Bookman* (Feb 1909), 235
Wealth at death £6070 11s. 7d.: probate, 27 Jan 1950, *CGPLA Eng. & Wales*

Knowles [*née* Morris], **Mary** (1733–1807), poet, was born on 5 May 1733, the eldest daughter of Moses and Mary Morris of Rugeley, Staffordshire. Her talent for needlework was brought to the attention of Queen Charlotte, for whom she was commissioned to produce worsted portraits of George III and the young princess, Charlotte. Mary married Thomas Knowles (*d.* 1784), physician and author of *Tentamen medicum* (1772). The couple, who had one son, George, travelled abroad and were received at The Hague and at Versailles. A brilliant conversationalist, Mary Knowles was on intimate terms with Samuel Johnson and said of Johnson's reading that 'he tore the heart out of a book' (Boswell, 942). About 1776 she wrote *Compendium of a Controversy on Water-Baptism*, in which she engaged with a Revd Mr Rand of Coventry. 'A Poetic Correspondence', between herself and a Captain Morris, was printed in the *British Friend* (April 1848); others of her verses appeared as small tracts without dates. James Boswell recorded her talents but declined to accept as authentic her account of a 'Dialogue between Dr Johnson and Mrs Knowles' (regarding the conversion to Quakerism of Jane Harry), which Mrs Knowles forwarded to Boswell while he was engaged on his biography of Johnson. After Anna Seward, who was

present at the interview, confirmed the authenticity of the account, Mary Knowles published it in the *Gentleman's Magazine* (June 1791) and it later appeared separately in 1799. Thomas Knowles died on 16 November 1784 at Lombard Street, London. Mary died, also in London, on 3 February 1807.

CHARLOTTE FELL-SMITH, *rev.* PHILIP CARTER

Sources J. Smith, ed., *A descriptive catalogue of Friends' books*, 2 vols. (1867); suppl. (1893) • J. Boswell, *Life of Johnson*, ed. R. W. Chapman, rev. J. D. Fleeman, rev. edn (1980) • *Monthly Repository*, 2 (1807), 160 • *Lady's Monthly Museum* (1803)
Archives Religious Society of Friends, Birmingham, papers and poems
Likenesses portrait, repro. in *Lady's Monthly Museum*

Knowles, Matilda Cullen (1864–1933), botanist, was born on 31 January 1864 at Ballymena, co. Antrim, one of three daughters of William James Knowles, an insurance agent and amateur archaeologist. From an early age she was interested in botany, and as a girl she became friendly with Robert Lloyd Praeger (1865–1953). They botanized together in Antrim and Londonderry, and in the late 1890s Miss Knowles undertook the survey of co. Tyrone for Praeger's *Irish Topographical Botany* (1901). She published her first paper in 1897 on the plants of co. Tyrone.

Subsequently, with her sister Catherine, Matilda Knowles went to Dublin and attended the natural history classes at the Royal College of Science. By June 1902 she had joined the staff of the Science and Art Museum, Dublin, on a temporary basis to assist Professor Thomas Johnson (1863–1954); in 1907 she was promoted to assistant in the botany section, working at first, under the direction of Johnson, on listing the flowering plants and ferns (vascular plants) native and naturalized in Ireland. In the preface to *Hand List of Irish Flowering Plants and Ferns* (1910), Johnson acknowledged that 'Though I am responsible for the List, and the form it takes, its preparation is due to my assistant, Miss M. C. Knowles'. When Johnson retired as custodian of the botany department in 1923, Miss Knowles was placed in charge of the collections, and although she was due to retire in 1929 she was granted extensions until her death.

Miss Knowles is highly regarded as a student of lichens, non-flowering, often microscopic plants formed by symbiotic fungi and algae. The stimulus that led her to study lichens was the Clare Island survey, initiated in 1908, during which she assisted Annie Lorrain Smith (1854–1937) of the British Museum (Natural History), London. They visited the island, situated off the south-west coast of co. Mayo, collecting and cataloguing lichens in 1909 and 1910. Smith's report on the island's lichen flora was published in the *Proceedings of the Royal Irish Academy* (1911).

Miss Knowles published her first paper on Irish lichens in 1912. She studied the zonation of the maritime and marine lichens on the rocky coast at Howth, co. Dublin, and in 1913 published her work in the *Proceedings of the Royal Dublin Society*. This paper is now recognized as a pioneering ecological study because Knowles defined for the first time three zones characterized by lichens of conspicuously different colours, grey highest up the shore, then orange, and black nearest the sea. Praeger prompted Matilda Knowles to list all Irish lichen species and record their distribution according to the vice-counties scheme of his *Irish Topographical Botany*. With the collaboration of about thirty naturalists she assembled data on 802 lichens, including about twenty new to Ireland. *Lichens of Ireland*, her principal work, was published in the *Proceedings of the Royal Irish Academy* in 1929.

Miss Knowles named three new species in her paper on the Howth lichen zones: *Acarospora benedarensis* (its name is derived from Ben Edar, the Irish name for Howth) is a synonym of *Acarospora smaragdula*; *Verrucaria lorrain-smithiae* is a synonym of *Verrucaria sandstedei*; *Lecania atrynoides* is accepted as distinct. While she received no academic recognition during her lifetime, two lichens, *Lecidea matildae*, named by A. H. Magnusson in 1956, and *Verrucaria knowlesiae* named by P. M. McCarthy in 1988, honour her. She was regarded as an 'accurate and energetic botanist, a charming companion, and a wise and trusty friend' (Praeger, *Irish Naturalists' Journal*, 193; *Journal of Botany*, 231). Following a short illness, Matilda Knowles died at the Mercer's Hospital, Dublin, on 27 April 1933.

E. CHARLES NELSON

Sources R. L. Praeger, 'Matilda Cullen Knowles', *Irish Naturalists' Journal*, 4 (1933), 191–3 · R. L. Praeger, 'Matilda Cullen Knowles, 1864–1933', *Journal of Botany, British and Foreign*, 71 (1933), 230–31 · C. E. O'Riordan, *The Natural History Museum, Dublin* (1983) · M. E. Mitchell, '150 years of Irish lichenology: a concise survey', *Glasra*, new ser., 2 (1993–5), 139–55 · M. R. D. Seaward, 'Census catalogue of Irish lichens', *Glasra*, 8 (1984), 1–32; repr. (Dublin, 1984) · H. Ross, 'Matilda Knowles, botanist', *More people and places in Irish science and technology*, ed. C. Mollan, W. Davis, and B. Finucane (1990), 52–3 · *CGPLA Ire.* (1933) · M. J. P. Scannell and P. Deevy, 'Inspired by lichens', *Stars, shells, and bluebells: women scientists and pioneers*, ed. [M. Mulvihill and P. Deevy] (Dublin, 1997), 84–97

Archives Archbishop Marsh's Library, Dublin · National Botanic Gardens, Glasnevin, Dublin, corresp., herbarium specimens, papers

Likenesses photograph, repro. in R. L. Praeger, *Some Irish naturalists* (1950) · photograph, repro. in Scannell and Deevy, 'Inspired by lichens'

Wealth at death £255 5s. 4d.: administration with will, 21 June 1933, *CGPLA NIre*

Knowles, Michael Clive [*name in religion* David] (1896–1974), Benedictine monk and historian of monasticism, was born at Eastfield, Studley, in Warwickshire, on 29 September 1896, the only surviving child of Herbert Henry (Harry) Knowles (1865–1944) and his wife, Caroline Morgan. His father was partner in William Hall & Co., a firm which made needles and pins, whose modest prosperity enabled him to send his son to school at Downside (1910–14). On 4 October 1914 he was received into the monastic community at Downside, and was a Benedictine monk for the remainder of his life, although he lived apart from his community from 1939.

At Downside, Knowles early came under the influence of the abbot, E. J. A. Butler (Dom Cuthbert), monastic reformer and scholar, and also met the elderly layman Edmund Bishop, one of the most distinguished medievalists of his generation. Knowles made his simple profession in 1915 and took solemn vows in 1918; he took David

as his name in religion. He was ordained subdeacon in 1920, deacon in 1921, and priest on 9 July 1922. Meanwhile he had spent three years at Christ's College, Cambridge (1919–22): he took a first in both parts of the classical tripos, with a distinction in philosophy in part two; he also received a college scholarship in 1920, and the Skeat prize for English literature. His love of reading and his exceptional memory gave him a rich store of literature, English, Latin, and Greek, on which he frequently drew in the writings and conversation of his later years.

For some years Knowles taught classics at Downside; but otherwise the main preoccupation of the 1920s was with theology and the religious life. In 1922–3 he completed his study of theology at the great Benedictine house of Sant-'Anselmo in Rome. In the late 1920s he began to show a deepening anxiety about what he believed to be the tension between the life of prayer and worship and the outward-looking, teaching function of the community, brought to a head in 1933. With a group of the younger monks he formed the idea of setting up a new community; when the plan was finally rejected at Rome in 1934, all but Knowles submitted, and most of the group remained at Downside. Knowles never accepted this verdict. In 1933 he had been moved to Ealing Priory in west London, still unreconciled, and in 1939 he left his community, to live apart for the rest of his life; however, a formal reconciliation was arranged in 1952, by which he was 'exclaustrated', that is, had permission to live outside the monastery. From 1939 until his death he was cared for by a devout Swedish doctor, a convert to the Catholic church, Dr Elizabeth Kornerup. He lived first in London; later he divided his time between London and Cambridge and, after his retirement in 1963, between Wimbledon and Linch, Sussex.

Long before 1939 Knowles had begun his life as a scholar. In 1926 he published *The American Civil War*, a remarkable essay in historical literature. Serious history began in 1929 when he started work on *The Monastic Order in England*, which was published by Cambridge University Press in 1940. He was already known to other scholars from his articles in the *Downside Review* and some personal contact, but *The Monastic Order* immediately established his reputation as a medieval historian. In 1941 he proceeded LittD at Cambridge; in 1944 he was elected to a teaching fellowship at Peterhouse (he remained a fellow until 1963); in 1947 he succeeded his friend Z. N. Brooke as professor of medieval history; in 1954 Sir Winston Churchill appointed him to the regius chair of modern history, from which he retired in 1963. He was a fellow of the Royal Historical Society, and president 1956–60; fellow of the Society of Antiquaries; and fellow of the British Academy (1947). In later years he was honorary fellow of Christ's and Peterhouse, and received honorary doctorates from eight universities, including his own.

During the years he taught in Cambridge, Knowles had a deep influence on many students who were inspired by his lectures and supervisions, and won an international reputation as one of the world's most eminent medievalists. As a lecturer, when on form, his still small voice and mastery of style could be spellbinding. But his fame rests, first and foremost, on *The Monastic Order in England … 940–1216* (1940; 2nd edn, 1963) and *The Religious Orders in England* (3 vols., 1948–59). These are very notable works of scholarship; they are also works of literature. The heart and core of *The Monastic Order* is the story of English monasticism in one of its golden eras, from the Norman conquest to the early thirteenth century: it is at once great narrative history and a deeply imaginative analysis of the qualities, both spiritual and worldly, revealed by the monastic literature of the period. In the third volume of *The Religious Orders* (1959), the monasteries are dissolved. To explain this involved cool analysis of evidence, events, and personalities, and searching criticism of the religious and their aspirations. There are memorable passages of romantic evocation, when Knowles recalls what dissolution meant to the religious and their homes; and there is a comic element which cuts Thomas Cromwell's visitors, and their victims, down to size. In the end the reader is left in no doubt that great issues were under discussion—yet by a historian who never ceased to be notably fair-minded.

Knowles wrote many other books on medieval ecclesiastical history, the Becket controversy, mysticism, and related themes; and his published lectures showed the range of his learning and culture. Austere yet richly gifted; conservative in theology yet abundantly charitable; reserved yet warm and deep in his affections; deeply serious yet capable of gaiety, wit, and a delicious vein of humour: to his friends and pupils and to many of his acquaintances he was one of the remarkable personalities of the British academic world of his day. His breach with Downside brought out a strength of purpose, as some thought a fierce obstinacy, which was hidden from many who knew him, and revealed some of the complexity of his nature. His closest friends recalled his fondness for walking and rambling, and the quality of his conversation; very characteristic was the tenacity of his memory for books read long ago (and even for long-departed steam engines), and the remarkable harmony in which these memories lived with an ordered, strict regime of spiritual life. To a wider public he is especially remembered as one of the greatest of Benedictine historians, a worthy successor of the Maurists, whom he so much admired. He died in hospital in Sussex on 21 November 1974, and was buried near Milland, Sussex.

                                       C. N. L. Brooke

Sources C. Brooke, R. Lovatt, D. Luscombe, and A. Sillem, *David Knowles remembered* (1991) • A. Morey, *David Knowles: a memoir* (1979) • W. A. Pantin, 'Curriculum vitae', in D. Knowles, *The historian and character and other essays*, ed. C. N. L. Brooke and G. Constable (1963), xvii–xxviii • [G. Constable], 'A bibliography of the writings of Dom David Knowles', in D. Knowles, *The historian and character and other essays*, ed. C. N. L. Brooke and G. Constable (1963), 363–73 • D. Knowles, 'Academic history', *History*, new ser., 47 (1962), 223–32 • A. Stacpoole, 'The making of a monastic historian', *Ampleforth Journal*, 80/1 (1975), 71–91; 80/2 (1975), 19–38; 80/3 (1976), 48–55; 81/1 (1976), 40 • K. Clark, *The other half: a self-portrait* (1977), 196–7 • B. Green, 'David Knowles's first book', *Downside Review*, 107 (1989), 79–85 • personal knowledge (2004)

Archives Downside Abbey, near Bath, Downside Abbey archives, letters and autobiography • Peterhouse, Cambridge | BL, corresp. with Sir Sydney Cockerell, Add. MS 52729 • CUL, corresp. with Sir Herbert Butterfield

Likenesses M. Noakes, drawing, 1961, Peterhouse, Cambridge; repro. in Morey, *David Knowles*, frontispiece • W. Bird, photograph, 1965, NPG; repro. in Brooke, Lovatt, Luscombe, and Sillem, *David Knowles remembered*, frontispiece • E. Leigh, photograph, repro. in Knowles, *Historian and character*, frontispiece • photographs, Downside Abbey archives, Somerset

Wealth at death £10,163: probate, 28 Feb 1975, *CGPLA Eng. & Wales*

Knowles, Reginald Lionel (1879–1950), book designer and illustrator, was born on 4 March 1879 at 16 Plimsoll Street, Poplar, in east London, the second son of Ebenezer Caleb Knowles, an author and musician who worked as a merchant's clerk, a native of Worcestershire, and his wife, Emma Dece Scutt, who became a teacher at the infant's department of Woolmore Street school, Poplar. He had four siblings: Charles Francis (1876–1936), an artist and writer; Marion Charlotte (1880–1882); Hubert George (1882–1949); and Horace John (1884–1954), an artist and illustrator. There is little published information about the Knowles family, but according to two manuscripts in the central library of Tower Hamlets, one by Horace Knowles and another by a former neighbour in Poplar, the three boys attended the Craft School in Aldgate. When Reginald left school, probably shortly before 1900, he began working as an artist for the publishing house of J. M. Dent. He was responsible for designing the title-page openings, the endpapers, and the hand-drawn lettering for the titles on the spines for Everyman's Library, the first fifty volumes of which were published in February 1906. The various borders, used for the frontispieces and title-pages of the different subject groups into which Everyman's Library was divided, featured intertwining leaves and flowers. Although Knowles's designs were clearly derived from the work of William Morris and Laurence Housman, they were distinctive and successful, and were used for thirty years, until 1935. At that time the elaborate art nouveau work was replaced by a series of small abstract designs by Eric Ravilious and the hand-drawn lettering by typeset titling in Eric Gill's Perpetua Roman typeface.

In 1911 the Society of the Divine Compassion and the Whitwell Press, which was owned by the society, began the publication of a high-quality religious journal, *Ecclesia*. Knowles was appointed art editor, and was responsible for many decorative borders, head- and tailpieces, and other illustrations, as well as for the overall design of the magazine. An extensive but incomplete file of the journal is held at the British Library: from this it appears that publication ceased in 1915 or soon after, and that Knowles held the post of art editor throughout its brief life. During the First World War, Knowles, with his brother Charles, worked for the Carlton Studios; Reginald was appointed art manager.

Knowles later founded his own studio, and continued to undertake commissioned work for Dent and for other publishers, including George Newnes, Jarrolds, Cassell, and George Allen, for whom he drew lettering for the title-pages and spines and designed bindings, many recognizable by their highly decorated, gold-blocked front boards.

At the time of his death, on 26 December 1950, at his home, 80 Pollard's Hill South, Croydon, he was working on a design for a series of books to be published by Frederick Muller. He was survived by his wife, Lena. Better known as a book designer and decorator, he also illustrated several books, some in colour but most in black and white. He collaborated with his brother Horace on at least two early books, both published by Freemantle, H. Lee's *Legends from Fairyland* (1907) and G. W. Dasent's translation of *Norse Fairy Tales* (1910). Many of his illustrations are rather static, and though some are quite effective, such as those for W. Brown's *My River* (1947), they are too derivative to be completely successful.

Reginald's younger brother, **Horace John Knowles** (1884–1954), was born on 22 July 1884 at 57 Bow Lane, Poplar. He was educated at George Green's school in Poplar and the Craft School in Aldgate. Although he was initially apprenticed as an engineering draughtsman, his early collaboration with his brother Reginald led to his becoming a full-time freelance artist some time later, first producing illuminated addresses on vellum and illustrating several church magazines before turning to book illustration proper. His best work was done in pen and ink, with which he produced very decorative, delicate drawings in black and white, often of scenes of the countryside. His finest production is perhaps *Countryside Treasures* (1946), which he wrote as well as illustrated, the text handwritten and decorated with initial capitals printed in green. The last major task of his career, which he worked on for five years, was to produce some 500 illustrations and maps for a commemorative edition of the Bible to celebrate the third jubilee of the British and Foreign Bible Society. He died on 21 August 1954 at his home, 82 Bishops Park Road, Croydon, and was survived by his wife, Laura.

ALAN HORNE

Sources 'The family of Knowles: some biographical notes set down by Horace John Knowles, artist, April 1951', Bancroft Road Library, Tower Hamlets, London • 'Transcript of reminiscences by Mr. G. N. Kent', 1960, Bancroft Road Library, Tower Hamlets, London • A. J. L. Hellicar, 'Charles, Reginald and Horace Knowles, artists', *East London Papers*, 2 (1959), 83–93 • J. M. Dent, *The house of Dent* (1938) • b. cert. • d. cert.
Archives Bancroft Road Library, Tower Hamlets, London, H. J. Knowles MS, 'The family of Knowles' (1951)
Wealth at death £3390 5s. 11d.: probate, 8 June 1951, CGPLA Eng. & Wales • £237 4s. 2d.—Horace John Knowles: administration, 18 Oct 1954, CGPLA Eng. & Wales

Knowles, Richard Brinsley Sheridan (1820–1882), journalist, son of James Sheridan *Knowles (1784–1862), dramatist and Baptist preacher, and Maria Charteris (d. 1841), actress, was born at Glasgow on 17 January 1820. From 1838 to 1841 he was a clerk in the registrar-general's office, Somerset House, London. He was admitted as a student of the Middle Temple on 14 November 1839 and called to the bar on 26 May 1843. Having inherited his father's love of the theatre, on 19 November 1845 he produced at the Haymarket Theatre a comedy entitled *The Maiden Aunt*, which had a run of thirty nights. In 1845–6 he edited the humorous magazines *Joe Miller the Younger* and *Mephystopheles*. On 25 October 1845 he married Eliza Mary,

youngest child of Peter and Elizabeth Crowley of Dublin, and sister of Nicholas Joseph Crowley (1819–1857), painter.

In 1849 Knowles became a Roman Catholic and was appointed editor of the *Catholic Standard*, subsequently purchased by Henry Wilberforce and renamed the *Weekly Register*. From 1853 to 1855 he edited the *Illustrated London Magazine*, a series of five volumes. He was a leading writer on *The Standard* from 1857 to 1860, but the anti-Catholic prejudice of the proprietors led to his dismissal. John Sherren Brewer, who was then editing the paper, at once resigned in protest. Knowles was editor of the *London Review*, but in later years his chief engagement was on the *Morning Post*, until ill health forced his resignation.

Turning to historical research, Knowles edited the *Chronicles of John of Oxenedes* from a manuscript in the duke of Newcastle's collection; this was published in 1859 in the Rolls Series. In 1871 he was appointed to the inspectorate of the Royal Commission on Historical Manuscripts, and catalogued many valuable collections, mainly belonging to Roman Catholic families. Among these were the papers of the marquess of Bute, the earl of Denbigh, the earl of Ashburnham, and Colonel John Towneley. His *Life of James Sheridan Knowles*, a limited edition privately printed in 1872, besides being a work of filial piety, vividly evokes the theatrical milieu of the early nineteenth century. Knowles died suddenly at his home, 29 North Bank, Regent's Park, London, on 28 January 1882, survived by his wife.

G. C. BOASE, rev. G. MARTIN MURPHY

Sources Boase, *Mod. Eng. biog.* • *The Athenaeum* (4 Feb 1882), 156 • *The Times* (30 Jan 1882), 7 • *Law Times* (25 Feb 1882), 304 • CGPLA Eng. & Wales (1882)
Archives PRO, corresp. as HMC inspector, HMC 1
Wealth at death £960 10s. 0d.: administration, 16 March 1882, CGPLA Eng. & Wales

Knowles, Thomas (1723–1802), religious writer, born at Ely, Cambridgeshire, was the son of John Knowles, a verger and master of the works of Ely Cathedral. He was educated at Ely grammar school and at Pembroke College, Cambridge, where he was admitted as a sizar on 6 July 1739; he graduated BA in 1744 and MA in 1747. He was elected a college fellow on 23 March 1749 and was ordained deacon at Ely in May 1746 and priest in Norwich in September 1748. He published *The Existence and Attributes of God not Demonstrable A Priori* (1746) in response to Samuel Clarke and his followers, in particular to Phillips Glover's *The Argument A Priori … Stated and Considered*. He subsequently published *The Scripture Doctrine of the Existence and Attributes of God … in Twelve Sermons* (1748), the preface of which was written in response to David Hume.

On 10 January 1748 Knowles became rector of Ickworth and of Chedburgh in Suffolk, the second of which he held until his death. He was also chaplain to the dowager Lady Hervey, of Ickworth. In 1752 he had a dispensation to hold the living of Teversham, Cambridgeshire, which he held until 1761. He was made DD by Archbishop Secker in 1753, apparently on the strength of his sermons in response to Bishop Robert Clayton's *An Essay on Spirit*. From 1771 onwards he was also lecturer of St Mary's Church, Bury St

Edmunds. On 10 October 1779 he was collated to a prebend at Ely, and in 1791 he became rector of Winston, Suffolk.

Knowles also wrote on practical religion: his *Preparatory Discourse on Confirmation* was hugely popular and went through ten editions by 1784, and in his final years he published anonymously a book of advice to young clergymen on entering the priesthood. He published two sermons on schools in 1772 and 1787, and works on the Tithe Bill and Test Act. His treatise *Primitive Christianity* (1789) drew forth *Observations* (1789) from Capel Lofft and *Strictures* (1790) from James Edward Hamilton.

Knowles died in Chedburgh on 6 October 1802, and was buried in his church there. He was married and one of his two daughters married Benjamin Underwood, rector of Great Barnet and of St Mary Abchurch, Abchurch Yard, London; the other, Eliza, married Sir Edmund Lacon, later baronet.   THOMPSON COOPER, *rev.* ADAM JACOB LEVIN

Sources Venn, *Alum. Cant.* · *Fasti Angl.* (Hardy), 1.362 · A. Chalmers, ed., *The general biographical dictionary*, new edn, 19 (1815), 408–9 · S. Tynams, *An architectural account of the church of St Mary, Bury St Edmunds* (1854), 131–2 · F. J. G. Robinson and others, *Eighteenth-century British books: an author union catalogue*, 3 (1981), 393 · R. Hawes, *The history of Framlingham*, ed. R. Loder (1798), 285

Knowlton, Thomas (1691–1781), gardener and botanist, was born at Chislehurst, Kent, and baptized there on 6 September 1691, the eldest of the five sons of William Knowlton and Ann Stokes. Little is known of his early life. In 1720 he was employed as a gardener by Sir Henry Penrice (1677–1752) at Offaly Palace, Hertfordshire. In the same year, on 27 June, he married Elizabeth Rice (*d.* 1738). They had two children, Elizabeth and Charles, the latter of whom attended St John's College, Cambridge, and pursued a career in the church. After leaving Penrice's service Knowlton superintended the botanic garden of Dr James Sherard at Eltham in Kent. After a short time working for the duke of Chandos in Canons he entered the service of Richard Boyle, third earl of Burlington, at Londesborough, Yorkshire, and there he remained for the rest of his life. His freelance work at other estates in Yorkshire appears to have made him a wealthy man, and he invested his profits in property.

Knowlton became known as a botanist of merit. He corresponded with E. M. Da Costa and other members of the Royal Society, and won the esteem of Sir Hans Sloane. He subscribed to Mark Catesby's *History of Carolina* and actively encouraged others to do the same. To him is due the first discovery in England of the 'moor-ball', a species of fresh-water algae of the Conferva family, called by Linnaeus *Aegagropila*. In order to find even a moderate number of these balls, he had to spend many hours wading in the lake at Walling Fen, in water from 2 to over 3 feet deep.

Knowlton was also something of an antiquary. He discovered the exact site of the ancient city of Delgovicia, near Pocklington in Yorkshire, and communicated some observations on this and other subjects to the *Philosophical Transactions* (44, 1748, 100–102, 124–7). Two large deer's horns which he discovered, one resembling the horn of an Irish elk, are figured in the same volume (plate 422). He

was at first distinguished by his interest in and knowledge of indigenous plants. In 1726 he travelled to Guernsey to study the cultivation of the Guernsey lily. He became increasingly interested in exotic species, for which he first built a hot house at Londesborough in 1729.

Knowlton died on 28 November 1781 at Londesborough. Toward the end of his life he was totally blind. He was buried in Londesborough churchyard. A botanical genus of the family Ranunculaceae, comprising five or six species of plants indigenous to the Cape of Good Hope, was named after him by Richard Anthony Salisbury in 1796. A John Knowlton, gardener to Earl Fitzwilliam, whose will was proved in February 1782 (PRO, PROB 11/1087, sig. 85), was perhaps a brother of the botanist.

THOMAS SECCOMBE, *rev.* P. E. KELL

Sources B. Henrey, *No ordinary gardener: Thomas Knowlton, 1691–1781*, ed. A. O. Chater (1986) · R. Pulteney, *Historical and biographical sketches of the progress of botany in England*, 2 (1790), 239–41 · Nichols, *Illustrations*, vol. 4 · F. E. Crackles, *Flora of the East Riding of Yorkshire* (1990) · *A selection of the correspondence of Linnaeus, and other naturalists, from the original manuscripts*, ed. J. E. Smith, 2 vols. (1821), vol. 2, pp. 78–80

Archives U. Glas. L., corresp. and diary | BL, corresp. with E. M. Da Costa, Add. MS 28539 · NHM, letters to Samuel Brewer

Knowlys, Newman (1758–1836), barrister and judge, was born in London, the fourth son of William Knowlys, merchant, of Harp Lane, Tower Street, London. Educated at Botesdale and Christ's College, Cambridge (he did not obtain a degree), Knowlys was admitted to the Middle Temple on 22 January 1774 and called to the bar on 8 February 1782. He was elected common serjeant of London in 1803 and became recorder in 1822. Knowlys was made a bencher of his inn in 1817, reader in 1819, and he was treasurer in 1826.

As a barrister Knowlys's practice lay chiefly in the criminal courts of metropolitan London and the City's customary courts. In the 1780s barristers began to appear in Old Bailey trials with some regularity, although the majority of cases continued to be heard without the involvement of counsel for either the prosecution or the defence. Knowlys was one of the roughly dozen men who formed a nascent criminal bar in London; he began to practise at the Old Bailey immediately after his call to the bar and between 1783 and 1803 he was engaged in over 1300 cases heard in that court. During the 1790s Knowlys shared the leadership of Old Bailey practice with Jerome William Knapp.

Although he enjoyed little success in Westminster Hall, Knowlys's purchase of a City common pleadership in 1787 made him one of four barristers who held the exclusive right to practise in the lord mayor's and sheriffs' courts of London. The majority of cases heard in these courts related to the recovery of small debts. The combination of a pleadership and Old Bailey practice was typical of the period. He was the second individual (the first being John Silvester) to hold successively the City offices of common pleader, common serjeant, and recorder of London. Advocates of what came to be known as the principle of rotation argued that practice in the City courts provided the best preparation for the subsequent positions, offering a solid grounding in London's municipal law. Critics pointed out that pleaderships were won not by talent but through purchase and that they were filled by an inferior grade of practitioner. City pleaderships provided a refuge for those barristers whose talents or connections were not such as to enable them to succeed in the superior courts. Yet the acquisition of a pleadership offered the recipient a ticket in the 'city lottery of law' (*The Times*, 23 April 1822), granting him a one in four chance of ultimately obtaining the recordership.

By the end of Knowlys's legal career both the system and its results were widely condemned. His recordership was bounded by negative publicity and did much to bring that office into disrepute. *The Times* had opposed his election, dismissing him as 'a mere practitioner in the courts' (1 April 1822), entirely lacking in the requisite personal dignity and legal ability, while the *Morning Chronicle* despised him for his reactionary opinions. Like his predecessor John Silvester, Knowlys was known to oppose reform of England's severe criminal law.

As common serjeant and later recorder of London, Knowlys's duties included sitting as a judge at the Old Bailey. The *Morning Chronicle* compared his common serjeantship with that of the notoriously brutal George Jeffreys. Shortly before his election as recorder that paper commented on his 'unparalleled severity' and 'bare-faced

system of *frightening* a jury into a verdict of conviction' in the trial for libel of Richard Carlile (*Morning Chronicle*, 6 March 1822). One critic claimed that he had turned the Old Bailey into a 'bear garden' (PRO, HO 73/4, 'Rudolph's and Wilson's case', Aug 1827). Knowlys was forced to resign in disgrace in 1833 after issuing a warrant of execution for one Job Cox, who had received a royal pardon. He remained steward of the borough court of Southwark until his death.

Little is known of Knowlys's family or personal life. He was married relatively late in life to Mrs Slope (*d*. 1837), a widow of Bath, on 15 August 1807. They had no children. Knowlys died on 5 January 1836 at his house in James Street, Buckingham Gate, London, and was buried in the Middle Temple vault. His wife died on 19 November of the following year.   ALLYSON N. MAY

Sources Venn, *Alum. Cant.*, 2/4.68 · *GM*, 2nd ser., 5 (1836), 211 · *GM*, 2nd ser., 8 (1837), 657 · *The Times* (9 Jan 1836) · *The Times* (1 April 1822) · *The Times* (12 April 1822) · *The Times* (23 April 1822) · *The Times* (25 June 1833) · *Morning Chronicle* (6 March 1822) · *Morning Chronicle* (7 March 1822) · *Morning Chronicle* (11 March 1822) · *Morning Chronicle* (28 March 1822) · *Morning Chronicle* (1 April 1822) · *Morning Chronicle* (6 April 1822) · *Morning Chronicle* (12 April 1822) · *Morning Chronicle* (13 April 1822) · *Morning Chronicle* (25 June 1833) · *Old Bailey session papers* (1783–1803) · *Browne's General Law List* (1783–97) · *New Law List* (1798–1802) · *Clarke's New Law List* (1803–36) · V. A. C. Gatrell, *The hanging tree: execution and the English people, 1770–1868* (1994), 359, 509–10 · 'Rudolph's and Wilson's case', Aug 1827, PRO, HO 73/4

PICTURE CREDITS

Keble, John (1792–1866)—by permission of the Warden and Fellows of Keble College, Oxford

Kedourie, Elie (1926–1992)—© reserved; private collection

Keeling, Enoch Bassett (1837–1886)—© National Portrait Gallery, London / Country Life Picture Library

Keene, Charles Samuel (1823–1891)—© National Portrait Gallery, London

Keightley, Sir Charles Frederic (1901–1974)—© National Portrait Gallery, London

Keir, Thelma Cazalet- (1899–1989)—© National Portrait Gallery, London

Keith, Sir Arthur (1866–1955)—© Estate of Sir William Rothenstein / National Portrait Gallery, London

Keith, George, styled tenth Earl Marischal (1692/3?–1778)—Scottish National Portrait Gallery

Keith, James Francis Edward (1696–1758)—private collection; photograph National Portrait Gallery, London

Keith, William, sixth Earl Marischal (1614–1671)—Scottish National Portrait Gallery

Kekewich, Sir Arthur (1832–1907)—© National Portrait Gallery, London

Kekewich, Robert George (1854–1914)—© National Portrait Gallery, London

Kell, Sir Vernon George Waldegrave (1873–1942)—Getty Images – F. A. Swaine

Keller, Hans Heinrich (1919–1985)—© George Newson; National Portrait Gallery, London

Kelly, Sir David Victor (1891–1959)—© National Portrait Gallery, London

Kelly, Edward [Ned] (c.1854–1880)—Mitchell Library, State Library of New South Wales

Kelly, Sir Fitzroy Edward (1796–1880)—© National Portrait Gallery, London

Kelly, Frances Maria (1790–1882)—© National Portrait Gallery, London

Kelly, James Fitzmaurice- (1857–1923)—by courtesy of Felix Rosenstiel's Widow & Son Ltd., London, on behalf of the Estate of Sir John Lavery; collection National Portrait Gallery, London

Keltie, Sir John Scott (1840–1927)—© National Portrait Gallery, London

Kelynack, Theophilus Nicholas (1866–1944)—© National Portrait Gallery, London

Kelyng, Sir John (bap. 1607, d. 1671)—Collection Plymouth City Art Gallery; © reserved in the photograph

Kem, Samuel (1604–1670)—© National Portrait Gallery, London

Kemble, Adelaide (1815–1879)—© National Portrait Gallery, London

Kemble, Charles (1775–1854)—© National Portrait Gallery, London

Kemble, Elizabeth (1762/3–1841)—Garrick Club / the art archive

Kemble, Frances Anne (1809–1893)—courtesy of the Pennsylvania

Academy of the Fine Arts, Philadelphia. Bequest of Henry C. Carey (The Carey Collection)

Kemble, John Philip (1757–1823)—© Tate, London, 2004

Kemble, Maria Theresa (1777–1838)—Garrick Club / the art archive

Kemble, Priscilla (1758–1845)—© National Portrait Gallery, London

Kemble, Roger (1722–1802)—© National Portrait Gallery, London

Kemble, Stephen George (1758–1822)—© National Portrait Gallery, London

Kemp, George Meikle (1795–1844)—Scottish National Portrait Gallery

Kemp, John (1380/81–1454)—The British Library

Kemp, Stanley Wells (1882–1945)—© National Portrait Gallery, London

Kempe, Sir Alfred Bray (1849–1922)—© National Portrait Gallery, London

Ken, Thomas (1637–1711)—© National Portrait Gallery, London

Kendal, Dame Madge (1848–1935)—© Tate, London, 2004

Kendall, Kay (1927–1959)—© Cecil Beaton Archive, Sotheby's; collection National Portrait Gallery, London

Kendrew, Sir John Cowdery (1917–1997)—© Nick Sinclair; collection National Portrait Gallery, London

Kennaway, Sir Ernest Laurence (1881–1958)—© National Portrait Gallery, London

Kennedy, Sir Alexander Blackie William (1847–1928)—courtesy of the Institution of Civil Engineers Archives

Kennedy, Benjamin Hall (1804–1889)—by permission of the Master and Fellows of St John's College, Cambridge

Kennedy, Douglas Neil (1893–1988)—courtesy EFDSS

Kennedy, Sir James Shaw (1788–1865)—V&A Images, The Victoria and Albert Museum

Kennedy, Marion Grace (1836–1914)—The Principal and Fellows, Newnham College, Cambridge

Kennedy, Thomas Francis (1788–1879)—© National Portrait Gallery, London / Country Life Picture Library

Kennett, White (1660–1728)—© National Portrait Gallery, London

Kenney, Annie (1879–1953)—Mary Evans / The Women's Library

Kennicott, Benjamin (1718–1783)—The Rector and Scholars of Exeter College, Oxford

Kenning, Sir George (1880–1956)—© National Portrait Gallery, London

Kenny, Elizabeth (1880–1952)—Getty Images – Hulton Archive

Kenrick, William (1729/30–1779)—© National Portrait Gallery, London

Kent, (William) Charles Mark (1823–1902)—© National Portrait Gallery, London

Kent, Sir Harold Simcox (1903–1998)—© National Portrait Gallery, London

Kent, William (bap. 1686, d. 1748)—© National Portrait Gallery, London

Kenyatta, Jomo (c.1895–1978)—Getty Images – Mohamed Amin

Kenyon, Sir Frederic George (1863–1952)—© National Portrait Gallery, London

Kenyon, Dame Kathleen Mary (1906–1978)—© Jorge Lewinski; collection National Portrait Gallery, London

Kenyon, Lloyd, first Baron Kenyon (1732–1802)—Property of the Rt. Hon. the Lord Kenyon

Keppel, Alice Frederica (1868–1947)—© National Portrait Gallery, London

Keppel, Arnold Joost van, first earl of Albemarle (1669/70–1718)—© National Portrait Gallery, London

Keppel, Augustus, Viscount Keppel (1725–1786)—© National Maritime Museum, London, Greenwich Hospital Collection

Keppel, Frederick (1729–1777)—by kind permission of the Bishop of Exeter and the Church Commissioners / Photograph The Paul Mellon Centre for Studies in British Art

Keppel, Sir George Olof Roos- (1866–1921)—The British Library

Keppel, Sir Henry (1809–1904)—© National Portrait Gallery, London

Keppel, William Anne, second earl of Albemarle (1702–1754)—© National Portrait Gallery, London

Ker, John, first duke of Roxburghe (c.1680–1741)—in the collection of the Duke of Buccleuch and Queensberry KT; photograph courtesy the Scottish National Portrait Gallery

Ker, John, third duke of Roxburghe (1740–1804)—Scottish National Portrait Gallery

Ker, Robert, first earl of Roxburghe (1569/70–1650)—reproduced by kind permission of the Duke of Roxburghe, Floors Castle, Kelso

Ker, William Paton (1855–1923)—© Estate of Sir William Rothenstein / National Portrait Gallery, London

Kérouaille, Louise Renée de Penancoët de, suo jure duchess of Portsmouth and suo jure duchess of Aubigny in the French nobility (1649–1734)—© The J. Paul Getty Museum, Los Angeles

Kerr, Archibald John Kerr Clark, Baron Inverchapel (1882–1951)—© Karsh / Camera Press; collection National Portrait Gallery, London

Kerr, Philip Henry, eleventh marquess of Lothian (1882–1940)—© National Portrait Gallery, London

Kerr, Robert, first marquess of Lothian (1636–1703)—V&A Images, The Victoria and Albert Museum

Kerr, Schomberg Henry, ninth marquess of Lothian (1833–1900)—The Royal Bank of Scotland Group Art Collection

Kerr, William, third earl of Lothian (c.1605–1675)—private collection

Kerrich, Thomas (1748–1828)—© National Portrait Gallery, London

Key, Sir Astley Cooper (1821–1888)—© National Portrait Gallery, London

Key, Charles Aston (1793–1849)—Heritage Images Partnership

Keyes, Roger John Brownlow, first Baron Keyes (1872–1945)—The de László Foundation / Witt Library, Courtauld Institute of Art, London

Keynes, Sir Geoffrey Langdon (1887–1982)—© National Portrait Gallery, London

Keynes, John Maynard, Baron Keynes (1883–1946)—© National Portrait Gallery, London

Keyser, Sir Polydor de (1832–1898)—Stedelijke Musea Dendermonde

Khama the Great (c.1835–1923)—© National Portrait Gallery, London

Khama, Sir Seretse (1921–1980)—Getty Images – Hulton Archive

Khan, Abdul Ghaffar (1890–1988)—© Nehru Memorial Museum and Library, New Delhi

Khan, Muhammad Iftikhar Ali, nawab of Pataudi (1910–1952)—Getty Images – Hulton Archive

Khan, Noor-un-Nisa Inayat (1914–1944)—© National Portrait Gallery, London

Kickham, Charles Joseph (1828–1882)—© National Portrait Gallery, London

Kidd, Benjamin (1858–1916)—© National Portrait Gallery, London

Kidd, Dame Margaret Henderson (1900–1989)—Scottish National Portrait Gallery / unknown private collection

Kiggell, Sir Launcelot Edward (1862–1954)—© National Portrait Gallery, London

Kilham, Alexander (1762–1798)—© National Portrait Gallery, London

Killigrew, Anne (1660–1685)—The Berkeley Castle Will Trust. Photograph: Photographic Survey, Courtauld Institute of Art, London

Killigrew, Thomas (1612–1683)—The Royal Collection © 2004 HM Queen Elizabeth II

Killigrew, Sir William (bap. 1606, d. 1695)—© reserved

Kilvert, (Robert) Francis (1840–1879)—Kilvert Society; photograph National Portrait Gallery, London

Kimber, William (1872–1961)—courtesy EFDSS

King, Cecil Harmsworth (1901–1987)—© National Portrait Gallery, London

King, Sir Edmund (bap. 1630, d. 1709)—© National Portrait Gallery, London

King, Frances Elizabeth (1757–1821)—© National Portrait Gallery, London

King, Henry (1592–1669)—Christ Church, Oxford

King, Horace Maybray, Baron Maybray-King (1901–1986)—© National Portrait Gallery, London

King, James (bap. 1750, d. 1784)—by permission of the National Library of Australia R3631

King, Jessie Marion (1875–1949)—Scottish National Portrait Gallery